Business Statistics
of the United States

Business
Statistics
of the United States
1997 Edition

Courtenay M. Slater, Editor

Bernan Press
Lanham, Maryland USA

Published 1998
Printed in the United States of America

99 98   4 3 2 1

Bernan Press
4611-F Assembly Drive
Lanham, MD 20706-4391
(800) 274-4447
e-mail: info@bernan.com

ISBN: 0-89059-083-4

Table of Contents

Business Statistics of the United States
1997 Edition

Courtenay M. Slater,
Editor

PART II: INDUSTRY PROFILES

CONTENTS

Part III: HISTORICAL DATA

Selected Monthly Data, 1969–1992

PART IV: STATE AND REGIONAL DATA

State and Regional Data, Annual, 1971-1996

Preface

Business Statistics of the United States is a basic desk reference for everyone requiring recent or historical information about the U.S. economy. It contains some 2,000 economic time series, predominantly from federal government sources, presenting a rich selection of the data most needed for analysis of economic trends and patterns. Of equal importance with the data themselves are the extensive background notes that enable the user to understand the data, to use them appropriately, and, if desired, to seek additional information from the source agencies.

Using This Book

Time period coverage. This 1997 edition of *Business Statistics* contains annual data for 1968 through 1996 and monthly data for 1993 through 1996. To make the volume even more timely, key data for the first six months of 1997 are found in Tables 2 and 3 of the lead article, "The 1960s to the 1990s: Three Decades of Economic Change," beginning on page xiii. Part III of this edition contains selected quarterly and monthly data for earlier time periods. In general, these quarterly data begin with 1960 and the monthly data with 1969.

Subject matter coverage. Part I covers the U.S. economy as a whole. It contains 10 chapters:

- Gross Domestic Product and Cyclical Indicators

- Consumer Income and Spending

- Industrial Production and Capacity Utilization

- Business Sales, Inventories, and Investment

- Prices

- Employment Costs, Productivity, and Profits

- Employment, Hours, and Earnings

- Money and Financial Markets

- U.S. Foreign Trade and Finance

- International Comparisons

Part II presents data by major industry group, following the structure of the Standard Industrial Classification (SIC). Basic data are repeated from Part I and are supplemented by additional industry detail. The user thus has the convenience of a profile of the industry in a single location. The industry groups covered are:

- Mining, Oil, and Gas

- Construction and Housing

- Total Manufacturing

- Durable Goods Manufacturing (nine 2-digit industries)

- Nondurable Goods Manufacturing (ten 2-digit industries)

- Transportation, Communications, and Utilities

- Retail and Wholesale Trade

- Finance, Insurance, Real Estate, and Private Services

- Government

Part III, as noted, contains additional historical data for selected series. Part IV contains annual data (1971 through 1996) for each state and region. The state data cover personal income and its major components, employment, and population.

Special features. Each chapter in Parts I and II begins with a chart and brief text highlighting some of the trends reflected in the data.

The lead article in the front section describes overall trends in the U.S. economy during the period covered by the book, with particular emphasis on the most recent few years. This analysis is carried through the first half of 1997.

Two additional articles describe recent and prospective developments in economic statistics. The first discusses issues that have been raised in the last few years about the suitability of the Consumer Price Index (CPI) as a cost-of-living measure and summarizes revisions to the CPI being introduced in 1998. The second describes the principal features of the newly-adopted North American Industry Classification System (NAICS) and statistical agencies' plans for implementing the new classifications.

The notes. The background notes beginning on page 337 contain definitions, descriptions of recent data revision, information about data availability and release schedules, and references to sources of additional technical information. They are arranged in the order in which the data appear in the book, with references to the data pages and the subject to which they pertain shown at the beginning of each group of notes.

The History of *Business Statistics*

The history of *Business Statistics* begins with the publication, many years ago, by the U.S. Commerce Department's Bureau of Economic Analysis (BEA) of the first edition of a volume of the same name and general purpose. After 27 periodic editions, the last of which appeared in 1992, the

BEA found it necessary, for budgetary and other reasons, to discontinue not only that publication but also maintenance of the database from which the publication was derived.

The individual statistical series in *Business Statistics* are publicly available. However, the task of gathering them from a number of sources within the government, plus a few private sources, and assembling them into one coherent database is highly impractical for most data users. Even when current data are more-or-less readily available, obtaining the full historical time series often is time consuming and difficult. Believing that a *Business Statistics* compilation was too valuable to be lost to the public, Bernan Press published the first edition of the present publication in 1995.

Sources and Acknowledgements

The great majority of the statistical data in this book are from federal government sources and are in the public domain. A few series are from private sources and further use may be subject to copyright restrictions. Sources for all the data are given in the notes.

The data in this volume meet the publication standards of the federal statistical agencies from which they were obtained. Every effort has been made to select data that are accurate, meaningful, and useful. All statistical data are subject to error arising from sampling variability, reporting errors, incomplete coverage, imputation, and other causes. The responsibility of the editor and publisher of this volume is limited to reasonable care in the reproduction and presentation of data obtained from established sources.

This volume has been edited by Courtenay M. Slater, Manager of Economic Publications for Bernan Associates and former Chief Economist for the Department of Commerce. In addition to overseeing preparation of the data and the background notes, Dr. Slater prepared the three introductory feature articles and the charts and texts that introduce each chapter. She assumes full responsibility for any interpretations or misinterpretations found in that material.

The editor is profoundly grateful to all of those who assisted in the preparation of this volume. Over the past year, Hongwei Zhang has maintained the database from which the data in this book are drawn, and she prepared all the data tables. This volume would not have been possible without her careful and reliable work. Assistance in reviewing the tables and fact-checking the text was provided by Steven Thomas and Candace Feit. The editor's longtime colleagues, George E. Hall and Cornelia J. Strawser reviewed the lead articles and provided much valuable advice. Renee Bocko-Dexter and others in the Bernan production department capably and cheerfully handled the substantial production work associated with a publication of this type.

Finally, special thanks are due to the many federal agency personnel who, as always, responded generously to our frequent need for assistance in obtaining data and background information.

The 1960s to the 1990s: Three Decades of Economic Change

The extraordinarily good performance of the U.S. economy in 1996 and early 1997 was marked by rapid employment growth, low inflation, strong export performance, and near-disappearance of the federal budget deficit. Pleased, but puzzled, observers asked "How did it happen?" and "How long can it last?"

Testifying to Congress in July 1997, Federal Reserve Chairman Alan Greenspan claimed "exceptional" performance by the U.S. economy.[1] In September, another Federal Reserve Board member spoke of the "good news" economy, and the Congressional Budget Office (CBO) used the terms "remarkable" and "stunning" to describe recent economic performance.[2] Meantime, an official assessment by the normally staid and cautious International Monetary Fund expressed satisfaction with the United States' "prudent macroeconomic policies," "exceptionally dynamic private sector," and "responsive labor market."[3]

Nineteen-ninety-six produced one of the happiest combinations of sturdy economic growth, high employment, and low inflation in many years, and the favorable trends continued into 1997. The combined value of the unemployment rate and the inflation rate, often referred to as the "misery index" was at an unusually low level from 1994 through 1996 and dipped further in the first half of 1997 (Chart 1). At the same time, growth of gross domestic product (GDP) accelerated. Despite the strong growth, there were few, if any, signs of the economic strains that traditionally have caused expansion to shift to inflation, stagnation, or recession. Perhaps the most frequently asked questions about the U.S. economy in mid-1997 were: "How did it happen?" and "How long can it last?"

The nearly 30 years covered by this book have been marked by rapid technological advance, major shifts in job requirements and work force composition, and dramatic changes in the global economic and political environment. These changes were not always easily digested. The past three decades have included periods of deep recession and high inflation and at times have evoked widespread expressions of concern about the strength, stability, and international competitiveness of the U.S. economy. Yet from these years of change and turbulence has emerged a prosperous, dynamic, and competitive economy, one widely viewed as a model for nations making the transition from managed to free market economies or seeking to join the ranks of wealthy industrialized nations.

This article briefly highlights major trends and events from 1968 to 1989 and then takes a closer look at the 1990s. The comprehensive statistical tables that form the main body of this book permit users to assemble additional information about the U.S. economy and to make their own assessments of the U.S. economic situation.

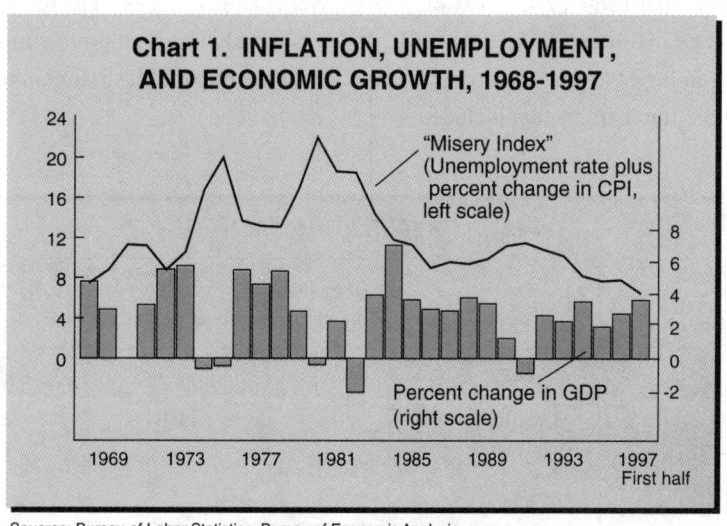

Chart 1. INFLATION, UNEMPLOYMENT, AND ECONOMIC GROWTH, 1968-1997

"Misery Index" (Unemployment rate plus percent change in CPI, left scale)

Percent change in GDP (right scale)

1969 1973 1977 1981 1985 1989 1993 1997 First half

Soucres: Bureau of Labor Statistics, Bureau of Economic Analysis

1968-1982: Wartime Strains, Inflation, Oil Shocks, and Recessions

In 1968, the first year covered by this volume, the U.S. economy, which had performed so well in the early 1960s, was showing unmistakable signs of the strains of financing the demands of the war in Vietnam without offsetting cutbacks in civilian production. Real output increased almost 5 percent during that year; the unemployment rate fell to 3.4 percent by the fourth quarter; the underlying rate of inflation (consumer prices other than food and energy) rose to 5.1 percent; and labor cost increases of more than 5 percent during the year signaled more inflation to come.

Inflationary pressures indeed did intensify, with the underlying inflation rate reaching 6.2 percent in 1969. An income tax surcharge and a leveling-off of defense spending in 1969 moved the federal budget into surplus, but this fiscal restraint came too late to slow the economic overheating without a recession.

The recession of 1969-1970 lasted 11 months (Table 1). Real output fell 0.7 percent and the unemployment rate rose to a peak of 6.1 percent. In retrospect, the 1969-1970 recession appears relatively mild, but it marked the beginning of a 13-year period of economic fluctuations that included

four recessions, two of them deep and prolonged.

The 1973 recession. Strains on productive capacity and renewed inflation were again a problem by the middle of 1973. The unemployment rate had dropped below 5 percent, industrial capacity utilization had reached an unusually high 89 percent, and the overall consumer price index (CPI) had risen 5.7 percent from July 1972 to July 1973, with the majority of the increase concentrated in food and energy prices. This overheating economy was then hit by large increases in world oil prices stemming from an oil embargo imposed by the Organization of Petroleum Exporting Countries (OPEC). The CPI for energy rose at a 67 percent annual rate from October 1973 to January 1974. Energy price increases quickly translated into higher overall producer costs and consumer prices. Coupled with production dislocations induced by oil shortages, this led to the deepest recession since the 1930s.

The 1973-1975 recession lasted 16 months. During that time real output fell 3.0 percent, and the unemployment rate reached a peak of 9 percent—a level unprecedented in the post-World War II United States. The recession was worldwide, with production falling in all the major industrial countries.

1980-1982: Two recessions in two years. The four and three-quarter years of recovery that began in March 1975 did not completely restore either full employment or reasonable price stability. The unemployment rate was still 6 percent at the end of 1979. When a new round of world oil price increases was initiated in 1979, the added strain helped bring on a new recession at the beginning of 1980.

The 1980 recession was sharp but brief. However, the subsequent abortive recovery lasted less than a year. The 1981-1982 recession that followed lasted sixteen months and brought the unemployment rate to an extraordinarily high 10.8 percent. In examining long-term trends, 1980-1982 can be viewed as a single recessionary period. Real output was no higher in 1982 than in 1979, and the unemployment rate remained above 9 percent until late in 1983.

1982-1990: Expansion, Inflation, and Deficits

The nearly eight years from late 1982 to mid-1990 were a period of uninterrupted economic growth, but also a period of accumulating structural imbalances. Output grew throughout the period, 20 million nonfarm jobs were added, and the unemployment rate came down from its 10.8 percent recession peak to 5.3 percent in mid-1990. The rate of price increase remained fairly high, however, with the underlying inflation rate dropping below 4 percent only briefly in 1986.

The long economic expansion of the 1980s was fueled by growth of consumer spending that exceeded the growth of disposable personal income. As a result, the personal savings rate, which had ranged between 7.0 and 9.5 percent from 1970 to 1985, dropped to a range of 5.0 to 5.5 percent from 1987 through 1990 (Chart 2).

Table 1: RECESSIONS, 1967-1995				
Onset	Trough	Duration (months)	Real output (percent change)	Peak Unemployment rate
December 1969	November 1970	11	-0.7	6.1
November 1973	March 1975	16	-3.0	9.0
January 1980	July 1980	6	-2.5	7.8
July 1981	November 1982	16	-3.0	10.8
July 1990	March 1991	8	-2.0	7.7

Sources: Bureau of Economic Analysis, Bureau of Labor Statistics

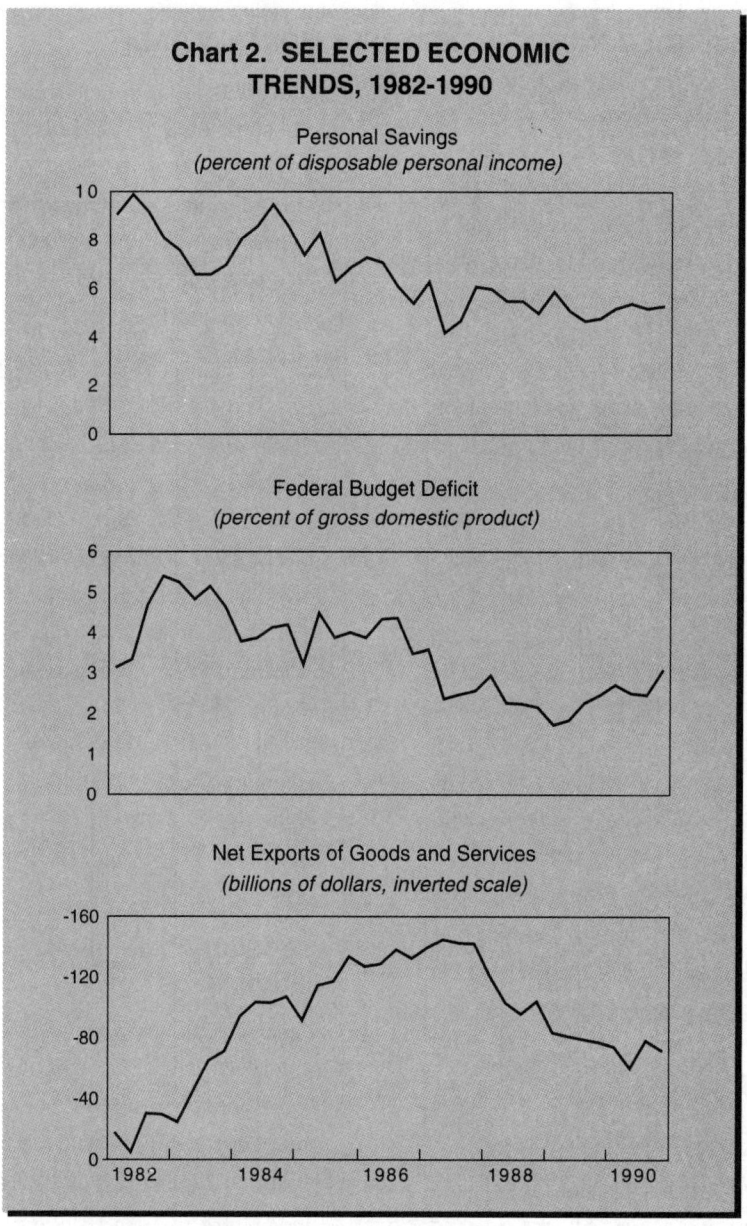

Chart 2. SELECTED ECONOMIC TRENDS, 1982-1990

Souce: Bureau of Economic Analysis

Iraqi invasion of Kuwait, though not on the scale of the oil shocks of the 1970s, combined with the structural imbalances built up during the 1980s to bring on the brief 1990-91 recession. The recession lasted eight months, with recovery beginning in March of 1991.

The recovery was weak at first, with the unemployment rate continuing to rise until June of 1992. In late 1993 the economy began to grow more briskly. This more rapid growth continued during 1994, producing relatively full employment by year's end and initiating the period of steady growth and moderating inflation which has continued into 1997. Real GDP grew at an annual rate of 2.7 percent from the fourth quarter of 1993 through the fourth quarter of 1996, and the GDP price index rose only 2.4 percent per year during those three years.

1997: Can the good news last? During the first half of 1997 real GDP grew at a 4.1 percent rate while the GDP price index rose at only a 2.1 percent rate. The unemployment rate averaged 5.1 percent, the lowest since early 1974 (Table 2). With both corporate and individual incomes growing, higher tax receipts were moving the federal budget rapidly toward balance, and, although the foreign trade deficit remained large, brisk growth of exports was demonstrating the global competitiveness of U.S. goods and services (Table 3). With manufacturers' new orders strong and inventories at reasonable levels, there seemed every reason to expect that healthy economic growth would continue during the remainder of the year.

Various aspects of economic performance during the 1990s and a brief discussion of some of the explanations that have been suggested for the economy's improved performance are discussed in the next sections.

Tax reductions and defense spending increases also stimulated economic growth during this period, but they were accompanied by a federal budget deficit that remained near or above 4 percent of GDP from mid-1982 through 1986.[4] Although economic growth helped lower the deficit to 2.0 percent of GDP by 1989, it climbed again to 2.7 percent in 1990 as the economy weakened.

The foreign trade deficit also burgeoned during the mid-1980s, and the United States became heavily dependent on an inflow of foreign funds to help finance government borrowing and business investment needs. Real interest rates were high and business investment grew slowly, especially from 1985 on.

The 1990s: The Road to the "Good News" Economy

By 1989 the economy had reached a high level of resource utilization, but the situation was not sustainable. Oil price increases stemming from the

Table 2: RECENT ECONOMIC INDICATORS: MONTHLY DATA
(seasonally adjusted, except as noted)

	1996						1997					
	Jul	Aug	Sep	Oct	Nov	Dec	Jan	Feb	Mar	Apr	May	Jun
Labor measures:												
Civilian labor force (thousands)	134,165	133,898	134,291	134,636	134,831	135,022	135,848	135,634	136,319	136,098	136,173	136,200
Civilian employment (thousands)	126,889	126,988	127,248	127,617	127,644	127,855	128,580	128,430	129,175	129,384	129,639	129,364
Unemployment rate (percent)	5.4	5.2	5.2	5.2	5.3	5.3	5.4	5.3	5.2	4.9	4.8	5.0
Nonagricultural payroll employment												
(thousands)	119,691	119,983	120,019	120,248	120,450	120,659	120,909	121,162	121,344	121,671	121,834	122,056
Production and nonsupervisory workers												
(private sector):												
Average weekly hours	34.3	34.5	34.7	34.4	34.5	34.7	34.4	34.8	34.8	34.5	34.5	34.6
Average hourly earnings (dollars)	11.81	11.86	11.91	11.91	11.98	12.03	12.05	12.10	12.14	12.14	12.19	12.23
Production and sales measures:												
Industrial production (1992=100)	115.5	115.8	116.0	116.2	117.2	117.7	117.8	118.4	118.8	119.3	119.5	119.9
Capacity utilization (percent of capacity)	83.2	83.2	83.1	83.0	83.4	83.5	83.3	83.5	83.6	83.6	83.5	83.5
Manufacturers' new orders ($ billions)	318.5	312.0	319.9	322.4	322.4	316.9	323.9	326.5	321.1	325.5	324.0	329.6
Manufacturers' inventory to sales ratio	1.37	1.38	1.37	1.37	1.36	1.37	1.36	1.36	1.36	1.35	1.37	1.35
Retail sales ($ billions)	203.1	203.0	204.7	206.3	205.8	206.9	210.2	213.0	212.3	209.9	209.4	210.9
Domestic new car sales												
(millions of units, annual rate)	7.1	7.6	7.5	6.7	6.6	6.9	7.5	7.1	7.3	6.6	6.8	6.6
New private housing units started												
(thousands, annual rate)	1,492	1,515	1,470	1,407	1,486	1,353	1,375	1,554	1,479	1,483	1,402	1,503
New one-family homes sold												
(thousands, annual rate)	782	814	768	706	788	794	822	826	825	765	764	815
Price measures:												
Consumer price index:												
All items	157.1	157.4	157.9	158.3	158.8	159.2	159.4	159.8	159.9	160.0	160.1	160.3
All items less food and energy	166.0	166.2	166.7	167.0	167.4	167.7	167.9	168.3	168.7	169.2	169.5	169.7
Producer price index: Finished goods	131.2	131.6	132.0	132.5	132.7	133.4	133.0	132.6	132.3	131.6	131.2	131.1
Interest rates (not seasonally adjusted):												
3-month treasury bill	5.2	5.1	5.2	5.0	5.0	4.9	5.1	5.0	5.1	5.2	5.1	4.9
U.S. treasury bonds, long-term composite	7.1	6.9	7.1	6.9	6.6	6.6	6.9	6.8	7.0	7.2	7.0	6.8
Fixed rate first mortgages	8.3	8.0	8.2	7.9	7.6	7.6	7.8	7.7	7.9	8.1	7.9	7.7

Sources: Bureau of Labor Statistics, Federal Reserve Board of Governors, Bureau of the Census, Bureau of Economic Analysis

Table 3: RECENT ECONOMIC INDICATORS: QUARTERLY DATA (seasonally adjusted, except as noted)				
	1996:III	1996:IV	1997:I	1997:II
National Income and Product Account Data:				
Percent changes:				
Quantity indexes:				
GDP	1.0	4.3	4.9	3.3
Personal consumption expenditures	0.5	3.3	5.3	0.9
Nonresidential fixed investment	16.5	5.9	4.1	14.6
Residential fixed investment	-4.5	-4.3	3.3	7.4
Price index: GDP	2.7	1.9	2.4	1.8
Billions of current dollars:				
Gross Domestic Product	7,676.0	7,792.9	7,933.6	8,034.3
Personal consumption expenditures	5,227.4	5,308.1	5,405.7	5,432.1
Nonresidential fixed investment	798.6	807.2	811.3	836.3
Residential fixed investment	313.5	312.0	316.2	324.6
Change in business inventories	37.1	31.9	66.1	81.1
Net exports of goods and services	-114.0	-88.6	-98.8	-88.7
Exports	863.7	904.6	922.2	960.3
Imports	977.6	993.2	1,021.0	1,049.0
Federal government:				
Receipts	1,598.6	1,641.6	1,675.3	1,709.3
Current expenditures	1,698.2	1,718.8	1,730.8	1,746.0
Current surplus or deficit (-)	-99.5	-77.1	-55.5	-36.8
Corporate profits before tax with inventory valuation adjustment	676.4	683.4	711.9	725.7
Personal income	6,541.9	6,618.4	6,746.2	6,829.1
Disposable personal income	5,644.6	5,695.8	5,790.5	5,849.9
Personal saving (% of disposable personal income)	4.5	3.9	3.7	4.2
Per capita disposable personal income:				
Current dollars	21,229	21,373	21,689	21,865
Chained 1992 dollars	19,161	19,152	19,331	19,439
Productivity and cost measures:				
Output per hour (1992=100):				
Nonfarm business	102.0	102.4	102.8	103.5
Manufacturing	112.4	113.5	114.2	114.9
Employment cost index (June 1989=100):				
Total compensation, private industry	129.7	130.6	131.4	132.5
Wages and salaries, private industry	126.4	127.4	128.5	129.7

Sources: Bureau of Economic Analysis, Bureau of Labor Statistics

Output and Employment

A striking characteristic of the U.S. economy during the 1970s and 1980s was the increasing number of people at work. Total employment increased by 39 million or 51 percent from 1969 to 1989. With more women entering paid employment, the labor force participation rate rose from 60.1 percent in 1969 to 66.5 percent in 1989.

Recent employment trends. For a time in the mid-1990s, it seemed that employment growth had slowed. In 1995 the labor force participation rate and the employment to population ratio were about where they were in 1989 and the unemployment rate was a bit higher (Table 4).[5] From the perspective of mid-1997, however, 1995 appears to have been merely a temporary breather during a quarter-century's strong upward march. Whether measured by total civilian employment or by the nonfarm payroll employment measure considered by some observers

to be more reliable, employment increased by more than 2 million per year from mid-1995 to mid-1997. The labor force participation rate and the employment to population ratio reached record highs in 1997.

All of the growth of employment since 1989 has occurred in private service-producing industries and in state and local government (Chart 3). Federal government employment fell about 10 percent from 1989 to mid-1997 and private goods-producing employment by 2 percent. The decline in goods-producing employment was centered in mining and manufacturing; employment in construction rose moderately.

The sustained ability of the U.S. economy to create new jobs and the willingness of the U.S. population to respond to employment opportunities represent remarkable success stories. Entry and reentry into the labor force, shifts by workers from declining to growing industries, and the absorption of immigrant labor into the work force all have demonstrated the responsiveness and flexibility of the U.S. economy. Concerns were being voiced in mid-1997, however, as to how much more the work force could expand in the near term without the lure of higher wages, which in turn could touch off price inflation.

Productivity and output gains. Output gains can be achieved through increases in hours worked or through labor productivity gains, that is, increases in the amount produced per worker hour. Productivity gains permit society to enjoy more goods and services for any given amount of time worked. Expressed differently, productivity gains help hold down price inflation; if increases in money wages are matched by increases in output, unit labor costs do not rise and prices need not be increased to cover increased labor costs.

Table 4: LABOR FORCE AND EMPLOYMENT MEASURES, 1989-1997

	1989	1990	1991	1992	1993	1994	1995	1996	1997 [1]
Civilian population, age 16 and over: [2]									
Population (thousands)	186,393	189,164	190,925	192,805	194,838	196,814	198,584	200,591	202,835
Labor force (thousands)	123,869	125,840	126,346	128,105	129,200	131,056	132,304	133,943	136,157
Employment (thousands)	117,342	118,793	117,718	118,492	120,259	123,060	124,900	126,708	129,462
Unemployment (thousands)	6,528	7,047	8,628	9,613	8,940	7,996	7,404	7,236	6,695
Unemployment rate (percent of labor force)	5.3	5.6	6.8	7.5	6.9	6.1	5.6	5.4	4.9
Employment to population ratio (percent)	63.0	62.8	61.7	61.5	61.7	62.5	62.9	63.2	63.8
Labor force participation rate (percent of population)	66.5	66.5	66.2	66.4	66.3	66.6	66.6	66.8	67.1
Nonfarm payroll employment:									
Total	107,884	109,403	108,249	108,601	110,713	114,163	117,191	119,523	121,854
Goods producing	25,254	24,905	23,745	23,231	23,352	23,908	24,265	24,431	24,694
Service producing	82,630	84,497	84,504	85,370	87,361	90,256	92,925	95,092	97,159
By sector:									
Private sector	90,105	91,098	89,847	89,956	91,872	95,036	97,885	100,076	102,259
Federal government	2,988	3,085	2,966	2,969	2,915	2,870	2,822	2,757	2,702
State and local government	14,791	15,219	15,436	15,675	15,926	16,258	16,484	16,690	16,893

1. Second quarter average

2. Data beginning with 1994 are not fully comparable with earlier periods because of changes in definnitions and methodology.

Source: Bureau of Labor Statistics

Ever since the mid-1970s, productivity gains have been suprisingly small by earlier historical standards. This disappointing performance continued during much of the 1990s, but data for the most recent few quarters have offered hints of improvement. For the nonfarm business sector, labor productivity in the second quarter of 1997 was 1.3 percent above the year earlier quarter. While this is a modest gain, it is an improvement over the near-zero productivity gains of 1993 through 1995.

Prices and Costs

During the 1990s the United States has moved closer to a situation of true price stability than at any time since the early 1960s. Three overall measures of price change, the GDP price index, the consumer price index (CPI), and the CPI for all items other than food and energy, each have shown diminishing rates of increase from 1990 through mid-1997. During the first half of 1997, prices rose at an annual rate of only 2.1 percent as measured by the GDP price index or 2.4 percent as measured by the CPI for all items other than food and energy (Table 5). Even more remarkable is the producer price index (PPI) for finished goods less food and energy, which rose only 0.6 percent during 1996 and actually declined during the first half of 1997.

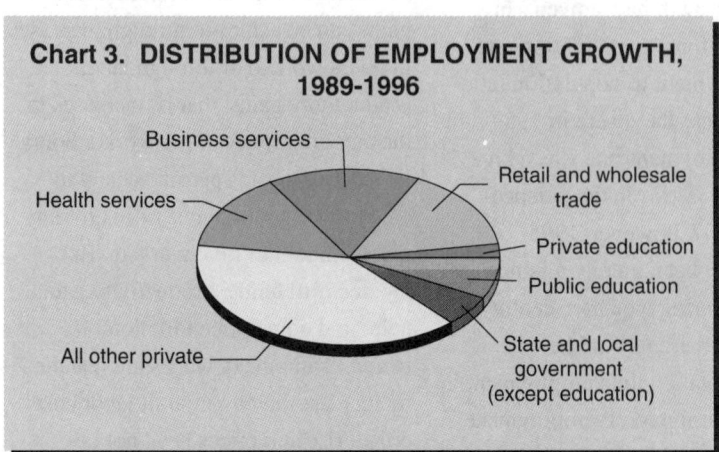

Chart 3. DISTRIBUTION OF EMPLOYMENT GROWTH, 1989-1996

Business services
Health services
Retail and wholesale trade
Private education
Public education
All other private
State and local government (except education)

Souce: Bureau of Labor Statistics

Table 5: PRICE AND COST MEASURES, 1989-1997
(annual percent change, fourth quarter to fourth quarter or December to December)

	1989	1990	1991	1992	1993	1994	1995	1996	1997[1]
Fourth quarter to fourth quarter:									
GDP price index	3.9	4.7	3.3	2.6	2.6	2.5	2.4	2.3	2.1
Employment cost index (all civilian workers):									
Total compensation	5.0	4.9	4.3	3.5	3.5	3.0	2.7	2.9	2.8
Wages and salaries	4.4	4.3	3.6	2.7	3.1	2.8	2.9	3.3	3.3
Productivity (output per worker hour):									
Nonfarm business	0.2	-0.6	2.2	3.5	-0.2	-0.1	0.4	1.2	2.0
Manufacturing	0.5	2.5	2.9	3.3	1.6	2.9	3.3	3.9	2.7
December to December:									
Consumer price indexes:									
All items	4.6	6.1	3.1	2.9	2.7	2.7	2.5	3.3	1.4
All items less food and energy	4.4	5.2	4.4	3.3	3.2	2.6	3.0	2.6	2.4
Food	5.6	5.3	1.9	1.5	2.9	2.9	2.1	4.3	0.9
Housing	3.9	4.5	3.4	2.6	2.7	2.2	3.0	2.9	2.3
Apparel and upkeep	1.0	5.1	3.4	1.4	0.9	-1.6	0.1	-0.2	2.3
Transportation	4.0	10.4	-1.5	3.0	2.4	3.8	1.5	4.4	-3.4
Medical care	8.5	9.6	7.9	6.6	5.4	4.9	3.9	3.0	3.0
Energy	5.1	18.1	-7.4	2.0	-1.4	2.2	-1.3	8.6	-8.9
Producer price indexes:									
Finished goods	4.9	5.7	-0.1	1.6	0.2	1.7	2.3	2.8	-3.4
Finished goods less food & energy	4.2	3.5	3.1	2.0	0.4	1.6	2.6	0.6	-0.3
Finished energy goods	9.5	30.7	-9.6	-0.3	-4.1	3.5	1.1	11.7	-16.0
Finished consumer foods	5.2	2.6	-1.5	1.6	2.4	1.1	1.9	3.4	-2.8
Intermediate materials, supplies, and components	2.3	4.3	-2.6	1.0	1.0	4.4	3.3	0.7	-1.7
Crude materials	7.1	6.0	-11.6	3.3	0.1	-0.5	5.5	14.7	-23.5
Crude foodstuffs and feedstuffs	2.8	-4.2	-5.8	3.0	7.2	-9.4	12.9	-1.0	-7.0
Crude nonfood materials	10.4	13.6	-14.6	3.4	-4.8	6.4	0.5	27.1	-33.2

1. Compound annual rate of change fourth quarter 1996 to second quarter 1997 or December 1996 to June 1997. Some data are peliminary.

Sources: Bureau of Economic Analysis, Bureau of Labor Statistics

Energy prices, a destabilizing factor during much of the 1970s and 1980s, held steady during the early 1990s, but showed a sharp increase during 1996. By mid-1997, however, most of the 1996 price increase had been reversed.

Food prices took a modest spurt in 1996, but in the first half of 1997, no major category of the CPI has shown a large increase. Medical care prices, which showed large increases in the early 1990s, rose at only a 3.0 percent rate in 1996 and the first half of 1997.

More fundamental factors in determining price levels are labor costs and labor productivity. The employment cost index, a comprehensive measure of labor costs, showed diminishing rates of increase from 1989 to 1995 and since has held to a moderate rate of increase of just under 3 percent. As noted above, even the small productivity gains of 1996 and early 1997 have been a welcome improvement over the three preceding years and may have helped hold down increases in labor costs during a period of increasingly full employment.

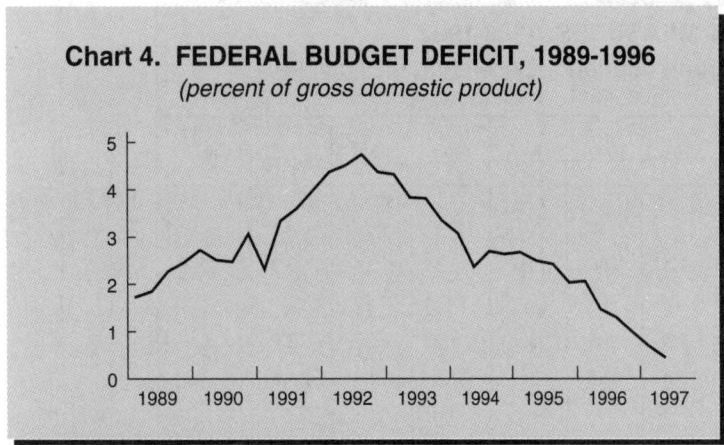

Chart 4. FEDERAL BUDGET DEFICIT, 1989-1996
(percent of gross domestic product)

Souce: Bureau of Economic Analysis

Federal Budget Trends

In the early 1990s a weak economy held down the growth of federal tax receipts while costs of Social Security benefits, Medicare, Medicaid and other programs of assistance to individuals grew rapidly. This combination resulted in a rapidly increasing federal deficit, which reached 4.5 percent of GDP in 1992 (Chart 4).

The size of the budget deficit, together with projections indicating its future growth, aroused great public concern, leading to highly-publicized efforts by Congress and the Administration to reach agreement on a plan to move toward a balanced budget. After much debate, two pieces of legislation—the Taxpayer Relief and Balanced Budget Acts of 1997—were enacted in the summer of 1997. These measures were intended to produce a balanced budget by the year 2002, although not all analysts agreed that the measures would, in fact, achieve that goal.

Meantime, while the budget debate was underway, the favorable impact of economic growth in increasing tax receipts and slowing the growth of spending on assistance programs was exerting a powerful short-run effect on the federal budget. By the second quarter of 1997 the deficit had fallen to 0.5 percent of GDP, the smallest since

the second quarter of 1979. Moreover, in its September 1997 report, the CBO projected small, but rising, budget surpluses from 2002 through 2007. These projected surpluses result from the combination of the budget legislation enacted in the summer and the favorable impact of the strong economy.[6]

Surprisingly large tax receipts were a principal factor in bringing down the deficit in 1997. Receipts in the second quarter were up 8 percent from the year earlier period, with personal tax and nontax receipts showing an 11 percent gain. Strong growth in receipts continued into the autumn. Detailed analysis of this welcome development was still underway in late 1997. The higher receipts clearly stemmed from the rising incomes associated with economic growth. Large capital gains due to the rapid rise in stock prices in 1996 and early 1997; executive bonuses based on good corporate performance; and the exercise of executive stock options may have been significant special factors.

The near balance achieved in the federal budget in 1997 will have some lasting effects, particularly in holding down future costs of debt service. However, continued control over the federal budget depends on a combina-

tion of sustained economic growth and sustained efforts to control the underlying trends in receipts and expenditures. The CBO projections showing a budget at, or close to, balance over the next 10 years assume (1) that the revenue and spending decisions reached in 1997 remain in place, and (2) that steady, moderate economic growth (about 2.4 percent per year) and moderate inflationary trends (about 3.0 percent per year) are sustained.

The United States in the World Economy

Economic growth in the 1990s has been stronger in the United States than in any of the other major industrial countries (Chart 5). Recession spread to all the major countries in the early 1990s, and recovery in most has been slower and less certain than in the United States. Recognition of the strength of the U.S. economy has contributed to a strong dollar and large inflows of foreign funds. U.S. purchases of imported goods and the nation's ability to sustain a large foreign trade deficit have helped sustain weaker economies abroad. At the same time, a strong dollar and the availability of imported goods have helped hold down the U.S. inflation rate.

Exports have become increasingly important to U.S. economic performance over the past three decades, constituting 12 percent of GDP in mid-1997, compared to only 5 percent in 1968. Recent strong growth of U.S. exports has demonstrated international competitiveness. Real (inflation-adjusted) U.S. exports grew almost 14 percent from the second quarter of 1996 to the second quarter of 1997. Imports grew by a similar amount, however, and the trade deficit remained large. The trade deficit stems entirely from trade in goods. U.S. trade in services, which include travel, transportation, royalties and license fees,

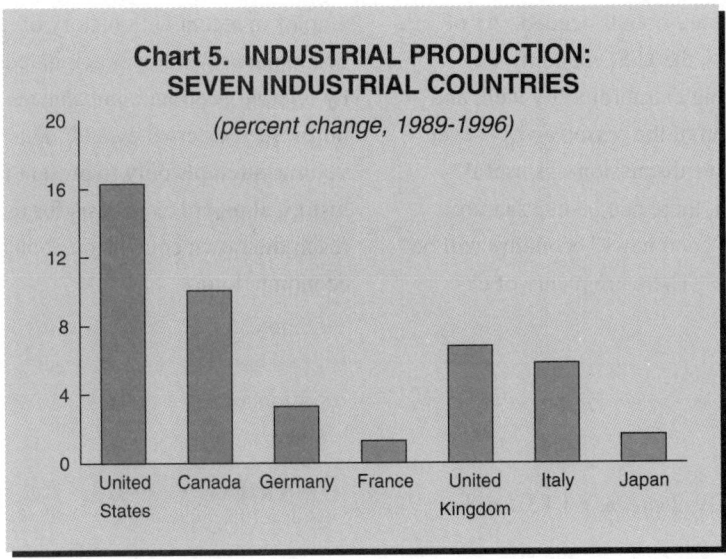

Chart 5. INDUSTRIAL PRODUCTION: SEVEN INDUSTRIAL COUNTRIES

(percent change, 1989-1996)

Source: The Conference Board

and other services, provides the United States with an increasingly important positive factor in its international balance. The surplus on trade in services reached $80 billion in 1996 and increased further, to an annual rate of about $82 billion, in the first half of 1997.

Understanding the "Good News" Economy

The seemingly new-found ability to combine high employment with near price stability presents a happy puzzle to observers. A widely-accepted theory about the U.S. economy had held that the lowest sustainable rate of unemployment was about 6 percent. Lower rates of unemployment would signal an overly-tight labor markets—markets in which wages would rise as employers competed for workers. Rising wages would, in turn, provoke accelerating price increases, leading eventually to recession and higher unemployment.

By mid-1997, the unemployment rate had remained consistently below 6 percent for almost three years—three years during which the inflation rate had diminished. Faced with this evidence, a number of economists centered new estimates of the lowest

sustainable rate of unemployment on a figure of about 5.5 percent.[7] However, since the unemployment rate in mid-1997 had been below 5.5 percent for over a year, while inflation continued to diminish, puzzles remained about how to explain the surprisingly good economic performance.

Labor markets considerations, investment performance, and international developments are among the factors which various analysts have suggested as possible contributors to the economy's ability to perform so well. Some of the more frequently made suggestions are summarized below, but with the caveat that these are merely possibilities which have been put forward as deserving further analysis.[8]

Labor markets. Two labor market factors frequently have been mentioned as possibly helping to restrain inflation. (1) *Fear of job loss.* Although total employment has grown rapidly, employment in some industries has declined. Corporate "downsizing" has enhanced the productivity of many firms, but has forced both managers and production workers to move to new, often less attractive, jobs in other industries. Many workers may have

come to feel that it is better to hang on to their current jobs than to risk unemployment by demanding higher wages. (2) *Reserve labor supply.* Some of the new jobs created in the last few years have been filled by young people just reaching working age and by reducing the number of unemployed. But these sources do not account for all the growth of employment. Jobs have also been filled by adult women entering or reentering the work force, retirees going back to work, welfare recipients being induced by stricter welfare rules to seek employment, and by immigrant labor.

Investment, capacity growth, and productivity. Investment in producers' durable equipment has grown strongly during the 1990s. Much of the spending has gone for computers and other "high tech" equipment. While labor markets grew tighter in 1996, the rate of industrial capacity utilization actually declined. There would appear to be few, if any, capacity bottlenecks pushing up prices. Beyond this, it has been suggested by some observers that actual productivity gains may significantly have exceeded those that can be measured in official statistics. It may be that the computer revolution has matured and that we are reaping important advantages not yet fully captured in traditional economic measures.

International factors. The strong dollar and the weak economic performance of some major U.S. trading partners have held down the prices of imports and this in turn has made it more difficult for domestic producers to raise prices.

Some of the above factors are temporary. Workers fear of job loss, for example, surely diminishes as the unemployment rate falls and competition for workers intensifies. Foreign economies will not remain weak and the dollar so strong indefinitely. Other factors may endure longer. There would seem to be no near-term limit on the potential availability of immigrant labor other than our willingness as a society to permit entry. And if we are reaping yet unmeasured benefits of new technology, this could represent an enduring improvement in the efficiency of our economy.

A cautionary note is needed. As of mid-1997, the U.S. economy was performing extraordinarily well, and discussion of the reasons why—even speculative discussion—is useful. However, there can be no assurance that the "good news" economy will be sustained. There are plenty of ex-amples in recent U.S. history of economic downturns precipitated either by internal economic imbalances or by unforeseen external events. This volume attempts only to present the historical record, as a basis for users to reach their own conclusion about the economic future.

---

[1] "Monetary Policy Report to the Congress," *Federal Reserve Bulletin*, Vol. 83, No. 8 (August 1997).

[2] Meyer, Laurence H., Member, Federal Reserve Board of Governors "Remarks before the 1998 Global Economic and Investment Outlook Conference," Carnegie Mellon Univeristy, Pittsburgh, PA, September 17, 1997 and Congressional Budget Office *The Economic and Budget Outlook: An Update* September 1997.

[3] International Monetary Fund, *World Economic Outlook*, October 1997.

[4] This and subsequent references to the federal budget deficit as a percent of GDP refer to the excess of current expenditure over receipts as published in the National Income and Product Accounts.

[5] Major 1994 changes in the design of the Current Population Survey, from which these data are derived, make precise comparisons inappropriate.

[6] Congressional Budget Office, *Op. Cit.*

[7] Meyer, *Op. Cit.* The Congressional Budget Office, however, placed its new estimate at 5.8 percent and assumed that within a few years the economy would revert to a situation in which 6 percent was the lowest sustainable unemployment rate. See Congressional Budget Office, *Op. Cit.*

[8] One source of additional discussion of these issues may be found in Greenspan, *Op. Cit.*

Developments in Economic Statistics: The Consumer Price Index

A revised consumer price index (CPI), based on consumer purchasing patterns during 1993-1995, will be introduced with the data for January 1998.

How well does the CPI measure inflation? Many economists long have argued that the actual cost of living rises more slowly than the CPI. However, the degree, if any, to which the CPI may overstate cost-of-living increases remains uncertain. The CPI was designed to be a measure of changes in the prices of a fixed market basket of goods. As such it can be only a partial measure of changes in the cost of living. However, recent and planned changes in the methods employed by the Bureau of Labor Statistics (BLS) to calculate the CPI will move the index toward a closer approximation of a cost-of-living measure.

A question that has received less attention is the extent to which the CPI provides comparably good measures of the cost of living for different income and age groups.

The consumer price index (CPI) is undergoing a comprehensive revision. An index based on consumer purchasing patterns in 1993 through 1995 will be initiated with the data for January 1998. Other important changes were introduced during 1997 or will be introduced from 1998 through 2000. Here we review the basic nature and uses of the CPI, recent public discussion of its adequacy, and the changes that are being introduced.

Recent Public Concern about the CPI

The consumer price index (CPI), always one of the most closely watched economic statistics, has attracted considerable controversy in the last few years. The questions recently raised about the CPI are not new; rather, the intensity of interest has stemmed largely from concerns about the growing impact of the CPI on the federal budget.

Many federal programs are indexed to the CPI; that is, various laws provide for automatic adjustment in tax obligations, benefit payments, and values of indexed treasury bonds based on the amount by which the CPI has increased. As concern has mounted about current and future costs of benefit programs, especially the Social Security benefits to which a growing retired population will be entitled, attention has been drawn to the budgetary savings that would be realized if the CPI rose more slowly— or if payments were indexed only by some fraction of the increase.

Does the CPI overstate increases in the cost of living? This question attracted congressional attention following well-publicized testimony by Federal Reserve Chairman Alan Greenspan, in which he presented estimates of overstatement and of the budgetary savings achievable if indexing of federal programs were adjusted downward to compensate for it. Subsequently, the Senate Finance Committee held hearings at which 15 economists presented their views on whether and, if so, by how much the CPI overstates cost-of-living increases.[1] The Finance Committee then appointed a commission, chaired by economist Michael Boskin, to study the question. The commission issued its report in December 1996.[2] In June 1997, the Bureau of Labor Statistics (BLS), responding to a congressional request, presented its analysis of the Boskin Commission recommendations and described recent and planned changes in the CPI.[3]

What is the CPI?

The CPI is a measure of the average change in the prices paid by urban consumers for a fixed market basket of goods and services. Representative prices are collected each month from large samples of housing units and retail and service establishments. This information is used to construct about 200 "item category" indexes, which subsequently are combined into broader categories and ultimately into the overall CPI.[4]

Selection of the items for inclusion in the market basket is based on information from the BLS' Consumer Expenditure Survey, a comprehensive household survey that collects data on the amounts consumers spend on various goods and services. Selection of the outlets from which CPI prices are collected is based on the BLS' Point of Purchase Survey, which provides estimates of consumer shopping patterns; that is, of relative reliance on traditional retail stores, discount outlets, catalog shopping, or other means of purchasing.

Thus the CPI is carefully designed to yield information on prices of the goods and services consumers actually buy in the places where they actually shop. In constructing the index, the price of each item is weighted to represent the share of consumer dollars actually spent for this item category in a base period. As part of the 1998 revision the base period will shift from the 1982-1984 base in use since 1987 to a new 1993-1995 base.

CPI data are published each month on a fixed schedule. In addition to the overall CPI, indexes are published for each major category of consumer spending and for subcategories and individual items within each broad group. The revised CPI will have eight broad groups: food and beverages,

housing, apparel, transportation, medical care, recreation, education and communication, and other goods and services. Table 1 provides an example of the hierarchy of groups, subgroups, and items used in the CPI program.

Uses of the CPI

The CPI serves both analytic and administrative uses. Analytically, it is looked to as one of the principal measures of the overall rate of price change as well as a source of information on which particular categories of goods and services are the principal contributors to this overall rate. Conclusions about current and prospective price increases enter importantly into the policy decisions of the fiscal and monetary authorities, and these decisions need to be based on accurate information. An overstatement of the seriousness of inflation, for example, could lead to an excessive tightening of monetary policy, producing an unnecessary choking off of economic growth. Conversely, an understatement of inflation could lead to failure to act in a timely manner to slow an overheating economy.

Private individuals also rely on information from the CPI as a factor in investment decisions. The nature and timing of bond offerings, stock market transactions, and personal savings decisions all are influenced by the CPI.

Administratively, the CPI is used not only for the indexing of federal programs, as already discussed, but for adjustment of private wages and salaries. These adjustments may be required under union contracts, or they may occur less formally in nonunion situations. The CPI also enters into many other

types of contracts, including alimony and child support agreements.

What is a Cost-of-Living Index?

However excellent the CPI may be as a measure of *price* change, it is still only a partial and imperfect measure of changes in the *cost of living*. Consumers do not purchase exactly the same goods and services month after month. Rather, they shift their purchasing patterns as the prices of some items rise faster than others; they take advantage of special sales at particular outlets; they continually introduce new items into their "market basket" and drop old ones. In addition, consumers pay for some items only indirectly, and these items are not included in the CPI. Examples of items not covered are "free" public schools and parks; these are paid for indirectly through tax dollars.[5]

As explained in the BLS' June 1997 report to Congress, a cost-of-living index:

> *compares the cost to the consumer at different points in time of maintaining a constant standard of well-being ... In the most general sense, the cost-of-living index answers the following question: "What is the minimum change in expenditure that would be required in order to leave a specified consumer unit indifferent (or as well off) between a specified reference period's prices and a comparison period's prices?" The cost-of-living index approximated by the CPI is a subindex of the all-encompassing cost-of-living concept ... The BLS defines the scope of the CPI to include only market goods and services or government-provided goods for which explicit user charges are assessed.[6]*

Concern about the lack of a true cost-of-living index and recognition of the difficulties of achieving such an index

---

Table 1. ILLUSTRATIVE EXTRACT FROM THE 1998 CPI ITEM STRUCTURE

MAJOR GROUP: FOOD AND BEVERAGE

FOOD
　FOOD AT HOME
　　Cereals and Bakery Products
　　　Cereals and cereal products
　　　　Flour and prepared flour mixes
　　　　Breakfast cereal
　　　　Rice, pasta, cornmeal

　　　Bakery Products
　　　　Bread
　　　　Fresh biscuits, rolls, muffins
　　　　Cakes, cupcakes, and cookies
　　　　Other bakery products

are not new. The results of perhaps the most comprehensive review of government price statistics ever undertaken were published in 1961 in a report usually referred to as the Stigler Committee Report after the committee's chairman, economist George Stigler.[7] This report outlined steps that could be taken to gradually move the CPI closer to a cost-of-living index.

Over the years since the Stigler Report was issued, the BLS has conducted a great deal of research; has adopted the concept of cost of living as a measurement objective; and has introduced a number of specific changes into the CPI. Important among the changes are extensive efforts to adjust for changes in the quality of products and the introduction of the Point of Purchase Survey mentioned earlier.[8]

The intent of the BLS to continue to work toward a cost-of-living index was reiterated in its recent report to Congress:

> ... the BLS long has said that it operates within a cost-of-living framework in producing the CPI. That framework has guided and will continue to guide, operational decisions about the construction of the index. Putting things slightly differently, if the BLS staff or other technical experts knew how to produce a true cost-of-living index on a monthly production schedule, that would be what we would produce.[9]

The CPI: Strengths and Limitations as a Cost-of-Living Index

The fact that the CPI is an imperfect measure of the cost of living does not necessarily mean that it *overstates* changes in the cost of living. Many economists believe that it does, but others argue that this is not necessarily the case.

The Boskin Commission concluded that, viewed as a cost-of-living measure, the present CPI is biased upward by about 1.1 percentage points per year; that is, that the actual cost of the goods and services purchased by consumers rises about 1.1 percentage points per year less than the rate of price increase as measured by the CPI. Some part of this upward bias could, in the commission's view, be removed by changes in BLS procedures. Much of it, however, as the commission acknowledged, lies outside the present ability of BLS to measure or adjust for in any precise, objective manner. Among the sources of bias identified by the commission were item substitution, measurement of quality change, and delays in introducing new products into the index. Each of these areas has attracted subsequent debate as to how accurately the commission measured the presumed bias in the CPI and, indeed, whether such bias exists and is amenable to measurement.

Substitution bias. The Boskin Commission estimated that substitution bias causes the CPI to overstate increases in the cost of living by .4 percentage points per year. By substitution bias is meant the failure of the CPI to take into account the extent to which consumers substitute some items for others when relative prices change, that is, when some prices increase more than others. Substitution may occur among individual items of the same type, as when one variety of apples is substituted for another, or among items of different types, as when oranges are purchased rather than apples.

There is no doubt that some substitution occurs in response to changes in relative prices. The questions revolve around how much substitution and how it can best be measured. While many consumers may substitute one variety

of apple for another, or oranges for apples, many others will continue to buy their favorite variety of apple unless its price rises by a very large amount. And some items that fall within the same broad category of goods or services are not realistically substitutable: dental care, for example, is not a substitute for heart surgery.

To account for substitution among individual items the Boskin Commission recommended a change in the formula used to calculate the individual CPI item indexes. In the judgment of BLS experts, the approach recommended by the commission (the geometric mean formula) may be appropriate where a high degree of substitution among items occurs. It is not appropriate for item categories where little or no substitution occurs. Since extensive substitution does not occur within all item groups, the BLS concluded that there is good reason to believe that the commission overestimated the effect on the CPI of this type of bias.

The BLS has begun issuing a monthly experimental measure that is constructed using a geometric mean formula for all index components and plans to make a decision by the end of 1997 as to which, if any, components of the official CPI should use this approach. The likely date for the introduction into the official CPI of any such changes would be with the release of the January 1999 data.[10]

With respect to substitution among broader categories of goods and services, the BLS is in general agreement with the Boskin Commission that such substitution occurs and that failure to account for it causes the CPI to somewhat overstate cost-of-living increases. However, the BLS concluded that methods and data for accurately computing an index that takes this substitution into account on a timely monthly basis are not presently available. The BLS plans to continue research in this area and, assuming funds are made available, presently plans to begin publishing an index that incorporates the effect of this "upper level" substitution in 2002.[11]

Quality change and new product introduction. Consumer goods and services are continually undergoing changes in their characteristics. Some of these changes represent clear improvements in quality, as when a change in the design of a household appliance increases its reliability and durability. Other changes may represent a deterioration in quality, and, in many cases, the question of whether a change is or is not an improvement may be very much a matter of opinion. Consumers are divided, for example, about whether the required inclusion of air bags in new automobiles is desirable. The question of whether the quality of private higher education has improved or deteriorated can provoke heated debate.

The BLS devotes much effort to measurement of quality changes and to corresponding adjustments in the CPI. These adjustments result in a substantial reduction in the measured rate of price increase. According to BLS estimates, a CPI subindex covering about 70 percent of the total CPI would have risen 3.9 percentage points in 1995 if quality adjustment procedures had not been applied. With the quality adjustments, the index rose only 2.2 percentage points. Thus, quality adjustments to items comprising about 70 percent of the CPI reduced the rate of increase in this broad subindex by about 1.7 percentage points in this single year.[12]

In addition to changes in the quality of existing goods and services, new products are continually being introduced and sometimes come into widespread use very quickly. Cellular phones, home computers, world wide web access, and automatic teller machines are just a few examples of products and services that have been widely adopted over a fairly short span of years. Although comprehensive revision of the CPI has occurred only once every 10 years or so, the BLS has established procedures for introducing new items into the index between these revisions. The specific stores in which prices are collected and the specific items priced are reselected on a five year cycle, with 20 percent of the sample replaced each year.[13]

Despite the efforts already made, the Boskin Commission concluded that there remains in the CPI an overstatement of cost-of-living increases of .6 percent (out of their estimated total overstatement of 1.1 percent) per year due to quality improvements for which inadequate adjustments are made and to new products that are not introduced into the CPI as quickly as they should be.

The BLS, however, has identified a number of problems with the analysis underlying this particular conclusion of the Boskin Commission. Some estimates of the value of quality improvements are simply judgments by the commission members, not backed by any quantitative studies. In other cases, the commission drew conclusions from partial evidence, one example being their comparison of the official CPI index for apparel with Sears catalogue prices for items whose characteristics remain unchanged from one year to the next.

The BLS makes the following general points with respect to the commission's findings in this area:

the commission's estimates of bias are made case by case using a variety of methods, without any clear statement of what methods are appropriate to use in each circumstance ... Also, in general, the commission's discussion of quality/new goods biases does not include explicit recommendations regarding the adoption of procedures to correct the problems it believes exist ... For production of the CPI and other national statistics the BLS must use methods that are objective, reproducible, and verifiable.

The commission also failed to make any systematic effort to explore the possible existence of negative biases in the CPI. Other analysts have hypothesized reduced convenience and comfort of air travel and deteriorating quality of higher education as examples of quality decreases that are ignored in the CPI. More generally, ... the BLS often hears complaints about broad-ranging declines in the quality of customer service ... [14]

For BLS, and for data users, the important question is not whether the Boskin Commission, or anyone else, has correctly measured any bias in the index, but what might be done to improve measurement of quality change and pricing of new items. Medical care is one difficult area, partly because of the rapid introduction of new, cost-saving treatment procedures. Here, the BLS has made recent changes in its methodology. Beginning in January 1997, the CPI for hospital services prices completed treatments rather than individual medical inputs.[15] Another area receiving attention is that of hi-tech consumer goods. In this category, it frequently becomes possible to purchase items that offer enhanced performance at lower prices. Personal computers are one of the most obvious examples. It is thus necessary to develop price indexes that measure the performance characteristics of the product rather than its physical characteristics. Projects are underway at BLS to expand the use of such measures.[16]

Equal CPI Representation for All Income Groups?

A question that has received less attention in recent public discussion is how well the CPI represents changes in the cost of living for households at different income levels.

The overall CPI is obtained by aggregating the indexes for the different categories of expenditures. This involves decisions on how much weight to give each category. Under present procedures the weights are based on total economy-wide spending in each category. This procedure gives relatively more weight to the spending patterns of upper-income households. Not only do upper-income household spend more per person than lower-income households, but the distribution of expenditure across categories is different. Car phones, personal computers, and air travel are examples of goods and services more likely to be purchased by upper-income households. Many of these items are ones that have been identified by the Boskin Commission or others as items for which failure to adequately account for quality change or new product introduction introduces upward bias into the CPI.

Thus, it is argued by some experts that the CPI may overstate cost-of-living increases for upper-income groups while possibly understanding cost-of-living changes for low-income households.[17] It is argued that this problem could be lessened if the CPI were weighted, not by total economy-wide spending, but by the average percent distribution of expenditures of indi-

vidual households. In other words, rather than giving each dollar of aggregate consumer expenditure equal weight, each household, regardless of income level, would be given equal weight.[18]

Can a Single CPI Serve All Uses?

As noted above, the CPI attempts to serve a multiplicity of analytic and administrative uses. Changes that might improve its usefulness for one purpose could make it less useful for others.

An index weighted by households rather than by aggregate consumer expenditure might, as discussed in the previous section, better measure cost-of-living changes for middle- and lower-income households. Thus, such an index might be especially suitable as a guide to adjusting federal benefit payments, but perhaps less suitable for adjusting tax obligations or indexed bonds. Furthermore, such an index would not be as useful as the present CPI for supplying the information needed to estimate real (inflation-adjusted) gross domestic product (GDP) and its components. The solution to this conflict may lie in computing different aggregations of the same basic price information for different purposes.

In another example, some uses of the CPI require that the estimate initially published each month be treated as the final estimate. Once adjustments to benefit payments, wage rates, or other contractual payments have been determined and payments made, it would be neither feasible nor desirable to revise these

payments based on a revised CPI. This has been a strong argument against moving to an index that continuously incorporate shifts in consumer purchasing, since the data needed to measure such shifts currently are not available on a timely monthly basis. However, an annual index taking shifting purchasing patterns into account could be constructed and revised periodically as more data became available. Such an index could be valuable for analytic purposes.

In yet another example, a CPI based on the spending patterns of the elderly might be more appropriate for adjusting social security benefits than one that represents an average for all age groups.

Considerations such as these that have led to suggestions for a family of indexes. The BLS has conducted and plans to continue conducting research on alternative indexes.[19]

A Summary of Recent and Forthcoming CPI Changes [20]

Some of the important CPI changes that have been or will be introduced as part of the "1998" revisions are summarized in Table 2 and described briefly below.

Table 2
MAJOR MILESTONES IN THE 1998 CPI REVISION

February 1997 (index for January 1997):
Introduce revised hospital services item structure and sample

February 1998 (index for January 1998):
Introduce new geographic sample and item structure
Update expenditure weights to 1993-1995

February 1999 (index for January 1999):
Introduce new housing sample and estimator
Rebase CPI to 1993-1995=100

Table 3. CPI MAJOR GROUPS, 1998 and 1987	
1998	**1987-1997**
Food and Beverages	Food and Beverages
Housing	Housing
Apparel	Apparel and Upkeep
Transportation	Transportation
Medical Care	Medical Care
Recreation	Entertainment
Education and Communication	Other Goods and Services
Other Goods and Services	

Item structure. Perhaps most immediately noticeable to users will be the regrouping of the CPI items into eight broad categories, as compared to the present seven (Table 3). There also will be shifts of individual items among major groups and additions, discontinuations, and redefinitions of individual items.[21] Among other changes, video and audio equipment are moved from Household Furnishings to the new Recreation Group and personal computers and other information processing equipment are moved from household furnishings to the new Education and Communication Group.

Expenditure weights and geographic sample. Two other basic changes introduced with the data for January 1998 will be the updating of the expenditure weights and the redesign of the geographic sample. The new expenditure weights assigned to each item category will be based on evidence from the Consumer Expenditure Survey showing how consumers allocated their spending during the three-year period 1993-1995. The new geographic sample, that is, the selection of the geographic areas where prices will be collected, will be based on the distribution of the U.S. population at the time of the 1990 Census. Prices will be collected in 87 urban areas throughout the United States ranging in size from the largest metropolitan areas to smaller urban areas that lie outside of metropolitan areas.

Hospital services. As mentioned, revised pricing procedures for hospital services went into effect with the data for January 1997. Previously, prices were collected for individual items, such as a unit of blood or a hospital inpatient day. The new procedure prices combined sets of charges for goods and services as shown on selected patient bills. This approach provides a better measure of actual transaction prices, that is, of what patients actually pay for the set of goods and services associated with a particular type of treatment. In many instances, the bundle of goods and services associated with the treatment of a particular medical condition is undergoing rapid change. The new pricing procedures are designed to better identify changes in the cost of treating a condition, as opposed to changes in the cost of individual goods and services.

Housing. Beginning with the index for January 1999, a new housing unit sample and a revised method of pricing homeowners' cost of shelter will be introduced. Since 1983 changes in the cost of owner-occupied housing have been represented by a BLS estimate of changes in the amounts home owners would have to pay if they were renting rather than buying their homes (i.e., the price of the shelter service provided by owner-occupied homes). This basic concept is being maintained; what will change is the sample from which the data are derived and the methodology used to obtain the estimates.

The new sample will consist entirely of rental units and will be based on data from the 1990 Census, augmented by information on housing constructed since the census was taken. Homeowners' costs of shelter will be obtained by reweighting the rent data to represent the type and location of owner-occupied housing. This represents a return to the method that was used from January 1983 through January 1987, but with an improved sample and collection method. After January 1987, BLS began using a sample of owner-occupied homes and matched them with the closest equivalent rental housing to determine the appropriate rent change for estimating homeowners' costs of shelter. This procedure led to a number of technical difficulties, and the BLS judges that the new sample and new procedures will provide better estimates.

The changes being made to the CPI represent continuing BLS improvement efforts and the periodic updating that occurs about once every ten years rather than specific responses to recent public discussion and recommendations. Nonetheless, they are important improvements in CPI which will, in fact, move the CPI in the direction of some of the recent recommendations.

1 *Consumer Price Index*, Hearings before the Committee on Finance, U.S. Senate, U.S. Government Printing Office, 1995.

2 *Toward a More Accurate Measure of the Cost of Living*, Final Report to the Senate Finance Committee from the Advisory Commission to Study the Consumer Price Index, December 4, 1996.

3 *Measurement Issues in the Consumer Price Index*, Bureau of Labor Statistics, U.S. Department of Labor, June, 1997.

4 In fact, two CPI's are published each month. The CPI-W represents prices paid by urban wage earners and clerical workers, and the CPI-U represents prices paid by all urban consumers. The CPI-U is the featured index in BLS data presentations, and it is used to index tax obligations and indexed bonds. It is the CPI-W, however, that is used to index many federal benefits.

5 The CPI includes the impact of property and sales taxes but not of income or payroll taxes, except to the extent that such taxes are passed on in higher prices.

6 BLS, *Op Cit.*

7 *Government Price Statistics*, U.S. Congress Joint Economic Committee, 87th Congress, 1st Session, January 24, 1961.

8 BLS, *Op. Cit._* and Popkin, Joel "Improving the CPI: The Record and Suggested Next Steps," *Business Economics*, Vol. XXXII, No 3. (July 1997), pp. 42-47.

9 BLS, *Op Cit.*

10 *Ibid.*

11 *Ibid.*

12 *Ibid.*

13 *Ibid.*

14 *Ibid.*

15 See Elaine M. Cardenas "Revision of the CPI Hospital Services Component." *Monthly Labor Review*, Vol. 19, No. 12 (December 1996).

16 BLS, *Op. Cit.*

17 Popkin, *Op. Cit.*

18 *Ibid.*

19 Some results of BLS research can be found in Thesia I. Garner, David S. Johnson, and Mary F. Kokoski, "An Experimental Consumer Price Index for the Poor," *Monthly Labor Review*, Vol. 119, No. 9 (September 1996); Nathan Amble and Kenneth Stewart, "Experimental Price Index for Elderly Consumers," *Monthly Labor Review*, Vol. 117, No. 5 (May 1994); Kenneth Stewart and Joseph Pavalone, "Experimental CPI for Americans 62 Years of Age and Older," *CPI Detailed Report,* April 1996; and Brent Moulton and Karin Smedley, "A Comparison of Estimates for Elementary Aggregates of the CPI," Bureau of Labor Statistics Working Paper, June 1995.

20 Material in this section is based on John S. Greenlees and Charles C. Mason, "Overview of the 1998 Revision of the Consumer Price Index," *Monthly Labor Review*, Vol. 119, No. 12 (December 1996). The same issue of the Monthly Labor Review also contains more detailed articles on the redesigned geographic sample, the revised item structure, the revised housing sample, the revised hospital component, the new method for selecting outlet samples, and publication plans for the revised CPI.

21 See Walter Lane "Changing the Item Structure of the Consumer Price Index*,*" *Monthly Labor Review* Vol. 119, No. 12 (December 1996). "Appendix 1: Item Structure 1987 and 1998" in the same issue provides a complete listing of the old and new item structure.

Developments in Economic Statistics: The North American Industry Classification System[1]

The United States, Canada, and Mexico have developed a common North American Industrial Classification System (NAICS). The revised system recognizes the information industries as a major economic sector and expands the classifications for service industries. In the United States, economic census data for 1997 will be collected in 1998 using the new classifications; publication of these data will begin in 1999. Full implementation of the NAICS by all the U.S. statistical agencies will take until 2004 or longer.

The North American Industry Classification System (NAICS) replaces the existing Standard Industrial Classification (SIC) system. The new system was officially adopted early in 1997, and the first publication of economic census data based on the new classifications is scheduled for early 1999.

Background

For more than 50 years, the SIC system has been used by federal agencies—and many private sources—to classify establishments by industry and to collect, tabulate, and publish statistical information. The purpose has been to provide analytically useful standardized groupings and to promote comparability of data from different sources.

Despite periodic revisions, the basic structure of the SIC has remained substantially the same over the past half-century. In recent years, the SIC has been criticized for having an over-emphasis on manufacturing, inadequate service categories, and a lack of adequate classifications for new industries.

In 1992 U.S. statistical agencies began working with their Canadian and Mexican counterparts to develop a common North American classification system. The objectives of this effort were much broader than for previous revisions of the U.S. SIC. Not only were new industries to be identified, but the system was to be reorganized according to a more consistent economic principle—according to types of production activities performed—

rather than the mixture of production-based and market-based categories in the SIC. Most importantly, the system was to accommodate the industrial classification needs of the three North American countries and provide them with a common basis for analyzing industrial structure and performance.

The new NAICS classifications now have been officially adopted by all three countries. The new U.S. code has been published in the *Federal Register*, and an official printed manual is scheduled for release by the Office of Management and Budget (OMB) around the end of 1997. Background papers explaining the principles on which the new system is based also have been made available.[2] The tasks that now remain—and they are daunting—are the actual implementation of the new system by the statistical agencies and the transition to the new concepts by suppliers and users of economic data.

The NAICS Structure

The NAICS classifications incorporate major changes from the familiar SIC. A number of new major sectors are created, and a new 6-digit industry numbering system is used.

The NAICS sectors. NAICS groups the economy into 20 broad sectors, compared to the 10 divisions of the SIC system (Table 1). Many of the new sectors consist largely of recognizable parts of SIC divisions. The transportation sector, for example, is broken out from the SIC Transportation, Communications, and Utilities

Code	NAICS Sector	SIC Divisions Making the Largest Contributions
	TABLE 1. NAICS SECTORS AND THEIR CORRESPONDING SIC DIVISIONS	
11	Agriculture, Forestry, Hunting, and Fishing	Agriculture, Forestry, and Fishing Manufacturing
21	Mining	Mineral Industries
22	Utilities	Transportation, Communications, and Utilities
23	Construction	Construction Industries
31-33	Manufacturing	Manufacturing
43	Wholesale Trade	Wholesale Trade
44-45	Retail Trade	Retail Trade Wholesale Trade
48-49	Transportation and Warehousing	Transportation, Communications, and Utilities
51	Information	Transportation, Communications, and Utilities Manufacturing Service Industries
52	Finance and Insurance	Finance, Insurance, and Real Estate
53	Real Estate and Rental and Leasing	Finance, Insurance, and Real Estate Service Industries
54	Professional, Scientific, and Technical Services	Service Industries
55	Management of Companies and Enterprises	Finance, Insurance, and Real Estate auxiliary establishments in all industries
57	Administrative and Support, Waste Management and Remediation Services	Service Industries Transportation, Communications, and Utilities Manufacturing Construction Industries
61	Education Services	Service Industries
62	Health Care and Social Assistance	Service Industries
71	Arts, Entertainment, and Recreation	Service Industries Retail Trade Finance, Insurance, and Real Estate
72	Accommodation and Food Services	Retail Trade Service Industries
81	Other Services (except Public Administration)	Service Industries Finance, Insurance, and Real Estate
93	Public Administration	Public Administration Service Industries

division. Similarly, the SIC division for Service Industries has been subdivided to form several sectors, including Professional, Scientific, and Technical Services; Education Services; and Health and Social Assistance.

Other sectors represent combinations of pieces from more than one SIC Division. The new Information sector includes major components from Transportation, Communications, and Utilities (broadcasting and telecommunications), Manufacturing (publishing), and Services Industries (software publishing, data processing, information services, motion picture, and sound recording). The Accommodations and Food Services sector brings together hotels and other lodging places from Service Industries and eating and drinking places from Retail Trade.

The NAICS numbering system. NAICS industries are identified by a 6-digit code, in contrast to the 4-digit SIC code. The longer code accommodates the larger number of sectors and allows more flexibility in designating subsectors. It also provides for additional detail not necessarily appropriate for all three NAICS countries. The international NAICS agreement fixes only the first five digits of the code. The sixth digit, where used, identifies subdivisions of NAICS industries that accommodate user needs in individual countries. Thus, 6-digit U.S. codes may differ from counterparts in Canada or Mexico, but at the 5-digit level they are standardized.

Table 2 illustrates the hierarchic structure of the NAICS codes.

Data Comparability

Because the NAICS is so different from the SIC, users wanting to con-

Table 2. EXAMPLES OF NAICS HIERARCHY

NAICS level	NAICS code	Description
		Example #1
Sector	31-33	Manufacturing
Subsector	334	Computer and electronic product manufacturing
Industry group	3346	Manufacturing and reproduction of magnetic and optical media
Industry	33461	Manufacturing and reproduction of magnetic and optical media
U.S. Industry	334611	Reproduction of software
		Example #2
Sector	51	Information
Subsector	513	Broadcasting and telecommunications
Industry group	5133	Telecommunications
Industry	51332	Wireless telecommunications carriers, except satellite
U.S. Industry	513321	Paging transmissions services

struct historical time series may face substantial difficulties with respect to some industries. Data for two-thirds of all 4-digit SICs will be derivable from the NAICS data, either because the industry is not being changed (other than in code) or because new industries are being defined as subdivisions of old ones. For the remaining industries, however, there will be breaks in series, and the broad sectors like manufacturing and retailing that we use to describe our economy in everyday conversation will lose some of their historical comparability.

The problem of data comparability was recognized, but the government committee working on the new industrial classification concluded that "it is unproductive to collect and maintain time series data that have questionable value. Thus, it may be preferable to accept a onetime break in historical continuity if the benefits of conversion to a new classification structure are apparent and accepted by users."[3]

Ideally, it would be desirable to retabulate historical data, such as the results of the 1992 Economic Censuses, using the new classifications. This will not be possible for all industries. Many of the new classifications require information that is not available from the 1992 Census questionnaires. However, as part of its publication plans for the 1997 Economic Censuses, the Census Bureau plans to construct bridge tables and comparative statistics tables to assist data users in making the best possible historical comparisons.[4]

Data Collection and Publication Plans

The first data collection using the new classifications will begin early in 1998. The first data publication is planned for 1999, but full implementation by all the statistical agencies will take until 2004 or longer.

The economic censuses. Early in 1998 the Census Bureau will begin the collection of data for the 1997 Economic Censuses, that is, data pertaining to the year 1997. The questionnaires will be designed to enable the bureau to classify each establishment according to both the SIC and the NAICS.

In early 1999, in its first "advance" report covering the entire economy, the bureau plans to publish national data for 1997 on a NAICS basis (3-digit sector detail), and comparative statistics for 1997 and 1992 on a 1987 SIC basis (2-digit detail). State level data also will be published, but in less detail; only data for the NAICS 2-digit sectors and comparative statistics for the 10 SIC divisions will be shown.

Roughly a year later, in early 2000, the bureau plans to publish detailed bridge tables covering all industries at the national level, and comparative statistics for all industries at both state and national levels. All other data will be published only on a new, NAICS basis. No comparability tables will be available for metropolitan areas, counties, or cities. All substate data from the 1997 Census will be published on a NAICS basis only.

The Census Bureau's ability to provide comparative and bridge tables is constrained not only by the inherent limitations of the available data, but also by the need for disclosure-avoidance procedures. Federal statistical agencies protect the confidentiality of the information provided by businesses by avoiding the publication of any data that could be identified with an individual establishment or company. Some of the SIC-to-NAICS comparisons may contain so few establishments that the comparisons are dominated by individual companies that could be identified. This would preclude publication of some parts of the comparative and bridge tables, even at the national level.

Budgetary limitations also constrain the ability of the Census Bureau and other statistical agencies to move quickly to fully implement the NAICS. For example, the agricultural services, forestry, and fisheries division of the SIC is not covered by the economic censuses. NAICS moves some activities from this division into other economic sectors. Veterinary services and landscape design, for example, are moved to the Professional, Scientific and Technical Services sector. Summaries for that sector in the economic censuses will be incomplete until funding is available to cover the industries not previously included.

Data collection and publication plans: other statistical programs. The introduction of NAICS will have a far-reaching impact on the entire U.S. statistical system. The Census Bureau's many annual and monthly economic statistics, the national accounts statistics from the Bureau of Economic Analysis, the Federal Reserve Board's industrial production statistics, and the employment, price, and productivity statistics from the Bureau of Labor Statistics all must be converted to the new system. Implementation will, at best, take several years. Table 3 summarizes agencies present time schedule for publishing NAICS-based data from some of the major statistical programs. Difficulties in obtaining funding could cause current conversion plans to be further stretched out.

Among presently-planned implementation activities are the following.

The Census Bureau will accelerate its business sample revision for the monthly and annual surveys of retail trade, wholesale trade, and service industries. This sample revision has occurred five years after the reference year for recent censuses; this time it is hoped to do it in three years to allow earlier implementation of NAICS for these current economic surveys.

The Census Bureau, in consultation with the Bureau of Economic Analysis (BEA) and other agencies, is considering possibilities for redefining the scope of its economic surveys. For example, Retail Sales will cover fewer industries under NAICS, particularly since eating and drinking places are moving to the Accommodations Sector. The Census Bureau may combine retail and service surveys so as to be able to report monthly changes in "personal consumption expenditures," consistent with concepts used by BEA in the national accounts. BEA's ability to maintain the quality of their estimates of national account aggregates will be dependent on continuing to receive economic survey data from the Census Bureau that is at least as comprehensive as that presently available, despite the shifts in the sectoral classifications for some industries.

The Bureau of Economic Analysis will use the 1997 Census data to develop NAICS-based input-output tables for 1997 and hopes to complete this process by 2002. In its surveys of foreign direct investment, BEA will begin data collection using the NAICS categories in 1998, with publication scheduled for the summer of 1999.

The Bureau of Labor Statistics (BLS) plans to have both NAICS and SIC codes assigned to all establishments in its employment and wages (ES-202) program by the end of the year 2000, assuming funding can be provided to states to accomplish the manual coding of 3.5 million establishments in industries being redefined. The dual-coded database will serve as the foundation for converting a number of other BLS programs. Converting the BLS productivity time series is dependent on the availability of NAICS-based input from Census and BEA, hence publication of these data is not expected until 2004.

The conversion of economic statistics from the SIC system to NAICS is a crucial step toward a strong foundation for statistical information in coming decades. However, the transition from the old to the new system can be obtained only at the cost of some loss of historical comparability in economic data. The conversion process will require major efforts on the part of the statistical agencies and much patience on the part of data users.

TABLE 3. TENTATIVE PUBLICATION SCHEDULE FOR SELECTED NAICS-BASED DATA

Bureau of the Census	
1997 Economic Census Reports	1999-2001
Export/Import Data Conversion	1998
County Business Patterns	2000
Annual Survey of Manufactures	2000
Other Current Economic Surveys	2001
Bureau of Economic Analysis	
Direct Investment Surveys	1999-2002
Benchmark Input-Output Accounts	2002
Corporate Profits	2001
State Personal Income	2001
Gross Product Originating by Industry	2002
Real Inventories and Sales	2002
Gross State Product by Industry	2003
Bureau Of Labor Statistics	
Employment and Wages Report	2001
Current Employment Statistics Survey	2003
Occupational Employment Statistics	2003
Producer Price Index/1997 Net Output Indexes	2004

[1] Much of the information in this article is adapted from Paul T. Zeisset and Mark E. Wallace, *How NAICS Will Affect Data Users*, U.S. Bureau of the Census, 1997. This and many other documents pertaining to NAICS may be found on the Bureau of the Census web site at the following address: http://www.census.gov/epcd/www/naics.html

[2] The Federal Register Notice containing the NAICS structure was published on April 9, 1997. This and previous notices and the background papers are available on the Bureau of the Census web site referenced in the note above.

[3] U.S. Economic Classification Policy Committee Issue Paper Number 5 "The Impact of Classification Revisions on Time Series," July 1993.

[4] "Comparative statistics" tables present new data according to the old system, along with data from one or more earlier censuses based on the same system for comparison. "Bridge" tables take interrelating the old and new classifications one step farther. They present new data cross-tabulated by both old and new classification systems at the same time, identifying the most detailed level of comparison between the two systems.

Part One

The U.S. Economy

Gross Domestic Product and Cyclical Indicators

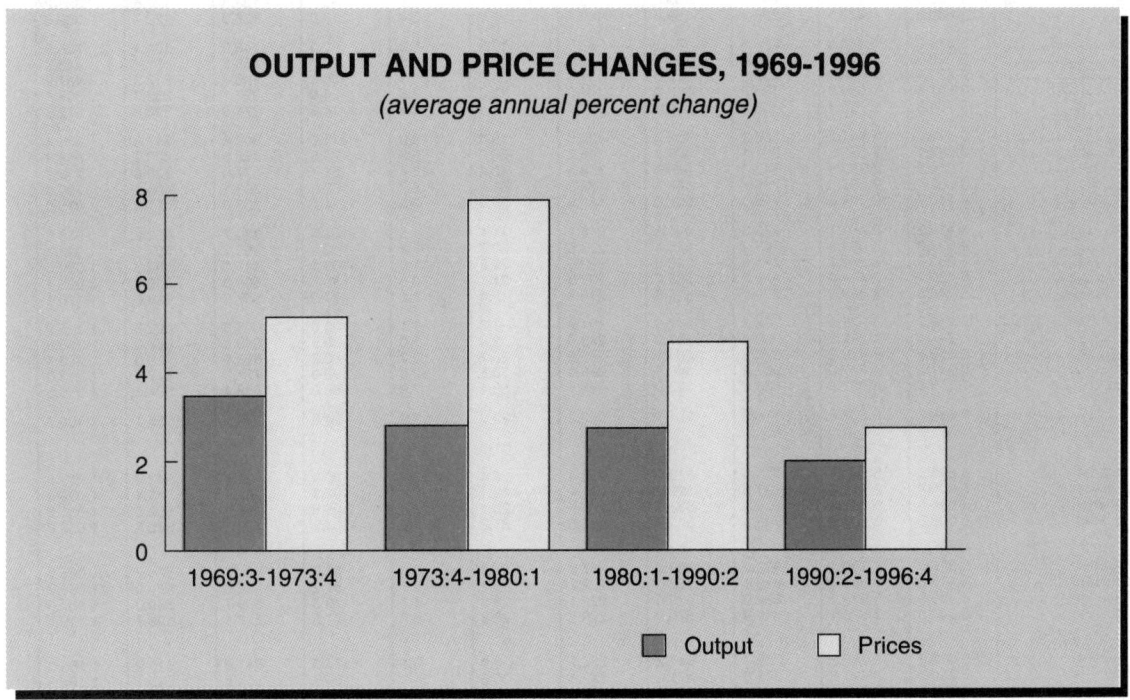

OUTPUT AND PRICE CHANGES, 1969-1996
(average annual percent change)

Output   Prices

B oth prices and real output increased more slowly from 1990-1996 than their average increases during the previous two decades. From mid-1990 through the end of 1996 output grew at an annual rate of 2.0 percent per year, while the annual rate of price increase was about 2.7 percent.

In the chart above, rates of economic growth and price change are shown from one business cycle peak to the next, except for the most recent period. The most recent period encom-passes the downturn which began in mid-1990 and the subsequent expansion from early 1991 through the end of 1996. This expansion was still ongoing at the end of 1996, so the comparison with earlier business cycles is not yet complete.

Output here is measured by the chain-type quantity index for gross domestic product and price change by the chain-type price index. Both indexes are based on 1992=100.

GROSS DOMESTIC PRODUCT
(Billions of dollars, quarterly data are at seasonally adjusted annual rates)

YEAR AND QUARTER	Gross domestic product	Personal consumption expenditures	Gross private domestic investment Total	Fixed investment Nonresidential	Fixed investment Residential	Change in business inventories Nonfarm	Change in business inventories Farm	Net exports	Exports	Imports	Government Total	Government Federal	Government State and local	Addendum: Final sales of domestic product
1968	910.6	559.8	139.9	92.1	38.7	7.8	1.4	-1.3	45.3	46.6	212.1	113.8	98.3	901.4
1969	982.2	604.7	155.0	102.9	42.6	9.5	0.0	-1.2	49.3	50.5	223.8	115.8	108.0	972.7
1970	1 035.6	648.1	150.2	106.7	41.4	3.0	-0.8	1.2	57.0	55.8	236.1	115.9	120.2	1 033.4
1971	1 125.4	702.5	176.0	111.7	55.8	6.8	1.7	-3.0	59.3	62.3	249.9	117.1	132.8	1 116.9
1972	1 237.3	770.7	205.6	126.1	69.7	9.6	0.3	-8.0	66.2	74.2	268.9	125.1	143.8	1 227.4
1973	1 382.6	851.6	242.9	150.0	75.3	15.9	1.5	0.6	91.8	91.2	287.6	128.2	159.4	1 365.2
1974	1 496.9	931.2	245.6	165.6	66.0	16.9	-2.8	-3.1	124.3	127.5	323.2	139.9	183.3	1 482.8
1975	1 630.6	1 029.1	225.4	169.0	62.7	-9.7	3.4	13.6	136.3	122.7	362.6	154.5	208.1	1 636.9
1976	1 819.0	1 148.8	286.6	187.2	82.5	17.8	-0.8	-2.3	148.9	151.1	385.9	162.7	223.1	1 802.0
1977	2 026.9	1 277.1	356.6	223.2	110.3	18.5	4.5	-23.7	158.8	182.4	416.9	178.4	238.5	2 003.8
1978	2 291.4	1 428.8	430.8	272.0	131.6	25.8	1.4	-26.1	186.1	212.3	457.9	194.4	263.4	2 264.2
1979	2 557.5	1 593.5	480.9	323.0	141.0	13.3	3.6	-24.0	228.7	252.7	507.1	215.0	292.0	2 540.6
1980	2 784.2	1 760.4	465.9	350.3	123.2	-1.5	-6.1	-14.9	278.9	293.8	572.8	248.4	324.4	2 791.9
1981	3 115.9	1 941.3	556.2	405.4	122.6	19.4	8.8	-15.0	302.8	317.8	633.4	284.1	349.2	3 087.8
1982	3 242.1	2 076.8	501.1	409.9	105.7	-20.2	5.8	-20.5	282.6	303.2	684.8	313.2	371.6	3 256.6
1983	3 514.5	2 283.4	547.1	399.4	152.5	10.4	-15.4	-51.7	277.0	328.6	735.7	344.5	391.2	3 519.4
1984	3 902.4	2 492.3	715.6	468.3	179.8	61.8	5.7	-102.0	303.1	405.1	796.6	372.6	424.0	3 835.0
1985	4 180.7	2 704.8	715.1	502.0	186.9	20.4	5.8	-114.2	303.0	417.2	875.0	410.1	464.9	4 154.5
1986	4 422.2	2 892.7	722.5	494.8	218.1	11.1	-1.5	-131.5	320.7	452.2	938.5	435.2	503.3	4 412.6
1987	4 692.3	3 094.5	747.2	495.4	227.6	30.7	-6.4	-142.1	365.7	507.9	992.8	455.7	537.2	4 668.1
1988	5 049.6	3 349.7	773.9	530.6	232.5	22.8	-11.9	-106.1	447.2	553.2	1 032.0	457.3	574.7	5 038.7
1989	5 438.7	3 594.8	829.2	566.2	231.3	31.7	0.0	-80.4	509.3	589.7	1 095.1	477.2	617.9	5 407.0
1990	5 743.8	3 839.3	799.7	575.9	215.7	5.4	2.6	-71.3	557.3	628.6	1 176.1	503.6	672.6	5 735.8
1991	5 916.7	3 975.1	736.2	547.3	191.2	-1.2	-1.1	-20.5	601.8	622.3	1 225.9	522.6	703.4	5 919.0
1992	6 244.4	4 219.8	790.4	557.9	225.6	2.0	5.0	-29.5	639.4	669.0	1 263.8	528.0	735.8	6 237.4
1993	6 558.1	4 459.2	876.2	604.1	251.6	26.7	-6.2	-60.7	658.6	719.3	1 283.4	518.3	765.0	6 537.6
1994	6 947.0	4 717.0	1 007.9	660.6	286.0	50.5	10.8	-90.9	721.2	812.1	1 313.0	510.2	802.8	6 885.7
1995	7 265.4	4 957.7	1 038.2	723.0	285.1	38.1	-7.9	-86.0	818.4	904.5	1 355.5	509.6	846.0	7 235.3
1996	7 636.0	5 207.6	1 116.5	781.4	309.2	23.0	2.9	-94.8	870.9	965.7	1 406.7	520.0	886.7	7 610.2
1988:														
1st quarter	4 898.2	3 247.1	756.5	515.9	228.4	14.4	-2.2	-120.9	421.1	542.0	1 015.5	456.3	559.1	4 886.0
2nd quarter	5 000.4	3 310.2	767.3	529.4	231.4	16.4	-9.9	-103.3	442.1	545.4	1 026.2	454.6	571.6	4 993.9
3rd quarter	5 094.5	3 382.3	776.5	533.2	233.6	23.1	-13.4	-95.8	456.2	552.0	1 031.5	453.5	578.1	5 084.8
4th quarter	5 205.3	3 459.2	795.5	543.7	236.6	37.2	-22.0	-104.2	469.3	573.5	1 054.8	465.0	589.9	5 190.1
1989:														
1st quarter	5 316.8	3 506.1	829.0	553.0	237.2	33.6	5.2	-83.7	492.6	576.3	1 065.3	465.5	599.9	5 277.9
2nd quarter	5 413.2	3 569.7	836.0	562.0	232.2	35.9	5.8	-81.2	512.8	594.0	1 088.7	476.5	612.1	5 371.4
3rd quarter	5 486.9	3 627.3	832.0	579.0	229.1	28.5	-4.7	-79.3	509.7	589.0	1 107.0	484.9	622.1	5 463.0
4th quarter	5 537.8	3 676.1	819.9	570.9	226.6	28.8	-6.5	-77.5	522.1	599.7	1 119.4	482.0	637.4	5 515.4
1990:														
1st quarter	5 660.6	3 759.2	822.7	581.2	232.7	8.9	-0.1	-74.3	541.6	615.9	1 153.0	496.4	656.6	5 651.8
2nd quarter	5 750.8	3 811.8	835.0	571.6	222.4	36.9	4.1	-60.3	554.8	615.1	1 164.3	500.1	664.2	5 709.8
3rd quarter	5 782.2	3 879.2	804.7	580.3	210.9	5.4	8.1	-78.5	555.5	634.1	1 176.9	501.2	675.7	5 768.7
4th quarter	5 781.7	3 907.0	736.3	570.6	196.9	-29.6	-1.7	-72.0	577.3	649.2	1 210.4	516.7	693.7	5 812.9
1991:														
1st quarter	5 821.9	3 910.7	723.5	555.4	184.3	-14.8	-1.5	-32.9	577.4	610.3	1 220.6	525.6	695.0	5 838.2
2nd quarter	5 892.5	3 961.0	716.4	550.2	185.9	-23.3	3.5	-12.3	602.7	615.0	1 227.4	528.2	699.2	5 912.2
3rd quarter	5 950.2	4 001.6	744.1	544.3	194.3	13.5	-8.1	-22.0	602.6	624.5	1 226.5	520.9	705.5	5 944.7
4th quarter	6 002.1	4 027.1	760.7	539.2	200.3	19.6	1.6	-14.8	624.4	639.3	1 229.2	515.5	713.6	5 980.9
1992:														
1st quarter	6 121.8	4 127.6	755.2	544.1	211.3	-7.5	7.3	-8.9	632.4	641.3	1 247.9	521.8	726.1	6 122.1
2nd quarter	6 201.2	4 183.0	790.7	556.8	223.7	1.1	9.1	-29.0	635.9	664.9	1 256.4	523.2	733.2	6 191.0
3rd quarter	6 271.7	4 238.9	799.7	561.0	227.1	6.8	4.8	-37.6	640.2	677.8	1 270.7	532.0	738.7	6 260.1
4th quarter	6 383.1	4 329.6	816.1	569.6	240.1	7.8	-1.3	-42.7	649.1	691.8	1 280.0	535.0	745.1	6 376.6
1993:														
1st quarter	6 444.5	4 365.4	854.3	580.5	243.0	37.1	-6.3	-46.6	647.1	693.7	1 271.5	521.3	750.1	6 413.8
2nd quarter	6 509.1	4 428.1	857.4	598.8	244.1	19.8	-5.3	-57.5	661.2	718.7	1 281.2	517.8	763.4	6 494.7
3rd quarter	6 574.6	4 488.6	872.8	606.4	252.4	25.2	-11.2	-72.1	646.8	718.9	1 285.3	515.7	769.6	6 560.6
4th quarter	6 704.2	4 554.9	920.3	630.6	266.8	24.8	-2.0	-66.6	679.4	746.0	1 295.5	518.5	777.0	6 681.3
1994:														
1st quarter	6 794.3	4 616.6	963.4	634.6	276.4	38.9	13.4	-76.6	678.5	755.1	1 291.0	506.9	784.1	6 741.9
2nd quarter	6 911.4	4 680.5	1 017.9	652.9	288.7	60.9	15.3	-87.9	710.1	797.9	1 300.8	505.3	795.5	6 835.1
3rd quarter	6 986.5	4 750.6	1 007.1	667.4	289.5	40.1	10.1	-103.4	732.6	836.0	1 332.3	520.4	811.9	6 936.3
4th quarter	7 095.7	4 820.2	1 043.1	687.5	289.5	62.0	4.2	-95.6	763.7	859.2	1 328.0	508.3	819.6	7 029.6
1995:														
1st quarter	7 168.9	4 871.7	1 050.8	710.9	287.8	58.4	-6.3	-98.3	784.5	882.8	1 344.7	513.6	831.1	7 116.8
2nd quarter	7 209.5	4 934.8	1 024.0	722.5	277.1	36.4	-12.0	-105.4	807.7	913.1	1 356.0	511.2	844.8	7 185.0
3rd quarter	7 301.3	4 990.6	1 028.8	725.4	284.0	31.8	-12.4	-80.4	831.6	912.0	1 362.2	512.9	849.3	7 281.8
4th quarter	7 381.9	5 033.8	1 049.1	733.1	291.4	25.6	-1.1	-60.1	849.9	909.9	1 359.2	500.6	858.6	7 357.4
1996:														
1st quarter	7 467.5	5 105.8	1 060.5	750.7	298.8	14.8	-3.8	-83.0	850.2	933.2	1 384.2	516.4	867.8	7 456.4
2nd quarter	7 607.7	5 189.1	1 105.4	769.3	312.7	17.2	6.2	-93.8	865.0	958.7	1 407.0	524.6	882.4	7 584.3
3rd quarter	7 676.0	5 227.4	1 149.2	798.6	313.5	31.3	5.8	-114.0	863.7	977.6	1 413.5	521.6	891.9	7 638.9
4th quarter	7 792.9	5 308.1	1 151.1	807.2	312.0	28.7	3.2	-88.6	904.6	993.2	1 422.3	517.6	904.7	7 761.0

REAL GROSS DOMESTIC PRODUCT
(Billions of chained (1992) dollars, quarterly data are at seasonally adjusted annual rates)

YEAR AND QUARTER	Gross domestic product	Personal consumption expenditures	Gross private domestic investment Total	Fixed investment Nonresidential	Fixed investment Residential	Change in business inventories Nonfarm	Change in business inventories Farm	Net exports	Exports	Imports	Government Total	Federal	State and local	Addendum: Final sales of domestic product
1968	3 293.9	2 070.2	433.3	266.4	154.0	23.0	3.7	-67.2	135.3	202.5	892.4	476.3	416.5	3 278.0
1969	3 393.6	2 147.5	458.3	285.6	158.6	27.3	0.0	-71.3	142.7	214.0	887.5	459.9	428.0	3 377.2
1970	3 397.6	2 197.8	426.1	282.8	149.1	8.3	-2.4	-65.0	158.1	223.1	866.8	427.2	440.0	3 406.5
1971	3 510.0	2 279.5	474.9	282.4	190.0	18.0	4.0	-75.8	159.2	235.0	851.0	397.0	454.4	3 499.8
1972	3 702.3	2 415.9	531.8	307.7	223.8	25.4	0.3	-89.0	172.0	261.0	854.1	390.2	464.5	3 689.5
1973	3 916.3	2 532.6	595.5	352.5	222.3	38.5	1.4	-63.0	209.6	272.6	848.4	371.1	478.5	3 883.9
1974	3 891.2	2 514.7	546.5	354.4	176.4	31.9	-4.7	-35.6	229.8	265.3	862.9	368.8	495.6	3 873.4
1975	3 873.9	2 570.0	446.6	317.3	153.5	-18.5	6.1	-7.2	228.2	235.4	876.3	367.9	510.0	3 906.4
1976	4 082.9	2 714.3	537.4	332.6	189.7	32.1	-1.3	-39.9	241.6	281.5	876.8	364.3	514.3	4 061.7
1977	4 273.6	2 829.8	622.1	371.8	229.8	31.7	6.8	-64.2	247.4	311.7	884.7	370.1	516.4	4 240.8
1978	4 503.0	2 951.6	693.4	422.6	245.0	41.4	2.6	-65.6	273.1	338.6	910.6	377.7	534.7	4 464.4
1979	4 630.6	3 020.2	709.8	463.3	236.0	19.3	3.8	-45.3	299.0	344.3	924.9	383.3	543.5	4 614.4
1980	4 615.0	3 009.7	628.3	461.1	186.1	-1.5	-7.1	10.1	331.4	321.3	941.4	399.3	543.6	4 641.9
1981	4 720.7	3 046.4	686.0	485.7	171.2	22.8	9.6	5.6	335.3	329.7	947.7	415.9	532.8	4 691.6
1982	4 620.3	3 081.5	587.2	464.3	140.1	-22.9	7.3	-14.1	311.4	325.5	960.1	429.4	531.4	4 651.2
1983	4 803.7	3 240.6	642.1	456.4	197.6	12.1	-16.9	-63.3	303.3	366.6	987.3	452.7	534.9	4 821.2
1984	5 140.1	3 407.6	833.4	535.4	226.4	69.1	6.4	-127.3	328.4	455.7	1 018.4	463.7	555.0	5 061.6
1985	5 323.5	3 566.5	823.9	568.5	229.5	23.3	6.9	-147.9	337.3	485.2	1 080.1	495.6	584.7	5 296.9
1986	5 487.7	3 708.7	811.8	548.5	257.0	12.5	-1.6	-163.9	362.2	526.1	1 135.0	518.4	616.9	5 480.9
1987	5 649.5	3 822.3	821.5	542.4	257.6	34.3	-8.8	-156.2	402.0	558.2	1 165.9	534.4	631.8	5 626.0
1988	5 865.2	3 972.7	828.2	566.0	252.5	24.7	-12.6	-114.4	465.8	580.2	1 180.9	524.6	656.6	5 855.1
1989	6 062.0	4 064.6	863.5	588.8	243.3	33.5	0.1	-82.7	520.2	603.0	1 213.9	531.5	682.6	6 028.7
1990	6 136.3	4 132.2	815.0	585.2	220.6	7.8	2.5	-61.9	564.4	626.3	1 250.4	541.9	708.6	6 126.7
1991	6 079.4	4 105.8	738.1	547.7	193.4	-1.2	-1.7	-22.3	599.9	622.2	1 258.1	539.4	718.7	6 082.6
1992	6 244.4	4 219.8	790.4	557.9	225.6	2.0	5.0	-29.5	639.4	669.0	1 263.8	528.0	735.8	6 237.4
1993	6 389.6	4 343.6	863.6	600.2	242.6	29.5	-7.3	-70.2	658.2	728.4	1 252.1	505.7	746.4	6 368.9
1994	6 610.7	4 486.0	975.7	648.4	267.0	49.0	11.7	-104.6	712.4	817.0	1 252.3	486.6	765.7	6 551.2
1995	6 742.1	4 595.3	991.5	706.5	257.0	35.7	-9.2	-98.8	791.2	890.1	1 251.9	470.3	781.6	6 712.7
1996	6 928.4	4 714.1	1 069.1	771.7	272.1	22.5	2.6	-114.4	857.0	971.5	1 257.9	464.2	793.7	6 901.0
1988:														
1st quarter	5 785.3	3 924.2	817.8	556.1	251.3	16.8	-3.3	-125.9	448.8	574.8	1 172.5	527.6	645.1	5 774.3
2nd quarter	5 844.1	3 952.2	823.2	567.1	252.2	17.7	-11.7	-106.9	461.4	568.3	1 177.0	522.3	655.0	5 840.1
3rd quarter	5 878.7	3 985.1	830.0	568.0	252.9	25.5	-13.6	-110.7	469.4	580.0	1 176.1	517.9	658.4	5 869.2
4th quarter	5 952.8	4 029.1	841.7	572.9	253.7	38.8	-21.8	-114.3	483.5	597.8	1 198.1	530.6	667.8	5 937.0
1989:														
1st quarter	6 011.0	4 032.8	870.5	579.5	252.6	36.2	5.0	-88.7	502.0	590.7	1 193.5	521.4	672.3	5 970.0
2nd quarter	6 055.6	4 047.4	873.1	586.6	244.3	37.8	6.1	-79.8	522.0	601.9	1 211.1	532.0	679.4	6 010.9
3rd quarter	6 088.0	4 083.2	864.0	600.5	240.1	30.4	-4.6	-84.5	521.3	605.8	1 222.6	537.7	685.1	6 063.1
4th quarter	6 093.5	4 095.0	846.3	588.8	236.0	29.6	-6.3	-77.9	535.5	613.5	1 228.4	535.0	693.7	6 070.8
1990:														
1st quarter	6 152.6	4 128.9	842.6	595.4	239.4	10.9	-0.1	-67.1	555.2	622.3	1 246.5	542.9	703.8	6 144.6
2nd quarter	6 171.6	4 134.7	853.4	583.4	227.8	39.2	4.2	-66.7	566.8	633.5	1 248.2	543.0	705.4	6 127.5
3rd quarter	6 142.1	4 148.5	817.9	588.1	214.9	6.8	7.9	-71.2	561.8	633.0	1 246.8	538.2	708.7	6 126.6
4th quarter	6 079.0	4 116.4	746.2	573.9	200.3	-25.9	-2.0	-42.5	573.9	616.4	1 259.9	543.5	716.5	6 108.1
1991:														
1st quarter	6 047.5	4 084.5	725.1	555.1	187.4	-15.0	-2.1	-24.3	572.3	596.6	1 262.6	547.3	715.5	6 065.4
2nd quarter	6 074.7	4 110.0	718.5	550.9	188.3	-23.4	2.7	-17.1	600.3	617.4	1 263.8	547.1	716.8	6 095.9
3rd quarter	6 090.1	4 119.5	745.8	545.3	195.6	13.6	-9.0	-29.8	603.6	633.4	1 255.1	536.3	718.8	6 085.4
4th quarter	6 105.3	4 109.1	763.2	539.5	202.4	19.9	1.4	-17.9	623.5	641.4	1 250.7	526.9	723.8	6 083.8
1992:														
1st quarter	6 175.7	4 173.8	758.2	544.4	213.9	-7.7	7.1	-14.8	633.0	647.8	1 258.5	525.1	733.5	6 175.8
2nd quarter	6 214.2	4 196.4	792.8	557.5	224.9	1.6	9.4	-32.5	635.8	668.3	1 257.5	523.3	734.2	6 203.8
3rd quarter	6 260.7	4 226.7	798.5	560.6	226.7	6.9	5.1	-30.8	639.7	670.5	1 266.5	529.6	736.9	6 249.5
4th quarter	6 327.1	4 282.3	812.2	569.1	236.7	7.4	-1.7	-40.0	649.1	689.1	1 272.5	534.0	738.5	6 320.7
1993:														
1st quarter	6 327.9	4 286.8	845.5	577.8	237.0	40.0	-7.6	-54.7	647.2	701.9	1 250.1	512.1	738.0	6 297.3
2nd quarter	6 359.9	4 322.8	846.1	595.1	236.1	23.4	-6.6	-62.6	660.1	722.7	1 253.1	507.8	745.3	6 344.9
3rd quarter	6 393.5	4 366.6	858.6	602.3	242.2	27.8	-12.3	-83.1	646.3	729.4	1 250.5	501.5	749.1	6 379.3
4th quarter	6 476.9	4 398.0	904.0	625.6	255.1	26.9	-2.6	-80.5	679.1	759.7	1 254.7	501.3	753.4	6 453.8
1994:														
1st quarter	6 524.5	4 439.4	939.9	626.2	261.3	39.6	13.8	-97.6	676.0	773.6	1 241.9	487.2	754.7	6 473.0
2nd quarter	6 600.3	4 472.2	987.8	641.2	271.5	59.6	16.6	-103.9	704.1	808.0	1 243.3	481.2	762.2	6 526.7
3rd quarter	6 629.5	4 498.2	972.2	653.2	269.4	38.2	11.6	-111.1	722.1	833.2	1 268.1	496.4	771.7	6 580.4
4th quarter	6 688.6	4 534.1	1 003.0	672.9	265.9	58.7	4.8	-105.9	747.3	853.2	1 255.8	481.7	774.1	6 624.8
1995:														
1st quarter	6 703.7	4 551.3	1 005.8	695.7	261.2	54.7	-7.3	-113.5	760.4	873.9	1 257.7	480.4	777.3	6 654.3
2nd quarter	6 708.8	4 583.5	977.5	705.4	250.4	34.0	-13.5	-112.8	777.4	890.3	1 257.3	474.9	782.3	6 685.3
3rd quarter	6 759.2	4 612.9	982.0	708.2	255.5	29.6	-13.6	-92.9	802.4	895.4	1 255.0	473.4	781.5	6 739.3
4th quarter	6 796.5	4 633.5	1 000.8	716.8	260.8	24.4	-2.3	-76.1	824.6	900.7	1 237.7	452.6	785.1	6 771.9
1996:														
1st quarter	6 826.4	4 669.4	1 012.2	736.9	266.1	14.5	-6.8	-100.8	828.2	929.0	1 243.2	460.9	782.4	6 815.0
2nd quarter	6 926.0	4 712.2	1 059.2	759.7	277.2	17.3	4.2	-112.6	847.4	960.0	1 265.1	470.7	794.4	6 902.3
3rd quarter	6 943.8	4 718.2	1 100.3	789.3	274.1	31.6	6.5	-138.9	851.4	990.2	1 261.5	465.7	795.9	6 905.0
4th quarter	7 017.4	4 756.4	1 104.8	800.8	271.1	26.5	6.4	-105.6	901.1	1 006.6	1 261.8	459.6	802.3	6 981.7

YEAR AND QUARTER	QUANTITY INDEXES FOR GROSS DOMESTIC PRODUCT (Index numbers, 1992=100)										
	Gross domestic product	Personal consumption expenditures	Private fixed investment			Exports and imports of goods and services		Government consumption expenditure and gross investment			Addendum: Final sales of domestic product
			Total	Nonresidential	Residential	Exports	Imports	Total	Federal	State and local	
1968	52.8	49.1	54.8	47.8	68.3	21.2	30.3	70.6	90.2	56.6	52.6
1969	54.4	50.9	58.0	51.2	70.3	22.3	32.0	70.2	87.1	58.2	54.1
1970	54.4	52.1	53.9	50.7	66.1	24.7	33.4	68.6	80.9	59.8	54.6
1971	56.2	54.0	60.1	50.6	84.2	24.9	35.1	67.3	75.2	61.8	56.1
1972	59.3	57.3	67.3	55.2	99.2	26.9	39.0	67.6	73.9	63.1	59.2
1973	62.7	60.0	75.3	63.2	98.6	32.8	40.8	67.1	70.3	65.0	62.3
1974	62.3	59.6	69.1	63.5	78.2	35.9	39.7	68.3	69.9	67.4	62.1
1975	62.0	60.9	56.5	56.9	68.1	35.7	35.2	69.3	69.7	69.3	62.6
1976	65.4	64.3	68.0	59.6	84.1	37.8	42.1	69.4	69.0	69.9	65.1
1977	68.4	67.1	78.7	66.7	101.9	38.7	46.6	70.0	70.1	70.2	68.0
1978	72.1	70.0	87.7	75.8	108.6	42.7	50.6	72.1	71.5	72.7	71.6
1979	74.2	71.6	89.8	83.1	104.7	46.8	51.5	73.2	72.6	73.9	74.0
1980	73.9	71.3	79.5	82.7	82.5	51.8	48.0	74.5	75.6	73.9	74.4
1981	75.6	72.2	86.8	87.1	75.9	52.4	49.3	75.0	78.8	72.4	75.2
1982	74.0	73.0	74.3	83.2	62.1	48.7	48.7	76.0	81.3	72.2	74.6
1983	76.9	76.8	81.2	81.8	87.6	47.4	54.8	78.1	85.7	72.7	77.3
1984	82.3	80.8	105.4	96.0	100.4	51.4	68.1	80.6	87.8	75.4	81.2
1985	85.3	84.5	104.2	101.9	101.8	52.8	72.5	85.5	93.9	79.5	84.9
1986	87.9	87.9	102.7	98.3	114.0	56.7	78.7	89.8	98.2	83.9	87.9
1987	90.5	90.6	103.9	97.2	114.2	62.9	83.4	92.3	101.2	85.9	90.2
1988	93.9	94.1	104.8	101.5	112.0	72.9	86.7	93.4	99.4	89.2	93.9
1989	97.1	96.3	109.2	105.6	107.8	81.4	90.1	96.1	100.7	92.8	96.7
1990	98.3	97.9	103.1	104.9	97.8	88.3	93.6	98.9	102.6	96.3	98.2
1991	97.4	97.3	93.4	98.2	85.8	93.8	93.0	99.6	102.2	97.7	97.5
1992	100.0	100.0	100.0	100.0	100.0	100.0	100.0	100.0	100.0	100.0	100.0
1993	102.3	102.9	109.3	107.6	107.6	102.9	108.9	99.1	95.8	101.5	102.1
1994	105.9	106.3	123.4	116.2	118.4	111.4	122.1	99.1	92.2	104.1	105.0
1995	108.0	108.9	125.4	126.7	113.9	123.7	133.1	99.1	89.1	106.2	107.6
1996	111.0	111.7	135.3	138.3	120.6	134.0	145.2	99.5	87.9	107.9	110.6
1988:											
1st quarter	92.7	93.0	103.5	99.7	111.4	70.2	85.9	92.8	99.9	87.7	92.6
2nd quarter	93.6	93.7	104.2	101.7	111.8	72.2	85.0	93.1	98.9	89.0	93.6
3rd quarter	94.1	94.4	105.0	101.8	112.1	73.4	86.7	93.1	98.1	89.5	94.1
4th quarter	95.3	95.5	106.5	102.7	112.5	75.6	89.4	94.8	100.5	90.8	95.2
1989:											
1st quarter	96.3	95.6	110.1	103.9	112.0	78.5	88.3	94.4	98.8	91.4	95.7
2nd quarter	97.0	95.9	110.5	105.2	108.3	81.6	90.0	95.8	100.8	92.3	96.4
3rd quarter	97.5	96.8	109.3	107.6	106.5	81.5	90.6	96.7	101.8	93.1	97.2
4th quarter	97.6	97.0	107.1	105.5	104.6	83.8	91.7	97.2	101.3	94.3	97.3
1990:											
1st quarter	98.5	97.9	106.6	106.7	106.1	86.8	93.0	98.6	102.8	95.7	98.5
2nd quarter	98.8	98.0	108.0	104.6	101.0	88.7	94.7	98.8	102.9	95.9	98.2
3rd quarter	98.4	98.3	103.5	105.4	95.3	87.9	94.6	98.7	101.9	96.3	98.2
4th quarter	97.4	97.6	94.4	102.9	88.8	89.8	92.1	99.7	103.0	97.4	97.9
1991:											
1st quarter	96.9	96.8	91.7	99.5	83.1	89.5	89.2	99.9	103.7	97.2	97.2
2nd quarter	97.3	97.4	90.9	98.8	83.5	93.9	92.3	100.0	103.6	97.4	97.7
3rd quarter	97.5	97.6	94.4	97.7	86.7	94.4	94.7	99.3	101.6	97.7	97.6
4th quarter	97.8	97.4	96.6	96.7	89.8	97.5	95.9	99.0	99.8	98.4	97.5
1992:											
1st quarter	98.9	98.9	95.9	97.6	94.8	99.0	96.8	99.6	99.5	99.7	99.0
2nd quarter	99.5	99.5	100.3	99.9	99.7	99.4	99.9	99.5	99.1	99.8	99.5
3rd quarter	100.3	100.2	101.0	100.5	100.5	100.1	100.2	100.2	100.3	100.2	100.2
4th quarter	101.3	101.5	102.8	102.0	104.9	101.5	103.0	100.7	101.1	100.4	101.3
1993:											
1st quarter	101.3	101.6	107.0	103.6	105.1	101.2	104.9	98.9	97.0	100.3	101.0
2nd quarter	101.9	102.4	107.1	106.7	104.7	103.2	108.0	99.2	96.2	101.3	101.7
3rd quarter	102.4	103.5	108.6	108.0	107.4	101.1	109.0	99.0	95.0	101.8	102.3
4th quarter	103.7	104.2	114.4	112.1	113.1	106.2	113.6	99.3	95.0	102.4	103.5
1994:											
1st quarter	104.5	105.2	118.9	112.3	115.8	105.7	115.7	98.3	92.3	102.6	103.8
2nd quarter	105.7	106.0	125.0	114.9	120.4	110.1	120.8	98.4	91.1	103.6	104.6
3rd quarter	106.2	106.6	123.0	117.1	119.4	112.9	124.6	100.4	94.0	104.9	105.5
4th quarter	107.1	107.5	126.9	120.6	117.9	116.9	127.5	99.4	91.2	105.2	106.2
1995:											
1st quarter	107.4	107.9	127.3	124.7	115.8	118.9	130.6	99.5	91.0	105.6	106.7
2nd quarter	107.4	108.6	123.7	126.4	111.0	121.6	133.1	99.5	90.0	106.3	107.2
3rd quarter	108.2	109.3	124.2	127.0	113.3	125.5	133.9	99.3	89.7	106.2	108.1
4th quarter	108.8	109.8	126.6	128.5	115.6	129.0	134.7	97.9	85.7	106.7	108.6
1996:											
1st quarter	109.3	110.7	128.1	132.1	118.0	129.5	138.9	98.4	87.3	106.3	109.3
2nd quarter	110.9	111.7	134.0	136.2	122.9	132.5	143.5	100.1	89.2	108.0	110.7
3rd quarter	111.2	111.8	139.2	141.5	121.5	133.2	148.0	99.8	88.2	108.2	110.7
4th quarter	112.4	112.7	139.8	143.5	120.2	140.9	150.5	99.9	87.0	109.0	111.9

YEAR AND QUARTER	Gross domestic product	Personal consumption expenditures	Private fixed investment			Exports and imports of goods and services		Government consumption expenditure and gross investment			Addendum: Final sales of domestic product
			Total	Nonresidential	Residential	Exports	Imports	Total	Federal	State and local	
1968	27.6	27.0	31.3	34.6	25.1	33.5	23.0	23.7	23.8	23.6	27.5
1969	28.9	28.2	32.9	36.0	26.9	34.5	23.6	25.2	25.1	25.2	28.8
1970	30.5	29.5	34.3	37.8	27.7	36.0	25.0	27.2	27.1	27.3	30.3
1971	32.1	30.8	36.1	39.6	29.4	37.3	26.5	29.3	29.4	29.2	31.9
1972	33.4	31.9	37.6	41.0	31.1	38.5	28.4	31.5	32.0	31.0	33.3
1973	35.3	33.6	39.7	42.6	33.9	43.8	33.4	33.9	34.5	33.3	35.2
1974	38.5	37.0	43.7	46.8	37.4	54.1	48.0	37.5	37.9	37.0	38.3
1975	42.1	40.0	49.2	53.3	40.9	59.7	52.1	41.4	42.0	40.8	41.9
1976	44.6	42.3	52.1	56.3	43.5	61.6	53.7	44.0	44.6	43.4	44.4
1977	47.4	45.1	56.2	60.1	48.0	64.2	58.5	47.1	48.2	46.2	47.3
1978	50.9	48.4	61.1	64.4	53.7	68.2	62.7	50.3	51.5	49.3	50.7
1979	55.2	52.8	66.7	69.7	59.8	76.5	73.4	54.8	56.1	53.7	55.1
1980	60.3	58.5	73.0	76.0	66.2	84.2	91.5	60.9	62.2	59.7	60.2
1981	66.0	63.7	79.9	83.5	71.6	90.3	96.4	66.8	68.3	65.6	65.8
1982	70.2	67.4	84.5	88.3	75.5	90.8	93.1	71.3	72.9	69.9	70.0
1983	73.2	70.5	85.2	87.5	77.2	91.3	89.6	74.5	76.1	73.2	73.0
1984	75.9	73.1	85.0	87.5	79.4	92.3	88.9	78.2	80.4	76.4	75.8
1985	78.5	75.8	86.2	88.3	81.5	89.8	86.0	81.0	82.7	79.5	78.4
1986	80.6	78.0	88.6	90.2	84.9	88.5	86.0	82.7	84.0	81.6	80.5
1987	83.1	81.0	90.4	91.3	88.3	91.0	91.0	85.2	85.3	85.0	83.0
1988	86.1	84.3	93.3	93.7	92.1	96.0	95.4	87.4	87.2	87.5	86.1
1989	89.7	88.4	95.9	96.2	95.1	97.9	97.8	90.2	89.8	90.5	89.7
1990	93.6	92.9	98.2	98.4	97.8	98.7	100.4	94.1	92.9	94.9	93.6
1991	97.3	96.8	99.6	99.9	98.9	100.3	100.0	97.5	96.9	97.9	97.3
1992	100.0	100.0	100.0	100.0	100.0	100.0	100.0	100.0	100.0	100.0	100.0
1993	102.6	102.7	101.5	100.7	103.7	100.1	98.8	102.5	102.5	102.5	102.7
1994	105.1	105.2	103.4	101.9	107.1	101.2	99.4	104.9	104.8	104.9	105.1
1995	107.8	107.9	104.8	102.3	110.9	103.4	101.6	108.3	108.3	108.2	107.8
1996	110.2	110.5	104.7	101.3	113.6	101.6	99.4	111.8	112.0	111.7	110.3
1988:											
1st quarter	84.7	82.8	92.2	92.8	90.9	93.9	94.3	86.6	86.5	86.7	84.6
2nd quarter	85.6	83.8	92.9	93.4	91.8	95.9	96.1	87.2	87.0	87.3	85.5
3rd quarter	86.7	84.9	93.4	93.9	92.4	97.2	95.1	87.7	87.5	87.8	86.6
4th quarter	87.5	85.9	94.4	94.9	93.2	97.1	95.9	88.1	87.7	88.3	87.4
1989:											
1st quarter	88.4	86.9	95.0	95.4	93.9	98.2	97.6	89.3	89.3	89.2	88.4
2nd quarter	89.4	88.2	95.6	95.8	95.0	98.3	98.8	89.9	89.6	90.1	89.4
3rd quarter	90.1	88.8	96.1	96.4	95.4	97.7	97.2	90.5	90.1	90.8	90.1
4th quarter	90.9	89.8	96.7	97.0	96.0	97.4	97.6	91.2	90.2	91.9	90.9
1990:											
1st quarter	92.0	91.1	97.5	97.6	97.2	97.5	98.8	92.5	91.4	93.3	92.0
2nd quarter	93.2	92.2	97.9	98.0	97.6	97.9	97.1	93.3	92.1	94.2	93.2
3rd quarter	94.2	93.5	98.5	98.7	98.1	98.9	100.0	94.4	93.1	95.3	94.2
4th quarter	95.1	94.9	99.1	99.4	98.3	100.6	105.6	96.1	95.0	96.8	95.1
1991:											
1st quarter	96.3	95.7	99.6	100.1	98.4	100.9	102.2	96.6	95.9	97.2	96.3
2nd quarter	97.0	96.4	99.6	100.0	98.7	100.5	99.7	97.2	96.6	97.6	97.0
3rd quarter	97.7	97.1	99.7	99.8	99.3	99.8	98.6	97.7	97.1	98.2	97.7
4th quarter	98.3	98.0	99.6	99.9	99.0	100.1	99.6	98.3	97.9	98.6	98.3
1992:											
1st quarter	99.1	98.9	99.6	99.9	98.8	99.9	99.0	99.2	99.4	99.0	99.1
2nd quarter	99.8	99.7	99.8	99.9	99.5	100.1	99.6	99.9	100.0	99.9	99.8
3rd quarter	100.2	100.3	100.1	100.1	100.2	100.1	101.0	100.3	100.4	100.3	100.2
4th quarter	100.9	101.1	100.5	100.1	101.5	100.0	100.4	100.6	100.2	100.9	100.9
1993:											
1st quarter	101.9	101.8	101.1	100.5	102.5	100.0	98.8	101.7	101.8	101.7	101.9
2nd quarter	102.4	102.5	101.5	100.7	103.4	100.2	99.5	102.2	101.9	102.4	102.4
3rd quarter	102.8	102.8	101.7	100.7	104.3	100.0	98.6	102.8	102.8	102.7	102.8
4th quarter	103.5	103.6	101.9	100.8	104.6	100.0	98.2	103.3	103.5	103.1	103.5
1994:											
1st quarter	104.2	104.0	102.6	101.4	105.8	100.4	97.6	104.0	104.0	103.9	104.2
2nd quarter	104.7	104.7	103.2	101.9	106.4	101.0	98.9	104.6	105.0	104.4	104.8
3rd quarter	105.4	105.6	103.7	102.2	107.5	101.4	100.3	105.1	104.8	105.2	105.4
4th quarter	106.1	106.3	104.0	102.1	108.8	102.1	100.7	105.8	105.5	105.9	106.1
1995:											
1st quarter	106.9	107.1	104.5	102.2	110.2	103.2	101.1	106.9	106.9	106.9	107.0
2nd quarter	107.5	107.7	104.9	102.6	110.7	104.1	102.8	107.9	107.6	108.0	107.5
3rd quarter	108.0	108.2	104.9	102.4	111.2	103.6	101.8	108.6	108.3	108.7	108.1
4th quarter	108.6	108.6	104.8	102.1	111.8	102.9	100.8	109.8	110.6	109.4	108.6
1996:											
1st quarter	109.4	109.3	104.7	101.7	112.3	102.5	100.3	111.3	111.9	110.9	109.4
2nd quarter	109.9	110.1	104.5	101.3	112.8	102.1	99.8	111.2	111.5	111.1	109.9
3rd quarter	110.6	110.8	104.9	101.2	114.4	101.5	98.8	112.1	112.1	112.1	110.7
4th quarter	111.1	111.6	104.8	100.8	115.1	100.4	98.8	112.8	112.7	112.8	111.2

PRICE INDEXES FOR GROSS DOMESTIC PRODUCT
(Index numbers, 1992=100)

SELECTED PER CAPITA PRODUCT AND INCOME SERIES AND U.S. POPULATION
(Dollars, except as noted, quarterly data are at seasonally adjusted annual rates)

YEAR AND QUARTER	Current dollars							Chained (1992) dollars						Population (Mid-period, thousands)
	Gross domestic product	Personal income	Disposable personal income	Personal consumption expenditures				Gross domestic product	Disposable personal income	Personal consumption expenditures				
				Total	Durable goods	Nondurable goods	Services			Total	Durable goods	Nondurable goods	Services	
1968	4 536	3 559	3 101	2 789	402	1 174	1 212	16 408	11 468	10 313	930	4 069	5 278	200 745
1969	4 845	3 844	3 302	2 982	424	1 249	1 310	16 739	11 726	10 593	953	4 136	5 479	202 736
1970	5 050	4 082	3 550	3 160	414	1 326	1 419	16 566	12 039	10 717	912	4 189	5 634	205 089
1971	5 419	4 334	3 811	3 383	467	1 375	1 541	16 900	12 366	10 975	990	4 211	5 768	207 692
1972	5 894	4 710	4 082	3 671	526	1 467	1 678	17 637	12 794	11 508	1 105	4 349	6 014	209 924
1973	6 524	5 226	4 562	4 018	583	1 619	1 816	18 479	13 566	11 950	1 207	4 449	6 225	211 939
1974	6 998	5 685	4 941	4 353	572	1 797	1 984	18 192	13 344	11 756	1 114	4 322	6 317	213 898
1975	7 550	6 107	5 383	4 765	618	1 948	2 199	17 936	13 444	11 899	1 103	4 344	6 474	215 981
1976	8 341	6 692	5 856	5 268	728	2 101	2 438	18 721	13 837	12 446	1 231	4 516	6 681	218 086
1977	9 201	7 336	6 383	5 797	822	2 256	2 719	19 400	14 142	12 846	1 332	4 587	6 892	220 289
1978	10 292	8 201	7 123	6 418	905	2 470	3 043	20 226	14 715	13 258	1 387	4 697	7 139	222 629
1979	11 361	9 133	7 888	7 079	950	2 772	3 357	20 571	14 951	13 417	1 365	4 752	7 285	225 106
1980	12 226	10 069	8 697	7 730	938	3 054	3 739	20 265	14 867	13 216	1 241	4 677	7 336	227 726
1981	13 547	11 167	9 601	8 440	1 002	3 296	4 142	20 524	15 064	13 245	1 243	4 671	7 374	230 008
1982	13 961	11 744	10 145	8 943	1 030	3 388	4 525	19 896	15 053	13 270	1 229	4 654	7 442	232 218
1983	14 998	12 379	10 803	9 744	1 194	3 543	5 007	20 499	15 332	13 829	1 397	4 747	7 720	234 332
1984	16 508	13 602	11 929	10 543	1 375	3 738	5 430	21 744	16 309	14 415	1 586	4 872	7 966	236 394
1985	17 529	14 464	12 629	11 341	1 514	3 889	5 938	22 320	16 654	14 954	1 725	4 941	8 290	238 506
1986	18 374	15 200	13 289	12 019	1 656	3 977	6 385	22 801	17 039	15 409	1 863	5 052	8 482	240 682
1987	19 323	16 013	13 896	12 743	1 716	4 175	6 851	23 264	17 164	15 740	1 873	5 103	8 758	242 842
1988	20 605	17 076	14 905	13 669	1 840	4 411	7 417	23 934	17 678	16 211	1 973	5 200	9 028	245 061
1989	21 984	18 194	15 790	14 531	1 911	4 704	7 915	24 504	17 854	16 430	2 006	5 269	9 145	247 387
1990	22 979	19 220	16 721	15 360	1 906	4 982	8 472	24 549	17 996	16 532	1 974	5 265	9 287	249 956
1991	23 416	19 715	17 242	15 732	1 802	5 056	8 874	24 060	17 809	16 249	1 828	5 156	9 265	252 680
1992	24 447	20 660	18 113	16 520	1 913	5 175	9 433	24 447	18 113	16 520	1 913	5 175	9 433	255 432
1993	25 403	21 379	18 706	17 273	2 054	5 309	9 910	24 750	18 221	16 825	2 029	5 233	9 563	258 161
1994	26 647	22 216	19 381	18 093	2 223	5 479	10 391	25 357	18 431	17 207	2 153	5 331	9 725	260 705
1995	27 605	23 370	20 349	18 837	2 312	5 607	10 917	25 616	18 861	17 460	2 217	5 367	9 877	263 194
1996	28 752	24 457	21 117	19 608	2 389	5 779	11 441	26 088	19 116	17 750	2 301	5 393	10 057	265 579
1988:														
1st quarter	20 057	16 691	14 582	13 296	1 819	4 281	7 197	23 690	17 623	16 069	1 969	5 139	8 951	244 208
2nd quarter	20 433	16 947	14 761	13 527	1 832	4 363	7 332	23 881	17 623	16 150	1 972	5 176	8 992	244 716
3rd quarter	20 764	17 196	15 026	13 785	1 822	4 459	7 504	23 960	17 704	16 242	1 948	5 221	9 067	245 354
4th quarter	21 163	17 467	15 248	14 064	1 888	4 542	7 634	24 202	17 761	16 381	2 003	5 264	9 102	245 966
1989:														
1st quarter	21 573	17 924	15 580	14 226	1 876	4 594	7 755	24 389	17 920	16 363	1 982	5 256	9 117	246 460
2nd quarter	21 914	18 135	15 703	14 451	1 913	4 694	7 844	24 515	17 804	16 385	2 011	5 245	9 117	247 017
3rd quarter	22 152	18 243	15 842	14 644	1 956	4 738	7 950	24 578	17 833	16 485	2 048	5 281	9 142	247 698
4th quarter	22 296	18 473	16 032	14 800	1 899	4 790	8 111	24 534	17 859	16 487	1 982	5 294	9 203	248 374
1990:														
1st quarter	22 740	18 882	16 420	15 102	1 982	4 904	8 216	24 716	18 035	16 587	2 053	5 299	9 222	248 928
2nd quarter	23 043	19 170	16 652	15 274	1 914	4 929	8 431	24 729	18 063	16 568	1 985	5 277	9 301	249 564
3rd quarter	23 101	19 381	16 860	15 498	1 891	5 019	8 589	24 539	18 031	16 574	1 959	5 273	9 338	250 299
4th quarter	23 032	19 446	16 947	15 564	1 840	5 076	8 648	24 216	17 856	16 398	1 897	5 212	9 287	250 299
1991:														
1st quarter	23 135	19 466	16 993	15 540	1 784	5 040	8 716	24 031	17 748	16 231	1 822	5 168	9 240	251 650
2nd quarter	23 355	19 673	17 214	15 700	1 794	5 072	8 833	24 078	17 861	16 290	1 825	5 185	9 281	252 295
3rd quarter	23 515	19 770	17 306	15 815	1 826	5 072	8 917	24 069	17 816	16 280	1 847	5 166	9 268	253 033
4th quarter	23 654	19 948	17 456	15 871	1 802	5 041	9 028	24 061	17 811	16 194	1 819	5 106	9 269	253 743
1992:														
1st quarter	24 070	20 304	17 801	16 229	1 864	5 124	9 241	24 281	18 000	16 410	1 872	5 168	9 370	254 338
2nd quarter	24 315	20 537	18 028	16 402	1 887	5 130	9 384	24 366	18 085	16 454	1 887	5 144	9 423	255 032
3rd quarter	24 516	20 631	18 088	16 570	1 925	5 185	9 460	24 474	18 036	16 522	1 923	5 144	9 435	255 815
4th quarter	24 881	21 163	18 533	16 877	1 973	5 260	9 643	24 663	18 330	16 692	1 968	5 223	9 502	256 543
1993:														
1st quarter	25 061	20 880	18 304	16 976	1 969	5 267	9 740	24 608	17 975	16 671	1 960	5 201	9 509	257 151
2nd quarter	25 250	21 351	18 692	17 177	2 033	5 300	9 844	24 671	18 247	16 769	2 014	5 228	9 527	257 785
3rd quarter	25 432	21 446	18 756	17 363	2 078	5 315	9 970	24 732	18 246	16 891	2 050	5 248	9 593	258 516
4th quarter	25 866	21 834	19 070	17 574	2 134	5 355	10 084	24 989	18 413	16 968	2 092	5 254	9 624	259 191
1994:														
1st quarter	26 158	21 623	18 878	17 774	2 168	5 407	10 199	25 120	18 154	17 092	2 120	5 307	9 667	259 738
2nd quarter	26 546	22 149	19 267	17 978	2 199	5 439	10 341	25 352	18 409	17 178	2 135	5 322	9 723	260 351
3rd quarter	26 764	22 365	19 530	18 199	2 235	5 514	10 450	25 396	18 493	17 232	2 152	5 337	9 745	261 040
4th quarter	27 115	22 722	19 844	18 419	2 290	5 555	10 574	25 559	18 667	17 326	2 203	5 359	9 767	261 692
1995:														
1st quarter	27 338	23 083	20 160	18 578	2 276	5 578	10 724	25 564	18 834	17 356	2 182	5 371	9 805	262 235
2nd quarter	27 428	23 264	20 239	18 774	2 293	5 602	10 879	25 524	18 798	17 438	2 198	5 370	9 871	262 847
3rd quarter	27 706	23 448	20 416	18 938	2 338	5 618	10 983	25 649	18 871	17 505	2 242	5 365	9 899	263 527
4th quarter	27 944	23 683	20 579	19 055	2 341	5 632	11 082	25 728	18 942	17 540	2 247	5 361	9 932	264 169
1996:														
1st quarter	28 213	24 027	20 853	19 291	2 368	5 698	11 225	25 791	19 071	17 642	2 269	5 374	9 999	264 680
2nd quarter	28 680	24 359	21 012	19 562	2 407	5 776	11 378	26 111	19 081	17 765	2 318	5 397	10 052	265 258
3rd quarter	28 869	24 604	21 229	19 660	2 386	5 786	11 488	26 116	19 161	17 745	2 301	5 393	10 052	265 887
4th quarter	29 243	24 835	21 373	19 919	2 395	5 854	11 669	26 333	19 152	17 848	2 316	5 408	10 125	266 491

COMPOSITE INDEXES OF ECONOMIC ACTIVITY AND INDEX COMPONENTS

YEAR AND MONTH	Index of leading economic indicators			Leading index components (Seasonally adjusted, except as noted)									
	Index (1992=100)	Percent changes		Average weekly hours, manufacturing production workers	Average weekly initial claims, unemployment insurance (Thousands)	Manufacturers' new orders, consumer goods and materials (Bil. 1992$)	Vendor performance, slower deliveries diffusion index (Percent)	Manufacturers' new orders, nondefense capital goods (Bil. 1992$)	Building permits, new private housing units (Thousands)	Stock prices: 500 common stocks, (Index, 1941-1943=10) [1]	Money supply (M2) (Bil. 1992$)	Interest rate spread, 10-year treasury bonds less federal funds [1]	Index of consumer expectations [1,2]
		From previous period	Over 6-month span, annual rate										
1968	86.2	1.8	2.1	40.7	195	1 053.70	52.6	266.41	1 524.1	98.70	2 016.6	-0.01	91.4
1969	86.7	0.5	-2.7	40.6	196	1 092.06	65.2	291.42	1 500.2	97.84	2 055.8	-1.53	88.5
1970	84.6	-2.1	-1.8	39.8	298	998.23	50.3	239.56	1 522.2	83.22	2 039.6	0.17	73.7
1971	87.2	2.6	4.9	39.9	293	1 052.43	48.0	254.02	2 158.2	98.29	2 187.9	1.50	77.1
1972	90.6	3.4	4.7	40.5	263	1 188.81	62.7	290.13	2 477.7	109.20	2 376.5	1.78	87.3
1973	91.3	0.7	-1.9	40.7	243	1 323.64	88.0	357.44	2 026.0	107.43	2 474.0	-1.89	67.6
1974	87.5	-3.8	-10.6	40.0	355	1 224.65	65.8	364.09	1 189.0	82.85	2 379.2	-2.95	56.0
1975	86.4	-1.1	8.0	39.4	474	1 007.26	30.2	277.28	1 043.0	86.16	2 407.1	2.16	65.5
1976	90.6	4.2	3.5	40.1	382	1 151.63	54.4	309.26	1 441.3	102.01	2 568.2	2.57	82.7
1977	92.3	1.7	1.0	40.3	374	1 267.46	55.7	343.84	1 867.6	98.20	2 707.8	1.88	81.3
1978	92.6	0.3	1.3	40.4	341	1 344.94	60.5	388.64	1 874.0	96.02	2 734.4	0.48	69.3
1979	91.2	-1.4	-3.7	40.2	383	1 307.62	57.9	406.38	1 593.9	103.01	2 704.7	-1.75	52.8
1980	89.4	-1.9	0.6	39.7	489	1 153.83	40.6	325.70	1 246.4	118.78	2 635.5	-1.90	56.8
1981	89.8	0.5	-4.0	39.9	450	1 165.63	46.3	326.87	1 031.8	128.05	2 637.0	-2.47	65.0
1982	89.6	-0.3	3.1	39.0	586	1 068.03	43.5	285.82	1 040.6	119.71	2 722.1	0.74	62.7
1983	94.5	4.9	7.9	40.1	439	1 205.31	56.8	283.63	1 690.4	160.41	2 923.1	2.02	84.7
1984	96.2	1.8	-1.8	40.7	373	1 301.60	57.3	336.15	1 737.2	160.46	3 041.0	2.21	92.7
1985	97.1	0.8	2.1	40.5	392	1 305.69	48.0	345.23	1 780.9	186.84	3 194.0	2.52	86.5
1986	98.4	1.4	2.7	40.7	377	1 332.90	50.6	332.27	1 820.6	236.35	3 357.5	0.88	85.8
1987	100.0	1.6	0.8	41.0	324	1 406.70	57.4	355.88	1 584.5	286.83	3 444.8	1.73	81.3
1988	100.3	0.3	0.9	41.0	311	1 455.80	57.7	412.53	1 492.7	265.79	3 485.9	1.28	85.2
1989	99.6	-0.7	-1.1	40.9	330	1 449.51	47.6	421.88	1 388.3	322.84	3 462.1	-0.72	85.3
1990	99.2	-0.5	-3.0	40.7	386	1 416.21	47.9	415.17	1 155.1	334.59	3 475.5	0.45	70.2
1991	99.0	-0.2	1.2	40.6	448	1 372.92	47.3	372.89	972.3	376.18	3 458.3	2.17	70.3
1992	100.0	1.0	1.5	41.1	406	1 442.10	50.2	377.89	1 128.8	415.74	3 413.2	3.49	70.3
1993	100.5	0.5	1.4	41.4	342	1 504.27	51.6	373.87	1 241.1	451.41	3 361.5	2.85	72.8
1994	101.4	0.9	2.3	41.9	342	1 635.99	60.1	415.56	1 366.9	460.33	3 327.4	2.88	83.8
1995	100.9	-0.5	....	41.6	358	1 670.61	52.8	465.44	1 335.8	541.64	3 311.1	0.74	83.2
1996	102.1	1.2	....	41.5	352	1 729.59	50.5	503.90	1 418.2	670.83	3 393.3	1.14	85.7
1993:													
January	100.7	-0.3	0.6	41.3	344	125.05	52.3	28.86	1 210.0	435.23	3 378.6	3.58	83.4
February	100.7	0.0	-0.4	41.5	337	127.13	51.7	32.97	1 180.0	441.70	3 360.7	3.23	80.6
March	100.1	-0.6	-1.4	41.1	353	124.71	52.7	29.62	1 086.0	450.16	3 351.5	2.91	75.8
April	100.4	0.3	-1.2	41.6	347	123.95	52.8	31.49	1 135.0	443.08	3 345.2	3.01	76.4
May	100.2	-0.2	-0.8	41.3	344	122.26	51.5	30.46	1 143.0	445.25	3 364.7	3.04	68.5
June	100.3	0.1	0.6	41.2	345	124.15	50.4	33.06	1 162.0	448.06	3 368.7	2.92	70.4
July	100.1	-0.2	0.2	41.4	351	123.07	51.0	29.18	1 207.0	447.29	3 364.9	2.75	64.7
August	100.3	0.2	1.2	41.4	337	122.49	51.8	30.98	1 264.0	454.13	3 362.3	2.65	65.8
September	100.4	0.1	1.8	41.6	337	125.98	51.3	29.75	1 286.0	459.24	3 363.9	2.27	66.8
October	100.5	0.1	2.2	41.5	351	127.00	50.7	31.24	1 323.0	463.90	3 354.7	2.34	72.5
November	100.8	0.3	1.4	41.6	341	128.38	50.9	33.01	1 395.0	462.89	3 359.3	2.70	70.3
December	101.2	0.4	2.2	41.7	324	130.11	51.5	33.27	1 502.0	465.95	3 363.0	2.81	78.8
1994:													
January	101.2	0.0	1.8	41.7	364	131.13	54.3	35.15	1 390.0	472.99	3 366.2	2.70	86.4
February	101.0	-0.2	1.2	41.2	347	131.30	56.7	33.69	1 269.0	471.58	3 357.6	2.72	83.5
March	101.5	0.5	0.4	42.0	334	136.16	55.4	33.74	1 342.0	463.81	3 351.1	3.14	85.1
April	101.4	-0.1	3.6	41.9	350	133.47	57.3	33.45	1 392.0	447.23	3 353.7	3.41	82.6
May	101.4	0.0	1.0	42.0	365	136.02	60.5	32.77	1 396.0	450.90	3 349.7	3.17	84.2
June	101.4	0.0	-0.2	42.0	348	136.30	60.2	35.82	1 357.0	454.83	3 330.1	2.85	82.7
July	101.2	-0.2	0.2	42.0	346	134.39	58.5	34.05	1 335.0	451.40	3 326.0	3.04	78.5
August	101.5	0.3	0.4	42.0	334	139.09	61.7	34.80	1 377.0	464.24	3 311.1	2.77	80.8
September	101.4	-0.1	0.4	41.9	328	137.99	62.3	35.39	1 412.0	466.96	3 303.9	2.73	83.5
October	101.5	0.1	0.6	42.1	333	136.97	64.7	34.85	1 397.0	463.81	3 296.9	2.98	85.1
November	101.6	0.1	-0.8	42.1	329	140.69	65.0	37.23	1 340.0	461.01	3 292.5	2.67	84.8
December	101.6	0.0	-1.4	42.1	324	142.50	64.5	34.61	1 396.0	455.19	3 289.8	2.36	88.8
1995:													
January	101.5	-0.1	-1.8	42.2	331	143.08	62.2	37.58	1 282.0	465.25	3 282.2	2.25	88.4
February	101.1	-0.4	-2.3	41.9	337	140.94	60.2	37.78	1 254.0	481.92	3 275.2	1.55	85.9
March	100.7	-0.4	-2.2	41.8	339	140.57	57.0	38.03	1 226.0	493.15	3 269.8	1.22	79.8
April	100.6	-0.1	-1.6	41.5	353	137.17	56.3	36.48	1 259.0	507.91	3 273.0	1.01	83.8
May	100.4	-0.2	-0.2	41.4	374	137.27	53.7	39.72	1 271.0	523.81	3 283.1	0.62	80.1
June	100.5	0.1	0.8	41.4	376	137.54	51.6	37.98	1 305.0	539.35	3 305.1	0.17	84.1
July	100.7	0.2	0.6	41.3	374	137.35	51.7	35.61	1 354.0	557.37	3 317.8	0.43	87.4
August	101.0	0.3	1.0	41.5	352	139.75	49.4	36.85	1 386.0	559.11	3 329.3	0.75	86.1
September	101.1	0.1	1.4	41.5	359	138.57	50.1	41.65	1 421.0	578.77	3 342.5	0.40	78.8
October	100.9	-0.2	-0.4	41.5	366	140.06	48.4	38.36	1 400.0	582.92	3 344.2	0.28	80.8
November	100.9	0.0	0.8	41.5	376	139.13	45.6	41.29	1 430.0	595.53	3 351.5	0.13	79.7
December	101.2	0.3	1.0	41.2	363	139.20	47.2	44.12	1 442.0	614.57	3 359.8	0.11	83.7
1996:													
January	100.5	-0.7	1.8	40.1	371	138.74	47.0	42.99	1 385.0	614.42	3 364.5	0.09	78.7
February	101.4	0.9	2.4	41.4	369	138.43	49.0	41.64	1 425.0	649.54	3 370.0	0.59	77.8
March	101.6	0.2	2.2	41.3	391	136.41	49.9	43.50	1 438.0	647.07	3 388.1	0.96	86.2
April	101.8	0.2	3.6	41.5	358	143.49	49.4	37.91	1 486.0	647.17	3 387.2	1.29	83.0
May	102.1	0.3	2.0	41.6	349	145.55	50.2	42.76	1 457.0	661.23	3 382.9	1.50	79.2
June	102.3	0.2	1.8	41.7	355	145.31	52.6	40.34	1 432.0	668.50	3 393.4	1.64	84.0
July	102.3	0.0	1.4	41.6	337	148.06	51.3	43.25	1 454.0	644.07	3 390.1	1.47	86.5
August	102.4	0.1	1.0	41.7	326	146.45	52.3	38.74	1 405.0	662.68	3 397.7	1.42	87.3
September	102.5	0.1	0.8	41.7	336	147.47	50.2	45.19	1 391.0	674.88	3 400.9	1.53	90.1
October	102.5	0.0	1.4	41.7	335	148.35	50.7	44.64	1 349.0	701.45	3 400.9	1.29	89.9
November	102.6	0.1	2.0	41.7	338	147.58	51.6	41.47	1 391.0	735.67	3 413.8	0.89	93.9
December	102.7	0.1	2.2	42.0	354	143.75	51.6	41.49	1 405.0	743.25	3 429.7	1.01	91.8

1. Not seasonally adjusted.
2. Copyright, University of Michigan; first quarter 1966=100.

YEAR AND MONTH	Diffusion indexes: 10 leading indicator components (Percent rising)		Index of coincident economic indicators			Coincident index components (Seasonally adjusted, except as noted)				Diffusion indexes: 4 coincident indicator components (Percent rising)	
			Index (1992=100)	Percent change		Employees on non-agricultural payrolls (Thousands)	Personal income less transfer payments (Bil. 1992$)	Index of industrial production (1992=100)	Manufacturing and trade sales (Mil. 1992$)		
	1-month span	6-month span		From previous period	Over 6-month span, annual rate					1-month span	6-month span
1968	....	....	58.5	4.3	....	67 889	2 404.9	58.0	3 719 541	....	....
1969	....	....	60.9	4.0	....	70 383	2 514.1	60.7	3 840 315	....	....
1970	....	....	60.9	0.1	....	70 889	2 548.6	58.7	3 792 043	....	....
1971	....	....	61.8	1.4	....	71 215	2 592.0	59.5	3 966 916	....	....
1972	....	....	65.2	5.5	....	73 667	2 744.3	65.3	4 317 895	....	....
1973	....	....	68.9	5.6	....	76 779	2 907.0	70.6	4 677 504	....	....
1974	....	....	69.1	0.3	....	78 273	2 868.4	69.5	4 649 449	....	....
1975	....	....	66.7	-3.4	....	76 940	2 810.8	63.4	4 309 736	....	....
1976	....	....	70.0	4.9	....	79 380	2 946.6	69.3	4 622 655	....	....
1977	....	....	73.4	4.9	....	82 469	3 075.6	74.9	4 944 799	....	....
1978	....	....	77.5	5.5	....	86 692	3 260.8	79.3	5 251 973	....	....
1979	....	....	80.2	3.4	....	89 826	3 371.9	81.9	5 377 659	....	....
1980	....	....	79.8	-0.4	....	90 418	3 358.2	79.7	5 211 474	....	....
1981	....	....	81.0	1.4	....	91 161	3 443.4	81.0	5 243 527	....	....
1982	....	....	79.3	-2.0	....	89 552	3 429.0	76.6	5 029 242	....	....
1983	....	....	80.7	1.8	....	90 145	3 480.3	79.5	5 276 272	....	....
1984	....	....	86.1	6.6	....	94 404	3 762.3	86.6	5 719 488	....	....
1985	....	....	88.6	3.0	....	97 387	3 894.2	88.0	5 884 621	....	....
1986	....	....	90.7	2.4	....	99 344	4 011.7	89.0	6 111 136	....	....
1987	....	....	93.5	3.1	....	101 953	4 117.9	93.1	6 335 344	....	....
1988	....	....	96.9	3.6	....	105 204	4 264.0	97.3	6 618 856	....	....
1989	....	....	99.1	2.3	....	107 890	4 368.5	99.0	6 735 633	....	....
1990	....	....	100.1	1.1	....	109 416	4 417.0	98.9	6 755 739	....	....
1991	....	....	98.7	-1.4	....	108 261	4 336.6	96.9	6 650 003	....	....
1992	....	....	100.0	1.3	....	108 591	4 390.4	100.0	6 884 702	....	....
1993	....	....	102.3	2.3	....	110 707	4 492.1	103.4	7 136 148	....	....
1994	....	....	106.1	3.7	....	114 145	4 612.8	108.6	7 535 664	....	....
1995	....	....	109.3	3.0	....	117 195	4 772.5	112.1	7 823 089	....	....
1996	....	....	112.3	2.8	....	119 517	4 913.8	115.2	8 140 538	....	....
1993:											
January	30.0	60.0	101.4	0.2	2.0	109 516	4 468.8	102.3	590 675	100.0	100.0
February	55.0	60.0	101.6	0.2	1.8	109 852	4 466.3	102.8	589 309	62.5	100.0
March	20.0	20.0	101.3	-0.3	1.6	109 757	4 446.5	102.8	586 076	12.5	100.0
April	70.0	30.0	101.6	0.3	1.4	110 071	4 472.1	103.2	587 741	100.0	100.0
May	50.0	40.0	101.9	0.3	1.6	110 386	4 501.2	102.6	588 943	75.0	100.0
June	65.0	70.0	102.0	0.1	2.8	110 550	4 486.6	102.8	594 310	75.0	100.0
July	30.0	40.0	102.1	0.1	2.8	110 759	4 487.3	103.1	590 970	75.0	100.0
August	65.0	70.0	102.4	0.3	2.8	110 983	4 511.2	102.8	594 487	87.5	100.0
September	60.0	80.0	102.7	0.3	3.4	111 220	4 504.7	103.9	599 211	75.0	100.0
October	60.0	70.0	103.0	0.3	3.0	111 541	4 503.9	104.1	601 917	100.0	100.0
November	80.0	70.0	103.3	0.3	3.7	111 795	4 518.1	104.7	604 857	100.0	87.5
December	100.0	80.0	103.7	0.4	4.3	112 050	4 539.0	105.4	607 652	100.0	100.0
1994:											
January	55.0	75.0	103.6	-0.1	4.3	112 284	4 511.1	105.7	607 096	75.0	100.0
February	40.0	60.0	104.3	0.7	4.7	112 577	4 557.4	106.2	612 942	100.0	100.0
March	65.0	60.0	104.9	0.6	4.5	112 988	4 572.0	107.0	622 541	100.0	100.0
April	40.0	50.0	105.2	0.3	5.1	113 355	4 586.9	107.4	619 502	75.0	100.0
May	60.0	70.0	105.7	0.5	4.7	113 704	4 615.5	108.1	621 016	100.0	100.0
June	45.0	60.0	106.0	0.3	3.8	113 991	4 605.8	108.6	625 859	87.5	100.0
July	25.0	80.0	106.2	0.2	4.2	114 335	4 612.3	109.1	623 279	50.0	100.0
August	75.0	70.0	106.7	0.5	3.8	114 685	4 613.8	109.2	637 837	87.5	100.0
September	55.0	70.0	106.9	0.2	4.2	114 992	4 634.9	109.3	635 339	75.0	100.0
October	40.0	70.0	107.4	0.5	4.4	115 247	4 675.3	109.9	638 197	100.0	100.0
November	60.0	40.0	107.7	0.3	3.6	115 674	4 674.2	110.6	643 789	100.0	100.0
December	55.0	30.0	108.2	0.5	3.4	115 906	4 694.6	111.6	648 267	100.0	100.0
1995:											
January	40.0	20.0	108.5	0.3	2.4	116 234	4 737.6	111.9	650 231	100.0	100.0
February	20.0	20.0	108.6	0.1	1.9	116 517	4 733.2	111.7	648 684	37.5	87.5
March	20.0	30.0	108.7	0.1	1.7	116 694	4 736.5	111.7	647 125	75.0	87.5
April	30.0	30.0	108.7	0.0	1.1	116 891	4 762.4	111.4	641 825	50.0	50.0
May	55.0	40.0	108.7	0.0	1.9	116 855	4 737.2	111.5	646 019	50.0	100.0
June	45.0	40.0	109.1	0.4	2.0	117 064	4 760.0	111.7	651 575	100.0	100.0
July	70.0	50.0	109.1	0.0	2.2	117 142	4 777.6	111.7	643 824	75.0	100.0
August	80.0	55.0	109.6	0.5	2.8	117 465	4 768.9	112.6	655 128	75.0	100.0
September	55.0	60.0	109.8	0.2	2.8	117 636	4 791.4	113.0	655 962	100.0	100.0
October	30.0	45.0	109.9	0.1	2.2	117 775	4 813.0	112.5	655 887	62.5	100.0
November	50.0	50.0	110.2	0.3	2.8	117 951	4 824.5	112.7	660 792	100.0	100.0
December	70.0	60.0	110.6	0.4	2.4	118 120	4 827.8	112.8	666 037	100.0	100.0
1996:											
January	20.0	90.0	110.3	-0.3	2.9	118 058	4 826.0	112.4	659 850	100.0	100.0
February	70.0	90.0	111.1	0.7	3.3	118 550	4 865.0	113.8	668 628	100.0	100.0
March	50.0	80.0	111.1	0.0	3.3	118 804	4 869.8	113.2	667 898	37.5	100.0
April	60.0	90.0	111.5	0.4	4.2	118 966	4 876.6	114.3	673 970	100.0	100.0
May	70.0	90.0	112.0	0.4	3.3	119 263	4 889.0	114.8	677 703	100.0	100.0
June	70.0	90.0	112.4	0.4	3.6	119 516	4 938.9	115.5	675 162	75.0	100.0
July	50.0	85.0	112.6	0.2	3.3	119 691	4 913.7	115.5	681 681	62.5	100.0
August	60.0	65.0	112.9	0.3	3.1	119 983	4 937.1	115.9	679 952	75.0	100.0
September	65.0	60.0	113.1	0.2	2.9	120 019	4 962.4	116.0	683 827	75.0	100.0
October	55.0	60.0	113.3	0.2	3.0	120 248	4 937.6	116.2	688 071	75.0	100.0
November	55.0	80.0	113.7	0.4	3.6	120 450	4 958.7	117.2	692 322	100.0	100.0
December	55.0	80.0	114.0	0.3	3.7	120 659	4 991.0	117.7	691 474	75.0	100.0

COMPOSITE INDEXES OF ECONOMIC ACTIVITY AND INDEX COMPONENTS—Continued

YEAR AND MONTH	Index of lagging economic indicators			Lagging index components (Seasonally adjusted, except as noted)							Diffusion indexes: 7 lagging indicator components (Percent rising)		Ratio: Coincident to lagging index (1992=100)
	Index (1992=100)	Percent changes		Average duration of unemployment (Weeks)	Ratio: Manufacturing and trade inventories to sales (1992$)	Manufacturing labor cost per unit of output [1]	Average prime interest rate [2]	Commercial and industrial loans outstanding (Mil. 1992$)	Consumer installment credit outstanding (Percent of personal income)	Consumer price index for services [1]	1-month span	6-month span	
		From previous period	Over 6-month span, annual rate										
1968	98.9	0.7	2.9	8.4	1.30	4.5	6.31	273 262	15.67	5.2	62.5	75.0	69.0
1969	101.2	2.4	3.7	7.9	1.33	4.5	7.95	309 606	15.84	6.9	64.9	82.2	69.3
1970	101.5	0.2	-2.2	8.7	1.39	4.5	7.91	301 912	15.35	8.0	38.7	31.6	68.7
1971	98.5	-3.0	-3.2	11.4	1.37	0.1	5.72	293 047	15.07	5.7	41.7	31.6	72.4
1972	96.7	-1.8	-0.2	12.0	1.30	1.1	5.25	284 348	14.98	3.8	45.3	57.1	77.9
1973	99.5	2.8	6.5	10.0	1.27	4.8	8.02	320 435	15.25	4.4	69.6	82.7	79.0
1974	103.0	3.4	3.4	9.7	1.35	12.6	10.80	361 206	15.05	9.2	53.0	64.9	75.7
1975	99.9	-3.1	-8.6	14.3	1.46	10.6	7.86	305 694	14.23	9.6	25.6	15.5	76.4
1976	96.9	-3.0	-1.1	15.8	1.39	3.2	6.84	285 460	14.02	8.3	48.2	50.6	83.5
1977	97.6	0.6	3.3	14.3	1.36	5.0	6.82	289 623	14.50	7.7	66.1	77.4	86.7
1978	100.0	2.4	3.8	11.9	1.36	5.7	9.06	305 402	15.09	8.6	73.2	75.0	88.4
1979	103.3	3.4	4.3	10.8	1.39	9.5	12.67	337 893	15.50	11.0	64.9	76.8	87.6
1980	103.8	0.5	-3.7	11.9	1.46	10.0	15.27	346 415	14.43	15.4	42.3	31.0	86.6
1981	102.7	-1.0	2.3	13.8	1.47	6.9	18.87	377 611	13.30	13.1	64.3	66.7	89.3
1982	101.2	-1.6	-5.5	15.6	1.52	4.2	14.86	384 868	13.02	9.0	39.9	20.9	88.9
1983	97.6	-3.6	-0.4	19.9	1.43	-3.0	10.79	373 005	13.17	3.5	47.0	51.2	94.8
1984	100.9	3.4	6.4	18.1	1.42	1.8	12.04	444 492	14.09	5.2	75.0	84.5	96.3
1985	103.7	2.8	2.0	15.6	1.45	2.2	9.93	451 587	15.77	5.1	55.9	62.5	96.0
1986	104.5	0.8	-0.1	15.0	1.43	....	8.33	454 505	16.89	5.0	47.6	42.3	97.0
1987	104.2	-0.4	1.1	14.5	1.40	-1.9	8.20	445 992	16.81	4.2	55.4	65.5	100.0
1988	105.0	0.8	2.1	13.5	1.39	3.6	9.32	536 687	16.80	4.6	57.8	76.2	101.4
1989	106.8	1.8	2.2	11.9	1.43	2.6	10.87	561 985	16.98	4.9	59.5	66.7	101.1
1990	106.6	-0.2	-0.6	12.0	1.47	2.8	10.01	544 757	16.53	5.5	42.3	38.7	101.9
1991	104.1	-2.5	-4.6	13.7	1.49	2.7	8.46	477 632	15.85	5.1	32.2	14.9	103.2
1992	100.0	-4.1	-3.6	17.8	1.44	-0.5	6.25	456 588	14.82	3.9	32.7	19.7	110.0
1993	99.5	-0.5	0.3	18.0	1.43	0.3	6.00	447 860	14.67	3.9	49.4	43.5	113.8
1994	100.2	0.7	3.1	18.8	1.40	-1.9	7.14	479 405	15.61	3.3	60.1	63.1	117.3
1995	103.8	3.6	....	16.6	1.41	0.7	8.83	523 895	16.89	3.4	57.2	61.9	115.8
1996	104.6	0.9	....	16.7	1.38	....	8.27	523 824	17.78	3.2	....	....	....
1993:													
January	99.2	0.2	0.4	18.3	1.42	-1.2	6.00	455 182	14.70	4.1	57.1	71.4	102.2
February	99.3	0.1	0.2	18.2	1.43	-1.6	6.00	453 838	14.76	4.1	50.0	71.4	102.3
March	99.4	0.1	1.0	17.6	1.44	-1.6	6.00	448 615	14.77	4.2	64.3	78.6	101.9
April	99.4	0.0	1.0	17.6	1.44	0.8	6.00	449 196	14.57	3.9	57.1	78.6	102.2
May	99.5	0.1	0.6	17.5	1.44	1.8	6.00	453 257	14.47	3.9	57.1	71.4	102.4
June	99.5	0.1	0.4	17.8	1.43	1.4	6.00	454 121	14.55	4.0	42.9	50.0	102.5
July	99.7	0.2	0.4	17.7	1.44	2.4	6.00	455 729	14.64	3.8	78.6	42.9	102.4
August	99.6	-0.1	-0.2	18.0	1.43	3.4	6.00	453 795	14.61	3.8	42.9	21.4	102.8
September	99.6	0.0	-0.2	18.1	1.43	3.5	6.00	452 153	14.73	3.9	28.6	21.4	103.1
October	99.6	0.0	0.2	18.1	1.42	2.0	6.00	448 584	14.81	3.6	50.0	21.4	103.4
November	99.4	-0.2	-0.6	18.6	1.42	1.4	6.00	447 104	14.88	3.5	21.4	21.4	103.9
December	99.4	0.1	-0.8	18.3	1.41	1.0	6.00	447 860	14.55	3.6	42.9	28.6	104.3
1994:													
January	99.8	0.4	-0.6	18.6	1.42	1.2	6.00	450 620	15.27	3.3	64.3	28.6	103.8
February	99.3	-0.5	0.4	19.0	1.41	-1.4	6.00	446 047	15.21	3.6	21.4	42.9	105.0
March	99.2	-0.1	1.2	19.0	1.39	-0.6	6.06	445 105	15.31	3.6	57.1	42.9	105.7
April	99.3	0.1	0.6	18.9	1.40	-1.6	6.45	444 652	15.27	3.4	71.4	42.9	105.9
May	99.6	0.3	2.2	19.4	1.41	-2.2	6.99	448 440	15.36	3.1	71.4	64.3	106.1
June	100.0	0.4	3.0	18.6	1.41	-1.6	7.25	451 804	15.53	2.9	71.4	85.7	106.0
July	100.1	0.1	3.2	19.0	1.42	-2.9	7.25	454 428	15.58	3.0	57.1	64.3	106.1
August	100.4	0.3	3.9	18.8	1.39	-1.2	7.51	457 190	15.75	3.1	85.7	85.7	106.3
September	100.7	0.3	3.4	18.8	1.40	-1.0	7.75	462 500	15.86	2.9	85.7	71.4	106.2
October	100.9	0.2	4.2	19.4	1.40	0.4	7.75	470 584	15.92	3.0	71.4	85.7	106.4
November	101.5	0.6	4.4	18.1	1.39	-0.2	8.15	472 955	16.06	3.2	78.6	100.0	106.1
December	101.7	0.2	4.2	17.9	1.39	-1.4	8.50	479 405	16.15	3.0	57.1	92.9	106.4
1995:													
January	102.2	0.5	5.0	17.1	1.40	-0.6	8.50	484 908	16.18	3.5	92.9	100.0	106.2
February	102.6	0.4	4.4	17.1	1.40	-0.6	9.00	493 170	16.26	3.3	71.4	100.0	105.8
March	102.8	0.2	5.0	17.2	1.41	-1.0	9.00	497 197	16.45	3.6	57.1	100.0	105.7
April	103.4	0.6	4.2	17.4	1.43	-0.2	9.00	505 939	16.52	3.8	78.6	100.0	105.1
May	103.7	0.3	3.3	16.9	1.42	1.0	9.00	506 672	16.76	3.7	64.3	78.6	104.8
June	104.2	0.5	3.3	15.7	1.41	0.8	9.00	511 050	16.86	4.0	78.6	71.4	104.7
July	104.3	0.1	2.1	16.5	1.43	1.8	8.80	513 043	16.92	3.5	57.1	42.9	104.6
August	104.3	-0.1	1.5	16.2	1.41	0.2	8.75	515 613	17.10	3.4	42.9	42.9	105.1
September	104.5	0.2	0.4	16.3	1.41	-0.6	8.75	517 858	17.29	3.1	57.1	28.6	105.1
October	104.5	0.0	0.6	16.2	1.42	0.6	8.75	521 116	17.31	3.2	71.4	42.9	105.2
November	104.5	0.0	0.2	16.5	1.41	1.0	8.75	517 242	17.49	3.1	35.7	28.6	105.5
December	104.4	-0.1	0.8	16.4	1.39	0.8	8.65	523 895	17.54	2.9	42.9	28.6	105.9
1996:													
January	104.6	0.2	-1.6	16.2	1.41	-1.2	8.50	523 303	17.57	3.1	71.4	28.6	105.4
February	104.4	-0.2	0.2	16.6	1.39	-1.4	8.25	521 329	17.59	3.2	28.6	42.9	106.4
March	104.5	0.1	0.2	17.2	1.39	1.2	8.25	526 221	17.68	3.2	57.1	42.9	106.3
April	104.5	0.0	0.2	17.3	1.38	0.6	8.25	527 726	17.74	3.0	35.7	57.1	106.7
May	104.6	0.1	0.8	16.9	1.38	-0.6	8.25	526 211	17.77	3.3	50.0	64.3	107.1
June	104.5	-0.1	0.6	17.2	1.38	-0.6	8.25	525 762	17.70	3.4	50.0	78.6	107.6
July	104.7	0.2	0.4	16.9	1.37	-0.4	8.25	524 691	17.90	3.5	64.3	64.3	107.5
August	104.8	0.1	0.2	17.2	1.38	0.4	8.25	524 879	17.92	3.3	50.0	57.1	107.7
September	104.8	0.0	0.6	16.9	1.37	-0.2	8.25	528 441	17.84	3.5	57.1	64.3	107.9
October	104.7	-0.1	0.4	16.7	1.37	-1.2	8.25	522 669	17.94	3.4	42.9	42.9	108.2
November	104.7	0.0	-0.8	16.0	1.37	-2.0	8.25	521 925	17.90	3.3	35.7	35.7	108.6
December	104.8	0.1	-0.2	15.8	1.36	-1.6	8.25	523 824	17.77	3.4	71.4	50.0	108.8

1. Annual data are annual average percent change; monthly data are six-month percent change at annual rate.
2. Not seasonally adjusted.

Consumer Income and Spending

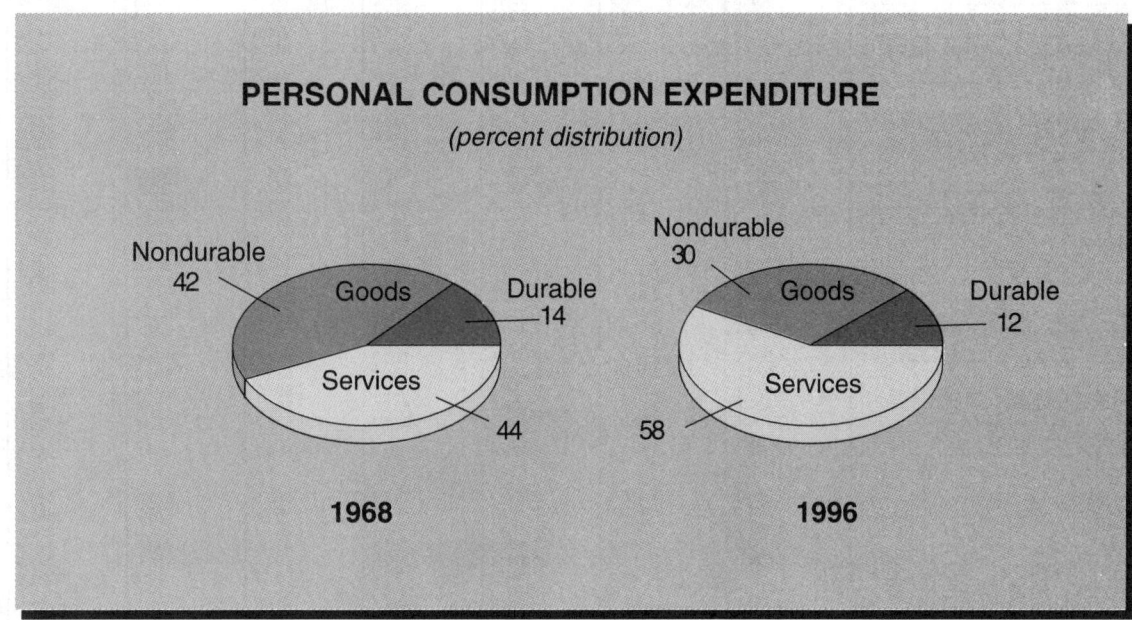

PERSONAL CONSUMPTION EXPENDITURE
(percent distribution)

1968

1996

In 1996, 58 percent of all consumer spending was for services, compared to 44 percent in 1968. The larger share of the consumer dollar spent for services reflected primarily the more rapid rate of price increase for services than for goods. Prices of services rose substantially faster than prices of nondurable goods from 1968 to 1996 and more than two and one-half times faster than prices of durable goods.

The slower rate of price increase for durable goods is explained in part by declining prices for many "high tech" electronic goods, such as CD players, VCRs, and home computers. Thus, using a slightly smaller share of each dollar spent, consumers were able to purchase a far larger real quantity of durable goods. After adjustment for price increase, total consumer purchasing rose 128 percent from 1968 to 1996, but the real quantity of durable goods purchased rose a much larger 227 percent. Real purchases of services were up 152 percent while purchases of nondurable goods rose only 75 percent.

CONSUMER INCOME AND SPENDING

PERSONAL INCOME BY SOURCE
(Billions of dollars, monthly data are at seasonally adjusted annual rates)

YEAR AND MONTH	Total	Wage and salary disbursements							Other labor income
		Total	Private industries					Government	
			Total	Commodity-producing industries		Distributive industries	Service industries		
				Total	Manufacturing				
1968	714.5	471.9	375.3	184.1	146.0	110.8	80.4	96.6	25.2
1969	779.3	518.3	412.7	200.4	157.7	121.7	90.6	105.5	28.5
1970	837.1	551.5	434.3	203.7	158.4	131.2	99.4	117.1	32.5
1971	900.2	583.9	457.4	209.1	160.5	140.4	107.9	126.5	36.7
1972	988.8	638.7	501.2	228.2	175.6	153.3	119.7	137.4	43.0
1973	1 107.5	708.7	560.0	255.9	196.6	170.3	133.9	148.7	49.2
1974	1 215.9	772.6	611.8	276.5	211.8	186.8	148.6	160.9	56.5
1975	1 319.0	814.6	638.6	277.1	211.6	198.1	163.4	176.0	65.9
1976	1 459.4	899.5	710.8	309.7	238.0	219.5	181.6	188.6	79.7
1977	1 616.1	993.9	791.6	346.1	266.7	242.7	202.8	202.3	94.7
1978	1 825.9	1 120.8	901.2	392.6	300.1	274.9	233.7	219.6	110.1
1979	2 055.8	1 255.9	1 018.8	442.5	335.3	308.5	267.8	237.1	124.3
1980	2 293.0	1 377.7	1 116.4	472.5	356.4	336.7	307.2	261.3	139.8
1981	2 568.5	1 517.6	1 232.0	514.9	388.0	368.5	348.6	285.6	153.0
1982	2 727.2	1 593.9	1 286.7	515.1	386.2	385.9	385.7	307.3	165.4
1983	2 900.8	1 685.3	1 360.3	528.2	401.2	405.7	426.4	325.0	177.2
1984	3 215.3	1 855.1	1 507.5	586.6	445.9	445.2	475.6	347.6	188.9
1985	3 449.8	1 995.9	1 622.1	620.7	468.9	476.5	525.0	373.8	203.1
1986	3 658.4	2 116.5	1 720.0	637.3	481.2	501.6	581.0	396.6	216.0
1987	3 888.7	2 272.7	1 849.5	660.4	497.2	535.4	653.7	423.1	235.4
1988	4 184.6	2 453.6	2 003.2	707.0	530.1	575.3	720.9	450.4	251.7
1989	4 501.0	2 598.1	2 118.7	732.4	548.1	606.8	779.5	479.4	273.1
1990	4 804.2	2 757.5	2 240.3	754.2	561.2	634.1	852.1	517.2	300.6
1991	4 981.6	2 827.6	2 281.5	746.3	562.5	646.6	888.6	546.1	322.7
1992	5 277.2	2 986.4	2 418.6	765.7	583.5	680.3	972.6	567.8	351.3
1993	5 519.2	3 089.6	2 505.3	781.2	592.9	699.4	1 024.7	584.3	385.1
1994	5 791.8	3 240.7	2 638.5	824.4	620.8	741.4	1 072.7	602.2	405.0
1995	6 150.8	3 429.5	2 806.5	864.4	648.4	783.1	1 159.0	623.0	406.8
1996	6 495.2	3 632.5	2 989.9	909.1	674.7	823.3	1 257.5	642.6	407.6
1993:									
January	5 366.1	2 975.2	2 390.9	748.2	566.5	679.1	963.6	584.3	371.3
February	5 375.0	2 979.4	2 399.9	752.4	568.2	678.7	968.8	579.4	374.4
March	5 367.2	2 971.7	2 392.3	748.4	565.3	674.8	969.1	579.4	375.7
April	5 483.3	3 064.6	2 484.4	780.1	594.5	693.4	1 010.9	580.2	375.7
May	5 518.3	3 091.9	2 510.3	780.5	592.2	702.0	1 027.9	581.6	379.2
June	5 510.6	3 081.5	2 498.7	779.2	591.9	697.7	1 021.9	582.8	383.9
July	5 517.7	3 097.5	2 513.1	783.2	594.2	702.6	1 027.2	584.4	383.8
August	5 556.9	3 119.4	2 533.2	785.3	595.7	706.3	1 041.7	586.1	386.9
September	5 558.1	3 116.3	2 528.1	791.0	601.5	704.0	1 033.1	588.3	390.6
October	5 580.3	3 130.0	2 542.4	793.2	601.1	708.5	1 040.7	587.6	390.9
November	5 603.7	3 137.7	2 549.6	797.5	604.7	707.2	1 044.9	588.1	393.3
December	5 793.4	3 310.1	2 720.5	835.0	639.0	738.8	1 146.7	589.6	394.6
									396.7
1994:									
January	5 562.0	3 138.4	2 543.8	793.5	598.6	715.7	1 034.6	594.6	399.8
February	5 628.0	3 128.5	2 532.1	794.9	598.4	711.9	1 025.3	596.4	398.3
March	5 658.9	3 148.0	2 551.1	802.9	605.2	719.9	1 028.3	596.9	400.4
April	5 740.4	3 214.5	2 615.4	816.1	615.2	732.8	1 066.5	599.1	402.2
May	5 776.6	3 241.8	2 638.1	821.2	618.9	738.9	1 078.1	603.7	405.0
June	5 782.8	3 239.7	2 638.6	824.1	621.2	742.1	1 072.4	601.1	403.9
July	5 811.5	3 256.6	2 654.5	829.0	624.1	745.7	1 079.8	602.1	406.8
August	5 834.2	3 262.2	2 658.7	832.0	626.8	746.4	1 080.3	603.4	406.4
September	5 868.5	3 281.9	2 677.0	837.6	629.8	752.0	1 087.4	604.9	407.5
October	5 928.8	3 319.6	2 713.1	842.9	633.7	764.1	1 106.1	606.5	411.0
November	5 937.6	3 318.6	2 710.8	847.5	637.1	761.3	1 101.9	607.8	409.1
December	5 972.0	3 338.5	2 728.7	851.3	640.6	765.4	1 112.0	609.8	409.3
1995:									
January	6 039.3	3 366.7	2 751.9	852.5	642.9	770.5	1 128.9	614.8	409.6
February	6 050.3	3 369.6	2 752.0	855.3	643.3	769.2	1 127.5	617.6	407.6
March	6 069.6	3 377.4	2 758.2	856.6	644.0	770.1	1 131.5	619.2	406.4
April	6 112.6	3 412.4	2 792.9	859.0	644.9	784.5	1 149.5	619.5	409.3
May	6 099.5	3 388.5	2 767.7	856.2	643.4	772.5	1 139.1	620.8	404.7
June	6 132.2	3 412.9	2 790.0	860.4	645.4	779.2	1 150.4	623.0	405.8
July	6 164.9	3 445.5	2 821.7	864.2	648.0	788.9	1 168.5	624.2	407.9
August	6 171.2	3 442.8	2 817.6	867.6	650.3	785.8	1 164.2	625.2	405.8
September	6 201.1	3 462.0	2 836.1	871.4	652.3	790.4	1 174.2	626.0	406.3
October	6 239.8	3 487.2	2 860.2	875.0	654.1	795.5	1 189.7	627.0	407.5
November	6 254.9	3 489.5	2 861.1	877.1	656.0	796.1	1 187.9	628.4	406.0
December	6 274.0	3 498.8	2 868.7	877.3	655.7	794.8	1 196.6	630.2	405.3
1996:									
January	6 311.0	3 504.2	2 869.8	874.9	652.9	793.9	1 201.0	634.3	402.8
February	6 371.1	3 550.6	2 915.0	891.4	664.4	806.9	1 216.6	635.6	406.3
March	6 396.0	3 562.8	2 926.0	888.5	660.0	812.3	1 225.2	636.8	406.0
April	6 424.7	3 581.6	2 943.0	901.5	671.5	810.4	1 231.1	638.7	406.4
May	6 446.8	3 598.3	2 957.8	905.6	673.5	814.6	1 237.5	640.6	406.5
June	6 512.4	3 653.6	3 011.8	911.9	677.3	832.6	1 267.4	641.7	410.9
July	6 504.9	3 633.3	2 989.6	912.5	677.3	821.0	1 256.1	643.7	406.9
August	6 538.9	3 660.6	3 015.3	918.6	681.4	829.1	1 267.6	645.4	408.2
September	6 582.0	3 694.6	3 047.1	920.6	681.8	836.9	1 289.6	647.5	410.2
October	6 575.6	3 683.5	3 035.4	921.7	681.8	832.1	1 281.6	648.1	407.2
November	6 615.2	3 713.4	3 064.4	926.5	684.7	840.8	1 297.1	649.1	408.7
December	6 664.4	3 753.7	3 104.0	935.2	690.4	848.9	1 319.9	649.7	411.4

YEAR AND MONTH	Proprietor's income [1]			Rental income of persons [2]	Personal dividend income	Personal interest income	Transfer payments to persons				Less: Personal contributions for social insurance
	Total	Farm	Nonfarm				Total	Social Security and Medicare	Unemployment insurance benefits	Other transfers	
1968	75.3	12.8	62.5	22.7	24.5	54.6	63.2	30.2	2.1	30.9	22.9
1969	79.1	14.6	64.6	23.4	25.1	60.8	70.3	32.9	2.2	35.2	26.2
1970	80.2	14.8	65.4	23.6	23.5	69.2	84.6	38.5	4.0	42.1	27.9
1971	86.5	15.4	71.1	24.6	23.5	75.7	100.1	44.5	5.8	49.8	30.7
1972	98.3	19.5	78.8	24.3	25.5	81.8	111.8	49.6	5.7	56.5	34.4
1973	116.8	32.6	84.2	25.8	27.6	94.1	127.9	60.4	4.4	63.1	42.6
1974	115.7	25.8	89.8	25.7	29.6	112.4	151.3	70.1	6.8	74.4	47.9
1975	121.8	24.1	97.7	24.7	29.2	123.0	190.2	81.4	17.6	91.2	50.4
1976	133.6	18.6	115.0	24.3	35.0	134.6	208.3	92.9	15.8	99.6	55.5
1977	147.4	17.5	129.9	22.8	39.5	155.7	223.3	104.9	12.7	105.7	61.2
1978	169.5	22.2	147.4	24.8	44.3	184.5	241.6	116.2	9.7	115.7	69.8
1979	185.0	25.3	159.7	26.9	50.5	223.6	270.7	131.8	9.8	129.1	81.0
1980	176.6	12.2	164.4	33.9	57.5	274.7	321.5	154.2	16.1	151.2	88.6
1981	187.6	21.9	165.7	44.5	67.2	337.2	365.9	182.0	15.9	168.0	104.5
1982	179.6	14.5	165.1	46.5	66.9	379.2	408.1	204.5	25.2	178.4	112.3
1983	191.9	4.1	187.8	46.1	77.4	403.2	439.4	221.7	26.3	191.4	119.7
1984	248.7	23.2	225.5	50.1	79.4	472.3	453.6	235.7	15.9	202.0	132.7
1985	268.6	23.6	245.0	48.1	88.3	508.4	486.5	253.4	15.7	217.4	149.0
1986	279.5	24.2	255.3	41.5	105.1	543.3	518.6	269.2	16.3	233.1	162.1
1987	305.1	31.5	273.6	44.8	101.1	560.0	543.3	282.9	14.5	245.9	173.7
1988	335.3	27.5	307.8	55.1	109.9	595.5	577.6	300.4	13.3	263.9	194.2
1989	357.4	36.3	321.1	51.7	130.9	674.5	626.0	325.1	14.4	286.5	210.8
1990	374.0	35.4	338.6	61.0	142.9	704.4	687.8	352.0	18.1	317.7	223.9
1991	376.5	29.3	347.2	67.9	153.6	699.2	769.9	382.3	26.8	360.8	235.8
1992	423.8	37.1	386.7	79.4	159.4	667.2	858.2	414.0	38.9	405.3	248.4
1993	450.8	32.4	418.4	105.7	185.3	651.0	912.0	444.4	34.0	433.6	260.3
1994	471.6	36.9	434.7	124.4	204.8	668.1	954.7	473.0	23.6	458.1	277.5
1995	489.0	23.4	465.5	132.8	251.9	718.9	1 015.0	507.8	21.4	485.8	293.1
1996	520.3	37.2	483.1	146.3	291.2	735.7	1 068.0	537.6	22.0	508.4	306.3
1993:											
January	439.5	30.0	409.5	99.5	176.5	661.3	897.6	440.9	34.6	422.1	254.9
February	441.5	29.2	412.3	102.3	177.9	660.4	894.7	436.5	32.9	425.3	255.6
March	439.9	29.9	410.0	97.4	179.1	659.3	899.4	435.4	35.9	428.1	255.2
April	450.0	36.1	413.9	104.6	180.4	656.3	906.3	441.7	34.2	430.4	258.1
May	455.4	37.5	417.9	105.6	182.0	653.3	906.2	441.5	32.6	432.1	260.1
June	451.3	35.2	416.1	106.6	183.9	651.3	911.7	442.3	36.5	432.9	259.5
July	444.5	26.8	417.7	100.6	185.8	649.8	913.2	445.2	33.8	434.2	260.6
August	446.3	23.4	422.9	108.3	187.7	647.7	918.9	445.8	35.5	437.6	262.1
September	447.9	26.6	421.3	109.5	189.8	645.9	919.8	448.1	34.7	437.0	262.0
October	454.5	32.2	422.3	107.6	191.9	644.2	921.9	449.4	32.4	440.1	263.1
November	465.8	39.0	426.8	111.8	193.7	641.0	922.9	450.3	31.8	440.8	263.8
December	473.0	42.7	430.3	115.0	194.8	641.1	931.2	455.6	33.6	442.0	268.7
1994:											
January	436.3	46.5	389.8	93.6	190.1	639.5	936.3	460.4	29.2	446.7	272.0
February	478.4	47.9	430.5	120.7	191.8	640.8	941.0	463.2	28.1	449.7	271.4
March	477.2	44.8	432.4	124.0	194.3	643.9	943.9	466.2	26.0	451.7	272.7
April	476.0	41.1	434.9	124.5	197.6	651.0	949.6	469.1	26.1	454.4	275.0
May	475.3	38.8	436.5	126.0	200.3	656.3	948.8	470.5	22.9	455.4	276.8
June	473.0	36.7	436.3	127.5	202.8	661.9	951.0	471.5	22.6	456.9	276.9
July	470.5	34.9	435.6	127.9	205.5	666.9	955.3	474.0	21.8	459.5	278.1
August	472.0	33.2	438.8	130.2	208.4	673.8	959.9	475.7	21.9	462.3	278.5
September	472.4	31.6	440.8	132.1	211.7	681.6	961.1	477.6	21.2	462.3	279.8
October	475.5	31.2	444.3	129.8	215.3	693.5	966.6	479.7	21.3	465.6	282.4
November	475.8	29.3	446.5	128.9	218.9	700.9	967.9	480.6	21.1	466.2	282.4
December	477.2	27.0	450.2	128.0	221.4	706.8	974.7	487.0	20.4	467.3	283.8
1995:											
January	477.8	22.1	455.8	130.0	241.8	710.6	991.4	494.7	21.2	475.5	288.7
February	477.7	20.3	457.4	130.5	243.3	714.2	996.5	498.6	20.9	477.0	289.0
March	479.0	19.5	459.5	131.1	245.2	717.0	1 003.1	502.0	20.8	480.3	289.5
April	480.2	21.0	459.2	132.1	247.1	718.5	1 005.1	503.4	20.3	481.4	291.9
May	484.3	21.3	462.9	132.4	248.5	719.6	1 012.1	506.5	21.6	484.0	290.4
June	488.9	21.8	467.2	132.4	250.1	720.1	1 014.0	507.6	21.2	485.2	292.1
July	486.9	21.8	465.2	130.5	252.1	717.3	1 018.4	509.0	22.2	487.2	294.2
August	492.4	22.8	469.7	131.2	254.1	717.7	1 021.3	510.5	21.6	489.2	294.0
September	495.6	24.3	471.3	132.7	256.4	718.6	1 024.8	513.8	21.6	489.4	295.3
October	499.3	27.3	471.9	132.3	259.0	722.6	1 028.9	513.6	22.5	492.8	296.9
November	502.1	29.0	473.1	138.6	261.7	724.9	1 029.3	514.3	22.3	492.7	297.0
December	503.2	30.3	472.9	140.4	263.7	725.2	1 035.0	520.2	21.1	493.7	297.6
1996:											
January	504.3	30.7	473.6	142.1	286.2	721.7	1 048.1	525.2	23.8	499.1	298.2
February	509.9	31.9	478.1	143.5	287.4	722.1	1 052.5	529.2	22.7	500.6	301.2
March	513.6	33.2	480.4	144.7	288.7	723.2	1 058.9	534.2	22.3	502.4	302.0
April	518.1	35.1	483.0	144.2	289.5	724.6	1 063.5	533.9	23.4	506.2	303.2
May	520.5	36.5	484.0	144.5	290.1	727.4	1 063.7	535.2	21.2	507.3	304.2
June	521.3	37.8	483.5	145.1	290.6	731.4	1 067.3	537.1	21.6	508.6	307.7
July	523.6	39.4	484.2	146.7	291.3	738.9	1 070.6	538.8	21.9	509.9	306.3
August	522.8	40.2	482.6	148.0	291.9	743.0	1 072.4	540.6	20.4	511.4	308.1
September	525.0	40.7	484.4	149.2	292.7	746.2	1 074.3	540.8	21.7	511.8	310.2
October	526.6	40.8	485.8	149.2	293.7	747.8	1 077.0	542.3	21.3	513.4	309.4
November	528.4	40.5	487.9	149.2	295.0	749.8	1 081.8	546.2	21.1	514.5	311.3
December	529.8	39.9	490.0	149.1	296.9	751.8	1 085.5	548.2	22.3	515.0	313.8

1. Includes inventory valuation and capital consumption adjustments.
2. Includes capital consumption adjustment.

DISPOSITION OF PERSONAL INCOME
(Billions of dollars, except as noted, monthly data are at seasonally adjusted annual rates)

YEAR AND MONTH	Total personal income	Less: Personal tax and nontax payments	Equals: Disposable personal income	Less: Personal outlays — Total	Personal consumption expenditures	Interest paid by persons	Personal transfer payments to rest of world, net	Personal savings — Billions of dollars	Percent of disposable personal income	Disposable personal income — Total, chained (1992) dollars	Per capita — Current dollars	Per capita — Chained 1992 dollars	Population (Thousands)
1968	714.6	92.1	622.5	574.6	559.8	13.8	1.0	47.8	7.7	2 302.1	3 101	11 468	200 745
1969	779.3	109.9	669.4	621.4	604.7	15.7	1.1	47.9	7.2	2 377.2	3 302	11 726	202 736
1970	837.1	109.0	728.1	666.1	648.1	16.8	1.2	62.0	8.5	2 469.0	3 550	12 039	205 089
1971	900.2	108.7	791.5	721.6	702.5	17.8	1.3	69.9	8.8	2 568.3	3 811	12 366	207 692
1972	988.8	132.0	856.8	791.6	770.7	19.6	1.3	65.2	7.6	2 685.7	4 082	12 794	209 924
1973	1 107.6	140.6	967.0	875.4	851.6	22.4	1.4	91.5	9.5	2 875.2	4 562	13 566	211 939
1974	1 215.9	159.1	1 056.8	956.6	931.2	24.2	1.2	100.2	9.5	2 854.2	4 941	13 344	213 898
1975	1 319.0	156.4	1 162.6	1 054.8	1 029.1	24.5	1.2	107.8	9.3	2 903.6	5 383	13 444	215 981
1976	1 459.4	182.3	1 277.1	1 176.7	1 148.8	26.7	1.2	100.4	7.9	3 017.6	5 856	13 837	218 086
1977	1 616.1	210.0	1 406.1	1 308.9	1 277.1	30.7	1.2	97.2	6.9	3 115.4	6 383	14 142	220 289
1978	1 825.9	240.1	1 585.8	1 467.6	1 428.8	37.5	1.3	118.2	7.5	3 276.0	7 123	14 715	222 629
1979	2 055.9	280.2	1 775.7	1 639.5	1 593.5	44.5	1.4	136.2	7.7	3 365.5	7 888	14 951	225 106
1980	2 292.9	312.4	1 980.5	1 811.5	1 760.4	49.4	1.6	169.1	8.5	3 385.7	8 697	14 867	227 726
1981	2 568.5	360.2	2 208.3	2 001.1	1 941.3	54.6	5.2	207.2	9.4	3 464.9	9 601	15 064	230 008
1982	2 727.2	371.4	2 355.8	2 141.8	2 076.8	58.8	6.2	214.0	9.1	3 495.6	10 145	15 053	232 200
1983	2 900.8	369.3	2 531.5	2 355.5	2 283.4	65.5	6.5	176.1	7.0	3 592.8	10 803	15 332	234 300
1984	3 215.3	395.5	2 819.8	2 574.4	2 492.3	74.7	7.4	245.5	8.7	3 855.4	11 929	16 309	236 400
1985	3 449.8	437.7	3 012.1	2 795.8	2 704.8	83.2	7.8	216.4	7.2	3 972.0	12 629	16 654	238 500
1986	3 658.4	459.9	3 198.5	2 991.1	2 892.7	90.3	8.1	207.4	6.5	4 101.0	13 289	17 039	240 700
1987	3 888.8	514.2	3 374.6	3 194.7	3 094.5	91.5	8.7	179.9	5.3	4 168.2	13 896	17 164	242 800
1988	4 184.6	532.0	3 652.6	3 451.7	3 349.7	92.9	9.1	200.9	5.5	4 332.1	14 905	17 678	245 100
1989	4 501.0	594.9	3 906.1	3 706.7	3 594.8	102.4	9.6	199.4	5.1	4 416.8	15 790	17 854	247 400
1990	4 804.2	624.8	4 179.4	3 958.1	3 839.3	108.9	9.9	221.3	5.3	4 498.2	16 721	17 996	250 000
1991	4 981.6	624.8	4 356.8	4 097.4	3 975.1	111.9	10.4	259.5	6.0	4 500.0	17 242	17 809	252 700
1992	5 277.2	650.5	4 626.7	4 341.0	4 219.8	111.7	9.6	285.6	6.2	4 626.7	18 113	18 113	255 432
1993	5 519.2	690.0	4 829.2	4 580.7	4 459.2	108.2	13.3	248.5	5.1	4 703.9	18 706	18 221	258 161
1994	5 791.8	739.1	5 052.7	4 842.1	4 717.0	110.9	14.2	210.6	4.2	4 805.1	19 381	18 431	260 705
1995	6 150.8	795.1	5 355.7	5 101.1	4 957.7	128.5	14.8	254.6	4.8	4 964.2	20 349	18 861	263 194
1996	6 495.2	886.9	5 608.3	5 368.8	5 207.6	145.2	15.9	239.6	4.3	5 076.9	21 117	19 116	265 579
1993:													
January	5 366.1	661.0	4 705.1	4 488.5	4 365.2	110.2	13.1	216.6	4.6	4 632.8	18 311	18 029	256 961
February	5 375.0	663.1	4 711.9	4 500.6	4 377.3	110.2	13.1	211.3	4.5	4 624.8	18 324	17 985	257 148
March	5 367.2	663.2	4 704.0	4 476.2	4 353.7	109.4	13.1	227.8	4.8	4 609.3	18 279	17 911	257 346
April	5 483.3	682.2	4 801.1	4 535.7	4 413.4	109.2	13.1	265.4	5.5	4 691.1	18 641	18 214	257 558
May	5 518.3	687.8	4 830.5	4 543.6	4 422.7	107.9	13.1	286.9	5.9	4 714.4	18 739	18 288	257 781
June	5 510.6	686.7	4 823.9	4 569.2	4 448.2	108.0	13.1	254.7	5.3	4 706.2	18 696	18 240	258 017
July	5 517.7	691.2	4 826.5	4 594.3	4 473.2	107.7	13.4	232.2	4.8	4 703.7	18 688	18 213	258 266
August	5 556.9	697.0	4 859.9	4 607.9	4 486.6	108.0	13.4	252.0	5.2	4 727.1	18 799	18 286	258 518
September	5 558.1	698.3	4 859.9	4 627.1	4 505.9	107.9	13.4	232.7	4.8	4 720.0	18 781	18 241	258 764
October	5 580.3	702.8	4 877.5	4 657.5	4 536.8	107.1	13.7	220.0	4.5	4 715.9	18 833	18 209	258 991
November	5 603.7	705.9	4 897.9	4 674.2	4 554.2	106.3	13.7	223.7	4.6	4 727.7	18 897	18 240	259 194
December	5 793.4	740.5	5 052.9	4 693.9	4 573.8	106.4	13.7	359.0	7.1	4 873.8	19 480	18 790	259 388
1994:													
January	5 562.0	711.8	4 850.2	4 681.6	4 559.6	107.9	14.0	168.7	3.5	4 677.1	18 686	18 019	259 560
February	5 628.0	711.0	4 917.0	4 757.2	4 635.8	107.3	14.0	159.9	3.3	4 728.3	18 932	18 205	259 726
March	5 658.9	715.8	4 943.0	4 775.8	4 654.4	107.4	14.0	167.2	3.4	4 740.4	19 017	18 238	259 928
April	5 740.4	780.6	4 959.7	4 784.7	4 662.8	107.8	14.1	175.0	3.5	4 748.3	19 066	18 253	260 138
May	5 776.6	735.7	5 040.9	4 797.8	4 675.3	108.5	14.1	243.1	4.8	4 818.9	19 362	18 510	260 345
June	5 782.8	735.2	5 047.6	4 827.3	4 703.5	109.8	14.1	220.3	4.4	4 811.2	19 371	18 464	260 571
July	5 811.5	737.5	5 074.0	4 841.7	4 718.0	109.6	14.2	232.3	4.6	4 818.9	19 455	18 477	260 804
August	5 834.2	738.8	5 095.3	4 886.3	4 760.9	111.3	14.2	209.0	4.1	4 822.8	19 519	18 475	261 040
September	5 868.5	743.2	5 125.3	4 900.4	4 772.9	113.3	14.2	224.9	4.4	4 840.3	19 616	18 526	261 275
October	5 928.8	751.6	5 177.2	4 935.0	4 806.4	114.2	14.4	242.2	4.7	4 877.5	19 799	18 653	261 494
November	5 937.6	751.8	5 185.8	4 953.7	4 823.2	116.1	14.4	232.1	4.5	4 877.1	19 816	18 637	261 695
December	5 972.0	755.7	5 216.3	4 963.4	4 830.9	118.1	14.4	252.9	4.8	4 900.0	19 918	18 710	261 888
1995:													
January	6 039.3	765.3	5 273.9	5 006.0	4 871.3	120.2	14.5	267.9	5.1	4 936.8	20 125	18 839	262 057
February	6 050.3	766.1	5 284.3	4 995.6	4 860.3	120.8	14.5	288.7	5.5	4 936.3	20 152	18 825	262 223
March	6 069.6	768.1	5 301.5	5 020.4	4 883.6	122.2	14.5	281.1	5.3	4 943.4	20 202	18 837	262 427
April	6 112.6	826.3	5 286.3	5 032.8	4 895.4	123.0	14.3	253.5	4.8	4 916.5	20 128	18 720	262 639
May	6 099.5	775.2	5 324.3	5 073.0	4 933.8	124.9	14.3	251.3	4.7	4 945.1	20 257	18 814	262 842
June	6 132.2	783.9	5 348.3	5 117.1	4 975.1	127.6	14.3	231.3	4.3	4 961.3	20 331	18 860	263 060
July	6 164.9	794.1	5 370.7	5 108.9	4 965.5	128.5	14.9	261.8	4.9	4 973.1	20 399	18 888	263 289
August	6 171.2	797.4	5 373.8	5 155.2	5 010.0	130.3	14.9	218.6	4.1	4 963.6	20 392	18 835	263 525
September	6 201.1	805.0	5 396.1	5 145.1	4 996.4	133.9	14.9	250.9	4.7	4 982.2	20 458	18 889	263 767
October	6 239.8	814.4	5 425.4	5 146.4	4 996.0	134.9	15.4	279.0	5.1	4 998.5	20 552	18 935	263 984
November	6 254.9	819.4	5 435.5	5 187.2	5 034.6	137.1	15.4	248.3	4.6	5 005.7	20 576	18 949	264 172
December	6 274.0	826.3	5 447.7	5 225.2	5 070.6	139.2	15.4	222.6	4.1	5 007.7	20 608	18 943	264 351
1996:													
January	6 311.0	827.6	5 483.4	5 223.8	5 068.9	139.5	15.4	259.7	4.7	5 027.2	20 731	19 006	264 505
February	6 371.1	842.2	5 528.9	5 278.2	5 122.8	140.0	15.4	250.7	4.5	5 056.3	20 890	19 105	264 667
March	6 396.0	850.1	5 545.8	5 281.8	5 125.8	140.7	15.4	264.0	4.8	5 059.2	20 938	19 101	264 870
April	6 424.7	909.4	5 515.3	5 333.4	5 176.1	141.5	15.8	181.9	3.3	5 015.7	20 807	18 923	265 066
May	6 446.8	868.8	5 578.0	5 359.2	5 200.5	142.9	15.8	218.8	3.9	5 065.0	21 029	19 095	265 253
June	6 512.4	885.1	5 627.3	5 350.8	5 190.6	144.4	15.8	276.5	4.9	5 103.2	21 199	19 224	265 456
July	6 504.5	885.9	5 619.0	5 379.5	5 216.8	146.8	15.9	239.5	4.3	5 079.7	21 150	19 120	265 669
August	6 538.9	897.0	5 641.9	5 389.2	5 226.4	146.9	15.9	252.6	4.5	5 094.4	21 219	19 160	265 886
September	6 582.0	909.1	5 673.0	5 403.2	5 238.8	148.5	15.9	269.8	4.8	5 110.3	21 318	19 204	266 106
October	6 575.6	909.4	5 666.2	5 450.0	5 285.4	147.9	16.7	216.3	3.8	5 087.2	21 277	19 103	266 308
November	6 615.2	921.7	5 693.5	5 470.2	5 302.7	150.8	16.7	223.3	3.9	5 101.1	21 364	19 142	266 492
December	6 664.4	936.8	5 727.6	5 505.9	5 336.4	152.8	16.7	221.7	3.9	5 123.0	21 478	19 211	266 672

DISPOSITION OF PERSONAL INCOME—Continued
(Billions of dollars, except as noted, monthly data are at seasonally adjusted annual rates)

YEAR AND MONTH	Personal consumption expenditure											
	Current dollars				Chained (1992) dollars				Implicit price deflators for personal consumption expenditure (1992=100)			
	Total	Durable goods	Nondurable goods	Services	Total	Durable goods	Nondurable goods	Services	Total	Durable goods	Nondurable goods	Services
1968	559.8	80.8	235.7	243.4	2 070.2	186.6	816.9	1 059.5	27.0	43.3	28.9	23.0
1969	604.7	85.9	253.2	265.5	2 147.6	193.3	838.6	1 110.7	28.2	44.5	30.2	23.9
1970	648.1	85.0	272.0	291.1	2 197.8	187.0	859.1	1 155.4	29.5	45.4	31.7	25.2
1971	702.5	96.9	285.5	320.1	2 279.5	205.7	874.5	1 197.9	30.8	47.1	32.6	26.7
1972	770.7	110.4	308.0	352.3	2 415.9	231.9	912.9	1 262.5	31.9	47.6	33.7	27.9
1973	851.6	123.5	343.1	384.9	2 532.6	255.8	942.9	1 319.4	33.6	48.3	36.4	29.2
1974	931.2	122.3	384.5	424.4	2 514.7	238.2	924.5	1 351.2	37.0	51.3	41.6	31.4
1975	1 029.1	133.5	420.6	475.0	2 570.0	238.1	938.3	1 398.3	40.0	56.0	44.8	34.0
1976	1 148.8	158.8	458.2	531.8	2 714.3	268.5	984.8	1 457.1	42.3	59.2	46.5	36.5
1977	1 277.1	181.1	496.9	599.0	2 829.8	293.4	1 010.4	1 518.2	45.1	61.7	49.2	39.5
1978	1 428.8	201.4	549.9	677.4	2 951.6	308.8	1 045.7	1 589.3	48.4	65.2	52.6	42.6
1979	1 593.5	213.9	624.0	755.6	3 020.1	307.3	1 069.7	1 639.8	52.8	69.6	58.3	46.1
1980	1 760.4	213.5	695.5	851.4	3 009.7	282.6	1 065.1	1 670.7	58.5	75.6	65.3	51.0
1981	1 941.3	230.5	758.2	952.6	3 046.4	285.8	1 074.3	1 696.1	63.7	80.6	70.6	56.2
1982	2 076.8	239.3	786.8	1 050.7	3 081.5	285.5	1 080.6	1 728.2	67.4	83.8	72.8	60.8
1983	2 283.4	279.8	830.3	1 173.3	3 240.6	327.4	1 112.4	1 809.0	70.5	85.5	74.6	64.9
1984	2 492.3	325.1	883.6	1 283.6	3 407.6	374.9	1 151.8	1 883.0	73.1	86.7	76.7	68.2
1985	2 704.8	361.1	927.6	1 416.1	3 566.5	411.4	1 178.3	1 977.3	75.8	87.8	78.7	71.6
1986	2 892.7	398.7	957.2	1 536.8	3 708.7	448.4	1 215.9	2 041.4	78.0	88.9	78.7	75.3
1987	3 094.5	416.7	1 014.0	1 663.8	3 822.3	454.9	1 239.3	2 126.9	81.0	91.6	81.8	78.2
1988	3 349.7	451.0	1 081.1	1 817.6	3 972.7	483.5	1 274.4	2 212.4	84.3	93.3	84.8	82.2
1989	3 594.8	472.8	1 163.8	1 958.1	4 064.6	496.2	1 303.5	2 262.3	88.4	95.3	89.3	86.6
1990	3 839.3	476.5	1 245.3	2 117.5	4 132.1	493.3	1 316.1	2 321.3	92.9	96.6	94.6	91.2
1991	3 975.1	455.2	1 277.6	2 242.3	4 105.8	462.0	1 302.9	2 341.0	96.8	98.5	98.1	95.8
1992	4 219.8	488.5	1 321.8	2 409.4	4 219.8	488.5	1 321.8	2 409.4	100.0	100.0	100.0	100.0
1993	4 459.2	530.2	1 370.7	2 558.4	4 343.6	523.8	1 351.0	2 468.9	102.7	101.2	101.5	103.6
1994	4 717.0	579.5	1 428.4	2 709.1	4 486.0	561.2	1 389.9	2 535.5	105.2	103.3	102.8	106.9
1995	4 957.7	608.5	1 475.8	2 873.4	4 595.3	583.6	1 412.6	2 599.6	107.9	104.3	104.5	110.5
1996	5 207.6	634.5	1 534.7	3 038.4	4 714.1	611.1	1 432.3	2 671.0	110.5	103.8	107.2	113.8
1993:												
January	4 365.2	519.8	1 359.1	2 486.3	4 298.1	517.2	1 346.1	2 435.0	101.6	100.5	101.0	102.1
February	4 377.3	501.9	1 361.3	2 514.0	4 296.4	499.5	1 342.6	2 454.3	101.9	100.5	101.4	102.4
March	4 353.7	497.4	1 342.9	2 513.4	4 266.0	495.4	1 323.8	2 446.7	102.1	100.4	101.4	102.7
April	4 413.4	520.0	1 365.6	2 527.8	4 312.3	515.1	1 345.5	2 451.8	102.3	101.0	101.5	103.1
May	4 422.7	525.0	1 366.6	2 531.1	4 316.4	520.4	1 347.0	2 449.2	102.5	100.9	101.5	103.3
June	4 448.2	527.6	1 366.7	2 554.0	4 339.7	522.3	1 350.9	2 466.6	102.5	101.0	101.2	103.5
July	4 473.2	539.0	1 372.0	2 562.2	4 359.4	533.0	1 355.6	2 471.1	102.6	101.1	101.2	103.7
August	4 486.6	535.8	1 372.4	2 578.3	4 364.0	528.4	1 354.0	2 481.7	102.8	101.4	101.4	103.9
September	4 505.9	536.8	1 377.3	2 591.8	4 376.2	528.2	1 360.8	2 487.3	103.0	101.6	101.2	104.2
October	4 536.8	548.1	1 385.6	2 603.0	4 386.4	537.3	1 360.7	2 488.6	103.4	102.0	101.8	104.6
November	4 554.2	553.6	1 387.9	2 612.8	4 396.0	542.2	1 361.0	2 493.0	103.6	102.1	102.0	104.8
December	4 573.8	557.6	1 390.6	2 625.6	4 411.7	546.8	1 363.6	2 501.5	103.7	102.0	102.0	105.0
1994:												
January	4 559.6	550.4	1 385.1	2 624.0	4 396.8	539.4	1 360.4	2 497.2	103.7	102.0	101.8	105.1
February	4 635.8	567.2	1 407.7	2 660.9	4 457.8	554.9	1 381.8	2 521.5	104.0	102.2	101.9	105.5
March	4 654.4	572.0	1 420.2	2 662.1	4 463.6	557.7	1 392.8	2 513.9	104.3	102.6	102.0	105.9
April	4 662.8	578.1	1 408.4	2 676.4	4 464.1	563.9	1 379.9	2 520.8	104.5	102.5	102.1	106.2
May	4 675.3	567.5	1 414.3	2 693.5	4 469.4	550.5	1 385.6	2 533.5	104.6	103.1	102.1	106.3
June	4 703.5	571.6	1 425.2	2 706.6	4 483.2	552.9	1 390.9	2 539.7	104.9	103.4	102.5	106.6
July	4 718.0	576.8	1 431.3	2 709.9	4 480.8	556.0	1 389.5	2 535.7	105.3	103.8	103.0	106.9
August	4 760.9	587.0	1 442.5	2 731.4	4 506.2	565.3	1 395.1	2 546.4	105.7	103.8	103.4	107.3
September	4 772.9	586.1	1 444.6	2 742.2	4 507.6	563.9	1 394.9	2 549.3	105.9	104.0	103.6	107.6
October	4 806.4	595.3	1 451.3	2 759.8	4 528.2	573.4	1 401.3	2 554.2	106.1	103.8	103.6	108.1
November	4 823.2	603.1	1 454.1	2 766.1	4 536.1	580.0	1 403.5	2 553.6	106.3	104.0	103.6	108.3
December	4 830.9	599.4	1 455.7	2 775.9	4 538.0	576.3	1 402.6	2 559.9	106.5	104.0	103.8	108.4
1995:												
January	4 871.3	604.0	1 474.1	2 793.2	4 560.0	579.7	1 420.5	2 561.0	106.8	104.2	103.8	109.1
February	4 860.3	587.3	1 454.6	2 818.4	4 540.2	563.0	1 400.5	2 576.7	107.1	104.3	103.9	109.4
March	4 883.6	599.5	1 459.2	2 824.8	4 553.7	574.0	1 404.0	2 576.1	107.2	104.5	103.9	109.7
April	4 895.4	588.6	1 464.7	2 842.1	4 553.0	562.9	1 406.1	2 583.9	107.5	104.6	104.2	110.0
May	4 933.8	603.4	1 474.5	2 855.9	4 582.4	578.6	1 412.9	2 591.3	107.7	104.3	104.4	110.2
June	4 975.1	616.4	1 478.0	2 880.7	4 615.1	591.6	1 415.7	2 608.3	107.8	104.2	104.4	110.4
July	4 965.5	608.6	1 476.6	2 880.3	4 597.9	584.2	1 411.8	2 602.2	108.0	104.2	104.6	110.7
August	5 010.0	626.4	1 479.7	2 903.9	4 627.6	600.5	1 413.1	2 614.8	108.3	104.3	104.7	111.1
September	4 996.4	613.1	1 484.9	2 898.4	4 613.2	587.6	1 416.9	2 609.2	108.3	104.3	104.8	111.1
October	4 996.0	608.2	1 478.8	2 909.1	4 602.9	583.5	1 407.8	2 611.6	108.5	104.2	105.1	111.4
November	5 034.6	616.8	1 487.6	2 930.3	4 636.5	592.8	1 417.6	2 626.4	108.6	104.0	104.9	111.6
December	5 070.6	630.4	1 497.1	2 943.1	4 661.0	604.8	1 423.7	2 633.4	108.8	104.2	105.2	111.8
1996:												
January	5 068.9	615.2	1 498.4	2 955.2	4 647.1	589.6	1 416.7	2 640.5	109.1	104.3	105.8	111.9
February	5 122.8	638.6	1 511.4	2 972.8	4 684.9	612.5	1 427.4	2 646.0	109.4	104.3	105.9	112.4
March	5 125.8	626.3	1 514.6	2 984.9	4 676.0	599.8	1 423.4	2 652.8	109.6	104.4	106.4	112.5
April	5 176.1	641.0	1 531.2	3 003.9	4 707.3	615.4	1 431.4	2 661.2	110.0	104.2	107.0	112.9
May	5 200.5	644.7	1 534.7	3 021.1	4 722.2	621.2	1 432.9	2 669.0	110.1	103.8	107.1	113.2
June	5 190.6	630.1	1 530.9	3 029.6	4 707.1	607.6	1 430.5	2 669.2	110.3	103.7	107.0	113.5
July	5 216.8	631.5	1 536.4	3 048.9	4 716.1	609.0	1 432.7	2 674.5	110.6	103.7	107.2	114.0
August	5 226.4	641.1	1 533.5	3 051.9	4 719.3	618.5	1 431.6	2 670.0	110.8	103.7	107.1	114.3
September	5 238.8	630.7	1 545.0	3 063.0	4 719.2	608.0	1 437.5	2 673.9	111.0	103.7	107.5	114.6
October	5 285.4	638.8	1 557.8	3 088.8	4 745.2	616.0	1 443.7	2 686.1	111.4	103.7	107.9	115.0
November	5 302.7	638.4	1 558.1	3 106.2	4 751.0	617.2	1 439.3	2 694.7	111.6	103.4	108.3	115.3
December	5 336.4	637.4	1 564.6	3 134.5	4 773.1	618.2	1 440.7	2 714.0	111.8	103.1	108.6	115.5

CONSUMER INSTALLMENT CREDIT
(Outstanding at end of period—Billions of dollars)

Not seasonally adjusted

YEAR AND MONTH	Total	By major holder						By major credit type						
		Commercial banks	Finance companies	Credit unions	Savings institutions	Non-financial businesses	Asset pools	Auto				Revolving		
								Total[1]	Commercial banks	Finance companies	Asset pools	Total[1]	Commercial banks	Non-financial businesses
1968	119.3	58.5	26.1	9.7	4.3	20.8		34.4	21.2	9.0		2.1	2.1	
1969	129.2	63.4	27.9	11.7	4.4	21.9		37.0	22.7	9.4		3.7	3.7	
1970	133.7	65.6	27.6	13.0	4.4	23.0		36.3	22.3	9.0		5.1	5.1	
1971	149.2	74.3	29.2	14.8	4.7	26.3		40.5	24.7	10.2		8.5	6.0	2.6
1972	168.8	87.0	31.9	17.0	5.2	27.8		47.9	28.9	10.5		9.7	7.2	2.5
1973	193.0	99.6	35.4	19.6	8.5	29.9		53.8	33.3	10.7		11.7	9.1	2.6
1974	201.9	103.0	36.1	21.9	9.1	31.8		54.3	32.8	10.6		13.7	11.1	2.6
1975	207.0	106.1	32.6	25.7	10.1	32.6		57.0	33.3	11.0		15.0	12.3	2.7
1976	229.0	118.0	33.7	31.2	10.8	35.2		66.8	39.6	11.9		17.2	14.4	2.8
1977	264.4	140.3	37.3	37.6	11.8	37.4		80.9	49.6	13.2		39.3	18.4	20.9
1978	310.4	166.5	44.5	45.2	13.1	41.2		98.7	60.5	17.0		48.3	24.3	24.0
1979	353.1	185.7	55.5	47.4	20.0	44.6		112.4	67.4	22.8		56.9	29.9	27.1
1980	355.4	180.2	62.3	44.1	22.7	46.2		112.0	61.5	29.4		58.5	29.8	28.7
1981	373.1	184.2	70.1	46.7	24.0	48.1		119.7	58.1	39.3		64.8	32.9	31.6
1982	390.3	190.9	75.3	48.8	26.6	48.7		127.5	59.6	44.1		70.5	36.7	33.0
1983	440.5	213.7	83.3	56.1	31.5	55.7		146.2	67.6	49.8		83.8	44.2	38.0
1984	521.0	258.8	89.9	67.9	44.2	60.2		175.3	83.9	51.9		106.3	60.6	41.1
1985	602.9	296.3	111.7	74.0	57.6	63.3		211.8	93.0	69.7		131.6	78.9	42.2
1986	659.1	321.1	134.0	77.1	62.9	64.0		247.9	101.6	92.9		148.9	90.7	41.5
1987	692.2	337.6	140.0	81.0	65.3	68.1		266.6	109.5	99.0		169.6	103.4	45.0
1988	741.9	370.7	144.7	88.3	66.8	71.4		285.4	123.4	98.3		194.5	123.0	47.5
1989	795.0	385.1	138.9	91.7	62.5	69.6	47.3	290.9	126.3	84.1	17.6	222.3	130.8	43.5
1990	810.2	387.0	133.4	91.6	49.7	71.9	76.7	283.9	124.9	75.8	24.2	250.9	133.4	44.9
1991	796.8	372.5	121.6	90.3	42.2	67.3	103.0	264.2	112.7	65.1	30.1	277.1	138.0	41.7
1992	801.0	365.5	118.1	89.4	37.4	70.3	120.3	263.8	109.6	62.0	34.7	292.0	133.0	44.5
1993	863.0	399.7	116.1	101.6	37.9	77.2	130.5	288.9	122.0	62.7	40.2	325.0	149.9	50.1
1994	988.1	462.9	134.4	119.6	38.5	86.6	146.1	328.6	141.9	70.2	36.7	383.2	182.0	56.8
1995	1 128.6	507.8	152.1	131.9	40.1	85.1	211.6	364.7	149.1	81.1	44.6	464.1	210.3	53.5
1996	1 214.9	529.4	152.4	144.2	44.7	77.8	266.5	393.2	154.0	86.7	52.4	522.9	228.6	44.9
1993:														
January	795.1	365.3	116.8	90.9	37.1	66.9	118.1	262.3	109.5	61.8	33.5	286.2	130.1	42.0
February	790.6	363.2	113.4	91.8	37.0	64.2	121.0	264.6	110.8	58.8	37.2	283.1	128.5	40.1
March	786.4	362.7	112.4	91.4	36.8	63.4	119.8	265.1	111.1	58.4	37.4	281.8	128.9	39.4
April	792.7	366.3	112.9	93.5	37.0	63.8	119.2	266.1	110.8	59.0	37.6	283.5	130.5	39.8
May	792.0	369.2	108.3	94.3	37.2	64.4	118.7	268.3	112.4	59.2	37.9	285.1	131.9	40.3
June	797.6	370.9	110.3	95.4	37.4	64.6	119.1	271.5	114.5	61.0	36.3	286.9	131.1	40.5
July	802.7	375.4	111.9	96.1	37.3	65.1	116.9	273.8	116.3	62.3	35.2	290.8	135.5	41.0
August	812.2	379.3	110.7	98.1	37.3	66.1	120.7	278.1	118.1	60.9	37.8	294.6	136.9	41.8
September	820.9	383.6	110.7	98.9	37.2	66.6	123.8	281.3	120.5	60.2	38.7	298.3	138.3	42.3
October	827.2	385.8	111.3	99.3	37.4	67.5	125.9	286.4	121.9	60.6	41.0	300.5	138.8	43.1
November	837.7	391.7	113.4	100.1	37.6	69.9	125.0	287.3	121.8	62.0	39.9	308.1	143.6	44.9
December	863.0	399.7	116.1	101.6	37.9	77.2	130.5	288.9	122.0	62.7	40.2	325.0	149.9	50.1
1994:														
January	855.8	398.6	117.2	100.2	37.6	74.1	128.1	288.8	122.4	64.3	38.0	318.1	146.2	47.9
February	853.0	398.4	117.7	100.3	37.4	71.8	127.5	289.3	122.2	65.2	37.4	315.0	144.9	46.3
March	859.3	401.1	119.8	101.6	37.1	71.7	128.0	293.2	124.2	66.1	37.3	316.4	146.5	46.1
April	869.3	408.4	122.5	102.7	37.5	72.2	126.0	296.9	126.9	67.9	35.4	321.0	150.2	46.6
May	880.3	411.8	121.9	105.7	37.8	73.0	130.2	301.9	129.4	66.8	36.7	325.4	151.0	47.2
June	893.5	417.4	124.0	108.2	38.1	73.3	132.6	307.3	132.0	67.4	36.7	331.3	154.2	47.4
July	899.7	423.9	122.8	109.7	38.1	73.9	131.3	308.4	134.4	65.9	35.7	335.9	158.3	47.9
August	918.6	432.7	124.8	112.9	38.0	75.1	135.2	314.9	137.5	66.5	35.8	345.6	162.9	48.6
September	933.6	438.2	130.0	114.3	38.4	74.7	137.9	321.5	138.8	68.6	37.4	348.6	166.3	48.2
October	944.3	443.0	131.2	116.0	38.1	75.0	141.0	323.8	140.3	69.0	36.6	351.5	164.8	48.3
November	958.8	449.0	132.5	117.5	38.3	78.1	143.3	326.9	141.6	69.8	36.5	364.6	172.3	50.6
December	988.1	462.9	134.4	119.6	38.5	86.6	146.1	328.6	141.9	70.2	36.7	383.2	182.0	56.8
1995:														
January	984.6	460.9	137.1	119.6	38.2	82.8	146.1	328.2	141.5	71.0	35.0	378.4	178.7	53.8
February	979.6	459.3	134.3	119.8	37.8	80.3	148.2	329.4	141.6	69.9	36.1	377.8	179.0	52.0
March	989.5	463.0	135.4	120.6	37.5	79.8	153.3	331.9	141.6	70.3	37.0	381.6	180.9	51.6
April	1 000.4	470.1	137.4	121.4	37.8	79.1	154.6	333.2	141.4	71.6	36.0	385.1	182.1	50.9
May	1 013.6	473.9	139.2	122.8	38.2	80.0	159.6	337.3	141.7	73.0	36.7	393.8	185.9	51.7
June	1 028.5	476.3	141.3	125.7	38.5	80.5	166.2	341.0	143.0	74.7	37.1	401.8	187.3	52.1
July	1 036.7	480.5	141.7	126.8	38.9	80.0	168.7	345.4	145.5	75.5	37.5	404.3	187.4	51.7
August	1 055.0	490.4	145.1	128.7	39.3	78.6	173.0	350.3	147.2	78.1	37.0	415.1	195.4	49.8
September	1 074.9	492.4	145.7	129.2	39.7	78.3	189.6	354.1	146.9	78.8	39.2	427.1	195.0	49.6
October	1 080.7	491.8	148.2	130.3	40.1	78.8	191.6	358.2	150.1	81.0	37.3	432.0	195.9	50.0
November	1 099.7	496.0	148.3	130.9	40.5	78.0	206.0	362.6	148.0	79.7	44.7	438.7	197.1	48.5
December	1 128.6	507.8	152.1	131.9	40.1	85.1	211.6	364.7	149.1	81.1	44.6	464.1	210.3	53.5
1996:														
January	1 117.9	499.5	152.1	131.5	40.2	80.7	213.9	363.1	148.2	82.0	42.6	454.7	200.1	50.5
February	1 115.8	497.2	153.9	131.2	40.5	78.1	215.0	364.3	147.7	84.1	41.8	453.5	198.9	48.6
March	1 120.5	497.7	152.5	131.5	40.7	76.7	221.4	367.6	148.5	84.3	43.5	455.1	196.8	47.4
April	1 129.0	503.9	154.3	132.8	41.2	73.7	223.0	369.9	150.1	86.5	41.3	460.5	201.1	44.5
May	1 135.9	502.4	156.1	134.6	41.6	74.1	227.2	374.2	150.5	87.4	42.6	466.6	203.4	44.7
June	1 146.9	505.7	153.9	136.1	42.1	72.0	237.2	380.7	152.9	86.3	46.8	470.3	204.1	42.6
July	1 157.6	510.2	155.8	137.9	43.0	69.9	240.8	385.6	153.9	88.0	47.8	474.7	207.3	40.5
August	1 171.6	516.7	154.7	140.0	44.0	71.0	245.3	388.4	154.5	87.2	48.8	480.7	209.8	41.3
September	1 177.3	517.2	154.6	140.9	44.9	68.5	251.2	390.4	153.1	88.7	49.5	483.3	211.2	38.8
October	1 180.2	521.3	151.4	143.0	44.9	68.0	251.8	392.7	154.8	88.0	49.2	487.5	215.0	38.1
November	1 190.3	523.0	151.0	143.3	44.8	69.8	258.5	392.1	154.8	87.6	49.3	497.8	217.9	39.3
December	1 214.9	529.4	152.4	144.2	44.7	77.8	266.5	393.2	154.0	86.7	52.4	522.9	228.6	44.9

1. Total includes amounts not shown separately by type.

CONSUMER INSTALLMENT CREDIT—Continued
(Outstanding at end of period—Billions of dollars)

YEAR AND MONTH	Not seasonally adjusted—Continued / By major credit type—Continued						Seasonally adjusted							
	Revolving—Continued	Other					Total	By major credit type			Net change during period			
		Total[1]	Commercial banks	Finance companies	Non-financial businesses	Asset pools		Automobile	Revolving	Other	Total	By major credit type		
	Asset pools											Automobile	Revolving	Other
1968		82.9	35.2	17.1	20.8		117.4	34.4	2.0	81.0	10.6	3.2		5.3
1969		88.6	37.0	18.4	21.9		127.1	37.0	3.6	86.6	9.7	2.6	1.5	5.6
1970		92.2	38.2	18.5	23.0		131.5	36.4	4.9	90.2	4.4	-0.6	1.3	3.6
1971		100.2	43.6	19.1	23.7		146.9	40.5	8.3	98.1	15.4	4.2	3.4	7.9
1972		111.2	50.9	21.4	25.2		166.1	47.8	9.4	108.9	19.3	7.3	1.1	10.8
1973		127.5	57.2	24.6	27.2		190.0	53.7	11.3	124.9	23.8	5.9	1.9	16.0
1974		134.0	59.1	25.5	29.2		198.8	54.2	13.2	131.3	8.8	0.5	1.9	6.4
1975		135.0	60.5	21.6	29.9		203.6	56.8	14.5	132.4	4.9	2.5	1.3	1.1
1976		145.0	64.1	21.8	32.4		224.8	65.9	16.6	142.3	21.2	9.2	2.1	10.0
1977		144.2	72.4	24.1	16.5		257.5	79.0	36.7	141.8	32.6	13.1	20.1	-0.5
1978		163.4	81.7	27.5	17.2		302.1	95.8	45.2	161.1	44.6	16.9	8.5	19.3
1979		183.8	88.5	32.6	17.5		343.5	108.7	53.4	181.5	41.5	12.8	8.2	20.5
1980		184.9	88.9	32.9	17.5		350.1	112.0	55.1	183.0	6.6	3.3	1.8	1.5
1981		188.5	93.2	30.8	16.5		367.6	119.8	61.1	186.8	17.5	7.8	6.0	3.7
1982		192.4	94.7	31.2	15.8		384.6	127.5	66.5	190.7	17.0	7.7	5.4	3.9
1983		210.3	101.9	33.5	17.7		433.7	146.2	79.1	208.4	49.1	18.7	12.6	17.7
1984		239.4	114.4	37.9	19.1		512.8	175.3	100.4	237.2	79.1	29.1	21.3	28.8
1985		259.6	124.5	39.3	21.0		592.5	210.9	124.6	257.0	79.7	35.7	24.2	19.8
1986		262.3	128.9	35.8	22.5		647.8	247.2	141.0	259.6	55.4	36.3	16.4	2.7
1987		256.0	124.8	33.2	23.2		680.4	266.2	160.7	253.5	32.6	19.0	19.7	-6.2
1988		262.1	124.3	35.9	23.9		729.4	285.5	184.3	259.6	49.1	19.3	23.6	6.2
1989	22.6	281.9	128.0	41.8	26.1	7.1	780.4	290.2	210.9	279.3	51.0	4.8	26.6	19.7
1990	44.6	275.4	128.7	42.0	27.0	7.9	793.9	283.1	238.2	272.7	13.5	-7.1	27.2	-6.6
1991	63.4	255.5	121.8	38.3	25.7	9.4	779.3	263.3	263.2	252.9	-14.6	-19.9	25.0	-19.8
1992	74.6	245.2	122.9	35.3	25.9	11.0	782.8	262.6	277.5	242.7	3.5	-0.7	14.4	-10.2
1993	79.8	249.1	127.8	30.1	27.1	10.5	842.9	287.1	309.1	246.7	60.1	24.6	31.6	4.0
1994	96.1	276.3	139.0	38.4	29.8	13.2	964.6	326.4	364.6	273.6	121.7	39.2	55.6	26.9
1995	147.9	299.8	148.4	42.6	31.5	19.1	1 100.7	362.1	441.9	296.8	136.1	35.7	77.3	23.2
1996	188.7	298.8	146.8	33.2	32.8	25.4	1 184.0	390.3	498.0	295.7	83.3	28.2	56.1	-1.0
1993:														
January	73.8	246.7	125.8	34.1	24.9	10.8	788.7	263.0	281.0	244.7	5.9	0.4	3.5	1.9
February	73.9	243.0	123.9	33.4	24.2	9.9	793.4	266.2	284.0	243.3	4.7	3.2	2.9	-1.4
March	72.7	239.6	122.8	32.7	23.9	9.7	792.9	266.8	285.4	240.6	-0.5	0.7	1.5	-2.6
April	71.7	243.2	125.0	32.3	23.9	9.9	799.1	268.1	287.6	243.4	6.3	1.4	2.2	2.8
May	70.8	238.6	125.0	27.3	24.1	10.0	798.4	269.9	288.4	240.1	-0.7	1.8	0.8	-3.3
June	72.5	239.3	125.3	27.3	24.0	10.2	801.9	272.3	289.5	240.2	3.5	2.3	1.1	0.1
July	71.5	238.1	123.5	27.4	24.1	10.2	807.7	274.5	294.0	239.3	5.8	2.2	4.5	-0.9
August	72.9	239.5	124.4	27.4	24.3	10.1	812.1	276.8	295.7	239.6	4.4	2.3	1.8	0.3
September	74.6	241.4	124.8	27.9	24.3	10.5	818.5	278.7	299.2	240.5	6.3	1.9	3.5	0.9
October	74.8	240.3	125.1	27.9	24.4	10.1	826.7	283.6	302.2	241.0	8.3	4.9	2.9	0.5
November	75.2	242.2	126.3	28.3	25.1	9.9	833.7	285.3	306.8	241.6	6.9	1.7	4.6	0.6
December	79.8	249.1	127.8	30.1	27.1	10.5	842.9	287.1	309.1	246.7	9.3	1.9	2.2	5.1
1994:														
January	79.3	248.9	130.0	29.4	26.2	10.8	849.1	289.7	312.6	246.9	6.2	2.5	3.5	0.2
February	79.5	248.8	131.3	28.8	25.6	10.6	856.3	291.3	316.1	249.0	7.2	1.6	3.5	2.1
March	79.7	249.7	130.4	29.7	25.6	11.1	866.6	295.3	320.5	250.8	10.3	4.0	4.4	1.9
April	79.8	251.3	131.3	30.4	25.6	10.8	876.8	299.6	325.7	251.5	10.2	4.3	5.2	0.7
May	82.2	253.0	131.4	30.6	25.8	11.3	887.5	303.9	329.0	254.6	10.7	4.3	3.3	3.1
June	84.3	255.0	131.3	32.0	25.9	11.6	898.2	308.1	334.0	256.0	10.7	4.2	5.0	1.4
July	84.2	255.3	131.2	32.2	26.0	11.4	905.3	309.0	339.6	256.7	7.1	0.9	5.5	0.7
August	88.1	258.1	132.4	33.3	26.4	11.2	918.6	313.4	347.1	258.2	13.3	4.4	7.5	1.5
September	87.8	263.5	133.1	36.2	26.5	12.7	930.9	318.6	349.7	262.6	12.3	5.2	2.7	4.4
October	91.5	268.9	137.8	36.7	26.7	12.9	943.6	320.5	353.4	269.7	12.7	1.9	3.7	7.2
November	94.1	267.3	135.1	37.1	27.5	12.7	953.8	324.2	363.0	266.6	10.1	3.7	9.6	-3.2
December	96.1	276.3	139.0	38.4	29.8	13.2	964.6	326.4	364.6	273.6	10.8	2.2	1.7	7.0
1995:														
January	97.6	278.0	140.8	39.9	28.9	13.5	976.9	329.3	372.0	275.6	12.3	2.9	7.4	2.0
February	98.3	272.5	138.7	38.1	28.2	13.8	983.7	331.9	379.1	272.7	6.8	2.7	7.1	-2.9
March	102.3	276.0	140.5	38.6	28.1	14.0	998.3	334.7	386.5	277.1	14.6	2.8	7.4	4.4
April	104.8	282.2	146.6	39.0	28.1	13.8	1 009.5	336.6	390.6	282.3	11.2	1.9	4.1	5.2
May	108.4	282.5	146.3	39.2	28.3	14.5	1 022.0	339.7	398.0	284.3	12.5	3.1	7.3	2.0
June	114.1	285.8	146.0	39.5	28.4	15.0	1 033.6	341.8	404.9	287.0	11.6	2.1	6.9	2.7
July	116.5	287.0	147.7	38.8	28.4	14.8	1 043.0	345.8	408.6	288.7	9.4	4.0	3.7	1.7
August	120.3	289.5	147.7	39.4	28.7	15.7	1 055.0	348.5	416.8	289.6	12.0	2.8	8.3	1.0
September	132.8	293.7	150.5	39.1	28.7	17.6	1 071.9	350.9	428.4	292.6	16.9	2.4	11.6	2.9
October	135.7	290.5	145.8	39.2	28.8	18.6	1 080.2	354.4	434.3	291.5	8.3	3.5	5.9	-1.1
November	141.9	298.3	150.9	40.3	29.4	19.4	1 093.8	359.4	436.9	297.5	13.6	5.0	2.6	6.1
December	147.9	299.8	148.4	42.6	31.5	19.1	1 100.7	362.1	441.9	296.8	7.0	2.7	5.0	-0.8
1996:														
January	151.6	300.1	151.2	41.4	30.2	19.6	1 109.0	364.2	447.2	297.5	8.2	2.1	5.4	0.8
February	153.4	298.0	150.6	40.9	29.5	19.8	1 120.7	367.3	455.2	298.2	11.8	3.1	8.0	0.7
March	157.9	297.8	152.4	39.1	29.3	20.0	1 131.1	371.0	461.0	299.0	10.3	3.7	5.8	0.8
April	161.4	298.6	152.7	38.6	29.2	20.4	1 139.8	374.0	467.2	298.6	8.7	2.9	6.2	-0.4
May	164.5	295.2	148.4	39.1	29.5	20.1	1 145.5	377.0	471.4	297.1	5.7	3.1	4.2	-1.5
June	169.2	295.8	148.7	37.8	29.4	21.2	1 152.4	381.6	473.7	297.2	6.9	4.5	2.3	0.1
July	171.6	297.3	149.1	37.9	29.4	21.4	1 164.5	385.7	479.6	299.2	12.2	4.2	6.0	2.0
August	174.6	302.6	152.5	38.3	29.7	21.8	1 171.6	386.2	482.5	302.8	7.1	0.5	2.9	3.7
September	178.0	303.5	152.8	36.5	29.7	23.7	1 173.9	386.9	484.8	302.2	2.3	0.7	2.3	-0.6
October	178.6	299.9	151.4	33.8	29.9	23.9	1 179.6	388.5	490.3	300.8	5.7	1.6	5.4	-1.4
November	184.0	300.4	150.2	33.6	30.5	25.1	1 183.8	388.5	495.7	299.6	4.2	0.0	5.5	-1.2
December	188.7	298.8	146.8	33.2	32.8	25.4	1 184.0	390.3	498.0	295.7	0.2	1.8	2.3	-3.8

1. Total includes amounts not shown separately by type.

Industrial Production and Capacity Utilization

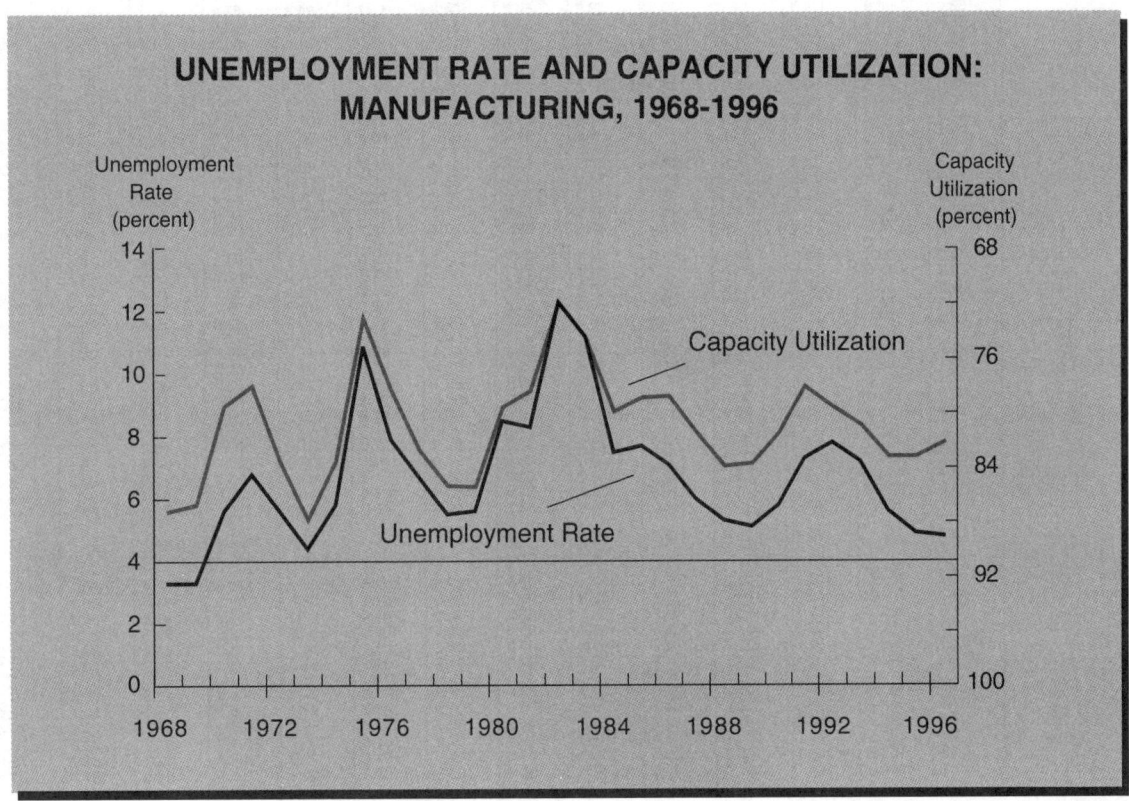

During the 1970s and early 1980s, the unemployment rate for workers last employed in manufacturing and the rate of manufacturing capacity utilization (shown inverted on the chart) moved in close correspondence to one another. In 1973, for example, strains on both physical capacity and labor supply became evident. The unemployment rate in manufacturing dropped to 4.4 percent, from 5.6 percent the previous year, while the capacity utilization rate rose from 83.4 percent in 1972 to 87.7 percent in 1973, its highest annual average during the period shown on the chart.

In contrast, when the unemployment rate fell from 5.6 percent in 1994 to 4.9 percent in 1995, the capacity utilization rate remained unchanged at 83.1 percent. In 1996, while the unemployment rate edged down further, the capacity utilization rate actually fell to 82.1 percent. Neither statistical series is a perfect measure of the extent of resource utilization, but their divergent movement in 1996 suggests that any limitations on further expansion of manufacturing output are more likely to come from constraints on labor supply than from shortages of plant capacity.

INDUSTRIAL PRODUCTION AND CAPACITY UTILIZATION SUMMARY
(Seasonally adjusted)

YEAR AND MONTH	Total industrial production	Products Total	Consumer goods	Business equipment	Construction supplies	Materials	Manufacturing Total	Durables	Non-durables	Mining	Utilities	Total industry	Mfg Total	Advanced processing	Primary processing	Mining	Utilities
1968	58.0	56.9	59.3	44.1	70.3	59.2	54.9	54.8	55.1	94.9	57.5	87.3	87.1	87.3	86.1	83.5	95.1
1969	60.7	59.0	61.5	47.0	73.4	62.8	57.4	57.0	58.0	98.6	62.6	87.3	86.6	86.4	86.5	86.5	96.7
1970	58.7	57.2	60.8	45.3	70.8	60.5	54.8	52.7	58.0	101.2	66.5	81.1	79.4	78.9	79.9	88.8	96.2
1971	59.5	58.0	64.3	43.1	73.0	61.4	55.6	52.4	60.3	98.7	69.6	79.4	77.9	77.1	78.7	87.3	94.6
1972	65.3	63.3	69.5	49.1	82.9	67.7	61.5	58.5	65.7	100.7	74.1	84.4	83.4	82.2	85.5	90.3	95.2
1973	70.6	67.9	72.6	57.5	88.7	74.2	66.9	65.3	69.0	101.6	77.0	88.4	87.7	86.2	90.5	92.3	93.5
1974	69.5	67.2	70.3	60.0	83.1	72.6	65.9	64.0	68.5	101.1	76.1	84.3	83.4	82.5	85.1	92.3	87.3
1975	63.4	62.7	67.7	53.6	71.4	63.8	59.4	56.1	64.2	98.9	76.8	74.6	72.9	73.3	72.1	89.7	84.4
1976	69.3	67.5	74.3	55.5	79.8	71.3	65.4	61.8	70.7	99.7	79.9	79.3	78.2	77.6	79.2	89.8	85.2
1977	74.9	73.1	79.5	62.0	87.0	76.9	71.2	68.1	75.7	102.8	82.0	83.5	82.6	81.9	83.8	90.9	85.0
1978	79.3	77.7	82.6	69.3	92.1	81.0	75.8	73.6	78.9	105.8	84.4	85.8	85.2	84.8	85.9	90.9	85.4
1979	81.9	80.1	81.5	77.3	93.1	83.9	78.5	77.4	79.9	107.6	86.8	86.0	85.3	84.9	86.0	91.4	86.6
1980	79.7	78.9	79.6	76.7	84.9	80.3	75.5	73.4	78.3	110.8	87.3	81.5	79.5	80.8	77.2	93.4	85.9
1981	81.0	80.4	80.1	78.0	82.3	81.4	76.7	74.6	79.5	114.8	85.0	80.8	78.3	78.8	77.2	93.9	82.5
1982	76.6	77.6	78.8	70.6	75.7	75.1	72.1	68.2	77.7	110.5	82.3	74.5	71.8	73.5	68.6	86.3	79.3
1983	79.5	80.2	83.2	68.3	84.2	78.3	76.3	72.2	81.9	105.9	83.7	75.7	74.4	74.4	74.5	80.4	79.7
1984	86.6	86.9	86.7	79.2	90.4	85.9	83.8	82.7	85.3	113.2	86.7	80.8	79.8	79.7	80.0	86.0	81.9
1985	88.0	89.1	87.6	82.5	93.5	86.3	85.7	85.6	86.0	110.3	88.8	79.8	78.8	78.6	79.1	84.3	83.5
1986	89.0	90.8	90.7	82.0	98.4	86.3	88.1	87.4	89.1	101.9	86.4	78.7	78.7	78.1	79.9	77.6	80.6
1987	93.1	95.0	93.7	85.1	104.7	90.4	92.8	92.0	93.8	101.5	89.4	81.3	81.3	79.9	84.5	80.0	82.5
1988	97.3	98.7	96.7	93.5	106.3	95.1	97.1	98.1	96.0	102.9	93.9	83.9	83.8	82.3	86.8	83.6	84.9
1989	99.0	100.4	97.7	98.8	105.5	97.0	99.0	100.5	97.3	101.5	97.1	84.0	83.6	82.5	86.1	85.5	86.3
1990	98.9	99.9	97.3	98.2	102.9	97.2	98.5	99.0	97.9	103.7	98.3	82.3	81.4	80.3	83.9	88.9	85.7
1991	96.9	97.5	97.0	95.7	96.2	95.9	96.2	95.5	97.0	101.6	100.4	79.2	78.0	77.2	79.6	87.6	86.3
1992	100.0	100.0	100.0	100.0	100.0	100.0	100.0	100.0	100.0	100.0	100.0	80.4	79.5	78.3	82.3	87.0	84.6
1993	103.4	103.0	103.2	105.1	103.3	103.9	103.7	105.5	101.7	98.9	103.9	81.6	80.8	79.3	84.1	86.7	87.2
1994	108.6	106.8	107.4	111.3	110.3	111.3	109.4	113.4	105.0	101.6	105.3	83.7	83.1	81.2	87.5	88.9	87.3
1995	112.1	109.3	108.9	119.4	111.6	116.6	113.2	119.7	106.2	100.9	109.1	83.8	83.1	81.2	87.3	88.2	89.1
1996	115.2	112.0	110.4	126.6	116.7	120.3	116.4	125.7	106.3	102.9	112.7	83.1	82.1	80.3	86.1	90.5	90.3
1993:																	
January	102.3	102.4	102.3	104.3	101.1	102.1	102.6	103.5	101.6	100.3	100.8	81.4	80.7	79.4	83.6	87.8	84.8
February	102.8	102.7	102.7	104.2	102.5	102.9	102.9	104.0	101.7	98.8	104.5	81.7	80.8	79.5	83.8	86.5	87.9
March	102.8	102.7	102.8	105.0	101.2	103.1	103.0	104.5	101.4	97.6	105.3	81.6	80.7	79.6	83.4	85.5	88.6
April	103.2	102.8	102.9	105.0	101.4	103.7	103.6	105.1	101.9	97.8	103.5	81.7	81.0	79.8	83.8	85.6	87.0
May	102.6	102.4	102.2	105.1	102.6	102.9	103.0	104.8	101.1	98.1	101.3	81.2	80.5	79.3	83.3	86.0	85.1
June	102.8	102.2	102.4	104.7	101.7	103.7	103.0	104.7	101.2	99.0	103.3	81.2	80.4	78.9	83.8	86.8	86.7
July	103.1	103.0	103.6	105.2	102.7	103.3	103.4	104.8	101.8	97.9	104.4	81.3	80.5	79.0	83.9	85.8	87.6
August	102.8	102.7	103.3	103.6	103.7	103.1	103.0	104.2	101.7	98.2	105.0	81.0	80.1	78.4	83.9	86.1	88.1
September	103.9	103.6	103.9	105.4	104.7	104.3	104.2	106.1	102.0	99.1	104.4	81.7	80.9	79.4	84.4	87.0	87.4
October	104.1	103.5	104.0	105.7	105.4	105.0	104.4	107.1	101.5	100.1	104.3	81.8	80.9	79.3	84.6	87.9	87.3
November	104.6	103.8	104.2	106.2	105.7	106.0	105.0	107.9	101.8	99.9	105.0	82.1	81.2	79.5	85.2	87.8	87.8
December	105.4	104.3	104.7	107.0	107.4	107.1	105.9	109.2	102.2	100.2	105.0	82.5	81.7	80.0	85.8	88.1	87.6
1994:																	
January	105.7	105.0	105.4	108.4	106.8	106.9	106.0	109.5	102.1	99.8	107.9	82.6	81.6	79.9	85.6	87.7	90.0
February	106.2	105.3	105.9	109.0	106.3	107.7	106.6	110.1	102.7	100.8	106.8	82.8	81.9	80.3	85.8	88.6	89.0
March	107.0	105.8	106.5	109.0	106.7	108.8	107.5	110.6	104.1	102.2	105.0	83.2	82.4	80.6	86.6	89.7	87.4
April	107.4	106.2	106.9	109.1	108.9	109.4	108.2	111.6	104.5	101.7	103.3	83.3	82.7	80.8	87.2	89.2	85.9
May	108.1	106.6	107.4	109.7	109.6	110.5	109.0	112.5	105.2	101.9	103.2	83.7	83.1	81.1	87.7	89.3	85.7
June	108.6	107.1	108.1	110.3	110.3	111.1	109.2	112.7	105.3	102.2	107.8	83.9	83.0	81.2	87.3	89.6	89.5
July	109.1	107.2	107.7	111.7	112.0	112.2	110.0	114.3	105.3	101.9	105.8	84.1	83.4	81.5	87.8	89.2	87.7
August	109.2	106.9	107.9	111.3	111.4	112.7	110.1	114.3	105.5	102.1	104.9	83.9	83.3	81.4	87.7	89.3	86.9
September	109.3	106.9	107.2	112.2	111.7	113.0	110.3	114.8	105.4	101.0	104.8	83.8	83.2	81.2	87.9	88.3	86.7
October	109.9	108.0	108.1	114.0	112.8	113.0	111.1	115.8	106.0	100.7	105.1	84.1	83.6	81.6	88.1	87.9	86.9
November	110.6	108.3	108.3	114.7	112.5	114.3	111.9	116.6	106.7	101.3	104.4	84.4	84.0	81.9	88.5	88.4	86.3
December	111.6	108.9	108.7	115.9	114.2	115.8	112.9	118.3	107.0	103.0	104.3	84.9	84.5	82.2	89.6	89.8	86.1
1995:																	
January	111.9	109.2	108.9	117.7	113.3	116.3	113.3	119.0	107.1	102.0	104.9	84.9	84.6	82.4	89.5	88.9	86.4
February	111.6	109.0	108.4	118.1	113.0	115.9	112.9	118.8	106.5	101.9	106.0	84.5	84.0	81.8	89.1	88.9	87.2
March	111.7	109.1	108.6	118.8	111.9	115.8	113.1	118.9	106.7	100.5	106.6	84.3	83.9	81.7	88.7	87.6	87.5
April	111.4	108.7	108.2	118.5	111.4	115.7	112.7	118.4	106.4	100.7	106.6	83.9	83.4	81.3	87.9	87.9	87.4
May	111.5	108.6	108.2	118.2	109.8	116.1	112.6	118.4	106.2	100.6	109.0	83.7	83.0	81.0	87.5	87.8	89.2
June	111.7	109.1	108.9	119.1	110.1	115.9	112.9	118.9	106.3	100.5	109.0	83.6	83.0	81.1	86.9	87.8	89.1
July	111.7	109.0	108.5	119.0	110.4	116.0	112.7	118.7	106.1	101.8	109.4	83.4	82.6	80.9	86.4	89.0	89.3
August	112.6	109.9	109.5	120.8	110.4	116.8	113.4	120.2	106.1	100.5	113.5	83.8	82.9	81.3	86.4	87.9	92.5
September	113.0	110.2	109.5	121.9	112.1	117.4	114.2	121.6	106.2	101.2	109.7	83.9	83.2	81.5	86.9	88.5	89.2
October	112.5	109.3	108.8	120.1	111.4	117.6	113.8	120.9	106.1	100.0	109.3	83.3	82.6	80.8	86.4	87.6	88.8
November	112.7	109.5	109.4	119.8	112.0	117.7	113.6	121.2	105.4	100.8	112.6	83.2	82.2	80.4	86.1	88.3	91.3
December	112.8	109.7	109.3	120.7	113.5	117.6	113.8	121.5	105.4	100.3	112.3	83.0	82.0	80.3	86.0	88.0	91.0
1996:																	
January	112.4	109.1	108.3	122.0	110.8	117.5	113.4	121.5	104.6	99.0	112.5	82.4	81.5	79.9	85.0	86.9	91.0
February	113.8	110.8	109.9	124.6	113.3	118.5	114.8	123.6	105.3	100.8	113.3	83.2	82.2	80.9	85.3	88.5	91.5
March	113.2	110.4	109.4	122.6	115.5	117.7	113.9	121.8	105.4	102.8	114.4	82.6	81.3	79.4	85.6	90.3	91.5
April	114.3	111.0	109.8	125.1	114.2	119.5	115.2	124.6	105.2	102.9	113.5	83.1	82.0	80.4	85.6	90.4	92.2
May	114.8	111.4	110.0	125.0	116.1	120.1	115.7	125.2	105.5	103.2	114.6	83.2	82.0	80.3	85.6	90.7	91.3
June	115.5	112.3	110.8	126.6	118.3	120.5	116.4	126.3	105.9	104.4	114.0	83.5	82.3	80.5	86.5	91.8	91.4
July	115.5	112.3	110.7	128.1	117.5	120.5	117.0	126.9	106.4	103.1	109.4	83.2	82.4	80.6	86.7	90.7	87.6
August	115.8	112.2	110.1	127.7	119.2	121.5	117.2	127.5	106.2	104.5	110.8	83.2	82.3	80.4	86.5	91.3	88.5
September	116.0	112.7	110.5	128.3	119.8	121.2	117.4	127.2	106.9	103.4	111.1	83.1	82.1	80.2	86.6	91.0	88.6
October	116.2	112.8	110.8	128.8	117.7	121.7	117.6	127.1	107.4	103.4	111.9	83.0	82.0	80.0	86.7	91.0	89.0
November	117.2	114.1	112.3	129.8	120.7	122.2	118.5	128.4	107.9	103.5	114.5	83.4	82.4	80.5	86.5	91.1	91.0
December	117.7	114.3	112.7	130.7	117.8	123.1	119.2	128.8	108.8	104.5	112.6	83.5	82.5	80.8	86.6	91.9	89.3

INDUSTRIAL PRODUCTION INDEXES BY MARKET GROUPS
(Seasonally adjusted, 1992=100)

YEAR AND MONTH	Total industrial production	Products Total	Final products Total	Total consumer goods	Durable consumer goods Total	Automotive products Total	Total autos and trucks	Autos	Trucks	Auto parts and allied products	Other consumer durables Total	Total appliances and electronics	Appliances and air conditions	Home electronics
1968	58.0	56.9	56.9	59.3	54.6	58.6	63.5	....	13.5	49.2	52.7	32.5	....	....
1969	60.7	59.0	58.7	61.5	57.1	59.1	62.5	....	15.2	52.7	56.3	34.7	....	....
1970	58.7	57.2	56.6	60.8	52.6	49.7	49.3	....	14.2	51.3	54.6	34.0	....	....
1971	59.5	58.0	57.1	64.3	59.6	63.3	67.7	....	20.0	55.1	57.7	35.8		
1972	65.3	63.3	62.0	69.5	66.7	68.4	72.3	130.9	25.8	61.2	66.1	40.8		
1973	70.6	67.9	66.6	72.6	71.8	75.2	82.8	140.8	33.6	62.8	70.0	45.7		
1974	69.5	67.2	66.4	70.3	64.4	65.0	66.1	102.0	31.5	61.7	64.7	42.2		
1975	63.4	62.7	62.5	67.7	58.7	61.8	60.7	94.7	28.5	61.6	56.9	34.4		
1976	69.3	67.5	66.9	74.3	68.8	76.3	82.8	126.5	40.1	65.4	63.8	38.5		
1977	74.9	73.1	72.3	79.5	77.9	87.2	95.4	136.2	50.1	73.6	71.8	44.4		
1978	79.3	77.7	77.1	82.6	80.7	89.6	97.8	133.6	55.7	75.8	74.9	47.1		
1979	81.9	80.1	79.6	81.5	76.7	81.4	87.5	123.1	45.8	70.4	73.6	47.3		
1980	79.7	78.9	79.2	79.6	66.9	62.3	61.5	97.1	24.6	59.3	69.7	45.9		
1981	81.0	80.4	81.2	80.1	67.2	61.6	61.2	93.7	26.8	58.3	70.7	46.2		
1982	76.6	77.6	78.2	78.8	62.5	59.1	57.2	78.3	34.0	57.4	64.4	40.6		
1983	79.5	80.2	80.0	83.2	73.8	74.3	79.9	111.0	45.9	64.7	73.1	54.0		
1984	86.6	86.9	86.9	86.7	84.1	89.4	96.0	127.1	60.8	77.8	80.1	61.7		
1985	88.0	89.1	89.2	87.6	84.7	95.4	103.9	134.9	68.2	81.6	77.3	58.1		
1986	89.0	90.8	90.3	90.7	88.7	97.5	104.1	132.4	71.0	85.8	82.6	66.8	90.4	48.6
1987	93.1	95.0	93.2	93.7	93.9	100.7	104.0	122.7	80.1	94.1	89.1	73.0	95.7	55.2
1988	97.3	98.7	97.6	96.7	99.8	107.1	111.1	130.0	86.7	99.3	94.5	84.2	100.2	70.7
1989	99.0	100.4	99.7	97.7	101.3	108.9	114.0	130.0	91.9	99.2	95.9	86.3	101.7	73.3
1990	98.9	99.9	99.4	97.3	98.0	100.9	103.3	115.0	87.7	96.1	96.0	87.7	98.2	78.9
1991	96.9	97.5	97.5	97.0	93.0	90.3	89.6	95.7	84.2	91.6	95.2	92.5	91.9	93.1
1992	100.0	100.0	100.0	100.0	100.0	100.0	100.0	100.0	100.6	100.3	100.0	100.0	100.0	100.0
1993	103.4	103.0	103.2	103.2	110.1	112.3	116.2	113.4	120.4	105.6	108.5	114.9	109.2	120.8
1994	108.6	106.8	107.1	107.4	120.4	123.7	132.7	126.4	138.5	109.6	118.0	136.9	122.8	152.2
1995	112.1	109.3	109.9	108.9	122.8	124.4	132.2	124.8	141.7	112.0	121.7	153.4	122.5	189.4
1996	115.2	112.0	112.8	110.4	126.2	125.8	132.7	122.5	149.9	114.5	126.3	173.0	129.7	224.9
1993:														
January	102.3	102.4	102.7	102.3	107.5	111.6	116.4	113.8	120.6	103.4	104.5	105.9	103.5	108.2
February	102.8	102.7	102.7	102.7	107.2	110.0	113.1	110.9	117.0	104.7	105.1	107.5	105.1	109.9
March	102.8	102.7	102.8	102.8	107.7	111.2	114.8	112.0	119.5	105.1	105.0	110.2	107.8	112.6
April	103.2	102.8	102.9	102.9	108.7	111.5	114.7	114.7	115.8	106.0	106.7	111.3	107.1	115.5
May	102.6	102.4	102.4	102.2	109.9	112.5	115.8	115.8	116.8	106.8	108.0	112.0	108.0	116.0
June	102.8	102.2	102.5	102.4	108.7	109.7	112.8	111.9	114.9	104.6	107.9	111.2	105.2	117.3
July	103.1	103.0	103.3	103.6	108.9	107.6	108.1	108.6	108.4	106.3	109.7	117.8	110.4	125.4
August	102.8	102.7	102.8	103.3	108.3	107.3	106.4	101.1	113.4	108.0	108.9	113.8	104.6	123.5
September	103.9	103.6	103.7	103.9	109.7	109.4	111.3	105.0	119.2	106.0	109.8	117.9	109.2	127.1
October	104.1	103.5	103.8	104.0	113.8	116.5	122.3	116.3	129.7	107.3	111.8	121.7	115.7	127.6
November	104.6	103.8	104.0	104.2	115.0	119.3	126.4	124.8	133.3	104.8	111.8	123.4	117.6	129.2
December	105.4	104.3	104.5	104.7	115.8	120.3	130.6	125.5	136.3	104.3	112.6	126.1	115.7	137.0
1994:														
January	105.7	105.0	105.3	105.4	118.2	124.8	134.8	131.0	138.6	109.3	113.4	127.7	118.4	137.5
February	106.2	105.3	105.7	105.9	119.1	127.1	139.1	134.4	143.6	108.7	113.4	127.9	118.9	137.2
March	107.0	105.8	106.1	106.5	118.4	123.4	133.2	128.5	137.5	108.0	114.8	130.7	120.4	141.5
April	107.4	106.2	106.4	106.9	119.4	123.6	133.4	129.0	137.1	108.2	116.3	131.0	122.1	140.0
May	108.1	106.6	106.8	107.4	119.2	121.6	129.5	124.9	133.2	109.1	117.4	135.6	121.9	150.2
June	108.6	107.1	107.3	108.1	119.9	121.9	129.7	123.7	135.0	109.6	118.4	136.9	124.0	150.7
July	109.1	107.2	107.3	107.7	120.6	119.6	124.4	117.4	130.9	111.3	121.1	142.1	128.6	156.5
August	109.2	106.9	107.1	107.9	121.8	123.5	133.9	122.4	145.5	107.4	120.6	143.6	130.5	157.4
September	109.3	106.9	107.0	107.2	121.2	122.5	131.0	121.3	140.4	109.3	120.2	142.2	125.7	160.4
October	109.9	108.0	108.1	108.1	122.2	124.9	133.3	127.0	139.1	111.6	120.2	139.5	119.7	161.8
November	110.6	108.3	108.4	108.3	121.6	125.1	133.9	125.8	141.9	111.1	119.2	139.0	117.2	164.1
December	111.6	108.9	109.1	108.7	123.4	126.5	135.8	131.7	139.4	112.0	121.1	146.1	125.5	169.5
1995:														
January	111.9	109.2	109.7	108.9	124.6	128.4	139.2	136.8	141.1	111.7	121.9	149.3	124.9	177.4
February	111.6	109.0	109.4	108.4	124.6	127.8	138.8	135.1	142.4	111.0	122.2	148.9	121.8	180.5
March	111.7	109.1	109.7	108.6	123.6	126.8	137.7	134.0	141.8	110.1	121.3	149.0	118.7	184.5
April	111.4	108.7	109.3	108.2	122.8	125.3	133.3	127.2	140.4	112.7	120.9	147.6	120.0	179.8
May	111.5	108.6	109.2	108.2	120.8	121.5	128.3	119.6	138.8	110.3	120.2	150.1	120.6	184.7
June	111.7	109.1	109.9	108.9	120.3	122.5	129.8	118.2	144.0	110.7	118.8	147.2	112.3	188.6
July	111.7	109.0	109.6	108.5	119.7	118.4	121.9	118.8	126.7	111.4	120.5	152.2	123.3	185.3
August	112.6	109.9	110.7	109.5	122.5	123.6	131.2	119.3	146.6	111.4	121.7	155.1	124.2	190.7
September	113.0	110.2	110.9	109.5	124.1	125.5	132.7	123.1	145.8	113.8	123.1	157.6	124.3	196.6
October	112.5	109.3	109.9	108.8	122.6	123.2	130.2	122.3	141.8	111.7	122.2	159.0	124.0	200.1
November	112.7	109.5	110.1	109.4	123.7	124.4	130.7	122.0	143.6	113.9	123.0	162.6	126.6	204.8
December	112.8	109.7	110.2	109.3	124.8	125.6	132.0	121.3	147.6	114.8	124.2	162.0	129.3	199.9
1996:														
January	112.4	109.1	109.8	108.3	121.1	121.1	126.2	115.3	142.3	112.1	121.1	157.4	120.2	201.5
February	113.8	110.8	111.7	109.9	124.7	125.6	133.0	121.6	150.3	113.7	123.9	164.4	124.6	211.6
March	113.2	110.4	111.1	109.4	120.8	115.1	111.2	93.5	135.4	117.7	124.7	165.8	129.5	208.3
April	114.3	111.0	112.1	109.8	125.7	126.0	135.0	126.1	150.3	111.9	125.3	170.2	127.2	221.4
May	114.8	111.4	112.2	110.0	126.9	126.9	135.0	129.0	147.4	114.0	126.7	172.0	128.7	223.7
June	115.5	112.3	113.1	110.8	129.9	130.0	137.7	133.3	148.7	117.4	129.7	180.1	139.4	227.8
July	115.5	112.3	113.4	110.7	129.7	132.1	145.7	137.8	161.3	112.4	128.0	181.1	137.4	233.3
August	115.8	112.2	113.0	110.1	128.0	128.7	138.7	132.5	152.3	113.5	127.5	175.9	134.7	224.8
September	116.0	112.7	113.3	110.5	127.1	127.7	134.6	129.9	146.6	116.2	126.6	174.2	129.2	228.7
October	116.2	112.8	113.6	110.8	124.5	122.0	125.7	112.3	147.4	114.4	126.2	176.5	123.6	242.4
November	117.2	114.1	114.8	112.3	127.1	127.4	133.8	123.5	152.4	116.4	126.8	176.9	125.6	240.4
December	117.7	114.3	115.3	112.7	128.4	127.2	135.5	115.9	164.9	114.0	129.1	181.1	136.4	234.5

INDUSTRIAL PRODUCTION INDEXES BY MARKET GROUPS—Continued
(Seasonally adjusted, 1992=100)

Final products—Continued

YEAR AND MONTH	Durable consumer goods		Nondurable consumer goods									Equipment			
				Nonenergy products					Energy products				Business equipment		
														Information processing and related	
	Carpeting and furniture	Miscellaneous	Total	Total	Foods and tobacco	Clothing	Chemical products	Paper products	Total	Fuels	Utilities	Total	Total	Total	Computer and office equipment
1968	64.3	67.4	61.1	....	59.8	97.3	40.2	59.0	63.8	75.2	53.8	54.9	44.1	13.3	1.8
1969	66.6	73.0	63.1	....	61.4	98.8	42.2	61.0	68.2	78.2	58.7	56.4	47.0	14.8	2.2
1970	64.2	70.5	64.2	....	62.3	95.9	45.9	58.9	72.1	81.8	62.7	52.4	45.3	15.3	2.3
1971	69.1	74.3	66.0	....	64.2	95.5	48.5	60.1	75.5	85.1	66.0	49.0	43.1	14.2	2.0
1972	83.3	83.3	70.3	....	67.8	103.9	53.0	60.6	79.8	89.3	69.9	53.7	49.1	16.6	2.4
1973	88.5	84.1	72.4	....	69.8	104.4	57.0	60.8	83.2	93.6	72.7	59.9	57.5	19.6	2.9
1974	80.4	78.7	72.4	....	70.2	99.3	59.7	62.1	82.3	90.4	72.8	61.9	60.0	21.8	3.5
1975	70.2	73.7	71.0	....	70.2	92.0	57.9	59.2	85.2	91.6	76.1	56.7	53.6	20.5	3.2
1976	79.3	82.5	76.2	....	74.3	103.8	63.2	63.4	86.8	97.2	76.0	58.6	55.5	22.3	3.9
1977	89.7	91.2	79.8	....	77.0	108.8	65.9	71.4	88.0	102.6	77.0	64.1	62.0	26.0	5.1
1978	95.8	92.7	82.9	....	80.0	111.4	70.1	76.1	89.8	102.6	79.7	70.8	69.3	31.8	7.5
1979	96.4	88.3	82.9	....	80.8	106.7	71.6	77.2	88.9	99.1	81.0	77.4	77.3	38.6	10.3
1980	88.9	83.4	83.8	....	82.4	107.5	75.0	77.9	85.8	91.1	82.7	78.9	76.7	43.3	13.9
1981	87.8	86.3	84.3	....	83.9	107.1	73.3	80.4	85.1	90.0	82.3	82.5	78.0	48.1	18.4
1982	78.8	81.2	84.2	....	84.7	105.8	71.0	82.1	85.2	89.1	83.3	77.5	70.6	51.2	21.3
1983	87.8	82.6	86.2	....	86.6	107.9	73.4	85.9	85.3	87.8	84.3	76.1	68.3	56.0	29.5
1984	94.2	88.6	87.5	....	88.2	106.4	73.5	90.1	87.7	91.6	86.0	87.3	79.2	67.9	42.0
1985	92.9	85.9	88.5	....	90.6	100.8	74.5	92.1	88.5	91.2	87.3	91.6	82.5	74.9	50.3
1986	98.3	86.8	91.3	91.5	92.8	102.1	80.3	94.7	90.7	95.4	88.8	89.7	82.0	73.8	53.7
1987	103.5	94.2	93.6	93.8	95.3	104.2	83.0	96.4	92.7	95.6	91.3	92.7	85.1	78.9	62.2
1988	103.4	97.5	95.9	95.7	96.9	102.2	87.6	98.3	97.0	97.9	96.5	99.1	93.5	86.3	74.6
1989	103.5	99.0	96.7	96.4	97.4	100.1	89.7	100.2	98.3	98.2	98.2	103.0	98.8	90.7	83.0
1990	100.8	99.4	97.1	97.1	98.3	96.6	92.4	100.6	97.7	98.5	97.2	102.7	98.2	90.5	81.4
1991	94.5	97.3	98.1	97.8	98.5	97.6	95.1	99.6	100.4	99.0	100.9	98.4	95.7	91.1	82.3
1992	100.0	100.0	100.0	100.0	100.0	100.0	100.0	100.0	100.0	100.0	100.0	100.0	100.0	100.0	100.0
1993	104.9	106.4	101.5	100.9	99.3	102.5	102.8	102.5	105.2	102.5	106.3	103.0	105.1	106.7	121.5
1994	110.0	110.8	104.1	103.9	103.4	105.4	106.0	101.2	105.1	101.9	106.3	106.6	111.3	113.6	152.1
1995	109.5	109.2	105.3	105.0	105.6	101.1	108.9	100.1	107.7	104.3	109.1	111.6	119.4	128.1	213.6
1996	109.9	107.9	106.5	105.6	106.1	95.5	112.8	101.1	111.9	106.6	114.1	116.8	126.6	143.2	296.9
1993:															
January	104.8	103.4	101.0	101.0	100.1	101.9	102.6	101.4	100.8	102.0	100.3	103.4	104.3	105.5	110.1
February	101.9	105.2	101.5	100.9	99.7	101.8	102.1	102.4	105.9	103.0	107.0	102.7	104.2	105.5	113.1
March	99.6	104.6	101.5	100.8	98.9	102.0	103.7	102.2	106.6	101.2	108.7	102.7	105.0	106.7	115.1
April	103.6	105.4	101.4	100.9	98.5	102.1	104.2	103.2	104.6	101.1	106.0	102.9	105.0	106.9	118.0
May	106.5	106.3	100.3	100.2	98.3	101.9	101.9	103.1	100.5	101.6	100.1	102.8	105.1	107.1	120.7
June	106.4	106.6	100.8	100.5	98.9	102.4	100.7	104.1	103.1	101.1	103.8	102.5	104.7	106.9	120.1
July	106.0	106.8	102.2	101.8	100.1	103.2	103.9	103.0	105.3	101.3	106.9	102.9	105.2	107.8	123.0
August	106.0	107.3	102.0	101.4	99.9	102.7	103.9	101.7	106.3	100.8	108.5	101.9	103.6	106.5	123.8
September	105.3	107.2	102.4	101.7	99.4	103.0	105.7	102.1	107.4	103.0	109.1	103.3	105.4	106.9	126.0
October	108.1	107.7	101.5	100.5	98.5	102.6	102.3	103.4	107.7	106.0	108.4	103.5	105.7	106.7	126.8
November	105.0	108.3	101.4	100.4	99.0	102.7	101.5	102.1	108.0	105.5	109.1	103.7	106.2	106.9	127.6
December	105.5	108.2	101.9	101.2	100.4	103.6	101.7	101.6	106.3	103.3	107.5	104.2	107.0	107.2	133.4
1994:															
January	107.3	108.0	102.2	101.0	100.3	102.8	101.4	101.5	110.0	101.5	113.5	105.2	108.4	108.7	135.8
February	106.8	108.1	102.6	101.7	100.3	102.7	104.8	101.1	108.6	100.4	111.9	105.4	109.0	110.0	138.1
March	106.9	109.3	103.5	103.1	102.4	105.0	104.9	101.3	106.0	101.0	108.1	105.5	109.0	110.2	140.0
April	110.6	110.4	103.7	103.8	103.2	105.9	105.3	102.1	102.8	102.4	103.0	105.5	109.1	110.3	140.9
May	109.5	110.5	104.4	104.5	103.2	106.1	108.3	102.1	103.9	102.8	104.3	105.7	109.7	111.4	145.5
June	110.2	111.6	105.2	104.9	103.5	105.8	109.2	102.3	107.1	102.2	109.2	106.0	110.3	112.2	147.8
July	111.8	113.3	104.5	104.3	103.5	106.7	106.6	101.5	106.1	100.9	108.2	106.5	111.7	113.5	151.9
August	110.5	112.0	104.4	104.5	104.0	105.8	106.5	101.8	104.2	100.2	104.9	105.9	111.3	114.1	154.4
September	110.4	112.0	103.7	103.8	104.4	106.0	103.3	101.1	103.1	101.6	103.5	106.6	112.2	116.4	162.0
October	113.1	112.2	104.6	104.8	105.5	106.7	105.6	99.9	103.4	100.8	104.4	108.1	114.0	116.4	162.0
November	110.9	111.4	104.9	105.2	105.8	105.5	107.3	100.0	103.0	104.2	102.3	108.7	114.7	117.7	165.5
December	112.1	110.9	105.0	105.4	105.2	106.4	109.0	100.0	102.7	102.7	102.5	109.8	115.9	118.3	168.4
1995:															
January	110.0	111.7	105.0	105.3	105.5	105.1	108.9	99.5	103.0	103.7	102.5	111.1	117.7	122.0	184.4
February	112.5	111.3	104.3	104.3	104.4	103.7	107.2	100.2	104.8	104.1	105.0	111.1	118.1	122.9	192.8
March	109.5	110.9	104.8	104.8	105.1	104.8	107.6	99.6	105.4	105.6	105.2	111.4	118.8	124.7	196.0
April	111.6	109.7	104.5	104.6	105.1	103.3	106.6	100.5	104.5	104.2	104.4	111.1	118.5	125.9	202.9
May	107.7	108.8	105.0	104.6	105.6	102.8	106.6	99.9	107.6	103.5	109.2	110.9	118.2	125.4	206.7
June	107.0	107.9	105.9	105.7	107.3	101.5	107.9	99.9	108.0	104.1	109.6	111.6	119.1	127.0	206.5
July	108.7	107.8	105.7	105.4	107.0	99.8	107.7	100.8	107.6	104.2	108.9	111.4	119.0	127.9	213.6
August	108.5	108.8	106.2	105.3	106.2	100.0	109.5	99.9	112.0	104.2	115.3	112.7	120.8	129.9	217.8
September	110.7	109.2	105.9	105.3	105.7	98.7	111.0	100.3	109.9	105.8	111.5	113.2	121.9	131.9	226.3
October	108.4	107.7	105.3	105.3	105.2	99.1	112.1	100.0	106.0	103.6	106.9	111.7	120.1	133.4	233.6
November	108.0	107.9	105.8	104.8	105.1	98.0	110.3	100.7	112.5	103.9	116.2	111.2	119.8	133.5	237.6
December	111.1	109.0	105.4	104.5	104.7	96.3	111.4	99.6	111.1	104.3	114.0	111.7	120.7	133.0	244.9
1996:															
January	106.8	107.2	105.1	104.0	104.6	94.5	111.1	98.5	111.8	104.4	115.0	112.4	122.0	135.9	251.8
February	108.0	108.6	106.2	105.1	105.8	96.5	111.3	99.8	112.8	106.7	115.4	114.8	124.6	139.4	263.6
March	110.8	108.0	106.6	105.3	106.8	95.8	110.5	99.7	114.1	106.9	117.1	113.9	122.6	139.8	270.8
April	109.1	108.0	105.9	104.7	105.7	96.1	110.0	100.0	112.8	106.4	115.5	115.9	125.1	140.5	277.3
May	112.4	108.1	105.8	104.7	105.3	95.9	110.5	100.7	112.8	106.8	115.4	116.0	125.0	140.8	284.7
June	114.6	108.7	106.0	104.9	105.8	95.6	110.6	100.2	113.2	106.7	116.0	117.1	126.6	143.9	294.3
July	107.0	108.5	106.0	105.5	105.9	95.4	112.6	101.4	109.1	106.7	109.9	118.1	128.1	144.1	306.5
August	111.1	108.0	105.6	105.1	105.4	95.4	111.3	101.8	109.4	107.7	110.0	117.9	127.7	144.6	310.8
September	110.5	107.6	106.3	105.9	106.1	95.1	113.5	101.9	109.4	105.4	110.9	118.1	128.3	146.3	319.0
October	108.6	106.5	107.3	106.8	106.7	95.5	115.5	102.9	110.7	108.1	111.7	118.1	128.8	147.4	323.6
November	110.7	106.4	108.5	107.4	107.2	95.0	117.3	102.9	115.3	107.8	118.5	119.0	129.8	147.1	328.3
December	109.3	109.6	108.7	108.3	108.2	94.9	118.8	103.0	111.8	106.0	114.2	119.6	130.7	148.5	332.5

YEAR AND MONTH	Business equipment—Continued Industrial equipment	Transit Total	Transit Autos and trucks	Other business equipment	Defense and space	Oil and gas well drilling	Manu-factured homes	Intermediate products Total	Con-struction supplies	Business supplies	Materials Total	Durable Total	Durable Consumer parts	Durable Equip-ment parts
1968	97.7	66.2	48.4	62.3	80.4	90.6	89.8	57.0	70.3	48.4	59.2	50.5	84.1	24.3
1969	104.1	65.3	49.3	65.9	76.5	93.7	109.8	60.1	73.4	51.4	62.8	53.2	84.6	26.0
1970	100.9	57.3	39.4	63.0	64.8	81.6	96.5	59.2	70.8	51.7	60.5	48.3	71.0	23.8
1971	94.4	55.3	46.7	64.7	58.2	78.1	118.6	61.0	73.0	53.2	61.4	48.4	78.6	23.9
1972	104.7	60.4	50.1	79.7	56.6	89.8	146.6	68.1	82.9	58.5	67.7	54.8	87.4	27.4
1973	120.0	72.8	59.7	93.9	55.3	97.2	144.0	72.5	88.7	61.9	74.2	62.6	100.0	32.4
1974	126.0	70.3	54.2	92.9	54.5	120.9	101.7	69.9	83.1	61.4	72.6	60.8	89.5	33.0
1975	109.5	64.2	50.5	77.4	53.5	137.2	81.5	63.1	71.4	57.8	63.8	50.6	72.7	28.0
1976	108.8	61.8	61.5	86.9	54.3	137.6	107.1	69.5	79.8	62.9	71.3	58.4	92.2	31.4
1977	118.2	65.8	71.4	94.9	54.4	167.2	118.7	75.7	87.0	68.4	76.9	64.6	104.7	36.1
1978	125.3	76.7	74.9	97.4	55.9	187.8	126.0	79.9	92.1	72.0	81.0	70.2	107.9	41.4
1979	130.8	88.1	70.9	106.0	57.7	182.1	121.2	82.0	93.1	74.9	83.9	73.3	103.0	47.1
1980	126.5	81.3	53.6	95.7	63.2	226.3	99.6	77.7	84.9	73.2	80.3	67.7	82.3	49.6
1981	126.5	74.6	55.5	94.9	64.5	301.1	101.8	77.6	82.3	74.7	81.4	70.4	81.2	53.2
1982	103.7	62.0	49.3	84.1	72.6	283.1	89.3	75.8	75.7	75.8	75.1	62.6	71.0	51.5
1983	87.3	58.4	64.2	85.3	80.4	244.7	110.5	81.0	84.2	79.1	78.3	68.2	81.7	54.7
1984	98.1	67.0	80.9	95.2	89.5	283.0	104.7	86.9	90.4	84.9	85.9	79.5	94.0	67.0
1985	97.4	73.0	91.6	90.5	103.8	248.6	102.5	89.1	93.5	86.4	86.3	80.9	95.1	68.9
1986	95.6	74.6	92.2	91.8	113.0	136.6	102.7	92.7	98.4	89.3	86.3	82.3	92.3	73.3
1987	95.4	75.4	92.5	98.4	117.5	124.0	106.2	100.7	104.7	98.4	90.4	87.5	95.0	78.6
1988	105.2	84.9	94.1	105.5	117.1	125.7	103.0	102.5	106.3	100.3	95.1	93.6	100.4	85.3
1989	109.6	94.4	96.0	109.5	117.4	116.6	96.9	102.9	105.5	101.3	97.0	95.7	99.6	89.6
1990	107.3	95.2	93.7	108.7	115.9	136.2	94.0	101.9	102.9	101.4	97.2	95.3	93.2	92.3
1991	100.9	96.4	91.6	98.2	106.7	116.8	84.3	97.5	96.2	98.3	95.9	93.2	89.5	93.3
1992	100.0	100.0	100.0	100.0	100.0	100.0	100.0	100.0	100.0	100.0	100.0	100.0	100.0	100.0
1993	106.5	98.4	109.6	107.3	93.5	107.3	115.5	102.5	103.3	102.0	103.9	107.0	111.6	107.5
1994	115.9	98.2	120.1	113.6	86.2	113.9	130.0	106.1	110.3	103.6	111.3	118.1	126.5	120.0
1995	124.8	95.9	119.5	116.0	80.7	109.1	148.9	107.5	111.6	105.0	116.6	126.7	126.2	141.5
1996	126.9	100.0	115.4	116.5	77.0	120.6	161.7	109.4	116.7	105.1	120.3	134.0	129.0	159.2
1993:														
January	102.9	104.7	113.1	103.3	96.8	116.2	116.6	101.5	101.1	101.7	102.1	103.7	104.9	104.7
February	102.9	102.3	109.4	106.3	96.1	102.5	114.9	102.7	102.5	102.8	102.9	104.9	108.7	104.9
March	104.2	101.5	109.6	107.2	94.8	94.4	110.5	102.4	101.2	103.1	103.1	105.3	110.2	105.7
April	105.0	100.5	108.6	106.6	95.0	96.0	111.4	102.7	101.4	103.5	103.7	106.4	111.9	107.0
May	105.2	99.6	108.8	106.9	93.8	100.9	110.6	102.1	102.6	101.9	102.9	105.7	109.2	107.0
June	106.4	97.3	107.9	105.4	93.1	104.7	111.2	101.3	101.7	101.1	103.7	106.5	111.1	106.9
July	108.8	92.8	100.1	108.1	92.2	107.8	115.9	101.8	102.7	101.3	103.3	106.2	107.6	107.2
August	107.2	92.2	100.4	103.8	92.3	113.3	115.6	102.2	103.7	101.4	103.1	105.8	104.5	107.9
September	108.9	93.7	105.2	107.9	92.5	114.1	117.5	103.2	104.7	102.2	104.3	108.3	112.7	108.7
October	107.7	97.9	114.1	110.8	92.2	113.7	118.0	102.8	105.4	101.3	105.0	109.2	117.0	109.2
November	109.1	99.6	119.4	110.3	91.9	111.7	120.9	103.3	105.7	101.8	106.0	110.2	118.5	109.8
December	110.3	98.9	119.1	111.4	90.9	112.9	122.8	103.8	107.4	101.6	107.1	112.2	122.8	110.9
1994:														
January	112.4	99.4	121.0	112.8	90.0	113.7	129.7	103.8	106.8	102.0	106.9	111.9	121.1	111.4
February	112.7	99.9	124.1	111.1	88.8	115.5	125.6	104.1	106.3	102.8	107.7	112.9	121.7	112.8
March	113.9	97.4	119.1	111.9	88.9	116.8	128.0	104.7	106.7	103.5	108.8	114.4	121.3	114.8
April	114.2	97.6	119.7	111.1	88.9	116.0	125.9	105.5	108.9	103.4	109.4	115.7	122.4	116.3
May	114.9	96.9	118.0	112.2	87.6	116.0	127.1	105.9	109.6	103.7	110.5	117.3	125.6	117.4
June	115.1	97.5	118.5	113.3	86.2	117.4	128.6	106.2	110.3	103.7	111.1	117.4	125.0	118.9
July	119.0	94.3	110.7	116.4	84.1	114.9	128.0	106.9	112.0	103.8	112.2	119.8	133.5	120.4
August	116.4	98.5	120.6	109.5	83.4	111.0	127.8	106.3	111.4	103.3	112.7	119.8	130.8	121.5
September	115.5	97.5	119.9	114.3	83.3	111.1	130.1	106.6	111.7	103.5	113.0	120.5	130.0	123.1
October	117.1	100.4	123.8	116.9	83.9	111.8	132.9	107.5	112.8	104.4	113.0	120.9	125.5	125.9
November	118.9	99.9	123.3	116.7	84.4	111.2	134.1	107.8	112.5	104.9	114.3	122.4	128.8	127.7
December	120.3	99.6	122.8	116.7	84.6	111.2	141.7	108.0	114.2	104.4	115.8	124.5	132.1	129.4
1995:														
January	122.2	101.8	127.9	117.7	84.2	111.6	148.9	107.5	113.3	104.1	116.3	125.0	130.9	131.7
February	122.7	102.0	127.5	116.9	82.9	111.9	141.2	107.6	113.0	104.4	115.9	124.7	127.8	133.3
March	122.8	101.6	125.8	117.4	82.5	108.9	140.8	107.4	111.9	104.8	115.8	124.8	125.3	135.4
April	122.6	99.6	120.6	114.6	81.8	110.4	142.2	107.0	111.4	104.3	115.7	124.5	123.1	137.0
May	123.2	97.8	117.2	114.7	82.0	111.2	144.8	106.8	109.8	105.1	116.1	125.1	123.9	138.8
June	123.9	97.9	117.7	116.5	81.8	108.2	146.5	106.6	110.1	104.6	115.9	125.5	123.8	140.3
July	124.1	95.6	114.5	116.1	81.1	109.2	147.5	107.2	110.4	105.2	116.0	125.6	123.4	142.5
August	126.9	96.7	117.5	114.5	80.6	110.2	151.7	107.6	110.4	105.9	116.8	127.2	124.5	145.0
September	127.0	97.5	120.2	116.6	79.4	107.9	153.5	108.0	112.1	105.6	117.4	129.1	127.7	147.2
October	127.0	86.7	116.0	115.3	78.7	106.1	154.8	107.5	111.4	105.2	117.6	129.2	127.3	148.1
November	127.2	84.8	114.8	115.4	77.3	106.4	157.3	107.8	112.0	105.3	117.7	130.0	127.8	149.2
December	128.0	88.2	114.7	116.8	76.0	107.2	157.2	108.3	113.5	105.2	117.6	129.6	128.3	149.2
1996:														
January	126.0	93.5	111.9	114.2	74.8	109.0	155.6	106.9	110.8	104.6	117.5	130.2	131.0	149.6
February	127.7	96.7	115.6	114.9	76.4	113.2	156.4	108.1	113.3	105.0	118.5	131.5	128.3	154.0
March	127.1	87.4	95.2	114.7	77.6	119.8	162.5	108.5	115.5	104.3	117.7	129.5	117.0	154.6
April	127.5	97.5	118.5	114.7	77.4	123.7	164.8	107.7	114.2	103.9	119.5	132.6	130.1	155.7
May	126.5	97.5	118.0	115.3	77.9	127.0	165.7	108.9	116.1	104.6	120.1	133.5	130.6	157.2
June	126.3	100.6	120.8	114.3	77.0	127.8	167.9	109.7	118.3	104.6	120.5	134.0	130.4	158.9
July	127.2	104.1	126.5	118.0	77.7	122.1	163.0	108.9	117.5	103.9	120.5	134.5	131.1	159.6
August	126.7	103.0	120.9	116.1	77.9	122.6	167.4	110.0	119.2	104.6	121.5	136.2	133.9	161.7
September	126.3	103.8	117.7	115.5	77.7	117.5	165.6	110.6	119.8	105.3	121.2	135.5	128.3	162.6
October	127.0	101.9	109.4	118.7	77.0	120.2	165.3	110.2	117.7	105.8	121.7	135.8	126.6	163.4
November	127.1	106.6	115.9	119.9	76.1	120.7	159.8	111.9	120.7	106.8	122.2	136.5	129.7	165.3
December	127.3	107.2	113.7	121.4	76.2	123.6	146.2	111.3	117.8	107.4	123.1	137.8	130.3	167.9

INDUSTRIAL PRODUCTION INDEXES BY MARKET GROUPS—Continued
(Seasonally adjusted, 1992=100)

YEAR AND MONTH	Durable—Continued Other Total	Basic metals	Nondurable Total	Textile	Paper	Chemical	Other	Energy Total	Primary	Converted fuel	Special aggregates Total excluding Autos and trucks	Motor vehicles and parts	Computers	Computers and semiconductors
1968	68.7	93.1	54.6	81.2	54.1	45.2	59.1	84.8	93.2	77.7	58.2	58.0	62.0	
1969	73.2	102.2	59.1	83.4	58.7	50.2	63.4	89.1	96.4	83.0	61.0	60.7	64.8	
1970	68.3	97.2	59.4	80.3	58.2	51.4	64.5	93.6	101.0	87.5	59.3	59.2	62.6	
1971	65.7	91.0	62.0	84.1	60.8	54.5	65.4	94.3	100.2	89.8	59.6	59.5	63.7	
1972	74.4	101.3	68.3	88.6	64.9	63.4	69.2	98.0	101.9	95.5	65.5	65.3	69.7	
1973	83.6	113.7	73.2	91.4	68.0	71.3	72.0	98.7	100.6	98.6	70.5	70.2	75.2	
1974	82.0	110.5	73.6	84.9	67.4	74.1	72.6	96.0	98.1	95.7	70.0	69.7	73.8	
1975	68.5	88.7	65.5	80.3	58.1	62.5	68.8	93.9	96.1	93.4	63.8	63.8	67.4	
1976	76.6	98.4	74.2	91.0	66.4	72.5	74.5	96.2	95.5	99.2	69.2	69.0	73.4	
1977	81.7	100.4	78.9	94.5	67.1	80.8	77.1	97.9	96.7	102.8	74.6	74.2	79.0	
1978	88.1	108.9	81.6	93.2	69.3	85.0	79.8	98.9	98.5	102.3	79.0	78.6	83.2	
1979	90.8	111.8	84.4	96.4	72.5	89.0	80.2	101.4	100.2	106.4	81.9	81.7	85.6	
1980	81.4	94.3	80.7	93.7	72.6	81.5	79.6	102.2	102.1	104.8	80.1	80.3	82.7	
1981	84.4	100.5	82.3	91.7	74.3	84.0	81.3	100.2	101.6	98.7	81.4	81.8	83.6	
1982	70.1	73.3	74.6	82.0	72.2	71.1	78.9	96.7	100.1	90.0	77.1	77.5	78.8	
1983	76.2	79.7	81.0	92.8	78.8	78.5	81.6	94.7	97.1	90.7	79.6	79.8	81.2	
1984	85.2	89.6	84.5	92.5	83.1	83.1	84.6	99.5	102.2	94.5	86.5	86.5	88.0	
1985	86.1	88.8	83.2	86.8	81.3	82.8	84.2	99.1	101.2	95.6	87.7	87.7	89.1	
1986	85.9	83.7	85.7	91.8	85.8	83.4	87.0	95.2	99.7	87.3	88.7	88.8	90.0	
1987	92.2	90.7	90.9	99.5	90.2	88.8	91.1	96.3	99.2	90.9	92.9	93.0	93.9	91.6
1988	97.9	99.6	94.8	98.6	93.7	95.2	93.1	98.5	100.5	94.9	97.1	97.1	97.8	95.3
1989	99.3	100.6	97.2	98.4	94.6	98.8	96.2	99.5	100.1	98.3	98.8	98.9	99.3	99.1
1990	98.8	100.9	98.1	94.4	96.3	100.3	97.3	100.6	101.7	98.5	98.8	99.0	99.2	100.4
1991	94.7	96.2	96.9	93.5	97.1	97.3	97.4	100.8	102.0	98.6	97.1	97.3	97.2	100.0
1992	100.0	100.0	100.0	100.0	100.0	100.0	100.0	100.0	100.0	100.0	100.0	100.0	100.0	100.0
1993	104.7	103.6	101.3	104.5	103.6	98.6	102.8	99.6	98.4	102.0	103.1	102.9	103.1	102.7
1994	113.1	109.6	105.8	110.3	108.2	102.9	106.9	101.4	100.2	103.6	108.0	107.5	107.9	106.8
1995	116.1	112.4	107.6	110.3	110.6	105.9	106.6	102.7	101.4	105.2	111.7	111.3	110.7	108.4
1996	118.2	113.2	106.4	106.3	107.4	105.9	106.1	103.8	102.6	106.1	114.9	114.6	112.9	109.8
1993:														
January	102.4	102.6	101.0	102.7	101.9	100.1	101.1	99.6	99.8	99.2	101.9	101.9	102.2	101.9
February	103.2	103.5	101.1	102.4	103.2	99.2	102.1	100.3	98.8	103.1	102.5	102.3	102.6	102.3
March	102.9	102.5	100.9	102.8	102.4	99.1	102.0	100.2	97.8	104.9	102.6	102.3	102.6	102.4
April	103.4	102.5	101.6	102.7	105.8	98.6	103.5	99.7	98.9	101.3	102.9	102.6	102.9	102.6
May	103.1	102.4	100.4	103.7	102.0	98.0	102.0	99.0	100.1	96.9	102.3	102.1	102.3	101.9
June	104.1	104.3	101.0	105.3	104.4	97.9	101.7	100.2	99.3	101.9	102.6	102.3	102.5	102.1
July	104.8	102.9	100.9	107.5	102.7	97.6	102.4	99.1	97.1	102.7	103.0	103.0	102.8	102.4
August	104.6	102.8	101.2	106.2	102.9	98.2	103.0	99.1	97.1	102.9	102.8	102.8	102.5	102.1
September	106.1	103.6	100.9	105.1	102.9	97.5	103.6	98.7	97.6	101.0	103.7	103.5	103.5	103.0
October	105.7	103.6	101.2	105.6	103.4	98.2	102.8	99.6	97.8	102.8	103.7	103.3	103.8	103.3
November	107.0	105.0	102.4	105.2	106.0	99.3	103.9	99.9	97.9	103.7	104.1	103.7	104.3	103.7
December	108.7	107.2	102.8	105.0	105.9	99.4	105.6	100.0	98.2	103.6	104.9	104.4	105.0	104.4
1994:														
January	108.2	105.5	102.2	105.7	105.5	99.3	103.2	100.3	97.5	105.5	105.1	104.6	105.2	104.6
February	109.1	107.0	103.0	106.8	105.0	100.7	103.8	100.6	99.0	103.6	105.5	105.1	105.7	105.0
March	111.1	107.5	104.2	107.6	107.6	101.3	105.3	100.9	100.0	102.7	106.4	106.0	106.5	105.7
April	112.2	109.8	104.0	108.1	105.7	101.8	104.5	100.8	100.0	102.2	106.9	106.5	106.9	106.0
May	113.5	110.6	105.1	108.1	106.8	103.1	105.7	100.5	100.1	101.4	107.6	107.1	107.5	106.6
June	112.9	109.4	105.6	109.9	107.7	103.3	105.8	102.3	99.5	107.5	108.2	107.7	108.0	107.0
July	113.4	110.2	106.3	111.3	106.1	103.9	108.4	101.2	100.4	102.7	108.9	108.1	108.5	107.4
August	113.8	108.2	107.2	110.8	110.1	104.5	108.2	102.1	101.3	103.7	108.7	108.0	108.5	107.3
September	114.5	110.2	107.2	112.7	110.7	103.5	108.6	101.9	100.6	104.4	108.8	108.2	108.5	107.2
October	115.1	112.2	106.8	112.7	109.8	102.9	109.1	101.5	100.2	104.0	109.4	109.0	109.1	107.7
November	115.7	111.0	108.0	115.5	112.0	104.0	108.9	102.0	101.5	103.0	110.1	109.5	109.8	108.3
December	117.4	113.2	109.5	114.7	111.3	106.4	111.4	102.6	102.3	103.2	111.0	110.4	110.6	109.1
1995:														
January	117.5	114.1	110.3	117.6	112.0	108.0	109.7	102.2	101.5	103.7	111.3	110.7	110.9	109.2
February	116.8	113.0	109.5	115.2	112.3	107.6	107.7	102.3	101.3	104.1	111.0	110.6	110.5	108.7
March	116.7	112.8	109.3	114.8	112.7	107.3	107.2	101.9	100.5	104.5	111.1	110.8	110.5	108.6
April	115.8	112.0	109.1	113.8	111.7	106.9	108.4	102.3	100.7	105.3	111.0	110.6	110.2	108.1
May	115.6	112.1	109.0	112.5	113.7	106.8	107.1	102.6	101.0	105.4	111.2	110.8	110.2	108.1
June	115.3	111.1	107.7	109.4	111.1	105.9	107.0	102.5	101.4	104.7	111.4	111.0	110.4	108.2
July	114.2	111.0	106.6	104.3	112.9	105.4	104.3	103.6	102.2	106.3	111.5	111.1	110.3	107.9
August	115.3	111.1	106.5	109.6	110.3	104.7	105.1	103.9	100.8	109.7	111.2	111.9	111.2	108.7
September	116.6	113.2	106.2	107.6	107.7	105.2	105.7	102.5	101.3	104.7	112.6	112.2	111.5	108.9
October	116.4	112.3	106.5	108.3	110.9	104.6	105.0	102.7	102.6	103.0	112.2	111.8	110.9	108.2
November	116.9	114.3	105.1	106.0	106.0	104.5	104.5	103.0	102.1	104.7	112.4	112.0	111.1	108.3
December	116.0	111.8	105.4	105.1	106.4	104.0	107.2	103.1	101.8	105.7	112.5	112.0	111.1	108.3
1996:														
January	115.9	109.0	104.1	102.2	104.7	103.7	104.7	102.5	100.9	105.4	112.1	111.6	110.6	107.7
February	116.8	111.3	104.5	103.6	104.9	103.5	105.9	103.5	102.6	105.3	113.5	113.1	111.9	108.9
March	116.8	112.1	104.4	104.6	104.4	103.5	105.4	104.5	103.9	105.7	113.4	113.5	111.2	108.2
April	117.2	112.1	105.5	105.6	106.9	104.1	106.5	104.2	104.0	104.6	113.9	113.5	112.2	109.2
May	117.8	112.2	105.9	106.1	106.4	104.7	107.1	104.6	103.5	106.7	114.4	114.0	112.6	109.6
June	117.9	112.6	106.2	106.3	105.2	105.3	108.0	104.8	103.5	107.2	115.1	114.7	113.2	110.1
July	118.2	112.9	107.4	109.9	109.1	106.1	107.1	102.4	101.7	103.9	114.9	114.6	113.1	110.0
August	119.2	113.6	106.5	107.4	108.2	106.2	104.7	104.0	103.2	105.4	115.4	115.0	113.4	110.2
September	119.2	114.7	106.9	107.1	107.0	106.8	106.2	103.9	102.2	107.0	115.7	115.4	113.5	110.2
October	120.0	117.2	108.0	108.4	108.0	109.3	103.9	103.9	102.0	107.5	116.1	115.9	113.7	110.4
November	119.1	114.4	108.4	108.5	110.9	107.7	106.8	104.0	101.6	108.5	116.9	116.6	114.6	111.2
December	119.9	115.7	109.5	105.9	112.5	110.2	106.3	103.9	102.6	106.3	117.4	117.2	115.1	111.6

INDUSTRIAL PRODUCTION INDEXES (1992=100)

| YEAR AND MONTH | Market Groups—Continued Seasonally adjusted Special aggregates—Continued | | | | | Industry groups Not seasonally adjusted | | | | | |
| | Consumer goods excluding | | Business equipment excluding | | Materials excluding energy | Total | Manufacturing | | | Mining | Utilities |
	Autos and trucks	Energy	Autos and trucks	Computer and office equipment			Total	Durables	Nondurables		
1968	59.0	58.7	44.3	63.2	51.3	58.0	54.9	54.9	54.9	95.1	57.6
1969	61.5	60.7	47.1	66.4	54.5	60.7	57.4	57.1	57.8	98.8	62.7
1970	61.9	59.5	45.8	63.4	51.3	58.7	54.8	52.7	57.8	101.4	66.5
1971	64.2	63.1	43.3	61.1	52.2	59.5	55.6	52.5	60.2	98.8	69.7
1972	69.4	68.3	49.4	68.9	58.5	65.3	61.5	58.6	65.5	100.9	74.2
1973	71.9	71.3	57.7	80.4	65.5	70.6	66.9	65.4	68.8	101.8	77.1
1974	70.8	69.0	60.8	82.8	64.3	69.5	65.9	64.1	68.3	101.3	76.1
1975	68.3	65.9	54.1	73.8	54.8	63.4	59.3	56.1	64.0	99.0	76.9
1976	73.7	72.9	55.5	75.0	62.7	69.2	65.4	61.9	70.5	99.9	79.9
1977	78.5	78.5	61.4	81.4	68.6	74.9	71.2	68.1	75.7	102.8	82.0
1978	81.6	81.7	69.0	88.6	73.4	79.3	75.8	73.6	78.9	105.8	84.4
1979	81.1	80.6	77.8	96.8	76.4	81.9	78.5	77.4	79.9	107.6	86.8
1980	80.5	78.8	78.4	93.0	71.4	79.7	75.5	73.4	78.3	110.8	87.3
1981	81.0	79.4	79.7	91.9	73.8	81.0	76.7	74.6	79.5	114.8	85.0
1982	79.9	78.0	72.2	80.7	66.0	76.6	72.1	68.2	77.7	110.5	82.3
1983	83.2	82.9	68.6	74.9	71.8	79.5	76.3	72.2	81.9	105.9	83.7
1984	86.1	86.6	79.0	84.1	80.9	86.6	83.8	82.7	85.3	113.2	86.7
1985	86.6	87.5	81.8	85.8	81.6	88.0	85.7	85.6	86.0	110.3	88.8
1986	89.9	90.7	81.2	85.2	83.3	89.0	88.1	87.4	89.1	101.9	86.4
1987	93.0	93.8	84.5	87.3	88.5	93.1	92.8	92.0	93.8	101.5	89.4
1988	95.8	96.7	93.5	95.3	94.0	97.3	97.1	98.1	96.0	102.9	93.9
1989	96.7	97.6	99.2	99.7	96.2	99.0	99.0	100.5	97.3	101.5	97.1
1990	97.0	97.3	98.6	99.6	96.1	98.9	98.5	99.0	97.9	103.7	98.3
1991	97.5	96.7	96.2	97.4	94.3	96.9	96.2	95.5	97.0	101.6	100.4
1992	100.0	100.0	100.0	100.0	100.0	100.0	100.0	100.0	100.0	100.0	100.0
1993	102.5	103.0	104.7	103.9	105.3	103.4	103.7	105.5	101.7	98.9	103.9
1994	106.0	107.6	110.4	108.6	114.4	108.6	109.4	113.4	105.0	101.6	105.3
1995	107.6	109.0	119.4	113.2	120.9	112.1	113.2	119.7	106.2	100.9	109.1
1996	109.2	110.2	127.7	115.8	125.4	115.2	116.4	125.7	106.3	102.9	112.8
1993:											
January	101.5	102.5	103.5	103.8	102.9	101.1	99.4	100.5	98.3	98.8	121.2
February	102.1	102.3	103.7	103.4	103.7	102.8	101.9	104.5	99.0	97.5	117.2
March	102.1	102.4	104.6	104.2	104.0	102.9	102.9	106.0	99.4	96.6	109.2
April	102.2	102.7	104.7	104.0	105.0	101.6	102.5	104.9	99.9	96.7	96.5
May	101.5	102.4	104.7	103.9	104.1	101.4	102.7	105.3	99.9	97.0	90.2
June	101.8	102.4	104.4	103.6	104.8	104.7	105.9	107.8	103.9	98.9	96.4
July	103.3	103.4	105.7	103.9	104.6	101.5	101.6	100.2	103.0	96.4	106.0
August	103.1	103.0	104.0	102.2	104.4	105.6	106.1	105.7	106.5	98.9	105.7
September	103.4	103.5	105.5	104.0	106.1	106.4	107.7	108.5	106.8	100.9	96.7
October	103.0	103.5	104.9	104.3	106.8	105.6	107.0	109.6	104.0	103.1	92.2
November	102.8	103.7	104.9	104.7	107.9	103.8	104.3	107.4	100.8	102.2	99.9
December	103.3	104.5	105.8	105.2	109.4	103.0	102.1	105.5	98.4	100.1	115.5
1994:											
January	103.8	104.9	107.2	106.6	109.0	104.6	102.8	106.5	98.7	97.9	131.0
February	104.2	105.6	107.5	107.0	109.9	106.3	105.5	110.6	99.9	99.2	120.6
March	105.0	106.6	108.0	107.0	111.4	107.0	107.3	112.2	102.0	100.8	108.8
April	105.4	107.3	108.1	107.0	112.2	106.0	107.4	111.7	102.6	100.7	95.6
May	106.2	107.8	108.9	107.3	113.6	106.8	108.7	113.0	103.9	101.0	91.2
June	107.0	108.3	109.6	107.8	113.9	110.7	112.3	115.9	108.3	102.5	100.5
July	106.8	107.9	111.8	109.0	115.7	107.0	107.5	108.3	106.6	100.6	107.1
August	106.5	108.4	110.4	108.4	116.1	112.0	113.3	115.7	110.5	103.3	104.8
September	105.9	107.7	111.4	108.9	116.5	112.2	114.3	117.9	110.4	103.2	97.1
October	106.8	108.7	113.1	110.6	116.7	111.4	113.7	118.3	108.7	103.6	92.9
November	106.9	108.9	113.9	111.1	118.1	109.6	111.0	116.0	105.5	103.4	99.3
December	107.3	109.5	115.3	112.0	119.9	109.1	109.2	114.9	103.0	102.4	114.5
1995:											
January	107.3	109.6	116.7	113.2	120.6	110.5	109.9	115.7	103.6	99.3	126.5
February	106.8	108.9	117.2	113.2	120.1	111.7	111.9	119.4	103.7	99.7	119.5
March	107.1	109.0	118.1	113.7	120.2	111.8	112.9	120.5	104.6	98.7	111.0
April	106.8	108.7	118.3	112.9	119.9	109.2	110.9	117.3	104.0	99.9	98.9
May	107.1	108.3	118.3	112.2	120.3	110.1	112.2	118.8	104.9	100.0	96.3
June	107.7	109.0	119.3	113.3	120.1	113.9	116.0	123.3	109.2	101.2	101.6
July	107.7	108.7	119.5	112.8	119.8	110.0	110.6	113.4	107.4	100.9	110.5
August	108.3	109.1	121.1	114.3	120.9	115.6	116.7	121.7	111.2	102.0	114.8
September	108.3	109.5	122.1	115.0	122.1	116.1	118.5	125.0	111.3	103.6	101.3
October	107.6	109.2	120.5	112.7	122.2	113.9	116.4	123.5	108.6	102.9	96.4
November	108.2	109.0	120.3	112.1	122.3	111.7	112.8	120.7	104.4	102.8	107.2
December	108.0	109.0	121.3	112.6	122.1	110.7	110.2	118.3	101.6	99.7	124.7
1996:											
January	107.3	107.8	123.0	113.6	122.1	111.3	110.0	118.3	101.1	96.2	137.5
February	108.6	109.5	125.5	115.6	123.1	113.9	113.7	124.3	102.5	98.3	128.7
March	109.2	108.8	125.3	113.1	121.7	113.3	113.6	123.3	103.2	100.8	120.4
April	108.4	109.4	125.8	115.3	124.2	112.6	114.1	124.3	103.2	102.1	105.2
May	108.7	109.6	125.7	114.7	124.9	113.3	115.2	125.6	104.2	102.5	101.2
June	109.3	110.4	127.2	115.8	125.4	117.6	119.7	129.8	108.8	105.1	106.1
July	108.9	110.9	128.2	116.8	126.1	113.6	114.7	121.0	107.8	102.5	110.3
August	108.6	110.2	128.3	116.1	127.0	118.9	120.6	129.2	111.4	106.1	110.8
September	109.2	110.6	129.3	116.3	126.6	119.1	121.7	130.7	112.0	105.9	101.9
October	109.9	110.8	130.8	116.6	127.1	117.5	120.2	129.7	110.0	106.4	98.0
November	111.0	111.8	131.2	117.5	127.8	116.1	117.6	127.7	106.8	105.6	108.9
December	111.4	112.8	132.4	118.2	129.0	115.3	115.2	124.9	104.8	103.7	124.8

INDUSTRIAL PRODUCTION INDEXES BY INDUSTRY GROUPS—Continued
(Seasonally adjusted, 1992=100)

YEAR AND MONTH	Total	Manufacturing			Durable goods manufacturing				Primary metals			
		Total	Primary process-ing	Advanced process-ing	Total	Lumber and products	Furniture and fixtures	Stone, clay, and glass products	Total	Iron and steel		Non-ferrous
										Total	Raw steel	
1968	58.0	54.9	65.8	49.6	54.8	69.1	57.5	76.2	111.0	136.8	140.0	77.6
1969	60.7	57.4	69.7	51.4	57.0	69.0	60.1	78.8	119.7	149.7	152.8	81.8
1970	58.7	54.8	67.2	48.9	52.7	68.6	56.2	74.8	111.2	139.0	139.2	75.9
1971	59.5	55.6	68.7	49.4	52.4	70.4	58.6	78.5	104.9	126.3	127.1	76.6
1972	65.3	61.5	77.3	54.3	58.5	80.6	70.7	86.9	118.3	141.5	143.9	87.0
1973	70.6	66.9	84.6	59.0	65.3	80.9	75.4	93.9	134.1	161.0	164.3	98.1
1974	69.5	65.9	82.0	58.6	64.0	73.4	70.1	92.4	129.7	155.7	163.1	94.8
1975	63.4	59.4	71.4	53.8	56.1	68.3	60.0	81.8	103.4	125.1	128.6	74.3
1976	69.3	65.4	80.3	58.6	61.8	77.8	67.0	91.5	115.7	137.9	140.9	85.7
1977	74.9	71.2	86.7	64.0	68.1	86.1	74.8	98.3	119.0	138.0	139.3	93.0
1978	79.3	75.8	90.7	68.9	73.6	87.5	80.4	106.0	128.0	147.5	154.9	101.1
1979	81.9	78.5	92.5	72.0	77.4	86.3	80.5	106.8	130.0	148.4	154.4	104.6
1980	79.7	75.5	84.4	71.4	73.4	80.4	79.1	96.5	108.0	119.0	126.9	92.4
1981	81.0	76.7	85.2	72.8	74.6	78.1	78.4	94.3	113.9	126.6	138.5	96.1
1982	76.6	72.1	75.7	70.5	68.2	70.3	74.6	84.2	80.5	80.5	82.6	80.7
1983	79.5	76.3	82.1	73.6	72.2	83.3	80.2	91.2	88.2	90.0	94.1	85.9
1984	86.6	83.8	88.4	81.7	82.7	89.9	88.6	98.6	98.7	98.9	102.6	98.6
1985	88.0	85.7	88.4	84.5	85.6	92.0	88.9	98.0	98.4	98.8	97.7	98.2
1986	89.0	88.1	90.0	87.2	87.4	99.6	93.3	101.7	91.2	86.8	89.4	97.6
1987	93.1	92.8	95.3	91.6	92.0	104.9	100.9	104.8	97.8	95.4	99.3	101.2
1988	97.3	97.1	99.0	96.2	98.1	105.1	101.1	107.5	106.2	107.6	111.3	104.6
1989	99.0	99.0	99.9	98.6	100.5	104.3	102.4	107.4	104.9	106.2	107.1	103.2
1990	98.9	98.5	99.3	98.2	99.0	101.6	100.9	105.0	104.0	106.4	108.4	100.9
1991	96.9	96.2	95.7	96.4	95.5	94.5	94.8	97.2	96.7	96.0	96.3	97.7
1992	100.0	100.0	100.0	100.0	100.0	100.0	100.0	100.0	100.0	100.0	100.0	100.0
1993	103.4	103.7	103.3	103.8	105.5	100.9	104.7	102.1	105.5	107.1	104.5	103.5
1994	108.6	109.4	109.2	109.5	113.4	105.9	107.9	107.9	113.0	113.2	106.7	112.6
1995	112.1	113.2	111.2	114.2	119.7	106.2	108.6	109.1	115.7	116.3	113.5	115.0
1996	115.2	116.4	112.2	118.4	125.7	109.7	108.8	110.9	117.2	116.4	112.4	118.1
1993:												
January	102.3	102.6	102.1	102.8	103.5	100.6	102.9	99.2	103.7	105.4	101.8	101.6
February	102.8	102.9	102.5	103.1	104.0	102.4	101.9	100.6	104.6	105.4	103.3	103.6
March	102.8	103.0	102.1	103.4	104.5	100.0	103.9	99.4	104.0	104.7	101.5	103.0
April	103.2	103.6	102.7	103.9	105.1	98.9	104.8	101.4	104.0	104.3	102.4	103.5
May	102.6	103.0	102.2	103.4	104.8	99.3	104.5	99.9	103.8	104.7	104.8	102.6
June	102.8	103.0	102.8	103.1	104.7	98.5	104.3	101.3	106.3	108.7	105.8	103.1
July	103.1	103.4	103.1	103.5	104.8	99.5	105.1	102.4	104.4	106.8	106.9	101.4
August	102.8	103.0	103.2	102.9	104.2	101.0	106.1	101.7	106.1	108.5	105.7	103.1
September	103.9	104.2	103.9	104.3	106.1	101.0	106.7	104.0	106.5	108.1	104.7	104.4
October	104.1	104.4	104.3	104.5	107.1	102.7	105.9	103.7	105.8	107.9	106.2	103.2
November	104.6	105.0	105.1	104.9	107.9	103.2	104.7	105.1	107.3	109.5	103.8	104.4
December	105.4	105.9	105.9	105.8	109.2	103.3	106.0	106.3	109.7	111.3	107.0	107.7
1994:												
January	105.7	106.0	105.9	106.0	109.5	105.0	104.3	104.7	107.5	106.1	100.7	109.4
February	106.2	106.6	106.3	106.8	110.1	103.8	105.6	104.7	110.2	111.2	103.8	108.9
March	107.0	107.5	107.4	107.6	110.6	103.6	106.3	106.8	110.3	111.0	104.1	109.3
April	107.4	108.2	108.3	108.2	111.6	104.2	107.4	107.4	113.5	115.9	104.5	110.5
May	108.1	109.0	109.2	108.9	112.5	106.3	108.2	107.9	114.5	117.3	105.4	111.0
June	108.6	109.2	108.9	109.3	112.7	106.2	108.6	107.2	111.7	111.6	105.5	111.8
July	109.1	110.0	109.7	110.2	114.3	107.0	108.2	107.5	113.7	114.2	105.1	113.0
August	109.2	110.1	109.8	110.3	114.3	106.0	109.4	109.4	110.3	106.4	106.5	114.9
September	109.3	110.3	110.1	110.4	114.8	106.9	107.5	108.6	113.9	113.1	108.6	115.0
October	109.9	111.1	110.6	111.3	115.8	106.3	110.3	108.7	116.2	117.0	108.4	115.4
November	110.6	111.9	111.4	112.1	116.6	106.1	109.3	109.7	115.5	115.2	111.4	115.9
December	111.6	112.9	112.9	112.8	118.3	109.3	109.3	111.6	118.1	119.6	116.8	116.5
1995:												
January	111.9	113.3	112.9	113.5	119.0	108.5	109.0	110.4	118.5	120.7	113.2	115.9
February	111.6	112.9	112.6	113.0	118.8	107.1	110.6	110.1	117.0	118.4	115.0	115.4
March	111.7	113.1	112.3	113.4	118.9	105.3	109.1	110.3	117.1	118.3	114.8	115.6
April	111.4	112.7	111.5	113.2	118.4	105.3	108.4	108.5	115.3	115.3	113.7	115.3
May	111.5	112.6	111.2	113.3	118.4	103.5	107.8	109.3	115.3	116.2	112.3	114.3
June	111.7	112.9	110.6	113.9	118.9	104.3	109.0	108.8	114.5	114.5	111.9	114.6
July	111.7	112.7	110.1	113.9	118.7	105.2	108.7	107.7	113.7	111.1	111.7	116.7
August	112.6	113.4	110.4	114.9	120.2	105.9	108.2	107.8	113.7	114.8	113.3	112.4
September	113.0	114.2	111.2	115.7	121.6	107.6	109.5	108.5	116.7	118.9	117.0	114.2
October	112.5	113.8	110.8	115.2	120.9	106.9	107.9	109.1	114.8	114.0	110.8	115.6
November	112.7	113.6	110.6	115.1	121.2	106.6	107.8	109.9	117.1	118.9	114.0	115.0
December	112.8	113.8	110.6	115.3	121.5	108.1	107.5	109.3	114.8	114.7	113.7	114.8
1996:												
January	112.4	113.4	109.5	115.2	121.5	105.3	107.4	110.1	111.7	112.3	112.3	111.0
February	113.8	114.8	110.1	117.1	123.6	106.3	107.9	109.1	114.6	113.9	111.2	115.3
March	113.2	113.9	110.8	115.4	121.8	109.7	105.8	108.7	115.6	113.8	112.7	117.6
April	114.3	115.2	111.0	117.3	124.6	110.3	108.1	108.5	116.1	114.6	112.1	117.9
May	114.8	115.7	111.7	117.6	125.2	110.4	110.3	109.8	116.3	115.7	112.9	117.0
June	115.5	116.4	112.6	118.3	126.3	112.4	109.5	111.3	117.0	117.1	114.9	116.8
July	115.5	117.0	113.0	118.9	126.9	109.3	108.1	114.1	118.0	118.0	113.3	117.9
August	115.8	117.2	113.1	119.2	127.5	111.4	108.8	111.8	118.3	118.2	113.6	118.5
September	116.0	117.4	113.5	119.3	127.2	110.7	108.8	113.1	119.5	117.4	112.6	121.8
October	116.2	117.6	113.8	119.5	127.1	109.2	110.4	111.7	122.1	123.2	111.5	120.7
November	117.2	118.5	113.8	120.8	128.4	113.1	110.5	111.8	118.5	115.9	108.7	121.4
December	117.7	119.2	114.0	121.7	128.8	108.0	110.5	111.3	118.8	116.7	112.5	121.2

INDUSTRIAL PRODUCTION INDEXES BY INDUSTRY GROUPS—Continued
(Seasonally adjusted, 1992=100)

Durable goods manufacturing—Continued

YEAR AND MONTH	Fabricated metal products	Industrial machinery and equipment		Electrical machinery		Transportation equipment				Instruments	Miscellaneous
		Total	Computer and office equipment	Total	Semiconductors	Total	Motor vehicles and parts		Aerospace and miscellaneous		
							Total	Autos and light trucks			
1968	82.4	39.3	1.8	25.7	....	64.8	64.2	....	72.4	34.0	70.3
1969	83.8	42.5	2.2	27.4	....	64.4	64.7	....	70.7	36.5	74.4
1970	77.7	41.1	2.3	26.2	....	54.1	52.0	....	62.3	36.2	72.1
1971	77.3	38.2	2.0	26.3	....	58.5	65.2	....	55.9	37.9	72.4
1972	84.8	44.3	2.4	30.1	....	62.4	71.1	....	57.7	42.5	84.6
1973	94.3	51.8	2.9	34.3	....	71.1	82.8	....	63.8	48.5	85.7
1974	90.5	55.2	3.5	33.9	....	64.6	71.4	....	62.0	51.4	81.9
1975	78.4	47.8	3.2	29.2	....	58.2	61.0	....	59.3	48.9	76.0
1976	86.9	50.2	3.9	32.8	....	66.3	80.0	....	56.6	53.7	82.5
1977	94.7	56.6	5.1	38.1	....	71.9	92.4	84.2	55.6	60.1	92.6
1978	98.2	63.3	7.5	42.2	....	77.5	96.8	87.5	62.2	66.2	92.7
1979	101.6	70.2	10.3	46.9	....	78.7	89.0	80.1	71.1	71.7	92.1
1980	94.4	70.5	13.9	48.6	....	70.3	65.8	58.1	74.3	73.6	86.9
1981	93.0	74.7	18.4	51.0	....	66.9	62.8	59.3	70.5	75.4	89.6
1982	84.9	65.8	21.3	51.7	....	63.0	56.9	54.4	68.3	76.3	85.5
1983	87.2	65.2	29.5	55.9	....	70.5	72.1	74.7	69.3	77.7	83.2
1984	95.2	78.9	42.0	66.7	....	80.5	87.3	90.7	75.1	86.0	87.6
1985	96.5	81.2	50.3	68.4	....	88.8	95.0	99.1	83.7	89.3	82.2
1986	95.6	81.8	53.7	71.0	42.9	94.1	94.2	99.2	94.2	88.8	83.5
1987	101.9	86.0	62.2	75.6	50.6	96.1	94.9	98.7	97.5	93.8	93.5
1988	106.1	97.1	74.6	82.5	57.3	101.1	100.2	103.1	102.1	97.2	99.8
1989	104.8	103.0	83.0	85.8	64.2	105.1	101.2	106.5	109.4	98.2	100.3
1990	101.2	100.1	81.4	87.7	71.8	102.3	95.3	99.3	109.8	98.4	100.0
1991	96.2	95.4	82.3	89.6	80.8	96.5	88.5	91.0	105.0	99.8	98.4
1992	100.0	100.0	100.0	100.0	100.0	100.0	100.0	100.0	100.0	100.0	100.0
1993	104.4	109.9	121.5	110.0	118.5	103.7	113.7	111.4	93.6	100.6	105.6
1994	112.0	125.3	152.1	126.3	152.8	107.4	129.7	125.8	85.6	99.9	109.1
1995	115.7	141.4	213.6	148.2	211.9	105.0	128.5	125.0	82.1	100.4	110.4
1996	118.6	156.4	296.9	163.3	258.2	106.1	127.1	124.6	85.6	102.8	112.9
1993:											
January	102.4	104.0	110.1	105.8	111.3	104.6	111.1	113.4	98.1	102.0	102.5
February	103.0	105.2	113.1	106.8	112.4	104.6	111.7	109.8	97.4	100.8	103.7
March	103.5	106.8	115.1	107.7	113.5	104.5	112.7	111.0	96.3	101.8	104.3
April	104.3	107.9	118.0	108.3	115.6	105.1	114.0	110.8	96.0	101.8	105.9
May	103.5	109.1	120.7	108.5	116.7	103.8	112.3	111.5	95.2	101.2	105.7
June	103.1	108.6	120.1	108.7	117.2	103.2	113.1	108.2	93.2	100.9	105.1
July	104.5	111.6	123.0	110.0	117.5	99.1	105.4	103.7	92.5	101.0	105.6
August	103.9	110.0	123.8	110.8	119.3	97.5	102.5	101.1	92.1	99.8	105.8
September	105.7	112.2	126.0	112.4	122.1	101.1	111.0	105.4	91.2	100.8	106.9
October	105.2	112.9	126.8	112.8	123.9	105.9	120.4	115.9	91.5	99.5	106.8
November	106.1	114.4	127.6	113.4	125.4	106.9	123.6	122.2	90.5	98.8	107.1
December	107.3	116.8	133.4	114.7	127.8	108.0	126.9	123.8	89.4	99.1	107.8
1994:											
January	107.8	118.2	135.8	116.2	131.6	107.4	127.4	128.0	87.8	100.0	107.3
February	107.8	118.3	138.1	117.9	134.5	107.9	130.3	132.0	86.1	100.8	107.4
March	109.6	120.3	140.0	120.0	138.6	105.6	125.6	126.4	86.1	100.4	108.2
April	110.7	121.2	140.9	121.9	142.7	106.1	126.4	126.7	86.3	100.0	109.4
May	111.1	123.4	145.5	123.3	145.6	106.6	127.3	123.0	86.4	99.3	108.9
June	111.6	124.5	147.8	124.9	149.4	106.5	127.6	123.1	86.0	99.4	108.5
July	113.0	127.9	151.9	127.5	153.8	107.3	130.5	117.9	84.7	99.8	111.5
August	113.1	126.6	154.4	129.1	157.8	108.8	133.9	126.3	84.5	98.9	109.5
September	113.2	128.2	162.0	130.2	162.1	107.5	131.7	123.8	83.9	99.9	108.8
October	114.1	129.8	165.5	132.7	167.9	106.9	129.4	126.6	85.0	100.1	110.2
November	114.9	131.5	168.4	134.1	172.3	108.5	132.5	126.8	85.1	100.0	110.2
December	116.5	133.2	175.0	137.4	177.5	109.3	134.2	129.2	85.0	100.6	109.7
1995:											
January	115.5	136.8	184.4	138.8	183.7	110.0	136.0	132.8	84.6	100.3	110.6
February	116.4	137.0	192.8	140.0	188.2	108.4	132.7	132.1	84.7	99.8	110.9
March	116.0	137.3	196.0	142.3	193.2	107.6	131.1	131.0	84.7	100.2	110.3
April	114.3	138.6	202.9	143.2	198.5	105.7	127.0	126.3	84.8	100.4	110.2
May	115.5	138.9	206.7	144.7	202.9	104.7	125.6	121.2	84.3	99.5	108.9
June	115.5	139.1	206.5	146.4	207.1	105.0	126.2	122.1	84.2	100.5	110.3
July	114.2	140.1	213.6	148.9	215.9	103.1	123.5	115.9	83.2	100.1	109.2
August	115.7	143.0	217.8	151.6	220.0	104.6	126.3	123.2	83.5	100.8	110.0
September	116.6	144.9	226.3	153.7	226.8	105.7	129.5	125.0	82.6	101.1	110.6
October	115.9	145.4	233.6	155.8	232.7	101.8	127.7	122.9	76.9	101.0	110.4
November	116.1	146.3	237.6	156.6	236.6	100.9	127.8	123.1	74.9	101.4	111.2
December	116.5	149.0	244.9	155.8	236.9	102.0	128.7	124.0	76.2	99.9	111.6
1996:											
January	116.7	148.3	251.8	155.8	238.9	103.3	127.6	118.4	79.7	101.0	110.3
February	117.9	151.4	263.6	161.0	247.5	104.4	127.4	124.8	81.9	102.9	112.4
March	117.6	152.5	270.8	160.3	247.2	94.9	106.8	103.0	82.8	102.9	112.5
April	117.8	153.3	277.3	161.1	249.7	106.4	130.3	127.1	83.2	102.3	112.0
May	118.4	154.3	284.7	161.8	252.8	106.8	130.5	127.6	83.8	102.4	112.2
June	118.9	156.1	294.3	164.0	256.5	107.1	130.4	130.4	84.3	103.3	113.1
July	119.1	157.7	306.5	163.8	258.4	109.5	134.1	137.3	85.7	102.3	113.0
August	119.4	159.6	310.8	164.6	262.6	109.3	132.8	131.0	86.5	103.0	112.9
September	119.3	159.4	319.0	165.2	265.4	107.3	127.0	127.4	87.9	103.0	113.0
October	119.3	159.9	323.6	165.6	266.5	105.3	121.2	117.3	89.4	103.4	113.0
November	119.1	161.7	328.3	167.2	272.5	109.5	128.9	125.7	90.3	103.0	114.1
December	119.5	162.9	332.5	168.8	280.4	109.6	127.9	125.6	91.5	104.1	116.6

YEAR AND MONTH	INDUSTRIAL PRODUCTION INDEXES BY INDUSTRY GROUPS—Continued (Seasonally adjusted, 1992=100) Nondurable goods manufacturing										
	Total	Foods	Tobacco products	Textile mill products	Apparel products	Paper and products	Printing and publishing	Chemicals and products	Petroleum and products	Rubber and plastic products	Leather and products
1968	55.1	57.7	93.8	69.8	82.4	53.1	53.3	43.3	75.2	32.1	274.7
1969	58.0	59.6	91.1	73.4	85.1	57.3	55.9	46.9	77.3	35.0	250.5
1970	58.0	60.6	94.3	71.8	81.8	56.7	54.4	48.8	80.8	33.0	235.0
1971	60.3	62.5	93.1	75.8	82.9	59.1	54.8	51.9	83.5	35.9	225.7
1972	65.7	65.8	96.6	83.1	87.9	64.3	58.5	58.4	87.4	43.7	234.2
1973	69.0	67.1	101.7	86.5	88.5	68.8	60.1	63.9	92.2	49.0	217.9
1974	68.5	68.0	99.4	78.7	84.5	68.2	59.1	66.2	89.0	47.9	207.2
1975	64.2	67.5	101.7	75.0	77.4	59.4	55.4	60.3	88.0	41.6	206.6
1976	70.7	71.4	106.8	83.3	91.1	67.4	60.5	67.5	93.6	48.1	205.1
1977	75.7	74.6	102.8	88.3	98.0	70.1	66.3	72.4	101.5	56.0	200.6
1978	78.9	77.2	107.4	88.6	100.4	73.4	70.1	76.4	104.9	59.3	201.6
1979	79.9	77.9	106.9	91.5	95.3	76.0	72.0	79.2	103.9	58.7	184.4
1980	78.3	79.7	108.5	89.0	95.4	75.2	72.4	75.9	95.9	53.3	181.6
1981	79.5	81.4	109.9	86.3	97.3	76.6	74.3	77.3	91.2	57.5	176.0
1982	77.7	82.4	106.2	80.1	96.3	74.3	77.5	71.0	86.6	56.8	163.1
1983	81.9	84.6	101.6	89.9	100.3	81.0	81.4	76.0	86.9	64.0	158.3
1984	85.3	86.4	101.7	90.4	102.2	85.0	87.0	79.3	89.9	72.1	141.9
1985	86.0	88.9	101.8	86.5	98.6	83.8	90.2	79.4	89.5	73.8	126.1
1986	89.1	91.2	100.3	90.5	101.8	88.3	93.4	82.4	95.7	78.2	115.0
1987	93.8	93.5	104.7	96.3	105.5	90.9	102.5	87.0	97.0	86.0	112.4
1988	96.0	94.9	106.5	95.0	103.6	93.8	103.4	92.2	98.8	88.2	112.0
1989	97.3	95.9	105.4	96.5	100.3	95.4	103.5	95.1	99.3	91.2	111.9
1990	97.9	97.0	105.4	93.2	97.2	96.0	103.1	97.3	100.3	92.2	107.8
1991	97.0	98.4	98.9	92.7	97.8	96.8	99.1	96.4	99.1	90.7	98.4
1992	100.0	100.0	100.0	100.0	100.0	100.0	100.0	100.0	100.0	100.0	100.0
1993	101.7	102.1	84.0	105.5	102.4	104.0	100.8	101.0	102.9	106.8	101.0
1994	105.0	103.7	103.7	110.8	106.5	108.4	100.5	104.1	103.0	116.1	93.6
1995	106.2	105.7	106.2	109.9	103.3	109.9	99.8	106.5	104.5	118.9	85.7
1996	106.3	106.3	105.6	106.6	98.2	108.0	98.4	108.9	106.5	120.5	80.0
1993:											
January	101.6	100.8	96.6	105.0	101.6	101.5	101.7	101.5	101.8	104.3	103.5
February	101.7	101.4	91.0	102.7	102.4	102.7	102.5	101.1	102.9	104.6	104.9
March	101.4	101.5	84.7	102.5	101.4	102.9	102.0	101.7	102.4	104.1	103.2
April	101.9	101.6	81.4	103.1	102.0	105.1	102.8	102.0	101.9	105.4	102.7
May	101.1	101.2	82.6	105.3	101.8	102.5	101.6	100.3	102.0	105.6	101.8
June	101.2	102.3	80.0	106.1	102.3	104.6	100.4	99.8	102.5	105.6	101.4
July	101.8	102.6	87.0	108.5	102.9	103.5	99.9	101.0	102.2	107.3	99.9
August	101.7	103.0	82.4	106.3	102.9	104.0	99.1	101.1	102.1	107.7	99.2
September	102.0	102.9	79.4	106.3	102.5	103.8	100.4	101.8	102.9	108.9	99.1
October	101.5	102.4	74.9	107.4	102.7	104.7	99.9	100.4	105.6	108.1	98.8
November	101.8	102.3	80.3	106.2	103.1	106.1	99.8	100.7	105.1	108.9	98.2
December	102.2	102.7	87.2	106.7	103.5	106.5	99.1	100.8	103.1	110.5	99.0
1994:											
January	102.1	102.4	88.9	108.2	102.7	106.1	98.7	100.6	102.2	111.4	98.4
February	102.7	101.5	95.2	107.6	103.2	106.3	99.7	102.4	101.8	111.5	95.5
March	104.1	103.9	94.7	109.1	105.0	107.0	101.2	103.0	101.4	114.3	95.8
April	104.5	103.7	100.6	110.6	106.0	106.0	101.0	103.4	104.5	114.6	96.5
May	105.2	103.3	102.9	109.6	106.5	107.6	100.9	105.3	105.0	115.9	94.4
June	105.3	103.6	103.4	110.6	107.1	107.9	101.0	105.3	102.7	115.9	93.2
July	105.3	104.0	101.8	112.6	107.3	107.2	101.2	104.6	101.6	117.1	93.3
August	105.5	103.8	107.7	110.6	107.2	110.4	100.0	105.0	103.2	116.5	92.1
September	105.4	104.1	109.3	111.9	107.9	109.7	100.5	103.4	102.1	117.3	92.3
October	106.0	104.1	116.1	112.7	108.7	109.7	100.9	103.9	102.4	118.8	90.7
November	106.7	104.9	113.3	112.8	108.1	111.5	101.0	105.2	104.3	119.3	90.5
December	107.0	104.7	111.0	113.8	108.6	111.2	100.4	106.7	104.2	120.5	90.3
1995:											
January	107.1	105.6	106.7	115.1	107.4	111.6	99.5	107.5	104.4	120.1	89.4
February	106.5	104.5	104.7	113.1	106.8	111.6	99.9	106.4	104.3	120.7	88.9
March	106.7	105.0	107.2	113.7	107.0	111.2	99.8	106.6	105.2	119.8	89.3
April	106.4	105.3	108.0	113.6	104.9	111.0	99.9	105.9	104.1	120.0	86.8
May	106.2	106.2	104.5	110.5	104.8	111.4	99.8	105.8	103.8	117.9	87.4
June	106.3	106.8	112.8	108.8	102.8	109.6	99.2	106.2	104.7	117.7	85.4
July	106.1	106.2	113.9	105.9	102.0	111.0	100.0	105.9	105.4	116.5	83.8
August	106.1	106.6	103.9	109.6	101.7	108.8	100.6	105.9	105.0	118.2	84.9
September	106.2	106.2	102.5	107.8	101.4	108.5	100.4	107.0	105.7	118.9	84.9
October	106.1	105.9	101.4	108.0	101.0	109.5	99.4	107.6	103.4	119.2	83.5
November	105.4	105.2	104.8	106.3	100.4	106.4	99.8	106.5	103.6	119.2	82.5
December	105.4	105.1	104.1	106.2	99.3	108.0	99.1	106.8	105.1	118.6	81.4
1996:											
January	104.6	104.8	104.1	102.5	96.8	105.3	98.2	106.8	105.2	118.2	80.1
February	105.3	105.7	107.4	104.0	99.2	104.6	99.2	107.0	106.0	118.6	81.7
March	105.4	106.2	111.3	107.0	98.1	105.8	97.6	106.6	105.7	119.3	81.2
April	105.2	105.9	106.3	105.3	99.0	107.5	96.9	106.9	105.6	118.0	81.1
May	105.5	105.6	103.7	106.1	99.0	107.8	97.9	107.2	106.2	119.8	80.7
June	105.9	106.1	105.1	108.0	99.0	108.5	97.1	107.9	106.3	120.9	81.0
July	106.4	106.5	102.5	108.7	98.3	110.2	97.6	109.0	105.3	120.7	80.0
August	106.2	105.5	104.1	107.7	98.5	108.1	97.9	108.7	107.8	122.0	79.5
September	106.9	106.2	104.9	107.2	98.2	108.8	99.1	109.7	106.9	122.8	79.4
October	107.4	107.1	104.0	107.6	97.8	107.6	99.7	111.3	108.4	121.4	78.4
November	107.9	107.6	105.4	108.2	97.3	110.1	100.0	111.8	107.4	121.7	77.4
December	108.8	108.2	108.9	106.3	97.2	111.6	99.8	114.0	107.3	122.6	80.1

INDUSTRIAL PRODUCTION INDEXES BY INDUSTRY GROUPS—Continued
(Seasonally adjusted, 1992=100)

YEAR AND MONTH	Mining					Utilities			Special aggregates — Manufacturing excluding:		
	Total	Metal mining	Coal mining	Oil and gas extraction	Stone and earth minerals	Total	Electric	Gas	Motor vehicles and parts	Computer and office equipment	Computers and semiconductors
1968	94.9	66.6	56.8	109.2	86.7	57.5	43.6	116.8			
1969	98.6	74.6	58.3	112.4	91.7	62.6	47.7	124.9			
1970	101.2	77.1	62.3	115.6	89.5	66.5	51.0	130.5			
1971	98.7	68.6	57.3	114.3	89.9	69.6	53.9	134.4			
1972	100.7	66.3	61.3	116.3	93.9	74.1	58.4	136.5			
1973	101.6	70.0	60.7	115.7	102.5	77.0	62.3	134.4			
1974	101.1	68.0	61.6	114.9	102.1	76.1	61.9	131.2			
1975	98.9	63.5	66.2	112.2	91.9	76.8	64.0	125.2			
1976	99.7	69.2	68.9	110.3	97.2	79.9	67.1	127.1			
1977	102.8	61.1	70.6	115.9	99.4	82.0	70.7	120.7			
1978	105.8	69.5	67.6	120.1	104.7	84.4	73.3	122.6			
1979	107.6	72.2	78.6	118.5	107.1	86.8	75.2	126.6			
1980	110.8	65.2	83.4	123.4	97.9	87.3	76.4	124.8			
1981	114.8	73.5	82.9	128.7	94.1	85.0	78.0	109.3			
1982	110.5	54.8	84.5	124.6	78.7	82.3	76.7	102.4			
1983	105.9	52.8	79.0	119.2	84.0	83.7	79.2	100.4			
1984	113.2	57.2	90.2	125.9	94.7	86.7	82.4	102.6			
1985	110.3	56.6	89.1	122.0	97.9	88.8	84.6	104.3			
1986	101.9	59.3	89.7	110.1	96.6	86.4	86.2	87.0	87.8	89.2	91.1
1987	101.5	61.9	92.5	108.0	100.9	89.4	89.4	89.0	92.7	93.7	95.4
1988	102.9	74.3	95.4	107.7	103.2	93.9	93.6	94.5	97.0	97.7	99.3
1989	101.5	85.6	98.9	103.6	101.8	97.1	96.8	98.1	98.9	99.4	100.7
1990	103.7	93.1	103.7	104.7	103.3	98.3	99.2	94.4	98.7	98.9	99.9
1991	101.6	93.3	100.1	103.3	96.7	100.4	101.2	97.3	96.7	96.5	97.0
1992	100.0	100.0	100.0	100.0	100.0	100.0	100.0	100.0	100.0	100.0	100.0
1993	98.9	98.7	95.1	99.4	102.2	103.9	103.8	104.3	103.1	103.3	102.9
1994	101.6	100.2	104.1	100.2	108.9	105.3	105.5	104.6	108.2	108.7	107.4
1995	100.9	101.9	104.3	98.4	113.3	109.1	109.5	107.4	112.3	111.6	109.0
1996	102.9	102.0	105.9	100.3	118.8	112.7	112.7	112.9	115.7	113.7	110.0
1993:											
January	100.3	98.5	99.1	100.5	102.3	100.8	101.3	98.9	102.1	102.4	102.2
February	98.8	101.0	96.4	99.0	100.1	104.5	104.1	106.1	102.4	102.7	102.4
March	97.6	97.9	94.4	98.4	97.0	105.3	104.2	109.7	102.5	102.8	102.5
April	97.8	98.7	94.8	98.2	98.6	103.5	103.5	103.6	102.9	103.3	102.9
May	98.1	99.2	95.4	98.2	101.1	101.3	102.8	95.5	102.5	102.7	102.3
June	99.0	99.5	98.8	98.8	101.1	103.3	103.3	103.4	102.5	102.7	102.3
July	97.9	99.1	91.1	98.6	102.6	104.4	105.0	102.3	103.2	103.0	102.6
August	98.2	91.3	89.0	100.4	102.2	105.0	105.8	101.9	103.0	102.6	102.1
September	99.1	95.6	94.0	99.9	104.6	104.4	104.2	104.9	103.8	103.8	103.2
October	100.1	99.4	96.7	100.3	104.4	104.3	102.9	109.5	103.5	104.0	103.4
November	99.9	101.1	95.4	100.1	105.4	105.0	103.7	109.6	103.9	104.6	104.0
December	100.2	103.7	96.0	99.9	107.1	105.0	104.7	106.1	104.6	105.4	104.7
1994:											
January	99.8	102.2	94.4	100.1	105.2	107.9	106.5	113.1	104.7	105.4	104.7
February	100.8	101.6	102.7	99.9	104.0	106.8	105.2	112.9	105.3	106.0	105.2
March	102.2	102.9	106.0	100.8	106.2	105.0	104.5	106.7	106.5	106.9	106.0
April	101.7	99.1	107.6	99.9	107.4	103.3	104.8	98.0	107.2	107.7	106.6
May	101.9	98.2	104.2	100.8	109.1	103.2	103.6	101.8	108.0	108.4	107.3
June	102.2	102.8	105.4	100.5	109.7	107.8	108.1	106.8	108.1	108.5	107.3
July	101.9	101.3	104.5	100.5	108.7	105.8	106.1	104.6	108.8	109.3	108.0
August	102.1	100.3	106.2	100.4	109.5	104.9	104.6	106.0	108.8	109.4	108.0
September	101.0	98.7	104.0	99.7	107.8	104.8	105.0	104.0	109.1	109.4	107.9
October	100.7	100.2	101.9	99.4	109.4	105.1	105.9	102.2	110.0	110.2	108.5
November	101.3	96.9	104.2	99.7	112.2	104.4	105.8	99.6	110.7	110.9	109.2
December	103.0	98.0	107.8	100.6	117.5	104.3	105.6	99.8	111.6	111.8	110.0
1995:											
January	102.0	100.6	107.0	99.1	116.2	104.9	105.8	101.4	112.0	112.2	110.2
February	101.9	102.1	106.2	99.4	113.4	106.0	106.7	103.6	111.8	111.6	109.5
March	100.5	100.0	102.6	98.3	113.5	106.6	107.3	103.8	112.0	111.7	109.5
April	100.7	100.8	102.8	98.8	110.8	106.6	107.2	104.4	111.8	111.2	108.9
May	100.6	100.6	101.7	99.1	110.4	109.0	108.7	109.9	111.8	111.1	108.6
June	100.5	101.6	102.9	98.4	111.2	109.0	109.4	107.4	112.1	111.3	108.8
July	101.8	102.7	107.7	98.6	115.1	109.4	109.6	108.6	112.0	111.1	108.3
August	100.5	102.8	100.4	98.5	112.9	113.5	115.2	107.2	112.7	111.8	108.9
September	101.2	102.2	102.6	97.8	116.0	109.7	110.3	107.5	113.3	112.5	109.4
October	100.0	103.9	105.4	96.7	112.3	109.3	111.3	102.3	112.9	111.9	108.8
November	100.8	103.5	104.3	98.1	112.4	112.6	111.2	117.3	112.8	111.7	108.5
December	100.3	101.7	103.4	97.5	115.0	112.3	111.6	115.0	112.9	111.8	108.5
1996:											
January	99.0	97.0	96.6	98.0	112.1	112.5	112.6	112.3	112.5	111.3	108.0
February	100.8	97.1	101.2	98.9	117.4	113.3	113.6	112.2	114.1	112.6	109.1
March	102.8	101.7	105.9	100.2	117.9	114.4	114.0	115.8	114.3	111.6	108.1
April	102.9	99.4	105.3	100.9	116.3	113.5	113.1	115.0	114.3	112.8	109.3
May	103.2	100.9	108.0	100.5	117.4	114.6	114.8	113.6	114.8	113.2	109.6
June	104.4	101.7	108.9	101.5	120.6	114.0	114.2	113.6	115.6	113.8	110.2
July	103.1	103.1	102.7	100.9	120.6	109.4	110.1	107.1	116.0	114.3	110.6
August	104.5	104.0	109.6	101.1	121.7	110.8	111.5	108.5	116.3	114.4	110.6
September	103.4	105.3	106.2	100.5	118.5	111.1	110.9	111.8	116.8	114.5	110.7
October	103.4	105.6	107.5	100.0	120.0	111.9	112.0	111.3	117.3	114.7	110.8
November	103.5	102.5	108.8	100.2	120.2	114.5	112.7	120.9	117.9	115.5	111.6
December	104.5	106.3	109.5	100.7	122.9	112.6	112.6	112.7	118.6	116.1	112.0

CAPACITY UTILIZATION
(Percent of capacity, seasonally adjusted)

YEAR AND MONTH	Total industry	Manufacturing			Durable goods				Primary metals					
		Total	Primary process-ing	Advanced process-ing	Total	Lumber and products	Furniture and fixtures	Stone, clay, and glass products	Total	Iron and steel		Nonferrous		
										Total	Raw steel	Total	Primary copper	Primary aluminum
1968	87.3	87.1	86.1	87.3	87.2	85.8	90.7	78.4	85.1	86.1	84.4	84.3	69.3	92.4
1969	87.3	86.6	86.5	86.4	86.7	83.3	90.7	79.7	89.3	92.8	91.8	84.1	87.7	99.6
1970	81.1	79.4	79.9	78.9	77.2	80.5	81.0	73.9	80.8	84.9	83.4	74.3	88.4	97.4
1971	79.4	77.9	78.7	77.1	74.7	80.0	80.7	75.6	74.8	76.6	76.0	71.7	74.9	88.1
1972	84.4	83.4	85.5	82.2	81.4	88.2	93.0	81.7	83.7	86.2	85.6	79.2	85.1	87.4
1973	88.4	87.7	90.5	86.2	88.0	85.5	93.9	86.0	94.5	98.0	97.1	88.1	85.0	94.0
1974	84.3	83.4	85.1	82.5	83.1	75.8	82.9	81.9	90.7	94.7	96.0	83.7	73.0	100.2
1975	74.6	72.9	72.1	73.3	70.6	69.5	68.9	70.3	71.7	75.9	75.2	64.1	61.9	78.4
1976	79.3	78.2	79.2	77.6	75.7	78.2	75.7	77.2	79.0	82.4	80.7	72.9	67.9	83.1
1977	83.5	82.6	83.8	81.9	80.8	85.7	82.1	81.8	80.1	80.7	78.6	79.4	63.2	87.4
1978	85.8	85.2	85.9	84.8	84.4	86.1	84.5	86.5	86.6	86.5	87.6	86.9	67.9	92.3
1979	86.0	85.3	86.0	84.9	85.6	83.8	81.0	85.5	88.4	88.6	88.3	88.0	71.8	95.7
1980	81.5	79.5	77.2	80.8	78.4	77.7	77.2	76.3	73.5	71.6	73.4	76.9	56.7	95.0
1981	80.8	78.3	77.2	78.8	76.8	74.9	74.7	75.0	77.6	76.4	80.5	79.1	72.0	90.3
1982	74.5	71.8	68.6	73.5	68.0	66.6	70.2	67.5	54.5	48.9	48.3	65.6	54.0	65.9
1983	75.7	74.4	74.5	74.4	70.1	78.8	74.9	73.1	61.7	56.9	57.4	69.6	56.8	67.4
1984	80.8	79.8	80.0	79.7	77.6	84.0	81.4	78.3	71.9	66.5	66.4	81.0	66.9	83.6
1985	79.8	78.8	79.1	78.6	76.8	84.0	79.5	76.3	73.2	68.9	65.8	80.3	71.9	74.9
1986	78.7	78.7	79.9	78.1	75.7	89.0	81.5	78.3	70.1	64.1	63.9	80.3	74.4	71.9
1987	81.3	81.3	84.5	79.9	77.9	92.1	86.0	79.8	79.2	76.2	77.7	84.1	77.2	84.1
1988	83.9	83.8	86.8	82.3	81.7	91.1	84.0	81.7	87.4	87.4	88.9	87.5	78.4	97.4
1989	84.0	83.6	86.1	82.5	82.0	88.7	83.1	81.1	85.2	84.7	84.1	85.9	76.3	98.6
1990	82.3	81.4	83.9	80.3	79.0	85.0	80.1	78.4	83.4	83.6	84.5	83.1	77.8	98.3
1991	79.2	78.0	79.6	77.2	74.7	78.5	74.7	72.2	77.6	75.7	75.8	80.1	81.3	99.6
1992	80.4	79.5	82.3	78.3	76.8	83.0	78.7	74.2	80.9	80.5	80.8	81.7	85.0	97.0
1993	81.6	80.8	84.1	79.3	79.2	83.6	81.6	75.6	85.9	87.6	87.7	83.8	86.8	88.6
1994	83.7	83.1	87.5	81.2	82.3	86.3	82.9	79.4	91.2	91.4	90.8	91.1	86.6	78.9
1995	83.8	83.1	87.3	81.2	82.7	84.6	82.4	79.5	91.9	91.6	94.1	92.3	82.6	80.7
1996	83.1	82.1	86.1	80.3	82.0	85.2	81.0	79.4	90.7	88.8	91.3	93.1	86.2	85.3
1993:														
January	81.4	80.7	83.6	79.4	78.6	83.5	80.7	73.5	84.4	85.9	83.6	82.7	85.9	94.3
February	81.7	80.8	83.8	79.5	78.9	85.0	79.8	74.5	85.1	85.9	85.2	84.2	89.6	91.2
March	81.6	80.7	83.4	79.6	79.0	82.9	81.3	73.6	84.6	85.4	84.1	83.7	90.4	91.0
April	81.7	81.0	83.8	79.8	79.3	82.0	81.9	75.1	84.6	85.1	85.1	84.0	90.7	91.8
May	81.2	80.5	83.3	79.3	79.0	82.3	81.6	74.0	84.4	85.5	87.4	83.2	84.9	91.6
June	81.2	80.4	83.8	78.9	78.7	81.6	81.3	75.0	86.5	88.9	88.6	83.5	92.6	91.8
July	81.3	80.5	83.9	79.0	78.6	82.4	81.9	75.8	85.0	87.4	89.8	82.1	85.3	89.2
August	81.0	80.1	83.9	78.4	78.0	83.6	82.5	75.3	86.3	88.8	89.1	83.4	82.0	85.7
September	81.7	80.9	84.4	79.4	79.3	83.6	83.0	77.0	86.7	88.6	88.6	84.4	86.3	85.2
October	81.8	80.9	84.6	79.3	79.8	85.0	82.2	76.8	86.1	88.4	90.3	83.4	82.1	85.5
November	82.1	81.2	85.2	79.5	80.2	85.4	81.2	77.8	87.3	89.8	88.6	84.3	83.9	83.2
December	82.5	81.7	85.8	80.0	81.0	85.3	82.1	78.7	89.3	91.4	91.6	86.9	87.8	82.6
1994:														
January	82.6	81.6	85.6	79.9	81.0	86.6	80.7	77.5	87.5	87.0	86.3	88.2	86.8	82.0
February	82.8	81.9	85.8	80.3	81.2	85.5	81.6	77.4	89.5	91.0	88.9	87.9	87.5	81.1
March	83.2	82.4	86.6	80.6	81.2	85.2	82.0	78.9	89.5	90.5	88.9	88.3	84.2	80.4
April	83.3	82.7	87.2	80.8	81.7	85.5	82.8	79.3	92.0	94.3	89.2	89.3	83.3	78.7
May	83.7	83.1	87.7	81.1	82.0	87.0	83.4	79.6	92.7	95.1	89.9	89.8	87.6	78.0
June	83.9	83.0	87.3	81.2	81.9	86.7	83.6	79.0	90.3	90.3	89.8	90.4	90.8	77.9
July	84.1	83.4	87.8	81.5	82.8	87.1	83.1	79.2	91.8	92.1	89.3	91.4	89.7	77.6
August	83.9	83.3	87.7	81.4	82.5	86.2	84.0	80.5	88.9	85.6	90.4	93.0	89.5	77.9
September	83.8	83.2	87.9	81.2	82.6	86.6	82.4	79.8	91.7	90.7	92.0	93.1	86.9	78.1
October	84.1	83.6	88.1	81.6	83.0	86.0	84.4	79.9	93.5	93.6	91.7	93.4	85.7	78.3
November	84.4	84.0	88.5	81.9	83.3	85.7	83.6	80.5	92.8	91.9	94.1	93.9	84.1	78.2
December	84.9	84.5	89.6	82.2	84.2	88.1	83.5	81.8	94.7	95.2	98.5	94.4	83.6	78.6
1995:														
January	84.9	84.6	89.5	82.4	84.4	87.2	83.2	80.8	94.9	95.9	95.4	93.8	84.2	78.7
February	84.5	84.0	89.1	81.8	83.8	85.9	84.3	80.6	93.5	93.9	96.6	93.2	82.6	78.6
March	84.3	83.9	88.7	81.7	83.5	84.4	83.1	80.6	93.4	93.7	96.1	93.3	86.0	78.7
April	83.9	83.4	87.9	81.3	82.8	84.2	82.4	79.2	91.9	91.2	95.0	92.8	81.4	79.5
May	83.7	83.0	87.5	81.0	82.4	82.6	81.9	79.7	91.8	91.8	93.6	91.9	86.1	80.2
June	83.6	83.0	86.9	81.1	82.4	83.1	82.8	79.3	91.0	90.3	93.0	91.9	81.9	80.7
July	83.4	82.6	86.4	80.9	81.9	83.7	82.4	78.4	90.2	87.4	92.6	93.5	81.5	81.0
August	83.8	82.9	86.4	81.3	82.5	84.1	81.9	78.4	90.1	90.3	93.6	89.9	82.4	81.2
September	83.9	83.2	86.9	81.5	83.1	85.3	82.8	78.8	92.3	93.3	96.4	91.3	77.2	82.0
October	83.3	82.6	86.4	80.8	82.2	84.7	81.6	79.1	90.7	89.4	91.0	92.3	83.8	81.7
November	83.2	82.2	86.1	80.4	82.0	84.3	81.3	79.7	92.3	93.0	93.5	91.7	83.8	82.6
December	83.0	82.0	86.0	80.3	81.8	85.3	81.0	79.1	90.4	89.6	92.9	91.4	80.4	83.7
1996:														
January	82.4	81.5	85.0	79.9	81.4	82.9	80.9	79.6	87.8	87.6	91.6	88.3	87.7	84.3
February	83.2	82.2	85.3	80.9	82.4	83.5	81.1	78.8	89.8	88.4	90.6	91.5	82.1	84.9
March	82.6	81.3	85.6	79.4	80.9	86.0	79.3	78.3	90.4	88.0	91.8	93.3	82.2	85.2
April	83.1	82.0	85.6	80.4	82.3	86.2	80.9	78.0	90.5	88.3	91.3	93.4	84.7	85.7
May	83.2	82.0	85.9	80.3	82.2	86.1	82.4	78.7	90.4	88.7	91.9	92.5	84.4	85.3
June	83.5	82.3	86.5	80.5	82.5	87.4	81.6	79.7	90.7	89.5	93.5	92.2	80.8	85.3
July	83.2	82.4	86.7	80.6	82.6	84.9	80.5	81.6	91.2	89.8	92.1	92.9	87.3	84.9
August	83.2	82.3	86.5	80.4	82.5	86.3	80.7	79.7	91.2	89.6	92.3	93.2	77.6	85.8
September	83.1	82.1	86.6	80.2	81.9	85.5	80.6	80.5	91.8	88.7	91.4	95.7	86.3	85.6
October	83.0	82.0	86.7	80.0	81.5	84.2	81.6	79.3	93.5	92.6	90.5	94.7	95.3	85.8
November	83.4	82.4	86.5	80.5	81.9	87.0	81.6	79.3	90.5	86.8	88.1	95.1	89.8	85.6
December	83.5	82.5	86.6	80.8	81.7	82.9	81.4	78.8	90.4	87.1	91.1	94.7	96.8	85.5

YEAR AND MONTH	CAPACITY UTILIZATION—Continued (Percent of capacity, seasonally adjusted)									
	Durable goods manufacturing—Continued									
	Fabricated metal products	Industrial machinery and equipment		Electrical machinery	Transportation equipment				Instruments	Miscellaneous
		Total	Computer and office equipment		Total	Motor vehicles and parts		Aerospace and miscellaneous		
						Total	Autos and light trucks			
1968	86.4	85.9	85.7	86.4	89.6	90.2	....	90.5	85.1	84.8
1969	83.8	87.8	92.9	85.3	86.4	86.9	....	87.3	83.9	84.8
1970	75.0	81.3	90.9	76.6	70.5	66.6	....	76.7	77.4	77.9
1971	73.7	73.0	70.9	73.5	74.2	79.5		68.7	76.3	74.3
1972	79.9	82.5	79.2	81.1	76.8	82.5		70.6	81.4	82.7
1973	86.8	93.0	86.3	88.0	84.7	91.6		77.3	87.6	79.9
1974	80.9	94.6	91.7	81.9	75.0	76.4		73.9	86.5	73.5
1975	68.6	78.4	74.0	67.0	65.8	63.1		69.6	77.1	66.9
1976	74.6	78.8	75.6	72.8	72.7	80.2	....	65.3	80.5	71.8
1977	79.9	83.9	78.1	80.1	76.4	90.3	89.8	63.2	86.1	79.5
1978	81.0	88.2	87.3	83.9	80.7	91.0	88.3	70.2	89.5	78.2
1979	82.0	91.6	89.3	87.7	80.2	82.0	78.3	78.4	90.6	76.1
1980	74.9	85.9	88.2	84.0	70.9	61.3	57.8	79.1	87.2	70.6
1981	73.2	84.8	85.7	81.2	66.1	59.3	60.3	72.2	84.8	72.4
1982	66.9	70.5	74.3	76.7	60.9	52.8	53.5	67.8	81.7	69.1
1983	68.4	66.2	78.7	77.8	66.7	66.2	71.9	67.2	79.7	67.3
1984	74.3	75.7	86.1	85.8	74.1	79.0	81.6	70.0	84.6	70.7
1985	74.9	72.8	80.0	80.5	77.9	83.1	81.5	73.8	83.6	65.9
1986	73.6	70.3	72.5	77.8	78.6	78.7	76.7	78.5	79.1	66.6
1987	78.1	72.1	74.6	78.7	77.5	76.8	74.7	78.1	80.2	74.0
1988	81.1	79.6	79.5	82.3	80.6	81.2	79.2	80.0	80.8	78.2
1989	80.0	83.4	81.2	81.3	81.8	79.5	79.8	84.4	79.8	77.4
1990	77.4	79.4	73.7	78.9	77.7	71.6	71.1	84.0	78.5	75.6
1991	73.7	74.3	68.8	76.4	71.7	64.0	64.4	80.8	78.7	73.1
1992	76.7	75.6	74.6	80.5	73.2	69.9	70.7	77.0	77.9	73.4
1993	79.4	79.6	77.2	82.5	75.3	77.3	78.3	72.9	77.7	76.4
1994	83.9	85.8	79.5	85.8	76.3	83.5	86.1	68.0	77.0	77.8
1995	84.8	89.8	88.2	87.8	72.4	76.9	80.4	66.8	77.3	77.6
1996	84.5	89.9	91.9	82.9	71.8	72.4	77.6	71.1	79.2	78.3
1993:										
January	78.5	76.9	76.0	82.3	76.1	76.5	79.6	75.6	78.9	74.6
February	78.9	77.6	76.9	82.5	76.1	76.8	77.1	75.2	78.0	75.4
March	79.2	78.4	77.2	82.7	76.0	77.3	78.0	74.5	78.8	75.8
April	79.6	78.9	77.9	82.6	76.4	78.0	77.8	74.5	78.7	76.8
May	78.9	79.4	78.5	82.2	75.4	76.7	78.3	74.0	78.2	76.6
June	78.5	78.7	77.0	81.8	75.0	77.1	76.0	72.6	78.0	76.0
July	79.4	80.7	77.7	82.2	71.9	71.7	72.8	72.2	78.0	76.4
August	78.9	79.2	77.0	82.3	70.7	69.5	71.0	72.0	77.1	76.4
September	80.1	80.4	77.3	82.9	73.3	75.1	74.1	71.3	77.8	77.1
October	79.6	80.6	76.6	82.7	76.7	81.2	81.5	71.7	76.8	76.9
November	80.2	81.4	75.9	82.5	77.4	83.1	86.0	71.0	76.2	77.0
December	81.0	82.8	78.2	82.9	78.0	85.0	87.2	70.2	76.4	77.5
1994:										
January	81.2	83.4	78.4	83.3	77.5	85.0	89.9	69.1	77.1	77.0
February	81.2	83.1	78.3	83.7	77.7	86.3	92.4	67.9	77.7	77.0
March	82.4	84.0	78.0	84.4	75.8	82.7	88.1	68.0	77.4	77.5
April	83.2	84.2	77.1	84.9	76.0	82.7	87.9	68.3	77.1	78.2
May	83.3	85.2	78.3	85.1	76.1	82.8	84.9	68.5	76.5	77.8
June	83.7	85.5	78.2	85.4	75.9	82.4	84.5	68.3	76.6	77.4
July	84.6	87.4	78.9	86.4	76.2	83.8	80.6	67.4	76.9	79.4
August	84.5	86.1	78.8	86.6	77.1	85.4	85.8	67.3	76.2	77.9
September	84.6	86.7	81.3	86.5	75.9	83.4	83.6	67.0	76.9	77.3
October	85.1	87.3	81.6	87.3	75.3	81.4	85.0	67.9	77.1	78.2
November	85.6	88.1	81.6	87.4	76.2	82.8	84.6	68.2	77.0	78.2
December	86.7	88.7	83.4	88.6	76.5	83.4	85.7	68.3	77.5	77.7
1995:										
January	85.8	90.5	86.1	88.5	76.8	84.0	87.5	68.1	77.3	78.2
February	86.3	90.0	88.1	88.1	75.5	81.5	86.7	68.3	76.8	78.3
March	85.8	89.5	87.7	88.4	74.8	80.1	85.6	68.4	77.1	77.8
April	84.3	89.7	88.8	87.8	73.3	77.1	82.2	68.7	77.3	77.7
May	85.0	89.2	88.5	87.6	72.5	75.8	78.4	68.4	76.6	77.3
June	84.8	88.7	86.5	87.4	72.5	75.7	78.6	68.5	77.4	77.6
July	83.7	88.6	87.6	87.8	71.1	73.7	74.4	67.8	77.0	76.7
August	84.5	89.8	87.4	88.2	72.0	74.9	78.7	68.2	77.6	77.2
September	85.0	90.4	88.9	88.3	72.5	76.4	79.4	67.6	77.9	77.5
October	84.3	90.0	89.7	88.3	69.7	74.9	77.8	63.1	77.7	77.3
November	84.2	89.9	89.3	87.6	68.9	74.5	77.6	61.6	78.0	77.7
December	84.4	90.8	90.1	85.9	69.5	74.6	77.8	62.8	77.0	77.9
1996:										
January	84.3	89.7	90.4	84.8	70.3	73.6	74.1	65.8	77.8	77.0
February	85.0	90.7	92.2	86.5	70.9	73.4	78.0	67.7	79.3	78.3
March	84.5	90.5	92.3	85.1	64.4	61.3	64.3	68.5	79.2	78.3
April	84.5	90.2	92.1	84.5	72.2	74.7	79.3	68.9	78.8	77.8
May	84.7	89.9	92.0	83.8	72.4	74.6	79.5	69.5	78.8	77.9
June	84.9	90.1	92.7	83.9	72.5	74.4	81.2	70.0	79.6	78.4
July	84.8	90.2	94.0	82.7	74.1	76.3	85.5	71.3	78.8	78.2
August	84.8	90.5	92.9	82.0	73.9	75.4	81.4	72.0	79.3	78.1
September	84.5	89.6	92.9	81.3	72.5	72.0	79.1	73.3	79.3	78.1
October	84.3	89.1	91.8	80.5	71.1	68.5	72.8	74.6	79.6	78.0
November	84.0	89.2	90.7	80.2	73.8	72.7	77.8	75.4	79.3	78.7
December	84.1	89.0	89.5	80.0	73.8	71.9	77.7	76.4	80.1	80.3

CAPACITY UTILIZATION—Continued
(Percent of capacity, seasonally adjusted)

Nondurable goods manufacturing

YEAR AND MONTH	Total	Foods	Textile mill products	Apparel products	Paper and products		Printing and publishing	Chemicals and products			Petroleum products
					Total	Pulp and paper		Total	Plastics materials	Synthetic fibers	
1968	86.6	84.4	90.8	85.6	89.4	91.9	90.5	80.5	90.8	94.6	95.2
1969	86.5	84.8	89.0	84.9	91.3	95.4	92.0	80.1	93.4	87.5	94.7
1970	82.8	83.6	83.5	78.9	86.5	92.2	86.9	77.7	82.3	81.9	93.9
1971	82.6	83.6	84.7	78.6	87.4	93.3	85.3	77.5	81.3	87.6	91.8
1972	86.4	85.5	88.6	82.0	91.9	95.8	88.3	82.3	98.5	87.6	92.8
1973	87.3	85.0	89.7	81.4	95.4	96.1	87.7	85.5	98.5	91.5	94.2
1974	83.9	83.6	80.5	76.5	91.9	93.5	83.9	84.4	93.8	89.9	87.1
1975	76.3	80.4	76.1	69.3	78.1	79.4	77.0	73.3	64.8	76.3	83.7
1976	81.8	82.4	83.6	80.3	87.0	89.8	82.6	78.4	74.5	77.7	85.2
1977	85.3	83.5	87.2	84.8	90.1	90.8	89.4	80.8	80.6	81.1	87.6
1978	86.4	83.6	86.0	85.9	92.5	92.4	91.7	82.7	85.3	86.5	87.6
1979	84.9	82.0	87.7	80.5	92.6	94.6	89.5	83.7	86.7	91.4	84.1
1980	81.0	81.6	84.8	79.4	88.4	92.2	85.8	78.4	75.2	65.3	74.7
1981	80.4	81.2	81.6	80.6	87.2	91.3	83.9	78.1	76.9	81.2	70.7
1982	77.5	80.2	75.5	79.7	83.1	86.2	83.8	70.7	71.2	68.6	70.1
1983	80.8	80.9	85.3	82.6	89.5	91.7	85.2	75.2	82.3	84.9	73.4
1984	82.9	81.5	85.8	84.1	92.1	93.4	87.7	77.4	86.3	85.4	77.8
1985	81.5	82.2	81.5	80.4	88.2	90.4	86.4	75.6	85.7	78.4	78.4
1986	82.8	82.9	85.4	82.3	90.3	94.0	85.6	77.6	89.4	86.3	83.7
1987	85.9	84.1	90.5	85.2	90.8	95.7	91.0	81.3	98.7	92.1	83.5
1988	86.4	84.4	88.0	83.6	92.2	95.6	89.5	84.0	95.5	91.7	85.3
1989	85.7	84.3	87.9	80.9	91.1	93.9	87.7	83.7	90.3	94.8	87.0
1990	84.4	83.9	83.4	78.3	88.9	93.9	85.2	83.0	87.1	86.7	87.6
1991	81.9	83.4	81.7	78.7	86.7	91.7	80.8	80.1	81.4	85.6	86.6
1992	82.8	82.8	87.1	80.3	87.8	92.1	81.1	80.3	89.1	86.0	88.6
1993	82.6	82.7	89.8	82.0	89.4	93.2	81.9	78.8	87.7	88.0	92.1
1994	84.0	82.4	91.6	84.9	91.5	94.9	82.1	79.1	96.3	86.7	91.3
1995	83.6	82.4	87.4	80.8	91.3	94.1	81.6	79.1	92.9	87.1	92.0
1996	82.2	81.2	82.1	75.2	88.1	90.7	80.8	78.6	93.7	87.6	93.8
1993:											
January	83.1	82.3	90.5	81.5	88.2	92.3	82.3	79.9	88.2	87.6	90.9
February	83.1	82.7	88.3	82.1	89.1	93.2	83.0	79.4	86.7	89.1	92.0
March	82.8	82.7	87.9	81.3	89.1	92.8	82.7	79.8	87.7	88.0	91.5
April	83.0	82.6	88.3	81.7	90.7	94.5	83.4	79.9	87.8	88.8	91.1
May	82.3	82.2	89.9	81.5	88.4	92.0	82.5	78.4	86.3	88.2	91.2
June	82.3	82.9	90.4	81.9	90.0	93.8	81.6	77.9	87.1	90.5	91.7
July	82.7	83.1	92.3	82.3	88.8	92.3	81.2	78.7	86.7	89.8	91.5
August	82.5	83.3	90.2	82.4	89.1	92.3	80.6	78.7	87.3	91.4	91.5
September	82.7	83.1	90.0	82.0	88.8	92.8	81.8	79.1	85.8	87.6	92.1
October	82.2	82.5	90.8	82.1	89.4	92.9	81.4	77.8	88.1	85.3	94.6
November	82.4	82.3	89.6	82.4	90.5	94.6	81.4	78.0	89.3	86.3	94.2
December	82.6	82.6	89.9	82.7	90.6	94.5	80.9	77.9	91.0	83.8	92.5
1994:											
January	82.5	82.2	90.9	82.0	90.2	93.9	80.6	77.6	91.3	88.7	91.6
February	82.8	81.3	90.2	82.4	90.2	93.8	81.5	78.8	93.6	86.7	91.1
March	83.8	83.1	91.1	83.8	90.7	94.8	82.6	79.0	95.2	87.1	90.5
April	84.0	82.8	92.1	84.6	89.7	93.4	82.5	79.1	94.5	87.3	93.2
May	84.4	82.4	91.0	84.9	91.0	94.3	82.4	80.3	96.9	87.0	93.4
June	84.3	82.4	91.5	85.3	91.2	94.3	82.5	80.2	97.0	83.7	91.2
July	84.2	82.6	92.9	85.5	90.5	92.9	82.7	79.4	97.9	85.4	90.1
August	84.2	82.3	91.0	85.4	93.0	96.3	81.7	79.5	98.1	89.4	91.3
September	84.0	82.4	91.8	85.9	92.3	96.2	82.1	78.1	97.5	85.6	90.1
October	84.3	82.3	92.1	86.5	92.2	95.2	82.4	78.3	93.1	86.7	90.2
November	84.8	82.7	91.9	86.0	93.7	97.2	82.5	79.1	97.6	85.6	91.8
December	84.9	82.5	92.4	86.4	93.3	96.3	82.0	80.1	102.6	86.9	91.5
1995:											
January	84.9	83.1	93.2	85.3	93.5	96.7	81.3	80.5	102.5	88.3	91.6
February	84.3	82.0	91.3	84.6	93.4	96.6	81.7	79.6	97.2	89.7	91.5
March	84.3	82.3	91.4	84.5	92.9	96.4	81.5	79.6	94.8	91.1	92.4
April	84.0	82.4	91.0	82.6	92.6	95.6	81.7	79.0	94.5	85.7	91.5
May	83.7	82.9	88.3	82.3	92.8	96.7	81.6	78.9	92.6	88.2	91.2
June	83.7	83.3	86.6	80.5	91.2	95.0	81.1	79.0	91.2	86.4	92.1
July	83.4	82.7	84.0	79.7	92.1	95.7	81.7	78.7	90.1	84.7	92.7
August	83.3	82.8	86.7	79.3	90.2	93.6	82.3	78.5	87.2	84.7	92.4
September	83.3	82.4	85.0	78.8	89.8	91.8	82.2	79.2	91.1	86.5	93.1
October	83.0	82.0	84.9	78.3	90.4	92.7	81.3	79.5	90.8	86.6	91.2
November	82.4	81.4	83.2	77.6	87.7	89.6	81.7	78.5	91.4	87.1	91.3
December	82.3	81.1	82.9	76.5	88.8	89.3	81.1	78.6	90.9	86.6	92.7
1996:											
January	81.6	80.8	79.8	74.5	86.5	88.6	80.4	78.4	91.6	84.5	92.8
February	82.0	81.3	80.8	76.2	85.8	88.4	81.2	78.3	91.9	83.1	93.5
March	81.9	81.6	83.0	75.3	86.6	88.2	80.0	77.7	92.9	83.4	93.1
April	81.6	81.2	81.5	76.0	87.9	90.1	79.5	77.7	93.6	82.8	93.0
May	81.8	80.9	82.0	75.9	88.1	89.9	80.3	77.7	94.3	84.5	93.6
June	82.0	81.1	83.3	75.9	88.5	89.3	79.7	78.0	95.0	85.3	93.6
July	82.2	81.3	83.7	75.2	89.8	92.7	80.1	78.6	94.9	91.1	92.7
August	82.0	80.4	82.7	75.3	88.0	91.7	80.5	78.1	94.9	87.6	94.8
September	82.4	80.8	82.2	75.0	88.4	91.2	81.4	78.6	95.4	89.2	94.0
October	82.7	81.3	82.4	74.7	87.4	91.5	82.0	79.5	94.0	95.4	95.3
November	82.9	81.7	82.7	74.2	89.3	92.7	82.2	79.6	92.4	90.4	94.4
December	83.5	82.0	81.1	74.1	90.4	94.0	82.2	81.0	94.0	93.8	94.2

CAPACITY UTILIZATION—Continued
(Percent of capacity, seasonally adjusted)

YEAR AND MONTH	Nondurable goods manufacturing—Continued		Mining						Utilities		
	Rubber and plastic products	Leather and products	Total	Metal mining	Coal mining	Oil and gas extraction		Stone and earth minerals	Total	Electric	Gas
						Total	Oil and gas well drilling				
1968	91.6	93.6	83.5	82.9	89.5	81.8	71.3	89.2	95.1	98.3	90.0
1969	91.7	85.9	86.5	91.8	90.7	84.6	77.8	91.5	96.7	99.8	91.6
1970	81.2	81.8	88.8	93.6	95.8	87.7	69.7	87.2	96.2	98.9	91.9
1971	82.6	79.9	87.3	83.2	86.0	88.5	68.6	85.9	94.6	96.5	92.3
1972	91.6	84.2	90.3	80.7	89.2	92.3	79.1	87.8	95.2	97.0	92.5
1973	93.3	79.6	92.3	84.6	85.7	94.8	85.2	92.8	93.5	95.4	90.7
1974	84.9	77.4	92.3	82.1	84.2	96.1	98.9	89.6	87.3	87.3	88.6
1975	70.1	79.7	89.7	76.4	87.5	93.8	99.2	79.1	84.4	84.8	84.8
1976	78.5	81.7	89.8	81.0	88.9	92.1	91.5	83.0	85.2	85.1	86.6
1977	88.3	83.3	90.9	69.4	88.2	94.2	101.7	85.4	85.0	86.0	83.2
1978	89.2	86.8	90.9	78.5	80.3	94.7	100.0	89.2	85.4	85.3	85.5
1979	84.2	82.2	91.4	81.4	88.8	92.8	88.2	90.6	86.6	85.3	89.5
1980	73.9	84.1	93.4	72.8	90.3	95.8	95.7	82.7	85.9	84.7	89.3
1981	77.9	83.9	93.9	79.1	86.7	96.1	98.0	79.8	82.5	84.3	79.1
1982	74.4	80.7	86.3	57.5	86.1	88.2	70.3	67.4	79.3	81.3	74.9
1983	79.2	82.8	80.4	57.9	79.1	81.7	52.6	72.6	79.7	82.3	74.4
1984	84.3	78.6	86.0	63.3	88.6	86.7	63.4	81.8	81.9	84.0	77.1
1985	82.1	74.1	84.3	62.7	85.7	84.9	58.5	84.4	83.5	84.7	79.8
1986	82.9	71.9	77.6	65.9	84.7	76.4	34.3	82.7	80.6	84.9	67.6
1987	89.0	74.7	80.0	70.9	85.7	78.9	36.4	85.7	82.5	86.1	69.9
1988	87.8	78.7	83.6	80.5	86.8	82.8	46.7	86.9	84.9	87.8	73.7
1989	87.4	82.5	85.5	85.4	88.3	85.0	53.1	85.2	86.3	89.4	75.7
1990	84.6	82.7	88.9	85.7	90.7	89.1	68.3	86.3	85.7	89.6	72.9
1991	80.3	78.8	87.6	82.9	85.7	89.2	63.1	81.1	86.3	89.1	75.1
1992	85.3	82.8	87.0	86.9	85.1	87.7	57.3	84.7	84.6	86.8	77.2
1993	88.0	85.5	86.7	83.9	80.5	88.6	66.3	85.1	87.2	88.8	80.4
1994	92.3	80.8	88.9	85.4	85.3	90.1	73.0	89.7	87.3	89.2	80.4
1995	91.5	75.3	88.2	87.3	84.3	88.8	71.0	91.8	89.1	91.1	82.2
1996	91.2	71.5	90.5	86.1	85.8	91.6	81.1	94.6	90.3	91.4	85.9
1993:											
January	87.2	86.8	87.8	84.3	84.5	89.0	69.5	86.0	84.8	87.2	76.3
February	87.3	88.1	86.5	86.3	82.1	87.8	61.6	84.0	87.9	89.5	81.9
March	86.6	86.9	85.5	83.5	80.3	87.4	57.1	81.2	88.6	89.5	84.6
April	87.5	86.6	85.6	84.2	80.5	87.3	58.4	82.4	87.0	88.8	79.9
May	87.4	86.0	86.0	84.5	80.9	87.4	61.7	84.3	85.1	88.1	73.7
June	87.2	85.8	86.8	84.6	83.7	88.0	64.4	84.2	86.7	88.4	79.7
July	88.4	84.6	85.8	84.2	77.1	88.0	66.7	85.3	87.6	89.8	78.8
August	88.4	84.3	86.1	77.4	75.2	89.7	70.5	84.9	88.1	90.4	78.6
September	89.2	84.3	87.0	81.0	79.3	89.4	71.4	86.8	87.4	88.9	80.9
October	88.4	84.2	87.9	84.1	81.5	89.9	71.6	86.5	87.3	87.7	84.3
November	88.8	83.8	87.8	85.5	80.2	89.9	70.8	87.3	87.8	88.3	84.4
December	89.9	84.6	88.1	87.6	80.6	89.8	71.9	88.7	87.6	89.0	81.7
1994:											
January	90.3	84.2	87.7	86.4	79.0	90.1	72.7	87.0	90.0	90.5	87.1
February	90.1	81.9	88.6	86.0	85.7	89.9	73.9	86.0	89.0	89.3	86.9
March	92.0	82.3	89.7	87.2	88.1	90.6	74.7	87.7	87.4	88.6	82.1
April	91.9	83.0	89.2	84.2	89.1	89.8	74.3	88.7	85.9	88.8	75.4
May	92.6	81.3	89.3	83.5	85.9	90.7	74.3	90.1	85.7	87.7	78.3
June	92.3	80.3	89.6	87.5	86.6	90.4	75.3	90.4	89.5	91.5	82.1
July	92.9	80.6	89.2	86.4	85.6	90.4	73.7	89.5	87.7	89.7	80.4
August	92.1	79.7	89.3	85.7	86.6	90.3	71.2	90.2	86.9	88.4	81.4
September	92.4	80.0	88.3	84.5	84.5	89.7	71.3	88.6	86.7	88.6	79.9
October	93.2	78.7	87.9	85.9	82.5	89.4	71.8	89.8	86.9	89.3	78.5
November	93.3	78.6	88.4	83.2	84.0	89.6	71.4	92.1	86.3	89.1	76.5
December	93.9	78.5	89.8	84.3	86.6	90.4	71.5	96.3	86.1	88.9	76.6
1995:											
January	93.3	77.8	88.9	86.6	85.9	89.1	71.9	95.1	86.4	89.0	77.8
February	93.6	77.5	88.9	87.9	85.4	89.4	72.2	92.6	87.2	89.5	79.4
March	92.8	78.0	87.6	86.0	82.6	88.5	70.4	92.5	87.5	89.9	79.5
April	92.8	76.0	87.9	86.6	82.8	89.0	71.5	90.2	87.4	89.6	80.0
May	91.0	76.7	87.8	86.5	82.1	89.3	72.1	89.7	89.2	90.7	84.2
June	90.6	75.0	87.8	87.2	83.1	88.7	70.3	90.2	89.1	91.1	82.2
July	89.6	73.6	89.0	88.0	87.2	89.0	71.1	93.2	89.3	91.1	83.1
August	90.8	74.8	87.9	88.0	81.3	89.0	71.9	91.3	92.5	95.6	82.0
September	91.2	74.9	88.5	87.3	86.5	88.4	70.5	93.7	89.2	91.3	82.2
October	91.3	73.8	87.6	88.6	85.6	87.6	69.5	90.6	88.8	92.0	78.2
November	91.1	73.1	88.3	88.1	84.9	88.9	69.8	90.5	91.3	91.7	89.6
December	90.5	72.2	88.0	86.4	84.2	88.5	70.5	92.5	91.0	91.8	87.8
1996:											
January	90.1	71.1	86.9	82.3	78.7	89.0	71.8	90.0	91.0	92.4	85.7
February	90.3	72.6	88.5	82.3	82.3	89.9	74.9	94.1	91.5	93.1	85.5
March	90.7	72.2	90.3	86.0	86.1	91.2	79.6	94.4	92.2	93.2	88.2
April	89.6	72.2	90.4	84.0	85.6	92.0	82.4	93.0	91.3	92.3	87.6
May	90.9	71.9	90.7	85.2	87.7	91.7	85.0	93.7	92.0	93.5	86.5
June	91.6	72.3	91.8	85.8	88.3	92.7	85.8	96.2	91.4	92.7	86.4
July	91.3	71.5	90.7	86.9	83.2	92.2	82.2	96.0	87.6	89.2	81.4
August	92.1	71.1	91.9	87.6	88.7	92.5	82.9	96.7	88.5	90.2	82.5
September	92.7	71.1	91.0	88.7	85.8	92.0	79.7	94.1	88.6	89.6	84.9
October	91.5	70.3	91.0	88.9	86.8	91.6	81.8	95.1	89.0	90.2	84.5
November	91.6	69.4	91.1	86.3	87.8	91.8	82.5	95.1	91.0	90.6	91.7
December	92.1	72.0	91.9	89.5	88.3	92.3	84.8	97.0	89.3	90.3	85.4

Business Sales, Inventories, and Investment

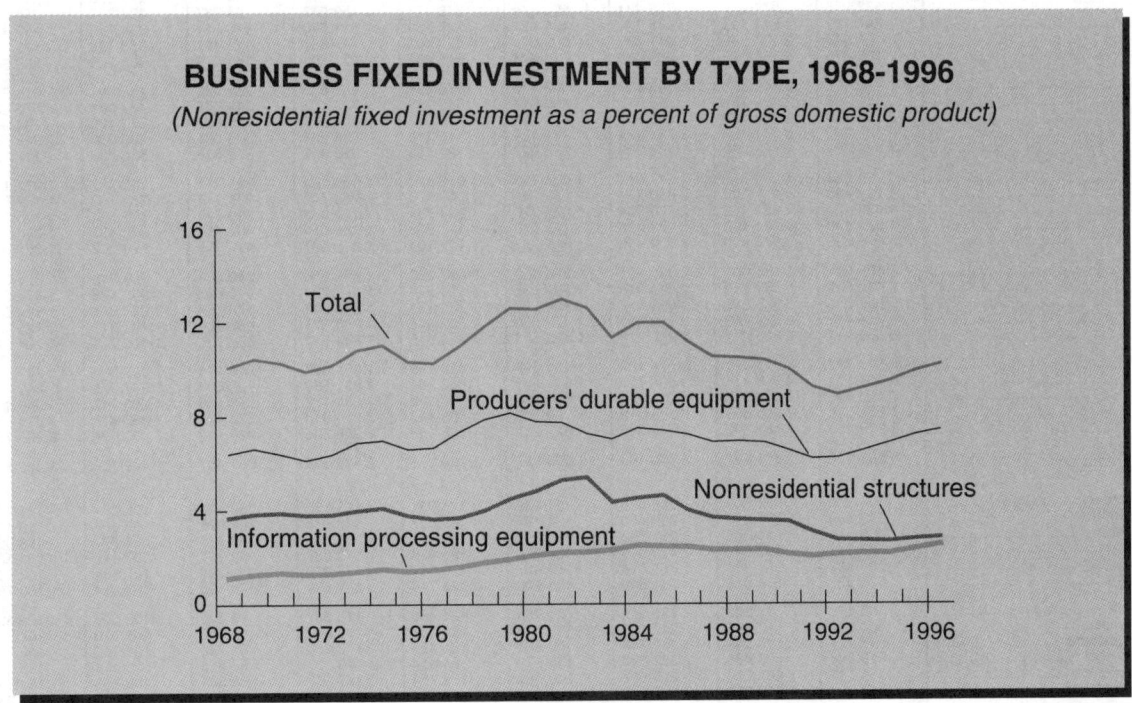

BUSINESS FIXED INVESTMENT BY TYPE, 1968-1996
(Nonresidential fixed investment as a percent of gross domestic product)

Over the 1968 to 1996 time span, total business fixed investment has varied from a peak of 13 percent of GDP in 1981 to a low of just under 9 percent in 1992—a year representing the early stages of recovery from the 1990-1991 recession. By 1996, business investment had recovered to more than 10 percent of GDP, with most of the gain since 1992 coming from investment in producers' durable equipment rather than in new structures.

By 1996, investment in the information processing category of producers' durable equipment slightly exceeded the 2.5 percent of GDP reached in the mid-1980s. Because prices of information processing equipment have fallen, the 2.6 percent of current dollar GDP going for information processing equipment in 1996 represented business acquisition of substantially greater real information processing capacity (relative to the size of the economy) than was the case in the earlier period.

MANUFACTURING AND TRADE SALES
(Millions of dollars)

YEAR AND MONTH	Total		Seasonally adjusted								
			Manufacturing			Retail trade			Merchant wholesalers		
	Not seasonally adjusted	Seasonally adjusted	Total	Durable goods industries	Nondurable goods industries	Total	Durable goods stores	Nondurable goods stores	Total	Durable goods establishments	Nondurable goods establishments
1968	1 184 225	1 184 225	602 744	331 490	271 254	329 336	106 023	223 313	252 145	116 297	135 848
1969	1 268 284	1 268 284	642 013	352 836	289 177	352 457	113 562	238 895	273 814	128 314	145 500
1970	1 298 651	1 298 651	633 663	337 876	295 787	374 989	114 586	260 403	289 999	133 778	156 221
1971	1 402 745	1 402 745	670 877	359 089	311 788	413 969	135 113	278 856	317 899	147 761	170 138
1972	1 572 976	1 572 976	756 321	407 844	348 477	458 267	155 937	302 330	358 388	168 879	189 509
1973	1 844 121	1 844 121	875 173	475 621	399 552	511 570	176 817	334 753	457 378	208 554	248 824
1974	2 134 949	2 134 949	1 017 477	530 074	487 403	541 686	172 497	369 189	575 786	255 863	319 923
1975	2 186 375	2 186 375	1 039 065	523 178	515 887	587 704	185 479	402 225	559 606	235 723	323 883
1976	2 449 803	2 449 803	1 185 563	607 475	578 088	655 859	219 908	435 951	608 381	263 605	344 776
1977	2 754 158	2 754 158	1 358 416	710 017	648 399	722 109	249 078	473 031	673 633	304 721	368 912
1978	3 123 838	3 123 838	1 522 858	812 776	710 082	804 019	280 899	523 120	796 961	372 176	424 785
1979	3 572 409	3 572 409	1 727 234	911 124	816 110	896 561	306 561	590 000	948 614	436 254	512 360
1980	3 926 797	3 926 797	1 852 689	929 027	923 662	956 921	298 618	658 303	1 117 187	486 509	630 678
1981	4 269 863	4 269 863	2 017 544	1 004 725	1 012 819	1 038 163	324 211	713 952	1 214 156	525 607	688 549
1982	4 171 496	4 171 496	1 960 214	950 541	1 009 673	1 068 747	335 587	733 160	1 142 535	480 318	662 217
1983	4 431 432	4 431 432	2 070 564	1 025 770	1 044 794	1 170 163	390 849	779 314	1 190 705	523 080	667 625
1984	4 921 490	4 921 490	2 288 184	1 175 276	1 112 908	1 286 914	454 481	832 433	1 346 392	622 361	724 031
1985	5 070 990	5 070 990	2 334 456	1 215 352	1 119 104	1 375 027	498 125	876 902	1 361 507	651 864	709 643
1986	5 165 031	5 165 031	2 335 881	1 238 859	1 097 022	1 449 636	540 688	908 948	1 379 514	681 691	697 823
1987	5 492 818	5 492 818	2 475 906	1 297 532	1 178 374	1 541 299	575 863	965 436	1 475 613	730 592	745 021
1988	5 965 883	5 965 883	2 695 432	1 421 501	1 273 931	1 656 202	629 154	1 027 048	1 614 249	801 751	812 498
1989	6 324 469	6 324 469	2 840 375	1 477 900	1 362 475	1 758 971	657 154	1 101 817	1 725 123	851 550	873 573
1990	6 550 911	6 550 911	2 912 228	1 485 313	1 426 915	1 844 611	668 835	1 175 776	1 794 072	880 767	913 305
1991	6 513 777	6 513 777	2 878 167	1 451 998	1 426 169	1 855 937	649 974	1 205 963	1 779 673	860 138	919 535
1992	6 806 114	6 806 114	3 004 727	1 541 866	1 462 861	1 951 589	703 604	1 247 985	1 849 798	908 917	940 881
1993	7 140 588	7 138 978	3 127 625	1 630 635	1 496 990	2 071 178	775 436	1 295 742	1 940 175	986 912	953 263
1994	7 651 022	7 648 610	3 348 019	1 789 576	1 558 443	2 224 913	872 495	1 352 418	2 075 678	1 082 312	993 366
1995	8 179 165	8 181 663	3 589 395	1 921 210	1 668 185	2 326 536	926 442	1 400 094	2 265 732	1 179 197	1 086 535
1996	8 601 158	8 595 397	3 735 183	2 005 997	1 729 186	2 439 535	990 407	1 449 128	2 420 679	1 245 781	1 174 898
1993:											
January	525 336	586 669	256 516	131 485	125 031	169 123	62 472	106 651	161 030	80 894	80 136
February	545 809	587 963	259 430	134 177	125 253	168 076	60 895	107 181	160 457	81 219	79 238
March	605 517	586 086	261 889	135 802	126 087	166 192	60 415	105 777	158 005	79 096	78 909
April	589 146	590 543	259 006	134 050	124 956	170 237	62 797	107 440	161 300	81 408	79 892
May	595 822	591 368	257 074	133 407	123 667	171 370	63 786	107 584	162 924	81 345	81 579
June	621 937	594 009	261 618	135 900	125 718	171 634	64 150	107 484	160 757	81 323	79 434
July	569 596	591 903	256 241	131 755	124 486	173 337	65 328	108 009	162 325	83 603	78 722
August	601 040	592 885	257 025	133 688	123 337	173 629	65 610	108 019	162 231	83 249	78 982
September	616 125	598 398	261 718	136 868	124 850	173 959	65 232	108 727	162 721	83 210	79 511
October	615 848	602 486	262 833	138 379	124 454	176 337	66 853	109 484	163 316	83 805	79 511
November	611 119	607 076	265 617	140 863	124 754	177 966	68 301	109 665	163 493	83 781	79 712
December	643 293	608 350	266 998	142 958	124 040	179 318	69 597	109 721	162 034	84 143	77 891
1994:											
January	545 893	610 034	267 287	142 969	124 318	178 005	68 668	109 337	164 742	84 690	80 052
February	572 965	616 147	269 138	143 474	125 664	180 976	69 865	111 111	166 033	85 607	80 426
March	651 225	627 161	273 780	146 016	127 764	183 962	71 716	112 246	169 419	87 448	81 971
April	616 705	623 510	272 114	145 486	126 628	183 096	72 019	111 077	168 300	87 242	81 058
May	634 825	626 051	274 359	146 528	127 831	182 621	71 189	111 432	169 071	87 814	81 257
June	665 093	634 069	278 167	148 906	129 261	184 382	71 920	112 462	171 520	89 215	82 305
July	598 723	634 022	276 826	148 108	128 718	184 578	71 680	112 898	172 618	89 975	82 643
August	667 209	650 098	285 457	152 969	132 488	187 336	73 545	113 791	177 305	93 270	84 035
September	667 468	647 973	283 375	151 282	132 093	187 935	74 037	113 898	176 663	92 915	83 748
October	665 047	652 475	283 203	151 165	132 038	190 464	76 005	114 459	178 808	93 708	85 100
November	664 435	660 369	289 842	155 369	134 473	190 727	75 936	114 791	179 800	94 357	85 443
December	701 434	668 144	293 999	157 079	136 920	190 831	75 915	114 916	183 314	96 283	87 031
1995:											
January	607 163	673 417	296 430	159 403	137 027	192 619	76 055	116 564	184 368	96 511	87 857
February	626 506	671 996	296 585	158 518	138 067	189 568	74 685	114 883	185 843	96 925	88 918
March	699 157	673 216	297 782	160 044	137 738	190 950	75 544	115 406	184 484	96 592	87 892
April	656 529	672 012	294 385	156 830	137 555	191 094	75 334	115 760	186 533	96 426	90 107
May	693 974	677 374	296 504	157 942	138 562	193 074	76 480	116 594	187 796	97 959	89 837
June	717 479	683 535	299 195	159 468	139 727	194 512	77 527	116 985	189 828	98 791	91 037
July	638 427	677 687	294 318	155 998	138 320	194 315	77 362	116 953	189 054	97 439	91 615
August	707 505	687 474	301 761	161 380	140 381	195 752	78 723	117 029	189 961	98 742	91 219
September	703 715	688 368	302 558	162 601	139 957	195 079	77 640	117 439	190 731	99 144	91 587
October	705 486	688 214	302 025	162 083	139 942	194 865	78 048	116 817	191 324	99 263	92 061
November	698 068	692 990	302 621	162 393	140 228	196 702	79 234	117 468	193 667	100 745	92 922
December	725 336	699 162	304 203	163 646	140 557	198 006	79 810	118 196	196 953	102 827	94 126
1996:											
January	632 955	693 216	300 439	160 363	140 076	197 714	79 640	118 074	195 063	100 951	94 112
February	667 030	699 473	303 090	162 473	140 617	201 085	81 931	119 154	195 298	101 055	94 243
March	715 517	700 685	301 666	160 768	140 898	201 685	82 641	119 044	197 334	102 421	94 913
April	706 583	711 705	309 477	165 496	143 981	202 375	81 580	120 795	199 853	102 829	97 024
May	736 916	717 503	313 247	168 781	144 466	204 177	83 239	120 938	200 079	103 580	96 499
June	732 971	712 727	310 052	167 524	142 528	202 698	82 315	120 383	199 977	103 174	96 803
July	690 594	721 396	313 851	168 762	145 089	203 291	82 531	120 760	204 254	104 447	99 807
August	737 011	718 782	313 854	168 960	144 894	203 036	82 487	120 549	201 892	102 804	99 088
September	734 806	724 103	315 971	171 415	144 556	204 713	83 091	121 622	203 419	104 520	98 899
October	755 229	727 725	316 461	169 368	147 093	206 277	83 871	122 406	204 987	104 966	100 021
November	731 366	730 646	319 296	171 426	147 870	205 789	83 485	122 304	205 561	105 568	99 993
December	760 180	728 760	316 306	169 504	146 802	206 894	83 785	123 109	205 560	105 051	100 509

MANUFACTURING AND TRADE INVENTORIES
(Book value, end of period—Millions of dollars)

YEAR AND MONTH	Total		Seasonally adjusted								
			Manufacturing [1]			Retail trade [1]			Merchant wholesalers		
	Not seasonally adjusted	Seasonally adjusted	Total	Durable goods industries	Nondurable goods industries	Total	Durable goods stores	Nondurable goods stores	Total	Durable goods establishments	Nondurable goods establishments
1968	....	....	90 560	58 732	31 828	38 945	16 580	22 365	....	....	....
1969	....	....	98 145	64 598	33 547	42 517	18 206	24 311	....	....	....
1970	....	....	101 599	66 651	34 948	43 867	17 908	25 959	....	....	....
1971	....	....	102 567	66 136	36 431	50 063	21 687	28 376	....	....	....
1972	....	....	108 121	70 067	38 054	55 079	24 238	30 841	....	....	....
1973	....	....	124 499	81 192	43 307	63 237	28 418	34 819	....	....	....
1974	....	....	157 625	101 493	56 132	71 067	32 861	38 206	....	....	....
1975	....	....	159 708	102 590	57 118	71 744	33 356	38 388	....	....	....
1976	....	....	174 636	111 988	62 648	79 273	37 841	41 432	....	....	....
1977	....	....	188 378	120 877	67 501	89 444	43 071	46 373	....	....	....
1978	....	....	211 691	138 181	73 510	102 694	50 136	52 558	....	....	....
1979	....	....	242 157	160 734	81 423	111 098	54 108	56 990	....	....	....
1980	503 572	508 924	265 215	174 788	90 427	121 078	55 799	65 279	122 631	79 372	43 259
1981	539 235	545 786	283 413	186 443	96 970	132 719	61 050	71 669	129 654	85 856	43 798
1982	566 523	573 908	311 852	200 444	111 408	134 628	61 316	73 312	127 428	85 222	42 206
1983	582 494	590 287	312 379	199 854	112 525	147 833	68 856	78 977	130 075	85 180	44 895
1984	640 467	649 780	339 516	221 330	118 186	167 812	79 074	88 738	142 452	95 474	46 978
1985	654 899	664 039	334 749	218 193	116 556	181 881	88 315	93 566	147 409	97 371	50 038
1986	653 299	662 738	322 654	211 997	110 657	186 510	89 983	96 527	153 574	102 349	51 225
1987	700 139	709 848	338 109	220 799	117 310	207 836	105 481	102 355	163 903	108 112	55 791
1988	757 952	767 222	369 374	242 468	126 906	219 047	112 453	106 594	178 801	117 045	61 756
1989	805 579	815 455	391 212	257 513	133 699	237 234	121 347	115 887	187 009	122 237	64 772
1990	830 883	840 396	405 073	263 209	141 864	239 773	121 105	118 668	195 550	126 200	69 350
1991	824 764	834 287	390 950	250 019	140 931	243 275	119 039	124 236	200 062	127 105	72 957
1992	832 779	842 204	382 547	238 166	144 381	251 994	122 948	129 046	207 663	131 090	76 573
1993	857 544	867 513	384 138	239 404	144 734	267 497	133 624	133 873	215 878	135 632	80 246
1994	918 291	930 049	405 028	253 691	151 337	290 128	149 840	140 288	234 893	149 028	85 865
1995	972 694	985 905	429 089	265 915	163 174	303 750	159 767	143 983	253 066	160 259	92 807
1996	989 987	1 004 425	434 434	271 329	163 105	314 183	165 997	148 186	255 808	161 480	94 328
1993:											
January	839 861	844 228	381 135	236 133	145 002	254 040	123 714	130 326	209 053	131 170	77 883
February	846 785	846 288	381 465	236 970	144 495	256 313	125 402	130 911	208 510	131 256	77 254
March	852 791	851 943	382 476	237 581	144 895	259 665	127 293	132 372	209 802	132 220	77 582
April	857 839	855 118	383 468	237 876	145 592	260 223	127 412	132 811	211 427	132 839	78 588
May	855 063	855 421	384 414	238 308	146 106	260 025	127 420	132 605	210 982	132 718	78 264
June	847 429	857 066	384 898	238 659	146 239	260 643	128 002	132 641	211 525	132 935	78 590
July	849 054	857 318	384 378	238 578	145 800	260 425	127 447	132 978	212 515	133 607	78 908
August	850 905	859 143	384 956	238 782	146 174	259 874	126 916	132 958	214 313	134 617	79 696
September	857 972	861 284	385 233	239 442	145 791	261 516	128 069	133 447	214 535	134 794	79 741
October	880 824	862 383	385 285	239 727	145 558	263 138	129 795	133 343	213 960	135 005	78 955
November	889 776	866 875	385 669	240 079	145 590	265 831	131 801	134 030	215 375	135 403	79 972
December	857 544	867 513	384 138	239 404	144 734	267 497	133 624	133 873	215 878	135 632	80 246
1994:											
January	864 562	868 946	385 351	240 938	144 413	266 600	134 293	132 307	216 995	136 387	80 608
February	873 767	872 958	386 381	241 504	144 877	268 027	134 929	133 098	218 550	137 381	81 169
March	873 793	873 363	386 832	241 519	145 313	269 053	135 179	133 874	217 478	136 327	81 151
April	880 189	877 409	387 667	242 107	145 560	270 682	136 296	134 386	219 060	137 867	81 193
May	887 209	887 465	390 037	243 779	146 258	274 784	138 587	136 197	222 644	140 856	81 788
June	882 657	892 898	391 312	244 791	146 521	278 979	140 977	138 002	222 607	141 255	81 352
July	889 983	898 291	395 438	247 026	148 412	277 595	140 705	136 890	225 258	143 556	81 702
August	897 687	906 279	396 936	248 433	148 503	282 903	145 122	137 781	226 440	143 931	82 509
September	907 410	911 531	397 096	248 563	148 533	286 591	147 538	139 053	227 844	144 833	83 011
October	937 038	917 295	399 162	249 661	149 501	286 993	147 578	139 415	231 140	146 955	84 185
November	947 967	923 142	401 665	251 374	150 291	288 450	148 729	139 721	233 027	147 780	85 247
December	918 291	930 049	405 028	253 691	151 337	290 128	149 840	140 288	234 893	149 028	85 865
1995:											
January	....	940 288	408 718	255 483	153 235	293 944	152 744	141 200	237 626	150 435	87 191
February	947 545	946 330	411 497	256 540	154 957	295 154	153 450	141 704	239 679	152 312	87 367
March	955 195	955 314	414 690	258 114	156 576	297 790	155 835	141 955	242 834	154 255	88 579
April	967 156	963 038	417 710	259 645	158 065	300 260	158 076	142 184	245 068	155 156	89 912
May	968 540	967 732	420 824	261 214	159 610	301 137	158 131	143 006	245 771	156 176	89 595
June	960 991	971 918	422 372	261 514	160 858	301 523	157 889	143 634	248 023	157 420	90 603
July	965 885	974 761	424 804	263 317	161 487	300 022	156 825	143 197	249 935	157 752	92 183
August	968 415	978 377	424 926	263 334	161 592	302 750	158 520	144 230	250 701	157 944	92 757
September	976 732	982 324	427 153	264 316	162 837	303 368	159 205	144 163	251 803	158 768	93 035
October	1 007 307	986 698	428 238	265 694	162 544	305 494	160 613	144 881	252 966	159 533	93 433
November	1 014 480	987 936	427 924	265 507	162 417	307 117	162 107	145 010	252 895	160 120	92 775
December	972 694	985 905	429 089	265 915	163 174	303 750	159 767	143 983	253 066	160 259	92 807
1996:											
January	986 170	990 600	431 192	267 964	163 228	305 094	160 493	144 601	254 314	161 180	93 134
February	993 200	990 843	431 462	268 245	163 217	305 336	160 667	144 669	254 045	161 002	93 043
March	988 633	989 251	431 363	268 392	162 971	303 737	159 306	144 431	254 151	160 700	93 451
April	997 542	993 599	431 352	268 648	162 704	304 635	159 966	144 669	257 612	161 840	95 772
May	993 097	992 630	430 298	268 657	161 641	305 592	160 893	144 699	256 740	160 921	95 819
June	980 412	992 101	429 802	268 294	161 508	306 177	161 528	144 649	256 122	160 820	95 302
July	987 418	996 796	430 543	269 493	161 050	309 786	163 433	146 353	256 467	161 237	95 230
August	989 105	999 357	431 647	270 537	161 110	311 112	164 862	146 250	256 598	161 809	94 789
September	995 092	1 000 431	432 674	270 794	161 880	312 969	166 530	146 439	254 788	162 323	92 465
October	1 026 279	1 004 990	434 038	271 616	162 422	315 281	168 146	147 135	255 671	161 436	94 235
November	1 031 242	1 004 540	435 200	272 198	163 002	313 490	165 865	147 625	255 850	161 764	94 086
December	989 987	1 004 425	434 434	271 329	163 105	314 183	165 997	148 186	255 808	161 480	94 328

1. Data from 1982 forward for manufacturing and from 1980 forward for retail trade are not comparable to earlier periods; see NOTES.

MANUFACTURING AND TRADE INVENTORY-SALES RATIOS
(Seasonally adjusted)

YEAR AND MONTH	Total	Manufacturing			Retail trade			Merchant wholesalers		
		Total	Durable goods industries	Nondurable goods industries	Total	Durable goods stores	Nondurable goods stores	Total	Durable goods establishments	Nondurable goods establishments
1968	.....	.....	.....	.....	.....	.....	.....	.....	.....	.....
1969	.....	.....	.....	.....	.....	.....	.....	.....	.....	.....
1970	.....	.....	.....	.....	.....	.....	.....	.....	.....	.....
1971	.....	.....	.....	.....	.....	.....	.....	.....	.....	.....
1972	.....	.....	.....	.....	.....	.....	.....	.....	.....	.....
1973	.....	.....	.....	.....	.....	.....	.....	.....	.....	.....
1974	.....	.....	.....	.....	.....	.....	.....	.....	.....	.....
1975	.....	.....	.....	.....	.....	.....	.....	.....	.....	.....
1976	.....	.....	.....	.....	.....	.....	.....	.....	.....	.....
1977	.....	.....	.....	.....	.....	.....	.....	.....	.....	.....
1978	.....	.....	.....	.....	.....	.....	.....	.....	.....	.....
1979	.....	.....	.....	.....	.....	.....	.....	.....	.....	.....
1980	.....	.....	.....	.....	.....	.....	.....	.....	.....	.....
1981	.....	.....	.....	.....	.....	.....	.....	.....	.....	.....
1982	.....	.....	.....	.....	.....	.....	.....	.....	.....	.....
1983	.....	.....	.....	.....	.....	.....	.....	.....	.....	.....
1984	.....	.....	.....	.....	.....	.....	.....	.....	.....	.....
1985	.....	.....	.....	.....	.....	.....	.....	.....	.....	.....
1986	.....	.....	.....	.....	.....	.....	.....	.....	.....	.....
1987	.....	.....	.....	.....	.....	.....	.....	.....	.....	.....
1988	.....	.....	.....	.....	.....	.....	.....	.....	.....	.....
1989	.....	.....	.....	.....	.....	.....	.....	.....	.....	.....
1990	.....	.....	.....	.....	.....	.....	.....	.....	.....	.....
1991	.....	.....	.....	.....	.....	.....	.....	.....	.....	.....
1992	.....	.....	.....	.....	.....	.....	.....	.....	.....	.....
1993	.....	.....	.....	.....	.....	.....	.....	.....	.....	.....
1994	.....	.....	.....	.....	.....	.....	.....	.....	.....	.....
1995	.....	.....	.....	.....	.....	.....	.....	.....	.....	.....
1996	.....	.....	.....	.....	.....	.....	.....	.....	.....	.....
1993:										
January	1.44	1.49	1.80	1.16	1.50	1.98	1.22	1.30	1.62	0.97
February	1.44	1.47	1.77	1.15	1.52	2.06	1.22	1.30	1.62	0.97
March	1.45	1.46	1.75	1.15	1.56	2.11	1.25	1.33	1.67	0.98
April	1.45	1.48	1.77	1.16	1.53	2.03	1.24	1.31	1.63	0.98
May	1.45	1.50	1.79	1.18	1.52	2.00	1.23	1.29	1.63	0.96
June	1.44	1.47	1.76	1.16	1.52	2.00	1.23	1.32	1.63	0.99
July	1.45	1.50	1.81	1.17	1.50	1.95	1.23	1.31	1.60	1.00
August	1.45	1.50	1.79	1.18	1.50	1.93	1.23	1.32	1.62	1.01
September	1.44	1.47	1.75	1.17	1.50	1.96	1.23	1.32	1.62	1.00
October	1.43	1.47	1.73	1.17	1.49	1.94	1.22	1.31	1.61	0.99
November	1.43	1.45	1.70	1.17	1.49	1.93	1.22	1.32	1.62	1.00
December	1.43	1.44	1.67	1.17	1.49	1.92	1.22	1.33	1.61	1.03
1994:										
January	1.42	1.44	1.68	1.16	1.50	1.96	1.21	1.32	1.61	1.01
February	1.42	1.44	1.68	1.15	1.48	1.93	1.20	1.32	1.60	1.01
March	1.39	1.41	1.65	1.14	1.46	1.88	1.19	1.28	1.56	0.99
April	1.41	1.42	1.66	1.15	1.48	1.89	1.21	1.30	1.58	1.00
May	1.42	1.42	1.66	1.14	1.50	1.95	1.22	1.32	1.60	1.01
June	1.41	1.41	1.64	1.13	1.51	1.96	1.23	1.30	1.58	0.99
July	1.42	1.43	1.67	1.15	1.50	1.96	1.21	1.30	1.60	0.99
August	1.39	1.39	1.62	1.12	1.51	1.97	1.21	1.28	1.54	0.98
September	1.41	1.40	1.64	1.12	1.52	1.99	1.22	1.29	1.56	0.99
October	1.41	1.41	1.65	1.13	1.51	1.94	1.22	1.29	1.57	0.99
November	1.40	1.39	1.62	1.12	1.51	1.96	1.22	1.30	1.57	1.00
December	1.39	1.38	1.62	1.11	1.52	1.97	1.22	1.28	1.55	0.99
1995:										
January	1.40	1.38	1.60	1.12	1.53	2.01	1.21	1.29	1.56	0.99
February	1.41	1.39	1.62	1.12	1.56	2.05	1.23	1.29	1.57	0.98
March	1.42	1.39	1.61	1.14	1.56	2.06	1.23	1.32	1.60	1.01
April	1.43	1.42	1.66	1.15	1.57	2.10	1.23	1.31	1.61	1.00
May	1.43	1.42	1.65	1.15	1.56	2.07	1.23	1.31	1.59	1.00
June	1.42	1.41	1.64	1.15	1.55	2.04	1.23	1.31	1.59	1.00
July	1.44	1.44	1.69	1.17	1.54	2.03	1.22	1.32	1.62	1.01
August	1.42	1.41	1.63	1.15	1.55	2.01	1.23	1.32	1.60	1.02
September	1.43	1.41	1.63	1.16	1.56	2.05	1.23	1.32	1.60	1.02
October	1.43	1.42	1.64	1.16	1.57	2.06	1.24	1.32	1.61	1.01
November	1.43	1.41	1.63	1.16	1.56	2.05	1.23	1.31	1.59	1.00
December	1.41	1.41	1.63	1.16	1.53	2.00	1.22	1.28	1.56	0.99
1996:										
January	1.43	1.44	1.67	1.16	1.54	2.02	1.22	1.30	1.60	0.99
February	1.42	1.42	1.65	1.16	1.52	1.96	1.21	1.30	1.59	0.99
March	1.41	1.43	1.67	1.16	1.51	1.93	1.21	1.29	1.57	0.98
April	1.40	1.39	1.62	1.13	1.50	1.96	1.20	1.29	1.57	0.99
May	1.38	1.37	1.59	1.12	1.50	1.93	1.20	1.28	1.55	0.99
June	1.39	1.39	1.60	1.13	1.51	1.96	1.20	1.28	1.56	0.98
July	1.38	1.37	1.60	1.11	1.52	1.98	1.21	1.26	1.54	0.95
August	1.39	1.38	1.60	1.11	1.53	2.00	1.21	1.27	1.57	0.96
September	1.38	1.37	1.58	1.12	1.53	2.00	1.20	1.25	1.55	0.93
October	1.38	1.37	1.60	1.10	1.53	2.00	1.20	1.25	1.54	0.94
November	1.37	1.36	1.59	1.10	1.52	1.99	1.21	1.24	1.53	0.94
December	1.38	1.37	1.60	1.11	1.52	1.98	1.20	1.24	1.54	0.94

REAL MANUFACTURING AND TRADE SALES AND INVENTORIES

YEAR AND MONTH	Billions of chained (1992) dollars, seasonally adjusted								Inventory-sales ratios (Based on chained (1992) dollars)			
	Sales				Inventories (Book value, end of period)							
	Total	Manufac-turing	Retail trade	Merchant whole-salers	Total	Manufac-turing	Retail trade	Merchant whole-salers	Total	Manufac-turing	Retail trade	Merchant whole-salers
1968	310.0	162.3	85.8	63.0	412.5	245.0	95.8	66.9	....	....	....	....
1969	320.0	166.6	88.5	66.0	435.4	256.0	102.3	72.3	....	....	....	....
1970	316.0	158.6	90.5	67.6	442.1	256.0	102.4	79.6	....	....	....	....
1971	330.6	162.9	96.7	71.4	458.3	253.1	116.1	85.8	....	....	....	....
1972	359.8	178.1	104.9	77.4	478.8	259.8	124.9	90.9	....	....	....	....
1973	389.8	192.4	110.3	87.4	509.4	277.7	134.8	93.4	....	....	....	....
1974	387.5	187.9	105.2	93.9	536.1	296.8	132.9	102.3	....	....	....	....
1975	359.1	169.0	105.9	84.5	516.8	289.7	126.4	96.6	....	....	....	....
1976	385.2	184.5	112.8	88.2	547.2	303.4	136.0	103.7	....	....	....	....
1977	412.1	199.4	118.2	94.6	573.7	311.8	143.7	114.5	....	....	....	....
1978	437.7	208.9	124.0	104.6	609.5	325.8	153.1	127.2	....	....	....	....
1979	448.1	211.6	126.1	110.0	629.3	338.5	153.1	133.8	....	....	....	....
1980	434.3	199.7	121.5	112.3	631.9	338.9	148.9	140.1	....	....	....	....
1981	437.0	201.1	122.0	113.0	647.8	343.5	157.2	143.5	....	....	....	....
1982	419.1	191.6	120.8	106.5	628.1	329.5	153.3	142.1	....	....	....	....
1983	439.7	200.5	129.8	109.5	639.5	329.5	166.2	141.9	....	....	....	....
1984	476.6	216.5	139.1	121.0	703.1	358.4	186.4	156.2	....	....	....	....
1985	490.4	220.4	145.2	124.9	718.7	353.9	201.3	162.5	....	....	....	....
1986	509.3	224.3	153.2	131.9	724.6	349.7	204.4	169.7	....	....	....	....
1987	528.0	234.1	157.6	136.4	755.9	354.8	223.9	177.0	....	....	....	....
1988	551.6	244.6	164.1	143.0	780.8	364.3	231.3	185.2	....	....	....	....
1989	561.3	246.6	167.7	147.0	817.6	383.5	245.0	189.2	....	....	....	....
1990	563.0	245.9	168.7	148.4	830.1	390.1	243.5	196.3	....	....	....	....
1991	554.2	241.8	164.5	147.9	829.2	384.0	243.3	201.9	....	....	....	....
1992	573.7	250.3	169.8	153.6	831.7	374.7	247.2	209.8	....	....	....	....
1993	594.7	256.8	177.5	160.4	859.1	380.9	263.0	215.1	....	....	....	....
1994	628.0	271.3	187.5	169.1	901.0	392.0	279.9	229.1	....	....	....	....
1995	651.9	281.0	192.5	178.5	928.1	399.8	288.6	239.7	....	....	....	....
1996	678.4	292.4	199.6	186.4	945.2	409.7	292.7	242.9	....	....	....	....
1993:												
January	590.7	254.6	175.4	160.6	837.1	374.2	248.9	211.1	1.42	1.47	1.42	1.32
February	589.3	256.6	173.6	159.1	840.6	375.0	252.7	210.3	1.43	1.46	1.46	1.32
March	586.1	258.1	171.4	156.3	846.1	376.1	256.5	211.2	1.44	1.46	1.50	1.35
April	587.7	254.3	175.2	158.7	848.3	376.8	257.0	212.4	1.44	1.48	1.47	1.34
May	588.9	252.8	176.5	160.1	848.2	377.6	257.0	211.8	1.44	1.49	1.46	1.32
June	594.3	257.6	177.0	160.1	850.5	378.4	258.0	212.5	1.43	1.47	1.46	1.33
July	591.0	251.7	178.5	161.3	851.3	378.5	258.0	213.6	1.44	1.50	1.45	1.33
August	594.5	253.8	178.4	162.2	851.5	379.6	255.7	215.3	1.43	1.50	1.43	1.33
September	599.2	258.1	178.8	162.3	855.8	380.5	259.6	215.0	1.43	1.47	1.45	1.33
October	601.9	258.8	180.1	162.5	855.7	381.1	260.0	214.1	1.42	1.47	1.44	1.32
November	604.9	261.4	181.5	161.8	859.1	381.6	262.1	215.2	1.42	1.46	1.44	1.33
December	607.7	263.8	183.1	160.2	859.1	380.9	263.0	215.1	1.41	1.44	1.44	1.34
1994:												
January	607.1	263.1	181.9	162.5	861.3	382.7	263.0	215.7	1.42	1.46	1.45	1.33
February	612.9	264.4	184.8	164.0	865.0	384.2	264.2	216.7	1.41	1.45	1.43	1.32
March	622.5	267.9	187.5	167.0	866.1	384.7	266.2	215.5	1.39	1.44	1.42	1.29
April	619.5	267.4	186.5	166.2	868.3	385.2	266.3	217.1	1.40	1.44	1.43	1.31
May	621.0	269.3	185.8	166.3	876.4	386.9	269.3	220.5	1.41	1.44	1.45	1.33
June	625.9	271.3	186.9	167.8	879.9	387.3	272.7	220.1	1.41	1.43	1.46	1.31
July	623.3	268.9	186.3	168.4	883.7	389.4	272.4	222.1	1.42	1.45	1.46	1.32
August	637.8	277.2	188.5	172.3	887.2	390.3	274.5	222.6	1.39	1.41	1.46	1.29
September	635.3	274.5	188.8	171.4	888.8	389.6	275.8	223.6	1.40	1.42	1.46	1.30
October	638.2	272.4	191.4	174.3	893.6	390.3	277.0	226.4	1.40	1.43	1.45	1.30
November	643.8	278.1	191.3	173.9	896.3	390.2	278.3	227.8	1.39	1.40	1.46	1.31
December	648.3	281.6	190.9	175.1	901.0	392.0	279.9	229.1	1.39	1.39	1.47	1.31
1995:												
January	650.2	282.3	192.3	176.2	906.9	393.2	282.6	231.0	1.40	1.39	1.47	1.31
February	648.7	281.3	188.9	177.6	908.3	392.6	283.5	232.1	1.40	1.40	1.50	1.31
March	647.1	281.1	189.9	175.4	911.8	393.1	284.5	234.0	1.41	1.40	1.50	1.33
April	641.8	276.7	189.8	175.3	915.2	393.7	286.4	235.0	1.43	1.42	1.51	1.34
May	646.0	278.1	191.6	176.3	916.1	394.5	286.9	234.6	1.42	1.42	1.50	1.33
June	651.6	279.9	193.0	178.5	919.5	395.1	288.2	236.1	1.41	1.41	1.49	1.32
July	643.8	273.9	192.7	177.4	921.7	396.8	287.4	237.4	1.43	1.45	1.49	1.34
August	655.1	282.6	194.0	178.8	922.3	395.7	288.8	237.7	1.41	1.40	1.49	1.33
September	656.0	283.6	193.3	178.8	925.1	397.8	288.7	238.5	1.41	1.40	1.49	1.33
October	655.9	282.5	192.9	180.6	929.5	399.1	290.8	239.6	1.42	1.41	1.51	1.33
November	660.8	283.9	195.0	182.4	929.5	398.4	291.6	239.5	1.41	1.40	1.50	1.31
December	666.0	286.2	196.0	184.4	928.1	399.8	288.6	239.7	1.39	1.40	1.47	1.30
1996:												
January	659.9	283.4	195.1	181.6	931.2	402.6	287.9	240.8	1.41	1.42	1.48	1.33
February	668.6	286.3	198.5	183.2	931.2	402.4	288.3	240.5	1.39	1.41	1.45	1.31
March	667.9	286.2	198.6	182.7	928.7	402.9	285.5	240.3	1.39	1.41	1.44	1.32
April	674.0	291.9	198.4	183.7	933.1	403.1	287.0	243.0	1.38	1.38	1.45	1.32
May	677.7	293.6	200.1	184.2	931.9	402.7	287.5	241.7	1.38	1.37	1.44	1.31
June	675.2	291.3	199.4	184.8	931.8	403.0	287.4	241.4	1.38	1.38	1.44	1.31
July	681.7	294.4	199.7	187.8	936.7	404.5	291.0	241.3	1.37	1.37	1.46	1.29
August	680.0	294.0	199.7	186.0	937.7	405.3	291.0	241.5	1.38	1.38	1.46	1.30
September	683.8	295.5	200.9	187.4	939.1	406.6	292.4	240.1	1.37	1.38	1.46	1.28
October	688.1	296.1	202.0	189.9	942.6	408.4	292.9	241.3	1.37	1.38	1.45	1.27
November	692.3	299.2	201.2	191.9	945.4	410.2	292.9	242.2	1.37	1.37	1.46	1.26
December	691.5	296.5	202.0	192.9	945.2	409.7	292.7	242.9	1.37	1.38	1.45	1.26

BUSINESS SALES, INVENTORIES, AND INVESTMENT

PRIVATE FIXED INVESTMENT BY TYPE
(Gross private domestic fixed investment—Billions of dollars, quarterly data are at seasonally adjusted annual rates)

YEAR AND QUARTER	Total	Nonresidential												
		Total	Structures					Producers' durable equipment						
			Total	Nonresidential buildings, including farm	Utilities	Mining exploration, shafts, and wells	Other structures	Total	Information processing and related equipment			Industrial equipment	Transportation and related equipment	Other
									Total	Computers and peripheral equipment [1]	Other			
1968	130.8	92.1	33.6	21.1	9.2	2.6	0.8	58.5	10.6	1.9	8.6	17.2	17.6	13.1
1969	145.5	102.9	37.7	24.4	9.6	2.8	0.9	65.2	12.9	2.4	10.4	18.9	18.9	14.5
1970	148.1	106.7	40.3	25.4	11.1	2.8	1.0	66.4	14.3	2.7	11.6	20.2	16.2	15.6
1971	167.5	111.7	42.7	27.1	11.9	2.7	1.0	69.1	14.9	2.8	12.1	19.4	18.4	16.4
1972	195.7	126.1	47.2	30.1	13.1	3.1	0.9	78.9	16.5	3.5	13.1	21.3	21.8	19.2
1973	225.4	150.0	55.0	35.5	15.0	3.5	1.0	95.1	19.8	3.5	16.3	25.9	26.6	22.8
1974	231.5	165.6	61.2	38.3	16.5	5.2	1.2	104.3	22.9	3.9	19.0	30.5	26.3	22.8
1975	231.7	169.0	61.4	35.6	17.1	7.4	1.3	107.6	23.5	3.6	19.9	31.1	25.2	27.9
1976	269.6	187.2	65.9	35.9	20.0	8.6	1.4	121.2	27.2	4.4	22.8	33.9	30.0	30.1
1977	333.5	223.2	74.6	39.9	21.5	11.5	1.8	148.7	33.1	5.7	27.5	39.2	39.3	37.1
1978	403.6	272.0	91.4	49.7	24.1	15.4	2.2	180.6	41.8	7.6	34.2	47.4	47.3	44.2
1979	464.0	323.0	114.9	65.7	27.5	19.0	2.6	208.1	49.9	10.2	39.8	55.8	53.6	48.7
1980	473.5	350.3	133.9	73.7	30.2	27.4	2.6	216.4	58.9	12.5	46.4	60.4	48.4	48.7
1981	528.1	405.4	164.6	86.3	33.0	42.5	2.8	240.9	69.5	17.1	52.3	65.2	50.6	55.7
1982	515.6	409.9	175.0	94.5	32.5	44.8	3.2	234.9	72.7	18.9	53.9	62.2	46.8	53.1
1983	552.0	399.4	152.7	90.5	28.7	30.0	3.5	246.7	82.0	23.9	58.1	58.2	53.7	52.7
1984	648.1	468.3	176.0	110.0	30.0	31.3	4.7	292.3	98.6	31.6	67.0	67.4	64.8	61.4
1985	688.9	502.0	193.3	128.0	30.6	27.9	6.8	308.7	104.2	33.7	70.5	71.7	69.7	63.0
1986	712.9	494.8	175.8	123.3	31.2	15.7	5.7	319.0	108.8	33.4	75.4	74.6	71.8	63.8
1987	722.9	495.4	172.1	126.0	26.5	13.1	6.5	323.3	109.8	35.8	74.0	75.9	70.4	67.2
1988	763.1	530.6	181.3	133.3	27.1	15.7	5.2	349.3	118.2	38.1	80.1	82.9	76.0	72.3
1989	797.5	566.2	192.3	142.7	29.4	14.4	6.0	373.9	127.1	43.3	83.8	91.5	75.5	84.1
1990	791.6	575.9	200.8	148.9	27.5	17.5	6.9	375.1	124.2	38.9	85.2	89.8	75.5	85.6
1991	738.5	547.3	181.7	126.1	31.6	17.1	6.9	365.6	122.6	38.1	84.5	86.4	79.5	77.1
1992	783.4	557.9	169.2	113.2	34.5	13.3	8.2	388.7	134.2	43.9	90.2	89.3	86.2	79.0
1993	855.7	604.1	176.4	119.2	32.8	16.6	7.8	427.7	141.6	48.6	93.0	97.9	99.9	88.3
1994	946.6	660.6	184.5	128.7	32.0	16.7	7.1	476.1	152.1	51.8	100.3	109.3	118.6	96.2
1995	1 008.1	723.0	200.6	143.8	33.2	16.3	7.3	522.4	172.8	65.6	107.2	121.5	125.7	102.4
1996	1 090.7	781.4	215.2	159.8	33.3	16.1	6.2	566.2	195.1	78.7	116.3	127.5	134.5	109.1
1988:														
1st quarter	744.3	515.9	177.4	130.6	26.1	15.3	5.3	338.5	114.3	36.7	77.6	78.4	74.5	71.3
2nd quarter	760.9	529.4	182.5	134.5	26.3	16.5	5.3	346.9	117.7	37.8	79.9	81.9	75.5	71.7
3rd quarter	766.8	533.2	181.9	133.6	27.7	15.7	4.9	351.3	119.3	38.7	80.6	84.5	74.9	72.6
4th quarter	780.3	543.7	183.3	134.6	28.2	15.2	5.3	360.4	121.3	39.0	82.3	86.7	79.0	73.4
1989:														
1st quarter	790.1	553.0	188.3	140.0	29.6	13.1	5.5	364.7	122.6	41.2	81.4	90.0	71.7	80.4
2nd quarter	794.2	562.0	188.0	138.3	29.6	14.4	5.7	374.0	127.7	44.0	83.7	91.2	72.3	82.7
3rd quarter	808.1	579.0	196.4	146.6	29.0	15.0	5.9	382.5	129.6	44.5	85.1	93.3	72.5	87.1
4th quarter	797.5	570.9	196.6	145.7	29.2	14.9	6.7	374.3	128.4	43.4	85.0	91.5	68.1	86.2
1990:														
1st quarter	813.9	581.2	201.9	150.8	27.0	16.8	7.3	379.3	127.8	41.3	86.5	91.7	74.0	85.8
2nd quarter	794.0	571.6	202.4	151.2	27.0	17.6	6.7	369.2	123.9	38.9	85.0	88.9	71.4	84.9
3rd quarter	791.2	580.3	203.5	151.4	27.5	17.6	7.0	376.7	121.5	36.8	84.7	90.3	78.5	86.4
4th quarter	767.5	570.6	195.4	142.1	28.4	18.1	6.8	375.1	123.4	38.6	84.7	88.1	78.3	85.4
1991:														
1st quarter	739.7	555.4	192.3	136.4	30.0	19.4	6.6	363.1	119.3	36.7	82.7	87.8	78.1	77.8
2nd quarter	736.2	550.2	187.6	130.9	31.3	18.9	6.6	362.6	121.6	37.2	84.5	86.4	77.3	77.2
3rd quarter	738.6	544.3	176.1	121.4	32.3	15.2	7.1	368.2	123.5	37.8	85.6	86.3	81.9	76.5
4th quarter	739.5	539.2	170.8	115.7	33.0	15.0	7.2	368.4	125.9	40.7	85.2	85.2	80.6	76.8
1992:														
1st quarter	755.4	544.1	171.6	117.2	34.3	12.8	7.3	372.5	129.2	41.9	87.3	86.2	79.5	77.6
2nd quarter	780.5	556.8	170.4	114.0	34.8	13.3	8.4	386.3	133.0	44.4	88.6	87.7	87.8	77.7
3rd quarter	788.1	561.0	167.6	110.6	34.7	13.3	9.0	393.4	137.7	44.6	93.1	90.5	85.5	79.7
4th quarter	809.7	569.6	167.1	111.0	34.2	13.8	8.1	402.5	136.8	44.9	91.9	92.8	91.9	81.1
1993:														
1st quarter	823.5	580.5	171.7	113.6	33.8	16.0	8.3	408.9	137.2	47.1	90.1	94.0	92.9	84.7
2nd quarter	842.9	598.8	175.2	117.6	32.7	16.8	8.1	423.6	138.1	47.1	91.0	95.4	102.9	87.3
3rd quarter	858.8	606.4	177.8	121.5	32.2	16.8	7.3	428.6	145.0	49.8	95.2	98.1	96.4	89.0
4th quarter	897.5	630.6	180.7	124.2	32.5	16.6	7.5	449.9	146.0	50.5	95.5	104.1	107.5	92.2
1994:														
1st quarter	911.0	634.6	175.4	120.7	32.1	15.7	6.8	459.3	147.6	49.9	97.7	105.4	113.1	93.3
2nd quarter	941.7	652.9	185.2	130.9	31.6	15.8	6.9	467.7	149.4	50.6	98.8	107.0	115.5	95.8
3rd quarter	956.9	667.4	186.8	130.0	32.0	17.0	7.7	480.6	152.8	51.5	101.2	110.8	119.8	97.3
4th quarter	977.0	687.5	190.7	133.2	32.4	18.1	7.0	496.8	158.5	55.1	103.4	114.0	126.1	98.3
1995:														
1st quarter	998.7	710.9	197.7	138.9	33.2	18.3	7.2	513.2	162.9	57.3	105.6	118.1	129.9	102.3
2nd quarter	999.6	722.5	201.1	144.1	33.5	16.1	7.4	521.4	173.0	64.7	108.3	123.0	123.6	101.8
3rd quarter	1 009.4	725.4	202.8	145.6	33.5	15.8	7.9	522.6	174.3	67.0	107.3	123.0	122.9	102.5
4th quarter	1 024.6	733.1	200.7	146.4	32.7	15.0	6.5	532.4	181.1	73.5	107.6	121.8	126.4	103.1
1996:														
1st quarter	1 049.4	750.7	205.7	149.8	33.4	15.7	6.7	545.0	188.0	76.4	111.6	124.7	127.1	105.3
2nd quarter	1 082.0	769.3	210.6	155.5	32.9	16.0	6.1	558.7	190.9	76.8	114.1	129.2	130.8	107.9
3rd quarter	1 112.0	798.6	217.7	162.5	32.7	16.5	6.0	580.9	201.1	80.9	120.3	128.2	140.0	111.5
4th quarter	1 119.2	807.2	227.0	171.2	34.1	16.0	5.8	580.2	200.3	81.0	119.3	127.9	140.1	111.9

1. New computers and peripheral equipment only.

YEAR AND QUARTER	PRIVATE FIXED INVESTMENT BY TYPE—Continued (Gross private domestic fixed investment—Billions of dollars, quarterly data are at seasonally adjusted annual rates)						REAL PRIVATE FIXED INVESTMENT BY TYPE (Gross private domestic fixed investment—Billions of chained (1992) dollars, quarterly data are at seasonally adjusted annual rates)						
	Residential							Nonresidential					
		Structures				Producers durable equipment	Total		Structures				
	Total	Total	Single family	Multi-family	Other structures			Total	Total	Nonresidential buildings, including farm	Utilities	Mining exploration, shafts, and wells	Other structures
1968	38.7	37.9	19.5	7.2	11.1	0.9	418.1	266.4	134.1	86.2	33.3	10.0	3.1
1969	42.6	41.6	19.7	9.5	12.4	1.0	442.9	285.6	141.3	92.7	33.4	10.4	3.4
1970	41.4	40.2	17.5	9.5	13.2	1.1	432.1	282.8	141.7	91.1	35.7	9.8	3.6
1971	55.8	54.5	25.8	12.9	15.8	1.3	464.9	282.4	139.4	89.4	36.1	9.1	3.2
1972	69.7	68.1	32.8	17.2	18.0	1.5	520.3	307.7	143.7	91.8	37.6	9.7	2.8
1973	75.3	73.6	35.2	19.4	19.0	1.7	567.5	352.5	155.4	100.3	40.0	10.4	2.9
1974	66.0	64.1	29.7	13.7	20.7	1.9	530.2	354.4	152.2	97.6	37.6	12.4	2.9
1975	62.7	60.8	29.6	6.7	24.5	1.9	471.0	317.3	136.2	82.5	34.4	14.4	2.8
1976	82.5	80.4	43.9	6.9	29.6	2.1	517.6	332.0	139.6	80.6	38.0	15.6	2.8
1977	110.3	107.9	62.2	10.0	35.7	2.4	593.7	371.8	146.4	83.6	38.2	18.1	3.5
1978	131.6	128.9	72.8	12.8	43.3	2.7	660.8	422.6	162.3	95.3	40.0	20.0	4.0
1979	141.0	137.9	72.3	17.0	48.6	3.2	695.6	463.3	182.7	113.5	41.3	21.3	4.5
1980	123.2	119.9	53.0	16.7	50.2	3.4	648.4	461.1	195.0	114.4	41.3	30.0	3.9
1981	122.6	119.0	52.0	17.5	49.5	3.6	660.6	485.7	210.4	122.8	42.0	34.9	3.8
1982	105.7	102.0	41.5	15.5	45.0	3.7	610.4	464.3	207.2	126.6	39.5	32.2	4.0
1983	152.5	148.3	72.2	22.4	53.7	4.2	654.2	456.4	185.8	117.6	34.2	26.7	4.3
1984	179.8	175.1	85.6	28.2	61.3	4.7	762.4	535.4	212.2	137.6	35.4	30.3	5.8
1985	186.9	181.9	86.1	28.5	67.2	5.1	799.3	568.5	227.8	155.2	35.6	27.0	8.3
1986	218.1	212.6	102.2	31.0	79.4	5.5	805.0	548.5	203.3	144.5	36.5	15.8	6.6
1987	227.6	221.8	114.5	25.5	81.9	5.8	799.5	542.4	195.9	142.4	30.7	15.5	7.3
1988	232.5	226.4	116.6	22.3	87.5	6.1	818.3	566.0	196.9	145.3	30.0	15.8	5.7
1989	231.3	225.1	116.9	22.3	85.9	6.2	832.0	588.8	201.2	150.2	30.9	13.9	6.4
1990	215.7	209.7	108.7	19.3	81.7	6.1	805.8	585.2	203.3	152.0	28.1	16.1	7.2
1991	191.2	185.4	95.4	15.1	74.8	5.8	741.3	547.7	181.6	126.9	32.0	15.7	6.9
1992	225.6	219.5	116.5	13.1	89.9	6.0	783.4	557.9	169.2	113.2	34.5	13.3	8.2
1993	251.6	245.2	133.3	10.8	101.1	6.4	842.8	600.2	170.8	115.3	31.8	16.0	7.7
1994	286.0	279.1	153.8	14.1	111.2	6.9	915.5	648.4	172.5	119.9	29.9	15.8	6.9
1995	285.1	277.8	145.2	17.9	114.8	7.2	962.1	706.5	179.9	128.8	30.0	14.3	6.7
1996	309.2	301.7	159.1	20.3	122.3	7.5	1 041.7	771.7	188.7	140.0	29.3	13.9	5.5
1988:													
1st quarter	228.4	222.5	114.5	23.1	84.9	5.9	807.1	556.1	195.9	144.0	29.7	16.3	5.9
2nd quarter	231.4	225.3	116.1	21.7	87.5	6.1	819.0	567.1	199.1	147.2	29.4	16.7	5.8
3rd quarter	233.6	227.4	116.2	21.9	89.3	6.1	820.6	568.0	196.4	145.1	30.5	15.5	5.3
4th quarter	236.6	230.3	119.8	22.4	88.1	6.2	826.4	572.9	195.9	144.9	30.6	14.7	5.8
1989:													
1st quarter	237.2	230.9	121.3	22.6	87.0	6.2	831.9	579.5	199.8	149.5	31.7	12.9	6.0
2nd quarter	232.2	226.0	117.7	23.1	85.2	6.2	830.9	586.6	197.2	145.9	31.3	14.0	6.2
3rd quarter	229.1	223.0	114.5	22.8	85.7	6.1	840.6	600.5	204.6	153.7	30.3	14.5	6.3
4th quarter	226.6	220.4	114.2	20.7	85.6	6.2	824.7	588.8	203.2	151.7	30.2	14.4	7.1
1990:													
1st quarter	232.7	226.4	120.2	20.0	86.2	6.2	834.7	595.4	206.5	155.4	27.7	15.8	7.7
2nd quarter	222.4	216.3	113.5	19.5	83.3	6.1	811.2	583.4	205.5	154.7	27.6	16.3	6.9
3rd quarter	210.9	204.9	104.7	19.2	81.0	6.0	803.1	588.1	205.2	153.8	28.1	16.1	7.2
4th quarter	196.9	191.0	96.5	18.3	76.2	6.0	774.4	573.9	196.0	143.9	28.9	16.3	6.9
1991:													
1st quarter	184.3	178.5	87.7	17.3	73.4	5.8	742.6	555.1	192.2	137.6	30.4	17.3	6.7
2nd quarter	185.9	180.0	89.8	15.3	75.0	5.9	739.4	550.9	187.2	131.7	31.7	17.0	6.6
3rd quarter	194.3	188.4	100.4	14.0	74.0	5.9	741.0	545.3	175.5	121.8	32.6	14.0	7.1
4th quarter	200.3	194.5	103.9	14.0	76.7	5.7	742.0	539.5	171.5	116.4	33.4	14.5	7.2
1992:													
1st quarter	211.3	205.4	108.8	13.1	83.4	6.0	758.3	544.4	172.7	118.1	34.6	12.7	7.3
2nd quarter	223.7	217.7	115.7	15.1	86.9	6.0	782.4	557.5	171.0	114.4	34.9	13.3	8.4
3rd quarter	227.1	221.1	117.9	12.5	90.7	6.1	787.3	560.6	167.4	110.4	34.6	13.4	9.0
4th quarter	240.1	233.9	123.6	11.6	98.6	6.2	805.8	569.1	165.6	109.8	33.9	13.7	8.1
1993:													
1st quarter	243.0	236.7	127.5	10.6	98.7	6.3	814.8	577.8	168.0	111.3	33.4	15.2	8.2
2nd quarter	244.1	237.7	128.5	10.3	98.9	6.4	831.1	595.1	170.3	114.4	31.7	16.2	8.0
3rd quarter	252.4	245.9	133.7	11.2	101.0	6.6	844.5	602.3	171.7	117.1	31.0	16.4	7.2
4th quarter	266.8	260.3	143.4	11.0	105.8	6.6	880.8	625.6	173.1	118.5	31.0	16.2	7.4
1994:													
1st quarter	276.4	269.7	150.4	11.7	107.6	6.6	887.8	626.2	166.3	114.3	30.3	15.1	6.7
2nd quarter	288.7	281.9	156.9	13.3	111.6	6.9	913.2	641.2	174.5	123.1	29.6	15.1	6.7
3rd quarter	289.5	282.5	155.0	15.1	112.4	7.0	922.7	653.2	174.0	120.6	29.8	16.2	7.4
4th quarter	289.5	282.3	153.0	16.2	113.1	7.2	938.5	672.9	175.0	121.8	29.8	16.7	6.7
1995:													
1st quarter	287.8	280.6	149.5	17.3	113.8	7.2	955.8	695.7	179.0	125.5	30.4	16.3	6.8
2nd quarter	277.1	269.9	140.5	17.2	112.3	7.1	954.0	705.4	180.9	129.4	30.4	14.2	6.8
3rd quarter	284.0	276.7	142.5	18.2	115.9	7.3	962.3	708.2	181.2	130.1	30.1	13.8	7.3
4th quarter	291.4	284.1	148.3	18.8	117.1	7.3	976.3	716.8	178.6	130.3	29.2	13.1	5.9
1996:													
1st quarter	298.8	291.5	153.4	20.2	117.9	7.3	1 001.5	736.9	182.1	132.7	29.7	13.6	6.0
2nd quarter	312.7	305.2	160.2	21.7	123.2	7.5	1 035.7	759.7	185.6	137.0	29.1	13.9	5.4
3rd quarter	313.5	305.9	162.2	19.2	124.5	7.5	1 060.9	789.3	190.0	141.7	28.7	14.1	5.4
4th quarter	312.0	304.4	160.6	20.1	123.7	7.6	1 068.7	800.8	196.9	148.4	29.5	13.8	5.1

REAL PRIVATE FIXED INVESTMENT BY TYPE—Continued
(Gross private domestic fixed investment—Billions of chained (1992) dollars, quarterly data are at seasonally adjusted annual rates)

YEAR AND QUARTER	Gross private domestic fixed investment												
	Nonresidential—Continued							Residential					
	Producers' durable equipment												
	Information processing and related equipment			Industrial equipment	Transportation and related equipment	Other		Total	Structures				Producers' durable equipment
	Total	Total	Computers and peripheral equipment [1]	Other						Total	Single family	Multi-family	Other structures	
1968	140.5	8.0	0.0	19.5	68.1	58.2	50.2	154.0	153.2	75.9	30.1	46.2	1.7
1969	152.2	9.7	0.1	22.8	72.6	60.5	53.5	158.6	157.4	72.1	37.5	47.3	2.0
1970	149.5	10.7	0.1	24.5	73.7	49.7	55.7	149.1	147.4	62.6	36.7	47.8	2.1
1971	150.7	11.4	0.1	24.7	67.7	53.6	55.7	190.0	188.4	86.9	46.7	54.3	2.4
1972	169.8	12.9	0.2	26.0	73.0	62.3	63.4	223.8	221.8	103.3	58.5	59.5	2.9
1973	201.2	15.4	0.2	31.7	86.2	75.0	73.8	222.3	219.8	101.1	60.1	58.2	3.2
1974	205.4	17.5	0.2	34.8	92.8	67.9	73.3	176.4	173.2	77.6	38.7	56.7	3.3
1975	183.9	16.9	0.2	33.3	78.6	58.5	68.2	153.5	150.4	70.8	17.3	61.4	3.1
1976	195.2	19.5	0.3	36.6	79.0	65.0	68.7	189.7	186.7	98.6	16.7	69.6	3.2
1977	225.6	24.1	0.5	43.8	83.6	79.1	77.7	229.8	226.8	126.2	21.9	76.3	3.5
1978	259.6	31.7	1.0	52.4	93.0	87.3	85.5	245.0	241.7	130.9	25.0	83.4	3.8
1979	280.7	38.6	1.5	59.5	99.8	91.0	86.2	236.0	232.2	116.0	30.5	84.2	4.2
1980	268.2	45.4	2.4	64.9	95.5	74.2	76.8	186.1	182.0	76.3	27.3	78.6	4.2
1981	278.2	52.5	3.8	68.5	94.1	72.0	78.9	171.2	167.0	69.5	26.3	71.6	4.2
1982	260.3	54.5	4.7	67.0	85.5	63.7	70.2	140.1	135.9	53.2	21.4	61.8	4.0
1983	272.4	63.4	7.1	70.4	78.5	71.7	68.0	197.6	193.2	92.0	29.3	71.7	4.5
1984	324.6	79.8	11.6	79.0	89.9	85.1	77.9	226.4	221.6	106.2	35.8	79.2	5.0
1985	342.4	88.0	14.5	81.9	94.1	88.4	78.3	229.5	224.2	104.8	34.9	84.3	5.4
1986	345.9	94.1	16.7	84.6	93.5	85.6	76.8	257.0	251.3	119.3	35.9	95.8	5.8
1987	346.9	97.5	21.0	80.2	91.1	82.1	79.0	257.6	251.6	128.3	28.3	94.8	6.1
1988	369.2	106.6	24.0	85.7	95.3	87.1	82.4	252.5	246.3	126.1	23.4	96.8	6.3
1989	387.6	116.2	29.4	88.1	101.5	78.9	92.3	243.3	237.0	121.9	23.3	91.8	6.3
1990	381.9	116.2	29.4	88.2	95.0	81.2	90.5	220.6	214.5	110.4	19.7	84.4	6.1
1991	366.2	117.8	32.5	86.0	88.3	81.7	78.8	193.4	187.6	96.4	15.4	75.7	5.9
1992	388.7	134.2	44.0	90.2	89.3	86.2	79.0	225.6	219.5	116.5	13.1	89.9	6.1
1993	429.6	147.9	56.1	92.3	96.5	98.3	86.8	242.6	236.2	127.1	10.6	98.6	6.4
1994	476.8	165.1	67.2	99.4	105.5	113.2	92.9	267.0	260.3	140.1	13.6	106.5	6.7
1995	528.3	201.8	102.8	107.0	113.4	118.9	97.0	257.0	250.0	126.9	16.9	106.7	7.0
1996	586.0	253.1	160.8	116.3	117.0	125.0	100.8	272.1	265.0	136.6	18.6	110.2	7.1
1988:													
1st quarter	360.3	102.1	22.5	83.0	91.5	87.0	82.4	251.3	245.2	124.9	24.5	95.7	6.2
2nd quarter	368.0	106.4	23.8	85.8	94.3	87.3	82.1	252.2	246.0	126.1	22.8	97.1	6.3
3rd quarter	371.6	108.3	24.7	86.6	97.2	85.3	82.7	252.9	246.6	125.4	22.9	98.4	6.3
4th quarter	377.0	109.7	25.1	87.5	98.1	88.9	82.4	253.7	247.4	128.0	23.3	96.1	6.4
1989:													
1st quarter	379.7	110.7	26.9	85.8	101.0	80.5	89.6	252.6	246.2	128.3	23.7	94.2	6.4
2nd quarter	389.4	116.6	29.8	88.1	102.0	80.5	91.5	244.3	238.0	122.6	24.0	91.4	6.4
3rd quarter	395.9	118.6	30.5	89.3	103.2	80.3	95.0	240.1	233.9	118.8	23.8	91.3	6.2
4th quarter	385.6	118.7	30.7	89.1	100.0	74.3	93.3	236.0	229.7	117.9	21.6	90.2	6.3
1990:													
1st quarter	388.8	119.2	30.6	89.8	98.6	80.3	91.6	239.4	233.1	122.8	20.6	89.7	6.3
2nd quarter	377.8	116.1	29.3	88.3	94.8	77.4	90.4	227.8	221.7	115.4	20.0	86.3	6.2
3rd quarter	383.0	113.9	27.9	87.6	95.1	84.3	91.0	214.9	208.8	105.8	19.5	83.6	6.1
4th quarter	377.9	115.8	29.9	87.1	91.4	82.8	88.8	200.3	194.4	97.6	18.6	78.1	6.0
1991:													
1st quarter	362.9	112.5	29.2	84.3	89.7	81.3	80.1	187.4	181.5	88.8	17.7	75.0	5.9
2nd quarter	363.8	116.2	30.8	86.2	88.7	79.9	79.3	188.3	182.3	90.8	15.6	76.0	6.0
3rd quarter	369.8	119.7	33.2	87.1	88.4	83.9	78.0	195.6	189.8	100.9	14.2	74.7	5.9
4th quarter	368.1	122.5	36.6	86.2	86.4	81.6	77.7	202.4	196.6	105.1	14.2	77.3	5.8
1992:													
1st quarter	371.7	126.7	39.2	87.7	86.8	79.9	78.2	213.9	207.9	110.4	13.3	84.3	6.0
2nd quarter	386.4	132.4	43.4	88.9	88.1	87.9	78.1	224.9	218.9	116.4	15.2	87.3	6.0
3rd quarter	393.1	138.6	45.7	92.8	89.8	85.4	79.3	226.7	220.7	117.7	12.5	90.6	6.0
4th quarter	403.5	138.9	47.5	91.5	92.6	91.5	80.5	236.7	230.5	121.6	11.5	97.5	6.2
1993:													
1st quarter	409.8	140.5	51.0	89.6	93.4	91.9	83.9	237.0	230.7	123.5	10.4	96.9	6.3
2nd quarter	424.9	143.2	53.2	90.3	94.2	101.5	85.8	236.1	229.8	123.6	10.1	96.1	6.3
3rd quarter	430.7	152.5	58.4	94.6	96.5	94.8	87.3	242.2	235.7	126.8	11.0	97.9	6.5
4th quarter	452.9	155.5	61.7	94.8	102.0	105.2	90.1	255.1	248.6	134.3	10.7	103.5	6.5
1994:													
1st quarter	460.6	158.1	62.2	96.8	102.8	108.8	90.9	261.3	254.8	139.4	11.4	103.8	6.5
2nd quarter	467.3	160.8	64.1	97.8	103.8	110.0	92.6	271.5	264.8	144.5	13.0	107.2	6.7
3rd quarter	480.0	166.1	67.1	100.2	106.7	113.5	93.7	269.4	262.7	140.5	14.7	107.6	6.7
4th quarter	499.1	175.6	75.3	102.8	108.9	120.5	94.5	265.9	259.0	136.1	15.5	107.6	6.9
1995:													
1st quarter	518.1	184.5	82.7	105.1	112.1	124.0	98.0	261.2	254.3	131.4	16.4	106.8	6.9
2nd quarter	525.9	199.3	97.2	107.9	114.9	117.3	96.6	250.4	243.6	123.1	16.3	104.7	6.9
3rd quarter	528.5	205.2	106.8	107.2	114.1	115.7	96.7	255.5	248.5	124.3	17.2	107.6	7.0
4th quarter	540.5	218.2	124.4	107.8	112.5	118.6	96.5	260.8	253.8	128.9	17.7	107.7	7.0
1996:													
1st quarter	557.4	232.8	138.7	111.7	114.8	119.2	97.9	266.1	259.1	133.1	18.9	107.5	7.0
2nd quarter	577.1	244.8	152.0	114.0	118.8	121.8	100.1	277.2	270.0	138.6	20.2	111.7	7.2
3rd quarter	602.9	264.3	170.0	120.3	117.6	129.5	102.8	274.1	266.9	138.3	17.5	111.5	7.2
4th quarter	606.7	270.4	182.4	119.3	116.9	129.7	102.5	271.1	263.9	136.2	18.0	110.0	7.2

1. New computers and peripheral equipment only.

Prices

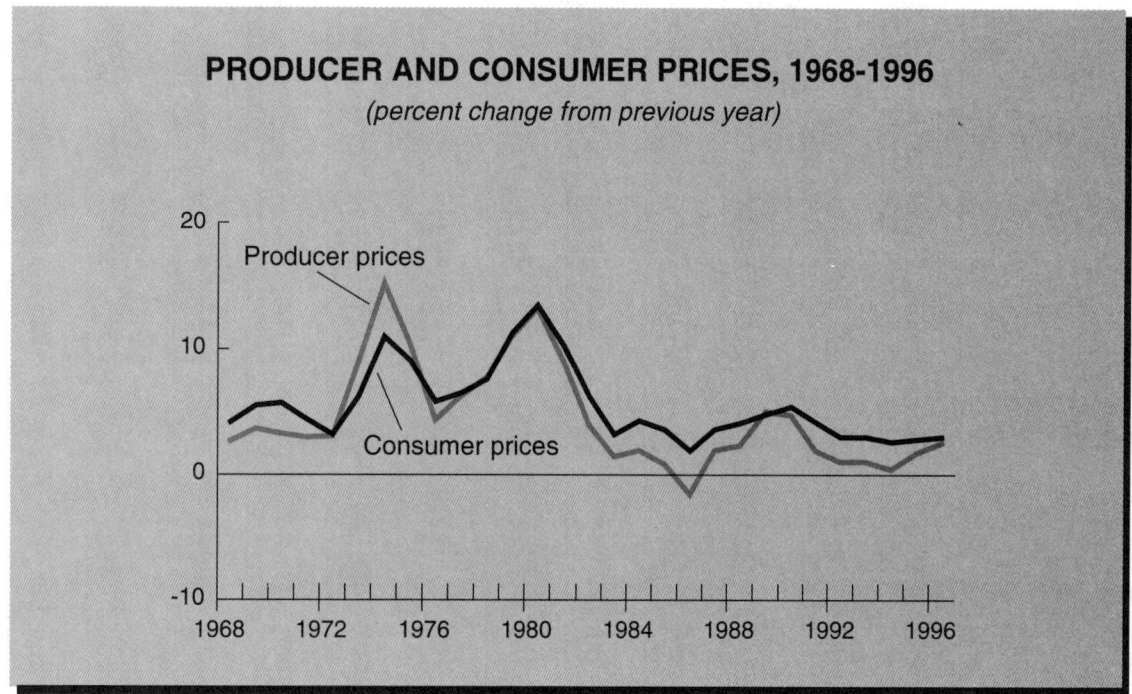

PRODUCER AND CONSUMER PRICES, 1968-1996
(percent change from previous year)

The United States has experienced two periods of severe inflation since 1967, both precipitated in part by large increases in world oil prices. In the first of these periods, the annual consumer price increase peaked in 1974 at 11.0 percent and the increase in producer prices of finished goods at 15.4 percent. Following the second round of oil price increases, both consumer prices and producer prices of finished goods rose more than 13 percent in 1980.

Inflation had eased by 1986, when consumer prices rose only 1.9 percent and producer prices of finished goods actually declined more than 1 percent. The rate of price increase then climbed gradually, reaching the 5 percent range by 1990. From 1990-1992, the inflation rate declined fairly steadily, and from 1993 through 1996 remained at a rate of 3 percent or less each year.

CONSUMER PRICE INDEXES
(All urban consumers—1982-1984=100)

YEAR AND MONTH	All items			Total	Total food	Food and beverages—Seasonally adjusted, excepted as noted									
						Food at home					Other food at home				
	Not seasonally adjusted	Seasonally adjusted				Total	Cereals and bakery products	Meats, poultry, fish, and eggs	Dairy products[1]	Fruits and vegetables	Total	Sugar and sweets	Fats and oils	Non-alcoholic beverages	Other prepared foods
		Index	Percent change												
1968	34.8	34.8	4.2	36.2	35.3	36.3	34.2	39.1	41.3	35.9	29.8	27.4	36.7	23.5	36.9
1969	36.7	36.7	5.5	38.1	37.1	38.0	35.2	42.6	42.7	36.4	30.7	28.9	36.8	24.2	38.1
1970	38.8	38.8	5.7	40.1	39.2	39.9	37.1	44.6	44.7	37.8	32.9	30.5	39.2	27.1	39.6
1971	40.5	40.5	4.4	41.4	40.4	40.9	38.8	44.1	46.1	39.7	34.3	31.6	42.7	28.1	40.8
1972	41.8	41.8	3.2	43.1	42.1	42.7	39.0	48.0	46.8	41.6	34.6	32.1	43.1	28.0	41.5
1973	44.4	44.4	6.2	48.8	48.2	49.7	43.5	60.9	51.2	47.4	36.7	34.0	46.8	30.1	43.0
1974	49.3	49.3	11.0	55.5	55.1	57.1	56.5	62.2	60.7	55.2	47.8	51.8	66.4	35.9	52.2
1975	53.8	53.8	9.1	60.2	59.8	61.8	62.9	67.0	62.6	56.9	55.4	65.3	73.5	41.3	58.9
1976	56.9	56.9	5.8	62.1	61.6	63.1	61.5	68.0	67.7	58.4	56.4	57.9	64.3	49.4	61.3
1977	60.6	60.6	6.5	65.8	65.5	66.8	62.5	67.4	69.5	63.8	68.4	60.8	70.8	74.4	63.4
1978	65.2	65.2	7.6	72.2	72.0	73.8	68.1	77.6	74.2	70.9	73.6	68.3	77.6	78.7	68.5
1979	72.6	72.6	11.3	79.9	79.9	81.8	74.9	89.0	82.8	76.6	79.0	73.6	83.7	82.6	75.4
1980	82.4	82.4	13.5	86.7	86.8	88.4	83.9	92.0	90.9	82.1	88.4	90.5	89.3	91.4	83.6
1981	90.9	90.9	10.3	93.5	93.6	94.8	92.3	96.0	97.4	92.0	94.9	97.7	98.8	95.3	92.2
1982	96.5	96.5	6.2	97.3	97.4	98.1	96.5	99.6	98.8	97.0	97.3	97.5	96.1	97.9	97.0
1983	99.6	99.6	3.2	99.5	99.4	99.1	99.6	99.2	100.0	97.3	99.5	99.3	97.4	99.8	100.0
1984	103.9	103.9	4.3	103.2	103.2	102.8	103.9	101.3	101.3	105.7	103.1	103.2	106.6	102.3	103.0
1985	107.6	107.6	3.6	105.6	105.6	104.3	107.9	100.1	103.2	108.4	105.7	105.8	108.9	104.3	106.4
1986	109.6	109.6	1.9	109.1	109.0	107.3	110.9	104.5	103.3	109.4	109.4	109.0	106.5	110.4	109.2
1987	113.6	113.6	3.6	113.5	113.5	111.9	114.8	110.5	105.9	119.1	110.5	111.0	108.1	107.5	113.8
1988	118.3	118.3	4.1	118.2	118.2	116.6	122.1	114.3	108.4	128.1	113.1	114.0	113.1	107.5	118.0
1989	124.0	124.0	4.8	124.9	125.1	124.2	132.4	121.3	115.6	138.0	119.1	119.4	121.2	111.3	125.5
1990	130.7	130.7	5.4	132.1	132.4	132.3	140.0	130.0	126.5	149.0	123.4	124.7	126.3	113.5	131.2
1991	136.2	136.2	4.2	136.8	136.3	135.8	145.8	132.6	125.1	155.8	127.3	129.3	131.7	114.1	137.1
1992	140.3	140.3	3.0	138.7	137.9	136.8	151.5	130.9	128.5	155.4	128.8	133.1	129.8	114.3	140.1
1993	144.5	144.5	3.0	141.6	140.9	140.1	156.6	135.5	129.4	159.0	130.5	133.4	130.0	114.6	143.7
1994	148.2	148.2	2.6	144.9	144.3	144.1	163.0	137.2	131.7	165.0	135.6	135.2	133.5	123.2	147.5
1995	152.4	152.4	2.8	148.9	148.4	148.8	167.5	138.8	132.8	177.7	140.8	137.5	137.3	131.7	151.1
1996	156.9	156.9	3.0	153.7	153.3	154.3	174.0	144.8	142.1	183.9	142.9	143.7	140.5	128.6	156.2
1993:															
January	142.6	142.8	0.3	140.0	139.2	137.9	153.3	132.9	129.5	155.0	129.1	133.1	129.7	113.1	141.9
February	143.1	143.2	0.3	140.4	139.7	138.5	154.6	133.1	128.8	157.5	129.6	133.1	129.9	113.8	142.5
March	143.6	143.5	0.2	140.5	139.8	138.6	154.9	133.9	128.8	156.2	129.7	132.6	129.9	114.2	142.6
April	144.0	143.9	0.3	140.8	140.2	139.0	155.0	135.5	128.0	155.6	129.7	133.1	129.7	114.1	142.7
May	144.2	144.3	0.3	141.7	141.2	140.5	156.3	135.5	128.0	162.9	130.2	133.0	129.1	114.8	143.4
June	144.4	144.4	0.1	141.3	140.7	139.7	156.3	135.7	129.8	156.1	130.2	133.1	130.0	114.6	143.3
July	144.4	144.6	0.1	141.4	140.8	139.6	156.8	136.0	130.2	154.1	130.7	133.0	130.1	115.0	144.2
August	144.8	144.9	0.2	141.9	141.3	140.3	156.9	136.1	130.5	157.9	130.5	133.5	130.1	114.6	144.0
September	145.1	145.1	0.1	142.2	141.6	140.6	157.8	136.0	129.6	159.8	130.5	133.3	130.2	114.0	144.4
October	145.7	145.7	0.4	142.8	142.2	141.5	158.3	136.7	129.5	162.2	131.3	133.9	130.0	115.3	145.1
November	145.8	146.0	0.2	143.0	142.5	141.8	158.8	137.1	129.5	162.7	131.6	134.4	130.3	115.7	145.2
December	145.8	146.4	0.3	143.5	142.9	142.4	159.6	136.9	130.2	165.4	131.7	134.4	130.7	115.8	145.4
1994:															
January	146.2	146.4	0.0	143.7	143.1	142.6	160.2	137.1	131.6	164.2	131.9	134.9	130.9	115.7	145.7
February	146.7	146.8	0.3	143.5	142.9	142.2	161.0	137.2	131.8	160.7	131.9	135.4	130.8	114.8	146.3
March	147.2	147.1	0.2	143.5	143.0	142.2	160.7	137.1	131.8	160.6	132.1	135.1	132.3	115.4	146.0
April	147.4	147.3	0.1	143.5	143.0	142.1	162.0	137.5	131.8	157.2	132.7	135.7	132.7	115.3	147.3
May	147.5	147.6	0.2	144.0	143.5	142.8	162.3	137.5	132.0	161.5	132.4	135.1	133.1	115.4	146.7
June	148.0	148.0	0.3	144.4	144.0	143.4	163.0	137.7	132.2	163.6	132.8	134.9	133.4	115.8	147.2
July	148.4	148.5	0.3	145.2	144.8	144.6	163.4	137.4	131.8	166.7	135.8	134.9	134.7	123.5	147.6
August	149.0	149.1	0.4	145.8	145.4	145.4	164.1	137.3	131.8	166.7	138.9	134.9	134.2	131.9	148.1
September	149.4	149.4	0.2	146.0	145.6	145.6	165.0	137.4	131.3	166.3	139.4	135.4	134.5	132.2	149.0
October	149.5	149.6	0.1	145.9	145.5	145.4	164.8	136.8	131.5	166.2	139.4	135.4	135.0	132.6	148.4
November	149.7	149.9	0.2	146.2	145.8	145.7	164.6	136.6	131.7	168.0	139.6	135.3	135.3	132.7	148.9
December	149.7	150.3	0.3	147.3	147.0	147.3	165.0	136.1	131.6	178.6	139.6	135.7	135.5	132.7	148.7
1995:															
January	150.3	150.6	0.2	147.2	146.9	147.0	164.5	136.6	132.7	174.8	140.0	135.5	136.0	132.9	149.4
February	150.9	151.0	0.3	147.7	147.4	147.6	165.5	137.3	132.1	176.8	140.0	135.6	136.1	132.5	149.6
March	151.4	151.3	0.2	147.6	147.3	147.0	165.7	137.7	132.2	172.0	140.2	136.2	136.4	132.3	150.1
April	151.9	151.8	0.3	148.2	147.9	148.1	166.4	137.7	132.1	177.5	140.5	136.5	136.7	132.5	150.4
May	152.2	152.1	0.2	148.7	148.4	148.6	166.6	137.9	132.8	179.5	140.5	136.9	136.9	131.5	151.0
June	152.5	152.5	0.3	148.7	148.4	148.6	167.1	137.7	132.2	179.6	140.5	137.3	136.3	131.6	151.1
July	152.5	152.6	0.1	149.0	148.7	148.8	167.7	138.2	132.9	178.8	140.8	137.8	137.6	131.6	151.3
August	152.9	153.0	0.3	149.3	149.0	149.1	168.2	139.0	132.8	177.8	141.2	138.5	137.6	131.8	151.9
September	153.2	153.2	0.1	149.7	149.4	149.7	168.6	139.5	132.3	180.6	141.1	138.3	137.7	131.8	151.7
October	153.7	153.7	0.3	150.1	149.8	150.1	169.3	140.7	133.2	179.9	141.1	138.9	138.3	130.9	152.0
November	153.6	153.8	0.1	150.2	149.9	150.1	169.9	141.2	133.7	177.6	141.1	139.3	138.8	130.8	151.9
December	153.5	154.1	0.2	150.4	150.1	150.3	170.4	141.5	135.0	176.7	141.4	139.7	138.8	130.4	152.7
1996:															
January	154.4	154.7	0.4	150.8	150.5	150.8	171.4	141.9	136.3	176.6	141.5	141.3	139.2	129.6	153.1
February	154.9	155.1	0.3	151.2	150.9	151.1	171.7	142.0	137.2	178.1	141.4	141.4	139.1	128.8	153.4
March	155.7	155.6	0.3	151.8	151.5	152.0	172.4	141.9	136.7	182.1	142.0	142.0	139.6	129.2	154.2
April	156.3	156.1	0.3	152.1	151.8	152.3	172.7	141.8	137.0	183.1	142.3	142.0	139.4	129.4	155.0
May	156.6	156.5	0.3	152.4	152.1	152.4	173.5	142.0	137.6	182.4	142.5	143.0	139.8	129.1	155.3
June	156.7	156.7	0.1	153.4	153.1	153.9	173.8	143.9	139.8	185.0	142.8	143.6	140.7	128.6	156.1
July	157.0	157.1	0.3	154.0	153.8	154.7	174.2	144.9	142.0	185.6	142.9	144.2	140.0	128.3	156.6
August	157.3	157.4	0.2	154.6	154.4	155.5	174.4	145.9	144.6	185.8	143.1	144.4	141.0	128.9	156.2
September	157.8	157.9	0.3	155.3	155.1	156.3	174.9	147.2	146.7	185.6	143.6	145.3	141.9	128.0	157.7
October	158.3	158.3	0.3	156.0	155.8	157.2	175.4	147.8	149.3	187.6	143.8	145.4	141.6	127.6	158.4
November	158.6	158.8	0.3	156.6	156.4	157.8	176.3	148.4	149.3	188.7	144.0	145.2	141.8	127.5	159.1
December	158.6	159.2	0.3	156.6	156.4	157.7	176.6	149.3	148.6	185.9	144.4	146.0	142.0	127.7	159.6

1. Not seasonally adjusted.

YEAR AND MONTH	Food and beverages—Continued		Total housing	Housing—Cost of shelter									
				Total	Renters' costs			Homeowners' costs					
											Maintenance and repair		
	Food away from home	Alcoholic beverages			Total[1]	Rent, residential	Other renters' costs	Total[1]	Owners' equivalent rent[1]	Household insurance[1]	Total[2]	Services[2]	Commodities[2]
1968	32.9	48.0	32.0	30.1	....	43.3	30.4	....	....	....	30.6	27.6	39.9
1969	34.9	49.7	34.0	32.6	....	44.7	32.7	....	....	....	33.2	30.2	42.6
1970	37.5	52.1	36.4	35.5	....	46.5	35.6	....	....	....	35.8	33.1	43.7
1971	39.4	54.2	38.0	37.0	....	48.7	37.0	....	....	....	38.6	36.1	45.8
1972	41.0	55.4	39.4	38.7	....	50.4	37.8	....	....	....	40.6	38.2	47.7
1973	44.2	56.8	41.2	40.5	....	52.5	39.5	....	....	....	43.6	40.6	52.4
1974	49.8	61.1	45.8	44.4	....	55.2	42.4	....	....	....	49.5	46.5	58.3
1975	54.5	65.9	50.7	48.8	....	58.0	45.5	....	....	....	54.1	51.3	61.9
1976	58.2	68.1	53.8	51.5	....	61.1	49.3	....	....	....	57.6	55.0	64.7
1977	62.6	70.0	57.4	54.9	....	64.8	53.3	....	....	....	62.0	59.3	69.1
1978	68.3	74.1	62.4	60.5	....	69.3	59.2	....	....	....	67.2	64.9	73.1
1979	75.9	79.9	70.1	68.9	....	74.3	66.7	....	....	....	74.0	71.7	79.4
1980	83.4	86.4	81.1	81.0	....	80.9	75.0	....	....	....	82.4	80.0	88.0
1981	90.9	92.5	90.4	90.5	....	87.9	83.6	....	....	....	90.7	88.5	94.9
1982	95.8	96.7	96.9	96.9	....	94.6	93.7	....	....	....	96.4	94.6	98.8
1983	100.0	100.4	99.5	99.1	103.0	100.1	99.9	102.5	102.5	103.2	99.9	99.7	100.2
1984	104.2	103.0	103.6	104.0	108.6	105.3	106.4	107.3	107.3	107.5	103.7	105.7	101.0
1985	108.3	106.4	107.7	109.8	115.4	111.8	113.5	113.1	113.2	112.4	106.5	108.7	103.7
1986	112.5	111.1	110.9	115.8	121.9	118.3	118.6	119.4	119.4	119.2	107.9	111.2	103.7
1987	117.0	114.1	114.2	121.3	128.1	123.1	127.4	124.8	124.8	124.0	111.8	114.8	107.8
1988	121.8	118.6	118.5	127.1	133.6	127.8	134.8	131.1	131.1	129.0	114.7	117.9	110.4
1989	127.4	123.5	123.0	132.8	138.9	132.8	140.7	137.3	137.4	132.6	118.0	120.6	114.6
1990	133.4	129.3	128.5	140.0	146.7	138.4	154.3	144.6	144.8	135.3	122.2	126.4	116.6
1991	137.9	142.8	133.6	146.3	155.6	143.3	174.6	150.2	150.4	138.4	126.3	130.3	121.0
1992	140.7	147.3	137.5	151.2	160.9	146.9	184.8	155.3	155.5	142.2	128.6	133.1	122.4
1993	143.2	149.6	141.2	155.7	165.0	150.3	190.3	160.2	160.5	146.9	130.6	135.0	124.6
1994	145.7	151.5	144.8	160.5	169.4	154.0	196.3	165.5	165.8	152.3	130.8	134.5	125.8
1995	149.0	153.9	148.5	165.7	174.3	157.8	204.3	171.0	171.3	157.4	135.0	139.8	128.5
1996	152.7	158.5	152.8	171.0	180.2	162.0	214.7	176.5	176.8	161.0	139.0	145.5	130.2
1993:													
January	142.1	149.1	139.5	153.6	162.4	148.9	187.4	158.2	158.5	144.2	129.7	135.1	122.5
February	142.3	149.1	139.5	153.9	162.6	149.1	187.7	158.5	158.8	144.8	130.5	135.2	124.0
March	142.4	149.0	139.9	154.1	162.8	149.2	188.1	158.8	159.1	145.1	131.5	135.8	125.8
April	142.7	149.2	140.5	154.7	163.5	149.7	189.6	159.4	159.7	145.6	131.8	134.9	127.7
May	142.9	149.2	140.7	155.0	163.9	150.0	190.1	159.7	160.0	145.8	131.6	135.4	126.6
June	143.1	149.3	141.1	155.5	164.2	150.4	189.9	160.2	160.5	146.5	131.2	136.0	124.8
July	143.4	149.5	141.2	155.6	164.3	150.4	190.3	160.4	160.7	147.0	131.3	136.2	124.7
August	143.6	149.8	141.5	155.9	164.4	150.8	189.6	160.8	161.1	147.6	131.6	136.5	124.9
September	143.8	150.0	141.9	156.3	164.8	150.9	190.8	161.1	161.4	148.6	131.3	137.4	122.8
October	144.0	150.2	142.2	156.6	165.4	151.3	192.1	161.4	161.7	148.8	130.8	136.4	123.1
November	144.2	150.4	142.5	157.0	165.8	151.5	193.2	161.8	162.1	149.1	127.9	130.2	124.9
December	144.3	150.9	142.9	157.6	166.5	151.9	194.7	162.4	162.7	149.1	127.6	130.8	123.5
1994:													
January	144.5	151.3	143.0	157.9	166.7	152.2	194.5	162.8	163.1	149.4	128.9	131.3	125.9
February	144.7	151.1	143.6	158.7	167.2	152.8	194.8	163.7	164.0	149.6	129.4	131.2	127.1
March	144.9	151.0	143.9	159.1	167.7	153.3	194.9	164.2	164.5	150.2	129.3	131.8	126.1
April	145.1	151.1	143.9	159.3	167.6	153.3	194.8	164.4	164.7	150.5	130.2	133.3	126.3
May	145.3	151.1	144.3	159.7	168.1	153.4	196.3	164.8	165.1	151.2	131.0	135.0	125.7
June	145.5	151.4	144.5	159.9	168.4	153.5	197.5	165.0	165.3	151.8	131.5	135.4	126.2
July	145.6	151.5	144.6	160.1	168.3	153.9	195.8	165.3	165.6	152.7	131.3	135.4	125.9
August	145.9	151.4	145.2	160.9	169.2	154.5	197.2	166.2	166.5	153.5	131.2	135.4	125.6
September	146.2	151.5	145.4	161.3	169.0	155.0	195.2	166.8	167.1	154.2	131.6	135.8	126.0
October	146.4	151.7	145.7	161.8	169.6	155.1	197.1	167.3	167.6	154.4	130.8	135.9	123.8
November	146.7	152.3	146.0	162.3	170.3	155.5	198.8	167.7	168.0	154.9	131.2	136.4	124.3
December	147.1	152.4	145.9	162.3	170.4	155.7	198.3	167.7	168.0	155.5	132.7	137.0	126.8
1995:													
January	147.4	152.3	146.5	162.8	170.7	156.1	198.3	168.3	168.6	156.2	133.1	137.3	127.5
February	147.7	152.3	146.8	163.3	171.2	156.3	199.6	168.8	169.1	156.4	133.8	137.9	128.2
March	148.2	152.7	147.1	163.8	171.9	156.7	201.5	169.3	169.6	157.3	134.2	138.8	128.2
April	148.3	153.1	147.5	164.3	172.6	157.0	203.1	169.7	170.0	157.6	134.2	139.0	127.6
May	148.6	153.5	147.8	164.9	173.1	157.3	204.5	170.3	170.6	157.8	134.6	139.4	128.1
June	148.8	153.7	148.1	165.3	173.5	157.6	205.1	170.8	171.1	157.9	135.0	139.4	129.0
July	149.1	153.8	148.5	165.7	173.9	158.0	205.5	171.2	171.5	157.7	135.1	139.8	128.7
August	149.4	154.7	148.9	166.0	173.9	158.2	204.6	171.7	172.0	158.1	135.4	140.3	128.8
September	149.6	154.7	149.1	166.5	174.7	158.5	207.0	172.2	172.5	156.9	135.4	140.3	128.9
October	149.9	155.0	149.7	167.1	175.2	158.8	208.0	172.8	173.1	157.0	136.3	141.8	128.9
November	150.1	155.6	149.9	167.5	175.3	159.2	207.4	173.3	173.6	157.5	136.2	141.8	128.7
December	150.4	155.5	150.3	168.0	175.7	159.6	207.4	173.9	174.2	158.4	136.6	142.1	129.1
1996:													
January	150.6	155.9	150.8	168.5	176.6	160.0	210.1	174.3	174.6	158.3	136.3	142.1	128.6
February	151.0	156.6	151.1	168.9	177.1	160.3	210.9	174.7	175.0	159.0	137.0	143.0	128.8
March	151.3	157.0	151.4	169.3	177.6	160.6	212.1	175.1	175.4	159.3	137.5	143.8	129.0
April	151.6	157.4	151.8	169.7	178.0	160.9	212.9	175.4	175.7	159.8	138.0	143.8	130.0
May	152.0	157.9	152.2	170.1	178.4	161.4	212.8	175.9	176.2	159.9	138.8	144.7	130.9
June	152.4	158.3	152.3	170.4	178.9	161.8	213.4	176.2	176.5	160.5	138.8	144.6	130.9
July	152.8	158.5	152.9	171.2	180.0	162.2	216.7	176.8	177.1	161.3	139.4	146.3	130.1
August	153.1	159.1	153.2	171.4	180.1	162.5	216.3	177.1	177.4	161.7	139.7	147.1	129.6
September	153.6	159.7	153.5	171.7	180.5	162.9	216.8	177.4	177.7	162.2	139.9	147.4	129.5
October	154.1	160.2	153.9	172.2	181.1	163.2	217.9	177.8	178.1	163.3	140.2	147.3	130.5
November	154.6	160.6	154.4	172.6	181.5	163.6	218.4	178.3	178.6	164.5	141.1	147.6	132.3
December	154.9	161.1	154.7	172.9	181.7	164.0	218.0	178.6	179.0	162.5	141.5	148.0	132.6

1. December 1982=100.
2. Not seasonally adjusted.

CONSUMER PRICE INDEXES—Continued
(All urban consumers—1982-1984=100, seasonally adjusted, except as noted)

YEAR AND MONTH	Housing—Other than shelter									Apparel and upkeep				
	Fuel and other utilities					Household furnishings and operation					Apparel commodities			
	Total	Fuels				Total	House-furnish-ings	House-keeping supplies	House-keeping services	Total	Total	Men's and boys'	Wom-en's and girls'	Infants' and toddlers' [1]
		Total	Fuel oil and other house-hold fuel com-modities	Gas (piped) and elec-tricity (energy services)	Other utility and public services									
1968	27.4	21.7	16.0	23.9	47.1	43.6	52.4	34.4	33.8	53.7	57.3	56.1	65.6	37.3
1969	28.0	22.1	16.3	24.3	48.4	45.2	54.1	35.1	35.8	56.8	60.8	59.7	69.2	38.4
1970	29.1	23.1	17.0	25.4	50.0	46.8	55.5	36.6	37.9	59.2	63.3	62.2	71.8	39.2
1971	31.1	24.7	18.2	27.1	53.4	48.6	56.8	38.2	40.6	61.1	65.2	63.9	74.4	40.0
1972	32.5	25.7	18.3	28.5	56.2	49.7	57.7	38.8	42.4	62.3	66.6	64.7	76.2	41.1
1973	34.3	27.5	21.1	29.9	57.8	51.1	58.8	39.9	44.6	64.6	69.0	67.1	78.8	42.5
1974	40.7	34.4	33.2	34.5	60.7	56.8	63.8	46.6	50.9	69.4	73.9	72.4	83.5	54.2
1975	45.4	39.4	36.4	40.1	63.9	63.4	69.8	56.9	55.9	72.5	76.7	75.5	85.5	64.5
1976	49.4	43.3	38.8	44.7	67.7	67.3	72.6	61.1	61.5	75.2	79.2	78.1	87.9	68.0
1977	54.7	49.0	43.9	50.5	70.8	70.4	75.0	65.4	65.1	78.6	82.3	81.7	90.6	74.6
1978	58.5	53.0	46.2	55.0	73.7	74.7	78.4	69.8	70.9	81.4	84.5	83.5	92.4	77.4
1979	64.8	61.3	62.4	61.0	74.3	79.9	82.9	75.2	77.9	84.9	87.5	85.4	94.0	79.0
1980	75.4	74.8	86.1	71.4	77.0	86.3	88.5	83.2	84.3	90.9	92.9	89.4	96.0	85.5
1981	86.4	87.2	104.6	81.9	84.3	93.0	94.1	91.3	91.9	95.3	96.5	94.2	97.5	92.9
1982	94.9	95.6	103.4	93.2	93.3	98.0	98.5	97.1	97.6	97.8	98.3	97.6	98.5	96.3
1983	100.2	100.5	97.2	101.5	99.5	100.2	100.4	100.3	99.8	100.2	100.2	100.3	100.2	101.1
1984	104.8	104.0	99.4	105.4	107.2	101.9	101.2	102.6	102.5	102.1	101.5	102.1	101.3	102.6
1985	106.5	104.5	95.9	107.1	112.1	103.8	101.7	106.2	106.1	105.0	104.0	105.0	104.9	107.2
1986	104.1	99.2	77.6	105.7	117.9	105.2	102.2	108.2	108.5	105.9	104.2	106.2	104.0	111.8
1987	103.0	97.3	77.9	103.8	120.1	107.1	103.6	111.5	110.6	110.6	108.9	109.1	110.4	112.1
1988	104.4	98.0	78.1	104.6	122.9	109.4	105.1	114.7	114.3	115.4	113.7	113.4	114.9	116.4
1989	107.8	100.9	81.7	107.5	127.1	111.2	105.5	120.9	117.3	118.6	116.7	117.0	116.4	119.1
1990	111.6	104.5	99.3	109.3	131.7	113.3	106.7	125.2	120.1	124.1	122.0	120.4	122.6	125.8
1991	115.3	106.7	94.6	112.6	137.9	116.0	107.5	128.9	127.5	128.7	126.4	124.2	127.6	128.9
1992	117.8	108.1	90.7	114.8	142.5	118.0	109.0	129.6	132.1	131.9	129.4	126.5	130.4	129.3
1993	121.3	111.2	90.3	118.5	147.0	119.3	109.5	130.7	135.8	133.7	131.0	127.5	132.6	127.1
1994	122.8	111.7	88.8	119.2	150.2	121.0	111.0	132.3	138.5	133.4	130.4	126.4	130.9	128.1
1995	123.7	111.5	88.1	119.2	152.8	123.0	112.2	137.1	143.7	132.0	128.7	126.2	126.9	127.2
1996	127.5	115.2	99.2	122.1	157.2	124.7	111.3	141.1	148.0	131.7	128.2	127.7	124.7	129.7
1993:														
January	119.5	108.9	89.5	116.1	144.3	118.4	109.0	130.1	134.2	132.7	130.0	126.7	130.6	127.9
February	119.0	107.7	89.6	114.7	145.3	118.5	108.9	130.5	134.4	134.1	131.5	127.6	133.8	127.0
March	120.2	109.1	90.5	116.3	146.3	118.4	108.9	129.8	134.5	134.0	131.4	127.9	134.0	125.9
April	120.7	110.1	91.2	117.3	146.2	118.9	109.3	130.6	134.9	134.1	131.5	127.7	133.6	126.5
May	121.0	110.4	90.9	117.7	146.3	118.9	109.1	131.2	135.2	133.5	130.8	127.2	132.3	127.7
June	121.4	110.9	91.6	118.2	146.5	119.0	109.1	131.1	135.6	132.9	130.2	127.0	131.2	128.1
July	121.7	111.0	91.6	118.4	147.1	118.6	108.8	129.6	135.8	132.9	130.1	127.2	131.3	126.7
August	122.0	111.2	90.8	118.6	147.8	119.1	109.5	129.3	136.5	133.9	131.2	127.6	133.5	128.4
September	122.5	111.6	90.7	119.2	148.1	119.5	109.7	130.8	136.7	133.7	130.9	127.3	132.5	126.5
October	122.7	111.6	90.2	119.3	148.4	120.0	110.1	131.9	137.0	133.7	130.8	127.4	132.1	126.3
November	122.4	111.1	89.6	118.7	148.6	120.4	110.6	131.8	137.3	134.4	131.6	128.6	132.8	127.5
December	122.5	111.0	87.4	118.9	148.8	120.5	110.8	132.0	137.3	134.1	131.2	127.6	132.7	127.1
1994:														
January	122.1	110.3	86.2	118.2	148.9	120.7	111.1	131.6	137.5	133.3	130.4	126.7	131.8	125.6
February	122.9	111.3	90.7	118.8	150.0	120.3	110.5	131.6	137.5	133.1	130.1	125.1	131.7	125.5
March	123.1	111.6	90.1	119.2	150.1	120.3	110.2	132.3	137.7	133.7	130.8	124.7	132.7	125.8
April	122.8	111.2	88.8	118.9	150.0	120.3	110.3	131.4	137.9	133.6	130.6	125.8	132.2	128.0
May	122.7	110.7	88.3	118.4	150.4	121.0	111.3	131.8	138.1	134.0	131.0	126.0	132.7	125.2
June	122.7	110.7	88.8	118.4	150.4	121.3	111.6	132.4	138.4	134.8	131.8	126.5	133.7	128.4
July	122.9	110.9	89.5	118.5	150.4	121.4	111.6	132.2	138.6	134.3	131.2	127.2	131.9	129.2
August	122.9	111.0	89.8	118.6	150.6	121.3	111.4	132.3	138.9	133.2	130.1	127.3	129.2	128.6
September	122.7	110.7	89.6	118.2	150.3	121.3	111.2	132.7	139.1	133.5	130.4	128.0	130.0	129.5
October	122.6	110.4	88.1	118.1	150.4	121.4	111.0	133.7	139.4	132.9	129.7	127.0	129.7	128.6
November	123.0	110.9	88.0	118.7	150.5	121.2	111.0	132.4	139.3	132.5	129.2	126.9	127.9	131.2
December	122.8	110.4	87.6	118.2	150.6	121.1	110.7	133.1	139.2	132.1	128.8	125.5	127.7	131.3
1995:														
January	123.3	110.5	86.7	118.4	152.1	121.9	110.8	133.9	142.5	132.2	128.9	126.5	127.5	129.0
February	123.2	110.7	86.8	118.7	151.8	122.3	111.1	134.5	142.7	131.8	128.4	126.6	126.5	126.8
March	123.0	110.4	86.6	118.3	151.9	122.3	110.9	135.6	142.7	132.1	128.7	126.1	127.1	127.1
April	123.4	110.7	87.0	118.6	152.2	122.3	110.8	135.8	142.9	132.1	128.7	125.9	127.1	127.1
May	122.9	109.9	87.9	117.5	152.3	122.6	110.9	136.3	143.3	131.8	128.3	126.4	127.2	123.6
June	123.4	110.5	89.0	118.0	152.7	122.5	110.8	136.4	143.1	131.4	128.0	126.1	126.1	121.6
July	123.5	110.5	89.5	118.0	153.0	122.9	111.0	137.4	143.6	131.6	128.2	125.8	126.9	123.0
August	124.2	111.5	89.6	119.2	153.1	123.3	111.4	138.1	143.9	132.4	129.0	126.0	127.3	128.0
September	123.5	110.1	89.5	117.6	153.2	123.6	111.6	138.5	144.4	132.2	128.8	126.4	126.1	131.2
October	124.2	111.1	88.0	118.9	153.5	123.9	111.8	139.2	144.7	132.3	129.0	126.6	127.0	131.0
November	124.4	111.2	88.0	119.1	153.6	123.7	111.3	139.7	145.1	132.0	128.7	126.1	126.8	129.7
December	124.6	111.4	88.9	119.1	153.9	124.0	111.5	140.1	145.5	132.1	128.7	126.3	126.6	128.7
1996:														
January	125.1	112.0	94.6	119.1	154.4	124.2	111.6	140.5	145.8	132.7	129.3	127.2	127.7	131.5
February	125.6	112.9	94.6	120.1	154.9	124.1	111.4	140.4	146.1	131.9	128.4	127.4	125.1	134.4
March	125.9	112.5	96.5	119.4	156.4	124.2	111.4	140.7	146.4	132.5	129.0	128.0	125.6	133.3
April	126.7	114.3	100.4	121.0	155.4	124.4	111.5	141.2	146.6	132.2	128.7	127.9	125.2	133.7
May	127.1	114.1	99.2	121.0	156.9	124.3	111.2	140.9	147.3	132.1	128.5	127.9	125.4	130.4
June	126.8	113.1	95.8	120.3	157.6	124.5	111.3	140.9	147.8	131.7	128.1	127.7	124.5	129.1
July	127.4	114.2	94.9	121.6	157.5	124.6	111.1	141.1	148.6	131.5	128.0	127.5	124.1	125.7
August	128.0	114.7	95.4	122.2	158.0	124.7	111.2	141.2	148.7	130.3	126.5	127.7	122.0	125.1
September	128.4	115.1	98.8	122.2	158.3	124.9	111.3	141.4	149.2	131.0	127.3	127.0	123.2	131.4
October	129.0	115.9	104.3	122.3	158.6	124.9	111.1	141.5	149.9	131.3	127.6	127.4	123.7	128.5
November	129.6	116.7	106.4	123.1	158.9	125.0	111.2	141.7	149.9	131.7	128.0	128.8	124.0	126.7
December	130.3	117.6	109.5	123.6	159.1	125.2	111.4	141.7	150.3	131.8	128.0	128.2	124.9	126.9

1. Not seasonally adjusted.

CONSUMER PRICE INDEXES—Continued
(All urban consumers—1982-1984=100, seasonally adjusted, except as noted)

YEAR AND MONTH	Apparel and upkeep—Continued			Transportation											
	Apparel commodities—Continued		Apparel services[1]	Total	Private transportation										Public transportation
	Footwear	Other apparel commodities			Total	New vehicles		Used cars	Motor fuel		Maintenance and repair	Other private transportation			
						Total	New cars		Total	Gasoline		Total	Commodities	Services	
1968	50.8	48.8	35.6	34.3	34.8	50.7	50.7	....	26.8	26.8	32.1	39.2	49.7	36.7	28.7
1969	53.9	52.1	37.2	35.7	36.0	51.5	51.5	30.9	27.6	27.7	34.1	41.6	51.6	39.2	30.9
1970	56.8	53.6	39.0	37.5	37.5	53.1	53.0	31.2	27.9	27.9	36.6	45.2	53.7	43.2	35.2
1971	58.6	54.5	40.5	39.5	39.4	55.3	55.2	33.0	28.1	28.1	39.3	48.6	55.5	47.1	37.8
1972	60.3	55.6	41.2	39.9	39.7	54.8	54.7	33.1	28.4	28.4	41.1	48.9	56.1	47.3	39.3
1973	62.8	57.4	42.8	41.2	41.0	54.8	54.8	35.2	31.2	31.2	43.2	48.4	55.8	46.8	39.7
1974	66.6	62.6	46.9	45.8	46.2	58.0	57.9	36.7	42.2	42.2	47.6	50.2	61.1	47.6	40.6
1975	69.6	66.6	51.0	50.1	50.6	63.0	62.9	43.8	45.1	45.1	53.7	53.5	66.8	50.4	43.5
1976	72.3	68.0	54.4	55.1	55.6	67.0	66.9	50.3	47.0	47.0	57.6	61.8	69.4	60.1	47.8
1977	75.7	70.7	58.3	59.0	59.7	70.5	70.4	54.7	49.7	49.7	61.9	67.2	72.8	66.0	50.0
1978	79.0	73.8	63.7	61.7	62.5	75.9	75.8	55.8	51.8	51.8	67.0	69.9	76.1	68.7	51.5
1979	85.3	79.3	70.8	70.5	71.7	81.9	81.8	60.2	70.1	70.2	73.7	75.2	83.3	73.7	54.9
1980	91.8	95.3	80.2	83.1	84.2	88.5	88.4	62.3	97.4	97.5	81.5	84.3	94.1	82.4	69.0
1981	96.7	99.6	88.7	93.2	93.8	93.9	93.7	76.9	108.5	108.5	89.2	91.4	100.2	89.7	85.6
1982	99.1	98.7	94.9	97.0	97.1	97.5	97.4	88.8	102.8	102.8	96.0	97.7	102.9	96.6	94.9
1983	99.8	100.3	100.1	99.3	99.3	99.9	99.9	98.7	99.4	99.4	100.3	98.8	100.8	98.4	99.5
1984	101.1	101.0	104.9	103.7	103.6	102.6	102.8	112.5	97.9	97.8	103.8	103.5	96.3	105.0	105.7
1985	102.3	100.6	110.4	106.4	106.2	106.1	106.1	113.7	98.7	98.6	106.8	109.0	96.8	111.3	110.5
1986	101.9	101.7	115.1	102.3	101.2	110.6	110.6	108.8	77.1	77.0	110.3	115.1	96.3	118.8	117.0
1987	105.1	108.0	119.6	105.4	104.2	114.4	114.6	113.1	80.2	80.1	114.8	120.8	96.9	125.6	121.1
1988	109.9	116.0	123.7	108.7	107.6	116.5	116.9	118.0	80.9	80.8	119.7	127.9	98.9	133.9	123.3
1989	114.4	122.1	129.4	114.1	112.9	119.2	119.2	120.4	88.5	88.5	124.9	135.8	101.5	143.2	129.5
1990	117.4	131.8	136.7	120.5	118.8	121.4	121.0	117.6	101.2	101.0	130.1	142.5	102.3	151.4	142.6
1991	120.9	137.7	142.9	123.8	121.9	126.0	125.3	118.1	99.4	99.2	136.0	149.1	104.1	159.2	148.9
1992	125.0	142.6	147.9	126.5	124.6	129.2	128.4	123.2	99.0	99.0	141.3	153.2	104.8	164.2	151.4
1993	125.9	145.6	151.7	130.4	127.5	132.7	131.5	133.9	98.0	97.7	145.9	156.8	103.4	169.1	167.0
1994	126.0	149.5	155.4	134.3	131.4	137.6	136.0	141.7	98.5	98.2	150.2	162.1	103.5	175.8	172.0
1995	125.4	152.4	157.3	139.1	136.3	141.0	139.0	156.5	100.0	99.8	154.0	170.6	104.8	186.0	175.9
1996	126.6	150.6	159.8	143.0	140.0	143.7	141.4	157.0	106.3	105.9	158.4	173.9	105.1	190.1	181.9
1993:															
January	126.0	146.8	149.7	129.3	127.1	130.7	129.8	128.2	101.6	101.6	143.6	155.4	104.5	167.2	159.8
February	126.1	145.3	150.2	129.8	127.4	131.0	129.9	128.0	101.8	101.7	144.3	155.9	104.2	167.9	162.2
March	125.6	142.9	150.6	129.6	127.3	131.2	130.1	129.8	100.8	100.7	144.6	155.7	103.8	167.8	160.8
April	125.5	146.6	150.8	129.8	127.5	131.7	130.6	130.9	100.1	99.9	145.1	156.0	103.9	168.1	161.4
May	126.1	145.8	150.9	129.9	127.2	132.2	131.0	132.2	97.8	97.6	145.4	156.3	103.6	168.6	166.0
June	125.5	145.4	151.3	129.7	127.0	132.3	131.1	133.6	96.4	96.1	145.9	156.3	103.2	168.7	166.1
July	125.4	144.1	151.7	130.0	127.2	132.9	131.6	134.8	95.6	95.3	146.3	156.5	103.2	168.9	168.3
August	125.0	144.1	152.0	130.4	127.5	133.5	132.1	136.2	95.3	95.1	146.3	156.9	102.9	169.5	169.9
September	126.1	146.1	152.4	130.4	127.5	133.8	132.3	137.3	94.3	94.0	146.6	157.2	103.1	169.8	169.9
October	126.0	147.4	152.9	132.0	129.2	134.3	132.9	138.2	99.3	98.8	146.9	157.5	103.0	170.3	169.9
November	126.6	146.9	153.6	132.2	129.1	134.6	133.2	139.2	97.8	97.2	147.3	158.2	102.6	171.3	173.3
December	127.0	145.4	153.8	132.1	128.8	134.8	133.4	138.3	96.5	96.0	147.8	158.2	103.0	171.1	176.2
1994:															
January	127.4	143.6	153.8	131.8	128.7	135.1	133.6	137.6	95.5	95.1	148.3	158.4	103.0	171.4	174.1
February	126.6	146.8	154.0	132.4	129.2	135.5	134.0	136.0	97.0	96.5	148.6	158.8	103.1	171.9	174.5
March	126.3	151.0	154.2	132.7	129.5	136.0	134.5	136.9	96.4	95.9	148.9	159.6	103.4	172.8	175.9
April	126.4	147.3	154.8	132.9	129.7	136.4	134.9	137.0	96.1	95.6	149.3	160.2	103.4	173.5	175.1
May	126.7	149.4	155.0	132.4	129.5	137.0	135.4	138.3	93.8	93.3	149.7	160.7	103.5	174.2	170.2
June	127.1	149.8	155.5	133.1	130.3	137.5	135.9	140.1	94.5	94.1	149.9	161.9	103.7	175.6	171.1
July	126.4	150.8	155.7	134.3	131.6	138.1	136.5	141.5	97.9	97.6	150.2	162.1	103.6	175.9	171.1
August	126.1	152.0	155.9	136.1	133.3	138.6	136.9	142.9	102.5	102.4	150.8	162.6	103.5	176.5	174.7
September	125.0	151.0	156.3	136.3	133.6	139.2	137.4	144.3	102.0	101.9	151.0	163.2	103.3	177.4	172.9
October	124.3	149.7	156.4	136.3	133.9	139.2	137.5	146.3	101.7	101.7	151.5	163.9	103.3	178.2	169.6
November	125.0	151.1	156.3	136.9	134.6	139.2	137.5	148.7	102.5	102.5	151.7	165.3	103.9	179.8	167.7
December	124.9	151.8	156.4	137.3	135.2	139.3	137.7	150.6	102.5	102.4	152.0	166.8	104.1	181.7	165.9
1995:															
January	125.4	151.3	157.0	137.7	135.5	139.6	137.9	153.0	101.7	101.6	152.1	167.8	103.8	183.0	167.9
February	125.3	151.1	157.3	138.0	135.8	139.7	138.1	155.1	101.4	101.3	152.4	168.5	104.3	183.7	169.2
March	125.1	153.0	157.6	138.6	136.1	139.9	138.2	158.4	100.5	100.3	152.7	169.5	104.4	185.0	172.3
April	125.6	152.7	157.7	139.2	136.6	140.6	138.8	158.0	100.5	100.3	153.1	170.6	104.5	186.3	175.2
May	124.8	149.8	157.7	139.7	136.9	140.9	139.0	157.8	101.4	101.3	153.8	170.5	104.8	186.1	176.9
June	124.4	153.6	156.9	140.3	137.1	141.1	139.2	157.4	101.8	101.9	153.8	170.4	104.9	186.0	183.3
July	124.7	151.9	157.2	139.8	136.7	141.0	139.0	156.6	100.9	100.7	154.2	170.1	105.1	185.6	180.9
August	125.3	154.9	157.3	139.5	136.6	141.2	139.2	156.2	99.7	99.5	154.6	171.0	105.2	186.6	178.4
September	126.8	153.8	157.4	139.3	136.5	141.7	139.5	155.7	98.4	98.2	154.9	171.3	105.1	187.1	177.0
October	126.3	151.5	157.0	139.7	136.7	141.7	139.5	156.1	98.7	98.4	155.1	171.7	105.2	187.5	179.6
November	126.0	151.7	157.2	139.3	136.4	142.0	139.9	156.6	96.7	96.3	155.6	171.8	105.1	187.7	178.4
December	125.5	154.0	157.7	139.3	137.0	142.0	139.9	157.5	98.5	98.2	155.8	171.7	105.0	187.6	171.5
1996:															
January	124.8	152.9	158.2	140.2	137.9	142.2	140.0	158.3	101.5	101.3	156.3	171.7	105.0	187.6	171.4
February	126.2	150.7	158.5	140.9	138.2	142.5	140.3	158.9	101.6	101.4	156.5	172.3	105.1	188.3	176.9
March	127.2	152.6	158.9	141.7	139.1	142.8	140.7	160.7	104.4	104.2	156.9	171.8	105.1	187.7	176.7
April	126.5	151.9	158.8	143.1	140.6	143.0	140.8	158.1	109.3	108.9	157.2	172.7	105.1	188.8	177.7
May	126.5	151.2	159.4	143.6	140.9	143.2	140.9	157.4	110.2	109.7	157.5	173.0	105.0	189.2	180.5
June	126.9	150.7	159.7	143.1	140.2	143.6	141.4	156.3	106.5	106.2	157.9	173.7	105.4	190.0	182.7
July	127.0	151.5	159.9	143.1	140.2	143.9	141.7	156.2	106.0	105.7	158.3	174.1	105.0	190.6	181.4
August	126.5	148.7	160.3	143.1	140.2	144.1	142.0	156.1	105.0	104.6	158.7	174.7	105.0	191.3	182.5
September	126.7	150.2	160.4	143.8	140.7	144.9	142.7	156.5	104.9	104.4	159.7	175.3	105.2	192.0	185.4
October	126.8	150.5	160.6	144.3	141.0	144.6	142.4	156.1	106.6	106.0	160.2	175.1	105.2	191.8	188.0
November	127.0	149.5	160.9	144.8	141.5	144.6	142.1	155.6	108.4	107.8	160.3	175.3	105.1	192.1	188.5
December	127.4	146.7	161.5	145.7	142.3	144.7	142.2	155.0	111.1	110.5	160.7	175.3	105.0	192.1	191.2

1. Not seasonally adjusted.

CONSUMER PRICE INDEXES—Continued
(All urban consumers—1982-1984=100, seasonally adjusted, except as noted)

| YEAR AND MONTH | Medical care | | | | Entertainment | | | Other goods and services | | | | | | | |
| | Total | Medical care commodities | Medical care services | | Total | Entertainment commodities | Entertainment services | Total | Tobacco and smoking products | Personal care [1] | | | Personal and educational expenses | | |
			Total	Professional medical services						Total	Toilet goods and personal care appliances	Personal care services	Total	School books and supplies	Personal and educational services
1968	29.9	45.0	27.9	32.5	43.0	42.3	43.9	36.9	37.8	40.0	39.8	40.1	31.9	35.4	31.2
1969	31.9	45.4	30.2	34.7	45.2	44.1	46.5	38.7	39.8	42.0	41.6	42.2	33.2	37.4	32.3
1970	34.0	46.5	32.3	37.0	47.5	46.1	49.4	40.9	43.1	43.5	42.7	44.2	35.5	38.8	34.8
1971	36.1	47.3	34.7	39.4	50.0	48.5	52.0	42.9	44.9	44.9	44.0	45.7	38.8	41.4	38.3
1972	37.3	47.4	35.9	40.8	51.5	50.0	53.3	44.7	47.4	46.0	45.2	46.8	41.0	44.2	40.4
1973	38.8	47.5	37.5	42.2	52.9	51.3	55.0	46.4	48.7	48.1	46.4	49.7	43.0	45.6	42.6
1974	42.4	49.2	41.4	45.8	56.9	55.7	58.4	49.8	51.1	52.8	51.5	53.9	45.4	47.2	45.2
1975	47.5	53.3	46.6	50.8	62.0	61.7	62.2	53.9	54.7	57.9	58.0	57.7	48.7	50.3	48.5
1976	52.0	56.5	51.3	55.5	65.1	65.1	64.9	57.0	57.0	61.7	61.3	61.9	51.9	53.7	51.7
1977	57.0	60.2	56.4	60.0	68.3	68.5	67.8	60.4	59.8	65.7	64.7	66.4	55.2	56.9	55.1
1978	61.8	64.4	61.2	64.5	71.9	72.1	71.6	64.3	63.0	69.9	68.2	71.3	59.4	61.6	59.1
1979	67.5	69.0	67.2	70.1	76.7	76.8	76.5	68.9	66.8	75.2	72.9	77.2	64.1	65.7	63.9
1980	74.9	75.4	74.8	77.9	83.6	84.5	82.3	75.2	72.0	81.9	79.6	83.7	70.9	71.4	70.8
1981	82.9	83.7	82.8	85.9	90.1	91.4	88.2	82.6	77.8	89.1	87.8	90.2	79.7	80.3	79.7
1982	92.5	92.3	92.6	93.2	96.0	97.0	94.6	91.1	86.5	95.4	95.1	95.7	90.3	91.0	90.2
1983	100.6	100.2	100.7	99.8	100.1	100.2	100.1	101.1	103.4	100.3	100.7	100.0	100.0	100.3	100.0
1984	106.8	107.5	106.7	107.0	103.8	102.8	105.4	107.9	110.1	104.3	104.2	104.4	109.7	108.7	109.8
1985	113.5	115.2	113.2	113.5	107.9	105.8	110.9	114.5	116.7	108.3	107.6	108.9	119.1	118.2	119.2
1986	122.0	122.8	121.9	120.8	111.6	107.9	116.8	121.4	124.7	111.9	111.3	112.5	128.6	128.1	128.7
1987	130.1	131.0	130.0	128.8	115.3	110.5	122.0	128.5	133.6	115.1	113.9	116.2	138.5	138.1	138.7
1988	138.6	139.9	138.3	137.5	120.3	115.0	127.7	137.0	145.8	119.4	118.1	120.7	147.9	148.1	148.0
1989	149.3	150.8	148.9	146.4	126.5	119.8	135.4	147.7	164.4	125.0	123.2	126.8	158.1	158.0	158.3
1990	162.8	163.4	162.7	156.1	132.4	124.0	143.2	159.0	181.5	130.4	128.2	132.8	170.2	171.3	170.4
1991	177.0	176.8	177.1	165.7	138.4	128.6	150.6	171.6	202.7	134.9	132.8	137.0	183.7	180.3	184.2
1992	190.1	188.1	190.5	175.8	142.3	131.3	155.9	183.3	219.8	138.3	136.5	140.0	197.4	190.3	198.1
1993	201.4	195.0	202.9	184.7	145.8	133.4	160.8	192.9	228.4	141.5	139.0	144.0	210.7	197.6	211.9
1994	211.0	200.7	213.4	192.5	150.1	136.1	166.8	198.5	220.0	144.6	141.5	147.9	223.2	205.5	224.8
1995	220.5	204.5	224.2	201.0	153.9	138.7	172.0	206.9	225.7	147.1	143.1	151.5	235.5	214.4	237.3
1996	228.2	210.4	232.4	208.3	159.1	143.0	178.1	215.4	232.8	150.1	144.3	156.6	247.5	226.9	249.3
1993:															
January	196.6	192.0	197.4	180.9	144.3	132.8	158.3	191.1	233.5	139.8	137.7	141.9	205.0	194.3	205.7
February	197.6	192.9	198.5	181.4	144.5	132.9	158.6	191.8	234.9	139.6	137.0	142.2	206.0	194.1	206.8
March	198.4	193.4	199.3	181.9	144.6	132.9	158.8	192.9	236.3	140.7	138.4	142.9	206.9	195.1	207.7
April	199.4	193.3	200.6	182.8	144.9	132.8	159.5	193.6	237.6	140.6	138.1	143.2	207.8	195.8	208.6
May	200.8	194.1	202.1	184.2	145.0	132.9	159.6	194.6	237.5	141.0	138.7	143.4	209.4	196.8	210.3
June	201.6	194.7	202.9	184.7	145.6	133.2	160.6	194.7	235.3	141.1	139.0	143.3	210.6	197.2	211.5
July	202.4	195.5	203.8	185.2	145.6	133.1	160.6	195.6	235.5	142.0	140.0	144.0	211.7	197.7	212.7
August	203.0	196.1	204.4	185.8	146.1	133.4	161.4	194.5	227.4	142.0	139.8	144.3	212.8	201.2	213.6
September	203.8	196.4	205.3	186.4	146.4	133.7	161.8	192.6	215.7	142.4	139.7	145.3	213.6	198.2	214.7
October	204.6	196.9	206.2	187.0	147.3	134.4	162.8	193.1	215.1	142.4	139.7	145.3	214.8	199.5	215.9
November	205.3	197.0	207.0	187.4	147.6	134.3	163.6	193.7	214.9	142.9	140.2	145.7	215.9	200.3	217.0
December	206.0	197.4	207.7	188.0	148.2	134.8	164.2	194.7	216.4	143.1	140.1	146.1	217.1	201.3	218.2
1994:															
January	206.5	197.9	208.3	188.5	148.4	134.6	164.9	195.3	216.8	143.3	140.5	146.3	217.9	201.9	219.0
February	207.4	198.4	209.2	189.1	148.9	134.4	166.1	195.7	217.0	143.0	140.0	146.2	218.8	202.4	219.9
March	208.1	198.7	210.0	189.9	149.3	135.0	166.3	196.4	217.8	143.0	139.7	146.6	219.6	203.2	220.8
April	209.3	199.4	211.3	191.2	149.4	135.4	166.0	197.6	218.4	144.2	141.4	147.1	221.2	203.8	222.4
May	210.0	200.1	212.0	191.5	149.8	136.1	166.2	198.5	220.0	144.4	141.7	147.2	222.2	204.7	223.4
June	210.8	200.5	212.9	192.2	150.0	136.2	166.5	199.2	219.8	145.2	141.8	148.8	223.4	205.5	224.6
July	211.6	201.1	213.8	192.8	150.5	136.6	167.1	199.9	221.0	145.0	141.9	148.3	224.3	206.5	225.5
August	212.4	201.7	214.6	193.4	150.6	136.6	167.2	200.4	221.3	145.0	141.9	148.3	225.0	206.9	226.3
September	213.3	201.9	215.7	194.2	150.7	137.1	166.9	200.8	221.2	145.1	141.8	148.7	225.8	207.6	227.1
October	214.3	202.4	216.8	195.3	151.0	137.1	167.7	201.6	222.0	145.3	142.0	148.7	226.9	207.6	228.2
November	215.1	203.0	217.7	195.8	151.5	137.2	168.5	202.3	221.7	145.7	142.3	149.2	228.1	208.2	229.5
December	216.1	203.3	218.8	196.6	151.5	137.2	168.6	203.0	222.9	145.8	142.6	149.2	229.0	208.6	230.4
1995:															
January	216.8	203.2	219.7	197.4	152.0	137.4	169.3	203.2	221.7	145.7	142.2	149.4	229.7	210.0	231.1
February	217.6	203.2	220.7	198.1	152.2	137.3	169.8	204.6	222.6	146.2	142.6	150.1	231.9	210.7	233.4
March	218.2	203.3	221.4	198.8	152.3	137.1	170.3	204.9	222.7	146.0	142.2	150.2	232.5	211.5	234.0
April	218.9	203.3	222.3	199.3	152.9	137.8	170.8	205.5	223.6	146.3	142.2	150.7	233.1	212.2	234.6
May	219.5	203.5	223.0	199.9	153.5	138.0	171.8	206.3	224.5	146.6	142.9	150.6	234.0	212.8	235.5
June	220.2	203.8	223.8	200.7	153.4	138.2	171.4	207.0	225.7	146.7	142.8	151.0	234.9	213.8	236.4
July	220.9	204.2	224.5	201.4	153.9	138.6	171.9	207.7	225.9	146.9	142.7	151.4	236.1	214.5	237.6
August	221.8	204.7	225.5	202.0	154.5	139.1	172.7	208.7	227.0	147.3	143.2	151.7	237.3	214.2	238.9
September	222.6	205.1	226.4	202.6	155.0	139.5	173.3	209.7	228.4	147.5	143.0	152.4	238.5	216.3	240.1
October	223.2	205.8	227.0	203.1	155.3	139.8	173.7	210.4	228.3	148.5	144.4	153.0	239.4	217.8	240.9
November	223.8	206.5	227.6	203.7	155.9	140.5	174.2	211.1	228.9	148.9	144.8	153.5	240.4	219.3	241.9
December	224.6	207.0	228.4	204.5	156.5	141.0	174.9	211.8	229.0	148.9	144.1	154.3	241.5	220.4	243.0
1996:															
January	225.3	207.7	229.1	205.2	156.9	141.2	175.4	212.4	229.1	149.1	143.7	155.0	242.6	221.6	244.1
February	225.9	208.2	229.7	205.7	158.0	142.4	176.5	213.2	230.0	149.3	144.1	155.2	243.6	222.6	245.1
March	226.4	208.6	230.3	206.2	158.1	142.5	176.5	213.9	231.1	149.4	144.0	155.3	244.5	223.8	246.0
April	227.0	209.3	230.9	206.8	158.2	142.5	176.7	214.6	231.3	149.7	144.2	155.7	245.6	224.8	247.1
May	227.7	209.8	231.6	207.4	158.7	142.7	177.5	215.5	232.2	150.3	145.3	155.8	246.6	225.4	248.1
June	228.3	210.5	232.2	207.8	159.1	143.0	178.1	215.8	232.2	149.6	143.9	155.9	247.6	226.0	249.1
July	228.9	210.8	232.8	208.5	159.3	143.0	178.5	216.6	232.9	150.0	144.4	156.3	248.6	226.5	250.1
August	229.3	211.1	233.3	209.2	159.6	143.4	178.7	217.4	233.1	150.5	145.0	156.5	249.7	228.7	251.2
September	229.9	211.5	233.9	209.8	159.8	143.5	179.1	217.7	234.2	150.8	145.1	157.2	249.9	229.5	251.3
October	230.4	212.4	234.3	210.5	160.3	143.8	179.7	218.4	235.4	150.9	144.6	157.9	250.6	230.6	252.0
November	231.0	212.1	235.1	211.2	160.6	144.0	180.2	219.2	236.0	151.2	144.7	158.6	251.7	231.5	253.1
December	231.5	212.4	235.6	211.6	161.1	144.4	180.8	219.4	235.3	150.5	142.8	159.2	252.7	232.5	254.1

1. Not seasonally adjusted.

CONSUMER PRICE INDEXES—COMMODITY AND SERVICE GROUPS
(All urban consumers—1982-1984=100, except as noted, seasonally adjusted, except as noted)

YEAR AND MONTH	Commodities Total	Food and beverages	Commodities less food and beverages Total	Nondurables Total	Apparel commodities	Less food, beverages, and apparel	Durables	Services Total	Rent of shelter [1,2]	Household services less rent of shelter [1]	Transportation services	Medical care services	Other services
1968	38.1	36.2	39.7	38.4	57.3	32.2	40.7	30.3	....	....	33.9	27.9	38.1
1969	39.9	38.1	41.4	40.2	60.8	33.4	42.2	32.4	....	....	36.3	30.2	40.0
1970	41.7	40.1	43.1	41.7	63.3	34.6	44.1	35.0	....	....	40.2	32.3	42.2
1971	43.2	41.4	44.7	43.1	65.2	35.9	46.0	37.0	....	....	43.4	34.7	44.4
1972	44.5	43.1	45.8	44.2	66.6	36.8	46.9	38.4	....	....	44.4	35.9	45.6
1973	47.8	48.8	47.3	46.1	69.0	38.6	48.1	40.1	....	....	44.7	37.5	47.7
1974	53.5	55.5	52.4	52.4	73.9	45.6	51.5	43.8	....	....	46.3	41.4	51.3
1975	58.2	60.2	57.3	56.3	76.7	50.3	57.4	48.0	....	....	49.8	46.6	55.1
1976	60.7	62.1	60.2	58.9	79.2	52.9	60.9	52.0	....	....	56.9	51.3	58.4
1977	64.2	65.8	63.6	62.1	82.3	56.2	64.4	56.0	....	....	61.5	56.4	62.1
1978	68.8	72.2	67.3	65.0	84.5	59.4	68.6	60.8	....	....	64.4	61.2	66.4
1979	76.6	79.9	75.2	74.3	87.5	70.5	75.4	67.5	....	....	69.5	67.2	71.9
1980	86.0	86.7	85.7	88.5	92.9	87.2	83.0	77.9	....	....	79.2	74.8	78.7
1981	93.2	93.5	93.1	97.0	96.5	97.1	89.6	88.1	....	....	88.6	82.8	86.1
1982	97.0	97.3	96.9	98.3	98.3	98.4	95.1	96.0	....	....	96.1	92.6	93.5
1983	99.8	99.5	100.0	100.0	100.2	100.0	99.8	99.4	102.7	103.4	99.1	100.7	100.0
1984	103.2	103.2	103.1	101.7	101.5	101.7	105.1	104.6	107.7	108.1	104.8	106.7	106.5
1985	105.4	105.6	105.2	104.0	104.0	104.0	106.8	109.9	113.9	111.2	110.0	113.2	113.0
1986	104.4	109.1	101.4	97.8	104.2	95.9	106.6	115.4	120.2	112.8	116.3	121.9	119.4
1987	107.7	113.5	104.0	101.1	108.9	99.5	108.2	120.2	125.9	113.1	121.9	130.0	125.7
1988	111.5	118.2	107.3	105.2	113.7	103.2	110.4	125.7	132.0	115.3	128.0	138.3	132.6
1989	116.7	124.9	111.6	111.2	116.7	111.0	112.2	131.9	138.0	118.7	135.6	148.9	140.9
1990	122.8	132.1	117.0	119.6	122.0	121.1	113.4	139.2	145.5	121.7	144.2	162.7	150.2
1991	126.6	136.8	120.4	123.5	126.4	124.8	116.0	146.3	152.1	126.7	151.2	177.1	159.8
1992	129.1	138.7	123.2	126.5	129.4	127.9	118.6	152.0	157.3	130.2	155.7	190.5	168.5
1993	131.5	141.6	125.3	128.1	131.0	129.6	121.3	157.9	162.0	134.2	162.9	202.9	177.0
1994	133.8	144.9	126.9	128.4	130.4	130.3	124.8	163.1	167.0	136.3	168.6	213.4	185.4
1995	136.4	148.9	128.9	129.5	128.7	132.9	128.0	168.7	172.4	138.3	175.9	224.2	193.3
1996	139.9	153.7	131.5	133.0	128.2	138.6	129.4	174.1	178.0	142.0	180.5	232.4	201.4
1993:													
January	130.7	140.0	125.0	128.5	130.0	130.7	119.7	155.3	159.9	132.3	159.7	197.4	173.5
February	131.2	140.4	125.4	129.4	131.5	131.3	119.7	155.7	160.6	131.8	160.7	198.5	174.2
March	131.2	140.5	125.5	129.4	131.4	131.4	120.1	156.1	161.0	132.9	160.5	199.3	174.7
April	131.4	140.8	125.7	129.5	131.5	131.4	120.5	156.7	161.2	133.5	160.9	200.6	175.4
May	131.6	141.7	125.4	128.8	130.8	130.7	120.7	157.3	161.2	133.8	162.2	202.1	176.2
June	131.3	141.3	125.1	128.2	130.2	130.1	121.0	157.8	162.0	134.3	162.4	202.9	177.1
July	131.3	141.4	125.0	127.7	130.1	129.4	121.2	158.2	162.6	134.6	163.1	203.8	177.8
August	131.6	141.9	125.2	127.4	131.2	128.6	121.7	158.6	163.1	135.0	163.8	204.4	178.5
September	131.4	142.2	124.8	126.5	130.9	126.9	122.1	159.1	162.9	135.5	164.0	205.3	179.3
October	132.2	142.8	125.8	127.7	130.8	128.8	122.5	159.5	163.1	135.8	164.4	206.2	180.2
November	132.4	143.0	125.9	127.6	131.6	128.5	122.9	160.0	163.1	135.6	165.8	207.0	181.1
December	132.4	143.5	125.7	127.4	131.2	128.3	123.0	160.6	163.5	135.7	166.4	207.7	181.9
1994:													
January	132.4	143.7	125.4	127.0	130.4	128.3	123.1	160.8	164.5	135.4	166.2	208.3	182.5
February	132.4	143.5	125.6	127.5	130.1	128.9	123.0	161.4	165.6	135.9	166.7	209.2	183.3
March	132.6	143.5	125.9	127.7	130.8	129.1	123.3	161.9	166.3	136.3	167.5	210.0	183.8
April	132.6	143.5	125.9	127.7	130.6	129.1	123.5	162.2	166.1	136.2	167.8	211.3	184.5
May	132.9	144.0	126.1	127.5	131.0	128.7	124.3	162.5	166.0	136.3	167.2	212.0	185.1
June	133.4	144.4	126.6	128.0	131.8	129.1	124.9	162.9	166.6	136.3	168.2	212.9	185.9
July	134.1	145.2	127.3	128.7	131.2	130.3	125.3	163.2	167.3	136.4	168.4	213.8	186.5
August	134.7	145.8	127.9	129.5	130.1	132.3	125.5	163.9	168.2	136.5	169.7	214.6	186.9
September	134.9	146.0	128.1	129.7	130.4	132.1	125.7	164.2	168.2	136.4	169.8	215.7	187.2
October	134.8	145.9	128.0	129.4	129.7	132.0	126.0	164.6	168.6	136.5	169.6	216.8	188.0
November	135.0	146.2	128.2	129.4	129.2	132.2	126.4	165.1	168.6	136.8	170.1	217.7	188.8
December	135.5	147.3	128.2	129.3	128.8	132.5	126.6	165.3	168.3	136.7	170.8	218.8	189.3
1995:													
January	135.5	147.2	128.3	129.0	128.9	132.3	126.9	166.0	169.4	137.8	171.9	219.7	189.9
February	135.7	147.7	128.3	129.1	128.4	132.5	127.3	166.6	170.4	137.6	172.7	220.7	191.2
March	135.7	147.6	128.5	129.0	128.7	132.2	127.5	167.1	171.2	137.7	174.1	221.4	191.7
April	136.1	148.2	128.6	129.0	128.7	132.4	127.9	167.7	171.3	137.9	175.6	222.3	192.2
May	136.4	148.7	128.9	129.6	128.3	133.3	128.0	168.1	171.5	137.7	176.0	223.0	192.9
June	136.5	148.7	129.0	129.8	128.0	133.7	128.0	168.6	172.2	138.1	177.4	223.8	193.1
July	136.6	149.0	129.0	129.7	128.2	133.2	128.0	168.9	173.2	138.2	176.7	224.5	193.9
August	136.8	149.3	129.2	129.7	129.0	133.1	128.2	169.4	173.6	138.7	176.8	225.5	194.8
September	136.9	149.7	129.1	129.6	128.8	132.7	128.3	169.7	173.6	138.2	176.8	226.4	195.6
October	137.2	150.1	129.3	129.9	129.0	133.0	128.5	170.4	174.1	139.0	177.7	227.0	196.1
November	137.1	150.2	129.1	129.5	128.7	132.4	128.6	170.7	174.1	139.1	177.6	227.6	196.8
December	137.4	150.4	129.5	130.2	128.7	133.9	128.8	171.0	174.2	139.5	176.1	228.4	197.6
1996:													
January	138.1	150.8	130.4	131.2	129.3	135.6	129.0	171.5	175.5	139.6	176.2	229.1	198.4
February	138.3	151.2	130.4	131.3	128.4	135.9	129.1	172.1	176.3	140.1	177.8	229.7	199.3
March	139.0	151.8	131.2	132.2	129.0	137.2	129.3	172.4	177.0	140.4	177.6	230.3	199.7
April	139.6	152.1	131.9	133.6	128.7	139.6	129.2	172.9	177.0	140.8	178.5	230.9	200.3
May	139.8	152.4	132.1	134.1	128.5	140.3	129.2	173.5	177.0	141.6	179.4	231.6	201.1
June	139.7	153.4	131.4	133.0	128.1	138.5	129.3	173.9	177.6	141.7	180.4	232.2	201.8
July	139.9	154.0	131.3	132.9	127.8	138.2	129.3	174.5	178.9	142.3	180.5	232.8	202.4
August	139.9	154.6	131.0	132.1	126.5	138.0	129.4	174.9	179.3	142.8	181.2	233.3	203.0
September	140.5	155.3	131.5	132.7	127.3	138.2	129.7	175.4	179.0	143.1	182.5	233.9	203.3
October	141.0	156.0	131.9	133.5	127.6	139.2	129.6	175.8	179.4	143.4	183.1	234.3	203.9
November	141.5	156.6	132.4	134.3	128.0	140.2	129.6	176.3	179.4	144.0	183.4	235.1	204.7
December	141.8	156.6	132.8	135.2	128.0	141.8	129.7	176.8	179.3	144.3	184.1	235.6	205.4

1. December 1982=100.
2. Not seasonally adjusted.

CONSUMER PRICE INDEXES—SPECIAL INDEXES
(All urban consumers—1982-1984=100, except as noted, seasonally adjusted)

YEAR AND MONTH	All items less Food	All items less Shelter	All items less Homeowners' cost[1]	All items less Medical care	Commodities less food	Nondurables less food	Nondurables less food and apparel[1]	Nondurables[1]	Services less rent of shelter[1]	Services less medical care services	Energy	All items less Energy	All items less Food and energy	Commodities less food and energy commodities	Energy commodities	Services less energy services
1968	34.9	36.7	....	35.1	40.0	39.1	33.7	37.1	....	30.8	24.2	35.9	36.3	42.9	24.4	30.9
1969	36.8	38.4	....	37.0	41.7	40.9	34.9	38.9	....	32.9	24.8	38.0	38.4	44.7	25.2	33.2
1970	39.0	40.3	....	39.2	43.4	42.5	36.3	40.8	....	35.6	25.5	40.3	40.8	46.7	25.6	36.0
1971	40.8	42.0	....	40.8	45.1	44.0	37.6	42.1	....	37.5	26.5	42.0	42.7	48.5	26.1	38.0
1972	42.0	43.3	....	42.1	46.1	45.0	38.6	43.5	....	38.9	27.2	43.4	44.0	49.7	26.4	39.4
1973	43.7	46.2	....	44.8	47.7	46.9	40.3	47.5	....	40.6	29.4	46.1	45.6	51.1	29.1	41.1
1974	48.0	51.4	....	49.8	52.8	52.9	46.9	54.0	....	44.3	38.1	50.6	49.4	55.0	40.4	44.8
1975	52.5	56.0	....	54.3	57.6	57.0	51.5	58.3	....	48.3	42.1	55.1	53.9	60.1	43.4	48.8
1976	56.0	59.3	....	57.2	60.5	59.5	54.1	60.5	....	52.2	45.1	58.2	57.4	63.2	45.4	52.7
1977	59.6	63.1	....	60.8	63.8	62.5	57.2	64.0	....	55.9	49.4	61.9	61.0	66.5	48.7	56.5
1978	63.9	67.4	....	65.4	67.5	65.5	60.4	68.6	....	60.7	52.5	66.7	65.5	70.5	51.0	61.3
1979	71.2	74.2	....	72.9	75.3	74.6	71.2	77.2	....	67.5	65.7	73.4	71.9	76.4	68.7	68.2
1980	81.5	82.9	....	82.8	85.7	88.4	87.1	87.6	....	78.2	86.0	81.9	80.8	83.5	95.2	78.5
1981	90.4	91.0	....	91.4	93.1	96.7	96.8	95.2	....	88.7	97.7	90.1	89.2	90.0	107.6	88.7
1982	96.3	96.2	....	96.8	96.9	98.3	98.2	97.8	....	96.4	99.2	96.1	95.8	95.3	102.9	96.3
1983	99.7	99.8	102.0	99.6	100.0	100.0	100.0	99.7	102.9	99.2	99.9	99.6	99.6	100.2	99.0	99.2
1984	104.0	103.9	106.3	103.7	103.1	101.7	101.8	102.5	108.5	104.4	100.9	104.3	104.6	104.4	98.1	104.5
1985	108.0	107.0	109.7	107.2	105.2	104.1	104.1	104.8	113.5	109.6	101.6	108.4	109.1	107.1	98.2	110.2
1986	109.8	108.0	111.2	108.8	101.7	98.5	96.9	103.5	118.7	114.6	88.2	112.6	113.5	108.6	77.2	116.5
1987	113.6	111.6	115.1	112.6	104.3	101.8	100.3	107.5	123.1	119.1	88.6	117.2	118.2	111.8	80.2	122.0
1988	118.3	115.9	119.5	117.0	107.7	105.8	104.0	111.8	128.3	124.3	89.3	122.3	123.4	115.8	80.8	127.9
1989	123.7	121.6	125.3	122.4	112.0	111.7	111.3	118.2	135.1	130.1	94.3	128.1	129.0	119.6	87.9	134.4
1990	130.3	128.2	132.1	128.8	117.4	119.9	120.9	126.0	142.7	136.8	102.1	134.7	135.5	123.6	101.2	142.3
1991	136.1	133.5	137.8	133.8	121.3	124.5	125.7	130.3	150.9	143.3	102.5	140.9	142.1	128.8	99.1	149.8
1992	140.8	137.3	141.9	137.5	124.2	127.6	128.9	132.8	157.6	148.4	103.0	145.4	147.3	132.5	98.3	155.9
1993	145.1	141.4	146.0	141.2	126.3	129.3	130.7	135.1	164.8	153.6	104.2	150.0	152.2	135.2	97.3	161.9
1994	149.0	144.8	149.5	144.7	127.9	129.7	131.6	136.8	170.7	158.4	104.6	154.1	156.5	137.1	97.6	167.6
1995	153.1	148.6	153.5	148.6	129.8	130.9	134.1	139.3	176.8	163.5	105.2	158.7	161.2	139.3	98.8	173.7
1996	157.5	152.8	157.9	152.8	132.6	134.5	139.5	143.5	182.5	168.7	110.1	163.1	165.6	141.3	105.7	179.4
1993:																
January	143.4	139.7	144.3	139.6	126.1	129.6	131.5	134.4	161.5	151.2	104.7	148.1	150.3	134.2	100.3	159.3
February	143.7	140.2	144.7	139.9	126.5	130.4	132.0	135.1	161.9	151.6	104.1	148.6	150.8	134.7	100.5	159.8
March	144.0	140.4	144.9	140.1	126.5	130.5	132.2	135.2	162.5	151.9	104.4	148.8	151.1	134.9	99.7	160.2
April	144.5	140.8	145.4	140.5	126.7	130.5	132.2	135.3	163.1	152.5	104.6	149.3	151.6	135.2	99.2	160.8
May	144.7	141.2	145.8	140.9	126.4	129.9	131.5	135.3	164.1	153.0	103.7	149.8	152.0	135.3	97.1	161.4
June	144.9	141.1	145.8	140.9	126.1	129.3	131.0	135.0	164.7	153.6	103.3	150.0	152.3	135.1	96.0	161.8
July	145.1	141.3	146.0	141.1	126.1	128.9	130.5	134.8	165.3	153.8	103.0	150.2	152.5	135.2	95.3	162.2
August	145.5	141.7	146.3	141.4	126.3	128.6	129.9	134.9	165.8	154.3	103.0	150.6	153.0	135.5	94.9	162.7
September	145.6	141.8	146.5	141.5	125.9	127.9	128.6	134.4	166.5	154.7	102.7	150.8	153.1	135.3	94.0	163.1
October	146.2	142.6	147.2	142.2	126.9	128.9	130.2	135.4	167.0	155.0	105.1	151.3	153.5	135.5	94.0	163.6
November	146.6	142.9	147.5	142.5	127.0	128.9	129.9	135.5	167.6	155.5	104.1	151.8	154.1	135.9	97.0	164.2
December	146.9	143.1	147.8	142.8	126.8	128.7	129.7	135.5	168.1	156.1	103.4	152.2	154.5	136.1	95.6	164.8
1994:																
January	146.9	143.1	147.8	142.8	126.6	128.4	129.7	135.6	168.1	156.2	102.6	152.3	154.6	136.0	94.6	165.1
February	147.4	143.3	148.0	143.2	126.8	128.8	130.3	135.6	168.8	156.8	103.8	152.6	155.0	136.3	96.4	165.8
March	147.8	143.6	148.4	143.5	127.0	129.0	130.4	135.8	169.4	157.3	103.7	153.0	155.5	136.2	95.8	166.3
April	148.0	143.8	148.5	143.6	127.0	129.0	130.3	135.8	169.7	157.6	103.3	153.2	155.8	136.4	95.4	166.6
May	148.2	144.0	148.8	143.8	127.2	128.9	129.8	135.8	169.9	157.8	102.0	153.7	156.2	137.0	93.3	166.9
June	148.6	144.5	149.3	144.3	127.8	129.3	130.2	136.4	170.4	158.1	102.3	154.1	156.7	137.5	94.0	167.4
July	149.0	145.1	149.8	144.7	128.4	130.0	131.5	137.1	170.8	158.4	104.0	154.5	156.9	137.7	97.1	167.7
August	149.7	145.7	150.4	145.4	129.0	130.6	133.4	137.8	171.5	159.0	106.2	154.8	157.4	137.8	101.2	168.5
September	150.0	145.9	150.6	145.6	129.1	130.9	133.3	137.9	171.7	159.3	105.8	155.3	157.7	137.9	100.7	168.5
October	150.2	146.0	150.7	145.7	129.1	130.6	133.2	137.7	172.1	159.6	105.5	155.5	158.0	137.9	100.3	169.3
November	150.6	146.3	151.1	146.0	129.2	130.6	133.6	138.0	172.6	160.1	106.2	155.9	158.4	137.9	101.0	169.8
December	150.7	146.7	151.5	146.3	129.3	130.7	133.6	138.3	173.1	160.2	105.9	156.3	158.6	138.0	100.9	170.1
1995:																
January	151.2	147.1	151.8	146.7	129.3	130.4	133.3	138.4	173.9	161.0	105.5	156.7	159.2	138.2	100.1	170.9
February	151.5	147.4	152.2	147.0	129.4	130.4	133.4	138.6	174.6	161.5	105.5	157.1	159.6	138.4	99.8	171.4
March	151.9	147.6	152.4	147.3	129.5	130.3	133.2	138.5	175.2	162.0	104.9	157.5	160.1	138.7	99.0	172.1
April	152.3	148.1	153.0	147.8	129.7	130.4	133.3	138.9	175.8	162.5	105.1	158.1	160.6	138.9	99.1	172.7
May	152.7	148.4	153.3	148.1	130.0	130.9	134.0	139.1	176.2	163.0	105.1	158.5	161.0	139.1	100.0	173.2
June	153.1	148.6	153.6	148.4	130.1	131.1	134.5	139.4	176.8	163.4	105.6	158.8	161.3	139.1	100.5	173.8
July	153.2	148.8	153.7	148.6	130.1	131.1	134.4	139.5	177.1	163.8	105.2	159.0	161.6	139.2	99.7	174.1
August	153.6	149.2	154.1	148.9	130.3	131.1	134.6	139.7	177.6	164.1	105.2	159.4	162.0	139.7	98.7	174.5
September	153.8	149.3	154.3	149.1	130.3	131.0	134.4	139.8	177.8	164.4	103.8	159.8	162.4	139.9	97.5	175.0
October	154.3	149.7	154.7	149.6	130.5	131.3	134.6	140.1	178.5	165.0	104.5	160.3	162.9	140.2	97.6	175.6
November	154.4	149.7	154.7	149.7	130.3	131.0	134.4	140.0	178.8	165.4	103.6	160.5	163.1	140.3	95.8	176.0
December	154.7	150.0	155.0	150.0	130.7	131.7	135.2	140.3	178.9	165.6	104.5	160.8	163.4	140.4	97.5	176.3
1996:																
January	155.3	150.6	155.6	150.5	131.5	132.6	136.4	141.3	179.2	166.0	106.3	161.2	163.8	140.7	100.8	176.7
February	155.7	151.0	156.0	150.9	131.6	132.7	136.9	141.5	180.1	166.6	106.8	161.6	164.2	140.8	100.9	177.4
March	156.2	151.5	156.6	151.4	132.3	133.6	138.0	142.3	180.5	167.0	107.9	162.0	164.6	141.2	103.6	177.8
April	156.8	152.1	157.2	151.9	133.1	135.0	139.9	143.1	180.9	167.4	111.1	162.3	164.9	141.1	108.4	178.1
May	157.2	152.5	157.6	152.3	133.2	135.4	140.4	143.2	181.8	168.0	111.4	162.7	165.3	141.2	109.1	178.8
June	157.2	152.6	157.7	152.5	132.6	134.5	139.2	143.4	182.2	168.4	109.2	163.1	165.6	141.2	105.4	179.3
July	157.6	152.9	158.1	152.9	132.5	134.4	139.3	143.6	182.9	169.0	109.5	163.6	166.0	141.2	104.9	179.9
August	157.8	153.2	158.4	153.1	132.3	133.6	139.4	143.6	183.4	169.4	109.3	163.8	166.2	141.1	104.0	180.3
September	158.2	153.7	158.9	153.6	132.8	134.2	139.9	144.1	184.0	169.9	109.5	164.4	166.7	141.6	104.3	180.8
October	158.7	154.2	159.4	154.1	133.2	135.0	140.8	144.8	184.5	170.3	110.7	164.8	167.0	141.7	106.5	181.2
November	159.1	154.7	159.9	154.5	133.6	135.8	141.8	145.5	185.1	170.8	112.0	165.2	167.4	141.8	108.3	181.7
December	159.6	155.1	160.3	154.9	134.1	136.7	142.8	146.0	185.7	171.3	113.7	165.4	167.7	141.9	111.1	182.2

1. December 1982=100.

PRODUCER PRICE INDEXES
(By stage of processing—1982=100, seasonally adjusted)

YEAR AND MONTH	Finished goods		Finished consumer goods				Finished consumer goods, except foods			Capital equipment		
	Index	Percent change from previous period	Total	Finished consumer foods			Total	Nondurable goods less foods	Durable goods	Total	Manufacturing industries	Nonmanufacturing industries
				Total	Crude	Processed						
1968	36.6	2.8	36.5	40.0	42.5	40.0	35.5	30.6	45.1	37.0	35.0	38.2
1969	38.0	3.8	37.9	42.4	45.9	42.3	36.3	31.5	45.9	38.3	36.2	39.5
1970	39.3	3.4	39.1	43.8	46.0	43.9	37.4	32.5	47.2	40.1	38.1	41.3
1971	40.5	3.1	40.2	44.5	45.8	44.7	38.7	33.5	48.9	41.7	39.6	43.0
1972	41.8	3.2	41.5	46.9	48.0	47.2	39.4	34.1	50.0	42.8	40.5	44.2
1973	45.6	9.1	46.0	56.5	63.6	55.8	41.2	36.1	50.9	44.2	42.2	45.3
1974	52.6	15.4	53.1	64.4	71.6	63.9	48.2	44.0	55.5	50.5	48.8	51.2
1975	58.2	10.6	58.2	69.8	71.7	70.3	53.2	48.9	61.0	58.2	56.5	58.9
1976	60.8	4.5	60.4	69.6	76.7	69.0	56.5	52.4	63.7	62.1	60.3	62.9
1977	64.7	6.4	64.3	73.3	79.5	72.7	60.6	56.8	67.4	66.1	64.5	66.8
1978	69.8	7.9	69.4	79.9	85.8	79.4	64.9	60.0	73.6	71.3	70.1	71.8
1979	77.6	11.2	77.5	87.3	92.3	86.8	73.5	69.3	80.8	77.5	77.1	77.7
1980	88.0	13.4	88.6	92.4	93.9	92.3	87.1	85.1	91.0	85.8	86.0	85.7
1981	96.1	9.2	96.6	97.8	104.4	97.2	96.1	95.8	96.4	94.6	94.9	94.4
1982	100.0	4.1	100.0	100.0	100.0	100.0	100.0	100.0	100.0	100.0	100.0	100.0
1983	101.6	1.6	101.3	101.0	102.4	100.9	101.2	100.5	102.8	102.8	102.3	103.0
1984	103.7	2.1	103.3	105.4	111.4	104.9	102.2	101.1	104.5	105.2	104.9	105.4
1985	104.7	1.0	103.8	104.6	102.9	104.8	103.3	101.7	106.5	107.5	107.4	107.6
1986	103.2	-1.4	101.4	107.3	105.6	107.4	98.5	93.3	108.9	109.7	109.7	109.7
1987	105.4	2.1	103.6	109.5	107.1	109.6	100.7	94.9	111.5	111.7	111.8	111.6
1988	108.0	2.5	106.2	112.6	109.8	112.7	103.1	97.3	113.8	114.3	115.5	113.9
1989	113.6	5.2	112.1	118.7	119.6	118.6	108.9	103.8	117.6	118.8	120.3	118.2
1990	119.2	4.9	118.2	124.4	123.0	124.4	115.3	111.5	120.4	122.9	124.5	122.2
1991	121.7	2.1	120.5	124.1	119.3	124.4	118.7	115.0	123.9	126.7	127.8	126.3
1992	123.2	1.2	121.7	123.3	107.6	124.4	120.8	117.3	125.7	129.1	129.3	129.0
1993	124.7	1.2	123.0	125.7	114.4	126.5	121.7	117.6	128.0	131.4	131.2	131.4
1994	125.5	0.6	123.3	126.8	111.3	127.9	121.6	116.2	130.9	134.1	133.2	134.3
1995	127.9	1.9	125.6	129.0	118.8	129.8	124.0	118.8	132.7	136.7	135.8	137.0
1996	131.3	2.7	129.5	133.6	129.2	133.8	127.6	123.3	134.2	138.3	137.2	138.6
1993:												
January	124.4	0.2	122.9	124.6	114.1	125.4	121.9	118.6	126.6	130.4	130.5	130.3
February	124.7	0.2	123.2	124.5	113.4	125.3	122.4	119.1	127.0	130.7	130.6	130.7
March	124.9	0.2	123.4	124.5	113.2	125.3	122.7	119.3	127.3	130.9	130.7	130.9
April	125.6	0.6	124.2	126.4	126.1	126.4	123.0	119.5	127.9	131.1	130.8	131.1
May	125.5	-0.1	124.1	126.5	125.4	126.5	122.9	119.4	127.9	131.2	130.9	131.2
June	125.1	-0.3	123.6	125.3	103.2	126.9	122.6	118.9	128.0	131.1	131.1	131.0
July	125.0	-0.1	123.4	124.9	100.9	126.7	122.5	118.6	128.3	131.5	131.2	131.5
August	124.0	-0.8	122.0	125.2	107.6	126.4	120.5	115.6	128.7	131.6	131.3	131.7
September	124.2	0.2	122.2	125.7	107.7	127.0	120.5	115.7	128.5	131.8	131.5	131.8
October	124.3	0.1	122.4	125.5	105.5	126.9	120.9	116.4	128.1	131.7	131.5	131.7
November	124.5	0.2	122.5	127.0	123.9	127.2	120.4	115.4	128.9	132.2	131.8	132.2
December	124.5	0.0	122.5	127.7	130.4	127.4	120.1	114.8	129.2	132.4	131.9	132.5
1994:												
January	124.7	0.2	122.5	127.3	123.1	127.6	120.4	114.9	129.9	132.9	132.3	133.1
February	125.0	0.2	122.9	126.7	109.0	128.0	121.0	115.9	129.9	133.1	132.4	133.3
March	125.1	0.1	122.9	127.3	111.9	128.4	120.9	115.5	130.1	133.3	132.6	133.5
April	125.1	0.0	122.8	127.1	105.1	128.7	120.8	115.3	130.3	133.7	132.9	133.9
May	125.0	-0.1	122.6	126.4	103.9	128.0	120.7	115.0	130.9	134.1	133.2	134.3
June	125.2	0.2	122.8	125.9	104.6	127.5	121.3	115.7	131.1	134.2	133.2	134.5
July	125.7	0.4	123.4	126.1	106.4	127.6	122.0	116.6	131.3	134.4	133.4	134.7
August	126.3	0.5	124.1	126.3	104.5	127.9	123.0	117.8	131.8	134.6	133.6	134.9
September	126.0	-0.2	123.6	126.2	105.8	127.7	122.3	116.8	131.8	135.0	133.8	135.3
October	125.5	-0.4	123.2	126.1	103.9	127.7	121.8	116.3	131.1	134.3	133.5	134.5
November	126.2	0.6	124.0	127.1	114.6	128.0	122.5	117.2	131.4	134.5	133.7	134.7
December	126.8	0.5	124.6	128.9	142.9	127.9	122.6	117.3	131.7	134.9	134.0	135.2
1995:												
January	126.9	0.1	124.6	128.2	120.1	128.8	122.9	117.6	132.0	135.5	134.5	135.8
February	127.1	0.2	124.8	128.4	116.8	129.2	123.2	117.9	132.2	135.8	134.8	136.0
March	127.3	0.2	125.0	128.4	118.3	129.1	123.3	118.2	132.1	135.9	135.0	136.1
April	127.5	0.2	125.2	128.7	130.4	128.6	123.6	118.4	132.3	136.2	135.3	136.5
May	127.7	0.2	125.4	128.0	123.9	128.3	124.1	119.2	132.3	136.4	135.5	136.7
June	127.7	0.0	125.4	127.5	112.1	128.6	124.3	119.4	132.2	136.5	135.7	136.7
July	127.9	0.2	125.6	128.5	110.2	129.8	124.2	119.2	132.5	136.8	136.0	137.0
August	127.9	0.0	125.5	128.5	107.8	130.0	124.1	119.0	132.6	136.9	136.1	137.1
September	128.3	0.3	125.9	129.9	122.2	130.4	124.1	119.0	132.5	137.0	136.2	137.2
October	128.5	0.2	126.1	129.8	112.7	131.0	124.3	119.1	133.2	137.6	136.9	137.8
November	128.8	0.2	126.3	131.2	126.5	131.5	124.1	118.4	134.0	138.1	137.2	138.3
December	129.6	0.6	127.4	131.4	124.9	131.8	125.5	120.4	134.1	138.0	136.8	138.3
1996:												
January	129.7	0.1	127.6	131.1	125.6	131.4	125.9	121.1	133.7	138.0	137.1	138.3
February	129.7	0.0	127.5	130.8	122.6	131.4	125.9	121.0	133.8	138.0	137.1	138.3
March	130.4	0.5	128.4	131.9	145.7	130.9	126.7	122.0	134.0	138.1	137.1	138.3
April	130.6	0.2	128.7	131.5	131.9	131.4	127.3	123.0	133.9	138.1	137.0	138.4
May	130.8	0.2	128.9	131.7	118.6	132.6	127.5	123.1	134.2	138.1	137.1	138.4
June	131.2	0.3	129.4	133.6	130.0	133.9	127.3	122.8	134.5	138.3	137.2	138.6
July	131.2	0.0	129.4	133.7	123.3	134.4	127.4	123.0	134.2	138.3	137.2	138.6
August	131.6	0.3	129.9	134.6	119.6	135.7	127.7	123.3	134.4	138.5	137.3	138.8
September	132.0	0.3	130.3	135.1	124.4	135.8	128.1	123.7	134.8	138.7	137.4	139.1
October	132.5	0.4	131.0	136.2	134.0	136.3	128.6	124.7	134.3	138.5	137.3	138.9
November	132.7	0.2	131.3	136.2	136.4	136.2	129.0	125.1	134.5	138.5	137.4	138.8
December	133.4	0.5	132.1	135.9	136.0	135.9	130.3	127.0	134.5	138.5	137.4	138.9

PRODUCER PRICE INDEXES—Continued
(By stage of processing—1982=100, seasonally adjusted)

Intermediate materials, supplies, and components

YEAR AND MONTH	Total	Materials and components for manufacturing					Materials and components for construction	Processed fuels and lubricants			Containers	Supplies	
		Total	Materials for food manufacturing	Materials for nondurable manufacturing	Materials for durable manufacturing	Components for manufacturing		Total	Manufacturing industries	Nonmanufacturing industries		Total	Manufacturing industries
1968	33.0	35.3	39.8	35.6	33.4	37.3	35.7	16.5	19.8	14.2	35.9	37.1	38.7
1969	34.1	36.5	42.0	36.0	35.2	38.5	37.7	16.6	20.0	14.4	37.2	37.8	39.8
1970	35.4	38.0	44.3	36.5	37.0	40.6	38.3	17.7	21.5	15.2	39.0	39.7	41.4
1971	36.8	38.9	45.7	37.0	38.1	41.9	40.8	19.5	23.6	16.6	40.8	40.8	42.5
1972	38.2	40.4	47.0	38.5	39.9	42.9	43.0	20.1	24.5	16.9	42.7	42.5	43.3
1973	42.4	44.1	57.2	42.6	43.1	44.3	46.5	22.2	26.4	19.4	45.2	51.7	45.6
1974	52.5	56.0	82.0	54.6	55.4	51.1	55.0	33.6	35.5	32.7	53.3	56.8	53.3
1975	58.0	61.7	82.1	61.4	60.8	57.8	60.1	39.4	41.9	38.0	60.0	61.8	59.4
1976	60.9	64.0	70.6	64.8	64.8	60.8	64.1	42.3	44.8	41.1	63.1	65.8	62.6
1977	64.9	67.4	71.9	66.8	70.2	64.5	69.3	47.7	51.0	46.2	65.9	69.3	66.6
1978	69.5	72.0	81.0	69.2	76.2	69.2	76.5	49.9	53.7	48.1	71.0	72.9	71.2
1979	78.4	80.9	89.9	78.3	87.3	75.8	84.2	61.6	64.3	60.4	79.4	80.2	78.1
1980	90.3	91.7	103.7	91.2	97.1	84.6	91.3	85.0	85.5	84.7	89.1	89.9	87.2
1981	98.6	98.7	102.1	100.5	100.7	94.7	97.9	100.6	100.2	101.0	96.7	96.9	95.2
1982	100.0	100.0	100.0	100.0	100.0	100.0	100.0	100.0	100.0	100.0	100.0	100.0	100.0
1983	100.6	101.2	101.3	98.5	103.0	102.4	102.8	95.4	96.2	94.9	100.0	101.8	100.0
1984	103.1	104.1	106.3	102.1	104.9	105.0	105.6	95.7	97.1	94.6	105.9	104.1	101.5
1985	102.7	103.3	101.5	100.5	103.3	106.4	107.3	92.8	93.8	92.0	109.0	104.4	107.3
1986	99.1	102.2	98.4	98.1	101.2	107.5	108.1	72.7	75.1	71.2	110.3	105.6	108.3
1987	101.5	103.5	100.8	102.2	106.2	108.8	109.8	73.3	75.9	71.7	114.5	107.7	110.0
1988	107.1	113.2	106.0	112.9	118.7	112.3	116.1	71.2	73.3	69.9	120.1	113.7	114.8
1989	112.0	118.1	112.7	118.5	123.6	116.4	121.3	76.4	78.3	75.3	125.4	118.1	119.8
1990	114.5	118.7	117.9	118.0	120.7	119.0	122.9	85.9	87.3	85.0	127.7	119.4	122.1
1991	114.4	118.1	115.3	116.7	117.2	121.0	124.5	85.3	88.4	83.4	128.1	121.4	124.4
1992	114.7	117.9	113.9	115.4	117.2	122.0	126.5	84.5	87.5	82.6	127.7	122.7	125.9
1993	116.2	118.9	115.6	115.5	119.1	123.0	132.0	84.7	88.1	82.6	126.4	125.0	128.5
1994	118.5	122.1	118.5	119.2	125.2	124.3	136.6	83.1	86.1	81.1	129.7	127.0	130.7
1995	124.9	130.4	119.5	135.1	135.6	126.5	142.1	84.2	87.1	82.3	148.8	132.1	137.0
1996	125.7	128.6	125.7	130.5	131.4	126.8	143.5	90.0	92.4	88.4	141.1	135.9	138.7
1993:													
January	115.5	118.4	114.0	115.7	118.0	122.6	129.1	84.6	88.2	82.3	126.8	124.1	127.7
February	115.9	118.7	113.3	115.7	119.0	122.8	130.8	85.3	88.7	83.1	126.9	124.2	128.0
March	116.3	118.8	113.5	115.5	119.7	122.8	132.3	85.8	88.8	83.8	126.8	124.2	128.1
April	116.6	119.0	114.8	115.9	119.6	123.0	132.6	86.0	89.3	83.9	126.6	124.7	128.5
May	116.2	118.8	115.2	115.7	118.7	123.0	131.8	85.4	88.1	83.6	126.5	124.6	128.2
June	116.3	118.8	114.8	115.8	118.6	123.0	131.2	86.3	89.2	84.4	126.5	124.7	128.3
July	116.3	118.9	116.0	115.7	118.8	123.0	131.1	85.3	88.7	83.1	126.4	125.2	128.4
August	116.2	119.0	115.4	115.6	119.2	123.1	131.7	84.2	88.0	81.8	126.1	125.6	128.6
September	116.3	119.0	116.0	115.3	119.4	123.1	132.5	84.4	88.1	82.0	126.1	125.5	128.9
October	116.5	119.0	116.9	115.2	119.1	123.2	132.7	85.0	88.5	82.7	126.1	125.6	129.0
November	116.5	119.2	117.7	115.4	119.4	123.3	133.5	83.7	86.9	81.6	126.2	125.8	129.2
December	116.3	119.3	119.3	114.8	120.1	123.3	134.3	81.3	85.0	78.9	126.2	126.2	129.3
1994:													
January	116.5	119.5	119.6	114.9	120.7	123.6	135.0	80.9	84.5	78.6	126.3	126.4	129.4
February	116.9	119.6	119.6	114.6	121.3	123.8	135.0	83.2	86.1	81.2	126.2	126.5	129.4
March	117.1	120.0	119.9	114.8	122.1	123.9	135.4	82.8	86.0	80.8	126.1	126.5	129.5
April	117.1	120.3	120.7	115.6	121.9	124.0	134.9	82.2	85.3	80.2	126.3	126.5	129.6
May	117.2	120.7	119.9	116.4	122.7	124.1	135.1	81.4	84.1	79.7	127.5	126.6	129.8
June	117.8	121.2	117.9	117.1	124.2	124.2	136.1	82.6	85.5	80.7	128.0	126.9	130.1
July	118.4	121.7	115.8	118.2	125.1	124.4	136.2	84.1	86.9	82.2	128.2	126.9	130.3
August	119.1	122.5	117.1	119.9	126.0	124.3	136.9	85.5	88.4	83.6	129.4	126.9	130.7
September	119.7	123.7	118.1	122.4	127.4	124.5	137.7	84.1	87.2	82.1	131.5	127.2	131.2
October	120.1	124.5	116.9	124.3	128.6	124.6	138.2	82.9	85.8	81.0	133.8	127.6	131.9
November	121.0	125.6	118.2	125.4	130.8	124.8	139.2	84.0	87.1	82.0	136.1	128.0	132.6
December	121.5	126.3	117.9	126.7	131.9	124.9	139.6	83.8	87.0	81.8	137.2	128.4	133.4
1995:													
January	122.8	128.1	118.5	129.6	134.7	125.7	140.5	83.8	87.0	81.8	140.1	129.4	134.6
February	123.7	129.3	118.8	132.0	136.0	126.0	140.9	84.4	87.7	82.3	144.7	129.9	135.2
March	124.2	129.8	119.0	133.1	136.5	126.1	141.6	84.5	87.7	82.4	146.1	130.5	135.8
April	124.9	130.6	117.3	135.7	136.8	126.3	142.1	84.9	87.5	83.2	146.9	131.2	136.4
May	125.2	130.9	116.4	136.8	136.3	126.3	142.1	85.3	87.9	83.5	149.0	131.4	136.8
June	125.5	131.0	117.2	137.2	135.9	126.4	141.9	85.4	88.5	83.5	151.4	131.9	137.3
July	125.6	131.4	119.2	137.5	136.4	126.5	142.6	84.4	87.3	82.6	152.0	132.4	137.7
August	125.7	131.4	119.3	137.3	136.4	126.6	143.0	84.1	86.9	82.2	152.0	132.8	137.9
September	125.5	131.3	120.1	137.0	136.0	126.7	143.3	82.9	85.2	81.4	151.6	133.2	138.1
October	125.5	131.0	122.2	136.2	134.8	126.9	142.9	83.3	86.3	81.3	151.2	133.6	138.1
November	125.3	130.5	123.0	134.9	134.0	127.1	142.5	82.9	86.0	80.8	151.0	134.4	138.3
December	125.5	130.1	123.2	134.2	133.2	127.1	142.2	84.9	87.5	83.2	150.3	134.8	138.3
1996:													
January	125.5	129.5	121.3	133.2	132.2	127.3	141.9	86.9	89.3	85.4	148.3	135.2	138.3
February	125.0	129.0	121.3	132.3	131.0	127.4	142.0	86.1	89.2	84.1	146.2	135.1	138.3
March	125.2	128.5	120.7	131.4	130.9	127.2	142.1	87.8	90.5	86.0	144.8	135.3	138.3
April	125.6	128.2	121.9	130.4	131.1	126.9	142.3	90.8	93.0	89.4	143.0	135.6	138.3
May	126.1	128.8	126.7	130.2	132.5	126.8	143.4	91.3	94.0	89.5	141.6	136.2	138.6
June	125.7	128.8	128.1	130.0	132.6	126.6	143.9	89.0	91.7	87.3	140.1	136.1	138.7
July	125.5	128.3	128.2	129.5	130.7	126.7	143.7	89.0	91.1	87.7	139.6	136.4	138.9
August	125.7	128.3	128.4	129.6	130.6	126.8	144.2	89.7	91.8	88.4	138.4	136.5	139.0
September	126.2	128.6	128.7	130.1	131.2	126.8	144.9	90.8	92.6	89.7	138.4	136.9	139.1
October	126.0	128.3	128.9	129.7	130.6	126.6	144.4	92.0	94.0	90.7	137.9	136.0	138.9
November	125.8	128.1	125.0	129.5	131.0	126.6	145.1	91.8	94.7	90.0	137.4	135.5	138.9
December	126.4	128.3	124.1	129.8	131.5	126.7	144.9	94.6	97.2	92.9	137.7	135.6	138.9

PRICES

PRODUCER PRICE INDEXES—Continued
(By stage of processing—1982=100, seasonally adjusted)

YEAR AND MONTH	Nonmfg Total	Feeds	Other supplies	Crude Total	Foodstuffs and feedstuffs	Nonfood Total	Except fuel Total[1]	Manufacturing[1]	Construction	Crude fuel Total[2]	Mfg industries	Nonmfg industries
1968	36.4	46.5	35.4	31.8	40.9	21.6	27.1	26.3	38.4	11.5	9.9	13.1
1969	36.9	46.4	36.0	33.9	44.1	22.5	28.4	27.6	39.8	12.0	10.2	13.8
1970	38.9	49.9	37.6	35.2	45.2	23.8	29.1	28.3	42.1	13.8	11.3	16.6
1971	39.9	50.4	38.9	36.0	46.1	24.7	29.4	28.4	44.1	15.7	12.6	19.3
1972	42.0	56.1	39.8	39.9	51.5	27.0	32.3	31.5	45.0	16.8	13.5	20.6
1973	54.7	97.3	42.7	54.5	72.6	34.3	42.9	42.7	46.2	18.6	14.8	22.9
1974	58.4	90.2	50.5	61.4	76.4	44.1	54.5	55.0	50.0	24.8	19.1	31.8
1975	62.9	84.0	58.9	61.6	77.4	43.7	50.0	49.7	55.9	30.6	24.4	38.0
1976	67.3	95.1	62.0	63.4	76.8	48.2	54.9	54.7	59.6	34.5	29.0	40.5
1977	70.7	99.3	65.2	65.5	77.5	51.7	56.3	56.0	63.1	42.0	37.2	47.4
1978	73.8	95.5	69.7	73.4	87.3	57.5	61.9	61.5	68.7	48.2	43.1	53.8
1979	81.2	106.9	76.3	85.9	100.0	69.6	75.5	75.6	76.6	57.3	53.1	62.0
1980	91.1	110.6	87.5	95.3	104.6	84.6	91.8	92.3	87.9	69.4	66.7	72.5
1981	97.8	111.3	95.4	103.0	103.9	101.8	109.8	110.9	96.8	84.8	83.6	86.2
1982	100.0	100.0	100.0	100.0	100.0	100.0	100.0	100.0	100.0	100.0	100.0	100.0
1983	102.0	109.1	101.0	101.3	101.8	100.7	98.8	98.6	100.1	105.1	105.8	104.4
1984	103.7	104.2	103.7	103.5	104.7	102.2	101.0	100.8	103.1	105.1	105.6	104.6
1985	103.0	86.6	105.3	95.8	94.8	96.9	94.3	93.1	105.7	102.7	102.7	102.5
1986	104.2	90.5	106.2	87.7	93.2	81.6	76.0	72.6	106.5	92.2	91.1	93.6
1987	106.6	94.6	108.3	93.7	96.2	87.9	88.5	84.7	114.8	84.1	82.1	86.3
1988	113.2	115.0	112.7	96.0	106.1	85.5	85.9	81.5	126.5	82.1	80.1	84.5
1989	117.2	114.4	117.5	103.1	111.2	93.4	95.8	91.0	136.9	85.3	83.9	87.0
1990	118.0	102.8	120.2	108.9	113.1	101.5	107.3	102.5	145.2	84.8	82.9	87.0
1991	119.9	101.3	122.5	101.2	105.5	94.6	97.5	92.2	147.5	82.9	82.3	84.1
1992	121.1	103.0	123.7	100.4	105.1	93.5	94.2	87.9	162.1	84.0	83.1	85.2
1993	123.2	105.4	125.8	102.4	108.4	94.7	94.1	85.6	193.6	87.1	85.9	88.6
1994	125.1	105.8	127.9	101.8	106.5	94.8	97.0	88.3	199.1	82.4	81.7	83.6
1995	129.5	103.4	133.2	102.7	105.8	96.8	105.8	97.3	201.7	72.1	72.5	72.9
1996	134.4	133.1	134.6	113.8	121.5	104.5	105.7	97.6	195.7	92.6	90.7	94.3
1993:												
January	122.3	104.3	124.8	101.7	106.1	94.9	92.5	85.2	174.9	90.6	88.9	92.2
February	122.3	102.0	125.1	101.3	105.8	94.6	96.1	88.5	181.4	83.4	82.6	84.6
March	122.1	100.9	125.2	101.9	106.6	94.9	97.7	89.9	186.1	81.4	80.8	82.5
April	122.7	102.4	125.6	103.4	109.4	95.7	98.2	89.5	200.0	82.4	81.7	83.6
May	122.8	102.6	125.6	105.8	110.5	98.7	98.9	89.7	206.9	89.4	87.8	91.0
June	122.8	102.1	125.7	103.9	106.4	98.2	95.1	86.1	201.5	94.9	92.7	96.7
July	123.6	108.1	125.8	101.5	107.5	93.8	93.7	84.7	199.6	85.5	84.4	86.9
August	124.0	110.1	126.0	100.7	108.2	92.0	91.7	83.0	193.2	84.4	83.5	85.7
September	123.8	107.4	126.1	101.2	108.2	92.8	91.0	82.3	193.8	87.6	86.2	89.1
October	123.8	106.1	126.3	103.7	107.6	97.2	95.8	87.3	194.8	90.8	89.1	92.4
November	124.1	107.9	126.4	102.9	111.5	93.4	92.1	83.2	196.4	87.5	86.1	89.0
December	124.6	111.1	126.5	101.4	112.9	90.2	87.0	78.0	194.4	87.9	86.6	89.3
1994:												
January	124.8	111.1	126.8	103.3	112.5	93.5	88.7	79.2	201.9	93.8	91.7	95.5
February	125.0	111.7	126.9	101.7	113.0	90.7	88.6	79.0	203.7	86.1	85.1	87.5
March	124.9	110.8	126.9	103.5	112.9	93.6	90.3	80.6	206.2	91.0	89.3	92.7
April	124.8	108.6	127.2	103.8	112.5	94.2	92.5	83.1	203.9	88.7	87.3	90.2
May	124.9	108.0	127.4	102.4	108.5	94.5	96.3	87.4	199.7	83.0	82.2	84.2
June	125.3	109.4	127.5	102.8	106.9	96.2	99.3	90.7	198.3	82.1	81.4	83.3
July	125.2	106.7	127.8	102.1	103.6	97.2	102.8	94.6	197.0	78.3	78.1	79.3
August	125.0	103.6	128.0	101.9	102.0	97.9	102.7	94.5	195.5	80.7	80.2	81.9
September	125.2	103.0	128.3	99.8	101.5	94.9	99.2	90.8	195.2	78.6	78.4	79.7
October	125.4	101.1	128.8	98.9	100.2	94.2	100.4	92.1	195.5	74.8	75.0	75.6
November	125.5	98.3	129.4	99.4	100.5	94.8	102.2	94.0	195.5	73.2	73.6	74.0
December	125.8	96.9	129.9	100.9	102.1	96.1	101.6	93.2	196.8	77.8	77.5	78.8
1995:												
January	126.7	97.4	130.8	101.6	102.3	97.2	103.6	95.2	199.2	77.1	76.8	78.1
February	127.0	95.8	131.4	102.5	104.0	97.6	106.8	98.3	203.7	72.3	72.6	73.1
March	127.7	97.2	131.9	101.9	102.4	97.6	107.6	99.1	204.6	71.0	71.5	71.8
April	128.4	98.8	132.5	103.4	101.6	100.4	111.4	102.9	206.8	71.9	72.3	72.7
May	128.5	97.1	132.9	102.5	99.2	100.7	111.3	102.9	206.5	72.6	72.9	73.4
June	129.1	98.5	133.4	103.0	101.5	100.0	109.4	100.8	206.5	74.1	74.3	75.0
July	129.5	99.7	133.7	102.0	104.3	96.5	104.9	96.5	201.2	72.9	73.3	73.6
August	130.1	102.8	133.9	100.4	104.7	93.8	104.4	96.1	199.1	66.5	67.6	67.0
September	130.6	105.0	134.2	102.5	108.8	94.6	105.0	96.7	199.3	67.4	68.4	68.0
October	131.3	110.1	134.3	102.5	111.1	93.1	101.6	93.1	198.5	69.7	70.4	70.3
November	132.3	116.9	134.5	104.0	114.2	93.6	100.7	92.3	197.0	72.5	72.8	73.3
December	133.0	121.8	134.6	106.3	115.3	96.5	102.3	94.0	197.6	77.6	77.3	78.6
1996:												
January	133.6	126.6	134.6	109.0	115.4	100.9	103.9	95.5	198.9	86.1	85.0	87.5
February	133.5	126.0	134.6	111.1	115.4	104.3	102.7	94.3	198.5	97.1	94.8	99.0
March	133.7	128.1	134.5	109.8	115.8	101.8	104.2	95.9	195.9	88.2	86.8	89.7
April	134.2	132.5	134.5	114.2	119.8	106.4	107.8	100.0	191.2	93.9	91.8	95.6
May	134.9	137.5	134.6	115.4	126.7	103.7	105.9	97.9	193.1	90.1	88.5	91.6
June	134.8	137.2	134.5	112.6	127.6	98.5	102.6	94.5	192.8	82.3	81.5	83.5
July	135.1	138.7	134.6	115.1	129.8	101.1	102.5	94.4	192.9	89.2	87.6	90.8
August	135.2	139.3	134.7	115.8	129.0	102.8	104.6	96.5	194.2	90.2	88.6	91.7
September	135.7	142.0	134.8	112.8	124.5	100.9	107.2	99.1	196.1	80.5	80.0	81.6
October	134.5	133.0	134.8	112.0	120.7	102.1	109.9	101.7	197.4	79.1	78.7	80.2
November	133.8	128.2	134.6	115.0	117.7	109.1	108.1	99.9	198.3	100.4	97.6	102.4
December	133.8	127.9	134.7	122.1	114.5	122.7	109.3	101.0	199.0	134.1	127.6	137.5

1. Includes crude petroleum.
2. Excludes crude petroleum.

55

PRICES

PRODUCER PRICE INDEXES—Continued
(By stage of processing—1982=100, seasonally adjusted)

Special groupings

YEAR AND MONTH	Finished goods, except foods	Intermediate materials less foods and feeds	Intermediate foods and feeds	Crude materials less agricultural products [1]	Finished energy goods	Finished goods less energy	Finished consumer goods less energy	Finished goods less foods and energy	Finished consumer goods less foods and energy	Consumer nondurable goods less foods and energy	Intermediate energy goods	Intermediate materials less: Energy	Intermediate materials less: Foods and energy	Crude energy materials [1]
1968	35.9	32.5	41.5	19.0										
1969	36.9	33.6	42.9	20.6										
1970	38.2	34.8	45.6	22.2										
1971	39.6	36.2	46.7	23.0										
1972	40.4	37.7	49.5	24.4										
1973	42.0	40.6	70.3	28.9				48.1	50.4				44.3	
1974	48.8	50.5	83.6	40.8	26.2		58.7	53.6	55.5	55.9	33.1	56.2	54.0	27.8
1975	54.7	56.6	81.6	42.0	30.7	62.4	63.9	59.7	60.6	60.8	38.7	61.7	60.2	33.3
1976	58.1	60.0	77.4	45.8	34.3	64.8	65.7	63.1	63.7	64.2	41.5	64.7	63.8	35.3
1977	62.2	64.1	79.6	49.6	39.7	68.6	69.4	66.9	67.3	67.9	46.8	68.5	67.6	40.4
1978	66.7	68.6	84.8	55.7	42.3	74.0	74.9	71.9	72.2	71.5	49.1	73.4	72.5	45.2
1979	74.6	77.4	94.5	68.3	57.1	80.7	81.7	78.3	78.8	77.5	61.1	81.7	80.7	54.9
1980	86.7	89.4	105.5	83.2	85.2	88.4	89.3	87.1	87.8	85.4	84.9	91.4	90.3	73.1
1981	95.6	98.2	104.6	101.7	101.5	95.4	95.7	94.6	94.6	93.3	100.5	98.2	97.7	97.7
1982	100.0	100.0	100.0	100.0	100.0	100.0	100.0	100.0	100.0	100.0	100.0	100.0	100.0	100.0
1983	101.8	100.5	103.6	100.4	95.2	102.5	102.4	103.0	103.1	103.4	95.3	101.7	101.6	98.7
1984	103.2	103.0	105.7	102.0	91.2	105.5	105.6	105.5	105.7	106.8	95.5	104.6	104.7	98.0
1985	104.6	103.0	97.3	96.7	87.6	107.2	107.0	108.1	108.4	110.0	92.6	104.7	105.2	93.3
1986	101.9	99.3	96.2	81.1	63.0	109.7	109.7	110.6	111.1	113.1	72.6	104.5	104.9	71.8
1987	104.0	101.7	99.2	87.3	61.8	112.3	112.5	113.3	114.2	116.3	73.0	107.3	107.8	75.0
1988	106.5	106.9	109.5	85.0	59.8	115.8	116.3	117.0	118.5	122.0	70.9	114.6	115.2	67.7
1989	111.8	111.9	113.8	92.9	65.7	121.2	122.1	122.1	124.0	128.8	76.1	119.5	120.2	75.9
1990	117.4	114.5	113.3	100.9	75.0	126.0	127.2	126.6	128.8	134.9	85.5	120.4	120.9	85.9
1991	120.9	114.6	111.1	94.0	78.1	129.1	130.0	131.1	133.7	140.8	85.1	120.8	121.4	80.4
1992	123.1	114.9	110.7	93.1	77.8	131.1	131.8	134.2	137.3	145.8	84.3	121.3	122.0	78.8
1993	124.4	116.4	112.7	94.3	78.0	132.9	133.5	135.8	138.5	146.1	84.6	123.2	123.8	76.7
1994	125.1	118.7	114.8	94.0	77.0	134.2	134.2	137.1	139.0	144.4	83.0	126.3	127.1	72.1
1995	127.5	125.5	114.8	95.4	78.1	136.9	136.9	140.0	141.9	148.5	84.1	134.0	135.2	69.4
1996	130.5	125.6	128.1	103.9	83.2	139.6	140.1	142.0	144.3	151.4	89.8	133.6	134.0	85.0
1993:														
January	124.3	115.7	111.2	94.4	78.3	132.5	133.2	135.6	138.7	147.8	84.5	122.2	122.9	78.6
February	124.7	116.3	110.0	94.1	79.0	132.7	133.4	135.8	139.0	147.9	85.2	122.7	123.5	77.5
March	124.9	116.6	109.8	94.4	79.3	132.8	133.5	136.1	139.2	148.1	85.7	122.9	123.8	77.7
April	125.2	116.8	111.2	95.4	79.1	133.7	134.6	136.5	139.9	148.8	85.9	123.2	124.0	78.0
May	125.2	116.5	111.5	98.6	78.7	133.7	134.7	136.6	139.9	148.9	85.3	123.0	123.7	81.3
June	124.9	116.6	111.1	98.2	78.5	133.3	134.1	136.4	139.6	148.3	86.1	122.9	123.7	80.9
July	125.0	116.4	113.8	93.6	78.0	133.3	134.0	136.6	139.7	148.1	85.2	123.1	123.7	75.0
August	123.6	116.4	113.9	91.7	77.4	132.2	132.4	135.0	137.1	142.9	84.1	123.3	123.9	73.6
September	123.6	116.5	113.6	92.4	77.6	132.3	132.5	135.0	137.0	142.8	84.3	123.4	124.0	74.5
October	123.9	116.7	113.7	96.7	78.5	132.3	132.5	134.9	136.9	143.1	84.8	123.4	124.0	79.4
November	123.7	116.6	114.9	92.9	76.8	133.0	133.2	135.3	137.3	143.1	83.6	123.7	124.3	74.4
December	123.5	116.3	117.0	89.5	75.2	133.5	133.8	135.8	137.8	143.9	81.2	124.0	124.5	70.0
1994:														
January	123.9	116.4	117.2	92.8	75.1	133.7	134.0	136.2	138.3	144.1	80.9	124.3	124.7	72.9
February	124.4	116.9	117.4	89.6	76.8	133.6	133.8	136.3	138.3	144.0	83.0	124.4	124.8	68.3
March	124.3	117.1	117.3	92.9	76.2	133.8	134.0	136.4	138.4	144.0	82.6	124.6	125.1	71.7
April	124.4	117.1	117.2	93.4	75.9	133.9	134.0	136.6	138.4	143.9	82.0	124.8	125.3	72.5
May	124.5	117.2	116.4	93.7	75.3	134.0	133.9	137.0	138.8	144.1	81.3	125.1	125.7	73.4
June	124.9	118.0	115.5	95.4	76.2	134.0	133.9	137.2	139.0	144.3	82.4	125.6	126.3	75.2
July	125.4	118.6	113.2	96.7	77.9	134.1	134.0	137.3	139.0	144.2	84.0	125.9	126.7	75.3
August	126.2	119.4	113.1	97.3	79.8	134.4	134.3	137.6	139.4	144.5	85.4	126.5	127.4	75.6
September	125.8	120.0	113.7	93.9	77.9	134.5	134.3	137.8	139.5	144.7	84.0	127.5	128.4	71.3
October	125.2	120.5	112.2	93.4	77.0	134.2	134.1	137.3	139.2	144.8	82.8	128.3	129.3	70.2
November	125.8	121.5	112.3	93.7	78.4	134.6	134.6	137.5	139.5	144.9	83.8	129.2	130.3	69.3
December	126.0	122.0	111.7	94.9	78.2	135.4	135.6	137.9	139.8	145.3	83.7	129.8	131.0	69.9
1995:														
January	126.4	123.3	112.2	95.9	78.3	135.5	135.5	138.4	140.2	145.8	83.7	131.4	132.6	69.8
February	126.7	124.3	111.9	96.2	78.5	135.8	135.8	138.7	140.5	146.2	84.3	132.4	133.7	69.6
March	126.8	124.8	112.5	96.0	78.3	136.0	136.0	139.0	140.9	147.0	84.3	133.0	134.3	69.1
April	127.1	125.6	111.9	99.2	78.3	136.3	136.3	139.3	141.2	147.4	84.8	133.8	135.1	72.0
May	127.5	125.9	110.7	99.6	79.0	136.4	136.3	139.7	141.7	148.3	85.1	134.0	135.5	72.4
June	127.7	126.2	111.6	98.6	79.1	136.3	136.2	139.8	141.8	148.6	85.3	134.3	135.7	71.5
July	127.7	126.3	113.4	95.1	78.3	136.8	136.8	140.1	142.1	149.0	84.3	134.7	136.1	68.2
August	127.7	126.3	114.4	92.6	78.0	136.9	136.9	140.2	142.2	149.1	84.0	134.9	136.2	65.6
September	127.7	126.0	115.7	93.1	77.5	137.5	137.6	140.4	142.5	149.7	82.8	135.0	136.2	67.4
October	128.0	125.8	118.7	91.7	77.3	137.8	137.8	140.9	143.0	150.0	83.2	134.8	135.8	66.9
November	128.0	125.5	121.4	92.0	76.0	138.5	138.6	141.4	143.4	150.1	82.7	134.7	135.5	68.3
December	129.0	125.6	123.1	95.2	79.1	138.7	138.9	141.5	143.7	150.5	84.8	134.5	135.2	72.5
1996:														
January	129.3	125.7	123.3	99.8	80.2	138.5	138.7	141.5	143.6	150.6	86.8	134.1	134.8	78.1
February	129.2	125.2	123.1	103.2	79.7	138.6	138.7	141.6	143.8	150.9	85.9	133.7	134.3	82.7
March	129.8	125.3	123.3	101.1	81.7	138.9	139.1	141.6	143.7	150.7	87.6	133.4	134.0	80.6
April	130.3	125.6	125.6	105.9	83.4	138.7	138.9	141.6	143.7	150.7	90.6	133.3	133.8	87.3
May	130.4	125.9	130.4	103.2	82.9	139.0	139.3	141.9	144.3	151.4	91.1	133.8	134.0	83.3
June	130.3	125.5	131.3	97.9	82.2	139.7	140.3	142.1	144.5	151.6	88.9	133.8	134.0	77.6
July	130.4	125.2	131.8	100.6	82.5	139.7	140.3	142.1	144.4	151.8	88.9	133.5	133.6	81.8
August	130.6	125.4	132.2	102.1	83.0	140.1	140.7	142.2	144.5	151.7	89.6	133.6	133.7	83.8
September	131.0	125.8	133.2	100.0	83.6	140.3	141.0	142.4	144.7	151.7	90.6	134.0	134.0	81.0
October	131.3	125.8	130.5	101.3	85.0	140.6	141.4	142.3	144.7	152.1	91.8	133.5	133.7	82.7
November	131.5	125.8	126.3	108.5	85.8	140.6	141.4	142.3	144.6	151.9	91.6	133.3	133.8	91.9
December	132.5	126.5	125.6	122.6	88.6	140.6	141.4	142.5	144.9	152.4	94.3	133.4	133.9	109.6

1. Includes crude petroleum.

YEAR AND MONTH	Crude materials less energy (SA)	Crude nonfood materials less energy[1] (SA)	Finished goods Total	Consumer goods Total	Foods	Goods except foods Total	Durable	Nondurable	Capital equipment	Intermediate materials, supplies, and components	Crude materials for further processing	Producer prices for finished goods (1982=$1.00)	Consumer prices (1982-1984=$1.00)
1968	...	...	36.6	36.5	40.0	35.5	45.1	30.6	37.0	33.0	31.8	2.732	2.873
1969	...	...	38.0	37.9	42.4	36.3	45.9	31.5	38.3	34.1	33.9	2.632	2.726
1970	...	...	39.3	39.1	43.8	37.4	47.2	32.5	40.1	35.4	35.2	2.545	2.574
1971	...	...	40.5	40.2	44.5	38.7	48.9	33.5	41.7	36.8	36.0	2.469	2.466
1972	...	...	41.8	41.5	46.9	39.4	50.0	34.1	42.8	38.2	39.9	2.392	2.391
1973	...	70.8	45.6	46.0	56.5	41.2	50.9	36.1	44.2	42.4	54.5	2.193	2.251
1974	78.4	83.3	52.6	53.1	64.4	48.2	55.5	44.0	50.5	52.5	61.4	1.901	2.029
1975	75.9	69.3	58.2	58.2	69.8	53.2	61.0	48.9	58.2	58.0	61.6	1.718	1.859
1976	77.6	80.2	60.8	60.4	69.6	56.5	63.7	52.4	62.1	60.9	63.4	1.645	1.757
1977	78.1	79.8	64.7	64.3	73.3	60.6	67.4	56.8	66.1	64.9	65.5	1.546	1.649
1978	87.5	87.8	69.8	69.4	79.9	64.9	73.6	60.0	71.3	69.5	73.4	1.433	1.532
1979	101.5	106.2	77.6	77.5	87.3	73.5	80.8	69.3	77.5	78.4	85.9	1.289	1.380
1980	106.5	113.1	88.0	88.6	92.4	87.1	91.0	85.1	85.8	90.3	95.3	1.136	1.215
1981	105.7	111.7	96.1	96.6	97.8	96.1	96.4	95.8	94.6	98.6	103.0	1.041	1.098
1982	100.0	100.0	100.0	100.0	100.0	100.0	100.0	100.0	100.0	100.0	100.0	1.000	1.035
1983	102.6	105.3	101.6	101.3	101.0	101.2	102.8	100.5	102.8	100.6	101.3	0.984	1.003
1984	106.3	111.7	103.7	103.3	105.4	102.2	104.5	101.1	105.2	103.1	103.5	0.964	0.961
1985	97.0	104.9	104.7	103.8	104.6	103.3	106.5	101.7	107.5	102.7	95.8	0.955	0.928
1986	95.4	103.1	103.2	101.4	107.3	98.5	108.9	93.3	109.7	99.1	87.7	0.969	0.913
1987	100.9	115.7	105.4	103.6	109.5	100.7	111.5	94.9	111.7	101.5	93.7	0.949	0.880
1988	112.6	133.0	108.0	106.2	112.6	103.1	113.8	97.3	114.3	107.1	96.0	0.926	0.846
1989	117.7	137.9	113.6	112.1	118.7	108.9	117.6	103.8	118.8	112.0	103.1	0.880	0.807
1990	118.6	136.3	119.2	118.2	124.4	115.3	120.4	111.5	122.9	114.5	108.9	0.839	0.766
1991	110.9	128.2	121.7	120.5	124.1	118.7	123.9	115.0	126.7	114.4	101.2	0.822	0.734
1992	110.7	128.4	123.2	121.7	123.3	120.8	125.7	117.3	129.1	114.7	100.4	0.812	0.713
1993	116.3	140.2	124.7	123.0	125.7	121.7	128.0	117.6	131.4	116.2	102.4	0.802	0.692
1994	119.3	156.2	125.5	123.3	126.8	121.6	130.9	116.2	134.1	118.5	101.8	0.797	0.675
1995	123.5	173.6	127.9	125.6	129.0	124.0	132.7	118.8	136.7	124.9	102.7	0.782	0.656
1996	130.0	155.8	131.3	129.5	133.5	127.6	134.2	123.2	138.3	125.7	113.5	0.762	0.638
1993:													
January	113.1	134.7	124.2	122.5	124.3	121.4	127.2	117.6	130.8	115.2	101.4	0.804	0.701
February	113.6	137.3	124.5	122.8	124.5	121.8	127.6	117.9	131.1	115.6	101.4	0.802	0.699
March	114.4	137.8	124.7	123.1	124.8	122.1	127.6	118.4	131.2	116.0	102.6	0.801	0.697
April	117.0	140.1	125.5	124.0	126.5	122.7	127.9	119.1	131.2	116.3	103.9	0.796	0.695
May	118.2	141.6	125.8	124.5	126.9	123.3	127.8	119.9	131.2	116.2	106.5	0.797	0.693
June	115.2	141.3	125.5	124.1	125.4	123.4	127.7	120.1	131.0	116.7	104.2	0.799	0.693
July	116.2	142.3	125.3	123.8	125.0	123.0	127.9	119.5	131.3	116.6	101.5	0.800	0.692
August	116.0	139.6	124.2	122.4	125.4	120.9	127.9	116.6	131.2	116.6	100.6	0.806	0.690
September	116.1	139.9	123.8	122.2	125.7	120.5	126.0	116.8	130.3	116.8	101.0	0.805	0.689
October	116.1	141.6	124.6	122.6	125.4	121.2	129.1	116.5	132.3	116.5	102.8	0.805	0.686
November	119.2	142.9	124.5	122.3	126.6	120.3	129.7	115.0	132.5	116.4	102.2	0.803	0.686
December	120.7	144.3	124.1	121.9	127.2	119.4	129.7	113.7	132.5	116.0	101.0	0.803	0.686
1994:													
January	121.4	148.2	124.5	122.2	127.0	119.9	130.5	114.0	133.3	116.2	103.2	0.802	0.684
February	122.8	151.8	124.8	122.5	126.7	120.5	130.5	114.9	133.5	116.6	101.8	0.800	0.682
March	122.9	152.6	124.9	122.6	127.5	120.4	130.5	114.7	133.6	116.8	104.1	0.799	0.679
April	122.6	152.4	125.0	122.7	127.1	120.7	130.4	115.1	133.8	116.9	104.1	0.799	0.679
May	119.3	150.8	125.3	122.9	126.6	121.2	130.9	115.6	134.1	117.2	103.0	0.800	0.678
June	118.4	151.9	125.6	123.3	125.9	122.0	130.8	116.9	134.2	118.2	103.2	0.799	0.676
July	116.9	155.3	126.0	123.8	126.2	122.5	130.9	117.5	134.2	118.7	102.2	0.796	0.674
August	116.4	157.8	126.5	124.5	126.6	123.4	131.0	118.7	134.3	119.5	101.9	0.792	0.671
September	116.5	159.4	125.6	123.5	126.3	122.2	129.2	117.8	133.5	120.1	99.7	0.794	0.669
October	115.9	160.4	125.8	123.4	126.1	122.0	132.1	116.3	134.8	120.0	98.2	0.797	0.669
November	117.5	165.7	126.1	123.8	126.9	122.3	132.1	116.7	134.8	120.9	99.1	0.792	0.668
December	119.7	169.3	126.2	123.9	128.6	121.8	132.2	115.9	135.1	121.1	100.5	0.789	0.668
1995:													
January	121.2	174.2	126.6	124.2	127.9	122.4	132.6	116.7	135.9	122.5	101.5	0.788	0.665
February	123.0	176.5	126.9	124.5	128.4	122.6	132.7	116.9	136.1	123.4	102.6	0.787	0.663
March	122.3	178.3	127.1	124.7	128.7	122.9	132.4	117.3	136.2	124.0	102.3	0.786	0.660
April	122.3	180.2	127.6	125.2	128.7	123.6	132.4	118.4	136.4	124.7	103.6	0.784	0.658
May	120.4	179.8	128.1	125.9	128.0	124.7	132.3	120.1	136.5	125.3	102.8	0.783	0.657
June	122.1	179.8	128.2	126.0	127.4	125.1	132.0	120.8	136.4	125.8	103.4	0.783	0.656
July	123.2	176.6	128.2	126.0	128.5	124.7	132.1	120.1	136.6	126.0	102.1	0.782	0.656
August	122.8	173.9	128.1	125.9	128.8	124.4	131.9	119.8	136.6	126.0	100.5	0.782	0.654
September	124.9	171.0	127.9	125.9	130.1	123.9	130.0	119.9	135.7	125.9	102.5	0.779	0.653
October	125.5	166.7	128.7	126.3	129.9	124.5	134.1	119.0	138.0	125.4	101.7	0.778	0.651
November	126.9	163.7	128.7	126.2	131.1	123.9	134.7	117.8	138.3	125.1	103.8	0.776	0.651
December	127.2	162.1	129.1	126.7	131.0	124.6	134.7	118.9	138.1	125.1	106.0	0.772	0.651
1996:													
January	127.3	162.2	129.4	127.1	130.7	125.4	134.2	120.1	138.3	125.2	108.8	0.771	0.648
February	127.3	161.9	129.4	127.0	130.7	125.3	134.3	119.9	138.4	124.7	111.1	0.771	0.645
March	126.6	158.5	130.1	128.0	132.0	126.1	134.3	121.2	138.3	124.9	110.0	0.767	0.642
April	128.9	156.4	130.6	128.7	131.2	127.4	134.0	123.1	138.3	125.4	114.4	0.766	0.640
May	134.2	157.5	131.1	129.3	131.5	128.2	134.2	124.1	138.2	126.2	115.9	0.765	0.639
June	134.0	154.7	131.7	130.0	133.6	128.3	134.4	124.2	138.2	126.2	113.3	0.762	0.638
July	134.9	152.2	131.5	129.9	133.9	128.0	133.8	124.0	138.1	125.9	115.6	0.762	0.637
August	134.5	152.9	131.9	130.4	135.3	128.1	133.7	124.2	138.2	126.1	116.0	0.760	0.636
September	131.5	153.7	131.8	130.4	135.6	128.0	132.4	124.6	137.3	126.7	112.9	0.758	0.634
October	128.7	153.5	132.7	131.2	136.6	128.8	135.2	124.5	138.9	126.0	111.3	0.755	0.632
November	126.5	153.2	132.6	131.1	136.1	128.8	135.2	124.5	138.7	125.7	114.8	0.754	0.631
December	124.2	153.2	132.7	131.2	135.5	129.2	135.0	125.2	138.7	126.0	121.6	0.750	0.631

1. Excludes crude petroleum.
2. Not seasonally adjusted.

PRICES RECEIVED AND PAID BY FARMERS
(1990-1992=100, not seasonally adjusted)

YEAR AND MONTH	All farm products	All crops	Food grains	Feed grains and hay	Cotton	To-bacco	Oil-bearing crops	Fruit and nuts	Commercial vegetables	Potatoes and dry beans	All livestock and products	Meat animals	Dairy products	Poultry and eggs	Food commodities	All commodities and services [2]	Production items	Ratio of prices received to prices paid
1968	.....	.....	.....	.....	.....	.....	.....	.....	.....	.....	.....	.....	.....	.....	.....	.....	.....	.....
1969	.....	.....	.....	.....	.....	.....	.....	.....	.....	.....	.....	.....	.....	.....	.....	.....	.....	.....
1970	.....	.....	.....	.....	.....	.....	.....	.....	.....	.....	.....	.....	.....	.....	.....	.....	.....	.....
1971	.....	.....	.....	.....	.....	.....	.....	.....	.....	.....	.....	.....	.....	.....	.....	.....	.....	.....
1972	.....	.....	.....	.....	.....	.....	.....	.....	.....	.....	.....	.....	.....	.....	.....	.....	.....	.....
1973	.....	.....	.....	.....	.....	.....	.....	.....	.....	.....	.....	.....	.....	.....	.....	.....	.....	.....
1974	.....	.....	.....	.....	.....	.....	.....	.....	.....	.....	.....	.....	.....	.....	.....	.....	.....	.....
1975	73	88	128	112	68	56	93	46	66	78	62	56	67	83	69	47	55	158
1976	75	87	105	105	99	63	97	45	67	75	64	57	74	83	71	50	59	150
1977	73	83	83	87	100	66	119	54	70	71	64	56	74	81	71	53	61	138
1978	83	89	102	88	91	72	110	72	74	73	78	75	81	87	83	58	67	144
1979	94	98	121	100	96	75	121	77	79	65	90	90	92	90	95	66	76	144
1980	98	107	136	115	114	80	118	73	80	93	89	84	100	91	96	75	85	131
1981	100	111	138	122	111	94	122	76	99	126	89	82	105	94	97	82	92	121
1982	94	98	119	103	92	99	103	78	92	88	90	86	104	89	93	86	94	109
1983	98	108	120	125	104	96	118	71	96	89	88	81	104	95	95	86	92	113
1984	101	111	117	127	108	98	125	85	97	111	91	83	103	109	98	89	94	114
1985	91	98	108	105	93	92	96	84	95	87	86	78	97	97	89	86	91	106
1986	87	87	89	84	91	82	89	83	92	81	88	80	96	105	87	85	86	103
1987	89	86	83	72	98	83	90	93	105	89	91	90	96	87	91	87	87	102
1988	99	104	113	102	95	86	126	96	104	88	93	91	93	98	99	91	90	108
1989	104	109	127	109	98	96	118	99	103	131	100	94	104	111	104	96	95	108
1990	104	103	100	105	107	97	105	97	102	133	105	105	105	105	104	99	99	105
1991	100	101	94	101	108	102	99	112	100	99	99	101	94	99	99	100	100	99
1992	98	101	113	98	88	101	100	99	111	88	97	96	100	97	99	101	101	97
1993	101	102	105	99	89	101	108	93	116	107	100	100	98	105	102	104	103	97
1994	100	105	119	106	109	101	110	90	109	110	95	90	99	106	98	106	106	94
1995	102	112	134	112	127	103	104	99	120	107	92	85	98	107	99	110	109	93
1996	112	126	157	146	122	105	128	118	111	114	99	87	114	120	108	115	115	98
1993:																		
January	97	96	110	90	87	104	100	72	119	94	98	99	96	99	98	103	102	94
February	98	97	106	91	89	115	100	72	125	94	99	101	93	99	99	103	102	95
March	99	97	104	94	93	106	101	69	108	104	101	104	93	105	100	103	102	96
April	104	107	102	97	91	91	102	73	164	119	102	104	96	106	105	104	104	100
May	103	103	99	99	90	.....	104	81	126	118	103	104	99	106	104	104	104	99
June	101	99	94	97	88	.....	105	97	100	107	102	102	100	107	101	104	104	97
July	101	102	95	99	89	91	117	101	105	123	100	99	98	105	101	103	104	97
August	102	104	98	100	86	91	117	113	109	105	100	100	95	108	103	103	104	98
September	102	105	101	98	85	99	109	121	112	94	100	99	98	106	103	103	104	98
October	101	103	106	100	86	100	106	119	95	93	99	96	100	106	103	103	104	98
November	102	106	116	107	88	104	113	106	102	117	98	94	104	107	102	104	104	97
December	103	109	123	115	93	104	119	86	124	111	97	92	103	105	102	104	104	99
1994:																		
January	105	110	122	117	103	105	120	79	114	112	98	95	104	103	102	106	106	99
February	104	110	126	119	108	116	120	80	111	115	100	97	103	104	102	106	106	98
March	105	110	129	118	110	98	121	85	92	132	101	98	103	107	103	106	106	99
April	102	106	125	116	111	98	118	87	87	118	100	97	103	107	100	107	108	95
May	101	107	120	115	114	.....	121	92	97	117	97	92	98	110	99	107	108	94
June	100	108	109	113	104	.....	121	96	104	118	94	87	96	110	98	107	108	93
July	97	103	103	103	97	86	106	100	98	131	92	87	93	108	96	106	106	92
August	97	101	109	99	110	92	100	104	94	112	94	90	95	107	97	106	106	92
September	97	103	118	98	108	102	99	102	104	93	91	84	98	107	96	106	106	92
October	95	99	121	92	109	104	95	95	117	89	89	82	100	104	94	106	106	92
November	95	101	120	90	113	106	97	85	123	91	90	83	100	103	94	105	105	90
December	99	106	122	96	121	105	98	76	163	91	90	83	98	102	96	106	105	93
1995:																		
January	98	103	120	97	130	108	98	73	120	92	93	89	96	101	95	107	108	90
February	97	102	116	99	132	113	96	73	115	89	94	92	96	100	95	107	108	89
March	99	107	113	102	136	99	98	76	147	96	93	89	96	100	97	109	108	91
April	99	112	113	104	128	88	99	81	172	100	89	84	94	100	97	109	108	91
May	100	116	119	108	126	.....	99	100	155	105	88	82	94	97	98	109	108	92
June	100	113	128	110	131	.....	102	104	122	121	90	85	93	101	98	110	108	92
July	102	115	137	114	132	101	105	114	98	144	90	85	92	105	100	110	108	94
August	103	115	141	115	119	101	104	127	101	116	92	85	95	112	101	110	109	94
September	105	115	148	116	123	105	104	122	117	98	93	85	98	115	102	110	109	95
October	105	114	154	122	122	104	107	122	98	106	92	83	103	113	101	111	110	95
November	106	117	157	125	124	106	113	106	98	108	94	82	107	119	101	111	110	95
December	108	119	161	131	125	106	119	94	101	108	96	84	106	117	103	112	112	96
1996:																		
January	108	121	158	133	126	109	120	94	93	111	94	82	108	117	102	113	112	96
February	106	123	159	140	125	118	125	98	108	116	93	82	106	113	101	113	113	94
March	109	128	161	146	127	100	125	103	140	125	94	83	106	112	104	114	114	96
April	108	128	168	159	130	92	132	103	118	132	93	81	106	112	102	114	114	95
May	112	131	184	170	127	.....	137	117	100	138	97	84	109	116	105	115	114	97
June	118	140	175	165	127	.....	133	133	115	139	100	85	113	122	113	115	115	102
July	119	136	159	169	121	92	136	131	97	139	102	89	118	122	113	115	116	103
August	117	133	153	166	119	100	138	130	114	106	104	91	122	123	113	115	116	102
September	116	125	147	147	118	109	124	141	100	94	105	92	126	123	112	115	116	100
October	112	119	140	125	118	110	118	139	107	91	103	91	126	121	110	115	116	97
November	110	117	139	117	115	111	119	124	119	90	102	90	116	126	109	115	115	96
December	110	115	137	116	115	111	124	101	123	84	103	90	109	130	108	115	114	96

1. Prior to 1995, monthly data available only for the first month of each quarter.
2. Includes commodities, services, interest, taxes, and wage rates.

Employment Costs, Productivity, and Profits

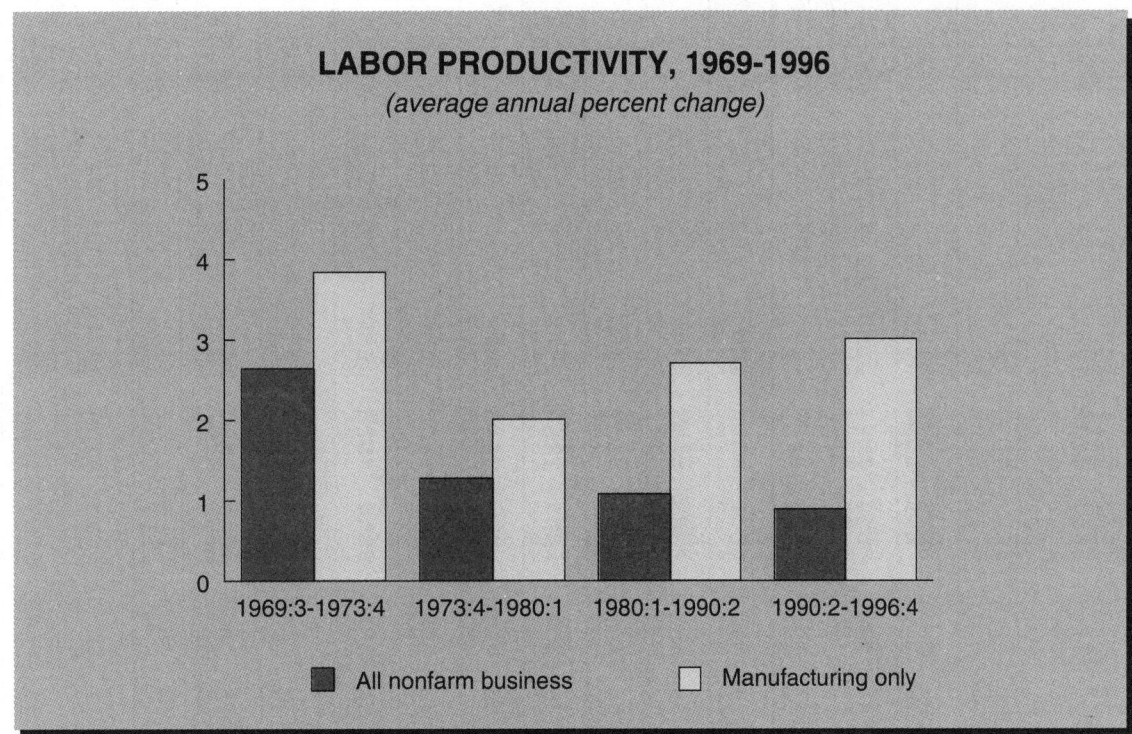

LABOR PRODUCTIVITY, 1969-1996
(average annual percent change)

Legend: ■ All nonfarm business   □ Manufacturing only

Categories: 1969:3-1973:4, 1973:4-1980:1, 1980:1-1990:2, 1990:2-1996:4

Between business cycle peaks in the third quarter of 1969 and the fourth quarter of 1973 labor productivity increased at an average annual rate of 2.6 percent for all nonfarm business and 3.8 percent for the manufacturing component, roughly in line with the gains of the 1960s. After 1973 productivity gains slowed abruptly and remained low by historical standards during the remainder of the 1970s and throughout the 1980s. From mid-1990 through the end of 1996 productivity gains in manufacturing recovered to an annual rate of 3.0 percent. For nonfarm business as a whole, however, productivity increases slowed further to an annual rate of just under 1 percent.

In the chart above, rates of productivity change are shown from one business cycle peak to the next, except for the most recent period. The most recent period encompasses the downturn which began in mid-1990 and the subsequent expansion from early 1991 through the end of 1996. This expansion was still ongoing at the end of 1996, so the comparison with earlier business cycles is not yet complete.

EMPLOYMENT COST INDEXES—TOTAL COMPENSATION
(June 1989=100, quarterly data, seasonally adjusted, except as noted)

YEAR AND QUARTER	Civilian workers	State and local government workers	All private industry workers	White-collar occupations	Blue-collar occupations	Service occupations	Goods-producing industries Total	Construction	Manufacturing Total	Durables	Nondurables	Service-producing industries Total	Transportation and utilities	Wholesale trade	Retail trade	Finance, insurance, and real estate [1]	Services	Nonmanufacturing industry
1982:																		
1st quarter	71.7	67.2	72.5	70.4	75.0	72.5	74.7	77.3	73.7	74.7	72.0	71.0	74.6	70.5	74.2	....	66.5	71.5
2nd quarter	72.8	68.2	73.5	71.3	76.1	74.0	75.7	78.4	74.8	75.7	73.2	72.8	75.7	71.6	74.9	....	68.0	72.6
3rd quarter	74.2	70.0	75.0	72.8	77.4	75.4	77.2	79.5	76.2	77.0	74.7	73.2	77.3	72.4	75.8	....	69.5	74.1
4th quarter	75.3	70.9	76.1	73.9	78.5	76.7	78.1	80.5	77.2	78.1	75.5	73.3	78.9	73.1	76.6	....	70.9	75.2
1983:																		
1st quarter	76.3	71.9	77.1	75.0	79.6	77.3	79.2	81.2	78.2	79.1	76.6	75.5	80.0	74.2	77.4	....	72.0	76.2
2nd quarter	77.4	73.0	78.2	76.0	80.7	78.5	80.1	82.6	79.2	79.9	77.8	77.2	81.6	75.4	78.8	....	72.9	77.4
3rd quarter	78.4	73.9	79.2	77.4	81.4	79.0	81.0	82.5	80.1	80.8	78.8	77.7	82.3	76.8	79.5	....	74.6	78.5
4th quarter	79.5	75.0	80.3	78.6	82.4	80.8	81.8	83.7	81.0	81.8	79.6	78.4	83.5	78.2	80.5	....	75.9	79.7
1984:																		
1st quarter	80.7	76.4	81.4	79.7	83.5	82.5	82.9	84.3	82.0	82.9	80.4	80.3	84.6	79.1	82.2	....	77.6	80.9
2nd quarter	81.7	77.5	82.4	80.8	84.2	83.1	83.6	84.5	83.0	84.0	81.2	81.6	85.4	80.3	83.2	....	78.5	81.8
3rd quarter	82.4	78.7	83.0	81.3	84.9	84.4	84.5	84.7	83.9	84.9	82.3	81.7	86.0	81.0	83.7	....	79.2	82.3
4th quarter	83.5	80.0	84.1	82.6	85.9	85.9	85.6	85.2	85.1	85.9	83.7	82.8	87.0	82.7	84.9	....	81.0	83.5
1985:																		
1st quarter	84.5	81.2	85.0	83.6	86.6	85.9	86.6	86.2	86.1	86.9	84.9	83.7	87.5	83.0	85.6	83.1	81.2	84.2
2nd quarter	85.4	82.2	85.9	84.6	87.3	86.7	87.2	86.9	86.8	87.6	85.4	84.8	88.3	84.4	86.5	83.6	82.4	85.1
3rd quarter	86.4	83.5	86.9	85.6	88.2	88.1	87.9	87.5	87.5	88.2	86.3	86.0	89.6	85.2	88.0	84.7	83.6	86.3
4th quarter	87.1	84.6	87.5	86.6	88.6	88.5	88.4	88.4	88.0	88.8	86.7	86.7	90.2	85.9	89.0	85.2	84.1	87.1
1986:																		
1st quarter	87.9	85.6	88.3	87.3	89.3	89.0	89.2	88.6	88.7	89.4	87.6	87.5	91.1	86.5	89.3	87.0	85.1	87.8
2nd quarter	88.5	86.8	89.0	88.2	89.8	89.8	90.1	89.7	89.7	90.1	88.9	88.2	91.3	87.0	89.7	87.6	86.1	88.5
3rd quarter	89.1	87.8	89.6	88.7	90.5	90.5	90.6	90.5	90.2	90.7	89.4	88.7	91.8	87.8	90.4	88.0	86.6	89.1
4th quarter	89.9	88.9	90.2	89.6	91.1	91.2	91.2	90.9	90.9	91.3	90.2	89.5	92.2	88.8	91.0	88.9	87.8	89.9
1987:																		
1st quarter	90.6	89.8	90.9	90.5	91.2	91.9	91.5	91.6	90.9	91.1	90.6	90.5	92.9	89.8	91.5	90.8	88.9	90.9
2nd quarter	91.4	90.9	91.6	91.1	92.1	92.6	92.1	92.5	91.7	91.9	91.2	91.2	93.8	90.8	92.3	91.1	89.8	91.5
3rd quarter	92.2	91.5	92.5	92.1	92.9	92.9	93.0	93.3	92.6	92.7	92.3	92.0	94.3	91.6	92.8	92.0	91.1	92.3
4th quarter	93.1	92.8	93.3	92.9	93.9	93.4	94.0	94.2	93.7	93.7	93.6	92.8	95.0	92.3	93.2	92.6	92.3	93.1
1988:																		
1st quarter	94.4	94.2	94.5	93.8	95.3	94.5	95.5	95.3	95.1	95.4	94.7	93.8	95.8	93.2	94.7	93.8	93.5	94.1
2nd quarter	95.5	95.3	95.7	95.0	96.3	95.7	96.5	96.2	96.1	96.4	95.5	95.0	96.6	94.4	96.1	94.6	94.8	95.4
3rd quarter	96.5	96.5	96.6	96.1	97.1	97.1	97.2	97.1	96.9	97.1	96.5	96.1	97.4	95.5	97.1	95.4	96.2	96.4
4th quarter	97.7	98.1	97.8	97.5	98.1	98.2	98.1	98.2	97.8	97.9	97.7	97.6	97.8	96.3	98.6	97.1	97.6	97.7
1989:																		
1st quarter	98.8	99.3	98.9	98.8	98.7	99.1	98.9	99.1	98.7	98.7	98.7	98.9	98.7	98.7	99.3	98.5	98.9	98.8
2nd quarter	100.0	100.8	100.0	99.9	99.9	100.1	100.0	99.9	99.9	99.9	99.9	100.0	99.8	99.8	99.8	100.0	100.3	99.9
3rd quarter	101.4	102.7	101.2	101.3	101.1	101.1	101.2	101.1	101.2	101.2	101.2	101.2	100.6	102.5	100.9	100.1	101.6	101.2
4th quarter	102.7	104.2	102.4	102.6	102.1	102.5	102.3	102.6	102.4	102.5	102.1	102.5	101.5	104.7	101.8	101.0	103.0	102.5
1990:																		
1st quarter	104.0	105.7	103.8	104.0	103.4	103.8	103.8	103.2	103.8	103.8	104.0	103.8	103.0	105.0	103.2	103.5	104.9	103.8
2nd quarter	105.4	107.3	105.1	105.4	104.6	105.0	105.1	104.1	105.1	105.0	105.4	105.1	103.1	105.2	104.6	104.7	106.7	105.0
3rd quarter	106.6	108.8	106.2	106.6	105.6	105.7	106.2	105.0	106.4	106.3	106.6	106.2	104.1	105.8	105.3	106.3	107.9	106.1
4th quarter	107.7	110.3	107.2	107.6	106.6	106.6	107.2	105.8	107.5	107.5	107.6	107.2	105.4	106.6	106.3	106.7	109.4	107.1
1991:																		
1st quarter	108.9	111.7	108.4	108.9	107.8	108.2	108.4	107.5	108.4	108.3	108.7	108.4	105.9	107.9	107.5	108.6	110.7	108.4
2nd quarter	110.2	112.7	109.7	110.2	108.9	110.0	109.7	108.4	109.9	109.8	110.0	109.7	107.6	109.3	108.7	109.5	111.7	109.7
3rd quarter	111.2	113.3	110.9	111.4	110.2	111.5	110.8	109.1	111.2	111.2	111.3	110.9	108.9	110.7	109.9	110.6	113.0	110.8
4th quarter	112.2	114.2	111.9	112.4	111.2	112.5	112.0	110.1	112.4	112.4	112.5	111.8	110.0	111.3	110.7	111.4	114.1	111.7
1992:																		
1st quarter	113.3	115.2	113.0	113.3	112.4	113.5	113.3	110.7	113.8	113.9	113.7	112.7	111.0	112.6	111.0	112.5	115.2	112.6
2nd quarter	114.1	116.4	113.7	114.1	113.3	114.3	114.1	111.6	114.7	114.7	114.5	113.5	111.8	113.2	111.9	112.2	116.6	113.5
3rd quarter	115.0	117.2	114.7	115.0	114.3	115.4	115.2	112.9	115.7	115.8	115.5	114.3	112.8	113.2	112.7	112.5	117.7	114.3
4th quarter	116.1	118.5	115.7	116.1	115.2	115.9	116.2	114.0	116.8	117.0	116.5	115.3	113.8	114.5	113.6	113.0	119.0	115.4
1993:																		
1st quarter	117.2	119.3	116.9	117.3	116.5	117.2	117.7	115.0	118.4	118.8	117.7	116.3	114.6	115.4	114.7	114.9	120.0	116.2
2nd quarter	118.2	120.1	117.9	118.2	117.6	118.1	118.8	115.9	119.6	119.9	118.8	117.2	116.0	116.1	115.4	116.4	121.0	117.2
3rd quarter	119.2	120.8	118.9	119.3	118.6	118.9	119.8	116.6	120.6	121.0	119.8	118.3	116.7	116.6	116.0	117.5	122.2	118.3
4th quarter	120.1	121.7	119.9	120.4	119.5	119.5	120.6	116.7	121.6	122.1	120.5	119.4	117.8	117.9	117.0	118.2	123.2	119.3
1994:																		
1st quarter	121.0	122.6	120.8	121.4	120.2	120.6	121.5	118.7	122.3	122.7	121.5	120.2	119.0	118.1	117.7	119.7	124.3	120.2
2nd quarter	122.0	123.6	121.8	122.4	121.1	121.1	122.8	120.1	123.3	123.7	122.6	121.1	119.8	119.4	119.0	120.3	125.0	121.1
3rd quarter	123.0	124.5	122.8	123.4	122.2	121.9	123.7	121.2	124.5	125.1	123.4	122.1	121.3	120.6	120.2	121.5	125.8	122.2
4th quarter	123.8	125.3	123.6	124.3	122.8	122.9	124.4	121.0	125.3	126.0	124.0	123.0	122.4	121.6	120.3	121.8	126.7	122.9
1995:																		
1st quarter	124.8	126.4	124.4	125.2	123.5	123.2	125.3	121.2	126.0	126.9	124.5	124.0	123.7	123.4	121.1	123.7	127.4	123.6
2nd quarter	125.7	127.4	125.2	126.1	124.3	123.9	126.0	121.9	126.7	127.6	125.2	124.9	124.7	124.5	121.6	124.6	128.2	124.5
3rd quarter	126.5	128.2	126.0	126.9	125.0	124.5	126.7	122.8	127.4	128.2	125.9	125.7	126.0	126.1	122.4	125.4	128.8	125.4
4th quarter	127.3	129.1	126.9	127.8	125.8	124.9	127.7	123.7	128.4	129.2	127.2	126.5	126.9	127.1	122.9	125.7	129.5	126.2
1996:																		
1st quarter	128.1	129.9	127.7	128.9	126.6	125.5	128.2	124.5	129.1	129.6	128.1	127.5	127.6	127.8	124.7	127.5	130.6	127.1
2nd quarter	129.2	130.7	128.8	129.9	127.5	126.4	129.4	125.1	130.2	131.1	128.7	128.5	128.5	129.0	124.6	128.5	131.7	128.1
3rd quarter	130.0	131.5	129.7	131.0	128.0	127.2	130.3	125.6	131.3	131.9	130.2	129.4	129.3	129.9	126.0	129.7	132.6	129.0
4th quarter	131.0	132.5	130.6	131.9	129.2	128.4	131.1	126.7	132.2	132.8	131.1	130.4	130.6	131.0	127.6	129.2	133.6	130.1

1. No identifiable seasonality was found for this series.

EMPLOYMENT COST INDEXES—WAGES AND SALARIES
(June 1989=100, quarterly data, seasonally adjusted, except as noted)

YEAR AND QUARTER	Civilian workers	State and local government workers	All private industry workers	White-collar occupations	Blue-collar occupations	Service occupations	Goods-producing Total	Construction	Manufacturing Total	Durables	Nondurables	Service-producing Total	Transportation and utilities	Wholesale trade	Retail trade	Finance, insurance, and real estate [1]	Services	Nonmanufacturing industry
1982:																		
1st quarter	73.7	69.2	74.6	72.2	77.6	75.1	77.1	80.7	76.3	77.4	74.3	72.6	78.1	71.3	75.7	71.4	68.7	73.6
2nd quarter	74.6	70.2	75.5	72.8	78.5	76.6	77.9	81.5	77.1	78.2	75.1	73.5	79.0	72.8	76.4	70.5	70.1	74.5
3rd quarter	75.9	71.9	76.8	74.1	79.9	77.9	79.2	82.6	78.4	79.4	76.5	74.7	80.9	73.2	77.4	73.1	71.1	75.7
4th quarter	76.9	72.6	77.7	75.2	80.7	79.3	79.9	83.5	79.1	80.3	77.2	75.9	82.2	74.0	78.1	75.1	72.5	76.9
1983:																		
1st quarter	77.8	73.6	78.6	76.3	81.5	79.5	80.7	84.1	80.0	80.9	78.2	76.9	83.4	75.0	78.8	76.2	73.3	77.8
2nd quarter	78.8	74.7	79.6	77.1	82.4	80.7	81.5	85.2	80.7	81.4	79.3	77.9	84.8	76.2	80.0	76.5	74.3	78.9
3rd quarter	79.7	75.4	80.6	78.5	83.2	81.0	82.3	85.0	81.6	82.2	80.3	79.1	85.5	77.7	80.5	78.2	76.0	80.0
4th quarter	80.7	76.4	81.6	79.7	83.8	82.8	83.1	85.9	82.5	83.3	81.0	80.2	86.4	78.5	81.3	80.5	77.3	81.1
1984:																		
1st quarter	81.8	77.8	82.5	80.5	84.8	84.5	84.0	86.3	83.4	84.3	81.7	81.3	87.6	79.3	83.0	80.0	78.5	82.0
2nd quarter	82.6	78.7	83.3	81.4	85.4	84.9	84.6	86.5	84.1	84.9	82.7	82.2	88.2	80.1	83.6	80.5	79.4	82.8
3rd quarter	83.2	79.8	83.9	81.9	86.0	86.2	85.4	86.7	85.0	85.7	83.7	82.6	88.5	81.0	84.2	79.4	80.2	83.2
4th quarter	84.3	81.0	84.9	83.1	86.9	87.8	86.3	87.0	86.1	86.7	85.0	83.7	89.4	82.8	85.5	79.8	82.2	84.3
1985:																		
1st quarter	85.3	82.1	85.9	84.3	87.7	87.5	87.4	88.0	87.2	87.8	85.8	84.6	89.9	83.1	86.0	84.0	82.1	85.2
2nd quarter	86.3	83.1	86.9	85.2	88.6	88.5	88.2	88.5	88.1	88.9	86.6	85.7	90.8	84.7	86.9	83.8	83.4	86.1
3rd quarter	87.3	84.4	87.9	86.3	89.7	89.8	89.0	88.9	88.8	89.4	87.5	87.0	92.1	85.7	88.5	85.5	84.6	87.4
4th quarter	88.0	85.5	88.5	87.2	89.9	89.9	89.4	89.7	89.2	89.9	88.1	87.8	92.7	86.3	89.6	87.1	85.1	88.1
1986:																		
1st quarter	88.9	86.6	89.4	88.0	90.7	90.5	90.3	90.0	90.3	90.9	89.0	88.5	93.3	87.1	90.1	87.2	86.2	88.7
2nd quarter	89.6	87.7	90.0	89.0	91.2	91.0	91.2	90.9	91.1	91.6	90.3	89.2	93.6	87.8	90.5	88.2	87.2	89.4
3rd quarter	90.2	89.0	90.5	89.5	91.9	91.6	91.7	91.5	91.6	92.1	90.6	89.7	94.0	88.5	91.1	88.8	87.3	90.0
4th quarter	91.0	90.1	91.2	90.2	92.4	92.3	92.2	91.9	92.1	92.6	91.4	90.4	94.4	89.5	91.5	89.5	88.5	90.7
1987:																		
1st quarter	91.9	91.0	92.0	91.4	92.8	93.1	92.8	92.6	92.7	93.0	92.1	91.5	94.7	90.7	92.2	91.9	89.8	91.7
2nd quarter	92.5	92.1	92.6	91.8	93.5	93.8	93.3	93.1	93.3	93.7	92.5	92.1	95.5	91.8	93.0	90.6	90.9	92.3
3rd quarter	93.3	92.6	93.5	92.9	94.3	94.1	94.3	94.0	94.2	94.5	93.8	92.9	96.0	92.4	93.6	90.8	92.2	93.2
4th quarter	94.1	93.9	94.2	93.5	95.1	94.5	95.1	94.9	95.2	95.5	94.8	93.5	96.4	93.1	93.9	90.6	93.2	93.8
1988:																		
1st quarter	95.0	95.0	95.0	94.4	95.9	95.4	96.0	95.8	96.0	96.2	95.7	94.3	97.1	93.5	95.1	91.5	94.1	94.5
2nd quarter	96.1	96.0	96.1	95.5	96.8	96.5	96.9	96.9	96.8	96.9	96.4	95.5	97.8	94.8	96.3	92.9	95.2	95.8
3rd quarter	97.0	97.0	96.9	96.6	97.4	97.7	97.4	97.6	97.3	97.4	97.2	96.5	98.5	96.1	97.5	92.9	96.6	96.8
4th quarter	98.1	98.5	98.0	97.9	98.1	98.6	98.1	98.4	98.1	98.0	98.3	97.9	98.8	96.6	98.7	96.3	97.9	97.9
1989:																		
1st quarter	99.2	99.5	99.1	99.0	99.0	99.4	99.0	99.3	99.0	99.0	98.9	99.2	99.5	99.2	99.4	98.3	99.0	99.1
2nd quarter	100.2	100.8	100.1	99.9	100.0	100.1	100.0	99.9	100.0	100.0	100.0	100.0	99.9	99.7	99.7	100.0	100.3	100.0
3rd quarter	101.4	102.4	101.1	101.3	101.0	100.9	100.9	101.0	100.9	100.7	101.1	101.2	100.6	102.8	100.9	100.6	101.3	101.3
4th quarter	102.5	103.7	102.2	102.5	101.7	102.2	101.9	101.8	101.9	101.9	101.9	102.3	101.4	105.3	101.8	101.3	102.5	102.3
1990:																		
1st quarter	103.6	105.1	103.2	103.6	102.8	103.1	103.1	102.2	103.3	103.2	103.5	103.3	102.6	104.9	103.0	101.8	104.1	103.2
2nd quarter	104.8	106.5	104.4	104.8	103.9	104.3	104.2	102.8	104.5	104.3	104.7	104.6	103.1	105.0	104.1	103.5	106.0	104.5
3rd quarter	105.8	107.9	105.4	105.9	104.7	104.8	105.1	103.3	105.4	105.3	105.7	105.6	104.0	105.3	104.8	104.9	106.9	105.3
4th quarter	106.8	109.3	106.2	106.7	105.4	106.4	105.8	103.9	106.2	106.1	106.4	106.4	104.8	106.3	105.5	104.8	108.4	106.2
1991:																		
1st quarter	107.9	110.6	107.3	107.9	106.6	106.9	107.0	105.3	107.4	107.3	107.5	107.5	105.4	107.6	106.6	107.0	109.4	107.3
2nd quarter	109.0	111.6	108.4	109.0	107.4	108.4	108.0	105.8	108.4	108.3	108.5	108.7	106.5	109.0	107.7	108.1	110.2	108.4
3rd quarter	109.8	112.2	109.2	110.0	108.2	109.7	108.8	106.1	109.3	109.2	109.5	109.6	107.6	110.3	108.7	108.0	111.3	109.2
4th quarter	110.6	113.1	110.1	110.8	108.9	110.6	109.7	106.9	110.3	110.2	110.7	110.3	108.9	110.3	109.4	108.4	112.2	109.9
1992:																		
1st quarter	111.5	113.8	111.0	111.7	109.8	111.2	110.7	107.4	111.5	111.2	111.7	111.1	109.7	111.7	109.7	109.5	113.1	110.7
2nd quarter	112.2	114.9	111.6	112.2	110.6	111.7	111.4	107.8	112.2	111.8	112.7	111.7	110.5	112.2	110.3	108.2	114.2	111.3
3rd quarter	112.7	115.3	112.1	112.8	111.3	112.4	112.2	108.5	112.9	112.7	113.3	112.2	111.2	111.9	111.1	108.2	115.0	111.8
4th quarter	113.7	116.5	113.0	113.8	111.9	112.8	112.9	109.0	113.7	113.4	114.5	113.1	111.9	113.5	111.9	108.3	116.2	112.7
1993:																		
1st quarter	114.5	117.2	113.9	114.7	112.7	113.5	113.8	109.7	114.7	114.4	115.4	113.9	112.9	114.2	112.9	109.3	116.9	113.4
2nd quarter	115.2	118.1	114.6	115.4	113.4	114.2	114.6	110.3	115.5	115.1	116.2	114.7	114.0	114.8	113.6	109.3	117.8	114.1
3rd quarter	116.2	118.8	115.6	116.6	114.4	114.9	115.4	111.1	116.3	115.9	117.0	115.8	114.7	115.2	114.3	112.3	118.8	115.3
4th quarter	117.1	119.5	116.5	116.6	115.0	115.2	116.2	111.2	117.3	117.2	117.7	116.8	115.5	116.4	115.1	112.9	119.7	116.2
1994:																		
1st quarter	117.8	120.4	117.1	118.3	116.3	116.3	117.0	112.4	118.0	117.8	118.2	117.3	116.3	116.5	115.5	113.7	120.7	116.8
2nd quarter	118.7	121.3	118.1	119.2	116.7	116.9	118.0	113.5	119.0	118.7	119.3	118.2	117.2	118.0	115.6	113.2	121.4	117.6
3rd quarter	119.6	122.3	119.0	120.1	117.8	117.6	119.0	114.3	120.0	119.8	120.4	119.1	118.9	119.0	117.8	113.8	122.1	118.6
4th quarter	120.4	123.2	119.8	120.9	118.2	118.7	119.6	114.8	120.8	120.8	121.0	119.9	119.7	119.8	117.9	114.2	123.1	119.3
1995:																		
1st quarter	121.3	124.3	120.6	121.7	119.2	119.4	120.5	115.1	121.9	121.9	121.8	120.7	121.1	121.2	119.0	115.0	123.8	120.0
2nd quarter	122.2	125.3	121.5	122.6	120.3	120.1	121.4	115.6	122.9	122.9	122.7	121.5	122.0	122.3	119.5	117.0	124.5	120.8
3rd quarter	123.1	126.1	122.4	123.5	121.1	120.8	122.1	116.5	123.5	123.6	123.4	122.5	123.0	124.0	120.3	118.0	125.3	121.8
4th quarter	123.9	127.1	123.2	124.4	121.7	121.3	122.9	117.5	124.3	124.3	124.6	123.4	123.7	125.4	120.6	118.4	126.1	122.7
1996:																		
1st quarter	125.1	127.8	124.4	125.8	122.8	122.2	123.9	118.6	125.4	125.1	125.7	124.7	124.5	126.5	123.1	119.8	127.4	123.9
2nd quarter	126.1	128.8	125.5	126.9	123.9	123.1	125.1	119.5	126.5	126.5	126.3	125.7	125.1	127.7	123.0	121.9	128.8	125.0
3rd quarter	127.0	129.6	126.4	127.9	124.5	124.2	126.1	120.1	127.7	127.7	127.7	126.6	126.0	128.6	124.2	122.2	129.7	125.8
4th quarter	128.0	130.6	127.4	128.9	125.4	125.5	126.8	120.9	128.4	128.4	128.7	127.7	127.0	129.5	125.8	122.2	130.6	127.0

1. No identifiable seasonality was found for this series.

PRODUCTIVITY AND RELATED DATA
(1992=100, quarterly data seasonally adjusted)

YEAR AND QUARTER	Business sector								Nonfarm business sector							
	Output per hour of all persons	Output	Hours of all persons	Compensation per hour	Real compensation per hour	Unit labor costs	Unit nonlabor payments	Implicit price deflator	Output per hour of all persons	Output	Hours of all persons	Compensation per hour	Real compensation per hour	Unit labor costs	Unit nonlabor payments	Implicit price deflator
1968	68.9	50.5	73.3	20.5	82.5	29.7	30.0	29.8	71.6	50.7	70.9	20.8	83.8	29.0	29.7	29.3
1969	69.2	52.0	75.2	21.9	83.7	31.7	30.0	31.1	71.6	52.3	72.9	22.2	84.9	31.0	29.6	30.5
1970	70.5	52.0	73.7	23.6	85.4	33.5	30.6	32.4	72.6	52.1	71.8	23.8	86.1	32.8	30.3	31.9
1971	73.6	54.0	73.3	25.1	87.0	34.1	33.4	33.9	75.6	54.1	71.5	25.4	87.8	33.5	33.0	33.3
1972	76.0	57.6	75.7	26.7	89.6	35.1	34.8	35.0	78.2	57.8	73.9	27.0	90.6	34.5	34.0	34.3
1973	78.4	61.6	78.5	29.0	91.6	37.0	36.6	36.8	80.7	62.0	76.9	29.2	92.3	36.2	34.3	35.5
1974	77.1	60.6	78.6	31.8	90.5	41.3	38.6	40.3	79.4	61.1	77.0	32.1	91.3	40.4	36.7	39.1
1975	79.8	60.0	75.2	35.1	91.5	44.0	44.5	44.2	81.5	60.0	73.6	35.3	92.1	43.3	43.0	43.2
1976	82.5	64.0	77.6	38.2	94.1	46.2	47.1	46.5	84.5	64.3	76.1	38.4	94.6	45.4	46.0	45.6
1977	83.9	67.6	80.6	41.2	95.3	49.0	50.0	49.4	85.8	67.9	79.2	41.5	96.0	48.3	49.0	48.6
1978	84.9	71.7	84.5	44.8	96.5	52.8	53.3	53.0	86.9	72.3	83.1	45.2	97.3	52.0	51.8	51.9
1979	84.5	73.9	87.4	49.2	95.0	58.2	56.5	57.6	86.3	74.3	86.1	49.5	95.7	57.4	54.7	56.4
1980	84.2	73.0	86.6	54.5	92.7	64.7	59.6	62.8	86.0	73.4	85.4	54.8	93.3	63.8	58.6	61.9
1981	85.7	74.8	87.2	59.6	92.0	69.5	67.1	68.7	86.9	74.8	86.1	60.1	92.8	69.2	65.6	67.9
1982	85.3	72.5	85.0	64.1	93.1	75.1	68.3	72.7	86.3	72.4	83.9	64.6	93.9	74.8	67.4	72.2
1983	88.0	76.1	86.5	66.7	94.0	75.8	74.6	75.4	89.9	76.8	85.5	67.3	94.8	74.9	74.3	74.7
1984	90.2	82.5	91.5	69.6	94.0	77.2	78.5	77.7	91.4	82.8	90.6	70.1	94.7	76.7	77.4	77.0
1985	91.7	85.7	93.5	73.0	95.2	79.7	80.5	80.0	92.3	85.8	92.9	73.4	95.7	79.5	79.9	79.6
1986	94.0	88.5	94.1	76.8	98.3	81.7	81.7	81.7	94.7	88.7	93.7	77.2	98.8	81.5	81.3	81.4
1987	94.0	91.1	97.0	79.8	98.5	84.9	81.9	83.8	94.5	91.3	96.7	80.1	98.9	84.7	81.4	83.6
1988	94.6	94.6	100.0	83.5	99.0	88.2	84.1	86.8	95.2	95.1	99.9	83.6	99.1	87.8	83.8	86.4
1989	95.4	97.8	102.5	85.8	97.1	89.9	91.3	90.4	95.7	98.1	102.5	85.8	97.1	89.7	90.7	90.0
1990	96.1	98.6	102.6	90.7	97.4	94.4	93.5	94.1	96.2	98.8	102.7	90.6	97.3	94.1	93.2	93.8
1991	96.7	96.9	100.2	95.1	97.9	98.3	96.6	97.7	96.9	97.1	100.2	95.1	97.9	98.1	96.8	97.6
1992	100.0	100.0	100.0	100.0	100.0	100.0	100.0	100.0	100.0	100.0	100.0	100.0	100.0	100.0	100.0	100.0
1993	100.2	102.7	102.6	102.6	99.6	102.4	102.7	102.5	100.1	103.0	102.8	102.3	99.3	102.2	103.1	102.5
1994	100.6	107.0	106.3	104.3	98.7	103.7	106.8	104.8	100.5	107.0	106.4	104.1	98.5	103.6	107.4	104.9
1995	100.5	109.5	108.9	106.9	98.4	106.3	108.7	107.2	100.7	109.8	109.0	106.7	98.3	106.0	109.7	107.3
1996	102.0	113.3	111.0	110.4	98.7	108.2	111.0	109.2	102.0	113.6	111.3	110.1	98.4	107.9	111.3	109.1
1988:																
1st quarter	94.6	93.3	98.7	82.0	98.9	86.7	82.6	85.2	94.8	93.4	98.5	82.1	99.1	86.6	81.9	84.9
2nd quarter	94.5	94.3	99.8	83.3	99.3	88.1	82.7	86.2	95.0	94.7	99.7	83.4	99.5	87.9	82.3	85.9
3rd quarter	94.7	94.8	100.1	84.2	99.2	88.9	84.8	87.4	95.4	95.4	100.0	84.2	99.3	88.3	84.3	86.9
4th quarter	94.9	96.0	101.2	84.7	98.7	89.3	86.3	88.2	95.9	96.9	101.1	84.9	98.9	88.5	86.5	87.8
1989:																
1st quarter	95.0	97.1	102.2	84.9	97.8	89.3	89.0	89.2	95.4	97.4	102.1	85.0	97.9	89.0	88.1	88.7
2nd quarter	95.5	97.8	102.3	85.4	96.8	89.4	91.6	90.2	95.7	98.0	102.4	85.3	96.8	89.1	91.0	89.8
3rd quarter	95.6	98.1	102.7	86.0	96.8	90.0	92.3	90.8	95.9	98.4	102.6	86.1	96.8	89.7	91.9	90.5
4th quarter	95.7	98.2	102.7	87.2	97.1	91.1	92.2	91.5	96.1	98.6	102.6	87.3	97.2	90.8	91.7	91.1
1990:																
1st quarter	96.1	99.3	103.3	88.6	97.1	92.2	93.1	92.5	96.4	99.6	103.3	88.6	97.0	91.9	92.7	92.2
2nd quarter	96.6	99.5	103.0	90.4	98.0	93.6	94.0	93.7	96.7	99.7	103.1	90.2	97.8	93.3	93.6	93.4
3rd quarter	96.3	98.6	102.4	91.6	97.6	95.1	93.7	94.6	96.4	98.8	102.5	91.4	97.4	94.8	93.3	94.3
4th quarter	95.4	97.1	101.8	92.4	96.9	96.9	93.2	95.6	95.5	97.2	101.8	92.4	96.8	96.7	93.1	95.4
1991:																
1st quarter	95.9	96.3	100.4	93.4	97.1	97.4	95.6	96.7	96.1	96.5	100.4	93.4	97.1	97.1	95.9	96.7
2nd quarter	96.7	96.9	100.2	94.7	97.9	97.9	96.5	97.4	96.8	97.0	100.1	94.7	97.9	97.8	96.4	97.3
3rd quarter	97.1	97.2	100.1	95.7	98.2	98.6	97.1	98.1	97.3	97.4	100.1	95.7	98.3	98.4	97.4	98.0
4th quarter	97.5	97.4	99.9	96.8	98.5	99.3	97.3	98.6	97.6	97.5	99.9	96.8	98.5	99.1	97.4	98.5
1992:																
1st quarter	99.4	98.8	99.5	98.6	99.7	99.3	99.2	99.3	99.3	98.8	99.5	98.6	99.7	99.2	99.2	99.2
2nd quarter	99.9	99.6	99.7	99.5	99.8	99.6	99.9	99.7	100.0	99.6	99.6	99.6	99.9	99.6	100.0	99.8
3rd quarter	99.7	99.8	100.1	100.7	100.2	101.0	98.6	100.1	99.7	99.8	100.1	100.7	100.2	101.0	98.4	100.1
4th quarter	101.0	101.7	100.7	101.2	99.9	100.1	102.2	100.9	101.1	101.8	100.7	101.2	99.9	100.1	102.3	100.9
1993:																
1st quarter	100.1	101.4	101.4	101.8	99.8	101.7	101.7	101.7	100.1	101.6	101.5	101.6	99.6	101.6	102.3	101.8
2nd quarter	99.7	102.1	102.4	102.4	99.7	102.7	101.5	102.3	99.6	102.3	102.6	102.1	99.4	102.5	101.8	102.3
3rd quarter	99.9	102.8	102.9	102.9	99.6	103.0	102.2	102.7	100.0	103.2	103.2	102.5	99.3	102.5	102.9	102.6
4th quarter	101.0	104.6	103.6	103.3	99.2	102.3	105.3	103.4	100.8	104.8	103.9	103.0	98.9	102.1	105.5	103.3
1994:																
1st quarter	100.7	105.2	104.5	104.0	99.5	103.3	104.9	103.9	100.6	105.2	104.6	103.8	99.2	103.2	105.0	103.8
2nd quarter	100.7	106.9	106.1	104.0	98.8	103.2	106.5	104.4	100.7	106.9	106.1	103.9	98.7	103.1	107.0	104.5
3rd quarter	100.5	107.3	106.7	104.4	98.3	103.9	107.4	105.1	100.4	107.3	106.8	104.2	98.1	103.8	108.1	105.3
4th quarter	100.7	108.5	107.7	105.1	98.3	104.3	108.3	105.8	100.8	108.6	107.8	105.0	98.2	104.2	109.2	106.0
1995:																
1st quarter	100.2	108.7	108.5	105.8	98.3	105.6	108.3	106.5	100.3	108.9	108.5	105.6	98.2	105.3	109.5	106.8
2nd quarter	100.4	108.7	108.3	106.6	98.3	106.1	108.4	107.0	100.5	108.9	108.4	106.4	98.1	105.8	109.6	107.2
3rd quarter	100.6	109.8	109.2	107.3	98.4	106.7	108.8	107.4	100.8	110.2	109.3	107.1	98.3	106.3	109.7	107.5
4th quarter	101.1	110.7	109.5	108.1	98.6	107.0	109.2	107.8	101.2	111.0	109.7	107.9	98.4	106.6	109.8	107.8
1996:																
1st quarter	101.6	111.4	109.6	108.9	98.4	107.1	110.6	108.4	101.7	111.7	109.8	108.7	98.3	106.9	111.1	108.4
2nd quarter	102.3	113.2	110.7	110.1	98.7	107.7	111.1	108.9	102.2	113.5	111.0	109.8	98.5	107.4	111.4	108.8
3rd quarter	102.0	113.5	111.3	111.0	98.9	108.8	110.8	109.6	102.0	113.8	111.6	110.6	98.6	108.5	111.0	109.4
4th quarter	102.5	115.0	112.2	111.9	98.9	109.2	111.4	110.0	102.4	115.3	112.6	111.5	98.5	108.9	111.6	109.8

PRODUCTIVITY AND RELATED DATA—Continued
(1992=100, quarterly data seasonally adjusted)

YEAR AND QUARTER	Nonfinancial corporations									Manufacturing					
	Output per hour of all employees	Output	Employee hours	Compensation per hour	Real compensation per hour	Unit costs			Implicit price deflator	Output per hour of all persons	Output	Hours of all persons	Compensation per hour	Real compensation per hour	Unit labor costs
						Total	Labor costs	Nonlabor costs							
1968	68.7	45.6	66.4	22.2	89.4	31.3	32.3	28.4	33.6	52.7	57.8	109.7	20.7	83.4	39.3
1969	68.7	47.4	69.0	23.7	90.5	33.5	34.5	30.6	35.1	53.4	59.3	111.0	22.2	85.0	41.6
1970	69.0	47.0	68.0	25.4	91.7	36.1	36.7	34.3	36.6	55.1	57.6	104.5	23.8	86.1	43.2
1971	71.9	48.9	67.9	27.0	93.4	37.1	37.5	36.0	38.0	58.7	59.1	100.6	25.3	87.5	43.0
1972	73.8	52.7	71.4	28.5	95.7	37.9	38.6	35.9	39.2	60.9	64.1	105.2	26.6	89.2	43.6
1973	74.4	55.8	74.9	30.7	97.2	40.3	41.3	37.5	41.5	62.6	69.2	110.5	28.6	90.5	45.7
1974	72.7	54.8	75.3	33.7	95.8	45.5	46.3	43.3	45.6	63.3	68.4	108.1	31.8	90.5	50.2
1975	75.5	53.9	71.4	37.0	96.6	49.0	49.0	48.9	50.1	65.3	63.5	97.3	35.6	93.0	54.6
1976	78.1	58.3	74.6	40.1	99.0	50.7	51.4	48.8	52.4	67.9	69.2	102.0	38.6	95.2	56.9
1977	80.1	62.6	78.1	43.3	100.2	53.1	54.0	50.4	55.1	70.2	74.6	106.2	42.0	97.2	59.8
1978	80.8	66.7	82.6	47.0	101.2	57.1	58.2	53.8	59.0	71.0	78.6	110.7	45.4	97.6	63.9
1979	79.4	68.2	85.9	51.4	99.3	63.4	64.7	59.8	64.3	70.6	79.7	112.8	49.8	96.2	70.5
1980	80.3	68.3	85.1	56.7	96.5	70.2	70.5	69.2	69.7	71.0	76.4	107.6	55.8	94.9	78.5
1981	82.8	71.5	86.3	61.8	95.5	75.8	74.7	79.0	75.8	71.9	77.0	107.1	61.3	94.6	85.2
1982	84.2	70.5	83.7	66.2	96.3	80.4	78.7	85.4	79.3	75.7	74.3	98.0	67.2	97.7	88.7
1983	86.8	73.7	84.9	68.7	96.8	80.9	79.1	85.8	81.1	78.4	77.7	99.0	69.0	97.2	88.0
1984	89.6	81.0	90.4	71.7	96.8	81.1	80.0	84.3	82.8	80.8	85.2	105.4	71.4	96.4	88.4
1985	91.0	84.2	92.5	74.9	97.7	83.1	82.3	85.2	84.4	83.8	87.8	104.7	75.3	98.1	89.8
1986	93.7	86.9	92.7	78.7	100.8	84.9	84.0	87.5	85.2	87.6	90.3	103.1	78.6	100.6	89.8
1987	95.1	91.1	95.8	81.6	100.7	86.2	85.7	87.5	87.1	90.0	93.5	103.9	80.8	99.8	89.8
1988	96.7	95.9	99.2	84.8	100.6	88.2	87.7	89.7	89.6	91.4	97.6	106.8	84.0	99.6	91.9
1989	95.4	97.5	102.2	86.9	98.4	92.5	91.1	96.3	92.8	92.6	99.2	107.2	86.8	98.2	93.7
1990	96.1	98.4	102.4	91.4	98.1	96.2	95.2	99.1	96.1	94.3	98.8	104.9	91.0	97.6	96.5
1991	97.5	97.1	99.6	95.6	98.5	99.3	98.0	103.0	98.8	96.4	96.9	100.6	95.7	98.6	99.3
1992	100.0	100.0	100.0	100.0	100.0	100.0	100.0	100.0	100.0	100.0	100.0	100.0	100.0	100.0	100.0
1993	101.2	103.4	102.2	102.1	99.1	100.5	100.9	99.4	101.7	102.2	103.6	101.4	102.9	99.9	100.7
1994	103.3	109.9	106.4	103.9	98.4	100.3	100.6	99.7	103.4	104.7	108.7	103.8	105.6	100.0	100.8
1995	104.1	114.0	109.5	106.3	97.9	101.4	102.1	99.5	105.0	108.1	112.5	104.1	108.7	100.1	100.6
1996	106.6	119.2	111.8	109.4	97.8	101.4	102.6	98.3	106.3	111.7	115.6	103.5	112.2	100.3	100.5
1988:															
1st quarter	96.3	94.3	97.9	83.3	100.4	87.0	86.4	88.6	88.3	90.7	96.1	106.1	82.8	99.9	91.3
2nd quarter	96.7	95.4	98.7	84.6	100.9	87.9	87.5	89.0	89.1	91.2	97.1	106.5	83.6	99.7	91.6
3rd quarter	96.7	96.2	99.4	85.4	100.7	88.8	88.4	90.1	90.2	91.7	98.0	106.8	84.4	99.5	92.0
4th quarter	97.3	97.9	100.6	86.0	100.2	89.1	88.4	91.2	90.8	92.3	99.2	107.4	85.6	99.8	92.8
1989:															
1st quarter	95.6	97.3	101.7	86.1	99.3	91.1	90.1	93.9	91.6	92.9	100.1	107.8	86.3	99.4	92.9
2nd quarter	95.2	97.2	102.0	86.4	98.0	92.1	90.8	95.9	92.6	92.9	99.8	107.5	86.0	97.6	92.6
3rd quarter	95.6	97.7	102.2	87.1	97.9	92.7	91.1	97.4	93.3	92.1	98.7	107.1	86.9	97.8	94.3
4th quarter	95.3	97.7	102.5	88.3	98.4	94.0	92.6	97.9	93.7	92.8	98.3	106.0	88.3	98.4	95.2
1990:															
1st quarter	95.5	98.3	103.0	89.4	98.0	94.7	93.7	97.6	94.9	93.7	99.0	105.7	89.0	97.5	95.0
2nd quarter	96.6	99.3	102.8	91.1	98.7	95.1	94.3	97.5	95.8	93.6	99.0	105.8	90.6	98.2	96.8
3rd quarter	96.0	98.2	102.4	92.3	98.4	97.2	96.2	99.9	96.5	94.8	99.4	104.8	91.6	97.6	96.6
4th quarter	96.5	97.7	101.3	93.2	97.7	97.9	96.6	101.6	97.2	95.1	97.9	103.0	92.8	97.2	97.6
1991:															
1st quarter	97.2	97.0	99.8	94.0	97.8	98.4	96.8	102.9	98.2	95.0	95.7	100.8	94.0	97.8	99.0
2nd quarter	97.4	96.8	99.4	95.3	98.6	99.2	97.8	103.2	98.8	95.7	96.1	100.3	95.2	98.5	99.5
3rd quarter	97.7	97.1	99.4	96.3	98.8	99.7	98.5	103.1	99.1	97.4	97.8	100.5	96.5	99.1	99.1
4th quarter	98.2	97.6	99.4	97.3	99.0	100.0	99.1	102.6	99.2	97.9	98.1	100.2	97.5	99.3	99.6
1992:															
1st quarter	99.2	98.6	99.4	98.6	99.7	99.7	99.5	100.4	99.5	98.7	98.3	99.5	98.6	99.7	99.9
2nd quarter	99.4	99.3	99.8	99.9	100.0	100.0	100.2	99.6	99.9	99.6	99.8	100.2	99.7	100.0	100.0
3rd quarter	100.1	100.1	100.0	100.6	100.2	100.7	100.5	101.3	100.1	100.4	100.4	100.0	100.6	100.2	100.2
4th quarter	101.3	102.0	100.7	101.2	99.9	99.6	99.9	98.8	100.4	101.1	101.6	100.4	101.0	99.7	99.9
1993:															
1st quarter	100.3	101.5	101.1	101.5	99.5	100.8	101.2	99.9	101.3	102.0	102.8	100.8	101.4	99.4	99.5
2nd quarter	100.8	102.8	101.9	101.9	99.1	100.6	101.1	99.1	101.4	102.0	103.2	101.2	102.5	99.7	100.5
3rd quarter	101.2	103.8	102.6	102.2	99.0	100.6	101.0	99.5	101.7	101.9	103.4	101.5	103.3	100.1	101.4
4th quarter	102.2	105.7	103.4	102.6	98.5	100.0	100.3	99.0	102.2	102.7	104.9	102.1	104.3	100.2	101.5
1994:															
1st quarter	103.6	108.1	104.3	103.6	99.0	100.4	100.0	101.5	102.8	103.7	106.2	102.4	105.1	100.5	101.3
2nd quarter	103.0	109.1	105.9	103.7	98.5	100.1	100.6	98.8	103.1	104.8	108.1	103.1	105.3	100.0	100.4
3rd quarter	103.1	110.2	106.8	104.0	97.9	100.5	100.9	99.5	103.7	105.2	109.3	104.0	105.9	99.8	100.7
4th quarter	103.8	112.3	108.3	104.6	97.9	100.3	100.8	99.1	104.1	105.7	111.1	105.1	106.6	99.8	100.9
1995:															
1st quarter	103.0	112.3	109.1	105.2	97.8	101.6	102.2	99.8	104.6	106.7	112.3	105.2	107.2	99.6	100.5
2nd quarter	103.5	112.9	109.1	106.0	97.7	101.8	102.4	100.1	104.8	107.6	111.9	104.0	108.2	99.8	100.5
3rd quarter	104.7	114.9	109.7	106.6	97.8	101.1	101.9	99.0	105.1	108.8	112.7	103.6	109.2	100.2	100.4
4th quarter	105.2	115.9	110.2	107.3	97.8	101.2	102.0	99.1	105.4	109.2	113.0	103.4	110.1	100.4	100.8
1996:															
1st quarter	105.6	116.5	110.4	107.8	97.5	101.4	102.1	99.2	106.0	110.3	113.3	102.7	110.8	100.2	100.4
2nd quarter	106.4	118.7	111.5	109.0	97.8	101.4	102.4	98.4	106.2	111.0	115.0	103.7	112.1	100.5	101.0
3rd quarter	107.0	120.0	112.1	109.9	97.9	101.5	102.7	98.1	106.4	112.4	116.4	103.6	112.9	100.6	100.4
4th quarter	107.6	121.5	113.0	110.7	97.8	101.5	102.9	97.4	106.5	113.5	117.7	103.7	113.5	100.3	100.0

YEAR AND QUARTER	CORPORATE PROFITS (Net profits after taxes—Millions of dollars)												
		Manufacturing											
		Nondurable goods											
								Chemicals					
	Total	Total	Food and tobacco [1]	Textiles	Apparel (including leather)	Paper	Printing	Total	Industrial chemicals and synthetics	Drugs	Other chemicals	Petroleum and coal products	Rubber
1968	32 069	....	2 209	654	....	889	....	3 525	....	....	....	5 794	....
1969	33 248	....	2 382	621	....	987	....	3 591	....	....	....	5 884	....
1970	28 572	....	2 549	413	....	719	....	3 434	....	....	....	5 893	....
1971	31 038	....	2 754	558	....	501	....	3 780	....	....	....	5 829	....
1972	36 467	....	3 021	659	....	941	....	4 499	....	....	....	5 151	....
1973	48 259	....	3 723	831	....	1 427	....	5 670	....	....	....	7 759	....
1974	58 747	....	4 601	780	....	2 287	....	7 175	....	....	....	14 483	....
1975	49 135	....	5 154	409	....	1 801	....	6 703	....	....	....	9 307	....
1976	64 519	....	5 826	809	....	2 270	....	7 610	....	....	....	11 725	....
1977	70 366	....	5 575	828	....	2 367	....	8 060	....	....	....	12 179	....
1978	81 148	....	6 213	1 170	....	2 598	....	9 117	....	....	....	12 805	....
1979	98 698	....	7 340	1 340	....	3 723	....	10 896	....	....	....	21 936	....
1980	92 579	....	8 222	977	....	2 789	....	11 578	....	....	....	25 133	....
1981	101 302	....	9 109	1 157	....	3 110	....	12 973	....	....	....	23 733	....
1982	71 028	....	8 383	851	....	1 460	....	10 324	....	....	....	19 666	....
1983	85 834	....	9 436	1 599	....	2 327	....	11 644	....	....	....	19 297	....
1984	107 648	....	9 760	1 635	....	3 015	....	13 883	....	....	....	17 154	....
1985	87 648	....	12 798	1 200	....	2 880	....	9 542	....	....	....	12 739	....
1986	83 121	....	13 292	1 706	....	3 280	....	12 900	....	....	....	8 823	....
1987	115 599	....	15 627	1 891	....	5 520	....	16 559	....	....	....	10 900	....
1988	154 583	87 472	20 671	1 560	1 862	8 081	7 490	23 651	10 243	7 378	....	21 225	2 931
1989	136 279	80 572	16 545	742	2 080	7 047	7 860	24 523	9 320	7 744	....	19 512	2 263
1990	111 561	70 615	16 073	433	1 276	4 882	5 180	23 393	7 842	9 312	....	18 012	1 369
1991	67 516	60 114	19 632	829	1 906	2 164	3 993	19 997	4 744	10 198	....	10 872	721
1992	23 212	46 952	17 576	2 102	3 483	1 196	4 855	12 996	-2582	9 482	6 096	3 209	1 535
1993	83 922	56 352	15 870	1 441	2 444	-201	5 548	15 550	4 218	10 199	1 133	13 067	2 635
1994	176 639	89 053	22 004	1 757	1 972	5 269	8 395	30 447	8 544	13 403	8 499	15 004	4 205
1995	200 178	105 361	24 967	891	1 962	11 929	10 043	36 878	10 990	15 607	10 282	14 123	4 572
1996	226 163	119 590	26 973	1 841	1 936	6 464	10 993	39 845	8 631	16 163	15 052	26 832	4 708
1988:													
1st quarter	37 060	21 574	4 469	394	532	1 745	1 979	6 484	2 478	2 313	....	5 050	921
2nd quarter	41 607	22 153	6 051	479	286	2 198	1 936	6 113	2 971	1 485	....	4 225	864
3rd quarter	38 506	22 651	5 400	310	502	2 227	2 025	5 493	2 744	1 404	....	5 911	783
4th quarter	37 410	21 094	4 751	377	542	1 911	1 550	5 561	2 050	2 176	....	6 039	363
1989:													
1st quarter	37 851	21 911	3 865	340	679	1 998	1 605	6 960	3 006	2 102	....	5 679	786
2nd quarter	36 568	19 869	3 939	487	316	2 017	1 802	6 829	2 860	1 928	....	3 830	648
3rd quarter	33 427	19 618	3 335	398	861	1 872	1 679	6 224	2 334	1 671	....	4 741	508
4th quarter	28 433	19 174	5 406	-483	224	1 160	2 774	4 510	1 120	2 043	....	5 262	321
1990:													
1st quarter	28 064	16 302	3 493	60	259	1 454	1 025	5 470	1 687	2 083	....	4 116	426
2nd quarter	35 143	19 458	5 169	257	269	1 600	1 237	6 347	2 675	1 993	....	3 992	588
3rd quarter	29 573	20 203	5 117	136	551	1 214	1 544	6 254	1 874	2 436	....	5 061	326
4th quarter	18 781	14 652	2 294	-20	197	614	1 374	5 322	1 606	2 800	....	4 843	29
1991:													
1st quarter	18 286	16 843	4 969	-32	321	860	696	5 224	1 836	2 244	....	4 860	-54
2nd quarter	23 080	15 447	5 160	189	337	821	715	5 385	1 280	2 160	....	2 528	311
3rd quarter	17 606	16 493	5 511	212	804	852	1 534	5 357	672	3 107	....	1 590	633
4th quarter	8 544	11 331	3 992	460	444	-369	1 048	4 031	956	2 687	....	1 894	-169
1992:													
1st quarter	-44163	-3968	3 125	296	750	-503	143	-3118	-5774	1 475	1 181	-3921	-740
2nd quarter	30 005	18 854	5 948	568	443	869	1 691	6 229	1 965	2 696	1 568	2 204	902
3rd quarter	27 729	18 799	4 605	570	1 713	726	1 793	6 228	1 599	2 819	1 810	2 350	814
4th quarter	9 641	13 267	3 898	668	577	104	1 228	3 657	-372	2 492	1 537	2 576	559
1993:													
1st quarter	11 148	12 842	2 915	227	645	726	971	4 325	1 561	3 016	-252	2 621	411
2nd quarter	25 222	15 864	4 829	596	577	815	1 637	3 125	2 037	2 609	-1521	3 274	1 012
3rd quarter	24 969	13 470	4 477	314	886	-1746	1 157	4 736	99	3 273	1 364	2 986	662
4th quarter	22 583	14 176	3 649	304	336	4	1 783	3 364	521	1 301	1 542	4 186	550
1994:													
1st quarter	35 460	19 209	5 521	338	178	688	1 926	7 603	2 132	3 901	1 569	2 289	667
2nd quarter	46 980	20 255	4 656	527	682	1 021	2 285	7 127	2 121	2 798	2 208	2 640	1 317
3rd quarter	46 904	24 485	5 827	661	734	1 301	2 263	8 230	2 555	3 162	2 513	4 290	1 179
4th quarter	47 295	25 104	6 000	231	378	2 259	1 921	7 487	1 736	3 542	2 209	5 785	1 042
1995:													
1st quarter	52 534	26 409	5 883	340	404	2 481	3 484	9 245	3 574	3 333	2 338	3 381	1 192
2nd quarter	57 560	28 372	6 713	390	198	3 228	2 090	10 523	4 009	3 942	2 573	3 798	1 432
3rd quarter	50 723	29 884	6 696	193	894	3 509	1 945	10 479	2 574	5 019	2 887	5 072	1 098
4th quarter	39 361	20 696	5 675	-32	466	2 711	2 524	6 631	833	3 313	2 484	1 872	850
1996:													
1st quarter	51 402	28 701	6 393	213	196	2 204	2 927	10 233	3 561	3 485	3 187	5 213	1 322
2nd quarter	59 410	28 345	6 170	596	255	1 948	1 948	7 998	-216	4 214	4 001	8 137	1 649
3rd quarter	62 273	34 518	7 123	657	816	1 751	2 942	13 288	3 415	4 293	5 580	6 530	1 412
4th quarter	53 078	28 026	7 287	375	669	917	3 176	8 326	1 871	4 171	2 284	6 952	325

1. The tobacco industry is included beginning with the data for 1985.

CORPORATE PROFITS—Continued
(Net profits after taxes—Millions of dollars)

Manufacturing—Continued

Durable goods

YEAR AND QUARTER	Total	Stone, clay, and glass products	Primary metals			Fabricated metal products	Machinery (except electrical)	Electrical and electronic equipment	Transportation equipment			Instruments
			Total	Iron and steel	Non-ferrous metals				Total	Motor vehicles and equipment	Aircraft, missiles, parts	
1968	....	769	....	1 186	1 149	1 320	2 947	2 518	....	3 222	....	....
1969	....	822	....	1 221	1 414	1 326	3 138	2 594	....	2 845	....	....
1970	....	627	....	692	1 297	1 066	2 689	2 349	....	1 424	....	....
1971	....	853	....	748	621	1 070	2 489	2 563	....	3 097	....	....
1972	....	1 060	....	1 022	687	1 569	3 481	2 999	....	3 639	....	....
1973	....	1 266	....	1 695	1 343	2 207	4 936	3 883	....	4 122	....	....
1974	....	1 204	....	3 149	2 035	2 837	5 648	2 940	....	1 957	....	....
1975	....	968	....	2 280	663	2 523	6 311	2 564	....	1 737	....	....
1976	....	1 447	....	2 085	913	3 196	7 889	4 073	....	5 099	....	....
1977	....	1 686	....	864	873	3 458	9 131	5 383	....	6 133	....	....
1978	....	2 353	....	2 124	1 362	3 815	10 746	6 500	....	6 211	....	....
1979	....	2 373	....	2 185	2 691	4 431	11 530	7 386	....	4 382	....	....
1980	....	1 833	....	2 334	2 768	3 967	11 459	7 114	....	-3424	....	....
1981	....	1 627	....	3 507	2 124	4 235	12 580	7 872	....	-209	....	....
1982	....	408	....	-3705	-333	2 320	8 038	6 449	....	734	....	....
1983	....	1 002	....	-3746	-288	2 693	7 680	6 367	....	7 168	....	....
1984	....	1 870	....	-379	-84	4 646	11 963	8 616	....	10 575	....	....
1985	....	1 627	....	-1349	-1000	3 388	9 676	6 886	....	9 087	....	....
1986	....	2 120	....	-3372	760	3 232	6 551	7 619	....	8 363	....	....
1987	....	2 911	....	1 356	1 077	4 427	10 203	9 570	....	10 647	....	....
1988	67 109	2 453	5 249	993	4 256	5 335	13 778	11 143	17 493	12 474	4 883	7 751
1989	55 708	1 968	5 298	1 512	3 785	5 514	9 694	9 663	13 111	8 801	3 861	6 098
1990	40 945	1 087	3 183	586	2 598	4 610	11 153	6 400	4 589	-548	4 487	6 739
1991	7 402	-1525	-452	-1438	986	3 361	-2737	4 695	-4825	-7605	2 482	6 754
1992	-23740	-374	-2382	-1211	-1171	4 058	-9228	8 354	-32402	-30731	-1836	4 317
1993	27 570	1 094	-794	-207	-585	2 788	-6725	12 508	7 791	2 758	4 618	5 798
1994	87 587	1 932	4 826	2 501	2 323	5 529	15 766	18 344	22 882	16 547	5 647	11 521
1995	94 815	2 959	8 144	2 686	5 459	5 519	16 294	26 428	21 438	15 429	4 347	9 414
1996	106 573	3 793	5 360	1 593	3 768	9 230	22 620	26 335	24 208	15 322	7 150	8 367
1988:												
1st quarter	15 485	96	1 233	369	864	1 567	3 122	2 399	4 521	3 294	1 216	1 754
2nd quarter	19 453	997	1 974	802	1 172	1 794	3 071	3 050	5 043	3 839	1 189	2 190
3rd quarter	15 855	804	411	-693	1 104	1 332	3 970	2 932	3 635	2 069	1 541	1 728
4th quarter	16 316	556	1 631	515	1 116	642	3 615	2 762	4 294	3 272	937	2 079
1989:												
1st quarter	15 940	-26	1 704	475	1 228	1 629	2 550	2 364	5 221	3 950	1 237	1 574
2nd quarter	16 699	836	1 650	447	1 203	1 654	2 392	2 496	4 835	3 491	983	1 580
3rd quarter	13 809	876	1 503	427	1 076	1 450	2 247	2 295	2 250	1 174	1 032	1 613
4th quarter	9 260	282	441	163	278	781	2 505	2 508	805	186	609	1 331
1990:												
1st quarter	11 762	-6	1 128	322	807	1 343	2 329	2 044	2 768	1 359	1 293	1 494
2nd quarter	15 684	1 003	1 398	466	932	1 496	2 902	2 032	3 401	2 131	1 160	2 252
3rd quarter	9 370	564	1 008	319	689	1 279	2 576	2 015	-345	-1933	1 587	1 276
4th quarter	4 129	-474	-351	-521	170	492	3 346	309	-1235	-2105	447	1 717
1991:												
1st quarter	1 443	-554	289	-258	547	502	-1244	1 874	-1019	-1976	944	1 507
2nd quarter	7 633	158	364	-50	414	1 491	87	2 243	215	-1294	1 370	2 225
3rd quarter	1 113	257	275	18	257	1 091	-317	-1320	-1596	-1679	-40	1 862
4th quarter	-2787	-1386	-1380	-1148	-232	277	-1263	1 898	-2425	-2656	208	1 160
1992:												
1st quarter	-40195	-1108	-2904	-1123	-1781	921	-3914	631	-34000	-28497	-5492	-515
2nd quarter	11 151	519	691	259	432	1 628	1 157	2 930	1 132	-72	1 077	1 988
3rd quarter	8 930	530	879	393	486	1 505	-450	2 717	41	-1223	1 192	2 257
4th quarter	-3626	-315	-1048	-740	-308	4	-6021	2 076	425	-939	1 387	587
1993:												
1st quarter	-1693	-759	-1407	-778	-628	703	-1079	2 070	-2279	-3566	1 183	23
2nd quarter	9 358	1 458	955	689	266	1 605	-7060	4 052	4 257	2 646	1 382	2 586
3rd quarter	11 498	723	204	46	158	1 321	379	3 320	1 977	694	1 153	2 060
4th quarter	8 407	-328	-546	-164	-381	-841	1 035	3 066	3 836	2 984	900	1 129
1994:												
1st quarter	16 251	-471	730	431	298	1 511	2 135	3 937	4 574	3 196	1 284	2 422
2nd quarter	26 725	1 045	1 195	666	528	1 904	5 340	5 038	7 142	5 427	1 501	3 182
3rd quarter	22 420	904	1 311	707	604	1 715	3 494	5 222	4 593	3 037	1 379	2 995
4th quarter	22 191	454	1 590	697	893	399	4 797	4 147	6 573	4 887	1 483	2 922
1995:												
1st quarter	26 124	253	2 429	845	1 585	1 813	4 719	5 565	6 614	5 030	1 243	3 471
2nd quarter	29 187	722	2 062	617	1 445	2 117	6 354	6 702	6 246	4 851	930	3 369
3rd quarter	20 839	1 343	2 038	718	1 320	1 353	2 033	6 811	4 063	2 006	1 600	2 050
4th quarter	18 665	641	1 615	506	1 109	236	3 188	7 350	4 515	3 542	574	524
1996:												
1st quarter	22 701	401	1 333	215	1 118	2 136	3 859	6 156	5 636	3 356	1 522	1 926
2nd quarter	31 066	1 247	1 780	666	1 114	2 412	6 448	6 489	8 225	5 624	2 108	2 563
3rd quarter	27 754	1 513	1 425	599	826	3 151	5 788	6 080	5 506	3 322	1 806	2 302
4th quarter	25 052	632	822	113	710	1 531	6 525	7 610	4 841	3 020	1 714	1 576

YEAR AND QUARTER	Other durable goods Total	Lumber and wood products	Furniture and fixtures	Mis-cellane-ous manu-facturing	Mining	Wholesale trade Total	Durable goods	Non-durable goods	Retail trade Total	General mer-chandise stores	Food stores	All oth-ers	DIVI-DENDS PAID, ALL MANU-FACTUR-ING (Millions of dollars)
1968	......	......	......	......	......	......	......	14 189	......	......	......	......	14 189
1969	......	......	......	......	......	......	......	15 058	......	......	......	......	15 058
1970	......	......	......	......	......	......	......	15 070	......	......	......	......	15 070
1971	......	......	......	......	......	......	......	15 252	......	......	......	......	15 252
1972	......	......	......	......	......	......	......	16 110	......	......	......	......	16 110
1973	......	......	......	......	......	......	......	17 734	......	......	......	......	17 734
1974	......	......	......	......	......	......	......	19 467	......	......	......	......	19 467
1975	......	......	......	......	......	......	......	19 968	......	......	......	......	19 968
1976	......	......	......	......	......	......	......	22 763	......	......	......	......	22 763
1977	......	......	......	......	......	......	......	26 585	......	......	......	......	26 585
1978	......	......	......	......	......	......	......	28 932	......	......	......	......	28 932
1979	......	......	......	......	......	......	......	32 491	......	......	......	......	32 491
1980	......	......	......	......	......	......	......	36 495	......	......	......	......	36 495
1981	......	......	......	......	......	......	......	40 317	......	......	......	......	40 317
1982	......	......	......	......	......	......	......	41 259	......	......	......	......	41 259
1983	......	......	......	......	......	......	......	41 624	......	......	......	......	41 624
1984	......	......	......	......	......	......	......	45 102	......	......	......	......	45 102
1985	......	......	......	......	......	......	......	45 517	......	......	......	......	45 517
1986	......	......	......	......	......	......	......	46 044	......	......	......	......	46 044
1987	......	......	......	......	......	......	......	49 512	......	......	......	......	49 512
1988	3 906	......	......	......	584	7 583	3 532	4 051	10 961	5 685	1 491	3 785	57 064
1989	4 364	......	......	......	1 613	7 275	2 731	4 543	8 380	3 560	540	4 281	65 243
1990	3 184	......	......	......	2 469	4 415	519	3 896	7 192	3 285	1 013	2 897	62 201
1991	2 131	......	......	......	759	3 916	333	3 584	6 798	2 747	1 601	2 450	60 231
1992	3 916	1 747	955	1 214	-240	5 121	1 355	3 766	6 170	2 288	1 007	2 872	63 061
1993	5 108	2 367	1 339	1 403	1 476	6 717	2 069	4 649	11 357	6 281	1 672	3 402	66 756
1994	6 789	3 300	1 615	1 874	820	5 698	1 433	4 266	18 144	7 468	2 981	7 693	69 977
1995	4 622	2 115	1 091	1 416	863	11 245	4 779	6 464	14 855	6 654	3 228	4 974	80 866
1996	6 661	2 705	2 300	1 656	5 749	13 238	5 535	7 702	18 073	6 931	3 659	7 486	94 822
1988:													
1st quarter	793	......	......	......	286	1 708	703	1 005	1 841	873	272	696	12 279
2nd quarter	1 333	......	......	......	407	1 669	718	951	2 165	784	560	821	13 745
3rd quarter	1 043	......	......	......	-125	2 172	1 162	1 010	2 018	929	339	749	14 531
4th quarter	737	......	......	......	16	2 034	949	1 085	4 937	3 099	320	1 519	16 509
1989:													
1st quarter	925	......	......	......	486	1 857	635	1 221	2 365	1 371	227	768	16 070
2nd quarter	1 257	......	......	......	441	2 014	629	1 385	2 029	704	436	889	17 585
3rd quarter	1 575	......	......	......	402	2 153	717	1 436	2 483	1 155	357	971	15 833
4th quarter	607	......	......	......	284	1 251	750	501	1 503	330	-480	1 653	15 755
1990:													
1st quarter	661	......	......	......	666	1 293	208	1 085	150	135	-383	399	15 149
2nd quarter	1 200	......	......	......	362	1 109	150	959	1 417	224	546	648	16 339
3rd quarter	998	......	......	......	658	1 269	61	1 208	1 518	567	244	707	14 759
4th quarter	325	......	......	......	783	744	100	644	4 107	2 359	606	1 143	15 954
1991:													
1st quarter	88	......	......	......	443	671	-264	935	731	388	331	12	14 722
2nd quarter	849	......	......	......	340	1 015	-58	1 073	1 887	658	654	575	14 982
3rd quarter	861	......	......	......	241	1 335	204	1 132	1 394	468	455	472	14 647
4th quarter	333	......	......	......	-265	895	451	444	2 786	1 233	161	1 391	15 880
1992:													
1st quarter	694	376	138	181	-684	621	-170	792	-735	-1220	264	221	14 765
2nd quarter	1 106	462	260	384	142	1 470	232	1 238	2 411	1 433	435	542	15 533
3rd quarter	1 451	560	423	468	170	1 447	423	1 024	1 551	719	292	539	15 519
4th quarter	665	349	134	181	132	1 583	870	712	2 943	1 356	16	1 570	17 244
1993:													
1st quarter	1 035	540	342	153	241	674	-167	841	1 511	1 020	-149	639	16 137
2nd quarter	1 504	749	348	407	779	2 474	908	1 566	3 661	1 927	670	1 064	16 982
3rd quarter	1 514	645	322	547	362	1 268	503	766	2 609	1 234	518	857	16 246
4th quarter	1 055	433	327	296	94	2 301	825	1 476	3 576	2 100	633	842	17 391
1994:													
1st quarter	1 414	724	221	469	-538	2 149	794	1 355	2 704	816	624	1 264	16 269
2nd quarter	1 880	999	483	397	694	2 535	1 312	1 223	4 143	1 563	851	1 729	17 187
3rd quarter	2 186	1 027	575	585	556	-890	-1841	951	3 805	1 398	783	1 623	17 533
4th quarter	1 309	550	336	423	108	1 904	1 168	737	7 492	3 691	723	3 077	18 988
1995:													
1st quarter	1 260	623	296	341	244	2 594	956	1 637	3 201	1 353	767	1 081	18 292
2nd quarter	1 615	738	600	277	646	2 606	874	1 731	3 621	1 422	894	1 306	20 646
3rd quarter	1 149	368	516	265	-438	2 930	1 437	1 493	3 593	1 284	706	1 603	20 980
4th quarter	598	386	-321	533	411	3 115	1 512	1 603	4 440	2 595	861	984	20 948
1996:													
1st quarter	1 253	374	421	459	794	3 388	1 473	1 915	2 943	941	888	1 114	20 048
2nd quarter	1 903	933	550	419	1 418	3 280	1 242	2 038	3 927	1 466	925	1 537	27 068
3rd quarter	1 990	994	619	377	1 970	3 401	1 970	1 431	4 834	1 665	891	2 279	23 268
4th quarter	1 515	404	710	401	1 567	3 169	850	2 318	6 369	2 859	955	2 556	24 438

Employment, Hours, and Earnings

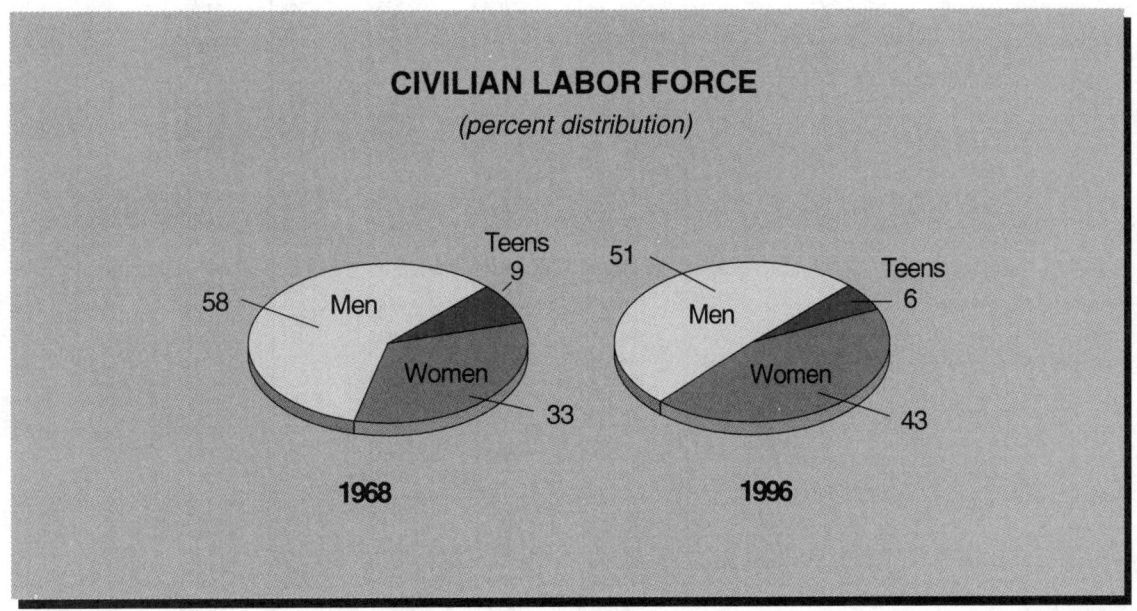

CIVILIAN LABOR FORCE
(percent distribution)

A dult women (age 20 and over) made up 43 percent of the civilian work force in 1996, compared to 33 percent in 1968. Increasing at a fairly steady rate over the period, the total number of women in the work force rose by 121 percent. The number of men in the work force rose 48 percent.

Young people ages 16 to 19 made up about 8.5 percent of the labor force in 1968, rising to more than 9 percent through most of the 1970s. Then, as members of the baby boom generation reached age 20 and above, the number of teenage workers dropped through 1985, not only as a percent of the work force, but also in absolute numbers. Since 1985, the number of teenagers in the labor force has fluctuated within a fairly narrow range and in 1996 remained almost 20 percent below the 1979 figure.

CIVILIAN POPULATION AND LABOR FORCE[1]
(Thousands of persons, 16 years of age and over)

YEAR AND MONTH	Not seasonally adjusted				Labor force (Seasonally adjusted)				
	Population	Labor force			Total		Persons 20 years and over		Both sexes, 16 to 19 years
		Total	Employed	Unemployed	Thousands of persons	Participation rate[2]	Men	Women	
1968	132 028	78 737	75 920	2 817	78 737	59.6	45 852	26 266	6 619
1969	134 335	80 734	77 902	2 832	80 734	60.1	46 351	27 413	6 970
1970	137 085	82 771	78 678	4 093	82 771	60.4	47 220	28 301	7 249
1971	140 216	84 382	79 367	5 016	84 382	60.2	48 009	28 904	7 470
1972	144 126	87 034	82 153	4 882	87 034	60.4	49 079	29 901	8 054
1973	147 096	89 429	85 064	4 365	89 429	60.8	49 932	30 991	8 507
1974	150 120	91 949	86 794	5 156	91 949	61.3	50 879	32 201	8 871
1975	153 153	93 775	85 846	7 929	93 775	61.2	51 494	33 410	8 870
1976	156 150	96 158	88 752	7 406	96 158	61.6	52 288	34 814	9 056
1977	159 033	99 009	92 017	6 991	99 009	62.3	53 348	36 310	9 351
1978	161 911	102 251	96 048	6 202	102 251	63.2	54 471	38 128	9 652
1979	164 863	104 962	98 824	6 137	104 962	63.7	55 615	39 708	9 638
1980	167 745	106 940	99 303	7 637	106 940	63.8	56 455	41 106	9 378
1981	170 130	108 670	100 397	8 273	108 670	63.9	57 197	42 485	8 988
1982	172 271	110 204	99 526	10 678	110 204	64.0	57 980	43 699	8 526
1983	174 215	111 550	100 834	10 717	111 550	64.0	58 744	44 636	8 171
1984	176 383	113 544	105 005	8 539	113 544	64.4	59 701	45 900	7 943
1985	178 206	115 461	107 150	8 312	115 461	64.8	60 277	47 283	7 901
1986	180 587	117 834	109 597	8 237	117 834	65.3	61 320	48 589	7 926
1987	182 753	119 865	112 440	7 425	119 865	65.6	62 095	49 783	7 988
1988	184 613	121 669	114 968	6 701	121 669	65.9	62 768	50 870	8 031
1989	186 393	123 869	117 342	6 528	123 869	66.5	63 704	52 212	7 954
1990	189 164	125 840	118 793	7 047	125 840	66.5	64 916	53 131	7 792
1991	190 925	126 346	117 718	8 628	126 346	66.2	65 374	53 708	7 265
1992	192 805	128 105	118 492	9 613	128 105	66.4	66 213	54 796	7 096
1993	194 838	129 200	120 259	8 940	129 200	66.3	66 642	55 388	7 170
1994	196 814	131 056	123 060	7 996	131 056	66.6	66 921	56 655	7 481
1995	198 584	132 304	124 900	7 404	132 304	66.6	67 324	57 215	7 765
1996	200 591	133 943	126 708	7 236	133 943	66.8	68 044	58 094	7 806
1993:									
January	193 962	127 186	117 027	10 158	128 400	66.2	66 329	54 982	7 089
February	194 108	127 651	117 646	10 004	128 458	66.2	66 363	54 951	7 144
March	194 248	127 829	118 350	9 478	128 598	66.2	66 496	54 970	7 132
April	194 398	127 616	118 781	8 835	128 584	66.1	66 429	55 064	7 091
May	194 549	128 949	120 142	8 807	129 264	66.4	66 676	55 344	7 244
June	194 719	131 060	121 587	9 473	129 411	66.5	66 801	55 496	7 114
July	194 882	131 574	122 352	9 223	129 397	66.4	66 846	55 346	7 205
August	195 063	130 673	122 018	8 655	129 619	66.4	66 864	55 491	7 264
September	195 259	128 975	120 673	8 302	129 268	66.2	66 625	55 463	7 180
October	195 444	129 685	121 389	8 296	129 573	66.3	66 754	55 648	7 171
November	195 625	129 662	121 568	8 094	129 711	66.3	66 681	55 782	7 248
December	195 794	129 537	121 578	7 959	129 941	66.4	66 701	56 062	7 178
1994:									
January	195 953	129 393	119 901	9 492	130 709	66.7	66 857	56 359	7 493
February	196 090	129 764	120 503	9 262	130 685	66.6	66 688	56 527	7 470
March	196 213	129 718	120 844	8 874	130 501	66.5	66 647	56 435	7 419
April	196 363	129 682	121 604	8 078	130 644	66.5	66 659	56 427	7 558
May	196 510	130 602	122 946	7 656	130 828	66.6	66 657	56 689	7 482
June	196 693	132 115	123 864	8 251	130 590	66.4	66 606	56 462	7 522
July	196 859	132 783	124 503	8 281	130 644	66.4	66 730	56 470	7 444
August	197 043	132 361	124 493	7 868	131 223	66.6	66 859	56 778	7 586
September	197 248	131 155	123 775	7 379	131 284	66.6	66 920	57 035	7 329
October	197 430	131 879	124 724	7 155	131 676	66.7	67 240	56 924	7 512
November	197 607	131 869	124 896	6 973	131 846	66.7	67 411	57 012	7 423
December	197 765	131 418	124 729	6 690	131 847	66.7	67 535	56 705	7 607
1995:									
January	197 753	130 698	122 597	8 101	132 198	66.9	67 605	56 934	7 659
February	197 886	131 028	123 343	7 685	132 140	66.8	67 447	57 002	7 691
March	198 007	131 423	123 943	7 480	132 271	66.8	67 506	56 962	7 803
April	198 148	131 657	124 278	7 378	132 613	66.9	67 504	57 331	7 778
May	198 286	131 739	124 554	7 185	131 935	66.5	67 220	57 010	7 705
June	198 453	133 447	125 720	7 727	131 978	66.5	67 237	56 902	7 839
July	198 615	134 440	126 548	7 892	132 300	66.6	67 196	57 339	7 765
August	198 801	133 383	125 926	7 457	132 246	66.5	67 122	57 276	7 848
September	199 005	132 341	125 173	7 167	132 450	66.6	67 305	57 354	7 791
October	199 192	132 863	125 979	6 884	132 564	66.6	67 277	57 555	7 732
November	199 355	132 622	125 599	7 024	132 533	66.5	67 237	57 534	7 762
December	199 508	132 008	125 136	6 872	132 422	66.4	67 303	57 334	7 785
1996:									
January	199 634	131 396	123 126	8 270	132 899	66.6	67 556	57 594	7 749
February	199 773	131 995	124 137	7 858	133 070	66.6	67 688	57 618	7 764
March	199 921	132 692	124 992	7 700	133 464	66.8	67 886	57 803	7 775
April	200 101	132 513	125 388	7 124	133 427	66.7	67 829	57 817	7 781
May	200 278	133 558	126 391	7 166	133 759	66.8	67 996	57 885	7 878
June	200 459	135 083	127 706	7 377	133 709	66.7	68 088	57 909	7 712
July	200 641	136 272	128 579	7 693	134 165	66.9	68 222	58 139	7 804
August	200 847	135 011	128 143	6 868	133 898	66.7	68 044	58 230	7 624
September	201 061	134 230	127 529	6 700	134 291	66.8	68 056	58 349	7 886
October	201 273	135 015	128 439	6 577	134 636	66.9	68 273	58 432	7 931
November	201 463	134 973	128 157	6 816	134 831	66.9	68 391	58 574	7 866
December	201 636	134 583	127 903	6 680	135 022	67.0	68 369	58 728	7 925

1. Changes in survey design, population coverage, or methodology in 1994, 1986, 1982, 1978, and 1972 affect year-to-year comparisions. See NOTES for more information.
2. Civilian labor force as a percent of the civilian population 16 years and over.

CIVILIAN EMPLOYMENT AND UNEMPLOYMENT[1]
(Thousands of persons, 16 years of age and over, seasonally adjusted)

YEAR AND MONTH	Employment — Total: Thousands of persons	Employment — Total: Ratio: Employment to population[2]	By age and sex: Men (20 and over)	By age and sex: Women (20 and over)	Both sexes, 16 to 19 years	By industry: Agricultural	By industry: Non-agricultural	Unemployment Total	Long term[3]	Men (20 and over)	Women (20 and over)	Both sexes, 16 to 19 years
1968	75 920	57.5	44 859	25 281	5 781	3 817	72 103	2 817	412	993	985	827
1969	77 902	58.0	45 388	26 397	6 117	3 606	74 296	2 832	375	963	1 015	849
1970	78 678	57.4	45 581	26 952	6 144	3 463	75 215	4 093	663	1 638	1 349	1 107
1971	79 367	56.6	45 912	27 246	6 208	3 394	75 972	5 016	1 187	2 097	1 658	1 263
1972	82 153	57.0	47 130	28 276	6 746	3 484	78 669	4 882	1 167	1 948	1 625	1 310
1973	85 064	57.8	48 310	29 484	7 271	3 470	81 594	4 365	826	1 624	1 507	1 237
1974	86 794	57.8	48 922	30 424	7 448	3 515	83 279	5 156	955	1 957	1 777	1 423
1975	85 846	56.1	48 018	30 726	7 104	3 408	82 438	7 929	2 505	3 476	2 684	1 768
1976	88 752	56.8	49 190	32 226	7 336	3 331	85 421	7 406	2 366	3 098	2 588	1 719
1977	92 017	57.9	50 555	33 775	7 688	3 283	88 734	6 991	1 942	2 794	2 535	1 662
1978	96 048	59.3	52 143	35 836	8 070	3 387	92 661	6 202	1 414	2 328	2 292	1 583
1979	98 824	59.9	53 308	37 434	8 083	3 347	95 477	6 137	1 241	2 308	2 276	1 554
1980	99 303	59.2	53 101	38 492	7 710	3 364	95 938	7 637	1 871	3 353	2 615	1 668
1981	100 397	59.0	53 582	39 590	7 225	3 368	97 030	8 273	2 285	3 615	2 895	1 762
1982	99 526	57.8	52 891	40 086	6 549	3 401	96 125	10 678	3 485	5 089	3 613	1 976
1983	100 834	57.9	53 487	41 004	6 342	3 383	97 450	10 717	4 210	5 257	3 632	1 829
1984	105 005	59.5	55 769	42 793	6 444	3 321	101 685	8 539	2 737	3 932	3 107	1 500
1985	107 150	60.1	56 562	44 154	6 434	3 179	103 971	8 312	2 305	3 715	3 129	1 469
1986	109 597	60.7	57 569	45 556	6 472	3 163	106 434	8 237	2 232	3 751	3 032	1 454
1987	112 440	61.5	58 726	47 074	6 640	3 208	109 232	7 425	1 983	3 369	2 709	1 347
1988	114 968	62.3	59 781	48 383	6 805	3 169	111 800	6 701	1 610	2 987	2 487	1 226
1989	117 342	63.0	60 837	49 745	6 759	3 199	114 142	6 528	1 375	2 867	2 467	1 194
1990	118 793	62.8	61 678	50 535	6 581	3 223	115 570	7 047	1 525	3 239	2 596	1 212
1991	117 718	61.7	61 178	50 634	5 906	3 269	114 449	8 628	2 357	4 195	3 074	1 359
1992	118 492	61.5	61 496	51 328	5 669	3 247	115 245	9 613	3 408	4 717	3 469	1 427
1993	120 259	61.7	62 355	52 099	5 805	3 115	117 144	8 940	3 094	4 287	3 288	1 365
1994	123 060	62.5	63 294	53 606	6 161	3 409	119 651	7 996	2 860	3 627	3 049	1 320
1995	124 900	62.9	64 085	54 396	6 419	3 440	121 460	7 404	2 363	3 239	2 819	1 346
1996	126 708	63.2	64 897	55 311	6 500	3 443	123 264	7 236	2 316	3 146	2 783	1 306
1993:												
January	119 075	61.4	61 895	51 505	5 675	3 222	115 853	9 325	3 346	4 434	3 477	1 414
February	119 275	61.4	61 963	51 573	5 739	3 125	116 150	9 183	3 190	4 400	3 378	1 405
March	119 542	61.5	62 007	51 808	5 727	3 119	116 423	9 056	3 115	4 489	3 162	1 405
April	119 474	61.5	62 032	51 732	5 710	3 074	116 400	9 110	3 014	4 397	3 332	1 381
May	120 115	61.7	62 309	51 996	5 810	3 100	117 015	9 149	3 101	4 367	3 348	1 434
June	120 290	61.8	62 409	52 183	5 698	3 108	117 182	9 121	3 141	4 392	3 313	1 416
July	120 467	61.8	62 497	52 088	5 882	3 126	117 341	8 930	3 046	4 349	3 258	1 323
August	120 856	62.0	62 634	52 294	5 928	3 026	117 830	8 763	3 026	4 230	3 197	1 336
September	120 554	61.7	62 437	52 241	5 876	3 174	117 380	8 714	3 042	4 188	3 222	1 304
October	120 823	61.8	62 614	52 379	5 830	3 084	117 739	8 750	3 029	4 140	3 269	1 341
November	121 169	61.9	62 732	52 531	5 906	3 157	118 012	8 542	2 986	3 949	3 251	1 342
December	121 464	62.0	62 760	52 813	5 891	3 116	118 348	8 477	2 968	3 941	3 249	1 287
1994:												
January	121 999	62.3	62 810	53 070	6 119	3 307	118 692	8 710	3 066	4 047	3 289	1 374
February	122 104	62.3	62 705	53 278	6 121	3 325	118 779	8 581	3 124	3 983	3 249	1 349
March	122 001	62.2	62 801	53 115	6 085	3 354	118 647	8 500	3 045	3 846	3 320	1 334
April	122 331	62.3	62 938	53 274	6 119	3 425	118 906	8 313	2 904	3 721	3 153	1 439
May	122 961	62.6	63 190	53 633	6 138	3 412	119 549	7 867	2 817	3 467	3 056	1 344
June	122 653	62.4	63 056	53 409	6 188	3 295	119 358	7 937	2 717	3 550	3 053	1 334
July	122 717	62.3	63 053	53 526	6 138	3 343	119 374	7 927	2 831	3 677	2 944	1 306
August	123 274	62.6	63 261	53 743	6 270	3 460	119 814	7 949	2 753	3 598	3 035	1 316
September	123 544	62.6	63 522	53 983	6 039	3 441	120 103	7 740	2 765	3 398	3 052	1 290
October	124 052	62.8	63 783	54 061	6 208	3 486	120 566	7 624	2 965	3 457	2 863	1 304
November	124 474	63.0	64 084	54 120	6 270	3 576	120 898	7 372	2 678	3 327	2 892	1 153
December	124 689	63.0	64 324	54 047	6 318	3 577	121 112	7 158	2 510	3 211	2 658	1 289
1995:												
January	124 766	63.1	64 222	54 151	6 393	3 530	121 236	7 432	2 399	3 383	2 783	1 266
February	124 937	63.1	64 369	54 223	6 345	3 579	121 358	7 203	2 354	3 078	2 779	1 346
March	125 070	63.2	64 355	54 169	6 546	3 625	121 445	7 201	2 255	3 151	2 793	1 257
April	125 023	63.1	64 228	54 366	6 429	3 572	121 451	7 590	2 436	3 276	2 965	1 349
May	124 577	62.8	63 926	54 292	6 359	3 350	121 227	7 358	2 541	3 294	2 718	1 346
June	124 533	62.8	64 001	54 038	6 494	3 455	121 078	7 445	2 280	3 236	2 864	1 345
July	124 804	62.8	63 978	54 458	6 368	3 398	121 406	7 496	2 325	3 218	2 881	1 397
August	124 729	62.7	63 831	54 419	6 479	3 387	121 342	7 517	2 395	3 291	2 857	1 369
September	124 927	62.8	64 031	54 495	6 401	3 307	121 620	7 523	2 341	3 274	2 859	1 390
October	125 235	62.9	64 183	54 657	6 395	3 427	121 808	7 329	2 286	3 094	2 898	1 337
November	125 124	62.8	63 948	54 770	6 406	3 340	121 784	7 409	2 355	3 289	2 764	1 356
December	125 068	62.7	63 997	54 680	6 391	3 344	121 724	7 354	2 367	3 306	2 654	1 394
1996:												
January	125 311	62.8	64 258	54 684	6 369	3 490	121 813	7 588	2 369	3 298	2 910	1 380
February	125 706	62.9	64 416	54 845	6 445	3 499	122 207	7 364	2 322	3 272	2 773	1 319
March	126 062	63.1	64 562	55 054	6 446	3 470	122 592	7 402	2 406	3 324	2 749	1 329
April	126 125	63.0	64 573	55 075	6 477	3 412	122 713	7 302	2 387	3 256	2 742	1 304
May	126 428	63.1	64 788	55 067	6 573	3 474	122 954	7 331	2 354	3 208	2 818	1 305
June	126 590	63.2	64 933	55 196	6 461	3 408	123 182	7 119	2 353	3 155	2 713	1 251
July	126 889	63.2	65 071	55 315	6 503	3 470	123 419	7 276	2 326	3 151	2 824	1 301
August	126 988	63.2	65 165	55 498	6 325	3 418	123 570	6 910	2 273	2 879	2 732	1 299
September	127 248	63.3	64 978	55 644	6 626	3 480	123 768	7 043	2 277	3 078	2 705	1 260
October	127 617	63.4	65 299	55 681	6 637	3 450	124 167	7 019	2 294	2 974	2 751	1 294
November	127 644	63.4	65 349	55 753	6 542	3 354	124 290	7 187	2 184	3 042	2 821	1 324
December	127 855	63.4	65 367	55 871	6 617	3 426	124 429	7 167	2 179	3 002	2 857	1 308

1. Changes in survey design, population coverage, or methodology in 1994, 1986, 1982, 1978, and 1972 affect year-to-year comparisions. See NOTES for more information.
2. Civilian employment as a percent of the civilian population 16 years and over.
3. Fifteen weeks and over.

UNEMPLOYMENT RATES[1]
(Percent of civilian labor force in group, seasonally adjusted)

YEAR AND MONTH	All civilian workers	By sex and age			By race		Persons of Hispanic origin	By marital or family status			By industry of last job	
		20 years and over		Both sexes, 16 to 19 years				Married men, spouse present	Married women, spouse present	Women who maintain families	Private non-agricultural wage and salary workers	
		Men	Women		White	Black					Total	Construction
1968	3.6	2.2	3.8	12.7	3.2	....	....	1.6	3.9	4.4	3.6	6.9
1969	3.5	2.1	3.7	12.2	3.1	....	....	1.5	3.9	4.4	3.5	6.0
1970	4.9	3.5	4.8	15.3	4.5	....	....	2.6	4.9	5.4	5.2	9.7
1971	5.9	4.4	5.7	16.9	5.4	....	....	3.2	5.7	7.3	6.2	10.4
1972	5.6	4.0	5.4	16.2	5.1	10.4	....	2.8	5.4	7.2	5.7	10.3
1973	4.9	3.3	4.9	14.5	4.3	9.4	7.5	2.3	4.7	7.1	4.9	8.9
1974	5.6	3.8	5.5	16.0	5.0	10.5	8.1	2.7	5.3	7.0	5.7	10.7
1975	8.5	6.8	8.0	19.9	7.8	14.8	12.2	5.1	7.9	10.0	9.1	18.0
1976	7.7	5.9	7.4	19.0	7.0	14.0	11.5	4.2	7.1	10.1	7.9	15.5
1977	7.1	5.2	7.0	17.8	6.2	14.0	10.1	3.6	6.5	9.4	7.1	12.7
1978	6.1	4.3	6.0	16.4	5.2	12.8	9.1	2.8	5.5	8.5	5.9	10.6
1979	5.8	4.2	5.7	16.1	5.1	12.3	8.3	2.8	5.1	8.3	5.8	10.3
1980	7.1	5.9	6.4	17.8	6.3	14.3	10.1	4.2	5.8	9.2	7.4	14.1
1981	7.6	6.3	6.8	19.6	6.7	15.6	10.4	4.3	6.0	10.4	7.7	15.6
1982	9.7	8.8	8.3	23.2	8.6	18.9	13.8	6.5	7.4	11.7	10.1	20.0
1983	9.6	8.9	8.1	22.4	8.4	19.5	13.7	6.5	7.0	12.2	9.9	18.4
1984	7.5	6.6	6.8	18.9	6.5	15.9	10.7	4.6	5.7	10.4	7.4	14.3
1985	7.2	6.2	6.6	18.6	6.2	15.1	10.5	4.3	5.6	10.4	7.2	13.1
1986	7.0	6.1	6.2	18.3	6.0	14.5	10.6	4.4	5.2	9.8	7.0	13.1
1987	6.2	5.4	5.4	16.9	5.3	13.0	8.8	3.9	4.3	9.2	6.2	11.6
1988	5.5	4.8	4.9	15.3	4.7	11.7	8.2	3.3	3.9	8.1	5.5	10.6
1989	5.3	4.5	4.7	15.0	4.5	11.4	8.0	3.0	3.7	8.1	5.3	10.0
1990	5.6	5.0	4.9	15.5	4.8	11.4	8.2	3.4	3.8	8.3	5.7	11.1
1991	6.8	6.4	5.7	18.7	6.1	12.5	10.0	4.4	4.5	9.3	7.1	15.5
1992	7.5	7.1	6.3	20.1	6.6	14.2	11.6	5.1	5.0	10.0	7.8	16.8
1993	6.9	6.4	5.9	19.0	6.1	13.0	10.8	4.4	4.6	9.7	7.1	14.4
1994	6.1	5.4	5.4	17.6	5.3	11.5	9.9	3.7	4.1	8.9	6.3	11.8
1995	5.6	4.8	4.9	17.3	4.9	10.4	9.3	3.3	3.9	8.0	5.7	11.5
1996	5.4	4.6	4.8	16.7	4.7	10.5	8.9	3.0	3.6	8.2	5.5	10.1
1993:												
January	7.3	6.7	6.3	19.9	6.3	14.1	11.3	4.6	5.0	10.4	7.4	14.5
February	7.1	6.6	6.1	19.7	6.2	13.5	11.5	4.6	4.6	10.2	7.3	14.3
March	7.0	6.8	5.8	19.7	6.1	13.7	11.3	4.6	4.4	9.2	7.2	14.9
April	7.1	6.6	6.1	19.5	6.1	14.0	11.0	4.6	5.0	9.6	7.3	14.6
May	7.1	6.5	6.0	19.8	6.2	13.1	10.2	4.6	4.7	10.0	7.3	15.2
June	7.0	6.6	6.0	19.9	6.2	13.4	10.4	4.5	4.7	9.9	7.2	15.0
July	6.9	6.5	5.9	18.4	6.1	12.7	10.7	4.5	4.7	9.7	7.1	16.2
August	6.8	6.3	5.8	18.4	6.0	12.3	9.8	4.4	4.4	9.2	7.0	14.8
September	6.7	6.3	5.8	18.2	5.9	12.5	10.0	4.3	4.6	9.2	7.0	14.2
October	6.8	6.2	5.9	18.7	6.2	11.8	11.4	4.4	4.7	9.4	7.0	13.9
November	6.6	5.9	5.8	18.5	5.7	12.6	10.5	4.1	4.5	9.6	6.8	12.8
December	6.5	5.9	5.8	17.9	5.8	11.7	10.6	4.0	4.5	10.0	6.7	13.1
1994:												
January	6.7	6.1	5.8	18.3	5.8	13.2	10.5	4.1	4.4	9.3	6.9	13.5
February	6.6	6.0	5.7	18.1	5.7	13.0	10.1	4.4	4.4	9.7	6.9	13.1
March	6.5	5.8	5.9	18.0	5.7	12.5	10.0	4.1	4.4	9.7	6.7	13.4
April	6.4	5.6	5.6	19.0	5.6	11.8	10.9	3.9	4.0	9.3	6.5	12.2
May	6.0	5.2	5.4	18.0	5.2	11.8	9.5	3.7	4.1	8.9	6.2	11.5
June	6.1	5.3	5.4	17.7	5.3	11.3	10.3	3.6	4.2	8.8	6.2	12.0
July	6.1	5.5	5.2	17.5	5.3	10.8	10.1	3.6	4.0	7.6	6.2	11.0
August	6.1	5.4	5.3	17.3	5.3	11.1	9.8	3.5	4.2	8.9	6.1	10.7
September	5.9	5.1	5.4	17.6	5.2	10.6	10.2	3.3	4.1	8.8	6.0	10.8
October	5.8	5.1	5.0	17.4	5.0	11.2	9.5	3.3	3.9	8.8	5.9	10.6
November	5.6	4.9	5.1	15.5	4.8	10.7	8.8	3.2	3.9	8.5	5.8	10.6
December	5.4	4.8	4.7	16.9	4.8	9.8	9.4	3.2	3.7	8.9	5.6	11.1
1995:												
January	5.6	5.0	4.9	16.5	4.9	10.4	10.2	3.3	3.7	8.9	5.6	11.6
February	5.5	4.6	4.9	17.5	4.7	10.4	8.9	3.2	3.7	8.4	5.5	10.4
March	5.4	4.7	4.9	16.1	4.8	9.8	9.0	3.2	3.9	7.9	5.5	11.1
April	5.7	4.9	5.2	17.3	5.0	10.6	9.0	3.3	4.0	9.2	5.8	11.6
May	5.6	4.9	4.8	17.5	4.9	10.0	9.6	3.4	3.8	8.0	5.8	12.4
June	5.6	4.8	5.0	17.2	4.9	10.6	9.1	3.4	3.9	8.5	5.6	11.1
July	5.7	4.8	5.0	18.0	4.9	10.8	8.9	3.4	4.0	8.0	5.8	11.0
August	5.7	4.9	5.0	17.4	4.9	11.0	9.5	3.3	4.2	7.0	5.8	12.3
September	5.7	4.9	5.0	17.8	4.9	11.1	9.1	3.4	4.0	8.0	5.9	12.7
October	5.5	4.6	5.0	17.3	4.9	9.9	9.5	3.1	3.9	7.9	5.7	11.5
November	5.6	4.9	4.8	17.5	5.0	9.6	9.3	3.2	3.8	7.7	5.7	11.7
December	5.6	4.9	4.6	17.9	4.9	10.2	9.6	3.2	3.7	6.8	5.8	11.3
1996:												
January	5.7	4.9	5.1	17.8	5.0	10.6	9.4	3.2	3.9	8.2	5.8	10.9
February	5.5	4.8	4.8	17.0	4.8	10.3	9.5	3.1	3.8	7.6	5.6	10.8
March	5.5	4.9	4.8	17.1	4.8	10.8	9.8	3.1	3.5	7.7	5.7	10.3
April	5.5	4.8	4.7	16.8	4.8	10.5	9.5	3.0	3.7	7.3	5.6	10.3
May	5.5	4.7	4.9	16.6	4.8	10.3	9.2	3.0	3.7	8.5	5.7	10.2
June	5.3	4.6	4.7	16.2	4.6	10.2	8.8	3.0	3.6	7.8	5.4	9.6
July	5.4	4.6	4.9	16.7	4.7	10.5	8.9	3.0	3.5	8.8	5.5	9.8
August	5.2	4.2	4.7	17.0	4.5	10.4	8.8	2.9	3.4	8.5	5.3	9.1
September	5.2	4.5	4.6	16.0	4.5	10.7	8.3	3.0	3.4	8.3	5.3	9.3
October	5.2	4.4	4.7	16.3	4.5	10.7	8.2	3.0	3.5	8.5	5.3	9.6
November	5.3	4.4	4.8	16.8	4.6	10.6	8.3	3.0	3.6	8.8	5.4	10.3
December	5.3	4.4	4.9	16.5	4.6	10.5	7.7	3.0	3.7	8.4	5.4	9.4

1. Changes in survey design, population coverage, or methodology in 1994, 1986, 1982, 1978, and 1972 affect year-to-year comparisions. See NOTES for more information.

UNEMPLOYMENT RATES[1]—Continued
(Percent of civilian labor force in group, seasonally adjusted)

YEAR AND MONTH	By industry of last job—Continued									By occupation				
	Private nonagricultural wage and salary workers—Continued								Agricultural wage and salary workers	Managerial and professional specialty	Technical, sales, and administrative support	Precision production, craft, and repair	Operators, fabricators, and laborers	Farming, forestry, and fishing
	Manufacturing			Transportation and utilities	Wholesale and retail trade	Finance, insurance, and real estate	Services	Government workers						
	Total	Durable goods	Nondurable goods												
1968	3.3	3.0	3.7	1.9	4.0	2.2	3.6	1.8	6.3	....	....	....	....	....
1969	3.3	3.0	3.7	2.1	4.1	2.1	3.5	1.9	6.1	....	....	....	....	....
1970	5.6	5.7	5.4	3.2	5.3	2.8	4.7	2.2	7.5	....	....	....	....	....
1971	6.8	7.0	6.5	3.8	6.4	3.3	5.6	2.9	7.9	....	....	....	....	....
1972	5.6	5.5	5.7	3.5	6.4	3.4	5.3	2.9	7.7	....	....	....	....	....
1973	4.4	3.9	4.9	3.0	5.6	2.7	4.8	2.7	7.0	....	....	....	....	....
1974	5.8	5.4	6.2	3.2	6.4	3.1	5.1	3.0	7.5	....	....	....	....	....
1975	10.9	11.3	10.4	5.6	8.7	4.9	7.1	4.1	10.4	....	....	....	....	....
1976	7.9	7.7	8.1	5.0	8.6	4.4	7.2	4.4	11.8	....	....	....	....	....
1977	6.7	6.2	7.4	4.7	8.0	3.9	6.6	4.2	11.2	....	....	....	....	....
1978	5.5	5.0	6.3	3.7	6.9	3.1	5.7	3.9	8.9	....	....	....	....	....
1979	5.6	5.0	6.4	3.7	6.5	3.0	5.4	3.7	9.3	....	....	....	....	....
1980	8.5	8.9	7.9	4.9	7.4	3.4	5.9	4.1	11.0	....	....	....	....	....
1981	8.3	8.2	8.4	5.2	8.1	3.5	6.6	4.7	12.1	....	....	....	....	....
1982	12.3	13.3	10.8	6.9	10.0	4.7	7.6	4.9	14.7	3.3	6.1	10.6	16.7	8.5
1983	11.2	12.1	10.0	7.4	10.0	4.5	7.9	5.3	16.0	3.3	6.3	10.6	15.5	10.0
1984	7.5	7.2	7.8	5.5	8.0	3.7	6.6	4.5	13.5	2.6	5.0	7.4	11.5	8.4
1985	7.7	7.6	7.8	5.2	7.7	3.5	6.2	3.9	13.2	2.4	4.8	7.2	11.3	8.3
1986	7.1	6.9	7.4	5.1	7.6	3.5	6.1	3.6	12.5	2.4	4.7	7.2	10.9	7.8
1987	6.0	5.8	6.3	4.5	6.9	3.1	5.4	3.5	10.5	2.3	4.3	6.1	9.4	7.1
1988	5.3	5.0	5.7	3.9	6.2	3.0	4.8	2.8	10.6	1.9	4.0	5.4	8.3	7.0
1989	5.1	4.8	5.5	3.9	6.0	3.1	4.7	2.7	9.6	2.0	3.9	5.2	8.0	6.4
1990	5.8	5.8	5.8	3.9	6.4	3.0	5.0	2.7	9.8	2.1	4.3	5.9	8.7	6.4
1991	7.3	7.5	6.9	5.3	7.6	4.0	5.8	3.3	11.8	2.8	5.2	8.0	10.6	7.9
1992	7.8	8.0	7.6	5.5	8.4	4.6	6.5	3.6	12.5	3.1	5.9	8.9	11.1	8.3
1993	7.2	7.1	7.4	5.1	7.8	4.1	6.1	3.3	11.7	3.0	5.4	7.9	10.0	8.4
1994	5.6	5.2	6.0	4.8	7.4	3.6	5.7	3.4	11.3	2.6	5.0	6.3	9.0	8.4
1995	4.9	4.4	5.7	4.5	6.5	3.3	5.2	2.9	11.1	2.4	4.5	6.0	8.2	7.9
1996	4.8	4.5	5.2	4.1	6.4	2.7	5.2	2.9	10.2	2.3	4.5	5.5	7.9	7.6
1993:														
January	7.5	7.7	7.3	4.9	8.0	4.6	6.6	3.6	11.4	3.2	5.6	8.1	10.1	8.6
February	7.4	7.3	7.5	4.8	7.9	4.4	6.5	3.7	12.2	3.4	5.4	8.1	10.3	9.0
March	7.4	7.2	7.6	5.0	7.9	4.5	6.0	3.6	11.6	3.1	5.2	8.2	10.5	8.5
April	7.4	7.2	7.5	4.8	8.2	4.4	6.2	3.5	12.3	3.1	5.5	8.7	9.9	8.9
May	7.2	7.0	7.4	5.9	8.3	4.0	6.0	3.3	11.3	3.0	5.3	8.1	10.2	7.9
June	7.5	7.7	7.2	4.8	8.0	4.1	6.1	3.3	11.9	2.8	5.6	8.3	10.3	8.0
July	7.2	6.8	7.6	4.7	7.5	3.9	6.0	3.5	12.0	2.7	5.4	8.4	9.9	8.2
August	7.4	7.1	7.9	5.4	7.6	4.1	5.6	3.2	12.4	2.8	5.4	7.2	10.3	7.9
September	7.2	7.2	7.3	5.4	7.5	4.0	6.0	2.9	10.8	2.8	5.3	7.6	10.1	8.1
October	6.8	6.7	7.0	5.8	7.8	3.8	6.0	3.2	12.3	2.8	5.4	8.0	9.8	8.3
November	6.6	6.4	6.9	5.2	7.8	3.8	5.9	3.2	11.0	2.9	5.3	7.0	9.3	8.3
December	6.7	6.5	6.9	5.2	7.5	3.8	5.9	3.2	11.5	2.9	5.2	7.3	9.2	8.9
1994:														
January	6.2	5.6	7.1	5.4	8.0	3.8	6.4	3.7	12.9	2.9	5.3	7.2	9.8	8.5
February	6.3	5.6	7.2	5.2	8.1	3.7	6.2	3.3	13.7	2.9	5.5	7.0	9.7	9.0
March	6.1	5.6	6.8	4.8	7.9	3.1	6.1	4.0	13.2	2.7	5.7	7.2	9.1	9.9
April	5.8	5.4	6.4	5.2	7.6	3.6	5.9	3.5	10.7	2.6	5.2	6.6	9.8	8.0
May	5.4	5.0	5.8	5.0	7.3	3.5	5.8	3.5	8.6	2.4	5.1	6.5	8.8	7.0
June	5.3	5.1	5.5	4.8	7.2	3.7	5.8	3.7	8.6	2.9	5.1	6.3	8.5	6.8
July	5.6	5.4	5.8	4.9	7.4	3.6	5.5	3.4	13.4	2.5	4.8	5.7	9.4	9.5
August	5.5	5.6	5.3	4.8	7.4	3.7	5.4	3.6	11.7	2.5	5.0	6.0	8.8	9.1
September	5.5	5.5	5.4	4.5	7.0	4.3	5.4	3.3	10.9	2.5	4.7	6.0	8.6	8.5
October	5.2	4.9	5.7	4.4	7.3	3.4	5.2	3.1	10.1	2.6	4.5	5.7	8.7	8.7
November	4.8	4.2	5.7	4.8	7.1	3.7	5.2	2.6	9.9	2.4	4.7	5.2	8.3	7.5
December	4.9	4.5	5.4	4.1	6.7	2.7	5.1	3.1	10.2	2.3	4.3	5.8	8.1	7.9
1995:														
January	4.8	4.3	5.4	4.8	6.5	2.9	5.0	3.1	10.8	2.3	4.5	6.0	8.1	7.7
February	4.5	4.0	5.3	4.6	6.5	3.5	5.0	2.9	9.7	2.3	4.4	5.5	7.9	7.5
March	4.5	4.1	5.0	4.5	6.2	3.4	5.2	2.9	10.4	2.5	4.4	5.5	7.6	8.0
April	4.8	4.3	5.6	4.5	6.7	3.5	5.3	3.0	11.2	2.5	4.8	6.0	8.0	8.2
May	5.3	4.9	5.8	4.2	6.5	3.6	5.2	2.8	11.9	2.2	4.5	6.2	8.5	8.2
June	5.0	4.2	6.2	4.4	6.2	3.4	5.3	3.1	11.9	2.4	4.5	6.0	8.4	8.1
July	5.2	4.8	5.8	4.5	6.6	3.4	5.4	2.8	10.8	2.5	4.4	6.4	8.4	8.0
August	4.9	4.3	5.8	4.3	6.5	3.4	5.5	3.0	8.9	2.6	4.4	6.6	8.5	7.4
September	5.0	4.4	6.0	4.5	7.2	2.9	5.0	2.8	11.4	2.4	4.5	6.1	8.6	7.4
October	4.8	4.3	5.6	4.1	6.4	3.2	5.3	2.9	12.1	2.4	4.5	5.9	8.0	8.8
November	5.1	4.6	5.7	4.1	6.3	2.9	5.4	3.0	11.4	2.5	4.1	6.1	8.3	7.7
December	5.0	4.4	5.8	4.8	6.5	2.9	5.4	2.7	12.3	2.5	4.4	5.8	8.4	7.6
1996:														
January	5.0	4.5	5.7	3.9	6.7	2.8	5.5	2.8	10.7	2.4	4.5	5.5	8.3	8.1
February	4.8	4.9	4.6	4.0	6.4	2.3	5.4	2.9	10.6	2.3	4.5	5.8	8.2	7.7
March	5.2	4.9	5.6	4.2	6.7	2.5	5.3	2.8	10.7	2.4	4.4	5.8	8.3	7.8
April	4.8	4.7	5.0	4.2	6.5	2.4	5.4	2.9	11.0	2.3	4.6	5.6	7.9	7.8
May	5.0	4.7	5.5	4.2	6.5	2.6	5.6	3.2	10.3	2.3	4.6	5.4	8.3	8.7
June	4.9	4.5	5.5	4.4	6.4	2.6	4.9	2.8	9.6	2.4	4.2	5.3	8.0	7.5
July	4.7	4.3	5.3	4.3	6.3	2.8	5.3	3.1	9.1	2.4	4.6	5.5	7.8	6.7
August	4.7	4.0	5.8	4.1	6.3	2.5	5.2	2.8	7.6	2.2	4.4	5.3	8.0	6.4
September	4.4	4.2	4.7	4.1	6.2	3.0	5.1	3.0	10.8	2.3	4.5	5.4	7.5	7.1
October	4.7	4.4	5.1	4.4	6.2	2.9	4.8	2.9	10.0	2.2	4.5	5.5	7.7	7.0
November	4.7	4.5	5.1	3.5	6.3	2.9	5.1	2.8	10.9	2.3	4.5	5.7	7.7	7.7
December	4.8	4.7	5.0	4.0	6.2	3.1	5.0	3.0	10.3	2.4	4.6	5.4	7.6	7.7

1. Changes in survey design, population coverage, or methodology in 1994, 1986, 1982, 1978, and 1972 affect year-to-year comparisions. See NOTES for more information.

EMPLOYMENT, HOURS, AND EARNINGS

	INSURED UNEMPLOYMENT (Weekly averages—Thousands of persons)								
YEAR AND MONTH	State programs (Seasonally adjusted)			Federal programs (Not seasonally adjusted)					
				Initial claims		Persons claiming benefits			
	Initial claims	Insured unemployed	Insured unemployment rate[1]	Federal employees	Newly discharged veterans	Federal employees	Newly discharged veterans	Railroad retirement	Extended benefits
1968	201	1 111	....	....	....	....	....	....	....
1969	197	1 093	....	....	....	....	....	....	....
1970	297	1 851	....	....	....	....	....	....	....
1971	296	2 152	4.07	....	....	....	....	....	....
1972	263	1 843	3.46	....	....	....	....	....	....
1973	244	1 628	2.74	....	....	....	....	....	....
1974	352	2 278	3.55	....	....	....	....	....	....
1975	473	3 958	5.97	....	....	....	....	....	....
1976	383	2 975	4.53	....	....	....	....	....	....
1977	374	2 645	3.91	....	....	....	....	....	....
1978	341	2 339	3.30	....	....	....	....	....	....
1979	383	2 427	2.99	....	....	....	....	....	....
1980	487	3 363	3.90	....	....	....	....	....	....
1981	452	3 034	3.49	....	....	....	....	....	....
1982	586	4 096	4.68	....	....	....	....	....	....
1983	441	3 341	3.87	....	....	....	....	....	....
1984	374	2 453	2.83	....	....	....	....	....	....
1985	392	2 585	2.85	....	....	....	....	....	....
1986	377	2 632	2.81	....	....	....	....	....	....
1987	324	2 273	2.38	2.14	2.54	21.24	17.65	....	8.64
1988	311	2 081	2.11	2.31	2.74	22.90	18.21	13.23	1.21
1989	329	2 175	2.14	2.13	2.31	22.21	15.11	10.46	0.60
1990	385	2 536	2.43	2.46	2.54	23.84	18.41	10.56	2.23
1991	446	3 339	3.15	2.57	2.93	30.57	22.19	10.81	32.05
1992	407	3 204	3.05	2.76	4.94	32.10	60.21	8.77	4.63
1993	343	2 768	2.64	2.53	3.92	32.11	54.83	7.43	8.02
1994	342	2 678	2.51	2.52	3.01	32.10	37.63	6.25	31.23
1995	358	2 591	2.36	4.54	2.51	31.71	29.88	5.51	14.31
1996	351	2 550	2.25	7.76	2.13	30.00	24.35	5.44	5.51
1993:									
January	344	2 689	2.56	2.93	5.12	35.65	70.81	10.60	0.01
February	337	2 611	2.50	2.27	4.30	33.93	69.07	11.50	0.01
March	353	2 665	2.55	1.96	4.15	32.43	65.05	10.50	0.01
April	354	2 760	2.65	2.25	3.93	30.11	60.18	9.00	0.01
May	344	2 778	2.64	2.27	3.68	27.84	55.27	6.60	0.01
June	348	2 838	2.73	2.49	3.62	28.10	51.34	5.75	0.01
July	348	2 816	2.68	2.89	3.98	29.97	50.52	5.00	0.01
August	337	2 818	2.70	2.29	3.99	31.31	49.93	5.00	0.01
September	338	2 836	2.68	2.49	3.66	30.60	47.67	5.00	0.01
October	347	2 833	2.68	3.00	3.81	32.55	46.73	6.00	9.53
November	341	2 820	2.68	2.74	3.22	34.70	44.86	6.75	35.40
December	322	2 756	2.60	2.75	3.56	38.09	46.49	7.50	51.20
1994:									
January	361	2 695	2.54	2.77	3.43	39.09	46.10	8.40	51.74
February	348	2 769	2.63	2.14	3.20	37.17	44.64	10.25	48.57
March	338	2 732	2.58	1.97	3.07	35.24	43.34	9.75	31.23
April	347	2 720	2.54	2.10	2.79	30.42	39.40	7.40	24.24
May	365	2 756	2.58	2.26	2.91	27.03	36.65	4.75	26.70
June	351	2 751	2.60	2.47	2.76	26.29	34.69	4.00	37.99
July	345	2 710	2.52	3.06	3.06	28.63	34.34	3.60	44.66
August	334	2 673	2.50	2.19	3.26	30.93	35.15	7.00	42.61
September	330	2 647	2.48	2.43	3.09	29.04	34.32	6.00	25.28
October	334	2 592	2.40	3.28	3.10	31.28	34.37	4.40	15.31
November	332	2 562	2.38	2.89	2.61	32.90	33.46	4.00	13.64
December	325	2 534	2.34	2.68	2.89	37.14	35.11	5.40	12.83
1995:									
January	331	2 493	2.30	3.29	2.96	37.59	36.36	7.50	12.71
February	333	2 499	2.30	2.14	2.49	35.94	35.18	8.50	13.15
March	338	2 500	2.30	1.87	2.50	33.78	33.02	8.00	15.92
April	351	2 490	2.28	1.89	2.23	29.44	30.15	6.00	16.62
May	373	2 561	2.35	1.86	2.33	25.77	28.03	4.25	20.63
June	378	2 625	2.40	2.43	2.44	24.42	27.00	3.25	18.73
July	373	2 680	2.42	2.93	2.95	27.05	27.68	3.80	15.09
August	349	2 627	2.40	2.15	2.77	29.48	29.26	4.00	11.79
September	356	2 638	2.40	2.65	2.46	27.75	28.40	4.00	10.99
October	366	2 680	2.40	3.59	2.37	33.28	28.05	4.50	12.10
November	377	2 680	2.40	17.29	2.20	35.20	27.22	5.50	11.23
December	365	2 624	2.36	12.38	2.38	40.83	28.18	6.80	12.72
1996:									
January	371	2 628	2.33	66.18	2.50	49.79	28.61	9.50	10.99
February	370	2 666	2.38	4.39	2.22	36.15	28.53	9.50	9.39
March	385	2 640	2.34	1.82	2.15	32.26	26.84	8.00	3.04
April	358	2 587	2.30	2.28	2.02	27.94	25.09	6.00	3.25
May	347	2 562	2.30	1.80	1.97	24.84	23.86	4.50	5.11
June	355	2 563	2.26	2.39	2.08	24.26	22.66	4.00	11.75
July	337	2 546	2.25	2.96	2.23	26.63	22.61	4.00	13.88
August	324	2 517	2.22	1.98	2.30	27.40	22.74	4.20	8.27
September	336	2 466	2.18	2.03	2.23	25.76	22.68	4.00	0.23
October	333	2 469	2.15	2.95	2.15	27.40	22.99	3.75	0.11
November	338	2 450	2.16	2.32	1.84	28.07	22.49	3.80	0.09
December	354	2 512	2.20	2.07	1.91	29.50	23.14	4.00	0.06

1. Insured unemployed as a percent of employment covered by state programs.

NONAGRICULTURAL EMPLOYMENT
(Wage and salary workers on nonagricultural payrolls—Thousands)

YEAR AND MONTH	Not seasonally adjusted		Seasonally adjusted		Goods-producing industries (Seasonally adjusted)						
					Total	Mining[1]	Construc-tion[1]	Manufacturing		Durable goods	
	Total	Private sector	Total	Private sector				Total	Production workers	Total	Production workers
1968	67 897	56 058	67 897	56 058	23 737	606	3 350	19 781	14 514	11 594	8 489
1969	70 384	58 189	70 384	58 189	24 361	619	3 575	20 167	14 767	11 862	8 683
1970	70 880	58 325	70 880	58 325	23 578	623	3 588	19 367	14 044	11 176	8 088
1971	71 211	58 331	71 211	58 331	22 935	609	3 704	18 623	13 544	10 604	7 697
1972	73 675	60 341	73 675	60 341	23 668	628	3 889	19 151	14 045	11 022	8 025
1973	76 790	63 058	76 790	63 058	24 893	642	4 097	20 154	14 834	11 863	8 699
1974	78 265	64 095	78 265	64 095	24 794	697	4 020	20 077	14 638	11 897	8 634
1975	76 945	62 259	76 945	62 259	22 600	752	3 525	18 323	13 043	10 662	7 532
1976	79 382	64 511	79 382	64 511	23 352	779	3 576	18 997	13 638	11 051	7 888
1977	82 471	67 344	82 471	67 344	24 346	813	3 851	19 682	14 135	11 570	8 280
1978	86 697	71 026	86 697	71 026	25 585	851	4 229	20 505	14 734	12 245	8 777
1979	89 823	73 876	89 823	73 876	26 461	958	4 463	21 040	15 068	12 730	9 082
1980	90 406	74 166	90 406	74 166	25 658	1 027	4 346	20 285	14 214	12 159	8 416
1981	91 152	75 121	91 152	75 121	25 497	1 139	4 188	20 170	14 020	12 082	8 270
1982	89 544	73 707	89 544	73 707	23 812	1 128	3 904	18 780	12 742	11 014	7 290
1983	90 152	74 282	90 152	74 282	23 330	952	3 946	18 432	12 528	10 707	7 095
1984	94 408	78 384	94 408	78 384	24 718	966	4 380	19 372	13 280	11 476	7 715
1985	97 387	80 992	97 387	80 992	24 842	927	4 668	19 248	13 084	11 458	7 618
1986	99 344	82 651	99 344	82 651	24 533	777	4 810	18 947	12 864	11 195	7 399
1987	101 958	84 948	101 958	84 948	24 674	717	4 958	18 999	12 952	11 154	7 409
1988	105 209	87 823	105 209	87 823	25 125	713	5 098	19 314	13 193	11 363	7 582
1989	107 884	90 105	107 884	90 105	25 254	692	5 171	19 391	13 230	11 394	7 594
1990	109 403	91 098	109 403	91 098	24 905	709	5 120	19 076	12 947	11 109	7 363
1991	108 249	89 847	108 249	89 847	23 745	689	4 650	18 406	12 434	10 569	6 967
1992	108 601	89 956	108 601	89 956	23 231	635	4 492	18 104	12 287	10 277	6 822
1993	110 713	91 872	110 713	91 872	23 352	610	4 668	18 075	12 341	10 221	6 849
1994	114 163	95 036	114 163	95 036	23 908	601	4 986	18 321	12 632	10 448	7 104
1995	117 191	97 885	117 191	97 885	24 265	581	5 160	18 524	12 826	10 683	7 317
1996	119 523	100 076	119 523	100 076	24 431	574	5 400	18 457	12 749	10 766	7 370
1993:											
January	107 883	89 197	109 516	90 782	23 245	623	4 519	18 103	12 331	10 251	6 846
February	108 496	89 455	109 852	91 085	23 335	614	4 613	18 108	12 341	10 251	6 851
March	108 935	89 790	109 757	90 991	23 261	616	4 551	18 094	12 335	10 236	6 844
April	109 927	90 784	110 071	91 295	23 262	612	4 577	18 073	12 324	10 215	6 832
May	110 885	91 703	110 386	91 578	23 321	613	4 641	18 067	12 326	10 203	6 825
June	111 476	92 583	110 550	91 722	23 304	608	4 650	18 046	12 309	10 185	6 814
July	110 604	92 749	110 759	91 928	23 313	606	4 677	18 030	12 302	10 189	6 815
August	110 713	93 034	110 983	92 123	23 345	600	4 699	18 046	12 316	10 189	6 822
September	111 690	93 031	111 220	92 335	23 387	602	4 713	18 072	12 352	10 214	6 855
October	112 371	93 192	111 541	92 630	23 435	603	4 756	18 076	12 357	10 227	6 870
November	112 716	93 382	111 795	92 861	23 476	601	4 780	18 095	12 388	10 244	6 892
December	112 860	93 562	112 050	93 086	23 534	615	4 806	18 113	12 414	10 268	6 919
1994:											
January	110 586	91 660	112 284	93 297	23 571	613	4 813	18 145	12 447	10 300	6 955
February	111 170	91 894	112 577	93 574	23 629	608	4 849	18 172	12 479	10 321	6 975
March	112 141	92 730	112 988	93 961	23 698	604	4 894	18 200	12 513	10 343	6 999
April	113 220	93 796	113 355	94 300	23 785	601	4 949	18 235	12 556	10 374	7 034
May	114 235	94 748	113 704	94 598	23 832	598	4 971	18 263	12 578	10 396	7 055
June	115 040	95 859	113 991	94 888	23 889	597	4 983	18 309	12 625	10 438	7 095
July	114 116	96 025	114 335	95 218	23 933	597	5 004	18 332	12 660	10 449	7 115
August	114 420	96 448	114 685	95 506	23 990	597	5 015	18 378	12 687	10 491	7 149
September	115 472	96 497	114 992	95 797	24 053	600	5 047	18 406	12 718	10 519	7 176
October	116 097	96 613	115 247	96 037	24 087	596	5 055	18 436	12 748	10 547	7 204
November	116 717	96 996	115 674	96 439	24 167	596	5 095	18 476	12 791	10 585	7 243
December	116 747	97 165	115 906	96 664	24 217	593	5 109	18 515	12 828	10 612	7 266
1995:											
January	114 435	95 243	116 234	96 973	24 264	592	5 129	18 543	12 857	10 633	7 288
February	115 093	95 524	116 517	97 250	24 282	587	5 134	18 561	12 867	10 664	7 312
March	115 849	96 175	116 694	97 413	24 278	587	5 130	18 561	12 871	10 676	7 327
April	116 674	97 009	116 891	97 592	24 297	585	5 140	18 572	12 878	10 691	7 334
May	117 409	97 743	116 855	97 579	24 244	582	5 114	18 548	12 851	10 684	7 322
June	118 138	98 761	117 064	97 762	24 251	581	5 137	18 533	12 835	10 676	7 310
July	116 926	98 673	117 142	97 842	24 230	579	5 149	18 502	12 806	10 674	7 306
August	117 180	99 062	117 465	98 123	24 261	577	5 173	18 511	12 810	10 689	7 318
September	118 083	98 987	117 636	98 328	24 290	577	5 205	18 508	12 809	10 696	7 322
October	118 665	99 052	117 775	98 440	24 284	576	5 225	18 483	12 782	10 689	7 310
November	118 917	99 172	117 951	98 616	24 287	573	5 236	18 478	12 771	10 694	7 313
December	118 918	99 221	118 120	98 774	24 308	573	5 232	18 503	12 801	10 738	7 359
1996:											
January	116 210	96 957	118 058	98 732	24 247	573	5 214	18 460	12 765	10 724	7 345
February	117 146	97 486	118 550	99 194	24 383	576	5 309	18 498	12 783	10 749	7 356
March	117 952	98 158	118 804	99 408	24 377	577	5 340	18 460	12 746	10 718	7 327
April	118 751	98 982	118 966	99 566	24 398	577	5 356	18 465	12 752	10 749	7 355
May	119 888	100 044	119 263	99 847	24 432	579	5 384	18 469	12 762	10 762	7 371
June	120 537	101 038	119 516	100 079	24 453	577	5 408	18 468	12 751	10 778	7 376
July	119 481	101 098	119 691	100 236	24 433	574	5 417	18 442	12 735	10 766	7 369
August	119 733	101 453	119 983	100 433	24 468	574	5 433	18 461	12 749	10 788	7 389
September	120 454	101 187	120 019	100 506	24 439	571	5 441	18 427	12 723	10 771	7 372
October	121 157	101 384	120 248	100 759	24 479	570	5 467	18 442	12 731	10 780	7 379
November	121 505	101 537	120 450	100 956	24 508	571	5 495	18 442	12 737	10 791	7 390
December	121 464	101 593	120 659	101 145	24 540	571	5 521	18 448	12 743	10 803	7 398

1. Additional industry detail available in individual industry profile sections.

NONAGRICULTURAL EMPLOYMENT—Continued
(Wage and salary workers on nonagricultural payrolls—Thousands, seasonally adjusted)

Manufacturing—Continued

Durable goods—Continued

YEAR AND MONTH	Lumber and products	Furniture and fixtures	Stone, clay, and glass products	Primary metal industries[1]	Fabricated metal products	Industrial machinery and equipment[1]	Electronic and electric equipment[1]	Transportation equipment[1]	Instruments and related products	Miscellaneous manufacturing
1968	674	450	602	1 261	1 609	1 988	1 629	2 133	814	433
1969	691	461	622	1 305	1 665	2 055	1 664	2 120	838	441
1970	658	440	610	1 260	1 559	2 003	1 584	1 833	804	426
1971	681	444	611	1 171	1 479	1 834	1 477	1 743	753	412
1972	740	483	645	1 173	1 541	1 909	1 535	1 777	786	433
1973	774	507	680	1 259	1 645	2 111	1 667	1 915	851	454
1974	727	489	673	1 289	1 632	2 230	1 666	1 853	885	452
1975	627	417	598	1 139	1 453	2 076	1 442	1 700	804	407
1976	693	444	613	1 155	1 505	2 085	1 503	1 785	840	429
1977	736	464	636	1 182	1 577	2 195	1 591	1 857	895	438
1978	770	494	664	1 215	1 667	2 347	1 699	1 987	952	452
1979	782	498	674	1 254	1 713	2 508	1 793	2 059	1 006	445
1980	704	466	629	1 142	1 609	2 517	1 771	1 881	1 022	418
1981	680	464	606	1 122	1 586	2 521	1 774	1 879	1 041	408
1982	610	432	548	922	1 424	2 264	1 701	1 718	1 013	382
1983	671	448	541	832	1 368	2 053	1 704	1 730	990	370
1984	718	486	562	857	1 462	2 218	1 869	1 883	1 040	382
1985	711	493	557	808	1 464	2 195	1 859	1 960	1 045	367
1986	724	498	554	751	1 422	2 074	1 790	2 003	1 018	361
1987	754	515	554	746	1 399	2 028	1 750	2 028	1 011	370
1988	767	527	567	770	1 428	2 089	1 764	2 036	1 031	383
1989	756	524	568	772	1 445	2 125	1 744	2 052	1 026	381
1990	733	506	556	756	1 419	2 095	1 673	1 989	1 006	375
1991	675	475	522	723	1 355	2 000	1 591	1 890	974	366
1992	680	478	513	695	1 329	1 929	1 528	1 830	929	368
1993	709	487	517	683	1 339	1 931	1 526	1 756	896	378
1994	754	505	532	698	1 388	1 990	1 571	1 761	861	389
1995	769	510	540	712	1 437	2 067	1 625	1 790	843	390
1996	780	504	541	711	1 448	2 112	1 651	1 781	854	387
1993:										
January	696	481	513	686	1 333	1 927	1 523	1 808	912	372
February	701	483	520	685	1 336	1 926	1 525	1 791	910	374
March	703	484	515	684	1 336	1 925	1 526	1 779	908	376
April	701	485	514	682	1 336	1 924	1 525	1 766	905	377
May	701	487	515	683	1 334	1 927	1 522	1 756	900	378
June	704	486	515	681	1 332	1 927	1 521	1 746	895	378
July	706	486	516	682	1 335	1 929	1 521	1 743	892	379
August	710	488	517	682	1 336	1 926	1 522	1 739	890	379
September	717	489	519	683	1 341	1 932	1 525	1 740	887	381
October	720	490	520	683	1 344	1 936	1 529	1 738	886	381
November	723	491	521	685	1 349	1 943	1 533	1 736	882	381
December	729	493	522	686	1 352	1 949	1 536	1 740	879	382
1994:										
January	734	495	524	687	1 357	1 954	1 538	1 749	878	384
February	740	495	525	690	1 362	1 961	1 544	1 743	876	385
March	742	498	526	691	1 367	1 968	1 551	1 742	872	386
April	746	499	531	689	1 373	1 978	1 559	1 743	869	387
May	750	502	531	690	1 378	1 984	1 561	1 747	865	388
June	754	506	531	696	1 387	1 992	1 569	1 754	861	388
July	759	509	533	698	1 391	1 987	1 572	1 750	857	393
August	761	509	534	700	1 397	1 999	1 581	1 764	855	391
September	763	510	534	704	1 401	2 004	1 586	1 772	854	391
October	764	512	536	707	1 408	2 008	1 588	1 781	850	393
November	768	512	537	708	1 415	2 016	1 595	1 792	850	392
December	769	513	539	710	1 422	2 022	1 601	1 797	848	391
1995:										
January	771	514	540	710	1 427	2 028	1 608	1 799	844	392
February	775	516	541	712	1 437	2 038	1 610	1 802	843	390
March	772	517	542	712	1 439	2 044	1 613	1 805	841	391
April	768	514	543	714	1 444	2 055	1 617	1 804	841	391
May	767	511	540	715	1 441	2 056	1 621	1 803	841	389
June	765	509	540	712	1 436	2 063	1 622	1 796	843	390
July	764	504	539	709	1 436	2 071	1 625	1 791	846	389
August	766	508	539	711	1 436	2 077	1 625	1 794	844	389
September	769	507	538	710	1 435	2 081	1 633	1 790	844	389
October	771	507	538	711	1 437	2 091	1 637	1 764	844	389
November	771	507	539	713	1 438	2 098	1 641	1 751	845	389
December	775	508	537	713	1 439	2 103	1 645	1 781	846	391
1996:										
January	766	506	536	713	1 440	2 105	1 648	1 772	849	389
February	774	505	540	713	1 442	2 105	1 653	1 778	850	389
March	773	504	540	712	1 440	2 111	1 652	1 745	853	388
April	777	501	539	710	1 439	2 111	1 652	1 780	853	387
May	778	503	541	711	1 441	2 112	1 653	1 781	855	387
June	781	503	540	713	1 445	2 113	1 653	1 787	856	387
July	781	503	540	706	1 449	2 113	1 655	1 778	854	387
August	783	502	540	712	1 451	2 114	1 654	1 791	855	386
September	782	503	541	711	1 452	2 108	1 652	1 783	854	385
October	785	503	542	707	1 455	2 115	1 650	1 783	855	385
November	787	504	541	708	1 457	2 115	1 649	1 790	854	386
December	788	505	543	707	1 458	2 119	1 647	1 793	856	387

1. Additional industry detail available in individual industry profile sections.

	NONAGRICULTURAL EMPLOYMENT—Continued (Wage and salary workers on nonagricultural payrolls—Thousands, seasonally adjusted)										
	Manufacturing—Continued										
YEAR AND MONTH	Nondurable goods										
	Total	Produc-tion workers	Food and products	Tobacco products	Textile mill products	Apparel and other textile products	Paper and prod-ucts	Printing and publishing	Chemi-cals and products	Petroleum and coal products	Rubber and mis-cellane-ous plastic products	Leather and products
1968	8 187	6 024	1 782	85	994	1 406	687	1 065	1 030	187	598	355
1969	8 304	6 084	1 791	83	1 003	1 409	706	1 094	1 060	182	634	343
1970	8 190	5 956	1 786	83	975	1 364	701	1 104	1 049	191	617	320
1971	8 019	5 847	1 766	77	955	1 343	677	1 081	1 011	194	617	299
1972	8 129	6 022	1 745	75	986	1 383	679	1 094	1 009	195	667	296
1973	8 291	6 138	1 715	78	1 010	1 438	694	1 111	1 038	193	731	284
1974	8 181	6 004	1 707	77	965	1 363	696	1 111	1 061	197	733	271
1975	7 661	5 510	1 658	76	868	1 243	633	1 083	1 015	194	643	248
1976	7 946	5 750	1 689	77	919	1 318	666	1 099	1 043	199	675	263
1977	8 112	5 855	1 711	71	910	1 316	682	1 141	1 074	202	750	255
1978	8 259	5 956	1 724	71	899	1 332	689	1 192	1 096	208	793	257
1979	8 310	5 986	1 733	70	885	1 304	697	1 235	1 109	210	821	246
1980	8 127	5 798	1 708	69	848	1 264	685	1 252	1 107	198	764	233
1981	8 089	5 751	1 671	70	823	1 244	681	1 266	1 109	214	772	238
1982	7 766	5 451	1 636	69	749	1 161	655	1 272	1 075	201	729	219
1983	7 725	5 433	1 614	68	741	1 163	654	1 298	1 043	196	743	205
1984	7 896	5 565	1 611	64	746	1 185	674	1 375	1 049	189	813	189
1985	7 790	5 466	1 601	64	702	1 120	671	1 426	1 044	179	818	165
1986	7 752	5 465	1 607	59	703	1 100	667	1 456	1 021	169	823	149
1987	7 845	5 543	1 617	55	725	1 097	674	1 503	1 025	164	842	143
1988	7 951	5 611	1 626	54	728	1 085	689	1 543	1 057	160	866	143
1989	7 997	5 636	1 644	50	720	1 076	696	1 556	1 074	156	888	138
1990	7 968	5 584	1 661	49	691	1 036	697	1 569	1 086	157	888	133
1991	7 837	5 467	1 667	49	670	1 006	688	1 536	1 076	160	862	124
1992	7 827	5 466	1 663	48	674	1 007	690	1 507	1 084	158	878	120
1993	7 854	5 492	1 680	44	675	989	692	1 517	1 081	152	909	117
1994	7 873	5 528	1 678	43	676	974	692	1 537	1 057	149	953	113
1995	7 841	5 508	1 692	42	663	936	693	1 546	1 038	145	980	106
1996	7 691	5 379	1 693	41	624	864	681	1 538	1 032	142	981	96
1993:											
January	7 852	5 485	1 676	45	677	1 002	692	1 510	1 084	154	894	118
February	7 857	5 490	1 678	44	677	1 002	693	1 511	1 083	154	897	118
March	7 858	5 491	1 679	43	676	1 000	693	1 512	1 083	152	902	118
April	7 858	5 492	1 677	44	678	998	692	1 514	1 081	152	904	118
May	7 864	5 501	1 677	44	678	996	693	1 516	1 083	152	907	118
June	7 861	5 495	1 678	44	676	993	692	1 517	1 082	152	909	118
July	7 841	5 487	1 672	44	675	979	692	1 518	1 082	151	911	117
August	7 857	5 494	1 685	42	673	985	692	1 520	1 080	150	913	117
September	7 858	5 497	1 683	43	675	982	693	1 520	1 081	151	914	116
October	7 849	5 487	1 687	43	673	978	690	1 521	1 077	150	914	116
November	7 851	5 496	1 684	44	672	976	690	1 523	1 075	151	920	116
December	7 845	5 495	1 683	43	672	971	690	1 522	1 075	149	924	116
1994:											
January	7 845	5 492	1 678	43	671	970	691	1 528	1 069	149	930	116
February	7 851	5 504	1 680	43	673	969	692	1 529	1 068	148	934	115
March	7 857	5 514	1 680	44	673	972	691	1 532	1 065	148	938	114
April	7 861	5 522	1 677	44	674	973	691	1 534	1 062	149	943	114
May	7 867	5 523	1 677	44	674	974	691	1 536	1 060	149	949	113
June	7 871	5 530	1 677	43	676	975	692	1 535	1 058	148	954	113
July	7 883	5 545	1 680	43	677	976	693	1 539	1 056	148	957	114
August	7 887	5 538	1 679	43	679	978	693	1 541	1 053	150	959	112
September	7 887	5 542	1 678	43	678	979	693	1 540	1 051	150	963	112
October	7 889	5 544	1 673	43	680	980	694	1 543	1 048	150	967	111
November	7 891	5 548	1 680	42	681	974	695	1 541	1 046	150	971	111
December	7 903	5 562	1 682	42	682	974	695	1 545	1 045	150	977	111
1995:											
January	7 910	5 569	1 689	43	679	970	695	1 546	1 044	148	985	111
February	7 897	5 555	1 682	42	681	965	695	1 548	1 042	148	985	109
March	7 885	5 544	1 682	41	679	960	695	1 547	1 040	148	984	109
April	7 881	5 544	1 684	42	679	955	696	1 547	1 039	147	984	108
May	7 864	5 529	1 686	42	672	948	695	1 546	1 038	147	983	107
June	7 857	5 525	1 699	42	667	940	694	1 547	1 037	146	980	105
July	7 828	5 500	1 693	42	659	934	693	1 547	1 036	145	975	104
August	7 822	5 492	1 692	43	658	929	694	1 545	1 036	144	977	104
September	7 812	5 487	1 699	42	653	922	692	1 544	1 036	143	977	104
October	7 794	5 472	1 700	42	648	910	690	1 544	1 037	143	977	103
November	7 784	5 458	1 702	42	646	902	688	1 544	1 037	142	978	103
December	7 765	5 442	1 702	42	640	896	688	1 543	1 034	142	978	100
1996:											
January	7 736	5 420	1 700	42	630	883	687	1 541	1 035	143	976	99
February	7 749	5 427	1 705	42	635	890	685	1 540	1 034	143	976	99
March	7 742	5 419	1 709	42	631	881	684	1 541	1 037	143	976	98
April	7 716	5 397	1 701	42	626	876	681	1 538	1 035	142	977	98
May	7 707	5 391	1 698	41	626	871	682	1 538	1 034	142	978	97
June	7 690	5 375	1 689	41	625	866	680	1 538	1 032	142	980	97
July	7 676	5 366	1 684	41	623	863	677	1 537	1 031	142	982	96
August	7 673	5 360	1 685	40	621	857	678	1 537	1 032	142	986	95
September	7 656	5 351	1 682	41	618	853	678	1 536	1 029	141	984	94
October	7 662	5 352	1 684	42	620	849	679	1 539	1 029	141	985	94
November	7 651	5 347	1 688	42	616	844	679	1 535	1 028	141	985	93
December	7 645	5 345	1 689	42	615	840	678	1 534	1 028	140	985	94

1. Additional industry detail available in individual industry profile sections.

NONAGRICULTURAL EMPLOYMENT—Continued
(Wage and salary workers on nonagricultural payrolls—Thousands, seasonally adjusted)

YEAR AND MONTH	Total	Transportation and public utilities¹	Wholesale trade¹	Retail trade¹ Total	General merchandise stores	Food stores	Automotive dealers and service stations	Eating and drinking places	Finance, insurance, and real estate¹ Total	Finance Total	Finance Depository institutions	Insurance	Real estate
1968	44 160	4 318	3 791	10 308	....	1 620	1 549	2 309	3 337	....	....	....	....
1969	46 023	4 442	3 919	10 785	....	1 683	1 611	2 466	3 512	....	....	....	....
1970	47 302	4 515	4 006	11 034	....	1 731	1 617	2 575	3 645	....	....	....	....
1971	48 278	4 476	4 014	11 338	....	1 752	1 642	2 700	3 772	....	....	....	....
1972	50 007	4 541	4 127	11 822	2 149	1 805	1 723	2 860	3 908	1 778	....	1 373	756
1973	51 897	4 656	4 291	12 315	2 229	1 856	1 778	3 054	4 046	1 866	....	1 401	778
1974	53 471	4 725	4 447	12 539	2 210	1 948	1 666	3 231	4 148	1 936	....	1 434	778
1975	54 345	4 542	4 430	12 630	2 113	2 007	1 677	3 380	4 165	1 964	....	1 442	760
1976	56 030	4 582	4 562	13 193	2 155	2 039	1 744	3 656	4 271	2 026	....	1 468	776
1977	58 125	4 713	4 723	13 792	2 204	2 106	1 801	3 949	4 467	2 113	....	1 528	826
1978	61 113	4 923	4 985	14 556	2 308	2 199	1 861	4 277	4 724	2 233	....	1 591	900
1979	63 363	5 136	5 221	14 972	2 287	2 297	1 812	4 513	4 975	2 369	....	1 643	963
1980	64 748	5 146	5 292	15 018	2 245	2 384	1 689	4 626	5 160	2 483	....	1 688	989
1981	65 655	5 165	5 375	15 171	2 230	2 448	1 653	4 749	5 298	2 593	....	1 713	992
1982	65 732	5 081	5 295	15 158	2 184	2 477	1 632	4 829	5 340	2 647	....	1 723	970
1983	66 821	4 952	5 283	15 587	2 165	2 556	1 674	5 038	5 466	2 741	....	1 728	997
1984	69 690	5 156	5 568	16 512	2 267	2 636	1 798	5 381	5 684	2 852	....	1 765	1 067
1985	72 544	5 233	5 727	17 315	2 323	2 774	1 889	5 699	5 948	2 974	....	1 840	1 135
1986	74 811	5 247	5 761	17 880	2 365	2 896	1 941	5 902	6 273	3 145	....	1 944	1 184
1987	77 284	5 362	5 848	18 422	2 411	2 958	2 001	6 086	6 533	3 264	....	2 027	1 242
1988	80 084	5 512	6 030	19 023	2 472	3 074	2 071	6 258	6 630	3 274	2 255	2 075	1 280
1989	82 630	5 614	6 187	19 475	2 544	3 164	2 092	6 402	6 668	3 283	2 273	2 090	1 296
1990	84 497	5 777	6 173	19 601	2 540	3 215	2 063	6 509	6 709	3 268	2 251	2 126	1 315
1991	84 504	5 755	6 081	19 284	2 453	3 204	1 984	6 476	6 646	3 187	2 164	2 161	1 299
1992	85 370	5 718	5 997	19 356	2 451	3 180	1 966	6 609	6 602	3 160	2 096	2 152	1 290
1993	87 361	5 811	5 981	19 773	2 488	3 224	2 014	6 821	6 757	3 238	2 089	2 197	1 322
1994	90 256	5 984	6 162	20 507	2 583	3 291	2 116	7 078	6 896	3 299	2 066	2 236	1 361
1995	92 925	6 132	6 378	21 187	2 681	3 366	2 190	7 354	6 806	3 231	2 025	2 225	1 351
1996	95 092	6 261	6 483	21 625	2 726	3 435	2 270	7 499	6 899	3 301	2 024	2 217	1 381
1993:													
January	86 271	5 766	5 957	19 512	2 471	3 192	1 982	6 702	6 658	3 189	2 089	2 166	1 303
February	86 517	5 768	5 951	19 592	2 490	3 200	1 986	6 731	6 670	3 192	2 088	2 170	1 308
March	86 496	5 772	5 945	19 535	2 486	3 201	1 990	6 686	6 673	3 195	2 086	2 173	1 305
April	86 809	5 779	5 954	19 645	2 480	3 207	1 993	6 773	6 695	3 206	2 087	2 178	1 311
May	87 065	5 794	5 973	19 710	2 481	3 213	2 000	6 805	6 719	3 217	2 089	2 187	1 315
June	87 246	5 811	5 967	19 745	2 477	3 227	2 006	6 817	6 741	3 228	2 089	2 195	1 318
July	87 446	5 823	5 986	19 790	2 486	3 232	2 012	6 833	6 765	3 242	2 093	2 201	1 322
August	87 638	5 820	5 981	19 853	2 488	3 238	2 021	6 860	6 782	3 253	2 091	2 207	1 322
September	87 833	5 835	5 998	19 900	2 494	3 247	2 030	6 878	6 808	3 265	2 090	2 214	1 329
October	88 106	5 847	6 008	19 971	2 500	3 251	2 038	6 917	6 832	3 279	2 090	2 217	1 336
November	88 319	5 865	6 024	19 991	2 502	3 245	2 047	6 924	6 857	3 290	2 089	2 225	1 342
December	88 516	5 854	6 039	20 055	2 498	3 241	2 058	6 957	6 877	3 300	2 087	2 229	1 348
1994:													
January	88 713	5 893	6 054	20 081	2 493	3 252	2 067	6 976	6 893	3 307	2 083	2 232	1 354
February	88 948	5 914	6 067	20 171	2 521	3 270	2 079	6 985	6 908	3 315	2 080	2 235	1 358
March	89 290	5 941	6 088	20 272	2 529	3 285	2 092	7 011	6 927	3 324	2 077	2 239	1 364
April	89 570	5 903	6 108	20 352	2 543	3 282	2 103	7 047	6 925	3 322	2 074	2 240	1 363
May	89 872	5 973	6 132	20 398	2 550	3 294	2 108	7 050	6 917	3 316	2 071	2 238	1 363
June	90 102	5 982	6 146	20 456	2 560	3 290	2 115	7 065	6 915	3 313	2 068	2 238	1 364
July	90 402	6 000	6 164	20 532	2 580	3 296	2 116	7 080	6 907	3 306	2 066	2 237	1 364
August	90 695	6 013	6 193	20 601	2 599	3 300	2 128	7 098	6 900	3 298	2 064	2 236	1 366
September	90 939	6 022	6 218	20 684	2 612	3 302	2 136	7 121	6 886	3 288	2 059	2 234	1 364
October	91 160	6 034	6 239	20 743	2 625	3 300	2 143	7 142	6 868	3 276	2 055	2 234	1 358
November	91 507	6 057	6 261	20 863	2 675	3 310	2 152	7 175	6 854	3 265	2 050	2 231	1 358
December	91 689	6 088	6 285	20 890	2 664	3 316	2 159	7 196	6 836	3 255	2 046	2 226	1 355
1995:													
January	91 970	6 089	6 312	21 003	2 677	3 329	2 166	7 261	6 823	3 244	2 040	2 228	1 351
February	92 235	6 109	6 341	21 060	2 676	3 336	2 173	7 280	6 812	3 235	2 035	2 228	1 349
March	92 416	6 116	6 358	21 059	2 644	3 342	2 180	7 302	6 809	3 232	2 034	2 233	1 344
April	92 594	6 119	6 366	21 130	2 680	3 354	2 183	7 310	6 801	3 225	2 032	2 232	1 344
May	92 611	6 111	6 370	21 125	2 675	3 358	2 183	7 312	6 792	3 222	2 027	2 226	1 344
June	92 813	6 112	6 382	21 188	2 684	3 366	2 185	7 353	6 788	3 217	2 022	2 224	1 347
July	92 912	6 111	6 393	21 207	2 685	3 369	2 184	7 372	6 793	3 222	2 022	2 221	1 350
August	93 204	6 139	6 393	21 249	2 681	3 380	2 192	7 389	6 801	3 225	2 020	2 223	1 353
September	93 346	6 140	6 397	21 293	2 685	3 382	2 198	7 416	6 804	3 228	2 019	2 221	1 355
October	93 491	6 182	6 401	21 274	2 697	3 379	2 205	7 401	6 812	3 233	2 017	2 222	1 357
November	93 664	6 195	6 405	21 321	2 684	3 395	2 210	7 428	6 819	3 240	2 018	2 219	1 360
December	93 812	6 179	6 416	21 340	2 677	3 405	2 219	7 436	6 828	3 248	2 019	2 216	1 364
1996:													
January	93 811	6 195	6 421	21 340	2 676	3 403	2 227	7 440	6 831	3 257	2 020	2 217	1 357
February	94 167	6 203	6 429	21 393	2 686	3 406	2 234	7 457	6 848	3 265	2 020	2 215	1 368
March	94 427	6 211	6 437	21 463	2 693	3 411	2 243	7 491	6 856	3 269	2 018	2 215	1 372
April	94 568	6 229	6 443	21 479	2 694	3 411	2 252	7 485	6 867	3 279	2 019	2 214	1 374
May	94 831	6 246	6 457	21 547	2 720	3 421	2 259	7 493	6 888	3 291	2 021	2 218	1 379
June	95 063	6 270	6 469	21 600	2 726	3 427	2 270	7 499	6 897	3 298	2 022	2 219	1 380
July	95 258	6 296	6 481	21 651	2 731	3 439	2 278	7 505	6 910	3 305	2 023	2 220	1 385
August	95 515	6 299	6 497	21 692	2 737	3 445	2 284	7 510	6 917	3 313	2 022	2 217	1 387
September	95 580	6 290	6 513	21 718	2 739	3 445	2 289	7 509	6 925	3 317	2 023	2 220	1 388
October	95 769	6 293	6 538	21 791	2 756	3 458	2 295	7 516	6 941	3 330	2 028	2 219	1 392
November	95 942	6 303	6 549	21 847	2 761	3 467	2 300	7 530	6 949	3 334	2 029	2 220	1 395
December	96 119	6 288	6 559	21 912	2 769	3 468	2 304	7 551	6 962	3 343	2 030	2 221	1 398

1. Additional industry detail available in individual industry profile sections.

NONAGRICULTURAL EMPLOYMENT—Continued
(Wage and salary workers on nonagricultural payrolls—Thousands, seasonally adjusted)

Service-producing industries—Continued

Services[1] (Private)

YEAR AND MONTH	Total	Hotels and other lodging places	Personal services	Business services[1] Total	Person-nel sup-ply	Help supply	Com-puter and data process-ing	Auto repair, services, and parking	Amuse-ment and recre-ation	Health services[1] Total	Offices and clin-ics of medical doctors	Nursing and per-sonal care fa-cilities	Hos-pitals
1968	10 567	.....	937	1 210	.....	.....	.....	.....	.....	2 639	.....	.....	1 654
1969	11 169	.....	931	1 329	.....	.....	.....	.....	.....	2 862	.....	.....	1 770
1970	11 548	.....	898	1 397	.....	.....	.....	.....	.....	3 053	.....	.....	1 863
1971	11 797	.....	848	1 402	.....	.....	.....	.....	.....	3 239	.....	.....	1 935
1972	12 276	813	828	1 491	214	.....	107	399	.....	3 412	467	591	1 980
1973	12 857	854	823	1 610	247	.....	120	422	.....	3 641	519	659	2 051
1974	13 441	878	807	1 686	257	.....	135	430	.....	3 887	567	708	2 160
1975	13 892	898	782	1 697	242	.....	143	439	.....	4 134	608	759	2 274
1976	14 551	929	790	1 806	293	.....	159	466	.....	4 350	644	809	2 363
1977	15 302	956	806	1 958	357	.....	187	498	.....	4 584	681	860	2 465
1978	16 252	988	827	2 181	438	.....	224	549	.....	4 792	720	911	2 538
1979	17 112	1 060	821	2 410	508	.....	271	575	.....	4 993	761	951	2 608
1980	17 890	1 076	818	2 564	543	.....	304	571	.....	5 278	802	997	2 750
1981	18 615	1 119	828	2 700	585	.....	337	574	.....	5 562	845	1 029	2 904
1982	19 021	1 133	844	2 722	541	417	365	589	.....	5 811	887	1 067	3 014
1983	19 664	1 172	869	2 948	619	488	416	619	.....	5 986	934	1 106	3 037
1984	20 746	1 263	918	3 353	797	643	474	682	.....	6 118	977	1 147	3 004
1985	21 927	1 331	957	3 679	891	732	542	730	.....	6 293	1 028	1 198	2 997
1986	22 957	1 378	991	3 957	990	837	588	762	.....	6 528	1 081	1 245	3 037
1987	24 110	1 464	1 027	4 278	1 177	989	629	794	.....	6 794	1 139	1 283	3 142
1988	25 504	1 540	1 056	4 638	1 350	1 126	673	834	977	7 105	1 200	1 311	3 294
1989	26 907	1 596	1 086	4 941	1 455	1 216	736	884	1 033	7 463	1 268	1 356	3 439
1990	27 934	1 631	1 104	5 139	1 535	1 288	772	914	1 076	7 814	1 338	1 415	3 549
1991	28 336	1 589	1 112	5 086	1 485	1 268	797	882	1 122	8 183	1 405	1 493	3 655
1992	29 052	1 576	1 116	5 315	1 629	1 411	836	881	1 188	8 490	1 463	1 533	3 750
1993	30 197	1 596	1 137	5 735	1 906	1 669	893	925	1 258	8 756	1 506	1 585	3 779
1994	31 579	1 631	1 140	6 281	2 272	2 017	959	968	1 334	8 992	1 545	1 649	3 763
1995	33 117	1 668	1 163	6 812	2 476	2 189	1 090	1 020	1 417	9 230	1 609	1 691	3 772
1996	34 377	1 716	1 184	7 254	2 646	2 341	1 208	1 084	1 466	9 469	1 679	1 732	3 814
1993:													
January	29 644	1 580	1 132	5 540	1 756	1 532	869	905	1 224	8 633	1 489	1 551	3 780
February	29 769	1 582	1 143	5 578	1 785	1 552	875	912	1 228	8 659	1 494	1 557	3 782
March	29 805	1 580	1 135	5 608	1 807	1 569	879	916	1 226	8 671	1 498	1 560	3 779
April	29 960	1 584	1 135	5 652	1 842	1 602	883	921	1 251	8 698	1 499	1 568	3 780
May	30 061	1 594	1 134	5 687	1 868	1 633	889	924	1 253	8 729	1 503	1 577	3 785
June	30 154	1 599	1 137	5 715	1 890	1 658	891	926	1 246	8 750	1 506	1 582	3 786
July	30 251	1 600	1 138	5 751	1 921	1 687	897	928	1 259	8 770	1 508	1 585	3 783
August	30 342	1 599	1 138	5 774	1 941	1 703	900	930	1 269	8 787	1 512	1 591	3 780
September	30 407	1 604	1 132	5 790	1 947	1 704	902	933	1 278	8 813	1 513	1 601	3 778
October	30 537	1 615	1 139	5 866	2 016	1 774	906	930	1 276	8 835	1 514	1 609	3 777
November	30 648	1 615	1 145	5 898	2 019	1 782	909	935	1 285	8 852	1 517	1 615	3 772
December	30 727	1 616	1 148	5 916	2 042	1 800	913	939	1 295	8 866	1 518	1 622	3 768
1994:													
January	30 805	1 617	1 152	5 952	2 059	1 826	920	940	1 297	8 884	1 523	1 626	3 767
February	30 885	1 614	1 142	6 005	2 114	1 876	921	945	1 301	8 889	1 522	1 629	3 764
March	31 035	1 624	1 140	6 072	2 163	1 924	927	952	1 313	8 919	1 527	1 635	3 765
April	31 227	1 629	1 144	6 150	2 212	1 964	935	959	1 322	8 945	1 531	1 640	3 767
May	31 346	1 630	1 134	6 185	2 227	1 977	942	961	1 333	8 964	1 537	1 644	3 763
June	31 500	1 631	1 133	6 254	2 266	2 009	952	967	1 345	8 979	1 541	1 649	3 759
July	31 682	1 637	1 135	6 318	2 303	2 044	959	969	1 347	9 007	1 547	1 654	3 763
August	31 809	1 638	1 139	6 366	2 321	2 060	969	976	1 346	9 028	1 556	1 657	3 762
September	31 934	1 638	1 143	6 410	2 332	2 064	980	982	1 343	9 042	1 554	1 658	3 762
October	32 066	1 634	1 144	6 468	2 368	2 101	990	985	1 351	9 061	1 563	1 660	3 760
November	32 237	1 636	1 146	6 546	2 400	2 136	1 001	991	1 353	9 077	1 567	1 663	3 760
December	32 348	1 646	1 146	6 564	2 413	2 138	1 010	994	1 358	9 100	1 573	1 667	3 761
1995:													
January	32 482	1 652	1 154	6 615	2 436	2 159	1 020	1 000	1 360	9 117	1 575	1 672	3 762
February	32 646	1 657	1 157	6 658	2 459	2 179	1 033	1 001	1 380	9 138	1 582	1 675	3 760
March	32 793	1 661	1 163	6 689	2 455	2 176	1 045	1 006	1 414	9 161	1 590	1 678	3 763
April	32 879	1 659	1 161	6 712	2 450	2 169	1 056	1 009	1 416	9 179	1 594	1 682	3 768
May	32 937	1 662	1 165	6 738	2 445	2 161	1 074	1 012	1 414	9 190	1 598	1 683	3 767
June	33 041	1 667	1 166	6 769	2 440	2 153	1 086	1 017	1 419	9 213	1 605	1 687	3 767
July	33 108	1 671	1 167	6 784	2 442	2 155	1 097	1 021	1 420	9 234	1 610	1 691	3 770
August	33 280	1 677	1 165	6 858	2 468	2 179	1 111	1 025	1 426	9 261	1 616	1 696	3 774
September	33 404	1 678	1 163	6 917	2 497	2 200	1 123	1 027	1 438	9 280	1 623	1 701	3 776
October	33 487	1 677	1 164	6 951	2 510	2 217	1 134	1 035	1 437	9 302	1 630	1 704	3 781
November	33 589	1 674	1 162	7 000	2 533	2 236	1 145	1 040	1 430	9 328	1 637	1 709	3 785
December	33 703	1 677	1 167	7 040	2 548	2 253	1 160	1 047	1 424	9 353	1 644	1 712	3 790
1996:													
January	33 698	1 683	1 170	6 993	2 486	2 191	1 164	1 052	1 433	9 356	1 646	1 714	3 792
February	33 938	1 691	1 174	7 109	2 569	2 271	1 174	1 059	1 450	9 386	1 655	1 717	3 798
March	34 064	1 701	1 176	7 141	2 582	2 283	1 183	1 066	1 455	9 411	1 661	1 722	3 801
April	34 150	1 709	1 179	7 173	2 592	2 294	1 189	1 070	1 460	9 429	1 668	1 725	3 804
May	34 277	1 715	1 182	7 216	2 634	2 332	1 195	1 075	1 465	9 453	1 674	1 730	3 809
June	34 390	1 731	1 184	7 252	2 663	2 359	1 199	1 079	1 466	9 466	1 679	1 733	3 809
July	34 465	1 718	1 184	7 288	2 683	2 376	1 209	1 087	1 472	9 478	1 682	1 735	3 812
August	34 560	1 718	1 187	7 330	2 699	2 392	1 218	1 094	1 474	9 493	1 687	1 737	3 813
September	34 621	1 722	1 189	7 354	2 706	2 398	1 226	1 097	1 471	9 514	1 691	1 739	3 823
October	34 717	1 726	1 193	7 379	2 711	2 398	1 236	1 104	1 478	9 532	1 695	1 742	3 829
November	34 800	1 731	1 194	7 398	2 706	2 391	1 246	1 107	1 481	9 552	1 700	1 745	3 834
December	34 884	1 738	1 194	7 437	2 721	2 406	1 256	1 112	1 483	9 567	1 703	1 747	3 839

1. Additional industry detail available in individual industry profile sections.

NONAGRICULTURAL EMPLOYMENT—Continued
(Wage and salary workers on nonagricultural payrolls—Thousands, seasonally adjusted)

Service-producing industries—Continued

YEAR AND MONTH	Services (Private)—Continued					Government					
	Legal services	Educational services	Social services	Membership organizations	Engineering and management services[1]	Total	Federal	State Total	State Education	Local Total	Local Education
1968		891				11 839	2 737	2 442	958	6 660	3 736
1969		930				12 195	2 758	2 533	1 042	6 904	3 874
1970		940				12 554	2 731	2 664	1 104	7 158	4 004
1971		948				12 881	2 696	2 747	1 149	7 437	4 188
1972	271	958	553	1 403		13 334	2 684	2 859	1 188	7 790	4 363
1973	296	975	552	1 410		13 732	2 663	2 923	1 205	8 146	4 537
1974	326	990	625	1 438		14 170	2 724	3 039	1 267	8 407	4 692
1975	341	1 001	690	1 452		14 686	2 748	3 179	1 323	8 758	4 834
1976	364	1 013	763	1 487		14 871	2 733	3 273	1 371	8 865	4 899
1977	394	1 031	855	1 495		15 127	2 727	3 377	1 385	9 023	4 974
1978	427	1 062	991	1 502		15 672	2 753	3 474	1 367	9 446	5 075
1979	460	1 090	1 081	1 516		15 947	2 773	3 541	1 378	9 633	5 107
1980	498	1 138	1 134	1 539		16 241	2 866	3 610	1 398	9 765	5 210
1981	532	1 179	1 149	1 527		16 031	2 772	3 640	1 420	9 619	5 216
1982	565	1 199	1 149	1 526		15 837	2 739	3 640	1 433	9 458	5 169
1983	602	1 225	1 188	1 510		15 869	2 774	3 662	1 450	9 434	5 139
1984	645	1 270	1 222	1 504		16 024	2 807	3 734	1 488	9 482	5 196
1985	692	1 359	1 325	1 517		16 394	2 875	3 832	1 540	9 687	5 344
1986	747	1 421	1 406	1 536		16 693	2 899	3 893	1 561	9 901	5 484
1987	801	1 449	1 454	1 614		17 010	2 943	3 967	1 586	10 100	5 598
1988	845	1 567	1 552	1 740	2 230	17 386	2 971	4 076	1 621	10 339	5 722
1989	880	1 647	1 644	1 836	2 389	17 779	2 988	4 182	1 668	10 609	5 875
1990	908	1 661	1 734	1 946	2 478	18 304	3 085	4 305	1 730	10 914	6 042
1991	912	1 710	1 845	1 982	2 433	18 402	2 966	4 355	1 768	11 081	6 136
1992	914	1 678	1 959	1 973	2 471	18 645	2 969	4 408	1 799	11 267	6 220
1993	924	1 711	2 070	2 035	2 521	18 841	2 915	4 488	1 834	11 438	6 353
1994	924	1 850	2 200	2 082	2 579	19 128	2 870	4 576	1 882	11 682	6 479
1995	921	1 965	2 336	2 146	2 731	19 305	2 822	4 635	1 919	11 849	6 606
1996	930	2 020	2 403	2 185	2 846	19 447	2 757	4 624	1 924	12 066	6 748
1993:											
January	918	1 668	2 014	2 015	2 499	18 734	2 942	4 451	1 813	11 341	6 293
February	920	1 671	2 026	2 022	2 504	18 767	2 944	4 457	1 817	11 366	6 316
March	922	1 670	2 036	2 024	2 511	18 766	2 935	4 462	1 818	11 369	6 318
April	923	1 683	2 047	2 032	2 515	18 776	2 924	4 472	1 823	11 380	6 316
May	924	1 692	2 052	2 031	2 520	18 808	2 916	4 482	1 830	11 410	6 343
June	925	1 702	2 070	2 037	2 522	18 828	2 906	4 477	1 824	11 445	6 366
July	925	1 716	2 079	2 039	2 525	18 831	2 901	4 480	1 824	11 450	6 370
August	925	1 729	2 098	2 039	2 524	18 860	2 906	4 488	1 834	11 466	6 368
September	927	1 738	2 087	2 040	2 528	18 885	2 902	4 505	1 845	11 478	6 372
October	927	1 742	2 093	2 041	2 531	18 911	2 901	4 511	1 849	11 499	6 384
November	926	1 758	2 105	2 046	2 536	18 934	2 900	4 514	1 851	11 520	6 395
December	924	1 768	2 117	2 048	2 536	18 964	2 898	4 521	1 855	11 545	6 408
1994:											
January	926	1 781	2 123	2 051	2 522	18 987	2 899	4 516	1 852	11 572	6 419
February	925	1 789	2 129	2 052	2 534	19 003	2 898	4 521	1 854	11 584	6 418
March	925	1 805	2 138	2 057	2 534	19 027	2 887	4 533	1 862	11 607	6 433
April	925	1 818	2 151	2 064	2 548	19 055	2 884	4 545	1 867	11 626	6 445
May	925	1 833	2 166	2 071	2 559	19 106	2 871	4 556	1 872	11 679	6 469
June	919	1 843	2 187	2 077	2 569	19 103	2 860	4 560	1 870	11 683	6 483
July	924	1 857	2 224	2 081	2 585	19 117	2 856	4 585	1 887	11 676	6 477
August	923	1 866	2 234	2 086	2 593	19 179	2 859	4 607	1 904	11 713	6 514
September	923	1 888	2 239	2 103	2 607	19 195	2 864	4 604	1 895	11 727	6 516
October	923	1 894	2 250	2 107	2 619	19 210	2 860	4 616	1 902	11 734	6 525
November	924	1 907	2 265	2 113	2 631	19 235	2 854	4 627	1 908	11 754	6 530
December	923	1 919	2 279	2 116	2 648	19 242	2 849	4 632	1 911	11 761	6 536
1995:											
January	924	1 924	2 297	2 123	2 667	19 261	2 842	4 643	1 917	11 776	6 553
February	924	1 942	2 307	2 127	2 683	19 267	2 836	4 648	1 923	11 783	6 558
March	923	1 948	2 318	2 133	2 695	19 281	2 831	4 651	1 925	11 799	6 571
April	923	1 953	2 325	2 135	2 711	19 299	2 828	4 649	1 924	11 822	6 587
May	921	1 961	2 330	2 139	2 714	19 276	2 829	4 639	1 921	11 808	6 583
June	919	1 966	2 330	2 145	2 734	19 302	2 831	4 638	1 921	11 833	6 593
July	920	1 968	2 323	2 149	2 741	19 300	2 826	4 626	1 921	11 848	6 605
August	920	1 983	2 338	2 158	2 751	19 342	2 824	4 620	1 913	11 898	6 654
September	921	1 978	2 364	2 154	2 757	19 308	2 812	4 623	1 914	11 873	6 629
October	921	1 985	2 359	2 152	2 766	19 335	2 803	4 627	1 916	11 905	6 633
November	921	1 985	2 363	2 164	2 775	19 335	2 797	4 623	1 916	11 915	6 644
December	921	1 993	2 371	2 170	2 781	19 346	2 791	4 622	1 914	11 933	6 659
1996:											
January	922	1 987	2 372	2 173	2 788	19 326	2 782	4 610	1 904	11 934	6 653
February	925	2 001	2 381	2 179	2 798	19 356	2 782	4 622	1 915	11 952	6 662
March	924	2 008	2 387	2 182	2 811	19 396	2 779	4 624	1 920	11 993	6 691
April	925	2 012	2 393	2 181	2 814	19 400	2 774	4 625	1 922	12 001	6 702
May	927	2 010	2 401	2 187	2 830	19 416	2 770	4 629	1 926	12 017	6 700
June	929	2 021	2 406	2 187	2 845	19 437	2 757	4 629	1 928	12 051	6 736
July	931	2 034	2 411	2 183	2 849	19 455	2 752	4 625	1 931	12 078	6 767
August	933	2 031	2 415	2 191	2 860	19 550	2 743	4 637	1 937	12 170	6 837
September	933	2 022	2 421	2 188	2 872	19 513	2 740	4 640	1 941	12 133	6 796
October	936	2 035	2 422	2 189	2 882	19 489	2 732	4 618	1 922	12 139	6 797
November	939	2 041	2 425	2 190	2 894	19 494	2 732	4 620	1 925	12 142	6 807
December	940	2 040	2 426	2 191	2 906	19 514	2 728	4 621	1 927	12 165	6 815

1. Additional industry detail available in individual industry profile sections.

AVERAGE WEEKLY HOURS
(Production or nonsupervisory workers on private nonagricultural payrolls—Seasonally adjusted, except as noted)

YEAR AND MONTH	All industries		Goods producing industries[1]	Mining	Construction	Total manufacturing		Durable goods manufacturing					
								Total		Lumber and products	Furniture and fixtures	Stone, clay, and glass products	Primary metal industries
	Not seasonally adjusted	Seasonally adjusted				Average weekly hours	Overtime hours	Average weekly hours	Overtime hours				
1968	37.8	37.8	40.2	42.6	37.3	40.7	3.6	41.4	3.8	40.6	40.6	41.8	41.6
1969	37.7	37.7	40.2	43.0	37.9	40.6	3.6	41.3	3.8	40.2	40.4	41.9	41.8
1970	37.1	37.1	39.4	42.7	37.3	39.8	3.0	40.3	3.0	39.6	39.2	41.2	40.4
1971	36.9	36.9	39.4	42.4	37.2	39.9	2.9	40.3	2.9	39.8	39.8	41.6	40.1
1972	37.0	37.0	39.9	42.6	36.5	40.5	3.5	41.2	3.6	40.4	40.2	42.0	41.4
1973	36.9	36.9	40.0	42.4	36.8	40.7	3.8	41.4	4.1	40.0	40.0	41.9	42.3
1974	36.5	36.5	39.5	41.9	36.6	40.0	3.3	40.6	3.4	39.2	39.1	41.3	41.6
1975	36.1	36.1	39.0	41.9	36.4	39.5	2.6	39.9	2.6	38.8	38.0	40.4	40.0
1976	36.1	36.1	39.6	42.4	36.8	40.1	3.1	40.6	3.2	39.9	38.8	41.1	40.8
1977	36.0	36.0	39.8	43.4	36.5	40.3	3.5	41.0	3.7	39.9	39.0	41.3	41.3
1978	35.8	35.8	39.9	43.4	36.8	40.4	3.6	41.1	3.8	39.8	39.3	41.6	41.8
1979	35.7	35.7	39.7	43.0	37.0	40.2	3.3	40.8	3.5	39.5	38.7	41.5	41.4
1980	35.3	35.3	39.3	43.3	37.0	39.7	2.8	40.1	2.8	38.6	38.1	40.8	40.1
1981	35.2	35.2	39.5	43.7	36.9	39.8	2.8	40.2	2.8	38.7	38.4	40.6	40.5
1982	34.8	34.8	38.7	42.7	36.7	38.9	2.3	39.3	2.2	38.1	37.2	40.1	38.6
1983	35.0	35.0	39.7	42.5	37.1	40.1	3.0	40.7	3.0	40.1	39.4	41.5	40.5
1984	35.2	35.2	40.2	43.3	37.8	40.7	3.4	41.4	3.6	39.9	39.7	42.0	41.7
1985	34.9	34.9	40.0	43.4	37.7	40.5	3.3	41.2	3.5	39.9	39.4	41.9	41.5
1986	34.8	34.8	40.1	42.2	37.4	40.7	3.4	41.3	3.5	40.4	39.8	42.2	41.9
1987	34.8	34.8	40.3	42.4	37.8	41.0	3.7	41.5	3.8	40.6	40.0	42.3	43.1
1988	34.7	34.7	40.4	42.3	37.9	41.1	3.9	41.8	4.1	40.1	39.4	42.3	43.5
1989	34.6	34.6	40.3	43.0	37.9	41.0	3.8	41.6	3.9	40.1	39.5	42.3	43.0
1990	34.5	34.5	40.3	44.1	38.2	40.8	3.6	41.3	3.7	40.2	39.1	42.0	42.7
1991	34.3	34.3	40.3	44.4	38.1	40.7	3.6	41.1	3.5	40.0	38.9	41.7	42.2
1992	34.4	34.4	40.5	43.9	38.0	41.0	3.8	41.5	3.7	40.6	39.7	42.2	43.0
1993	34.5	34.5	40.9	44.3	38.5	41.4	4.1	42.1	4.3	40.8	40.1	42.7	43.7
1994	34.7	34.7	41.4	44.8	38.9	42.0	4.7	42.9	5.0	41.2	40.4	43.4	44.7
1995	34.5	34.5	41.0	44.7	38.9	41.6	4.4	42.4	4.7	40.6	39.6	43.0	44.0
1996	34.4	34.4	41.1	45.3	39.0	41.6	4.5	42.4	4.8	40.8	39.4	43.3	44.2
1993:													
January	34.0	34.4	40.7	44.4	38.2	41.3	4.0	41.9	4.0	40.7	40.3	42.5	43.5
February	34.1	34.4	40.8	44.0	38.0	41.5	4.1	42.1	4.1	40.9	40.4	42.6	43.7
March	34.0	34.2	40.5	43.3	38.1	41.1	3.9	41.8	4.0	40.5	40.1	42.0	43.6
April	34.2	34.4	41.0	44.2	38.4	41.6	4.3	42.3	4.4	40.6	40.6	42.5	44.0
May	34.7	34.6	40.8	44.5	38.5	41.3	4.1	41.9	4.2	40.6	39.9	42.7	43.6
June	34.6	34.4	40.7	44.0	38.4	41.2	4.1	41.9	4.2	40.5	39.6	42.6	43.6
July	34.8	34.5	40.9	44.6	38.6	41.4	4.1	42.1	4.2	40.7	40.0	42.6	43.6
August	35.1	34.6	40.9	44.6	38.6	41.4	4.1	42.1	4.3	40.8	40.3	42.8	43.6
September	34.5	34.5	41.1	44.4	38.8	41.6	4.3	42.4	4.5	41.4	40.4	42.9	43.7
October	34.6	34.5	40.9	45.0	38.4	41.5	4.3	42.3	4.5	40.9	40.2	42.8	43.7
November	34.5	34.5	41.1	44.3	38.9	41.6	4.3	42.4	4.6	41.2	40.3	43.3	44.0
December	34.7	34.5	41.1	44.3	38.7	41.7	4.4	42.5	4.7	41.1	40.2	43.1	44.0
1994:													
January	34.4	34.8	41.1	44.3	38.6	41.7	4.4	42.6	4.7	41.6	39.8	43.2	44.1
February	34.0	34.3	40.4	44.2	37.4	41.2	4.4	42.1	4.7	40.3	38.9	42.3	44.0
March	34.4	34.6	41.3	44.3	38.8	42.0	4.7	42.9	5.0	41.3	40.7	43.5	44.6
April	34.5	34.6	41.1	44.6	38.4	41.9	4.5	42.6	4.7	41.2	40.2	43.4	44.4
May	34.8	34.7	41.4	44.6	39.0	42.0	4.6	42.9	4.9	41.4	40.5	43.7	44.7
June	34.8	34.6	41.3	44.7	38.7	42.0	4.6	42.8	4.9	41.3	40.6	43.5	44.5
July	34.9	34.6	41.4	45.1	38.7	42.0	4.7	42.8	5.0	41.3	40.6	43.5	44.8
August	35.0	34.5	41.3	44.9	38.7	42.0	4.7	42.8	5.0	41.1	40.4	43.4	44.7
September	34.8	34.6	41.2	44.8	38.7	41.9	4.6	42.6	4.9	41.0	40.5	43.4	44.8
October	35.0	34.8	41.3	44.6	38.6	42.1	4.7	42.8	5.0	41.1	40.7	43.5	44.8
November	34.6	34.6	41.4	45.1	38.8	42.1	4.8	42.9	5.1	41.0	40.3	43.5	45.0
December	34.8	34.6	41.5	44.8	39.1	42.1	4.8	42.9	5.1	41.2	40.3	43.5	44.9
1995:													
January	34.4	34.9	41.6	45.2	39.4	42.2	4.8	43.1	5.2	41.5	40.5	43.6	44.9
February	34.2	34.5	41.1	44.6	38.0	41.9	4.7	42.7	5.1	40.8	40.3	42.9	44.7
March	34.2	34.5	41.2	44.2	38.8	41.8	4.6	42.7	5.0	40.7	39.8	43.1	44.5
April	34.3	34.6	40.9	44.9	38.5	41.5	4.4	42.2	4.7	40.6	39.1	42.9	44.2
May	34.2	34.2	40.7	44.4	37.8	41.4	4.2	42.1	4.5	40.3	39.3	42.6	43.8
June	34.6	34.4	40.9	44.7	38.7	41.4	4.2	42.2	4.5	40.4	39.4	42.9	43.8
July	34.8	34.5	40.9	44.7	38.9	41.3	4.2	42.1	4.5	40.3	39.2	43.0	43.2
August	34.8	34.4	40.9	44.5	38.7	41.5	4.3	42.3	4.6	40.6	39.7	43.1	43.6
September	34.6	34.4	40.9	44.8	38.7	41.5	4.4	42.3	4.7	40.6	39.5	43.1	43.6
October	34.7	34.5	41.0	44.9	39.1	41.5	4.4	42.3	4.7	40.6	39.5	43.0	43.8
November	34.4	34.4	40.9	44.6	38.7	41.5	4.4	42.4	4.7	40.6	39.6	43.0	44.0
December	34.4	34.3	40.6	44.7	38.4	41.2	4.2	41.9	4.5	40.1	39.3	42.8	43.7
1996:													
January	33.4	33.9	39.8	44.2	38.3	40.1	4.2	41.1	4.5	39.4	35.8	42.1	43.3
February	34.1	34.4	41.0	45.2	39.2	41.4	4.4	42.2	4.6	40.6	39.2	43.4	44.1
March	34.2	34.4	40.8	45.2	38.7	41.3	4.3	42.0	4.5	40.7	39.4	43.3	43.8
April	34.1	34.3	40.9	45.0	38.8	41.5	4.5	42.3	4.8	40.7	39.3	43.3	43.9
May	34.3	34.3	41.0	45.3	38.5	41.6	4.6	42.5	4.9	40.9	39.6	43.3	44.1
June	34.9	34.7	41.1	45.6	38.8	41.7	4.5	42.5	4.8	41.1	39.6	43.4	44.2
July	34.6	34.3	41.0	45.0	38.7	41.6	4.5	42.4	4.7	41.0	39.7	43.2	44.0
August	34.8	34.5	41.1	45.2	38.8	41.7	4.5	42.5	4.8	40.9	39.6	43.2	44.3
September	34.9	34.7	41.1	45.3	38.7	41.7	4.5	42.5	4.8	40.9	39.6	43.2	44.4
October	34.5	34.4	41.1	45.4	38.9	41.7	4.5	42.4	4.7	40.8	39.6	43.3	44.4
November	34.5	34.5	41.1	45.3	38.8	41.7	4.6	42.5	4.8	40.9	39.8	43.2	44.3
December	34.9	34.7	41.3	45.7	38.9	42.0	4.7	42.7	4.9	41.0	40.1	43.4	44.6

1. Includes mining, construction, and manufacturing. Additional industry detail available in individual industry profile section.

AVERAGE WEEKLY HOURS—Continued
(Production or nonsupervisory workers on private nonagricultural payrolls—Seasonally adjusted)

YEAR AND MONTH	Durable goods manufacturing—Continued						Nondurable goods manufacturing					
	Fabricated metal products	Industrial machinery and equipment	Electronic and electric equipment	Transportation equipment[1]	Instruments and related products	Miscellaneous manufacturing	Total		Food and products	Tobacco products[2]	Textile mill products	Apparel and other textile products
							Average weekly hours	Overtime hours				
1968	41.7	42.0	....	42.2	....	39.4	39.8	3.3	40.8	37.9	41.2	36.1
1969	41.6	42.5	....	41.5	....	39.0	39.7	3.4	40.8	37.4	40.8	35.9
1970	40.7	41.1	....	40.3	....	38.7	39.1	3.0	40.5	37.8	39.9	35.3
1971	40.4	40.6	....	40.7	....	38.9	39.3	3.0	40.3	37.8	40.6	35.6
1972	41.2	42.1	....	41.7	....	39.5	39.7	3.3	40.5	37.6	41.3	36.0
1973	41.6	42.8	....	42.1	....	39.0	39.6	3.4	40.4	38.6	40.9	35.9
1974	40.8	42.1	....	40.5	....	38.7	39.1	3.0	40.4	38.3	39.5	35.2
1975	40.1	40.8	....	40.4	....	38.5	38.8	2.7	40.3	38.2	39.3	35.2
1976	40.8	41.2	....	41.7	....	38.8	39.4	3.0	40.5	37.5	40.1	35.8
1977	41.0	41.5	....	42.5	....	38.8	39.4	3.2	40.0	37.8	40.4	35.6
1978	41.0	42.0	....	42.2	....	38.8	39.4	3.2	39.7	38.1	40.4	35.6
1979	40.7	41.7	....	41.1	....	38.8	39.3	3.1	39.9	38.0	40.4	35.3
1980	40.4	41.0	....	40.6	....	38.7	39.0	2.8	39.7	38.1	40.1	35.4
1981	40.3	40.9	....	40.9	....	38.8	39.2	2.8	39.7	38.8	39.6	35.7
1982	39.2	39.7	....	40.5	....	38.4	38.4	2.5	39.4	37.8	37.5	34.7
1983	40.6	40.5	....	42.1	....	39.1	39.4	3.0	39.5	37.4	40.4	36.2
1984	41.4	41.9	....	42.7	....	39.4	39.7	3.1	39.8	38.9	39.9	36.4
1985	41.3	41.5	....	42.6	....	39.4	39.6	3.1	40.0	37.2	39.7	36.4
1986	41.3	41.6	....	42.3	....	39.6	39.9	3.3	40.0	37.4	41.1	36.7
1987	41.6	42.2	....	42.0	....	39.4	40.2	3.6	40.2	39.0	41.8	37.0
1988	41.9	42.7	41.0	42.7	41.4	39.2	40.2	3.6	40.3	39.8	41.0	37.0
1989	41.6	42.4	40.8	42.4	41.1	39.4	40.2	3.6	40.7	38.6	40.9	36.9
1990	41.3	41.9	40.8	42.0	41.1	39.5	40.0	3.6	40.8	39.2	39.9	36.4
1991	41.2	41.7	40.7	41.9	41.0	39.7	40.2	3.7	40.6	39.1	40.6	37.0
1992	41.6	42.2	41.2	41.8	41.1	39.9	40.4	3.8	40.6	38.6	41.1	37.2
1993	42.1	43.0	41.8	43.0	41.1	39.8	40.6	4.0	40.7	37.4	41.4	37.2
1994	42.9	43.7	42.2	44.3	41.7	40.0	40.9	4.3	41.3	39.3	41.6	37.5
1995	42.4	43.4	41.6	43.8	41.4	39.9	40.5	4.0	41.1	39.6	40.8	37.0
1996	42.4	43.1	41.5	44.0	41.7	39.7	40.5	4.1	41.0	40.0	40.6	37.0
1993:												
January	41.8	42.7	41.7	42.2	41.2	39.9	40.6	3.9	40.6	38.6	41.7	37.5
February	42.0	42.8	41.8	42.6	41.2	40.0	40.7	4.0	40.7	37.3	41.8	37.6
March	41.7	42.6	41.5	42.5	40.9	39.8	40.1	3.7	40.4	36.0	39.8	36.9
April	42.3	43.2	42.0	43.0	41.5	40.3	40.8	4.2	40.7	35.5	41.9	37.8
May	41.8	42.8	41.7	42.6	41.2	39.7	40.5	3.9	40.5	36.7	41.5	37.2
June	41.9	42.8	41.4	42.6	41.1	39.6	40.4	3.9	40.6	38.6	41.2	37.0
July	42.0	43.1	41.7	42.9	41.2	39.6	40.6	4.0	40.8	36.0	41.2	37.2
August	42.1	43.0	41.8	42.8	41.0	39.7	40.5	3.9	40.7	37.4	41.4	37.2
September	42.3	43.3	41.9	43.5	41.3	40.0	40.6	4.0	40.8	38.1	41.6	37.2
October	42.2	43.2	41.9	43.4	41.0	39.8	40.6	4.0	40.9	38.6	41.5	36.9
November	42.3	43.2	41.9	43.6	41.0	39.9	40.6	4.0	40.8	37.6	41.8	37.1
December	42.5	43.4	41.9	43.9	41.2	40.1	40.6	4.1	40.8	37.4	41.7	37.1
1994:												
January	42.6	43.4	42.1	43.8	41.3	39.9	40.7	4.1	41.0	37.5	41.4	37.1
February	42.2	43.0	41.6	43.8	41.2	38.9	40.1	4.0	40.7	35.4	40.2	35.7
March	42.7	43.6	42.3	44.5	41.6	40.0	40.9	4.3	41.2	37.9	41.8	37.4
April	42.5	43.4	42.2	43.9	41.6	40.0	40.9	4.2	41.1	39.4	41.8	37.5
May	42.8	43.6	42.2	44.2	41.7	40.1	40.9	4.2	41.1	38.8	41.8	37.7
June	42.6	43.7	42.2	43.9	41.7	40.0	41.0	4.3	41.2	40.2	41.9	37.7
July	42.8	43.7	42.3	43.7	41.9	40.4	41.1	4.3	41.5	37.9	41.8	37.6
August	42.8	43.5	42.1	44.1	41.8	39.9	41.0	4.2	41.3	39.4	41.6	37.6
September	42.6	43.5	41.7	43.9	41.7	39.6	40.9	4.2	41.4	41.2	41.5	37.4
October	42.8	43.7	42.1	44.2	41.8	40.1	41.0	4.3	41.3	41.9	41.8	37.7
November	42.9	43.7	42.0	44.6	41.7	40.0	41.0	4.3	41.5	39.8	41.4	37.5
December	42.9	43.8	42.0	44.7	41.7	40.0	41.1	4.3	41.7	41.1	41.5	37.6
1995:												
January	43.4	44.1	42.3	44.5	41.6	40.1	41.1	4.3	41.8	39.1	41.6	37.6
February	42.8	43.7	41.5	44.5	41.4	40.1	40.8	4.2	41.3	38.5	41.6	37.4
March	42.7	43.6	41.6	44.6	41.5	39.9	40.7	4.1	41.2	38.1	41.2	37.3
April	42.0	43.1	41.5	43.6	41.3	39.9	40.6	4.0	40.9	38.4	41.1	37.1
May	42.1	43.3	41.5	43.3	41.3	39.7	40.5	3.9	41.1	40.0	40.5	37.0
June	42.1	43.2	41.4	43.5	41.3	39.9	40.4	3.9	41.2	41.6	40.4	36.8
July	42.0	43.0	41.4	43.5	41.3	39.8	40.4	3.9	41.2	39.3	40.4	36.8
August	42.2	43.4	41.6	43.5	41.5	39.9	40.4	4.0	41.2	40.4	40.7	36.7
September	42.4	43.2	41.7	43.5	41.4	39.8	40.4	3.9	41.1	40.0	40.6	36.8
October	42.3	43.2	42.0	43.5	41.5	39.8	40.3	3.9	40.9	40.4	40.5	36.6
November	42.2	43.5	41.7	44.0	41.4	39.7	40.3	3.9	40.7	40.6	40.5	36.8
December	42.1	42.9	41.1	42.9	41.1	39.4	40.2	3.8	40.5	39.1	40.3	36.8
1996:												
January	41.2	42.2	40.4	42.5	40.2	37.7	38.7	3.8	40.0	35.8	36.1	33.6
February	42.1	43.0	41.5	43.3	41.7	39.4	40.5	4.0	41.1	38.7	40.6	36.8
March	42.1	43.0	41.4	42.3	41.6	39.7	40.5	4.0	41.1	39.4	40.7	36.9
April	42.3	43.1	41.2	44.1	41.5	39.6	40.4	4.1	41.0	39.3	40.4	36.7
May	42.5	43.1	41.4	44.3	41.6	39.8	40.5	4.1	41.0	39.9	40.7	37.1
June	42.6	43.1	41.6	44.1	41.9	39.7	40.7	4.1	41.0	41.0	40.9	37.5
July	42.4	43.0	41.3	44.0	41.6	39.7	40.5	4.1	40.8	38.6	40.9	37.1
August	42.4	43.0	41.6	44.4	41.8	39.7	40.6	4.1	40.8	40.0	40.9	37.4
September	42.4	43.1	41.6	44.4	41.8	39.9	40.7	4.1	41.0	42.0	40.9	37.3
October	42.3	43.0	41.5	44.0	41.8	39.8	40.6	4.1	41.1	41.2	40.9	37.3
November	42.3	43.1	41.5	44.3	41.9	39.9	40.7	4.2	41.1	41.2	41.2	37.3
December	42.4	43.3	41.8	44.6	42.0	40.4	40.9	4.3	41.3	41.9	41.5	37.4

1. Additional industry detail available in individual industry profile section.
2. Not seasonally adjusted.

AVERAGE WEEKLY HOURS—Continued
(Production or nonsupervisory workers on private nonagricultural payrolls—Seasonally adjusted)

YEAR AND MONTH	Nondurable goods manufacturing—Continued						Service producing industries					
	Paper and products	Printing and publishing	Chemicals and products	Petroleum and coal products[1]	Rubber and miscellaneous plastic products	Leather and products	Total	Transportation and public utilities	Wholesale trade	Retail trade	Finance, insurance, and real estate[1]	Services[1]
1968	42.9	38.3	41.8	42.5	41.5	38.3	36.3	40.6	40.1	34.7	37.0	34.7
1969	43.0	38.3	41.8	42.6	41.2	37.2	36.1	40.7	40.2	34.2	37.1	34.7
1970	41.9	37.7	41.6	42.8	40.3	37.2	35.8	40.5	39.9	33.8	36.7	34.4
1971	42.1	37.5	41.6	42.8	40.4	37.7	35.5	40.1	39.4	33.7	36.6	33.9
1972	42.8	37.7	41.7	42.7	41.2	38.3	35.4	40.4	39.4	33.4	36.6	33.9
1973	42.9	37.7	41.8	42.4	41.2	37.8	35.2	40.5	39.2	33.1	36.6	33.8
1974	42.2	37.5	41.5	42.1	40.6	36.9	34.9	40.2	38.8	32.7	36.5	33.6
1975	41.6	36.9	41.0	41.2	39.9	37.1	34.7	39.7	38.6	32.4	36.5	33.5
1976	42.5	37.5	41.6	42.1	40.7	37.4	34.4	39.8	38.7	32.1	36.4	33.3
1977	42.9	37.7	41.7	42.7	41.1	36.9	34.2	39.9	38.8	31.6	36.4	33.0
1978	42.9	37.6	41.9	43.6	40.9	37.1	33.9	40.0	38.8	31.0	36.4	32.8
1979	42.6	37.5	41.9	43.8	40.6	36.5	33.7	39.9	38.8	30.6	36.2	32.7
1980	42.2	37.1	41.5	41.8	40.0	36.7	33.5	39.6	38.4	30.2	36.2	32.6
1981	42.5	37.3	41.6	43.2	40.3	36.7	33.5	39.4	38.5	30.1	36.3	32.6
1982	41.8	37.1	40.9	43.9	39.6	35.6	33.3	39.0	38.3	29.9	36.2	32.6
1983	42.6	37.6	41.6	43.9	41.2	36.8	33.3	39.0	38.5	29.8	36.2	32.7
1984	43.1	37.9	41.9	43.7	41.7	36.8	33.3	39.4	38.5	29.8	36.5	32.6
1985	43.1	37.8	41.9	43.0	41.1	37.2	33.1	39.5	38.4	29.4	36.4	32.5
1986	43.2	38.0	41.9	43.8	41.4	36.9	32.9	39.2	38.3	29.2	36.4	32.5
1987	43.4	38.0	42.3	44.0	41.6	38.2	32.9	39.2	38.1	29.2	36.3	32.5
1988	43.3	38.0	42.2	44.4	41.7	37.5	32.8	38.2	38.1	29.1	35.9	32.6
1989	43.3	37.9	42.4	44.3	41.4	37.9	32.7	38.3	38.0	28.9	35.8	32.6
1990	43.3	37.9	42.6	44.6	41.1	37.4	32.7	38.4	38.1	28.8	35.8	32.5
1991	43.3	37.7	42.9	44.1	41.1	37.5	32.5	38.1	38.1	28.6	35.7	32.4
1992	43.6	38.1	43.1	43.8	41.7	38.0	32.7	38.3	38.2	28.8	35.8	32.5
1993	43.6	38.3	43.1	44.2	41.8	38.6	32.7	39.3	38.2	28.8	35.8	32.5
1994	43.9	38.6	43.2	44.4	42.2	38.5	32.8	39.7	38.4	28.9	35.8	32.5
1995	43.1	38.2	43.2	43.7	41.5	38.0	32.7	39.4	38.3	28.8	35.9	32.4
1996	43.3	38.2	43.2	43.6	41.5	38.1	32.7	39.6	38.3	28.8	35.9	32.4
1993:												
January	43.5	38.3	43.0	44.1	41.8	39.4	32.6	39.2	38.1	28.8	35.7	32.1
February	43.7	38.3	43.0	43.9	42.0	40.0	32.6	39.1	38.1	28.7	35.7	32.3
March	43.4	38.1	42.8	43.3	41.6	38.6	32.4	39.3	38.0	28.2	35.5	32.2
April	43.9	38.5	43.0	44.9	42.2	39.3	32.6	39.2	38.1	28.7	35.7	32.3
May	43.6	38.1	43.2	44.7	41.7	38.5	32.9	39.4	38.3	28.9	36.2	32.7
June	43.6	38.3	43.1	44.1	41.7	37.8	32.7	39.2	38.2	28.7	35.6	32.6
July	43.5	38.4	43.4	44.0	41.8	38.1	32.7	39.3	38.2	28.9	35.6	32.8
August	43.6	38.2	43.2	44.1	41.8	38.2	32.9	39.5	38.3	28.9	36.4	33.0
September	43.6	38.3	43.3	44.1	41.9	38.5	32.7	39.5	38.1	28.8	35.6	32.3
October	43.7	38.4	43.2	45.7	41.8	38.4	32.7	39.4	38.2	28.9	35.7	32.4
November	43.8	38.3	43.0	43.9	42.0	38.4	32.7	39.3	38.2	28.7	35.7	32.4
December	43.6	38.3	43.3	43.4	41.9	38.5	32.7	39.7	38.2	28.8	35.7	32.4
1994:												
January	43.6	38.4	43.3	44.0	42.0	38.8	33.1	39.7	38.4	29.1	36.4	32.5
February	43.2	38.1	42.8	43.6	41.4	38.2	32.6	39.6	38.1	28.6	35.8	32.2
March	43.9	38.4	43.3	44.6	42.5	38.6	32.7	39.7	38.3	28.9	35.7	32.3
April	43.9	38.6	43.2	45.1	42.0	38.7	32.8	39.9	38.3	28.9	35.7	32.4
May	44.0	38.7	43.3	43.8	42.2	38.3	32.9	39.9	38.4	28.9	36.1	32.6
June	44.0	38.7	43.2	44.0	42.2	38.3	32.8	39.8	38.4	29.0	35.6	32.5
July	44.1	38.7	43.4	43.8	42.3	38.3	32.8	39.7	38.4	29.0	35.7	32.7
August	44.1	38.6	43.3	43.5	42.3	38.3	32.6	39.6	38.2	28.9	35.5	32.7
September	44.0	38.6	43.0	46.3	42.0	38.2	32.7	39.6	38.3	28.9	35.4	32.4
October	44.1	38.7	43.4	45.1	42.2	38.7	33.0	39.8	38.6	29.2	36.2	32.7
November	43.9	38.7	43.4	44.4	42.2	38.5	32.7	39.6	38.3	28.9	35.7	32.3
December	43.9	38.7	43.3	44.2	42.2	38.4	32.7	39.4	38.4	28.8	35.7	32.4
1995:												
January	43.9	38.5	43.4	43.8	42.3	38.1	33.0	39.6	38.5	29.0	36.3	32.4
February	43.6	38.4	43.3	44.4	42.0	38.4	32.6	39.4	38.3	28.7	35.8	32.3
March	43.4	38.4	43.3	43.3	41.8	38.3	32.6	39.3	38.2	28.7	35.5	32.2
April	43.2	38.4	43.4	43.9	41.6	38.2	32.9	39.6	38.4	29.2	36.3	32.5
May	43.0	38.3	43.2	43.2	41.5	38.3	32.4	39.1	38.0	28.7	35.4	32.1
June	42.9	38.2	43.3	43.7	41.4	38.1	32.6	39.4	38.2	28.7	35.6	32.5
July	43.0	38.2	43.1	44.1	41.0	37.2	32.6	39.6	38.4	28.9	36.3	32.8
August	42.9	38.1	43.1	43.2	41.3	38.1	32.6	39.3	38.2	28.7	35.6	32.7
September	43.0	38.1	43.1	43.8	41.4	37.9	32.6	39.2	38.2	28.8	35.7	32.3
October	42.9	38.1	43.2	44.3	41.4	37.8	32.7	39.4	38.4	28.8	36.4	32.6
November	42.9	38.2	43.0	43.8	41.4	37.6	32.7	39.3	38.2	28.9	35.7	32.3
December	42.9	37.9	43.0	43.2	41.3	37.6	32.5	39.2	38.1	28.7	35.7	32.3
1996:												
January	41.5	37.1	42.5	43.1	40.4	35.0	32.3	38.9	38.0	28.4	35.5	31.8
February	43.1	38.2	43.3	42.8	41.3	37.6	32.6	39.5	38.2	28.8	35.7	32.2
March	43.1	38.1	43.1	42.9	41.3	38.0	32.7	39.7	38.2	28.9	35.7	32.2
April	43.3	38.1	43.0	43.3	41.4	37.8	32.5	39.2	38.1	28.7	35.6	32.2
May	43.3	38.2	43.1	42.6	41.5	38.2	32.5	39.4	38.1	28.8	35.6	32.2
June	43.4	38.2	43.4	44.7	41.5	38.4	33.0	39.9	38.6	29.0	36.5	32.8
July	43.3	38.2	43.2	44.3	41.5	38.3	32.5	39.4	38.1	28.7	35.6	32.5
August	43.4	38.3	43.2	43.9	41.6	38.6	32.7	39.7	38.3	28.8	36.3	32.7
September	43.5	38.3	43.1	44.2	41.6	38.7	32.9	39.8	38.4	28.9	36.5	32.6
October	43.4	38.2	43.1	43.6	41.5	38.6	32.6	39.6	38.2	28.8	35.7	32.4
November	43.6	38.2	43.3	44.0	41.3	38.9	32.7	39.8	38.3	28.9	35.8	32.4
December	43.7	38.4	43.5	43.9	41.8	38.8	33.0	39.9	38.5	29.0	36.7	32.7

1. Not seasonally adjusted.

INDEXES OF AGGREGATE WEEKLY HOURS
(Production or nonsupervisory workers on private nonagricultural payrolls—1982=100, seasonally adjusted)

YEAR AND MONTH	Total private	Goods-producing industries									
		Total	Mining	Construction	Manufacturing						
					Total	Durable goods					
						Total	Lumber and products	Furniture and fixtures	Stone, clay, and glass products	Primary metal industries[1]	Fabricated metal products
1968	84.9	111.7	56.0	95.6	119.2	121.7	124.8	118.6	121.9	158.1	128.8
1969	87.7	114.5	57.9	103.6	121.0	124.2	126.5	121.5	126.4	165.1	132.6
1970	86.3	107.8	57.6	101.3	112.8	113.0	117.9	111.6	120.9	152.9	120.3
1971	85.8	105.0	54.9	103.6	108.8	107.4	123.8	114.0	122.2	140.5	113.2
1972	89.2	110.5	57.8	107.9	114.8	115.4	136.1	126.6	131.1	146.3	121.9
1973	93.2	116.9	58.8	113.7	121.7	125.8	140.6	132.0	138.4	161.8	131.8
1974	93.2	113.7	63.4	109.5	118.1	122.4	128.2	123.4	134.5	162.4	127.4
1975	88.8	99.9	68.3	92.7	103.8	104.9	107.8	100.7	115.6	134.3	108.4
1976	92.3	105.4	71.5	94.0	110.3	111.9	123.5	111.0	120.8	140.0	115.3
1977	96.0	110.3	76.5	100.2	115.0	118.4	132.0	117.2	125.9	144.2	121.9
1978	100.7	116.5	79.0	112.2	120.1	125.9	138.3	125.6	132.1	151.3	129.3
1979	104.0	119.9	88.2	119.9	122.1	129.1	138.6	123.5	132.8	154.8	131.4
1980	102.8	112.9	94.1	115.1	113.8	117.8	119.9	112.4	119.8	133.4	119.8
1981	104.1	111.6	104.8	109.3	112.5	116.1	115.1	112.7	114.1	132.5	117.1
1982	100.0	100.0	100.0	100.0	100.0	100.0	100.0	100.0	100.0	100.0	100.0
1983	101.5	100.5	81.5	102.2	101.4	100.7	117.7	110.3	103.2	95.2	100.3
1984	107.7	109.0	84.9	116.8	109.0	111.5	126.3	121.6	109.5	102.9	111.0
1985	110.5	108.7	81.4	125.3	106.9	109.5	124.9	121.9	108.1	96.1	111.2
1986	112.3	107.3	65.7	128.2	105.7	106.8	129.2	124.2	108.7	89.8	107.8
1987	115.6	109.0	61.8	132.7	107.0	107.4	134.9	129.5	109.7	91.8	107.1
1988	119.3	111.4	61.7	136.9	109.3	110.5	135.6	130.1	113.3	97.2	110.5
1989	122.1	111.7	60.5	138.9	109.3	110.1	132.6	129.6	113.5	96.0	110.6
1990	123.0	109.5	63.9	138.0	106.4	106.1	128.2	122.8	109.7	93.0	107.1
1991	120.4	103.4	62.0	122.8	102.1	99.3	116.9	113.9	101.4	87.2	101.4
1992	121.2	102.1	56.2	118.4	101.7	98.2	119.9	117.6	101.2	85.6	100.7
1993	124.6	104.2	54.3	125.4	103.1	100.0	126.1	121.3	102.9	86.2	103.3
1994	130.0	109.2	54.6	136.3	107.0	105.5	135.9	127.0	107.9	90.9	110.5
1995	133.4	110.3	54.1	140.8	107.5	107.5	135.8	125.6	108.8	92.1	113.6
1996	136.4	111.2	55.1	148.1	106.9	108.3	138.3	123.2	110.1	92.6	114.5
1993:											
January	122.7	103.1	56.0	119.5	102.7	100.0	123.3	120.4	101.7	86.1	101.8
February	123.1	103.9	54.3	122.7	103.2	100.5	124.6	121.0	103.5	86.1	102.6
March	122.2	102.7	53.5	120.7	102.1	99.8	124.0	120.4	100.8	85.9	101.9
April	123.5	104.0	54.6	122.4	103.5	100.8	123.7	122.2	101.5	86.6	103.4
May	124.6	103.8	55.2	124.6	102.6	99.9	123.7	120.7	102.5	85.9	102.1
June	124.1	103.5	53.8	124.5	102.4	99.6	123.8	119.5	102.0	85.8	102.3
July	124.8	104.1	54.5	126.1	102.7	100.0	125.0	120.4	102.5	85.8	102.8
August	125.5	104.2	53.8	126.6	102.8	100.2	126.2	121.6	103.0	85.8	103.2
September	125.4	105.1	53.8	127.8	103.7	101.4	129.1	122.9	104.0	86.1	104.2
October	125.7	104.9	54.4	127.5	103.5	101.3	128.5	122.6	103.8	86.3	104.3
November	126.1	105.7	53.6	130.1	104.0	102.0	130.0	123.2	105.2	87.2	105.1
December	126.5	106.1	55.3	130.4	104.3	102.6	130.6	123.2	105.0	87.4	106.0
1994:											
January	128.0	106.4	54.7	130.3	104.8	103.3	133.7	122.6	105.5	87.9	106.5
February	126.4	105.1	54.2	127.6	103.7	102.5	129.8	119.8	103.8	88.2	106.0
March	128.3	107.9	54.0	133.7	106.0	104.7	133.9	126.0	106.8	89.6	107.9
April	128.7	108.0	54.2	134.1	106.0	104.6	134.4	125.1	107.6	89.0	108.0
May	129.6	108.8	53.9	136.0	106.6	105.5	135.7	126.7	108.6	89.8	109.3
June	129.7	108.9	54.1	135.5	106.9	105.8	136.0	128.0	108.1	90.2	109.6
July	130.2	109.4	54.5	136.0	107.3	106.3	136.9	128.6	108.3	91.2	110.6
August	130.2	109.4	54.4	136.2	107.4	106.6	136.5	128.0	108.4	91.3	111.3
September	130.7	109.6	54.7	137.1	107.4	106.7	136.4	128.3	108.4	92.2	111.1
October	132.0	110.1	54.3	136.6	108.1	107.7	136.9	129.6	108.6	92.7	112.4
November	131.8	110.8	55.3	139.0	108.5	108.4	137.4	128.6	109.4	93.5	113.3
December	132.1	111.4	55.0	140.6	109.0	108.8	138.5	128.9	109.4	93.6	113.9
1995:											
January	133.6	112.2	55.4	142.6	109.5	109.6	139.8	129.6	109.9	93.6	115.8
February	132.6	110.8	54.3	138.2	108.7	108.9	137.4	129.5	108.4	93.5	114.8
March	132.8	111.0	53.8	140.2	108.5	109.1	137.3	127.9	109.2	93.3	115.0
April	133.7	110.2	54.6	138.9	107.8	108.0	135.7	125.1	108.7	93.0	113.4
May	131.9	109.3	53.8	135.7	107.3	107.6	134.2	124.8	107.6	92.0	113.3
June	133.0	109.9	53.9	139.6	107.2	107.6	133.9	124.5	108.4	92.0	112.7
July	133.6	109.7	53.9	140.6	106.7	107.2	133.8	122.9	108.4	90.1	112.2
August	133.4	110.0	53.7	140.6	107.2	108.0	135.0	125.1	108.7	91.2	113.0
September	133.9	110.1	53.9	141.5	107.1	108.0	135.2	124.2	108.9	91.1	113.4
October	134.4	110.3	54.1	143.5	106.9	107.9	135.7	124.2	108.7	91.5	113.3
November	134.3	110.0	53.4	142.1	106.9	108.2	135.7	124.5	108.7	92.4	113.2
December	133.9	109.3	53.7	140.7	106.3	107.6	135.1	123.9	107.9	91.8	112.9
1996:											
January	132.5	106.9	53.1	140.9	103.1	105.2	131.2	112.3	105.6	90.9	110.5
February	135.1	110.9	54.9	146.7	106.8	108.3	135.9	122.9	109.9	92.6	112.9
March	135.4	110.2	55.2	145.5	106.3	107.4	136.4	122.9	109.9	92.0	113.0
April	135.1	110.6	54.8	146.1	106.7	108.6	137.1	122.0	109.7	91.9	113.5
May	135.7	111.0	55.4	145.8	107.2	109.2	138.2	123.9	109.9	92.4	114.2
June	137.6	111.4	55.8	147.4	107.3	109.4	139.5	123.6	110.2	93.2	114.9
July	136.1	110.9	54.7	147.4	106.8	108.9	139.0	124.2	109.7	91.6	114.7
August	137.1	111.4	55.1	148.2	107.2	109.5	139.3	123.9	109.9	93.2	115.0
September	137.9	111.3	54.9	148.1	107.1	109.4	138.6	123.9	109.9	93.2	115.1
October	137.2	111.4	55.0	149.4	106.9	109.2	139.4	123.6	110.7	92.9	114.9
November	137.9	111.7	55.2	150.0	107.2	109.6	140.1	124.5	110.2	92.7	115.1
December	139.1	112.4	55.7	151.2	107.8	110.3	140.9	125.7	111.0	93.3	115.5

1. Additional industry detail available in individual industry profile sections.

INDEXES OF AGGREGATE WEEKLY HOURS—Continued
(Production or nonsupervisory workers on private nonagricultural payrolls—1982=100, seasonally adjusted)

YEAR AND MONTH	Manufacturing—Continued										
	Durable goods—Continued					Nondurable goods					
	Industrial machinery and equipment	Electronic and electric equipment	Transportation equipment[1]	Instruments and products	Miscellaneous manufacturing	Total	Food and products	Tobacco products	Textile mill products	Apparel and other textile products	Paper and products
1968	105.2	....	141.7	....	126.1	115.7	109.5	134.8	150.6	131.3	111.4
1969	109.4	....	138.5	....	126.5	116.5	110.5	128.8	150.0	130.5	114.6
1970	101.2	....	114.1	....	119.8	112.4	110.2	129.2	141.8	123.9	110.2
1971	89.5	....	112.6	....	116.2	110.8	109.3	118.7	141.3	122.9	106.4
1972	97.8	....	118.4	....	126.2	114.1	108.7	115.9	148.9	127.8	110.3
1973	111.8	....	129.1	....	130.9	116.0	106.3	124.0	150.7	131.7	112.7
1974	116.1	....	117.9	....	128.8	112.1	106.0	120.9	138.5	121.3	111.2
1975	101.6	....	106.8	....	112.5	102.1	101.8	118.1	122.9	110.2	96.8
1976	102.6	....	117.9		120.1	108.1	104.4	118.2	133.3	119.3	104.7
1977	109.8	....	125.6		122.2	110.2	104.6	106.8	132.9	117.9	107.6
1978	119.4	....	133.6		125.9	112.0	105.1	106.1	131.6	119.5	109.0
1979	126.9	....	134.1		123.8	112.3	107.0	104.4	129.3	115.6	110.5
1980	122.1	....	114.6		113.9	108.1	105.1	101.2	122.7	112.2	106.9
1981	120.2	....	114.2		110.5	107.6	102.8	105.1	117.3	111.0	106.8
1982	100.0	....	100.0		100.0	100.0	100.0	100.0	100.0	100.0	100.0
1983	90.1	....	105.7		98.1	102.4	99.1	96.3	107.4	104.5	102.1
1984	103.8	....	118.9		102.9	105.5	100.3	93.5	107.0	107.2	106.8
1985	101.0	....	122.7		97.8	103.4	100.6	88.4	100.1	100.7	106.8
1986	94.7	....	123.3		97.5	104.2	101.7	81.6	103.8	99.7	106.9
1987	93.8	....	124.3		99.9	106.6	103.7	80.1	109.4	100.1	108.5
1988	98.8	113.1	125.8	89.9	103.5	107.7	105.0	80.1	107.7	99.0	108.9
1989	100.3	111.5	125.3	89.6	103.0	108.2	107.8	70.6	105.6	98.3	109.9
1990	97.5	106.5	119.1	87.6	101.1	106.8	109.7	70.6	98.4	92.9	110.4
1991	91.8	100.7	113.3	84.0	98.1	105.9	110.2	70.2	97.0	91.3	109.3
1992	89.6	99.1	110.9	80.2	99.4	106.6	110.9	68.2	98.6	92.2	110.5
1993	92.7	100.9	111.4	77.0	101.6	107.4	112.6	60.7	98.9	90.4	110.9
1994	99.3	105.7	118.5	75.2	104.2	109.2	114.6	64.1	99.4	89.7	112.3
1995	103.5	107.8	121.6	73.7	103.3	107.6	115.5	62.8	94.9	84.2	110.5
1996	104.8	108.0	122.7	75.2	101.8	105.1	115.9	63.2	88.9	76.9	109.1
1993:											
January	91.4	100.1	112.2	78.9	100.3	106.4	112.1	64.7	100.1	92.2	110.7
February	91.6	100.8	112.3	78.6	101.3	106.8	112.4	64.1	100.2	92.6	111.2
March	91.2	100.3	111.3	77.8	101.1	105.3	111.6	58.1	95.1	90.8	110.7
April	92.6	101.4	111.9	78.8	102.8	107.1	112.3	59.7	100.4	92.8	111.7
May	92.0	100.4	110.0	77.5	101.3	106.4	111.7	60.3	99.7	91.2	111.0
June	92.1	99.7	109.0	77.0	101.0	106.2	112.1	61.0	98.4	90.4	111.0
July	92.9	100.2	109.7	76.5	101.0	106.4	112.4	58.6	98.3	90.1	110.9
August	92.6	100.5	109.5	76.3	101.3	106.4	113.0	58.6	98.6	90.0	110.8
September	93.7	101.1	111.9	76.6	102.8	106.7	113.2	59.4	99.0	89.7	111.2
October	93.8	101.5	111.5	75.9	102.3	106.5	113.7	58.8	98.6	88.6	110.8
November	94.3	101.8	112.3	75.6	102.1	106.7	113.5	61.6	99.2	89.1	111.0
December	95.3	102.0	113.9	75.6	103.0	106.7	113.4	60.1	98.9	88.6	110.8
1994:											
January	95.8	102.6	115.1	75.8	102.5	106.8	113.4	60.1	98.2	88.3	110.8
February	95.7	101.8	114.6	75.6	100.3	105.4	112.9	58.9	95.5	85.0	110.2
March	97.4	104.2	116.4	76.1	103.5	107.8	114.6	63.6	99.3	89.2	111.9
April	97.6	104.8	115.3	75.8	103.9	107.9	114.1	67.2	99.5	89.6	112.2
May	98.6	104.8	116.5	75.8	104.2	108.1	113.9	65.7	99.7	90.1	112.4
June	99.4	105.5	116.6	75.2	103.9	108.3	114.2	63.9	99.9	90.3	112.6
July	99.4	105.7	116.6	75.4	106.5	108.8	115.4	63.1	100.0	90.4	112.9
August	99.8	106.3	118.1	74.9	105.1	108.4	114.7	65.8	99.6	90.2	112.9
September	100.2	105.9	118.7	74.5	103.6	108.3	114.9	65.0	99.1	89.8	112.6
October	101.1	106.8	120.6	74.5	105.3	108.7	114.2	66.0	100.2	90.6	113.1
November	101.5	107.4	122.8	74.3	104.7	108.7	115.4	63.1	99.4	89.7	112.8
December	101.9	107.9	123.7	74.2	104.3	109.1	116.1	66.2	99.7	90.1	112.8
1995:											
January	103.0	109.2	123.7	73.8	104.9	109.3	117.2	65.0	99.6	89.6	112.8
February	102.6	107.3	124.3	73.5	104.5	108.4	115.3	62.5	99.6	88.4	111.8
March	102.8	107.6	124.9	73.5	104.0	107.8	114.9	62.0	98.3	87.6	111.5
April	102.5	107.2	122.1	73.3	104.0	107.5	114.3	62.9	98.0	86.6	111.4
May	102.9	107.2	121.2	73.3	103.1	106.9	115.0	61.6	95.6	85.7	110.7
June	103.0	106.8	121.2	73.6	103.6	106.8	116.4	64.0	94.5	84.4	110.0
July	102.8	107.0	121.4	73.8	101.9	106.1	115.9	63.5	93.3	83.6	110.5
August	104.0	107.5	121.4	74.2	102.9	106.0	115.7	65.5	93.9	82.7	110.0
September	103.9	108.0	121.2	74.0	103.0	105.9	116.2	61.2	92.9	82.2	110.1
October	104.4	109.1	118.8	74.3	102.6	105.5	115.8	61.8	92.0	80.8	109.4
November	105.5	108.5	119.0	74.2	103.1	105.1	115.4	63.4	91.7	80.3	109.2
December	104.3	107.2	119.4	73.6	102.3	104.5	114.7	60.9	90.6	79.6	109.0
1996:											
January	102.6	105.4	118.1	72.0	97.6	100.3	113.4	58.1	79.5	71.7	105.4
February	104.4	108.5	120.7	74.9	102.0	104.9	116.9	62.8	90.4	78.8	109.1
March	104.5	108.1	114.8	75.1	102.4	104.8	117.3	64.2	90.1	78.3	108.8
April	104.8	107.5	123.1	74.7	101.8	104.2	116.3	63.2	88.8	77.4	108.9
May	104.8	108.1	124.1	75.2	102.3	104.4	116.3	62.8	89.3	77.7	108.9
June	104.8	108.4	123.5	75.6	102.0	104.5	115.6	62.5	89.7	78.0	109.0
July	104.5	107.8	123.0	74.7	101.6	103.9	114.7	62.6	89.4	77.2	108.5
August	104.6	108.4	124.9	75.4	101.3	104.0	114.7	61.0	89.2	76.9	109.0
September	104.4	108.1	124.2	75.4	101.8	103.9	115.1	64.0	89.0	76.4	109.4
October	104.6	107.5	123.1	75.4	101.5	103.9	115.7	63.1	89.2	76.0	109.4
November	104.9	107.4	124.7	75.6	101.8	103.9	116.0	66.4	89.4	75.5	109.9
December	105.7	108.0	125.5	75.8	103.4	104.5	116.9	65.1	90.0	75.3	110.2

1. Additional industry detail available in individual industry profile sections.

INDEXES OF AGGREGATE WEEKLY HOURS—Continued
(Production or nonsupervisory workers on private nonagricultural payrolls—1982=100, seasonally adjusted)

YEAR AND MONTH	Nondurable goods manufacturing—Continued					Service-producing industries					
	Printing and publishing	Chemicals and products	Petroleum and coal products	Rubber and miscellaneous plastic products	Leather and products	Total	Transportation and public utilities	Wholesale trade	Retail trade	Finance, insurance, and real estate	Services
1968	98.5	104.1	95.4	87.0	180.0	72.8	93.4	77.7	80.1	67.8	61.3
1969	100.9	106.2	90.9	91.6	168.1	75.7	96.3	80.6	82.6	71.6	64.2
1970	98.9	102.5	96.2	86.3	156.4	76.7	96.9	81.7	83.4	73.0	65.3
1971	95.3	99.8	100.9	87.5	148.7	77.2	95.1	80.4	85.3	74.3	65.6
1972	96.5	100.9	101.5	97.8	150.7	79.6	97.3	82.5	88.2	76.5	68.0
1973	97.4	104.2	99.9	107.9	142.3	82.5	99.9	85.6	90.9	78.9	71.3
1974	95.5	105.7	100.9	105.8	131.8	84.0	100.4	87.6	91.0	79.8	73.9
1975	88.9	97.1	96.3	89.0	121.3	83.9	94.6	86.4	90.6	79.9	76.0
1976	90.3	102.0	102.3	96.1	130.6	86.4	95.5	89.1	93.9	81.5	78.8
1977	94.1	105.0	106.6	109.2	123.9	89.5	97.9	92.5	96.5	85.4	82.0
1978	97.5	107.4	112.2	115.3	125.5	93.6	101.3	97.7	100.0	90.3	86.3
1979	101.0	108.3	114.0	118.2	117.1	96.9	104.9	102.0	101.5	94.4	90.2
1980	100.1	106.0	99.1	106.7	110.7	98.3	104.1	101.9	100.1	97.8	94.3
1981	100.6	106.8	110.0	109.0	113.6	100.8	103.3	103.3	100.6	105.5	98.2
1982	100.0	100.0	100.0	100.0	100.0	100.0	100.0	100.0	100.0	100.0	100.0
1983	103.3	98.3	98.4	107.2	96.8	102.0	97.3	99.9	102.7	101.6	103.6
1984	110.9	99.8	92.5	119.6	89.3	107.1	102.8	105.3	108.2	106.4	108.2
1985	114.9	98.9	88.7	117.6	78.1	111.3	104.6	108.4	111.7	110.9	114.0
1986	119.6	97.3	88.1	119.6	69.5	114.6	104.0	108.5	114.3	116.7	119.2
1987	123.2	99.3	89.4	123.1	70.3	118.5	106.5	109.4	117.9	120.1	124.9
1988	126.7	102.9	88.1	127.3	67.9	122.8	108.2	113.3	121.0	119.2	132.2
1989	126.2	104.5	85.7	129.6	66.4	126.8	111.1	116.1	122.9	119.5	139.3
1990	127.5	104.3	87.2	127.9	62.8	129.1	114.5	115.7	123.0	120.2	144.2
1991	123.3	101.6	86.7	123.2	57.7	128.0	113.4	113.7	119.5	118.3	145.3
1992	122.3	100.0	86.0	127.8	56.6	129.7	113.6	112.8	120.6	118.1	149.3
1993	123.9	100.9	83.1	133.2	55.6	133.7	118.2	112.8	123.4	121.2	155.4
1994	125.9	102.0	81.4	141.9	53.0	139.3	122.4	116.9	128.6	124.0	162.9
1995	125.0	102.5	77.9	143.4	48.3	143.8	123.9	121.1	132.2	122.9	170.5
1996	123.7	101.3	76.1	142.8	43.4	147.8	127.6	122.9	134.8	124.8	176.8
1993:											
January	123.5	99.3	85.6	131.0	57.5	131.5	115.6	112.1	122.0	118.4	152.4
February	123.7	99.3	84.9	132.2	58.4	131.8	115.4	111.9	122.1	118.9	153.1
March	123.1	99.2	82.5	131.5	56.3	131.0	116.1	111.6	119.6	118.7	152.8
April	124.5	99.8	84.8	133.8	56.8	132.3	115.8	112.1	122.2	119.2	154.1
May	123.8	100.8	84.6	132.6	55.6	134.0	116.8	113.1	123.6	121.7	156.0
June	124.2	100.7	82.8	132.8	54.6	133.3	116.5	112.7	122.9	120.5	155.5
July	124.5	101.8	83.0	133.5	54.4	134.0	117.2	113.0	124.0	121.1	156.0
August	123.9	101.3	82.9	133.9	54.6	135.1	117.8	113.2	124.4	124.3	157.4
September	124.2	102.1	81.8	134.4	55.0	134.4	118.1	113.0	124.3	122.1	156.4
October	124.4	101.7	83.2	133.7	54.9	135.0	118.1	113.5	125.1	122.3	157.0
November	124.0	101.9	81.0	135.3	54.3	135.3	118.1	113.8	124.3	123.5	158.1
December	123.9	102.8	80.4	135.7	54.4	135.6	118.5	114.1	125.1	123.2	158.0
1994:											
January	124.8	102.4	81.9	137.0	54.8	137.6	119.9	114.9	126.6	125.5	160.9
February	123.8	101.4	80.1	135.9	54.0	136.0	120.0	114.3	125.0	124.0	158.5
March	125.1	102.4	81.8	140.3	54.0	137.4	120.9	115.2	127.1	124.4	160.0
April	125.9	102.2	81.6	139.6	54.1	138.0	120.5	115.7	127.4	123.9	161.3
May	126.1	102.3	80.1	141.3	53.0	139.0	122.3	116.3	127.8	125.4	162.5
June	126.1	102.0	80.3	142.2	53.0	139.0	122.1	116.6	128.5	124.1	162.2
July	126.4	102.3	80.8	143.1	53.5	139.5	122.0	117.0	129.0	124.0	163.1
August	126.2	101.6	80.8	143.1	52.4	139.5	122.0	117.0	129.0	123.5	163.3
September	126.2	101.2	85.0	142.9	51.7	140.2	122.3	117.8	129.5	123.2	164.5
October	126.7	102.0	81.9	144.1	52.3	141.9	123.0	119.2	131.2	124.2	166.7
November	126.4	102.1	81.3	144.5	51.5	141.2	122.9	118.7	130.6	122.9	166.0
December	126.8	101.9	81.9	145.6	51.9	141.4	122.6	119.6	130.4	122.3	166.7
1995:											
January	126.2	102.3	80.3	147.1	50.9	143.3	123.8	120.5	131.9	123.8	169.3
February	125.8	102.1	81.4	146.3	50.7	142.3	123.2	120.5	130.9	122.2	168.2
March	125.7	101.9	79.8	145.2	50.6	142.6	123.2	120.4	131.0	121.8	168.9
April	125.7	102.5	78.7	144.7	49.9	144.3	124.1	121.3	133.6	123.8	170.4
May	125.4	102.0	78.7	144.0	49.4	142.1	122.5	120.0	131.3	121.0	168.1
June	125.2	102.6	78.1	143.1	48.6	143.4	123.5	121.0	131.6	122.5	170.1
July	125.0	102.3	78.6	140.8	46.9	144.4	124.1	121.9	132.7	124.2	171.1
August	124.7	102.5	76.9	142.0	48.0	143.9	123.8	121.3	132.0	122.7	170.8
September	124.6	102.5	76.9	142.3	47.7	144.6	123.6	121.3	132.7	123.1	172.2
October	124.1	103.1	77.1	142.5	47.0	145.3	125.1	122.0	132.7	123.9	173.1
November	124.6	102.4	75.3	142.5	45.6	145.3	125.1	121.4	133.3	123.0	173.0
December	123.5	102.3	74.7	142.0	45.1	145.0	124.5	121.2	132.5	122.8	173.1
1996:											
January	120.7	101.1	75.7	138.7	41.4	144.0	123.9	120.9	131.0	121.4	172.2
February	124.2	102.8	75.2	141.4	44.5	146.0	126.1	121.7	133.5	123.1	174.3
March	124.0	102.1	75.9	141.4	44.4	146.7	127.0	121.9	134.5	123.7	174.9
April	123.5	101.6	74.4	142.0	44.1	146.1	125.7	121.6	133.5	122.9	174.8
May	123.9	101.6	75.4	142.5	44.0	146.8	126.7	121.9	134.5	123.6	175.5
June	123.7	102.0	78.2	142.9	43.7	149.3	128.9	123.7	135.6	127.6	178.8
July	123.7	101.0	77.1	143.0	43.0	147.5	127.6	122.2	134.5	124.0	176.5
August	124.0	101.0	77.1	144.1	43.3	148.6	128.7	123.2	135.2	125.2	178.0
September	123.7	100.6	76.8	143.8	42.8	149.9	129.0	123.9	135.8	128.1	179.9
October	123.6	100.4	75.0	143.4	42.7	148.7	128.5	123.7	135.9	123.8	178.2
November	123.4	100.7	76.6	142.9	42.4	149.7	129.2	124.2	136.7	126.0	179.1
December	123.9	101.0	77.0	144.5	43.5	151.0	129.3	125.0	137.6	128.3	181.1

AVERAGE HOURLY EARNINGS
(Earnings per production or nonsupervisory worker on private nonagricultural payrolls—Dollars, seasonally adjusted)

YEAR AND MONTH	Total private		Good-producing industries					Service-producing industries					
			Total	Mining[1]	Con-struc-tion[1]	Manufacturing		Total	Trans-portation and pub-lic utilities[1]	Whole-sale trade[1]	Retail trade[1]	Finance, insur-ance, and real estate[1]	Serv-ices[1]
	Current dollars	1982 dollars				Total	Exclud-ing over-time						
1968	2.85	7.89	3.22	3.35	4.41	3.01	2.88	2.59	3.42	3.04	2.16	2.75	2.42
1969	3.04	7.98	3.45	3.60	4.79	3.19	3.05	2.77	3.63	3.23	2.30	2.93	2.61
1970	3.23	8.03	3.67	3.85	5.24	3.35	3.23	2.95	3.85	3.43	2.44	3.07	2.81
1971	3.45	8.21	3.94	4.06	5.69	3.57	3.45	3.15	4.21	3.64	2.60	3.22	3.04
1972	3.70	8.53	4.22	4.44	6.06	3.82	3.66	3.38	4.65	3.85	2.75	3.36	3.27
1973	3.94	8.55	4.50	4.75	6.41	4.09	3.91	3.59	5.02	4.07	2.91	3.53	3.47
1974	4.24	8.28	4.84	5.23	6.81	4.42	4.25	3.87	5.41	4.38	3.14	3.77	3.75
1975	4.53	8.12	5.27	5.95	7.31	4.83	4.67	4.14	5.88	4.72	3.36	4.06	4.02
1976	4.86	8.24	5.65	6.46	7.71	5.22	5.02	4.43	6.45	5.02	3.57	4.27	4.31
1977	5.25	8.36	6.10	6.94	8.10	5.68	5.44	4.77	6.99	5.39	3.85	4.54	4.65
1978	5.69	8.40	6.64	7.67	8.66	6.17	5.91	5.17	7.57	5.88	4.20	4.89	4.99
1979	6.16	8.17	7.21	8.49	9.27	6.70	6.43	5.58	8.16	6.39	4.53	5.27	5.36
1980	6.66	7.78	7.83	9.17	9.94	7.27	7.02	6.06	8.87	6.95	4.88	5.79	5.85
1981	7.25	7.69	8.57	10.04	10.82	7.99	7.72	6.59	9.70	7.55	5.25	6.31	6.41
1982	7.68	7.68	9.16	10.77	11.63	8.49	8.25	7.02	10.32	8.08	5.48	6.78	6.92
1983	8.02	7.79	9.48	11.28	11.94	8.83	8.52	7.37	10.79	8.54	5.74	7.29	7.31
1984	8.32	7.80	9.83	11.63	12.13	9.19	8.82	7.62	11.12	8.88	5.85	7.63	7.59
1985	8.57	7.77	10.19	11.98	12.32	9.54	9.16	7.86	11.40	9.15	5.94	7.94	7.90
1986	8.76	7.81	10.39	12.46	12.48	9.73	9.34	8.08	11.70	9.34	6.03	8.36	8.18
1987	8.98	7.73	10.58	12.54	12.71	9.91	9.48	8.32	12.03	9.59	6.12	8.73	8.49
1988	9.28	7.69	10.88	12.80	13.08	10.19	9.73	8.64	12.24	9.98	6.31	9.06	8.88
1989	9.66	7.64	11.22	13.26	13.54	10.48	10.02	9.04	12.57	10.39	6.53	9.53	9.38
1990	10.01	7.52	11.56	13.68	13.77	10.83	10.37	9.42	12.92	10.79	6.75	9.97	9.83
1991	10.32	7.45	11.86	14.19	14.00	11.18	10.71	9.77	13.20	11.15	6.94	10.39	10.23
1992	10.57	7.41	12.09	14.54	14.15	11.46	10.95	10.04	13.43	11.39	7.12	10.82	10.54
1993	10.83	7.39	12.37	14.60	14.38	11.74	11.18	10.30	13.55	11.74	7.29	11.35	10.78
1994	11.12	7.40	12.71	14.88	14.73	12.07	11.43	10.56	13.78	12.06	7.49	11.83	11.04
1995	11.43	7.39	13.04	15.30	15.09	12.37	11.74	10.88	14.13	12.43	7.69	12.32	11.39
1996	11.81	7.43	13.47	15.61	15.46	12.78	12.12	11.25	14.44	12.87	7.99	12.79	11.79
1993:													
January	10.71	7.39	12.20	14.58	14.21	11.59	11.06	10.18	13.51	11.56	7.22	11.10	10.69
February	10.73	7.38	12.23	14.50	14.23	11.62	11.09	10.20	13.48	11.59	7.24	11.13	10.71
March	10.76	7.39	12.26	14.65	14.34	11.63	11.11	10.24	13.57	11.63	7.26	11.14	10.72
April	10.77	7.38	12.30	14.81	14.34	11.67	11.13	10.23	13.55	11.68	7.25	11.21	10.73
May	10.81	7.39	12.34	14.75	14.36	11.70	11.15	10.28	13.56	11.76	7.28	11.34	10.77
June	10.80	7.38	12.34	14.59	14.34	11.72	11.17	10.27	13.57	11.72	7.28	11.31	10.75
July	10.83	7.39	12.39	14.57	14.42	11.75	11.19	10.29	13.59	11.76	7.29	11.39	10.77
August	10.86	7.39	12.40	14.57	14.41	11.77	11.21	10.33	13.57	11.82	7.31	11.46	10.82
September	10.87	7.39	12.42	14.58	14.38	11.81	11.25	10.33	13.58	11.81	7.31	11.44	10.83
October	10.89	7.37	12.45	14.60	14.43	11.83	11.24	10.35	13.54	11.85	7.34	11.52	10.85
November	10.92	7.38	12.49	14.47	14.46	11.87	11.28	10.37	13.54	11.84	7.35	11.55	10.86
December	10.95	7.38	12.53	14.64	14.46	11.92	11.32	10.39	13.62	11.86	7.36	11.59	10.89
1994:													
January	10.98	7.40	12.55	14.88	14.43	11.94	11.33	10.44	13.67	11.93	7.40	11.71	10.92
February	11.02	7.41	12.62	14.81	14.58	12.01	11.41	10.46	13.70	11.93	7.42	11.69	10.93
March	11.02	7.40	12.61	14.77	14.55	11.99	11.36	10.46	13.71	11.93	7.43	11.70	10.94
April	11.05	7.41	12.62	14.88	14.60	11.98	11.34	10.50	13.69	11.99	7.46	11.79	10.98
May	11.08	7.42	12.66	14.86	14.66	12.01	11.38	10.53	13.73	12.03	7.47	11.81	11.02
June	11.09	7.39	12.67	14.81	14.69	12.03	11.39	10.53	13.72	12.04	7.49	11.77	11.03
July	11.11	7.38	12.69	14.79	14.73	12.04	11.40	10.55	13.75	12.06	7.50	11.81	11.05
August	11.13	7.36	12.73	14.82	14.75	12.08	11.44	10.57	13.79	12.06	7.51	11.81	11.07
September	11.16	7.37	12.77	14.96	14.82	12.11	11.47	10.60	13.80	12.10	7.53	11.88	11.10
October	11.22	7.40	12.82	15.03	14.93	12.15	11.49	10.66	13.89	12.21	7.55	12.02	11.17
November	11.22	7.38	12.84	15.00	14.87	12.18	11.52	10.65	13.91	12.18	7.56	11.95	11.14
December	11.25	7.38	12.85	15.03	14.86	12.19	11.53	10.68	13.96	12.21	7.59	11.99	11.18
1995:													
January	11.27	7.38	12.85	15.04	14.71	12.23	11.56	10.72	13.96	12.27	7.58	12.09	11.23
February	11.31	7.39	12.93	15.09	14.96	12.28	11.62	10.74	13.95	12.28	7.61	12.09	11.25
March	11.32	7.37	12.93	15.16	14.98	12.27	11.63	10.75	14.00	12.29	7.61	12.15	11.26
April	11.36	7.38	12.96	15.20	15.02	12.29	11.76	10.81	14.03	12.42	7.63	12.23	11.34
May	11.36	7.36	12.96	15.23	15.04	12.30	11.68	10.80	14.04	12.35	7.65	12.21	11.33
June	11.40	7.37	13.01	15.31	15.12	12.32	11.71	10.85	14.11	12.40	7.68	12.28	11.36
July	11.46	7.41	13.08	15.41	15.11	12.40	11.78	10.91	14.17	12.47	7.71	12.42	11.43
August	11.46	7.39	13.09	15.43	15.14	12.41	11.78	10.90	14.16	12.46	7.73	12.36	11.41
September	11.50	7.41	13.11	15.40	15.16	12.43	11.80	10.94	14.22	12.51	7.76	12.42	11.45
October	11.55	7.42	13.16	15.46	15.19	12.47	11.84	11.00	14.30	12.55	7.75	12.51	11.52
November	11.56	7.42	13.18	15.45	15.22	12.50	11.87	11.00	14.31	12.56	7.77	12.49	11.53
December	11.58	7.41	13.19	15.48	15.18	12.52	11.90	11.03	14.28	12.60	7.80	12.55	11.55
1996:													
January	11.62	7.41	13.31	15.43	15.26	12.64	12.00	11.06	14.28	12.60	7.83	12.53	11.59
February	11.64	7.40	13.28	15.47	15.25	12.60	11.96	11.08	14.32	12.65	7.85	12.59	11.60
March	11.66	7.39	13.24	15.46	15.27	12.54	11.92	11.12	14.35	12.71	7.88	12.66	11.65
April	11.71	7.40	13.38	15.46	15.32	12.71	12.09	11.14	14.38	12.73	7.90	12.66	11.67
May	11.74	7.40	13.40	15.50	15.37	12.73	12.06	11.17	14.42	12.76	7.93	12.73	11.70
June	11.81	7.44	13.45	15.59	15.41	12.77	12.11	11.26	14.47	12.94	8.00	12.82	11.77
July	11.81	7.42	13.49	15.61	15.47	12.80	12.14	11.25	14.45	12.84	7.98	12.80	11.78
August	11.86	7.44	13.54	15.52	15.52	12.85	12.19	11.29	14.50	12.91	8.01	12.84	11.83
September	11.91	7.45	13.57	15.70	15.59	12.87	12.20	11.35	14.51	13.03	8.04	12.91	11.89
October	11.91	7.42	13.57	15.67	15.58	12.87	12.21	11.35	14.43	12.93	8.10	12.86	11.91
November	11.98	7.44	13.62	15.77	15.58	12.93	12.26	11.43	14.53	13.08	8.13	12.98	11.99
December	12.03	7.45	13.69	15.88	15.69	12.99	12.29	11.47	14.56	13.17	8.16	13.00	12.04

1. Additional industry detail available in individual industry profile section.

AVERAGE HOURLY EARNINGS
(Earnings per production or nonsupervisory worker on private nonagricultural payrolls—Dollars, not seasonally adjusted)

YEAR AND MONTH	Total private	Goods-producing industries Total	Mining	Construction	Manufacturing Total	Durable goods Total	Lumber and products	Furniture and fixtures	Stone, clay, and glass products	Primary metal industries[1]
1968	2.85	3.22	3.35	4.41	3.01	3.18	2.58	2.47	2.99	3.55
1969	3.04	3.45	3.60	4.79	3.19	3.38	2.75	2.62	3.19	3.79
1970	3.23	3.67	3.85	5.24	3.35	3.55	2.97	2.77	3.40	3.93
1971	3.45	3.94	4.06	5.69	3.57	3.79	3.18	2.90	3.67	4.23
1972	3.70	4.22	4.44	6.06	3.82	4.07	3.34	3.08	3.94	4.66
1973	3.94	4.50	4.75	6.41	4.09	4.35	3.62	3.29	4.22	5.04
1974	4.24	4.84	5.23	6.81	4.42	4.70	3.90	3.53	4.54	5.60
1975	4.53	5.27	5.95	7.31	4.83	5.15	4.28	3.78	4.92	6.18
1976	4.86	5.65	6.46	7.71	5.22	5.57	4.74	3.99	5.33	6.77
1977	5.25	6.10	6.94	8.10	5.68	6.06	5.11	4.34	5.81	7.40
1978	5.69	6.64	7.67	8.66	6.17	6.58	5.62	4.68	6.32	8.20
1979	6.16	7.21	8.49	9.27	6.70	7.12	6.08	5.06	6.85	8.98
1980	6.66	7.83	9.17	9.94	7.27	7.75	6.57	5.49	7.50	9.77
1981	7.25	8.57	10.04	10.82	7.99	8.53	7.02	5.91	8.27	10.81
1982	7.68	9.16	10.77	11.63	8.49	9.03	7.46	6.31	8.87	11.33
1983	8.02	9.48	11.28	11.94	8.83	9.38	7.82	6.62	9.27	11.35
1984	8.32	9.83	11.63	12.13	9.19	9.73	8.05	6.84	9.57	11.47
1985	8.57	10.19	11.98	12.32	9.54	10.09	8.25	7.17	9.84	11.67
1986	8.76	10.39	12.46	12.48	9.73	10.28	8.37	7.46	10.04	11.86
1987	8.98	10.58	12.54	12.71	9.91	10.43	8.43	7.67	10.25	11.94
1988	9.28	10.88	12.80	13.08	10.19	10.71	8.59	7.95	10.56	12.16
1989	9.66	11.22	13.26	13.54	10.48	11.01	8.84	8.25	10.82	12.43
1990	10.01	11.56	13.68	13.77	10.83	11.35	9.08	8.52	11.12	12.92
1991	10.32	11.86	14.19	14.00	11.18	11.75	9.24	8.76	11.36	13.33
1992	10.57	12.09	14.54	14.15	11.46	12.02	9.44	9.01	11.60	13.66
1993	10.83	12.37	14.60	14.38	11.74	12.33	9.61	9.27	11.85	13.99
1994	11.12	12.71	14.88	14.73	12.07	12.68	9.84	9.55	12.13	14.34
1995	11.43	13.04	15.30	15.09	12.37	12.94	10.12	9.82	12.41	14.62
1996	11.81	13.47	15.61	15.46	12.78	13.34	10.44	10.15	12.82	14.97
1993:										
January	10.76	12.16	14.73	14.21	11.61	12.18	9.46	9.16	11.63	13.74
February	10.76	12.15	14.60	14.13	11.61	12.19	9.51	9.12	11.67	13.81
March	10.79	12.21	14.71	14.29	11.63	12.20	9.50	9.11	11.69	13.81
April	10.79	12.30	14.89	14.27	11.70	12.25	9.51	9.14	11.80	13.94
May	10.82	12.35	14.72	14.33	11.71	12.30	9.56	9.17	11.81	13.93
June	10.76	12.35	14.59	14.25	11.71	12.31	9.56	9.23	11.83	14.02
July	10.76	12.40	14.48	14.38	11.72	12.28	9.65	9.28	11.90	14.06
August	10.78	12.40	14.44	14.46	11.70	12.29	9.68	9.33	11.90	14.00
September	10.91	12.51	14.53	14.54	11.85	12.44	9.73	9.40	12.04	14.21
October	10.94	12.49	14.46	14.57	11.80	12.40	9.71	9.40	11.93	14.01
November	10.96	12.50	14.43	14.49	11.87	12.49	9.67	9.44	12.00	14.09
December	10.97	12.58	14.67	14.48	12.00	12.62	9.73	9.44	11.97	14.27
1994:										
January	11.06	12.51	15.06	14.43	11.96	12.56	9.75	9.41	11.97	14.17
February	11.06	12.54	14.92	14.48	12.00	12.61	9.71	9.41	11.98	14.25
March	11.04	12.55	14.84	14.48	11.99	12.59	9.70	9.38	11.94	14.21
April	11.07	12.61	14.96	14.52	12.01	12.61	9.74	9.45	12.04	14.22
May	11.09	12.67	14.83	14.63	12.02	12.63	9.80	9.45	12.11	14.25
June	11.03	12.68	14.73	14.60	12.03	12.64	9.84	9.48	12.15	14.32
July	11.05	12.76	14.72	14.76	12.05	12.63	9.87	9.54	12.17	14.42
August	11.04	12.73	14.68	14.81	12.01	12.64	9.87	9.57	12.19	14.36
September	11.21	12.87	14.91	14.99	12.15	12.78	9.95	9.69	12.27	14.42
October	11.27	12.86	14.89	15.08	12.11	12.72	9.96	9.70	12.22	14.39
November	11.26	12.85	14.95	14.90	12.18	12.80	9.93	9.68	12.22	14.47
December	11.27	12.89	15.08	14.87	12.27	12.90	9.97	9.77	12.22	14.56
1995:										
January	11.35	12.81	15.23	14.71	12.25	12.84	9.95	9.68	12.20	14.57
February	11.35	12.83	15.24	14.87	12.26	12.86	9.94	9.67	12.24	14.46
March	11.34	12.87	15.22	14.88	12.27	12.86	9.94	9.68	12.26	14.45
April	11.38	12.94	15.30	14.93	12.30	12.84	9.97	9.76	12.44	14.76
May	11.35	12.97	15.19	15.01	12.30	12.87	10.01	9.71	12.32	14.53
June	11.33	13.02	15.23	15.04	12.32	12.89	10.11	9.78	12.37	14.61
July	11.39	13.14	15.34	15.15	12.40	12.94	10.21	9.83	12.46	14.69
August	11.36	13.10	15.29	15.20	12.35	12.93	10.20	9.89	12.47	14.63
September	11.54	13.22	15.35	15.35	12.47	13.06	10.28	9.95	12.55	14.70
October	11.59	13.20	15.33	15.35	12.43	12.98	10.27	9.92	12.54	14.64
November	11.58	13.19	15.35	15.26	12.49	13.03	10.22	9.95	12.57	14.73
December	11.60	13.22	15.54	15.15	12.60	13.13	10.29	10.00	12.54	14.69
1996:										
January	11.70	13.27	15.63	15.26	12.66	13.17	10.28	10.01	12.60	14.84
February	11.68	13.19	15.61	15.16	12.57	13.12	10.23	9.95	12.56	14.70
March	11.68	13.17	15.50	15.16	12.54	13.05	10.29	10.00	12.60	14.73
April	11.74	13.36	15.55	15.22	12.73	13.28	10.33	10.06	12.77	14.98
May	11.72	13.37	15.44	15.29	12.71	13.27	10.34	10.08	12.74	14.82
June	11.75	13.45	15.58	15.34	12.75	13.33	10.45	10.11	12.82	14.91
July	11.73	13.54	15.54	15.51	12.79	13.35	10.47	10.13	12.94	15.08
August	11.76	13.54	15.51	15.57	12.79	13.39	10.54	10.19	12.92	15.02
September	11.95	13.66	15.73	15.75	12.90	13.52	10.57	10.27	12.99	15.18
October	11.95	13.62	15.54	15.75	12.83	13.42	10.56	10.28	12.91	15.09
November	12.00	13.63	15.67	15.62	12.93	13.49	10.57	10.28	12.96	15.18
December	12.06	13.73	15.95	15.66	13.07	13.64	10.61	10.43	12.93	15.15

1. Additional industry detail available in individual industry profile section.

AVERAGE HOURLY EARNINGS—Continued
(Earnings per production or nonsupervisory worker on private nonagricultural payrolls—Dollars, not seasonally adjusted)

YEAR AND MONTH	Manufacturing—Continued										
	Durable goods by industry—Continued						Nondurable goods				
	Fabricated metal products	Industrial machinery and equipment[1]	Electronic and electric equipment[1]	Transportation equipment[1]	Instruments and products	Miscellaneous manufacturing	Total	Food and products	Tobacco products	Textile mill products	Apparel and other textile products
1968	3.16	3.36	....	3.69	....	2.50	2.74	2.80	2.48	2.21	2.21
1969	3.34	3.58	....	3.89	....	2.66	2.91	2.96	2.62	2.35	2.31
1970	3.53	3.77	....	4.06	....	2.83	3.08	3.16	2.91	2.45	2.39
1971	3.77	4.02	....	4.45	....	2.97	3.27	3.38	3.16	2.57	2.49
1972	4.05	4.32	....	4.81	....	3.11	3.48	3.60	3.47	2.75	2.60
1973	4.29	4.60	....	5.15	....	3.29	3.70	3.85	3.76	2.95	2.76
1974	4.61	4.94	....	5.54	....	3.53	4.01	4.19	4.12	3.20	2.97
1975	5.05	5.37	....	6.07	....	3.81	4.37	4.61	4.55	3.42	3.17
1976	5.50	5.79	....	6.62	....	4.04	4.71	4.98	4.98	3.69	3.40
1977	5.91	6.26	....	7.29	....	4.36	5.11	5.37	5.54	3.99	3.62
1978	6.35	6.78	....	7.91	....	4.69	5.54	5.80	6.13	4.30	3.94
1979	6.85	7.32	....	8.53	....	5.03	6.01	6.27	6.67	4.66	4.23
1980	7.45	8.00	....	9.35	....	5.46	6.56	6.85	7.74	5.07	4.56
1981	8.20	8.81	....	10.39	....	5.97	7.19	7.44	8.88	5.52	4.97
1982	8.77	9.26	....	11.11	....	6.42	7.75	7.92	9.79	5.83	5.20
1983	9.12	9.56	....	11.67	....	6.81	8.09	8.19	10.38	6.18	5.38
1984	9.40	9.97	....	12.20	....	7.05	8.39	8.39	11.22	6.46	5.55
1985	9.71	10.30	....	12.71	....	7.30	8.72	8.57	11.96	6.70	5.73
1986	9.89	10.58	....	12.81	....	7.55	8.95	8.75	12.88	6.93	5.84
1987	10.01	10.73	....	12.94	....	7.76	9.19	8.93	14.07	7.17	5.94
1988	10.29	11.08	9.79	13.29	10.60	8.00	9.45	9.12	14.67	7.38	6.12
1989	10.57	11.40	10.05	13.67	10.83	8.29	9.75	9.38	15.31	7.67	6.35
1990	10.83	11.77	10.30	14.08	11.29	8.61	10.12	9.62	16.23	8.02	6.57
1991	11.19	12.15	10.70	14.75	11.64	8.85	10.44	9.90	16.77	8.30	6.77
1992	11.42	12.41	11.00	15.20	11.89	9.15	10.73	10.20	16.92	8.60	6.95
1993	11.69	12.73	11.24	15.80	12.23	9.39	10.98	10.45	16.89	8.88	7.09
1994	11.93	13.00	11.50	16.51	12.47	9.67	11.24	10.66	19.07	9.13	7.34
1995	12.13	13.24	11.69	16.74	12.71	10.05	11.58	10.93	19.41	9.41	7.64
1996	12.52	13.59	12.18	17.20	13.14	10.38	11.97	11.20	19.34	9.69	7.96
1993:											
January	11.54	12.59	11.14	15.46	12.08	9.35	10.87	10.33	15.69	8.80	7.05
February	11.55	12.61	11.10	15.50	12.09	9.33	10.86	10.30	16.23	8.81	7.04
March	11.55	12.59	11.12	15.59	12.13	9.29	10.88	10.34	16.89	8.75	7.05
April	11.62	12.65	11.15	15.65	12.19	9.35	10.98	10.47	17.46	8.88	7.06
May	11.69	12.65	11.18	15.79	12.20	9.34	10.94	10.47	17.89	8.86	7.05
June	11.69	12.68	11.25	15.77	12.18	9.36	10.95	10.47	18.06	8.86	7.07
July	11.65	12.76	11.25	15.52	12.24	9.39	11.01	10.49	18.47	8.87	7.01
August	11.67	12.74	11.26	15.67	12.25	9.32	10.95	10.42	17.30	8.90	7.07
September	11.81	12.84	11.31	15.98	12.33	9.43	11.09	10.50	16.32	8.95	7.15
October	11.74	12.82	11.28	15.98	12.32	9.42	11.02	10.38	16.05	8.95	7.14
November	11.82	12.87	11.36	16.18	12.36	9.48	11.07	10.55	16.43	8.97	7.18
December	11.91	13.00	11.51	16.41	12.46	9.58	11.16	10.63	16.80	9.00	7.25
1994:											
January	11.87	12.92	11.40	16.25	12.42	9.58	11.15	10.58	17.00	9.03	7.22
February	11.89	12.95	11.44	16.35	12.43	9.57	11.18	10.56	18.21	9.03	7.22
March	11.89	12.95	11.45	16.36	12.42	9.56	11.17	10.61	18.67	9.02	7.25
April	11.90	12.94	11.45	16.43	12.43	9.61	11.19	10.63	19.58	9.09	7.28
May	11.89	12.95	11.48	16.42	12.37	9.61	11.19	10.64	20.22	9.06	7.28
June	11.90	12.95	11.52	16.45	12.42	9.61	11.21	10.65	20.75	9.11	7.33
July	11.86	12.95	11.56	16.44	12.46	9.63	11.28	10.68	20.57	9.11	7.31
August	11.87	12.93	11.52	16.47	12.47	9.65	11.19	10.59	18.87	9.12	7.36
September	11.99	13.05	11.57	16.75	12.54	9.73	11.30	10.64	18.84	9.20	7.45
October	11.92	13.04	11.51	16.57	12.54	9.75	11.29	10.64	18.69	9.18	7.44
November	12.03	13.12	11.53	16.68	12.53	9.82	11.34	10.81	19.41	9.26	7.46
December	12.09	13.20	11.59	16.89	12.62	9.94	11.41	10.85	18.55	9.30	7.48
1995:											
January	12.04	13.16	11.58	16.68	12.53	10.01	11.43	10.85	18.60	9.34	7.55
February	12.03	13.17	11.53	16.78	12.62	9.98	11.41	10.82	19.53	9.31	7.49
March	12.05	13.17	11.54	16.75	12.62	9.94	11.44	10.87	20.30	9.29	7.53
April	12.03	13.07	11.52	16.56	12.67	9.98	11.56	10.92	19.98	9.35	7.62
May	12.08	13.17	11.56	16.65	12.65	10.02	11.50	10.90	20.97	9.34	7.57
June	12.05	13.17	11.63	16.71	12.68	9.98	11.53	10.92	21.85	9.37	7.62
July	12.11	13.23	11.74	16.72	12.76	10.06	11.65	10.92	21.71	9.39	7.64
August	12.11	13.25	11.76	16.66	12.70	9.98	11.56	10.89	18.49	9.45	7.68
September	12.22	13.34	11.81	16.95	12.81	10.11	11.65	10.97	17.57	9.50	7.72
October	12.19	13.33	11.79	16.74	12.76	10.13	11.67	10.92	18.09	9.49	7.73
November	12.26	13.39	11.83	16.79	12.83	10.15	11.73	11.05	19.48	9.53	7.77
December	12.42	13.47	11.93	16.88	12.89	10.27	11.84	11.17	17.71	9.57	7.83
1996:											
January	12.38	13.44	11.95	16.88	13.00	10.30	11.91	11.08	18.38	9.56	7.87
February	12.32	13.40	11.88	16.95	12.94	10.25	11.79	11.03	18.13	9.55	7.82
March	12.32	13.36	11.91	16.64	12.96	10.24	11.83	11.10	19.34	9.55	7.86
April	12.47	13.44	12.01	17.22	13.03	10.33	11.93	11.19	20.40	9.65	7.95
May	12.46	13.45	12.09	17.19	13.04	10.34	11.89	11.18	21.04	9.62	7.94
June	12.53	13.51	12.19	17.23	13.09	10.33	11.92	11.22	21.37	9.68	7.99
July	12.51	13.55	12.26	17.29	13.18	10.37	12.00	11.25	20.98	9.68	7.95
August	12.54	13.63	12.28	17.28	13.18	10.37	11.95	11.16	20.27	9.72	7.94
September	12.67	13.77	12.35	17.45	13.31	10.48	12.01	11.19	18.37	9.78	8.00
October	12.55	13.70	12.33	17.25	13.27	10.47	12.00	11.16	17.73	9.73	8.03
November	12.62	13.80	12.36	17.35	13.34	10.52	12.12	11.38	18.60	9.77	8.01
December	12.79	13.97	12.54	17.57	13.39	10.59	12.24	11.46	18.67	9.92	8.15

1. Additional industry detail available in individual industry profile section.

AVERAGE HOURLY EARNINGS—Continued
(Earnings per production or nonsupervisory worker on private nonagricultural payrolls—Dollars, not seasonally adjusted)

| YEAR AND MONTH | Manufacturing—Continued | | | | | | Service-producing industries | | | | | |
| | Nondurable goods by industry—Continued | | | | | | | | | | | |
	Paper and products	Printing and publishing	Chemicals and products	Petroleum and coal products	Rubber and miscellaneous plastic products	Leather and products	Total	Transportation and public utilities[1]	Wholesale trade[1]	Retail trade[1]	Finance, insurance, and real estate[1]	Services[1]
1968	3.05	3.48	3.26	3.75	2.93	2.23	2.59	3.42	3.04	2.16	2.75	2.42
1969	3.24	3.69	3.47	4.00	3.08	2.36	2.77	3.63	3.23	2.30	2.93	2.61
1970	3.44	3.92	3.69	4.28	3.21	2.49	2.95	3.85	3.43	2.44	3.07	2.81
1971	3.67	4.20	3.97	4.57	3.41	2.59	3.15	4.21	3.64	2.60	3.22	3.04
1972	3.95	4.51	4.26	4.96	3.63	2.68	3.38	4.65	3.85	2.75	3.36	3.27
1973	4.20	4.75	4.51	5.28	3.84	2.79	3.59	5.02	4.07	2.91	3.53	3.47
1974	4.53	5.03	4.88	5.68	4.09	2.99	3.87	5.41	4.38	3.14	3.77	3.75
1975	5.01	5.38	5.39	6.48	4.42	3.21	4.14	5.88	4.72	3.36	4.06	4.02
1976	5.47	5.71	5.91	7.21	4.71	3.40	4.43	6.45	5.02	3.57	4.27	4.31
1977	5.96	6.12	6.43	7.83	5.21	3.61	4.77	6.99	5.39	3.85	4.54	4.65
1978	6.52	6.51	7.02	8.63	5.57	3.89	5.17	7.57	5.88	4.20	4.89	4.99
1979	7.13	6.94	7.60	9.36	6.02	4.22	5.58	8.16	6.39	4.53	5.27	5.36
1980	7.84	7.53	8.30	10.10	6.58	4.58	6.06	8.87	6.95	4.88	5.79	5.85
1981	8.60	8.19	9.12	11.38	7.22	4.99	6.59	9.70	7.55	5.25	6.31	6.41
1982	9.32	8.74	9.96	12.46	7.70	5.33	7.02	10.32	8.08	5.48	6.78	6.92
1983	9.93	9.11	10.58	13.28	8.06	5.54	7.37	10.79	8.54	5.74	7.29	7.31
1984	10.41	9.41	11.07	13.44	8.35	5.71	7.62	11.12	8.88	5.85	7.63	7.59
1985	10.83	9.71	11.56	14.06	8.60	5.83	7.86	11.40	9.15	5.94	7.94	7.90
1986	11.18	9.99	11.98	14.19	8.79	5.92	8.08	11.70	9.34	6.03	8.36	8.18
1987	11.43	10.28	12.37	14.58	8.98	6.08	8.32	12.03	9.59	6.12	8.73	8.49
1988	11.69	10.53	12.71	14.97	9.19	6.28	8.64	12.24	9.98	6.31	9.06	8.88
1989	11.96	10.88	13.09	15.41	9.46	6.59	9.04	12.57	10.39	6.53	9.53	9.38
1990	12.31	11.24	13.54	16.24	9.76	6.91	9.42	12.92	10.79	6.75	9.97	9.83
1991	12.72	11.48	14.04	17.04	10.07	7.18	9.77	13.20	11.15	6.94	10.39	10.23
1992	13.07	11.74	14.51	17.90	10.36	7.42	10.04	13.43	11.39	7.12	10.82	10.54
1993	13.42	11.93	14.82	18.53	10.57	7.63	10.30	13.55	11.74	7.29	11.35	10.78
1994	13.77	12.14	15.13	19.07	10.70	7.97	10.56	13.78	12.06	7.49	11.83	11.04
1995	14.23	12.33	15.62	19.36	10.91	8.17	10.88	14.13	12.43	7.69	12.32	11.39
1996	14.67	12.65	16.17	19.32	11.24	8.56	11.25	14.44	12.87	7.99	12.79	11.79
1993:												
January	13.17	11.84	14.75	18.39	10.53	7.50	10.28	13.50	11.61	7.26	11.14	10.80
February	13.18	11.82	14.77	18.40	10.51	7.49	10.29	13.52	11.63	7.26	11.21	10.80
March	13.22	11.87	14.73	18.66	10.46	7.51	10.29	13.55	11.61	7.27	11.19	10.78
April	13.39	11.86	14.81	18.57	10.59	7.59	10.27	13.53	11.72	7.26	11.23	10.74
May	13.36	11.82	14.76	18.56	10.55	7.60	10.28	13.50	11.76	7.27	11.36	10.76
June	13.39	11.83	14.74	18.46	10.54	7.57	10.20	13.49	11.67	7.26	11.23	10.65
July	13.50	11.91	14.80	18.42	10.58	7.56	10.19	13.57	11.74	7.25	11.27	10.61
August	13.41	11.96	14.74	18.35	10.53	7.64	10.22	13.55	11.77	7.25	11.39	10.65
September	13.67	12.09	14.94	18.67	10.66	7.70	10.34	13.61	11.82	7.32	11.41	10.82
October	13.55	12.04	14.86	18.55	10.60	7.68	10.38	13.58	11.84	7.35	11.52	10.86
November	13.54	12.01	14.92	18.65	10.62	7.81	10.41	13.61	11.83	7.36	11.57	10.91
December	13.62	12.11	15.02	18.68	10.67	7.88	10.42	13.61	11.88	7.36	11.65	10.97
1994:												
January	13.57	12.06	14.96	18.80	10.71	7.90	10.56	13.72	11.99	7.45	11.79	11.05
February	13.61	12.05	15.00	19.23	10.71	7.94	10.56	13.73	11.97	7.45	11.77	11.03
March	13.62	12.11	14.98	19.32	10.68	7.99	10.52	13.68	11.91	7.45	11.75	11.00
April	13.67	12.06	15.04	18.93	10.70	7.96	10.53	13.67	12.04	7.47	11.81	10.99
May	13.71	12.05	15.04	18.76	10.69	7.96	10.53	13.66	12.03	7.47	11.84	11.01
June	13.68	12.08	15.07	18.87	10.72	7.95	10.44	13.63	11.99	7.46	11.67	10.89
July	13.83	12.13	15.15	18.93	10.75	7.97	10.45	13.75	12.05	7.46	11.72	10.89
August	13.79	12.13	15.06	18.75	10.65	7.96	10.44	13.77	12.01	7.44	11.73	10.89
September	13.95	12.27	15.25	19.32	10.65	7.97	10.61	13.83	12.11	7.54	11.85	11.09
October	13.89	12.24	15.28	19.30	10.65	8.01	10.70	13.94	12.21	7.57	12.02	11.19
November	13.91	12.20	15.26	19.25	10.68	8.03	10.69	13.99	12.17	7.57	11.98	11.20
December	13.97	12.26	15.39	19.32	10.79	8.04	10.71	13.95	12.23	7.59	12.05	11.27
1995:												
January	14.00	12.25	15.37	19.18	10.81	8.10	10.84	14.01	12.33	7.63	12.17	11.36
February	14.01	12.25	15.39	19.55	10.75	8.11	10.84	13.97	12.31	7.63	12.20	11.35
March	14.02	12.27	15.39	19.37	10.79	8.10	10.82	13.98	12.27	7.63	12.21	11.32
April	14.26	12.22	15.69	19.55	10.76	8.28	10.86	14.04	12.47	7.65	12.32	11.38
May	14.15	12.23	15.49	19.17	10.85	8.15	10.79	13.96	12.35	7.64	12.24	11.31
June	14.13	12.25	15.49	19.16	10.90	8.10	10.74	14.02	12.34	7.65	12.19	11.22
July	14.41	12.33	15.68	19.25	11.01	8.01	10.80	14.16	12.46	7.66	12.32	11.26
August	14.20	12.36	15.56	19.14	10.93	8.14	10.76	14.14	12.41	7.65	12.27	11.22
September	14.33	12.50	15.71	19.41	10.99	8.24	10.95	14.25	12.52	7.77	12.39	11.45
October	14.31	12.44	15.79	19.68	11.01	8.23	11.03	14.35	12.56	7.77	12.52	11.54
November	14.38	12.41	15.88	19.46	11.01	8.23	11.02	14.34	12.55	7.78	12.48	11.57
December	14.51	12.50	16.03	19.44	11.15	8.33	11.06	14.32	12.63	7.80	12.56	11.66
1996:												
January	14.58	12.49	16.08	19.41	11.13	8.51	11.18	14.32	12.66	7.89	12.61	11.73
February	14.43	12.49	15.96	19.54	11.14	8.41	11.18	14.34	12.68	7.87	12.69	11.72
March	14.44	12.53	16.00	19.21	11.15	8.46	11.18	14.33	12.69	7.90	12.73	11.72
April	14.61	12.53	16.15	19.32	11.20	8.40	11.20	14.39	12.78	7.92	12.75	11.71
May	14.59	12.54	16.04	18.99	11.20	8.42	11.15	14.34	12.75	7.92	12.74	11.67
June	14.63	12.54	16.11	18.88	11.16	8.47	11.18	14.40	12.88	7.98	12.75	11.66
July	14.79	12.63	16.16	19.02	11.25	8.43	11.12	14.44	12.82	7.93	12.69	11.60
August	14.69	12.70	16.22	18.98	11.23	8.62	11.15	14.48	12.85	7.95	12.71	11.63
September	14.74	12.82	16.25	19.35	11.31	8.69	11.36	14.57	13.03	8.06	12.89	11.89
October	14.74	12.81	16.28	19.35	11.28	8.71	11.37	14.49	12.94	8.12	12.87	11.93
November	14.86	12.83	16.38	19.61	11.33	8.73	11.45	14.57	13.06	8.13	12.97	12.04
December	14.95	12.90	16.45	20.26	11.51	8.83	11.50	14.60	13.20	8.16	13.02	12.16

1. Additional industry detail available in individual industry profile section.

AVERAGE WEEKLY EARNINGS
(Earnings per production or nonsupervisory worker on private nonagricultural payrolls—Dollars)

YEAR AND MONTH	Total private		Goods-producing[1]	Mining[2]	Construction[2]	Manufacturing					
						Total	Durable goods				
	Seasonally adjusted	Not seasonally adjusted					Total	Lumber and products	Furniture and fixtures	Stone, clay, and glass products	Primary metal industries[2]
1968	107.73	107.73	129.44	142.71	164.49	122.51	131.65	104.75	100.28	124.98	147.68
1969	114.61	114.61	138.69	154.80	181.54	129.51	139.59	110.55	105.85	133.66	158.42
1970	119.83	119.83	144.60	164.40	195.45	133.33	143.07	117.61	108.58	140.08	158.77
1971	127.31	127.31	155.24	172.14	211.67	142.44	152.74	126.56	115.42	152.67	169.62
1972	136.90	136.90	168.38	189.14	221.19	154.71	167.68	134.94	123.82	165.48	192.92
1973	145.39	145.39	180.00	201.40	235.89	166.46	180.09	144.80	131.60	176.82	213.19
1974	154.76	154.76	191.18	219.14	249.25	176.80	190.82	152.88	138.02	187.50	232.96
1975	163.53	163.53	205.53	249.31	266.08	190.79	205.49	166.06	143.64	198.77	247.20
1976	175.45	175.45	223.74	273.90	283.73	209.32	226.14	189.13	154.81	219.06	276.22
1977	189.00	189.00	242.78	301.20	295.65	228.90	248.46	203.89	169.26	239.95	305.62
1978	203.70	203.70	264.94	332.88	318.69	249.27	270.44	223.68	183.92	262.91	342.76
1979	219.91	219.91	286.24	365.07	342.99	269.34	290.50	240.16	195.82	284.28	371.77
1980	235.10	235.10	307.72	397.06	367.78	288.62	310.78	253.60	209.17	306.00	391.78
1981	255.20	255.20	338.52	438.75	399.26	318.00	342.91	271.67	226.94	335.76	437.81
1982	267.26	267.26	354.49	459.88	426.82	330.26	354.88	284.23	234.73	355.69	437.34
1983	280.70	280.70	376.36	479.40	442.97	354.08	381.77	313.58	260.83	384.71	459.68
1984	292.86	292.86	395.17	503.58	458.51	374.03	402.82	321.20	271.55	401.94	478.30
1985	299.09	299.09	407.60	519.93	464.46	386.37	415.71	329.18	282.50	412.30	484.31
1986	304.85	304.85	416.64	525.81	466.75	396.01	424.56	338.15	296.91	423.69	496.93
1987	312.50	312.50	426.37	531.70	480.44	406.31	432.85	342.26	306.80	433.58	514.61
1988	322.02	322.02	439.55	541.44	495.73	418.81	447.68	344.46	313.23	446.69	528.96
1989	334.24	334.24	452.17	570.18	513.17	429.68	458.02	354.48	325.88	457.69	534.49
1990	345.35	345.35	465.87	603.29	526.01	441.86	468.76	365.02	333.13	467.04	551.68
1991	353.98	353.98	477.96	630.04	533.40	455.03	482.93	369.60	340.76	473.71	562.53
1992	363.61	363.61	489.65	638.31	537.70	469.86	498.83	383.26	357.70	489.52	587.38
1993	373.64	373.64	505.93	646.78	553.63	486.04	519.09	392.09	371.73	506.00	611.36
1994	385.86	385.86	526.19	666.62	573.00	506.94	543.97	405.41	385.82	526.44	641.00
1995	394.34	394.34	534.64	683.91	587.00	514.59	548.66	410.87	388.87	533.63	643.28
1996	406.26	406.26	553.62	707.13	602.94	531.65	565.62	425.95	399.91	555.11	661.67
1993:											
January	368.42	365.84	488.83	649.59	514.40	477.17	507.91	376.51	364.57	476.83	599.06
February	369.11	366.92	489.65	636.56	518.57	477.17	508.32	383.25	361.15	483.14	600.74
March	367.99	366.86	492.06	632.53	535.88	475.67	508.74	381.90	361.67	483.97	600.74
April	370.49	369.02	496.92	650.69	539.41	479.70	509.60	382.30	361.94	497.96	607.78
May	374.03	375.45	505.12	652.10	561.74	483.62	516.60	391.00	361.30	509.01	607.35
June	371.52	372.30	506.35	643.42	560.03	484.79	518.25	390.05	366.43	511.06	614.08
July	373.64	374.45	504.68	638.57	569.45	480.52	510.85	391.79	368.42	510.51	611.61
August	375.76	378.38	509.64	646.91	574.06	485.55	517.41	398.82	379.73	516.46	607.60
September	375.02	376.40	511.66	646.59	556.88	491.78	523.72	401.85	377.88	521.33	620.98
October	375.71	378.52	515.84	657.93	574.06	493.24	527.00	401.99	382.58	518.96	612.24
November	376.74	378.12	516.25	645.02	559.31	498.54	534.57	400.34	386.10	523.20	622.78
December	377.78	380.66	523.33	654.28	556.03	508.80	547.71	404.77	390.82	513.51	637.87
1994:											
January	382.10	380.46	509.16	664.15	535.35	496.34	532.54	398.78	375.46	502.74	626.31
February	377.99	376.04	501.60	653.50	524.18	490.80	527.10	386.46	358.52	492.38	625.58
March	381.29	379.78	517.06	652.96	553.14	502.38	538.85	397.70	378.01	512.23	632.35
April	382.33	381.92	519.53	665.72	557.57	504.42	540.97	402.26	378.95	522.54	635.63
May	384.48	385.93	525.81	659.94	580.81	504.84	541.83	407.68	377.06	534.05	638.40
June	383.71	383.84	527.49	661.38	579.62	507.67	543.52	409.34	385.84	537.03	640.10
July	384.41	385.65	525.71	660.93	587.45	501.28	532.99	404.67	383.51	533.05	640.25
August	383.99	386.40	529.57	662.07	589.44	504.42	539.73	410.59	390.46	536.36	639.02
September	386.14	390.11	539.25	678.41	599.60	515.16	550.82	412.93	399.23	542.33	648.90
October	390.46	394.45	536.26	673.03	597.17	512.25	548.23	414.34	399.64	540.12	643.23
November	388.21	389.60	535.85	678.73	573.65	517.65	554.24	409.12	396.88	534.01	654.04
December	389.25	392.20	541.38	680.11	576.96	526.38	565.02	415.75	406.43	529.13	665.39
1995:											
January	393.32	390.44	527.77	683.83	556.04	514.50	550.84	404.97	393.01	516.06	655.65
February	390.20	388.17	523.46	678.18	550.19	511.24	547.84	397.60	383.90	512.86	646.36
March	390.54	387.83	527.67	668.16	568.42	511.66	547.83	401.58	381.39	522.28	643.03
April	393.06	390.33	516.31	677.79	562.86	496.92	526.44	400.79	367.95	526.21	639.11
May	388.51	388.17	529.18	672.92	577.89	509.22	543.11	406.41	375.78	530.99	637.87
June	392.16	392.02	536.42	685.35	595.58	512.51	546.54	412.49	386.31	539.33	642.84
July	395.37	396.37	534.80	682.63	606.00	505.92	535.72	408.40	381.40	538.27	628.73
August	394.22	395.33	539.72	683.46	604.96	512.53	546.94	419.22	396.59	544.94	634.94
September	395.60	399.28	549.95	696.89	612.47	523.74	558.97	422.51	399.99	552.20	643.86
October	398.48	402.17	546.48	697.52	615.54	518.33	552.95	423.12	397.79	549.25	639.77
November	397.66	398.35	543.43	687.68	590.56	523.33	557.68	415.95	399.99	543.02	652.54
December	397.19	399.04	544.66	697.75	577.22	529.20	561.96	415.72	407.00	534.20	652.24
1996:											
January	393.92	390.78	521.51	686.16	560.04	503.87	538.65	396.81	359.36	515.34	644.06
February	400.42	398.29	536.83	704.01	579.11	519.14	552.35	407.15	384.07	532.54	648.27
March	401.10	399.46	536.02	697.50	577.60	517.90	548.10	415.72	390.00	538.02	645.17
April	401.65	400.33	543.75	698.20	589.01	524.48	557.76	420.43	389.32	551.66	653.13
May	402.68	402.00	548.17	697.89	594.78	528.74	562.65	426.01	394.13	555.46	653.56
June	409.81	410.08	556.83	716.68	607.46	534.23	569.19	434.72	399.35	565.36	660.51
July	405.08	405.86	552.43	696.19	617.30	525.67	556.70	426.13	398.11	562.89	657.49
August	409.17	409.25	560.56	702.60	621.24	534.62	569.08	436.36	408.62	568.48	662.38
September	413.28	417.06	570.99	722.01	625.28	545.67	582.71	439.71	414.91	575.46	680.06
October	409.70	412.28	565.23	713.29	628.43	537.58	573.03	437.18	414.28	568.04	670.00
November	413.31	414.00	564.28	712.99	606.06	544.35	578.72	433.37	416.34	563.76	675.51
December	417.44	420.89	573.91	733.70	604.48	559.40	594.70	437.13	433.89	557.28	686.30

1. Includes mining, construction and manufacturing.
2. Additional industry detail available in individual industry profile section.

AVERAGE WEEKLY EARNINGS—Continued
(Earnings per production or nonsupervisory worker on private nonagricultural payrolls—Dollars, not seasonally adjusted)

YEAR AND MONTH	Manufacturing—Continued										
	Durable goods—Continued						Nondurable goods by industry				
	Fabricated metal products	Industrial machinery and equipment	Electronic and electric equipment[1]	Transportation equipment[1]	Instruments and products	Miscellaneous manufacturing	Total	Food and products	Tobacco products	Textile mill products	Apparel and other textile products
1968	131.77	141.12	141.12	155.72	155.72	98.50	109.05	114.24	93.99	91.05	79.78
1969	138.94	152.15	152.15	161.44	161.44	103.74	115.53	120.77	97.99	95.88	82.93
1970	143.67	154.95	154.95	163.62	163.62	109.52	120.43	127.98	110.00	97.76	84.37
1971	152.31	163.21	163.21	181.12	181.12	115.53	128.51	136.21	119.45	104.34	88.64
1972	166.86	181.87	181.87	200.58	200.58	122.85	138.16	145.80	130.47	113.58	93.60
1973	178.46	196.88	196.88	216.82	216.82	128.31	146.52	155.54	145.14	120.66	99.08
1974	188.09	207.97	207.97	224.37	224.37	136.61	156.79	169.28	157.80	126.40	104.54
1975	202.51	219.10	219.10	245.23	245.23	146.69	169.56	185.78	173.81	134.41	111.58
1976	224.40	238.55	238.55	276.05	276.05	156.75	185.57	201.69	186.75	147.97	121.72
1977	242.31	259.79	259.79	309.83	309.83	169.17	201.33	214.80	209.41	161.20	128.87
1978	260.35	284.76	284.76	333.80	333.80	181.97	218.28	230.26	233.55	173.72	140.26
1979	278.80	305.24	305.24	350.58	350.58	195.16	236.19	250.17	253.46	188.26	149.32
1980	300.98	328.00	328.00	379.61	379.61	211.30	255.84	271.95	294.89	203.31	161.42
1981	330.46	360.33	360.33	424.95	424.95	231.64	281.85	295.37	344.54	218.59	177.43
1982	343.78	367.62	367.62	449.96	449.96	246.53	297.60	312.05	370.06	218.63	180.44
1983	370.27	387.18	387.18	491.31	491.31	266.27	318.75	323.51	388.21	249.67	194.76
1984	389.16	417.74	417.74	520.94	520.94	277.77	333.08	333.92	436.46	257.75	202.02
1985	401.02	427.45	427.45	541.45	541.45	287.62	345.31	342.80	444.91	265.99	208.57
1986	408.46	440.13	440.13	541.86	541.86	298.98	357.11	350.00	481.71	284.82	214.33
1987	416.42	452.81	452.81	543.48	543.48	305.74	369.44	358.99	548.73	299.71	219.78
1988	431.15	473.12	401.39	567.48	438.84	313.60	379.89	367.54	583.87	302.58	226.44
1989	439.71	483.36	410.04	579.61	445.11	326.63	391.95	381.77	590.97	313.70	234.32
1990	447.28	493.16	420.24	591.36	464.02	340.10	404.80	392.50	636.22	320.00	239.15
1991	461.03	506.66	435.49	618.03	477.24	351.35	419.69	401.94	655.71	336.98	250.49
1992	475.07	523.70	453.20	635.36	488.68	365.09	433.49	414.12	653.11	353.46	258.54
1993	492.15	547.39	469.83	679.40	502.65	373.72	445.79	425.32	631.69	367.63	263.75
1994	511.80	568.10	485.30	731.39	520.00	386.80	459.72	440.26	749.45	379.81	275.25
1995	514.31	574.62	486.30	733.21	526.19	401.00	468.99	449.22	768.64	383.93	282.68
1996	530.85	585.73	505.47	756.80	547.94	412.09	484.79	459.20	773.60	393.41	294.52
1993:											
January	481.22	540.11	464.54	652.41	498.90	368.39	439.15	416.30	605.63	363.44	262.97
February	481.64	539.71	461.76	655.65	495.69	369.47	437.66	412.00	605.38	362.09	262.59
March	479.33	538.85	460.37	662.58	498.54	369.74	434.11	411.53	608.04	346.50	260.85
April	481.07	537.63	460.50	660.43	498.57	372.13	440.30	416.71	619.83	364.97	257.69
May	489.81	542.69	465.09	680.55	500.20	369.86	441.98	420.89	656.56	368.58	262.26
June	493.32	543.97	466.88	679.69	503.03	369.72	444.57	424.04	697.12	370.35	264.42
July	482.31	543.58	462.38	648.74	496.94	365.27	443.70	425.89	664.92	362.78	258.67
August	491.31	542.72	469.54	670.68	498.58	370.94	445.67	429.30	647.02	372.02	264.42
September	492.48	546.98	471.63	688.74	504.30	376.26	453.58	434.70	621.79	375.01	263.84
October	500.12	553.82	474.89	699.92	505.12	379.63	450.72	429.73	619.53	373.22	265.61
November	507.08	558.56	482.80	711.92	511.70	384.89	454.98	436.77	617.77	378.53	269.97
December	518.09	577.20	494.93	736.81	524.57	388.95	459.79	439.02	628.32	379.80	272.60
1994:											
January	503.29	562.02	479.94	710.13	515.43	380.33	450.46	426.37	637.50	372.04	265.70
February	498.19	556.85	473.62	712.86	509.63	368.45	442.73	423.46	644.63	357.59	255.59
March	505.33	568.51	484.34	728.02	519.16	383.36	454.62	430.77	707.59	376.13	271.15
April	508.13	565.48	484.34	731.14	515.85	386.32	456.55	430.52	771.45	380.87	273.00
May	508.89	565.92	483.31	732.33	514.59	384.40	456.55	433.05	784.54	378.71	274.46
June	510.51	567.21	487.30	730.38	517.91	385.36	460.73	437.72	834.15	386.26	278.54
July	498.12	558.15	479.74	698.70	515.84	380.39	460.22	444.29	779.60	375.33	273.39
August	508.04	557.28	483.84	726.33	517.51	385.04	459.91	442.66	743.48	382.13	278.94
September	517.97	570.29	488.25	750.40	524.17	390.17	467.82	450.07	776.21	386.40	281.61
October	514.94	569.85	486.87	737.37	524.17	395.85	466.28	445.82	783.11	385.56	282.72
November	523.31	577.28	491.18	752.27	526.26	400.66	470.61	456.18	772.52	387.07	283.48
December	531.96	591.36	500.69	771.87	537.61	402.57	475.80	457.87	762.41	390.60	284.99
1995:											
January	518.92	581.67	488.68	738.92	525.01	399.40	465.20	445.94	727.26	387.61	280.86
February	513.68	579.48	478.50	746.71	523.73	398.20	462.11	439.29	751.91	382.64	280.13
March	512.13	578.16	480.06	747.05	526.25	397.60	463.32	441.32	773.43	382.75	280.87
April	484.81	546.33	463.10	698.83	513.14	388.22	457.78	434.62	767.23	373.07	271.27
May	508.57	571.58	477.43	729.27	521.18	397.79	463.45	444.72	838.80	378.27	280.09
June	509.72	570.26	482.65	733.57	523.68	399.20	466.97	449.90	908.96	382.30	283.46
July	498.93	560.95	476.64	705.58	520.61	391.33	467.17	449.90	853.20	373.72	278.86
August	511.04	569.75	488.04	724.71	523.24	398.20	468.18	454.11	747.00	387.45	284.16
September	524.24	578.96	498.38	752.58	530.33	407.43	477.65	461.84	702.80	390.45	287.18
October	519.29	575.86	497.54	731.54	528.26	408.24	473.80	452.09	730.84	385.29	285.24
November	525.95	585.14	500.41	743.80	536.29	410.06	478.58	457.47	790.89	389.78	288.27
December	536.54	594.03	504.64	741.03	543.96	411.83	483.07	460.20	692.46	389.50	292.06
1996:											
January	506.34	568.51	482.78	714.02	525.20	386.25	457.34	435.44	658.00	344.16	262.07
February	517.44	580.22	494.21	733.94	540.89	402.83	472.78	445.61	701.63	383.91	287.78
March	516.21	578.49	494.27	703.87	543.02	407.55	476.75	449.55	762.00	388.69	290.82
April	521.25	573.89	490.01	759.40	538.14	405.97	477.20	449.84	801.72	386.97	289.38
May	527.06	578.35	496.90	764.96	541.16	408.43	480.36	455.03	839.50	390.57	296.16
June	536.28	584.98	507.10	766.74	549.78	410.10	486.34	458.90	876.17	400.75	302.82
July	520.42	574.52	497.76	738.28	540.38	402.36	482.40	460.13	809.83	389.14	292.56
August	534.20	582.00	510.85	765.50	548.29	412.73	488.76	463.14	810.80	401.44	299.34
September	546.08	596.24	518.70	787.00	559.02	423.39	496.01	472.22	771.54	404.89	300.80
October	535.89	587.73	514.16	762.45	553.36	420.89	490.80	465.37	730.48	399.90	301.93
November	542.66	597.54	520.36	772.08	562.95	427.11	499.34	475.68	766.32	407.41	301.98
December	557.64	620.27	537.97	801.19	575.77	435.25	509.18	481.32	782.27	416.64	308.89

1. Additional industry detail available in individual industry profile section.

AVERAGE WEEKLY EARNINGS—Continued
(Earnings per production or nonsupervisory worker on private nonagricultural payrolls—Dollars, not seasonally adjusted)

YEAR AND MONTH	Manufacturing—Continued Nondurable goods by industry—Continued						Service-producing industries					
	Paper and products	Printing and publishing	Chemicals and products	Petroleum and coal products	Rubber and miscellaneous plastic products	Leather and products	Total	Transportation and public utilities[1]	Wholesale trade[1]	Retail trade[1]	Finance, insurance, and real estate[1]	Services[1]
1968	130.85	133.28	136.27	159.38	121.60	85.41	94.04	138.85	121.90	74.95	101.75	83.97
1969	139.32	141.33	145.05	170.40	126.90	87.79	100.00	147.74	129.85	78.66	108.70	90.57
1970	144.14	147.78	153.50	183.18	129.36	92.63	105.37	155.93	136.86	82.47	112.67	96.66
1971	154.51	157.50	165.15	195.60	137.76	97.64	111.84	168.82	143.42	87.62	117.85	103.06
1972	169.06	170.03	177.64	211.79	149.56	102.64	119.65	187.86	151.69	91.85	122.98	110.85
1973	180.18	179.08	188.52	223.87	158.21	105.46	126.37	203.31	159.54	96.32	129.20	117.29
1974	191.17	188.63	202.52	239.13	166.05	110.33	135.06	217.48	169.94	102.68	137.61	126.00
1975	208.42	198.52	220.99	266.98	176.36	119.09	143.66	233.44	182.19	108.86	148.19	134.67
1976	232.48	214.13	245.86	303.54	191.70	127.16	152.39	256.71	194.27	114.60	155.43	143.52
1977	255.68	230.72	268.13	334.34	214.13	133.21	163.13	278.90	209.13	121.66	165.26	153.45
1978	279.71	244.78	294.14	376.27	227.81	144.32	175.26	302.80	228.14	130.20	178.00	163.67
1979	303.74	260.25	318.44	409.97	244.41	154.03	188.05	325.58	247.93	138.62	190.77	175.27
1980	330.85	279.36	344.45	422.18	263.20	168.09	203.01	351.25	266.88	147.38	209.60	190.71
1981	365.50	305.49	379.39	491.62	290.97	183.13	220.77	382.18	290.68	158.03	229.05	208.97
1982	389.58	324.25	407.36	546.99	304.92	189.75	233.77	402.48	309.46	163.85	245.44	225.59
1983	423.02	342.54	440.13	582.99	332.07	203.87	245.42	420.81	328.79	171.05	263.90	239.04
1984	448.67	356.64	463.83	587.33	348.20	210.13	253.75	438.13	341.88	174.33	278.50	247.43
1985	466.77	367.04	484.36	604.58	353.46	216.88	260.17	450.30	351.36	174.64	289.02	256.75
1986	482.98	379.62	501.96	621.52	363.91	218.45	265.83	458.64	357.72	176.08	304.30	265.85
1987	496.06	390.64	523.25	641.52	373.57	232.26	273.73	471.58	365.38	178.70	316.90	275.93
1988	506.18	400.14	536.36	664.67	383.22	235.50	283.39	467.57	380.24	183.62	325.25	289.49
1989	517.87	412.35	555.02	682.66	391.64	249.76	295.61	481.43	394.82	188.72	341.17	305.79
1990	533.02	426.00	576.80	724.30	401.14	258.43	308.03	496.13	411.10	194.40	356.93	319.48
1991	550.78	432.80	602.32	751.46	413.88	269.25	317.53	502.92	424.82	198.48	370.92	331.45
1992	569.85	447.29	625.38	784.02	432.01	281.96	328.31	514.37	435.10	205.06	387.36	342.55
1993	585.11	456.92	638.74	819.03	441.83	294.52	336.81	532.52	448.47	209.95	406.33	350.35
1994	604.50	468.60	653.62	846.71	451.54	306.85	346.37	547.07	463.10	216.46	423.51	358.80
1995	613.31	471.01	674.78	846.03	452.77	310.46	355.78	556.72	476.07	221.47	442.29	369.04
1996	635.21	483.23	698.54	842.35	466.46	326.14	367.88	571.82	492.92	230.11	459.16	382.00
1993:												
January	572.90	448.74	634.25	811.00	442.26	292.50	331.02	522.45	438.86	202.55	397.70	346.68
February	570.69	447.98	632.16	807.76	440.37	292.11	333.40	524.58	440.78	204.73	400.20	348.84
March	568.46	453.43	628.97	807.98	434.09	287.63	331.34	528.45	438.86	202.11	397.25	347.12
April	581.13	451.87	635.35	833.79	441.60	291.46	333.78	527.67	445.36	206.18	400.91	346.90
May	581.16	446.80	636.16	829.63	440.99	293.36	338.21	531.90	451.58	210.10	411.23	351.85
June	583.80	449.54	635.29	814.09	442.68	291.45	334.56	531.51	446.96	210.54	399.79	347.19
July	583.20	453.77	636.40	810.48	434.84	288.79	337.29	538.73	449.64	214.60	401.21	348.01
August	581.99	459.26	632.35	809.24	439.10	294.14	341.35	540.65	451.97	215.33	414.60	351.45
September	602.85	467.88	648.40	823.35	444.52	295.68	338.12	536.23	450.34	211.55	406.20	349.49
October	596.20	464.74	641.95	847.74	444.14	297.22	339.43	536.41	453.47	211.68	411.26	351.86
November	597.11	465.99	647.53	818.74	449.23	303.03	339.37	534.87	451.91	210.50	413.05	353.48
December	606.09	471.08	660.88	810.71	454.54	307.32	341.78	538.96	455.00	215.65	415.91	355.43
1994:												
January	593.01	458.28	646.27	827.20	448.75	304.15	344.26	540.57	458.02	210.09	429.16	359.13
February	582.51	454.29	639.00	838.43	442.32	296.16	342.14	539.59	453.66	209.35	421.37	355.17
March	593.83	466.24	648.63	861.67	452.83	306.82	342.95	538.99	453.77	212.33	419.48	355.30
April	598.75	465.52	648.22	853.74	453.68	307.26	344.33	542.70	461.13	214.39	421.62	356.08
May	600.50	462.72	649.73	821.69	452.19	305.66	346.44	545.03	464.36	215.88	427.42	358.93
June	601.92	463.87	651.02	830.28	455.60	309.26	343.48	545.20	461.62	218.58	415.45	353.93
July	607.14	465.79	652.97	829.13	447.20	302.06	346.94	551.38	462.72	222.31	418.40	356.10
August	605.38	469.43	646.07	815.63	448.37	307.26	345.56	552.18	459.98	220.97	416.42	356.10
September	619.38	479.76	657.28	894.52	450.50	310.03	348.01	551.82	465.02	218.66	419.49	359.32
October	615.33	477.36	663.15	870.43	451.56	313.99	353.10	556.21	473.75	220.29	435.12	365.91
November	614.82	477.02	666.86	854.70	454.97	313.17	348.49	554.00	467.33	217.26	425.29	361.76
December	625.86	481.82	677.16	853.94	463.97	312.76	351.29	548.24	470.86	222.39	430.19	365.15
1995:												
January	616.00	466.73	665.52	840.08	456.18	306.18	352.30	549.19	471.01	215.17	441.77	368.06
February	606.63	467.95	664.85	868.02	451.50	307.37	351.22	547.62	469.01	214.40	436.76	366.61
March	604.26	471.17	666.39	838.72	451.02	308.61	350.57	546.62	467.49	215.93	433.46	364.50
April	603.20	461.92	679.38	858.25	434.70	307.19	356.21	554.58	467.60	221.09	447.22	369.85
May	605.62	464.74	667.62	828.14	451.36	313.78	349.60	545.84	470.54	219.27	433.30	363.05
June	606.18	464.28	670.72	837.29	454.53	313.47	352.27	553.79	472.62	222.62	433.96	364.65
July	616.75	467.31	671.10	848.93	443.70	293.17	358.56	566.40	479.71	227.50	447.22	369.33
August	606.34	472.15	665.97	826.85	449.22	314.20	355.08	561.36	475.30	225.68	436.81	366.89
September	621.92	482.50	678.67	850.16	459.38	318.06	356.97	562.88	479.52	224.55	442.32	369.84
October	616.76	476.45	682.13	871.82	456.92	314.39	361.78	566.83	483.56	223.78	455.73	376.20
November	624.09	480.27	689.19	852.35	460.22	312.74	358.15	563.56	479.41	222.51	445.54	373.71
December	634.09	481.25	703.72	839.81	470.53	317.37	360.56	562.78	483.73	226.20	448.39	376.62
1996:												
January	607.99	458.38	681.79	836.57	448.54	294.45	356.64	551.32	476.02	216.98	447.66	373.01
February	617.60	473.37	687.88	836.31	460.08	312.01	362.23	563.56	481.84	221.93	453.03	377.38
March	618.03	478.65	689.60	824.11	460.50	319.79	363.35	564.60	483.49	225.15	454.46	377.38
April	626.77	474.89	691.22	836.56	460.32	315.00	362.88	562.65	486.92	224.93	453.90	377.06
May	627.37	476.52	689.72	808.97	465.92	321.64	362.38	562.13	487.05	227.30	453.54	375.77
June	634.94	475.27	699.17	843.94	465.37	331.18	371.18	577.44	499.74	234.61	465.38	382.45
July	638.93	479.94	693.26	842.59	459.00	317.81	365.85	573.27	488.44	233.14	451.76	377.00
August	637.55	490.22	695.84	833.22	467.17	335.32	367.95	579.20	493.44	234.53	453.75	380.30
September	648.56	497.42	703.63	855.27	476.15	340.65	374.88	587.17	502.96	234.55	470.49	387.61
October	642.66	491.90	703.30	843.66	469.25	339.69	370.66	575.25	495.60	233.04	459.46	386.53
November	655.33	496.52	715.81	862.84	471.33	343.09	373.27	579.89	500.20	232.52	464.33	390.10
December	665.28	503.10	730.38	889.41	490.33	347.02	379.50	582.54	510.84	239.09	477.83	397.63

1. Additional industry detail available in individual industry profile section.

Money and Financial Markets

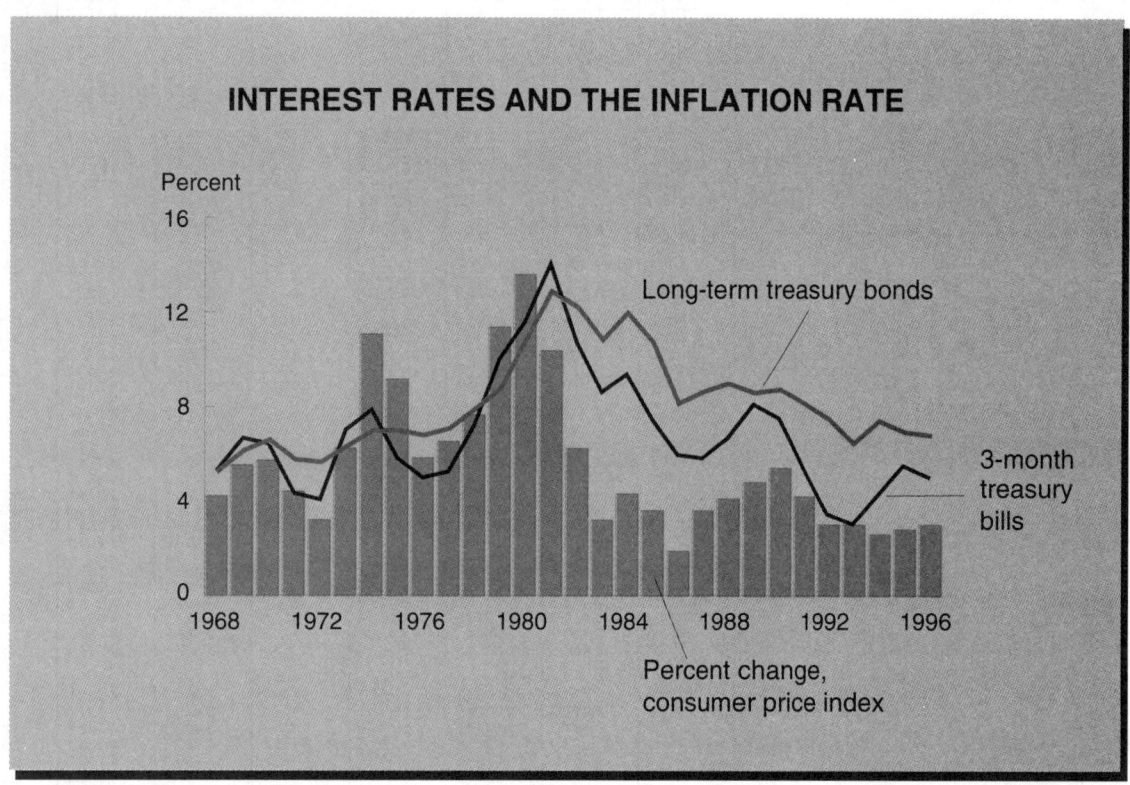

INTEREST RATES AND THE INFLATION RATE

Percent

Long-term treasury bonds

3-month treasury bills

Percent change, consumer price index

1968 1972 1976 1980 1984 1988 1992 1996

Except for the inflationary spike in 1974 and 1975, short-term interest rates tracked the rate of price increase fairly closely from 1968 to 1980. Long-term rates adjusted more slowly, so that the 3-month bill rate went above the long-term treasury bond composite during several periods of escalating inflation. Neither long nor short rates provided much positive return after adjustment for inflation.

From 1980 to 1996 the decline in interest rates generally lagged behind the drop in the inflation rate. The real rate of return was higher, and a positive spread between long and short rates was maintained.

MONEY AND FINANCIAL MARKETS

MONEY STOCK, LIQUID ASSETS, AND DEBT[1]
(Billions of dollars)

YEAR AND MONTH	Money stock measures (Averages of daily figures) Seasonally adjusted				Not seasonally adjusted				Debt (Monthly average, seasonally adjusted)	
	M1	M2	M3	L	M1	M2	M3	L	Federal	Non-Federal
1968	197.4	566.9	607.2	729.9	202.8	569.7	610.1	731.9	290.1	946.7
1969	203.9	587.9	615.9	764.4	209.4	590.1	618.2	765.9	288.8	1 037.9
1970	214.4	626.6	677.2	814.8	220.1	627.9	678.2	815.7	298.9	1 117.2
1971	228.3	710.2	776.0	902.6	234.5	711.2	776.6	903.0	321.0	1 228.6
1972	249.2	802.3	886.0	1 022.9	256.2	803.2	886.2	1 023.1	338.0	1 367.7
1973	262.8	855.5	985.0	1 141.5	270.2	856.5	985.2	1 141.7	345.6	1 545.2
1974	274.3	902.5	1 070.1	1 248.6	281.9	903.9	1 071.1	1 249.1	356.4	1 707.1
1975	287.4	1 017.0	1 172.0	1 366.5	295.4	1 018.3	1 173.7	1 368.1	440.5	1 810.7
1976	306.3	1 152.7	1 312.0	1 516.6	314.5	1 154.1	1 314.2	1 518.5	510.6	1 984.9
1977	331.3	1 271.5	1 472.5	1 705.4	340.0	1 273.9	1 476.9	1 709.0	565.2	2 246.3
1978	358.4	1 368.0	1 646.8	1 911.4	368.0	1 371.9	1 653.0	1 916.0	621.0	2 580.6
1979	382.8	1 475.7	1 806.5	2 121.1	393.1	1 480.1	1 811.8	2 124.0	653.4	2 937.8
1980	409.0	1 601.1	1 992.3	2 330.0	419.5	1 606.2	1 997.0	2 331.9	729.7	3 204.1
1981	436.8	1 756.2	2 240.9	2 601.9	447.0	1 761.9	2 245.1	2 602.7	814.3	3 516.5
1982	474.7	1 910.9	2 442.3	2 846.0	485.8	1 919.9	2 450.4	2 850.6	967.7	3 792.3
1983	521.2	2 127.7	2 684.8	3 150.6	533.2	2 139.1	2 695.5	3 157.9	1 162.3	4 165.5
1984	552.2	2 312.2	2 979.8	3 518.6	564.6	2 324.2	2 992.9	3 529.1	1 354.2	4 758.5
1985	619.9	2 497.6	3 198.3	3 827.0	633.4	2 510.1	3 212.2	3 841.1	1 575.0	5 450.4
1986	724.4	2 733.9	3 486.4	4 122.3	740.0	2 747.3	3 501.4	4 140.2	1 793.3	6 113.1
1987	749.7	2 832.7	3 672.5	4 339.9	765.5	2 845.4	3 685.8	4 358.0	1 943.6	6 720.5
1988	787.0	2 996.3	3 912.9	4 663.5	803.3	3 008.7	3 925.3	4 683.4	2 097.0	7 344.6
1989	794.2	3 160.9	4 065.9	4 892.8	811.0	3 173.0	4 077.9	4 914.9	2 245.0	7 926.6
1990	825.8	3 279.5	4 125.9	4 976.6	843.2	3 291.7	4 138.5	5 000.2	2 488.0	8 365.1
1991	897.3	3 379.6	4 180.4	5 006.2	916.0	3 393.2	4 195.2	5 031.1	2 760.4	8 575.7
1992	1 025.0	3 434.0	4 190.4	5 078.0	1 046.0	3 450.4	4 207.8	5 105.6	3 064.3	8 816.0
1993	1 129.8	3 486.6	4 254.4	5 167.8	1 153.7	3 506.6	4 274.8	5 197.7	3 323.3	9 185.4
1994	1 150.7	3 502.1	4 327.3	5 308.4	1 174.4	3 522.5	4 347.4	5 338.8	3 492.2	9 658.7
1995	1 129.0	3 655.0	4 592.5	5 697.6	1 152.8	3 675.3	4 612.0	5 729.5	3 638.8	10 228.1
1996	1 081.0	3 834.3	4 933.0	6 098.7	1 103.0	3 852.8	4 950.0	6 128.1	3 780.4	10 833.6
1993:										
January	1 032.0	3 431.3	4 174.3	5 064.7	1 040.2	3 433.8	4 178.5	5 078.3	3 082.6	8 837.0
February	1 034.0	3 424.0	4 174.4	5 063.1	1 022.3	3 410.2	4 165.9	5 058.1	3 096.4	8 855.1
March	1 038.4	3 420.4	4 173.2	5 057.6	1 030.8	3 420.7	4 174.8	5 065.4	3 122.6	8 876.4
April	1 047.8	3 423.6	4 181.9	5 069.2	1 057.8	3 441.6	4 194.8	5 080.2	3 154.0	8 903.4
May	1 067.5	3 447.6	4 210.1	5 109.1	1 057.2	3 435.7	4 198.4	5 090.7	3 180.0	8 932.0
June	1 075.4	3 452.9	4 209.9	5 115.2	1 072.2	3 450.2	4 206.1	5 105.5	3 204.3	8 973.3
July	1 084.7	3 452.7	4 207.4	5 112.2	1 083.6	3 453.8	4 203.2	5 102.8	3 222.5	9 018.4
August	1 094.5	3 456.8	4 209.8	5 118.3	1 088.6	3 453.1	4 207.7	5 111.9	3 242.4	9 047.8
September	1 104.2	3 463.6	4 220.0	5 119.0	1 099.2	3 455.8	4 209.6	5 104.8	3 262.4	9 085.2
October	1 114.3	3 469.7	4 229.9	5 132.1	1 112.0	3 464.5	4 225.3	5 122.7	3 265.5	9 124.2
November	1 123.6	3 480.2	4 244.3	5 150.1	1 129.5	3 486.2	4 254.7	5 164.4	3 287.7	9 150.6
December	1 129.8	3 486.6	4 254.4	5 167.8	1 153.7	3 506.6	4 274.8	5 197.7	3 323.3	9 185.4
1994:										
January	1 132.8	3 490.8	4 258.5	5 184.1	1 142.2	3 494.2	4 263.6	5 196.9	3 340.0	9 229.6
February	1 137.3	3 491.7	4 244.6	5 182.3	1 124.1	3 475.1	4 231.6	5 172.8	3 355.1	9 267.6
March	1 140.1	3 494.3	4 249.6	5 186.5	1 131.4	3 492.8	4 248.5	5 192.6	3 375.7	9 304.1
April	1 142.4	3 503.0	4 262.8	5 201.5	1 152.5	3 520.7	4 275.2	5 213.9	3 388.6	9 341.0
May	1 143.5	3 504.0	4 264.8	5 217.7	1 132.4	3 490.9	4 252.0	5 198.1	3 399.1	9 381.3
June	1 144.7	3 493.7	4 264.0	5 212.8	1 141.9	3 491.7	4 262.1	5 203.9	3 409.4	9 421.4
July	1 150.2	3 502.1	4 285.0	5 238.7	1 150.7	3 504.7	4 282.3	5 230.7	3 414.0	9 451.2
August	1 149.7	3 498.2	4 284.5	5 247.4	1 144.1	3 495.7	4 282.6	5 242.8	3 430.3	9 488.7
September	1 150.8	3 498.4	4 293.0	5 248.3	1 146.6	3 491.3	4 283.7	5 234.3	3 448.2	9 532.5
October	1 150.4	3 499.4	4 301.7	5 268.4	1 148.0	3 492.9	4 298.2	5 258.6	3 464.5	9 573.8
November	1 150.4	3 500.9	4 313.1	5 288.2	1 156.1	3 506.1	4 323.3	5 301.4	3 485.3	9 619.6
December	1 150.7	3 502.1	4 327.3	5 308.4	1 174.4	3 522.5	4 347.4	5 338.8	3 492.2	9 658.7
1995:										
January	1 150.3	3 506.3	4 348.3	5 336.8	1 159.3	3 510.2	4 353.8	5 349.4	3 506.5	9 698.3
February	1 148.4	3 506.1	4 356.2	5 369.2	1 135.1	3 489.7	4 342.4	5 358.7	3 535.1	9 745.5
March	1 147.1	3 506.7	4 369.6	5 397.9	1 139.1	3 506.6	4 369.7	5 406.7	3 551.9	9 796.5
April	1 150.4	3 519.1	4 395.9	5 431.5	1 160.1	3 536.9	4 407.1	5 445.3	3 555.7	9 854.4
May	1 145.1	3 534.9	4 425.9	5 465.3	1 133.8	3 520.9	4 412.0	5 445.0	3 571.8	9 916.3
June	1 142.7	3 562.9	4 462.0	5 503.5	1 140.8	3 560.8	4 460.1	5 493.0	3 593.5	9 971.1
July	1 145.0	3 583.1	4 493.7	5 554.9	1 145.6	3 586.6	4 491.7	5 546.5	3 608.5	10 010.0
August	1 144.0	3 604.4	4 525.5	5 591.4	1 139.3	3 603.6	4 524.4	5 588.7	3 613.7	10 045.3
September	1 141.6	3 620.1	4 548.8	5 637.1	1 138.5	3 613.5	4 539.3	5 621.8	3 616.4	10 089.8
October	1 135.7	3 629.8	4 565.0	5 666.9	1 132.9	3 621.5	4 561.5	5 654.0	3 626.4	10 140.0
November	1 133.1	3 639.3	4 578.3	5 674.2	1 138.7	3 643.2	4 587.1	5 685.4	3 635.9	10 187.5
December	1 129.0	3 655.0	4 592.5	5 697.6	1 152.8	3 675.3	4 612.0	5 729.5	3 638.8	10 228.1
1996:										
January	1 122.2	3 669.9	4 620.1	5 720.8	1 130.1	3 673.3	4 626.4	5 734.9	3 639.6	10 278.2
February	1 119.8	3 685.0	4 652.9	5 739.5	1 105.6	3 668.6	4 641.0	5 731.4	3 658.0	10 334.9
March	1 126.2	3 713.9	4 689.4	5 789.7	1 117.7	3 715.6	4 691.9	5 802.6	3 685.1	10 384.4
April	1 123.5	3 724.5	4 706.2	5 825.9	1 131.2	3 741.5	4 715.6	5 838.9	3 698.0	10 437.3
May	1 117.1	3 725.6	4 728.9	5 846.5	1 105.2	3 709.2	4 712.7	5 824.0	3 704.3	10 486.6
June	1 115.5	3 741.9	4 751.4	5 889.6	1 114.2	3 739.5	4 748.7	5 876.0	3 710.7	10 539.6
July	1 108.8	3 750.0	4 770.0	5 914.7	1 109.7	3 753.9	4 768.1	5 906.1	3 729.4	10 593.8
August	1 099.8	3 762.7	4 790.5	5 945.0	1 096.4	3 764.0	4 791.0	5 944.4	3 743.4	10 636.0
September	1 093.2	3 775.2	4 822.0	5 987.0	1 090.1	3 768.0	4 810.8	5 969.6	3 746.4	10 682.3
October	1 080.2	3 788.0	4 858.0	6 013.5	1 076.8	3 777.7	4 853.8	5 999.9	3 758.2	10 735.6
November	1 080.0	3 810.0	4 887.8	6 057.0	1 085.2	3 812.9	4 895.9	6 067.3	3 771.4	10 791.1
December	1 081.0	3 834.3	4 933.0	6 098.7	1 103.0	3 852.8	4 950.0	6 128.1	3 780.4	10 833.6

1. See NOTES for definitions of M1, M2, M3, L, and debt.

SELECTED COMPONENTS OF THE MONEY STOCK
(Averages of daily figures—Billions of dollars)

YEAR AND MONTH	Currency	Demand deposits	Other checkable deposits	Overnight RPs	Eurodollars	Money market funds		Savings deposits	Small time deposits	Large time deposits
						Retail	Institutional			
1968	43.0	153.6	0.1	....	2.9	....	....	268.9	100.6	37.4
1969	45.7	157.3	0.2	4.9	2.7	....	....	263.6	120.4	20.4
1970	48.6	164.8	0.1	3.0	2.4	....	....	260.9	151.2	45.1
1971	52.0	175.1	0.2	5.2	2.9	....	....	292.2	189.8	57.6
1972	56.2	191.6	0.2	6.6	3.9	....	....	321.4	231.7	73.3
1973	60.8	200.3	0.3	12.8	5.8	0.1	....	326.7	265.8	111.0
1974	67.0	205.2	0.4	14.2	8.5	1.7	0.2	338.6	287.9	144.7
1975	72.8	211.6	0.9	14.7	10.2	2.8	0.5	388.8	337.8	129.7
1976	79.5	221.6	2.7	25.1	15.4	2.5	0.6	453.2	390.7	118.1
1977	87.4	236.8	4.2	32.9	21.9	2.6	1.0	492.2	445.5	145.2
1978	96.0	250.7	8.5	44.6	35.1	6.7	3.4	481.9	520.9	195.6
1979	104.8	257.7	16.8	47.7	49.8	34.8	10.2	423.8	634.2	223.1
1980	115.4	261.5	28.1	57.4	57.7	63.4	15.9	400.2	728.5	260.2
1981	122.6	231.4	78.7	65.3	77.0	152.4	38.6	343.9	823.1	303.8
1982	132.5	234.0	104.1	67.4	89.8	185.2	49.4	400.1	850.9	324.8
1983	146.1	238.3	132.1	94.5	104.8	137.5	41.4	684.9	784.0	316.4
1984	156.1	243.7	147.4	105.4	96.9	166.5	62.1	704.7	888.8	403.2
1985	167.9	266.6	179.8	119.9	94.0	176.8	64.5	815.2	885.7	422.4
1986	180.7	302.1	235.6	143.3	103.9	210.4	85.1	940.9	858.3	420.2
1987	196.8	286.8	259.5	172.6	108.2	224.6	92.0	937.4	921.0	467.0
1988	212.3	286.8	280.9	189.0	117.0	245.9	92.3	926.3	1 037.1	518.3
1989	222.7	279.3	285.3	158.0	95.2	321.7	110.3	893.7	1 151.4	541.5
1990	246.8	277.4	293.9	138.8	88.7	357.1	138.0	923.8	1 172.8	480.9
1991	267.3	289.6	332.5	119.5	79.3	371.9	185.5	1 045.0	1 065.4	416.5
1992	292.9	339.5	384.4	128.6	67.0	353.5	207.5	1 187.3	868.3	353.4
1993	322.2	385.2	414.5	158.6	66.4	354.9	209.5	1 219.2	782.6	333.4
1994	354.4	384.1	403.8	182.9	80.8	384.3	198.5	1 149.6	817.5	363.1
1995	372.6	391.1	356.5	182.1	88.7	455.2	246.9	1 137.1	933.7	419.8
1996	395.2	402.4	274.8	194.0	113.9	536.6	299.3	1 271.0	945.7	491.5
1993:										
January	294.8	341.0	388.1	128.1	64.5	352.6	203.4	1 188.2	858.5	346.9
February	297.0	341.5	387.4	130.6	66.3	350.3	209.4	1 188.8	850.8	344.1
March	299.0	342.9	388.5	136.2	67.8	351.7	208.5	1 187.8	842.5	340.2
April	301.4	348.5	389.9	139.4	67.5	350.1	207.6	1 191.0	834.7	343.7
May	304.2	358.6	396.6	140.1	66.1	352.8	211.9	1 200.2	827.2	344.3
June	307.0	361.4	399.0	143.7	63.6	352.9	207.3	1 205.3	819.4	342.5
July	309.7	364.6	402.5	151.3	60.2	350.7	204.4	1 206.4	811.1	338.7
August	312.4	369.7	404.5	148.2	62.7	349.6	203.1	1 209.0	803.8	338.8
September	315.5	374.2	406.7	151.8	63.5	350.6	204.2	1 210.9	797.9	336.8
October	317.8	378.5	410.1	153.2	64.6	350.6	206.1	1 212.4	792.4	336.1
November	319.8	383.4	412.4	155.3	67.9	353.5	207.3	1 216.0	787.2	333.6
December	322.2	385.2	414.5	158.6	66.4	354.9	209.5	1 219.2	782.6	333.4
1994:										
January	325.3	387.3	412.2	158.4	65.8	356.7	206.0	1 224.5	776.8	337.5
February	329.1	388.5	411.7	156.1	67.3	357.3	195.7	1 226.6	770.6	333.7
March	331.7	387.6	412.8	161.1	66.9	361.4	195.4	1 227.2	765.5	331.9
April	334.0	388.2	412.2	164.5	67.2	371.0	195.6	1 226.3	763.3	332.4
May	337.2	385.2	413.1	164.2	70.7	374.7	190.8	1 221.4	764.4	335.1
June	339.9	384.4	412.3	168.0	74.5	369.5	189.6	1 211.5	767.9	338.3
July	342.9	386.3	413.4	171.6	79.3	373.1	190.4	1 205.9	772.3	341.5
August	345.2	385.1	411.0	171.0	78.6	372.6	190.8	1 197.3	778.6	345.9
September	347.4	386.0	408.9	173.7	78.6	373.1	190.4	1 189.3	785.2	351.8
October	349.9	386.2	405.9	172.0	79.8	375.7	196.2	1 177.8	795.4	354.4
November	353.0	384.3	404.7	174.9	80.9	379.4	197.6	1 164.6	806.5	358.8
December	354.4	384.1	403.8	182.9	80.8	384.3	198.5	1 149.6	817.5	363.1
1995:										
January	357.1	384.4	400.3	187.7	84.7	387.2	204.2	1 135.3	833.5	365.4
February	359.0	383.9	397.5	191.9	83.7	387.0	201.9	1 118.1	852.6	372.6
March	362.1	381.6	394.7	191.5	85.0	385.4	208.2	1 100.4	873.9	378.2
April	365.1	381.5	394.8	192.5	87.7	389.3	214.1	1 089.3	890.1	382.6
May	367.9	380.9	387.3	196.2	89.0	397.2	220.2	1 089.0	903.5	385.6
June	367.3	383.8	382.7	190.8	89.7	412.0	229.6	1 096.7	911.7	389.0
July	367.2	387.0	381.8	188.4	91.5	423.8	235.2	1 096.6	917.5	395.5
August	368.4	388.0	378.6	193.3	92.2	435.5	235.9	1 103.6	921.3	399.7
September	369.3	389.0	374.4	192.6	92.6	442.2	239.5	1 112.0	924.2	404.0
October	370.5	390.0	366.4	190.4	90.8	446.7	242.6	1 120.5	926.8	411.4
November	371.2	389.7	363.3	187.5	89.0	451.2	244.7	1 124.2	930.7	417.7
December	372.6	391.1	356.5	182.1	88.7	455.2	246.9	1 137.1	933.7	419.8
1996:										
January	373.0	394.4	345.9	187.2	92.0	459.6	250.1	1 153.8	934.3	420.9
February	373.4	397.3	340.3	188.9	93.0	466.0	259.7	1 165.1	934.1	426.2
March	375.4	404.5	337.3	187.8	91.5	476.8	263.7	1 180.2	930.8	432.6
April	376.4	404.5	333.9	188.9	94.0	481.4	263.4	1 190.1	929.5	435.4
May	377.7	407.1	323.5	202.7	94.5	484.5	263.6	1 195.6	928.5	442.5
June	379.9	410.6	316.4	195.3	95.6	493.6	269.7	1 204.1	928.8	448.9
July	382.8	408.7	308.7	194.2	95.8	499.6	274.0	1 211.0	930.5	455.9
August	385.2	405.8	300.4	192.4	96.3	506.1	278.8	1 222.7	934.1	460.3
September	387.6	404.9	292.2	194.4	98.9	513.2	285.2	1 231.5	937.4	468.3
October	390.2	398.2	283.2	196.0	105.1	520.5	288.1	1 246.4	941.0	480.9
November	392.5	402.1	276.8	195.3	107.1	527.1	292.0	1 259.0	943.9	483.4
December	395.2	402.4	274.8	194.0	113.9	536.6	299.3	1 271.0	945.7	491.5

YEAR AND MONTH	AGGREGATE RESERVES OF DEPOSITORY INSTITUTIONS AND MONETARY BASE (Averages of daily figures, millions of dollars— seasonally adjusted and adjusted for changes in reserve requirements)					ASSETS AND LIABILITIES OF COMMERCIAL BANKS (All commercial banks in the United States— Billions of dollars, seasonally adjusted)			
	Reserves				Monetary base	Assets			
						Bank credit			
							Securities in bank credit		
	Total	Non-borrowed	Non-borrowed plus extended credit	Required		Total	Total	U.S. government securities	Other securities
1968	13 767	13 021	13 021	13 341	58 357	....	....	....	....
1969	14 168	13 049	13 049	13 882	61 569	....	....	....	....
1970	14 558	14 225	14 225	14 309	65 013	....	....	....	....
1971	15 230	15 104	15 104	15 049	69 108	....	....	....	....
1972	16 645	15 595	15 595	16 361	75 167	....	....	....	....
1973	17 021	15 723	15 723	16 717	81 073	....	....	....	....
1974	17 550	16 823	16 970	17 292	87 535	....	....	....	....
1975	17 822	17 692	17 704	17 556	93 887	....	....	....	....
1976	18 388	18 335	18 335	18 115	101 515	....	....	....	....
1977	18 990	18 420	18 420	18 800	110 324	....	....	....	....
1978	19 753	18 885	18 885	19 521	120 445	....	....	....	....
1979	20 720	19 248	19 248	20 279	131 143	....	....	....	....
1980	22 015	20 325	20 328	21 501	142 004	....	....	....	....
1981	22 443	21 807	21 956	22 124	149 021	....	....	....	....
1982	23 600	22 966	23 152	23 100	160 127	....	....	....	....
1983	25 367	24 593	24 595	24 806	175 467	....	....	....	....
1984	26 854	23 668	26 272	26 000	187 333	....	....	....	....
1985	31 463	30 144	30 643	30 426	203 609	....	....	....	....
1986	38 972	38 146	38 449	37 603	223 651	....	....	....	....
1987	38 895	38 118	38 601	37 849	239 799	....	....	....	....
1988	40 428	38 712	39 957	39 381	256 905	2 435.7	562.0	366.8	195.2
1989	40 522	40 257	40 277	39 600	267 625	2 608.9	584.5	400.0	184.5
1990	41 797	41 471	41 494	40 132	293 190	2 751.5	633.7	455.6	178.1
1991	45 563	45 371	45 371	44 584	317 403	2 856.2	745.0	565.2	179.8
1992	54 383	54 260	54 260	53 228	351 347	2 956.7	843.5	666.8	176.7
1993	60 545	60 463	60 463	59 482	386 880	3 113.6	918.8	733.9	184.9
1994	59 404	59 195	59 195	58 236	418 484	3 326.2	952.3	732.1	220.2
1995	56 386	56 129	56 129	55 109	434 523	3 610.1	1 001.9	710.5	291.4
1996	50 063	49 908	49 908	48 639	452 669	3 770.2	989.9	706.7	283.2
1993:									
January	54 787	54 622	54 623	53 527	353 526	2 959.0	846.0	669.7	176.3
February	54 842	54 797	54 797	53 739	355 929	2 971.3	859.6	681.4	178.2
March	55 123	55 032	55 032	53 910	358 224	2 984.5	869.8	689.4	180.4
April	55 319	55 246	55 246	54 223	360 640	2 989.3	875.9	694.3	181.6
May	56 701	56 580	56 580	55 705	364 965	3 011.9	880.1	697.9	182.2
June	57 090	56 909	56 909	56 180	368 229	3 036.8	889.2	707.5	181.7
July	57 617	57 373	57 373	56 528	371 383	3 054.2	893.7	711.8	181.9
August	58 012	57 660	57 660	57 060	374 434	3 059.7	899.0	715.4	183.7
September	58 783	58 355	58 355	57 693	378 231	3 068.9	903.5	719.9	183.6
October	59 712	59 427	59 427	58 623	381 248	3 076.7	902.2	720.3	181.9
November	60 316	60 226	60 226	59 215	384 384	3 096.8	909.8	727.0	182.8
December	60 545	60 463	60 463	59 482	386 880	3 113.6	918.8	733.9	184.9
1994:									
January	60 720	60 646	60 646	59 272	389 868	3 156.1	952.7	742.9	209.8
February	60 707	60 637	60 637	59 567	393 937	3 161.0	949.8	744.3	205.5
March	60 486	60 431	60 431	59 519	396 412	3 182.8	961.3	755.2	206.1
April	60 492	60 368	60 368	59 340	398 537	3 204.3	973.9	763.8	210.2
May	60 084	59 884	59 884	59 169	401 590	3 207.4	967.8	757.3	210.5
June	60 002	59 669	59 669	58 898	404 359	3 221.8	971.9	758.7	213.2
July	60 147	59 689	59 689	59 040	407 321	3 252.9	977.3	757.3	219.9
August	59 812	59 343	59 343	58 808	409 389	3 263.7	967.5	752.2	215.3
September	59 753	59 266	59 266	58 693	411 375	3 277.7	966.8	750.3	216.5
October	59 517	59 136	59 136	58 713	413 564	3 291.5	961.3	740.9	220.4
November	59 448	59 199	59 199	58 440	417 197	3 302.4	955.4	734.8	220.6
December	59 404	59 195	59 195	58 236	418 484	3 326.2	952.3	732.1	220.2
1995:									
January	59 206	59 070	59 074	57 866	420 668	3 355.5	952.3	730.3	222.0
February	58 839	58 780	58 780	57 893	422 393	3 370.5	944.2	727.0	217.1
March	58 409	58 341	58 341	57 615	424 883	3 398.0	949.3	715.0	234.3
April	57 985	57 874	57 874	57 232	427 427	3 474.7	1 001.9	708.0	294.0
May	57 779	57 629	57 629	56 899	430 696	3 495.5	993.6	709.7	283.9
June	57 381	57 109	57 109	56 417	429 755	3 517.0	995.5	708.5	286.9
July	57 722	57 351	57 351	56 632	429 827	3 536.8	987.8	701.7	286.1
August	57 475	57 193	57 193	56 488	430 747	3 548.3	989.1	705.8	283.3
September	57 320	57 043	57 043	56 370	431 366	3 568.5	992.4	705.4	286.9
October	56 857	56 612	56 612	55 776	432 277	3 588.0	996.9	712.3	284.6
November	56 345	56 141	56 141	55 402	433 049	3 598.7	999.1	714.1	285.0
December	56 386	56 129	56 129	55 109	434 523	3 610.1	1 001.9	710.5	291.4
1996:									
January	55 691	55 653	55 653	54 206	434 518	3 628.4	989.9	702.1	287.8
February	54 810	54 775	54 775	53 959	433 584	3 650.4	1 005.0	713.3	291.7
March	55 613	55 592	55 592	54 476	436 733	3 643.5	988.5	703.3	285.2
April	55 155	55 064	55 064	54 035	437 075	3 667.6	990.4	707.8	282.6
May	54 168	54 040	54 040	53 308	437 881	3 665.6	992.2	711.6	280.6
June	54 038	53 652	53 652	52 888	439 686	3 672.0	983.2	707.4	275.8
July	53 221	52 854	52 854	52 156	442 262	3 685.6	984.7	708.2	276.5
August	52 181	51 847	51 847	51 221	443 999	3 674.5	972.1	702.2	269.9
September	51 280	50 912	50 912	50 242	445 812	3 692.8	968.8	703.2	265.6
October	50 076	49 789	49 789	49 082	447 077	3 718.2	969.3	703.2	266.1
November	49 811	49 597	49 597	48 776	449 365	3 743.1	980.7	707.3	273.4
December	50 063	49 908	49 908	48 639	452 669	3 770.2	989.9	706.7	283.2

ASSETS AND LIABILITIES OF COMMERCIAL BANKS—Continued
(All commercial banks in the United States—Billions of dollars, seasonally adjusted)

YEAR AND MONTH	Assets—Continued / Bank credit—Continued / Loans and leases in bank credit Total	Commercial and industrial	Real estate Total	Revolving home equity	Other	Consumer	Security	Other	Interbank loans	Cash assets	Other assets	Total assets
1968												
1969												
1970												
1971												
1972												
1973												
1974												
1975												
1976												
1977												
1978												
1979												
1980												
1981												
1982												
1983												
1984												
1985												
1986												
1987												
1988	1 873.8	608.0	675.0	39.9	635.1	357.7	40.7	192.4	158.4	223.2	185.0	2 940.3
1989	2 024.4	639.3	770.1	50.1	719.9	378.1	41.4	195.6	179.9	227.4	188.9	3 139.4
1990	2 117.8	640.9	855.1	62.1	793.1	383.2	45.0	193.5	191.7	212.7	206.3	3 297.5
1991	2 111.2	619.5	879.9	69.5	810.4	366.5	54.4	190.9	166.2	212.9	210.7	3 382.4
1992	2 113.3	596.2	901.2	73.4	827.8	358.9	64.1	192.8	161.3	212.5	216.1	3 484.6
1993	2 194.8	585.9	940.4	72.9	867.5	390.4	87.5	190.6	152.4	218.9	217.9	3 644.2
1994	2 373.9	645.1	1 002.4	75.2	927.2	451.2	76.2	199.0	172.2	209.3	220.9	3 872.3
1995	2 608.1	716.4	1 077.5	79.1	998.4	493.1	83.0	238.1	193.7	223.6	226.0	4 197.0
1996	2 780.3	783.2	1 127.9	85.2	1 042.6	520.9	78.7	269.7	204.9	231.0	265.4	4 415.0
1993:												
January	2 113.0	595.6	898.9	73.4	825.6	361.6	64.0	192.8	156.6	209.5	214.8	3 478.5
February	2 111.7	594.9	898.8	73.6	825.2	363.8	63.4	190.7	152.9	208.4	216.7	3 487.9
March	2 114.7	592.2	901.5	74.3	827.1	364.9	66.0	190.3	154.5	207.1	218.1	3 502.9
April	2 113.4	586.7	902.6	74.7	827.8	366.2	64.8	193.1	149.6	210.6	219.7	3 508.3
May	2 131.8	589.9	908.7	74.7	834.0	369.1	69.1	195.1	155.4	214.2	217.9	3 538.7
June	2 147.6	592.0	913.9	74.7	839.2	371.5	72.5	197.6	161.5	214.6	218.4	3 570.7
July	2 160.5	589.3	916.8	74.4	842.5	374.7	81.8	197.8	160.5	216.4	219.4	3 590.5
August	2 160.7	588.6	919.8	74.1	845.7	377.2	79.7	195.3	156.5	221.7	217.6	3 595.7
September	2 165.4	587.1	921.6	73.8	847.9	379.9	82.4	194.5	153.4	225.7	221.8	3 610.4
October	2 174.5	587.2	926.7	73.4	853.3	383.8	81.7	195.0	151.4	218.9	220.7	3 608.5
November	2 187.0	586.1	931.6	73.1	858.5	387.7	88.2	193.4	152.7	220.4	220.8	3 631.8
December	2 194.8	585.9	940.4	72.9	867.5	390.4	87.5	190.6	152.4	218.9	217.9	3 644.2
1994:												
January	2 203.4	590.6	942.3	72.8	869.5	394.7	85.5	190.3	152.9	218.5	200.2	3 669.9
February	2 211.2	592.1	941.8	72.9	868.9	398.6	88.4	190.2	154.4	220.8	209.4	3 688.0
March	2 221.5	595.6	944.1	72.9	871.2	402.4	89.0	190.5	149.5	218.7	213.7	3 707.3
April	2 230.3	601.1	947.7	72.9	874.8	407.6	82.2	191.8	150.6	212.1	218.2	3 727.9
May	2 239.6	605.5	951.9	73.0	878.9	412.0	80.4	189.8	156.6	216.6	222.2	3 745.8
June	2 249.9	609.5	957.8	73.4	884.4	416.4	78.4	187.7	155.2	215.0	219.8	3 754.8
July	2 275.6	616.3	965.0	73.4	891.6	422.9	80.5	190.8	158.6	210.9	225.3	3 790.7
August	2 296.2	621.9	972.8	73.7	899.0	428.3	80.2	193.0	160.0	207.4	225.4	3 799.6
September	2 310.9	626.9	980.4	74.0	906.4	433.7	75.0	194.9	161.1	204.1	222.0	3 808.2
October	2 330.3	633.7	985.8	74.4	911.4	440.6	75.0	195.2	163.3	209.3	222.0	3 829.5
November	2 347.0	639.6	991.7	74.8	916.9	444.6	74.2	197.0	169.6	208.3	224.6	3 848.6
December	2 373.9	645.1	1 002.4	75.2	927.2	451.2	76.2	199.0	172.2	209.3	220.9	3 872.3
1995:												
January	2 403.2	655.7	1 013.7	75.7	938.0	457.3	73.2	203.4	175.8	218.1	224.6	3 917.1
February	2 426.3	668.0	1 021.6	76.0	945.6	459.9	73.0	203.9	175.9	211.9	228.9	3 930.5
March	2 448.7	670.8	1 028.6	76.1	952.5	465.0	75.4	208.9	178.5	208.1	227.5	3 955.6
April	2 472.7	680.8	1 035.4	76.6	958.8	470.1	77.7	208.7	183.2	210.4	216.6	4 027.9
May	2 501.8	687.6	1 041.3	77.1	964.2	472.5	88.1	212.4	187.8	211.2	216.7	4 054.2
June	2 521.5	691.6	1 049.4	77.7	971.7	478.0	87.7	214.8	191.7	212.3	218.1	4 081.9
July	2 549.0	696.9	1 062.0	78.0	984.0	480.8	87.1	222.3	193.7	213.3	216.9	4 103.8
August	2 559.2	699.0	1 067.3	78.3	989.0	485.2	84.2	223.5	192.0	210.6	217.5	4 111.6
September	2 576.2	703.8	1 071.0	78.5	992.5	488.8	86.6	225.9	195.4	213.5	220.4	4 141.1
October	2 591.1	709.4	1 075.3	78.4	996.9	489.1	86.7	230.6	192.9	222.3	219.3	4 165.7
November	2 599.6	713.6	1 076.7	78.8	997.9	490.9	86.3	232.1	193.7	216.1	220.0	4 172.0
December	2 608.1	716.4	1 077.5	79.1	998.4	493.1	83.0	238.1	193.7	223.6	226.0	4 197.0
1996:												
January	2 638.4	721.8	1 086.0	79.4	1 006.5	497.5	88.1	245.1	203.6	230.0	230.9	4 236.2
February	2 645.4	725.6	1 089.0	79.7	1 009.2	499.4	85.9	245.5	194.2	219.3	232.3	4 239.6
March	2 655.0	724.9	1 096.1	79.7	1 016.4	500.8	85.3	247.9	206.1	216.8	236.6	4 246.2
April	2 677.2	732.1	1 100.1	80.1	1 020.0	504.7	85.0	255.3	208.9	221.4	240.6	4 281.4
May	2 673.4	736.3	1 101.7	79.9	1 021.8	504.1	76.6	254.7	207.6	220.1	236.7	4 273.2
June	2 688.8	740.2	1 104.1	79.4	1 024.7	508.7	78.8	257.1	205.0	219.3	245.2	4 284.7
July	2 700.9	744.7	1 104.8	80.1	1 024.7	511.8	77.9	261.7	197.7	220.5	247.7	4 294.0
August	2 702.4	746.9	1 109.4	80.5	1 028.9	512.8	72.3	261.0	197.6	223.3	257.8	4 295.8
September	2 724.0	761.1	1 112.0	81.2	1 030.8	515.9	73.8	261.3	205.4	224.2	260.0	4 325.1
October	2 748.9	770.6	1 115.6	83.3	1 032.2	519.5	76.9	266.4	204.6	226.1	253.3	4 345.5
November	2 762.4	775.0	1 121.5	84.2	1 037.3	520.5	76.9	268.5	212.0	232.6	260.0	4 391.2
December	2 780.3	783.2	1 127.9	85.2	1 042.6	520.9	78.7	269.7	204.9	231.0	265.4	4 415.0

ASSETS AND LIABILITIES OF COMMERCIAL BANKS—Continued
(All commercial banks in the United States—Billions of dollars, seasonally adjusted)

YEAR AND MONTH	Liabilities											Residual (Assets less liabilities)
	Deposits					Borrowings				Other liabilities	Total liabilities	
	Total	Trans- action	Nontransaction			Total	From banks in the U.S.	From nonbanks in the U.S.	Net due foreign offices			
			Total	Large time	Other							
1968												
1969												
1970												
1971												
1972												
1973												
1974												
1975												
1976												
1977												
1978												
1979												
1980												
1981												
1982												
1983												
1984												
1985												
1986												
1987												
1988	2 117.2	610.0	1 507.2	442.3	1 064.9	480.6	243.8	236.7	11.9	139.2	2 748.9	191.5
1989	2 242.2	611.2	1 631.0	475.2	1 155.8	543.2	273.8	269.3	13.5	144.5	2 943.3	196.1
1990	2 340.1	612.6	1 727.5	449.6	1 277.9	562.3	286.4	275.8	37.8	147.5	3 087.6	209.9
1991	2 470.5	652.8	1 817.7	446.8	1 371.0	488.6	215.4	273.2	41.8	144.7	3 145.7	236.7
1992	2 503.8	747.6	1 756.2	380.1	1 376.1	493.0	208.1	284.9	71.3	147.9	3 216.0	268.6
1993	2 533.4	817.4	1 716.1	348.0	1 368.1	525.0	208.7	316.3	130.1	147.5	3 336.0	308.2
1994	2 528.7	797.9	1 730.8	361.6	1 369.2	609.5	241.7	367.8	228.7	174.7	3 541.6	330.7
1995	2 670.8	775.7	1 895.2	421.4	1 473.7	681.7	280.3	401.5	263.5	230.2	3 846.3	350.7
1996	2 859.9	719.5	2 140.4	519.6	1 620.8	705.5	304.7	400.7	231.3	259.8	4 056.5	358.6
1993:												
January	2 490.7	743.7	1 747.0	373.9	1 373.0	487.8	206.9	280.9	73.8	145.0	3 197.3	281.2
February	2 496.1	747.6	1 748.5	370.4	1 378.1	490.6	210.1	280.5	73.0	145.9	3 205.6	282.3
March	2 495.5	752.9	1 742.6	365.5	1 377.1	498.7	211.3	287.4	79.9	148.5	3 222.6	280.3
April	2 496.7	757.8	1 738.9	364.8	1 374.0	490.1	197.8	292.3	89.5	146.9	3 223.2	285.1
May	2 516.5	775.3	1 741.2	365.2	1 375.9	501.0	204.2	296.9	87.5	147.1	3 252.1	286.6
June	2 521.4	783.6	1 737.8	363.3	1 374.5	515.3	211.7	303.7	92.0	149.5	3 278.2	292.5
July	2 518.2	788.0	1 730.2	356.0	1 374.2	525.2	216.8	308.4	104.8	148.4	3 296.6	293.9
August	2 520.1	798.3	1 721.8	350.2	1 371.7	525.0	216.4	308.6	116.2	147.9	3 309.3	286.4
September	2 521.2	806.5	1 714.7	345.9	1 368.8	529.3	222.6	306.6	123.3	146.4	3 320.1	290.3
October	2 516.8	805.6	1 711.2	346.3	1 364.9	526.2	219.2	307.0	128.3	146.0	3 317.4	291.1
November	2 528.0	814.2	1 713.8	345.7	1 368.1	526.1	214.5	311.7	130.0	146.3	3 330.4	301.4
December	2 533.4	817.4	1 716.1	348.0	1 368.1	525.0	208.7	316.3	130.1	147.5	3 336.0	308.2
1994:												
January	2 531.5	812.7	1 718.8	348.3	1 370.5	542.0	219.1	322.9	124.5	163.0	3 361.0	308.9
February	2 527.1	814.9	1 712.2	341.5	1 370.7	536.2	222.7	313.5	142.7	171.0	3 377.0	311.0
March	2 517.4	814.3	1 703.1	334.0	1 369.1	550.3	230.0	320.2	164.7	168.4	3 400.8	306.5
April	2 510.4	806.4	1 704.0	336.2	1 367.8	563.4	231.6	331.7	175.6	173.6	3 422.9	305.0
May	2 517.1	812.8	1 704.3	337.3	1 367.0	561.8	237.3	324.5	179.0	175.4	3 433.3	312.5
June	2 507.5	811.0	1 696.5	336.1	1 360.5	568.1	240.0	328.0	186.4	172.1	3 434.2	320.7
July	2 512.9	809.9	1 703.0	340.2	1 362.8	576.3	244.1	332.2	196.6	180.6	3 466.4	324.3
August	2 515.8	807.5	1 708.3	343.5	1 364.8	587.9	248.8	339.1	204.4	178.5	3 486.7	312.9
September	2 515.6	801.9	1 713.7	348.0	1 365.7	589.4	255.4	334.0	209.9	177.8	3 492.7	315.5
October	2 522.6	802.4	1 720.2	354.4	1 365.8	590.7	251.7	339.1	214.1	181.1	3 508.6	320.9
November	2 521.0	797.7	1 723.3	357.6	1 365.7	599.0	247.6	351.4	214.0	180.7	3 514.7	333.9
December	2 528.7	797.9	1 730.8	361.6	1 369.2	609.5	241.7	367.8	228.7	174.7	3 541.6	330.7
1995:												
January	2 533.9	804.0	1 730.0	365.9	1 364.1	638.0	263.6	374.4	244.6	166.5	3 583.0	334.0
February	2 537.1	799.5	1 737.6	373.5	1 364.1	639.1	269.9	369.2	247.6	170.1	3 593.9	336.6
March	2 541.9	793.1	1 748.8	380.2	1 368.6	648.3	275.3	373.1	242.7	187.0	3 619.9	335.6
April	2 562.3	793.3	1 768.9	386.9	1 382.0	672.0	279.9	392.1	236.9	232.0	3 703.1	324.8
May	2 577.4	788.8	1 788.6	391.4	1 397.2	675.3	287.5	387.9	242.1	226.4	3 721.2	333.0
June	2 600.8	786.4	1 814.4	397.3	1 417.1	672.0	286.3	385.7	246.0	226.4	3 745.1	336.8
July	2 607.1	791.3	1 815.8	401.8	1 414.0	687.1	295.9	391.2	235.8	218.4	3 748.4	355.4
August	2 616.5	783.3	1 833.2	408.3	1 424.9	687.4	294.8	392.7	244.8	221.4	3 770.1	341.5
September	2 634.8	782.9	1 851.9	414.9	1 437.0	689.3	302.7	386.5	252.0	228.0	3 804.1	337.0
October	2 645.2	778.3	1 866.9	423.0	1 443.9	687.0	299.7	387.3	257.8	222.9	3 812.9	352.8
November	2 648.1	768.7	1 879.4	423.2	1 456.2	674.0	291.4	382.6	264.4	222.9	3 809.4	362.5
December	2 670.8.	775.7	1 895.2	421.4	1 473.7	681.7	280.3	401.5	263.5	230.2	3 846.3	350.7
1996:												
January	2 681.2	780.3	1 900.9	421.4	1 479.5	693.4	297.8	395.6	267.7	235.2	3 877.4	358.8
February	2 673.2	764.1	1 909.1	425.8	1 483.3	687.2	286.6	400.5	276.6	235.0	3 872.0	367.6
March	2 697.6	765.5	1 932.1	430.0	1 502.1	695.9	297.6	398.3	256.7	227.6	3 877.7	368.5
April	2 712.2	764.6	1 947.6	433.7	1 513.9	706.4	301.4	405.0	258.0	226.2	3 902.8	378.6
May	2 724.4	756.2	1 968.2	434.6	1 533.6	709.2	295.5	413.7	257.4	214.7	3 905.7	367.5
June	2 731.8	750.7	1 981.1	439.4	1 541.7	703.4	290.7	412.8	258.5	220.1	3 913.8	370.9
July	2 743.0	743.9	1 999.1	447.3	1 551.8	701.1	287.1	414.0	257.4	219.9	3 921.5	372.6
August	2 751.0	733.3	2 017.6	458.8	1 558.8	701.5	290.1	411.4	247.7	222.2	3 922.4	373.3
September	2 771.9	725.2	2 046.7	471.7	1 575.0	706.8	296.1	410.8	251.0	221.4	3 951.1	374.0
October	2 774.2	712.7	2 061.5	479.6	1 581.9	689.4	292.0	397.4	244.2	242.7	3 950.6	395.0
November	2 831.4	721.3	2 110.0	500.8	1 609.2	708.5	300.4	408.1	238.1	252.2	4 030.2	361.0
December	2 859.9	719.5	2 140.4	519.6	1 620.8	705.5	304.7	400.7	231.3	259.8	4 056.5	358.6

SELECTED INTEREST RATES AND BOND YIELDS
(Percent per annum)

YEAR AND MONTH	Short-term rates									U.S. Treasury securities			
	Federal funds	Federal Reserve discount rate[1]	Eurodollar deposits, 1-month	U.S. Treasury bills, 3-month	Bankers' accept-ances, 3-month	CDs (Second-ary mar-ket), 3-month	Commer-cial paper, 6-month	Finance company paper, 6-month	Bank prime rate	One year	Ten year	Thirty year	Long-term compos-ite[2]
1968	5.66	5.16	....	5.35	5.75	5.86	5.90	5.68	6.31	5.69	5.65	....	5.26
1969	8.20	5.87	....	6.69	7.63	7.76	7.83	7.09	7.95	7.12	6.67	....	6.12
1970	7.18	5.95	....	6.44	7.27	7.56	7.71	7.20	7.91	6.90	7.35	....	6.58
1971	4.66	4.88	6.39	4.34	4.84	5.01	5.11	4.89	5.72	4.88	6.16	....	5.74
1972	4.43	4.50	5.01	4.07	4.47	4.67	4.73	4.56	5.25	4.96	6.21	....	5.63
1973	8.73	6.44	9.28	7.03	8.08	8.42	8.15	7.38	8.02	7.31	6.84	....	6.30
1974	10.50	7.83	10.74	7.88	9.94	10.24	9.84	8.61	10.80	8.18	7.56	....	6.98
1975	5.82	6.25	6.34	5.83	6.31	6.44	6.32	6.16	7.86	6.76	7.99	....	6.98
1976	5.05	5.50	5.26	5.00	5.08	5.27	5.35	5.22	6.84	5.87	7.61	....	6.78
1977	5.54	5.46	5.74	5.26	5.54	5.64	5.61	5.50	6.82	6.09	7.42	....	7.06
1978	7.93	7.46	8.36	7.22	8.06	8.22	7.99	7.78	9.06	8.34	8.41	8.49	7.89
1979	11.19	10.28	11.67	10.04	10.99	11.23	10.91	10.25	12.67	10.67	9.44	9.29	8.74
1980	13.36	11.77	13.81	11.62	12.72	13.07	12.29	11.28	15.27	12.05	11.46	11.30	10.81
1981	16.38	13.42	16.72	14.08	15.32	15.91	14.76	13.73	18.87	14.78	13.91	13.44	12.89
1982	12.26	11.02	12.78	10.73	11.89	12.27	11.89	11.20	14.86	12.28	13.00	12.76	12.23
1983	9.09	8.50	9.37	8.62	8.90	9.07	8.89	8.69	10.79	9.57	11.11	11.18	10.84
1984	10.23	8.80	10.43	9.39	10.14	10.37	10.16	9.65	12.04	10.89	12.44	12.39	11.99
1985	8.10	7.69	8.12	7.49	7.92	8.05	8.01	7.75	9.93	8.43	10.62	10.79	10.75
1986	6.81	6.33	6.79	5.97	6.39	6.52	6.39	6.31	8.33	6.46	7.68	7.80	8.14
1987	6.66	5.66	6.88	5.83	6.74	6.86	6.84	6.37	8.20	6.76	8.38	8.58	8.63
1988	7.57	6.20	7.69	6.67	7.56	7.73	7.68	7.15	9.32	7.65	8.85	8.96	8.98
1989	9.22	6.92	9.16	8.12	8.87	9.09	8.80	8.16	10.87	8.54	8.50	8.45	8.59
1990	8.10	6.98	8.16	7.51	7.93	8.15	7.95	7.52	10.01	7.88	8.55	8.61	8.73
1991	5.69	5.45	5.82	5.41	5.71	5.84	5.85	5.60	8.46	5.86	7.86	8.14	8.16
1992	3.52	3.25	3.63	3.46	3.62	3.68	3.80	3.63	6.25	3.89	7.01	7.67	7.52
1993	3.02	3.00	3.07	3.02	3.13	3.17	3.31	3.16	6.00	3.43	5.87	6.60	6.46
1994	4.20	3.60	4.34	4.27	4.62	4.63	4.93	4.56	7.14	5.31	7.08	7.37	7.41
1995	5.84	5.21	5.84	5.51	5.82	5.88	5.93	5.69	8.83	5.95	6.58	6.88	6.94
1996	5.30	5.02	5.32	5.03	5.30	5.39	5.44	5.23	8.28	5.51	6.43	6.70	6.80
1993:													
January	3.02	3.00	3.09	3.06	3.14	3.19	3.35	3.29	6.00	3.50	6.60	7.34	7.17
February	3.03	3.00	3.03	2.95	3.06	3.12	3.27	3.21	6.00	3.39	6.26	7.09	6.89
March	3.07	3.00	3.06	2.97	3.07	3.11	3.24	3.14	6.00	3.33	5.98	6.82	6.65
April	2.96	3.00	3.04	2.89	3.05	3.09	3.19	3.07	6.00	3.24	5.97	6.85	6.64
May	3.00	3.00	3.02	2.96	3.06	3.10	3.20	3.07	6.00	3.36	6.04	6.92	6.68
June	3.04	3.00	3.09	3.10	3.16	3.21	3.38	3.16	6.00	3.54	5.96	6.81	6.55
July	3.06	3.00	3.05	3.05	3.12	3.16	3.35	3.15	6.00	3.47	5.81	6.63	6.34
August	3.03	3.00	3.06	3.05	3.10	3.14	3.33	3.16	6.00	3.44	5.68	6.32	6.18
September	3.09	3.00	3.05	2.96	3.07	3.12	3.25	3.11	6.00	3.36	5.36	6.00	5.94
October	2.99	3.00	3.06	3.04	3.19	3.24	3.27	3.13	6.00	3.39	5.33	5.94	5.90
November	3.02	3.00	3.06	3.12	3.29	3.35	3.43	3.19	6.00	3.58	5.72	6.21	6.25
December	2.96	3.00	3.22	3.08	3.23	3.26	3.40	3.18	6.00	3.61	5.77	6.25	6.27
1994:													
January	3.05	3.00	3.03	3.02	3.10	3.15	3.30	3.15	6.00	3.54	5.75	6.29	6.24
February	3.25	3.00	3.27	3.21	3.40	3.43	3.62	3.39	6.00	3.87	5.97	6.49	6.44
March	3.34	3.00	3.50	3.52	3.73	3.77	4.08	3.70	6.06	4.32	6.48	6.91	6.90
April	3.56	3.00	3.71	3.74	3.96	4.01	4.40	4.03	6.45	4.82	6.97	7.27	7.32
May	4.01	3.24	4.18	4.19	4.45	4.51	4.92	4.45	6.99	5.31	7.18	7.41	7.47
June	4.25	3.50	4.27	4.18	4.45	4.52	4.86	4.50	7.25	5.27	7.10	7.40	7.43
July	4.26	3.50	4.43	4.39	5.01	4.73	5.13	4.67	7.25	5.48	7.30	7.58	7.61
August	4.47	3.76	4.57	4.50	5.03	4.81	5.19	4.79	7.51	5.56	7.24	7.49	7.55
September	4.73	4.00	4.82	4.64	4.95	5.03	5.32	4.99	7.75	5.76	7.46	7.71	7.81
October	4.76	4.00	4.96	4.96	5.41	5.51	5.70	5.30	7.75	6.11	7.74	7.94	8.02
November	5.29	4.40	5.36	5.25	5.71	5.79	6.01	5.58	8.15	6.54	7.96	8.08	8.16
December	5.45	4.75	5.99	5.64	6.18	6.29	6.62	6.17	8.50	7.14	7.81	7.87	7.97
1995:													
January	5.53	4.75	5.82	5.81	6.12	6.24	6.63	6.25	8.50	7.05	7.78	7.85	7.93
February	5.92	5.25	5.99	5.80	6.05	6.16	6.38	6.10	9.00	6.70	7.47	7.61	7.69
March	5.98	5.25	6.01	5.73	6.04	6.15	6.30	6.04	9.00	6.43	7.20	7.45	7.52
April	6.05	5.25	6.02	5.67	6.00	6.11	6.19	6.01	9.00	6.27	7.06	7.36	7.41
May	6.01	5.25	5.98	5.70	5.91	6.07	6.07	5.81	9.00	6.00	6.63	6.95	6.99
June	6.00	5.25	5.95	5.50	5.80	5.90	5.79	5.47	9.00	5.64	6.17	6.57	6.59
July	5.85	5.25	5.81	5.47	5.66	5.77	5.68	5.39	8.80	5.59	6.28	6.72	6.71
August	5.74	5.25	5.78	5.41	5.68	5.77	5.75	5.51	8.75	5.75	6.49	6.86	6.90
September	5.80	5.25	5.73	5.26	5.66	5.73	5.66	5.45	8.75	5.62	6.20	6.55	6.63
October	5.76	5.25	5.74	5.30	5.71	5.79	5.71	5.51	8.75	5.59	6.04	6.37	6.43
November	5.80	5.25	5.72	5.35	5.64	5.74	5.59	5.35	8.75	5.43	5.93	6.26	6.31
December	5.60	5.25	5.74	5.16	5.52	5.14	5.43	5.43	8.65	5.31	5.71	6.06	6.11
1996:													
January	5.56	5.24	5.45	5.02	5.31	5.39	5.23	5.01	8.50	5.09	5.65	6.05	6.07
February	5.22	5.00	5.20	4.87	5.07	5.15	5.15	5.00	8.25	4.94	5.81	6.24	6.28
March	5.31	5.00	5.26	4.96	5.21	5.29	5.26	5.04	8.25	5.34	6.27	6.60	6.72
April	5.22	5.00	5.32	4.99	5.28	5.36	5.38	5.20	8.25	5.54	6.51	6.79	6.94
May	5.24	5.00	5.30	5.02	5.29	5.36	5.42	5.23	8.25	5.64	6.74	6.93	7.08
June	5.27	5.00	5.33	5.11	5.38	5.46	5.57	5.35	8.25	5.81	6.91	7.06	7.20
July	5.40	5.00	5.31	5.17	5.45	5.53	5.67	5.44	8.25	5.85	6.87	7.03	7.13
August	5.22	5.00	5.28	5.09	5.32	5.40	5.51	5.33	8.25	5.67	6.64	6.84	6.94
September	5.30	5.00	5.40	5.20	5.40	5.50	5.70	5.40	8.30	5.80	6.80	7.00	7.10
October	5.20	5.00	5.30	5.00	5.30	5.40	5.50	5.30	8.30	5.60	6.50	6.80	6.90
November	5.31	5.00	5.26	5.03	5.29	5.38	5.40	5.23	8.25	5.42	6.20	6.48	6.55
December	5.29	5.00	5.48	4.87	5.35	5.44	5.44	5.25	8.25	5.47	6.30	6.55	6.63

1. Discount window borrowing, Federal Reserve Bank of New York.
2. Maturities of more than ten years.

YEAR AND MONTH	SELECTED INTEREST RATES AND BOND YIELDS— Continued (Percent per annum)					COMMON STOCK PRICES AND YIELDS							
	Bond yields				Fixed-rate first mort- gages	Dow Jones industrials (30 stocks)	Standard and Poor's composite, (500 stocks)[1]	Stock price indexes					Stock dividend- price ratio, Standard and Poor's composite (Percent)
	Domestic corporate (Moody's)		A-rated utility bonds	State and local bonds (Bond Buyer)					New York Stock Exchange (December 31, 1965=50, except as noted)				
	Aaa	Baa						Compos- ite	Industrial	Transpor- tation	Utility (Dec. 31, 1965=100)	Finance	
1968	6.18	6.94	....	....	....	906.00	98.69	55.37	58.00	50.58	88.38	65.85	3.07
1969	7.03	7.81	....	....	....	876.72	97.84	54.67	57.44	46.96	85.60	70.49	3.24
1970	8.04	9.11	9.17	....	....	753.20	83.22	45.72	48.03	32.14	74.48	60.00	3.83
1971	7.39	8.56	8.01	....	....	884.76	98.29	54.22	57.92	44.35	79.04	70.38	3.14
1972	7.21	8.16	7.55	....	7.38	950.71	109.20	60.29	65.73	50.17	76.96	78.35	2.84
1973	7.44	8.24	8.01	....	8.04	923.88	107.43	57.42	63.08	37.74	75.38	70.12	3.06
1974	8.57	9.50	10.11	....	9.19	759.37	82.85	43.84	48.08	31.89	59.58	49.67	4.47
1975	8.83	10.61	10.57	....	9.04	802.49	86.16	45.73	50.52	31.10	63.00	47.14	4.31
1976	8.43	9.75	9.07	....	8.87	974.92	102.01	54.46	60.44	39.57	73.94	52.94	3.77
1977	8.02	8.97	8.56	....	8.84	894.62	98.20	53.69	57.86	41.08	81.84	55.25	4.62
1978	8.73	9.49	9.36	....	9.64	820.23	96.02	53.70	58.23	43.50	78.44	56.65	5.28
1979	9.63	10.69	10.67	....	11.19	844.40	103.01	58.32	64.75	47.34	76.40	61.42	5.47
1980	11.94	13.67	13.81	....	13.77	891.41	118.78	68.10	78.70	60.61	74.70	64.25	5.26
1981	14.17	16.04	16.63	11.33	16.63	932.92	128.04	74.02	85.44	72.61	77.82	73.52	5.20
1982	13.79	16.11	15.51	11.66	16.08	884.36	119.71	68.93	78.18	60.41	79.48	71.99	5.81
1983	12.04	13.55	12.73	9.51	13.23	1 190.34	160.41	92.63	107.45	89.36	94.00	95.34	4.40
1984	12.71	14.19	13.81	10.10	13.87	1 178.48	160.46	92.46	108.01	85.63	92.88	89.28	4.64
1985	11.37	12.72	12.06	9.10	12.42	1 328.23	186.84	108.09	123.78	104.10	113.48	114.21	4.25
1986	9.02	10.39	9.61	7.32	10.18	1 792.76	236.34	136.00	155.85	119.87	142.72	147.20	3.48
1987	9.38	10.58	9.95	7.64	10.20	2 275.99	286.83	161.70	195.31	140.39	148.59	146.48	3.08
1988	9.71	10.83	10.20	7.68	10.34	2 060.82	265.79	149.91	180.95	134.12	143.53	127.26	3.64
1989	9.26	10.18	9.79	7.23	10.32	2 508.91	322.84	180.02	216.23	175.28	174.87	151.88	3.45
1990	9.32	10.36	10.01	7.27	10.13	2 678.94	334.59	183.46	225.78	158.62	181.20	133.26	3.61
1991	8.77	9.80	9.32	6.92	9.25	2 929.33	376.17	206.33	258.14	173.99	185.32	150.82	3.24
1992	8.14	8.98	8.52	6.44	8.40	3 284.29	415.74	229.01	284.62	201.09	198.91	179.26	2.99
1993	7.22	7.93	7.46	5.60	7.33	3 522.06	451.41	249.58	299.99	242.49	228.90	216.42	2.78
1994	7.96	8.62	8.28	6.18	8.36	3 793.77	460.33	254.12	315.25	247.29	209.06	209.73	2.82
1995	7.59	8.20	7.86	5.95	7.95	4 493.76	541.64	291.15	367.34	269.41	220.30	238.45	2.56
1996	7.37	8.05	7.76	5.75	7.80	5 742.89	670.83	358.17	453.98	327.33	249.77	303.89	2.19
1993:													
January	7.91	8.67	8.13	6.15	8.02	3 277.71	435.23	239.67	292.07	221.00	211.02	203.38	2.88
February	7.71	8.39	7.80	5.87	7.68	3 367.26	441.70	243.41	294.40	226.96	218.88	209.92	2.81
March	7.58	8.15	7.61	5.64	7.50	3 440.73	450.16	248.11	298.75	229.41	225.06	217.01	2.76
April	7.46	8.14	7.66	5.76	7.47	3 423.62	443.08	244.72	292.16	237.97	227.58	216.02	2.82
May	7.43	8.21	7.75	5.73	7.47	3 478.17	445.25	246.02	297.83	237.80	222.41	209.40	2.80
June	7.33	8.07	7.59	5.63	7.42	3 513.81	448.06	247.16	298.78	234.30	226.53	209.74	2.81
July	7.17	7.93	7.43	5.57	7.21	3 529.43	447.29	247.85	295.34	238.30	232.55	218.94	2.81
August	6.85	7.60	7.16	5.45	7.11	3 597.01	454.13	251.93	298.83	250.82	237.44	224.95	2.76
September	6.66	7.34	6.94	5.29	6.92	3 592.28	459.24	254.86	300.92	248.15	244.21	229.34	2.73
October	6.67	7.31	6.91	5.25	6.83	3 625.80	463.90	257.53	306.61	254.04	240.97	228.17	2.72
November	6.93	7.66	7.25	5.47	7.16	3 674.69	462.89	255.93	310.84	262.96	230.12	214.08	2.72
December	6.93	7.69	7.28	5.35	7.17	3 743.62	465.95	257.73	313.22	268.11	229.95	216.00	2.72
1994:													
January	6.92	7.65	7.24	5.31	7.06	3 868.36	472.99	262.11	320.92	278.29	225.15	218.71	2.69
February	7.08	7.76	7.45	5.40	7.15	3 905.62	471.58	261.97	322.40	276.67	220.85	217.12	2.70
March	7.48	8.13	7.82	5.91	7.68	3 816.98	463.81	257.32	318.48	265.68	215.45	211.02	2.78
April	7.88	8.52	8.20	6.23	8.32	3 661.48	447.23	247.97	304.48	250.43	210.08	208.12	2.90
May	7.99	8.62	8.37	6.19	8.60	3 707.99	450.90	249.56	307.58	244.75	205.77	211.30	2.89
June	7.97	8.65	8.30	6.11	8.40	3 737.58	454.83	251.21	308.66	246.64	206.54	215.89	2.84
July	8.11	8.80	8.45	6.23	8.61	3 718.30	451.40	249.29	307.34	244.21	205.46	210.91	2.87
August	8.07	8.74	8.36	6.21	8.51	3 797.48	464.24	255.08	316.55	244.67	211.26	214.77	2.78
September	8.34	8.98	8.62	6.28	8.64	3 880.60	466.96	257.61	322.19	239.10	204.60	211.90	2.80
October	8.57	9.20	8.80	6.52	8.93	3 868.10	463.81	255.22	321.53	230.71	203.34	203.33	2.82
November	8.68	9.32	8.95	6.97	9.17	3 792.43	461.01	252.48	319.33	227.45	200.13	198.38	2.86
December	8.46	9.10	8.78	6.80	9.20	3 770.31	455.19	248.65	313.95	218.93	200.02	193.25	2.91
1995:													
January	8.46	9.08	8.75	6.53	9.15	3 872.46	465.25	253.56	319.93	230.25	201.16	201.05	2.87
February	8.26	8.85	8.55	6.22	8.83	3 953.72	481.92	261.86	328.98	237.29	207.73	211.76	2.81
March	8.12	8.70	8.40	6.10	8.46	4 062.78	493.15	266.81	337.96	244.45	204.16	213.29	2.76
April	8.03	8.60	8.31	6.02	8.32	4 230.66	507.91	274.37	347.69	254.36	208.93	219.38	2.68
May	7.65	8.20	7.89	5.95	7.96	4 391.57	523.81	281.81	357.01	254.69	211.58	228.55	2.60
June	7.30	7.90	7.60	5.84	7.57	4 510.76	539.35	289.52	366.75	256.80	216.27	236.26	2.55
July	7.41	8.04	7.72	5.92	7.61	4 684.76	557.37	298.18	379.13	279.15	219.18	240.50	2.50
August	7.57	8.19	7.84	6.06	7.86	4 639.27	559.11	300.05	379.79	285.63	221.99	245.27	2.49
September	7.32	7.93	7.55	5.91	7.64	4 746.76	578.77	310.41	390.42	295.54	229.64	260.72	2.42
October	7.12	7.75	7.36	5.80	7.48	4 760.46	582.92	311.78	389.63	291.16	236.43	265.12	2.41
November	7.02	7.68	7.30	5.64	7.38	4 935.81	595.53	317.58	398.66	300.06	238.98	266.12	2.37
December	6.82	7.49	7.10	5.45	7.20	5 136.10	614.57	327.90	412.11	303.53	247.59	273.36	2.30
1996:													
January	6.80	7.47	7.09	5.43	7.03	5 179.37	614.42	329.22	412.71	300.03	254.07	273.73	2.31
February	6.99	7.63	7.31	5.43	7.08	5 518.73	649.54	346.46	435.92	315.29	257.80	290.97	2.22
March	7.35	8.03	7.75	5.79	7.62	5 612.24	647.07	346.73	439.56	324.76	245.77	290.45	2.22
April	7.50	8.19	7.90	5.94	7.93	5 579.86	647.17	347.50	441.99	326.42	244.87	287.92	2.24
May	7.62	8.20	7.90	5.87	8.07	5 616.71	661.23	354.84	452.63	334.66	249.73	290.43	2.21
June	7.71	8.40	8.13	6.02	8.32	5 671.51	668.50	358.32	458.30	331.57	247.20	294.42	2.21
July	7.65	8.35	8.07	5.92	8.25	5 496.26	644.07	345.52	438.58	316.66	245.31	287.89	2.28
August	7.46	8.18	7.87	5.76	8.00	5 685.50	662.68	354.59	449.41	321.61	244.74	302.95	2.22
September	7.70	8.40	8.10	5.90	8.23	5 804.01	674.88	360.96	459.69	323.12	242.25	308.16	2.20
October	7.40	8.10	7.80	5.70	7.92	5 996.21	701.46	373.54	473.98	332.93	249.61	324.42	2.11
November	7.10	7.79	7.54	5.59	7.62	6 318.36	735.67	388.75	490.60	348.32	258.85	345.30	2.01
December	7.20	7.89	7.63	5.64	7.60	6 435.87	743.25	391.61	494.38	352.28	257.09	350.01	2.01

1. 1941-1943=10.

U.S. Foreign Trade and Finance

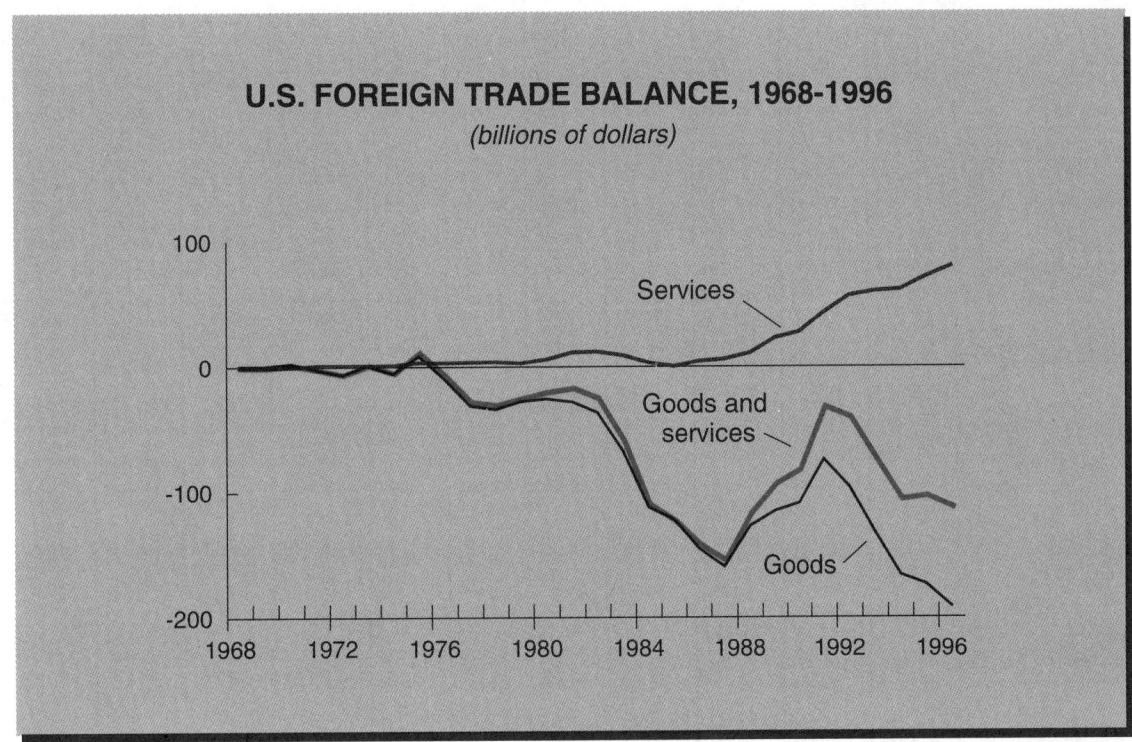

U.S. FOREIGN TRADE BALANCE, 1968-1996
(billions of dollars)

Since the mid 1980s the United States has had a rapidly growing surplus on trade in services. This surplus reached $80 billion in 1996, offsetting 42 percent of the deficit on trade in goods.

Travel and passenger fares have been among the rapidly growing categories of U.S. service exports and have surpassed imports in these categories since 1989. In 1996, earnings from foreign travel to the United States and from passenger fares exceeded U.S. expenditures abroad in these categories by $26 billion, accounting for 32 percent of the total surplus on trade in services.

U.S. INTERNATIONAL TRANSACTIONS
(Millions of dollars, seasonally adjusted)

YEAR AND QUARTER	Exports of goods, services, and income							Imports of goods, services, and income [1]						
	Total	Goods, adjusted, excluding military	Services	Income receipts on U.S. assets abroad				Total	Goods, adjusted, excluding military	Services	Income payments on foreign assets in the United States			
				Total	Direct investment receipts	Other private receipts	U.S. government receipts				Total	Direct investment payments	Other private payments	U.S. government payments
1968	54 911	33 626	11 917	9 367	6 591	2 021	756	-48 671	-32 991	-12 302	-3 378	-876	-1 800	-702
1969	60 132	36 414	12 806	10 913	7 649	2 338	925	-53 998	-35 807	-13 322	-4 869	-848	-3 244	-777
1970	68 387	42 469	14 171	11 748	8 169	2 671	907	-59 901	-39 866	-14 520	-5 515	-875	-3 617	-1 024
1971	72 384	43 319	16 358	12 707	9 160	2 641	906	-66 414	-45 579	-15 400	-5 435	-1 164	-2 428	-1 844
1972	81 986	49 381	17 841	14 765	10 949	2 949	866	-79 237	-55 797	-16 868	-6 572	-1 284	-2 604	-2 684
1973	113 050	71 410	19 832	21 808	16 542	4 330	936	-98 997	-70 499	-18 843	-9 655	-1 610	-4 209	-3 836
1974	148 484	98 306	22 591	27 587	19 157	7 356	1 074	-137 274	-103 811	-21 379	-12 084	-1 331	-6 491	-4 262
1975	157 936	107 088	25 497	25 351	16 595	7 644	1 112	-132 745	-98 185	-21 996	-12 564	-2 234	-5 788	-4 542
1976	172 090	114 745	27 971	29 375	18 999	9 043	1 332	-162 109	-124 228	-24 570	-13 311	-3 110	-5 681	-4 520
1977	184 655	120 816	31 485	32 354	19 673	11 057	1 625	-193 764	-151 907	-27 640	-14 217	-2 834	-5 841	-5 542
1978	220 516	142 075	36 353	42 088	25 458	14 788	1 843	-229 870	-176 002	-32 189	-21 680	-4 211	-8 795	-8 674
1979	287 965	184 439	39 692	63 834	38 183	23 356	2 295	-281 657	-212 007	-36 689	-32 961	-6 357	-15 481	-11 122
1980	344 440	224 250	47 584	72 606	37 146	32 898	2 562	-333 774	-249 750	-41 491	-42 532	-8 635	-21 214	-12 684
1981	380 928	237 044	57 354	86 529	32 549	50 300	3 680	-364 196	-265 067	-45 503	-53 626	-6 898	-29 415	-17 313
1982	361 436	211 157	64 079	86 200	23 922	58 160	4 118	-355 804	-247 642	-51 749	-56 412	-1 943	-35 187	-19 282
1983	351 306	201 799	64 307	85 200	26 950	53 418	4 832	-377 573	-268 901	-54 973	-53 700	-4 206	-30 501	-18 993
1984	395 850	219 926	71 168	104 756	31 262	68 267	5 227	-474 203	-332 418	-67 748	-74 036	-8 723	-44 158	-21 155
1985	382 749	215 915	73 155	93 679	30 547	57 633	5 499	-484 037	-338 088	-72 862	-73 087	-7 213	-42 745	-23 129
1986	400 842	223 344	86 312	91 186	31 968	52 806	6 413	-529 356	-368 425	-81 836	-79 095	-7 058	-47 412	-24 625
1987	449 272	250 208	98 553	100 511	39 608	55 592	5 311	-593 416	-409 765	-92 349	-91 302	-7 425	-57 659	-26 218
1988	560 620	320 230	111 024	129 366	52 092	70 571	6 703	-662 876	-447 189	-99 965	-115 722	-11 693	-72 314	-31 715
1989	642 921	362 120	127 142	153 659	55 368	92 638	5 653	-720 189	-477 365	-104 185	-138 639	-6 507	-93 768	-38 364
1990	700 455	389 307	147 824	163 324	58 740	94 072	10 512	-757 758	-498 337	-120 019	-139 402	-2 871	-95 489	-41 042
1991	722 557	416 913	164 236	141 408	52 198	81 186	8 023	-733 335	-490 981	-121 195	-121 159	3 433	-83 063	-41 529
1992	743 358	440 352	177 154	125 852	51 912	66 826	7 114	-764 549	-536 458	-120 255	-107 836	-302	-67 054	-40 480
1993	773 387	456 832	186 711	129 844	61 241	63 495	5 108	-826 020	-589 441	-126 403	-110 176	-5 574	-63 041	-41 561
1994	854 156	502 398	197 248	154 510	70 911	79 498	4 101	-948 849	-668 590	-135 472	-144 787	-20 154	-77 614	-47 019
1995	991 490	575 871	218 739	196 880	90 349	101 836	4 695	-1 086 539	-749 431	-147 036	-190 072	-30 345	-98 448	-61 279
1996	1 055 233	612 069	236 764	206 400	98 890	102 866	4 644	-1 163 450	-803 239	-156 634	-203 577	-32 132	-100 103	-71 342
1988:														
1st quarter	133 067	75 655	26 605	30 807	12 165	15 936	2 706	-161 534	-109 963	-24 852	-26 719	-3 044	-16 441	-7 234
2nd quarter	138 160	79 542	27 590	31 028	13 492	16 227	1 309	-163 018	-110 836	-24 657	-27 525	-2 981	-16 814	-7 730
3rd quarter	142 089	80 941	28 487	32 661	12 954	18 502	1 205	-165 704	-110 901	-24 921	-29 882	-2 807	-18 842	-8 233
4th quarter	147 305	84 092	28 342	34 871	13 483	19 906	1 482	-172 622	-115 489	-25 538	-31 595	-2 860	-20 217	-8 518
1989:														
1st quarter	155 053	87 426	30 593	37 034	13 618	22 363	1 053	-175 851	-116 477	-25 545	-33 829	-2 223	-22 369	-9 237
2nd quarter	162 257	92 208	31 125	38 924	13 988	23 870	1 066	-182 462	-120 907	-25 663	-35 892	-2 473	-23 893	-9 526
3rd quarter	161 091	90 163	32 332	38 596	13 862	22 898	1 836	-180 066	-118 873	-26 207	-34 986	-1 738	-23 478	-9 770
4th quarter	164 522	92 323	33 094	39 105	13 900	23 507	1 698	-181 810	-121 108	-26 771	-33 931	-72	-24 028	-9 831
1990:														
1st quarter	170 110	95 301	35 021	39 788	14 849	23 001	1 938	-185 633	-122 447	-28 785	-34 401	-988	-23 407	-10 006
2nd quarter	173 486	97 573	35 998	39 915	14 882	23 073	1 960	-186 179	-122 169	-29 309	-34 701	-947	-23 604	-10 150
3rd quarter	173 414	96 339	37 402	39 673	14 016	23 660	1 997	-191 531	-125 389	-30 509	-35 633	-1 305	-24 011	-10 317
4th quarter	183 444	100 094	39 404	43 946	14 992	24 338	4 616	-194 412	-128 332	-31 412	-34 668	368	-24 467	-10 569
1991:														
1st quarter	179 343	101 345	37 918	40 080	14 790	22 679	2 611	-183 007	-120 141	-30 411	-32 455	1 079	-22 953	-10 581
2nd quarter	180 518	104 529	40 767	35 222	12 883	20 486	1 853	-181 720	-120 705	-30 302	-30 713	484	-20 837	-10 360
3rd quarter	179 217	103 732	41 849	33 636	11 872	19 821	1 943	-183 658	-123 479	-29 890	-30 289	255	-20 091	-10 453
4th quarter	183 486	107 307	43 706	32 473	12 656	18 200	1 617	-184 951	-126 656	-30 594	-27 701	1 616	-19 182	-10 135
1992:														
1st quarter	184 610	108 344	44 118	32 148	13 250	17 262	1 636	-183 097	-126 284	-30 274	-26 539	1 131	-17 618	-10 052
2nd quarter	185 967	109 025	44 075	32 867	14 133	16 929	1 805	-191 301	-133 277	-30 024	-28 000	-715	-17 141	-10 144
3rd quarter	184 924	109 593	44 578	30 753	12 880	16 015	1 858	-193 033	-136 887	-29 145	-27 001	-535	-16 336	-10 130
4th quarter	187 856	113 390	44 383	30 083	11 649	16 620	1 814	-197 118	-140 010	-30 811	-26 297	-184	-15 959	-10 154
1993:														
1st quarter	189 422	111 862	46 135	31 425	14 734	15 370	1 321	-197 041	-141 069	-30 647	-25 325	518	-15 650	-10 193
2nd quarter	192 533	114 185	46 633	31 715	15 245	15 145	1 325	-206 335	-147 571	-31 319	-27 445	-1 774	-15 464	-10 207
3rd quarter	191 354	111 429	46 887	33 038	15 641	16 077	1 320	-206 720	-147 926	-31 494	-27 300	-999	-15 749	-10 552
4th quarter	200 077	119 356	47 056	33 665	15 621	16 903	1 141	-215 928	-152 875	-32 947	-30 106	-3 319	-16 178	-10 609
1994:														
1st quarter	200 670	118 382	47 249	35 039	16 118	17 883	1 038	-218 852	-155 009	-33 270	-30 573	-3 192	-16 576	-10 805
2nd quarter	208 713	123 025	49 071	36 617	16 546	19 094	977	-231 438	-163 852	-33 611	-33 975	-4 328	-18 426	-11 221
3rd quarter	217 714	127 629	50 095	39 990	18 709	20 318	963	-244 405	-171 977	-34 236	-38 192	-5 965	-20 393	-11 834
4th quarter	227 062	133 362	50 833	42 867	19 540	22 203	1 124	-254 154	-177 752	-34 355	-42 047	-6 669	-22 219	-13 159
1995:														
1st quarter	237 587	138 389	51 980	47 218	21 425	24 611	1 182	-263 845	-182 790	-35 884	-45 171	-7 035	-23 897	-14 239
2nd quarter	246 787	143 181	53 303	50 303	23 416	25 522	1 365	-274 363	-190 739	-36 544	-47 080	-7 379	-24 640	-15 061
3rd quarter	250 734	145 360	56 244	49 130	22 347	25 740	1 043	-275 019	-188 180	-37 308	-49 531	-8 883	-24 841	-15 807
4th quarter	256 382	148 941	57 211	50 230	23 162	25 963	1 105	-273 316	-187 722	-37 304	-48 290	-7 048	-25 070	-16 172
1996:														
1st quarter	256 382	150 048	57 057	49 277	23 389	24 643	1 245	-278 860	-192 973	-38 671	-47 216	-6 842	-24 210	-16 164
2nd quarter	262 335	153 411	58 736	50 188	23 929	25 053	1 206	-289 231	-200 973	-38 953	-49 305	-7 873	-24 600	-16 832
3rd quarter	261 979	150 764	59 322	51 893	24 675	25 938	1 280	-295 865	-203 257	-39 345	-53 263	-9 612	-25 158	-18 493
4th quarter	274 545	157 846	61 656	55 043	26 898	27 232	913	-299 493	-206 036	-39 664	-53 793	-7 805	-26 135	-19 853

1. A minus sign indicates capital outflow, that is, an increase in assets abroad.

U.S. INTERNATIONAL TRANSACTIONS—Continued
(Millions of dollars, seasonally adjusted)

YEAR AND QUARTER	Unilateral transfers, net				U.S. assets abroad, net [1]						
	Total	U.S. government		Private remittances and other transfers	Total	U.S. official reserve assets, net					
		Grants	Pensions and other transfers			Total	Gold	Special drawing rights	Reserve position in the IMF	Foreign currencies
1968	-5 629	-4 256	-537	-836	-10 977	-870	1 173	....	-870	-1 173
1969	-5 735	-4 259	-537	-939	-11 585	-1 179	-967	....	-1 034	822
1970	-6 156	-4 449	-611	-1 096	-9 337	2 481	787	-851	389	2 156
1971	-7 402	-5 589	-696	-1 117	-12 475	2 349	866	-249	1 350	382
1972	-8 544	-6 665	-770	-1 109	-14 497	-4	547	-703	153	-1
1973	-6 913	-4 748	-915	-1 250	-22 874	158	....	9	-33	182
1974	-9 249	-7 293	-939	-1 017	-34 745	-1 467	....	-172	-1 265	-30
1975	-7 075	-5 101	-1 068	-906	-39 703	-849	....	-66	-466	-317
1976	-5 686	-3 519	-1 250	-917	-51 269	-2 558	....	-78	-2 212	-268
1977	-5 227	-2 990	-1 378	-859	-34 785	-375	-118	-121	-294	158
1978	-5 788	-3 412	-1 532	-844	-61 130	732	-65	1 249	4 231	-4 683
1979	-6 593	-4 015	-1 658	-920	-66 054	-1 133	-65	-1 136	-189	257
1980	-8 348	-5 486	-1 818	-1 044	-86 967	-8 155	....	-16	-1 667	-6 472
1981	-11 702	-5 145	-2 041	-4 516	-114 147	-5 175	....	-1 824	-2 491	-861
1982	-17 076	-6 087	-2 251	-8 738	-122 335	-4 965	....	-1 371	-2 552	-1 041
1983	-17 719	-6 469	-2 207	-9 043	-61 573	-1 196	....	-66	-4 434	3 304
1984	-20 597	-8 696	-2 159	-9 742	-36 313	-3 131	....	-979	-995	-1 156
1985	-22 701	-11 268	-2 138	-9 295	-39 889	-3 858	....	-897	908	-3 869
1986	-24 679	-11 883	-2 372	-10 424	-106 753	312	....	-246	1 501	-942
1987	-23 910	-10 309	-2 409	-11 192	-72 617	9 149	....	-509	2 070	7 588
1988	-25 988	-10 537	-2 709	-12 742	-100 221	-3 912	....	127	1 025	-5 064
1989	-26 963	-10 911	-2 744	-13 308	-168 744	-25 293	....	-535	471	-25 229
1990	-34 589	-17 433	-3 184	-13 972	-74 011	-2 158	....	-192	731	-2 697
1991	5 121	24 160	-3 730	-15 309	-57 881	5 763	....	-177	-367	6 307
1992	-35 192	-15 826	-4 018	-15 348	-68 774	3 901	....	2 316	-2 692	4 277
1993	-38 137	-16 821	-4 081	-17 235	-194 537	-1 379	....	-537	-44	-797
1994	-38 845	-15 671	-4 544	-18 630	-160 516	5 346	....	-441	494	5 293
1995	-34 046	-11 096	-3 420	-19 530	-307 207	-9 742	....	-808	-2 466	-6 468
1996	-39 968	-14 933	-4 331	-20 704	-352 444	6 668	....	370	-1 280	7 578
1988:										
1st quarter	-6 236	-2 298	-678	-3 260	4 515	1 502	....	155	446	901
2nd quarter	-5 854	-1 981	-677	-3 196	-21 828	39	....	180	69	-210
3rd quarter	-6 085	-2 395	-677	-3 013	-48 389	-7 380	....	-35	202	-7 547
4th quarter	-7 813	-3 863	-677	-3 273	-34 521	1 925	....	-173	307	1 791
1989:										
1st quarter	-6 250	-2 409	-688	-3 153	-52 028	-4 000	....	-188	316	-4 128
2nd quarter	-5 874	-1 956	-660	-3 258	-6 529	-12 095	....	68	-159	-12 004
3rd quarter	-6 724	-2 735	-706	-3 283	-50 013	-5 996	....	-211	337	-6 122
4th quarter	-8 117	-3 813	-690	-3 614	-60 176	-3 202	....	-204	-23	-2 975
1990:										
1st quarter	-6 904	-2 725	-796	-3 383	39 529	-3 177	....	-247	234	-3 164
2nd quarter	-7 829	-3 569	-798	-3 462	-35 403	371	....	-216	493	94
3rd quarter	-7 523	-3 030	-794	-3 699	-41 844	1 739	....	363	8	1 368
4th quarter	-12 335	-8 110	-797	-3 428	-36 291	-1 091	....	-93	-4	-995
1991:										
1st quarter	13 748	18 367	-861	-3 758	-8 819	-353	....	31	-341	-43
2nd quarter	3 545	8 227	-863	-3 819	2 419	1 014	....	-190	72	1 132
3rd quarter	-6 929	-2 246	-860	-3 823	-14 331	3 877	....	6	-114	3 986
4th quarter	-5 244	-189	-1 146	-3 909	-37 151	1 225	....	-23	17	1 232
1992:										
1st quarter	-7 625	-2 941	-901	-3 783	-9 963	-1 057	....	-172	111	-996
2nd quarter	-8 462	-3 398	-1 189	-3 875	-14 813	1 464	....	-168	1	1 631
3rd quarter	-7 867	-3 025	-1 011	-3 831	-12 185	1 952	....	-173	-118	2 243
4th quarter	-11 237	-6 461	-917	-3 859	-31 812	1 542	....	2 829	-2 685	1 398
1993:										
1st quarter	-8 502	-3 504	-900	-4 098	-20 024	-983	....	-140	-228	-615
2nd quarter	-8 501	-3 243	-1 061	-4 197	-44 338	822	....	-166	313	675
3rd quarter	-9 347	-3 904	-1 061	-4 382	-51 461	-545	....	-118	-48	-378
4th quarter	-11 787	-6 169	-1 060	-4 558	-78 714	-673	....	-113	-80	-480
1994:										
1st quarter	-7 971	-2 387	-963	-4 621	-38 839	-59	....	-101	-3	45
2nd quarter	-9 275	-3 709	-971	-4 595	-32 429	3 537	....	-108	251	3 394
3rd quarter	-9 671	-3 478	-1 550	-4 643	-28 835	-165	....	-111	273	-327
4th quarter	-11 928	-6 097	-1 060	-4 771	-60 415	2 033	....	-121	-27	2 181
1995:										
1st quarter	-8 451	-2 865	-758	-4 828	-59 625	-5 318	....	-867	-526	-3 925
2nd quarter	-8 128	-2 399	-967	-4 762	-110 548	-2 722	....	-156	-786	-1 780
3rd quarter	-8 847	-2 987	-964	-4 896	-40 679	-1 893	....	362	-991	-1 264
4th quarter	-8 620	-2 845	-731	-5 044	-96 356	191	....	-147	-163	501
1996:										
1st quarter	-10 406	-4 321	-1 136	-4 949	-70 768	17	....	-199	-849	1 065
2nd quarter	-8 689	-2 423	-1 081	-5 185	-49 698	-523	....	-133	-220	-170
3rd quarter	-8 947	-2 690	-1 064	-5 193	-77 542	7 489	....	848	-183	6 824
4th quarter	-11 926	-5 499	-1 050	-5 377	-154 436	-315	....	-146	-28	-141

1. A minus sign indicates capital outflow, that is, an increase in assets abroad.

U.S. FOREIGN TRADE AND FINANCE

U.S. INTERNATIONAL TRANSACTIONS—Continued
(Millions of dollars, seasonally adjusted)

U.S. assets abroad, net [1]—Continued

YEAR AND QUARTER	U.S. government assets other than official reserve assets, net				U.S. private assets, net				
	Total	U.S. credits and other long-term assets	Repayments on U.S. credits and other long-term assets	U.S. foreign currency holdings and short-term assets, net	Total	Direct investment	Foreign securities	U.S. claims On unaffiliated foreigners reported by U.S. nonbanking concerns	U.S. claims Reported by U.S. banks, not included elsewhere
1968	-2 274	-3 722	1 386	62	-7 833	-5 295	-1 569	-1 203	233
1969	-2 200	-3 489	1 200	89	-8 206	-5 960	-1 549	-126	-570
1970	-1 589	-3 293	1 721	-16	-10 229	-7 590	-1 076	-596	-967
1971	-1 884	-4 181	2 115	182	-12 940	-7 618	-1 113	-1 229	-2 980
1972	-1 568	-3 819	2 086	165	-12 925	-7 747	-618	-1 054	-3 506
1973	-2 644	-4 638	2 596	-602	-20 388	-11 353	-671	-2 383	-5 980
1974	366	-5 001	4 826	541	-33 643	-9 052	-1 854	-3 221	-19 516
1975	-3 474	-5 941	2 475	-9	-35 380	-14 244	-6 247	-1 357	-13 532
1976	-4 214	-6 943	2 596	133	-44 498	-11 949	-8 885	-2 296	-21 368
1977	-3 693	-6 445	2 719	33	-30 717	-11 890	-5 460	-1 940	-11 427
1978	-4 660	-7 470	2 941	-131	-57 202	-16 056	-3 626	-3 853	-33 667
1979	-3 746	-7 697	3 926	25	-61 176	-25 222	-4 726	-5 014	-26 213
1980	-5 162	-9 860	4 456	242	-73 651	-19 222	-3 568	-4 023	-46 838
1981	-5 097	-9 674	4 413	164	-103 875	-9 624	-5 699	-4 377	-84 175
1982	-6 131	-10 063	4 292	-360	-111 239	991	-7 983	6 823	-111 070
1983	-5 006	-9 967	5 012	-51	-55 372	-7 728	-6 762	-10 954	-29 928
1984	-5 489	-9 599	4 490	-379	-27 694	-12 344	-4 756	533	-11 127
1985	-2 821	-7 657	4 719	117	-33 211	-14 065	-7 481	-10 342	-1 323
1986	-2 022	-9 084	6 089	973	-105 044	-19 025	-4 271	-21 773	-59 975
1987	1 006	-6 506	7 625	-113	-82 771	-28 355	-5 251	-7 046	-42 119
1988	2 967	-7 680	10 370	277	-99 275	-16 175	-7 980	-21 193	-53 927
1989	1 259	-5 590	6 723	125	-144 710	-36 834	-22 070	-27 646	-58 160
1990	2 307	-8 430	10 867	-130	-74 160	-29 950	-28 765	-27 824	12 379
1991	2 911	-12 874	16 776	-992	-66 555	-31 369	-45 673	11 097	-610
1992	-1 657	-7 398	5 807	-66	-71 018	-42 640	-49 166	-387	21 175
1993	-342	-6 299	6 270	-313	-192 817	-77 945	-146 253	766	30 615
1994	-352	-5 212	5 045	-185	-165 510	-69 262	-60 309	-31 739	-4 200
1995	-549	-4 803	4 115	139	-296 916	-86 737	-100 074	-34 997	-75 108
1996	-690	-4 930	4 134	106	-358 422	-87 813	-108 189	-64 234	-98 186
1988:									
1st quarter	-1 597	-2 814	1 109	108	4 610	-3 414	-4 504	-3 454	15 982
2nd quarter	-854	-2 021	1 144	23	-21 013	-994	1 318	-9 954	-11 383
3rd quarter	1 960	-1 458	3 358	60	-42 969	-6 215	-1 500	-5 217	-30 037
4th quarter	3 457	-1 388	4 759	86	-39 903	-5 552	-3 294	-2 568	-28 489
1989:									
1st quarter	964	-1 007	1 965	6	-48 992	-10 464	-2 225	-9 293	-27 010
2nd quarter	-303	-1 174	815	56	5 869	-6 016	-6 192	-5 767	23 844
3rd quarter	505	-2 136	2 670	-29	-44 522	-7 055	-9 149	-5 924	-22 394
4th quarter	92	-1 274	1 273	93	-57 066	-13 300	-4 504	-6 662	-32 600
1990:									
1st quarter	-743	-1 869	1 200	-74	43 449	-8 703	-8 580	3 019	57 713
2nd quarter	-793	-2 016	1 209	14	-34 981	-2 853	-11 037	-5 069	-16 022
3rd quarter	-338	-1 349	1 039	-28	-43 245	-16 026	-1 037	-15 514	-10 668
4th quarter	4 181	-3 195	7 419	-43	-39 380	-2 365	-8 111	-10 260	-18 644
1991:									
1st quarter	549	-2 018	2 630	-63	-9 015	-12 567	-9 960	-40	13 552
2nd quarter	-418	-1 056	840	-202	1 823	439	-12 021	7 902	5 503
3rd quarter	3 238	-8 724	12 417	-455	-21 447	-7 769	-12 550	3 341	-4 469
4th quarter	-459	-1 077	890	-272	-37 918	-11 474	-11 142	-106	-15 196
1992:									
1st quarter	-258	-1 516	1 326	-68	-8 648	-19 231	-8 668	7 562	11 689
2nd quarter	-295	-1 240	1 084	-139	-15 982	-8 853	-8 196	-6 620	7 687
3rd quarter	-390	-1 978	1 359	229	-13 747	-3 774	-13 059	-3 737	6 823
4th quarter	-714	-2 663	2 038	-89	-32 640	-10 781	-19 243	2 408	-5 024
1993:									
1st quarter	489	-943	1 763	-331	-19 530	-13 517	-28 208	-6 130	28 325
2nd quarter	-293	-764	891	-420	-44 867	-21 770	-29 863	-725	7 461
3rd quarter	-197	-1 666	2 036	-567	-50 720	-11 638	-51 940	5 896	6 962
4th quarter	-340	-2 926	1 580	1 006	-77 701	-31 021	-36 272	1 725	-12 133
1994:									
1st quarter	399	-757	1 120	36	-39 179	-28 364	-19 540	-1 504	10 229
2nd quarter	490	-984	1 642	-168	-36 456	-15 188	-9 229	-10 080	-1 959
3rd quarter	-298	-1 223	1 346	-421	-28 372	-6 947	-12 405	-9 204	184
4th quarter	-943	-2 248	937	368	-61 505	-18 765	-19 135	-10 951	-12 654
1995:									
1st quarter	-158	-1 622	1 069	395	-54 149	-14 126	-7 631	-4 044	-28 348
2nd quarter	-184	-815	642	-11	-107 642	-13 662	-23 313	-23 147	-47 520
3rd quarter	266	-1 014	1 522	-242	-39 052	-14 385	-36 144	6 988	4 489
4th quarter	-473	-1 352	882	-3	-96 074	-44 565	-32 986	-14 794	-3 729
1996:									
1st quarter	-210	-1 076	1 013	-147	-70 575	-22 210	-34 455	-15 778	1 868
2nd quarter	-358	-1 489	870	261	-48 817	-23 634	-20 328	-5 047	192
3rd quarter	162	-1 127	1 206	83	-85 193	-11 104	-23 206	-17 294	-33 589
4th quarter	-284	-1 238	1 045	-91	-153 837	-30 865	-30 200	-26 115	-66 657

1. A minus sign indicates capital outflow, that is, an increase in assets abroad.

U.S. INTERNATIONAL TRANSACTIONS—Continued
(Millions of dollars, seasonally adjusted)

YEAR AND QUARTER	Total	Foreign official assets in the United States, net							Other foreign assets in the United States, net				U.S. liabilities	
		Total	U.S. government securities			Other U.S. government liabilities	U.S. liabilities reported by U.S. banks, not included elsewhere	Other foreign official assets	Total	Direct investment	U.S. treasury securities and U.S. currency flows	U.S. securities other than treasury securities	To unaffiliated foreigners reported by U.S. nonbanking concerns	Reported by U.S. banks, not included elsewhere
			Total	U.S. Treasury securities	Other									
1968	9 928	-774	-769	-798	29	-15	10	....	10 703	807	136	4 414	1 475	3 871
1969	12 702	-1 301	-2 343	-2 269	-74	251	792	....	14 002	1 263	-68	3 130	792	8 886
1970	6 359	6 908	9 439	9 411	28	-456	-2 075	....	-550	1 464	81	2 189	2 014	-6 298
1971	22 970	26 879	26 570	26 578	-8	-510	819	....	-3 909	367	-24	2 289	369	-6 911
1972	21 461	10 475	8 470	8 213	257	182	1 638	185	10 986	949	-39	4 507	815	4 754
1973	18 388	6 026	641	59	582	936	4 126	323	12 362	2 800	-216	4 041	1 035	4 702
1974	35 341	10 546	4 172	3 270	902	301	5 818	254	24 796	4 760	1 797	378	1 844	16 017
1975	17 170	7 027	5 563	4 658	905	1 517	-2 158	2 104	10 143	2 603	4 090	2 503	319	628
1976	38 018	17 693	9 892	9 319	573	4 627	969	2 205	20 326	4 347	4 283	1 284	-578	10 990
1977	53 219	36 816	32 538	30 230	2 308	1 400	773	2 105	16 403	3 728	2 434	2 437	1 086	6 719
1978	67 036	33 678	24 221	23 555	666	2 476	5 551	1 430	33 358	7 897	5 178	2 254	1 889	16 141
1979	40 852	-13 665	-21 972	-22 435	463	-40	7 213	1 135	54 516	11 877	7 060	1 351	1 621	32 607
1980	62 612	15 497	11 895	9 708	2 187	615	-159	3 145	47 115	16 918	7 145	5 457	6 852	10 743
1981	86 232	4 960	6 322	5 019	1 303	-338	-3 670	2 646	81 272	25 195	6 127	6 905	917	42 128
1982	96 418	3 593	5 085	5 779	-694	605	-1 747	-350	92 826	12 464	11 027	6 085	-2 383	65 633
1983	88 780	5 845	6 496	6 972	-476	602	545	-1 798	82 934	10 457	14 089	8 164	-118	50 342
1984	118 032	3 140	4 703	4 690	13	739	555	-2 857	114 892	24 748	27 101	12 568	16 626	33 849
1985	146 383	-1 119	-1 139	-838	-301	844	645	-1 469	147 501	20 010	25 633	50 962	9 851	41 045
1986	230 211	35 648	33 150	34 364	-1 214	2 195	1 187	-884	194 563	35 623	7 909	70 969	3 325	76 737
1987	248 383	45 387	44 802	43 238	1 564	-2 326	3 918	-1 007	202 996	58 219	-2 243	42 120	18 363	86 537
1988	246 065	39 758	43 050	41 741	1 309	-467	-319	-2 506	206 307	57 278	26 039	26 353	32 893	63 744
1989	224 390	8 503	1 532	149	1 383	160	4 976	1 835	215 887	67 736	35 518	38 767	22 086	51 780
1990	140 992	33 910	30 243	29 576	667	1 868	3 385	-1 586	107 082	47 915	16 266	1 592	45 133	-3 824
1991	109 641	17 389	16 147	14 846	1 301	1 367	-1 484	1 359	92 253	22 004	34 226	35 144	-3 115	3 994
1992	168 776	40 477	22 403	18 454	3 949	2 191	16 571	-688	128 299	17 936	50 531	30 043	13 573	16 216
1993	279 671	71 753	53 014	48 952	4 062	1 313	14 841	2 585	207 918	48 993	43 281	80 092	10 489	25 063
1994	297 337	40 385	36 827	30 750	6 077	2 366	3 665	-2 473	256 952	45 679	57 674	56 971	-7 710	104 338
1995	451 234	110 729	72 712	68 977	3 735	744	34 008	3 265	340 505	67 526	111 848	96 367	34 588	30 176
1996	547 555	122 354	115 634	111 253	4 381	720	4 722	1 278	425 201	76 955	172 878	133 798	31 786	9 784
1988:														
1st quarter	31 877	24 925	27 568	27 730	-162	-48	-1 751	-844	6 952	8 274	6 511	2 423	12 593	-22 849
2nd quarter	74 408	6 006	6 055	5 853	202	-442	810	-417	68 402	13 594	7 673	9 702	6 742	30 691
3rd quarter	52 699	-1 974	-3 197	-3 769	572	-155	1 886	-508	54 673	13 680	4 743	7 464	6 399	22 387
4th quarter	87 080	10 801	12 624	11 927	697	178	-1 264	-737	76 279	21 729	7 112	6 764	7 159	33 515
1989:														
1st quarter	66 562	7 700	5 355	4 634	721	-307	2 197	455	58 862	18 480	10 961	8 544	6 637	14 240
2nd quarter	10 829	-5 115	-9 823	-9 726	-97	314	3 823	572	15 943	15 174	4 789	9 365	12 000	-25 385
3rd quarter	73 908	13 060	12 966	12 776	190	-338	-211	643	60 848	11 359	12 744	10 270	-1 121	27 596
4th quarter	73 092	-7 142	-6 966	-7 535	569	492	-833	165	80 234	22 723	7 024	10 588	4 570	35 329
1990:														
1st quarter	-22 947	-6 421	-6 698	-6 177	-521	-195	598	-126	-16 526	15 651	1 709	1 311	12 904	-48 101
2nd quarter	41 100	6 207	4 081	3 735	346	1 160	1 240	-274	34 893	13 658	6 257	2 114	6 713	6 151
3rd quarter	63 090	13 937	12 469	12 335	134	-408	2 141	-265	49 153	8 172	6 044	-2 874	16 838	20 973
4th quarter	59 749	20 186	20 391	19 683	708	1 310	-594	-921	39 563	10 435	2 256	1 041	8 678	17 153
1991:														
1st quarter	8 129	5 569	126	155	-29	769	3 908	766	2 560	3 858	9 539	5 023	-586	-15 274
2nd quarter	12 417	-4 914	-3 764	-3 545	-219	253	-1 517	115	17 330	13 117	15 661	14 872	-2 549	-23 771
3rd quarter	32 923	3 854	6 095	5 621	474	771	-3 107	95	29 069	-1 667	3 004	10 310	4 761	12 661
4th quarter	56 174	12 879	13 690	12 615	1 075	-426	-768	383	43 295	6 697	6 022	4 939	-4 741	30 378
1992:														
1st quarter	30 624	20 988	15 380	14 916	464	-73	5 568	113	9 636	1 631	1 986	4 569	5 689	-4 239
2nd quarter	49 814	20 879	12 950	11 251	1 699	518	7 486	-75	28 935	5 426	11 331	10 467	3 954	-2 243
3rd quarter	34 979	-7 524	593	-319	912	607	-7 724	-1 000	42 503	2 408	11 008	2 531	4 854	21 702
4th quarter	53 357	6 133	-6 520	-7 394	874	1 138	11 241	274	47 224	8 470	26 206	12 476	-924	996
1993:														
1st quarter	24 541	10 937	1 745	1 080	665	-469	8 257	1 404	13 604	7 502	16 363	9 694	-215	-19 740
2nd quarter	58 453	17 466	6 750	5 668	1 082	132	9 485	1 099	40 987	10 801	5 608	15 205	6 531	2 842
3rd quarter	85 088	19 073	20 443	19 098	1 345	932	-2 486	184	66 015	11 082	9 658	17 782	288	27 205
4th quarter	111 590	24 277	24 076	23 106	970	718	-415	-102	87 313	19 609	11 652	37 411	3 885	14 756
1994:														
1st quarter	79 804	10 841	1 074	897	177	932	9 588	-753	68 963	-1 464	15 412	21 070	2 454	31 491
2nd quarter	51 978	9 639	8 282	5 922	2 360	179	2 143	-965	42 339	6 689	-798	12 352	-1 701	25 797
3rd quarter	87 242	19 516	18 697	16 475	2 222	442	1 177	-800	67 726	19 567	10 361	13 389	-2 328	26 737
4th quarter	78 313	389	8 774	7 456	1 318	813	-9 243	45	77 924	20 887	32 699	10 160	-6 135	20 313
1995:														
1st quarter	97 652	22 098	11 258	10 132	1 126	-420	10 995	265	75 554	12 873	36 411	15 734	9 075	1 461
2nd quarter	122 714	37 138	26 560	25 234	1 326	120	7 510	2 948	85 576	10 209	32 339	20 606	7 286	15 136
3rd quarter	125 839	39 585	21 116	20 598	518	-221	18 918	-228	86 254	24 568	39 195	32 128	6 968	-16 605
4th quarter	105 029	11 908	13 778	13 013	765	1 265	-3 415	280	93 121	19 876	3 903	27 899	11 259	30 184
1996:														
1st quarter	88 233	52 014	55 652	55 600	52	-143	-3 284	-211	36 219	15 877	10 602	36 475	6 800	-33 535
2nd quarter	106 114	13 154	-2 125	-3 383	1 258	-204	14 198	1 285	92 960	17 440	36 152	29 761	7 288	2 319
3rd quarter	158 629	24 089	26 689	25 472	1 217	907	-1 922	-1 585	134 540	25 977	50 798	35 115	20 610	2 040
4th quarter	194 579	33 097	35 418	33 564	1 854	160	-4 270	1 789	161 482	17 661	75 326	32 447	-2 912	38 960

1. A minus sign indicates capital outflow, that is, an increase in assets abroad.

U.S. FOREIGN TRADE AND FINANCE

U.S. INTERNATIONAL TRANSACTIONS—Continued
(Millions of dollars, seasonally adjusted)

YEAR AND QUARTER	Allocation of special drawing rights	Statistical discrepancy		Balance on [1]						
		Total	Seasonal adjustment discrepancy	Goods	Services	Goods and services	Investment income	Goods, services, and income	Unilateral transfers	Current account
1968	....	438	....	635	-385	250	5 990	6 240	-5 629	611
1969		-1 516		607	-516	91	6 044	6 135	-5 735	399
1970	867	-219		2 603	-349	2 254	6 233	8 486	-6 156	2 331
1971	717	-9 779		-2 260	957	-1 303	7 272	5 969	-7 402	-1 433
1972	710	-1 879		-6 416	973	-5 443	8 192	2 749	-8 544	-5 795
1973		-2 654		911	989	1 900	12 153	14 053	-6 913	7 140
1974		-2 558		-5 505	1 213	-4 292	15 503	11 210	-9 249	1 962
1975		4 417		8 903	3 501	12 404	12 787	25 191	-7 075	18 116
1976		8 955		-9 483	3 401	-6 082	16 063	9 982	-5 686	4 295
1977		-4 099		-31 091	3 845	-27 246	18 137	-9 109	-5 226	-14 335
1978		9 236		-33 927	4 164	-29 763	20 408	-9 355	-5 788	-15 143
1979	1 139	24 349		-27 568	3 003	-24 565	30 873	6 308	-6 593	-285
1980	1 152	20 886		-25 500	6 093	-19 407	30 073	10 666	-8 349	2 317
1981	1 093	21 792		-28 023	11 852	-16 172	32 903	16 732	-11 702	5 030
1982		37 359		-36 485	12 329	-24 156	29 788	5 632	-17 075	-11 443
1983		16 779		-67 102	9 335	-57 767	31 500	-26 267	-17 718	-43 985
1984		17 231		-112 492	3 419	-109 073	30 720	-78 353	-20 598	-98 951
1985		17 494		-122 173	294	-121 880	20 592	-101 288	-22 700	-123 987
1986		29 735		-145 081	4 476	-140 605	12 091	-128 514	-24 679	-153 193
1987		-7 713		-159 557	6 204	-153 353	9 209	-144 144	-23 909	-168 053
1988		-17 600		-126 959	11 059	-115 900	13 644	-102 256	-25 988	-128 245
1989		48 585		-115 245	22 957	-92 288	15 020	-77 268	-26 963	-104 231
1990		24 911		-109 030	27 805	-81 225	23 921	-57 304	-34 588	-91 892
1991		-46 103		-74 068	43 041	-31 027	20 249	-10 779	5 122	-5 657
1992		-43 619		-96 106	56 899	-39 207	18 016	-21 191	-35 192	-56 383
1993		5 637		-132 609	60 308	-72 301	19 668	-52 634	-38 137	-90 771
1994		-3 283		-166 192	61 776	-104 416	9 723	-94 693	-38 845	-133 538
1995		-14 931		-173 560	71 703	-101 857	6 808	-95 049	-34 046	-129 095
1996		-46 927		-191 170	80 130	-111 040	2 824	-108 216	-39 968	-148 184
1988:										
1st quarter		-1 689	4 121	-34 308	1 753	-32 555	4 088	-28 467	-6 236	-34 703
2nd quarter		-21 868	-2 916	-31 294	2 933	-28 361	3 503	-24 858	-5 854	-30 712
3rd quarter		25 390	-5 663	-29 960	3 566	-26 394	2 779	-23 615	-6 085	-29 700
4th quarter		-19 429	4 461	-31 397	2 804	-28 593	3 276	-25 317	-7 813	-33 130
1989:										
1st quarter		12 514	3 013	-29 051	5 048	-24 003	3 205	-20 798	-6 250	-27 048
2nd quarter		21 779	-1 561	-28 699	5 462	-23 237	3 032	-20 205	-5 874	-26 079
3rd quarter		1 804	-7 187	-28 710	6 125	-22 585	3 610	-18 975	-6 724	-25 699
4th quarter		12 489	5 736	-28 785	6 323	-22 462	5 174	-17 288	-8 117	-25 405
1990:										
1st quarter		5 845	4 116	-27 146	6 236	-20 910	5 387	-15 523	-6 904	-22 427
2nd quarter		14 825	100	-24 596	6 689	-17 907	5 214	-12 693	-7 829	-20 522
3rd quarter		4 394	-5 569	-29 050	6 893	-22 157	4 040	-18 117	-7 523	-25 640
4th quarter		-155	1 352	-28 238	7 992	-20 246	9 278	-10 968	-12 335	-23 303
1991:										
1st quarter		-9 354	4 633	-18 796	7 507	-11 289	7 625	-3 664	13 748	10 084
2nd quarter		-17 179	44	-16 176	10 465	-5 711	4 509	-1 202	3 545	2 343
3rd quarter		-7 222	-6 028	-19 747	11 959	-7 788	3 347	-4 441	-6 929	-11 370
4th quarter		-12 314	1 346	-19 349	13 112	-6 237	4 772	-1 465	-5 244	-6 709
1992:										
1st quarter		-14 549	4 438	-17 940	13 844	-4 096	5 609	1 513	-7 625	-6 112
2nd quarter		-21 205	464	-24 252	14 051	-10 201	4 867	-5 334	-8 462	-13 796
3rd quarter		-6 818	-6 628	-27 294	15 433	-11 861	3 752	-8 109	-7 867	-15 976
4th quarter		-1 046	1 367	-26 620	13 572	-13 048	3 786	-9 262	-11 237	-20 499
1993:										
1st quarter		11 604	5 570	-29 207	15 488	-13 719	6 100	-7 619	-8 502	-16 121
2nd quarter		8 188	76	-33 386	15 314	-18 072	4 270	-13 802	-8 501	-22 303
3rd quarter		-8 914	-6 249	-36 497	15 393	-21 104	5 738	-15 366	-9 347	-24 713
4th quarter		-5 238	607	-33 519	14 109	-19 410	3 559	-15 851	-11 787	-27 638
1994:										
1st quarter		-14 812	4 345	-36 627	13 979	-22 648	4 466	-18 182	-7 971	-26 153
2nd quarter		12 451	-103	-40 827	15 460	-25 367	2 642	-22 725	-9 275	-32 000
3rd quarter		-22 045	-6 923	-44 348	15 859	-28 489	1 798	-26 691	-9 671	-36 362
4th quarter		21 122	2 681	-44 390	16 478	-27 912	820	-27 092	-11 928	-39 020
1995:										
1st quarter		-3 318	5 658	-44 401	16 096	-28 305	2 047	-26 258	-8 451	-34 709
2nd quarter		23 538	-775	-47 558	16 759	-30 799	3 223	-27 576	-8 128	-35 704
3rd quarter		-52 028	-6 985	-42 820	18 936	-23 884	-401	-24 285	-8 847	-33 132
4th quarter		16 881	2 106	-38 781	19 907	-18 874	1 940	-16 934	-8 620	-25 554
1996:										
1st quarter		15 419	6 228	-42 925	18 386	-24 539	2 061	-22 478	-10 406	-32 884
2nd quarter		-20 831	-1 076	-47 562	19 783	-27 779	883	-26 896	-8 689	-35 585
3rd quarter		-38 254	-7 830	-52 493	19 977	-32 516	-1 370	-33 886	-8 947	-42 833
4th quarter		-3 269	2 669	-48 190	21 992	-26 198	1 250	-24 948	-11 926	-36 874

1. A minus sign inicates capital outflow, that is, an increase in assets abroad.

U.S. EXPORTS AND IMPORTS OF GOODS AND SERVICES
(Balance of payments basis—Millions of dollars, seasonally adjusted)

YEAR AND MONTH	Goods and services			Goods			Services		
	Exports	Imports	Balance	Exports	Imports	Balance	Exports	Imports	Balance
1968	45 543	45 293	250	33 626	32 991	635	11 917	12 302	-385
1969	49 220	49 129	91	36 414	35 807	607	12 806	13 322	-516
1970	56 640	54 386	2 254	42 469	39 866	2 603	14 171	14 520	-349
1971	59 677	60 979	-1 302	43 319	45 579	-2 260	16 358	15 400	958
1972	67 222	72 665	-5 443	49 381	55 797	-6 416	17 841	16 868	973
1973	91 242	89 342	1 900	71 410	70 499	911	19 832	18 843	989
1974	120 897	125 190	-4 293	98 306	103 811	-5 505	22 591	21 379	1 212
1975	132 585	120 181	12 404	107 088	98 185	8 903	25 497	21 996	3 501
1976	142 716	148 798	-6 082	114 745	124 228	-9 483	27 971	24 570	3 401
1977	152 301	179 547	-27 246	120 816	151 907	-31 091	31 485	27 640	3 845
1978	178 428	208 191	-29 763	142 075	176 002	-33 927	36 353	32 189	4 164
1979	224 131	248 696	-24 565	184 439	212 007	-27 568	39 692	36 689	3 003
1980	271 834	291 241	-19 407	224 250	249 750	-25 500	47 584	41 491	6 093
1981	294 398	310 570	-16 172	237 044	265 067	-28 023	57 354	45 503	11 851
1982	275 236	299 391	-24 155	211 157	247 642	-36 485	64 079	51 749	12 330
1983	266 106	323 874	-57 768	201 799	268 901	-67 102	64 307	54 973	9 334
1984	291 094	400 166	-109 072	219 926	332 418	-112 492	71 168	67 748	3 420
1985	289 070	410 950	-121 880	215 915	338 088	-122 173	73 155	72 862	293
1986	309 656	450 261	-140 605	223 344	368 425	-145 081	86 312	81 836	4 476
1987	348 761	502 114	-153 353	250 208	409 765	-159 557	98 553	92 349	6 204
1988	431 254	547 154	-115 900	320 230	447 189	-126 959	111 024	99 965	11 059
1989	489 262	581 550	-92 288	362 120	477 365	-115 245	127 142	104 185	22 957
1990	537 131	618 356	-81 225	389 307	498 337	-109 030	147 824	120 019	27 805
1991	581 149	612 176	-31 027	416 913	490 981	-74 068	164 236	121 195	43 041
1992	617 506	656 713	-39 207	440 352	536 458	-96 106	177 154	120 255	56 899
1993	643 543	715 844	-72 301	456 832	589 441	-132 609	186 711	126 403	60 308
1994	699 646	804 062	-104 416	502 398	668 590	-166 192	197 248	135 472	61 776
1995	794 610	896 467	-101 857	575 871	749 431	-173 560	218 739	147 036	71 703
1996	848 833	959 873	-111 040	612 069	803 239	-191 170	236 764	156 634	80 130
1993:									
January	52 153	56 151	-3 998	36 954	45 980	-9 026	15 199	10 171	5 028
February	51 920	55 329	-3 409	36 400	45 284	-8 884	15 520	10 045	5 475
March	53 887	60 033	-6 146	38 509	49 806	-11 297	15 378	10 227	5 151
April	53 587	59 746	-6 158	38 040	49 267	-11 227	15 547	10 479	5 068
May	54 326	58 985	-4 659	38 900	48 717	-9 817	15 426	10 268	5 158
June	52 756	59 974	-7 217	37 245	49 587	-12 341	15 511	10 387	5 124
July	52 220	59 316	-7 095	36 688	48 930	-12 242	15 533	10 386	5 147
August	52 606	59 028	-6 422	37 044	48 695	-11 651	15 563	10 333	5 230
September	53 125	60 801	-7 677	37 697	50 302	-12 605	15 428	10 499	4 929
October	55 377	62 852	-7 475	39 333	51 868	-12 536	16 045	10 984	5 061
November	54 492	61 682	-7 190	39 317	50 844	-11 528	15 175	10 838	4 337
December	56 503	61 092	-4 590	40 707	50 162	-9 456	15 796	10 930	4 866
1994:									
January	54 230	61 201	-6 971	39 097	50 432	-11 335	15 133	10 769	4 364
February	53 066	62 419	-9 353	37 577	51 189	-13 612	15 489	11 230	4 259
March	58 336	64 659	-6 323	41 708	53 388	-11 680	16 628	11 271	5 357
April	56 601	64 634	-8 033	40 500	53 519	-13 019	16 101	11 115	4 986
May	56 801	65 609	-8 808	40 507	54 391	-13 884	16 294	11 218	5 076
June	58 694	67 223	-8 529	42 018	55 942	-13 924	16 676	11 281	5 395
July	57 948	67 661	-9 713	41 142	56 350	-15 208	16 806	11 311	5 495
August	60 067	69 196	-9 129	43 371	57 760	-14 389	16 696	11 436	5 260
September	59 711	69 360	-9 649	43 116	57 867	-14 751	16 595	11 493	5 102
October	59 781	69 611	-9 830	43 210	58 234	-15 024	16 571	11 377	5 194
November	61 282	71 521	-10 239	44 214	60 050	-15 836	17 068	11 471	5 597
December	63 132	70 972	-7 840	45 937	59 468	-13 531	17 195	11 504	5 691
1995:									
January	62 621	72 714	-10 093	45 060	60 854	-15 794	17 561	11 860	5 701
February	62 515	71 570	-9 054	45 544	59 678	-14 133	16 971	11 892	5 079
March	65 233	74 389	-9 156	47 785	62 258	-14 473	17 448	12 131	5 317
April	65 468	75 292	-9 825	47 508	63 168	-15 661	17 960	12 124	5 836
May	66 019	75 919	-9 900	47 953	63 773	-15 820	18 066	12 146	5 920
June	64 998	76 072	-11 074	47 720	63 798	-16 078	17 278	12 274	5 004
July	65 583	74 988	-9 405	47 062	62 612	-15 550	18 521	12 376	6 145
August	67 272	74 807	-7 535	48 663	62 338	-13 675	18 609	12 469	6 140
September	68 751	75 692	-6 942	49 635	63 229	-13 595	19 116	12 463	6 653
October	68 074	74 977	-6 903	49 277	62 640	-13 363	18 797	12 337	6 460
November	68 480	74 751	-6 271	49 408	62 268	-12 860	19 072	12 483	6 589
December	69 599	75 301	-5 703	50 256	62 814	-12 559	19 343	12 487	6 856
1996:									
January	67 630	77 140	-9 510	48 899	64 407	-15 508	18 731	12 733	5 998
February	68 818	76 476	-7 657	50 433	63 514	-13 080	18 385	12 962	5 423
March	70 657	78 030	-7 372	50 716	65 052	-14 335	19 941	12 978	6 963
April	69 982	79 658	-9 676	50 794	66 691	-15 897	19 188	12 967	6 221
May	71 277	81 250	-9 973	51 282	68 108	-16 826	19 995	13 142	6 853
June	70 889	79 021	-8 132	51 335	66 174	-14 839	19 554	12 847	6 707
July	68 500	80 123	-11 623	49 087	66 844	-17 757	19 413	13 279	6 134
August	71 150	81 157	-10 007	51 254	68 013	-16 759	19 896	13 144	6 752
September	70 435	81 323	-10 887	50 423	68 400	-17 976	20 012	12 923	7 089
October	73 088	81 023	-7 935	52 503	67 823	-15 320	20 585	13 200	7 385
November	73 969	81 634	-7 665	53 209	68 385	-15 176	20 760	13 249	7 511
December	72 444	83 045	-10 601	52 133	69 828	-17 695	20 311	13 217	7 094

U.S. EXPORTS OF GOODS BY SELECTED COUNTRIES AND REGIONS
(Census basis, except as noted—Millions of dollars, not seasonally adjusted)

YEAR AND MONTH	Total exports of goods — Total: Balance of payments basis	Net adjustments	Total: Census basis	North America — Total	Canada	Mexico	Central and South America [1] — Total [2]	Argentina	Brazil	Chile	Colombia	Dominican Republic	Venezuela
1968	33 626				8 072	1 378			705				655
1969	36 414				9 137	1 450			672				708
1970	42 469				9 596	1 704			841				759
1971	43 319				10 903	1 620			966				787
1972	49 381				13 070	1 982			1 243				924
1973	71 410				16 146	2 937			1 916				1 033
1974	98 306				21 281	4 855			3 088				1 768
1975	107 088				22 948	5 141			3 056				2 243
1976	114 745				25 677	4 990			2 809				2 628
1977	120 816				27 738	4 806			2 490				3 171
1978	142 075				30 540	6 680			2 981				3 728
1979	184 439				37 599	9 847			3 442				3 934
1980	224 250				40 331	15 145		2 625	4 344		1 736		4 573
1981	237 044				44 602	17 789		2 192	3 798		1 771		5 445
1982	211 157				37 887	11 817		1 294	3 423		1 903		5 206
1983	201 799	91	201 708		43 345	9 082		965	2 557		1 514		2 811
1984	219 926	1 183	218 743		51 777	11 992		900	2 640		1 450		3 377
1985	215 915	3 294	212 621	66 922	53 287	13 635		721	3 140		1 468		3 399
1986	223 344	-3 127	226 471	67 904	55 512	12 392		944	3 885		1 319		3 141
1987	250 208	-3 696	253 904	74 396	59 814	14 582		1 090	4 040		1 412		3 586
1988	320 230	-3 105	323 335	92 250	71 622	20 628		1 054	4 267		1 754		4 612
1989	362 120	-1 716	363 836	103 791	78 809	24 982		1 039	4 804		1 924		3 025
1990	389 307	-3 617	392 924	112 241	83 866	28 375		1 179	5 062		2 029		3 107
1991	416 913	-4 851	421 764	118 427	85 150	33 277		2 045	6 148	1 839	1 952	1 743	4 656
1992	440 352	-7 809	448 161	131 186	90 594	40 592	35 204	3 223	5 751	2 466	3 286	2 100	5 444
1993	456 832	-8 258	465 090	142 025	100 444	41 581	36 842	3 776	6 058	2 599	3 235	2 350	4 590
1994	502 398	-10 228	512 626	165 283	114 439	50 844	41 708	4 462	8 102	2 774	4 064	2 799	4 039
1995	575 871	-8 871	584 742	173 518	127 226	46 292	49 992	4 189	11 439	3 615	4 624	3 015	4 640
1996	612 069	-13 006	625 075	191 002	134 210	56 792	52 599	4 517	12 718	4 140	4 714	3 191	4 750
1993:													
January	35 296	-662	35 958	10 071	6 878	3 193	2 717	216	437	221	235	151	407
February	35 404	-667	36 070	11 036	7 747	3 289	2 705	216	409	189	235	167	407
March	41 464	-534	41 999	13 253	9 498	3 755	3 043	275	474	208	305	223	412
April	38 736	-684	39 421	12 395	8 781	3 614	3 106	257	565	188	295	210	452
May	39 168	-702	39 870	12 296	8 792	3 504	3 210	302	476	240	273	186	397
June	37 934	-690	38 624	12 718	9 070	3 648	2 943	268	442	220	273	200	338
July	34 737	-728	35 465	10 238	7 058	3 180	3 139	413	474	216	251	209	373
August	36 102	-774	36 876	11 581	8 327	3 254	3 024	332	488	227	233	201	352
September	37 255	-700	37 956	11 964	8 572	3 392	3 044	327	488	214	248	210	386
October	40 489	-658	41 148	12 252	8 906	3 346	3 366	388	556	222	303	211	378
November	39 574	-719	40 294	12 867	8 911	3 956	3 182	383	443	221	297	195	383
December	40 707	-705	41 412	11 357	7 906	3 451	3 363	400	806	234	285	187	306
1994:													
January	36 814	-746	37 561	11 377	7 578	3 799	2 984	365	647	181	248	149	345
February	36 410	-716	37 126	11 865	8 183	3 682	2 863	380	496	186	243	202	310
March	45 360	-779	46 139	14 787	10 409	4 378	3 341	379	583	234	325	224	360
April	40 836	-751	41 587	13 205	9 383	3 822	3 301	386	528	222	356	287	357
May	41 343	-872	42 215	14 399	10 018	4 381	3 215	370	542	211	284	249	351
June	42 593	-832	43 425	14 605	10 188	4 417	3 470	350	568	238	310	240	336
July	38 405	-813	39 218	11 849	7 642	4 207	3 326	332	673	234	349	218	289
August	42 583	-1 006	43 589	14 367	9 912	4 455	3 430	364	657	216	354	255	315
September	42 880	-886	43 766	14 601	10 220	4 381	3 670	369	644	218	432	241	312
October	44 322	-992	45 314	14 990	10 490	4 500	3 821	410	756	243	445	263	343
November	44 846	-828	45 674	15 147	10 590	4 557	3 956	356	966	255	351	230	313
December	46 006	-1 008	47 013	14 089	9 825	4 264	4 333	400	1 043	334	368	242	409
1995:													
January	42 998	-635	43 633	14 103	10 101	4 001	3 731	400	853	251	329	204	333
February	44 319	-680	44 999	13 834	10 162	3 672	3 694	301	895	243	367	218	339
March	51 809	-770	52 579	15 639	11 719	3 921	4 477	372	1 102	283	442	266	372
April	47 160	-649	47 808	13 984	10 601	3 383	4 232	350	1 082	247	401	284	365
May	49 100	-755	49 855	15 201	11 420	3 781	4 350	325	981	397	391	289	387
June	48 550	-843	49 393	14 642	10 938	3 704	4 137	316	968	291	373	260	456
July	43 672	-718	44 390	11 901	8 435	3 466	3 945	282	818	295	386	231	438
August	48 221	-751	48 972	15 021	10 834	4 187	4 203	327	915	353	357	261	444
September	49 061	-662	49 723	14 840	10 778	4 062	4 232	395	854	316	403	246	422
October	51 024	-804	51 828	15 742	11 429	4 313	4 254	376	912	314	407	267	405
November	49 906	-805	50 710	15 046	11 078	3 968	4 331	342	1 015	255	383	267	356
December	50 052	-801	50 853	13 567	9 732	3 835	4 406	403	1 046	308	388	223	325
1996:													
January	47 072	-695	47 767	14 578	10 301	4 276	3 773	311	829	287	380	209	332
February	50 322	-791	51 112	15 476	11 212	4 265	3 965	327	858	390	402	247	335
March	54 048	-904	54 952	16 059	11 600	4 459	4 100	346	941	280	373	259	412
April	51 029	-843	51 872	15 858	11 500	4 359	4 015	334	879	309	403	256	376
May	52 230	-1 130	53 359	16 196	11 456	4 740	4 396	383	990	308	407	294	466
June	50 939	-882	51 821	15 881	11 320	4 560	4 404	439	1 116	296	395	237	393
July	46 158	-1 440	47 598	14 214	9 647	4 567	4 463	387	1 033	403	377	271	378
August	50 223	-1 352	51 575	15 765	10 935	4 830	4 614	389	1 239	323	385	297	453
September	49 289	-1 309	50 598	16 623	11 673	4 950	4 447	395	1 203	317	387	262	371
October	55 042	-1 065	56 107	17 747	12 120	5 627	4 905	404	1 238	379	447	306	436
November	53 737	-1 279	55 016	17 261	12 145	5 116	4 773	421	1 244	356	386	305	440
December	51 980	-1 316	53 295	15 344	10 302	5 041	4 745	380	1 147	492	372	247	359

1. Includes Caribbean
2. Includes countries not shown separately. See NOTES for list of included countries.

U.S. EXPORTS OF GOODS BY SELECTED COUNTRIES AND REGIONS—Continued
(Census basis—Millions of dollars, not seasonally adjusted)

YEAR AND MONTH	Total¹	Western Europe — European Union									
		Total¹	Belgium	France	Germany	Ireland	Italy	Netherlands	Spain	Sweden	United Kingdom
1968	....	....	....	1 095	1 709	....	1 121	....	....	....	2 289
1969	....	....	....	1 195	2 142	....	1 262	....	....	....	2 335
1970	....	....	....	1 483	2 741	....	1 353	....	....	....	2 536
1971	....	....	....	1 373	2 831	....	1 314	....	....	....	2 369
1972	....	....	....	1 609	2 808	....	1 434	....	....	....	2 658
1973	....	....	....	2 263	3 756	....	2 119	....	....	....	3 564
1974	28 639	28 268	....	2 942	4 985	....	2 752	3 979	....	....	4 574
1975	29 939	22 862	....	3 031	5 194	....	2 867	4 183	....	....	4 527
1976	32 401	25 406	....	3 446	5 731	....	3 071	4 645	....	....	4 801
1977	33 752	26 476	....	3 503	5 989	....	2 790	4 796	....	....	5 951
1978	39 936	32 051	....	4 166	6 957	....	3 361	5 683	....	....	7 116
1979	54 331	42 582	....	5 587	8 478	....	4 362	6 907	....	....	10 635
1980	67 512	53 679	....	7 485	10 960	....	5 511	8 669	3 340	1 767	12 694
1981	65 377	52 363	....	7 341	10 277	....	5 360	8 595	3 563	1 842	12 439
1982	60 054	47 932	....	7 110	9 291	....	4 616	8 604	3 590	1 689	10 645
1983	55 980	44 311	....	5 961	8 737	....	3 908	7 767	2 915	1 581	10 621
1984	58 019	46 976	....	6 037	9 084	....	4 375	7 554	2 561	1 542	12 210
1985	56 763	48 994	....	6 096	9 050	....	4 625	7 269	2 524	1 925	11 273
1986	61 642	53 154	....	7 216	10 561	....	4 838	7 848	2 615	1 871	11 418
1987	69 718	60 575	....	7 943	11 748	....	5 530	8 217	3 148	1 894	14 114
1988	87 858	75 755	....	9 970	14 348	....	6 775	10 117	4 215	2 700	18 364
1989	100 165	86 331	....	11 579	16 862	....	7 215	11 364	4 796	3 138	20 837
1990	112 975	98 027	....	13 652	18 693	....	7 987	13 016	5 213	3 405	23 484
1991	118 682	103 123	10 572	15 346	21 302	2 681	8 570	13 511	5 474	3 287	22 046
1992	117 100	102 958	9 775	14 593	21 249	2 862	8 721	13 752	5 537	2 845	22 800
1993	113 681	96 973	8 878	13 267	18 932	2 728	6 464	12 839	4 168	2 354	26 438
1994	118 177	102 818	10 939	13 619	19 229	3 419	7 183	13 582	4 622	2 518	26 900
1995	134 863	123 671	12 466	14 245	22 394	4 109	8 862	16 558	5 526	3 080	28 857
1996	141 543	127 710	12 532	14 455	23 495	3 669	8 797	16 662	5 500	3 431	30 962
1993:											
January	9 895	8 769	723	1 290	1 748	256	582	1 158	375	217	2 339
February	9 460	8 260	725	1 299	1 561	254	581	1 179	386	185	2 045
March	10 806	9 563	793	1 348	1 962	234	574	1 252	422	200	2 693
April	9 933	8 033	659	1 047	1 638	243	680	1 131	344	239	2 047
May	9 624	7 822	718	1 225	1 643	194	556	1 058	316	211	1 861
June	8 529	7 382	708	1 074	1 456	199	576	970	355	173	1 784
July	8 155	6 748	660	949	1 335	196	428	903	290	148	1 802
August	8 334	7 041	717	924	1 371	232	367	869	342	186	1 978
September	8 977	7 591	753	967	1 419	210	436	1 028	285	179	2 276
October	10 091	8 567	819	1 012	1 704	243	540	1 134	347	227	2 508
November	9 677	8 442	843	1 004	1 487	226	537	951	340	197	2 655
December	10 200	8 758	760	1 128	1 608	244	608	1 207	365	193	2 451
1994:											
January	8 802	7 670	726	1 043	1 454	299	535	1 223	357	178	1 792
February	8 794	7 848	712	998	1 461	267	501	984	329	181	2 373
March	11 875	10 225	912	1 300	1 827	285	585	1 295	434	224	3 254
April	10 299	8 618	870	1 044	1 657	307	611	1 082	349	251	2 443
May	9 587	8 462	786	1 040	1 565	275	733	991	368	206	2 360
June	9 605	8 356	934	1 173	1 454	276	709	1 090	390	199	2 101
July	8 712	7 525	797	1 094	1 433	247	526	893	398	156	1 894
August	9 147	7 888	929	1 062	1 424	261	467	950	472	186	2 002
September	9 463	8 316	1 061	1 087	1 594	280	575	1 138	315	217	2 042
October	10 197	8 934	1 075	1 145	1 678	291	580	1 156	381	230	2 227
November	10 139	8 810	1 102	1 310	1 743	320	552	1 219	403	254	1 934
December	11 558	10 168	1 036	1 324	1 939	311	808	1 560	427	237	2 478
1995:											
January	9 648	8 986	886	1 166	1 709	326	640	1 174	456	209	1 949
February	10 266	9 505	977	1 256	1 740	310	707	1 209	391	208	2 065
March	12 571	11 295	1 140	1 288	1 906	403	780	1 506	589	247	2 750
April	11 767	11 017	1 139	1 236	1 944	337	727	1 481	483	269	2 802
May	11 755	10 528	1 066	1 267	1 825	295	717	1 597	499	247	2 410
June	11 023	9 658	966	1 159	1 756	272	862	1 212	415	237	2 239
July	9 910	9 168	929	1 044	1 699	307	580	1 198	363	226	2 172
August	10 729	9 937	1 039	1 075	1 760	347	690	1 400	382	262	2 307
September	11 114	10 324	1 063	1 112	1 912	310	727	1 217	526	268	2 557
October	12 029	10 996	1 115	1 215	2 070	357	873	1 491	451	308	2 451
November	11 745	10 911	1 100	1 159	1 914	442	741	1 580	423	267	2 510
December	12 306	11 348	1 045	1 268	2 160	404	819	1 494	548	332	2 647
1996:											
January	10 993	10 208	978	1 204	1 903	334	745	1 249	589	257	2 342
February	11 727	10 729	1 087	1 221	1 932	317	900	1 374	535	276	2 481
March	12 869	11 285	1 048	1 313	2 169	327	807	1 593	502	307	2 613
April	12 590	11 367	1 004	1 252	1 964	342	871	1 231	428	268	3 346
May	12 771	11 483	1 085	1 154	2 044	332	756	1 340	499	277	3 150
June	11 971	10 613	1 000	1 157	1 927	247	734	1 377	432	251	2 708
July	9 805	8 775	890	953	1 662	225	602	1 025	363	221	2 155
August	11 169	10 042	1 087	1 106	1 853	253	613	1 322	362	254	2 620
September	11 125	9 868	1 051	1 112	1 907	303	614	1 238	373	268	2 360
October	12 620	11 412	1 102	1 346	2 043	336	733	1 826	465	313	2 467
November	12 031	11 013	1 067	1 316	2 086	299	694	1 554	466	379	2 410
December	11 873	10 916	1 134	1 322	2 007	355	730	1 533	484	360	2 310

1. Includes countries not shown separately. See NOTES for list of included countries.

U.S. EXPORTS OF GOODS BY SELECTED COUNTRIES AND REGIONS—Continued
(Census basis—Millions of dollars, not seasonally adjusted)

YEAR AND MONTH	Western Europe—Continued: European Free Trade Association			Eastern Europe and former Soviet Republics			Former Soviet Republics		Selected Near and Middle Eastern countries		
	Total [1]	Norway	Switzerland	Total [1]	Hungary	Poland	Total [1]	Russia	Israel	Saudi Arabi	Turkey
1968							58				
1969							106				
1970							119				
1971							161				
1972							542				
1973							1 194				
1974				1 432			609				835
1975				2 788			1 835				1 502
1976				3 502			2 310				2 774
1977				2 544			1 628				3 575
1978				3 679			2 252				4 370
1979				5 683			3 607				4 875
1980		843	3 781	3 860	80	714	1 513				5 769
1981		892	3 022	4 338	78	681	2 431				7 327
1982		950	2 707	3 610	68	295	2 587				9 026
1983		813	2 960	2 891	110	324	2 003				7 903
1984		859	2 562	4 188	88	318	3 284				5 564
1985		666	2 288	3 215	94	238	2 423				4 474
1986		937	2 976	1 989	98	151	1 248				3 449
1987		842	3 151	2 200	95	239	1 480				3 373
1988		929	4 196	3 650	76	304	2 769				3 776
1989		1 037	4 911	5 307	122	413	4 284				3 574
1990		1 281	4 943	4 263	156	406	3 088				4 035
1991	12 507	1 489	5 557	4 787	256	459	3 578		3 911	6 557	2 468
1992	10 837	1 279	4 540	4 069	295	641	2 764	2 112	4 077	7 167	2 735
1993	12 704	1 212	6 806	6 104	435	912	3 984	2 970	4 429	6 661	3 429
1994	11 975	1 267	5 624	5 301	309	625	3 562	2 578	4 996	6 013	2 752
1995	7 706	1 293	6 227	5 701	295	776	3 807	2 823	5 621	6 155	2 768
1996	10 198	1 559	8 373	7 267	331	968	5 078	3 346	6 012	7 311	2 847
1993:											
January	855	106	359	348	18	74	210	152	405	551	232
February	883	112	278	359	24	73	193	139	332	504	268
March	896	130	371	443	23	123	255	148	453	682	274
April	1 337	94	789	732	177	114	389	224	342	635	495
May	1 438	95	910	566	31	77	393	313	381	579	302
June	782	80	366	456	17	110	256	180	334	491	326
July	1 086	82	710	497	17	82	346	242	348	455	288
August	960	82	525	412	39	41	275	203	399	447	288
September	1 128	126	644	395	28	46	256	189	308	484	219
October	1 262	119	717	650	18	60	449	366	423	639	223
November	977	94	512	633	18	58	496	416	309	559	222
December	1 101	93	626	614	26	54	466	398	395	638	292
1994:											
January	804	99	348	346	16	36	247	188	356	552	268
February	750	122	283	346	18	45	238	143	352	517	158
March	1 348	111	809	461	22	102	279	209	383	515	269
April	1 332	89	687	590	25	46	472	389	488	424	304
May	874	94	372	433	23	74	288	204	486	436	207
June	942	79	480	360	22	38	253	175	336	415	261
July	965	105	530	394	58	48	234	155	504	453	166
August	953	102	446	493	35	40	341	176	433	547	239
September	895	147	319	571	23	49	447	350	372	469	190
October	964	112	386	384	21	48	253	182	462	627	243
November	1 055	94	461	507	22	45	250	196	415	519	214
December	1 093	114	503	417	25	54	260	211	411	541	234
1995:											
January	453	90	354	368	27	45	225	178	415	733	167
February	432	85	338	369	26	38	245	195	421	398	268
March	1 003	115	874	434	25	52	285	217	634	411	210
April	515	109	391	436	24	54	292	220	406	402	185
May	889	107	765	536	22	134	319	249	608	629	244
June	1 044	94	933	490	22	54	346	266	432	619	268
July	457	97	342	421	23	55	291	230	428	406	226
August	499	97	385	454	19	58	319	233	445	368	246
September	523	106	399	516	26	67	354	258	425	526	209
October	731	157	554	508	24	62	350	250	435	543	244
November	566	111	437	597	27	73	411	271	434	589	208
December	596	125	455	573	29	84	371	257	538	531	294
1996:											
January	513	106	393	491	25	69	323	243	443	428	219
February	650	126	509	757	31	63	596	355	531	501	266
March	1 258	137	1 044	620	28	78	448	330	540	732	257
April	903	118	769	590	29	73	401	277	475	565	257
May	997	113	867	544	25	94	363	273	524	561	227
June	1 072	146	908	498	25	65	328	238	554	449	202
July	795	125	653	504	23	98	316	232	448	787	192
August	817	125	670	743	24	69	575	323	486	734	251
September	911	100	792	532	27	81	360	248	424	609	271
October	946	156	774	666	26	80	488	282	488	658	195
November	720	191	510	748	42	120	491	272	574	710	236
December	617	118	484	573	27	78	389	272	524	578	274

1. Includes countries not shown separately. See NOTES for list of included countries.

YEAR AND MONTH	U.S. EXPORTS OF GOODS BY SELECTED COUNTRIES AND REGIONS—Continued (Census basis—Millions of dollars, not seasonally adjusted) Selected Asian and Oceanic countries											
	Australia	China	Hong Kong	India	Indonesia	Japan	South Korea	Malaysia	Phil- ippines	Singapore	Thailand	Taiwan
1968	....	....	....	....	....	2 954	....	....	....	....	....	....
1969	....	....	....	....	....	3 490	....	....	....	....	....	....
1970	....	....	....	....	....	4 652	....	....	....	....	....	....
1971	....	....	....	....	....	4 055	....	....	....	....	....	....
1972	....	....	....	....	....	4 963	....	....	....	....	....	....
1973	....	....	....	....	....	8 313	....	....	....	....	....	....
1974	2 157	807	882	....	....	10 679	....	....	....	988	....	1 427
1975	1 816	304	808	....	....	9 563	....	....	....	994	....	1 660
1976	2 185	135	1 115	....	....	10 145	....	....	....	965	....	1 635
1977	2 356	171	1 292	....	....	10 529	....	....	....	1 172	....	1 798
1978	2 910	824	1 625	....	....	12 885	....	....	....	1 462	....	2 340
1979	3 617	1 724	2 083	....	....	17 581	....	....	....	2 331	....	3 271
1980	4 093	3 755	2 686	....	1 545	20 790	....	....	....	3 033	....	4 337
1981	5 242	3 603	2 635	....	1 302	21 823	....	....	....	3 003	....	4 305
1982	4 535	2 912	2 453	....	2 025	20 966	....	....	....	3 214	....	4 367
1983	3 954	2 173	2 564	....	1 466	21 894	....	....	....	3 759	....	4 667
1984	4 793	3 004	3 062	....	1 216	23 575	....	....	....	3 675	....	5 003
1985	5 441	3 856	2 786	....	795	22 631	5 956	....	....	3 476	....	4 700
1986	5 551	3 106	3 030	....	946	26 882	6 355	....	....	3 380	....	5 524
1987	5 495	3 497	3 983	....	767	28 249	8 099	....	....	4 053	....	7 413
1988	6 973	5 021	5 687	....	1 059	37 725	11 232	....	....	5 768	....	12 129
1989	8 331	5 755	6 246	....	1 247	44 494	13 478	....	....	7 345	....	11 335
1990	8 535	4 807	6 841	....	1 897	48 585	14 399	....	....	8 019	....	11 482
1991	8 404	6 278	8 137	1 999	1 891	48 125	15 505	3 900	2 265	8 804	3 753	13 182
1992	8 876	7 418	9 077	1 917	2 779	47 813	14 639	4 363	2 759	9 626	3 989	15 250
1993	8 277	8 763	9 874	2 778	2 770	47 892	14 782	6 064	3 529	11 678	3 766	16 168
1994	9 781	9 282	11 441	2 294	2 809	53 488	18 025	6 969	3 886	13 020	4 865	17 109
1995	10 789	11 754	14 232	3 296	3 360	64 343	25 380	8 816	5 295	15 333	6 665	19 290
1996	12 008	11 993	13 966	3 328	3 977	67 607	26 621	8 546	6 142	16 720	7 198	18 460
1993:												
January	591	621	748	184	211	3 719	1 202	450	279	950	303	1 266
February	627	684	710	146	159	3 858	1 119	377	220	882	308	1 079
March	747	622	878	189	230	4 395	1 120	655	274	903	292	1 375
April	644	728	871	250	176	3 683	1 259	443	249	825	304	1 325
May	721	586	1 019	254	171	4 092	1 172	575	261	934	323	1 480
June	707	755	776	228	153	4 274	1 274	412	219	1 018	273	1 483
July	685	712	715	186	177	4 127	1 342	490	269	950	259	1 283
August	687	767	883	327	146	3 732	1 189	501	292	1 108	281	1 085
September	713	836	783	205	157	3 994	1 237	399	274	967	319	1 388
October	751	624	806	168	472	4 001	1 222	706	287	1 116	465	1 490
November	665	782	744	298	259	3 761	1 233	590	458	880	285	1 415
December	740	1 048	941	342	458	4 257	1 413	466	448	1 145	355	1 500
1994:												
January	702	551	752	170	381	3 839	1 392	626	297	1 070	339	1 559
February	668	878	727	168	149	4 309	1 211	486	280	845	325	1 130
March	756	784	886	158	202	4 843	1 420	718	313	1 176	399	1 605
April	746	713	916	164	197	4 260	1 334	484	299	932	361	1 464
May	779	757	944	178	393	4 069	1 337	520	303	1 144	364	1 247
June	823	1 009	1 231	328	206	4 571	1 341	538	340	1 035	382	1 386
July	915	970	978	166	209	4 358	1 566	566	297	969	430	1 292
August	1 029	926	1 054	194	195	4 895	1 604	534	338	1 120	461	1 469
September	806	629	978	190	191	4 556	1 616	690	375	1 290	393	1 405
October	860	618	1 007	185	205	4 712	1 622	594	335	1 212	405	1 291
November	795	648	970	198	214	4 412	1 686	623	375	1 033	559	1 621
December	901	798	999	195	268	4 663	1 897	592	335	1 195	448	1 639
1995:												
January	829	745	1 030	200	252	4 492	1 645	603	366	950	461	1 453
February	847	1 086	1 027	208	262	4 987	1 956	581	327	1 187	538	1 529
March	972	1 070	1 235	260	285	5 581	2 481	687	415	1 305	516	1 793
April	832	896	1 133	249	241	5 287	2 046	628	514	1 110	477	1 530
May	915	831	1 397	273	242	5 035	2 056	687	397	1 113	454	1 726
June	989	947	1 231	293	241	5 542	2 238	754	455	1 299	515	1 864
July	857	986	1 237	353	311	5 474	2 111	806	405	1 267	516	1 475
August	852	881	1 156	318	262	5 435	2 202	834	514	1 417	498	1 716
September	964	960	1 181	345	311	5 685	2 065	805	438	1 306	640	1 654
October	958	1 097	1 223	285	339	5 510	2 126	780	514	1 541	678	1 389
November	869	1 125	1 202	267	323	5 442	2 055	796	490	1 317	831	1 459
December	904	1 130	1 181	247	290	5 873	2 399	857	460	1 521	540	1 702
1996:												
January	1 013	929	996	250	336	5 222	1 925	832	469	1 276	527	1 571
February	966	1 147	970	252	307	5 875	2 067	665	455	1 439	710	1 341
March	1 076	1 093	1 192	298	350	6 412	2 567	765	496	1 713	565	1 606
April	952	841	1 126	242	386	5 440	2 144	687	617	1 340	678	1 613
May	1 099	882	1 267	257	290	5 903	2 195	693	518	1 349	535	1 719
June	946	772	1 228	229	327	5 644	2 260	649	467	1 540	664	1 432
July	950	998	997	259	281	5 432	2 053	677	460	1 437	505	1 440
August	1 062	778	1 215	250	281	5 741	2 419	605	503	1 335	524	1 400
September	957	753	1 129	273	240	5 359	2 025	580	475	1 250	480	1 422
October	1 025	928	1 392	387	311	5 810	2 221	868	569	1 309	670	1 484
November	1 019	1 586	1 197	390	339	5 372	2 269	792	575	1 393	467	1 612
December	943	1 286	1 257	240	531	5 398	2 476	733	539	1 341	873	1 821

U.S. EXPORTS OF GOODS BY SELECTED COUNTRIES AND REGIONS—Continued
(Census basis—Millions of dollars, not seasonally adjusted)

YEAR AND MONTH	Selected African countries				Special country groupings [1]					
	Angola	Egypt	Nigeria	South Africa	ASEAN [2]	MERCOSUR [3]	Central American Common Market	Newly industrialized countries	OPEC [4]	Pacific rim countries
1968				456						
1969				506						
1970				563						
1971				622						
1972				603						
1973				746						
1974			286	1 160					6 723	
1975			536	1 302					10 767	
1976			770	1 348					12 566	
1977			958	1 054					14 019	
1978			985	1 080					16 655	
1979			632	1 413					15 051	
1980		1 874	1 150	2 464					17 759	
1981		2 159	1 523	2 912					21 533	
1982		2 875	1 295	2 368					22 863	
1983		2 813	864	2 129					16 905	
1984		2 704	577	2 265					14 387	
1985		2 323	676	1 205				16 918	12 480	
1986		1 982	409	1 158				18 289	10 844	
1987		2 210	295	1 281				23 548	11 058	
1988		2 332	357	1 688				34 816	13 994	
1989		2 612	490	1 659				38 404	13 196	
1990		2 249	552	1 732				40 741	13 679	
1991	186	2 720	831	2 113	20 775	8 783	3 287	45 628	19 054	117 767
1992	158	3 088	1 001	2 434	23 969	9 620	4 300	48 592	21 960	124 451
1993	174	2 768	895	2 188	28 281	10 609	4 777	52 502	19 500	131 595
1994	197	2 855	509	2 174	31 925	13 663	87 805	59 595	17 868	147 779
1995	260	2 985	603	2 751	39 659	17 017	6 023	74 234	19 533	180 552
1996	268	3 153	818	3 112	42 958	18 615	6 362	75 768	22 275	188 243
1993:										
January	9	226	75	168	2 198	709	356	4 166	1 610	10 127
February	7	311	87	199	1 952	678	412	3 791	1 512	9 807
March	28	167	107	170	2 447	818	408	4 275	1 841	11 395
April	16	263	60	178	2 015	883	397	4 280	1 668	10 309
May	15	244	70	159	2 276	848	493	4 606	1 688	11 119
June	10	208	47	166	2 087	772	400	4 551	1 422	11 199
July	18	245	68	162	2 183	947	394	4 290	1 334	10 901
August	16	267	68	222	2 421	884	373	4 264	1 374	10 691
September	17	185	96	153	2 202	877	397	4 375	1 446	10 937
October	12	211	86	313	3 054	1 032	393	4 635	1 958	11 591
November	12	196	70	132	2 534	893	378	4 271	1 733	10 951
December	14	246	63	166	2 912	1 268	378	4 998	1 913	12 568
1994:										
January	7	239	53	159	2 807	1 086	346	4 773	1 726	11 366
February	21	221	33	144	2 090	942	333	3 912	1 379	10 781
March	28	220	50	201	2 815	1 035	440	5 087	1 546	12 821
April	20	331	43	165	2 280	982	6 726	4 646	1 338	11 452
May	8	160	46	183	2 866	993	7 231	4 672	1 529	11 759
June	8	244	38	194	2 554	998	7 474	4 994	1 293	12 649
July	17	171	30	178	2 483	1 082	7 156	4 805	1 317	12 264
August	18	210	24	201	2 673	1 134	7 519	5 247	1 396	13 332
September	25	175	72	167	2 947	1 130	7 539	5 289	1 356	12 676
October	13	333	34	198	2 756	1 306	7 943	5 131	1 593	12 681
November	9	263	39	177	2 810	1 436	8 113	5 309	1 668	12 593
December	23	290	48	207	2 845	1 542	8 144	5 730	1 730	13 408
1995:										
January	18	226	46	177	2 640	1 366	442	5 078	1 872	12 493
February	14	224	47	217	2 900	1 317	421	5 700	1 364	13 916
March	9	265	48	224	3 212	1 598	553	6 813	1 633	15 991
April	15	237	37	238	2 973	1 545	537	5 818	1 427	14 425
May	16	229	47	212	2 898	1 427	516	6 292	1 797	14 533
June	30	201	55	239	3 376	1 407	501	6 633	1 766	15 819
July	16	234	78	210	3 311	1 224	517	6 090	1 550	15 083
August	28	254	59	254	3 534	1 364	528	6 491	1 470	15 434
September	24	245	48	280	3 507	1 371	461	6 205	1 615	15 528
October	23	309	57	265	3 863	1 405	536	6 278	1 726	15 623
November	24	217	45	221	3 769	1 456	527	6 033	1 742	15 235
December	43	345	36	214	3 678	1 539	485	6 803	1 571	16 471
1996:										
January	20	212	68	268	3 453	1 246	487	5 768	1 512	14 719
February	47	294	56	253	3 622	1 284	471	5 816	1 572	15 415
March	19	239	68	275	4 050	1 409	527	7 078	1 944	17 587
April	14	223	60	243	3 795	1 318	497	6 223	1 708	15 388
May	20	201	57	236	3 394	1 497	506	6 530	1 777	16 086
June	17	216	47	286	3 657	1 676	530	6 460	1 886	15 419
July	13	293	75	250	3 370	1 577	534	5 928	2 124	14 882
August	26	320	74	294	3 258	1 733	527	6 368	1 936	15 524
September	17	269	79	285	3 029	1 708	555	5 826	1 801	14 343
October	32	231	67	257	3 733	1 757	591	6 406	2 027	16 084
November	22	287	122	222	3 571	1 778	594	6 471	1 950	16 320
December	23	370	46	245	4 028	1 631	542	6 896	2 038	16 477

1. See NOTES for list of countries included in each group.
2. Association of Southeast Asian Nations.
3. Argentina, Brazil, Paraguay, Uruguay.
4. Organization of Petroleum Exporting Countries.

U.S. IMPORTS OF GOODS BY SELECTED COUNTRIES AND REGIONS
(Census basis, except as noted—Millions of dollars, not seasonally adjusted)

YEAR AND MONTH	Total: Balance of payments basis	Net adjustments	Total: Census basis	North America Total	Canada	Mexico	Total [1]	Argentina	Brazil	Chile	Colombia	Dominican Republic	Venezuela
1968	32 991	....	....	....	9 005	910	....	....	670	....	....	....	950
1969	35 807	....	....	....	10 384	1 029	....	....	617	....	....	....	940
1970	39 866	....	....	....	11 092	1 219	....	....	670	....	....	....	1 082
1971	45 579	....	....	....	12 692	1 262	....	....	762	....	....	....	1 216
1972	55 797	....	....	....	14 927	1 632	....	....	942	....	....	....	1 298
1973	70 499	....	....	....	17 715	2 306	....	....	1 189	....	....	....	1 787
1974	103 811	....	....	....	21 924	3 390	....	....	1 700	....	....	....	4 671
1975	98 185	....	....	....	21 747	3 059	....	....	1 464	....	....	....	3 624
1976	124 228	....	....	....	26 237	3 598	....	....	1 737	....	....	....	3 574
1977	151 907	....	....	....	29 599	4 694	....	....	2 241	....	....	....	4 084
1978	176 002	....	....	....	33 525	6 094	....	....	2 826	....	....	....	3 545
1979	212 007	....	....	....	38 046	8 800	....	....	3 118	....	....	....	5 166
1980	249 750	....	....	....	41 455	12 520	....	741	3 715	....	1 248	....	5 297
1981	265 067	....	....	....	46 414	13 765	....	1 125	4 475	....	822	....	5 566
1982	247 642	....	....	....	46 477	15 566	....	1 128	4 285	....	801	....	4 768
1983	268 901	7 178	261 723	....	52 130	16 776	....	853	4 946	....	970	....	4 938
1984	332 418	1 908	330 510	....	66 478	18 020	....	954	7 621	....	1 146	....	6 543
1985	338 088	1 705	336 383	....	69 006	19 132	....	1 069	7 526	....	1 331	....	6 537
1986	368 425	2 753	365 672	....	68 253	17 302	....	856	6 813	....	1 874	....	5 097
1987	409 765	3 482	406 283	....	71 085	20 271	....	1 080	7 865	....	2 232	....	5 579
1988	447 189	5 263	441 926	....	81 398	23 260	....	1 436	9 294	....	2 161	....	5 157
1989	477 365	3 718	473 647	....	87 953	27 162	....	1 391	8 410	....	2 555	....	6 771
1990	498 337	2 357	495 980	....	91 372	30 172	....	1 511	7 976	....	3 168	....	9 446
1991	490 981	2 529	488 452	....	91 064	31 130	....	1 287	6 717	1 302	2 736	2 008	8 179
1992	536 458	3 795	532 663	133 841	98 630	35 211	33 531	1 256	7 609	1 388	2 837	2 373	8 181
1993	589 441	8 783	580 658	151 133	111 216	39 917	34 456	1 206	7 479	1 462	3 032	2 672	8 140
1994	668 590	5 334	663 256	177 900	128 406	49 494	38 461	1 725	8 683	1 821	3 171	3 091	8 371
1995	749 431	5 888	743 543	207 033	145 349	61 684	42 255	1 761	8 830	1 931	3 751	3 399	9 721
1996	803 239	7 950	795 289	230 190	155 893	74 297	49 547	2 279	8 773	2 262	4 424	3 575	13 173
1993:													
January	42 546	488	42 058	10 706	7 910	2 796	2 601	115	537	144	282	119	686
February	42 001	185	41 817	11 512	8 520	2 992	2 457	71	376	147	263	191	595
March	51 584	839	50 745	13 629	10 174	3 455	3 081	101	630	180	293	241	697
April	48 546	695	47 851	12 915	9 560	3 355	2 847	107	612	146	256	225	708
May	47 106	776	46 331	12 880	9 616	3 264	2 887	98	591	119	233	221	692
June	50 758	397	50 362	13 622	10 095	3 527	3 068	94	653	116	244	243	792
July	49 133	816	48 317	10 929	7 845	3 084	2 994	100	710	105	253	247	741
August	49 402	792	48 611	11 939	8 781	3 158	2 926	87	698	101	210	263	685
September	51 743	1 217	50 526	13 191	9 718	3 473	2 983	110	716	89	236	233	707
October	54 935	1 045	53 889	13 997	10 249	3 748	2 994	111	713	108	249	230	665
November	52 340	905	51 434	13 747	9 972	3 775	2 855	103	621	83	288	237	640
December	49 348	629	48 719	12 070	8 778	3 292	2 763	109	622	124	225	222	530
1994:													
January	46 919	405	46 514	12 109	8 613	3 496	2 641	122	686	158	197	130	529
February	47 444	790	46 654	12 689	9 075	3 614	2 719	91	569	162	252	207	559
March	55 783	1 120	54 663	15 137	10 930	4 207	3 288	157	741	199	253	264	666
April	52 055	583	51 472	14 185	10 357	3 828	2 861	100	645	176	256	229	598
May	53 549	561	52 987	14 695	10 662	4 033	3 136	168	739	157	197	243	695
June	57 349	211	57 139	15 540	11 346	4 194	3 422	193	762	150	243	298	806
July	55 062	254	54 807	12 673	9 059	3 614	3 238	128	768	132	261	291	704
August	59 668	364	59 304	15 310	10 955	4 355	3 638	147	783	110	352	285	847
September	59 107	227	58 880	15 888	11 511	4 377	3 567	184	842	151	298	299	733
October	62 254	284	61 970	16 631	12 050	4 581	3 382	134	801	135	277	300	729
November	61 606	272	61 334	17 342	12 412	4 930	3 285	142	677	125	283	289	776
December	57 795	264	57 531	15 703	11 438	4 265	3 285	159	671	167	301	255	730
1995:													
January	57 536	243	57 293	16 286	11 579	4 707	3 261	121	805	160	266	159	772
February	55 447	230	55 217	16 281	11 494	4 787	3 168	119	633	176	264	247	727
March	64 454	870	63 583	18 161	12 688	5 473	3 784	145	745	216	334	321	864
April	60 672	880	59 792	16 813	12 100	4 713	3 216	158	647	195	282	257	719
May	64 351	1 153	63 198	17 869	12 602	5 267	3 720	175	702	146	333	306	901
June	64 997	907	64 090	17 702	12 499	5 204	3 647	162	732	170	321	317	859
July	62 064	210	61 854	14 469	9 748	4 722	3 539	132	715	158	279	298	854
August	64 684	232	64 452	17 572	12 285	5 287	3 691	172	812	133	374	322	768
September	63 648	231	63 417	17 892	12 542	5 350	3 471	150	692	116	294	298	859
October	67 810	420	67 390	18 943	13 264	5 680	3 578	162	775	142	340	318	729
November	63 885	308	63 577	18 402	12 762	5 639	3 638	131	775	152	319	309	849
December	59 883	204	59 679	16 644	11 787	4 857	3 543	134	797	166	344	248	821
1996:													
January	62 184	275	61 910	17 819	12 211	5 607	3 734	195	741	211	301	178	956
February	60 968	388	60 580	17 978	12 396	5 582	3 444	122	633	207	302	275	802
March	64 577	1 213	63 364	18 462	12 761	5 701	3 817	158	686	210	403	277	914
April	66 277	1 613	64 664	19 041	13 047	5 994	4 104	184	716	253	374	290	1 058
May	68 104	1 247	66 857	20 169	13 749	6 420	4 325	206	723	195	350	309	1 223
June	65 070	874	64 196	19 645	13 479	6 166	3 925	207	737	181	335	307	990
July	68 107	425	67 682	17 636	11 595	6 041	4 341	176	729	172	386	354	1 160
August	68 795	770	68 025	19 635	13 163	6 472	4 148	205	859	162	344	328	1 030
September	68 616	307	68 309	19 985	13 488	6 497	4 353	250	732	143	379	306	1 262
October	74 433	315	74 118	20 617	13 501	7 116	4 595	233	706	136	437	356	1 314
November	68 304	289	68 016	20 376	13 773	6 603	4 087	152	747	162	384	284	1 108
December	67 805	235	67 570	18 828	12 729	6 099	4 674	192	764	229	429	313	1 357

1. Includes countries not shown separately. See NOTES for list of included countries.

U.S. IMPORTS OF GOODS BY SELECTED COUNTRIES AND REGIONS—Continued
(Census basis—Millions of dollars, not seasonally adjusted)

YEAR AND MONTH	Total[1]	Western Europe — European Union									
		Total[1]	Belgium	France	Germany	Ireland	Italy	Netherlands	Spain	Sweden	United Kingdom
1968				842	2 721		1 102				2 058
1969				842	2 603		1 204				2 120
1970				942	3 127		1 316				2 194
1971				1 088	3 651		1 406				2 499
1972				1 369	4 250		1 757				2 987
1973				1 732	5 345		2 002				3 657
1974	23 522	19 035		2 257	6 324		2 585	1 433			4 061
1975	20 735	16 610		2 137	5 382		2 397	1 083			3 784
1976	22 784	17 848		2 509	5 592		2 530	1 080			4 254
1977	27 417	22 087		3 032	7 238		3 037	1 477			5 141
1978	36 485	29 009		4 051	9 962		4 102	1 603			6 514
1979	41 684	33 295		4 768	10 955		4 918	1 852			8 028
1980	46 416	35 958		5 247	11 681		4 313	1 910	1 230	1 631	9 755
1981	51 855	41 624		5 851	11 379		5 189	2 366	1 537	1 714	12 835
1982	52 346	42 509		5 545	11 975		5 301	2 494	1 508	1 992	13 095
1983	53 884	43 892		6 025	12 695		5 455	2 970	1 536	2 429	12 470
1984	71 153	57 360		8 113	16 996		7 935	4 069	2 391	3 244	14 492
1985	79 756	67 822		9 482	20 239		9 674	4 081	2 515	4 124	14 937
1986	89 825	75 736		10 129	25 124		10 607	4 066	2 702	4 419	15 396
1987	95 496	81 188		10 730	27 069		11 040	3 964	2 839	4 758	17 341
1988	100 443	84 939		12 509	26 362		11 576	4 559	3 204	4 985	17 976
1989	101 764	85 153		13 013	24 832		11 933	4 810	3 317	4 892	18 319
1990	108 901	91 868		13 124	28 109		12 723	4 972	3 311	4 937	20 288
1991	102 262	86 481	3 929	13 333	26 137	1 948	11 764	4 811	2 848	4 524	18 413
1992	110 727	93 993	4 476	14 797	28 820	2 262	12 314	5 300	3 002	4 716	20 093
1993	115 557	97 941	5 149	15 279	28 562	2 519	13 216	5 443	2 992	4 534	21 730
1994	130 730	110 875	6 354	16 699	31 744	2 894	14 802	6 007	3 555	5 041	25 058
1995	145 320	131 871	6 054	17 209	36 844	4 079	16 348	6 405	3 880	6 256	26 930
1996	157 601	142 947	6 776	18 646	38 945	4 804	18 325	6 583	4 280	7 153	28 979
1993:											
January	7 998	6 870	409	1 012	1 944	189	916	423	237	320	1 504
February	8 217	6 990	363	1 121	2 202	166	867	371	204	309	1 487
March	10 358	8 688	434	1 354	2 555	203	1 172	496	253	439	1 932
April	9 450	7 968	396	1 269	2 330	179	974	437	251	368	1 879
May	9 317	7 881	415	1 217	2 344	178	963	432	252	388	1 851
June	10 186	8 593	448	1 340	2 429	211	1 203	502	279	422	1 920
July	10 006	8 431	493	1 212	2 433	225	1 247	487	265	377	1 804
August	9 117	7 809	299	1 188	2 242	218	1 146	490	276	281	1 709
September	9 290	7 821	453	1 211	2 291	244	935	432	214	281	1 785
October	10 653	9 014	489	1 316	2 559	244	1 533	485	239	389	1 878
November	10 438	8 791	493	1 402	2 599	251	1 133	399	253	424	1 990
December	10 527	9 084	458	1 639	2 633	211	1 126	489	269	372	1 991
1994:											
January	8 721	7 401	497	1 039	2 071	183	1 039	443	233	336	1 653
February	9 323	7 933	500	1 178	2 260	280	983	455	256	368	1 751
March	11 508	9 813	581	1 482	2 744	284	1 249	687	315	466	2 169
April	10 490	8 880	544	1 450	2 542	205	1 124	513	282	403	1 916
May	11 001	9 440	552	1 361	2 804	309	1 137	520	320	396	2 157
June	11 303	9 565	554	1 402	2 684	243	1 345	535	332	409	2 116
July	11 126	9 496	571	1 365	2 772	201	1 419	480	306	368	2 081
August	10 684	9 110	435	1 302	2 632	214	1 368	475	332	307	2 064
September	10 966	9 207	489	1 384	2 454	256	1 013	468	271	398	2 361
October	11 711	9 848	589	1 714	2 783	218	1 309	490	304	487	2 131
November	12 162	10 224	555	1 540	2 936	283	1 478	446	310	554	2 374
December	11 736	9 958	489	1 483	3 063	218	1 340	496	293	549	2 284
1995:											
January	10 814	9 875	503	1 367	2 689	263	1 300	484	290	514	1 875
February	10 632	9 657	538	1 225	2 576	265	1 198	436	288	496	2 053
March	12 638	11 467	545	1 609	3 006	277	1 375	501	350	629	2 538
April	12 204	11 093	468	1 507	3 246	309	1 300	532	320	531	2 225
May	12 678	11 391	555	1 526	3 116	360	1 320	542	325	593	2 394
June	12 699	11 473	445	1 384	3 306	392	1 472	558	360	532	2 332
July	13 064	11 855	592	1 496	3 633	347	1 576	565	338	493	2 110
August	11 450	10 388	346	1 471	2 992	272	1 420	492	341	312	2 075
September	11 135	10 068	461	1 264	2 665	398	1 056	492	269	494	2 313
October	13 221	12 033	552	1 708	2 937	430	1 529	716	363	549	2 566
November	12 505	11 404	578	1 419	3 161	398	1 439	543	343	551	2 294
December	12 282	11 166	473	1 235	3 520	368	1 362	544	292	562	2 156
1996:											
January	11 960	10 862	494	1 294	2 914	455	1 526	457	315	567	2 182
February	11 899	10 773	532	1 354	2 857	345	1 420	501	333	581	2 217
March	13 306	12 018	577	1 679	3 312	366	1 537	568	353	623	2 328
April	13 276	11 958	566	1 491	3 225	394	1 466	544	371	636	2 470
May	13 595	12 346	575	1 607	3 423	412	1 476	578	360	643	2 583
June	12 674	11 474	548	1 560	2 970	389	1 536	533	328	593	2 364
July	14 267	12 974	682	1 621	3 613	381	1 785	560	403	629	2 475
August	12 637	11 503	422	1 533	3 268	378	1 680	542	335	338	2 329
September	12 236	11 061	570	1 531	2 958	430	1 204	554	302	565	2 246
October	14 404	13 067	692	1 815	3 448	399	1 598	636	419	682	2 624
November	13 353	12 077	556	1 509	3 404	450	1 537	558	378	639	2 366
December	13 994	12 835	562	1 653	3 555	407	1 560	553	381	658	2 795

1. Includes countries not shown separately. See NOTES for list of included countries.

YEAR AND MONTH	U.S. IMPORTS OF GOODS BY SELECTED COUNTRIES AND REGIONS—Continued (Census basis—Millions of dollars, not seasonally adjusted)										
	Western Europe—Continued			Eastern Europe and former Soviet Republics					Selected Near and Middle Eastern countries		
	European Free Trade Association			Total[1]	Hungary	Poland	Former Soviet Republics		Israel	Saudi Arabi	Turkey
	Total[1]	Norway	Switzerland				Total[1]	Russia			
1968							58				
1969							52				
1970							72				
1971							57				
1972							95				
1973							220				
1974				890			350				
1975				731			254				
1976				856			220				
1977				914			453				
1978				1 503			539				
1979				1 865			874				
1980		2 633	2 796	1 433	107	417	453				
1981		2 478	2 448	1 555	129	365	348				
1982		1 973	2 340	1 067	133	212	228				
1983		1 358	2 494	1 359	158	189	347				
1984		1 904	3 117	2 154	221	220	554				
1985		1 164	3 476	1 936	218	220	409			1 907	
1986		1 079	5 253	2 001	225	233	558			3 612	
1987		1 404	4 249	1 923	279	296	425			4 433	
1988		1 446	4 611	2 163	293	377	586			5 620	
1989		1 991	4 714	2 064	328	387	710			7 181	
1990		1 830	5 587	2 275	348	408	1 065			9 974	
1991	14 302	1 624	5 576	1 800	367	357	813		3 484	10 900	1 006
1992	15 021	1 969	5 645	1 551	347	375	658	481	3 816	10 371	1 110
1993	15 816	1 958	5 973	3 526	401	454	2 094	1 743	4 420	7 708	1 198
1994	17 665	2 353	6 373	5 832	470	651	3 848	3 245	5 229	7 688	1 575
1995	11 039	3 087	7 594	7 020	547	664	4 896	4 030	5 709	8 377	1 798
1996	12 112	3 993	7 792	6 987	676	628	4 690	3 577	6 434	10 467	1 778
1993:											
January	995	126	345	172	37	26	64	47	386	881	84
February	1 068	87	453	173	23	25	94	79	335	705	113
March	1 498	150	615	248	30	40	138	120	385	776	124
April	1 330	166	515	277	28	40	156	131	298	837	99
May	1 319	211	455	263	31	34	151	133	331	751	66
June	1 447	183	517	340	33	36	218	193	354	678	92
July	1 431	242	503	363	39	42	231	194	396	541	93
August	1 160	151	456	276	35	41	156	113	335	532	98
September	1 324	161	493	305	31	42	186	158	395	529	99
October	1 494	175	590	357	34	42	230	202	389	513	95
November	1 444	177	502	369	40	38	234	181	454	489	147
December	1 307	128	530	384	42	49	237	191	363	476	89
1994:											
January	1 158	131	412	308	38	48	173	139	450	481	114
February	1 243	135	472	352	31	44	226	194	390	349	100
March	1 500	164	539	433	44	69	257	213	429	437	137
April	1 424	175	527	473	35	52	336	296	400	635	148
May	1 398	179	502	498	42	53	339	296	429	630	104
June	1 574	235	578	438	33	48	285	241	410	716	110
July	1 472	227	531	496	42	61	320	280	468	783	111
August	1 346	207	488	541	40	54	344	296	430	715	171
September	1 577	288	582	404	37	47	248	187	402	714	126
October	1 664	277	566	613	45	66	400	344	504	762	150
November	1 710	177	621	601	43	62	431	348	478	743	176
December	1 600	159	555	676	41	48	490	412	440	723	128
1995:											
January	720	208	494	626	45	57	449	385	519	647	172
February	775	190	557	550	41	58	391	313	434	656	147
March	923	274	620	784	50	57	579	497	513	745	191
April	912	241	626	683	45	52	515	430	388	717	157
May	1 070	287	748	571	45	60	390	317	482	766	167
June	1 031	326	673	704	45	52	539	478	469	638	146
July	964	228	706	526	49	55	339	253	544	685	181
August	888	310	558	590	42	48	423	345	455	624	134
September	891	249	611	509	43	50	341	272	493	745	128
October	1 032	235	761	454	51	59	282	219	450	634	102
November	893	244	621	552	48	59	358	294	531	760	145
December	942	295	619	471	45	57	290	227	431	761	127
1996:											
January	885	260	592	416	44	54	244	184	538	747	154
February	908	242	646	466	44	47	297	237	507	571	151
March	1 078	322	721	468	48	48	301	232	486	750	152
April	1 091	400	663	581	49	50	414	340	434	910	163
May	1 051	353	668	564	52	60	389	288	534	911	140
June	1 023	370	633	538	47	48	366	254	494	635	120
July	1 079	398	654	519	54	53	323	232	661	916	148
August	927	344	553	663	59	53	467	357	498	932	140
September	994	337	638	588	59	51	392	299	565	1 068	126
October	1 095	377	687	714	67	61	509	394	613	939	161
November	1 046	323	697	685	77	51	438	331	567	823	166
December	936	268	641	784	78	52	551	430	538	1 265	156

1. Includes countries not shown separately. See NOTES for list of included countries.

U.S. IMPORTS OF GOODS BY SELECTED COUNTRIES AND REGIONS—Continued
(Census basis—Millions of dollars, not seasonally adjusted)

Selected Asian and Oceanic countries

YEAR AND MONTH	Australia	China	Hong Kong	India	Indonesia	Japan	South Korea	Malaysia	Phil- ippines	Singapore	Thailand	Taiwan
1968						4 054						
1969						4 888						
1970						5 875						
1971						7 259						
1972						9 064						
1973						9 676						
1974						12 338						
1975						11 268						
1976						15 504						
1977						18 550						
1978						24 458						
1979						26 248						
1980					5 183	30 701						
1981					6 022	37 612						
1982					4 224	37 744						
1983					5 285	41 183						
1984					5 461	57 135						
1985	2 837	3 862	8 396		4 569	68 783	10 031			4 260		16 396
1986	2 632	4 771	8 891		3 312	81 911	12 729			4 725		19 791
1987	3 007	6 294	9 854		3 394	84 575	16 987			6 201		24 622
1988	3 541	8 511	10 238		3 150	89 519	20 105			7 973		24 714
1989	3 898	11 989	9 739		3 529	93 586	19 742			8 950		24 326
1990	4 442	15 224	9 488		3 341	89 655	18 493			9 839		22 667
1991	3 988	18 969	9 279	3 193	3 241	91 511	17 019	6 102	3 471	9 957	6 122	23 023
1992	3 688	25 728	9 793	3 780	4 529	97 414	16 682	8 294	4 355	11 313	7 529	24 596
1993	3 297	31 540	9 554	4 554	5 435	107 246	17 118	10 563	4 894	12 798	8 542	25 102
1994	3 202	38 787	9 696	5 310	6 547	119 156	19 629	13 982	5 719	15 358	10 306	26 706
1995	3 323	45 543	10 291	5 726	7 435	123 479	24 184	17 455	7 007	18 560	11 348	28 972
1996	3 869	51 513	9 865	6 170	8 250	115 187	22 655	17 829	8 161	20 343	11 336	29 907
1993:												
January	340	2 188	789	335	413	7 637	1 366	706	355	851	651	1 970
February	208	1 862	560	378	373	8 015	1 171	690	362	823	583	1 661
March	250	2 083	683	461	455	9 663	1 391	828	399	1 116	707	2 116
April	251	2 226	659	388	377	9 196	1 355	733	353	922	601	2 003
May	255	2 376	731	330	365	7 792	1 412	804	364	986	599	1 986
June	258	2 754	821	364	440	8 624	1 550	871	417	1 159	677	2 161
July	298	2 981	893	407	460	8 865	1 559	896	437	1 138	845	2 109
August	298	3 223	871	410	503	9 050	1 474	1 022	468	1 120	774	2 330
September	301	3 339	921	407	449	9 280	1 541	985	467	1 226	753	2 258
October	307	3 278	958	411	619	10 113	1 482	1 097	449	1 200	809	2 239
November	275	2 900	889	343	480	9 467	1 455	985	411	1 077	758	2 144
December	254	2 330	780	320	501	9 545	1 363	947	412	1 181	784	2 126
1994:												
January	265	2 763	876	383	528	8 470	1 393	992	452	1 117	749	2 148
February	226	2 499	613	405	435	8 888	1 291	933	400	929	691	1 948
March	236	2 183	581	510	486	10 595	1 503	1 024	474	1 295	799	2 008
April	244	2 492	615	403	447	9 780	1 461	988	402	1 161	704	2 018
May	262	2 979	704	416	445	8 509	1 646	1 053	428	1 268	794	2 202
June	278	3 463	813	427	518	10 112	1 633	1 109	488	1 305	825	2 224
July	281	3 645	880	474	690	9 990	1 795	1 205	489	1 270	889	2 163
August	298	4 166	959	511	612	10 697	1 827	1 262	536	1 321	1 014	2 450
September	279	4 134	946	490	597	9 909	1 741	1 335	545	1 452	986	2 445
October	299	4 101	1 078	534	618	11 316	1 756	1 412	551	1 395	994	2 453
November	311	3 534	895	391	607	10 629	1 850	1 358	477	1 392	964	2 400
December	224	2 827	736	365	563	10 262	1 732	1 311	478	1 452	897	2 247
1995:												
January	272	3 451	903	467	577	9 234	1 870	1 278	507	1 392	908	2 387
February	298	3 002	661	458	532	9 733	1 499	1 107	489	1 064	770	1 898
March	259	2 910	656	524	592	11 732	1 819	1 200	554	1 438	934	2 351
April	261	3 148	670	433	494	11 180	1 747	1 268	468	1 355	846	2 186
May	299	3 655	811	452	612	10 510	1 983	1 404	536	1 376	859	2 448
June	265	3 961	881	458	677	10 885	2 003	1 429	590	1 609	944	2 363
July	294	4 312	950	518	736	10 549	2 132	1 524	608	1 592	1 006	2 492
August	283	4 805	1 013	551	691	10 459	2 310	1 625	666	1 688	1 087	2 667
September	271	4 584	1 024	527	657	10 050	2 181	1 723	675	1 793	1 029	2 554
October	261	4 714	1 077	543	672	10 235	2 395	1 750	705	1 819	1 099	2 745
November	305	3 868	901	437	594	9 552	2 260	1 583	628	1 728	976	2 503
December	256	3 134	746	360	601	9 360	1 986	1 562	582	1 708	892	2 378
1996:												
January	255	3 658	912	489	617	8 955	2 268	1 504	663	1 665	937	2 453
February	289	3 540	720	471	629	9 575	1 996	1 301	636	1 417	829	2 252
March	283	2 864	640	495	567	10 241	1 940	1 423	657	1 980	915	2 165
April	277	3 248	669	514	630	9 913	1 919	1 426	569	1 699	890	2 304
May	303	3 954	806	474	593	9 082	1 937	1 443	615	1 713	817	2 476
June	302	4 111	763	446	679	8 964	1 660	1 348	655	1 611	900	2 467
July	315	4 817	953	564	751	9 781	1 816	1 500	726	1 695	1 004	2 648
August	353	5 496	889	584	736	9 453	1 770	1 596	733	1 699	1 008	2 567
September	325	5 481	902	590	715	9 205	1 725	1 638	767	1 801	1 000	2 731
October	365	5 813	1 017	638	898	10 741	1 912	1 685	783	1 759	1 110	2 818
November	407	4 585	835	479	715	9 620	1 826	1 496	655	1 601	997	2 493
December	396	3 947	758	426	722	9 657	1 887	1 469	704	1 704	931	2 533

YEAR AND MONTH	U.S. IMPORTS OF GOODS BY SELECTED COUNTRIES AND REGIONS—Continued (Census basis—Millions of dollars, not seasonally adjusted)									
	Selected African countries				Special country groupings [1]					
	Angola	Egypt	Nigeria	South Africa	ASEAN [2]	MERCOSUR [3]	Central American Common Market	Newly industrialized countries	OPEC [4]	Pacific rim countries
1968	....	....	....	256	....	....	....	....	....	....
1969	....	....	....	246	....	....	....	....	....	....
1970	....	....	....	290	....	....	....	....	....	....
1971	....	....	....	287	....	....	....	....	....	....
1972	....	....	....	325	....	....	....	....	....	....
1973	....	....	....	377	....	....	....	....	....	....
1974	....	....	....	609	....	....	....	....	....	....
1975	....	....	....	841	....	....	....	....	....	....
1976	....	....	....	925	....	....	....	....	....	....
1977	....	....	....	1 261	....	....	....	....	....	....
1978	....	....	....	2 259	....	....	....	....	....	....
1979	....	....	....	2 616	....	....	....	....	....	....
1980	....	459	....	3 321	....	....	....	....	....	....
1981	....	397	....	2 445	....	....	....	....	....	....
1982	....	547	....	1 967	....	....	....	....	....	....
1983	....	303	....	2 027	....	....	....	....	....	....
1984	....	169	....	2 488	....	....	....	....	....	....
1985	....	79	3 002	2 071	....	....	....	....	22 800	....
1986	....	112	2 530	2 365	....	....	....	....	19 750	....
1987	....	465	3 573	1 346	....	....	....	....	23 953	....
1988	....	220	3 279	1 513	....	....	....	....	22 962	....
1989	....	226	5 226	1 529	....	....	....	....	30 601	....
1990	....	398	5 977	1 701	....	....	....	....	38 017	....
1991	1 775	206	5 168	1 728	28 918	8 284	2 972	59 277	32 644	188 407
1992	2 303	434	5 103	1 727	36 050	9 166	3 727	62 384	33 200	208 424
1993	2 092	613	5 301	1 845	42 262	9 001	4 266	64 572	31 739	229 552
1994	2 061	549	4 430	2 031	51 957	10 656	4 804	71 388	31 685	261 153
1995	2 232	606	4 931	2 208	61 844	10 813	5 862	82 008	35 197	288 685
1996	2 902	680	5 978	2 323	65 968	11 355	6 774	82 770	44 285	290 033
1993:										
January	225	34	460	138	2 977	684	285	4 975	2 733	16 745
February	171	37	443	120	2 832	460	360	4 215	2 486	15 855
March	224	34	543	166	3 510	751	414	5 305	2 890	19 175
April	171	39	665	165	2 988	735	336	4 938	3 056	18 232
May	196	32	452	157	3 119	744	347	5 115	2 709	17 256
June	117	88	536	152	3 566	807	370	5 692	2 794	19 262
July	195	83	521	185	3 779	830	358	5 699	2 711	19 831
August	113	50	368	151	3 890	805	369	5 796	2 566	20 555
September	169	63	320	153	3 882	845	386	5 945	2 495	20 946
October	202	51	331	146	4 178	846	360	5 879	2 682	21 916
November	181	60	348	141	3 715	747	333	5 564	2 459	20 221
December	130	41	315	172	3 827	748	349	5 450	2 159	19 557
1994:										
January	177	63	182	166	3 841	822	296	5 534	2 086	19 187
February	119	33	305	108	3 389	674	348	4 781	2 026	18 316
March	147	55	262	174	4 079	949	423	5 387	2 229	20 563
April	152	36	364	161	3 705	763	337	5 255	2 413	19 788
May	151	44	398	169	3 990	923	384	5 821	2 562	19 700
June	160	45	475	190	4 263	974	420	5 975	2 949	22 194
July	170	49	447	186	4 547	914	407	6 109	3 099	22 613
August	208	38	546	172	4 749	952	455	6 556	3 139	24 318
September	227	52	433	181	4 918	1 047	436	6 585	2 814	23 565
October	174	53	293	127	4 974	953	435	6 682	2 807	25 176
November	197	34	368	186	4 800	841	432	6 537	2 834	23 707
December	180	48	358	211	4 704	845	431	6 167	2 727	22 027
1995:										
January	113	59	396	182	4 665	942	404	6 552	2 700	22 095
February	183	51	336	143	3 966	772	476	5 122	2 697	20 458
March	193	49	467	165	4 721	907	551	6 264	3 025	23 689
April	201	53	307	163	4 433	819	431	5 957	2 617	22 957
May	250	63	492	201	4 790	896	493	6 618	3 187	23 861
June	163	41	431	216	5 250	912	499	6 855	3 062	24 882
July	231	43	412	186	5 470	862	489	7 165	3 123	25 412
August	147	62	417	191	5 762	1 007	541	7 679	2 965	26 432
September	207	42	454	198	5 880	870	505	7 552	3 024	25 712
October	206	40	444	166	6 050	956	489	8 036	2 874	26 586
November	173	48	336	206	5 511	924	506	7 392	2 939	24 112
December	167	58	439	190	5 346	947	480	6 816	2 984	22 490
1996:										
January	197	62	549	146	5 392	1 008	454	7 298	3 280	23 163
February	165	56	405	156	4 815	771	537	6 385	2 809	22 534
March	128	62	367	191	5 54'	857	547	6 725	2 964	22 930
April	224	81	484	239	5 216	918	538	6 591	3 555	22 842
May	278	46	552	215	5 184	946	565	6 933	3 896	23 162
June	214	47	523	165	5 196	963	550	6 501	3 401	22 763
July	204	79	667	223	5 679	928	617	7 113	4 090	25 243
August	270	42	499	204	5 777	1 086	580	6 925	3 835	25 516
September	293	32	648	184	5 925	1 003	586	7 159	4 235	25 498
October	353	58	523	194	6 241	963	619	7 505	4 263	27 996
November	289	65	414	226	5 468	926	565	6 756	3 643	24 420
December	287	51	349	180	5 532	986	618	6 882	4 313	23 967

1. See NOTES for list of countries included in each group.
2. Association of Southeast Asian Nations.
3. Argentina, Brazil, Paraguay, Uruguay.
4. Organization of Petroleum Exporting Countries.

YEAR AND MONTH	U.S. EXPORTS OF GOODS BY PRINCIPAL END-USE CATEGORY (Census basis, except as noted—Billions of dollars, seasonally adjusted)								
	Total exports of goods			Foods, feeds, and beverages	Industrial supplies and materials	Capital goods, except automotive	Automotive vehicles, engines, and parts	Consumer goods (nonfood), except automotive	Other goods
	Total: Balance of payments basis	Net adjustments	Total: Census basis						
1968	33.63								
1969	36.41								
1970	42.47								
1971	43.32								
1972	49.38								
1973	71.41								
1974	98.31								
1975	107.09								
1976	114.75								
1977	120.82								
1978	142.08			25.57	39.05	46.81	14.56	11.20	
1979	184.44			30.26	57.30	58.71	16.56	13.58	
1980	224.25			36.01	70.59	74.65	15.98	17.31	
1981	237.04			38.57	67.79	82.47	18.23	17.26	
1982	211.16			31.96	62.13	75.03	15.94	15.75	
1983	201.80	0.09	201.71	31.83	57.43	70.02	17.02	14.50	
1984	219.93	1.18	218.74	31.93	62.59	75.41	20.99	14.64	
1985	215.92	3.29	212.62	24.42	59.17	76.89	22.99	14.01	
1986	223.34	-3.13	226.47	22.84	61.89	79.47	22.16	15.86	
1987	250.21	-3.70	253.90	24.74	67.84	90.66	25.74	19.76	
1988	320.23	-3.11	323.34	32.86	86.73	115.42	30.21	26.00	
1989	362.12	-1.72	363.84	37.06	99.33	138.71	34.94	36.57	
1990	389.31	-3.62	392.92	34.95	104.92	152.12	36.50	42.78	20.73
1991	416.91	-4.85	421.76	35.74	109.57	165.96	40.01	46.86	23.66
1992	440.35	-7.81	448.16	40.27	109.14	175.92	47.03	51.42	24.39
1993	456.83	-8.26	465.09	40.63	111.81	181.70	52.40	54.66	23.89
1994	502.40	-10.23	512.63	41.96	121.40	205.02	57.78	59.98	26.50
1995	575.87	-8.87	584.74	50.47	146.25	233.05	61.83	64.43	28.72
1996	612.07	-13.01	625.08	55.53	147.65	252.90	65.02	70.14	33.84
1993:									
January	36.95	-0.66	37.62	3.31	9.44	14.38	4.09	4.45	1.96
February	36.40	-0.66	37.06	3.46	8.68	14.29	4.32	4.38	1.93
March	38.51	-0.52	39.03	3.50	9.24	15.52	4.34	4.52	1.92
April	38.04	-0.68	38.72	3.52	9.16	15.20	4.44	4.43	1.98
May	38.90	-0.69	39.59	3.39	9.72	15.36	4.52	4.71	1.90
June	37.25	-0.69	37.93	3.25	8.81	15.26	4.18	4.51	1.92
July	36.69	-0.74	37.42	3.25	9.18	14.27	4.22	4.57	1.94
August	37.04	-0.79	37.83	3.07	8.92	15.08	4.11	4.52	2.15
September	37.70	-0.72	38.41	3.35	9.50	14.68	4.30	4.60	1.99
October	39.33	-0.67	40.01	3.41	9.89	15.50	4.62	4.56	2.03
November	39.32	-0.73	40.05	3.48	9.60	15.42	4.83	4.76	1.96
December	40.71	-0.71	41.42	3.66	9.69	16.74	4.45	4.67	2.22
1994:									
January	39.10	-0.75	39.84	3.36	9.04	16.32	4.41	4.69	2.03
February	37.58	-0.72	38.29	3.22	8.67	15.58	4.34	4.50	1.97
March	41.71	-0.78	42.49	3.44	10.49	16.94	4.79	4.87	1.96
April	40.50	-0.75	41.25	3.14	9.62	16.92	4.73	4.78	2.07
May	40.51	-0.87	41.38	3.25	9.93	16.54	4.69	4.91	2.07
June	42.02	-0.83	42.85	3.13	9.81	17.62	4.83	5.19	2.28
July	41.14	-0.81	41.96	3.10	10.35	16.48	4.69	4.96	2.37
August	43.37	-1.01	44.38	3.58	10.64	17.62	4.89	5.17	2.49
September	43.12	-0.89	44.00	3.64	10.29	17.83	4.92	5.11	2.22
October	43.21	-0.99	44.20	3.84	10.61	16.88	5.01	5.26	2.60
November	44.21	-0.83	45.04	4.07	10.64	17.81	5.10	5.28	2.15
December	45.94	-1.01	46.95	4.20	11.31	18.50	5.39	5.27	2.28
1995:									
January	45.06	-0.64	45.70	3.85	11.53	17.24	5.47	5.15	2.46
February	45.54	-0.68	46.22	3.96	11.65	18.11	5.18	5.23	2.10
March	47.79	-0.77	48.56	4.10	12.51	18.86	5.29	5.34	2.47
April	47.51	-0.65	48.16	4.06	12.37	19.09	5.16	5.26	2.22
May	47.95	-0.76	48.71	3.98	12.41	19.29	5.14	5.47	2.43
June	47.72	-0.84	48.56	3.85	12.68	19.51	4.77	5.43	2.33
July	47.06	-0.72	47.78	4.11	12.07	19.29	4.85	5.23	2.22
August	48.66	-0.75	49.41	4.46	12.10	20.02	5.07	5.49	2.28
September	49.64	-0.66	50.30	4.78	12.53	19.85	5.31	5.47	2.35
October	49.28	-0.80	50.08	4.40	12.46	20.07	5.22	5.45	2.48
November	49.41	-0.81	50.21	4.43	11.81	20.56	5.06	5.42	2.93
December	50.26	-0.80	51.06	4.49	12.12	21.17	5.32	5.50	2.47
1996:									
January	48.90	-0.70	49.59	4.68	11.91	20.04	5.27	5.55	2.14
February	50.43	-0.79	51.22	4.49	12.10	21.07	5.31	5.80	2.45
March	50.72	-0.90	51.62	4.86	12.60	20.77	5.09	5.73	2.57
April	50.79	-0.84	51.64	4.60	12.71	21.11	5.05	5.73	2.44
May	51.28	-1.13	52.41	4.68	12.45	21.05	5.43	5.86	2.94
June	51.34	-0.88	52.22	4.48	12.34	20.86	5.57	5.89	3.08
July	49.09	-1.44	50.53	4.68	11.62	20.11	5.35	5.59	3.19
August	51.25	-1.35	52.61	4.69	12.34	21.16	5.49	5.87	3.07
September	50.42	-1.31	51.73	4.42	12.19	20.42	5.72	5.89	3.09
October	52.50	-1.07	53.57	4.55	12.68	22.05	5.41	6.14	2.74
November	53.21	-1.28	54.49	5.01	12.25	22.21	5.88	6.07	3.06
December	52.13	-1.32	53.45	4.40	12.46	22.05	5.47	6.02	3.06

U.S. IMPORTS OF GOODS BY PRINCIPAL END-USE CATEGORY
(Census basis, except as noted—Billions of dollars, seasonally adjusted)

YEAR AND MONTH	Total imports of goods			Foods, feeds, and beverages	Industrial supplies and materials	Capital goods, except automotive	Automotive vehicles, engines, and parts	Consumer goods (nonfood), except automotive	Other goods
	Total: Balance of payments basis	Net adjustments	Total: Census basis						
1968	32.99	....	....	....	....	....	....	....	....
1969	35.81	....	....	....	....	....	....	....	....
1970	39.87	....	....	....	....	....	....	....	....
1971	45.58	....	....	....	....	....	....	....	....
1972	55.80	....	....	....	....	....	....	....	....
1973	70.50	....	....	....	....	....	....	....	....
1974	103.81	....	....	....	....	....	....	....	....
1975	98.19	....	....	....	....	....	....	....	....
1976	124.23	....	....	....	....	....	....	....	....
1977	151.91	....	....	....	....	....	....	....	....
1978	176.00	....	....	15.84	79.26	19.29	25.11	29.40	....
1979	212.01	....	....	18.01	102.67	24.49	26.51	31.22	....
1980	249.75	....	....	18.55	124.96	30.72	28.13	34.22	....
1981	265.07	....	....	18.53	131.10	36.86	30.80	38.30	....
1982	247.64	....	....	17.47	107.82	38.22	34.26	39.66	....
1983	268.90	7.18	261.72	18.56	105.63	42.61	42.04	46.59	....
1984	332.42	1.91	330.51	21.92	122.72	60.15	56.77	61.19	....
1985	338.09	1.71	336.38	21.89	112.48	60.81	65.21	66.43	....
1986	368.43	2.75	365.67	24.40	101.37	71.86	78.25	79.43	....
1987	409.77	3.48	406.28	24.81	110.67	84.77	85.17	88.82	....
1988	447.19	5.26	441.93	24.93	118.06	101.79	87.95	96.42	....
1989	477.37	3.72	473.65	25.08	132.40	112.45	87.38	102.26	....
1990	498.34	2.36	495.98	26.65	143.41	116.04	87.69	105.29	16.09
1991	490.98	2.53	488.45	26.21	131.38	120.80	84.94	107.78	15.94
1992	536.46	3.80	532.66	27.61	138.64	134.25	91.79	122.66	17.71
1993	589.44	8.78	580.66	27.87	145.61	152.37	102.42	134.02	18.39
1994	668.59	5.33	663.26	27.87	145.61	152.37	102.42	134.02	18.39
1995	749.43	5.89	743.54	33.18	181.85	221.43	123.80	159.91	23.39
1996	803.24	7.95	795.29	35.71	204.48	229.05	128.94	171.01	26.10
1993:									
January	45.98	0.49	45.50	2.26	11.64	11.68	8.04	10.47	1.40
February	45.28	0.18	45.10	2.17	11.06	11.86	8.37	10.34	1.31
March	49.81	0.84	48.97	2.38	12.50	12.38	8.61	11.48	1.63
April	49.27	0.69	48.57	2.26	12.63	12.48	8.65	11.10	1.45
May	48.72	0.78	47.94	2.30	12.42	12.36	8.36	10.85	1.66
June	49.59	0.40	49.19	2.33	12.77	12.96	8.41	11.15	1.57
July	48.93	0.82	48.11	2.25	12.23	12.86	8.06	11.20	1.51
August	48.70	0.79	47.90	2.30	11.81	12.55	8.38	11.44	1.42
September	50.30	1.22	49.08	2.41	12.18	12.76	8.77	11.46	1.51
October	51.87	1.05	50.82	2.53	12.55	13.45	9.05	11.65	1.59
November	50.84	0.91	49.94	2.33	12.31	13.14	8.93	11.56	1.66
December	50.16	0.63	49.53	2.33	11.50	13.88	8.79	11.32	1.70
1994:									
January	50.43	0.41	50.03	2.44	11.68	14.03	8.67	11.52	1.69
February	51.19	0.79	50.40	2.36	11.92	14.00	8.90	11.52	1.69
March	53.39	1.12	52.27	2.56	12.62	14.47	9.40	11.44	1.78
April	53.52	0.58	52.94	2.52	12.63	14.76	9.32	11.91	1.79
May	54.39	0.56	53.83	2.54	13.10	14.90	9.53	12.00	1.76
June	55.94	0.21	55.73	2.59	14.00	15.20	9.98	12.17	1.79
July	56.35	0.25	56.10	2.59	14.36	15.31	9.96	12.14	1.72
August	57.76	0.36	57.40	2.69	14.74	15.41	10.41	12.41	1.73
September	57.87	0.23	57.64	2.70	14.29	16.32	9.96	12.53	1.84
October	58.23	0.28	57.95	2.65	13.92	16.32	10.51	12.73	1.82
November	60.05	0.27	59.78	2.65	14.56	16.94	10.81	13.01	1.81
December	59.47	0.26	59.20	2.66	14.28	16.71	10.82	12.87	1.86
1995:									
January	60.85	0.24	60.61	2.85	14.46	16.99	11.06	13.34	1.92
February	59.68	0.23	59.45	2.79	14.36	16.78	10.66	13.05	1.80
March	62.26	0.87	61.39	2.91	15.33	17.54	10.63	13.21	1.77
April	63.17	0.88	62.29	2.74	15.38	17.98	10.99	13.47	1.74
May	63.77	1.15	62.62	2.71	15.88	18.11	10.34	13.61	1.97
June	63.80	0.91	62.89	2.75	15.82	18.72	10.22	13.42	1.96
July	62.61	0.21	62.40	2.72	15.33	18.81	10.03	13.50	2.02
August	62.34	0.23	62.11	2.72	15.01	18.90	10.00	13.43	2.05
September	63.23	0.23	63.00	2.80	15.42	19.27	10.15	13.37	2.00
October	62.64	0.42	62.22	2.76	14.81	19.64	9.54	13.36	2.11
November	62.27	0.31	61.96	2.72	15.04	19.36	9.81	13.06	1.98
December	62.81	0.20	62.61	2.71	15.02	19.32	10.40	13.08	2.08
1996:									
January	64.41	0.28	64.13	2.82	15.88	19.34	10.41	13.59	2.10
February	63.51	0.39	63.13	2.81	14.95	18.98	10.48	13.79	2.11
March	65.05	1.21	63.84	2.98	15.63	19.46	10.12	13.57	2.10
April	66.69	1.61	65.08	3.05	16.89	18.71	10.49	13.69	2.25
May	68.11	1.25	66.86	3.02	17.36	19.02	11.03	14.27	2.17
June	66.17	0.87	65.30	2.91	16.70	18.84	10.76	13.94	2.15
July	66.84	0.43	66.42	2.95	17.35	18.70	11.04	14.10	2.28
August	68.01	0.77	67.24	3.02	17.38	19.01	11.22	14.44	2.18
September	68.40	0.31	68.09	2.99	17.84	19.13	11.16	14.77	2.20
October	67.82	0.32	67.51	3.01	18.25	18.94	10.16	14.95	2.20
November	68.39	0.29	68.10	2.98	17.56	19.33	11.23	14.75	2.25
December	69.83	0.24	69.59	3.19	18.70	19.58	10.85	15.15	2.13

U.S. EXPORTS AND IMPORTS OF GOODS BY PRINCIPAL END-USE CATEGORY IN CONSTANT DOLLARS
(Census basis—Billions of 1992 dollars, seasonally adjusted)

YEAR AND MONTH	Exports							Imports						
	Total	Foods, feeds, and beverages	Industrial supplies and materials	Capital goods, except automotive	Automotive vehicles, engines, and parts	Consumer goods (nonfood), except automotive	Other goods	Total	Foods, feeds, and beverages	Industrial supplies and materials	Capital goods, except automotive	Automotive vehicles, engines, and parts	Consumer goods (nonfood), except automotive	Other goods
1968														
1969														
1970														
1971														
1972														
1973														
1974														
1975														
1976														
1977														
1978														
1979														
1980														
1981														
1982														
1983														
1984														
1985														
1986	227.20	22.30	57.30	75.80	21.70			365.40	24.40	101.30	71.80	78.20	79.40	
1987	254.10	24.30	66.70	86.20	24.60			406.20	24.80	111.00	84.50	85.00	88.70	
1988	322.40	32.30	85.10	109.20	29.30			441.00	24.80	118.30	101.40	87.70	95.90	
1989	363.80	37.20	99.30	138.80	34.80			473.20	25.10	132.30	113.30	86.10	102.90	
1990	393.60	35.10	104.40	152.70	37.40	39.22	18.70	495.30	26.60	146.20	116.40	87.30	105.70	14.46
1991	421.70	35.70	109.70	166.70	40.00	40.42	21.11	488.50	26.50	131.60	120.70	85.70	108.00	14.15
1992	448.20	40.30	109.10	175.90	47.00	43.60	21.71	532.70	27.60	138.60	134.30	91.80	122.70	15.46
1993	471.17	40.19	111.08	190.02	51.93	54.03	23.91	591.45	28.03	151.26	160.16	100.73	132.92	18.35
1994	522.29	40.43	114.17	225.76	56.54	58.97	26.41	675.05	29.52	168.80	199.56	112.13	144.22	20.82
1995	590.48	44.85	121.27	274.43	59.84	62.35	27.74	747.37	30.04	173.50	252.46	114.00	155.12	22.25
1996	692.27	43.95	128.96	355.63	62.27	67.00	34.46	857.72	32.96	184.32	331.08	117.92	165.07	26.37
1993:														
January	37.93	3.33	9.44	14.75	4.06	4.40	1.96	46.26	2.29	12.03	12.05	8.04	10.45	1.41
February	37.35	3.51	8.65	14.67	4.27	4.31	1.93	45.85	2.24	11.33	12.29	8.35	10.33	1.31
March	39.45	3.54	9.20	16.01	4.30	4.48	1.93	49.59	2.47	12.58	12.84	8.59	11.47	1.63
April	39.14	3.57	9.08	15.73	4.40	4.39	1.98	49.07	2.32	12.64	13.04	8.57	11.05	1.45
May	39.80	3.36	9.55	15.88	4.47	4.65	1.89	48.16	2.34	12.37	12.82	8.24	10.74	1.65
June	38.40	3.31	8.69	15.87	4.15	4.47	1.92	49.80	2.35	13.00	13.57	8.28	11.04	1.56
July	37.81	3.16	9.06	14.94	4.19	4.52	1.94	49.10	2.27	12.80	13.53	7.92	11.08	1.50
August	38.44	2.99	8.85	15.90	4.08	4.47	2.15	49.03	2.28	12.46	13.31	8.23	11.33	1.42
September	39.10	3.28	9.47	15.55	4.26	4.55	1.99	50.13	2.38	12.87	13.45	8.59	11.33	1.50
October	40.80	3.34	9.85	16.50	4.57	4.51	2.04	51.89	2.47	13.21	14.38	8.77	11.49	1.57
November	40.82	3.35	9.58	16.44	4.79	4.70	1.96	51.24	2.31	13.26	13.95	8.65	11.42	1.65
December	42.14	3.45	9.66	17.79	4.41	4.61	2.22	51.34	2.30	12.72	14.93	8.51	11.20	1.69
1994:														
January	40.87	3.09	9.11	17.67	4.34	4.61	2.05	52.11	2.42	13.08	15.20	8.32	11.41	1.67
February	39.36	3.07	8.66	16.94	4.28	4.43	1.99	52.53	2.38	13.16	15.33	8.56	11.41	1.68
March	43.27	3.21	10.31	18.29	4.70	4.79	1.96	54.20	2.54	13.97	15.59	9.00	11.34	1.76
April	42.17	2.99	9.43	18.33	4.64	4.70	2.07	54.65	2.50	13.72	15.98	8.91	11.78	1.77
May	42.20	3.04	9.64	18.03	4.60	4.82	2.07	55.03	2.49	13.85	16.03	9.08	11.85	1.73
June	43.69	3.03	9.40	19.15	4.73	5.10	2.28	56.64	2.50	14.48	16.38	9.50	12.02	1.76
July	42.62	3.03	9.68	18.07	4.58	4.89	2.36	56.65	2.48	14.49	16.55	9.47	11.97	1.69
August	45.03	3.52	9.84	19.32	4.79	5.09	2.47	57.51	2.48	14.75	16.52	9.85	12.23	1.69
September	44.74	3.59	9.41	19.70	4.81	5.02	2.20	58.13	2.44	14.59	17.55	9.42	12.34	1.79
October	44.96	3.81	9.55	18.97	4.88	5.16	2.58	58.27	2.45	14.06	17.69	9.82	12.50	1.76
November	45.81	3.99	9.35	20.19	4.96	5.18	2.13	59.90	2.46	14.45	18.41	10.08	12.76	1.75
December	47.59	4.06	9.77	21.09	5.24	5.17	2.25	59.45	2.38	14.21	18.34	10.10	12.63	1.79
1995:														
January	46.22	3.76	9.72	19.98	5.32	5.04	2.41	60.86	2.49	14.18	18.92	10.33	13.10	1.84
February	46.69	3.84	9.68	21.01	5.02	5.09	2.05	59.53	2.53	13.89	18.70	9.93	12.76	1.73
March	48.82	3.92	10.34	21.84	5.14	5.19	2.40	61.31	2.55	14.79	19.51	9.87	12.90	1.69
April	48.03	3.78	10.04	21.97	5.01	5.10	2.13	61.73	2.55	14.38	19.90	10.15	13.11	1.65
May	48.66	3.67	10.01	22.38	4.99	5.28	2.33	61.70	2.47	14.65	20.04	9.50	13.17	1.86
June	48.55	3.51	10.25	22.68	4.63	5.25	2.23	62.43	2.51	14.79	20.89	9.40	12.99	1.85
July	47.95	3.58	9.81	22.68	4.71	5.04	2.13	62.29	2.42	14.60	21.14	9.19	13.04	1.91
August	49.92	3.89	9.99	23.64	4.92	5.29	2.19	62.66	2.48	14.46	21.64	9.18	12.97	1.94
September	50.87	4.03	10.48	23.68	5.15	5.28	2.26	63.98	2.53	14.86	22.46	9.30	12.93	1.90
October	50.84	3.62	10.51	24.06	5.01	5.26	2.39	63.50	2.56	14.18	23.08	8.72	12.95	2.01
November	51.49	3.61	10.08	24.90	4.85	5.23	2.84	63.43	2.50	14.46	23.00	8.95	12.62	1.89
December	52.42	3.65	10.36	25.63	5.10	5.30	2.38	63.97	2.46	14.27	23.18	9.49	12.59	1.98
1996:														
January	52.83	3.72	10.13	26.47	5.05	5.33	2.13	66.97	2.69	14.81	24.83	9.52	13.07	2.05
February	54.65	3.61	10.41	27.55	5.09	5.55	2.43	66.31	2.54	14.08	24.76	9.58	13.29	2.06
March	55.49	3.81	10.93	27.82	4.88	5.49	2.56	67.42	2.76	14.44	25.84	9.26	13.07	2.07
April	55.91	3.49	11.08	28.58	4.85	5.47	2.43	68.42	2.71	15.12	25.84	9.26	13.20	2.22
May	56.94	3.47	10.88	28.84	5.20	5.61	2.95	70.97	2.71	15.79	26.47	9.60	13.75	2.15
June	57.19	3.41	10.82	28.91	5.33	5.62	3.10	70.12	2.74	15.46	26.45	9.86	13.46	2.16
July	56.04	3.54	10.23	28.57	5.13	5.33	3.24	71.88	2.78	16.04	27.03	10.11	13.63	2.30
August	58.48	3.57	10.89	30.04	5.25	5.60	3.12	73.35	2.86	15.88	28.17	10.26	13.96	2.22
September	58.60	3.58	10.74	30.00	5.48	5.62	3.19	74.16	2.72	15.91	28.85	10.17	14.25	2.25
October	60.80	3.77	11.09	32.07	5.17	5.86	2.85	74.26	2.74	15.86	29.62	9.29	14.45	2.29
November	62.88	4.22	10.81	33.23	5.61	5.79	3.22	75.93	2.75	15.17	31.12	10.26	14.28	2.36
December	62.47	3.76	10.95	33.57	5.22	5.73	3.25	77.92	2.98	15.76	32.36	9.90	14.67	2.25

YEAR AND MONTH	U.S. EXPORTS OF SERVICES (Balance of payments basis—Millions of dollars, seasonally adjusted)								U.S. IMPORTS OF SERVICES (Balance of payments basis—Millions of dollars, seasonally adjusted)			
	Total	Travel	Passenger fares	Other transportation	Royalties and license fees	Other private services	Transfers under U.S. military sales contracts[1]	U.S. government miscellaneous services	Total	Travel	Passenger fares	Other transportation
1968	11 917	1 775	411	2 548	1 867	1 024	3 939	353	12 302	3 030	885	2 367
1969	12 806	2 043	450	2 652	2 019	1 160	4 138	343	13 322	3 373	1 080	2 455
1970	14 171	2 331	544	3 125	2 331	1 294	4 214	332	14 520	3 980	1 215	2 843
1971	16 358	2 534	615	3 299	2 545	1 546	5 472	347	15 400	4 373	1 290	3 130
1972	17 841	2 817	699	3 579	2 770	1 764	5 856	357	16 868	5 042	1 596	3 520
1973	19 832	3 412	975	4 465	3 225	1 985	5 369	401	18 843	5 526	1 790	4 694
1974	22 591	4 032	1 104	5 697	3 821	2 321	5 197	419	21 379	5 980	2 095	5 942
1975	25 497	4 697	1 039	5 840	4 300	2 920	6 256	446	21 996	6 417	2 263	5 708
1976	27 971	5 742	1 229	6 747	4 353	3 584	5 826	489	24 570	6 856	2 568	6 852
1977	31 485	6 150	1 366	7 090	4 920	3 848	7 554	557	27 640	7 451	2 748	7 972
1978	36 353	7 183	1 603	8 136	5 885	4 717	8 209	620	32 189	8 475	2 896	9 124
1979	39 692	8 441	2 156	9 971	6 184	5 439	6 981	520	36 689	9 413	3 184	10 906
1980	47 584	10 588	2 591	11 618	7 085	6 276	9 029	398	41 491	10 397	3 607	11 790
1981	57 354	12 913	3 111	12 560	7 284	10 250	10 720	517	45 503	11 479	4 487	12 474
1982	64 079	12 393	3 174	12 317	5 603	17 444	12 572	576	51 749	12 394	4 772	11 710
1983	64 307	10 947	3 610	12 590	5 778	18 192	12 524	666	54 973	13 149	6 003	12 222
1984	71 168	17 177	4 067	13 809	6 177	19 255	9 969	714	67 748	22 913	5 735	14 843
1985	73 155	17 762	4 411	14 674	6 678	20 035	8 718	878	72 862	24 558	6 444	15 643
1986	86 312	20 385	5 582	15 784	8 113	27 303	8 549	595	81 836	25 913	6 505	17 817
1987	98 553	23 563	7 003	17 471	10 183	28 701	11 106	526	92 349	29 310	7 283	19 057
1988	111 024	29 434	8 976	19 811	12 146	30 709	9 284	664	99 965	32 114	7 729	20 969
1989	127 142	36 205	10 657	21 106	13 818	36 204	8 564	587	104 185	33 416	8 249	22 260
1990	147 824	43 007	15 298	22 745	16 634	39 540	9 932	668	120 019	37 349	10 531	25 168
1991	164 236	48 385	15 854	23 331	17 819	47 024	11 135	690	121 195	35 322	10 012	25 204
1992	177 154	54 742	16 618	22 616	19 656	50 294	12 387	841	120 255	38 552	10 556	24 894
1993	186 711	57 875	16 611	23 050	20 304	54 517	13 471	883	126 403	40 713	11 313	25 746
1994	197 248	58 417	17 083	24 941	22 661	61 093	12 166	887	135 472	43 782	12 885	27 255
1995	218 739	63 395	19 125	27 412	27 383	66 850	13 756	818	147 036	46 053	14 433	28 249
1996	236 764	69 908	20 557	27 216	29 974	73 569	14 647	893	156 634	48 739	15 776	28 453
1993:												
January	15 199	4 687	1 374	1 985	1 645	4 263	1 184	62	10 171	3 347	933	2 104
February	15 520	4 853	1 404	1 926	1 654	4 330	1 285	70	10 045	3 287	910	2 056
March	15 378	4 664	1 353	2 042	1 669	4 366	1 207	78	10 227	3 196	899	2 296
April	15 547	4 872	1 379	2 025	1 724	4 337	1 116	94	10 479	3 372	935	2 234
May	15 426	4 828	1 389	1 969	1 731	4 349	1 061	97	10 268	3 217	899	2 177
June	15 511	4 769	1 362	1 983	1 724	4 395	1 181	96	10 387	3 238	905	2 270
July	15 533	4 906	1 425	1 944	1 671	4 418	1 087	83	10 386	3 330	949	2 170
August	15 563	4 807	1 383	1 926	1 663	4 470	1 237	76	10 333	3 305	933	2 154
September	15 428	4 773	1 385	1 992	1 668	4 523	1 017	70	10 499	3 411	970	2 186
October	16 045	5 219	1 474	2 067	1 712	4 595	920	57	10 984	3 676	1 003	2 279
November	15 175	4 548	1 289	1 983	1 726	4 668	906	56	10 838	3 615	982	2 224
December	15 796	4 949	1 394	2 053	1 736	4 723	882	59	10 930	3 720	996	2 178
1994:												
January	15 133	4 504	1 320	1 847	1 752	4 807	820	83	10 769	3 516	1 018	2 083
February	15 489	4 637	1 369	1 868	1 771	4 865	893	86	11 230	3 650	1 058	2 094
March	16 628	5 259	1 548	2 078	1 791	4 969	901	82	11 271	3 714	1 076	2 287
April	16 101	4 838	1 408	2 032	1 823	4 967	961	72	11 115	3 611	1 069	2 202
May	16 294	4 804	1 381	2 062	1 848	5 128	1 033	38	11 218	3 650	1 072	2 242
June	16 676	5 071	1 464	2 075	1 872	5 042	1 112	40	11 281	3 622	1 064	2 310
July	16 806	5 023	1 477	2 076	1 913	5 053	1 195	69	11 311	3 649	1 087	2 310
August	16 696	4 769	1 397	2 169	1 936	5 110	1 239	76	11 436	3 671	1 093	2 414
September	16 595	4 701	1 404	2 098	1 955	5 147	1 209	81	11 493	3 725	1 119	2 354
October	16 571	4 698	1 369	2 197	1 971	5 287	962	87	11 377	3 618	1 067	2 366
November	17 068	5 072	1 472	2 162	1 997	5 334	943	88	11 471	3 672	1 081	2 329
December	17 195	5 040	1 475	2 279	2 033	5 385	898	85	11 504	3 686	1 082	2 263
1995:												
January	17 561	5 338	1 612	2 158	2 127	5 282	971	73	11 860	3 780	1 115	2 318
February	16 971	4 789	1 485	2 122	2 165	5 333	1 010	67	11 892	3 762	1 122	2 284
March	17 448	4 737	1 476	2 325	2 195	5 385	1 268	62	12 131	3 739	1 121	2 487
April	17 960	5 325	1 601	2 304	2 219	5 394	1 067	50	12 124	3 866	1 201	2 322
May	18 066	5 223	1 574	2 339	2 244	5 477	1 158	51	12 146	3 772	1 186	2 406
June	17 278	4 494	1 396	2 265	2 273	5 566	1 227	57	12 274	3 856	1 218	2 360
July	18 521	5 368	1 608	2 241	2 341	5 646	1 232	85	12 376	3 807	1 226	2 378
August	18 609	5 304	1 589	2 315	2 364	5 677	1 271	89	12 469	3 805	1 241	2 432
September	19 116	5 686	1 692	2 309	2 373	5 713	1 255	88	12 463	3 885	1 239	2 343
October	18 797	5 537	1 644	2 306	2 346	5 763	1 136	65	12 337	3 889	1 239	2 391
November	19 072	5 696	1 703	2 372	2 356	5 776	1 106	63	12 483	3 923	1 262	2 314
December	19 343	5 901	1 745	2 359	2 380	5 835	1 055	68	12 487	3 973	1 263	2 214
1996:												
January	18 731	5 426	1 657	2 199	2 462	5 881	1 011	95	12 733	4 026	1 255	2 328
February	18 385	5 179	1 613	2 125	2 483	5 950	936	99	12 962	4 256	1 327	2 194
March	19 941	6 107	1 817	2 231	2 487	6 059	1 145	95	12 978	4 203	1 278	2 294
April	19 188	5 512	1 557	2 310	2 450	5 994	1 298	67	12 967	4 022	1 298	2 443
May	19 995	6 090	1 747	2 270	2 445	6 067	1 315	61	13 142	4 113	1 347	2 460
June	19 554	5 754	1 648	2 225	2 450	6 070	1 348	59	12 847	3 965	1 298	2 351
July	19 413	5 667	1 682	2 193	2 483	6 091	1 228	69	13 279	3 915	1 291	2 445
August	19 896	5 945	1 766	2 293	2 498	6 145	1 179	70	13 144	4 046	1 324	2 403
September	20 012	6 047	1 789	2 230	2 514	6 196	1 165	71	12 923	3 955	1 305	2 372
October	20 585	6 145	1 791	2 400	2 559	6 321	1 299	70	13 200	4 025	1 344	2 478
November	20 760	6 215	1 801	2 393	2 570	6 370	1 342	69	13 249	4 156	1 367	2 323
December	20 311	5 823	1 690	2 349	2 574	6 426	1 381	68	13 217	4 061	1 342	2 366

1. Contains goods that cannot be separately identified.

YEAR AND MONTH	U.S. IMPORTS OF SERVICES—Continued (Balance of payments basis—Millions of dollars, seasonally adjusted)				U.S. EXPORT AND IMPORT PRICE INDEXES (1990=100)					
					Exports			Imports		
	Royalties and license fees	Other private services	Direct defense expenditures[1]	U.S. government miscellaneous services	All commodities	Agricultural	Non-agricultural	All commodities	Petroleum[2]	Non-petroleum
1968	186	668	4 535	631	....	....	....	....	....	....
1969	221	751	4 856	586	....	....	....	....	....	....
1970	224	827	4 855	576	....	....	....	....	....	....
1971	241	956	4 819	592	....	....	....	....	....	....
1972	294	1 043	4 784	589	....	....	....	....	....	....
1973	385	1 180	4 629	640	....	....	....	....	....	....
1974	346	1 262	5 032	722	....	....	....	....	....	....
1975	472	1 551	4 795	789	....	....	....	....	....	....
1976	482	2 006	4 895	911	....	....	....	....	....	....
1977	504	2 190	5 823	951	....	....	....	....	....	....
1978	671	2 573	7 352	1 099	....	....	....	....	....	....
1979	831	2 822	8 294	1 239	....	....	....	....	....	....
1980	724	2 909	10 851	1 214	....	....	....	....	....	....
1981	650	3 562	11 564	1 287	....	....	....	....	....	....
1982	795	8 159	12 460	1 460	....	....	....	....	....	....
1983	943	8 001	13 087	1 568	....	....	....	....	....	....
1984	1 168	9 040	12 516	1 534	....	....	....	....	....	....
1985	1 170	10 203	13 108	1 735	....	....	....	....	....	....
1986	1 401	14 785	13 730	1 686	....	....	....	....	....	....
1987	1 857	17 999	14 950	1 893	....	....	....	....	....	....
1988	2 601	19 028	15 604	1 921	....	....	....	....	....	....
1989	2 528	20 548	15 313	1 871	91.1	92.8	90.5	90.6	102.3	89.5
1990	3 135	24 387	17 531	1 919	91.9	88.3	92.1	93.5	126.3	90.5
1991	4 035	28 098	16 409	2 116	92.6	86.9	93.1	93.7	112.6	92.0
1992	5 089	25 066	13 835	2 263	92.7	86.1	93.4	94.3	105.3	93.3
1993	4 819	29 356	12 202	2 255	93.2	87.7	93.9	94.0	95.8	93.8
1994	5 560	33 138	10 292	2 560	95.2	91.9	95.6	95.7	90.8	96.2
1995	6 503	39 285	9 890	2 623	100.0	100.0	100.0	100.0	100.0	100.0
1996	7 322	42 796	10 861	2 687	100.5	111.4	99.2	101.0	118.7	99.2
1993:										
January	363	2 157	1 070	197	92.8	86.4	93.6	93.7	98.9	93.2
February	362	2 176	1 056	198	93.0	85.9	93.9	93.7	100.7	93.0
March	366	2 222	1 050	198	92.9	85.6	93.9	94.2	103.9	93.2
April	390	2 281	1 077	190	93.1	85.9	94.1	94.6	105.9	93.4
May	396	2 320	1 068	191	93.4	86.8	94.3	94.9	105.5	93.8
June	400	2 330	1 049	195	93.2	84.3	94.3	94.4	100.9	93.8
July	409	2 328	990	210	93.4	88.7	93.9	93.9	94.8	93.9
August	399	2 361	970	211	93.3	88.9	93.9	93.9	93.3	94.0
September	404	2 363	959	206	93.2	88.4	93.8	93.9	92.2	94.1
October	421	2 447	980	178	93.2	88.2	93.8	94.4	93.5	94.6
November	425	2 443	973	176	93.4	90.3	93.7	93.9	88.8	94.4
December	428	2 468	959	181	93.7	92.9	93.7	93.0	79.0	94.5
1994:										
January	427	2 602	920	203	94.3	95.3	94.1	93.0	77.4	94.7
February	690	2 622	905	211	94.3	94.0	94.3	93.3	81.5	94.6
March	422	2 659	897	216	94.5	94.6	94.4	93.5	80.0	95.0
April	409	2 700	914	210	94.5	92.6	94.7	94.2	84.2	95.2
May	409	2 728	905	212	94.8	94.0	94.9	95.0	91.3	95.4
June	429	2 749	889	216	94.8	91.9	95.2	95.8	96.3	95.7
July	462	2 724	852	227	95.0	89.8	95.7	96.6	101.2	96.2
August	442	2 757	831	228	95.2	88.8	96.0	97.1	100.0	96.8
September	452	2 807	812	224	95.4	89.2	96.2	96.7	92.5	97.1
October	461	2 873	788	204	95.9	89.2	96.8	97.3	93.2	97.8
November	472	2 929	785	203	96.6	90.5	97.4	98.0	97.1	98.0
December	485	2 990	792	206	97.2	92.7	97.8	97.9	95.0	98.2
1995:										
January	492	3 091	835	229	98.0	92.7	98.7	98.2	96.2	98.4
February	505	3 142	845	232	98.6	93.1	99.3	98.8	98.7	98.8
March	514	3 192	847	231	99.1	94.4	99.7	99.4	100.7	99.2
April	513	3 182	826	214	100.0	96.2	100.5	100.3	105.4	99.8
May	520	3 229	822	211	100.3	96.9	100.8	101.3	108.8	100.4
June	530	3 279	820	211	100.5	98.3	100.8	100.8	105.2	100.4
July	564	3 353	827	221	100.8	102.0	100.7	100.5	98.6	100.7
August	559	3 386	825	221	100.3	100.6	100.3	100.3	96.0	100.7
September	567	3 392	817	220	100.5	103.6	100.1	100.3	97.8	100.5
October	578	3 226	802	212	100.6	105.6	99.9	99.8	95.7	100.3
November	581	3 387	806	210	100.6	107.9	99.6	100.0	96.3	100.4
December	581	3 427	818	211	100.5	108.8	99.4	100.4	100.7	100.4
1996:										
January	579	3 478	850	217	101.0	110.6	99.7	100.6	105.5	100.2
February	575	3 520	870	220	100.8	110.4	99.5	100.4	104.0	100.1
March	570	3 525	887	221	100.6	111.9	99.2	101.0	112.9	99.9
April	566	3 516	905	217	101.2	117.3	99.2	101.9	122.5	99.8
May	561	3 525	917	219	101.6	120.9	99.1	101.2	118.0	99.5
June	557	3 530	925	221	101.4	118.3	99.2	100.1	111.1	99.1
July	930	3 542	927	229	100.9	116.0	99.0	100.0	113.2	98.7
August	658	3 554	928	231	100.7	115.8	98.8	100.1	115.7	98.6
September	556	3 578	925	232	99.9	107.4	99.0	101.3	124.4	99.0
October	577	3 640	909	227	99.7	104.6	99.0	101.8	133.2	98.7
November	589	3 680	907	227	99.3	102.2	99.0	101.6	132.1	98.6
December	604	3 707	911	226	99.3	101.3	99.1	101.9	134.7	98.7

1. Contains goods that cannot be separately identified.
2. Petroleum and petroleum products.

International Comparisons

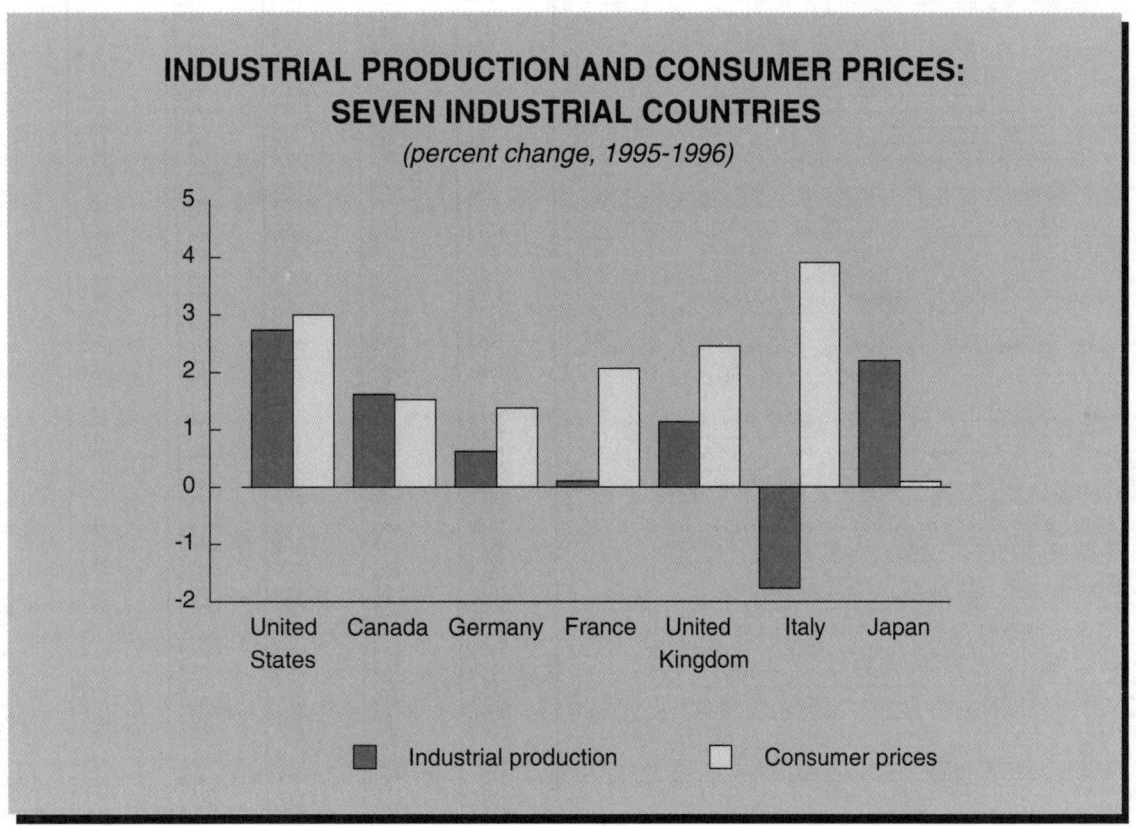

**INDUSTRIAL PRODUCTION AND CONSUMER PRICES:
SEVEN INDUSTRIAL COUNTRIES**
(percent change, 1995-1996)

Industrial production · Consumer prices

In 1996, the United States achieved a sturdy 2.7 percent gain in industrial production. None of the other countries shown in the chart had as large a gain. Industrial production in Japan rose 2.2 percent, and the other countries were each below 2 percent, with an actual drop of about 1.75 percent in Italy.

Price increases ranged from near zero in Japan to a still modest 3 percent in the United States, but nearly 4 percent in Italy.

YEAR AND MONTH	INDUSTRIAL PRODUCTION INDEXES (1990=100, seasonally adjusted)							
	United States	OECD, European countries [1]	Japan	Germany	France	United Kingdom	Italy	Canada
1968	58.7	56.0	34.2	57.8	56.1	70.7	56.4	55.2
1969	61.4	61.2	39.6	65.0	62.6	73.1	58.4	58.9
1970	59.4	64.5	45.0	69.1	66.1	73.5	62.2	58.0
1971	60.2	65.7	46.2	69.8	69.1	73.1	62.2	61.3
1972	66.1	69.1	49.6	72.3	74.2	74.4	64.9	66.7
1973	71.4	74.6	57.0	76.6	79.8	81.0	71.2	74.6
1974	70.3	75.8	54.8	75.3	81.8	79.4	74.4	76.0
1975	64.2	70.7	48.7	70.7	74.5	75.1	67.5	70.5
1976	70.1	75.8	54.1	76.0	81.5	77.6	76.0	75.2
1977	75.8	77.7	56.4	77.6	82.9	81.6	76.8	77.7
1978	80.2	79.4	59.9	79.0	84.8	83.9	78.2	80.4
1979	82.9	83.2	64.3	82.8	88.6	87.2	83.5	84.3
1980	80.6	83.3	67.3	82.9	87.6	81.5	88.1	81.5
1981	81.9	82.0	68.0	81.5	86.7	78.9	86.7	83.1
1982	77.5	80.8	68.3	79.0	86.0	80.4	84.0	75.0
1983	80.4	81.4	70.4	79.2	86.0	83.3	81.4	79.8
1984	87.6	83.4	77.0	81.7	87.5	83.4	84.1	89.5
1985	89.0	86.2	79.8	85.5	88.1	88.0	85.0	94.5
1986	90.0	88.2	79.7	87.3	89.1	90.1	88.1	93.8
1987	94.2	90.3	82.4	87.7	90.9	93.7	91.5	98.4
1988	98.4	94.2	90.7	90.7	94.6	98.2	97.0	103.6
1989	100.2	97.9	96.0	95.1	98.0	100.3	100.0	103.4
1990	100.0	100.0	100.0	100.0	100.0	100.0	100.0	100.0
1991	98.0	99.9	101.9	103.1	98.8	96.1	99.3	95.8
1992	101.2	98.8	96.1	101.2	97.6	95.6	99.1	96.9
1993	104.6	95.7	92.0	93.8	93.9	97.9	96.7	101.2
1994	109.8	100.3	92.5	97.0	97.5	103.1	101.6	108.3
1995	113.4	103.8	95.4	97.6	99.2	105.9	107.7	112.0
1996	116.5	104.5	97.5	98.2	99.3	107.1	105.8	113.8
1993:								
January	103.5	96.0	92.4	94.7	94.9	96.2	99.1	98.9
February	104.0	95.9	93.3	92.9	95.5	97.2	97.7	100.0
March	104.0	95.8	95.6	93.8	94.9	96.5	96.2	101.2
April	104.4	95.3	93.6	92.9	94.1	96.5	93.7	100.5
May	103.8	95.2	92.2	93.8	93.5	97.8	97.9	99.8
June	104.0	94.9	92.4	93.8	93.7	96.9	96.0	101.3
July	104.3	95.1	91.6	92.9	92.4	98.3	97.1	100.4
August	104.0	95.9	91.6	94.7	92.4	98.4	98.8	101.2
September	105.1	96.4	91.8	94.7	94.3	98.4	94.9	102.5
October	105.3	96.4	89.1	93.8	93.9	99.5	96.7	102.9
November	105.9	96.5	90.4	93.7	93.8	99.9	96.8	102.9
December	106.6	96.9	89.8	94.1	93.9	99.4	95.4	102.9
1994:								
January	106.9	96.5	89.7	93.2	94.8	100.7	94.6	103.8
February	107.5	97.8	89.3	94.8	93.5	100.9	97.3	104.0
March	108.2	98.1	93.1	95.3	95.0	100.6	97.4	105.2
April	108.7	99.9	91.1	96.0	96.5	102.3	101.8	106.3
May	109.3	99.4	90.2	96.2	96.5	103.5	99.5	106.7
June	109.9	100.2	92.5	96.9	96.4	103.1	101.0	108.3
July	110.4	101.0	91.6	98.8	99.1	103.4	103.1	109.1
August	110.5	101.2	95.4	96.9	99.1	104.6	105.2	109.9
September	110.5	101.9	93.5	97.6	99.0	105.1	103.4	110.4
October	111.2	102.4	92.7	98.8	98.8	104.6	103.2	110.7
November	111.9	102.5	95.4	99.0	99.9	103.7	103.4	112.1
December	112.8	104.2	95.0	100.5	100.8	104.4	109.5	112.8
1995:								
January	113.2	103.1	93.9	96.2	99.4	104.5	104.6	112.9
February	112.9	103.2	95.8	97.6	98.7	105.3	105.2	112.7
March	113.0	104.2	97.3	97.0	100.1	105.9	106.5	112.0
April	112.7	103.6	96.4	97.5	98.8	105.5	107.4	111.8
May	112.8	104.5	95.9	99.3	99.6	105.9	106.0	111.9
June	113.0	104.2	95.1	98.3	99.9	105.5	106.4	111.4
July	113.0	104.3	93.0	99.7	100.0	106.0	107.3	112.0
August	113.9	104.4	96.0	97.0	100.0	106.4	114.9	112.1
September	114.3	104.3	93.5	98.3	99.1	106.9	108.2	112.1
October	113.8	103.2	94.8	96.0	97.8	105.9	107.4	111.7
November	114.0	103.7	96.1	96.9	97.7	106.4	107.4	111.9
December	114.1	104.9	97.0	97.1	98.7	106.8	111.4	111.6
1996:								
January	113.7	103.7	97.0	97.4	98.3	106.0	105.9	112.2
February	115.1	103.2	98.1	96.1	98.4	106.3	105.7	112.5
March	114.5	104.5	94.0	97.3	98.7	107.2	108.2	112.3
April	115.6	103.6	96.1	97.1	99.0	106.0	104.6	112.2
May	116.1	104.5	97.5	98.2	99.4	107.5	105.7	112.4
June	116.8	104.7	94.3	98.2	99.0	106.7	108.1	113.2
July	116.8	105.5	98.1	99.4	100.3	107.5	104.8	114.7
August	117.1	104.7	96.8	99.2	100.3	107.1	106.7	114.8
September	117.3	105.0	98.2	98.9	99.7	107.7	105.8	115.2
October	117.5	104.9	100.5	98.3	99.4	107.3	105.0	115.1
November	118.6	105.1	99.7	99.3	99.3	107.9	105.5	116.5
December	119.1	105.0	99.7	99.1	99.9	108.4	103.5	115.0

1. European member countries of the Organization for Economic Cooperation and Development.

CONSUMER PRICE INDEXES
(1990=100, indexes: not seasonally adjusted, percent changes: seasonally adjusted)

YEAR AND MONTH	United States Index	United States 6-month percent change, annual rate[1]	Japan Index	Japan 6-month percent change, annual rate[1]	Germany Index	Germany 6-month percent change, annual rate[1]	France Index	France 6-month percent change, annual rate[1]	United Kingdom Index	United Kingdom 6-month percent change, annual rate[1]	Italy Index	Italy 6-month percent change, annual rate[1]	Canada Index	Canada 6-month percent change, annual rate[1]
1968	26.6	4.3	30.5	5.6	44.7	1.6	19.3	4.6	13.1	5.0	9.7	1.3	24.0	4.1
1969	28.1	5.4	32.2	5.7	45.6	2.0	20.4	5.9	13.8	5.5	10.0	3.2	25.1	4.6
1970	29.7	5.8	34.6	7.3	47.1	3.4	21.6	5.8	14.7	6.2	10.6	5.2	26.0	3.5
1971	31.0	4.3	36.8	6.4	49.6	5.3	22.8	5.6	16.1	9.5	11.1	4.7	26.7	2.8
1972	32.0	3.3	38.6	4.9	52.3	5.5	24.2	6.0	17.2	6.9	11.7	5.9	28.0	4.8
1973	34.0	6.1	43.0	11.6	56.0	7.1	26.0	7.3	18.8	9.4	12.9	10.3	30.1	7.7
1974	37.7	11.1	53.0	23.2	59.9	7.0	29.5	13.8	21.8	15.9	15.4	19.3	33.4	10.8
1975	41.2	9.2	59.3	11.8	63.5	6.0	33.0	11.6	27.1	24.3	18.1	17.4	37.0	10.8
1976	43.6	5.7	64.8	9.4	66.2	4.3	36.1	9.7	31.6	16.5	21.0	16.4	39.8	7.5
1977	46.4	6.5	70.1	8.2	68.6	3.7	39.6	9.4	36.6	15.9	25.1	19.5	42.9	8.0
1978	49.9	7.6	73.1	4.2	70.5	2.7	43.2	9.3	39.6	8.2	28.2	12.3	46.7	8.9
1979	55.5	11.3	75.8	3.7	73.4	4.1	47.8	10.6	44.9	13.5	32.7	15.7	51.0	9.2
1980	63.1	13.6	81.7	7.8	77.4	5.5	54.3	13.6	53.0	18.0	39.6	21.1	56.2	10.2
1981	69.6	10.3	85.7	4.9	82.3	6.3	61.5	13.3	59.3	11.9	47.2	19.3	63.2	12.4
1982	73.9	6.1	88.0	2.7	86.6	5.3	68.9	11.9	64.4	8.6	55.0	16.4	70.1	10.8
1983	76.2	3.2	89.7	1.9	89.4	3.3	75.4	9.5	67.4	4.6	63.2	15.0	74.1	5.8
1984	79.5	4.3	91.7	2.3	91.6	2.4	81.2	7.6	70.7	5.0	69.9	10.6	77.3	4.4
1985	82.3	3.5	93.6	2.1	93.5	2.1	85.9	5.9	75.0	6.1	75.9	8.6	80.4	3.9
1986	83.9	1.9	94.2	0.6	93.3	-0.1	88.1	2.5	77.6	3.4	80.5	6.2	83.8	4.2
1987	87.0	3.7	94.3	0.1	93.6	0.2	91.0	3.3	80.8	4.2	84.2	4.6	87.4	4.4
1988	90.5	4.1	94.9	0.7	94.8	1.3	93.4	2.7	84.8	4.9	88.4	5.0	90.9	4.0
1989	94.9	4.8	97.1	2.3	97.4	2.8	96.7	3.5	91.3	7.7	94.2	6.6	95.5	5.0
1990	100.0	5.4	100.0	3.0	100.0	2.7	100.0	3.4	100.0	9.6	100.0	6.2	100.0	4.8
1991	104.2	4.2	103.3	3.3	103.5	3.5	103.1	3.1	105.9	5.9	106.4	6.4	105.7	5.6
1992	107.4	3.0	105.1	1.7	107.6	4.0	105.6	2.4	109.8	3.7	112.0	5.3	107.2	1.5
1993	110.6	3.0	106.4	1.3	111.7	3.8	107.8	2.1	111.5	1.6	116.8	4.2	109.2	1.9
1994	113.5	2.6	107.1	0.7	114.6	2.7	109.6	1.7	114.3	2.5	121.4	3.9	109.4	0.2
1995	116.6	2.8	107.0	-0.1	116.7	1.8	111.6	1.8	118.2	3.4	127.9	5.4	111.8	2.2
1996	120.1	3.0	107.1	0.1	118.3	1.4	113.9	2.1	121.1	2.4	132.9	3.9	113.5	1.6
1993:														
January	109.1	3.2	105.4	1.5	109.9	5.0	106.7	2.8	109.3	1.1	114.6	4.1	108.5	2.2
February	109.5	3.2	105.4	2.1	110.7	4.4	107.0	3.0	110.1	2.2	115.0	3.9	108.8	1.7
March	109.9	3.5	105.7	1.9	111.0	4.8	107.6	2.8	110.5	2.6	115.3	4.4	108.8	1.7
April	110.2	2.6	106.4	2.5	111.2	4.4	107.6	2.3	111.5	4.3	115.7	4.6	108.8	1.5
May	110.4	2.4	106.5	3.3	111.5	3.1	107.9	1.7	111.9	3.5	116.2	4.0	109.0	1.1
June	110.5	2.2	106.4	2.7	111.8	2.2	107.8	1.1	111.8	3.7	116.7	3.7	109.0	1.1
July	110.5	2.4	106.7	1.3	112.3	1.8	107.9	1.7	111.6	1.6	117.2	4.4	109.3	1.5
August	110.8	2.2	107.1	-0.2	112.4	1.6	107.9	1.1	112.0	0.7	117.3	4.3	109.4	2.0
September	111.1	2.0	107.1	0.2	112.2	1.4	108.2	1.3	112.5	1.3	117.4	3.5	109.4	1.7
October	111.5	2.5	107.1	-0.2	112.2	1.6	108.5	1.3	112.4	0.7	118.2	3.8	109.6	1.1
November	111.6	2.7	106.4	-0.9	112.4	2.9	108.5	1.9	112.3	1.3	118.7	4.5	110.1	-0.5
December	111.6	2.9	106.5	0.7	112.6	3.4	108.5	1.7	112.5	0.9	118.7	4.7	109.9	-0.7
1994:														
January	111.9	2.3	106.6	0.4	113.2	3.6	108.6	1.7	112.0	3.4	119.4	3.8	109.9	-1.1
February	112.3	2.3	106.6	1.9	114.0	3.6	108.9	2.2	112.7	4.3	119.9	3.7	109.1	-2.3
March	112.7	3.1	107.1	1.1	114.1	3.9	109.1	2.2	113.0	3.9	120.1	4.1	109.0	-1.6
April	112.8	3.1	107.3	-0.2	114.2	3.4	109.4	2.0	114.3	4.0	120.4	3.2	109.0	-0.9
May	112.9	3.1	107.4	0.8	114.4	2.3	109.7	1.5	114.7	3.6	120.9	3.0	108.8	0.7
June	113.3	2.9	107.1	0.4	114.8	1.8	109.7	1.7	114.7	3.6	121.1	3.2	109.0	1.1
July	113.6	2.9	106.5	0.9	115.1	1.4	109.7	1.7	114.2	1.4	121.3	3.9	109.4	0.7
August	114.0	3.0	107.0	0.2	115.3	1.2	109.7	1.1	114.7	0.9	121.7	3.7	109.5	2.2
September	114.3	2.3	107.3	0.2	115.1	1.0	110.0	0.7	115.0	1.8	122.0	4.2	109.6	2.2
October	114.4	2.5	107.8	1.3	115.0	0.9	110.3	1.3	115.1	2.6	122.7	4.5	109.4	2.2
November	114.6	2.6	107.5	-0.2	115.1	1.6	110.3	2.2	115.2	3.2	123.1	5.5	110.0	2.9
December	114.6	2.8	107.2	-0.9	115.4	1.9	110.1	2.2	115.7	3.3	123.6	6.8	110.2	3.1
1995:														
January	115.0	3.3	107.2	-1.3	115.6	2.4	110.4	1.6	115.7	5.5	124.0	6.6	110.6	4.1
February	115.5	3.3	106.9	-0.4	116.2	2.6	110.9	2.2	116.5	6.0	125.0	7.3	111.1	3.5
March	115.9	3.7	106.8	-0.5	116.2	2.6	111.2	2.6	116.9	5.4	126.1	7.6	111.3	3.1
April	116.3	3.0	107.1	-0.9	116.4	3.0	111.2	1.5	118.2	4.4	126.7	7.1	111.6	2.9
May	116.5	2.6	107.3	-0.2	116.6	1.4	111.5	1.6	118.6	4.0	127.5	6.0	111.9	1.8
June	116.7	2.4	107.2	1.1	116.9	1.2	111.5	1.6	118.8	4.3	128.2	4.8	111.9	1.4
July	116.7	2.2	106.7	0.2	117.3	0.7	111.2	1.8	118.2	1.0	128.3	5.0	112.2	0.9
August	117.0	1.9	106.8	-0.9	117.0	0.3	111.8	1.6	118.8	0.3	128.7	4.8	112.1	0.5
September	117.3	1.4	107.4	-0.7	116.9	0.5	112.1	1.6	119.4	1.2	129.1	4.1	112.1	0.4
October	117.6	2.6	107.1	-0.2	116.8	0.5	112.2	2.7	118.8	1.5	129.8	4.3	112.1	0.4
November	117.6	2.8	106.8	-0.7	116.8	1.5	112.4	2.3	118.8	1.4	130.5	4.2	112.2	0.7
December	117.5	3.3	106.8	-1.3	117.2	1.7	112.4	3.1	119.5	1.2	130.8	4.2	112.1	1.6
1996:														
January	118.2	3.6	106.7	0.4	117.3	2.1	112.7	3.2	119.1	3.7	131.0	4.2	112.4	2.2
February	118.6	3.9	106.4	1.3	117.9	2.6	113.1	3.2	119.6	4.1	131.4	3.9	112.5	2.7
March	119.2	4.3	106.7	0.8	117.9	2.2	113.8	3.0	120.1	3.0	131.8	3.9	113.0	2.5
April	119.7	3.4	107.3	0.8	118.0	2.6	114.0	2.1	121.0	3.0	132.5	3.1	113.3	2.0
May	119.9	3.1	107.5	1.1	118.3	1.4	114.2	0.9	121.2	3.0	133.0	2.6	113.7	2.1
June	120.0	2.7	107.2	1.3	118.5	1.2	114.1	0.4	121.3	3.0	133.3	2.8	113.5	1.4
July	120.2	2.5	107.1	0.7	118.8	1.0	113.9	0.5	120.9	1.5	133.0	1.8	113.5	1.2
August	120.4	2.5	107.0	-0.4	118.7	0.3	113.6	0.7	121.4	1.3	133.1	1.7	113.7	1.4
September	120.8	2.3	107.4	0.4	118.6	0.5	114.0	0.5	121.9	1.8	133.6	1.4	113.8	1.8
October	121.2	2.7	107.7	0.4	118.6	1.0	114.3	1.4	121.9	2.5	133.7	2.1	114.0	2.3
November	121.4	3.0	107.3	0.2	118.5	2.0	114.2	2.3	122.0	2.5	134.1	2.3	114.5	2.3
December	121.4	2.8	107.4	-0.4	118.8	2.0	114.4	1.8	122.4	2.1	134.2	1.7	114.5	2.5

1. Annual data are annual average percent change from previous year.

YEAR AND MONTH	STOCK PRICE INDEXES (1990=100, not seasonally adjusted)							EXCHANGE RATES (Not seasonally adjusted)						
	United States	Japan	Germany	France	United Kingdom	Italy	Canada	Exchange value of the U.S. dollar[1]	Foreign currency per U.S. dollar					
									Japanese yen	German mark	French franc	British pound	Italian lira	Canadian dollar
1968	29.6	5.4	39.9	12.6	14.1	19.9	27.1	122.06	....	....	....	....	....	....
1969	29.3	6.9	41.3	15.0	13.7	22.3	30.5	122.39	....	....	....	....	....	....
1970	25.1	7.6	34.2	16.4	12.4	21.4	27.7	121.07	....	....	....	....	....	....
1971	29.6	8.4	32.9	15.7	15.4	16.7	29.1	117.81	346.62	3.4700	5.4900	0.4100	615.90	1.0100
1972	33.0	13.4	36.0	17.7	19.8	16.0	34.0	109.07	303.11	3.1900	5.0400	0.4000	583.73	0.9900
1973	32.0	16.7	32.2	19.5	16.9	20.5	36.1	99.14	271.40	2.6700	4.4500	0.4100	582.40	1.0000
1974	24.5	14.8	27.2	14.6	9.6	18.5	30.3	101.42	291.94	2.5900	4.8100	0.4300	651.18	0.9800
1975	26.2	14.8	33.7	16.1	12.6	14.1	30.0	98.50	296.77	2.4600	4.2900	0.4500	653.24	1.0200
1976	30.9	16.3	36.3	15.5	14.0	12.3	30.5	105.63	296.48	2.5200	4.7800	0.5600	832.76	0.9900
1977	29.3	17.4	36.8	12.5	18.0	10.0	29.5	103.35	268.38	2.3200	4.9100	0.5700	882.69	1.0600
1978	28.7	19.4	39.0	16.3	19.9	10.2	33.9	92.39	210.46	2.0100	4.5100	0.5200	849.10	1.1400
1979	31.1	21.9	36.7	20.7	22.7	12.6	46.1	88.07	219.21	1.8300	4.2500	0.4700	830.92	1.1700
1980	35.9	23.9	34.3	23.9	25.3	19.2	62.1	87.39	226.58	1.8200	4.2300	0.4300	856.52	1.1700
1981	38.4	26.2	33.7	21.1	28.6	35.1	63.1	103.26	220.45	2.2600	5.4300	0.5000	1 137.42	1.2000
1982	36.2	25.7	34.1	20.5	31.8	27.5	48.0	116.50	249.05	2.4300	6.5800	0.5700	1 353.47	1.2300
1983	48.3	30.9	45.1	28.1	40.5	30.5	69.2	125.33	237.45	2.5500	7.6200	0.6600	1 519.71	1.2300
1984	48.2	37.0	50.0	37.3	48.1	33.7	68.4	138.34	237.59	2.8500	8.7400	0.7500	1 757.82	1.3000
1985	56.8	43.8	69.9	43.6	58.7	54.2	79.3	143.23	238.47	2.9400	8.9900	0.7800	1 909.45	1.3700
1986	71.8	57.9	96.8	66.8	73.1	109.8	88.0	112.27	168.50	2.1700	6.9300	0.6800	1 491.49	1.3900
1987	86.0	80.3	83.9	75.4	94.5	100.8	104.3	96.95	144.63	1.8000	6.0100	0.6100	1 296.61	1.3300
1988	80.6	95.0	70.7	70.1	86.1	82.0	96.6	92.75	128.14	1.7600	5.9600	0.5600	1 301.67	1.2300
1989	98.1	119.7	88.8	97.7	103.4	100.9	111.1	98.52	138.00	1.8800	6.3800	0.6100	1 371.31	1.1800
1990	100.0	100.0	100.0	100.0	100.0	100.0	100.0	89.05	144.82	1.6200	5.4400	0.5600	1 198.05	1.1700
1991	114.7	84.6	90.7	98.2	110.2	86.0	101.4	89.73	134.51	1.6600	5.6400	0.5700	1 239.62	1.1500
1992	125.4	62.8	89.2	102.3	114.1	71.5	99.5	86.64	126.75	1.5600	5.3000	0.5700	1 233.21	1.2100
1993	136.3	66.1	97.5	112.6	136.2	85.9	114.1	93.16	111.23	1.6500	5.6600	0.6700	1 571.92	1.2900
1994	138.5	69.4	110.4	112.5	144.7	106.9	125.2	91.32	102.19	1.6200	5.5500	0.6500	1 611.75	1.3700
1995	164.4	60.0	108.4	102.1	152.6	95.8	129.6	84.30	94.11	1.4300	4.9900	0.6300	1 628.92	1.3700
1996	202.9	72.9	127.6	116.0	175.8	98.0	154.0	87.34	108.81	1.5000	5.1200	0.6400	1 542.65	1.3600
1993:														
January	131.9	59.1	84.3	97.5	126.0	75.8	96.6	92.36	124.99	1.6100	5.4800	0.6500	1 491.07	1.2800
February	133.3	58.8	90.2	109.1	129.0	79.9	100.9	93.82	120.76	1.6400	5.5600	0.6900	1 550.43	1.2600
March	135.8	64.5	91.2	111.8	130.1	73.9	105.3	93.65	117.02	1.6500	5.5900	0.6800	1 591.35	1.2500
April	132.3	72.6	88.1	106.7	128.3	81.9	110.8	90.62	112.41	1.6000	5.4000	0.6500	1 536.14	1.2600
May	135.3	71.3	88.0	103.9	129.6	83.9	113.5	90.24	110.34	1.6100	5.4200	0.6500	1 475.66	1.2700
June	135.4	68.0	90.6	108.5	132.3	83.5	115.9	91.81	107.41	1.6500	5.5700	0.6600	1 505.05	1.2800
July	134.7	70.7	96.6	114.8	133.8	87.7	116.0	94.59	107.69	1.7200	5.8500	0.6700	1 586.02	1.2800
August	139.3	72.9	102.8	122.0	142.0	98.4	120.9	94.32	103.77	1.6900	5.9300	0.6700	1 603.75	1.3100
September	137.9	69.7	101.4	116.4	139.2	92.8	116.6	92.07	105.57	1.6200	5.6700	0.6600	1 569.10	1.3200
October	140.6	68.4	110.0	120.1	144.6	90.8	124.4	93.29	107.02	1.6400	5.7500	0.6700	1 600.93	1.3300
November	138.8	56.9	109.3	116.1	143.8	85.4	122.2	95.47	107.88	1.7000	5.9100	0.6800	1 666.31	1.3200
December	140.2	60.4	117.5	124.8	155.4	96.4	126.3	95.73	109.91	1.7100	5.8500	0.6700	1 687.17	1.3300
1994:														
January	144.8	70.2	115.1	128.4	161.3	103.1	133.1	96.54	111.44	1.7400	5.9200	0.6700	1 699.45	1.3200
February	140.4	69.4	110.7	123.1	154.8	102.5	129.3	95.79	106.30	1.7400	5.9000	0.6800	1 685.96	1.3400
March	134.0	66.3	112.3	114.6	144.3	112.6	126.6	94.35	105.10	1.6900	5.7600	0.6700	1 666.63	1.3600
April	135.5	68.4	117.8	119.2	146.0	124.5	124.7	94.39	103.48	1.7000	5.8200	0.6700	1 626.07	1.3800
May	137.2	72.8	109.7	111.7	138.7	113.8	126.5	92.79	103.75	1.6600	5.6700	0.6600	1 594.56	1.3800
June	133.5	71.6	106.4	104.1	135.2	107.4	117.7	91.60	102.53	1.6300	5.5600	0.6600	1 592.22	1.3800
July	137.7	70.9	111.5	114.2	142.8	110.5	122.2	89.06	98.45	1.5700	5.3700	0.6500	1 562.31	1.3800
August	142.9	71.6	114.5	113.8	150.3	107.5	127.1	89.26	99.94	1.5600	5.3600	0.6500	1 582.15	1.3800
September	139.1	67.9	105.2	103.4	139.6	105.8	127.3	88.08	98.77	1.5500	5.3000	0.6400	1 565.79	1.3500
October	142.0	69.3	107.7	104.9	141.9	98.9	125.4	86.66	98.35	1.5200	5.2000	0.6200	1 548.29	1.3500
November	136.4	66.2	105.9	108.7	141.2	97.4	119.7	87.71	98.04	1.5400	5.2900	0.6300	1 583.81	1.3600
December	138.1	68.4	108.3	103.5	140.5	98.5	123.2	89.64	100.18	1.5700	5.4100	0.6400	1 633.71	1.3900
1995:														
January	141.4	64.7	103.8	98.9	136.8	102.8	117.4	88.30	99.77	1.5300	5.2900	0.6400	1 611.53	1.4100
February	146.5	59.2	108.2	97.8	137.4	97.5	120.6	87.29	98.24	1.5000	5.2300	0.6400	1 620.58	1.4000
March	150.5	56.0	98.6	102.3	142.1	93.3	126.1	83.69	90.52	1.4100	4.9800	0.6200	1 688.99	1.4100
April	154.7	58.3	103.5	105.6	145.8	99.8	125.1	81.81	83.69	1.3800	4.8500	0.6200	1 710.89	1.3800
May	160.3	53.6	106.6	107.2	150.8	98.8	130.0	82.73	85.11	1.4100	4.9900	0.6300	1 652.78	1.3600
June	163.7	50.4	106.6	102.3	150.0	94.9	132.3	82.27	84.64	1.4000	4.9200	0.6300	1 639.75	1.3800
July	168.9	57.9	112.8	105.6	157.3	98.8	134.9	81.90	87.40	1.3900	4.8300	0.6300	1 609.71	1.3600
August	168.9	62.9	113.7	103.6	158.8	99.0	132.0	84.59	94.74	1.4500	4.9700	0.6400	1 607.18	1.3600
September	175.7	62.1	111.4	98.4	160.2	96.1	132.4	85.69	100.55	1.4600	5.0400	0.6400	1 613.41	1.3500
October	174.8	61.2	109.3	99.8	160.2	90.5	130.3	84.10	100.84	1.4100	4.9400	0.6300	1 605.69	1.3500
November	182.0	65.0	111.9	100.6	165.2	86.1	136.2	84.14	101.94	1.4200	4.8900	0.6400	1 592.67	1.3500
December	185.1	68.9	114.0	103.0	166.6	91.8	137.8	85.07	101.85	1.4400	4.9600	0.6500	1 593.88	1.3700
1996:														
January	191.2	72.2	123.7	111.2	170.2	96.5	145.2	86.23	105.75	1.4600	5.0100	0.6500	1 584.87	1.3700
February	192.5	69.8	123.2	109.5	170.0	94.5	144.2	86.41	105.79	1.4700	5.0400	0.6500	1 570.00	1.3800
March	194.0	74.3	123.3	112.5	170.3	90.4	145.3	86.57	105.95	1.4800	5.0600	0.6500	1 562.43	1.3700
April	196.6	76.5	123.0	118.1	176.9	102.4	150.4	87.46	107.20	1.5000	5.1000	0.6600	1 565.60	1.3600
May	201.1	76.2	124.4	116.1	174.2	104.1	153.4	88.28	106.34	1.5300	5.1900	0.6600	1 556.71	1.3700
June	201.6	78.2	126.3	116.9	171.5	102.4	147.4	88.16	108.96	1.5300	5.1800	0.6500	1 542.30	1.3700
July	192.4	71.8	122.1	109.8	169.6	93.4	144.1	87.25	109.19	1.5000	5.0900	0.6400	1 526.82	1.3700
August	196.0	70.0	125.6	108.4	177.0	93.2	150.3	86.54	107.87	1.4800	5.0600	0.6500	1 516.62	1.3700
September	206.6	74.8	130.4	117.4	179.7	99.0	154.7	87.46	109.93	1.5100	5.1300	0.6400	1 520.48	1.3700
October	212.0	71.0	130.6	117.8	180.8	94.0	163.7	87.98	112.41	1.5300	5.1700	0.6300	1 523.82	1.3500
November	227.6	72.9	139.0	127.4	183.4	102.4	175.9	86.98	112.30	1.5100	5.1200	0.6000	1 513.66	1.3400
December	222.7	67.2	139.7	127.4	186.0	103.7	173.2	88.71	113.98	1.5500	5.2400	0.6000	1 528.44	1.3600

1. March 1973=100. Weighted average value of the dollar against a group of currencies; see NOTES for more information.

Part Two

Industry Profiles

Mining, Oil, and Gas

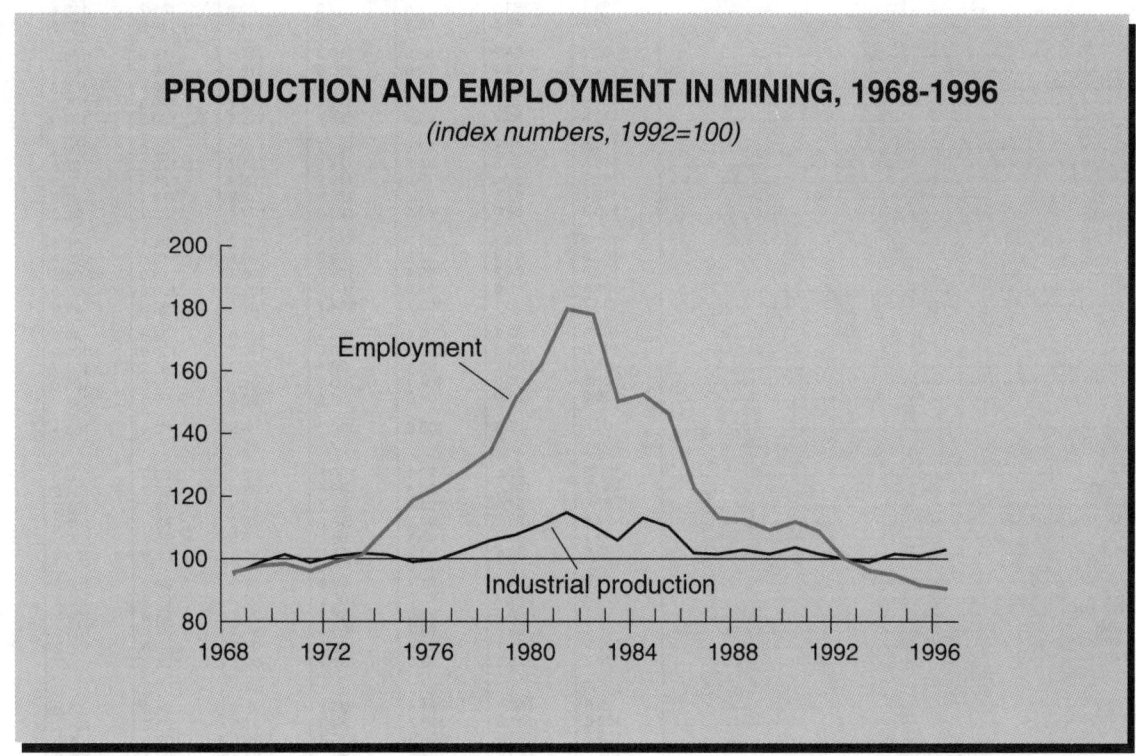

PRODUCTION AND EMPLOYMENT IN MINING, 1968-1996
(index numbers, 1992=100)

Employment in mining (including oil and gas production) rose rapidly during the 1970s and peaked in 1981 at over 1,100,000 workers. The subsequent decline was equally precipitous. By 1996, only 574,000 workers were employed in mining, one-half the 1981 level and 5 percent fewer than in 1968.

Industrial production also declined from 1981 to 1986, though much less dramatically than employment. From 1986 to 1996 production was fairly stable, despite the continuing decline in employment.

MINING INDUSTRIES—INDUSTRIAL PRODUCTION
(Seasonally adjusted, 1992=100)

YEAR AND MONTH	Total mining	Metal mining	Coal mining	Oil and gas extraction Total	Crude oil and natural gas Total	Crude oil	Natural gas	Natural gas liquids	Oil and gas well drilling	Stone and earth minerals
1968	94.9	66.6	56.8	109.2	120.9	129.8	103.5	84.8	90.6	86.7
1969	98.6	74.6	58.3	112.4	124.0	131.8	110.8	89.5	93.7	91.7
1970	101.2	77.1	62.3	115.6	130.0	137.7	117.6	93.6	81.6	89.5
1971	98.7	68.6	57.3	114.3	128.7	135.2	120.6	94.8	78.1	89.9
1972	100.7	66.3	61.3	116.3	128.9	135.1	121.4	97.5	89.8	93.9
1973	101.6	70.0	60.7	115.7	126.6	131.6	122.0	98.0	97.2	102.5
1974	101.1	68.0	61.6	114.9	120.9	125.7	116.6	95.3	120.9	102.1
1975	98.9	63.5	66.2	112.2	114.3	119.9	107.5	92.0	137.2	91.9
1976	99.7	69.2	68.9	110.3	111.5	116.5	106.2	91.7	137.6	97.2
1977	102.8	61.1	70.6	115.9	112.3	116.8	107.5	93.2	167.2	99.4
1978	105.8	69.5	67.6	120.1	115.4	122.8	106.3	90.7	187.8	104.7
1979	107.6	72.2	78.6	118.5	113.7	120.3	105.8	94.1	182.1	107.1
1980	110.8	65.2	83.4	123.4	115.1	120.5	109.0	93.8	226.3	97.9
1981	114.8	73.5	82.9	128.7	114.5	120.0	108.4	92.9	301.1	94.1
1982	110.5	54.8	84.5	124.6	111.7	120.9	99.5	90.3	283.1	78.7
1983	105.9	52.8	79.0	119.2	108.4	121.4	90.3	90.5	244.7	84.0
1984	113.2	57.2	90.2	125.9	112.9	124.1	97.6	92.6	283.0	94.7
1985	110.3	56.6	89.1	122.0	111.4	125.1	92.3	90.5	248.6	97.9
1986	101.9	59.3	89.7	110.1	108.2	121.1	90.1	87.6	136.6	96.6
1987	101.5	61.9	92.5	108.0	106.6	116.5	92.9	91.4	124.0	100.9
1988	102.9	74.3	95.4	107.7	106.1	113.9	95.3	93.5	125.7	103.2
1989	101.5	85.6	98.9	103.6	102.5	106.5	97.0	90.0	116.6	101.8
1990	103.7	93.1	103.7	104.7	101.6	102.9	99.6	90.8	136.2	103.3
1991	101.6	93.3	100.1	103.3	101.9	103.8	99.2	97.8	116.8	96.7
1992	100.0	100.0	100.0	100.0	100.0	100.0	100.0	100.0	100.0	100.0
1993	98.9	98.7	95.1	99.4	98.0	95.2	101.7	102.1	107.3	102.2
1994	101.6	100.2	104.1	100.2	98.1	92.6	105.6	101.5	113.9	108.9
1995	100.9	101.9	104.3	98.4	96.5	90.6	104.6	103.8	109.1	113.3
1996	102.9	102.0	105.9	100.3	96.5	89.0	106.9	108.7	120.6	118.8
1993:										
January	100.3	98.5	99.1	100.5	98.0	96.3	100.2	103.6	116.2	102.3
February	98.8	101.0	96.4	99.0	98.0	95.7	101.2	104.9	102.5	100.1
March	97.6	97.9	94.4	98.4	98.4	96.3	101.3	105.8	94.4	97.0
April	97.8	98.7	94.8	98.2	98.0	95.7	101.0	106.3	96.0	98.6
May	98.1	99.2	95.4	98.2	97.5	95.3	100.5	102.1	100.9	101.1
June	99.0	99.5	98.8	98.8	97.5	95.0	100.9	103.7	104.7	101.1
July	97.9	99.1	91.1	98.6	97.0	94.3	100.6	102.8	107.8	102.6
August	98.2	91.3	89.0	100.4	98.2	95.2	102.4	103.2	113.3	102.2
September	99.1	95.6	94.0	99.9	97.6	93.9	102.6	101.9	114.1	104.6
October	100.1	99.4	96.7	100.3	98.1	94.6	103.0	102.7	113.7	104.4
November	99.9	101.1	95.4	100.1	98.7	95.8	102.7	95.5	111.7	105.4
December	100.2	103.7	96.0	99.9	98.5	94.7	103.7	92.6	112.9	107.1
1994:										
January	99.8	102.2	94.4	100.1	98.4	94.3	103.9	95.9	113.7	105.2
February	100.8	101.6	102.7	99.9	97.8	93.2	104.2	96.0	115.5	104.0
March	102.2	102.9	106.0	100.8	98.6	93.2	106.0	97.2	116.8	106.2
April	101.7	99.1	107.6	99.9	97.6	92.1	105.2	97.4	116.0	107.4
May	101.9	98.2	104.2	100.8	98.6	93.0	106.3	100.1	116.0	109.1
June	102.2	102.8	105.4	100.5	97.8	92.4	105.4	102.3	117.4	109.7
July	101.9	101.3	104.5	100.5	98.1	92.1	106.5	103.5	114.9	108.7
August	102.1	100.3	106.2	100.4	98.7	92.1	107.7	104.0	111.0	109.5
September	101.0	98.7	104.0	99.7	97.8	92.6	105.0	105.7	111.1	107.8
October	100.7	100.2	101.9	99.4	97.4	92.1	104.8	102.0	111.8	109.4
November	101.3	96.9	104.2	99.7	97.7	91.3	106.5	105.8	111.2	112.2
December	103.0	98.0	107.8	100.6	98.6	93.0	106.3	108.5	111.2	117.5
1995:										
January	102.0	100.6	107.0	99.1	96.8	92.0	103.5	107.3	111.6	116.2
February	101.9	102.1	106.2	99.4	97.1	92.9	103.1	106.4	111.9	113.4
March	100.5	100.0	102.6	98.3	96.4	90.9	104.1	104.1	108.9	113.5
April	100.7	100.8	102.8	98.8	96.8	91.6	104.0	104.8	110.4	110.8
May	100.6	100.6	101.7	99.1	96.9	91.4	104.6	105.2	111.2	110.4
June	100.5	101.6	102.9	98.4	96.8	91.1	104.5	102.2	108.2	111.2
July	101.8	102.7	107.7	98.6	96.8	90.5	105.5	102.9	109.2	115.1
August	100.5	102.8	100.4	98.5	96.6	90.2	105.5	102.1	110.2	112.9
September	101.2	102.2	106.6	97.8	96.1	89.3	105.4	102.9	107.9	116.0
October	100.0	103.9	105.4	96.7	95.1	88.6	104.0	102.3	106.1	112.3
November	100.8	103.5	104.3	98.1	96.5	90.2	105.4	104.2	106.4	112.4
December	100.3	101.7	103.4	97.5	95.9	89.2	105.2	100.8	107.2	115.0
1996:										
January	99.0	97.0	96.6	98.0	96.0	89.0	105.8	103.3	109.0	112.1
February	100.8	97.1	101.2	98.9	96.7	89.3	106.8	99.8	113.2	117.4
March	102.8	101.7	105.9	100.2	96.6	89.6	106.4	106.8	119.8	117.9
April	102.9	99.4	105.3	100.9	96.8	89.2	107.4	108.0	123.7	116.3
May	103.2	100.9	108.0	100.5	95.7	88.2	106.2	106.8	127.0	117.4
June	104.4	101.7	108.9	101.5	96.7	89.7	106.4	108.7	127.8	120.6
July	103.1	103.1	102.7	100.9	97.0	89.3	107.6	108.5	122.1	120.6
August	104.5	104.0	109.6	101.1	97.1	88.8	108.4	110.9	122.6	121.7
September	103.4	105.3	106.2	100.5	97.2	90.3	106.7	111.2	117.5	118.5
October	103.4	105.6	107.5	100.0	96.0	88.9	105.8	113.0	120.2	120.0
November	103.5	102.5	108.8	100.2	96.1	88.2	107.0	112.7	120.7	120.2
December	104.5	106.3	109.5	100.7	96.1	87.8	107.6	114.3	123.6	122.9

MINING INDUSTRIES—CAPACITY UTILIZATION AND PRODUCER PRICES

YEAR AND MONTH	Capacity utilization (Percent of capacity seasonally adjusted)						Producer prices (December 1984=100, except as noted, not seasonally adjusted)						
				Oil and gas extraction							Crude materials [2]		Non-metallic minerals, except fuels
	Total mining	Metal mining	Coal mining	Total	Oil and gas well drilling	Stone and earth minerals	Total mining industries	Metal mining	Coal mining [1]	Oil and gas extraction [1]	Natural gas (To pipelines)	Crude petroleum	
1968	83.5	82.9	89.5	81.8	71.3	89.2					7.6	13.7	
1969	86.5	91.8	90.7	84.6	77.8	91.5					7.7	14.3	
1970	88.8	93.6	95.8	87.7	69.7	87.2					7.9	14.5	
1971	87.3	83.2	86.0	88.5	68.6	85.9					8.4	15.6	
1972	90.3	80.7	89.2	92.3	79.1	87.8					9.0	15.5	
1973	92.3	84.6	85.7	94.8	85.2	92.8					9.8	17.2	
1974	92.3	82.1	84.2	96.1	98.9	89.6					11.6	28.9	
1975	89.7	76.4	87.5	93.8	99.2	79.1					16.1	33.5	
1976	89.8	81.0	88.9	92.1	91.5	83.0					21.8	34.6	
1977	90.9	69.4	88.2	94.2	101.7	85.4					30.8	37.4	
1978	90.9	78.5	80.3	94.7	100.0	89.2					36.5	40.9	
1979	91.4	81.4	88.8	92.8	88.2	90.6					47.6	51.3	
1980	93.4	72.8	90.3	95.8	95.7	82.7					63.3	75.9	
1981	93.9	79.1	86.7	96.1	98.0	79.8					82.1	109.6	
1982	86.3	57.5	86.1	88.2	70.3	67.4					100.0	100.0	
1983	80.4	57.9	79.1	81.7	52.6	72.6					106.6	92.9	
1984	86.0	63.3	88.6	86.7	63.4	81.8					106.1	91.3	
1985	84.3	62.7	85.7	84.9	58.5	84.4					102.9	84.5	102.8
1986	77.6	65.9	84.7	76.4	34.3	82.7	77.0	91.2	99.5	76.9	89.6	46.9	104.2
1987	80.0	70.9	85.7	78.9	36.4	85.7	75.0	100.1	96.0	74.3	79.5	55.5	105.1
1988	83.6	80.5	86.8	82.8	46.7	86.9	70.6	100.7	94.6	68.5	77.4	46.2	108.0
1989	85.5	85.4	88.3	85.0	53.1	85.2	76.4	100.3	94.3	75.7	82.0	56.3	111.2
1990	88.9	85.7	90.7	89.1	68.3	86.3	81.8	93.4	96.5	82.7	80.4	71.0	113.7
1991	87.6	82.9	85.7	89.2	63.1	81.1	78.4	82.2	96.3	77.9	79.1	61.9	116.3
1992	87.0	86.9	85.1	87.7	57.3	84.7	76.9	76.6	94.0	76.5	80.6	58.0	117.5
1993	86.7	83.9	80.5	88.6	66.3	85.1	76.4	69.7	93.3	76.2	84.7	51.4	118.8
1994	88.9	85.4	85.3	90.1	73.0	89.7	73.3	81.4	93.2	71.1	78.8	47.1	120.5
1995	88.2	87.3	84.3	88.8	71.0	91.8	71.0	101.4	91.6	66.6	66.6	51.1	123.8
1996	90.5	86.1	85.8	91.6	81.1	94.6	84.4	92.1	91.4	84.8	91.2	62.6	127.1
1993:													
January	87.8	84.3	84.5	89.0	69.5	86.0	78.3	73.7	93.0	78.7	89.1	52.0	118.6
February	86.5	86.3	82.1	87.8	61.6	84.0	76.2	72.6	93.4	75.8	80.0	56.1	118.4
March	85.5	83.5	80.3	87.4	57.1	81.2	75.8	70.1	93.2	75.3	77.6	58.1	118.3
April	85.6	84.2	80.5	87.3	58.4	82.4	76.1	68.9	92.9	75.9	78.9	57.7	118.6
May	86.0	84.5	80.9	87.4	61.7	84.3	79.5	67.9	92.7	80.7	87.6	57.9	118.3
June	86.8	84.6	83.7	88.0	64.4	84.2	80.5	68.7	93.1	82.0	94.2	52.9	118.6
July	85.8	84.2	77.1	88.0	66.7	85.3	75.2	69.8	92.9	74.6	82.8	50.2	118.7
August	86.1	77.4	75.2	89.7	70.5	84.9	74.2	71.4	93.1	73.0	81.4	48.3	118.7
September	87.0	81.0	79.3	89.4	71.4	86.8	75.2	70.5	93.2	74.5	85.5	46.5	118.9
October	87.9	84.1	81.5	89.9	71.6	86.5	78.3	66.9	94.4	78.8	89.2	51.8	119.6
November	87.8	85.5	80.2	89.9	70.8	87.3	74.8	66.5	94.1	74.0	85.2	46.0	119.1
December	88.1	87.6	80.6	89.8	71.9	88.7	72.7	69.5	94.0	70.9	85.5	38.9	119.2
1994:													
January	87.7	86.4	79.0	90.1	72.7	87.0	75.8	70.5	93.8	75.1	92.9	39.3	119.8
February	88.6	86.0	85.7	89.9	73.9	86.0	71.5	72.6	92.5	69.3	83.3	37.8	120.0
March	89.7	87.2	88.1	90.6	74.7	87.7	74.5	73.2	92.6	73.4	89.5	39.6	120.2
April	89.2	84.2	89.1	89.8	74.3	88.7	74.4	73.7	93.0	73.1	86.7	42.7	120.7
May	89.3	83.5	85.9	90.7	74.3	90.1	73.7	74.6	93.2	72.0	79.4	48.9	120.6
June	89.6	87.5	86.6	90.4	75.3	90.4	74.9	81.4	92.0	73.5	78.6	52.9	120.5
July	89.2	86.4	85.6	90.4	73.7	89.5	74.3	84.9	92.1	72.4	73.9	56.2	120.5
August	89.3	85.7	86.6	90.3	71.2	90.2	75.0	84.4	92.7	73.3	76.9	54.4	120.4
September	88.3	84.5	84.5	89.7	71.3	88.6	72.4	87.6	94.3	69.2	74.2	48.3	120.5
October	87.9	85.9	82.5	89.4	71.8	89.8	71.0	88.3	95.0	67.1	69.5	49.3	120.7
November	88.4	83.2	84.0	89.6	71.4	92.1	70.5	91.1	94.9	66.2	67.7	49.1	120.8
December	89.8	84.3	86.6	90.4	71.5	96.3	72.0	94.2	92.0	68.6	73.5	47.1	120.9
1995:													
January	88.9	86.6	85.9	89.1	71.9	95.1	72.1	101.9	88.4	68.7	72.8	48.4	122.4
February	88.9	87.9	85.4	89.4	72.2	92.6	71.2	102.3	91.3	66.9	67.0	51.0	123.3
March	87.6	86.0	82.6	88.5	70.4	92.5	70.7	103.7	93.7	65.7	65.3	50.6	123.6
April	87.9	86.6	82.8	89.0	71.5	90.2	72.6	105.1	92.6	68.3	66.3	55.3	123.5
May	87.8	86.5	82.1	89.3	72.1	89.7	72.8	100.9	90.4	69.2	67.3	56.0	123.3
June	87.8	87.2	83.1	88.7	70.3	90.2	72.8	101.8	90.7	69.1	68.9	53.3	123.8
July	89.0	88.0	87.2	89.0	71.1	93.2	70.6	103.6	92.5	65.7	67.2	48.3	124.2
August	87.9	88.0	81.3	89.0	71.9	91.3	67.6	101.2	91.8	61.8	59.6	49.1	124.2
September	88.5	87.3	86.5	88.4	70.5	93.7	68.7	99.3	91.7	63.5	60.8	51.4	124.5
October	87.6	88.6	85.6	87.6	69.5	90.6	69.0	97.0	93.0	63.7	63.5	48.3	124.3
November	88.3	88.1	84.9	88.9	69.8	90.5	70.5	100.0	91.4	66.0	67.0	49.0	124.4
December	88.0	86.4	84.2	88.5	70.5	92.5	74.1	100.0	91.3	71.0	73.3	52.2	124.4
1996:													
January	86.9	82.3	78.7	89.0	71.8	90.0	79.1	98.2	89.9	78.0	83.5	56.0	125.9
February	88.5	82.3	82.3	89.9	74.9	94.1	83.4	97.5	91.9	82.6	96.5	52.8	126.4
March	90.3	86.0	86.1	91.2	79.6	94.4	80.9	96.7	92.2	79.2	85.8	57.7	126.7
April	90.4	84.0	85.6	92.0	82.4	93.0	86.0	96.4	91.1	86.2	92.8	66.0	127.1
May	90.7	85.2	87.7	91.7	85.0	93.7	82.9	97.1	93.1	81.8	88.0	61.0	127.6
June	91.8	85.8	88.3	92.7	85.8	96.2	78.1	93.3	91.7	75.9	78.9	57.7	128.1
July	90.7	86.9	83.2	92.2	82.2	96.0	81.0	89.2	90.5	80.7	87.3	59.9	127.2
August	91.9	87.6	88.7	92.5	82.9	96.7	82.6	87.5	92.6	82.7	88.2	62.0	127.2
September	91.0	88.7	85.8	92.0	79.7	94.1	81.3	86.8	90.9	81.3	76.6	67.2	127.5
October	91.0	88.9	86.8	91.6	81.8	95.1	83.0	86.6	90.5	83.7	75.2	72.0	127.3
November	91.1	86.3	87.8	91.8	82.5	95.1	90.4	88.4	91.3	93.4	100.6	68.5	127.3
December	91.9	89.5	88.3	92.3	84.8	97.0	104.2	87.3	90.7	112.1	140.7	70.9	127.1

1. December 1985=100.
2. 1982=100.

MINING INDUSTRIES—EMPLOYMENT, HOURS, AND EARNINGS

YEAR AND MONTH	Total mining (Seasonally adjusted)						Total mining (Not seasonally adjusted)					
	Total payroll employees (Thousands)	Production workers					Total payroll employees (Thousands)	Production workers				
		Employees	Weekly hours worked		Average earnings (Dollars)			Employees	Weekly hours worked		Average earnings (Dollars)	
			Average hours	Aggregate hours index (1982=100)	Hourly	Weekly			Average hours	Aggregate hours index (1982=100)	Hourly	Weekly
1968	606	461	42.6	56.0	3.35	142.71	606	461	42.6	56.0	3.35	142.71
1969	619	472	43.0	57.9	3.60	154.80	619	472	43.0	57.9	3.60	154.80
1970	623	473	42.7	57.6	3.85	164.40	623	473	42.7	57.6	3.85	164.40
1971	609	455	42.4	54.9	4.06	172.14	609	455	42.4	54.9	4.06	172.14
1972	628	475	42.6	57.8	4.44	189.14	628	475	42.6	57.8	4.44	189.14
1973	642	486	42.4	58.8	4.75	201.40	642	486	42.4	58.8	4.75	201.40
1974	697	530	41.9	63.4	5.23	219.14	697	530	41.9	63.4	5.23	219.14
1975	752	571	41.9	68.3	5.95	249.31	752	571	41.9	68.3	5.95	249.31
1976	779	592	42.4	71.5	6.46	273.90	779	592	42.4	71.5	6.46	273.90
1977	813	618	43.4	76.5	6.94	301.20	813	618	43.4	76.5	6.94	301.20
1978	851	638	43.4	79.0	7.67	332.88	851	638	43.4	79.0	7.67	332.88
1979	958	719	43.0	88.2	8.49	365.07	958	719	43.0	88.2	8.49	365.07
1980	1 027	762	43.3	94.1	9.17	397.06	1 027	762	43.3	94.1	9.17	397.06
1981	1 139	841	43.7	104.8	10.04	438.75	1 139	841	43.7	104.8	10.04	438.75
1982	1 128	821	42.7	100.0	10.77	459.88	1 128	821	42.7	100.0	10.77	459.88
1983	952	673	42.5	81.5	11.28	479.40	952	673	42.5	81.5	11.28	479.40
1984	966	686	43.3	84.9	11.63	503.58	966	686	43.3	84.9	11.63	503.58
1985	927	658	43.4	81.4	11.98	519.93	927	658	43.4	81.4	11.98	519.93
1986	777	545	42.2	65.7	12.46	525.81	777	545	42.2	65.7	12.46	525.81
1987	717	511	42.4	61.8	12.54	531.70	717	511	42.4	61.8	12.54	531.70
1988	713	512	42.3	61.7	12.80	541.44	713	512	42.3	61.7	12.80	541.44
1989	692	493	43.0	60.5	13.26	570.18	692	493	43.0	60.5	13.26	570.18
1990	709	509	44.1	63.9	13.68	603.29	709	509	44.1	63.9	13.68	603.29
1991	689	489	44.4	62.0	14.19	630.04	689	489	44.4	62.0	14.19	630.04
1992	635	448	43.9	56.2	14.54	638.31	635	448	43.9	56.2	14.54	638.31
1993	610	431	44.3	54.3	14.60	646.78	610	431	44.3	54.3	14.60	646.78
1994	601	427	44.8	54.6	14.88	666.62	601	427	44.8	54.6	14.88	666.62
1995	581	424	44.7	54.1	15.30	683.91	581	424	44.7	54.1	15.30	683.91
1996	574	426	45.3	55.1	15.61	707.13	574	426	45.3	55.1	15.61	707.13
1993:												
January	623	442	44.4	56.0	14.58	647.35	611	431	44.1	54.2	14.73	649.59
February	614	433	44.0	54.3	14.50	638.00	598	419	43.6	52.1	14.60	636.56
March	616	433	43.3	53.5	14.65	634.35	603	422	43.0	51.7	14.71	632.53
April	612	433	44.2	54.6	14.81	654.60	607	428	43.7	53.3	14.89	650.69
May	613	435	44.5	55.2	14.75	656.38	613	434	44.3	54.9	14.72	652.10
June	608	429	44.0	53.8	14.59	641.96	612	433	44.1	54.5	14.59	643.42
July	606	428	44.6	54.5	14.57	649.82	616	436	44.1	54.9	14.48	638.57
August	600	423	44.6	53.8	14.57	649.82	611	433	44.8	55.4	14.44	646.91
September	602	425	44.4	53.8	14.58	647.35	611	433	44.5	55.0	14.53	646.59
October	603	424	45.0	54.4	14.60	657.00	610	431	45.5	55.9	14.46	657.93
November	601	424	44.3	53.6	14.47	641.02	608	429	44.7	54.7	14.43	645.02
December	615	438	44.3	55.3	14.64	648.55	616	437	44.6	55.6	14.67	654.28
1994:												
January	613	433	44.3	54.7	14.88	659.18	601	423	44.1	53.2	15.06	664.15
February	608	430	44.2	54.2	14.81	654.60	594	416	43.8	52.0	14.92	653.50
March	604	427	44.3	54.0	14.77	654.31	592	416	44.0	52.3	14.84	652.96
April	601	426	44.6	54.2	14.88	663.65	596	421	44.5	53.4	14.96	665.72
May	598	424	44.6	53.9	14.86	662.76	597	423	44.5	53.7	14.83	659.94
June	597	424	44.7	54.1	14.81	662.01	606	430	44.9	55.1	14.73	661.38
July	597	424	45.1	54.5	14.79	667.03	607	433	44.9	55.4	14.72	660.93
August	597	425	44.9	54.4	14.82	665.42	609	435	45.1	56.0	14.68	662.07
September	600	428	44.8	54.7	14.96	670.21	608	436	45.5	56.6	14.91	678.41
October	596	427	44.6	54.3	15.03	670.34	603	434	45.2	55.9	14.89	673.03
November	596	430	45.1	55.3	15.00	676.50	601	434	45.4	56.2	14.95	678.73
December	593	430	44.8	55.0	15.03	673.34	594	428	45.1	55.1	15.08	680.11
1995:												
January	592	430	45.2	55.4	15.04	679.81	581	419	44.9	53.6	15.23	683.83
February	587	427	44.6	54.3	15.09	673.01	573	414	44.5	52.5	15.24	678.18
March	587	427	44.2	53.8	15.16	670.07	576	417	43.9	52.3	15.22	668.16
April	585	426	44.9	54.6	15.20	682.48	578	420	44.3	53.1	15.30	677.79
May	582	425	44.4	53.8	15.23	676.21	582	424	44.3	53.5	15.19	672.92
June	581	423	44.7	53.9	15.31	684.36	588	430	45.0	55.2	15.23	685.35
July	579	423	44.7	53.9	15.41	688.83	590	432	44.5	54.9	15.34	682.63
August	577	423	44.5	53.7	15.43	686.64	588	433	44.7	55.2	15.29	683.46
September	577	422	44.8	53.9	15.40	689.92	585	430	45.4	55.7	15.35	696.89
October	576	422	44.9	54.1	15.46	694.15	582	428	45.5	55.5	15.33	697.52
November	573	420	44.6	53.4	15.45	689.07	577	424	44.8	54.2	15.35	687.68
December	573	421	44.7	53.7	15.48	691.96	573	420	44.9	53.8	15.54	697.75
1996:												
January	573	421	44.2	53.1	15.43	682.01	562	410	43.9	51.3	15.63	686.16
February	576	426	45.2	54.9	15.47	699.24	563	413	45.1	53.2	15.61	704.01
March	577	428	45.2	55.2	15.46	698.79	566	418	45.0	53.7	15.50	697.50
April	577	427	45.0	54.8	15.46	695.70	571	422	44.9	54.0	15.55	698.20
May	579	429	45.3	55.4	15.50	702.15	576	427	45.2	55.0	15.44	697.89
June	577	429	45.6	55.8	15.59	710.90	582	434	46.0	56.9	15.58	716.68
July	574	426	45.0	54.7	15.61	702.45	585	435	44.8	55.6	15.54	696.19
August	574	427	45.2	55.1	15.65	707.38	584	436	45.3	56.4	15.51	702.60
September	571	425	45.3	54.9	15.70	711.21	577	432	45.9	56.6	15.73	722.01
October	570	425	45.4	55.0	15.67	711.42	576	431	45.9	56.5	15.54	713.29
November	571	427	45.3	55.2	15.77	714.38	575	431	45.5	56.0	15.67	712.99
December	571	427	45.7	55.7	15.88	725.72	570	426	46.0	55.9	15.95	733.70

MINING INDUSTRIES—EMPLOYMENT, HOURS, AND EARNINGS
(Not seasonally adjusted)

YEAR AND MONTH	Metal mining					Coal mining				
	Employment (Thousands)		Average weekly hours	Average earnings (Dollars)		Employment (Thousands)		Average weekly hours	Average earnings (Dollars)	
	Total payroll employees	Production workers		Hourly	Weekly	Total payroll employees	Production workers		Hourly	Weekly
1968	82	65	43.3	3.42	148.09	132	114	40.0	3.83	153.20
1969	89	72	43.1	3.64	156.88	135	117	39.7	4.20	166.74
1970	93	75	43.1	3.88	167.23	145	127	40.5	4.54	183.87
1971	87	69	42.8	4.12	176.34	146	123	40.3	4.78	192.63
1972	83	66	41.4	4.56	188.78	161	140	40.7	5.27	214.49
1973	87	69	41.7	4.84	201.83	162	140	39.8	5.70	226.86
1974	95	76	41.4	5.44	225.22	180	154	37.7	6.22	234.49
1975	94	73	40.7	6.13	249.49	213	182	39.5	7.21	284.80
1976	94	73	41.0	6.76	277.16	225	192	39.8	7.74	308.05
1977	90	68	40.8	7.28	297.02	225	192	41.9	8.25	345.68
1978	94	72	41.3	8.23	339.90	210	173	40.5	9.51	385.16
1979	101	77	41.2	9.27	381.92	259	216	40.7	10.28	418.40
1980	98	74	40.5	10.26	415.53	246	204	40.1	10.86	435.49
1981	104	78	40.5	11.55	467.78	225	186	40.5	11.91	482.36
1982	73	53	39.3	12.31	483.78	237	194	39.9	12.69	506.33
1983	56	41	39.3	12.58	494.39	194	156	39.9	13.73	547.83
1984	55	40	40.5	13.05	528.53	196	158	40.7	14.82	603.17
1985	46	34	40.9	13.38	547.24	187	153	41.1	15.24	626.36
1986	41	31	41.1	13.19	542.11	176	144	40.6	15.40	625.24
1987	44	33	41.9	12.94	542.19	162	132	42.0	15.76	661.92
1988	50	39	42.3	13.24	560.05	151	123	42.2	16.06	677.73
1989	56	44	42.8	13.58	581.22	144	116	43.4	16.26	705.68
1990	58	46	42.8	14.05	601.34	147	119	44.0	16.71	735.24
1991	56	44	43.0	14.87	639.41	136	110	44.6	17.06	760.88
1992	53	42	42.9	15.26	654.65	127	103	44.0	17.15	754.60
1993	50	40	43.1	15.29	659.00	109	86	44.4	17.27	766.79
1994	49	39	43.5	16.08	699.48	112	90	45.2	17.76	802.75
1995	51	41	43.8	16.77	734.53	104	84	44.9	18.45	828.41
1996	54	42	44.0	17.35	763.40	96	79	45.8	18.75	858.75
1993:										
January	51	40	43.1	15.23	656.41	121	98	45.5	17.49	795.80
February	51	40	43.0	15.19	653.17	114	91	45.0	17.19	773.55
March	51	41	42.2	15.20	641.44	118	94	43.7	17.29	755.57
April	51	41	43.6	15.30	667.08	118	95	44.7	17.53	783.59
May	50	40	43.0	15.21	654.03	116	94	44.3	17.34	768.16
June	51	41	43.2	15.26	659.23	109	86	43.7	17.15	749.46
July	50	40	43.0	15.08	648.44	103	82	42.6	17.20	732.72
August	46	37	42.6	15.13	644.54	99	78	44.7	17.13	765.71
September	50	40	43.7	15.44	674.73	98	77	44.4	17.10	759.24
October	50	40	42.9	15.42	661.52	97	75	45.6	17.09	779.30
November	49	39	42.7	15.53	663.13	97	75	45.0	17.16	772.20
December	49	40	43.8	15.44	676.27	113	91	44.1	17.39	766.90
1994:										
January	48	38	43.7	15.86	693.08	113	91	45.2	17.89	808.63
February	48	38	43.0	15.76	677.68	113	90	45.2	17.63	796.88
March	48	38	43.1	15.79	680.55	112	90	45.8	17.65	808.37
April	48	38	43.5	15.82	688.17	112	90	45.3	17.65	799.55
May	48	39	42.9	16.02	687.26	111	90	45.7	17.65	806.61
June	49	40	43.5	15.84	689.04	113	91	45.0	17.67	795.15
July	49	40	44.1	16.01	706.04	113	91	42.7	17.55	749.39
August	50	40	43.5	15.99	695.57	112	90	45.2	17.50	791.00
September	49	40	44.3	16.42	727.41	110	89	45.4	17.67	802.22
October	49	40	43.4	16.50	716.10	110	89	45.3	17.71	802.26
November	49	40	43.0	16.49	709.07	111	90	45.2	18.10	818.12
December	49	40	44.2	16.44	726.65	110	90	46.0	18.39	845.94
1995:										
January	49	40	43.7	16.64	727.17	109	88	46.7	18.51	864.42
February	49	40	43.0	16.57	712.51	107	86	46.1	18.37	846.86
March	50	40	43.5	16.62	722.97	107	86	44.9	18.37	824.81
April	50	41	44.1	16.98	748.82	106	86	44.1	18.34	808.79
May	51	41	42.7	16.61	709.25	105	84	44.5	18.31	814.80
June	52	42	43.5	16.44	715.14	105	84	44.8	18.36	822.53
July	53	43	44.2	16.71	738.58	104	84	41.8	18.38	768.28
August	53	43	43.4	16.84	730.86	104	84	44.8	18.48	827.90
September	52	42	44.7	16.89	754.98	103	84	45.7	18.52	846.36
October	52	41	44.1	16.92	746.17	102	83	45.4	18.46	838.08
November	52	41	44.4	17.06	757.46	102	83	44.8	18.58	832.38
December	52	41	44.5	16.94	753.83	100	82	45.1	18.78	846.98
1996:										
January	52	41	44.4	16.97	753.47	99	81	44.7	18.92	845.72
February	52	41	44.6	16.92	754.63	99	80	47.0	18.79	883.13
March	53	42	44.0	17.14	754.16	98	80	46.7	18.77	876.56
April	53	42	44.7	17.31	773.76	97	79	45.4	18.71	849.43
May	54	43	43.2	17.30	747.36	97	79	45.6	18.61	848.62
June	55	44	43.9	17.24	756.84	97	79	46.7	18.66	871.42
July	55	44	43.6	17.28	753.41	98	79	43.6	18.65	813.14
August	56	44	43.0	17.41	748.63	96	78	45.3	18.61	843.03
September	55	43	44.9	17.57	788.89	95	78	46.1	18.76	864.84
October	54	42	43.6	17.46	761.26	95	77	45.8	18.59	851.42
November	54	42	43.6	17.75	773.90	95	77	46.0	18.83	866.18
December	54	42	44.4	17.79	789.88	94	77	46.2	19.14	884.27

MINING INDUSTRIES—EMPLOYMENT, HOURS, AND EARNINGS
(Not seasonally adjusted)

YEAR AND MONTH	Oil and gas extraction					Nonmetallic minerals, except fuels				
	Employment (Thousands)		Average weekly hours	Average earnings (Dollars)		Employment (Thousands)		Average weekly hours	Average earnings (Dollars)	
	Total payroll employees	Production workers		Hourly	Weekly	Total payroll employees	Production workers		Hourly	Weekly
1968	276	186	42.8	3.22	137.82	116	95	44.9	3.04	136.50
1969	280	188	43.8	3.43	150.23	115	94	45.6	3.27	149.11
1970	270	178	43.2	3.57	154.22	115	94	44.7	3.47	155.11
1971	264	173	43.2	3.78	163.30	115	93	44.9	3.70	166.13
1972	268	177	43.4	4.04	175.34	116	93	44.7	3.95	176.57
1973	274	182	43.0	4.33	186.19	119	95	45.5	4.22	192.01
1974	300	203	43.8	4.87	213.31	122	98	45.0	4.50	202.50
1975	329	223	43.7	5.38	235.11	117	92	43.5	4.95	215.33
1976	346	237	44.1	5.85	257.99	115	90	44.2	5.36	236.91
1977	381	267	44.7	6.37	284.74	116	92	44.6	5.81	259.13
1978	429	299	45.0	7.01	315.45	119	94	44.8	6.33	283.58
1979	474	327	44.4	7.72	342.77	124	98	45.0	6.90	310.50
1980	560	389	45.4	8.59	389.99	123	96	43.6	7.52	327.87
1981	692	486	45.6	9.50	433.20	119	91	43.0	8.28	356.04
1982	708	491	44.2	10.25	453.05	110	83	42.7	8.90	380.03
1983	598	398	43.6	10.67	465.21	104	79	43.6	9.31	405.92
1984	606	405	44.4	10.72	475.97	109	83	44.7	9.87	441.19
1985	583	387	44.2	11.06	488.85	110	84	44.5	10.18	453.01
1986	450	287	42.6	11.61	494.59	110	83	44.5	10.38	461.91
1987	402	261	41.7	11.53	480.80	110	85	45.4	10.60	481.24
1988	400	265	41.3	11.85	489.41	112	85	45.5	10.94	497.77
1989	381	248	42.0	12.50	525.00	111	85	45.6	11.25	513.00
1990	395	261	43.9	12.94	568.07	110	83	45.3	11.58	524.57
1991	393	258	44.5	13.53	602.09	105	78	44.5	11.93	530.89
1992	353	228	43.8	14.01	613.64	102	76	44.9	12.26	550.47
1993	350	228	43.8	14.14	619.33	102	76	46.1	12.70	585.47
1994	337	220	44.2	14.13	624.55	104	78	46.5	13.11	609.62
1995	320	218	44.2	14.52	641.78	105	80	46.6	13.39	623.97
1996	317	224	44.7	14.85	663.80	106	81	47.1	13.76	648.10
1993:										
January	347	225	44.2	14.10	623.22	92	68	42.4	12.34	523.22
February	340	219	43.2	14.09	608.69	94	69	43.3	12.34	534.32
March	338	216	42.4	14.24	603.78	96	71	44.0	12.45	547.80
April	338	218	42.5	14.47	614.98	101	76	45.6	12.55	572.28
May	343	222	43.6	14.31	623.92	104	79	47.1	12.66	596.29
June	348	226	43.3	14.22	615.73	105	80	47.3	12.68	599.76
July	357	233	43.7	14.09	615.73	106	80	47.3	12.77	604.02
August	360	237	44.4	14.03	622.93	106	80	47.7	12.82	611.51
September	358	236	43.7	14.11	616.61	105	80	47.3	12.95	612.54
October	358	236	45.4	14.03	636.96	105	80	47.3	12.87	608.75
November	357	236	44.3	13.93	617.10	104	79	47.3	12.86	599.28
December	353	232	44.6	14.07	627.52	100	75	46.6	12.89	590.36
1994:										
January	345	224	44.0	14.41	634.04	95	70	43.4	12.87	558.56
February	338	219	43.7	14.26	623.16	95	70	42.5	12.86	546.55
March	334	216	43.2	14.11	609.55	98	73	45.0	12.89	580.05
April	333	215	43.7	14.38	628.41	103	78	46.4	13.02	604.13
May	332	214	43.0	14.10	606.30	106	81	47.7	13.04	622.01
June	336	217	44.0	13.95	613.80	108	82	48.0	13.08	627.84
July	337	220	44.8	13.99	626.75	108	82	48.1	13.18	633.96
August	339	222	44.2	13.89	613.94	108	82	48.0	13.17	632.16
September	341	225	44.8	14.18	635.26	108	82	47.9	13.27	635.63
October	337	223	44.6	14.08	627.97	107	82	47.6	13.33	634.51
November	335	223	45.5	14.06	639.73	106	81	46.9	13.25	621.43
December	332	221	44.6	14.11	629.31	103	78	45.9	13.24	607.72
1995:										
January	326	219	44.4	14.30	634.92	97	72	44.8	13.09	586.43
February	319	215	44.4	14.38	638.47	98	73	43.7	13.17	575.53
March	318	213	43.1	14.39	620.21	102	77	45.7	13.19	602.78
April	316	213	43.9	14.55	638.75	106	80	45.7	13.25	605.53
May	319	216	43.6	14.46	630.46	108	82	46.6	13.30	619.78
June	323	220	44.3	14.54	644.12	109	83	47.8	13.39	640.04
July	323	222	44.3	14.77	654.31	110	84	48.0	13.43	644.64
August	322	223	43.8	14.50	635.10	109	84	47.9	13.51	647.13
September	321	222	44.3	14.51	642.79	109	83	48.6	13.66	663.88
October	320	221	44.9	14.55	653.30	108	83	47.7	13.61	649.20
November	317	218	44.4	14.50	643.80	107	82	46.2	13.50	623.70
December	319	219	44.9	14.81	664.97	103	78	45.3	13.41	607.47
1996:										
January	314	216	43.8	14.79	647.80	97	72	42.5	13.53	575.03
February	314	218	44.6	14.89	664.09	98	74	45.0	13.40	603.00
March	315	220	44.2	14.67	648.41	102	77	46.3	13.50	625.05
April	316	220	44.0	14.80	651.20	105	81	46.9	13.59	637.37
May	317	222	44.7	14.64	654.41	108	83	47.1	13.69	644.80
June	320	226	45.3	14.85	672.71	110	85	48.2	13.81	665.64
July	321	227	44.0	14.80	651.20	111	85	48.5	13.88	673.18
August	322	230	44.5	14.73	655.49	111	85	48.5	13.93	675.61
September	317	227	45.1	15.01	676.95	110	84	48.9	14.04	686.56
October	318	228	45.4	14.79	671.47	109	84	48.6	13.94	677.48
November	318	229	45.2	14.88	672.58	108	83	46.8	13.88	649.58
December	318	229	45.9	15.29	701.81	105	79	46.7	13.83	645.86

PETROLEUM AND PETROLEUM PRODUCTS—IMPORTS AND STOCKS
(Not seasonally adjusted)

YEAR AND MONTH	Imports						Stocks (End of period—millions of barrels)		
	Total energy-related petroleum products		Crude petroleum					Crude petroleum	
			Quantity (Thousands of barrels)		Value (Millions of dollars)	Unit price (Dollars per barrel)	All oils		
	Quantity (Thousands of barrels)	Value (Millions of dollars)	Total	Average per day				Total	Strategic petroleum reserve
1968	....	....	....	....	....	....	1 000	272	....
1969	....	....	....	....	....	....	980	265	....
1970	....	....	....	....	....	....	1 018	276	....
1971	....	....	....	....	....	....	1 044	260	....
1972	....	....	....	....	....	....	959	246	....
1973	....	....	....	....	....	....	1 008	242	....
1974	....	....	....	....	....	....	1 074	265	....
1975	....	....	....	....	....	....	1 133	271	....
1976	....	....	....	....	....	....	1 112	285	....
1977	....	....	....	....	....	....	1 312	348	7
1978	....	....	....	....	....	....	1 278	376	67
1979	....	....	....	....	....	....	1 341	430	91
1980	....	....	....	....	....	....	1 392	466	108
1981	....	....	....	....	....	....	1 484	594	230
1982	....	....	....	....	....	....	1 430	644	294
1983	....	....	....	....	....	....	1 454	723	379
1984	....	....	....	....	....	....	1 556	796	451
1985	....	....	....	....	....	....	1 519	814	493
1986	....	....	....	....	....	....	1 593	843	512
1987	....	....	....	....	....	....	1 607	890	541
1988	....	....	....	....	....	....	1 597	890	560
1989	....	....	....	....	....	....	1 581	921	580
1990	....	....	....	....	....	....	1 621	908	586
1991	2 828 953	50 646	2 146 064	5 880	37 463	17.46	1 617	893	569
1992	2 947 582	50 537	2 294 570	6 269	38 553	16.80	1 592	893	575
1993	3 257 008	50 210	2 543 374	6 968	38 469	15.13	1 647	922	587
1994	3 416 045	49 533	2 704 196	7 409	38 479	14.23	1 653	929	592
1995	3 361 882	53 835	2 767 312	7 582	43 750	15.81	1 563	895	592
1996	3 622 385	70 199	2 893 647	7 906	54 931	18.98	1 507	850	566
1993:									
January	266 997	4 230	211 974	6 838	3 286	15.50	1 618	902	575
February	226 799	3 661	175 907	6 282	2 764	15.71	1 602	908	576
March	266 422	4 452	206 109	6 649	3 400	16.49	1 590	915	578
April	278 989	4 755	220 275	7 343	3 677	16.69	1 617	930	582
May	266 018	4 561	211 342	6 817	3 532	16.71	1 650	935	582
June	282 280	4 622	222 528	7 418	3 575	16.07	1 667	935	583
July	287 498	4 379	229 523	7 404	3 435	14.96	1 682	935	583
August	264 478	3 907	204 153	6 586	2 961	14.51	1 676	920	584
September	271 272	3 975	206 735	6 891	2 971	14.37	1 665	906	586
October	293 942	4 361	223 416	7 207	3 260	14.59	1 688	917	586
November	286 793	4 024	228 292	7 610	3 131	13.72	1 686	924	587
December	265 521	3 283	203 121	6 552	2 478	12.20	1 647	922	587
1994:									
January	267 794	3 210	205 957	6 644	2 398	11.64	1 620	922	587
February	246 832	3 168	176 918	6 319	2 138	12.09	1 581	917	587
March	291 130	3 620	219 839	7 092	2 585	11.76	1 578	928	590
April	276 807	3 689	217 213	7 240	2 792	12.85	1 585	926	591
May	279 542	4 010	216 618	6 988	3 044	14.05	1 612	923	591
June	303 935	4 672	248 057	8 269	3 767	15.18	1 615	912	592
July	309 733	5 039	245 642	7 924	3 952	16.09	1 654	924	592
August	310 550	5 067	242 485	7 822	3 873	15.97	1 659	920	592
September	309 759	4 683	260 423	8 681	3 905	15.00	1 677	921	592
October	268 835	4 004	221 030	7 130	3 270	14.80	1 673	935	592
November	281 242	4 348	229 157	7 639	3 508	15.31	1 687	938	592
December	269 889	4 024	220 858	7 124	3 248	14.70	1 654	929	592
1995:									
January	260 988	3 994	212 270	6 847	3 196	15.06	1 643	922	592
February	244 696	3 864	195 944	6 998	3 043	15.53	1 608	921	592
March	288 005	4 584	239 741	7 734	3 782	15.78	1 601	931	592
April	251 431	4 247	212 013	7 067	3 553	16.76	1 601	928	592
May	287 411	5 066	240 514	7 759	4 184	17.40	1 612	924	592
June	291 331	4 980	241 982	8 066	4 061	16.78	1 609	920	592
July	299 639	4 717	245 447	7 918	3 807	15.51	1 624	907	592
August	294 480	4 542	240 839	7 769	3 665	15.22	1 614	899	592
September	300 142	4 644	244 875	8 163	3 780	15.44	1 620	898	592
October	274 218	4 232	226 375	7 302	3 451	15.25	1 607	903	592
November	285 510	4 383	231 567	7 719	3 498	15.10	1 604	911	592
December	284 030	4 582	235 746	7 605	3 730	15.82	1 563	895	592
1996:									
January	306 887	5 196	238 990	7 709	3 927	16.43	1 544	895	592
February	252 634	4 181	198 120	6 832	3 189	16.10	1 500	893	592
March	255 345	4 544	201 663	6 505	3 492	17.31	1 482	889	589
April	297 886	5 861	238 198	7 940	4 589	19.27	1 502	890	586
May	323 841	6 274	261 641	8 440	4 945	18.90	1 520	890	586
June	309 546	5 637	253 014	8 434	4 544	17.96	1 546	899	584
July	339 099	6 221	275 225	8 878	4 998	18.16	1 550	891	583
August	307 806	5 844	250 957	8 095	4 681	18.65	1 545	891	578
September	316 593	6 402	260 375	8 679	5 200	19.97	1 551	876	574
October	314 661	6 842	250 694	8 087	5 367	21.41	1 533	882	574
November	275 355	5 998	216 953	7 232	4 638	21.38	1 522	869	570
December	322 733	7 199	247 816	7 994	5 361	21.63	1 507	850	566

Construction and Housing

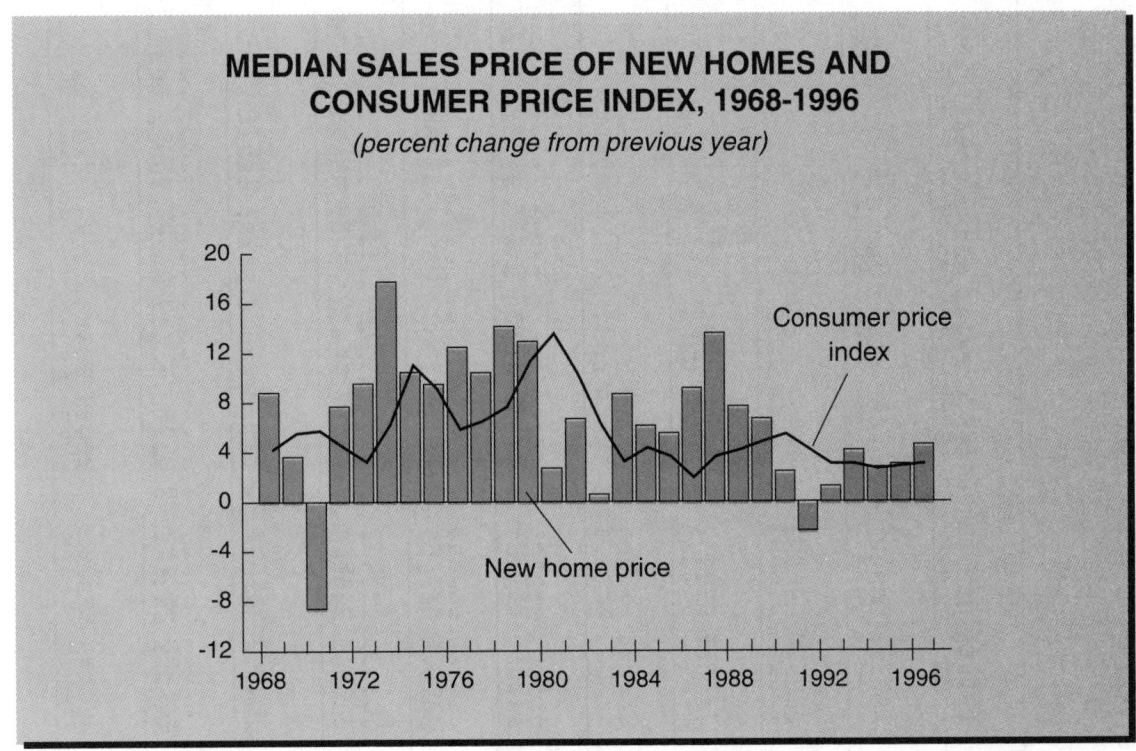

**MEDIAN SALES PRICE OF NEW HOMES AND
CONSUMER PRICE INDEX, 1968-1996**

(percent change from previous year)

During the 1970s and much of the 1980s, increases in the prices of new homes were substantially more rapid than the overall rate of consumer price increase. From 1990-1996, in contrast, the rise in new-home prices was more nearly in line with the overall increase in consumer prices. Factors contributing to the slowdown in the rate of increase in new-home prices may have included reduced rates of new household formation and changed perceptions of the likely rate of return on investment in a new home.

CONSTRUCTION AND HOUSING

CONSTRUCTION COSTS, PRICES, EMPLOYMENT, HOURS, AND EARNINGS

YEAR AND MONTH	Construction cost indexes (1992=100)		Producer price index (June 1986=100, not seasonally adjusted)			Employment, hours, and earnings (Seasonally adjusted)									
						Employment (Thousands)					Production workers			
											Hours worked		Average earnings (Dollars)	
	Fixed weight index	Implicit deflator	Inputs to construction industries	Maintenance and repair construction	New construction	Total	Production workers	General building contractors	Heavy construction, except building	Special trade contractors	Average weekly hours	Aggregate weekly hours index (1982=100)	Hourly	Weekly
1968	25.2	25.0	....	....	....	3 350	2 822	976	....	....	37.3	95.6	4.41	164.49
1969	26.9	26.8	....	....	....	3 575	3 012	1 071	....	....	37.9	103.6	4.79	181.54
1970	28.4	28.4	....	....	....	3 588	2 990	1 066	....	....	37.3	101.3	5.24	195.45
1971	30.4	30.3	....	....	....	3 704	3 071	1 102	....	....	37.2	103.6	5.69	211.67
1972	32.4	32.2	....	....	....	3 889	3 257	1 165	774	1 951	36.5	107.9	6.06	221.19
1973	35.3	35.0	....	....	....	4 097	3 405	1 221	790	2 087	36.8	113.7	6.41	235.89
1974	39.7	39.7	....	....	....	4 020	3 294	1 192	799	2 029	36.6	109.5	6.81	249.25
1975	43.2	43.4	....	....	....	3 525	2 808	1 012	734	1 779	36.4	92.7	7.31	266.08
1976	45.5	45.5	....	....	....	3 576	2 814	1 022	747	1 806	36.8	94.0	7.71	283.73
1977	49.2	49.1	....	....	....	3 851	3 021	1 108	760	1 983	36.5	100.2	8.10	295.65
1978	54.4	54.6	....	....	....	4 229	3 354	1 229	828	2 173	36.8	112.2	8.66	318.69
1979	61.3	61.1	....	....	....	4 463	3 565	1 272	898	2 293	37.0	119.9	9.27	342.99
1980	68.6	67.8	....	....	....	4 346	3 421	1 173	895	2 278	37.0	115.1	9.94	367.78
1981	74.0	72.9	....	....	....	4 188	3 261	1 094	865	2 229	36.9	109.3	10.82	399.26
1982	76.0	75.7	....	....	....	3 904	2 998	990	795	2 119	36.7	100.0	11.63	426.82
1983	77.7	77.1	....	....	....	3 946	3 031	1 019	753	2 174	37.1	102.2	11.94	442.97
1984	80.6	79.7	....	....	....	4 380	3 404	1 161	758	2 462	37.8	116.8	12.13	458.51
1985	82.9	81.8	....	....	....	4 668	3 655	1 251	765	2 652	37.7	125.3	12.32	464.46
1986	86.2	84.8	....	....	....	4 810	3 770	1 289	750	2 771	37.4	128.2	12.48	466.75
1987	89.4	87.9	101.5	101.3	101.6	4 958	3 870	1 318	739	2 901	37.8	132.7	12.71	480.44
1988	92.6	91.2	106.1	106.0	106.1	5 098	3 980	1 350	743	3 005	37.9	136.9	13.08	495.73
1989	95.8	94.8	111.0	110.9	111.0	5 171	4 035	1 332	767	3 072	37.9	138.9	13.54	513.17
1990	98.5	97.8	113.4	113.6	113.3	5 120	3 974	1 298	770	3 051	38.2	138.0	13.77	526.01
1991	99.3	98.7	114.8	115.1	114.6	4 650	3 549	1 140	727	2 783	38.1	122.8	14.00	533.40
1992	100.0	100.0	116.7	116.2	116.9	4 492	3 431	1 077	711	2 704	38.0	118.4	14.15	537.70
1993	103.7	103.8	121.4	119.4	122.2	4 668	3 589	1 120	713	2 836	38.5	125.4	14.38	553.63
1994	108.0	108.1	125.0	122.3	125.9	4 986	3 858	1 188	740	3 058	38.9	136.3	14.73	573.00
1995	112.5	112.4	129.1	127.1	129.8	5 160	3 993	1 207	752	3 201	38.9	140.8	15.09	587.00
1996	115.0	115.2	131.2	129.3	131.8	5 400	4 184	1 254	770	3 377	39.0	148.1	15.46	602.94
1993:														
January	101.8	102.1	119.0	117.7	119.5	4 519	3 446	1 085	690	2 744	38.2	119.5	14.21	542.82
February	102.2	102.4	120.5	118.5	121.1	4 613	3 555	1 099	714	2 800	38.0	122.7	14.23	540.74
March	103.0	103.1	121.8	119.3	122.6	4 551	3 489	1 091	699	2 761	38.1	120.7	14.34	546.35
April	103.4	103.5	122.2	119.7	123.0	4 577	3 511	1 103	697	2 777	38.4	122.4	14.34	550.66
May	103.1	103.2	121.6	119.4	122.4	4 641	3 565	1 115	709	2 817	38.5	124.6	14.36	552.86
June	102.9	103.0	121.1	119.2	121.8	4 650	3 571	1 117	717	2 816	38.4	124.5	14.34	550.66
July	103.4	103.5	120.9	119.1	121.5	4 677	3 597	1 121	718	2 838	38.6	126.1	14.42	556.61
August	104.0	104.1	121.1	119.3	121.8	4 699	3 612	1 123	718	2 858	38.6	126.6	14.41	556.23
September	104.4	104.5	121.8	119.7	122.5	4 713	3 628	1 127	718	2 868	38.8	127.8	14.38	557.94
October	104.7	104.7	122.0	119.9	122.7	4 756	3 655	1 142	722	2 892	38.4	127.5	14.43	554.11
November	105.3	105.3	122.5	120.1	123.3	4 780	3 683	1 149	723	2 908	38.9	130.1	14.46	562.49
December	105.8	105.6	122.8	120.2	123.7	4 806	3 709	1 158	724	2 924	38.7	130.4	14.46	559.60
1994:														
January	106.2	106.2	123.6	120.7	124.6	4 813	3 716	1 158	725	2 930	38.6	130.3	14.43	557.00
February	106.3	106.5	123.7	121.0	124.7	4 849	3 757	1 156	727	2 966	37.4	127.6	14.58	545.29
March	106.5	106.6	124.0	121.2	125.0	4 894	3 793	1 174	723	2 997	38.8	133.7	14.55	564.54
April	106.7	106.7	123.8	121.2	124.7	4 949	3 845	1 182	739	3 028	38.4	134.1	14.60	560.64
May	107.1	107.0	123.9	121.4	124.8	4 971	3 841	1 185	743	3 043	39.0	136.0	14.66	571.74
June	107.5	107.4	124.7	122.1	125.6	4 983	3 855	1 186	739	3 058	38.7	135.5	14.69	568.50
July	107.9	107.8	124.8	122.3	125.7	5 004	3 869	1 188	745	3 071	38.7	136.0	14.73	570.05
August	108.4	108.3	125.4	122.9	126.3	5 015	3 876	1 196	742	3 077	38.7	136.2	14.75	570.83
September	108.9	108.8	125.8	123.2	126.7	5 047	3 902	1 202	744	3 101	38.7	137.1	14.82	573.53
October	109.5	109.5	126.0	123.4	126.9	5 055	3 898	1 207	741	3 107	38.6	136.6	14.93	576.30
November	110.3	110.2	126.8	124.1	127.7	5 095	3 944	1 209	747	3 139	38.8	139.0	14.87	576.96
December	111.1	111.0	126.9	124.2	127.8	5 109	3 959	1 210	748	3 151	39.1	140.6	14.86	581.03
1995:														
January	111.7	111.6	127.6	125.2	128.5	5 129	3 984	1 212	750	3 167	39.4	142.6	14.71	579.57
February	111.7	111.7	127.9	125.7	128.7	5 134	4 004	1 203	746	3 185	38.0	138.2	14.96	568.48
March	111.7	111.7	128.6	126.4	129.3	5 130	3 978	1 207	752	3 171	38.8	140.2	14.98	581.22
April	111.8	111.9	129.1	127.1	129.8	5 140	3 974	1 205	750	3 185	38.5	138.9	15.02	578.27
May	112.1	112.1	129.3	127.4	130.0	5 114	3 954	1 196	743	3 175	37.8	135.7	15.04	568.51
June	112.6	112.5	129.2	127.5	129.8	5 137	3 971	1 199	746	3 192	38.7	139.6	15.12	585.14
July	112.6	112.6	129.5	127.6	130.2	5 149	3 981	1 203	750	3 196	38.9	140.6	15.11	587.78
August	112.6	112.7	129.7	127.8	130.4	5 173	4 001	1 205	753	3 215	38.7	140.6	15.14	585.92
September	113.0	113.1	130.0	127.9	130.6	5 205	4 025	1 209	759	3 237	38.7	141.5	15.16	586.69
October	113.3	113.4	129.6	127.6	130.2	5 225	4 040	1 215	761	3 249	39.1	143.5	15.19	593.93
November	113.2	113.4	129.2	127.4	129.9	5 236	4 043	1 220	759	3 257	38.7	142.1	15.22	589.01
December	113.3	113.5	129.2	127.5	129.8	5 232	4 036	1 222	754	3 256	38.4	140.7	15.18	582.91
1996:														
January	113.6	113.8	129.4	127.8	129.9	5 214	4 051	1 221	744	3 249	38.3	140.9	15.26	584.46
February	113.8	113.9	129.4	127.8	130.0	5 309	4 121	1 234	768	3 307	39.2	146.7	15.25	597.80
March	113.8	114.1	129.8	128.2	130.4	5 340	4 141	1 242	775	3 323	38.7	145.5	15.27	590.95
April	113.7	114.0	130.3	128.7	130.9	5 356	4 146	1 247	768	3 341	38.8	146.1	15.32	594.42
May	114.1	114.3	131.3	129.5	132.0	5 384	4 170	1 254	771	3 359	38.5	145.8	15.37	591.75
June	114.5	114.8	131.5	129.5	132.2	5 408	4 183	1 260	775	3 373	38.8	147.4	15.41	597.91
July	115.2	115.5	131.2	129.4	131.9	5 417	4 193	1 258	773	3 386	38.7	147.4	15.47	598.69
August	115.5	115.7	131.6	129.7	132.3	5 433	4 206	1 261	774	3 398	38.8	148.2	15.52	602.18
September	116.0	116.1	132.3	130.2	133.1	5 441	4 214	1 259	771	3 411	38.7	148.1	15.59	603.33
October	116.3	116.2	132.0	130.1	132.7	5 467	4 229	1 265	771	3 431	38.9	149.4	15.58	606.06
November	116.4	116.3	132.6	130.4	133.3	5 495	4 256	1 272	773	3 450	38.8	150.0	15.58	604.50
December	116.7	116.6	132.5	130.4	133.3	5 521	4 281	1 281	772	3 468	38.9	151.2	15.69	610.34

	General building contractors				Heavy construction, except building				Special trade contractors			
CONSTRUCTION EMPLOYMENT, HOURS, AND EARNINGS—Continued (Not seasonally adjusted)												
YEAR AND MONTH	Production workers (Thousands)	Average weekly hours	Average earnings		Production workers (Thousands)	Average weekly hours	Average earnings		Production workers (Thousands)	Average weekly hours	Average earnings	
			Hourly	Weekly			Hourly	Weekly			Hourly	Weekly
1968	846	36.1	4.24	153.06	....	....	....	....	....	....	....	....
1969	929	36.6	4.62	169.09	....	....	....	....	....	....	....	....
1970	910	36.3	5.02	182.23	....	....	....	....	....	....	....	....
1971	936	36.1	5.33	192.41	....	....	....	....	....	....	....	....
1972	976	35.7	5.58	199.21	666	39.3	5.57	218.90	1 615	35.8	6.58	235.56
1973	1 009	35.8	5.87	210.15	665	39.9	5.85	233.42	1 731	36.1	6.97	251.62
1974	967	35.9	6.24	224.02	663	39.7	6.31	250.51	1 663	35.8	7.36	263.49
1975	799	35.9	6.78	243.40	593	39.2	6.81	266.95	1 416	35.5	7.85	278.68
1976	800	36.4	7.15	260.26	597	39.3	7.31	287.28	1 417	36.0	8.20	295.20
1977	865	36.3	7.52	272.98	594	38.8	7.56	293.33	1 562	35.8	8.65	309.67
1978	955	35.8	8.00	286.40	669	40.1	8.10	324.81	1 730	36.2	9.26	335.21
1979	989	35.9	8.61	309.10	743	40.2	8.65	347.73	1 833	36.4	9.90	360.36
1980	900	36.1	9.22	332.84	720	40.3	9.20	370.76	1 802	36.2	10.63	384.81
1981	825	36.0	9.85	354.60	693	40.1	10.31	413.43	1 743	36.1	11.50	415.15
1982	734	36.2	10.53	381.19	631	40.0	11.45	458.00	1 632	35.7	12.20	435.54
1983	751	36.6	10.73	392.72	604	40.4	11.86	479.14	1 676	36.2	12.53	453.59
1984	862	37.1	10.89	404.02	618	41.5	11.90	493.85	1 925	36.8	12.78	470.30
1985	935	37.1	11.23	416.63	629	41.4	12.08	500.11	2 092	36.9	12.89	475.64
1986	953	37.0	11.43	422.91	623	40.8	12.00	489.60	2 194	36.7	13.09	480.40
1987	963	37.3	11.72	437.16	618	41.5	12.07	500.91	2 290	37.0	13.31	492.47
1988	989	37.5	12.18	456.75	621	41.5	12.46	517.09	2 370	37.1	13.64	506.04
1989	969	37.5	12.71	476.63	639	41.5	13.19	547.39	2 427	37.1	13.98	518.66
1990	938	37.7	13.01	490.48	643	42.0	13.34	560.28	2 393	37.4	14.20	531.08
1991	811	37.6	13.27	498.95	600	41.6	13.77	572.83	2 137	37.4	14.35	536.69
1992	761	37.5	13.45	504.38	588	41.6	13.96	580.74	2 083	37.2	14.47	538.28
1993	790	37.7	13.64	514.23	593	42.1	14.10	593.61	2 206	37.8	14.73	556.79
1994	843	38.1	13.97	532.26	618	42.6	14.44	615.14	2 397	38.3	15.08	577.56
1995	856	38.3	14.33	548.84	626	42.5	14.65	622.63	2 511	38.1	15.47	589.41
1996	886	38.2	14.67	560.39	643	42.8	15.10	646.28	2 656	38.3	15.82	605.91
1993:												
January	707	36.1	13.62	491.68	458	38.1	13.59	517.78	1 908	35.7	14.60	521.22
February	705	36.7	13.54	496.92	476	39.6	13.52	535.39	1 909	36.0	14.52	522.72
March	704	37.0	13.63	504.31	494	41.2	13.94	574.33	1 927	36.7	14.63	536.92
April	738	37.4	13.63	509.76	553	41.0	13.86	568.26	2 071	37.1	14.62	542.40
May	784	38.1	13.58	517.40	618	43.1	14.16	610.30	2 220	38.6	14.65	565.49
June	821	38.0	13.46	511.48	646	43.2	14.04	606.53	2 297	38.6	14.60	563.56
July	845	38.2	13.53	516.85	655	43.5	14.12	614.22	2 376	39.0	14.76	575.64
August	849	38.5	13.63	524.76	664	44.1	14.28	629.75	2 413	38.9	14.81	576.11
September	836	37.4	13.71	512.75	672	42.2	14.43	608.95	2 383	37.6	14.86	558.74
October	842	38.4	13.78	529.15	674	43.2	14.49	625.97	2 387	38.6	14.87	573.98
November	836	37.9	13.74	520.75	638	42.3	14.26	603.20	2 338	37.9	14.82	561.68
December	817	37.8	13.78	520.88	566	41.0	13.94	571.54	2 246	37.9	14.89	564.33
1994:												
January	764	36.6	13.75	503.25	490	39.8	13.89	552.82	2 053	36.6	14.83	542.78
February	744	36.0	13.86	498.96	486	38.5	13.93	536.31	2 027	35.7	14.85	530.15
March	767	37.7	13.84	521.77	517	41.0	13.93	571.13	2 115	37.7	14.85	559.85
April	802	37.8	13.87	524.29	595	41.8	14.10	589.38	2 288	37.7	14.87	560.60
May	835	38.6	13.84	534.22	652	44.0	14.40	633.60	2 422	39.0	14.97	583.83
June	875	38.5	13.73	528.61	673	43.7	14.40	629.28	2 517	39.0	14.96	583.44
July	895	38.6	13.85	534.61	687	43.7	14.57	636.71	2 589	39.2	15.13	593.10
August	906	38.7	13.95	539.87	690	44.3	14.66	649.44	2 612	39.0	15.15	590.85
September	894	38.8	14.19	550.57	699	44.7	14.86	664.24	2 594	39.2	15.31	600.15
October	893	38.7	14.27	552.25	692	43.3	15.06	652.10	2 574	38.9	15.37	597.89
November	883	38.3	14.22	544.63	659	41.9	14.54	609.23	2 541	37.7	15.25	574.93
December	859	38.6	14.20	548.12	582	41.4	14.30	592.02	2 431	38.2	15.25	582.55
1995:												
January	803	37.7	14.17	534.21	503	40.6	13.82	561.09	2 239	37.1	15.12	560.95
February	780	37.1	14.23	527.93	499	39.3	14.15	556.10	2 191	36.4	15.28	556.19
March	791	37.9	14.15	536.29	539	41.2	14.26	587.51	2 275	37.5	15.31	574.13
April	820	37.5	14.21	532.88	603	40.7	14.38	585.27	2 406	37.0	15.33	567.21
May	845	38.0	14.24	541.12	648	41.8	14.56	608.61	2 513	37.8	15.39	581.74
June	886	38.5	14.14	544.39	676	43.8	14.76	646.49	2 618	38.9	15.42	599.84
July	906	38.7	14.26	551.86	688	44.6	14.90	664.54	2 675	39.3	15.51	609.54
August	912	38.8	14.31	555.23	697	44.1	14.95	659.30	2 704	39.0	15.58	607.62
September	898	38.9	14.51	564.44	710	44.4	15.14	672.22	2 684	39.1	15.69	613.48
October	894	39.1	14.57	569.69	709	44.8	15.09	676.03	2 684	39.2	15.69	615.05
November	880	38.3	14.57	558.03	659	41.7	14.76	615.49	2 630	38.0	15.63	593.94
December	857	38.0	14.58	554.04	583	41.2	14.27	587.92	2 511	37.4	15.58	582.69
1996:												
January	803	36.7	14.67	538.39	498	39.8	14.52	577.90	2 320	36.1	15.65	564.97
February	798	38.1	14.57	555.12	517	41.2	14.35	591.22	2 339	37.6	15.57	585.43
March	811	37.9	14.58	552.58	558	41.4	14.35	594.09	2 393	37.5	15.57	583.88
April	845	38.4	14.56	559.10	622	42.4	14.70	623.28	2 532	37.8	15.58	588.92
May	883	38.2	14.60	557.72	671	42.2	14.91	629.20	2 661	38.2	15.63	597.07
June	925	38.6	14.48	558.93	699	43.7	15.20	664.24	2 762	38.9	15.67	609.56
July	942	38.6	14.57	562.40	711	44.2	15.46	683.33	2 840	39.1	15.83	618.95
August	948	38.6	14.58	562.79	719	44.2	15.51	685.54	2 861	39.2	15.91	623.67
September	931	38.5	14.85	571.73	724	44.5	15.69	698.21	2 839	38.9	16.06	624.73
October	927	38.6	14.76	569.74	719	44.5	15.70	698.65	2 839	39.2	16.08	630.34
November	920	38.1	14.81	564.26	675	42.4	15.24	646.18	2 793	38.2	15.98	610.44
December	902	38.1	14.96	569.98	602	41.4	14.76	611.06	2 688	38.1	16.12	614.17

NEW CONSTRUCTION PUT IN PLACE
(Billions of dollars, not seasonally adjusted)

YEAR AND MONTH	Total	Private Total[1]	Residential Total	Residential New housing units	Nonresidential buildings[1] Total	Industrial	Office	Hotels, motels	Other commercial buildings	Tele-communications	Public Total[1]	Housing and re-development	Industrial	Military facilities	Highways and streets
1968	96.8	69.4	34.2	26.7	23.8	8.5	7.8	1.3	9.1	1.7	27.4	0.8	0.4	0.8	9.3
1969	104.9	77.2	37.2	29.2	27.7	9.6	9.4	1.5	11.1	2.2	27.8	1.1	0.4	0.9	9.3
1970	105.9	78.0	35.9	27.1	28.2	9.3	9.9	1.5	11.6	3.0	27.9	1.1	0.3	0.7	10.0
1971	122.4	92.7	48.5	38.7	29.3	7.8	11.8	1.5	13.8	3.0	29.7	1.1	0.4	0.9	10.7
1972	139.1	109.1	60.7	50.1	32.4	6.7	6.8	2.2	9.8	3.3	30.0	0.9	0.4	1.1	10.4
1973	153.8	121.4	65.1	54.6	37.6	9.0	7.8	2.5	11.4	4.0	32.4	0.9	0.5	1.2	10.5
1974	155.2	117.0	56.0	43.4	39.9	11.5	8.0	1.8	11.9	4.3	38.1	1.0	0.6	1.2	12.1
1975	152.6	109.3	51.6	36.3	35.4	11.7	6.5	1.2	9.5	3.8	43.3	1.4	0.7	1.4	13.2
1976	172.1	128.2	68.3	50.8	34.6	10.5	6.3	1.0	9.7	3.9	44.0	1.3	0.7	1.6	12.4
1977	200.5	157.4	92.0	72.2	38.3	11.3	7.0	1.1	11.6	4.5	43.1	1.5	0.8	1.4	12.5
1978	239.9	189.7	109.8	85.6	48.8	16.2	8.7	1.4	14.7	5.6	50.2	1.4	0.9	1.5	14.2
1979	272.9	216.2	116.4	89.3	64.8	22.0	12.6	2.5	19.0	6.9	56.7	1.7	1.1	1.7	17.1
1980	273.9	210.3	100.4	69.6	72.5	20.5	17.8	3.4	20.5	7.8	63.7	2.0	1.4	1.9	18.2
1981	289.1	224.4	99.2	69.4	85.6	25.4	23.5	4.3	20.8	8.2	64.7	2.4	1.7	2.0	18.4
1982	279.3	216.3	84.7	57.0	92.7	26.1	31.3	4.8	17.8	8.5	63.1	2.3	1.6	2.2	17.3
1983	311.6	248.1	125.5	94.7	87.1	19.5	28.3	6.1	18.9	7.6	63.5	2.6	1.8	2.5	17.9
1984	369.0	298.8	153.9	113.8	107.7	20.9	35.6	8.0	28.0	8.1	70.2	2.7	1.8	2.8	21.6
1985	401.4	323.6	158.5	114.7	127.5	24.1	43.6	8.8	35.7	8.4	77.8	2.9	2.0	3.2	23.7
1986	429.9	345.3	187.2	133.2	120.9	21.0	39.4	8.9	35.8	9.1	84.6	3.0	1.7	3.9	25.3
1987	441.7	351.0	194.7	139.9	123.3	21.2	36.9	8.9	37.3	9.2	90.7	3.3	1.5	4.3	27.1
1988	455.6	360.9	198.1	139.0	130.9	23.2	39.3	8.3	38.9	9.6	94.7	3.3	1.4	3.6	29.1
1989	469.8	371.6	196.6	139.2	140.0	28.8	40.1	9.3	39.8	9.6	98.2	3.4	1.3	3.5	28.8
1990	468.5	361.1	182.9	128.0	143.5	33.6	35.1	10.7	40.1	9.8	107.5	3.8	1.4	2.7	32.1
1991	424.2	314.1	157.8	110.6	116.6	31.4	26.0	6.9	29.4	9.0	110.1	3.6	1.8	1.8	32.0
1992	452.1	336.2	187.8	129.6	105.7	29.0	20.3	3.7	29.2	9.0	115.9	4.1	1.9	2.5	33.1
1993	478.7	362.7	210.5	144.1	110.6	26.5	20.9	4.6	32.5	9.6	116.0	4.0	1.7	2.5	34.3
1994	519.9	399.4	238.9	167.9	120.3	29.0	22.2	4.7	37.6	10.1	120.5	3.7	1.5	2.3	37.4
1995	534.1	406.8	230.7	162.9	135.0	32.5	25.6	7.1	42.7	11.1	127.3	4.3	1.5	3.0	36.5
1996	568.6	437.1	247.2	179.5	149.4	32.1	27.6	11.8	47.3	12.0	131.5	4.5	1.4	2.5	37.8
1993:															
January	31.2	24.3	13.3	9.3	7.9	2.1	1.7	0.3	2.2	0.6	6.9	0.3	0.2	0.2	1.2
February	30.6	23.6	12.5	8.8	7.9	2.0	1.7	0.3	2.1	0.6	7.0	0.4	0.1	0.2	1.3
March	34.4	26.7	14.7	10.3	8.6	2.3	1.8	0.4	2.3	0.8	7.7	0.4	0.2	0.2	1.5
April	37.1	28.2	16.1	10.8	8.6	2.0	1.9	0.3	2.4	0.8	8.9	0.4	0.2	0.2	2.1
May	40.1	30.6	17.8	11.7	9.3	2.2	1.9	0.5	2.7	0.7	9.5	0.4	0.1	0.2	2.8
June	43.6	32.6	19.4	12.7	9.6	2.2	1.8	0.5	2.8	0.9	11.0	0.4	0.1	0.2	3.8
July	44.1	32.8	19.9	13.3	9.3	2.2	1.7	0.4	2.7	0.8	11.3	0.3	0.1	0.2	3.7
August	45.9	34.1	20.5	13.8	10.0	2.3	1.8	0.4	3.0	0.8	11.9	0.3	0.1	0.2	4.0
September	45.9	33.7	19.9	13.9	10.2	2.3	1.7	0.5	3.2	0.8	12.2	0.3	0.2	0.2	4.4
October	44.5	33.8	20.2	13.9	10.0	2.3	1.7	0.4	3.2	0.8	10.8	0.3	0.1	0.2	4.0
November	42.9	32.8	19.4	13.7	9.9	2.2	1.7	0.4	3.2	0.9	10.0	0.3	0.1	0.2	3.3
December	38.4	29.6	16.8	11.9	9.5	2.4	1.7	0.3	2.8	1.0	8.8	0.3	0.2	0.2	2.4
1994:															
January	32.8	25.8	15.1	11.0	7.9	1.9	1.5	0.3	2.2	0.6	6.9	0.2	0.1	0.2	1.5
February	31.9	25.0	14.2	10.3	8.0	2.0	1.6	0.4	2.1	0.7	6.9	0.2	0.1	0.1	1.4
March	37.2	29.6	17.0	12.4	9.3	2.1	1.9	0.4	2.6	0.9	7.6	0.3	0.1	0.1	1.8
April	40.5	32.1	18.9	13.2	9.8	2.3	1.9	0.5	2.9	0.7	8.4	0.3	0.1	0.2	2.3
May	44.7	34.8	21.0	14.4	10.4	2.5	2.0	0.5	3.1	0.8	9.9	0.3	0.1	0.2	3.3
June	48.0	36.6	22.5	15.3	10.5	2.4	1.8	0.4	3.4	0.9	11.4	0.3	0.1	0.2	3.9
July	48.5	36.6	22.9	15.8	10.2	2.4	1.7	0.3	3.5	0.8	12.0	0.3	0.1	0.2	4.4
August	50.8	37.9	23.3	16.1	10.9	2.5	1.9	0.4	3.7	1.0	12.9	0.3	0.1	0.2	4.8
September	50.3	37.4	22.7	16.1	11.2	2.7	2.0	0.4	3.8	0.9	12.9	0.3	0.2	0.3	4.5
October	48.7	36.7	22.3	15.5	10.9	2.6	1.9	0.4	3.8	0.9	12.0	0.4	0.1	0.2	4.3
November	45.9	35.4	21.0	15.0	11.0	2.9	2.1	0.4	3.4	0.9	10.5	0.3	0.1	0.2	3.1
December	40.8	31.4	18.0	12.9	10.2	2.7	1.8	0.4	3.1	1.0	9.3	0.4	0.1	0.2	2.1
1995:															
January	36.2	28.3	15.9	11.7	9.3	2.2	1.9	0.5	2.8	0.8	7.9	0.3	0.1	0.2	1.5
February	35.2	27.6	14.8	10.8	9.7	2.4	1.9	0.5	2.9	0.7	7.6	0.3	0.1	0.2	1.4
March	39.6	31.0	17.0	12.3	10.5	2.6	2.1	0.6	3.3	0.9	8.6	0.3	0.1	0.3	1.8
April	42.1	32.6	18.2	12.6	10.9	2.8	2.2	0.5	3.3	0.9	9.5	0.4	0.1	0.2	2.2
May	45.7	34.7	19.7	13.3	11.4	2.9	2.4	0.6	3.4	0.9	10.9	0.4	0.1	0.3	3.2
June	48.4	36.2	20.8	13.9	11.8	2.8	2.2	0.6	3.9	1.1	12.1	0.4	0.1	0.3	3.7
July	48.7	36.8	21.3	14.7	11.9	2.8	2.3	0.6	3.8	1.0	12.0	0.4	0.1	0.3	4.0
August	50.9	37.6	22.0	15.3	12.0	2.7	2.3	0.6	3.9	1.0	13.3	0.4	0.1	0.3	4.7
September	50.4	37.2	21.6	15.5	12.2	2.9	2.2	0.6	4.1	1.0	13.2	0.4	0.2	0.4	4.3
October	49.5	37.3	21.6	15.4	12.2	2.8	2.1	0.6	4.1	1.0	12.2	0.4	0.1	0.2	4.4
November	46.4	35.5	20.4	14.8	11.8	2.8	2.1	0.8	3.8	1.0	10.9	0.4	0.1	0.3	3.2
December	41.0	31.9	17.5	12.7	11.4	2.8	2.0	0.8	3.5	0.9	9.1	0.4	0.1	0.3	2.2
1996:															
January	37.4	29.2	15.7	11.7	10.5	2.5	1.8	0.8	3.2	0.8	8.2	0.4	0.1	0.3	1.6
February	36.2	28.6	14.9	11.2	10.6	2.4	1.9	0.9	3.2	0.9	7.6	0.3	0.1	0.2	1.6
March	40.1	31.6	17.6	13.2	10.9	2.5	1.9	0.9	3.3	0.9	8.4	0.3	0.1	0.2	1.8
April	44.6	34.7	19.7	14.3	11.7	2.6	2.1	1.0	3.7	1.0	9.9	0.3	0.1	0.2	2.5
May	48.5	37.0	21.7	15.3	12.1	2.5	2.4	0.9	3.9	1.0	11.5	0.4	0.1	0.2	3.3
June	51.3	39.4	23.2	16.4	12.9	2.7	2.5	1.0	4.1	0.9	11.9	0.4	0.1	0.2	3.7
July	52.5	39.9	23.7	16.9	12.7	2.6	2.4	1.0	4.1	1.0	12.7	0.4	0.1	0.2	4.2
August	54.5	41.4	24.2	17.3	13.5	2.6	2.5	1.1	4.5	1.1	13.1	0.4	0.1	0.2	4.3
September	54.8	40.8	23.4	17.1	13.8	2.9	2.6	1.1	4.5	1.0	14.0	0.5	0.2	0.3	4.5
October	54.1	41.1	23.1	16.7	14.3	3.1	2.5	1.1	4.7	1.1	13.0	0.4	0.1	0.2	4.5
November	50.6	39.0	21.7	16.0	13.8	2.9	2.6	1.1	4.4	1.1	11.6	0.4	0.1	0.2	3.3
December	44.1	34.6	18.3	13.4	12.9	2.7	2.4	1.1	3.9	1.3	9.5	0.4	0.1	0.2	2.4

1. Includes categories not shown separately.

YEAR AND MONTH	Total	Private										Public				
		Total[1]	Residential		Nonresidential buildings[1]					Tele-com-munica-tions		Total[1]	Housing and re-develop-ment	Industrial	Military facilities	High-ways and streets
			Total	New housing units	Total	Industrial	Office	Hotels, motels	Other commer-cial buildings							
1968	96.8	69.4	34.2	26.7	23.8	8.5	7.8	1.3	9.1	1.7		27.4	0.8	0.4	0.8	9.3
1969	104.9	77.2	37.2	29.2	27.7	9.6	9.4	1.5	11.1	2.2		27.8	1.1	0.4	0.9	9.3
1970	105.9	78.0	35.9	27.1	28.2	9.3	9.9	1.5	11.6	3.0		27.9	1.1	0.3	0.7	10.0
1971	122.4	92.7	48.5	38.7	29.3	7.8	11.8	1.5	13.8	3.0		29.7	1.1	0.4	0.9	10.7
1972	139.1	109.1	60.7	50.1	32.4	6.7	6.8	2.2	9.8	3.3		30.0	0.9	0.4	1.1	10.4
1973	153.8	121.4	65.1	54.6	37.6	9.0	7.8	2.5	11.4	4.0		32.4	0.9	0.5	1.2	10.5
1974	155.2	117.0	56.0	43.4	39.9	11.5	8.0	1.8	11.9	4.3		38.1	1.0	0.6	1.2	12.1
1975	152.6	109.3	51.6	36.3	35.4	11.7	6.5	1.2	9.5	3.8		43.3	1.4	0.7	1.4	13.2
1976	172.1	128.2	68.3	50.8	34.6	10.5	6.3	1.0	9.7	3.9		44.0	1.3	0.7	1.6	12.4
1977	200.5	157.4	92.0	72.2	38.3	11.3	7.0	1.1	11.6	4.5		43.1	1.5	0.8	1.4	12.5
1978	239.9	189.7	109.8	85.6	48.8	16.2	8.7	1.4	14.7	5.6		50.2	1.4	0.9	1.5	14.2
1979	272.9	216.2	116.4	89.3	64.8	22.0	12.6	2.5	19.0	6.9		56.7	1.7	1.1	1.7	17.1
1980	273.9	210.3	100.4	69.6	72.5	20.5	17.8	3.4	20.5	7.8		63.7	2.0	1.4	1.9	18.2
1981	289.1	224.4	99.2	69.4	85.6	25.4	23.5	4.3	20.8	8.2		64.7	2.4	1.7	2.0	18.4
1982	279.3	216.3	84.7	57.0	92.7	26.1	31.3	4.8	17.8	8.5		63.1	2.3	1.6	2.2	17.3
1983	311.6	248.1	125.5	94.7	87.1	19.5	28.3	6.1	18.9	7.6		63.5	2.6	1.8	2.5	17.9
1984	369.0	298.8	153.9	113.8	107.7	20.9	35.6	8.0	28.0	8.1		70.2	2.7	1.8	2.8	21.6
1985	401.4	323.6	158.5	114.7	127.5	24.1	43.6	8.8	35.7	8.4		77.8	2.9	2.0	3.2	23.7
1986	429.9	345.3	187.2	133.2	120.9	21.0	39.4	8.9	35.8	9.1		84.6	3.0	1.7	3.9	25.3
1987	441.7	351.0	194.7	139.9	123.3	21.2	36.9	8.9	37.3	9.2		90.7	3.3	1.5	4.3	27.1
1988	455.6	360.9	198.1	139.0	130.9	23.2	39.3	8.3	38.9	9.6		94.7	3.3	1.4	3.6	29.1
1989	469.8	371.6	196.6	139.2	140.0	28.8	40.1	9.3	39.8	9.6		98.2	3.4	1.3	3.5	28.8
1990	468.5	361.1	182.9	128.0	143.5	33.6	35.1	10.7	40.1	9.8		107.5	3.8	1.4	2.7	32.1
1991	424.2	314.1	157.8	110.6	116.6	31.4	26.0	6.9	29.4	9.0		110.1	3.6	1.8	1.8	32.0
1992	452.1	336.2	187.8	129.6	105.7	29.0	20.3	3.7	29.2	9.0		115.9	4.1	1.9	2.5	37.9
1993	478.7	362.7	210.5	144.1	110.6	26.5	20.9	4.6	32.5	9.6		116.0	4.0	1.7	2.5	34.3
1994	519.9	399.4	238.9	167.9	120.3	29.0	22.2	4.7	37.6	10.1		120.5	3.7	1.5	2.3	37.4
1995	534.1	406.8	230.7	162.9	135.0	32.5	25.6	7.1	42.7	11.1		127.3	4.3	1.5	3.0	36.5
1996	568.6	437.1	247.2	179.5	149.4	32.1	27.6	11.8	47.3	12.0		131.5	4.5	1.4	2.5	37.8
1993:																
January	463.9	355.2	204.5	136.7	106.8	27.5	21.7	3.6	31.2	10.0		108.7	4.5	1.9	2.6	27.6
February	467.5	353.2	203.5	138.1	107.0	27.1	21.7	3.6	31.1	9.3		114.3	4.8	1.9	2.9	31.4
March	468.3	354.9	204.3	138.2	108.7	28.4	21.2	4.6	31.1	10.0		113.4	4.5	2.0	2.7	31.3
April	468.6	349.8	202.6	137.3	105.4	25.2	22.0	3.6	30.0	9.2		118.8	5.1	2.0	2.7	32.5
May	469.2	356.7	204.1	138.1	111.3	27.0	21.5	5.3	32.5	9.1		112.5	4.5	1.5	2.4	32.2
June	476.3	358.9	207.0	140.4	110.5	25.1	21.2	5.3	32.3	9.4		117.4	4.7	1.4	2.3	37.0
July	477.3	359.8	208.3	142.5	109.0	26.5	21.0	4.7	29.9	9.6		117.5	4.0	1.6	2.5	34.5
August	477.2	362.5	210.4	144.7	111.7	26.6	20.3	4.9	31.3	9.2		114.7	3.3	1.7	2.6	32.0
September	483.5	367.0	212.7	147.0	113.8	26.3	19.7	5.5	33.8	9.3		116.6	3.3	1.6	2.2	36.1
October	483.1	368.8	216.2	149.7	112.1	25.7	19.9	4.8	33.8	9.5		114.3	3.3	1.7	2.3	36.4
November	493.2	376.4	221.7	153.8	113.9	25.4	19.6	5.0	36.3	10.0		116.8	3.3	1.5	2.3	35.7
December	505.4	384.9	227.7	159.5	115.5	27.4	21.1	2.9	35.3	10.8		120.6	3.3	2.0	2.2	36.7
1994:																
January	490.1	376.9	228.6	160.2	108.4	26.2	19.0	4.2	31.7	9.7		113.2	3.1	1.3	2.7	35.8
February	490.0	376.6	228.6	159.7	107.6	27.0	20.2	4.4	30.6	10.2		113.4	2.9	1.5	1.9	34.3
March	507.6	393.6	234.9	165.4	118.5	26.7	23.6	4.8	35.2	10.1		114.0	3.5	1.7	2.0	36.5
April	513.1	399.5	238.7	168.4	121.0	28.0	22.8	5.3	37.3	9.4		113.6	3.6	1.4	2.2	36.0
May	520.0	403.8	241.3	170.8	122.9	29.2	23.0	5.1	37.3	9.6		116.2	3.6	1.4	2.2	37.6
June	524.9	404.3	241.8	170.6	121.9	28.7	21.6	4.6	38.4	10.2		120.6	3.7	1.3	2.3	38.3
July	526.5	401.2	241.5	169.9	119.5	28.3	21.1	3.8	38.9	10.0		125.3	3.4	1.3	2.5	41.0
August	526.1	404.0	241.0	169.3	121.8	29.5	22.1	4.2	39.1	10.7		122.1	3.5	1.5	2.5	38.2
September	529.9	406.8	242.9	170.5	123.9	30.2	23.1	4.5	40.0	10.0		123.1	3.6	1.5	2.4	37.1
October	529.6	402.1	239.5	167.5	122.9	29.6	22.7	4.5	40.8	10.1		127.5	4.3	1.6	2.2	37.7
November	528.8	405.8	240.0	168.4	126.0	32.2	23.8	5.2	38.7	10.4		123.1	3.9	1.5	2.3	35.9
December	537.3	409.3	242.3	171.2	125.8	31.3	23.1	5.3	40.1	11.2		128.0	4.4	1.5	2.8	34.8
1995:																
January	535.1	409.6	241.0	170.0	126.2	29.8	24.3	6.0	39.8	11.2		125.5	4.1	1.7	2.8	34.9
February	536.9	412.7	237.7	166.3	131.3	32.3	24.4	6.0	42.0	10.7		124.3	4.1	1.7	2.7	34.0
March	538.3	411.0	235.1	164.5	133.8	32.2	25.2	7.4	43.6	11.3		127.4	4.2	1.6	3.3	36.3
April	536.9	407.3	229.6	160.3	135.3	34.4	26.0	5.5	42.2	12.0		129.6	4.3	1.6	2.8	35.8
May	528.9	401.8	226.6	157.9	134.4	33.8	27.2	6.2	40.6	10.4		127.1	4.1	1.4	2.9	35.9
June	529.6	400.6	222.9	155.1	136.4	33.1	26.5	6.6	43.7	11.7		129.0	4.5	1.3	3.1	35.9
July	532.3	406.7	224.8	157.6	139.5	34.3	28.3	6.9	42.9	12.3		125.7	4.3	1.4	3.1	36.6
August	529.2	401.8	227.6	161.3	134.2	31.9	26.3	6.9	41.7	10.8		127.3	4.4	1.5	3.1	37.7
September	533.2	406.1	230.0	163.7	136.0	32.2	25.3	7.3	43.3	11.1		127.1	4.2	1.6	3.3	36.3
October	534.7	407.5	231.4	165.6	136.3	31.6	24.6	7.6	44.0	10.8		127.2	4.5	1.5	2.3	37.9
November	536.6	408.7	232.7	166.6	136.8	32.4	24.0	9.4	43.6	10.7		127.9	4.4	1.4	3.1	36.8
December	541.9	414.7	235.4	169.2	139.1	32.1	25.1	9.7	44.4	10.7		127.2	4.4	1.4	3.3	37.8
1996:																
January	550.8	420.3	237.4	171.1	141.7	33.4	23.5	10.5	45.3	12.0		130.5	4.7	1.3	3.1	37.7
February	546.1	421.8	239.3	173.5	140.6	32.1	23.8	10.9	45.4	11.7		124.3	4.1	1.4	2.9	39.5
March	548.6	421.2	243.0	176.5	139.0	31.4	23.7	10.5	45.4	11.3		127.3	4.0	1.5	2.4	37.4
April	562.9	431.1	248.8	181.4	143.4	31.9	25.2	11.3	46.7	11.8		131.8	4.0	1.5	2.7	38.1
May	562.3	428.5	249.7	181.8	141.8	30.2	26.5	10.2	46.0	11.6		133.8	4.8	1.4	2.6	37.2
June	568.2	438.6	250.2	182.4	150.4	32.0	29.8	11.2	46.9	10.8		129.6	4.0	1.5	2.5	37.2
July	567.0	436.9	249.4	181.2	146.9	30.5	28.9	11.5	45.4	10.9		130.2	4.8	1.5	2.3	37.6
August	571.0	443.6	249.2	181.1	152.6	31.0	29.0	12.9	48.6	11.9		127.4	4.4	1.6	2.3	35.2
September	580.0	444.4	249.0	180.7	153.5	32.9	29.7	12.7	47.1	11.5		135.6	5.1	1.7	2.5	38.3
October	584.1	449.0	247.9	179.9	159.3	34.7	30.0	12.7	49.9	11.9		135.2	4.7	0.9	2.5	38.4
November	586.2	448.9	248.3	180.0	159.9	33.2	30.0	13.1	50.2	13.0		137.3	5.0	1.1	2.4	38.6
December	579.1	447.1	247.9	179.1	157.4	30.8	29.5	13.8	48.9	14.6		132.1	4.5	1.1	2.2	39.6

1. Includes categories not shown separately.

YEAR AND MONTH	HOUSING STARTS AND BUILDING PERMITS								NEW HOMES				
	New private housing units (Thousands)						Manufacturers' shipments of mobile homes (Thousands)		Seasonally adjusted			Sales price (Dollars)	
	Started (Not seasonally adjusted)		Seasonally adjusted annual rate										
			Started		Authorized by building permits [1]								
	Total	One-family structures	Total	One-family structures	Total	One-family structures	Not seasonally adjusted	Seasonally adjusted annual rate	Sold (Thousands)	For sale, end-of-period (Thousands)	Months supply at current rate (Months)	Median	Average
1968	1 507.6	899.4	1 508	899	1 353	695	318.0	318	....	....	....	24 700	26 600
1969	1 466.8	810.6	1 467	811	1 324	626	412.7	413	....	....	....	25 600	27 900
1970	1 433.6	812.9	1 434	813	1 352	647	401.2	401	....	....	....	23 400	26 600
1971	2 052.2	1 151.0	2 052	1 151	1 925	906	496.6	497	....	....	....	25 200	28 300
1972	2 356.6	1 309.2	2 357	1 309	2 219	1 033	575.9	576	....	....	....	27 600	30 500
1973	2 045.3	1 132.0	2 045	1 132	1 820	882	566.9	567	634	422	....	32 500	35 500
1974	1 337.7	888.1	1 338	888	1 074	644	329.3	329	519	350	....	35 900	38 900
1975	1 160.4	892.2	1 160	892	939	676	212.7	213	549	316	....	39 300	42 600
1976	1 537.5	1 162.4	1 538	1 162	1 296	894	246.1	246	646	358	....	44 200	48 000
1977	1 987.1	1 450.9	1 987	1 451	1 690	1 126	277.0	277	819	408	....	48 800	54 200
1978	2 020.3	1 433.3	2 020	1 433	1 800	1 183	275.9	276	817	419	....	55 700	62 500
1979	1 745.1	1 194.1	1 745	1 194	1 552	982	277.4	277	709	402	....	62 900	71 800
1980	1 292.2	852.2	1 292	852	1 191	710	221.6	222	545	342	....	64 600	76 400
1981	1 084.2	705.4	1 084	705	986	564	241.0	241	436	278	....	68 900	83 000
1982	1 062.2	662.6	1 062	663	1 000	546	239.6	240	412	255	....	69 300	83 900
1983	1 703.0	1 067.6	1 703	1 068	1 605	902	295.7	296	623	304	....	75 300	89 800
1984	1 749.5	1 084.2	1 750	1 084	1 682	922	295.7	296	639	358	....	79 900	97 600
1985	1 741.8	1 072.4	1 742	1 072	1 733	957	283.9	284	688	350	....	84 300	100 800
1986	1 805.4	1 179.4	1 805	1 179	1 769	1 078	244.4	244	750	361	....	92 000	111 900
1987	1 620.5	1 146.4	1 621	1 146	1 535	1 024	232.9	233	671	370	....	104 500	127 200
1988	1 488.1	1 081.3	1 488	1 081	1 456	994	218.3	218	676	371	....	112 500	138 300
1989	1 376.1	1 003.3	1 376	1 003	1 338	932	198.0	198	650	366	....	120 000	148 800
1990	1 192.7	894.8	1 193	895	1 111	794	188.1	188	534	321	....	122 900	149 800
1991	1 013.9	840.4	1 014	840	949	754	170.9	171	509	284	....	120 000	147 200
1992	1 199.7	1 029.9	1 200	1 030	1 095	911	210.3	210	610	267	....	121 500	144 100
1993	1 287.6	1 125.7	1 288	1 126	1 199	987	254.2	254	666	295	....	126 500	147 700
1994	1 457.0	1 198.4	1 457	1 198	1 363	1 061	305.0	305	670	340	....	130 000	154 500
1995	1 354.1	1 076.2	1 354	1 076	1 333	997	340.0	341	667	374	....	133 900	158 700
1996	1 476.8	1 160.9	1 477	1 161	1 426	1 070	368.1	363	757	326	....	140 000	166 400
1993:													
January	70.5	62.8	1 210	1 091	1 177	989	17.2	267	596	266	5.4	118 000	138 900
February	74.6	65.5	1 210	1 063	1 148	953	18.2	262	604	267	5.3	129 400	149 400
March	95.5	84.9	1 083	950	1 056	881	21.0	247	602	270	5.4	125 000	146 600
April	117.8	104.4	1 258	1 110	1 104	922	21.4	241	701	272	4.7	127 000	148 400
May	120.9	109.2	1 260	1 128	1 112	911	20.3	230	626	275	5.3	129 900	152 300
June	128.5	110.1	1 280	1 081	1 130	932	22.6	238	653	275	5.2	124 500	145 700
July	115.3	100.4	1 254	1 086	1 174	977	19.9	246	655	278	5.3	123 900	143 400
August	121.8	108.3	1 300	1 162	1 230	1 000	23.8	247	645	286	5.5	126 600	150 600
September	118.5	100.6	1 343	1 143	1 251	1 028	23.4	254	726	287	4.9	129 400	150 100
October	123.2	105.5	1 392	1 209	1 287	1 071	23.6	261	704	290	5.0	125 000	146 900
November	102.3	90.6	1 376	1 228	1 357	1 125	22.3	285	769	293	4.8	130 000	152 500
December	98.7	83.3	1 533	1 316	1 461	1 161	20.5	292	812	293	4.5	125 000	146 400
1994:													
January	76.2	67.2	1 272	1 140	1 390	1 112	20.9	302	619	294	5.9	126 000	153 400
February	83.5	70.8	1 337	1 133	1 269	1 065	21.6	301	686	295	5.0	129 900	150 700
March	134.3	114.6	1 564	1 306	1 342	1 078	26.6	304	747	298	4.8	132 300	152 800
April	137.6	114.3	1 465	1 206	1 392	1 084	24.8	318	692	297	5.2	129 000	152 900
May	148.8	122.3	1 526	1 244	1 396	1 110	26.0	296	691	302	5.3	129 900	151 800
June	136.4	117.6	1 409	1 193	1 357	1 067	27.9	295	621	315	6.2	133 500	158 400
July	127.8	110.4	1 439	1 231	1 335	1 041	23.3	289	628	319	6.3	124 400	144 400
August	139.8	110.1	1 450	1 149	1 377	1 054	29.0	295	656	323	6.1	133 300	154 900
September	130.1	105.2	1 474	1 201	1 412	1 056	27.4	307	677	331	6.0	129 700	157 200
October	130.6	101.3	1 450	1 152	1 397	1 042	28.0	310	715	330	5.6	132 000	153 000
November	113.4	87.8	1 511	1 187	1 340	1 014	26.0	322	646	333	6.3	129 900	155 400
December	98.5	76.8	1 455	1 151	1 396	1 086	23.5	347	629	336	6.6	130 000	154 500
1995:													
January	84.5	63.6	1 383	1 079	1 282	967	25.7	361	633	341	6.7	127 900	147 400
February	81.6	65.3	1 325	1 063	1 254	916	24.3	335	565	345	7.2	135 000	160 200
March	103.8	85.3	1 246	991	1 226	914	29.2	326	614	346	6.8	130 000	153 300
April	116.9	93.9	1 278	1 019	1 259	925	26.1	318	619	347	6.8	134 000	157 800
May	130.5	102.3	1 309	1 020	1 271	958	30.0	329	667	347	6.3	133 900	158 000
June	123.4	100.5	1 294	1 025	1 305	982	30.7	333	718	348	5.9	133 700	160 200
July	129.1	102.0	1 464	1 144	1 354	1 019	24.7	319	769	345	5.6	131 000	154 200
August	135.8	108.5	1 404	1 129	1 386	1 045	33.2	344	703	351	6.1	134 900	162 000
September	122.4	97.7	1 378	1 110	1 421	1 079	29.7	346	682	353	6.4	130 000	155 600
October	126.2	101.5	1 382	1 132	1 400	1 052	32.9	354	688	360	6.4	135 200	156 200
November	107.2	82.0	1 451	1 130	1 430	1 060	29.4	355	673	367	6.7	137 000	160 700
December	92.8	73.7	1 404	1 129	1 442	1 091	24.1	370	697	370	6.5	138 600	165 600
1996:													
January	90.7	68.9	1 444	1 138	1 385	1 047	27.1	350	727	370	6.3	131 900	155 300
February	95.9	74.2	1 520	1 188	1 425	1 083	27.1	346	778	354	5.1	139 400	163 700
March	116.0	96.9	1 429	1 156	1 438	1 119	30.1	368	711	367	6.2	136 800	161 200
April	146.6	117.9	1 522	1 215	1 486	1 128	37.3	378	741	368	6.0	140 000	170 000
May	143.9	111.6	1 476	1 142	1 457	1 101	33.5	366	732	362	5.9	136 400	163 300
June	138.0	115.0	1 488	1 214	1 432	1 094	31.2	372	732	355	5.9	140 000	166 500
July	137.5	109.1	1 492	1 164	1 454	1 077	29.1	372	782	352	5.6	144 200	168 400
August	144.2	115.6	1 515	1 222	1 405	1 061	34.3	369	814	343	5.2	137 000	159 700
September	128.7	99.3	1 470	1 148	1 391	1 029	31.5	373	768	331	5.3	139 000	167 400
October	130.8	101.0	1 407	1 104	1 349	1 003	36.0	369	706	330	5.7	143 800	168 400
November	111.5	82.6	1 486	1 133	1 391	1 016	28.0	354	788	327	5.1	143 500	172 000
December	93.1	68.8	1 353	1 024	1 405	999	22.9	338	794	322	5.0	144 900	171 800

1. Data beginning with 1994 cover 19,000 permit issuing places; 1984-1993: 17,000 places; 1978-1983: 16,000 places; 1972-1977: 14,000 places; 1967-1971: 13,000 places.

Manufacturing

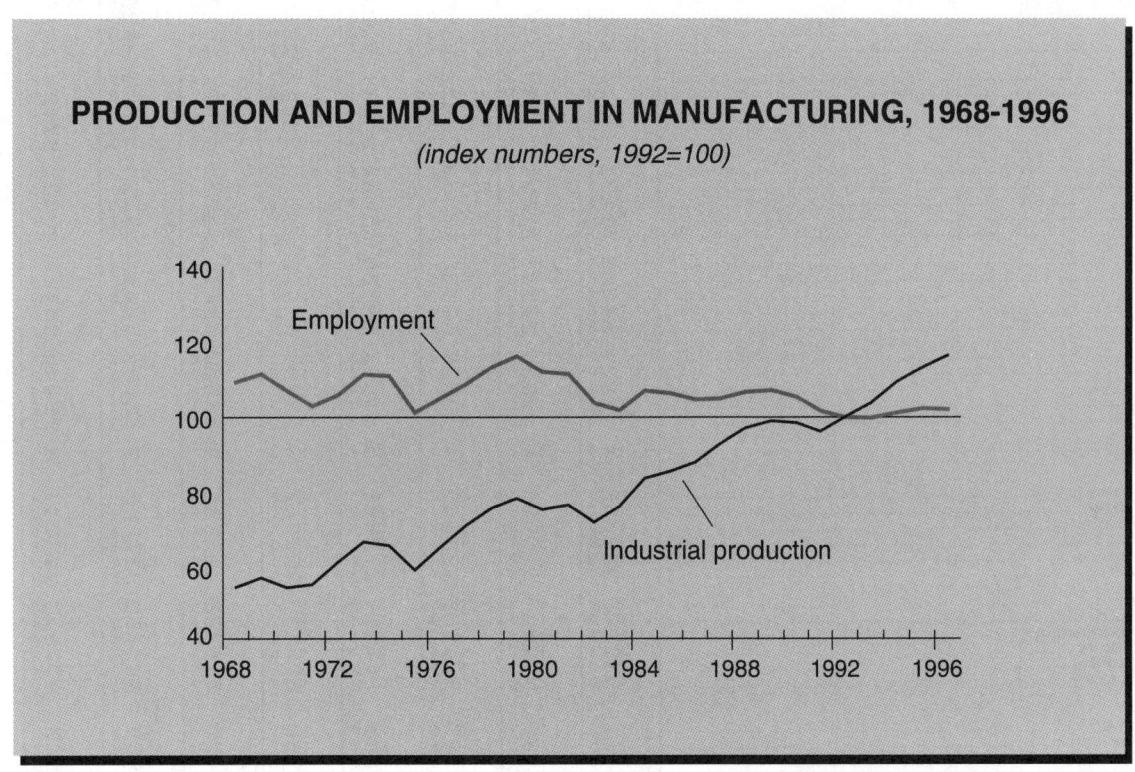

PRODUCTION AND EMPLOYMENT IN MANUFACTURING, 1968-1996
(index numbers, 1992=100)

Industrial production in manufacturing grew 112 percent from 1968 to 1996, while employment declined after 1979.

Employment in manufacturing peaked at 21 million in 1979 and, apart from cyclical ups and downs, has since been declining. In 1996 manufacturing employment was 12 percent below 1979 and 7 percent below 1968. Viewed as a percent of all private nonfarm employment, manufacturing employment fell from 35 percent in 1968 to 28 percent in 1979 and 18 percent in 1996.

MANUFACTURING

TOTAL MANUFACTURING—PRODUCTION, CAPACITY, AND PRICES
(Seasonally adjusted)

YEAR AND MONTH	Industrial production (1992=100)					Capacity utilization (Percent of capacity)					Producer price index, total manufacturing industries [1]
	Total manufacturing	Primary processing	Advanced processing	Durable goods	Non-durable goods	Total manufacturing	Primary processing	Advanced processing	Durable goods	Non-durable goods	
1968	54.9	65.8	49.6	54.8	55.1	87.1	86.1	87.3	87.2	86.6	....
1969	57.4	69.7	51.4	57.0	58.0	86.6	86.5	86.4	86.7	86.5	....
1970	54.8	67.2	48.9	52.7	58.0	79.4	79.9	78.9	77.2	82.8	....
1971	55.6	68.7	49.4	52.4	60.3	77.9	78.7	77.1	74.7	82.6	....
1972	61.5	77.3	54.3	58.5	65.7	83.4	85.5	82.2	81.4	86.4	....
1973	66.9	84.6	59.0	65.3	69.0	87.7	90.5	86.2	88.0	87.3	....
1974	65.9	82.0	58.6	64.0	68.5	83.4	85.1	82.5	83.1	83.9	....
1975	59.4	71.4	53.8	56.1	64.2	72.9	72.1	73.3	70.6	76.3	....
1976	65.4	80.3	58.6	61.8	70.7	78.2	79.2	77.6	75.7	81.8	....
1977	71.2	86.7	64.0	68.1	75.7	82.6	83.8	81.9	80.8	85.3	....
1978	75.8	90.7	68.9	73.6	78.9	85.2	85.9	84.8	84.4	86.4	....
1979	78.5	92.5	72.0	77.4	79.9	85.3	86.0	84.9	85.6	84.9	....
1980	75.5	84.4	71.4	73.4	78.3	79.5	77.2	80.8	78.4	81.0	....
1981	76.7	85.2	72.8	74.6	79.5	78.3	77.2	78.8	76.8	80.4	....
1982	72.1	75.7	70.5	68.2	77.7	71.8	68.6	73.5	68.0	77.5	....
1983	76.3	82.1	73.6	72.2	81.9	74.4	74.5	74.4	70.1	80.8	....
1984	83.8	88.4	81.7	82.7	85.3	79.8	80.0	79.7	77.6	82.9	....
1985	85.7	88.4	84.5	85.6	86.0	78.8	79.1	78.6	76.8	81.5	....
1986	88.1	90.0	87.2	87.4	89.1	78.7	79.9	78.1	75.7	82.8	98.4
1987	92.8	95.3	91.6	92.0	93.8	81.3	84.5	79.9	77.9	85.9	100.9
1988	97.1	99.0	96.2	98.1	96.0	83.8	86.8	82.3	81.7	86.4	104.4
1989	99.0	99.9	98.6	100.5	97.3	83.6	86.1	82.5	82.0	85.7	109.6
1990	98.5	99.3	98.2	99.0	97.9	81.4	83.9	80.3	79.0	84.4	114.5
1991	96.2	95.7	96.4	95.5	97.0	78.0	79.6	77.2	74.7	81.9	115.9
1992	100.0	100.0	100.0	100.0	100.0	79.5	82.3	78.3	76.8	82.8	117.4
1993	103.7	103.3	103.8	105.5	101.7	80.8	84.1	79.3	79.2	82.6	119.1
1994	109.4	109.2	109.5	113.4	105.0	83.1	87.5	81.2	82.3	84.0	120.7
1995	113.2	111.2	114.2	119.7	106.2	83.1	87.3	81.2	82.7	83.6	124.2
1996	116.4	112.2	118.4	125.7	106.3	82.1	86.1	80.3	82.0	82.2	127.1
1993:											
January	102.6	102.1	102.8	103.5	101.6	80.7	83.6	79.4	78.6	83.1	118.4
February	102.9	102.5	103.1	104.0	101.7	80.8	83.8	79.5	78.9	83.1	118.9
March	103.0	102.1	103.4	104.5	101.4	80.7	83.4	79.6	79.0	82.8	119.3
April	103.6	102.7	103.9	105.1	101.9	81.0	83.8	79.8	79.3	83.0	119.7
May	103.0	102.2	103.4	104.8	101.1	80.5	83.3	79.3	79.0	82.3	119.8
June	103.0	102.8	103.1	104.7	101.2	80.4	83.8	78.9	78.7	82.3	119.5
July	103.4	103.1	103.5	104.8	101.8	80.5	83.9	79.0	78.6	82.7	119.3
August	103.0	103.2	102.9	104.2	101.7	80.1	83.9	78.4	78.0	82.5	118.6
September	104.2	103.9	104.3	106.1	102.0	80.9	84.4	79.4	79.3	82.7	118.4
October	104.4	104.3	104.5	107.1	101.5	80.9	84.6	79.3	79.8	82.2	119.4
November	105.0	105.1	104.9	107.9	101.8	81.2	85.2	79.5	80.2	82.4	119.3
December	105.9	105.9	105.8	109.2	102.2	81.7	85.8	80.0	81.0	82.6	118.8
1994:											
January	106.0	105.9	106.0	109.5	102.1	81.6	85.6	79.9	81.0	82.5	119.3
February	106.6	106.3	106.8	110.1	102.7	81.9	85.8	80.3	81.2	82.8	119.8
March	107.5	107.4	107.6	110.6	104.1	82.4	86.6	80.6	81.2	83.8	119.9
April	108.2	108.3	108.2	111.6	104.5	82.7	87.2	80.8	81.7	84.0	120.1
May	109.0	109.2	108.9	112.5	105.2	83.1	87.7	81.1	82.0	84.4	120.4
June	109.2	108.9	109.3	112.7	105.3	83.0	87.3	81.2	81.9	84.3	120.4
July	110.0	109.7	110.2	114.3	105.3	83.4	87.8	81.5	82.8	84.2	120.9
August	110.1	109.8	110.3	114.3	105.5	83.3	87.7	81.4	82.5	84.2	121.5
September	110.3	110.1	110.4	114.8	105.4	83.2	87.9	81.2	82.6	84.0	121.1
October	111.1	110.6	111.3	115.8	106.0	83.6	88.1	81.6	83.0	84.3	121.5
November	111.9	111.4	112.1	116.6	106.7	84.0	88.5	81.9	83.3	84.7	121.9
December	112.9	112.9	112.8	118.3	107.0	84.5	89.6	82.2	84.2	84.9	121.7
1995:											
January	113.3	112.9	113.5	119.0	107.1	84.6	89.5	82.4	84.4	84.9	122.6
February	112.9	112.6	113.0	118.8	106.5	84.0	89.1	81.8	83.8	84.3	123.1
March	113.1	112.3	113.4	118.9	106.7	83.9	88.7	81.7	83.5	84.3	123.4
April	112.7	111.5	113.2	118.4	106.4	83.4	87.9	81.3	82.8	84.0	124.1
May	112.6	111.2	113.3	118.4	106.2	83.0	87.5	81.0	82.4	83.7	124.5
June	112.9	110.6	113.9	118.9	106.3	83.0	86.9	81.1	82.4	83.7	124.4
July	112.7	110.1	113.9	118.7	106.1	82.6	86.4	80.9	81.9	83.4	124.4
August	113.4	110.4	114.9	120.2	106.1	82.9	86.4	81.3	82.5	83.3	124.4
September	114.2	111.2	115.7	121.6	106.2	83.2	86.9	81.5	83.1	83.3	124.3
October	113.8	110.8	115.2	120.9	106.1	82.6	86.4	80.8	82.2	83.0	125.1
November	113.6	110.6	115.1	121.2	105.4	82.2	86.1	80.4	82.0	82.4	125.1
December	113.8	110.6	115.3	121.5	105.4	82.0	86.0	80.3	81.8	82.3	125.3
1996:											
January	113.4	109.5	115.2	121.5	104.6	81.5	85.0	79.9	81.4	81.6	125.8
February	114.8	110.1	117.1	123.6	105.3	82.2	85.3	80.9	82.4	82.0	125.7
March	113.9	110.8	115.4	121.8	105.4	81.3	85.6	79.4	80.9	81.9	126.0
April	115.2	111.0	117.3	124.6	105.2	82.0	85.6	80.4	82.3	81.6	126.8
May	115.7	111.7	117.6	125.2	105.5	82.0	85.9	80.3	82.2	81.8	127.4
June	116.4	112.6	118.3	126.3	105.9	82.3	86.5	80.5	82.5	82.0	127.1
July	117.0	113.0	118.9	126.9	106.4	82.4	86.7	80.6	82.6	82.2	127.1
August	117.2	113.1	119.2	127.5	106.2	82.3	86.5	80.4	82.5	82.0	127.4
September	117.4	113.5	119.3	127.2	106.9	82.1	86.6	80.2	81.9	82.4	127.5
October	117.6	113.8	119.5	127.1	107.4	82.0	86.7	80.0	81.5	82.7	128.2
November	118.5	113.8	120.8	128.4	107.9	82.4	86.5	80.5	81.9	82.9	128.0
December	119.2	114.0	121.7	128.8	108.8	82.5	86.6	80.8	81.7	83.5	128.0

1. December 1984=100, not seasonally adjusted.

	TOTAL MANUFACTURING—EMPLOYMENT AND HOURS WORKED											
YEAR AND MONTH	Employment (Thousands, seasonally adjusted)						Hours worked (Production workers—seasonally adjusted)					
	Total payroll employees			Production workers			Average weekly hours			Average overtime hours		
	Total manufacturing	Durable goods	Nondurable goods	Total manufacturing	Durable goods	Nondurable goods	Total manufacturing	Durable goods	Nondurable goods	Total manufacturing	Durable goods	Nondurable goods
1968	19 781	11 594	8 187	14 514	8 489	6 024	40.7	41.4	39.8	3.6	3.8	3.3
1969	20 167	11 862	8 304	14 767	8 683	6 084	40.6	41.3	39.7	3.6	3.8	3.4
1970	19 367	11 176	8 190	14 044	8 088	5 956	39.8	40.3	39.1	3.0	3.0	3.0
1971	18 623	10 604	8 019	13 544	7 697	5 847	39.9	40.3	39.3	2.9	2.9	3.0
1972	19 151	11 022	8 129	14 045	8 025	6 022	40.5	41.2	39.7	3.5	3.6	3.3
1973	20 154	11 863	8 291	14 834	8 699	6 138	40.7	41.4	39.6	3.8	4.1	3.4
1974	20 077	11 897	8 181	14 638	8 634	6 004	40.0	40.6	39.1	3.3	3.4	3.0
1975	18 323	10 662	7 661	13 043	7 532	5 510	39.5	39.9	38.8	2.6	2.6	2.7
1976	18 997	11 051	7 946	13 638	7 888	5 750	40.1	40.6	39.4	3.1	3.2	3.0
1977	19 682	11 570	8 112	14 135	8 280	5 855	40.3	41.0	39.4	3.5	3.7	3.2
1978	20 505	12 245	8 259	14 734	8 777	5 956	40.4	41.1	39.4	3.6	3.8	3.2
1979	21 040	12 730	8 310	15 068	9 082	5 986	40.2	40.8	39.3	3.3	3.5	3.1
1980	20 285	12 159	8 127	14 214	8 416	5 798	39.7	40.1	39.0	2.8	2.8	2.8
1981	20 170	12 082	8 089	14 020	8 270	5 751	39.8	40.2	39.2	2.8	2.8	2.8
1982	18 780	11 014	7 766	12 742	7 290	5 451	38.9	39.3	38.4	2.3	2.2	2.5
1983	18 432	10 707	7 725	12 528	7 095	5 433	40.1	40.7	39.4	3.0	3.0	3.0
1984	19 372	11 476	7 896	13 280	7 715	5 565	40.7	41.4	39.7	3.4	3.4	3.1
1985	19 248	11 458	7 790	13 084	7 618	5 466	40.5	41.2	39.6	3.3	3.5	3.1
1986	18 947	11 195	7 752	12 864	7 399	5 465	40.7	41.3	39.9	3.4	3.5	3.3
1987	18 999	11 154	7 845	12 952	7 409	5 543	41.0	41.5	40.2	3.7	3.8	3.6
1988	19 314	11 363	7 951	13 193	7 582	5 611	41.1	41.8	40.2	3.9	4.1	3.6
1989	19 391	11 394	7 997	13 230	7 594	5 636	41.0	41.6	40.2	3.8	3.9	3.6
1990	19 076	11 109	7 968	12 947	7 363	5 584	40.8	41.3	40.0	3.6	3.7	3.6
1991	18 406	10 569	7 837	12 434	6 967	5 467	40.7	41.1	40.2	3.6	3.5	3.7
1992	18 104	10 277	7 827	12 287	6 822	5 466	41.0	41.5	40.4	3.8	3.7	3.8
1993	18 075	10 221	7 854	12 341	6 849	5 492	41.4	42.1	40.6	4.1	4.3	4.0
1994	18 321	10 448	7 873	12 632	7 104	5 528	42.0	42.9	40.9	4.7	5.0	4.3
1995	18 524	10 683	7 841	12 826	7 317	5 508	41.6	42.4	40.5	4.4	4.7	4.0
1996	18 457	10 766	7 691	12 749	7 370	5 379	41.6	42.4	40.5	4.5	4.8	4.1
1993:												
January	18 103	10 251	7 852	12 331	6 846	5 485	41.3	41.9	40.6	4.0	4.0	3.9
February	18 108	10 251	7 857	12 341	6 851	5 490	41.5	42.1	40.7	4.1	4.1	4.0
March	18 094	10 236	7 858	12 335	6 844	5 491	41.1	41.8	40.1	3.9	4.0	3.7
April	18 073	10 215	7 858	12 324	6 832	5 492	41.6	42.3	40.8	4.3	4.4	4.2
May	18 067	10 203	7 864	12 326	6 825	5 501	41.3	41.9	40.5	4.1	4.2	3.9
June	18 046	10 185	7 861	12 309	6 814	5 495	41.2	41.9	40.4	4.1	4.2	3.9
July	18 030	10 189	7 841	12 302	6 815	5 487	41.4	42.1	40.6	4.1	4.2	4.0
August	18 046	10 189	7 857	12 316	6 822	5 494	41.4	42.1	40.5	4.1	4.3	3.9
September	18 072	10 214	7 858	12 352	6 855	5 497	41.6	42.4	40.6	4.3	4.5	4.0
October	18 076	10 227	7 849	12 357	6 870	5 487	41.5	42.3	40.6	4.3	4.5	4.0
November	18 095	10 244	7 851	12 388	6 892	5 496	41.6	42.4	40.6	4.4	4.6	4.0
December	18 113	10 268	7 845	12 414	6 919	5 495	41.7	42.5	40.6	4.4	4.7	4.1
1994:												
January	18 145	10 300	7 845	12 447	6 955	5 492	41.7	42.6	40.7	4.4	4.7	4.1
February	18 172	10 321	7 851	12 479	6 975	5 504	41.2	42.1	40.1	4.4	4.7	4.0
March	18 200	10 343	7 857	12 513	6 999	5 514	42.0	42.9	40.9	4.7	5.0	4.3
April	18 235	10 374	7 861	12 556	7 034	5 522	41.9	42.6	40.9	4.5	4.7	4.2
May	18 263	10 396	7 867	12 578	7 055	5 523	42.0	42.9	40.9	4.6	4.9	4.2
June	18 309	10 438	7 871	12 625	7 095	5 530	42.0	42.8	41.0	4.6	4.9	4.3
July	18 332	10 449	7 883	12 660	7 115	5 545	42.0	42.8	41.1	4.7	5.0	4.3
August	18 378	10 491	7 887	12 687	7 149	5 538	42.0	42.8	41.0	4.7	5.0	4.2
September	18 406	10 519	7 887	12 718	7 176	5 542	41.9	42.6	40.9	4.6	4.9	4.2
October	18 436	10 547	7 889	12 748	7 204	5 544	42.1	42.8	41.0	4.7	5.0	4.3
November	18 476	10 585	7 891	12 791	7 243	5 548	42.1	42.9	41.0	4.8	5.1	4.3
December	18 515	10 612	7 903	12 828	7 266	5 562	42.1	42.9	41.1	4.8	5.1	4.3
1995:												
January	18 543	10 633	7 910	12 857	7 288	5 569	42.2	43.1	41.1	4.8	5.2	4.3
February	18 561	10 664	7 897	12 867	7 312	5 555	41.9	42.7	40.8	4.7	5.1	4.2
March	18 561	10 676	7 885	12 871	7 327	5 544	41.8	42.7	40.7	4.6	5.0	4.1
April	18 572	10 691	7 881	12 878	7 334	5 544	41.5	42.2	40.6	4.4	4.7	4.0
May	18 548	10 684	7 864	12 851	7 322	5 529	41.4	42.1	40.5	4.2	4.5	3.9
June	18 533	10 676	7 857	12 835	7 310	5 525	41.4	42.2	40.4	4.2	4.5	3.9
July	18 502	10 674	7 828	12 806	7 306	5 500	41.3	42.1	40.4	4.2	4.5	3.9
August	18 511	10 689	7 822	12 810	7 318	5 492	41.5	42.3	40.4	4.3	4.6	4.0
September	18 508	10 696	7 812	12 809	7 322	5 487	41.5	42.3	40.4	4.4	4.7	3.9
October	18 483	10 689	7 794	12 782	7 310	5 472	41.5	42.3	40.3	4.4	4.7	3.9
November	18 478	10 694	7 784	12 771	7 313	5 458	41.5	42.4	40.3	4.4	4.7	3.9
December	18 503	10 738	7 765	12 801	7 359	5 442	41.2	41.9	40.2	4.2	4.5	3.8
1996:												
January	18 460	10 724	7 736	12 765	7 345	5 420	40.1	41.1	38.7	4.2	4.5	3.8
February	18 498	10 749	7 749	12 783	7 356	5 427	41.4	42.2	40.5	4.4	4.6	4.0
March	18 460	10 718	7 742	12 746	7 327	5 419	41.3	42.0	40.5	4.3	4.5	4.0
April	18 465	10 749	7 716	12 752	7 355	5 397	41.5	42.3	40.4	4.5	4.8	4.1
May	18 469	10 762	7 707	12 762	7 371	5 391	41.6	42.5	40.5	4.6	4.9	4.1
June	18 468	10 778	7 690	12 751	7 376	5 375	41.7	42.5	40.7	4.5	4.8	4.1
July	18 442	10 766	7 676	12 735	7 369	5 366	41.6	42.4	40.5	4.5	4.7	4.1
August	18 461	10 788	7 673	12 749	7 389	5 360	41.7	42.5	40.6	4.5	4.8	4.1
September	18 427	10 771	7 656	12 723	7 372	5 351	41.7	42.5	40.7	4.5	4.8	4.1
October	18 442	10 780	7 662	12 731	7 379	5 352	41.7	42.4	40.6	4.5	4.7	4.1
November	18 442	10 791	7 651	12 737	7 390	5 347	41.7	42.5	40.7	4.6	4.8	4.2
December	18 448	10 803	7 645	12 743	7 398	5 345	42.0	42.7	40.9	4.7	4.9	4.3

MANUFACTURING

YEAR AND MONTH	Aggregate weekly hours index (Seasonally adjusted, 1982=100)			Average hourly earnings					Average weekly earnings (Not seasonally adjusted)		
				Seasonally adjusted		Not seasonally adjusted					
	Total manufacturing	Durable goods	Nondurable goods	Total	Excluding overtime	Total manufacturing	Durable goods	Nondurable goods	Total manufacturing	Durable goods	Nondurable goods
1968	119.2	121.7	115.7	3.01	2.88	3.01	3.18	2.74	122.51	131.65	109.05
1969	121.0	124.2	116.5	3.19	3.05	3.19	3.38	2.91	129.51	139.59	115.53
1970	112.8	113.0	112.4	3.35	3.23	3.35	3.55	3.08	133.33	143.07	120.43
1971	108.8	107.4	110.8	3.57	3.45	3.57	3.79	3.27	142.44	152.74	128.51
1972	114.8	115.4	114.1	3.82	3.66	3.82	4.07	3.48	154.71	167.68	138.16
1973	121.7	125.8	116.0	4.09	3.91	4.09	4.35	3.70	166.46	180.09	146.52
1974	118.1	122.4	112.1	4.42	4.25	4.42	4.70	4.01	176.80	190.82	156.79
1975	103.8	104.9	102.1	4.83	4.67	4.83	5.15	4.37	190.79	205.49	169.56
1976	110.3	111.9	108.1	5.22	5.02	5.22	5.57	4.71	209.32	226.14	185.57
1977	115.0	118.4	110.2	5.68	5.44	5.68	6.06	5.11	228.90	248.46	201.33
1978	120.1	125.9	112.0	6.17	5.91	6.17	6.58	5.54	249.27	270.44	218.28
1979	122.1	129.1	112.3	6.70	6.43	6.70	7.12	6.01	269.34	290.50	236.19
1980	113.8	117.8	108.1	7.27	7.02	7.27	7.75	6.56	288.62	310.78	255.84
1981	112.5	116.1	107.6	7.99	7.72	7.99	8.53	7.19	318.00	342.91	281.85
1982	100.0	100.0	100.0	8.49	8.25	8.49	9.03	7.75	330.26	354.88	297.60
1983	101.4	100.7	102.4	8.83	8.52	8.83	9.38	8.09	354.08	381.77	318.75
1984	109.0	111.5	105.5	9.19	8.82	9.19	9.73	8.39	374.03	402.82	333.08
1985	106.9	109.5	103.4	9.54	9.16	9.54	10.09	8.72	386.37	415.71	345.31
1986	105.7	106.8	104.2	9.73	9.34	9.73	10.28	8.95	396.01	424.56	357.11
1987	107.0	107.4	106.6	9.91	9.48	9.91	10.43	9.19	406.31	432.85	369.44
1988	109.3	110.5	107.7	10.19	9.73	10.19	10.71	9.45	418.81	447.68	379.89
1989	109.3	110.1	108.2	10.48	10.02	10.48	11.01	9.75	429.68	458.02	391.95
1990	106.4	106.1	106.8	10.83	10.37	10.83	11.35	10.12	441.86	468.76	404.80
1991	102.1	99.3	105.9	11.18	10.71	11.18	11.75	10.44	455.03	482.93	419.69
1992	101.7	98.2	106.6	11.46	10.95	11.46	12.02	10.73	469.86	498.83	433.49
1993	103.1	100.0	107.4	11.74	11.18	11.74	12.33	10.98	486.04	519.09	445.79
1994	107.0	105.5	109.2	12.07	11.43	12.07	12.68	11.24	506.94	543.97	459.72
1995	107.5	107.5	107.6	12.37	11.74	12.37	12.94	11.58	514.59	548.66	468.99
1996	106.9	108.3	105.1	12.78	12.12	12.78	13.34	11.97	531.65	565.62	484.79
1993:											
January	102.7	100.0	106.4	11.59	11.06	11.61	12.18	10.87	477.17	507.91	439.15
February	103.2	100.5	106.8	11.62	11.09	11.61	12.19	10.86	477.17	508.32	437.66
March	102.1	99.8	105.3	11.63	11.11	11.63	12.20	10.88	475.67	508.74	434.11
April	103.5	100.8	107.1	11.67	11.13	11.70	12.25	10.98	479.70	509.60	440.30
May	102.6	99.9	106.4	11.70	11.15	11.71	12.30	10.94	483.62	516.60	441.98
June	102.4	99.6	106.2	11.72	11.17	11.71	12.31	10.95	484.79	518.25	444.57
July	102.7	100.0	106.4	11.75	11.19	11.72	12.28	11.01	480.52	510.85	443.70
August	102.8	100.2	106.4	11.77	11.21	11.70	12.29	10.95	485.55	517.41	445.67
September	103.7	101.4	106.7	11.81	11.25	11.85	12.44	11.09	491.78	523.72	453.58
October	103.5	101.3	106.5	11.83	11.24	11.80	12.40	11.02	493.24	527.00	450.72
November	104.0	102.0	106.7	11.87	11.28	11.87	12.49	11.07	498.54	534.57	454.98
December	104.3	102.6	106.7	11.92	11.32	12.00	12.62	11.16	508.80	547.71	459.79
1994:											
January	104.8	103.3	106.8	11.94	11.33	11.96	12.56	11.15	496.34	532.54	450.46
February	103.7	102.5	105.4	12.01	11.41	12.00	12.61	11.18	490.80	527.10	442.73
March	106.0	104.7	107.8	11.99	11.36	11.99	12.59	11.17	502.38	538.85	454.62
April	106.0	104.6	107.9	11.98	11.34	12.01	12.61	11.19	504.42	540.97	456.55
May	106.6	105.5	108.1	12.01	11.38	12.02	12.63	11.19	504.84	541.83	456.55
June	106.9	105.8	108.3	12.03	11.39	12.03	12.64	11.21	507.67	543.52	460.73
July	107.3	106.3	108.8	12.04	11.40	12.05	12.63	11.28	501.28	532.99	460.22
August	107.4	106.6	108.4	12.08	11.44	12.01	12.64	11.19	504.42	539.73	459.91
September	107.4	106.7	108.3	12.11	11.47	12.15	12.78	11.30	515.16	550.82	467.82
October	108.1	107.7	108.7	12.15	11.49	12.11	12.72	11.29	512.25	548.23	466.28
November	108.5	108.4	108.7	12.18	11.52	12.18	12.80	11.34	517.65	554.24	470.61
December	109.0	108.8	109.1	12.19	11.53	12.27	12.90	11.41	526.38	565.02	475.80
1995:											
January	109.5	109.6	109.3	12.23	11.56	12.25	12.84	11.43	514.50	550.84	465.20
February	108.7	108.9	108.4	12.28	11.62	12.26	12.86	11.41	511.24	547.84	462.11
March	108.5	109.1	107.8	12.27	11.63	12.27	12.86	11.44	511.66	547.83	463.32
April	107.8	108.0	107.5	12.29	11.76	12.30	12.84	11.56	496.92	526.44	457.78
May	107.3	107.6	106.9	12.30	11.68	12.30	12.87	11.50	509.22	543.11	463.45
June	107.2	107.6	106.8	12.32	11.71	12.32	12.89	11.53	512.51	546.54	466.97
July	106.7	107.2	106.1	12.40	11.78	12.40	12.94	11.65	505.92	535.72	467.17
August	107.2	108.0	106.0	12.41	11.78	12.35	12.93	11.56	512.53	546.94	468.18
September	107.1	108.0	105.9	12.43	11.80	12.47	13.06	11.65	523.74	558.97	477.65
October	106.9	107.9	105.5	12.47	11.84	12.43	12.98	11.67	518.33	552.95	473.80
November	106.9	108.2	105.1	12.50	11.87	12.49	13.03	11.73	523.33	557.68	478.58
December	106.3	107.6	104.5	12.52	11.90	12.60	13.13	11.84	529.20	561.96	483.07
1996:											
January	103.1	105.2	100.3	12.64	12.00	12.66	13.17	11.91	503.87	538.65	457.34
February	106.8	108.3	104.9	12.60	11.96	12.57	13.12	11.79	519.14	552.35	472.78
March	106.3	107.4	104.8	12.54	11.92	12.54	13.05	11.83	517.90	548.10	476.75
April	106.7	108.6	104.2	12.71	12.09	12.73	13.28	11.93	524.48	557.76	477.20
May	107.2	109.2	104.4	12.73	12.06	12.71	13.27	11.89	528.74	562.65	480.36
June	107.3	109.4	104.5	12.77	12.11	12.75	13.33	11.92	534.23	569.19	486.34
July	106.8	108.9	103.9	12.80	12.14	12.79	13.35	12.00	525.67	556.70	482.40
August	107.2	109.5	104.0	12.85	12.19	12.79	13.39	11.95	534.62	569.08	488.76
September	107.1	109.4	103.9	12.87	12.20	12.90	13.52	12.01	545.67	582.71	496.01
October	106.9	109.2	103.9	12.87	12.21	12.83	13.42	12.00	537.58	573.03	490.80
November	107.2	109.6	103.9	12.93	12.26	12.93	13.49	12.12	544.35	578.72	499.34
December	107.8	110.3	104.5	12.99	12.29	13.07	13.64	12.24	559.40	594.70	509.18

MANUFACTURERS' SHIPMENTS—NOT SEASONALLY ADJUSTED
(Millions of dollars, adjusted for trading-day and calendar-month variation, but without seasonal adjustment)

YEAR AND MONTH	Total	Durable goods									Instruments and products
		Total[1]	Stone, clay, and glass products	Primary metals Total	Blast furnaces, steel mills	Fabricated metal products	Industrial machinery and equipment	Electronic and electric equipment	Transportation equipment Total	Motor vehicles and parts	
1968	602 744	331 490	15 465	48 717	24 908	43 638	51 370	39 372	83 527	49 465	17 645
1969	642 013	352 836	16 499	53 534	26 412	46 104	56 584	41 560	85 175	50 943	18 662
1970	633 663	337 876	16 454	51 995	25 189	44 210	56 893	41 408	74 539	42 538	18 367
1971	670 877	359 089	18 220	51 585	25 791	45 478	56 445	42 377	88 857	58 247	18 613
1972	756 321	407 844	20 875	58 490	28 712	51 487	66 156	47 502	94 706	63 923	21 043
1973	875 173	475 621	23 141	72 791	36 301	58 804	78 207	54 569	110 587	74 799	23 627
1974	1 017 477	530 074	25 503	95 686	49 718	67 212	93 041	58 684	108 244	68 631	27 454
1975	1 039 065	523 178	26 233	80 890	42 281	68 411	96 354	56 068	113 503	70 033	29 547
1976	1 185 563	607 475	29 618	93 082	46 764	77 560	105 847	65 151	141 028	95 380	33 238
1977	1 358 416	710 017	34 209	103 267	50 670	89 938	122 749	77 845	166 954	117 747	38 803
1978	1 522 858	812 776	40 238	118 175	59 228	101 245	143 919	88 679	188 773	131 999	44 655
1979	1 727 234	911 124	44 287	137 488	67 414	113 494	167 014	102 361	201 623	131 378	50 702
1980	1 852 689	929 027	44 473	134 057	61 612	116 071	180 564	112 864	186 516	104 560	59 825
1981	2 017 544	1 004 725	46 220	142 072	70 254	123 535	201 102	122 084	205 223	116 981	66 613
1982	1 960 214	950 541	43 515	104 874	46 928	119 236	186 773	125 728	201 347	112 270	74 918
1983	2 070 564	1 025 770	47 697	109 240	46 398	123 083	178 446	136 138	245 392	148 296	79 637
1984	2 288 184	1 175 276	53 101	120 315	51 978	138 107	211 075	162 362	284 593	181 993	89 398
1985	2 334 456	1 215 352	55 821	112 265	48 904	143 268	218 408	163 951	307 380	193 445	96 207
1986	2 335 881	1 238 859	59 254	107 865	45 718	143 063	213 574	164 811	322 688	198 811	100 798
1987	2 475 906	1 297 532	61 477	120 248	51 815	147 367	217 671	171 287	332 936	205 923	107 325
1988	2 695 432	1 421 501	63 145	149 837	64 294	159 505	244 365	187 301	354 849	222 353	116 009
1989	2 840 375	1 477 900	63 729	155 718	64 783	164 073	256 212	194 598	369 675	233 232	121 523
1990	2 912 228	1 485 313	63 728	148 787	62 826	165 064	259 367	195 898	370 328	217 295	127 978
1991	2 878 167	1 451 998	59 957	136 378	57 267	159 760	247 508	199 278	367 235	209 210	132 836
1992	3 004 727	1 541 866	62 521	138 287	58 449	166 532	258 662	216 764	399 270	238 384	134 941
1993	3 127 625	1 630 635	65 610	142 685	62 466	175 118	278 063	233 622	414 694	267 365	137 387
1994	3 348 019	1 789 576	71 230	161 188	69 887	190 544	313 047	266 405	450 809	314 637	138 400
1995	3 589 395	1 921 210	75 991	180 303	74 547	204 820	351 113	299 838	462 849	326 415	140 911
1996	3 735 183	2 005 997	83 365	173 619	72 268	215 427	378 366	323 001	471 661	334 633	146 199
1993:											
January	230 017	115 269	4 260	11 071	4 826	12 707	18 943	15 893	29 862	19 985	9 807
February	256 363	133 800	4 918	12 005	5 157	14 226	21 718	18 517	36 396	23 973	10 905
March	274 123	145 608	5 103	12 417	5 447	15 309	26 603	19 964	38 478	24 417	12 201
April	257 069	133 692	5 550	12 041	5 251	14 292	21 969	18 085	36 163	23 733	10 594
May	258 973	135 215	5 452	11 815	5 209	14 787	22 329	18 610	36 088	23 778	11 117
June	281 112	148 968	5 989	12 764	5 514	15 772	26 085	21 081	38 647	24 140	12 591
July	232 105	112 585	5 228	10 585	4 744	12 812	19 584	17 223	22 911	13 194	10 242
August	257 785	131 617	5 818	11 838	5 282	14 531	21 090	19 390	31 871	19 995	11 195
September	279 163	146 534	6 423	12 452	5 414	15 545	25 761	22 005	35 124	22 606	12 590
October	271 704	142 762	6 143	12 258	5 413	15 761	22 805	20 199	37 702	25 883	11 366
November	266 609	141 362	5 757	12 049	5 241	15 007	23 667	20 983	35 781	24 429	12 041
December	262 602	143 223	4 969	11 390	4 968	14 369	27 509	21 672	35 671	21 232	12 678
1994:											
January	240 456	126 292	4 762	11 596	5 158	13 910	20 376	18 290	32 996	23 632	10 150
February	266 827	143 780	5 211	12 785	5 737	15 300	24 404	20 692	38 552	27 807	11 053
March	287 241	156 789	5 910	13 264	5 852	16 555	29 193	22 305	40 915	27 380	12 049
April	269 943	144 725	6 111	13 022	5 675	15 553	24 519	20 768	38 000	27 145	10 897
May	276 779	148 758	5 958	13 437	5 855	16 023	25 430	21 315	38 730	28 229	11 450
June	298 639	162 998	6 506	14 007	6 011	16 711	29 838	23 933	41 591	28 486	12 782
July	248 184	124 818	5 756	12 000	5 200	14 094	22 328	19 732	25 368	15 808	10 271
August	287 158	151 312	6 490	13 901	6 070	16 571	25 020	22 344	38 343	27 298	11 355
September	301 788	161 866	6 562	14 246	6 076	17 045	29 051	24 798	39 593	27 436	12 720
October	291 598	155 324	6 382	14 413	6 125	17 000	26 332	23 130	38 746	28 081	11 289
November	290 820	156 088	6 125	14 279	5 981	16 515	26 271	24 262	39 787	28 260	11 707
December	288 586	156 826	5 457	14 238	6 147	15 267	30 285	24 836	38 188	25 075	12 677
1995:											
January	267 787	141 574	5 372	14 721	6 078	15 691	23 524	20 700	35 499	26 128	10 525
February	294 613	159 319	5 849	15 670	6 534	16 977	27 977	22 883	41 733	30 535	11 458
March	312 565	172 069	6 112	16 296	6 876	17 741	33 251	25 313	43 269	30 605	12 617
April	291 505	155 344	6 024	15 448	6 327	16 757	27 703	22 468	39 356	27 988	10 931
May	298 684	159 738	6 329	15 651	6 482	17 261	28 692	23 736	39 481	28 439	11 773
June	320 422	174 221	6 844	15 905	6 454	17 965	33 494	27 200	41 924	28 658	12 765
July	263 819	131 193	6 191	13 241	5 375	15 060	24 193	21 605	25 291	15 610	10 026
August	304 142	159 957	6 974	15 013	6 220	17 730	27 684	25 419	37 381	26 926	11 629
September	322 181	174 452	6 990	15 268	6 333	18 126	32 770	28 804	41 029	28 960	12 702
October	310 665	166 353	7 008	15 174	6 407	18 319	29 183	26 067	40 560	30 238	11 425
November	303 562	163 026	6 564	14 437	5 988	17 041	29 213	27 029	39 405	27 977	12 067
December	299 450	163 964	5 734	13 479	5 473	16 152	33 429	28 614	37 921	24 351	12 993
1996:											
January	271 841	142 526	5 809	13 675	5 812	16 006	25 648	22 446	33 706	25 688	10 529
February	300 906	163 218	6 025	14 638	6 183	17 372	31 082	25 337	40 858	30 462	11 804
March	316 450	173 195	6 514	14 940	6 097	17 872	36 590	28 046	38 765	26 457	12 799
April	306 714	163 846	6 979	14 934	6 170	18 012	29 611	24 911	40 751	30 192	11 332
May	315 731	170 750	7 266	15 144	6 212	18 653	30 732	25 876	43 026	31 346	12 221
June	331 597	182 994	7 640	14 891	6 269	19 163	36 489	29 242	42 733	30 094	13 367
July	280 761	141 288	7 050	13 154	5 551	15 968	26 289	23 166	27 765	18 510	10 982
August	316 500	167 484	7 557	14 463	6 056	18 836	29 817	26 037	39 759	28 543	12 070
September	336 555	184 229	7 564	14 786	6 220	19 291	35 574	30 164	43 625	30 485	13 173
October	325 541	173 673	7 901	14 900	6 252	19 262	30 728	27 781	41 227	30 434	11 976
November	320 385	172 028	7 081	14 495	5 847	18 290	30 464	29 403	40 958	29 064	12 668
December	312 202	170 766	5 979	13 599	5 599	16 702	35 342	30 592	38 488	23 358	13 278

1. Includes categories not shown separately.

YEAR AND MONTH	MANUFACTURERS' SHIPMENTS—NOT SEASONALLY ADJUSTED—Continued (Millions of dollars, adjusted for trading-day and calendar-month variation, but without seasonal adjustment) Nondurable goods industries								MANUFACTURERS' SHIPMENTS—SEASONALLY ADJUSTED (Millions of dollars, adjusted for seasonality and for trading-day and calendar-month variation) Durable goods industries				
	Total[1]	Food and products	Tobacco products	Textile mill products	Paper and products	Chemicals and products	Petroleum and coal products	Rubber and plastics products	Total[1]	Total	Stone, clay, and glass products	Primary metals Total	Primary metals Blast furnaces, steel mills
1968	271 254	87 328	4 937	21 970	22 093	45 491	22 548	15 585	602 744	331 490	15 465	48 717	24 908
1969	289 177	93 385	4 992	22 978	24 188	48 096	23 721	16 935	642 013	352 836	16 499	53 534	26 412
1970	295 787	98 535	5 350	22 614	24 573	49 195	24 200	16 754	633 663	337 876	16 454	51 995	25 189
1971	311 788	103 637	5 528	24 034	25 182	51 681	26 198	18 409	670 877	359 089	18 220	51 585	25 791
1972	348 477	115 054	5 919	28 065	28 004	58 130	27 918	21 662	756 321	407 844	20 875	58 490	28 712
1973	399 552	135 585	6 341	31 073	32 495	66 003	33 903	25 191	875 173	475 621	23 141	72 791	36 301
1974	487 403	161 884	7 139	32 790	41 514	85 387	57 229	28 828	1 017 477	530 074	25 503	95 686	49 718
1975	515 887	172 054	8 058	31 065	41 497	91 710	67 496	28 128	1 039 065	523 178	26 233	80 890	42 281
1976	578 088	180 830	8 786	36 387	47 939	106 467	80 022	32 880	1 185 563	607 475	29 618	93 082	46 764
1977	648 399	192 913	9 051	40 550	51 881	120 905	94 702	40 944	1 358 416	710 017	34 209	103 267	50 670
1978	710 082	215 989	9 951	42 281	56 777	132 262	100 967	44 823	1 522 858	812 776	40 238	118 175	59 228
1979	816 110	235 976	10 602	45 137	64 957	151 887	144 156	48 694	1 727 234	911 124	44 287	137 488	67 414
1980	923 662	256 191	12 194	47 256	72 553	168 220	192 969	49 157	1 852 689	929 027	44 473	134 057	61 612
1981	1 012 819	272 140	13 130	50 260	79 970	186 909	217 681	55 178	2 017 544	1 004 725	46 220	142 072	70 254
1982	1 009 673	280 529	16 061	47 516	79 698	176 254	203 404	57 307	1 960 214	950 541	43 515	104 874	46 928
1983	1 044 794	289 314	16 268	53 733	84 817	189 552	187 788	62 870	2 070 564	1 025 770	47 697	109 240	46 398
1984	1 112 908	304 584	17 473	56 336	95 525	205 963	184 488	72 938	2 288 184	1 175 276	53 101	120 315	51 978
1985	1 119 104	308 606	18 559	54 605	94 679	204 790	176 574	75 590	2 334 456	1 215 352	55 821	112 265	48 904
1986	1 097 022	318 203	19 146	57 188	99 865	205 711	122 605	78 379	2 335 881	1 238 859	59 254	107 865	45 718
1987	1 178 374	329 725	20 757	62 787	108 989	229 546	130 414	86 634	2 475 906	1 297 532	61 477	120 248	51 815
1988	1 273 931	354 084	23 809	64 627	122 882	261 238	131 682	95 485	2 695 432	1 421 501	63 145	149 837	64 294
1989	1 362 475	380 160	25 875	67 265	131 896	283 196	146 487	101 236	2 840 375	1 477 900	63 729	155 718	64 783
1990	1 426 915	391 728	29 856	65 533	132 424	292 802	173 389	105 250	2 912 228	1 485 313	63 728	148 787	62 826
1991	1 426 169	397 893	31 943	65 440	130 131	298 545	159 144	105 804	2 878 167	1 451 998	59 957	136 378	57 267
1992	1 462 861	406 964	35 198	70 753	133 201	305 420	150 227	113 593	3 004 727	1 541 866	62 521	138 287	58 449
1993	1 496 990	422 220	28 383	73 955	133 263	314 907	144 834	122 777	3 127 625	1 630 635	65 610	142 685	62 466
1994	1 558 443	430 963	30 021	78 027	143 649	333 905	143 328	135 145	3 348 019	1 789 576	71 230	161 188	69 887
1995	1 668 185	448 406	32 984	79 743	172 637	362 127	151 261	145 426	3 589 395	1 921 210	75 991	180 303	74 547
1996	1 729 186	471 633	34 492	78 505	161 968	372 848	180 122	143 888	3 735 183	2 005 997	83 365	173 619	72 268
1993:													
January	114 748	31 794	1 965	5 427	10 690	24 653	11 502	9 271	256 516	131 485	5 019	11 674	4 986
February	122 563	33 684	2 060	5 982	10 977	26 310	11 753	10 299	259 430	134 177	5 340	11 797	5 049
March	128 515	35 658	3 503	6 182	11 285	27 965	11 846	10 548	261 889	135 802	5 235	11 843	5 168
April	123 377	34 260	1 716	5 919	10 833	27 378	12 391	10 220	259 006	134 050	5 404	11 749	5 141
May	123 758	34 741	2 519	6 112	11 003	26 126	12 888	10 359	257 074	133 407	5 380	11 502	5 078
June	132 144	36 535	3 039	6 838	11 575	28 764	12 999	11 144	261 618	135 900	5 455	12 087	5 228
July	119 520	33 805	2 294	5 487	10 878	24 909	12 294	9 390	256 241	131 755	5 326	11 602	5 199
August	126 168	36 232	1 646	6 645	11 236	25 555	12 269	10 382	257 025	133 688	5 387	11 770	5 238
September	132 629	37 879	2 746	6 775	11 700	27 265	12 184	10 823	261 718	136 868	5 840	12 090	5 283
October	128 942	36 453	1 924	6 617	11 242	25 372	12 634	10 749	262 833	138 379	5 633	11 911	5 277
November	125 247	35 747	2 255	6 364	11 045	25 435	11 629	10 114	265 617	140 863	5 743	12 258	5 383
December	119 379	35 432	2 716	5 607	10 799	25 175	10 445	9 478	266 998	142 958	5 786	12 444	5 488
1994:													
January	114 164	32 207	2 319	5 307	10 596	24 883	9 933	9 754	267 287	142 969	5 608	12 211	5 328
February	123 047	35 035	2 401	6 164	11 309	26 002	10 403	10 681	269 138	143 474	5 657	12 476	5 555
March	130 452	37 059	2 349	6 714	11 566	29 081	10 596	11 569	273 780	146 016	6 033	12 633	5 550
April	125 218	33 878	2 501	6 151	11 060	28 404	11 473	11 250	272 114	145 486	5 947	12 717	5 571
May	128 021	35 267	2 468	6 469	11 546	27 866	12 031	11 454	274 359	146 528	5 867	13 054	5 700
June	135 641	36 942	2 519	7 262	12 259	29 594	13 000	12 191	278 167	148 906	5 922	13 292	5 726
July	123 366	33 562	2 338	5 758	11 567	25 863	12 758	10 203	276 826	148 108	5 861	13 262	5 716
August	135 846	36 435	2 686	7 025	12 620	28 201	13 409	11 720	285 457	152 969	6 008	13 827	6 010
September	139 922	38 323	2 571	7 298	12 804	29 973	12 602	11 966	283 375	151 282	5 987	13 856	5 943
October	136 274	37 406	2 515	6 981	12 870	27 687	12 359	12 071	283 203	151 165	5 886	14 062	5 981
November	134 732	37 021	2 625	6 691	12 834	28 024	12 658	11 372	289 842	155 369	6 112	14 505	6 151
December	131 760	37 828	2 729	6 207	12 618	28 327	12 106	10 914	293 999	157 079	6 334	15 470	6 751
1995:													
January	126 213	33 642	2 386	5 839	13 190	28 231	11 235	11 399	296 430	159 403	6 305	15 499	6 275
February	135 294	35 860	2 612	6 569	14 137	29 802	11 898	12 240	296 585	158 518	6 348	15 264	6 302
March	140 496	37 255	2 799	7 166	14 417	31 880	11 602	12 880	297 782	160 044	6 256	15 536	6 537
April	136 161	35 569	2 657	6 430	13 926	30 284	13 010	12 442	294 385	156 830	5 870	15 088	6 214
May	138 946	36 477	2 979	6 728	14 661	30 454	13 579	12 595	296 504	157 942	6 197	15 165	6 293
June	146 201	37 923	2 812	7 394	15 614	32 473	13 702	12 999	299 195	159 468	6 227	15 123	6 185
July	132 626	35 265	2 688	5 817	14 122	28 880	12 817	10 766	294 318	155 998	6 300	14 690	5 914
August	144 185	38 363	2 796	7 108	15 035	30 552	13 114	12 556	301 761	161 380	6 454	14 955	6 169
September	147 729	40 585	2 697	7 389	15 031	31 332	12 756	12 738	302 558	162 601	6 413	14 850	6 188
October	144 312	39 780	2 749	6 807	14 655	29 864	12 474	12 536	302 025	162 083	6 456	14 818	6 229
November	140 536	39 085	2 988	6 632	14 197	29 114	12 515	11 645	302 621	162 393	6 565	14 659	6 164
December	135 486	38 602	2 821	5 864	13 652	29 261	12 559	10 630	304 203	163 646	6 649	14 602	6 000
1996:													
January	129 315	36 001	2 526	5 352	13 299	28 796	12 060	10 738	300 439	160 363	6 787	14 375	5 990
February	137 688	37 535	2 720	6 242	13 932	29 716	12 652	11 936	303 090	162 473	6 540	14 255	5 969
March	143 255	38 920	2 955	6 886	13 814	31 580	13 371	12 511	301 666	160 768	6 686	14 283	5 838
April	142 868	37 978	2 729	6 147	13 365	31 715	15 519	12 434	309 477	165 496	6 818	14 549	6 037
May	144 981	39 397	2 851	6 578	13 530	31 797	15 773	12 681	313 247	168 781	7 070	14 633	6 012
June	148 603	39 506	2 870	7 580	14 027	32 468	15 382	12 958	310 052	167 524	6 958	14 153	6 023
July	139 473	38 044	2 938	5 857	13 199	29 919	15 091	11 186	313 851	168 762	7 173	14 630	6 105
August	149 016	40 413	3 119	6 923	13 614	31 217	15 620	12 340	313 854	168 960	7 000	14 415	6 018
September	152 326	41 648	2 815	7 332	13 702	32 368	15 959	12 465	315 971	171 415	6 968	14 377	6 069
October	151 868	41 927	3 013	6 804	13 523	31 744	16 627	12 395	316 461	169 368	7 237	14 565	6 066
November	148 357	41 144	2 958	6 666	13 141	30 699	16 251	11 627	319 296	171 426	7 092	14 719	6 025
December	141 436	39 120	2 998	6 138	12 822	30 829	15 817	10 617	316 306	169 504	6 944	14 743	6 134

1. Includes categories not shown separately.

MANUFACTURERS' SHIPMENTS—SEASONALLY ADJUSTED—Continued
(Millions of dollars, adjusted for seasonality and for trading-day and calendar-month variation)

YEAR AND MONTH	Durable goods industries—Continued						Nondurable goods industries							
	Fabricated metal products	Industrial machinery and equipment	Electronic and electric equipment	Transportation equipment		Instruments and products	Total¹	Food and products	Tobacco products	Textile mill products	Paper and products	Chemicals and products	Petroleum and coal products	Rubber and plastics products
				Total	Motor vehicles and parts									
1968	43 638	51 370	39 372	83 527	49 465	17 645	271 254	87 328	4 937	21 970	22 093	45 491	22 548	15 585
1969	46 104	56 584	41 560	85 175	50 943	18 662	289 177	93 385	4 992	22 978	24 188	48 096	23 721	16 935
1970	44 210	56 893	41 408	74 539	42 538	18 367	295 787	98 535	5 350	22 614	24 573	49 195	24 200	16 754
1971	45 478	56 445	42 377	88 857	58 247	18 613	311 788	103 637	5 528	24 034	25 182	51 681	26 198	18 409
1972	51 487	66 156	47 502	94 706	63 923	21 043	348 477	115 054	5 919	28 065	28 004	58 130	27 918	21 662
1973	58 804	78 207	54 569	110 587	74 799	23 627	399 552	135 585	6 341	31 073	32 495	66 003	33 903	25 191
1974	67 212	93 041	58 684	108 244	68 631	27 454	487 403	161 884	7 139	32 790	41 514	85 387	57 229	28 828
1975	68 411	96 354	56 068	113 503	70 033	29 547	515 887	172 054	8 058	31 065	41 497	91 710	67 496	28 128
1976	77 560	105 847	65 151	141 028	95 380	33 238	578 088	180 830	8 786	36 387	47 939	106 467	80 022	32 880
1977	89 938	122 749	77 845	166 954	117 747	38 803	648 399	192 913	9 051	40 550	51 881	120 905	94 702	40 944
1978	101 245	143 919	88 679	188 773	131 999	44 655	710 082	215 989	9 951	42 281	56 777	132 262	100 967	44 823
1979	113 494	167 014	102 361	201 623	131 378	50 702	816 110	235 976	10 602	45 137	64 957	151 887	144 156	48 694
1980	116 071	180 564	112 864	186 516	104 560	59 825	923 662	256 191	12 194	47 256	72 553	168 220	192 969	49 157
1981	123 535	201 102	122 084	205 223	116 981	66 613	1 012 819	272 140	13 130	50 260	79 970	186 909	217 681	55 178
1982	119 236	186 773	125 728	201 347	112 270	74 918	1 009 673	280 529	16 061	47 516	79 698	176 254	203 404	57 307
1983	123 083	178 446	136 138	245 392	148 296	79 637	1 044 794	289 314	16 268	53 733	84 817	189 552	187 788	62 870
1984	138 107	211 075	162 362	284 593	181 993	89 398	1 112 908	304 584	17 473	56 336	95 525	205 963	184 488	72 938
1985	143 268	218 408	163 951	307 380	193 445	96 207	1 119 104	308 606	18 559	54 605	94 679	204 790	176 574	75 590
1986	143 063	213 574	164 811	322 688	198 811	100 798	1 097 022	318 203	19 146	57 188	99 865	205 711	122 605	78 379
1987	147 367	217 671	171 287	332 936	205 923	107 325	1 178 374	329 725	20 757	62 787	108 989	229 546	130 414	86 634
1988	159 505	244 365	187 301	354 849	222 353	116 009	1 273 931	354 084	23 809	64 627	122 882	261 238	131 682	95 485
1989	164 073	256 212	194 598	369 675	233 232	121 523	1 362 475	380 160	25 875	67 265	131 896	283 196	146 487	101 236
1990	165 064	259 367	195 898	370 328	217 295	127 978	1 426 915	391 728	29 856	65 533	132 424	292 802	173 389	105 250
1991	159 760	247 508	199 278	367 235	209 210	132 836	1 426 169	397 893	31 943	65 440	130 131	298 545	159 144	105 804
1992	166 532	258 662	216 764	399 270	238 384	134 941	1 462 861	406 964	35 198	70 753	133 201	305 420	150 227	113 593
1993	175 118	278 063	233 622	414 694	267 365	137 387	1 496 990	422 220	28 383	73 955	133 263	314 907	144 834	122 777
1994	190 544	313 047	266 405	450 809	314 637	138 400	1 558 443	430 963	30 021	78 027	143 649	333 905	143 328	135 145
1995	204 820	351 113	299 838	462 849	326 415	140 911	1 668 185	448 406	32 984	79 743	172 637	362 127	151 261	145 426
1996:	215 427	378 366	323 001	471 661	334 633	146 199	1 729 186	471 633	34 492	78 505	161 968	372 848	180 122	143 888
1993:														
January	14 145	22 528	18 190	34 386	21 714	11 213	125 031	34 608	2 545	6 328	11 098	26 087	12 880	9 971
February	14 272	22 280	18 827	35 024	22 186	11 332	125 253	34 393	2 455	6 153	10 968	26 476	12 890	10 210
March	14 553	22 966	18 989	35 587	22 751	11 419	126 087	34 902	2 983	5 917	11 080	26 542	12 934	10 079
April	14 328	22 448	18 920	34 929	22 171	11 221	124 956	35 342	2 161	6 110	11 085	26 351	12 562	9 959
May	14 393	22 631	19 029	34 260	21 371	11 243	123 667	34 450	2 443	6 130	11 098	25 690	12 479	10 085
June	14 743	22 535	19 607	35 001	22 090	11 503	125 718	35 413	2 590	6 162	11 051	26 788	12 130	10 265
July	14 271	22 954	19 426	31 680	20 711	11 436	124 486	35 472	2 510	6 188	11 098	26 135	11 906	10 105
August	14 361	22 814	19 695	33 021	20 610	11 476	123 337	35 800	1 632	6 198	10 984	25 745	11 690	10 194
September	14 755	23 636	19 953	33 550	21 929	11 593	124 850	35 564	2 459	6 117	11 331	25 986	11 620	10 398
October	14 874	23 539	19 862	35 549	23 248	11 517	124 454	35 110	2 139	6 245	11 066	25 958	11 911	10 358
November	15 062	24 412	20 206	35 366	23 897	11 808	124 754	35 331	2 098	6 243	11 196	26 477	11 388	10 597
December	15 342	24 912	20 274	36 299	24 444	11 640	124 040	35 555	2 455	6 178	11 172	26 215	10 834	10 621
1994:														
January	15 330	24 110	21 001	37 146	25 258	11 550	124 318	35 019	2 743	6 214	11 035	26 322	11 219	10 472
February	15 347	24 932	21 170	36 419	25 341	11 416	125 664	35 813	2 681	6 353	11 276	26 228	11 349	10 637
March	15 772	24 996	21 176	37 870	25 588	11 299	127 764	36 358	2 088	6 382	11 371	27 445	11 509	10 976
April	15 592	25 308	21 851	36 524	25 377	11 518	126 628	34 931	2 896	6 383	11 355	27 316	11 507	10 960
May	15 625	25 780	21 823	36 460	25 579	11 476	127 831	35 097	2 412	6 468	11 599	27 402	11 580	11 085
June	15 685	25 785	22 148	37 971	26 225	11 630	129 261	35 938	2 289	6 535	11 702	27 614	12 078	11 236
July	15 789	26 369	22 431	36 439	25 620	11 549	128 718	35 276	2 441	6 479	11 839	27 211	12 364	11 121
August	16 233	26 934	22 687	39 132	27 678	11 628	132 488	35 885	2 606	6 557	12 332	28 369	12 825	11 454
September	16 182	26 660	22 450	37 889	26 560	11 712	132 093	35 965	2 443	6 572	12 396	28 798	12 086	11 493
October	16 035	27 181	22 823	36 856	25 814	11 499	132 038	35 956	2 676	6 646	12 678	28 413	11 875	11 670
November	16 583	27 107	23 316	39 203	27 554	11 533	134 473	36 494	2 548	6 606	12 976	29 155	12 526	11 889
December	16 410	27 480	23 117	39 356	28 490	11 708	136 920	37 814	2 564	6 811	13 062	29 550	12 504	12 233
1995:														
January	17 141	27 784	23 825	39 375	27 602	11 899	137 027	36 560	2 649	6 839	13 762	29 750	12 545	12 240
February	17 024	28 404	23 456	39 108	27 583	11 732	138 067	36 728	2 780	6 768	14 082	30 090	12 907	12 208
March	16 951	28 361	23 997	40 077	28 578	11 815	137 738	36 704	2 605	6 777	14 207	30 089	12 491	12 212
April	16 768	28 956	23 770	37 921	26 206	11 537	137 555	36 674	2 879	6 700	14 300	29 334	12 915	12 110
May	16 853	29 339	24 341	37 414	25 978	11 773	138 562	36 412	2 890	6 703	14 671	29 993	13 035	12 105
June	16 885	29 113	25 095	38 462	26 570	11 628	139 727	37 014	2 698	6 626	14 906	30 446	12 824	12 025
July	16 956	28 879	24 697	36 398	25 314	11 298	138 320	37 022	2 740	6 537	14 464	30 400	12 426	11 772
August	17 266	29 631	25 877	37 968	27 105	11 884	140 381	37 682	2 686	6 654	14 701	30 661	12 545	12 234
September	17 207	29 805	25 998	39 229	28 003	11 725	139 957	38 118	2 694	6 645	14 548	30 337	12 279	12 240
October	17 304	30 101	25 745	38 700	27 987	11 703	139 942	38 105	2 809	6 523	14 437	30 574	12 115	12 137
November	17 123	30 257	25 991	38 803	27 263	11 901	140 228	38 429	2 929	6 560	14 334	30 302	12 482	12 146
December	17 437	30 698	26 302	38 986	27 782	12 055	140 557	38 633	2 748	6 438	14 127	30 389	12 946	11 930
1996:														
January	17 443	30 261	25 885	37 098	26 991	11 840	140 076	39 053	2 692	6 273	13 890	30 235	13 292	11 540
February	17 381	31 622	25 997	38 096	27 418	11 994	140 617	38 555	2 844	6 419	13 881	30 078	13 620	11 898
March	17 081	31 076	26 559	35 873	24 721	12 002	140 898	38 513	2 810	6 497	13 630	29 897	14 229	11 890
April	17 980	30 913	26 422	39 249	28 262	11 945	143 981	39 145	2 851	6 425	13 711	30 674	15 297	12 098
May	18 217	31 308	26 574	40 870	28 755	12 199	144 466	39 336	2 784	6 532	13 541	31 297	15 108	12 154
June	18 035	31 682	26 933	39 428	28 104	12 181	142 528	38 609	2 841	6 770	13 390	30 628	14 563	12 022
July	18 005	31 518	26 655	40 203	29 480	12 386	145 089	39 744	2 954	6 580	13 538	31 423	14 706	12 212
August	18 298	31 789	26 663	40 331	28 665	12 316	144 894	39 673	2 970	6 508	13 311	31 257	14 988	12 027
September	18 310	32 243	27 176	41 667	29 388	12 206	144 556	39 204	2 902	6 594	13 250	31 272	15 461	11 978
October	18 215	31 623	27 494	39 560	28 287	12 310	147 093	40 036	2 998	6 544	13 299	32 269	16 220	12 005
November	18 385	31 659	28 273	40 319	28 312	12 490	147 870	40 385	2 903	6 605	13 269	31 895	16 250	12 103
December	18 067	32 292	27 756	39 117	26 934	12 371	146 802	39 286	2 976	6 725	13 294	31 956	16 285	11 959

1. Includes categories not shown separately.

MANUFACTURERS' SHIPMENTS—SEASONALLY ADJUSTED—Continued
(Millions of dollars, adjusted for seasonality and for trading-day and calendar-month variation)

YEAR AND MONTH	Home goods and apparel	Consumer staples	Machinery and equipment	Automotive equipment	Construction materials and supplies	Other materials, supplies, and intermediate products	Household durables	Capital goods industries Total	Nondefense	Defense
1968	57 804	122 085	91 899	25 719	39 621	200 751	23 794	99 702	72 405	27 297
1969	61 072	130 509	99 397	26 836	42 493	214 859	24 838	105 773	79 568	26 205
1970	59 987	136 616	96 531	23 038	41 945	210 904	24 259	102 285	78 907	23 378
1971	63 664	143 858	103 931	31 257	45 559	219 088	25 682	98 643	79 148	19 495
1972	72 839	158 995	117 214	34 568	54 119	249 670	29 968	107 198	87 762	19 436
1973	79 588	183 532	137 154	39 808	62 228	295 929	33 285	124 912	103 997	20 915
1974	81 310	225 831	152 937	36 687	69 146	360 524	34 445	143 828	122 674	21 154
1975	81 417	246 958	158 401	37 803	66 984	349 019	34 003	149 687	126 363	23 324
1976	91 278	269 428	176 828	50 088	77 948	408 132	39 178	162 172	135 540	26 632
1977	104 862	294 653	206 927	60 310	91 883	471 894	45 450	185 541	155 956	29 585
1978	113 615	326 611	239 871	67 007	106 017	530 773	50 495	217 165	186 427	30 738
1979	119 089	378 177	278 174	67 095	118 024	605 503	54 211	254 754	222 069	32 685
1980	125 155	437 351	294 260	54 491	118 429	635 014	56 392	287 132	246 797	40 335
1981	132 795	477 583	320 239	60 747	122 844	692 461	59 269	317 628	269 774	47 854
1982	132 768	486 145	304 441	58 940	115 777	640 923	56 074	312 298	252 098	60 200
1983	142 230	491 169	309 553	76 794	127 781	684 315	60 118	316 125	242 297	73 828
1984	152 189	510 658	354 591	92 959	141 230	774 635	65 833	361 205	278 900	82 305
1985	153 541	518 004	372 580	97 313	147 103	766 196	67 080	388 763	293 420	95 343
1986	159 393	503 297	373 230	101 143	154 113	759 975	70 319	396 158	289 969	106 189
1987	162 547	531 790	384 526	105 027	164 865	824 206	69 444	404 738	295 334	109 404
1988	168 547	568 799	427 220	112 479	175 594	926 983	73 667	438 089	333 402	104 687
1989	173 813	616 035	454 632	118 728	180 083	971 901	78 138	450 863	350 870	99 993
1990	174 969	658 793	471 815	110 537	180 604	974 478	78 456	473 175	370 804	102 371
1991	175 357	667 740	469 599	105 892	171 876	953 641	78 122	467 419	369 796	97 623
1992	185 588	678 502	500 554	120 632	184 498	1 000 209	82 276	481 257	389 448	91 809
1993	195 574	691 290	524 481	134 229	199 228	1 048 320	88 522	484 967	400 884	84 083
1994	205 984	706 035	569 332	155 405	217 556	1 154 364	95 167	506 368	429 273	77 095
1995	210 752	743 516	611 998	160 464	228 364	1 279 763	99 063	546 185	473 290	72 895
1996	219 057	802 092	653 894	166 342	235 093	1 288 415	108 875	576 403	503 781	72 622
1993:										
January	16 353	57 537	43 173	11 059	15 702	84 879	7 209	39 820	32 693	7 127
February	16 333	57 360	42 567	11 271	16 450	87 010	7 324	39 801	32 416	7 385
March	16 087	58 572	43 781	11 302	16 500	87 144	7 221	40 790	33 496	7 294
April	15 900	57 838	42 891	11 049	16 348	86 830	7 141	39 952	32 722	7 230
May	16 075	56 797	43 214	10 787	16 492	85 822	7 173	40 482	33 286	7 196
June	16 446	58 128	43 589	11 040	16 660	87 659	7 381	40 571	33 450	7 121
July	16 053	57 994	41 791	10 569	16 109	85 925	7 431	38 904	31 739	7 165
August	16 351	56 932	43 377	10 386	16 307	86 533	7 351	40 255	33 624	6 631
September	16 449	58 002	43 306	10 941	16 862	88 308	7 546	40 163	33 116	7 047
October	16 408	57 462	44 226	11 629	16 834	87 990	7 463	40 928	33 664	7 264
November	16 736	57 090	45 133	11 879	17 204	89 969	7 636	41 114	34 384	6 730
December	16 163	57 434	46 466	12 213	17 594	90 057	7 539	41 732	35 393	6 339
1994:										
January	16 440	57 317	45 634	12 516	17 275	90 458	7 626	41 070	34 286	6 784
February	16 646	58 041	45 790	12 546	17 358	91 264	7 687	40 918	34 476	6 442
March	16 969	58 345	46 841	12 648	18 022	92 991	7 755	41 809	35 217	6 592
April	17 024	57 927	46 301	12 562	17 843	92 915	7 883	41 397	34 870	6 527
May	17 191	57 719	46 601	12 565	17 826	94 176	7 935	41 434	35 039	6 395
June	17 021	58 739	47 728	12 981	17 941	95 490	7 941	42 334	35 914	6 420
July	17 118	58 322	46 775	12 581	18 019	95 709	7 853	42 035	35 608	6 427
August	17 358	59 901	48 679	13 600	18 372	98 516	8 043	43 011	36 385	6 626
September	17 554	59 303	48 357	13 117	18 327	98 228	8 079	42 696	36 514	6 182
October	17 487	59 060	47 778	12 807	18 390	99 124	8 084	42 764	36 311	6 453
November	17 282	59 992	49 133	13 675	18 935	101 761	8 006	43 605	37 144	6 461
December	17 649	61 159	48 995	13 955	19 213	104 176	8 156	42 758	36 678	6 080
1995:										
January	17 993	60 294	50 004	13 620	19 405	105 522	8 422	44 459	37 970	6 489
February	17 472	61 043	50 362	13 583	19 454	105 483	8 088	44 521	38 395	6 126
March	17 476	60 473	50 419	13 935	19 160	107 032	8 062	44 684	38 496	6 188
April	17 267	61 065	50 441	12 902	18 663	104 885	7 959	45 336	39 207	6 129
May	17 340	61 276	50 540	12 859	18 714	106 337	8 013	45 642	39 462	6 180
June	17 556	61 880	51 490	13 085	18 787	106 725	8 107	46 174	40 098	6 076
July	17 435	61 666	49 490	12 560	18 749	104 948	8 161	44 583	38 484	6 099
August	17 693	62 746	50 959	13 415	19 191	107 872	8 432	45 553	39 435	6 118
September	17 582	62 603	51 574	13 671	19 276	108 145	8 340	46 068	40 041	6 027
October	17 668	62 846	51 547	13 645	19 177	107 354	8 450	45 799	39 794	6 005
November	17 639	63 310	52 423	13 338	18 959	107 357	8 561	46 473	40 768	5 705
December	17 526	64 039	52 478	13 655	18 851	107 573	8 396	46 793	40 860	5 933
1996:										
January	17 215	64 511	50 833	13 259	18 931	105 576	8 511	44 987	38 849	6 138
February	17 610	64 411	53 114	13 599	18 484	105 734	8 487	47 032	41 139	5 893
March	18 068	65 080	52 546	12 571	18 712	104 430	8 989	47 177	41 057	6 120
April	18 204	66 574	53 328	13 984	19 300	107 066	9 025	46 761	40 743	6 018
May	18 334	66 833	55 112	14 249	19 681	108 195	9 119	48 230	42 237	5 993
June	18 307	65 648	54 634	13 935	19 619	106 903	9 209	48 329	42 099	6 230
July	18 295	67 371	54 571	14 513	20 211	107 992	9 093	47 332	41 478	5 854
August	18 273	67 474	55 233	14 153	20 033	107 726	9 076	48 433	42 446	5 987
September	18 367	67 215	56 638	14 714	19 955	107 983	9 205	49 397	43 255	6 142
October	18 497	69 210	55 058	14 100	20 113	108 763	9 271	47 955	42 186	5 769
November	18 888	69 265	55 932	14 071	20 038	109 485	9 331	49 404	43 132	6 272
December	18 762	68 257	55 860	13 467	19 807	108 635	9 394	49 875	43 709	6 166

MANUFACTURERS' INVENTORIES [1]
(Book value, end of period—Millions of dollars)

YEAR AND MONTH	Not seasonally adjusted			Seasonally adjusted											
					Durable goods industries										
	Total	Durable goods industries	Nondurable goods industries	Total	Total	Stone, clay, and glass products	Primary metals		Fabricated metal products	Industrial machinery and equipment	Electronic and electric equipment	Transportation equipment		Instruments and products
							Total	Blast furnaces, steel mills				Total	Motor vehicles and parts	
1968	90 235	58 341	31 894	90 560	58 732	1 918	7 547	4 207	7 506	11 628	7 297	14 413	3 879	3 825
1969	97 749	64 133	33 616	98 145	64 598	2 051	8 066	4 451	7 666	13 408	8 072	15 942	4 067	4 088
1970	101 246	66 187	35 059	101 599	66 651	2 239	8 995	4 990	7 907	14 500	8 410	14 648	4 178	4 196
1971	102 267	65 664	36 603	102 567	66 136	2 302	9 084	4 926	8 098	14 344	8 058	13 799	4 173	4 201
1972	107 900	69 583	38 317	108 121	70 067	2 430	9 617	5 387	8 408	15 142	8 528	14 775	4 670	4 435
1973	124 327	80 608	43 719	124 499	81 192	2 712	10 034	5 302	9 864	18 411	10 532	16 458	5 708	5 233
1974	157 595	100 763	56 832	157 625	101 493	3 403	13 447	6 820	13 387	24 189	12 231	19 197	6 688	6 486
1975	159 844	101 958	57 886	159 708	102 590	3 594	15 742	8 597	13 091	24 156	11 110	19 620	6 101	6 547
1976	174 867	111 366	63 501	174 636	111 988	3 841	17 699	10 035	14 304	25 245	12 594	20 886	7 814	7 214
1977	188 435	120 131	68 304	188 378	120 877	4 095	18 261	10 004	15 527	27 282	13 922	22 423	9 078	8 185
1978	209 113	136 015	73 098	211 691	138 181	4 710	19 420	10 719	17 296	32 086	16 163	26 170	10 357	9 682
1979	239 101	158 146	80 955	242 157	160 734	5 183	22 446	12 012	19 145	37 464	19 566	31 638	10 978	11 415
1980	261 700	171 864	89 836	265 215	174 788	5 674	23 055	12 153	19 532	40 958	21 838	35 900	9 864	13 376
1981	279 453	183 268	96 185	283 413	186 443	6 106	25 794	13 359	20 209	43 652	23 608	37 527	9 047	14 760
1982	307 212	196 663	110 549	311 852	200 444	6 506	24 174	12 556	21 440	47 908	25 100	43 005	8 534	17 038
1983	307 675	196 002	111 673	312 379	199 854	6 628	22 308	11 065	21 752	44 586	26 922	43 791	10 433	17 769
1984	334 236	217 049	117 187	339 516	221 330	7 042	22 444	11 087	23 330	48 760	31 636	50 770	11 680	20 206
1985	329 555	213 978	115 577	334 749	218 193	7 040	19 974	9 709	22 880	46 526	30 549	52 634	11 809	21 569
1986	317 567	207 865	109 702	322 654	211 997	7 093	18 436	8 567	22 094	42 409	28 632	53 363	11 445	22 461
1987	332 619	216 343	116 276	338 109	220 799	7 154	19 076	8 620	22 920	43 141	29 859	56 461	11 937	23 692
1988	363 300	237 510	125 790	369 374	242 468	7 496	22 422	10 495	24 950	47 707	31 645	63 202	12 310	25 346
1989	384 539	252 058	132 481	391 212	257 513	7 792	22 838	10 942	25 427	50 342	33 623	70 968	12 503	26 541
1990	397 850	257 363	140 487	405 073	263 209	8 205	22 560	11 045	25 044	49 673	32 913	77 640	13 504	26 552
1991	383 509	244 121	139 388	390 950	250 019	7 928	20 703	10 236	23 922	47 880	30 981	73 019	13 163	25 778
1992	374 906	232 318	142 588	382 547	238 166	8 009	19 975	9 802	23 824	47 096	30 731	63 310	13 065	24 685
1993	375 982	233 306	142 676	384 138	239 404	7 611	20 134	9 833	23 842	48 632	31 874	60 964	14 066	23 212
1994	395 974	247 001	148 973	405 028	253 691	7 879	22 613	10 704	25 601	52 943	35 855	61 332	15 615	22 974
1995	419 188	258 699	160 489	429 089	265 915	8 593	24 089	11 519	27 427	59 121	39 259	58 346	16 101	23 383
1996	424 462	263 937	160 525	434 434	271 329	8 607	24 767	12 279	27 440	58 177	39 450	62 723	16 493	24 367
1993:														
January	380 058	234 827	145 231	381 135	236 133	7 972	19 920	9 790	23 683	46 493	30 742	62 487	12 960	24 406
February	383 573	238 461	145 112	381 465	236 970	7 953	19 924	9 791	23 654	46 309	30 875	63 018	13 178	24 439
March	382 115	237 348	144 767	382 476	237 581	7 940	19 875	9 651	23 879	46 080	31 063	63 024	13 319	24 404
April	384 987	238 961	146 026	383 468	237 876	7 905	19 700	9 532	23 728	46 334	31 265	62 727	13 430	24 317
May	387 094	240 557	146 537	384 414	238 308	7 852	19 847	9 616	23 765	46 424	31 546	62 577	13 413	24 146
June	383 121	237 782	145 339	384 898	238 659	7 801	19 792	9 592	23 667	46 898	31 458	62 721	13 581	24 079
July	385 339	239 537	145 802	384 378	238 578	7 793	19 819	9 699	23 730	47 146	31 620	62 350	13 180	23 865
August	387 883	241 077	146 806	384 956	238 782	7 726	20 076	9 707	24 010	47 378	31 667	61 648	13 763	23 744
September	384 850	239 076	145 774	385 233	239 442	7 685	20 030	9 663	24 099	47 716	31 544	62 001	13 799	23 694
October	386 527	240 199	146 328	385 285	239 727	7 709	20 120	9 758	24 011	48 182	31 687	61 373	13 919	23 783
November	385 940	240 541	145 399	385 669	240 079	7 666	19 988	9 782	23 897	48 268	31 921	61 983	13 952	23 397
December	375 982	233 306	142 676	384 138	239 404	7 611	20 134	9 833	23 842	48 632	31 874	60 964	14 066	23 212
1994:														
January	384 104	239 694	144 410	385 351	240 938	7 677	20 197	9 905	23 902	49 094	32 184	61 085	14 120	23 182
February	388 639	243 174	145 465	386 381	241 504	7 635	20 324	9 930	24 029	49 359	32 433	60 851	14 253	23 024
March	386 411	241 104	145 307	386 832	241 519	7 654	20 399	9 909	23 807	49 965	32 666	60 093	14 224	22 934
April	389 204	243 094	146 110	387 667	242 107	7 605	20 468	9 911	23 874	50 236	32 974	60 223	14 201	22 849
May	392 962	246 133	146 829	390 037	243 779	7 583	20 692	10 079	24 059	50 427	33 403	60 713	14 618	23 060
June	389 527	243 722	145 805	391 312	244 791	7 467	20 844	10 147	24 204	51 119	33 679	60 517	14 784	23 057
July	396 578	248 081	148 497	395 438	247 026	7 567	21 136	10 254	24 829	51 440	34 072	60 928	15 023	22 902
August	400 092	250 887	149 205	396 936	248 433	7 550	21 295	10 259	24 993	52 032	34 376	60 926	14 943	22 951
September	396 721	248 078	148 643	397 096	248 563	7 607	21 446	10 309	24 960	52 120	34 694	60 529	15 133	22 928
October	400 319	250 011	150 308	399 162	249 661	7 681	21 907	10 544	25 107	52 340	35 054	60 515	15 069	22 815
November	401 830	251 818	150 012	401 665	251 374	7 749	22 295	10 647	25 333	52 742	35 404	60 572	15 303	22 900
December	395 974	247 001	148 973	405 028	253 691	7 879	22 613	10 704	25 601	52 943	35 855	61 332	15 615	22 974
1995:														
January	407 331	254 335	152 996	408 718	255 483	7 941	23 038	10 834	25 935	54 344	36 361	60 568	15 712	22 733
February	414 129	258 578	155 551	411 497	256 540	7 990	23 319	11 060	26 271	54 630	36 967	59 887	15 771	22 807
March	414 292	257 687	156 605	414 690	258 114	8 115	23 498	11 123	26 879	55 025	37 190	60 102	15 904	22 762
April	419 587	260 853	158 734	417 710	259 645	8 332	23 783	11 352	27 175	55 292	37 355	60 025	16 028	22 794
May	424 260	263 927	160 333	420 824	261 214	8 529	23 812	11 391	27 458	55 991	37 489	60 369	16 247	22 629
June	420 575	260 374	160 201	422 372	261 514	8 629	23 994	11 503	27 690	56 331	37 739	59 337	16 173	22 896
July	426 312	264 582	161 730	424 804	263 317	8 742	24 238	11 553	27 836	56 710	38 354	59 403	16 256	22 906
August	428 261	265 910	162 351	424 926	263 334	8 787	24 171	11 576	27 863	56 984	38 562	59 031	16 062	22 922
September	426 575	263 573	163 002	427 153	264 316	8 821	24 097	11 533	27 723	57 516	38 871	59 018	15 903	22 984
October	429 109	265 855	163 254	428 238	265 694	8 754	24 086	11 480	27 738	57 879	39 402	59 123	16 030	23 088
November	427 816	265 883	161 933	427 924	265 507	8 710	24 131	11 390	27 671	58 652	38 871	58 473	16 076	23 284
December	419 188	258 699	160 489	429 089	265 915	8 593	24 089	11 519	27 427	59 121	39 259	58 346	16 101	23 383
1996:														
January	429 719	266 871	162 848	431 192	267 964	8 577	24 175	11 650	27 411	59 785	39 646	59 174	16 440	23 547
February	434 546	270 602	163 944	431 462	268 245	8 586	24 109	11 621	27 570	59 888	39 307	59 472	16 279	23 711
March	430 993	267 835	163 158	431 363	268 392	8 573	24 326	11 899	27 428	59 660	38 962	60 187	16 749	23 912
April	433 470	269 951	163 519	431 352	268 648	8 514	24 133	11 703	27 304	60 059	39 276	60 198	16 625	24 066
May	434 015	271 624	162 391	430 298	268 657	8 439	24 133	11 627	27 170	59 918	39 152	60 312	16 534	24 118
June	427 726	266 934	160 792	429 802	268 294	8 447	24 253	11 668	26 948	59 018	39 342	60 919	16 387	23 935
July	431 983	270 828	161 155	430 543	269 493	8 373	24 085	11 662	27 277	59 463	39 245	61 425	16 745	24 310
August	434 755	273 129	161 626	431 647	270 537	8 423	24 077	11 775	27 415	59 573	39 341	61 612	16 662	24 446
September	431 950	269 918	162 032	432 674	270 794	8 435	24 374	11 990	27 335	59 024	39 389	61 940	16 628	24 438
October	434 837	271 704	163 133	434 038	271 616	8 478	24 310	12 019	27 376	58 980	39 454	62 541	16 747	24 636
November	435 162	272 612	162 550	435 200	272 198	8 507	24 479	12 153	27 410	59 196	39 760	62 638	16 357	24 311
December	424 462	263 937	160 525	434 434	271 329	8 607	24 767	12 279	27 440	58 177	39 450	62 723	16 493	24 367

1. Data prior to 1982 are not comparable to subsequent periods due to change in inventory valuation methods; see NOTES.

MANUFACTURERS' INVENTORIES [1]—Continued
(Book value, end of period—Millions of dollars, seasonally adjusted)

YEAR AND MONTH	Durable goods industries by stage of fabrication			Nondurable goods industries										
	Materials and supplies	Work in process	Finished goods	Total	Food and products	Tobacco products	Textile mill products	Paper and products	Chemicals and products	Petroleum and coal products	Rubber and plastics products	By stage of fabrication		
												Materials and supplies	Work in process	Finished goods
1968	17 344	27 213	14 175	31 828	8 009	2 218	3 610	2 309	5 542	2 035	2 018	12 328	4 852	14 648
1969	18 636	30 282	15 680	33 547	8 329	2 188	3 670	2 399	6 173	2 085	2 215	12 753	5 120	15 674
1970	19 149	29 745	17 757	34 948	8 738	2 052	3 676	2 735	6 749	2 161	2 386	13 168	5 271	16 509
1971	19 679	28 550	17 907	36 431	9 258	2 099	3 866	2 828	6 923	2 260	2 453	13 686	5 678	17 067
1972	20 807	30 713	18 547	38 054	9 673	2 355	4 056	2 896	7 079	2 142	2 695	14 677	5 998	17 379
1973	25 944	35 490	19 758	43 307	11 627	2 426	4 592	3 317	7 553	2 476	3 103	18 147	6 729	18 431
1974	35 070	42 530	23 893	56 132	14 625	3 024	5 044	4 816	11 579	3 945	4 023	23 744	8 189	24 199
1975	33 903	43 227	25 460	57 118	14 467	3 290	4 794	4 849	12 073	4 426	4 085	23 565	8 834	24 719
1976	37 457	46 074	28 457	62 648	15 695	3 416	5 232	5 299	13 319	4 711	4 581	25 847	9 929	26 872
1977	40 186	50 226	30 465	67 501	16 329	3 511	5 649	5 667	14 633	5 439	5 116	27 387	10 961	29 153
1978	45 198	58 848	34 135	73 510	18 073	3 669	5 935	6 114	16 018	5 330	5 801	29 619	12 085	31 806
1979	52 670	69 325	38 739	81 423	19 879	3 517	6 148	6 926	17 690	7 458	6 399	32 814	13 910	34 699
1980	55 173	76 945	42 670	90 427	21 710	3 721	6 648	7 802	20 066	9 693	6 435	36 606	15 884	37 937
1981	57 998	80 998	47 447	96 970	21 483	4 436	6 896	8 593	22 438	10 420	6 968	38 165	16 194	42 611
1982	59 136	86 707	54 601	111 408	23 016	6 873	6 723	9 022	24 448	17 009	7 748	44 039	18 612	48 757
1983	60 325	86 899	52 630	112 525	23 609	6 746	7 514	9 192	24 698	14 843	8 070	44 816	18 691	49 018
1984	66 031	98 251	57 048	118 186	24 182	6 533	7 827	10 299	26 420	14 260	8 904	45 692	19 328	53 166
1985	63 904	98 162	56 127	116 556	24 015	5 943	7 439	10 140	26 119	13 975	9 213	44 106	19 442	53 008
1986	61 331	97 000	53 666	110 657	23 884	5 449	7 191	10 254	25 743	8 791	9 285	42 335	18 124	50 198
1987	63 562	102 393	54 844	117 310	24 860	5 331	7 939	11 163	26 585	9 973	10 065	45 319	19 270	52 721
1988	69 611	112 958	59 899	126 906	27 122	5 286	8 384	12 495	29 792	9 196	11 367	49 396	20 559	56 951
1989	72 435	122 251	62 827	133 699	28 459	5 570	8 721	13 404	31 725	10 743	11 533	50 674	21 653	61 372
1990	73 559	124 130	65 520	141 864	29 714	5 974	8 732	13 640	34 001	13 432	12 292	52 645	22 817	66 402
1991	70 834	114 960	64 225	140 931	30 099	6 342	8 484	13 796	34 529	11 671	12 121	53 011	22 815	65 105
1992	69 427	104 572	64 167	144 381	30 986	6 670	8 714	14 012	35 721	11 330	12 534	53 995	23 536	66 850
1993	72 544	102 632	64 228	144 734	31 185	6 322	9 268	13 979	35 778	10 268	12 816	55 069	23 394	66 271
1994	78 401	107 244	68 046	151 337	32 306	5 776	9 804	14 481	37 038	11 159	14 228	58 163	24 685	68 489
1995	85 040	105 810	75 065	163 174	34 411	5 768	10 268	17 384	39 939	11 523	15 264	62 530	26 185	74 459
1996	83 846	110 559	76 924	163 105	34 626	6 254	10 029	16 230	41 380	12 469	15 697	60 741	26 668	75 696
1993:														
January	69 186	103 321	63 626	145 002	31 138	6 650	8 735	14 054	36 034	11 349	12 450	54 200	23 446	67 356
February	69 546	103 567	63 857	144 495	31 104	6 651	8 718	14 068	35 747	11 347	12 379	53 944	23 704	66 847
March	70 074	103 478	64 029	144 895	30 965	6 771	8 785	14 084	35 836	11 379	12 443	54 124	23 599	67 172
April	70 264	103 105	64 507	145 592	31 181	6 685	8 873	14 084	35 852	11 617	12 539	54 556	23 678	67 338
May	70 877	102 840	64 591	146 106	31 331	6 786	8 965	14 078	35 934	11 401	12 679	54 830	23 474	67 802
June	70 763	103 381	64 515	146 239	31 472	6 896	8 927	14 038	35 918	11 223	12 691	55 082	23 512	67 645
July	71 157	103 066	64 355	145 800	31 375	6 796	8 925	14 042	35 836	11 051	12 700	54 790	23 470	67 540
August	71 673	102 979	64 130	146 174	31 153	6 783	8 948	14 137	36 103	11 028	12 750	54 866	23 529	67 779
September	71 691	103 661	64 090	145 791	30 950	6 763	9 038	14 009	36 106	10 758	12 803	54 826	23 461	67 504
October	71 882	104 066	63 779	145 558	30 936	6 612	9 066	14 006	36 021	10 898	12 771	54 843	23 467	67 248
November	72 211	103 187	64 681	145 590	31 103	6 615	9 177	13 960	36 031	10 752	12 855	55 281	23 446	66 863
December	72 544	102 632	64 228	144 734	31 185	6 322	9 268	13 979	35 778	10 268	12 816	55 069	23 394	66 271
1994:														
January	71 831	103 598	65 509	144 413	31 268	6 031	9 463	13 870	35 844	10 128	12 858	54 651	23 432	66 330
February	72 448	103 568	65 488	144 877	31 164	5 880	9 483	14 003	36 051	10 359	12 925	54 696	23 466	66 715
March	72 731	103 276	65 512	145 313	31 414	6 167	9 524	14 000	35 909	10 389	12 963	55 044	23 666	66 603
April	73 255	103 195	65 657	145 560	31 661	6 091	9 534	14 051	35 975	10 370	12 942	55 073	23 599	66 888
May	73 865	103 992	65 922	146 258	31 885	6 135	9 563	14 130	35 996	10 541	12 989	55 414	23 810	67 034
June	74 526	105 133	65 132	146 521	31 810	6 124	9 561	14 143	35 912	10 721	13 083	55 629	23 996	66 896
July	75 346	105 788	65 892	148 412	32 315	6 039	9 608	14 209	36 413	11 108	13 305	55 954	24 261	68 197
August	75 684	106 297	66 452	148 503	32 388	5 838	9 586	14 258	36 269	11 169	13 413	56 148	24 184	68 171
September	76 297	106 066	66 200	148 533	32 386	5 819	9 602	14 275	36 221	10 818	13 676	56 860	24 301	67 372
October	76 666	106 334	66 661	149 501	32 504	5 678	9 671	14 265	36 397	11 040	13 919	57 110	24 523	67 868
November	77 615	106 489	67 270	150 291	32 410	5 735	9 752	14 366	36 639	11 204	13 809	57 295	24 817	68 179
December	78 401	107 244	68 046	151 337	32 306	5 776	9 804	14 481	37 038	11 159	14 228	58 163	24 685	68 489
1995:														
January	78 468	108 838	68 177	153 235	32 866	5 692	9 836	14 771	37 264	11 446	14 471	58 726	24 825	69 684
February	79 508	108 235	68 797	154 957	32 931	5 750	9 882	15 040	37 566	11 608	14 895	59 367	25 043	70 547
March	79 868	107 917	70 329	156 576	33 099	5 613	10 009	15 379	37 660	11 540	15 044	60 612	25 117	70 847
April	80 750	107 958	70 937	158 065	33 063	5 593	10 085	15 706	38 271	11 615	15 313	61 041	25 214	71 810
May	81 437	108 219	71 558	159 610	33 139	5 543	10 162	15 981	38 851	11 737	15 391	61 583	25 487	72 540
June	82 127	106 783	72 604	160 858	33 262	5 562	10 222	16 479	39 245	11 643	15 465	62 286	25 680	72 892
July	82 844	107 317	73 156	161 487	33 359	5 638	10 237	16 731	39 610	11 280	15 507	62 426	25 831	73 230
August	83 569	106 705	73 060	161 592	33 293	5 744	10 244	16 805	39 701	11 175	15 436	62 555	25 744	73 293
September	83 703	106 642	73 971	162 837	33 908	5 925	10 281	17 084	40 012	11 192	15 351	62 820	26 020	73 997
October	85 172	106 091	74 431	162 544	34 163	5 803	10 292	17 296	39 821	10 931	15 299	62 420	25 971	74 153
November	85 021	105 930	74 556	162 417	34 256	5 719	10 309	17 266	39 651	11 071	15 247	62 755	25 951	73 711
December	85 040	105 810	75 065	163 174	34 411	5 768	10 268	17 384	39 939	11 523	15 264	62 530	26 185	74 459
1996:														
January	85 722	106 519	75 723	163 228	34 378	5 814	10 192	17 354	40 037	11 563	15 225	62 561	26 358	74 309
February	86 049	106 456	75 740	163 217	34 477	5 788	10 178	17 394	40 061	11 642	15 236	62 422	26 253	74 542
March	85 891	107 003	75 498	162 971	34 485	5 807	10 089	17 294	40 271	12 008	15 278	61 779	26 266	74 926
April	85 844	107 500	75 304	162 704	34 780	5 760	10 059	16 975	40 439	12 006	15 196	61 682	26 334	74 688
May	85 483	107 734	75 440	161 641	34 572	5 781	10 012	16 705	40 294	11 940	15 162	61 187	26 318	74 136
June	84 397	108 228	75 669	161 508	34 589	5 805	9 963	16 504	40 410	11 876	15 258	60 727	26 373	74 408
July	85 307	108 368	75 818	161 050	34 538	5 737	9 958	16 458	40 267	11 957	15 301	60 635	26 240	74 175
August	84 805	108 874	76 858	161 110	34 455	5 854	10 039	16 497	40 390	11 931	15 354	60 506	26 568	74 036
September	85 018	108 712	77 064	161 880	34 790	5 957	10 000	16 454	40 701	12 139	15 479	60 638	26 489	74 753
October	84 227	109 806	77 583	162 422	34 685	6 092	9 997	16 369	40 875	12 191	15 557	61 028	26 652	74 742
November	84 154	110 655	77 389	163 002	34 814	6 258	10 034	16 275	40 940	12 307	15 625	60 852	26 728	75 422
December	83 846	110 559	76 924	163 105	34 626	6 254	10 029	16 230	41 380	12 469	15 697	60 741	26 668	75 696

1. Data prior to 1982 are not comparable to subsequent periods due to change in inventory valuation methods; see NOTES.

YEAR AND MONTH	By market category						Supplementary series			
	Home goods and apparel	Consumer staples	Machinery and equipment	Automotive equipment	Construction materials and supplies	Other materials, supplies, and intermediate products	Household durables	Capital goods industries		
								Total	Nondefense	Defense
1968	9 180	13 104	19 218	2 035	5 805	29 653	4 148	25 709	18 158	7 551
1969	9 908	13 732	22 095	2 191	6 378	31 836	4 544	28 652	20 883	7 769
1970	10 162	14 176	24 032	2 355	6 867	34 271	4 711	27 859	22 810	5 049
1971	10 642	14 865	23 978	2 387	7 145	34 562	4 829	26 587	22 455	4 132
1972	11 498	15 596	25 239	2 703	7 603	36 142	5 311	27 667	23 337	4 330
1973	13 398	17 990	29 787	3 174	8 696	41 134	6 319	32 032	27 460	4 572
1974	14 470	23 571	37 403	3 695	11 076	54 267	7 393	39 605	34 583	5 022
1975	13 586	24 083	37 041	3 455	11 267	55 960	6 649	40 181	34 289	5 892
1976	15 324	25 758	37 766	4 163	12 540	63 175	7 453	41 046	34 449	6 597
1977	16 556	27 541	41 529	4 795	13 509	68 042	8 070	44 014	37 781	6 233
1978	18 715	30 063	49 266	5 353	15 100	75 494	9 161	52 237	45 660	6 577
1979	19 157	33 648	58 623	5 630	16 908	87 232	9 533	63 816	55 393	8 423
1980	20 106	37 689	66 157	5 145	17 513	94 117	9 967	74 531	63 692	10 839
1981	21 591	39 589	69 413	4 814	18 328	101 503	10 565	81 112	67 616	13 496
1982	21 738	48 183	76 522	4 865	18 580	106 625	10 926	92 601	73 748	18 853
1983	22 682	47 337	72 066	5 494	19 309	107 999	10 845	89 562	68 420	21 142
1984	24 999	48 555	79 058	6 192	20 552	115 702	12 270	102 615	75 466	27 149
1985	24 229	48 134	75 592	6 214	20 555	111 881	11 704	102 843	71 763	31 080
1986	23 647	44 983	70 923	5 930	20 348	108 766	11 325	99 104	67 631	31 473
1987	25 379	47 186	72 400	6 322	21 158	113 976	12 190	103 167	68 734	34 433
1988	26 723	50 289	81 687	6 448	22 925	125 688	12 948	114 207	77 448	36 759
1989	27 255	54 029	90 697	6 479	23 326	131 807	13 541	124 850	86 897	37 953
1990	27 153	58 161	95 055	6 934	23 714	134 811	13 446	128 997	90 894	38 103
1991	26 303	58 657	93 404	6 559	22 509	130 000	12 678	121 629	88 958	32 671
1992	26 822	60 692	89 635	6 699	22 780	128 420	12 521	110 333	84 393	25 940
1993	28 670	60 233	89 628	6 918	23 985	129 250	13 040	107 115	83 535	23 580
1994	30 798	62 117	96 051	7 475	25 468	139 013	14 439	110 919	90 335	20 584
1995	31 835	66 226	102 141	7 779	27 031	150 815	15 288	113 830	96 742	17 088
1996	31 453	67 511	106 554	8 023	26 793	151 944	15 841	117 371	100 942	16 429
1993:										
January	26 876	61 085	88 761	6 659	22 675	127 836	12 499	108 890	83 387	25 503
February	26 969	60 935	89 315	6 786	22 839	127 737	12 425	108 954	83 699	25 255
March	27 443	61 068	89 424	6 880	23 207	128 014	12 673	108 356	83 435	24 921
April	27 745	61 261	89 504	6 943	23 454	128 088	12 809	108 224	83 547	24 677
May	28 078	61 569	89 406	6 906	23 419	128 209	13 022	108 279	83 461	24 818
June	28 260	61 661	89 764	6 957	23 497	128 194	13 043	108 580	83 817	24 763
July	28 448	61 304	89 840	6 689	23 484	128 457	13 137	108 765	84 361	24 404
August	28 603	61 174	89 088	6 891	23 672	129 146	13 154	107 628	83 168	24 460
September	28 548	60 895	89 741	6 932	23 766	128 964	12 999	108 292	83 805	24 487
October	28 658	60 725	90 058	6 876	23 754	129 277	13 069	108 075	84 019	24 056
November	28 531	60 865	90 074	6 876	23 979	129 255	13 000	108 130	83 903	24 227
December	28 670	60 233	89 628	6 918	23 985	129 250	13 040	107 115	83 535	23 580
1994:										
January	28 808	59 999	90 005	6 957	24 402	129 765	13 132	107 625	84 011	23 614
February	28 956	60 061	90 180	6 934	24 462	130 346	13 273	107 677	84 223	23 454
March	28 996	60 505	90 552	6 870	24 536	130 553	13 326	107 619	84 857	22 762
April	28 955	60 762	90 963	6 787	24 334	131 010	13 307	108 233	85 441	22 792
May	29 076	61 124	92 098	6 908	24 434	132 022	13 362	108 756	86 518	22 238
June	29 336	61 247	92 737	6 981	24 575	132 542	13 493	109 079	87 318	21 761
July	29 632	62 263	93 376	7 105	24 797	133 864	13 724	109 557	87 761	21 796
August	30 040	62 155	94 139	7 074	24 844	134 585	14 039	110 071	88 624	21 447
September	30 193	61 866	94 121	7 175	24 872	135 242	14 054	109 358	88 444	20 914
October	30 298	61 894	94 243	7 182	25 005	136 528	14 096	109 727	88 700	21 027
November	30 760	62 057	94 967	7 310	25 100	137 543	14 341	109 963	89 255	20 708
December	30 798	62 117	96 051	7 475	25 468	139 013	14 439	110 919	90 335	20 584
1995:										
January	31 032	62 695	96 448	7 537	25 462	141 213	14 584	111 448	91 131	20 317
February	31 340	63 097	96 853	7 581	25 640	142 751	14 734	111 431	91 535	19 896
March	31 724	63 312	97 481	7 645	25 966	143 990	14 719	111 788	92 198	19 590
April	32 000	63 544	97 664	7 698	26 340	145 960	14 988	111 671	92 407	19 264
May	32 113	63 897	98 313	7 744	26 637	147 240	15 017	112 359	93 118	19 241
June	32 131	64 338	98 204	7 703	26 636	148 458	15 103	111 786	92 919	18 867
July	32 073	64 343	98 953	7 752	26 904	150 113	15 092	112 214	93 638	18 576
August	31 918	64 391	99 268	7 725	26 904	150 331	14 942	112 189	93 897	18 292
September	31 922	65 304	100 096	7 624	26 964	150 910	15 052	113 157	94 886	18 271
October	31 983	65 360	101 136	7 738	27 106	151 046	15 160	113 790	95 886	17 904
November	31 941	65 299	101 448	7 768	27 108	151 069	15 178	113 328	96 060	17 268
December	31 835	66 226	102 141	7 779	27 031	150 815	15 288	113 830	96 742	17 088
1996:										
January	31 937	66 504	103 556	7 909	26 961	151 348	15 370	114 822	97 873	16 949
February	32 104	66 449	103 739	7 930	26 806	151 425	15 570	115 128	98 067	17 061
March	31 579	66 775	103 758	8 118	26 655	151 579	15 400	114 931	97 704	17 227
April	31 495	66 864	104 705	8 200	26 401	151 014	15 438	115 761	98 749	17 012
May	31 308	66 622	104 848	8 224	26 430	150 341	15 415	115 793	98 826	16 967
June	31 222	66 577	104 625	8 151	26 406	150 283	15 392	115 608	98 522	17 086
July	31 037	66 363	105 556	8 378	26 423	150 395	15 171	116 375	99 292	17 083
August	31 291	66 334	106 297	8 357	26 479	150 561	15 525	117 101	100 133	16 968
September	31 526	66 935	106 149	8 304	26 556	150 903	15 761	117 017	100 141	16 876
October	31 636	67 079	106 836	8 295	26 577	151 079	15 816	117 676	100 893	16 783
November	31 537	67 469	107 462	8 051	26 734	151 328	15 882	118 665	102 033	16 632
December	31 453	67 511	106 554	8 023	26 793	151 944	15 841	117 371	100 942	16 429

1. Data prior to 1982 are not comparable to subsequent periods due to change in inventory valuation methods; see NOTES.

MANUFACTURING

MANUFACTURERS' NEW ORDERS
(Net, millions of dollars)

YEAR AND MONTH	Not seasonally adjusted			Seasonally adjusted									
				Total	Durable goods industries								
						Primary metals						Transportation equipment	
	Total	Durable goods industries	Nondurable goods industries		Total[1]	Total	Blast furnaces, steel mills	Non-ferrous and other primary metals	Fabricated metal products	Industrial machinery and equipment	Electronic and electric equipment	Total	Aircraft, missiles, and parts
1968	607 881	336 614	271 267	607 881	336 614	48 089	24 416	19 182	45 158	52 286	39 182	85 893	28 195
1969	647 874	358 509	289 365	647 874	358 509	54 880	27 247	22 496	47 446	60 226	42 438	83 945	24 704
1970	624 263	328 079	296 184	624 263	328 079	51 793	25 521	21 883	43 990	55 322	41 117	67 380	17 417
1971	671 051	358 856	312 195	671 051	358 856	51 284	25 571	20 704	44 305	55 886	42 639	89 900	22 459
1972	770 181	420 455	349 726	770 181	420 455	61 447	30 996	24 607	52 879	70 941	48 702	96 501	20 963
1973	912 039	511 525	400 514	912 039	511 525	78 395	39 413	31 417	64 733	89 162	58 275	118 194	26 669
1974	1 047 924	562 339	485 585	1 047 924	562 339	98 831	51 047	38 394	74 281	106 101	58 884	114 081	29 934
1975	1 021 662	503 485	518 177	1 021 662	503 485	75 034	38 611	27 864	64 349	92 863	54 610	109 050	26 869
1976	1 194 151	615 680	578 471	1 194 151	615 680	94 491	47 212	37 378	76 372	107 595	66 864	143 502	31 851
1977	1 381 302	732 422	648 880	1 381 302	732 422	105 689	52 103	42 400	92 028	126 235	80 010	175 446	40 625
1978	1 579 542	867 335	712 207	1 579 542	867 335	124 741	62 648	48 319	105 182	154 051	92 781	213 539	54 600
1979	1 771 243	953 796	817 447	1 771 243	953 796	139 783	66 968	58 420	117 428	174 660	107 314	223 226	67 818
1980	1 876 304	952 701	923 603	1 876 304	952 701	134 416	62 473	60 399	116 195	179 750	115 335	202 584	72 514
1981	2 016 298	1 003 845	1 012 453	2 016 298	1 003 845	137 286	67 457	57 545	123 245	201 576	123 053	203 482	63 530
1982	1 945 684	936 764	1 008 920	1 945 684	936 764	98 445	43 013	46 942	113 399	169 274	127 630	209 325	73 365
1983	2 105 410	1 057 677	1 047 733	2 105 410	1 057 677	113 884	49 123	55 566	122 760	178 879	142 131	261 359	86 952
1984	2 314 549	1 201 964	1 112 585	2 314 549	1 201 964	118 354	50 719	56 030	141 650	212 109	165 541	295 202	91 620
1985	2 348 477	1 228 268	1 120 209	2 348 477	1 228 268	112 276	49 079	52 275	142 300	218 395	163 352	311 482	100 889
1986	2 342 444	1 243 761	1 098 683	2 342 444	1 243 761	108 218	46 408	51 294	143 541	208 567	164 282	327 541	107 993
1987	2 512 663	1 329 712	1 182 951	2 512 663	1 329 712	125 989	54 763	60 302	150 716	221 171	173 210	348 224	114 835
1988	2 739 240	1 464 916	1 274 324	2 739 240	1 464 916	152 578	64 002	75 997	158 170	250 055	189 211	389 635	137 443
1989	2 874 861	1 512 664	1 362 197	2 874 861	1 512 664	152 814	62 752	77 249	160 037	257 051	192 482	411 434	153 430
1990	2 934 086	1 507 001	1 427 085	2 934 086	1 507 001	149 338	63 369	72 944	163 285	258 894	195 748	395 737	150 329
1991	2 865 665	1 438 187	1 427 478	2 865 665	1 438 187	134 657	56 366	66 778	158 401	243 450	197 659	363 366	132 645
1992	2 978 548	1 515 694	1 462 854	2 978 548	1 515 694	136 849	58 002	67 337	165 793	258 608	217 966	377 147	110 830
1993	3 092 381	1 596 974	1 495 407	3 092 381	1 596 974	144 018	63 604	67 112	172 121	277 416	233 991	386 643	88 070
1994	3 356 797	1 794 508	1 562 289	3 356 797	1 794 508	167 685	70 960	81 963	191 099	325 788	266 386	440 817	90 217
1995	3 604 239	1 937 624	1 666 615	3 604 239	1 937 624	178 681	75 372	88 273	205 894	356 282	305 736	472 332	114 099
1996	3 770 368	2 039 558	1 730 810	3 770 368	2 039 558	174 865	72 295	85 221	217 468	379 817	321 390	502 861	134 097
1993:													
January	234 245	118 979	115 266	255 593	130 444	12 753	5 808	5 810	14 189	22 503	18 438	31 426	6 293
February	258 421	135 345	123 076	260 024	134 637	12 574	5 794	5 737	14 197	22 474	18 525	34 637	10 042
March	269 549	140 736	128 813	255 935	130 256	12 078	5 404	5 676	14 124	22 364	18 193	31 896	7 047
April	255 804	132 183	123 621	256 829	131 828	11 722	4 999	5 600	14 050	22 160	18 623	32 178	8 110
May	252 941	129 282	123 659	252 132	128 690	11 420	5 033	5 285	14 126	22 410	18 579	31 270	7 931
June	275 107	142 979	132 128	258 492	132 870	11 758	5 196	5 567	14 093	21 930	19 889	34 419	9 883
July	231 267	111 983	119 284	254 196	130 082	11 463	5 021	5 390	14 011	22 885	20 005	30 342	6 469
August	253 474	127 527	125 947	254 050	130 933	11 588	5 076	5 468	14 191	22 973	19 846	30 701	7 793
September	271 193	139 292	131 901	257 220	132 585	11 957	5 278	5 447	14 793	23 467	20 766	29 604	4 715
October	267 903	140 434	127 469	258 908	135 066	12 136	5 414	5 463	14 536	23 448	20 465	32 486	6 385
November	262 412	137 712	124 700	263 344	138 719	12 233	5 325	5 676	14 518	24 920	20 092	33 973	8 023
December	260 065	140 522	119 543	264 303	140 010	12 487	5 444	5 956	15 275	25 430	19 996	33 959	5 824
1994:													
January	249 092	134 295	114 797	270 317	145 722	12 459	5 308	5 936	15 071	24 829	21 282	39 835	12 308
February	267 917	144 202	123 715	268 586	142 567	12 653	5 685	5 853	15 208	25 667	21 254	34 809	7 149
March	288 612	156 639	131 973	273 825	145 201	14 058	5 831	6 876	16 294	26 299	21 169	34 714	5 599
April	270 669	144 819	125 850	271 819	144 844	13 053	5 840	6 115	15 552	26 835	22 552	34 271	6 298
May	276 057	147 431	128 626	274 927	146 618	13 974	5 761	6 953	15 797	26 662	21 660	35 458	7 849
June	296 673	160 888	135 785	279 454	150 118	13 816	5 868	6 684	15 668	27 310	21 804	36 829	8 250
July	248 301	124 836	123 465	275 565	146 869	13 503	5 643	6 707	15 932	27 455	21 186	34 727	5 780
August	284 142	148 091	136 051	283 747	150 992	13 788	5 912	6 788	16 330	28 362	21 993	36 906	6 869
September	299 030	159 553	139 477	284 880	152 658	14 789	6 360	7 212	16 046	27 852	22 924	37 452	7 400
October	292 790	156 859	135 931	283 893	151 307	14 998	6 105	7 646	15 959	28 385	21 816	35 839	6 731
November	290 512	156 012	134 500	291 450	156 885	14 935	6 171	7 519	16 739	28 667	24 255	38 230	8 815
December	293 002	160 883	132 119	298 208	160 805	15 951	6 659	7 728	16 551	26 984	24 287	42 213	7 245
1995:													
January	276 929	149 877	127 052	299 495	161 929	15 847	6 462	8 106	17 435	29 270	24 529	38 850	7 446
February	299 264	163 293	135 971	299 555	161 044	15 107	6 298	7 430	17 272	29 513	24 025	40 204	9 975
March	315 301	174 072	141 229	299 157	161 385	15 301	6 800	7 258	17 002	30 041	25 673	39 194	7 966
April	291 331	154 447	136 884	292 785	154 969	14 748	6 170	7 264	16 919	29 048	24 725	35 824	7 287
May	298 191	158 977	139 214	297 451	158 883	14 368	6 186	7 041	17 187	29 627	25 604	37 989	9 698
June	314 020	167 945	146 075	296 429	156 936	14 361	6 003	7 228	16 866	30 108	24 943	36 013	6 357
July	265 281	132 252	133 029	294 040	155 362	14 115	5 772	7 147	16 985	28 290	26 369	35 454	8 054
August	302 190	159 084	143 106	301 449	161 945	15 227	6 366	7 575	17 194	29 667	25 615	38 623	9 221
September	320 200	174 209	145 991	305 828	166 946	14 909	6 071	7 534	17 295	29 851	26 345	43 877	12 736
October	312 976	170 002	142 974	302 899	163 442	14 988	6 450	7 203	17 247	29 698	26 656	39 485	9 537
November	303 396	163 012	140 384	304 567	164 232	14 900	6 479	7 136	17 385	31 208	24 922	40 318	10 498
December	305 160	170 454	134 706	309 948	170 076	14 729	6 275	7 304	17 233	30 181	25 949	46 101	15 213
1996:													
January	286 915	156 859	130 056	308 892	168 420	14 362	6 033	6 905	17 444	30 961	26 058	44 307	13 592
February	303 501	165 811	137 690	303 957	163 553	14 510	5 921	7 099	17 449	32 526	25 019	38 387	8 785
March	322 813	179 595	143 218	306 561	166 267	13 782	5 596	6 860	17 134	30 428	26 706	42 684	15 658
April	307 060	163 620	143 440	308 467	164 329	14 649	5 934	7 295	18 062	30 995	26 031	37 999	7 644
May	316 493	171 243	145 250	315 764	171 209	14 977	6 382	7 212	18 598	31 599	25 853	43 213	12 251
June	331 043	182 129	148 914	313 081	170 382	14 889	6 120	7 188	18 190	31 346	26 567	42 598	9 931
July	287 081	147 034	140 047	318 488	173 087	15 135	6 357	7 223	18 190	32 424	27 930	42 196	10 293
August	312 787	164 086	148 701	311 958	167 204	14 934	6 058	7 378	18 379	32 098	26 712	38 272	7 269
September	335 124	183 300	151 824	319 894	175 113	14 468	6 125	6 886	18 716	32 115	26 556	45 692	13 296
October	333 193	181 955	151 238	322 392	175 015	14 264	5 959	7 051	18 548	31 424	30 901	41 936	11 871
November	321 484	172 506	148 978	322 400	173 636	14 338	5 758	7 102	18 597	31 487	28 307	43 049	11 671
December	312 874	171 420	141 454	316 898	170 016	14 590	6 032	7 033	18 198	31 979	24 086	42 701	11 357

1. Includes categories not shown separately.

YEAR AND MONTH	Nondurable goods industries		By market category						Supplementary series		
	Total	Industries with unfilled orders	Home goods and apparel	Consumer staples	Machinery and equipment	Automotive equipment	Construction materials and supplies	Other materials, supplies, and intermediate products	Household durables	Capital goods industries	
										Nondefense	Defense
1968	271 267	67 586	58 025	122 093	87 705	25 812	40 326	184 872	24 064	69 451	26 251
1969	289 365	72 452	60 905	130 473	104 287	26 889	43 170	217 388	24 676	84 549	23 790
1970	296 184	72 794	60 053	136 650	90 920	22 920	41 976	208 527	24 360	72 866	21 311
1971	312 195	75 322	63 910	143 889	104 615	31 325	44 769	219 246	25 887	80 185	18 787
1972	349 726	85 481	73 471	159 032	121 439	34 668	54 858	256 608	30 564	92 943	20 467
1973	400 514	95 225	80 190	183 637	151 221	40 271	65 713	310 891	33 804	119 108	23 409
1974	485 585	106 139	80 399	225 842	168 767	36 721	71 972	367 873	33 582	139 131	26 033
1975	518 177	110 975	81 682	247 066	151 278	37 452	64 582	339 984	34 140	118 635	24 765
1976	578 471	126 068	91 453	269 537	179 180	50 230	76 851	411 296	39 289	137 875	30 616
1977	648 880	140 721	105 613	294 776	214 944	60 614	92 881	480 457	46 181	164 168	34 624
1978	712 207	155 601	114 334	326 735	261 585	67 579	107 563	552 092	51 123	211 056	41 511
1979	817 447	172 861	119 157	378 236	305 432	66 949	118 946	619 405	54 117	253 844	33 795
1980	923 603	188 221	124 929	437 370	299 968	54 244	118 449	636 198	56 099	253 619	58 256
1981	1 012 453	206 535	132 987	477 650	312 509	60 834	122 619	688 321	59 342	261 666	58 881
1982	1 008 920	210 918	132 729	486 180	285 408	58 757	112 605	629 399	56 055	230 555	81 415
1983	1 047 733	233 594	143 390	491 092	303 922	77 638	128 440	702 743	60 924	235 489	96 105
1984	1 112 585	255 393	151 993	510 701	359 604	92 714	141 669	776 636	65 706	284 022	103 504
1985	1 120 209	263 955	153 711	518 109	374 954	97 164	147 149	763 711	66 904	294 544	109 505
1986	1 098 683	279 953	159 615	503 299	371 101	101 263	154 725	761 205	70 749	287 786	111 879
1987	1 182 951	308 101	163 728	531 778	400 962	105 265	165 396	838 571	69 526	313 127	111 639
1988	1 274 324	329 100	168 005	569 099	462 470	112 298	176 043	936 836	73 599	373 294	102 728
1989	1 362 197	345 474	174 574	616 054	496 955	118 385	179 546	970 570	78 242	395 855	93 398
1990	1 427 085	353 047	175 162	658 631	500 441	110 181	180 616	972 911	77 946	399 966	96 638
1991	1 427 478	350 693	175 921	667 789	462 856	106 058	172 621	956 041	78 314	365 655	87 213
1992	1 462 854	362 809	185 713	678 613	491 195	120 525	184 385	997 721	82 175	378 293	76 155
1993	1 495 407	370 132	194 976	691 347	505 543	134 526	198 463	1 045 794	88 914	380 331	71 902
1994	1 562 289	392 875	205 506	706 180	567 922	155 704	219 305	1 166 983	95 500	428 365	71 682
1995	1 666 615	429 098	211 076	743 712	625 988	160 532	228 339	1 281 309	98 950	486 726	70 317
1996	1 730 810	432 089	219 062	802 369	674 135	166 309	235 777	1 294 738	108 715	526 951	79 998
1993:											
January	125 149	31 130	16 573	57 534	39 774	11 085	15 872	85 951	7 350	29 032	8 135
February	125 387	31 174	16 507	57 413	43 416	11 288	16 766	87 742	7 444	33 182	5 803
March	125 679	30 562	16 010	58 583	40 329	11 288	16 307	86 182	7 080	29 832	6 095
April	125 001	31 096	15 723	57 829	41 754	11 023	16 248	86 641	7 305	31 748	6 633
May	123 442	30 674	15 810	56 827	41 043	10 859	16 566	85 032	6 979	30 848	5 463
June	125 622	30 604	16 539	58 118	43 879	11 040	16 284	86 696	7 387	33 598	4 947
July	124 114	30 574	15 999	57 938	39 998	10 617	16 079	86 085	7 504	29 685	7 082
August	123 117	30 325	16 225	56 897	41 497	10 381	16 305	85 673	7 455	31 500	6 465
September	124 635	30 944	16 307	58 058	40 913	10 939	16 639	87 470	7 540	30 256	6 154
October	123 842	30 696	16 092	57 439	42 628	11 705	16 660	87 776	7 466	31 906	5 335
November	124 625	30 908	16 658	57 081	44 474	11 922	17 185	89 721	7 671	33 754	5 667
December	124 293	31 187	16 255	57 489	44 860	12 284	17 426	90 721	7 676	34 074	4 840
1994:											
January	124 595	31 142	16 489	57 289	47 469	12 522	17 231	90 958	7 608	36 125	7 054
February	126 019	31 539	16 669	58 057	45 585	12 561	17 421	91 560	7 677	34 633	5 346
March	128 624	32 213	17 106	58 394	46 250	12 690	18 476	95 780	7 764	34 611	3 379
April	126 975	31 422	16 895	57 945	45 469	12 579	17 985	94 655	7 796	34 168	5 580
May	128 309	32 707	17 431	57 728	44 936	12 578	17 971	95 686	8 172	33 496	6 588
June	129 336	32 339	16 985	58 727	48 929	13 042	18 201	95 559	7 977	36 702	6 014
July	128 696	32 278	17 094	58 288	46 294	12 590	18 143	95 032	7 861	34 958	6 150
August	132 755	33 549	17 221	59 947	48 161	13 628	18 342	99 072	8 041	35 871	5 182
September	132 222	33 243	17 496	59 304	48 045	13 124	18 384	99 678	8 274	36 480	6 598
October	132 586	33 779	17 361	59 093	47 485	12 838	18 747	99 788	8 057	36 052	6 258
November	134 565	33 949	17 088	60 035	50 326	13 695	19 049	103 831	8 068	38 508	4 745
December	137 403	34 521	17 369	61 162	48 390	14 011	19 350	106 007	8 172	35 860	9 088
1995:											
January	137 566	35 479	18 328	60 328	50 869	13 618	19 750	107 079	8 267	39 249	6 066
February	138 511	35 666	17 543	61 106	51 261	13 601	19 474	107 054	7 929	39 479	6 339
March	137 772	35 468	17 480	60 503	51 516	13 979	19 030	107 435	8 119	39 676	5 926
April	137 816	35 751	17 293	61 088	49 216	12 930	18 548	105 350	7 660	37 700	5 108
May	138 568	35 977	17 906	61 306	51 504	12 846	18 807	106 277	8 201	41 076	5 481
June	139 493	36 239	17 480	61 944	50 733	13 123	18 529	106 197	8 266	39 381	4 900
July	138 678	36 225	17 300	61 765	47 988	12 549	18 902	106 335	8 300	37 109	5 442
August	139 504	35 609	17 478	62 742	50 381	13 446	19 382	107 360	8 340	38 636	6 773
September	138 882	35 149	17 283	62 464	55 722	13 693	19 105	106 705	8 345	43 743	7 232
October	139 457	35 677	17 472	62 911	53 230	13 644	19 169	107 107	8 339	40 426	5 604
November	140 335	36 192	17 928	63 315	54 790	13 272	18 926	107 390	8 731	43 449	4 936
December	139 872	35 302	17 638	63 965	58 632	13 638	18 731	106 583	8 404	46 612	6 631
1996:											
January	140 472	36 059	17 201	64 576	56 866	13 298	18 927	105 992	8 426	45 260	8 086
February	140 404	35 466	17 676	64 428	55 851	13 581	18 639	104 406	8 512	43 748	5 154
March	140 294	35 046	18 169	65 036	56 883	12 550	18 676	102 835	9 038	45 608	8 406
April	144 138	36 081	18 188	66 632	52 387	13 963	19 265	106 684	9 038	39 593	6 092
May	144 555	35 891	18 263	66 902	57 364	14 231	19 652	108 374	9 107	44 488	6 009
June	142 699	36 149	18 158	65 666	54 848	13 919	19 653	107 814	9 122	41 982	8 265
July	145 401	36 364	18 035	67 599	57 510	14 546	20 269	110 333	8 896	45 044	5 110
August	144 754	35 859	18 220	67 382	53 544	14 171	20 053	108 520	9 027	40 314	5 134
September	144 781	36 035	18 540	67 134	59 893	14 717	20 195	109 132	9 192	46 931	5 511
October	147 377	35 860	18 962	69 119	57 687	14 063	20 057	112 444	9 648	46 293	4 962
November	148 764	36 871	18 637	69 365	55 038	14 090	19 903	111 085	8 876	43 081	8 684
December	146 882	36 266	18 675	68 289	55 341	13 459	20 264	107 071	9 547	43 162	8 522

MANUFACTURERS' UNFILLED ORDERS
(End of period—Millions of dollars)

YEAR AND MONTH	Not seasonally adjusted			Seasonally adjusted									
				Total	Durable goods industries								
					Total	Primary metals			Fabricated metal products	Industrial machinery and equipment	Electronic and electric equipment	Transportation equipment	
	Total	Durable goods industries	Nondurable goods industries			Total	Blast furnaces, steel mills	Non-ferrous and other primary metals				Total	Aircraft, missiles, and parts
1968	108 222	104 263	3 959	108 377	104 393	6 591	3 416	2 472	13 813	19 673	11 296	43 023	35 362
1969	114 083	109 936	4 147	114 341	110 161	7 991	4 283	2 876	15 128	23 319	12 171	41 812	33 233
1970	104 683	100 139	4 544	105 008	100 412	7 796	4 617	2 663	14 877	21 737	11 881	34 720	26 198
1971	104 857	99 906	4 951	105 247	100 225	7 478	4 380	2 552	13 688	21 170	12 148	35 793	26 259
1972	118 717	112 517	6 200	119 349	113 034	10 470	6 681	3 116	15 077	25 968	13 376	37 627	26 151
1973	155 583	148 421	7 162	156 561	149 204	16 129	9 794	4 962	21 019	36 959	17 111	45 248	27 842
1974	186 030	180 686	5 344	187 043	181 519	19 225	11 054	5 952	28 100	50 084	17 319	51 118	30 506
1975	168 627	160 993	7 634	169 546	161 664	13 266	7 345	4 015	24 008	46 580	15 857	46 633	28 244
1976	177 215	169 198	8 017	178 128	169 857	14 684	7 776	4 891	22 810	48 321	17 584	49 078	29 421
1977	200 101	191 603	8 498	202 024	193 323	17 298	9 435	5 483	25 152	52 026	19 999	57 101	37 325
1978	256 785	246 162	10 623	259 169	248 281	23 969	12 932	7 393	29 137	62 233	24 219	81 782	54 417
1979	300 794	288 834	11 960	303 593	291 321	26 320	12 485	9 457	33 131	69 844	29 261	103 555	74 034
1980	324 409	312 508	11 901	327 416	315 202	26 815	13 418	10 096	33 296	68 979	31 751	119 700	88 051
1981	323 163	311 628	11 535	326 547	314 707	22 024	10 589	8 784	33 036	69 405	32 718	118 008	86 794
1982	308 633	297 851	10 782	311 887	300 798	15 500	6 574	7 418	27 117	51 864	34 639	125 879	93 703
1983	343 479	329 758	13 721	347 273	333 114	20 400	9 431	9 594	26 752	52 351	40 794	141 637	105 504
1984	369 844	356 446	13 398	373 529	359 651	18 362	8 103	8 694	30 254	53 466	43 967	152 189	117 923
1985	383 865	369 362	14 503	387 196	372 097	18 331	8 248	8 361	29 197	53 516	43 366	156 155	127 282
1986	390 428	374 264	16 164	393 515	376 699	18 590	8 897	7 783	29 633	48 416	42 793	161 145	133 565
1987	427 185	406 444	20 741	430 426	408 688	24 340	11 828	10 300	32 973	51 868	44 711	176 588	144 987
1988	470 993	449 859	21 134	474 154	452 150	27 079	11 508	12 974	31 661	57 583	46 702	211 575	174 721
1989	505 479	484 623	20 856	508 849	487 098	24 120	9 479	11 824	27 629	58 369	44 616	253 517	217 557
1990	527 337	506 311	21 026	531 131	509 124	24 768	10 120	11 258	25 859	57 872	44 501	279 082	242 208
1991	514 835	492 500	22 335	519 199	495 802	23 075	9 290	10 609	24 516	53 812	42 988	275 260	242 798
1992	488 656	466 328	22 328	493 184	469 654	21 644	8 902	9 928	23 782	53 677	44 337	253 260	222 389
1993	453 412	432 667	20 745	458 245	436 442	23 086	10 176	9 628	20 786	52 986	44 776	225 499	194 405
1994	462 190	437 599	24 591	467 369	441 677	29 698	11 337	14 533	21 350	65 651	44 965	215 517	181 307
1995	477 034	454 013	23 021	482 605	458 520	28 049	12 199	12 226	22 455	70 825	51 226	225 008	192 800
1996	512 219	487 574	24 645	517 647	491 911	29 250	12 188	12 661	24 543	72 221	49 565	256 231	223 121
1993:													
January	492 884	470 038	22 846	492 261	468 613	22 723	9 724	10 092	23 826	53 652	44 585	250 300	218 472
February	494 942	471 583	23 359	492 855	469 073	23 500	10 469	10 133	23 751	53 846	44 283	249 913	218 427
March	490 368	466 711	23 657	486 901	463 527	23 735	10 705	10 213	23 322	53 244	43 487	246 222	215 245
April	489 103	465 202	23 901	484 724	461 305	23 708	10 563	10 280	23 044	52 956	43 190	243 471	213 107
May	483 071	459 269	23 802	479 782	456 588	23 626	10 518	10 178	22 777	52 735	42 740	240 481	210 564
June	477 066	453 280	23 786	476 656	453 558	23 297	10 486	9 971	22 127	52 130	43 022	239 899	210 021
July	476 228	452 678	23 550	474 611	451 885	23 158	10 308	9 876	21 867	52 061	43 601	238 561	208 004
August	471 917	448 588	23 329	471 636	449 130	22 976	10 146	9 870	21 697	52 220	43 752	236 241	205 750
September	463 947	441 346	22 601	467 138	444 847	22 843	10 141	9 601	21 735	52 051	44 565	232 295	201 498
October	460 146	439 018	21 128	463 213	441 534	23 068	10 278	9 556	21 397	51 960	45 168	229 232	198 231
November	455 949	435 368	20 581	460 940	439 390	23 043	10 220	9 497	20 853	52 468	45 054	227 839	197 704
December	453 412	432 667	20 745	458 245	436 442	23 086	10 176	9 628	20 786	52 986	44 776	225 499	194 405
1994:													
January	462 048	440 670	21 378	461 275	439 195	23 334	10 156	9 827	20 527	53 705	45 057	228 188	197 314
February	463 138	441 092	22 046	460 723	438 288	23 511	10 286	9 909	20 388	54 440	45 141	226 578	196 103
March	464 509	440 942	23 567	460 768	437 473	24 936	10 567	10 867	20 910	55 743	45 134	223 422	192 029
April	465 235	441 036	24 199	460 473	436 831	25 272	10 836	10 985	20 870	57 270	45 835	221 169	189 943
May	464 513	439 709	24 804	461 041	436 921	26 192	10 897	11 730	21 042	58 152	45 672	220 167	189 651
June	462 547	437 599	24 948	462 328	438 133	26 716	11 039	12 021	21 025	59 677	45 328	219 025	189 278
July	462 664	437 617	25 047	461 067	436 894	26 957	10 966	12 322	21 168	60 763	44 083	217 313	186 778
August	459 648	434 396	25 252	459 357	434 917	26 918	10 868	12 482	21 265	62 191	43 389	215 087	184 926
September	456 890	432 083	24 807	460 862	436 293	27 851	11 285	12 974	21 129	63 383	43 863	214 650	183 836
October	458 082	433 618	24 464	461 552	436 435	28 787	11 409	13 752	21 053	64 587	42 856	213 633	182 262
November	457 774	433 542	24 232	463 160	437 951	29 217	11 429	14 162	21 209	66 147	43 795	212 660	182 214
December	462 190	437 599	24 591	467 369	441 677	29 698	11 337	14 533	21 350	65 651	44 965	215 517	181 307
1995:													
January	471 332	445 902	25 430	470 434	444 203	30 046	11 524	14 703	21 644	67 137	45 669	214 992	179 983
February	475 983	449 876	26 107	473 404	446 729	29 889	11 520	14 460	21 892	68 246	46 238	216 088	181 164
March	478 719	451 879	26 840	474 779	448 070	29 654	11 783	14 014	21 943	69 926	47 914	215 205	180 631
April	478 545	450 982	27 563	473 179	446 209	29 314	11 739	13 642	22 094	70 018	48 869	213 108	178 947
May	478 052	450 221	27 831	474 126	447 150	28 517	11 632	13 066	22 428	70 306	50 132	213 683	180 142
June	471 650	443 945	27 705	471 360	444 618	27 755	11 450	12 586	22 409	71 301	49 980	211 234	177 690
July	473 112	445 004	28 108	471 082	443 982	27 180	11 308	12 215	22 438	70 712	51 652	210 290	177 365
August	471 160	444 131	27 029	470 770	444 547	27 452	11 505	12 285	22 366	70 748	51 390	210 945	178 388
September	469 179	443 888	25 291	474 040	448 892	27 511	11 388	12 429	22 454	70 794	51 737	215 593	182 630
October	471 490	447 537	23 953	474 914	450 251	27 681	11 609	12 310	22 397	70 391	52 648	216 378	183 990
November	471 324	447 523	23 801	476 860	452 090	27 922	11 924	12 218	22 659	71 342	51 579	217 893	185 780
December	477 034	454 013	23 021	482 605	458 520	28 049	12 199	12 226	22 455	70 825	51 226	225 008	192 800
1996:													
January	492 108	468 346	23 762	491 058	466 577	28 036	12 242	12 039	22 456	71 525	51 399	232 217	198 963
February	494 703	470 939	23 764	491 925	467 657	28 291	12 194	12 152	22 524	72 429	50 421	232 508	199 876
March	501 066	477 339	23 727	496 820	473 156	27 790	11 952	11 870	22 577	71 781	50 568	239 319	207 316
April	501 412	477 113	24 299	495 810	471 989	27 890	11 849	12 036	22 659	71 863	50 177	238 069	206 696
May	502 174	477 606	24 568	498 327	474 417	28 234	12 219	12 032	23 040	72 154	49 456	240 412	209 555
June	501 620	476 741	24 879	501 356	477 275	28 970	12 316	12 475	23 195	71 818	49 090	243 582	211 159
July	507 940	482 487	25 453	505 993	481 600	29 475	12 568	12 697	23 380	72 724	50 365	245 575	213 277
August	504 227	479 089	25 138	504 097	479 844	29 994	12 608	13 093	23 461	73 033	50 414	243 516	211 449
September	502 796	478 160	24 636	508 020	483 542	30 085	12 664	13 099	23 867	72 905	49 794	247 541	215 524
October	510 448	486 442	24 006	513 951	489 189	29 784	12 557	13 051	24 200	72 706	53 201	249 917	218 733
November	511 547	486 920	24 627	517 055	491 399	29 403	12 290	12 859	24 412	72 534	53 235	252 647	221 118
December	512 219	487 574	24 645	517 647	491 911	29 250	12 188	12 661	24 543	72 221	49 565	256 231	223 121

YEAR AND MONTH	Nondurable goods industries	By market category						Supplementary series		
		Home goods and apparel	Consumer staples	Machinery and equipment	Automotive equipment	Construction materials and supplies	Other materials, supplies, and intermediate products	Household durables	Capital goods industries	
									Nondefense	Defense
1968	3 984	2 331	281	43 432	776	8 205	30 784	2 129	47 608	23 152
1969	4 180	2 167	244	48 324	827	8 873	33 349	1 967	52 591	20 809
1970	4 596	2 245	284	42 704	714	8 880	30 991	2 078	46 544	18 804
1971	5 022	2 509	314	43 386	785	8 073	31 149	2 292	47 576	18 158
1972	6 315	3 168	355	47 635	886	8 810	38 198	2 914	52 781	19 261
1973	7 357	3 831	466	61 767	1 354	12 311	53 339	3 471	67 947	21 756
1974	5 524	2 891	480	77 672	1 400	15 125	60 751	2 582	84 495	26 558
1975	7 882	3 179	596	70 549	1 058	12 694	51 673	2 740	76 773	27 936
1976	8 271	3 376	708	72 941	1 209	11 592	54 856	2 862	79 121	31 826
1977	8 701	4 670	846	81 172	1 481	12 821	63 498	4 135	87 552	36 692
1978	10 888	5 493	978	103 005	2 046	14 408	85 040	4 864	112 277	47 425
1979	12 272	5 547	1 036	130 361	1 899	15 360	99 144	4 754	144 114	48 656
1980	12 214	5 226	1 054	136 142	1 656	15 410	100 488	4 388	150 973	66 636
1981	11 840	5 668	1 113	128 411	1 742	15 213	96 356	4 729	142 802	77 793
1982	11 089	5 784	1 140	109 196	1 563	11 981	84 771	4 860	121 082	99 052
1983	14 159	7 131	1 047	103 626	2 406	12 673	103 680	5 810	114 280	121 177
1984	13 878	6 890	1 083	108 659	2 172	13 102	105 750	5 603	119 424	142 324
1985	15 099	6 996	1 177	111 055	2 036	13 124	103 383	5 253	120 687	156 188
1986	16 816	7 357	1 171	108 830	2 159	13 677	104 644	5 815	118 429	161 705
1987	21 738	8 735	1 148	125 209	2 397	14 140	119 288	5 842	136 171	163 786
1988	22 004	7 999	1 431	160 441	2 220	14 557	129 322	5 703	176 069	161 878
1989	21 751	8 893	1 438	202 960	1 887	13 992	127 879	5 854	221 152	155 314
1990	22 007	9 067	1 276	231 612	1 531	14 021	126 374	5 215	250 314	149 844
1991	23 397	9 810	1 324	224 767	1 705	14 828	128 935	5 498	246 093	139 666
1992	23 530	9 879	1 437	215 369	1 600	14 735	126 421	5 151	234 866	124 175
1993	21 803	9 222	1 498	196 418	1 907	14 011	123 986	5 593	214 298	112 265
1994	25 692	8 685	1 642	195 145	2 212	15 792	136 787	6 012	213 320	106 858
1995	24 085	9 168	1 840	209 261	2 283	15 757	138 423	5 922	226 846	104 221
1996	25 736	9 072	2 118	229 614	2 257	16 427	144 623	5 641	250 020	111 574
1993:										
January	23 648	10 099	1 434	211 969	1 626	14 905	127 494	5 292	231 205	125 183
February	23 782	10 273	1 487	212 818	1 643	15 220	128 228	5 412	231 971	123 601
March	23 374	10 195	1 498	209 366	1 629	15 028	127 267	5 271	228 307	122 402
April	23 419	10 018	1 489	208 229	1 604	14 927	127 078	5 435	227 333	121 805
May	23 194	9 754	1 519	206 057	1 676	15 002	126 286	5 241	224 895	120 072
June	23 098	9 847	1 509	206 347	1 676	14 626	125 323	5 247	225 043	117 898
July	22 726	9 793	1 454	204 554	1 724	14 597	125 480	5 320	222 989	117 815
August	22 506	9 667	1 418	202 674	1 719	14 594	124 621	5 424	220 865	117 649
September	22 291	9 525	1 474	200 280	1 717	14 372	123 784	5 418	218 005	116 756
October	21 679	9 209	1 451	198 683	1 793	14 197	123 570	5 421	216 247	114 827
November	21 550	9 130	1 443	198 024	1 836	14 178	123 322	5 456	215 617	113 764
December	21 803	9 222	1 498	196 418	1 907	14 011	123 986	5 593	214 298	112 265
1994:										
January	22 080	9 271	1 470	198 253	1 914	13 966	124 486	5 575	216 137	112 535
February	22 435	9 293	1 486	198 047	1 929	14 029	124 785	5 565	216 294	111 439
March	23 295	9 430	1 535	197 456	1 971	14 483	127 573	5 574	215 688	108 226
April	23 642	9 300	1 553	196 624	1 987	14 625	129 316	5 487	214 986	107 279
May	24 120	9 540	1 562	194 959	2 001	14 770	130 825	5 724	213 443	107 472
June	24 195	9 505	1 550	196 160	2 061	15 030	130 894	5 760	214 231	107 066
July	24 173	9 481	1 516	195 679	2 071	15 154	130 216	5 768	213 581	106 789
August	24 440	9 344	1 562	195 161	2 099	15 125	130 772	5 766	213 067	105 345
September	24 569	9 285	1 564	194 849	2 106	15 183	132 221	5 961	213 033	105 761
October	25 117	9 159	1 597	194 556	2 136	15 540	132 886	5 934	212 774	105 566
November	25 209	8 965	1 640	195 749	2 156	15 654	134 957	5 996	214 138	103 850
December	25 692	8 685	1 642	195 145	2 212	15 792	136 787	6 012	213 320	106 858
1995:										
January	26 231	9 020	1 676	196 010	2 210	16 136	138 345	5 857	214 599	106 435
February	26 675	9 091	1 739	196 909	2 228	16 156	139 915	5 698	215 683	106 648
March	26 709	9 095	1 769	198 006	2 271	16 027	140 318	5 755	216 863	106 386
April	26 970	9 122	1 793	196 782	2 300	15 912	140 780	5 456	215 356	105 365
May	26 976	9 688	1 823	197 746	2 287	16 005	140 720	5 644	216 970	104 666
June	26 742	9 611	1 887	196 989	2 326	15 747	140 191	5 803	216 253	103 490
July	27 100	9 476	1 987	195 488	2 315	15 899	141 578	5 942	214 878	102 833
August	26 223	9 262	1 983	194 909	2 346	16 090	141 066	5 850	214 079	103 488
September	25 148	8 963	1 844	199 057	2 368	15 919	139 626	5 855	217 781	104 693
October	24 663	8 767	1 909	200 740	2 367	15 911	139 379	5 744	218 413	104 292
November	24 770	9 056	1 914	203 107	2 301	15 878	139 412	5 914	221 094	103 523
December	24 085	9 168	1 840	209 261	2 283	15 757	138 423	5 922	226 846	104 221
1996:										
January	24 481	9 154	1 904	215 294	2 321	15 754	138 839	5 837	233 257	106 169
February	24 268	9 220	1 921	218 032	2 304	15 909	137 511	5 862	235 866	105 430
March	23 664	9 320	1 876	222 369	2 283	15 874	135 916	5 911	240 417	107 716
April	23 821	9 305	1 934	221 428	2 262	15 838	135 533	5 924	239 267	107 790
May	23 910	9 234	2 004	223 680	2 244	15 809	135 712	5 912	241 518	107 806
June	24 081	9 085	2 022	223 894	2 228	15 843	136 623	5 825	241 401	109 841
July	24 393	8 824	2 249	226 834	2 261	15 901	138 965	5 628	244 967	109 097
August	24 253	8 772	2 158	225 145	2 279	15 921	139 756	5 579	242 835	108 244
September	24 478	8 945	2 077	228 400	2 283	16 161	140 905	5 566	246 511	107 613
October	24 762	9 410	1 987	231 028	2 245	16 105	144 586	5 943	250 618	106 806
November	25 656	9 159	2 087	230 134	2 264	15 971	146 186	5 488	250 567	109 218
December	25 736	9 072	2 118	229 614	2 257	16 427	144 623	5 641	250 020	111 574

Manufacturing by Industry: Durable Goods

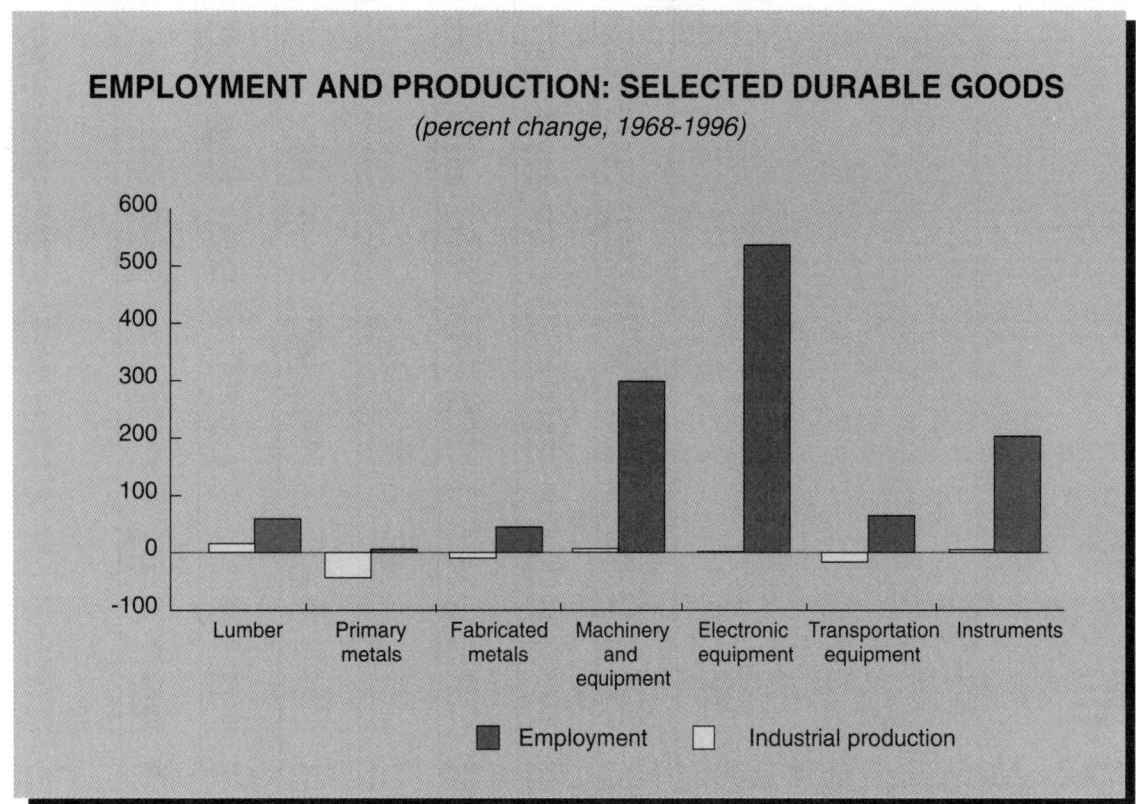

EMPLOYMENT AND PRODUCTION: SELECTED DURABLE GOODS
(percent change, 1968-1996)

Lumber | Primary metals | Fabricated metals | Machinery and equipment | Electronic equipment | Transportation equipment | Instruments

■ Employment   □ Industrial production

Several durable goods industries had dramatic gains in production from 1968 to 1996. Industrial production was up 200 percent or more in machinery and equipment (which includes computers), electronic and electric equipment, and instruments. These output increases were achieved with little or no increase in employment. In none of these three industries did employment grow by as much as 7 percent.

In no durable goods industry did production decline over this period, but the gain for primary metals (which includes iron and steel) was a scant 6 percent. Employment in primary metals fell 44 percent, from 1,261,000 workers in 1968 to 711,000 in 1996. Most of the decline in employment occurred during the 1980s, a period when production also showed a declining trend. By 1996, production was 10 percent above its most recent cyclical peak in 1988, but employment was down 8 percent over the same period.

LUMBER AND WOOD PRODUCTS—PRODUCTION, CAPACITY, AND PRICES

YEAR AND MONTH	Industrial production (1992=100, seasonally adjusted)							Capacity utilization (Percent of capacity, seasonally adjusted)	Producer prices (1982=100, except as noted, not seasonally adjusted)		
	Total	Logging and lumber		Lumber products					Lumber and wood products industry [1]	Intermediate materials	
		Total	Logging	Total	Millwork and plywood		Manu-factured homes			Softwood lumber	Hard-wood lumber
					Total	Plywood					
1968	69.1	76.3	71.5	65.5	56.9	71.3	....	85.8	....	37.5	39.8
1969	69.0	74.0	68.8	67.1	57.2	70.7	....	83.3	....	41.8	45.8
1970	68.6	75.0	70.6	65.8	56.0	70.5	....	80.5	....	35.2	43.7
1971	70.4	71.4	62.2	71.9	62.9	80.1	....	80.0	....	44.0	43.2
1972	80.6	83.2	74.4	81.3	72.9	88.7	146.6	88.2	....	52.1	48.1
1973	80.9	80.8	75.6	83.5	76.0	88.9	144.0	85.5	....	66.6	64.4
1974	73.4	79.3	81.7	71.2	64.1	77.6	101.7	75.8	....	65.7	72.2
1975	68.3	75.5	76.6	65.1	62.1	75.7	81.5	69.5	....	62.4	61.1
1976	77.8	83.6	82.5	75.6	70.5	86.5	107.1	78.2	....	77.1	67.1
1977	86.1	88.6	95.4	84.3	81.3	92.3	118.7	85.7	....	92.5	76.3
1978	87.5	87.8	91.0	87.5	84.4	95.1	126.0	86.1	....	107.6	89.9
1979	86.3	86.9	93.1	86.0	82.0	90.4	121.2	83.8	....	118.1	99.1
1980	80.4	83.6	112.2	77.9	74.8	84.4	99.6	77.7	....	107.3	96.0
1981	78.1	78.2	104.3	77.9	74.4	85.7	101.8	74.9	....	106.6	97.3
1982	70.3	70.0	89.9	70.4	65.7	80.0	89.3	66.6	....	100.0	100.0
1983	83.3	82.0	104.8	84.1	80.3	92.5	110.5	78.8	....	115.0	108.1
1984	89.9	88.3	112.0	90.8	89.8	95.2	104.7	84.0	....	110.0	121.8
1985	92.0	91.9	109.1	92.0	93.9	97.8	102.5	84.0	100.3	107.4	117.1
1986	99.6	102.4	118.5	97.7	102.9	109.4	102.7	89.0	101.5	108.4	118.2
1987	104.9	105.8	118.2	104.2	111.8	115.9	106.2	92.1	105.3	116.1	126.8
1988	105.1	106.7	115.4	103.9	111.5	115.5	103.0	91.1	109.2	120.0	131.0
1989	104.3	105.0	113.9	103.7	109.3	111.7	96.9	88.7	115.3	127.1	128.2
1990	101.6	100.5	103.6	102.2	105.4	107.2	94.0	85.0	117.0	123.8	131.0
1991	94.5	95.6	97.9	93.8	95.2	98.2	84.3	78.5	119.4	125.7	128.5
1992	100.0	100.0	100.0	100.0	100.0	100.0	100.0	83.0	129.7	148.6	140.7
1993	100.9	96.5	97.5	104.2	101.6	98.5	115.5	83.6	148.3	193.0	163.3
1994	105.9	100.5	99.3	110.0	107.1	100.7	130.0	86.3	154.4	198.1	168.3
1995	106.2	98.6	99.8	112.0	106.6	99.8	148.9	84.6	154.1	178.5	167.0
1996	109.7	99.8	95.9	117.1	111.0	101.8	161.7	85.2	153.5	189.5	163.9
1993:											
January	100.6	96.2	93.0	104.0	101.0	96.3	116.6	83.5	139.2	171.1	153.0
February	102.4	98.9	101.5	105.1	103.6	100.8	114.9	85.0	145.4	192.2	156.1
March	100.0	95.2	97.5	103.6	101.6	100.6	110.5	82.9	151.1	212.0	157.9
April	98.9	94.2	95.7	102.5	99.6	98.9	111.4	82.0	152.6	212.2	161.4
May	99.3	95.6	96.3	102.2	99.2	97.1	110.6	82.3	150.4	200.1	164.5
June	98.5	94.0	95.9	102.0	98.6	96.9	111.2	81.6	147.1	185.8	166.3
July	99.5	95.5	97.5	102.5	100.0	97.7	115.9	82.4	145.7	177.7	167.4
August	101.0	97.3	97.5	103.8	101.3	97.3	115.6	83.6	146.3	181.8	167.2
September	101.0	96.1	99.3	104.7	102.3	98.1	117.5	83.6	148.2	185.9	167.0
October	102.7	99.0	97.9	105.5	103.6	98.8	118.0	85.0	149.0	189.5	166.4
November	103.2	99.4	99.7	106.2	103.8	98.7	120.9	85.4	151.3	199.0	166.3
December	103.3	97.1	98.5	108.0	105.0	100.1	122.8	85.3	153.5	208.8	166.1
1994:											
January	105.0	100.3	98.8	108.5	104.3	98.0	129.7	86.6	156.6	216.8	166.5
February	103.8	99.0	98.9	107.4	104.0	99.7	125.6	85.5	155.5	209.6	166.5
March	103.6	99.2	102.3	107.0	103.7	101.5	128.0	85.2	155.9	210.2	167.9
April	104.2	98.3	99.4	108.8	106.8	101.9	125.9	85.5	153.2	197.9	167.9
May	106.3	101.6	100.5	109.9	107.6	102.4	127.1	87.0	152.5	194.4	168.5
June	106.2	100.7	98.2	110.4	108.3	103.1	128.6	86.7	153.7	199.8	168.6
July	107.0	101.2	99.3	111.4	108.5	100.2	128.0	87.1	152.7	192.6	168.8
August	106.0	100.3	100.5	110.4	108.0	100.3	127.8	86.2	153.3	193.9	169.2
September	106.9	101.9	99.6	110.6	107.8	100.5	130.1	86.6	154.1	192.9	168.8
October	106.3	99.6	94.9	111.5	108.2	98.9	132.9	86.0	153.9	188.7	168.7
November	106.1	98.8	98.6	111.8	109.0	100.3	134.1	85.7	155.9	191.3	168.7
December	109.3	104.9	100.5	112.7	108.6	101.3	141.7	88.1	155.5	188.8	169.1
1995:											
January	108.5	102.7	102.7	113.0	107.7	102.1	148.9	87.2	155.7	189.1	169.9
February	107.1	99.2	100.4	113.1	109.6	100.1	141.2	85.9	155.0	183.4	169.8
March	105.3	97.5	102.6	111.2	106.9	99.5	140.8	84.4	155.5	185.4	170.0
April	105.3	99.4	96.8	109.9	105.3	97.3	142.2	84.2	155.0	180.9	169.3
May	103.5	95.7	96.6	109.4	105.4	96.8	144.8	82.6	154.5	178.1	167.9
June	104.3	97.7	98.0	109.3	104.4	97.4	146.5	83.1	153.0	173.7	167.2
July	105.2	98.6	98.4	110.2	104.6	98.9	147.5	83.7	154.2	178.1	166.5
August	105.9	97.1	100.8	112.5	107.0	103.0	151.7	84.1	154.2	177.2	165.9
September	107.6	99.9	99.9	113.4	106.8	99.8	153.5	85.3	155.1	179.9	165.5
October	106.9	98.1	100.6	113.6	107.0	99.9	154.8	84.7	153.8	175.9	164.9
November	106.6	97.3	101.2	113.7	107.1	99.6	157.3	84.3	152.1	170.8	164.2
December	108.1	99.9	100.0	114.3	107.9	103.6	157.2	85.3	151.4	169.3	163.4
1996:											
January	105.3	95.9	98.7	112.4	105.8	100.8	155.6	82.9	150.6	169.2	163.5
February	106.3	97.9	99.0	112.6	107.1	100.7	156.4	83.5	150.7	170.6	164.0
March	109.7	102.2	98.6	115.4	108.3	101.7	162.5	86.0	150.9	174.6	164.4
April	110.3	101.1	100.1	117.1	110.6	104.2	164.8	86.2	151.0	178.5	163.8
May	110.4	100.5	97.5	117.9	111.7	106.3	165.7	86.1	153.8	192.1	163.2
June	112.4	101.8	98.2	120.3	113.3	105.6	167.9	87.4	154.5	196.8	163.5
July	109.3	97.8	95.3	117.9	113.1	106.6	163.0	84.9	153.3	191.6	163.1
August	111.4	101.8	93.1	118.6	112.7	103.6	167.4	86.3	154.4	196.6	163.1
September	110.7	99.6	91.2	119.1	112.4	97.9	165.6	85.5	156.6	203.9	163.5
October	109.2	95.7	91.6	119.3	113.6	100.4	165.3	84.2	154.6	193.7	164.3
November	113.1	104.8	94.7	119.4	112.8	101.1	159.8	87.0	156.2	204.4	164.9
December	108.0	99.0	93.2	114.8	110.8	92.8	146.2	82.9	155.9	202.4	166.0

1. December 1984=100.

YEAR AND MONTH	LUMBER AND WOOD PRODUCTS—PRICES, EMPLOYMENT, HOURS, AND EARNINGS										FURNITURE AND FIXTURES—INDUSTRIAL PRODUCTION (1992=100, seasonally adjusted)	
	Producer prices—Continued (1982=100, not seasonally adjusted)			Employment (Thousands, seasonally adjusted)		Production workers						
	Intermediate materials—Continued		Crude materials: Logs and timber [1]	Total payroll employees	Production workers	Weekly hours worked (Seasonally adjusted)		Average earnings (Dollars, not seasonally adjusted)				
	Millwork	Plywood				Average hours	Aggregate hours index (1982=100)	Hourly	Weekly	Total	Household furniture
1968	37.9	49.8	....	674	581	40.6	124.8	2.58	104.75	57.5	71.7
1969	42.2	52.8	....	691	594	40.2	126.5	2.75	110.55	60.1	72.6
1970	41.5	46.7	....	658	564	39.6	117.9	2.97	117.61	56.2	69.2
1971	43.2	49.4	....	681	588	39.8	123.8	3.18	126.56	58.6	73.9
1972	46.0	56.3	....	740	637	40.4	136.1	3.34	134.94	70.7	90.1
1973	51.6	66.9	....	774	665	40.0	140.6	3.62	144.80	75.4	95.0
1974	56.2	69.4	....	727	618	39.2	128.2	3.90	152.88	70.1	87.5
1975	57.4	69.4	....	627	526	38.8	107.8	4.28	166.06	60.0	75.3
1976	63.3	80.6	....	693	585	39.9	123.5	4.74	189.13	67.0	84.4
1977	69.3	91.4	....	736	626	39.9	132.0	5.11	203.89	74.8	91.8
1978	84.3	101.5	....	770	657	39.8	138.3	5.62	223.68	80.4	98.5
1979	91.0	107.9	....	782	664	39.5	138.6	6.08	240.16	80.5	96.4
1980	93.2	106.2	....	704	587	38.6	119.9	6.57	253.60	79.1	90.0
1981	97.8	105.9	....	680	563	38.7	115.1	7.02	271.67	78.4	90.3
1982	100.0	100.0	100.0	610	497	38.1	100.0	7.46	284.23	74.6	79.6
1983	108.2	105.2	96.6	671	555	40.1	117.7	7.82	313.58	80.2	86.8
1984	110.2	104.1	97.0	718	598	39.9	126.3	8.05	321.20	88.6	92.7
1985	111.7	99.6	96.0	711	592	39.9	124.9	8.25	329.18	88.9	91.1
1986	113.7	101.4	92.3	724	605	40.4	129.2	8.37	338.15	93.3	96.6
1987	117.7	102.6	101.8	754	628	40.6	134.9	8.43	342.26	100.9	103.0
1988	121.9	103.4	117.7	767	639	40.1	135.6	8.59	344.46	101.1	102.5
1989	127.3	115.9	131.9	756	626	40.1	132.6	8.84	354.48	102.4	103.0
1990	130.4	114.2	142.8	733	603	40.2	128.2	9.08	365.02	100.9	100.8
1991	135.5	114.3	144.1	675	553	40.0	116.9	9.24	369.60	94.8	96.6
1992	143.3	133.3	164.8	680	558	40.6	119.9	9.44	383.26	100.0	100.0
1993	156.6	152.8	212.3	709	584	40.8	126.1	9.61	392.09	104.7	104.5
1994	162.4	158.6	219.1	754	623	41.2	135.9	9.84	405.41	107.9	109.7
1995	163.8	165.3	220.4	769	632	40.6	135.8	10.12	410.87	108.6	110.0
1996	166.6	156.4	206.8	780	641	40.8	138.3	10.44	425.95	108.8	111.3
1993:											
January	148.0	154.9	183.2	696	573	40.7	123.3	9.46	376.51	102.9	101.4
February	151.8	164.8	193.8	701	576	40.9	124.6	9.51	383.25	101.9	100.9
March	155.9	168.9	200.9	703	579	40.5	124.0	9.50	381.90	103.9	102.5
April	158.8	158.7	222.6	701	576	40.6	123.7	9.51	382.30	104.8	104.9
May	158.2	148.5	233.5	701	576	40.6	123.7	9.56	391.00	104.5	104.8
June	156.6	144.0	224.9	704	578	40.5	123.8	9.56	390.05	104.3	106.0
July	155.7	143.3	222.5	706	581	40.7	125.0	9.65	391.79	105.1	103.5
August	156.1	146.4	212.6	710	585	40.8	126.2	9.68	398.82	106.1	106.0
September	158.7	149.6	212.6	717	590	41.4	129.1	9.73	401.85	106.7	106.1
October	159.1	147.9	212.9	720	594	40.9	128.5	9.71	401.99	105.9	106.7
November	159.9	150.8	215.6	723	597	41.2	130.0	9.67	400.34	104.7	105.1
December	160.7	155.5	212.4	729	601	41.1	130.6	9.73	404.77	106.0	106.5
1994:											
January	162.8	159.7	223.7	734	608	41.6	133.7	9.75	398.78	104.3	104.6
February	163.4	153.8	226.5	740	609	40.3	129.8	9.71	386.46	105.6	107.0
March	163.2	152.5	230.7	742	613	41.3	133.9	9.70	397.70	106.3	107.6
April	162.4	147.8	227.2	746	617	41.2	134.4	9.74	402.26	107.4	108.9
May	161.5	149.2	220.7	750	620	41.4	135.7	9.80	407.68	108.2	109.6
June	161.7	153.8	218.1	754	623	41.3	136.0	9.84	409.34	108.6	110.5
July	161.5	153.7	215.5	759	627	41.3	136.9	9.87	404.67	108.2	110.6
August	161.3	157.6	213.5	761	628	41.1	136.5	9.87	410.59	109.4	111.6
September	161.6	165.7	212.6	763	629	41.0	136.4	9.95	412.93	107.5	110.9
October	162.6	164.6	213.3	764	630	41.1	136.9	9.96	414.34	110.3	112.6
November	163.3	172.5	212.8	768	634	41.0	137.4	9.93	409.12	109.3	111.5
December	163.3	172.0	214.5	769	636	41.2	138.5	9.97	415.75	109.3	110.7
1995:											
January	163.9	166.0	218.1	771	637	41.5	139.8	9.95	404.97	109.0	110.4
February	163.4	162.8	224.5	775	637	40.8	137.4	9.94	397.60	110.6	111.8
March	163.8	164.5	225.9	772	638	40.7	137.3	9.94	401.58	109.1	109.1
April	163.8	164.0	229.3	768	632	40.6	135.7	9.97	400.79	108.4	110.7
May	163.7	165.2	228.4	767	630	40.3	134.2	10.01	406.41	107.8	109.6
June	163.7	159.3	228.8	765	627	40.4	133.9	10.11	412.49	109.0	110.5
July	163.9	167.6	219.9	764	628	40.3	133.8	10.21	408.40	108.7	108.7
August	164.0	171.1	216.0	766	629	40.6	135.0	10.20	419.22	108.2	109.2
September	164.2	173.4	216.0	769	630	40.6	135.2	10.28	422.51	109.5	110.4
October	164.0	169.9	214.6	771	632	40.6	135.7	10.27	423.12	107.9	110.7
November	163.4	161.7	211.5	771	632	40.6	135.7	10.22	415.95	107.8	109.3
December	163.6	157.4	212.3	775	637	40.1	135.1	10.29	415.72	107.5	110.0
1996:											
January	163.6	154.0	214.5	766	630	39.4	131.2	10.28	396.81	107.4	110.3
February	163.8	154.2	214.0	774	633	40.6	135.9	10.23	407.15	107.9	110.5
March	164.1	152.1	209.3	773	634	40.7	136.4	10.29	415.72	105.8	107.7
April	164.6	151.6	200.2	777	637	40.7	137.1	10.33	420.43	108.1	111.9
May	165.8	158.3	202.8	778	639	40.9	138.2	10.34	426.01	110.3	115.4
June	166.7	155.8	201.5	781	642	41.1	139.5	10.45	434.72	109.5	113.3
July	167.0	154.0	201.7	781	641	41.0	139.0	10.47	426.13	108.1	109.5
August	167.9	157.4	203.6	783	644	40.9	139.3	10.54	436.36	108.8	112.3
September	168.7	166.7	206.0	782	641	40.9	138.6	10.57	439.71	108.8	111.2
October	168.7	160.1	208.8	785	646	40.8	139.4	10.56	437.18	110.4	111.5
November	169.3	157.9	209.8	787	648	40.9	140.1	10.57	433.37	110.5	111.2
December	169.3	155.3	209.5	788	650	41.0	140.9	10.61	437.13	110.5	110.3

1. Logs, bolts, timber, and pulpwood.

FURNITURE AND FIXTURES—CAPACITY, PRICES, EMPLOYMENT, HOURS, AND EARNINGS

YEAR AND MONTH	Capacity utilization (Percent of capacity, seasonally adjusted)	Producer prices (1982=100, except as noted, not seasonally adjusted)				Employment (Thousands, seasonally adjusted)		Production workers			
		Furniture and fixtures industry [1]	Finished goods			Total payroll employees	Production workers	Weekly hours worked (Seasonally adjusted)		Average earnings (Dollars, not seasonally adjusted)	
			Household furniture	Floor coverings	Household appliances			Average hours	Aggregate hours index (1982=100)	Hourly	Weekly
1968	90.7	....	45.2	55.9	51.1	450	372	40.6	118.6	2.47	100.28
1969	90.7	....	47.2	55.4	51.7	461	383	40.4	121.5	2.62	105.85
1970	81.0	....	48.6	54.9	52.9	440	362	39.2	111.6	2.77	108.58
1971	80.7		50.0	54.6	54.0	444	365	39.8	114.0	2.90	115.42
1972	93.0		51.0	54.4	54.0	483	400	40.2	126.6	3.08	123.82
1973	93.9		53.5	56.4	54.5	507	420	40.0	132.0	3.29	131.60
1974	82.9		59.4	63.7	59.2	489	402	39.1	123.4	3.53	138.02
1975	68.9		63.6	69.0	66.5	417	337	38.0	100.7	3.78	143.64
1976	75.7		66.8	72.5	69.9	444	364	38.8	111.0	3.99	154.81
1977	82.1		70.6	75.3	72.9	464	382	39.0	117.2	4.34	169.26
1978	84.5		75.5	78.2	76.8	494	406	39.3	125.6	4.68	183.92
1979	81.0		81.0	81.7	80.8	498	406	38.7	123.5	5.06	195.82
1980	77.2		89.1	90.0	87.5	466	376	38.1	112.4	5.49	209.17
1981	74.7		95.4	98.7	94.1	464	374	38.4	112.7	5.91	226.94
1982	70.2		100.0	100.0	100.0	432	342	37.2	100.0	6.31	234.73
1983	74.9		102.1	102.4	103.9	448	356	39.4	110.3	6.62	260.83
1984	81.4	....	105.3	105.6	106.0	486	390	39.7	121.6	6.84	271.55
1985	79.5	101.9	108.5	105.6	106.7	493	394	39.4	121.9	7.17	282.50
1986	81.5	103.9	110.3	108.3	105.7	498	397	39.8	124.2	7.46	296.91
1987	86.0	106.4	113.0	110.7	105.6	515	412	40.0	129.5	7.67	306.80
1988	84.0	111.4	117.6	114.7	106.0	527	420	39.4	130.1	7.95	313.23
1989	83.1	115.6	121.8	117.6	108.7	524	418	39.5	129.6	8.25	325.88
1990	80.1	119.1	125.1	119.0	110.8	506	400	39.1	122.8	8.52	333.13
1991	74.7	121.6	128.0	120.4	111.3	475	373	38.9	113.9	8.76	340.76
1992	78.7	122.9	130.0	120.3	111.4	478	377	39.7	117.6	9.01	357.72
1993	81.6	125.4	133.4	120.2	112.9	487	385	40.1	121.3	9.27	371.73
1994	82.9	129.7	138.0	121.5	112.8	505	400	40.4	127.0	9.55	385.82
1995	82.4	133.3	141.8	123.7	112.4	510	403	39.6	125.6	9.82	388.87
1996	81.0	136.2	144.5	126.6	112.7	504	398	39.4	123.2	10.15	399.91
1993:											
January	80.7	123.5	131.2	119.4	112.0	481	380	40.3	120.4	9.16	364.57
February	79.8	124.3	131.6	119.5	112.3	483	381	40.4	121.0	9.12	361.15
March	81.3	124.3	131.7	119.5	112.5	484	382	40.1	120.4	9.11	361.67
April	81.9	124.5	132.2	119.4	112.8	485	383	40.6	122.2	9.14	361.94
May	81.6	125.1	132.6	119.2	113.0	487	385	39.9	120.7	9.17	361.30
June	81.3	125.4	133.0	119.1	113.4	486	384	39.6	119.5	9.23	366.43
July	81.9	125.5	133.2	120.0	113.4	486	383	40.0	120.4	9.28	368.42
August	82.5	125.7	133.3	120.8	113.4	488	384	40.3	121.6	9.33	379.73
September	83.0	125.8	133.6	121.2	113.4	489	387	40.4	122.9	9.40	377.88
October	82.2	126.6	135.8	121.3	113.0	490	388	40.2	122.6	9.40	382.58
November	81.2	126.7	136.4	121.4	113.0	491	389	40.3	123.2	9.44	386.10
December	82.1	127.2	135.8	121.2	112.7	493	390	40.2	123.2	9.44	390.82
1994:											
January	80.7	127.6	136.1	121.4	112.8	495	392	39.8	122.6	9.41	375.46
February	81.6	128.1	136.9	121.3	112.8	495	392	38.9	119.8	9.41	358.52
March	82.0	128.3	137.2	120.9	113.0	498	394	40.7	126.0	9.38	378.01
April	82.8	128.9	137.4	121.1	113.1	499	396	40.2	125.1	9.45	378.95
May	83.4	130.1	137.8	121.0	113.2	502	398	40.5	126.7	9.45	377.06
June	83.6	130.1	138.0	121.3	112.9	506	401	40.6	128.0	9.48	385.84
July	83.1	130.2	138.1	121.9	112.9	509	403	40.6	128.6	9.54	383.51
August	84.0	130.1	138.1	121.8	112.7	509	403	40.4	128.0	9.57	390.46
September	82.4	130.3	138.6	121.2	112.7	510	403	40.5	128.3	9.69	399.23
October	84.4	130.5	138.9	121.7	112.9	512	405	40.7	129.6	9.70	399.64
November	83.6	130.9	139.2	122.4	112.7	512	406	40.3	128.6	9.68	396.88
December	83.5	131.0	139.4	122.2	112.4	513	407	40.3	128.9	9.77	406.43
1995:											
January	83.2	131.5	140.0	122.6	112.3	514	407	40.5	129.6	9.68	393.01
February	84.3	132.0	140.4	122.9	112.3	516	409	40.3	129.5	9.67	383.90
March	83.1	132.1	140.7	122.7	112.1	517	409	39.8	127.9	9.68	381.39
April	82.4	132.6	141.0	123.1	112.4	514	407	39.1	125.1	9.76	367.95
May	81.9	132.8	141.6	123.8	112.4	511	404	39.3	124.8	9.71	375.78
June	82.8	133.4	141.8	123.3	112.2	509	402	39.4	124.5	9.78	386.31
July	82.4	133.4	142.0	123.5	112.3	504	399	39.2	122.9	9.83	381.40
August	81.9	133.9	142.2	123.6	112.2	508	401	39.7	125.1	9.89	396.59
September	82.8	133.8	142.5	124.0	112.6	507	400	39.5	124.2	9.95	399.99
October	81.6	134.4	142.7	125.1	112.6	507	400	39.5	124.2	9.92	397.79
November	81.3	134.9	143.2	124.8	112.7	507	400	39.6	124.5	9.95	399.99
December	81.0	134.9	143.2	125.0	112.5	508	401	39.3	123.9	10.00	407.00
1996:											
January	80.9	135.2	143.6	124.9	112.4	506	399	35.8	112.3	10.01	359.36
February	81.1	135.7	143.8	125.2	112.5	505	399	39.2	122.9	9.95	384.07
March	79.3	135.6	144.1	125.8	112.6	504	397	39.4	122.9	10.00	390.00
April	80.9	135.8	144.2	124.8	113.0	501	395	39.3	122.0	10.06	389.32
May	82.4	135.7	144.4	126.4	113.1	503	398	39.6	123.9	10.08	394.13
June	81.6	135.9	144.5	125.6	113.1	503	397	39.6	123.6	10.11	399.35
July	80.5	136.2	144.6	126.8	113.0	503	398	39.7	124.2	10.13	398.11
August	80.7	136.1	144.5	127.3	113.0	502	398	39.6	123.9	10.19	408.62
September	80.6	136.4	144.7	128.0	112.5	503	398	39.6	123.9	10.27	414.91
October	81.6	137.1	144.9	128.1	112.4	503	397	39.6	123.6	10.27	414.28
November	81.6	137.3	145.2	128.2	112.4	504	398	39.8	124.5	10.28	416.34
December	81.4	137.4	145.2	127.8	111.9	505	399	40.1	125.7	10.43	433.89

1. December 1984=100.

STONE, CLAY, AND GLASS PRODUCTS—PRODUCTION, CAPACITY, SHIPMENTS, AND INVENTORIES

YEAR AND MONTH	Industrial production (1992=100, seasonally adjusted)						Capacity utilization (Percent of capacity, seasonally adjusted)	Manufacturers' shipments and inventories (Millions of dollars, seasonally adjusted)	
	Total	Pressed and blown glass		Cement	Structural clay products	Concrete and miscellaneous		Shipments	Inventories (Book value, end of period)
		Total	Glass containers						
1968	76.2	76.1	103.6	104.7	120.5	79.0	78.4	15 465	1 918
1969	78.8	81.7	118.2	108.7	123.2	80.5	79.7	16 499	2 051
1970	74.8	81.5	121.3	102.1	110.4	76.2	73.9	16 454	2 239
1971	78.5	83.4	118.6	110.5	113.8	78.6	75.6	18 220	2 302
1972	86.9	88.8	120.3	117.1	120.9	88.4	81.7	20 875	2 430
1973	93.9	95.0	125.3	125.5	128.4	95.4	86.0	23 141	2 712
1974	92.4	95.8	128.0	115.5	123.2	95.6	81.9	25 503	3 403
1975	81.8	90.2	128.2	97.5	104.8	83.7	70.3	26 233	3 594
1976	91.5	97.9	136.6	102.4	113.7	93.3	77.2	29 618	3 841
1977	98.3	102.2	137.5	110.4	123.3	100.9	81.8	34 209	4 095
1978	106.0	108.0	139.1	117.0	131.2	108.9	86.5	40 238	4 710
1979	106.8	110.0	135.7	118.0	130.4	111.2	85.5	44 287	5 183
1980	96.5	109.2	131.4	100.9	111.1	99.2	76.3	44 473	5 674
1981	94.3	111.3	129.0	102.6	102.5	95.0	75.0	46 220	6 106
1982	84.2	101.4	128.6	89.6	81.5	84.0	67.5	43 515	6 506
1983	91.2	101.8	122.1	99.2	96.8	92.1	73.1	47 697	6 628
1984	98.6	102.8	118.3	110.1	111.2	100.6	78.3	53 101	7 042
1985	98.0	97.0	108.8	109.7	105.3	100.8	76.3	55 821	7 040
1986	101.7	100.4	111.3	112.4	111.8	104.4	78.3	59 254	7 093
1987	104.8	99.1	107.1	113.6	113.4	107.9	79.8	61 477	7 154
1988	107.5	101.8	106.9	113.2	115.2	111.3	81.7	63 145	7 496
1989	107.4	103.3	108.2	111.8	118.7	110.2	81.1	63 729	7 792
1990	105.0	102.4	106.9	111.5	114.2	107.0	78.4	63 728	8 205
1991	97.2	96.7	99.3	96.2	100.3	98.3	72.2	59 957	7 928
1992	100.0	100.0	100.0	100.0	100.0	100.0	74.2	62 521	8 009
1993	102.1	98.3	93.3	96.6	101.6	102.6	75.6	65 610	7 611
1994	107.9	102.2	93.1	106.0	112.1	107.9	79.4	71 230	7 879
1995	109.1	98.6	85.7	106.2	109.9	110.7	79.5	75 991	8 593
1996	110.9	95.8	79.6	110.0	111.6	113.9	79.4	83 365	8 607
1993:									
January	99.2	94.1	89.7	93.4	102.4	99.7	73.5	4 260	7 972
February	100.6	97.9	93.3	92.4	102.7	101.5	74.5	4 918	7 953
March	99.4	99.1	93.6	90.6	102.9	99.3	73.6	5 103	7 940
April	101.4	104.3	105.3	93.2	103.1	100.8	75.1	5 550	7 905
May	99.9	95.0	89.9	97.0	103.0	100.6	74.0	5 452	7 852
June	101.3	98.0	90.3	96.3	102.7	102.1	75.0	5 989	7 801
July	102.4	98.4	93.2	97.9	101.9	103.6	75.8	5 228	7 793
August	101.7	95.7	90.2	98.7	100.8	102.7	75.3	5 818	7 726
September	104.0	100.1	93.6	97.2	99.4	104.4	77.0	6 423	7 685
October	103.7	94.9	88.9	99.3	98.7	105.1	76.8	6 143	7 709
November	105.1	98.4	91.4	101.0	99.6	105.9	77.8	5 757	7 666
December	106.3	104.3	100.1	102.0	102.6	105.7	78.7	4 969	7 611
1994:									
January	104.7	95.5	87.9	94.9	106.5	105.5	77.5	4 762	7 677
February	104.7	100.0	91.6	97.1	109.7	104.3	77.4	5 211	7 635
March	106.8	100.7	92.0	110.6	111.3	106.1	78.9	5 910	7 654
April	107.4	101.6	94.6	106.1	111.7	107.5	79.3	6 111	7 605
May	107.9	101.6	92.2	109.2	111.8	108.1	79.6	5 958	7 583
June	107.2	104.0	96.0	107.3	112.1	106.5	79.0	6 506	7 467
July	107.5	103.9	94.7	105.4	112.7	107.2	79.2	5 756	7 567
August	109.4	103.5	91.3	107.2	113.0	109.9	80.5	6 490	7 550
September	108.6	102.7	93.7	108.0	112.9	108.5	79.8	6 562	7 607
October	108.7	104.0	94.7	104.3	113.0	108.8	79.9	6 382	7 681
November	109.7	104.9	94.3	108.9	114.1	109.7	80.5	6 125	7 749
December	111.6	104.0	93.8	112.8	116.4	112.1	81.8	5 457	7 879
1995:									
January	110.4	102.4	91.5	108.9	119.2	110.2	80.8	5 372	7 941
February	110.1	100.3	88.7	108.7	120.8	111.1	80.6	5 849	7 990
March	110.3	102.5	90.9	110.9	120.4	110.2	80.6	6 112	8 115
April	108.5	99.9	86.4	103.7	118.1	108.9	79.2	6 024	8 332
May	109.3	100.3	88.1	101.0	114.5	110.3	79.7	6 329	8 529
June	108.8	98.8	87.0	106.2	110.2	110.1	79.3	6 844	8 629
July	107.7	97.7	83.8	105.0	106.1	109.6	78.4	6 191	8 742
August	107.8	99.5	86.0	104.8	103.2	109.3	78.4	6 974	8 787
September	108.5	95.2	80.6	105.2	102.2	111.7	78.8	6 990	8 821
October	109.1	96.2	83.5	107.7	102.2	111.3	79.1	7 008	8 754
November	109.9	94.7	80.7	106.2	101.8	113.6	79.7	6 564	8 710
December	109.3	96.0	81.6	106.1	100.3	112.6	79.1	5 734	8 593
1996:									
January	110.1	100.8	89.5	107.9	98.5	112.4	79.6	5 809	8 577
February	109.1	99.0	85.1	110.1	97.7	111.0	78.8	6 025	8 586
March	108.7	94.5	80.4	109.1	98.9	112.4	78.3	6 514	8 573
April	108.5	95.5	80.8	113.7	102.0	111.1	78.0	6 979	8 514
May	109.8	98.1	85.8	111.0	106.7	112.0	78.7	7 266	8 439
June	111.3	92.9	75.7	109.8	112.4	115.7	79.7	7 640	8 447
July	114.1	95.9	77.3	112.6	117.5	118.1	81.6	7 050	8 373
August	111.8	95.2	78.4	111.8	120.6	114.1	79.7	7 557	8 423
September	113.1	95.9	77.8	108.2	120.6	116.5	80.5	7 564	8 435
October	111.7	93.0	73.3	110.9	122.1	114.7	79.3	7 901	8 478
November	111.8	94.9	77.8	109.9	121.1	114.5	79.3	7 081	8 507
December	111.3	93.3	73.4	105.4	121.0	114.8	78.8	5 979	8 607

STONE, CLAY, AND GLASS—PRICES, EMPLOYMENT, HOURS, AND EARNINGS

Year and month	Stone, clay, and glass products industry [1]	Producer prices (1982=100, except as noted, not seasonally adjusted) — Intermediate materials						Crude materials: Construction sand, gravel, and crushed stone	Employment (Thousands, seasonally adjusted)		Production workers — Weekly hours worked (Seasonally adjusted)		Production workers — Average earnings (Dollars, not seasonally adjusted)	
		Flat glass	Cement	Concrete products	Asphalt felts and coatings	Gypsum products	Glass containers		Total payroll employees	Production workers	Average hours	Aggregate hours index (1982=100)	Hourly	Weekly
1968	....	47.1	....	34.5	25.9	40.5	30.2	37.3	602	482	41.8	121.9	2.99	124.98
1969	....	49.5	....	35.8	25.8	40.5	32.3	38.7	622	499	41.9	126.4	3.19	133.66
1970	....	52.2	....	37.7	25.8	38.9	33.9	40.9	610	485	41.2	120.9	3.40	140.08
1971	....	55.6	36.8	40.5	31.5	42.7	37.0	42.8	611	486	41.6	122.2	3.67	152.67
1972	....	55.3	....	42.2	32.9	44.8	38.0	43.7	645	516	42.0	131.1	3.94	165.48
1973	....	54.8	....	44.2	34.0	47.2	39.1	44.9	680	546	41.9	138.4	4.22	176.82
1974	....	58.2	....	50.9	49.2	53.7	43.7	48.6	673	539	41.3	134.5	4.54	187.50
1975	....	62.8	57.1	57.3	56.7	56.2	50.5	54.3	598	473	40.4	115.6	4.92	198.77
1976	....	67.7	62.9	60.5	59.8	60.3	55.0	57.9	613	486	41.1	120.8	5.33	219.06
1977	....	72.6	67.6	64.4	63.5	71.7	60.2	61.3	636	505	41.3	125.9	5.81	239.95
1978	....	78.0	74.3	71.9	73.3	89.5	68.7	66.7	664	525	41.6	132.1	6.32	262.91
1979	....	83.0	83.7	82.0	81.7	98.5	73.4	74.4	674	529	41.5	132.8	6.85	284.28
1980	....	88.7	91.9	92.0	99.6	100.1	82.3	85.3	629	486	40.8	119.8	7.50	306.00
1981	....	96.0	97.4	97.8	102.3	100.1	92.5	94.0	606	465	40.6	114.1	8.27	335.76
1982	....	100.0	100.0	100.0	100.0	100.0	100.0	100.0	548	413	40.1	100.0	8.87	355.69
1983	....	103.7	100.4	101.4	96.4	111.7	99.1	101.7	541	412	41.5	103.2	9.27	384.71
1984	....	101.4	104.0	103.9	100.3	135.4	101.4	106.0	562	431	42.0	109.5	9.57	401.94
1985	102.1	101.7	106.1	107.5	102.6	132.3	106.8	110.7	557	427	41.9	108.1	9.84	412.30
1986	103.8	104.5	104.2	109.2	97.9	137.0	111.9	114.2	554	426	42.2	108.7	10.04	423.69
1987	104.5	107.2	101.9	109.4	92.4	125.2	113.0	118.1	554	429	42.3	109.7	10.25	433.58
1988	105.8	109.7	102.2	110.0	94.7	112.9	112.3	120.6	567	443	42.3	113.3	10.56	446.69
1989	107.9	109.7	102.1	111.2	95.8	110.0	115.2	122.8	568	444	42.3	113.5	10.82	457.69
1990	110.0	107.5	103.7	113.5	97.1	105.2	120.4	125.4	556	432	42.0	109.7	11.12	467.04
1991	112.3	105.9	106.8	116.6	98.2	99.3	125.4	128.6	522	403	41.7	101.4	11.36	473.71
1992	112.8	106.5	106.3	117.2	96.2	99.9	125.1	130.6	513	396	42.2	101.2	11.60	489.52
1993	115.4	107.3	111.7	120.2	96.8	108.3	125.8	134.0	517	399	42.7	102.9	11.85	506.00
1994	119.6	110.5	119.5	124.6	95.3	136.1	127.5	137.9	532	411	43.4	107.9	12.13	526.44
1995	124.3	113.2	128.1	129.4	100.0	154.5	130.5	142.3	540	418	43.0	108.8	12.41	533.63
1996	125.8	110.0	134.0	133.2	100.0	154.0	129.1	145.6	541	421	43.3	110.1	12.82	555.11
1993:														
January	113.8	106.8	107.0	118.7	98.2	99.4	124.5	132.7	513	396	42.5	101.7	11.63	476.83
February	114.1	107.2	107.7	118.9	97.3	102.0	124.9	132.6	520	402	42.6	103.5	11.67	483.14
March	114.5	106.8	107.8	119.2	97.6	103.4	125.0	132.9	515	397	42.0	100.8	11.69	483.97
April	115.0	107.1	111.7	119.5	96.9	108.8	124.9	133.6	514	395	42.5	101.5	11.80	497.96
May	115.1	107.3	112.2	119.7	96.7	108.2	125.4	133.2	515	397	42.7	102.5	11.81	509.01
June	115.3	107.4	112.6	120.0	96.8	107.6	126.0	133.6	515	396	42.6	102.0	11.83	511.06
July	115.5	107.4	112.8	120.2	97.0	106.7	126.4	133.8	516	398	42.6	102.5	11.90	510.51
August	115.9	107.9	113.1	120.3	97.1	110.2	126.5	133.8	517	398	42.8	103.0	11.90	516.46
September	116.1	107.6	113.4	120.7	96.5	112.5	126.7	134.7	519	401	42.9	104.0	12.04	521.33
October	116.1	106.6	113.9	121.0	96.1	112.6	126.7	136.0	520	401	42.8	103.8	11.93	518.96
November	116.5	107.3	114.1	121.7	95.6	114.2	126.6	135.3	521	402	43.3	105.2	12.00	523.20
December	116.6	107.5	114.1	122.1	95.8	114.2	126.5	135.5	522	403	43.1	105.0	11.97	513.51
1994:														
January	116.9	107.5	114.6	122.5	95.8	113.0	126.6	136.7	524	404	43.2	105.5	11.97	502.74
February	117.4	108.2	115.2	122.7	94.9	117.9	126.4	136.9	525	406	42.3	103.8	11.98	492.38
March	118.2	108.6	116.1	123.4	94.5	128.8	126.4	137.2	526	406	43.5	106.8	11.94	512.23
April	118.5	108.7	118.5	123.7	94.6	130.7	126.4	138.0	531	410	43.4	107.6	12.04	522.54
May	119.1	110.0	119.2	124.0	94.9	131.3	127.9	137.5	531	411	43.7	108.6	12.11	534.05
June	119.8	110.9	120.3	124.2	95.2	139.5	127.9	137.8	531	411	43.5	108.1	12.15	537.03
July	120.1	111.3	120.4	124.7	95.2	139.8	127.9	138.1	533	412	43.5	108.3	12.17	533.05
August	120.4	111.8	121.5	125.1	95.8	140.7	127.9	138.3	534	413	43.4	108.4	12.19	536.36
September	120.7	111.4	121.7	125.3	95.6	146.2	128.2	138.3	534	413	43.4	108.4	12.27	542.33
October	121.1	112.0	122.3	125.8	95.7	149.0	128.2	138.5	536	413	43.5	108.6	12.22	540.12
November	121.4	113.7	122.2	126.5	95.8	146.3	128.2	138.5	537	416	43.5	108.6	12.22	540.12
December	121.6	112.2	122.1	127.0	95.8	149.4	128.3	138.6	539	416	43.5	109.4	12.22	529.13
1995:														
January	122.4	112.9	123.3	127.8	96.1	148.4	128.7	140.3	540	417	43.6	109.9	12.20	516.06
February	123.1	113.9	124.0	128.1	96.6	151.9	128.6	140.7	541	418	42.9	108.4	12.24	512.86
March	123.8	114.4	124.0	128.5	97.7	157.6	130.1	141.2	542	419	43.1	109.2	12.26	522.28
April	124.5	115.5	128.9	129.1	99.8	161.2	129.9	141.5	543	419	42.9	108.7	12.44	526.21
May	124.6	115.5	129.4	129.3	100.9	159.9	130.7	141.8	540	418	42.6	107.6	12.32	530.99
June	124.4	112.5	129.3	129.3	101.4	158.7	130.7	142.5	540	418	42.9	108.4	12.37	539.33
July	124.5	112.8	129.6	129.6	101.6	154.8	131.0	143.1	539	417	43.0	108.4	12.46	538.27
August	124.6	112.4	129.7	129.7	101.1	153.5	131.0	143.0	539	417	43.1	108.7	12.47	544.94
September	124.8	112.3	129.9	130.0	101.1	152.7	131.2	143.3	538	418	43.1	108.9	12.55	552.20
October	124.8	112.3	129.7	130.2	101.3	152.5	131.2	143.2	538	418	43.0	108.7	12.54	549.25
November	124.9	112.1	129.7	130.8	101.1	151.5	131.2	143.6	539	418	43.0	108.7	12.57	543.02
December	124.9	111.6	129.4	131.0	100.8	150.9	131.2	143.6	537	417	42.8	107.9	12.54	534.20
1996:														
January	125.1	112.0	129.3	131.5	100.8	149.8	130.2	144.5	536	415	42.1	105.6	12.60	515.34
February	125.3	111.9	130.1	132.0	100.4	149.5	130.2	144.4	540	419	43.4	109.9	12.56	532.54
March	125.3	110.8	130.1	132.4	100.3	146.4	129.2	144.9	540	420	43.3	109.9	12.60	538.02
April	125.4	110.0	133.3	132.8	99.9	145.3	129.7	145.5	539	419	43.3	109.9	12.77	551.66
May	125.5	109.4	134.8	133.0	100.2	148.0	129.6	145.6	541	420	43.3	109.9	12.74	555.46
June	125.5	109.3	135.0	133.2	99.3	152.3	129.6	145.5	540	420	43.4	110.2	12.82	565.36
July	125.8	109.5	135.0	133.6	99.7	152.5	129.6	145.9	540	420	43.2	109.7	12.94	562.89
August	125.9	109.4	135.3	133.5	99.8	157.4	129.6	145.6	540	421	43.2	109.9	12.92	568.48
September	126.3	109.2	136.3	133.8	100.1	159.3	129.3	146.1	541	421	43.2	109.9	12.99	575.46
October	126.2	109.2	136.4	133.8	100.1	162.2	127.4	146.1	542	423	43.3	110.7	12.91	568.04
November	126.6	109.6	136.4	134.5	100.4	165.0	127.4	146.3	541	422	43.2	110.2	12.96	563.76
December	126.5	109.9	135.9	134.7	99.7	160.8	127.4	146.3	543	423	43.4	111.0	12.93	557.28

1. December 1984=100.

PRIMARY METALS—INDUSTRIAL PRODUCTION
(1992=100, seasonally adjusted)

YEAR AND MONTH	Total	Iron and steel Total	Basic steel and mill products Total	Basic iron and steel Total	Pig iron	Raw steel	Steel mill products Total	Consumer durable steel	Equipment steel	Construction steel	Can and closure steel	Miscellaneous steel	Iron and steel foundries
1968	111.0	136.8	127.8	167.8	171.9	140.0	106.9	160.9	211.1	177.0	183.4	49.2	177.7
1969	119.7	149.7	140.7	181.0	185.4	152.8	119.3	166.3	220.3	180.3	185.9	63.7	191.3
1970	111.2	139.0	132.6	170.3	178.2	139.2	112.6	130.7	189.3	167.2	186.3	67.5	167.5
1971	104.9	126.3	118.0	152.5	156.9	127.1	99.8	141.5	182.9	137.8	166.2	54.9	164.0
1972	118.3	141.5	133.0	169.5	172.8	143.9	113.4	164.1	206.0	148.4	164.9	64.8	180.7
1973	134.1	161.0	152.2	191.3	196.0	164.3	131.0	196.0	229.2	174.8	182.8	74.7	201.6
1974	129.7	155.7	148.7	185.8	185.4	163.1	128.6	160.8	234.3	181.0	194.3	77.1	187.8
1975	103.4	125.1	119.4	153.0	154.8	128.6	101.4	134.6	205.1	135.2	160.1	55.8	151.9
1976	115.7	137.9	131.2	164.9	166.9	140.9	112.9	186.5	231.0	123.5	171.1	57.7	168.5
1977	119.0	138.0	126.3	158.8	157.1	139.3	108.7	178.6	233.9	117.0	159.1	54.9	180.3
1978	128.0	147.5	137.5	168.6	170.0	154.9	120.6	184.3	265.0	134.3	159.3	64.9	182.4
1979	130.0	148.4	138.4	170.7	168.3	154.4	120.8	159.5	268.9	140.5	156.9	70.3	182.4
1980	108.0	119.0	112.8	139.2	133.5	126.9	98.5	105.9	236.7	119.4	128.3	60.8	138.5
1981	113.9	126.6	121.4	145.7	142.0	138.5	108.6	120.4	252.6	125.8	124.3	70.0	142.0
1982	80.5	80.5	75.9	88.2	83.6	82.6	69.8	81.8	132.9	84.6	108.8	47.0	94.8
1983	88.2	90.0	85.5	95.1	94.3	94.1	81.5	109.7	118.4	91.4	113.9	61.9	104.7
1984	98.7	98.9	92.8	104.0	99.6	102.6	88.1	113.2	132.3	90.1	106.6	70.3	118.9
1985	98.4	98.8	95.0	99.7	96.8	97.7	93.3	124.5	121.1	99.9	104.9	77.1	110.7
1986	91.2	86.8	87.5	88.8	84.6	89.4	87.2	108.2	102.3	93.5	102.8	76.4	86.0
1987	97.8	95.4	93.5	97.7	93.7	99.3	92.3	102.3	107.1	91.8	106.8	86.1	102.6
1988	106.2	107.6	106.4	111.0	107.8	111.3	105.0	116.1	125.7	96.4	114.3	99.3	112.0
1989	104.9	106.2	104.9	109.5	107.8	107.1	103.5	107.3	116.9	102.2	112.8	99.5	110.9
1990	104.0	106.4	106.5	108.5	106.2	108.4	106.0	100.0	123.8	108.1	114.5	103.4	106.0
1991	96.7	96.0	95.7	95.7	93.7	96.3	95.7	88.7	97.6	93.7	110.2	96.6	96.9
1992	100.0	100.0	100.0	100.0	100.0	100.0	100.0	100.0	100.0	100.0	100.0	100.0	100.0
1993	105.5	107.1	107.4	102.8	102.9	104.5	108.8	115.6	108.5	113.0	108.7	106.7	106.2
1994	113.0	113.2	113.2	103.7	103.9	106.7	116.0	132.2	112.6	125.3	108.9	111.7	113.2
1995	115.7	116.3	117.3	109.1	108.7	113.5	119.7	125.0	119.4	128.8	100.1	118.5	112.9
1996	117.2	116.4	118.7	106.2	105.0	112.4	122.4	132.6	125.8	136.6	106.2	118.3	108.7
1993:													
January	103.7	105.4	106.1	102.0	102.7	101.8	107.4	112.5	103.3	102.4	122.6	106.9	103.1
February	104.6	105.4	105.8	102.9	103.5	103.3	106.6	112.2	104.6	109.2	113.9	104.9	104.1
March	104.0	104.7	104.8	100.9	100.9	101.5	105.9	112.0	103.1	106.2	106.5	105.1	104.6
April	104.0	104.3	104.2	101.8	102.0	102.4	104.9	110.3	105.6	109.6	105.1	102.9	104.6
May	103.8	104.7	104.9	103.7	103.9	104.8	105.2	108.5	104.0	110.1	100.5	104.5	104.0
June	106.3	108.7	109.4	103.4	102.9	105.8	111.2	117.1	112.5	117.6	110.1	108.9	106.5
July	104.4	106.8	106.5	104.4	104.0	106.9	107.1	110.5	108.7	112.1	118.4	104.6	108.2
August	106.1	108.5	109.9	104.1	104.3	105.7	111.6	117.1	112.2	117.1	111.8	109.5	103.9
September	106.5	108.1	108.5	103.8	104.6	104.7	110.9	115.6	112.5	117.5	109.4	107.1	106.9
October	105.8	107.9	108.3	105.0	106.1	106.2	109.3	117.5	111.8	114.7	102.0	106.7	106.7
November	107.3	109.5	109.4	99.4	98.1	103.8	112.4	124.4	112.2	119.3	115.7	108.2	110.0
December	109.7	111.3	111.2	102.7	102.3	107.0	113.7	129.7	115.5	120.0	88.7	111.1	111.8
1994:													
January	107.5	106.1	105.2	99.7	100.2	100.7	106.8	123.6	102.8	116.9	112.9	101.4	109.1
February	110.2	111.2	111.6	97.4	94.6	103.8	115.8	136.6	111.2	121.1	112.6	110.9	110.2
March	110.3	111.0	110.3	97.2	94.1	104.1	114.2	132.7	112.3	123.8	102.7	109.2	113.4
April	113.5	115.9	116.5	105.2	107.4	104.5	119.8	134.1	109.8	136.4	107.2	116.2	114.3
May	114.5	117.3	118.2	107.0	109.8	105.4	121.5	134.6	114.9	129.6	118.3	118.4	114.3
June	111.7	111.6	111.6	105.0	106.4	105.5	113.5	129.2	107.1	116.4	104.4	111.1	111.8
July	113.7	114.2	114.5	103.7	104.6	105.1	117.7	132.5	115.5	128.2	100.1	114.0	113.4
August	110.3	106.4	105.3	103.2	103.3	106.5	105.9	120.2	98.5	110.2	99.4	103.6	110.0
September	113.9	113.1	112.5	104.0	103.7	108.6	115.0	132.1	113.4	126.9	101.5	110.0	115.1
October	116.2	117.0	117.4	104.5	104.6	108.4	121.2	132.1	125.3	131.2	109.2	117.0	115.4
November	115.5	115.2	115.3	106.9	107.0	111.4	117.8	131.8	119.0	130.2	108.6	112.7	114.6
December	118.1	119.6	120.4	110.9	110.7	116.8	123.2	146.4	121.0	132.3	130.1	115.6	116.8
1995:													
January	118.5	120.7	122.8	109.1	108.9	113.2	126.8	134.6	119.1	143.2	92.2	126.2	113.7
February	117.0	118.4	119.7	110.5	110.2	115.0	122.5	134.2	121.1	131.9	99.1	119.9	113.8
March	117.1	118.3	119.2	110.5	110.3	114.8	121.8	135.4	118.3	127.9	105.0	119.3	115.0
April	115.3	115.3	115.6	109.3	108.8	113.7	117.4	123.5	111.2	127.4	97.4	116.9	114.5
May	115.3	116.2	116.3	108.2	107.9	112.3	118.7	124.7	117.7	126.0	101.5	117.5	115.8
June	114.5	114.5	115.5	107.1	106.3	111.9	118.0	120.5	134.4	122.8	97.3	115.3	110.8
July	113.7	111.1	111.0	107.1	106.4	111.7	112.2	116.8	115.4	125.2	95.4	109.4	111.1
August	113.7	114.8	115.6	109.0	108.8	113.3	117.6	123.1	117.8	124.8	102.4	116.1	112.1
September	116.7	118.9	120.8	112.6	113.0	117.0	123.2	125.0	124.9	130.6	108.6	122.5	112.5
October	114.8	114.0	114.5	107.8	107.8	110.8	116.5	120.4	114.9	124.8	101.5	115.7	112.3
November	117.1	118.9	121.1	109.6	109.3	114.0	124.6	123.9	119.4	129.6	97.2	127.2	111.3
December	114.8	114.7	115.4	107.9	106.8	113.7	117.6	117.6	118.9	131.5	104.0	116.2	112.2
1996:													
January	111.7	112.3	113.2	108.2	108.2	112.3	114.7	118.9	115.4	132.4	94.8	112.1	109.2
February	114.6	113.9	115.1	107.2	107.1	111.2	117.5	119.9	117.3	129.0	102.0	116.3	109.9
March	115.6	113.8	116.1	107.8	107.6	112.7	118.5	117.4	120.8	132.0	103.2	117.5	106.5
April	116.1	114.6	117.4	106.6	105.8	112.1	120.6	128.7	124.2	132.8	102.1	117.4	105.4
May	116.3	115.7	118.8	106.8	105.9	112.9	122.3	130.2	126.1	132.0	100.1	119.9	105.6
June	117.0	117.1	121.6	108.9	108.5	114.9	125.3	133.6	128.9	140.7	101.7	122.0	102.7
July	118.0	118.0	123.3	106.7	105.2	113.3	128.1	149.0	133.8	138.5	123.9	120.6	101.0
August	118.3	118.2	120.8	106.1	104.3	113.6	125.1	140.4	137.6	137.9	118.1	117.6	109.5
September	119.5	117.4	119.5	106.2	104.9	112.6	123.4	140.0	131.2	135.0	111.6	117.0	110.4
October	122.1	123.2	126.1	104.4	102.2	111.5	132.5	146.0	142.2	147.4	125.2	125.6	113.6
November	118.5	115.9	115.6	101.6	99.1	108.7	119.7	130.6	119.7	143.9	104.9	114.2	116.6
December	118.8	116.7	117.5	104.1	101.5	112.5	121.5	135.8	112.1	137.7	86.9	119.7	113.7

PRIMARY METALS—INDUSTRIAL PRODUCTION—(Continued) AND CAPACITY UTILIZATION
(Seasonally adjusted)

YEAR AND MONTH	Industrial production—Continued (1992=100)								Capacity utilization (Percent of capacity, seasonally adjusted)					
	Nonferrous metals													
	Total	Primary nonferrous metals			Nonferrous products			Non-ferrous found-ries	Total	Iron and steel		Nonferrous metals		
		Total	Copper	Alu-minum	Total	Nonferrous mill products				Total	Raw steel	Total	Primary copper	Primary alu-minum
						Total	Alu-minum							
1968	77.6	88.6	83.9	73.0	81.0	81.0	75.7	85.6	85.1	86.1	84.4	84.3	69.3	92.4
1969	81.8	105.8	107.6	85.4	84.0	84.7	71.8	86.8	89.3	92.8	91.8	84.1	87.7	99.6
1970	75.9	107.2	108.7	89.5	77.5	79.3	67.0	76.3	80.8	84.9	83.4	74.3	88.4	97.4
1971	76.6	101.4	93.2	88.3	78.9	82.4	74.5	72.5	74.8	76.6	76.0	71.7	74.9	88.1
1972	87.0	107.8	107.4	92.5	90.7	93.9	84.9	86.0	83.7	86.2	85.6	79.2	85.1	87.4
1973	98.1	113.6	107.4	101.9	105.2	108.8	106.4	100.1	94.5	98.0	97.1	88.1	85.0	94.0
1974	94.8	112.9	92.9	110.3	101.1	105.5	111.8	93.8	90.7	94.7	96.0	83.7	73.0	100.2
1975	74.3	93.9	82.2	87.3	76.2	79.4	78.9	70.8	71.7	75.9	75.2	64.1	61.9	78.4
1976	85.7	103.1	93.2	95.4	89.9	94.3	92.6	81.6	79.0	82.4	80.7	72.9	67.9	83.1
1977	93.0	101.9	85.5	102.2	98.7	104.8	102.1	86.0	80.1	80.7	78.6	79.4	63.2	87.4
1978	101.1	108.2	91.2	108.2	108.4	115.4	116.3	93.9	86.6	86.5	87.6	86.9	67.9	92.3
1979	104.6	116.1	98.0	113.1	110.0	116.2	118.5	97.3	88.4	88.6	88.3	88.0	67.9	92.3
1980	92.4	106.4	75.9	115.2	95.5	104.8	107.3	74.4	73.5	71.6	73.4	76.9	56.7	95.0
1981	96.1	107.5	91.1	111.4	100.0	110.0	110.3	77.5	77.6	76.4	80.5	79.1	72.0	90.3
1982	80.7	84.4	66.1	81.2	85.3	93.6	86.2	66.8	54.5	48.9	48.3	65.6	54.0	65.9
1983	85.9	86.9	68.6	83.2	92.9	100.7	98.8	75.6	61.7	56.9	57.4	69.6	56.8	67.4
1984	98.6	95.5	77.6	101.5	107.5	109.4	101.1	103.1	71.9	66.5	66.4	81.0	66.9	83.6
1985	98.2	92.2	79.7	86.9	107.4	106.6	97.0	110.0	73.2	68.9	65.8	80.3	71.9	74.9
1986	97.6	80.4	79.4	75.4	108.2	107.1	103.0	111.8	70.1	64.1	63.9	80.3	74.4	71.9
1987	101.2	83.8	80.1	83.0	111.3	112.1	110.6	108.9	79.2	76.2	77.7	84.1	77.2	84.1
1988	104.6	97.3	80.0	97.6	109.2	107.5	107.7	114.8	85.2	87.4	88.9	87.5	78.4	97.4
1989	103.2	98.7	79.0	100.0	106.0	104.1	106.2	112.3	85.2	84.7	84.1	85.9	76.3	98.6
1990	100.9	96.4	81.6	100.4	102.7	102.1	104.0	104.7	83.4	83.6	84.5	83.1	77.8	98.3
1991	97.7	103.2	88.3	102.2	97.4	97.2	102.0	98.1	77.6	75.7	75.8	80.1	81.3	99.6
1992	100.0	100.0	100.0	100.0	100.0	100.0	100.0	100.0	80.9	80.5	80.8	81.7	85.0	97.0
1993	103.5	100.1	109.5	91.7	104.7	104.4	98.6	106.0	85.9	87.6	87.7	83.8	86.8	88.6
1994	112.6	97.8	111.3	81.8	115.2	113.7	107.6	120.2	91.2	91.4	90.8	91.1	86.6	78.9
1995	115.0	98.3	106.7	83.7	117.2	114.8	105.7	125.1	91.9	91.6	94.1	92.3	82.6	80.7
1996	118.1	100.9	111.1	88.5	119.7	116.1	101.2	131.8	90.7	88.8	91.3	93.1	86.2	85.3
1993:														
January	101.6	101.2	105.9	97.4	102.1	101.6	98.5	103.8	84.4	85.9	83.6	82.7	85.9	94.3
February	103.6	100.9	111.0	94.2	104.1	104.3	101.0	103.8	85.1	85.9	85.2	84.2	89.6	91.2
March	103.0	101.7	112.4	94.0	104.0	103.8	98.3	104.8	84.6	85.4	84.1	83.7	90.4	91.0
April	103.5	102.4	113.2	94.9	104.2	104.0	99.9	105.3	84.6	85.1	85.1	84.0	90.7	91.8
May	102.6	100.8	106.5	94.7	103.3	103.0	99.6	104.3	84.4	85.5	87.4	83.2	84.9	91.6
June	103.1	105.7	116.6	94.9	104.1	104.0	93.5	104.5	86.5	88.9	88.6	83.5	92.6	91.8
July	101.4	94.2	107.8	92.4	103.5	103.2	95.8	104.7	85.0	87.4	89.8	82.1	85.3	89.2
August	103.1	95.8	104.1	88.7	104.8	104.8	97.0	104.9	86.3	88.8	89.1	83.4	82.0	85.7
September	104.4	102.3	110.0	88.3	105.9	105.9	102.9	105.9	86.7	88.6	88.6	84.4	86.3	85.2
October	103.2	98.5	105.0	88.6	104.2	102.8	97.1	108.7	86.1	88.4	90.3	83.4	82.1	85.5
November	104.4	98.0	107.8	86.3	105.9	104.4	93.6	110.6	87.3	89.8	88.6	84.3	83.9	83.2
December	107.7	100.1	113.3	85.6	110.4	110.4	105.8	110.3	89.3	91.4	91.6	86.9	87.8	82.6
1994:														
January	109.4	97.7	112.2	85.1	112.6	112.8	106.5	111.7	87.5	87.0	86.3	88.2	86.8	82.0
February	108.9	99.6	113.0	84.1	110.8	110.1	106.3	113.2	89.5	91.0	88.9	87.9	87.5	81.1
March	109.3	96.4	108.6	83.5	111.5	109.9	102.2	116.3	89.5	90.5	88.9	88.3	84.2	80.4
April	110.5	94.7	107.3	81.7	112.9	111.2	101.7	118.2	92.0	94.3	89.2	89.3	83.3	78.7
May	111.0	97.7	112.7	80.9	113.4	111.8	103.4	118.4	92.7	95.1	89.9	89.8	87.6	78.0
June	111.8	101.6	116.7	80.8	113.4	111.2	103.0	120.4	90.3	90.3	89.8	90.4	90.8	77.9
July	113.0	99.0	115.1	80.5	114.3	111.8	104.4	122.4	91.8	92.1	89.3	91.4	89.7	77.6
August	114.9	99.0	114.8	80.8	117.9	116.5	113.2	122.3	88.9	85.6	90.4	93.0	89.5	77.9
September	115.0	97.9	111.2	81.1	117.9	115.9	111.6	124.0	91.7	90.7	92.0	93.1	86.9	78.1
October	115.4	97.3	109.6	81.2	118.9	117.1	110.4	124.7	93.5	93.6	91.7	93.4	85.7	78.3
November	115.9	96.9	107.5	81.2	119.3	117.5	117.2	125.2	92.8	91.9	94.1	93.9	84.1	78.2
December	116.5	96.3	106.6	81.5	120.0	118.2	110.8	125.8	94.7	95.2	98.5	94.4	83.6	78.6
1995:														
January	115.9	96.7	107.5	81.7	118.6	116.0	110.9	127.3	94.9	95.9	95.4	93.8	84.2	78.7
February	115.4	96.1	105.7	81.6	118.5	116.1	111.1	126.4	93.5	93.9	96.6	93.2	82.6	78.6
March	115.6	98.3	110.2	81.7	118.4	116.1	109.9	126.0	93.4	93.7	96.1	93.3	86.0	78.7
April	115.3	97.6	104.6	82.4	118.0	116.3	112.8	123.5	91.9	91.2	95.0	92.8	81.4	79.5
May	114.3	99.7	110.9	83.2	116.9	114.7	105.4	124.1	91.8	91.8	93.6	91.9	86.1	80.2
June	114.6	98.4	105.7	83.7	116.8	114.8	106.4	123.2	91.0	90.3	93.0	91.9	81.9	80.7
July	116.7	98.7	105.4	84.0	118.3	117.8	108.4	119.8	90.2	87.4	92.6	93.5	81.5	81.0
August	112.4	99.1	106.8	84.2	114.1	111.3	97.8	123.7	90.1	90.3	93.6	89.9	82.4	81.2
September	114.2	96.8	100.4	85.1	115.9	113.2	101.0	125.2	92.3	93.3	96.4	91.3	77.2	82.0
October	115.6	99.6	109.2	84.8	117.9	115.7	106.7	125.5	90.7	89.4	91.0	92.3	83.8	81.7
November	115.0	99.7	109.3	85.7	116.7	113.4	97.9	127.9	92.3	93.0	93.5	91.7	83.8	82.6
December	114.8	99.3	105.2	86.8	116.3	112.7	99.8	128.2	90.4	89.6	92.9	91.4	80.4	83.7
1996:														
January	111.0	103.7	114.7	87.4	110.3	105.2	84.4	127.9	87.8	87.6	91.6	88.3	87.7	84.3
February	115.3	100.1	107.1	88.1	117.9	114.3	97.2	130.0	89.8	88.4	90.6	91.5	82.1	84.9
March	117.6	99.5	107.0	88.3	120.1	117.7	108.6	127.9	90.4	88.0	91.8	93.3	82.2	85.2
April	117.9	100.9	109.9	88.9	119.9	117.1	101.3	129.3	90.5	88.3	91.3	93.4	84.7	85.7
May	117.0	99.8	109.3	88.5	119.3	115.9	102.1	130.5	90.4	88.7	91.9	92.5	84.4	85.3
June	116.8	98.0	104.3	88.5	118.5	114.5	98.4	131.9	90.7	89.5	93.5	92.2	80.8	85.3
July	117.9	101.9	112.3	88.1	119.5	116.8	101.2	128.7	91.2	89.8	92.1	92.9	87.3	84.9
August	118.5	96.4	99.6	89.0	121.1	117.1	104.5	134.4	91.2	89.6	92.3	93.2	77.6	85.8
September	121.8	100.6	110.5	88.8	123.6	120.4	111.1	134.2	91.8	88.7	91.4	95.7	86.3	85.6
October	120.7	103.1	121.6	89.1	121.7	117.6	97.9	135.1	93.5	92.6	90.5	94.7	95.3	85.8
November	121.4	103.5	114.3	88.8	122.5	118.8	102.7	134.7	90.5	86.8	88.1	95.1	89.8	85.6
December	121.2	103.8	122.9	88.7	122.5	118.2	104.7	136.9	90.4	87.1	91.1	94.7	96.8	85.5

	Shipments		Inventories (Book value, end of period)		New orders, net			Unfilled orders (End of period)		
YEAR AND MONTH	Total	Blast furnaces, steel mills	Total	Blast furnaces, steel mills	Total[1]	Blast furnaces, steel mills	Non-ferrous and other primary metals	Total	Blast furnaces, steel mills	Non-ferrous and other primary metals
1968	48 717	24 908	7 547	4 207	48 089	24 416	19 182	6 591	3 416	2 472
1969	53 534	26 412	8 066	4 451	54 880	27 247	22 496	7 991	4 283	2 876
1970	51 995	25 189	8 995	4 990	51 793	25 521	21 883	7 796	4 617	2 663
1971	51 585	25 791	9 084	4 926	51 284	25 571	20 704	7 478	4 380	2 552
1972	58 490	28 712	9 617	5 387	61 447	30 996	24 607	10 470	6 681	3 116
1973	72 791	36 301	10 034	5 302	78 395	39 413	31 417	16 129	9 794	4 962
1974	95 686	49 718	13 447	6 820	98 831	51 047	38 394	19 225	11 054	5 952
1975	80 890	42 281	15 742	8 597	75 034	38 611	27 864	13 266	7 345	4 015
1976	93 082	46 764	17 699	10 035	94 491	47 212	37 378	14 684	7 776	4 891
1977	103 267	50 670	18 261	10 004	105 689	52 103	42 400	17 298	9 435	5 483
1978	118 175	59 228	19 420	10 719	124 741	62 648	48 319	23 969	12 932	7 393
1979	137 488	67 414	22 446	12 012	139 783	66 968	58 420	26 320	12 485	9 457
1980	134 057	61 612	23 055	12 153	134 416	62 473	60 399	26 815	13 418	10 096
1981	142 072	70 254	25 794	13 359	137 286	67 457	57 545	22 024	10 589	8 784
1982	104 874	46 928	24 174	12 556	98 445	43 013	46 942	15 500	6 574	7 418
1983	109 240	46 398	22 308	11 065	113 884	49 123	55 566	20 400	9 431	9 594
1984	120 315	51 978	22 444	11 087	118 354	50 719	56 030	18 362	8 103	8 694
1985	112 265	48 904	19 974	9 709	112 276	49 079	52 275	18 331	8 248	8 361
1986	107 865	45 718	18 436	8 567	108 218	46 408	51 294	18 590	8 897	7 783
1987	120 248	51 815	19 076	8 620	125 989	54 763	60 302	24 340	11 828	10 300
1988	149 837	64 294	22 422	10 495	152 578	64 002	75 997	27 079	11 508	12 974
1989	155 718	64 783	22 838	10 942	152 814	62 752	77 249	24 120	9 479	11 824
1990	148 787	62 826	22 560	11 045	149 338	63 369	72 944	24 768	10 120	11 258
1991	136 378	57 267	20 703	10 236	134 657	56 366	66 778	23 075	9 290	10 609
1992	138 287	58 449	19 975	9 802	136 849	58 002	67 337	21 644	8 902	9 928
1993	142 685	62 466	20 134	9 833	144 018	60 442	67 112	23 086	10 176	9 628
1994	161 188	69 887	22 613	10 704	167 685	70 960	81 963	29 698	11 337	14 533
1995	180 303	74 547	24 089	11 519	178 681	75 372	88 273	28 049	12 199	12 226
1996	173 619	72 268	24 767	12 279	174 865	72 295	85 221	29 250	12 188	12 661
1993:										
January	11 674	4 986	19 920	9 790	12 753	5 808	5 810	22 723	9 724	10 092
February	11 797	5 049	19 924	9 791	12 574	5 794	5 737	23 500	10 469	10 133
March	11 843	5 168	19 875	9 651	12 078	5 404	5 676	23 735	10 705	10 213
April	11 749	5 141	19 700	9 532	11 722	4 999	5 600	23 708	10 563	10 280
May	11 502	5 078	19 847	9 616	11 420	5 033	5 285	23 626	10 518	10 178
June	12 087	5 228	19 792	9 592	11 758	5 196	5 567	23 297	10 486	9 971
July	11 602	5 199	19 819	9 699	11 463	5 021	5 390	23 158	10 308	9 876
August	11 770	5 238	20 076	9 707	11 588	5 076	5 468	22 976	10 146	9 870
September	12 090	5 283	20 030	9 663	11 957	5 278	5 447	22 843	10 141	9 601
October	11 911	5 277	20 120	9 758	12 136	5 414	5 463	23 068	10 278	9 556
November	12 258	5 383	19 988	9 782	12 233	5 325	5 676	23 043	10 220	9 497
December	12 444	5 488	20 134	9 833	12 487	5 444	5 956	23 086	10 176	9 628
1994:										
January	12 211	5 328	20 197	9 905	12 459	5 308	5 936	23 334	10 156	9 827
February	12 476	5 555	20 324	9 930	12 653	5 685	5 853	23 511	10 286	9 909
March	12 633	5 550	20 399	9 909	14 058	5 831	6 876	24 936	10 567	10 867
April	12 717	5 571	20 468	9 911	13 053	5 840	6 115	25 272	10 836	10 985
May	13 054	5 700	20 692	10 079	13 974	5 761	6 953	26 192	10 897	11 730
June	13 292	5 726	20 844	10 147	13 816	5 868	6 684	26 716	11 039	12 021
July	13 262	5 716	21 136	10 254	13 503	5 643	6 707	26 957	10 966	12 322
August	13 827	6 010	21 295	10 259	13 788	5 912	6 788	26 918	10 868	12 482
September	13 856	5 943	21 446	10 309	14 789	6 360	7 212	27 851	11 285	12 974
October	14 062	5 981	21 907	10 544	14 998	6 105	7 646	28 787	11 409	13 752
November	14 505	6 151	22 295	10 647	14 935	6 171	7 519	29 217	11 429	14 162
December	15 470	6 751	22 613	10 704	15 951	6 659	7 728	29 698	11 337	14 533
1995:										
January	15 499	6 275	23 038	10 834	15 847	6 462	8 106	30 046	11 524	14 703
February	15 264	6 302	23 319	11 060	15 107	6 298	7 430	29 889	11 520	14 460
March	15 536	6 537	23 498	11 123	15 301	6 800	7 258	29 654	11 783	14 014
April	15 088	6 214	23 783	11 352	14 748	6 170	7 264	29 314	11 739	13 642
May	15 165	6 293	23 812	11 391	14 368	6 186	7 041	28 517	11 632	13 066
June	15 123	6 185	23 994	11 503	14 361	6 003	7 228	27 755	11 450	12 586
July	14 690	5 914	24 238	11 553	14 115	5 772	7 147	27 180	11 308	12 215
August	14 955	6 169	24 171	11 576	15 227	6 366	7 575	27 452	11 505	12 285
September	14 850	6 188	24 097	11 533	14 909	6 071	7 534	27 511	11 388	12 429
October	14 818	6 229	24 086	11 480	14 988	6 450	7 203	27 681	11 609	12 310
November	14 659	6 164	24 131	11 390	14 900	6 479	7 136	27 922	11 924	12 218
December	14 602	6 000	24 089	11 519	14 729	6 275	7 304	28 049	12 199	12 226
1996:										
January	14 375	5 990	24 175	11 650	14 362	6 033	6 905	28 036	12 242	12 039
February	14 255	5 969	24 109	11 621	14 510	5 921	7 099	28 291	12 194	12 152
March	14 283	5 838	24 326	11 899	13 782	5 596	6 860	27 790	11 952	11 870
April	14 549	6 037	24 133	11 703	14 649	5 934	7 295	27 890	11 849	12 036
May	14 633	6 012	24 133	11 627	14 977	6 382	7 212	28 234	12 219	12 032
June	14 153	6 023	24 253	11 668	14 889	6 120	7 188	28 970	12 316	12 475
July	14 630	6 105	24 085	11 662	15 135	6 357	7 223	29 475	12 568	12 697
August	14 415	6 018	24 077	11 775	14 934	6 058	7 378	29 994	12 608	13 093
September	14 377	6 069	24 374	11 990	14 468	6 125	6 886	30 085	12 664	13 099
October	14 565	6 066	24 310	12 019	14 264	5 959	7 051	29 784	12 557	13 051
November	14 719	6 025	24 479	12 153	14 338	5 758	7 102	29 403	12 290	12 859
December	14 743	6 134	24 767	12 279	14 590	6 032	7 033	29 250	12 188	12 661

1. Also includes iron and steel foundries not shown separately.

PRIMARY METALS—PRODUCER PRICES
(1982=100, except as noted, not seasonally adjusted)

YEAR AND MONTH	Primary metal industries (December 1984=100)	Intermediate materials						Crude materials				
		Foundry and forge shop products	Steel mill products	Primary nonferrous metals	Aluminum mill shapes	Copper and brass mill shapes	Nonferrous wire and cable	Iron ore	Iron and steel scrap	Nonferrous metal ores (December 1983=100)	Copper base scrap	Aluminum base scrap
1968	....	29.7	29.3	37.5	33.9	52.1	49.3	35.2	39.9	....	78.1	30.9
1969	....	30.7	30.7	40.2	35.6	57.9	52.9	35.2	47.6	....	99.8	33.2
1970	....	32.4	32.7	44.9	36.7	63.4	62.6	35.9	59.6	....	100.9	34.4
1971	....	34.6	35.2	40.2	36.4	57.5	57.2	37.0	49.1	....	80.7	32.7
1972	....	36.0	37.3	40.7	36.9	60.3	57.4	37.0	52.3	....	79.3	31.1
1973	....	38.1	38.4	48.9	37.9	68.8	61.5	38.3	80.7	....	120.1	46.8
1974	....	46.7	48.6	69.5	50.1	88.7	84.0	44.2	151.6	....	138.0	70.9
1975	....	56.2	56.4	65.0	54.9	72.8	75.2	55.4	105.4	....	87.3	44.4
1976	....	63.3	60.0	67.4	59.4	79.6	74.7	61.3	111.2	....	96.1	74.0
1977	....	66.7	65.8	72.4	67.7	80.8	77.1	66.8	99.2	....	90.1	90.2
1978	....	72.2	72.8	76.8	75.9	83.3	76.6	69.9	113.6	....	100.3	117.1
1979	....	80.2	80.2	103.9	82.8	105.0	92.1	77.8	146.8	....	129.3	169.6
1980	....	89.7	86.6	132.7	89.3	112.6	107.5	87.8	140.9	....	138.9	183.9
1981	....	95.4	96.6	114.7	98.3	107.8	102.5	96.3	140.6	....	126.3	141.7
1982	....	100.0	100.0	100.0	100.0	100.0	100.0	100.0	100.0	....	100.0	100.0
1983	....	101.6	100.9	106.8	102.2	105.7	100.7	101.2	107.4	....	110.2	142.3
1984	....	104.4	104.7	101.3	112.0	106.9	99.9	101.2	123.7	103.5	101.5	167.6
1985	99.4	105.2	104.7	93.6	107.8	106.9	100.9	97.5	112.6	73.2	95.4	123.4
1986	97.0	105.2	99.8	93.8	102.6	106.9	101.8	91.5	109.6	75.7	93.6	124.5
1987	101.0	105.7	102.3	109.3	105.6	121.8	107.0	84.2	128.4	106.0	113.0	156.4
1988	113.0	109.6	110.7	144.3	130.9	162.7	129.6	82.8	177.1	108.1	157.9	219.5
1989	118.8	114.6	114.5	149.2	135.4	182.0	146.1	82.8	173.7	109.6	179.8	204.4
1990	116.5	117.2	112.1	133.4	127.9	174.6	142.6	83.3	166.0	98.3	181.3	172.6
1991	113.1	119.0	109.5	114.0	123.2	160.5	139.2	83.6	147.6	82.6	170.0	143.1
1992	111.7	120.1	106.4	108.1	121.9	166.0	136.7	83.7	139.2	75.4	162.9	137.6
1993	111.4	121.3	108.2	98.1	120.4	150.7	133.1	82.7	172.5	67.2	136.1	129.2
1994	117.0	123.9	113.4	115.7	127.7	167.3	139.8	82.7	192.9	81.4	155.5	172.9
1995	128.2	129.3	120.1	146.8	160.4	195.2	151.5	91.8	202.7	101.6	193.5	209.4
1996	123.7	132.6	115.6	126.2	144.8	179.0	147.5	96.7	191.1	90.2	166.3	173.4
1993:												
January	110.8	120.8	105.1	104.6	120.5	161.3	137.2	83.6	151.9	71.5	162.1	137.9
February	111.0	121.0	105.6	104.2	121.1	162.6	136.6	82.8	160.8	70.2	160.2	136.8
March	110.9	121.2	106.1	103.0	121.1	158.7	135.8	82.8	159.9	67.3	153.1	133.6
April	110.9	121.1	106.7	100.5	120.7	155.5	133.9	82.5	157.4	65.9	143.9	129.4
May	110.8	121.1	107.3	96.5	120.1	144.9	131.8	82.5	160.2	64.9	132.4	127.1
June	111.2	121.1	108.0	95.4	119.8	150.8	132.2	82.5	170.1	66.4	132.7	127.5
July	111.7	121.3	108.4	97.0	120.3	152.5	132.5	82.5	176.4	67.7	134.2	132.3
August	112.0	121.4	109.2	98.6	120.6	150.7	132.1	82.5	172.9	69.6	132.8	132.1
September	111.9	121.5	109.8	97.5	121.2	146.7	131.7	82.7	174.5	68.2	127.0	128.0
October	111.8	121.5	110.2	94.7	120.1	141.6	131.1	82.8	189.4	63.7	117.9	123.7
November	111.8	121.8	110.6	92.4	119.6	140.1	131.2	82.6	196.0	63.6	115.2	119.8
December	112.4	121.9	111.1	93.1	119.4	142.8	131.5	82.6	200.8	67.3	122.1	122.6
1994:												
January	112.7	122.4	111.4	94.2	119.4	146.0	132.5	82.6	203.8	68.6	127.0	128.7
February	113.6	122.8	111.9	98.3	121.0	151.0	134.7	82.6	206.2	71.3	134.6	143.1
March	114.2	123.1	111.9	102.8	122.9	153.5	135.4	82.6	204.0	71.9	138.8	150.9
April	114.4	123.4	111.9	103.8	124.1	150.7	134.8	82.6	198.5	72.3	138.7	156.9
May	115.1	123.6	112.5	106.0	124.4	157.7	136.9	82.6	185.7	73.3	145.4	153.9
June	116.0	123.7	112.3	113.3	125.3	172.1	139.1	82.6	168.1	81.3	157.8	163.1
July	117.0	123.9	113.4	117.3	127.7	171.5	139.6	82.6	176.5	85.6	163.2	177.0
August	117.5	124.1	114.1	120.7	128.7	169.4	139.8	82.6	190.6	85.2	162.1	178.5
September	118.7	124.4	114.8	122.9	129.1	177.1	143.2	82.6	193.3	88.9	165.4	182.2
October	119.7	124.7	115.3	129.0	131.6	176.4	144.2	82.6	190.0	89.8	166.1	193.5
November	121.7	125.0	115.8	136.2	136.7	188.5	147.6	82.9	196.1	92.3	180.8	218.4
December	122.9	125.2	115.8	143.6	141.3	194.2	149.7	82.9	202.0	95.8	185.9	228.5
1995:												
January	126.6	126.6	117.9	150.8	158.4	196.3	151.6	82.9	210.6	99.8	188.7	237.9
February	128.2	127.6	119.7	152.5	164.9	194.0	151.3	82.9	208.1	100.2	185.0	237.7
March	129.1	128.4	121.0	151.9	165.1	198.2	150.8	93.5	201.3	100.1	182.0	220.1
April	129.7	128.9	121.7	149.7	165.1	197.7	152.0	93.5	202.9	106.2	191.4	216.7
May	128.9	128.9	121.9	146.0	163.7	188.7	150.0	93.5	202.8	102.8	185.1	208.8
June	128.9	128.9	121.9	145.0	160.9	195.2	151.2	93.5	200.7	103.1	195.1	207.3
July	128.8	129.4	121.9	147.0	159.5	197.6	152.7	93.5	201.0	104.9	200.8	208.5
August	128.8	129.9	121.2	147.9	159.4	197.1	153.2	93.5	210.2	102.1	202.7	212.3
September	128.2	130.1	120.2	146.9	160.3	194.9	150.4	93.5	206.3	100.2	200.4	205.0
October	127.4	130.6	119.1	142.4	158.5	189.1	149.7	93.5	201.4	100.2	199.9	194.1
November	127.1	130.8	117.9	140.6	156.0	194.8	152.6	93.5	193.1	97.5	199.0	183.9
December	126.8	131.0	117.3	141.1	152.4	198.2	152.1	94.0	193.7	100.9	192.5	181.0
1996:												
January	125.7	131.6	116.6	137.5	150.8	188.8	150.0	97.6	199.7	97.9	181.1	179.3
February	124.4	132.1	115.2	131.8	148.0	183.8	148.6	97.6	201.4	96.7	176.7	178.6
March	124.2	132.5	114.7	132.4	148.3	186.3	148.3	97.6	197.8	95.9	179.9	179.3
April	124.1	132.4	114.9	132.4	147.3	182.4	148.6	97.7	197.8	95.5	180.0	183.8
May	124.6	132.6	115.2	135.2	145.3	191.4	150.8	94.8	199.5	97.2	182.9	179.9
June	124.6	132.7	115.6	136.9	147.1	180.9	149.3	94.6	194.8	92.4	167.8	174.6
July	123.2	132.7	115.5	122.4	145.7	172.3	145.9	96.7	190.5	86.6	157.9	167.2
August	122.8	132.8	115.9	117.2	143.2	170.0	145.0	96.7	191.6	84.3	153.2	168.1
September	122.7	132.7	116.3	116.5	142.0	169.6	145.0	96.7	191.7	83.5	151.9	168.4
October	122.7	133.0	116.0	114.4	140.3	169.6	145.6	96.7	183.4	83.2	151.8	160.0
November	122.6	133.0	115.7	115.9	139.0	175.2	145.6	96.7	172.4	85.3	154.5	166.7
December	123.0	133.0	115.6	121.5	140.3	177.1	147.4	96.7	172.2	83.9	157.9	174.8

PRIMARY METALS—EMPLOYMENT, HOURS, AND EARNINGS

YEAR AND MONTH	Primary metals						Blast furnaces and basic steel					
	Employment (Thousands, seasonally adjusted)		Production workers				Seasonally adjusted			Not seasonally adjusted		
			Weekly hours worked (Seasonally adjusted)		Average earnings (Dollars, not seasonally adjusted)							
	Total payroll employees	Production workers	Average hours	Aggregate hours index (1982=100)	Hourly	Weekly	Total payroll employees (Thousands)	Average weekly hours	Aggregate hours index (1982=100)	Production workers (Thousands)	Average earnings (Dollars)	
											Hourly	Weekly
1968	1 261	1 003	41.6	158.1	3.55	147.68	636	41.0	186.1	506	3.76	154.16
1969	1 305	1 042	41.8	165.1	3.79	158.42	644	41.3	190.5	514	4.02	166.03
1970	1 260	1 000	40.4	152.9	3.93	158.77	627	40.0	179.5	500	4.16	166.40
1971	1 171	923	40.1	140.5	4.23	169.62	574	39.6	161.5	455	4.49	177.80
1972	1 173	933	41.4	146.3	4.66	192.92	568	40.6	165.1	453	5.08	206.25
1973	1 259	1 011	42.3	161.8	5.04	213.19	605	41.7	181.5	485	5.51	229.77
1974	1 289	1 030	41.6	162.4	5.60	232.96	610	41.3	180.7	487	6.27	258.95
1975	1 139	887	40.0	134.3	6.18	247.20	548	39.5	151.8	428	6.94	274.13
1976	1 155	904	40.8	140.0	6.77	276.22	549	40.3	155.6	431	7.59	305.88
1977	1 182	922	41.3	144.2	7.40	305.62	554	40.5	157.2	433	8.36	338.58
1978	1 215	954	41.8	151.3	8.20	342.76	561	41.5	164.6	442	9.39	389.69
1979	1 254	986	41.4	154.8	8.98	371.77	571	41.2	167.0	451	10.41	428.89
1980	1 142	878	40.1	133.4	9.77	391.78	512	39.4	139.8	396	11.39	448.77
1981	1 122	862	40.5	132.5	10.81	437.81	506	40.4	141.9	392	12.60	509.04
1982	922	683	38.6	100.0	11.33	437.34	396	37.9	100.0	294	13.35	505.97
1983	832	620	40.5	95.2	11.35	459.68	341	39.5	90.8	256	12.89	509.16
1984	857	651	41.7	102.9	11.47	478.30	334	40.7	93.7	257	12.98	528.29
1985	808	611	41.5	96.1	11.67	484.31	303	41.1	85.3	232	13.33	547.86
1986	751	565	41.9	89.8	11.86	496.93	273	41.7	78.2	209	13.73	572.54
1987	746	562	43.1	91.8	11.94	514.61	268	43.4	79.0	203	13.77	597.62
1988	770	589	43.5	97.2	12.16	528.96	278	44.0	85.1	215	13.98	615.12
1989	772	589	43.0	96.0	12.43	534.49	279	43.4	83.9	215	14.25	618.45
1990	756	574	42.7	93.0	12.92	551.68	276	43.4	82.6	212	14.82	643.19
1991	723	545	42.2	87.2	13.33	562.53	263	42.7	76.4	200	15.36	655.87
1992	695	525	43.0	85.6	13.66	587.38	250	43.5	73.7	189	15.87	690.35
1993	683	520	43.7	86.2	13.99	611.36	240	44.1	72.6	183	16.36	721.48
1994	698	537	44.7	90.9	14.34	641.00	239	44.9	73.4	182	16.85	756.57
1995	712	553	44.0	92.1	14.62	643.28	242	44.4	73.6	185	17.33	769.45
1996	711	554	44.2	92.6	14.97	661.67	240	44.5	73.7	185	17.79	791.66
1993:												
January	686	522	43.5	86.1	13.74	599.06	242	44.0	72.7	184	15.95	698.61
February	685	520	43.7	86.1	13.81	600.74	242	44.2	73.0	183	16.20	711.18
March	684	520	43.6	85.9	13.81	600.74	241	44.2	73.0	183	16.18	708.68
April	682	519	44.0	86.6	13.94	607.78	241	44.3	73.2	183	16.31	720.90
May	683	520	43.6	85.9	13.93	607.35	241	44.1	72.8	183	16.25	715.00
June	681	519	43.6	85.8	14.02	614.08	239	44.2	72.6	183	16.49	733.81
July	682	519	43.6	85.8	14.06	611.61	239	44.3	72.8	183	16.48	736.66
August	682	519	43.6	85.8	14.00	607.60	239	44.1	72.4	183	16.40	721.60
September	683	520	43.7	86.1	14.21	620.98	240	43.9	72.1	183	16.57	734.05
October	683	521	43.7	86.3	14.01	612.24	240	43.8	71.9	183	16.41	715.48
November	685	523	44.0	87.2	14.09	622.78	241	44.1	72.4	184	16.51	726.44
December	686	524	44.0	87.4	14.27	637.87	241	44.1	72.4	184	16.56	738.58
1994:												
January	687	526	44.1	87.9	14.17	626.31	241	43.6	72.0	184	16.55	723.24
February	690	529	44.0	88.2	14.25	625.58	240	44.1	72.4	183	16.57	725.77
March	691	530	44.6	89.6	14.21	632.35	240	44.5	72.7	182	16.62	736.27
April	689	529	44.4	89.0	14.22	635.63	236	44.7	71.8	178	16.64	743.81
May	690	530	44.7	89.8	14.25	638.40	235	44.9	71.7	178	16.74	749.95
June	696	535	44.5	90.2	14.32	640.10	239	44.8	72.8	182	16.79	752.19
July	698	537	44.8	91.2	14.42	640.25	240	45.1	73.7	183	16.93	766.93
August	700	539	44.7	91.3	14.36	639.02	238	45.2	73.8	182	16.95	764.45
September	704	543	44.8	92.2	14.42	648.90	239	45.4	74.2	183	17.04	780.43
October	707	546	44.8	92.7	14.39	643.23	240	45.4	74.6	183	17.07	771.56
November	708	548	45.0	93.5	14.54	654.04	240	45.6	74.9	184	17.12	778.96
December	710	550	44.9	93.6	14.56	665.39	241	45.4	75.0	185	17.15	787.19
1995:												
January	710	550	44.9	93.6	14.57	655.65	240	45.3	74.4	183	17.29	784.97
February	712	552	44.7	93.5	14.46	646.36	241	45.4	75.0	184	17.08	768.60
March	712	553	44.5	93.3	14.45	643.03	241	44.8	74.0	184	17.02	760.79
April	714	555	44.2	93.0	14.76	639.11	242	45.6	75.7	184	17.48	793.59
May	715	554	43.8	92.0	14.53	637.87	242	44.1	73.6	185	17.22	757.68
June	712	554	43.8	92.0	14.61	642.84	242	44.0	73.5	187	17.33	762.52
July	709	550	43.2	90.1	14.69	628.73	241	43.5	71.8	185	17.39	758.20
August	711	552	43.6	91.2	14.63	634.94	242	44.0	73.1	185	17.41	762.56
September	710	551	43.6	91.1	14.70	643.86	240	43.9	72.5	184	17.54	775.27
October	711	551	43.8	91.5	14.64	639.77	241	44.2	73.0	184	17.41	766.04
November	713	554	44.0	92.4	14.73	652.54	242	44.2	73.4	185	17.52	781.39
December	713	554	43.7	91.8	14.69	652.24	242	44.2	73.4	186	17.31	772.03
1996:												
January	713	554	43.3	90.9	14.84	644.06	242	44.2	73.4	185	17.62	780.57
February	713	554	44.1	92.6	14.70	648.27	242	44.9	74.6	185	17.46	778.72
March	712	554	43.8	92.0	14.73	645.17	242	44.4	73.7	185	17.57	778.35
April	710	552	43.9	91.9	14.98	653.13	242	44.3	73.6	184	17.87	786.28
May	711	553	44.1	92.4	14.82	653.56	242	44.3	74.0	185	17.52	776.14
June	713	556	44.2	93.2	14.91	660.51	241	44.4	74.1	187	17.64	784.98
July	706	549	44.0	91.6	15.08	657.49	241	44.3	74.0	186	17.96	797.42
August	712	555	44.3	93.2	15.02	662.38	241	44.3	74.0	186	17.83	784.52
September	711	554	44.4	93.2	15.18	680.06	241	44.3	74.0	186	18.10	807.26
October	707	552	44.4	92.9	15.09	670.00	236	44.6	72.9	182	17.94	796.54
November	708	552	44.3	92.7	15.18	675.51	236	44.6	72.9	183	18.05	814.06
December	707	552	44.6	93.3	15.15	686.30	236	44.6	72.9	183	17.92	808.19

FABRICATED METAL PRODUCTS—PRODUCTION, CAPACITY, SHIPMENTS, INVENTORIES, AND ORDERS
(Seasonally adjusted)

YEAR AND MONTH	Industrial production (1992=100)							Capacity utilization (Percent of capacity)	Manufacturers' shipments, inventories, and orders (Millions of dollars)			
	Total	Metal containers	Hardware, tools, and cutlery		Structural metal products	Other fabricated metal products			Shipments	Inventories (Book value, end of period)	New orders (Net)	Unfilled orders (End of period)
			Total	Hardware and tools		Total	Fasteners, stampings, etc.					
1968	82.4	68.7	86.5	88.5	85.1	83.7	93.5	86.4	43 638	7 506	45 158	13 813
1969	83.8	78.3	90.0	92.1	85.9	82.8	92.1	83.8	46 104	7 666	47 446	15 128
1970	77.7	84.4	83.7	84.4	85.8	70.9	75.3	75.0	44 210	7 907	43 990	14 877
1971	77.3	81.7	88.0	89.5	84.6	69.8	72.1	73.7	45 478	8 098	44 305	13 688
1972	84.8	84.4	98.4	99.7	93.0	76.8	79.3	79.9	51 487	8 408	52 879	15 077
1973	94.3	93.4	105.6	107.3	103.7	86.3	89.5	86.8	58 804	9 864	64 733	21 019
1974	90.5	94.0	101.1	100.4	99.2	83.3	84.4	80.9	67 212	13 387	74 281	28 100
1975	78.4	90.1	87.5	87.4	85.3	71.0	69.8	68.6	68 411	13 091	64 349	24 008
1976	86.9	93.1	102.5	102.4	91.6	79.9	81.2	74.6	77 560	14 304	76 372	22 810
1977	94.7	98.1	110.7	111.0	98.9	88.8	91.2	79.9	89 938	15 527	92 028	25 152
1978	98.2	97.8	109.7	109.8	101.8	93.8	96.4	81.0	101 245	17 296	105 182	29 137
1979	101.6	100.8	115.8	117.9	107.0	96.0	96.8	82.0	113 494	19 145	117 428	33 131
1980	94.4	94.3	99.0	100.2	104.2	88.6	86.1	74.9	116 071	19 532	116 195	33 296
1981	93.0	93.2	100.0	101.6	101.8	87.5	84.5	73.2	123 535	20 209	123 245	33 036
1982	84.9	94.5	85.4	85.3	94.1	79.0	72.8	66.9	119 236	21 440	113 399	27 117
1983	87.2	95.1	91.5	92.0	91.4	82.7	80.3	68.4	123 083	21 752	122 760	26 752
1984	95.2	94.3	99.5	100.8	94.6	93.8	93.9	74.3	138 107	23 330	141 650	30 254
1985	96.5	91.8	100.1	101.1	99.0	94.3	93.1	74.9	143 268	22 880	142 300	29 197
1986	95.6	88.0	100.3	101.6	97.5	93.7	91.4	73.6	143 063	22 094	143 541	29 633
1987	101.9	92.1	105.4	107.8	105.5	99.9	97.9	78.1	147 367	22 920	150 716	32 973
1988	106.1	95.4	107.2	108.9	106.8	106.0	104.3	81.1	159 505	24 950	158 170	31 661
1989	104.8	97.5	107.6	109.3	106.2	103.7	102.4	80.0	164 073	25 427	160 037	27 629
1990	101.2	100.2	102.2	102.6	103.5	99.8	98.0	77.4	165 064	25 044	163 285	25 859
1991	96.2	100.0	96.6	96.8	99.1	94.2	91.4	73.7	159 760	23 922	158 401	24 516
1992	100.0	100.0	100.0	100.0	100.0	100.0	100.0	76.7	166 532	23 824	165 793	23 782
1993	104.4	98.4	105.1	105.0	102.9	105.3	108.9	79.4	175 118	23 842	172 121	20 786
1994	112.0	104.3	115.2	115.2	110.9	112.2	118.2	83.9	190 544	25 601	191 099	21 350
1995	115.7	98.5	115.3	115.3	118.1	116.3	122.4	84.8	204 820	27 427	205 894	22 455
1996	118.6	95.6	116.6	117.0	123.3	119.0	126.6	84.5	215 427	27 440	217 468	24 543
1993:												
January	102.4	99.0	101.7	102.1	99.8	103.9	106.1	78.5	14 145	23 683	14 189	23 826
February	103.0	97.6	102.2	101.8	101.7	104.2	106.5	78.9	14 272	23 654	14 197	23 751
March	103.5	98.7	103.0	103.0	100.1	105.5	109.5	79.2	14 553	23 879	14 124	23 322
April	104.3	99.2	105.0	105.2	101.2	106.0	110.0	79.6	14 328	23 728	14 050	23 044
May	103.5	97.4	103.9	103.8	101.6	104.6	108.3	78.9	14 393	23 765	14 126	22 777
June	103.1	98.2	103.1	102.6	102.0	103.8	106.6	78.5	14 743	23 667	14 093	22 127
July	104.5	98.5	105.2	105.0	102.9	105.5	109.1	79.4	14 271	23 730	14 011	21 867
August	103.9	96.5	104.6	104.2	103.4	104.5	107.5	78.9	14 361	24 010	14 191	21 697
September	105.7	99.0	107.8	108.2	104.8	106.1	110.6	80.1	14 755	24 099	14 793	21 735
October	105.2	96.5	106.4	106.5	105.4	105.5	109.5	79.6	14 874	24 011	14 536	21 397
November	106.1	99.0	107.6	107.7	105.7	106.5	111.0	80.2	15 062	23 897	14 518	20 853
December	107.3	100.9	110.1	110.5	106.4	107.5	112.5	81.0	15 342	23 842	15 275	20 786
1994:												
January	107.8	99.6	111.1	111.5	105.4	108.6	114.5	81.2	15 330	23 902	15 071	20 527
February	107.8	99.6	111.3	111.3	106.0	107.9	113.3	81.2	15 347	24 029	15 208	20 388
March	109.6	103.4	113.4	113.4	108.0	109.8	115.2	82.4	15 772	23 807	16 294	20 910
April	110.7	100.8	115.8	116.0	109.3	111.4	117.3	83.2	15 592	23 874	15 552	20 870
May	111.1	102.3	115.6	115.8	110.1	111.4	117.0	83.3	15 625	24 059	15 797	21 042
June	111.6	102.8	115.1	115.0	110.7	111.9	117.8	83.7	15 685	24 204	15 668	21 025
July	113.0	101.4	117.2	116.7	112.6	113.0	119.4	84.6	15 789	24 829	15 932	21 168
August	113.1	104.3	115.9	116.0	112.2	113.3	119.2	84.5	16 233	24 993	16 330	21 265
September	113.2	104.5	115.0	115.1	112.4	113.6	120.0	84.6	16 182	24 960	16 046	21 129
October	114.1	103.2	115.6	115.8	113.9	114.5	120.7	85.1	16 035	25 107	15 959	21 053
November	114.9	106.0	118.1	118.4	114.3	115.0	121.0	85.6	16 583	25 333	16 739	21 209
December	116.5	124.1	117.5	117.4	115.3	116.3	123.1	86.7	16 410	25 601	16 551	21 350
1995:												
January	115.5	97.3	117.4	117.3	117.0	115.6	121.1	85.8	17 141	25 935	17 435	21 644
February	116.4	94.1	116.7	117.0	117.9	117.4	124.1	86.3	17 024	26 271	17 272	21 892
March	116.0	98.3	113.8	114.2	118.1	116.9	123.1	85.8	16 951	26 879	17 002	21 943
April	114.3	98.1	115.3	116.1	116.4	114.4	120.7	84.3	16 768	27 175	16 919	22 094
May	115.5	99.4	114.8	115.2	117.6	116.1	122.0	85.0	16 853	27 458	17 187	22 428
June	115.4	102.4	116.1	116.4	117.3	115.8	121.8	84.8	16 885	27 690	16 866	22 409
July	114.2	95.8	112.4	112.9	115.0	115.0	120.6	83.7	16 956	27 836	16 985	22 438
August	115.7	101.7	114.0	113.9	118.1	116.3	122.4	84.5	17 266	27 863	17 194	22 366
September	116.6	97.3	115.9	115.6	119.1	117.5	124.0	85.0	17 207	27 723	17 295	22 454
October	115.9	101.1	115.1	114.9	118.5	116.6	122.8	84.3	17 304	27 738	17 247	22 397
November	116.1	99.8	115.0	114.5	119.4	116.8	123.3	84.2	17 123	27 671	17 385	22 659
December	116.5	97.1	116.8	117.0	120.4	116.8	123.3	84.4	17 437	27 427	17 233	22 455
1996:												
January	116.7	100.9	116.5	116.8	119.5	117.6	126.5	84.3	17 443	27 411	17 444	22 456
February	117.9	100.7	116.9	117.5	121.2	118.6	126.1	85.0	17 381	27 570	17 449	22 524
March	117.6	97.7	113.4	113.3	122.5	118.1	124.9	84.5	17 081	27 428	17 134	22 577
April	117.8	99.2	114.7	114.7	122.7	118.1	125.1	84.5	17 980	27 304	18 062	22 659
May	118.4	98.8	115.5	115.6	122.7	118.9	126.1	84.7	18 217	27 170	18 598	23 040
June	118.9	96.3	117.0	117.6	123.6	119.1	125.9	84.9	18 035	26 948	18 190	23 195
July	119.1	99.5	115.3	115.7	123.4	120.3	127.9	84.8	18 005	27 277	18 190	23 380
August	119.4	92.1	118.0	118.8	123.9	120.1	127.7	84.8	18 298	27 415	18 379	23 461
September	119.3	81.2	117.6	118.4	124.4	120.3	127.8	84.5	18 310	27 335	18 716	23 867
October	119.3	94.9	118.6	119.1	124.5	119.4	126.9	84.3	18 215	27 376	18 548	24 200
November	119.1	93.9	117.3	118.1	125.5	118.7	126.2	84.0	18 385	27 410	18 597	24 412
December	119.5	91.6	118.9	118.5	125.9	119.2	127.3	84.1	18 067	27 440	18 198	24 543

FABRICATED METAL PRODUCTS—PRICES, EMPLOYMENT, HOURS, AND EARNINGS

YEAR AND MONTH	Producer prices (1982=100, except as noted, not seasonally adjusted)								Employment (Thousands, seasonally adjusted)		Production workers			
	Fabricated metal products industry [1]	Intermediate materials							Total payroll employees	Production workers	Weekly hours worked (Seasonally adjusted)		Average earnings (Dollars, not seasonally adjusted)	
		Metal containers	Hardware	Plumbing fixtures and brass fittings	Heating equipment	Fabricated structural metal products	Fabricated ferrous wire products (June 1982=100)	Other miscellaneous metal products			Average hours	Aggregate hours index (1982=100)	Hourly	Weekly
1968	....	31.6	36.6	37.1	43.3	33.5	....	35.3	1 609	1 244	41.7	128.8	3.16	131.77
1969	....	32.5	37.9	38.5	44.4	34.7	....	36.9	1 665	1 284	41.6	132.6	3.34	138.94
1970	....	34.3	39.8	39.9	46.6	36.7	....	39.4	1 559	1 188	40.7	120.3	3.53	143.67
1971	....	37.1	41.7	41.8	48.6	38.8	....	41.3	1 479	1 128	40.4	113.2	3.77	152.31
1972	....	39.2	42.9	43.0	49.8	40.2	....	43.2	1 541	1 189	41.2	121.9	4.05	166.86
1973	....	41.0	44.5	45.1	50.8	41.8	....	45.1	1 645	1 277	41.6	131.8	4.29	178.46
1974	....	50.1	50.2	53.5	56.9	52.9	....	54.8	1 632	1 256	40.8	127.4	4.61	188.09
1975	....	58.5	58.2	58.2	63.5	62.0	....	63.2	1 453	1 090	40.1	108.4	5.05	202.51
1976	....	61.5	61.8	62.5	66.6	63.6	....	66.1	1 505	1 138	40.8	115.3	5.50	224.40
1977	....	66.4	66.2	67.0	69.8	67.8	....	69.9	1 577	1 198	41.0	121.9	5.91	242.31
1978	....	74.1	71.5	71.4	73.5	74.3	....	76.1	1 667	1 269	41.0	129.3	6.35	260.35
1979	....	81.9	78.0	77.9	78.9	81.6	....	82.9	1 713	1 298	40.7	131.4	6.85	278.80
1980	....	90.9	85.8	88.5	87.0	88.8	....	89.2	1 609	1 194	40.4	119.8	7.45	300.98
1981	....	96.1	93.9	96.0	94.5	96.9	....	96.2	1 586	1 171	40.3	117.1	8.20	330.46
1982	....	100.0	100.0	100.0	100.0	100.0	....	100.0	1 424	1 028	39.2	100.0	8.77	343.78
1983	....	102.1	103.7	103.8	102.7	99.6	96.2	101.0	1 368	994	40.6	100.3	9.12	370.27
1984	....	106.5	105.9	108.6	106.6	101.9	97.5	105.8	1 462	1 078	41.4	111.0	9.40	389.16
1985	100.6	109.0	109.1	111.9	109.5	103.2	99.3	108.6	1 464	1 083	41.3	111.2	9.71	401.02
1986	101.0	110.2	109.5	115.5	113.0	103.6	100.3	108.5	1 422	1 051	41.3	107.8	9.89	408.46
1987	102.1	109.5	109.6	119.7	115.5	105.4	101.0	109.5	1 399	1 038	41.6	107.1	10.01	416.42
1988	107.4	110.2	113.7	128.7	119.2	114.3	107.0	114.1	1 428	1 062	41.9	110.5	10.29	431.15
1989	112.6	111.5	120.4	137.7	125.1	120.3	111.9	119.0	1 445	1 070	41.6	110.6	10.57	439.71
1990	115.1	114.0	125.9	144.3	131.6	121.8	114.6	120.7	1 419	1 045	41.3	107.1	10.83	447.28
1991	116.6	115.5	130.2	149.7	134.1	122.4	115.9	121.0	1 355	991	41.2	101.4	11.19	461.03
1992	117.2	113.9	132.7	153.1	137.3	122.1	117.5	121.1	1 329	975	41.6	100.7	11.42	475.07
1993	118.2	109.7	135.2	155.9	140.4	123.2	119.3	121.4	1 339	988	42.1	103.3	11.69	492.15
1994	120.3	108.1	137.5	159.6	142.5	127.3	122.6	122.7	1 388	1 037	42.9	110.5	11.93	511.80
1995	124.8	117.2	141.1	166.0	147.5	135.1	125.7	124.9	1 437	1 080	42.4	113.6	12.13	514.31
1996	126.2	110.0	143.8	171.1	151.2	137.8	126.8	125.7	1 448	1 088	42.4	114.5	12.52	530.85
1993:														
January	117.4	109.9	134.1	153.7	139.2	121.8	117.7	121.0	1 333	981	41.8	101.8	11.54	481.22
February	117.7	110.2	134.3	153.3	139.3	122.1	117.8	121.1	1 336	984	42.0	102.6	11.55	481.64
March	117.8	109.5	134.6	155.2	139.4	122.4	117.7	121.1	1 336	984	41.7	101.9	11.55	479.33
April	118.0	109.2	134.8	156.2	140.6	122.7	118.3	121.3	1 336	984	42.3	103.4	11.62	481.07
May	118.0	109.1	134.8	156.3	140.7	122.9	118.7	121.3	1 334	983	41.8	102.1	11.69	489.81
June	118.1	109.1	135.2	156.5	141.2	123.1	118.9	121.2	1 332	983	41.9	102.3	11.69	493.32
July	118.3	109.2	135.3	155.9	140.9	123.4	119.8	121.4	1 335	985	42.0	102.8	11.65	482.31
August	118.4	108.8	135.5	156.5	140.7	123.6	120.5	121.4	1 336	987	42.1	103.2	11.67	491.31
September	118.6	109.8	135.6	156.5	140.4	123.8	120.6	121.4	1 341	992	42.3	104.2	11.81	492.48
October	118.6	110.1	135.7	156.8	140.6	124.1	120.5	121.5	1 344	995	42.2	104.3	11.74	500.12
November	118.9	111.0	135.9	156.9	140.7	124.4	120.5	121.8	1 349	1 000	42.3	105.1	11.82	507.08
December	118.9	110.1	136.2	156.8	140.7	124.6	121.2	122.0	1 352	1 004	42.5	106.0	11.91	518.09
1994:														
January	119.1	109.0	136.4	157.4	141.2	124.9	121.7	122.1	1 357	1 007	42.6	106.5	11.87	503.29
February	119.3	108.5	136.5	157.8	141.8	125.0	121.9	122.1	1 362	1 011	42.2	106.0	11.89	498.19
March	119.4	107.7	136.7	158.6	142.1	125.2	122.0	122.3	1 367	1 017	42.7	107.9	11.89	505.33
April	119.7	108.0	137.2	159.2	142.4	125.7	122.3	122.3	1 373	1 023	42.5	108.0	11.90	508.13
May	119.8	108.0	137.4	159.3	142.6	126.3	122.1	122.4	1 378	1 028	42.8	109.3	11.89	508.89
June	120.0	106.6	137.5	160.3	142.4	127.1	122.3	122.6	1 387	1 036	42.6	109.6	11.90	510.51
July	120.3	106.9	137.6	159.7	142.6	127.4	122.3	122.7	1 391	1 040	42.8	110.6	11.86	498.12
August	120.6	108.1	137.8	160.3	142.9	128.0	122.6	122.8	1 397	1 047	42.8	111.3	11.87	508.04
September	120.8	108.2	138.0	160.3	143.0	128.7	122.9	122.9	1 401	1 050	42.6	111.1	11.99	517.97
October	121.2	108.6	138.1	160.5	143.0	129.2	123.4	123.1	1 408	1 057	42.8	112.4	11.92	514.94
November	121.6	108.8	138.5	161.1	143.1	130.1	123.7	123.3	1 415	1 063	42.9	113.3	12.03	523.31
December	121.8	108.9	138.6	161.1	143.3	130.4	123.8	123.5	1 422	1 069	42.9	113.9	12.09	531.96
1995:														
January	122.6	109.6	139.4	161.7	145.3	131.9	124.5	124.2	1 427	1 074	43.4	115.8	12.04	518.92
February	123.6	117.8	139.7	164.8	146.5	132.5	125.5	124.4	1 437	1 080	42.8	114.8	12.03	513.68
March	124.1	117.8	140.4	165.7	147.0	133.6	125.4	124.6	1 439	1 084	42.7	115.0	12.05	512.13
April	124.4	118.1	140.8	165.9	147.2	134.4	125.6	124.6	1 444	1 087	42.0	113.4	12.03	484.81
May	124.6	118.1	140.9	166.5	147.4	134.6	126.1	124.8	1 441	1 084	42.1	113.3	12.08	508.57
June	125.0	118.3	141.4	166.5	147.6	135.2	126.3	124.8	1 436	1 078	42.1	112.7	12.05	509.72
July	125.2	118.0	141.5	166.5	147.7	135.8	125.6	125.1	1 436	1 076	42.0	112.2	12.11	498.93
August	125.5	118.0	141.6	166.7	148.1	136.0	126.0	125.4	1 436	1 078	42.2	113.0	12.11	511.04
September	125.6	117.8	141.7	166.8	148.2	136.5	126.3	125.3	1 435	1 077	42.4	113.4	12.22	524.24
October	125.8	117.9	141.7	167.2	148.4	136.6	125.7	125.3	1 437	1 078	42.3	113.3	12.19	519.29
November	125.8	117.7	141.9	166.7	148.4	136.7	125.7	125.4	1 438	1 080	42.2	113.2	12.26	525.95
December	125.9	117.8	142.2	166.6	148.5	136.7	125.4	125.3	1 439	1 080	42.1	112.9	12.42	536.54
1996:														
January	125.9	115.1	142.8	167.6	150.1	136.8	125.8	125.5	1 440	1 080	41.2	110.5	12.38	506.34
February	125.7	110.5	143.1	170.2	150.5	136.9	126.0	125.3	1 442	1 080	42.1	112.9	12.32	517.44
March	125.9	110.5	143.5	170.9	150.5	137.1	126.4	125.4	1 440	1 081	42.1	113.0	12.32	516.21
April	126.0	110.5	143.5	171.0	150.6	137.2	126.8	125.6	1 439	1 080	42.3	113.5	12.47	521.25
May	126.0	109.7	143.6	171.5	150.8	137.5	127.2	125.6	1 441	1 082	42.5	114.2	12.46	527.06
June	126.2	109.5	143.7	171.8	151.1	138.0	127.2	125.6	1 445	1 086	42.6	114.9	12.53	536.28
July	126.2	109.6	143.7	171.6	151.5	138.0	127.2	125.6	1 449	1 089	42.4	114.7	12.51	520.42
August	126.4	109.6	144.2	171.5	151.8	138.2	127.0	125.8	1 451	1 092	42.4	115.0	12.54	534.20
September	126.4	109.5	144.2	171.6	151.8	138.4	127.1	125.9	1 452	1 093	42.4	115.1	12.67	546.08
October	126.5	108.5	144.6	171.6	151.8	138.6	126.9	126.0	1 455	1 094	42.3	114.9	12.55	535.89
November	126.5	108.4	144.1	171.8	151.8	138.6	126.6	125.9	1 457	1 096	42.3	115.1	12.62	542.66
December	126.6	109.1	144.2	171.4	151.9	138.6	127.0	126.1	1 458	1 097	42.4	115.5	12.79	557.64

1. Except machinery and transportation equipment, December 1984=100.

YEAR AND MONTH	INDUSTRIAL MACHINERY AND EQUIPMENT—PRODUCTION, AND CAPACITY									
	Industrial production (1992=100, seasonally adjusted)								Capacity utilization (Percent of capacity, seasonally adjusted)	
	Total	Engines and turbines	Construction and allied	Metal-working	Special industry	General industrial	Computer and office equipment	Service industry machines	Total	Computer and office equipment
1968	39.3	82.9	106.7	108.3	99.0	83.0	1.8	49.9	85.9	85.7
1969	42.5	95.7	116.9	111.9	105.9	88.9	2.2	58.8	87.8	92.9
1970	41.1	95.9	114.6	99.7	100.1	83.8	2.3	57.7	81.3	90.9
1971	38.2	102.7	114.5	82.9	88.5	76.9	2.0	60.4	73.0	70.9
1972	44.3	109.9	131.6	96.9	98.8	86.9	2.4	74.2	82.5	79.2
1973	51.8	120.9	151.0	116.0	112.2	101.8	2.9	89.1	93.0	86.3
1974	55.2	132.8	168.3	118.7	115.4	106.7	3.5	81.9	94.6	91.7
1975	47.8	110.3	150.9	96.5	98.2	95.7	3.2	60.0	78.4	74.0
1976	50.2	120.6	140.9	95.6	97.0	97.4	3.9	74.1	78.8	75.6
1977	56.6	129.1	163.6	106.0	96.2	105.4	5.1	81.8	83.9	78.1
1978	63.3	138.5	181.8	111.1	102.0	109.1	7.5	89.3	88.2	87.3
1979	70.2	139.7	184.8	120.5	103.4	117.2	10.3	90.9	91.6	89.3
1980	70.5	127.0	176.5	119.0	100.8	111.1	13.9	78.6	85.9	88.2
1981	74.7	127.5	189.0	116.3	94.8	109.9	18.4	82.5	84.8	85.7
1982	65.8	101.5	145.2	87.3	88.0	93.5	21.3	73.7	70.5	74.3
1983	65.2	90.1	101.2	74.2	81.7	89.6	29.5	79.7	66.2	78.7
1984	78.9	115.8	115.8	90.4	90.5	101.3	42.0	89.2	75.7	86.1
1985	81.2	108.2	113.4	92.3	90.4	96.3	50.3	86.3	72.8	80.0
1986	81.8	104.7	105.4	98.2	88.9	92.8	53.7	91.4	70.3	72.5
1987	86.0	97.9	101.4	96.9	96.7	92.9	62.2	96.7	72.1	74.6
1988	97.1	107.6	114.8	106.2	105.5	102.2	74.6	103.3	79.6	79.5
1989	103.0	107.2	121.8	113.9	110.7	103.3	83.0	108.0	83.4	81.2
1990	100.1	100.5	117.6	109.4	107.7	104.0	81.4	97.6	79.4	73.7
1991	95.4	98.4	104.4	98.8	102.2	100.1	82.3	91.9	74.3	68.8
1992	100.0	100.0	100.0	100.0	100.0	100.0	100.0	100.0	75.6	74.6
1993	109.9	109.9	110.5	106.2	107.8	104.5	121.5	106.3	79.6	77.2
1994	125.3	123.4	121.0	115.5	121.4	109.8	152.1	118.0	85.8	79.5
1995	141.4	123.6	139.6	124.6	135.4	114.2	213.6	121.4	89.8	88.2
1996	156.4	115.7	152.0	125.0	132.4	115.2	296.9	130.6	89.9	91.9
1993:										
January	104.0	104.5	103.8	103.2	104.2	102.5	110.1	100.4	76.9	76.0
February	105.2	104.3	103.6	103.3	104.1	102.2	113.1	103.0	77.6	76.9
March	106.8	105.5	105.9	105.8	103.4	104.4	115.1	104.4	78.4	77.2
April	107.9	108.4	106.7	106.3	106.1	104.4	118.0	103.8	78.9	77.9
May	109.1	107.0	109.4	104.8	106.7	103.2	120.7	109.8	79.4	78.5
June	108.6	107.7	111.1	105.9	107.4	104.6	120.1	100.8	78.7	77.0
July	111.6	111.5	119.9	107.6	108.0	105.4	123.0	105.2	80.7	77.7
August	110.0	109.3	109.7	108.0	109.7	104.5	123.8	103.0	79.2	77.0
September	112.2	114.2	111.3	108.6	110.3	106.6	126.0	106.0	80.4	77.3
October	112.9	113.7	114.0	105.3	109.4	104.4	126.8	110.1	80.6	76.6
November	114.4	114.4	115.2	107.3	111.8	105.3	127.6	113.5	81.4	75.9
December	116.8	117.9	115.5	108.7	112.9	106.6	133.4	115.7	82.8	78.2
1994:										
January	118.2	118.0	123.1	110.8	113.9	105.8	135.8	110.5	83.4	78.4
February	118.3	119.7	119.7	111.2	114.6	107.2	138.1	109.5	83.1	78.3
March	120.3	122.1	120.1	112.0	118.2	107.4	140.0	113.2	84.0	78.0
April	121.2	123.8	120.2	112.8	118.6	108.0	140.9	116.0	84.2	77.1
May	123.4	123.0	120.6	113.9	119.3	108.6	145.5	117.0	85.2	78.3
June	124.5	125.8	120.4	113.6	119.7	109.9	147.8	118.2	85.5	78.2
July	127.9	124.1	135.4	116.4	121.2	109.6	151.9	122.4	87.4	78.9
August	126.6	123.6	119.9	116.8	122.4	110.9	154.4	124.9	86.1	78.8
September	128.2	123.7	110.9	118.0	123.3	111.8	162.0	123.9	86.7	81.3
October	129.8	124.9	111.9	120.3	126.6	113.4	165.5	122.0	87.3	81.6
November	131.5	126.6	122.8	120.0	128.7	112.0	168.4	119.9	88.1	81.6
December	133.2	125.9	127.2	120.4	131.1	112.6	175.0	118.2	88.7	83.4
1995:										
January	136.8	129.1	135.2	121.4	132.2	113.7	184.4	125.8	90.5	86.1
February	137.0	130.5	132.9	122.2	133.8	113.4	192.8	118.7	90.0	88.1
March	137.3	129.5	132.8	122.0	133.6	113.5	196.0	116.2	89.5	87.7
April	138.6	127.3	132.9	123.7	133.8	112.9	202.9	121.5	89.7	88.8
May	138.9	123.8	133.5	123.5	134.8	113.4	206.7	117.2	89.2	88.5
June	139.1	119.3	135.1	123.5	135.5	114.8	206.5	117.3	88.7	86.5
July	140.1	121.9	136.1	123.2	136.7	114.0	213.6	116.2	88.6	87.6
August	143.0	125.7	143.6	126.9	137.5	115.9	217.8	119.7	89.8	87.4
September	144.9	121.1	145.1	127.1	137.6	115.1	226.3	123.2	90.4	88.9
October	145.4	118.7	148.0	125.5	136.5	115.4	233.6	124.9	90.0	89.7
November	146.3	118.0	148.1	127.4	136.8	114.8	237.6	124.8	89.9	89.3
December	149.0	118.0	151.5	128.8	135.4	114.2	244.9	130.8	90.8	90.1
1996:										
January	148.3	117.4	146.2	124.6	132.8	113.7	251.8	125.6	89.7	90.4
February	151.4	112.2	149.4	125.6	134.8	117.8	263.6	130.5	90.7	92.2
March	152.5	113.0	149.2	126.1	134.3	115.7	270.8	131.7	90.5	92.3
April	153.3	113.1	151.1	126.9	134.3	115.1	277.3	128.0	90.2	92.1
May	154.3	114.6	151.7	124.2	134.0	115.0	284.7	129.0	89.9	92.0
June	156.1	115.7	152.2	123.1	133.0	114.9	294.3	138.7	90.1	92.7
July	157.7	112.4	157.2	123.3	132.5	115.4	306.5	128.7	90.2	94.0
August	159.6	116.7	153.0	124.8	130.6	115.5	310.8	135.6	90.5	92.9
September	159.4	117.1	153.2	124.1	130.6	114.5	319.0	132.4	89.6	92.9
October	159.9	118.5	153.5	124.5	131.3	115.3	323.6	123.2	89.1	91.8
November	161.7	117.9	153.9	126.8	129.5	114.4	328.3	131.7	89.2	90.7
December	162.9	119.3	152.7	125.9	130.6	115.6	332.5	132.2	89.0	89.5

INDUSTRIAL MACHINERY AND EQUIPMENT—SHIPMENTS, INVENTORIES, ORDERS AND PRICES

YEAR AND MONTH	Manufacturers' shipments, inventories, and orders (Millions of dollars, seasonally adjusted)				Producer prices (1982=100, except as noted, not seasonally adjusted)					
	Shipments	Inventories (Book value, end of period)	New orders (Net)	Unfilled orders (End of period)	Machinery, except electrical [1]	Electronic computers [2]	Commodity groups			
							Metalworking machinery and equipment	General purpose machinery and equipment	Special industry machinery	Miscellaneous machinery and equipment
1968	51 370	11 628	52 286	19 673	....	....	32.4	34.0	32.4	38.9
1969	56 584	13 408	60 226	23 319	....	....	33.7	35.2	33.8	40.3
1970	56 893	14 500	55 322	21 737	....	....	35.6	37.4	35.6	42.0
1971	56 445	14 344	55 886	21 170	....	....	36.7	39.2	37.2	43.7
1972	66 156	15 142	70 941	25 968	....	....	37.5	40.3	38.0	44.8
1973	78 207	18 411	89 162	36 959	....	....	39.1	41.8	40.0	46.2
1974	93 041	24 189	106 101	50 084	....	....	45.8	49.7	46.4	52.0
1975	96 354	24 156	92 863	46 580	....	....	53.5	58.7	53.8	60.5
1976	105 847	25 245	107 595	48 321	....	....	56.9	62.4	58.0	64.1
1977	122 749	27 282	126 235	52 026	....	....	61.9	66.4	62.3	67.3
1978	143 919	32 086	154 051	62 233	....	....	67.6	71.2	68.6	72.5
1979	167 014	37 464	174 660	69 844	....	....	75.2	77.8	76.0	77.8
1980	180 564	40 958	179 750	68 979	....	....	85.5	87.0	84.8	85.7
1981	201 102	43 652	201 576	69 405	....	....	93.9	95.0	94.7	94.1
1982	186 773	47 908	169 274	51 864	....	....	100.0	100.0	100.0	100.0
1983	178 446	44 586	178 879	52 351	....	....	101.7	101.4	103.7	102.1
1984	211 075	48 760	212 109	53 466	....	....	104.1	103.3	107.3	102.2
1985	218 408	46 526	218 395	53 516	101.0	....	106.6	105.7	110.8	103.3
1986	213 574	42 409	208 567	48 416	102.0	....	108.4	107.2	114.2	104.2
1987	217 671	43 141	221 171	51 868	103.2	....	110.1	108.3	117.3	105.7
1988	244 365	47 707	250 055	57 583	106.4	....	113.5	112.8	121.7	108.6
1989	256 212	50 342	257 051	58 369	110.7	....	118.2	119.0	127.0	112.7
1990	259 367	49 673	258 894	57 872	113.9	....	123.0	123.7	131.5	116.7
1991	247 508	47 880	243 450	53 812	116.4	88.9	127.6	127.8	135.9	120.3
1992	258 662	47 096	258 608	53 677	116.7	74.5	130.9	129.9	139.5	121.7
1993	278 063	48 632	277 416	52 986	116.8	65.4	133.5	132.2	143.7	122.7
1994	313 047	52 943	325 788	65 651	117.5	60.1	136.5	134.8	146.2	124.7
1995	351 113	59 121	356 282	70 825	119.0	53.8	139.8	139.1	149.8	127.0
1996	378 366	58 177	379 817	72 221	119.2	45.2	143.1	142.5	153.3	129.2
1993:										
January	22 528	46 493	22 503	53 652	117.1	69.4	132.4	131.2	141.9	122.3
February	22 280	46 309	22 474	53 846	117.0	69.2	132.5	131.4	142.6	122.4
March	22 966	46 080	22 364	53 244	117.0	67.7	133.0	131.5	143.0	122.5
April	22 448	46 334	22 160	52 956	116.8	66.7	132.8	131.7	143.3	122.4
May	22 631	46 424	22 410	52 735	116.7	65.9	133.0	131.8	143.4	122.5
June	22 535	46 898	21 930	52 130	116.7	65.2	133.3	132.1	143.7	122.4
July	22 954	47 146	22 885	52 061	116.6	64.3	133.7	132.3	143.9	122.6
August	22 814	47 378	22 973	52 220	116.6	63.4	133.8	132.6	143.9	122.9
September	23 636	47 716	23 467	52 051	116.8	63.7	134.3	132.7	144.1	123.0
October	23 539	48 182	23 448	51 960	116.7	63.1	134.4	132.8	144.5	123.2
November	24 412	48 268	24 920	52 468	116.7	63.0	134.5	133.0	144.7	123.1
December	24 912	48 632	25 430	52 986	116.8	62.9	134.6	133.2	144.7	123.3
1994:										
January	24 110	49 094	24 829	53 705	117.1	62.6	134.8	133.6	145.1	123.9
February	24 932	49 359	25 667	54 440	117.0	61.1	135.0	133.7	145.5	124.2
March	24 996	49 965	26 299	55 743	117.3	61.1	135.4	134.1	145.7	124.2
April	25 308	50 236	26 835	57 270	117.3	60.7	136.5	134.2	145.9	124.2
May	25 780	50 427	26 662	58 152	117.4	60.5	136.7	134.3	146.0	124.2
June	25 785	51 119	27 310	59 677	117.5	60.3	136.5	134.6	146.2	124.4
July	26 369	51 440	27 455	60 763	117.6	59.9	136.7	134.9	146.4	124.5
August	26 934	52 032	28 362	62 191	117.6	59.5	136.8	135.1	146.4	124.7
September	26 660	52 120	27 852	63 383	117.7	59.8	137.0	135.2	146.5	125.2
October	27 181	52 340	28 385	64 587	117.7	59.0	137.1	135.7	146.6	125.5
November	27 107	52 742	28 667	66 147	117.7	58.3	137.4	135.9	146.8	125.6
December	27 480	52 943	26 984	65 651	117.8	58.3	137.4	136.1	147.0	125.7
1995:										
January	27 784	54 344	29 270	67 137	118.3	57.6	137.9	136.9	148.1	126.2
February	28 404	54 630	29 513	68 246	118.6	56.8	138.6	137.7	148.6	126.4
March	28 361	55 025	30 041	69 926	118.7	56.3	138.9	138.1	149.0	126.4
April	28 956	55 292	29 048	70 018	119.0	55.8	139.2	138.5	149.3	126.6
May	29 339	55 991	29 627	70 306	119.1	55.0	139.7	138.7	149.7	126.7
June	29 113	56 331	30 108	71 301	119.1	53.9	139.8	138.9	150.0	126.8
July	28 879	56 710	28 290	70 712	119.2	53.7	140.4	139.3	150.2	127.2
August	29 631	56 984	29 667	70 748	119.1	52.4	140.5	139.5	150.3	127.2
September	29 805	57 516	29 851	70 794	119.1	51.7	140.5	139.7	150.5	127.3
October	30 101	57 879	29 698	70 391	119.2	51.1	140.6	140.0	150.7	127.4
November	30 257	58 652	31 208	71 342	119.3	50.6	140.8	140.5	150.8	127.6
December	30 698	59 121	30 181	70 825	119.4	50.3	140.9	140.8	151.0	127.7
1996:										
January	30 261	59 785	30 961	71 525	119.7	49.7	142.0	141.6	152.0	128.2
February	31 622	59 888	32 526	72 429	119.7	48.4	142.2	141.9	152.4	128.6
March	31 076	59 660	30 428	71 781	119.7	47.6	142.5	142.2	152.7	128.7
April	30 913	60 059	30 995	71 863	119.3	46.6	142.7	142.3	152.9	128.8
May	31 308	59 918	31 599	72 154	119.3	46.1	143.1	142.3	153.0	128.8
June	31 682	59 018	31 346	71 818	119.1	45.6	143.3	142.4	153.2	128.9
July	31 518	59 463	32 424	72 724	119.1	44.5	143.3	142.6	153.4	129.5
August	31 789	59 573	32 098	73 033	119.1	44.1	143.4	142.7	153.8	129.5
September	32 243	59 024	32 115	72 905	119.1	43.8	143.5	142.7	153.9	129.8
October	31 623	58 980	31 424	72 706	118.9	42.9	143.6	143.0	154.0	129.8
November	31 659	59 196	31 487	72 534	118.9	42.1	144.0	143.3	154.4	129.9
December	32 292	58 177	31 979	72 221	118.7	41.2	144.1	143.4	154.4	130.1

1. December 1984=100.
2. December 1990=100.

INDUSTRIAL MACHINERY AND EQUIPMENT—EMPLOYMENT, HOURS, AND EARNINGS

YEAR AND MONTH	Industrial machinery and equipment — Employment (Thousands, seasonally adjusted)		Industrial machinery and equipment — Production workers: Weekly hours worked (Seasonally adjusted)		Industrial machinery and equipment — Average earnings (Dollars, not seasonally adjusted)		Computer and office equipment (Not seasonally adjusted) — Employment (Thousands)		Computer and office equipment — Production workers	Computer and office equipment — Production workers: Average earnings (Dollars)	
	Total payroll employees	Production workers	Average hours	Aggregate hours index (1982=100)	Hourly	Weekly	Total payroll employees	Production workers	Average weekly hours worked	Hourly	Weekly
1968	1 988	1 358	42.0	....	3.36	141.12	244	133	41.5	3.32	137.80
1969	2 055	1 397	42.5	....	3.58	152.15	269	141	41.9	3.59	150.40
1970	2 003	1 336	41.1	....	3.77	154.95	281	138	41.0	3.69	151.30
1971	1 834	1 195	40.6		4.02	163.21	257	116	41.4	3.85	159.40
1972	1 909	1 258	42.1		4.32	181.87	252	112	42.1	3.94	165.90
1973	2 111	1 416	42.8		4.60	196.88	276	127	41.3	4.12	170.20
1974	2 230	1 494	42.1		4.94	207.97	296	137	40.9	4.37	178.70
1975	2 076	1 350	40.8		5.37	219.10	278	119	40.3	4.82	194.30
1976	2 085	1 352	41.2		5.79	238.55	278	119	41.6	5.15	214.20
1977	2 195	1 435	41.5		6.26	259.79	303	136	40.9	5.36	219.20
1978	2 347	1 540	42.0		6.78	284.76	340	154	41.4	5.62	232.70
1979	2 508	1 648	41.7		7.32	305.24	386	173	41.6	6.10	253.80
1980	2 517	1 614	41.0		8.00	328.00	420	181	41.4	6.75	279.50
1981	2 521	1 592	40.9		8.81	360.33	447	182	41.2	7.46	307.40
1982	2 264	1 367	39.7		9.26	367.62	460	184	41.1	7.93	325.90
1983	2 053	1 207	40.5		9.56	387.18	474	190	41.5	8.52	353.60
1984	2 218	1 342	41.9		9.97	417.74	515	205	42.2	8.94	377.30
1985	2 195	1 320	41.5		10.30	427.45	500	184	41.6	9.34	388.50
1986	2 074	1 234	41.6		10.58	440.13	469	163	42.1	9.97	419.70
1987	2 028	1 203	42.2	93.8	10.73	452.81	461	155	42.6	10.28	437.90
1988	2 089	1 256	42.7	98.8	11.08	473.12	459	148	41.7	10.65	444.10
1989	2 125	1 282	42.4	100.3	11.40	483.36	459	145	42.3	10.99	464.90
1990	2 095	1 260	41.9	97.5	11.77	493.16	438	137	42.0	11.51	483.40
1991	2 000	1 193	41.7	91.8	12.15	506.66	415	135	41.5	12.13	503.40
1992	1 929	1 152	42.2	89.6	12.41	523.70	391	128	42.0	12.33	517.90
1993	1 931	1 170	43.0	92.7	12.73	547.39	363	121	41.9	12.54	525.40
1994	1 990	1 233	43.7	99.3	13.00	568.10	354	123	42.7	13.08	558.50
1995	2 067	1 295	43.4	103.5	13.24	574.62	352	123	43.0	13.59	584.40
1996	2 112	1 319	43.1	104.8	13.59	585.73	363	128	42.2	13.86	584.90
1993:											
January	1 927	1 161	42.7	91.4	12.59	540.11	376	125	41.5	12.27	509.20
February	1 926	1 161	42.8	91.6	12.61	539.71	372	124	41.5	12.39	514.20
March	1 925	1 161	42.6	91.2	12.59	538.85	368	123	41.7	12.36	515.40
April	1 924	1 162	43.2	92.6	12.65	537.63	367	122	41.1	12.55	515.80
May	1 927	1 165	42.8	92.0	12.65	542.69	367	122	41.9	12.36	517.90
June	1 927	1 167	42.8	92.1	12.68	543.97	365	121	41.9	12.41	520.00
July	1 929	1 169	43.1	92.9	12.76	543.58	363	120	41.7	12.65	527.50
August	1 926	1 168	43.0	92.6	12.74	542.72	359	118	42.3	12.76	539.80
September	1 932	1 173	43.3	93.7	12.84	546.98	356	117	42.3	12.69	536.80
October	1 936	1 177	43.2	93.8	12.82	553.82	355	117	42.1	12.57	529.20
November	1 943	1 184	43.2	94.3	12.87	558.56	356	118	42.3	12.66	535.50
December	1 949	1 191	43.4	95.3	13.00	577.20	355	119	43.0	12.79	550.00
1994:											
January	1 954	1 197	43.4	95.8	12.92	562.02	356	121	42.0	12.69	533.00
February	1 961	1 207	43.0	95.7	12.95	556.85	354	123	42.3	12.82	542.30
March	1 968	1 212	43.6	97.4	12.95	568.51	355	123	42.8	12.91	552.60
April	1 978	1 220	43.4	97.6	12.94	565.48	355	123	42.7	13.00	555.10
May	1 984	1 226	43.6	98.6	12.95	565.92	356	122	43.0	13.08	562.40
June	1 992	1 234	43.7	99.4	12.95	567.21	359	124	43.3	13.14	569.00
July	1 987	1 233	43.7	99.4	12.95	558.15	358	124	41.9	13.04	546.40
August	1 999	1 244	43.5	99.8	12.93	557.28	355	123	42.0	13.12	551.00
September	2 004	1 249	43.5	100.2	13.05	570.29	354	124	42.9	13.40	574.90
October	2 008	1 254	43.7	101.1	13.04	569.85	349	121	42.5	13.22	561.90
November	2 016	1 259	43.7	101.5	13.12	577.28	350	121	43.2	13.21	570.70
December	2 022	1 262	43.8	101.9	13.20	591.36	349	121	43.7	13.30	581.20
1995:											
January	2 028	1 267	44.1	103.0	13.16	581.67	350	121	42.8	13.39	573.10
February	2 038	1 273	43.7	102.6	13.17	579.48	349	120	43.3	13.48	583.70
March	2 044	1 279	43.6	102.8	13.17	578.16	347	119	43.2	13.59	587.10
April	2 055	1 289	43.1	102.5	13.07	546.33	347	120	42.7	13.64	582.40
May	2 056	1 289	43.3	102.9	13.17	571.58	348	120	42.8	13.74	588.10
June	2 063	1 293	43.2	103.0	13.17	570.26	352	122	43.0	13.67	587.80
July	2 071	1 297	43.0	102.8	13.23	560.95	353	122	43.1	13.57	584.90
August	2 077	1 300	43.4	104.0	13.25	569.75	353	123	42.5	13.78	585.70
September	2 081	1 304	43.2	103.9	13.34	578.96	354	123	43.0	13.63	586.10
October	2 091	1 310	43.2	104.4	13.33	575.86	357	125	43.0	13.48	579.60
November	2 098	1 315	43.5	105.5	13.39	585.14	359	127	43.1	13.46	580.10
December	2 103	1 319	42.9	104.3	13.47	594.03	360	128	43.4	13.62	591.10
1996:											
January	2 105	1 319	42.2	102.6	13.44	568.51	360	129	41.7	13.42	559.60
February	2 105	1 317	43.0	104.4	13.40	580.22	359	128	42.9	13.65	585.60
March	2 111	1 318	43.0	104.5	13.36	578.49	361	127	43.4	13.61	590.70
April	2 111	1 319	43.1	104.8	13.44	573.89	361	127	42.1	13.70	576.80
May	2 112	1 319	43.1	104.8	13.45	578.35	363	128	42.0	13.76	577.90
June	2 113	1 318	43.1	104.8	13.51	584.98	366	128	42.7	13.99	597.40
July	2 113	1 318	43.0	104.5	13.55	574.52	364	128	41.4	13.93	576.70
August	2 114	1 319	43.0	104.6	13.63	582.00	364	128	41.0	13.95	572.00
September	2 108	1 314	43.1	104.4	13.77	596.24	363	127	42.4	14.05	595.70
October	2 115	1 319	43.0	104.6	13.70	587.73	364	127	41.5	13.94	578.50
November	2 115	1 320	43.1	104.9	13.80	597.54	365	128	42.0	14.06	590.50
December	2 119	1 324	43.3	105.7	13.97	620.27	366	130	43.2	14.31	618.20

YEAR AND MONTH	Electrical machinery	Major electrical equipment and parts		Household appliances							Audio and video equipment
								Miscellaneous			
		Total	Electric distribution equipment	Total	Cooking equipment	Refrigerators and freezers	Laundry	Total	Electrical housewares	Appliances, not elsewhere classified	

ELECTRONIC AND ELECTRIC EQUIPMENT—INDUSTRIAL PRODUCTION (1992=100, seasonally adjusted)

YEAR AND MONTH	Electrical machinery	Total	Electric distribution equipment	Total	Cooking equipment	Refrigerators and freezers	Laundry	Total	Electrical housewares	Appliances, not elsewhere classified	Audio and video equipment
1968	25.7	84.5	92.4	53.7	43.7	64.5	70.7	48.6	66.9	45.3	41.8
1969	27.4	89.8	99.7	56.6	45.9	66.2	71.1	53.1	76.2	46.8	43.6
1970	26.2	82.5	98.8	57.2	45.0	70.6	67.0	53.1	73.7	48.1	39.0
1971	26.3	83.3	98.2	60.2	50.2	73.8	72.0	55.0	75.1	49.5	43.9
1972	30.1	91.4	106.7	70.6	60.0	86.2	82.4	65.2	91.9	54.6	49.3
1973	34.3	106.2	121.2	79.3	68.1	91.3	88.8	76.1	102.0	65.7	54.1
1974	33.9	107.2	116.3	75.6	60.0	89.2	75.7	76.1	105.3	61.8	47.6
1975	29.2	84.6	91.5	63.1	56.8	69.8	63.6	63.2	92.0	50.1	41.0
1976	32.8	91.0	95.2	70.3	73.9	63.6	68.4	73.3	105.7	59.0	44.6
1977	38.1	99.3	108.0	78.9	80.0	75.9	75.7	80.8	117.2	68.2	51.6
1978	42.2	108.4	115.5	79.1	87.8	77.1	73.7	79.0	112.4	67.4	58.2
1979	46.9	112.6	120.3	81.4	83.9	76.9	74.1	85.4	118.5	74.4	56.7
1980	48.6	105.0	115.6	77.6	88.7	66.6	67.1	82.9	125.7	66.3	57.8
1981	51.0	105.5	110.7	76.9	98.9	69.2	65.3	77.9	111.0	67.7	58.4
1982	51.7	91.8	99.4	68.2	83.2	57.5	58.0	72.2	105.4	59.2	51.8
1983	55.9	87.8	97.3	82.4	121.3	69.2	71.0	81.0	106.0	75.5	69.6
1984	66.7	100.6	106.1	90.3	119.9	83.8	75.1	90.7	107.1	87.1	83.0
1985	68.4	96.9	102.6	83.5	94.1	72.2	79.1	87.9	102.7	88.6	74.8
1986	71.0	96.6	100.9	89.9	105.3	84.6	88.3	88.4	97.7	93.9	77.9
1987	75.6	97.0	101.5	93.6	104.7	88.4	92.6	93.1	100.7	97.9	80.0
1988	82.5	105.8	114.0	96.9	111.2	96.1	94.1	94.2	100.3	94.8	86.8
1989	85.8	105.3	108.8	97.2	101.6	98.5	94.6	96.6	105.3	94.1	93.7
1990	87.7	103.6	107.0	95.3	97.2	87.1	96.1	98.0	105.0	91.7	92.8
1991	89.6	98.4	99.6	92.1	94.7	88.5	92.1	92.9	100.2	87.6	95.9
1992	100.0	100.0	100.0	100.0	100.0	100.0	100.0	100.0	100.0	100.0	100.0
1993	110.0	106.8	99.7	110.1	101.2	105.4	120.4	110.8	106.3	119.9	107.8
1994	126.3	113.0	107.7	121.7	126.7	122.1	141.6	111.1	106.0	126.1	124.5
1995	148.2	116.4	105.4	121.2	120.3	122.2	138.7	113.9	107.1	125.7	131.2
1996	163.3	114.6	105.1	127.6	120.6	127.9	148.2	122.1	109.7	135.6	123.3
1993:											
January	105.8	102.8	100.7	104.5	102.4	94.5	110.6	106.9	98.6	111.8	104.9
February	106.8	102.8	101.6	105.5	99.9	101.9	110.3	106.9	101.4	116.1	103.1
March	107.7	104.1	97.7	108.2	101.5	108.0	114.8	107.8	103.3	119.7	104.6
April	108.3	105.6	97.1	107.2	107.9	103.6	109.7	107.4	104.0	117.1	105.2
May	108.5	106.6	97.4	108.6	102.3	106.3	114.2	109.4	105.2	119.9	100.6
June	108.7	107.0	97.8	106.6	93.0	101.1	116.4	109.6	104.8	119.6	102.2
July	110.0	107.1	99.6	111.0	99.5	101.5	130.2	110.9	105.6	121.9	114.2
August	110.8	109.6	101.0	107.5	93.9	101.3	117.9	110.7	109.7	116.7	107.7
September	112.4	109.8	102.0	111.3	95.0	109.8	121.1	113.7	110.0	122.3	111.0
October	112.8	108.3	101.1	116.1	107.8	111.6	126.6	116.5	111.5	126.6	110.9
November	113.4	109.4	99.7	117.5	105.8	111.0	139.8	115.1	110.0	123.6	111.1
December	114.7	108.9	100.7	116.7	105.1	114.4	133.8	114.7	111.5	123.2	119.2
1994:											
January	116.2	107.6	103.8	119.0	133.0	103.3	135.6	113.1	102.9	129.0	116.1
February	117.9	109.9	105.2	119.4	123.9	112.4	142.3	110.8	103.3	124.6	111.9
March	120.0	111.9	109.1	120.3	117.8	120.5	145.9	110.4	106.0	121.6	118.0
April	121.9	112.9	108.8	122.6	119.6	127.0	146.3	112.0	106.6	124.5	113.2
May	123.3	112.6	109.3	121.4	127.8	125.0	135.6	111.4	105.5	123.7	128.6
June	124.9	113.9	110.7	123.1	128.5	127.2	140.8	111.7	104.3	126.3	126.3
July	127.5	114.1	110.0	127.7	130.2	129.1	160.5	112.4	105.2	128.7	132.9
August	129.1	114.1	108.7	127.4	122.2	149.7	151.3	110.2	105.2	125.9	131.6
September	130.2	114.2	108.6	123.3	132.9	128.1	142.4	109.4	106.2	125.5	128.3
October	132.7	115.2	106.7	117.6	124.1	109.8	139.9	109.0	108.3	124.3	127.0
November	134.1	115.7	105.3	114.8	125.1	108.0	124.2	109.8	109.3	125.2	128.3
December	137.4	113.3	105.7	123.4	134.9	124.8	134.7	113.7	108.7	133.5	131.7
1995:											
January	138.8	113.1	102.0	122.6	127.6	119.6	144.1	113.0	111.1	126.7	136.8
February	140.0	113.4	105.8	121.9	128.5	120.9	139.4	112.5	109.7	123.9	133.2
March	142.3	116.8	106.7	119.2	123.7	114.9	135.6	112.5	109.2	123.3	138.2
April	143.2	115.4	103.5	118.7	127.1	113.5	133.5	111.5	107.3	122.2	120.7
May	144.7	118.1	105.0	119.5	120.6	118.5	139.3	111.4	108.5	121.0	127.1
June	146.4	118.8	105.1	110.2	100.3	114.4	121.1	108.1	105.0	114.3	136.5
July	148.9	117.0	105.3	123.5	137.7	118.7	138.7	113.1	101.9	127.5	123.0
August	151.6	119.1	106.2	124.4	119.9	144.6	134.1	113.6	103.6	125.7	130.1
September	153.7	117.1	105.6	120.9	114.6	121.2	140.5	115.3	106.6	126.2	133.2
October	155.8	116.3	107.1	121.9	108.8	127.0	141.3	117.2	108.6	128.9	133.2
November	156.6	117.1	106.2	124.7	114.0	129.1	146.3	118.3	106.0	133.1	139.4
December	155.8	115.0	106.2	126.5	120.0	124.3	150.8	120.0	107.8	136.2	123.0
1996:											
January	155.8	116.6	106.2	117.4	88.6	127.7	139.3	116.3	105.4	128.4	119.9
February	161.0	117.9	108.2	121.0	104.9	126.2	138.1	118.7	110.6	129.4	128.1
March	160.3	117.0	105.7	126.5	127.5	127.5	133.7	123.1	109.4	139.1	115.3
April	161.1	117.4	106.6	124.1	112.0	126.3	141.8	121.0	106.6	133.7	135.1
May	161.8	115.7	104.8	126.4	115.5	125.4	140.8	125.9	110.8	142.1	132.8
June	164.0	114.0	103.4	135.3	136.2	134.6	155.5	127.1	114.6	143.8	131.7
July	163.8	113.1	105.6	134.9	129.0	121.9	182.3	123.0	117.2	134.7	130.8
August	164.6	112.7	103.4	136.3	136.5	154.9	156.8	119.7	116.6	128.8	111.6
September	165.2	113.3	104.2	129.6	132.9	117.7	153.9	123.3	111.3	141.7	110.7
October	165.6	111.8	104.3	123.7	111.5	116.3	147.8	122.5	107.4	136.0	131.6
November	167.2	113.2	104.6	126.8	122.3	129.0	142.2	121.8	104.9	134.4	123.7
December	168.8	112.0	104.8	128.9	130.0	127.5	145.7	122.4	101.9	135.6	108.7

ELECTRONIC AND ELECTRIC EQUIPMENT— PRODUCTION, CAPACITY, SHIPMENTS, INVENTORIES, AND ORDERS

YEAR AND MONTH	Industrial production—Continued (1992=100, seasonally adjusted)				Capacity utilization—Electrical machinery (Percent of capacity, seasonally adjusted)	Manufacturers' shipments, inventories, and orders (Millions of dollars, seasonally adjusted)			
	Commu- nications equip- ment	Electronic compo- nents	Miscellaneous electrical supplies			Ship- ments	Inven- tories (Book value, end of period)	New orders (Net)	Unfilled orders (End of period)
			Total	Storage batteries					
1968	33.6	3.9	43.8	44.3	86.4	39 372	7 297	39 182	11 296
1969	33.9	4.5	45.9	48.2	85.3	41 560	8 072	42 438	12 171
1970	31.8	4.4	47.0	51.4	76.6	41 408	8 410	41 117	11 881
1971	29.0	4.7	48.9	52.2	73.5	42 377	8 058	42 639	12 148
1972	31.8	5.9	53.8	60.5	81.1	47 502	8 528	48 702	13 376
1973	34.6	7.4	60.6	65.7	88.0	54 569	10 532	58 275	17 111
1974	35.7	7.3	60.5	66.9	81.9	58 684	12 231	58 884	17 319
1975	34.8	6.0	54.7	64.4	67.0	56 068	11 110	54 610	15 857
1976	34.8	7.8	64.6	75.8	72.8	65 151	12 594	66 864	17 584
1977	38.9	9.9	78.6	86.2	80.1	77 845	13 922	80 010	19 999
1978	43.8	12.0	82.2	91.0	83.9	88 679	16 163	92 781	24 219
1979	51.2	15.3	80.9	89.4	87.7	102 361	19 566	107 314	29 261
1980	56.8	18.1	71.3	78.5	84.0	112 864	21 838	115 335	31 751
1981	57.9	21.5	74.4	80.1	81.2	122 084	23 608	123 053	32 718
1982	60.7	25.6	74.1	76.0	76.7	125 728	25 100	127 630	34 639
1983	62.1	29.8	80.9	86.0	77.8	136 138	26 922	142 131	40 794
1984	70.4	40.6	99.3	101.1	85.8	162 362	31 636	165 541	43 967
1985	78.1	41.2	95.8	97.9	80.5	163 951	30 549	163 352	43 366
1986	80.5	44.2	96.9	103.9	77.8	164 811	28 632	164 282	42 793
1987	82.9	51.9	101.4	107.8	78.7	171 287	29 859	173 210	44 741
1988	90.0	58.5	109.3	105.8	82.3	187 301	31 645	189 211	46 702
1989	91.4	65.2	108.1	104.8	81.3	194 598	33 623	192 482	44 616
1990	94.7	72.1	97.3	105.4	78.9	195 898	32 913	195 748	44 501
1991	90.6	80.9	102.5	98.7	76.4	199 278	30 981	197 659	42 988
1992	100.0	100.0	100.0	100.0	80.5	216 764	30 731	217 966	44 337
1993	104.2	117.8	108.0	110.7	82.5	233 622	31 874	233 991	44 776
1994	109.5	151.3	116.0	122.4	85.8	266 405	35 855	266 386	44 965
1995	119.0	208.0	119.2	116.8	87.8	299 838	39 259	305 736	51 226
1996	121.0	252.4	126.9	117.8	82.9	323 001	39 450	321 390	49 565
1993:									
January	104.0	110.6	100.9	99.1	82.3	18 190	30 742	18 438	44 585
February	104.9	111.8	104.3	108.3	82.5	18 827	30 875	18 525	44 283
March	104.0	112.8	107.0	122.9	82.7	18 989	31 063	18 193	43 487
April	104.0	114.6	106.2	114.6	82.6	18 920	31 265	18 623	43 190
May	103.4	116.1	107.0	114.5	82.2	19 029	31 546	18 579	42 740
June	103.9	116.4	106.5	105.7	81.8	19 607	31 458	19 889	43 022
July	104.5	116.8	109.3	110.4	82.2	19 426	31 620	20 005	43 601
August	104.5	118.7	110.6	115.9	82.3	19 695	31 667	19 846	43 752
September	104.9	121.4	110.5	111.2	82.9	19 953	31 544	20 766	44 565
October	104.1	122.9	111.4	114.5	82.7	19 862	31 687	20 465	45 168
November	104.1	124.4	111.3	111.0	82.5	20 206	31 921	20 092	45 054
December	104.4	126.8	110.6	100.1	82.9	20 274	31 874	19 996	44 776
1994:									
January	104.0	130.7	116.9	145.0	83.3	21 001	32 184	21 282	45 057
February	104.4	133.4	116.9	144.0	83.7	21 170	32 433	21 254	45 141
March	106.4	137.8	115.5	123.7	84.4	21 176	32 666	21 169	45 134
April	107.3	141.7	115.0	116.7	84.9	21 851	32 974	22 552	45 835
May	108.4	144.3	114.9	113.9	85.1	21 823	33 403	21 660	45 672
June	108.1	148.0	113.4	112.4	85.4	22 148	33 679	21 804	45 328
July	108.2	152.3	116.8	122.7	86.4	22 431	34 072	21 186	44 083
August	110.5	156.2	114.5	110.6	86.6	22 687	34 376	21 993	43 389
September	110.6	160.2	116.1	119.8	86.5	22 450	34 694	22 924	43 863
October	113.1	165.8	117.3	122.4	87.3	22 823	35 054	21 816	42 856
November	115.3	169.8	115.9	117.2	87.4	23 316	35 404	24 255	43 795
December	117.6	175.1	118.4	120.5	88.6	23 117	35 855	24 287	44 965
1995:									
January	116.6	181.0	119.8	120.1	88.5	23 825	36 361	24 529	45 669
February	114.7	185.6	119.4	110.8	88.1	23 456	36 967	24 025	46 238
March	117.1	190.4	117.4	105.7	88.4	23 997	37 190	25 673	47 914
April	117.4	194.8	120.5	119.1	87.8	23 770	37 355	24 725	48 869
May	117.3	199.2	116.3	112.3	87.6	24 341	37 489	25 604	50 132
June	118.5	203.4	117.2	117.7	87.4	25 095	37 739	24 943	49 980
July	119.1	211.7	116.4	113.0	87.8	24 697	38 354	26 369	51 652
August	121.3	215.7	117.4	115.1	88.2	25 877	38 562	25 615	51 390
September	122.3	222.3	120.9	129.0	88.3	25 998	38 871	26 345	51 737
October	124.6	227.7	119.9	112.5	88.3	25 745	39 402	26 656	52 648
November	120.2	231.6	121.3	116.3	87.6	25 991	38 871	24 922	51 579
December	119.4	232.0	123.9	130.2	85.9	26 302	39 259	25 949	51 226
1996:									
January	119.8	233.8	119.3	111.4	84.8	25 885	39 646	26 058	51 399
February	122.9	241.8	127.0	127.4	86.5	25 997	39 307	25 019	50 421
March	122.4	241.7	126.8	129.7	85.1	26 559	38 962	26 706	50 568
April	122.0	244.2	124.5	106.7	84.5	26 422	39 276	26 031	50 177
May	120.2	247.4	127.0	122.2	83.8	26 574	39 152	25 853	49 456
June	122.5	250.9	130.4	133.0	83.9	26 933	39 342	26 567	49 090
July	121.6	252.8	127.0	111.5	82.7	26 655	39 245	27 930	50 365
August	120.2	256.9	128.7	116.6	82.0	26 663	39 341	26 712	50 414
September	120.8	259.0	128.7	117.0	81.3	27 176	39 389	26 556	49 794
October	120.5	260.8	126.7	108.8	80.5	27 494	39 454	30 901	53 201
November	118.9	266.5	128.3	119.1	80.2	28 273	39 760	28 307	53 235
December	120.1	273.3	127.9	109.8	80.0	27 756	39 450	24 086	49 565

ELECTRONIC AND ELECTRIC EQUIPMENT—PRICES, EMPLOYMENT, HOURS, AND EARNINGS

| YEAR AND MONTH | Producer prices (1982=100, except as noted, not seasonally adjusted) | | | | Employment (Thousands, seasonally adjusted) | | Production workers | | | |
| | Electrical and electronic machinery, equipment, and supplies [1] | Finished goods: Communications and related equipment (December 1985=100) | Intermediate materials | | | | Weekly hours worked (Seasonally adjusted) | | Average earnings (Dollars, not seasonally adjusted) | |
			Switchgear, switchboard, etc.	Electronic components and accessories	Total payroll employees	Production workers	Average hours	Aggregate hours index (1982=100)	Hourly	Weekly
1968	.....	.....	38.4	56.3	1 629	.....	.....	.....	.....	.....
1969	.....	.....	38.4	57.2	1 664	.....	.....	.....	.....	.....
1970	.....	.....	40.5	57.4	1 584	.....	.....	.....	.....	.....
1971	.....	.....	42.3	58.2	1 477	.....	.....	.....	.....	.....
1972	.....	.....	42.2	58.7	1 535	.....	.....	.....	.....	.....
1973	.....	.....	42.9	59.3	1 667	.....	.....	.....	.....	.....
1974	.....	.....	50.3	63.3	1 666	.....	.....	.....	.....	.....
1975	.....	.....	58.6	65.6	1 442	.....	.....	.....	.....	.....
1976	.....	.....	61.9	65.8	1 503	.....	.....	.....	.....	.....
1977	.....	.....	65.9	67.9	1 591	.....	.....	.....	.....	.....
1978	.....	.....	69.8	72.1	1 699	.....	.....	.....	.....	.....
1979	.....	.....	75.8	77.1	1 793	.....	.....	.....	.....	.....
1980	.....	.....	88.4	88.8	1 771	.....	.....	.....	.....	.....
1981	.....	.....	95.1	95.5	1 774	.....	.....	.....	.....	.....
1982	.....	.....	100.0	100.0	1 701	.....	.....	.....	.....	.....
1983	.....	.....	103.3	104.3	1 704	.....	.....	.....	.....	.....
1984	.....	.....	105.0	109.8	1 869	.....	.....	.....	.....	.....
1985	.....	.....	106.7	112.4	1 859	.....	.....	.....	.....	.....
1986	102.1	101.2	108.1	114.5	1 790	.....	.....	.....	.....	.....
1987	103.3	102.5	110.1	115.0	1 750	.....	.....	.....	.....	.....
1988	104.6	102.8	113.2	117.5	1 764	1 112	41.0	113.1	9.79	401.39
1989	107.1	104.7	119.0	119.4	1 744	1 102	40.8	111.5	10.05	410.04
1990	108.9	106.1	124.4	118.4	1 673	1 055	40.8	106.5	10.30	420.24
1991	110.1	107.4	128.5	118.6	1 591	999	40.7	100.7	10.70	435.49
1992	110.8	107.9	131.5	117.5	1 528	971	41.2	99.1	11.00	453.20
1993	112.0	109.1	134.6	117.7	1 526	975	41.8	100.9	11.24	469.83
1994	112.7	110.8	136.8	116.6	1 571	1 010	42.2	105.7	11.50	485.30
1995	113.3	112.1	140.3	113.6	1 625	1 045	41.6	107.8	11.69	486.30
1996	113.2	113.0	142.6	108.9	1 651	1 051	41.5	108.0	12.18	505.47
1993:										
January	111.4	108.8	133.9	117.2	1 523	969	41.7	100.1	11.14	464.54
February	111.8	108.6	134.5	117.8	1 525	973	41.8	100.8	11.10	461.76
March	111.8	108.7	134.5	117.8	1 526	975	41.5	100.3	11.12	460.37
April	111.9	109.0	134.5	118.3	1 525	974	42.0	101.4	11.15	460.50
May	111.8	109.0	134.7	118.0	1 522	972	41.7	100.4	11.18	465.09
June	111.9	108.9	134.6	118.0	1 521	972	41.4	99.7	11.25	466.88
July	111.9	109.1	134.6	117.7	1 521	970	41.7	100.2	11.25	462.38
August	112.0	109.2	134.6	117.7	1 522	970	41.8	100.5	11.26	469.54
September	112.1	109.3	134.8	117.6	1 525	974	41.9	101.1	11.31	471.63
October	112.2	109.8	134.7	117.4	1 529	978	41.9	101.5	11.28	474.89
November	112.3	109.6	134.7	117.6	1 533	981	41.9	101.8	11.36	482.80
December	112.4	109.7	135.4	117.2	1 536	983	41.9	102.0	11.51	494.93
1994:										
January	112.5	110.0	135.1	117.4	1 538	984	42.1	102.6	11.40	479.94
February	112.6	110.1	136.4	117.5	1 544	988	41.6	101.8	11.44	473.62
March	112.8	110.2	136.4	117.6	1 551	994	42.3	104.2	11.45	484.34
April	112.8	110.9	137.0	117.4	1 559	1 002	42.2	104.8	11.45	484.34
May	112.9	111.0	137.1	117.4	1 561	1 002	42.2	104.8	11.48	483.31
June	112.7	111.1	136.5	117.5	1 569	1 009	42.2	105.5	11.52	487.30
July	112.8	111.1	136.4	117.4	1 572	1 009	42.3	105.7	11.56	479.74
August	112.7	110.8	137.1	116.5	1 581	1 019	42.1	106.3	11.52	483.84
September	112.6	110.8	137.1	115.9	1 586	1 025	41.7	105.9	11.57	488.25
October	112.6	110.7	137.0	115.2	1 588	1 024	42.1	106.8	11.51	486.87
November	112.6	111.1	137.4	115.1	1 595	1 032	42.0	107.4	11.53	491.18
December	112.7	111.2	138.1	114.8	1 601	1 037	42.0	107.9	11.59	500.69
1995:										
January	113.1	111.9	139.4	114.6	1 608	1 042	42.3	109.2	11.58	488.68
February	113.3	112.1	139.5	115.0	1 610	1 044	41.5	107.3	11.53	478.50
March	113.1	112.1	140.3	114.3	1 613	1 044	41.6	107.6	11.54	480.06
April	113.3	112.2	140.3	114.4	1 617	1 043	41.5	107.2	11.52	463.10
May	113.3	112.1	139.6	114.0	1 621	1 043	41.5	107.2	11.56	477.43
June	113.2	111.9	139.7	113.7	1 622	1 041	41.4	106.8	11.63	482.65
July	113.2	111.8	140.4	113.1	1 625	1 043	41.4	107.0	11.74	476.64
August	113.1	111.9	139.9	112.9	1 625	1 043	41.6	107.5	11.76	488.04
September	113.2	112.3	140.7	112.9	1 633	1 045	41.7	108.0	11.81	498.38
October	113.3	112.3	140.5	112.9	1 637	1 048	42.0	109.1	11.79	497.54
November	113.5	112.3	141.7	113.1	1 641	1 050	41.7	108.5	11.83	500.41
December	113.5	112.2	141.2	112.9	1 645	1 053	41.1	107.2	11.93	504.64
1996:										
January	113.8	112.9	142.0	112.5	1 648	1 053	40.4	105.4	11.95	482.78
February	113.9	113.1	142.0	112.2	1 653	1 055	41.5	108.5	11.88	494.21
March	113.5	113.0	142.3	110.8	1 652	1 054	41.4	108.1	11.91	494.27
April	113.3	113.0	141.7	109.4	1 652	1 053	41.2	107.5	12.01	490.01
May	113.1	112.7	142.1	108.5	1 653	1 054	41.4	108.1	12.09	496.90
June	113.0	112.6	142.6	107.9	1 653	1 052	41.6	108.4	12.19	507.10
July	113.0	112.9	142.1	108.0	1 655	1 054	41.3	107.8	12.26	497.76
August	113.1	113.1	142.7	108.0	1 654	1 052	41.6	108.4	12.28	510.85
September	113.0	113.1	142.6	108.1	1 652	1 049	41.6	108.1	12.35	518.70
October	112.7	113.2	142.7	107.3	1 650	1 046	41.5	107.5	12.33	514.16
November	112.8	113.0	144.8	107.3	1 649	1 045	41.5	107.4	12.36	520.36
December	112.7	113.9	144.0	107.2	1 647	1 043	41.8	108.0	12.54	537.97

1. December 1984=100.

TRANSPORTATION EQUIPMENT—INDUSTRIAL PRODUCTION
(1992=100, seasonally adjusted)

YEAR AND MONTH	Total	Motor vehicles and parts								Aerospace and miscellaneous transportation equipment			
		Total	Autos	Trucks and truck trailers				Motor vehicle parts	Motor homes	Total	Aircraft and parts	Ships and boats	Railroad and miscellaneous
				Total	Trucks and buses								
					Total	Consumer trucks	Business vehicles						
1968	64.8	64.2	84.0	28.2	27.4	13.5	59.3	73.6	....	72.4	70.2	95.5	47.7
1969	64.4	64.7	81.8	30.2	28.6	15.2	60.0	75.2	....	70.7	65.7	96.7	58.9
1970	54.1	52.0	63.4	25.0	24.1	14.2	48.0	61.8	....	62.3	57.1	90.5	53.2
1971	58.5	65.2	86.9	30.5	30.3	20.0	57.1	71.8	....	55.9	47.9	88.3	59.8
1972	62.4	71.1	90.5	36.2	34.9	25.8	61.2	79.6	....	57.7	47.6	102.3	65.2
1973	71.1	82.8	100.5	45.2	44.0	33.6	72.1	92.9	....	63.8	52.7	115.0	71.4
1974	64.6	71.4	78.4	42.8	40.8	31.5	65.5	82.9	....	62.0	51.2	116.2	68.0
1975	58.2	61.0	74.6	35.3	35.8	28.5	52.8	65.8	....	59.3	48.1	120.9	65.0
1976	66.3	80.0	96.4	47.9	48.6	40.1	65.0	86.1	....	56.6	43.9	124.6	63.6
1977	71.9	92.4	107.3	59.5	59.2	50.1	73.2	98.3	....	55.6	45.0	127.4	58.3
1978	77.5	96.8	108.0	65.2	64.2	55.7	76.4	103.7	....	62.2	52.8	131.4	62.6
1979	78.7	89.0	102.8	57.0	54.8	45.8	66.6	95.1	....	71.1	64.2	129.8	68.6
1980	70.3	65.8	82.5	33.6	31.5	24.6	42.3	72.3	....	74.3	69.7	135.8	65.9
1981	66.9	62.8	82.7	34.5	32.8	26.8	41.6	65.1	....	70.5	65.1	142.8	61.4
1982	63.0	56.9	68.8	37.9	37.3	34.0	42.3	58.7	....	68.3	61.9	131.0	63.6
1983	70.5	72.1	95.2	48.9	48.3	45.9	52.4	69.3	....	69.3	63.7	109.6	68.9
1984	80.5	87.3	111.7	67.0	64.5	60.8	70.6	81.3	....	75.1	66.7	113.6	81.0
1985	88.8	95.0	120.8	75.1	73.6	68.2	82.2	87.9	....	83.7	73.8	109.1	96.9
1986	94.1	94.2	118.9	77.3	76.5	71.0	85.2	85.9	....	94.2	86.4	103.9	107.7
1987	96.1	94.9	111.0	86.2	85.2	80.1	92.9	87.1	115.1	97.5	92.9	107.3	104.2
1988	101.1	100.2	113.7	93.3	92.5	86.7	100.9	92.9	123.1	102.1	95.7	111.2	113.0
1989	105.1	101.2	115.6	96.4	95.7	91.9	100.4	91.9	108.9	109.4	103.9	112.9	120.1
1990	102.3	95.3	106.1	90.9	90.9	87.7	94.6	88.9	88.6	109.8	105.1	113.0	119.0
1991	96.5	88.5	95.7	83.5	83.6	84.2	83.9	85.8	80.5	105.0	105.4	101.3	105.7
1992	100.0	100.0	100.0	100.0	100.0	100.0	100.0	100.0	100.0	100.0	100.0	100.0	100.0
1993	103.7	113.7	105.9	122.6	123.0	120.4	126.9	114.3	107.3	93.6	90.6	94.9	99.7
1994	107.4	129.7	117.5	139.8	139.7	138.5	140.1	133.3	112.1	85.6	80.2	94.0	94.7
1995	105.0	128.5	114.9	143.1	141.9	141.7	142.5	130.8	102.8	82.1	75.0	90.9	95.4
1996	106.1	127.1	111.1	141.9	143.1	149.9	137.2	130.6	108.8	85.6	83.0	88.2	89.7
1993:													
January	104.6	111.1	109.1	122.3	122.6	120.6	125.9	105.1	111.6	98.1	96.7	98.0	101.0
February	104.6	111.7	105.6	118.9	119.2	117.0	122.8	112.0	106.7	97.4	95.1	98.0	102.0
March	104.5	112.7	106.0	120.9	121.1	119.5	123.9	113.1	95.7	96.3	93.8	94.5	102.3
April	105.1	114.0	107.9	117.3	117.5	115.8	120.4	116.7	110.1	96.0	93.0	95.4	103.1
May	103.8	112.3	108.4	118.6	118.5	116.8	121.2	111.4	103.6	95.2	91.8	95.2	102.8
June	103.2	113.1	104.2	118.5	118.9	114.9	125.1	116.9	103.0	93.2	89.8	93.3	100.7
July	99.1	105.4	100.8	109.5	109.4	108.4	111.1	106.3	106.5	92.5	89.6	95.6	97.8
August	97.5	102.5	93.6	117.0	117.1	113.4	122.5	100.2	109.6	92.1	88.9	94.9	98.1
September	101.1	111.0	97.1	123.3	123.6	119.2	130.0	114.3	107.0	91.2	88.0	93.5	97.2
October	105.9	120.4	107.4	132.7	133.4	129.7	138.6	123.1	115.4	91.5	88.4	93.4	97.5
November	106.9	123.6	115.2	135.6	136.7	133.3	141.3	123.1	109.5	90.5	86.9	93.4	97.2
December	108.0	126.9	115.9	136.7	138.0	136.3	139.8	129.8	108.8	89.4	85.4	93.7	96.6
1994:													
January	107.4	127.4	121.1	138.5	138.4	138.6	137.5	126.0	108.6	87.8	83.5	93.1	95.5
February	107.9	130.3	124.4	143.0	142.8	143.6	140.8	127.5	110.6	86.1	81.3	92.6	94.5
March	105.6	125.6	119.1	137.1	137.1	137.5	135.6	123.9	110.0	86.1	81.0	94.9	94.3
April	106.1	126.4	119.8	137.2	137.1	137.1	135.9	125.2	112.3	86.3	80.6	95.5	95.7
May	106.6	127.3	116.1	134.8	135.2	133.2	136.7	131.6	113.2	86.4	80.8	96.2	95.7
June	106.5	127.6	115.1	137.3	137.3	135.0	139.1	131.3	118.9	86.0	80.3	94.7	95.8
July	107.3	130.5	109.3	130.9	130.0	130.9	127.3	146.4	114.1	84.7	79.1	95.6	93.2
August	108.8	133.9	114.0	146.1	146.5	145.5	146.2	142.3	106.0	84.5	78.8	93.5	94.2
September	107.5	131.7	113.0	143.1	143.2	140.4	145.7	139.3	115.7	83.9	77.7	93.0	94.8
October	106.9	129.4	118.2	143.6	143.4	139.1	148.1	129.5	119.0	85.0	79.9	92.0	93.8
November	108.5	132.5	117.0	145.4	145.3	141.9	148.7	137.1	106.6	85.1	79.7	93.4	94.3
December	109.3	134.2	122.4	140.4	139.9	139.4	139.4	140.0	109.9	85.0	79.3	93.8	95.0
1995:													
January	110.0	136.0	127.0	144.6	143.7	141.1	146.1	138.4	110.7	84.6	77.9	93.9	96.8
February	108.4	132.7	125.2	146.0	145.0	142.4	147.7	131.1	107.0	84.7	77.9	92.3	97.7
March	107.6	131.1	124.0	145.4	143.5	141.8	145.1	128.7	105.6	84.7	77.3	91.8	99.3
April	105.7	127.0	117.5	142.6	140.9	140.4	141.2	125.7	98.0	84.8	78.0	90.5	98.6
May	104.7	125.6	110.4	141.9	140.7	138.8	143.1	128.0	96.3	84.3	77.8	90.3	97.1
June	105.0	126.2	108.8	146.2	145.2	144.0	146.7	128.2	94.3	84.2	77.9	89.9	96.7
July	103.1	123.5	109.2	133.0	131.1	126.7	137.5	129.1	96.8	83.2	76.6	90.9	95.7
August	104.6	126.3	109.4	146.4	145.9	146.6	145.5	127.7	101.6	83.5	77.6	91.4	94.2
September	105.7	129.5	112.8	147.1	146.1	145.8	147.6	132.5	100.5	82.6	76.4	92.4	93.3
October	101.8	127.7	111.9	140.1	139.5	141.8	137.5	132.8	95.9	76.9	68.2	90.7	92.7
November	100.9	127.8	111.4	140.5	139.5	143.6	135.3	132.9	112.0	74.9	65.8	88.8	91.7
December	102.0	128.7	110.6	143.2	142.1	147.6	136.2	133.9	114.5	76.2	68.1	88.4	91.1
1996:													
January	103.3	127.6	105.0	138.7	139.4	142.3	137.5	138.3	106.1	79.7	74.3	86.2	89.9
February	104.4	127.4	110.6	143.3	144.4	150.3	138.8	131.1	106.3	81.9	77.5	86.9	89.9
March	94.9	106.8	84.9	128.8	129.6	135.4	124.1	109.6	121.1	82.8	78.6	89.1	89.9
April	106.4	130.3	114.1	143.1	144.9	150.3	140.5	135.1	107.0	83.2	79.4	89.4	89.1
May	106.8	130.5	116.9	139.5	140.9	147.4	135.2	135.4	113.1	83.8	80.5	89.5	88.7
June	107.1	130.4	120.7	141.6	142.2	148.7	136.7	131.3	114.8	84.3	81.2	90.6	88.3
July	109.5	134.1	124.7	151.2	153.0	161.3	145.9	132.3	88.7	85.7	82.9	89.7	90.1
August	109.3	132.8	119.9	143.8	144.6	152.3	138.0	136.7	95.3	86.5	83.9	89.0	90.7
September	107.3	127.0	117.5	138.4	139.1	146.6	132.9	127.3	120.6	87.9	86.2	88.1	90.6
October	105.3	121.2	101.6	139.3	141.0	147.4	136.4	125.3	111.5	89.4	89.1	86.7	89.9
November	109.5	128.9	111.7	143.1	144.3	152.4	137.6	133.2	120.2	90.3	90.7	87.7	88.6
December	109.6	127.9	104.8	151.9	153.7	164.9	143.0	131.8	101.2	91.5	92.0	85.9	90.6

TRANSPORTATION EQUIPMENT—CAPACITY, SHIPMENTS, INVENTORIES AND ORDERS

YEAR AND MONTH	Capacity utilization (Percent of capacity, seasonally adjusted)				Manufacturers' shipments, inventories and orders (Millions of dollars, seasonally adjusted)							
	Total	Motor vehicles and parts		Aero-space and miscellane-ous	Shipments		Inventories (Book value, end of period)		New orders (Net)		Unfilled orders (End of period)	
		Total	Autos and light trucks		Total	Motor vehicles and parts	Total	Motor vehicles and parts	Total	Aircraft, missiles, and parts	Total	Aircraft, missiles, and parts
1968	89.6	90.2	....	90.5	83 527	49 465	14 413	3 879	85 893	28 195	43 023	35 362
1969	86.4	86.9	....	87.3	85 175	50 943	15 942	4 067	83 945	24 704	41 812	33 233
1970	70.5	66.6	....	76.7	74 539	42 538	14 648	4 178	67 380	17 417	34 720	26 198
1971	74.2	79.5	....	68.7	88 857	58 247	13 799	4 173	89 900	22 459	35 793	26 259
1972	76.8	82.5	....	70.6	94 706	63 923	14 775	4 670	96 501	20 963	37 627	26 151
1973	84.7	91.6	....	77.3	110 587	74 799	16 458	5 708	118 194	26 669	45 248	27 842
1974	75.0	76.4	....	73.9	108 244	68 631	19 197	6 688	114 081	29 934	51 118	30 506
1975	65.8	63.1	....	69.6	113 503	70 033	19 620	6 101	109 050	26 869	46 633	28 244
1976	72.7	80.2	....	65.3	141 028	95 380	20 886	7 814	143 502	31 851	49 078	29 421
1977	76.4	90.3	89.8	63.2	166 954	117 747	22 423	9 078	175 446	40 625	57 101	37 325
1978	80.7	91.0	88.3	70.2	188 773	131 999	26 170	10 357	213 539	54 600	81 782	54 417
1979	80.2	82.0	78.3	78.4	201 623	131 378	31 638	10 978	223 226	67 818	103 555	74 034
1980	70.9	61.3	57.8	79.1	186 516	104 560	35 900	9 864	202 584	72 514	119 700	88 051
1981	66.1	59.3	60.3	72.2	205 223	116 981	37 527	9 047	203 482	63 530	118 008	86 794
1982	60.9	52.8	53.5	67.8	201 347	112 270	43 005	8 534	209 325	73 365	125 879	93 703
1983	66.7	66.2	71.9	67.2	245 392	148 296	43 791	10 433	261 359	86 952	141 637	105 504
1984	74.1	79.0	81.6	70.0	284 593	181 993	50 770	11 680	295 202	91 620	152 189	117 923
1985	77.9	83.1	81.5	73.8	307 380	193 445	52 634	11 809	311 482	100 889	156 155	127 282
1986	78.6	78.7	76.7	78.5	322 688	198 811	53 363	11 445	327 541	107 993	161 145	133 565
1987	77.5	76.8	74.7	78.1	332 936	205 923	56 461	11 937	348 224	114 835	176 588	144 987
1988	80.6	81.2	79.2	80.0	354 849	222 353	63 202	12 310	389 635	137 443	211 575	174 721
1989	81.8	79.5	79.8	84.4	369 675	233 232	70 968	12 503	411 434	153 430	253 517	217 557
1990	77.7	71.6	71.1	84.0	370 328	217 295	77 640	13 504	395 737	150 329	279 082	242 208
1991	71.7	64.0	64.4	80.8	367 235	209 210	73 019	13 163	363 366	132 645	275 260	242 798
1992	73.2	69.9	70.7	77.0	399 270	238 384	63 310	13 065	377 147	110 830	253 260	222 389
1993	75.3	77.3	78.3	72.9	414 694	267 365	60 964	14 066	386 643	88 070	225 499	194 405
1994	76.3	83.5	86.1	68.0	450 809	314 637	61 332	15 615	440 817	90 217	215 517	181 307
1995	72.4	76.9	80.4	66.8	462 849	326 415	58 346	16 101	472 332	114 099	225 008	192 800
1996	71.8	72.4	77.6	71.1	471 661	334 633	62 723	16 493	502 861	134 097	256 231	223 121
1993:												
January	76.1	76.5	79.6	75.6	34 386	21 714	62 487	12 960	31 426	6 293	250 300	218 472
February	76.1	76.8	77.1	75.2	35 024	22 186	63 018	13 178	34 637	10 042	249 913	218 427
March	76.0	77.3	78.0	74.5	35 587	22 751	63 024	13 319	31 896	7 047	246 222	215 245
April	76.4	78.0	77.8	74.5	34 929	22 171	62 727	13 430	32 178	8 110	243 471	213 107
May	75.4	76.7	78.3	74.0	34 260	21 371	62 577	13 413	31 270	7 931	240 481	210 564
June	75.0	77.1	76.0	72.6	35 001	22 090	62 721	13 581	34 419	9 883	239 899	210 021
July	71.9	71.7	72.8	72.2	31 680	20 711	62 350	13 180	30 342	6 469	238 561	208 004
August	70.7	69.5	71.0	72.0	33 021	20 610	61 648	13 763	30 701	7 793	236 241	205 750
September	73.3	75.1	74.1	71.3	33 550	21 929	62 001	13 799	29 604	4 715	232 295	201 498
October	76.7	81.2	81.5	71.7	35 549	23 248	61 373	13 919	32 486	6 385	229 232	198 231
November	77.4	83.1	86.0	71.0	35 366	23 897	61 983	13 952	33 973	8 023	227 839	197 704
December	78.0	85.0	87.2	70.2	36 299	24 444	60 964	14 066	33 959	5 824	225 499	194 405
1994:												
January	77.5	85.0	89.9	69.1	37 146	25 258	61 085	14 120	39 835	12 308	228 188	197 314
February	77.7	86.3	92.4	67.9	36 419	25 341	60 851	14 253	34 809	7 149	226 578	196 103
March	75.8	82.7	88.1	68.0	37 870	25 588	60 093	14 224	34 714	5 599	223 422	192 029
April	76.0	82.7	87.9	68.3	36 524	25 377	60 223	14 201	34 271	6 298	221 169	189 943
May	76.1	82.8	84.9	68.5	36 460	25 579	60 713	14 618	35 458	7 849	220 167	189 651
June	75.9	82.4	84.5	68.3	37 971	26 225	60 517	14 784	36 829	8 250	219 025	189 278
July	76.2	83.8	80.6	67.4	36 439	25 620	60 928	15 023	34 727	5 780	217 313	186 778
August	77.1	85.4	85.8	67.3	39 132	27 678	60 926	14 943	36 906	6 869	215 087	184 926
September	75.9	83.4	83.6	67.0	37 889	26 560	60 529	15 133	37 452	7 400	214 650	183 836
October	75.3	81.4	85.0	67.9	36 856	25 814	60 515	15 069	35 839	6 731	213 633	182 262
November	76.2	82.8	84.6	68.2	39 203	27 554	60 572	15 303	38 230	8 815	212 660	182 214
December	76.5	83.4	85.7	68.3	39 356	28 490	61 332	15 615	42 213	7 245	215 517	181 307
1995:												
January	76.8	84.0	87.5	68.1	39 375	27 602	60 568	15 712	38 850	7 446	214 992	179 983
February	75.5	81.5	86.7	68.3	39 108	27 583	59 887	15 771	40 204	9 975	216 088	181 164
March	74.8	80.1	85.6	68.4	40 077	28 578	60 102	15 904	39 194	7 966	215 205	180 631
April	73.3	77.1	82.2	68.7	37 921	26 206	60 025	16 028	35 824	7 287	213 108	178 947
May	72.5	75.8	78.4	68.4	37 414	25 978	60 369	16 247	37 989	9 698	213 683	180 142
June	72.5	75.7	78.6	68.5	38 462	26 570	59 337	16 173	36 013	6 357	211 234	177 690
July	71.1	73.7	74.4	67.8	36 398	25 314	59 403	16 256	35 454	8 054	210 290	177 365
August	72.0	74.9	78.7	68.2	37 968	27 105	59 031	16 062	38 623	9 221	210 945	178 388
September	72.5	76.4	79.4	67.6	39 229	28 003	59 018	15 903	43 877	12 736	215 593	182 630
October	69.7	74.9	77.8	63.1	38 700	27 987	59 123	16 030	39 485	9 537	216 378	183 990
November	68.9	74.5	77.6	61.6	38 803	27 263	58 473	16 076	40 318	10 498	217 893	185 780
December	69.5	74.6	77.8	62.8	38 986	27 782	58 346	16 101	46 101	15 213	225 008	192 800
1996:												
January	70.3	73.6	74.1	65.8	37 098	26 991	59 174	16 440	44 307	13 592	232 217	198 963
February	70.9	73.4	78.0	67.7	38 096	27 418	59 472	16 279	38 387	8 785	232 508	199 876
March	64.4	61.3	64.3	68.5	35 873	24 721	60 187	16 749	42 684	15 658	239 319	207 316
April	72.2	74.7	79.3	68.9	39 249	28 262	60 198	16 625	37 999	7 644	238 069	206 696
May	72.4	74.6	79.5	69.5	40 870	28 755	60 312	16 534	43 213	12 251	240 412	209 555
June	72.5	74.4	81.2	70.0	39 428	28 104	60 919	16 387	42 598	9 931	243 582	211 159
July	74.1	76.3	85.5	71.3	40 203	29 480	61 425	16 745	42 196	10 293	245 575	213 277
August	73.9	75.4	81.4	72.0	40 331	28 665	61 612	16 662	38 272	7 269	243 516	211 449
September	72.5	72.0	79.1	73.3	41 667	29 388	61 940	16 628	45 692	13 296	247 541	215 524
October	71.1	68.5	72.8	74.6	39 560	28 287	62 541	16 747	41 936	11 871	249 917	218 733
November	73.8	72.7	77.8	75.4	40 319	28 312	62 638	16 357	43 049	11 671	252 647	221 118
December	73.8	71.9	77.7	76.4	39 117	26 934	62 723	16 493	42 701	11 357	256 231	223 121

TRANSPORTATION EQUIPMENT—MOTOR VEHICLE SALES AND INVENTORIES

YEAR AND MONTH	Retail sales of new passenger cars						Retail inventories of new domestic passenger cars (Thousands of units)		
	Thousands of units, not seasonally adjusted			Millions of units, seasonally adjusted annual rate			Not seasonally adjusted	Seasonally adjusted	Inventory to sales ratio
	Total	Domestics	Imports	Total	Domestics	Imports			
1968	9 655	8 625	1 030	9.7	8.6	1.0	1 449	1 525	2.0
1969	9 582	8 464	1 117	9.6	8.5	1.1	1 467	1 542	2.2
1970	8 403	7 119	1 283	8.4	7.1	1.3	1 220	1 294	2.4
1971	10 228	8 662	1 566	10.2	8.7	1.6	1 447	1 512	2.1
1972	10 873	9 253	1 621	10.9	9.3	1.6	1 311	1 379	1.7
1973	11 350	9 589	1 762	11.4	9.6	1.8	1 600	1 654	2.5
1974	8 774	7 362	1 412	8.8	7.4	1.4	1 672	1 730	3.4
1975	8 538	6 951	1 587	8.5	7.0	1.6	1 419	1 468	2.2
1976	9 994	8 492	1 502	10.0	8.5	1.5	1 465	1 494	1.9
1977	11 046	8 971	2 075	11.1	9.0	2.1	1 731	1 743	2.3
1978	11 164	9 164	2 000	11.2	9.2	2.0	1 729	1 731	2.3
1979	10 559	8 230	2 329	10.6	8.2	2.3	1 691	1 667	2.4
1980	8 982	6 581	2 400	9.0	6.6	2.4	1 448	1 440	2.6
1981	8 534	6 209	2 326	8.5	6.2	2.3	1 471	1 495	3.6
1982	7 979	5 758	2 221	8.0	5.8	2.2	1 126	1 127	2.2
1983	9 179	6 793	2 386	9.2	6.8	2.4	1 352	1 350	2.0
1984	10 390	7 952	2 439	10.4	8.0	2.4	1 415	1 411	2.1
1985	10 978	8 205	2 774	11.0	8.2	2.8	1 630	1 619	2.5
1986	11 406	8 215	3 191	11.4	8.2	3.2	1 499	1 515	2.0
1987	10 171	7 081	3 090	10.2	7.1	3.1	1 680	1 716	2.8
1988	10 546	7 539	3 006	10.6	7.5	3.0	1 601	1 601	2.3
1989	9 777	7 078	2 699	9.8	7.1	2.7	1 669	1 687	3.1
1990	9 300	6 897	2 403	9.3	6.9	2.4	1 408	1 418	2.6
1991	8 175	6 137	2 038	8.2	6.1	2.0	1 283	1 296	2.6
1992	8 214	6 277	1 938	8.2	6.3	1.9	1 276	1 288	2.3
1993	8 518	6 734	1 784	8.5	6.7	1.8	1 365	1 378	2.4
1994	8 990	7 255	1 735	9.0	7.3	1.7	1 437	1 449	2.3
1995	8 636	7 129	1 507	8.6	7.1	1.5	1 619	1 631	2.6
1996	8 527	7 254	1 273	8.5	7.3	1.3	1 363	1 376	2.4
1993:									
January	562	436	126	8.4	6.5	1.9	1 300	1 303	2.4
February	593	466	127	7.7	5.9	1.8	1 396	1 379	2.8
March	735	582	154	8.0	6.3	1.7	1 491	1 429	2.7
April	769	607	162	8.7	6.9	1.9	1 483	1 441	2.5
May	812	640	173	8.7	6.8	1.9	1 465	1 434	2.5
June	836	671	164	8.7	6.9	1.8	1 453	1 410	2.4
July	764	599	165	8.7	6.8	1.8	1 206	1 400	2.5
August	697	537	160	8.4	6.7	1.7	1 169	1 396	2.5
September	704	554	150	8.3	6.6	1.7	1 221	1 370	2.5
October	717	582	136	9.0	7.2	1.7	1 253	1 347	2.2
November	668	538	129	8.9	7.2	1.7	1 355	1 361	2.3
December	661	522	139	8.7	7.0	1.8	1 365	1 378	2.4
1994:									
January	606	489	118	8.7	7.0	1.7	1 434	1 422	2.4
February	699	573	125	9.1	7.4	1.8	1 476	1 410	2.3
March	876	701	176	9.1	7.3	1.8	1 490	1 429	2.4
April	786	638	148	9.5	7.6	1.9	1 456	1 399	2.2
May	815	661	153	8.8	7.1	1.7	1 458	1 408	2.4
June	871	703	169	8.7	6.9	1.8	1 472	1 438	2.5
July	713	563	150	8.7	6.9	1.8	1 228	1 452	2.5
August	782	604	179	9.1	7.2	1.9	1 209	1 422	2.4
September	742	600	142	9.1	7.4	1.7	1 184	1 406	2.3
October	738	605	133	9.1	7.4	1.7	1 308	1 413	2.3
November	671	553	117	9.0	7.4	1.6	1 392	1 410	2.3
December	692	566	126	9.1	7.5	1.6	1 437	1 449	2.3
1995:									
January	582	472	110	8.8	7.2	1.6	1 530	1 520	2.6
February	649	532	117	8.4	6.8	1.6	1 686	1 601	2.8
March	799	655	144	8.5	7.0	1.6	1 789	1 700	2.9
April	686	562	124	8.1	6.6	1.5	1 808	1 736	3.2
May	825	674	151	8.6	6.9	1.7	1 794	1 706	3.0
June	853	702	151	8.8	7.2	1.6	1 763	1 698	2.9
July	721	594	128	8.5	7.0	1.5	1 505	1 694	2.9
August	806	659	148	9.3	7.8	1.5	1 475	1 633	2.5
September	715	593	122	8.7	7.3	1.4	1 504	1 642	2.7
October	702	593	108	8.6	7.2	1.4	1 580	1 661	2.8
November	645	544	101	8.6	7.3	1.4	1 621	1 657	2.8
December	654	550	105	8.9	7.5	1.4	1 619	1 631	2.6
1996:									
January	567	479	88	8.0	6.8	1.2	1 661	1 630	2.9
February	691	596	95	8.8	7.5	1.3	1 683	1 599	2.6
March	793	674	119	8.8	7.5	1.3	1 514	1 445	2.3
April	761	657	104	8.8	7.6	1.2	1 493	1 427	2.3
May	871	753	118	9.0	7.7	1.3	1 461	1 398	2.2
June	792	677	115	8.5	7.2	1.3	1 473	1 432	2.4
July	732	624	109	8.4	7.2	1.3	1 277	1 498	2.5
August	750	621	129	8.8	7.5	1.3	1 299	1 531	2.5
September	697	593	104	8.7	7.4	1.3	1 326	1 514	2.5
October	678	576	102	8.2	6.9	1.3	1 329	1 446	2.5
November	590	496	95	8.1	6.9	1.3	1 417	1 456	2.6
December	605	508	97	8.3	7.0	1.3	1 363	1 376	2.4

YEAR AND MONTH	TRANSPORTATION EQUIPMENT—MOTOR VEHICLE SALES						
	Retail sales of new trucks and buses						
	Thousands of units, not seasonally adjusted				Millions of units, seasonally adjusted annual rate		
	Total	0-10,000 pounds		10,001 pounds and over	Total	0-10,000 pounds		10,001 pounds and over
		Domestic	Imports			Domestic	Imports	
1968	....	1 464.2	....	343.3	....	1.5	....	0.3
1969	....	1 551.1	....	384.5	....	1.6	....	0.4
1970	....	1 408.5	....	337.3	....	1.4	....	0.3
1971	....	1 592.5	....	338.9	....	1.7	....	0.3
1972	....	2 122.5	....	437.4	....	2.1	....	0.4
1973	....	2 509.4	....	495.7	....	2.5	....	0.5
1974	....	2 180.1	....	423.9	....	2.2	....	0.4
1975	....	2 052.6	....	298.3	....	2.1	....	0.3
1976	3 300.5	2 738.3	237.5	324.7	3.3	2.7	0.2	0.3
1977	3 813.0	3 112.8	323.1	377.1	3.8	3.1	0.3	0.4
1978	4 256.8	3 481.1	335.9	439.8	4.3	3.5	0.3	0.4
1979	3 589.7	2 730.2	469.4	390.1	3.6	2.7	0.5	0.4
1980	2 487.4	1 731.1	484.6	271.7	2.5	1.7	0.5	0.3
1981	2 255.6	1 581.7	447.6	226.3	2.3	1.6	0.4	0.2
1982	2 562.8	1 967.5	410.4	184.9	2.6	2.0	0.4	0.2
1983	3 117.3	2 465.2	463.3	188.8	3.1	2.5	0.5	0.2
1984	4 093.1	3 207.2	607.7	278.2	4.1	3.2	0.6	0.3
1985	4 741.7	3 618.4	828.3	295.0	4.8	3.6	0.8	0.3
1986	4 811.8	3 671.4	866.9	273.5	4.9	3.7	1.0	0.3
1987	5 000.6	3 786.1	912.2	302.3	5.0	3.8	0.9	0.3
1988	5 242.4	4 195.8	697.9	348.7	5.2	4.2	0.7	0.4
1989	5 067.8	4 107.0	630.3	330.5	5.1	4.1	0.6	0.3
1990	4 848.4	3 947.4	602.7	298.3	4.9	4.0	0.6	0.3
1991	4 365.8	3 594.8	528.8	242.2	4.4	3.6	0.5	0.2
1992	4 903.3	4 232.7	395.9	274.7	4.9	4.2	0.4	0.3
1993	5 681.1	4 980.9	364.5	335.7	5.7	5.0	0.4	0.3
1994	6 422.4	5 638.0	396.3	388.1	6.4	5.6	0.4	0.4
1995	6 483.8	5 662.7	392.9	428.2	6.5	5.7	0.4	0.4
1996	6 931.4	6 087.6	433.2	410.6	6.9	6.1	0.4	0.4
1993:								
January	353.9	306.9	26.9	20.1	5.1	4.5	0.4	0.3
February	383.8	333.4	28.5	21.9	5.2	4.5	0.4	0.3
March	495.3	433.1	32.7	29.5	5.3	4.6	0.4	0.3
April	506.2	444.8	30.8	30.6	5.8	5.0	0.4	0.3
May	531.2	471.7	31.3	28.2	5.7	5.0	0.4	0.3
June	548.7	486.5	30.5	31.7	5.8	5.1	0.4	0.3
July	504.1	441.7	34.2	28.2	5.8	5.1	0.4	0.3
August	462.9	400.9	34.2	27.8	5.6	4.9	0.3	0.3
September	461.8	400.2	32.5	29.1	5.6	4.9	0.4	0.4
October	466.1	410.3	26.5	29.3	5.9	5.2	0.3	0.3
November	474.3	415.8	28.4	30.1	6.1	5.4	0.4	0.4
December	492.8	435.6	28.0	29.2	6.3	5.6	0.3	0.4
1994:								
January	440.3	389.1	26.1	25.1	6.2	5.5	0.4	0.4
February	474.0	423.0	24.8	26.2	6.4	5.7	0.4	0.4
March	597.9	533.4	31.1	33.4	6.4	5.7	0.4	0.4
April	553.8	492.1	27.7	34.0	6.5	5.8	0.4	0.4
May	569.0	505.6	31.8	31.6	6.2	5.5	0.4	0.4
June	609.5	536.0	36.1	37.4	6.3	5.4	0.4	0.4
July	507.2	445.3	30.6	31.3	6.1	5.4	0.4	0.4
August	548.1	470.7	42.4	35.0	6.4	5.5	0.4	0.4
September	511.2	441.8	36.8	32.6	6.5	5.7	0.5	0.4
October	554.8	482.3	37.9	34.6	6.6	5.8	0.5	0.4
November	528.2	461.6	35.0	31.6	6.8	5.9	0.4	0.4
December	528.4	457.1	36.0	35.3	6.6	5.8	0.4	0.4
1995:								
January	450.2	384.1	32.8	33.3	6.8	5.8	0.5	0.5
February	481.1	418.1	30.3	32.7	6.4	5.6	0.4	0.4
March	604.7	530.2	34.0	40.5	6.5	5.7	0.4	0.5
April	530.3	463.0	29.0	38.3	6.2	5.4	0.4	0.4
May	602.5	528.8	34.5	39.2	6.4	5.5	0.4	0.5
June	624.5	551.0	32.6	40.9	6.6	5.8	0.4	0.4
July	534.2	472.0	28.9	33.3	6.4	5.6	0.3	0.4
August	559.0	487.3	36.9	34.8	6.6	5.8	0.4	0.4
September	499.7	430.6	36.4	32.7	6.3	5.5	0.4	0.4
October	524.5	457.2	31.1	36.2	6.3	5.5	0.4	0.4
November	524.6	461.8	31.9	30.9	6.7	5.9	0.4	0.4
December	548.5	478.6	34.5	35.4	7.1	6.2	0.4	0.4
1996:								
January	483.7	428.9	25.2	29.6	6.7	6.0	0.3	0.4
February	547.6	487.0	28.4	32.2	7.2	6.4	0.4	0.4
March	611.5	537.8	37.8	35.9	6.9	6.0	0.4	0.4
April	598.6	526.6	34.3	37.7	6.8	6.0	0.4	0.4
May	652.0	572.9	40.8	38.3	6.9	6.0	0.5	0.4
June	612.1	535.4	37.3	39.4	6.7	5.9	0.4	0.4
July	584.8	513.9	35.2	35.7	6.7	5.8	0.4	0.4
August	583.8	505.1	44.8	33.9	7.0	6.1	0.5	0.4
September	535.0	470.9	32.1	32.0	6.9	6.2	0.4	0.4
October	618.8	546.1	37.2	35.5	7.3	6.4	0.5	0.4
November	556.0	487.0	40.9	28.1	7.1	6.2	0.5	0.4
December	547.5	476.0	39.2	32.3	7.0	6.2	0.5	0.4

TRANSPORTATION EQUIPMENT—PRODUCER AND CONSUMER PRICES

YEAR AND MONTH	Transportation equipment industry [1]	Producer prices (1982=100, except as noted, not seasonally adjusted) — Finished goods							Intermediate materials		Commodity group: Motor vehicles and equipment	Consumer prices (1982-84=100, seasonally adjusted) — New vehicles		Used cars
		Passenger cars	Light motor trucks	Heavy motor trucks	Truck trailers	Civilian aircraft [2]	Ships [2]	Railroad equipment	Aircraft engines [3]	Aircraft parts [4]		Total	New cars	
1968		47.9	39.0	34.0				29.8			40.9	50.7	50.7	
1969		48.5	40.1	35.0				31.4			41.7	51.5	51.5	30.9
1970		50.0	42.0	36.3				33.2			43.3	53.1	53.0	31.2
1971		52.6	45.3	38.4				34.9			45.7	55.3	55.2	33.0
1972		54.0	46.2	39.3				37.1			47.0	54.8	54.7	33.1
1973		54.2	47.0	39.8				38.9			47.4	54.8	54.8	35.2
1974		57.8	52.3	44.5				47.3			51.4	58.0	57.9	36.7
1975		63.0	56.9	50.7				58.1			57.6	63.0	62.9	43.8
1976		66.8	60.4	56.1				62.5			61.2	67.0	66.9	50.3
1977		70.7	64.8	61.2				67.4			65.2	70.5	70.4	54.7
1978		75.9	70.5	66.8				73.0			70.0	75.9	75.8	55.8
1979		81.9	76.4	73.4				80.0			75.8	81.9	81.8	60.2
1980		88.9	83.3	82.3				90.4			83.1	88.5	88.4	62.3
1981		96.2	95.0	92.9	96.9			97.0			94.6	93.9	93.7	76.9
1982		100.0	100.0	100.0	100.0			100.0			100.0	97.5	97.4	88.8
1983		102.2	102.6	103.6	100.6			101.1			102.2	99.9	99.9	98.7
1984		104.0	106.7	108.0	104.0			102.6			104.1	102.6	102.8	112.5
1985		106.9	112.2	108.8	106.2			104.9			106.4	106.1	106.1	113.7
1986	104.4	110.2	117.7	113.4	104.3	100.9	100.5	105.4	99.7	103.4	109.1	110.6	110.6	108.8
1987	105.9	112.9	121.1	111.8	103.4	102.9	100.7	104.7	99.7	105.8	111.7	114.4	114.6	113.1
1988	107.8	113.0	125.0	112.4	106.6	104.5	101.0	107.5	103.2	110.3	113.1	116.5	116.9	118.0
1989	112.1	115.5	129.5	117.2	110.4	108.8	105.4	114.0	106.7	114.5	116.2	119.2	119.2	120.4
1990	115.6	118.3	130.0	120.3	110.8	115.3	110.1	118.6	113.5	117.7	118.2	121.4	121.0	117.6
1991	119.8	124.1	135.5	123.6	112.1	123.0	114.6	122.2	119.2	121.8	122.1	126.0	125.3	118.1
1992	123.0	126.9	142.4	128.6	115.1	128.8	122.1	123.7	125.0	128.0	124.9	129.2	128.4	123.2
1993	126.3	129.8	150.3	133.9	118.2	131.5	129.1	125.2	127.7	131.2	128.0	132.7	131.5	133.9
1994	130.1	133.9	157.1	138.7	122.2	135.4	131.1	129.2	130.7	134.0	131.4	137.6	136.0	141.7
1995	132.2	134.1	159.0	144.1	131.7	141.8	132.8	134.8	132.8	135.7	133.0	141.0	139.0	156.5
1996	134.2	135.4	160.3	144.5	130.7	147.3	138.7	137.2	134.7	139.3	134.1	143.7	141.4	157.0
1993:														
January	125.0	129.0	148.4	132.0	117.0	130.0	128.7	123.6	127.1	130.5	127.1	130.7	129.8	128.2
February	125.7	129.6	150.1	132.7	117.0	130.5	128.7	124.2	127.1	130.2	127.8	131.0	129.9	128.0
March	125.8	129.6	150.2	133.2	117.0	131.3	128.7	124.3	127.3	130.4	127.8	131.2	130.1	129.8
April	125.9	129.8	149.1	133.2	117.1	132.5	129.2	124.5	127.4	130.3	127.7	131.7	130.6	130.9
May	126.1	129.3	149.3	133.1	117.1	132.4	129.2	124.5	127.8	130.5	127.6	132.2	131.0	132.2
June	126.1	129.6	149.5	133.1	118.0	129.0	129.2	124.6	128.0	130.8	127.7	132.3	131.1	133.6
July	126.3	129.6	149.6	134.6	118.0	131.1	129.3	125.0	128.2	131.4	127.8	132.9	131.6	134.8
August	126.2	129.1	149.5	134.7	118.1	130.9	129.3	125.8	128.3	132.1	127.7	133.5	132.1	136.2
September	124.1	124.5	143.4	134.2	119.5	131.9	129.3	126.1	127.5	131.8	124.9	133.8	132.3	137.3
October	128.1	131.6	155.2	134.9	119.9	132.0	129.3	125.7	127.3	132.2	129.7	134.3	132.9	138.2
November	128.3	132.7	154.3	135.6	119.9	133.6	129.3	125.7	127.6	132.1	129.9	134.6	133.2	139.2
December	128.5	132.9	154.5	135.6	120.0	133.1	129.3	127.6	128.6	132.1	130.0	134.8	133.4	138.3
1994:														
January	129.4	133.7	155.9	137.2	119.9	133.8	130.4	127.9	130.6	133.0	130.7	135.1	133.6	137.6
February	129.5	133.7	156.3	137.7	120.1	134.1	130.4	128.1	130.9	133.3	130.9	135.5	134.0	136.0
March	129.5	133.6	156.3	137.6	120.1	134.6	131.3	128.5	130.9	133.4	130.8	136.0	134.5	136.9
April	129.6	133.3	156.4	138.1	120.3	135.5	131.3	128.5	130.7	133.5	130.8	136.4	134.9	137.0
May	130.1	134.1	157.7	138.6	120.3	134.8	131.3	128.7	130.7	133.7	131.4	137.0	135.4	138.3
June	129.9	133.8	157.7	139.6	120.5	135.3	131.3	129.0	130.6	133.6	131.3	137.5	135.9	140.1
July	130.1	134.1	157.3	139.2	120.5	135.3	131.3	129.1	130.4	134.3	131.5	138.1	136.5	141.5
August	130.1	134.0	157.4	139.9	120.6	135.6	131.3	129.8	130.5	134.1	131.6	138.6	136.9	142.9
September	128.2	129.2	152.3	140.5	124.3	136.1	131.3	129.9	130.6	134.3	129.1	139.2	137.4	144.3
October	131.5	135.8	160.5	137.6	124.4	136.6	131.3	130.0	130.5	134.8	132.8	139.2	137.5	146.3
November	131.2	135.6	158.0	138.6	126.0	137.0	131.3	130.1	130.8	135.1	132.5	139.2	137.5	148.7
December	131.6	135.7	159.6	139.7	129.2	136.4	131.3	130.2	131.6	135.1	133.0	139.3	137.7	150.6
1995:														
January	132.2	135.8	160.0	140.4	130.5	139.1	131.9	130.9	131.7	137.5	133.4	139.6	137.9	153.0
February	132.2	135.4	159.5	141.4	130.7	139.7	133.1	132.7	131.6	137.0	133.3	139.7	138.1	155.1
March	132.0	134.5	159.1	142.9	131.3	139.8	133.1	133.2	131.7	136.2	133.1	139.9	138.2	158.4
April	131.9	134.0	159.5	143.3	131.5	140.1	133.1	134.2	131.4	136.1	132.9	140.6	138.8	158.0
May	131.8	133.3	159.5	143.8	131.6	140.7	133.1	134.7	132.4	135.2	132.7	140.9	139.0	157.8
June	131.5	132.3	158.2	144.6	132.1	141.1	133.1	135.2	133.1	135.3	132.2	141.1	139.2	157.4
July	131.4	132.3	158.0	144.6	132.1	142.4	132.3	135.5	133.0	134.4	132.2	141.0	139.0	156.6
August	131.3	131.3	158.1	144.9	132.1	142.6	132.9	135.7	133.6	134.4	131.9	141.2	139.2	156.2
September	129.3	127.2	151.5	144.9	132.0	142.8	132.9	135.6	133.6	134.6	129.1	141.7	139.5	155.7
October	133.9	137.4	160.9	146.3	132.1	144.1	132.9	136.1	133.6	135.3	134.8	141.7	139.5	156.1
November	134.4	138.2	161.7	146.2	132.2	144.5	132.9	136.6	133.8	136.0	135.5	142.0	139.9	156.6
December	134.4	138.0	162.0	145.4	132.1	144.7	132.9	136.9	133.8	136.0	135.4	142.0	139.9	157.5
1996:														
January	134.2	136.2	161.2	145.7	132.1	145.2	135.3	136.7	135.0	139.3	134.5	142.2	140.0	158.3
February	134.2	136.1	160.8	146.6	132.1	145.4	135.3	137.7	134.8	139.6	134.5	142.5	140.3	158.9
March	134.3	136.1	160.6	147.3	132.0	145.6	135.3	137.6	135.5	139.5	134.5	142.8	140.7	160.7
April	134.1	135.2	160.4	147.2	130.5	146.1	138.8	137.8	133.9	139.4	134.1	143.0	140.8	158.1
May	134.1	135.4	159.8	147.9	130.4	146.3	138.3	137.7	134.0	139.4	134.1	143.2	140.9	157.4
June	134.3	135.9	160.1	145.4	130.6	146.9	138.3	137.3	134.1	139.4	134.2	143.6	141.4	156.3
July	133.8	134.1	159.3	145.4	130.6	147.4	138.6	137.3	134.4	139.0	133.5	143.9	141.7	156.2
August	133.8	133.9	158.9	145.7	130.0	148.2	139.6	137.2	134.6	139.1	133.3	144.1	142.0	156.1
September	132.1	130.4	154.1	142.6	130.0	148.5	139.2	137.0	134.7	139.3	131.0	144.9	142.7	156.5
October	135.4	137.3	163.2	142.3	130.0	148.8	144.7	137.0	134.8	139.3	135.2	144.6	142.4	156.1
November	135.2	137.3	162.7	139.5	130.2	149.4	140.7	136.5	135.0	139.3	134.9	144.6	142.1	155.6
December	135.1	136.9	162.4	138.9	130.2	149.3	141.0	136.3	135.6	139.5	134.8	144.7	142.2	155.0

1. December 1984=100.
2. December 1985=100.
3. Aircraft engines and engine parts, December 1985=100.
4. Aircraft parts and auxiliary equipment, not elsewhere classified, June 1985=100.

TRANSPORTATION EQUIPMENT—EMPLOYMENT, HOURS, AND EARNINGS

YEAR AND MONTH	Employment (Thousands, seasonally adjusted)					Production workers							
	Total payroll employees			Production workers		Weekly hours worked (Seasonally adjusted)				Average earnings (Dollars, not seasonally adjusted)			
						Average hours		Aggregate hours index (1982=100)		Hourly		Weekly	
	Total transportation equipment	Motor vehicles	Aircraft and parts	Total transportation equipment	Motor vehicles	Total transportation equipment	Motor vehicles	Total transportation equipment	Motor vehicles	Total transportation equipment	Motor vehicles	Total transportation equipment	Motor vehicles
1968	2 133	874	821	1 450	681	42.2	43.1	141.7	141.6	3.69	3.89	155.72	167.66
1969	2 120	911	775	1 443	708	41.5	41.7	138.5	142.4	3.89	4.10	161.44	170.97
1970	1 833	799	644	1 223	605	40.3	40.3	114.1	117.7	4.06	4.22	163.62	170.07
1971	1 743	849	509	1 196	655	40.7	41.2	112.6	130.3	4.45	4.72	181.12	194.46
1972	1 777	875	481	1 226	676	41.7	43.0	118.4	140.5	4.81	5.13	200.58	220.59
1973	1 915	977	510	1 324	755	42.1	43.5	129.1	158.5	5.15	5.46	216.82	237.51
1974	1 853	908	524	1 256	688	40.5	40.6	117.9	134.9	5.54	5.87	224.37	238.32
1975	1 700	792	499	1 142	602	40.4	40.3	106.8	117.3	6.07	6.44	245.23	259.53
1976	1 785	881	473	1 223	682	41.7	42.9	117.9	141.2	6.62	7.09	276.05	304.16
1977	1 857	947	467	1 277	735	42.5	44.0	125.6	156.0	7.29	7.85	309.83	345.40
1978	1 987	1 005	511	1 370	782	42.2	43.3	133.6	163.3	7.91	8.50	333.80	368.05
1979	2 059	990	593	1 409	764	41.1	41.1	134.1	151.8	8.53	9.06	350.58	372.37
1980	1 881	789	633	1 220	575	40.6	40.0	114.6	111.0	9.35	9.85	379.61	394.00
1981	1 879	789	626	1 207	586	40.9	40.9	114.2	115.7	10.39	11.02	424.95	450.72
1982	1 718	699	584	1 068	512	40.5	40.5	100.0	100.0	11.11	11.62	449.96	470.61
1983	1 730	754	562	1 085	568	42.1	43.3	105.7	118.9	11.67	12.14	491.31	525.66
1984	1 883	862	575	1 203	664	42.7	43.8	118.9	140.2	12.20	12.73	520.94	557.57
1985	1 960	883	616	1 244	685	42.6	43.5	122.7	143.6	12.71	13.39	541.45	582.47
1986	2 003	872	656	1 258	670	42.3	42.6	123.3	137.7	12.81	13.45	541.86	572.97
1987	2 028	866	678	1 278	673	42.0	42.2	124.3	137.2	12.94	13.53	543.48	570.97
1988	2 036	856	684	1 273	667	42.7	43.5	125.8	140.0	13.29	13.99	567.48	608.57
1989	2 052	859	711	1 278	664	42.4	43.1	125.3	138.0	13.67	14.25	579.61	614.18
1990	1 989	812	712	1 224	617	42.0	42.4	119.1	126.2	14.08	14.56	591.36	617.34
1991	1 890	789	669	1 169	602	41.9	42.3	113.3	122.9	14.75	15.23	618.03	644.23
1992	1 830	813	612	1 147	622	41.8	42.4	110.9	127.3	15.20	15.45	635.36	655.08
1993	1 756	837	542	1 120	642	43.0	44.3	111.4	137.4	15.80	16.10	679.40	713.23
1994	1 761	909	482	1 154	704	44.3	46.0	118.5	156.2	16.51	17.02	731.39	782.92
1995	1 790	971	451	1 200	761	43.8	44.9	121.6	164.9	16.74	17.34	733.21	778.57
1996	1 781	963	460	1 206	760	44.0	44.9	122.7	164.8	17.20	17.75	756.80	796.98
1993:													
January	1 808	842	575	1 149	649	42.2	42.9	112.2	134.4	15.46	15.62	652.41	668.54
February	1 791	832	572	1 139	640	42.6	43.7	112.3	135.0	15.50	15.67	655.65	678.51
March	1 779	831	564	1 131	638	42.5	43.7	111.3	134.6	15.59	15.84	662.58	695.38
April	1 766	825	559	1 124	634	43.0	44.7	111.9	136.8	15.65	15.96	660.43	697.45
May	1 756	826	550	1 116	636	42.6	43.8	110.0	134.5	15.79	16.11	680.55	720.12
June	1 746	826	544	1 106	634	42.6	43.9	109.0	134.3	15.77	16.11	679.69	720.12
July	1 743	831	537	1 105	638	42.9	43.9	109.7	135.2	15.52	15.66	648.74	665.55
August	1 739	832	531	1 105	637	42.8	44.1	109.5	135.6	15.67	15.89	670.68	700.75
September	1 740	838	529	1 111	642	43.5	45.1	111.9	139.7	15.98	16.34	688.74	728.76
October	1 738	846	522	1 110	647	43.4	45.0	111.5	140.5	15.98	16.34	699.92	741.84
November	1 736	851	515	1 113	651	43.6	45.4	112.3	142.6	16.18	16.57	711.92	758.91
December	1 740	862	507	1 121	660	43.9	45.8	113.9	145.9	16.41	16.89	736.81	787.07
1994:													
January	1 749	881	502	1 135	678	43.8	45.9	115.1	150.2	16.25	16.70	710.13	758.18
February	1 743	878	496	1 130	675	43.8	45.9	114.6	149.5	16.35	16.79	712.86	767.30
March	1 742	882	492	1 130	678	44.5	46.2	116.4	151.2	16.36	16.82	728.02	780.45
April	1 743	886	488	1 135	684	43.9	45.4	115.3	149.9	16.43	16.97	731.14	787.41
May	1 747	892	485	1 139	688	44.2	45.6	116.5	151.4	16.42	16.94	732.33	787.71
June	1 754	901	480	1 148	696	43.9	45.3	116.6	152.2	16.45	16.96	730.38	781.86
July	1 750	905	478	1 153	702	43.7	44.9	116.6	152.1	16.44	16.93	698.70	731.38
August	1 764	917	476	1 157	712	44.1	45.6	118.1	156.7	16.47	16.96	726.33	773.38
September	1 772	929	473	1 168	723	43.9	45.3	118.7	158.1	16.75	17.33	750.40	805.85
October	1 781	940	471	1 179	732	44.2	45.7	120.6	161.5	16.57	17.04	737.37	783.84
November	1 792	949	469	1 190	740	44.6	46.2	122.8	165.0	16.68	17.19	752.27	801.05
December	1 797	952	467	1 196	742	44.7	46.1	123.7	165.1	16.89	17.46	771.87	822.37
1995:													
January	1 799	962	464	1 201	751	44.5	46.1	123.7	167.1	16.68	17.22	738.92	786.95
February	1 802	967	463	1 207	757	44.5	45.9	124.3	167.7	16.78	17.36	746.71	796.82
March	1 805	971	462	1 210	761	44.6	45.8	124.9	168.2	16.75	17.35	747.05	798.10
April	1 804	973	461	1 210	763	43.6	44.8	122.1	165.0	16.56	17.13	698.83	736.59
May	1 803	973	459	1 209	763	43.3	44.1	121.2	162.4	16.65	17.23	729.27	773.63
June	1 796	971	456	1 204	760	43.5	44.2	121.2	162.1	16.71	17.27	733.57	775.42
July	1 791	973	451	1 206	763	43.5	44.3	121.4	163.1	16.72	17.27	705.58	733.98
August	1 794	975	450	1 206	765	43.5	44.2	121.4	163.2	16.66	17.17	724.71	760.63
September	1 790	973	449	1 204	763	43.5	44.3	121.2	163.1	16.95	17.55	752.58	798.53
October	1 764	976	424	1 180	767	43.5	44.5	118.8	164.7	16.74	17.47	731.54	782.66
November	1 751	966	420	1 169	758	44.0	45.3	119.0	165.7	16.79	17.51	743.80	794.95
December	1 781	973	449	1 203	769	42.9	44.3	119.4	164.4	16.88	17.55	741.03	798.53
1996:													
January	1 772	965	450	1 201	764	42.5	43.7	118.1	161.1	16.88	17.42	714.02	756.03
February	1 778	969	451	1 204	766	43.3	44.2	120.7	163.4	16.95	17.47	733.94	770.43
March	1 745	934	451	1 173	735	42.3	42.1	114.8	149.4	16.64	17.04	703.87	720.79
April	1 780	967	453	1 206	765	44.1	45.3	123.1	167.3	17.22	17.89	759.40	812.21
May	1 781	968	455	1 210	765	44.3	45.7	124.1	168.7	17.19	17.84	764.96	818.86
June	1 787	974	452	1 210	770	44.1	45.3	123.5	168.4	17.23	17.84	766.74	817.07
July	1 778	960	458	1 208	760	44.0	45.2	123.0	165.8	17.29	17.89	738.28	776.43
August	1 791	968	459	1 215	764	44.4	45.6	124.9	168.1	17.28	17.80	765.50	809.90
September	1 783	965	461	1 209	762	44.4	45.3	124.2	166.6	17.45	18.04	787.00	833.45
October	1 783	959	470	1 209	757	44.0	44.8	123.1	163.7	17.25	17.73	762.45	797.85
November	1 790	960	475	1 216	758	44.3	44.9	124.7	164.3	17.35	17.85	772.08	806.82
December	1 793	961	479	1 216	759	44.6	45.2	125.5	165.6	17.57	18.12	801.19	842.58

INSTRUMENTS AND RELATED PRODUCTS— PRODUCTION, CAPACITY, SHIPMENTS, INVENTORIES, PRICES, EMPLOYMENT, HOURS, AND EARNINGS

YEAR AND MONTH	Industrial production— Instruments (1992=100, seasonally adjusted)			Capacity utilization— Instruments (Percent of capacity, seasonally adjusted)	Manufacturers' shipments, and inventories (Millions of dollars, seasonally adjusted)		Producer prices (1984=100, not seasonally adjusted)[1]	Employment (Thousands, seasonally adjusted)		Production workers			
	Total	Scientific and medical			Ship- ments	Inven- tories (Book value, end of period)		Total payroll employ- ees	Produc- tion workers (Not sea- sonally adjusted)	Weekly hours worked (Seasonally adjusted)		Average earnings (Dollars, not sea- sonally adjusted)	
		Total	Medical							Average hours	Aggregate hours index (1982=100)	Hourly	Weekly
1968	34.0	30.6	22.1	85.1	17 645	3 825		814					
1969	36.5	32.4	24.6	83.9	18 662	4 088		838					
1970	36.2	32.2	23.6	77.4	18 367	4 196		804					
1971	37.9	33.3	26.0	76.3	18 613	4 201		753					
1972	42.5	36.6	27.9	81.4	21 043	4 435		786					
1973	48.5	41.6	30.0	87.6	23 627	5 233		851					
1974	51.4	43.5	30.6	86.5	27 454	6 486		885					
1975	48.9	43.0	32.9	77.1	29 547	6 547		804					
1976	53.7	46.1	34.5	80.5	33 238	7 214		840					
1977	60.1	52.6	36.3	86.1	38 803	8 185		895					
1978	66.2	57.2	38.5	89.5	44 655	9 682		952					
1979	71.7	62.5	41.3	90.6	50 702	11 415		1 006					
1980	73.6	67.9	42.4	87.2	59 825	13 376		1 022					
1981	75.4	69.8	46.0	84.8	66 613	14 760		1 041					
1982	76.3	72.2	52.3	81.7	74 918	17 038		1 013					
1983	77.7	72.6	53.2	79.7	79 637	17 769		990					
1984	86.0	80.8	57.8	84.6	89 398	20 206		1 040					
1985	89.3	84.3	62.0	83.6	96 207	21 569	100.7	1 045					
1986	88.8	85.7	64.2	79.1	100 798	22 461	102.4	1 018					
1987	93.8	92.9	72.3	80.2	107 325	23 692	105.1	1 011					
1988	97.2	95.4	76.4	80.8	116 009	25 346	107.0	1 031	508	41.4	89.9	10.60	438.84
1989	98.2	96.2	79.1	79.8	121 523	26 541	110.8	1 026	509	41.1	89.6	10.83	445.11
1990	98.4	99.2	87.7	78.5	127 978	26 552	114.6	1 006	499	41.1	87.6	11.29	464.02
1991	99.8	99.8	94.7	78.7	132 836	25 778	116.8	974	479	41.0	84.0	11.64	477.24
1992	100.0	100.0	100.0	77.9	134 941	24 685	118.7	929	457	41.1	80.2	11.89	488.68
1993	100.6	99.6	104.3	77.7	137 387	23 212	120.8	896	438	41.1	77.0	12.23	502.65
1994	99.9	98.6	103.3	77.0	138 400	22 974	122.1	861	422	41.7	75.2	12.47	520.00
1995	100.4	98.6	106.6	77.3	140 911	23 383	124.0	843	417	41.4	73.7	12.71	526.19
1996	102.8	100.3	108.4	79.2	146 199	24 367	125.1	854	422	41.7	75.2	13.14	547.94
1993:													
January	102.0	101.7	106.4	78.9	11 213	24 406	120.4	912	447	41.2	78.9	12.08	498.90
February	100.8	100.2	104.0	78.0	11 332	24 439	120.4	910	446	41.2	78.6	12.09	495.69
March	101.8	101.0	107.0	78.8	11 419	24 404	120.6	908	446	40.9	77.8	12.13	498.54
April	101.8	101.0	105.9	78.7	11 221	24 317	120.9	905	444	41.5	78.8	12.19	498.57
May	101.2	100.1	106.1	78.2	11 243	24 146	120.8	900	439	41.2	77.5	12.20	500.20
June	100.9	99.9	105.5	78.0	11 503	24 079	120.7	895	439	41.1	77.0	12.18	503.03
July	101.0	100.0	106.9	78.0	11 436	23 865	121.0	892	434	41.2	76.5	12.24	496.94
August	99.8	98.3	102.3	77.1	11 476	23 744	121.2	890	435	41.0	76.3	12.25	498.58
September	100.8	99.9	106.2	77.8	11 593	23 694	121.2	887	433	41.3	76.6	12.33	504.30
October	99.5	98.4	102.5	76.8	11 517	23 783	120.9	886	433	41.0	75.9	12.32	505.12
November	98.8	97.5	99.4	76.2	11 808	23 397	121.1	882	432	41.0	75.6	12.36	511.70
December	99.1	97.6	99.2	76.4	11 640	23 212	121.1	879	431	41.2	75.6	12.46	524.57
1994:													
January	100.0	98.1	101.1	77.1	11 550	23 182	121.8	878	429	41.3	75.8	12.42	515.43
February	100.8	99.5	104.1	77.7	11 416	23 024	121.7	876	429	41.2	75.6	12.43	509.63
March	100.4	99.2	102.0	77.4	11 299	22 934	121.6	872	429	41.6	76.1	12.42	519.16
April	100.0	98.9	101.8	77.1	11 518	22 849	122.2	869	426	41.6	75.8	12.43	515.85
May	99.3	97.9	101.3	76.5	11 476	23 060	122.0	865	424	41.7	75.8	12.37	514.59
June	99.4	98.1	102.8	76.6	11 630	23 057	122.1	861	423	41.7	75.2	12.42	517.91
July	99.8	98.6	104.4	76.9	11 549	22 902	122.3	857	418	41.9	75.4	12.46	515.84
August	98.9	97.3	102.1	76.2	11 628	22 951	122.2	855	418	41.8	74.9	12.47	517.51
September	99.9	98.2	105.0	76.9	11 712	22 928	122.0	854	417	41.7	74.5	12.54	524.17
October	100.1	98.7	105.4	77.1	11 499	22 815	122.3	850	417	41.8	74.5	12.54	524.17
November	100.0	98.7	104.1	77.0	11 533	22 900	122.6	850	417	41.8	74.5	12.54	526.26
December	100.6	99.4	105.2	77.5	11 708	22 974	122.6	848	419	41.7	74.3	12.53	537.61
										41.7	74.2	12.62	
1995:													
January	100.3	99.1	106.3	77.3	11 899	22 733	122.9	844	415	41.6	73.8	12.53	525.01
February	99.8	98.5	106.6	76.8	11 732	22 807	123.4	843	415	41.4	73.5	12.62	523.73
March	100.2	98.8	107.9	77.1	11 815	22 762	123.4	841	414	41.5	73.5	12.62	526.25
April	100.4	98.9	107.7	77.3	11 537	22 794	123.6	841	415	41.3	73.3	12.67	513.14
May	99.5	97.8	103.8	76.6	11 773	22 629	123.7	841	414	41.3	73.3	12.65	521.18
June	100.5	99.0	107.4	77.4	11 628	22 896	123.9	843	417	41.3	73.6	12.68	523.68
July	100.1	98.0	104.9	77.0	11 298	22 906	124.2	846	415	41.3	73.8	12.76	520.61
August	100.8	98.9	107.2	77.6	11 884	22 922	124.2	844	418	41.5	74.2	12.70	523.24
September	101.1	98.9	106.8	77.9	11 725	22 984	124.3	844	418	41.4	74.0	12.81	530.33
October	101.0	98.9	106.5	77.7	11 703	23 088	125.3	844	419	41.5	74.3	12.76	528.26
November	101.4	99.2	108.9	78.0	11 901	23 284	125.2	845	419	41.4	74.2	12.83	536.29
December	99.9	97.6	105.4	77.0	12 055	23 383	124.4	846	419	41.1	73.6	12.89	543.96
1996:													
January	101.0	98.8	110.2	77.8	11 840	23 547	125.1	849	419	40.2	72.0	13.00	525.20
February	102.9	101.0	111.6	79.3	11 994	23 711	125.3	850	420	41.7	74.9	12.94	540.89
March	102.9	101.0	110.2	79.2	12 002	23 912	125.2	853	422	41.6	75.1	12.96	543.02
April	102.3	99.9	108.4	78.8	11 945	24 066	125.1	853	422	41.5	74.7	13.03	538.14
May	102.4	99.9	107.5	78.8	12 199	24 118	125.1	855	424	41.6	75.2	13.04	541.16
June	103.3	101.0	110.0	79.6	12 181	23 935	124.9	856	424	41.9	75.6	13.09	549.78
July	102.3	99.8	106.6	78.8	12 386	24 310	125.2	854	418	41.6	74.7	13.18	540.38
August	103.0	100.4	106.8	79.3	12 316	24 446	125.0	855	422	41.8	75.4	13.18	548.29
September	103.0	100.0	107.0	79.3	12 206	24 436	125.0	854	422	41.8	75.4	13.31	559.02
October	103.4	100.7	108.8	79.6	12 310	24 636	125.1	855	423	41.8	75.4	13.27	553.36
November	103.0	99.9	106.8	79.3	12 490	24 311	124.7	854	422	41.9	75.6	13.34	562.95
December	104.1	100.9	107.5	80.1	12 371	24 367	125.2	856	423	42.0	75.8	13.39	575.77

1. Covers measuring and controlling instruments; photographic, medical, and optical goods; watches and clocks.

Manufacturing by Industry: Nondurable Goods

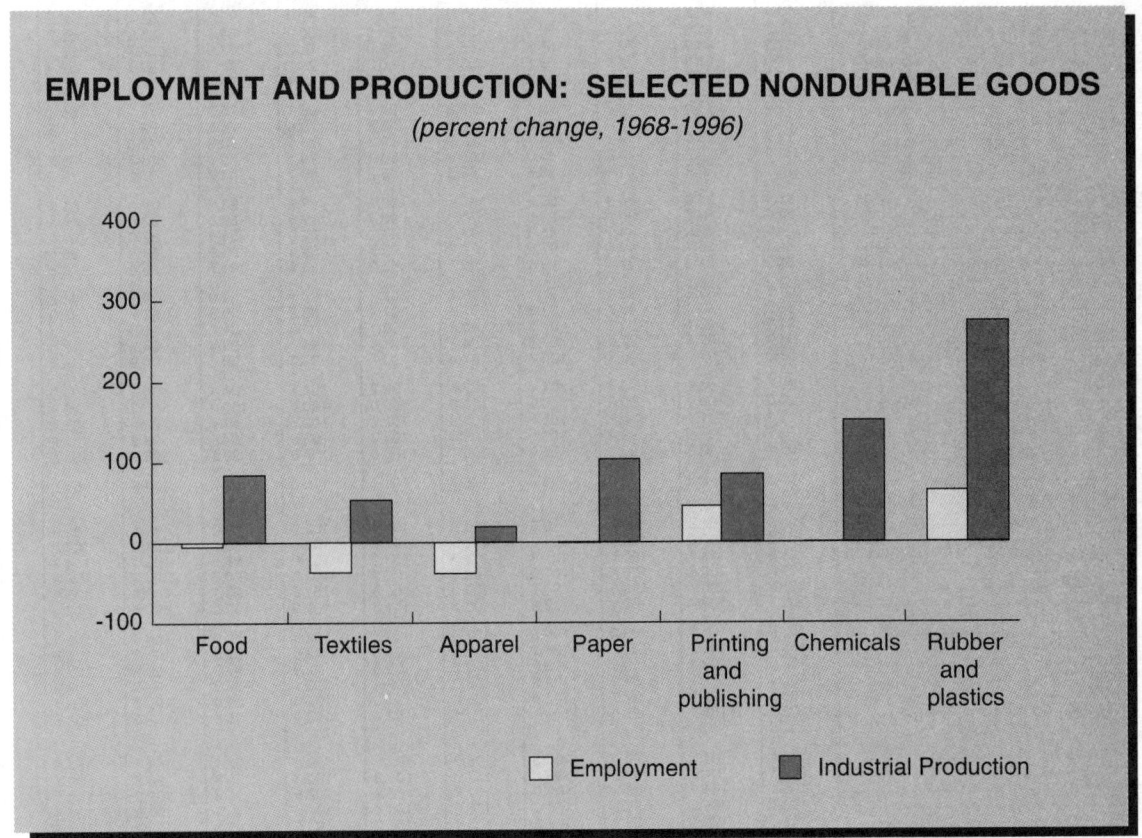

EMPLOYMENT AND PRODUCTION: SELECTED NONDURABLE GOODS
(percent change, 1968-1996)

Industrial production of rubber and plastic products increased 275 percent from 1968 to 1996. Several other nondurable goods industry groups also had strong production gains: chemicals were up 150 percent, and production in the food, paper, and printing and publishing groups also rose.

Significant employment gains took place only in rubber and plastics (64 percent) and printing and publishing (44 percent). Employment in textiles and apparel declined by more than one-third. Even larger drops in employment occurred in two smaller industry groups not shown on the chart: leather (73 percent) and tobacco (52 percent)

Measured by employment, food and food products remained the largest of the nondurable industry groups with 1,700,000 workers in 1996. Printing and publishing, with over 1,500,000 workers, was the second largest.

FOOD AND FOOD PRODUCTS—PRODUCTION, CAPACITY, SHIPMENTS, AND INVENTORIES

YEAR AND MONTH	Industrial production (1992=100, seasonally adjusted)										Capacity utiliza-tion—Total foods (Percent of capacity, seasonally adjusted)	Manufacturers' shipments and inventories (Millions of dollars, seasonally adjusted)	
	Total foods	Meat products	Dairy products	Canned and frozen foods	Grain mill products	Bakery products	Sugar and confection-ery	Fats and oils	Bev-erages	Coffee and mis-cellane-ous		Shipments	Inventories (Book value, end of period)
1968	57.7	59.6	66.3	52.6	46.5	95.9	64.3	59.1	44.8	55.8	84.4	87 328	8 009
1969	59.6	58.9	66.4	56.3	48.7	101.2	64.4	62.2	47.2	56.9	84.8	93 385	8 329
1970	60.6	60.5	66.2	58.2	50.4	94.6	66.4	65.8	49.5	56.6	83.6	98 535	8 738
1971	62.5	62.8	67.5	61.2	51.0	93.7	67.9	70.5	52.7	56.2	83.6	103 637	9 258
1972	65.8	67.8	72.3	66.1	53.3	98.0	69.9	66.5	55.2	58.8	85.5	115 054	9 673
1973	67.1	63.9	72.7	68.8	55.1	98.0	72.3	67.0	57.9	63.3	85.0	135 585	11 627
1974	68.0	67.3	74.5	69.3	55.0	96.8	74.1	71.7	63.3	59.7	83.6	161 884	14 625
1975	67.5	64.0	75.0	69.3	56.2	97.5	64.4	70.3	59.7	60.0	80.4	172 054	14 467
1976	71.4	71.8	76.3	72.9	58.9	97.7	68.1	75.3	65.1	65.1	82.4	180 830	15 695
1977	74.6	75.1	78.0	80.5	62.5	98.8	78.4	72.5	69.1	64.6	83.5	192 913	16 329
1978	77.2	75.5	78.1	85.1	62.9	98.2	79.5	78.6	73.0	72.2	83.6	215 989	18 073
1979	77.9	76.2	78.8	83.0	62.8	99.1	79.1	79.6	75.4	75.2	82.0	235 976	19 879
1980	79.7	79.2	81.8	83.6	65.5	96.2	80.7	81.7	77.2	78.3	81.6	256 191	21 710
1981	81.4	81.0	86.8	80.9	67.6	97.7	83.6	83.2	79.3	81.0	81.2	272 140	21 483
1982	82.4	78.8	90.1	83.5	71.6	99.4	79.6	85.6	80.0	80.4	80.2	280 529	23 016
1983	84.6	82.4	94.1	85.4	74.2	97.7	82.9	85.4	82.0	83.1	80.9	289 314	23 609
1984	86.4	83.1	90.1	87.6	77.8	99.7	85.4	85.9	84.4	86.5	81.5	304 584	24 182
1985	88.9	84.4	97.4	88.1	83.5	102.9	83.9	91.7	86.6	86.8	82.2	308 606	24 015
1986	91.2	85.6	98.6	91.1	85.2	106.1	87.1	89.6	89.3	90.2	82.9	318 203	23 884
1987	93.5	87.2	96.7	92.6	91.6	107.4	88.9	90.9	91.7	94.0	84.1	329 725	24 860
1988	94.9	90.1	100.3	93.9	90.8	103.1	91.6	94.7	94.6	96.6	84.4	354 084	27 122
1989	95.9	92.4	97.0	97.6	94.2	101.4	93.1	98.4	94.3	97.0	84.3	380 160	28 459
1990	97.0	93.2	95.9	100.7	97.4	100.7	94.0	99.2	94.9	98.3	83.9	391 728	29 714
1991	98.4	96.1	96.1	104.4	97.6	98.7	95.2	104.4	96.2	100.0	83.4	397 893	30 099
1992	100.0	100.0	100.0	100.0	100.0	100.0	100.0	100.0	100.0	100.0	82.8	406 964	30 986
1993	102.1	101.6	100.7	101.6	103.9	102.2	102.7	98.4	100.0	105.7	82.7	422 220	31 185
1994	103.7	107.4	99.4	103.5	105.6	105.7	102.6	94.9	103.9	101.2	82.4	430 963	32 306
1995	105.7	110.9	100.1	105.9	106.1	106.8	107.0	98.5	105.9	103.5	82.4	448 406	34 411
1996	106.3	112.0	97.8	103.7	105.7	104.7	110.0	95.7	109.8	107.6	81.2	471 633	34 626
1993:													
January	100.8	101.3	100.7	99.5	100.6	101.4	102.9	99.0	99.3	102.9	82.3	34 608	31 138
February	101.4	99.8	102.6	101.0	102.5	99.6	104.4	100.1	101.1	102.2	82.7	34 393	31 104
March	101.5	98.9	100.5	101.4	103.3	103.1	102.0	98.9	100.1	104.3	82.7	34 902	30 965
April	101.6	100.8	101.4	101.0	103.2	100.0	102.8	100.6	99.1	106.9	82.6	35 342	31 181
May	101.2	100.7	102.0	99.2	103.0	100.9	101.0	99.1	99.2	105.9	82.2	34 450	31 331
June	102.3	103.2	102.1	102.2	103.3	101.3	102.9	100.0	99.4	106.4	82.9	35 413	31 472
July	102.6	101.7	103.0	100.5	103.5	104.5	102.8	98.0	100.0	108.4	83.1	35 472	31 375
August	103.0	102.2	101.0	104.1	105.3	102.8	103.6	97.9	101.0	105.9	83.3	35 800	31 153
September	102.9	102.1	100.0	103.1	105.2	105.3	102.9	97.8	99.8	107.1	83.1	35 564	30 950
October	102.4	102.1	99.1	102.8	105.0	103.4	103.1	97.7	98.8	106.9	82.5	35 110	30 936
November	102.3	102.9	97.7	102.9	106.0	101.3	102.4	96.8	100.5	105.1	82.3	35 331	31 103
December	102.7	103.2	98.6	101.1	106.1	103.4	102.3	95.3	101.5	106.8	82.6	35 555	31 185
1994:													
January	102.4	104.5	99.0	100.3	105.3	102.5	99.8	92.1	103.4	104.6	82.2	35 019	31 268
February	101.5	104.5	98.5	99.9	107.3	103.9	100.3	96.8	98.8	99.1	81.3	35 813	31 164
March	103.9	104.9	99.6	104.0	107.9	106.2	102.8	95.3	103.3	103.1	83.1	36 358	31 414
April	103.7	106.5	99.3	105.2	106.0	105.0	101.3	93.4	104.0	101.8	82.8	34 931	31 661
May	103.3	105.7	99.9	105.3	105.1	105.0	98.5	93.2	103.3	102.5	82.4	35 097	31 885
June	103.6	107.0	97.9	107.1	104.2	106.9	100.7	92.7	104.2	99.1	82.4	35 938	31 810
July	104.0	108.0	98.4	101.3	105.5	108.4	103.9	93.4	105.0	101.9	82.6	35 276	32 315
August	103.8	108.1	99.8	103.1	106.0	105.5	104.2	95.2	103.7	101.0	82.3	35 885	32 388
September	104.1	108.7	99.8	103.3	104.7	106.2	104.5	95.6	104.4	101.8	82.4	35 965	32 386
October	104.1	110.6	99.9	102.5	103.2	106.8	104.2	95.7	105.1	101.5	82.3	35 956	32 504
November	104.9	109.4	100.8	105.4	105.1	105.9	104.3	97.0	106.8	100.4	82.7	36 494	32 410
December	104.7	110.9	99.4	105.2	106.7	106.5	107.0	98.3	104.2	98.1	82.5	37 814	32 306
1995:													
January	105.6	108.7	100.8	106.1	107.7	107.6	106.0	98.8	105.1	103.2	83.1	36 560	32 866
February	104.5	109.0	99.4	107.8	108.0	107.2	103.2	99.5	100.8	100.3	82.0	36 728	32 931
March	105.0	110.8	100.5	105.0	107.8	107.3	105.3	99.9	102.5	101.8	82.3	36 704	33 099
April	105.3	109.4	99.9	106.5	105.6	105.9	111.5	99.7	105.2	100.7	82.4	36 674	33 063
May	106.2	111.4	99.6	110.1	104.6	106.7	109.8	100.9	105.3	102.4	82.9	36 412	33 139
June	106.8	113.1	101.1	105.7	106.6	108.2	109.6	98.3	106.4	105.6	83.3	37 014	33 262
July	106.2	110.7	100.7	106.6	105.8	106.9	109.0	98.0	107.2	103.6	82.7	37 022	33 359
August	106.6	109.4	100.0	107.5	105.2	108.1	106.6	99.0	109.1	106.1	82.8	37 682	33 293
September	106.2	111.4	99.8	104.2	107.3	107.7	104.3	96.8	109.3	104.4	82.4	38 118	33 908
October	105.9	110.7	100.5	103.9	106.4	107.8	105.2	97.7	107.5	104.4	82.0	38 105	34 163
November	105.2	113.1	99.5	102.4	105.3	104.7	104.6	97.1	107.0	104.9	81.4	38 429	34 256
December	105.1	113.3	99.5	104.7	103.0	104.1	109.1	96.5	105.6	104.1	81.1	38 633	34 411
1996:													
January	104.8	113.3	98.4	104.7	102.5	106.3	103.9	95.3	104.9	105.2	80.8	39 099	34 378
February	105.7	116.0	98.8	102.9	104.1	105.3	109.4	94.3	107.3	104.4	81.3	38 555	34 477
March	106.2	113.8	98.0	104.6	103.8	105.4	112.1	93.6	109.5	104.4	81.6	38 513	34 485
April	105.9	115.2	97.8	102.3	105.7	103.6	110.9	95.8	107.2	106.9	81.2	39 145	34 780
May	105.6	113.8	96.9	101.3	105.2	102.5	113.9	95.1	107.3	107.9	80.9	39 336	34 572
June	106.1	111.8	96.6	101.1	105.5	105.1	110.7	95.3	110.6	108.0	81.1	38 609	34 589
July	106.5	111.7	95.8	103.7	107.7	105.2	106.2	98.2	110.5	108.9	81.3	39 744	34 538
August	105.5	111.8	95.8	100.6	104.8	104.0	108.0	95.0	110.6	108.4	80.4	39 673	34 455
September	106.2	108.2	97.5	103.7	105.6	105.1	109.2	92.4	111.3	109.9	80.8	39 204	34 790
October	107.1	109.6	98.2	105.2	107.1	105.9	109.4	96.1	112.4	107.8	81.3	40 036	34 685
November	107.6	109.3	99.3	106.9	107.3	103.9	111.2	97.0	112.8	110.0	81.7	40 385	34 814
December	108.2	109.0	100.7	107.0	108.5	104.1	114.5	100.3	113.2	109.2	82.0	39 286	34 626

FOOD AND FOOD PRODUCTS—PRICES, EMPLOYMENT, HOURS, AND EARNINGS

YEAR AND MONTH	Producer prices (1982=100, except as noted, not seasonally adjusted)				Consumer prices— Food and beverages (1982-1984=100, seasonally adjusted)					Employment (Thousands, seasonally adjusted)		Production workers			
	Food and food products industry [1]	Finished consumer foods	Intermediate materials for food manufacturing	Crude foodstuffs and feedstuffs	Total	Food				Total payroll employees	Production workers	Weekly hours worked (Production workers, seasonally adjusted)		Average earnings (Dollars, not seasonally adjusted)	
						Total	Food at home	Food away from home				Average hours	Aggregate hours index (1982=100)	Hourly	Weekly
1968	....	40.0	39.8	40.9	36.2	35.3	36.3	32.9	1 782	1 192	40.8	109.5	2.80	114.24
1969	....	42.4	42.0	44.1	38.1	37.1	38.0	34.9	1 791	1 202	40.8	110.5	2.96	120.77
1970	....	43.8	44.3	45.2	40.1	39.2	39.9	37.5	1 786	1 207	40.5	110.2	3.16	127.98
1971	....	44.5	45.7	46.1	41.4	40.4	40.9	39.4	1 766	1 203	40.3	109.3	3.38	136.21
1972	....	46.9	47.0	51.5	43.1	42.1	42.7	41.0	1 745	1 192	40.5	108.7	3.60	145.80
1973	....	56.5	57.2	72.6	48.8	48.2	49.7	44.2	1 715	1 167	40.4	106.3	3.85	155.54
1974	....	64.4	82.0	76.4	55.5	55.1	57.1	49.8	1 707	1 164	40.4	106.0	4.19	169.28
1975	....	69.8	82.1	77.4	60.2	59.8	61.8	54.5	1 658	1 120	40.3	101.8	4.61	185.78
1976		69.6	70.6	76.8	62.1	61.6	63.1	58.2	1 689	1 145	40.5	104.4	4.98	201.69
1977		73.3	71.9	77.5	65.8	65.5	66.8	62.6	1 711	1 161	40.0	104.6	5.37	214.80
1978		79.9	81.0	87.3	72.2	72.0	73.8	68.3	1 724	1 174	39.7	105.1	5.80	230.26
1979		87.3	89.9	100.0	79.9	79.9	81.8	75.9	1 733	1 191	39.9	107.0	6.27	250.17
1980		92.4	103.7	104.6	86.7	86.8	88.4	83.4	1 708	1 175	39.7	105.1	6.85	271.95
1981		97.8	102.1	103.9	93.5	93.6	94.8	90.9	1 671	1 150	39.7	102.8	7.44	295.37
1982		100.0	100.0	100.0	97.3	97.4	98.1	95.8	1 636	1 126	39.4	100.0	7.92	312.05
1983		101.0	101.3	101.8	99.5	99.4	99.1	100.0	1 614	1 114	39.5	99.1	8.19	323.51
1984	99.0	105.4	106.3	104.7	103.2	103.2	102.8	104.2	1 611	1 119	39.8	100.3	8.39	333.92
1985	99.0	104.6	101.5	94.8	105.6	105.6	104.3	108.3	1 601	1 117	40.0	100.6	8.57	342.80
1986	100.3	107.3	98.4	93.2	109.1	109.0	107.3	112.5	1 607	1 129	40.0	101.7	8.75	350.00
1987	102.6	109.5	100.8	96.2	113.5	113.5	111.9	117.0	1 617	1 145	40.2	103.7	8.93	358.99
1988	107.1	112.6	106.0	106.1	118.2	118.2	116.6	121.8	1 626	1 155	40.3	105.0	9.12	367.54
1989	112.2	118.7	112.7	111.2	124.9	125.1	124.2	127.4	1 644	1 176	40.7	107.8	9.38	381.77
1990	116.2	124.4	117.9	113.1	132.1	132.4	132.3	133.4	1 661	1 194	40.8	109.7	9.62	392.50
1991	116.5	124.1	115.3	105.5	136.8	136.3	135.8	137.9	1 667	1 205	40.6	110.2	9.90	401.94
1992	116.9	123.3	113.9	105.1	138.7	137.9	136.8	140.7	1 663	1 212	40.6	110.9	10.20	414.12
1993	118.7	125.7	115.6	108.4	141.6	140.9	140.1	143.2	1 680	1 228	40.7	112.6	10.45	425.32
1994	120.1	126.8	118.5	106.5	144.9	144.3	144.1	145.7	1 678	1 231	41.3	114.6	10.66	440.26
1995	121.7	129.0	119.5	105.8	148.9	148.4	148.8	149.0	1 692	1 248	41.1	115.5	10.93	449.22
1996	127.1	133.6	125.3	121.5	153.7	153.3	154.3	152.7	1 693	1 254	41.0	115.9	11.20	459.20
1993:														
January	117.5	124.3	113.3	105.6	140.0	139.2	137.9	142.1	1 676	1 225	40.6	112.1	10.33	416.30
February	117.6	124.5	112.8	106.0	140.4	139.7	138.5	142.3	1 678	1 226	40.7	112.4	10.30	412.00
March	117.8	124.8	113.5	108.3	140.5	139.8	138.6	142.4	1 679	1 226	40.4	111.6	10.34	411.53
April	118.6	126.5	114.9	110.4	140.8	140.2	139.0	142.7	1 677	1 224	40.7	112.3	10.47	416.71
May	119.0	126.9	115.6	112.2	141.7	141.2	140.5	142.9	1 677	1 224	40.5	111.7	10.47	420.89
June	118.9	125.4	115.0	107.2	141.3	140.7	139.7	143.1	1 678	1 225	40.6	112.1	10.47	424.04
July	119.1	125.0	116.5	107.5	141.4	140.8	139.6	143.4	1 672	1 222	40.8	112.4	10.49	425.89
August	119.1	125.4	116.1	108.0	141.9	141.3	140.3	143.6	1 685	1 232	40.7	113.0	10.42	429.30
September	119.0	125.7	116.3	107.7	142.2	141.6	140.6	143.8	1 683	1 231	40.8	113.2	10.50	434.70
October	119.0	125.4	116.7	105.7	142.8	142.2	141.5	144.0	1 687	1 234	40.9	113.7	10.38	429.73
November	119.4	126.6	117.3	110.2	143.0	142.5	141.8	144.2	1 684	1 234	40.8	113.5	10.55	436.77
December	119.8	127.2	118.8	112.1	143.5	142.9	142.4	144.3	1 683	1 233	40.8	113.4	10.63	439.02
1994:														
January	120.0	127.0	118.9	112.2	143.7	143.1	142.6	144.5	1 678	1 227	41.0	113.4	10.58	426.37
February	120.5	126.7	119.2	113.1	143.5	142.9	142.2	144.7	1 680	1 231	40.7	112.9	10.56	423.46
March	121.0	127.5	119.9	114.2	143.5	143.0	142.2	144.9	1 680	1 234	41.2	114.6	10.61	430.77
April	120.9	127.1	120.7	113.1	143.5	143.0	142.1	145.1	1 677	1 232	41.1	114.1	10.63	430.52
May	120.6	126.6	120.1	109.7	144.0	143.5	142.8	145.3	1 677	1 230	41.1	113.9	10.64	433.05
June	119.8	125.9	118.0	107.8	144.4	144.0	143.4	145.5	1 677	1 230	41.2	114.2	10.65	437.72
July	119.7	126.2	116.2	103.6	145.2	144.8	144.6	145.6	1 680	1 234	41.5	115.4	10.68	444.29
August	120.1	126.6	117.8	101.8	145.8	145.4	145.4	145.9	1 679	1 232	41.3	114.7	10.59	442.66
September	119.9	126.3	118.5	101.3	146.0	145.6	145.6	146.2	1 678	1 232	41.4	114.9	10.64	450.07
October	119.6	126.1	116.8	98.9	145.9	145.5	145.4	146.4	1 673	1 227	41.3	114.2	10.64	445.82
November	119.6	126.9	118.0	100.4	146.2	145.8	145.7	146.7	1 680	1 234	41.5	115.4	10.81	456.18
December	119.4	128.6	117.5	101.6	147.3	147.0	147.3	147.1	1 682	1 236	41.7	116.1	10.85	457.87
1995:														
January	120.2	127.9	117.8	102.2	147.2	146.9	147.0	147.4	1 689	1 244	41.8	117.2	10.85	445.94
February	120.8	128.4	118.4	104.1	147.7	147.4	147.6	147.7	1 682	1 239	41.3	115.3	10.82	439.29
March	121.1	128.7	119.0	103.2	147.6	147.3	147.0	148.2	1 682	1 238	41.2	114.9	10.87	441.32
April	120.5	128.7	117.2	101.8	148.2	147.9	148.1	148.3	1 684	1 240	40.9	114.3	10.92	434.62
May	120.3	128.0	116.5	99.6	148.7	148.4	148.6	148.6	1 686	1 242	41.1	115.0	10.90	444.72
June	120.4	127.4	117.3	102.1	148.7	148.4	148.6	148.8	1 699	1 254	41.2	116.4	10.92	449.90
July	121.4	128.5	119.5	104.6	149.0	148.7	148.8	149.1	1 693	1 248	41.2	115.9	10.92	449.90
August	122.0	128.8	120.0	104.8	149.3	149.0	149.1	149.4	1 692	1 246	41.2	115.7	10.89	454.11
September	122.4	130.1	120.5	108.8	149.7	149.4	149.7	149.6	1 699	1 255	41.1	116.2	10.97	461.84
October	123.2	129.9	122.2	109.6	150.1	149.8	150.1	149.9	1 700	1 256	40.9	115.8	10.92	452.09
November	123.8	131.1	122.8	114.2	150.2	149.9	150.1	150.1	1 702	1 258	40.7	115.4	11.05	457.47
December	124.2	131.0	122.9	114.7	150.4	150.1	150.3	150.4	1 702	1 257	40.5	114.7	11.17	460.20
1996:														
January	124.2	130.7	120.7	114.7	150.8	150.5	150.8	150.6	1 700	1 258	40.0	113.4	11.08	435.44
February	124.4	130.7	121.0	115.0	151.2	150.9	151.1	151.0	1 705	1 262	41.1	116.9	11.03	445.61
March	124.3	132.0	120.6	116.2	151.8	151.5	152.0	151.3	1 709	1 266	41.1	117.3	11.10	449.55
April	124.6	131.2	121.6	119.6	152.1	151.8	152.3	151.6	1 701	1 259	41.0	116.3	11.19	449.84
May	126.3	131.5	122.6	127.7	152.4	152.1	152.4	152.0	1 698	1 259	41.0	116.3	11.18	455.03
June	127.6	133.6	123.2	129.0	153.4	153.1	153.9	152.4	1 689	1 251	41.0	115.6	11.22	458.90
July	128.3	133.9	128.5	130.9	154.0	153.8	154.7	152.8	1 684	1 248	40.8	114.7	11.25	460.13
August	129.7	135.3	129.4	129.5	154.6	154.4	155.5	153.1	1 685	1 247	40.8	114.7	11.16	463.14
September	129.7	135.6	129.2	124.9	155.3	155.1	156.3	153.6	1 682	1 246	41.0	115.1	11.19	472.22
October	129.8	136.6	129.2	119.6	156.0	155.8	157.2	154.1	1 684	1 249	41.1	115.7	11.16	465.37
November	128.5	136.1	124.8	117.7	156.6	156.4	157.8	154.6	1 688	1 252	41.1	116.0	11.38	475.68
December	128.2	135.5	123.8	113.6	156.6	156.4	157.7	154.9	1 689	1 256	41.3	116.9	11.46	481.32

1. December 1984=100.

TOBACCO PRODUCTS—PRODUCTION, SHIPMENTS, INVENTORIES, PRICES, EMPLOYMENT, HOURS, AND EARNINGS

YEAR AND MONTH	Industrial production (1992=100, seasonally adjusted)	Manufacturers' shipments and inventories (Millions of dollars, seasonally adjusted)		Producer prices (Not seasonally adjusted)		Employment (Thousands, seasonally adjusted)		Production workers			
								Weekly hours worked (Seasonally adjusted)		Average earnings (Dollars, not seasonally adjusted)	
		Shipments	Inventories (Book value, end of period)	Tobacco manufactures[1]	Leaf tobacco (1982=100)	Total payroll employees	Production workers	Average hours[2]	Aggregate hours index (1982=100)	Hourly	Weekly
1968	93.8	4 937	2 218	....	37.9	85	72	37.9	134.8	2.48	93.99
1969	91.1	4 992	2 188	....	39.7	83	70	37.4	128.8	2.62	97.99
1970	94.3	5 350	2 052	....	40.3	83	69	37.8	129.2	2.91	110.00
1971	93.1	5 528	2 099	....	41.9	77	63	37.8	118.7	3.16	119.45
1972	96.6	5 919	2 355	....	45.7	75	62	37.6	115.9	3.47	130.47
1973	101.7	6 341	2 426	....	47.7	78	65	38.6	124.0	3.76	145.14
1974	99.4	7 139	3 024	....	54.7	77	64	38.3	120.9	4.12	157.80
1975	101.7	8 058	3 290	....	....	76	62	38.2	118.1	4.55	173.81
1976	106.8	8 786	3 416	....	60.6	77	64	37.5	118.2	4.98	186.75
1977	102.8	9 051	3 511	....	65.1	71	57	37.8	106.8	5.54	209.41
1978	107.4	9 951	3 669	....	70.8	71	56	38.1	106.1	6.13	233.55
1979	106.9	10 602	3 517	....	76.7	70	56	38.0	104.4	6.67	253.46
1980	108.5	12 194	3 721	....	82.1	69	54	38.1	101.2	7.74	294.89
1981	109.9	13 130	4 436	....	91.2	70	55	38.8	105.1	8.88	344.54
1982	106.2	16 061	6 873	....	100.0	69	53	37.8	100.0	9.79	370.06
1983	101.6	16 268	6 746	....	101.3	68	52	37.4	96.3	10.38	388.21
1984	101.7	17 473	6 533	....	101.5	64	49	38.9	93.5	11.22	436.46
1985	101.8	18 559	5 943	106.6	101.2	64	48	37.2	88.4	11.96	444.91
1986	100.3	19 146	5 449	115.5	89.8	59	44	37.4	81.6	12.88	481.71
1987	104.7	20 757	5 331	126.5	85.8	55	42	39.0	80.1	14.07	548.73
1988	106.5	23 809	5 286	141.8	87.2	54	41	39.8	80.1	14.67	583.87
1989	105.4	25 875	5 570	161.4	93.8	50	37	38.6	70.6	15.31	590.97
1990	105.4	29 856	5 974	183.2	95.8	49	36	39.2	70.6	16.23	636.22
1991	98.9	31 943	6 342	207.5	101.1	49	36	39.1	70.2	16.77	655.71
1992	100.0	35 198	6 670	230.2	101.0	48	36	38.6	68.2	16.92	653.11
1993	84.0	28 383	6 322	218.0	100.3	44	33	37.4	60.7	16.89	631.69
1994	103.7	30 021	5 776	187.8	100.2	43	33	39.3	64.1	19.07	749.45
1995	106.2	32 984	5 768	193.2	102.5	42	32	39.6	62.8	19.41	768.64
1996	105.6	34 492	6 254	199.1	105.1	41	32	40.0	63.2	19.34	773.60
1993:											
January	96.6	2 545	6 650	244.6	104.8	45	34	38.6	64.7	15.69	605.63
February	91.0	2 455	6 651	244.8	110.0	44	33	37.3	64.1	16.23	605.38
March	84.7	2 983	6 771	244.8	108.7	43	32	36.0	58.1	16.89	608.04
April	81.4	2 161	6 685	248.3	97.6	44	33	35.5	59.7	17.46	619.83
May	82.6	2 443	6 786	248.8	91.8	44	33	36.7	60.3	17.89	656.56
June	80.0	2 590	6 896	242.4	91.8	44	33	38.6	61.0	18.06	697.12
July	87.0	2 510	6 796	240.8	91.8	44	32	36.0	58.6	18.47	664.92
August	82.4	1 632	6 783	178.5	93.1	42	32	37.4	58.6	17.30	647.02
September	79.4	2 459	6 763	178.5	100.9	43	32	38.1	59.4	16.32	621.79
October	74.9	2 139	6 612	178.7	102.2	43	32	38.6	58.8	16.05	619.53
November	80.3	2 098	6 615	178.7	105.5	44	33	37.6	61.6	16.43	617.77
December	87.2	2 455	6 322	187.4	105.5	43	33	37.4	60.1	16.80	628.32
1994:											
January	88.9	2 743	6 031	187.6	105.5	43	32	37.5	60.1	17.00	637.50
February	95.2	2 681	5 880	187.7	109.4	43	32	35.4	58.9	18.21	644.63
March	94.7	2 088	6 167	187.7	91.8	44	33	37.9	63.6	18.67	707.59
April	100.6	2 896	6 091	187.7	98.9	44	34	39.4	67.2	19.58	771.45
May	102.9	2 412	6 135	187.7	98.9	44	34	38.8	65.7	20.22	784.54
June	103.4	2 289	6 124	187.7	98.9	43	33	40.2	63.9	20.75	834.15
July	101.8	2 441	6 039	187.7	87.2	43	33	37.9	63.1	20.57	779.60
August	107.7	2 606	5 838	187.7	91.1	43	34	39.4	65.8	18.87	743.48
September	109.3	2 443	5 819	187.9	102.8	43	33	41.2	65.0	18.84	776.21
October	116.1	2 676	5 678	187.6	104.8	43	33	41.9	66.0	18.69	783.11
November	113.3	2 548	5 735	188.1	106.1	42	32	39.8	63.1	19.41	772.52
December	111.0	2 564	5 776	187.9	107.4	42	33	41.1	66.2	18.55	762.41
1995:											
January	106.7	2 649	5 692	188.1	110.5	43	33	39.1	65.0	18.60	727.26
February	104.7	2 780	5 750	188.7	112.5	42	32	38.5	62.5	19.53	751.91
March	107.2	2 605	5 613	190.6	100.2	41	32	38.1	62.0	20.30	773.43
April	108.0	2 879	5 593	190.7	90.0	42	32	38.4	62.9	19.98	767.23
May	104.5	2 890	5 543	195.3	....	42	31	40.0	61.6	20.97	838.80
June	112.8	2 698	5 562	195.3	....	42	32	41.6	64.0	21.85	908.96
July	113.9	2 740	5 638	195.2	103.5	42	32	39.3	63.5	21.71	853.20
August	103.9	2 686	5 744	195.0	102.0	43	33	40.4	65.5	18.49	747.00
September	102.5	2 694	5 925	195.0	107.6	42	32	40.0	61.2	17.57	702.80
October	101.4	2 809	5 803	195.0	106.7	42	32	40.4	61.8	18.09	730.84
November	104.8	2 929	5 719	195.0	108.5	42	32	40.6	63.4	19.48	790.89
December	104.1	2 748	5 768	195.0	108.5	42	32	39.1	60.9	17.71	692.46
1996:											
January	104.1	2 692	5 814	195.1	111.4	42	32	35.8	58.1	18.38	658.00
February	107.4	2 844	5 788	195.0	118.8	42	32	38.7	62.8	18.13	701.63
March	111.3	2 810	5 807	195.1	102.6	42	32	39.4	64.2	19.34	762.00
April	106.3	2 851	5 760	195.1	94.4	42	32	39.3	63.2	20.40	801.72
May	103.7	2 784	5 781	201.1	....	41	32	39.9	62.8	21.04	839.50
June	105.1	2 841	5 805	201.0	....	41	32	41.0	62.5	21.37	876.17
July	102.5	2 954	5 737	201.1	94.1	41	32	38.6	62.6	20.98	809.83
August	104.1	2 970	5 854	201.4	102.6	40	31	40.0	61.0	20.27	810.80
September	104.9	2 902	5 957	201.0	110.5	41	32	42.0	64.0	18.37	771.54
October	104.0	2 998	6 092	201.1	112.6	42	32	41.2	63.1	17.73	730.48
November	105.4	2 903	6 258	201.1	112.9	42	33	41.2	66.4	18.60	766.32
December	108.9	2 976	6 254	201.2	113.2	42	32	41.9	65.1	18.67	782.27

1. December 1984=100.
2. Not seasonally adjusted.

TEXTILE MILL PRODUCTS—PRODUCTION, CAPACITY, SHIPMENTS, AND INVENTORIES

YEAR AND MONTH	Industrial production (1992=100, seasonally adjusted)					Capacity utilization (Percent of capacity, seasonally adjusted)	Manufacturers' shipments and inventories (Millions of dollars, seasonally adjusted)	
	Total	Fabrics	Knit goods	Carpeting	Yarns and miscellaneous		Shipments	Inventories (Book value, end of period)
1968	69.8	112.0	54.5	46.5	59.1	90.8	21 970	3 610
1969	73.4	113.0	59.8	52.0	61.2	89.0	22 978	3 670
1970	71.8	105.9	60.4	52.4	60.3	83.5	22 614	3 676
1971	75.8	103.7	63.9	57.6	67.2	84.7	24 034	3 866
1972	83.1	101.6	75.7	66.9	74.8	88.6	28 065	4 056
1973	86.5	108.4	79.4	73.2	73.7	89.7	31 073	4 592
1974	78.7	101.3	69.7	63.2	67.4	80.5	32 790	5 044
1975	75.0	92.5	68.7	58.1	66.5	76.1	31 065	4 794
1976	83.3	106.5	71.8	67.3	75.2	83.6	36 387	5 232
1977	88.3	107.5	76.0	82.8	78.8	87.2	40 550	5 649
1978	88.6	100.3	78.5	87.0	82.7	86.0	42 281	5 935
1979	91.5	107.2	78.5	96.5	83.8	87.7	45 137	6 148
1980	89.0	107.7	79.5	84.8	77.4	84.8	47 256	6 648
1981	86.3	105.3	76.3	79.2	76.1	81.6	50 260	6 896
1982	80.1	92.2	76.7	75.8	69.7	75.5	47 516	6 723
1983	89.9	102.5	82.6	91.0	80.4	85.3	53 733	7 514
1984	90.4	100.1	81.9	99.6	82.0	85.8	56 336	7 827
1985	86.5	91.9	80.9	99.5	79.4	81.5	54 605	7 439
1986	90.5	95.0	82.2	104.7	86.6	85.4	57 188	7 191
1987	96.3	100.6	85.6	105.2	96.6	90.5	62 787	7 939
1988	95.0	102.4	82.0	106.7	95.7	88.0	64 627	8 384
1989	96.5	100.1	88.8	105.2	97.9	87.9	67 265	8 721
1990	93.2	94.4	87.7	100.9	96.4	83.4	65 533	8 732
1991	92.7	96.3	92.6	88.0	92.7	81.7	65 440	8 484
1992	100.0	100.0	100.0	100.0	100.0	87.1	70 753	8 714
1993	105.5	104.9	107.5	105.8	104.0	89.8	73 955	9 268
1994	110.8	109.9	112.0	111.1	111.9	91.6	78 027	9 804
1995	109.9	111.1	109.8	107.8	110.5	87.4	79 743	10 268
1996	106.6	105.9	107.5	105.8	109.3	82.1	78 505	10 029
1993:								
January	105.0	101.9	105.9	115.0	102.9	90.5	6 328	8 735
February	102.7	103.5	102.5	104.9	100.7	88.3	6 153	8 718
March	102.5	105.7	106.8	90.6	99.1	87.9	5 917	8 785
April	103.1	104.0	105.5	99.6	101.4	88.3	6 110	8 873
May	105.3	102.2	106.3	111.3	105.0	89.9	6 130	8 965
June	106.1	107.1	107.1	107.5	102.8	90.4	6 162	8 927
July	108.5	109.8	108.7	113.2	103.5	92.3	6 188	8 925
August	106.3	106.7	106.8	106.0	104.8	90.2	6 198	8 948
September	106.3	104.5	110.4	102.9	106.4	90.0	6 117	9 038
October	107.4	104.8	109.1	112.3	107.0	90.8	6 245	9 066
November	106.2	105.6	109.1	104.4	106.0	89.6	6 243	9 177
December	106.7	103.2	112.4	102.4	108.4	89.9	6 178	9 268
1994:								
January	108.2	106.3	110.5	115.3	106.9	90.9	6 214	9 463
February	107.6	107.1	110.2	106.3	107.4	90.2	6 353	9 483
March	109.1	107.3	114.3	104.9	109.1	91.1	6 382	9 524
April	110.6	107.1	113.9	115.8	111.1	92.1	6 383	9 534
May	109.6	107.2	113.3	109.1	110.9	91.0	6 468	9 563
June	110.6	108.7	112.8	109.2	112.3	91.5	6 535	9 561
July	112.6	110.3	114.3	115.7	113.4	92.9	6 479	9 608
August	110.6	110.3	111.8	107.4	113.3	91.0	6 557	9 586
September	111.9	113.1	111.4	109.1	112.8	91.8	6 572	9 602
October	112.7	112.5	112.1	114.5	113.8	92.1	6 646	9 671
November	112.8	114.8	108.4	109.2	117.0	91.9	6 606	9 752
December	113.8	114.4	110.8	116.2	114.6	92.4	6 811	9 804
1995:								
January	115.1	117.3	112.6	108.7	117.9	93.2	6 839	9 836
February	113.1	115.1	108.2	114.4	115.4	91.3	6 768	9 882
March	113.7	115.1	112.5	110.6	115.4	91.4	6 777	10 009
April	113.6	112.3	112.8	114.3	115.4	91.0	6 700	10 085
May	110.5	114.1	109.9	102.1	111.3	88.3	6 703	10 162
June	108.8	110.6	112.7	96.2	110.1	86.6	6 626	10 222
July	105.9	106.5	108.3	108.8	103.6	84.0	6 537	10 237
August	109.6	110.5	111.0	106.7	109.8	86.7	6 654	10 244
September	107.8	108.2	106.7	111.6	109.5	85.0	6 645	10 281
October	108.0	110.0	110.4	101.4	106.1	84.9	6 523	10 292
November	106.3	106.9	107.8	104.2	105.8	83.2	6 560	10 309
December	106.2	106.8	105.2	114.7	105.9	82.9	6 438	10 268
1996:								
January	102.5	103.1	106.1	95.8	103.1	79.8	6 273	10 192
February	104.0	103.4	106.3	100.5	106.6	80.8	6 419	10 178
March	107.0	104.4	106.8	120.6	107.6	83.0	6 497	10 089
April	105.3	106.9	106.9	100.3	106.1	81.5	6 425	10 059
May	106.1	106.4	107.6	103.2	107.6	82.0	6 532	10 012
June	108.0	106.1	107.0	118.9	109.3	83.3	6 770	9 963
July	108.7	110.7	110.3	99.3	110.2	83.7	6 580	9 958
August	107.7	105.8	108.3	107.6	110.6	82.7	6 508	10 039
September	107.2	107.2	107.0	108.5	109.7	82.2	6 594	10 000
October	107.6	107.7	109.4	99.3	111.7	82.4	6 544	9 997
November	108.2	106.1	107.1	109.1	113.7	82.7	6 605	10 034
December	106.3	102.7	107.4	106.2	115.3	81.1	6 725	10 029

TEXTILE MILL PRODUCTS—PRICES, EMPLOYMENT, HOURS, AND EARNINGS

YEAR AND MONTH	Producer prices (1982=100, except as noted, not seasonally adjusted)							Employment (Thousands, seasonally adjusted)		Production workers			
	Textile mill products [1]	Intermediate materials					Crude materials: Raw cotton	Total payroll employees	Production workers	Weekly hours worked (Seasonally adjusted)		Average earnings (Dollars, not seasonally adjusted)	
		Synthetic fibers	Processed yarns and thread	Gray fabrics	Finished fabrics	Industrial textile products				Average hours	Aggregate hours index (1982=100)	Hourly	Weekly
1968							51.9	994	881	41.2	150.6	2.21	91.05
1969							44.3	1 003	884	40.8	150.0	2.35	95.88
1970							43.6	975	855	39.9	141.8	2.45	97.76
1971							47.2	955	837	40.6	141.3	2.57	104.34
1972							57.0	986	867	41.3	148.9	2.75	113.58
1973							93.4	1 010	886	40.9	150.7	2.95	120.66
1974							96.4	965	843	39.5	138.5	3.20	126.40
1975							75.1	868	752	39.3	122.9	3.42	134.41
1976		63.2	71.9	73.0	81.2		113.3	919	800	40.1	133.3	3.69	147.97
1977		66.2	73.0	72.1	83.3		101.1	910	792	40.4	132.9	3.99	161.20
1978		67.6	74.0	81.6	83.3	77.7	96.0	899	783	40.4	131.6	4.30	173.72
1979		73.4	78.9	87.5	86.2	82.4	104.2	885	771	40.4	129.3	4.66	188.26
1980		83.1	88.6	95.0	92.9	91.7	135.7	848	737	40.1	122.7	5.07	203.31
1981		96.5	99.8	101.0	100.5	98.5	120.0	823	713	39.6	117.3	5.52	218.59
1982		100.0	100.0	100.0	100.0	100.0	100.0	749	642	37.5	100.0	5.83	218.63
1983		96.7	100.1	101.2	98.9	99.9	114.0	741	639	40.4	107.4	6.18	249.67
1984		98.5	103.2	105.8	101.7	100.2	113.5	746	646	39.9	107.0	6.46	257.75
1985	99.7	95.5	102.1	104.4	101.4	102.5	97.7	702	606	39.7	100.1	6.70	265.99
1986	100.3	92.5	101.7	103.7	101.4	106.5	88.0	703	608	41.1	103.8	6.93	284.82
1987	102.6	91.8	103.8	107.2	104.2	106.1	105.8	725	630	41.8	109.4	7.17	299.71
1988	106.8	97.3	108.0	114.0	109.4	107.7	95.5	728	632	41.0	107.7	7.38	302.58
1989	109.3	104.8	110.4	115.2	113.6	109.2	105.6	720	622	40.9	105.6	7.67	313.70
1990	111.6	106.7	112.6	117.2	116.0	112.0	118.2	691	593	39.9	98.4	8.02	320.00
1991	112.5	105.3	112.6	117.4	117.5	113.8	116.2	670	574	40.6	97.0	8.30	336.98
1992	113.6	103.4	110.8	120.6	118.8	114.7	89.8	674	577	41.1	98.6	8.60	353.46
1993	113.6	103.6	107.8	118.6	119.5	115.5	91.9	675	575	41.4	98.9	8.88	367.63
1994	113.6	104.1	108.4	116.8	119.2	116.6	121.3	676	575	41.6	99.4	9.13	379.81
1995	116.5	109.4	112.8	121.2	121.7	119.0	156.2	663	560	40.8	94.9	9.41	383.93
1996	118.2	111.3	114.7	121.4	123.6	125.6	130.0	624	528	40.6	88.9	9.69	393.41
1993:													
January	113.5	102.6	108.5	120.1	119.4	115.1	89.8	677	578	41.7	100.1	8.80	363.44
February	113.5	102.3	108.2	119.8	119.4	115.6	89.9	677	577	41.8	100.2	8.81	362.09
March	113.5	102.4	108.0	119.5	119.4	115.5	94.8	676	575	39.8	95.1	8.75	346.50
April	113.5	102.8	107.9	119.6	119.5	115.5	92.2	678	577	41.9	100.4	8.88	364.97
May	113.4	102.9	107.7	118.4	120.0	115.5	93.9	678	578	41.5	99.7	8.86	368.58
June	113.4	103.5	107.9	119.0	119.8	115.5	91.0	676	575	41.2	98.4	8.86	370.35
July	113.6	103.8	107.9	118.8	119.6	115.6	91.4	675	574	41.2	98.3	8.87	362.78
August	113.7	105.1	107.7	118.8	119.5	115.6	89.0	673	573	41.4	98.6	8.90	372.02
September	113.8	104.5	107.8	117.5	119.4	115.3	90.0	675	573	41.6	99.0	8.95	375.01
October	113.7	104.4	107.7	118.1	119.4	115.3	92.6	673	572	41.5	98.6	8.95	373.22
November	113.7	104.2	107.3	117.0	119.3	115.7	89.3	672	571	41.8	99.2	8.97	378.53
December	113.5	104.2	107.1	116.9	119.1	115.8	98.8	672	571	41.7	98.9	9.00	379.80
1994:													
January	113.5	103.8	107.1	116.5	119.2	115.6	107.9	671	571	41.4	98.2	9.03	372.04
February	113.1	103.5	107.0	116.3	118.9	115.8	120.0	673	572	40.2	95.5	9.03	357.59
March	113.1	103.1	107.1	116.4	118.9	115.9	121.6	673	572	41.8	99.3	9.02	376.13
April	113.3	103.0	107.2	116.6	119.2	116.1	124.1	674	573	41.8	99.5	9.09	380.87
May	113.2	103.2	107.3	116.4	119.2	116.0	129.9	674	574	41.8	99.7	9.06	378.71
June	113.5	103.4	108.4	116.4	119.2	116.1	130.1	676	574	41.9	99.9	9.11	386.26
July	113.6	104.6	109.1	116.3	119.1	116.8	114.8	677	576	41.8	100.0	9.11	375.33
August	113.8	105.6	108.9	117.2	119.1	117.1	119.2	679	576	41.6	99.6	9.12	382.13
September	113.8	105.9	109.0	117.6	119.1	117.5	122.5	678	575	41.5	99.1	9.20	386.40
October	113.9	104.8	109.4	116.5	119.5	117.4	111.4	680	577	41.8	100.2	9.18	385.56
November	114.2	104.2	109.8	117.2	119.6	117.4	120.8	681	578	41.4	99.4	9.26	387.07
December	114.3	104.3	109.9	117.7	119.5	117.4	133.3	682	578	41.5	99.7	9.30	390.60
1995:													
January	114.7	106.8	110.6	118.6	120.0	118.0	144.4	679	576	41.6	99.6	9.34	387.61
February	115.5	107.0	111.1	120.5	120.6	117.7	150.2	681	576	41.6	99.6	9.31	382.64
March	115.7	106.4	112.0	120.7	121.0	118.1	181.4	679	574	41.2	98.3	9.29	382.75
April	116.1	108.4	112.2	121.0	121.3	118.2	176.2	679	574	41.1	98.0	9.35	373.07
May	116.6	108.6	113.1	121.7	121.7	118.5	166.4	672	568	40.5	95.6	9.34	378.27
June	116.6	108.4	113.2	122.0	121.8	119.0	179.9	667	563	40.4	94.5	9.37	382.30
July	116.8	109.6	112.9	121.4	122.0	118.8	164.4	659	556	40.4	93.3	9.39	373.72
August	116.9	111.0	113.5	121.4	122.3	119.1	139.7	658	555	40.7	93.9	9.45	387.45
September	117.2	111.6	113.4	122.5	122.3	119.2	148.3	653	551	40.6	92.9	9.50	390.45
October	117.4	112.4	113.5	121.8	122.4	119.6	143.4	648	547	40.5	92.0	9.49	385.29
November	117.2	111.8	113.9	120.9	122.3	120.8	140.8	646	545	40.5	91.7	9.53	389.78
December	117.3	110.9	113.8	121.6	122.3	121.0	138.9	640	541	40.3	90.6	9.57	389.50
1996:													
January	117.4	111.0	114.4	120.8	123.1	121.7	137.0	630	530	36.1	79.5	9.56	344.16
February	117.5	111.2	114.5	120.8	123.2	121.5	136.0	635	536	40.6	90.4	9.55	383.91
March	117.7	111.2	114.1	121.9	123.1	121.5	133.0	631	533	40.7	90.1	9.55	388.69
April	118.1	111.2	114.7	122.4	123.6	121.5	143.5	626	529	40.4	88.8	9.65	386.97
May	118.3	111.0	114.5	121.6	123.5	127.4	138.2	626	528	40.7	89.3	9.62	390.57
June	118.0	109.5	114.6	120.9	123.7	127.3	136.5	625	528	40.9	89.7	9.68	400.75
July	118.3	111.7	114.5	121.1	123.7	127.4	128.8	623	526	40.9	89.4	9.68	389.14
August	118.4	111.8	114.3	121.4	123.9	127.8	128.9	621	525	40.9	89.2	9.72	401.44
September	118.5	112.1	114.6	121.3	123.8	128.1	123.2	618	524	40.9	89.0	9.78	404.89
October	118.6	112.0	114.9	121.6	123.7	128.1	120.3	620	525	40.9	89.2	9.73	399.90
November	118.6	111.7	114.8	121.2	123.9	127.1	113.3	616	522	41.2	89.4	9.77	407.41
December	118.6	111.6	114.6	121.5	123.6	127.5	120.8	615	522	41.5	90.0	9.92	416.64

1. December 1984=100.

APPAREL—PRODUCTION, CAPACITY, PRICES, EMPLOYMENT, HOURS, AND EARNINGS

YEAR AND MONTH	Apparel products (Seasonally adjusted)		Producer prices (1982=100, except as noted, not seasonally adjusted)				Consumer prices: Apparel commodities (1982-1984=100, seasonally adjusted)	Employment (Thousands, seasonally adjusted)		Production workers			
			Apparel industry [1]	Finished apparel						Weekly hours worked— (Production workers, seasonally adjusted)		Average earnings (Dollars, not seasonally adjusted)	
	Industrial production (1992=100)	Capacity utilization (Percent of capacity)		Women's	Men's and boys'	Girls', children's, and infants'		Total payroll employees	Production workers	Average hours	Aggregate hours index (1982=100)	Hourly	Weekly
1968	82.4	85.6	....	59.4	47.2	54.2	57.3	1 406	1 240	36.1	131.3	2.21	79.78
1969	85.1	84.9	....	61.4	49.3	56.2	60.8	1 409	1 238	35.9	130.5	2.31	82.93
1970	81.8	78.9	....	62.8	51.2	58.8	63.3	1 364	1 196	35.3	123.9	2.39	84.37
1971	82.9	78.6	....	64.1	52.7	60.3	65.2	1 343	1 178	35.6	122.9	2.49	88.64
1972	87.9	82.0	....	64.6	53.6	60.7	66.6	1 383	1 208	36.0	127.8	2.60	93.60
1973	88.5	81.4	....	66.7	56.1	61.9	69.0	1 438	1 250	35.9	131.7	2.76	99.08
1974	84.5	76.5	....	70.0	63.4	68.9	73.9	1 363	1 175	35.2	121.3	2.97	104.54
1975	77.4	69.3	....	71.3	66.3	70.0	76.7	1 243	1 067	35.2	110.2	3.17	111.58
1976	91.1	80.3	....	73.5	71.1	72.1	79.2	1 318	1 134	35.8	119.3	3.40	121.72
1977	98.0	84.8	....	75.6	77.1	73.2	82.3	1 316	1 129	35.6	117.9	3.62	128.87
1978	100.4	85.9	....	77.4	80.2	76.6	84.5	1 332	1 145	35.6	119.5	3.94	140.26
1979	95.3	80.5	....	81.1	84.7	81.0	87.5	1 304	1 117	35.3	115.6	4.23	149.32
1980	95.4	79.4	....	86.9	91.3	87.1	92.9	1 264	1 079	35.4	112.2	4.56	161.42
1981	97.3	80.6		95.0	96.0	97.1	96.5	1 244	1 060	35.7	111.0	4.97	177.43
1982	96.3	79.7		100.0	100.0	100.0	98.3	1 161	981	34.7	100.0	5.20	180.44
1983	100.3	82.6		102.1	101.3	100.5	100.2	1 163	984	36.2	104.5	5.38	194.76
1984	102.2	84.1	101.1	103.7	103.5	103.2	101.5	1 185	1 002	36.4	107.2	5.55	202.02
1985	98.6	80.4	101.1	105.4	105.0	103.1	104.0	1 120	944	36.4	100.7	5.73	208.57
1986	101.8	82.3	102.3	106.8	106.4	103.8	104.2	1 100	926	36.7	99.7	5.84	214.33
1987	105.5	85.2	103.9	108.4	108.6	106.7	108.9	1 097	922	37.0	100.1	5.94	219.78
1988	103.6	83.6	107.2	111.3	113.0	107.5	113.7	1 085	912	37.0	99.0	6.12	226.44
1989	100.3	80.9	110.2	113.5	116.8	110.5	116.7	1 076	907	36.9	98.3	6.35	234.32
1990	97.2	78.3	113.3	116.1	120.2	115.3	122.0	1 036	869	36.4	92.9	6.57	239.15
1991	97.8	78.7	116.0	117.9	122.7	117.8	126.4	1 006	841	37.0	91.3	6.77	250.49
1992	100.0	80.3	118.0	119.9	126.0	119.0	129.4	1 007	844	37.2	92.2	6.95	258.54
1993	102.4	82.0	119.2	120.2	127.7	120.1	131.0	989	829	37.2	90.4	7.09	263.75
1994	106.5	84.9	119.7	119.7	128.5	119.9	130.4	974	815	37.5	89.7	7.34	275.25
1995	103.3	80.8	120.6	119.6	130.3	121.6	128.7	936	776	37.0	84.2	7.64	282.68
1996	98.2	75.2	122.3	119.9	132.1	122.4	128.2	864	708	37.0	76.9	7.96	294.52
1993:													
January	101.6	81.5	118.9	120.7	127.2	120.2	130.0	1 002	838	37.5	92.2	7.05	262.97
February	102.4	82.1	118.9	120.2	127.5	120.6	131.5	1 002	839	37.6	92.6	7.04	262.59
March	101.4	81.3	119.1	120.3	127.6	120.2	131.4	1 000	838	36.9	90.8	7.05	260.85
April	102.0	81.7	119.1	120.5	127.7	120.2	131.5	998	836	37.8	92.8	7.06	257.69
May	101.8	81.5	119.2	120.4	127.7	120.3	130.8	996	835	37.2	91.2	7.05	262.26
June	102.3	81.9	119.1	120.1	127.7	118.5	130.2	993	832	37.0	90.4	7.07	264.42
July	102.9	82.3	119.4	120.5	127.6	120.4	130.1	979	825	37.2	90.1	7.01	258.67
August	102.9	82.4	119.4	120.1	127.9	120.5	131.2	985	824	37.2	90.0	7.07	264.42
September	102.5	82.0	119.3	120.1	127.9	119.7	130.9	982	822	37.2	89.7	7.15	263.84
October	102.7	82.1	119.3	120.1	128.0	119.9	130.8	978	818	36.9	88.6	7.14	265.61
November	103.1	82.4	119.4	119.9	127.7	120.5	131.6	976	818	37.1	89.1	7.18	269.97
December	103.5	82.7	119.3	119.6	127.7	120.6	131.2	971	814	37.1	88.6	7.25	272.60
1994:													
January	102.7	82.0	119.5	119.9	128.0	120.4	130.4	970	811	37.1	88.3	7.22	265.70
February	103.2	82.4	119.6	120.1	128.1	120.6	130.1	969	811	35.7	85.0	7.22	255.59
March	105.0	83.8	119.7	120.1	128.3	120.5	130.8	972	813	37.4	89.2	7.25	271.15
April	106.0	84.6	119.6	119.5	128.4	120.4	130.6	973	814	37.5	89.6	7.28	273.00
May	106.5	84.9	119.7	119.9	128.5	120.3	131.0	974	814	37.7	90.1	7.28	274.46
June	107.1	85.3	119.5	119.5	128.4	120.3	131.8	975	816	37.7	90.3	7.33	278.54
July	107.3	85.5	119.8	119.9	128.6	121.0	131.2	976	819	37.6	90.4	7.31	273.39
August	107.2	85.4	119.7	119.4	128.7	120.6	130.1	978	817	37.6	90.2	7.36	278.94
September	107.9	85.9	119.7	119.6	128.8	119.2	130.4	979	818	37.4	89.8	7.45	281.61
October	108.7	86.5	119.8	119.8	128.8	118.6	129.7	980	819	37.7	90.6	7.44	282.72
November	108.1	86.0	119.7	119.5	128.8	118.6	129.2	974	815	37.5	89.7	7.46	283.48
December	108.6	86.4	119.8	119.8	129.1	118.5	128.8	974	816	37.6	90.1	7.48	284.99
1995:													
January	107.4	85.3	120.0	119.9	129.2	119.1	128.9	970	812	37.6	89.6	7.55	280.86
February	106.8	84.6	120.3	120.1	129.8	121.2	128.4	965	805	37.4	88.4	7.49	280.13
March	107.0	84.5	120.6	120.2	129.9	120.9	128.7	960	800	37.3	87.6	7.53	280.87
April	104.9	82.6	120.4	119.4	130.1	121.1	128.7	955	795	37.1	86.6	7.62	271.27
May	104.8	82.3	120.5	119.8	130.1	121.6	128.3	948	789	37.0	85.7	7.57	280.09
June	102.8	80.5	120.4	119.4	130.0	122.1	128.0	940	781	36.8	84.4	7.62	283.46
July	102.0	79.7	120.7	120.1	130.3	121.4	128.2	934	774	36.8	83.6	7.64	278.86
August	101.7	79.3	120.6	119.4	130.4	121.4	129.0	929	768	36.7	82.7	7.68	284.16
September	101.4	78.8	120.9	120.2	130.4	122.7	128.8	922	761	36.8	82.2	7.72	287.18
October	101.0	78.3	121.0	120.2	130.8	122.8	129.0	910	752	36.6	80.8	7.73	285.24
November	100.4	77.6	120.7	118.2	130.9	122.8	128.7	902	743	36.8	80.3	7.77	288.27
December	99.3	76.5	120.7	118.7	130.8	122.7	128.7	896	737	36.8	79.6	7.83	292.06
1996:													
January	96.8	74.5	121.4	119.7	131.7	122.4	129.3	883	727	33.6	71.7	7.87	262.07
February	99.2	76.2	121.6	119.9	132.1	121.7	128.4	890	730	36.8	78.8	7.82	287.78
March	98.1	75.3	121.6	119.9	132.2	121.8	129.0	881	723	36.9	78.3	7.86	290.82
April	99.0	76.0	121.5	118.9	132.2	121.8	128.7	876	719	36.7	77.4	7.95	289.38
May	99.0	75.9	122.2	119.5	132.2	121.8	128.5	871	714	37.1	77.7	7.94	296.16
June	99.0	75.9	122.5	120.2	132.3	121.8	128.1	866	709	37.5	78.0	7.99	302.82
July	98.3	75.2	122.6	120.2	132.4	121.8	127.8	863	709	37.1	77.2	7.95	292.56
August	98.5	75.3	122.5	119.4	132.0	121.8	126.5	857	701	37.4	76.9	7.94	299.34
September	98.2	75.0	123.0	120.4	131.9	123.1	127.3	853	698	37.3	76.4	8.00	300.80
October	97.8	74.7	123.1	120.6	132.2	123.5	127.6	849	694	37.3	76.0	8.03	301.93
November	97.3	74.2	122.9	120.0	132.4	123.5	128.0	844	690	37.3	75.5	8.01	301.98
December	97.2	74.1	123.1	120.1	132.3	123.9	128.0	840	686	37.4	75.3	8.15	308.89

1. December 1984=100.

PAPER AND PAPER PRODUCTS—PRODUCTION, CAPACITY, SHIPMENTS, AND INVENTORIES
(Seasonally adjusted)

YEAR AND MONTH	Industrial production (1992=100)								Capacity utilization (Percent of capacity)		Manufacturers' shipments and inventories (Millions of dollars)	
	Total	Pulp and paper				Paper products			Total	Pulp and paper	Shipments	Inventories (Book value, end of period)
		Total	Wood pulp	Paper	Paper-board	Total	Paper-board containers	Con-verted paper products				
1968	53.1	55.9	57.8	54.8	56.5	51.4	52.0	49.6	89.4	91.9	22 093	2 309
1969	57.3	60.7	62.8	58.4	63.4	55.1	56.0	53.1	91.3	95.4	24 188	2 399
1970	56.7	60.3	63.9	57.3	61.9	54.3	55.7	51.8	86.5	92.2	24 573	2 735
1971	59.1	62.8	67.2	59.1	64.8	56.7	57.9	54.2	87.4	93.3	25 182	2 828
1972	64.3	67.2	71.1	63.0	70.8	62.6	64.1	60.0	91.9	95.8	28 004	2 896
1973	68.8	69.7	73.8	65.7	73.0	68.3	68.4	67.0	95.4	96.1	32 495	3 317
1974	68.2	69.1	73.0	66.4	71.0	67.7	64.6	69.1	91.9	93.5	41 514	4 816
1975	59.4	59.4	62.4	58.1	60.1	59.5	57.9	60.0	78.1	79.4	41 497	4 849
1976	67.4	67.8	71.6	65.6	69.0	67.2	65.0	68.3	87.0	89.8	47 939	5 299
1977	70.1	68.6	71.6	67.9	69.0	71.5	68.1	72.3	90.1	90.8	51 881	5 667
1978	73.4	70.7	71.9	69.7	72.2	75.6	73.1	75.8	92.5	92.4	56 777	6 114
1979	76.0	74.4	76.0	74.2	74.4	77.4	74.9	77.5	92.6	94.6	64 957	6 926
1980	75.2	74.7	77.6	74.2	74.6	75.8	72.0	77.0	88.4	92.2	72 553	7 802
1981	76.6	76.4	79.1	76.2	75.8	76.9	73.6	77.8	87.2	91.3	79 970	8 593
1982	74.3	73.6	75.4	75.1	69.4	75.0	70.4	77.0	83.1	86.2	79 698	9 022
1983	81.0	79.8	80.3	81.1	76.9	82.1	75.7	85.4	89.5	91.7	84 817	9 192
1984	85.0	83.7	84.6	85.0	80.5	86.2	80.0	89.3	92.1	93.4	95 525	10 299
1985	83.8	82.4	82.7	84.0	78.6	85.1	80.0	87.7	88.2	90.4	94 679	10 140
1986	88.3	86.8	87.2	87.8	84.5	89.6	84.9	92.2	90.3	94.0	99 865	10 254
1987	90.9	90.6	91.1	91.1	89.5	91.3	89.3	92.5	90.8	95.7	108 989	11 163
1988	93.8	93.4	93.3	94.5	91.3	94.1	92.3	95.3	92.2	95.6	122 882	12 495
1989	95.4	94.3	94.9	95.2	92.1	96.6	94.3	97.9	91.1	93.9	131 896	13 404
1990	96.0	96.7	96.9	97.8	94.2	95.5	95.2	95.7	88.9	93.9	132 424	13 640
1991	96.8	97.3	97.7	97.6	96.6	96.4	95.8	96.8	86.7	91.7	130 131	13 796
1992	100.0	100.0	100.0	100.0	100.0	100.0	100.0	100.0	87.8	92.1	133 201	14 012
1993	104.0	103.3	98.7	104.0	103.4	104.5	106.0	103.8	89.4	93.2	133 263	13 979
1994	108.4	107.1	101.1	106.8	109.4	109.3	112.5	107.7	91.5	94.9	143 649	14 481
1995	109.9	108.9	103.0	108.3	111.6	110.6	112.0	110.0	91.3	94.1	172 637	17 384
1996	108.0	107.6	100.4	105.2	114.0	108.2	113.3	105.5	88.1	90.7	161 968	16 230
1993:												
January	101.5	101.4	99.2	101.3	102.5	101.5	102.9	100.9	88.2	92.3	11 098	14 054
February	102.7	102.6	99.0	103.0	103.0	102.8	104.0	102.2	89.1	93.2	10 968	14 068
March	102.9	102.3	98.7	102.9	102.2	103.4	104.3	103.0	89.1	92.8	11 080	14 084
April	105.1	104.4	99.5	106.5	101.8	105.6	105.0	106.1	90.7	94.5	11 085	14 084
May	102.5	101.8	98.4	102.1	102.4	103.1	105.4	101.9	88.4	92.0	11 098	14 078
June	104.6	104.0	98.8	105.6	102.6	105.1	104.4	105.7	90.0	93.8	11 051	14 038
July	103.5	102.4	96.7	103.5	102.1	104.2	105.8	103.5	88.8	92.3	11 098	14 042
August	104.0	102.6	96.7	103.7	102.3	105.0	107.4	103.8	89.1	92.3	10 984	14 137
September	103.8	103.2	95.5	104.0	103.9	104.2	107.0	102.8	88.8	92.8	11 331	14 009
October	104.7	103.5	97.5	104.0	104.3	105.5	107.8	104.4	89.4	92.9	11 066	14 006
November	106.1	105.5	101.0	105.3	107.3	106.6	109.0	105.4	90.5	94.6	11 196	13 960
December	106.5	105.6	103.1	105.5	106.6	107.1	109.2	106.1	90.6	94.5	11 172	13 979
1994:												
January	106.1	105.1	98.4	105.6	106.1	106.9	108.1	106.4	90.2	93.9	11 035	13 870
February	106.3	105.1	100.1	105.7	105.7	107.2	108.6	106.5	90.2	93.8	11 276	14 003
March	107.0	106.4	99.5	106.6	108.0	107.4	110.0	106.1	90.7	94.8	11 371	14 000
April	106.0	105.0	100.8	104.6	107.0	106.7	110.0	105.1	89.7	93.4	11 355	14 051
May	107.6	106.2	100.0	106.5	107.5	108.6	111.9	106.9	91.0	94.3	11 599	14 130
June	107.9	106.3	99.6	106.3	108.3	109.1	111.8	107.7	91.2	94.3	11 702	14 143
July	107.2	105.0	100.1	103.9	108.3	108.8	115.6	105.1	90.5	92.9	11 839	14 209
August	110.4	108.9	102.3	108.5	111.7	111.4	114.4	109.8	93.0	96.3	12 332	14 258
September	109.7	109.0	102.0	107.8	113.1	110.1	113.6	108.2	92.3	96.2	12 396	14 275
October	109.7	108.1	103.2	106.3	112.5	110.8	115.9	108.1	92.2	95.2	12 678	14 265
November	111.5	110.6	104.3	110.1	113.2	112.2	114.6	111.1	93.7	97.2	12 976	14 366
December	111.2	109.6	103.4	109.4	111.9	112.3	115.1	110.8	93.3	96.3	13 062	14 481
1995:												
January	111.6	110.3	104.0	108.7	114.9	112.6	118.2	109.5	93.5	96.7	13 762	14 771
February	111.6	110.4	105.0	109.7	113.4	112.4	115.5	110.9	93.4	96.6	14 082	15 040
March	111.2	110.6	104.5	109.5	114.2	111.7	112.7	111.3	92.9	96.4	14 207	15 379
April	111.0	109.8	103.5	108.6	113.8	111.8	113.5	111.1	92.6	95.6	14 300	15 706
May	111.4	111.5	104.0	111.0	114.4	111.3	110.5	111.9	92.8	96.7	14 671	15 981
June	109.6	109.7	104.8	107.8	114.3	109.5	110.7	109.0	91.2	95.0	14 906	16 479
July	111.0	110.8	104.6	110.6	112.9	111.0	108.2	112.9	92.1	95.7	14 464	16 731
August	108.8	108.7	103.5	108.1	111.1	108.8	108.4	109.3	90.2	93.6	14 701	16 805
September	108.5	106.9	102.4	106.6	108.7	109.6	112.7	108.1	89.8	91.8	14 548	17 084
October	109.5	108.2	101.6	108.6	109.4	110.4	109.3	111.2	90.4	92.7	14 437	17 296
November	106.4	104.8	99.1	104.3	107.2	107.5	109.9	106.3	87.7	89.6	14 334	17 266
December	108.0	104.7	99.2	105.8	104.5	110.3	114.7	108.0	88.8	89.3	14 127	17 384
1996:												
January	105.3	104.1	99.1	103.1	107.4	106.1	108.6	104.9	86.5	88.6	13 890	17 354
February	104.6	104.1	97.8	102.0	109.5	104.9	110.1	102.2	85.8	88.4	13 881	17 394
March	105.8	104.0	98.8	102.6	108.0	106.9	112.7	103.8	86.6	88.2	13 630	17 294
April	107.5	106.4	98.8	105.6	110.1	108.1	111.8	106.2	87.9	90.1	13 711	16 975
May	107.8	106.5	100.4	104.6	111.5	108.7	113.2	106.3	88.1	89.9	13 541	16 705
June	108.5	105.9	99.5	105.2	109.0	110.2	117.9	106.0	88.5	89.3	13 390	16 504
July	110.2	110.1	101.7	107.6	116.8	110.2	114.5	107.9	89.8	92.7	13 538	16 458
August	108.1	109.1	103.6	104.3	119.5	107.4	113.0	104.4	88.0	91.7	13 311	16 497
September	108.8	108.6	101.7	104.7	117.6	108.9	119.0	103.3	88.4	91.2	13 250	16 454
October	107.6	109.3	100.2	104.9	119.5	106.5	109.7	104.8	87.4	91.5	13 299	16 369
November	110.1	110.8	104.5	107.5	118.7	109.7	115.3	106.6	89.3	92.7	13 269	16 275
December	111.6	112.6	98.9	110.0	120.5	110.9	114.3	109.1	90.4	94.0	13 294	16 230

PAPER AND PAPER PRODUCTS—PRICES, EMPLOYMENT, HOURS, AND EARNINGS

YEAR AND MONTH	Paper and paper products [1]	Producer prices (1982=100, except as noted, not seasonally adjusted)					Crude materials: Wastepaper	Employment (Thousands, seasonally adjusted)		Production workers			
		Intermediate materials						Total payroll employees	Production workers	Weekly hours worked (Seasonally adjusted)		Average earnings (Dollars, not seasonally adjusted)	
		Woodpulp	Paper	Paperboard	Paper boxes and containers	Building paper and board				Average hours	Aggregate hours index (1982=100)	Hourly	Weekly
1968	....	26.4	35.6	37.6	40.7	42.1	107.3	687	533	42.9	111.4	3.05	130.85
1969	....	26.4	36.8	39.0	41.8	44.1	114.5	706	547	43.0	114.6	3.24	139.32
1970	....	28.9	38.8	39.7	43.3	42.2	103.2	701	540	41.9	110.2	3.44	144.14
1971	....	29.6	39.9	40.2	44.7	42.9	92.5	677	518	42.1	106.4	3.67	154.51
1972	....	29.4	40.6	41.4	46.4	44.4	110.3	679	528	42.8	110.3	3.95	169.06
1973	....	33.8	42.4	45.2	49.9	47.1	162.9	694	540	42.9	112.7	4.20	180.18
1974	....	57.5	51.9	59.7	58.5	51.6	219.2	696	541	42.2	111.2	4.53	191.17
1975	....	74.8	60.4	66.8	63.3	53.1	90.9	633	477	41.6	96.8	5.01	208.42
1976	....	75.5	63.7	69.1	66.0	57.9	152.6	666	505	42.5	104.7	5.47	232.48
1977	....	74.2	67.8	69.1	67.1	65.6	154.6	682	515	42.9	107.6	5.96	255.68
1978	....	70.3	72.0	70.5	69.9	78.2	157.8	689	521	42.9	109.0	6.52	279.71
1979	....	82.9	80.2	79.3	79.1	76.2	170.5	697	532	42.6	110.5	7.13	303.74
1980	....	100.3	89.7	92.0	89.4	86.1	172.2	685	519	42.2	106.9	7.84	330.85
1981	....	104.8	97.7	101.2	97.7	96.7	145.0	681	515	42.5	106.8	8.60	365.50
1982	....	100.0	100.0	100.0	100.0	100.0	100.0	655	491	41.8	100.0	9.32	389.58
1983	....	91.5	98.5	98.4	99.5	104.4	....	654	491	42.6	102.1	9.93	423.02
1984	....	104.8	105.8	110.4	105.7	108.2	198.2	674	508	43.1	106.8	10.41	448.67
1985	98.8	91.4	106.0	107.7	108.8	107.4	122.9	671	508	43.1	106.8	10.83	466.77
1986	99.5	94.7	107.0	106.6	107.8	108.8	142.6	667	507	43.2	106.9	11.18	482.98
1987	104.9	111.5	111.5	118.1	115.4	111.2	181.4	674	512	43.4	108.5	11.43	496.06
1988	113.7	136.7	123.2	133.2	123.5	* 113.3	183.6	689	516	43.3	108.9	11.69	506.18
1989	120.8	157.4	129.6	140.1	129.8	115.6	157.1	696	521	43.3	109.9	11.96	517.87
1990	121.9	151.3	128.8	135.7	129.9	112.2	138.9	697	522	43.3	110.4	12.31	533.02
1991	121.1	119.2	126.9	130.2	128.6	111.8	121.4	688	517	43.3	109.3	12.72	550.78
1992	121.2	118.9	123.2	134.3	130.6	119.6	117.5	690	520	43.6	110.5	13.07	569.85
1993	120.2	104.2	123.8	130.0	129.9	132.7	117.4	692	522	43.6	110.9	13.42	585.11
1994	123.7	115.9	126.0	140.5	136.1	144.1	209.5	692	524	43.9	112.3	13.77	604.50
1995	146.7	183.2	159.0	183.1	163.8	144.9	371.1	693	525	43.1	110.5	14.23	613.31
1996	138.6	133.1	149.4	155.1	153.9	137.2	141.6	681	517	43.3	109.1	14.67	635.21
1993:													
January	120.6	111.7	122.7	133.0	130.5	124.9	124.3	692	522	43.5	110.7	13.17	572.90
February	120.5	108.3	122.9	131.6	130.4	129.0	125.1	693	522	43.7	111.2	13.18	570.69
March	120.7	105.3	123.4	131.3	130.4	133.9	128.1	693	523	43.4	110.7	13.22	568.46
April	120.6	106.4	123.6	130.6	130.3	135.4	126.7	692	522	43.9	111.7	13.39	581.13
May	120.6	107.0	123.8	129.9	130.2	133.8	123.3	693	522	43.6	111.0	13.36	581.16
June	120.5	106.7	124.2	128.9	130.0	132.0	119.9	692	522	43.6	111.0	13.39	583.80
July	120.0	104.5	124.5	128.6	130.0	131.2	116.7	692	523	43.5	110.9	13.50	583.20
August	119.9	102.5	124.5	128.0	129.8	131.6	111.0	692	521	43.6	110.8	13.41	581.99
September	119.7	101.8	124.4	128.0	129.3	134.7	109.1	693	523	43.6	111.2	13.67	602.85
October	120.1	99.6	124.3	129.7	129.3	133.8	109.0	690	520	43.7	110.8	13.55	596.20
November	119.9	98.8	123.8	130.2	129.3	135.1	107.6	690	520	43.8	111.0	13.54	597.11
December	120.0	98.5	123.5	130.5	129.9	137.5	108.1	690	521	43.6	110.8	13.62	606.09
1994:													
January	119.9	100.9	122.6	130.2	130.2	138.7	108.8	691	521	43.6	110.8	13.57	593.01
February	120.0	101.1	122.4	130.1	130.5	139.2	118.3	692	523	43.2	110.2	13.61	582.51
March	120.1	103.3	122.1	131.1	130.6	140.4	131.0	691	523	43.9	111.9	13.62	593.83
April	120.2	106.7	121.7	133.4	131.0	140.9	138.2	691	524	43.9	112.2	13.67	598.75
May	120.7	108.3	121.8	133.1	132.8	142.3	158.0	691	524	44.0	112.4	13.71	600.50
June	121.6	112.6	122.4	133.5	134.1	142.9	209.3	692	525	44.0	112.6	13.68	601.92
July	122.1	113.5	123.5	137.8	134.2	143.2	282.1	693	525	44.1	112.9	13.83	607.14
August	123.3	118.9	124.6	143.5	135.9	146.0	290.8	693	525	44.1	112.9	13.79	605.38
September	125.5	123.4	128.0	146.9	139.1	148.6	260.1	693	525	44.0	112.6	13.95	619.38
October	128.2	131.6	131.4	153.6	142.5	146.9	250.4	694	526	44.1	113.1	13.89	615.33
November	130.4	134.3	134.5	156.0	145.6	149.8	265.5	695	527	43.9	112.8	13.91	614.82
December	132.8	136.0	137.4	156.7	147.0	149.6	302.2	695	527	43.9	112.8	13.97	625.86
1995:													
January	136.0	144.6	141.9	165.3	151.0	147.3	343.5	695	527	43.9	112.8	14.00	616.00
February	139.1	158.8	146.9	170.5	155.6	148.0	387.5	695	526	43.6	111.8	14.01	606.63
March	141.4	168.4	150.6	172.3	157.3	147.3	465.0	695	527	43.4	111.5	14.02	604.26
April	143.9	173.7	155.2	183.8	159.0	146.6	508.9	696	529	43.2	111.4	14.26	603.20
May	146.2	181.1	157.5	188.2	162.9	145.4	544.9	695	528	43.0	110.7	14.15	605.62
June	148.8	191.7	161.0	189.6	167.6	141.3	511.3	694	526	42.9	110.0	14.13	606.18
July	150.3	196.3	164.2	189.9	169.0	141.4	452.4	693	527	43.0	110.5	14.41	616.75
August	150.9	200.5	164.8	190.6	169.4	142.3	394.2	694	526	42.9	110.0	14.20	606.34
September	151.2	198.2	166.4	190.3	168.8	145.8	310.6	692	525	43.0	110.1	14.33	621.92
October	151.2	198.7	167.3	188.8	168.6	146.3	215.8	690	523	42.9	109.4	14.31	616.76
November	150.8	195.4	166.6	185.7	168.8	145.5	170.5	688	522	42.9	109.2	14.38	624.09
December	150.2	191.3	165.6	182.2	167.8	141.9	148.5	688	521	42.9	109.0	14.51	634.09
1996:													
January	147.8	176.6	163.1	175.7	165.3	138.5	163.4	687	521	41.5	105.4	14.58	607.99
February	146.1	160.4	160.9	172.6	163.9	138.2	163.0	685	519	43.1	109.1	14.43	617.60
March	143.0	141.4	157.5	166.6	161.1	136.3	142.0	684	518	43.1	108.8	14.44	618.03
April	140.5	120.3	152.6	161.8	157.6	136.2	123.1	681	516	43.3	108.9	14.61	626.77
May	138.2	114.1	149.4	154.0	155.3	137.9	124.1	682	516	43.3	108.9	14.59	627.37
June	137.2	120.0	148.4	150.6	152.3	135.9	128.6	680	515	43.4	109.0	14.63	634.94
July	136.3	125.5	146.4	148.0	151.1	137.4	134.9	677	514	43.3	108.5	14.79	638.93
August	135.3	127.3	144.5	145.5	148.5	137.3	136.9	678	515	43.4	109.0	14.69	637.55
September	135.1	127.8	143.5	145.6	148.6	140.5	142.2	678	516	43.5	109.4	14.74	648.56
October	134.9	128.2	142.3	146.6	148.0	138.7	146.2	679	517	43.4	109.4	14.74	642.66
November	134.6	127.6	141.7	146.9	147.3	136.2	147.8	679	517	43.6	109.9	14.86	655.33
December	134.7	128.2	142.1	147.6	147.4	133.7	146.6	678	517	43.7	110.2	14.95	665.28

1. December 1984=100.

PRINTING AND PUBLISHING—PRODUCTION, CAPACITY, PRICES, EMPLOYMENT, HOURS, AND EARNINGS

YEAR AND MONTH	Industrial production (1992=100, seasonally adjusted)			Capacity utilization (Percent of capacity, seasonally adjusted)	Producer prices (December 1984=100, not seasonally adjusted)	Employment (Thousands, seasonally adjusted)		Production workers			
								Weekly hours worked (Seasonally adjusted)		Average earnings (Dollars, not seasonally adjusted)	
	Total	News-papers	Commer-cial printing			Total payroll employ-ees	Produc-tion workers	Average hours	Aggregate hours index (1982=100)	Hourly	Weekly
1968	53.3	87.1	37.4	90.5	....	1 065	667	38.3	98.5	3.48	133.28
1969	55.9	92.8	39.2	92.0	....	1 094	682	38.3	100.9	3.69	141.33
1970	54.4	89.8	38.9	86.9	....	1 104	679	37.7	98.9	3.92	147.78
1971	54.8	90.2	38.7	85.3	....	1 081	658	37.5	95.3	4.20	157.50
1972	58.5	95.9	43.7	88.3	....	1 094	664	37.7	96.5	4.51	170.03
1973	60.1	98.4	46.0	87.7	....	1 111	670	37.7	97.4	4.75	179.08
1974	59.1	98.6	44.2	83.9	....	1 111	660	37.5	95.5	5.03	188.63
1975	55.4	92.8	41.2	77.0	....	1 083	624	36.9	88.9	5.38	198.52
1976	60.5	95.0	46.8	82.6	....	1 099	625	37.5	90.3	5.71	214.13
1977	66.3	97.6	52.2	89.4	....	1 141	647	37.7	94.1	6.12	230.72
1978	70.1	103.6	54.3	91.7	....	1 192	672	37.6	97.5	6.51	244.78
1979	72.0	107.3	56.3	89.5	....	1 235	697	37.5	101.0	6.94	260.25
1980	72.4	105.8	56.8	85.8	....	1 252	699	37.1	100.1	7.53	279.36
1981	74.3	106.9	58.0	83.9	....	1 266	699	37.3	100.6	8.19	305.49
1982	77.5	106.4	63.0	83.8	....	1 272	699	37.1	100.0	8.74	324.25
1983	81.4	111.3	66.9	85.2	....	1 298	712	37.6	103.3	9.11	342.54
1984	87.0	119.8	71.7	87.7	....	1 375	758	37.9	110.9	9.41	356.64
1985	90.2	121.7	75.6	86.4	103.6	1 426	788	37.8	114.9	9.71	367.04
1986	93.4	125.3	78.5	85.6	107.8	1 456	816	38.0	119.6	9.99	379.62
1987	102.5	129.3	93.2	91.0	112.2	1 503	839	38.0	123.2	10.28	390.64
1988	103.4	124.9	95.5	89.5	118.2	1 543	864	38.0	126.7	10.53	400.14
1989	103.5	121.9	96.8	87.7	124.7	1 556	863	37.9	126.2	10.88	412.35
1990	103.1	116.0	97.8	85.2	130.5	1 569	871	37.9	127.5	11.24	426.00
1991	99.1	105.9	95.2	80.8	136.4	1 536	847	37.7	123.3	11.48	432.80
1992	100.0	100.0	100.0	81.1	140.8	1 507	833	38.1	122.3	11.74	447.29
1993	100.8	98.6	100.6	81.9	145.6	1 517	839	38.3	123.9	11.93	456.92
1994	100.5	98.5	101.9	82.1	149.7	1 537	846	38.6	125.9	12.14	468.60
1995	99.8	95.0	103.4	81.6	159.0	1 546	848	38.2	125.0	12.33	471.01
1996	98.4	85.1	104.9	80.8	165.6	1 538	839	38.2	123.7	12.65	483.23
1993:											
January	101.7	103.7	100.6	82.3	144.7	1 510	835	38.3	123.5	11.84	448.74
February	102.5	104.0	101.3	83.0	145.0	1 511	837	38.3	123.7	11.82	447.98
March	102.0	103.7	101.1	82.7	145.1	1 512	837	38.1	123.1	11.87	453.43
April	102.8	102.6	101.9	83.4	145.4	1 514	838	38.5	124.5	11.86	451.87
May	101.6	100.4	101.0	82.5	145.5	1 516	842	38.1	123.8	11.82	446.80
June	100.4	98.2	98.9	81.6	145.0	1 517	840	38.3	124.2	11.83	449.54
July	99.9	96.1	99.6	81.2	145.3	1 518	840	38.4	124.5	11.91	453.77
August	99.1	95.0	99.7	80.6	145.7	1 520	840	38.2	123.9	11.96	459.26
September	100.4	94.5	101.8	81.8	145.9	1 520	840	38.3	124.2	12.09	467.88
October	99.9	94.8	100.2	81.4	146.5	1 521	839	38.4	124.4	12.04	464.74
November	99.8	95.2	100.6	81.4	146.5	1 523	839	38.3	124.0	12.01	465.99
December	99.1	95.5	100.0	80.9	146.8	1 522	838	38.3	123.9	12.11	471.08
1994:											
January	98.7	96.0	98.8	80.6	148.4	1 528	842	38.4	124.8	12.06	458.28
February	99.7	96.7	101.1	81.5	148.4	1 529	842	38.1	123.8	12.05	454.29
March	101.2	97.4	103.1	82.6	148.7	1 532	844	38.4	125.1	12.11	466.24
April	101.0	97.4	102.6	82.5	148.7	1 534	845	38.6	125.9	12.06	465.52
May	100.9	97.7	102.4	82.4	149.2	1 536	844	38.7	126.1	12.05	462.72
June	101.0	98.2	101.9	82.5	149.2	1 535	844	38.7	126.1	12.08	463.87
July	101.2	99.5	102.7	82.7	149.4	1 539	846	38.7	126.4	12.13	465.79
August	100.0	100.0	99.7	81.7	149.6	1 541	847	38.6	126.2	12.13	469.43
September	100.5	100.4	101.0	82.1	150.3	1 540	847	38.6	126.2	12.27	479.76
October	100.9	99.9	103.1	82.4	150.8	1 543	848	38.7	126.7	12.24	477.36
November	101.0	99.7	103.6	82.5	151.7	1 541	846	38.7	126.4	12.22	477.02
December	100.4	98.6	102.8	82.0	152.4	1 545	849	38.7	126.8	12.26	481.82
1995:											
January	99.5	98.0	101.6	81.3	154.7	1 546	849	38.5	126.2	12.25	466.73
February	99.9	96.8	102.6	81.7	155.6	1 548	849	38.4	125.8	12.25	467.95
March	99.8	96.4	102.8	81.5	156.4	1 547	848	38.4	125.7	12.27	471.17
April	99.9	95.7	103.0	81.7	157.2	1 547	848	38.4	125.7	12.22	461.92
May	99.8	95.4	103.0	81.6	157.9	1 546	848	38.3	125.4	12.23	464.74
June	99.2	95.4	101.6	81.1	158.9	1 547	849	38.2	125.2	12.25	464.28
July	100.0	95.8	103.0	81.7	159.7	1 547	848	38.2	125.0	12.33	467.31
August	100.6	96.0	104.5	82.3	160.1	1 545	848	38.1	124.7	12.36	472.15
September	100.4	94.9	104.7	82.2	160.5	1 544	847	38.1	124.6	12.50	482.50
October	99.4	92.9	103.6	81.3	161.6	1 544	844	38.1	124.1	12.44	476.45
November	99.8	91.5	104.9	81.7	162.6	1 544	845	38.2	124.6	12.41	480.27
December	99.1	90.5	105.0	81.1	163.0	1 543	844	37.9	123.5	12.50	481.25
1996:											
January	98.2	89.5	104.4	80.4	164.5	1 541	843	37.1	120.7	12.49	458.38
February	99.2	87.0	106.3	81.2	164.8	1 540	842	38.2	124.2	12.49	473.37
March	97.6	84.1	104.7	80.0	164.8	1 541	843	38.1	124.0	12.53	478.65
April	96.9	81.7	104.2	79.5	165.1	1 538	840	38.1	123.5	12.53	474.89
May	97.9	80.9	106.4	80.3	165.3	1 538	840	38.2	123.9	12.54	476.52
June	97.1	81.6	104.8	79.7	165.4	1 538	839	38.2	123.7	12.54	475.27
July	97.6	83.1	104.2	80.1	165.2	1 537	839	38.2	123.7	12.63	479.94
August	97.9	85.0	103.4	80.5	165.5	1 537	839	38.3	124.0	12.70	490.22
September	99.1	87.3	104.6	81.4	166.1	1 536	837	38.3	123.7	12.82	497.42
October	99.7	88.9	104.4	82.0	166.4	1 539	838	38.2	123.6	12.81	491.90
November	100.0	86.5	106.0	82.2	166.7	1 535	837	38.2	123.4	12.83	496.52
December	99.8	86.0	105.9	82.2	166.9	1 534	836	38.4	123.9	12.90	503.10

CHEMICALS AND CHEMICAL PRODUCTS—PRODUCTION AND CAPACITY
(Seasonally adjusted)

YEAR AND MONTH	Industrial production (1992=100)								Capacity utilization (Percent of capacity)		
	Total	Basic chemicals	Inorganic chemicals, not elsewhere classified	Synthetic materials	Drugs and medicines	Soap and toiletries	Industrial organic chemicals	Agricultural chemicals	Total	Plastic materials	Synthetic fibers
1968	43.3	59.5	75.3	33.3	31.1	55.4	....	43.2	80.5	90.8	94.6
1969	46.9	66.4	83.5	36.4	33.0	57.4	....	45.4	80.1	93.4	87.5
1970	48.8	69.4	81.1	35.9	36.0	62.2	....	43.5	77.7	82.3	81.9
1971	51.9	71.9	74.8	40.0	40.0	62.1	....	45.2	77.5	81.3	87.6
1972	58.4	81.4	81.5	49.1	42.0	71.0	63.0	50.6	82.3	98.5	87.6
1973	63.9	85.0	83.5	55.6	45.7	75.4	73.5	58.0	85.5	98.5	91.5
1974	66.2	89.1	88.8	59.0	48.3	78.5	74.0	63.4	84.4	93.8	89.9
1975	60.3	74.4	72.3	50.0	49.0	72.4	61.4	66.5	73.3	64.8	76.3
1976	67.5	79.6	77.3	57.7	53.4	79.1	75.2	67.8	78.4	74.5	77.7
1977	72.4	83.9	84.2	64.3	55.7	82.1	85.1	73.2	80.8	80.6	81.1
1978	76.4	85.6	84.9	71.2	59.0	87.7	86.5	74.4	82.7	85.3	86.5
1979	79.2	88.1	86.4	77.5	60.4	89.4	89.5	77.7	83.7	86.7	91.4
1980	75.9	83.1	81.0	64.0	62.8	94.5	81.5	80.4	78.4	75.2	65.3
1981	77.3	83.6	82.2	71.9	63.4	89.2	85.2	85.8	78.1	76.9	81.2
1982	71.0	75.0	74.6	64.5	64.8	81.5	71.2	74.6	70.7	71.2	68.6
1983	76.0	79.8	78.8	75.7	67.4	83.4	79.0	73.6	75.2	82.3	84.9
1984	79.3	84.0	81.9	80.1	68.1	82.7	82.1	85.7	77.4	86.3	85.4
1985	79.4	83.3	81.1	78.7	69.4	83.4	82.7	80.7	75.6	85.7	78.4
1986	82.4	81.8	78.0	82.9	75.8	88.3	83.5	74.8	77.6	89.4	86.3
1987	87.0	85.4	81.7	90.7	78.4	91.3	87.6	84.6	81.3	98.7	92.1
1988	92.2	89.4	84.6	94.5	82.2	97.1	98.0	90.0	84.0	95.5	91.7
1989	95.1	92.6	88.0	97.5	85.1	98.1	103.5	97.2	83.7	90.3	94.8
1990	97.3	101.2	101.1	95.9	88.3	99.9	104.9	100.4	83.0	87.1	86.7
1991	96.4	97.7	97.4	92.9	93.1	98.8	99.9	97.6	80.1	81.4	85.6
1992	100.0	100.0	100.0	100.0	100.0	100.0	100.0	100.0	80.3	89.1	86.0
1993	101.0	96.5	93.1	101.0	100.5	107.1	96.1	100.7	78.8	87.7	88.0
1994	104.1	91.3	86.2	108.8	105.9	105.9	101.5	99.8	79.1	96.3	86.7
1995	106.5	91.2	86.3	111.8	111.1	104.1	103.9	103.6	79.1	92.9	87.1
1996	108.9	87.5	81.0	117.6	116.9	104.2	102.1	103.2	78.6	93.7	87.6
1993:											
January	101.5	100.1	98.5	101.5	100.5	106.5	99.0	103.5	79.9	88.2	87.6
February	101.1	99.3	96.2	100.8	100.3	105.5	97.8	102.4	79.4	86.7	89.1
March	101.7	99.2	95.6	101.5	101.2	108.3	96.5	102.0	79.8	87.7	88.0
April	102.0	98.5	95.7	101.2	102.9	106.7	95.3	104.4	79.9	87.8	88.8
May	100.3	97.8	95.7	100.7	99.0	107.3	94.5	103.0	78.4	86.3	88.2
June	99.8	97.8	95.1	101.6	96.8	108.0	94.1	102.9	77.9	87.1	90.5
July	101.0	95.3	91.9	101.1	100.5	110.2	94.1	99.2	78.7	86.7	89.8
August	101.1	93.5	88.2	101.9	102.4	106.4	94.6	97.6	78.7	87.3	91.4
September	101.8	92.8	88.4	99.3	103.9	108.9	95.5	97.2	79.1	85.8	87.6
October	100.4	94.2	90.6	100.0	98.9	108.4	96.5	98.6	77.8	88.1	85.3
November	100.7	95.6	91.6	101.3	99.7	104.6	97.4	99.0	78.0	89.3	86.3
December	100.8	94.3	90.0	101.4	99.9	104.8	98.1	98.9	77.9	91.0	83.8
1994:											
January	100.6	91.9	88.0	102.6	100.4	103.2	98.7	99.9	77.6	91.3	88.7
February	102.4	92.4	87.2	104.9	103.7	106.8	99.3	97.6	78.8	93.6	86.7
March	103.0	92.7	87.8	106.4	103.7	107.0	100.0	100.5	79.0	95.2	87.1
April	103.4	92.0	87.2	106.3	105.2	105.2	100.8	98.8	79.1	94.5	87.3
May	105.3	91.3	87.5	108.6	108.5	107.6	101.6	99.9	80.3	96.9	87.0
June	105.3	92.2	86.7	107.8	109.5	108.4	102.2	99.4	80.2	97.0	83.7
July	104.6	91.5	87.2	109.8	107.2	105.2	102.6	99.2	79.4	97.9	85.4
August	105.0	91.8	86.9	111.9	104.3	110.6	102.7	100.1	79.5	98.1	89.4
September	103.4	90.8	84.9	110.3	103.3	103.0	102.6	99.7	78.1	97.5	85.6
October	103.9	88.8	82.8	108.2	106.8	102.9	102.4	101.6	78.3	93.1	86.7
November	105.2	89.4	83.3	111.8	109.1	103.6	102.5	100.6	79.1	97.6	85.6
December	106.7	91.1	85.5	116.8	109.4	107.9	103.0	100.9	80.1	102.6	86.9
1995:											
January	107.5	93.9	89.3	117.7	111.3	103.7	103.8	102.1	80.5	102.5	88.3
February	106.4	94.6	91.3	114.6	109.5	102.3	104.6	101.5	79.6	97.2	89.7
March	106.6	95.0	91.7	112.6	110.1	102.2	105.0	101.3	79.6	94.8	91.1
April	105.9	93.9	89.6	111.9	108.8	102.0	105.2	102.9	79.0	94.5	85.7
May	105.8	92.2	86.5	112.0	109.4	100.6	105.2	103.8	78.9	92.6	88.2
June	106.2	91.0	85.8	110.7	110.5	102.4	105.0	104.0	79.0	91.2	86.4
July	105.9	91.7	86.3	109.0	110.1	102.5	104.6	104.6	78.7	90.1	84.7
August	105.9	89.4	83.6	107.6	111.4	105.4	104.0	104.5	78.5	87.2	84.7
September	107.0	88.9	83.7	111.0	113.1	106.5	103.3	103.7	79.2	91.1	86.5
October	107.6	89.4	83.4	110.9	114.1	107.7	102.5	105.5	79.5	90.8	86.6
November	106.5	88.2	82.8	111.7	111.8	106.8	101.9	104.6	78.5	91.4	87.1
December	106.8	86.7	81.5	111.4	113.5	106.8	101.6	104.6	78.6	90.9	86.6
1996:											
January	106.8	87.0	81.2	112.0	112.8	107.3	101.5	104.3	78.4	91.6	84.5
February	107.0	86.4	80.7	111.4	114.0	105.7	101.4	103.7	78.3	91.9	83.1
March	106.6	84.9	79.7	113.3	113.8	103.8	101.3	103.1	77.7	92.9	83.4
April	106.9	86.6	80.1	114.3	114.0	101.6	101.2	100.8	77.7	93.6	82.8
May	107.2	87.4	80.5	115.5	114.4	102.5	101.0	100.0	77.7	94.3	84.5
June	107.9	87.2	81.1	117.3	114.5	102.7	100.9	102.6	78.0	95.0	85.3
July	109.0	87.1	80.8	120.1	116.9	103.6	100.9	102.6	78.6	94.9	91.1
August	108.7	87.3	80.8	118.9	115.2	103.4	100.9	104.9	78.1	94.9	87.6
September	109.7	88.1	82.1	120.6	118.9	102.5	100.8	103.7	78.6	95.4	89.2
October	111.3	90.4	82.3	123.3	120.5	105.3	103.9	104.0	79.5	94.0	95.4
November	111.8	87.8	81.4	119.9	122.9	105.7	105.0	103.3	79.6	92.4	90.4
December	114.0	89.4	81.6	124.1	124.8	106.6	107.0	105.8	81.0	94.0	93.8

CHEMICALS AND CHEMICAL PRODUCTS—SHIPMENTS, INVENTORIES, PRICES, EMPLOYMENT, HOURS, AND EARNINGS

YEAR AND MONTH	Manufacturers' shipments and inventories (Millions of dollars, seasonally adjusted)		Producer prices (1982=100, except as noted, not seasonally adjusted)				Employment (Thousands, seasonally adjusted)		Production workers			
			Chemi-cal industry [1]	Commodity groups			Total payroll employ-ees	Produc-tion workers	Weekly hours worked (Seasonally adjusted)		Average earnings (Dollars, not seasonally adjusted)	
	Shipments	Inventories (Book value, end of period)		Drugs and pharma-ceuticals	Agricul-tural chemi-cals	Other chemicals and chemical products			Average hours	Aggregate hours index (1982=100)	Hourly	Weekly
1968	45 491	5 542	....	47.3	32.9	37.6	1 030	610	41.8	104.1	3.26	136.27
1969	48 096	6 173	....	47.6	29.6	38.6	1 060	622	41.8	106.2	3.47	145.05
1970	49 195	6 749	....	48.2	30.3	40.2	1 049	604	41.6	102.5	3.69	153.50
1971	51 681	6 923	....	48.8	31.5	41.5	1 011	588	41.6	99.8	3.97	165.15
1972	58 130	7 079	....	49.0	31.4	42.0	1 009	593	41.7	100.9	4.26	177.64
1973	66 003	7 553	....	49.6	33.0	43.7	1 038	611	41.8	104.2	4.51	188.52
1974	85 387	11 579	....	53.6	47.1	54.6	1 061	623	41.5	105.7	4.88	202.52
1975	91 710	12 073	....	60.3	69.6	62.4	1 015	580	41.0	97.1	5.39	220.99
1976	106 467	13 319	....	63.8	64.4	63.2	1 043	600	41.6	102.0	5.91	245.86
1977	120 905	14 633	....	66.9	64.2	65.1	1 074	616	41.7	105.0	6.43	268.13
1978	132 262	16 018	....	70.5	67.8	67.3	1 096	628	41.9	107.4	7.02	294.14
1979	151 887	17 690	....	75.9	73.3	71.0	1 109	633	41.9	108.3	7.60	318.44
1980	168 220	20 066	....	83.0	87.9	83.1	1 107	626	41.5	106.0	8.30	344.45
1981	186 909	22 438	....	92.1	97.4	94.1	1 109	628	41.6	106.8	9.12	379.39
1982	176 254	24 448	....	100.0	100.0	100.0	1 075	599	40.9	100.0	9.96	407.36
1983	189 552	24 698	....	107.6	95.9	101.3	1 043	579	41.6	98.3	10.58	440.13
1984	205 963	26 420	....	114.2	97.4	102.7	1 049	583	41.9	99.8	11.07	463.83
1985	204 790	26 119	100.7	122.0	96.2	105.2	1 044	577	41.9	98.9	11.56	484.36
1986	205 711	25 743	100.5	130.1	94.2	105.8	1 021	568	41.9	97.3	11.98	501.96
1987	229 546	26 585	103.6	139.1	96.4	107.0	1 025	575	42.3	99.3	12.37	523.25
1988	261 238	29 792	113.0	148.4	104.5	111.9	1 057	596	42.2	102.9	12.71	536.36
1989	283 196	31 725	119.6	160.0	108.7	117.3	1 074	603	42.4	104.5	13.09	555.02
1990	292 802	34 001	121.0	170.8	107.4	118.9	1 086	600	42.6	104.3	13.54	576.80
1991	298 545	34 529	124.4	182.6	111.7	121.5	1 076	580	42.9	101.6	14.04	602.32
1992	305 420	35 721	125.8	192.2	110.3	123.3	1 084	567	43.1	100.0	14.51	625.38
1993	314 907	35 778	127.2	200.9	109.9	125.5	1 081	573	43.1	100.9	14.82	638.74
1994	333 905	37 038	130.0	206.0	119.9	127.1	1 057	578	43.2	102.0	15.13	653.62
1995	362 127	39 939	143.4	210.9	130.1	130.6	1 038	580	43.2	102.5	15.62	674.78
1996	372 848	41 380	145.8	214.7	133.7	132.4	1 032	574	43.2	101.3	16.17	698.54
1993:												
January	26 087	36 034	127.3	197.9	110.6	124.9	1 084	565	43.0	99.3	14.75	634.25
February	26 476	35 747	127.5	199.1	110.2	125.3	1 083	565	43.0	99.3	14.77	632.16
March	26 542	35 836	127.2	199.2	110.3	125.1	1 083	567	42.8	99.2	14.73	628.97
April	26 351	35 852	127.7	200.5	109.6	125.5	1 081	568	43.0	99.8	14.81	635.35
May	25 690	35 934	127.2	200.3	109.3	125.6	1 083	571	43.2	100.8	14.76	636.16
June	26 788	35 918	127.2	201.0	109.6	125.7	1 082	572	43.1	100.7	14.74	635.29
July	26 135	35 836	127.2	201.5	109.3	125.6	1 082	574	43.4	101.8	14.80	636.40
August	25 745	36 103	126.9	202.3	107.7	125.6	1 080	574	43.2	101.3	14.74	632.35
September	25 986	36 106	127.1	202.1	108.0	125.5	1 081	577	43.3	102.1	14.94	648.40
October	25 958	36 021	127.1	202.6	109.2	125.6	1 077	576	43.2	101.7	14.86	641.95
November	26 477	36 031	127.3	202.2	113.0	125.6	1 075	580	43.0	101.9	14.92	647.53
December	26 215	35 778	126.7	202.3	112.1	125.8	1 075	581	43.3	102.8	15.02	660.88
1994:												
January	26 322	35 844	126.9	204.6	113.8	126.0	1 069	579	43.3	102.4	14.96	646.27
February	26 228	36 051	126.8	204.5	115.6	126.1	1 068	580	42.8	101.4	15.00	639.00
March	27 445	35 909	126.7	204.7	116.3	125.9	1 065	579	43.3	102.4	14.98	648.63
April	27 316	35 975	127.5	205.3	119.0	126.0	1 062	579	43.2	102.2	15.04	648.22
May	27 402	35 996	128.0	206.2	120.3	126.6	1 060	578	43.3	102.3	15.04	649.73
June	27 614	35 912	128.4	206.2	119.8	126.5	1 058	578	43.2	102.0	15.07	651.02
July	27 211	36 413	129.2	206.0	120.5	126.6	1 056	577	43.4	102.3	15.15	652.97
August	28 369	36 269	130.3	206.3	120.1	127.9	1 053	574	43.3	101.6	15.06	646.07
September	28 798	36 221	132.0	206.6	121.4	127.6	1 051	576	43.0	101.2	15.25	657.28
October	28 413	36 397	133.6	206.4	123.5	128.4	1 048	575	43.4	102.0	15.28	663.15
November	29 155	36 639	134.4	207.3	124.4	128.3	1 046	576	43.4	102.1	15.26	666.86
December	29 550	37 038	136.1	207.3	124.7	129.1	1 045	576	43.3	101.9	15.39	677.16
1995:												
January	29 750	37 264	138.4	207.8	126.9	129.8	1 044	577	43.4	102.3	15.37	665.52
February	30 090	37 566	140.6	208.9	129.6	129.5	1 042	577	43.3	102.1	15.39	664.85
March	30 089	37 660	141.4	208.9	131.5	130.6	1 040	576	43.3	101.9	15.39	666.39
April	29 334	38 271	144.8	210.4	132.5	130.5	1 039	578	43.4	102.5	15.69	679.38
May	29 993	38 851	145.0	210.4	132.1	130.7	1 038	578	43.2	102.0	15.49	667.62
June	30 446	39 245	143.9	210.2	131.1	130.7	1 037	580	43.3	102.6	15.49	670.72
July	30 400	39 610	144.5	210.8	129.4	130.8	1 036	581	43.1	102.3	15.68	671.10
August	30 661	39 701	144.3	210.9	127.9	130.3	1 036	582	43.1	102.5	15.56	665.97
September	30 337	40 012	144.7	211.9	128.2	130.8	1 036	582	43.1	102.5	15.71	678.67
October	30 574	39 821	144.7	213.1	128.7	130.6	1 037	584	43.2	103.1	15.79	682.13
November	30 302	39 651	144.6	213.4	130.7	131.4	1 037	583	43.0	102.4	15.88	689.19
December	30 389	39 939	144.3	213.8	132.7	131.5	1 034	582	43.0	102.3	16.03	703.72
1996:												
January	30 235	40 037	144.6	213.5	135.2	132.1	1 035	582	42.5	101.1	16.08	681.79
February	30 078	40 061	144.5	213.4	136.3	132.5	1 034	581	43.3	102.8	15.96	687.88
March	29 897	40 271	145.0	214.4	138.2	132.1	1 037	580	43.1	102.1	16.00	689.60
April	30 674	40 439	145.3	214.1	136.9	132.2	1 035	578	43.0	101.6	16.15	691.22
May	31 297	40 294	146.0	214.8	134.9	132.5	1 034	577	43.1	101.6	16.04	689.72
June	30 628	40 410	146.0	215.0	132.9	132.4	1 032	575	43.4	102.0	16.11	699.17
July	31 423	40 267	145.9	215.4	129.9	132.5	1 031	572	43.2	101.0	16.16	693.26
August	31 257	40 390	146.1	215.1	129.9	132.3	1 032	572	43.2	101.0	16.22	695.84
September	31 272	40 701	146.8	215.1	131.1	132.7	1 029	571	43.1	100.6	16.25	703.63
October	32 269	40 875	146.8	215.4	132.2	132.8	1 029	570	43.1	100.4	16.28	703.30
November	31 895	40 940	146.3	214.8	132.7	132.3	1 028	569	43.3	100.7	16.38	715.81
December	31 956	41 380	146.4	215.4	133.7	132.3	1 028	568	43.5	101.0	16.45	730.38

1. Chemicals and products, December 1984=100.

PETROLEUM AND COAL PRODUCTS—PRODUCTION, CAPACITY, SHIPMENTS, AND INVENTORIES
(Seasonally adjusted)

YEAR AND MONTH	Industrial production—Petroleum products (1992=100)								Capacity utilization: Petroleum products (Percent of capacity)	Manufacturers' shipments and inventories: Petroleum and coal products (Millions of dollars)	
	Total	Petroleum refining and miscellaneous						Paving and roofing materials		Shipments	Inventories (Book value, end of period)
		Total	Miscellaneous petroleum products	Distillate fuel oil	Residual fuel oil	Aviation fuel and kerosene	Automotive gasoline				
1968	75.2	76.2	75.3	77.1	84.9	85.4	73.7	61.0	95.2	22 548	2 035
1969	77.3	77.7	77.8	78.0	82.1	75.7	77.4	68.1	94.7	23 721	2 085
1970	80.8	80.8	79.9	82.5	79.2	78.6	80.7	74.8	93.9	24 200	2 161
1971	83.5	83.5	82.0	83.9	84.1	77.2	84.6	78.2	91.8	26 198	2 260
1972	87.4	87.3	86.2	88.3	89.3	76.2	88.9	82.0	92.8	27 918	2 142
1973	92.2	92.3	92.0	94.9	109.3	77.0	92.4	85.7	94.2	33 903	2 476
1974	89.0	89.9	90.4	89.5	120.7	71.1	90.0	79.2	87.1	57 229	3 945
1975	88.0	89.9	83.4	89.0	138.8	72.7	92.0	71.8	83.7	67 496	4 426
1976	93.6	95.6	87.6	98.2	154.6	75.8	96.8	76.0	85.2	80 022	4 711
1977	101.5	103.3	97.3	110.5	196.9	81.1	99.6	83.4	87.6	94 702	5 439
1978	104.9	105.9	109.9	106.5	186.9	79.6	101.5	94.0	87.6	100 967	5 330
1979	103.9	104.9	112.7	106.1	188.8	84.1	96.9	93.2	84.1	144 156	7 458
1980	95.9	97.2	105.6	89.6	177.1	80.0	92.1	81.8	74.7	192 969	9 693
1981	91.2	92.3	95.0	88.0	148.0	76.4	90.7	78.0	70.7	217 681	10 420
1982	86.6	87.5	80.7	87.6	120.2	76.3	89.7	76.5	70.1	203 404	17 009
1983	86.9	86.0	81.7	82.5	95.6	78.9	89.8	95.0	73.4	187 788	14 843
1984	89.9	89.5	83.4	90.2	99.8	86.9	91.5	95.0	77.8	184 488	14 260
1985	89.5	89.7	84.7	90.1	98.7	88.7	90.9	90.2	78.4	176 574	13 975
1986	95.7	94.9	92.0	94.1	99.7	96.7	95.6	103.0	83.7	122 605	8 791
1987	97.0	95.8	94.6	91.5	99.3	98.8	96.8	107.0	83.5	130 414	9 973
1988	98.8	97.9	95.5	96.0	103.7	100.8	98.5	107.1	85.3	131 682	9 196
1989	99.3	98.5	95.6	97.3	106.9	102.7	98.6	106.0	87.0	146 487	10 743
1990	100.3	99.6	98.7	98.2	106.4	106.4	98.6	106.8	87.6	173 389	13 432
1991	99.1	99.2	97.2	99.5	104.6	102.6	98.7	98.7	86.6	159 144	11 671
1992	100.0	100.0	100.0	100.0	100.0	100.0	100.0	100.0	88.6	150 227	11 330
1993	102.9	102.0	101.7	105.1	93.5	102.2	101.4	108.8	92.1	144 834	10 268
1994	103.0	101.9	102.5	107.7	92.4	104.6	99.6	110.3	91.3	143 328	11 159
1995	104.5	103.6	104.7	106.1	88.2	101.9	103.5	111.3	92.0	151 261	11 523
1996	106.5	105.0	102.6	111.7	80.6	109.4	104.6	117.3	93.8	180 122	12 469
1993:											
January	101.8	101.3	101.3	100.9	89.7	101.0	102.2	104.5	90.9	12 880	11 349
February	102.9	102.2	100.7	101.7	91.0	104.4	103.3	107.5	92.0	12 890	11 347
March	102.4	101.9	103.8	103.2	90.0	108.2	100.3	104.8	91.5	12 934	11 379
April	101.9	101.4	100.3	103.1	102.3	105.6	100.2	105.4	91.1	12 562	11 617
May	102.0	101.0	98.0	101.2	100.6	103.8	101.6	108.0	91.2	12 479	11 401
June	102.5	101.3	99.0	103.3	92.1	112.2	100.1	109.9	91.7	12 130	11 223
July	102.2	100.9	100.7	105.8	89.5	102.9	99.5	111.0	91.5	11 906	11 051
August	102.1	100.4	103.5	104.8	85.8	96.8	99.1	114.3	91.5	11 690	11 028
September	102.9	101.6	101.2	105.3	94.8	95.5	102.0	111.2	92.1	11 620	10 758
October	105.6	104.9	105.9	113.2	99.6	96.6	103.2	109.9	94.6	11 911	10 898
November	105.1	104.3	104.6	110.4	96.2	98.3	103.6	109.6	94.2	11 388	10 752
December	103.1	102.1	100.8	108.6	90.3	101.0	101.3	109.9	92.5	10 834	10 268
1994:											
January	102.2	100.4	97.4	108.2	89.3	103.8	98.9	115.4	91.6	11 219	10 128
February	101.8	100.6	101.7	108.7	93.3	102.1	97.2	110.6	91.1	11 349	10 359
March	101.4	100.1	99.2	108.9	95.5	96.8	98.0	110.7	90.5	11 509	10 389
April	104.5	103.3	104.8	109.3	95.9	108.9	99.7	113.8	93.2	11 507	10 370
May	105.0	104.1	109.3	112.0	95.3	105.3	99.3	111.4	93.4	11 580	10 541
June	102.7	102.0	102.1	109.8	90.5	105.1	99.2	107.2	91.2	12 078	10 721
July	101.6	100.6	99.3	106.5	94.2	103.3	98.7	109.4	90.1	12 364	11 108
August	103.2	102.5	100.4	107.8	95.4	111.7	100.0	108.5	91.3	12 825	11 169
September	102.1	101.3	100.6	107.7	91.2	104.2	99.2	108.0	90.1	12 086	10 818
October	102.4	101.5	104.7	105.9	89.1	104.4	98.7	108.9	90.2	11 875	11 040
November	104.3	103.5	104.4	104.0	88.7	102.6	104.2	109.6	91.8	12 526	11 204
December	104.2	103.4	106.4	104.2	90.7	106.7	102.0	109.9	91.5	12 504	11 159
1995:											
January	104.4	103.7	106.0	106.2	100.2	99.5	102.6	108.8	91.6	12 545	11 446
February	104.3	103.7	107.2	106.0	85.5	100.4	103.2	107.9	91.5	12 907	11 608
March	105.2	104.4	107.6	111.0	87.6	95.4	103.5	110.2	92.4	12 491	11 540
April	104.1	103.0	103.0	104.8	89.5	99.3	103.9	111.9	91.5	12 915	11 615
May	103.8	102.9	105.9	104.8	83.2	100.2	102.9	109.7	91.2	13 035	11 737
June	104.7	103.5	105.5	104.0	86.6	101.1	104.1	113.0	92.1	12 824	11 643
July	105.4	104.3	107.3	102.4	92.5	102.2	104.8	112.7	92.7	12 426	11 280
August	105.0	103.9	106.0	106.3	91.0	102.0	103.4	112.0	92.4	12 545	11 175
September	105.7	105.0	104.6	107.6	91.7	105.4	105.1	109.0	93.1	12 279	11 192
October	103.4	102.2	99.5	105.0	85.1	105.1	102.9	112.5	91.2	12 115	10 931
November	103.6	102.4	101.0	106.6	74.6	106.8	102.7	112.2	91.3	12 482	11 071
December	105.1	103.7	102.9	108.0	91.2	106.0	102.8	115.8	92.7	12 946	11 523
1996:											
January	105.2	103.7	101.7	108.1	86.1	110.7	102.9	115.8	92.8	13 292	11 563
February	106.0	104.5	98.9	112.3	85.7	108.6	104.5	117.3	93.5	13 620	11 642
March	105.7	104.5	98.8	109.1	79.4	110.1	106.1	113.9	93.1	14 229	12 008
April	105.6	104.4	100.8	110.7	76.0	110.1	104.6	113.9	93.0	15 297	12 006
May	106.2	104.7	102.6	109.6	81.7	104.0	105.7	117.3	93.6	15 108	11 940
June	106.3	105.0	101.6	110.2	84.9	108.4	105.3	116.1	93.6	14 563	11 876
July	105.3	103.9	100.0	105.6	74.8	105.0	106.9	116.3	92.7	14 706	11 957
August	107.8	106.2	104.5	111.2	83.0	109.2	106.2	120.1	94.8	14 988	11 931
September	106.9	105.4	104.2	111.1	80.3	118.4	103.2	118.1	94.0	15 461	12 139
October	108.4	106.8	105.5	120.3	81.3	111.4	103.4	120.5	95.3	16 220	12 191
November	107.4	105.8	104.0	117.3	75.2	108.6	104.2	119.3	94.4	16 250	12 307
December	107.3	105.7	108.3	115.0	78.7	108.7	102.5	119.3	94.2	16 285	12 469

PETROLEUM AND COAL PRODUCTS—PRICES, EMPLOYMENT, HOURS, AND EARNINGS

YEAR AND MONTH	Producer prices (1982=100, except as noted, not seasonally adjusted)							Consumer prices: Motor fuel (1982-1984=100, seasonally adjusted)		Employment (Thousands, seasonally adjusted)		Production workers			
	Petroleum refining and related industries [1]	Intermediate materials				Finished goods				Total payroll employees	Production workers	Weekly hours worked (Seasonally adjusted)		Average earnings (Dollars, not seasonally adjusted)	
		Liquefied petroleum gas	Jet fuels	Number 2 diesel fuel	Residual fuel	Gasoline	Number 2 fuel oil	Total	Gasoline			Average hours [2]	Aggregate hours index (1982=100)	Hourly	Weekly
1968	.....	.....	.....	.....	8.1	14.3	.....	26.8	26.8	187	118	42.5	95.4	3.75	159.38
1969	.....	.....	.....	.....	7.9	14.6	.....	27.6	27.7	182	112	42.6	90.9	4.00	170.40
1970	.....	.....	.....	.....	10.6	14.4	.....	27.9	27.9	191	118	42.8	96.2	4.28	183.18
1971	.....	15.2	.....	.....	14.0	15.1	.....	28.1	28.1	194	124	42.8	100.9	4.57	195.60
1972	.....	14.9	.....	.....	13.4	15.5	.....	28.4	28.4	195	125	42.7	101.5	4.96	211.79
1973	.....	18.0	.....	14.3	16.1	18.2	13.9	31.2	31.2	193	124	42.4	99.9	5.28	223.87
1974	.....	29.2	.....	27.7	41.1	29.2	26.3	42.2	42.2	197	126	42.1	100.9	5.68	239.13
1975	.....	35.2	28.4	31.2	41.9	34.5	30.1	45.1	45.1	194	123	41.2	96.3	6.48	266.98
1976	.....	45.8	31.1	34.1	38.3	38.0	32.7	47.0	47.0	199	128	42.1	102.3	7.21	303.54
1977	.....	57.3	35.7	38.5	44.2	41.3	37.6	49.7	49.7	202	131	42.7	106.6	7.83	334.34
1978	.....	54.7	39.6	39.7	42.1	43.4	39.0	51.8	51.8	208	136	43.6	112.2	8.63	376.27
1979	.....	64.7	53.7	57.1	57.9	60.0	56.4	70.1	70.2	210	137	43.8	114.0	9.36	409.97
1980	.....	102.3	87.5	85.8	81.3	93.3	82.8	97.4	97.5	198	125	41.8	99.1	10.10	422.18
1981	.....	112.0	104.5	105.0	104.8	108.0	104.1	108.5	108.5	214	134	43.2	110.0	11.38	491.62
1982	.....	100.0	100.0	100.0	100.0	100.0	100.0	102.8	102.8	201	120	43.9	100.0	12.46	546.99
1983	.....	113.5	91.5	87.9	89.6	90.2	87.8	99.4	99.4	196	118	43.9	98.4	13.28	582.99
1984	.....	99.1	87.0	86.3	94.7	84.6	87.3	97.9	97.8	189	111	43.7	92.5	13.44	587.33
1985	.....	86.3	81.0	81.2	83.2	83.3	84.5	98.7	98.6	179	109	43.0	88.7	14.06	604.58
1986	66.6	61.0	53.8	48.6	44.5	54.7	50.5	77.1	77.0	169	106	43.8	88.1	14.19	621.52
1987	70.5	57.4	54.2	55.4	53.1	58.8	55.9	80.2	80.1	164	107	44.0	89.4	14.58	641.52
1988	67.7	51.6	52.1	49.7	41.1	57.3	49.5	80.9	80.8	160	104	44.4	88.1	14.97	664.67
1989	75.7	52.7	58.1	58.9	47.6	65.1	58.0	88.5	88.5	156	102	44.3	85.7	15.41	682.66
1990	91.4	77.4	76.0	74.1	57.7	78.7	73.3	101.2	101.0	157	103	44.6	87.2	16.24	724.30
1991	83.1	75.4	66.4	65.6	49.1	69.9	65.2	99.4	99.2	160	103	44.1	86.7	17.04	751.46
1992	80.3	65.8	61.9	61.9	45.9	68.1	61.7	99.0	99.0	158	103	43.8	86.0	17.90	784.02
1993	77.6	63.6	59.0	60.5	49.6	63.9	59.1	98.0	97.7	152	99	44.2	83.1	18.53	819.03
1994	74.8	58.2	53.9	56.0	48.2	61.7	56.0	98.5	98.2	149	97	44.4	81.4	19.07	846.71
1995	77.2	65.1	55.0	57.0	52.6	63.7	56.6	100.0	99.8	145	94	43.7	77.9	19.36	846.03
1996	87.4	84.7	66.7	70.0	59.8	72.8	69.5	106.3	105.9	142	92	43.6	76.1	19.32	842.35
1993:															
January	77.3	65.6	59.8	60.6	49.6	63.4	57.2	101.6	101.6	154	101	44.1	85.6	18.39	811.00
February	78.2	67.2	60.3	60.3	51.6	64.0	61.0	101.8	101.7	154	101	43.9	84.9	18.40	807.76
March	79.7	67.4	61.2	63.1	48.3	65.5	63.8	100.8	100.7	152	100	43.3	82.5	18.66	807.98
April	81.1	67.1	59.6	63.2	53.1	67.9	61.7	100.1	99.9	152	100	44.9	84.8	18.57	833.79
May	82.5	66.3	61.2	63.4	53.1	69.9	62.1	97.8	97.6	152	100	44.7	84.6	18.56	829.63
June	80.3	64.7	60.2	61.6	51.4	67.8	60.0	96.4	96.1	152	99	44.1	82.8	18.46	814.09
July	77.7	63.9	57.7	57.7	51.6	65.0	56.1	95.6	95.3	151	99	44.0	83.0	18.42	810.48
August	75.8	62.5	55.5	55.2	48.9	63.8	53.8	95.3	95.1	150	98	44.1	82.9	18.35	809.24
September	76.7	61.7	57.0	60.8	46.5	63.3	57.9	94.3	94.0	151	98	44.1	81.8	18.67	823.35
October	78.7	60.5	60.5	66.5	47.9	63.7	64.5	99.3	98.8	150	97	45.7	83.2	18.55	847.74
November	75.9	59.5	61.3	63.0	46.7	60.4	59.5	97.8	97.2	151	98	43.9	81.0	18.65	818.74
December	67.5	57.0	53.8	51.2	46.2	52.5	51.8	96.5	96.0	149	97	43.4	80.4	18.68	810.71
1994:															
January	67.5	55.4	49.3	51.4	42.4	53.4	52.0	95.5	95.1	149	97	44.0	81.9	18.80	827.20
February	71.2	55.6	53.9	56.6	44.3	56.4	58.4	97.0	96.5	148	96	43.6	80.1	19.23	838.43
March	70.7	55.8	51.9	56.9	46.5	56.2	55.6	96.4	95.9	148	96	44.6	81.8	19.32	861.67
April	72.0	55.4	50.7	54.6	43.7	59.5	54.7	96.1	95.6	149	96	45.1	81.6	18.93	853.74
May	73.5	55.8	51.7	54.8	43.6	61.2	54.9	93.8	93.3	149	96	43.8	80.1	18.76	821.69
June	74.7	57.2	52.3	54.2	47.5	62.9	54.4	94.5	94.1	148	96	44.0	80.3	18.87	830.28
July	78.0	58.4	54.5	56.4	51.3	66.5	56.6	97.9	97.6	148	97	43.8	80.8	18.93	829.13
August	82.5	59.6	56.5	57.4	56.6	72.4	58.0	102.5	102.4	150	97	43.5	80.8	18.75	815.63
September	79.5	60.0	55.6	57.7	54.7	67.0	57.8	102.0	101.9	150	97	46.3	85.0	19.32	894.52
October	76.2	59.6	55.9	58.4	48.2	62.1	56.9	101.7	101.7	150	97	45.1	81.9	19.30	870.43
November	77.8	61.9	58.0	59.5	49.0	64.1	57.8	102.5	102.5	150	97	44.4	81.3	19.25	854.70
December	73.5	64.4	56.1	54.2	50.9	58.4	55.4	102.5	102.4	150	97	44.2	81.9	19.32	853.94
1995:															
January	74.3	63.8	53.3	54.0	50.4	60.2	56.4	101.7	101.6	148	96	43.8	80.3	19.18	840.08
February	74.6	67.0	53.0	53.1	54.0	60.4	54.2	101.4	101.3	148	96	44.4	81.4	19.55	868.02
March	75.3	65.5	52.2	55.0	54.8	61.6	54.0	100.5	100.3	148	96	43.3	79.8	19.37	838.72
April	80.2	65.7	53.6	58.2	54.7	67.7	56.3	100.5	100.3	147	95	43.9	78.7	19.55	858.25
May	83.4	65.9	55.4	59.4	56.9	71.8	59.3	101.4	101.3	147	95	43.2	78.7	19.17	828.14
June	81.9	68.5	53.9	56.8	61.2	70.6	54.5	101.8	101.9	146	94	43.7	78.1	19.16	837.29
July	78.1	64.5	53.7	53.7	57.1	65.9	53.2	100.9	100.7	145	94	44.1	78.6	19.25	848.93
August	77.5	61.7	53.9	56.0	54.0	64.5	55.3	99.7	99.5	144	93	43.2	76.9	19.14	826.85
September	77.6	62.4	55.8	58.5	45.9	64.2	58.1	98.4	98.2	143	93	43.8	76.9	19.41	850.16
October	75.4	64.4	56.5	58.8	46.8	60.8	56.8	98.7	98.4	143	93	44.3	77.1	19.68	871.82
November	73.4	65.2	58.5	59.7	47.0	57.2	59.6	96.7	96.3	142	91	43.8	75.3	19.46	852.35
December	75.4	66.9	59.5	60.2	48.5	59.8	62.0	98.5	98.2	142	91	43.2	74.7	19.44	839.81
1996:															
January	79.4	73.0	62.8	62.2	55.8	64.1	64.3	101.5	101.3	143	92	43.1	75.7	19.41	836.57
February	77.3	76.0	57.0	59.4	57.1	62.2	61.1	101.6	101.4	143	92	42.8	75.2	19.54	836.31
March	81.8	77.4	58.9	62.6	56.8	68.0	65.9	104.4	104.2	143	92	42.9	75.9	19.21	824.11
April	90.5	81.0	66.7	75.4	56.2	76.4	75.6	109.3	108.9	142	91	43.3	74.4	19.32	836.56
May	92.8	76.3	68.8	74.5	61.9	80.1	69.4	110.2	109.7	142	92	42.6	75.4	18.99	808.97
June	87.3	74.7	62.1	64.9	61.0	75.8	60.1	106.5	106.2	142	92	44.7	78.2	18.88	843.94
July	86.3	76.0	62.0	66.1	61.5	73.6	62.6	106.0	105.7	142	92	44.3	77.1	19.02	842.59
August	86.9	80.8	66.0	66.6	61.6	72.6	67.2	105.0	104.6	142	92	43.9	77.1	18.98	833.22
September	89.9	88.4	73.0	74.7	58.4	73.6	72.8	104.9	104.4	141	92	44.2	76.8	19.35	855.27
October	92.0	95.4	75.5	80.2	61.7	74.1	80.6	106.6	106.0	141	92	43.6	75.0	19.35	843.66
November	92.5	102.5	72.6	77.0	61.7	76.6	77.1	108.4	107.8	141	92	44.0	76.6	19.61	862.84
December	92.5	114.7	75.0	76.0	64.4	76.0	77.5	111.1	110.5	140	92	43.9	77.0	20.26	889.41

1. December 1984=100.
2. Not seasonally adjusted.

YEAR AND MONTH	RUBBER AND PLASTIC PRODUCTS—PRODUCTION, CAPACITY, SHIPMENTS, AND INVENTORIES (Seasonally adjusted)						
	Industrial production (1992=100)				Capacity utilization (Percent of capacity)	Manufacturers' shipments and inventories (Millions of dollars)	
	Total	Tires	Other rubber products	Plastic products, not elsewhere classified		Shipments	Inventories (Book value, end of period)
1968	32.1	45.9	77.3	20.3	91.6	15 585	2 018
1969	35.0	46.3	77.8	24.1	91.7	16 935	2 215
1970	33.0	41.7	69.5	23.8	81.2	16 754	2 386
1971	35.9	48.1	70.1	26.1	82.6	18 409	2 453
1972	43.7	54.5	79.4	33.6	91.6	21 662	2 695
1973	49.0	55.9	87.4	39.6	93.3	25 191	3 103
1974	47.9	59.1	86.2	37.3	84.9	28 828	4 023
1975	41.6	54.5	74.0	31.7	70.1	28 128	4 085
1976	48.1	54.0	80.4	40.0	78.5	32 880	4 581
1977	56.0	70.2	85.1	47.1	88.3	40 944	5 116
1978	59.3	69.9	88.0	51.4	89.2	44 823	5 801
1979	58.7	68.9	88.6	50.7	84.2	48 694	6 399
1980	53.3	55.3	78.0	48.1	73.9	49 157	6 435
1981	57.5	64.2	82.0	51.1	77.9	55 178	6 968
1982	56.8	63.4	73.1	52.0	74.4	57 307	7 748
1983	64.0	68.2	77.1	60.3	79.2	62 870	8 070
1984	72.1	78.8	85.7	67.9	84.3	72 938	8 904
1985	73.8	76.8	85.3	70.6	82.1	75 590	9 213
1986	78.2	75.0	86.6	76.8	82.9	78 379	9 285
1987	86.0	83.3	93.5	84.7	89.0	86 634	10 065
1988	88.2	88.2	98.3	85.8	87.8	95 485	11 367
1989	91.2	91.8	97.2	89.6	87.4	101 236	11 533
1990	92.2	91.0	97.6	91.1	84.6	105 250	12 292
1991	90.7	87.3	92.9	90.8	80.3	105 804	12 121
1992	100.0	100.0	100.0	100.0	85.3	113 593	12 534
1993	106.8	105.3	106.1	107.1	88.0	122 777	12 816
1994	116.1	110.0	112.9	117.8	92.3	135 145	14 228
1995	118.9	117.1	112.6	120.7	91.5	145 426	15 264
1996	120.5	116.7	113.8	122.7	91.2	143 888	15 697
1993:							
January	104.3	104.3	104.9	104.1	87.2	9 971	12 450
February	104.6	104.0	103.8	104.9	87.3	10 210	12 379
March	104.1	102.9	104.6	104.1	86.6	10 079	12 443
April	105.4	105.2	105.3	105.4	87.5	9 959	12 539
May	105.6	108.8	104.3	105.4	87.4	10 085	12 679
June	105.6	102.8	105.0	106.2	87.2	10 265	12 691
July	107.3	105.4	107.1	107.7	88.4	10 105	12 700
August	107.7	108.4	106.9	107.7	88.4	10 194	12 750
September	108.9	105.9	106.6	109.9	89.2	10 398	12 803
October	108.1	106.3	106.3	108.8	88.4	10 358	12 771
November	108.9	104.2	107.2	110.1	88.8	10 597	12 855
December	110.5	105.5	111.4	111.1	89.9	10 621	12 816
1994:							
January	111.4	109.6	112.2	111.5	90.3	10 472	12 858
February	111.5	108.6	110.6	112.2	90.1	10 637	12 925
March	114.3	110.0	113.8	115.1	92.0	10 976	12 963
April	114.6	110.1	111.7	116.0	91.9	10 960	12 942
May	115.9	113.3	115.8	116.3	92.6	11 085	12 989
June	115.9	110.2	112.8	117.6	92.3	11 236	13 083
July	117.1	112.0	114.7	118.5	92.9	11 121	13 305
August	116.5	103.1	112.1	119.5	92.1	11 454	13 413
September	117.3	103.7	113.9	120.2	92.4	11 493	13 676
October	118.8	110.9	112.5	121.5	93.2	11 670	13 919
November	119.3	112.9	112.2	122.0	93.3	11 889	13 809
December	120.5	115.5	113.0	123.1	93.9	12 233	14 228
1995:							
January	120.1	112.9	111.8	123.2	93.3	12 240	14 471
February	120.7	114.7	113.7	123.2	93.6	12 208	14 895
March	119.8	114.3	114.0	122.1	92.8	12 212	15 044
April	120.0	120.5	112.5	121.8	92.8	12 110	15 313
May	117.9	113.6	111.5	120.1	91.0	12 105	15 391
June	117.7	116.1	112.7	119.1	90.6	12 025	15 465
July	116.5	121.4	110.5	117.3	89.6	11 772	15 507
August	118.2	118.2	113.5	119.4	90.8	12 234	15 436
September	118.9	119.3	112.9	120.4	91.2	12 240	15 351
October	119.2	117.6	113.4	120.9	91.3	12 137	15 299
November	119.2	120.8	113.0	120.5	91.1	12 146	15 247
December	118.6	115.5	112.2	120.5	90.5	11 930	15 264
1996:							
January	118.2	116.7	113.0	119.7	90.1	11 540	15 225
February	118.6	113.8	113.2	120.6	90.3	11 898	15 236
March	119.3	119.6	112.5	121.0	90.7	11 890	15 278
April	118.0	111.9	112.3	120.2	89.6	12 098	15 196
May	119.8	111.7	113.2	122.6	90.9	12 154	15 162
June	120.9	116.8	113.3	123.4	91.6	12 022	15 258
July	120.7	114.5	113.3	123.3	91.3	12 212	15 301
August	122.0	116.7	113.6	124.7	92.1	12 027	15 354
September	122.8	123.9	114.7	124.7	92.7	11 978	15 479
October	121.4	118.0	115.5	123.4	91.5	12 005	15 557
November	121.7	120.8	114.9	123.6	91.6	12 103	15 625
December	122.6	115.4	115.8	125.3	92.1	11 959	15 697

RUBBER AND PLASTIC PRODUCTS—PRICES, EMPLOYMENT, HOURS, AND EARNINGS

YEAR AND MONTH	Producer prices (1982=100, except as noted, not seasonally adjusted)						Employment (Thousands, seasonally adjusted)		Production workers			
	Rubber and plastic products[1]	Finished tires and tubes[2]	Intermediate materials				Total payroll employees	Production workers	Weekly hours worked (Seasonally adjusted)		Average earnings (Dollars, not seasonally adjusted)	
			Synthetic rubber	Plastic construction products	Plastic film and sheet[3]	Plastic parts for manufacturing			Average hours	Aggregate hours index (1982=100)	Hourly	Weekly
1968	....	40.3	33.4	....	....	....	598	463	41.5	87.0	2.93	121.60
1969	....	40.1	33.9	....	....	....	634	491	41.2	91.6	3.08	126.90
1970	....	42.7	34.0	65.5	....	....	617	473	40.3	86.3	3.21	129.36
1971	....	42.8	34.0	63.7	47.3	....	617	479	40.4	87.5	3.41	137.76
1972	....	42.8	34.1	62.9	46.2	....	667	525	41.2	97.8	3.63	149.56
1973	....	43.7	34.3	63.4	46.9	....	731	579	41.2	107.9	3.84	158.21
1974	....	52.3	44.1	80.1	61.6	....	733	577	40.6	105.8	4.09	166.05
1975	....	58.2	49.3	83.5	69.6	....	643	493	39.9	89.0	4.42	176.36
1976	....	63.3	52.6	85.7	72.5	....	675	522	40.7	96.1	4.71	191.70
1977	....	66.6	56.1	89.7	75.0	....	750	588	41.1	109.2	5.21	214.13
1978	....	70.2	60.4	91.8	76.2	....	793	622	40.9	115.3	5.57	227.81
1979	....	80.7	70.3	99.4	81.4	82.5	821	643	40.6	118.2	6.02	244.41
1980	....	92.8	85.3	103.9	89.3	90.8	764	588	40.0	106.7	6.58	263.20
1981	....	98.2	98.0	104.3	95.7	96.6	772	597	40.3	109.0	7.22	290.97
1982	....	100.0	100.0	100.0	100.0	100.0	729	558	39.6	100.0	7.70	304.92
1983	....	96.1	97.0	110.1	102.4	101.8	743	574	41.2	107.2	8.06	332.07
1984	....	94.9	96.8	115.5	106.6	103.5	813	632	41.7	119.6	8.35	348.20
1985	100.0	93.0	96.8	108.6	106.1	103.5	818	632	41.1	117.6	8.60	353.46
1986	100.3	91.7	91.5	106.4	105.1	107.9	823	639	41.4	119.6	8.79	363.91
1987	100.9	91.0	98.0	108.4	106.8	108.1	842	653	41.6	123.1	8.98	373.57
1988	106.7	94.0	108.9	121.1	113.9	110.0	866	674	41.7	127.3	9.19	383.22
1989	110.2	97.2	108.5	120.1	119.9	111.3	888	692	41.4	129.6	9.46	391.64
1990	111.3	96.8	111.9	117.2	119.0	112.9	888	687	41.1	127.9	9.76	401.14
1991	113.7	98.2	106.1	115.1	120.6	113.5	862	662	41.1	123.2	10.07	413.88
1992	114.2	98.9	103.8	112.7	120.3	113.3	878	677	41.7	127.8	10.36	432.01
1993	115.4	98.9	105.7	116.6	121.4	113.9	909	703	41.8	133.2	10.57	441.83
1994	117.1	98.6	108.9	122.9	122.8	113.5	953	742	42.2	141.9	10.70	451.54
1995	123.3	100.2	126.3	133.8	135.6	115.9	980	763	41.5	143.4	10.91	452.77
1996	123.1	97.0	122.2	130.9	132.7	117.5	981	761	41.5	142.8	11.24	466.46
1993:												
January	115.0	98.8	104.6	113.3	121.7	114.1	894	692	41.8	131.0	10.53	442.26
February	115.1	98.6	105.0	114.6	122.5	114.3	897	695	42.0	132.2	10.51	440.37
March	115.1	98.8	104.1	115.4	122.5	114.0	902	698	41.6	131.5	10.46	434.09
April	115.3	99.7	104.7	115.5	122.5	114.3	904	700	42.2	133.8	10.59	441.60
May	115.2	99.7	104.5	115.5	122.5	114.6	907	702	41.7	132.6	10.55	440.99
June	115.4	99.8	105.0	116.1	121.6	113.2	909	703	41.7	132.8	10.54	442.68
July	115.4	98.9	106.6	116.7	121.0	113.2	911	705	41.8	133.5	10.58	434.84
August	115.4	98.7	106.7	117.7	120.5	113.5	913	707	41.8	133.9	10.53	439.10
September	115.7	98.6	107.5	118.3	120.6	113.8	914	708	41.9	134.4	10.66	444.52
October	115.8	98.6	107.1	118.7	120.5	113.9	914	706	41.8	133.7	10.60	444.14
November	115.7	98.4	106.5	118.9	120.5	113.9	920	711	42.0	135.3	10.62	449.23
December	115.9	98.7	106.1	119.0	120.8	113.6	924	715	41.9	135.7	10.67	454.54
1994:												
January	115.7	98.4	105.6	118.5	120.2	113.5	930	720	42.0	137.0	10.71	448.75
February	115.8	98.3	104.7	118.8	120.1	113.7	934	725	41.4	135.9	10.71	442.32
March	115.8	98.3	104.8	118.9	120.0	113.6	938	729	42.5	140.3	10.68	452.83
April	115.9	98.9	104.5	119.7	120.5	113.5	943	734	42.0	139.6	10.70	453.68
May	116.0	99.1	105.0	120.4	120.2	113.3	949	739	42.2	141.3	10.69	452.19
June	116.4	98.9	107.7	120.6	120.3	113.3	954	744	42.2	142.2	10.72	455.60
July	116.7	98.9	108.5	121.9	121.1	113.2	957	747	42.3	143.1	10.75	447.20
August	117.0	98.4	109.5	123.3	121.6	113.3	959	747	42.3	143.1	10.65	448.37
September	117.9	98.3	110.9	126.1	123.5	113.5	963	751	42.0	142.9	10.65	450.50
October	118.8	98.5	114.6	128.2	126.0	113.6	967	754	42.2	144.1	10.65	451.56
November	119.5	98.8	115.4	129.1	128.6	113.7	971	756	42.2	144.5	10.68	454.97
December	120.1	98.7	115.5	129.5	131.6	113.8	977	762	42.2	145.6	10.79	463.97
1995:												
January	121.3	98.7	118.9	129.9	132.7	114.3	985	768	42.3	147.1	10.81	456.18
February	121.8	98.8	121.9	131.8	134.4	114.5	985	769	42.0	146.3	10.75	451.50
March	122.5	99.8	124.7	132.9	135.2	114.6	984	767	41.8	145.2	10.79	451.02
April	123.2	99.9	126.2	134.8	135.4	115.6	984	768	41.6	144.7	10.76	434.70
May	123.6	99.8	127.4	136.1	135.9	115.8	983	766	41.5	144.0	10.85	451.36
June	124.1	101.0	127.3	135.3	136.9	115.8	980	763	41.4	143.1	10.90	454.53
July	124.1	101.3	127.9	135.2	136.4	115.8	975	758	41.0	140.8	11.01	443.70
August	124.2	101.0	129.0	136.3	136.0	116.4	977	759	41.3	142.0	10.93	449.22
September	124.2	101.0	129.1	134.8	137.0	116.8	977	759	41.4	142.3	10.99	459.38
October	124.0	101.0	128.3	134.0	137.0	116.8	977	760	41.4	142.5	11.01	456.92
November	123.6	101.0	127.8	132.6	136.0	116.8	978	760	41.4	142.5	11.01	460.22
December	123.2	99.7	126.6	131.8	134.7	117.0	978	759	41.3	142.0	11.15	470.53
1996:												
January	123.0	98.4	124.5	130.5	133.8	117.0	976	758	40.4	138.7	11.13	448.54
February	122.9	97.7	123.0	130.9	133.6	117.6	976	756	41.3	141.4	11.14	460.08
March	122.8	97.2	123.2	129.8	133.5	117.7	976	756	41.3	141.4	11.15	460.50
April	122.6	96.9	122.3	130.7	131.3	117.7	977	757	41.4	142.0	11.20	460.32
May	123.0	97.4	122.0	130.6	131.6	117.7	978	758	41.5	142.5	11.20	465.92
June	123.0	96.2	122.0	131.7	132.0	117.7	980	760	41.5	142.9	11.16	465.37
July	123.2	96.3	122.1	131.8	133.3	117.6	982	761	41.5	143.0	11.25	459.00
August	123.4	97.2	122.0	131.9	132.4	117.4	986	765	41.6	144.1	11.23	467.17
September	123.5	97.3	121.4	131.2	132.8	117.4	984	763	41.6	143.8	11.31	476.15
October	123.1	96.2	121.5	130.5	132.5	117.4	985	763	41.5	143.4	11.28	469.25
November	123.3	95.9	120.8	131.4	133.1	117.4	985	764	41.3	142.9	11.33	471.33
December	123.3	97.2	121.2	130.3	133.0	117.4	985	763	41.8	144.5	11.51	490.33

1. December 1984=100.
2. Includes tires, tubes, tread, and repair materials.
3. Includes plastic film, sheet, and other shapes.

LEATHER AND LEATHER PRODUCTS—PRODUCTION, CAPACITY, PRICES, EMPLOYMENT, HOURS, AND EARNINGS

YEAR AND MONTH	Industrial production (1992=100, seasonally adjusted)		Capacity utilization (Percent of capacity, seasonally adjusted)	Producer prices (1982=100, except as noted, not seasonally adjusted)				Employment (Thousands, seasonally adjusted)		Production workers			
										Weekly hours worked (Seasonally adjusted)		Average earnings (Dollars, not seasonally adjusted)	
	Total	Shoes		Leather and leather products[1]	Finished footwear	Leather	Cattle hides	Total payroll employees	Production workers	Average hours	Aggregate hours index (1982=100)	Hourly	Weekly
1968	274.7	339.3	93.6	....	42.8	32.8	26.6	355	306	38.3	180.0	2.23	85.41
1969	250.5	308.1	85.9	....	44.7	34.9	34.2	343	294	37.2	168.1	2.36	87.79
1970	235.0	296.8	81.8	....	46.2	34.6	30.4	320	273	37.2	156.4	2.49	92.63
1971	225.7	283.1	79.9	....	47.7	36.2	32.3	299	257	37.7	148.7	2.59	97.64
1972	234.2	280.2	84.2	....	50.8	45.1	69.4	296	256	38.3	150.7	2.68	102.64
1973	217.9	258.9	79.6	....	53.3	51.4	76.9	284	245	37.8	142.3	2.79	105.46
1974	207.2	235.1	77.4	....	57.1	49.6	55.1	271	232	36.9	131.8	2.99	110.33
1975	206.6	230.9	79.7	....	60.3	48.7	51.8	248	213	37.1	121.3	3.21	119.09
1976	205.1	223.2	81.7	....	64.8	60.4	78.1	263	227	37.4	130.6	3.40	127.16
1977	200.6	223.1	83.3	....	68.8	64.6	85.8	255	218	36.9	123.9	3.61	133.21
1978	201.6	223.4	86.8	....	74.7	76.6	111.2	257	220	37.1	125.5	3.89	144.32
1979	184.4	211.2	82.2	....	89.0	114.6	169.3	246	209	36.5	117.1	4.22	154.03
1980	181.6	204.0	84.1	....	95.2	99.8	104.6	233	197	36.7	110.7	4.58	168.09
1981	176.0	197.3	83.9	....	98.3	102.7	104.5	238	201	36.7	113.6	4.99	183.13
1982	163.1	190.5	80.7	....	100.0	100.0	100.0	219	183	35.6	100.0	5.33	189.75
1983	158.3	180.4	82.8	....	102.1	106.2	109.8	205	171	36.8	96.8	5.54	203.87
1984	141.9	160.4	78.6	....	102.7	119.6	143.8	189	158	36.8	89.3	5.71	210.13
1985	126.1	140.5	74.1	101.3	104.8	113.4	126.1	165	137	37.2	78.1	5.83	216.88
1986	115.0	127.9	71.9	103.0	106.9	122.9	147.7	149	123	36.9	69.5	5.92	218.45
1987	112.4	119.4	74.7	106.6	109.4	140.9	179.9	143	120	38.2	70.3	6.08	232.26
1988	112.0	121.6	78.7	113.4	115.1	167.5	205.8	143	118	37.5	67.9	6.28	235.50
1989	111.9	117.0	82.5	118.0	120.8	170.4	213.1	138	114	37.9	66.4	6.59	249.76
1990	107.8	112.5	82.7	122.6	125.6	177.5	217.8	133	109	37.4	62.8	6.91	258.43
1991	98.4	96.6	78.8	124.8	128.6	168.4	173.4	124	100	37.5	57.7	7.18	269.25
1992	100.0	100.2	82.8	127.0	132.0	163.7	171.4	120	97	38.0	56.6	7.42	281.96
1993	101.0	100.0	85.5	129.0	134.4	168.6	180.2	117	94	38.6	55.6	7.63	294.52
1994	93.6	97.5	80.8	130.6	135.5	179.6	200.9	113	90	38.5	53.0	7.97	306.85
1995	85.7	90.4	75.3	134.1	139.2	191.4	209.9	106	83	38.0	48.3	8.17	310.46
1996	80.0	81.4	71.5	134.7	141.6	177.9	186.5	96	74	38.1	43.4	8.56	326.14
1993:													
January	103.5	103.5	86.8	128.7	133.5	166.6	184.9	118	95	39.4	57.5	7.50	292.50
February	104.9	105.1	88.1	128.4	133.8	169.0	175.0	118	95	40.0	58.4	7.49	292.11
March	103.2	101.0	86.9	128.5	133.9	169.0	177.5	118	95	38.6	56.3	7.51	287.63
April	102.7	100.1	86.6	128.8	134.5	168.3	182.7	118	94	39.3	56.8	7.59	291.46
May	101.8	99.7	86.0	128.8	134.1	169.7	183.5	118	94	38.5	55.6	7.60	293.36
June	101.4	97.6	85.8	129.3	134.2	168.7	178.6	118	94	37.8	54.6	7.57	291.45
July	99.9	97.2	84.6	128.9	134.8	167.2	180.4	117	93	38.1	54.4	7.56	288.79
August	99.2	97.7	84.3	129.8	134.8	168.7	174.3	117	93	38.2	54.6	7.64	294.14
September	99.1	99.2	84.3	129.0	134.9	169.0	182.2	116	93	38.5	55.0	7.70	295.68
October	98.8	99.6	84.2	129.0	134.7	168.6	179.1	116	93	38.4	54.9	7.68	297.22
November	98.2	99.6	83.8	129.1	134.9	168.9	181.5	116	92	38.4	54.3	7.81	303.03
December	99.0	99.8	84.6	129.3	135.1	169.1	183.3	116	92	38.5	54.4	7.88	307.32
1994:													
January	98.4	100.6	84.2	130.1	135.5	171.2	179.8	116	92	38.8	54.8	7.90	304.15
February	95.5	98.9	81.9	129.2	135.1	171.0	175.5	115	92	38.2	54.0	7.94	296.16
March	95.8	98.3	82.3	129.5	135.4	172.9	178.6	114	91	38.6	54.0	7.99	306.82
April	96.5	100.6	83.0	129.6	135.2	173.6	191.3	114	91	38.7	54.1	7.96	307.26
May	94.4	98.4	81.3	129.8	135.4	174.9	194.0	113	90	38.3	53.0	7.96	305.66
June	93.2	96.9	80.3	130.1	135.2	178.5	193.0	113	90	38.3	53.0	7.95	309.26
July	93.3	96.6	80.6	130.3	135.3	180.7	202.3	114	91	38.3	53.5	7.97	302.06
August	92.1	96.6	79.7	130.6	135.3	181.2	204.5	112	89	38.3	52.4	7.96	307.26
September	92.3	96.3	80.0	131.3	135.6	184.4	211.5	112	88	38.2	51.7	7.97	310.03
October	90.7	96.0	78.7	131.7	135.8	186.8	229.8	111	88	38.7	52.3	8.01	313.99
November	90.5	94.9	78.6	132.1	136.1	189.4	228.1	111	87	38.5	51.5	8.03	313.17
December	90.3	96.1	78.5	132.5	136.6	190.4	223.1	111	88	38.4	51.9	8.04	312.76
1995:													
January	89.4	93.9	77.8	133.3	137.5	192.2	221.2	111	87	38.1	50.9	8.10	306.18
February	88.9	93.6	77.5	133.7	138.6	194.7	223.7	109	86	38.4	50.7	8.11	307.37
March	89.3	94.2	78.0	133.8	138.7	195.2	232.0	109	86	38.3	50.6	8.10	308.61
April	86.8	92.4	76.0	134.2	138.8	198.4	223.7	108	85	38.2	49.9	8.28	307.19
May	87.4	92.0	76.7	134.4	138.9	199.5	236.8	107	84	38.3	49.4	8.15	313.78
June	85.4	90.3	75.0	134.3	139.0	195.3	216.7	105	83	38.1	48.6	8.10	313.47
July	83.8	89.2	73.6	134.3	139.2	193.9	217.7	104	82	37.2	46.9	8.01	293.17
August	84.9	90.1	74.8	134.2	139.3	190.0	207.1	104	82	38.1	48.0	8.14	314.20
September	84.9	90.7	74.9	134.1	139.3	186.5	200.1	104	82	37.9	47.7	8.24	318.06
October	83.5	87.3	73.8	134.4	140.1	184.6	185.8	103	81	37.8	47.0	8.23	314.39
November	82.5	86.6	73.1	134.4	140.4	183.5	176.7	103	79	37.6	45.6	8.23	312.74
December	81.4	84.5	72.2	134.5	140.5	182.4	177.4	100	78	37.6	45.1	8.33	317.37
1996:													
January	80.1	82.2	71.1	134.6	140.6	182.3	172.7	99	77	35.0	41.4	8.51	294.45
February	81.7	83.5	72.6	134.6	141.1	181.0	175.7	99	77	37.6	44.5	8.41	312.01
March	81.2	83.2	72.2	134.8	141.3	181.2	177.1	98	76	38.0	44.4	8.46	319.79
April	81.1	81.9	72.2	134.1	141.2	176.1	175.6	98	76	37.8	44.1	8.40	315.00
May	80.7	81.7	71.9	134.5	141.2	178.1	178.1	97	75	38.2	44.0	8.42	321.64
June	81.0	81.7	72.3	134.4	141.6	175.2	181.2	97	74	38.4	43.7	8.47	331.18
July	80.0	80.3	71.5	134.1	141.7	172.7	186.0	96	73	38.3	43.0	8.43	317.81
August	79.5	80.0	71.1	134.2	142.0	173.4	190.7	95	73	38.6	43.3	8.62	335.32
September	79.4	80.3	71.1	135.3	142.0	176.0	186.3	94	72	38.7	42.8	8.69	340.65
October	78.4	80.7	70.3	135.1	142.2	177.4	204.8	94	72	38.6	42.7	8.71	339.69
November	77.4	79.5	69.4	135.2	142.2	179.4	204.4	93	71	38.9	42.4	8.73	343.09
December	80.1	81.2	72.0	136.0	142.3	182.5	205.4	94	73	38.8	43.5	8.83	347.02

1. December 1984=100.

Transportation, Communications, and Utilities

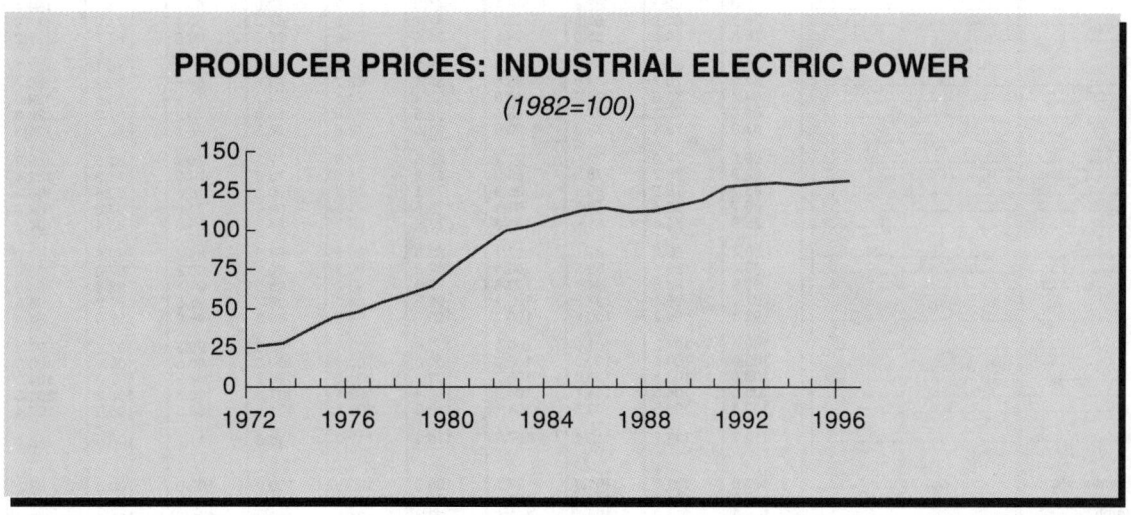

PRODUCER PRICES: INDUSTRIAL ELECTRIC POWER
(1982=100)

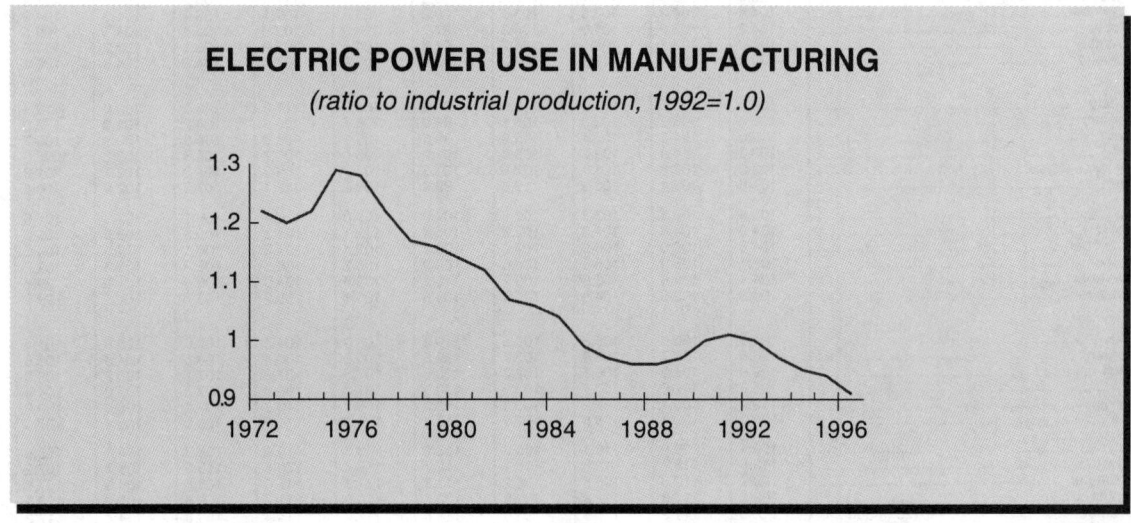

ELECTRIC POWER USE IN MANUFACTURING
(ratio to industrial production, 1992=1.0)

Electricity prices rose sharply from 1973 to 1982, and, after a lag, the ratio of electric power use to manufacturing production fell between 1976 and 1987. Industrial electricity prices were rela-tively stable from 1991-1996, but the decline in the ratio of electricity use to output resumed. In part, the decline reflects a shifting production mix toward industries with less intensive power use.

ELECTRIC AND GAS UTILITIES—INDUSTRIAL PRODUCTION
(1992=100, seasonally adjusted)

YEAR AND MONTH	Total	Electric Total	Generation Total	Generation Fossil fuel	Generation Hydro and nuclear	Sales Total	Sales Residential	Nonresidential Total	Nonresidential Industrial	Gas Total	Gas Residential	Gas Commercial and other	Gas transmission
1968	57.5	43.6	46.1	56.1	27.3	41.7	40.7	42.5	53.6	116.8	96.2	78.0	148.3
1969	62.6	47.7	50.2	60.7	30.8	45.9	45.4	46.1	58.0	124.9	102.0	84.6	159.3
1970	66.5	51.0	53.4	65.1	31.4	49.4	49.8	49.0	59.4	130.5	104.1	90.0	169.6
1971	69.6	53.9	56.3	67.5	35.5	52.3	53.2	51.5	61.0	134.4	106.6	94.2	175.2
1972	74.1	58.4	61.0	73.3	38.1	56.7	57.6	55.8	65.9	136.5	108.8	94.6	177.8
1973	77.0	62.3	63.6	76.1	41.3	61.2	62.0	60.3	71.1	134.4	106.0	97.8	176.7
1974	76.1	61.9	62.6	73.3	47.1	61.0	62.0	60.1	71.3	131.2	106.3	97.6	169.5
1975	76.8	64.0	65.0	74.5	54.6	62.9	65.5	60.9	67.7	125.2	108.8	95.0	158.6
1976	79.9	67.1	69.8	80.8	55.3	65.2	64.5	65.5	76.1	127.1	111.9	100.9	157.6
1977	82.0	70.7	73.9	85.6	55.1	68.7	68.6	68.7	80.2	120.7	102.3	92.4	156.9
1978	84.4	73.3	76.0	84.9	65.4	71.5	71.7	71.4	83.5	122.6	105.1	93.8	158.8
1979	86.8	75.2	77.8	88.5	62.6	73.6	73.0	73.9	87.2	126.6	105.6	99.1	166.5
1980	87.3	76.4	78.9	90.6	61.5	74.8	76.5	73.6	84.2	124.8	103.2	94.2	166.5
1981	85.0	78.0	79.5	91.1	62.4	77.0	77.3	76.7	85.5	109.3	97.9	91.5	127.1
1982	82.3	76.7	78.3	85.8	69.2	75.6	78.0	74.0	77.3	102.4	98.8	92.7	115.7
1983	83.7	79.2	80.4	86.9	73.1	78.3	80.7	76.5	80.4	100.4	94.4	87.2	124.2
1984	86.7	82.4	83.8	91.1	75.5	81.5	82.6	81.0	87.0	102.6	97.2	90.6	118.9
1985	88.8	84.6	85.9	93.3	77.6	83.7	84.7	83.0	85.4	104.3	93.6	86.1	130.0
1986	86.4	86.2	87.1	92.1	82.5	85.5	87.5	84.2	83.8	87.0	92.5	82.6	84.6
1987	89.4	89.4	89.5	96.4	82.3	89.3	90.7	88.2	87.6	89.0	92.1	85.4	86.9
1988	93.9	93.6	94.1	100.6	87.3	93.2	95.0	91.7	92.8	94.5	96.7	95.2	91.2
1989	97.1	96.8	97.9	103.1	92.8	96.0	96.7	95.5	96.0	98.1	100.3	96.1	95.7
1990	98.3	99.2	100.5	100.7	100.0	98.2	98.3	98.0	97.0	94.4	94.2	94.7	94.9
1991	100.4	101.2	101.9	100.1	103.6	100.6	102.3	99.3	97.8	97.3	96.4	97.4	97.2
1992	100.0	100.0	100.0	100.0	100.0	100.0	100.0	100.0	100.0	100.0	100.0	100.0	100.0
1993	103.9	103.8	103.0	103.7	102.2	104.3	106.2	102.9	102.0	104.3	105.0	101.3	103.4
1994	105.3	105.5	104.1	104.9	103.4	106.4	107.5	105.6	102.9	104.6	100.9	102.1	106.0
1995	109.1	109.5	109.3	104.7	113.0	109.8	111.5	108.5	105.0	107.4	103.0	108.6	110.9
1996	112.7	112.7	112.4	107.1	116.9	112.9	115.5	111.2	105.5	112.9	109.5	116.2	112.8
1993:													
January	100.8	101.3	101.9	97.7	106.0	100.9	100.9	100.9	100.3	98.9	99.6	95.6	100.0
February	104.5	104.1	104.3	105.4	103.0	104.0	106.3	102.2	101.3	106.1	108.6	105.6	104.4
March	105.3	104.2	103.6	108.5	98.4	104.6	107.3	102.7	101.6	109.7	111.7	111.0	107.2
April	103.5	103.5	103.0	100.6	104.9	104.0	106.1	102.4	102.1	103.6	105.0	101.5	102.9
May	101.3	102.8	103.3	94.7	111.5	102.5	101.6	102.9	102.4	95.5	95.8	97.9	93.3
June	103.3	103.3	104.1	102.8	105.0	102.7	102.9	102.5	102.3	103.4	104.5	98.5	103.1
July	104.4	105.0	104.2	105.8	102.4	105.6	108.5	103.3	102.6	102.3	101.6	97.8	102.9
August	105.0	105.8	104.1	107.8	100.3	107.0	111.4	103.8	101.7	101.9	100.0	94.5	104.8
September	104.4	104.2	102.0	103.6	100.3	105.7	109.1	103.1	101.3	104.9	106.7	100.1	102.7
October	104.3	102.9	101.0	104.3	97.7	104.3	106.0	102.8	101.7	109.5	111.0	104.3	106.9
November	105.0	103.7	102.1	106.7	97.6	104.8	107.0	103.1	102.9	109.6	110.6	105.6	106.7
December	105.0	104.7	102.9	107.2	98.9	105.8	107.3	104.6	104.3	106.1	104.7	102.7	105.3
1994:													
January	107.9	106.5	104.3	111.6	97.5	108.0	111.8	105.1	102.0	113.1	113.9	109.8	110.8
February	106.8	105.2	103.0	106.5	99.9	106.7	109.9	104.2	101.0	112.9	112.8	110.3	111.2
March	105.0	104.5	102.4	105.9	99.5	105.9	108.3	104.0	100.9	106.7	104.3	105.6	105.6
April	103.3	104.8	103.0	105.3	101.2	106.0	106.7	105.3	102.2	98.0	91.9	95.2	100.9
May	103.2	103.6	101.8	102.8	101.3	104.7	105.2	104.3	102.1	101.8	99.3	101.1	101.2
June	107.8	108.1	106.3	113.8	99.8	109.3	112.1	107.2	102.9	106.8	99.6	106.4	110.6
July	105.8	106.1	103.3	102.5	104.0	108.0	110.4	106.1	102.9	104.6	100.2	105.8	104.8
August	104.9	104.6	104.0	102.8	105.2	105.1	104.3	105.5	103.5	106.0	103.1	102.8	106.9
September	104.8	105.0	104.5	102.2	106.4	105.4	104.3	106.1	104.5	104.0	99.3	97.9	108.4
October	105.1	105.9	105.5	104.0	106.9	106.2	106.5	105.9	103.8	102.2	97.4	99.0	105.3
November	104.4	105.8	105.8	100.7	110.2	105.8	104.9	106.4	104.0	99.6	94.7	95.2	103.3
December	104.3	105.6	104.8	100.4	108.6	106.1	105.2	106.7	104.5	99.8	94.9	96.5	103.2
1995:													
January	104.9	105.8	105.8	100.3	110.4	106.0	104.3	107.0	105.3	101.4	97.0	98.8	104.2
February	106.0	106.7	106.9	103.7	109.5	106.6	106.4	106.5	104.4	103.6	100.4	103.6	105.7
March	106.6	107.3	106.7	102.0	110.5	107.8	107.8	107.7	105.2	103.8	98.4	102.6	108.0
April	106.6	107.2	107.1	103.3	110.3	107.3	106.6	107.5	105.2	104.4	98.8	102.5	110.2
May	109.0	108.7	108.2	103.3	112.2	109.1	110.8	107.8	105.4	109.9	104.9	114.4	113.4
June	109.0	109.4	108.6	102.9	113.2	110.0	111.8	108.6	105.4	107.4	104.1	107.7	111.2
July	109.4	109.6	110.1	106.3	113.2	109.5	110.8	108.3	104.5	108.6	104.1	108.8	113.7
August	113.5	115.2	113.6	115.1	112.7	116.4	123.8	110.9	105.7	107.2	97.0	110.0	117.6
September	109.7	110.3	108.8	105.2	111.8	111.3	115.0	108.6	104.3	107.5	103.4	108.7	111.4
October	109.3	111.3	112.8	102.8	120.6	110.5	111.7	109.6	105.0	102.3	96.1	106.2	106.1
November	112.6	111.2	110.8	105.0	115.5	111.6	114.4	109.6	104.4	117.3	118.7	120.5	114.5
December	112.3	111.6	111.9	106.2	116.4	111.5	114.0	109.5	105.3	115.0	112.8	119.5	115.0
1996:													
January	112.5	112.6	112.4	106.4	117.2	112.8	116.5	110.1	105.3	112.3	110.4	115.1	112.3
February	113.3	113.6	113.1	104.7	119.7	114.1	117.3	111.8	107.4	112.2	110.0	114.9	112.5
March	114.4	114.0	114.7	105.7	121.9	113.7	117.3	111.0	106.6	115.8	115.0	120.3	113.6
April	113.5	113.1	114.2	104.3	122.0	112.5	116.3	109.8	103.5	115.0	112.1	120.3	113.9
May	114.6	114.8	115.5	109.2	120.6	114.5	117.6	112.4	105.1	113.6	108.8	119.3	113.6
June	114.0	114.2	113.5	108.4	117.7	114.7	119.5	111.3	104.5	113.6	106.8	117.0	116.8
July	109.4	110.1	109.4	104.1	113.7	110.6	112.3	109.4	104.5	107.1	103.0	106.2	108.6
August	110.8	111.5	111.2	106.3	115.2	111.8	113.2	110.9	104.2	108.5	101.5	112.0	112.0
September	111.1	110.9	110.6	108.0	113.2	111.2	111.5	111.1	106.7	111.8	107.7	113.6	112.3
October	111.9	112.0	112.0	109.5	114.4	112.2	112.5	112.0	107.1	111.3	108.2	113.4	110.0
November	114.5	112.7	111.1	111.5	111.6	113.8	116.0	112.3	105.5	120.9	121.2	124.2	116.3
December	112.6	112.6	111.3	106.9	115.0	113.5	115.5	112.1	105.8	112.7	109.3	118.3	111.2

TRANSPORTATION, COMMUNICATIONS, AND UTILITIES—CAPACITY AND PRICES

YEAR AND MONTH	Capacity utilization—Electric and gas utilities (Percent of capacity, seasonally adjusted)			Producer Prices							
				Industries				Intermediate materials			
								Electric power		Natural gas (December 1990=100)	
	Total	Electric	Gas	Motor freight transportation and warehousing[1]	Water transportation[2]	Transportation by air[2]	Pipe lines, except natural gas[3]	Commercial	Industrial	Commercial	Industrial
1968	95.1	98.3	90.0					29.6	21.3		
1969	96.7	99.8	91.6					29.7	21.6		
1970	96.2	98.9	91.9					30.8	22.5		
1971	94.6	96.5	92.3					33.7	24.8		
1972	95.2	97.0	92.5					34.8	26.2		
1973	93.5	95.4	90.7					36.8	28.0		
1974	87.3	87.3	88.6					44.8	36.4		
1975	84.4	84.8	84.8					51.4	44.3		
1976	85.2	85.1	86.6					54.7	47.9		
1977	85.0	86.0	83.2					60.7	54.3		
1978	85.4	85.3	85.5					64.6	59.1		
1979	86.6	85.3	89.5					68.7	64.5		
1980	85.9	84.7	89.3					80.6	77.8		
1981	82.5	84.3	79.1					91.6	89.2		
1982	79.3	81.3	74.9					100.0	100.0		
1983	79.7	82.3	74.4					102.5	103.1		
1984	81.9	84.0	77.1					108.0	108.4		
1985	83.5	84.7	79.8					110.3	112.8		
1986	80.6	84.9	67.6					110.5	114.5		
1987	82.5	86.1	69.9				97.9	108.9	111.9		
1988	84.9	87.8	73.7				94.8	109.5	112.6		
1989	86.3	89.4	75.7				94.4	113.0	116.2		
1990	85.7	89.6	72.9				95.8	115.3	119.6		
1991	86.3	89.1	75.1				96.1	122.3	128.1	95.9	93.6
1992	84.6	86.8	77.2				96.4	124.4	129.6	96.7	94.2
1993	87.2	88.8	80.4		99.7	105.6	96.6	127.2	130.6	102.7	101.6
1994	87.3	89.2	80.4	101.9	100.0	108.5	102.6	128.8	129.2	103.7	99.5
1995	89.1	91.1	82.2	104.5	103.0	113.7	110.8	131.7	130.8	96.5	90.9
1996	90.3	91.4	85.9	106.3	103.7	121.1	104.6	131.6	131.6	103.2	98.9
1993:											
January	84.8	87.2	76.3		100.2	103.6	96.5	121.0	127.1	103.0	101.0
February	87.9	89.5	81.9		100.2	104.2	96.5	120.8	126.4	102.0	100.1
March	88.6	89.5	84.6		99.7	104.3	96.5	120.9	126.7	101.5	99.4
April	87.0	88.8	79.9		100.1	104.5	96.5	121.6	126.8	100.9	99.5
May	85.1	88.1	73.7		99.9	104.5	96.5	122.4	127.5	102.2	102.4
June	86.7	88.4	79.7	100.0	99.7	104.5	96.5	135.8	136.9	101.0	100.7
July	87.6	89.8	78.8	99.5	100.2	105.2	96.5	136.0	137.1	100.7	102.0
August	88.1	90.4	78.6	99.9	99.0	106.0	96.5	136.1	137.2	101.6	102.5
September	87.4	88.9	80.9	99.9	99.0	106.3	96.5	136.7	137.6	102.8	102.5
October	87.3	87.7	84.3	100.0	99.9	108.0	96.7	127.2	131.9	102.9	101.0
November	87.8	88.3	84.4	100.1	99.6	108.6	96.7	124.3	126.3	105.9	104.0
December	87.6	89.0	81.7	100.2	99.1	108.2	97.1	124.1	126.0	108.5	104.7
1994:											
January	90.0	90.5	87.1	100.6	98.4	109.2	100.8	124.1	126.2	108.9	104.0
February	89.0	89.3	86.9	101.1	98.5	108.1	100.8	124.1	125.9	108.8	104.8
March	87.4	88.6	82.1	101.3	98.5	108.5	100.8	123.9	125.8	109.2	105.2
April	85.9	88.8	75.4	101.5	99.5	108.0	100.9	123.7	125.4	107.3	102.4
May	85.7	87.7	78.3	101.7	99.9	108.0	100.9	124.6	126.0	104.8	102.7
June	89.5	91.5	82.1	101.9	99.1	109.1	101.0	134.8	133.5	100.8	97.9
July	87.7	89.7	80.4	102.1	99.5	109.0	102.3	135.8	134.5	100.4	97.2
August	86.9	88.4	81.4	102.2	100.1	109.0	102.9	136.0	134.5	100.3	97.6
September	86.7	88.6	79.9	102.3	100.3	108.5	103.0	136.9	134.9	99.8	95.3
October	86.9	89.3	78.5	102.7	102.9	108.3	103.7	128.7	129.1	99.2	94.0
November	86.3	89.1	76.5	102.7	101.4	108.1	106.5	126.3	127.0	102.0	96.2
December	86.1	88.9	76.6	102.9	101.6	107.9	107.0	126.9	127.4	102.5	96.8
1995:											
January	86.4	89.0	77.8	103.1	102.6	108.1	110.9	127.2	127.6	102.6	97.6
February	87.2	89.5	79.4	104.2	102.8	109.6	110.9	127.6	128.0	101.3	95.4
March	87.5	89.9	79.5	104.4	102.6	110.1	110.9	127.7	128.3	99.9	93.6
April	87.4	89.6	80.0	104.3	102.0	110.0	110.9	126.5	126.4	98.0	92.3
May	89.2	90.7	84.2	104.4	102.3	113.2	110.9	129.8	130.2	94.2	89.5
June	89.1	91.1	82.2	104.7	102.2	114.1	110.7	138.5	135.3	94.3	90.2
July	89.3	91.1	83.1	104.4	102.4	115.2	110.7	139.7	136.6	93.8	88.4
August	92.5	95.6	82.0	104.8	103.3	115.8	110.7	139.7	136.5	92.7	87.2
September	89.2	91.3	82.2	104.7	104.5	117.1	110.7	137.8	133.7	93.0	86.4
October	88.8	92.0	78.2	104.9	104.2	117.2	110.6	131.3	131.4	92.5	86.8
November	91.3	91.7	89.6	104.9	103.7	118.0	110.6	127.1	127.6	97.4	91.0
December	91.0	91.8	87.8	104.7	104.0	115.9	110.6	127.6	127.7	98.5	92.3
1996:											
January	91.0	92.4	85.7	105.1	103.9	117.2	110.6	127.6	127.9	101.8	95.4
February	91.5	93.1	85.5	105.9	103.8	119.1	110.6	126.0	127.1	103.0	96.8
March	92.2	93.2	88.2	105.8	104.2	119.9	110.6	126.8	127.8	104.2	98.0
April	91.3	92.3	87.6	105.9	103.8	120.2	103.7	126.6	129.1	102.6	96.6
May	92.0	93.5	86.5	106.0	103.0	120.8	103.7	129.6	135.0	100.3	97.0
June	91.4	92.7	86.4	106.9	102.9	121.4	103.7	138.4	137.5	100.5	97.2
July	87.6	89.2	81.4	106.2	103.0	122.5	104.0	139.1	136.0	101.2	98.0
August	88.5	90.2	82.5	106.4	103.0	121.8	104.0	139.6	136.2	102.3	99.0
September	88.6	89.6	84.9	106.6	103.8	121.9	101.0	139.5	136.2	99.7	96.9
October	89.0	90.2	84.5	106.9	104.6	122.4	100.9	131.3	131.2	99.4	96.1
November	91.0	90.6	91.7	107.1	104.5	123.5	100.9	126.8	127.1	108.3	103.5
December	89.3	90.3	85.4	107.2	104.2	122.7	100.9	127.5	127.7	115.0	112.9

1. June 1993=100.
2. December 1992=100.
3. December 1986=100.

TRANSPORTATION, COMMUNICATIONS, AND UTILITIES—EMPLOYMENT, HOURS, AND EARNINGS

| YEAR AND MONTH | Total payroll employment (Thousands, seasonally adjusted) | | | | | | Production and nonsupervisory workers | | | | |
| | Total | Transportation | | | Commu-nications | Electric, gas, and sanitary services | Seasonally adjusted | | | Average earnings (Dollars, not seasonally adjusted) | |
		Total	Trucking and warehousing	Transpor-tation by air			Employ-ment	Average hours	Aggregate hours index (1982=100)	Hourly	Weekly
1968	4 318	2 680	1 045	329	982	656	3 757	40.6	93.4	3.42	138.85
1969	4 442	2 722	1 083	353	1 049	672	3 863	40.7	96.3	3.63	147.74
1970	4 515	2 694	1 083	352	1 129	692	3 914	40.5	96.9	3.85	155.93
1971	4 476	2 639	1 077	345	1 143	698	3 872	40.1	95.1	4.21	168.82
1972	4 541	2 676	1 124	348	1 152	713	3 943	40.4	97.3	4.65	187.86
1973	4 656	2 746	1 184	366	1 180	731	4 034	40.5	99.9	5.02	203.31
1974	4 725	2 779	1 190	368	1 203	744	4 079	40.2	100.4	5.41	217.48
1975	4 542	2 634	1 108	363	1 176	733	3 894	39.7	94.6	5.88	233.44
1976	4 582	2 678	1 149	374	1 169	735	3 918	39.8	95.5	6.45	256.71
1977	4 713	2 781	1 220	386	1 185	747	4 008	39.9	97.9	6.99	278.90
1978	4 923	2 905	1 303	408	1 240	778	4 142	40.0	101.3	7.57	302.80
1979	5 136	3 019	1 339	438	1 309	807	4 299	39.9	104.9	8.16	325.58
1980	5 146	2 960	1 280	453	1 357	829	4 293	39.6	104.1	8.87	351.25
1981	5 165	2 920	1 256	455	1 391	854	4 283	39.4	103.3	9.70	382.18
1982	5 081	2 787	1 210	444	1 417	877	4 190	39.0	100.0	10.32	402.48
1983	4 952	2 742	1 216	455	1 324	886	4 072	39.0	97.3	10.79	420.81
1984	5 156	2 914	1 317	488	1 340	902	4 258	39.4	102.8	11.12	438.13
1985	5 233	2 997	1 361	522	1 319	916	4 335	39.5	104.6	11.40	450.30
1986	5 247	3 051	1 394	566	1 275	921	4 339	39.2	104.0	11.70	458.64
1987	5 362	3 156	1 465	603	1 282	925	4 446	39.2	106.5	12.03	471.58
1988	5 512	3 301	1 351	850	1 280	931	4 555	38.2	108.2	12.24	467.57
1989	5 614	3 404	1 379	897	1 272	938	4 655	38.3	111.1	12.57	481.43
1990	5 777	3 511	1 395	968	1 309	957	4 781	38.4	114.5	12.92	496.13
1991	5 755	3 495	1 378	962	1 299	961	4 774	38.1	113.4	13.20	502.92
1992	5 718	3 495	1 385	964	1 269	954	4 768	38.3	113.6	13.43	514.37
1993	5 811	3 598	1 444	988	1 269	944	4 862	38.3	118.2	13.55	532.52
1994	5 984	3 761	1 526	1 023	1 295	928	5 012	39.7	122.4	13.78	547.07
1995	6 132	3 904	1 587	1 068	1 318	911	5 140	39.4	123.9	14.13	556.72
1996	6 261	4 038	1 641	1 122	1 338	885	5 269	39.6	127.6	14.44	571.82
1993:											
January	5 766	3 553	1 422	973	1 267	946	4 819	39.2	115.6	13.50	522.45
February	5 768	3 557	1 419	979	1 264	947	4 825	39.1	115.4	13.52	524.58
March	5 772	3 560	1 422	981	1 265	947	4 827	39.3	116.1	13.55	528.45
April	5 779	3 567	1 426	982	1 267	945	4 829	39.2	115.8	13.53	527.67
May	5 794	3 581	1 432	987	1 267	946	4 847	39.4	116.8	13.50	531.90
June	5 811	3 595	1 436	993	1 269	947	4 858	39.2	116.5	13.49	531.51
July	5 823	3 610	1 445	992	1 267	946	4 873	39.3	117.2	13.57	538.73
August	5 820	3 604	1 453	988	1 270	946	4 875	39.5	117.8	13.55	540.65
September	5 835	3 620	1 459	995	1 271	944	4 888	39.5	118.1	13.61	536.23
October	5 847	3 632	1 467	992	1 273	942	4 898	39.4	118.1	13.58	536.41
November	5 865	3 651	1 475	998	1 275	939	4 913	39.3	118.1	13.61	534.87
December	5 854	3 639	1 468	987	1 277	938	4 878	39.7	118.5	13.61	538.96
1994:											
January	5 893	3 677	1 490	1 001	1 279	937	4 938	39.7	119.9	13.72	540.57
February	5 914	3 694	1 502	999	1 285	935	4 953	39.6	120.0	13.73	539.59
March	5 941	3 721	1 513	1 004	1 286	934	4 977	39.7	120.9	13.68	538.99
April	5 903	3 682	1 463	1 015	1 289	932	4 936	39.9	120.5	13.67	542.70
May	5 973	3 750	1 528	1 014	1 293	930	5 012	39.9	122.3	13.66	545.03
June	5 982	3 761	1 530	1 018	1 293	928	5 015	39.8	122.1	13.63	545.20
July	6 000	3 778	1 536	1 023	1 295	927	5 025	39.7	122.0	13.75	551.38
August	6 013	3 787	1 540	1 028	1 301	925	5 037	39.6	122.0	13.77	552.18
September	6 022	3 799	1 545	1 033	1 299	924	5 050	39.6	122.3	13.83	551.82
October	6 034	3 809	1 546	1 039	1 302	923	5 053	39.8	123.0	13.94	556.21
November	6 057	3 828	1 556	1 044	1 305	924	5 072	39.6	122.9	13.99	554.00
December	6 088	3 853	1 564	1 058	1 311	924	5 087	39.4	122.6	13.95	548.24
1995:											
January	6 089	3 869	1 574	1 055	1 299	921	5 110	39.6	123.8	14.01	549.19
February	6 109	3 876	1 579	1 055	1 314	919	5 113	39.4	123.2	13.97	547.62
March	6 116	3 883	1 585	1 054	1 317	916	5 123	39.3	123.2	13.98	546.62
April	6 119	3 888	1 590	1 052	1 316	915	5 123	39.6	124.1	14.04	554.58
May	6 111	3 883	1 581	1 058	1 315	913	5 120	39.1	122.5	13.96	545.84
June	6 112	3 886	1 580	1 064	1 315	911	5 123	39.4	123.5	14.02	553.79
July	6 111	3 883	1 574	1 064	1 318	910	5 121	39.6	124.1	14.16	566.40
August	6 139	3 913	1 587	1 071	1 317	909	5 148	39.3	123.8	14.14	561.36
September	6 140	3 910	1 577	1 077	1 322	908	5 154	39.2	123.6	14.25	562.88
October	6 182	3 950	1 608	1 086	1 325	907	5 190	39.4	125.1	14.35	566.83
November	6 195	3 966	1 610	1 099	1 326	903	5 202	39.3	125.1	14.34	563.56
December	6 179	3 953	1 597	1 098	1 324	902	5 190	39.2	124.5	14.32	562.78
1996:											
January	6 195	3 971	1 617	1 098	1 326	898	5 206	38.9	123.9	14.32	551.32
February	6 203	3 982	1 619	1 102	1 326	895	5 219	39.5	126.1	14.34	563.56
March	6 211	3 992	1 624	1 106	1 327	892	5 227	39.7	127.0	14.33	564.60
April	6 229	4 011	1 630	1 117	1 329	889	5 242	39.2	125.7	14.39	562.65
May	6 246	4 027	1 641	1 119	1 332	887	5 257	39.4	126.7	14.34	562.13
June	6 270	4 047	1 651	1 122	1 338	885	5 279	39.9	128.9	14.40	577.44
July	6 296	4 073	1 659	1 131	1 341	882	5 295	39.4	127.6	14.44	573.27
August	6 299	4 075	1 656	1 134	1 344	880	5 299	39.7	128.7	14.48	579.20
September	6 290	4 066	1 651	1 134	1 345	879	5 297	39.8	129.0	14.57	587.17
October	6 293	4 072	1 648	1 140	1 343	878	5 302	39.6	128.5	14.49	575.25
November	6 303	4 078	1 649	1 142	1 347	878	5 308	39.8	129.2	14.57	579.89
December	6 288	4 065	1 642	1 133	1 347	876	5 298	39.9	129.3	14.60	582.54

TRANSPORTATION, COMMUNICATIONS, AND UTILITIES—EMPLOYMENT, HOURS, AND EARNINGS

Production and nonsupervisory workers—Continued
(Not seasonally adjusted)

YEAR AND MONTH	Trucking and warehousing				Communications				Electric, gas, and sanitary services			
	Employment (Thousands)	Average weekly hours	Average earnings		Employment (Thousands)	Average weekly hours	Average earnings		Employment (Thousands)	Average weekly hours	Average earnings	
			Hourly	Weekly			Hourly	Weekly			Hourly	Weekly
1968	946	41.8	3.42	142.96	769	39.6	3.11	123.16	....	....	....	....
1969	982	41.8	3.63	151.73	825	40.1	3.29	131.93	....	....	....	....
1970	975	41.4	3.85	159.39	886	39.3	3.41	134.01	....	....	....	....
1971	964	41.7	4.34	180.98	896	38.1	3.69	140.59	....	....	....	....
1972	1 005	41.9	4.86	203.63	909	39.3	4.15	163.10	609	41.5	4.82	200.03
1973	1 061	41.8	5.27	220.29	934	39.6	4.48	177.41	620	41.8	5.13	214.43
1974	1 062	40.8	5.64	230.11	943	39.6	4.91	194.44	628	41.5	5.52	229.08
1975	978	40.2	6.00	241.20	911	38.9	5.54	215.51	614	41.1	6.03	247.83
1976	1 013	40.5	6.47	262.04	902	38.9	6.19	240.79	611	41.2	6.58	271.10
1977	1 078	40.5	7.10	287.55	907	39.6	6.74	266.90	618	41.3	7.11	293.64
1978	1 154	40.4	7.76	313.50	939	39.9	7.33	292.47	637	41.8	7.65	319.77
1979	1 184	39.7	8.34	331.10	987	39.8	7.85	312.43	660	41.7	8.25	344.03
1980	1 121	39.2	9.13	357.90	1 014	39.9	8.50	339.15	678	41.7	8.90	371.13
1981	1 094	39.1	9.90	387.09	1 040	39.8	9.48	377.30	699	41.4	9.89	409.45
1982	1 049	38.4	10.23	392.83	1 072	39.5	10.19	402.51	711	41.4	10.78	446.29
1983	1 057	38.5	10.40	400.40	996	39.4	10.77	424.34	712	41.4	11.50	476.10
1984	1 148	38.9	10.47	407.28	1 018	39.9	11.26	449.27	719	41.5	12.20	506.30
1985	1 185	38.5	10.52	405.02	1 005	40.2	11.75	472.35	730	41.7	12.83	535.01
1986	1 212	38.1	10.71	408.05	972	40.1	12.15	487.22	733	41.8	13.39	559.70
1987	1 275	38.3	10.82	414.41	972	40.0	12.45	498.00	733	41.5	13.79	572.29
1988	1 176	38.3	10.95	419.39	951	39.8	12.85	511.43	736	41.5	14.27	592.21
1989	1 203	38.4	11.35	435.84	950	39.4	13.18	519.29	742	41.9	14.72	616.77
1990	1 215	38.5	11.68	449.68	978	39.4	13.51	532.29	759	41.6	15.23	633.57
1991	1 197	38.4	11.83	454.27	986	39.2	13.96	547.23	762	41.6	15.69	652.70
1992	1 205	38.7	12.07	467.11	981	39.4	14.42	568.15	753	41.9	16.08	673.75
1993	1 254	39.5	12.26	484.27	985	39.6	14.91	590.44	744	42.3	16.71	706.83
1994	1 328	39.9	12.50	498.75	993	39.6	15.24	603.50	734	42.4	17.24	730.98
1995	1 382	39.6	12.73	504.11	1 017	39.8	15.56	619.29	719	42.4	17.68	749.63
1996	1 429	39.8	12.94	515.01	1 049	40.4	16.02	647.21	700	42.2	18.28	771.42
1993:												
January	1 210	38.4	12.04	462.34	981	39.6	14.90	590.04	740	41.6	16.39	681.82
February	1 204	38.5	12.12	466.62	981	39.3	14.77	580.46	739	41.5	16.54	686.41
March	1 208	38.7	12.17	470.98	981	39.3	14.70	577.71	738	42.6	16.80	715.68
April	1 216	38.8	12.24	474.91	981	39.4	14.74	580.76	738	42.1	16.60	698.86
May	1 234	39.6	12.26	485.50	984	39.5	14.79	584.21	743	42.2	16.63	701.79
June	1 253	39.7	12.20	484.34	990	39.7	14.86	589.94	753	42.5	16.57	704.23
July	1 267	39.7	12.21	484.74	991	40.0	14.86	594.40	757	42.5	16.70	709.75
August	1 274	40.3	12.26	494.08	992	40.1	14.97	600.30	757	42.3	16.62	703.03
September	1 285	39.9	12.35	492.77	988	39.8	15.11	601.38	745	42.4	16.78	711.47
October	1 297	40.0	12.37	494.80	988	39.4	15.02	591.79	743	42.5	16.95	720.38
November	1 303	40.0	12.43	497.20	989	39.4	15.10	594.94	739	42.5	16.98	721.65
December	1 303	39.7	12.46	494.66	974	39.3	15.08	592.64	737	42.4	16.90	716.56
1994:												
January	1 271	38.7	12.37	478.72	974	39.3	15.13	594.61	734	43.0	17.10	735.30
February	1 276	38.3	12.41	475.30	976	39.2	15.10	591.92	734	43.0	17.24	741.32
March	1 288	39.1	12.48	487.97	979	39.1	15.07	589.24	733	42.2	17.14	723.31
April	1 241	39.7	12.38	491.49	981	39.2	15.09	591.53	733	42.4	17.16	727.58
May	1 323	40.3	12.51	504.15	988	39.4	15.07	593.76	733	42.2	17.20	725.84
June	1 341	40.5	12.41	502.61	997	39.6	15.17	600.73	741	42.4	17.06	723.34
July	1 347	40.2	12.37	497.27	999	39.9	15.19	606.08	742	42.3	17.23	728.83
August	1 355	40.6	12.46	505.88	1 006	39.9	15.39	614.06	739	41.8	17.08	713.94
September	1 365	40.3	12.63	508.99	999	39.8	15.41	613.32	730	42.3	17.22	728.41
October	1 369	40.4	12.65	511.06	1 004	40.0	15.38	615.20	728	42.8	17.54	750.71
November	1 375	40.0	12.68	507.20	1 006	39.9	15.47	617.25	729	42.5	17.48	742.90
December	1 384	39.9	12.66	505.13	1 007	39.7	15.44	612.97	728	42.3	17.43	737.29
1995:												
January	1 341	38.6	12.57	485.20	997	40.2	15.53	624.31	723	42.1	17.42	733.38
February	1 342	38.6	12.63	487.52	1 007	39.1	15.39	601.75	719	42.1	17.42	733.38
March	1 350	38.9	12.67	492.86	1 010	39.1	15.47	604.88	719	41.7	17.44	727.25
April	1 360	39.1	12.60	492.66	1 009	39.4	15.38	605.97	716	42.6	17.61	750.19
May	1 368	39.3	12.66	497.54	1 010	39.4	15.34	604.40	718	42.0	17.51	735.42
June	1 389	40.2	12.64	508.13	1 017	39.6	15.40	609.84	726	42.2	17.48	737.66
July	1 384	39.9	12.64	504.34	1 019	40.4	15.51	626.60	727	42.6	17.75	756.15
August	1 401	40.3	12.77	514.63	1 021	40.4	15.56	628.62	725	42.3	17.56	742.79
September	1 394	40.4	12.88	520.35	1 021	40.1	15.63	626.76	717	42.4	17.73	751.75
October	1 427	40.4	12.87	519.95	1 027	40.2	15.88	638.38	718	42.8	17.96	768.69
November	1 421	39.9	12.91	515.11	1 031	39.9	15.79	630.02	714	43.2	18.13	783.22
December	1 410	39.9	12.84	512.32	1 029	40.0	15.79	631.60	712	42.6	18.11	771.49
1996:												
January	1 377	37.7	12.75	480.68	1 021	39.9	15.80	630.42	705	42.0	17.98	755.16
February	1 382	39.1	12.82	501.26	1 031	39.9	15.77	629.22	701	42.4	18.09	767.02
March	1 385	39.5	12.88	508.76	1 035	39.8	15.82	629.64	698	42.2	18.06	762.13
April	1 397	39.4	12.89	507.87	1 036	39.9	15.89	634.01	698	42.1	18.11	762.43
May	1 422	39.7	12.94	513.72	1 042	40.1	15.87	636.39	699	41.9	18.12	759.23
June	1 450	40.4	12.86	519.54	1 052	41.2	15.99	658.79	705	42.2	18.03	760.87
July	1 459	39.9	12.85	512.72	1 057	40.9	15.97	653.17	705	41.9	18.04	755.88
August	1 465	40.4	12.96	523.58	1 062	40.9	16.09	658.08	703	41.9	18.16	760.90
September	1 459	40.4	13.08	528.43	1 063	41.4	16.22	671.51	696	42.5	18.56	788.80
October	1 459	40.3	13.11	528.33	1 062	40.2	16.14	648.83	696	42.2	18.57	783.65
November	1 454	40.2	13.09	526.22	1 064	40.0	16.21	648.40	696	42.5	18.85	801.13
December	1 445	40.1	13.05	523.31	1 059	40.4	16.41	662.96	695	42.1	18.79	791.06

ELECTRIC POWER USE IN MINING AND MANUFACTURING
(1992=100, seasonally adjusted)

YEAR AND MONTH	Total	Mining					Manufacturing								
								Durable goods industries							
		Total	Metal mining	Coal mining	Oil and gas extraction	Stone and earth minerals	Total	Total	Lumber and products	Furniture and fixtures	Stone, clay, and glass products	Primary metals	Fabricated metal products	Industrial machinery and equipment	Electrical machinery
1968															
1969															
1970															
1971															
1972	74.0	62.4	48.4	55.2	70.9	72.9	74.8	83.1	65.4	60.8	80.0	100.3	71.8	65.1	72.1
1973	79.3	65.9	54.8	56.9	72.9	77.9	80.2	90.6	70.5	67.7	85.5	111.0	77.5	72.0	78.2
1974	79.7	67.0	55.3	55.6	75.4	80.0	80.6	91.0	68.6	66.5	86.1	117.3	75.0	72.2	74.1
1975	76.1	70.7	56.7	65.4	78.4	80.8	76.5	81.4	64.0	59.5	79.6	99.0	70.8	72.3	69.1
1976	83.1	74.5	56.1	71.8	83.5	85.4	83.8	88.3	72.5	66.1	86.3	107.7	75.9	76.3	72.8
1977	86.7	80.1	67.1	73.5	86.6	93.2	87.2	92.3	75.7	69.2	92.2	110.9	79.4	80.2	76.2
1978	88.2	85.0	83.7	71.0	88.3	97.2	88.4	97.1	80.4	71.7	98.1	117.8	84.1	83.1	78.8
1979	91.3	91.2	92.7	88.1	87.7	101.3	91.3	101.1	80.8	72.2	100.2	123.9	87.9	86.5	85.1
1980	86.8	92.1	87.3	92.3	90.2	103.6	86.4	94.7	71.8	70.6	94.8	114.6	83.1	87.6	82.0
1981	86.6	93.9	93.0	92.5	92.4	100.4	86.1	94.7	71.1	70.7	92.4	113.5	83.8	89.3	83.7
1982	77.5	85.9	60.5	97.4	97.5	83.2	76.9	79.0	65.5	66.4	83.7	83.5	75.9	81.1	77.8
1983	81.3	88.5	73.6	89.6	97.4	89.2	80.8	82.4	77.1	72.5	89.0	85.5	79.4	81.3	82.6
1984	87.8	97.1	77.0	99.9	107.7	99.7	87.1	92.5	80.5	76.8	96.0	99.7	86.9	91.5	89.5
1985	85.9	96.7	71.0	96.5	112.6	99.1	85.1	89.6	79.8	77.8	94.5	91.2	88.2	91.3	88.6
1986	85.9	89.0	63.4	97.9	101.9	86.8	85.7	88.9	88.1	84.5	94.6	85.3	89.8	90.8	91.8
1987	89.2	90.0	72.9	98.6	96.5	89.7	89.2	93.1	94.2	93.3	97.4	90.7	94.4	93.7	94.3
1988	93.3	94.7	85.4	100.2	97.0	96.2	93.2	100.1	96.8	98.2	99.7	102.2	100.6	101.3	97.9
1989	96.5	95.6	94.1	99.6	92.5	100.2	96.5	101.7	98.8	100.0	100.4	103.2	101.0	103.2	100.1
1990	98.6	99.4	94.9	104.3	97.7	103.7	98.5	102.0	100.4	100.6	100.5	103.2	101.0	105.1	101.8
1991	97.8	99.9	96.2	98.1	103.0	100.6	97.6	99.4	96.4	98.2	96.3	99.5	100.7	101.5	100.5
1992	100.0	100.0	100.0	100.0	100.0	100.0	100.0	100.0	100.0	100.0	100.0	100.0	100.0	100.0	100.0
1993	100.4	97.0	96.2	96.8	98.9	94.0	100.7	100.9	105.6	107.2	102.8	98.5	103.2	102.1	101.5
1994	104.1	98.7	98.8	100.9	96.6	100.7	104.4	103.2	110.9	113.4	105.1	98.7	108.1	104.8	106.2
1995	105.6	99.3	107.4	99.0	91.8	104.7	106.1	105.3	113.8	112.7	106.7	100.6	110.1	107.2	111.3
1996	105.7	102.5	115.0	97.9	93.6	110.0	105.9	105.7	117.9	113.6	108.2	98.6	111.7	107.2	116.5
1993:															
January	99.3	95.9	92.5	102.8	97.6	88.2	99.5	99.4	104.0	103.4	100.3	97.5	100.9	100.3	99.1
February	99.6	98.5	95.8	98.0	102.1	94.7	99.7	99.1	103.6	103.0	100.4	97.3	100.8	101.0	98.4
March	100.7	99.9	102.7	101.7	99.0	95.2	100.7	101.1	104.6	105.3	102.3	99.1	103.6	101.3	99.9
April	101.0	99.0	101.4	101.7	98.3	93.7	101.1	101.3	105.1	106.6	102.5	100.0	103.8	102.6	101.1
May	100.2	98.8	99.8	97.8	100.1	95.3	100.3	100.9	103.9	106.6	102.7	99.1	103.0	102.4	100.0
June	100.6	96.9	99.9	98.2	98.3	87.1	100.9	101.4	103.9	106.9	104.0	100.7	101.2	101.6	100.7
July	100.5	96.3	97.3	93.7	97.4	95.5	100.8	101.7	105.4	107.3	104.2	100.2	103.1	103.2	102.0
August	99.5	91.5	82.4	91.8	95.7	95.0	100.1	100.4	105.0	108.6	100.8	98.5	102.6	100.4	102.5
September	100.7	94.8	91.0	92.3	97.3	97.9	101.2	101.6	105.7	110.0	104.3	98.2	105.1	104.3	103.3
October	100.2	97.4	95.4	91.1	103.5	94.5	100.5	100.4	106.2	109.5	103.2	96.7	103.4	102.0	102.3
November	101.1	96.8	97.5	94.0	99.5	92.9	101.4	101.3	107.0	108.5	104.7	98.2	104.0	102.0	102.5
December	101.5	97.4	98.2	94.2	98.8	97.1	101.8	101.6	112.5	110.3	105.1	96.2	106.4	104.0	105.6
1994:															
January	101.5	97.3	93.8	101.2	97.1	98.2	101.8	101.7	108.6	108.4	103.4	98.1	106.0	102.9	102.1
February	102.0	96.5	94.3	97.8	97.0	96.9	102.4	102.0	109.8	110.4	103.6	98.2	105.4	103.2	103.2
March	103.2	98.1	97.5	101.7	95.9	99.5	103.6	103.7	112.0	111.3	105.8	100.5	106.4	103.6	105.6
April	102.5	98.1	95.2	101.5	96.8	101.4	102.9	101.4	109.3	112.8	104.2	95.7	106.0	103.6	105.6
May	103.2	97.5	97.3	101.5	95.4	97.7	103.7	102.2	111.0	113.8	105.9	97.1	106.9	104.3	105.1
June	103.5	99.3	100.0	101.5	96.2	102.5	103.8	103.2	112.1	113.9	104.7	98.6	106.7	104.9	106.1
July	103.9	98.9	98.7	101.7	97.7	98.4	104.3	102.8	110.8	113.9	103.9	98.2	108.1	105.4	105.7
August	105.5	100.3	99.4	102.2	98.7	103.1	105.8	104.2	111.4	115.2	107.9	99.2	109.5	106.2	108.6
September	105.4	100.2	100.8	100.8	97.4	105.2	105.8	103.9	111.9	113.7	104.6	99.7	109.6	106.2	107.8
October	105.6	99.2	101.0	100.7	96.6	100.3	106.1	104.4	109.7	116.3	104.8	99.9	110.0	106.3	108.2
November	106.3	99.2	103.1	98.0	95.9	102.2	106.8	104.8	112.4	115.7	106.7	99.8	110.4	106.6	107.8
December	106.0	99.7	103.7	101.6	94.7	102.5	106.4	104.9	111.9	115.2	106.6	100.2	111.8	106.5	107.9
1995:															
January	106.5	100.1	105.7	100.1	94.0	105.9	107.0	105.8	114.5	112.5	111.0	101.0	110.9	107.6	109.9
February	105.3	98.6	103.4	100.6	92.1	104.2	105.7	104.6	113.0	114.2	107.5	98.3	110.5	107.7	109.4
March	106.3	99.0	106.4	97.7	93.6	102.0	106.8	105.1	113.3	112.5	108.1	99.1	110.8	107.5	111.6
April	105.4	97.9	103.6	97.9	92.1	102.5	105.9	104.5	111.5	112.9	105.8	100.4	108.9	106.2	108.1
May	106.8	99.8	108.6	99.3	93.2	102.3	107.3	106.5	115.2	112.1	106.7	103.1	110.1	107.1	112.2
June	106.0	99.6	106.3	99.2	92.7	106.1	106.5	105.7	114.3	113.3	106.8	101.2	109.8	107.8	111.9
July	105.1	98.3	107.8	98.8	89.3	104.3	105.6	104.3	113.3	111.9	105.6	100.4	107.9	108.2	108.6
August	105.1	97.8	103.6	98.4	91.7	102.6	105.6	105.8	113.0	112.3	105.9	100.9	111.4	108.1	113.3
September	105.0	99.2	106.5	99.5	91.0	106.4	105.4	105.4	112.8	113.9	106.2	101.0	110.9	106.9	111.7
October	105.5	100.2	111.7	97.8	91.3	106.2	105.8	105.6	115.7	112.6	105.7	100.7	110.0	106.8	113.0
November	105.0	100.3	111.5	99.5	90.5	106.8	105.4	104.9	114.5	111.9	105.7	99.9	109.9	106.4	112.7
December	105.1	100.9	113.4	97.4	91.2	108.7	105.4	105.8	114.1	112.0	106.9	101.8	109.8	106.5	112.8
1996:															
January	106.0	101.2	109.3	97.1	94.1	110.6	106.3	107.1	115.6	112.6	108.2	102.0	111.3	107.2	116.1
February	106.5	102.8	115.8	98.9	93.8	108.9	106.8	107.6	115.6	112.6	107.6	103.8	111.3	107.7	114.6
March	105.0	103.6	117.0	98.3	94.2	111.8	105.1	105.5	116.0	110.4	104.9	100.8	110.0	106.8	114.9
April	105.6	102.3	113.4	96.2	94.2	112.3	105.8	105.8	118.1	113.0	107.0	100.6	110.4	107.6	114.4
May	105.0	102.4	116.3	96.9	94.0	107.5	105.2	105.3	118.4	115.5	106.5	98.5	110.4	107.1	115.5
June	104.3	101.3	110.4	97.2	94.7	107.7	104.6	104.5	119.3	114.7	107.2	96.2	110.8	106.1	115.6
July	105.9	104.5	120.0	99.5	95.2	108.9	106.0	106.5	117.9	112.7	109.3	100.1	112.1	107.0	116.2
August	105.3	102.3	119.2	99.6	92.6	106.5	105.5	105.6	118.8	113.8	109.7	98.0	112.5	108.0	116.0
September	106.0	102.1	114.0	99.1	91.7	111.8	106.2	105.4	117.3	113.7	110.5	96.4	112.4	107.8	118.8
October	106.4	102.6	118.3	96.9	92.3	109.7	106.7	105.4	118.8	114.9	110.1	96.4	112.6	107.4	117.1
November	106.0	101.0	111.1	96.9	92.7	110.4	106.3	104.7	119.7	114.5	108.7	95.0	112.3	107.7	119.5
December	106.3	104.0	115.4	100.6	94.1	114.0	106.5	104.4	119.9	114.6	108.7	94.9	114.1	106.4	118.9

ELECTRIC POWER USE IN MINING AND MANUFACTURING—Continued
(1992=100, seasonally adjusted)

YEAR AND MONTH	Durable goods industries—Continued			Manufacturing—Continued Nondurable goods industries										
	Transportation equipment	Instruments	Miscellaneous	Total	Foods	Tobacco products	Textile mill products	Apparel products	Paper and products	Printing and publishing	Chemicals and products	Petroleum and products	Rubber and plastic products	Leather and products
1968	....	....	....	....	....	....	....	....	....	....	....	....	....	....
1969	....	....	....	....	....	....	....	....	....	....	....	....	....	....
1970	....	....	....	....	....	....	....	....	....	....	....	....	....	....
1971														
1972	77.1	49.8	74.0	68.2	61.0	66.2	82.8	96.3	55.7	47.5	79.4	57.3	47.6	152.6
1973	81.7	53.1	74.5	71.9	63.5	68.4	85.5	107.1	58.0	50.3	84.6	59.1	51.6	155.2
1974	72.2	50.3	71.8	72.2	63.0	66.0	80.0	98.9	58.7	47.9	87.1	58.3	51.2	143.5
1975	68.0	50.8	71.4	72.5	65.1	67.6	73.6	97.1	55.1	48.7	90.3	59.2	47.5	139.4
1976	75.1	53.4	76.9	80.1	67.7	72.5	80.8	99.1	62.7	50.1	101.3	62.9	54.0	148.2
1977	82.0	56.9	80.8	83.1	70.6	76.5	81.6	100.9	65.1	52.5	103.6	67.5	61.5	146.7
1978	83.5	59.3	84.1	81.4	72.1	79.5	86.8	100.7	66.6	54.5	96.3	70.2	64.1	144.5
1979	83.7	61.0	85.6	83.3	74.3	79.7	87.5	95.4	69.9	57.1	97.4	72.7	68.4	136.8
1980	75.6	63.4	81.8	79.8	75.9	89.6	85.9	95.6	72.4	58.1	87.5	74.1	65.3	135.9
1981	76.8	66.3	85.9	79.1	76.0	96.1	82.6	94.3	73.0	59.6	85.5	75.3	66.6	138.7
1982	71.2	67.2	82.4	75.2	76.6	91.5	74.4	91.7	71.0	61.0	79.1	75.0	61.8	131.1
1983	76.4	69.4	80.5	79.5	80.1	90.5	83.3	96.5	75.6	64.4	83.7	74.2	69.0	132.1
1984	85.0	74.6	83.0	82.8	81.2	95.2	84.8	99.4	79.6	67.7	87.4	76.8	76.0	126.6
1985	89.3	77.4	80.7	81.5	82.3	95.0	82.9	98.0	78.7	71.3	84.4	76.9	77.2	118.4
1986	92.6	82.5	83.0	83.2	86.2	91.0	86.6	100.0	82.1	77.0	82.6	82.6	80.5	113.0
1987	96.6	87.4	87.1	86.0	88.9	103.2	91.7	103.1	86.6	82.6	83.5	85.8	86.3	115.4
1988	98.8	91.0	92.4	87.7	92.4	100.5	92.9	103.3	91.1	88.1	83.3	86.3	90.1	115.2
1989	102.1	96.9	94.9	92.3	94.2	96.7	96.2	102.4	91.6	92.2	92.3	88.1	91.6	112.2
1990	100.3	99.8	97.0	95.7	96.0	108.5	95.3	102.8	95.3	97.5	97.1	90.3	94.6	103.2
1991	98.8	100.8	97.5	96.2	98.7	107.7	96.0	100.7	98.5	98.3	95.9	92.0	94.4	99.2
1992	100.0	100.0	100.0	100.0	100.0	100.0	100.0	100.0	100.0	100.0	100.0	100.0	100.0	100.0
1993	101.2	101.5	105.9	100.5	103.9	92.6	103.6	101.5	100.6	103.4	97.5	102.0	106.5	99.7
1994	104.6	103.1	116.0	105.4	109.1	88.5	107.9	106.4	102.8	107.8	103.1	105.5	115.8	99.0
1995	105.4	102.9	120.1	106.6	112.4	97.2	108.2	105.1	104.7	109.6	102.5	109.6	119.9	93.0
1996	106.1	102.0	125.9	106.1	112.9	99.6	105.9	102.3	102.5	111.0	102.4	107.7	123.0	93.6
1993:														
January	100.5	100.7	103.3	99.6	101.2	97.6	101.0	99.2	100.6	101.6	98.5	96.9	103.0	102.0
February	99.7	100.6	103.4	100.1	101.1	91.6	100.0	98.8	100.0	102.6	99.3	99.7	104.1	100.8
March	103.1	102.8	102.9	100.5	102.5	94.8	102.2	101.1	101.4	102.6	97.7	102.7	104.6	101.0
April	100.9	100.5	103.7	101.0	102.9	85.5	102.9	100.6	101.7	103.9	98.9	101.0	105.8	100.5
May	101.6	102.2	103.2	99.9	102.5	87.4	101.5	100.7	100.3	103.0	96.8	102.9	105.1	99.2
June	100.5	102.0	103.5	100.5	103.8	90.2	105.0	100.5	98.5	101.9	98.2	102.5	105.6	98.4
July	100.1	103.0	107.8	99.9	105.5	91.6	102.4	103.2	100.2	103.8	96.0	102.2	105.6	100.7
August	100.2	100.3	108.1	99.8	105.6	93.1	105.6	103.0	99.9	103.6	94.3	103.6	107.9	99.2
September	101.0	103.9	110.0	100.9	106.2	93.8	106.1	104.7	102.4	105.4	95.7	102.8	108.0	100.1
October	101.5	100.5	107.7	100.5	103.8	92.5	103.1	102.3	100.3	103.5	97.1	103.0	107.8	99.8
November	102.6	98.9	107.5	101.5	104.8	92.8	103.2	101.5	101.0	104.1	98.8	102.1	109.0	96.0
December	102.8	101.6	108.2	102.1	106.0	98.4	108.5	100.9	101.0	105.0	97.9	104.2	111.2	96.7
1994:														
January	104.5	100.5	108.2	101.9	108.5	88.8	102.5	101.8	101.1	103.6	98.6	103.1	109.6	96.2
February	104.2	102.2	108.6	102.7	107.2	93.1	108.4	103.0	102.2	105.2	99.3	102.2	110.9	97.0
March	105.0	102.4	112.7	103.5	108.4	92.0	108.8	105.9	101.3	107.5	100.8	102.2	111.9	98.4
April	103.7	102.4	113.1	104.0	109.4	89.6	106.6	106.8	101.8	107.5	100.5	106.6	113.6	100.3
May	103.1	102.7	112.4	104.9	109.0	86.0	108.3	107.6	104.5	107.9	101.8	103.9	114.5	102.6
June	105.0	104.9	115.8	104.3	109.6	85.1	105.3	108.2	103.2	108.6	100.9	103.9	116.4	101.5
July	103.5	103.7	115.5	105.4	108.8	84.9	106.2	107.7	102.1	109.9	103.2	107.1	116.4	103.1
August	103.6	104.6	118.5	107.1	109.0	88.3	110.0	106.3	103.7	107.5	105.5	107.5	119.3	99.2
September	103.8	104.7	119.9	107.3	110.2	87.0	108.1	107.7	103.2	107.7	105.7	109.1	118.4	99.4
October	105.5	103.1	122.0	107.5	108.7	88.1	108.8	106.5	104.2	109.5	106.7	106.2	119.4	97.2
November	106.8	102.7	121.4	108.4	110.8	87.8	110.6	107.6	103.1	109.4	107.8	108.6	119.2	95.4
December	105.9	102.6	122.4	107.6	110.3	91.5	110.4	106.0	103.1	109.0	106.8	105.6	119.6	96.1
1995:														
January	104.8	103.2	120.9	107.9	111.5	95.5	111.8	106.2	103.3	107.6	106.1	108.9	119.5	95.4
February	106.8	105.0	122.7	106.6	110.3	94.7	108.5	106.3	103.6	108.6	104.8	105.2	119.5	93.7
March	106.2	102.7	123.0	108.2	111.7	90.6	109.0	106.9	104.2	108.5	105.6	113.2	120.0	95.8
April	105.1	101.6	120.3	107.1	110.9	95.6	109.0	105.6	106.0	108.4	104.0	107.6	120.0	89.3
May	106.1	102.0	121.7	107.9	113.3	96.0	112.7	106.6	106.0	109.2	104.0	108.6	120.6	92.3
June	105.8	102.7	120.6	107.1	112.9	100.0	107.6	105.2	107.1	108.3	102.4	110.9	119.3	92.6
July	102.5	102.6	118.8	106.6	112.1	102.4	107.4	101.9	105.6	109.1	102.8	108.9	117.6	91.9
August	106.0	105.0	118.3	105.5	114.1	100.9	107.1	107.1	104.6	112.3	99.3	109.1	120.4	94.7
September	105.2	101.3	119.3	105.5	113.8	97.4	106.6	105.1	106.0	110.6	99.7	107.2	119.8	94.6
October	106.2	102.6	119.0	106.1	113.2	99.1	108.9	104.7	104.1	110.4	100.2	111.1	121.2	92.2
November	104.6	103.1	118.3	105.8	112.4	95.7	106.9	104.1	103.4	111.3	100.2	112.5	120.3	91.3
December	104.7	102.3	118.0	105.2	111.8	96.3	102.5	101.3	102.5	111.0	100.1	112.9	119.9	90.5
1996:														
January	108.0	105.8	120.5	105.7	113.1	94.5	103.6	102.8	103.0	111.3	100.9	111.3	120.6	93.7
February	107.5	104.4	121.0	106.1	112.3	99.4	106.1	103.5	101.5	111.7	102.4	110.5	120.9	94.3
March	104.0	103.1	121.8	104.9	111.9	98.2	103.7	102.1	101.0	110.4	100.7	108.7	121.2	91.3
April	104.2	103.7	125.5	105.8	112.1	98.9	105.4	102.1	102.4	109.8	102.0	107.5	123.1	94.3
May	106.3	102.8	126.1	105.1	112.2	98.7	103.6	103.7	101.1	111.3	101.6	105.0	124.1	93.7
June	106.2	103.5	126.3	104.6	112.0	96.1	103.8	100.7	100.7	110.8	100.8	105.2	123.0	93.5
July	107.0	102.0	129.0	105.6	113.1	100.2	106.0	100.8	103.3	110.6	101.1	106.3	123.2	96.7
August	105.9	99.8	123.2	105.5	111.7	101.2	105.8	104.0	102.6	109.0	101.4	106.5	123.8	95.2
September	107.0	99.4	126.5	106.9	112.2	104.3	108.9	101.7	104.1	110.6	103.3	106.8	123.9	92.0
October	107.6	100.1	129.3	107.7	114.3	99.6	106.1	101.8	104.5	110.4	103.8	110.1	125.4	94.6
November	105.7	98.6	129.6	107.6	114.2	105.1	108.6	103.6	102.1	113.8	104.6	108.8	123.4	92.8
December	103.7	100.2	132.0	108.2	115.3	98.8	109.1	100.3	103.8	112.7	106.0	105.4	123.9	91.5

Retail and Wholesale Trade

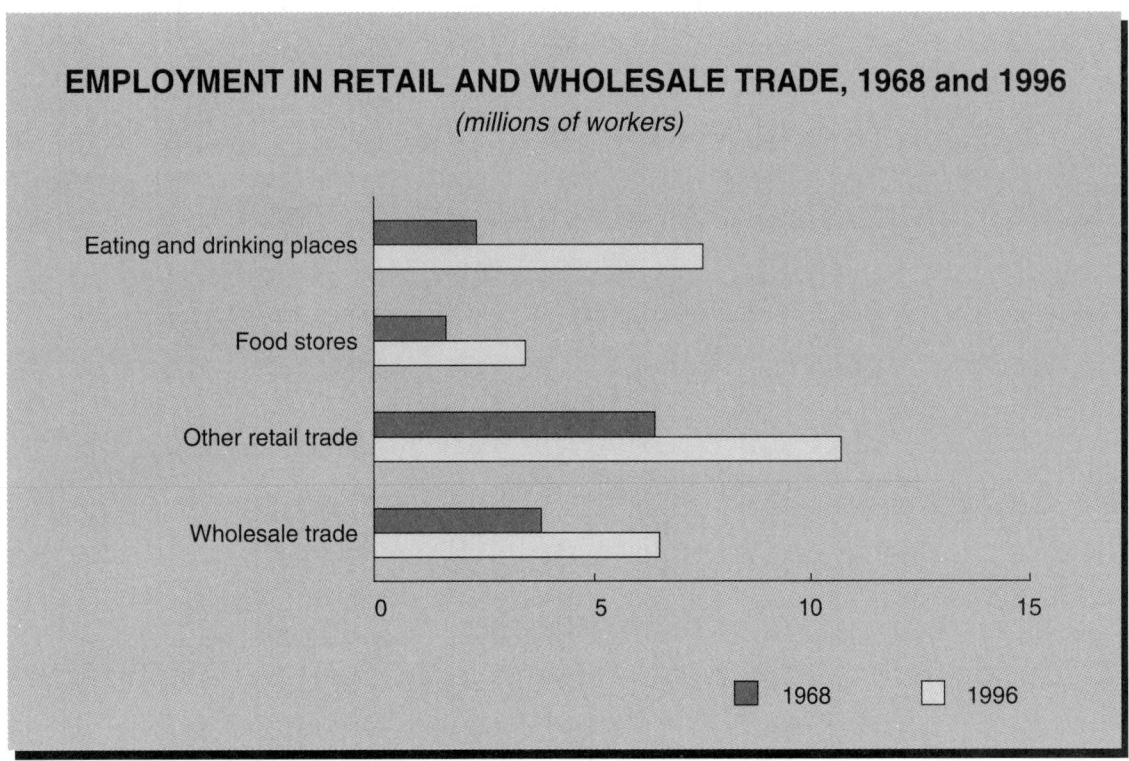

EMPLOYMENT IN RETAIL AND WHOLESALE TRADE, 1968 and 1996
(millions of workers)

Eating and drinking places

Food stores

Other retail trade

Wholesale trade

0   5   10   15

■ 1968   □ 1996

Employment in retail and wholesale trade doubled from 1968 to 1996, from 14 to 28 million workers. Growth of employment in eating and drinking places was especially strong, with the number of workers increasing from 2.3 million in 1968 to 7.5 million in 1996.

Additional evidence of American's increased penchant for dining out can be found in the increased share of eating and drinking places in total retail sales. Eating and drinking places accounted for 10 percent of total retail sales in 1996, compared with 8 percent in 1968.

RETAIL AND WHOLESALE TRADE

YEAR AND MONTH	RETAIL AND WHOLESALE TRADE—EMPLOYMENT										
	Total payroll employment (Thousands, seasonally adjusted)										
	Wholesale trade			Retail trade						Production and non-supervisory workers	
	Total	Durable goods	Nondurable goods	Total	General merchandise stores	Food stores	Auto dealers and service stations	Apparel and accessory stores	Eating and drinking places	Wholesale trade	Retail trade
1968	3 791	....	....	10 308	....	1 620	1 549	725	2 309	3 164	9 378
1969	3 919	....	....	10 785	....	1 683	1 611	753	2 466	3 271	9 822
1970	4 006	....	....	11 034	....	1 731	1 617	761	2 575	3 340	10 034
1971	4 014	....	....	11 338	....	1 752	1 642	779	2 700	3 327	10 288
1972	4 127	2 336	1 791	11 822	2 149	1 805	1 723	784	2 860	3 418	10 717
1973	4 291	2 457	1 835	12 315	2 229	1 856	1 778	795	3 054	3 560	11 155
1974	4 447	2 578	1 869	12 539	2 210	1 948	1 666	811	3 231	3 683	11 316
1975	4 430	2 539	1 891	12 630	2 113	2 007	1 677	806	3 380	3 650	11 373
1976	4 562	2 615	1 946	13 193	2 155	2 039	1 744	842	3 656	3 759	11 890
1977	4 723	2 732	1 991	13 792	2 204	2 106	1 801	870	3 949	3 892	12 424
1978	4 985	2 917	2 068	14 556	2 308	2 199	1 861	909	4 277	4 109	13 110
1979	5 221	3 098	2 123	14 972	2 287	2 297	1 812	949	4 513	4 290	13 458
1980	5 292	3 139	2 153	15 018	2 245	2 384	1 689	957	4 626	4 328	13 484
1981	5 375	3 182	2 193	15 171	2 230	2 448	1 653	968	4 749	4 375	13 582
1982	5 295	3 107	2 188	15 158	2 184	2 477	1 632	942	4 829	4 261	13 594
1983	5 283	3 087	2 197	15 587	2 165	2 556	1 674	963	5 038	4 239	13 989
1984	5 568	3 291	2 277	16 512	2 267	2 636	1 798	1 008	5 381	4 466	14 736
1985	5 727	3 402	2 325	17 315	2 323	2 774	1 889	1 039	5 699	4 607	15 421
1986	5 761	3 395	2 365	17 880	2 365	2 896	1 941	1 075	5 902	4 623	15 925
1987	5 848	3 437	2 411	18 422	2 411	2 958	2 001	1 123	6 086	4 685	16 378
1988	6 030	3 564	2 466	19 023	2 472	3 074	2 071	1 165	6 258	4 858	16 869
1989	6 187	3 653	2 534	19 475	2 544	3 164	2 092	1 197	6 402	4 981	17 262
1990	6 173	3 614	2 559	19 601	2 540	3 215	2 063	1 183	6 509	4 959	17 358
1991	6 081	3 531	2 550	19 284	2 453	3 204	1 984	1 151	6 476	4 872	17 006
1992	5 997	3 446	2 552	19 356	2 451	3 180	1 966	1 131	6 609	4 817	17 048
1993	5 981	3 433	2 549	19 773	2 488	3 224	2 014	1 144	6 821	4 823	17 428
1994	6 162	3 559	2 604	20 507	2 583	3 291	2 116	1 144	7 078	4 972	18 056
1995	6 378	3 715	2 663	21 187	2 681	3 366	2 190	1 125	7 354	5 163	18 639
1996	6 483	3 804	2 679	21 625	2 726	3 435	2 270	1 101	7 499	5 239	19 025
1993:											
January	5 957	3 411	2 546	19 512	2 471	3 192	1 982	1 140	6 702	4 800	17 214
February	5 951	3 408	2 543	19 592	2 490	3 200	1 986	1 147	6 731	4 794	17 285
March	5 945	3 405	2 540	19 535	2 486	3 201	1 990	1 141	6 686	4 792	17 239
April	5 954	3 412	2 542	19 645	2 480	3 207	1 990	1 141	6 686	4 792	17 239
May	5 973	3 417	2 556	19 710	2 481	3 213	2 000	1 146	6 805	4 816	17 386
June	5 967	3 423	2 544	19 745	2 477	3 227	2 006	1 145	6 817	4 812	17 403
July	5 986	3 433	2 553	19 790	2 486	3 232	2 012	1 143	6 833	4 827	17 441
August	5 981	3 435	2 546	19 853	2 488	3 238	2 021	1 147	6 860	4 823	17 495
September	5 998	3 449	2 549	19 900	2 494	3 247	2 030	1 145	6 878	4 838	17 533
October	6 008	3 455	2 553	19 971	2 500	3 251	2 038	1 140	6 917	4 849	17 592
November	6 024	3 465	2 559	19 991	2 502	3 245	2 047	1 137	6 924	4 860	17 593
December	6 039	3 479	2 560	20 055	2 498	3 241	2 058	1 148	6 957	4 873	17 654
1994:											
January	6 054	3 488	2 566	20 081	2 493	3 252	2 067	1 131	6 976	4 881	17 680
February	6 067	3 496	2 571	20 171	2 521	3 270	2 079	1 135	6 985	4 896	17 762
March	6 088	3 508	2 580	20 272	2 529	3 285	2 092	1 143	7 011	4 908	17 867
April	6 108	3 522	2 586	20 352	2 543	3 282	2 103	1 137	7 047	4 928	17 912
May	6 132	3 536	2 596	20 398	2 550	3 294	2 108	1 139	7 050	4 940	17 971
June	6 146	3 547	2 599	20 456	2 560	3 290	2 115	1 141	7 065	4 953	18 011
July	6 164	3 562	2 602	20 532	2 580	3 296	2 116	1 145	7 080	4 972	18 076
August	6 193	3 579	2 614	20 601	2 599	3 300	2 128	1 146	7 098	4 998	18 134
September	6 218	3 593	2 625	20 684	2 612	3 302	2 136	1 152	7 121	5 017	18 208
October	6 239	3 608	2 631	20 743	2 625	3 300	2 143	1 156	7 142	5 037	18 260
November	6 261	3 625	2 636	20 863	2 675	3 310	2 152	1 150	7 175	5 055	18 359
December	6 285	3 642	2 643	20 890	2 664	3 316	2 159	1 146	7 196	5 080	18 392
1995:											
January	6 312	3 662	2 650	21 003	2 677	3 329	2 166	1 146	7 261	5 105	18 486
February	6 341	3 682	2 659	21 060	2 676	3 336	2 173	1 148	7 280	5 133	18 539
March	6 358	3 697	2 661	21 059	2 644	3 342	2 180	1 140	7 302	5 144	18 543
April	6 366	3 702	2 664	21 130	2 680	3 354	2 183	1 139	7 310	5 153	18 590
May	6 370	3 706	2 664	21 125	2 675	3 358	2 183	1 128	7 312	5 153	18 584
June	6 382	3 716	2 666	21 188	2 684	3 366	2 185	1 130	7 353	5 170	18 634
July	6 393	3 721	2 672	21 207	2 685	3 369	2 184	1 124	7 372	5 179	18 659
August	6 393	3 725	2 668	21 249	2 681	3 380	2 192	1 125	7 389	5 179	18 692
September	6 397	3 732	2 665	21 293	2 685	3 382	2 198	1 110	7 416	5 183	18 726
October	6 401	3 739	2 662	21 274	2 697	3 379	2 205	1 105	7 401	5 182	18 717
November	6 405	3 745	2 660	21 321	2 684	3 395	2 210	1 106	7 428	5 184	18 743
December	6 416	3 753	2 663	21 340	2 677	3 405	2 219	1 103	7 436	5 191	18 755
1996:											
January	6 421	3 759	2 662	21 340	2 676	3 403	2 227	1 097	7 440	5 192	18 748
February	6 429	3 766	2 663	21 393	2 686	3 406	2 234	1 097	7 457	5 198	18 831
March	6 437	3 773	2 664	21 463	2 693	3 411	2 243	1 098	7 491	5 205	18 906
April	6 443	3 779	2 664	21 479	2 694	3 411	2 252	1 096	7 485	5 208	18 905
May	6 457	3 788	2 669	21 547	2 720	3 421	2 259	1 097	7 493	5 219	18 971
June	6 469	3 798	2 671	21 600	2 726	3 427	2 270	1 099	7 499	5 228	19 006
July	6 481	3 806	2 675	21 651	2 731	3 439	2 278	1 101	7 505	5 234	19 046
August	6 497	3 816	2 681	21 692	2 737	3 445	2 284	1 101	7 510	5 248	19 072
September	6 513	3 826	2 687	21 718	2 739	3 445	2 289	1 101	7 509	5 263	19 094
October	6 538	3 837	2 701	21 791	2 756	3 458	2 295	1 107	7 516	5 284	19 180
November	6 549	3 847	2 702	21 847	2 761	3 467	2 300	1 107	7 530	5 292	19 216
December	6 559	3 855	2 704	21 912	2 769	3 468	2 304	1 106	7 551	5 298	19 277

RETAIL AND WHOLESALE TRADE—HOURS, AND EARNINGS
(Production and nonsupervisory workers)

YEAR AND MONTH	Weekly hours worked (Seasonally adjusted)				Average earnings (Dollars, not seasonally adjusted)								
	Average hours		Aggregate hours index (1982=100)		Hourly							Weekly	
	Wholesale trade	Retail trade	Wholesale trade	Retail trade	Wholesale trade	Retail trade	General merchandise stores	Food stores	Auto dealer and service stations	Apparel and accessary stores	Eating and drinking places	Wholesale trade	Retail trade
1968	40.1	34.7	77.7	80.1	3.04	2.16	....	2.38	....	2.04	1.62	121.90	74.95
1969	40.2	34.2	80.6	82.6	3.23	2.30	....	2.55	....	2.15	1.74	129.85	78.66
1970	39.9	33.8	81.7	83.4	3.43	2.44	....	2.71	....	2.26	1.86	136.86	82.47
1971	39.4	33.7	80.4	85.3	3.64	2.60	....	2.94	....	2.36	1.96	143.42	87.62
1972	39.4	33.4	82.5	88.2	3.85	2.75	2.62	3.18	3.18	2.52	2.07	151.69	91.85
1973	39.2	33.1	85.6	90.9	4.07	2.91	2.76	3.38	3.38	2.63	2.18	159.54	96.32
1974	38.8	32.7	87.6	91.0	4.38	3.14	2.98	3.74	3.64	2.83	2.37	169.94	102.68
1975	38.6	32.4	86.4	90.6	4.72	3.36	3.21	4.08	3.84	3.03	2.55	182.19	108.86
1976	38.7	32.1	89.1	93.9	5.02	3.57	3.41	4.41	4.14	3.26	2.69	194.27	114.60
1977	38.8	31.6	92.5	96.5	5.39	3.85	3.71	4.77	4.49	3.45	2.93	209.13	121.66
1978	38.8	31.0	97.7	100.0	5.88	4.20	4.05	5.23	4.93	3.72	3.22	228.14	130.20
1979	38.8	30.6	102.0	101.5	6.39	4.53	4.38	5.67	5.31	4.01	3.45	247.93	138.62
1980	38.4	30.2	101.9	100.1	6.95	4.88	4.77	6.24	5.66	4.30	3.69	266.88	147.38
1981	38.5	30.1	103.3	100.6	7.55	5.25	5.15	6.85	6.07	4.65	3.95	290.68	158.03
1982	38.3	29.9	100.0	100.0	8.08	5.48	5.39	7.22	6.31	4.85	4.09	309.46	163.85
1983	38.5	29.8	99.9	102.7	8.54	5.74	5.61	7.51	6.76	5.02	4.27	328.79	171.05
1984	38.5	29.8	105.3	108.2	8.88	5.85	5.64	7.64	7.13	5.11	4.26	341.88	174.33
1985	38.4	29.4	108.4	111.7	9.15	5.94	5.92	7.35	7.41	5.25	4.33	351.36	174.64
1986	38.3	29.2	108.5	114.3	9.34	6.03	6.30	7.06	7.68	5.37	4.35	357.72	176.08
1987	38.1	29.2	109.4	117.9	9.59	6.12	6.47	6.95	7.81	5.56	4.42	365.38	178.70
1988	38.1	29.1	113.3	121.0	9.98	6.31	6.45	7.01	8.24	5.79	4.57	380.24	183.62
1989	38.0	28.9	116.1	122.9	10.39	6.53	6.64	7.15	8.57	6.01	4.75	394.82	188.72
1990	38.1	28.8	115.7	123.0	10.79	6.75	6.83	7.31	8.92	6.25	4.97	411.10	194.40
1991	38.1	28.6	113.7	119.5	11.15	6.94	7.04	7.33	9.07	6.60	5.18	424.82	198.48
1992	38.2	28.8	112.8	120.6	11.39	7.12	7.18	7.56	9.34	6.88	5.29	435.10	205.06
1993	38.2	28.8	112.8	123.4	11.74	7.29	7.29	7.80	9.66	7.01	5.35	448.47	209.95
1994	38.4	28.9	116.9	128.6	12.06	7.49	7.44	7.94	10.09	7.17	5.47	463.10	216.46
1995	38.3	28.8	121.1	132.2	12.43	7.69	7.53	8.15	10.41	7.47	5.59	476.07	221.47
1996	38.3	28.8	122.9	134.8	12.87	7.99	7.87	8.40	10.90	7.73	5.78	492.92	230.11
1993:													
January	38.1	28.8	112.1	122.0	11.61	7.26	7.26	7.74	9.36	7.04	5.34	438.86	202.55
February	38.1	28.7	111.9	122.1	11.63	7.26	7.32	7.75	9.43	7.02	5.34	440.78	204.73
March	38.0	28.2	111.6	119.6	11.61	7.27	7.32	7.80	9.43	7.00	5.34	438.86	202.11
April	38.1	28.7	112.1	122.2	11.72	7.26	7.26	7.78	9.62	7.06	5.34	445.36	206.18
May	38.3	28.9	113.1	123.6	11.76	7.27	7.30	7.79	9.74	7.05	5.34	451.58	210.10
June	38.2	28.7	112.7	122.9	11.67	7.26	7.29	7.79	9.67	7.01	5.33	446.96	210.54
July	38.2	28.9	113.0	124.0	11.74	7.25	7.26	7.74	9.75	6.96	5.31	449.64	214.60
August	38.3	28.9	113.2	124.4	11.77	7.25	7.30	7.72	9.77	6.90	5.33	451.97	215.33
September	38.1	28.8	113.0	124.3	11.82	7.32	7.30	7.83	9.78	7.04	5.36	450.34	211.55
October	38.2	28.9	113.5	125.1	11.84	7.35	7.30	7.87	9.79	7.07	5.38	453.47	211.68
November	38.2	28.7	113.8	124.3	11.83	7.36	7.28	7.90	9.76	7.06	5.40	451.91	210.50
December	38.2	28.8	114.1	125.1	11.88	7.36	7.26	7.85	9.75	6.97	5.43	455.00	215.65
1994:													
January	38.4	29.1	114.9	126.6	11.99	7.45	7.41	7.88	9.78	7.18	5.43	458.02	210.09
February	38.1	28.6	114.3	125.0	11.97	7.45	7.46	7.90	9.85	7.16	5.42	453.66	209.35
March	38.3	28.9	115.2	127.1	11.91	7.45	7.46	7.91	9.94	7.12	5.41	453.77	212.33
April	38.3	28.9	115.7	127.4	12.04	7.47	7.41	7.94	10.14	7.16	5.43	461.13	214.39
May	38.4	28.9	116.3	127.8	12.03	7.47	7.48	7.93	10.12	7.17	5.44	464.36	215.88
June	38.4	29.0	116.6	128.5	11.99	7.46	7.50	7.89	10.11	7.13	5.44	461.62	218.58
July	38.4	29.0	117.0	129.0	12.05	7.46	7.45	7.88	10.19	7.11	5.44	462.72	222.31
August	38.2	28.9	117.0	129.0	12.01	7.44	7.42	7.88	10.10	7.07	5.46	459.98	220.97
September	38.3	28.9	117.8	129.5	12.11	7.54	7.45	7.99	10.26	7.22	5.50	465.02	218.66
October	38.6	29.2	119.2	131.2	12.21	7.57	7.47	7.99	10.23	7.28	5.53	473.75	220.29
November	38.3	28.9	118.7	130.6	12.17	7.57	7.40	8.03	10.18	7.25	5.54	467.33	217.26
December	38.4	28.8	119.6	130.4	12.23	7.59	7.40	8.02	10.19	7.23	5.59	470.86	222.39
1995:													
January	38.5	29.0	120.5	131.9	12.33	7.63	7.44	8.08	10.15	7.42	5.52	471.01	215.17
February	38.3	28.7	120.5	130.9	12.31	7.63	7.50	8.11	10.15	7.43	5.52	469.01	214.40
March	38.2	28.7	120.4	131.0	12.27	7.63	7.53	8.10	10.18	7.47	5.53	467.49	215.93
April	38.4	29.2	121.3	133.6	12.47	7.65	7.51	8.06	10.43	7.49	5.53	477.60	221.09
May	38.0	28.7	120.0	131.3	12.35	7.64	7.51	8.13	10.31	7.48	5.57	470.54	219.27
June	38.2	28.7	121.0	131.6	12.34	7.65	7.51	8.08	10.47	7.49	5.56	472.62	222.62
July	38.4	28.9	121.9	132.7	12.46	7.66	7.53	8.11	10.54	7.44	5.57	479.71	227.50
August	38.2	28.7	121.3	132.0	12.41	7.65	7.51	8.11	10.45	7.39	5.60	475.30	225.68
September	38.2	28.8	121.3	132.7	12.52	7.77	7.59	8.23	10.62	7.52	5.64	479.52	224.55
October	38.4	28.8	122.0	132.7	12.56	7.77	7.59	8.27	10.50	7.55	5.65	483.56	223.78
November	38.2	28.9	121.4	133.3	12.55	7.78	7.54	8.27	10.51	7.50	5.66	479.41	222.51
December	38.1	28.7	121.2	132.5	12.63	7.80	7.55	8.25	10.57	7.47	5.70	483.73	226.20
1996:													
January	38.0	28.4	120.9	131.0	12.66	7.89	7.73	8.38	10.38	7.73	5.69	476.02	216.98
February	38.2	28.8	121.7	133.5	12.68	7.87	7.74	8.38	10.53	7.73	5.69	481.84	221.93
March	38.2	28.9	121.9	134.5	12.69	7.90	7.81	8.38	10.77	7.71	5.69	483.49	225.15
April	38.1	28.7	121.6	133.5	12.78	7.92	7.91	8.40	10.79	7.74	5.70	486.92	224.93
May	38.1	28.8	121.9	134.5	12.75	7.92	7.88	8.37	10.87	7.73	5.72	487.05	227.30
June	38.6	29.0	123.7	135.6	12.88	7.98	7.89	8.30	11.19	7.77	5.76	499.74	234.61
July	38.1	28.7	122.2	134.5	12.82	7.93	7.86	8.28	10.88	7.65	5.76	488.44	233.14
August	38.3	28.8	123.2	135.2	12.85	7.95	7.87	8.31	10.96	7.62	5.78	493.44	234.53
September	38.4	28.9	123.9	135.8	13.03	8.06	7.94	8.44	11.07	7.76	5.82	502.96	234.55
October	38.2	28.8	123.7	135.9	12.94	8.12	7.94	8.51	11.01	7.79	5.91	495.60	233.04
November	38.3	28.9	124.2	136.7	13.06	8.13	7.86	8.53	11.12	7.78	5.92	500.20	232.52
December	38.5	29.0	125.0	137.6	13.20	8.16	7.93	8.52	11.09	7.76	5.97	510.84	239.09

RETAIL SALES—UNADJUSTED
(All retail stores—Millions of dollars, unadjusted for seasonal variation or for holiday and trading day differences)

YEAR AND MONTH	Total	Durable goods stores				Nondurable goods stores							
		Total	Building materials¹	Automotive dealers	Furniture and home furnishings and equipment	Total	General merchandise group stores	Food stores	Gasoline service stations	Apparel and accessory stores	Eating and drinking places	Drug and proprietary stores	Liquor stores
1968	329 336	106 023	15 602	64 314	15 257	223 313	44 019	75 899	24 750	19 707	25 279	12 378	7 258
1969	352 457	113 562	17 175	67 745	16 152	238 895	46 559	81 258	26 301	21 384	27 173	13 200	7 739
1970	374 989	114 586	18 080	65 241	17 043	260 403	49 163	89 990	28 903	22 095	30 476	14 567	8 412
1971	413 969	135 113	20 924	80 718	18 183	278 856	54 365	94 002	30 620	24 178	32 321	15 143	9 294
1972	458 267	155 937	24 123	92 335	21 199	302 330	59 656	100 589	33 072	26 367	35 738	16 139	9 814
1973	511 570	176 817	27 466	104 893	24 244	334 753	65 825	111 817	36 942	29 109	40 290	17 190	10 288
1974	541 686	172 497	27 347	97 551	25 982	369 189	69 540	126 312	43 054	30 077	44 606	17 190	10 288
1975	587 704	185 479	27 299	107 348	27 046	402 225	73 759	138 665	47 603	32 398	51 067	19 995	11 896
1976	655 859	219 908	33 259	130 169	30 300	435 951	79 500	148 218	52 037	34 706	57 331	21 710	12 442
1977	722 109	249 078	38 913	150 129	33 308	473 031	87 824	158 444	56 638	37 165	63 370	23 381	13 031
1978	804 019	280 899	45 170	168 065	36 832	523 120	97 215	175 425	59 889	42 649	71 828	25 607	13 630
1979	896 561	306 561	51 016	178 641	42 417	590 000	103 817	197 985	73 521	46 070	82 110	28 455	15 194
1980	956 921	298 618	50 794	164 149	44 238	658 303	108 955	220 224	94 093	49 296	90 058	30 951	16 882
1981	1 038 163	324 211	52 230	181 903	46 900	713 952	120 534	236 188	103 072	53 998	98 118	33 999	17 702
1982	1 068 747	335 587	50 994	192 440	46 761	733 160	124 624	246 122	97 440	55 570	104 593	36 440	18 146
1983	1 170 163	390 849	58 739	229 979	54 691	779 314	135 959	256 018	102 927	60 192	113 281	40 591	19 121
1984	1 286 914	454 481	67 077	273 320	61 432	832 433	150 283	271 909	107 565	64 341	121 321	44 011	18 273
1985	1 375 027	498 125	71 196	303 199	68 287	876 902	158 636	285 062	113 341	70 195	127 949	46 994	19 532
1986	1 449 636	540 688	77 104	326 138	75 714	908 948	169 397	297 019	102 093	75 626	139 415	50 546	19 929
1987	1 541 506	575 863	83 454	342 896	78 072	965 436	181 970	309 461	104 769	79 322	153 461	54 142	19 826
1988	1 656 202	629 154	91 056	372 570	85 390	1 027 048	192 521	325 493	110 341	85 307	167 993	57 842	19 638
1989	1 758 971	657 154	92 379	386 011	91 301	1 101 817	206 306	347 045	122 882	92 341	177 829	63 343	20 099
1990	1 844 611	668 835	94 640	387 605	91 545	1 175 776	215 514	368 333	138 504	95 819	190 149	70 558	21 722
1991	1 855 937	649 974	91 496	372 647	91 676	1 205 963	226 730	374 523	137 295	97 441	194 424	75 540	22 454
1992	1 951 589	703 604	100 838	406 935	96 947	1 247 985	246 420	377 099	136 950	104 212	200 164	77 788	21 698
1993	2 072 788	776 126	109 444	456 332	105 399	1 296 662	264 613	384 978	138 172	107 176	213 461	79 615	21 532
1994	2 227 325	873 408	122 342	518 492	118 649	1 353 917	283 203	398 845	141 671	109 862	223 485	81 809	22 078
1995	2 324 038	925 017	125 831	551 330	127 270	1 399 021	299 169	409 617	146 080	110 429	232 060	85 554	21 966
1996	2 445 296	993 336	134 485	592 919	133 486	1 451 960	312 792	423 318	154 967	113 668	236 526	90 682	22 850
1993:													
January	147 772	52 640	6 594	31 107	7 836	95 132	16 031	30 792	10 779	6 623	16 058	6 171	1 599
February	144 335	52 205	6 610	31 671	7 276	92 130	16 287	28 905	10 387	6 453	15 468	6 203	1 520
March	163 943	61 393	8 174	38 028	8 116	102 550	18 992	31 288	11 314	7 795	17 249	6 644	1 670
April	169 634	64 807	9 513	39 720	7 951	104 827	20 103	31 676	11 474	8 784	17 669	6 653	1 709
May	175 371	66 825	10 595	40 006	8 174	108 546	21 440	32 770	12 084	8 747	18 521	6 589	1 794
June	174 825	69 169	10 415	41 648	8 459	105 656	20 436	32 216	11 988	8 289	18 415	6 512	1 793
July	176 995	68 588	9 949	41 499	8 718	108 407	20 497	33 868	12 292	8 446	18 949	6 528	1 953
August	176 208	67 548	9 810	40 160	8 685	108 660	21 655	32 141	12 042	9 268	19 188	6 542	1 781
September	170 202	65 205	9 637	38 749	8 591	104 997	20 473	31 593	11 293	8 747	17 938	6 402	1 712
October	175 510	65 330	9 732	38 737	8 813	110 180	22 444	32 277	11 811	9 058	17 938	6 297	1 712
November	180 364	65 800	9 214	37 478	9 898	114 564	26 622	31 799	11 373	10 105	18 558	6 465	1 763
December	217 629	76 616	9 201	37 529	12 882	141 013	39 633	35 653	11 335	14 861	17 274	6 518	1 789
1994:													
January	154 400	57 416	7 170	34 998	8 135	96 984	16 959	31 458	10 533	6 318	15 947	6 486	2 449
February	155 596	59 970	7 051	37 642	8 024	95 626	17 565	29 645	10 217	6 659	16 381	6 188	1 549
March	183 782	73 596	9 509	46 929	9 175	110 186	21 529	33 177	11 306	8 786	18 607	6 907	1 505
April	181 209	73 444	10 773	45 768	8 820	107 765	21 224	32 368	11 328	8 628	18 625	6 605	1 713
May	186 395	75 176	11 936	45 215	9 082	111 219	22 242	33 411	11 932	8 573	19 259	6 771	1 756
June	189 244	77 751	11 649	47 380	9 488	111 493	22 420	33 718	12 240	8 559	19 309	6 653	1 828
July	184 978	73 101	10 856	43 814	9 465	111 877	21 593	34 440	12 572	8 424	20 046	6 558	1 854
August	192 925	77 533	11 474	46 166	10 037	115 392	23 283	33 867	13 025	9 702	19 831	6 814	1 978
September	184 957	74 542	11 131	44 444	9 810	110 415	21 852	33 121	12 183	8 854	18 710	6 557	1 855
October	188 454	73 896	10 857	44 061	10 120	114 558	23 839	33 200	12 280	9 299	19 177	6 764	1 820
November	193 411	73 347	10 225	41 573	11 465	120 064	28 496	33 244	11 932	10 487	18 128	6 788	1 802
December	231 974	83 636	9 711	40 502	15 028	148 338	42 201	37 196	12 123	15 573	19 465	8 718	1 843
1995:													
January	166 188	64 096	8 071	38 638	9 552	102 092	18 335	32 602	11 244	6 506	17 291	6 822	2 575
February	162 959	63 992	7 839	39 519	8 860	98 967	18 490	30 606	10 711	6 651	16 931	6 608	1 556
March	190 844	77 744	10 073	49 250	9 941	113 100	22 386	33 949	11 949	8 572	19 323	7 127	1 502
April	186 287	74 251	10 708	45 660	9 232	112 036	22 842	33 382	11 840	8 854	19 381	6 945	1 727
May	199 980	82 517	12 436	50 337	9 951	117 463	24 010	34 810	12 971	8 926	20 184	7 263	1 699
June	201 079	84 428	12 007	52 371	10 131	116 651	24 067	34 652	13 201	8 798	20 210	7 019	1 808
July	193 423	78 198	11 087	47 577	10 054	115 225	23 280	35 150	12 998	8 398	20 491	6 773	1 862
August	202 572	83 320	11 455	50 716	10 786	119 252	24 763	34 972	13 141	9 661	20 833	7 010	1 884
September	191 213	77 195	10 952	46 357	10 519	114 018	23 297	33 796	12 223	9 216	19 506	6 827	1 857
October	192 351	76 716	11 171	45 901	10 608	115 635	24 215	33 555	12 190	8 926	19 626	7 044	1 839
November	200 800	76 827	10 329	43 516	12 183	123 973	30 201	34 200	11 680	10 664	18 589	7 162	1 781
December	236 342	85 733	9 703	41 488	15 453	150 609	43 283	37 943	11 932	15 257	19 695	8 954	1 869
1996:													
January	173 264	68 706	8 062	42 364	9 904	104 558	18 670	33 580	11 488	6 516	17 424	7 062	2 582
February	180 251	73 420	8 232	46 817	9 641	106 831	20 597	32 580	11 248	7 397	18 187	7 108	1 660
March	199 413	82 506	9 776	52 785	10 617	116 907	23 358	34 982	12 454	8 843	19 940	7 417	1 630
April	198 610	82 958	11 936	51 163	10 143	115 652	23 479	34 031	12 887	9 026	19 489	7 329	1 811
May	213 754	90 210	13 348	55 088	10 639	123 544	25 904	36 348	14 039	9 435	20 742	7 651	1 772
June	204 705	85 962	12 892	51 960	10 507	118 743	24 866	35 310	13 642	8 941	20 219	7 164	1 927
July	204 817	86 024	12 718	52 014	10 686	118 793	23 695	36 289	13 629	8 616	20 470	7 381	1 927
August	212 247	87 258	12 300	52 396	11 326	124 989	26 416	36 716	13 795	10 366	21 250	7 526	2 002
September	195 749	80 509	11 634	48 378	10 721	115 240	23 819	34 096	12 724	9 052	19 278	7 114	2 032
October	207 531	84 794	12 316	51 058	11 211	122 737	25 978	35 498	13 264	9 569	20 083	7 715	1 757
November	210 236	80 826	10 921	45 364	12 483	129 410	31 075	35 880	12 807	10 777	20 219	7 613	1 837
December	244 719	90 163	10 350	43 532	15 608	154 556	44 935	38 008	12 990	15 130	19 822	9 602	1 970

1. Includes building materials, hardware and garden supply stores, and mobile home dealers.

RETAIL SALES—ADJUSTED [1]
(All retail stores—Millions of dollars, adjusted for seasonal variation and for holiday and trading day differences)

YEAR AND MONTH	Total	Durable goods stores											Nondurable goods stores, total
		Total	Building materials			Automotive dealers			Furniture and home furnishings and equipment				
			Total [2]	Building materials and supply stores	Hardware stores	Total	Motor vehicle and miscellaneous automotive dealers	Auto and home supply stores	Total	Furniture and home furnishings	Household appliances, radio, and TV		
1968	329 336	106 023	15 602	10 370	2 841	64 314	59 426	4 888	15 257	9 309	5 005		223 313
1969	352 457	113 562	17 175	11 005	3 000	67 745	62 323	5 422	16 152	10 012	5 220		238 895
1970	374 989	114 586	18 080	11 343	2 979	65 241	59 243	5 998	17 043	10 442	5 571		260 403
1971	413 969	135 113	20 924	13 070	3 230	80 718	73 747	6 971	18 183	11 439	5 634		278 856
1972	458 267	155 937	24 123	15 112	3 620	92 335	84 477	7 858	21 199	13 480	6 274		302 330
1973	511 570	176 817	27 466	17 314	4 187	104 893	96 121	8 772	24 244	15 430	7 210		334 753
1974	541 686	172 497	27 347	17 874	4 604	97 551	88 310	9 241	25 982	18 544	7 427		369 189
1975	587 704	185 479	27 299	17 947	5 165	107 348	97 275	10 073	27 046	16 460	8 218		402 225
1976	655 859	219 908	33 259	22 484	5 591	130 169	119 063	11 116	30 300	18 383	9 129		435 951
1977	722 109	249 078	38 913	27 123	6 139	150 129	150 129	13 095	33 308	20 384	10 046		473 031
1978	804 019	280 899	45 170	31 910	6 652	168 065	168 065	14 165	36 832	22 538	10 780		523 120
1979	896 561	306 561	51 016	36 245	7 937	178 641	152 458	16 183	42 417	25 642	12 936		590 000
1980	956 921	298 618	50 794	34 997	8 349	164 149	146 190	17 959	44 238	26 332	14 010		658 303
1981	1 038 163	324 211	52 230	35 738	8 475	181 903	162 271	19 632	46 900	27 499	15 402		713 952
1982	1 068 747	335 587	50 994	35 144	8 727	192 440	172 359	20 081	46 761	27 093	15 774		733 160
1983	1 170 163	390 849	58 739	41 256	9 140	229 979	207 871	22 108	54 691	31 296	19 280		779 314
1984	1 286 914	454 481	67 077	47 127	10 354	273 320	250 193	23 127	61 432	35 587	21 474		832 433
1985	1 375 027	498 125	71 196	50 766	10 471	303 199	277 995	25 204	68 287	38 270	25 147		876 902
1986	1 449 636	540 688	77 104	56 510	10 734	326 138	301 083	25 055	75 714	43 030	27 037		908 948
1987	1 541 299	575 863	83 454	61 302	11 036	342 896	316 274	26 622	78 072	44 477	27 121		965 436
1988	1 656 202	629 154	91 056	66 796	11 894	372 570	343 217	29 353	85 390	47 617	30 608		1 027 048
1989	1 758 971	657 154	92 379	67 457	12 637	386 011	356 485	29 526	91 301	51 202	32 666		1 101 817
1990	1 844 611	668 835	94 640	70 341	12 524	387 605	356 764	30 841	91 545	50 524	33 035		1 175 776
1991	1 855 937	649 974	91 496	68 196	12 148	372 647	343 018	29 629	91 676	49 469	33 569		1 205 963
1992	1 951 589	703 604	100 838	75 358	12 729	406 935	377 118	29 817	96 947	52 348	35 802		1 247 985
1993	2 071 178	775 436	109 298	82 325	13 207	456 662	425 861	30 801	104 946	55 437	40 274		1 295 742
1994	2 224 913	872 495	121 961	92 690	14 162	519 150	486 166	32 984	117 928	60 601	47 324		1 352 418
1995	2 326 536	926 442	126 231	95 825	14 291	552 535	518 355	34 180	127 200	63 795	52 909		1 400 094
1996	2 439 535	990 407	133 690	101 342	15 125	591 661	555 734	35 927	133 199	66 439	56 009		1 449 128
1993:													
January	169 123	62 472	8 787	6 600	1 073	36 254	33 753	2 501	8 563	4 602	3 137		106 651
February	168 076	60 895	8 796	6 703	1 073	35 446	32 880	2 566	8 374	4 469	3 101		107 181
March	166 192	60 415	8 623	6 535	1 066	35 283	32 771	2 512	8 367	4 429	3 141		105 777
April	170 237	62 797	8 799	6 638	1 062	36 893	34 354	2 539	8 530	4 532	3 210		107 440
May	171 370	63 786	9 103	6 838	1 116	37 580	35 025	2 555	8 602	4 574	3 240		107 584
June	171 634	64 150	9 002	6 766	1 104	37 504	34 936	2 568	8 730	4 602	3 298		107 484
July	173 337	65 328	9 013	6 782	1 104	38 549	35 960	2 589	8 854	4 667	3 504		108 009
August	173 629	65 610	9 134	6 857	1 116	38 704	36 086	2 618	8 843	4 659	3 461		108 019
September	173 959	65 232	9 194	6 920	1 118	38 281	35 696	2 585	8 938	4 667	3 545		108 727
October	176 337	66 853	9 439	7 006	1 117	39 577	36 968	2 609	8 983	4 724	3 498		109 484
November	177 966	68 301	9 478	7 207	1 117	40 987	38 384	2 603	9 048	4 747	3 549		109 665
December	179 318	69 597	9 930	7 473	1 141	41 604	39 048	2 556	9 114	4 765	3 590		109 721
1994:													
January	178 005	68 668	9 613	7 213	1 174	41 226	38 551	2 675	8 893	4 520	3 627		109 337
February	180 976	69 865	9 412	7 167	1 174	42 051	39 316	2 735	9 302	4 830	3 694		111 111
March	183 962	71 716	9 993	7 596	1 161	43 126	40 341	2 785	9 484	4 936	3 751		112 246
April	183 096	72 019	10 098	7 677	1 191	43 156	40 432	2 724	9 538	4 963	3 751		111 077
May	182 621	71 189	10 074	7 646	1 157	42 053	39 356	2 697	9 648	5 021	3 799		111 432
June	184 382	71 920	10 139	7 731	1 170	42 526	39 796	2 730	9 842	5 070	3 925		112 462
July	184 578	71 680	10 161	7 721	1 176	42 052	39 318	2 734	9 888	5 104	3 927		112 898
August	187 336	73 545	10 443	7 960	1 192	43 406	40 655	2 751	10 033	5 192	3 986		113 791
September	187 935	74 037	10 511	7 945	1 191	43 590	40 816	2 774	10 142	5 219	4 057		113 898
October	190 464	76 005	10 513	7 996	1 209	45 388	42 628	2 760	10 305	5 239	4 205		114 459
November	190 727	75 936	10 533	7 969	1 198	45 368	42 546	2 822	10 376	5 227	4 286		114 791
December	190 831	75 915	10 471	8 069	1 169	45 208	42 411	2 797	10 477	5 280	4 316		114 916
1995:													
January	192 619	76 055	10 658	8 237	1 095	45 029	42 198	2 831	10 475	5 267	4 328		116 564
February	189 568	74 685	10 492	8 017	1 158	44 085	41 326	2 759	10 317	5 175	4 294		114 883
March	190 950	75 544	10 674	8 083	1 177	44 854	42 025	2 829	10 280	5 158	4 284		115 406
April	191 094	75 334	10 383	7 906	1 156	44 748	41 936	2 812	10 271	5 194	4 244		115 760
May	193 074	76 480	10 307	7 804	1 183	45 637	42 833	2 804	10 440	5 222	4 367		116 594
June	194 512	77 527	10 369	7 840	1 236	46 557	43 773	2 804	10 521	5 281	4 378		116 985
July	194 315	77 362	10 423	7 897	1 197	46 260	43 432	2 828	10 605	5 315	4 412		116 953
August	195 752	78 723	10 424	7 819	1 204	47 384	44 525	2 859	10 775	5 339	4 497		117 029
September	195 079	77 640	10 457	7 916	1 208	46 299	43 421	2 878	10 812	5 440	4 465		117 439
October	194 865	78 048	10 580	8 042	1 194	46 633	43 721	2 912	10 806	5 420	4 501		116 817
November	196 702	79 234	10 697	8 057	1 251	47 282	44 343	2 939	10 960	5 505	4 554		117 468
December	198 006	79 810	10 767	8 207	1 232	47 747	44 822	2 925	10 938	5 479	4 585		118 196
1996:													
January	197 714	79 640	10 440	7 890	1 235	48 073	45 134	2 939	10 709	5 270	4 549		118 074
February	201 085	81 931	10 580	7 994	1 263	49 948	46 979	2 969	10 821	5 387	4 524		119 154
March	201 685	82 641	10 683	8 137	1 239	49 920	46 935	2 985	11 128	5 570	4 637		119 044
April	202 375	81 580	11 048	8 326	1 283	48 460	45 470	2 990	11 118	5 524	4 673		120 795
May	204 177	83 239	11 224	8 578	1 271	49 478	46 456	3 022	11 175	5 539	4 714		120 938
June	202 698	82 315	11 500	8 665	1 257	48 665	45 663	3 002	11 140	5 548	4 673		120 383
July	203 017	82 332	11 474	8 705	1 263	48 709	45 692	3 017	11 136	5 568	4 670		120 685
August	203 036	82 487	11 302	8 587	1 244	49 009	46 013	2 996	11 235	5 576	4 759		120 549
September	204 713	83 091	11 336	8 597	1 244	49 839	46 851	2 988	11 232	5 554	4 811		121 622
October	206 277	83 871	11 386	8 601	1 279	50 114	47 033	3 081	11 214	5 620	4 727		122 406
November	205 789	83 485	11 339	8 627	1 266	49 520	46 564	2 956	11 142	5 632	4 647		122 304
December	206 894	83 785	11 319	8 558	1 299	50 044	47 068	2 976	11 125	5 657	4 600		123 109

1. Annual data prior to 1993 are totals of the unadjusted monthly figures. 1993 and later years are totals of the adjusted figures.
2. Includes building materials, hardware and garden supply stores, and mobile home dealers.

RETAIL SALES—ADJUSTED [1]—Continued
(All retail stores—Millions of dollars, adjusted for seasonal variation and for holiday and trading day differences)

YEAR AND MONTH	General merchandise group stores			Food stores		Gasoline service stations	Apparel and accessory stores				Eating and drinking places	Drug and proprietary stores	Liquor stores
	Total	Department stores	Variety stores	Total	Grocery stores		Total	Men's and boys' clothing and furnishings	Women's clothing, specialty, and fur	Shoe stores			
1968	44 019	32 431	5 302	75 899	69 873	24 750	19 707	3 916	7 435	4 062	25 279	12 378	7 258
1969	46 559	34 754	5 597	81 258	74 836	26 301	21 384	4 382	7 842	4 577	27 173	13 200	7 739
1970	49 163	36 187	6 082	89 990	82 558	28 903	22 095	4 544	8 239	4 458	30 476	14 567	8 412
1971	54 365	40 472	6 111	94 002	86 419	30 620	24 178	4 903	9 222	4 524	32 321	15 143	9 294
1972	59 656	44 451	6 598	100 589	92 856	33 072	26 367	5 684	9 739	4 884	35 738	16 139	9 814
1973	65 825	49 342	7 207	111 817	103 555	36 942	29 109	6 193	10 732	5 600	40 290	17 190	10 288
1974	69 540	52 059	7 594	126 312	117 182	43 054	30 077	6 190	11 338	5 405	44 606	18 595	11 087
1975	73 759	55 702	7 893	138 665	129 087	47 603	32 398	6 619	12 438	5 751	51 067	19 995	11 896
1976	79 500	61 500	7 101	148 218	137 992	52 037	34 706	6 815	13 426	8 249	57 331	21 710	12 442
1977	87 824	68 856	6 987	158 444	148 116	56 638	37 165	7 042	12 537	7 058	63 370	23 381	13 031
1978	97 215	76 137	7 176	175 425	164 234	59 889	42 649	7 537	15 995	8 305	71 828	25 607	13 630
1979	103 817	81 161	7 770	197 985	185 318	73 521	46 070	7 763	17 030	9 693	82 110	28 455	15 194
1980	108 955	85 464	7 791	220 224	205 630	94 093	49 296	7 664	17 592	10 530	90 058	30 951	16 882
1981	120 534	95 638	8 202	236 188	220 580	103 072	53 998	7 910	19 060	11 821	98 118	33 999	17 702
1982	124 624	99 841	8 211	246 122	230 696	97 440	55 570	7 803	20 017	11 419	104 593	36 440	18 146
1983	135 959	108 637	8 367	256 018	240 402	102 927	60 192	7 958	21 847	11 949	113 281	40 591	19 121
1984	150 283	120 487	8 700	271 909	258 465	107 565	64 341	8 206	23 764	12 306	121 321	44 011	18 273
1985	158 636	126 412	8 459	285 062	269 546	113 341	70 195	8 458	26 149	13 054	127 949	46 994	19 532
1986	169 397	134 486	7 447	297 019	280 833	102 093	75 626	8 646	28 600	13 947	139 415	50 546	19 929
1987	181 970	144 017	7 134	309 461	290 979	104 769	79 322	9 017	29 208	14 594	153 461	54 142	19 826
1988	192 521	151 523	7 458	325 493	307 173	110 341	85 307	9 826	30 567	15 444	167 993	57 842	19 638
1989	206 306	160 524	7 936	347 045	328 072	122 882	92 341	10 507	32 231	17 290	177 829	63 343	20 099
1990	215 514	165 808	8 306	368 333	348 243	138 504	95 819	10 450	32 812	18 043	190 149	70 558	21 722
1991	226 730	172 922	8 341	374 523	354 331	137 295	97 441	10 435	32 865	17 504	194 424	75 540	22 454
1992	246 420	186 423	9 516	377 099	358 148	136 950	104 212	10 197	35 750	18 122	200 164	77 788	21 698
1993	264 106	204 105	9 099	385 000	365 511	138 371	107 095	10 268	36 948	18 181	213 401	79 607	21 530
1994	282 336	222 078	8 091	398 680	378 269	141 792	109 416	10 653	35 832	18 677	223 386	81 869	22 024
1995	299 100	236 526	7 745	410 105	388 527	146 306	110 453	10 259	35 152	18 793	232 135	85 722	21 982
1996	312 080	247 905	8 309	422 752	399 953	154 576	113 639	10 202	33 334	19 155	236 153	90 434	22 817
1993:													
January	21 534	16 597	791	31 718	30 165	11 628	9 194	848	3 343	1 515	17 379	6 435	1 809
February	21 547	16 465	779	32 100	30 507	11 857	8 803	845	3 067	1 480	17 321	6 670	1 816
March	21 058	16 155	765	31 606	30 084	11 724	8 380	836	2 878	1 413	17 406	6 572	1 802
April	21 692	16 651	772	31 984	30 379	11 756	8 919	858	3 094	1 509	17 564	6 626	1 797
May	21 858	16 829	786	31 923	30 295	11 653	8 949	848	3 117	1 523	17 673	6 596	1 794
June	21 882	16 900	771	31 975	30 334	11 461	8 889	850	3 075	1 543	17 827	6 658	1 797
July	22 157	17 121	779	32 101	30 455	11 466	8 966	867	3 146	1 506	17 743	6 716	1 792
August	22 221	17 219	780	32 090	30 442	11 244	8 942	851	3 059	1 549	18 017	6 600	1 785
September	22 356	17 394	753	32 076	30 443	11 259	9 013	857	3 096	1 545	18 230	6 649	1 781
October	22 612	17 611	721	32 377	30 708	11 478	9 048	871	3 065	1 531	18 088	6 624	1 786
November	22 618	17 515	723	32 446	30 772	11 476	9 040	855	3 050	1 518	18 069	6 658	1 782
December	22 571	17 648	679	32 604	30 927	11 369	8 952	882	2 958	1 549	18 084	6 803	1 789
1994:													
January	22 740	17 736	672	32 627	30 965	11 424	8 850	869	2 933	1 527	17 486	6 749	1 780
February	23 037	17 985	687	32 894	31 242	11 650	9 047	879	3 067	1 542	18 344	6 639	1 805
March	23 460	18 485	687	33 027	31 362	11 704	9 083	901	3 013	1 546	18 644	6 752	1 817
April	23 123	18 053	693	32 740	31 087	11 524	9 025	878	2 988	1 519	18 441	6 699	1 835
May	23 119	18 086	680	33 036	31 357	11 462	8 987	879	2 919	1 543	18 465	6 764	1 856
June	23 441	18 467	679	33 192	31 527	11 657	9 060	899	2 961	1 535	18 674	6 782	1 852
July	23 471	18 565	651	33 112	31 435	11 816	9 171	903	2 923	1 597	18 823	6 846	1 856
August	23 740	18 754	663	33 463	31 761	12 071	9 215	897	3 017	1 558	18 691	6 911	1 835
September	23 789	18 736	669	33 608	31 872	12 098	9 064	876	2 930	1 567	18 785	6 902	1 861
October	24 104	19 018	668	33 544	31 779	12 027	9 315	897	3 008	1 582	18 894	6 930	1 848
November	24 159	19 115	677	33 772	31 998	12 151	9 340	900	3 034	1 593	18 962	6 948	1 845
December	24 153	19 078	665	33 665	31 884	12 208	9 259	875	3 039	1 568	19 177	6 947	1 834
1995:													
January	24 967	19 450	731	34 243	32 478	12 208	9 354	889	3 043	1 544	19 127	7 069	1 820
February	24 134	19 039	615	33 928	32 159	12 199	9 000	868	2 946	1 453	18 981	7 083	1 805
March	24 486	19 394	603	33 753	31 998	12 230	9 178	854	2 991	1 590	19 189	7 029	1 835
April	24 612	19 425	629	33 961	32 180	12 181	9 070	845	2 936	1 578	19 304	7 080	1 811
May	24 761	19 465	640	34 100	32 356	12 330	9 196	838	2 968	1 593	19 408	7 128	1 810
June	25 056	19 779	640	34 034	32 274	12 430	9 246	840	2 953	1 613	19 358	7 126	1 822
July	25 262	20 114	636	34 113	32 311	12 262	9 197	841	2 947	1 588	19 460	7 077	1 791
August	25 039	19 811	624	34 230	32 419	12 236	9 113	851	2 896	1 557	19 525	7 131	1 828
September	25 313	20 050	658	34 204	32 368	12 126	9 353	857	2 919	1 561	19 506	7 224	1 852
October	25 003	19 793	649	34 382	32 545	11 986	9 117	852	2 856	1 553	19 451	7 202	1 857
November	25 207	20 185	653	34 435	32 586	11 967	9 321	872	2 839	1 595	19 384	7 293	1 873
December	25 260	20 021	667	34 722	32 853	12 151	9 308	852	2 858	1 568	19 442	7 280	1 878
1996:													
January	25 225	19 870	658	34 882	33 020	12 353	9 230	843	2 732	1 577	19 360	7 184	1 912
February	25 588	20 277	673	34 703	32 853	12 388	9 585	864	2 857	1 600	19 662	7 328	1 889
March	25 284	20 102	680	34 823	32 949	12 747	9 322	846	2 686	1 588	19 607	7 380	1 902
April	26 074	20 539	681	35 092	33 206	13 057	9 565	840	2 822	1 645	19 646	7 411	1 901
May	26 130	20 843	685	35 009	33 108	13 320	9 559	861	2 839	1 631	19 661	7 464	1 899
June	25 949	20 546	698	35 113	33 188	12 992	9 502	834	2 859	1 597	19 479	7 470	1 910
July	25 983	20 651	715	35 371	33 474	12 737	9 457	849	2 738	1 626	19 589	7 578	1 907
August	26 187	20 808	705	35 148	33 241	12 750	9 482	866	2 731	1 602	19 549	7 617	1 928
September	26 295	20 896	689	35 633	33 731	12 827	9 585	879	2 792	1 553	19 651	7 649	1 877
October	26 511	21 016	714	35 691	33 787	13 004	9 522	856	2 774	1 573	19 845	7 785	1 882
November	26 253	20 936	702	35 627	33 688	13 082	9 344	852	2 726	1 555	20 084	7 768	1 892
December	26 674	21 382	711	35 761	33 806	13 242	9 402	811	2 768	1 584	20 002	7 800	1 910

1. Annual data prior to 1993 are totals of the unadjusted monthly figures. 1993 and later years are totals of the adjusted figures.

RETAIL INVENTORIES[1]
(All retail stores—Book value, end of period, millions of dollars)

YEAR AND MONTH	Not seasonally adjusted										Seasonally adjusted		
	Total	Durable goods stores				Nondurable goods stores					Total	Durable goods stores	
		Total	Building materials[2]	Automotive dealers	Furniture and home furnishings and equipment	Total	General merchandise group stores		Food stores	Apparel and accessory stores		Total	Building materials[2]
							Total	Department stores					
1968	38 113	16 290	2 796	8 253	2 940	21 823	7 388	5 217	4 561	3 808	38 945	16 580	2 885
1969	41 610	17 877	2 807	9 193	3 171	23 733	8 004	5 556	4 972	4 249	42 517	18 206	2 900
1970	42 808	17 482	2 877	8 410	3 330	25 326	8 834	6 283	5 166	4 245	43 867	17 908	2 981
1971	48 895	21 273	3 547	11 136	3 546	27 622	10 013	6 997	5 685	4 618	50 063	21 687	3 683
1972	53 791	23 820	4 097	11 665	4 379	29 971	10 928	7 639	6 071	4 976	55 079	24 238	4 268
1973	61 835	28 065	4 641	14 270	4 776	33 770	12 173	8 349	7 050	5 530	63 237	28 418	4 844
1974	69 644	32 590	4 910	16 770	5 428	37 054	12 595	8 890	8 164	5 798	71 067	32 861	5 131
1975	70 273	33 130	5 239	16 478	5 711	37 143	12 426	9 070	8 190	5 758	71 744	33 356	5 474
1976	77 617	37 607	6 215	18 623	6 115	40 010	13 643	10 143	8 840	6 229	79 273	37 841	6 481
1977	87 411	42 742	7 179	22 142	6 511	44 669	15 821	12 067	9 474	7 340	89 444	43 071	7 502
1978	100 242	49 717	8 036	25 490	7 750	50 525	18 110	13 598	10 305	8 566	102 694	50 136	8 397
1979	108 408	53 630	8 604	27 256	8 533	54 778	19 139	14 353	11 456	9 143	111 098	54 108	8 981
1980	117 857	55 084	9 307	25 667	9 097	62 773	20 984	15 301	13 589	10 383	121 078	55 799	9 685
1981	129 073	60 261	9 793	28 137	9 687	68 812	23 509	17 544	14 866	11 598	132 719	61 050	10 180
1982	130 797	60 492	9 805	28 437	9 607	70 305	24 068	17 897	15 473	11 698	134 628	61 316	10 203
1983	143 513	67 921	11 224	33 030	11 105	75 592	25 996	19 331	16 488	12 658	147 833	68 856	11 716
1984	162 773	78 125	12 310	39 280	12 334	84 648	31 236	23 510	17 826	13 675	167 812	79 074	12 890
1985	176 941	87 630	13 054	46 399	13 693	89 311	31 517	23 330	19 480	14 575	181 881	88 315	13 683
1986	181 651	89 586	13 373	46 190	14 297	92 065	32 528	24 167	19 772	14 830	186 510	89 983	14 033
1987	203 210	105 654	14 184	57 800	15 005	97 556	34 874	26 032	20 019	15 880	207 836	105 481	14 868
1988	214 824	112 970	15 462	60 915	16 295	101 854	35 768	27 468	21 812	16 524	219 047	112 453	16 157
1989	233 143	122 220	16 437	66 436	17 297	110 923	39 487	30 916	23 821	17 713	237 234	121 347	17 122
1990	236 152	122 141	16 368	65 517	17 477	114 011	38 969	30 716	25 402	17 957	239 773	121 105	17 015
1991	239 478	119 977	16 099	63 134	17 737	119 501	42 168	33 257	26 045	18 500	243 275	119 039	16 735
1992	248 198	124 046	16 596	66 501	18 077	124 152	44 938	35 104	26 275	20 336	251 994	122 948	17 252
1993	263 297	134 506	17 787	71 716	20 127	128 791	48 371	37 983	26 624	20 849	267 497	133 624	18 451
1994	285 757	150 773	19 601	81 626	22 431	134 984	51 098	40 365	27 388	22 015	290 128	149 840	20 312
1995	299 071	160 609	20 334	88 585	23 238	138 462	53 878	42 868	28 131	21 795	303 750	159 767	21 050
1996	309 184	166 527	21 776	90 852	22 525	142 657	54 596	44 222	29 435	21 786	314 183	165 997	22 542
1993:													
January	246 341	122 392	17 008	65 508	17 419	123 949	45 760	35 930	25 828	20 218	254 040	123 714	17 534
February	251 403	125 587	17 695	68 092	16 897	125 816	47 193	37 201	25 517	21 299	256 313	125 402	17 677
March	259 196	129 258	18 344	70 247	17 443	129 938	50 055	39 392	25 843	22 079	259 665	127 293	17 707
April	260 206	129 423	18 345	69 848	17 554	130 783	50 800	39 772	25 924	22 284	260 223	127 412	17 639
May	258 315	129 274	18 546	69 078	17 590	129 041	50 013	39 427	25 676	21 898	260 025	127 420	17 713
June	255 917	128 204	18 176	68 230	17 942	127 713	48 747	38 326	25 688	21 676	260 643	128 002	17 767
July	253 889	123 493	17 854	63 054	18 185	130 396	49 803	39 153	25 433	23 094	260 425	127 447	17 836
August	253 921	121 287	17 556	60 680	18 567	132 634	51 284	40 359	25 205	23 785	259 874	126 916	17 769
September	262 624	124 293	17 484	61 429	19 606	138 331	54 895	43 103	25 686	24 632	261 516	128 069	17 914
October	278 958	131 983	17 873	65 130	20 941	146 975	60 013	46 898	26 686	25 744	263 138	129 795	18 201
November	286 457	137 523	17 866	69 228	21 941	148 934	61 379	48 018	27 102	25 789	265 831	131 801	18 343
December	263 297	134 506	17 787	71 716	20 127	128 791	48 371	37 983	26 624	20 849	267 497	133 624	18 451
1994:													
January	258 692	132 902	18 188	70 187	19 644	125 790	46 642	36 692	26 229	20 243	266 600	134 293	18 751
February	263 068	135 196	18 981	71 643	19 278	127 872	48 305	38 156	25 785	21 336	268 027	134 929	19 000
March	268 518	137 321	19 723	72 755	19 143	131 197	50 138	39 456	26 210	22 169	269 053	135 179	19 056
April	270 621	138 639	20 045	72 833	19 766	131 982	50 978	40 272	25 922	22 562	270 682	136 296	19 256
May	273 116	140 702	20 406	74 011	20 030	132 414	51 619	40 764	25 836	22 293	274 784	138 587	19 509
June	273 911	141 106	20 011	73 981	20 206	132 805	51 585	40 676	26 110	22 193	278 979	140 977	19 599
July	269 960	135 837	19 707	68 353	20 017	134 123	51 559	40 811	26 059	23 323	277 595	140 705	19 687
August	275 883	138 438	19 729	69 569	20 858	137 445	53 257	42 167	25 866	24 294	282 903	145 122	19 989
September	287 144	142 823	19 393	72 026	22 303	144 321	57 486	45 548	26 432	25 363	286 591	147 538	19 870
October	304 049	150 082	19 723	74 560	24 634	153 967	62 782	49 605	27 415	27 060	286 993	147 578	20 023
November	310 961	155 380	19 785	78 521	25 429	155 581	64 125	50 653	27 916	27 087	288 450	148 729	20 251
December	285 757	150 773	19 601	81 626	22 431	134 984	51 098	40 365	27 388	22 015	290 128	149 840	20 312
1995:													
January	285 422	151 426	19 831	82 716	21 631	133 996	51 284	40 482	26 931	21 609	293 944	152 744	20 465
February	290 404	154 338	20 117	85 353	21 323	136 066	53 165	42 136	26 522	22 867	295 154	153 450	20 178
March	297 481	158 547	21 021	88 307	21 701	138 934	54 540	42 895	26 676	24 027	297 790	155 835	20 330
April	300 569	161 150	21 444	89 213	21 881	139 419	54 824	43 189	26 552	24 320	300 260	158 076	20 589
May	299 657	160 665	21 421	88 596	21 818	138 992	54 767	43 277	26 431	23 921	301 137	158 131	20 499
June	296 254	158 082	20 860	86 500	22 028	138 172	54 311	42 856	26 529	23 298	301 523	157 889	20 431
July	291 012	150 828	20 579	79 356	21 736	140 184	55 135	43 617	26 582	24 296	300 022	156 825	20 558
August	295 071	151 080	20 605	77 221	22 845	143 991	56 890	45 080	26 569	25 316	302 750	158 520	20 876
September	303 850	154 064	20 738	77 865	24 100	149 786	60 768	48 253	27 031	26 041	303 368	159 205	21 270
October	323 454	163 184	21 060	82 964	25 804	160 270	66 776	53 089	28 024	27 744	305 494	160 613	21 337
November	331 164	169 318	20 748	87 413	26 967	161 846	68 403	54 484	28 524	27 614	307 117	162 107	21 193
December	299 071	160 609	20 334	88 585	23 238	138 462	53 878	42 868	28 131	21 795	303 750	159 767	21 050
1996:													
January	296 503	159 430	20 435	88 524	22 264	137 073	53 513	42 580	27 569	21 324	305 094	160 493	21 089
February	300 875	161 920	21 070	89 899	22 338	138 955	54 640	43 868	27 224	22 450	305 336	160 667	21 176
March	302 771	161 773	22 100	87 905	22 488	140 998	56 102	45 081	27 416	23 357	303 737	159 306	21 394
April	304 538	162 959	22 399	87 183	23 013	141 579	56 541	45 488	27 519	22 875	304 635	159 966	21 455
May	303 736	163 110	22 478	87 326	22 929	140 626	56 156	45 158	27 382	22 341	305 592	160 893	21 551
June	300 383	161 280	22 365	86 317	22 438	139 103	55 332	44 452	27 262	22 130	306 177	161 528	21 948
July	300 137	157 004	22 045	81 286	22 582	143 133	56 792	45 599	27 471	23 449	309 786	163 433	22 045
August	303 023	157 087	21 550	80 468	23 125	145 936	58 718	47 359	27 374	24 246	311 112	164 862	21 834
September	313 263	161 115	21 547	82 303	24 173	152 148	62 677	50 463	27 932	24 946	312 969	166 530	22 077
October	333 919	171 129	21 882	86 430	26 261	162 790	68 354	55 131	29 284	26 801	315 281	168 146	22 170
November	338 080	173 277	21 835	88 245	26 157	164 803	69 654	56 509	30 002	27 240	313 490	165 865	22 281
December	309 184	166 527	21 776	90 852	22 525	142 657	54 596	44 222	29 435	21 786	314 183	165 997	22 542

1. Data prior to 1980 are not comparable to subsequent periods due to change in inventory valuation methods; see NOTES.

	RETAIL INVENTORIES [1]—Continued (All retail stores—Book value, end of period, millions of dollars)							MERCHANT WHOLESALERS—SALES AND INVENTORIES (Millions of dollars, not seasonally adjusted)					
	Seasonally adjusted—Continued							Sales			Inventories (Book value, end of period)		
	Durable goods stores—Continued		Nondurable goods stores										
YEAR AND MONTH	Automotive dealers	Furniture and home furnishings and equipment	Total	General merchandise group stores		Food stores	Apparel and accessory stores	Total	Durable goods establishments	Nondurable goods establishments	Total	Durable goods establishments	Nondurable goods establishments
				Total	Department stores								
1968	8 404	2 988	22 365	7 875	5 556	4 511	3 967	252 145	116 297	135 848	....	....	....
1969	9 381	3 216	24 311	8 538	5 923	4 908	4 421	273 814	128 314	145 500	....	....	....
1970	8 679	3 374	25 959	9 438	6 713	5 095	4 422	289 999	133 778	156 221	....	....	....
1971	11 363	3 585	28 376	10 728	7 499	5 601	4 820	317 899	147 761	170 138	....	....	....
1972	11 855	4 414	30 841	11 743	8 214	5 981	5 200	358 388	168 879	189 509	....	....	....
1973	14 356	4 800	34 819	13 137	9 016	6 946	5 791	457 378	208 554	248 824	....	....	....
1974	16 737	5 439	38 206	13 647	9 632	8 043	6 071	575 786	255 863	319 923	....	....	....
1975	16 347	5 717	38 388	13 521	9 848	8 069	6 029	559 606	235 723	323 883	....	....	....
1976	18 420	6 115	41 432	14 886	11 037	8 709	6 516	608 381	263 605	344 776	....	....	....
1977	21 879	6 610	46 373	17 307	13 145	9 362	7 646	673 633	304 721	368 912	....	....	....
1978	25 188	7 876	52 558	19 853	14 829	10 193	8 914	796 961	372 176	424 785	....	....	....
1979	26 933	8 681	56 990	21 033	15 686	11 343	9 514	948 614	436 254	512 360	....	....	....
1980	25 553	9 207	65 279	23 171	16 814	13 390	10 929	1 117 187	486 509	630 678	124 015	78 849	45 166
1981	28 026	9 795	71 669	25 951	19 279	14 649	12 234	1 214 156	525 607	688 549	130 709	85 371	45 338
1982	28 352	9 714	73 312	26 548	19 645	15 248	12 392	1 142 535	480 318	662 217	128 514	84 806	43 708
1983	32 919	11 217	78 977	28 651	21 196	16 282	13 466	1 190 705	523 080	667 625	131 306	84 709	46 597
1984	39 004	12 433	88 738	34 392	25 750	17 624	14 641	1 346 392	622 361	724 031	143 458	94 895	48 563
1985	45 798	13 762	93 566	34 683	25 525	19 283	15 689	1 361 507	651 864	709 643	148 403	96 659	51 744
1986	45 246	14 340	96 527	35 743	26 412	19 612	16 067	1 379 514	681 691	697 823	154 081	101 369	52 712
1987	56 161	15 050	102 355	38 285	28 450	19 898	17 280	1 475 613	730 592	745 021	164 310	106 820	57 490
1988	58 907	16 311	106 594	39 179	29 987	21 601	18 079	1 614 249	801 751	812 498	179 828	115 613	64 215
1989	64 072	17 280	115 887	43 107	33 678	23 543	19 422	1 725 123	851 550	873 573	187 897	120 701	67 196
1990	63 053	17 407	118 668	42 423	33 423	25 039	19 690	1 794 072	880 767	913 305	196 881	124 839	72 042
1991	60 774	17 614	124 236	45 775	36 110	25 606	20 263	1 779 673	860 138	919 535	201 777	125 921	75 856
1992	64 016	17 880	129 046	48 671	38 074	25 764	22 225	1 849 798	908 917	940 881	209 675	130 044	79 631
1993	69 224	19 928	133 873	52 265	41 107	26 034	22 811	1 940 175	986 912	953 263	218 265	134 658	83 607
1994	78 875	22 231	140 288	55 095	43 591	26 735	24 113	2 075 678	1 082 312	993 366	236 560	147 398	89 162
1995	85 754	23 076	143 983	58 095	46 294	27 433	23 898	2 265 732	1 179 197	1 086 535	254 435	158 360	96 075
1996	88 051	22 413	148 186	58 823	47 704	28 701	23 914	2 420 679	1 245 781	1 174 898	256 341	159 406	96 935
1993:													
January	64 575	17 866	130 326	49 640	38 885	25 748	22 615	147 547	72 468	75 079	213 462	131 407	82 055
February	65 955	17 712	130 911	50 156	39 366	25 844	22 467	145 111	72 743	72 368	211 809	131 837	79 972
March	67 341	17 927	132 372	51 271	40 278	25 969	22 599	167 451	84 571	82 880	211 480	132 531	78 949
April	67 436	18 004	132 811	51 648	40 337	26 140	22 578	162 443	81 851	80 592	212 646	133 993	78 653
May	66 947	18 134	132 605	51 704	40 688	25 919	22 622	161 478	79 961	81 517	209 654	133 675	75 979
June	67 238	18 554	132 641	51 415	40 514	25 928	22 793	166 000	84 989	81 011	208 391	132 474	75 917
July	66 096	18 943	132 978	51 435	40 489	25 836	23 002	160 496	82 490	78 006	209 826	134 361	75 465
August	65 916	18 965	132 958	51 747	40 767	25 858	22 870	167 047	86 481	80 566	209 101	134 447	74 654
September	66 192	19 109	133 447	51 897	40 856	25 971	23 042	166 760	86 527	80 233	210 498	133 918	76 580
October	67 176	19 089	133 343	52 003	40 745	25 976	22 884	168 634	87 641	80 993	215 339	134 657	80 682
November	68 480	19 520	134 030	52 500	41 041	25 949	22 883	164 146	83 901	80 245	217 379	134 514	82 865
December	69 224	19 928	133 873	52 265	41 107	26 034	22 811	163 062	83 289	79 773	218 265	134 658	83 607
1994:													
January	68 994	20 189	132 307	50 615	39 753	26 126	22 669	151 037	75 911	75 126	221 766	136 363	85 403
February	69 131	20 229	133 098	51 325	40 377	26 095	22 578	150 542	76 951	73 591	222 060	137 724	84 336
March	69 505	19 735	133 874	51 521	40 509	26 341	22 668	180 202	93 880	86 322	218 864	136 266	82 598
April	70 016	20 335	134 386	52 044	41 052	26 143	22 906	165 553	85 472	80 081	220 364	138 890	81 474
May	71 518	20 714	136 197	53 340	42 068	26 164	23 078	171 651	88 599	83 052	221 131	141 945	79 186
June	72 819	20 961	138 002	54 351	42 952	26 406	23 361	177 210	92 737	84 473	219 219	140 939	78 280
July	72 146	20 916	136 890	53 327	42 247	26 498	23 230	165 561	86 027	79 534	223 445	144 922	78 523
August	75 847	21 284	137 781	53 741	42 550	26 532	23 405	187 126	99 134	87 992	221 712	143 962	77 750
September	77 909	21 696	139 053	54 312	43 092	26 679	23 726	180 723	96 754	83 969	223 545	143 936	79 609
October	77 074	22 354	139 415	54 371	43 060	26 660	23 947	184 995	98 271	86 724	232 670	146 753	85 917
November	77 810	22 464	139 721	54 687	43 182	26 700	23 928	180 204	94 535	85 669	235 176	146 980	88 196
December	78 875	22 231	140 288	55 095	43 591	26 735	24 113	180 874	94 041	86 833	236 560	147 398	89 162
1995:													
January	81 076	22 277	141 200	55 734	43 954	26 803	24 198	173 188	88 671	84 517	242 583	150 441	92 142
February	81 987	22 351	141 704	56 439	44 541	26 822	24 249	168 934	87 305	81 629	243 012	152 760	90 252
March	84 286	22 465	141 955	56 149	44 131	26 804	24 542	195 748	103 173	92 575	243 422	153 693	89 729
April	85 594	22 558	142 184	56 119	44 161	26 772	24 715	178 737	91 773	86 964	247 000	156 382	90 618
May	85 514	22 609	143 006	56 569	44 662	26 822	24 814	195 310	100 899	94 411	244 623	157 348	87 275
June	85 046	22 922	143 634	57 211	45 254	26 856	24 550	195 978	102 667	93 311	244 162	156 917	87 245
July	84 091	22 784	143 197	57 098	45 199	27 059	24 199	181 185	93 010	88 175	248 561	159 765	88 796
August	84 279	23 287	144 230	57 339	45 398	27 252	24 413	200 611	104 998	95 613	245 083	158 215	86 868
September	84 318	23 375	144 163	57 392	45 608	27 273	24 360	190 321	101 227	89 094	246 307	157 514	88 793
October	85 867	23 331	144 881	57 832	46 084	27 250	24 466	202 470	106 641	95 829	254 744	159 334	95 410
November	86 778	23 718	145 010	58 196	46 330	27 284	24 308	193 706	100 471	93 235	255 500	159 413	96 087
December	85 754	23 076	143 983	58 095	46 294	27 433	23 898	189 544	98 362	91 182	254 435	158 360	96 075
1996:													
January	86 452	22 976	144 601	58 256	46 333	27 440	23 906	187 850	94 766	93 084	259 948	161 153	98 795
February	86 044	23 391	144 669	57 931	46 323	27 536	23 832	185 873	95 179	90 694	257 779	161 412	96 367
March	83 940	23 376	144 431	57 932	46 523	27 569	23 907	199 654	104 758	94 896	254 869	160 165	94 704
April	83 666	23 798	144 669	58 061	46 654	27 798	23 200	201 259	102 990	98 269	259 534	162 920	96 614
May	84 577	23 736	144 699	58 096	46 699	27 814	23 151	207 431	105 911	101 520	255 346	162 273	93 073
June	85 146	23 373	144 649	58 309	46 940	27 653	23 295	196 669	102 546	94 123	255 303	160 718	91 585
July	86 350	23 696	146 353	58 877	47 302	27 964	23 379	205 016	104 395	100 621	255 298	163 449	91 849
August	87 883	23 549	146 250	59 167	47 693	28 085	23 403	208 264	106 886	101 378	251 327	162 167	89 160
September	89 119	23 423	146 439	59 164	47 652	28 182	23 336	202 502	106 447	96 055	249 879	161 013	88 866
October	89 363	23 680	147 135	59 185	47 815	28 482	23 592	222 157	115 259	106 898	257 523	161 276	96 247
November	87 695	22 965	147 625	59 208	48 011	28 677	23 937	200 745	103 239	97 506	258 000	161 049	96 951
December	88 051	22 413	148 186	58 823	47 704	28 701	23 914	203 259	103 405	99 854	256 341	159 406	96 935

1. Data prior to 1980 are not comparable to subsequent periods due to change in inventory valuation methods; see NOTES.

Finance, Insurance, Real Estate, and Private Services

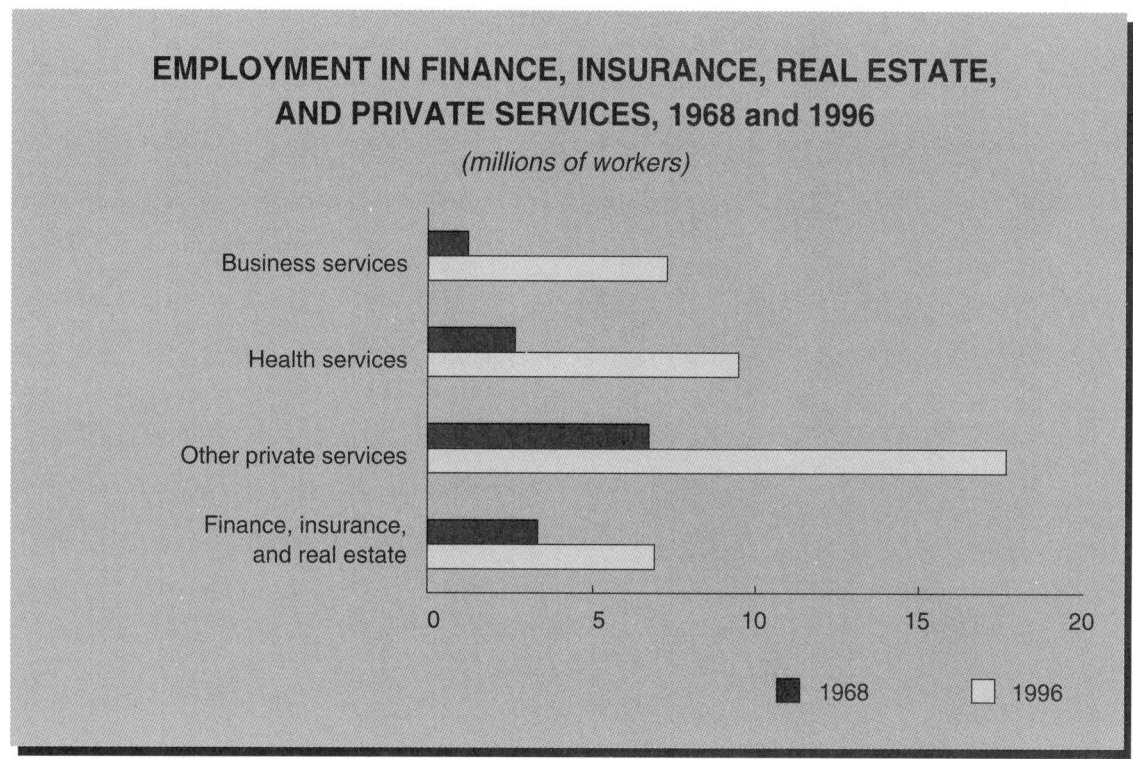

EMPLOYMENT IN FINANCE, INSURANCE, REAL ESTATE, AND PRIVATE SERVICES, 1968 and 1996

(millions of workers)

Employment in services increased rapidly throughout the 1968-1996 period, with business and health services showing especially rapid growth. Jobs in business services increased sixfold, and those in health services more than tripled. Employment in other private services grew less dramatically, but even so increased by over 160 percent. Employment in finance, insurance, and real estate more than doubled.

In 1996, private services (including finance, insurance, and real estate) provided over one-third of all U.S.

nonfarm payroll jobs, compared with only 20 percent in 1968.

The industry groups shown here—finance, insurance, real estate, and private services—constitute only part of the broader "service-producing" category, which also includes transportation, communications, and utilities; wholesale and retail trade; and government. In 1968, this broad service-producing category already provided 65 percent of all nonfarm payroll jobs. By 1996 the service producing share had reached 80 percent.

	FINANCE, INSURANCE, AND REAL ESTATE—EMPLOYMENT, HOURS, AND EARNINGS										
	Payroll employment (Thousands, seasonally adjusted)					Production and nonsupervisory workers					
YEAR AND MONTH						Employ-ment (Thou-sands, season-ally ad-justed)	Weekly hours worked		Average earnings (Dollars, not seasonally adjusted)			
							Average hours, not sea-sonally adjusted	Aggregate hours index (1982=100, seasonally adjusted)	Hourly		Weekly	
	Total	Finance		Insur-ance	Real estate				Total	Deposi-tory insti-tutions	Total	Deposi-tory insti-tutions
		Total	Deposi-tory in-stitutions									
1968	3 337	....	....	....	....	2 651	37.0	67.8	2.75	....	101.75	....
1969	3 512	....	....	....	....	2 797	37.1	71.6	2.93	....	108.70	....
1970	3 645	....	....	....	....	2 879	36.7	73.0	3.07	....	112.67	....
1971	3 772	....	....	....	....	2 936	36.6	74.3	3.22	....	117.85	....
1972	3 908	1 778	....	1 373	756	3 024	36.6	76.5	3.36	....	122.98	....
1973	4 046	1 866	....	1 401	778	3 121	36.6	78.9	3.53	....	129.20	....
1974	4 148	1 936	....	1 434	778	3 169	36.5	79.8	3.77	....	137.61	....
1975	4 165	1 964	....	1 442	760	3 173	36.5	79.9	4.06	....	148.19	....
1976	4 271	2 026	....	1 468	776	3 243	36.4	81.5	4.27	....	155.43	....
1977	4 467	2 113	....	1 528	826	3 397	36.4	85.4	4.54	....	165.26	....
1978	4 724	2 233	....	1 591	900	3 593	36.4	90.3	4.89	....	178.00	....
1979	4 975	2 369	....	1 643	963	3 776	36.2	94.4	5.27	....	190.77	....
1980	5 160	2 483	....	1 688	989	3 907	36.2	97.8	5.79	....	209.60	....
1981	5 298	2 593	....	1 713	992	3 999	36.3	105.5	6.31	....	229.05	....
1982	5 340	2 647	....	1 723	970	3 996	36.2	100.0	6.78	....	245.44	....
1983	5 466	2 741	....	1 728	997	4 066	36.2	101.6	7.29	....	263.90	....
1984	5 684	2 852	....	1 765	1 067	4 226	36.5	106.4	7.63	....	278.50	....
1985	5 948	2 974	....	1 840	1 135	4 410	36.4	110.9	7.94	....	289.02	....
1986	6 273	3 145	....	1 944	1 184	4 637	36.4	116.7	8.36	....	304.30	....
1987	6 533	3 264	....	2 027	1 242	4 797	36.3	120.1	8.73	....	316.90	....
1988	6 630	3 274	2 255	2 075	1 280	4 811	35.9	119.2	9.06	7.77	325.25	277.39
1989	6 668	3 283	2 273	2 090	1 296	4 829	35.8	119.5	9.53	8.13	341.17	289.43
1990	6 709	3 268	2 251	2 126	1 315	4 860	35.8	120.2	9.97	8.43	356.93	300.11
1991	6 646	3 187	2 164	2 161	1 299	4 795	35.7	118.3	10.39	8.70	370.92	307.98
1992	6 602	3 160	2 096	2 152	1 290	4 772	35.8	118.1	10.82	8.90	387.36	315.06
1993	6 757	3 238	2 089	2 197	1 322	4 908	35.8	121.2	11.35	9.10	406.33	320.32
1994	6 896	3 299	2 066	2 236	1 361	5 018	35.8	124.0	11.83	9.37	423.51	329.82
1995	6 806	3 231	2 025	2 225	1 351	4 961	35.9	122.9	12.32	9.62	442.29	341.51
1996	6 899	3 301	2 024	2 217	1 381	5 034	35.9	124.8	12.79	9.91	459.16	348.83
1993:												
January	6 658	3 189	2 089	2 166	1 303	4 830	35.7	118.4	11.14	9.02	397.70	317.50
February	6 670	3 192	2 088	2 170	1 308	4 835	35.7	118.9	11.21	9.10	400.20	319.41
March	6 673	3 195	2 086	2 173	1 305	4 841	35.5	118.7	11.19	9.07	397.25	314.73
April	6 695	3 206	2 087	2 178	1 311	4 850	35.7	119.2	11.23	9.07	400.91	318.36
May	6 719	3 217	2 089	2 187	1 315	4 870	36.2	121.7	11.36	9.17	411.23	325.54
June	6 741	3 228	2 089	2 195	1 318	4 889	35.6	120.5	11.23	9.03	399.79	316.05
July	6 765	3 242	2 093	2 201	1 322	4 912	35.6	121.1	11.27	9.06	401.21	318.91
August	6 782	3 253	2 091	2 207	1 322	4 930	36.4	124.3	11.39	9.08	414.60	327.79
September	6 808	3 265	2 090	2 214	1 329	4 952	35.6	122.1	11.41	9.09	406.20	318.15
October	6 832	3 279	2 090	2 217	1 336	4 974	35.7	122.3	11.52	9.14	411.26	319.90
November	6 857	3 290	2 089	2 225	1 342	4 997	35.7	123.5	11.57	9.16	413.05	319.68
December	6 877	3 300	2 087	2 229	1 348	5 011	35.7	123.2	11.65	9.18	415.91	321.30
1994:												
January	6 893	3 307	2 083	2 232	1 354	5 021	36.4	125.5	11.79	9.30	429.16	331.08
February	6 908	3 315	2 080	2 235	1 358	5 030	35.8	124.0	11.77	9.35	421.37	326.32
March	6 927	3 324	2 077	2 239	1 364	5 045	35.7	124.4	11.75	9.30	419.48	324.57
April	6 925	3 322	2 074	2 240	1 363	5 040	35.7	123.9	11.81	9.32	421.62	328.06
May	6 917	3 316	2 071	2 238	1 363	5 031	36.1	125.4	11.84	9.38	427.42	333.93
June	6 915	3 313	2 068	2 238	1 364	5 033	35.6	124.1	11.67	9.26	415.45	325.03
July	6 907	3 306	2 066	2 237	1 364	5 028	35.7	124.0	11.72	9.32	418.40	328.06
August	6 900	3 298	2 064	2 236	1 366	5 022	35.5	123.5	11.73	9.33	416.42	326.55
September	6 886	3 288	2 059	2 234	1 364	5 010	35.4	123.2	11.85	9.38	419.49	327.36
October	6 868	3 276	2 055	2 234	1 358	4 996	36.2	124.2	12.02	9.48	435.12	338.44
November	6 854	3 265	2 050	2 231	1 358	4 985	35.5	122.9	11.98	9.47	425.29	332.40
December	6 836	3 255	2 046	2 226	1 355	4 973	35.7	122.3	12.05	9.49	430.19	335.00
1995:												
January	6 823	3 244	2 040	2 228	1 351	4 964	36.3	123.8	12.17	9.58	441.77	347.75
February	6 812	3 235	2 035	2 228	1 349	4 957	35.8	122.2	12.20	9.59	436.76	338.53
March	6 809	3 232	2 034	2 233	1 344	4 955	35.5	121.8	12.21	9.61	433.46	336.35
April	6 801	3 225	2 032	2 232	1 344	4 951	36.3	123.8	12.32	9.62	447.22	348.24
May	6 792	3 222	2 027	2 226	1 344	4 948	35.4	121.0	12.24	9.60	433.30	335.04
June	6 788	3 217	2 022	2 224	1 347	4 953	35.6	122.5	12.19	9.54	433.96	336.76
July	6 793	3 222	2 022	2 221	1 350	4 954	36.3	124.2	12.32	9.61	447.22	347.88
August	6 801	3 225	2 020	2 223	1 353	4 961	35.6	122.7	12.27	9.56	436.81	337.47
September	6 804	3 228	2 019	2 221	1 355	4 966	35.7	123.1	12.39	9.63	442.32	338.98
October	6 812	3 233	2 017	2 222	1 357	4 971	36.4	123.9	12.52	9.70	455.73	350.17
November	6 819	3 240	2 018	2 219	1 360	4 976	35.7	123.0	12.48	9.68	445.54	338.80
December	6 828	3 248	2 019	2 216	1 364	4 981	35.7	122.8	12.56	9.73	448.39	340.55
1996:												
January	6 831	3 257	2 020	2 217	1 357	4 980	35.5	121.4	12.61	9.77	447.66	340.00
February	6 848	3 265	2 020	2 215	1 368	4 994	35.7	123.1	12.69	9.84	453.03	344.40
March	6 856	3 269	2 018	2 215	1 372	5 002	35.7	123.7	12.73	9.86	454.46	344.11
April	6 867	3 279	2 019	2 214	1 374	5 014	35.6	122.9	12.75	9.84	453.90	343.42
May	6 888	3 291	2 021	2 218	1 379	5 028	35.6	123.6	12.74	9.86	453.54	343.13
June	6 897	3 298	2 022	2 219	1 380	5 035	36.5	127.6	12.75	9.88	465.38	357.66
July	6 910	3 305	2 023	2 220	1 385	5 044	35.6	124.0	12.69	9.84	451.76	345.38
August	6 917	3 313	2 022	2 217	1 387	5 049	35.7	125.2	12.71	9.88	453.75	347.78
September	6 925	3 317	2 023	2 220	1 388	5 055	36.5	128.1	12.89	10.01	470.49	361.36
October	6 941	3 330	2 028	2 219	1 392	5 066	35.7	123.8	12.87	9.98	459.46	347.30
November	6 949	3 334	2 029	2 220	1 395	5 069	35.8	126.0	12.97	10.06	464.33	352.10
December	6 962	3 343	2 030	2 221	1 398	5 077	36.7	128.3	13.02	10.11	477.83	364.97

	Total		By industry group									
						Business services						
YEAR AND MONTH	All workers	Production and nonsupervisory workers	Agricultural services	Hotels and other lodging places	Personal services	Total	Personnel supply services	Computer and data processing	Auto repair services and parking	Miscellaneous repair services	Motion pictures	Amusement and recreation
1968	10 567	9 727	....	....	937	1 210	....	....	....	174	....	....
1969	11 169	10 205	....	....	931	1 329	....	....	....	184	....	....
1970	11 548	10 481	....	....	898	1 397	....	....	....	189	....	....
1971	11 797	10 655	....	....	848	1 402	....	....	....	193	....	....
1972	12 276	11 059	....	813	828	1 491	214	107	399	199	....	....
1973	12 857	11 606	....	854	823	1 610	247	120	422	205	....	....
1974	13 441	12 100	....	878	807	1 686	257	135	430	217	....	....
1975	13 892	12 479	....	898	782	1 697	242	143	439	218	....	....
1976	14 551	13 043	184	929	790	1 806	293	159	466	227	....	....
1977	15 302	13 683	197	956	806	1 958	357	187	498	241	....	....
1978	16 252	14 476	217	988	827	2 181	438	224	549	261	....	....
1979	17 112	15 193	234	1 060	821	2 410	508	271	575	282	....	....
1980	17 890	15 921	246	1 076	818	2 564	543	304	571	289	....	....
1981	18 615	16 562	258	1 119	828	2 700	585	337	574	293	....	....
1982	19 021	16 867	267	1 133	844	2 722	541	365	589	287	....	....
1983	19 664	17 429	287	1 172	869	2 948	619	416	619	287	....	....
1984	20 746	18 284	328	1 263	918	3 353	797	474	682	310	....	....
1985	21 927	19 305	361	1 331	957	3 679	891	542	730	319	....	....
1986	22 957	20 163	389	1 378	991	3 957	990	588	762	322	....	....
1987	24 110	21 132	411	1 464	1 027	4 278	1 177	629	794	321	....	....
1988	25 504	22 323	447	1 540	1 056	4 638	1 350	673	834	350	341	977
1989	26 907	23 532	465	1 596	1 086	4 941	1 455	736	884	374	375	1 033
1990	27 934	24 387	490	1 631	1 104	5 139	1 535	772	914	374	408	1 076
1991	28 336	24 712	487	1 589	1 112	5 086	1 485	797	882	341	411	1 122
1992	29 052	25 347	490	1 576	1 116	5 315	1 629	836	881	347	401	1 188
1993	30 197	26 380	519	1 596	1 137	5 735	1 906	893	925	349	412	1 258
1994	31 579	27 632	564	1 631	1 140	6 281	2 272	959	968	338	441	1 334
1995	33 117	28 979	582	1 668	1 163	6 812	2 476	1 090	1 020	359	488	1 417
1996	34 377	30 073	625	1 716	1 184	7 254	2 646	1 208	1 084	375	522	1 466
1993:												
January	29 644	25 890	497	1 580	1 132	5 540	1 756	869	905	356	413	1 224
February	29 769	26 003	508	1 582	1 143	5 578	1 785	875	912	357	409	1 228
March	29 805	26 039	499	1 580	1 135	5 608	1 807	879	916	357	402	1 226
April	29 960	26 172	509	1 584	1 135	5 652	1 842	883	921	356	405	1 251
May	30 061	26 267	513	1 594	1 134	5 687	1 868	889	924	353	406	1 253
June	30 154	26 340	516	1 599	1 137	5 715	1 890	891	926	351	408	1 246
July	30 251	26 425	517	1 600	1 138	5 751	1 921	897	928	347	408	1 259
August	30 342	26 503	521	1 599	1 138	5 774	1 941	900	930	345	414	1 269
September	30 407	26 577	529	1 604	1 132	5 790	1 947	902	933	343	416	1 278
October	30 537	26 676	532	1 615	1 139	5 866	2 016	906	930	342	419	1 276
November	30 648	26 771	541	1 615	1 145	5 898	2 019	909	935	339	418	1 285
December	30 727	26 851	544	1 616	1 148	5 916	2 042	913	939	337	425	1 295
1994:												
January	30 805	26 926	548	1 617	1 152	5 952	2 059	920	940	336	427	1 297
February	30 885	27 005	544	1 614	1 142	6 005	2 114	921	945	335	432	1 301
March	31 035	27 174	542	1 624	1 140	6 072	2 163	927	952	330	435	1 313
April	31 227	27 327	552	1 629	1 144	6 150	2 212	935	959	332	438	1 322
May	31 346	27 438	562	1 630	1 134	6 185	2 227	942	961	335	436	1 333
June	31 500	27 564	563	1 631	1 133	6 254	2 266	952	967	337	441	1 345
July	31 682	27 717	567	1 637	1 135	6 318	2 303	959	969	339	436	1 347
August	31 809	27 827	570	1 638	1 139	6 366	2 321	969	976	340	446	1 346
September	31 934	27 949	574	1 638	1 143	6 410	2 332	980	982	341	442	1 343
October	32 066	28 066	575	1 634	1 144	6 468	2 368	990	985	343	451	1 351
November	32 237	28 205	581	1 636	1 146	6 546	2 400	1 001	991	345	458	1 353
December	32 348	28 319	582	1 646	1 146	6 564	2 413	1 010	994	348	460	1 358
1995:												
January	32 482	28 417	567	1 652	1 154	6 615	2 436	1 020	1 000	351	465	1 360
February	32 646	28 572	570	1 657	1 157	6 658	2 459	1 033	1 001	356	477	1 380
March	32 793	28 692	579	1 661	1 163	6 689	2 455	1 045	1 006	356	476	1 414
April	32 879	28 774	584	1 659	1 161	6 712	2 450	1 056	1 009	357	482	1 416
May	32 937	28 824	574	1 662	1 165	6 738	2 445	1 074	1 012	357	486	1 414
June	33 041	28 897	576	1 667	1 166	6 769	2 440	1 086	1 017	358	486	1 419
July	33 108	28 972	581	1 671	1 167	6 784	2 442	1 097	1 021	360	490	1 420
August	33 280	29 115	583	1 677	1 165	6 858	2 468	1 111	1 025	361	492	1 426
September	33 404	29 255	585	1 678	1 163	6 917	2 497	1 123	1 027	362	497	1 438
October	33 487	29 316	590	1 677	1 164	6 951	2 510	1 134	1 035	362	501	1 437
November	33 589	29 394	589	1 674	1 162	7 000	2 533	1 145	1 040	365	504	1 430
December	33 703	29 504	598	1 677	1 167	7 040	2 548	1 160	1 047	367	504	1 424
1996:												
January	33 698	29 445	600	1 683	1 170	6 993	2 486	1 164	1 052	367	509	1 433
February	33 938	29 703	611	1 691	1 174	7 109	2 569	1 174	1 059	370	509	1 450
March	34 064	29 813	614	1 701	1 176	7 141	2 582	1 183	1 066	372	517	1 455
April	34 150	29 883	617	1 709	1 179	7 173	2 592	1 189	1 070	373	516	1 460
May	34 277	29 999	618	1 715	1 182	7 216	2 634	1 195	1 075	375	523	1 465
June	34 390	30 095	625	1 731	1 184	7 252	2 663	1 199	1 079	375	524	1 466
July	34 465	30 178	628	1 718	1 184	7 288	2 683	1 209	1 087	375	527	1 472
August	34 560	30 247	631	1 718	1 187	7 330	2 699	1 218	1 094	376	526	1 474
September	34 621	30 282	630	1 722	1 189	7 354	2 706	1 226	1 097	377	530	1 471
October	34 717	30 369	635	1 726	1 193	7 379	2 711	1 236	1 104	376	529	1 478
November	34 800	30 421	639	1 731	1 194	7 398	2 706	1 246	1 107	380	528	1 481
December	34 884	30 491	638	1 738	1 194	7 437	2 721	1 256	1 112	380	530	1 483

								Health services			

PRIVATE SERVICES—EMPLOYMENT—Continued
(Thousands, seasonally adjusted)

By industry group—Continued

YEAR AND MONTH	Legal services	Edu-cational services	Social services	Museums, botanical gardens, and zoos	Member-ship orga-nizations	Engineer-ing and manage-ment	Total	Hospitals	Offices and clin-ics of medical doctors	Nursing and per-sonal care facili-ties	Home health care serv-ices
1968	....	891	....	....	....	....	2 639	1 654	....	....	....
1969	....	930	....	....	....	....	2 862	1 770	....	....	....
1970	....	940	....	....	....	....	3 053	1 863	....	....	....
1971	....	948	....	....	....	....	3 239	1 935	....	....	....
1972	271	958	553	....	1 403	....	3 412	1 980	467	591	....
1973	296	975	552	....	1 410	....	3 641	2 051	519	659	....
1974	326	990	625	....	1 438	....	3 887	2 160	567	708	....
1975	341	1 001	690	....	1 452	....	4 134	2 274	608	759	....
1976	364	1 013	763	....	1 487	....	4 350	2 363	644	809	....
1977	394	1 031	855	....	1 495	....	4 584	2 465	681	860	....
1978	427	1 062	991	....	1 502	....	4 792	2 538	720	911	....
1979	460	1 090	1 081	....	1 516	....	4 993	2 608	761	951	....
1980	498	1 138	1 134	....	1 539	....	5 278	2 750	802	997	....
1981	532	1 179	1 149	....	1 527	....	5 562	2 904	845	1 029	....
1982	565	1 199	1 149	....	1 526	....	5 811	3 014	887	1 067	....
1983	602	1 225	1 188	....	1 510	....	5 986	3 037	934	1 106	....
1984	645	1 270	1 222	....	1 504	....	6 118	3 004	977	1 147	....
1985	692	1 359	1 325	....	1 517	....	6 293	2 997	1 028	1 198	....
1986	747	1 421	1 406	....	1 536	....	6 528	3 037	1 081	1 245	....
1987	801	1 449	1 454	....	1 614	....	6 794	3 142	1 139	1 283	....
1988	845	1 567	1 552	58	1 740	2 230	7 105	3 294	1 200	1 311	216
1989	880	1 647	1 644	62	1 836	2 389	7 463	3 439	1 268	1 356	244
1990	908	1 661	1 734	66	1 946	2 478	7 814	3 549	1 338	1 415	291
1991	912	1 710	1 845	69	1 982	2 433	8 183	3 655	1 405	1 493	345
1992	914	1 678	1 959	73	1 973	2 471	8 490	3 750	1 463	1 533	398
1993	924	1 711	2 070	76	2 035	2 521	8 756	3 779	1 506	1 585	469
1994	924	1 850	2 200	79	2 082	2 579	8 992	3 763	1 545	1 649	559
1995	921	1 965	2 336	80	2 146	2 731	9 230	3 772	1 609	1 691	629
1996	930	2 020	2 403	85	2 185	2 846	9 469	3 814	1 679	1 732	665
1993:											
January	918	1 668	2 014	74	2 015	2 499	8 633	3 780	1 489	1 551	429
February	920	1 671	2 026	74	2 022	2 504	8 659	3 782	1 494	1 557	434
March	922	1 670	2 036	73	2 024	2 511	8 671	3 779	1 498	1 560	440
April	923	1 683	2 047	74	2 032	2 515	8 698	3 780	1 499	1 568	447
May	924	1 692	2 052	75	2 031	2 520	8 729	3 785	1 503	1 577	457
June	925	1 702	2 070	76	2 037	2 522	8 750	3 786	1 506	1 582	464
July	925	1 716	2 079	75	2 039	2 525	8 770	3 783	1 508	1 585	473
August	925	1 729	2 098	76	2 039	2 524	8 787	3 780	1 512	1 591	481
September	927	1 738	2 087	77	2 040	2 528	8 813	3 778	1 513	1 601	489
October	927	1 742	2 093	77	2 041	2 531	8 835	3 777	1 514	1 609	499
November	926	1 758	2 105	77	2 046	2 536	8 852	3 772	1 517	1 615	504
December	924	1 768	2 117	77	2 048	2 536	8 866	3 768	1 518	1 622	511
1994:											
January	926	1 781	2 123	78	2 051	2 522	8 884	3 767	1 523	1 626	518
February	925	1 789	2 129	78	2 052	2 534	8 889	3 764	1 522	1 629	525
March	925	1 805	2 138	78	2 057	2 534	8 919	3 765	1 527	1 635	536
April	925	1 818	2 151	78	2 064	2 548	8 945	3 767	1 531	1 640	543
May	925	1 833	2 166	79	2 071	2 559	8 964	3 763	1 537	1 644	551
June	919	1 843	2 187	79	2 077	2 569	8 979	3 759	1 541	1 649	558
July	924	1 857	2 224	79	2 081	2 585	9 007	3 763	1 547	1 654	564
August	923	1 866	2 234	79	2 086	2 593	9 028	3 762	1 556	1 657	572
September	923	1 888	2 239	79	2 103	2 607	9 042	3 762	1 554	1 658	580
October	923	1 894	2 250	79	2 107	2 619	9 061	3 760	1 563	1 660	584
November	924	1 907	2 265	79	2 113	2 631	9 077	3 760	1 567	1 663	587
December	923	1 919	2 279	79	2 116	2 648	9 100	3 761	1 573	1 667	596
1995:											
January	924	1 924	2 297	79	2 123	2 667	9 117	3 762	1 575	1 672	602
February	924	1 942	2 307	79	2 127	2 683	9 138	3 760	1 582	1 675	608
March	923	1 948	2 318	80	2 133	2 695	9 161	3 763	1 590	1 678	611
April	923	1 953	2 325	80	2 135	2 711	9 179	3 768	1 594	1 682	614
May	921	1 961	2 330	80	2 139	2 714	9 190	3 767	1 598	1 683	618
June	919	1 966	2 330	80	2 145	2 734	9 213	3 767	1 605	1 687	625
July	920	1 968	2 323	81	2 149	2 741	9 234	3 770	1 610	1 691	632
August	920	1 983	2 338	81	2 158	2 751	9 261	3 774	1 616	1 696	641
September	921	1 978	2 364	81	2 154	2 757	9 280	3 776	1 623	1 701	644
October	921	1 985	2 359	81	2 152	2 766	9 302	3 781	1 630	1 704	648
November	921	1 985	2 363	82	2 164	2 775	9 328	3 785	1 637	1 709	651
December	921	1 993	2 371	82	2 170	2 781	9 353	3 790	1 644	1 712	656
1996:											
January	922	1 987	2 372	83	2 173	2 788	9 356	3 792	1 646	1 714	653
February	925	2 001	2 381	83	2 179	2 798	9 386	3 798	1 655	1 717	660
March	924	2 008	2 387	84	2 182	2 811	9 411	3 801	1 661	1 722	662
April	925	2 012	2 393	84	2 181	2 814	9 429	3 804	1 668	1 725	665
May	927	2 010	2 401	85	2 187	2 830	9 453	3 809	1 674	1 730	665
June	929	2 021	2 406	85	2 187	2 845	9 466	3 809	1 679	1 733	666
July	931	2 034	2 411	85	2 183	2 849	9 478	3 812	1 682	1 735	665
August	933	2 031	2 415	85	2 191	2 860	9 493	3 813	1 687	1 737	667
September	933	2 022	2 421	85	2 188	2 872	9 514	3 823	1 691	1 739	668
October	936	2 035	2 422	86	2 189	2 882	9 532	3 829	1 695	1 742	670
November	939	2 041	2 425	86	2 190	2 894	9 552	3 834	1 700	1 745	674
December	940	2 040	2 426	87	2 191	2 906	9 567	3 839	1 703	1 747	673

PRIVATE SERVICES—HOURS AND EARNINGS
(Production and nonsupervisory workers)

YEAR AND MONTH	Weekly hours worked (Seasonally adjusted)		Average earnings (Dollars, not seasonally adjusted)											
			Hourly						Weekly					
	Average hours (Not seasonally adjusted)	Aggregate hours index (1982=100)	All private services	Business services			Auto repair services and parking	Amusement and recreation	All private services	Business services			Auto repair services and parking	Amusement and recreation
				Total	Personnel supply	Computer and data processing				Total	Personnel supply	Computer and data processing		
1968	34.7	61.3	2.42	....	....	....	....	....	83.97	....	....	....	....	....
1969	34.7	64.2	2.61	....	....	....	....	....	90.57	....	....	....	....	....
1970	34.4	65.3	2.81	....	....	....	....	....	96.66	....	....	....	....	....
1971	33.9	65.6	3.04	....	....	....	....	....	103.06	....	....	....	....	....
1972	33.9	68.0	3.27	....	....	4.53	3.26	....	110.85	....	....	163.53	122.25	....
1973	33.8	71.3	3.47	....	....	4.79	3.47	....	117.29	....	....	173.88	130.13	....
1974	33.6	73.9	3.75	....	....	5.02	3.75	....	126.00	....	....	184.74	140.25	....
1975	33.5	76.0	4.02	....	....	5.26	3.99	....	134.67	....	....	196.20	150.02	....
1976	33.3	78.8	4.31	....	....	5.18	4.31	....	143.52	....	....	190.62	163.35	....
1977	33.0	82.0	4.65	....	....	5.32	4.61	....	153.45	....	....	197.90	172.41	....
1978	32.8	86.3	4.99	....	....	5.76	5.03	....	163.67	....	....	211.39	188.12	....
1979	32.7	90.2	5.36	....	....	6.35	5.59	....	175.27	....	....	231.78	209.63	....
1980	32.6	94.3	5.85	....	....	7.16	6.10	....	190.71	....	....	260.62	229.36	....
1981	32.6	98.2	6.41	....	....	7.92	6.44	....	208.97	....	....	294.62	244.08	....
1982	32.6	100.0	6.92	....	....	9.00	6.76	....	225.59	....	....	338.40	254.85	....
1983	32.7	103.6	7.31	....	....	10.10	6.94	....	239.04	....	....	387.84	260.94	....
1984	32.6	108.2	7.59	....	....	10.50	7.21	....	247.43	....	....	400.05	270.38	....
1985	32.5	114.0	7.90	....	....	10.98	7.40	....	256.75	....	....	422.73	276.76	....
1986	32.5	119.2	8.18	....	....	11.63	7.55	....	265.85	....	....	444.27	282.37	....
1987	32.5	124.9	8.49	....	....	12.29	7.78	....	275.93	....	....	460.88	285.53	....
1988	32.6	132.2	8.88	8.61	....	13.21	8.16	7.39	289.49	286.71	....	499.34	299.47	201.01
1989	32.6	139.3	9.38	9.08	....	14.19	8.47	7.82	305.79	301.46	....	539.22	310.85	214.27
1990	32.5	144.2	9.83	9.48	....	15.11	8.77	8.11	319.48	313.79	....	575.69	320.98	220.59
1991	32.4	145.3	10.23	9.76	....	15.57	8.96	8.04	331.45	322.08	....	591.66	326.14	215.47
1992	32.5	149.3	10.54	9.97	....	15.81	9.16	8.08	342.55	329.01	....	602.36	333.42	218.16
1993	32.5	155.4	10.78	10.12	....	16.46	9.33	8.32	350.35	333.96	....	627.13	338.68	227.97
1994	32.5	162.9	11.04	10.31	....	17.17	9.58	8.49	358.80	341.26	....	649.03	347.75	228.38
1995	32.4	170.5	11.39	10.71	....	17.79	9.92	8.74	369.04	354.50	....	672.46	356.13	235.98
1996	32.4	176.8	11.79	11.21	....	18.72	10.20	8.82	382.00	372.17	....	705.74	368.22	237.26
1993:														
January	32.1	152.4	10.80	10.08	....	15.98	9.32	8.69	346.68	331.63	....	605.64	331.79	227.68
February	32.3	153.1	10.80	10.14	....	16.15	9.30	8.70	348.84	335.63	....	620.16	332.01	230.55
March	32.2	152.8	10.78	10.10	....	16.17	9.27	8.69	347.12	334.31	....	616.08	333.72	226.81
April	32.3	154.1	10.74	10.12	....	16.33	9.28	8.45	346.90	332.95	....	618.91	336.86	227.31
May	32.7	156.0	10.76	10.14	....	16.54	9.28	8.39	351.85	338.68	....	636.79	340.58	227.37
June	32.6	155.5	10.65	10.08	....	16.42	9.28	7.87	347.19	333.65	....	620.68	339.65	221.15
July	32.8	156.0	10.61	10.10	....	16.37	9.26	7.60	348.01	333.30	....	620.42	342.62	224.96
August	33.0	157.4	10.65	10.14	....	16.63	9.28	7.65	351.45	337.66	....	638.59	343.36	225.68
September	32.3	156.4	10.82	10.18	....	16.61	9.37	8.24	349.49	329.83	....	629.52	340.13	223.30
October	32.4	157.0	10.86	10.10	....	16.68	9.39	8.57	351.86	331.28	....	635.51	341.80	227.96
November	32.4	158.1	10.91	10.11	....	16.72	9.41	8.86	353.48	334.64	....	637.03	340.64	237.45
December	32.4	158.0	10.97	10.17	....	16.85	9.47	8.91	355.43	338.66	....	640.30	342.81	237.90
1994:														
January	32.5	160.9	11.05	10.34	....	17.00	9.45	8.78	359.13	344.32	....	652.80	341.15	230.04
February	32.2	158.5	11.03	10.35	....	17.09	9.49	8.71	355.17	338.45	....	646.00	339.74	225.59
March	32.3	160.0	11.00	10.29	....	16.92	9.46	8.67	355.30	339.57	....	637.88	341.51	227.15
April	32.4	161.3	10.99	10.25	....	16.96	9.53	8.64	356.08	339.28	....	639.39	344.99	228.10
May	32.6	162.5	11.01	10.31	....	17.23	9.54	8.50	358.93	343.32	....	659.91	348.21	224.40
June	32.5	162.2	10.89	10.22	....	16.99	9.52	8.14	353.93	338.28	....	638.82	349.38	222.22
July	32.7	163.1	10.89	10.29	....	17.12	9.53	7.83	356.10	338.54	....	642.00	350.70	226.29
August	32.7	163.3	10.89	10.26	....	17.17	9.58	7.87	356.10	339.61	....	640.44	350.63	223.51
September	32.4	164.5	11.09	10.34	....	17.31	9.63	8.55	359.32	341.22	....	647.39	348.61	225.72
October	32.7	166.7	11.19	10.37	....	17.46	9.68	8.80	365.91	345.32	....	670.46	351.38	234.96
November	32.3	166.0	11.20	10.34	....	17.37	9.74	8.96	361.76	341.22	....	651.38	348.69	236.54
December	32.4	166.7	11.27	10.40	....	17.34	9.82	9.10	365.15	346.32	....	655.45	353.52	242.97
1995:														
January	32.4	169.3	11.36	10.60	....	17.55	9.84	9.07	368.06	351.92	....	675.68	350.30	238.54
February	32.3	168.2	11.35	10.62	....	17.65	9.79	9.09	366.61	350.46	....	667.17	347.55	240.89
March	32.2	168.9	11.32	10.58	....	17.51	9.82	9.01	364.50	350.20	....	654.87	350.57	236.06
April	32.5	170.4	11.38	10.72	....	17.80	9.85	8.90	369.85	351.62	....	678.18	353.62	242.08
May	32.1	168.1	11.31	10.62	....	17.69	9.90	8.82	363.05	348.34	....	656.30	352.44	231.97
June	32.5	170.1	11.22	10.63	....	17.76	9.88	8.33	364.65	351.85	....	662.45	358.64	233.24
July	32.8	171.1	11.26	10.80	....	17.97	9.90	8.15	369.33	356.40	....	682.86	359.37	236.35
August	32.7	170.8	11.22	10.64	....	17.68	9.94	8.18	366.89	352.18	....	663.00	360.82	233.13
September	32.3	172.2	11.45	10.74	....	17.83	9.97	8.80	369.84	354.42	....	673.97	357.92	232.32
October	32.6	173.1	11.54	10.79	....	17.99	10.02	8.90	376.20	358.23	....	694.41	360.72	234.07
November	32.3	173.0	11.57	10.77	....	17.87	10.01	9.11	373.71	358.64	....	675.49	358.36	239.59
December	32.3	173.1	11.66	10.91	....	18.13	10.04	9.18	376.62	362.21	....	679.88	356.42	241.43
1996:														
January	31.8	172.2	11.73	11.08	....	18.15	10.05	9.09	373.01	356.78	....	675.18	354.77	236.34
February	32.2	174.3	11.72	11.09	....	18.25	10.07	9.13	377.38	363.75	....	686.20	361.51	241.03
March	32.2	174.9	11.72	11.08	....	18.32	10.12	9.05	377.38	367.86	....	688.83	365.33	236.21
April	32.2	174.8	11.71	11.13	....	18.34	10.12	8.90	377.06	366.18	....	691.42	363.31	237.63
May	32.2	175.5	11.67	11.09	....	18.42	10.17	8.80	375.77	367.08	....	690.75	366.12	229.68
June	32.8	178.8	11.66	11.18	....	18.76	10.14	8.38	382.45	375.65	....	718.51	371.12	232.96
July	32.5	176.5	11.60	11.14	....	18.63	10.17	8.26	377.00	368.73	....	693.04	369.17	233.76
August	32.7	178.0	11.63	11.15	....	18.80	10.18	8.25	380.30	372.41	....	706.88	372.59	235.13
September	32.6	179.9	11.89	11.30	....	19.08	10.26	8.88	387.61	377.42	....	730.76	372.44	233.54
October	32.4	178.2	11.93	11.25	....	19.05	10.29	9.06	386.53	374.63	....	718.19	373.53	239.18
November	32.4	179.1	12.04	11.40	....	19.21	10.36	9.30	390.10	379.62	....	726.14	375.03	246.45
December	32.7	181.1	12.16	11.55	....	19.53	10.43	9.43	397.63	386.93	....	746.05	375.48	252.72

Government

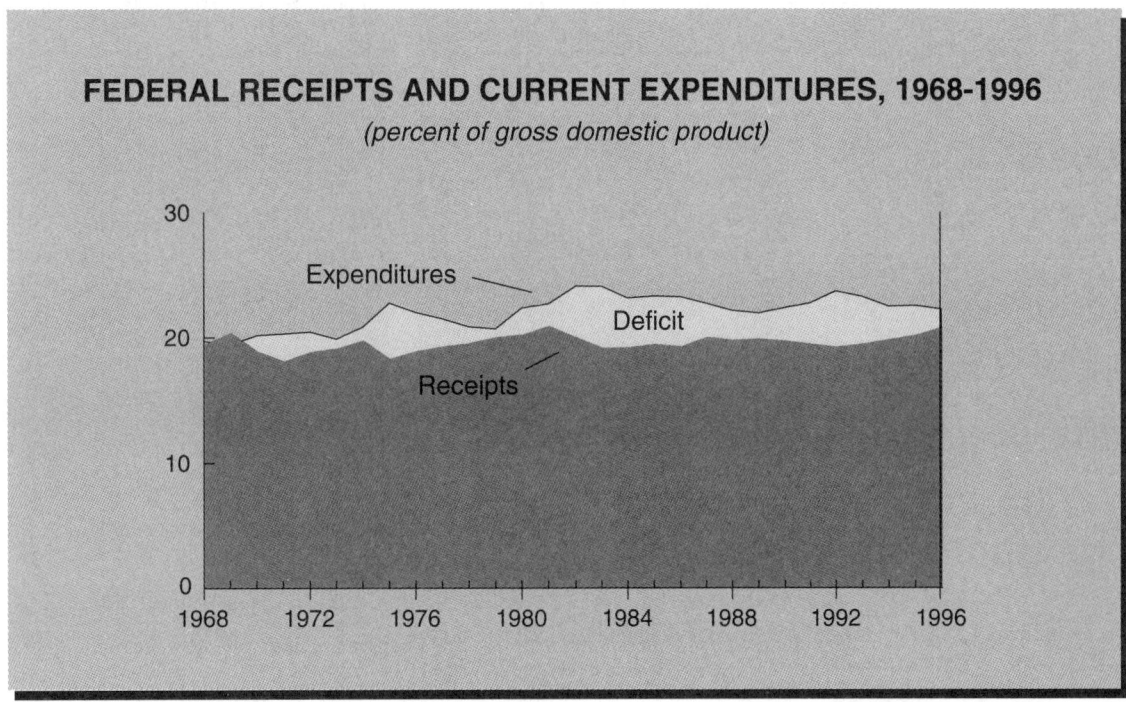

FEDERAL RECEIPTS AND CURRENT EXPENDITURES, 1968-1996
(percent of gross domestic product)

From 1992 to 1996, a growing economy boosted federal receipts, while current federal expenditures declined relative to gross domestic product. As a result, the federal deficit, measured on a national income and product account basis, fell from 4.5 percent of GDP in 1992 to 1.4 percent in 1996.

"Current federal expenditures" as shown in the national income and product accounts (NIPAs) excludes gross fixed investment but includes an allowance for consumption of fixed capital (depreciation). This treatment of the government sector was introduced in the comprehensive 1996 revisions of the NIPAs.

FEDERAL GOVERNMENT RECEIPTS AND CURRENT EXPENDITURES
(Calendar years—Billions of dollars, quarterly data are at seasonally adjusted annual rates)

YEAR AND QUARTER	Receipts					Current Expenditures						Surplus or deficit (—), national income and product accounts		
	Total	Personal tax and nontax receipts	Corporate profits tax accruals	Indirect business tax and nontax accruals	Contributions for social insurance	Total	Consumption expenditures	Transfer payments (Net)	Grants-in-aid to state and local governments	Net interest paid	Subsidies less surplus of government enterprises	Total	Social insurance funds	Other
1968	176.8	79.3	36.1	18.2	43.2	179.7	97.0	48.1	18.6	11.3	4.6	-2.8	5.2	-8.1
1969	199.5	94.7	36.1	19.2	49.5	190.8	100.1	52.6	20.3	12.7	5.1	8.7	7.7	1.0
1970	195.1	92.2	30.6	19.5	52.8	209.1	100.5	63.6	24.4	14.1	6.5	-14.1	3.6	-17.7
1971	203.3	89.9	33.5	20.5	59.4	228.6	103.8	75.4	29.0	13.8	6.6	-25.3	0.7	-26.1
1972	232.6	107.8	36.6	20.1	68.1	253.1	110.1	83.5	37.5	14.4	8.0	-20.5	3.0	-23.6
1973	264.0	114.3	43.3	21.5	84.9	275.1	112.9	96.2	40.6	18.0	7.4	-11.1	9.3	-20.4
1974	295.1	130.9	45.1	22.1	97.1	312.0	123.3	118.2	43.9	20.7	5.5	-16.9	7.0	-23.9
1975	297.4	125.4	43.6	24.2	104.2	371.3	135.0	150.3	54.6	23.0	8.6	-73.9	-11.2	-62.7
1976	343.1	146.6	54.6	23.8	118.2	400.3	141.7	163.0	61.1	26.8	7.8	-57.2	-9.7	-47.5
1977	389.6	169.1	61.6	25.6	133.3	435.9	155.4	173.6	67.5	29.1	10.4	-46.3	-5.6	-40.7
1978	446.5	193.8	71.4	28.9	152.4	478.1	168.8	186.2	77.3	34.6	11.4	-31.7	3.7	-35.4
1979	511.1	229.7	74.4	30.1	176.8	529.5	185.9	209.7	80.5	42.1	11.3	-18.4	9.8	-28.2
1980	561.5	256.2	70.3	39.7	195.3	622.5	215.2	252.0	88.7	52.7	13.9	-61.0	-4.4	-56.6
1981	649.3	297.2	65.7	57.3	229.1	707.1	246.0	287.1	87.9	71.7	14.4	-57.8	-1.3	-56.5
1982	646.4	302.9	49.0	49.7	244.8	781.0	270.0	323.4	83.9	84.4	19.4	-134.7	-19.8	-114.8
1983	671.9	293.0	61.3	53.3	264.2	846.3	293.0	347.7	87.0	92.8	25.4	-174.4	-20.7	-153.6
1984	746.9	308.3	75.2	57.9	305.3	902.9	314.1	354.3	94.4	113.3	27.1	-156.0	21.9	-177.9
1985	811.3	343.7	76.3	58.2	333.1	974.2	342.5	379.0	100.3	126.9	25.2	-162.9	33.1	-196.0
1986	850.1	358.3	83.8	53.2	354.7	1 027.6	362.3	399.1	107.6	130.5	28.0	-177.5	40.0	-217.5
1987	937.4	402.4	103.2	57.8	374.1	1 066.3	378.2	413.0	102.9	137.8	34.4	-128.9	49.7	-178.6
1988	997.2	414.4	111.0	60.9	410.9	1 118.5	387.8	437.2	111.2	148.4	33.8	-121.3	73.8	-195.1
1989	1 079.3	463.4	117.1	61.7	437.1	1 192.7	405.2	471.7	118.2	166.7	30.8	-113.4	80.9	-194.2
1990	1 129.8	485.7	118.0	65.1	461.1	1 284.5	426.6	513.3	132.4	179.9	32.4	-154.7	80.1	-234.8
1991	1 149.0	476.9	109.8	79.7	482.6	1 345.0	445.9	522.2	153.4	192.7	30.8	-196.0	65.0	-261.0
1992	1 198.5	490.8	118.6	81.9	507.1	1 479.4	451.0	625.1	172.2	195.8	35.1	-280.9	48.4	-329.3
1993	1 275.1	522.6	138.3	86.9	527.3	1 525.7	447.3	659.9	185.8	192.7	40.1	-250.7	44.6	-295.2
1994	1 374.8	562.3	156.7	98.7	557.1	1 561.4	443.2	683.0	199.2	200.0	35.9	-186.7	59.2	-245.8
1995	1 463.2	605.8	182.1	93.5	581.8	1 637.6	443.5	720.9	211.9	224.8	36.4	-174.4	54.1	-228.6
1996	1 587.6	686.7	194.5	95.8	610.5	1 698.1	451.5	763.5	218.3	227.1	37.7	-110.5	55.3	-165.8
1988:														
1st quarter	966.9	401.6	102.9	60.6	401.8	1 110.7	388.7	433.0	108.8	143.1	37.1	-143.8	63.8	-207.5
2nd quarter	995.8	418.0	109.5	60.2	408.1	1 109.2	384.4	433.1	111.6	147.2	33.0	-113.4	70.8	-184.3
3rd quarter	1 002.1	414.0	113.0	61.4	413.7	1 116.8	383.9	437.0	112.2	150.0	33.7	-114.7	77.2	-191.9
4th quarter	1 023.9	423.9	118.6	61.5	419.9	1 137.1	394.3	445.8	112.3	153.1	31.6	-113.2	83.4	-196.6
1989:														
1st quarter	1 072.6	451.8	127.0	62.1	431.6	1 164.6	395.4	459.4	115.9	162.6	31.3	-92.0	81.4	-173.5
2nd quarter	1 084.2	469.1	119.1	60.8	435.2	1 184.4	406.2	463.7	117.1	166.6	30.8	-100.2	82.0	-182.2
3rd quarter	1 073.7	461.6	110.3	62.6	439.1	1 198.4	409.0	475.3	118.4	165.4	30.4	-124.7	80.9	-205.6
4th quarter	1 086.9	471.1	111.8	61.5	442.4	1 223.3	410.1	488.6	121.4	172.4	30.7	-136.5	79.1	-215.6
1990:														
1st quarter	1 107.3	477.4	111.6	63.2	455.1	1 261.5	421.7	504.2	128.4	176.2	30.9	-154.1	76.7	-230.8
2nd quarter	1 132.7	490.7	118.5	64.2	459.3	1 276.9	423.7	509.6	132.2	179.7	31.7	-144.1	82.2	-226.3
3rd quarter	1 144.1	489.7	124.3	65.5	464.5	1 286.7	423.2	513.2	131.8	185.8	32.7	-142.6	84.1	-226.7
4th quarter	1 135.2	484.9	117.4	67.4	465.6	1 313.0	437.7	526.1	137.1	177.8	34.4	-177.7	77.5	-255.2
1991:														
1st quarter	1 140.1	478.4	107.3	77.2	477.2	1 274.7	450.5	461.7	144.8	186.3	31.6	-134.6	66.0	-200.6
2nd quarter	1 142.6	474.3	108.9	79.1	480.3	1 339.3	449.1	515.5	151.8	192.6	30.0	-196.7	63.6	-260.3
3rd quarter	1 152.3	476.0	111.8	79.9	484.7	1 366.3	443.7	545.6	154.4	191.9	30.7	-214.0	66.8	-280.8
4th quarter	1 160.9	479.0	111.1	82.8	488.1	1 399.8	440.5	565.8	162.7	200.0	30.9	-238.8	63.7	-302.5
1992:														
1st quarter	1 183.4	481.0	119.6	80.8	502.0	1 450.7	445.8	611.1	165.4	196.8	31.8	-267.4	48.2	-315.6
2nd quarter	1 193.1	481.6	125.3	80.2	506.1	1 472.8	446.3	621.9	173.0	198.4	33.1	-279.6	47.6	-327.2
3rd quarter	1 187.0	490.7	106.0	80.2	510.1	1 484.5	454.4	624.2	174.2	196.4	35.3	-297.5	50.2	-347.7
4th quarter	1 230.5	510.0	123.7	86.5	510.3	1 509.5	457.7	643.3	176.3	191.8	40.3	-279.0	47.6	-326.6
1993:														
1st quarter	1 227.1	500.8	125.2	82.6	518.5	1 505.3	447.1	647.1	177.2	192.2	41.7	-278.2	41.0	-319.2
2nd quarter	1 268.8	519.1	138.5	85.5	525.8	1 518.0	445.8	655.7	181.9	193.1	41.6	-249.2	44.6	-293.8
3rd quarter	1 277.2	527.1	135.0	85.9	529.3	1 527.8	447.0	661.3	187.3	192.9	39.2	-250.6	44.3	-294.9
4th quarter	1 327.2	543.4	154.5	93.8	535.5	1 551.9	449.2	675.5	196.9	192.5	37.8	-224.6	48.3	-273.0
1994:														
1st quarter	1 324.5	542.0	136.9	98.2	547.4	1 533.5	442.4	670.6	194.5	189.9	36.0	-209.0	54.6	-263.6
2nd quarter	1 381.1	574.3	153.4	98.1	555.3	1 544.3	439.2	676.9	196.2	196.6	35.4	-163.2	58.7	-221.9
3rd quarter	1 383.8	561.6	163.4	99.3	559.5	1 571.4	450.5	683.8	199.6	202.8	34.8	-187.6	60.7	-248.3
4th quarter	1 409.5	571.1	173.2	99.0	566.2	1 596.4	440.8	700.7	206.6	210.8	37.5	-186.8	62.7	-249.6
1995:														
1st quarter	1 429.0	581.4	179.0	94.3	574.3	1 620.6	444.8	709.5	212.2	218.8	35.3	-191.5	55.5	-247.0
2nd quarter	1 459.0	608.2	178.7	93.8	578.3	1 638.5	444.0	718.0	216.5	223.9	36.1	-179.5	52.2	-231.7
3rd quarter	1 472.8	607.5	186.9	93.7	584.7	1 649.3	449.0	725.1	210.6	227.5	37.0	-176.5	53.7	-230.3
4th quarter	1 491.9	626.0	183.8	92.2	589.9	1 642.0	436.3	731.1	208.5	229.0	37.2	-150.2	55.1	-205.3
1996:														
1st quarter	1 526.3	644.9	192.1	91.7	597.6	1 679.9	444.6	757.6	213.7	226.6	37.4	-153.6	49.1	-202.7
2nd quarter	1 583.8	688.8	197.2	90.0	607.8	1 695.4	453.7	757.5	223.2	223.5	37.5	-111.6	53.3	-165.0
3rd quarter	1 598.6	695.7	196.7	91.5	614.8	1 698.2	454.0	761.5	218.7	226.6	37.4	-99.5	58.2	-157.8
4th quarter	1 641.6	717.5	192.0	110.2	622.0	1 718.8	453.6	777.3	217.5	231.8	38.5	-77.1	60.6	-137.7

STATE AND LOCAL GOVERNMENT RECEIPTS AND CURRENT EXPENDITURES
(Calendar years—Billions of dollars, quarterly data are at seasonally adjusted annual rates)

YEAR AND QUARTER	Receipts						Current Expenditures						Surplus or deficit (—), national income and product accounts		
	Total	Personal tax and nontax receipts	Corporate profits tax accruals	Indirect business tax and nontax accruals	Contributions for social insurance	Federal grants-in-aid	Total	Consumption expenditures	Transfer payments to persons	Net interest paid	Less: Dividends received by government	Subsidies less surplus of government enterprises	Total	Social insurance funds	Other
1968	102.7	12.7	3.3	60.8	7.2	18.6	82.6	70.8	14.5	-1.0	0.1	-1.6	20.0	5.2	14.8
1969	114.8	15.2	3.6	67.4	8.3	20.3	93.7	79.8	16.7	-1.2	0.2	-1.5	21.1	5.8	15.3
1970	129.0	16.7	3.7	74.8	9.2	24.4	108.2	91.6	20.1	-1.8	0.2	-1.6	20.8	6.9	13.9
1971	145.3	18.7	4.3	83.1	10.2	29.0	123.7	102.9	24.0	-1.4	0.3	-1.4	21.7	7.6	14.1
1972	169.7	24.2	5.3	91.2	11.5	37.5	137.5	113.4	27.5	-1.5	0.3	-1.6	32.2	8.7	23.5
1973	185.3	26.3	6.0	99.5	13.0	40.6	152.0	126.4	30.4	-2.9	0.5	-1.5	33.4	9.6	23.8
1974	200.6	28.2	6.7	107.2	14.6	43.9	170.2	144.0	32.3	-4.4	0.9	-0.9	30.5	10.9	19.5
1975	225.6	31.0	7.3	115.8	16.8	54.6	198.0	164.9	38.9	-4.5	0.9	-0.4	27.6	13.1	14.5
1976	253.9	35.8	9.6	127.8	19.5	61.1	217.9	179.7	43.6	-4.1	0.9	-0.4	35.9	15.6	20.4
1977	281.9	41.0	11.4	139.9	22.1	67.5	237.1	196.1	47.4	-4.7	1.3	-0.3	44.7	17.9	26.8
1978	309.3	46.3	12.1	148.9	24.7	77.3	256.7	214.5	52.4	-8.1	1.7	-0.3	52.6	20.2	32.4
1979	330.6	50.5	13.6	158.6	27.4	80.5	278.3	235.9	57.2	-13.3	2.0	0.4	52.3	23.7	28.6
1980	361.4	56.2	14.5	172.3	29.7	88.7	307.0	261.3	65.7	-19.3	1.9	1.2	54.4	26.9	27.5
1981	390.8	63.0	15.4	192.0	32.5	87.9	335.4	285.3	73.6	-23.6	2.3	2.4	55.4	29.8	25.6
1982	409.0	68.5	14.0	206.8	35.8	83.9	357.7	307.9	79.9	-28.9	2.9	1.7	51.3	36.6	14.7
1983	443.6	76.2	15.9	226.8	37.7	87.0	378.8	326.2	86.6	-31.0	3.4	0.2	64.9	41.6	23.3
1984	492.0	87.1	18.8	251.5	40.2	94.4	405.1	350.8	93.9	-34.1	3.9	-1.6	86.9	42.9	44.0
1985	528.7	94.0	20.2	271.4	42.8	100.3	437.8	382.6	101.9	-38.9	4.5	-3.3	91.0	47.0	44.0
1986	570.6	101.6	22.7	291.5	47.3	107.6	475.7	412.7	111.8	-40.7	5.1	-3.0	94.9	52.8	42.1
1987	594.9	111.8	23.9	307.1	49.2	102.9	511.1	441.1	120.7	-41.5	5.9	-3.4	83.8	54.8	29.0
1988	631.4	117.6	26.0	324.6	51.9	111.2	545.5	471.3	131.0	-44.6	6.9	-5.3	85.9	56.7	29.2
1989	681.0	131.4	24.2	353.0	54.1	118.2	585.9	507.2	144.5	-51.2	8.1	-6.6	95.1	60.2	34.9
1990	728.9	139.1	22.5	377.6	57.4	132.4	648.8	550.1	166.5	-51.7	9.0	-7.1	80.1	59.9	20.2
1991	784.2	147.8	23.6	398.4	60.9	153.4	708.4	579.4	199.0	-53.3	9.5	-7.2	75.8	64.3	11.5
1992	844.3	159.7	24.4	423.7	64.3	172.2	758.0	603.6	227.2	-54.7	10.1	-8.0	86.3	68.0	18.3
1993	894.4	167.4	26.9	445.6	68.7	185.8	807.0	631.6	247.2	-52.4	10.5	-9.0	87.4	67.8	19.7
1994	949.2	176.8	29.9	469.8	73.4	199.2	852.3	663.8	264.3	-55.1	11.4	-9.3	96.8	68.9	27.9
1995	999.0	189.4	31.1	489.3	77.3	211.9	895.9	698.6	280.6	-59.6	12.5	-11.2	103.1	70.5	32.5
1996	1 043.4	200.2	34.5	508.9	81.4	218.3	938.0	730.9	294.8	-61.7	13.6	-12.3	105.3	71.3	34.1
1988:															
1st quarter	613.6	113.4	24.1	316.4	50.9	108.8	533.0	459.7	126.9	-42.6	6.4	-4.6	80.6	55.5	25.1
2nd quarter	627.6	117.1	25.8	321.5	51.7	111.6	541.6	467.8	129.4	-43.7	6.9	-5.1	86.1	56.3	29.7
3rd quarter	636.0	118.3	26.5	326.7	52.2	112.2	548.9	474.6	132.3	-45.3	7.1	-5.6	87.1	57.0	30.1
4th quarter	648.2	121.7	27.7	333.7	52.8	112.3	558.4	483.1	135.5	-47.0	7.2	-6.0	89.9	57.8	32.1
1989:															
1st quarter	663.6	125.9	26.8	341.7	53.2	115.9	568.0	493.3	138.5	-49.8	7.6	-6.4	95.6	59.5	36.1
2nd quarter	677.5	131.6	24.7	350.5	53.7	117.1	579.2	502.7	142.2	-51.0	8.0	-6.7	98.3	60.2	38.1
3rd quarter	686.5	133.0	22.6	358.1	54.4	118.4	590.6	511.0	146.5	-51.7	8.2	-6.9	95.9	60.5	35.4
4th quarter	696.3	135.3	22.9	361.6	55.1	121.4	605.9	522.0	150.9	-52.2	8.5	-6.3	90.4	60.5	29.9
1990:															
1st quarter	710.3	135.6	21.4	368.9	56.0	128.4	624.8	535.3	156.5	-51.2	8.7	-7.1	85.5	59.3	26.2
2nd quarter	721.3	137.5	22.7	371.9	56.9	132.2	638.5	543.9	162.4	-51.7	9.0	-7.1	82.8	59.5	23.3
3rd quarter	736.2	141.2	23.7	381.8	57.9	131.8	655.5	554.0	169.3	-51.8	9.0	-7.0	80.7	60.0	20.7
4th quarter	748.0	142.3	22.2	387.7	58.7	137.1	676.5	567.3	177.7	-52.0	9.3	-7.1	71.5	60.9	10.6
1991:															
1st quarter	758.5	143.9	22.8	387.5	59.6	144.8	689.8	572.1	186.9	-52.6	9.4	-7.2	68.8	62.5	6.3
2nd quarter	775.8	146.3	23.4	393.8	60.5	151.8	702.1	576.9	195.0	-53.0	9.5	-7.2	73.7	63.9	9.8
3rd quarter	791.4	147.7	24.3	403.8	61.3	154.4	714.3	581.5	203.1	-53.6	9.5	-7.2	77.1	64.9	12.2
4th quarter	811.0	153.5	24.2	408.4	62.2	162.7	727.2	587.3	210.8	-54.0	9.6	-7.2	83.8	66.0	17.7
1992:															
1st quarter	823.4	155.7	24.3	414.9	63.1	165.4	738.6	592.6	217.7	-54.7	9.8	-7.2	84.8	67.1	17.6
2nd quarter	838.8	158.4	25.7	417.7	64.0	173.0	752.2	600.8	224.1	-54.9	10.1	-7.7	86.6	68.1	18.5
3rd quarter	847.3	159.9	21.6	427.0	64.7	174.2	765.4	607.4	231.2	-54.8	10.1	-8.3	82.0	68.4	13.6
4th quarter	867.7	164.9	25.9	435.2	65.4	176.3	775.9	613.6	235.8	-54.2	10.3	-8.9	91.7	68.4	23.3
1993:															
1st quarter	867.6	161.6	24.1	438.0	66.8	177.2	789.8	621.4	240.4	-53.1	10.2	-8.7	77.8	67.8	10.0
2nd quarter	883.9	166.5	26.9	440.4	68.2	181.9	802.6	628.9	245.2	-52.3	10.4	-8.8	81.3	67.7	13.6
3rd quarter	899.9	168.4	26.3	448.5	69.4	187.3	812.9	635.0	249.5	-51.9	10.5	-9.1	86.9	67.7	19.3
4th quarter	926.3	172.9	30.4	455.5	70.6	196.9	822.6	641.1	253.8	-52.3	10.8	-9.2	103.7	67.9	35.9
1994:															
1st quarter	922.0	170.8	26.1	458.7	71.8	194.5	837.2	651.6	257.9	-53.2	11.1	-7.9	84.7	68.4	16.3
2nd quarter	941.0	176.1	29.4	466.3	72.9	196.2	846.2	659.2	262.3	-54.5	11.3	-9.5	94.8	68.9	25.9
3rd quarter	956.9	178.3	31.3	473.8	73.9	199.6	858.4	668.6	266.6	-55.6	11.4	-9.7	98.4	69.0	29.4
4th quarter	976.8	182.0	32.9	480.4	74.9	206.6	867.5	676.0	270.5	-57.2	11.7	-10.1	109.3	69.4	40.0
1995:															
1st quarter	988.4	185.1	30.6	484.6	75.8	212.2	880.6	686.9	274.9	-58.6	12.1	-10.6	107.7	70.0	37.7
2nd quarter	997.7	187.0	30.4	487.1	76.8	216.5	892.1	696.2	278.6	-59.4	12.3	-11.0	105.6	70.3	35.3
3rd quarter	1 002.0	191.3	32.0	490.4	77.7	210.6	900.9	702.4	282.6	-60.0	12.6	-11.4	101.1	70.8	30.3
4th quarter	1 007.8	194.0	31.5	495.1	78.7	208.5	910.0	708.8	286.3	-60.5	12.9	-11.7	97.8	71.0	26.8
1996:															
1st quarter	1 024.9	195.0	34.1	502.3	79.7	213.7	920.8	717.6	289.1	-60.5	13.3	-12.1	104.1	70.8	33.2
2nd quarter	1 046.2	198.9	35.0	508.9	80.9	223.2	932.5	727.0	292.7	-61.2	13.6	-12.3	114.4	71.3	43.1
3rd quarter	1 046.7	201.7	34.9	509.4	82.0	218.7	944.2	735.9	296.6	-62.2	13.7	-12.4	102.6	71.5	31.1
4th quarter	1 054.9	205.1	34.0	515.1	83.1	217.5	954.5	743.3	300.6	-63.0	14.0	-12.5	100.4	71.4	28.9

GOVERNMENT CONSUMPTION EXPENDITURES AND GROSS INVESTMENT [1]
(Calendar years—Billions of dollars, quarterly data are at seasonally adjusted annual rates)

YEAR AND QUARTER	Total	Federal Total	Defense Total	Defense Consumption expenditures [2] Total	Defense Consumption expenditures Capital consumption [3]	Defense Gross investment	Nondefense Total	Nondefense Consumption expenditures [2] Total	Nondefense Consumption expenditures Capital consumption [3]	Nondefense Gross investment	State and local Total	State and local Consumption expenditures [2] Total	State and local Consumption expenditures Capital consumption [3]	State and local Gross investment
1968	.....	.....	.....	.....	.....	.....	.....	.....	.....	.....	.....	.....	.....	.....
1969	.....	.....	.....	.....	.....	.....	.....	.....	.....	.....	.....	.....	.....	.....
1970	.....	.....	.....	.....	.....	.....	.....	.....	.....	.....	.....	.....	.....	.....
1971	.....	.....	.....	.....	.....	.....	.....	.....	.....	.....	.....	.....	.....	.....
1972	268.9	125.1	93.2	82.3	15.6	10.9	31.9	27.8	2.2	4.0	143.8	113.4	9.2	30.4
1973	287.6	128.2	94.7	83.7	17.1	11.0	33.5	29.2	2.3	4.3	159.4	126.4	10.2	33.0
1974	323.2	139.9	101.9	90.1	18.9	11.9	38.0	33.2	2.5	4.8	183.3	144.0	12.6	39.3
1975	362.6	154.5	110.9	97.0	20.5	14.0	43.6	38.0	2.8	5.5	208.1	164.9	14.3	43.2
1976	385.9	162.7	116.1	101.3	21.7	14.8	46.6	40.4	2.9	6.2	223.1	179.7	15.0	43.4
1977	416.9	178.4	125.8	109.6	23.1	16.2	52.6	45.7	3.1	6.9	238.5	196.1	15.9	42.4
1978	457.9	194.4	135.6	118.4	24.8	17.1	58.9	50.4	3.3	8.5	263.4	214.5	17.2	48.9
1979	507.1	215.0	151.2	130.7	26.9	20.6	63.8	55.2	3.6	8.6	292.0	235.9	19.3	56.1
1980	572.8	248.4	174.2	150.9	28.9	23.3	74.2	64.3	4.1	9.9	324.4	261.3	22.2	63.1
1981	633.4	284.1	202.0	174.3	31.3	27.7	82.2	71.7	4.6	10.5	349.2	285.3	25.3	64.0
1982	684.8	313.2	230.9	197.6	33.6	33.3	82.3	72.3	5.0	9.9	371.6	307.9	27.4	63.6
1983	735.7	344.5	255.0	214.9	35.9	40.2	89.4	78.2	5.3	11.3	391.2	326.2	28.3	65.0
1984	796.6	372.6	282.7	236.3	35.8	46.4	89.9	77.9	5.6	12.0	424.0	350.8	29.2	73.2
1985	875.0	410.1	312.4	257.6	38.6	54.8	97.7	84.9	6.0	12.8	464.9	382.6	30.7	82.3
1986	938.5	435.2	332.4	272.7	41.6	59.7	102.9	89.7	6.4	13.2	503.3	412.7	32.8	90.6
1987	992.8	455.7	350.4	287.6	43.3	62.8	105.3	90.7	6.8	14.6	537.2	441.1	35.2	96.0
1988	1 032.0	457.3	354.0	297.9	45.3	56.1	103.3	89.9	7.2	13.4	574.7	471.3	37.3	103.4
1989	1 095.1	477.2	360.6	303.3	47.3	57.3	116.7	101.9	7.8	14.7	617.9	507.2	39.7	110.6
1990	1 176.1	503.6	373.1	312.7	50.2	60.4	130.4	113.9	8.4	16.6	672.6	550.1	42.3	122.5
1991	1 225.9	522.6	383.5	325.4	52.8	58.1	139.1	120.6	8.9	18.5	703.4	579.4	44.7	123.9
1992	1 263.8	528.0	375.8	319.7	54.2	56.1	152.2	131.4	9.3	20.8	735.8	603.6	46.6	132.2
1993	1 283.4	518.3	360.7	311.1	55.7	49.6	157.7	136.2	9.7	21.5	765.0	631.6	48.8	133.4
1994	1 313.0	510.2	349.2	301.6	56.7	47.6	161.0	141.6	10.2	19.5	802.8	663.8	51.3	138.9
1995	1 355.5	509.6	344.6	298.6	57.5	46.0	165.0	144.9	10.7	20.1	846.0	698.6	54.2	147.4
1996	1 406.7	520.0	352.8	305.7	57.3	47.0	167.3	145.7	11.2	21.5	886.7	730.9	56.6	155.7
1988:														
1st quarter	1 015.5	456.3	354.6	300.0	44.4	54.6	101.7	88.7	7.0	13.0	559.1	459.7	36.5	99.5
2nd quarter	1 026.2	454.6	353.2	296.1	44.9	57.1	101.4	88.3	7.2	13.1	571.6	467.8	37.0	103.7
3rd quarter	1 031.5	453.5	351.5	295.7	45.8	55.8	102.0	88.2	7.3	13.8	578.1	474.6	37.5	103.5
4th quarter	1 054.8	465.0	356.7	299.8	46.2	56.9	108.2	94.5	7.4	13.8	589.9	483.1	38.1	106.8
1989:														
1st quarter	1 065.3	465.5	352.8	297.0	46.6	55.9	112.7	98.5	7.5	14.2	599.9	493.3	38.7	106.6
2nd quarter	1 088.7	476.5	360.6	304.4	47.0	56.2	115.9	101.8	7.7	14.2	612.1	502.7	39.4	109.5
3rd quarter	1 107.0	484.9	367.6	306.2	47.6	61.4	117.3	102.8	7.8	14.6	622.1	511.0	40.0	111.1
4th quarter	1 119.4	482.0	361.3	305.5	48.0	55.8	120.7	104.7	8.0	16.1	637.4	522.0	40.7	115.3
1990:														
1st quarter	1 153.0	496.4	369.7	311.7	49.2	58.0	126.7	110.0	8.1	16.7	656.6	535.3	41.3	121.3
2nd quarter	1 164.3	500.1	370.6	310.8	49.4	59.8	129.5	112.9	8.3	16.5	664.2	543.9	41.9	120.4
3rd quarter	1 176.9	501.2	368.9	307.3	50.3	61.6	132.3	115.9	8.4	16.4	675.7	554.0	42.8	121.7
4th quarter	1 210.4	516.7	383.3	321.0	52.1	62.3	133.3	116.7	8.6	16.6	693.7	567.3	43.4	126.5
1991:														
1st quarter	1 220.6	525.6	389.7	331.3	51.7	58.4	136.0	119.3	8.7	16.7	695.0	572.1	43.9	123.0
2nd quarter	1 227.4	528.2	389.3	328.6	52.8	60.7	138.9	120.5	8.8	18.4	699.2	576.9	44.5	122.4
3rd quarter	1 226.5	520.9	382.1	323.1	53.1	59.0	138.8	120.6	8.9	18.2	705.5	581.5	45.0	124.1
4th quarter	1 229.2	515.5	373.0	318.5	53.5	54.5	142.6	122.0	9.0	20.6	713.6	587.3	45.5	126.3
1992:														
1st quarter	1 247.9	521.8	372.8	317.2	53.7	55.6	149.0	128.5	9.1	20.4	726.1	592.6	45.8	133.5
2nd quarter	1 256.4	523.2	374.1	317.3	54.2	56.9	149.1	129.1	9.2	20.0	733.2	600.8	46.4	132.4
3rd quarter	1 270.7	532.0	380.9	323.5	54.3	57.4	151.1	130.9	9.4	20.2	738.7	607.4	46.9	131.3
4th quarter	1 280.0	535.0	375.3	320.7	54.7	54.6	159.7	137.0	9.4	22.6	745.1	613.6	47.4	131.5
1993:														
1st quarter	1 271.5	521.3	363.6	312.4	55.1	51.2	157.7	134.7	9.6	23.0	750.1	621.4	48.0	128.7
2nd quarter	1 281.2	517.8	361.7	311.5	55.3	50.3	156.1	134.3	9.7	21.7	763.4	628.9	48.6	134.5
3rd quarter	1 285.3	515.7	358.0	310.6	56.1	47.4	157.7	136.4	9.8	21.4	769.6	635.0	49.1	134.6
4th quarter	1 295.5	518.5	359.4	309.8	56.4	49.6	159.1	139.4	9.9	19.7	777.0	641.1	49.6	135.9
1994:														
1st quarter	1 291.0	506.9	344.9	299.8	56.6	45.1	162.0	142.6	10.0	19.4	784.1	651.6	50.3	132.5
2nd quarter	1 300.8	505.3	348.5	300.7	56.9	47.7	156.8	138.5	10.2	18.3	795.5	659.2	50.9	136.3
3rd quarter	1 332.3	520.4	359.7	308.7	56.5	51.1	160.7	141.8	10.3	18.9	811.9	668.6	51.7	143.3
4th quarter	1 328.0	508.3	343.6	297.3	56.8	46.3	164.7	143.5	10.4	21.2	819.6	676.0	52.3	143.6
1995:														
1st quarter	1 344.7	513.6	346.3	299.9	57.2	46.5	167.3	144.9	10.5	22.4	831.1	686.9	53.1	144.2
2nd quarter	1 356.0	511.2	348.1	299.8	57.6	48.4	163.0	144.2	10.7	18.8	844.8	696.2	53.8	148.6
3rd quarter	1 362.2	512.9	347.3	303.2	57.5	44.1	165.5	145.8	10.8	19.8	849.3	702.4	54.5	147.0
4th quarter	1 359.2	500.6	336.5	291.6	57.7	45.0	164.1	144.7	11.0	19.3	858.6	708.8	55.3	149.8
1996:														
1st quarter	1 384.2	516.4	348.4	298.2	57.2	50.2	168.0	146.4	11.1	21.5	867.8	717.6	56.0	150.3
2nd quarter	1 407.0	524.6	357.3	307.8	57.6	49.5	167.3	145.9	11.2	21.4	882.4	727.0	56.3	155.3
3rd quarter	1 413.5	521.6	354.8	309.3	57.2	45.5	166.8	144.6	11.3	22.1	891.9	735.9	56.8	156.0
4th quarter	1 422.3	517.6	350.6	307.6	57.1	42.9	167.0	146.0	11.4	21.0	904.7	743.3	57.3	161.4

1. Gross government investment consists of general government and government enterprise expenditures for fixed assets; inventory investment is included in government consumption expenditures.
2. Consumption expenditures excludes expenditures classified as investment, except for goods transferred to foreign countries by the federal government.
3. Consumption of general government fixed capital, or depreciation, is included in government consumption expenditures as a partial measure of the value of the services of general government fixed assets; use of depreciation assumes a zero net rate of return on these assets.

REAL GOVERNMENT CONSUMPTION EXPENDITURES AND GROSS INVESTMENT [1], [2]
(Calendar years—Billions of dollars, quarterly data are at seasonally adjusted annual rates)

YEAR AND QUARTER	Total	Federal									State and local			
		Total	Defense				Nondefense				Total	Consumption expenditures [3]		Gross invest-ment
			Total	Consumption expenditures [3]		Gross invest-ment	Total	Consumption expenditures [3]		Gross invest-ment		Total	Capital con-sump-tion [4]	
				Total	Capital con-sump-tion [4]			Total	Capital con-sump-tion [4]					
1968	892.4	476.3	400.9	376.7	55.5	32.5	82.5	71.4	5.2	10.7	416.5	307.5	20.8	102.0
1969	887.5	459.9	381.6	361.6	55.7	29.4	84.3	75.1	5.3	9.4	428.0	324.4	21.9	97.6
1970	866.8	427.2	349.0	330.1	55.1	27.2	83.1	74.6	5.4	8.8	440.0	344.1	23.0	91.3
1971	851.0	397.0	313.7	304.7	53.3	20.1	86.3	77.5	5.3	9.1	454.4	362.1	23.9	88.6
1972	854.1	390.2	300.3	285.3	51.4	22.9	91.9	83.0	5.3	9.4	464.5	376.0	24.8	85.6
1973	848.4	371.1	281.2	265.5	49.3	22.4	91.5	82.3	5.3	9.5	478.5	389.9	25.7	86.0
1974	862.9	368.8	273.6	256.5	47.3	23.0	96.4	87.3	5.3	9.6	495.6	406.8	26.6	86.7
1975	876.3	367.9	269.7	248.9	45.7	25.5	99.1	89.9	5.2	9.8	510.0	423.2	27.5	85.8
1976	876.8	364.3	264.7	242.5	44.3	26.2	100.4	90.2	5.2	10.6	514.3	429.5	28.3	84.3
1977	884.7	370.1	266.4	243.7	43.2	26.7	104.3	93.6	5.3	11.1	516.4	437.7	29.0	79.3
1978	910.6	377.7	266.8	244.7	42.0	26.2	111.4	98.1	5.4	13.2	534.7	448.1	29.8	86.4
1979	924.9	383.3	271.0	245.9	40.9	28.7	112.7	100.4	5.5	12.5	543.5	452.3	30.7	90.5
1980	941.4	399.3	280.7	254.0	40.2	30.2	119.0	106.0	5.7	13.2	543.6	451.7	31.5	91.1
1981	947.7	415.9	296.0	266.4	39.7	32.9	120.4	107.9	5.8	12.8	532.8	450.3	32.2	83.0
1982	960.1	429.4	316.5	282.0	39.8	37.4	113.3	102.3	5.9	11.5	531.4	455.6	32.7	77.4
1983	987.3	452.7	334.6	293.3	40.3	43.4	118.5	105.9	6.2	12.9	534.9	458.2	33.4	78.3
1984	1 018.4	463.7	348.1	301.3	41.6	48.1	115.9	102.3	6.5	13.8	555.0	468.0	34.5	87.9
1985	1 080.1	495.6	374.1	318.2	43.7	56.3	121.8	107.4	6.9	14.5	584.7	487.8	35.7	97.3
1986	1 135.0	518.4	393.4	331.1	46.2	62.2	125.2	110.6	7.2	14.7	616.9	513.3	37.1	103.9
1987	1 165.9	534.4	409.2	341.1	48.5	67.6	125.3	109.2	7.5	16.1	631.8	525.5	38.5	106.5
1988	1 180.9	524.6	405.5	345.3	50.2	60.3	119.1	104.8	7.8	14.4	656.6	545.3	39.9	111.5
1989	1 213.9	531.5	401.6	340.9	51.6	60.7	130.1	114.8	8.2	15.3	682.6	566.3	41.6	116.5
1990	1 250.4	541.9	401.5	338.9	53.0	62.5	140.5	123.9	8.6	16.8	708.6	583.2	43.2	125.4
1991	1 258.1	539.4	397.5	338.7	53.9	58.9	142.0	123.6	9.0	18.4	718.7	593.8	44.9	124.9
1992	1 263.8	528.0	375.8	319.7	54.2	56.1	152.2	131.4	9.3	20.8	735.8	603.6	46.6	132.2
1993	1 252.1	505.7	354.4	306.0	54.2	48.5	151.2	129.9	9.6	21.3	746.4	615.8	48.1	130.6
1994	1 252.3	486.6	336.9	292.2	53.5	44.8	149.5	130.4	9.9	19.0	765.7	633.4	49.4	132.2
1995	1 251.9	470.3	322.6	280.6	52.5	42.1	147.5	128.0	10.3	19.4	781.6	646.0	50.7	135.6
1996	1 257.9	464.2	317.8	275.5	51.4	42.3	146.1	125.3	10.8	21.0	793.7	653.6	52.0	140.1
1988:														
1st quarter	1 172.5	527.6	409.3	350.7	49.6	58.8	118.4	104.3	7.7	14.1	645.1	537.4	39.3	108.1
2nd quarter	1 177.0	522.3	405.6	343.6	50.0	61.9	116.7	102.7	7.8	14.1	655.0	542.8	39.7	112.3
3rd quarter	1 176.1	517.9	401.1	341.2	50.4	60.0	116.8	102.1	7.9	14.8	658.4	547.3	40.1	111.4
4th quarter	1 198.1	530.6	406.1	345.5	50.7	60.6	124.6	110.1	7.9	14.6	667.8	553.6	40.5	114.4
1989:														
1st quarter	1 193.5	521.4	394.4	335.1	51.1	59.3	127.1	112.3	8.0	14.9	672.3	559.2	41.0	113.4
2nd quarter	1 211.1	532.0	402.4	343.1	51.4	59.4	129.7	115.1	8.1	14.8	679.4	563.9	41.4	115.7
3rd quarter	1 222.6	537.7	407.4	342.9	51.8	64.4	130.5	115.5	8.2	15.1	685.1	568.6	41.8	116.7
4th quarter	1 228.4	535.0	402.1	342.5	52.1	59.7	133.0	116.5	8.3	16.5	693.7	573.5	42.2	120.3
1990:														
1st quarter	1 246.5	542.9	404.1	343.6	52.5	60.6	139.0	122.0	8.4	17.0	703.8	578.1	42.6	125.6
2nd quarter	1 248.2	543.0	402.8	340.0	52.8	62.7	140.4	123.7	8.5	16.8	705.4	581.6	43.0	123.8
3rd quarter	1 246.8	538.2	396.1	332.4	53.1	63.5	142.2	125.8	8.6	16.5	708.7	585.0	43.4	123.8
4th quarter	1 259.9	543.5	403.1	339.7	53.4	63.3	140.5	124.0	8.7	16.7	716.5	588.2	43.8	128.3
1991:														
1st quarter	1 262.6	547.3	408.4	348.9	53.7	59.5	139.1	122.5	8.8	16.7	715.5	590.9	44.3	124.6
2nd quarter	1 263.8	547.1	405.0	343.8	53.9	61.2	142.2	123.9	8.9	18.4	716.8	593.5	44.7	123.3
3rd quarter	1 255.1	536.3	395.0	335.2	54.1	59.8	141.4	123.2	9.0	18.2	718.8	594.2	45.1	124.7
4th quarter	1 250.7	526.9	381.7	326.7	54.2	55.0	145.3	124.7	9.1	20.6	723.8	596.7	45.6	127.1
1992:														
1st quarter	1 258.5	525.1	374.2	318.3	53.6	56.0	150.9	130.4	9.2	20.5	733.5	599.0	46.0	134.4
2nd quarter	1 257.5	523.3	373.3	316.5	54.4	56.8	150.0	129.9	9.3	20.1	734.2	601.7	46.4	132.6
3rd quarter	1 266.5	529.6	378.7	321.3	54.5	57.5	150.9	130.7	9.3	20.2	736.9	605.9	46.9	131.0
4th quarter	1 272.5	534.0	376.9	322.6	54.4	54.2	157.1	134.5	9.4	22.6	738.5	607.9	47.3	130.6
1993:														
1st quarter	1 250.1	512.1	359.2	308.5	54.4	50.6	152.9	130.0	9.5	23.0	738.0	610.8	47.6	127.1
2nd quarter	1 253.1	507.8	356.7	307.1	54.3	49.5	151.1	129.5	9.6	21.6	745.3	613.5	47.9	131.8
3rd quarter	1 250.5	501.5	351.1	305.0	54.1	46.1	150.3	129.1	9.6	21.2	749.1	617.5	48.3	131.5
4th quarter	1 254.7	501.3	350.8	303.2	54.0	47.6	150.4	130.8	9.7	19.5	753.4	621.5	48.6	131.9
1994:														
1st quarter	1 241.9	487.2	335.1	292.4	53.8	42.9	151.9	132.7	9.8	19.1	754.7	627.2	48.9	127.6
2nd quarter	1 243.3	481.2	335.9	291.5	53.6	44.5	145.1	127.1	9.9	18.0	762.2	631.6	49.2	130.6
3rd quarter	1 268.1	496.4	347.0	298.7	53.4	48.3	149.4	130.8	9.9	18.4	771.7	635.9	49.5	135.8
4th quarter	1 255.8	481.7	329.6	286.2	53.1	43.4	151.7	131.1	10.0	20.7	774.1	639.0	49.9	135.0
1995:														
1st quarter	1 257.7	480.4	328.7	285.6	52.9	43.2	151.4	129.8	10.1	21.7	777.3	643.2	50.2	134.1
2nd quarter	1 257.3	474.9	327.4	283.1	52.6	44.3	147.3	129.0	10.2	18.2	782.3	645.0	50.5	137.3
3rd quarter	1 255.0	473.4	324.0	283.8	52.4	40.3	149.1	130.0	10.3	19.0	781.5	646.8	50.9	134.7
4th quarter	1 237.7	452.6	310.3	269.7	52.1	40.6	142.1	123.4	10.4	18.6	785.1	648.9	51.2	136.2
1996:														
1st quarter	1 243.2	460.9	314.9	271.3	51.8	43.6	145.7	125.0	10.6	20.8	782.4	646.6	51.5	135.7
2nd quarter	1 265.1	470.7	323.2	278.4	51.6	44.9	147.2	126.5	10.7	20.8	794.4	654.2	51.9	140.2
3rd quarter	1 261.5	465.7	319.4	278.1	51.3	41.4	146.0	124.6	10.8	21.6	795.9	655.7	52.2	140.1
4th quarter	1 261.8	459.6	313.6	274.4	51.0	39.2	145.7	125.1	11.0	20.6	802.3	657.8	52.6	144.5

1. Components do not add to total. See NOTES.
2. Gross government investment consists of general government and government enterprise expenditures for fixed assets; inventory investment is included in government consumption expenditures.
3. Consumption expenditures excludes expenditures classified as investment, except for goods transferred to foreign countries by the federal government.
4. Consumption of general government fixed capital, or depreciation, is included in government consumption expenditures as a partial measure of the value of the services of general government fixed assets; use of depreciation assumes a zero net rate of return on these assets.

NATIONAL DEFENSE CONSUMPTION EXPENDITURES AND GROSS INVESTMENT [1]
(Calendar years—Billions of dollars, quarterly data are at seasonally adjusted annual rates)

YEAR AND QUARTER	Total	Consumption expenditures [2]												
		Total	Durable goods [2]						Nondurable goods			Services		
			Aircraft	Missiles	Ships	Vehicles	Electronics	Other durable goods	Petroleum products	Ammunition	Other nondurable goods	Employee compensation	Capital consumption [3]	Research and development
1968	....	....	....	....	....	....	....	....	....	....	....	....	....	....
1969	....	....	....	....	....	....	....	....	....	....	....	....	....	....
1970	....	....	....	....	....	....	....	....	....	....	....	....	....	....
1971	....	....	....	....	....	....	....	....	....	....	....	....	....	....
1972	93.2	82.3	3.0	1.2	0.2	0.4	0.8	0.2	1.8	2.0	0.9	40.5	15.6	5.2
1973	94.7	83.7	2.8	1.2	0.2	0.4	0.8	-0.1	1.7	1.7	0.9	41.4	17.1	5.4
1974	101.9	90.1	2.2	1.4	0.2	0.5	0.8	-0.5	2.8	1.4	1.1	44.1	18.9	5.9
1975	110.9	97.0	2.3	1.6	0.3	0.8	0.9	0.6	2.9	1.1	1.1	47.9	20.5	6.1
1976	116.1	101.3	2.2	1.3	0.3	0.6	0.7	0.9	2.5	0.6	1.4	50.2	21.7	6.6
1977	125.8	109.6	3.3	1.5	0.5	0.8	0.8	0.9	2.4	0.8	1.3	53.6	23.1	7.1
1978	135.6	118.4	3.6	2.3	0.7	1.1	1.0	1.0	2.5	1.0	1.3	57.5	24.8	7.4
1979	151.2	130.7	4.9	2.2	0.9	1.2	1.1	1.3	3.6	1.2	1.5	61.7	26.9	8.1
1980	174.2	150.9	5.6	2.3	0.7	1.5	1.4	1.3	6.8	1.4	1.9	68.5	28.9	10.4
1981	202.0	174.3	7.8	2.7	0.6	1.7	1.7	1.5	7.7	1.6	2.6	78.8	31.3	12.6
1982	230.9	197.6	10.3	3.0	0.4	1.7	2.0	1.7	6.8	2.1	2.7	87.4	33.6	14.4
1983	255.0	214.9	13.6	3.7	1.2	2.3	2.4	1.9	6.4	2.5	2.5	92.4	35.9	16.4
1984	282.7	236.3	14.0	4.0	1.0	2.8	2.7	2.4	5.9	2.2	2.3	107.5	35.8	18.7
1985	312.4	257.6	15.4	3.9	0.8	2.9	3.2	3.0	5.8	1.3	2.9	115.3	38.6	23.0
1986	332.4	272.7	17.2	4.6	0.8	3.2	3.3	2.7	3.6	3.6	3.1	118.7	41.6	25.4
1987	350.4	287.6	18.2	4.7	1.0	3.1	3.7	3.0	3.9	2.8	3.6	124.4	43.3	26.9
1988	354.0	297.9	18.3	5.1	1.1	2.6	3.6	3.1	3.5	3.5	3.6	126.4	45.3	32.4
1989	360.6	303.3	16.0	5.1	1.0	1.6	3.8	3.7	4.2	3.1	3.6	131.4	47.3	32.6
1990	373.1	312.7	16.3	5.3	1.7	1.5	3.8	3.5	5.3	2.8	2.9	134.8	50.2	30.8
1991	383.5	325.1	16.5	5.5	1.9	1.7	3.4	4.8	4.7	2.7	3.4	142.3	52.8	25.0
1992	375.8	319.7	14.0	4.8	2.1	1.3	3.3	4.6	3.5	2.6	3.4	143.1	54.2	26.1
1993	360.7	311.1	11.4	4.1	2.3	1.3	3.5	4.4	3.2	2.4	2.8	138.8	55.7	26.0
1994	349.2	301.6	9.4	3.5	1.6	0.8	3.1	4.6	3.0	1.7	2.8	133.8	56.7	25.0
1995	344.6	298.6	8.7	3.1	1.2	1.1	2.5	4.5	2.8	1.2	2.4	131.5	57.5	20.9
1996	352.8	305.7	9.7	3.2	0.9	1.0	2.6	5.0	3.4	1.1	3.4	135.2	57.3	23.5
1988:														
1st quarter	354.6	300.0	19.3	4.8	1.0	2.4	3.6	2.8	3.5	3.3	3.8	126.2	44.4	33.3
2nd quarter	353.2	296.1	17.9	5.0	1.0	2.9	3.7	2.8	3.3	4.1	3.7	126.6	44.9	31.3
3rd quarter	351.5	295.7	19.7	4.4	1.0	3.0	3.4	3.4	3.4	3.1	3.5	126.7	45.8	30.2
4th quarter	356.7	299.8	16.5	6.1	1.2	2.1	3.9	3.4	3.9	3.3	3.4	126.0	46.2	34.9
1989:														
1st quarter	352.8	297.0	16.8	4.9	0.9	1.9	3.7	3.3	3.8	3.8	3.4	130.4	46.6	29.9
2nd quarter	360.6	304.4	15.9	5.5	1.2	1.9	3.7	3.9	4.2	3.0	4.0	131.6	47.0	33.0
3rd quarter	367.6	306.2	15.9	5.4	1.1	1.5	4.2	4.0	4.0	3.2	3.8	132.7	47.6	33.6
4th quarter	361.3	305.5	15.4	4.8	1.1	1.4	3.6	3.7	4.6	2.2	3.3	130.7	48.0	34.0
1990:														
1st quarter	369.7	311.7	15.8	5.7	1.4	1.3	4.1	4.0	4.4	2.9	2.8	133.7	49.2	34.0
2nd quarter	370.6	310.8	15.9	4.9	1.8	1.5	3.4	4.7	4.1	2.9	3.1	134.0	49.4	32.3
3rd quarter	368.9	307.3	15.4	5.6	1.7	1.5	4.2	3.0	4.1	2.4	2.9	134.6	50.3	28.4
4th quarter	383.3	321.0	18.1	4.9	1.9	1.6	3.4	2.3	8.7	3.0	2.9	137.0	52.1	28.5
1991:														
1st quarter	389.7	331.3	16.4	5.7	1.7	1.6	3.7	5.3	6.6	2.8	3.8	143.9	51.7	24.8
2nd quarter	389.3	328.6	16.5	5.7	2.0	2.2	4.0	4.2	3.9	2.7	3.2	143.3	52.8	24.6
3rd quarter	382.1	323.1	16.4	5.9	2.2	1.6	3.3	4.7	4.5	2.4	3.0	141.7	53.1	24.4
4th quarter	373.0	318.5	16.6	4.8	1.9	1.4	2.8	4.8	3.6	2.7	3.5	140.1	53.5	26.3
1992:														
1st quarter	372.8	317.2	15.0	4.8	2.0	1.2	3.2	4.8	3.3	1.8	3.6	144.6	53.7	26.2
2nd quarter	374.1	317.3	13.8	4.6	1.9	1.3	3.1	4.2	3.6	3.4	3.3	145.4	54.2	23.2
3rd quarter	380.9	323.5	13.8	5.1	2.1	1.3	3.5	4.7	4.0	2.5	3.5	144.0	54.3	26.2
4th quarter	375.3	320.7	13.2	4.6	2.4	1.4	3.3	4.8	3.1	2.4	3.3	138.4	54.7	28.8
1993:														
1st quarter	363.6	312.4	11.4	4.3	1.9	1.3	3.6	4.4	3.0	2.4	2.7	142.4	55.1	26.0
2nd quarter	361.7	311.5	12.3	4.2	3.6	1.5	3.9	4.6	3.5	2.6	2.7	139.4	55.3	25.1
3rd quarter	358.0	310.6	11.6	4.1	1.7	1.2	3.4	4.3	3.4	2.6	3.1	138.1	56.1	25.2
4th quarter	359.4	309.8	10.3	4.0	1.8	1.0	3.0	4.3	2.9	2.1	2.6	135.4	56.4	27.7
1994:														
1st quarter	344.9	299.8	9.1	3.9	1.7	0.8	3.3	4.4	2.5	1.8	2.5	135.6	56.6	24.4
2nd quarter	348.5	300.7	8.5	3.3	1.6	0.8	3.2	4.7	3.4	1.5	2.2	135.2	56.9	26.0
3rd quarter	359.7	308.7	10.7	3.8	1.6	0.8	3.1	4.9	3.5	1.4	3.2	133.2	56.5	26.1
4th quarter	343.6	297.3	9.1	2.9	1.5	0.9	2.9	4.6	2.8	2.3	3.1	131.5	56.8	23.6
1995:														
1st quarter	346.3	299.9	9.6	2.9	1.1	1.0	2.6	4.2	2.6	1.1	2.3	132.1	57.2	22.5
2nd quarter	348.1	299.8	6.8	3.3	1.3	1.2	2.4	4.9	2.8	1.3	2.5	131.2	57.6	20.8
3rd quarter	347.3	303.2	10.0	3.6	1.6	1.3	2.7	4.4	3.3	1.3	2.2	131.7	57.5	20.9
4th quarter	336.5	291.6	8.4	2.7	0.8	0.9	2.2	4.6	2.4	0.9	2.4	130.8	57.7	19.3
1996:														
1st quarter	348.4	298.2	8.7	2.9	0.7	0.9	2.3	4.7	3.1	1.2	3.3	134.9	57.2	20.9
2nd quarter	357.3	307.8	10.2	3.2	0.9	1.0	2.9	5.5	3.4	1.5	3.4	135.4	57.6	22.9
3rd quarter	354.8	309.3	10.6	3.8	1.3	1.1	2.9	5.0	4.1	1.1	3.3	135.9	57.2	24.2
4th quarter	350.6	307.6	9.2	2.8	0.6	0.9	2.3	4.8	3.0	0.7	3.6	134.7	57.1	26.2

1. Gross government investment consists of general government and government enterprise expenditures for fixed assets; inventory investment is included in government consumption expenditures.
2. Consumption expenditures for durable goods excludes expenditures classified as investment, except for goods transferred to foreign countries by the federal government.
3. Consumption of general government fixed capital, or depreciation, is included in government consumption expenditures as a partial measure of the value of the services of general government fixed assets; use of depreciation assumes a zero net rate of return on these assets.

NATIONAL DEFENSE CONSUMPTION EXPENDITURES AND GROSS INVESTMENT [1]—Continued
(Calendar years—Billions of chained (1992) dollars, quarterly data are at seasonally adjusted annual rates)

YEAR AND QUARTER	Consumption expenditures—Continued / Services—Continued						Gross investment							
	Installation support	Weapons support	Personnel support	Transportation of material	Travel of persons	Other services	Total	Structures	Aircraft	Missiles	Ships	Vehicles	Electronics	Other equipment
1968	....	....	....	....	....	....	....	....	....	....	....	....	....	....
1969	....	....	....	....	....	....	....	....	....	....	....	....	....	....
1970	....	....	....	....	....	....	....	....	....	....	....	....	....	....
1971	4.4	1.6	1.9	1.8	0.9	-0.2	10.9	1.8	2.6	1.5	1.8	0.4	0.6	2.2
1972	4.3	1.6	1.8	1.6	1.0	-0.1	11.0	2.1	2.3	1.5	1.6	0.3	0.6	2.5
1973	4.7	1.8	2.0	1.7	1.1	-0.2	11.9	2.2	2.3	1.7	2.2	0.3	0.6	2.6
1974	4.9	1.7	2.2	1.8	1.0	-0.8	14.0	2.3	3.6	1.3	2.2	0.3	0.7	3.6
1975														
1976	5.4	1.9	2.4	1.8	1.0	-0.2	14.8	2.1	3.4	1.4	2.4	0.5	0.8	4.2
1977	6.2	2.1	2.4	1.9	1.2	-0.4	16.2	2.4	3.7	1.2	3.1	0.6	0.9	4.2
1978	6.3	2.4	2.8	1.9	1.4	-0.5	17.1	2.5	3.7	1.1	3.9	0.8	1.1	4.0
1979	7.3	2.9	3.0	2.2	1.3	-0.5	20.6	2.5	4.8	1.8	4.3	0.9	1.2	5.0
1980	8.8	4.4	3.4	2.6	1.6	-0.7	23.3	3.2	6.1	2.3	4.1	1.2	1.6	4.8
1981	9.9	5.2	4.5	2.8	2.1	-0.8	27.7	3.2	7.5	2.8	5.1	1.1	2.0	6.1
1982	14.0	6.0	6.3	3.1	2.6	-0.7	33.3	4.0	8.4	3.4	6.2	2.1	2.4	6.8
1983	14.3	7.3	6.8	3.4	2.4	-0.5	40.2	4.8	10.1	4.6	7.1	3.4	2.9	7.3
1984	15.5	8.6	7.2	3.3	2.9	-0.7	46.4	4.9	10.9	5.7	8.0	4.2	3.4	9.3
1985	17.2	9.8	8.9	3.1	3.1	-0.7	54.8	6.2	13.4	6.6	9.0	3.7	4.3	11.5
1986	18.6	10.4	9.9	3.4	3.3	-0.8	59.7	6.8	17.9	7.9	8.9	3.8	4.6	9.9
1987	20.1	11.0	11.6	3.5	3.7	-0.8	62.8	7.7	17.6	8.7	8.8	4.3	5.1	10.6
1988	20.3	10.7	12.1	3.6	3.7	-1.1	56.1	7.4	13.6	7.8	8.6	3.7	4.9	10.1
1989	20.0	9.9	12.7	4.0	4.0	-1.0	57.3	6.4	12.2	8.9	10.0	3.1	4.7	12.0
1990	21.9	10.7	13.4	4.8	4.1	-1.1	60.4	6.1	12.2	10.9	10.8	3.2	4.7	12.5
1991	23.5	9.7	13.4	8.8	7.0	-1.6	58.1	4.6	9.6	10.7	10.2	3.4	4.2	15.4
1992	23.3	8.8	15.7	5.9	5.4	-2.3	56.1	5.2	8.7	10.5	10.1	2.8	4.2	14.7
1993	25.3	7.4	15.5	4.6	4.9	-2.6	49.6	5.1	9.3	7.9	8.7	1.9	4.0	12.3
1994	26.1	8.4	16.9	3.8	4.4	-4.0	47.6	5.8	10.4	5.7	8.1	1.0	4.0	12.6
1995	27.7	8.3	18.3	4.3	4.5	-1.7	46.0	6.4	9.0	4.6	8.0	0.9	3.5	13.5
1996	27.4	6.3	19.0	4.7	4.3	-2.1	47.0	6.8	9.3	4.1	6.8	0.9	3.6	15.5
1988:														
1st quarter	20.9	11.6	12.6	3.5	4.0	-0.8	54.6	7.2	14.5	6.6	8.4	3.9	5.0	9.0
2nd quarter	20.1	10.3	12.1	3.8	3.7	-1.0	57.1	7.9	14.4	8.3	8.1	3.9	5.0	9.6
3rd quarter	19.7	10.7	11.8	4.1	3.6	-1.8	55.8	7.0	12.4	8.1	8.3	3.9	4.6	11.5
4th quarter	20.7	10.1	12.0	3.2	3.6	-0.7	56.9	7.3	13.0	8.4	9.6	3.1	4.9	10.5
1989:														
1st quarter	19.3	9.2	11.4	4.3	4.4	-1.1	55.9	6.5	11.9	8.2	10.2	3.3	4.6	11.2
2nd quarter	19.5	10.1	12.9	4.1	3.8	-1.0	56.2	6.2	11.2	8.8	9.3	3.0	4.7	13.0
3rd quarter	20.1	9.5	12.8	4.2	3.7	-1.0	61.4	6.4	12.2	10.4	10.6	3.7	5.1	13.0
4th quarter	21.1	11.0	13.8	3.5	4.0	-0.7	55.8	6.2	13.4	8.1	9.9	2.6	4.6	11.0
1990:														
1st quarter	22.6	10.4	13.5	3.7	3.4	-1.1	58.0	6.3	10.8	10.4	10.0	3.1	5.0	12.3
2nd quarter	20.7	10.8	13.8	4.4	4.2	-1.1	59.8	6.3	12.9	9.6	10.6	3.3	4.4	12.7
3rd quarter	21.9	10.6	12.5	5.2	4.2	-1.1	61.6	6.4	13.0	11.3	10.3	3.5	5.0	12.1
4th quarter	22.4	11.1	13.8	5.9	4.5	-1.0	62.3	5.3	12.2	12.4	12.2	2.9	4.2	13.0
1991:														
1st quarter	24.4	11.3	13.6	9.5	6.1	-1.6	58.4	4.8	9.0	11.6	9.8	2.9	4.5	15.7
2nd quarter	23.2	9.7	12.6	11.0	8.4	-1.5	60.7	4.8	10.6	11.1	10.6	4.3	4.8	14.5
3rd quarter	21.9	8.6	12.7	9.6	9.4	-2.2	59.0	4.5	10.1	10.6	10.2	4.3	4.0	15.3
4th quarter	24.6	8.9	14.7	5.1	4.1	-1.0	54.5	4.5	8.4	9.4	10.2	2.3	3.6	16.0
1992:														
1st quarter	22.2	8.9	15.2	4.7	4.1	-2.1	55.6	5.2	7.9	9.8	10.7	2.4	4.4	15.2
2nd quarter	22.0	8.1	14.2	8.0	6.1	-3.1	56.9	5.5	10.1	10.9	10.4	2.2	3.7	14.0
3rd quarter	22.3	8.8	15.3	7.6	7.1	-2.8	57.4	4.8	9.0	11.0	9.9	3.4	4.5	14.9
4th quarter	26.6	9.4	18.0	3.5	4.2	-1.4	54.6	5.5	7.7	10.2	9.3	3.1	4.1	14.6
1993:														
1st quarter	24.6	8.2	16.2	3.3	4.2	-2.5	51.2	4.8	8.2	8.7	9.2	3.0	4.7	12.7
2nd quarter	24.9	6.4	14.8	4.3	5.0	-2.6	50.3	4.9	7.9	8.4	9.0	1.8	5.0	13.4
3rd quarter	25.2	6.6	15.5	6.2	5.8	-3.6	47.4	5.4	9.6	6.5	8.2	1.4	4.3	12.0
4th quarter	26.3	8.4	15.6	4.8	4.8	-1.7	49.6	5.3	11.8	8.0	8.2	1.3	3.8	11.3
1994:														
1st quarter	26.5	7.9	15.5	3.9	3.6	-4.1	45.1	5.4	7.9	6.6	7.6	1.1	4.3	12.3
2nd quarter	26.0	8.2	16.1	4.0	4.4	-5.2	47.7	5.5	9.9	5.6	8.7	1.2	4.0	12.8
3rd quarter	25.7	9.5	18.1	3.7	5.8	-2.8	51.1	6.1	12.5	5.7	8.8	0.8	4.1	13.0
4th quarter	26.2	7.9	17.8	3.6	3.8	-4.0	46.3	6.1	11.5	4.8	7.1	1.0	3.7	12.2
1995:														
1st quarter	27.1	8.6	18.0	4.0	4.6	-1.8	46.5	7.0	9.3	4.1	8.7	1.0	4.0	12.4
2nd quarter	28.4	9.3	19.0	4.1	4.7	-1.8	48.4	6.2	9.0	5.8	8.5	0.9	3.3	14.7
3rd quarter	28.5	8.5	18.2	4.2	4.4	-1.2	44.1	6.0	8.0	5.1	7.6	1.0	3.7	12.8
4th quarter	26.8	7.0	17.9	4.7	4.2	-2.0	45.0	6.5	9.5	3.6	7.2	0.8	3.2	14.2
1996:														
1st quarter	26.5	6.1	18.0	4.5	4.5	-2.1	50.2	6.7	13.7	4.2	7.0	1.0	3.3	14.3
2nd quarter	28.2	5.9	18.5	5.0	4.3	-2.0	49.5	7.3	10.0	4.3	7.2	0.9	3.7	16.0
3rd quarter	28.3	5.4	18.8	4.7	4.2	-2.6	45.5	6.6	7.6	4.3	6.6	0.9	4.0	15.5
4th quarter	26.4	8.0	20.5	4.7	4.1	-1.9	42.9	6.6	5.9	3.7	6.3	0.8	3.2	16.3

1. Gross government investment consists of general government and government enterprise expenditures for fixed assets; inventory investment is included in government consumption expenditures.

FEDERAL GOVERNMENT RECEIPTS AND OUTLAYS BY FISCAL YEAR [1]
(Millions of dollars)

Column groups: *Receipts, outlays, deficit, and financing* covers Receipts (Net), Outlays (Net), Budget surplus or deficit (—), and Sources of financing (Borrowing from the public, Other financing). *Receipts by source* covers Individual income taxes, Corporate income taxes, Social insurance taxes and contributions (Employment taxes and contributions, Unemployment insurance, Other retirement contributions), Excise taxes, Estate and gift taxes, Customs deposits, and Miscellaneous receipts.

Year and month	Receipts (Net)	Outlays (Net)	Budget surplus or deficit (—)	Borrowing from the public	Other financing	Individual income taxes	Corporate income taxes	Employment taxes and contributions	Unemployment insurance	Other retirement contributions	Excise taxes	Estate and gift taxes	Customs deposits	Miscellaneous receipts
1968	152 973	178 134	-25 161	22 919	2 242	68 726	28 665	29 224	3 346	1 354	14 079	3 051	2 038	2 491
1969	186 882	183 640	3 242	-11 437	8 195	87 249	36 678	34 236	3 328	1 451	15 222	3 491	2 319	2 909
1970	192 807	195 649	-2 842	5 090	-2 248	90 412	32 829	39 133	3 464	1 765	15 705	3 644	2 430	3 424
1971	187 139	210 172	-23 033	19 839	3 194	86 230	26 785	41 699	3 674	1 952	16 614	3 735	2 591	3 858
1972	207 309	230 681	-23 373	19 340	4 032	94 737	32 166	46 120	4 357	2 097	15 477	5 436	3 287	3 632
1973	230 799	245 707	-14 908	18 533	-3 625	103 246	36 153	54 876	6 051	2 187	16 260	4 917	3 188	3 920
1974	263 224	269 359	-6 135	2 789	3 346	118 952	38 620	65 888	6 837	2 347	16 844	5 035	3 334	5 368
1975	279 090	332 332	-53 242	51 001	2 241	122 386	40 621	75 199	6 771	2 565	16 551	4 611	3 676	6 712
1976	298 060	371 792	-73 732	82 704	-8 972	131 603	41 409	79 901	8 054	2 814	16 963	5 216	4 074	8 027
1977	355 559	409 218	-53 659	71 699	-18 040	157 626	54 892	92 199	11 312	2 974	17 548	7 327	5 150	6 531
1978	399 561	458 746	-59 186	58 022	1 163	180 988	59 952	103 881	13 850	3 237	18 376	5 285	6 573	7 419
1979	463 302	504 032	-40 729	33 183	7 547	217 841	65 677	120 058	15 387	3 494	18 745	5 411	7 439	9 252
1980	517 112	590 947	-73 835	69 530	4 305	244 069	64 600	138 748	15 336	3 719	24 329	6 389	7 174	12 748
1981	599 272	678 249	-78 976	75 500	3 477	285 917	61 137	162 973	15 763	3 984	40 839	6 787	8 083	13 790
1982	617 766	745 755	-127 989	134 447	-6 458	297 744	49 207	180 686	16 600	4 212	36 311	7 991	8 854	16 161
1983	600 562	808 380	-207 818	211 811	-3 993	288 938	37 022	185 766	18 799	4 429	35 300	6 053	8 655	15 600
1984	666 499	851 888	-185 388	168 902	16 487	298 415	56 893	209 658	25 138	4 580	37 361	6 010	11 370	17 073
1985	734 165	946 499	-212 334	199 410	12 924	334 531	61 331	234 646	25 758	4 759	35 992	6 422	12 079	18 647
1986	769 260	990 505	-221 245	236 801	-15 556	348 959	63 143	255 062	24 098	4 742	32 919	6 958	13 327	20 053
1987	854 396	1 004 164	-149 769	151 971	-2 203	392 557	83 926	273 028	25 575	4 715	32 457	7 493	15 085	19 560
1988	909 303	1 064 489	-155 187	162 119	-6 933	401 181	94 508	305 093	24 584	4 658	35 227	7 594	16 198	20 259
1989	991 190	1 143 671	-152 481	139 083	13 398	445 690	103 291	332 859	22 011	4 546	34 386	8 745	16 334	23 328
1990	1 031 969	1 253 163	-221 194	220 840	544	466 884	93 507	353 891	21 635	4 522	35 345	11 500	16 707	27 978
1991	1 055 041	1 324 400	-269 359	277 415	-8 246	467 827	98 086	370 526	20 922	4 568	42 402	11 138	15 949	23 623
1992	1 090 453	1 380 793	-290 339	310 696	-20 294	475 964	100 270	385 491	23 410	4 788	45 569	11 143	17 359	27 284
1993	1 153 226	1 408 532	-255 306	248 594	6 503	509 680	117 520	396 939	26 556	4 805	48 057	12 577	18 802	19 465
1994	1 258 411	1 461 359	-202 948	184 583	18 427	543 055	140 385	428 810	28 004	4 661	55 225	15 225	20 099	23 164
1995	1 351 495	1 515 410	-163 916	171 363	-4 247	590 244	157 004	451 045	28 878	4 550	57 484	14 763	19 301	28 226
1996	1 452 763	1 560 040	-107 277	129 657	-22 380	656 417	171 824	476 361	28 584	4 469	54 014	17 189	18 670	25 232
1993:														
January	112 716	82 899	29 817	-8 355	-21 462	73 704	3 212	28 209	844	363	3 307	888	1 310	971
February	65 979	114 477	-48 498	30 689	17 809	23 947	792	31 623	2 259	369	3 342	822	1 347	1 695
March	83 288	127 263	-43 975	37 727	6 248	27 935	12 724	32 980	240	432	4 514	977	1 598	2 051
April	132 017	124 200	7 817	5 464	-13 281	56 137	17 795	45 164	3 581	431	4 168	1 898	1 544	1 404
May	70 642	107 605	-36 963	30 832	6 131	17 919	2 376	33 062	8 849	365	3 502	1 009	1 419	2 257
June	128 570	117 471	11 099	24 757	-35 856	56 463	24 949	37 738	301	366	4 565	900	1 642	1 668
July	80 630	120 207	-39 577	1 055	38 522	37 489	2 695	30 156	1 709	419	4 214	944	1 761	1 252
August	86 737	109 815	-23 078	54 301	-31 223	39 444	1 943	31 447	4 810	400	4 295	1 150	1 828	1 429
September	127 504	118 939	8 565	-9 346	781	55 653	24 510	36 908	413	447	4 385	1 049	1 646	2 456
October	78 662	124 085	-45 423	4 255	41 168	37 680	2 158	29 440	1 046	343	3 597	990	1 708	1 708
November	83 102	121 483	-38 381	71 028	-32 647	37 634	2 208	31 525	2 773	385	4 808	1 305	1 688	781
December	125 403	133 108	-7 705	13 995	-6 290	54 183	28 239	33 273	259	423	4 695	1 179	1 584	1 582
1994:														
January	122 961	107 713	15 248	-6 933	-8 315	74 167	3 916	35 831	794	358	4 011	1 105	1 526	1 260
February	73 186	114 752	-41 566	31 633	9 933	28 107	1 594	32 957	2 664	367	3 249	1 093	1 419	1 491
March	93 108	125 423	-32 315	26 511	5 804	29 917	15 574	35 976	522	459	5 285	1 211	1 745	2 418
April	141 326	123 872	17 454	-21 801	4 347	60 038	20 586	47 348	2 605	370	4 050	1 479	1 479	2 472
May	83 546	115 602	-32 056	27 649	4 407	24 384	2 817	35 749	10 426	364	5 253	1 342	1 620	1 589
June	138 124	123 275	14 849	2 098	-16 947	58 123	29 114	40 853	290	366	4 596	1 068	1 711	2 003
July	84 827	118 025	-33 198	-3 245	36 443	37 372	3 805	32 222	1 399	424	4 175	1 060	1 782	2 587
August	97 338	121 608	-24 270	52 427	-28 157	43 170	3 108	34 020	4 880	391	5 989	1 239	2 039	2 502
September	135 895	131 903	3 992	-12 154	8 162	57 964	27 265	39 614	346	411	5 518	1 254	1 799	1 725
October	89 024	120 365	-31 341	32 457	-1 116	43 659	3 055	31 263	1 073	351	4 272	1 202	1 848	2 300
November	87 673	124 915	-37 242	40 528	-3 286	37 414	1 497	33 786	3 249	352	5 518	1 220	1 827	2 811
December	130 810	134 941	-4 131	-13 316	17 447	53 736	31 915	35 708	230	420	4 587	1 092	1 747	1 375
1995:														
January	131 801	115 171	16 630	13 337	-29 967	79 162	3 258	38 990	1 069	383	4 555	1 005	1 539	1 839
February	82 544	120 527	-37 983	38 964	-981	33 863	2 060	35 667	2 630	357	3 485	916	1 435	2 131
March	92 532	143 074	-50 542	13 645	36 897	26 846	14 863	38 646	320	413	5 143	1 218	1 470	3 612
April	165 392	115 673	49 719	-27 638	-22 081	76 441	23 482	50 423	3 061	354	4 602	1 906	1 349	3 774
May	90 405	129 958	-39 553	44 740	-5 187	29 729	2 193	37 226	10 601	355	4 770	1 339	1 471	2 719
June	147 868	135 054	12 814	8 491	-21 305	61 457	35 876	40 605	320	416	4 897	1 040	1 583	1 674
July	92 749	106 328	-13 579	10 627	2 952	42 819	3 397	34 514	1 636	349	5 074	1 037	1 603	2 320
August	96 560	130 411	-33 851	16 071	17 780	44 122	2 501	34 914	4 454	436	4 757	1 500	1 794	2 081
September	143 219	135 933	7 286	-9 845	2 559	60 909	32 989	39 304	235	364	5 706	1 289	1 634	789
October	95 674	118 252	-22 578	13 353	9 406	51 840	2 180	30 549	1 214	342	4 453	1 160	1 786	2 070
November	90 086	128 538	-38 452	38 339	-26 580	39 524	1 694	34 919	2 940	340	5 154	1 349	1 593	2 496
December	138 347	133 064	5 283	-18 358	13 071	53 179	38 021	37 123	223	416	4 870	1 383	1 439	1 618
1996:														
January	142 999	123 543	19 456	……	……	86 192	5 158	40 742	1 081	374	4 241	1 288	1 482	2 364
February	89 428	133 775	-44 347	47 022	-2 727	40 327	1 692	36 011	2 546	403	4 308	1 090	1 456	1 517
March	89 087	136 158	-47 071	38 189	9 086	……	……	56 615	3 628	346	4 577	2 704	1 388	1 680
April	203 468	131 064	72 404	-35 466	-10 478	107 513	24 937	……	……	……	……	……	……	……
May	90 122	143 173	-53 051	20 633	-11 145	29 914	2 570	29 938	10 155	417	4 113	1 415	1 427	1 929
June	151 995	117 655	34 340	-8 619	8 037	60 816	36 957	44 888	400	295	4 310	1 141	1 450	1 663
July	103 893	130 749	-26 856	29 098	-3 263	49 814	4 975	36 946	1 939	372	4 508	1 259	1 712	2 287
August	99 996	141 828	-41 832	16 160	1 966	46 105	3 074	36 562	3 994	397	4 033	1 566	1 807	2 459
September	157 668	121 965	35 703	-5 892	1 680	68 672	35 105	42 817	206	348	5 315	1 698	1 604	1 902
October	99 656	139 915	-40 259	15 588	24 671	53 600	863	34 428	1 330	346	3 923	1 547	1 432	2 187
November	97 849	135 727	-37 878	45 459	-7 581	46 271	2 339	36 967	2 574	411	4 678	1 394	1 219	1 997
December	148 489	129 666	18 823	-12 321	-7 041	59 423	38 956	40 057	259	371	4 559	1 371	1 520	1 973

1. Fiscal years through 1976 are from July 1 through June 30. Beginning with October 1976 (fiscal year 1977), fiscal years are from October 1 through September 30. The period from July 1 through September 30, 1976 (not shown here) is a separate fiscal period known as the transition quarter and not included in any fiscal year.

FEDERAL GOVERNMENT OUTLAYS BY FISCAL YEAR [1]—Continued
(Millions of dollars)

YEAR AND MONTH	National defense	International affairs	General science, space, and technology	Energy	Natural resources and environment	Agriculture	Commerce and housing credit	Transportation	Community and regional development	Education, employment, and social services	Health	Medicare	Income security	Social Security
1968	81 926	5 301	5 524	1 037	2 988	4 545	4 280	6 316	1 382	7 634	4 390	4 649	11 816	23 854
1969	82 497	4 600	5 020	1 010	2 900	5 826	-119	6 526	1 552	7 548	5 162	5 695	13 076	27 298
1970	81 692	4 330	4 511	997	3 065	5 166	2 112	7 008	2 392	8 634	5 907	6 213	15 655	30 270
1971	78 872	4 159	4 182	1 035	3 915	4 290	2 366	8 052	2 917	9 849	6 843	6 622	22 946	35 872
1972	79 174	4 781	4 175	1 296	4 241	5 259	2 222	8 392	3 423	12 529	8 674	7 479	27 650	40 157
1973	76 681	4 149	4 032	1 237	4 775	4 854	931	9 066	4 605	12 745	9 356	8 052	28 276	49 090
1974	79 347	5 710	3 980	1 303	5 697	2 230	4 705	9 172	4 229	12 457	10 733	9 639	33 713	55 867
1975	86 509	7 097	3 991	2 916	7 346	3 036	9 947	10 918	4 322	16 022	12 930	12 875	50 176	64 658
1976	89 619	6 433	4 373	4 204	8 184	3 170	7 619	13 739	5 442	18 910	15 734	15 834	60 799	73 899
1977	97 241	6 353	4 736	5 770	10 032	6 787	3 093	14 829	7 021	21 104	17 302	19 345	61 060	85 061
1978	104 495	7 482	4 926	7 992	10 983	11 357	6 254	15 521	11 841	26 710	18 524	22 768	61 505	93 861
1979	116 342	7 459	5 235	9 180	12 135	11 236	4 686	18 079	10 480	30 223	20 494	26 495	66 376	104 073
1980	133 995	12 714	5 832	10 156	13 858	8 839	9 390	21 329	11 252	31 843	23 169	32 090	86 557	118 547
1981	157 513	13 104	6 469	15 166	13 568	11 323	8 206	23 379	10 568	33 709	26 866	39 149	99 742	139 584
1982	185 309	12 300	7 200	13 527	12 998	15 944	6 256	20 625	8 347	27 029	27 445	46 567	107 737	155 964
1983	209 903	11 848	7 935	9 353	12 672	22 901	6 681	21 334	7 560	26 606	28 641	52 588	122 621	170 724
1984	227 413	15 876	8 317	7 086	12 593	13 613	6 959	23 669	7 673	27 579	30 417	57 540	112 694	178 223
1985	252 748	16 176	8 627	5 685	13 357	25 565	4 337	25 838	7 680	29 342	33 542	65 822	128 230	188 623
1986	273 375	14 152	8 976	4 735	13 639	31 449	5 059	28 117	7 233	30 585	35 936	70 164	119 824	198 757
1987	281 999	11 649	9 216	4 115	13 363	26 606	6 435	26 222	5 051	29 724	39 967	75 120	123 282	207 353
1988	290 361	10 471	10 841	2 297	14 606	17 210	19 164	27 272	5 294	31 938	44 487	78 878	129 374	219 341
1989	303 559	9 573	12 838	2 706	16 182	16 919	29 710	27 608	5 362	36 674	48 390	84 964	136 066	232 542
1990	299 331	13 764	14 444	3 341	17 080	11 958	67 600	29 485	8 498	38 755	57 716	98 102	147 076	248 623
1991	273 292	15 851	16 111	2 436	18 559	15 183	76 271	31 099	6 811	43 354	71 183	104 489	170 320	269 015
1992	298 350	16 107	16 409	4 500	20 025	15 205	10 919	33 333	6 838	45 248	89 497	119 024	197 022	287 585
1993	291 086	17 248	17 030	4 319	20 239	20 363	-21 853	35 004	9 052	50 012	99 415	130 552	207 299	304 585
1994	281 642	17 083	16 227	5 219	21 064	15 046	-4 228	38 066	10 454	46 307	107 122	144 747	214 089	319 565
1995	272 066	16 434	16 724	4 936	22 078	9 778	-17 808	39 350	10 641	54 263	115 418	159 855	220 493	335 846
1996	265 748	13 496	16 709	2 836	21 614	9 159	-10 646	39 565	10 685	52 001	119 378	174 225	225 989	349 676
1993:														
January	19 683	1 161	1 395	15	1 372	1 206	-1 832	2 363	650	4 360	7 828	9 645	16 225	25 731
February	22 903	1 253	1 325	399	1 282	1 145	-3 532	2 093	690	4 068	8 053	9 935	21 317	25 070
March	25 511	1 181	1 103	560	1 549	4 244	-1 368	3 383	760	4 607	8 379	11 954	21 056	25 281
April	27 192	536	1 444	431	1 709	2 666	-3 961	2 591	987	3 695	8 883	11 816	20 408	25 420
May	20 460	1 410	1 382	453	1 071	1 739	-1 896	2 398	862	3 433	7 758	9 732	15 900	25 288
June	24 786	1 024	1 347	604	1 605	824	-2 523	3 281	986	3 820	8 981	12 337	13 801	28 724
July	25 916	1 241	1 521	198	1 421	206	-2 014	3 250	962	3 113	8 023	12 103	18 665	25 567
August	21 278	493	1 556	400	1 487	171	-2 703	3 270	876	4 937	8 632	10 883	14 925	25 451
September	24 903	1 556	1 388	-276	1 907	205	3 003	3 760	1 168	4 326	9 080	11 074	15 696	25 623
October	24 281	4 732	1 421	345	1 911	1 442	377	3 133	898	3 586	9 315	10 729	17 342	25 538
November	22 990	1 964	1 522	510	2 784	2 237	-1 361	3 248	930	5 098	8 675	11 491	16 764	25 556
December	26 809	548	1 496	385	1 567	3 074	1 126	3 714	772	4 455	8 906	13 803	19 771	25 917
1994:														
January	18 861	1 103	1 299	465	1 447	1 122	-1 124	2 503	906	2 693	7 665	9 858	16 196	26 151
February	21 996	948	1 269	159	1 449	1 817	-4 608	2 784	445	2 666	8 229	10 897	22 466	26 325
March	24 476	696	1 685	510	1 631	1 439	-1 260	2 845	1 276	2 285	10 014	13 843	20 549	26 507
April	24 501	1 554	1 238	316	1 463	1 641	-702	2 620	938	3 694	8 410	11 245	20 957	26 627
May	19 509	917	1 415	325	1 519	1 112	1 564	2 869	843	3 841	9 074	11 430	15 796	26 525
June	24 197	582	1 596	261	1 670	320	1 016	3 151	1 184	3 797	9 729	13 279	13 139	30 088
July	22 147	893	1 236	464	1 635	309	277	3 226	1 081	2 948	8 189	12 599	17 037	26 698
August	23 711	990	1 654	390	1 745	382	-3 026	3 719	1 138	4 342	9 426	12 540	16 848	26 722
September	27 657	2 323	1 772	987	2 156	236	2 623	3 583	1 469	5 088	9 106	13 032	17 101	26 912
October	18 801	4 339	1 115	525	3 418	2 048	858	3 434	1 171	3 705	8 631	11 099	15 275	26 702
November	22 428	2 177	1 673	166	1 797	2 784	-1 244	3 506	1 109	4 025	9 525	12 687	16 151	26 612
December	26 348	1 334	1 529	417	1 622	1 938	-2 166	3 021	1 102	5 779	9 246	14 058	19 331	27 158
1995:														
January	18 499	999	1 194	488	1 571	1 049	-1 469	3 080	1 140	4 650	9 440	11 923	16 326	27 811
February	21 461	1 108	1 374	260	1 374	1 264	-2 978	2 799	228	4 078	8 918	11 829	20 583	27 632
March	26 533	425	1 628	569	1 951	1 195	-1 853	3 167	971	4 678	10 625	15 409	24 708	27 800
April	17 753	95	1 298	196	1 587	623	-1 092	2 560	896	3 647	9 281	11 510	18 963	27 953
May	22 194	1 282	1 596	244	1 820	236	-1 988	3 154	860	4 205	9 472	14 390	20 633	27 997
June	26 148	818	1 521	601	1 698	328	-3 041	3 432	1 035	4 480	10 543	15 663	16 426	32 058
July	18 069	517	1 355	547	1 811	-482	-733	3 324	1 191	2 869	8 777	12 016	15 310	27 998
August	23 882	1 877	1 668	13	2 116	-462	-2 592	3 359	909	5 785	10 422	14 840	16 919	27 950
September	26 040	1 479	1 612	969	1 915	-102	2 490	3 719	1 043	4 802	9 401	14 430	19 591	28 175
October	18 353	1 074	1 427	348	2 835	1 109	-1 661	3 128	943	3 556	9 657	12 671	14 522	28 061
November	21 234	1 616	1 474	489	2 245	2 291	-1 465	3 284	1 087	4 185	10 189	14 058	18 134	27 889
December	25 376	431	1 274	-163	1 711	708	-451	3 117	912	3 623	8 567	14 794	19 738	28 505
1996:														
January	....	....	....	....	....	....	....	....	....	....	....	....	....	....
February	21 691	2 604	1 326	54	1 817	345	-1 024	2 960	396	4 498	9 542	14 117	23 812	28 833
March	22 479	1 391	1 381	131	1 592	-62	-1 443	2 864	1 007	4 270	10 306	14 123	25 968	29 116
April	22 725	988	1 534	17	1 660	-249	-1 741	2 864	1 026	4 014	10 458	15 124	21 417	29 092
May	26 609	1 165	1 584	216	1 757	-175	256	3 324	826	3 961	11 201	17 571	21 407	29 156
June	19 769	837	1 536	822	1 543	-124	-1 368	3 185	896	3 903	9 762	12 049	11 332	32 682
July	22 541	497	1 660	187	2 062	843	-304	3 648	959	3 108	10 077	16 111	18 189	29 265
August	26 000	969	1 526	153	1 821	627	-1 678	3 583	1 021	5 037	10 352	16 983	20 125	29 222
September	19 738	1 007	1 689	563	1 914	3 309	1 559	3 540	1 191	5 082	10 004	12 546	13 664	29 147
October	22 284	4 112	1 447	-207	1 758	2 347	-167	3 870	1 247	4 176	10 067	16 067	18 544	29 353
November	24 911	814	1 586	-96	1 888	1 405	-4 535	3 386	990	4 973	10 060	16 479	19 714	29 457
December	23 085	1 371	1 590	201	2 150	2 240	-1 335	3 209	706	3 799	10 558	15 220	17 278	29 559

1. Fiscal years through 1976 are from July 1 through June 30. Beginning with October 1976 (fiscal year 1977), fiscal years are from October 1 through September 30. The period from July 1 through September 30, 1976 (not shown here) is a separate fiscal period known as the transition quarter and not included in any fiscal year.

YEAR AND MONTH	FEDERAL GOVERNMENT OUTLAYS BY FISCAL YEAR [1]—Continued (Millions of dollars)					GOVERNMENT EMPLOYMENT (Payroll employment—Thousands, seasonally adjusted)					
	Outlays by function—Continued							State		Local	
	Veterans benefits and services	Administration of justice	General government	Interest	Undistributed offsetting receipts	Total	Federal	Total	Education	Total	Education
1968	7 032	659	1 757	11 090	-8 045	11 839	2 737	2 442	958	6 660	3 736
1969	7 631	766	1 939	12 699	-7 986	12 195	2 758	2 533	1 042	6 904	3 874
1970	8 669	959	2 320	14 380	-8 632	12 554	2 731	2 664	1 104	7 158	4 004
1971	9 768	1 306	2 442	14 841	-10 107	12 881	2 696	2 747	1 149	7 437	4 188
1972	10 720	1 653	2 960	15 478	-9 583	13 334	2 684	2 859	1 188	7 790	4 363
1973	12 003	2 141	9 774	17 349	-13 409	13 732	2 663	2 923	1 205	8 146	4 537
1974	13 374	2 470	10 032	21 449	-16 749	14 170	2 724	3 039	1 267	8 407	4 692
1975	16 584	2 955	10 408	23 244	-13 602	14 686	2 748	3 179	1 323	8 758	4 834
1976	18 419	3 328	9 747	26 727	-14 386	14 871	2 733	3 273	1 371	8 865	4 899
1977	18 022	3 605	12 833	29 901	-14 879	15 127	2 727	3 377	1 385	9 023	4 974
1978	18 961	3 813	12 015	35 458	-15 720	15 672	2 753	3 474	1 367	9 446	5 075
1979	19 914	4 173	12 293	42 636	-17 476	15 947	2 773	3 541	1 378	9 633	5 107
1980	21 169	4 584	13 028	52 538	-19 942	16 241	2 866	3 610	1 398	9 765	5 210
1981	22 973	4 769	11 429	68 774	-28 041	16 031	2 772	3 640	1 420	9 619	5 216
1982	23 938	4 712	10 914	85 044	-26 099	15 837	2 739	3 640	1 433	9 458	5 169
1983	24 824	5 105	11 235	89 828	-33 976	15 869	2 774	3 662	1 450	9 434	5 139
1984	25 588	5 663	11 817	111 123	-31 957	16 024	2 807	3 734	1 488	9 482	5 196
1985	26 262	6 270	11 588	129 504	-32 698	16 394	2 875	3 832	1 540	9 687	5 344
1986	26 327	6 572	12 564	136 047	-33 007	16 693	2 899	3 893	1 561	9 901	5 484
1987	26 750	7 553	7 565	138 652	-36 455	17 010	2 943	3 967	1 586	10 100	5 598
1988	29 386	9 236	9 464	151 838	-36 967	17 386	2 971	4 076	1 621	10 339	5 722
1989	30 031	9 474	9 017	169 266	-37 212	17 779	2 988	4 182	1 668	10 609	5 875
1990	29 058	9 993	10 734	184 221	-36 615	18 304	3 085	4 305	1 730	10 914	6 042
1991	31 305	12 276	11 661	194 541	-39 356	18 402	2 966	4 355	1 768	11 081	6 136
1992	34 064	14 426	12 990	199 421	-39 280	18 645	2 969	4 408	1 799	11 267	6 220
1993	35 671	14 955	13 009	198 811	-37 386	18 841	2 915	4 488	1 834	11 438	6 353
1994	37 585	15 256	11 303	202 957	-37 772	19 128	2 870	4 576	1 882	11 682	6 479
1995	37 890	16 216	13 835	232 169	-44 455	19 305	2 822	4 635	1 919	11 849	6 606
1996	36 985	17 548	11 892	241 090	-37 620	19 447	2 757	4 624	1 924	12 066	6 748
1993:											
January	1 641	1 222	133	17 858	-2 660	18 734	2 942	4 451	1 813	11 341	6 293
February	2 649	1 060	994	15 893	-2 809	18 767	2 944	4 457	1 817	11 366	6 316
March	4 090	1 270	1 040	16 415	-2 987	18 766	2 935	4 462	1 818	11 369	6 318
April	4 332	1 581	655	16 585	....	18 776	2 924	4 472	1 823	11 380	6 316
May	801	1 199	886	17 420	-2 579	18 808	2 916	4 482	1 830	11 410	6 343
June	2 871	1 131	1 497	15 464	-3 065	18 828	2 906	4 477	1 824	11 445	6 366
July	4 289	1 350	340	17 159	-3 094	18 831	2 901	4 480	1 824	11 450	6 370
August	2 063	1 122	848	17 473	-3 187	18 860	2 906	4 488	1 834	11 466	6 368
September	3 010	1 415	1 712	15 440	-5 823	18 885	2 902	4 505	1 845	11 478	6 372
October	2 819	1 011	640	17 082	-2 593	18 911	2 901	4 511	1 849	11 499	6 384
November	3 198	1 306	1 317	16 171	-2 910	18 934	2 900	4 514	1 851	11 520	6 395
December	4 469	1 244	1 708	16 638	-2 737	18 964	2 898	4 521	1 855	11 545	6 408
1994:											
January	2 151	1 210	669	17 095	-2 914	18 987	2 899	4 516	1 852	11 572	6 419
February	3 135	1 105	782	15 524	-2 815	19 003	2 898	4 521	1 854	11 584	6 418
March	2 793	1 760	779	16 594	-2 999	19 027	2 887	4 533	1 862	11 607	6 433
April	3 930	1 230	-148	17 080	-2 721	19 055	2 884	4 545	1 867	11 626	6 445
May	1 666	1 277	1 279	17 671	-3 032	19 106	2 871	4 556	1 872	11 679	6 469
June	3 011	1 136	1 715	15 880	-2 827	19 103	2 860	4 560	1 870	11 683	6 483
July	3 079	1 440	-13	17 956	-3 176	19 117	2 856	4 585	1 887	11 676	6 477
August	3 130	1 204	1 325	18 322	-3 051	19 179	2 859	4 607	1 904	11 713	6 514
September	4 257	1 362	1 292	16 944	-5 996	19 195	2 864	4 604	1 895	11 727	6 516
October	1 677	1 340	1 261	18 669	-2 596	19 210	2 860	4 616	1 902	11 734	6 525
November	3 337	1 176	1 556	18 242	-2 575	19 235	2 854	4 627	1 908	11 754	6 530
December	4 277	1 278	1 972	19 302	-2 671	19 242	2 849	4 632	1 911	11 761	6 536
1995:											
January	1 996	1 568	-233	19 568	-2 911	19 261	2 842	4 643	1 917	11 776	6 553
February	3 023	1 099	1 170	18 002	-2 688	19 267	2 836	4 648	1 923	11 783	6 558
March	4 642	1 488	1 680	19 671	-2 829	19 281	2 831	4 651	1 925	11 799	6 571
April	1 850	1 359	299	20 017	-3 121	19 299	2 828	4 649	1 924	11 822	6 587
May	3 204	1 129	1 109	20 295	-2 956	19 276	2 829	4 639	1 921	11 808	6 583
June	4 552	1 419	1 781	18 617	-3 127	19 302	2 831	4 638	1 921	11 833	6 593
July	1 591	1 664	421	20 245	-10 163	19 300	2 826	4 626	1 921	11 848	6 605
August	3 267	1 400	1 464	20 619	-3 022	19 342	2 824	4 620	1 913	11 898	6 654
September	4 517	1 335	1 385	18 929	-5 796	19 308	2 812	4 623	1 914	11 873	6 629
October	1 594	1 223	1 712	20 565	-2 765	19 335	2 803	4 627	1 916	11 905	6 633
November	3 280	1 258	717	19 058	-2 565	19 335	2 797	4 623	1 916	11 915	6 644
December	4 435	1 233	1 924	19 934	-2 683	19 346	2 791	4 622	1 914	11 933	6 659
1996:											
January	....	....	....	....	....	19 326	2 782	4 610	1 904	11 934	6 653
February	2 901	1 281	1 575	19 771	-2 855	19 356	2 782	4 622	1 915	11 952	6 662
March	3 300	1 342	766	20 244	-2 490	19 396	2 779	4 624	1 920	11 993	6 691
April	2 974	1 585	-25	20 463	-2 932	19 400	2 774	4 625	1 922	12 001	6 702
May	5 254	1 683	180	20 359	-2 991	19 416	2 770	4 629	1 926	12 017	6 700
June	1 570	1 327	1 755	18 977	-2 636	19 437	2 757	4 629	1 928	12 051	6 736
July	3 255	1 989	53	20 311	-3 543	19 455	2 752	4 625	1 931	12 078	6 767
August	4 657	1 460	1 390	21 460	-2 880	19 550	2 743	4 637	1 937	12 170	6 837
September	1 641	1 382	1 548	19 243	-6 466	19 513	2 740	4 640	1 941	12 133	6 796
October	3 336	1 311	1 657	21 472	140 209	19 489	2 732	4 618	1 922	12 139	6 797
November	5 156	1 897	200	20 144	-2 635	19 494	2 732	4 620	1 925	12 142	6 807
December	3 088	1 563	1 687	19 997	-6 839	19 514	2 728	4 621	1 927	12 165	6 815

1. Fiscal years through 1976 are from July 1 through June 30. Beginning with October 1976 (fiscal year 1977), fiscal years are from October 1 through September 30. The period from July 1 through September 30, 1976 (not shown here) is a separate fiscal period known as the transition quarter and not included in any fiscal year.

Part Three

Historical Data

GROSS DOMESTIC PRODUCT
(Billions of dollars, quarterly data are at seasonally adjusted annual rates)

| YEAR AND QUARTER | Gross domestic product | Personal consumption expenditures | Gross private domestic investment | | | | | Exports and imports of goods and services | | | Government consumption expenditures and gross investment | | | Addendum: Final sales of domestic product |
| | | | Total | Fixed investment | | Change in business inventories | | Net exports | Exports | Imports | Total | Federal | State and local | |
				Nonres-idential	Residen-tial	Nonfarm	Farm							
1960	526.6	332.2	78.8	49.2	26.3	2.7	0.6	2.4	25.3	22.8	113.2	65.6	47.6	523.3
1961	544.8	342.6	77.9	48.6	26.4	2.0	0.9	3.4	26.0	22.7	120.9	69.1	51.8	541.9
1962	585.2	363.4	87.9	52.8	29.0	5.5	0.6	2.4	27.4	25.0	131.4	76.5	55.0	579.1
1963	617.4	383.0	93.4	55.6	32.1	5.2	0.5	3.3	29.4	26.1	137.7	78.1	59.6	611.7
1964	663.0	411.4	101.7	62.4	34.3	6.2	-1.2	5.5	33.6	28.1	144.4	79.4	65.0	658.0
1965	719.1	444.3	118.0	74.1	34.2	8.9	0.8	3.9	35.4	31.5	153.0	81.8	71.2	709.4
1966	787.8	481.9	130.4	84.4	32.3	14.3	-0.5	1.9	38.9	37.1	173.6	94.1	79.5	774.0
1967	833.6	509.5	128.0	85.2	32.4	9.6	0.9	1.4	41.4	39.9	194.6	106.6	88.1	823.1
1968	910.6	559.8	139.9	92.1	38.7	7.8	1.4	-1.3	45.3	46.6	212.1	113.8	98.3	901.4
1969	982.2	604.7	155.0	102.9	42.6	9.5	0.0	-1.2	49.3	50.5	223.8	115.8	108.0	972.7
1970	1 035.6	648.1	150.2	106.7	41.4	3.0	-0.8	1.2	57.0	55.8	236.1	115.9	120.2	1 033.4
1971	1 125.4	702.5	176.0	111.7	55.8	6.8	1.7	-3.0	59.3	62.3	249.9	117.1	132.8	1 116.9
1972	1 237.3	770.7	205.6	126.1	69.7	9.6	0.3	-8.0	66.2	74.2	268.9	125.1	143.8	1 227.4
1973	1 382.6	851.6	242.9	150.0	75.3	15.9	1.5	0.6	91.8	91.2	287.6	128.2	159.4	1 365.2
1974	1 496.9	931.2	245.6	165.6	66.0	16.9	-2.8	-3.1	124.3	127.5	323.2	139.9	183.3	1 482.8
1975	1 630.6	1 029.1	225.4	169.0	62.7	-9.7	3.4	13.6	136.3	122.7	362.6	154.5	208.1	1 636.9
1976	1 819.0	1 148.8	286.6	187.2	82.5	17.8	-0.8	-2.3	148.9	151.1	385.9	162.7	223.1	1 802.0
1977	2 026.9	1 277.1	356.6	223.2	110.3	18.5	4.5	-23.7	158.8	182.4	416.9	178.4	238.5	2 003.8
1978	2 291.4	1 428.8	430.8	272.0	131.6	25.8	1.4	-26.1	186.1	212.3	457.9	194.4	263.4	2 264.2
1979	2 557.5	1 593.5	480.9	323.0	141.0	13.3	3.6	-24.0	228.7	252.7	507.1	215.0	292.0	2 540.6
1980	2 784.2	1 760.4	465.9	350.3	123.2	-1.5	-6.1	-14.9	278.9	293.8	572.8	248.4	324.4	2 791.9
1981	3 115.9	1 941.3	556.2	405.4	122.6	19.4	8.8	-15.0	302.8	317.8	633.4	284.1	349.2	3 087.8
1982	3 242.1	2 076.8	501.1	409.9	105.7	-20.2	5.8	-20.5	282.6	303.2	684.8	313.2	371.6	3 256.6
1983	3 514.5	2 283.4	547.1	399.4	152.5	10.4	-15.4	-51.7	277.0	328.6	735.7	344.5	391.2	3 519.4
1984	3 902.4	2 492.3	715.6	468.3	179.8	61.8	5.7	-102.0	303.1	405.1	796.6	372.6	424.0	3 835.0
1985	4 180.7	2 704.8	715.1	502.0	186.9	20.4	5.8	-114.2	303.0	417.2	875.0	410.1	464.9	4 154.5
1986	4 422.2	2 892.7	722.5	494.8	218.1	11.1	-1.5	-131.5	320.7	452.2	938.5	435.2	503.3	4 412.6
1987	4 692.3	3 094.5	747.2	495.4	227.6	30.7	-6.4	-142.1	365.7	507.9	992.8	455.7	537.2	4 668.1
1960:														
1st quarter	527.3	327.3	89.1	49.4	28.4	10.7	0.6	0.9	24.2	23.3	110.0	64.0	46.0	516.0
2nd quarter	526.1	333.2	79.4	50.2	26.1	2.2	0.9	1.7	25.2	23.5	111.8	64.5	47.3	523.0
3rd quarter	529.0	333.1	78.4	48.9	25.3	3.2	1.0	3.0	25.9	22.9	114.5	66.2	48.2	524.8
4th quarter	523.9	335.0	68.1	48.5	25.3	-5.4	-0.2	4.0	25.8	21.7	116.7	67.7	49.0	529.6
1961:														
1st quarter	528.1	335.7	70.1	47.4	25.3	-3.2	0.6	4.4	26.1	21.7	117.8	67.1	50.8	530.7
2nd quarter	538.9	340.6	75.4	48.3	25.5	1.0	0.6	3.3	25.2	21.9	119.7	68.7	50.9	537.3
3rd quarter	549.6	343.5	82.2	48.6	26.9	5.7	0.9	2.8	26.1	23.3	121.0	69.3	51.7	542.9
4th quarter	562.6	350.7	84.0	50.2	27.8	4.6	1.4	2.9	26.8	23.9	124.9	71.3	53.6	556.6
1962:														
1st quarter	575.3	355.3	89.3	51.4	28.4	8.0	1.5	2.3	26.6	24.3	128.4	74.5	53.9	565.8
2nd quarter	582.8	361.3	87.9	53.0	29.2	5.4	0.2	3.2	28.1	24.9	130.4	75.9	54.5	577.1
3rd quarter	589.9	365.4	89.1	53.7	29.2	5.9	0.2	2.9	28.0	25.1	132.6	77.3	55.3	583.7
4th quarter	592.9	371.7	85.4	53.2	29.1	2.7	0.4	1.5	27.0	25.6	134.3	78.1	56.2	589.8
1963:														
1st quarter	602.2	375.1	90.3	53.1	30.2	5.1	1.9	2.0	27.2	25.2	134.7	76.9	57.8	595.1
2nd quarter	610.9	379.4	91.8	54.7	32.2	4.8	0.1	3.7	29.6	25.9	135.9	77.3	58.7	606.0
3rd quarter	623.7	386.4	94.7	56.3	32.5	6.6	-0.6	3.1	29.8	26.7	139.5	79.1	60.4	617.8
4th quarter	632.8	391.1	96.6	58.1	33.7	4.2	0.6	4.4	31.1	26.8	140.7	79.0	61.7	627.9
1964:														
1st quarter	649.4	400.5	100.6	59.6	35.4	6.2	-0.6	5.9	32.9	27.0	142.4	79.4	62.9	643.8
2nd quarter	658.4	408.3	100.4	61.4	34.2	6.1	-1.2	4.9	32.6	27.7	144.8	80.1	64.6	653.6
3rd quarter	669.2	417.1	101.5	63.5	33.7	6.1	-1.8	5.4	33.9	28.4	145.1	79.4	65.7	664.9
4th quarter	675.1	419.8	104.4	65.2	33.8	6.5	-1.1	5.7	35.0	29.3	145.3	78.6	66.7	669.7
1965:														
1st quarter	695.6	430.6	115.8	69.7	33.9	11.9	0.3	3.0	31.5	28.5	146.2	78.3	67.9	683.4
2nd quarter	708.2	437.8	115.8	72.4	34.2	8.0	1.1	4.7	36.3	31.7	149.9	79.9	70.1	699.0
3rd quarter	725.0	447.2	119.1	75.3	34.3	8.7	0.8	3.7	35.7	32.0	155.0	82.4	72.7	715.5
4th quarter	747.7	461.5	121.3	78.9	34.5	6.8	1.0	4.1	38.0	33.9	160.9	86.5	74.3	739.9
1966:														
1st quarter	770.5	472.0	130.5	82.2	34.8	12.8	0.6	3.2	38.2	35.0	164.8	88.5	76.3	757.0
2nd quarter	780.0	477.1	129.9	84.2	33.2	14.1	-1.7	2.0	38.2	36.2	171.1	92.9	78.2	767.5
3rd quarter	793.6	486.4	129.4	85.3	31.9	12.7	-0.6	0.8	39.0	38.2	176.9	96.7	80.2	781.4
4th quarter	807.1	492.0	132.0	85.7	29.2	17.4	-0.4	1.5	40.4	38.8	181.6	98.4	83.3	790.1
1967:														
1st quarter	817.5	496.8	127.7	84.3	28.3	13.3	1.7	2.3	41.7	39.4	190.8	105.1	85.6	802.5
2nd quarter	823.3	506.2	123.0	84.5	31.6	4.6	2.1	2.1	41.1	39.0	191.9	105.0	87.0	816.5
3rd quarter	838.9	513.7	128.5	84.7	33.4	9.9	0.5	1.1	40.7	39.5	195.6	107.0	88.6	828.5
4th quarter	854.7	521.2	133.0	87.2	36.0	10.6	-0.9	0.2	41.9	41.7	200.3	109.1	91.2	845.0
1968:														
1st quarter	880.5	539.5	135.7	90.6	36.9	5.1	3.0	-1.2	43.2	44.4	206.6	112.4	94.2	872.4
2nd quarter	904.9	553.2	141.9	89.9	38.2	9.6	4.3	-0.6	44.8	45.4	210.4	113.1	97.3	891.0
3rd quarter	920.1	569.1	138.7	91.8	38.9	7.8	0.2	-1.3	47.0	48.2	213.6	114.2	99.5	912.1
4th quarter	936.8	577.5	143.5	96.0	40.9	8.6	-2.0	-1.9	46.2	48.2	217.7	115.5	102.3	930.2
1969:														
1st quarter	960.0	588.8	154.7	99.5	43.2	10.2	1.8	-1.9	41.9	43.8	218.4	114.1	104.3	948.1
2nd quarter	974.1	599.4	154.4	101.4	43.4	8.3	1.4	-1.8	50.9	52.7	222.0	114.8	107.2	964.5
3rd quarter	993.6	609.2	159.0	105.1	43.2	11.9	-1.2	-1.3	51.0	52.4	226.7	117.6	109.2	982.9
4th quarter	1 001.0	621.1	152.0	105.6	40.7	7.7	-1.9	0.1	53.2	53.1	227.8	116.7	111.1	995.2
1970:														
1st quarter	1 013.9	632.4	148.5	105.8	40.7	0.4	1.6	1.1	54.7	53.5	231.8	117.1	114.7	1 011.9
2nd quarter	1 029.5	642.7	151.1	107.1	39.4	4.2	0.4	2.4	57.6	55.2	233.4	115.5	117.9	1 025.0
3rd quarter	1 047.8	655.2	153.8	108.2	40.4	7.1	-1.8	0.9	57.3	56.4	237.9	115.3	122.5	1 042.6
4th quarter	1 051.3	662.1	147.6	105.7	45.0	0.4	-3.5	0.4	58.3	57.9	241.2	115.7	125.5	1 054.4

YEAR AND QUARTER	Gross domestic product	Personal con-sumption expendi-tures	Gross private domestic investment						Exports and imports of goods and services			Government consumption expendi-tures and gross investment			Adden-dum: Final sales of domestic product
			Total	Fixed investment		Change in business inventories			Net exports	Exports	Imports	Total	Federal	State and local	
				Nonres-idential	Residen-tial	Nonfarm	Farm								
1971:															
1st quarter	1 096.8	681.6	169.3	108.2	48.6	9.9	2.5		0.8	59.5	58.7	245.1	116.2	128.8	1 084.3
2nd quarter	1 117.7	695.8	177.1	111.1	54.6	7.3	4.2		-3.8	59.5	63.3	248.7	116.8	131.9	1 106.3
3rd quarter	1 137.3	708.2	181.1	112.4	58.3	8.1	2.3		-3.1	62.4	65.5	251.1	117.3	133.8	1 126.9
4th quarter	1 149.8	724.5	176.6	115.3	61.5	2.1	-2.3		-6.0	56.0	61.9	254.6	117.8	136.8	1 150.0
1972:															
1st quarter	1 190.2	741.9	191.8	120.6	66.6	5.0	-0.5		-8.6	63.5	72.2	265.2	125.2	140.0	1 185.6
2nd quarter	1 224.4	759.9	204.2	123.5	68.2	10.4	2.0		-8.3	63.1	71.4	268.6	127.3	141.3	1 211.9
3rd quarter	1 247.8	778.1	209.8	126.3	69.6	13.0	1.0		-7.9	66.2	74.1	267.9	123.1	144.7	1 233.8
4th quarter	1 286.8	802.9	216.8	133.8	74.3	10.1	-1.4		-7.1	72.1	79.2	274.1	124.7	149.4	1 278.1
1973:															
1st quarter	1 337.5	827.2	232.9	141.2	77.9	18.1	-4.2		-4.4	81.0	85.4	281.8	128.3	153.5	1 323.6
2nd quarter	1 369.4	842.1	242.4	149.0	75.8	12.7	5.0		-1.1	88.3	89.5	286.0	129.1	157.0	1 351.7
3rd quarter	1 391.4	860.8	240.3	153.7	75.0	9.0	2.6		3.2	94.3	91.1	287.1	126.0	161.1	1 379.8
4th quarter	1 432.3	876.1	255.8	156.4	72.7	24.0	2.8		4.7	103.4	98.7	295.6	129.6	166.1	1 405.6
1974:															
1st quarter	1 446.5	894.4	241.2	159.0	69.0	16.6	-3.3		4.3	114.6	110.3	306.6	133.7	172.9	1 433.3
2nd quarter	1 482.5	922.4	247.5	163.7	67.5	15.3	1.0		-5.6	123.8	129.4	318.2	137.2	181.0	1 466.2
3rd quarter	1 511.7	950.1	242.8	168.5	67.4	6.9	-0.1		-9.1	124.5	133.6	328.0	140.9	187.1	1 504.9
4th quarter	1 546.8	957.8	251.0	171.0	60.0	28.7	-8.7		-2.2	134.4	136.6	340.1	147.8	192.3	1 526.8
1975:															
1st quarter	1 560.3	982.7	212.2	166.3	57.7	-18.8	7.1		13.1	138.0	124.9	352.3	150.5	201.8	1 572.1
2nd quarter	1 597.8	1 012.4	211.2	166.0	59.9	-17.8	3.1		16.6	131.8	115.2	357.7	153.0	204.6	1 612.5
3rd quarter	1 657.1	1 046.3	234.3	169.7	64.6	-0.8	0.8		11.6	133.7	122.1	364.9	154.7	210.2	1 657.1
4th quarter	1 707.3	1 075.1	243.7	173.9	68.7	-1.3	2.5		12.9	141.7	128.7	375.5	159.7	215.9	1 706.1
1976:															
1st quarter	1 767.3	1 110.2	271.3	179.1	76.2	16.5	-0.5		4.2	143.1	138.9	381.7	159.3	222.3	1 751.3
2nd quarter	1 797.9	1 130.2	285.8	183.4	80.7	23.6	-1.8		-1.1	146.0	147.1	383.0	160.8	222.2	1 776.1
3rd quarter	1 830.4	1 159.8	289.5	189.8	80.6	17.1	2.0		-5.0	150.9	155.8	386.0	163.1	222.9	1 811.3
4th quarter	1 880.3	1 195.0	299.8	196.4	92.5	13.9	-3.0		-7.2	155.4	162.7	392.8	167.7	225.0	1 869.4
1977:															
1st quarter	1 934.4	1 230.7	321.3	208.8	97.6	16.2	-1.3		-21.6	154.8	176.4	403.9	172.7	231.2	1 919.4
2nd quarter	2 005.1	1 259.1	353.2	218.5	111.7	17.7	5.3		-21.7	161.3	183.0	414.6	177.8	236.8	1 982.1
3rd quarter	2 063.2	1 290.3	373.8	226.8	115.0	27.6	4.4		-21.1	161.8	182.9	420.2	179.5	240.7	2 031.3
4th quarter	2 104.7	1 328.1	378.0	238.8	116.9	12.5	9.8		-30.3	157.1	187.4	428.9	183.7	245.2	2 082.5
1978:															
1st quarter	2 147.7	1 358.3	392.9	243.8	121.1	28.7	-0.6		-39.3	164.0	203.3	435.8	186.3	249.5	2 119.6
2nd quarter	2 273.7	1 417.4	425.6	268.2	130.5	26.5	0.4		-23.3	185.6	208.8	453.9	192.5	261.4	2 246.8
3rd quarter	2 333.9	1 450.6	443.5	281.3	135.8	19.2	7.2		-24.6	190.5	215.1	464.4	196.1	268.3	2 307.5
4th quarter	2 410.2	1 488.7	461.2	294.8	139.1	28.9	-1.5		-17.3	204.5	221.8	477.5	202.9	274.6	2 382.8
1979:															
1st quarter	2 464.5	1 529.3	471.1	308.2	138.6	20.1	4.2		-19.2	210.7	229.8	483.3	206.5	276.8	2 440.2
2nd quarter	2 522.3	1 563.9	482.4	314.2	140.9	24.2	3.1		-23.4	219.7	243.1	499.3	212.0	287.3	2 495.0
3rd quarter	2 592.8	1 617.4	486.4	331.4	143.5	4.9	6.6		-24.4	232.9	257.3	513.4	216.0	297.4	2 581.2
4th quarter	2 650.4	1 663.5	483.5	338.0	141.2	4.0	0.3		-29.0	251.5	280.5	532.3	225.6	306.6	2 646.1
1980:															
1st quarter	2 722.3	1 713.1	493.0	350.0	134.5	9.0	-0.6		-37.2	267.1	304.3	553.4	236.3	317.1	2 713.9
2nd quarter	2 719.4	1 716.9	449.8	338.9	111.2	4.9	-5.2		-16.7	275.9	292.6	569.5	247.8	321.7	2 719.8
3rd quarter	2 783.4	1 774.9	430.8	348.7	115.9	-21.3	-12.5		3.3	282.5	279.2	574.5	248.5	325.9	2 817.2
4th quarter	2 911.8	1 836.8	490.1	363.5	131.3	1.4	-6.1		-8.9	290.3	299.2	593.8	261.1	332.8	2 916.5
1981:															
1st quarter	3 040.2	1 890.3	549.9	379.7	132.0	31.5	6.8		-17.0	302.8	319.7	616.9	271.3	345.6	3 001.9
2nd quarter	3 070.3	1 923.5	534.7	396.4	128.9	-0.4	9.9		-16.4	305.5	322.0	628.5	282.8	345.7	3 060.8
3rd quarter	3 167.7	1 967.4	576.1	413.4	120.2	30.7	11.8		-10.2	299.7	309.9	634.4	285.4	348.9	3 125.2
4th quarter	3 185.5	1 983.9	564.1	432.2	109.6	15.8	6.5		-16.3	303.2	319.4	653.7	296.9	356.8	3 163.1
1982:															
1st quarter	3 178.6	2 021.4	511.1	426.7	104.8	-25.5	5.1		-17.2	292.3	309.5	663.4	301.5	361.9	3 199.1
2nd quarter	3 231.6	2 046.1	514.1	415.0	102.8	-8.1	4.3		-5.0	294.2	299.1	676.3	307.6	368.7	3 235.3
3rd quarter	3 259.1	2 091.1	509.3	402.6	102.3	-4.7	9.0		-30.3	279.0	309.3	689.1	314.8	374.3	3 254.8
4th quarter	3 299.1	2 148.7	469.8	395.1	112.8	-42.7	4.6		-29.7	265.1	294.9	710.3	328.9	381.4	3 337.2
1983:															
1st quarter	3 361.0	2 185.0	481.3	383.7	130.9	-26.0	-7.3		-24.6	270.6	295.3	719.4	334.5	384.8	3 394.3
2nd quarter	3 469.2	2 257.2	526.0	385.8	148.2	4.9	-13.0		-45.5	272.5	318.0	731.5	343.8	387.7	3 477.2
3rd quarter	3 563.3	2 316.8	561.7	400.9	162.6	30.6	-32.4		-65.2	278.2	343.4	750.0	355.5	394.5	3 565.0
4th quarter	3 664.6	2 374.7	619.4	427.4	168.5	32.2	-8.8		-71.3	286.7	358.0	741.9	344.0	397.9	3 641.2
1984:															
1st quarter	3 791.1	2 422.5	695.6	440.4	175.6	74.0	5.5		-94.3	293.7	388.0	767.4	358.1	409.3	3 711.6
2nd quarter	3 879.7	2 475.6	716.2	464.0	181.4	65.2	5.6		-103.5	303.0	406.5	791.4	372.6	418.8	3 808.9
3rd quarter	3 942.2	2 510.5	731.7	478.4	180.8	65.6	6.8		-103.1	306.5	409.6	803.1	373.3	429.8	3 869.8
4th quarter	3 996.7	2 560.6	718.8	490.3	181.3	42.2	5.0		-107.1	309.2	416.4	824.5	386.3	438.2	3 949.5
1985:															
1st quarter	4 081.2	2 623.8	705.6	496.6	183.4	17.7	7.9		-91.4	305.9	397.3	843.1	395.2	448.0	4 055.6
2nd quarter	4 134.8	2 673.4	711.2	504.1	182.8	20.1	4.2		-114.7	303.9	418.6	864.8	404.4	460.4	4 110.5
3rd quarter	4 221.4	2 742.3	706.3	498.2	187.7	13.9	6.6		-117.2	297.0	414.2	890.0	418.6	471.4	4 201.0
4th quarter	4 285.3	2 779.6	737.2	508.9	193.9	30.0	4.3		-133.6	305.3	438.9	902.1	422.2	479.9	4 250.9
1986:															
1st quarter	4 358.2	2 823.3	752.1	502.4	204.5	42.5	2.5		-126.9	312.2	439.1	909.7	418.6	491.1	4 313.2
2nd quarter	4 385.6	2 855.6	729.7	492.6	218.3	22.3	-3.5		-128.8	314.5	443.4	929.1	431.1	498.0	4 366.8
3rd quarter	4 443.3	2 926.2	699.4	488.6	224.1	-10.1	-3.1		-138.0	320.5	458.5	955.7	448.4	507.3	4 456.5
4th quarter	4 501.7	2 965.6	708.9	495.6	225.6	-10.5	-1.8		-132.3	335.4	467.7	959.5	442.8	516.7	4 513.9
1987:															
1st quarter	4 565.7	3 002.4	729.6	480.0	225.3	31.9	-7.7		-139.4	337.4	476.9	973.2	447.9	525.3	4 541.5
2nd quarter	4 645.1	3 070.0	732.3	490.1	229.2	23.7	-10.7		-144.7	356.9	501.6	987.4	454.9	532.6	4 632.1
3rd quarter	4 722.6	3 134.2	734.0	504.6	227.4	6.0	-4.0		-142.4	373.9	516.4	996.8	456.5	540.4	4 720.6
4th quarter	4 835.9	3 171.3	792.8	506.8	228.4	61.0	-3.3		-142.0	394.7	536.7	1 013.8	463.4	550.4	4 778.2

REAL GROSS DOMESTIC PRODUCT
(Billions of chained (1992) dollars, quarterly data are at seasonally adjusted annual rates)

YEAR AND QUARTER	Gross domestic product	Personal consumption expenditures	Gross private domestic investment						Exports and imports of goods and services			Government consumption expenditures and gross investment			Addendum: Final sales of domestic product
			Total	Fixed investment		Change in business inventories			Net exports	Exports	Imports	Total	Federal	State and local	
				Nonresidential	Residential	Nonfarm	Farm								
1960	2 262.9	1 432.6	270.5	155.9	121.8	8.8	1.6		-21.3	86.8	108.1	617.2	349.4	267.2	2 264.2
1961	2 314.3	1 461.5	267.6	154.5	122.2	6.2	2.2		-19.1	88.3	107.3	647.2	363.0	283.8	2 318.0
1962	2 454.8	1 533.8	302.1	168.0	133.9	18.1	1.5		-26.5	93.0	119.5	686.0	393.2	292.1	2 445.4
1963	2 559.4	1 596.6	321.6	176.4	149.6	16.4	1.3		-22.7	100.0	122.7	701.9	391.8	309.7	2 552.4
1964	2 708.4	1 692.3	348.3	197.2	158.3	19.5	-3.7		-15.9	113.3	129.2	715.9	385.2	330.9	2 705.1
1965	2 881.1	1 799.1	397.2	231.3	153.7	27.7	2.4		-27.4	115.6	143.0	737.6	385.2	353.2	2 860.4
1966	3 069.2	1 902.0	430.6	259.4	140.0	44.7	-1.3		-40.9	123.4	164.2	804.6	429.1	375.9	3 033.5
1967	3 147.2	1 958.6	411.8	255.3	135.6	29.6	2.5		-50.1	126.1	176.2	865.6	471.7	394.2	3 125.1
1968	3 293.9	2 070.2	433.3	266.4	154.0	23.0	3.7		-67.2	135.3	202.5	892.4	476.3	416.5	3 278.0
1969	3 393.6	2 147.5	458.3	285.6	158.6	27.3	0.0		-71.3	142.7	214.0	887.5	459.9	428.0	3 377.2
1970	3 397.6	2 197.8	426.1	282.8	149.1	8.3	-2.4		-65.0	158.1	223.1	866.8	427.2	440.0	3 406.5
1971	3 510.0	2 279.5	474.9	282.4	190.0	18.0	4.0		-75.8	159.2	235.0	851.0	397.0	454.4	3 499.8
1972	3 702.3	2 415.9	531.8	307.7	223.8	25.4	0.3		-89.0	172.0	261.0	854.1	390.2	464.5	3 689.5
1973	3 916.3	2 532.6	595.5	352.5	222.3	38.5	1.4		-63.0	209.6	272.6	848.4	371.1	478.5	3 883.9
1974	3 891.2	2 514.7	546.5	354.4	176.4	31.9	-4.7		-35.6	229.8	265.3	862.9	368.8	495.6	3 873.4
1975	3 873.9	2 570.0	446.6	317.3	153.5	-18.5	6.1		-7.2	228.2	235.4	876.3	367.9	510.0	3 906.4
1976	4 082.9	2 714.3	537.4	332.6	189.7	32.1	-1.3		-39.9	241.6	281.5	876.8	364.3	514.3	4 061.7
1977	4 273.6	2 829.8	622.1	371.8	229.8	31.7	6.8		-64.2	247.4	311.7	884.7	370.1	516.4	4 240.8
1978	4 503.0	2 951.6	693.4	422.6	245.0	41.4	2.6		-65.6	273.1	338.6	910.6	377.7	534.7	4 464.4
1979	4 630.6	3 020.2	709.8	463.3	236.0	19.3	3.8		-45.3	299.0	344.3	924.9	383.3	543.5	4 614.4
1980	4 615.0	3 009.7	628.3	461.1	186.1	-1.5	-7.1		10.1	331.4	321.3	941.4	399.3	543.6	4 641.9
1981	4 720.7	3 046.4	686.0	485.7	171.2	22.8	9.6		5.6	335.3	329.7	947.7	415.9	532.8	4 691.6
1982	4 620.3	3 081.5	587.2	464.3	140.1	-22.9	7.3		-14.1	311.4	325.5	960.1	429.4	531.4	4 651.2
1983	4 803.7	3 240.6	642.1	456.4	197.6	12.1	-16.9		-63.3	303.3	366.6	987.3	452.7	534.9	4 821.2
1984	5 140.1	3 407.6	833.4	535.4	226.4	69.1	6.4		-127.3	328.4	455.7	1 018.4	463.7	555.0	5 061.6
1985	5 323.5	3 566.5	823.9	568.5	229.5	23.3	6.9		-147.9	337.4	485.2	1 080.1	495.6	584.7	5 296.9
1986	5 487.7	3 708.7	811.8	548.5	257.0	12.5	-1.6		-163.9	362.2	526.1	1 135.0	518.4	616.9	5 480.9
1987	5 649.5	3 822.3	821.5	542.4	257.6	34.3	-8.8		-156.2	402.0	558.2	1 165.9	534.4	631.8	5 626.0
1960:															
1st quarter	2 279.2	1 422.5	304.3	156.7	131.8	34.6	0.1		-27.3	83.2	110.5	605.5	345.0	259.9	2 248.5
2nd quarter	2 265.5	1 439.6	271.7	158.7	121.0	6.9	1.7		-24.5	86.7	111.2	613.6	347.1	266.0	2 268.4
3rd quarter	2 268.3	1 433.5	269.4	154.6	117.3	10.8	2.9		-19.2	88.7	107.8	621.6	351.1	270.0	2 265.1
4th quarter	2 238.6	1 434.8	236.6	153.7	117.2	-17.1	1.7		-14.1	88.7	102.7	627.9	354.5	273.0	2 274.7
1961:															
1st quarter	2 251.7	1 434.2	241.7	150.6	117.6	-10.2	2.3		-13.0	89.3	102.3	635.6	353.6	281.8	2 277.7
2nd quarter	2 292.0	1 455.7	258.6	153.2	118.0	2.3	2.1		-18.6	85.1	103.6	641.2	360.6	280.1	2 301.1
3rd quarter	2 332.6	1 463.5	282.2	154.6	124.4	18.1	2.3		-21.8	88.6	110.4	648.0	364.9	282.6	2 320.4
4th quarter	2 381.0	1 492.8	288.0	159.8	128.6	14.5	2.2		-23.0	90.1	113.1	663.9	373.0	290.5	2 372.8
1962:															
1st quarter	2 422.6	1 508.4	305.2	163.3	130.9	26.3	2.2		-27.0	89.5	116.5	674.9	386.2	288.0	2 400.3
2nd quarter	2 448.0	1 526.7	301.9	168.6	135.0	17.0	0.6		-23.6	95.4	119.0	682.4	391.7	290.0	2 440.7
3rd quarter	2 471.9	1 539.6	306.5	170.8	134.9	19.7	1.1		-25.4	95.2	120.5	691.4	397.0	293.6	2 462.0
4th quarter	2 476.7	1 560.6	295.0	169.3	134.7	9.3	1.9		-30.2	91.9	122.0	695.4	398.0	296.7	2 478.7
1963:															
1st quarter	2 508.7	1 571.2	313.1	168.7	139.6	17.0	6.9		-27.0	92.1	119.2	691.1	388.3	302.3	2 492.4
2nd quarter	2 538.1	1 586.3	316.2	173.7	149.6	14.9	0.9		-21.4	100.6	122.0	694.5	388.8	305.3	2 533.8
3rd quarter	2 586.3	1 607.6	327.4	178.8	152.4	21.2	-1.4		-23.7	101.3	125.0	713.3	399.5	313.4	2 578.0
4th quarter	2 604.6	1 621.1	329.7	184.5	157.0	12.7	-1.0		-18.7	106.0	124.7	708.6	390.5	317.9	2 605.3
1964:															
1st quarter	2 666.7	1 653.6	346.1	189.4	166.7	19.6	-3.8		-12.8	111.7	124.6	712.5	389.5	322.9	2 663.1
2nd quarter	2 697.5	1 683.1	344.2	194.1	158.2	19.3	-4.3		-16.6	110.8	127.4	721.4	391.6	329.9	2 695.0
3rd quarter	2 729.6	1 713.9	349.1	200.6	155.7	18.7	-4.1		-16.6	114.2	130.8	714.9	381.7	333.6	2 727.6
4th quarter	2 739.8	1 718.6	353.9	204.5	152.8	20.3	-2.7		-17.6	116.6	134.2	714.7	377.9	337.3	2 734.5
1965:															
1st quarter	2 808.9	1 756.2	392.0	218.7	153.4	38.2	0.6		-26.9	102.5	129.4	713.9	374.2	340.4	2 777.2
2nd quarter	2 846.5	1 776.1	391.6	226.6	154.6	26.0	2.8		-26.0	118.7	144.7	728.4	380.2	349.0	2 826.8
3rd quarter	2 898.8	1 806.1	400.9	235.0	155.2	25.6	3.2		-28.8	116.6	145.3	746.3	388.2	359.1	2 879.8
4th quarter	2 970.5	1 858.0	404.3	244.9	151.8	21.1	3.0		-27.8	124.7	152.5	761.7	398.3	364.2	2 957.8
1966:															
1st quarter	3 042.4	1 885.6	436.1	255.6	155.2	41.4	0.6		-33.3	123.1	156.3	776.3	407.7	369.4	3 008.8
2nd quarter	3 055.5	1 890.9	429.8	259.3	142.8	43.6	-2.9		-38.0	122.2	160.2	800.0	428.1	372.3	3 023.1
3rd quarter	3 076.5	1 912.4	426.7	262.0	138.2	39.7	-1.7		-46.3	123.0	169.3	812.5	436.6	376.3	3 047.2
4th quarter	3 102.4	1 919.1	429.8	260.8	123.7	53.9	-1.3		-46.0	125.2	171.1	829.6	444.2	385.8	3 054.9
1967:															
1st quarter	3 127.2	1 931.2	415.8	255.0	120.0	39.9	5.5		-46.6	127.0	173.6	864.4	474.4	390.2	3 085.6
2nd quarter	3 129.5	1 957.5	399.3	254.4	133.6	15.0	7.0		-46.8	125.6	172.4	860.2	468.3	392.2	3 119.0
3rd quarter	3 154.2	1 967.1	411.5	253.4	140.3	30.8	0.5		-50.4	124.4	174.8	865.4	471.8	393.9	3 134.2
4th quarter	3 178.0	1 978.5	420.6	258.6	148.4	32.5	-3.0		-56.6	127.4	184.0	872.5	472.3	400.6	3 161.5
1968:															
1st quarter	3 236.2	2 025.1	425.2	266.4	149.3	15.4	6.5		-64.5	130.3	194.7	887.3	480.5	407.1	3 225.3
2nd quarter	3 292.1	2 056.4	442.9	261.6	153.1	27.7	11.5		-65.2	132.5	197.7	892.2	477.7	414.9	3 258.0
3rd quarter	3 316.1	2 095.1	430.1	264.9	155.9	23.1	0.9		-68.9	140.7	209.6	893.6	473.6	420.4	3 303.9
4th quarter	3 331.2	2 104.4	434.9	272.7	157.8	25.6	-4.4		-70.2	137.6	207.8	896.6	473.5	423.6	3 325.1
1969:															
1st quarter	3 381.9	2 128.0	463.3	280.4	163.5	29.7	3.8		-65.1	123.2	188.3	891.6	466.4	425.7	3 357.5
2nd quarter	3 390.2	2 141.4	458.9	283.2	161.7	24.3	3.8		-75.9	149.5	225.3	890.8	462.5	428.8	3 373.0
3rd quarter	3 409.7	2 152.0	468.2	290.6	160.5	33.9	-2.9		-74.8	147.7	222.4	888.7	459.8	429.3	3 389.6
4th quarter	3 392.6	2 168.8	442.6	288.4	148.7	21.4	-4.6		-69.6	150.4	220.0	878.8	451.0	428.2	3 388.9
1970:															
1st quarter	3 386.5	2 182.3	427.6	285.9	149.0	0.4	2.3		-65.6	153.8	219.4	871.8	439.7	432.5	3 397.6
2nd quarter	3 391.6	2 192.9	427.3	284.3	139.1	11.6	0.9		-64.6	159.0	223.6	863.2	428.5	435.0	3 391.9
3rd quarter	3 423.0	2 211.6	435.9	285.8	146.4	19.8	-4.6		-64.3	158.7	223.0	866.7	422.0	445.0	3 421.9
4th quarter	3 389.4	2 204.6	413.8	275.3	161.9	1.2	-8.1		-65.6	160.9	226.5	865.5	418.3	447.5	3 414.8

SELECTED ANNUAL AND QUARTERLY DATA, 1960-1987

REAL GROSS DOMESTIC PRODUCT—Continued
(Billions of chained (1992) dollars, quarterly data are at seasonally adjusted annual rates)

YEAR AND QUARTER	Gross domestic product	Personal consumption expenditures	Gross private domestic investment						Exports and imports of goods and services			Government expenditures and gross investment			Addendum: Final sales of domestic product
			Total	Fixed investment		Change in business inventories			Net exports	Exports	Imports	Total	Federal	State and local	
				Nonresidential	Residential	Nonfarm	Farm								
1971:															
1st quarter	3 481.4	2 246.5	465.0	277.9	170.6	25.5	5.7		-64.3	159.6	223.9	856.4	406.7	450.0	3 458.9
2nd quarter	3 501.0	2 266.5	480.6	281.8	187.8	18.7	9.8		-81.5	159.4	240.9	852.6	399.7	453.1	3 481.2
3rd quarter	3 523.8	2 283.9	484.1	282.3	197.0	18.8	5.4		-78.1	168.1	246.1	848.8	394.8	454.3	3 509.4
4th quarter	3 533.8	2 321.1	470.0	287.7	204.6	9.1	-5.1		-79.5	149.7	229.2	846.4	386.8	460.0	3 549.5
1972:															
1st quarter	3 604.7	2 352.0	502.4	297.6	218.3	14.4	-1.6		-95.6	167.4	263.0	858.8	397.0	462.2	3 608.1
2nd quarter	3 687.9	2 394.9	533.3	302.5	222.6	27.4	4.6		-88.3	164.8	253.1	859.9	399.7	460.5	3 665.7
3rd quarter	3 726.2	2 430.6	542.4	307.3	223.1	35.8	1.3		-85.7	172.4	258.2	848.4	384.8	464.3	3 700.0
4th quarter	3 790.4	2 486.1	549.1	323.6	231.1	24.0	-2.9		-86.1	183.5	269.6	849.2	379.3	470.8	3 784.3
1973:															
1st quarter	3 892.2	2 530.4	588.6	339.0	238.8	47.0	-7.3		-81.2	200.3	281.5	854.6	381.8	473.8	3 867.0
2nd quarter	3 919.0	2 527.5	601.0	352.5	226.7	29.2	9.3		-64.7	209.0	273.8	852.3	378.6	474.7	3 884.5
3rd quarter	3 907.1	2 539.9	583.0	358.2	217.0	22.2	2.1		-55.9	210.3	266.2	839.1	360.6	479.9	3 890.9
4th quarter	3 947.1	2 532.6	609.2	360.5	206.8	55.6	1.4		-50.3	218.8	269.1	847.7	363.6	485.5	3 893.1
1974:															
1st quarter	3 908.2	2 512.7	565.5	360.2	191.6	35.0	-6.4		-34.1	226.4	260.6	857.5	367.6	491.3	3 889.1
2nd quarter	3 922.6	2 522.7	561.1	359.2	183.2	27.7	-0.7		-34.7	236.4	271.2	866.9	370.7	497.6	3 899.7
3rd quarter	3 880.0	2 532.4	530.3	354.5	177.1	11.0	-1.0		-41.1	225.0	266.1	861.8	366.6	496.7	3 882.5
4th quarter	3 854.1	2 490.9	529.2	343.7	153.9	53.7	-10.8		-32.3	231.1	263.4	865.6	370.4	496.6	3 822.2
1975:															
1st quarter	3 800.9	2 513.2	431.2	321.5	144.3	-39.5	10.5		-6.8	230.5	237.3	875.7	368.5	508.8	3 848.3
2nd quarter	3 835.2	2 556.3	419.9	312.8	147.4	-32.8	6.4		2.5	220.9	218.4	871.6	368.2	504.9	3 887.9
3rd quarter	3 907.0	2 591.8	462.5	315.9	157.7	-0.7	3.6		-11.9	224.7	236.6	875.7	366.9	510.5	3 922.7
4th quarter	3 952.5	2 618.7	472.8	319.1	164.6	-1.1	3.9		-12.7	236.7	249.3	882.2	368.1	515.9	3 966.7
1976:															
1st quarter	4 044.6	2 674.2	519.7	324.9	181.4	31.1	-1.3		-29.2	236.0	265.2	886.2	365.3	522.8	4 027.0
2nd quarter	4 072.2	2 697.9	540.5	328.4	186.7	42.6	-2.1		-38.4	238.1	276.5	876.8	364.4	514.1	4 039.1
3rd quarter	4 088.5	2 724.4	539.9	335.4	183.6	29.9	2.7		-42.8	244.7	287.5	872.8	363.6	511.0	4 061.7
4th quarter	4 126.4	2 760.8	549.6	341.6	207.0	25.0	-4.7		-49.2	247.7	296.8	871.5	363.8	509.4	4 119.0
1977:															
1st quarter	4 176.3	2 794.3	577.7	357.6	212.8	28.4	-2.2		-67.0	243.8	310.8	878.1	366.0	513.9	4 161.4
2nd quarter	4 260.1	2 810.3	622.7	367.8	236.6	30.3	7.9		-63.2	250.1	313.3	887.6	372.3	517.0	4 228.4
3rd quarter	4 329.5	2 836.9	652.8	374.6	236.4	47.5	11.1		-56.9	252.2	309.1	887.4	372.2	516.9	4 270.0
4th quarter	4 328.3	2 877.7	635.3	387.1	233.5	20.7	10.3		-69.9	243.6	313.5	885.8	369.8	517.7	4 303.3
1978:															
1st quarter	4 345.5	2 893.1	650.5	389.1	235.1	48.4	-0.9		-84.9	249.5	334.4	887.5	370.8	518.5	4 306.0
2nd quarter	4 510.7	2 954.6	691.0	421.0	246.2	42.8	1.2		-59.7	275.5	335.1	910.9	378.6	534.2	4 474.6
3rd quarter	4 552.1	2 968.3	710.7	433.8	249.7	30.3	10.8		-62.0	278.3	340.3	917.8	379.3	540.5	4 511.6
4th quarter	4 603.7	2 990.6	721.5	446.5	249.0	44.2	-0.9		-55.7	289.1	344.7	925.9	382.2	545.7	4 565.4
1979:															
1st quarter	4 605.7	3 008.1	717.8	456.8	243.2	28.8	5.9		-55.7	288.9	344.6	916.2	381.3	536.8	4 579.0
2nd quarter	4 615.6	3 003.5	722.9	455.9	238.9	34.4	5.0		-56.1	289.7	345.7	924.8	384.8	541.9	4 577.0
3rd quarter	4 644.9	3 028.7	708.2	470.3	235.7	7.2	6.7		-40.2	299.8	340.0	925.6	383.1	544.5	4 639.2
4th quarter	4 656.2	3 040.2	690.1	470.2	226.4	6.6	-2.2		-29.1	317.8	346.9	932.9	384.0	550.9	4 662.5
1980:															
1st quarter	4 679.0	3 037.2	689.6	475.9	210.3	13.2	-2.7		-20.0	327.7	347.8	946.5	395.1	553.2	4 675.3
2nd quarter	4 566.6	2 968.8	614.5	450.4	169.9	6.8	-6.2		11.3	333.9	322.7	948.3	403.7	546.1	4 579.0
3rd quarter	4 562.3	2 998.6	570.7	454.1	173.0	-28.0	-14.0		33.4	332.8	299.4	936.4	399.3	538.6	4 637.1
4th quarter	4 651.9	3 034.2	638.3	464.3	191.3	1.9	-5.3		15.7	331.1	315.4	934.4	399.2	536.6	4 676.2
1981:															
1st quarter	4 739.2	3 045.6	699.8	471.3	188.0	37.4	6.8		8.3	336.8	328.5	946.1	406.7	540.7	4 692.9
2nd quarter	4 696.8	3 045.9	662.4	479.5	180.8	-0.2	10.3		9.5	338.9	329.4	947.7	418.4	530.3	4 699.0
3rd quarter	4 753.0	3 058.8	704.6	490.7	166.5	35.9	13.4		5.5	331.4	325.9	945.5	418.1	528.2	4 702.5
4th quarter	4 693.8	3 035.3	677.1	501.4	149.6	18.3	7.8		-0.9	334.1	335.0	951.7	420.5	532.0	4 672.0
1982:															
1st quarter	4 615.9	3 054.0	605.8	488.0	141.1	-29.0	7.0		-5.3	320.4	325.7	949.0	420.2	529.6	4 655.4
2nd quarter	4 634.9	3 062.1	601.6	469.6	136.5	-9.6	5.7		2.6	322.8	320.2	954.7	424.3	531.2	4 651.2
3rd quarter	4 612.1	3 080.1	593.7	454.2	134.8	-4.9	11.5		-26.5	308.2	334.7	961.2	431.0	530.8	4 616.9
4th quarter	4 618.3	3 129.7	547.6	445.5	147.9	-47.9	5.0		-27.3	294.4	321.7	975.6	442.1	533.8	4 681.3
1983:															
1st quarter	4 663.0	3 156.5	563.9	435.9	170.8	-29.7	-8.6		-29.8	298.9	328.8	978.4	444.6	534.1	4 719.4
2nd quarter	4 763.6	3 220.0	617.7	440.6	192.9	5.3	-14.6		-54.7	299.8	354.5	985.0	452.5	532.7	4 785.3
3rd quarter	4 849.0	3 267.1	661.4	459.2	210.5	35.9	-34.8		-78.0	304.3	382.2	1 001.8	465.1	536.6	4 860.7
4th quarter	4 939.2	3 318.6	725.3	490.0	216.3	36.9	-9.8		-90.8	310.2	401.0	984.1	448.5	536.0	4 919.5
1984:															
1st quarter	5 053.6	3 354.0	812.2	505.5	224.0	83.5	4.5		-115.5	317.5	433.0	994.1	450.8	543.8	4 961.0
2nd quarter	5 132.9	3 397.5	835.6	530.8	229.6	72.5	7.2		-125.5	325.7	451.2	1 016.6	465.9	550.9	5 050.0
3rd quarter	5 170.3	3 418.4	850.8	546.3	226.6	72.6	7.8		-130.5	332.0	462.5	1 022.5	463.1	559.9	5 085.6
4th quarter	5 203.7	3 460.6	834.9	558.8	225.5	47.8	6.2		-137.7	338.4	476.1	1 040.4	475.1	565.6	5 149.9
1985:															
1st quarter	5 257.3	3 511.2	816.6	504.6	226.9	20.7	8.7		-127.3	338.7	466.0	1 053.2	482.3	571.1	5 231.7
2nd quarter	5 283.7	3 540.8	821.1	572.7	225.7	23.5	3.6		-151.6	337.4	489.0	1 072.8	491.5	581.5	5 261.0
3rd quarter	5 359.6	3 602.5	816.0	563.5	230.2	16.1	9.6		-152.6	332.0	484.7	1 095.7	505.2	590.6	5 336.9
4th quarter	5 393.6	3 612.1	841.8	572.9	235.1	32.9	5.6		-160.0	341.4	501.3	1 098.9	503.4	595.7	5 358.0
1986:															
1st quarter	5 460.8	3 644.1	855.3	563.8	245.1	50.5	2.2		-149.7	351.3	501.0	1 108.3	500.1	608.7	5 410.5
2nd quarter	5 467.0	3 683.0	824.0	548.0	259.2	27.6	-5.2		-167.1	355.9	523.0	1 129.6	514.8	615.1	5 448.4
3rd quarter	5 496.3	3 742.8	781.3	538.7	262.6	-12.7	-3.7		-173.9	364.1	538.1	1 154.5	533.9	620.8	5 518.2
4th quarter	5 526.8	3 764.8	786.7	543.4	261.2	-15.6	0.1		-164.9	377.5	542.3	1 147.7	524.8	623.2	5 546.6
1987:															
1st quarter	5 561.8	3 765.8	808.6	526.3	258.8	36.3	-7.7		-161.2	377.7	538.8	1 153.4	526.9	626.8	5 535.8
2nd quarter	5 618.0	3 814.0	807.1	537.6	260.8	27.4	-14.1		-160.2	393.5	553.7	1 162.8	534.3	628.8	5 608.4
3rd quarter	5 667.4	3 852.9	806.4	553.8	256.2	7.7	-6.9		-152.2	411.1	563.2	1 165.9	534.2	632.0	5 671.5
4th quarter	5 750.6	3 856.5	864.0	552.0	254.7	65.6	-6.3		-151.3	425.7	577.0	1 181.5	542.2	639.6	5 688.3

QUANTITY INDEXES FOR GROSS DOMESTIC PRODUCT
(Index numbers, 1992=100)

YEAR AND QUARTER	Gross domestic product	Personal consumption expenditures	Private fixed investment Total	Nonresidential	Residential	Exports and imports of goods and services Exports	Imports	Government expenditures and gross investment Total	Federal	State and local	Addendum: Final sales of domestic product
1960	36.2	34.0	34.2	28.0	54.0	13.6	16.2	48.8	66.2	36.3	36.3
1961	37.1	34.6	33.9	27.7	54.2	13.8	16.1	51.2	68.8	38.6	37.2
1962	39.3	36.4	38.2	30.1	59.4	14.5	17.9	54.3	74.5	39.7	39.2
1963	41.0	37.8	40.7	31.6	66.3	15.6	18.3	55.5	74.2	42.1	40.9
1964	43.4	40.1	44.1	35.3	70.2	17.7	19.3	56.7	73.0	45.0	43.4
1965	46.1	42.6	50.3	41.5	68.2	18.1	21.4	58.4	73.0	48.0	45.9
1966	49.2	45.1	54.5	46.5	62.1	19.3	24.6	63.7	81.3	51.1	48.6
1967	50.4	46.4	52.1	45.8	60.1	19.7	26.3	68.5	89.3	53.6	50.1
1968	52.8	49.1	54.8	47.8	68.3	21.2	30.3	70.6	90.2	56.6	52.6
1969	54.4	50.9	58.0	51.2	70.3	22.3	32.0	70.2	87.1	58.2	54.1
1970	54.4	52.1	53.9	50.7	66.1	24.7	33.4	68.6	80.9	59.8	54.6
1971	56.2	54.0	60.1	50.6	84.2	24.9	35.1	67.3	75.2	61.8	56.1
1972	59.3	57.3	67.3	55.2	99.2	26.9	39.0	67.6	73.9	63.1	59.2
1973	62.7	60.0	75.3	63.2	98.6	32.8	40.8	67.1	70.3	65.0	62.3
1974	62.3	59.6	69.1	63.5	78.2	35.9	39.7	68.3	69.9	67.4	62.1
1975	62.0	60.9	56.5	56.9	68.1	35.7	35.2	69.3	69.7	69.3	62.6
1976	65.4	64.3	68.0	59.6	84.1	37.8	42.1	69.4	69.0	69.9	65.1
1977	68.4	67.1	78.7	66.7	101.9	38.7	46.6	70.0	70.1	70.2	68.0
1978	72.1	70.0	87.7	75.8	108.6	42.7	50.6	72.1	71.5	72.7	71.6
1979	74.2	71.6	89.8	83.1	104.7	46.8	51.5	73.2	72.6	73.9	74.0
1980	73.9	71.3	79.5	82.7	82.5	51.8	48.0	74.5	75.6	73.9	74.4
1981	75.6	72.2	86.8	87.1	75.9	52.4	49.3	75.0	78.8	72.4	75.2
1982	74.0	73.0	74.3	83.2	62.1	48.7	48.7	76.0	81.3	72.2	74.6
1983	76.9	76.8	81.2	81.8	87.6	47.4	54.8	78.1	85.7	72.7	77.3
1984	82.3	80.8	105.4	96.0	100.4	51.4	68.1	80.6	87.8	75.4	81.2
1985	85.3	84.5	104.2	101.9	101.8	52.8	72.5	85.5	93.9	79.5	84.9
1986	87.9	87.9	102.7	98.3	114.0	56.7	78.7	89.8	98.2	83.9	87.9
1987	90.5	90.6	103.9	97.2	114.2	62.9	83.4	92.3	101.2	85.9	90.2
1960:											
1st quarter	36.5	33.7	38.5	28.1	58.4	13.0	16.5	47.9	65.3	35.3	36.1
2nd quarter	36.3	34.1	34.4	28.5	53.6	13.6	16.6	48.6	65.7	36.2	36.4
3rd quarter	36.3	34.0	34.1	27.7	52.0	13.9	16.1	49.2	66.5	36.7	36.3
4th quarter	35.9	34.0	29.9	27.5	51.9	13.9	15.4	49.7	67.1	37.1	36.5
1961:											
1st quarter	36.1	34.0	30.6	27.0	52.1	14.0	15.3	50.3	67.0	38.3	36.5
2nd quarter	36.7	34.5	32.7	27.5	52.3	13.3	15.5	50.7	68.3	38.1	36.9
3rd quarter	37.4	34.7	35.7	27.7	55.2	13.9	16.5	51.3	69.1	38.4	37.2
4th quarter	38.1	35.4	36.4	28.6	57.0	14.1	16.9	52.5	70.6	39.5	38.0
1962:											
1st quarter	38.8	35.8	38.6	29.3	58.0	14.0	17.4	53.4	73.1	39.1	38.5
2nd quarter	39.2	36.2	38.2	30.2	59.9	14.9	17.8	54.0	74.2	39.4	39.1
3rd quarter	39.6	36.5	38.8	30.6	59.8	14.9	18.0	54.7	75.2	39.9	39.5
4th quarter	39.7	37.0	37.3	30.3	59.7	14.4	18.2	55.0	75.4	40.3	39.7
1963:											
1st quarter	40.2	37.2	39.6	30.2	61.9	14.4	17.8	54.7	73.6	41.1	40.0
2nd quarter	40.7	37.6	40.0	31.1	66.3	15.7	18.2	55.0	73.7	41.5	40.6
3rd quarter	41.4	38.1	41.4	32.1	67.6	15.9	18.7	56.5	75.7	42.6	41.3
4th quarter	41.7	38.4	41.7	33.1	69.6	16.6	18.6	56.1	74.0	43.2	41.8
1964:											
1st quarter	42.7	39.2	43.8	33.9	73.9	17.5	18.6	56.4	73.8	43.9	42.7
2nd quarter	43.2	39.9	43.5	34.8	70.2	17.3	19.0	57.1	74.2	44.8	43.2
3rd quarter	43.7	40.6	44.2	36.0	69.0	17.9	19.6	56.6	72.3	45.3	43.7
4th quarter	43.9	40.7	44.8	36.7	67.8	18.2	20.1	56.6	71.6	45.8	43.8
1965:											
1st quarter	45.0	41.6	49.6	39.2	68.0	16.0	19.4	56.5	70.9	46.3	44.5
2nd quarter	45.6	42.1	49.5	40.6	68.5	18.6	21.6	57.6	72.0	47.4	45.3
3rd quarter	46.4	42.8	50.7	42.1	68.8	18.2	21.7	59.1	73.5	48.8	46.2
4th quarter	47.6	44.0	51.1	43.9	67.3	19.5	22.8	60.3	75.4	49.5	47.4
1966:											
1st quarter	48.7	44.7	55.2	45.8	68.8	19.3	23.4	61.4	77.2	50.2	48.2
2nd quarter	48.9	44.8	54.4	46.5	63.3	19.1	24.0	63.3	81.1	50.6	48.5
3rd quarter	49.3	45.3	54.0	47.0	61.3	19.2	25.3	64.3	82.7	51.2	48.9
4th quarter	49.7	45.5	54.4	46.8	54.8	19.6	25.6	65.6	84.1	52.4	49.0
1967:											
1st quarter	50.1	45.8	52.6	45.7	53.2	19.9	26.0	68.4	89.9	53.0	49.5
2nd quarter	50.1	46.4	50.5	45.6	59.2	19.7	25.8	68.1	88.7	53.3	50.0
3rd quarter	50.5	46.6	52.1	45.4	62.2	19.5	26.1	68.5	89.4	53.5	50.3
4th quarter	50.9	46.9	53.2	46.4	65.8	19.9	27.5	69.0	89.5	54.5	50.7
1968:											
1st quarter	51.8	48.0	53.8	47.8	66.2	20.4	29.1	70.2	91.0	55.3	51.7
2nd quarter	52.7	48.7	56.0	46.9	67.9	20.7	29.6	70.6	90.5	56.4	52.2
3rd quarter	53.1	49.7	54.4	47.5	69.1	22.0	31.3	70.7	89.7	57.1	53.0
4th quarter	53.4	49.9	55.0	48.9	70.0	21.5	31.1	71.0	89.7	57.6	53.3
1969:											
1st quarter	54.2	50.4	58.6	50.3	72.5	19.3	28.1	70.6	88.3	57.9	53.8
2nd quarter	54.3	50.8	58.1	50.8	71.7	23.4	33.7	70.5	87.6	58.3	54.1
3rd quarter	54.6	51.0	59.2	52.1	71.1	23.1	33.3	70.3	87.1	58.4	54.3
4th quarter	54.3	51.4	56.0	51.7	65.9	23.5	32.9	69.5	85.4	58.2	54.3
1970:											
1st quarter	54.2	51.7	54.1	51.3	66.1	24.1	32.8	69.0	83.3	58.8	54.5
2nd quarter	54.3	52.0	54.1	51.0	61.7	24.9	33.4	68.3	81.2	59.1	54.4
3rd quarter	54.8	52.4	55.1	51.2	64.9	24.8	33.3	68.6	79.9	60.5	54.9
4th quarter	54.3	52.3	52.4	49.3	71.8	25.2	33.9	68.5	79.2	60.8	54.8

SELECTED ANNUAL AND QUARTERLY DATA, 1960-1987

YEAR AND QUARTER	QUANTITY INDEXES FOR GROSS DOMESTIC PRODUCT—Continued (Index numbers,1992=100)										
	Gross domestic product	Personal consumption expenditures	Private fixed investment			Exports and imports of goods and services		Government expenditures and gross investment			Addendum: Final sales of domestic product
			Total	Nonresidential	Residential	Exports	Imports	Total	Federal	State and local	
1971:											
1st quarter	55.8	53.2	58.8	49.8	75.6	25.0	33.5	67.8	77.0	61.2	55.5
2nd quarter	56.1	53.7	60.8	50.5	83.3	24.9	36.0	67.5	75.7	61.6	55.8
3rd quarter	56.4	54.1	61.2	50.6	87.3	26.3	36.8	67.2	74.8	61.7	56.3
4th quarter	56.6	55.0	59.5	51.6	90.7	23.4	34.3	67.0	73.3	62.5	56.9
1972:											
1st quarter	57.7	55.7	63.6	53.3	96.8	26.2	39.3	68.0	75.2	62.8	57.9
2nd quarter	59.1	56.8	67.5	54.2	98.7	25.8	37.8	68.0	75.7	62.6	58.8
3rd quarter	59.7	57.6	68.6	55.1	98.9	27.0	38.6	67.1	72.9	63.1	59.3
4th quarter	60.7	58.9	69.5	58.0	102.4	28.7	40.3	67.2	71.8	64.0	60.7
1973:											
1st quarter	62.3	60.0	74.5	60.8	105.9	31.3	42.1	67.6	72.3	64.4	62.0
2nd quarter	62.8	59.9	76.0	63.2	100.5	32.7	40.9	67.4	71.7	64.5	62.3
3rd quarter	62.6	60.2	73.8	64.2	96.2	32.9	39.8	66.4	68.3	65.2	62.4
4th quarter	63.2	60.0	77.1	64.6	91.7	34.2	40.2	67.1	68.9	66.0	62.4
1974:											
1st quarter	62.6	59.6	71.6	64.6	84.9	35.4	39.0	67.9	69.6	66.8	62.4
2nd quarter	62.8	59.8	71.0	64.4	81.2	37.0	40.5	68.6	70.2	67.6	62.5
3rd quarter	62.1	60.0	67.1	63.6	78.5	35.2	39.8	68.2	69.4	67.5	62.3
4th quarter	61.7	59.0	67.0	61.6	68.2	36.2	39.4	68.5	70.2	67.5	61.3
1975:											
1st quarter	60.9	59.6	54.6	57.6	64.0	36.1	35.5	69.3	69.8	69.2	61.7
2nd quarter	61.4	60.6	53.1	56.1	65.4	34.6	32.7	69.0	69.7	68.6	62.3
3rd quarter	62.6	61.4	58.5	56.6	69.9	35.2	35.4	69.3	69.5	69.4	62.9
4th quarter	63.3	62.1	59.8	57.2	73.0	37.0	37.3	69.8	69.7	70.1	63.6
1976:											
1st quarter	64.8	63.4	65.8	58.2	80.4	36.9	39.6	70.1	69.2	71.1	64.6
2nd quarter	65.2	63.9	68.4	58.9	82.8	37.2	41.3	69.4	69.0	69.9	64.8
3rd quarter	65.5	64.6	68.3	60.1	81.4	38.3	43.0	69.1	68.9	69.5	65.1
4th quarter	66.1	65.4	69.5	61.2	91.8	38.7	44.4	69.0	68.9	69.2	66.0
1977:											
1st quarter	66.9	66.2	73.1	64.1	94.4	38.1	46.5	69.5	69.3	69.8	66.7
2nd quarter	68.2	66.6	78.8	65.9	104.9	39.1	46.8	70.2	70.5	70.3	67.8
3rd quarter	69.3	67.2	82.6	67.2	104.8	39.4	46.2	70.2	70.5	70.3	68.5
4th quarter	69.3	68.2	80.4	69.4	103.5	38.1	46.9	70.1	70.0	70.4	69.0
1978:											
1st quarter	69.6	68.6	82.3	69.7	104.2	39.0	50.0	70.2	70.2	70.5	69.0
2nd quarter	72.2	70.0	87.4	75.5	109.2	43.1	50.1	72.1	71.7	72.6	71.7
3rd quarter	72.9	70.3	89.9	77.8	110.7	43.5	50.9	72.6	71.8	73.5	72.3
4th quarter	73.7	70.9	91.3	80.0	110.4	45.2	51.5	73.3	72.4	74.2	73.2
1979:											
1st quarter	73.8	71.3	90.8	81.9	107.8	45.2	51.5	72.5	72.2	73.0	73.4
2nd quarter	73.9	71.2	91.5	81.7	105.9	45.3	51.7	73.2	72.9	73.7	73.4
3rd quarter	74.4	71.8	89.6	84.3	104.5	46.9	50.8	73.2	72.6	74.0	74.4
4th quarter	74.6	72.1	87.3	84.3	100.4	49.7	51.9	73.8	72.7	74.9	74.8
1980:											
1st quarter	74.9	72.0	87.3	85.3	93.3	51.3	52.0	74.9	74.8	75.2	75.0
2nd quarter	73.1	70.4	77.7	80.7	75.3	52.2	48.2	75.0	76.5	74.2	73.4
3rd quarter	73.1	71.1	72.2	81.4	76.7	52.1	44.8	74.1	75.6	73.2	74.3
4th quarter	74.5	71.9	80.8	83.2	84.8	51.8	47.2	73.9	75.6	72.9	75.0
1981:											
1st quarter	75.9	72.2	88.5	84.5	83.4	52.7	49.1	74.9	77.0	73.5	75.2
2nd quarter	75.2	72.2	83.8	86.0	80.2	53.0	49.2	75.0	79.2	72.1	75.3
3rd quarter	76.1	72.5	89.1	88.0	73.8	51.8	48.7	74.8	79.2	71.8	75.4
4th quarter	75.2	71.9	85.7	89.9	66.3	52.2	50.1	75.3	79.6	72.3	74.9
1982:											
1st quarter	73.9	72.4	76.6	87.5	62.6	50.1	48.7	75.1	79.6	72.0	74.6
2nd quarter	74.2	72.6	76.1	84.2	60.5	50.5	47.9	75.5	80.4	72.2	74.6
3rd quarter	73.9	73.0	75.1	81.4	59.8	48.2	50.0	76.1	81.6	72.1	74.0
4th quarter	74.0	74.2	69.3	79.9	65.6	46.0	48.1	77.2	83.7	72.6	75.1
1983:											
1st quarter	74.7	74.8	71.3	78.1	75.7	46.8	49.2	77.4	84.2	72.6	75.7
2nd quarter	76.3	76.3	78.2	79.0	85.5	46.9	53.0	77.9	85.7	72.4	76.7
3rd quarter	77.7	77.4	83.7	82.3	93.3	47.6	57.1	79.3	88.1	72.9	77.9
4th quarter	79.1	78.6	91.8	87.8	95.9	48.5	59.9	77.9	84.9	72.9	78.9
1984:											
1st quarter	80.9	79.5	102.8	90.6	99.3	49.7	64.7	78.7	85.4	73.9	79.5
2nd quarter	82.2	80.5	105.7	95.2	101.8	50.9	67.5	80.4	88.2	74.9	81.0
3rd quarter	82.8	81.0	107.6	97.9	100.5	51.9	69.1	80.9	87.7	76.1	81.5
4th quarter	83.3	82.0	105.6	100.2	100.0	52.9	71.2	82.3	90.0	76.9	82.6
1985:											
1st quarter	84.2	83.2	103.3	101.2	100.6	53.0	69.7	83.3	91.4	77.6	83.9
2nd quarter	84.6	83.9	103.9	102.7	100.1	52.8	73.1	84.9	93.1	79.0	84.4
3rd quarter	85.8	85.4	103.2	101.0	102.1	51.9	72.5	86.7	95.7	80.3	85.6
4th quarter	86.4	85.6	106.5	102.7	104.2	53.4	74.9	87.0	95.4	81.0	85.9
1986:											
1st quarter	87.5	86.4	108.2	101.1	108.7	55.0	74.9	87.7	94.7	82.7	86.7
2nd quarter	87.6	87.3	104.3	98.2	114.9	55.7	78.2	89.4	97.5	83.6	87.4
3rd quarter	88.0	88.7	98.8	96.6	116.4	57.0	80.4	91.4	101.1	84.4	88.5
4th quarter	88.5	89.2	99.5	97.4	115.8	59.0	81.1	90.8	99.4	84.7	88.9
1987:											
1st quarter	89.1	89.2	102.3	94.3	114.7	59.1	80.6	91.3	99.8	85.2	88.8
2nd quarter	90.0	90.4	102.1	96.4	115.6	61.5	82.8	92.0	101.2	85.5	89.9
3rd quarter	90.8	91.3	102.0	99.3	113.6	64.3	84.2	92.3	101.2	85.9	90.9
4th quarter	92.1	91.4	109.3	98.9	112.9	66.6	86.3	93.5	102.7	86.9	91.2

PRICE INDEXES FOR GROSS DOMESTIC PRODUCT
(Index numbers, 1992=100)

YEAR AND QUARTER	Gross domestic product	Personal consumption expenditures	Private fixed investment Total	Nonresidential	Residential	Exports	Imports	Government expenditures and gross investment Total	Federal	State and local	Addendum: Final sales of domestic product
1960	23.3	23.2	28.1	31.6	21.6	29.1	21.1	18.3	18.8	17.8	23.1
1961	23.5	23.4	28.0	31.5	21.6	29.5	21.1	18.7	19.0	18.2	23.4
1962	23.8	23.7	28.0	31.5	21.7	29.5	20.9	19.2	19.4	18.8	23.7
1963	24.1	24.0	28.0	31.5	21.5	29.4	21.3	19.6	19.9	19.3	24.0
1964	24.5	24.3	28.2	31.7	21.7	29.6	21.8	20.2	20.6	19.6	24.3
1965	25.0	24.7	28.6	32.1	22.3	30.6	22.1	20.7	21.2	20.2	24.8
1966	25.7	25.3	29.3	32.6	23.1	31.6	22.6	21.6	21.9	21.1	25.5
1967	26.5	26.0	30.1	33.4	23.9	32.8	22.7	22.5	22.6	22.4	26.3
1968	27.6	27.0	31.3	34.6	25.1	33.5	23.0	23.7	23.8	23.6	27.5
1969	28.9	28.2	32.9	36.0	26.9	34.5	23.6	25.2	25.1	25.2	28.8
1970	30.5	29.5	34.3	37.8	27.7	36.0	25.0	27.2	27.1	27.3	30.3
1971	32.1	30.8	36.1	39.6	29.4	37.3	26.5	29.3	29.4	29.2	31.9
1972	33.4	31.9	37.6	41.0	31.1	38.5	28.4	31.5	32.0	31.0	33.3
1973	35.3	33.6	39.7	42.6	33.9	43.8	33.4	33.9	34.5	33.3	35.2
1974	38.5	37.0	43.7	46.8	37.4	54.1	48.0	37.5	37.9	37.0	38.3
1975	42.1	40.0	49.2	53.3	40.9	59.7	52.1	41.4	42.0	40.8	41.9
1976	44.6	42.3	52.1	56.3	43.5	61.6	53.7	44.0	44.6	43.4	44.4
1977	47.4	45.1	56.2	60.1	48.0	64.2	58.5	47.1	48.2	46.2	47.3
1978	50.9	48.4	61.1	64.4	53.7	68.2	62.7	50.3	51.5	49.3	50.7
1979	55.2	52.8	66.7	69.7	59.8	76.5	73.4	54.8	56.1	53.7	55.1
1980	60.3	58.5	73.0	76.0	66.2	84.2	91.5	60.9	62.2	59.7	60.2
1981	66.0	63.7	79.9	83.5	71.6	90.3	96.4	66.8	68.3	65.6	65.8
1982	70.2	67.4	84.5	88.3	75.5	90.8	93.1	71.3	72.9	69.9	70.0
1983	73.2	70.5	85.2	87.5	77.2	91.3	89.6	74.5	76.1	73.2	73.0
1984	75.9	73.1	85.0	87.5	79.4	92.3	88.9	78.2	80.4	76.4	75.8
1985	78.5	75.8	86.2	88.3	81.5	89.8	86.0	81.0	82.7	79.5	78.4
1986	80.6	78.0	88.6	90.2	84.9	88.5	86.0	82.7	84.0	81.6	80.5
1987	83.1	81.0	90.4	91.3	88.3	91.0	91.0	85.2	85.3	85.0	83.0
1960:											
1st quarter	23.1	23.0	28.0	31.6	21.5	29.1	21.1	18.2	18.5	17.7	23.0
2nd quarter	23.2	23.1	28.1	31.6	21.6	29.1	21.1	18.2	18.6	17.8	23.1
3rd quarter	23.3	23.2	28.1	31.6	21.6	29.2	21.2	18.4	18.9	17.9	23.2
4th quarter	23.4	23.4	28.1	31.6	21.6	29.1	21.2	18.6	19.1	17.9	23.3
1961:											
1st quarter	23.5	23.4	28.0	31.5	21.6	29.2	21.2	18.6	19.0	18.0	23.3
2nd quarter	23.5	23.4	28.1	31.6	21.6	29.6	21.2	18.6	19.0	18.2	23.4
3rd quarter	23.6	23.5	28.0	31.4	21.6	29.5	21.1	18.7	19.0	18.3	23.4
4th quarter	23.6	23.5	28.0	31.5	21.6	29.7	21.1	18.8	19.1	18.5	23.5
1962:											
1st quarter	23.7	23.6	28.1	31.5	21.7	29.7	20.9	19.0	19.3	18.7	23.6
2nd quarter	23.8	23.7	28.1	31.5	21.7	29.4	20.9	19.1	19.3	18.8	23.7
3rd quarter	23.9	23.7	28.0	31.5	21.7	29.4	20.8	19.2	19.4	18.8	23.7
4th quarter	24.0	23.8	28.0	31.4	21.6	29.4	20.9	19.3	19.6	19.0	23.8
1963:											
1st quarter	24.0	23.9	28.0	31.5	21.6	29.5	21.1	19.5	19.8	19.1	23.9
2nd quarter	24.1	23.9	28.0	31.5	21.5	29.5	21.2	19.6	19.8	19.2	23.9
3rd quarter	24.1	24.0	27.9	31.6	21.3	29.4	21.4	19.5	19.8	19.3	24.0
4th quarter	24.3	24.1	28.0	31.5	21.4	29.4	21.5	19.9	20.2	19.4	24.1
1964:											
1st quarter	24.3	24.2	27.9	31.5	21.2	29.5	21.7	20.0	20.4	19.5	24.2
2nd quarter	24.4	24.3	28.1	31.7	21.6	29.4	21.8	20.1	20.5	19.6	24.3
3rd quarter	24.5	24.3	28.2	31.7	21.6	29.7	21.8	20.3	20.8	19.7	24.4
4th quarter	24.6	24.4	28.5	31.9	22.1	30.0	21.8	20.3	20.7	19.8	24.5
1965:											
1st quarter	24.8	24.5	28.5	31.9	22.1	30.7	22.0	20.5	20.9	20.0	24.6
2nd quarter	24.9	24.7	28.6	32.0	22.1	30.6	21.9	20.6	21.0	20.1	24.7
3rd quarter	25.0	24.8	28.6	32.1	22.1	30.6	22.1	20.8	21.2	20.2	24.9
4th quarter	25.2	24.8	28.9	32.2	22.7	30.5	22.3	21.1	21.7	20.4	25.0
1966:											
1st quarter	25.3	25.0	28.8	32.2	22.4	31.0	22.4	21.2	21.7	20.7	25.2
2nd quarter	25.5	25.2	29.3	32.5	23.2	31.3	22.6	21.3	21.6	21.0	25.4
3rd quarter	25.8	25.4	29.3	32.6	23.1	31.7	22.6	21.8	22.2	21.3	25.7
4th quarter	26.0	25.6	29.7	32.9	23.6	32.3	22.7	21.9	22.1	21.6	25.9
1967:											
1st quarter	26.2	25.7	29.8	33.1	23.6	32.8	22.7	22.1	22.1	22.0	26.0
2nd quarter	26.3	25.9	29.9	33.3	23.7	32.8	22.6	22.3	22.4	22.2	26.2
3rd quarter	26.6	26.1	30.1	33.5	23.8	32.7	22.6	22.6	22.6	22.5	26.4
4th quarter	26.9	26.4	30.5	33.8	24.3	32.9	22.7	22.9	23.1	22.8	26.7
1968:											
1st quarter	27.2	26.7	30.8	34.1	24.7	33.1	22.8	23.3	23.3	23.2	27.1
2nd quarter	27.5	26.9	31.1	34.4	25.0	33.8	23.0	23.6	23.6	23.5	27.4
3rd quarter	27.8	27.2	31.3	34.7	25.0	33.4	23.0	23.9	24.1	23.7	27.6
4th quarter	28.1	27.4	32.0	35.3	25.9	33.6	23.2	24.3	24.4	24.2	28.0
1969:											
1st quarter	28.4	27.7	32.4	35.5	26.4	34.1	23.3	24.5	24.4	24.5	28.2
2nd quarter	28.7	28.0	32.7	35.8	26.8	34.1	23.4	24.9	24.8	25.0	28.6
3rd quarter	29.1	28.3	33.0	36.2	26.9	34.6	23.6	25.5	25.5	25.4	29.0
4th quarter	29.5	28.6	33.4	36.6	27.3	35.4	24.2	25.9	25.8	26.0	29.4
1970:											
1st quarter	29.9	29.0	33.7	37.0	27.3	35.5	24.4	26.6	26.6	26.5	29.8
2nd quarter	30.4	29.3	34.5	37.7	28.3	36.3	24.7	27.0	26.9	27.1	30.2
3rd quarter	30.6	29.6	34.3	37.9	27.6	36.1	25.3	27.4	27.3	27.5	30.5
4th quarter	31.0	30.0	34.7	38.4	27.8	36.2	25.6	27.8	27.6	28.1	30.9

SELECTED ANNUAL AND QUARTERLY DATA, 1960-1987

PRICE INDEXES FOR GROSS DOMESTIC PRODUCT—Continued
(Index numbers, 1992=100)

YEAR AND QUARTER	Gross domestic product	Personal consumption expenditures	Private fixed investment			Exports and imports of goods and services		Government expenditures and gross investment			Addendum: Final sales of domestic product
			Total	Nonresidential	Residential	Exports	Imports	Total	Federal	State and local	
1971:											
1st quarter	31.5	30.3	35.3	39.0	28.5	37.3	26.2	28.6	28.6	28.6	31.4
2nd quarter	31.9	30.7	35.9	39.5	29.1	37.3	26.3	29.1	29.2	29.1	31.8
3rd quarter	32.3	31.0	36.3	39.8	29.7	37.1	26.6	29.5	29.6	29.5	32.1
4th quarter	32.5	31.2	36.7	40.1	30.1	37.3	27.0	30.0	30.4	29.7	32.4
1972:											
1st quarter	33.0	31.6	37.1	40.6	30.5	37.9	27.5	30.8	31.5	30.3	32.9
2nd quarter	33.2	31.7	37.4	40.9	30.7	38.3	28.2	31.2	31.8	30.7	33.1
3rd quarter	33.5	32.0	37.7	41.1	31.2	38.4	28.7	31.5	31.9	31.2	33.4
4th quarter	33.9	32.3	38.3	41.4	32.1	39.4	29.4	32.2	32.8	31.7	33.8
1973:											
1st quarter	34.4	32.7	38.7	41.7	32.6	40.6	30.2	32.9	33.5	32.4	34.2
2nd quarter	35.0	33.3	39.4	42.3	33.4	42.4	32.6	33.6	34.1	33.1	34.8
3rd quarter	35.6	33.9	40.2	43.0	34.5	44.9	34.2	34.2	34.9	33.6	35.5
4th quarter	36.2	34.6	40.7	43.4	35.1	47.2	36.7	34.8	35.5	34.2	36.1
1974:											
1st quarter	37.0	35.6	41.5	44.1	35.9	50.6	42.6	35.7	36.2	35.2	36.8
2nd quarter	37.8	36.6	42.7	45.6	36.8	52.3	47.7	36.7	37.1	36.4	37.6
3rd quarter	38.9	37.5	44.4	47.5	37.9	55.3	50.1	38.1	38.4	37.7	38.8
4th quarter	40.1	38.4	46.2	49.8	39.0	58.2	51.7	39.3	39.9	38.8	40.0
1975:											
1st quarter	41.0	39.1	47.9	51.7	40.0	60.0	52.6	40.2	40.8	39.7	40.9
2nd quarter	41.7	39.6	49.0	53.1	40.7	59.7	52.7	41.0	41.5	40.5	41.5
3rd quarter	42.4	40.4	49.6	53.8	41.1	59.4	51.6	41.6	42.1	41.2	42.3
4th quarter	43.2	41.1	50.4	54.6	41.8	59.8	51.6	42.6	43.4	41.8	43.0
1976:											
1st quarter	43.7	41.5	50.9	55.2	42.0	60.6	52.4	43.1	43.6	42.5	43.5
2nd quarter	44.2	41.9	51.8	55.9	43.3	61.3	53.3	43.7	44.1	43.2	44.0
3rd quarter	44.8	42.6	52.5	56.7	44.0	61.7	54.2	44.2	44.8	43.6	44.6
4th quarter	45.6	43.3	53.4	57.5	44.7	62.8	54.8	45.0	46.1	44.2	45.4
1977:											
1st quarter	46.3	44.0	54.4	58.5	45.9	63.6	56.8	46.0	47.1	45.0	46.1
2nd quarter	47.1	44.8	55.6	59.5	47.3	64.6	58.4	46.7	47.7	45.8	46.9
3rd quarter	47.7	45.5	56.8	60.6	48.7	64.1	59.2	47.3	48.2	46.6	47.6
4th quarter	48.6	46.2	58.0	61.7	50.1	64.5	59.8	48.4	49.6	47.4	48.4
1978:											
1st quarter	49.4	47.0	59.2	62.6	51.6	65.8	60.8	49.1	50.2	48.1	49.2
2nd quarter	50.4	48.0	60.5	63.9	53.1	67.5	62.3	49.9	50.9	49.0	50.3
3rd quarter	51.3	48.9	61.7	64.9	54.4	68.6	63.3	50.6	51.7	49.6	51.2
4th quarter	52.4	49.8	63.0	66.1	55.9	70.9	64.4	51.6	53.1	50.3	52.2
1979:											
1st quarter	53.5	50.9	64.3	67.5	57.0	73.0	66.9	52.8	54.2	51.6	53.3
2nd quarter	54.7	52.1	66.0	69.0	58.9	76.0	70.5	54.0	55.1	53.0	54.5
3rd quarter	55.8	53.4	67.6	70.5	60.8	77.8	75.6	55.5	56.4	54.6	55.7
4th quarter	56.9	54.7	69.0	71.8	62.3	79.2	80.7	57.0	58.6	55.7	56.8
1980:											
1st quarter	58.3	56.4	70.6	73.4	63.9	81.5	87.2	58.5	59.8	57.3	58.1
2nd quarter	59.6	57.8	72.3	75.2	65.4	82.6	90.7	60.1	61.4	58.9	59.4
3rd quarter	60.9	59.2	73.8	76.8	66.9	84.9	93.2	61.3	62.2	60.5	60.7
4th quarter	62.6	60.5	75.4	78.4	68.6	87.7	94.7	63.6	65.4	62.0	62.4
1981:											
1st quarter	64.2	62.1	77.4	80.6	70.1	90.0	97.2	65.2	66.8	63.9	64.0
2nd quarter	65.4	63.2	79.3	82.8	71.2	90.3	97.8	66.3	67.5	65.2	65.1
3rd quarter	66.7	64.3	80.7	84.3	72.1	90.4	95.2	67.2	68.4	66.1	66.5
4th quarter	67.9	65.4	82.3	86.2	73.2	90.6	95.5	68.7	70.5	67.1	67.7
1982:											
1st quarter	68.9	66.2	83.5	87.4	74.2	91.2	95.2	69.9	71.7	68.3	68.7
2nd quarter	69.7	66.8	84.5	88.3	75.3	91.2	93.5	70.9	72.5	69.4	69.6
3rd quarter	70.7	67.9	84.9	88.7	76.0	90.5	92.3	71.7	73.1	70.5	70.5
4th quarter	71.5	68.7	85.0	88.7	76.3	90.1	91.6	72.8	74.4	71.5	71.3
1983:											
1st quarter	72.1	69.2	84.6	88.1	76.7	90.6	89.7	73.5	75.3	72.1	72.0
2nd quarter	72.8	70.1	84.3	87.6	76.9	91.0	89.8	74.3	76.0	72.8	72.7
3rd quarter	73.5	70.9	84.2	87.3	77.3	91.4	89.8	74.8	76.3	73.5	73.3
4th quarter	74.2	71.6	84.4	87.2	77.9	92.3	89.3	75.4	76.8	74.2	74.0
1984:											
1st quarter	75.0	72.3	84.5	87.1	78.4	92.5	89.6	77.2	79.4	75.3	74.8
2nd quarter	75.6	72.9	84.9	87.5	79.0	93.2	90.1	77.9	80.0	76.1	75.5
3rd quarter	76.3	73.4	85.2	87.6	79.8	92.2	88.5	78.6	80.7	76.8	76.1
4th quarter	76.8	74.0	85.5	87.7	80.4	91.3	87.4	79.2	81.3	77.5	76.7
1985:											
1st quarter	77.6	74.7	85.8	87.9	80.8	90.3	85.4	80.1	81.9	78.5	77.5
2nd quarter	78.3	75.5	85.9	88.0	81.0	90.2	85.7	80.7	82.4	79.2	78.2
3rd quarter	78.8	76.1	86.3	88.4	81.5	89.4	85.5	81.2	82.8	79.8	78.7
4th quarter	79.4	77.0	86.9	88.8	82.5	89.3	87.3	82.1	83.9	80.6	79.4
1986:											
1st quarter	79.8	77.5	87.4	89.2	83.5	88.9	87.5	82.1	83.7	80.7	79.7
2nd quarter	80.3	77.6	88.2	89.9	84.3	88.5	84.7	82.3	83.8	81.0	80.2
3rd quarter	80.8	78.2	89.0	90.7	85.4	88.0	85.4	82.8	83.9	81.7	80.7
4th quarter	81.4	78.8	89.7	91.1	86.4	88.8	86.3	83.6	84.4	82.9	81.4
1987:											
1st quarter	82.1	79.7	89.9	91.1	87.1	89.3	88.5	84.4	85.0	83.8	82.0
2nd quarter	82.7	80.5	90.2	91.2	87.9	90.7	90.8	85.0	85.2	84.7	82.6
3rd quarter	83.4	81.4	90.5	91.2	88.8	91.2	91.6	85.5	85.4	85.5	83.3
4th quarter	84.1	82.3	91.2	91.9	89.6	92.8	93.1	85.8	85.5	86.1	84.0

SELECTED PER CAPITA PRODUCT AND INCOME SERIES AND U.S. POPULATION
(Dollars, except as noted, quarterly data are at seasonally adjusted annual rates)

YEAR AND QUARTER	Current dollars							Chained (1992) dollars						Population (Mid-period, thousands)
	Gross domestic product	Personal income	Disposable personal income	Personal consumption expenditures				Gross domestic product	Disposable personal income	Personal consumption expenditures				
				Total	Durable goods	Nondurable goods	Services			Total	Durable goods	Nondurable goods	Services	
1960	2 913	2 282	2 013	1 838	240	846	752	12 519	8 681	7 926	582	3 405	3 969	180 760
1961	2 965	2 340	2 066	1 865	227	852	785	12 595	8 814	7 954	551	3 411	4 063	183 742
1962	3 136	2 449	2 156	1 948	251	873	824	13 156	9 098	8 220	606	3 465	4 199	186 590
1963	3 261	2 536	2 229	2 023	273	888	862	13 520	9 294	8 434	655	3 487	4 325	189 300
1964	3 455	2 681	2 389	2 144	295	931	918	14 112	9 825	8 817	706	3 608	4 525	191 927
1965	3 700	2 864	2 546	2 286	325	986	975	14 825	10 311	9 257	785	3 753	4 706	194 347
1966	4 007	3 081	2 720	2 451	347	1 062	1 042	15 612	10 735	9 674	842	3 913	4 888	196 599
1967	4 194	3 274	2 882	2 563	354	1 092	1 117	15 835	11 081	9 854	846	3 932	5 069	198 752
1968	4 536	3 559	3 101	2 789	402	1 174	1 212	16 408	11 468	10 313	930	4 069	5 278	200 745
1969	4 845	3 844	3 302	2 982	424	1 249	1 310	16 739	11 726	10 593	953	4 136	5 479	202 736
1970	5 050	4 082	3 550	3 160	414	1 326	1 419	16 566	12 039	10 717	912	4 189	5 634	205 089
1971	5 419	4 334	3 811	3 383	467	1 375	1 541	16 900	12 366	10 975	990	4 211	5 768	207 692
1972	5 894	4 710	4 082	3 671	526	1 467	1 678	17 637	12 794	11 508	1 105	4 349	6 014	209 924
1973	6 524	5 226	4 562	4 018	583	1 619	1 816	18 479	13 566	11 950	1 207	4 449	6 225	211 939
1974	6 998	5 685	4 941	4 353	572	1 797	1 984	18 192	13 344	11 756	1 114	4 322	6 317	213 898
1975	7 550	6 107	5 383	4 765	618	1 948	2 199	17 936	13 444	11 899	1 103	4 344	6 474	215 981
1976	8 341	6 692	5 856	5 268	728	2 101	2 438	18 721	13 837	12 446	1 231	4 516	6 681	218 086
1977	9 201	7 336	6 383	5 797	822	2 256	2 719	19 400	14 142	12 846	1 332	4 587	6 892	220 289
1978	10 292	8 201	7 123	6 418	905	2 470	3 043	20 226	14 715	13 258	1 387	4 697	7 139	222 629
1979	11 361	9 133	7 888	7 079	950	2 772	3 357	20 571	14 951	13 417	1 365	4 752	7 285	225 106
1980	12 226	10 069	8 697	7 730	938	3 054	3 739	20 265	14 867	13 216	1 241	4 677	7 336	227 726
1981	13 547	11 167	9 601	8 440	1 002	3 296	4 142	20 524	15 064	13 245	1 243	4 671	7 374	230 008
1982	13 961	11 744	10 145	8 943	1 030	3 388	4 525	19 896	15 053	13 270	1 229	4 654	7 442	232 218
1983	14 998	12 379	10 803	9 744	1 194	3 543	5 007	20 499	15 332	13 829	1 397	4 747	7 720	234 332
1984	16 508	13 602	11 929	10 543	1 375	3 738	5 430	21 744	16 309	14 415	1 586	4 872	7 966	236 394
1985	17 529	14 464	12 629	11 341	1 514	3 889	5 938	22 320	16 654	14 954	1 725	4 941	8 290	238 506
1986	18 374	15 200	13 289	12 019	1 656	3 977	6 385	22 801	17 039	15 409	1 863	5 052	8 482	240 682
1987	19 323	16 013	13 896	12 743	1 716	4 175	6 851	23 264	17 164	15 740	1 873	5 103	8 758	242 842
1960:														
1st quarter	2 934	2 269	2 003	1 821	240	839	742	12 684	8 707	7 916	582	3 406	3 957	179 694
2nd quarter	2 917	2 286	2 016	1 848	245	852	751	12 563	8 710	7 983	593	3 434	3 978	180 335
3rd quarter	2 921	2 288	2 017	1 839	241	845	754	12 526	8 681	7 916	586	3 396	3 960	181 094
4th quarter	2 880	2 286	2 014	1 842	233	846	763	12 306	8 626	7 887	567	3 383	3 981	181 915
1961:														
1st quarter	2 892	2 298	2 027	1 838	218	850	770	12 329	8 659	7 853	532	3 392	4 005	182 634
2nd quarter	2 939	2 321	2 049	1 858	223	851	784	12 502	8 759	7 940	541	3 414	4 062	183 337
3rd quarter	2 985	2 351	2 077	1 866	229	850	787	12 670	8 846	7 949	552	3 402	4 065	184 103
4th quarter	3 043	2 389	2 112	1 897	239	858	800	12 878	8 987	8 074	578	3 436	4 118	184 894
1962:														
1st quarter	3 101	2 410	2 128	1 915	243	866	806	13 056	9 033	8 129	588	3 453	4 142	185 553
2nd quarter	3 130	2 443	2 152	1 940	249	870	821	13 147	9 093	8 199	601	3 458	4 192	186 203
3rd quarter	3 156	2 461	2 164	1 955	251	874	829	13 224	9 117	8 236	605	3 470	4 213	186 926
4th quarter	3 159	2 481	2 178	1 980	261	881	839	13 196	9 147	8 315	630	3 478	4 247	187 680
1963:														
1st quarter	3 198	2 498	2 193	1 992	266	883	843	13 323	9 187	8 344	641	3 480	4 255	188 299
2nd quarter	3 234	2 516	2 211	2 008	271	884	853	13 436	9 243	8 397	653	3 483	4 289	188 906
3rd quarter	3 289	2 545	2 238	2 038	274	893	870	13 638	9 309	8 477	659	3 497	4 356	189 631
4th quarter	3 324	2 583	2 276	2 054	279	893	883	13 682	9 434	8 516	667	3 486	4 398	190 362
1964:														
1st quarter	3 401	2 622	2 322	2 097	289	912	897	13 965	9 587	8 660	690	3 542	4 453	190 954
2nd quarter	3 437	2 660	2 379	2 132	295	926	910	14 082	9 807	8 786	706	3 596	4 503	191 560
3rd quarter	3 481	2 701	2 412	2 170	304	941	924	14 198	9 909	8 915	727	3 648	4 548	192 256
4th quarter	3 499	2 739	2 442	2 176	292	945	939	14 200	9 996	8 908	701	3 647	4 593	192 938
1965:														
1st quarter	3 596	2 784	2 468	2 226	320	956	950	14 519	10 067	9 077	765	3 680	4 624	193 467
2nd quarter	3 650	2 828	2 506	2 257	318	973	966	14 672	10 167	9 155	765	3 711	4 678	193 994
3rd quarter	3 725	2 892	2 578	2 297	327	989	981	14 893	10 412	9 279	790	3 751	4 725	194 647
4th quarter	3 829	2 953	2 632	2 363	337	1 024	1 002	15 211	10 595	9 515	821	3 869	4 795	195 279
1966:														
1st quarter	3 936	3 005	2 667	2 411	352	1 044	1 015	15 541	10 656	9 632	858	3 894	4 828	195 763
2nd quarter	3 974	3 047	2 689	2 431	338	1 060	1 033	15 567	10 657	9 634	820	3 918	4 875	196 277
3rd quarter	4 031	3 106	2 738	2 471	350	1 072	1 049	15 627	10 764	9 714	846	3 932	4 902	196 877
4th quarter	4 087	3 166	2 785	2 492	350	1 072	1 069	15 710	10 864	9 718	843	3 905	4 946	197 481
1967:														
1st quarter	4 129	3 212	2 828	2 509	342	1 080	1 088	15 796	10 995	9 755	825	3 926	4 999	197 967
2nd quarter	4 148	3 240	2 859	2 551	358	1 087	1 107	15 769	11 054	9 864	860	3 935	5 049	198 455
3rd quarter	4 215	3 299	2 903	2 581	357	1 095	1 128	15 849	11 116	9 884	850	3 927	5 103	199 012
4th quarter	4 283	3 344	2 939	2 612	361	1 107	1 144	15 924	11 157	9 914	849	3 937	5 126	199 572
1968:														
1st quarter	4 403	3 434	3 018	2 697	386	1 140	1 171	16 181	11 329	10 126	900	4 015	5 181	199 995
2nd quarter	4 514	3 526	3 093	2 760	394	1 164	1 202	16 423	11 499	10 259	916	4 056	5 256	200 452
3rd quarter	4 578	3 606	3 123	2 831	415	1 191	1 226	16 498	11 497	10 423	955	4 109	5 311	200 997
4th quarter	4 648	3 670	3 168	2 865	415	1 201	1 250	16 529	11 544	10 442	947	4 097	5 363	201 538
1969:														
1st quarter	4 754	3 728	3 194	2 916	424	1 220	1 272	16 746	11 543	10 537	961	4 127	5 410	201 955
2nd quarter	4 812	3 808	3 259	2 961	424	1 241	1 296	16 749	11 641	10 579	957	4 138	5 455	202 419
3rd quarter	4 895	3 891	3 352	3 001	424	1 257	1 320	16 797	11 838	10 602	952	4 134	5 495	202 986
4th quarter	4 917	3 947	3 402	3 051	423	1 277	1 351	16 664	11 878	10 653	944	4 147	5 555	203 584
1970:														
1st quarter	4 968	3 988	3 447	3 099	416	1 304	1 379	16 593	11 895	10 693	925	4 180	5 595	204 086
2nd quarter	5 029	4 076	3 532	3 139	420	1 318	1 401	16 567	12 051	10 711	931	4 176	5 609	204 721
3rd quarter	5 101	4 116	3 598	3 190	423	1 332	1 434	16 663	12 144	10 766	931	4 190	5 656	205 419
4th quarter	5 100	4 145	3 623	3 212	398	1 351	1 463	16 443	12 063	10 695	861	4 209	5 675	206 130

SELECTED PER CAPITA PRODUCT AND INCOME SERIES AND U.S. POPULATION-Continued
(Dollars, except as noted, quarterly data are at seasonally adjusted annual rates)

YEAR AND QUARTER	Current dollars							Chained (1992) dollars						Population (Mid-period, thousands)
	Gross domestic product	Personal income	Disposable personal income	Personal consumption expenditures				Gross domestic product	Disposable personal income	Personal consumption expenditures				
				Total	Durable goods	Nondurable goods	Services			Total	Durable goods	Nondurable goods	Services	
1971:														
1st quarter	5 304	4 221	3 716	3 296	448	1 355	1 492	16 838	12 249	10 865	954	4 209	5 706	206 763
2nd quarter	5 390	4 318	3 802	3 355	461	1 370	1 525	16 883	12 387	10 930	973	4 212	5 743	207 362
3rd quarter	5 468	4 366	3 842	3 405	470	1 378	1 556	16 941	12 391	10 980	997	4 200	5 776	208 000
4th quarter	5 511	4 431	3 882	3 473	487	1 395	1 592	16 937	12 436	11 125	1 037	4 221	5 845	208 642
1972:														
1st quarter	5 691	4 554	3 938	3 547	502	1 415	1 631	17 236	12 484	11 246	1 060	4 237	5 925	209 142
2nd quarter	5 840	4 621	3 996	3 625	516	1 452	1 658	17 592	12 594	11 424	1 084	4 332	5 973	209 637
3rd quarter	5 937	4 740	4 110	3 702	530	1 482	1 690	17 728	12 839	11 564	1 110	4 381	6 030	210 181
4th quarter	6 106	4 926	4 281	3 810	555	1 521	1 734	17 987	13 256	11 797	1 164	4 445	6 127	210 737
1973:														
1st quarter	6 333	5 025	4 384	3 917	593	1 564	1 760	18 430	13 411	11 981	1 239	4 482	6 168	211 192
2nd quarter	6 470	5 151	4 504	3 979	586	1 592	1 800	18 515	13 520	11 941	1 216	4 434	6 220	211 663
3rd quarter	6 557	5 269	4 600	4 057	583	1 638	1 835	18 413	13 572	11 970	1 204	4 455	6 246	212 191
4th quarter	6 734	5 457	4 760	4 119	569	1 680	1 869	18 556	13 760	11 906	1 170	4 425	6 267	212 708
1974:														
1st quarter	6 786	5 518	4 809	4 196	558	1 732	1 906	18 336	13 509	11 789	1 136	4 361	6 268	213 144
2nd quarter	6 940	5 610	4 875	4 318	576	1 781	1 962	18 364	13 332	11 810	1 144	4 336	6 312	213 602
3rd quarter	7 059	5 768	5 007	4 437	601	1 829	2 006	18 118	13 346	11 825	1 151	4 331	6 325	214 147
4th quarter	7 204	5 842	5 071	4 461	553	1 848	2 061	17 951	13 189	11 602	1 025	4 260	6 363	214 700
1975:														
1st quarter	7 253	5 891	5 119	4 568	573	1 880	2 116	17 668	13 091	11 682	1 048	4 272	6 403	215 135
2nd quarter	7 409	6 019	5 417	4 694	595	1 927	2 173	17 784	13 679	11 854	1 067	4 351	6 470	215 652
3rd quarter	7 662	6 177	5 428	4 837	638	1 977	2 222	18 064	13 447	11 983	1 132	4 375	6 484	216 289
4th quarter	7 873	6 339	5 565	4 958	666	2 006	2 286	18 227	13 556	12 076	1 162	4 379	6 539	216 848
1976:														
1st quarter	8 132	6 493	5 704	5 109	709	2 049	2 350	18 612	13 739	12 306	1 222	4 456	6 608	217 314
2nd quarter	8 256	6 606	5 785	5 190	718	2 078	2 394	18 699	13 809	12 388	1 222	4 507	6 638	217 776
3rd quarter	8 383	6 758	5 907	5 312	731	2 118	2 463	18 725	13 875	12 478	1 231	4 535	6 695	218 338
4th quarter	8 589	6 909	6 026	5 459	755	2 158	2 546	18 849	13 923	12 611	1 249	4 564	6 782	218 917
1977:														
1st quarter	8 815	7 064	6 127	5 609	791	2 204	2 613	19 033	13 910	12 735	1 298	4 583	6 823	219 427
2nd quarter	9 116	7 226	6 288	5 724	813	2 237	2 675	19 368	14 035	12 777	1 327	4 569	6 841	219 956
3rd quarter	9 354	7 413	6 464	5 850	830	2 260	2 760	19 628	14 213	12 862	1 342	4 563	6 923	220 573
4th quarter	9 515	7 640	6 651	6 004	855	2 322	2 828	19 567	14 410	13 009	1 361	4 631	6 978	221 201
1978:														
1st quarter	9 687	7 821	6 819	6 126	842	2 364	2 920	19 599	14 523	13 048	1 325	4 645	7 060	221 719
2nd quarter	10 229	8 098	7 048	6 376	920	2 441	3 016	20 293	14 691	13 292	1 423	4 681	7 142	222 281
3rd quarter	10 469	8 317	7 210	6 507	918	2 504	3 085	20 419	14 753	13 315	1 397	4 711	7 170	222 933
4th quarter	10 780	8 567	7 413	6 659	939	2 571	3 149	20 590	14 891	13 376	1 403	4 750	7 182	223 583
1979:														
1st quarter	10 995	8 800	7 620	6 823	942	2 648	3 233	20 547	14 988	13 420	1 385	4 759	7 249	224 152
2nd quarter	11 223	8 978	7 764	6 959	934	2 715	3 310	20 538	14 911	13 365	1 350	4 724	7 283	224 737
3rd quarter	11 502	9 246	7 977	7 175	969	2 818	3 388	20 606	14 938	13 436	1 384	4 750	7 282	225 418
4th quarter	11 721	9 503	8 189	7 357	957	2 906	3 494	20 592	14 966	13 445	1 341	4 775	7 324	226 117
1980:														
1st quarter	12 006	9 773	8 465	7 555	968	2 995	3 592	20 635	15 007	13 394	1 320	4 746	7 334	226 754
2nd quarter	11 959	9 831	8 490	7 551	876	3 017	3 658	20 083	14 681	13 056	1 169	4 669	7 269	227 389
3rd quarter	12 204	10 128	8 744	7 782	931	3 064	3 787	20 004	14 772	13 147	1 220	4 642	7 334	228 070
4th quarter	12 733	10 539	9 086	8 032	975	3 139	3 918	20 341	15 009	13 268	1 255	4 652	7 407	228 689
1981:														
1st quarter	13 267	10 838	9 335	8 249	1 015	3 251	3 982	20 681	15 041	13 290	1 291	4 684	7 340	229 155
2nd quarter	13 368	10 981	9 427	8 375	990	3 290	4 095	20 450	14 928	13 262	1 235	4 681	7 391	229 674
3rd quarter	13 754	11 380	9 766	8 543	1 035	3 311	4 197	20 638	15 183	13 282	1 271	4 664	7 385	230 301
4th quarter	13 796	11 466	9 873	8 592	968	3 333	4 291	20 328	15 105	13 145	1 175	4 654	7 379	230 903
1982:														
1st quarter	13 737	11 510	9 910	8 736	1 008	3 351	4 377	19 948	14 972	13 198	1 212	4 648	7 393	231 395
2nd quarter	13 935	11 729	10 105	8 823	1 016	3 354	4 453	19 986	15 123	13 204	1 213	4 639	7 408	231 906
3rd quarter	14 018	11 794	10 216	8 994	1 024	3 407	4 562	19 837	15 048	13 248	1 219	4 649	7 438	232 498
4th quarter	14 155	11 943	10 346	9 219	1 073	3 440	4 705	19 815	15 070	13 428	1 273	4 678	7 528	233 074
1983:														
1st quarter	14 391	12 013	10 442	9 356	1 090	3 448	4 818	19 966	15 085	13 515	1 284	4 690	7 594	233 546
2nd quarter	14 824	12 259	10 652	9 645	1 174	3 517	4 954	20 355	15 196	13 759	1 379	4 721	7 698	234 028
3rd quarter	15 188	12 456	10 910	9 875	1 223	3 587	5 066	20 669	15 385	13 926	1 428	4 774	7 754	234 603
4th quarter	15 584	12 786	11 205	10 098	1 290	3 620	5 189	21 004	15 659	14 113	1 497	4 803	7 832	235 153
1984:														
1st quarter	16 091	13 162	11 555	10 282	1 337	3 673	5 272	21 449	15 998	14 236	1 553	4 820	7 874	235 605
2nd quarter	16 434	13 490	11 848	10 486	1 374	3 739	5 373	21 742	16 260	14 391	1 586	4 887	7 923	236 082
3rd quarter	16 658	13 801	12 104	10 608	1 373	3 755	5 481	21 847	16 481	14 445	1 579	4 886	7 990	236 657
4th quarter	16 847	13 949	12 205	10 793	1 416	3 783	5 594	21 935	16 495	14 587	1 626	4 895	8 074	237 232
1985:														
1st quarter	17 171	14 215	12 316	11 040	1 472	3 826	5 742	22 120	16 481	14 773	1 680	4 913	8 185	237 673
2nd quarter	17 360	14 359	12 647	11 224	1 488	3 875	5 861	22 184	16 750	14 866	1 696	4 933	8 241	238 176
3rd quarter	17 679	14 514	12 663	11 484	1 578	3 902	6 004	22 445	16 632	15 085	1 799	4 948	8 331	238 789
4th quarter	17 901	14 767	12 889	11 611	1 517	3 953	6 141	22 531	16 749	15 089	1 724	4 968	8 404	239 387
1986:														
1st quarter	18 170	14 999	13 134	11 771	1 544	3 986	6 241	22 767	16 952	15 192	1 752	5 020	8 422	239 861
2nd quarter	18 245	15 109	13 231	11 880	1 601	3 950	6 330	22 744	17 065	15 322	1 811	5 057	8 447	240 368
3rd quarter	18 440	15 292	13 374	12 144	1 751	3 966	6 427	22 810	17 107	15 533	1 961	5 051	8 495	240 962
4th quarter	18 637	15 399	13 416	12 278	1 729	4 007	6 542	22 881	17 032	15 587	1 927	5 080	8 561	241 539
1987:														
1st quarter	18 866	15 644	13 683	12 406	1 629	4 103	6 674	22 982	17 162	15 560	1 801	5 096	8 665	242 009
2nd quarter	19 153	15 862	13 649	12 659	1 706	4 166	6 786	23 165	16 957	15 726	1 870	5 115	8 735	242 520
3rd quarter	19 425	16 073	13 959	12 892	1 788	4 198	6 906	23 311	17 160	15 848	1 942	5 100	8 794	243 120
4th quarter	19 842	16 471	14 291	13 012	1 740	4 234	7 038	23 595	17 379	15 823	1 881	5 101	8 838	243 721

YEAR AND QUARTER	Total	Nonresidential									Residential			
		Structures				Producers' durable equipment								
							Information processing and related equipment							
		Total[1]	Nonresidential buildings, including farms	Utilities	Mining exploration, shafts, and wells	Total[2]	Computers and peripheral equipment[3]	Other	Industrial equipment	Transportation and related equipment	Structures[1]			Producers' durable equipment
											Total	Single family	Multi-family	

PRIVATE FIXED INVESTMENT BY TYPE (Gross private domestic fixed investment-Billions of dollars, quarterly data are at seasonally adjusted annual rates)

YEAR AND QUARTER	Total	Total[1]	Nonres. bldgs incl. farms	Utilities	Mining	Total[2]	Computers	Other	Industrial	Transportation	Total	Single family	Multi-family	PDE
1960	75.5	19.6	12.0	5.0	2.3	29.7	0.2	4.5	9.3	8.5	25.8	14.9	2.6	0.5
1961	75.0	19.7	12.7	4.6	2.3	28.9	0.3	4.8	8.7	8.0	25.9	14.1	3.3	0.5
1962	81.8	20.8	13.7	4.6	2.5	32.1	*0.3	5.1	9.2	9.8	28.4	15.1	4.8	0.5
1963	87.7	21.2	13.9	5.0	2.3	34.4	0.7	5.3	10.0	9.4	31.5	16.0	6.4	0.6
1964	96.7	23.7	15.8	5.4	2.4	38.7	0.9	5.8	11.4	10.6	33.6	17.6	6.4	0.6
1965	108.3	28.3	19.5	6.1	2.4	45.8	1.2	6.6	13.6	13.2	33.5	17.8	6.0	0.7
1966	116.7	31.3	21.3	7.1	2.5	53.0	1.7	7.9	16.1	14.5	31.6	16.6	5.2	0.7
1967	117.6	31.5	20.6	7.8	2.4	53.7	1.9	8.1	16.8	14.3	31.6	16.8	4.7	0.7
1968	130.8	33.6	21.1	9.2	2.6	58.5	1.9	8.6	17.2	17.6	37.9	19.5	7.2	0.9
1969	145.5	37.7	24.4	9.6	2.8	65.2	2.4	10.4	18.9	18.9	41.6	19.7	9.5	1.0
1970	148.1	40.3	25.4	11.1	2.8	66.4	2.7	11.6	20.2	16.2	40.2	17.5	9.5	1.1
1971	167.5	42.7	27.1	11.9	2.7	69.1	2.8	12.1	19.4	18.4	54.5	25.8	12.9	1.3
1972	195.7	47.2	30.1	13.1	3.1	78.9	3.5	13.1	21.3	21.8	68.1	32.8	17.2	1.5
1973	225.4	55.0	35.5	15.0	3.5	95.1	3.5	16.3	25.9	26.6	73.6	35.2	19.4	1.7
1974	231.5	61.2	38.3	16.5	5.2	104.3	3.9	19.0	30.5	26.3	64.1	29.7	13.7	1.9
1975	231.7	61.4	35.6	17.1	7.4	107.6	3.6	19.9	31.1	25.2	60.8	29.6	6.7	1.9
1976	269.6	65.9	35.9	20.0	8.6	121.2	4.4	22.8	33.9	30.0	80.4	43.9	6.9	2.1
1977	333.5	74.6	39.9	21.5	11.5	148.7	5.7	27.5	39.2	39.3	107.9	62.2	10.0	2.4
1978	403.6	91.4	49.7	24.1	15.4	180.6	7.6	34.2	47.4	47.3	128.9	72.8	12.8	2.7
1979	464.0	114.9	65.7	27.5	19.0	208.1	10.2	39.8	55.8	53.6	137.9	72.3	17.0	3.2
1980	473.5	133.9	73.7	30.2	27.4	216.4	12.5	46.4	60.4	48.4	119.9	53.0	16.7	3.4
1981	528.1	164.6	86.3	33.0	42.5	240.9	17.1	52.3	65.2	50.6	119.0	52.0	17.5	3.6
1982	515.6	175.0	94.5	32.5	44.8	234.9	18.9	53.9	62.2	46.8	102.0	41.5	15.5	3.7
1983	552.0	152.7	90.5	28.7	30.0	246.7	23.9	58.1	58.2	53.7	148.3	72.2	22.4	4.2
1984	648.1	176.0	110.0	30.0	31.3	292.3	31.6	67.0	67.4	64.8	175.1	85.6	28.2	4.7
1985	688.9	193.3	128.0	30.6	27.9	308.7	33.7	70.5	71.7	69.7	181.9	86.1	28.5	5.1
1986	712.9	175.8	123.3	31.2	15.7	319.0	33.4	75.4	74.6	71.8	212.6	102.2	31.0	5.5
1987	722.9	172.1	126.0	26.5	13.1	323.3	35.8	74.0	75.9	70.4	221.8	114.5	25.5	5.8
1960:														
1st quarter	77.8	19.4	11.7	5.0	2.4	30.1	0.1	4.4	9.2	9.0	27.8	16.7	2.8	0.5
2nd quarter	76.3	19.5	11.8	5.1	2.4	30.7	0.2	4.6	9.9	8.6	25.6	14.9	2.6	0.5
3rd quarter	74.2	19.4	12.0	4.9	2.3	29.5	0.2	4.4	9.3	8.7	24.8	14.1	2.5	0.5
4th quarter	73.8	20.0	12.6	5.0	2.3	28.4	0.3	4.7	8.9	7.7	24.8	13.7	2.7	0.5
1961:														
1st quarter	72.7	19.9	12.8	4.7	2.3	27.5	0.2	4.4	8.4	7.4	24.8	13.5	2.8	0.5
2nd quarter	73.8	19.6	12.6	4.6	2.3	28.7	0.3	4.9	8.6	7.7	25.0	13.6	3.1	0.5
3rd quarter	75.5	19.7	12.6	4.7	2.3	28.9	0.3	4.9	8.7	8.0	26.4	14.3	3.5	0.5
4th quarter	78.0	19.6	12.7	4.5	2.4	30.6	0.3	5.0	9.3	9.0	27.3	14.9	3.9	0.5
1962:														
1st quarter	79.8	20.0	12.8	4.6	2.5	31.4	0.3	5.3	9.4	9.3	27.8	15.0	4.3	0.5
2nd quarter	82.2	20.8	13.6	4.6	2.6	32.2	0.3	5.2	9.5	9.6	28.7	15.3	4.7	0.5
3rd quarter	82.9	21.4	14.2	4.6	2.5	32.3	0.4	4.9	9.1	10.1	28.6	15.2	5.1	0.6
4th quarter	82.4	20.9	13.9	4.6	2.3	32.3	0.4	4.9	8.9	10.1	28.6	15.0	5.3	0.6
1963:														
1st quarter	83.3	20.2	13.2	4.7	2.3	32.9	0.6	5.1	9.3	9.5	29.6	15.2	5.8	0.6
2nd quarter	86.9	21.2	13.9	5.0	2.3	33.5	0.7	5.3	9.8	9.0	31.6	15.9	6.4	0.6
3rd quarter	88.8	21.4	14.1	5.0	2.3	34.9	0.8	5.4	10.2	9.3	31.9	16.0	6.6	0.6
4th quarter	91.8	21.9	14.5	5.2	2.2	36.2	0.8	5.4	10.5	9.9	33.1	16.8	6.9	0.6
1964:														
1st quarter	95.0	22.4	14.8	5.3	2.3	37.2	1.0	5.6	10.8	10.2	34.8	18.4	6.8	0.6
2nd quarter	95.6	23.4	15.5	5.4	2.4	38.0	0.9	5.7	10.8	10.6	33.5	17.5	6.5	0.6
3rd quarter	97.2	24.3	16.2	5.4	2.4	39.3	0.9	5.7	11.4	11.3	33.1	17.2	6.3	0.6
4th quarter	99.0	24.8	16.6	5.5	2.5	40.3	0.9	6.2	12.4	10.3	33.2	17.5	6.1	0.6
1965:														
1st quarter	103.5	26.1	17.7	5.8	2.4	43.5	1.0	6.2	12.6	12.9	33.2	17.2	6.2	0.7
2nd quarter	106.6	28.2	19.3	6.0	2.6	44.3	1.1	6.5	13.3	12.8	33.5	17.5	6.1	0.7
3rd quarter	109.6	28.5	19.7	6.1	2.4	46.8	1.2	6.8	14.1	13.3	33.6	18.1	5.9	0.7
4th quarter	113.4	30.4	21.2	6.4	2.3	48.5	1.3	7.0	14.4	13.8	33.8	18.5	5.8	0.7
1966:														
1st quarter	117.0	31.1	21.2	6.7	2.5	51.1	1.4	7.5	15.0	14.7	34.1	18.7	5.9	0.7
2nd quarter	117.4	31.2	21.1	7.1	2.4	53.0	1.6	7.8	16.0	14.7	32.5	17.7	5.6	0.7
3rd quarter	117.3	31.9	21.6	7.3	2.5	53.4	1.8	8.0	16.4	14.2	31.2	15.8	5.1	0.7
4th quarter	114.9	31.2	21.1	7.2	2.4	54.5	2.0	8.2	16.7	14.4	28.5	14.0	4.4	0.7
1967:														
1st quarter	112.7	31.7	21.4	7.3	2.4	52.7	1.9	8.0	17.1	13.3	27.7	14.3	4.1	0.7
2nd quarter	116.2	30.9	20.2	7.7	2.5	53.6	1.9	8.1	17.0	14.0	31.0	15.8	4.2	0.7
3rd quarter	118.1	31.5	20.4	7.9	2.4	53.2	1.8	8.0	16.3	14.7	32.7	17.9	4.9	0.7
4th quarter	123.3	32.0	20.5	8.4	2.4	55.3	1.9	8.5	16.9	15.1	35.2	19.2	5.7	0.8
1968:														
1st quarter	127.5	33.1	20.9	8.8	2.5	57.6	1.9	8.7	17.2	17.2	36.1	19.0	6.3	0.8
2nd quarter	128.0	33.2	21.0	9.0	2.5	56.7	1.9	8.5	17.0	16.6	37.3	19.6	6.9	0.8
3rd quarter	130.7	33.2	20.6	9.4	2.6	58.6	2.0	8.7	17.0	17.7	38.0	19.3	7.5	0.9
4th quarter	137.0	34.8	21.8	9.5	2.7	61.3	1.9	8.7	17.6	19.0	40.0	20.2	8.0	0.9
1969:														
1st quarter	142.7	35.8	23.1	9.5	2.6	63.7	2.1	9.4	18.2	19.4	42.3	21.0	9.0	0.9
2nd quarter	144.8	36.7	23.6	9.4	2.8	64.7	2.4	10.1	18.7	19.1	42.4	20.2	9.7	1.0
3rd quarter	148.3	38.9	25.2	9.6	2.9	66.1	2.6	10.8	19.4	19.0	42.2	19.2	9.7	1.0
4th quarter	146.2	39.4	25.4	10.1	2.9	66.2	2.7	11.3	19.4	18.1	39.6	18.3	9.7	1.1
1970:														
1st quarter	146.5	39.5	25.5	10.2	2.8	66.4	3.1	11.4	20.1	16.8	39.6	17.0	9.4	1.1
2nd quarter	146.5	40.3	25.7	10.9	2.8	66.8	3.0	11.7	20.2	16.5	38.3	16.5	9.2	1.1
3rd quarter	148.6	40.6	25.2	11.6	2.7	67.6	2.4	11.6	20.4	17.1	39.3	17.4	9.4	1.1
4th quarter	150.6	40.8	25.1	11.6	2.8	64.9	2.4	11.8	20.0	14.6	43.8	19.3	10.1	1.2

1. Includes the category other structures, not shown separately.
2. Includes the category other producers' durable equipment, not shown separately.
3. Includes new computers and peripheral equipment only.

PRIVATE FIXED INVESTMENT BY TYPE-Continued
(Gross private domestic fixed investment-Billions of dollars, quarterly data are at seasonally adjusted annual rates)

YEAR AND QUARTER	Total	Nonresidential — Structures				Nonresidential — Producers' durable equipment					Residential — Structures [1]			Residential — Producers' durable equipment
		Total [1]	Nonresidential buildings, including farm	Utilities	Mining exploration, shafts, and wells	Total [2]	Computers and peripheral equipment [3]	Other	Industrial equipment	Transportation and related equipment	Total	Single family	Multi-family	
1971:														
1st quarter	156.8	41.5	25.8	11.8	2.7	66.7	2.3	11.6	19.2	17.7	47.4	22.0	11.0	1.2
2nd quarter	165.7	42.3	26.7	12.1	2.5	68.8	2.8	12.2	19.1	18.3	53.3	25.3	12.2	1.3
3rd quarter	170.7	43.1	27.5	12.0	2.7	69.3	2.9	12.2	19.3	18.2	57.1	27.1	13.7	1.3
4th quarter	176.8	43.8	28.2	11.9	2.8	71.5	3.1	12.5	19.9	19.5	60.2	28.7	14.6	1.4
1972:														
1st quarter	187.2	45.8	29.0	12.8	2.9	74.9	3.7	12.6	19.9	21.0	65.1	31.4	16.2	1.5
2nd quarter	191.7	46.6	29.5	13.0	3.0	76.9	3.4	12.7	20.9	21.2	66.7	32.2	17.1	1.5
3rd quarter	195.8	47.3	30.3	13.1	3.1	78.9	3.5	13.0	21.8	21.0	68.0	33.0	17.2	1.6
4th quarter	208.1	49.0	31.4	13.5	3.2	84.9	3.2	13.9	22.6	24.2	72.7	34.9	18.5	1.6
1973:														
1st quarter	219.0	51.3	33.3	13.9	3.2	89.9	3.4	15.1	23.6	25.2	76.1	36.9	19.3	1.7
2nd quarter	224.7	54.1	35.2	14.6	3.3	94.9	3.7	15.9	25.3	26.9	74.0	36.9	19.6	1.7
3rd quarter	228.7	56.8	36.6	15.5	3.6	96.8	3.4	16.6	26.5	27.1	73.3	35.1	20.1	1.7
4th quarter	229.1	57.7	36.9	15.9	3.8	98.6	3.7	17.5	28.1	27.0	71.0	31.8	18.7	1.8
1974:														
1st quarter	228.0	59.0	37.6	16.2	4.1	100.0	3.5	18.0	29.1	26.8	67.1	29.7	16.8	1.9
2nd quarter	231.2	61.3	38.7	16.3	5.1	102.3	3.2	18.6	30.3	26.8	65.6	30.5	14.8	1.9
3rd quarter	235.9	61.4	37.8	16.8	5.5	107.1	4.4	19.3	31.1	27.4	65.4	30.3	13.0	1.9
4th quarter	231.0	63.2	39.1	16.8	5.9	107.8	4.4	20.3	31.5	24.2	58.2	28.3	10.3	1.8
1975:														
1st quarter	223.9	61.7	37.2	16.6	6.6	104.6	4.1	20.0	30.3	24.0	55.8	26.4	8.5	1.8
2nd quarter	225.9	60.4	35.1	16.9	7.1	105.6	3.5	19.8	30.7	23.9	58.0	27.3	6.4	1.9
3rd quarter	234.4	61.3	35.0	17.1	7.6	108.4	3.3	19.8	31.5	25.8	62.7	30.8	5.8	1.9
4th quarter	242.6	62.0	34.9	17.7	8.1	111.8	3.5	19.8	31.9	27.0	66.7	34.0	6.0	2.0
1976:														
1st quarter	255.2	64.1	36.5	17.8	8.4	115.0	3.7	20.6	33.1	28.3	74.1	38.2	6.0	2.0
2nd quarter	264.0	65.1	35.7	19.8	8.2	118.3	4.4	21.9	33.6	29.0	78.6	42.8	6.3	2.1
3rd quarter	270.4	66.7	35.6	21.2	8.7	123.1	4.5	23.5	34.0	30.2	78.5	45.6	7.1	2.2
4th quarter	288.9	67.8	35.9	21.3	9.2	128.6	5.0	25.2	35.0	32.4	90.3	48.8	8.3	2.2
1977:														
1st quarter	306.4	69.7	37.3	20.7	10.2	139.1	5.2	25.9	36.5	36.9	95.5	53.7	8.9	2.1
2nd quarter	330.2	73.6	39.2	21.8	11.2	144.8	5.6	27.0	37.6	38.4	109.4	62.8	10.1	2.3
3rd quarter	341.8	76.4	40.9	21.6	12.0	150.4	5.8	27.7	40.1	39.3	112.5	65.0	10.6	2.5
4th quarter	355.7	78.5	42.1	21.7	12.5	160.3	6.1	29.2	42.5	42.6	114.3	67.3	10.5	2.7
1978:														
1st quarter	364.8	79.2	43.3	22.2	11.8	164.5	6.3	31.0	44.0	43.1	118.5	68.3	10.8	2.6
2nd quarter	398.8	88.6	47.9	23.7	14.7	179.6	7.3	33.7	46.4	48.4	127.8	71.5	12.6	2.7
3rd quarter	417.1	95.8	52.4	24.7	16.4	185.6	8.0	35.4	49.0	48.3	133.0	75.1	13.8	2.8
4th quarter	433.9	102.0	55.2	25.9	18.8	192.8	8.7	36.7	50.2	49.6	136.2	76.3	14.1	2.9
1979:														
1st quarter	446.8	104.8	57.5	26.2	18.9	203.4	9.3	38.3	53.7	54.1	135.6	73.8	14.6	2.9
2nd quarter	455.1	110.0	63.6	27.2	16.7	204.3	9.8	38.5	54.6	52.5	137.7	72.8	16.5	3.1
3rd quarter	474.9	119.0	68.7	28.3	19.3	212.2	10.4	40.2	55.9	55.4	140.2	73.3	17.9	3.3
4th quarter	479.2	125.7	73.2	28.4	21.2	212.3	11.1	42.1	59.1	52.6	137.9	69.3	19.0	3.3
1980:														
1st quarter	484.6	130.3	75.3	29.7	22.4	219.7	10.9	45.1	60.0	51.7	131.2	60.7	18.9	3.4
2nd quarter	450.1	129.8	73.5	30.1	23.4	209.1	11.9	45.4	59.4	45.6	107.9	46.5	16.2	3.3
3rd quarter	464.6	133.6	71.6	30.2	29.3	215.1	13.5	47.3	59.7	48.1	112.5	47.2	15.2	3.4
4th quarter	494.8	141.9	74.3	30.9	34.4	221.6	13.8	47.9	62.5	48.1	127.9	57.5	16.6	3.5
1981:														
1st quarter	511.6	147.5	81.2	32.4	31.5	232.1	15.4	50.2	63.8	50.5	128.4	59.6	18.7	3.6
2nd quarter	525.3	158.3	84.4	32.7	38.5	238.1	15.9	52.2	64.6	50.0	125.3	56.6	18.5	3.6
3rd quarter	533.6	166.8	89.1	33.4	41.2	246.6	17.2	53.4	66.0	52.0	116.5	49.7	17.0	3.7
4th quarter	541.8	185.7	90.3	33.6	58.6	246.5	20.0	53.5	66.4	49.8	105.9	42.3	15.7	3.7
1982:														
1st quarter	531.5	183.8	92.6	34.0	54.1	242.9	20.8	54.6	64.2	49.5	101.2	39.0	15.6	3.6
2nd quarter	517.8	179.6	95.1	33.2	48.1	235.4	18.1	53.8	63.6	46.8	99.1	38.9	14.9	3.7
3rd quarter	505.0	170.4	94.9	32.1	40.1	232.2	18.3	54.2	61.9	43.9	98.6	39.6	15.5	3.7
4th quarter	507.9	166.2	95.3	30.8	36.7	228.9	18.2	52.9	59.0	47.1	109.0	48.3	16.2	3.8
1983:														
1st quarter	514.6	156.7	90.2	28.8	34.2	227.0	21.3	54.5	56.2	47.2	126.9	59.1	18.8	4.0
2nd quarter	534.0	147.8	86.7	29.2	28.2	238.0	23.3	56.7	56.7	49.6	144.1	70.3	21.2	4.1
3rd quarter	563.4	151.0	92.2	26.9	28.4	249.9	25.2	57.3	59.1	55.1	158.2	78.7	23.7	4.3
4th quarter	596.0	155.5	92.9	30.1	29.2	272.0	25.8	64.0	60.9	63.1	164.1	80.7	26.1	4.5
1984:														
1st quarter	616.0	164.5	101.5	29.0	30.5	275.9	27.7	63.1	64.6	60.8	171.0	85.1	26.8	4.6
2nd quarter	645.4	174.4	109.5	30.1	30.6	289.6	30.1	67.0	66.8	64.8	176.7	87.9	27.2	4.7
3rd quarter	659.3	181.0	112.6	30.9	32.3	297.5	32.9	67.5	68.2	66.5	176.1	85.5	29.4	4.7
4th quarter	671.6	184.2	116.4	30.1	31.7	306.1	35.7	70.2	70.2	67.2	176.5	83.9	29.4	4.8
1985:														
1st quarter	680.0	193.5	123.7	30.9	32.3	303.1	33.3	70.1	69.5	67.1	178.5	86.1	29.1	4.9
2nd quarter	686.9	194.1	128.2	30.7	28.1	310.0	35.0	70.2	71.9	69.6	177.8	83.8	28.5	5.0
3rd quarter	685.8	191.0	128.5	30.2	25.9	307.2	32.4	70.1	71.3	71.4	182.6	85.7	28.4	5.1
4th quarter	702.8	194.6	131.5	30.4	25.4	314.3	34.2	71.4	74.3	70.7	188.6	88.9	28.2	5.3
1986:														
1st quarter	707.0	190.9	128.3	31.7	23.4	311.5	33.7	72.1	74.0	68.1	199.2	94.0	29.9	5.4
2nd quarter	710.9	173.9	121.9	32.1	14.6	318.7	34.3	74.0	73.8	72.0	212.9	100.1	32.2	5.4
3rd quarter	712.6	168.3	120.1	31.2	12.2	320.3	32.3	76.1	75.4	74.0	218.5	106.7	31.2	5.6
4th quarter	721.1	170.1	122.8	29.7	12.6	325.5	33.3	79.5	75.3	73.0	219.9	107.8	30.9	5.6
1987:														
1st quarter	705.3	165.4	120.5	27.6	11.8	314.6	35.0	72.9	75.1	67.5	219.7	110.9	27.7	5.6
2nd quarter	719.3	167.3	123.1	26.3	11.1	322.8	35.1	73.2	74.9	73.8	223.5	114.0	25.5	5.7
3rd quarter	732.0	175.3	128.7	26.0	13.8	329.3	36.3	75.2	76.2	72.3	221.5	115.6	24.1	5.9
4th quarter	735.1	180.3	131.8	26.0	15.5	326.5	36.7	74.7	77.2	68.2	222.4	117.3	24.6	6.0

1. Includes the category other structures, not shown separately.
2. Includes the category other producers' durable equipment, not shown separately.
3. Includes new computers and peripheral equipment only.

REAL PRIVATE FIXED INVESTMENT BY TYPE
(Gross private domestic fixed investment-Billions of chained (1992) dollars, quarterly data are at seasonally adjusted annual rates)

YEAR AND QUARTER	Total	Nonresidential									Residential			
		Structures				Producers' durable equipment					Structures			Producers' durable equipment
		Total[1]	Nonresidential buildings, including farms	Utilities	Mining exploration, shafts, and wells	Total[2]	Computers and peripheral equipment[3]	Other	Industrial equipment	Transportation and related equipment	Total[1]	Single family	Multi-family	
1960	269.2	92.6	59.9	20.4	10.3	74.3	0.0	11.1	41.9	28.8	122.0	68.4	13.0	1.0
1961	267.9	93.9	63.3	18.9	10.5	72.6	0.0	11.8	39.7	27.0	122.4	64.8	16.4	1.0
1962	292.0	98.1	67.4	19.0	11.1	81.0	0.0	12.5	41.8	33.4	134.2	69.1	23.9	1.0
1963	313.7	99.2	67.5	20.4	10.4	87.1	0.0	13.0	45.1	32.1	150.0	73.8	32.1	1.2
1964	343.7	109.5	75.0	22.2	11.1	98.1	0.0	14.1	51.0	36.3	158.7	81.0	31.9	1.2
1965	378.5	126.9	89.4	24.4	11.0	115.9	0.0	16.0	60.2	45.5	153.6	79.1	28.6	1.4
1966	399.1	135.6	94.2	27.8	10.4	133.8	0.0	18.9	69.2	50.1	139.5	70.5	24.0	1.4
1967	391.0	132.2	88.7	29.8	9.9	132.5	0.0	18.9	69.5	48.4	135.0	69.1	20.9	1.4
1968	418.1	134.1	86.2	33.3	10.0	140.5	0.0	19.5	68.1	58.2	153.2	75.9	30.1	1.7
1969	442.9	141.3	92.7	33.4	10.4	152.2	0.1	22.8	72.6	60.5	157.4	72.1	37.5	2.0
1970	432.1	141.7	91.1	35.7	9.8	149.5	0.1	24.5	73.7	49.7	147.4	62.6	36.7	2.1
1971	464.9	139.4	89.4	36.1	9.1	150.7	0.1	24.7	67.7	53.6	188.4	86.9	46.7	2.4
1972	520.3	143.7	91.8	37.6	9.7	169.8	0.2	26.0	73.0	62.3	221.8	103.3	58.5	2.9
1973	567.5	155.4	100.3	40.0	10.4	201.2	0.2	31.7	86.2	75.0	219.8	101.1	60.1	3.2
1974	530.2	152.2	97.6	37.6	12.4	205.4	0.2	34.8	92.8	67.9	173.2	77.6	38.7	3.3
1975	471.0	136.2	82.5	34.4	14.4	183.9	0.2	33.3	78.6	58.5	150.4	70.8	17.3	3.1
1976	517.6	139.6	80.6	38.0	15.6	195.2	0.3	36.6	79.0	65.0	186.7	98.6	16.7	3.2
1977	593.7	146.4	83.6	38.2	18.1	225.6	0.5	43.8	83.6	79.1	226.8	126.2	21.9	3.5
1978	660.8	162.3	95.3	40.0	20.0	259.6	1.0	52.4	93.0	87.3	241.7	130.9	25.0	3.8
1979	695.6	182.7	113.5	41.3	21.3	280.7	1.5	59.5	99.8	91.0	232.2	116.0	30.5	4.2
1980	648.4	195.0	114.4	41.3	30.0	268.2	2.4	64.9	95.5	74.2	182.0	76.3	27.3	4.2
1981	660.6	210.4	122.8	42.0	34.9	278.2	3.8	68.5	94.1	72.0	167.0	69.5	26.3	4.2
1982	610.4	207.2	126.6	39.5	32.2	260.3	4.7	67.0	85.5	63.7	135.9	53.2	21.4	4.0
1983	654.2	185.8	117.6	34.2	26.7	272.4	7.1	70.4	78.5	71.7	193.2	92.0	29.3	4.5
1984	762.4	212.2	137.6	35.4	30.3	324.6	11.6	79.0	89.9	85.1	221.6	106.2	35.8	5.0
1985	799.3	227.8	155.2	35.6	27.0	342.4	14.5	81.9	94.1	88.4	224.2	104.8	34.9	5.4
1986	805.0	203.3	144.5	36.5	15.8	345.9	16.7	84.6	93.5	85.6	251.3	119.3	35.9	5.8
1987	799.5	195.9	142.4	30.7	15.5	346.9	21.0	80.2	91.1	82.1	251.6	128.3	28.3	6.1
1960:														
1st quarter	277.8	90.8	57.7	20.5	10.5	75.6	0.0	10.8	41.3	29.8	132.2	77.1	13.8	1.0
2nd quarter	271.7	91.9	58.7	20.8	10.3	76.8	0.0	11.4	44.4	29.3	121.2	68.5	12.6	1.0
3rd quarter	264.2	92.1	59.8	20.0	10.3	73.7	0.0	10.9	41.7	29.8	117.4	64.9	12.6	1.0
4th quarter	263.0	95.6	63.3	20.4	10.2	71.2	0.0	11.5	40.3	26.4	117.3	63.0	13.1	1.0
1961:														
1st quarter	259.9	95.2	64.5	19.1	10.1	68.7	0.0	10.9	37.8	24.9	117.8	62.4	14.1	0.9
2nd quarter	263.2	93.6	63.1	18.9	10.3	71.7	0.0	12.0	39.3	25.7	118.2	62.3	15.4	1.0
3rd quarter	269.6	93.6	62.8	19.2	10.7	72.7	0.0	12.0	39.4	26.9	124.6	65.8	17.2	1.0
4th quarter	278.7	93.1	63.0	18.5	11.0	77.1	0.0	12.3	42.4	30.5	128.9	68.6	19.0	1.0
1962:														
1st quarter	284.5	94.8	63.7	19.1	11.3	79.0	0.0	13.1	42.7	31.5	131.3	68.4	21.1	1.0
2nd quarter	293.6	98.3	67.3	19.1	11.3	81.4	0.0	12.7	43.1	33.1	135.4	69.9	23.4	1.0
3rd quarter	296.0	100.9	70.4	19.0	11.0	81.7	0.0	12.2	41.4	34.6	135.1	69.6	25.1	1.1
4th quarter	294.1	98.4	68.2	19.0	10.6	81.8	0.0	12.1	40.1	34.3	134.9	68.5	26.0	1.1
1963:														
1st quarter	297.2	95.0	64.5	19.3	10.4	83.2	0.0	12.5	42.2	32.1	139.8	69.4	28.6	1.1
2nd quarter	310.5	99.4	67.6	20.6	10.5	84.7	0.0	12.9	44.2	30.6	150.0	73.0	31.8	1.1
3rd quarter	318.4	100.1	68.2	20.4	10.5	88.4	0.0	13.3	46.4	31.8	152.8	75.0	33.4	1.2
4th quarter	328.5	102.1	69.6	21.4	10.1	92.0	0.0	13.2	47.6	34.1	157.5	77.8	34.5	1.2
1964:														
1st quarter	341.4	104.8	71.7	21.7	10.5	94.4	0.0	13.7	48.7	34.9	167.2	86.5	34.5	1.2
2nd quarter	340.2	108.4	73.8	22.1	11.2	96.2	0.0	14.0	48.7	36.3	158.6	80.2	32.2	1.2
3rd quarter	345.5	112.0	77.1	22.3	11.2	99.5	0.0	13.9	51.3	38.8	155.9	79.0	31.2	1.3
4th quarter	347.7	112.8	77.5	22.5	11.6	102.2	0.0	14.9	55.4	35.3	153.0	78.1	29.5	1.2
1965:														
1st quarter	364.0	118.6	82.6	23.4	11.0	110.4	0.0	15.0	56.2	44.3	153.4	77.2	29.6	1.3
2nd quarter	373.8	126.9	88.9	24.1	11.8	112.1	0.0	15.7	58.8	44.1	154.6	78.4	29.3	1.3
3rd quarter	383.8	128.2	90.8	24.6	10.7	118.2	0.0	16.5	62.2	45.9	155.1	81.3	28.6	1.4
4th quarter	392.2	134.1	95.4	25.5	10.4	122.9	0.0	17.0	63.5	47.8	151.5	79.6	27.1	1.5
1966:														
1st quarter	406.8	137.3	96.4	26.6	10.7	129.7	0.0	18.1	65.8	51.0	155.0	82.3	28.1	1.4
2nd quarter	401.2	134.6	93.3	27.9	10.2	134.3	0.0	18.8	69.6	50.9	142.4	74.5	25.3	1.4
3rd quarter	400.5	137.6	95.6	28.6	10.7	134.7	0.0	19.2	70.4	49.1	137.7	67.3	23.1	1.4
4th quarter	387.7	133.0	91.7	28.2	10.0	136.5	0.0	19.4	70.8	49.2	123.1	57.9	19.6	1.4
1967:														
1st quarter	378.3	134.3	92.7	28.5	9.9	130.9	0.0	18.7	71.7	45.7	119.3	59.3	18.3	1.4
2nd quarter	388.4	130.5	87.2	29.5	10.2	132.7	0.0	18.8	70.5	47.7	133.1	65.5	18.8	1.4
3rd quarter	392.6	131.9	88.0	30.0	9.9	131.0	0.0	18.5	67.1	49.7	139.8	73.8	21.6	1.4
4th quarter	404.9	132.1	86.8	31.4	9.8	135.2	0.0	19.6	68.6	50.6	147.8	77.6	24.7	1.6
1968:														
1st quarter	414.3	134.7	87.2	32.5	10.1	140.1	0.0	19.9	69.6	57.5	148.6	75.2	27.1	1.6
2nd quarter	412.0	133.5	86.6	32.8	9.7	136.8	0.0	19.3	67.7	55.1	152.4	76.7	29.3	1.7
3rd quarter	417.9	132.6	84.4	33.8	10.0	140.2	0.1	19.6	66.8	58.4	155.0	75.8	31.7	1.8
4th quarter	428.1	135.4	86.7	34.1	10.2	145.0	0.1	19.4	68.4	61.8	156.9	75.9	32.4	1.8
1969:														
1st quarter	441.2	137.4	90.1	33.5	9.9	150.2	0.1	20.8	70.6	63.1	162.6	77.8	35.9	1.9
2nd quarter	442.8	138.5	90.7	32.7	10.4	151.8	0.1	22.2	72.0	61.9	160.5	74.1	38.4	2.0
3rd quarter	449.9	145.1	95.5	33.2	10.8	153.9	0.1	23.6	74.2	60.3	159.2	70.4	38.0	2.0
4th quarter	437.9	144.1	94.4	34.0	10.6	152.7	0.1	24.4	73.5	56.8	147.1	66.0	37.6	2.0
1970:														
1st quarter	435.5	143.0	94.2	34.0	10.1	151.4	0.1	24.4	75.0	52.1	147.4	61.6	36.8	2.1
2nd quarter	425.6	141.5	91.4	35.4	9.9	150.9	0.1	24.8	74.1	51.0	137.3	57.1	34.3	2.1
3rd quarter	433.2	142.1	90.4	37.1	9.3	151.8	0.1	24.3	73.9	52.1	144.7	62.9	36.7	2.1
4th quarter	434.1	140.4	88.2	36.3	9.9	143.9	0.1	24.6	71.6	43.6	160.2	69.0	39.0	2.2

1. Includes the category other structures, not shown separately.
2. Includes the category other producers' durable equipment, not shown separately.
3. Includes new computers and peripheral equipment only.

REAL PRIVATE FIXED INVESTMENT BY TYPE—Continued
(Gross private domestic fixed investment—Billions of chained (1992) dollars, quarterly data are at seasonally adjusted annual rates)

YEAR AND QUARTER	Total	Nonresidential — Structures Total[1]	Nonresidential buildings, including farms	Utilities	Mining exploration, shafts, and wells	Producers' durable equipment Total[2]	Computers and peripheral equipment[3]	Other	Industrial equipment	Transportation and related equipment	Residential — Structures Total[1]	Single family	Multi-family	Residential Producers' durable equipment
1971:														
1st quarter	444.0	140.0	88.3	36.5	9.6	146.3	0.1	24.0	68.2	51.6	168.9	76.8	41.5	2.3
2nd quarter	462.3	139.7	89.2	36.9	8.6	149.9	0.1	24.9	67.0	52.9	186.2	86.3	44.7	2.4
3rd quarter	470.5	139.2	89.8	35.8	9.0	150.7	0.1	24.7	67.0	52.9	195.5	90.6	49.1	2.4
4th quarter	482.7	138.8	90.3	35.1	9.1	155.7	0.1	25.2	68.5	57.2	203.0	94.1	51.5	2.5
1972:														
1st quarter	504.7	142.4	90.7	37.3	9.6	161.8	0.2	25.1	68.4	60.3	216.5	101.1	56.0	2.7
2nd quarter	513.6	143.2	91.4	37.3	9.7	165.5	0.2	25.4	71.6	60.7	220.8	103.0	59.0	2.8
3rd quarter	519.2	143.5	92.3	37.4	9.6	169.6	0.2	25.8	74.6	59.5	221.0	103.5	58.3	2.9
4th quarter	543.6	145.7	93.0	38.4	10.1	182.5	0.2	27.5	77.2	68.9	228.9	105.7	60.5	3.0
1973:														
1st quarter	566.8	150.5	97.4	38.9	9.9	192.7	0.2	29.6	80.1	72.6	236.5	110.3	62.2	3.2
2nd quarter	571.2	155.2	100.7	39.8	10.1	201.4	0.2	31.0	84.9	76.5	224.1	107.7	61.7	3.2
3rd quarter	569.1	158.7	102.1	40.9	10.7	203.8	0.2	32.3	87.8	75.9	214.4	98.7	61.0	3.2
4th quarter	562.7	157.3	101.0	40.3	11.0	207.0	0.2	33.9	92.1	74.9	204.0	87.7	55.4	3.3
1974:														
1st quarter	549.4	156.4	101.2	39.3	11.3	207.4	0.2	34.5	93.9	72.3	188.4	80.2	48.8	3.4
2nd quarter	541.0	155.8	100.7	38.0	12.7	206.9	0.2	34.4	95.0	70.3	179.8	80.8	42.1	3.4
3rd quarter	530.9	149.2	94.4	37.4	12.7	207.9	0.3	34.7	93.3	69.6	173.9	78.1	36.0	3.3
4th quarter	499.6	147.3	94.0	35.8	12.8	199.4	0.3	35.5	89.1	59.2	150.9	71.2	27.9	3.0
1975:														
1st quarter	467.8	139.8	87.2	34.4	13.6	185.0	0.2	34.2	80.9	57.4	141.3	64.8	22.5	3.0
2nd quarter	461.1	134.4	81.5	34.2	14.0	181.2	0.2	33.2	78.3	55.6	144.4	65.6	16.6	3.0
3rd quarter	473.0	135.3	81.0	34.2	14.9	183.3	0.2	33.1	77.9	59.7	154.6	73.4	14.8	3.1
4th quarter	482.2	135.4	80.4	34.8	15.2	186.2	0.2	32.7	77.4	61.1	161.5	79.5	15.2	3.1
1976:														
1st quarter	502.4	139.1	83.7	34.5	15.8	188.6	0.3	33.6	79.0	62.7	178.5	89.5	15.2	3.1
2nd quarter	510.6	138.6	80.4	37.8	15.0	192.2	0.3	35.2	79.0	63.7	183.7	96.7	15.3	3.2
3rd quarter	515.5	140.1	79.2	39.9	15.5	197.4	0.3	37.5	78.7	65.1	180.6	101.4	16.9	3.2
4th quarter	541.9	140.5	79.0	39.7	16.0	202.7	0.4	40.2	79.2	68.3	204.1	106.9	19.6	3.3
1977:														
1st quarter	564.2	141.8	80.7	37.8	17.2	216.3	0.4	41.1	81.0	77.0	210.3	114.5	20.5	3.1
2nd quarter	595.2	146.3	83.2	39.0	18.0	222.1	0.5	43.0	81.2	79.0	233.8	130.0	22.6	3.4
3rd quarter	602.3	148.3	84.9	38.1	18.4	226.8	0.5	44.2	84.4	78.6	233.2	129.4	22.7	3.7
4th quarter	613.1	149.2	85.6	37.7	18.6	237.5	0.6	46.8	87.8	81.8	230.1	130.7	21.8	3.9
1978:														
1st quarter	616.6	147.1	86.0	38.0	16.8	241.0	0.7	48.3	88.9	81.3	231.8	128.5	21.9	3.7
2nd quarter	660.2	159.8	93.0	39.8	19.7	260.3	0.9	51.9	92.2	90.0	242.9	130.1	24.7	3.9
3rd quarter	676.8	168.3	99.7	40.6	20.9	265.2	1.0	53.9	95.3	88.3	246.4	133.3	26.7	3.8
4th quarter	689.5	174.3	102.3	41.6	22.9	272.1	1.2	55.6	95.5	89.5	245.6	131.7	26.6	3.9
1979:														
1st quarter	695.1	174.3	104.3	41.0	22.0	281.6	1.3	57.8	99.8	94.8	239.7	124.9	27.3	4.0
2nd quarter	690.4	177.6	111.5	41.4	19.0	278.1	1.4	57.9	98.9	89.7	235.1	118.3	30.1	4.2
3rd quarter	702.6	186.5	116.8	41.8	21.2	284.1	1.6	60.2	98.7	93.2	231.7	114.9	31.7	4.3
4th quarter	694.1	192.5	121.3	40.9	23.2	279.0	1.8	62.2	101.8	86.1	222.4	106.1	32.9	4.3
1980:														
1st quarter	685.5	195.8	121.4	41.8	25.1	281.5	1.9	65.4	99.5	82.1	206.2	90.5	31.8	4.3
2nd quarter	622.5	191.1	115.6	41.4	26.1	261.5	2.2	64.1	95.3	70.7	165.7	68.1	26.9	4.1
3rd quarter	629.3	193.5	109.9	40.9	32.4	262.9	2.7	65.2	92.7	72.5	168.9	67.3	24.5	4.2
4th quarter	656.3	199.8	110.9	40.9	36.4	267.1	2.9	64.8	94.6	71.4	187.1	79.5	26.0	4.2
1981:														
1st quarter	660.7	198.6	118.7	41.8	29.6	274.9	3.3	67.1	94.7	74.2	183.8	80.8	28.8	4.3
2nd quarter	662.6	205.9	121.2	41.9	33.2	276.4	3.4	68.7	93.8	71.4	176.7	75.8	28.0	4.2
3rd quarter	661.6	210.8	125.9	42.1	33.2	282.7	3.8	69.6	94.3	73.3	162.3	65.9	25.3	4.2
4th quarter	657.6	226.4	125.4	41.9	43.4	278.7	4.6	68.7	93.5	69.1	145.4	55.5	22.9	4.2
1982:														
1st quarter	636.0	219.2	126.4	41.8	38.6	272.3	5.1	68.7	89.6	68.0	136.9	50.6	22.2	4.0
2nd quarter	612.8	211.9	128.0	40.5	34.0	261.2	4.5	67.0	87.4	63.9	132.3	50.0	20.7	4.0
3rd quarter	595.0	200.9	126.2	38.8	28.9	256.3	4.5	67.2	84.6	59.3	130.6	50.6	21.0	4.0
4th quarter	597.8	197.0	125.8	37.0	27.5	251.5	4.5	65.3	80.4	63.5	143.7	61.7	21.7	4.1
1983:														
1st quarter	608.4	189.0	118.3	34.3	28.3	249.5	5.7	66.6	76.1	63.4	166.5	75.5	24.8	4.3
2nd quarter	633.4	179.9	113.1	34.8	24.9	262.5	6.7	69.1	76.3	66.3	188.6	89.8	27.8	4.4
3rd quarter	668.9	184.2	119.5	32.0	25.8	276.5	7.7	69.3	79.6	73.4	206.0	100.4	30.9	4.6
4th quarter	706.1	189.9	119.4	35.8	27.7	301.1	8.2	76.8	81.9	83.7	211.7	102.2	33.7	4.7
1984:														
1st quarter	729.4	200.8	128.9	34.5	29.8	306.2	9.4	75.3	86.7	80.1	219.3	106.7	34.5	4.8
2nd quarter	760.7	210.8	137.9	35.5	29.5	321.5	10.8	79.2	89.0	85.2	224.7	109.6	34.8	5.0
3rd quarter	773.9	217.4	140.1	36.4	31.3	330.5	12.3	79.4	90.7	87.2	221.7	105.5	37.1	5.0
4th quarter	785.7	219.9	143.6	35.3	30.7	340.3	13.8	82.2	93.3	87.7	220.5	103.1	36.9	5.1
1985:														
1st quarter	792.9	229.4	151.5	36.1	31.1	337.3	13.5	81.9	92.3	86.7	221.8	105.5	36.0	5.2
2nd quarter	800.1	229.5	156.2	35.8	27.3	345.0	14.8	81.8	94.9	89.0	220.5	102.5	35.0	5.3
3rd quarter	794.9	224.6	155.3	35.2	25.1	340.6	14.2	81.5	93.1	90.2	224.9	104.2	34.6	5.4
4th quarter	809.1	227.6	157.6	35.4	24.7	346.9	15.7	82.4	96.1	87.9	229.5	107.0	33.9	5.6
1986:														
1st quarter	809.3	222.3	152.6	37.1	22.9	343.0	16.6	82.3	94.0	83.7	239.4	112.1	35.4	5.7
2nd quarter	806.6	201.5	143.5	37.6	14.5	347.2	17.4	83.6	92.8	86.2	253.5	117.8	37.5	5.8
3rd quarter	800.4	194.2	140.1	36.5	12.5	344.9	16.1	84.5	93.9	87.4	256.8	124.0	35.8	5.9
4th quarter	803.9	195.2	141.7	34.7	13.4	348.5	16.7	88.1	93.3	84.9	255.4	123.5	35.1	5.9
1987:														
1st quarter	784.2	190.0	137.9	32.2	13.8	336.7	19.2	79.4	91.5	78.6	252.9	125.8	31.3	5.9
2nd quarter	797.7	191.3	139.7	30.6	13.4	346.5	20.5	79.4	90.3	86.1	254.9	128.3	28.5	6.0
3rd quarter	809.5	199.4	145.0	30.1	16.7	354.7	22.1	81.6	91.6	84.1	250.1	129.3	26.7	6.2
4th quarter	806.3	202.8	147.2	29.7	18.1	349.6	22.2	80.3	91.2	79.8	248.6	130.0	26.9	6.2

1. Includes the category other structures, not shown separately.
2. Includes the category other producers' durable equipment, not shown separately.
3. Includes new computers and peripheral equipment only.

FEDERAL GOVERNMENT RECEIPTS AND CURRENT EXPENDITURES
(Calendar years-Billions of dollars, quarterly data are at seasonally adjusted annual rates)

YEAR AND QUARTER	Receipts					Current expenditures						Surplus or deficit (—), national income and product accounts		
	Total	Personal tax and nontax receipts	Corporate profits tax accruals	Indirect business tax and nontax accruals	Contributions for social insurance	Total	Consumption expenditures	Transfer payments (Net)	Grants-in-aid to state and local governments	Net interest paid	Subsidies less surplus of government enterprises	Total	Social insurance funds	Other
1960	97.0	43.5	21.4	13.5	18.5	89.6	51.3	23.4	6.5	6.8	1.6	7.4	1.6	5.8
1961	99.0	44.6	21.5	13.7	19.2	96.1	52.9	27.1	7.2	6.3	2.6	2.9	-1.1	4.0
1962	107.2	48.5	22.5	14.7	21.5	104.4	59.1	27.7	8.0	6.8	2.9	2.8	0.7	2.1
1963	115.5	51.3	24.6	15.4	24.3	110.2	62.0	29.1	9.1	7.3	2.6	5.4	2.2	3.2
1964	116.2	48.4	26.1	16.3	25.4	115.4	63.9	30.0	10.4	8.0	3.1	0.9	2.8	-1.9
1965	125.8	53.7	28.9	16.6	26.6	122.4	67.2	32.4	11.1	8.4	3.4	3.4	2.0	1.4
1966	143.5	61.5	31.4	15.7	34.9	140.9	77.0	35.7	14.4	9.2	4.6	2.6	7.5	-4.8
1967	152.6	67.2	30.0	16.5	38.9	160.9	88.3	42.3	15.9	9.8	4.5	-8.3	6.1	-14.5
1968	176.8	79.3	36.1	18.2	43.2	179.7	97.0	48.1	18.6	11.3	4.6	-2.8	5.2	-8.1
1969	199.5	94.7	36.1	19.2	49.5	190.8	100.1	52.6	20.3	12.7	5.1	8.7	7.7	1.0
1970	195.1	92.2	30.6	19.5	52.8	209.1	100.5	63.6	24.4	14.1	6.5	-14.1	3.6	-17.7
1971	203.3	89.9	33.5	20.5	59.4	228.6	103.8	75.4	29.0	13.8	6.6	-25.3	0.7	-26.1
1972	232.6	107.8	36.6	20.1	68.1	253.1	110.1	83.5	37.5	14.4	8.0	-20.5	3.0	-23.6
1973	264.0	114.3	43.3	21.5	84.9	275.1	112.9	96.2	40.6	18.0	7.4	-11.1	9.3	-20.4
1974	295.1	130.9	45.1	22.1	97.1	312.0	123.3	118.2	43.9	20.7	5.5	-16.9	7.0	-23.9
1975	297.4	125.4	43.6	24.2	104.2	371.3	135.0	150.3	54.6	23.0	8.6	-73.9	-11.2	-62.7
1976	343.1	146.6	54.6	23.8	118.2	400.3	141.7	163.0	61.1	26.8	7.8	-57.2	-9.7	-47.5
1977	389.6	169.1	61.6	25.6	133.3	435.9	155.4	173.6	67.5	29.1	10.4	-46.3	-5.6	-40.7
1978	446.5	193.8	71.4	28.9	152.4	478.1	168.8	186.2	77.3	34.6	11.4	-31.7	3.7	-35.4
1979	511.1	229.7	74.4	30.1	176.8	529.5	185.9	209.7	80.5	42.1	11.3	-18.4	9.8	-28.2
1980	561.5	256.2	70.3	39.7	195.3	622.5	215.2	252.0	88.7	52.7	13.9	-61.0	-4.4	-56.6
1981	649.3	297.2	65.7	57.3	229.1	707.1	246.0	287.1	87.9	71.7	14.4	-57.8	-1.3	-56.5
1982	646.4	302.9	49.0	49.7	244.8	781.0	270.0	323.4	83.9	84.4	19.4	-134.7	-19.8	-114.8
1983	671.9	293.0	61.3	53.3	264.2	846.3	293.0	347.7	87.0	92.8	25.4	-174.4	-20.7	-153.6
1984	746.9	308.3	75.2	57.9	305.3	902.9	314.1	354.3	94.4	113.3	27.1	-156.0	21.9	-177.9
1985	811.3	343.7	76.3	58.2	333.1	974.2	342.5	379.0	100.3	126.9	25.2	-162.9	33.1	-196.0
1986	850.1	358.3	83.8	53.2	354.7	1 027.6	362.3	399.1	107.6	130.5	28.0	-177.5	40.0	-217.5
1987	937.4	402.4	103.2	57.8	374.1	1 066.3	378.2	413.0	102.9	137.8	34.4	-128.9	49.7	-178.6
1960:														
1st quarter	98.3	42.7	23.7	13.7	18.3	86.5	49.7	22.1	6.2	7.1	1.3	11.9	2.6	9.3
2nd quarter	97.3	43.5	21.7	13.6	18.4	89.0	50.8	22.9	6.6	7.1	1.6	8.3	1.9	6.5
3rd quarter	96.6	43.9	20.7	13.5	18.6	90.2	51.5	23.8	6.7	6.6	1.5	6.5	1.4	5.1
4th quarter	95.7	44.1	19.7	13.4	18.5	92.8	53.2	24.8	6.6	6.4	1.8	2.8	0.4	2.5
1961:														
1st quarter	95.7	44.1	19.4	13.4	18.9	93.2	50.9	26.6	7.2	6.3	2.2	2.6	-0.8	3.4
2nd quarter	97.6	44.2	20.7	13.5	19.1	96.6	53.1	27.4	7.2	6.2	2.7	1.1	-1.4	2.5
3rd quarter	99.7	44.7	21.9	13.7	19.3	96.7	52.9	27.4	7.3	6.3	2.8	3.0	-1.3	4.3
4th quarter	102.9	45.3	23.9	14.2	19.6	98.0	54.5	27.0	7.4	6.2	2.8	5.0	-0.7	5.7
1962:														
1st quarter	104.4	46.3	22.3	14.5	21.2	101.8	57.2	27.6	7.8	6.4	2.8	2.5	0.7	1.9
2nd quarter	106.1	48.0	22.1	14.5	21.5	103.7	59.0	27.2	7.9	6.6	3.0	2.5	0.7	1.8
3rd quarter	108.4	49.2	22.7	15.0	21.6	104.9	59.6	27.6	7.9	6.9	2.8	3.5	1.0	2.6
4th quarter	109.9	50.4	22.8	14.9	21.8	107.3	60.6	28.4	8.3	7.1	2.9	2.6	0.5	2.1
1963:														
1st quarter	112.7	50.9	22.9	15.0	23.9	108.3	61.0	29.4	8.5	7.1	2.4	4.4	1.1	3.4
2nd quarter	115.2	51.2	24.5	15.4	24.2	108.7	61.5	28.6	8.8	7.2	2.6	6.5	2.5	4.0
3rd quarter	116.4	51.4	25.2	15.4	24.4	110.6	62.3	28.9	9.4	7.4	2.7	5.8	2.7	3.1
4th quarter	117.8	51.7	25.8	15.6	24.8	113.1	63.3	29.5	9.9	7.6	2.7	4.7	2.6	2.1
1964:														
1st quarter	116.7	50.2	25.9	15.7	24.9	114.7	63.6	30.1	10.1	7.8	3.0	2.0	1.8	0.2
2nd quarter	113.4	46.2	26.0	16.0	25.2	116.0	64.7	29.8	10.4	7.9	3.2	-2.6	2.8	-5.3
3rd quarter	116.5	47.9	26.6	16.5	25.6	115.6	64.0	29.9	10.5	8.0	3.3	1.0	3.0	-2.1
4th quarter	118.3	49.5	26.1	17.0	25.8	115.2	63.1	30.1	10.7	8.4	2.9	3.1	3.5	-0.4
1965:														
1st quarter	124.1	53.2	27.5	17.5	26.0	116.5	63.5	31.0	10.5	8.1	3.3	7.7	2.3	5.3
2nd quarter	125.9	54.4	28.4	16.8	26.3	119.2	65.6	31.0	11.0	8.3	3.3	6.7	3.3	3.4
3rd quarter	124.6	53.1	28.9	15.9	26.7	124.9	67.6	34.3	11.3	8.4	3.4	-0.3	0.4	-0.8
4th quarter	128.7	54.4	30.8	16.2	27.4	129.2	72.0	33.1	11.6	8.8	3.7	-0.5	2.0	-2.5
1966:														
1st quarter	138.0	57.4	31.7	15.1	33.8	132.7	71.9	34.7	13.3	8.7	4.1	5.3	7.6	-2.3
2nd quarter	142.9	61.0	31.7	15.9	34.3	138.5	76.6	34.0	14.4	9.0	4.6	4.4	7.9	-3.5
3rd quarter	145.4	62.6	31.4	15.8	35.5	144.0	79.4	35.5	14.9	9.3	4.9	1.4	8.0	-6.6
4th quarter	147.8	64.9	30.8	16.2	35.9	148.4	80.3	38.5	15.0	9.7	5.0	-0.6	6.4	-7.0
1967:														
1st quarter	149.0	65.7	29.7	16.1	37.5	157.9	86.7	41.3	15.3	9.9	4.7	-8.9	5.4	-14.3
2nd quarter	149.7	65.4	29.4	16.4	38.5	158.3	87.5	41.9	14.9	9.6	4.5	-8.6	5.9	-14.6
3rd quarter	153.6	68.2	29.6	16.5	39.3	161.2	88.1	43.1	16.0	9.7	4.3	-7.5	6.4	-13.9
4th quarter	158.0	69.6	31.4	16.8	40.2	166.2	90.9	43.1	17.5	10.2	4.6	-8.2	6.8	-15.1
1968:														
1st quarter	166.1	71.4	35.3	17.5	41.9	172.6	95.1	44.8	17.6	10.6	4.5	-6.5	6.6	-13.1
2nd quarter	171.2	74.3	35.9	18.1	42.9	178.7	96.3	47.9	18.7	11.3	4.6	-7.6	4.8	-12.3
3rd quarter	182.4	84.0	36.1	18.6	43.7	181.7	97.6	49.3	18.8	11.4	4.7	0.7	5.0	-4.2
4th quarter	187.7	87.7	36.9	18.7	44.4	185.6	99.2	50.4	19.3	11.9	4.7	2.1	4.7	-2.5
1969:														
1st quarter	197.8	93.6	37.5	18.6	48.1	183.9	96.8	51.0	19.0	12.2	5.0	13.9	7.1	6.8
2nd quarter	201.1	96.5	36.5	19.2	48.9	189.6	99.6	52.7	19.8	12.5	5.1	11.5	6.9	4.6
3rd quarter	198.8	93.8	35.3	19.6	50.1	192.8	101.5	52.8	20.6	12.7	5.2	6.0	8.4	-2.3
4th quarter	200.2	95.0	35.0	19.3	51.0	196.9	102.3	53.9	22.0	13.5	5.1	3.4	8.5	-5.1
1970:														
1st quarter	195.6	94.0	30.4	19.2	51.9	197.7	101.7	55.7	23.1	13.8	5.9	-2.1	9.1	-11.2
2nd quarter	197.5	94.8	30.5	19.5	52.6	211.8	100.0	65.1	24.1	13.9	6.7	-14.4	1.3	-15.7
3rd quarter	193.8	89.6	31.4	19.5	53.2	211.7	100.2	65.2	25.0	14.5	6.5	-17.9	3.3	-21.2
4th quarter	193.4	90.6	30.1	19.5	53.2	215.3	100.0	68.5	25.7	14.3	6.9	-22.0	0.8	-22.8

FEDERAL GOVERNMENT RECEIPTS AND CURRENT EXPENDITURES-Continued
(Calendar years-Billions of dollars, quarterly data are at seasonally adjusted annual rates)

YEAR AND QUARTER	Receipts					Current expenditures						Surplus or deficit (—), national income and product accounts		
	Total	Personal tax and nontax receipts	Corporate profits tax accruals	Indirect business tax and nontax accruals	Contributions for social insurance	Total	Consumption expenditures	Transfer payments (Net)	Grants-in-aid to state and local governments	Net interest paid	Subsidies less surplus of government enterprises	Total	Social insurance funds	Other
1971:														
1st quarter	199.1	87.0	33.3	20.8	58.1	220.4	102.6	69.6	27.0	14.3	6.9	-21.2	4.5	-25.8
2nd quarter	201.7	88.5	34.0	20.2	59.1	229.9	103.7	76.9	29.5	13.5	6.3	-28.1	-1.8	-26.4
3rd quarter	203.4	90.0	33.2	20.4	59.9	230.5	104.1	77.0	29.2	13.8	6.4	-27.1	0.4	-27.5
4th quarter	208.8	94.3	33.4	20.5	60.5	233.6	104.9	78.2	30.3	13.7	6.6	-24.8	-0.2	-24.6
1972:														
1st quarter	228.0	106.3	35.0	19.8	66.9	243.7	110.3	80.4	31.4	14.2	7.3	-15.7	3.7	-19.4
2nd quarter	229.3	106.7	35.2	19.9	67.6	253.5	111.8	80.5	39.1	14.2	7.8	-24.2	4.9	-29.0
3rd quarter	232.7	107.8	36.3	20.2	68.5	246.3	108.3	81.4	33.5	14.4	8.8	-13.7	5.5	-19.1
4th quarter	240.3	110.5	39.9	20.6	69.3	268.9	110.2	91.6	46.1	14.9	8.2	-28.6	-2.0	-26.6
1973:														
1st quarter	256.9	109.8	43.1	21.3	82.6	270.1	112.3	92.7	41.3	16.3	7.6	-13.2	11.7	-24.9
2nd quarter	260.3	111.2	43.6	21.8	83.8	274.6	113.3	95.3	40.9	17.4	7.6	-14.3	9.5	-23.8
3rd quarter	264.4	115.4	42.1	21.2	85.6	274.1	111.9	97.1	39.2	18.8	7.0	-9.7	8.2	-17.9
4th quarter	274.4	120.8	44.3	21.7	87.6	281.7	114.2	99.8	40.8	19.6	7.4	-7.4	7.8	-15.2
1974:														
1st quarter	282.5	124.3	42.5	21.6	94.0	294.1	119.0	107.6	42.4	19.7	5.4	-11.6	12.0	-23.6
2nd quarter	292.3	129.3	44.8	22.1	96.1	305.2	120.1	115.6	44.0	20.2	4.8	-12.9	8.0	-20.9
3rd quarter	304.4	134.0	49.5	22.3	98.7	317.4	124.2	121.7	43.3	21.2	5.5	-13.0	6.0	-18.9
4th quarter	301.4	136.0	43.7	22.3	99.5	331.5	129.7	128.1	46.0	21.5	6.2	-30.1	2.2	-32.3
1975:														
1st quarter	296.7	136.5	36.6	21.9	101.8	348.5	131.7	138.0	49.4	21.8	7.7	-51.8	-4.4	-47.4
2nd quarter	264.6	99.3	39.3	23.4	102.6	370.1	134.1	152.1	53.6	22.2	8.1	-105.5	-10.1	-95.4
3rd quarter	309.6	130.6	48.7	25.4	104.9	378.5	135.1	154.2	57.3	23.1	8.9	-68.9	-16.1	-52.8
4th quarter	318.5	135.1	49.7	26.1	107.6	388.0	139.2	156.7	57.9	24.8	9.5	-69.4	-14.3	-55.1
1976:														
1st quarter	331.2	137.6	55.7	23.1	114.8	389.6	138.7	159.0	58.7	25.7	7.6	-58.4	-9.4	-49.0
2nd quarter	339.1	143.6	54.9	23.7	117.0	392.5	141.0	158.6	59.2	26.3	7.5	-53.4	-7.0	-46.4
3rd quarter	347.2	149.4	54.4	24.1	119.3	404.5	141.4	167.6	61.0	26.9	7.8	-57.3	-11.3	-46.0
4th quarter	354.8	155.6	53.3	24.2	121.7	414.5	145.9	166.6	65.5	28.4	8.2	-59.7	-11.0	-48.7
1977:														
1st quarter	376.7	166.7	56.9	24.5	128.6	419.3	149.8	169.6	63.2	28.0	8.7	-42.5	-6.4	-36.1
2nd quarter	384.9	165.9	61.7	25.2	132.1	427.9	154.0	170.3	66.2	28.5	9.0	-43.0	-3.9	-39.1
3rd quarter	392.7	167.7	63.9	26.3	134.8	442.0	156.2	176.1	70.9	28.8	10.0	-49.3	-6.2	-43.1
4th quarter	404.0	176.0	63.9	26.4	137.7	454.2	161.4	178.1	69.9	30.9	14.0	-50.2	-5.7	-44.5
1978:														
1st quarter	412.7	178.1	60.4	27.3	147.0	463.8	163.4	181.2	74.4	32.7	12.2	-51.1	2.7	-53.8
2nd quarter	440.2	187.5	73.0	28.9	150.8	470.8	167.3	181.4	77.6	33.5	11.2	-30.6	6.6	-37.2
3rd quarter	456.9	199.9	74.0	29.2	153.7	481.5	169.7	189.3	77.4	35.2	10.1	-24.7	2.1	-26.8
4th quarter	476.1	209.8	78.2	30.2	157.9	496.4	174.9	192.8	79.6	37.1	12.0	-20.3	3.6	-23.9
1979:														
1st quarter	492.7	216.3	75.4	29.9	171.1	505.7	179.7	197.6	78.0	39.7	10.5	-13.0	13.7	-26.7
2nd quarter	505.0	224.6	75.6	30.2	174.5	517.2	184.4	202.1	78.0	41.4	11.3	-12.2	13.9	-26.1
3rd quarter	517.5	234.1	74.8	29.9	178.7	536.5	184.0	216.9	81.9	42.3	11.3	-19.0	5.8	-24.8
4th quarter	529.1	243.7	71.9	30.5	183.0	558.7	195.3	222.3	84.1	44.9	12.1	-29.6	5.7	-35.3
1980:														
1st quarter	546.3	243.4	79.9	32.8	190.2	583.5	203.2	232.3	85.5	49.9	12.6	-37.3	8.5	-45.8
2nd quarter	543.0	249.8	61.8	39.1	192.4	606.1	214.8	236.9	87.4	53.4	13.5	-63.1	3.1	-66.2
3rd quarter	563.1	258.9	66.4	41.9	195.9	638.5	216.1	266.2	89.3	52.3	14.6	-75.5	-16.2	-59.3
4th quarter	593.7	272.9	73.2	44.8	202.7	661.7	226.6	272.4	92.5	55.2	15.1	-68.1	-13.0	-55.0
1981:														
1st quarter	639.3	283.9	73.8	57.8	223.8	683.1	236.4	274.7	90.4	66.8	14.7	-43.8	4.5	-48.3
2nd quarter	645.5	294.9	64.4	58.8	227.4	694.5	244.9	277.5	90.2	68.8	13.1	-49.0	5.6	-54.6
3rd quarter	663.2	307.7	67.6	56.6	231.4	717.5	246.2	296.6	86.7	73.1	15.2	-54.2	-7.0	-47.2
4th quarter	649.2	302.4	56.9	55.9	234.0	733.3	256.5	299.8	84.2	78.1	14.7	-84.1	-8.4	-75.7
1982:														
1st quarter	645.8	303.9	48.4	51.9	241.7	745.8	262.1	305.1	82.7	80.5	15.4	-100.1	-5.2	-94.8
2nd quarter	653.0	309.1	50.9	48.7	244.2	761.0	263.1	313.3	84.9	83.4	16.3	-108.0	-12.3	-95.7
3rd quarter	642.8	296.9	50.8	48.9	246.2	795.6	271.8	328.8	83.5	87.0	24.5	-152.7	-24.7	-128.0
4th quarter	643.8	301.6	46.0	49.2	247.0	821.8	282.8	346.4	84.3	86.8	21.5	-178.0	-37.1	-140.8
1983:														
1st quarter	649.6	295.5	46.5	49.6	257.9	826.1	286.8	343.3	86.5	86.9	22.6	-176.4	-25.9	-150.6
2nd quarter	680.7	301.6	63.0	54.0	262.1	848.2	293.8	350.5	86.9	90.0	25.8	-167.5	-28.0	-139.5
3rd quarter	675.0	284.4	70.4	54.4	265.9	858.5	302.7	345.8	87.7	95.2	26.7	-183.5	-16.8	-166.7
4th quarter	682.4	290.7	65.4	55.3	271.1	852.6	288.8	351.4	86.9	99.0	26.5	-170.1	-12.3	-157.9
1984:														
1st quarter	732.6	294.8	82.7	57.3	298.0	876.3	301.5	349.4	91.9	104.6	29.2	-143.7	14.4	-158.0
2nd quarter	743.7	301.0	81.2	58.1	303.5	893.8	314.8	351.5	94.7	107.8	25.1	-150.1	19.7	-169.8
3rd quarter	750.4	313.7	70.0	58.3	308.4	913.1	317.3	355.4	93.2	117.6	29.4	-162.7	25.0	-187.6
4th quarter	760.7	323.9	67.1	58.1	311.6	928.3	322.9	360.8	97.6	123.0	24.5	-167.6	28.7	-196.3
1985:														
1st quarter	820.4	360.0	75.6	57.6	327.2	951.2	332.9	373.3	96.2	124.6	24.3	-130.8	29.4	-160.2
2nd quarter	781.1	314.5	73.6	62.3	330.7	966.6	338.0	376.2	99.4	127.7	24.2	-185.5	32.4	-218.0
3rd quarter	818.3	347.8	78.7	57.4	334.4	982.0	346.9	382.1	101.2	126.3	25.5	-163.6	32.8	-196.5
4th quarter	825.2	352.5	77.1	55.5	340.1	997.0	352.4	384.5	104.3	128.9	26.9	-171.7	37.7	-209.4
1986:														
1st quarter	834.2	348.9	81.3	54.1	349.8	1 003.3	351.6	389.6	104.5	130.3	27.3	-169.1	39.8	-208.9
2nd quarter	837.3	352.0	80.8	52.4	352.1	1 027.7	360.8	397.9	109.5	131.4	28.1	-190.4	39.5	-229.9
3rd quarter	850.5	360.1	82.0	52.5	356.0	1 044.6	369.7	404.5	113.1	128.9	28.4	-194.1	38.2	-232.3
4th quarter	878.3	372.2	91.3	53.9	360.9	1 034.8	367.3	404.6	103.2	131.5	28.3	-156.5	42.6	-199.0
1987:														
1st quarter	881.4	367.4	90.3	55.6	368.1	1 045.5	373.6	406.4	100.9	132.9	31.7	-164.1	46.1	-210.2
2nd quarter	952.5	420.2	103.2	57.6	371.6	1 062.5	376.4	412.2	105.4	134.3	34.3	-110.0	45.8	-155.8
3rd quarter	948.2	404.5	109.3	58.3	376.1	1 065.2	376.2	413.3	102.8	138.2	35.0	-117.1	50.6	-167.6
4th quarter	967.7	417.3	110.0	59.5	380.9	1 092.0	386.7	420.3	102.5	145.9	36.4	-124.3	56.3	-180.6

STATE AND LOCAL GOVERNMENT RECEIPTS AND CURRENT EXPENDITURES
(Calendar years-Billions of dollars, quarterly data are at seasonally adjusted annual rates)

YEAR AND QUARTER	Receipts						Current expenditures						Surplus or deficit (—), national income and product accounts		
	Total	Personal tax and nontax receipts	Corporate profits tax accruals	Indirect business tax and nontax accruals	Contributions for social insurance	Federal grants-in-aid	Total	Consumption expenditures	Transfer payments to persons	Net interest paid	Less: Dividends received by government	Subsidies less surplus of government enterprises	Total	Social insurance funds	Other
1960	48.3	5.2	1.2	32.0	3.4	6.5	38.4	33.7	5.9	0.1	....	-1.3	9.9	2.3	7.6
1961	52.4	5.7	1.3	34.4	3.7	7.2	42.0	36.7	6.5	0.1	....	-1.4	10.4	2.4	7.9
1962	56.6	6.3	1.5	37.0	3.9	8.0	44.8	39.1	7.0	0.2	....	-1.4	11.7	2.6	9.1
1963	61.1	6.7	1.7	39.4	4.2	9.1	48.1	42.2	7.5	0.1	....	-1.7	13.0	2.8	10.2
1964	67.1	7.5	1.8	42.6	4.7	10.4	52.4	46.0	8.2	-0.1	....	-1.7	14.7	3.2	11.5
1965	72.3	8.1	2.0	46.1	5.0	11.1	57.2	50.5	8.8	-0.3	....	-1.7	15.1	3.4	11.6
1966	81.5	9.5	2.2	49.7	5.7	14.4	64.3	56.5	10.1	-0.6	....	-1.7	17.3	4.0	13.3
1967	89.8	10.6	2.6	53.9	6.7	15.9	72.5	62.9	12.1	-0.9	....	-1.6	17.3	4.8	12.5
1968	102.7	12.7	3.3	60.8	7.2	18.6	82.6	70.8	14.5	-1.0	0.1	-1.6	20.0	5.2	14.8
1969	114.8	15.2	3.6	67.4	8.3	20.3	93.7	79.8	16.7	-1.2	0.2	-1.5	21.1	5.8	15.3
1970	129.0	16.7	3.7	74.8	9.2	24.4	108.2	91.6	20.1	-1.8	0.2	-1.6	20.8	6.9	13.9
1971	145.3	18.7	4.3	83.1	10.2	29.0	123.7	102.9	24.0	-1.4	0.3	-1.4	21.7	7.6	14.1
1972	169.7	24.2	5.3	91.2	11.5	37.5	137.5	113.4	27.5	-1.5	0.3	-1.6	32.2	8.7	23.5
1973	185.3	26.3	6.0	99.5	13.0	40.6	152.0	126.4	30.4	-2.9	0.5	-1.5	33.4	9.6	23.8
1974	200.6	28.2	6.7	107.2	14.6	43.9	170.2	144.0	32.3	-4.4	0.9	-0.9	30.5	10.9	19.5
1975	225.6	31.0	7.3	115.8	16.8	54.6	198.0	164.9	38.9	-4.5	0.9	-0.4	27.6	13.1	14.5
1976	253.9	35.8	9.6	127.8	19.5	61.1	217.9	179.7	43.6	-4.1	0.9	-0.4	35.9	15.6	20.4
1977	281.9	41.0	11.4	139.9	22.1	67.5	237.1	196.1	47.4	-4.7	1.3	-0.3	44.7	17.9	26.8
1978	309.3	46.3	12.1	148.9	24.7	77.3	256.7	214.5	52.4	-8.1	1.7	-0.3	52.6	20.2	32.4
1979	330.6	50.5	13.6	158.6	27.4	80.5	278.3	235.9	57.2	-13.3	2.0	0.4	52.3	23.7	28.6
1980	361.4	56.2	14.5	172.3	29.7	88.7	307.0	261.3	65.7	-19.3	1.9	1.2	54.4	26.9	27.5
1981	390.8	63.0	15.4	192.0	32.5	87.9	335.4	285.3	73.6	-23.6	2.3	2.4	55.4	29.8	25.6
1982	409.0	68.5	14.0	206.8	35.8	83.9	357.7	307.9	79.9	-28.9	2.9	1.7	51.3	36.6	14.7
1983	443.6	76.2	15.9	226.8	37.7	87.0	378.8	326.2	86.6	-31.0	3.4	0.2	64.9	41.6	23.3
1984	492.0	87.1	18.8	251.5	40.2	94.4	405.1	350.8	93.9	-34.1	3.9	-1.6	86.9	42.9	44.0
1985	528.7	94.0	20.2	271.4	42.8	100.3	437.8	382.6	101.9	-38.9	4.5	-3.3	91.0	47.0	44.0
1986	570.6	101.6	22.7	291.5	47.3	107.6	475.7	412.7	111.8	-40.7	5.1	-3.0	94.9	52.8	42.1
1987	594.9	111.8	23.9	307.1	49.2	102.9	511.1	441.1	120.7	-41.5	5.9	-3.4	83.8	54.8	29.0
1960:															
1st quarter	46.8	5.0	1.4	30.9	3.3	6.2	37.2	32.6	5.8	0.1	....	-1.2	9.6	2.2	7.4
2nd quarter	48.1	5.1	1.3	31.7	3.4	6.6	38.2	33.5	5.9	0.1	....	-1.3	9.9	2.3	7.6
3rd quarter	49.0	5.2	1.2	32.3	3.5	6.7	38.8	34.0	6.0	0.1	....	-1.3	10.2	2.3	7.9
4th quarter	49.5	5.3	1.1	33.0	3.5	6.6	39.5	34.7	6.1	0.1	....	-1.3	10.0	2.3	7.7
1961:															
1st quarter	50.9	5.4	1.2	33.5	3.6	7.2	40.7	35.6	6.3	0.1	....	-1.3	10.2	2.4	7.9
2nd quarter	51.7	5.6	1.2	34.1	3.6	7.2	41.8	36.6	6.4	0.1	....	-1.4	9.9	2.4	7.5
3rd quarter	52.8	5.8	1.3	34.7	3.7	7.3	42.3	37.0	6.6	0.1	....	-1.4	10.5	2.5	8.0
4th quarter	54.0	5.9	1.4	35.5	3.8	7.4	43.2	37.7	6.7	0.2	....	-1.4	10.8	2.5	8.3
1962:															
1st quarter	55.3	6.0	1.5	36.2	3.8	7.8	44.0	38.3	6.8	0.2	....	-1.4	11.3	2.5	8.8
2nd quarter	56.1	6.2	1.5	36.7	3.8	7.9	44.6	38.9	6.9	0.1	....	-1.4	11.5	2.5	9.0
3rd quarter	56.9	6.4	1.5	37.2	3.9	7.9	45.0	39.3	7.0	0.1	....	-1.4	11.9	2.6	9.3
4th quarter	58.0	6.5	1.5	37.7	4.0	8.3	45.8	40.0	7.1	0.2	....	-1.5	12.2	2.6	9.6
1963:															
1st quarter	58.9	6.5	1.5	38.2	4.1	8.5	46.6	40.8	7.3	0.2	....	-1.6	12.2	2.7	9.6
2nd quarter	60.1	6.6	1.6	38.9	4.2	8.8	47.5	41.7	7.4	0.1	....	-1.6	12.6	2.8	9.9
3rd quarter	61.9	6.8	1.7	39.8	4.3	9.4	48.4	42.5	7.5	0.0	....	-1.7	13.5	2.9	10.7
4th quarter	63.4	6.9	1.7	40.5	4.4	9.9	49.7	43.6	7.7	0.1	....	-1.7	13.8	2.9	10.8
1964:															
1st quarter	65.0	7.2	1.8	41.4	4.5	10.1	50.9	44.6	7.9	0.0	....	-1.6	14.1	3.1	11.0
2nd quarter	66.5	7.5	1.8	42.1	4.7	10.4	51.9	45.5	8.1	0.0	....	-1.6	14.5	3.2	11.3
3rd quarter	68.0	7.7	1.9	43.2	4.7	10.5	52.8	46.4	8.2	-0.1	....	-1.7	15.2	3.2	12.0
4th quarter	68.9	7.9	1.8	43.7	4.8	10.7	54.0	47.5	8.4	-0.2	....	-1.8	14.9	3.2	11.7
1965:															
1st quarter	69.9	8.0	1.9	44.6	4.9	10.5	55.2	48.6	8.5	-0.2	....	-1.7	14.7	3.3	11.4
2nd quarter	71.4	8.0	1.9	45.5	4.9	11.0	56.4	49.7	8.7	-0.3	....	-1.8	15.0	3.4	11.6
3rd quarter	73.1	8.1	2.0	46.6	5.1	11.3	58.1	51.1	8.9	-0.2	....	-1.7	15.0	3.4	11.6
4th quarter	74.9	8.3	2.1	47.7	5.2	11.6	59.3	52.4	9.0	-0.4	....	-1.7	15.5	3.6	12.0
1966:															
1st quarter	78.0	8.8	2.3	48.4	5.4	13.3	61.2	54.0	9.3	-0.5	....	-1.6	16.8	3.7	13.1
2nd quarter	80.6	9.3	2.3	49.1	5.6	14.4	63.3	55.6	9.9	-0.6	....	-1.6	17.4	3.8	13.5
3rd quarter	82.9	9.8	2.2	50.2	5.8	14.9	65.2	57.3	10.3	-0.7	....	-1.6	17.7	4.1	13.6
4th quarter	84.6	10.3	2.2	51.1	6.1	15.0	67.4	59.0	10.9	-0.8	....	-1.7	17.2	4.3	12.9
1967:															
1st quarter	86.3	10.3	2.6	51.8	6.3	15.3	68.9	60.3	11.2	-0.9	....	-1.6	17.3	4.3	13.0
2nd quarter	87.2	10.3	2.6	52.8	6.6	14.9	71.2	61.8	11.8	-0.8	....	-1.7	16.0	4.5	11.5
3rd quarter	90.9	10.8	2.6	54.7	6.8	16.0	73.7	63.8	12.4	-1.0	....	-1.5	17.1	5.0	12.1
4th quarter	94.7	11.1	2.7	56.4	6.9	17.5	76.1	65.6	13.1	-1.0	....	-1.6	18.6	5.3	13.4
1968:															
1st quarter	98.1	11.8	3.2	58.4	7.0	17.6	78.7	67.8	13.6	-1.0	0.1	-1.6	19.5	5.2	14.3
2nd quarter	101.5	12.4	3.3	60.0	7.1	18.7	81.3	69.6	14.4	-1.0	0.1	-1.6	20.1	5.2	15.0
3rd quarter	104.1	13.0	3.3	61.7	7.3	18.8	83.8	71.6	14.7	-0.9	0.1	-1.5	20.3	5.2	15.0
4th quarter	106.9	13.6	3.4	63.1	7.5	19.3	86.6	74.0	15.2	-1.0	0.1	-1.5	20.3	5.4	14.9
1969:															
1st quarter	109.4	14.2	3.8	64.6	7.8	19.0	89.1	75.9	15.9	-1.1	0.1	-1.5	20.3	5.4	14.8
2nd quarter	112.7	14.7	3.7	66.4	8.1	19.8	91.9	78.4	16.3	-1.1	0.1	-1.5	20.8	5.7	15.1
3rd quarter	116.7	15.7	3.5	68.4	8.5	20.6	95.2	81.0	17.0	-1.1	0.2	-1.5	21.5	5.9	15.6
4th quarter	120.4	16.1	3.4	70.2	8.7	22.0	98.4	83.9	17.7	-1.5	0.2	-1.6	22.0	6.2	15.8
1970:															
1st quarter	124.2	16.4	3.8	72.0	8.9	23.1	102.4	87.3	18.6	-1.7	0.2	-1.6	21.8	6.6	15.3
2nd quarter	127.5	16.7	3.7	73.9	9.1	24.1	106.1	90.1	19.6	-1.9	0.2	-1.6	21.4	6.8	14.6
3rd quarter	130.8	16.9	3.8	75.8	9.4	25.0	110.1	93.0	20.7	-1.7	0.3	-1.6	20.7	7.1	13.7
4th quarter	133.4	17.0	3.6	77.5	9.6	25.7	114.1	95.9	21.8	-1.8	0.3	-1.5	19.2	7.2	12.0

YEAR AND QUARTER	Receipts						Current expenditures						Surplus or deficit (—), national income and product accounts		
	Total	Personal tax and nontax receipts	Corporate profits tax accruals	Indirect business tax and nontax accruals	Contributions for social insurance	Federal grants-in-aid	Total	Consumption expenditures	Transfer payments to persons	Net interest paid	Less: Dividends received by government	Subsidies less surplus of government enterprises	Total	Social insurance funds	Other
1971:															
1st quarter	138.1	17.4	4.1	79.8	9.8	27.0	118.7	99.3	22.7	-1.6	0.3	-1.5	19.4	7.3	12.1
2nd quarter	144.0	18.4	4.2	81.8	10.1	29.5	122.4	101.8	23.6	-1.4	0.3	-1.4	21.6	7.5	14.1
3rd quarter	147.3	19.0	4.4	84.5	10.3	29.2	125.5	104.3	24.4	-1.2	0.3	-1.4	21.9	7.7	14.2
4th quarter	151.9	20.2	4.5	86.4	10.5	30.3	128.1	106.3	25.3	-1.3	0.3	-1.4	23.8	7.9	15.9
1972:															
1st quarter	158.1	22.6	5.0	88.1	11.0	31.4	133.2	109.4	26.4	-1.3	0.3	-1.5	24.9	8.3	16.6
2nd quarter	170.0	24.2	5.0	90.3	11.3	39.1	135.6	111.8	27.0	-1.4	0.3	-1.6	34.4	8.6	25.9
3rd quarter	167.1	24.6	5.2	92.2	11.6	33.5	139.4	114.8	28.1	-1.5	0.3	-1.7	27.7	8.8	18.9
4th quarter	183.7	25.4	5.7	94.4	12.0	46.1	142.0	117.6	28.3	-1.9	0.3	-1.7	41.7	9.0	32.6
1973:															
1st quarter	182.2	25.4	6.0	97.0	12.4	41.3	146.0	121.0	29.3	-2.2	0.4	-1.6	36.1	9.3	26.9
2nd quarter	183.8	25.6	6.1	98.4	12.8	40.9	150.2	124.6	30.2	-2.7	0.5	-1.6	33.6	9.5	24.1
3rd quarter	185.6	26.5	5.8	100.8	13.1	39.2	153.7	128.2	30.6	-3.1	0.5	-1.5	31.9	9.7	22.2
4th quarter	189.8	27.5	6.1	101.9	13.6	40.8	157.9	131.8	31.5	-3.4	0.6	-1.4	31.9	10.0	21.9
1974:															
1st quarter	192.8	26.8	6.3	103.3	14.0	42.4	160.6	136.3	30.2	-3.9	0.7	-1.3	32.2	10.4	21.8
2nd quarter	199.1	27.7	6.6	106.3	14.4	44.0	166.7	141.3	31.6	-4.3	0.8	-1.1	32.4	10.7	21.7
3rd quarter	203.5	28.9	7.3	109.2	14.8	43.3	173.2	146.5	33.0	-4.6	0.9	-0.8	30.3	11.1	19.2
4th quarter	207.1	29.4	6.4	110.0	15.3	46.0	180.2	151.8	34.5	-4.6	0.9	-0.6	26.9	11.6	15.4
1975:															
1st quarter	212.4	29.6	6.0	111.5	15.8	49.4	188.5	157.5	36.8	-4.6	0.9	-0.4	23.9	12.1	11.7
2nd quarter	221.5	30.5	6.6	114.2	16.5	53.6	195.8	163.3	38.4	-4.6	0.8	-0.4	25.7	12.7	12.9
3rd quarter	231.6	31.4	8.3	117.5	17.2	57.3	201.1	167.8	39.2	-4.5	0.9	-0.4	30.5	13.4	17.1
4th quarter	236.8	32.6	8.5	119.9	17.8	57.9	206.4	171.0	41.2	-4.3	0.9	-0.6	30.4	14.0	16.4
1976:															
1st quarter	244.4	33.9	9.7	123.6	18.5	58.7	211.5	174.6	42.4	-4.1	0.8	-0.5	32.9	14.6	18.3
2nd quarter	249.6	35.2	9.6	126.3	19.2	59.2	215.4	178.0	42.8	-4.1	0.9	-0.4	34.1	15.3	18.8
3rd quarter	255.8	36.4	9.7	128.9	19.9	61.0	220.3	181.3	44.3	-4.0	0.9	-0.3	35.4	15.9	19.6
4th quarter	265.7	37.6	9.6	132.5	20.5	65.5	224.4	184.9	44.8	-4.0	1.0	-0.3	41.3	16.5	24.8
1977:															
1st quarter	269.5	39.0	10.5	135.7	21.1	63.2	229.3	189.2	45.6	-4.1	1.1	-0.3	40.2	17.0	23.1
2nd quarter	278.2	40.5	11.4	138.4	21.7	66.2	235.2	193.5	47.6	-4.5	1.2	-0.3	43.0	17.6	25.4
3rd quarter	287.9	41.4	11.9	141.3	22.4	70.9	239.6	198.5	47.7	-4.9	1.4	-0.3	48.3	18.2	30.1
4th quarter	291.9	42.9	11.9	144.1	23.1	69.9	244.4	203.2	48.5	-5.4	1.5	-0.4	47.4	18.8	28.7
1978:															
1st quarter	298.8	44.2	10.5	146.0	23.7	74.4	249.9	208.2	50.3	-6.5	1.7	-0.4	48.9	19.4	29.5
2nd quarter	311.1	45.9	12.4	150.9	24.3	77.6	254.9	212.0	52.4	-7.5	1.7	-0.3	56.2	19.8	36.4
3rd quarter	309.4	46.9	12.5	147.6	25.0	77.4	258.8	216.6	53.1	-8.6	1.8	-0.2	50.7	20.5	30.2
4th quarter	317.7	48.2	13.1	151.2	25.7	79.6	263.0	221.2	53.8	-9.7	1.8	-0.1	54.7	21.1	33.6
1979:															
1st quarter	320.7	48.3	13.8	154.3	26.4	78.0	268.9	227.4	54.8	-11.3	1.9	0.1	51.8	22.2	29.6
2nd quarter	323.9	48.4	13.8	156.5	27.1	78.0	275.5	232.5	56.2	-12.5	1.9	0.4	48.4	23.2	25.2
3rd quarter	335.1	51.9	13.6	159.9	27.8	81.9	281.1	239.0	57.5	-13.9	2.0	0.5	54.0	24.2	29.8
4th quarter	342.6	53.4	13.0	163.7	28.4	84.1	287.7	244.7	60.2	-15.5	2.1	0.6	55.0	25.2	29.7
1980:															
1st quarter	351.1	53.4	16.3	167.0	28.8	85.5	296.6	252.1	62.8	-17.2	2.0	0.7	54.5	26.0	28.5
2nd quarter	352.8	55.1	12.7	168.9	28.8	87.4	302.0	258.5	63.2	-18.7	1.9	1.0	50.8	26.1	24.8
3rd quarter	364.4	56.9	13.8	174.0	30.3	89.3	311.0	264.5	67.1	-20.1	1.8	1.3	53.3	27.5	25.8
4th quarter	377.3	59.3	15.0	179.4	31.1	92.5	318.4	270.0	69.5	-21.2	1.8	1.8	58.9	28.1	30.8
1981:															
1st quarter	386.0	60.5	17.3	186.3	31.5	90.4	327.1	277.4	71.3	-21.9	2.0	2.3	58.9	28.2	30.7
2nd quarter	389.4	62.0	15.2	189.9	32.1	90.2	334.0	282.8	73.6	-22.8	2.2	2.6	55.4	29.0	26.5
3rd quarter	393.9	64.0	15.7	194.7	32.8	86.7	338.4	287.9	74.5	-24.1	2.4	2.6	55.5	30.2	25.3
4th quarter	394.0	65.5	13.5	197.2	33.6	84.2	342.2	293.1	74.9	-25.6	2.6	2.3	51.8	32.0	19.9
1982:															
1st quarter	398.1	66.3	14.1	200.4	34.7	82.7	348.9	299.8	76.9	-27.2	2.8	2.2	49.3	34.2	15.1
2nd quarter	407.1	67.3	14.4	204.9	35.6	84.9	355.6	305.8	79.5	-28.5	2.9	1.8	51.5	36.0	15.5
3rd quarter	412.7	70.0	14.4	208.6	36.3	83.5	360.6	310.5	81.2	-29.5	3.0	1.5	52.1	37.5	14.6
4th quarter	418.1	70.5	13.3	213.1	36.8	84.3	365.8	315.7	82.1	-30.2	3.1	1.3	52.3	38.8	13.5
1983:															
1st quarter	424.4	71.3	12.4	217.1	37.1	86.5	373.0	320.6	85.0	-30.3	3.2	0.8	51.4	40.3	11.1
2nd quarter	438.8	74.4	16.4	223.8	37.4	86.9	376.3	324.2	85.8	-30.7	3.3	0.4	62.4	41.4	21.0
3rd quarter	451.9	78.3	18.1	230.1	37.8	87.7	380.5	328.1	87.0	-31.1	3.4	0.0	71.4	42.1	29.3
4th quarter	459.5	81.0	16.8	236.3	38.4	86.9	385.3	332.0	88.8	-31.8	3.5	-0.2	74.2	42.5	31.8
1984:															
1st quarter	479.1	84.0	20.6	243.4	39.2	91.9	394.8	340.1	91.6	-32.5	3.7	-0.7	84.3	42.2	42.1
2nd quarter	490.8	86.7	20.2	249.3	39.9	94.7	401.7	347.0	93.1	-33.5	3.8	-1.2	89.2	42.5	46.6
3rd quarter	493.1	87.9	17.5	253.9	40.6	93.2	408.6	354.5	94.4	-34.6	3.9	-1.8	84.5	43.1	41.4
4th quarter	505.1	89.9	16.8	259.6	41.1	97.6	415.4	361.6	96.4	-35.9	4.1	-2.6	89.6	43.7	45.9
1985:															
1st quarter	512.6	91.2	19.9	263.8	41.6	96.2	423.7	369.7	98.7	-37.4	4.2	-3.0	89.0	45.0	44.0
2nd quarter	523.7	93.3	19.4	269.3	42.3	99.4	432.0	377.7	100.6	-38.6	4.5	-3.3	91.7	46.1	45.6
3rd quarter	534.2	94.3	21.0	274.5	43.2	101.2	442.5	387.1	102.9	-39.4	4.6	-3.5	91.7	47.7	44.1
4th quarter	544.4	97.0	20.7	278.1	44.3	104.3	452.9	395.9	105.2	-40.1	4.7	-3.4	91.5	49.0	42.5
1986:															
1st quarter	560.9	98.3	21.2	291.3	45.5	104.5	462.0	402.5	107.9	-40.3	4.9	-3.2	98.9	50.5	48.3
2nd quarter	564.0	99.3	21.9	286.8	46.5	109.5	469.5	407.5	110.7	-40.6	5.0	-3.1	94.5	51.9	42.6
3rd quarter	577.0	102.1	22.4	292.1	47.4	113.1	478.9	414.8	113.1	-40.8	5.2	-2.9	98.1	53.1	45.0
4th quarter	580.6	106.7	25.1	295.7	49.9	103.2	492.4	426.1	115.4	-41.0	5.4	-2.7	88.2	55.8	32.4
1987:															
1st quarter	576.8	107.3	20.8	299.4	48.4	100.9	498.9	431.1	117.3	-41.0	5.6	-2.9	77.9	54.2	23.7
2nd quarter	599.4	116.6	23.9	304.7	48.9	105.4	507.6	438.1	119.6	-41.2	5.8	-3.1	91.8	54.6	37.2
3rd quarter	597.7	109.4	25.4	310.7	49.4	102.8	514.7	443.6	121.9	-41.5	5.9	-3.4	83.0	55.0	28.0
4th quarter	605.6	114.0	25.5	313.4	50.1	102.5	523.1	451.7	124.0	-42.3	6.1	-4.1	82.4	55.4	27.0

STATE AND LOCAL GOVERNMENT RECEIPTS AND CURRENT EXPENDITURES-Continued
(Calendar years-Billions of dollars, quarterly data are at seasonally adjusted annual rates)

YEAR AND QUARTER	Exports of goods, services, and income				Imports of goods, services, and income				Unilateral transfers, net	U.S. assets abroad, net [1]				
												U.S. government assets other than official reserve assets, net	U.S. private assets, net	
	Total	Merchandise, adjusted, excluding military	Services	Income receipts on U.S. assets abroad	Total	Merchandise, adjusted, excluding military	Services	Income payments on foreign assets in the U.S.		Total	U.S. official reserve assets, net		Total	Direct investment
1961	31 402	20 108	6 295	4 999	-23 453	-14 537	-7 671	-1 245	-4 127	-5 538	607	-910	-5 235	-2 653
1962	33 340	20 781	6 941	5 618	-25 676	-16 260	-8 092	-1 324	-4 277	-4 174	1 535	-1 085	-4 623	-2 851
1963	35 776	22 272	7 348	6 157	-26 970	-17 048	-8 362	-1 560	-4 392	-7 270	378	-1 662	-5 986	-3 483
1964	40 165	25 501	7 840	6 824	-29 102	-18 700	-8 619	-1 783	-4 240	-9 560	171	-1 680	-8 050	-3 760
1965	42 722	26 461	8 824	7 437	-32 708	-21 510	-9 111	-2 088	-4 583	-5 716	1 225	-1 605	-5 336	-5 011
1966	46 454	29 310	9 616	7 528	-38 468	-25 493	-10 494	-2 481	-4 955	-7 321	570	-1 543	-6 347	-5 418
1967	49 353	30 666	10 667	8 021	-41 476	-26 866	-11 863	-2 747	-5 294	-9 757	53	-2 423	-7 386	-4 805
1968	54 911	33 626	11 917	9 367	-48 671	-32 991	-12 302	-3 378	-5 629	-10 977	-870	-2 274	-7 833	-5 295
1969	60 132	36 414	12 806	10 913	-53 998	-35 807	-13 322	-4 869	-5 735	-11 585	-1 179	-2 200	-8 206	-5 960
1970	68 387	42 469	14 171	11 748	-59 901	-39 866	-14 520	-5 515	-6 156	-9 337	2 481	-1 589	-10 229	-7 590
1971	72 384	43 319	16 358	12 707	-66 414	-45 579	-15 400	-5 435	-7 402	-12 475	2 349	-1 884	-12 940	-7 618
1972	81 986	49 381	17 841	14 765	-79 237	-55 797	-16 868	-6 572	-8 544	-14 497	-4	-1 568	-12 925	-7 747
1973	113 050	71 410	19 832	21 808	-98 997	-70 499	-18 843	-9 655	-6 913	-22 874	158	-2 644	-20 388	-11 353
1974	148 484	98 306	22 591	27 587	-137 274	-103 811	-21 379	-12 084	-9 249	-34 745	-1 467	366	-33 643	-9 052
1975	157 936	107 088	25 497	25 351	-132 745	-98 185	-21 996	-12 564	-7 075	-39 703	-849	-3 474	-35 380	-14 244
1976	172 090	114 745	27 971	29 375	-162 109	-124 228	-24 570	-13 311	-5 686	-51 269	-2 558	-4 214	-44 498	-11 949
1977	184 655	120 816	31 485	32 354	-193 764	-151 907	-27 640	-14 217	-5 226	-34 785	-375	-3 693	-30 717	-11 890
1978	220 516	142 075	36 353	42 088	-229 870	-176 002	-32 189	-21 680	-5 788	-61 130	732	-4 660	-57 202	-16 056
1979	287 965	184 439	39 692	63 834	-281 657	-212 007	-36 689	-32 961	-6 593	-66 054	-1 133	-3 746	-61 176	-25 222
1980	344 440	224 250	47 584	72 606	-333 774	-249 750	-41 491	-42 532	-8 349	-86 967	-8 155	-5 162	-73 651	-19 222
1981	380 928	237 044	57 354	86 529	-364 196	-265 067	-45 503	-53 626	-11 702	-114 147	-5 175	-5 097	-103 875	-9 624
1982	361 436	211 157	64 079	86 200	-355 804	-247 642	-51 749	-56 412	-17 075	-122 335	-4 965	-6 131	-111 239	991
1983	351 306	201 799	64 307	85 200	-377 573	-268 901	-54 973	-53 700	-17 718	-61 573	-1 196	-5 006	-55 372	-7 728
1984	395 850	219 926	71 168	104 756	-474 203	-332 418	-67 748	-74 036	-20 598	-36 313	-3 131	-5 489	-27 694	-12 344
1985	382 749	215 915	73 155	93 679	-484 037	-338 088	-72 862	-73 087	-22 700	-39 889	-3 858	-2 821	-33 211	-14 065
1986	400 842	223 344	86 312	91 186	-529 356	-368 425	-81 836	-79 095	-24 679	-106 753	312	-2 022	-105 044	-19 025
1987	449 272	250 208	98 553	100 511	-593 416	-409 765	-92 349	-91 302	-23 909	-72 617	9 149	1 006	-82 771	-28 355
1961:														
1st quarter	7 827	5 095	1 481	1 251	-5 599	-3 394	-1 912	-293	-989	-1 320	371	-381	-1 310	-774
2nd quarter	7 773	4 806	1 758	1 209	-5 659	-3 438	-1 922	-299	-1 208	-1 029	-320	471	-1 180	-551
3rd quarter	7 757	5 038	1 468	1 251	-6 026	-3 809	-1 900	-317	-887	-1 928	-212	-486	-1 230	-737
4th quarter	8 047	5 169	1 590	1 288	-6 171	-3 896	-1 939	-336	-1 043	-1 260	768	-513	-1 515	-592
1962:														
1st quarter	8 015	5 077	1 666	1 272	-6 256	-3 966	-1 971	-319	-1 113	-1 301	427	-406	-1 322	-545
2nd quarter	8 719	5 336	2 004	1 379	-6 402	-4 080	-1 992	-330	-1 272	-1 461	-163	-381	-917	-716
3rd quarter	8 295	5 331	1 567	1 397	-6 455	-4 116	-2 005	-334	-879	-279	881	8	-1 168	-811
4th quarter	8 315	5 037	1 709	1 569	-6 567	-4 098	-2 126	-343	-1 016	-1 134	390	-306	-1 218	-779
1963:														
1st quarter	8 428	5 063	1 849	1 516	-6 478	-4 064	-2 057	-357	-1 107	-1 922	32	-482	-1 472	-980
2nd quarter	9 244	5 599	2 150	1 495	-6 674	-4 226	-2 066	-382	-1 371	-2 631	124	-654	-2 101	-874
3rd quarter	8 832	5 671	1 620	1 541	-6 893	-4 372	-2 122	-399	-918	-887	227	-86	-1 028	-721
4th quarter	9 275	5 939	1 731	1 605	-6 926	-4 386	-2 118	-422	-999	-1 831	-5	-440	-1 386	-908
1964:														
1st quarter	9 885	6 242	1 922	1 721	-6 982	-4 416	-2 140	-426	-993	-2 086	-51	-288	-1 747	-822
2nd quarter	9 975	6 199	2 088	1 688	-7 179	-4 598	-2 142	-439	-1 269	-2 018	303	-386	-1 935	-970
3rd quarter	10 009	6 423	1 851	1 735	-7 349	-4 756	-2 153	-440	-935	-2 255	70	-414	-1 911	-1 018
4th quarter	10 299	6 637	1 982	1 680	-7 594	-4 930	-2 186	-478	-1 043	-3 200	-151	-592	-2 457	-949
1965:														
1st quarter	9 689	5 768	2 047	1 874	-7 395	-4 711	-2 187	-497	-1 037	-1 576	843	-374	-2 045	-1 606
2nd quarter	11 263	6 876	2 448	1 939	-8 208	-5 428	-2 269	-511	-1 478	-1 270	69	-536	-803	-1 250
3rd quarter	10 625	6 643	2 120	1 862	-8 307	-5 516	-2 263	-528	-1 013	-1 454	42	-254	-1 242	-1 030
4th quarter	11 149	7 174	2 212	1 763	-8 802	-5 855	-2 393	-554	-1 058	-1 416	271	-441	-1 246	-1 125
1966:														
1st quarter	11 190	7 242	2 124	1 824	-9 068	-6 012	-2 483	-573	-1 140	-1 465	424	-321	-1 568	-1 115
2nd quarter	11 726	7 169	2 705	1 852	-9 390	-6 195	-2 601	-594	-1 547	-1 967	68	-504	-1 531	-1 373
3rd quarter	11 470	7 290	2 301	1 879	-9 912	-6 576	-2 693	-643	-1 073	-1 681	83	-339	-1 425	-1 314
4th quarter	12 068	7 609	2 487	1 972	-10 098	-6 710	-2 717	-671	-1 194	-2 208	-5	-380	-1 823	-1 616
1967:														
1st quarter	12 439	7 751	2 731	1 957	-10 248	-6 708	-2 866	-674	-1 315	-1 203	1 027	-643	-1 587	-1 186
2nd quarter	12 275	7 693	2 666	1 916	-10 136	-6 475	-2 986	-675	-1 472	-2 339	-419	-543	-1 377	-964
3rd quarter	12 134	7 530	2 540	2 064	-10 262	-6 526	-3 059	-677	-1 309	-3 155	-375	-551	-2 229	-1 359
4th quarter	12 506	7 692	2 731	2 083	-10 833	-7 157	-2 955	-721	-1 199	-3 060	-180	-685	-2 195	-1 297
1968:														
1st quarter	13 016	7 998	2 816	2 202	-11 571	-7 796	-2 997	-778	-1 249	-1 299	912	-706	-1 505	-981
2nd quarter	13 577	8 324	2 936	2 317	-11 885	-8 051	-2 990	-844	-1 363	-2 427	-135	-632	-1 660	-1 172
3rd quarter	14 195	8 745	3 039	2 411	-12 611	-8 612	-3 129	-870	-1 445	-3 447	-572	-568	-2 307	-1 573
4th quarter	14 126	8 559	3 129	2 438	-12 604	-8 532	-3 185	-887	-1 573	-3 803	-1 075	-368	-2 360	-1 568
1969:														
1st quarter	12 921	7 468	2 884	2 569	-11 622	-7 444	-3 174	-1 004	-1 177	-2 595	-45	-406	-2 144	-1 556
2nd quarter	15 492	9 536	3 283	2 673	-13 978	-9 527	-3 303	-1 148	-1 645	-3 428	-298	-632	-2 498	-1 663
3rd quarter	15 439	9 400	3 245	2 794	-14 072	-9 380	-3 368	-1 324	-1 319	-3 361	-685	-703	-1 973	-1 548
4th quarter	16 279	10 010	3 394	2 875	-14 329	-9 456	-3 481	-1 392	-1 593	-2 199	-151	-459	-1 589	-1 192
1970:														
1st quarter	16 461	10 258	3 235	2 968	-14 458	-9 587	-3 449	-1 422	-1 383	-2 828	264	-399	-2 693	-1 958
2nd quarter	17 419	10 744	3 645	3 030	-14 861	-9 766	-3 690	-1 405	-1 586	-1 942	808	-348	-2 402	-2 144
3rd quarter	17 267	10 665	3 625	2 977	-15 141	-10 049	-3 715	-1 377	-1 611	-2 363	585	-423	-2 525	-1 718
4th quarter	17 241	10 802	3 666	2 773	-15 443	-10 464	-3 668	-1 311	-1 576	-2 205	824	-419	-2 610	-1 771

1. A minus sign indicates capital outflow, that is, an increase in assets abroad.

U.S. INTERNATIONAL TRANSACTIONS—Continued
(Millions of dollars, seasonally adjusted)

Year and quarter	Exports of goods, services, and income				Imports of goods, services, and income				Unilateral transfers, net	U.S. assets abroad, net[1]				
	Total	Merchandise, adjusted, excluding military	Services	Income receipts on U.S. assets abroad	Total	Merchandise, adjusted, excluding military	Services	Income payments on foreign assets in the U.S.		Total	U.S. official reserve assets, net	U.S. government assets other than official reserve assets, net	U.S. private assets, net — Total	U.S. private assets, net — Direct investment
1971:														
1st quarter	17 980	10 920	4 048	3 012	-15 551	-10 600	-3 724	-1 227	-1 746	-2 927	688	-573	-3 042	-2 033
2nd quarter	18 163	10 878	4 087	3 198	-16 764	-11 614	-3 867	-1 283	-1 808	-2 713	660	-567	-2 806	-1 949
3rd quarter	18 676	11 548	3 972	3 156	-17 460	-12 171	-3 861	-1 428	-1 752	-3 569	1 198	-387	-4 380	-2 308
4th quarter	17 564	9 973	4 251	3 340	-16 639	-11 194	-3 948	-1 497	-2 098	-3 263	-197	-355	-2 711	-1 327
1972:														
1st quarter	19 757	11 833	4 473	3 451	-19 153	-13 501	-4 173	-1 479	-2 297	-3 763	442	-212	-3 993	-2 187
2nd quarter	19 427	11 618	4 233	3 576	-19 105	-13 254	-4 228	-1 623	-2 011	-2 303	-238	-271	-1 794	-1 481
3rd quarter	20 788	12 351	4 634	3 803	-19 767	-14 022	-4 095	-1 650	-2 306	-4 129	-81	-518	-3 530	-2 435
4th quarter	22 015	13 579	4 503	3 933	-21 212	-15 020	-4 371	-1 821	-1 933	-4 302	-127	-566	-3 609	-1 644
1973:														
1st quarter	24 681	15 474	4 579	4 628	-23 000	-16 285	-4 613	-2 102	-1 536	-7 886	213	-572	-7 527	-3 785
2nd quarter	27 127	17 112	4 828	5 187	-24 301	-17 168	-4 741	-2 392	-1 953	-4 154	11	-423	-3 742	-2 691
3rd quarter	29 329	18 271	5 145	5 913	-24 841	-17 683	-4 640	-2 518	-1 751	-3 189	-23	-608	-2 558	-2 159
4th quarter	31 912	20 553	5 279	6 080	-26 855	-19 363	-4 849	-2 643	-1 674	-7 646	-43	-1 042	-6 561	-2 718
1974:														
1st quarter	34 698	22 614	5 189	6 895	-29 643	-21 952	-4 985	-2 706	-3 443	-5 914	-246	1 389	-7 057	900
2nd quarter	37 295	24 500	5 691	7 104	-34 710	-26 346	-5 359	-3 005	-2 475	-10 318	-358	267	-10 227	-1 790
3rd quarter	37 385	24 629	5 633	7 123	-36 004	-27 368	-5 360	-3 276	-1 676	-7 694	-1 002	-354	-6 338	-4 385
4th quarter	39 105	26 563	6 078	6 464	-36 918	-28 145	-5 675	-3 098	-1 656	-10 818	139	-938	-10 019	-3 776
1975:														
1st quarter	40 047	27 480	6 454	6 113	-33 797	-24 980	-5 580	-3 237	-2 043	-10 576	-327	-877	-9 372	-4 022
2nd quarter	38 675	25 866	6 807	6 002	-31 284	-22 832	-5 309	-3 143	-2 377	-9 591	-28	-875	-8 688	-3 990
3rd quarter	38 347	26 109	5 886	6 352	-33 078	-24 487	-5 379	-3 212	-1 189	-5 099	-333	-745	-4 021	-1 495
4th quarter	40 868	27 633	6 351	6 884	-34 588	-25 886	-5 729	-2 973	-1 467	-14 436	-161	-977	-13 298	-4 736
1976:														
1st quarter	41 183	27 575	6 556	7 052	-37 464	-28 176	-5 883	-3 405	-1 153	-12 364	-777	-749	-10 838	-3 923
2nd quarter	42 309	28 256	6 660	7 393	-39 494	-30 182	-5 980	-3 332	-1 141	-11 701	-1 580	-914	-9 207	-2 017
3rd quarter	43 818	29 056	7 311	7 451	-41 737	-32 213	-6 231	-3 293	-2 165	-10 618	-408	-1 428	-8 782	-3 327
4th quarter	44 780	29 858	7 444	7 478	-43 416	-33 657	-6 478	-3 281	-1 201	-16 588	207	-1 124	-15 671	-2 682
1977:														
1st quarter	44 916	29 668	7 494	7 754	-46 360	-36 585	-6 676	-3 099	-1 243	-1 198	-420	-1 062	284	-1 880
2nd quarter	46 796	30 852	7 901	8 043	-48 401	-38 063	-6 940	-3 398	-1 426	-12 182	-24	-885	-11 273	-3 783
3rd quarter	47 125	30 752	7 991	8 382	-48 511	-38 005	-6 894	-3 612	-1 371	-6 297	112	-1 001	-5 408	-2 762
4th quarter	45 818	29 544	8 098	8 176	-50 495	-39 254	-7 133	-4 108	-1 185	-15 109	-43	-746	-14 320	-3 466
1978:														
1st quarter	48 847	30 470	8 704	9 673	-54 471	-42 487	-7 612	-4 372	-1 396	-15 219	187	-1 009	-14 397	-4 771
2nd quarter	54 213	35 674	8 772	9 767	-56 513	-43 419	-7 768	-5 326	-1 477	-5 606	248	-1 257	-4 597	-3 720
3rd quarter	56 058	36 523	9 203	10 332	-58 300	-44 422	-8 248	-5 630	-1 425	-9 703	115	-1 394	-8 424	-2 753
4th quarter	61 399	39 408	9 673	12 318	-60 587	-45 674	-8 561	-6 352	-1 491	-30 601	182	-999	-29 784	-4 812
1979:														
1st quarter	64 530	41 475	9 664	13 391	-63 492	-47 582	-8 649	-7 261	-1 462	-8 980	-3 585	-1 094	-4 301	-5 465
2nd quarter	68 445	43 885	9 713	14 847	-67 584	-50 778	-8 960	-7 846	-1 552	-15 565	322	-970	-14 917	-7 220
3rd quarter	74 411	47 104	9 936	17 371	-71 856	-54 002	-9 329	-8 525	-1 632	-27 156	2 779	-779	-29 156	-7 166
4th quarter	80 577	51 975	10 378	18 224	-78 726	-59 645	-9 751	-9 330	-1 949	-14 353	-649	-904	-12 800	-5 370
1980:														
1st quarter	85 274	54 237	10 997	20 040	-86 559	-65 815	-10 335	-10 409	-2 174	-13 814	-3 268	-1 441	-9 105	-5 188
2nd quarter	83 441	55 967	11 491	15 983	-82 734	-62 274	-10 106	-10 354	-1 648	-24 724	502	-1 159	-24 067	-2 659
3rd quarter	86 148	55 830	12 543	17 775	-79 906	-59 010	-10 292	-10 604	-1 909	-19 666	-1 109	-1 382	-17 175	-4 156
4th quarter	89 578	58 216	12 554	18 808	-84 577	-62 651	-10 760	-11 166	-2 618	-28 761	-4 279	-1 178	-23 304	-7 219
1981:														
1st quarter	94 665	60 317	13 684	20 664	-91 024	-67 004	-11 360	-12 660	-2 678	-23 015	-4 529	-1 361	-17 125	-2 044
2nd quarter	96 294	60 141	14 392	21 761	-92 303	-67 181	-11 447	-13 675	-2 763	-24 158	-905	-1 491	-21 762	-5 709
3rd quarter	95 013	58 031	14 835	22 147	-89 787	-64 407	-11 236	-14 144	-3 145	-17 945	-4	-1 268	-16 673	-1 124
4th quarter	94 958	58 555	14 446	21 957	-91 082	-66 475	-11 460	-13 147	-3 117	-49 028	262	-976	-48 314	-745
1982:														
1st quarter	92 646	55 163	16 032	21 451	-90 276	-63 502	-12 749	-14 025	-4 091	-34 975	-1 089	-800	-33 086	-1 335
2nd quarter	94 629	55 344	16 187	23 098	-88 258	-60 580	-13 096	-14 582	-4 080	-41 323	-1 132	-1 727	-38 464	2 505
3rd quarter	89 512	52 089	16 003	21 420	-90 886	-63 696	-12 794	-14 396	-4 160	-22 133	-794	-2 524	-18 815	2 317
4th quarter	84 650	48 561	15 857	20 232	-86 380	-59 864	-13 109	-13 407	-4 744	-23 903	-1 950	-1 080	-20 874	-2 495
1983:														
1st quarter	84 792	49 198	16 239	19 355	-85 078	-59 757	-12 951	-12 370	-3 672	-27 537	-787	-1 136	-25 614	491
2nd quarter	85 967	49 340	16 093	20 534	-91 109	-64 783	-13 557	-12 769	-4 061	-1 727	16	-1 263	-480	-595
3rd quarter	88 775	50 324	16 308	22 143	-98 508	-70 370	-14 133	-14 005	-4 449	-11 047	529	-1 171	-10 405	-3 717
4th quarter	91 775	52 937	15 671	23 167	-102 885	-73 991	-14 337	-14 557	-5 536	-21 262	-953	-1 436	-18 873	-3 906
1984:														
1st quarter	94 914	52 991	17 353	24 570	-112 663	-79 740	-16 131	-16 792	-4 434	-7 252	-657	-2 033	-4 562	-751
2nd quarter	99 229	54 626	18 045	26 558	-119 297	-83 798	-16 885	-18 614	-4 544	-24 690	-566	-1 342	-22 783	-939
3rd quarter	101 311	55 893	17 936	27 482	-120 590	-83 918	-17 168	-19 504	-5 209	16 283	-799	-1 392	18 474	-2 224
4th quarter	100 397	56 416	17 834	26 147	-121 651	-84 962	-17 564	-19 125	-6 411	-20 654	-1 110	-720	-18 825	-8 432
1985:														
1st quarter	96 595	54 866	18 227	23 502	-116 271	-80 319	-17 707	-18 245	-5 170	-4 291	-233	-760	-3 298	-1 583
2nd quarter	96 229	54 154	18 214	23 861	-120 924	-84 565	-18 276	-18 083	-5 398	-1 131	-356	-1 053	278	-3 165
3rd quarter	93 549	52 836	17 961	22 752	-120 349	-83 909	-18 151	-18 289	-6 007	-4 555	-121	-453	-3 981	-3 477
4th quarter	96 378	54 059	18 756	23 563	-126 499	-89 295	-18 732	-18 472	-6 125	-29 912	-3 148	-555	-26 210	-5 839
1986:														
1st quarter	98 821	53 536	20 935	24 350	-129 152	-89 220	-20 298	-19 634	-5 318	-16 231	-115	-266	-15 850	-8 606
2nd quarter	100 666	56 828	20 804	23 034	-131 516	-91 743	-19 492	-20 281	-6 341	-23 736	16	-230	-23 522	-6 089
3rd quarter	99 708	55 645	21 879	22 184	-132 680	-92 801	-20 847	-19 032	-6 610	-31 355	280	-1 554	-30 081	-3 715
4th quarter	101 649	57 335	22 697	21 617	-136 010	-94 661	-21 200	-20 149	-6 409	-35 427	132	29	-35 588	-612
1987:														
1st quarter	102 839	56 696	23 544	22 599	-138 677	-96 023	-21 691	-20 963	-5 286	9 785	1 956	-5	7 834	-4 939
2nd quarter	109 693	60 202	24 703	24 788	-145 847	-100 648	-22 957	-22 242	-5 675	-25 074	3 419	-168	-28 325	-5 877
3rd quarter	114 722	64 217	24 970	25 535	-150 813	-104 412	-23 192	-23 209	-5 863	-26 091	32	310	-26 433	-7 095
4th quarter	122 016	69 093	25 334	27 589	-158 082	-108 682	-24 512	-24 888	-7 084	-31 235	3 742	868	-35 845	-10 442

1. A minus sign indicates capital outflow, that is, an increase in assets abroad.

U.S. INTERNATIONAL TRANSACTIONS—Continued
(Millions of dollars, seasonally adjusted)

YEAR AND QUARTER	U.S. assets abroad, net—Continued [1]			Foreign assets in the United States, net								Statistical discrepancy	Balance on	
	U.S. private assets, net—Continued					Other foreign assets in the United States, net								
		U.S. claims								U.S. liabilities				
	Foreign securities	On unaffiliated foreigners reported by U.S. nonbanking concerns	Reported by U.S. banks, not included elsewhere	Total	Foreign official assets in the United States, net	Total	Direct investment	U.S. treasury securities and U.S. currency flows	U.S. securities other than U.S. treasury securities	To unaffiliated foreigners reported by U.S. nonbanking concerns	Reported by U.S. banks, not included elsewhere		Goods and services	Current account
1961	-762	-558	-1 261	2 705	765	1 939	311	151	324	226	928	-989	4 195	3 822
1962	-969	-354	-450	1 911	1 270	641	346	-66	134	-110	336	-1 124	3 370	3 387
1963	-1 105	157	-1 556	3 217	1 986	1 231	231	-149	287	-37	898	-360	4 210	4 414
1964	-677	-1 108	-2 505	3 643	1 660	1 983	322	-146	-85	75	1 818	-907	6 022	6 823
1965	-759	341	93	742	134	607	415	-131	-358	178	503	-457	4 664	5 431
1966	-720	-442	233	3 661	-672	4 333	425	-356	906	476	2 882	629	2 940	3 031
1967	-1 308	-779	-495	7 379	3 451	3 928	698	-135	1 016	584	1 765	-205	2 604	2 583
1968	-1 569	-1 203	233	9 928	-774	10 703	807	136	4 414	1 475	3 871	438	250	611
1969	-1 549	-126	-570	12 702	-1 301	14 002	1 263	-68	3 130	792	8 886	-1 516	91	399
1970	-1 076	-596	-967	6 359	6 908	-550	1 464	81	2 189	2 014	-6 298	-219	2 254	2 331
1971	-1 113	-1 229	-2 980	22 970	26 879	-3 909	367	-24	2 289	369	-6 911	-9 779	-1 303	-1 433
1972	-618	-1 054	-3 506	21 461	10 475	10 986	949	-39	4 507	815	4 754	-1 879	-5 443	-5 795
1973	-671	-2 383	-5 980	18 388	6 026	12 362	2 800	-216	4 041	1 035	4 702	-2 654	1 900	7 140
1974	-1 854	-3 221	-19 516	35 341	10 546	24 796	4 760	1 797	378	1 844	16 017	-2 558	-4 292	1 962
1975	-6 247	-1 357	-13 532	17 170	7 027	10 143	2 603	4 090	2 503	319	628	4 417	12 404	18 116
1976	-8 885	-2 296	-21 368	38 018	17 693	20 326	4 347	4 283	1 284	-578	10 990	8 955	-6 082	4 295
1977	-5 460	-1 940	-11 427	53 219	36 816	16 403	3 728	2 434	2 437	1 086	6 719	-4 099	-27 246	-14 335
1978	-3 626	-3 853	-33 667	67 036	33 678	33 358	7 897	5 178	2 254	1 889	16 141	9 236	-29 763	-15 143
1979	-4 726	-5 014	-26 213	40 852	-13 665	54 516	11 877	7 060	1 351	1 621	32 607	24 349	-24 565	-285
1980	-3 568	-4 023	-46 838	62 612	15 497	47 115	16 918	7 145	5 457	6 852	10 743	20 886	-19 407	2 317
1981	-5 699	-4 377	-84 175	86 232	4 960	81 272	25 195	6 127	6 905	917	42 128	21 792	-16 172	5 030
1982	-7 983	6 823	-111 070	96 418	3 593	92 826	12 464	11 027	6 085	-2 383	65 633	37 359	-24 156	-11 443
1983	-6 762	-10 954	-29 928	88 780	5 845	82 934	10 457	14 089	8 164	-118	50 342	16 779	-57 767	-43 985
1984	-4 756	533	-11 127	118 032	3 140	114 892	24 748	27 101	12 568	16 626	33 849	17 231	-109 073	-98 951
1985	-7 481	-10 342	-1 323	146 383	-1 119	147 501	20 010	25 633	50 962	9 851	41 045	17 494	-121 880	-123 987
1986	-4 271	-21 773	-59 975	230 211	35 648	194 563	35 623	7 909	70 969	3 325	76 737	29 735	-140 605	-153 193
1987	-5 251	-7 046	-42 119	248 383	45 387	202 996	58 219	-2 243	42 120	18 363	86 537	-7 713	-153 353	-168 053
1961:														
1st quarter	-135	-117	-284	435	438	-3	68	-82	104	73	-166	-354	1 270	1 239
2nd quarter	-246	-164	-219	620	-307	927	86	-38	152	72	655	-497	1 204	906
3rd quarter	-124	-149	-220	934	673	261	58	83	3	14	103	150	797	844
4th quarter	-257	-128	-538	715	-41	756	99	188	66	67	336	-288	924	833
1962:														
1st quarter	-196	-186	-395	737	0	737	89	193	145	-14	324	-82	806	646
2nd quarter	-308	-5	112	675	503	172	130	-51	7	-64	150	-259	1 268	1 045
3rd quarter	-87	-181	-89	-277	178	-455	59	-109	-23	16	-398	-405	777	961
4th quarter	-378	17	-78	779	591	188	68	-99	6	-47	260	-377	522	732
1963:														
1st quarter	-522	-27	57	1 191	946	245	40	25	14	-36	202	-112	791	843
2nd quarter	-536	-108	-583	1 527	910	617	108	-109	119	69	430	-95	1 457	1 199
3rd quarter	-100	47	-254	205	56	149	105	1	52	11	-20	-339	797	1 021
4th quarter	53	245	-776	295	75	220	-22	-66	102	-80	286	186	1 166	1 350
1964:														
1st quarter	20	-206	-739	462	393	69	87	32	-42	0	-8	-286	1 608	1 910
2nd quarter	-206	-166	-593	630	227	403	109	-108	14	19	369	-139	1 547	1 527
3rd quarter	2	-532	-363	769	275	494	56	-65	-30	37	496	-239	1 365	1 725
4th quarter	-494	-204	-810	1 781	763	1 018	70	-5	-27	19	961	-243	1 503	1 662
1965:														
1st quarter	-198	286	-527	208	-202	410	184	60	57	3	106	111	917	1 257
2nd quarter	-147	165	429	-330	-194	-136	-21	64	-243	63	1	23	1 627	1 577
3rd quarter	-209	-19	16	587	115	472	147	-149	-227	49	652	-438	984	1 305
4th quarter	-205	-91	175	280	421	-141	104	-106	54	63	-256	-153	1 138	1 289
1966:														
1st quarter	-437	-159	143	458	-164	622	143	-102	173	68	340	25	871	982
2nd quarter	-115	-68	25	961	-57	1 018	133	-316	518	78	605	217	1 078	789
3rd quarter	-115	-105	109	909	-342	1 251	-37	66	107	195	920	287	322	485
4th quarter	-53	-110	-44	1 332	-111	1 443	187	-4	108	135	1 017	100	669	776
1967:														
1st quarter	-265	-107	-29	401	708	-307	169	-6	133	219	-822	-74	908	876
2nd quarter	-261	-69	-83	1 884	1 100	784	174	-61	329	66	276	-212	898	667
3rd quarter	-419	-40	-411	2 513	548	1 965	127	-36	520	164	1 190	79	485	563
4th quarter	-363	-563	28	2 584	1 098	1 486	228	-32	34	135	1 121	2	311	474
1968:														
1st quarter	-449	-231	156	1 374	-533	1 907	367	22	855	207	456	-271	21	196
2nd quarter	-283	-567	362	2 192	-2 007	4 199	133	86	1 122	478	2 380	-94	219	329
3rd quarter	-318	-213	-203	2 809	442	2 367	148	-8	1 124	315	788	499	43	139
4th quarter	-519	-191	-82	3 550	1 321	2 229	160	36	1 312	474	247	304	-29	-51
1969:														
1st quarter	-366	-132	-90	3 664	-1 117	4 781	359	-125	1 388	90	3 069	-1 191	-266	122
2nd quarter	-498	-21	-316	3 896	-766	4 662	267	-35	365	181	3 884	-337	-11	-131
3rd quarter	-546	141	-20	3 833	1 256	2 577	261	79	396	345	1 496	-520	-103	48
4th quarter	-139	-114	-144	1 311	-672	1 983	376	13	981	176	437	531	467	357
1970:														
1st quarter	-306	-366	-63	2 160	2 830	-670	592	16	304	222	-1 804	-169	457	620
2nd quarter	80	-73	-265	848	694	154	212	-35	374	534	-931	-95	933	972
3rd quarter	-517	-157	-133	1 940	1 411	529	357	1	720	510	-1 059	-309	526	515
4th quarter	-333	0	-506	1 413	1 975	-562	303	99	792	748	-2 504	354	336	222

1. A minus sign indicates capital outflow, that is, an increase in assets abroad.

U.S. INTERNATIONAL TRANSACTIONS—Continued
(Millions of dollars, seasonally adjusted)

YEAR AND QUARTER	U.S. assets abroad, net—Continued [1]			Foreign assets in the United States, net								Statistical discrepancy	Balance on	
	U.S. private assets, net—Continued				Foreign official assets in the United States, net	Other foreign assets in the United States, net								
		U.S. claims		Total		Total	Direct investment	U.S. treasury securities and U.S. currency flows	U.S. securities other than U.S. treasury securities	U.S. liabilities				
	Foreign securities	On unaffiliated foreigners reported by U.S. nonbanking concerns	Reported by U.S. banks, not included elsewhere							To unaffiliated foreigners reported by U.S. nonbanking concerns	Reported by U.S. banks, not included elsewhere		Goods and services	Current account
1971:														
1st quarter	-408	-355	-246	3 092	5 178	-2 086	196	179	559	-62	-2 958	-1 028	644	683
2nd quarter	-368	-131	-358	5 154	5 630	-476	140	1 862	196	-34	-2 640	-2 211	-516	-409
3rd quarter	-346	-337	-1 389	8 726	10 367	-1 641	-293	-795	626	79	-1 258	-4 800	-512	-536
4th quarter	9	-406	-987	5 997	5 704	293	324	-1 270	908	386	-55	-1 740	-918	-1 173
1972:														
1st quarter	-476	-248	-1 082	4 367	2 762	1 605	-136	-3	1 059	-14	699	911	-1 368	-1 693
2nd quarter	-318	-185	190	4 277	1 103	3 174	373	-83	961	250	1 673	-463	-1 631	-1 689
3rd quarter	203	-241	-1 057	6 382	4 740	1 642	310	-12	718	216	410	-1 145	-1 132	-1 285
4th quarter	-28	-380	-1 557	6 437	1 871	4 566	403	59	1 769	363	1 972	-1 182	-1 309	-1 130
1973:														
1st quarter	55	-809	-2 988	10 743	9 937	806	631	-119	1 718	246	-1 670	-3 002	-845	145
2nd quarter	-86	-202	-763	3 056	-403	3 458	835	-185	489	54	2 265	225	31	873
3rd quarter	-196	-502	299	2 168	-772	2 940	539	-205	1 173	454	979	-1 716	1 093	2 737
4th quarter	-445	-870	-2 528	2 423	-2 736	5 159	795	293	662	281	3 128	1 840	1 620	3 383
1974:														
1st quarter	-600	-2 113	-5 244	6 514	-1 138	7 652	1 784	336	712	354	4 466	-2 212	866	1 612
2nd quarter	-272	-588	-7 577	9 962	4 434	5 528	539	60	363	390	4 176	246	-1 514	110
3rd quarter	-282	273	-1 944	9 303	3 062	6 241	1 610	400	227	239	3 765	-1 314	-2 466	-295
4th quarter	-699	-793	-4 751	9 563	4 188	5 375	828	1 001	-925	861	3 610	724	-1 179	531
1975:														
1st quarter	-1 931	353	-3 772	2 788	3 419	-631	278	892	344	359	-2 504	3 581	3 374	4 207
2nd quarter	-985	112	-3 825	4 371	2 244	2 127	870	10	385	55	807	206	4 532	5 014
3rd quarter	-938	-939	-649	2 991	-1 731	4 722	86	2 424	737	-163	1 638	-1 972	2 129	4 080
4th quarter	-2 393	-883	-5 286	7 021	3 095	3 926	1 369	764	1 038	68	687	2 602	2 369	4 813
1976:														
1st quarter	-2 467	-747	-3 701	7 769	3 699	4 070	1 471	737	1 036	154	672	2 029	72	2 566
2nd quarter	-1 405	-999	-4 786	8 453	4 039	4 414	1 086	-91	134	-231	3 516	1 600	-1 246	1 648
3rd quarter	-2 751	616	-3 320	9 120	2 958	6 162	999	3 325	64	-184	1 958	1 582	-2 077	-84
4th quarter	-2 262	-1 166	-9 561	12 677	6 997	5 680	790	312	51	-317	4 844	3 748	-2 833	163
1977:														
1st quarter	-749	-771	3 684	3 062	5 554	-2 492	980	1 181	749	-98	-5 304	823	-6 099	-2 687
2nd quarter	-1 784	-1 124	-4 582	14 781	7 888	6 893	965	-799	589	-102	6 240	432	-6 250	-3 031
3rd quarter	-2 177	1 310	-1 779	14 676	8 257	6 419	1 023	1 651	337	768	2 640	-5 622	-6 156	-2 757
4th quarter	-749	-1 355	-8 750	20 703	15 117	5 586	761	401	763	518	3 143	268	-8 745	-5 862
1978:														
1st quarter	-1 115	-2 241	-6 270	18 684	15 448	3 236	1 356	1 381	396	507	-404	3 555	-10 925	-7 020
2nd quarter	-1 094	315	-98	1 551	-5 113	6 664	2 313	1 493	1 082	304	1 472	7 832	-6 741	-3 777
3rd quarter	-510	-29	-5 132	17 582	4 903	12 679	2 620	-368	296	912	9 219	-4 212	-6 944	-3 667
4th quarter	-907	-1 898	-22 167	29 220	18 440	10 780	1 608	2 672	480	166	5 854	2 060	-5 154	-679
1979:														
1st quarter	-908	-3 854	5 926	2 707	-8 697	11 404	1 554	2 964	409	-296	6 773	5 558	-5 092	-424
2nd quarter	-492	716	-7 921	7 663	-9 775	17 438	3 354	743	524	799	12 018	8 593	-6 140	-691
3rd quarter	-2 331	-1 826	-17 833	25 349	6 036	19 313	3 382	2 402	166	210	13 153	884	-6 291	923
4th quarter	-995	-50	-6 385	5 134	-1 228	6 362	3 588	951	252	908	663	9 317	-7 043	-98
1980:														
1st quarter	-787	-1 927	-1 203	9 582	-7 413	16 995	3 321	4 300	2 435	340	6 599	6 539	-10 916	-3 459
2nd quarter	-1 387	144	-20 165	11 373	7 731	3 643	229	5 756	496	1 671	-4 509	14 292	-4 922	-941
3rd quarter	-944	365	-12 440	14 930	7 564	7 366	4 713	222	263	1 252	916	403	-929	4 333
4th quarter	-450	-2 605	-13 030	26 726	7 614	19 112	3 128	2 394	2 263	3 590	7 737	-348	-2 641	2 383
1981:														
1st quarter	-473	-2 944	-11 664	9 819	5 502	4 317	3 146	2 486	2 357	121	-3 793	11 140	-4 363	963
2nd quarter	-1 564	513	-15 002	15 364	-3 159	18 523	5 294	1 641	3 512	13	8 063	7 566	-4 095	1 228
3rd quarter	-697	458	-15 310	17 531	-5 992	23 523	5 505	-248	704	1 084	16 478	-1 667	-2 777	2 081
4th quarter	-2 966	-2 404	-42 199	43 519	8 609	34 910	11 251	2 248	332	-301	21 380	4 750	-4 934	759
1982:														
1st quarter	-628	2 220	-33 343	27 184	-3 265	30 449	2 098	1 297	1 263	-65	25 856	9 512	-5 056	-1 721
2nd quarter	-471	-1 095	-39 403	35 200	1 534	33 666	2 885	4 193	2 486	-2 023	26 125	3 832	-2 145	2 291
3rd quarter	-3 397	3 670	-21 405	18 621	2 694	15 927	2 807	2 091	555	-282	10 756	9 046	-8 398	-5 534
4th quarter	-3 488	2 028	-16 919	15 412	2 629	12 783	4 673	3 446	1 781	-13	2 896	14 965	-8 555	-6 474
1983:														
1st quarter	-1 549	-4 253	-20 303	16 249	-38	16 287	1 237	3 713	2 873	-2 763	11 227	15 246	-7 271	-3 958
2nd quarter	-2 813	-590	3 518	16 339	1 612	14 727	3 301	4 616	2 470	-64	4 404	-5 409	-12 907	-9 203
3rd quarter	-1 308	-1 764	-3 616	20 458	-2 689	23 147	4 097	2 308	1 777	1 311	13 654	4 771	-17 871	-14 182
4th quarter	-1 093	-4 347	-9 527	35 734	6 960	28 774	1 823	3 452	1 044	1 398	21 057	2 174	-19 720	-16 646
1984:														
1st quarter	758	-3 012	-1 557	23 391	-2 956	26 347	4 947	2 450	1 333	6 092	11 525	6 044	-25 527	-22 183
2nd quarter	-764	-934	-20 146	42 770	-156	42 926	8 706	8 036	362	4 232	21 590	6 532	-28 012	-24 612
3rd quarter	-1 106	3 987	17 817	7 633	-884	8 517	4 497	6 103	1 447	1 662	-5 192	572	-27 257	-24 488
4th quarter	-3 644	492	-7 241	44 237	7 136	37 101	6 597	10 512	9 426	4 640	5 926	4 082	-28 276	-27 665
1985:														
1st quarter	-2 474	475	284	18 365	-10 962	29 327	4 936	3 390	9 615	-720	12 106	10 772	-24 933	-24 846
2nd quarter	-2 219	2 337	3 325	29 370	8 502	20 868	4 412	6 888	7 194	1 724	650	1 854	-30 473	-30 093
3rd quarter	-1 572	-2 779	3 847	38 339	2 506	35 833	4 915	9 136	11 669	2 801	7 312	-977	-31 263	-30 807
4th quarter	-1 217	-10 375	-8 779	60 311	-1 165	61 476	5 750	6 219	22 484	6 046	20 977	5 847	-35 212	-36 246
1986:														
1st quarter	-5 930	-6 230	4 916	41 557	2 712	38 845	3 499	6 420	18 730	696	9 500	10 323	-35 047	-35 649
2nd quarter	-1 051	-2 722	-13 660	53 797	15 918	37 879	5 607	4 620	22 752	1 635	3 265	7 130	-33 603	-37 191
3rd quarter	181	-7 638	-18 909	70 935	15 789	55 146	8 805	-854	17 107	1 947	28 141	2	-36 124	-39 582
4th quarter	2 529	-5 183	-32 322	63 923	1 229	62 694	17 713	-2 277	12 380	-953	35 831	12 274	-35 829	-40 770
1987:														
1st quarter	-1 749	-5 715	20 237	42 271	14 199	28 072	12 907	-2 326	18 372	6 151	-7 032	-10 932	-37 474	-41 124
2nd quarter	-287	712	-22 873	57 276	10 444	46 832	8 538	-731	15 960	5 595	17 470	9 627	-38 700	-41 829
3rd quarter	-1 159	-1 319	-16 860	83 041	764	82 277	20 659	-1 835	12 676	6 656	44 121	-14 996	-38 417	-41 954
4th quarter	-2 056	-724	-22 623	65 795	19 980	45 815	16 115	2 649	-4 888	-39	31 978	8 590	-38 767	-43 150

1. A minus sign indicates capital outflow, that is, an increase in assets abroad.

PRODUCTIVITY AND RELATED DATA
(1992=100, quarterly data seasonally adjusted)

YEAR AND QUARTER	Business sector								Nonfarm business sector							
	Output per hour of all persons	Output	Hours of all persons	Compensation per hour	Real compensation per hour	Unit labor costs	Unit nonlabor payments	Implicit price deflator	Output per hour of all persons	Output	Hours of all persons	Compensation per hour	Real compensation per hour	Unit labor costs	Unit nonlabor payments	Implicit price deflator
1960	51.4	34.3	66.7	13.6	64.7	26.6	24.6	25.8	54.8	34.0	62.0	14.3	67.7	26.1	24.0	25.3
1961	53.2	34.9	65.7	14.2	66.6	26.7	25.0	26.1	56.5	34.7	61.3	14.8	69.3	26.1	24.5	25.6
1962	55.7	37.2	66.8	14.8	68.9	26.6	25.7	26.3	59.1	37.0	62.6	15.4	71.5	26.0	25.3	25.8
1963	57.9	38.9	67.2	15.4	70.5	26.6	26.3	26.5	61.2	38.7	63.3	15.9	73.0	26.0	25.9	26.0
1964	60.5	41.4	68.3	16.2	73.2	26.7	26.8	26.8	63.8	41.3	64.8	16.7	75.4	26.1	26.6	26.3
1965	62.7	44.2	70.6	16.8	74.8	26.8	28.0	27.2	65.7	44.2	67.3	17.2	76.7	26.2	27.6	26.7
1966	65.2	47.2	72.5	17.9	77.5	27.5	28.6	27.9	68.0	47.4	69.7	18.2	78.8	26.8	28.2	27.3
1967	66.6	48.1	72.3	18.9	79.5	28.4	29.2	28.7	69.2	48.2	69.7	19.3	80.9	27.8	28.8	28.2
1968	68.9	50.5	73.3	20.5	82.5	29.7	30.0	29.8	71.6	50.7	70.9	20.8	83.8	29.0	29.7	29.3
1969	69.2	52.0	75.2	21.9	83.7	31.7	30.0	31.1	71.6	52.3	72.9	22.2	84.9	31.0	29.9	30.5
1970	70.5	52.0	73.7	23.6	85.4	33.5	30.6	32.4	72.6	52.1	71.8	23.8	86.1	32.8	30.3	31.9
1971	73.6	54.0	73.3	25.1	87.0	34.1	33.4	33.9	75.6	54.1	71.5	25.4	87.8	33.5	33.0	33.3
1972	76.0	57.6	75.7	26.7	89.6	35.1	34.8	35.0	78.2	57.8	73.9	27.0	90.6	34.5	34.0	34.3
1973	78.4	61.6	78.5	29.0	91.6	37.0	36.6	36.8	80.7	62.0	76.9	29.2	92.3	36.2	34.3	35.5
1974	77.1	60.6	78.6	31.8	90.5	41.3	38.6	40.3	79.4	61.1	77.0	32.1	91.3	40.4	36.7	39.1
1975	79.8	60.0	75.2	35.1	91.5	44.0	44.5	44.2	81.5	60.0	73.6	35.3	92.1	43.3	43.0	43.2
1976	82.5	64.0	77.6	38.2	94.1	46.2	47.1	46.5	84.5	64.3	76.1	38.4	94.6	45.4	46.0	45.6
1977	83.9	67.6	80.6	41.2	95.3	49.0	50.0	49.4	85.8	67.9	79.2	41.5	96.0	48.3	49.0	48.6
1978	84.9	71.7	84.5	44.8	96.5	52.8	53.3	53.0	86.9	72.3	83.1	45.2	97.3	52.0	51.8	51.9
1979	84.5	73.9	87.4	49.2	95.0	58.2	56.5	57.6	86.3	74.3	86.1	49.5	95.7	57.4	54.7	56.4
1980	84.2	73.0	86.6	54.5	92.7	64.7	59.6	62.8	86.0	73.4	85.4	54.8	93.3	63.8	58.6	61.9
1981	85.7	74.8	87.2	59.6	92.0	69.5	67.1	68.7	86.9	74.8	86.1	60.1	92.8	69.2	65.6	67.9
1982	85.3	72.5	85.0	64.1	93.1	75.1	68.3	72.7	86.3	72.4	83.9	64.6	93.9	74.8	67.4	72.2
1983	88.0	76.1	86.5	66.7	94.0	75.8	74.6	75.4	89.9	76.8	85.5	67.3	94.8	74.9	74.3	74.7
1984	90.2	82.5	91.5	69.6	94.0	77.2	78.5	77.7	91.4	82.8	90.6	70.1	94.7	76.7	77.4	77.0
1985	91.7	85.7	93.5	73.0	95.2	79.7	80.5	80.0	92.3	85.8	92.9	73.4	95.7	79.5	79.9	79.6
1986	94.0	88.5	94.1	76.8	98.3	81.7	81.7	81.7	94.7	88.7	93.7	77.2	98.8	81.5	81.3	81.4
1987	94.0	91.1	97.0	79.8	98.5	84.9	81.9	83.8	94.5	91.3	96.7	80.1	98.9	84.7	81.4	83.6
1960:																
1st quarter	52.3	34.8	66.5	13.7	65.2	26.1	25.0	25.7	55.6	34.6	62.3	14.2	67.6	25.5	24.7	25.2
2nd quarter	51.2	34.4	67.2	13.6	64.5	26.6	24.4	25.8	54.7	34.1	62.4	14.2	67.6	26.0	23.9	25.3
3rd quarter	51.2	34.4	67.1	13.6	64.4	26.5	24.7	25.9	54.8	34.0	62.0	14.3	68.0	26.1	24.0	25.4
4th quarter	50.9	33.7	66.2	13.7	64.8	27.0	24.1	25.9	54.2	33.2	61.3	14.4	68.0	26.6	23.4	25.5
1961:																
1st quarter	51.5	33.9	65.8	13.9	65.3	27.0	24.3	26.0	54.9	33.5	61.0	14.6	68.5	26.5	23.7	25.5
2nd quarter	53.2	34.6	65.1	14.2	66.7	26.7	24.9	26.0	56.3	34.3	60.9	14.7	69.3	26.2	24.5	25.6
3rd quarter	53.8	35.3	65.6	14.3	66.8	26.5	25.2	26.1	57.1	35.0	61.3	14.8	69.5	26.0	24.8	25.6
4th quarter	54.5	36.0	66.2	14.5	67.6	26.5	25.4	26.1	57.8	35.8	62.0	15.0	70.0	25.9	24.9	25.6
1962:																
1st quarter	55.0	36.7	66.8	14.6	68.0	26.5	25.6	26.2	58.9	36.6	62.2	15.2	70.9	25.9	25.3	25.6
2nd quarter	55.3	37.1	67.2	14.8	68.6	26.7	25.5	26.3	58.6	36.9	63.0	15.3	71.1	26.1	25.2	25.8
3rd quarter	56.1	37.5	66.9	14.9	68.9	26.6	25.7	26.3	59.3	37.3	62.9	15.4	71.4	26.0	25.5	25.8
4th quarter	56.5	37.5	66.3	15.1	69.7	26.7	25.7	26.3	59.8	37.3	62.4	15.6	72.0	26.1	25.4	25.8
1963:																
1st quarter	57.0	38.1	66.8	15.2	69.9	26.6	25.9	26.4	60.2	37.8	62.7	15.7	72.5	26.1	25.5	25.9
2nd quarter	57.3	38.5	67.2	15.2	70.0	26.6	26.1	26.4	60.7	38.3	63.2	15.8	72.6	26.0	25.7	25.9
3rd quarter	58.5	39.3	67.2	15.5	70.6	26.4	26.6	26.5	61.8	39.2	63.4	16.0	72.9	25.8	26.3	26.0
4th quarter	58.7	39.6	67.5	15.6	71.2	26.7	26.6	26.6	61.9	39.5	63.8	16.2	73.7	26.1	26.1	26.1
1964:																
1st quarter	60.3	40.7	67.5	16.0	72.4	26.5	26.9	26.6	63.5	40.7	64.2	16.4	74.4	25.8	26.7	26.1
2nd quarter	60.4	41.2	68.2	16.1	72.7	26.6	26.8	26.7	63.9	41.2	64.5	16.5	74.9	25.9	26.8	26.2
3rd quarter	60.9	41.7	68.5	16.3	73.6	26.7	26.8	26.8	64.3	41.7	64.9	16.8	75.9	26.1	26.7	26.3
4th quarter	60.6	41.8	69.0	16.4	73.8	27.1	26.6	26.9	63.6	41.7	65.6	16.9	76.0	26.6	26.2	26.4
1965:																
1st quarter	61.7	43.1	69.8	16.6	74.2	26.9	27.4	27.0	64.6	43.0	66.6	17.0	76.0	26.2	27.1	26.6
2nd quarter	61.8	43.7	70.7	16.7	74.2	27.0	27.5	27.2	65.1	43.7	67.2	17.1	76.2	26.3	27.2	26.6
3rd quarter	63.1	44.5	70.5	16.9	75.0	26.7	28.2	27.3	66.1	44.5	67.3	17.3	76.8	26.1	27.8	26.7
4th quarter	64.1	45.7	71.4	17.0	75.3	26.6	28.8	27.4	67.2	45.8	68.1	17.5	77.3	26.0	28.2	26.8
1966:																
1st quarter	65.2	47.0	72.1	17.4	76.4	26.8	28.9	27.5	68.2	47.1	69.1	17.8	77.9	26.1	28.3	26.9
2nd quarter	65.0	47.1	72.5	17.8	77.2	27.4	28.4	27.7	67.9	47.3	69.7	18.1	78.6	26.7	28.1	27.2
3rd quarter	65.0	47.3	72.7	18.1	77.6	27.8	28.5	28.0	67.8	47.5	70.1	18.3	78.9	27.0	28.1	27.4
4th quarter	65.5	47.6	72.6	18.3	78.2	28.0	28.7	28.3	68.2	47.7	69.9	18.6	79.3	27.2	28.6	27.7
1967:																
1st quarter	66.2	47.9	72.4	18.5	78.9	28.0	29.0	28.4	68.8	48.0	69.7	18.9	80.3	27.4	28.7	27.9
2nd quarter	66.7	47.9	71.8	18.8	79.7	28.3	28.9	28.5	69.1	47.9	69.4	19.1	81.0	27.7	28.6	28.0
3rd quarter	66.7	48.2	72.3	19.0	79.8	28.6	29.3	28.8	69.4	48.3	69.6	19.4	81.2	28.0	28.9	28.3
4th quarter	66.9	48.6	72.6	19.3	79.8	28.8	29.5	29.1	69.6	48.7	70.0	19.7	81.4	28.3	29.2	28.6
1968:																
1st quarter	68.3	49.6	72.6	19.9	81.6	29.1	29.8	29.4	71.1	49.8	70.0	20.2	83.0	28.5	29.6	28.9
2nd quarter	69.1	50.5	73.1	20.3	82.4	29.3	30.3	29.7	71.9	50.8	70.6	20.6	83.7	28.7	30.1	29.2
3rd quarter	69.1	50.9	73.6	20.6	82.7	29.9	29.9	29.9	71.7	51.1	71.2	20.9	83.9	29.2	29.7	29.4
4th quarter	69.0	51.1	74.0	21.1	83.4	30.5	29.9	30.3	71.6	51.3	71.7	21.4	84.6	29.8	29.6	29.7
1969:																
1st quarter	69.2	52.0	75.1	21.2	82.7	30.6	30.6	30.6	72.2	52.2	72.3	21.6	84.7	30.0	30.2	30.0
2nd quarter	69.2	52.0	75.2	21.7	83.6	31.4	30.1	30.9	71.6	52.2	73.0	22.0	84.7	30.7	29.7	30.4
3rd quarter	69.3	52.3	75.5	22.2	84.2	32.0	29.9	31.2	71.5	52.5	73.4	22.4	85.0	31.3	29.6	30.7
4th quarter	69.1	51.9	75.1	22.6	84.7	32.8	29.5	31.6	71.2	52.1	73.1	22.8	85.4	32.1	29.0	31.0
1970:																
1st quarter	69.3	51.8	74.7	23.1	85.0	33.3	29.5	31.9	71.4	52.0	72.9	23.2	85.6	32.6	29.1	31.3
2nd quarter	70.1	51.9	74.0	23.4	84.8	33.3	30.6	32.3	72.4	52.1	71.9	23.6	85.7	32.6	30.3	31.8
3rd quarter	71.6	52.5	73.3	23.9	85.8	33.3	31.1	32.5	73.6	52.7	71.4	24.1	86.6	32.7	30.7	32.0
4th quarter	71.2	51.7	72.7	24.2	85.6	33.9	31.3	33.0	73.1	51.9	70.9	24.3	86.2	33.3	31.0	32.4

SELECTED ANNUAL AND QUARTERLY DATA, 1960-1987

YEAR AND QUARTER	Business sector								Nonfarm business sector							
	Output per hour of all persons	Output	Hours of all persons	Compensation per hour	Real compensation per hour	Unit labor costs	Unit nonlabor payments	Implicit price deflator	Output per hour of all persons	Output	Hours of all persons	Compensation per hour	Real compensation per hour	Unit labor costs	Unit nonlabor payments	Implicit price deflator
1971:																
1st quarter	73.3	53.5	72.9	24.6	86.5	33.6	33.0	33.4	75.3	53.6	71.2	24.8	87.2	33.0	32.5	32.8
2nd quarter	73.4	53.8	73.4	24.9	86.7	34.0	33.4	33.8	75.6	54.0	71.4	25.2	87.8	33.4	33.0	33.2
3rd quarter	74.2	54.2	73.1	25.4	87.6	34.2	33.9	34.1	76.2	54.4	71.3	25.6	88.3	33.6	33.5	33.6
4th quarter	73.4	54.3	74.0	25.5	87.4	34.8	33.5	34.3	75.4	54.5	72.3	25.8	88.1	34.2	32.9	33.7
1972:																
1st quarter	74.4	55.7	74.9	26.2	88.8	35.2	33.8	34.7	76.8	56.1	73.1	26.4	89.6	34.4	33.4	34.0
2nd quarter	76.0	57.3	75.4	26.5	89.3	34.8	34.8	34.8	78.2	57.6	73.7	26.7	90.2	34.2	34.1	34.2
3rd quarter	76.4	58.0	75.9	26.8	89.6	35.1	35.1	35.1	78.7	58.3	74.1	27.1	90.8	34.5	34.1	34.3
4th quarter	77.2	59.2	76.6	27.4	90.6	35.4	35.6	35.5	79.2	59.3	74.9	27.7	91.6	34.9	34.2	34.6
1973:																
1st quarter	78.9	61.2	77.5	28.2	92.0	35.8	36.0	35.8	81.3	61.8	75.9	28.5	92.8	35.0	34.5	34.8
2nd quarter	78.7	61.7	78.4	28.6	91.5	36.4	36.5	36.4	81.0	62.1	76.8	28.9	92.2	35.7	34.4	35.2
3rd quarter	77.9	61.3	78.8	29.2	91.6	37.6	36.5	37.2	80.5	62.1	77.2	29.4	92.2	36.6	33.9	35.6
4th quarter	78.2	62.0	79.3	29.8	91.1	38.1	37.5	37.9	79.9	62.1	77.7	30.1	91.8	37.6	34.4	36.4
1974:																
1st quarter	77.0	61.1	79.3	30.4	90.1	39.4	37.4	38.7	79.7	61.6	77.3	30.8	91.3	38.6	34.8	37.2
2nd quarter	77.6	61.3	79.0	31.4	90.7	40.5	37.9	39.5	79.7	61.7	77.4	31.7	91.5	39.7	36.3	38.5
3rd quarter	76.7	60.3	78.6	32.4	91.0	42.2	38.6	40.9	78.8	60.8	77.2	32.6	91.5	41.3	36.9	39.7
4th quarter	77.0	59.8	77.6	33.1	90.2	43.0	40.7	42.2	79.3	60.2	76.0	33.4	91.0	42.1	38.7	40.9
1975:																
1st quarter	78.2	58.6	75.0	34.2	91.2	43.7	42.1	43.1	80.0	58.8	73.4	34.4	91.7	42.9	40.8	42.2
2nd quarter	79.6	59.2	74.4	34.8	91.7	43.7	43.8	43.7	81.4	59.3	72.8	35.0	92.4	43.0	42.5	42.8
3rd quarter	80.6	60.6	75.2	35.3	91.2	43.8	45.8	44.5	82.4	60.6	73.5	35.6	92.2	43.2	44.1	43.5
4th quarter	80.6	61.5	76.3	36.0	91.5	44.7	46.2	45.3	82.3	61.6	74.8	36.3	92.1	44.1	44.5	44.2
1976:																
1st quarter	82.0	63.3	77.2	37.0	92.9	45.1	46.8	45.7	83.9	63.6	75.8	37.2	93.3	44.3	45.4	44.7
2nd quarter	82.5	63.8	77.4	37.7	93.9	45.8	46.7	46.1	84.5	64.1	75.9	37.9	94.4	44.9	45.7	45.2
3rd quarter	82.5	64.1	77.7	38.5	94.3	46.7	46.9	46.8	84.6	64.4	76.1	38.8	95.0	45.9	45.9	45.9
4th quarter	83.1	64.8	78.0	39.3	95.0	47.4	47.9	47.5	84.8	65.0	76.7	39.5	95.4	46.6	47.0	46.7
1977:																
1st quarter	83.5	65.8	78.8	40.1	94.9	48.0	48.8	48.3	85.3	66.1	77.5	40.2	95.4	47.2	47.8	47.4
2nd quarter	83.7	67.4	80.5	40.7	94.7	48.6	49.9	49.0	85.9	67.9	78.9	41.0	95.6	47.7	49.0	48.2
3rd quarter	84.7	68.7	81.2	41.5	95.4	49.1	50.6	49.6	86.6	69.1	79.8	41.8	96.1	48.3	49.9	48.9
4th quarter	83.8	68.6	81.9	42.3	95.8	50.5	50.6	50.5	85.4	68.7	80.5	42.7	96.6	50.0	49.4	49.8
1978:																
1st quarter	83.5	68.7	82.3	43.5	96.7	52.1	50.2	51.4	85.5	69.2	80.9	43.9	97.6	51.3	48.8	50.4
2nd quarter	85.1	72.0	84.7	44.2	96.3	52.0	53.4	52.5	87.2	72.6	83.2	44.6	97.1	51.2	51.7	51.4
3rd quarter	85.3	72.7	85.2	45.2	96.2	53.0	54.2	53.4	87.3	73.1	83.8	45.6	96.9	52.2	52.7	52.4
4th quarter	85.4	73.5	86.1	46.3	96.3	54.2	55.2	54.6	87.6	74.3	84.8	46.7	97.0	53.3	53.8	53.4
1979:																
1st quarter	84.6	73.5	86.9	47.5	96.3	56.2	55.1	55.8	86.5	74.0	85.5	47.8	97.0	55.3	53.1	54.6
2nd quarter	84.6	73.6	87.0	48.6	95.4	57.4	56.4	57.0	86.4	74.1	85.8	48.9	96.0	56.5	54.6	55.9
3rd quarter	84.5	74.2	87.8	49.7	94.5	58.8	57.2	58.2	86.2	74.6	86.5	50.0	95.1	58.0	55.4	57.1
4th quarter	84.2	74.2	88.1	50.8	93.8	60.4	57.3	59.3	86.0	74.6	86.7	51.2	94.5	59.6	55.6	58.2
1980:																
1st quarter	84.8	74.4	87.7	52.4	92.9	61.7	58.7	60.6	86.5	74.9	86.6	52.6	93.4	60.9	57.6	59.7
2nd quarter	83.6	71.9	86.0	53.8	92.5	64.4	58.0	62.1	85.2	72.3	84.9	54.2	93.0	63.6	57.8	61.5
3rd quarter	83.8	71.8	85.7	55.2	93.0	65.8	59.7	63.6	85.6	72.3	84.5	55.5	93.6	64.9	58.6	62.6
4th quarter	84.6	73.6	87.0	56.4	92.6	66.7	62.2	65.1	86.5	74.2	85.8	56.9	93.3	65.8	60.4	63.9
1981:																
1st quarter	85.9	75.3	87.6	57.8	92.3	67.3	65.7	66.7	87.6	75.6	86.4	58.3	93.1	66.6	64.1	65.7
2nd quarter	85.3	74.4	87.2	59.1	92.3	69.3	65.8	68.0	86.5	74.5	86.1	59.5	93.0	68.8	64.2	67.2
3rd quarter	86.4	75.4	87.3	60.3	91.7	69.8	68.7	69.4	87.4	75.2	86.1	60.8	92.5	69.6	66.9	68.7
4th quarter	85.2	74.1	87.0	61.2	91.6	71.8	68.2	70.5	86.2	73.9	85.7	61.7	92.4	71.6	67.1	70.0
1982:																
1st quarter	84.4	72.5	85.9	62.5	92.7	74.1	66.8	71.4	85.4	72.3	84.7	63.0	93.5	73.8	65.8	71.0
2nd quarter	85.2	72.8	85.4	63.7	93.1	74.7	68.0	72.3	86.2	72.7	84.4	64.1	93.7	74.4	67.1	71.8
3rd quarter	85.3	72.3	84.8	64.7	93.0	75.8	68.5	73.2	86.4	72.2	83.6	65.2	93.7	75.5	67.5	72.6
4th quarter	86.1	72.4	84.1	65.4	93.6	75.9	70.1	73.8	87.1	72.3	83.0	65.9	94.4	75.7	69.3	73.4
1983:																
1st quarter	86.7	73.3	84.5	65.9	94.4	76.0	71.5	74.4	88.1	73.5	83.4	66.5	95.2	75.5	70.6	73.8
2nd quarter	88.1	75.3	85.5	66.5	94.2	75.5	74.3	75.1	89.9	76.0	84.5	67.1	95.0	74.6	73.8	74.3
3rd quarter	88.3	77.0	87.2	66.8	93.7	75.7	75.7	75.7	90.6	78.0	86.1	67.5	94.6	74.5	75.9	75.0
4th quarter	88.8	78.7	88.7	67.6	93.8	76.2	76.7	76.4	90.8	79.7	87.8	68.1	94.4	75.0	76.6	75.5
1984:																
1st quarter	89.7	81.0	90.3	68.5	93.7	76.4	77.8	76.9	91.1	81.5	89.4	69.0	94.4	75.7	76.6	76.0
2nd quarter	90.3	82.5	91.3	69.3	93.9	76.7	78.6	77.4	91.6	82.8	90.5	69.8	94.6	76.2	77.5	76.7
3rd quarter	90.3	83.1	91.9	70.0	94.1	77.5	78.7	77.9	91.5	83.3	91.0	70.6	94.8	77.1	77.8	77.4
4th quarter	90.5	83.5	92.4	70.7	94.3	78.2	78.9	78.5	91.5	83.7	91.5	71.2	94.9	77.9	77.9	77.9
1985:																
1st quarter	90.8	84.6	93.2	71.6	94.5	78.8	79.8	79.2	91.7	84.7	92.4	72.0	95.1	78.6	78.8	78.7
2nd quarter	91.0	85.0	93.4	72.4	94.7	79.5	80.2	79.8	91.8	85.1	92.7	72.8	95.2	79.3	79.5	79.4
3rd quarter	92.4	86.4	93.5	73.5	95.5	79.5	81.3	80.2	92.8	86.4	93.0	73.8	95.9	79.5	81.0	80.0
4th quarter	92.5	86.9	94.0	74.7	96.2	80.7	80.9	80.8	93.0	87.0	93.6	74.9	96.5	80.6	80.4	80.5
1986:																
1st quarter	93.9	88.2	93.9	75.5	96.7	80.5	82.1	81.0	94.5	88.3	93.4	75.9	97.2	80.3	81.9	80.9
2nd quarter	94.2	88.2	93.6	76.3	98.2	81.0	82.0	81.4	94.9	88.4	93.1	76.7	98.7	80.8	81.8	81.1
3rd quarter	94.1	88.7	94.2	77.1	98.7	81.9	81.8	81.9	94.8	88.8	93.7	77.5	99.1	81.8	81.3	81.6
4th quarter	93.9	89.1	94.9	78.2	99.3	83.2	80.9	82.4	94.6	89.3	94.4	78.5	99.8	83.1	80.3	82.1
1987:																
1st quarter	93.4	89.7	96.0	78.7	98.6	84.2	80.7	82.9	94.0	89.9	95.6	79.0	99.1	84.1	80.2	82.7
2nd quarter	93.9	90.7	96.5	79.3	98.3	84.4	81.8	83.4	94.6	90.9	96.2	79.6	98.7	84.2	81.3	83.2
3rd quarter	93.9	91.4	97.3	79.8	97.9	85.0	82.5	84.1	94.4	91.6	97.0	80.1	98.2	84.8	82.0	83.8
4th quarter	94.6	92.8	98.1	81.4	98.9	86.0	82.6	84.8	95.0	93.0	97.8	81.6	99.2	85.9	82.1	84.5

PRODUCTIVITY AND RELATED DATA—Continued
(1992=100, quarterly data seasonally adjusted)

PRODUCTIVITY AND RELATED DATA—Continued
(1992=100, quarterly data seasonally adjusted)

YEAR AND QUARTER	Nonfinancial corporations									Manufacturing					
	Output per hour of all employees	Output	Employee hours	Compensation per hour	Real compensation per hour	Unit costs			Implicit price deflator	Output per hour of all persons	Output	Hours of all persons	Compensation per hour	Real compensation per hour	Unit labor costs
						Total	Labor costs	Nonlabor costs							
1960	54.5	28.8	52.9	15.6	73.9	27.8	28.6	25.3	29.6	41.2	38.0	92.2	14.9	70.6	36.1
1961	56.2	29.4	52.4	16.1	75.6	27.9	28.7	25.8	29.7	42.6	38.3	89.8	15.3	72.0	36.0
1962	58.6	31.9	54.5	16.7	77.7	27.7	28.6	25.4	29.9	43.7	40.9	93.5	15.9	74.0	36.4
1963	60.6	33.7	55.7	17.3	79.2	27.7	28.5	25.3	30.1	45.5	43.0	94.5	16.4	75.2	36.1
1964	63.1	36.1	57.3	18.0	81.6	27.7	28.6	25.2	30.4	47.4	45.7	96.5	17.1	77.3	36.1
1965	64.5	39.1	60.6	18.5	82.6	27.8	28.7	25.1	30.9	48.4	49.4	102.1	17.5	77.7	36.1
1966	65.5	41.8	63.9	19.5	84.6	28.6	29.8	25.1	31.6	49.0	53.2	108.7	18.2	79.0	37.3
1967	66.4	42.9	64.6	20.6	86.6	29.9	31.0	26.6	32.4	50.9	55.1	108.1	19.2	80.8	37.8
1968	68.7	45.6	66.4	22.2	89.4	31.3	32.3	28.4	33.6	52.7	57.8	109.7	20.7	83.4	39.3
1969	68.7	47.4	69.0	23.7	90.5	33.5	34.5	30.6	35.1	53.4	59.3	111.0	22.2	85.0	41.6
1970	69.0	47.0	68.0	25.4	91.7	36.1	36.7	34.3	36.6	55.1	57.6	104.5	23.8	86.1	43.2
1971	71.9	48.9	67.9	27.0	93.4	37.1	37.5	36.0	38.0	58.7	59.1	100.6	25.3	87.5	43.0
1972	73.8	52.7	71.4	28.5	95.7	37.9	38.6	35.9	39.2	60.9	64.1	105.2	26.6	89.2	43.6
1973	74.4	55.8	74.9	30.7	97.2	40.3	41.3	37.5	41.5	62.6	69.2	110.5	28.6	90.5	45.7
1974	72.7	54.8	75.3	33.7	95.8	45.5	46.3	43.3	45.6	63.3	68.4	108.1	31.8	90.5	50.2
1975	75.5	53.9	71.4	37.0	96.6	49.0	49.0	48.9	50.1	65.3	63.5	97.3	35.6	93.0	54.6
1976	78.1	58.3	74.6	40.1	99.0	50.7	51.4	48.8	52.4	67.9	69.2	102.0	38.6	95.2	56.9
1977	80.1	62.6	78.1	43.3	100.2	53.1	54.0	50.4	55.1	70.2	74.6	106.2	42.0	97.2	59.8
1978	80.8	66.7	82.6	47.0	101.2	57.1	58.2	53.8	59.0	71.0	78.6	110.7	45.4	97.6	63.9
1979	79.4	68.2	85.9	51.4	99.3	63.4	64.7	59.8	64.3	70.6	79.7	112.8	49.8	96.2	70.5
1980	80.3	68.3	85.1	56.7	96.5	70.2	70.5	69.2	69.7	71.0	76.4	107.6	55.8	94.9	78.5
1981	82.8	71.5	86.3	61.8	95.5	75.8	74.7	79.0	75.8	71.9	77.0	107.1	61.3	94.6	85.2
1982	84.2	70.5	83.7	66.2	96.3	80.4	78.7	85.4	79.3	75.7	74.3	98.0	67.2	97.7	88.7
1983	86.8	73.7	84.9	68.7	96.8	80.9	79.1	85.8	81.1	78.4	77.7	99.0	69.0	97.2	88.0
1984	89.6	81.0	90.4	71.7	96.8	81.1	80.0	84.3	82.8	80.8	85.2	105.4	71.4	96.4	88.4
1985	91.0	84.2	92.5	74.9	97.7	83.1	82.3	85.2	84.4	83.8	87.8	104.7	75.3	98.1	89.8
1986	93.7	86.9	92.7	78.7	100.8	84.9	84.0	87.5	85.2	87.6	90.3	103.1	78.6	100.6	89.8
1987	95.1	91.1	95.8	81.6	100.7	86.2	85.7	87.5	87.1	90.0	93.5	103.9	80.8	99.8	89.8
1960:															
1st quarter	54.7	29.2	53.3	15.4	73.7	27.3	28.2	24.6	29.5	41.5	39.4	94.8	14.7	70.4	35.5
2nd quarter	54.1	28.9	53.3	15.6	73.8	27.8	28.7	25.1	29.6	41.1	38.4	93.3	14.9	70.6	36.2
3rd quarter	54.3	28.8	53.0	15.6	74.0	27.9	28.7	25.5	29.6	41.1	37.7	91.7	14.9	70.7	36.3
4th quarter	54.6	28.5	52.1	15.8	74.3	28.1	28.9	26.0	29.6	41.2	36.7	89.0	15.1	71.1	36.6
1961:															
1st quarter	54.7	28.2	51.6	15.9	74.7	28.3	29.1	26.3	29.7	41.2	36.2	87.9	15.2	71.4	36.9
2nd quarter	56.0	29.1	52.0	16.1	75.5	27.9	28.7	25.8	29.7	42.3	37.7	89.1	15.3	71.9	36.1
3rd quarter	56.5	29.7	52.7	16.2	75.7	27.8	28.6	25.7	29.7	43.2	39.0	90.2	15.4	72.0	35.6
4th quarter	57.5	30.7	53.4	16.3	76.3	27.6	28.4	25.4	29.8	43.7	40.2	92.0	15.5	72.5	35.5
1962:															
1st quarter	58.3	31.4	53.8	16.6	77.1	27.6	28.4	25.3	29.9	43.7	40.5	92.6	15.8	73.4	36.0
2nd quarter	58.1	31.7	54.6	16.7	77.3	27.8	28.7	25.3	29.9	43.3	40.7	94.0	15.9	73.6	36.6
3rd quarter	58.6	32.1	54.8	16.8	77.7	27.8	28.6	25.5	29.9	43.6	41.0	93.9	16.0	73.9	36.6
4th quarter	59.3	32.5	54.7	16.9	78.2	27.7	28.6	25.4	30.0	44.1	41.2	93.6	16.1	74.4	36.6
1963:															
1st quarter	59.7	32.8	55.0	17.1	78.6	27.8	28.6	25.4	30.0	44.6	41.8	93.8	16.2	74.6	36.3
2nd quarter	60.3	33.6	55.7	17.1	78.6	27.6	28.4	25.2	30.1	45.5	42.9	94.4	16.3	74.9	35.8
3rd quarter	60.9	34.1	55.9	17.3	79.1	27.6	28.4	25.3	30.1	45.6	43.2	94.7	16.4	75.0	36.1
4th quarter	61.5	34.5	56.1	17.5	79.9	27.7	28.5	25.3	30.3	46.2	43.9	95.0	16.7	76.0	36.1
1964:															
1st quarter	62.8	35.3	56.2	17.8	80.7	27.5	28.4	25.1	30.3	46.9	44.6	95.1	16.9	76.5	36.0
2nd quarter	62.9	35.9	57.0	17.9	81.2	27.6	28.5	25.1	30.3	47.4	45.6	96.2	17.0	77.1	35.9
3rd quarter	63.5	36.6	57.5	18.2	82.0	27.7	28.6	25.2	30.4	47.5	46.2	97.1	17.2	77.8	36.2
4th quarter	63.0	36.8	58.3	18.2	81.9	28.0	28.9	25.5	30.6	47.8	46.7	97.6	17.3	77.7	36.1
1965:															
1st quarter	64.2	38.1	59.4	18.3	82.1	27.6	28.5	25.2	30.7	48.1	48.2	100.4	17.3	77.6	36.0
2nd quarter	64.3	38.7	60.1	18.4	82.1	27.7	28.7	25.1	30.8	48.5	49.0	101.1	17.4	77.5	35.9
3rd quarter	64.5	39.2	60.8	18.6	82.6	27.9	28.8	25.1	30.9	48.6	49.9	102.5	17.5	77.7	35.9
4th quarter	65.1	40.3	61.9	18.8	83.1	27.9	28.9	25.0	31.0	48.4	50.5	104.4	17.6	77.9	36.4
1966:															
1st quarter	65.5	41.2	63.0	19.1	83.6	28.0	29.2	24.6	31.2	48.5	51.8	106.8	17.9	78.2	36.8
2nd quarter	65.4	41.7	63.7	19.4	84.2	28.4	29.6	24.9	31.5	48.7	52.9	108.7	18.1	78.6	37.2
3rd quarter	65.3	42.0	64.3	19.7	84.7	28.9	30.1	25.3	31.7	49.1	53.7	109.5	18.4	79.0	37.4
4th quarter	65.6	42.4	64.6	19.9	85.1	29.2	30.4	25.6	32.0	49.6	54.5	110.0	18.6	79.4	37.6
1967:															
1st quarter	65.8	42.4	64.4	20.2	86.0	29.5	30.7	26.0	32.1	50.0	54.5	109.0	18.8	80.2	37.7
2nd quarter	66.3	42.5	64.1	20.5	86.7	29.7	30.9	26.4	32.2	50.6	54.4	107.6	19.1	80.7	37.7
3rd quarter	66.5	42.9	64.6	20.7	86.9	30.1	31.2	26.9	32.5	51.0	54.8	107.6	19.4	81.2	38.1
4th quarter	67.0	43.7	65.2	21.0	87.0	30.3	31.3	27.3	32.8	52.1	56.5	108.4	19.6	81.3	37.6
1968:															
1st quarter	67.9	44.4	65.3	21.6	88.7	30.8	31.9	27.7	33.2	52.5	57.2	108.9	20.2	82.8	38.4
2nd quarter	68.7	45.3	66.0	22.0	89.4	31.0	32.0	28.0	33.5	52.8	57.7	109.3	20.6	83.7	39.0
3rd quarter	68.9	46.1	66.8	22.3	89.4	31.4	32.4	28.6	33.7	52.5	57.8	110.0	20.8	83.3	39.6
4th quarter	69.2	46.6	67.4	22.7	90.1	31.9	32.9	29.1	34.2	52.9	58.5	110.6	21.2	84.1	40.1
1969:															
1st quarter	68.9	47.0	68.3	23.0	90.1	32.4	33.4	29.5	34.5	53.3	59.1	110.9	21.6	84.6	40.5
2nd quarter	68.8	47.4	68.9	23.4	90.3	33.1	34.1	30.2	34.9	53.1	59.1	111.3	22.0	84.6	41.4
3rd quarter	68.6	47.7	69.5	23.9	90.7	33.8	34.8	30.9	35.3	53.5	59.7	111.5	22.4	85.2	41.9
4th quarter	68.4	47.5	69.5	24.4	91.1	34.6	35.6	31.7	35.7	53.8	59.4	110.3	22.9	85.6	42.5
1970:															
1st quarter	67.9	46.9	69.1	24.7	91.1	35.5	36.4	33.0	36.1	53.5	58.0	108.5	23.2	85.4	43.4
2nd quarter	68.8	47.0	68.3	25.1	91.2	35.9	36.5	34.0	36.6	54.8	57.9	105.7	23.7	86.0	43.2
3rd quarter	69.9	47.4	67.8	25.6	92.1	36.1	36.7	34.5	36.7	55.8	57.8	103.7	24.1	86.5	43.2
4th quarter	69.7	46.6	66.9	25.9	91.9	36.9	37.2	35.8	37.1	56.6	56.6	100.0	24.4	86.3	43.0

PRODUCTIVITY AND RELATED DATA—Continued
(1992=100, quarterly data seasonally adjusted)

YEAR AND QUARTER	Nonfinancial corporations									Manufacturing					
	Output per hour of all employees	Output	Employee hours	Compensation per hour	Real compensation per hour	Unit costs Total	Unit costs Labor costs	Unit costs Nonlabor costs	Implicit price deflator	Output per hour of all persons	Output	Hours of all persons	Compensation per hour	Real compensation per hour	Unit labor costs
1971:															
1st quarter	71.5	48.1	67.3	26.5	92.9	36.6	37.0	35.6	37.6	57.8	58.2	100.7	24.9	87.4	43.1
2nd quarter	71.5	48.5	67.8	26.8	93.3	37.0	37.5	35.8	38.0	58.4	58.8	100.7	25.2	87.6	43.1
3rd quarter	72.2	49.0	67.8	27.2	93.7	37.3	37.7	36.2	38.2	58.9	59.0	100.1	25.4	87.6	43.1
4th quarter	72.5	49.9	68.8	27.4	93.7	37.4	37.8	36.3	38.4	59.8	60.5	101.1	25.6	87.7	42.8
1972:															
1st quarter	73.0	51.1	70.0	28.0	95.0	37.7	38.4	35.7	38.8	60.5	62.4	103.0	26.1	88.6	43.1
2nd quarter	73.5	52.3	71.1	28.3	95.4	37.9	38.5	36.1	38.9	60.6	63.5	104.8	26.4	89.0	43.6
3rd quarter	74.0	53.0	71.7	28.6	95.8	37.9	38.7	35.8	39.2	60.8	64.1	105.3	26.7	89.3	43.9
4th quarter	74.7	54.4	72.8	29.2	96.5	38.2	39.0	35.9	39.7	61.8	66.5	107.5	27.1	89.9	43.9
1973:															
1st quarter	75.6	55.9	73.9	30.0	97.7	38.7	39.6	36.0	40.2	62.1	68.1	109.6	27.9	90.9	44.9
2nd quarter	74.5	55.7	74.8	30.4	97.1	39.9	40.8	37.2	41.0	62.4	68.9	110.5	28.3	90.4	45.4
3rd quarter	74.0	55.6	75.1	31.0	97.1	40.9	41.9	38.1	41.9	63.2	69.8	110.5	28.9	90.4	45.7
4th quarter	73.7	55.9	75.9	31.6	96.5	41.8	42.9	38.8	42.8	62.9	70.1	111.5	29.4	89.9	46.8
1974:															
1st quarter	72.9	55.3	75.9	32.3	95.8	43.3	44.3	40.4	43.7	62.0	68.3	110.2	30.2	89.7	48.8
2nd quarter	73.4	55.6	75.7	33.2	96.0	44.4	45.3	41.9	44.6	63.3	68.9	108.9	31.3	90.5	49.5
3rd quarter	72.4	54.8	75.6	34.1	95.9	46.4	47.1	44.2	46.3	63.9	69.4	108.6	32.3	90.6	50.5
4th quarter	72.0	53.4	74.2	35.0	95.5	48.1	48.6	46.7	47.9	64.1	67.1	104.6	33.4	91.2	52.1
1975:															
1st quarter	73.2	52.1	71.2	36.0	96.2	49.0	49.2	48.5	49.0	63.5	61.9	97.4	34.6	92.3	54.5
2nd quarter	75.3	53.0	70.4	36.7	96.7	48.8	48.7	49.2	49.6	64.7	61.9	95.7	35.4	93.3	54.7
3rd quarter	76.8	54.8	71.4	37.3	96.5	48.7	48.6	48.9	50.4	66.2	64.2	97.0	36.0	93.1	54.4
4th quarter	76.8	55.7	72.5	38.1	96.7	49.5	49.6	49.1	51.2	66.5	66.0	99.3	36.6	92.9	55.0
1976:															
1st quarter	77.9	57.5	73.9	38.9	97.6	49.4	50.0	47.9	51.6	66.9	67.9	101.4	37.4	93.9	55.9
2nd quarter	77.9	58.0	74.4	39.6	98.6	50.3	50.9	48.5	51.9	67.4	68.6	101.8	38.2	95.1	56.7
3rd quarter	78.4	58.6	74.8	40.6	99.3	51.0	51.8	48.9	52.5	68.1	69.5	102.1	39.0	95.5	57.3
4th quarter	78.3	58.9	75.3	41.4	100.0	52.1	52.9	49.9	53.3	69.0	70.7	102.5	39.8	96.1	57.7
1977:															
1st quarter	78.6	59.9	76.3	42.0	99.5	52.6	53.4	50.4	54.1	69.7	72.4	103.9	40.7	96.5	58.4
2nd quarter	80.0	62.2	77.9	42.8	99.8	52.7	53.6	50.0	54.8	70.3	74.6	106.2	41.5	96.7	59.0
3rd quarter	81.4	64.1	78.8	43.7	100.4	52.7	53.7	49.9	55.2	70.7	75.6	107.0	42.5	97.6	60.1
4th quarter	80.3	64.1	79.7	44.5	100.8	54.4	55.4	51.4	56.4	70.3	75.9	107.9	43.2	97.9	61.5
1978:															
1st quarter	80.1	64.2	80.2	45.6	101.4	56.0	56.9	53.4	57.2	70.1	75.9	108.3	44.1	98.1	62.9
2nd quarter	81.1	66.9	82.6	46.4	101.0	56.2	57.3	53.2	58.4	71.0	78.6	110.7	44.7	97.3	62.9
3rd quarter	80.9	67.4	83.4	47.4	100.8	57.4	58.6	53.8	59.4	71.4	79.6	111.5	45.6	97.1	64.0
4th quarter	80.9	68.4	84.5	48.5	100.9	58.7	60.0	54.9	60.8	71.4	80.4	112.6	46.8	97.3	65.6
1979:															
1st quarter	79.7	68.1	85.4	49.6	100.6	60.9	62.2	56.9	62.3	70.7	80.4	113.8	47.8	97.0	67.7
2nd quarter	79.4	67.9	85.6	50.8	99.8	62.6	63.9	59.0	63.7	71.0	80.0	112.8	49.3	96.8	69.4
3rd quarter	79.0	68.1	86.1	51.9	99.8	64.4	65.7	60.7	65.0	70.2	79.3	113.0	50.3	95.8	71.7
4th quarter	79.4	68.6	86.4	53.1	98.0	65.7	66.9	62.5	66.0	70.4	79.0	112.2	51.7	95.3	73.3
1980:															
1st quarter	79.9	69.0	86.3	54.5	96.7	67.3	68.2	64.6	67.4	70.9	79.1	111.5	53.1	94.3	74.9
2nd quarter	79.6	67.4	84.6	56.0	96.1	69.9	70.3	68.8	68.8	70.5	75.3	106.8	55.0	94.4	78.0
3rd quarter	80.4	67.5	84.0	57.4	96.7	71.4	71.4	71.3	70.5	70.7	74.3	105.1	56.7	95.5	80.1
4th quarter	81.3	69.5	85.5	58.8	96.4	72.3	72.3	72.3	72.1	71.6	76.9	107.4	58.2	95.4	81.3
1981:															
1st quarter	82.1	70.8	86.3	60.0	95.7	73.7	73.0	75.4	73.8	71.3	76.9	107.9	59.2	94.4	82.9
2nd quarter	82.4	71.1	86.3	61.3	95.7	75.3	74.4	78.0	75.2	71.8	77.6	108.1	60.6	94.8	84.4
3rd quarter	83.8	72.5	86.5	62.6	95.1	75.9	74.7	79.4	76.5	72.3	77.8	107.6	61.9	94.2	85.6
4th quarter	83.0	71.5	86.0	63.6	95.1	78.2	76.5	83.0	77.6	72.0	75.7	105.1	63.3	94.7	87.9
1982:															
1st quarter	83.2	70.7	85.0	64.8	96.1	79.4	77.9	83.7	78.4	73.7	75.1	101.9	65.2	96.7	88.5
2nd quarter	84.3	70.8	84.1	65.9	96.3	80.0	78.2	85.0	79.1	75.9	75.1	99.0	67.0	98.0	88.3
3rd quarter	84.6	70.4	83.3	66.8	96.0	80.7	79.0	85.5	79.8	76.9	74.2	96.6	68.1	97.8	88.6
4th quarter	84.7	69.9	82.5	67.4	96.6	81.6	79.6	87.4	80.0	76.6	72.6	94.8	68.5	98.2	89.5
1983:															
1st quarter	85.3	70.6	82.8	67.8	97.1	81.1	79.5	85.8	80.3	77.6	74.1	95.5	68.8	98.5	88.6
2nd quarter	86.8	72.9	84.0	68.4	96.8	80.5	78.8	85.3	80.9	78.1	76.3	97.8	68.8	97.4	88.1
3rd quarter	87.3	74.6	85.5	68.8	96.4	80.4	78.8	84.8	81.3	79.0	79.2	100.2	69.0	96.7	87.3
4th quarter	87.9	76.8	87.4	69.8	96.8	81.5	79.4	87.5	81.8	79.0	81.1	102.7	69.5	96.5	88.0
1984:															
1st quarter	88.6	78.8	89.0	70.3	96.2	80.5	79.4	83.8	82.3	80.0	83.7	104.6	70.1	95.9	87.6
2nd quarter	89.6	80.7	90.1	71.2	96.6	80.6	79.5	83.5	82.6	80.5	85.1	105.7	70.8	96.0	88.0
3rd quarter	89.9	81.6	90.9	72.2	97.0	81.3	80.3	84.2	83.0	81.2	85.9	105.8	71.9	96.6	88.5
4th quarter	90.2	82.6	91.6	72.8	97.0	82.0	80.7	85.7	83.3	81.3	86.0	105.7	72.8	97.0	89.5
1985:															
1st quarter	90.2	83.1	92.2	73.5	97.1	82.3	81.5	84.5	83.9	82.1	86.6	105.5	74.0	97.7	90.1
2nd quarter	90.3	83.5	92.5	74.3	97.3	83.2	82.3	85.8	84.3	83.8	87.7	104.7	74.6	97.7	89.1
3rd quarter	92.0	85.1	92.6	75.3	97.9	82.6	81.9	84.8	84.5	84.4	88.1	104.3	75.6	98.3	89.5
4th quarter	91.6	85.1	92.8	76.6	98.6	84.2	83.6	85.9	84.9	85.0	88.6	104.2	76.8	98.8	90.3
1986:															
1st quarter	93.7	87.0	92.8	77.5	99.3	83.8	82.7	87.0	84.9	86.4	89.7	103.9	77.6	99.3	89.8
2nd quarter	93.5	86.4	92.4	78.3	100.7	84.6	83.7	87.1	84.9	87.3	90.1	103.1	78.1	100.5	89.4
3rd quarter	93.3	86.4	92.7	79.0	101.1	85.7	84.7	88.3	85.4	87.8	90.2	102.8	78.9	100.9	89.9
4th quarter	94.3	87.8	93.1	80.1	101.7	85.7	85.0	87.8	85.7	88.8	91.3	102.8	79.8	101.3	89.9
1987:															
1st quarter	94.1	88.9	94.4	80.6	101.0	86.1	85.6	87.4	86.2	89.1	91.8	103.1	80.3	100.7	90.2
2nd quarter	94.9	90.4	95.3	81.0	100.4	86.0	85.4	87.5	86.8	90.2	92.9	103.1	80.5	99.8	89.3
3rd quarter	95.4	92.0	96.4	81.5	100.0	85.9	85.4	87.2	87.3	90.2	93.9	104.1	81.0	99.4	89.8
4th quarter	96.1	93.3	97.1	83.1	101.0	86.9	86.5	88.0	87.9	90.7	95.5	105.4	81.4	99.0	89.8

YEAR AND QUARTER	Mining	NEW PLANT AND EQUIPMENT SPENDING[1] (Billions of dollars, seasonally adjusted annual rates)								
		Manufacturing								
		Total	Durables							
			Total	Stone, clay and glass products	Primary metals	Blast furnaces and steel mills	Non-ferrous metals	Fab-ricated metals	Machinery except electrical	Electrical machinery
1961	1.26	15.53	7.43	0.70	1.28	0.86	0.29	0.52	1.11	1.05
1962	1.41	16.03	7.81	0.72	1.25	0.76	0.34	0.59	1.26	0.99
1963	1.26	17.27	8.64	0.70	1.51	0.88	0.46	0.69	1.24	1.02
1964	1.33	21.23	10.98	0.81	2.22	1.44	0.56	0.85	1.61	1.17
1965	1.36	25.41	13.49	0.86	2.57	1.59	0.71	0.86	2.24	1.69
1966	1.42	31.37	17.23	1.13	3.06	1.72	1.01	1.14	2.91	2.51
1967	1.38	32.25	17.83	0.92	3.31	1.90	1.11	1.29	3.02	3.13
1968	1.44	32.34	17.93	0.89	3.45	2.01	1.11	1.36	2.90	3.16
1969	1.77	36.27	19.97	1.12	3.29	1.83	1.06	1.34	3.63	3.27
1970	2.02	36.99	19.80	1.06	3.24	1.63	1.18	1.22	3.78	3.49
1971	2.67	33.60	16.78	0.94	2.69	1.27	1.02	1.20	3.15	3.03
1972	2.88	35.42	18.22	1.34	2.44	1.07	0.97	1.43	3.23	2.83
1973	3.30	42.35	22.63	1.58	2.94	1.25	1.22	1.81	3.95	3.48
1974	4.58	52.48	26.77	1.65	4.27	1.97	1.77	1.93	5.13	3.80
1975	6.12	53.66	25.37	1.67	5.43	3.08	1.72	1.96	4.86	3.08
1976	7.63	58.53	27.50	1.91	5.32	3.13	1.42	2.20	5.43	3.61
1977	9.81	67.48	32.77	2.30	4.97	2.88	1.30	2.45	6.35	4.61
1978	10.55	78.13	39.02	3.05	5.07	2.65	1.45	2.93	7.19	5.92
1979	11.05	95.13	47.72	3.69	5.96	3.36	1.60	3.17	9.80	7.69
1980	12.71	112.60	54.82	3.69	6.65	3.70	2.02	3.26	10.68	10.20
1981	15.81	128.68	58.93	3.03	7.19	3.87	2.34	3.42	12.39	11.41
1982	14.11	123.97	54.58	2.70	6.78	4.27	1.72	2.81	12.28	12.21
1983	10.64	117.35	51.61	2.62	5.89	3.66	1.57	2.56	11.98	12.68
1984	11.86	139.61	64.57	3.13	6.83	3.99	1.96	3.14	13.62	16.22
1985	12.00	152.88	70.87	3.58	7.45	4.66	1.75	3.25	13.83	17.09
1986	8.15	137.95	65.68	3.13	6.74	3.76	1.75	3.61	11.36	15.64
1987	8.28	141.06	68.03	3.32	8.59	5.30	1.98	3.62	11.87	16.84
1988	9.29	163.45	77.04	3.63	10.99	7.01	2.51	3.91	13.70	20.84
1989	9.21	183.80	82.56	4.00	12.03	7.87	2.64	4.17	14.58	20.46
1990	9.88	192.61	82.58	3.29	12.16	7.78	2.88	4.39	13.66	22.04
1991	10.02	182.81	77.64	2.89	10.74	6.53	2.81	4.03	12.68	20.97
1992	8.88	174.02	73.32	3.36	9.76	5.64	2.67	3.67	10.64	20.42
1993	10.08	179.47	81.45	4.31	9.87	5.64	2.59	3.92	9.71	24.41
1985:										
1st quarter	12.13	147.69	68.84	3.36	7.22	4.34	1.87	3.13	13.87	17.66
2nd quarter	12.56	155.97	72.87	3.77	7.33	4.61	1.71	3.03	14.69	18.73
3rd quarter	12.14	154.76	70.77	3.69	7.46	4.68	1.73	3.38	13.65	16.78
4th quarter	11.19	151.98	70.61	3.47	7.69	4.88	1.72	3.44	13.20	15.72
1986:										
1st quarter	9.71	142.28	65.33	3.18	7.19	4.29	1.71	3.65	12.02	14.42
2nd quarter	8.16	138.09	65.38	2.81	6.57	3.42	1.82	3.62	11.07	16.26
3rd quarter	7.35	133.95	65.53	2.95	6.29	3.61	1.55	3.52	11.25	14.97
4th quarter	7.52	138.07	66.31	3.51	6.95	3.75	1.89	3.64	11.18	16.55
1987:										
1st quarter	7.49	135.22	67.34	3.07	7.47	4.57	1.59	3.57	11.12	16.51
2nd quarter	7.86	137.20	66.48	3.18	8.17	4.95	1.94	3.51	11.00	16.35
3rd quarter	8.60	142.75	68.57	3.57	8.81	5.44	2.09	3.61	12.29	17.07
4th quarter	9.03	146.91	69.43	3.42	9.53	5.94	2.24	3.79	12.72	17.29
1988:										
1st quarter	9.29	155.63	73.68	3.44	10.29	6.35	2.49	3.86	13.68	19.40
2nd quarter	9.59	159.99	76.04	3.71	10.66	6.80	2.41	4.05	13.45	21.05
3rd quarter	9.25	165.72	77.43	3.53	11.61	7.48	2.59	3.88	13.01	21.04
4th quarter	9.01	169.85	80.02	3.78	11.22	7.21	2.57	3.87	14.48	21.60
1989:										
1st quarter	8.99	173.07	79.84	4.03	11.10	7.15	2.48	4.00	14.26	20.46
2nd quarter	9.18	180.51	82.14	4.13	11.88	7.72	2.61	4.10	14.77	19.95
3rd quarter	9.22	185.92	83.80	4.12	12.17	7.97	2.67	4.38	14.49	21.14
4th quarter	9.39	191.98	83.86	3.78	12.66	8.40	2.78	4.19	14.77	20.36
1990:										
1st quarter	9.70	191.73	85.75	3.61	12.60	8.23	2.90	4.52	14.64	23.07
2nd quarter	9.76	194.70	83.74	3.32	12.32	7.92	2.87	4.43	14.50	22.09
3rd quarter	9.89	195.06	83.16	3.26	11.91	7.46	2.91	4.44	13.85	22.15
4th quarter	10.13	189.25	79.01	3.02	11.94	7.63	2.84	4.20	12.16	21.25
1991:										
1st quarter	10.05	190.50	80.31	2.92	11.91	7.54	2.92	4.18	13.12	21.18
2nd quarter	10.09	187.18	78.89	2.78	11.03	6.79	2.88	4.05	12.67	20.81
3rd quarter	9.97	178.24	75.54	2.82	10.75	6.70	2.69	4.01	12.59	21.08
4th quarter	9.98	178.33	76.85	3.02	9.72	5.53	2.75	3.89	12.49	20.95
1992:										
1st quarter	8.99	173.14	73.26	3.00	9.82	5.76	2.67	3.65	10.31	20.27
2nd quarter	9.20	172.52	73.74	3.13	10.01	5.92	2.54	3.62	11.46	20.93
3rd quarter	8.96	173.05	72.63	3.32	9.58	5.58	2.64	3.49	10.54	20.55
4th quarter	8.43	176.74	73.64	3.83	9.67	5.41	2.80	3.88	10.29	20.08
1993:										
1st quarter	8.98	173.99	78.19	4.16	8.94	5.22	2.26	3.54	10.39	24.04
2nd quarter	9.10	177.55	80.33	4.32	9.62	5.52	2.58	3.95	8.48	24.30
3rd quarter	11.09	182.48	82.74	4.27	10.16	5.80	2.64	4.02	9.93	23.91
4th quarter	10.92	182.15	83.64	4.44	10.53	5.88	2.81	4.12	10.05	25.20
1994:										
1st quarter	11.43	185.04	86.03	5.03	11.28	6.93	2.31	3.99	9.10	25.33
2nd quarter	10.70	193.99	91.71	5.42	12.08	7.26	2.55	3.92	9.17	28.36

1. These series were discontinued in mid-1994; see NOTES.

YEAR AND QUARTER	NEW PLANT AND EQUIPMENT SPENDING[1] (Billions of dollars, seasonally adjusted annual rates)									
	Durables—Continued			Nondurables						
	Transportation equipment	Motor vehicles	Aircraft	Total	Food and beverages	Textiles	Paper	Chemicals	Petroleum	Rubber
1961	1.78	1.38	0.30	8.10	1.50	0.35	0.62	1.60	2.97	0.36
1962	1.98	1.45	0.40	8.22	1.45	0.39	0.62	1.58	3.08	0.38
1963	2.37	1.82	0.44	8.63	1.50	0.43	0.70	1.72	3.10	0.39
1964	3.08	2.48	0.41	10.25	1.75	0.59	0.91	2.10	3.51	0.47
1965	3.74	3.00	0.53	11.92	1.87	0.79	1.07	2.82	3.88	0.59
1966	4.61	3.13	1.17	14.15	2.11	0.96	1.32	3.35	4.48	0.65
1967	4.44	2.85	1.25	14.42	2.05	0.77	1.49	3.08	4.84	0.67
1968	4.25	2.67	1.23	14.40	2.20	0.65	1.27	2.80	4.96	0.96
1969	4.80	2.99	1.29	16.31	2.76	0.86	1.62	3.01	5.26	1.07
1970	4.65	3.05	0.88	17.19	3.32	0.80	1.74	3.38	5.16	0.92
1971	3.54	2.42	0.63	16.82	3.35	0.90	1.29	3.27	5.21	0.79
1972	4.41	3.00	0.68	17.20	3.28	1.06	1.46	3.38	4.79	1.03
1973	5.60	3.83	0.79	19.72	3.74	1.02	1.99	4.17	4.61	1.56
1974	6.60	4.29	1.21	25.71	4.25	1.06	2.88	6.18	7.04	1.61
1975	5.46	3.33	1.19	28.28	4.38	0.86	2.93	7.12	9.07	1.20
1976	5.79	3.60	1.02	31.03	5.39	0.98	2.99	7.37	10.02	1.37
1977	8.32	5.82	1.14	34.71	5.72	1.18	3.48	7.35	11.82	1.77
1978	10.97	7.10	1.77	39.10	6.59	1.32	3.78	7.58	13.68	2.22
1979	13.47	8.06	2.71	47.41	7.42	1.45	5.18	9.24	16.77	2.18
1980	16.10	8.54	3.60	57.77	8.51	1.60	6.39	10.62	22.75	1.68
1981	16.91	9.10	3.40	69.75	10.13	1.76	5.95	11.99	31.94	1.77
1982	13.55	7.13	3.45	69.39	9.43	1.55	5.47	11.44	33.50	1.72
1983	11.86	6.56	2.95	65.74	8.46	1.63	5.73	11.59	29.47	2.05
1984	16.63	10.17	3.63	75.04	9.71	2.00	6.90	13.46	32.56	2.62
1985	19.61	13.39	3.51	82.01	11.35	1.82	8.14	14.35	34.06	3.34
1986	18.86	12.79	3.86	72.28	11.62	1.71	8.26	14.54	23.05	3.30
1987	16.73	10.88	3.60	73.03	12.10	2.00	8.54	13.92	22.06	2.94
1988	15.76	9.75	3.49	86.41	14.16	2.18	10.92	16.62	26.03	3.26
1989	18.71	11.49	4.17	101.24	15.89	2.25	15.58	18.47	30.08	3.79
1990	17.89	11.28	4.02	110.04	16.36	2.18	16.53	20.63	34.79	3.48
1991	17.19	10.20	4.05	105.17	17.43	1.96	11.50	21.52	35.59	3.43
1992	16.06	8.67	4.36	100.69	18.95	2.05	10.53	23.15	29.59	3.85
1993	19.16	12.28	3.23	98.02	18.78	2.27	10.31	21.83	28.71	3.32
1985:										
1st quarter	17.87	11.32	3.59	78.85	10.70	2.06	7.58	14.28	32.98	2.99
2nd quarter	19.32	13.16	3.46	83.10	11.45	1.87	7.74	14.70	35.72	3.03
3rd quarter	19.59	12.97	3.79	83.99	11.46	1.78	8.23	14.45	35.10	3.34
4th quarter	20.89	15.26	3.22	81.37	11.62	1.55	8.75	14.00	32.34	3.89
1986:										
1st quarter	18.73	12.67	3.87	76.95	10.62	1.54	8.52	13.85	29.34	3.92
2nd quarter	18.59	12.60	3.89	72.71	11.47	1.77	8.50	14.26	23.59	3.46
3rd quarter	20.46	14.62	3.69	68.41	11.96	1.58	8.35	14.07	19.50	3.16
4th quarter	17.85	11.43	3.98	71.76	12.26	1.92	7.77	15.67	20.79	2.81
1987:										
1st quarter	18.93	13.27	3.57	67.88	12.13	1.94	7.79	12.78	19.43	2.71
2nd quarter	17.49	11.47	3.71	70.72	11.85	2.10	8.14	13.76	20.47	3.03
3rd quarter	15.88	9.92	3.69	74.17	12.09	1.91	8.56	14.33	23.05	3.03
4th quarter	15.32	9.54	3.45	77.48	12.36	2.03	9.35	14.54	24.14	2.94
1988:										
1st quarter	15.25	9.47	3.32	81.95	13.80	2.11	9.60	15.53	25.19	3.25
2nd quarter	15.26	9.35	3.44	83.95	13.84	2.14	10.48	16.54	25.42	2.82
3rd quarter	16.02	10.01	3.57	88.28	14.04	2.26	11.10	18.02	25.89	3.53
4th quarter	16.36	10.04	3.60	89.83	14.83	2.19	12.01	16.29	26.95	3.43
1989:										
1st quarter	17.39	9.93	4.49	93.23	14.91	2.16	13.81	17.46	26.58	3.40
2nd quarter	18.54	11.62	3.95	98.37	16.26	2.20	14.39	17.90	28.31	3.82
3rd quarter	18.65	11.75	3.74	102.12	15.73	2.29	15.67	18.35	30.52	3.96
4th quarter	19.83	12.27	4.50	108.12	16.45	2.33	17.75	19.75	33.26	3.90
1990:										
1st quarter	18.80	12.03	4.30	105.98	15.98	2.23	17.30	20.08	31.50	3.52
2nd quarter	18.19	11.33	4.12	110.95	16.89	2.17	18.53	20.24	33.80	3.59
3rd quarter	18.28	11.63	4.03	111.90	16.36	2.21	16.72	20.40	36.01	3.50
4th quarter	16.63	10.43	3.69	110.24	16.21	2.10	14.20	21.44	36.61	3.33
1991:										
1st quarter	17.50	10.99	3.63	110.19	17.21	2.09	12.85	20.97	39.34	3.52
2nd quarter	17.86	11.23	3.84	108.29	16.82	1.95	11.64	21.51	38.74	3.34
3rd quarter	16.09	8.97	4.07	102.70	17.69	1.85	11.39	21.75	33.80	3.26
4th quarter	17.56	9.89	4.66	101.48	18.02	1.95	10.57	21.61	32.17	3.58
1992:										
1st quarter	17.02	9.26	4.93	99.87	18.65	1.94	11.01	22.02	30.15	3.73
2nd quarter	15.42	7.96	4.52	98.78	18.59	2.17	9.84	22.75	29.01	3.64
3rd quarter	15.69	8.23	4.46	100.42	18.72	2.12	10.25	23.31	29.56	3.81
4th quarter	16.16	9.28	3.56	103.09	19.81	1.98	10.94	24.05	29.67	4.15
1993:										
1st quarter	17.23	10.22	3.51	95.80	19.79	2.05	10.60	21.42	26.07	3.00
2nd quarter	19.95	13.02	3.40	97.22	19.24	2.16	10.37	21.57	28.38	3.24
3rd quarter	20.27	13.68	3.00	99.74	18.99	2.37	9.79	22.10	30.44	3.41
4th quarter	18.86	11.89	3.02	98.51	17.29	2.50	10.45	22.09	29.30	3.54
1994:										
1st quarter	21.49	15.16	2.52	99.02	17.01	2.20	10.01	21.93	29.60	3.44
2nd quarter	21.07	14.10	2.81	102.28	18.77	2.41	10.35	22.91	28.83	4.30

1. These series were discontinued in mid-1994; see NOTES.

YEAR AND QUARTER	NEW PLANT AND EQUIPMENT SPENDING[1] (Billions of dollars, seasonally adjusted annual rates)										
	Transportation				Public Utilities			Commu-nications	Whole-sale and retail trade	Finance and Insur-ance	Personal and busi-ness services
	Total	Railroads	Air	Other	Total	Electric	Gas and other				
1961	3.14	1.19	0.73	1.22	5.20	3.78	1.42	3.59	4.14	1.39	4.08
1962	3.59	1.43	0.53	1.63	5.12	3.76	1.36	4.02	4.53	1.46	4.69
1963	3.64	1.72	0.35	1.57	5.33	4.01	1.32	4.19	4.91	1.68	5.39
1964	4.71	2.20	0.92	1.60	5.80	4.27	1.53	4.75	5.72	1.90	5.84
1965	5.66	2.60	1.08	1.98	6.49	4.76	1.73	5.47	6.51	2.21	6.41
1966	6.68	3.09	1.66	1.93	7.82	5.73	2.09	6.23	7.09	2.23	7.57
1967	6.57	2.50	2.28	1.79	9.33	7.30	2.03	6.61	6.88	2.46	7.27
1968	6.91	2.15	2.54	2.23	10.52	7.97	2.54	7.07	7.04	3.03	8.09
1969	7.23	2.61	2.28	2.34	11.70	9.05	2.65	8.57	7.62	3.62	8.96
1970	7.17	2.48	2.50	2.18	13.03	10.56	2.46	10.40	8.78	3.91	9.62
1971	6.42	2.39	1.33	2.71	14.70	12.28	2.42	10.96	9.32	4.66	10.58
1972	7.14	2.35	1.93	2.86	16.26	13.60	2.66	12.27	10.95	6.37	12.11
1973	8.00	2.91	1.89	3.21	17.99	15.07	2.92	13.30	13.18	7.75	14.16
1974	9.16	3.63	1.80	3.73	19.96	16.85	3.11	14.46	15.02	8.45	15.56
1975	9.95	3.88	1.54	4.53	20.23	16.94	3.29	12.90	14.77	9.96	14.83
1976	11.10	4.25	1.13	5.72	22.90	19.29	3.61	13.66	17.61	9.19	17.83
1977	12.20	4.67	2.15	5.38	27.83	23.24	4.58	16.27	20.84	10.13	20.28
1978	12.07	4.93	3.00	4.14	32.10	26.70	5.40	19.79	26.14	13.52	24.52
1979	13.91	5.86	3.73	4.32	37.53	30.78	6.75	23.55	30.81	18.23	25.06
1980	13.56	5.91	3.66	3.98	41.32	33.30	8.01	26.80	31.95	22.57	24.89
1981	12.67	5.03	3.48	4.15	47.17	37.37	9.80	30.09	35.68	28.38	26.26
1982	11.75	4.28	3.61	3.86	53.58	43.65	9.93	30.06	36.78	30.35	25.58
1983	10.81	3.85	3.38	3.57	52.95	44.87	8.08	27.85	44.45	32.04	25.08
1984	13.44	5.32	3.31	4.81	57.53	45.18	12.35	31.60	53.39	37.89	28.52
1985	14.57	5.65	4.11	4.81	59.58	44.01	15.58	37.08	60.10	45.15	28.76
1986	15.05	5.33	5.17	4.55	56.61	41.03	15.58	38.22	65.37	49.57	28.44
1987	15.07	4.72	5.34	5.01	56.26	39.10	17.17	37.17	68.53	54.06	30.07
1988	16.63	5.52	5.63	5.48	60.37	40.90	19.47	37.24	76.37	59.22	32.93
1989	18.84	6.26	6.73	5.85	66.28	44.81	21.47	39.83	84.52	70.30	34.62
1990	21.47	6.40	8.87	6.20	67.21	44.10	23.11	43.13	95.63	68.96	33.72
1991	22.66	5.95	10.17	6.54	66.57	43.76	22.82	42.68	104.99	63.98	34.67
1992	22.64	6.67	8.93	7.04	72.21	48.22	23.99	41.53	116.23	72.76	38.32
1993	21.77	6.14	6.42	9.22	75.98	52.55	23.43	45.02	131.37	80.47	42.57
1985:											
1st quarter	13.50	5.35	3.40	4.75	59.17	44.80	14.37	36.07	58.32	41.74	28.61
2nd quarter	14.29	5.79	3.33	5.17	59.52	44.13	15.39	37.56	60.57	43.31	28.54
3rd quarter	14.86	5.86	4.60	4.39	59.50	43.48	16.02	38.50	60.24	46.41	27.96
4th quarter	15.35	5.47	5.00	4.88	59.66	43.51	16.15	36.08	61.01	48.07	29.89
1986:											
1st quarter	14.82	5.25	5.31	4.26	57.86	42.31	15.55	39.33	62.15	49.84	28.17
2nd quarter	15.28	5.38	5.50	4.39	56.98	41.26	15.72	40.24	64.68	46.18	28.04
3rd quarter	14.77	5.50	4.69	4.58	56.30	40.85	15.46	36.33	66.13	50.92	28.54
4th quarter	15.11	5.16	5.10	4.84	55.44	39.78	15.66	37.17	67.97	50.86	29.00
1987:											
1st quarter	14.70	4.49	5.58	4.64	54.52	38.59	15.93	36.26	66.16	52.40	28.88
2nd quarter	14.53	4.66	4.94	4.93	54.49	39.03	15.46	36.15	67.72	51.78	29.72
3rd quarter	15.27	4.84	5.14	5.29	57.47	38.97	18.50	37.87	67.72	54.23	30.39
4th quarter	15.58	4.84	5.64	5.11	57.76	39.47	18.29	38.08	71.96	56.84	31.25
1988:											
1st quarter	15.97	5.32	5.32	5.33	57.43	38.86	18.56	36.25	73.68	56.20	32.06
2nd quarter	16.50	5.54	5.44	5.52	58.67	39.62	19.05	37.81	74.84	61.36	33.27
3rd quarter	16.65	5.43	5.74	5.48	61.08	41.54	19.54	37.44	77.50	59.51	32.83
4th quarter	17.26	5.73	5.94	5.58	63.21	42.77	20.44	37.22	79.05	59.28	33.55
1989:											
1st quarter	17.60	6.10	5.56	5.94	65.92	43.86	22.06	39.46	81.63	65.46	35.07
2nd quarter	18.42	5.81	6.79	5.83	68.74	46.70	22.05	38.16	83.71	68.10	35.05
3rd quarter	20.68	6.29	8.44	5.96	65.30	44.62	20.67	39.77	86.33	71.07	35.43
4th quarter	18.69	6.81	6.22	5.66	65.23	43.91	21.33	41.49	85.97	75.21	33.10
1990:											
1st quarter	21.74	6.51	9.07	6.16	65.45	43.68	21.77	42.41	94.11	71.68	34.33
2nd quarter	21.72	6.64	9.23	5.85	65.05	42.96	22.09	43.44	94.63	72.39	33.93
3rd quarter	20.47	5.55	9.08	5.85	67.96	44.12	23.84	42.78	94.42	68.82	33.98
4th quarter	22.06	6.95	8.25	6.85	69.39	45.18	24.21	43.55	99.10	64.32	32.68
1991:											
1st quarter	23.00	5.74	10.88	6.39	67.15	43.56	23.59	43.14	100.80	65.82	33.19
2nd quarter	22.79	6.29	9.93	6.57	65.02	43.09	21.93	41.84	104.36	60.86	33.25
3rd quarter	21.93	6.49	8.99	6.45	67.10	43.67	23.43	42.54	107.29	64.88	35.13
4th quarter	23.13	5.18	11.23	6.73	66.76	44.37	22.39	43.13	106.65	64.88	37.01
1992:											
1st quarter	21.82	6.79	8.73	6.30	69.09	46.06	23.03	39.26	110.90	73.49	37.54
2nd quarter	23.32	6.40	9.77	7.15	72.56	48.45	24.12	41.35	113.18	71.61	37.55
3rd quarter	23.66	6.87	9.36	7.43	72.48	48.37	24.11	42.18	117.79	72.02	37.68
4th quarter	21.66	6.64	7.80	7.22	73.79	49.37	24.42	42.72	121.83	73.87	40.35
1993:											
1st quarter	22.38	6.16	7.26	8.96	73.78	49.98	23.79	43.79	124.11	77.60	38.84
2nd quarter	21.50	5.94	6.63	8.92	74.45	50.61	23.83	45.68	127.91	79.13	43.63
3rd quarter	21.32	5.89	6.70	8.74	75.94	52.96	22.98	45.06	133.21	82.46	43.01
4th quarter	21.84	6.55	5.06	10.23	78.87	55.60	23.27	45.28	138.74	82.29	44.42
1994:											
1st quarter	22.47	7.46	4.23	10.77	73.20	48.68	24.51	43.56	145.46	88.51	49.67
2nd quarter	19.59	5.36	4.53	9.70	76.51	53.55	22.96	42.97	152.63	91.53	49.16

1. These series were discontinued in mid-1994; see NOTES.

PERSONAL INCOME AND ITS DISPOSITION—Continued
(Billions of dollars, monthly data are at seasonally adjusted annual rates)

YEAR AND MONTH	Personal income	Wage and salary disburse-ments	Other labor income	Proprietors' income [1] Farm	Proprietors' income [1] Nonfarm	Rental income of per-sons [2]	Personal dividend income	Personal interest income	Transfer pay-ments to persons	Less: Personal contribu-tions for social insur-ance	Personal tax and nontax pay-ments	Dispos-able personal income
1969:												
January	746.8	495.5	27.1	12.9	64.2	22.8	25.0	57.4	67.4	25.4	104.4	642.4
February	752.5	498.2	27.3	13.0	64.7	23.0	25.0	58.4	68.3	25.5	108.2	644.3
March	759.4	503.3	27.5	13.3	64.6	23.3	25.2	59.2	68.7	25.7	111.0	648.4
April	765.2	507.2	27.7	14.0	64.7	23.5	25.1	59.6	69.3	25.8	114.5	650.7
May	770.8	511.3	27.9	14.3	64.9	23.6	25.0	60.0	69.7	26.0	110.3	660.4
June	776.5	515.5	28.2	14.5	64.9	23.7	25.5	60.6	69.7	26.1	108.7	667.8
July	783.8	521.8	28.5	14.6	64.8	23.7	25.1	61.1	70.5	26.4	108.5	675.2
August	790.4	526.9	28.8	14.9	65.2	23.6	25.0	61.7	70.9	26.6	109.5	681.0
September	795.2	530.3	29.2	15.2	65.0	23.5	25.0	62.3	71.3	26.7	110.4	684.7
October	799.7	533.9	29.5	15.9	64.1	23.4	25.0	62.6	72.1	26.8	110.7	689.0
November	803.0	536.4	29.8	16.2	63.7	23.3	24.9	63.2	72.5	26.9	110.7	692.3
December	808.1	538.9	30.2	16.2	63.9	23.3	25.1	64.0	73.6	27.0	111.7	696.4
1970:												
January	809.6	539.9	30.5	16.0	63.8	23.3	24.7	64.5	74.3	27.3	110.0	699.6
February	814.0	542.2	30.9	15.7	64.3	23.2	24.2	65.3	75.4	27.4	110.2	703.7
March	818.3	545.5	31.2	15.4	64.2	23.3	24.0	66.3	76.0	27.5	111.0	707.3
April	836.6	550.4	31.5	14.4	64.5	23.4	23.8	66.9	89.6	27.8	112.0	724.6
May	833.1	551.9	31.9	14.1	64.8	23.6	23.7	67.5	83.3	27.8	110.4	722.6
June	833.7	551.0	32.3	14.2	64.6	23.5	23.4	68.7	83.8	27.7	111.9	721.9
July	840.7	554.2	32.7	15.0	65.4	23.2	23.2	70.0	85.0	28.1	106.2	734.4
August	845.3	556.2	33.1	15.1	65.8	23.0	23.0	71.1	86.2	28.2	106.3	739.1
September	850.8	557.5	33.5	15.0	66.4	23.2	23.0	72.0	88.5	28.2	107.0	743.8
October	850.8	554.3	33.9	14.3	66.6	23.8	23.1	72.3	90.5	28.0	107.1	743.7
November	852.9	555.1	34.2	14.2	67.0	24.4	23.1	72.5	90.5	28.1	107.8	745.1
December	859.4	559.4	34.4	14.2	67.5	24.7	22.3	73.2	91.9	28.2	107.8	751.6
1971:												
January	868.4	567.4	34.5	14.8	68.0	24.4	23.8	73.7	92.0	30.1	103.5	764.9
February	871.8	570.0	34.8	15.1	67.4	23.5	23.6	74.4	93.3	30.2	104.5	767.3
March	878.1	572.7	35.1	15.2	68.7	24.3	23.3	74.9	94.2	30.3	105.1	773.0
April	884.1	576.3	35.6	15.3	69.6	24.6	23.3	74.9	94.9	30.4	106.2	777.9
May	890.7	581.1	36.0	15.3	70.2	24.9	23.4	75.0	95.5	30.6	107.0	783.7
June	911.4	582.6	36.4	15.3	70.8	24.9	23.5	75.3	113.1	30.6	107.5	803.9
July	902.1	584.2	36.8	14.8	71.6	24.9	23.5	76.0	101.0	30.7	107.9	794.2
August	909.2	589.8	37.3	14.8	72.0	24.7	23.6	76.6	101.3	31.0	108.8	800.4
September	913.2	590.0	37.7	15.1	72.5	24.7	23.6	77.0	103.5	30.9	110.1	803.0
October	916.2	591.6	38.2	16.3	73.1	24.6	23.7	76.9	102.9	30.9	111.6	804.6
November	923.5	595.2	38.7	16.4	74.3	24.6	23.9	77.0	104.5	31.0	115.2	808.2
December	933.6	605.5	39.2	16.4	74.7	24.9	22.5	77.4	104.6	31.5	116.6	817.0
1972:												
January	942.6	613.4	39.6	14.8	75.7	25.4	24.6	77.7	104.9	33.5	126.1	816.5
February	954.2	620.5	40.2	14.9	75.3	25.8	24.8	78.2	108.3	33.9	129.1	825.1
March	960.6	624.0	40.9	15.4	75.9	25.7	24.8	78.9	109.0	33.9	131.6	829.0
April	967.1	627.9	41.8	17.0	77.1	25.2	24.9	79.5	107.6	34.0	132.4	834.7
May	972.6	630.5	42.4	17.8	77.6	24.7	25.2	80.1	108.4	34.1	130.2	842.4
June	966.3	633.9	43.0	18.6	75.4	14.6	25.3	81.0	108.8	34.2	130.3	836.1
July	984.6	636.1	43.5	19.5	79.0	24.4	25.7	81.9	109.5	35.1	130.8	853.7
August	998.0	642.8	44.1	20.7	81.1	24.4	25.8	82.9	110.8	34.6	132.5	865.5
September	1 005.9	648.6	44.5	21.9	80.2	24.7	25.8	84.0	110.7	34.7	133.6	872.3
October	1 026.0	656.2	44.9	23.8	81.4	25.2	26.0	84.6	118.9	35.0	135.1	891.0
November	1 040.0	661.9	45.4	24.6	83.0	25.6	26.1	85.7	122.9	35.2	136.0	904.0
December	1 048.0	668.2	45.9	24.9	83.8	25.4	26.4	87.2	121.5	35.3	136.3	911.7
1973:												
January	1 051.2	676.1	46.6	23.4	84.5	24.6	26.3	88.5	122.6	41.3	137.5	913.8
February	1 061.6	684.2	47.1	23.9	84.3	24.1	26.6	89.6	123.4	41.7	134.9	926.7
March	1 070.6	689.2	47.6	25.4	83.6	24.4	26.9	90.3	124.9	41.8	133.3	937.3
April	1 078.9	695.3	47.9	29.0	82.5	23.6	27.3	90.2	125.1	42.0	134.3	944.6
May	1 091.5	699.9	48.3	30.7	83.4	26.7	27.2	90.6	126.8	42.2	137.7	953.8
June	1 100.4	705.5	48.8	32.0	83.8	26.8	27.4	91.9	126.6	42.4	138.6	961.8
July	1 106.5	711.4	49.2	31.2	84.4	25.1	27.5	93.6	126.8	42.8	140.2	966.3
August	1 117.3	715.1	49.8	33.2	84.3	24.8	27.9	95.6	129.6	43.0	141.7	975.6
September	1 130.0	721.7	50.3	35.3	84.5	25.3	28.1	97.5	130.6	43.3	144.0	986.1
October	1 149.1	728.5	50.9	42.2	84.6	27.3	28.3	98.6	131.9	43.3	145.9	1 003.2
November	1 163.0	736.7	51.5	43.2	85.1	28.4	28.6	100.1	133.0	43.7	148.5	1 014.5
December	1 170.3	740.7	52.1	41.9	85.2	29.0	29.5	102.2	133.4	43.7	150.4	1 019.9
1974:												
January	1 171.1	744.1	52.6	35.9	85.9	28.6	29.2	103.7	137.7	46.5	149.1	1 022.0
February	1 176.3	748.3	53.2	32.5	87.4	28.0	28.9	105.6	139.3	46.8	151.5	1 024.8
March	1 180.8	751.8	53.8	28.9	88.6	27.4	29.2	107.5	140.4	46.9	152.8	1 027.9
April	1 185.5	756.6	54.4	23.8	88.2	25.2	29.3	109.1	146.0	47.1	153.8	1 031.7
May	1 199.3	766.0	55.2	21.7	89.5	26.6	29.6	110.5	147.8	47.6	157.4	1 041.9
June	1 209.9	774.6	55.9	20.9	89.5	26.4	29.9	112.2	148.6	48.0	159.9	1 050.0
July	1 227.5	780.9	56.8	22.8	91.3	26.6	29.9	113.4	154.2	48.4	161.8	1 065.7
August	1 234.6	783.3	57.6	23.4	92.1	26.4	29.8	114.9	155.4	48.5	162.7	1 071.8
September	1 243.5	789.1	58.5	24.0	92.0	25.4	30.0	116.2	157.2	48.8	164.1	1 079.3
October	1 253.5	795.1	59.4	25.6	91.0	23.6	29.8	117.9	160.0	49.0	165.6	1 087.9
November	1 251.5	790.6	60.2	25.6	90.9	22.3	29.7	118.5	162.4	48.7	165.1	1 086.3
December	1 257.6	791.2	60.9	24.9	91.7	22.1	29.3	119.1	167.1	48.7	165.5	1 092.1

1. Includes inventory valuation and capital consumption adjustments.
2. Includes capital consumption adjustment.

PERSONAL INCOME AND ITS DISPOSITION—Continued
(Billions of dollars, monthly data are at seasonally adjusted annual rates)

YEAR AND MONTH	Personal income	Wage and salary disburse- ments	Other labor income	Proprietors' income [1] Farm	Proprietors' income [1] Nonfarm	Rental income of per- sons [2]	Personal dividend income	Personal interest income	Transfer pay- ments to persons	Less: Personal contribu- tions for social insur- ance	Personal tax and nontax pay- ments	Dispos- able personal income
1975:												
January	1 262.1	792.3	61.3	22.0	94.0	23.1	29.2	119.2	170.6	49.6	166.1	1 096.0
February	1 267.7	790.0	61.9	21.2	94.2	24.1	29.1	119.8	176.8	49.4	165.8	1 101.9
March	1 272.3	792.7	62.6	20.9	93.1	24.8	29.1	120.3	178.4	49.5	166.4	1 105.8
April	1 279.0	793.5	63.2	21.3	94.3	24.9	28.9	120.3	182.0	49.5	147.5	1 131.5
May	1 291.7	800.6	64.1	21.8	95.6	25.0	28.8	120.9	184.6	49.8	87.4	1 204.3
June	1 323.2	806.3	65.0	22.8	96.6	25.0	28.8	122.0	207.0	50.0	154.5	1 168.8
July	1 321.0	810.9	66.1	25.3	98.1	24.9	28.9	123.0	193.8	50.2	159.7	1 161.4
August	1 337.8	823.1	67.2	26.3	98.7	24.8	29.1	124.2	195.2	50.7	162.6	1 175.2
September	1 349.3	829.1	68.3	26.9	100.0	24.8	29.6	125.3	196.5	51.0	163.6	1 185.7
October	1 364.6	837.8	69.4	27.4	101.4	24.8	29.9	126.4	199.1	51.4	165.9	1 198.7
November	1 374.4	846.1	70.6	26.9	102.7	25.0	30.3	127.0	197.6	51.8	167.8	1 206.7
December	1 384.7	852.6	71.8	25.8	104.2	25.2	29.0	127.8	200.4	52.1	169.6	1 215.2
1976:												
January	1 401.2	864.9	73.1	22.8	106.0	25.5	31.2	128.3	203.5	53.9	171.0	1 230.2
February	1 412.3	871.7	74.3	21.4	108.3	25.6	32.3	128.7	204.1	54.2	171.7	1 240.6
March	1 419.6	876.2	75.5	20.1	110.4	25.4	32.5	130.1	203.7	54.4	172.0	1 247.6
April	1 429.9	883.3	76.8	19.2	111.3	25.1	33.4	131.5	203.7	54.7	176.5	1 253.4
May	1 439.3	890.7	78.0	18.5	112.4	24.8	34.5	132.9	202.5	55.0	179.0	1 260.3
June	1 446.7	893.3	79.2	17.9	114.1	23.4	35.0	134.4	204.9	55.1	180.8	1 265.9
July	1 464.2	900.6	80.4	17.6	116.3	23.9	35.6	134.7	210.9	55.6	183.3	1 280.9
August	1 476.1	909.4	81.6	17.3	117.3	23.4	36.0	135.5	211.3	56.0	185.9	1 290.2
September	1 486.0	914.6	82.8	17.1	119.1	23.4	36.4	137.1	211.9	56.2	188.2	1 297.8
October	1 493.7	920.1	83.8	16.9	118.7	23.5	37.1	138.7	211.5	56.5	190.5	1 303.1
November	1 515.2	930.9	85.0	17.0	122.4	23.7	37.7	140.6	215.0	57.0	193.5	1 321.6
December	1 528.6	938.0	86.3	17.4	123.4	23.9	38.1	142.3	216.6	57.3	195.6	1 333.0
1977:												
January	1 533.8	939.3	87.9	19.0	124.0	23.9	37.8	144.9	215.9	58.7	196.6	1 337.2
February	1 550.8	950.5	89.2	18.9	124.7	23.8	38.3	146.9	217.8	59.3	216.3	1 334.5
March	1 565.4	959.5	90.4	18.4	125.7	23.7	38.7	148.8	219.9	59.7	204.1	1 361.3
April	1 577.3	969.8	91.3	16.3	127.3	22.1	38.8	150.3	221.5	60.2	205.2	1 372.2
May	1 590.1	981.5	92.6	15.5	128.4	23.0	38.4	152.2	219.3	60.7	208.5	1 381.5
June	1 600.8	990.6	93.8	15.0	127.7	22.7	39.3	154.1	218.6	61.1	205.5	1 395.3
July	1 620.5	999.5	95.3	14.5	131.1	22.4	39.9	155.9	223.5	61.6	207.1	1 413.3
August	1 634.2	1 005.4	96.6	14.7	131.9	22.2	40.1	158.1	227.1	61.8	208.6	1 425.6
September	1 650.3	1 016.8	98.0	16.1	131.8	22.2	40.3	160.4	227.0	62.3	211.7	1 438.6
October	1 669.6	1 030.5	99.2	19.0	131.9	22.2	40.5	163.2	226.0	62.9	216.4	1 453.2
November	1 692.7	1 038.5	100.5	21.0	135.6	22.4	40.9	165.7	231.4	63.2	219.0	1 473.6
December	1 707.9	1 044.7	101.9	21.7	138.9	22.8	41.3	168.2	231.9	63.4	221.3	1 486.6
1978:												
January	1 714.5	1 051.5	103.2	21.3	136.2	23.7	41.7	170.6	232.9	66.7	223.0	1 491.4
February	1 731.8	1 062.2	104.5	21.0	138.4	24.0	41.8	173.1	233.8	67.1	222.7	1 509.1
March	1 756.0	1 078.1	105.9	21.2	141.1	24.0	42.1	175.6	235.7	67.8	221.1	1 534.9
April	1 782.2	1 096.4	107.3	22.8	145.5	23.1	42.5	178.2	234.9	68.6	227.6	1 554.6
May	1 799.3	1 104.0	108.6	23.6	147.2	23.3	42.8	180.7	238.0	68.9	232.3	1 567.1
June	1 818.3	1 118.2	109.8	23.9	148.8	23.7	43.5	183.1	236.8	69.6	240.4	1 577.9
July	1 837.1	1 128.2	111.0	23.7	145.7	25.0	44.1	185.3	244.4	70.2	243.8	1 593.3
August	1 854.9	1 136.3	112.1	23.1	148.8	25.6	45.2	187.8	246.5	70.5	246.7	1 608.2
September	1 870.3	1 147.5	113.2	22.6	149.3	26.0	46.0	190.5	246.2	71.0	250.0	1 620.3
October	1 897.5	1 164.8	114.2	19.9	156.8	25.9	46.6	192.9	248.2	71.8	254.5	1 642.9
November	1 914.0	1 174.9	115.3	20.8	155.1	26.3	47.3	196.1	250.6	72.3	257.8	1 656.2
December	1 934.7	1 187.5	116.5	22.1	155.4	26.8	48.0	199.7	251.7	72.9	261.6	1 673.1
1979:												
January	1 953.0	1 198.1	117.8	26.6	151.7	28.5	48.2	204.5	255.7	78.1	261.9	1 691.0
February	1 970.6	1 208.7	118.9	27.6	153.7	28.6	48.7	208.2	254.7	78.6	264.2	1 706.4
March	1 994.1	1 223.3	120.1	27.8	155.8	28.3	49.0	211.6	257.6	79.4	267.6	1 726.5
April	2 000.0	1 225.1	121.1	24.7	158.3	24.6	49.4	214.3	262.0	79.6	268.4	1 731.6
May	2 018.0	1 236.0	122.3	24.7	159.5	25.6	50.0	217.4	262.5	80.0	272.3	1 745.7
June	2 035.4	1 250.2	123.5	24.8	160.5	25.2	50.3	220.5	261.0	80.7	278.1	1 757.3
July	2 066.6	1 261.3	124.8	26.0	161.3	25.0	50.5	222.7	276.4	81.3	282.8	1 783.8
August	2 085.3	1 269.5	126.0	25.7	164.6	25.3	50.6	226.5	278.7	81.7	285.7	1 799.6
September	2 100.8	1 282.0	127.3	25.3	163.1	23.3	51.2	230.9	280.1	82.3	289.7	1 811.1
October	2 125.1	1 292.7	128.5	25.3	161.9	28.0	51.8	236.0	283.6	82.8	293.3	1 831.8
November	2 147.7	1 305.3	129.9	23.9	162.0	29.3	52.5	241.7	286.3	83.3	297.0	1 850.7
December	2 173.5	1 318.8	131.3	21.6	164.2	30.7	53.3	248.1	289.5	84.0	301.0	1 872.5
1980:												
January	2 203.4	1 326.6	133.0	17.9	168.6	33.5	55.2	257.7	297.6	86.7	293.3	1 910.1
February	2 216.7	1 338.2	134.3	14.3	165.7	33.9	55.4	263.5	298.3	86.9	296.5	1 920.2
March	2 228.4	1 350.7	135.6	10.5	161.3	35.3	56.3	267.9	297.5	86.9	300.6	1 927.8
April	2 225.1	1 349.7	136.7	2.4	158.7	35.4	56.7	270.7	301.1	86.4	301.9	1 923.2
May	2 232.1	1 353.4	137.9	0.8	157.4	33.9	57.0	272.9	305.4	86.7	304.7	1 927.4
June	2 249.4	1 361.3	139.1	1.8	159.3	34.4	57.6	274.0	309.2	87.3	308.1	1 941.3
July	2 284.9	1 364.4	140.2	9.1	162.5	33.1	57.7	270.2	335.8	88.0	310.6	1 974.4
August	2 307.0	1 381.9	141.4	12.4	163.3	30.9	58.0	272.2	336.0	89.2	316.1	1 990.9
September	2 338.0	1 395.2	142.8	15.4	166.8	30.0	58.2	276.1	343.3	89.8	320.5	2 017.5
October	2 380.3	1 420.3	144.4	19.1	169.7	31.5	58.5	284.2	343.6	91.1	327.2	2 053.0
November	2 409.9	1 439.0	145.7	21.0	168.7	36.0	59.0	290.2	342.2	91.9	332.7	2 077.2
December	2 440.4	1 451.2	146.9	21.7	170.4	39.0	59.9	296.5	347.3	92.5	336.9	2 103.5

1. Includes inventory valuation and capital consumption adjustments.
2. Includes capital consumption adjustment.

SELECTED MONTHLY DATA, 1969-1992

PERSONAL INCOME AND ITS DISPOSITION—Continued
(Billions of dollars, monthly data are at seasonally adjusted annual rates)

YEAR AND MONTH	Personal income	Sources of personal income									Disposition of personal income	
		Wage and salary disbursements	Other labor income	Proprietors' income [1]		Rental income of persons [2]	Personal dividend income	Personal interest income	Transfer payments to persons	Less: Personal contributions for social insurance	Personal tax and nontax payments	Disposable personal income
				Farm	Nonfarm							
1981:												
January	2 464.2	1 465.8	148.1	20.4	174.0	43.9	61.0	304.2	348.2	101.4	340.6	2 123.6
February	2 481.7	1 473.5	149.0	20.4	173.5	43.8	62.4	309.9	350.9	101.8	344.0	2 137.7
March	2 504.9	1 485.1	149.9	20.4	174.4	43.6	63.6	314.9	355.4	102.4	348.5	2 156.4
April	2 503.4	1 494.0	150.3	19.7	164.1	42.8	65.2	315.4	354.9	102.9	352.1	2 151.3
May	2 519.7	1 501.1	151.1	20.6	162.2	42.7	66.6	321.8	356.9	103.3	357.4	2 162.3
June	2 543.0	1 512.4	152.1	22.1	160.8	42.8	67.9	330.4	358.4	103.9	361.1	2 181.9
July	2 599.2	1 522.8	153.3	27.5	164.7	43.2	69.5	348.0	375.2	104.9	367.0	2 232.2
August	2 625.3	1 538.0	154.4	27.9	165.4	43.8	69.8	355.9	375.9	105.7	372.8	2 252.5
September	2 637.8	1 544.3	155.5	26.8	164.9	44.7	70.3	361.0	376.5	106.1	375.4	2 262.4
October	2 639.7	1 554.3	156.5	20.9	162.2	46.8	70.3	358.6	376.8	106.8	364.1	2 275.6
November	2 652.0	1 560.5	157.6	18.6	162.5	47.6	70.2	361.3	380.8	107.2	368.3	2 283.7
December	2 651.1	1 559.1	158.7	16.9	160.0	48.1	69.7	364.5	381.3	107.1	371.4	2 279.7
1982:												
January	2 649.7	1 567.6	159.9	16.6	150.5	47.1	68.1	368.1	382.4	110.6	366.1	2 283.6
February	2 665.9	1 576.2	161.0	15.6	151.9	46.7	66.9	372.4	386.4	111.1	372.5	2 293.4
March	2 674.3	1 577.1	162.1	14.9	152.8	46.1	66.2	377.3	389.0	111.2	371.9	2 302.4
April	2 705.5	1 577.8	163.2	14.3	166.6	45.7	65.6	387.5	396.1	111.2	366.6	2 338.9
May	2 724.2	1 590.5	164.2	14.0	169.2	45.3	65.2	390.1	397.7	112.1	378.3	2 345.9
June	2 730.3	1 593.5	165.2	13.6	168.4	45.5	65.1	389.8	401.4	112.3	384.6	2 345.7
July	2 736.5	1 601.0	166.2	14.0	162.3	45.5	65.4	382.0	413.0	113.0	365.1	2 371.4
August	2 742.3	1 604.2	167.1	13.2	164.6	46.2	65.8	379.4	414.8	113.1	367.6	2 374.8
September	2 747.2	1 602.2	167.9	12.5	166.9	46.8	66.6	377.4	419.9	112.9	367.8	2 379.4
October	2 768.1	1 606.8	168.5	13.9	174.4	49.4	67.8	375.7	424.9	113.1	369.9	2 398.2
November	2 785.3	1 609.9	169.2	15.6	175.9	48.5	69.1	375.1	435.3	113.2	371.7	2 413.6
December	2 797.1	1 620.3	169.8	15.2	177.9	45.2	70.6	375.3	436.4	113.7	374.7	2 422.4
1983:												
January	2 795.8	1 629.3	169.8	9.9	177.0	46.7	71.8	376.1	432.1	116.9	365.0	2 430.8
February	2 800.6	1 624.7	170.8	15.0	174.0	46.2	73.3	378.3	434.8	116.5	366.6	2 434.0
March	2 820.2	1 635.6	172.3	15.2	172.9	45.9	74.5	381.7	439.2	117.0	368.8	2 451.5
April	2 844.9	1 647.9	175.3	9.4	182.5	45.9	75.5	386.5	439.6	117.6	367.4	2 477.4
May	2 874.8	1 666.6	176.9	7.0	183.9	45.9	76.7	391.8	444.7	118.7	378.5	2 496.3
June	2 887.1	1 675.4	178.2	2.9	185.6	46.0	77.4	397.9	442.9	119.1	382.0	2 505.0
July	2 909.8	1 690.9	178.9	-2.4	192.6	46.3	78.5	406.4	438.4	119.9	360.3	2 549.5
August	2 911.7	1 697.3	179.7	-5.7	190.5	39.6	79.4	412.8	438.3	120.3	362.6	2 549.0
September	2 945.0	1 710.6	180.4	-4.5	196.5	47.0	80.0	418.8	437.1	121.0	365.0	2 580.0
October	2 977.4	1 738.7	180.6	-4.7	196.4	47.8	80.5	424.7	436.1	122.6	369.7	2 607.7
November	3 005.7	1 745.7	181.3	0.4	199.1	48.1	80.7	429.6	443.9	123.0	371.2	2 634.5
December	3 036.9	1 760.6	182.2	6.9	202.4	48.2	80.5	433.8	446.1	123.8	374.4	2 662.5
1984:												
January	3 066.3	1 781.5	183.5	16.0	204.2	48.4	80.1	434.4	446.8	128.6	375.3	2 691.0
February	3 104.1	1 793.8	184.5	22.7	218.1	48.2	79.6	439.4	447.1	129.3	379.4	2 724.6
March	3 132.9	1 806.4	185.4	26.4	221.9	47.7	79.4	446.0	449.7	130.1	381.4	2 751.5
April	3 167.1	1 828.8	186.4	24.1	226.4	45.8	79.2	455.8	451.9	131.4	383.6	2 783.5
May	3 177.8	1 833.2	187.3	23.4	225.2	45.8	78.7	464.1	451.6	131.6	386.9	2 791.0
June	3 209.7	1 851.7	188.2	23.9	228.0	46.5	78.6	472.6	452.9	132.7	392.8	2 816.9
July	3 234.2	1 866.8	188.6	22.6	224.6	48.6	78.4	484.7	453.3	133.5	398.0	2 836.2
August	3 266.7	1 874.2	189.7	22.5	238.0	50.2	78.2	491.0	456.7	133.9	400.9	2 865.9
September	3 297.5	1 891.9	190.9	22.8	244.8	51.9	79.2	495.0	455.9	134.8	406.0	2 891.5
October	3 286.6	1 894.1	192.7	23.9	222.8	54.4	79.7	493.9	459.9	134.9	408.2	2 878.4
November	3 312.3	1 910.3	194.2	24.5	224.9	56.8	80.3	495.1	461.9	135.6	413.7	2 898.7
December	3 328.7	1 928.0	195.6	25.0	227.6	56.6	81.0	496.0	455.4	136.5	419.6	2 909.0
1985:												
January	3 358.2	1 933.3	197.1	26.1	240.0	53.5	82.6	494.8	476.0	145.1	419.3	2 938.9
February	3 376.0	1 942.6	198.3	26.1	243.7	52.3	83.4	496.2	479.1	145.6	452.1	2 923.9
March	3 401.2	1 963.5	199.4	25.5	244.0	51.1	84.4	498.4	481.6	146.8	482.2	2 918.9
April	3 404.6	1 964.9	200.0	23.6	242.4	49.4	85.4	503.4	482.4	146.9	425.8	2 978.8
May	3 416.9	1 974.7	201.1	22.8	242.1	48.6	86.5	505.8	482.8	147.5	359.0	3 058.0
June	3 438.3	1 993.0	202.3	22.2	242.1	48.3	87.8	507.6	483.7	148.6	438.6	2 999.7
July	3 451.6	1 994.4	203.7	21.4	244.7	49.3	88.8	506.6	491.4	148.8	438.8	3 012.8
August	3 465.5	2 008.7	204.9	21.3	244.9	49.3	89.8	508.8	487.6	149.8	442.2	3 023.3
September	3 480.4	2 025.1	206.0	21.8	245.3	39.7	90.9	512.2	490.5	150.9	445.5	3 034.9
October	3 515.2	2 036.1	207.2	24.2	250.1	47.9	92.1	516.9	492.4	151.7	447.0	3 068.2
November	3 525.2	2 045.1	208.1	24.3	250.3	39.7	93.5	522.1	494.5	152.4	448.6	3 076.6
December	3 564.4	2 069.3	208.9	23.6	250.3	47.7	94.3	527.9	496.5	154.1	452.8	3 111.7
1986:												
January	3 580.0	2 067.4	209.0	20.8	251.9	47.1	97.7	538.4	505.9	158.1	446.1	3 133.9
February	3 594.6	2 075.5	209.8	20.0	251.3	46.4	100.6	542.9	507.1	158.9	447.4	3 147.2
March	3 618.1	2 091.5	210.7	19.6	252.1	45.6	102.7	545.3	510.8	160.2	448.3	3 169.8
April	3 617.6	2 087.1	211.9	19.3	255.3	44.9	104.6	542.4	512.1	160.1	447.7	3 169.8
May	3 630.2	2 094.5	213.2	20.2	255.0	43.8	105.8	543.0	515.4	160.7	450.0	3 180.2
June	3 647.2	2 105.4	214.6	21.9	255.4	42.6	107.0	543.8	517.9	161.5	456.0	3 191.1
July	3 669.8	2 113.9	216.3	26.7	255.1	40.6	107.4	546.4	525.5	162.2	458.0	3 211.8
August	3 684.7	2 128.1	217.9	28.4	258.1	39.3	107.7	546.6	521.7	163.1	462.7	3 222.0
September	3 700.2	2 135.0	219.5	29.3	264.0	38.2	107.8	545.9	524.2	163.6	465.9	3 234.4
October	3 702.7	2 153.8	221.2	27.8	252.6	36.1	107.4	542.4	526.2	164.8	471.1	3 231.6
November	3 716.5	2 169.5	222.9	27.9	251.3	35.1	107.0	541.3	527.1	165.7	477.6	3 238.9
December	3 739.4	2 176.9	224.7	28.2	261.2	38.1	105.9	540.8	529.7	166.1	488.1	3 251.2

1. Includes inventory valuation and capital consumption adjustments.
2. Includes capital consumption adjustment.

PERSONAL INCOME AND ITS DISPOSITION—Continued
(Billions of dollars, monthly data are at seasonally adjusted annual rates)

YEAR AND MONTH	Personal income	Wage and salary disburse-ments	Other labor income	Proprietors' income [1] Farm	Proprietors' income [1] Nonfarm	Rental income of per-sons [2]	Personal dividend income	Personal interest income	Transfer pay-ments to persons	Less: Personal contribu-tions for social insur-ance	Personal tax and nontax pay-ments	Dispos-able personal income
1987:												
January	3 759.5	2 192.2	226.5	27.8	264.2	40.7	104.6	539.8	533.0	169.3	474.3	3 285.2
February	3 789.0	2 210.6	228.3	29.8	268.4	42.7	102.7	540.9	535.8	170.2	471.3	3 317.7
March	3 809.4	2 226.0	230.1	30.5	268.7	43.8	101.4	543.1	536.9	171.0	478.4	3 331.0
April	3 821.4	2 231.4	232.4	32.2	268.6	41.1	100.1	548.0	539.0	171.4	608.3	3 213.1
May	3 853.7	2 250.1	233.8	31.6	271.6	41.2	100.1	551.6	546.2	172.5	499.5	3 354.2
June	3 865.7	2 259.2	234.8	30.9	273.1	42.3	99.6	555.2	543.4	172.9	502.5	3 363.3
July	3 877.8	2 267.2	234.1	31.2	275.3	41.0	99.7	557.5	545.3	173.5	507.3	3 370.5
August	3 913.0	2 294.0	235.5	31.5	276.6	43.0	99.8	562.4	545.3	175.0	515.1	3 397.9
September	3 932.0	2 299.9	237.5	31.9	277.7	44.9	100.3	568.5	546.7	175.2	519.5	3 412.5
October	3 981.0	2 323.3	242.0	32.5	278.1	50.8	100.9	580.8	548.9	176.3	523.4	3 457.5
November	4 006.7	2 340.4	244.1	32.6	278.9	52.3	101.7	585.4	548.6	177.3	528.6	3 478.1
December	4 055.3	2 377.9	245.4	35.9	281.4	53.6	102.3	587.3	550.8	179.4	541.9	3 513.4
1988:												
January	4 051.1	2 364.7	244.9	37.9	287.7	52.1	103.1	583.1	566.2	188.7	518.0	3 533.1
February	4 075.8	2 382.4	245.8	39.1	291.1	52.6	103.9	582.3	568.3	189.7	509.1	3 566.7
March	4 101.0	2 395.6	246.9	39.6	294.8	52.5	104.8	581.5	575.8	190.4	517.8	3 583.2
April	4 129.7	2 421.4	248.4	34.5	305.5	54.5	106.0	577.3	574.0	191.9	551.5	3 578.2
May	4 142.4	2 433.4	249.7	29.7	307.8	54.1	107.1	579.0	574.2	192.6	529.8	3 612.7
June	4 169.5	2 452.3	250.9	27.5	311.9	54.0	108.4	583.3	575.0	193.8	524.0	3 645.5
July	4 200.6	2 471.1	251.9	30.5	309.7	51.4	110.0	593.6	577.6	195.2	529.6	3 671.0
August	4 216.4	2 471.6	253.2	29.3	313.0	51.9	112.1	600.3	580.2	195.2	531.4	3 685.0
September	4 240.3	2 486.2	254.7	24.0	315.2	54.9	113.6	606.9	581.0	196.2	536.0	3 704.3
October	4 274.9	2 517.8	256.4	12.2	317.3	58.9	115.5	611.1	584.0	198.3	542.9	3 732.0
November	4 287.3	2 515.2	258.0	9.0	318.8	62.1	117.0	619.1	586.4	198.3	544.3	3 743.0
December	4 326.5	2 531.3	259.7	16.4	321.1	62.5	117.5	628.9	588.8	199.6	549.7	3 776.8
1989:												
January	4 387.4	2 552.2	261.3	29.9	323.5	58.1	122.1	643.4	604.1	207.3	580.8	3 806.6
February	4 412.4	2 550.3	263.1	41.9	322.3	57.1	123.7	653.9	607.2	207.3	571.0	3 841.4
March	4 452.7	2 565.4	265.2	45.3	322.9	56.0	125.6	663.7	617.2	208.5	581.4	3 871.3
April	4 473.7	2 581.3	267.5	39.3	319.3	58.2	127.5	675.3	615.0	209.6	618.5	3 855.2
May	4 472.7	2 570.5	269.7	38.6	317.8	56.8	128.9	681.4	618.0	209.0	596.0	3 876.7
June	4 492.3	2 582.6	271.9	37.3	317.1	55.5	130.4	684.8	622.5	209.9	587.6	3 904.7
July	4 510.0	2 604.9	274.2	33.9	316.2	51.6	132.2	682.1	626.3	211.4	592.2	3 917.8
August	4 518.1	2 601.2	276.5	32.9	321.3	50.7	133.5	682.4	630.9	211.2	593.7	3 924.4
September	4 527.8	2 615.1	278.7	32.6	320.0	40.9	134.6	682.4	635.5	212.1	598.0	3 929.8
October	4 558.7	2 646.9	280.6	34.1	320.4	33.4	136.4	680.4	640.7	214.2	604.2	3 954.6
November	4 592.7	2 647.3	283.0	34.6	325.5	50.5	137.8	681.2	647.0	214.2	605.5	3 987.2
December	4 613.0	2 659.7	285.6	34.9	327.3	51.8	137.8	683.1	647.7	214.8	609.3	4 003.7
1990:												
January	4 667.2	2 678.4	288.9	36.9	333.6	54.1	140.6	687.4	668.8	221.5	607.7	4 059.5
February	4 703.8	2 707.8	291.5	33.4	332.3	55.2	142.0	690.6	670.4	219.4	613.6	4 090.2
March	4 730.0	2 725.7	293.8	36.2	330.6	56.2	143.4	693.9	672.4	222.1	617.5	4 112.5
April	4 771.1	2 748.8	295.7	38.3	335.9	56.3	144.8	697.5	674.1	220.3	624.4	4 146.8
May	4 774.2	2 744.4	297.8	38.5	337.5	57.5	142.2	701.0	676.8	221.6	627.9	4 146.2
June	4 806.8	2 765.7	299.9	38.1	338.0	59.0	143.3	704.6	683.3	225.0	632.4	4 174.4
July	4 837.1	2 782.4	302.1	35.8	341.4	62.6	143.4	709.3	686.0	225.9	631.4	4 205.7
August	4 842.0	2 775.7	304.0	34.8	344.5	64.4	143.3	711.9	688.6	225.4	629.5	4 212.5
September	4 873.8	2 795.2	305.9	34.1	345.1	66.0	143.3	713.7	697.1	226.5	631.6	4 242.2
October	4 868.2	2 780.0	307.8	34.4	341.2	66.1	143.1	715.0	706.2	225.7	627.1	4 241.1
November	4 875.9	2 782.8	309.3	33.3	341.9	66.9	142.9	714.6	710.0	226.0	625.6	4 250.2
December	4 900.4	2 803.0	310.6	31.6	340.8	67.1	142.1	712.9	719.9	227.6	628.7	4 271.7
1991:												
January	4 890.3	2 788.9	310.7	27.7	333.6	66.7	147.0	707.5	741.2	232.9	625.3	4 265.0
February	4 895.4	2 787.6	312.2	25.0	336.3	66.3	150.3	705.2	745.5	232.9	621.6	4 273.8
March	4 910.0	2 791.6	314.2	26.8	338.0	66.1	150.5	703.5	752.5	233.1	620.1	4 290.0
April	4 937.0	2 799.0	317.4	32.0	342.4	65.9	151.5	703.6	758.8	233.5	619.9	4 317.1
May	4 960.1	2 809.1	319.7	34.8	345.5	66.0	153.2	702.3	763.6	234.1	619.1	4 340.9
June	4 993.4	2 837.3	322.0	33.3	348.2	66.2	154.5	700.8	767.3	236.1	622.6	4 370.8
July	4 982.3	2 825.2	324.1	28.0	350.9	65.8	155.8	698.7	769.8	236.0	620.7	4 361.6
August	4 999.6	2 835.9	326.3	27.0	351.2	66.8	156.4	697.0	775.7	236.7	622.8	4 376.8
September	5 025.8	2 855.3	328.4	26.9	352.8	68.6	157.0	695.4	779.3	237.9	627.5	4 398.3
October	5 030.2	2 848.5	330.1	27.6	352.1	66.8	156.6	695.9	790.5	237.8	629.7	4 400.5
November	5 053.5	2 862.2	332.4	30.9	354.8	74.1	155.9	692.8	788.8	238.4	631.0	4 422.4
December	5 101.6	2 890.7	334.9	31.5	360.4	75.9	154.5	688.3	805.9	240.5	636.9	4 464.7
1992:												
January	5 129.1	2 889.3	338.2	34.6	372.8	76.4	152.7	677.7	830.9	243.4	634.7	4 494.4
February	5 175.1	2 925.3	340.8	37.5	374.3	77.2	152.1	673.5	840.1	245.8	642.1	4 533.0
March	5 188.4	2 934.9	343.3	35.4	375.9	78.0	152.0	671.2	844.0	246.4	633.3	4 555.2
April	5 214.3	2 942.2	345.1	34.6	382.4	78.3	153.0	674.9	850.3	246.5	637.5	4 576.7
May	5 239.2	2 959.0	347.5	36.0	383.6	79.4	154.3	673.4	853.6	247.6	640.2	4 599.1
June	5 259.5	2 967.5	350.1	40.6	385.4	80.7	156.2	670.6	856.5	248.1	642.3	4 617.2
July	5 271.2	2 974.3	353.6	40.0	387.3	82.3	158.2	663.5	860.8	248.8	646.5	4 624.8
August	5 258.8	2 996.5	356.0	39.1	387.0	45.2	160.9	660.8	863.6	250.2	652.2	4 606.6
September	5 303.2	2 993.7	358.0	37.8	388.5	81.1	163.2	659.3	871.6	250.0	653.3	4 649.9
October	5 348.4	3 010.5	358.4	37.8	399.9	88.6	166.3	660.7	877.5	251.4	658.9	4 689.4
November	5 373.0	3 032.7	360.8	36.6	403.5	91.0	169.7	660.4	870.8	252.5	663.7	4 709.3
December	5 566.5	3 210.9	363.9	35.0	399.6	94.1	174.2	660.0	879.2	250.4	701.9	4 864.6

1. Includes inventory valuation and capital consumption adjustments.
2. Includes capital consumption adjustment.

PERSONAL INCOME AND ITS DISPOSITION—Continued
(Billions of dollars, except as noted, monthly data are at seasonally adjusted annual rates)

YEAR AND MONTH	Personal outlays					Personal saving		Constant (1992) dollars				
	Total	Personal consumption expenditure				Billions of dollars	Percent of disposable personal income	Disposable personal income	Personal consumption expenditure			
		Total	Durable goods	Nondurable goods	Services				Total	Durable goods	Nondurable goods	Services
1969:												
January	601.4	585.6	85.7	244.7	255.2	41.0	6.4	2 328.4	2 122.2	195.3	829.6	1 088.3
February	606.5	590.5	86.3	247.0	257.2	37.8	5.9	2 330.0	2 135.4	195.9	836.5	1 094.3
March	606.5	590.4	84.7	247.4	258.3	41.8	6.5	2 335.2	2 126.4	191.3	834.4	1 094.8
April	611.7	595.2	85.8	249.5	259.9	39.0	6.0	2 333.8	2 134.8	193.7	836.6	1 097.5
May	618.0	601.3	85.9	252.4	263.0	42.4	6.4	2 360.0	2 149.0	193.8	842.6	1 106.4
June	618.6	601.8	86.0	251.5	264.3	49.1	7.4	2 375.3	2 140.6	193.4	833.6	1 108.6
July	620.3	603.4	84.1	253.7	265.6	54.9	8.1	2 393.0	2 138.4	189.0	837.0	1 110.0
August	627.5	610.5	86.1	256.6	267.8	53.4	7.8	2 406.8	2 157.9	193.2	844.5	1 115.6
September	631.0	613.8	88.1	255.4	270.3	53.8	7.9	2 409.3	2 159.7	197.5	835.8	1 120.8
October	636.4	619.0	86.9	259.2	273.0	52.6	7.6	2 416.5	2 171.1	193.8	846.3	1 127.8
November	638.4	621.0	86.1	259.8	275.1	53.8	7.8	2 417.1	2 168.3	191.7	844.1	1 131.3
December	640.8	623.3	85.7	260.8	276.9	55.6	8.0	2 421.0	2 167.0	190.9	842.2	1 133.5
1970:												
January	647.2	629.6	84.5	265.5	279.5	52.3	7.5	2 422.0	2 179.7	188.3	854.0	1 138.1
February	652.4	634.6	86.3	265.9	282.4	51.3	7.3	2 427.2	2 189.0	191.8	851.0	1 146.6
March	650.8	633.0	83.8	267.1	282.2	56.5	8.0	2 433.7	2 178.1	185.9	854.2	1 140.7
April	654.8	636.9	85.1	267.4	284.5	69.8	9.6	2 480.6	2 180.2	188.7	848.9	1 144.7
May	661.5	643.5	86.2	270.7	286.6	61.1	8.5	2 465.3	2 195.5	190.9	857.4	1 147.9
June	665.6	647.6	86.9	271.4	289.4	56.2	7.8	2 455.5	2 202.9	192.4	858.5	1 152.5
July	668.1	650.0	86.3	271.9	291.8	66.3	9.0	2 487.9	2 202.1	190.6	857.2	1 156.4
August	672.8	654.7	87.3	273.0	294.4	66.3	9.0	2 495.9	2 210.9	192.1	859.5	1 161.2
September	679.1	660.9	87.2	276.0	297.7	64.7	8.7	2 500.3	2 221.7	191.2	865.4	1 168.0
October	678.5	660.2	84.5	276.5	299.2	65.2	8.8	2 487.0	2 207.9	184.0	863.5	1 167.1
November	676.7	658.5	80.0	277.5	301.1	68.3	9.2	2 481.1	2 192.9	172.8	865.1	1 167.6
December	685.9	667.6	81.9	281.2	304.6	65.7	8.7	2 491.7	2 213.2	175.9	874.1	1 174.6
1971:												
January	696.9	678.5	92.1	280.6	305.8	68.1	8.9	2 529.2	2 243.4	196.5	872.9	1 174.4
February	700.3	681.8	91.9	281.0	308.9	67.0	8.7	2 529.4	2 247.6	195.3	873.0	1 181.4
March	703.0	684.4	94.2	279.2	311.0	70.0	9.1	2 539.3	2 248.4	200.1	865.2	1 183.3
April	710.0	691.2	94.9	282.7	313.7	67.9	8.7	2 544.7	2 261.3	200.9	872.6	1 187.6
May	712.5	693.7	94.2	283.2	316.3	71.2	9.1	2 553.5	2 260.2	199.2	870.9	1 191.7
June	721.3	702.4	97.5	286.4	318.5	82.6	10.3	2 607.4	2 278.0	205.5	876.9	1 193.6
July	720.6	701.4	95.5	284.9	321.0	73.6	9.3	2 567.8	2 267.8	201.0	871.3	1 196.6
August	726.8	707.5	96.6	287.2	323.7	73.6	9.2	2 579.3	2 280.0	204.6	874.4	1 200.5
September	735.2	715.7	101.3	288.0	326.5	67.9	8.4	2 584.8	2 303.7	216.3	874.9	1 206.9
October	738.3	718.6	101.5	288.0	329.1	66.4	8.2	2 584.6	2 308.4	216.7	873.6	1 213.1
November	743.6	723.8	101.5	291.3	331.0	64.6	8.0	2 591.2	2 320.4	216.6	882.5	1 216.2
December	751.2	731.2	101.6	293.6	336.0	65.8	8.0	2 608.4	2 334.6	216.0	886.1	1 229.1
1972:												
January	754.5	734.6	104.7	291.5	338.4	61.9	7.6	2 596.9	2 336.5	221.6	876.2	1 233.6
February	759.1	739.0	103.5	295.0	340.5	66.0	8.0	2 613.6	2 341.0	218.8	882.3	1 236.2
March	772.3	752.0	106.4	301.1	344.5	56.8	6.8	2 622.3	2 378.6	224.6	900.2	1 247.5
April	775.7	755.2	106.9	301.8	346.5	59.0	7.1	2 635.6	2 384.6	225.0	901.7	1 251.8
May	781.2	760.5	108.5	305.4	346.6	61.3	7.3	2 654.8	2 396.6	228.1	910.6	1 249.3
June	784.9	764.0	108.8	305.9	349.4	51.2	6.1	2 629.9	2 403.3	228.5	911.8	1 255.1
July	793.2	772.2	110.5	309.2	352.6	60.5	7.1	2 676.2	2 420.6	231.6	917.7	1 262.4
August	799.8	778.6	112.1	310.9	355.6	65.7	7.6	2 704.6	2 433.2	234.7	920.4	1 268.3
September	804.8	783.4	111.7	314.3	357.4	67.5	7.7	2 714.5	2 438.0	233.4	924.0	1 271.6
October	818.9	797.3	115.7	319.8	361.8	72.1	8.1	2 767.0	2 476.3	242.6	937.7	1 283.2
November	824.6	802.8	117.0	320.2	365.6	79.4	8.8	2 799.1	2 485.9	245.4	935.8	1 292.1
December	830.5	808.5	118.4	321.5	368.6	81.2	8.9	2 814.4	2 495.9	248.0	936.5	1 298.3
1973:												
January	840.9	818.8	122.9	326.9	369.0	72.8	8.0	2 812.2	2 519.9	257.3	946.1	1 298.4
February	850.4	828.0	125.2	331.3	371.5	76.3	8.2	2 836.7	2 534.5	261.5	950.4	1 302.8
March	857.5	834.8	127.6	332.8	374.4	79.8	8.5	2 848.1	2 536.7	266.2	942.9	1 306.9
April	860.4	837.4	125.4	334.6	377.4	84.3	8.9	2 849.5	2 525.9	260.6	938.6	1 309.2
May	866.4	843.1	126.1	336.3	380.7	87.4	9.2	2 864.3	2 531.8	261.4	936.8	1 316.8
June	869.4	845.8	120.9	340.1	384.8	92.4	9.6	2 871.0	2 524.8	250.3	940.1	1 323.4
July	879.6	855.8	123.0	346.7	386.1	86.8	9.0	2 875.2	2 546.3	254.1	956.1	1 321.3
August	879.1	855.1	121.7	345.0	388.5	96.5	9.9	2 872.9	2 518.2	251.0	933.7	1 322.4
September	895.5	871.4	126.7	351.2	393.6	90.5	9.2	2 891.4	2 555.2	261.3	946.3	1 332.3
October	896.0	870.3	122.3	352.9	395.1	107.2	10.7	2 923.5	2 536.3	251.9	941.3	1 332.2
November	904.9	879.1	121.9	359.1	398.1	109.6	10.8	2 933.0	2 541.4	250.4	945.1	1 335.8
December	904.9	879.0	119.0	360.3	399.7	115.0	11.3	2 924.0	2 520.1	244.1	937.5	1 331.1
1974:												
January	912.0	887.1	119.0	365.1	403.0	110.0	10.8	2 904.5	2 521.2	243.5	935.7	1 335.5
February	917.3	892.2	117.0	369.2	405.8	107.5	10.5	2 878.4	2 506.0	238.4	929.3	1 334.5
March	928.9	903.8	120.6	373.0	410.2	99.0	9.6	2 855.7	2 510.9	244.5	923.4	1 337.8
April	938.2	913.0	121.4	377.3	414.3	93.5	9.1	2 847.2	2 519.6	244.0	927.3	1 343.7
May	949.8	924.4	124.3	380.7	419.4	92.1	8.8	2 848.2	2 527.0	247.5	925.9	1 348.5
June	955.3	929.8	123.3	383.0	423.5	94.7	9.0	2 847.6	2 521.6	241.5	925.6	1 352.4
July	964.9	939.4	126.1	387.5	425.7	100.8	9.5	2 870.0	2 529.8	243.9	929.7	1 352.7
August	981.5	955.8	133.4	393.0	429.4	90.3	8.4	2 856.0	2 546.9	255.4	930.0	1 353.6
September	980.9	955.2	126.8	394.4	433.9	98.4	9.1	2 848.0	2 520.4	240.0	922.8	1 357.2
October	984.2	958.5	122.6	396.7	439.2	103.7	9.5	2 849.5	2 510.4	228.5	921.6	1 365.8
November	980.5	954.8	116.8	397.6	440.5	105.8	9.7	2 825.3	2 483.3	216.6	916.3	1 360.4
December	985.6	960.0	116.5	396.0	447.5	106.5	9.7	2 820.2	2 479.1	215.0	905.8	1 372.1

PERSONAL INCOME AND ITS DISPOSITION—Continued
(Billions of dollars, except as noted, monthly data are at seasonally adjusted annual rates)

YEAR AND MONTH	Personal outlays Total	Personal consumption expenditure Total	Durable goods	Nondurable goods	Services	Personal saving Billions of dollars	Percent of disposable personal income	Constant (1992) dollars Disposable personal income	Personal consumption expenditure Total	Durable goods	Nondurable goods	Services
1975:												
January	998.6	973.0	121.0	402.1	450.0	97.4	8.9	2 815.2	2 499.3	223.0	915.6	1 369.7
February	1 012.5	986.8	126.2	404.7	456.0	89.4	8.1	2 816.5	2 522.3	231.0	919.0	1 379.3
March	1 013.9	988.3	122.5	406.3	459.5	91.9	8.3	2 817.4	2 518.1	222.2	922.8	1 383.7
April	1 018.7	993.4	123.8	405.4	464.2	112.8	10.0	2 871.5	2 521.0	222.4	919.3	1 391.5
May	1 043.0	1 017.7	129.6	419.5	468.7	161.3	13.4	3 043.6	2 572.1	232.8	948.5	1 396.0
June	1 051.2	1 025.9	131.4	421.6	472.9	117.6	10.1	2 934.5	2 575.8	235.4	947.1	1 398.0
July	1 064.5	1 038.9	136.2	424.8	477.8	96.8	8.3	2 890.9	2 585.9	243.1	943.9	1 401.6
August	1 071.8	1 046.1	136.5	429.3	480.3	103.4	8.8	2 911.4	2 591.5	242.3	948.6	1 403.1
September	1 079.8	1 053.9	141.1	429.0	483.8	105.9	8.9	2 922.9	2 598.0	249.2	946.2	1 402.8
October	1 085.6	1 059.6	139.2	429.7	490.8	113.1	9.4	2 938.1	2 597.2	244.4	941.7	1 415.4
November	1 100.8	1 074.6	144.1	436.2	494.2	105.9	8.8	2 938.7	2 617.1	252.0	951.9	1 413.0
December	1 117.4	1 091.0	149.9	439.2	502.0	97.8	8.0	2 942.4	2 641.8	259.7	954.9	1 425.5
1976:												
January	1 133.7	1 107.0	152.1	446.9	507.9	96.6	7.9	2 968.1	2 670.7	262.7	969.9	1 434.8
February	1 134.9	1 108.0	155.0	443.5	509.6	105.7	8.5	2 988.4	2 668.9	266.9	964.6	1 432.8
March	1 142.7	1 115.6	155.3	445.5	514.8	104.9	8.4	3 000.4	2 682.9	267.4	970.6	1 440.6
April	1 153.2	1 126.0	158.1	450.1	517.8	100.2	8.0	3 006.6	2 701.0	270.5	980.9	1 443.4
May	1 150.8	1 123.4	152.7	449.8	520.9	109.5	8.7	3 007.8	2 681.1	259.9	975.2	1 444.7
June	1 169.0	1 141.3	158.1	457.8	525.5	96.9	7.7	3 007.6	2 711.6	268.3	988.8	1 449.0
July	1 178.3	1 150.3	159.6	459.2	531.5	102.6	8.0	3 026.3	2 717.8	269.6	987.5	1 455.9
August	1 187.1	1 158.9	158.4	462.9	537.6	103.1	8.0	3 030.7	2 722.4	267.2	991.0	1 460.6
September	1 198.6	1 170.1	160.8	465.3	544.0	99.3	7.6	3 031.4	2 733.1	269.3	991.6	1 468.7
October	1 207.7	1 179.0	160.7	469.9	548.4	95.4	7.3	3 026.4	2 738.0	266.2	997.5	1 472.0
November	1 220.5	1 191.6	163.1	470.5	557.9	101.1	7.6	3 054.5	2 753.9	270.0	995.2	1 487.0
December	1 243.7	1 214.4	172.1	476.7	565.6	89.3	6.7	3 063.0	2 790.5	284.0	1 004.6	1 495.2
1977:												
January	1 247.4	1 217.6	167.9	479.5	570.2	89.8	6.7	3 056.1	2 782.8	275.2	1 005.5	1 499.1
February	1 263.8	1 233.8	173.6	486.4	573.8	70.7	5.3	3 027.3	2 798.9	285.0	1 008.5	1 498.2
March	1 271.2	1 240.8	179.4	485.2	576.3	90.1	6.6	3 073.3	2 801.3	293.9	1 002.6	1 494.3
April	1 280.8	1 250.0	178.3	489.9	581.7	91.4	6.7	3 079.9	2 805.6	292.3	1 006.4	1 497.1
May	1 291.5	1 260.3	178.1	493.6	588.6	90.1	6.5	3 083.8	2 813.1	290.9	1 008.0	1 505.9
June	1 298.5	1 266.9	179.7	492.6	594.6	96.8	6.9	3 097.3	2 812.2	292.6	1 000.7	1 511.3
July	1 315.5	1 283.6	181.0	498.8	603.9	97.8	6.9	3 120.4	2 834.0	293.2	1 009.8	1 524.0
August	1 321.5	1 289.1	183.2	497.5	608.4	104.2	7.3	3 133.6	2 833.6	296.1	1 003.9	1 526.2
September	1 331.0	1 298.2	184.9	499.2	614.0	107.7	7.5	3 150.8	2 843.3	298.5	1 005.9	1 531.2
October	1 348.0	1 314.8	185.7	507.3	621.7	105.2	7.2	3 166.0	2 864.4	297.3	1 017.8	1 542.3
November	1 364.0	1 330.3	189.2	517.1	624.0	109.7	7.4	3 192.3	2 881.7	301.8	1 030.9	1 538.9
December	1 373.6	1 339.3	192.3	516.1	630.9	112.9	7.6	3 204.1	2 886.7	303.8	1 024.4	1 549.5
1978:												
January	1 368.5	1 333.3	180.1	514.9	638.3	122.9	8.2	3 194.5	2 855.8	284.3	1 017.0	1 553.7
February	1 395.2	1 359.4	187.0	523.9	648.5	114.0	7.6	3 215.5	2 896.5	294.5	1 030.4	1 567.6
March	1 418.7	1 382.3	193.2	533.5	655.6	116.2	7.6	3 250.0	2 926.9	302.8	1 042.2	1 574.9
April	1 438.1	1 401.0	201.9	535.6	663.6	116.5	7.5	3 265.2	2 942.7	314.4	1 036.5	1 582.0
May	1 455.7	1 417.9	205.2	543.0	669.7	111.4	7.1	3 265.9	2 955.0	317.5	1 041.0	1 585.7
June	1 471.8	1 433.2	206.2	549.2	677.8	106.2	6.7	3 265.6	2 966.1	317.0	1 044.2	1 595.1
July	1 473.9	1 434.7	203.3	552.0	679.3	119.4	7.5	3 278.2	2 952.0	310.8	1 043.7	1 589.0
August	1 495.3	1 455.4	209.9	556.8	688.7	112.9	7.0	3 291.2	2 978.5	319.1	1 048.0	1 601.4
September	1 502.0	1 461.6	201.0	565.6	695.0	118.2	7.3	3 297.0	2 974.2	304.2	1 059.2	1 605.1
October	1 515.7	1 474.6	208.2	565.9	700.5	127.2	7.7	3 318.6	2 978.6	313.1	1 052.2	1 605.4
November	1 529.1	1 487.3	209.7	575.1	702.6	127.1	7.7	3 327.3	2 988.1	313.4	1 062.5	1 602.8
December	1 546.7	1 504.2	211.6	583.6	709.0	126.4	7.6	3 342.5	3 005.2	314.7	1 071.7	1 609.0
1979:												
January	1 555.6	1 512.9	208.4	585.1	719.4	135.4	8.0	3 349.8	2 996.9	308.7	1 062.7	1 619.9
February	1 574.3	1 531.1	212.0	592.4	726.6	132.1	7.7	3 357.1	3 012.2	311.7	1 065.6	1 629.3
March	1 587.7	1 543.9	213.0	602.8	728.2	138.8	8.0	3 371.8	3 015.2	311.2	1 071.7	1 625.8
April	1 591.5	1 547.2	210.6	599.0	737.6	140.0	8.1	3 354.4	2 997.3	305.4	1 054.1	1 636.2
May	1 609.2	1 564.3	212.2	608.9	743.2	136.5	7.8	3 351.4	3 003.1	306.8	1 059.3	1 634.3
June	1 625.7	1 580.3	206.9	622.4	751.0	131.6	7.5	3 347.2	3 010.1	298.3	1 071.4	1 639.9
July	1 637.5	1 591.4	213.5	622.5	755.3	146.3	8.2	3 367.4	3 004.2	306.1	1 058.8	1 637.2
August	1 667.6	1 620.8	218.8	637.3	764.7	132.1	7.3	3 372.2	3 037.1	312.6	1 075.0	1 644.6
September	1 687.3	1 639.9	222.9	646.0	771.0	123.8	6.8	3 362.8	3 044.9	316.9	1 078.5	1 642.6
October	1 697.1	1 648.8	215.8	648.8	784.1	134.7	7.4	3 373.9	3 036.9	304.8	1 075.1	1 655.6
November	1 714.7	1 665.7	216.1	659.8	789.8	136.1	7.4	3 384.7	3 046.3	303.0	1 085.1	1 656.6
December	1 725.4	1 676.0	217.0	662.7	796.3	147.1	7.9	3 393.6	3 037.5	302.0	1 078.9	1 655.9
1980:												
January	1 758.7	1 708.6	226.9	675.2	806.5	151.4	7.9	3 423.6	3 062.4	312.6	1 082.7	1 663.7
February	1 762.9	1 712.5	220.3	677.9	814.3	157.2	8.2	3 405.4	3 037.0	300.2	1 076.1	1 661.5
March	1 768.9	1 718.3	211.1	684.4	822.8	158.9	8.2	3 379.5	3 012.3	285.2	1 069.7	1 663.8
April	1 757.6	1 707.1	199.6	684.8	822.7	165.6	8.6	3 349.9	2 973.6	267.9	1 065.1	1 651.2
May	1 762.8	1 712.4	195.7	686.5	830.3	164.6	8.5	3 330.8	2 959.4	261.2	1 062.3	1 648.4
June	1 781.6	1 731.2	202.2	686.8	842.1	159.7	8.2	3 334.1	2 973.2	268.3	1 057.8	1 659.4
July	1 809.8	1 759.1	213.7	691.6	853.8	164.6	8.3	3 364.1	2 997.3	282.6	1 056.8	1 667.3
August	1 826.6	1 775.5	211.0	701.7	862.8	164.3	8.3	3 363.8	2 999.9	276.5	1 062.7	1 671.8
September	1 841.4	1 790.0	212.5	703.4	874.1	176.1	8.7	3 379.5	2 998.5	275.6	1 056.4	1 679.3
October	1 875.8	1 823.9	223.1	713.1	887.8	177.2	8.6	3 414.9	3 033.9	288.7	1 064.2	1 690.7
November	1 883.8	1 831.6	223.7	714.7	893.2	193.4	9.3	3 429.3	3 023.8	287.5	1 059.1	1 687.3
December	1 907.5	1 854.7	222.3	725.5	906.9	195.9	9.3	3 453.2	3 044.8	284.8	1 068.1	1 703.9

PERSONAL INCOME AND ITS DISPOSITION—Continued
(Billions of dollars, except as noted, monthly data are at seasonally adjusted annual rates)

YEAR AND MONTH	Personal outlays Total	Personal consumption expenditure Total	Durable goods	Nondurable goods	Services	Personal saving Billions of dollars	Percent of disposable personal income	Constant (1992) dollars Disposable personal income	Personal consumption expenditure Total	Durable goods	Nondurable goods	Services
1981:												
January	1 929.9	1 873.5	226.6	740.3	906.6	193.8	9.1	3 453.1	3 046.4	289.2	1 079.6	1 684.7
February	1 945.8	1 888.9	233.9	744.8	910.1	191.9	9.0	3 440.8	3 040.3	297.0	1 071.0	1 677.2
March	1 966.2	1 908.5	237.3	750.1	921.1	190.3	8.8	3 446.1	3 050.0	301.0	1 069.4	1 684.4
April	1 968.2	1 909.8	228.1	754.0	927.7	183.1	8.5	3 422.6	3 038.3	286.6	1 074.0	1 686.3
May	1 978.5	1 919.5	226.3	753.2	939.9	183.8	8.5	3 423.5	3 039.1	282.0	1 072.3	1 696.1
June	2 000.6	1 941.2	227.8	759.3	954.1	181.2	8.3	3 439.4	3 060.0	282.3	1 079.3	1 710.5
July	2 009.9	1 949.8	231.6	759.1	959.1	222.3	10.0	3 494.9	3 052.6	285.8	1 073.8	1 704.0
August	2 036.1	1 975.5	246.9	763.0	965.6	216.4	9.6	3 502.2	3 071.5	303.1	1 074.9	1 699.4
September	2 038.6	1 976.9	236.6	765.4	974.9	223.8	9.9	3 492.9	3 052.1	289.3	1 073.4	1 698.9
October	2 036.5	1 974.2	223.9	767.7	982.7	239.1	10.5	3 498.7	3 035.4	272.8	1 074.7	1 701.8
November	2 042.5	1 980.0	223.7	766.9	989.3	241.2	10.6	3 491.6	3 027.2	271.2	1 070.9	1 699.4
December	2 060.2	1 997.6	223.2	773.9	1 000.5	219.5	9.6	3 473.1	3 043.4	269.7	1 078.3	1 710.6
1982:												
January	2 068.2	2 004.7	227.9	770.2	1 006.6	215.4	9.4	3 459.2	3 036.7	274.3	1 069.9	1 706.9
February	2 092.1	2 028.8	235.7	780.9	1 012.1	201.3	8.8	3 463.7	3 064.0	283.5	1 081.9	1 709.8
March	2 094.0	2 030.6	235.8	775.2	1 019.6	208.4	9.1	3 470.8	3 061.2	283.5	1 074.8	1 715.4
April	2 096.8	2 033.0	231.4	775.3	1 026.3	242.1	10.4	3 523.6	3 062.7	277.5	1 080.4	1 718.8
May	2 115.3	2 051.0	243.1	777.9	1 030.0	230.6	9.8	3 511.7	3 070.3	290.1	1 077.4	1 713.1
June	2 119.1	2 054.4	232.4	780.3	1 041.7	226.7	9.7	3 486.1	3 053.2	276.6	1 069.8	1 722.3
July	2 143.3	2 078.4	233.7	794.8	1 049.9	228.1	9.6	3 502.8	3 069.9	277.6	1 084.5	1 721.7
August	2 150.9	2 085.6	234.7	789.7	1 061.2	223.9	9.4	3 498.7	3 072.7	279.4	1 077.8	1 730.1
September	2 175.0	2 109.3	246.0	792.1	1 071.2	204.4	8.6	3 494.5	3 097.8	293.0	1 080.3	1 736.1
October	2 196.5	2 130.2	240.0	801.4	1 088.9	201.7	8.4	3 501.6	3 110.2	284.5	1 090.1	1 750.0
November	2 219.7	2 152.5	254.0	799.9	1 098.5	193.9	8.0	3 513.6	3 133.5	301.7	1 086.7	1 756.3
December	2 230.9	2 163.3	256.4	804.3	1 102.6	191.5	7.9	3 522.1	3 145.4	304.0	1 094.0	1 757.6
1983:												
January	2 242.4	2 174.6	254.0	802.8	1 117.8	188.4	7.8	3 517.3	3 146.6	299.7	1 091.6	1 767.4
February	2 244.7	2 176.2	252.6	800.8	1 122.9	189.3	7.8	3 516.6	3 144.2	297.6	1 090.6	1 768.7
March	2 273.3	2 204.3	257.1	812.4	1 134.7	178.2	7.3	3 535.0	3 178.6	302.3	1 104.2	1 784.2
April	2 302.4	2 232.8	267.0	814.3	1 151.5	175.1	7.1	3 548.2	3 197.8	313.7	1 097.7	1 797.3
May	2 325.3	2 255.3	274.0	822.9	1 158.5	171.0	6.8	3 560.1	3 216.4	322.2	1 102.9	1 800.3
June	2 354.5	2 283.5	283.0	832.2	1 168.3	150.5	6.0	3 561.0	3 246.1	332.1	1 113.6	1 807.1
July	2 377.6	2 305.3	288.0	839.1	1 178.2	171.9	6.7	3 609.0	3 263.4	337.1	1 119.4	1 812.9
August	2 389.2	2 316.0	285.5	840.5	1 189.9	159.9	6.3	3 594.6	3 266.0	333.3	1 118.1	1 822.1
September	2 402.8	2 329.0	287.0	844.7	1 197.3	177.1	6.9	3 624.6	3 271.9	334.4	1 122.5	1 822.2
October	2 430.8	2 355.6	297.9	848.8	1 208.9	176.9	6.8	3 652.5	3 299.5	346.6	1 126.3	1 831.7
November	2 445.7	2 369.0	299.8	853.0	1 216.2	188.8	7.2	3 679.9	3 309.0	347.6	1 132.6	1 833.6
December	2 476.9	2 399.4	312.3	851.6	1 235.5	185.7	7.0	3 714.5	3 347.4	361.9	1 129.5	1 860.0
1984:												
January	2 506.2	2 428.8	320.3	869.6	1 238.9	184.8	6.9	3 739.5	3 375.2	371.8	1 146.0	1 858.6
February	2 485.4	2 406.6	312.3	860.8	1 233.5	239.3	8.8	3 770.9	3 330.8	362.9	1 128.5	1 842.1
March	2 511.3	2 431.9	312.6	865.7	1 253.7	240.2	8.7	3 796.9	3 356.0	362.9	1 132.5	1 864.8
April	2 536.9	2 456.9	319.4	876.2	1 261.3	246.6	8.9	3 827.5	3 378.4	368.8	1 145.1	1 867.0
May	2 555.5	2 474.2	324.8	879.6	1 269.8	235.4	8.4	3 831.0	3 396.2	374.9	1 150.0	1 872.8
June	2 578.3	2 495.8	329.0	892.5	1 274.3	238.6	8.5	3 857.7	3 417.9	379.4	1 166.4	1 871.8
July	2 574.1	2 491.4	324.6	882.7	1 284.1	262.1	9.2	3 874.2	3 403.2	374.3	1 151.8	1 879.0
August	2 591.8	2 508.6	322.8	886.2	1 299.6	274.1	9.6	3 901.1	3 414.8	371.4	1 153.1	1 893.6
September	2 615.3	2 531.6	327.3	896.9	1 307.5	276.2	9.6	3 925.9	3 437.3	375.5	1 164.4	1 899.9
October	2 616.1	2 531.5	325.7	890.4	1 315.5	262.3	9.1	3 897.3	3 427.6	374.3	1 152.3	1 904.5
November	2 656.8	2 571.7	340.5	902.2	1 328.9	241.8	8.3	3 917.3	3 475.4	390.4	1 167.5	1 918.5
December	2 664.5	2 578.5	341.9	899.9	1 336.7	244.5	8.4	3 924.7	3 478.8	392.6	1 163.7	1 923.5
1985:												
January	2 693.9	2 607.0	347.6	901.7	1 357.6	245.0	8.3	3 950.2	3 504.1	398.5	1 163.3	1 943.6
February	2 716.5	2 628.7	346.8	913.0	1 368.9	207.4	7.1	3 912.5	3 517.5	395.5	1 172.6	1 951.3
March	2 724.8	2 635.8	354.9	913.2	1 367.7	194.2	6.7	3 889.3	3 512.0	404.1	1 167.1	1 940.8
April	2 739.0	2 649.4	347.1	923.4	1 379.0	239.8	8.1	3 958.3	3 520.7	395.2	1 177.0	1 950.2
May	2 778.1	2 687.9	365.4	924.4	1 398.1	279.9	9.2	4 050.6	3 560.4	416.8	1 177.8	1 964.7
June	2 773.5	2 682.8	350.8	921.4	1 410.6	226.2	7.5	3 959.8	3 541.4	400.1	1 170.2	1 973.6
July	2 796.3	2 704.9	357.1	925.7	1 422.1	216.5	7.2	3 968.8	3 563.2	407.6	1 174.6	1 982.6
August	2 828.8	2 737.1	370.5	931.9	1 434.8	194.5	6.4	3 971.8	3 595.8	421.9	1 182.4	1 991.0
September	2 877.9	2 784.9	402.9	937.5	1 444.5	157.1	5.2	3 974.6	3 647.1	459.3	1 187.4	1 994.3
October	2 846.1	2 752.8	359.0	939.3	1 454.5	222.1	7.2	4 002.9	3 591.5	407.9	1 185.7	1 999.7
November	2 866.7	2 772.8	360.2	948.7	1 463.8	210.0	6.8	3 997.9	3 603.0	409.2	1 192.8	2 002.7
December	2 907.8	2 813.2	370.3	950.9	1 492.0	203.8	6.6	4 028.0	3 641.6	420.7	1 189.3	2 033.0
1986:												
January	2 922.7	2 826.8	380.3	959.9	1 486.6	211.2	6.7	4 041.6	3 645.6	431.0	1 198.3	2 015.1
February	2 916.1	2 819.6	368.2	953.1	1 498.2	231.1	7.3	4 059.0	3 636.5	418.0	1 197.5	2 022.0
March	2 920.4	2 823.6	362.5	955.3	1 505.8	249.4	7.9	4 097.7	3 650.1	412.0	1 216.3	2 023.4
April	2 934.6	2 837.3	381.9	942.4	1 513.0	235.3	7.4	4 101.7	3 671.3	434.2	1 210.3	2 025.3
May	2 959.7	2 861.8	391.4	951.3	1 519.1	220.5	6.9	4 103.1	3 692.4	442.8	1 218.2	2 028.4
June	2 965.8	2 867.8	380.9	954.5	1 532.4	225.3	7.1	4 100.7	3 685.2	429.0	1 217.9	2 037.8
July	2 987.6	2 888.9	392.7	955.1	1 541.1	224.2	7.0	4 120.5	3 706.3	441.0	1 219.0	2 044.3
August	3 006.7	2 907.8	410.7	953.3	1 543.8	215.4	6.7	4 123.7	3 721.6	459.7	1 215.2	2 042.1
September	3 081.5	2 981.0	462.6	958.2	1 561.0	152.9	4.7	4 122.3	3 800.4	517.0	1 216.7	2 054.7
October	3 044.9	2 944.3	411.2	966.0	1 567.1	186.7	5.8	4 111.6	3 746.0	459.5	1 227.8	2 054.4
November	3 041.8	2 941.3	396.7	962.5	1 582.1	197.1	6.1	4 111.8	3 733.9	442.5	1 221.3	2 068.7
December	3 111.4	3 011.2	445.0	974.9	1 591.3	139.9	4.3	4 118.6	3 814.6	494.2	1 231.8	2 080.4

	PERSONAL INCOME AND ITS DISPOSITION—Continued (Billions of dollars, except as noted, monthly data are at seasonally adjusted annual rates)											
YEAR AND MONTH	Personal outlays					Personal saving		Constant (1992) dollars				
	Total	Personal consumption expenditure				Billions of dollars	Percent of disposable personal income	Disposable personal income	Personal consumption expenditure			
		Total	Durable goods	Nondurable goods	Services				Total	Durable goods	Nondurable goods	Services
1987:												
January	3 055.5	2 956.3	376.0	976.6	1 603.6	229.7	7.0	4 135.4	3 721.4	416.6	1 221.3	2 086.3
February	3 120.2	3 021.0	402.4	1 003.6	1 615.0	197.5	6.0	4 159.3	3 787.3	445.1	1 244.6	2 096.6
March	3 129.2	3 029.9	404.3	998.5	1 627.1	201.8	6.1	4 165.1	3 788.6	445.8	1 234.2	2 108.0
April	3 155.4	3 055.4	412.4	1 006.0	1 637.0	57.7	1.8	4 004.3	3 807.7	453.0	1 239.2	2 114.1
May	3 164.9	3 065.0	409.1	1 010.4	1 645.5	189.3	5.6	4 168.2	3 808.7	448.8	1 241.6	2 117.6
June	3 190.0	3 089.8	419.8	1 015.0	1 655.0	173.2	5.2	4 164.2	3 825.5	458.8	1 241.0	2 123.9
July	3 212.0	3 110.9	426.4	1 016.3	1 668.2	158.6	4.7	4 162.4	3 841.7	464.5	1 239.6	2 135.5
August	3 249.4	3 148.3	442.9	1 022.6	1 682.8	148.6	4.4	4 176.5	3 869.7	481.2	1 241.4	2 143.1
September	3 244.6	3 143.5	434.7	1 023.1	1 685.7	167.9	4.9	4 176.7	3 847.4	470.7	1 238.5	2 135.4
October	3 255.0	3 154.5	417.6	1 026.2	1 710.7	202.5	5.9	4 214.7	3 845.3	451.5	1 238.9	2 155.0
November	3 264.4	3 164.2	421.2	1 030.7	1 712.3	213.7	6.1	4 227.1	3 845.5	454.7	1 241.1	2 149.2
December	3 295.7	3 195.3	433.3	1 038.9	1 723.0	217.7	6.2	4 264.8	3 878.6	468.9	1 249.7	2 158.1
1988:												
January	3 333.3	3 232.5	444.8	1 039.1	1 748.6	199.8	5.7	4 278.3	3 914.2	481.8	1 247.5	2 182.1
February	3 336.4	3 235.4	442.1	1 038.2	1 755.1	230.2	6.5	4 314.0	3 913.4	479.2	1 248.3	2 183.4
March	3 374.7	3 273.5	445.6	1 058.9	1 768.9	208.5	5.8	4 318.4	3 945.1	481.6	1 268.8	2 192.0
April	3 382.4	3 281.1	442.2	1 061.0	1 777.9	195.8	5.5	4 289.6	3 933.4	477.1	1 261.8	2 192.5
May	3 414.3	3 312.8	450.3	1 068.9	1 793.7	198.4	5.5	4 314.4	3 956.4	484.9	1 268.9	2 199.8
June	3 438.5	3 336.7	452.2	1 073.5	1 811.0	207.0	5.7	4 333.9	3 966.7	485.7	1 269.6	2 208.9
July	3 464.3	3 362.8	448.2	1 084.8	1 829.7	206.7	5.6	4 342.8	3 978.2	480.6	1 274.3	2 221.5
August	3 489.1	3 387.1	446.9	1 094.5	1 845.6	195.9	5.3	4 344.4	3 993.2	478.0	1 283.7	2 230.1
September	3 499.1	3 397.0	446.2	1 102.6	1 848.2	205.2	5.5	4 344.3	3 984.0	475.3	1 285.0	2 222.2
October	3 541.5	3 438.7	456.2	1 112.0	1 870.5	190.6	5.1	4 359.8	4 017.2	484.5	1 292.5	2 238.3
November	3 558.3	3 454.8	459.6	1 119.9	1 875.3	184.7	4.9	4 360.8	4 025.1	487.5	1 298.5	2 236.7
December	3 588.6	3 484.1	477.6	1 119.4	1 887.1	188.2	5.0	4 384.9	4 045.1	506.0	1 293.5	2 241.7
1989:												
January	3 611.0	3 503.4	472.8	1 135.5	1 895.1	195.5	5.1	4 394.7	4 044.7	499.4	1 304.9	2 236.9
February	3 612.2	3 503.6	456.9	1 128.5	1 918.2	229.1	6.0	4 420.1	4 031.5	481.8	1 292.6	2 255.6
March	3 620.7	3 511.4	457.7	1 132.8	1 920.9	250.6	6.5	4 434.6	4 022.2	483.8	1 288.4	2 248.4
April	3 669.1	3 558.8	478.4	1 151.2	1 929.2	186.1	4.8	4 385.8	4 048.6	503.8	1 291.5	2 249.9
May	3 679.9	3 568.7	468.1	1 161.8	1 938.7	196.8	5.1	4 392.4	4 043.4	492.3	1 296.0	2 252.8
June	3 693.3	3 581.6	471.0	1 165.8	1 944.8	211.4	5.4	4 415.5	4 050.1	494.4	1 299.3	2 253.3
July	3 713.4	3 601.3	476.8	1 167.1	1 957.4	204.4	5.2	4 418.0	4 061.0	499.4	1 299.1	2 259.8
August	3 752.2	3 639.3	498.0	1 172.2	1 969.1	172.2	4.4	4 421.3	4 100.2	521.7	1 309.3	2 265.1
September	3 754.4	3 641.2	479.0	1 181.4	1 980.8	175.4	4.5	4 412.6	4 088.5	501.0	1 316.2	2 268.3
October	3 772.4	3 657.6	473.8	1 182.7	2 001.0	182.2	4.6	4 418.0	4 086.2	494.6	1 309.4	2 279.9
November	3 780.0	3 664.7	469.7	1 186.6	2 008.3	207.2	5.2	4 441.9	4 082.6	489.5	1 311.7	2 279.5
December	3 821.7	3 705.9	471.7	1 200.1	2 034.1	182.0	4.5	4 446.8	4 116.1	492.5	1 323.8	2 297.9
1990:												
January	3 867.4	3 751.4	514.8	1 208.2	2 028.4	192.1	4.7	4 479.0	4 139.1	534.6	1 312.7	2 287.4
February	3 866.9	3 750.1	483.4	1 224.4	2 042.3	223.3	5.5	4 493.7	4 120.1	500.2	1 322.2	2 295.4
March	3 893.0	3 776.1	481.6	1 229.5	2 065.0	219.5	5.3	4 495.3	4 127.6	498.7	1 322.5	2 304.4
April	3 914.7	3 797.7	484.8	1 226.8	2 086.1	232.0	5.6	4 515.1	4 135.1	502.5	1 317.2	2 313.4
May	3 918.0	3 800.4	474.0	1 222.3	2 104.2	228.2	5.5	4 499.6	4 124.4	491.2	1 310.3	2 322.0
June	3 955.5	3 837.3	473.8	1 241.4	2 122.1	218.9	5.2	4 508.8	4 144.7	492.4	1 323.2	2 328.0
July	3 974.3	3 854.7	475.4	1 245.5	2 133.3	231.4	5.5	4 527.8	4 150.0	493.3	1 322.7	2 332.8
August	4 001.1	3 881.0	469.3	1 257.1	2 154.6	211.4	5.0	4 504.6	4 150.1	486.5	1 321.4	2 341.3
September	4 022.5	3 901.9	474.9	1 266.1	2 160.9	219.7	5.2	4 507.0	4 145.5	491.4	1 315.4	2 337.8
October	4 029.0	3 908.2	466.2	1 273.3	2 168.7	212.1	5.0	4 477.4	4 125.9	480.0	1 310.0	2 335.4
November	4 030.8	3 909.7	463.6	1 278.5	2 167.6	219.4	5.2	4 477.4	4 118.6	477.8	1 313.4	2 326.8
December	4 024.0	3 903.1	455.8	1 270.5	2 176.7	247.7	5.8	4 492.3	4 104.6	471.1	1 301.8	2 331.5
1991:												
January	4 001.3	3 879.8	432.3	1 264.6	2 183.0	263.8	6.2	4 463.1	4 060.0	443.5	1 293.2	2 323.9
February	4 026.2	3 904.4	444.3	1 266.9	2 193.3	247.6	5.8	4 460.6	4 075.1	452.8	1 298.9	2 323.7
March	4 069.9	3 947.9	470.4	1 273.3	2 204.1	220.1	5.1	4 475.1	4 118.3	479.4	1 309.9	2 328.3
April	4 064.0	3 941.8	450.7	1 273.2	2 217.8	253.1	5.9	4 491.3	4 100.8	458.1	1 304.4	2 338.4
May	4 089.2	3 966.8	450.8	1 284.2	2 231.8	251.8	5.8	4 502.0	4 114.0	458.0	1 312.0	2 344.0
June	4 096.7	3 974.4	456.5	1 281.8	2 236.2	274.1	6.3	4 525.7	4 115.3	465.3	1 307.8	2 342.1
July	4 119.0	3 996.7	462.8	1 286.1	2 247.8	242.7	5.6	4 504.4	4 127.6	468.6	1 313.0	2 345.9
August	4 116.9	3 994.4	457.8	1 282.5	2 254.1	259.9	5.9	4 506.3	4 112.6	463.6	1 305.8	2 343.2
September	4 135.8	4 013.7	465.3	1 281.5	2 266.9	262.5	6.0	4 512.9	4 118.3	469.9	1 302.5	2 345.9
October	4 122.5	3 999.8	454.0	1 273.5	2 272.3	277.9	6.3	4 505.9	4 095.6	457.3	1 295.0	2 343.4
November	4 153.2	4 030.6	457.1	1 280.4	2 293.1	269.3	6.1	4 510.6	4 111.0	460.2	1 296.3	2 354.6
December	4 173.6	4 050.8	460.7	1 283.3	2 306.8	291.1	6.5	4 541.8	4 120.7	466.9	1 295.8	2 358.1
1992:												
January	4 234.2	4 112.1	473.3	1 303.7	2 335.0	260.2	5.8	4 558.1	4 170.3	477.3	1 317.5	2 375.5
February	4 247.8	4 125.2	478.7	1 303.7	2 342.9	285.2	6.3	4 584.2	4 171.9	480.3	1 315.5	2 375.8
March	4 267.8	4 145.6	470.2	1 302.0	2 373.3	287.3	6.3	4 592.0	4 179.1	470.6	1 310.1	2 398.5
April	4 279.3	4 157.3	469.3	1 304.2	2 383.8	297.5	6.5	4 601.3	4 179.6	469.6	1 310.8	2 399.3
May	4 308.0	4 186.3	483.3	1 311.6	2 391.4	291.1	6.3	4 614.1	4 199.9	482.5	1 316.0	2 401.3
June	4 327.1	4 205.6	491.4	1 309.4	2 404.7	290.1	6.3	4 621.7	4 209.7	491.3	1 309.2	2 409.1
July	4 352.8	4 232.1	487.8	1 318.4	2 425.9	272.0	5.9	4 611.9	4 220.4	487.4	1 314.7	2 418.2
August	4 329.2	4 208.6	492.8	1 329.5	2 386.3	277.4	6.0	4 605.2	4 207.3	492.1	1 324.4	2 390.9
September	4 396.4	4 276.0	496.9	1 331.0	2 448.1	253.4	5.5	4 624.1	4 252.3	496.3	1 324.3	2 431.7
October	4 428.4	4 307.5	505.4	1 344.8	2 457.3	261.0	5.6	4 645.1	4 266.8	503.5	1 336.1	2 427.2
November	4 444.6	4 324.3	496.8	1 349.3	2 478.3	264.7	5.6	4 657.6	4 276.8	494.7	1 340.2	2 441.9
December	4 476.9	4 357.0	516.4	1 354.3	2 486.2	387.8	8.0	4 804.8	4 303.4	516.7	1 343.1	2 443.7

SELECTED MONTHLY DATA, 1969-1992

INDUSTRIAL PRODUCTION AND CAPACITY UTILIZATION
(Seasonally adjusted)

YEAR AND MONTH	Total industrial production	Major market groups — Products — Total	Consumer goods	Business equipment	Construction supplies	Materials	Manufacturing Total	Durables	Nondurables	Mining	Utilities	Total industry	Manufacturing Total	Advanced processing	Primary processing	Mining	Utilities
1969:																	
January	59.8	58.6	61.0	46.1	73.5	61.1	56.6	56.6	56.7	96.0	60.4	87.8	87.3	87.5	86.3	84.5	96.3
February	60.2	58.8	61.5	46.0	74.2	61.8	57.1	56.8	57.4	95.9	60.9	88.0	87.7	87.6	87.2	84.3	96.5
March	60.7	59.4	62.0	46.5	74.5	62.1	57.5	57.2	57.9	96.4	61.5	88.4	88.0	88.1	87.3	84.7	97.0
April	60.5	58.9	61.1	47.0	73.8	62.3	57.3	57.1	57.6	97.0	61.2	87.8	87.3	87.2	86.8	85.3	96.0
May	60.2	58.6	60.6	46.7	73.3	62.1	57.0	56.5	57.8	98.4	61.3	87.1	86.6	86.3	86.4	86.4	95.5
June	60.8	59.0	61.3	47.1	73.7	63.0	57.4	57.1	57.9	101.2	62.4	87.6	86.8	86.7	86.4	88.8	96.8
July	61.2	59.5	62.4	47.6	73.0	63.0	57.8	57.3	58.6	98.8	63.4	87.8	87.1	87.0	86.6	86.7	97.8
August	61.3	59.4	62.3	47.4	73.0	63.6	57.9	57.5	58.5	98.6	63.8	87.7	86.9	86.7	86.7	86.5	97.8
September	61.3	59.3	61.8	47.9	73.0	63.8	57.8	57.6	58.2	99.7	63.1	87.3	86.5	86.1	86.4	87.3	96.3
October	61.3	59.3	61.8	48.0	73.2	63.8	57.9	57.7	58.2	99.8	63.6	87.1	86.2	85.9	86.3	87.4	96.5
November	60.7	58.6	61.3	46.9	72.8	63.5	57.3	56.6	58.3	100.2	64.5	85.9	85.0	84.0	86.1	87.7	97.4
December	60.6	58.6	61.4	46.7	72.4	63.1	57.0	55.9	58.5	101.5	64.6	85.4	84.2	83.5	85.0	88.8	96.9
1970:																	
January	59.4	57.7	60.3	46.1	70.1	61.6	55.7	54.0	58.1	100.6	64.7	83.5	82.1	81.6	82.5	88.0	96.6
February	59.4	57.8	60.9	46.3	69.9	61.3	55.8	54.0	58.3	99.8	64.7	83.2	81.9	81.6	82.1	87.4	96.0
March	59.3	57.8	60.8	46.4	70.5	61.1	55.6	54.0	57.9	100.0	65.6	82.8	81.4	81.2	81.4	87.6	96.8
April	59.2	57.8	61.1	46.4	71.2	60.7	55.4	53.6	58.0	100.1	65.9	82.4	80.9	80.8	80.7	87.7	96.8
May	59.1	57.8	61.4	46.3	71.3	60.5	55.3	53.5	57.9	100.1	67.2	82.0	80.4	80.4	80.1	87.8	98.0
June	58.9	57.7	61.6	46.0	71.0	60.2	55.1	53.3	57.8	100.0	65.8	81.5	79.9	79.9	79.6	87.7	95.5
July	59.1	57.7	61.7	45.9	71.8	60.5	55.3	53.2	58.3	98.9	66.8	81.4	79.9	79.6	80.0	86.8	96.4
August	58.9	57.1	60.7	45.8	71.5	61.3	54.9	53.1	57.6	101.1	67.6	81.0	79.2	78.4	80.0	88.8	97.0
September	58.5	56.7	60.4	44.8	71.3	60.9	54.4	52.1	57.9	102.5	68.0	80.2	78.2	77.4	79.2	90.1	97.0
October	57.4	55.8	59.7	43.3	70.6	59.2	53.2	50.0	57.9	104.0	66.9	78.4	76.3	75.2	77.7	91.5	95.0
November	57.0	55.5	59.3	43.1	69.7	58.9	52.9	49.6	57.7	104.0	67.2	77.7	75.6	74.3	77.2	91.6	94.8
December	58.3	56.8	61.9	43.7	70.5	60.2	54.3	51.6	58.2	103.3	67.1	79.2	77.3	76.7	77.9	90.9	94.1
1971:																	
January	58.8	57.0	62.8	42.7	70.6	61.1	54.7	52.0	58.7	101.8	68.7	79.6	77.7	76.9	78.7	89.7	95.9
February	58.7	57.1	62.7	42.9	71.0	60.7	54.8	52.1	58.6	100.4	68.3	79.2	77.6	76.8	78.6	88.5	94.8
March	58.6	56.9	62.9	42.5	70.7	60.8	54.7	51.9	58.6	100.9	68.9	78.9	77.2	76.2	78.5	89.0	95.2
April	58.9	57.2	63.4	42.3	71.4	61.2	54.9	51.9	59.3	101.4	69.1	79.2	77.4	76.2	79.0	89.6	95.0
May	59.2	57.2	63.5	42.0	71.7	61.9	55.3	52.6	59.3	101.3	69.7	79.4	77.8	76.4	79.5	89.6	95.4
June	59.5	57.4	64.0	42.2	72.5	62.2	55.5	52.4	59.9	100.9	70.3	79.5	77.8	76.4	79.5	89.3	95.7
July	59.3	58.1	65.0	42.2	73.2	60.7	55.5	52.1	60.5	97.5	70.0	79.1	77.7	77.0	78.1	86.4	94.9
August	59.0	57.8	64.2	42.9	71.9	60.4	54.9	51.0	60.5	98.7	69.5	78.4	76.6	76.5	75.9	87.5	93.7
September	59.9	58.6	64.8	43.9	74.6	61.5	56.0	52.4	61.2	98.4	70.0	79.5	77.9	77.4	78.1	87.3	93.9
October	60.4	59.2	65.7	44.3	75.6	61.7	56.8	53.3	61.9	89.8	71.1	79.9	78.9	78.3	79.2	79.7	94.9
November	60.6	59.5	66.2	44.5	75.9	61.8	57.0	53.4	62.3	93.4	70.2	80.0	79.0	78.5	79.0	83.0	93.3
December	61.3	59.9	66.7	44.8	77.2	63.1	57.6	53.9	62.9	99.4	69.9	80.7	79.5	79.0	79.8	88.4	92.5
1972:																	
January	62.7	60.9	67.6	45.9	79.1	64.9	58.9	55.5	63.9	99.7	71.7	82.3	81.2	80.7	82.8	88.8	94.3
February	63.1	61.5	67.8	46.5	79.5	65.1	59.4	56.1	64.0	99.5	73.0	82.6	81.5	81.1	82.7	88.7	95.7
March	63.6	61.9	68.1	47.3	80.2	65.7	59.9	56.6	64.6	100.0	73.0	83.1	82.0	81.2	83.5	89.3	95.2
April	64.7	62.9	69.4	48.3	81.4	66.8	60.9	57.7	65.4	101.4	74.4	84.2	83.1	82.3	84.5	90.6	96.6
May	64.5	62.6	68.7	48.4	81.8	66.9	60.7	57.7	65.1	99.9	73.1	83.8	82.7	81.4	84.9	89.4	94.5
June	64.7	62.9	69.0	48.6	82.3	66.9	60.9	57.7	65.6	100.5	73.0	83.8	82.7	81.5	84.7	90.0	94.0
July	64.6	62.7	68.7	48.4	82.8	67.0	60.9	57.9	65.4	101.1	73.1	83.5	82.5	81.0	84.9	90.6	93.7
August	65.5	63.5	69.9	49.1	83.7	68.0	61.8	58.6	66.3	100.7	74.0	84.4	83.4	81.8	85.8	90.5	94.4
September	66.2	64.1	70.2	50.2	84.8	68.9	62.3	59.4	66.4	102.1	74.5	85.1	83.9	82.3	86.4	91.8	94.7
October	67.2	65.0	71.1	51.2	85.8	70.0	63.3	60.8	66.9	101.8	76.1	86.1	85.0	83.4	87.8	91.6	96.2
November	68.0	65.7	71.4	52.5	87.0	70.9	64.1	61.9	67.2	101.3	76.7	86.9	85.9	84.2	88.8	91.2	96.6
December	68.6	66.2	72.2	53.0	86.4	71.8	64.9	62.6	68.0	100.8	76.8	87.5	86.7	85.3	89.3	90.9	96.3
1973:																	
January	68.7	66.2	71.5	54.1	86.8	71.9	65.0	63.2	67.5	100.7	76.1	87.3	86.6	85.2	89.1	90.9	95.0
February	69.6	67.2	72.5	55.0	89.8	72.8	65.9	64.2	68.2	101.3	77.4	88.3	87.6	85.9	90.6	91.6	96.2
March	69.6	67.2	72.6	55.3	88.7	72.7	66.1	64.2	68.6	99.6	75.5	88.0	87.5	86.0	90.4	90.2	93.3
April	69.9	67.3	72.4	56.1	88.1	73.2	66.3	64.4	68.7	99.5	76.4	88.1	87.5	86.0	90.3	90.2	93.9
May	70.2	67.6	72.5	56.8	88.6	73.6	66.5	64.8	68.8	100.2	76.6	88.3	87.6	86.1	90.5	90.9	93.7
June	70.7	68.0	72.7	57.6	88.8	74.2	67.0	65.5	68.9	101.2	77.7	88.7	87.9	86.6	90.4	91.9	94.6
July	71.1	68.3	72.6	58.0	88.7	75.0	67.3	65.8	69.3	102.8	77.9	89.0	88.1	86.6	91.1	93.4	94.3
August	71.1	68.1	72.5	58.2	88.9	75.1	67.4	65.7	69.6	103.0	77.6	88.7	88.0	86.5	91.0	93.7	93.5
September	71.6	69.1	73.8	59.5	89.1	75.0	67.8	66.5	69.4	102.6	79.6	89.2	88.2	87.1	90.5	93.5	95.3
October	71.9	69.1	73.4	60.0	89.1	75.6	68.2	66.8	70.0	102.9	78.1	89.2	88.5	87.2	90.9	93.8	93.2
November	71.9	69.2	73.3	60.1	89.5	75.7	68.3	67.1	69.9	102.7	76.7	89.0	88.5	87.0	91.2	93.8	91.0
December	70.8	67.7	71.2	58.7	88.9	75.1	67.1	65.7	68.8	103.1	74.5	87.4	86.6	84.7	90.2	94.3	88.0
1974:																	
January	69.8	66.8	70.2	58.4	86.7	74.0	66.3	64.3	68.9	102.3	74.5	85.9	85.3	83.6	88.4	93.6	87.5
February	69.5	66.7	69.7	58.6	86.2	73.5	66.0	63.9	68.9	102.8	74.0	85.4	84.7	83.1	87.7	94.0	86.5
March	69.9	67.3	70.6	59.1	86.3	73.4	66.3	63.9	69.7	102.1	75.4	85.5	84.8	83.4	87.4	93.3	87.8
April	69.7	67.4	70.4	59.7	86.8	72.7	66.0	63.8	69.0	101.9	75.9	85.1	84.2	82.7	87.0	93.1	88.0
May	70.5	68.0	71.0	60.8	86.6	73.9	66.8	64.9	69.5	102.8	77.5	85.8	85.0	83.8	87.3	93.9	89.5
June	70.8	68.4	71.5	61.0	85.9	73.9	67.1	65.2	69.6	101.7	77.8	85.8	85.1	84.0	87.1	92.9	89.5
July	70.4	67.9	71.0	61.1	83.6	73.8	66.7	64.7	69.5	102.9	75.4	85.2	84.3	83.2	86.4	94.0	86.4
August	70.2	67.8	71.4	60.1	82.7	73.4	66.7	64.7	69.4	100.1	76.7	84.7	84.1	83.1	85.9	91.3	87.4
September	70.5	68.1	71.2	61.6	81.9	73.7	66.8	65.0	69.1	101.4	77.3	84.8	83.9	83.2	85.3	92.5	87.7
October	70.0	67.6	70.9	61.4	79.5	73.1	66.2	64.6	68.3	102.6	77.0	83.9	83.0	82.6	83.5	93.6	87.1
November	68.0	66.3	69.0	60.9	77.3	69.8	64.4	62.8	66.5	96.2	75.8	81.3	80.4	80.6	80.1	87.8	85.3
December	65.1	64.0	67.1	57.4	73.6	66.1	61.3	59.5	63.8	96.5	75.9	77.7	76.3	77.2	74.9	88.0	85.0

INDUSTRIAL PRODUCTION AND CAPACITY UTILIZATION—Continued
(Seasonally adjusted)

YEAR AND MONTH	Industrial production indexes (1992=100)											Capacity utilization (Percent of capacity)					
	Total industrial production	Major market groups				Materials	Major industry groups					Total industry	Manufacturing			Mining	Utilities
		Products					Manufacturing			Mining	Utilities						
		Total	Consumer goods	Business equipment	Construction supplies		Total	Durables	Non durables				Total	Advanced processing	Primary processing		
1975:																	
January	63.4	62.2	64.3	56.4	71.7	64.7	59.5	57.5	62.2	100.7	74.5	75.5	73.9	74.5	72.7	91.7	83.3
February	62.4	61.7	64.4	55.2	71.3	62.8	58.3	56.0	61.5	100.5	75.6	74.1	72.3	73.0	71.0	91.5	84.2
March	61.3	60.8	64.0	53.7	69.7	61.2	57.0	54.9	59.9	99.3	77.6	72.6	70.5	71.8	68.2	90.3	86.2
April	61.9	61.5	65.7	53.5	69.7	61.6	57.6	55.1	61.2	98.6	78.7	73.1	71.1	72.3	68.9	89.6	87.1
May	61.7	61.5	66.1	52.9	69.3	61.1	57.5	54.6	61.7	98.0	76.3	72.7	70.8	71.8	69.0	89.0	84.2
June	62.5	62.2	67.4	52.6	69.7	62.0	58.4	54.6	63.8	99.4	76.7	73.5	71.7	72.4	70.2	90.2	84.3
July	62.9	62.7	68.8	52.4	70.3	62.1	58.9	54.9	64.8	97.3	76.6	73.8	72.3	72.7	71.2	88.2	84.0
August	64.0	63.4	69.3	52.9	72.1	64.1	59.9	56.0	65.7	97.7	77.9	75.0	73.3	73.4	73.1	88.5	85.2
September	64.6	63.7	70.0	52.9	72.9	65.3	60.7	56.7	66.6	97.6	77.4	75.6	74.1	73.6	74.9	88.3	84.4
October	65.0	63.8	69.9	53.1	73.4	66.0	61.1	57.0	67.2	98.6	76.3	75.8	74.5	74.1	75.0	89.1	83.0
November	65.6	64.4	70.7	53.5	73.5	66.7	61.6	57.4	67.9	99.6	77.5	76.4	74.9	74.5	75.5	89.9	84.0
December	66.1	64.7	71.3	53.6	73.3	67.5	62.2	58.1	68.4	99.3	76.7	76.8	75.5	75.2	76.1	89.6	82.9
1976:																	
January	66.8	65.3	72.0	53.5	75.9	68.4	62.9	58.9	68.8	99.7	78.4	77.5	76.2	75.6	77.2	89.9	84.6
February	68.0	66.6	73.5	54.7	77.9	69.4	64.3	60.5	70.0	99.2	77.1	78.7	77.7	77.2	78.8	89.4	83.0
March	67.8	66.2	72.9	54.5	77.5	69.7	64.1	60.3	69.6	98.4	78.0	78.3	77.2	76.6	78.5	88.7	83.8
April	68.1	66.3	73.1	54.5	77.2	70.2	64.3	60.6	69.7	98.2	78.9	78.4	77.2	76.7	78.5	88.5	84.6
May	68.9	67.1	74.0	55.0	79.0	71.0	65.1	61.8	69.9	99.4	79.3	79.1	78.1	77.7	78.9	89.6	84.8
June	68.9	66.9	74.0	54.8	79.3	71.3	65.0	61.6	70.0	99.3	79.3	79.0	77.8	77.2	79.1	89.5	84.6
July	69.3	67.5	74.3	55.4	80.5	71.5	65.6	62.3	70.6	98.7	79.7	79.3	78.3	77.8	79.3	88.9	84.8
August	69.7	67.8	74.7	55.5	81.2	72.1	65.9	63.0	70.2	99.1	79.8	79.6	78.5	78.0	79.5	89.3	84.8
September	70.0	68.0	74.4	55.6	81.4	72.4	66.2	62.3	71.8	101.0	79.5	79.7	78.6	77.6	80.2	90.9	84.3
October	70.2	68.3	74.7	56.0	82.0	72.4	66.4	62.4	72.4	100.9	80.8	79.8	78.7	77.7	80.2	90.8	85.6
November	71.4	69.7	76.7	57.9	82.8	73.1	67.3	63.8	72.5	101.0	84.0	80.9	79.6	79.2	80.0	90.9	88.8
December	71.9	70.3	77.4	58.9	81.9	73.7	68.0	64.5	73.1	101.0	83.9	81.4	80.2	79.8	80.5	90.8	88.4
1977:																	
January	72.3	70.9	78.1	59.1	81.6	73.8	68.5	64.9	73.8	99.7	83.0	81.6	80.6	80.5	80.5	89.6	87.3
February	72.4	70.5	77.3	59.1	81.9	74.5	68.7	65.2	73.7	101.5	79.9	81.5	80.6	79.9	81.5	91.0	83.7
March	73.2	71.1	78.0	59.3	84.0	75.8	69.6	65.9	74.9	102.9	78.8	82.3	81.4	80.5	82.8	92.0	82.4
April	74.3	72.3	78.7	60.9	86.2	76.5	70.6	67.3	75.3	103.8	79.9	83.3	82.3	81.5	83.8	92.5	83.4
May	75.0	72.9	79.2	61.1	87.5	77.5	71.2	67.9	76.0	104.0	81.9	83.9	82.9	81.8	84.7	92.4	85.2
June	75.6	73.5	79.7	61.8	88.5	78.0	71.8	68.6	76.3	104.7	82.7	84.3	83.3	82.2	85.2	92.7	85.8
July	75.6	73.8	80.0	62.4	89.3	77.7	71.8	68.9	75.9	103.9	83.7	84.2	83.2	82.2	84.7	91.7	86.7
August	75.9	74.2	80.7	62.8	89.4	77.8	72.4	69.4	76.7	101.2	83.1	84.3	83.6	82.8	85.0	89.1	85.8
September	76.3	74.5	80.4	64.4	88.8	78.4	72.5	69.8	76.2	106.1	82.8	84.6	83.5	83.1	84.2	93.2	85.4
October	76.1	74.3	80.7	64.0	89.0	78.2	72.4	69.7	76.2	104.8	83.0	84.2	83.2	82.5	84.4	91.7	85.4
November	76.2	74.4	80.8	64.4	88.7	78.2	72.5	69.5	76.8	104.4	81.9	84.1	83.2	82.6	84.2	91.0	84.1
December	75.9	74.9	81.0	65.1	89.0	76.7	72.8	70.2	76.5	96.2	82.8	83.5	83.4	83.0	84.0	83.6	84.8
1978:																	
January	75.6	74.4	79.6	64.6	89.2	76.9	72.6	69.5	77.0	95.4	83.0	83.0	82.9	82.1	84.2	82.7	84.9
February	75.6	74.8	80.6	65.0	89.4	76.3	72.6	69.5	76.9	95.3	83.5	82.8	82.6	82.2	83.4	82.5	85.2
March	76.4	75.7	81.4	65.8	89.3	76.9	73.1	70.2	77.1	99.7	83.7	83.4	83.0	83.0	82.9	86.1	85.3
April	79.0	77.4	83.1	67.9	92.0	80.7	75.2	72.6	78.9	109.2	83.6	86.0	85.2	84.9	85.7	94.1	85.0
May	79.0	77.2	82.4	67.9	91.8	81.1	75.3	72.7	78.8	108.7	84.5	85.8	85.0	84.2	86.3	93.6	85.7
June	79.9	78.4	83.8	69.1	93.1	81.5	76.2	73.6	79.8	109.3	84.7	86.6	85.8	85.4	86.4	93.9	85.8
July	80.1	78.5	83.5	69.6	92.7	82.0	76.4	74.3	79.4	109.7	84.5	86.6	85.8	85.6	86.2	94.1	85.3
August	80.3	78.6	83.3	70.9	92.2	82.2	76.8	74.9	79.3	108.6	84.5	86.6	85.9	85.6	86.5	93.0	85.3
September	80.7	79.0	83.7	71.1	93.0	82.7	77.2	75.4	79.7	108.3	85.3	86.7	86.2	85.8	86.8	92.6	85.9
October	81.1	79.2	83.4	72.1	93.3	83.4	77.6	76.0	79.6	109.2	85.5	86.9	86.3	85.8	87.3	93.2	85.8
November	81.6	79.7	83.2	73.6	93.4	83.7	78.2	76.8	80.1	108.7	84.9	87.2	86.8	86.3	87.6	92.6	85.1
December	81.9	80.0	83.4	73.8	95.0	84.1	78.6	77.4	80.2	108.0	85.3	87.3	86.9	86.3	88.1	91.9	85.3
1979:																	
January	81.5	80.0	82.8	75.7	93.5	83.1	78.3	77.4	79.4	106.0	85.5	86.7	86.4	86.5	86.2	90.1	85.4
February	82.1	80.5	82.7	76.6	94.3	84.0	78.9	78.2	79.6	105.7	88.5	87.1	86.7	86.6	87.0	89.8	88.4
March	82.4	80.6	82.8	77.3	94.1	84.3	79.2	78.5	80.0	105.5	87.8	87.1	86.9	86.7	87.1	89.6	87.6
April	81.6	79.6	81.1	76.4	93.3	83.9	78.0	76.5	80.0	107.5	89.3	86.1	85.3	84.6	86.6	91.3	89.1
May	82.5	80.7	82.4	78.1	93.7	84.5	79.2	78.3	80.3	107.0	88.6	86.9	86.4	86.1	86.8	90.9	88.4
June	82.6	80.5	82.2	78.2	93.4	84.8	79.3	78.7	80.0	107.3	86.7	86.7	86.3	85.8	87.0	91.1	86.5
July	82.0	80.0	80.9	77.9	93.9	84.2	78.9	78.0	80.0	105.7	85.2	85.9	85.6	84.6	87.0	89.8	85.0
August	81.6	79.6	80.3	77.3	92.3	83.9	78.1	76.8	79.8	108.6	85.9	85.4	84.5	83.7	85.8	92.2	85.6
September	81.7	79.8	80.5	77.8	92.4	83.7	78.1	77.1	79.4	109.4	85.8	85.3	84.3	83.8	85.1	92.9	85.5
October	82.0	80.3	80.9	78.3	92.7	83.9	78.5	77.2	80.2	109.3	86.2	85.5	84.5	84.2	85.0	92.8	85.8
November	81.6	79.9	80.5	77.2	92.2	83.5	77.9	76.4	79.9	109.9	86.8	84.9	83.6	83.3	84.2	93.3	86.4
December	81.5	79.8	81.0	76.5	91.6	83.2	77.8	76.3	79.9	109.2	86.0	84.5	83.3	83.1	83.7	92.7	85.5
1980:																	
January	81.8	79.6	80.3	76.9	90.9	84.4	78.0	76.1	80.5	113.1	84.2	84.7	83.3	82.9	83.9	96.0	83.6
February	81.9	80.3	80.7	78.3	91.2	83.6	78.2	76.7	80.0	111.3	85.2	84.6	83.3	83.5	82.9	94.3	84.5
March	81.9	80.3	81.0	77.8	90.4	83.5	77.9	76.5	79.6	112.3	87.8	84.4	82.7	83.1	82.1	95.0	86.9
April	80.3	78.8	79.6	77.3	84.2	81.8	76.2	74.5	78.6	111.0	86.1	82.6	80.8	81.8	79.2	93.8	85.0
May	78.3	77.3	77.8	75.9	80.9	79.2	73.9	71.7	76.8	111.7	85.6	80.4	78.1	80.0	74.8	94.3	84.4
June	77.3	76.9	77.7	75.2	79.8	77.4	72.8	70.3	76.2	110.8	86.0	79.2	76.7	79.0	72.8	93.4	84.6
July	76.8	77.1	78.1	75.2	79.1	76.0	72.2	69.6	75.9	109.1	88.1	78.5	75.9	78.9	71.0	91.9	86.5
August	77.7	78.1	79.0	75.5	82.7	76.8	73.4	70.9	76.9	107.9	88.8	79.3	77.0	79.6	72.7	90.7	87.1
September	78.8	78.8	80.1	75.7	83.9	78.5	74.5	71.9	78.2	109.8	89.3	80.3	77.9	79.9	74.5	92.2	87.4
October	79.4	79.2	80.3	76.7	84.4	79.3	75.4	73.2	78.4	109.0	88.8	80.7	78.6	80.3	75.7	91.4	86.8
November	80.7	79.8	80.4	77.5	85.8	81.4	76.7	75.0	78.8	110.7	89.3	81.8	79.7	80.5	78.3	92.8	87.2
December	81.1	80.1	80.5	78.2	85.7	82.0	76.9	74.9	79.5	112.8	88.9	82.1	79.7	80.4	78.4	94.4	86.7

INDUSTRIAL PRODUCTION AND CAPACITY UTILIZATION—Continued
(Seasonally adjusted)

YEAR AND MONTH	Industrial production indexes (1992=100)											Capacity utilization (Percent of capacity)					
	Total industrial production	Major market groups					Major industry groups					Total industry	Manufacturing			Mining	Utilities
		Products				Materials	Manufacturing			Mining	Utilities						
		Total	Consumer goods	Business equipment	Construction supplies		Total	Durables	Non durables				Total	Advanced processing	Primary processing		
1981:																	
January	80.4	79.6	80.2	76.5	85.6	81.1	76.4	74.2	79.4	112.3	84.6	81.2	79.0	79.2	78.6	93.8	82.5
February	80.8	80.1	80.6	78.0	84.6	81.3	76.9	74.7	79.8	113.4	83.0	81.4	79.2	79.4	78.9	94.3	80.8
March	81.1	80.3	80.4	78.2	85.6	81.9	77.1	75.1	79.8	114.5	84.1	81.6	79.3	79.6	78.8	94.9	81.9
April	80.6	80.4	80.3	78.1	85.4	80.5	77.2	75.2	79.9	108.9	82.9	80.9	79.3	79.5	78.8	90.0	80.7
May	81.3	81.2	81.0	79.2	85.1	81.1	77.8	76.0	80.2	109.6	85.2	81.4	79.6	80.1	78.8	90.3	82.8
June	81.8	81.1	80.3	80.0	83.3	82.3	77.7	75.9	80.0	114.3	86.6	81.8	79.3	79.9	78.3	93.7	84.1
July	82.5	81.5	81.1	79.8	83.0	83.4	78.2	76.3	80.7	117.0	86.9	82.3	79.6	80.1	78.8	95.6	84.4
August	82.1	80.9	80.4	78.4	83.0	83.4	77.5	75.8	79.9	118.7	85.6	81.8	78.8	78.8	78.9	96.6	83.1
September	81.5	80.4	79.8	78.0	80.4	82.5	76.9	74.9	79.7	117.8	84.5	80.9	78.0	78.4	77.4	95.5	82.0
October	80.9	80.1	79.4	77.9	79.0	81.5	76.1	74.1	78.7	117.9	85.6	80.1	77.0	77.8	75.4	95.2	82.9
November	79.7	79.4	78.9	76.0	77.2	79.8	74.9	72.4	78.3	116.6	85.2	78.8	75.6	76.8	73.5	93.7	82.5
December	78.8	79.0	78.2	75.6	74.9	78.3	73.7	71.1	77.3	117.0	85.5	77.7	74.2	76.1	70.7	93.7	82.8
1982:																	
January	77.6	78.0	77.8	72.9	74.0	76.7	72.2	68.8	76.9	116.1	86.3	76.3	72.6	74.3	69.3	92.6	83.5
February	79.2	79.9	79.4	75.0	77.3	78.1	74.3	71.1	78.7	116.9	84.2	77.8	74.6	76.2	71.5	92.9	81.4
March	78.7	79.5	78.9	74.8	75.8	77.5	73.8	70.6	78.3	116.0	83.8	77.1	73.9	75.7	70.4	91.9	81.0
April	77.9	78.9	78.7	73.5	75.4	76.5	73.1	69.9	77.6	114.4	83.8	76.2	73.1	75.1	69.3	90.2	80.9
May	77.3	78.3	78.8	72.3	76.5	75.9	72.8	69.6	77.4	112.4	82.0	75.4	72.7	74.7	68.7	88.3	79.1
June	77.1	78.1	79.4	71.7	76.4	75.5	72.8	69.5	77.5	110.4	81.6	75.0	72.6	74.4	68.9	86.3	78.7
July	76.5	77.6	79.1	70.9	76.3	74.7	72.2	68.8	77.0	109.0	81.6	74.2	71.8	73.8	68.0	85.0	78.6
August	76.0	77.2	79.5	68.9	76.6	74.4	71.9	67.7	77.8	107.7	81.8	73.7	71.4	72.9	68.4	83.6	78.7
September	75.5	76.7	78.9	68.3	76.0	73.8	71.5	67.0	77.9	106.2	80.7	73.0	70.9	72.2	68.2	82.1	77.6
October	74.9	75.9	78.7	66.6	75.2	73.3	70.7	65.6	78.0	106.3	81.1	72.2	69.9	71.2	67.5	81.8	77.9
November	74.7	75.9	78.7	65.8	75.9	72.9	70.5	65.2	77.9	105.8	81.7	71.9	69.6	70.8	67.2	81.0	78.4
December	74.1	75.6	77.8	66.4	73.7	71.9	70.0	65.1	77.0	105.2	79.2	71.1	69.0	70.4	66.2	80.3	75.9
1983:																	
January	75.6	76.7	79.6	65.6	77.8	74.1	71.8	66.8	78.9	106.4	79.4	72.5	70.6	71.4	69.0	81.0	76.1
February	75.5	76.4	79.8	65.1	79.0	74.0	72.1	67.4	78.8	103.8	77.6	72.3	70.8	71.3	69.9	79.0	74.2
March	76.2	77.0	80.1	65.7	79.6	75.0	73.1	68.6	79.6	102.4	78.7	72.9	71.8	72.0	71.2	77.9	75.2
April	77.2	78.0	81.4	65.8	82.1	75.9	74.0	69.5	80.3	103.5	81.1	73.7	72.5	72.5	72.3	78.7	77.4
May	78.1	78.7	82.3	66.1	83.0	77.0	75.0	70.5	81.4	103.4	82.7	74.5	73.4	73.1	73.9	78.6	78.9
June	78.5	79.5	83.1	66.6	84.2	77.0	75.6	71.2	81.9	103.4	81.8	74.8	73.9	73.7	74.1	78.6	77.9
July	79.9	80.5	83.9	67.3	86.6	79.0	76.7	72.7	82.4	105.5	85.5	76.1	74.8	74.5	75.5	80.1	81.3
August	81.0	81.5	85.1	68.3	86.5	80.1	77.6	73.6	83.2	107.2	88.0	77.0	75.6	75.4	76.1	81.3	83.6
September	82.4	83.1	86.3	71.1	87.1	81.2	79.3	75.7	84.4	108.4	86.2	78.2	77.2	77.0	77.4	82.2	81.8
October	83.0	83.2	85.5	71.7	88.5	82.6	79.8	76.6	84.3	109.7	87.4	78.7	77.6	77.2	78.4	83.2	82.9
November	82.9	83.4	85.2	72.7	88.0	82.2	80.1	77.0	84.3	109.1	84.5	78.6	77.7	77.5	78.2	82.7	80.1
December	83.4	84.2	85.7	73.6	87.3	82.1	80.0	77.5	83.5	108.3	91.9	78.9	77.5	77.4	77.8	82.0	87.0
1984:																	
January	85.1	85.3	86.9	76.0	89.0	84.6	82.0	80.1	84.6	112.2	88.0	80.4	79.3	79.2	79.5	84.9	83.3
February	85.0	85.2	86.5	75.6	90.3	84.4	82.4	80.5	85.1	110.9	83.3	80.1	79.5	79.2	80.2	84.0	78.8
March	85.9	85.9	86.6	77.1	90.9	85.7	83.0	81.3	85.4	111.6	88.5	80.8	79.8	79.4	80.7	84.5	83.7
April	86.4	86.5	87.5	77.4	91.0	86.0	83.4	81.9	85.5	113.0	88.3	81.0	80.0	79.8	80.5	85.6	83.4
May	86.9	86.7	86.8	78.2	90.4	86.7	83.7	82.4	85.6	114.8	88.8	81.3	80.1	79.7	80.9	87.1	83.9
June	87.3	87.4	87.2	79.5	90.6	86.7	84.3	83.0	86.0	115.3	87.5	81.5	80.3	80.1	81.0	87.5	82.6
July	87.4	87.7	87.1	80.6	90.6	86.8	84.5	83.6	85.8	116.3	85.8	81.5	80.4	80.4	80.3	88.4	81.1
August	87.4	87.5	86.0	81.2	90.2	87.1	84.6	84.2	85.2	114.9	86.8	81.3	80.2	80.2	80.2	87.4	82.0
September	87.3	87.3	86.2	80.8	90.0	87.0	84.4	83.9	85.2	115.4	86.3	81.0	79.8	79.7	80.1	87.9	81.4
October	86.9	87.5	86.6	81.1	90.1	85.8	84.5	83.8	85.4	111.6	86.0	80.5	79.6	79.8	79.4	85.1	81.1
November	87.0	87.9	86.8	81.2	90.9	85.5	84.5	83.9	85.4	111.3	86.4	80.4	79.5	79.6	79.2	85.0	81.5
December	86.6	87.4	86.4	81.4	90.4	85.2	84.3	83.8	85.0	110.5	85.0	79.8	79.0	79.4	78.2	84.6	80.2
1985:																	
January	86.9	87.6	86.4	81.4	89.4	85.7	84.4	84.1	84.7	109.4	89.8	79.9	78.9	79.1	78.5	83.7	84.6
February	87.6	88.2	87.0	81.9	90.8	86.6	84.9	84.6	85.2	111.4	91.5	80.4	79.1	79.0	79.2	85.4	86.3
March	87.8	88.6	87.2	82.3	92.0	86.6	85.4	85.2	85.7	111.4	88.7	80.4	79.3	79.4	79.3	85.4	83.6
April	88.0	88.9	86.8	83.2	93.3	86.6	85.6	85.5	85.7	111.4	89.1	80.3	79.2	79.1	79.6	85.4	83.9
May	88.2	89.5	87.5	83.4	94.1	86.2	86.0	85.7	86.3	111.4	87.2	80.3	79.4	79.5	79.2	85.5	82.1
June	88.0	89.2	87.6	82.1	94.0	86.1	85.7	85.6	86.0	111.5	86.9	79.9	78.9	78.7	79.2	85.5	81.8
July	87.6	88.7	87.0	82.5	93.8	85.9	85.4	85.4	85.5	110.0	87.4	79.4	78.3	78.0	79.0	84.2	82.2
August	88.1	89.6	87.9	82.9	95.0	86.0	86.1	86.2	86.1	109.3	87.2	79.6	78.8	78.5	79.4	83.6	82.0
September	88.6	90.1	88.6	83.0	95.1	86.6	86.4	86.0	87.0	110.1	89.7	79.9	78.8	78.5	79.4	84.1	84.2
October	87.9	89.2	88.1	81.3	94.4	86.0	85.7	85.3	86.4	109.2	88.5	79.0	77.9	77.4	79.0	83.2	83.1
November	88.4	90.0	88.3	83.4	95.4	86.0	86.7	86.7	86.7	107.5	87.3	79.2	78.5	78.3	79.0	81.8	81.8
December	89.0	90.2	88.6	82.8	94.3	87.1	86.6	86.5	86.8	110.5	92.0	79.5	78.2	77.9	78.9	83.9	86.2
1986:																	
January	89.6	91.3	90.0	83.5	97.8	87.0	87.9	87.4	88.4	110.3	86.9	79.8	79.1	78.8	79.9	83.6	81.3
February	88.9	90.3	89.7	82.5	96.8	86.8	87.4	87.0	88.0	108.1	86.3	79.2	78.6	78.2	79.6	81.9	80.7
March	88.0	89.5	88.7	82.0	96.1	85.9	86.6	86.3	87.0	105.8	85.7	78.2	77.8	77.4	78.6	80.2	80.1
April	88.7	90.6	90.8	82.2	97.3	86.0	87.8	87.3	88.6	102.7	85.3	78.7	78.7	78.4	79.5	77.8	79.7
May	88.5	90.2	90.4	81.9	97.0	86.0	87.7	87.1	88.6	101.6	85.4	78.4	78.5	78.0	79.6	77.0	79.7
June	88.2	89.9	90.7	80.3	96.9	85.7	87.5	86.4	88.9	100.1	85.9	78.1	78.1	77.6	79.4	75.9	80.1
July	88.5	90.4	90.8	81.6	97.3	85.8	87.7	86.9	88.8	99.9	87.0	78.2	78.2	77.9	79.0	75.9	81.2
August	88.7	90.6	90.9	81.9	98.1	86.0	88.2	87.3	89.5	99.1	85.5	78.3	78.6	77.9	80.2	75.4	79.7
September	88.7	90.6	90.5	82.3	99.1	85.8	88.2	87.8	88.9	97.6	85.8	78.2	78.4	77.7	80.1	74.5	80.0
October	89.5	91.5	91.3	82.2	100.4	86.5	88.9	87.9	90.3	98.7	87.3	78.8	78.9	78.2	80.4	75.5	81.3
November	89.9	91.8	91.6	81.4	101.8	87.2	89.3	88.2	90.6	100.0	88.0	79.1	79.1	78.1	81.3	76.7	82.0
December	90.7	93.0	93.0	82.3	102.5	87.5	90.3	89.1	91.8	99.4	87.9	79.7	79.9	79.0	81.8	76.5	81.9

INDUSTRIAL PRODUCTION AND CAPACITY UTILIZATION—Continued
(Seasonally adjusted)

YEAR AND MONTH	Industrial production indexes (1992=100)											Capacity utilization (Percent of capacity)					
	Total indus-trial produc-tion	Major market groups				Mate-rials	Major industry groups					Total industry	Manufacturing			Mining	Utilities
		Products					Manufacturing			Mining	Utilities						
		Total	Con-sumer goods	Busi-ness equip-ment	Con-struc-tion sup-plies		Total	Dura-bles	Non dura-bles				Total	Ad-vanced proc-essing	Primary proc-essing		
1987:																	
January	90.2	92.1	91.5	81.4	101.5	87.4	89.6	88.5	91.0	100.1	87.6	79.1	79.1	78.3	81.1	77.3	81.5
February	91.2	93.3	92.8	83.2	102.3	88.2	91.0	90.2	92.0	100.0	86.2	80.0	80.2	79.4	82.1	77.6	80.1
March	91.5	93.6	93.3	83.0	102.4	88.5	91.2	90.3	92.4	99.9	88.4	80.2	80.3	79.3	82.5	77.9	82.0
April	91.9	93.8	92.8	83.4	103.4	89.1	91.6	90.8	92.8	100.0	88.2	80.5	80.6	79.3	83.5	78.3	81.7
May	92.3	94.3	93.2	83.3	103.6	89.5	91.9	90.8	93.3	100.5	89.8	80.7	80.7	79.3	83.8	79.0	83.1
June	93.1	95.2	93.9	85.4	106.0	90.1	92.8	91.9	94.1	100.6	89.9	81.3	81.4	80.0	84.4	79.4	83.0
July	93.7	95.7	94.1	85.5	105.9	90.9	93.4	92.1	95.2	100.2	90.9	81.8	81.8	80.1	85.6	79.4	83.8
August	93.8	95.7	94.4	85.0	106.5	91.0	93.3	92.2	94.7	102.2	91.7	81.7	81.5	80.0	85.0	81.2	84.5
September	93.7	95.5	93.6	86.0	105.3	91.1	93.4	92.4	94.6	102.5	89.3	81.6	81.5	79.8	85.5	81.5	82.2
October	94.9	96.7	94.7	87.8	106.9	92.4	94.6	94.6	94.8	103.4	91.1	82.6	82.5	80.8	86.1	82.4	83.7
November	95.2	96.8	94.8	88.1	106.8	92.9	95.0	94.9	95.3	104.1	89.4	82.7	82.8	80.9	86.7	83.0	82.0
December	95.8	97.1	95.0	89.0	106.3	93.8	95.6	95.5	95.8	104.0	90.1	83.1	83.1	81.2	87.5	83.1	82.5
1988:																	
January	95.8	97.5	95.9	89.4	105.2	93.4	95.4	95.6	95.3	102.7	94.0	83.1	82.9	81.3	86.4	82.2	85.9
February	96.1	97.9	96.0	90.3	106.1	93.6	95.8	95.9	95.8	102.8	93.9	83.3	83.1	81.4	86.8	82.5	85.7
March	96.2	97.7	95.6	90.0	106.2	93.9	95.7	95.8	95.7	104.2	93.9	83.2	82.9	81.1	86.9	83.8	85.6
April	96.7	98.5	96.6	91.9	106.7	94.2	96.7	97.2	96.2	103.4	91.4	83.6	83.7	82.1	87.0	83.3	83.2
May	96.8	98.3	96.2	92.9	106.9	94.5	96.6	97.7	95.3	103.8	92.7	83.6	83.5	82.0	86.7	83.9	84.1
June	96.8	98.1	96.0	93.1	106.2	94.9	96.6	97.8	95.1	103.4	93.5	83.5	83.4	81.9	86.5	83.8	84.7
July	97.4	98.6	96.3	94.1	106.9	95.7	97.2	98.4	96.0	103.1	94.7	84.0	83.8	82.4	86.9	83.8	85.6
August	98.0	99.4	97.3	95.1	105.9	95.9	97.5	98.5	96.4	103.5	98.0	84.3	84.0	82.8	86.5	84.4	88.4
September	97.6	99.1	96.8	95.3	106.1	95.5	97.7	99.2	96.0	101.9	93.0	84.0	84.0	82.8	86.6	83.4	83.7
October	97.9	99.4	97.5	95.2	106.3	95.7	97.9	99.3	96.4	102.1	93.9	84.1	84.1	82.9	86.6	83.9	84.4
November	98.6	99.9	97.9	97.1	106.2	96.6	98.9	100.7	96.7	101.6	93.6	84.6	84.8	83.6	87.3	83.8	83.9
December	99.1	100.6	98.5	97.9	107.2	97.0	99.4	101.2	97.4	102.0	93.7	85.0	85.1	83.8	87.9	84.5	83.8
1989:																	
January	99.7	101.1	98.8	98.5	109.3	97.5	100.3	102.4	97.9	101.5	91.7	85.3	85.7	84.2	88.9	84.4	81.9
February	98.9	100.3	98.0	97.5	106.7	96.9	99.1	101.0	97.0	100.3	95.6	84.5	84.5	83.4	87.0	83.6	85.3
March	99.8	101.3	99.1	98.4	106.4	97.7	99.9	101.3	98.4	100.3	98.4	85.1	85.0	83.7	87.9	83.8	87.7
April	100.1	101.6	98.8	100.5	106.2	97.9	100.0	101.9	97.9	103.1	98.0	85.2	84.9	83.9	87.1	86.4	87.2
May	99.5	100.7	98.0	99.2	105.1	97.6	99.4	101.0	97.6	103.0	97.2	84.6	84.2	83.1	86.6	86.6	86.5
June	99.3	100.9	97.6	100.9	104.8	97.0	99.4	101.1	97.5	101.7	96.0	84.3	84.1	83.0	86.3	85.7	85.3
July	98.3	99.5	96.0	99.4	104.9	96.5	98.3	100.0	96.5	100.7	95.6	83.3	83.0	81.8	85.6	85.0	84.8
August	98.7	100.0	96.6	99.6	104.5	96.8	98.7	100.4	96.8	102.0	96.1	83.5	83.1	82.0	85.4	86.3	85.2
September	98.5	100.0	96.6	99.2	104.3	96.3	98.4	100.1	96.5	102.3	96.6	83.2	82.7	81.8	84.6	86.7	85.6
October	98.1	99.1	97.1	96.2	104.2	96.5	97.9	98.4	97.3	101.2	97.6	82.7	82.1	80.7	85.1	86.0	86.4
November	98.5	99.7	97.2	97.2	104.7	96.6	98.2	98.7	97.7	102.0	98.1	82.9	82.2	81.0	84.9	86.8	86.7
December	98.9	100.8	98.4	99.5	105.1	96.3	98.3	99.6	96.9	99.9	104.8	83.2	82.2	81.4	83.7	85.1	92.6
1990:																	
January	98.5	100.0	96.8	97.6	105.6	96.2	98.1	98.0	98.2	103.7	97.3	82.6	81.8	80.5	84.8	88.5	85.8
February	99.0	100.4	97.7	98.0	105.7	96.9	99.0	99.4	98.6	103.1	94.8	82.9	82.4	81.2	85.2	88.0	83.4
March	99.4	100.9	98.2	98.4	105.5	97.3	99.3	100.2	98.4	102.9	97.6	83.2	82.6	81.5	84.8	88.0	85.7
April	98.9	99.8	97.4	96.8	104.6	97.4	98.6	99.2	97.8	103.7	97.9	82.6	81.8	80.5	84.7	88.8	85.8
May	99.3	100.4	97.5	98.3	103.6	97.6	99.0	99.9	97.9	103.9	98.6	82.8	82.0	80.8	84.6	89.0	86.2
June	99.3	100.3	98.2	97.8	103.2	97.8	98.9	100.0	97.6	103.9	99.8	82.7	81.8	80.6	84.3	89.1	87.0
July	99.2	100.2	97.6	98.9	102.5	97.7	98.8	99.8	97.8	104.0	99.0	82.5	81.6	80.6	84.0	89.2	86.2
August	99.4	100.3	97.8	99.7	101.5	98.0	99.1	100.1	98.0	103.2	99.3	82.5	81.7	80.5	84.3	88.6	86.3
September	99.5	100.5	98.4	99.5	101.7	98.0	99.1	100.1	97.9	104.0	100.6	82.5	81.5	80.5	83.8	89.4	87.3
October	99.0	99.9	97.2	99.3	101.0	97.6	98.5	99.1	97.8	104.7	99.5	81.9	80.9	79.9	83.1	90.0	86.2
November	97.7	98.5	95.9	97.3	100.0	96.4	97.2	96.9	97.5	104.0	97.3	80.7	79.7	78.6	82.1	89.5	84.1
December	97.1	98.1	95.4	96.3	99.2	95.6	96.6	95.7	97.5	102.8	97.8	80.1	79.1	78.2	81.0	88.5	84.4
1991:																	
January	96.7	97.6	95.9	95.9	95.5	95.3	95.8	94.7	96.9	103.4	100.4	79.6	78.2	77.5	79.9	89.0	86.6
February	95.9	96.7	94.8	95.8	94.6	94.6	95.1	93.9	96.4	104.8	97.0	78.9	77.6	76.8	79.2	90.2	83.6
March	95.0	96.0	94.8	94.8	93.9	93.5	94.1	93.1	95.1	103.4	97.6	78.1	76.6	76.1	77.8	89.1	84.1
April	95.3	96.3	95.0	95.3	95.0	93.8	94.4	93.7	95.2	102.3	98.9	78.2	76.8	76.3	78.0	88.1	85.2
May	96.0	97.0	96.7	94.9	94.8	94.6	95.0	94.0	96.2	101.5	102.2	78.7	77.2	76.8	78.1	87.4	87.9
June	97.2	98.4	98.1	96.1	98.2	95.3	96.3	95.7	97.0	101.7	102.1	79.5	78.1	77.6	79.3	87.6	87.8
July	97.2	97.8	97.9	95.1	96.8	96.4	96.6	95.9	97.3	100.8	101.7	79.5	78.2	77.4	80.0	86.9	87.4
August	97.4	97.6	97.4	95.2	97.1	97.1	96.8	96.1	97.5	100.6	101.5	79.6	78.3	77.3	80.4	86.7	87.1
September	98.3	98.8	98.9	97.1	97.7	97.5	97.8	97.5	98.2	100.5	101.4	80.1	79.0	78.2	80.9	86.7	86.9
October	98.2	98.4	98.6	96.7	96.3	97.9	97.8	97.3	98.3	100.5	100.9	79.9	78.9	78.0	80.9	86.7	86.3
November	98.1	98.4	98.6	96.6	97.6	97.5	97.6	97.4	97.7	99.7	102.3	79.7	78.6	77.7	80.6	86.1	87.4
December	97.4	97.6	97.9	95.4	96.4	97.2	97.1	96.4	97.7	100.0	99.3	79.1	78.1	77.1	80.4	86.4	84.8
1992:																	
January	97.5	97.2	97.3	94.9	97.4	98.0	97.2	96.4	98.2	99.7	98.3	79.0	78.1	76.9	80.9	86.2	83.8
February	98.1	98.1	98.2	97.3	99.3	98.2	98.0	97.9	98.1	99.1	98.9	79.4	78.6	77.4	81.1	85.8	84.1
March	98.9	98.8	99.0	97.6	99.4	99.1	98.9	98.6	99.2	99.2	99.3	79.9	79.1	77.9	82.0	86.0	84.3
April	99.6	99.6	99.9	99.3	99.8	99.6	99.5	99.4	99.6	100.1	100.5	80.4	79.5	78.3	82.3	86.9	85.3
May	100.0	100.0	100.0	99.6	101.1	100.0	100.0	100.3	99.5	101.1	99.6	80.6	79.7	78.5	82.4	87.9	84.4
June	99.7	99.4	99.1	99.9	99.7	100.3	99.9	99.9	99.8	99.5	98.2	80.2	79.5	78.1	82.7	86.6	83.0
July	100.4	100.3	100.0	101.1	101.1	100.6	100.5	100.4	100.6	101.0	98.7	80.6	79.9	78.4	83.2	87.9	83.4
August	100.1	100.2	100.1	100.7	101.1	99.8	100.2	100.2	100.3	99.5	98.5	80.2	79.5	78.3	82.3	86.7	83.1
September	100.5	100.5	100.3	101.3	100.0	100.5	100.6	100.5	100.8	99.6	99.9	80.5	79.7	78.4	82.5	86.9	84.2
October	101.3	101.5	101.7	102.0	100.4	101.0	101.4	101.5	101.2	100.1	101.4	81.0	80.1	78.9	82.8	87.4	85.5
November	101.9	102.1	102.1	103.1	100.6	101.6	102.0	102.2	101.6	100.3	102.4	81.3	80.4	79.3	83.2	87.6	86.2
December	101.9	102.2	102.2	103.3	100.1	101.5	101.8	102.5	101.1	100.8	104.3	81.2	80.2	79.2	82.6	88.1	87.8

CIVILIAN POPULATION, LABOR FORCE, EMPLOYMENT, AND UNEMPLOYMENT
(Thousands of persons, 16 years of age and over, seasonally adjusted, except as noted)

YEAR AND MONTH	Population (Not seasonally adjusted)	Labor force		Employed		Unemployed		Men 20 years and over		Women 20 years and over		Both sexes, 16 to 19 years	
		Thousands of persons	Participation rate [1]	Thousands of persons	Ratio: Employment to population [2]	Total	Long term [3]	Employed	Unemployed	Employed	Unemployed	Employed	Unemployed
1969:													
January	133 324	79 523	59.6	76 805	57.6	2 718	339	45 154	927	25 777	993	5 874	798
February	133 465	80 019	60.0	77 327	57.9	2 692	358	45 339	903	26 092	992	5 896	797
March	133 639	80 079	59.9	77 367	57.9	2 712	353	45 305	900	26 115	981	5 947	831
April	133 821	80 281	60.0	77 523	57.9	2 758	386	45 262	904	26 233	1 029	6 028	825
May	134 027	80 125	59.8	77 412	57.8	2 713	387	45 278	904	26 283	979	5 851	830
June	134 213	80 696	60.1	77 880	58.0	2 816	368	45 313	923	26 429	1 038	6 138	855
July	134 414	80 827	60.1	77 959	58.0	2 868	377	45 305	985	26 516	979	6 138	904
August	134 597	81 106	60.3	78 250	58.1	2 856	373	45 513	957	26 556	1 043	6 181	856
September	134 774	81 290	60.3	78 250	58.1	3 040	391	45 447	1 072	26 572	1 068	6 231	900
October	135 012	81 494	60.4	78 445	58.1	3 049	374	45 488	1 064	26 658	1 074	6 299	911
November	135 239	81 397	60.2	78 541	58.1	2 856	392	45 505	1 003	26 652	1 013	6 384	840
December	135 489	81 624	60.2	78 740	58.1	2 884	413	45 577	1 062	26 832	977	6 331	845
1970:													
January	135 713	81 981	60.4	78 780	58.0	3 201	431	45 654	1 188	26 908	1 046	6 218	967
February	135 957	82 151	60.4	78 698	57.9	3 453	470	45 627	1 334	26 828	1 160	6 243	959
March	136 179	82 498	60.6	78 863	57.9	3 635	534	45 668	1 382	26 933	1 284	6 262	969
April	136 416	82 727	60.6	78 930	57.9	3 797	602	45 679	1 494	27 114	1 243	6 137	1 060
May	136 686	82 483	60.3	78 564	57.5	3 919	591	45 666	1 553	26 739	1 344	6 159	1 022
June	136 928	82 484	60.2	78 413	57.3	4 071	657	45 554	1 624	26 904	1 290	5 955	1 157
July	137 196	82 901	60.4	78 726	57.4	4 175	662	45 516	1 735	27 083	1 380	6 127	1 060
August	137 455	82 880	60.3	78 624	57.2	4 256	705	45 495	1 755	27 011	1 364	6 118	1 137
September	137 717	82 954	60.2	78 498	57.0	4 456	788	45 535	1 830	26 784	1 435	6 179	1 191
October	137 988	83 276	60.4	78 685	57.0	4 591	771	45 508	1 890	27 058	1 473	6 119	1 228
November	138 264	83 548	60.4	78 650	56.9	4 898	871	45 540	2 023	27 020	1 596	6 090	1 279
December	138 529	83 670	60.4	78 594	56.7	5 076	1 102	45 466	2 192	27 038	1 625	6 090	1 259
1971:													
January	138 795	83 850	60.4	78 864	56.8	4 986	1 113	45 527	2 100	27 173	1 637	6 164	1 249
February	139 021	83 603	60.1	78 700	56.6	4 903	1 068	45 455	2 069	27 040	1 629	6 205	1 205
March	139 285	83 575	60.0	78 588	56.4	4 987	1 098	45 520	2 055	26 967	1 687	6 101	1 245
April	139 566	83 946	60.1	78 987	56.6	4 959	1 149	45 789	2 049	26 984	1 700	6 214	1 210
May	139 826	84 135	60.2	79 139	56.6	4 996	1 173	45 917	2 093	27 056	1 662	6 166	1 241
June	140 090	83 706	59.8	78 757	56.2	4 949	1 167	45 879	2 061	27 013	1 623	5 865	1 265
July	140 343	84 340	60.1	79 305	56.5	5 035	1 251	46 000	2 079	27 054	1 610	6 251	1 346
August	140 596	84 673	60.2	79 539	56.6	5 134	1 261	46 041	2 160	27 171	1 694	6 327	1 280
September	140 869	84 731	60.1	79 689	56.6	5 042	1 239	46 090	2 142	27 390	1 657	6 209	1 243
October	141 146	84 872	60.1	79 918	56.6	4 954	1 268	46 132	2 029	27 538	1 650	6 248	1 275
November	141 393	85 458	60.4	80 297	56.8	5 161	1 277	46 209	2 166	27 721	1 701	6 367	1 294
December	141 666	85 625	60.4	80 471	56.8	5 154	1 283	46 280	2 178	27 791	1 674	6 400	1 302
1972:													
January	142 736	85 978	60.2	80 959	56.7	5 019	1 257	46 471	2 071	27 956	1 624	6 532	1 324
February	143 017	86 036	60.2	81 108	56.7	4 928	1 292	46 600	1 993	28 016	1 506	6 492	1 429
March	143 263	86 611	60.5	81 573	56.9	5 038	1 232	46 821	2 034	28 126	1 625	6 626	1 379
April	143 483	86 614	60.4	81 655	56.9	4 959	1 203	46 863	2 019	28 114	1 619	6 678	1 321
May	143 760	86 809	60.4	81 887	57.0	4 922	1 168	46 950	2 006	28 184	1 698	6 753	1 218
June	144 033	87 006	60.4	82 083	57.0	4 923	1 141	47 147	1 981	28 175	1 666	6 761	1 276
July	144 285	87 143	60.4	82 230	57.0	4 913	1 154	47 244	1 960	28 225	1 702	6 761	1 251
August	144 522	87 517	60.6	82 578	57.1	4 939	1 156	47 321	1 898	28 382	1 684	6 875	1 357
September	144 761	87 392	60.4	82 543	57.0	4 849	1 131	47 394	1 878	28 417	1 657	6 732	1 314
October	144 988	87 491	60.3	82 616	57.0	4 875	1 123	47 354	1 910	28 438	1 689	6 824	1 276
November	145 211	87 592	60.3	82 990	57.2	4 602	1 040	47 529	1 791	28 567	1 523	6 894	1 288
December	145 446	87 943	60.5	83 400	57.3	4 543	1 006	47 747	1 742	28 698	1 512	6 955	1 289
1973:													
January	145 720	87 487	60.0	83 161	57.1	4 326	947	47 701	1 688	28 596	1 552	6 864	1 086
February	145 943	88 364	60.5	83 912	57.5	4 452	894	47 884	1 693	28 995	1 492	7 033	1 267
March	146 230	88 846	60.8	84 452	57.8	4 394	889	48 117	1 695	29 110	1 498	7 225	1 201
April	146 459	89 018	60.8	84 559	57.7	4 459	809	48 098	1 670	29 304	1 480	7 157	1 309
May	146 719	88 977	60.6	84 648	57.7	4 329	816	48 068	1 671	29 432	1 403	7 148	1 255
June	146 981	89 548	60.9	85 185	58.0	4 363	779	48 244	1 628	29 505	1 541	7 436	1 194
July	147 233	89 604	60.9	85 299	57.9	4 305	756	48 452	1 566	29 592	1 532	7 255	1 207
August	147 471	89 509	60.7	85 204	57.8	4 305	788	48 353	1 575	29 578	1 546	7 273	1 184
September	147 731	89 838	60.8	85 488	57.9	4 350	785	48 408	1 543	29 710	1 539	7 370	1 268
October	147 980	90 131	60.9	85 987	58.1	4 144	793	48 631	1 467	29 885	1 416	7 471	1 261
November	148 219	90 716	61.2	86 320	58.2	4 396	832	48 764	1 560	30 071	1 518	7 485	1 318
December	148 479	90 890	61.2	86 401	58.2	4 489	767	48 902	1 628	29 991	1 573	7 508	1 288
1974:													
January	148 753	91 199	61.3	86 555	58.2	4 644	799	49 107	1 755	29 893	1 598	7 555	1 291
February	148 982	91 485	61.4	86 754	58.2	4 731	829	49 057	1 809	30 146	1 600	7 551	1 322
March	149 225	91 453	61.3	86 819	58.2	4 634	849	48 986	1 735	30 293	1 581	7 540	1 318
April	149 478	91 287	61.1	86 669	58.0	4 618	889	48 853	1 796	30 376	1 579	7 440	1 243
May	149 750	91 596	61.2	86 891	58.0	4 705	880	49 039	1 736	30 424	1 618	7 428	1 351
June	150 012	91 868	61.2	86 941	58.0	4 927	926	48 946	1 800	30 512	1 670	7 483	1 457
July	150 248	92 212	61.4	87 149	58.0	5 063	924	48 883	1 833	30 869	1 733	7 397	1 497
August	150 493	92 059	61.2	87 037	57.8	5 022	960	48 950	1 957	30 662	1 764	7 425	1 301
September	150 753	92 488	61.4	87 051	57.7	5 437	1 021	48 978	1 978	30 569	1 918	7 504	1 541
October	151 009	92 518	61.3	86 995	57.6	5 523	1 072	48 959	2 129	30 570	1 846	7 466	1 548
November	151 256	92 766	61.3	86 626	57.3	6 140	1 128	48 833	2 380	30 424	2 166	7 369	1 594
December	151 494	92 780	61.2	86 144	56.9	6 636	1 326	48 458	2 727	30 431	2 295	7 255	1 614

1. Civilian labor force as a percent of the civilian population 16 years and over.
2. Civilian employment as a percent of the civilian population 16 years and over.
3. Fifteen weeks and over.

CIVILIAN POPULATION, LABOR FORCE, EMPLOYMENT, AND UNEMPLOYMENT—Continued
(Thousands of persons, 16 years of age and over, seasonally adjusted, except as noted)

YEAR AND MONTH	Population (Not seasonally adjusted)	Labor force		Employed		Unemployed		By age and sex					
		Thousands of persons	Participation rate [1]	Thousands of persons	Ratio: Employment to population [2]	Total	Long term [3]	Men 20 years and over: Employed	Unemployed	Women 20 years and over: Employed	Unemployed	Both sexes, 16 to 19 years: Employed	Unemployed
1975:													
January	151 755	93 128	61.4	85 627	56.4	7 501	1 555	48 086	3 127	30 343	2 629	7 198	1 745
February	151 990	92 776	61.0	85 256	56.1	7 520	1 841	47 927	3 214	30 215	2 595	7 114	1 711
March	152 217	93 165	61.2	85 187	56.0	7 978	2 074	47 776	3 476	30 334	2 742	7 077	1 760
April	152 443	93 399	61.3	85 189	55.9	8 210	2 442	47 759	3 632	30 410	2 831	7 020	1 747
May	152 704	93 884	61.5	85 451	56.0	8 433	2 643	47 835	3 772	30 483	2 838	7 133	1 823
June	152 976	93 575	61.2	85 355	55.8	8 220	2 843	47 754	3 627	30 618	2 753	6 983	1 840
July	153 309	94 021	61.3	85 894	56.0	8 127	2 943	48 050	3 611	30 794	2 679	7 050	1 837
August	153 580	94 162	61.3	86 234	56.1	7 928	2 862	48 239	3 453	30 966	2 643	7 029	1 832
September	153 848	94 202	61.2	86 279	56.1	7 923	2 906	48 126	3 585	30 979	2 600	7 174	1 738
October	154 082	94 267	61.2	86 370	56.1	7 897	2 689	48 165	3 489	31 121	2 657	7 084	1 751
November	154 338	94 250	61.1	86 456	56.0	7 794	2 789	48 203	3 497	31 135	2 624	7 118	1 673
December	154 589	94 409	61.1	86 665	56.1	7 744	2 868	48 266	3 346	31 268	2 638	7 131	1 760
1976:													
January	154 853	94 934	61.3	87 400	56.4	7 534	2 713	48 592	3 161	31 595	2 619	7 213	1 754
February	155 066	94 998	61.3	87 672	56.5	7 326	2 519	48 721	3 041	31 680	2 575	7 271	1 710
March	155 306	95 215	61.3	87 985	56.7	7 230	2 441	48 836	3 012	31 842	2 518	7 307	1 700
April	155 529	95 746	61.6	88 416	56.8	7 330	2 210	49 097	3 002	31 951	2 545	7 368	1 783
May	155 765	95 847	61.5	88 794	57.0	7 053	2 115	49 193	2 968	32 147	2 384	7 454	1 701
June	156 027	95 885	61.5	88 563	56.8	7 322	2 332	49 010	3 167	32 267	2 498	7 286	1 657
July	156 276	96 583	61.8	89 093	57.0	7 490	2 316	49 236	3 136	32 334	2 673	7 523	1 681
August	156 525	96 741	61.8	89 223	57.0	7 518	2 378	49 417	3 046	32 437	2 673	7 369	1 799
September	156 779	96 553	61.6	89 173	56.9	7 380	2 296	49 485	3 075	32 390	2 635	7 298	1 670
October	156 993	96 704	61.6	89 274	56.9	7 430	2 292	49 524	3 076	32 412	2 638	7 338	1 716
November	157 235	97 254	61.9	89 634	57.0	7 620	2 354	49 561	3 241	32 753	2 644	7 320	1 735
December	157 438	97 348	61.8	89 803	57.0	7 545	2 375	49 599	3 227	32 914	2 597	7 290	1 721
1977:													
January	157 688	97 208	61.6	89 928	57.0	7 280	2 200	49 738	3 046	32 872	2 527	7 318	1 707
February	157 913	97 785	61.9	90 342	57.2	7 443	2 174	49 838	3 136	32 997	2 616	7 507	1 691
March	158 131	98 115	62.0	90 808	57.4	7 307	2 057	50 031	2 939	33 246	2 642	7 531	1 726
April	158 371	98 330	62.1	91 271	57.6	7 059	1 936	50 185	2 824	33 470	2 562	7 616	1 673
May	158 657	98 665	62.2	91 754	57.8	6 911	1 928	50 280	2 847	33 851	2 408	7 623	1 656
June	158 929	99 093	62.4	91 959	57.9	7 134	1 918	50 544	2 769	33 678	2 577	7 737	1 788
July	159 185	98 913	62.1	92 084	57.8	6 829	1 907	50 597	2 698	33 749	2 492	7 738	1 639
August	159 430	99 366	62.3	92 441	58.0	6 925	1 836	50 745	2 720	33 809	2 542	7 887	1 663
September	159 674	99 453	62.3	92 702	58.1	6 751	1 853	50 825	2 532	34 218	2 538	7 659	1 681
October	159 915	99 815	62.4	93 052	58.2	6 763	1 789	51 046	2 679	34 187	2 462	7 819	1 622
November	160 129	100 576	62.8	93 761	58.6	6 815	1 804	51 316	2 584	34 536	2 589	7 909	1 642
December	160 377	100 491	62.7	94 105	58.7	6 386	1 717	51 492	2 509	34 668	2 416	7 945	1 461
1978:													
January	160 617	100 873	62.8	94 384	58.8	6 489	1 643	51 542	2 535	34 948	2 375	7 894	1 579
February	160 831	100 837	62.7	94 519	58.8	6 318	1 584	51 578	2 483	35 118	2 210	7 823	1 625
March	161 038	101 092	62.8	94 755	58.8	6 337	1 531	51 635	2 468	35 310	2 238	7 810	1 631
April	161 263	101 574	63.0	95 394	59.2	6 180	1 502	51 912	2 335	35 546	2 263	7 936	1 582
May	161 518	101 896	63.1	95 769	59.3	6 127	1 420	52 050	2 298	35 597	2 283	8 122	1 546
June	161 795	102 371	63.3	96 343	59.5	6 028	1 352	52 240	2 200	35 828	2 322	8 275	1 506
July	162 034	102 399	63.2	96 090	59.3	6 309	1 373	52 190	2 232	35 764	2 464	8 136	1 613
August	162 259	102 511	63.2	96 431	59.4	6 080	1 242	52 228	2 229	35 856	2 295	8 347	1 556
September	162 502	102 795	63.3	96 670	59.5	6 125	1 308	52 284	2 229	36 274	2 308	8 112	1 588
October	162 783	103 080	63.3	97 133	59.7	5 947	1 319	52 448	2 222	36 525	2 158	8 160	1 567
November	163 017	103 562	63.5	97 485	59.8	6 077	1 242	52 802	2 216	36 559	2 281	8 124	1 580
December	163 272	103 809	63.6	97 581	59.8	6 228	1 269	52 807	2 330	36 686	2 278	8 088	1 620
1979:													
January	163 516	104 057	63.6	97 948	59.9	6 109	1 250	53 072	2 277	36 697	2 262	8 179	1 570
February	163 726	104 502	63.8	98 329	60.1	6 173	1 297	53 233	2 291	36 904	2 312	8 192	1 570
March	164 027	104 589	63.8	98 480	60.0	6 109	1 365	53 120	2 270	37 159	2 289	8 201	1 550
April	164 162	104 172	63.5	98 103	59.8	6 069	1 272	53 085	2 253	36 944	2 238	8 074	1 578
May	164 459	104 171	63.3	98 331	59.8	5 840	1 239	53 178	2 117	37 134	2 189	8 019	1 534
June	164 721	104 638	63.5	98 679	59.9	5 959	1 171	53 309	2 193	37 221	2 251	8 149	1 515
July	164 970	105 002	63.6	99 006	60.0	5 996	1 123	53 384	2 302	37 514	2 196	8 108	1 498
August	165 198	105 096	63.6	98 776	59.8	6 320	1 203	53 336	2 350	37 548	2 406	7 892	1 564
September	165 431	105 530	63.8	99 340	60.0	6 190	1 172	53 510	2 345	37 798	2 254	8 032	1 591
October	165 813	105 700	63.7	99 404	59.9	6 296	1 219	53 478	2 417	37 931	2 300	7 995	1 579
November	166 051	105 812	63.7	99 574	60.0	6 238	1 239	53 435	2 449	38 065	2 264	8 074	1 525
December	166 300	106 258	63.9	99 933	60.1	6 325	1 277	53 555	2 435	38 259	2 319	8 119	1 571
1980:													
January	166 544	106 562	64.0	99 879	60.0	6 683	1 353	53 501	2 724	38 367	2 380	8 011	1 579
February	166 759	106 697	64.0	99 995	60.0	6 702	1 358	53 686	2 726	38 389	2 395	7 920	1 581
March	166 984	106 442	63.7	99 713	59.7	6 729	1 457	53 353	2 842	38 406	2 341	7 954	1 546
April	167 197	106 591	63.8	99 233	59.4	7 358	1 694	53 035	3 292	38 427	2 565	7 771	1 501
May	167 407	106 929	63.9	98 945	59.1	7 984	1 740	52 915	3 598	38 335	2 624	7 695	1 762
June	167 643	106 780	63.7	98 682	58.9	8 098	1 760	52 712	3 662	38 312	2 656	7 658	1 780
July	167 932	107 159	63.8	98 796	58.8	8 363	1 995	52 733	3 820	38 374	2 733	7 689	1 810
August	168 103	107 105	63.7	98 824	58.8	8 281	2 162	52 815	3 770	38 511	2 762	7 498	1 749
September	168 297	107 098	63.6	99 077	58.9	8 021	2 309	52 866	3 747	38 595	2 601	7 616	1 673
October	168 503	107 405	63.7	99 317	58.9	8 088	2 306	53 094	3 584	38 620	2 788	7 603	1 716
November	168 695	107 568	63.8	99 545	59.0	8 023	2 329	53 210	3 550	38 795	2 767	7 540	1 706
December	168 883	107 352	63.6	99 634	59.0	7 718	2 406	53 333	3 332	38 737	2 775	7 564	1 611

1. Civilian labor force as a percent of the civilian population 16 years and over.
2. Civilian employment as a percent of the civilian population 16 years and over.
3. Fifteen weeks and over.

CIVILIAN POPULATION, LABOR FORCE, EMPLOYMENT, AND UNEMPLOYMENT—Continued
(Thousands of persons, 16 years of age and over, seasonally adjusted, except as noted)

YEAR AND MONTH	Population (Not seasonally adjusted)	Labor force — Thousands of persons	Labor force — Participation rate[1]	Employed — Thousands of persons	Employed — Ratio: Employment to population[2]	Unemployed — Total	Unemployed — Long term[3]	Men 20 years and over — Employed	Men 20 years and over — Unemployed	Women 20 years and over — Employed	Women 20 years and over — Unemployed	Both sexes, 16 to 19 years — Employed	Both sexes, 16 to 19 years — Unemployed
1981:													
January	169 104	108 026	63.9	99 955	59.1	8 071	2 389	53 392	3 468	39 042	2 824	7 521	1 779
February	169 280	108 242	63.9	100 191	59.2	8 051	2 344	53 445	3 483	39 280	2 777	7 466	1 791
March	169 453	108 553	64.1	100 571	59.4	7 982	2 276	53 662	3 445	39 464	2 770	7 445	1 767
April	169 641	108 925	64.2	101 056	59.6	7 869	2 231	53 886	3 350	39 628	2 772	7 542	1 747
May	169 829	109 222	64.3	101 048	59.5	8 174	2 221	53 879	3 580	39 759	2 844	7 410	1 750
June	170 042	108 396	63.7	100 298	59.0	8 098	2 250	53 576	3 526	39 682	2 832	7 040	1 740
July	170 246	108 556	63.8	100 693	59.1	7 863	2 166	53 814	3 365	39 683	2 855	7 196	1 643
August	170 399	108 725	63.8	100 689	59.1	8 036	2 241	53 718	3 519	39 723	2 834	7 248	1 683
September	170 593	108 294	63.5	100 064	58.7	8 230	2 261	53 625	3 550	39 342	2 942	7 097	1 738
October	170 809	109 024	63.8	100 378	58.8	8 646	2 303	53 482	3 819	39 843	3 029	7 053	1 798
November	170 996	109 236	63.9	100 207	58.6	9 029	2 345	53 335	4 026	39 908	3 115	6 964	1 888
December	171 166	108 912	63.6	99 645	58.2	9 267	2 374	53 149	4 280	39 708	3 173	6 788	1 814
1982:													
January	171 335	109 089	63.7	99 692	58.2	9 397	2 409	53 103	4 358	39 821	3 131	6 768	1 908
February	171 489	109 467	63.8	99 762	58.2	9 705	2 758	53 172	4 435	39 859	3 304	6 731	1 966
March	171 667	109 567	63.8	99 672	58.1	9 895	2 965	53 054	4 624	39 936	3 403	6 682	1 868
April	171 844	109 820	63.9	99 576	57.9	10 244	3 086	53 081	4 742	39 848	3 544	6 647	1 958
May	172 026	110 451	64.2	100 116	58.2	10 335	3 276	53 234	4 788	40 121	3 555	6 761	1 992
June	172 190	110 081	63.9	99 543	57.8	10 538	3 451	52 933	5 072	40 219	3 564	6 391	1 902
July	172 364	110 342	64.0	99 493	57.7	10 849	3 555	52 896	5 183	40 228	3 655	6 369	2 011
August	172 511	110 514	64.1	99 633	57.8	10 881	3 696	52 797	5 240	40 336	3 627	6 500	2 014
September	172 690	110 721	64.1	99 504	57.6	11 217	3 889	52 760	5 536	40 275	3 681	6 469	2 000
October	172 881	110 744	64.1	99 215	57.4	11 529	4 185	52 624	5 711	40 105	3 805	6 486	2 013
November	173 058	111 050	64.2	99 112	57.3	11 938	4 485	52 537	5 853	40 111	4 029	6 464	2 056
December	173 199	111 083	64.1	99 032	57.2	12 051	4 662	52 497	5 903	40 164	4 122	6 371	2 026
1983:													
January	173 354	110 695	63.9	99 161	57.2	11 534	4 668	52 487	5 618	40 268	3 987	6 406	1 929
February	173 505	110 634	63.8	99 089	57.1	11 545	4 641	52 453	5 738	40 336	3 948	6 300	1 859
March	173 656	110 587	63.7	99 179	57.1	11 408	4 612	52 615	5 630	40 368	3 876	6 196	1 902
April	173 794	110 828	63.8	99 560	57.3	11 268	4 370	52 814	5 643	40 542	3 735	6 204	1 890
May	173 953	110 796	63.7	99 642	57.3	11 154	4 538	52 922	5 609	40 538	3 721	6 182	1 824
June	174 125	111 879	64.3	100 633	57.8	11 246	4 470	53 515	5 347	40 695	3 874	6 423	2 025
July	174 306	111 756	64.1	101 208	58.1	10 548	4 329	53 835	5 170	41 041	3 503	6 332	1 875
August	174 440	112 231	64.3	101 608	58.2	10 623	4 070	53 837	5 162	41 314	3 539	6 457	1 922
September	174 602	112 298	64.3	102 016	58.4	10 282	3 854	53 983	5 036	41 650	3 482	6 383	1 764
October	174 779	111 926	64.0	102 039	58.4	9 887	3 648	54 146	4 817	41 597	3 356	6 296	1 714
November	174 951	112 228	64.1	102 729	58.7	9 499	3 535	54 499	4 605	41 788	3 261	6 442	1 633
December	175 121	112 327	64.1	102 996	58.8	9 331	3 379	54 662	4 422	41 852	3 302	6 482	1 607
1984:													
January	175 533	112 209	63.9	103 201	58.8	9 008	3 254	54 975	4 275	41 812	3 182	6 414	1 551
February	175 679	112 615	64.1	103 824	59.1	8 791	2 991	55 213	4 128	42 196	3 120	6 415	1 543
March	175 824	112 713	64.1	103 967	59.1	8 746	2 881	55 281	4 052	42 328	3 126	6 358	1 568
April	175 969	113 098	64.3	104 336	59.3	8 762	2 858	55 373	4 077	42 512	3 148	6 451	1 537
May	176 123	113 649	64.5	105 193	59.7	8 456	2 884	55 661	3 879	43 071	3 094	6 461	1 483
June	176 284	113 817	64.6	105 591	59.9	8 226	2 612	55 996	3 754	42 944	2 992	6 651	1 480
July	176 440	113 972	64.6	105 435	59.8	8 537	2 638	55 921	3 869	42 979	3 158	6 535	1 510
August	176 583	113 682	64.4	105 163	59.6	8 519	2 604	55 930	3 876	42 885	3 182	6 348	1 461
September	176 763	113 857	64.4	105 490	59.7	8 367	2 538	56 095	3 851	42 967	2 993	6 428	1 523
October	176 956	114 019	64.4	105 638	59.7	8 381	2 526	56 183	3 745	43 052	3 177	6 403	1 459
November	177 135	114 170	64.5	105 972	59.8	8 198	2 438	56 274	3 734	43 244	3 074	6 454	1 390
December	177 306	114 581	64.6	106 223	59.9	8 358	2 401	56 313	3 812	43 472	3 051	6 438	1 495
1985:													
January	177 384	114 725	64.7	106 302	59.9	8 423	2 284	56 184	3 765	43 589	3 151	6 529	1 507
February	177 516	114 876	64.7	106 555	60.0	8 321	2 389	56 216	3 739	43 787	3 114	6 552	1 468
March	177 667	115 328	64.9	106 989	60.2	8 339	2 394	56 356	3 715	44 035	3 160	6 598	1 464
April	177 799	115 331	64.9	106 936	60.1	8 395	2 393	56 374	3 812	44 000	3 187	6 562	1 396
May	177 944	115 234	64.8	106 932	60.1	8 302	2 292	56 531	3 640	43 905	3 192	6 496	1 470
June	178 096	114 965	64.6	106 505	59.8	8 460	2 310	56 288	3 861	43 958	3 178	6 259	1 421
July	178 263	115 320	64.7	106 807	59.9	8 513	2 329	56 435	3 757	43 975	3 140	6 397	1 616
August	178 405	115 291	64.6	107 095	60.0	8 196	2 258	56 655	3 675	44 103	3 144	6 337	1 377
September	178 572	115 905	64.9	107 657	60.3	8 248	2 242	56 845	3 694	44 395	3 153	6 417	1 401
October	178 770	116 145	65.0	107 847	60.3	8 298	2 295	56 969	3 678	44 565	3 044	6 313	1 576
November	178 940	116 135	64.9	108 007	60.4	8 128	2 207	56 972	3 642	44 617	3 052	6 418	1 434
December	179 112	116 354	65.0	108 216	60.4	8 138	2 208	56 995	3 606	44 889	3 038	6 332	1 494
1986:													
January	179 670	116 682	64.9	108 887	60.6	7 795	2 089	57 637	3 489	44 944	2 908	6 306	1 398
February	179 821	116 882	65.0	108 480	60.3	8 402	2 308	57 269	3 758	44 804	3 156	6 407	1 488
March	179 985	117 220	65.1	108 837	60.5	8 383	2 261	57 353	3 766	44 960	3 164	6 524	1 453
April	180 148	117 316	65.1	108 952	60.5	8 364	2 162	57 358	3 700	45 081	3 119	6 513	1 545
May	180 311	117 528	65.2	109 089	60.5	8 439	2 232	57 287	3 836	45 289	3 119	6 513	1 484
June	180 503	118 084	65.4	109 576	60.7	8 508	2 320	57 471	3 832	45 621	3 136	6 484	1 540
July	180 682	118 129	65.4	109 810	60.8	8 319	2 269	57 514	3 859	45 837	3 005	6 459	1 455
August	180 828	118 150	65.3	110 015	60.8	8 135	2 276	57 597	3 701	45 926	3 068	6 492	1 428
September	180 997	118 395	65.4	110 085	60.8	8 310	2 318	57 630	3 862	45 972	2 986	6 483	1 462
October	181 186	118 516	65.4	110 273	60.9	8 243	2 188	57 660	3 823	46 046	3 010	6 567	1 410
November	181 363	118 634	65.4	110 475	60.9	8 159	2 202	57 941	3 775	46 070	2 957	6 464	1 427
December	181 547	118 611	65.3	110 728	61.0	7 883	2 161	58 185	3 713	46 132	2 812	6 411	1 358

1. Civilian labor force as a percent of the civilian population 16 years and over.
2. Civilian employment as a percent of the civilian population 16 years and over.
3. Fifteen weeks and over.

CIVILIAN POPULATION, LABOR FORCE, EMPLOYMENT, AND UNEMPLOYMENT—Continued
(Thousands of persons, 16 years of age and over, seasonally adjusted, except as noted)

YEAR AND MONTH	Population (Not seasonally adjusted)	Labor force		Employed		Unemployed		By age and sex					
								Men 20 years and over		Women 20 years and over		Both sexes, 16 to 19 years	
		Thousands of persons	Participation rate [1]	Thousands of persons	Ratio: Employment to population [2]	Total	Long term [3]	Employed	Unemployed	Employed	Unemployed	Employed	Unemployed
1987:													
January	181 827	118 845	65.4	110 953	61.0	7 892	2 168	58 264	3 635	46 219	2 866	6 470	1 391
February	181 998	119 122	65.5	111 257	61.1	7 865	2 117	58 279	3 596	46 444	2 834	6 534	1 435
March	182 179	119 270	65.5	111 408	61.2	7 862	2 070	58 362	3 539	46 549	2 907	6 497	1 416
April	182 344	119 336	65.4	111 794	61.3	7 542	2 091	58 503	3 415	46 746	2 756	6 545	1 371
May	182 533	120 008	65.7	112 434	61.6	7 574	2 104	58 713	3 462	47 052	2 706	6 669	1 406
June	182 703	119 644	65.5	112 246	61.4	7 398	2 087	58 581	3 477	47 102	2 627	6 563	1 294
July	182 885	119 902	65.6	112 634	61.6	7 268	1 921	58 740	3 380	47 229	2 642	6 665	1 246
August	183 002	120 318	65.7	113 057	61.8	7 261	1 878	58 810	3 294	47 322	2 660	6 925	1 307
September	183 161	120 011	65.5	112 909	61.6	7 102	1 866	58 964	3 147	47 285	2 670	6 660	1 285
October	183 311	120 509	65.7	113 282	61.8	7 227	1 794	59 073	3 200	47 533	2 629	6 676	1 398
November	183 470	120 540	65.7	113 505	61.9	7 035	1 797	59 210	3 102	47 622	2 604	6 673	1 329
December	183 620	120 729	65.7	113 793	62.0	6 936	1 767	59 217	3 051	47 781	2 588	6 795	1 297
1988:													
January	183 822	120 969	65.8	114 016	62.0	6 953	1 714	59 346	3 077	47 862	2 574	6 808	1 302
February	183 969	121 156	65.9	114 227	62.1	6 929	1 738	59 535	3 049	47 919	2 628	6 773	1 252
March	184 111	120 913	65.7	114 037	61.9	6 876	1 744	59 393	3 086	48 090	2 490	6 554	1 300
April	184 232	121 251	65.8	114 650	62.2	6 601	1 563	59 832	2 869	48 147	2 466	6 671	1 266
May	184 374	121 071	65.7	114 292	62.0	6 779	1 647	59 644	3 080	47 946	2 489	6 702	1 210
June	184 562	121 473	65.8	114 927	62.3	6 546	1 531	59 751	2 930	48 146	2 453	7 030	1 163
July	184 729	121 665	65.9	115 060	62.3	6 605	1 601	59 888	2 876	48 186	2 517	6 986	1 212
August	184 830	122 125	66.1	115 282	62.4	6 843	1 639	59 877	3 117	48 467	2 463	6 938	1 263
September	184 962	121 960	65.9	115 356	62.4	6 604	1 569	59 980	2 877	48 511	2 468	6 865	1 259
October	185 114	122 206	66.0	115 638	62.5	6 568	1 562	60 023	2 932	48 859	2 431	6 756	1 205
November	185 244	122 637	66.2	116 100	62.7	6 537	1 468	60 042	2 989	49 254	2 448	6 804	1 100
December	185 402	122 622	66.1	116 104	62.6	6 518	1 490	60 059	2 945	49 257	2 395	6 788	1 178
1989:													
January	185 644	123 390	66.5	116 708	62.9	6 682	1 480	60 477	2 898	49 529	2 467	6 702	1 317
February	185 777	123 135	66.3	116 776	62.9	6 359	1 304	60 588	2 838	49 497	2 341	6 691	1 180
March	185 897	123 227	66.3	117 022	62.9	6 205	1 353	60 795	2 710	49 503	2 410	6 724	1 085
April	186 024	123 565	66.4	117 097	62.9	6 468	1 397	60 764	2 864	49 565	2 443	6 768	1 161
May	186 181	123 474	66.3	117 099	62.9	6 375	1 348	60 795	2 720	49 583	2 486	6 721	1 169
June	186 329	123 995	66.5	117 418	63.0	6 577	1 300	61 054	2 787	49 542	2 518	6 822	1 272
July	186 483	123 967	66.5	117 472	63.0	6 495	1 435	60 947	2 804	49 693	2 562	6 832	1 129
August	186 598	124 166	66.5	117 655	63.1	6 511	1 302	60 915	2 849	49 804	2 472	6 936	1 190
September	186 726	123 944	66.4	117 354	62.8	6 590	1 360	60 668	3 002	50 015	2 389	6 671	1 199
October	186 871	124 211	66.5	117 581	62.9	6 630	1 392	60 958	2 935	49 871	2 507	6 752	1 188
November	187 017	124 637	66.6	117 912	63.0	6 725	1 418	60 958	2 992	50 221	2 502	6 733	1 231
December	187 165	124 497	66.5	117 830	63.0	6 667	1 375	61 068	2 962	50 116	2 500	6 646	1 205
1990:													
January	188 413	125 833	66.8	119 081	63.2	6 752	1 412	61 742	3 063	50 436	2 489	6 903	1 200
February	188 516	125 710	66.7	119 059	63.2	6 651	1 350	61 805	2 946	50 438	2 506	6 816	1 199
March	188 630	125 801	66.7	119 203	63.2	6 598	1 331	61 832	2 974	50 463	2 471	6 908	1 153
April	188 778	125 649	66.6	118 852	63.0	6 797	1 376	61 579	3 107	50 457	2 519	6 816	1 171
May	188 913	125 893	66.6	119 151	63.1	6 742	1 415	61 778	3 043	50 646	2 515	6 727	1 184
June	189 058	125 573	66.4	118 983	62.9	6 590	1 436	61 762	3 066	50 550	2 412	6 671	1 112
July	189 188	125 732	66.5	118 810	62.8	6 922	1 534	61 683	3 183	50 514	2 575	6 613	1 164
August	189 342	125 990	66.5	118 802	62.7	7 188	1 607	61 715	3 291	50 635	2 641	6 452	1 256
September	189 528	125 892	66.4	118 524	62.5	7 368	1 695	61 608	3 387	50 587	2 735	6 329	1 246
October	189 710	125 995	66.4	118 536	62.5	7 459	1 689	61 606	3 487	50 616	2 721	6 314	1 251
November	189 872	126 070	66.4	118 306	62.3	7 764	1 831	61 545	3 700	50 541	2 778	6 220	1 286
December	190 017	126 142	66.4	118 241	62.2	7 901	1 804	61 506	3 794	50 530	2 796	6 205	1 311
1991:													
January	190 163	125 955	66.2	117 940	62.0	8 015	1 866	61 383	3 766	50 472	2 856	6 085	1 393
February	190 271	126 020	66.2	117 755	61.9	8 265	1 955	61 117	4 051	50 422	2 924	6 115	1 290
March	190 381	126 238	66.3	117 652	61.8	8 586	2 137	61 144	4 206	50 422	3 019	6 086	1 361
April	190 517	126 548	66.4	118 109	62.0	8 439	2 206	61 280	4 183	50 760	2 944	6 069	1 312
May	190 650	126 176	66.2	117 440	61.6	8 736	2 252	61 052	4 168	50 457	3 196	5 931	1 372
June	190 800	126 331	66.2	117 639	61.7	8 692	2 533	61 147	4 229	50 585	3 122	5 907	1 341
July	190 946	126 154	66.1	117 568	61.6	8 586	2 388	61 179	4 245	50 636	2 956	5 753	1 385
August	191 116	126 150	66.0	117 484	61.5	8 666	2 460	61 122	4 235	50 601	3 087	5 761	1 344
September	191 302	126 650	66.2	117 928	61.6	8 722	2 497	61 279	4 307	50 864	3 077	5 785	1 338
October	191 497	126 642	66.1	117 800	61.5	8 842	2 638	61 174	4 276	50 811	3 196	5 815	1 370
November	191 657	126 701	66.1	117 770	61.4	8 931	2 718	61 201	4 332	50 759	3 240	5 810	1 359
December	191 798	126 664	66.0	117 466	61.2	9 198	2 892	61 074	4 453	50 728	3 305	5 664	1 440
1992:													
January	191 953	127 261	66.3	117 978	61.5	9 283	3 060	61 116	4 651	51 095	3 261	5 767	1 371
February	192 067	127 207	66.2	117 753	61.3	9 454	3 182	61 062	4 657	51 033	3 372	5 658	1 425
March	192 204	127 604	66.4	118 144	61.5	9 460	3 196	61 363	4 650	51 204	3 389	5 577	1 421
April	192 354	127 841	66.5	118 426	61.6	9 415	3 130	61 468	4 699	51 323	3 441	5 635	1 275
May	192 503	128 119	66.6	118 375	61.5	9 744	3 444	61 513	4 859	51 245	3 474	5 617	1 411
June	192 663	128 459	66.7	118 419	61.5	10 040	3 758	61 537	4 890	51 383	3 512	5 499	1 638
July	192 826	128 563	66.7	118 713	61.6	9 850	3 614	61 641	4 779	51 458	3 598	5 614	1 473
August	193 018	128 613	66.6	118 826	61.6	9 787	3 579	61 681	4 768	51 386	3 584	5 759	1 435
September	193 229	128 501	66.5	118 720	61.4	9 781	3 504	61 663	4 723	51 359	3 540	5 698	1 518
October	193 442	128 026	66.2	118 628	61.3	9 398	3 505	61 550	4 709	51 373	3 409	5 705	1 280
November	193 621	128 441	66.3	118 876	61.4	9 565	3 397	61 644	4 666	51 535	3 432	5 697	1 467
December	193 784	128 554	66.3	118 997	61.4	9 557	3 651	61 721	4 529	51 524	3 606	5 752	1 422

1. Civilian labor force as a percent of the civilian population 16 years and over.
2. Civilian employment as a percent of the civilian population 16 years and over.
3. Fifteen weeks and over.

CIVILIAN EMPLOYMENT AND SELECTED UNEMPLOYMENT RATES
(Seasonally adjusted)

YEAR AND MONTH	Employment by industry (Thousands of persons)		Selected unemployment rates (Percent of civilian labor force in group)													
			All civilian workers	By sex and age			By race		Persons of His-panic origin	By marital or family status			Wage and salary workers, by industry of last job			
				20 years and over		Both sexes, 16-19 years							Private nonagricultural			
	Agricultural	Non-agricultural		Men	Women		White	Black		Married men, spouse present	Married women, spouse present	Women who main-tain families	Total	Con-struc-tion	Manu-factur-ing	Agricultural
1969:																
January	3 704	73 101	3.4	2.0	3.7	12.0	3.0	....	....	1.4	3.9	4.5	3.5	5.7	3.3	6.0
February	3 770	73 557	3.4	2.0	3.7	11.9	3.0			1.4	3.8	4.0	3.4	5.6	3.0	5.3
March	3 668	73 699	3.4	1.9	3.6	12.3	3.0			1.4	3.7	4.4	3.4	6.0	3.1	6.3
April	3 629	73 894	3.4	2.0	3.8	12.0	3.0			1.4	3.8	5.0	3.5	6.4	3.2	6.2
May	3 706	73 706	3.4	2.0	3.6	12.4	3.0			1.5	3.8	4.3	3.4	5.3	3.1	5.3
June	3 663	74 217	3.5	2.0	3.8	12.2	3.1			1.5	4.1	4.6	3.5	4.8	3.3	5.7
July	3 548	74 411	3.5	2.1	3.6	12.8	3.2			1.6	3.9	4.2	3.4	5.7	3.0	8.0
August	3 613	74 637	3.5	2.1	3.8	12.2	3.1			1.5	4.0	4.8	3.6	6.5	3.0	6.0
September	3 551	74 699	3.7	2.3	3.9	12.6	3.4			1.7	4.0	4.5	3.7	6.8	3.6	5.5
October	3 517	74 928	3.7	2.3	3.9	12.6	3.4			1.6	3.9	4.2	3.7	7.1	3.6	6.3
November	3 477	75 064	3.5	2.2	3.7	11.6	3.2			1.5	3.9	4.2	3.6	6.4	3.7	5.7
December	3 409	75 331	3.5	2.3	3.5	11.8	3.3			1.7	3.8	4.4	3.6	6.3	3.7	6.1
1970:																
January	3 422	75 358	3.9	2.5	3.7	13.5	3.6			1.9	3.8	4.4	4.0	7.4	3.9	6.4
February	3 439	75 259	4.2	2.8	4.1	13.3	3.8			2.0	4.3	4.5	4.3	7.9	4.6	6.5
March	3 499	75 364	4.4	2.9	4.6	13.4	4.0			2.2	4.9	5.3	4.6	8.1	4.7	7.1
April	3 568	75 362	4.6	3.2	4.4	14.7	4.1			2.3	4.6	3.8	4.8	8.7	4.8	6.5
May	3 547	75 017	4.8	3.3	4.8	14.2	4.4			2.5	4.8	4.9	5.1	10.8	5.1	9.1
June	3 555	74 858	4.9	3.4	4.6	16.3	4.5			2.5	4.7	4.7	5.3	10.5	5.5	5.7
July	3 517	75 209	5.0	3.7	4.8	14.7	4.6			2.7	5.0	5.9	5.5	10.7	5.9	7.9
August	3 418	75 206	5.1	3.7	4.8	15.7	4.7			2.8	4.9	6.0	5.5	11.3	5.9	7.6
September	3 451	75 047	5.4	3.9	5.1	16.2	5.0			2.9	5.3	5.6	5.8	12.0	6.1	8.6
October	3 337	75 348	5.5	4.0	5.2	16.7	5.2			3.0	5.2	6.5	6.0	11.2	6.7	8.5
November	3 372	75 278	5.9	4.3	5.6	17.4	5.4			3.2	5.6	6.4	6.3	10.6	7.1	8.2
December	3 380	75 214	6.1	4.6	5.7	17.1	5.6			3.4	5.6	6.2	6.6	11.6	7.4	9.6
1971:																
January	3 393	75 471	5.9	4.4	5.7	16.8	5.5			3.3	5.7	6.4	6.4	11.5	6.9	8.7
February	3 288	75 412	5.9	4.4	5.7	16.3	5.3			3.2	5.7	7.3	6.3	11.1	6.9	9.3
March	3 356	75 232	6.0	4.3	5.9	16.9	5.5			3.2	6.0	6.9	6.3	11.1	6.8	7.4
April	3 574	75 413	5.9	4.3	5.9	16.3	5.4			3.1	6.0	7.1	6.3	10.1	7.0	6.8
May	3 449	75 690	5.9	4.4	5.8	16.8	5.4			3.2	5.7	7.8	6.4	9.9	6.8	7.2
June	3 334	75 423	5.9	4.3	5.7	17.7	5.5			3.1	5.7	7.3	6.3	10.5	6.7	6.3
July	3 386	75 919	6.0	4.3	5.6	17.7	5.5			3.1	5.6	7.2	6.2	9.5	6.7	8.4
August	3 395	76 144	6.1	4.5	5.9	16.8	5.6			3.2	5.6	7.3	6.3	9.6	7.1	8.9
September	3 367	76 322	6.0	4.4	5.7	16.7	5.4			3.3	5.6	7.6	6.3	9.4	7.1	8.3
October	3 405	76 513	5.8	4.2	5.7	16.9	5.4			3.0	5.7	7.3	6.1	9.8	6.5	7.3
November	3 410	76 887	6.0	4.5	5.8	16.9	5.6			3.4	5.7	7.3	6.3	10.3	6.7	8.2
December	3 371	77 100	6.0	4.5	5.7	16.9	5.4			3.2	5.5	8.5	6.3	10.9	6.7	7.8
1972:																
January	3 366	77 593	5.8	4.3	5.5	16.9	5.2	11.2		3.0	5.3	7.2	6.0	10.3	6.1	8.6
February	3 358	77 750	5.7	4.1	5.1	18.0	5.1	11.2		2.9	5.3	7.0	6.0	10.8	6.0	8.1
March	3 438	78 135	5.8	4.2	5.5	17.2	5.2	10.7		2.8	5.4	7.0	6.0	10.3	6.0	6.9
April	3 382	78 273	5.7	4.1	5.4	16.5	5.3	9.8		2.8	5.5	7.2	5.9	10.5	5.8	6.3
May	3 412	78 475	5.7	4.1	5.7	15.3	5.1	10.2		2.8	5.6	7.0	5.9	10.9	5.9	8.0
June	3 402	78 681	5.7	4.0	5.6	15.9	5.1	10.2		2.8	5.6	7.7	5.7	9.7	5.7	7.6
July	3 461	78 769	5.6	4.0	5.7	15.6	5.1	10.5		2.8	5.7	7.3	5.9	10.4	5.9	6.7
August	3 603	78 975	5.6	3.9	5.6	16.5	5.1	10.6		2.7	5.6	7.3	5.9	11.3	5.6	6.7
September	3 568	78 975	5.5	3.8	5.5	16.3	5.0	10.4		2.8	5.3	7.2	5.6	8.9	5.3	8.9
October	3 634	78 982	5.6	3.9	5.6	15.8	5.1	10.6		2.8	5.2	8.3	5.8	10.1	5.4	9.9
November	3 517	79 473	5.3	3.6	5.1	15.7	4.7	10.0		2.5	5.0	6.5	5.3	10.1	4.8	8.2
December	3 596	79 804	5.2	3.5	5.0	15.6	4.6	9.4		2.4	5.0	6.3	5.1	9.7	4.6	7.1
1973:																
January	3 456	79 705	4.9	3.4	5.1	13.7	4.5	9.1		2.4	4.9	7.1	5.0	9.4	4.8	6.8
February	3 415	80 497	5.0	3.4	4.9	15.3	4.5	9.5		2.4	4.8	6.6	5.1	9.3	4.4	7.3
March	3 469	80 983	4.9	3.4	4.9	14.3	4.4	9.4	7.3	2.4	4.6	7.0	4.9	8.9	4.4	6.6
April	3 407	81 152	5.0	3.4	4.8	15.5	4.5	9.9	7.9	2.4	4.6	6.9	4.9	9.1	4.3	7.4
May	3 376	81 272	4.9	3.4	4.6	14.9	4.3	9.6	8.1	2.3	4.6	6.7	4.8	8.8	4.5	8.9
June	3 509	81 676	4.9	3.3	5.0	13.8	4.3	9.8	7.9	2.2	4.7	8.0	4.8	8.0	4.4	7.0
July	3 540	81 759	4.8	3.1	4.9	14.3	4.2	9.8	7.2	2.1	4.7	7.0	4.8	9.1	4.0	5.7
August	3 425	81 779	4.8	3.2	5.0	14.0	4.3	9.2	7.4	2.2	5.0	6.5	4.9	8.4	4.2	7.5
September	3 342	82 146	4.8	3.1	4.9	14.7	4.3	9.7	7.7	2.1	4.7	6.8	4.8	9.0	4.4	6.4
October	3 424	82 563	4.6	2.9	4.5	14.4	4.1	8.8	8.0	2.2	4.3	7.0	4.6	8.9	4.1	6.8
November	3 593	82 727	4.8	3.1	4.8	15.0	4.3	9.3	8.1	2.2	4.6	8.0	4.9	9.0	4.4	7.4
December	3 658	82 743	4.9	3.2	5.0	14.6	4.4	9.0	7.6	2.3	4.7	7.1	5.0	8.4	4.4	6.7
1974:																
January	3 756	82 799	5.1	3.5	5.1	14.6	4.6	9.5	7.6	2.4	4.8	6.7	5.1	9.5	4.8	6.7
February	3 824	82 930	5.2	3.6	5.0	14.9	4.6	9.8	7.8	2.4	5.0	6.4	5.3	8.5	5.1	6.9
March	3 726	83 093	5.1	3.4	5.0	14.9	4.5	9.8	7.6	2.3	4.7	6.5	5.1	8.6	5.0	7.0
April	3 582	83 087	5.1	3.5	4.9	14.3	4.5	9.5	7.0	2.4	4.5	6.6	5.2	9.9	4.9	7.3
May	3 529	83 362	5.1	3.4	5.0	15.4	4.6	9.7	7.3	2.2	4.7	7.0	5.2	9.5	4.8	7.0
June	3 386	83 555	5.4	3.5	5.2	16.3	4.8	10.1	8.6	2.5	4.8	6.7	5.5	9.9	5.2	7.4
July	3 436	83 713	5.5	3.6	5.3	16.8	4.9	10.4	8.8	2.7	5.1	6.2	5.6	10.2	5.4	8.3
August	3 429	83 608	5.5	3.8	5.4	14.9	5.0	9.9	8.1	2.8	5.3	6.6	5.7	10.9	5.7	7.4
September	3 460	83 591	5.9	3.9	5.9	17.0	5.4	10.8	8.1	2.8	5.8	7.4	6.1	11.6	6.0	7.3
October	3 431	83 564	6.0	4.2	5.7	17.2	5.4	11.5	8.2	3.0	5.3	7.3	6.2	12.1	6.5	8.3
November	3 405	83 221	6.6	4.6	6.6	17.8	6.0	12.4	8.6	3.4	6.5	8.5	6.9	13.6	7.5	7.6
December	3 361	82 783	7.2	5.3	7.0	18.2	6.4	13.1	9.1	3.8	7.0	8.3	7.7	15.3	8.7	7.7

CIVILIAN EMPLOYMENT AND SELECTED UNEMPLOYMENT RATES—Continued
(Seasonally adjusted)

YEAR AND MONTH	Employment by industry (Thousands of persons)		Selected unemployment rates (Percent of civilian labor force in group)													
			All civilian workers	By sex and age			By race		Persons of Hispanic origin	By marital or family status			Wage and salary workers, by industry of last job			
				20 years and over		Both sexes, 16-19 years				Married men, spouse present	Married women, spouse present	Women who maintain families	Private nonagricultural			Agricultural
	Agricultural	Non-agricultural		Men	Women		White	Black					Total	Construction	Manufacturing	
1975:																
January	3 401	82 226	8.1	6.1	8.0	19.5	7.4	14.1	10.7	4.6	8.1	9.0	8.7	15.7	10.4	10.7
February	3 361	81 895	8.1	6.3	7.9	19.4	7.4	14.4	11.2	4.7	8.0	9.7	8.7	16.3	10.7	9.1
March	3 358	81 829	8.6	6.8	8.3	19.9	7.8	15.1	12.1	5.1	8.4	9.9	9.3	17.8	11.3	10.6
April	3 315	81 874	8.8	7.1	8.5	19.9	8.0	15.3	12.4	5.5	8.7	9.6	9.8	19.2	12.0	11.3
May	3 560	81 891	9.0	7.3	8.5	20.4	8.4	15.1	14.3	5.7	8.7	10.5	10.1	21.5	12.3	9.4
June	3 368	81 987	8.8	7.1	8.2	20.9	8.1	15.0	11.7	5.5	8.2	10.2	9.8	19.8	12.1	10.4
July	3 457	82 437	8.6	7.0	8.0	20.7	8.0	14.1	11.6	5.4	7.6	10.4	9.5	19.5	11.4	9.0
August	3 429	82 805	8.4	6.7	7.9	20.7	7.7	15.2	12.1	5.2	7.6	9.8	9.2	19.1	10.7	11.3
September	3 508	82 771	8.4	6.9	7.7	19.5	7.7	15.4	12.7	5.3	7.6	9.8	9.1	18.5	10.5	11.1
October	3 397	82 973	8.4	6.8	7.9	19.8	7.7	14.9	13.0	5.2	7.5	10.4	9.0	17.8	10.1	10.8
November	3 331	83 125	8.3	6.8	7.8	19.0	7.6	14.6	12.4	4.9	7.3	10.1	8.9	17.4	9.9	10.3
December	3 259	83 406	8.2	6.5	7.8	19.8	7.4	14.5	12.1	4.7	7.2	10.4	8.7	16.8	9.2	11.7
1976:																
January	3 387	84 013	7.9	6.1	7.7	19.6	7.2	14.3	11.4	4.4	7.2	10.6	8.3	15.5	8.5	11.4
February	3 304	84 368	7.7	5.9	7.5	19.0	6.9	14.4	10.7	4.2	7.2	10.2	8.0	15.4	8.2	10.6
March	3 296	84 689	7.6	5.8	7.3	18.9	6.9	13.5	11.0	4.2	6.9	9.5	7.8	15.7	7.7	10.9
April	3 438	84 978	7.7	5.8	7.4	19.5	6.9	13.8	11.7	4.1	7.0	9.6	7.7	15.6	7.8	11.5
May	3 367	85 427	7.4	5.7	6.9	18.6	6.7	13.2	10.5	4.1	6.8	9.2	7.7	14.7	7.7	12.9
June	3 310	85 253	7.6	6.1	7.2	18.5	6.9	14.3	11.1	4.4	7.0	9.6	7.9	16.3	7.8	11.5
July	3 358	85 735	7.8	6.0	7.6	18.3	7.1	13.9	11.7	4.4	7.3	10.1	8.1	16.8	7.7	11.7
August	3 380	85 843	7.8	5.8	7.6	19.6	7.1	14.3	12.4	4.1	7.4	10.5	8.1	16.6	7.8	11.0
September	3 278	85 895	7.6	5.9	7.5	18.6	7.0	13.7	11.8	4.4	7.2	10.6	8.0	15.7	7.7	11.3
October	3 316	85 958	7.7	5.8	7.5	19.0	7.0	13.9	11.6	4.2	7.2	10.5	7.9	14.7	7.8	11.2
November	3 263	86 371	7.8	6.1	7.5	19.2	7.1	14.0	11.7	4.3	7.0	9.8	8.0	15.4	7.7	13.5
December	3 251	86 552	7.8	6.1	7.3	19.1	7.0	14.1	11.7	4.2	6.9	10.3	7.9	14.3	8.1	13.6
1977:																
January	3 185	86 743	7.5	5.8	7.1	18.9	6.8	13.8	11.2	4.1	6.6	9.5	7.6	14.8	7.3	13.0
February	3 222	87 120	7.6	5.9	7.3	18.4	6.9	14.2	11.4	4.1	6.9	9.5	7.7	14.7	7.5	12.8
March	3 212	87 596	7.4	5.5	7.4	18.6	6.7	13.9	11.2	3.8	7.0	9.7	7.6	13.9	7.0	12.7
April	3 313	87 958	7.2	5.3	7.1	18.0	6.4	12.8	9.6	3.7	6.7	9.3	7.1	12.5	6.9	12.5
May	3 432	88 322	7.0	5.4	6.6	17.8	6.3	13.5	9.9	3.6	6.5	8.9	7.2	13.4	6.5	11.6
June	3 340	88 619	7.2	5.2	7.1	18.8	6.4	13.9	10.1	3.5	6.7	9.4	7.0	12.6	6.5	11.8
July	3 247	88 837	6.9	5.1	6.9	17.5	6.0	13.9	9.5	3.4	6.5	9.2	6.9	12.0	6.5	9.4
August	3 260	89 181	7.0	5.1	7.0	17.4	6.0	15.1	9.4	3.4	6.4	9.9	6.9	11.5	6.6	10.1
September	3 201	89 501	6.8	4.7	6.9	18.0	6.0	14.5	9.7	3.3	6.4	10.4	6.7	10.5	6.7	10.5
October	3 272	89 780	6.8	5.0	6.7	17.2	5.9	14.5	9.4	3.6	6.2	9.3	6.8	11.8	6.6	10.0
November	3 375	90 386	6.8	4.8	7.0	17.2	5.8	14.7	9.3	3.3	6.4	9.4	6.7	11.4	6.4	9.6
December	3 320	90 785	6.4	4.6	6.5	15.5	5.5	13.6	8.8	3.2	6.0	8.1	6.3	10.8	5.8	10.0
1978:																
January	3 434	90 950	6.4	4.7	6.4	16.7	5.5	13.9	9.3	3.1	5.8	8.3	6.4	11.6	5.9	9.4
February	3 320	91 199	6.3	4.6	5.9	17.2	5.5	13.1	9.9	3.0	5.5	7.8	6.3	11.1	6.0	9.8
March	3 351	91 404	6.3	4.6	6.0	17.3	5.4	13.1	9.5	3.1	5.4	8.7	6.2	11.0	5.7	10.1
April	3 349	92 045	6.1	4.3	6.0	16.6	5.3	12.9	8.5	2.8	5.1	9.9	6.0	9.8	5.4	8.2
May	3 325	92 444	6.0	4.2	6.0	16.0	5.2	13.0	9.6	2.8	5.8	9.1	5.9	9.7	5.6	8.0
June	3 483	92 860	5.9	4.0	6.1	15.4	5.0	12.8	9.1	2.8	5.5	8.7	5.7	9.6	5.6	8.9
July	3 441	92 649	6.2	4.1	6.4	16.5	5.3	13.0	9.5	2.6	5.6	9.9	5.9	9.8	5.4	9.2
August	3 401	93 030	5.9	4.1	6.0	15.7	5.1	12.3	9.1	2.7	5.6	8.2	5.7	9.2	5.4	8.5
September	3 400	93 270	6.0	4.1	6.0	16.4	5.2	11.9	8.9	2.7	5.7	8.4	5.9	10.9	5.3	8.7
October	3 409	93 724	5.8	4.1	5.6	16.1	5.0	11.8	8.5	2.6	5.2	7.6	5.6	11.2	5.1	9.4
November	3 284	94 201	5.9	4.0	5.9	16.3	5.0	12.7	8.4	2.5	5.5	7.8	5.7	10.8	5.2	8.2
December	3 396	94 185	6.0	4.2	5.8	16.7	5.2	12.4	8.7	2.7	5.6	8.0	5.9	12.2	5.3	8.3
1979:																
January	3 305	94 643	5.9	4.1	5.8	16.1	5.1	12.4	8.2	2.7	5.4	7.9	5.8	10.8	5.2	7.5
February	3 373	94 956	5.9	4.1	5.9	16.1	5.1	13.1	7.7	2.8	5.3	8.5	5.8	11.5	5.1	9.0
March	3 368	95 112	5.8	4.1	5.8	15.9	5.1	12.5	7.9	2.7	5.3	8.3	5.8	10.3	5.4	8.1
April	3 291	94 812	5.8	4.1	5.7	16.3	5.0	12.9	8.2	2.7	5.2	8.1	5.7	10.3	5.5	8.9
May	3 272	95 059	5.6	3.8	5.6	16.1	4.8	12.4	7.9	2.4	5.0	8.6	5.6	9.5	5.3	9.3
June	3 331	95 348	5.7	4.0	5.7	15.7	4.9	12.2	8.4	2.6	5.1	9.0	5.6	9.7	5.3	8.3
July	3 335	95 671	5.7	4.1	5.5	15.6	4.9	12.1	8.1	2.8	4.9	8.1	5.7	9.7	5.6	9.9
August	3 374	95 402	6.0	4.2	6.0	16.5	5.3	12.4	8.7	2.9	5.4	8.2	6.0	9.1	6.0	9.6
September	3 371	95 969	5.9	4.2	5.6	16.5	5.2	11.7	7.6	2.8	5.0	8.1	5.9	9.1	6.1	10.4
October	3 325	96 079	6.0	4.3	5.7	16.5	5.2	12.3	8.7	2.9	5.2	8.4	5.9	10.0	6.0	9.5
November	3 436	96 138	5.9	4.4	5.6	15.9	5.2	11.9	9.2	3.0	4.8	8.4	5.9	10.5	6.0	10.6
December	3 400	96 533	6.0	4.3	5.7	16.2	5.2	12.2	9.1	2.9	5.1	8.4	5.9	11.1	6.0	9.7
1980:																
January	3 316	96 563	6.3	4.8	5.8	16.5	5.5	13.0	8.7	3.5	5.3	8.9	6.3	11.7	6.8	10.1
February	3 397	96 598	6.3	4.8	5.9	16.6	5.5	12.9	8.9	3.3	5.4	8.8	6.3	11.4	6.8	9.6
March	3 418	96 295	6.3	5.1	5.7	16.3	5.6	12.9	9.2	3.5	5.3	8.8	6.4	13.2	6.7	10.3
April	3 326	95 907	6.9	5.8	6.3	16.2	6.1	13.8	10.4	4.1	5.7	9.0	7.1	14.6	8.2	12.0
May	3 382	95 563	7.5	6.4	6.4	18.6	6.6	14.4	10.1	4.5	5.9	8.3	7.9	16.1	9.6	11.4
June	3 296	95 386	7.6	6.5	6.5	18.9	6.7	14.6	10.1	4.7	6.1	8.4	8.0	15.4	9.5	10.1
July	3 319	95 477	7.8	6.8	6.6	19.1	6.9	15.3	10.8	4.9	6.2	8.9	8.2	15.8	9.9	11.6
August	3 234	95 590	7.7	6.7	6.7	18.9	6.9	14.6	10.8	4.9	6.2	9.4	8.1	16.5	9.5	13.2
September	3 443	95 634	7.5	6.6	6.3	18.0	6.6	14.8	11.4	4.7	5.9	9.1	7.9	15.5	9.2	11.7
October	3 372	95 945	7.5	6.3	6.7	18.4	6.6	15.1	10.6	4.5	6.0	10.1	7.8	14.1	9.1	11.3
November	3 396	96 149	7.5	6.3	6.7	18.5	6.5	15.1	9.9	4.3	5.8	9.8	7.8	14.5	8.8	10.1
December	3 492	96 142	7.2	5.9	6.7	17.6	6.3	15.0	10.3	4.1	5.8	10.2	7.5	13.6	8.5	10.5

CIVILIAN EMPLOYMENT AND SELECTED UNEMPLOYMENT RATES—Continued
(Seasonally adjusted)

YEAR AND MONTH	Employment by industry (Thousands of persons)		All civilian workers	By sex and age			By race		Persons of Hispanic origin	By marital or family status			Wage and salary workers, by industry of last job			
				20 years and over		Both sexes, 16-19 years				Married men, spouse present	Married women, spouse present	Women who maintain families	Private nonagricultural			Agricultural
	Agricultural	Non-agricultural		Men	Women		White	Black					Total	Construction	Manufacturing	
1981:																
January	3 429	96 526	7.5	6.1	6.7	19.1	6.7	14.6	10.6	4.2	6.1	10.3	7.6	13.7	8.4	10.8
February	3 345	96 846	7.4	6.1	6.6	19.3	6.6	14.7	11.3	4.2	5.8	10.0	7.7	13.8	8.5	12.4
March	3 365	97 206	7.4	6.0	6.6	19.2	6.5	15.1	10.2	4.2	5.9	9.7	7.5	14.9	8.2	12.1
April	3 529	97 527	7.2	5.9	6.5	18.8	6.4	14.7	9.5	3.8	5.8	9.8	7.3	14.5	7.7	9.5
May	3 369	97 679	7.5	6.2	6.7	19.1	6.6	14.8	10.0	4.0	5.7	10.4	7.7	15.9	7.8	10.9
June	3 334	96 964	7.5	6.2	6.7	19.8	6.5	15.7	10.3	4.3	5.7	10.5	7.4	16.3	7.5	12.6
July	3 296	97 397	7.2	5.9	6.7	18.6	6.3	15.0	10.0	4.0	5.7	11.3	7.3	15.3	7.5	11.4
August	3 379	97 310	7.4	6.1	6.7	18.8	6.3	16.3	10.0	4.1	5.5	10.3	7.4	16.1	7.3	12.4
September	3 361	96 703	7.6	6.2	7.0	19.7	6.6	15.9	9.6	4.3	6.0	10.6	7.7	15.8	7.9	11.7
October	3 412	96 966	7.9	6.7	7.1	20.3	6.9	16.7	10.7	4.6	6.1	10.6	8.0	17.4	8.5	13.3
November	3 415	96 792	8.3	7.0	7.2	21.3	7.3	16.8	11.2	4.9	6.5	10.9	8.4	17.6	9.3	13.8
December	3 227	96 418	8.5	7.5	7.4	21.1	7.5	17.2	11.7	5.4	6.5	10.4	8.9	17.6	10.5	14.0
1982:																
January	3 393	96 299	8.6	7.6	7.3	22.0	7.6	17.3	11.7	5.4	6.3	10.4	8.9	18.8	10.4	15.0
February	3 375	96 387	8.9	7.7	7.7	22.6	7.8	17.7	12.1	5.4	6.9	10.4	9.1	18.3	10.6	13.4
March	3 372	96 300	9.0	8.0	7.9	21.8	8.0	18.1	12.2	5.7	7.0	10.6	9.4	18.3	10.8	13.9
April	3 351	96 225	9.3	8.2	8.2	22.8	8.3	18.2	12.9	6.0	7.7	11.3	9.8	19.3	11.3	14.8
May	3 434	96 682	9.4	8.3	8.1	22.8	8.2	18.5	13.9	6.1	7.2	11.9	9.9	18.8	11.6	18.0
June	3 331	96 212	9.6	8.7	8.1	22.9	8.5	18.5	13.8	6.5	7.0	12.1	10.1	19.5	12.4	15.2
July	3 402	96 091	9.8	8.9	8.3	24.0	8.7	18.8	14.2	6.7	7.3	12.3	10.3	20.4	12.4	14.6
August	3 408	96 225	9.8	9.0	8.3	23.7	8.7	18.9	14.8	6.8	7.2	11.8	10.3	20.4	12.4	14.7
September	3 385	96 119	10.1	9.5	8.4	23.6	9.0	19.7	14.4	7.1	7.5	12.2	10.6	21.7	13.6	13.4
October	3 489	95 726	10.4	9.8	8.7	23.7	9.2	20.1	15.0	7.4	7.9	11.3	11.0	22.6	13.8	12.5
November	3 510	95 602	10.8	10.0	9.1	24.1	9.6	20.2	15.2	7.5	8.5	12.6	11.4	21.7	14.5	15.7
December	3 414	95 618	10.8	10.1	9.3	24.1	9.7	20.9	15.7	7.5	8.2	13.5	11.5	21.5	14.3	16.2
1983:																
January	3 439	95 722	10.4	9.7	9.0	23.1	9.1	21.2	15.3	7.2	7.8	13.3	10.9	20.4	13.0	15.6
February	3 382	95 707	10.4	9.9	8.9	22.8	9.3	19.9	15.5	7.2	7.6	13.0	10.9	19.8	13.3	16.3
March	3 360	95 819	10.3	9.7	8.8	23.5	9.1	20.1	15.6	7.2	7.5	13.2	10.8	20.5	12.9	16.1
April	3 341	96 219	10.2	9.7	8.4	23.4	8.9	20.4	14.8	7.1	7.3	13.0	10.6	20.4	12.4	17.6
May	3 328	96 314	10.1	9.6	8.4	22.8	8.8	20.3	14.0	7.0	7.4	12.8	10.5	20.2	12.4	17.2
June	3 462	97 171	10.1	9.1	8.7	24.0	8.7	20.7	14.3	6.6	7.8	12.6	10.1	18.2	11.6	17.3
July	3 481	97 727	9.4	8.8	7.9	22.8	8.2	19.4	12.4	6.1	6.9	12.1	9.6	17.8	10.8	14.5
August	3 502	98 106	9.5	8.7	7.9	22.9	8.2	19.7	13.0	6.4	6.8	11.6	9.8	18.0	11.1	15.0
September	3 347	98 669	9.2	8.5	7.7	21.7	8.0	18.8	12.9	6.0	6.7	11.8	9.3	17.9	10.0	15.8
October	3 303	98 736	8.8	8.2	7.5	21.4	7.7	18.2	12.1	5.7	6.3	11.3	9.0	15.6	9.5	16.0
November	3 291	99 438	8.5	7.8	7.2	20.2	7.4	17.5	12.3	5.5	6.2	10.4	8.6	15.2	8.9	15.6
December	3 332	99 664	8.3	7.5	7.3	19.9	7.1	17.8	11.6	5.2	6.3	11.2	8.3	16.3	8.5	15.7
1984:																
January	3 293	99 908	8.0	7.2	7.1	19.5	6.9	17.3	11.4	5.0	5.9	10.9	7.9	15.3	8.2	15.4
February	3 353	100 471	7.8	7.0	6.9	19.4	6.8	16.2	10.4	4.8	5.9	10.7	7.8	14.9	7.7	13.8
March	3 233	100 734	7.8	6.8	6.9	19.8	6.7	16.6	11.5	4.7	5.8	10.8	7.6	13.5	7.6	15.1
April	3 291	101 045	7.7	6.9	6.9	19.2	6.7	16.5	11.6	4.7	5.8	10.5	7.7	14.6	7.6	13.0
May	3 343	101 850	7.4	6.5	6.7	18.7	6.4	15.7	10.6	4.6	5.7	9.9	7.2	14.9	7.1	13.9
June	3 383	102 208	7.2	6.3	6.5	18.2	6.2	15.6	10.3	4.5	5.7	9.7	7.0	14.7	7.3	12.8
July	3 344	102 091	7.5	6.5	6.8	18.8	6.3	16.7	10.4	4.5	5.8	10.0	7.4	14.6	7.5	13.9
August	3 286	101 877	7.5	6.5	6.9	18.7	6.4	16.0	10.7	4.6	5.9	10.1	7.4	14.2	7.4	12.5
September	3 393	102 097	7.3	6.4	6.5	19.2	6.4	15.0	10.5	4.6	5.7	9.7	7.2	13.8	7.3	13.9
October	3 194	102 444	7.4	6.2	6.9	18.6	6.3	15.3	10.8	4.5	5.8	10.4	7.3	13.4	7.3	13.6
November	3 394	102 578	7.2	6.2	6.6	17.7	6.2	15.0	10.2	4.4	5.5	10.9	7.2	13.9	7.2	11.3
December	3 385	102 838	7.3	6.3	6.6	18.8	6.3	15.2	10.4	4.5	5.5	10.1	7.3	13.7	7.4	12.9
1985:																
January	3 317	102 985	7.3	6.3	6.7	18.8	6.3	15.2	10.5	4.5	5.7	10.2	7.3	13.5	7.5	15.9
February	3 317	103 238	7.2	6.2	6.6	18.3	6.2	15.8	9.8	4.4	5.3	10.9	7.2	13.3	7.6	13.2
March	3 250	103 739	7.2	6.2	6.7	18.2	6.2	15.1	10.5	4.2	5.8	10.2	7.2	13.3	7.6	12.8
April	3 306	103 630	7.3	6.3	6.8	17.5	6.3	15.1	10.4	4.3	5.8	10.9	7.3	13.7	8.0	13.5
May	3 280	103 652	7.2	6.0	6.8	18.5	6.2	15.2	10.6	4.0	5.7	10.6	7.1	10.5	7.7	11.3
June	3 161	103 344	7.4	6.4	6.7	18.5	6.5	14.4	10.7	4.6	5.9	9.7	7.3	13.9	7.7	12.9
July	3 143	103 664	7.4	6.2	6.7	20.2	6.4	15.2	11.2	4.4	5.6	10.4	7.2	13.5	8.0	13.9
August	3 121	103 974	7.1	6.1	6.7	17.9	6.2	14.3	10.4	4.3	5.4	10.7	7.2	13.3	7.9	13.3
September	3 064	104 593	7.1	6.1	6.6	17.9	6.1	15.2	10.4	4.4	5.7	11.1	7.2	13.7	7.7	12.8
October	3 051	104 796	7.1	6.1	6.4	20.0	6.1	15.0	11.1	4.1	5.4	10.5	7.1	13.2	7.6	13.0
November	3 062	104 945	7.0	6.0	6.4	18.3	5.9	15.6	10.6	4.2	5.4	10.1	7.1	13.2	7.7	13.1
December	3 141	105 075	7.0	6.0	6.3	19.1	6.0	15.0	10.5	4.3	5.3	9.7	7.0	12.5	7.3	11.0
1986:																
January	3 287	105 600	6.7	5.7	6.1	18.1	5.7	14.5	10.2	4.3	5.0	9.9	6.7	12.8	6.9	11.2
February	3 083	105 397	7.2	6.2	6.6	18.8	6.3	14.4	11.9	4.4	5.4	9.9	7.2	13.2	7.2	13.8
March	3 200	105 637	7.2	6.2	6.6	18.2	6.2	14.6	10.7	4.5	5.5	10.1	7.2	13.0	7.1	12.2
April	3 153	105 799	7.1	6.1	6.5	19.2	6.1	14.8	10.3	4.2	5.3	9.6	7.2	12.4	6.9	13.9
May	3 150	105 939	7.2	6.3	6.4	18.6	6.2	14.6	10.8	4.5	5.5	9.9	7.2	12.9	7.3	15.1
June	3 193	106 383	7.2	6.3	6.4	19.2	6.2	15.1	10.6	4.5	5.4	9.9	7.2	12.5	7.5	13.7
July	3 141	106 669	7.0	6.3	6.2	18.4	6.1	14.4	10.7	4.5	5.2	9.3	7.2	13.3	7.0	11.5
August	3 082	106 933	6.9	6.0	6.1	18.0	5.9	14.8	10.9	4.3	5.1	10.1	7.0	12.2	7.0	12.9
September	3 171	106 914	7.0	6.3	6.1	18.4	6.0	14.9	11.1	4.3	5.1	9.8	7.0	12.9	7.0	12.7
October	3 128	107 145	7.0	6.2	6.1	17.7	6.0	14.6	10.4	4.5	5.0	8.9	7.0	13.5	7.4	11.7
November	3 220	107 255	6.9	6.1	6.0	18.1	6.0	14.3	9.3	4.4	4.9	9.9	7.0	14.9	7.2	9.9
December	3 148	107 580	6.6	6.0	5.7	17.5	5.8	13.7	10.5	4.3	4.7	9.9	6.7	13.5	6.9	12.0

CIVILIAN EMPLOYMENT AND SELECTED UNEMPLOYMENT RATES—Continued
(Seasonally adjusted)

YEAR AND MONTH	Employment by industry (Thousands of persons)		All civilian workers	By sex and age			By race		Persons of Hispanic origin	By marital or family status			Wage and salary workers, by industry of last job			
				20 years and over		Both sexes, 16-19 years				Married men, spouse present	Married women, spouse present	Women who maintain families	Private nonagricultural			Agricultural
	Agricultural	Non-agricultural		Men	Women		White	Black					Total	Construction	Manufacturing	
1987:																
January	3 143	107 810	6.6	5.9	5.8	17.7	5.7	14.0	10.6	4.2	4.7	9.7	6.6	12.2	6.6	11.3
February	3 208	108 049	6.6	5.8	5.8	18.0	5.7	13.8	9.8	4.1	4.7	9.6	6.6	11.6	6.7	11.3
March	3 214	108 194	6.6	5.7	5.9	17.9	5.7	13.8	9.3	4.1	4.5	9.7	6.6	12.5	6.8	10.9
April	3 246	108 548	6.3	5.5	5.6	17.3	5.4	12.9	8.9	4.0	4.5	9.4	6.3	12.1	6.3	9.4
May	3 345	109 089	6.3	5.6	5.4	17.4	5.4	13.6	8.6	4.0	4.2	9.4	6.3	12.2	6.3	8.3
June	3 216	109 030	6.2	5.6	5.3	16.5	5.4	12.9	8.5	4.1	4.1	9.6	6.2	11.8	5.8	9.2
July	3 235	109 399	6.1	5.4	5.3	15.8	5.2	12.9	8.1	3.9	4.2	9.1	6.1	10.9	6.0	11.5
August	3 112	109 945	6.0	5.3	5.3	15.9	5.1	12.6	7.9	3.7	4.2	9.1	5.9	11.1	5.5	10.4
September	3 189	109 720	5.9	5.1	5.3	16.2	5.1	12.6	8.3	3.7	4.2	8.8	5.9	12.3	5.7	8.2
October	3 219	110 063	6.0	5.1	5.2	17.3	5.2	12.3	8.4	3.7	4.2	8.9	5.9	11.3	5.8	10.8
November	3 145	110 360	5.8	5.0	5.2	16.6	5.0	12.1	8.8	3.5	4.2	8.6	5.8	10.5	5.5	11.6
December	3 213	110 580	5.7	4.9	5.1	16.0	4.9	12.1	8.1	3.4	4.3	8.2	5.6	10.6	5.1	11.6
1988:																
January	3 247	110 769	5.7	4.9	5.1	16.1	5.0	12.0	7.6	3.5	4.1	8.9	5.7	11.8	5.4	11.4
February	3 201	111 026	5.7	4.9	5.2	15.6	4.9	12.4	8.5	3.4	4.0	8.4	5.7	10.9	5.6	10.7
March	3 169	110 868	5.7	4.9	4.9	16.6	4.8	12.7	8.4	3.4	4.0	7.6	5.6	10.8	5.3	11.0
April	3 224	111 426	5.4	4.6	4.9	16.0	4.6	12.2	8.8	3.0	3.8	8.6	5.3	10.6	5.2	10.4
May	3 121	111 171	5.6	4.9	4.9	15.3	4.7	12.3	8.8	3.3	3.9	8.3	5.6	10.7	5.4	12.0
June	3 111	111 816	5.4	4.7	4.8	14.2	4.6	11.5	8.8	3.2	3.8	7.9	5.4	10.3	4.9	9.6
July	3 060	112 000	5.4	4.6	5.0	14.8	4.7	11.6	7.9	3.1	4.0	8.1	5.4	10.4	5.2	11.1
August	3 119	112 163	5.6	4.9	4.8	15.4	4.8	11.4	8.1	3.4	4.0	7.5	5.6	10.7	5.5	11.1
September	3 165	112 191	5.4	4.6	4.8	15.5	4.8	11.0	7.4	3.1	3.8	8.1	5.5	9.6	5.6	11.1
October	3 231	112 407	5.4	4.7	4.7	15.1	4.7	11.1	7.8	3.1	3.7	7.9	5.5	10.1	5.3	10.2
November	3 241	112 859	5.3	4.7	4.7	13.9	4.6	11.0	7.9	3.3	3.8	7.7	5.5	10.6	5.2	9.5
December	3 194	112 910	5.3	4.7	4.6	14.8	4.6	11.3	7.6	3.1	3.6	8.2	5.3	10.2	5.1	8.8
1989:																
January	3 287	113 421	5.4	4.6	4.7	16.4	4.6	11.8	8.6	3.1	3.7	8.1	5.5	10.3	5.2	9.5
February	3 234	113 542	5.2	4.5	4.5	15.0	4.3	11.9	7.0	3.1	3.4	8.1	5.2	10.1	4.8	9.2
March	3 198	113 824	5.0	4.3	4.6	13.9	4.2	11.1	6.6	2.9	3.5	7.9	5.1	9.7	4.8	8.8
April	3 162	113 935	5.2	4.5	4.7	14.6	4.5	11.1	8.1	3.1	4.1	7.7	5.2	9.7	4.8	10.1
May	3 125	113 974	5.2	4.3	4.8	14.8	4.4	11.2	7.9	2.9	3.8	8.4	5.2	9.5	5.0	10.1
June	3 068	114 350	5.3	4.4	4.8	15.7	4.5	11.7	8.2	2.8	3.8	8.0	5.3	10.0	5.1	10.2
July	3 227	114 245	5.2	4.4	4.9	14.2	4.5	11.0	8.8	3.0	3.9	8.2	5.4	10.2	5.1	8.5
August	3 284	114 371	5.2	4.5	4.7	14.6	4.5	11.1	8.8	3.1	3.8	7.9	5.3	10.3	5.2	8.8
September	3 219	114 135	5.3	4.7	4.6	15.2	4.5	11.7	8.1	3.3	3.8	7.7	5.5	10.4	5.3	8.0
October	3 215	114 366	5.3	4.6	4.8	15.0	4.5	11.7	8.0	3.1	4.0	7.7	5.4	9.1	5.4	10.1
November	3 132	114 780	5.4	4.7	4.7	15.5	4.6	11.7	7.9	3.1	3.7	8.2	5.5	9.8	5.4	12.0
December	3 188	114 642	5.4	4.6	4.8	15.3	4.6	11.6	8.3	3.1	3.8	8.0	5.4	9.7	5.6	9.5
1990:																
January	3 210	115 871	5.4	4.7	4.7	14.8	4.6	11.1	7.3	3.4	3.7	7.9	5.5	9.2	6.0	8.9
February	3 188	115 871	5.3	4.5	4.7	15.0	4.6	11.0	7.5	3.1	3.7	7.8	5.4	9.2	5.6	9.1
March	3 260	115 943	5.2	4.6	4.7	14.3	4.5	10.9	7.4	3.1	3.6	8.2	5.3	10.0	5.5	9.3
April	3 231	115 621	5.4	4.8	4.8	14.7	4.7	10.7	8.5	3.3	3.6	7.6	5.6	10.3	5.6	12.3
May	3 266	115 885	5.4	4.7	4.7	15.0	4.6	10.6	7.9	3.2	3.6	7.9	5.5	11.4	5.6	8.8
June	3 245	115 738	5.2	4.7	4.6	14.3	4.5	10.5	7.7	3.1	3.6	8.2	5.3	9.8	5.0	9.4
July	3 192	115 618	5.5	4.9	4.9	15.0	4.7	11.4	8.0	3.4	3.8	8.4	5.6	10.5	5.8	9.8
August	3 197	115 605	5.7	5.1	5.0	16.3	4.9	11.7	8.3	3.5	4.0	8.3	5.8	11.6	5.9	9.9
September	3 206	115 318	5.9	5.2	5.1	16.4	5.0	12.1	8.3	3.5	4.0	9.0	6.0	12.1	6.1	10.0
October	3 270	115 266	5.9	5.4	5.1	16.5	5.1	12.1	8.5	3.7	4.1	8.7	6.1	13.0	5.9	9.3
November	3 189	115 117	6.2	5.7	5.2	17.1	5.3	12.4	8.9	3.9	4.2	9.0	6.4	13.8	6.3	9.6
December	3 245	114 996	6.3	5.8	5.2	17.4	5.4	12.4	9.9	3.9	4.1	9.0	6.5	14.2	6.8	11.9
1991:																
January	3 208	114 732	6.4	5.8	5.4	18.6	5.6	11.9	9.1	4.1	4.1	9.3	6.5	14.4	6.9	12.0
February	3 270	114 485	6.6	6.2	5.5	17.4	5.8	12.2	9.2	4.3	4.4	9.2	6.9	15.4	7.2	11.2
March	3 177	114 475	6.8	6.4	5.6	18.3	6.0	12.5	9.8	4.4	4.7	9.0	7.0	14.1	7.6	13.0
April	3 241	114 868	6.7	6.4	5.5	17.8	5.9	12.7	9.8	4.5	4.6	9.5	7.0	14.8	7.5	11.7
May	3 275	114 165	6.9	6.4	6.0	18.8	6.1	12.8	10.0	4.4	4.7	9.5	7.1	14.9	7.5	12.2
June	3 300	114 339	6.9	6.5	5.8	18.5	6.2	12.5	10.1	4.5	4.6	9.2	7.2	15.2	7.7	11.7
July	3 319	114 249	6.8	6.5	5.5	19.4	6.2	11.9	9.6	4.3	4.5	8.3	7.2	16.4	7.0	10.8
August	3 313	114 171	6.9	6.5	5.7	18.9	6.2	12.4	10.5	4.4	4.5	9.5	7.1	15.4	7.3	11.8
September	3 319	114 609	6.9	6.6	5.7	18.8	6.2	12.3	10.9	4.5	4.6	9.4	7.1	15.9	7.0	11.9
October	3 289	114 511	7.0	6.5	5.9	19.1	6.2	13.3	10.7	4.3	4.5	9.7	7.1	16.2	6.9	12.4
November	3 296	114 474	7.0	6.6	6.0	19.0	6.3	12.5	10.4	4.7	4.6	9.5	7.4	16.9	7.2	12.0
December	3 146	114 320	7.3	6.8	6.1	20.3	6.5	12.9	10.2	4.9	4.9	9.2	7.6	16.8	7.5	11.2
1992:																
January	3 155	114 823	7.3	7.1	6.0	19.2	6.4	13.5	11.0	4.9	4.8	9.2	7.5	17.1	7.5	11.2
February	3 239	114 514	7.4	7.1	6.2	20.1	6.5	14.2	11.3	5.1	5.0	9.6	7.7	17.9	7.7	11.2
March	3 236	114 908	7.4	7.0	6.2	20.3	6.5	14.1	11.2	4.8	5.0	10.0	7.7	17.2	7.5	10.1
April	3 245	115 181	7.4	7.1	6.3	18.5	6.5	14.1	11.0	4.9	5.1	10.0	7.7	16.5	7.7	11.9
May	3 213	115 162	7.6	7.3	6.3	20.1	6.6	14.7	11.7	5.1	5.1	10.1	7.9	16.8	8.2	14.6
June	3 297	115 122	7.8	7.4	6.4	23.0	6.9	14.6	12.1	5.2	5.2	10.2	7.9	17.1	8.2	13.0
July	3 285	115 428	7.7	7.2	6.5	20.8	6.7	14.4	11.7	5.2	5.2	10.4	7.9	16.5	8.1	13.9
August	3 279	115 547	7.6	7.2	6.5	19.9	6.7	14.2	11.7	5.3	5.0	10.7	8.0	16.8	7.9	11.1
September	3 274	115 446	7.6	7.1	6.4	21.0	6.7	13.9	11.8	5.3	5.0	9.6	7.9	17.4	8.0	16.0
October	3 254	115 374	7.3	7.1	6.2	18.3	6.5	14.3	11.8	5.2	5.0	9.4	7.8	16.0	8.1	13.1
November	3 207	115 669	7.4	7.0	6.2	20.5	6.5	14.1	12.0	5.0	5.0	11.0	7.6	15.4	7.9	14.2
December	3 259	115 738	7.4	6.8	6.5	19.8	6.5	14.3	11.5	4.9	5.0	10.1	7.7	16.3	7.5	12.3

YEAR AND MONTH	NONAGRICULTURAL EMPLOYMENT (Wage and salary workers on nonagricultural payrolls—Thousands, seasonally adjusted)													
	Total	Goods-producing industries [1]					Service-producing industries							
		Total	Con-struction	Manufacturing			Total	Trans-portation and public utilities	Whole-sale trade	Retail trade	Finance, insur-ance, and real estate	Services (Private)	Government	
				Total	Durable goods	Nondurable goods							Total	Federal
1969:														
January	69 272	24 121	3 485	20 019	11 799	8 220	45 151	4 332	3 860	10 562	3 431	10 912	12 054	2 760
February	69 542	24 231	3 514	20 101	11 826	8 275	45 311	4 338	3 870	10 610	3 448	10 962	12 083	2 761
March	69 791	24 307	3 529	20 164	11 860	8 304	45 484	4 363	3 876	10 660	3 462	11 035	12 088	2 751
April	69 948	24 309	3 538	20 157	11 856	8 301	45 639	4 398	3 884	10 693	3 478	11 076	12 110	2 755
May	70 180	24 358	3 574	20 170	11 864	8 306	45 822	4 417	3 900	10 746	3 490	11 117	12 152	2 751
June	70 498	24 444	3 595	20 235	11 911	8 324	46 054	4 471	3 920	10 794	3 508	11 152	12 209	2 779
July	70 668	24 495	3 594	20 282	11 939	8 343	46 173	4 484	3 931	10 819	3 525	11 197	12 217	2 770
August	70 799	24 487	3 576	20 289	11 951	8 338	46 312	4 492	3 939	10 854	3 542	11 237	12 248	2 760
September	70 833	24 482	3 603	20 251	11 943	8 308	46 351	4 507	3 944	10 856	3 546	11 263	12 235	2 752
October	70 993	24 447	3 599	20 220	11 926	8 294	46 546	4 502	3 956	10 919	3 557	11 333	12 279	2 742
November	70 941	24 302	3 618	20 058	11 739	8 319	46 639	4 506	3 969	10 946	3 569	11 353	12 296	2 727
December	71 127	24 354	3 655	20 072	11 751	8 321	46 773	4 510	3 985	10 961	3 582	11 395	12 340	2 727
1970:														
January	71 018	24 190	3 562	20 004	11 669	8 335	46 828	4 487	3 997	10 968	3 597	11 432	12 347	2 714
February	71 165	24 198	3 636	19 940	11 617	8 323	46 967	4 475	4 002	11 015	3 608	11 481	12 386	2 713
March	71 347	24 202	3 646	19 934	11 630	8 304	47 145	4 489	4 006	11 060	3 625	11 496	12 469	2 787
April	71 251	24 026	3 617	19 788	11 517	8 271	47 225	4 465	4 006	11 024	3 632	11 525	12 573	2 863
May	70 993	23 745	3 567	19 558	11 364	8 194	47 248	4 485	4 009	11 024	3 637	11 553	12 540	2 791
June	70 905	23 647	3 570	19 456	11 262	8 194	47 258	4 543	4 002	11 018	3 640	11 537	12 518	2 724
July	70 969	23 597	3 574	19 403	11 198	8 205	47 372	4 585	4 024	11 027	3 647	11 516	12 573	2 695
August	70 789	23 468	3 579	19 265	11 103	8 162	47 321	4 565	4 007	11 022	3 650	11 494	12 583	2 684
September	70 857	23 380	3 552	19 202	11 073	8 129	47 477	4 565	4 010	11 046	3 662	11 593	12 601	2 690
October	70 416	22 836	3 562	18 646	10 574	8 072	47 580	4 544	4 010	11 078	3 670	11 632	12 646	2 685
November	70 296	22 707	3 585	18 493	10 432	8 061	47 589	4 531	4 004	11 033	3 683	11 653	12 685	2 688
December	70 666	23 019	3 623	18 768	10 714	8 054	47 647	4 472	4 003	11 109	3 695	11 667	12 701	2 687
1971:														
January	70 718	22 944	3 582	18 737	10 694	8 043	47 774	4 465	3 996	11 176	3 709	11 692	12 736	2 684
February	70 657	22 840	3 542	18 679	10 650	8 029	47 817	4 481	3 999	11 194	3 716	11 683	12 744	2 682
March	70 746	22 827	3 604	18 602	10 586	8 016	47 919	4 480	3 995	11 225	3 725	11 714	12 780	2 680
April	70 936	22 915	3 676	18 616	10 591	8 025	48 021	4 470	3 997	11 265	3 739	11 729	12 821	2 685
May	71 129	22 980	3 681	18 673	10 633	8 040	48 149	4 491	4 010	11 293	3 751	11 758	12 846	2 685
June	71 163	22 919	3 695	18 599	10 594	8 005	48 244	4 515	3 990	11 315	3 773	11 787	12 864	2 685
July	71 219	22 886	3 717	18 564	10 568	7 996	48 333	4 511	4 003	11 353	3 779	11 801	12 886	2 693
August	71 220	22 851	3 718	18 513	10 518	7 995	48 369	4 469	4 011	11 395	3 787	11 786	12 921	2 707
September	71 527	22 989	3 746	18 617	10 593	8 024	48 538	4 501	4 029	11 423	3 801	11 857	12 927	2 708
October	71 532	22 940	3 793	18 589	10 589	8 000	48 592	4 461	4 037	11 436	3 813	11 877	12 968	2 706
November	71 734	23 046	3 846	18 637	10 607	8 030	48 688	4 454	4 048	11 437	3 829	11 915	13 005	2 702
December	71 996	23 073	3 791	18 654	10 624	8 030	48 923	4 486	4 058	11 530	3 840	11 956	13 053	2 698
1972:														
January	72 303	23 210	3 852	18 730	10 691	8 039	49 093	4 485	4 059	11 585	3 848	11 990	13 126	2 703
February	72 525	23 260	3 810	18 824	10 762	8 062	49 265	4 497	4 067	11 653	3 854	12 024	13 170	2 698
March	72 808	23 384	3 847	18 909	10 822	8 087	49 424	4 527	4 090	11 677	3 865	12 065	13 200	2 691
April	73 061	23 487	3 877	18 989	10 883	8 106	49 574	4 519	4 102	11 703	3 878	12 133	13 239	2 695
May	73 341	23 590	3 897	19 069	10 942	8 127	49 751	4 522	4 108	11 745	3 886	12 201	13 289	2 691
June	73 643	23 677	3 911	19 139	10 985	8 154	49 966	4 543	4 132	11 791	3 914	12 330	13 256	2 676
July	73 636	23 586	3 878	19 086	10 972	8 114	50 050	4 535	4 129	11 805	3 917	12 320	13 344	2 645
August	73 929	23 700	3 911	19 161	11 039	8 122	50 229	4 533	4 142	11 852	3 926	12 367	13 409	2 666
September	74 115	23 797	3 918	19 244	11 101	8 143	50 318	4 564	4 151	11 871	3 933	12 362	13 437	2 671
October	74 527	24 003	3 951	19 418	11 247	8 171	50 524	4 578	4 161	11 943	3 945	12 440	13 457	2 674
November	74 881	24 121	3 930	19 558	11 353	8 205	50 760	4 584	4 181	12 035	3 959	12 499	13 502	2 678
December	75 235	24 179	3 848	19 703	11 470	8 233	51 056	4 611	4 200	12 174	3 967	12 562	13 542	2 684
1973:														
January	75 474	24 368	3 932	19 808	11 555	8 253	51 106	4 598	4 216	12 139	3 976	12 630	13 547	2 673
February	75 908	24 610	4 020	19 957	11 677	8 280	51 298	4 605	4 241	12 176	4 000	12 689	13 587	2 665
March	76 137	24 690	4 027	20 031	11 734	8 297	51 447	4 623	4 249	12 211	4 015	12 730	13 619	2 664
April	76 312	24 754	4 045	20 077	11 769	8 308	51 558	4 630	4 258	12 226	4 021	12 759	13 664	2 667
May	76 516	24 814	4 078	20 104	11 811	8 293	51 702	4 644	4 261	12 295	4 033	12 773	13 696	2 670
June	76 738	24 928	4 125	20 167	11 863	8 304	51 810	4 643	4 290	12 314	4 045	12 793	13 725	2 655
July	76 758	24 940	4 154	20 145	11 887	8 258	51 818	4 645	4 300	12 314	4 059	12 779	13 721	2 624
August	77 018	24 992	4 143	20 202	11 925	8 277	52 026	4 663	4 319	12 324	4 064	12 885	13 771	2 645
September	77 164	24 978	4 145	20 185	11 921	8 264	52 186	4 693	4 318	12 372	4 072	12 981	13 750	2 654
October	77 502	25 113	4 138	20 323	12 024	8 299	52 389	4 711	4 335	12 413	4 075	13 021	13 834	2 659
November	77 833	25 214	4 147	20 408	12 081	8 327	52 619	4 703	4 350	12 483	4 089	13 099	13 895	2 668
December	77 992	25 264	4 168	20 431	12 102	8 329	52 728	4 716	4 360	12 500	4 100	13 133	13 919	2 680
1974:														
January	77 953	25 175	4 144	20 359	12 043	8 316	52 778	4 737	4 399	12 420	4 113	13 172	13 937	2 683
February	78 177	25 211	4 251	20 284	11 986	8 298	52 966	4 738	4 419	12 431	4 131	13 239	14 008	2 699
March	78 177	25 134	4 216	20 242	11 958	8 284	53 043	4 737	4 422	12 437	4 133	13 280	14 034	2 705
April	78 261	25 102	4 156	20 260	12 004	8 256	53 159	4 731	4 430	12 479	4 137	13 303	14 079	2 711
May	78 407	25 067	4 131	20 244	11 987	8 257	53 340	4 733	4 441	12 529	4 145	13 390	14 102	2 719
June	78 434	25 017	4 064	20 258	12 017	8 241	53 417	4 734	4 455	12 541	4 157	13 444	14 086	2 723
July	78 517	24 925	3 975	20 250	12 035	8 215	53 592	4 740	4 461	12 563	4 158	13 515	14 155	2 729
August	78 478	24 833	3 966	20 157	11 951	8 206	53 645	4 734	4 468	12 542	4 158	13 533	14 210	2 732
September	78 498	24 721	3 921	20 089	11 915	8 174	53 777	4 713	4 463	12 608	4 161	13 552	14 280	2 739
October	78 569	24 582	3 882	19 978	11 874	8 104	53 987	4 716	4 476	12 685	4 164	13 616	14 330	2 737
November	78 238	24 216	3 827	19 663	11 666	7 997	54 022	4 704	4 481	12 647	4 164	13 646	14 380	2 738
December	77 565	23 653	3 774	19 185	11 345	7 840	53 912	4 688	4 459	12 574	4 158	13 636	14 397	2 738

1. Includes mining, not shown separately.

NONAGRICULTURAL EMPLOYMENT—Continued
(Wage and salary workers on nonagricultural payrolls—Thousands, seasonally adjusted)

| YEAR AND MONTH | Total | Goods-producing industries [1] | | | | | Service-producing industries | | | | | | | |
| | | Total | Con-struction | Manufacturing | | | Total | Trans-portation and public utilities | Whole-sale trade | Retail trade | Finance, insur-ance, and real estate | Services (Private) | Government | |
				Total	Durable goods	Nondurable goods							Total	Federal
1975:														
January	77 145	23 266	3 757	18 769	11 076	7 693	53 879	4 645	4 438	12 478	4 151	13 649	14 518	2 735
February	76 742	22 781	3 641	18 397	10 831	7 566	53 961	4 596	4 418	12 500	4 144	13 696	14 607	2 736
March	76 419	22 481	3 522	18 216	10 716	7 500	53 938	4 565	4 402	12 491	4 141	13 722	14 617	2 737
April	76 298	22 335	3 461	18 134	10 617	7 517	53 963	4 548	4 405	12 443	4 149	13 769	14 649	2 737
May	76 459	22 359	3 471	18 139	10 581	7 558	54 100	4 543	4 402	12 524	4 150	13 813	14 668	2 739
June	76 388	22 291	3 454	18 091	10 524	7 567	54 097	4 519	4 400	12 595	4 151	13 792	14 640	2 738
July	76 626	22 254	3 447	18 060	10 455	7 605	54 372	4 521	4 416	12 636	4 157	13 947	14 695	2 750
August	76 980	22 448	3 484	18 205	10 529	7 676	54 532	4 519	4 427	12 696	4 169	14 018	14 703	2 750
September	77 188	22 607	3 508	18 350	10 613	7 737	54 581	4 522	4 449	12 717	4 178	14 001	14 714	2 756
October	77 499	22 723	3 516	18 447	10 638	7 809	54 776	4 520	4 456	12 772	4 192	14 058	14 778	2 757
November	77 619	22 765	3 527	18 473	10 640	7 833	54 854	4 519	4 469	12 805	4 194	14 103	14 764	2 754
December	77 915	22 891	3 547	18 567	10 700	7 867	55 024	4 496	4 482	12 883	4 207	14 159	14 797	2 753
1976:														
January	78 326	23 070	3 588	18 703	10 793	7 910	55 256	4 539	4 497	12 934	4 211	14 242	14 833	2 750
February	78 606	23 165	3 589	18 798	10 856	7 942	55 441	4 550	4 516	13 029	4 218	14 293	14 835	2 744
March	78 819	23 237	3 572	18 887	10 929	7 958	55 582	4 559	4 528	13 051	4 228	14 367	14 849	2 739
April	79 134	23 360	3 587	18 999	11 005	7 994	55 774	4 568	4 549	13 137	4 240	14 435	14 845	2 736
May	79 192	23 320	3 564	18 985	11 050	7 935	55 872	4 568	4 560	13 177	4 250	14 481	14 836	2 733
June	79 258	23 315	3 555	18 992	11 069	7 923	55 943	4 575	4 562	13 168	4 262	14 541	14 835	2 723
July	79 485	23 359	3 564	19 015	11 078	7 937	56 126	4 595	4 569	13 207	4 266	14 622	14 867	2 723
August	79 581	23 356	3 567	19 031	11 117	7 914	56 225	4 595	4 570	13 261	4 275	14 639	14 885	2 724
September	79 842	23 498	3 565	19 152	11 177	7 975	56 344	4 615	4 587	13 307	4 300	14 665	14 870	2 727
October	79 842	23 406	3 571	19 049	11 094	7 955	56 436	4 597	4 592	13 315	4 319	14 708	14 905	2 726
November	80 141	23 555	3 601	19 161	11 196	7 965	56 586	4 605	4 600	13 341	4 330	14 775	14 935	2 732
December	80 338	23 580	3 590	19 186	11 218	7 968	56 758	4 631	4 611	13 386	4 347	14 836	14 947	2 728
1977:														
January	80 517	23 628	3 542	19 276	11 276	8 000	56 889	4 647	4 624	13 441	4 363	14 893	14 921	2 723
February	80 794	23 803	3 665	19 321	11 288	8 033	56 991	4 656	4 633	13 475	4 375	14 939	14 913	2 724
March	81 221	24 000	3 739	19 436	11 381	8 055	57 221	4 657	4 653	13 580	4 401	15 014	14 916	2 729
April	81 610	24 186	3 813	19 546	11 446	8 100	57 424	4 678	4 675	13 634	4 422	15 086	14 929	2 723
May	81 977	24 308	3 843	19 639	11 520	8 119	57 669	4 701	4 692	13 704	4 437	15 147	14 988	2 724
June	82 381	24 431	3 879	19 723	11 582	8 141	57 950	4 707	4 713	13 762	4 454	15 232	15 082	2 724
July	82 760	24 515	3 908	19 799	11 658	8 141	58 245	4 725	4 735	13 806	4 469	15 336	15 174	2 720
August	82 974	24 508	3 911	19 796	11 656	8 140	58 466	4 727	4 754	13 872	4 484	15 411	15 218	2 726
September	83 431	24 612	3 935	19 851	11 704	8 147	58 819	4 766	4 776	13 942	4 513	15 529	15 293	2 731
October	83 661	24 656	3 944	19 878	11 731	8 147	59 005	4 747	4 787	13 998	4 538	15 600	15 335	2 729
November	84 031	24 739	3 967	19 926	11 762	8 164	59 292	4 764	4 809	14 091	4 565	15 693	15 370	2 731
December	84 271	24 746	3 991	20 057	11 868	8 189	59 525	4 784	4 831	14 169	4 581	15 750	15 410	2 746
1978:														
January	84 464	24 780	3 941	20 145	11 942	8 203	59 684	4 804	4 848	14 222	4 600	15 745	15 465	2 739
February	84 808	24 870	3 968	20 203	11 987	8 216	59 938	4 825	4 872	14 249	4 631	15 837	15 524	2 740
March	85 338	25 055	4 065	20 277	12 034	8 243	60 283	4 858	4 898	14 338	4 650	15 947	15 592	2 740
April	86 083	25 458	4 220	20 358	12 100	8 258	60 625	4 896	4 930	14 402	4 666	16 066	15 665	2 748
May	86 404	25 507	4 211	20 413	12 153	8 260	60 897	4 908	4 956	14 485	4 688	16 153	15 707	2 752
June	86 811	25 656	4 283	20 491	12 212	8 279	61 155	4 938	4 983	14 560	4 718	16 237	15 719	2 757
July	87 037	25 717	4 304	20 523	12 258	8 265	61 320	4 906	4 991	14 613	4 740	16 330	15 740	2 760
August	87 324	25 778	4 310	20 570	12 308	8 262	61 546	4 929	5 020	14 651	4 755	16 435	15 756	2 761
September	87 434	25 820	4 311	20 616	12 363	8 253	61 614	4 953	5 039	14 688	4 772	16 475	15 687	2 764
October	87 797	25 972	4 336	20 729	12 462	8 267	61 825	4 993	5 069	14 752	4 794	16 496	15 721	2 764
November	88 249	26 116	4 347	20 851	12 548	8 303	62 133	5 021	5 095	14 835	4 827	16 612	15 743	2 764
December	88 559	26 235	4 352	20 956	12 624	8 332	62 324	5 044	5 122	14 860	4 845	16 691	15 762	2 746
1979:														
January	88 728	26 264	4 309	21 019	12 677	8 342	62 464	5 062	5 148	14 914	4 871	16 692	15 777	2 757
February	88 985	26 319	4 324	21 043	12 717	8 326	62 666	5 082	5 160	14 938	4 891	16 799	15 796	2 757
March	89 426	26 511	4 456	21 102	12 768	8 334	62 915	5 101	5 182	15 004	4 907	16 908	15 813	2 754
April	89 363	26 462	4 423	21 092	12 766	8 326	62 901	5 005	5 188	14 968	4 924	16 955	15 861	2 758
May	89 681	26 527	4 467	21 110	12 781	8 329	63 154	5 109	5 206	14 958	4 952	17 042	15 887	2 769
June	89 955	26 599	4 493	21 162	12 828	8 334	63 356	5 166	5 230	14 931	4 971	17 120	15 938	2 776
July	90 019	26 606	4 505	21 148	12 819	8 329	63 413	5 163	5 235	14 881	4 986	17 148	16 000	2 782
August	90 159	26 474	4 506	21 003	12 698	8 305	63 685	5 188	5 242	14 901	5 015	17 221	16 118	2 811
September	90 149	26 471	4 495	21 012	12 745	8 267	63 678	5 178	5 247	14 945	5 014	17 261	16 033	2 776
October	90 360	26 467	4 496	20 998	12 705	8 293	63 893	5 183	5 264	15 033	5 039	17 337	16 037	2 775
November	90 466	26 383	4 497	20 908	12 631	8 277	64 083	5 198	5 280	15 098	5 055	17 390	16 062	2 778
December	90 617	26 451	4 533	20 929	12 655	8 274	64 166	5 196	5 266	15 083	5 068	17 471	16 082	2 785
1980:														
January	90 729	26 448	4 570	20 892	12 614	8 278	64 281	5 195	5 290	15 095	5 092	17 506	16 103	2 790
February	90 876	26 386	4 550	20 834	12 611	8 223	64 490	5 186	5 310	15 125	5 108	17 617	16 144	2 820
March	90 995	26 307	4 461	20 833	12 617	8 216	64 688	5 182	5 315	15 142	5 122	17 703	16 224	2 881
April	90 780	25 979	4 380	20 573	12 384	8 189	64 801	5 165	5 296	15 025	5 125	17 746	16 444	3 111
May	90 316	25 630	4 333	20 258	12 117	8 141	64 686	5 151	5 280	14 986	5 139	17 804	16 326	2 958
June	89 974	25 331	4 287	20 003	11 925	8 078	64 643	5 126	5 266	14 942	5 152	17 847	16 310	2 946
July	89 676	25 042	4 246	19 777	11 761	8 016	64 634	5 120	5 263	14 921	5 161	17 919	16 250	2 891
August	89 964	25 197	4 259	19 929	11 852	8 077	64 767	5 118	5 270	14 955	5 173	17 990	16 261	2 829
September	90 046	25 254	4 271	19 959	11 894	8 065	64 792	5 120	5 288	14 967	5 184	18 051	16 232	2 783
October	90 334	25 371	4 286	20 048	11 974	8 074	64 963	5 136	5 297	14 992	5 211	18 095	16 232	2 794
November	90 550	25 485	4 282	20 146	12 066	8 080	65 065	5 130	5 310	15 019	5 223	18 156	16 227	2 797
December	90 774	25 585	4 306	20 199	12 112	8 087	65 189	5 139	5 325	15 045	5 230	18 240	16 210	2 799

1. Includes mining, not shown separately.

NONAGRICULTURAL EMPLOYMENT—Continued
(Wage and salary workers on nonagricultural payrolls—Thousands, seasonally adjusted)

| YEAR AND MONTH | Total | Goods-producing industries [1] | | | | | Service-producing industries | | | | | | | |
| | | Total | Con-struction | Manufacturing | | | Total | Trans-portation and public utilities | Whole-sale trade | Retail trade | Finance, insur-ance, and real estate | Services (Private) | Government | |
				Total	Durable goods	Nondurable goods							Total	Federal
1981:														
January	91 003	25 594	4 265	20 236	12 151	8 085	65 409	5 150	5 347	15 096	5 261	18 357	16 198	2 797
February	91 095	25 575	4 272	20 197	12 105	8 092	65 520	5 159	5 358	15 146	5 271	18 400	16 186	2 789
March	91 206	25 654	4 306	20 227	12 132	8 095	65 552	5 163	5 365	15 163	5 277	18 439	16 145	2 781
April	91 219	25 567	4 313	20 274	12 173	8 101	65 652	5 161	5 381	15 208	5 290	18 487	16 125	2 780
May	91 142	25 511	4 240	20 277	12 167	8 110	65 631	5 157	5 376	15 204	5 297	18 533	16 064	2 774
June	91 285	25 634	4 194	20 286	12 174	8 112	65 651	5 163	5 380	15 185	5 298	18 581	16 044	2 780
July	91 410	25 630	4 168	20 278	12 151	8 127	65 780	5 180	5 381	15 170	5 305	18 624	16 120	2 787
August	91 320	25 559	4 144	20 219	12 104	8 115	65 761	5 184	5 381	15 199	5 310	18 682	16 005	2 772
September	91 191	25 564	4 119	20 240	12 120	8 120	65 627	5 176	5 380	15 217	5 311	18 725	15 818	2 752
October	91 216	25 443	4 117	20 119	12 048	8 071	65 773	5 169	5 385	15 203	5 315	18 805	15 896	2 756
November	91 014	25 264	4 092	19 960	11 916	8 044	65 750	5 170	5 388	15 135	5 316	18 848	15 893	2 751
December	90 831	25 044	4 075	19 756	11 751	8 005	65 787	5 151	5 382	15 145	5 318	18 896	15 895	2 743
1982:														
January	90 448	24 695	3 930	19 555	11 621	7 934	65 753	5 147	5 368	15 090	5 325	18 945	15 878	2 740
February	90 474	24 709	4 014	19 479	11 553	7 926	65 765	5 139	5 358	15 128	5 327	18 964	15 849	2 738
March	90 337	24 544	3 981	19 344	11 467	7 877	65 793	5 128	5 353	15 134	5 333	18 977	15 868	2 736
April	90 031	24 292	3 953	19 136	11 308	7 828	65 739	5 108	5 333	15 140	5 331	18 954	15 873	2 737
May	89 965	24 165	3 977	19 013	11 211	7 802	65 800	5 113	5 324	15 177	5 332	18 984	15 870	2 724
June	89 703	23 898	3 919	18 828	11 075	7 753	65 805	5 095	5 303	15 175	5 342	18 996	15 894	2 742
July	89 380	23 670	3 888	18 663	10 967	7 696	65 710	5 079	5 288	15 172	5 341	19 025	15 805	2 749
August	89 177	23 479	3 867	18 519	10 807	7 712	65 698	5 065	5 272	15 182	5 341	19 035	15 803	2 743
September	88 995	23 396	3 853	18 471	10 761	7 710	65 599	5 043	5 254	15 191	5 345	19 040	15 726	2 718
October	88 787	23 126	3 837	18 242	10 558	7 684	65 661	5 033	5 241	15 175	5 348	19 059	15 805	2 740
November	88 649	22 964	3 844	18 095	10 446	7 649	65 685	5 023	5 231	15 139	5 356	19 118	15 818	2 748
December	88 675	22 894	3 840	18 047	10 412	7 635	65 781	5 016	5 220	15 209	5 360	19 152	15 824	2 746
1983:														
January	88 826	22 930	3 877	18 062	10 424	7 638	65 896	4 977	5 214	15 254	5 375	19 202	15 874	2 772
February	88 758	22 846	3 820	18 060	10 427	7 633	65 912	4 969	5 213	15 264	5 389	19 217	15 860	2 766
March	88 946	22 826	3 793	18 077	10 435	7 642	66 120	4 977	5 209	15 333	5 398	19 337	15 866	2 765
April	89 211	22 911	3 808	18 159	10 495	7 664	66 300	4 989	5 225	15 383	5 421	19 430	15 852	2 763
May	89 497	23 041	3 841	18 260	10 575	7 685	66 456	4 995	5 239	15 427	5 432	19 496	15 867	2 768
June	89 886	23 172	3 902	18 330	10 620	7 710	66 714	4 994	5 263	15 505	5 444	19 622	15 886	2 769
July	90 313	23 334	3 946	18 443	10 712	7 731	66 979	4 999	5 278	15 608	5 470	19 729	15 895	2 775
August	89 973	23 430	3 993	18 495	10 750	7 745	66 543	4 366	5 299	15 687	5 494	19 819	15 878	2 775
September	91 088	23 628	4 031	18 654	10 868	7 786	67 460	5 045	5 325	15 781	5 517	19 922	15 870	2 784
October	91 408	23 809	4 069	18 788	10 978	7 810	67 599	5 047	5 349	15 846	5 529	19 976	15 852	2 786
November	91 727	23 961	4 108	18 901	11 069	7 832	67 766	5 034	5 377	15 910	5 548	20 048	15 849	2 778
December	92 110	24 058	4 132	18 972	11 130	7 842	68 052	5 037	5 406	16 024	5 571	20 150	15 864	2 781
1984:														
January	92 524	24 199	4 174	19 066	11 202	7 864	68 325	5 087	5 443	16 121	5 585	20 221	15 868	2 778
February	93 043	24 430	4 296	19 172	11 287	7 885	68 613	5 103	5 480	16 201	5 603	20 337	15 889	2 784
March	93 312	24 496	4 269	19 263	11 360	7 903	68 816	5 117	5 500	16 258	5 624	20 422	15 895	2 788
April	93 650	24 586	4 294	19 329	11 403	7 926	69 064	5 127	5 521	16 325	5 634	20 520	15 937	2 794
May	93 952	24 675	4 334	19 372	11 446	7 926	69 277	5 144	5 536	16 353	5 651	20 627	15 966	2 802
June	94 325	24 783	4 387	19 420	11 498	7 922	69 542	5 164	5 555	16 447	5 670	20 718	15 988	2 806
July	94 647	24 865	4 405	19 484	11 554	7 930	69 782	5 166	5 587	16 522	5 685	20 768	16 054	2 813
August	94 885	24 897	4 421	19 498	11 584	7 914	69 988	5 186	5 602	16 568	5 705	20 825	16 102	2 817
September	95 186	24 893	4 455	19 462	11 580	7 882	70 293	5 184	5 626	16 663	5 725	20 986	16 109	2 817
October	95 499	24 909	4 467	19 480	11 598	7 882	70 590	5 196	5 642	16 768	5 752	21 082	16 150	2 824
November	95 829	24 917	4 495	19 467	11 596	7 871	70 912	5 196	5 656	16 929	5 773	21 181	16 177	2 831
December	95 997	24 963	4 535	19 483	11 614	7 869	71 034	5 200	5 671	16 958	5 798	21 257	16 150	2 834
1985:														
January	96 249	24 968	4 550	19 472	11 616	7 856	71 281	5 213	5 687	16 972	5 817	21 391	16 201	2 834
February	96 397	24 914	4 549	19 420	11 580	7 840	71 483	5 223	5 689	17 034	5 836	21 477	16 224	2 835
March	96 734	24 953	4 615	19 393	11 568	7 825	71 781	5 204	5 707	17 150	5 859	21 598	16 263	2 846
April	96 896	24 918	4 640	19 328	11 520	7 808	71 978	5 220	5 710	17 209	5 884	21 670	16 285	2 856
May	97 163	24 893	4 664	19 285	11 497	7 788	72 270	5 231	5 717	17 291	5 907	21 795	16 329	2 868
June	97 280	24 843	4 659	19 246	11 469	7 777	72 437	5 232	5 725	17 343	5 928	21 858	16 351	2 878
July	97 465	24 786	4 659	19 200	11 428	7 772	72 679	5 241	5 728	17 353	5 950	21 915	16 492	2 888
August	97 696	24 795	4 688	19 186	11 407	7 779	72 901	5 227	5 737	17 413	5 978	22 055	16 491	2 896
September	97 878	24 761	4 724	19 124	11 358	7 766	73 117	5 243	5 745	17 443	6 008	22 186	16 492	2 894
October	98 098	24 768	4 740	19 124	11 365	7 759	73 330	5 253	5 756	17 475	6 038	22 287	16 521	2 895
November	98 286	24 754	4 750	19 108	11 351	7 757	73 532	5 254	5 761	17 511	6 071	22 405	16 530	2 903
December	98 500	24 765	4 765	19 110	11 342	7 768	73 735	5 257	5 762	17 579	6 103	22 482	16 552	2 910
1986:														
January	98 599	24 787	4 793	19 105	11 341	7 764	73 812	5 260	5 756	17 584	6 116	22 527	16 569	2 914
February	98 718	24 738	4 789	19 077	11 313	7 764	73 980	5 255	5 755	17 618	6 150	22 588	16 614	2 914
March	98 796	24 679	4 795	19 039	11 283	7 756	74 117	5 246	5 744	17 684	6 174	22 663	16 606	2 914
April	98 974	24 651	4 823	19 016	11 266	7 750	74 323	5 242	5 755	17 734	6 208	22 762	16 622	2 911
May	99 096	24 567	4 800	18 986	11 238	7 748	74 529	5 251	5 763	17 801	6 235	22 833	16 646	2 901
June	98 973	24 472	4 784	18 924	11 177	7 747	74 501	5 148	5 730	17 836	6 262	22 895	16 630	2 885
July	99 276	24 431	4 792	18 883	11 152	7 731	74 845	5 250	5 779	17 903	6 294	22 978	16 641	2 879
August	99 435	24 429	4 811	18 881	11 148	7 733	75 006	5 222	5 767	17 985	6 320	23 061	16 651	2 888
September	99 747	24 415	4 812	18 879	11 130	7 749	75 332	5 261	5 767	18 051	6 343	23 153	16 757	2 896
October	99 980	24 407	4 827	18 860	11 105	7 755	75 573	5 259	5 768	18 092	6 365	23 255	16 834	2 895
November	100 145	24 407	4 831	18 860	11 097	7 763	75 738	5 285	5 770	18 111	6 383	23 334	16 855	2 895
December	100 394	24 446	4 868	18 867	11 093	7 774	75 948	5 290	5 776	18 159	6 419	23 431	16 873	2 901

1. Includes mining, not shown separately.

NONAGRICULTURAL EMPLOYMENT—Continued
(Wage and salary workers on nonagricultural payrolls—Thousands, seasonally adjusted)

Year and Month	Total	Goods-producing industries [1] Total	Construction	Manufacturing Total	Durable goods	Nondurable goods	Service Total	Transportation and public utilities	Wholesale trade	Retail trade	Finance, insurance, and real estate	Services (Private)	Government Total	Federal
1987:														
January	100 543	24 444	4 884	18 852	11 080	7 772	76 099	5 297	5 786	18 139	6 434	23 554	16 889	2 909
February	100 772	24 512	4 916	18 890	11 109	7 781	76 260	5 310	5 802	18 197	6 453	23 620	16 878	2 913
March	101 005	24 517	4 911	18 899	11 108	7 791	76 488	5 314	5 809	18 247	6 474	23 737	16 907	2 922
April	101 367	24 542	4 925	18 909	11 101	7 808	76 825	5 342	5 822	18 325	6 507	23 861	16 968	2 932
May	101 564	24 586	4 951	18 924	11 109	7 815	76 978	5 343	5 827	18 342	6 524	23 973	16 969	2 938
June	101 713	24 584	4 951	18 920	11 103	7 817	77 129	5 343	5 834	18 394	6 534	24 047	16 977	2 945
July	102 047	24 643	4 951	18 976	11 107	7 869	77 404	5 351	5 844	18 438	6 555	24 186	17 030	2 945
August	102 266	24 706	4 965	19 021	11 159	7 862	77 560	5 367	5 858	18 455	6 566	24 296	17 018	2 948
September	102 430	24 761	4 962	19 072	11 194	7 878	77 669	5 394	5 874	18 500	6 573	24 350	16 978	2 953
October	102 980	24 856	5 007	19 117	11 225	7 892	78 124	5 410	5 891	18 627	6 590	24 472	17 134	2 962
November	103 200	24 933	5 020	19 183	11 261	7 922	78 267	5 429	5 902	18 666	6 584	24 539	17 147	2 971
December	103 544	24 992	5 047	19 216	11 287	7 929	78 552	5 439	5 923	18 722	6 599	24 669	17 200	2 976
1988:														
January	103 623	24 910	4 979	19 204	11 266	7 938	78 713	5 450	5 918	18 747	6 608	24 779	17 211	2 972
February	104 046	24 990	5 022	19 240	11 294	7 946	79 056	5 458	5 944	18 875	6 608	24 920	17 251	2 973
March	104 311	25 057	5 073	19 261	11 308	7 953	79 254	5 476	5 964	18 867	6 619	25 026	17 302	2 973
April	104 537	25 098	5 092	19 285	11 334	7 951	79 439	5 482	5 983	18 906	6 620	25 145	17 303	2 967
May	104 811	25 111	5 091	19 302	11 340	7 962	79 700	5 496	6 003	18 962	6 623	25 275	17 341	2 963
June	105 132	25 156	5 118	19 325	11 363	7 962	79 976	5 506	6 027	19 010	6 630	25 440	17 363	2 962
July	105 400	25 170	5 125	19 333	11 385	7 948	80 230	5 519	6 048	19 062	6 634	25 591	17 376	2 961
August	105 599	25 136	5 125	19 300	11 362	7 938	80 463	5 535	6 058	19 102	6 633	25 715	17 420	2 964
September	105 814	25 157	5 132	19 321	11 384	7 937	80 657	5 537	6 076	19 121	6 632	25 846	17 445	2 976
October	106 091	25 193	5 128	19 363	11 410	7 953	80 898	5 544	6 094	19 165	6 639	25 962	17 494	2 983
November	106 368	25 236	5 131	19 410	11 445	7 965	81 132	5 562	6 108	19 202	6 648	26 085	17 527	2 986
December	106 691	25 265	5 135	19 437	11 469	7 968	81 426	5 573	6 135	19 283	6 651	26 218	17 566	2 985
1989:														
January	106 993	25 340	5 182	19 466	11 485	7 981	81 653	5 578	6 160	19 336	6 649	26 334	17 596	2 982
February	107 244	25 303	5 143	19 471	11 486	7 985	81 941	5 607	6 185	19 414	6 656	26 448	17 631	2 985
March	107 438	25 308	5 134	19 483	11 482	8 001	82 130	5 581	6 205	19 448	6 658	26 586	17 652	2 986
April	107 637	25 323	5 159	19 472	11 477	7 995	82 314	5 600	6 199	19 467	6 659	26 708	17 681	2 986
May	107 738	25 303	5 160	19 453	11 453	8 000	82 435	5 610	6 194	19 469	6 662	26 767	17 733	3 000
June	107 838	25 254	5 153	19 421	11 420	8 001	82 584	5 618	6 186	19 470	6 668	26 878	17 764	3 000
July	107 933	25 222	5 170	19 382	11 380	8 002	82 711	5 627	6 190	19 480	6 672	26 951	17 791	3 001
August	108 048	25 251	5 181	19 374	11 370	8 004	82 797	5 526	6 190	19 491	6 679	27 039	17 872	2 994
September	108 178	25 200	5 177	19 327	11 330	7 997	82 978	5 614	6 183	19 489	6 680	27 144	17 868	2 984
October	108 290	25 183	5 201	19 284	11 290	7 994	83 107	5 629	6 183	19 522	6 676	27 213	17 884	2 984
November	108 571	25 216	5 226	19 290	11 287	8 003	83 355	5 649	6 185	19 564	6 683	27 347	17 927	2 983
December	108 692	25 137	5 170	19 268	11 269	7 999	83 555	5 734	6 182	19 571	6 685	27 433	17 950	2 978
1990:														
January	108 946	25 114	5 270	19 140	11 139	8 001	83 832	5 741	6 191	19 626	6 687	27 549	18 038	3 002
February	109 263	25 267	5 307	19 254	11 259	7 995	83 996	5 760	6 177	19 617	6 699	27 670	18 073	3 007
March	109 461	25 212	5 269	19 238	11 244	7 994	84 249	5 762	6 168	19 622	6 694	27 801	18 202	3 093
April	109 499	25 123	5 194	19 220	11 219	8 001	84 376	5 770	6 173	19 631	6 701	27 811	18 290	3 155
May	109 790	25 074	5 183	19 181	11 196	7 985	84 716	5 785	6 173	19 623	6 708	27 998	18 529	3 349
June	109 869	25 031	5 159	19 159	11 181	7 978	84 838	5 788	6 184	19 635	6 716	27 958	18 557	3 340
July	109 707	24 950	5 120	19 118	11 148	7 970	84 757	5 781	6 185	19 638	6 719	28 008	18 426	3 168
August	109 543	24 861	5 085	19 067	11 096	7 971	84 682	5 773	6 183	19 621	6 726	28 048	18 331	3 042
September	109 457	24 783	5 056	19 016	11 051	7 965	84 674	5 783	6 176	19 605	6 723	28 075	18 312	2 992
October	109 274	24 657	4 993	18 955	11 012	7 943	84 617	5 787	6 163	19 559	6 718	28 084	18 306	2 981
November	109 074	24 460	4 953	18 797	10 884	7 913	84 614	5 780	6 154	19 538	6 709	28 125	18 304	2 964
December	108 965	24 375	4 909	18 754	10 860	7 894	84 590	5 799	6 148	19 499	6 702	28 138	18 304	2 943
1991:														
January	108 759	24 175	4 805	18 660	10 783	7 877	84 584	5 812	6 121	19 423	6 707	28 203	18 318	2 952
February	108 500	24 058	4 799	18 549	10 688	7 861	84 442	5 774	6 106	19 362	6 699	28 169	18 332	2 951
March	108 330	23 926	4 744	18 473	10 633	7 840	84 404	5 758	6 093	19 336	6 699	28 172	18 346	2 950
April	108 145	23 822	4 685	18 432	10 613	7 819	84 323	5 757	6 084	19 271	6 680	28 165	18 366	2 954
May	108 107	23 791	4 677	18 413	10 597	7 816	84 316	5 753	6 077	19 249	6 665	28 200	18 372	2 957
June	108 200	23 741	4 661	18 383	10 562	7 821	84 459	5 742	6 078	19 275	6 651	28 278	18 435	2 973
July	108 131	23 688	4 634	18 365	10 552	7 813	84 443	5 754	6 081	19 254	6 631	28 297	18 426	2 970
August	108 215	23 687	4 619	18 384	10 543	7 841	84 528	5 756	6 070	19 265	6 619	28 384	18 434	2 973
September	108 223	23 648	4 612	18 360	10 519	7 841	84 575	5 746	6 076	19 256	6 610	28 469	18 418	2 979
October	108 209	23 574	4 578	18 326	10 487	7 839	84 635	5 744	6 069	19 237	6 605	28 535	18 445	2 984
November	108 115	23 467	4 520	18 285	10 447	7 838	84 648	5 738	6 060	19 223	6 598	28 549	18 480	2 983
December	108 121	23 409	4 522	18 229	10 395	7 834	84 712	5 725	6 055	19 233	6 594	28 604	18 501	2 981
1992:														
January	108 084	23 317	4 513	18 151	10 324	7 827	84 767	5 706	6 045	19 245	6 578	28 670	18 523	2 978
February	108 077	23 263	4 489	18 125	10 315	7 810	84 814	5 709	6 038	19 253	6 583	28 681	18 550	2 982
March	108 119	23 239	4 488	18 103	10 295	7 808	84 880	5 708	6 036	19 253	6 575	28 726	18 582	2 984
April	108 301	23 258	4 482	18 133	10 306	7 827	85 043	5 711	6 024	19 319	6 583	28 807	18 599	2 983
May	108 495	23 274	4 493	18 140	10 310	7 830	85 221	5 709	6 016	19 362	6 593	28 917	18 624	2 984
June	108 541	23 247	4 481	18 132	10 298	7 834	85 294	5 715	6 005	19 353	6 599	28 996	18 626	2 976
July	108 595	23 227	4 473	18 123	10 290	7 833	85 368	5 712	5 985	19 362	6 593	29 072	18 644	2 965
August	108 741	23 209	4 487	18 097	10 268	7 829	85 532	5 718	5 975	19 373	6 601	29 149	18 716	2 962
September	108 807	23 178	4 483	18 074	10 247	7 827	85 629	5 726	5 964	19 380	6 613	29 236	18 710	2 969
October	108 941	23 179	4 493	18 064	10 234	7 830	85 762	5 732	5 965	19 423	6 622	29 333	18 687	2 949
November	109 119	23 182	4 500	18 060	10 233	7 827	85 937	5 732	5 965	19 471	6 631	29 433	18 705	2 944
December	109 266	23 209	4 518	18 069	10 230	7 839	86 057	5 738	5 948	19 463	6 648	29 541	18 719	2 945

1. Includes mining, not shown separately.

AVERAGE HOURS AND EARNINGS
(Production or nonsupervisory workers on private nonagricultural payrolls—Seasonally adjusted, except as noted)

YEAR AND MONTH	Average weekly hours — All industries[1]	Construction	Manufacturing Average weekly hours	Manufacturing Overtime hours	Retail trade	Indexes of aggregate weekly hours (1982=100) All industries[1]	Manufacturing	Average hourly earnings All industries[1] Current dollars	1982 dollars	Construction	Manufacturing	Retail trade	Average weekly earnings (Dollars) All industries[1]	Not seasonally adjusted Construction	Manufacturing	Retail trade
1969:																
January	37.8	38.0	40.7	3.7	34.5	86.7	120.6	2.95	7.97	4.56	3.11	2.23	111.51	167.99	126.05	76.16
February	37.6	37.8	40.4	3.6	34.3	86.6	120.2	2.97	7.98	4.56	3.12	2.25	111.67	166.81	124.80	76.39
March	37.7	37.6	40.8	3.6	34.4	87.1	121.7	2.98	7.95	4.65	3.13	2.26	112.35	171.77	127.39	76.95
April	37.7	37.8	40.7	3.7	34.2	87.3	121.3	3.00	7.96	4.69	3.15	2.28	113.10	174.38	127.58	77.06
May	37.8	38.1	40.7	3.6	34.3	87.8	121.3	3.02	7.99	4.73	3.16	2.28	114.16	179.83	128.61	77.63
June	37.6	37.6	40.7	3.6	34.2	87.7	121.8	3.04	8.00	4.79	3.18	2.30	114.30	181.63	129.65	79.35
July	37.7	37.7	40.6	3.6	34.1	88.2	121.7	3.05	7.98	4.80	3.20	2.30	114.99	184.21	129.20	80.96
August	37.7	37.9	40.6	3.6	34.2	88.3	121.6	3.07	8.02	4.83	3.23	2.32	115.74	188.07	129.51	81.19
September	37.7	38.0	40.7	3.6	34.1	88.4	121.7	3.08	8.00	4.88	3.23	2.33	116.12	192.86	132.84	79.69
October	37.6	37.5	40.6	3.5	33.9	88.3	121.1	3.10	8.01	4.92	3.26	2.35	116.56	190.35	131.87	79.20
November	37.5	37.9	40.4	3.5	33.9	87.9	119.2	3.12	8.02	4.95	3.26	2.36	117.00	184.26	132.36	79.30
December	37.6	38.1	40.5	3.5	33.8	88.4	119.5	3.13	8.01	5.00	3.27	2.37	117.69	189.50	134.89	80.14
1970:																
January	37.4	37.0	40.4	3.4	33.9	87.7	118.7	3.14	7.99	5.04	3.28	2.37	117.44	180.85	131.60	79.49
February	37.4	38.1	40.2	3.2	33.8	87.8	117.5	3.16	8.00	5.07	3.29	2.39	118.18	186.94	130.54	79.92
March	37.3	37.7	40.1	3.2	33.8	87.7	117.4	3.18	8.01	5.11	3.31	2.40	118.61	188.98	132.40	80.25
April	37.2	38.0	39.9	3.0	33.6	87.2	115.8	3.18	7.97	5.16	3.32	2.40	118.30	193.16	131.80	80.01
May	37.2	37.9	39.8	3.0	33.8	86.7	113.8	3.20	8.00	5.14	3.34	2.42	119.04	194.56	132.93	81.16
June	37.1	37.6	39.9	3.1	33.8	86.4	113.7	3.22	8.01	5.21	3.36	2.43	119.46	196.86	134.34	82.86
July	37.2	37.5	40.0	3.0	33.7	86.6	113.7	3.24	8.02	5.26	3.38	2.44	120.53	200.45	134.06	84.91
August	37.1	37.2	39.8	2.9	33.9	86.1	112.2	3.26	8.05	5.34	3.39	2.46	120.95	203.90	133.73	85.40
September	36.8	35.0	39.3	2.7	33.7	85.4	110.6	3.27	8.03	5.32	3.42	2.48	120.34	193.86	135.04	83.82
October	36.9	36.8	39.5	2.7	33.7	84.8	106.8	3.27	8.00	5.37	3.38	2.48	120.66	203.63	133.45	83.08
November	36.9	37.0	39.5	2.6	33.7	84.5	105.7	3.29	8.00	5.40	3.39	2.48	121.40	196.93	134.58	82.83
December	36.9	37.9	39.5	2.7	33.6	85.2	108.2	3.31	8.01	5.40	3.44	2.49	122.14	203.46	138.05	83.73
1971:																
January	36.9	37.5	39.9	2.8	33.6	85.3	109.2	3.34	8.07	5.48	3.47	2.51	123.25	198.36	137.86	83.74
February	36.9	36.7	39.7	2.8	33.6	85.2	108.4	3.36	8.10	5.52	3.51	2.53	123.98	196.32	137.94	84.07
March	36.9	37.4	39.8	2.8	33.6	85.3	108.3	3.39	8.17	5.54	3.52	2.54	125.09	203.87	139.74	84.41
April	36.9	37.1	39.7	2.8	33.7	85.6	108.2	3.40	8.15	5.58	3.53	2.56	125.46	204.06	139.48	85.58
May	36.9	36.8	39.9	2.9	33.6	85.8	109.3	3.43	8.21	5.64	3.55	2.58	126.57	207.38	141.65	86.25
June	36.9	37.2	40.0	2.9	33.6	85.8	109.2	3.44	8.19	5.68	3.57	2.59	126.94	212.24	143.51	88.06
July	36.7	37.1	39.9	2.9	33.7	85.3	108.7	3.45	8.18	5.70	3.58	2.61	126.62	214.70	142.09	90.83
August	36.9	37.1	39.8	2.9	33.7	85.7	108.0	3.48	8.23	5.74	3.59	2.62	128.41	218.50	142.09	90.48
September	36.6	35.8	39.4	2.9	33.7	85.5	107.8	3.48	8.23	5.77	3.59	2.63	127.37	214.54	143.32	88.89
October	36.9	37.3	39.9	2.9	33.8	86.1	109.0	3.50	8.25	5.80	3.60	2.64	129.15	223.65	144.00	88.70
November	37.0	38.5	40.0	2.9	33.7	86.6	109.6	3.51	8.26	5.82	3.60	2.65	129.87	221.51	145.12	88.18
December	37.0	36.7	40.2	3.0	33.9	86.9	110.3	3.54	8.29	5.84	3.66	2.67	130.98	213.81	150.22	90.63
1972:																
January	36.9	37.0	40.2	3.1	33.7	87.4	111.0	3.61	8.43	5.91	3.71	2.69	133.21	211.23	148.06	89.70
February	37.0	36.9	40.4	3.2	33.5	87.7	112.2	3.61	8.41	5.93	3.73	2.70	133.57	211.46	149.20	89.43
March	37.0	36.8	40.4	3.3	33.6	88.3	112.9	3.64	8.47	5.96	3.75	2.71	134.68	215.49	151.13	90.03
April	37.1	36.5	40.7	3.6	33.6	88.8	114.3	3.66	8.51	6.00	3.78	2.72	135.79	215.39	153.09	90.64
May	36.9	36.2	40.5	3.4	33.4	88.6	114.2	3.67	8.52	6.03	3.79	2.72	135.42	217.80	153.50	90.36
June	37.0	36.4	40.6	3.5	33.5	89.2	114.9	3.67	8.50	6.02	3.80	2.74	135.79	219.78	155.04	92.89
July	36.9	36.4	40.5	3.4	33.4	88.9	114.2	3.69	8.50	6.03	3.81	2.75	136.16	223.05	153.52	94.88
August	36.9	36.6	40.6	3.5	33.3	89.3	114.9	3.72	8.55	6.07	3.85	2.77	137.27	228.09	155.09	94.33
September	37.0	36.7	40.6	3.5	33.3	89.6	115.5	3.74	8.56	6.10	3.87	2.78	138.38	231.99	158.69	92.85
October	37.1	36.7	40.7	3.6	33.4	90.5	117.0	3.77	8.59	6.17	3.89	2.79	139.87	234.00	158.30	92.63
November	37.0	36.0	40.8	3.7	33.3	90.9	118.3	3.78	8.59	6.21	3.91	2.81	139.86	221.25	159.92	92.40
December	36.8	35.3	40.5	3.7	33.3	90.8	118.6	3.81	8.62	6.27	3.95	2.83	140.21	220.92	163.58	94.42
1973:																
January	36.8	36.0	40.4	3.9	33.3	91.4	118.8	3.83	8.63	6.37	3.98	2.82	140.94	221.15	159.60	92.87
February	37.0	35.8	40.9	4.0	33.3	92.3	121.5	3.84	8.61	6.29	3.99	2.85	142.08	218.61	161.60	93.81
March	37.1	36.6	40.8	3.8	33.3	92.8	121.7	3.86	8.58	6.31	4.00	2.86	143.21	226.97	162.80	94.14
April	37.1	36.8	40.9	4.1	33.1	93.0	122.1	3.89	8.59	6.33	4.03	2.88	144.32	228.86	164.02	94.79
May	37.0	36.9	40.7	3.9	33.2	93.0	121.7	3.90	8.55	6.34	4.05	2.89	144.30	233.10	164.84	95.08
June	37.0	36.9	40.6	3.8	33.2	93.3	121.8	3.92	8.56	6.35	4.06	2.91	145.04	236.88	166.05	97.78
July	37.0	36.8	40.7	3.8	33.2	93.2	121.7	3.96	8.63	6.39	4.10	2.92	146.52	239.02	166.65	99.86
August	36.9	36.8	40.5	3.7	33.0	93.3	121.4	3.96	8.46	6.40	4.12	2.93	146.12	241.16	165.65	98.94
September	36.9	36.7	40.7	3.8	33.0	93.4	121.8	3.99	8.51	6.46	4.14	2.95	147.23	244.60	170.15	97.65
October	36.8	36.5	40.6	3.8	32.9	93.6	122.4	4.01	8.48	6.50	4.17	2.96	147.57	246.09	169.31	96.79
November	37.0	37.8	40.7	3.9	33.0	94.5	123.2	4.04	8.47	6.54	4.19	2.98	149.48	245.15	171.37	97.12
December	36.8	36.7	40.6	3.7	32.9	94.1	123.1	4.06	8.46	6.56	4.21	3.01	149.41	239.94	174.69	98.94
1974:																
January	36.7	36.1	40.5	3.6	32.9	93.8	122.0	4.07	8.39	6.55	4.22	3.01	149.37	227.01	169.60	97.57
February	36.8	37.2	40.4	3.5	32.8	94.1	121.2	4.10	8.35	6.60	4.24	3.02	150.88	237.60	170.02	97.87
March	36.7	36.5	40.4	3.5	32.8	93.8	120.7	4.12	8.31	6.62	4.26	3.04	151.20	237.83	171.25	98.82
April	36.4	35.9	39.3	2.8	33.0	93.1	117.4	4.13	8.29	6.65	4.27	3.05	150.33	234.60	166.96	100.06
May	36.7	36.4	40.3	3.5	32.7	93.9	120.4	4.19	8.31	6.69	4.36	3.11	153.77	242.36	175.71	101.08
June	36.6	36.7	40.2	3.4	32.7	93.9	120.0	4.24	8.35	6.75	4.42	3.14	155.18	249.83	178.16	103.93
July	36.6	36.7	40.2	3.4	32.6	93.7	119.8	4.25	8.30	6.76	4.45	3.16	155.55	252.30	177.60	106.18
August	36.5	36.4	40.2	3.3	32.6	93.5	119.0	4.29	8.28	6.92	4.50	3.19	156.59	257.74	179.25	106.51
September	36.6	36.8	40.0	3.2	32.7	93.4	118.1	4.33	8.25	7.00	4.54	3.21	158.48	264.79	183.37	104.97
October	36.4	36.8	40.0	3.2	32.5	93.1	117.0	4.36	8.24	7.00	4.60	3.22	158.70	266.92	184.06	104.01
November	36.2	36.8	39.5	2.8	32.5	91.7	113.4	4.36	8.15	7.04	4.61	3.23	157.83	258.08	183.02	103.68
December	36.1	37.0	39.3	2.7	32.5	90.4	109.2	4.40	8.16	7.09	4.64	3.25	158.84	262.41	186.73	105.62

1. Includes industries not shown separately.

AVERAGE HOURS AND EARNINGS—Continued
(Production or nonsupervisory workers on private nonagricultural payrolls—Seasonally adjusted, except as noted)

YEAR AND MONTH	Average weekly hours					Indexes of aggregate weekly hours (1982=100)		Average hourly earnings					Average weekly earnings (Dollars)			
	All indus- tries [1]	Con- struc- tion	Manufacturing		Retail trade	All in- dustries [1]	Manu- facturing	All industries [1]		Con- struction	Manu- facturing	Retail trade	All indus- tries [1]	Not seasonally adjusted		
			Aver- age weekly hours	Over- time hours				Current dollars	1982 dollars					Con- struction	Manu- facturing	Retail trade
1975:																
January	36.1	37.1	39.2	2.5	32.4	89.7	105.9	4.41	8.12	7.13	4.66	3.26	159.20	253.46	181.12	104.29
February	35.9	35.9	38.9	2.4	32.4	88.3	102.3	4.43	8.11	7.11	4.70	3.29	159.04	248.86	180.95	105.27
March	35.8	35.2	38.8	2.4	32.4	87.4	101.0	4.45	8.12	7.29	4.74	3.30	159.31	250.16	183.44	105.92
April	35.9	36.1	39.2	2.4	32.2	87.4	101.6	4.46	8.11	7.26	4.76	3.32	160.11	259.56	184.78	106.23
May	35.9	36.5	39.0	2.3	32.4	87.7	101.2	4.48	8.13	7.28	4.78	3.34	160.83	264.97	186.03	107.55
June	36.0	35.8	39.2	2.5	32.4	87.8	101.4	4.51	8.13	7.35	4.81	3.35	162.36	263.90	189.60	109.88
July	36.0	36.2	39.4	2.6	32.3	88.2	101.8	4.53	8.09	7.36	4.83	3.36	163.08	271.57	188.94	111.89
August	36.2	36.8	39.7	2.8	32.5	89.2	103.8	4.57	8.13	7.34	4.87	3.38	165.43	275.98	192.15	112.22
September	36.2	36.9	39.9	2.8	32.3	89.5	105.3	4.60	8.11	7.36	4.90	3.39	166.52	278.26	197.38	109.50
October	36.2	36.3	39.8	2.8	32.3	89.8	105.9	4.61	8.09	7.33	4.92	3.41	166.88	276.02	196.80	109.46
November	36.2	36.4	39.9	2.9	32.4	90.1	106.2	4.66	8.12	7.41	4.96	3.43	168.69	269.31	198.90	109.78
December	36.3	36.6	40.2	3.0	32.3	90.7	107.9	4.67	8.09	7.44	4.99	3.45	169.52	273.39	205.73	111.83
1976:																
January	36.3	37.7	40.5	3.1	32.5	91.5	109.5	4.70	8.10	7.44	5.02	3.47	170.61	268.17	201.60	111.30
February	36.3	37.1	40.3	3.1	32.4	91.8	109.8	4.73	8.16	7.48	5.06	3.47	171.70	269.69	202.40	111.33
March	36.1	36.9	40.2	3.2	32.2	91.6	110.1	4.75	8.18	7.53	5.10	3.49	171.48	265.19	204.11	111.30
April	36.1	36.6	39.6	2.6	32.4	92.0	109.2	4.77	8.18	7.59	5.11	3.50	172.20	275.23	199.92	112.67
May	36.2	36.6	40.3	3.3	32.2	92.4	110.9	4.81	8.22	7.68	5.16	3.53	174.12	280.42	207.55	112.96
June	36.2	36.9	40.2	3.2	32.1	92.3	110.6	4.84	8.23	7.65	5.19	3.54	175.21	284.25	209.79	115.05
July	36.2	36.6	40.3	3.2	32.0	92.7	111.0	4.87	8.24	7.73	5.23	3.55	176.29	288.75	209.32	117.15
August	36.1	36.6	40.1	3.1	31.9	92.5	110.3	4.91	8.27	7.77	5.28	3.60	177.25	290.60	210.53	117.10
September	36.0	36.2	39.8	3.2	31.9	92.6	110.5	4.94	8.26	7.80	5.32	3.64	177.84	289.14	214.13	116.12
October	36.0	37.1	40.0	3.1	31.8	92.6	109.9	4.97	8.27	7.86	5.32	3.67	178.92	302.48	213.33	115.66
November	36.0	37.0	40.1	3.2	31.8	92.8	110.9	5.01	8.31	7.88	5.38	3.69	180.36	290.24	216.81	115.61
December	36.0	36.8	40.0	3.2	31.8	93.0	110.8	5.04	8.32	7.91	5.42	3.72	181.44	291.77	222.22	118.50
1977:																
January	35.8	35.6	39.7	3.3	31.7	92.8	110.5	5.06	8.30	7.99	5.48	3.71	181.15	271.88	215.05	116.25
February	36.1	37.5	40.3	3.3	31.7	94.0	112.4	5.10	8.29	7.99	5.48	3.75	184.11	289.38	218.65	117.94
March	36.0	36.9	40.2	3.3	31.7	94.5	113.3	5.13	8.30	8.01	5.52	3.77	184.68	289.38	221.90	118.63
April	36.0	36.7	40.4	3.6	31.6	95.2	114.5	5.17	8.31	8.03	5.58	3.79	186.12	291.77	222.96	118.94
May	36.1	36.7	40.4	3.5	31.7	95.7	115.1	5.20	8.32	8.03	5.61	3.82	187.72	294.09	226.24	120.33
June	36.0	36.3	40.5	3.5	31.5	96.1	116.0	5.23	8.31	8.08	5.66	3.84	188.28	296.37	230.52	122.50
July	36.0	36.4	40.3	3.5	31.6	96.4	115.8	5.27	8.34	8.07	5.70	3.87	189.72	300.27	228.17	125.45
August	36.0	36.1	40.4	3.5	31.5	96.5	115.7	5.28	8.33	8.10	5.73	3.88	190.08	299.26	229.31	124.74
September	36.0	36.2	40.4	3.5	31.5	97.0	116.2	5.32	8.35	8.15	5.77	3.91	191.52	303.14	235.65	122.85
October	36.0	36.3	40.5	3.5	31.6	97.4	116.4	5.36	8.39	8.20	5.82	3.93	192.96	308.39	236.29	123.09
November	35.9	36.5	40.4	3.6	31.3	97.7	116.7	5.39	8.38	8.22	5.85	3.96	193.50	298.19	238.10	122.53
December	35.9	36.2	40.4	3.5	31.3	97.8	117.3	5.41	8.37	8.26	5.88	3.99	194.22	299.27	243.72	124.90
1978:																
January	35.5	34.7	39.6	3.4	31.0	97.0	115.8	5.47	8.42	8.32	5.95	4.05	194.19	275.55	234.02	124.23
February	35.6	35.7	39.9	3.7	30.9	97.7	117.0	5.50	8.42	8.37	5.98	4.06	195.80	288.22	236.81	124.64
March	35.9	36.6	40.5	3.5	31.2	99.1	118.9	5.54	8.42	8.45	6.01	4.09	198.89	304.08	242.80	126.59
April	36.0	36.9	40.8	3.9	31.1	100.4	120.3	5.60	8.45	8.48	6.05	4.13	201.60	309.96	244.02	127.82
May	35.9	36.6	40.4	3.5	31.1	100.3	119.6	5.63	8.42	8.57	6.09	4.16	202.12	312.68	245.23	128.54
June	35.9	37.2	40.5	3.6	31.1	101.1	120.2	5.67	8.41	8.63	6.12	4.18	203.55	324.80	249.29	130.94
July	35.9	37.3	40.6	3.6	31.1	101.3	120.6	5.71	8.41	8.67	6.18	4.21	204.99	330.05	249.05	134.40
August	35.8	37.2	40.5	3.5	31.0	101.4	120.4	5.74	8.40	8.73	6.21	4.23	205.49	331.25	249.27	133.56
September	35.8	37.0	40.6	3.6	30.9	101.6	121.1	5.79	8.42	8.78	6.27	4.27	207.28	333.38	256.00	131.63
October	35.9	37.1	40.5	3.6	30.9	102.1	121.6	5.84	8.39	8.81	6.33	4.30	209.66	337.31	257.00	132.13
November	35.8	36.9	40.6	3.7	30.8	102.6	122.7	5.87	8.39	8.87	6.39	4.33	210.15	324.85	261.35	131.89
December	35.8	37.1	40.6	3.6	30.9	103.0	123.4	5.91	8.38	8.91	6.43	4.36	211.58	331.67	268.27	134.90
1979:																
January	35.7	36.5	40.5	3.6	30.6	102.9	123.5	5.95	8.38	8.95	6.47	4.42	212.42	311.95	260.65	133.95
February	35.7	36.7	40.5	3.6	30.7	103.3	123.6	6.00	8.36	9.06	6.53	4.43	214.20	320.57	262.51	134.55
March	35.8	37.4	40.6	3.7	30.7	104.2	124.0	6.03	8.32	9.03	6.56	4.45	215.87	333.53	266.34	135.74
April	35.4	35.7	39.2	2.9	30.9	102.6	119.9	6.03	8.22	9.12	6.56	4.48	213.46	321.82	254.80	137.70
May	35.7	37.2	40.2	3.4	30.6	103.9	122.9	6.09	8.21	9.20	6.65	4.49	217.41	341.30	265.86	136.50
June	35.7	37.2	40.2	3.4	30.7	104.4	123.1	6.13	8.17	9.21	6.68	4.51	218.84	347.32	269.47	139.50
July	35.7	36.9	40.2	3.4	30.7	104.3	123.0	6.18	8.14	9.29	6.72	4.53	220.63	350.03	268.13	142.38
August	35.7	37.4	40.1	3.2	30.6	104.2	121.4	6.21	8.11	9.33	6.75	4.56	221.70	355.85	268.00	142.24
September	35.7	37.4	40.2	3.2	30.6	104.3	121.6	6.27	8.10	9.42	6.79	4.59	223.84	361.76	274.04	140.61
October	35.6	36.9	40.2	3.2	30.5	104.3	121.4	6.28	8.04	9.40	6.82	4.61	223.57	357.77	274.85	139.54
November	35.6	37.0	40.1	3.2	30.6	104.5	120.4	6.32	8.01	9.48	6.87	4.64	224.99	348.07	277.55	140.45
December	35.6	37.2	40.2	3.2	30.6	104.8	120.7	6.38	7.99	9.54	6.93	4.67	227.13	356.00	285.48	142.91
1980:																
January	35.5	36.4	40.0	3.1	30.5	104.7	120.0	6.40	7.90	9.42	6.94	4.73	227.84	334.29	277.41	142.44
February	35.5	36.9	40.1	3.0	30.4	104.7	119.4	6.45	7.88	9.61	7.00	4.74	228.98	342.72	278.60	142.44
March	35.3	36.4	39.8	3.1	30.3	104.1	118.4	6.51	7.82	9.70	7.07	4.79	229.80	349.69	281.39	143.82
April	35.2	36.8	39.5	2.9	29.9	103.1	116.1	6.54	7.79	9.77	7.11	4.79	230.86	355.62	279.74	142.56
May	35.1	36.8	39.3	2.6	30.1	102.1	112.5	6.57	7.75	9.83	7.16	4.82	231.26	361.86	280.60	144.12
June	35.2	37.4	39.2	2.4	30.2	101.5	110.1	6.63	7.74	9.89	7.22	4.85	232.71	372.78	284.07	147.14
July	35.0	36.9	39.1	2.5	30.0	100.9	108.4	6.66	7.76	9.95	7.29	4.91	233.10	374.98	282.85	150.61
August	35.2	36.9	39.4	2.6	30.1	101.6	110.3	6.71	7.77	10.05	7.36	4.93	235.52	376.24	288.01	151.41
September	35.2	37.2	39.6	2.7	30.1	102.2	111.1	6.76	7.76	10.10	7.42	4.96	237.95	387.60	295.71	149.49
October	35.3	37.5	39.8	2.8	30.2	102.7	111.9	6.83	7.76	10.18	7.51	4.99	241.10	390.26	298.50	149.90
November	35.4	37.6	40.0	3.0	30.2	103.1	113.2	6.90	7.75	10.26	7.60	5.02	243.57	378.96	305.52	150.60
December	35.4	37.3	40.3	3.1	30.0	103.5	114.1	6.94	7.73	10.33	7.64	5.03	244.98	385.39	314.16	152.20

1. Includes industries not shown separately.

AVERAGE HOURS AND EARNINGS—Continued
(Production or nonsupervisory workers on private nonagricultural payrolls—Seasonally adjusted, except as noted)

YEAR AND MONTH	Average weekly hours					Indexes of aggregate weekly hours (1982=100)		Average hourly earnings					Average weekly earnings (Dollars)			
	All industries[1]	Construction	Manufacturing		Retail trade	All industries[1]	Manufacturing	All industries[1]		Construction	Manufacturing	Retail trade	All industries[1]	Not seasonally adjusted		
			Average weekly hours	Overtime hours				Current dollars	1982 dollars					Construction	Manufacturing	Retail trade
1981:																
January	35.5	37.5	40.1	3.1	30.3	104.2	114.3	6.99	7.72	10.37	7.69	5.13	248.15	381.79	308.43	152.52
February	35.4	36.5	40.0	3.0	30.3	104.1	113.6	7.05	7.71	10.41	7.75	5.16	249.57	366.80	306.13	153.62
March	35.4	37.5	40.0	3.0	30.3	104.3	113.8	7.11	7.74	10.48	7.81	5.18	251.69	390.90	311.62	154.96
April	35.4	37.2	40.1	2.9	30.2	104.3	114.4	7.14	7.72	10.54	7.87	5.21	252.76	387.76	312.84	156.60
May	35.3	36.6	40.1	3.0	30.0	103.7	114.3	7.18	7.71	10.64	7.93	5.21	253.45	391.46	317.59	156.08
June	35.2	36.6	39.9	2.9	30.0	103.8	113.8	7.22	7.70	10.77	7.97	5.23	254.14	396.55	320.39	158.17
July	35.3	36.8	39.9	2.9	30.1	104.1	113.4	7.26	7.65	10.88	8.01	5.26	256.28	408.62	317.59	161.92
August	35.3	36.7	39.9	2.9	30.2	104.0	113.1	7.34	7.67	10.97	8.09	5.29	259.10	409.16	320.40	162.23
September	35.1	36.8	39.7	2.7	30.1	103.7	112.6	7.39	7.66	11.02	8.16	5.36	259.39	397.38	322.32	161.87
October	35.1	37.2	39.7	2.6	29.9	103.7	111.5	7.41	7.65	11.10	8.19	5.30	260.09	419.63	323.95	157.64
November	35.2	37.8	39.5	2.6	30.1	103.4	109.8	7.46	7.67	11.26	8.22	5.30	262.59	414.77	325.94	158.24
December	35.0	37.3	39.4	2.5	29.6	102.4	107.7	7.46	7.65	11.21	8.23	5.35	261.10	418.86	329.97	160.89
1982:																
January	34.4	34.2	38.0	2.3	29.8	100.2	102.5	7.52	7.69	11.57	8.38	5.38	258.69	388.61	312.38	157.18
February	35.2	37.2	39.6	2.5	30.1	102.6	106.5	7.54	7.69	11.36	8.33	5.38	265.41	408.12	326.93	159.35
March	34.9	37.2	39.1	2.4	29.8	101.6	104.2	7.57	7.72	11.42	8.37	5.40	264.17	422.17	327.27	159.35
April	34.8	36.9	38.9	2.2	29.9	100.8	102.3	7.59	7.72	11.43	8.41	5.43	264.13	417.28	325.85	161.02
May	34.9	37.1	39.0	2.4	29.9	100.8	101.7	7.65	7.71	11.57	8.46	5.45	266.99	431.63	329.55	162.71
June	34.9	36.9	39.1	2.3	29.8	100.3	100.7	7.67	7.64	11.60	8.51	5.48	267.68	430.50	334.05	164.65
July	34.8	37.0	39.2	2.3	29.8	99.9	99.8	7.71	7.64	11.68	8.54	5.49	268.31	441.18	332.60	167.38
August	34.8	36.9	39.0	2.3	29.9	99.6	98.6	7.75	7.66	11.72	8.56	5.51	269.70	439.17	331.50	167.38
September	34.8	37.0	39.0	2.3	30.0	99.3	98.2	7.75	7.66	11.67	8.58	5.51	269.70	433.94	333.76	165.85
October	34.7	36.8	38.9	2.3	29.9	98.7	96.5	7.78	7.65	11.80	8.58	5.55	269.97	441.49	333.45	165.09
November	34.8	36.9	39.1	2.3	29.9	98.6	96.0	7.80	7.68	11.78	8.61	5.57	271.44	423.45	337.98	165.17
December	34.8	37.0	39.1	2.4	29.8	98.6	95.8	7.83	7.74	11.88	8.63	5.59	272.48	440.13	344.60	169.28
1983:																
January	35.0	37.9	39.4	2.4	30.1	99.5	96.7	7.88	7.78	11.85	8.66	5.63	275.80	439.39	341.04	166.13
February	34.6	36.8	39.3	2.4	29.4	98.4	96.5	7.91	7.81	11.95	8.72	5.67	273.69	424.80	338.72	163.88
March	34.8	36.7	39.6	2.5	29.7	99.1	97.6	7.92	7.80	11.95	8.72	5.67	275.62	434.62	345.71	166.72
April	34.9	36.7	39.8	2.7	29.8	99.8	98.6	7.95	7.77	11.95	8.74	5.69	277.46	435.17	348.25	168.15
May	35.0	37.0	40.0	2.8	29.8	100.4	99.7	7.99	7.78	11.89	8.78	5.72	279.65	442.44	349.92	169.88
June	35.0	37.2	40.1	2.9	29.8	101.1	100.7	8.01	7.78	11.91	8.80	5.74	280.35	446.84	354.24	172.47
July	35.0	37.2	40.3	3.0	29.9	101.9	101.9	8.04	7.79	11.91	8.83	5.76	281.40	451.91	353.60	175.34
August	35.0	37.2	40.3	3.1	29.8	101.0	102.4	8.01	7.72	11.93	8.84	5.77	280.35	451.82	352.96	174.46
September	35.1	37.1	40.6	3.3	29.8	103.3	104.3	8.09	7.79	11.97	8.90	5.78	283.96	457.45	362.71	172.82
October	35.2	37.0	40.7	3.3	30.0	104.1	105.4	8.14	7.81	11.99	8.94	5.80	286.53	450.96	362.23	173.12
November	35.1	37.1	40.7	3.3	29.9	104.4	106.2	8.14	7.80	12.00	8.98	5.80	285.71	433.79	366.38	172.56
December	35.2	37.1	40.6	3.4	30.1	104.9	106.5	8.16	7.81	11.99	9.00	5.81	287.23	444.18	372.86	177.45
1984:																
January	35.2	37.4	40.7	3.5	30.0	105.4	107.4	8.21	7.81	12.08	9.05	5.82	288.99	441.41	369.05	171.70
February	35.3	38.4	41.1	3.5	30.0	106.5	109.0	8.21	7.80	12.03	9.06	5.82	289.81	446.59	369.15	171.70
March	35.1	37.1	40.7	3.5	29.9	106.2	108.6	8.23	7.82	12.07	9.09	5.83	288.87	442.60	370.37	172.58
April	35.3	37.6	40.9	3.5	30.0	107.1	109.6	8.28	7.85	12.10	9.11	5.85	292.28	451.88	373.01	174.04
May	35.2	37.6	40.7	3.4	29.9	107.2	109.2	8.27	7.82	12.14	9.13	5.84	291.10	460.63	371.18	174.03
June	35.2	38.0	40.7	3.4	29.9	107.6	109.3	8.31	7.84	12.15	9.16	5.85	292.51	464.74	373.32	176.95
July	35.1	37.5	40.6	3.4	29.8	107.9	109.4	8.34	7.83	12.17	9.19	5.85	292.73	465.08	370.36	177.51
August	35.1	37.6	40.5	3.3	29.8	107.9	109.3	8.34	7.77	12.15	9.23	5.84	292.73	465.02	370.06	176.60
September	35.1	37.6	40.5	3.3	29.7	108.5	109.0	8.38	7.77	12.16	9.26	5.84	294.14	472.01	377.40	174.33
October	35.0	37.6	40.5	3.3	29.6	108.5	108.8	8.38	7.75	12.15	9.29	5.86	293.30	465.50	374.63	172.58
November	35.1	38.1	40.5	3.4	29.6	109.1	108.6	8.41	7.78	12.15	9.32	5.89	295.19	452.08	379.32	173.46
December	35.1	38.0	40.6	3.4	29.7	109.4	108.8	8.44	7.79	12.21	9.36	5.87	296.24	461.73	387.69	177.26
1985:																
January	35.0	37.6	40.4	3.3	29.6	109.4	108.4	8.44	7.77	12.26	9.39	5.88	295.40	448.81	380.43	171.09
February	34.9	37.9	40.1	3.3	29.6	109.3	107.0	8.47	7.76	12.33	9.43	5.90	295.60	452.74	375.17	171.67
March	35.0	38.2	40.5	3.2	29.6	110.1	107.8	8.50	7.76	12.27	9.45	5.91	297.50	461.83	382.18	173.16
April	34.9	37.9	40.3	3.3	29.3	109.8	106.8	8.52	7.76	12.30	9.49	5.91	297.35	464.28	380.95	172.27
May	34.9	37.6	40.4	3.1	29.6	110.4	106.8	8.52	7.75	12.29	9.50	5.93	297.35	466.73	382.45	174.94
June	34.9	37.5	40.5	3.2	29.5	110.5	106.7	8.57	7.77	12.28	9.53	5.93	299.09	464.06	387.46	176.71
July	34.9	37.7	40.4	3.2	29.4	110.2	106.3	8.57	7.76	12.31	9.55	5.94	299.09	471.69	382.96	177.59
August	34.9	37.6	40.6	3.3	29.4	110.8	106.7	8.59	7.77	12.33	9.57	5.95	299.79	471.94	384.75	177.29
September	34.9	37.7	40.6	3.3	29.4	111.0	106.3	8.63	7.80	12.38	9.58	5.97	301.19	481.73	390.46	175.81
October	34.9	37.8	40.7	3.3	29.3	111.3	106.5	8.63	7.76	12.34	9.60	5.96	301.19	476.45	390.05	174.03
November	34.9	37.4	40.7	3.4	29.3	111.4	106.3	8.65	7.74	12.32	9.63	5.97	301.89	451.41	394.28	174.02
December	34.9	37.4	41.0	3.6	29.2	111.9	107.2	8.71	7.76	12.44	9.70	6.02	303.98	462.50	406.58	178.80
1986:																
January	35.1	38.5	40.8	3.5	29.4	112.5	106.9	8.68	7.71	12.32	9.66	6.00	304.67	461.77	394.79	173.35
February	34.8	36.5	40.6	3.4	29.2	111.7	106.2	8.71	7.76	12.37	9.69	6.01	303.11	436.13	391.31	173.03
March	34.9	36.9	40.8	3.5	29.3	112.1	106.2	8.73	7.82	12.29	9.72	6.01	304.68	447.49	396.01	174.27
April	34.8	37.5	40.6	3.4	29.1	111.9	105.7	8.72	7.85	12.37	9.70	6.01	303.46	462.38	393.26	173.98
May	34.8	37.4	40.7	3.5	29.2	112.1	105.8	8.74	7.85	12.42	9.73	6.01	304.15	469.20	394.63	174.89
June	34.7	37.2	40.6	3.4	29.1	111.6	105.2	8.75	7.83	12.45	9.73	6.02	303.63	467.21	396.17	177.00
July	34.7	37.4	40.6	3.5	29.1	112.0	104.8	8.75	7.83	12.45	9.74	6.02	303.63	472.15	391.55	178.20
August	34.8	37.6	40.8	3.5	29.2	112.5	105.4	8.77	7.84	12.50	9.75	6.03	305.20	478.46	393.98	178.50
September	34.7	37.7	40.7	3.5	29.1	112.6	105.3	8.77	7.81	12.52	9.74	6.04	304.32	485.87	399.34	176.35
October	34.6	37.2	40.6	3.5	29.1	112.6	104.9	8.80	7.83	12.60	9.76	6.06	304.48	481.33	396.58	175.74
November	34.7	37.1	40.8	3.5	29.2	113.1	105.4	8.85	7.85	12.68	9.78	6.07	307.10	462.82	401.39	176.32
December	34.7	37.3	40.9	3.6	28.9	113.2	105.7	8.85	7.83	12.74	9.80	6.08	307.10	471.04	409.76	178.46

1. Includes industries not shown separately.

AVERAGE HOURS AND EARNINGS—Continued
(Production or nonsupervisory workers on private nonagricultural payrolls—Seasonally adjusted, except as noted)

YEAR AND MONTH	Average weekly hours					Indexes of aggregate weekly hours (1982=100)		Average hourly earnings					Average weekly earnings (Dollars)			
	All indus-tries[1]	Con-struc-tion	Manufacturing		Retail trade	All in-dustries[1]	Manu-facturing	All industries[1]		Con-struction	Manu-facturing	Retail trade	All indus-tries[1]	Not seasonally adjusted		
			Aver-age weekly hours	Over-time hours				Current dollars	1982 dollars					Con-struction	Manu-facturing	Retail trade
1987:																
January	34.7	38.5	40.9	3.6	29.0	113.7	105.8	8.87	7.80	12.58	9.81	6.05	307.79	469.84	401.88	172.35
February	34.9	38.2	41.2	3.7	29.3	114.5	106.7	8.89	7.78	12.55	9.83	6.05	310.26	463.10	401.88	174.50
March	34.8	37.8	41.0	3.7	29.3	114.5	106.3	8.91	7.77	12.67	9.85	6.06	310.07	472.74	403.27	175.42
April	34.7	37.3	40.9	3.7	29.3	114.6	106.4	8.92	7.74	12.66	9.86	6.08	309.52	471.99	398.75	177.83
May	34.8	38.2	41.0	3.7	29.3	115.4	106.7	8.95	7.75	12.71	9.88	6.09	311.46	489.06	403.68	177.83
June	34.8	37.7	41.0	3.7	29.3	115.4	106.6	8.95	7.72	12.76	9.88	6.10	311.46	483.99	405.66	179.97
July	34.7	37.8	41.0	3.8	29.2	115.6	107.0	8.96	7.70	12.69	9.87	6.12	310.91	486.75	400.72	182.40
August	34.9	37.8	41.0	3.8	29.4	116.4	107.3	9.02	7.72	12.73	9.93	6.13	314.80	489.83	403.27	183.31
September	34.8	37.7	40.9	3.8	29.5	116.3	107.5	9.03	7.70	12.71	9.99	6.18	314.24	467.57	407.59	182.90
October	34.8	37.9	41.1	3.8	29.2	116.8	108.3	9.06	7.70	12.74	9.98	6.15	315.29	498.19	410.94	179.26
November	34.8	37.6	41.1	3.9	29.2	117.2	108.7	9.10	7.72	12.85	10.00	6.16	316.68	477.11	414.41	179.22
December	34.7	38.1	41.1	3.9	28.8	117.1	108.8	9.12	7.72	12.79	10.02	6.19	316.46	482.78	420.93	181.37
1988:																
January	34.7	37.7	41.1	3.9	29.1	117.2	108.7	9.14	7.72	13.02	10.05	6.21	317.16	468.50	413.28	177.22
February	34.7	37.4	41.0	3.8	29.1	118.0	108.8	9.13	7.70	12.92	10.05	6.22	316.81	464.61	409.44	178.46
March	34.6	37.8	41.0	3.8	29.1	117.8	108.6	9.15	7.69	12.86	10.07	6.24	316.59	481.50	412.27	178.46
April	34.6	37.6	40.8	3.7	29.1	118.2	108.3	9.20	7.70	12.99	10.12	6.26	318.32	491.18	415.33	181.83
May	34.6	37.7	41.0	3.8	29.1	118.5	108.9	9.24	7.71	12.99	10.15	6.28	319.70	495.84	416.15	182.12
June	34.6	37.9	41.0	3.8	29.1	118.9	109.2	9.26	7.69	13.04	10.17	6.30	320.40	501.94	419.00	184.97
July	34.7	37.6	41.0	3.8	29.2	119.4	109.2	9.28	7.67	13.09	10.18	6.32	322.02	502.43	414.33	189.03
August	34.5	37.6	40.9	3.8	29.0	119.0	108.7	9.30	7.65	13.11	10.21	6.32	320.85	503.58	414.73	186.55
September	34.6	37.5	40.9	3.8	29.1	119.5	108.9	9.35	7.66	13.15	10.24	6.36	323.51	508.24	423.74	185.66
October	34.7	37.8	41.0	3.9	29.2	120.3	109.5	9.40	7.67	13.17	10.28	6.38	326.18	517.92	424.15	186.59
November	34.6	37.9	41.1	3.9	29.1	120.3	110.1	9.40	7.65	13.15	10.31	6.41	325.24	496.32	428.70	185.18
December	34.6	37.6	41.0	3.9	29.2	120.8	109.9	9.44	7.67	13.27	10.33	6.41	326.62	495.13	432.22	190.67
1989:																
January	34.8	37.8	41.1	3.9	29.3	121.7	110.4	9.49	7.67	13.34	10.37	6.43	330.25	487.64	425.99	184.40
February	34.5	37.2	41.0	4.0	29.0	121.2	110.3	9.52	7.67	13.37	10.41	6.46	328.44	481.21	424.32	183.10
March	34.5	37.7	41.1	3.9	28.9	121.5	110.3	9.54	7.64	13.41	10.42	6.47	329.13	500.41	427.22	184.40
April	34.7	37.8	41.3	4.0	28.9	122.3	110.7	9.59	7.62	13.47	10.43	6.49	332.77	509.38	427.22	188.14
May	34.5	37.1	40.9	3.7	28.9	121.4	109.6	9.58	7.58	13.45	10.43	6.48	330.51	506.31	426.59	186.62
June	34.5	37.0	40.9	3.7	28.9	121.5	109.2	9.62	7.59	13.48	10.45	6.50	331.89	507.86	429.50	188.92
July	34.6	38.1	40.9	3.7	29.0	122.1	109.0	9.68	7.62	13.54	10.49	6.52	334.93	525.15	424.85	193.10
August	34.4	37.9	40.9	3.7	28.8	121.6	108.8	9.68	7.62	13.54	10.52	6.55	332.99	526.32	427.41	191.81
September	34.4	37.7	40.8	3.6	28.9	121.7	108.2	9.71	7.62	13.55	10.53	6.57	334.02	528.05	435.07	190.45
October	34.6	38.0	40.7	3.7	28.9	122.3	107.7	9.76	7.63	13.63	10.55	6.59	337.70	538.61	430.68	190.74
November	34.4	38.1	40.7	3.6	28.8	122.3	107.8	9.77	7.61	13.69	10.58	6.60	336.09	522.73	433.78	189.33
December	34.3	37.5	40.6	3.6	28.8	122.0	107.3	9.81	7.61	13.85	10.61	6.64	336.48	514.95	440.67	193.89
1990:																
January	34.5	39.0	40.7	3.7	28.9	122.8	106.7	9.81	7.54	13.62	10.57	6.67	338.45	512.86	429.95	188.55
February	34.4	38.3	40.7	3.6	28.9	123.1	107.5	9.87	7.56	13.69	10.69	6.69	339.53	508.77	431.07	188.94
March	34.5	38.3	40.8	3.7	28.9	123.5	107.6	9.91	7.55	13.72	10.73	6.71	341.90	518.85	437.12	190.85
April	34.5	37.8	40.8	3.5	29.0	123.4	107.5	9.94	7.56	13.67	10.75	6.72	342.93	508.40	427.45	194.79
May	34.4	37.8	40.9	3.7	28.8	122.9	107.4	9.96	7.57	13.75	10.80	6.73	342.62	525.86	441.72	193.15
June	34.5	38.2	40.9	3.7	28.9	123.3	107.3	10.01	7.57	13.77	10.83	6.75	345.35	534.89	445.52	196.52
July	34.5	37.5	40.9	3.7	28.8	123.1	107.1	10.04	7.55	13.77	10.86	6.76	346.38	528.00	440.24	199.58
August	34.4	38.0	40.7	3.6	28.7	122.6	106.2	10.04	7.49	13.79	10.87	6.77	345.38	537.42	441.05	197.57
September	34.5	38.2	40.8	3.7	28.7	122.9	106.1	10.09	7.47	13.87	10.91	6.78	348.11	545.84	451.41	196.13
October	34.1	36.9	40.6	3.6	28.4	121.5	105.3	10.10	7.43	13.84	10.96	6.80	344.41	531.50	447.45	193.40
November	34.3	38.2	40.5	3.5	28.6	121.6	103.7	10.12	7.42	13.83	10.96	6.81	347.12	529.45	447.17	193.29
December	34.5	38.8	40.6	3.5	28.8	122.3	103.7	10.15	7.43	13.87	10.99	6.81	350.18	534.14	456.37	198.85
1991:																
January	34.1	37.6	40.4	3.4	28.5	120.7	102.6	10.16	7.41	13.99	11.03	6.83	346.46	506.80	443.81	189.61
February	34.2	38.1	40.2	3.3	28.5	120.3	101.4	10.18	7.43	13.96	11.04	6.84	348.16	515.69	439.30	191.12
March	34.1	37.8	40.2	3.3	28.5	119.9	101.0	10.21	7.44	13.93	11.06	6.85	348.16	518.47	443.51	193.05
April	34.1	37.8	40.4	3.4	28.3	119.4	101.2	10.25	7.45	14.01	11.11	6.90	349.53	528.07	445.51	195.14
May	34.2	38.0	40.4	3.4	28.6	119.8	101.2	10.29	7.45	14.00	11.15	6.91	351.92	533.90	449.35	196.94
June	34.5	37.9	40.7	3.6	28.8	120.8	101.9	10.34	7.47	13.95	11.19	6.94	356.73	537.77	457.26	202.06
July	34.1	37.8	40.7	3.6	28.5	119.6	102.0	10.33	7.45	13.97	11.22	6.96	352.25	538.86	453.29	202.76
August	34.2	37.8	40.8	3.6	28.6	120.1	102.4	10.35	7.45	14.02	11.23	6.96	353.97	544.36	457.26	202.46
September	34.4	38.2	40.9	3.7	28.6	120.6	102.4	10.39	7.46	14.04	11.26	6.98	357.42	552.87	466.99	201.19
October	34.2	38.1	40.9	3.7	28.5	120.0	102.2	10.38	7.44	14.01	11.28	6.99	355.00	553.90	462.79	198.80
November	34.3	37.8	40.9	3.7	28.7	120.1	102.1	10.41	7.43	13.98	11.32	7.01	357.06	529.20	467.10	199.65
December	34.4	38.4	41.0	3.7	28.7	120.5	101.9	10.45	7.44	14.09	11.32	7.03	359.48	535.15	474.55	204.28
1992:																
January	34.2	38.7	40.8	3.5	28.6	119.9	101.0	10.43	7.42	14.07	11.28	7.03	356.71	516.37	458.78	195.84
February	34.5	37.9	41.0	3.7	28.8	120.7	101.6	10.48	7.44	13.99	11.34	7.04	361.56	510.50	460.00	199.80
March	34.4	37.9	41.0	3.7	28.8	120.6	101.4	10.51	7.43	14.12	11.37	7.07	361.54	524.81	465.03	200.36
April	34.3	38.8	41.0	3.8	28.7	120.5	101.7	10.52	7.43	14.11	11.40	7.09	360.84	537.09	461.37	202.35
May	34.3	38.2	41.1	3.9	28.7	120.8	102.1	10.53	7.42	14.12	11.44	7.09	361.18	548.49	470.60	203.48
June	34.3	38.1	41.1	3.8	28.6	120.7	101.9	10.56	7.42	14.22	11.46	7.11	362.21	551.07	473.30	204.90
July	34.3	38.1	41.1	3.8	28.6	120.8	101.9	10.59	7.42	14.15	11.49	7.13	363.24	548.49	466.42	207.74
August	34.5	38.1	41.1	3.8	28.8	121.6	101.8	10.63	7.43	14.20	11.51	7.15	366.74	556.78	470.60	209.57
September	34.3	37.8	41.0	3.7	28.9	121.0	101.5	10.62	7.40	14.12	11.51	7.19	364.27	527.93	472.73	209.09
October	34.3	38.1	41.1	3.8	28.8	121.5	101.7	10.65	7.40	14.18	11.53	7.18	365.30	559.52	474.54	205.35
November	34.5	37.8	41.2	3.8	28.8	122.4	101.9	10.67	7.39	14.23	11.54	7.19	368.12	534.38	480.48	205.92
December	34.3	37.6	41.2	3.9	28.8	121.9	102.0	10.67	7.37	14.27	11.57	7.20	365.98	531.59	487.30	209.95

1. Includes industries not shown separately.

SELECTED MONTHLY DATA, 1969-1992

CONSUMER PRICE INDEXES
(All urban consumers—1982-1984=100, seasonally adjusted, except as noted)

YEAR AND MONTH	All items	Food	Housing					Apparel and upkeep	Transportation			Medical care	Enter-tain-ment	Per-sonal care¹	Energy	All items less food and energy
			Total	Shelter		Fuel and other utilities	House-hold furnish-ings and op-eration		Total	New cars	Motor fuel					
				Total	Mainte-nance and repair¹											
1969:																
January	35.7	36.1	33.0	31.3	31.7	27.7	44.4	55.5	34.7	50.8	27.1	30.9	44.1	41.1	24.4	37.3
February	35.8	36.1	33.1	31.4	31.9	27.7	44.6	55.7	35.2	50.9	27.2	31.2	44.2	41.3	24.4	37.6
March	36.1	36.2	33.4	31.8	32.4	27.8	44.7	55.9	35.8	51.2	27.6	31.4	44.4	41.5	24.7	37.8
April	36.3	36.4	33.6	32.1	32.7	27.9	44.9	56.2	35.8	51.2	27.9	31.6	44.7	41.8	24.9	38.1
May	36.4	36.6	33.7	32.3	32.9	27.9	45.0	56.4	35.5	51.2	27.8	31.8	44.9	41.8	24.8	38.1
June	36.6	37.0	33.9	32.4	33.2	28.0	45.2	56.7	35.6	51.4	28.0	31.9	45.1	42.0	25.0	38.3
July	36.8	37.3	34.1	32.7	33.4	28.0	45.3	57.0	35.6	51.5	27.8	32.1	45.2	42.1	24.9	38.5
August	36.9	37.5	34.3	32.9	33.6	28.1	45.5	57.0	35.7	51.7	27.8	32.2	45.5	42.2	24.9	38.7
September	37.1	37.7	34.5	33.2	33.9	28.2	45.6	57.4	35.6	51.6	27.7	32.5	45.7	42.3	25.0	38.9
October	37.3	37.8	34.7	33.4	34.1	28.3	45.7	57.6	35.9	51.9	27.7	32.3	45.8	42.3	25.0	39.1
November	37.5	38.2	34.8	33.6	34.2	28.4	45.7	57.9	36.0	52.1	27.5	32.5	46.0	42.5	25.0	39.2
December	37.7	38.6	35.0	33.8	34.4	28.4	45.9	58.0	36.2	52.0	27.7	32.6	46.2	42.6	25.1	39.4
1970:																
January	37.9	38.7	35.1	34.0	34.5	28.4	46.0	58.2	36.6	52.0	27.6	32.8	46.4	42.8	25.1	39.6
February	38.1	38.9	35.4	34.4	34.7	28.5	46.3	58.5	36.7	52.0	27.7	33.0	46.6	42.9	25.1	39.8
March	38.3	38.9	35.8	34.8	35.0	28.6	46.5	58.5	36.6	52.2	27.2	33.2	46.7	43.1	25.0	40.1
April	38.5	39.0	35.9	35.0	35.1	28.8	46.5	58.7	37.1	52.3	28.3	33.5	46.9	43.2	25.5	40.4
May	38.6	39.2	36.1	35.3	35.4	28.9	46.7	58.8	37.2	52.3	28.1	33.7	47.1	43.3	25.4	40.5
June	38.8	39.2	36.3	35.5	35.7	28.9	46.8	59.0	37.4	52.3	27.8	33.9	47.3	43.3	25.3	40.8
July	38.9	39.2	36.5	35.6	36.0	29.2	46.8	59.1	37.6	52.5	28.0	34.1	47.5	43.5	25.5	40.9
August	39.0	39.2	36.6	35.9	36.2	29.3	47.0	59.3	37.5	52.9	27.5	34.3	47.8	43.7	25.4	41.1
September	39.2	39.4	36.9	36.2	36.4	29.5	47.1	59.6	37.7	53.4	27.7	34.5	48.1	43.8	25.6	41.3
October	39.4	39.5	37.1	36.3	36.6	29.7	47.3	59.8	38.1	54.3	28.1	34.6	48.4	44.0	25.9	41.5
November	39.6	39.5	37.3	36.5	36.8	30.0	47.5	60.1	38.5	54.9	28.2	34.8	48.6	44.0	26.0	41.8
December	39.8	39.5	37.4	36.8	37.0	30.1	47.6	60.3	38.9	55.6	28.4	35.1	48.8	44.2	26.2	42.0
1971:																
January	39.9	39.4	37.5	36.8	37.2	30.3	47.7	60.4	39.2	56.1	28.5	35.2	49.1	44.3	26.3	42.1
February	39.9	39.5	37.5	36.6	37.3	30.5	47.8	60.6	39.4	56.2	28.1	35.4	49.3	44.3	26.2	42.2
March	40.0	39.8	37.4	36.4	37.6	30.7	47.9	60.6	39.4	56.0	27.9	35.6	49.4	44.5	26.2	42.2
April	40.1	40.1	37.4	36.4	37.8	30.7	48.1	60.7	39.4	56.0	27.5	35.8	49.7	44.7	26.1	42.4
May	40.3	40.3	37.6	36.5	38.1	30.9	48.5	61.1	39.4	56.1	27.5	36.0	49.9	44.8	26.2	42.6
June	40.5	40.5	37.9	36.9	38.7	31.0	48.7	61.2	39.6	56.2	27.6	36.2	50.1	44.9	26.3	42.8
July	40.6	40.6	38.1	37.0	38.9	31.3	48.8	61.3	39.6	56.5	27.3	36.4	50.3	45.0	26.3	42.9
August	40.7	40.6	38.2	37.2	39.2	31.5	49.0	61.1	39.7	54.7	28.4	36.5	50.4	44.9	26.8	43.0
September	40.8	40.6	38.4	37.4	39.5	31.6	49.0	61.3	39.5	53.6	28.5	36.7	50.5	45.2	26.9	43.0
October	40.9	40.7	38.5	37.5	39.5	31.7	49.1	61.4	39.5	53.5	28.6	36.5	50.5	45.3	27.0	43.1
November	41.0	40.9	38.6	37.7	39.6	31.7	49.1	61.5	39.4	53.6	28.4	36.6	50.7	45.3	26.9	43.2
December	41.1	41.3	38.7	37.8	39.7	31.9	49.2	61.6	39.4	54.0	28.5	36.7	50.7	45.3	27.0	43.3
1972:																
January	41.2	41.1	38.9	38.0	39.8	32.0	49.2	61.7	39.7	54.6	28.2	36.8	50.9	45.4	27.0	43.5
February	41.4	41.7	39.0	38.1	39.8	32.1	49.2	61.9	39.6	54.7	28.1	36.9	51.0	45.5	26.8	43.6
March	41.4	41.6	39.0	38.2	40.0	32.2	49.4	61.9	39.6	54.8	28.1	37.0	51.1	45.6	26.9	43.6
April	41.5	41.6	39.1	38.3	40.2	32.3	49.4	62.1	39.6	55.0	27.8	37.1	51.3	45.8	26.9	43.8
May	41.6	41.7	39.2	38.4	40.4	32.4	49.6	62.2	39.7	54.9	28.0	37.2	51.3	46.0	27.0	43.9
June	41.7	41.9	39.4	38.6	40.6	32.5	49.6	62.2	39.7	54.9	27.7	37.3	51.6	46.1	27.0	44.0
July	41.8	42.1	39.6	38.8	40.7	32.6	49.7	62.2	39.8	55.0	28.0	37.3	51.6	46.1	27.1	44.1
August	41.9	42.2	39.7	39.0	41.0	32.7	49.8	62.0	40.0	55.3	28.4	37.4	51.6	46.2	27.3	44.3
September	42.1	42.5	39.8	39.0	41.0	32.8	49.9	62.5	40.2	55.5	29.0	37.4	51.8	46.3	27.6	44.3
October	42.2	42.8	39.8	39.1	41.1	32.9	49.9	62.8	40.1	54.1	29.1	37.8	51.9	46.4	27.7	44.4
November	42.4	43.0	39.9	39.2	41.2	33.0	50.0	63.0	40.3	54.0	29.3	37.8	52.0	46.5	27.9	44.4
December	42.5	43.2	40.1	39.3	41.6	33.0	50.2	63.2	40.4	54.1	29.3	37.9	52.0	46.7	27.8	44.6
1973:																
January	42.7	44.0	40.1	39.4	41.8	33.1	50.2	63.2	40.4	54.1	29.4	38.0	52.1	46.8	27.9	44.6
February	43.0	44.6	40.2	39.5	41.9	33.4	50.3	63.4	40.6	54.3	29.6	38.1	52.2	47.0	28.2	44.8
March	43.4	45.8	40.4	39.6	42.3	33.5	50.4	63.8	40.7	54.4	29.7	38.2	52.4	47.3	28.3	45.0
April	43.7	46.5	40.5	39.7	42.7	33.7	50.6	64.2	41.0	54.7	30.2	38.3	52.6	47.6	28.6	45.1
May	43.9	47.1	40.6	39.9	43.2	33.8	50.7	64.4	41.0	54.8	30.4	38.5	52.8	47.8	28.8	45.3
June	44.2	47.6	40.9	40.0	43.7	34.0	51.0	64.6	41.2	54.8	31.0	38.6	52.9	48.0	29.2	45.4
July	44.2	47.7	41.0	40.1	43.9	34.1	51.1	64.6	41.2	55.0	31.0	38.6	53.1	48.1	29.2	45.5
August	45.0	50.5	41.3	40.5	44.2	34.4	51.3	64.9	41.2	55.2	31.0	38.7	53.1	48.3	29.4	45.7
September	45.2	50.4	41.7	41.0	44.4	34.5	51.5	65.2	41.1	55.1	30.8	38.9	53.2	48.5	29.4	46.0
October	45.6	50.7	42.1	41.6	44.6	35.1	51.7	65.4	41.4	55.0	32.2	39.6	53.4	48.9	30.3	46.3
November	45.9	51.4	42.5	41.8	44.8	35.8	52.0	65.7	41.8	54.9	33.7	39.7	53.6	49.2	31.5	46.5
December	46.3	51.9	42.8	42.1	45.3	36.7	52.2	66.0	42.2	54.8	35.2	39.9	53.7	49.6	32.5	46.7
1974:																
January	46.8	52.5	43.3	42.4	45.7	37.9	52.7	66.3	42.8	55.0	37.2	40.1	54.1	49.9	34.1	46.9
February	47.3	53.6	43.6	42.7	46.1	38.6	53.1	67.0	43.4	55.2	39.3	40.3	54.5	50.3	35.4	47.2
March	47.8	54.2	44.1	43.0	46.8	38.9	53.9	67.5	44.2	55.4	42.1	40.7	54.8	50.6	36.9	47.6
April	48.1	54.1	44.4	43.2	47.6	39.6	54.4	68.2	44.7	55.7	42.7	41.0	55.2	51.1	37.6	47.9
May	48.6	54.5	44.9	43.5	48.4	40.1	55.5	68.7	45.3	56.5	43.6	41.4	56.0	51.8	38.3	48.5
June	49.0	54.5	45.4	43.9	49.4	40.5	56.3	69.2	45.9	57.5	43.6	42.1	56.8	52.4	38.6	49.0
July	49.3	54.3	45.9	44.4	50.2	41.0	57.1	69.5	46.4	58.6	43.7	42.6	57.4	52.9	38.9	49.5
August	49.9	55.1	46.5	44.9	50.9	41.6	58.1	70.8	46.6	58.9	43.4	43.2	57.8	53.5	39.2	50.2
September	50.6	56.2	47.1	45.5	51.8	42.0	59.0	71.0	47.0	59.7	43.2	43.7	58.4	54.2	39.3	50.7
October	51.0	56.8	47.7	46.0	52.1	42.3	59.8	71.2	47.3	60.8	42.6	44.1	58.7	54.9	39.2	51.2
November	51.5	57.5	48.1	46.3	52.4	42.6	60.6	71.7	47.6	60.9	42.4	44.4	59.3	55.4	39.2	51.6
December	51.9	58.2	48.6	46.9	52.6	42.8	61.2	71.7	47.9	61.0	42.5	44.8	59.8	55.8	39.6	52.0

1. Not seasonally adjusted.

CONSUMER PRICE INDEXES—Continued
(All urban consumers—1982-1984=100, seasonally adjusted, except as noted)

YEAR AND MONTH	All items	Food	Housing Total	Shelter Total	Shelter Mainte-nance and repair [1]	Fuel and other utilities	House-hold furnish-ings and op-eration	Apparel and upkeep	Transportation Total	Transportation New cars	Transportation Motor fuel	Medical care	Enter-tain-ment	Per-sonal care [1]	Energy	All items less food and energy
1975:																
January	52.3	58.4	49.0	47.3	52.9	43.4	61.6	71.8	48.0	60.2	42.8	45.3	60.5	56.3	40.0	52.3
February	52.6	58.5	49.4	47.7	53.1	43.8	62.1	72.0	48.3	61.0	42.8	45.8	60.9	56.8	40.3	52.8
March	52.8	58.4	49.7	47.9	53.1	44.0	62.4	72.1	48.7	62.6	43.0	46.3	60.9	57.2	40.6	53.0
April	53.0	58.3	50.0	48.2	53.4	44.5	62.8	72.1	48.8	62.9	43.0	46.7	61.7	57.4	41.0	53.3
May	53.1	58.6	50.2	48.3	53.6	44.8	63.1	72.2	48.9	62.6	43.5	47.0	61.7	57.6	41.3	53.5
June	53.5	59.2	50.5	48.7	53.9	45.2	63.4	72.2	49.4	62.8	44.5	47.4	61.8	57.7	41.7	53.8
July	54.0	60.3	50.7	48.9	54.3	45.4	63.6	72.6	50.2	62.8	46.1	47.8	62.0	58.1	42.5	54.0
August	54.2	60.3	51.0	49.0	54.4	45.8	63.8	72.6	50.6	63.2	46.5	48.1	62.3	58.2	42.8	54.2
September	54.6	60.7	51.3	49.3	54.8	46.4	64.1	72.7	51.4	63.6	46.9	48.5	62.6	58.4	43.2	54.5
October	54.9	61.3	51.5	49.6	55.1	46.7	64.4	73.0	51.7	63.9	47.3	48.9	62.7	58.7	43.5	54.8
November	55.3	61.7	52.0	50.0	55.4	47.4	64.6	73.2	52.4	64.1	47.3	48.8	63.1	59.0	43.9	55.2
December	55.6	62.1	52.3	50.3	55.5	47.7	64.8	73.4	52.6	65.2	47.2	49.3	63.3	59.4	44.1	55.5
1976:																
January	55.8	61.9	52.6	50.5	55.8	48.0	65.7	73.7	53.0	65.4	47.1	49.7	63.7	59.8	44.5	55.9
February	55.9	61.3	52.8	50.6	55.9	48.3	66.1	74.0	53.3	65.8	46.7	50.2	63.8	60.3	44.4	56.2
March	56.0	60.9	52.9	50.7	56.2	48.4	66.5	74.2	53.8	66.0	46.3	50.7	64.0	60.5	44.1	56.5
April	56.1	60.9	53.1	50.7	56.6	48.6	66.7	74.3	54.0	66.2	45.7	51.0	64.1	60.8	43.9	56.7
May	56.4	61.1	53.2	50.9	57.0	48.7	66.8	74.6	54.3	66.3	46.1	51.4	64.6	61.1	44.1	57.0
June	56.7	61.3	53.5	51.2	57.5	48.8	67.1	74.9	54.8	66.4	46.7	51.8	64.9	61.4	44.4	57.2
July	57.0	61.6	53.8	51.6	57.9	49.1	67.4	75.3	55.1	66.6	46.8	52.3	65.2	61.7	44.8	57.6
August	57.3	61.8	54.1	51.9	58.2	49.6	67.6	75.8	55.4	67.0	46.9	52.6	65.4	62.1	45.2	57.9
September	57.6	62.1	54.4	52.2	58.6	50.0	67.8	76.1	56.0	67.5	47.2	53.0	65.7	62.5	45.7	58.2
October	57.9	62.4	54.6	52.3	58.9	50.5	68.1	76.2	56.6	68.6	47.8	53.2	66.0	63.0	46.1	58.5
November	58.1	62.3	54.8	52.4	59.2	51.4	68.4	76.5	57.0	68.3	48.2	53.9	66.5	63.3	46.8	58.7
December	58.4	62.5	55.1	52.4	59.4	52.3	68.6	76.8	57.3	68.6	48.3	54.2	66.6	63.5	47.5	58.9
1977:																
January	58.7	62.7	55.6	52.9	59.7	53.3	68.9	77.2	57.8	68.8	48.5	54.6	66.9	63.9	48.1	59.3
February	59.3	63.9	55.9	53.2	60.0	53.5	69.2	77.6	58.2	68.9	49.2	54.9	67.1	64.0	48.1	59.7
March	59.6	64.2	56.2	53.5	60.5	53.9	69.4	77.5	58.7	69.3	49.7	55.5	67.3	64.3	48.4	60.0
April	60.0	65.0	56.5	54.0	60.9	54.1	69.5	77.6	59.0	69.3	49.7	56.0	67.2	64.7	48.6	60.3
May	60.2	65.3	56.8	54.3	61.4	54.0	69.8	78.1	59.1	69.6	50.0	56.5	67.6	65.1	48.9	60.6
June	60.5	65.7	57.1	54.7	62.0	54.1	70.2	78.5	59.1	69.9	49.7	57.0	68.1	65.5	48.9	61.0
July	60.8	65.9	57.6	55.2	62.3	54.5	70.5	79.1	59.0	70.2	49.4	57.3	68.3	65.8	49.1	61.2
August	61.1	66.2	57.9	55.5	62.7	55.0	70.8	79.2	58.9	70.5	49.4	57.7	68.6	66.1	49.5	61.5
September	61.3	66.4	58.3	55.9	63.1	55.4	71.0	79.1	59.1	70.8	49.6	58.2	69.1	66.4	49.8	61.8
October	61.6	66.6	58.6	56.2	63.4	55.7	71.3	79.3	59.3	72.0	50.1	58.4	69.4	66.8	50.5	62.0
November	62.0	67.1	59.0	56.6	63.6	56.8	71.5	79.8	59.5	72.5	50.5	58.6	69.6	67.4	51.3	62.3
December	62.3	67.4	59.4	57.0	63.7	56.8	71.9	80.1	59.8	73.5	50.9	59.0	69.8	67.7	51.6	62.7
1978:																
January	62.7	67.9	59.7	57.5	64.2	56.7	72.2	80.1	60.1	74.2	50.9	59.3	70.1	68.1	51.1	63.1
February	63.0	68.6	60.1	57.8	64.5	57.1	72.3	79.5	60.2	74.4	50.6	59.9	70.5	68.3	50.6	63.4
March	63.4	69.5	60.5	58.3	65.1	57.5	72.8	79.9	60.3	74.7	50.7	60.2	70.8	68.5	51.0	63.8
April	63.9	70.6	61.0	58.8	65.9	58.0	73.3	80.7	60.4	74.6	50.4	60.7	71.2	68.8	51.4	64.3
May	64.5	71.6	61.6	59.4	66.3	58.3	73.8	81.3	60.7	74.8	50.5	61.1	71.6	69.3	51.7	64.7
June	65.0	72.7	62.1	60.0	66.9	58.4	74.4	81.6	61.1	75.3	50.7	61.5	71.6	69.6	51.9	65.2
July	65.5	73.0	62.7	60.7	67.6	58.4	74.8	81.5	61.6	75.6	51.1	61.9	72.0	70.1	52.1	65.6
August	65.9	73.3	63.1	61.3	68.1	58.6	75.3	81.7	62.0	76.0	51.8	62.4	72.3	70.3	52.6	66.1
September	66.5	73.6	63.8	62.1	68.5	58.8	75.8	81.9	62.6	76.5	52.5	62.8	72.7	71.0	53.2	66.7
October	67.1	74.2	64.5	62.8	69.5	59.4	76.4	82.4	63.3	77.2	53.5	63.3	73.1	71.3	54.1	67.2
November	67.5	74.7	64.9	63.3	69.9	59.6	76.9	82.6	63.9	77.8	54.4	63.8	73.4	71.8	54.9	67.6
December	67.9	75.1	65.2	63.5	70.2	60.0	77.4	82.6	64.5	78.5	55.4	64.1	73.9	72.0	55.9	68.0
1979:																
January	68.5	76.4	65.7	64.0	70.8	60.4	77.9	83.0	64.6	78.9	56.0	64.8	74.4	72.6	55.8	68.5
February	69.2	77.7	66.5	64.9	71.0	60.8	78.2	83.3	65.2	79.7	56.4	65.2	74.6	73.2	55.9	69.2
March	69.9	78.4	67.0	65.5	71.4	61.3	78.6	83.6	66.4	80.2	59.0	65.7	75.1	73.8	57.4	69.8
April	70.6	79.0	67.7	66.3	72.3	61.9	79.0	84.0	67.8	81.1	62.1	66.1	75.6	74.0	59.5	70.3
May	71.4	79.7	68.4	67.1	72.8	62.7	79.3	84.5	69.1	81.5	65.2	66.6	76.2	74.5	62.0	70.8
June	72.2	80.0	69.3	68.0	73.7	64.0	79.7	84.7	70.5	81.8	69.1	67.1	76.5	74.9	64.7	71.3
July	73.0	80.5	70.2	69.0	74.4	65.1	80.0	84.8	71.7	82.3	72.7	67.7	77.0	75.5	67.3	71.9
August	73.7	80.4	71.2	70.1	74.9	66.4	80.4	85.0	72.7	82.6	75.9	68.2	77.5	75.9	69.7	72.7
September	74.4	80.9	72.1	71.1	75.8	67.4	80.7	85.6	73.5	82.8	78.8	68.7	77.9	76.5	71.9	73.3
October	75.2	81.5	73.1	72.3	76.4	68.2	81.2	86.1	74.0	83.1	80.4	69.2	78.3	76.8	73.5	74.0
November	76.0	82.0	74.2	73.5	76.9	68.8	82.0	86.6	74.7	83.3	81.7	69.8	78.8	77.2	74.8	74.8
December	76.9	82.8	75.2	74.6	77.4	69.6	82.5	87.3	75.8	84.1	83.8	70.6	79.0	78.0	76.8	75.7
1980:																
January	78.0	83.3	76.2	75.9	78.1	70.4	83.0	88.1	78.0	85.1	89.8	71.4	79.7	78.5	79.1	76.7
February	79.0	83.4	77.2	76.8	79.0	71.5	83.6	88.7	79.8	86.2	94.1	72.3	80.5	79.3	81.9	77.5
March	80.1	84.1	78.3	78.1	80.5	72.6	84.4	89.7	81.8	86.4	99.6	73.0	81.4	80.0	84.5	78.6
April	80.9	84.7	79.4	79.3	81.6	73.7	84.9	90.1	82.2	87.3	98.7	73.6	82.2	80.6	85.4	79.5
May	81.7	85.2	80.5	80.5	82.2	74.5	85.5	90.3	82.8	87.9	98.7	74.2	82.8	81.3	86.4	80.1
June	82.5	85.7	82.0	82.3	82.5	75.5	86.1	90.6	82.7	87.8	98.1	74.7	83.5	81.6	86.5	81.0
July	82.6	86.6	81.5	81.3	83.0	76.3	86.6	90.9	83.1	88.4	97.9	75.2	84.1	82.4	86.7	80.8
August	83.2	88.0	81.8	81.4	83.3	76.9	87.2	91.4	83.7	89.7	97.8	75.6	84.7	82.8	87.2	81.3
September	83.9	89.1	82.3	82.0	84.2	77.3	87.9	92.0	84.6	90.4	97.7	76.3	85.5	83.3	87.5	82.1
October	84.7	89.8	83.4	83.4	84.5	77.5	88.3	92.7	85.3	90.2	98.5	76.9	86.0	83.7	88.0	83.0
November	85.6	90.8	84.4	84.7	84.9	78.1	88.6	93.1	86.1	90.5	98.7	77.3	86.2	84.1	88.8	83.9
December	86.4	91.3	85.5	85.8	85.7	79.2	89.1	93.3	86.8	90.4	99.4	77.8	86.6	84.9	90.7	84.9

1. Not seasonally adjusted.

SELECTED MONTHLY DATA, 1969-1992

CONSUMER PRICE INDEXES—Continued
(All urban consumers—1982-1984=100, seasonally adjusted, except as noted)

YEAR AND MONTH	All items	Food	Housing					Apparel and upkeep	Transportation			Medical care	Entertainment	Personal care[1]	Energy	All items less food and energy
			Total	Shelter		Fuel and other utilities	Household furnishings and operation		Total	New cars	Motor fuel					
				Total	Maintenance and repair[1]											
1981:																
January	87.2	91.6	86.1	86.3	85.7	80.7	89.6	93.4	88.5	90.8	103.5	78.6	87.5	85.5	92.1	85.4
February	88.0	92.1	86.6	86.3	87.4	82.7	90.3	93.9	90.7	90.8	109.9	79.2	88.2	86.3	95.2	85.9
March	88.6	92.6	87.1	86.7	88.3	83.8	90.9	94.3	91.8	90.2	113.0	79.9	88.6	87.2	97.4	86.4
April	89.1	92.8	87.8	87.3	89.3	84.8	91.7	94.7	91.7	91.8	110.6	80.7	88.9	87.9	97.6	87.0
May	89.7	92.8	88.8	88.6	90.3	85.2	92.1	94.8	92.2	93.8	109.0	81.4	89.4	88.6	97.9	87.8
June	90.5	93.2	89.8	89.9	91.0	85.7	92.7	95.0	92.7	94.6	107.8	82.3	89.8	89.2	97.3	88.6
July	91.5	93.9	91.3	91.5	92.1	87.0	93.3	95.4	93.5	95.0	107.2	83.4	90.0	89.7	97.3	89.8
August	92.2	94.4	92.2	92.5	92.5	87.9	93.9	95.9	93.9	94.8	107.2	84.3	90.5	90.3	97.8	90.7
September	93.1	94.8	93.4	93.9	92.8	88.8	94.4	96.1	94.6	95.0	107.7	85.1	91.3	90.8	98.6	91.8
October	93.4	95.0	93.4	93.8	92.6	88.9	94.8	96.4	95.5	95.5	108.3	85.9	91.9	91.0	99.2	92.1
November	93.8	95.1	93.8	94.0	93.2	89.9	95.5	96.4	96.2	96.0	108.9	86.8	92.5	91.3	100.5	92.5
December	94.1	95.3	94.1	94.3	93.5	90.4	95.8	96.7	96.4	96.7	108.6	87.5	92.8	91.9	101.5	93.0
1982:																
January	94.4	95.6	94.4	94.4	94.3	91.3	96.2	96.7	96.7	96.8	108.1	88.2	93.5	92.6	100.6	93.3
February	94.7	96.3	94.7	94.7	94.7	91.7	96.7	97.0	96.2	96.2	106.0	88.8	94.1	93.1	98.0	93.8
March	94.7	96.2	94.6	94.2	94.4	92.6	97.1	97.3	95.8	95.9	103.6	89.6	94.5	93.6	96.6	93.9
April	95.0	96.4	95.4	95.3	95.7	93.1	97.3	97.5	94.5	96.7	97.3	90.5	94.9	94.5	94.2	94.7
May	95.9	97.2	96.7	96.8	96.5	93.8	97.8	97.6	95.1	97.1	97.8	91.3	95.2	94.7	95.7	95.4
June	97.0	98.1	97.7	98.0	97.0	94.5	98.0	97.7	97.2	97.6	102.8	92.2	95.8	95.2	98.4	96.1
July	97.5	98.2	98.1	98.5	96.6	94.9	98.3	98.1	98.1	98.0	104.3	93.0	96.4	95.8	99.3	96.7
August	97.7	98.0	98.4	98.9	96.9	95.4	98.3	98.1	98.2	98.1	104.1	93.9	96.7	96.3	99.8	97.1
September	97.7	98.2	98.2	98.4	97.7	96.1	98.5	98.1	98.0	98.1	103.2	94.7	97.1	96.5	100.3	97.2
October	98.1	98.2	98.6	98.4	97.9	97.7	98.9	98.3	98.2	97.9	103.2	95.5	97.9	97.2	101.7	97.5
November	98.0	98.2	98.3	97.9	97.8	98.4	98.8	98.3	98.2	97.8	102.8	96.5	97.8	97.7	102.5	97.3
December	97.7	98.2	97.5	96.5	97.5	98.9	99.1	98.2	97.7	98.2	100.4	97.2	98.0	97.9	102.8	97.3
1983:																
January	97.9	98.1	98.0	97.2	99.0	99.4	99.3	98.6	97.6	98.5	99.0	97.9	98.3	98.4	99.6	97.6
February	98.0	98.2	98.2	97.5	97.9	99.2	99.4	99.1	96.9	98.8	95.9	98.8	99.0	99.0	97.7	98.0
March	98.1	98.8	98.3	97.6	98.1	99.0	99.6	99.1	96.5	99.0	94.2	99.0	99.6	99.0	96.8	98.2
April	98.8	99.2	98.9	98.4	99.2	99.5	100.0	99.3	97.8	99.2	98.0	99.4	99.6	99.5	98.9	98.6
May	99.2	99.5	99.1	98.7	99.4	99.9	99.9	99.9	98.6	99.4	100.5	99.9	99.7	99.7	100.4	98.9
June	99.4	99.6	99.3	99.0	99.6	99.9	100.1	100.3	99.0	99.6	101.0	100.4	99.9	100.2	100.6	99.2
July	99.8	99.6	99.7	99.4	99.9	100.3	100.3	100.9	99.6	99.8	101.3	100.8	100.1	100.9	100.9	99.8
August	100.1	99.7	99.8	99.6	100.4	100.2	100.3	101.0	100.4	100.2	102.1	101.4	100.4	100.7	101.2	100.1
September	100.4	100.0	100.1	100.1	100.0	100.6	100.3	100.8	100.7	100.6	101.2	101.8	100.8	101.0	101.0	100.5
October	100.8	100.3	100.4	100.3	100.3	100.8	100.6	100.6	101.1	100.9	100.7	102.3	101.4	101.2	100.8	101.0
November	101.1	100.3	100.8	100.7	102.0	101.3	100.9	100.9	101.5	101.1	99.5	102.8	101.6	102.0	100.5	101.5
December	101.4	100.6	101.0	101.1	102.4	101.2	101.2	101.1	101.5	101.3	98.6	103.4	101.6	102.3	100.0	101.8
1984:																
January	102.1	102.0	101.5	101.4	102.9	102.4	101.2	101.5	102.0	101.6	98.9	104.0	101.7	102.5	100.2	102.5
February	102.6	102.7	102.1	101.8	102.0	104.2	101.0	101.2	102.2	101.7	99.4	105.0	102.4	102.9	101.4	102.8
March	102.9	102.9	102.3	102.3	102.5	103.6	101.2	101.3	102.9	102.0	100.1	105.2	102.5	102.9	101.4	103.2
April	103.3	102.9	102.9	103.0	102.8	104.3	101.4	101.2	103.3	102.3	99.9	105.8	103.3	103.3	101.7	103.7
May	103.5	102.7	103.1	103.2	103.1	104.4	101.6	101.4	103.7	102.4	99.5	106.2	103.2	103.5	101.6	104.1
June	103.7	103.1	103.3	103.6	103.6	104.3	101.7	101.3	103.9	102.6	98.3	106.7	103.6	104.0	100.8	104.5
July	104.1	103.3	103.9	104.3	104.0	105.3	101.5	101.9	103.7	102.9	96.4	107.2	103.9	104.4	100.5	105.0
August	104.4	103.9	104.2	104.7	103.9	105.6	102.0	102.5	103.8	103.2	95.4	107.7	104.4	104.4	100.1	105.4
September	104.7	103.8	104.7	105.1	104.7	106.0	102.5	102.7	104.1	103.4	96.1	108.1	104.7	105.1	100.6	105.8
October	105.1	104.0	104.9	105.5	104.4	105.8	102.6	103.0	104.8	103.5	97.4	108.7	105.2	105.1	101.1	106.2
November	105.3	104.1	105.1	105.8	104.7	105.9	102.6	103.0	104.9	103.7	97.0	109.3	105.4	106.2	100.8	106.4
December	105.5	104.5	105.3	106.4	105.2	105.4	102.7	103.1	104.7	103.8	96.0	109.8	105.9	106.3	100.1	106.8
1985:																
January	105.7	104.7	105.5	106.7	105.6	105.6	102.5	103.2	105.1	104.5	96.4	110.2	106.3	106.5	100.3	107.1
February	106.3	105.2	106.0	107.4	105.9	105.3	103.3	104.1	105.6	105.0	96.5	110.8	106.4	106.9	100.3	107.7
March	106.8	105.5	106.4	107.8	106.8	106.0	103.6	104.5	106.3	105.3	98.1	111.4	106.7	107.1	101.3	108.1
April	107.0	105.4	106.7	108.1	106.2	106.3	104.0	104.5	106.3	105.3	99.8	112.0	106.7	107.5	102.3	108.4
May	107.2	105.2	107.4	109.2	105.7	106.4	103.9	104.4	106.5	105.7	99.4	112.6	107.3	107.9	102.2	108.8
June	107.5	105.5	107.6	109.6	106.1	106.6	103.7	105.1	106.5	106.0	99.8	113.3	107.8	108.2	102.2	109.1
July	107.7	105.5	107.9	110.1	106.1	106.7	103.5	105.2	106.6	106.1	100.0	113.9	108.2	108.5	101.7	109.4
August	107.9	105.6	108.3	110.8	107.0	106.4	103.7	105.3	106.2	106.4	98.7	114.6	108.2	108.8	101.2	109.8
September	108.1	105.8	108.5	111.0	106.4	106.8	103.8	105.5	106.2	106.7	98.2	115.2	108.6	109.2	101.2	110.0
October	108.5	105.8	108.9	111.5	106.3	106.8	104.4	105.7	106.5	106.9	98.2	115.8	109.3	109.5	101.2	110.5
November	109.0	106.5	109.5	112.3	107.6	107.3	104.6	106.0	107.0	107.2	98.9	116.5	109.5	109.7	101.8	111.1
December	109.5	107.3	109.8	112.7	107.8	107.7	104.5	106.1	107.5	107.2	99.7	117.1	109.2	110.0	102.4	111.4
1986:																
January	109.9	107.5	110.1	113.2	109.4	107.8	104.5	106.1	108.0	107.8	100.1	118.0	110.2	110.7	102.6	111.9
February	109.7	107.3	110.0	113.5	109.5	106.4	104.6	105.4	107.0	108.1	95.9	118.8	110.7	111.1	99.5	112.2
March	109.1	107.5	110.3	114.3	106.1	105.3	104.9	105.0	103.6	108.4	83.5	119.7	110.7	111.1	92.6	112.5
April	108.7	107.7	110.4	115.0	106.1	104.4	105.0	105.0	101.0	108.9	74.3	120.4	110.9	111.6	87.2	112.9
May	109.0	108.2	110.4	115.2	105.9	103.7	105.0	104.9	101.4	109.9	75.5	121.2	111.1	111.8	87.2	113.1
June	109.4	108.3	110.9	115.6	105.8	104.7	105.1	104.9	102.3	110.7	77.9	121.8	111.5	111.8	88.8	113.4
July	109.5	109.1	110.9	115.9	106.5	103.6	105.2	105.5	101.1	111.2	72.9	122.5	111.7	111.8	85.6	113.8
August	109.6	110.1	111.1	116.3	108.6	103.6	105.2	106.4	101.1	111.5	69.0	123.2	111.8	112.3	83.6	114.2
September	110.0	110.2	111.5	116.9	108.6	103.4	105.7	106.9	100.6	111.8	70.8	124.0	112.1	112.2	84.3	114.6
October	110.2	110.5	111.6	117.5	109.4	102.4	105.7	106.6	100.5	112.3	69.2	124.7	112.6	112.6	84.4	115.0
November	110.4	111.1	111.6	117.8	108.8	101.7	105.5	106.9	100.8	113.2	68.6	125.5	112.9	112.7	82.1	115.3
December	110.8	111.4	111.9	118.1	109.7	101.8	106.1	107.2	101.1	113.6	69.1	126.2	112.9	112.8	82.5	115.6

1. Not seasonally adjusted.

YEAR AND MONTH	All items	Food	Housing	Shelter		Fuel and other utilities	House-hold furnish-ings and op-eration	Apparel and upkeep	Transportation			Medical care	Enter-tain-ment	Per-sonal care [1]	Energy	All items less food and energy
			Total	Total	Mainte-nance and repair [1]				Total	New cars	Motor fuel					
1987:																
January	111.5	111.9	112.2	118.4	110.3	102.2	106.3	108.0	102.7	114.1	74.1	126.8	113.3	113.6	85.1	116.1
February	111.9	112.3	112.6	118.9	110.2	102.2	106.5	108.6	103.6	112.9	78.4	127.3	113.5	113.9	87.1	116.4
March	112.3	112.5	112.9	119.3	110.7	102.4	106.8	109.2	103.9	112.8	78.7	127.9	113.9	113.9	87.3	116.8
April	112.8	112.7	113.4	120.1	110.3	102.3	107.2	109.8	104.4	113.5	79.3	128.7	114.5	114.2	87.3	117.5
May	113.1	113.3	113.7	120.5	110.2	102.5	107.1	110.3	104.5	114.0	77.8	129.3	114.8	114.9	86.8	117.9
June	113.6	114.0	114.0	120.8	111.1	103.1	107.1	110.3	105.2	114.5	79.5	130.1	114.9	114.9	88.2	118.1
July	113.9	113.8	114.2	120.9	113.2	103.3	107.2	110.3	106.0	115.1	81.2	130.7	115.4	115.3	88.9	118.5
August	114.4	114.0	114.8	121.7	112.9	104.0	107.3	111.0	106.7	115.3	83.1	131.3	115.6	115.6	90.2	118.9
September	114.8	114.5	115.1	122.2	112.7	104.0	107.5	111.6	107.0	115.5	82.7	132.0	116.1	116.0	90.0	119.4
October	115.1	114.7	115.4	122.9	112.8	103.3	107.4	112.3	107.1	115.6	82.6	132.5	116.9	116.2	89.3	120.0
November	115.5	114.7	115.7	123.2	113.5	103.7	107.4	113.0	107.4	116.2	82.7	133.1	117.3	116.3	89.7	120.3
December	115.7	115.3	116.0	123.9	113.3	103.4	107.3	112.7	107.3	115.7	82.1	133.6	117.4	116.5	89.2	120.6
1988:																
January	116.1	115.8	116.3	124.4	113.7	103.2	107.5	113.2	107.1	115.1	81.2	134.6	118.1	117.3	88.5	121.1
February	116.2	115.8	116.7	124.9	114.3	103.5	107.7	112.1	107.1	115.4	80.8	135.4	118.3	117.8	88.4	121.3
March	116.6	116.0	117.1	125.3	113.3	103.5	108.3	113.4	107.1	115.5	80.0	136.3	119.0	118.1	88.1	121.9
April	117.2	116.6	117.6	125.8	115.3	103.9	109.1	115.1	107.5	115.7	80.6	136.8	119.6	118.5	88.5	122.5
May	117.6	117.0	117.8	126.1	114.3	103.7	109.3	115.1	108.0	116.1	80.3	137.7	119.7	118.7	88.2	122.9
June	118.1	117.7	118.2	126.6	114.7	104.2	109.6	115.5	108.4	116.6	80.2	138.4	120.1	119.0	88.6	123.4
July	118.6	118.9	118.5	127.0	114.5	104.3	109.8	115.9	108.9	117.0	81.2	139.3	120.5	119.2	89.1	123.8
August	119.0	119.6	118.9	127.6	115.0	104.4	109.7	114.5	109.7	117.5	82.5	139.9	120.7	119.0	89.8	124.1
September	119.6	120.2	119.4	128.1	115.3	105.0	110.1	116.3	110.0	118.5	81.4	140.7	121.3	120.3	89.5	124.8
October	120.0	120.5	119.8	128.4	115.0	105.7	110.3	117.5	110.0	118.5	80.8	141.6	121.8	121.0	89.5	125.3
November	120.4	120.7	120.1	129.0	115.4	105.6	110.6	117.7	110.3	118.3	80.8	142.1	122.2	121.8	89.5	125.8
December	120.8	121.2	120.5	129.4	115.8	106.2	110.6	118.2	110.4	118.2	80.3	142.9	122.8	122.4	89.3	126.2
1989:																
January	121.3	121.8	120.8	129.6	116.1	106.6	111.0	118.4	111.0	118.4	81.1	144.0	123.7	122.8	89.9	126.7
February	121.7	122.6	121.1	130.1	117.1	106.4	110.7	117.1	111.7	118.6	82.6	145.1	124.3	123.2	90.5	127.0
March	122.3	123.4	121.4	130.8	117.1	106.7	110.3	118.1	112.5	118.9	84.4	145.9	124.6	123.6	91.5	127.5
April	123.2	124.1	121.8	131.1	117.3	107.1	110.5	118.6	115.1	119.1	93.8	146.8	125.2	124.1	96.2	128.0
May	123.8	124.9	122.2	131.8	117.4	107.4	110.6	118.9	115.9	119.3	95.7	147.6	125.5	124.8	97.0	128.5
June	124.1	125.3	122.6	132.2	118.3	107.5	111.0	118.7	115.8	119.2	94.4	148.8	126.3	124.5	96.5	128.9
July	124.6	125.8	123.3	133.0	118.4	108.1	111.1	118.3	115.4	119.2	93.2	149.7	126.9	124.8	96.3	129.4
August	124.6	126.1	123.6	133.4	118.5	108.3	111.4	117.1	114.5	118.9	89.1	150.8	127.4	125.6	94.6	129.7
September	124.9	126.5	123.8	133.7	118.6	108.3	111.5	118.7	114.0	118.7	86.9	151.9	127.8	125.9	93.4	130.1
October	125.5	127.0	124.4	134.6	118.6	108.4	111.9	119.6	114.6	119.5	87.8	152.9	128.2	126.4	94.1	130.8
November	125.9	127.5	124.8	135.2	119.3	108.8	111.9	120.0	114.5	120.2	86.2	154.2	128.7	127.0	93.6	131.3
December	126.4	128.0	125.3	135.7	119.5	109.3	112.0	119.8	114.8	120.9	86.1	155.1	129.4	127.1	93.9	131.8
1990:																
January	127.6	129.8	126.0	136.1	120.4	111.1	112.4	119.9	117.1	121.2	93.5	156.2	129.8	127.6	98.6	132.3
February	128.1	131.0	126.1	136.4	120.8	110.7	112.6	122.0	117.3	121.0	93.3	157.2	130.3	128.4	97.8	132.9
March	128.6	131.2	126.7	137.4	121.2	110.7	112.6	123.8	117.3	120.7	92.5	158.5	130.9	129.0	97.2	133.7
April	129.0	131.0	127.0	138.0	121.2	110.5	112.6	124.1	117.8	120.4	92.9	159.8	131.1	130.3	97.2	134.2
May	129.2	131.3	127.3	138.4	122.2	110.2	112.8	124.0	117.6	120.5	91.8	146.8	131.7	130.2	96.4	134.6
June	130.0	132.3	128.0	139.4	121.8	110.7	113.0	124.2	118.1	120.4	92.7	162.2	132.1	131.0	97.0	135.3
July	130.6	133.0	128.6	140.5	122.1	109.9	113.2	124.2	118.5	120.4	93.1	163.6	132.8	130.6	96.8	136.0
August	131.7	133.4	129.6	141.6	121.2	111.4	113.3	124.5	120.8	120.7	101.2	165.0	133.3	130.6	101.3	136.8
September	132.6	133.7	130.1	141.9	124.6	112.6	113.8	125.4	123.3	120.7	109.6	166.1	134.0	131.3	106.2	137.3
October	133.5	134.3	130.5	142.2	123.4	113.7	114.3	125.4	125.7	121.3	117.2	167.4	134.1	131.7	110.5	137.8
November	133.8	134.7	130.7	142.4	123.9	114.1	114.0	125.4	126.2	121.8	117.4	168.9	134.5	131.9	110.8	138.2
December	134.3	134.8	130.9	143.0	123.8	113.4	114.0	126.2	126.9	122.6	117.8	170.0	134.9	132.4	110.6	138.8
1991:																
January	134.8	135.2	131.9	143.9	124.1	115.0	114.4	126.9	125.6	123.5	110.9	171.2	135.5	133.1	108.1	139.7
February	134.9	135.3	132.3	144.2	125.1	115.1	115.4	127.3	123.9	124.3	102.6	172.3	136.2	134.1	104.2	140.4
March	134.9	135.5	132.5	144.6	124.2	114.9	115.5	127.0	122.8	124.6	97.7	173.4	136.6	133.6	101.5	140.7
April	135.2	136.3	132.6	145.0	126.1	114.2	115.6	127.5	122.6	124.9	97.6	174.5	137.4	134.7	100.8	141.1
May	135.7	136.8	133.0	145.3	126.9	114.7	116.0	128.0	123.3	125.1	99.4	175.4	137.8	134.9	101.8	141.5
June	136.1	137.6	133.1	145.7	126.2	114.4	115.8	127.9	123.5	125.4	98.2	176.6	138.2	134.7	100.8	142.0
July	136.3	136.8	133.5	146.1	126.9	115.0	116.0	128.7	123.4	125.6	96.4	177.6	138.7	135.2	100.3	142.5
August	136.7	136.3	133.7	146.4	127.2	115.0	116.2	129.9	124.1	125.7	97.7	179.0	139.4	135.5	100.8	143.1
September	137.1	136.5	134.2	146.9	126.8	115.5	116.4	130.0	124.1	125.7	97.8	180.1	140.1	135.6	101.1	143.6
October	137.3	136.4	134.6	147.4	126.6	116.0	116.4	130.1	124.0	126.0	97.3	181.0	140.3	135.7	101.2	143.9
November	137.9	136.9	135.1	148.0	127.6	116.5	116.6	131.0	124.5	126.3	98.4	182.1	140.5	135.7	102.0	144.4
December	138.3	137.2	135.5	148.6	128.1	116.8	116.6	130.7	125.2	126.8	99.5	183.3	140.3	135.7	102.7	144.9
1992:																
January	138.4	136.7	135.8	149.1	128.0	116.4	117.0	130.9	124.6	126.9	97.1	184.5	140.1	136.5	101.2	145.3
February	138.7	137.3	136.0	149.3	128.3	116.4	117.1	131.0	124.6	127.1	96.7	185.8	140.7	137.5	100.8	145.6
March	139.2	137.7	136.3	149.8	128.4	116.4	117.4	131.3	125.1	127.4	97.0	187.0	141.2	137.9	100.8	146.1
April	139.5	137.6	136.6	150.0	128.0	117.0	117.7	130.7	125.6	127.7	96.8	188.1	141.7	138.5	101.1	146.5
May	139.8	137.4	136.8	150.3	128.1	117.2	117.6	131.6	126.0	128.1	97.6	188.9	142.0	138.0	101.6	147.0
June	140.2	137.7	137.3	150.9	128.5	117.5	118.1	132.1	126.5	128.3	99.8	189.8	142.2	137.8	102.9	147.3
July	140.6	137.6	137.6	151.1	128.8	117.9	118.2	132.7	126.9	128.5	100.4	190.8	142.5	138.8	103.3	147.8
August	140.9	138.5	137.8	151.5	128.1	118.1	118.2	132.3	127.0	128.9	99.8	191.7	142.8	138.7	103.1	148.1
September	141.2	139.1	138.0	151.6	128.5	118.4	118.2	132.2	127.1	129.1	99.5	192.6	143.1	138.6	103.2	148.3
October	141.8	139.1	138.5	152.3	129.4	118.7	118.4	132.4	128.2	129.2	100.8	193.7	143.4	138.7	103.9	149.0
November	142.2	138.9	138.9	152.7	129.5	119.5	118.6	132.7	128.7	129.5	101.2	194.7	143.7	139.0	104.7	149.4
December	142.4	139.0	139.1	152.9	129.3	119.5	118.5	132.8	128.9	129.7	101.7	195.5	144.2	139.6	104.9	149.8

1. Not seasonally adjusted.

PRODUCER PRICE INDEXES
(By stage of processing—1982=100, seasonally adjusted)

YEAR AND MONTH	Finished goods								Intermediate materials, supplies, and components					Crude materials for further processing		
			Consumer goods													
					Consumer goods, except foods											
	Total	Total less foods and energy	Total	Foods	Total	Nondurable goods, except foods	Durable goods	Capital equipment	Total	Materials and components for manufacturing	Materials and components for construction	Processed fuels and lubricants	Supplies	Total	Foodstuffs and feedstuffs	Nonfood materials
1969:																
January	37.2	....	37.2	41.0	35.8	31.0	45.3	37.6	33.6	....	....	....	....	32.6	42.1	21.7
February	37.2	....	37.1	40.8	35.9	31.0	45.4	37.7	33.7	....	....	....	....	32.3	41.5	21.7
March	37.4	....	37.3	41.1	36.0	31.2	45.6	37.8	33.9	....	....	....	....	32.7	42.3	21.9
April	37.6	....	37.5	41.5	36.1	31.2	45.7	37.9	33.8	....	....	....	....	33.1	42.9	22.1
May	37.8	....	37.8	42.3	36.1	31.3	45.7	38.0	33.9	....	....	....	....	34.0	44.7	22.3
June	38.0	....	38.0	42.7	36.3	31.4	45.8	38.1	34.0	....	....	....	....	34.5	45.2	22.5
July	38.1	....	38.0	42.5	36.4	31.5	45.9	38.3	34.0	....	....	....	....	34.1	44.5	22.7
August	38.2	....	38.1	42.8	36.4	31.6	45.9	38.4	34.2	....	....	....	....	34.4	44.8	22.9
September	38.3	....	38.2	42.9	36.5	31.7	46.0	38.5	34.2	....	....	....	....	34.4	44.4	23.1
October	38.5	....	38.5	43.3	36.7	31.8	46.2	38.7	34.4	....	....	....	....	34.8	45.2	23.1
November	38.8	....	38.8	44.1	36.7	31.9	46.3	39.0	34.6	....	....	....	....	35.2	46.0	23.2
December	38.9	....	38.8	44.1	36.8	32.0	46.4	39.2	34.7	....	....	....	....	35.1	45.9	23.3
1970:																
January	39.1	....	39.0	44.4	36.9	32.1	46.4	39.3	35.0	....	....	....	....	35.1	45.4	23.3
February	39.0	....	38.9	44.1	37.0	32.1	46.6	39.4	35.0	....	....	....	....	35.2	45.2	23.6
March	39.1	....	39.0	44.2	37.0	32.1	46.7	39.6	34.9	....	....	....	....	35.6	46.1	23.6
April	39.1	....	39.0	44.0	37.1	32.2	46.7	39.7	35.1	....	....	....	....	35.5	46.0	23.8
May	39.1	....	38.9	43.5	37.2	32.3	46.8	39.8	35.2	....	....	....	....	35.0	45.0	23.8
June	39.2	....	39.0	43.7	37.2	32.3	46.9	39.9	35.3	....	....	....	....	35.0	44.7	23.9
July	39.2	....	39.0	43.8	37.3	32.4	47.0	40.0	35.5	....	....	....	....	35.1	45.3	23.8
August	39.2	....	39.0	43.3	37.5	32.6	47.1	40.2	35.5	....	....	....	....	34.7	44.8	23.6
September	39.6	....	39.4	44.1	37.6	32.7	47.4	40.3	35.6	....	....	....	....	35.5	45.7	23.9
October	39.6	....	39.3	43.6	37.9	32.7	48.1	40.8	35.8	....	....	....	....	35.5	45.6	24.2
November	39.8	....	39.5	43.8	38.0	32.9	48.2	41.0	35.9	....	....	....	....	35.1	45.0	23.9
December	39.8	....	39.4	43.0	38.3	33.2	48.2	41.1	35.9	....	....	....	....	34.5	43.9	24.2
1971:																
January	39.9	....	39.5	43.2	38.5	33.4	48.4	41.3	36.0	....	....	....	....	34.8	44.2	24.2
February	40.1	....	39.7	43.6	38.5	33.3	48.6	41.4	36.1	....	....	....	....	35.9	46.1	24.3
March	40.2	....	39.8	43.9	38.5	33.3	48.6	41.5	36.3	....	....	....	....	35.4	45.3	24.2
April	40.3	....	40.0	44.4	38.4	33.2	48.7	41.6	36.3	....	....	....	....	36.0	46.4	24.5
May	40.5	....	40.1	44.7	38.5	33.3	48.8	41.7	36.5	....	....	....	....	36.0	46.3	24.4
June	40.6	....	40.3	45.0	38.6	33.4	48.9	41.7	36.7	....	....	....	....	36.2	46.4	24.6
July	40.4	....	40.1	44.1	38.8	33.5	49.0	41.9	36.9	....	....	....	....	35.9	45.8	24.7
August	40.7	....	40.4	44.7	38.8	33.6	49.1	42.0	37.2	....	....	....	....	35.8	45.9	24.6
September	40.7	....	40.3	44.5	38.9	33.7	49.1	41.9	37.2	....	....	....	....	35.7	45.0	24.9
October	40.7	....	40.4	44.9	38.9	33.7	48.9	41.8	37.1	....	....	....	....	36.4	46.4	25.1
November	40.8	....	40.6	45.2	38.9	33.7	49.0	41.8	37.2	....	....	....	....	37.0	47.4	25.2
December	41.1	....	40.9	45.7	39.1	33.8	49.5	42.1	37.4	....	....	....	....	37.2	47.6	25.6
1972:																
January	41.0	....	40.7	45.5	39.0	33.6	49.6	42.3	37.5	....	....	....	....	37.8	48.4	25.8
February	41.3	....	40.9	45.9	39.1	33.6	49.8	42.5	37.7	....	....	....	....	38.1	48.9	26.0
March	41.3	....	40.9	45.7	39.2	33.7	49.9	42.6	37.8	....	....	....	....	38.1	48.4	26.4
April	41.3	....	40.9	45.7	39.2	33.8	49.9	42.7	37.9	....	....	....	....	38.7	49.4	26.6
May	41.5	....	41.1	46.3	39.3	33.9	49.9	42.8	38.0	....	....	....	....	39.3	50.1	26.9
June	41.7	....	41.4	46.8	39.4	33.9	50.0	42.8	38.0	....	....	....	....	39.4	50.4	27.0
July	41.8	....	41.6	47.1	39.5	34.0	50.1	42.9	38.1	....	....	....	....	40.0	51.5	27.1
August	42.0	....	41.7	47.3	39.6	34.1	50.4	42.9	38.2	....	....	....	....	40.3	52.2	27.2
September	42.2	....	42.0	47.8	39.8	34.3	50.6	43.0	38.5	....	....	....	....	40.5	52.4	27.1
October	42.0	....	41.9	47.6	39.6	34.4	49.7	42.8	38.7	....	....	....	....	40.9	53.0	27.3
November	42.3	....	42.1	48.3	39.7	34.6	49.7	42.9	39.0	....	....	....	....	42.0	54.6	28.1
December	42.7	....	42.6	49.3	39.8	34.6	50.0	43.0	39.6	....	....	....	....	43.8	57.7	28.6
1973:																
January	43.0	....	43.0	50.5	39.9	34.7	49.8	43.0	39.8	41.5	44.1	20.8	....	45.0	59.3	29.1
February	43.5	....	43.5	51.2	40.3	35.2	50.0	43.3	40.4	41.9	44.7	21.0	....	47.1	62.5	30.0
March	44.4	....	44.7	53.9	40.5	35.4	50.2	43.6	41.1	42.6	45.6	21.2	....	49.3	66.1	30.6
April	44.7	....	45.0	54.5	40.8	35.6	50.6	43.8	41.3	43.1	46.3	21.3	....	50.1	67.3	31.0
May	45.0	....	45.3	55.0	40.9	35.8	50.9	44.1	42.2	43.5	46.8	21.6	....	52.5	70.5	32.6
June	45.5	....	45.9	56.2	41.1	36.0	51.0	44.2	43.0	44.0	46.7	22.0	....	55.0	74.0	34.0
July	45.4	....	45.7	55.7	41.2	36.0	51.2	44.3	42.3	44.1	46.3	22.1	....	52.5	69.7	33.4
August	47.0	....	47.7	61.0	41.4	36.1	51.4	44.4	43.5	44.8	46.5	22.2	....	64.1	89.9	35.9
September	46.9	....	47.5	60.3	41.5	36.3	51.4	44.6	43.0	45.0	47.0	22.5	....	60.9	81.3	38.2
October	46.8	....	47.4	59.6	41.7	36.8	51.0	44.7	43.4	45.4	47.4	23.1	....	58.5	76.9	38.0
November	47.2	....	47.9	59.8	42.2	37.4	51.4	44.9	43.8	45.9	48.3	23.8	....	59.0	77.4	38.6
December	47.6	....	48.3	60.1	42.8	38.1	51.7	45.3	44.8	46.9	48.9	25.1	....	59.1	75.7	40.4
1974:																
January	48.8	49.7	49.6	62.2	43.7	39.2	52.4	45.8	45.9	48.2	49.7	26.4	....	63.3	82.3	42.0
February	49.7	50.0	50.7	63.8	44.6	40.2	52.7	46.2	46.8	49.1	50.3	28.6	....	64.3	83.5	42.8
March	50.2	50.5	51.1	63.5	45.5	41.3	53.1	46.8	48.1	50.7	51.4	30.5	....	62.3	78.9	43.4
April	50.7	51.1	51.5	63.0	46.4	42.3	53.6	47.4	49.0	52.1	52.7	31.6	....	60.6	74.7	44.2
May	51.3	52.2	52.0	62.9	47.2	43.2	54.4	48.7	50.6	53.9	54.2	33.1	....	58.3	71.8	42.6
June	51.3	53.1	51.8	60.8	48.0	44.2	55.0	49.7	51.5	55.4	55.2	33.8	....	55.4	65.8	43.0
July	52.7	54.0	53.2	63.1	49.0	45.0	55.9	50.7	53.4	57.3	56.4	35.7	....	59.8	72.4	45.0
August	53.7	55.0	54.1	64.6	49.6	45.7	56.4	52.1	55.8	59.2	57.4	36.7	....	62.9	78.1	45.3
September	54.3	55.7	54.6	65.1	50.1	46.2	56.9	53.1	55.9	59.9	58.0	35.9	....	60.9	74.3	45.3
October	55.3	56.7	55.6	66.3	50.9	46.7	58.3	54.2	57.2	60.9	58.0	36.9	....	63.2	78.6	45.6
November	56.4	57.4	56.7	69.1	51.2	47.0	58.8	55.0	57.8	62.6	58.3	37.0	....	64.2	80.4	45.7
December	56.4	57.9	56.6	68.0	51.6	47.3	59.3	55.5	57.8	62.3	58.6	37.3	....	61.5	76.8	44.1

PRODUCER PRICE INDEXES—Continued
(By stage of processing—1982=100, seasonally adjusted)

YEAR AND MONTH	Finished goods								Intermediate materials, supplies, and components					Crude materials for further processing		
	Total	Total less foods and energy	Consumer goods		Consumer goods, except foods			Capital equipment	Total	Materials and components for manufacturing	Materials and components for construction	Processed fuels and lubricants	Supplies	Total	Foodstuffs and feedstuffs	Nonfood materials
			Total	Foods	Total	Nondurable goods, except foods	Durable goods									
1975:																
January	56.7	58.3	56.8	68.0	51.9	47.6	59.6	56.2	58.0	62.5	58.9	38.1	....	59.6	74.0	43.0
February	56.6	58.7	56.6	67.3	52.0	47.6	60.0	56.7	57.8	62.2	59.2	37.5	....	57.9	70.9	42.9
March	56.6	59.0	56.4	66.7	52.1	47.6	60.3	57.2	57.4	61.6	59.2	37.9	....	57.1	70.0	42.2
April	57.1	59.2	56.9	67.8	52.3	47.8	60.4	57.5	57.5	61.4	59.3	38.3	....	59.5	74.4	42.5
May	57.4	59.3	57.3	68.5	52.5	48.1	60.5	57.8	57.3	60.9	59.6	38.2	....	61.2	76.8	43.4
June	57.9	59.5	57.8	69.5	52.7	48.4	60.7	58.0	57.3	60.9	60.0	38.5	....	61.5	77.4	43.3
July	58.4	59.8	58.4	70.5	53.1	48.8	60.7	58.4	57.5	61.0	60.0	38.9	....	62.4	79.3	43.3
August	58.9	59.9	59.0	71.3	53.5	49.3	61.1	58.5	58.0	61.3	60.1	39.9	....	63.0	80.2	43.6
September	59.3	60.2	59.4	71.8	53.9	49.7	61.3	58.9	58.2	61.5	60.3	40.5	....	64.5	81.9	44.7
October	59.8	60.6	59.9	72.4	54.3	50.1	61.8	59.3	58.8	62.0	61.0	41.0	....	65.1	83.0	44.8
November	60.0	61.0	60.1	72.3	54.8	50.5	62.4	59.7	59.0	62.2	61.2	41.8	....	64.4	81.6	44.8
December	60.1	61.4	60.1	71.9	55.1	50.8	62.5	60.0	59.2	62.3	61.9	41.8	....	64.0	80.1	45.7
1976:																
January	60.0	61.7	59.9	70.9	55.2	51.0	62.7	60.4	59.4	62.7	62.1	41.6	63.3	63.0	78.4	45.5
February	59.9	61.9	59.6	69.7	55.4	51.1	63.0	60.7	59.6	62.6	62.3	41.5	63.6	62.1	77.2	44.8
March	60.0	62.2	59.6	69.5	55.5	51.2	63.1	61.1	59.8	62.8	62.9	41.4	63.5	61.5	75.8	45.3
April	60.3	62.3	60.0	70.7	55.5	51.3	62.9	61.3	60.0	63.0	63.1	41.5	63.5	63.9	79.0	46.5
May	60.4	62.4	60.0	70.6	55.5	51.3	62.9	61.5	60.3	63.2	63.5	41.3	64.3	63.6	77.8	47.4
June	60.5	62.8	60.1	69.8	56.0	51.9	63.3	61.8	60.8	63.7	63.7	41.5	66.0	65.2	79.9	48.3
July	60.7	63.1	60.3	69.5	56.4	52.4	63.4	62.1	61.1	64.2	64.1	41.9	66.8	64.8	77.7	50.0
August	60.9	63.5	60.4	68.9	56.8	52.9	63.8	62.5	61.3	64.4	64.5	42.3	67.0	63.6	76.1	49.4
September	61.1	63.9	60.5	68.5	57.2	53.1	64.4	62.9	61.9	64.9	65.1	42.9	68.3	63.4	75.6	49.5
October	61.4	64.1	60.9	68.7	57.7	53.7	64.7	63.1	62.0	65.0	65.6	43.2	67.7	63.0	74.0	50.5
November	61.9	64.6	61.4	68.6	58.4	54.6	65.2	63.4	62.4	65.4	66.1	43.9	67.4	63.7	73.9	51.3
December	62.4	64.9	61.9	70.1	58.4	54.5	65.3	64.0	62.8	65.7	66.7	44.2	68.3	64.5	76.8	50.3
1977:																
January	62.5	65.1	62.1	70.2	58.6	54.7	65.6	64.0	63.0	65.7	66.8	44.8	68.6	64.3	77.6	49.1
February	63.2	65.4	62.8	71.5	59.2	55.4	65.9	64.3	63.3	65.8	66.7	46.0	68.8	65.7	78.6	50.9
March	63.7	65.7	63.4	72.6	59.5	55.8	66.2	64.7	63.9	66.3	67.3	46.6	69.0	66.6	79.9	51.4
April	64.0	65.9	63.7	72.8	59.9	56.2	66.3	65.0	64.4	66.6	67.7	47.2	70.3	68.3	82.6	51.9
May	64.4	66.1	64.2	73.7	60.1	56.5	66.6	65.3	64.9	67.1	68.2	47.5	70.8	67.6	81.0	52.4
June	64.6	66.5	64.2	73.2	60.4	56.7	67.0	65.7	64.9	67.3	68.7	47.8	70.0	65.5	77.6	51.5
July	64.8	66.8	64.5	73.7	60.6	56.9	67.2	66.0	65.1	67.7	69.5	48.2	68.5	64.7	76.4	51.3
August	65.2	67.3	64.8	74.1	60.9	57.1	67.8	66.6	65.4	68.0	70.1	48.5	68.8	63.9	74.3	51.8
September	65.5	67.8	65.0	73.7	61.4	57.5	68.4	67.0	65.7	68.3	71.1	48.7	68.9	63.7	73.8	52.1
October	65.9	68.2	65.3	73.9	61.7	57.7	68.9	67.6	65.8	68.4	71.3	49.1	68.7	64.0	74.4	52.1
November	66.4	68.8	65.8	74.6	62.2	58.1	69.4	68.1	66.3	68.8	71.5	49.2	69.9	65.4	76.6	52.5
December	66.7	69.0	66.1	74.9	62.4	58.3	69.6	68.6	66.6	69.1	72.1	49.3	69.9	66.4	77.7	53.5
1978:																
January	67.0	69.2	66.4	75.6	62.6	58.4	70.0	68.8	66.9	69.3	72.8	49.5	70.3	67.3	79.3	53.6
February	67.5	69.5	66.9	77.1	62.6	58.4	70.3	69.1	67.4	69.7	73.7	49.4	70.3	68.4	81.2	53.7
March	67.8	69.9	67.3	77.6	63.0	58.6	70.8	69.6	67.8	70.2	74.2	49.3	71.2	69.8	83.5	54.1
April	68.6	70.6	68.2	79.1	63.6	58.8	72.3	69.9	68.1	70.7	74.9	49.1	71.5	72.1	86.9	55.3
May	69.1	71.1	68.6	79.4	64.1	59.0	73.0	70.5	68.7	71.2	75.6	49.6	72.3	72.8	87.4	56.2
June	69.7	71.7	69.3	80.5	64.6	59.5	73.5	71.0	69.2	71.7	76.4	50.2	72.5	74.6	89.8	57.4
July	70.3	72.3	69.9	80.7	65.2	60.0	74.5	71.5	69.4	72.0	76.8	49.6	72.9	74.2	88.1	58.3
August	70.4	72.8	69.9	80.0	65.6	60.2	75.2	72.0	69.9	72.6	77.5	49.5	73.7	73.7	86.8	58.6
September	71.1	73.5	70.6	80.8	66.3	60.7	76.1	72.6	70.5	73.2	77.9	49.8	74.1	75.1	88.7	59.5
October	71.4	73.4	71.0	82.2	66.3	61.3	75.3	72.8	71.3	74.0	78.6	50.4	75.0	77.0	91.4	60.4
November	72.0	74.1	71.5	82.4	66.9	62.0	75.6	73.5	71.9	74.6	79.6	51.0	75.3	77.4	91.6	61.1
December	72.8	74.7	72.5	83.6	67.7	62.7	76.6	74.0	72.4	75.0	79.8	51.5	76.1	78.0	92.4	61.7
1979:																
January	73.7	75.3	73.3	85.0	68.4	63.3	77.4	74.5	73.1	76.0	80.9	51.8	76.5	80.1	95.8	62.0
February	74.4	75.9	74.2	86.5	69.0	63.8	78.2	75.2	73.7	76.6	81.4	52.0	77.4	82.1	98.4	63.5
March	75.0	76.4	74.8	87.2	69.6	64.4	78.8	75.7	74.6	77.6	82.1	52.9	77.6	83.8	100.0	65.2
April	75.8	77.0	75.6	87.6	70.5	65.5	79.2	76.4	75.7	78.8	82.9	54.7	78.0	84.4	100.7	65.7
May	76.2	77.4	75.9	86.8	71.4	66.6	79.7	76.8	76.6	79.5	83.4	57.1	78.6	84.7	99.8	67.4
June	76.6	78.0	76.4	85.9	72.4	67.9	80.4	77.3	77.5	80.2	83.7	59.5	79.4	85.6	99.1	70.0
July	77.4	78.5	77.3	86.2	73.6	69.5	80.9	77.8	78.7	81.4	84.2	61.9	80.9	86.5	100.5	70.3
August	78.2	78.8	78.3	86.7	74.7	71.4	80.7	77.8	79.8	82.1	84.8	65.2	81.3	85.5	98.6	70.6
September	79.5	79.7	79.8	87.8	76.4	73.1	82.4	78.7	81.1	83.1	86.0	68.3	82.0	87.9	100.9	73.0
October	80.4	80.4	80.6	87.8	77.7	74.6	83.2	79.2	82.4	84.2	87.1	70.8	83.1	88.8	101.1	74.6
November	81.4	81.0	81.8	89.5	78.6	75.6	84.1	79.8	83.2	85.1	87.1	72.4	83.3	90.0	102.0	76.1
December	82.2	81.7	82.6	90.0	79.5	76.6	84.8	80.6	84.0	86.0	87.1	73.4	84.3	91.2	102.9	77.7
1980:																
January	83.4	83.3	83.9	89.5	81.6	78.3	87.6	81.7	86.0	88.2	88.1	76.8	84.7	90.9	100.0	80.2
February	84.6	84.2	85.2	89.3	83.6	80.6	89.0	82.3	87.6	89.5	89.2	80.0	87.1	92.6	101.8	81.9
March	85.5	84.7	86.1	90.0	84.7	82.4	88.7	83.1	88.2	89.5	90.3	82.5	87.8	90.8	99.1	81.2
April	86.2	85.5	86.7	88.6	86.1	84.6	89.1	84.4	88.5	89.6	89.8	84.0	87.8	88.3	94.0	81.7
May	86.6	85.7	87.1	89.1	86.4	85.0	89.0	84.6	89.0	90.4	89.9	84.2	88.2	89.5	96.3	81.5
June	87.3	86.6	87.9	89.8	87.2	85.6	90.3	85.1	89.8	91.3	90.7	84.7	88.6	90.1	97.1	81.8
July	88.7	87.7	89.4	92.8	88.1	86.2	91.7	86.2	90.5	91.6	91.6	86.2	90.1	94.6	104.2	83.4
August	89.7	88.4	90.5	95.2	88.6	86.7	92.2	87.0	91.5	92.8	92.2	86.4	91.3	99.0	110.9	85.3
September	90.1	88.8	90.8	95.3	89.0	87.0	92.8	87.5	91.9	92.9	92.6	87.3	92.3	100.4	111.9	87.1
October	90.8	89.6	91.3	96.1	89.5	87.4	93.5	88.8	92.8	94.2	93.1	87.4	92.8	102.2	113.9	88.6
November	91.4	90.1	92.0	96.5	90.2	88.3	93.7	89.3	93.5	94.9	93.9	88.9	93.8	103.5	114.6	90.6
December	91.8	90.4	92.4	96.6	90.7	89.3	93.7	89.7	94.4	95.5	94.8	91.5	93.8	102.7	111.7	92.3

PRODUCER PRICE INDEXES—Continued
(By stage of processing—1982=100, seasonally adjusted)

YEAR AND MONTH	Finished goods								Intermediate materials, supplies, and components					Crude materials for further processing		
	Total	Total less foods and energy	Consumer goods					Capital equipment	Total	Materials and components for manufacturing	Materials and components for construction	Processed fuels and lubricants	Supplies	Total	Foodstuffs and feedstuffs	Nonfood materials
			Total	Foods	Consumer goods, except foods											
					Total	Nondurable goods, except foods	Durable goods									
1981:																
January	92.8	91.4	93.3	96.8	92.0	91.0	93.9	90.8	95.6	96.3	95.4	94.0	94.6	103.4	111.1	94.4
February	93.6	92.0	94.1	96.5	93.1	92.5	94.4	91.7	96.1	96.5	95.2	96.7	94.6	104.2	107.6	100.1
March	94.7	92.6	95.3	97.2	94.6	94.6	94.6	92.4	97.1	97.1	96.0	100.6	95.1	103.8	106.0	101.1
April	95.7	93.5	96.4	97.2	96.1	96.4	95.5	93.1	98.3	97.8	97.6	103.1	96.2	104.2	105.6	102.4
May	96.0	94.0	96.6	97.4	96.2	96.2	96.2	93.8	98.7	98.2	97.9	103.3	97.0	103.8	103.8	103.7
June	96.5	94.6	97.0	98.0	96.6	96.5	96.6	94.4	99.0	98.7	98.4	102.4	97.4	104.9	105.8	103.8
July	96.7	94.8	97.1	99.0	96.4	96.3	96.4	95.0	99.2	99.4	98.7	100.9	97.8	105.0	105.6	104.0
August	96.8	95.3	97.1	98.9	96.4	96.3	96.7	95.4	99.7	100.0	98.8	101.6	97.9	104.0	104.6	103.1
September	97.2	95.9	97.5	98.7	97.1	97.0	97.2	96.1	99.7	100.1	98.8	101.2	97.9	102.7	102.2	103.1
October	97.6	96.5	97.8	98.5	97.5	97.1	98.1	96.9	99.8	100.0	99.2	101.1	98.1	101.2	100.5	101.8
November	97.9	97.0	98.0	98.1	98.0	97.6	98.7	97.5	99.9	100.2	99.4	101.1	98.2	99.7	98.2	101.3
December	98.3	97.6	98.4	98.1	98.5	98.3	98.9	98.1	100.0	100.2	99.6	101.3	98.7	98.8	96.1	101.7
1982:																
January	98.9	98.1	99.0	98.9	99.0	98.9	99.1	98.6	100.4	100.0	99.7	102.7	99.0	99.7	99.2	100.4
February	98.8	98.1	99.0	99.2	98.8	99.0	98.4	98.2	100.3	100.3	99.6	101.2	99.4	100.0	100.1	99.8
March	98.8	98.7	98.8	99.0	98.7	98.5	98.9	98.7	99.9	100.2	99.7	99.7	99.6	99.7	100.4	98.9
April	99.0	99.0	98.9	100.2	98.4	98.1	98.9	99.0	99.7	100.2	99.6	98.6	99.8	100.2	101.9	98.4
May	99.0	99.4	98.8	100.9	98.0	97.3	99.3	99.5	99.7	100.4	99.7	97.3	100.4	101.9	104.4	99.2
June	99.8	99.9	99.8	101.6	99.0	98.5	99.9	100.0	99.8	100.1	100.1	98.4	100.6	101.8	104.0	99.5
July	100.2	100.1	100.1	100.1	100.1	100.1	100.2	100.3	100.0	99.8	100.0	100.6	100.4	100.7	101.1	100.3
August	100.6	100.6	100.5	100.1	100.7	100.8	100.7	100.7	99.9	99.6	99.7	100.9	100.2	99.8	99.6	100.0
September	100.7	100.8	100.7	100.1	100.9	101.1	100.6	101.0	100.0	99.9	100.4	99.5	100.1	99.2	98.1	100.3
October	101.0	101.3	101.0	100.0	101.3	101.6	100.9	101.1	99.9	99.9	100.4	99.7	100.1	98.7	97.1	100.5
November	101.4	101.6	101.4	100.0	102.0	102.4	101.4	101.3	100.1	99.9	100.6	100.2	100.3	99.2	97.2	101.3
December	101.8	102.2	101.7	100.1	102.4	102.8	101.7	101.9	100.1	99.8	100.7	100.5	100.4	98.8	97.3	100.4
1983:																
January	101.0	101.8	100.8	99.6	101.2	101.1	101.7	101.8	99.8	99.8	101.2	98.3	100.4	98.8	97.7	100.1
February	101.1	102.2	100.8	100.3	100.9	100.2	102.4	102.1	100.0	100.5	101.6	96.1	100.6	100.0	100.2	99.8
March	101.0	102.5	100.7	100.5	100.5	99.6	102.5	102.2	99.7	100.1	101.9	95.1	100.7	100.5	100.4	100.7
April	101.1	102.4	100.7	101.1	100.3	99.3	102.5	102.3	99.5	100.3	102.0	92.7	101.0	101.2	102.2	99.9
May	101.4	102.6	101.0	101.1	100.8	99.8	102.8	102.5	99.8	100.5	102.3	93.7	101.1	100.9	101.6	100.1
June	101.6	102.8	101.3	100.7	101.4	100.8	102.9	102.6	100.2	100.8	102.6	95.2	101.3	100.5	100.3	100.6
July	101.6	103.1	101.3	100.2	101.5	100.8	103.1	102.8	100.5	101.4	102.9	95.0	101.4	99.5	98.5	100.6
August	101.9	103.5	101.6	100.6	101.8	101.2	103.3	103.1	100.9	101.6	103.0	95.5	102.2	102.2	103.1	101.2
September	102.2	103.5	101.8	101.5	101.8	101.1	103.3	103.3	101.6	102.3	103.4	96.3	103.1	103.3	104.9	101.6
October	102.2	103.6	101.9	102.4	101.5	101.0	102.8	103.4	101.7	102.3	103.7	97.0	103.2	103.2	105.2	101.0
November	102.0	103.8	101.5	101.6	101.3	100.5	103.2	103.5	101.8	102.5	104.0	95.6	103.5	102.3	103.2	101.3
December	102.3	104.1	101.9	102.3	101.5	100.6	103.5	103.8	101.9	102.9	104.2	94.8	103.6	103.5	104.9	101.9
1984:																
January	103.0	104.5	102.7	104.8	101.6	100.6	103.7	104.1	102.1	103.2	104.2	94.6	103.8	104.6	106.8	102.2
February	103.4	104.7	103.1	105.3	101.9	101.0	103.9	104.5	102.5	103.5	104.8	95.5	103.8	103.8	104.5	103.0
March	103.8	105.2	103.6	106.2	102.2	101.1	104.5	104.6	103.0	104.2	105.3	95.8	104.1	105.7	108.4	102.8
April	103.9	105.3	103.5	105.2	102.5	101.6	104.4	105.3	103.2	104.4	105.4	96.2	104.2	105.2	107.0	103.1
May	103.8	105.3	103.5	104.7	102.7	102.0	104.4	105.1	103.4	104.5	105.3	97.2	104.3	104.5	105.3	103.6
June	103.8	105.5	103.4	104.5	102.6	101.9	104.4	105.2	103.6	104.6	105.4	97.5	104.3	103.3	103.3	103.2
July	104.0	105.7	103.6	105.9	102.3	101.3	104.6	105.5	103.4	104.5	105.7	96.4	104.1	104.0	105.2	102.8
August	103.8	105.9	103.3	105.8	102.0	100.7	104.7	105.6	103.2	104.4	106.0	95.0	104.5	103.3	104.0	102.4
September	103.8	106.2	103.2	105.5	101.9	100.4	105.0	105.9	103.1	104.1	106.2	94.9	104.2	102.8	103.5	102.1
October	103.6	105.9	103.1	105.2	101.9	100.9	104.2	105.6	103.2	104.0	106.4	95.2	104.2	101.5	101.5	101.4
November	104.0	106.2	103.4	105.6	102.2	101.1	104.7	105.8	103.3	104.2	106.5	95.2	104.0	101.9	103.3	100.4
December	104.0	106.3	103.5	105.6	102.3	101.0	105.0	105.6	103.2	104.1	106.7	94.7	104.1	101.4	102.9	99.8
1985:																
January	104.0	106.9	103.4	105.4	102.3	100.6	105.7	106.3	103.1	103.9	106.8	94.5	104.3	99.9	101.2	98.5
February	104.1	107.3	103.4	106.0	102.0	100.0	105.9	106.9	102.8	103.7	106.7	92.9	104.4	99.4	100.5	98.1
March	104.1	107.6	103.3	105.4	102.1	100.2	106.0	107.1	102.7	103.5	106.6	92.5	104.4	97.6	97.8	97.4
April	104.6	107.6	103.9	104.8	103.3	101.9	106.1	107.1	102.9	103.6	106.6	94.4	104.1	96.7	95.8	97.8
May	104.9	107.8	104.2	103.8	104.1	103.0	106.5	107.4	103.2	103.5	107.4	95.6	104.1	95.8	93.6	98.1
June	104.6	108.2	103.8	103.7	103.6	102.0	106.8	107.6	102.6	103.5	107.9	91.7	104.1	95.2	93.5	97.1
July	104.7	108.4	103.8	103.4	103.4	101.6	106.9	107.7	102.3	103.3	107.7	90.6	104.3	94.9	92.9	97.1
August	104.5	108.5	103.6	103.8	103.3	101.4	107.1	107.9	102.3	103.2	107.7	90.4	104.5	92.9	89.9	96.1
September	103.8	107.9	102.9	102.5	102.9	101.6	105.6	107.2	102.2	103.1	107.5	90.5	104.6	91.8	87.9	96.0
October	104.9	108.9	103.9	103.9	103.7	102.1	107.0	108.3	102.3	102.9	107.6	91.3	104.8	94.1	92.2	96.1
November	105.5	109.1	104.6	105.3	104.1	102.5	107.3	108.5	102.5	102.9	107.6	92.5	104.9	95.7	96.0	95.4
December	106.0	109.1	105.3	106.1	104.6	103.4	107.4	108.6	102.9	103.0	107.8	94.3	105.0	95.5	95.9	95.1
1986:																
January	105.5	109.3	104.6	105.8	103.8	102.2	107.1	108.6	102.4	102.6	107.8	92.0	105.2	94.2	93.3	95.2
February	104.1	109.5	102.8	104.8	101.6	98.8	107.4	108.7	101.2	102.3	107.9	85.5	105.3	90.5	91.8	89.2
March	102.8	109.6	101.0	104.8	99.1	94.9	107.6	108.9	99.9	102.3	107.8	77.6	105.5	88.2	91.0	85.1
April	102.3	110.1	100.3	105.0	97.9	92.7	108.4	109.2	98.9	101.9	108.2	73.0	105.5	85.6	89.0	82.0
May	102.8	110.2	101.0	106.1	98.4	93.4	108.4	109.3	98.7	101.7	108.2	71.7	105.4	86.5	91.2	81.5
June	103.1	110.5	101.2	106.2	98.7	93.8	108.6	109.6	98.6	101.7	108.1	71.2	105.6	86.2	90.9	81.1
July	102.3	110.7	100.2	107.6	96.5	90.3	108.9	109.7	98.0	101.9	108.0	66.7	105.6	86.4	93.5	78.3
August	102.7	110.8	100.7	109.5	96.4	90.2	108.9	109.8	98.0	102.1	108.0	65.7	105.8	86.7	96.3	75.8
September	102.9	110.7	100.9	109.0	97.0	91.3	108.4	109.7	98.5	102.3	108.2	68.1	105.8	86.6	94.9	77.1
October	103.5	111.8	101.5	109.8	97.4	90.7	110.7	110.6	98.3	102.4	108.2	66.8	105.6	87.4	95.9	77.7
November	103.4	112.0	101.4	109.5	97.4	90.6	110.9	110.8	98.3	102.5	108.3	66.7	105.8	87.6	96.0	78.2
December	103.6	112.1	101.5	109.3	97.7	91.0	111.1	110.9	98.5	102.5	108.1	67.5	105.9	86.9	94.4	78.3

PRODUCER PRICE INDEXES—Continued
(By stage of processing—1982=100, seasonally adjusted)

YEAR AND MONTH	Finished goods								Intermediate materials, supplies, and components					Crude materials for further processing		
			Consumer goods													
					Consumer goods, except foods					Materials and components for manufacturing	Materials and components for construction	Processed fuels and lubricants	Supplies			
	Total	Total less foods and energy	Total	Foods	Total	Nondurable goods, except foods	Durable goods	Capital equipment	Total					Total	Foodstuffs and feedstuffs	Nonfood materials
1987:																
January	104.1	112.5	102.1	108.0	99.2	92.7	111.5	111.3	99.0	102.8	108.1	69.5	106.1	89.3	92.6	83.2
February	104.4	112.3	102.5	108.6	99.5	93.5	110.5	111.1	99.8	103.1	108.3	71.7	106.5	90.2	93.6	84.1
March	104.5	112.4	102.6	108.3	99.8	94.0	110.7	111.1	99.9	103.4	108.4	71.5	106.5	90.5	93.1	84.8
April	105.1	112.9	103.3	109.6	100.2	94.3	111.4	111.6	100.3	103.9	108.5	72.0	106.8	92.5	97.4	85.4
May	105.2	113.0	103.4	110.5	100.0	94.0	111.3	111.6	100.8	104.5	108.7	72.8	107.3	93.8	99.1	86.3
June	105.5	113.1	103.8	110.4	100.5	94.7	111.3	111.5	101.4	105.1	109.2	73.7	107.5	94.5	98.2	87.9
July	105.7	113.3	104.0	110.2	100.9	95.3	111.5	111.7	101.9	105.5	109.7	75.1	107.7	95.6	97.1	90.3
August	105.9	113.6	104.2	109.4	101.4	96.2	111.6	112.0	102.4	105.9	110.2	76.2	107.8	96.5	96.8	91.9
September	106.2	113.9	104.5	110.3	101.0	96.0	112.0	112.0	102.6	106.4	110.8	74.7	108.2	96.0	97.4	90.8
October	106.0	114.0	104.4	109.9	102.1	96.0	112.0	112.0	103.1	107.2	111.3	74.5	108.8	95.8	97.3	90.6
November	106.0	114.2	104.3	109.9	101.8	95.9	112.0	112.1	103.5	107.6	112.0	74.3	109.5	95.1	96.2	90.1
December	105.8	114.3	104.1	109.1	101.8	96.1	111.6	112.2	103.8	108.3	112.6	73.3	110.0	94.9	96.9	89.3
1988:																
January	106.4	115.0	104.6	110.7	101.6	95.8	112.4	112.8	104.1	109.4	113.7	70.6	110.5	94.2	98.5	87.3
February	106.3	115.3	104.4	109.9	101.8	95.9	112.6	113.0	104.4	109.9	113.9	70.7	110.7	95.2	100.7	87.5
March	106.6	115.6	104.7	110.3	102.0	96.1	112.7	113.2	104.8	110.5	114.3	70.4	111.1	94.1	99.8	86.3
April	107.0	115.9	105.2	110.4	102.7	97.1	112.8	113.5	105.5	111.5	114.8	70.8	111.8	95.4	100.9	87.8
May	107.2	116.2	105.4	110.7	102.8	97.1	113.2	113.8	106.2	112.2	115.2	71.4	112.2	95.8	101.3	88.1
June	107.5	116.6	105.7	111.7	102.8	97.0	113.3	114.0	107.4	112.9	115.7	74.1	113.7	97.0	106.3	87.0
July	108.4	117.2	106.6	113.0	103.5	97.9	113.9	114.4	108.3	114.1	116.4	74.1	115.1	96.7	108.4	85.2
August	108.8	117.7	107.1	113.7	103.8	97.9	114.6	114.9	108.5	114.5	116.7	73.6	115.1	97.0	110.5	84.5
September	109.0	118.1	107.3	115.3	103.4	97.3	114.8	115.2	108.7	115.0	117.1	72.4	115.6	97.0	112.9	83.0
October	109.2	118.4	107.5	114.9	103.8	97.8	115.0	115.5	108.6	115.4	117.7	69.3	116.0	96.6	113.6	82.0
November	109.6	118.7	107.9	115.1	104.3	98.5	115.1	115.7	108.8	116.2	118.3	68.1	116.2	95.2	109.7	82.1
December	110.0	119.2	108.3	115.7	104.7	98.8	115.5	116.1	109.4	117.0	118.9	69.2	116.3	98.1	111.3	85.6
1989:																
January	111.1	119.9	109.5	116.9	105.9	100.2	116.3	116.9	110.8	117.8	119.5	72.6	117.2	102.0	114.1	90.1
February	111.9	120.5	110.5	117.6	106.9	101.4	116.7	117.3	111.3	118.3	120.0	73.6	117.5	101.7	112.2	90.7
March	112.3	120.7	110.9	118.2	107.4	102.1	116.6	117.5	111.9	118.6	120.4	75.2	118.1	102.9	113.2	92.0
April	113.1	120.8	111.9	117.8	109.0	104.5	116.5	117.6	112.5	118.7	120.7	78.4	118.1	104.1	111.2	95.1
May	114.0	121.6	112.9	118.3	110.3	105.9	117.2	118.3	112.6	118.8	121.1	78.5	118.1	104.5	110.9	95.9
June	114.0	122.2	112.7	118.0	110.1	105.5	117.7	118.9	112.5	118.5	121.4	78.2	118.0	103.2	109.4	94.7
July	113.8	122.1	112.4	118.4	109.5	104.8	117.2	118.9	112.2	118.2	121.5	77.2	118.3	103.5	108.9	95.5
August	113.4	122.7	111.7	118.7	108.3	102.9	117.9	119.3	111.8	117.9	121.7	75.5	118.3	101.2	110.1	91.2
September	114.0	123.1	112.5	118.7	109.4	104.1	118.7	119.7	112.1	117.8	122.0	76.4	118.5	102.5	109.6	93.5
October	114.6	123.5	113.1	119.9	109.8	104.6	118.6	120.0	112.2	117.9	122.5	76.8	118.4	102.7	109.3	94.0
November	114.8	123.9	113.2	120.5	109.6	104.4	118.7	120.4	112.0	117.8	122.3	76.1	118.4	103.5	112.2	93.6
December	115.5	124.2	114.1	121.8	110.3	105.2	119.1	120.6	112.2	117.5	122.1	78.0	118.4	105.1	114.6	94.5
1990:																
January	117.7	124.5	116.9	124.2	113.3	109.5	118.7	121.0	113.7	117.7	121.9	85.9	118.7	106.7	114.6	97.0
February	117.6	124.9	116.7	124.9	112.7	108.5	119.0	121.4	112.8	117.5	121.9	81.5	118.4	106.8	114.6	97.2
March	117.5	125.3	116.3	124.5	112.4	108.0	119.1	121.8	112.9	117.8	122.4	80.4	118.6	105.1	114.1	94.8
April	117.4	125.5	116.1	123.3	112.6	108.2	119.4	122.1	113.1	118.1	122.9	80.3	118.8	102.7	114.3	91.1
May	117.5	126.0	116.3	123.8	112.5	108.1	119.5	122.1	113.1	118.3	123.0	79.0	119.4	103.1	113.4	92.3
June	117.6	126.4	116.3	123.6	112.8	108.0	120.5	122.5	112.9	118.3	122.7	78.4	119.2	100.6	113.5	88.2
July	117.9	126.6	116.6	124.5	112.7	107.9	120.7	122.9	112.8	118.4	122.9	76.9	119.6	101.0	114.4	88.3
August	119.2	127.1	118.2	124.7	115.0	111.0	120.8	123.3	114.0	118.6	123.0	83.5	119.4	110.5	113.1	103.9
September	120.7	127.7	120.0	124.3	117.9	114.5	121.9	123.8	115.8	119.3	123.4	90.9	119.8	115.8	111.7	113.1
October	121.9	128.0	121.5	124.7	120.0	117.6	121.5	124.1	117.4	120.0	123.5	97.7	120.1	125.8	112.3	128.3
November	122.6	128.4	122.3	125.4	120.7	118.4	122.0	124.5	117.7	120.2	123.6	98.2	120.3	117.8	111.3	116.4
December	122.0	128.6	121.4	124.7	119.8	117.0	122.4	124.8	116.9	119.9	123.7	94.3	120.5	110.8	109.5	106.6
1991:																
January	122.6	129.5	122.0	125.0	120.5	117.8	123.0	125.6	116.9	119.9	124.0	93.7	120.9	113.3	108.3	110.9
February	121.8	129.8	120.8	124.7	118.9	115.5	123.4	125.8	115.9	119.5	123.8	89.8	121.1	104.1	107.3	98.0
March	121.3	130.1	120.2	125.0	117.9	114.0	123.7	126.0	114.7	118.8	123.9	85.1	121.2	100.5	108.0	92.3
April	121.3	130.4	120.2	125.2	117.8	114.0	123.7	126.1	114.2	118.5	124.2	83.7	121.3	100.2	107.7	92.0
May	121.6	130.6	120.4	125.3	118.1	114.5	123.4	126.5	114.1	118.0	124.4	84.0	121.3	100.9	105.8	94.0
June	121.4	130.7	120.1	124.9	117.8	114.1	123.4	126.6	113.9	117.8	125.1	83.4	121.4	99.2	105.9	91.3
July	121.1	131.0	119.6	124.3	117.4	113.5	123.4	126.7	113.6	117.4	125.3	82.5	121.2	99.4	104.7	92.3
August	121.3	131.3	119.9	123.0	118.3	114.7	123.6	126.8	113.8	117.3	124.7	83.7	121.6	99.1	102.7	93.0
September	121.5	131.8	120.1	122.8	118.7	115.0	124.2	127.2	114.0	117.3	124.8	84.7	121.7	98.4	104.1	91.2
October	121.9	132.3	120.5	123.1	119.2	115.4	124.9	127.6	114.0	117.5	124.6	84.1	121.6	100.8	104.9	94.3
November	122.4	132.5	121.0	123.4	119.8	116.2	124.9	127.8	114.1	117.4	124.5	84.7	121.8	100.7	103.9	94.7
December	122.3	132.6	120.8	122.8	119.8	116.1	125.0	128.0	114.0	117.4	124.6	84.7	121.8	98.2	102.6	91.6
1992:																
January	122.0	133.0	120.4	122.8	119.1	115.2	125.2	128.2	113.4	117.2	124.9	81.5	122.0	97.2	104.5	88.9
February	122.3	133.1	120.8	123.5	119.4	115.7	124.9	128.3	113.8	117.4	125.8	82.6	122.0	98.6	106.1	90.1
March	122.4	133.4	120.8	123.1	119.6	115.7	125.4	128.6	113.9	117.4	126.5	82.0	122.3	97.1	105.4	88.1
April	122.5	133.8	120.9	122.6	119.9	116.2	125.6	129.0	114.1	117.6	126.6	82.5	122.4	98.1	104.1	90.5
May	122.9	134.3	121.4	122.5	120.7	117.2	125.7	129.0	114.5	117.8	126.6	83.9	122.6	100.3	106.2	92.6
June	123.4	134.1	121.9	122.9	121.3	118.1	125.5	129.0	115.1	118.2	126.3	86.4	122.7	101.6	106.4	94.7
July	123.3	134.3	121.9	122.7	121.3	118.0	125.8	129.1	115.2	118.2	126.3	86.6	122.7	101.6	105.0	95.6
August	123.4	134.3	121.9	123.3	121.1	117.6	126.0	129.4	115.1	118.3	126.4	86.0	122.8	100.7	103.9	94.7
September	123.7	134.6	122.3	123.5	121.5	118.3	125.8	129.4	115.3	118.4	126.9	86.2	123.1	102.8	103.9	98.0
October	124.2	134.9	122.8	123.9	122.0	119.0	126.0	129.7	115.3	118.2	126.9	86.6	123.3	102.8	105.8	96.9
November	124.1	135.1	122.6	123.8	121.9	118.6	126.3	129.9	115.1	118.1	127.1	85.3	123.4	102.5	104.3	97.4
December	124.2	135.2	122.7	124.7	121.7	118.3	126.4	130.1	115.1	118.1	127.9	84.8	123.6	101.3	105.4	94.8

YEAR AND MONTH	Money stock measures[1]				Selected components					
	M1	M2	M3	L	Currency	Demand deposits	Other checkable deposits	Savings deposits	Small time deposits	Large time deposits
1969:										
January	198.7	569.3	607.9	732.8	43.1	154.7	0.1	268.7	102.0	35.8
February	199.3	571.9	609.1	736.7	43.4	155.1	0.1	268.2	104.4	34.3
March	200.0	574.4	610.8	741.0	43.6	155.5	0.1	268.9	105.4	33.5
April	200.7	575.7	611.5	743.9	43.8	156.1	0.1	267.9	107.1	32.8
May	200.8	576.5	611.6	744.4	43.9	156.0	0.1	267.4	108.3	32.1
June	201.3	578.5	612.1	746.8	44.2	156.2	0.1	267.9	109.3	30.8
July	201.7	579.5	610.0	746.3	44.5	156.3	0.1	265.9	111.9	27.7
August	201.7	580.1	607.7	746.7	44.7	156.2	0.1	264.4	113.9	24.8
September	202.1	582.1	608.5	750.5	44.9	156.3	0.1	264.5	115.4	23.7
October	202.9	583.4	608.9	752.7	45.2	156.8	0.1	263.5	117.1	22.5
November	203.6	585.4	613.5	759.7	45.5	157.2	0.1	263.3	118.5	21.3
December	203.9	587.9	615.9	764.4	45.7	157.3	0.2	263.6	120.4	20.4
1970:										
January	206.2	589.6	616.2	767.6	46.0	159.4	0.1	262.7	120.6	19.1
February	205.0	586.4	613.3	766.6	46.1	158.0	0.2	257.9	123.4	19.3
March	205.8	587.3	615.8	769.7	46.3	158.5	0.2	254.4	127.0	20.7
April	206.7	588.3	619.5	773.1	46.5	159.3	0.2	251.4	130.2	24.1
May	207.2	591.5	624.1	778.4	46.9	159.4	0.2	250.1	134.1	25.4
June	207.5	595.2	627.0	778.9	47.2	159.5	0.2	250.4	137.2	25.1
July	208.0	599.1	635.7	786.3	47.4	159.7	0.2	251.5	139.7	30.8
August	209.9	604.9	644.9	793.4	47.6	161.3	0.2	252.9	142.1	34.5
September	211.8	611.2	654.4	799.0	47.9	163.0	0.2	255.1	144.3	37.8
October	212.9	616.4	662.3	806.0	48.1	163.8	0.1	257.0	146.6	40.3
November	213.7	621.1	669.3	810.4	48.3	164.3	0.1	258.8	148.8	42.8
December	214.4	626.6	677.2	814.8	48.6	164.8	0.1	260.9	151.2	45.1
1971:										
January	215.5	632.9	685.6	823.3	48.9	165.6	0.1	263.6	153.8	47.1
February	217.4	641.0	695.8	830.7	49.2	167.1	0.2	266.1	157.5	49.4
March	218.8	649.9	706.6	838.2	49.4	168.2	0.2	269.4	161.7	51.0
April	220.0	658.4	713.7	845.1	49.7	169.1	0.2	272.6	165.8	48.9
May	222.0	666.7	723.2	852.4	50.0	170.9	0.2	275.7	169.0	49.8
June	223.4	672.9	730.1	858.1	50.4	171.9	0.2	278.2	171.3	51.0
July	224.9	679.6	738.3	869.0	50.9	172.8	0.2	280.8	174.0	52.3
August	225.6	685.5	744.1	874.7	51.2	173.2	0.2	283.4	176.6	52.0
September	226.5	692.5	751.7	881.1	51.4	173.8	0.2	286.0	180.0	52.4
October	227.2	698.4	760.2	888.6	51.7	174.3	0.2	288.2	183.0	54.6
November	227.8	704.6	768.3	895.0	51.8	174.7	0.2	290.3	186.6	55.9
December	228.3	710.2	776.0	902.6	52.0	175.1	0.2	292.2	189.8	57.6
1972:										
January	230.1	717.7	783.8	911.6	52.3	176.6	0.2	294.7	192.9	58.3
February	232.3	725.7	792.9	920.9	52.7	178.4	0.2	297.2	196.2	59.2
March	234.3	733.5	800.6	930.2	53.0	180.1	0.2	299.5	199.8	58.8
April	235.6	738.4	807.9	937.8	53.1	181.2	0.2	301.1	201.7	60.5
May	235.9	743.3	815.9	946.3	53.4	181.2	0.2	302.7	204.8	63.9
June	236.7	749.7	824.6	955.5	53.7	181.7	0.2	304.9	208.1	65.4
July	238.8	759.5	835.5	965.9	54.0	183.4	0.2	307.7	213.0	66.0
August	240.9	768.7	846.6	976.1	54.4	185.3	0.2	311.1	216.6	67.5
September	243.2	778.3	856.4	987.1	54.8	187.0	0.2	314.3	221.0	68.4
October	245.0	786.9	865.8	998.5	55.3	188.4	0.2	316.6	225.3	69.2
November	246.4	793.9	875.8	1 010.7	55.7	189.3	0.2	319.2	228.4	71.7
December	249.2	802.3	886.0	1 022.9	56.2	191.6	0.2	321.4	231.7	73.3
1973:										
January	251.5	810.3	896.3	1 034.6	56.6	193.4	0.2	322.7	236.2	74.3
February	252.2	814.1	906.1	1 045.0	56.8	193.8	0.3	323.0	238.9	79.3
March	251.6	815.3	915.0	1 054.9	57.2	192.9	0.3	323.6	240.1	86.9
April	252.8	819.7	922.5	1 064.3	57.8	193.4	0.3	323.8	243.1	90.2
May	254.9	826.8	932.1	1 076.6	58.1	195.2	0.3	325.1	246.8	92.7
June	256.7	833.2	940.7	1 087.4	58.5	196.6	0.3	326.6	250.0	93.4
July	257.5	836.5	950.3	1 097.5	58.8	197.1	0.3	327.4	251.6	98.0
August	257.8	838.8	959.0	1 108.7	59.1	197.0	0.3	325.8	255.1	104.0
September	257.9	839.3	965.8	1 117.7	59.6	196.7	0.3	325.1	256.4	109.0
October	259.0	842.6	972.0	1 126.6	59.9	197.5	0.3	325.5	258.1	110.4
November	261.0	848.9	977.4	1 133.2	60.3	199.0	0.3	325.9	262.0	110.2
December	262.8	855.5	985.0	1 141.5	60.8	200.3	0.3	326.7	265.8	111.0
1974:										
January	263.8	859.7	994.0	1 154.5	61.3	200.7	0.3	327.5	268.3	115.1
February	265.3	864.2	1 002.4	1 165.4	61.8	201.6	0.3	327.8	271.0	118.4
March	266.7	870.1	1 010.7	1 174.6	62.3	202.5	0.4	328.8	274.6	119.5
April	267.2	873.0	1 020.9	1 186.4	63.0	202.4	0.4	329.6	276.1	126.8
May	267.6	874.6	1 029.0	1 195.9	63.4	202.3	0.4	329.7	277.1	132.7
June	268.4	877.8	1 037.7	1 205.2	63.7	202.8	0.4	330.4	278.7	136.8
July	269.4	881.5	1 044.0	1 213.6	64.1	203.4	0.4	331.7	280.0	139.5
August	270.0	884.1	1 048.4	1 221.3	64.7	203.4	0.4	332.0	281.4	140.9
September	271.1	888.2	1 053.1	1 229.3	65.2	203.9	0.4	332.7	283.5	141.4
October	272.4	893.6	1 058.8	1 236.4	65.8	204.4	0.4	334.3	285.8	142.2
November	273.7	898.8	1 063.9	1 241.9	66.5	205.1	0.4	336.2	287.4	141.7
December	274.3	902.5	1 070.1	1 248.6	67.0	205.2	0.4	338.6	287.9	144.7

1. See NOTES to pages 94-95 for definitions of M1, M2, M3, and L.

YEAR AND MONTH	MONEY STOCK AND SELECTED COMPONENTS—Continued (Averages of daily figures—Billions of dollars, seasonally adjusted)									
	Money stock measures[1]				Selected components					
	M1	M2	M3	L	Currency	Demand deposits	Other checkable deposits	Savings deposits	Small time deposits	Large time deposits
1975:										
January	273.8	906.4	1 076.1	1 254.6	67.4	204.2	0.5	341.0	289.5	147.0
February	274.7	914.1	1 082.5	1 259.0	67.8	204.6	0.5	343.9	293.0	145.7
March	276.6	925.6	1 090.3	1 267.0	68.4	205.8	0.6	348.4	297.9	142.4
April	276.2	935.5	1 096.1	1 274.9	68.5	205.2	0.6	353.5	302.9	137.9
May	278.8	947.8	1 106.2	1 286.1	69.1	207.1	0.6	358.8	307.2	135.8
June	282.4	963.4	1 118.8	1 298.5	70.0	209.8	0.7	365.6	312.3	133.1
July	283.2	975.1	1 128.2	1 310.0	70.5	210.0	0.7	370.6	318.2	130.2
August	284.5	983.9	1 135.2	1 320.0	71.0	210.9	0.7	374.2	322.3	128.6
September	285.5	991.7	1 145.8	1 331.8	71.2	211.5	0.7	377.7	325.6	129.0
October	285.0	997.9	1 153.5	1 342.6	71.7	210.5	0.8	380.6	329.4	130.3
November	287.7	1 008.3	1 164.9	1 357.0	72.3	212.4	0.8	384.6	333.1	131.2
December	287.4	1 017.0	1 172.0	1 366.5	72.8	211.6	0.9	388.8	337.8	129.7
1976:										
January	288.5	1 027.2	1 182.5	1 379.3	73.2	212.2	1.0	394.3	341.6	127.2
February	290.9	1 041.0	1 194.0	1 393.6	73.9	213.7	1.1	402.7	344.8	124.6
March	292.3	1 050.1	1 204.5	1 404.2	74.7	214.1	1.2	408.5	346.6	125.2
April	294.2	1 060.8	1 216.7	1 415.9	75.5	215.0	1.4	413.8	350.3	125.0
May	296.0	1 072.8	1 228.4	1 429.6	76.1	216.0	1.5	418.4	355.8	122.2
June	295.8	1 077.7	1 235.9	1 439.3	76.6	215.2	1.7	420.0	359.4	124.9
July	297.0	1 086.7	1 245.9	1 452.1	77.1	215.6	1.8	423.4	363.7	125.5
August	298.9	1 099.1	1 258.8	1 462.4	77.6	216.9	2.0	428.5	369.3	122.5
September	299.6	1 111.3	1 268.3	1 471.1	78.1	216.8	2.2	433.5	375.8	120.7
October	302.8	1 126.4	1 281.7	1 486.7	78.6	219.3	2.3	439.8	381.4	118.8
November	303.6	1 138.9	1 294.9	1 500.9	79.1	219.4	2.5	447.2	385.7	117.8
December	306.3	1 152.7	1 312.0	1 516.6	79.5	221.6	2.7	453.2	390.7	118.1
1977:										
January	309.1	1 166.7	1 324.3	1 530.2	80.2	223.5	2.8	459.1	396.1	117.6
February	311.5	1 178.2	1 336.2	1 545.7	80.8	225.0	3.0	463.3	401.0	118.3
March	313.5	1 188.8	1 348.6	1 560.7	81.3	226.4	3.1	466.3	406.6	118.5
April	315.9	1 200.2	1 361.1	1 575.5	82.1	228.0	3.1	470.0	411.9	118.8
May	316.5	1 209.0	1 374.0	1 589.4	82.5	228.0	3.2	472.7	417.6	120.3
June	318.0	1 217.7	1 387.3	1 604.7	83.1	228.8	3.3	474.5	423.0	123.4
July	320.4	1 227.7	1 401.0	1 620.2	83.9	230.2	3.5	477.6	427.5	126.1
August	322.0	1 237.6	1 414.7	1 637.8	84.5	231.2	3.6	481.8	431.4	129.5
September	324.3	1 246.8	1 428.1	1 653.1	85.2	232.5	3.7	484.9	435.3	132.2
October	327.3	1 255.7	1 443.0	1 670.7	85.9	234.7	3.9	487.2	438.7	136.5
November	329.2	1 263.7	1 458.2	1 687.3	86.6	235.7	4.0	490.5	441.5	140.9
December	331.3	1 271.5	1 472.5	1 705.4	87.4	236.8	4.2	492.2	445.5	145.2
1978:										
January	334.8	1 280.9	1 487.4	1 723.0	88.0	239.5	4.3	494.6	448.8	149.1
February	335.3	1 286.3	1 498.7	1 735.9	88.7	239.2	4.4	496.4	451.8	153.2
March	336.8	1 292.9	1 513.4	1 751.5	89.4	239.8	4.6	497.5	455.5	158.6
April	339.9	1 301.2	1 529.0	1 769.1	90.0	242.2	4.7	498.6	459.4	164.8
May	343.5	1 310.1	1 543.6	1 783.8	90.8	244.8	4.9	499.7	463.3	170.8
June	345.6	1 318.1	1 554.6	1 795.1	91.5	246.1	4.9	498.4	470.3	173.7
July	347.5	1 324.9	1 567.4	1 810.8	92.0	247.3	5.0	494.2	479.2	177.1
August	349.2	1 334.0	1 582.7	1 828.6	92.7	248.2	5.1	494.4	486.0	180.8
September	353.1	1 346.8	1 598.3	1 848.3	93.6	251.2	5.2	495.1	493.7	182.5
October	354.3	1 354.3	1 612.0	1 864.8	94.4	251.4	5.3	493.4	501.2	184.5
November	356.2	1 360.9	1 631.3	1 889.2	95.2	251.0	6.7	488.8	510.0	191.8
December	358.4	1 368.0	1 646.8	1 911.4	96.0	250.7	8.5	481.9	520.9	195.6
1979:										
January	358.7	1 372.7	1 657.2	1 924.3	96.8	248.6	10.0	472.6	533.3	198.6
February	359.9	1 378.8	1 669.3	1 939.8	97.4	248.1	11.1	466.6	542.9	201.0
March	362.5	1 388.9	1 683.3	1 961.5	98.0	248.8	12.3	463.2	552.3	201.7
April	367.3	1 402.5	1 699.8	1 984.1	98.8	251.7	13.4	459.2	563.3	201.3
May	367.7	1 409.4	1 708.8	2 000.3	99.5	250.8	14.0	455.8	571.2	201.0
June	372.5	1 423.2	1 726.0	2 027.2	100.3	253.9	14.9	456.2	577.7	199.4
July	376.4	1 435.0	1 741.2	2 045.7	101.2	256.1	15.7	456.3	582.9	200.9
August	378.5	1 447.3	1 759.3	2 064.2	102.1	256.8	16.1	457.1	589.8	204.0
September	380.9	1 456.8	1 782.5	2 090.8	103.1	257.9	16.4	452.6	598.8	210.6
October	381.9	1 462.5	1 794.8	2 104.7	103.9	257.9	16.5	441.6	611.1	217.4
November	382.0	1 468.1	1 797.5	2 108.7	104.3	257.7	16.5	429.2	625.7	220.3
December	382.8	1 475.7	1 806.5	2 121.1	104.8	257.7	16.8	423.8	634.2	223.1
1980:										
January	385.8	1 483.7	1 819.1	2 136.0	106.0	258.9	17.4	417.2	641.5	225.7
February	389.6	1 495.4	1 837.7	2 154.9	106.7	261.2	18.0	410.5	650.6	229.5
March	389.1	1 501.8	1 847.2	2 169.0	107.5	259.4	18.5	400.1	665.5	233.5
April	383.0	1 502.8	1 850.7	2 180.2	107.9	252.4	19.0	386.4	686.3	238.6
May	382.9	1 511.8	1 862.0	2 190.3	108.7	251.4	19.2	382.2	696.0	239.5
June	388.3	1 529.6	1 879.2	2 202.1	109.6	254.4	20.6	390.8	694.9	233.6
July	392.8	1 545.7	1 897.9	2 215.7	110.7	256.5	22.0	402.7	691.1	228.8
August	400.0	1 563.5	1 917.6	2 241.6	111.7	261.4	23.2	414.6	688.4	229.0
September	405.6	1 576.0	1 931.7	2 259.5	112.5	264.8	24.5	419.0	690.5	232.9
October	410.3	1 587.3	1 950.0	2 278.6	113.5	267.4	25.7	419.8	695.7	238.3
November	413.1	1 599.3	1 973.7	2 308.1	114.8	266.6	27.9	414.7	709.1	247.1
December	409.0	1 601.1	1 992.3	2 330.0	115.4	261.5	28.1	400.2	728.5	260.2

1. See NOTES to pages 94-95 for definitions of M1, M2, M3, and L.

SELECTED MONTHLY DATA, 1969-1992

YEAR AND MONTH	Money stock measures[1]				Selected components					
	M1	M2	M3	L	Currency	Demand deposits	Other checkable deposits	Savings deposits	Small time deposits	Large time deposits
1981:										
January	411.5	1 608.4	2 015.9	2 357.4	115.4	248.3	43.8	382.2	748.7	271.7
February	414.3	1 619.7	2 033.2	2 378.6	116.3	240.8	53.3	375.0	758.0	276.4
March	418.9	1 638.0	2 051.9	2 393.1	117.0	238.6	59.3	372.0	765.6	275.2
April	426.4	1 659.8	2 078.7	2 413.2	118.0	238.4	66.0	372.5	767.5	274.3
May	423.7	1 664.8	2 094.1	2 435.0	118.3	235.4	66.0	367.0	775.5	281.2
June	423.9	1 670.5	2 108.4	2 453.8	118.8	233.2	67.9	360.9	784.3	286.0
July	426.0	1 682.4	2 128.2	2 475.7	119.5	232.7	69.8	360.0	786.1	290.5
August	427.5	1 696.4	2 149.4	2 499.8	119.9	232.9	70.7	354.0	796.3	295.5
September	427.9	1 708.4	2 170.8	2 526.7	120.2	231.4	72.3	348.2	804.4	298.7
October	429.6	1 724.4	2 192.4	2 554.0	120.5	231.6	73.4	343.6	815.9	299.0
November	432.5	1 738.7	2 214.4	2 579.9	121.2	231.3	76.0	343.1	820.6	300.3
December	436.8	1 756.2	2 240.9	2 601.9	122.6	231.4	78.7	343.9	823.1	303.8
1982:										
January	443.4	1 772.6	2 265.2	2 632.5	123.3	234.3	81.8	346.5	824.7	307.1
February	441.2	1 775.5	2 271.1	2 647.5	123.9	230.6	82.6	345.3	833.1	312.6
March	442.2	1 787.6	2 290.2	2 668.6	124.5	229.2	84.4	344.2	843.9	316.1
April	446.2	1 804.7	2 316.3	2 696.8	125.5	228.9	87.6	344.3	853.2	320.3
May	446.1	1 816.5	2 328.8	2 714.8	126.6	228.1	87.1	344.0	860.6	319.4
June	446.9	1 827.0	2 342.8	2 732.3	127.4	226.9	88.3	343.5	865.4	320.8
July	447.5	1 835.5	2 353.9	2 747.1	128.1	226.3	88.9	342.0	873.9	323.9
August	451.6	1 851.2	2 378.7	2 767.0	129.0	227.5	91.0	344.2	876.3	325.7
September	457.4	1 865.4	2 396.0	2 782.5	129.8	229.5	93.9	346.7	877.6	325.4
October	466.1	1 877.9	2 418.3	2 813.0	130.8	232.4	98.6	355.3	870.4	329.0
November	472.1	1 890.4	2 431.5	2 826.8	131.5	233.9	102.5	362.6	866.8	330.6
December	474.7	1 910.9	2 442.3	2 846.0	132.5	234.0	104.1	400.1	850.9	324.8
1983:										
January	477.7	1 965.5	2 476.2	2 885.4	133.6	234.1	106.0	521.5	794.8	302.4
February	483.7	2 001.8	2 505.0	2 913.7	134.9	233.6	111.0	601.8	755.0	289.8
March	489.6	2 019.7	2 522.0	2 935.1	136.3	234.6	114.4	639.2	736.6	285.3
April	493.1	2 033.8	2 541.6	2 964.4	137.4	234.4	116.9	660.7	731.8	287.1
May	499.2	2 047.7	2 556.6	2 980.2	138.6	236.3	120.0	678.1	726.6	284.4
June	503.1	2 057.8	2 571.4	3 000.4	139.5	236.9	122.3	687.1	726.0	288.2
July	508.2	2 070.2	2 583.7	3 025.7	140.4	238.8	124.6	688.9	733.5	289.0
August	510.3	2 078.8	2 597.4	3 047.8	141.3	238.8	125.8	687.6	742.1	294.5
September	512.7	2 088.0	2 615.3	3 067.5	142.6	238.7	126.9	687.3	750.3	300.0
October	518.2	2 105.1	2 635.5	3 085.6	144.0	239.9	129.7	686.3	763.2	302.4
November	519.5	2 117.8	2 661.9	3 115.1	145.2	238.9	130.8	684.9	776.0	309.4
December	521.2	2 127.7	2 684.8	3 150.6	146.1	238.3	132.1	684.9	784.0	316.4
1984:										
January	525.0	2 143.1	2 702.5	3 173.6	147.4	240.2	132.7	685.5	793.2	322.1
February	527.3	2 163.2	2 730.3	3 206.0	148.1	240.3	134.2	690.8	802.2	327.0
March	530.9	2 179.8	2 757.1	3 247.6	149.2	240.6	136.3	696.7	807.6	333.7
April	533.8	2 195.6	2 785.5	3 286.6	150.1	241.6	137.2	702.1	813.7	341.4
May	536.2	2 209.0	2 814.1	3 321.9	150.9	241.0	139.4	701.9	822.0	353.5
June	540.2	2 220.4	2 835.4	3 358.7	152.0	242.6	140.8	698.1	832.0	365.0
July	541.0	2 228.9	2 858.7	3 392.1	152.8	242.1	141.2	693.1	843.1	375.7
August	540.9	2 235.5	2 872.5	3 413.8	153.6	241.1	141.3	686.3	857.7	381.5
September	544.3	2 250.7	2 893.1	3 447.8	154.4	242.3	142.7	685.5	868.9	385.5
October	544.0	2 264.6	2 918.8	3 473.8	154.9	240.9	143.4	687.1	878.2	395.4
November	547.6	2 287.0	2 947.6	3 496.8	155.6	242.1	145.1	694.4	884.4	398.7
December	552.2	2 312.2	2 979.8	3 518.6	156.1	243.7	147.4	704.7	888.8	403.2
1985:										
January	556.2	2 337.2	3 004.9	3 548.9	157.0	244.6	149.5	720.2	887.9	402.4
February	563.2	2 359.1	3 028.5	3 581.0	157.9	247.5	152.7	736.1	884.7	403.3
March	566.6	2 371.5	3 044.2	3 609.1	158.5	247.9	155.1	744.3	883.9	407.1
April	569.8	2 380.3	3 050.6	3 620.3	159.4	248.3	156.9	748.4	886.1	410.9
May	574.8	2 395.1	3 068.1	3 633.9	160.5	250.3	158.6	755.8	890.1	410.9
June	583.3	2 419.4	3 093.7	3 663.3	161.7	253.8	162.4	767.9	891.6	408.3
July	589.2	2 435.2	3 104.0	3 682.2	162.9	255.3	165.5	780.1	888.7	404.5
August	596.5	2 450.0	3 121.5	3 707.7	164.3	257.6	169.1	791.6	884.1	405.9
September	604.0	2 462.9	3 140.6	3 731.5	165.2	261.5	171.8	798.7	882.4	410.7
October	607.7	2 473.7	3 157.9	3 755.6	166.3	261.2	174.6	806.6	881.9	414.4
November	612.7	2 483.9	3 174.7	3 792.1	167.1	262.3	177.7	812.7	881.9	418.3
December	619.9	2 497.6	3 198.3	3 827.0	167.9	266.6	179.8	815.2	885.7	422.4
1986:										
January	620.9	2 507.2	3 221.5	3 848.1	168.6	264.9	181.8	817.2	889.6	431.5
February	625.1	2 518.3	3 240.4	3 867.5	169.5	266.0	183.9	819.7	891.7	435.1
March	633.7	2 538.6	3 266.6	3 892.5	170.7	270.3	186.9	824.1	895.0	434.5
April	640.9	2 563.2	3 297.4	3 915.8	171.5	272.8	190.8	835.1	895.6	433.9
May	651.9	2 590.7	3 320.2	3 947.5	172.8	276.9	196.5	850.5	891.9	430.0
June	661.0	2 611.2	3 339.4	3 968.9	173.6	280.1	201.4	863.2	887.0	428.2
July	670.1	2 632.5	3 371.1	3 996.8	174.8	283.0	206.3	875.2	884.7	429.6
August	679.8	2 653.9	3 397.6	4 025.6	176.0	285.7	212.0	889.4	881.2	430.1
September	687.3	2 674.2	3 424.7	4 050.1	177.0	287.3	216.9	903.9	877.6	429.1
October	694.9	2 694.1	3 443.0	4 070.4	178.3	287.7	222.7	919.6	870.0	424.1
November	706.5	2 708.8	3 456.7	4 088.2	179.4	292.2	228.8	931.1	861.8	421.2
December	724.4	2 733.9	3 486.4	4 122.3	180.7	302.1	235.6	940.9	858.3	420.2

1. See NOTES to pages 94-95 for definitions of M1, M2, M3, and L.

YEAR AND MONTH	MONEY STOCK AND SELECTED COMPONENTS—Continued (Averages of daily figures—Billions of dollars, seasonally adjusted)									
	Money stock measures[1]				Selected components					
	M1	M2	M3	L	Currency	Demand deposits	Other checkable deposits	Savings deposits	Small time deposits	Large time deposits
1987:										
January	730.1	2 749.9	3 511.3	4 151.7	182.1	299.3	242.6	952.1	855.9	423.0
February	730.8	2 753.9	3 520.1	4 167.1	183.4	296.2	245.0	959.1	852.2	424.4
March	733.4	2 759.3	3 526.6	4 165.9	184.1	294.9	248.0	964.5	850.1	426.6
April	743.5	2 773.4	3 546.6	4 180.2	185.4	298.9	252.9	970.2	847.9	428.9
May	746.7	2 780.0	3 564.2	4 206.0	186.5	299.2	254.6	972.8	847.5	435.0
June	742.7	2 780.2	3 576.4	4 223.6	187.7	293.8	254.8	969.8	853.9	440.1
July	742.8	2 785.1	3 584.8	4 228.5	188.8	291.9	255.6	966.0	862.1	441.7
August	745.7	2 795.1	3 607.9	4 255.7	190.0	291.6	257.5	962.9	870.0	444.6
September	747.6	2 805.8	3 631.4	4 289.2	191.5	290.2	259.3	960.4	877.8	448.2
October	756.4	2 821.1	3 654.6	4 319.2	193.2	295.4	261.3	953.0	889.7	454.7
November	753.3	2 825.5	3 666.5	4 323.5	195.2	291.3	260.3	941.4	908.1	462.4
December	749.7	2 832.7	3 672.5	4 339.9	196.8	286.8	259.5	937.4	921.0	467.0
1988:										
January	757.1	2 855.3	3 698.1	4 366.0	197.9	289.9	262.6	936.5	933.0	465.9
February	757.8	2 877.5	3 724.8	4 396.5	199.1	287.4	264.5	938.0	949.5	470.1
March	761.4	2 897.4	3 749.5	4 423.4	200.6	287.3	266.7	941.2	960.9	474.1
April	768.6	2 918.3	3 778.4	4 477.0	202.2	289.6	270.0	945.0	968.6	476.0
May	771.9	2 933.0	3 802.5	4 506.7	203.5	288.2	273.3	949.7	974.7	478.7
June	778.5	2 945.2	3 820.4	4 524.3	205.0	290.8	275.9	952.6	979.3	484.3
July	782.7	2 955.9	3 838.5	4 559.2	206.4	290.5	278.9	952.0	985.3	491.7
August	783.3	2 959.6	3 849.2	4 576.9	207.6	289.8	279.0	946.2	993.5	498.3
September	783.5	2 964.6	3 861.4	4 588.0	208.9	288.6	279.0	938.4	1 006.0	506.4
October	784.4	2 974.7	3 879.1	4 610.1	210.0	288.0	279.4	933.4	1 019.2	511.9
November	785.1	2 988.6	3 899.1	4 638.4	211.2	286.8	280.1	931.9	1 028.3	513.5
December	787.0	2 996.3	3 912.9	4 663.5	212.3	286.8	280.9	926.3	1 037.1	518.3
1989:										
January	786.0	2 999.8	3 920.1	4 678.6	213.2	285.0	280.8	916.3	1 050.0	524.3
February	784.2	3 000.4	3 927.5	4 696.8	213.7	283.4	280.2	904.3	1 061.8	531.2
March	782.9	3 007.2	3 947.0	4 722.3	214.9	282.5	278.6	894.1	1 073.6	537.7
April	780.1	3 014.3	3 956.7	4 746.0	215.5	280.4	277.3	881.1	1 091.2	545.8
May	774.9	3 019.1	3 961.3	4 757.7	216.5	278.8	272.7	866.1	1 110.3	548.9
June	773.4	3 034.8	3 982.9	4 782.8	217.5	276.7	272.4	861.9	1 124.1	549.4
July	778.7	3 060.2	4 007.8	4 805.9	218.2	279.6	274.0	863.6	1 132.9	549.6
August	779.3	3 081.5	4 016.1	4 826.7	218.9	277.9	275.6	867.8	1 140.1	547.7
September	781.6	3 100.8	4 025.0	4 838.6	219.5	277.4	277.9	872.9	1 142.7	545.4
October	787.0	3 122.5	4 036.0	4 857.8	220.1	279.3	280.8	879.0	1 145.8	543.3
November	788.1	3 141.1	4 052.0	4 871.7	221.0	277.8	282.5	887.2	1 147.7	542.6
December	794.2	3 160.9	4 065.9	4 892.8	222.7	279.3	285.3	893.7	1 151.4	541.5
1990:										
January	795.3	3 173.1	4 072.0	4 901.8	224.4	278.1	285.8	900.5	1 150.6	538.9
February	798.2	3 185.3	4 074.9	4 902.9	225.9	278.1	287.1	904.9	1 151.6	531.9
March	801.7	3 196.9	4 080.5	4 918.1	227.8	277.5	289.3	908.7	1 154.5	526.9
April	806.3	3 209.3	4 086.1	4 929.0	229.8	277.3	292.0	912.3	1 157.0	520.5
May	804.6	3 207.0	4 084.9	4 915.4	231.6	274.2	291.5	911.5	1 158.9	516.6
June	810.3	3 221.0	4 094.3	4 936.5	233.8	275.7	293.3	914.7	1 161.3	512.8
July	810.4	3 230.2	4 105.1	4 943.3	235.9	275.6	291.4	917.3	1 164.5	511.6
August	816.0	3 248.4	4 117.7	4 951.8	238.7	277.8	291.8	920.7	1 166.0	506.0
September	821.6	3 262.3	4 125.2	4 975.0	241.6	279.3	292.8	922.8	1 167.1	498.0
October	819.8	3 265.3	4 125.7	4 974.4	243.9	276.6	291.4	922.6	1 169.3	493.8
November	822.0	3 269.6	4 119.2	4 966.2	245.4	276.3	292.5	922.8	1 170.8	490.1
December	825.8	3 279.5	4 125.9	4 976.6	246.8	277.4	293.9	923.8	1 172.8	480.9
1991:										
January	826.7	3 293.4	4 148.9	5 007.3	251.1	273.5	294.3	927.1	1 174.7	483.2
February	832.8	3 311.1	4 168.0	5 021.5	254.0	274.5	296.6	934.5	1 174.3	483.9
March	839.8	3 329.4	4 176.0	5 021.9	255.9	275.7	300.7	946.0	1 169.2	478.6
April	842.5	3 337.9	4 180.7	5 000.7	256.2	275.4	303.3	957.8	1 161.2	472.4
May	849.1	3 348.0	4 179.0	4 980.3	256.8	277.2	307.5	970.6	1 151.4	466.9
June	858.6	3 359.1	4 180.3	5 005.1	258.0	281.2	311.9	983.1	1 139.3	462.5
July	861.3	3 361.0	4 174.6	5 015.6	259.5	279.9	314.5	993.1	1 128.6	455.2
August	867.2	3 360.5	4 170.4	5 005.8	261.2	280.3	318.3	999.9	1 119.9	447.9
September	870.6	3 360.0	4 163.0	4 993.7	262.3	279.6	321.3	1 007.0	1 109.7	441.6
October	877.5	3 363.9	4 166.0	4 995.4	264.1	281.9	323.9	1 018.9	1 096.2	432.1
November	888.6	3 372.5	4 174.4	5 007.3	265.8	286.1	329.2	1 031.2	1 081.7	423.3
December	897.3	3 379.6	4 180.4	5 006.2	267.3	289.6	332.5	1 045.0	1 065.4	416.5
1992:										
January	910.0	3 387.7	4 187.0	5 005.3	268.9	295.9	337.5	1 064.9	1 044.1	412.0
February	926.2	3 407.1	4 207.5	5 027.0	270.9	303.1	344.5	1 087.1	1 020.5	405.8
March	936.8	3 410.5	4 207.6	5 041.6	272.0	308.7	348.5	1 102.9	1 000.9	403.1
April	944.3	3 408.8	4 197.0	5 041.0	273.7	311.6	351.4	1 116.3	982.3	395.7
May	952.4	3 407.4	4 192.2	5 029.8	275.3	314.0	355.5	1 125.7	964.4	388.8
June	954.2	3 401.3	4 188.3	5 040.8	277.0	312.8	356.7	1 132.4	950.6	383.6
July	963.2	3 402.2	4 188.7	5 036.9	279.6	316.7	359.2	1 141.2	937.3	379.3
August	975.4	3 408.9	4 201.0	5 052.9	282.5	321.3	363.8	1 151.2	922.7	375.0
September	988.2	3 418.2	4 205.9	5 073.0	285.7	327.2	367.2	1 163.5	909.9	370.3
October	1 003.9	3 432.0	4 202.9	5 075.2	287.9	334.0	373.8	1 174.6	894.8	362.9
November	1 016.7	3 435.3	4 200.2	5 084.1	290.0	337.5	381.1	1 182.7	880.0	357.0
December	1 025.0	3 434.0	4 190.4	5 078.0	292.9	339.5	384.4	1 187.3	868.3	353.4

1. See NOTES to pages 94-95 for definitions of M1, M2, M3, and L.

SELECTED MONTHLY DATA, 1969-1992

INTEREST RATES, BOND YIELDS, AND STOCK PRICE INDEXES
(Not seasonally adjusted)

YEAR AND MONTH	Short-term rates					U.S. Treasury securities			Bond yields				Fixed-rate first mort-gages	Stock price indexes	
	Federal funds	Federal Reserve discount rate [1]	U.S. Treasury bills, 3-month	Com-mercial paper, 6-month	Bank prime rate	One year	Ten year	Long-term compos-ite [2]	Domestic corporate (Moody's)		A-rated utility bonds	State and local bonds (Bond Buyer)		Dow Jones industrials (30 stocks)	Standard and Poor's composite, (500 stocks) [3]
									Aaa	Baa					
1969:															
January	6.30	5.50	6.18	6.53	6.95	6.34	6.04	5.74	6.59	7.32	....	4.85	....	934.99	102.04
February	6.61	5.50	6.16	6.62	7.00	6.41	6.19	5.86	6.66	7.30	....	4.98	....	931.29	101.46
March	6.79	5.50	6.08	6.82	7.24	6.34	6.30	6.05	6.85	7.51	....	5.26	....	916.52	99.30
April	7.41	5.95	6.16	7.04	7.50	6.26	6.17	5.84	6.89	7.54	....	5.19	....	927.38	101.26
May	8.67	6.00	6.08	7.35	7.50	6.42	6.32	5.85	6.79	7.52	....	5.33	....	954.86	104.62
June	8.90	6.00	6.49	8.23	8.23	7.04	6.57	6.06	6.98	7.70	....	5.75	....	896.61	99.14
July	8.61	6.00	7.01	8.65	8.50	7.60	6.72	6.07	7.08	7.84	....	5.75	....	844.02	94.71
August	9.19	6.00	7.01	8.33	8.50	7.54	6.69	6.02	6.97	7.86	....	6.00	....	825.46	94.18
September	9.15	6.00	7.13	8.48	8.50	7.82	7.16	6.32	7.14	8.05	....	6.26	....	826.71	94.51
October	9.00	6.00	7.04	8.56	8.50	7.64	7.10	6.27	7.33	8.22	....	6.09	....	832.51	95.52
November	8.85	6.00	7.20	8.46	8.50	7.89	7.14	6.51	7.35	8.25	....	6.30	....	841.08	96.21
December	8.97	6.00	7.72	8.84	8.50	8.17	7.65	6.81	7.72	8.65	....	6.82	....	789.22	91.11
1970:															
January	8.98	6.00	7.92	8.78	8.50	8.10	7.79	6.86	7.91	8.86	9.24	6.63	....	782.96	90.31
February	8.98	6.00	7.16	8.55	8.50	7.59	7.24	6.44	7.93	8.78	9.01	6.22	....	756.21	87.16
March	7.76	6.00	6.71	8.33	8.39	6.97	7.07	6.39	7.84	8.63	8.90	6.05	....	777.62	88.65
April	8.10	6.00	6.48	8.06	8.00	7.06	7.39	6.53	7.83	8.70	9.01	6.65	....	771.65	85.95
May	7.94	6.00	7.03	8.24	8.00	7.75	7.91	6.94	8.11	8.98	9.33	7.00	....	691.96	76.06
June	7.60	6.00	6.74	8.21	8.00	7.55	7.84	6.99	8.48	9.25	9.50	6.93	....	699.30	75.59
July	7.21	6.00	6.47	8.29	8.00	7.10	7.46	6.57	8.44	9.40	9.42	6.42	....	712.80	75.72
August	6.61	6.00	6.41	7.90	8.00	6.98	7.53	6.75	8.13	9.44	9.35	6.17	....	731.97	77.92
September	6.29	6.00	6.24	7.32	7.83	6.73	7.39	6.63	8.09	9.39	9.39	6.31	....	759.38	82.58
October	6.20	6.00	5.93	6.85	7.50	6.43	7.33	6.59	8.03	9.33	9.20	6.37	....	763.72	84.37
November	5.60	5.85	5.29	6.29	7.28	5.51	6.84	6.24	8.05	9.38	9.04	5.71	....	769.27	84.28
December	4.90	5.52	4.86	5.73	6.92	5.00	6.39	5.97	7.64	9.12	8.63	5.47	....	821.51	90.05
1971:															
January	4.14	5.23	4.49	5.11	6.29	4.57	6.24	5.91	7.36	8.74	8.06	5.35	....	849.04	93.49
February	3.72	4.91	3.78	4.47	5.88	3.89	6.11	5.84	7.08	8.39	7.68	5.23	....	879.69	97.11
March	3.71	4.75	3.33	4.19	5.44	3.69	5.70	5.71	7.21	8.46	7.91	5.17	....	901.29	99.60
April	4.15	4.75	3.78	4.57	5.28	4.30	5.83	5.75	7.25	8.45	7.87	5.37	7.31	932.54	103.04
May	4.63	4.75	4.14	5.10	5.46	5.04	6.39	5.96	7.53	8.62	8.31	5.90	7.43	925.49	101.64
June	4.91	4.75	4.70	5.46	5.50	5.64	6.52	5.94	7.64	8.75	8.33	5.95	7.53	900.43	99.72
July	5.31	4.88	5.41	5.75	5.91	6.04	6.73	5.91	7.64	8.76	8.50	6.06	7.60	887.81	99.00
August	5.56	5.00	5.08	5.74	6.00	5.80	6.58	5.78	7.59	8.76	8.24	5.82	7.70	875.40	97.24
September	5.55	5.00	4.67	5.75	6.00	5.41	6.14	5.56	7.44	8.59	7.94	5.37	7.69	901.22	99.40
October	5.20	5.00	4.49	5.54	5.90	4.91	5.93	5.46	7.39	8.48	7.96	5.06	7.63	872.15	97.29
November	4.91	4.90	4.19	4.92	5.53	4.67	5.81	5.44	7.26	8.38	7.77	5.20	7.55	822.11	92.78
December	4.14	4.63	4.02	4.74	5.49	4.60	5.93	5.62	7.25	8.38	7.54	5.21	7.48	869.90	99.17
1972:															
January	3.50	4.50	3.41	4.08	5.18	4.28	5.95	5.62	7.19	8.23	7.44	5.12	7.44	904.65	103.30
February	3.29	4.50	3.18	3.94	4.75	4.27	6.08	5.67	7.27	8.23	7.49	5.28	7.33	914.37	105.24
March	3.83	4.50	3.72	4.16	4.75	4.67	6.07	5.66	7.24	8.24	7.57	5.31	7.30	939.23	107.69
April	4.17	4.50	3.72	4.58	4.97	4.96	6.19	5.74	7.30	8.24	7.63	5.43	7.29	958.16	108.81
May	4.27	4.50	3.65	4.51	5.00	4.64	6.13	5.64	7.30	8.23	7.67	5.30	7.37	948.22	107.65
June	4.46	4.50	3.87	4.64	5.04	4.93	6.11	5.59	7.23	8.20	7.58	5.33	7.37	943.43	108.01
July	4.55	4.50	4.06	4.85	5.25	4.96	6.11	5.57	7.21	8.23	7.54	5.41	7.40	925.92	107.21
August	4.80	4.50	4.01	4.81	5.27	4.98	6.21	5.54	7.19	8.19	7.58	5.30	7.40	958.34	111.01
September	4.87	4.50	4.65	5.15	5.50	5.52	6.55	5.70	7.22	8.09	7.62	5.36	7.42	950.58	109.39
October	5.04	4.50	4.72	5.30	5.73	5.52	6.48	5.69	7.21	8.06	7.66	5.18	7.42	944.10	109.56
November	5.06	4.50	4.78	5.25	5.75	5.27	6.28	5.50	7.12	7.99	7.41	5.02	7.43	1 001.19	115.05
December	5.33	4.50	5.06	5.45	5.79	5.52	6.36	5.63	7.08	7.93	7.44	5.05	7.44	1 020.32	117.50
1973:															
January	5.94	4.77	5.31	5.78	6.00	5.89	6.46	5.94	7.15	7.90	7.57	5.05	7.44	1 026.82	118.42
February	6.58	5.05	5.56	6.22	6.02	6.19	6.64	6.14	7.22	7.97	7.62	5.13	7.44	974.04	114.16
March	7.09	5.50	6.05	6.85	6.30	6.85	6.71	6.20	7.29	8.03	7.74	5.29	7.46	957.35	112.42
April	7.12	5.50	6.29	7.14	6.61	6.85	6.67	6.11	7.26	8.09	7.67	5.15	7.54	944.10	110.27
May	7.84	5.90	6.35	7.27	7.01	6.89	6.85	6.22	7.29	8.06	7.65	5.15	7.65	922.41	107.22
June	8.49	6.33	7.19	7.99	7.49	7.31	6.90	6.32	7.37	8.13	7.82	5.17	7.73	893.90	104.75
July	10.40	6.98	8.02	9.19	8.30	8.39	7.13	6.53	7.45	8.24	8.20	5.40	8.05	903.61	105.83
August	10.50	7.29	8.67	10.21	9.23	8.82	7.40	6.81	7.68	8.53	8.67	5.48	8.50	883.73	103.80
September	10.78	7.50	8.48	10.23	9.86	8.31	7.09	6.42	7.63	8.63	8.41	5.10	8.82	909.98	105.61
October	10.01	7.50	7.16	8.92	9.94	7.40	6.79	6.26	7.60	8.41	8.24	5.05	8.77	967.62	109.84
November	10.03	7.50	7.87	8.94	9.75	7.57	6.73	6.31	7.67	8.42	8.24	5.18	8.58	878.98	102.03
December	9.95	7.50	7.37	9.08	9.75	7.27	6.74	6.35	7.68	8.48	8.34	5.12	8.54	824.08	94.78
1974:															
January	9.65	7.50	7.76	8.67	9.73	7.42	6.99	6.56	7.83	8.48	8.57	5.22	8.54	857.24	96.11
February	8.97	7.50	7.06	7.83	9.21	6.88	6.96	6.54	7.85	8.53	8.58	5.20	8.46	831.34	93.45
March	9.35	7.50	7.99	8.42	8.85	7.76	7.21	6.81	8.01	8.62	8.89	5.40	8.41	874.00	97.44
April	10.51	7.60	8.23	9.79	10.02	8.62	7.51	7.04	8.25	8.87	9.29	5.73	8.58	847.79	92.46
May	11.31	8.00	8.43	10.62	11.25	8.78	7.58	7.07	8.37	9.05	9.53	6.02	8.97	829.84	89.67
June	11.93	8.00	8.15	10.97	11.54	8.67	7.54	7.03	8.47	9.27	10.25	6.13	9.09	831.43	89.79
July	12.92	8.00	7.75	11.72	11.97	8.80	7.81	7.18	8.72	9.48	11.29	6.68	9.28	783.00	82.82
August	12.01	8.00	8.75	11.65	12.00	9.36	8.04	7.33	9.00	9.77	11.44	6.71	9.59	729.30	76.03
September	11.34	8.00	8.37	11.23	12.00	8.87	8.04	7.30	9.24	10.18	11.04	6.76	9.96	651.28	68.12
October	10.06	8.00	7.24	9.37	11.68	8.05	7.90	7.22	9.27	10.48	11.43	6.57	9.98	638.62	69.44
November	9.45	8.00	7.59	8.81	10.83	7.66	7.68	6.93	8.89	10.60	10.21	6.61	9.79	642.10	71.74
December	8.53	7.81	7.18	8.98	10.50	7.31	7.43	6.78	8.89	10.63	10.76	7.05	9.62	596.50	67.07

1. Discount window borrowing, Federal Reserve Bank of New York.
2. Maturities of more than ten years.
3. 1941-1943=10.

INTEREST RATES, BOND YIELDS, AND STOCK PRICE INDEXES—Continued
(Not seasonally adjusted)

YEAR AND MONTH	Short-term rates					U.S. Treasury securities			Bond yields				Fixed-rate first mort-gages	Stock price indexes	
	Federal funds	Federal Reserve discount rate [1]	U.S. Treasury bills, 3-month	Commercial paper, 6-month	Bank prime rate	One year	Ten year	Long-term composite [2]	Domestic corporate (Moody's)		A-rated utility bonds	State and local bonds (Bond Buyer)		Dow Jones industrials (30 stocks)	Standard and Poor's composite, (500 stocks) [3]
									Aaa	Baa					
1975:															
January	7.13	7.40	6.49	7.30	10.05	6.83	7.50	6.68	8.83	10.81	10.45	6.82	9.43	659.09	72.56
February	6.24	6.82	5.59	6.34	8.96	5.98	7.39	6.61	8.62	10.65	10.19	6.39	9.11	724.89	80.10
March	5.54	6.40	5.55	6.06	7.93	6.11	7.73	6.73	8.67	10.48	10.35	6.73	8.90	765.06	83.78
April	5.49	6.25	5.69	6.15	7.50	6.90	8.23	7.03	8.95	10.58	10.90	6.95	8.82	790.93	84.72
May	5.22	6.12	5.32	5.82	7.40	6.39	8.06	6.99	8.90	10.69	10.95	6.97	8.91	836.56	90.10
June	5.55	6.00	5.20	5.79	7.07	6.29	7.86	6.86	8.77	10.62	10.62	6.94	8.89	845.70	92.40
July	6.10	6.00	6.17	6.45	7.15	7.11	8.06	6.89	8.84	10.55	10.57	7.07	8.89	856.28	92.49
August	6.14	6.00	6.46	6.70	7.66	7.70	8.40	7.06	8.95	10.59	10.74	7.17	8.94	815.51	85.71
September	6.24	6.00	6.38	6.86	7.88	7.75	8.43	7.29	8.95	10.61	10.97	7.44	9.13	818.28	84.67
October	5.82	6.00	6.08	6.49	7.96	6.95	8.14	7.29	8.86	10.62	10.63	7.39	9.22	831.26	88.57
November	5.22	6.00	5.47	5.92	7.53	6.49	8.05	7.21	8.78	10.56	10.21	7.43	9.15	845.51	90.07
December	5.20	6.00	5.50	5.97	7.26	6.60	8.00	7.17	8.79	10.56	10.21	7.31	9.10	840.80	88.70
1976:															
January	4.87	5.79	4.96	5.27	7.00	5.81	7.74	6.94	8.60	10.41	9.69	7.07	9.02	929.34	96.86
February	4.77	5.50	4.85	5.23	6.75	5.91	7.79	6.92	8.55	10.24	9.48	6.94	8.81	971.70	100.64
March	4.84	5.50	5.05	5.37	6.75	6.21	7.73	6.87	8.52	10.12	9.21	6.91	8.76	988.55	101.08
April	4.82	5.50	4.88	5.23	6.75	5.92	7.56	6.73	8.40	9.94	8.97	6.60	8.73	992.51	101.93
May	5.29	5.50	5.19	5.55	6.75	6.40	7.90	6.99	8.58	9.86	9.27	6.87	8.77	988.82	101.16
June	5.48	5.50	5.45	5.94	7.20	6.52	7.86	6.92	8.62	9.89	9.33	6.87	8.85	985.59	101.77
July	5.31	5.50	5.28	5.67	7.25	6.20	7.83	6.85	8.56	9.82	9.25	6.79	8.93	993.20	104.20
August	5.29	5.50	5.15	5.47	7.01	6.00	7.77	6.79	8.45	9.64	9.10	6.61	9.00	981.63	103.29
September	5.25	5.50	5.08	5.45	7.00	5.84	7.59	6.70	8.38	9.40	8.88	6.51	8.98	994.37	105.45
October	5.02	5.50	4.93	5.22	6.77	5.50	7.41	6.65	8.32	9.29	8.69	6.30	8.93	951.95	101.89
November	4.95	5.43	4.81	5.05	6.50	5.29	7.29	6.62	8.25	9.23	8.58	6.29	8.81	944.58	101.19
December	4.65	5.25	4.36	4.70	6.35	4.89	6.87	6.39	7.98	9.12	8.41	5.94	8.79	976.86	104.66
1977:															
January	4.61	5.25	4.60	4.75	6.25	5.29	7.21	6.68	7.96	9.08	8.59	5.87	8.72	970.62	103.81
February	4.68	5.25	4.66	4.82	6.25	5.47	7.39	7.15	8.04	9.12	8.54	5.88	8.67	941.77	100.96
March	4.69	5.25	4.61	4.87	6.25	5.50	7.46	7.20	8.10	9.12	8.59	5.89	8.69	946.11	100.57
April	4.73	5.25	4.54	4.87	6.25	5.44	7.37	7.13	8.04	9.07	8.55	5.72	8.75	929.10	99.05
May	5.35	5.25	4.94	5.35	6.41	5.84	7.46	7.17	8.05	9.01	8.74	5.75	8.82	926.31	98.76
June	5.39	5.25	5.00	5.49	6.75	5.80	7.28	6.99	7.95	8.91	8.62	5.62	8.86	916.56	99.29
July	5.42	5.25	5.14	5.41	6.75	5.94	7.33	6.97	7.94	8.87	8.52	5.63	8.94	908.20	100.18
August	5.90	5.27	5.50	5.84	6.83	6.37	7.40	7.00	7.98	8.82	8.40	5.62	8.94	872.26	97.75
September	6.14	5.75	5.77	6.17	7.13	6.53	7.34	6.94	7.92	8.80	8.37	5.51	8.90	853.30	96.23
October	6.47	5.80	6.19	6.56	7.52	6.97	7.52	7.08	8.04	8.89	8.54	5.64	8.91	823.96	93.74
November	6.51	6.00	6.16	6.59	7.75	6.95	7.58	7.14	8.08	8.95	8.57	5.49	8.92	828.51	94.28
December	6.56	6.00	6.06	6.64	7.75	6.96	7.69	7.23	8.19	8.99	8.73	5.57	8.96	818.80	93.82
1978:															
January	6.70	6.37	6.45	6.79	7.93	7.28	7.96	7.50	8.41	9.17	9.00	5.71	9.02	781.09	90.25
February	6.78	6.50	6.46	6.80	8.00	7.34	8.03	7.60	8.47	9.20	9.02	5.62	9.16	763.57	88.98
March	6.79	6.50	6.32	6.80	8.00	7.31	8.04	7.63	8.47	9.22	8.92	5.61	9.20	756.37	88.82
April	6.89	6.50	6.31	6.86	8.00	7.45	8.15	7.74	8.56	9.32	9.10	5.79	9.36	794.66	92.71
May	7.36	6.84	6.43	7.11	8.27	7.82	8.35	7.87	8.69	9.49	9.43	6.03	9.58	838.56	97.41
June	7.60	7.00	6.71	7.63	8.63	8.09	8.46	7.94	8.76	9.60	9.57	6.22	9.71	840.26	97.66
July	7.81	7.23	7.08	7.91	9.00	8.39	8.64	8.09	8.88	9.60	9.73	6.28	9.74	831.71	97.19
August	8.04	7.43	7.04	7.90	9.01	8.31	8.41	7.87	8.69	9.48	9.31	6.12	9.78	887.93	103.92
September	8.45	7.83	7.84	8.44	9.41	8.64	8.42	7.82	8.69	9.42	9.16	6.09	9.76	878.64	103.86
October	8.96	8.26	8.13	9.03	9.94	9.14	8.64	8.07	8.89	9.59	9.48	6.13	9.86	857.69	100.58
November	9.76	9.50	8.79	10.23	10.94	10.01	8.81	8.16	9.03	9.83	9.72	6.19	10.11	804.29	94.71
December	10.03	9.50	9.12	10.43	11.55	10.30	9.01	8.35	9.16	9.94	9.84	6.50	10.35	807.94	96.11
1979:															
January	10.07	9.50	9.35	10.32	11.75	10.41	9.10	8.43	9.25	10.13	9.98	6.46	10.39	837.39	99.71
February	10.06	9.50	9.27	10.01	11.75	10.24	9.10	8.43	9.26	10.08	10.06	6.31	10.41	825.18	98.23
March	10.09	9.50	9.46	9.96	11.75	10.25	9.12	8.45	9.37	10.26	10.27	6.33	10.43	847.84	100.11
April	10.01	9.50	9.49	9.87	11.75	10.12	9.18	8.44	9.38	10.33	10.24	6.28	10.50	864.96	102.07
May	10.24	9.50	9.58	9.98	11.75	10.12	9.25	8.55	9.50	10.47	10.54	6.25	10.69	837.41	99.73
June	10.29	9.50	9.05	9.71	11.65	9.57	8.91	8.32	9.29	10.38	10.00	6.12	11.04	838.65	101.73
July	10.47	9.69	9.27	9.82	11.54	9.64	8.95	8.35	9.20	10.29	10.03	6.13	11.09	836.95	102.71
August	10.94	10.24	9.45	10.39	11.91	9.98	9.03	8.42	9.23	10.35	9.94	6.20	11.09	873.55	107.36
September	11.43	10.70	10.18	11.60	12.90	10.84	9.33	8.68	9.44	10.54	10.47	6.52	11.30	878.50	108.60
October	13.77	11.77	11.47	13.23	14.39	12.44	10.30	9.44	10.13	11.40	11.56	7.08	11.64	840.39	104.47
November	13.18	12.00	11.87	13.26	15.55	12.39	10.65	9.80	10.76	11.99	12.46	7.30	12.83	815.78	103.66
December	13.78	12.00	12.07	12.80	15.30	11.98	10.39	9.59	10.74	12.06	12.45	7.22	12.90	836.14	107.78
1980:															
January	13.82	12.00	12.04	12.66	15.25	12.06	10.80	10.03	11.09	12.42	12.82	7.35	12.88	860.74	110.87
February	14.13	12.52	12.82	13.60	15.63	13.92	12.41	11.55	12.38	13.57	14.35	8.16	13.04	878.22	115.34
March	17.19	13.00	15.53	16.50	18.31	15.82	12.75	11.87	12.96	14.45	15.03	9.16	15.28	803.56	104.69
April	17.61	13.00	14.00	14.93	19.77	13.30	11.47	10.83	12.04	14.19	14.29	8.63	16.33	786.33	102.97
May	10.98	12.94	9.15	9.29	16.57	9.39	10.18	9.82	10.99	13.17	12.64	7.59	14.26	828.19	107.69
June	9.47	11.40	7.00	8.03	12.63	8.16	9.78	9.40	10.58	12.71	11.99	7.63	12.71	869.86	114.55
July	9.03	10.87	8.13	8.29	11.48	8.65	10.25	9.83	11.07	12.65	12.41	8.13	12.19	909.79	119.83
August	9.61	10.00	9.26	9.61	11.12	10.24	11.10	10.53	11.64	13.15	13.56	8.67	12.56	947.33	123.50
September	10.87	10.17	10.32	11.04	12.23	11.52	11.51	10.94	12.02	13.70	13.72	8.94	13.20	946.67	126.51
October	12.81	11.00	11.58	12.32	13.79	12.49	11.75	11.20	12.31	14.23	14.18	9.11	13.79	949.17	130.22
November	15.85	11.47	13.89	14.73	16.06	14.15	12.68	11.83	12.97	14.64	15.04	9.56	14.21	971.08	135.65
December	18.90	12.87	15.66	16.49	20.35	14.88	12.84	11.89	13.21	15.14	15.64	10.20	14.79	945.96	133.48

1. Discount window borrowing, Federal Reserve Bank of New York.
2. Maturities of more than ten years.
3. 1941-1943=10.

SELECTED MONTHLY DATA, 1969-1992

INTEREST RATES, BOND YIELDS, AND STOCK PRICE INDEXES—Continued
(Not seasonally adjusted)

YEAR AND MONTH	Short-term rates					U.S. Treasury securities			Bond yields				Fixed-rate first mort-gages	Stock price indexes	
	Federal funds	Federal Reserve discount rate [1]	U.S. Treasury bills, 3-month	Com-mercial paper, 6-month	Bank prime rate	One year	Ten year	Long-term compos-ite [2]	Domestic corporate (Moody's) Aaa	Baa	A-rated utility bonds	State and local bonds (Bond Buyer)		Dow Jones industrials (30 stocks)	Standard and Poor's composite, (500 stocks) [3]
1981:															
January	19.08	13.00	14.73	15.10	20.16	14.08	12.57	11.65	12.81	15.03	15.17	9.66	14.90	962.13	132.97
February	15.93	13.00	14.91	14.87	19.43	14.57	13.19	12.23	13.35	15.37	15.95	10.09	15.13	945.50	128.40
March	14.70	13.00	13.48	13.59	18.05	13.71	13.12	12.15	13.33	15.34	15.41	10.16	15.40	987.18	133.19
April	15.72	13.00	13.63	14.17	17.15	14.32	13.68	12.62	13.88	15.56	16.48	10.62	15.58	1 004.86	134.43
May	18.52	13.87	16.29	16.66	19.61	16.20	14.10	12.96	14.32	15.95	16.48	10.77	16.40	979.52	131.73
June	19.10	14.00	14.56	15.22	20.03	14.86	13.47	12.39	13.75	15.80	15.94	10.67	16.70	996.27	132.28
July	19.04	14.00	14.70	16.09	20.39	15.72	14.28	13.05	14.38	16.17	16.86	11.14	16.83	947.94	129.13
August	17.82	14.00	15.61	16.62	20.50	16.72	14.94	13.78	14.89	16.34	17.69	12.26	17.29	926.25	129.63
September	15.87	14.00	14.95	15.93	20.08	16.52	15.32	14.14	15.49	16.92	18.33	12.92	18.16	853.38	118.27
October	15.08	14.00	13.87	14.72	18.45	15.38	15.15	14.13	15.40	17.11	18.24	12.83	18.45	853.24	119.80
November	13.31	13.03	11.27	11.96	16.84	12.41	13.39	12.68	14.22	16.39	16.62	11.89	17.83	860.44	122.92
December	12.37	12.10	10.93	12.14	15.75	12.85	13.72	12.88	14.23	16.55	16.44	12.91	16.92	878.28	123.79
1982:															
January	13.22	12.00	12.41	13.35	15.75	14.32	14.59	13.73	15.18	17.10	17.09	13.28	17.40	853.41	117.28
February	14.78	12.00	13.78	14.27	16.56	14.73	14.43	13.63	15.27	17.18	17.23	12.97	17.60	833.15	114.50
March	14.68	12.00	12.49	13.47	16.50	13.95	13.86	12.98	14.58	16.82	16.67	12.82	17.16	812.33	110.84
April	14.94	12.00	12.82	13.64	16.50	13.98	13.87	12.84	14.46	16.78	16.62	12.58	16.89	844.96	116.31
May	14.45	12.00	12.15	13.02	16.50	13.34	13.62	12.67	14.26	16.64	16.23	11.95	16.68	846.72	116.35
June	14.15	12.00	12.11	13.79	16.50	14.07	14.30	13.32	14.81	16.92	16.72	12.44	16.70	804.37	109.70
July	12.59	11.81	11.92	13.00	16.26	13.24	13.95	12.97	14.61	16.80	16.45	12.28	16.82	818.41	109.38
August	10.12	10.68	9.01	10.80	14.39	11.43	13.06	12.15	13.71	16.32	15.49	11.23	16.27	832.11	109.65
September	10.31	10.00	8.20	10.86	13.50	10.85	12.34	11.48	12.94	15.63	14.53	10.66	15.43	917.27	122.43
October	9.71	9.68	7.75	9.21	12.52	9.32	10.91	10.51	12.12	14.73	13.29	9.68	14.61	988.71	132.66
November	9.20	9.35	8.04	8.72	11.85	9.16	10.55	10.18	11.68	14.30	12.79	10.06	13.83	1 027.76	138.10
December	8.95	8.73	8.02	8.50	11.50	8.91	10.54	10.33	11.83	14.14	12.99	9.96	13.62	1 033.08	139.37
1983:															
January	8.68	8.50	7.81	8.15	11.16	8.62	10.46	10.37	11.79	13.94	12.74	9.50	13.25	1 064.29	144.27
February	8.51	8.50	8.13	8.39	10.98	8.92	10.72	10.60	12.01	13.95	12.90	9.58	13.04	1 087.43	146.80
March	8.77	8.50	8.30	8.48	10.50	9.04	10.51	10.34	11.73	13.61	12.47	9.20	12.80	1 129.58	151.88
April	8.80	8.50	8.25	8.48	10.50	8.98	10.40	10.19	11.51	13.29	12.04	9.04	12.78	1 168.43	157.71
May	8.63	8.50	8.19	8.31	10.50	8.90	10.38	10.21	11.46	13.09	11.92	9.11	12.63	1 212.86	164.10
June	8.98	8.50	8.82	9.03	10.50	9.66	10.85	10.64	11.74	13.37	12.40	9.52	12.87	1 221.47	166.39
July	9.37	8.50	9.12	9.36	10.50	10.20	11.38	11.10	12.15	13.39	12.79	9.53	13.42	1 213.93	166.96
August	9.56	8.50	9.39	9.68	10.89	10.53	11.85	11.42	12.51	13.64	13.16	9.72	13.81	1 189.21	162.42
September	9.45	8.50	9.05	9.28	11.00	10.16	11.65	11.26	12.37	13.55	12.98	9.58	13.73	1 237.04	167.16
October	9.48	8.50	8.71	8.98	11.00	9.81	11.54	11.21	12.25	13.46	12.89	9.66	13.54	1 252.20	167.65
November	9.34	8.50	8.71	9.09	11.00	9.94	11.69	11.32	12.41	13.61	13.14	9.74	13.44	1 250.00	165.23
December	9.47	8.50	8.96	9.50	11.00	10.11	11.83	11.44	12.57	13.75	13.29	9.89	13.42	1 257.64	164.36
1984:															
January	9.56	8.50	7.14	9.18	11.00	9.90	11.67	11.29	12.20	13.65	12.99	9.63	13.37	1 258.89	166.39
February	9.59	8.50	9.03	9.31	11.00	10.04	11.84	11.44	12.08	13.59	13.05	9.64	13.23	1 164.46	157.25
March	9.91	8.50	9.08	9.86	11.21	10.59	12.32	11.90	12.57	13.99	13.63	9.94	13.39	1 161.97	157.44
April	10.29	8.87	9.69	10.22	11.93	10.90	12.63	12.17	12.81	14.31	13.96	9.96	13.65	1 152.71	157.60
May	10.32	9.00	9.90	10.87	12.39	11.66	13.41	12.89	13.28	14.74	14.79	10.49	13.94	1 143.42	156.55
June	11.06	9.00	9.94	11.23	12.60	12.08	13.56	13.04	13.55	15.05	15.00	10.67	14.42	1 121.14	153.12
July	11.23	9.00	10.13	11.34	13.00	12.03	13.36	12.82	13.44	15.15	14.93	10.42	14.67	1 113.27	151.08
August	11.64	9.00	10.49	11.16	13.00	11.82	12.72	12.23	12.87	14.63	14.12	9.99	14.47	1 212.82	164.42
September	11.30	9.00	10.41	10.94	12.97	11.58	12.52	11.97	12.66	14.35	13.86	10.10	14.35	1 213.51	166.11
October	9.99	9.00	9.97	10.16	12.58	10.90	12.16	11.66	12.63	13.94	13.52	10.25	14.13	1 199.30	164.82
November	9.43	8.83	8.79	9.06	11.77	9.82	11.57	11.25	12.29	13.48	12.98	10.17	13.64	1 211.30	166.27
December	8.38	8.37	8.16	8.55	11.06	9.33	11.50	11.21	12.13	13.40	12.88	9.95	13.18	1 188.96	164.48
1985:															
January	8.35	8.00	7.76	8.15	10.61	9.02	11.38	11.15	12.08	13.26	12.78	9.51	13.08	1 238.16	171.61
February	8.50	8.00	8.17	8.69	10.50	9.29	11.51	11.35	12.13	13.23	12.76	9.65	12.92	1 283.23	180.88
March	8.58	8.00	8.57	9.23	10.50	9.86	11.86	11.78	12.56	13.69	13.17	9.77	13.17	1 268.83	179.42
April	8.27	8.00	8.00	8.47	10.50	9.14	11.43	11.42	12.23	13.51	12.75	9.42	13.20	1 266.36	180.62
May	7.97	7.81	7.56	7.88	10.31	8.46	10.85	10.96	11.72	13.15	12.25	9.01	12.91	1 279.40	184.90
June	7.53	7.50	7.01	7.38	9.78	7.80	10.16	10.36	10.94	12.40	11.62	8.69	12.22	1 314.00	188.89
July	7.88	7.50	7.05	7.57	9.50	7.86	10.31	10.51	10.97	12.43	11.60	8.81	12.03	1 343.17	192.54
August	7.90	7.50	7.18	7.74	9.50	8.05	10.33	10.59	11.05	12.50	11.77	9.08	12.19	1 326.18	188.31
September	7.92	7.50	7.08	7.86	9.50	8.07	10.37	10.67	11.07	12.48	11.87	9.27	12.19	1 317.95	184.06
October	7.99	7.50	7.17	7.79	9.50	8.01	10.24	10.56	11.02	12.36	11.82	9.08	12.14	1 351.58	186.18
November	8.05	7.50	7.20	7.69	9.50	7.88	9.78	10.08	10.55	11.99	11.38	8.54	11.78	1 432.88	197.45
December	8.27	7.50	7.07	7.62	9.50	7.67	9.26	9.59	10.16	11.58	10.91	8.42	11.26	1 517.02	207.26
1986:															
January	8.14	7.50	7.04	7.62	9.50	7.73	9.19	9.51	10.05	11.44	10.74	8.08	10.88	1 534.86	208.19
February	7.86	7.50	7.03	7.54	9.50	7.61	8.70	9.07	9.67	11.11	10.20	7.44	10.71	1 652.73	219.37
March	7.48	7.10	6.59	7.08	9.10	7.03	7.78	8.13	9.00	10.50	9.41	7.08	10.08	1 757.35	232.33
April	6.99	6.83	6.06	6.47	8.83	6.44	7.30	7.59	8.79	10.19	9.26	7.19	9.94	1 807.05	237.98
May	6.85	6.50	6.12	6.53	8.50	6.65	7.71	8.02	9.09	10.29	9.50	7.54	10.14	1 801.80	238.46
June	6.92	6.50	6.21	6.63	8.50	6.73	7.80	8.23	9.13	10.34	9.65	7.87	10.68	1 867.70	245.30
July	6.56	6.16	5.84	6.24	8.16	6.27	7.30	7.86	8.88	10.16	9.56	7.51	10.51	1 809.92	240.18
August	6.17	5.82	5.57	5.83	7.90	5.93	7.17	7.72	8.72	10.18	9.51	7.21	10.20	1 843.45	245.00
September	5.89	5.50	5.19	5.61	7.50	5.77	7.45	8.08	8.89	10.20	9.57	7.11	10.01	1 813.47	238.27
October	5.85	5.50	5.18	5.61	7.50	5.72	7.43	8.04	8.86	10.24	9.48	7.08	9.97	1 817.04	237.36
November	6.04	5.50	5.35	5.69	7.50	5.80	7.25	7.81	8.68	10.07	9.31	6.84	9.70	1 883.65	245.09
December	6.91	5.50	5.49	5.88	7.50	5.87	7.11	7.67	8.49	9.97	9.08	6.87	9.31	1 924.07	248.61

1. Discount window borrowing, Federal Reserve Bank of New York.
2. Maturities of more than ten years.
3. 1941-1943=10.

INTEREST RATES, BOND YIELDS, AND STOCK PRICE INDEXES—Continued
(Not seasonally adjusted)

YEAR AND MONTH	Short-term rates					U.S. Treasury securities			Bond yields				Fixed-rate first mort-gages	Stock price indexes	
	Federal funds	Federal Reserve discount rate[1]	U.S. Treasury bills, 3-month	Com-mercial paper, 6-month	Bank prime rate	One year	Ten year	Long-term compos-ite[2]	Domestic corporate (Moody's) Aaa	Baa	A-rated utility bonds	State and local bonds (Bond Buyer)		Dow Jones industrials (30 stocks)	Standard and Poor's composite, (500 stocks)[3]
1987:															
January	6.43	5.50	5.45	5.76	7.50	5.78	7.08	7.60	8.36	9.72	8.92	6.66	9.20	2 065.13	264.51
February	6.10	5.50	5.59	5.99	7.50	5.96	7.25	7.69	8.38	9.65	8.82	6.61	9.08	2 202.34	280.93
March	6.13	5.50	5.56	6.10	7.50	6.03	7.25	7.62	8.36	9.61	8.84	6.65	9.04	2 292.61	292.47
April	6.37	5.50	5.76	6.50	7.75	6.50	8.02	8.31	8.85	10.04	9.51	7.55	9.83	2 302.64	289.32
May	6.85	5.50	5.75	7.04	8.14	7.00	8.61	8.79	9.33	10.51	10.05	8.00	10.60	2 291.11	289.12
June	6.73	5.50	5.69	7.00	8.25	6.80	8.40	8.63	9.32	10.52	10.05	7.79	10.54	2 384.02	301.38
July	6.58	5.50	5.78	6.72	8.25	6.68	8.45	8.70	9.42	10.61	10.17	7.72	10.28	2 481.72	310.09
August	6.73	5.50	6.00	6.81	8.25	7.03	8.76	8.97	9.67	10.80	10.37	7.82	10.33	2 655.01	329.36
September	7.22	5.95	6.32	7.55	8.70	7.67	9.42	9.58	10.18	11.31	10.84	8.26	10.89	2 570.80	318.66
October	7.29	6.00	6.40	7.96	9.07	7.59	9.52	9.61	10.52	11.62	11.07	8.70	11.26	2 224.59	280.16
November	6.69	6.00	5.81	7.17	8.78	6.96	8.86	8.99	10.01	11.23	10.39	7.95	10.65	1 931.86	245.01
December	6.77	6.00	5.80	7.49	8.75	7.17	8.99	9.12	10.11	11.29	10.42	7.96	10.65	1 910.07	240.96
1988:															
January	6.83	6.00	5.90	6.92	8.75	6.99	8.67	8.82	9.88	11.07	10.05	7.69	10.49	1 947.35	250.48
February	6.58	6.00	5.69	6.58	8.51	6.64	8.21	8.41	9.40	10.62	9.75	7.49	9.89	1 980.65	258.13
March	6.58	6.00	5.69	6.64	8.50	6.71	8.37	8.61	9.39	10.57	9.91	7.74	9.93	2 044.31	265.74
April	6.87	6.00	5.92	6.92	8.50	7.01	8.72	8.91	9.67	10.90	10.23	7.81	10.20	2 036.13	262.61
May	7.09	6.00	6.27	7.31	8.84	7.40	9.09	9.24	9.90	11.04	10.61	7.91	10.46	1 988.91	256.12
June	7.51	6.00	6.50	7.53	9.00	7.49	8.92	9.04	9.86	11.00	10.41	7.78	10.46	2 104.94	270.68
July	7.75	6.00	6.73	7.90	9.29	7.75	9.06	9.20	9.96	11.11	10.40	7.76	10.43	2 104.22	269.05
August	8.01	6.37	7.02	8.36	9.84	8.17	9.26	9.33	10.11	11.21	10.45	7.79	10.60	2 051.29	263.73
September	8.19	6.50	7.23	8.23	10.00	8.09	8.98	9.06	9.82	10.90	10.26	7.66	10.48	2 080.06	267.97
October	8.30	6.50	7.34	8.24	10.00	8.11	8.80	8.89	9.51	10.41	10.11	7.46	10.30	2 144.31	277.40
November	8.35	6.50	7.68	8.55	10.05	8.48	8.96	9.07	9.45	10.48	10.12	7.46	10.27	2 099.04	271.02
December	8.76	6.50	8.09	8.97	10.50	8.99	9.11	9.13	9.57	10.65	10.08	7.61	10.61	2 148.58	276.51
1989:															
January	9.12	6.50	8.29	9.02	10.50	9.05	9.09	9.07	9.62	10.65	10.09	7.35	10.73	2 234.68	285.41
February	9.36	6.59	8.48	9.35	10.93	9.25	9.17	9.16	9.64	10.61	10.25	7.44	10.65	2 304.30	294.01
March	9.85	7.00	8.83	9.97	11.50	9.57	9.36	9.33	9.80	10.67	10.37	7.59	11.03	2 283.11	292.71
April	9.84	7.00	8.70	9.78	11.50	9.36	9.18	9.18	9.79	10.61	10.33	7.48	11.05	2 348.91	302.25
May	9.81	7.00	8.40	9.29	11.50	8.98	8.86	8.95	9.57	10.46	10.09	7.25	10.77	2 439.55	313.93
June	9.53	7.00	8.22	8.80	11.07	8.44	8.28	8.40	9.10	10.03	9.65	7.02	10.20	2 494.90	323.73
July	9.24	7.00	7.92	8.35	10.98	7.89	8.02	8.19	8.93	9.87	9.54	6.96	9.88	2 554.03	331.93
August	8.99	7.00	7.91	8.32	10.50	8.18	8.11	8.26	8.96	9.88	9.55	7.06	9.98	2 691.11	346.61
September	9.02	7.00	7.72	8.50	10.50	8.22	8.19	8.31	9.01	9.91	9.55	7.26	10.13	2 693.41	347.33
October	8.84	7.00	7.63	8.24	10.50	7.99	8.01	8.15	8.92	9.81	9.39	7.22	9.95	2 692.01	347.40
November	8.55	7.00	7.65	8.00	10.50	7.77	7.87	8.03	8.89	9.81	9.28	7.14	9.77	2 642.49	340.22
December	8.45	7.00	7.64	7.93	10.50	7.72	7.84	8.02	8.86	9.82	9.36	6.98	9.74	2 728.47	348.57
1990:															
January	8.23	7.00	7.64	7.96	10.11	7.92	8.21	8.39	8.99	9.94	9.63	7.10	9.90	2 679.24	339.97
February	8.24	7.00	7.76	8.04	10.00	8.11	8.47	8.66	9.22	10.14	9.84	7.22	10.20	2 614.18	330.45
March	8.28	7.00	7.87	8.23	10.00	8.35	8.59	8.74	9.37	10.21	9.92	7.29	10.27	2 700.13	338.47
April	8.26	7.00	7.78	8.29	10.00	8.40	8.79	8.92	9.46	10.30	10.09	7.39	10.37	2 708.26	338.18
May	8.18	7.00	7.78	8.23	10.00	8.32	8.76	8.90	9.47	10.41	10.04	7.35	10.48	2 793.81	350.25
June	8.29	7.00	7.74	8.06	10.00	8.10	8.48	8.62	9.26	10.22	9.85	7.24	10.16	2 894.82	360.39
July	8.15	7.00	7.66	7.90	10.00	7.94	8.47	8.64	9.24	10.20	9.96	7.19	10.04	2 934.23	360.03
August	8.13	7.00	7.44	7.77	10.00	7.78	8.75	8.97	9.41	10.41	10.29	7.32	10.10	2 681.89	330.75
September	8.20	7.00	7.38	7.83	10.00	7.76	8.89	9.11	9.56	10.64	10.28	7.43	10.18	2 550.69	315.41
October	8.11	7.00	7.19	7.81	10.00	7.55	8.72	8.93	9.53	10.74	10.23	7.49	10.18	2 460.54	307.12
November	7.81	7.00	7.07	7.74	10.00	7.31	8.39	8.60	9.30	10.62	10.07	7.18	10.01	2 518.56	315.29
December	7.31	6.79	6.81	7.49	10.00	7.05	8.08	8.31	9.05	10.43	9.95	7.09	9.67	2 610.92	328.75
1991:															
January	6.91	6.50	6.30	7.02	9.52	6.64	8.09	8.33	9.04	10.45	9.83	7.08	9.64	2 587.60	325.49
February	6.25	6.00	5.95	6.41	9.05	6.27	7.85	8.12	8.83	10.07	9.54	6.91	9.37	2 863.04	362.26
March	6.12	6.00	5.91	6.36	9.00	6.40	8.11	8.38	8.93	10.09	9.58	7.10	9.50	2 920.11	372.28
April	5.91	5.98	5.67	6.07	9.00	6.24	8.04	8.29	8.86	9.94	9.46	7.02	9.49	2 925.53	379.68
May	5.78	5.50	5.51	5.94	8.50	6.13	8.07	8.33	8.86	9.86	9.45	6.95	9.47	2 928.42	377.99
June	5.90	5.50	5.60	6.16	8.50	6.36	8.28	8.54	9.01	9.96	9.53	7.13	9.62	2 968.13	378.29
July	5.82	5.50	5.58	6.14	8.50	6.31	8.27	8.50	9.00	9.89	9.55	7.05	9.57	2 978.18	380.23
August	5.66	5.50	5.39	5.76	8.50	5.78	7.90	8.17	8.75	9.65	9.25	6.90	9.24	3 006.08	389.40
September	5.45	5.20	5.25	5.59	8.20	5.57	7.65	7.96	8.61	9.51	9.05	6.80	9.01	3 010.35	387.20
October	5.21	5.00	5.03	5.33	8.00	5.33	7.53	7.88	8.55	9.49	9.02	6.68	8.86	3 019.73	386.88
November	4.81	4.58	4.60	4.93	7.58	4.89	7.42	7.83	8.48	9.45	8.95	6.73	8.71	2 986.12	385.92
December	4.43	4.11	4.12	4.49	7.21	4.38	7.09	7.58	8.31	9.26	8.68	6.69	8.50	2 958.64	388.51
1992:															
January	4.03	3.50	3.84	4.06	6.50	4.15	7.03	7.48	8.20	9.13	8.57	6.54	8.43	3 227.06	416.08
February	4.06	3.50	3.84	4.13	6.50	4.29	7.34	7.78	8.29	9.23	8.79	6.73	8.76	3 257.27	412.56
March	3.98	3.50	4.05	4.38	6.50	4.63	7.54	7.93	8.35	9.25	8.91	6.76	8.94	3 247.41	407.36
April	3.73	3.50	3.81	4.13	6.50	4.30	7.48	7.88	8.33	9.21	8.82	6.67	8.85	3 294.08	407.41
May	3.82	3.50	3.66	3.97	6.50	4.19	7.39	7.80	8.28	9.13	8.70	6.57	8.67	3 376.78	414.81
June	3.76	3.50	3.70	3.99	6.50	4.17	7.26	7.72	8.22	9.05	8.62	6.49	8.51	3 337.79	408.27
July	3.25	3.02	3.28	3.53	6.02	3.60	6.84	7.40	8.07	8.84	8.38	6.13	8.13	3 329.40	415.05
August	3.30	3.00	3.14	3.44	6.00	3.47	6.59	7.19	7.95	8.65	8.16	6.16	7.98	3 307.45	417.93
September	3.22	3.00	2.97	3.26	6.00	3.18	6.42	7.08	7.92	8.62	8.11	6.25	7.92	3 293.92	418.48
October	3.10	3.00	2.84	3.33	6.00	3.30	6.59	7.26	7.99	8.84	8.40	6.41	8.09	3 198.69	412.50
November	3.09	3.00	3.14	3.67	6.00	3.68	6.87	7.43	8.10	8.96	8.51	6.36	8.31	3 238.49	422.84
December	2.92	3.00	3.25	3.70	6.00	3.71	6.77	7.30	7.98	8.81	8.27	6.22	8.22	3 303.15	435.64

1. Discount window borrowing, Federal Reserve Bank of New York.
2. Maturities of more than ten years.
3. 1941-1943=10.

Part Four
State and Regional Data

State and Regional Data, Annual, 1971-1996

This appendix contains annual time-series data on personal income and employment for the United States, each state, the District of Columbia, and eight geographic regions. All data are from the Bureau of Economic Analysis, U.S. Department of Commerce. All revisions available through September 1997 are included.

These data utilize the same concepts and definitions as the personal income estimates contained in the national income and product accounts (NIPAs). Summaries of these definitions can be found in the Notes for pages 14–17 of this volume.

Additional Notes on the State and Regional Data

The U.S. data that accompany the state data differ from those in the NIPAs in that the NIPA totals include the labor income of U.S. residents temporarily working and living abroad.

The population estimates shown are the ones used in the calculation of per capita amounts. They are midyear estimates from the Bureau of the Census.

The dividends, interest, and rent total includes the capital consumption adjustment for rental income of persons.

The states are divided into regions as follows:

- **New England**: Connecticut, Maine, Massachusetts, New Hampshire, Rhode Island, Vermont

- **Mideast**: Delaware, District of Columbia, Maryland, New Jersey, New York, Pennsylvania

- **Great Lakes**: Illinois, Indiana, Michigan, Ohio, Wisconsin

- **Plains**: Iowa, Kansas, Minnesota, Missouri, Nebraska, North Dakota, South Dakota

- **Southeast**: Alabama, Arkansas, Florida, Georgia, Kentucky, Louisiana, Mississippi, North Carolina, South Carolina, Tennessee, Virginia, West Virginia

- **Southwest**: Arizona, New Mexico, Oklahoma, Texas

- **Rocky Mountain**: Colorado, Idaho, Montana, Utah, Wyoming

- **Far West**: Alaska, California, Hawaii, Nevada, Oregon, Washington

These regional groupings are the ones used by the Bureau of Economic Analysis. They differ from the region and division definitions used by the U.S. Bureau of the Census.

The data provided here are from a larger data set maintained by the Bureau of Economic Analysis. The data are described in "State Personal Income, Revised Estimates for 1958-1996," *Survey of Current Business* (September 1997)

YEAR	PERSONAL INCOME (Millions of dollars, except as noted)													TOTAL EM-PLOY-MENT (Thou-sands)
	Total	Farm	Nonfarm	Derivation of personal income						Per capita (Dollars)		Popu-lation (Thou-sands)		
				Earnings by place of work	Less: Personal contributions for social insurance	Plus: Adjust-ment for resi-dence	Equals: Net earn-ings by place of residence	Dividends, interest, and rent	Transfer payments	Total	Dispos-able			
UNITED STATES														
1971	894 815	19 112	875 703	701 512	30 457	-210	670 845	123 763	100 207	4 327	3 804	206 818		91 586
1972	983 311	23 214	960 097	774 294	34 247	-244	739 803	131 529	111 979	4 699	4 071	209 275		94 317
1973	1 101 241	35 924	1 065 317	868 143	42 376	-263	825 504	147 560	128 177	5 211	4 548	211 349		98 433
1974	1 210 981	31 144	1 179 837	939 618	47 695	-282	891 641	167 661	151 679	5 676	4 933	213 334		100 118
1975	1 314 384	29 942	1 284 442	997 365	50 184	-336	946 845	176 931	190 608	6 100	5 377	215 457		98 907
1976	1 455 441	25 900	1 429 541	1 108 418	55 250	-358	1 052 810	193 828	208 803	6 690	5 854	217 554		101 597
1977	1 611 733	25 150	1 586 583	1 231 242	60 966	-402	1 169 874	217 993	223 866	7 334	6 381	219 761		105 049
1978	1 820 240	29 175	1 791 065	1 394 282	69 478	-441	1 324 363	253 571	242 306	8 196	7 117	222 098		109 688
1979	2 047 659	30 914	2 016 745	1 556 345	80 661	-427	1 475 257	300 895	271 507	9 118	7 874	224 564		113 288
1980	2 286 358	21 274	2 265 084	1 686 882	88 283	-488	1 598 111	366 045	322 202	10 062	8 690	227 225		114 231
1981	2 557 139	27 954	2 529 185	1 846 125	104 069	-487	1 741 569	448 858	366 712	11 144	9 578	229 466		115 304
1982	2 717 124	24 529	2 692 595	1 928 363	111 843	-559	1 815 961	492 511	408 652	11 729	10 130	231 664		114 521
1983	2 895 249	17 089	2 878 160	2 048 345	119 234	-553	1 928 558	526 719	439 972	12 384	10 808	233 792		116 020
1984	3 204 432	31 374	3 173 058	2 281 282	132 207	-617	2 148 458	601 787	454 187	13 588	11 915	235 825		121 051
1985	3 437 411	31 279	3 406 132	2 454 846	148 470	-647	2 305 729	644 751	486 931	14 448	12 613	237 924		124 473
1986	3 646 346	32 229	3 614 117	2 599 801	161 501	-622	2 437 678	689 878	518 790	15 185	13 274	240 133		126 941
1987	3 874 096	37 946	3 836 150	2 798 603	173 054	-656	2 624 893	705 928	543 275	15 990	13 873	242 289		130 371
1988	4 171 650	36 800	4 134 850	3 027 680	193 506	-689	2 833 485	760 582	577 583	17 062	14 891	244 499		134 676
1989	4 485 191	43 556	4 441 635	3 212 991	210 125	-740	3 002 126	857 102	625 963	18 172	15 767	246 819		137 318
1990	4 786 293	44 073	4 742 220	3 414 296	223 152	-790	3 190 354	908 201	687 738	19 191	16 692	249 398		139 185
1991	4 963 545	39 006	4 924 539	3 508 762	235 010	-785	3 272 967	920 772	769 806	19 689	17 213	252 102		138 786
1992	5 260 922	44 935	5 215 987	3 745 439	247 816	-778	3 496 845	905 933	858 144	20 631	18 084	255 003		139 411
1993	5 507 622	44 564	5 463 058	3 916 307	259 745	-2 836	3 653 726	942 002	911 894	21 365	18 693	257 783		142 007
1994	5 774 806	42 833	5 731 973	4 103 099	276 992	-3 227	3 822 880	997 326	954 600	22 180	19 345	260 356		145 650
1995	6 137 875	34 432	6 103 443	4 315 345	292 597	-3 375	4 019 373	1 103 603	1 014 899	23 348	20 327	262 890		149 446
1996	6 479 914	46 649	6 433 265	4 548 138	305 842	-3 395	4 238 901	1 173 114	1 067 899	24 426	21 087	265 284		152 317
ALABAMA														
1971	11 174	310	10 863	8 867	400	155	8 621	1 103	1 449	3 195	2 862	3 497		1 423
1972	12 404	382	12 022	9 899	455	178	9 622	1 158	1 624	3 504	3 113	3 540		1 471
1973	14 027	566	13 462	11 178	567	194	10 804	1 317	1 906	3 917	3 484	3 581		1 526
1974	15 599	370	15 229	12 220	652	204	11 772	1 542	2 285	4 300	3 816	3 628		1 552
1975	17 323	436	16 887	13 201	714	216	12 703	1 702	2 918	4 707	4 222	3 681		1 543
1976	19 565	496	19 069	15 050	827	234	14 457	1 872	3 236	5 235	4 669	3 737		1 594
1977	21 630	397	21 233	16 687	916	262	16 033	2 123	3 474	5 718	5 089	3 783		1 651
1978	24 523	523	24 000	19 038	1 040	284	18 282	2 458	3 783	6 396	5 682	3 834		1 714
1979	27 385	541	26 844	20 955	1 186	310	20 080	2 927	4 379	7 077	6 256	3 869		1 739
1980	30 179	231	29 948	22 322	1 299	343	21 365	3 663	5 151	7 738	6 822	3 900		1 736
1981	33 418	506	32 912	24 169	1 492	379	23 056	4 568	5 794	8 528	7 495	3 919		1 724
1982	35 130	416	34 714	24 825	1 589	404	23 641	5 059	6 430	8 950	7 938	3 925		1 692
1983	37 451	293	37 158	26 551	1 733	400	25 217	5 299	6 934	9 519	8 479	3 934		1 721
1984	41 199	482	40 717	29 486	1 914	431	28 003	5 992	7 204	10 425	9 324	3 952		1 786
1985	44 304	469	43 835	31 847	2 132	440	30 156	6 467	7 681	11 153	9 908	3 973		1 830
1986	47 007	452	46 554	33 750	2 215	461	31 995	6 949	8 063	11 777	10 472	3 992		1 867
1987	49 868	517	49 352	36 156	2 355	480	34 281	7 203	8 384	12 420	10 996	4 015		1 922
1988	53 529	791	52 739	38 921	2 622	483	36 783	7 839	8 908	13 303	11 900	4 024		1 983
1989	57 544	929	56 615	41 301	2 851	502	38 952	8 822	9 770	14 278	12 707	4 030		2 020
1990	61 667	832	60 834	43 914	3 029	513	41 397	9 313	10 957	15 233	13 573	4 048		2 058
1991	65 166	1 125	64 041	46 245	3 234	516	43 527	9 591	12 048	15 946	14 252	4 087		2 075
1992	69 794	976	68 818	49 527	3 434	546	46 639	9 677	13 479	16 896	15 152	4 131		2 113
1993	73 309	1 039	72 270	51 983	3 638	556	48 900	9 954	14 454	17 531	15 680	4 182		2 174
1994	77 344	1 018	76 326	54 768	3 908	602	51 463	10 675	15 206	18 349	16 344	4 215		2 189
1995	82 067	730	81 338	57 355	4 160	637	53 832	11 882	16 353	19 327	17 202	4 246		2 248
1996	86 021	886	85 135	59 680	4 300	687	56 067	12 622	17 332	20 131	17 821	4 273		2 272
ALASKA														
1971	1 685	2	1 683	1 579	71	-62	1 447	127	110	5 324	4 606	316		153
1972	1 844	2	1 842	1 734	79	-77	1 579	138	128	5 648	4 811	326		158
1973	2 164	2	2 162	1 916	96	-95	1 725	161	277	6 493	5 623	333		167
1974	2 671	2	2 669	2 573	132	-212	2 229	192	250	7 748	6 533	345		189
1975	3 759	4	3 755	4 066	204	-619	3 243	222	293	10 132	8 464	371		227
1976	4 520	4	4 516	5 101	251	-893	3 957	257	306	11 498	9 600	393		243
1977	4 647	5	4 642	4 682	233	-460	3 989	298	360	11 695	9 781	397		237
1978	4 735	5	4 730	4 553	229	-332	3 992	352	391	11 773	10 000	402		237
1979	4 998	4	4 994	4 718	248	-292	4 178	423	397	12 523	10 454	399		241
1980	5 611	4	5 607	5 268	280	-332	4 656	482	473	13 843	11 771	405		244
1981	6 497	2	6 495	6 150	346	-445	5 359	579	558	15 524	12 893	418		253
1982	7 785	2	7 783	7 125	395	-536	6 194	688	903	17 315	14 630	450		278
1983	8 782	2	8 780	7 972	444	-596	6 932	863	987	17 981	15 277	488		298
1984	9 291	2	9 289	8 497	478	-607	7 412	996	884	18 087	15 808	514		310
1985	10 080	2	10 078	8 893	517	-602	7 774	1 122	1 184	18 930	16 700	532		318
1986	10 068	7	10 060	8 672	510	-547	7 615	1 171	1 281	18 497	16 527	544		311
1987	9 731	10	9 721	8 234	499	-514	7 221	1 174	1 336	18 043	15 892	539		312
1988	10 001	11	9 990	8 421	540	-540	7 342	1 210	1 449	18 452	16 309	542		319
1989	10 928	6	10 922	9 245	604	-615	8 025	1 317	1 586	19 973	17 269	547		331
1990	11 665	8	11 657	9 818	643	-653	8 522	1 400	1 742	21 089	18 141	553		341
1991	12 250	8	12 242	10 295	683	-694	8 918	1 432	1 901	21 517	18 698	569		350
1992	12 978	8	12 969	10 838	706	-724	9 409	1 477	2 092	22 102	19 307	587		354
1993	13 613	10	13 603	11 216	742	-736	9 738	1 573	2 302	22 776	19 965	598		361
1994	14 125	8	14 118	11 466	766	-752	9 948	1 786	2 392	23 487	20 364	601		367
1995	14 563	10	14 553	11 607	775	-757	10 074	1 968	2 521	24 170	21 002	603		368
1996	14 810	9	14 801	11 586	782	-758	10 047	2 059	2 705	24 398	21 050	607		371

YEAR	PERSONAL INCOME (Millions of dollars, except as noted)												TOTAL EMPLOYMENT (Thousands)
				Derivation of personal income						Per capita (Dollars)		Population (Thousands)	
	Total	Farm	Nonfarm	Earnings by place of work	Less: Personal contributions for social insurance	Plus: Adjustment for residence	Equals: Net earnings by place of residence	Dividends, interest, and rent	Transfer payments	Total	Disposable		
ARIZONA													
1971	7 786	213	7 573	5 955	266	-28	5 660	1 283	843	4 106	3 626	1 896	786
1972	8 946	220	8 726	6 892	314	-32	6 546	1 425	975	4 453	3 896	2 009	850
1973	10 384	253	10 131	8 006	405	-31	7 570	1 643	1 170	4 886	4 335	2 125	925
1974	11 716	404	11 313	8 922	464	-41	8 417	1 886	1 413	5 267	4 646	2 224	955
1975	12 465	229	12 235	9 084	484	-46	8 554	1 992	1 919	5 452	4 916	2 286	935
1976	14 013	348	13 664	10 281	550	-46	9 685	2 191	2 137	5 968	5 344	2 348	976
1977	15 798	282	15 516	11 680	646	-55	10 979	2 490	2 329	6 508	5 780	2 427	1 047
1978	18 704	336	18 369	13 883	767	-67	13 049	3 019	2 636	7 429	6 551	2 518	1 149
1979	22 205	412	21 793	16 485	937	-69	15 479	3 720	3 005	8 415	7 374	2 639	1 241
1980	25 626	494	25 131	18 562	1 059	-79	17 425	4 573	3 628	9 360	8 234	2 738	1 285
1981	29 157	434	28 723	20 571	1 265	-12	19 294	5 633	4 230	10 376	9 045	2 810	1 317
1982	30 629	412	30 217	21 227	1 344	-5	19 879	6 029	4 720	10 599	9 261	2 890	1 319
1983	33 575	331	33 244	23 137	1 472	5	21 670	6 746	5 158	11 309	10 031	2 969	1 383
1984	38 016	555	37 460	26 603	1 676	9	24 937	7 652	5 427	12 394	10 971	3 067	1 511
1985	42 415	521	41 895	29 717	1 922	22	27 817	8 553	6 046	13 323	11 753	3 184	1 631
1986	46 545	499	46 046	32 422	2 123	42	30 341	9 614	6 590	14 069	12 424	3 308	1 711
1987	50 463	634	49 829	35 214	2 246	68	33 036	10 220	7 206	14 682	12 921	3 437	1 777
1988	53 988	770	53 218	37 880	2 507	111	35 484	10 700	7 803	15 272	13 541	3 535	1 851
1989	57 733	684	57 048	39 550	2 674	168	37 044	11 872	8 817	15 939	14 034	3 622	1 883
1990	61 223	640	60 584	41 681	2 799	233	39 116	12 248	9 860	16 640	14 663	3 679	1 907
1991	64 094	725	63 368	43 513	3 013	224	40 724	12 363	11 007	17 104	15 085	3 747	1 921
1992	68 328	647	67 682	46 525	3 208	242	43 559	12 234	12 535	17 809	15 789	3 837	1 945
1993	73 564	824	72 740	50 152	3 452	218	46 918	13 108	13 537	18 641	16 471	3 946	2 030
1994	79 868	510	79 359	54 859	3 838	215	51 235	14 115	14 519	19 562	17 205	4 083	2 167
1995	87 518	687	86 831	60 061	4 213	217	56 065	15 986	15 467	20 329	17 860	4 305	2 289
1996	94 596	687	93 908	65 124	4 527	248	60 845	17 405	16 345	21 363	18 633	4 428	2 396
ARKANSAS													
1971	6 081	421	5 660	4 673	199	15	4 488	710	883	3 084	2 781	1 972	831
1972	6 862	505	6 357	5 340	229	13	5 123	752	987	3 400	3 051	2 018	867
1973	8 142	934	7 208	6 369	289	9	6 089	859	1 194	3 955	3 542	2 058	902
1974	9 097	852	8 245	6 945	333	2	6 613	1 032	1 451	4 331	3 850	2 100	927
1975	9 934	807	9 127	7 318	356	0	6 962	1 150	1 822	4 603	4 164	2 158	905
1976	11 036	647	10 388	8 166	401	-12	7 753	1 269	2 013	5 089	4 542	2 169	941
1977	12 355	728	11 627	9 177	450	-19	8 708	1 475	2 172	5 597	5 011	2 207	981
1978	14 387	1 195	13 192	10 803	516	-25	10 262	1 741	2 384	6 420	5 754	2 241	1 022
1979	15 851	1 010	14 841	11 668	589	-29	11 049	2 081	2 721	6 986	6 212	2 269	1 033
1980	17 129	384	16 745	11 980	638	-19	11 323	2 580	3 225	7 484	6 617	2 289	1 035
1981	19 330	870	18 459	13 293	741	-41	12 511	3 175	3 643	8 429	7 461	2 293	1 030
1982	20 137	643	19 493	13 459	786	-41	12 632	3 531	3 974	8 777	7 708	2 294	1 014
1983	21 409	397	21 012	14 331	846	-70	13 416	3 707	4 286	9 285	8 205	2 306	1 043
1984	23 834	862	22 972	16 357	934	-90	15 333	4 084	4 417	10 274	9 205	2 320	1 083
1985	25 459	843	24 616	17 350	1 044	-94	16 213	4 484	4 762	10 940	9 802	2 327	1 104
1986	26 705	775	25 930	18 164	1 126	-117	16 921	4 759	5 025	11 452	10 303	2 332	1 116
1987	27 797	936	26 861	19 261	1 179	-135	17 946	4 651	5 200	11 867	10 634	2 342	1 143
1988	29 640	1 275	28 365	20 711	1 306	-164	19 242	4 916	5 483	12 652	11 352	2 343	1 178
1989	31 360	1 171	30 189	21 731	1 430	-167	20 134	5 277	5 949	13 366	11 962	2 346	1 197
1990	33 065	892	32 173	22 830	1 516	-212	21 102	5 525	6 438	14 045	12 562	2 354	1 210
1991	35 093	992	34 101	24 296	1 622	-232	22 443	5 577	7 073	14 799	13 278	2 371	1 239
1992	37 967	1 248	36 719	26 638	1 761	-270	24 607	5 504	7 856	15 846	14 243	2 396	1 265
1993	39 923	1 248	38 675	27 984	1 866	-309	25 809	5 682	8 431	16 451	14 777	2 427	1 305
1994	42 079	1 353	40 726	29 761	2 022	-343	27 396	5 910	8 773	17 142	15 316	2 455	1 335
1995	45 039	1 403	43 635	31 525	2 159	-321	29 045	6 599	9 394	18 126	16 155	2 485	1 379
1996	47 584	1 847	45 737	33 278	2 237	-322	30 719	6 972	9 893	18 959	16 872	2 510	1 402
CALIFORNIA													
1971	101 679	1 734	99 945	77 505	3 596	-46	73 863	15 328	12 487	4 998	4 442	20 346	9 036
1972	111 196	2 216	108 980	85 663	4 217	-35	81 411	16 227	13 559	5 402	4 707	20 585	9 369
1973	122 804	2 963	119 841	94 713	5 095	-31	89 587	18 226	14 990	5 885	5 185	20 868	9 844
1974	137 198	3 671	133 526	104 529	5 561	-24	98 944	20 529	17 724	6 480	5 698	21 173	10 163
1975	150 729	3 297	147 432	112 967	5 919	123	107 172	21 583	21 974	6 999	6 225	21 537	10 286
1976	169 161	3 488	165 674	127 102	6 508	228	120 823	23 789	24 549	7 712	6 793	21 935	10 633
1977	188 443	3 563	184 880	142 483	7 312	76	135 248	26 733	26 462	8 431	7 372	22 350	11 119
1978	216 040	3 509	212 531	163 369	8 358	47	155 057	32 241	28 742	9 459	8 242	22 839	11 802
1979	247 641	4 647	242 994	186 412	9 856	32	176 587	39 385	31 669	10 649	9 229	23 255	12 462
1980	281 590	5 742	275 847	207 494	10 411	14	197 097	47 655	36 837	11 831	10 233	23 801	12 777
1981	315 376	4 454	310 922	226 309	12 745	137	213 701	58 549	43 126	12 986	11 254	24 286	12 969
1982	336 460	4 687	331 773	239 570	13 951	155	225 773	63 322	47 365	13 556	11 824	24 820	12 896
1983	362 338	4 289	358 049	259 288	15 096	170	244 362	67 579	50 396	14 288	12 552	25 360	13 215
1984	403 455	5 002	398 452	290 820	17 060	135	273 895	77 797	51 763	15 611	13 698	25 844	13 848
1985	437 964	5 030	432 934	317 109	19 233	99	297 975	82 844	57 145	16 564	14 437	26 441	14 356
1986	469 932	5 493	464 438	341 654	21 478	68	320 244	88 282	61 406	17 339	15 113	27 102	14 785
1987	506 180	6 630	499 550	374 269	23 852	11	350 428	91 122	64 630	18 223	15 683	27 777	15 392
1988	548 999	6 985	542 014	407 650	26 814	-11	380 825	99 328	68 846	19 287	16 697	28 464	16 164
1989	591 509	6 808	584 702	435 993	28 998	-6	406 990	110 070	74 450	20 245	17 356	29 218	16 578
1990	640 268	7 006	633 262	469 357	31 082	-44	438 230	119 374	82 663	21 413	18 438	29 901	16 955
1991	655 102	5 890	649 212	476 911	32 610	-6	444 295	119 503	91 304	21 552	18 755	30 396	16 907
1992	687 242	6 706	680 536	498 152	33 823	34	464 363	118 155	104 723	22 253	19 532	30 883	16 554
1993	702 415	7 780	694 635	506 523	34 561	-581	471 381	120 897	110 137	22 533	19 806	31 172	16 533
1994	722 002	6 813	715 189	517 995	36 011	-675	481 309	126 623	114 070	23 022	20 158	31 362	16 735
1995	764 435	6 566	757 869	541 103	37 257	-724	503 122	142 004	119 309	24 217	21 087	31 565	17 154
1996	807 975	7 419	800 556	570 329	38 767	-728	530 834	151 522	125 620	25 346	21 826	31 878	17 571

| YEAR | PERSONAL INCOME (Millions of dollars, except as noted) | | | | | | | | | | | | TOTAL EMPLOYMENT (Thousands) |
| | Total | Farm | Nonfarm | Derivation of personal income | | | | | | Per capita (Dollars) | | Population (Thousands) | |
				Earnings by place of work	Less: Personal contributions for social insurance	Plus: Adjustment for residence	Equals: Net earnings by place of residence	Dividends, interest, and rent	Transfer payments	Total	Disposable		
COLORADO													
1971	10 146	318	9 828	7 933	329	3	7 606	1 515	1 024	4 404	3 867	2 304	1 072
1972	11 483	353	11 130	9 094	381	4	8 717	1 621	1 145	4 775	4 129	2 405	1 149
1973	13 204	459	12 745	10 463	485	3	9 981	1 880	1 343	5 290	4 597	2 496	1 243
1974	14 809	558	14 251	11 644	558	4	11 090	2 151	1 567	5 827	5 041	2 541	1 276
1975	16 250	486	15 763	12 578	589	8	11 997	2 315	1 938	6 283	5 509	2 586	1 285
1976	18 047	354	17 693	13 994	653	8	13 349	2 548	2 150	6 856	5 985	2 632	1 339
1977	20 232	281	19 951	15 728	752	11	14 988	2 888	2 356	7 504	6 498	2 696	1 411
1978	23 449	218	23 231	18 326	875	20	17 471	3 404	2 574	8 475	7 334	2 767	1 505
1979	27 169	217	26 952	21 176	1 056	20	20 140	4 143	2 886	9 536	8 207	2 849	1 594
1980	31 261	288	30 973	23 972	1 209	27	22 790	5 093	3 378	10 747	9 260	2 909	1 654
1981	35 974	271	35 703	27 193	1 460	6	25 739	6 290	3 945	12 080	10 350	2 978	1 722
1982	39 370	166	39 204	29 538	1 629	2	27 911	6 992	4 468	12 860	10 984	3 062	1 765
1983	42 276	346	41 929	31 485	1 731	-1	29 754	7 610	4 911	13 491	11 827	3 134	1 794
1984	46 335	430	45 905	34 569	1 907	7	32 669	8 570	5 095	14 617	12 880	3 170	1 891
1985	48 966	395	48 572	36 531	2 123	16	34 423	9 131	5 413	15 260	13 403	3 209	1 926
1986	50 649	396	50 253	37 447	2 255	20	35 212	9 587	5 850	15 645	13 789	3 237	1 924
1987	52 788	487	52 301	39 082	2 317	32	36 797	9 710	6 281	16 190	14 235	3 260	1 914
1988	55 485	576	54 909	41 164	2 518	46	38 692	10 152	6 641	17 008	14 961	3 262	1 986
1989	59 385	616	58 769	43 390	2 725	62	40 726	11 403	7 256	18 128	15 819	3 276	2 019
1990	63 842	910	62 932	46 760	2 920	81	43 921	12 043	7 877	19 323	16 790	3 304	2 052
1991	67 918	643	67 275	49 564	3 186	80	46 457	12 674	8 787	20 159	17 493	3 369	2 105
1992	72 989	624	72 365	53 848	3 431	81	50 499	12 741	9 749	21 070	18 218	3 464	2 154
1993	79 356	964	78 392	58 795	3 723	61	55 133	13 707	10 517	22 243	19 188	3 568	2 252
1994	84 643	481	84 162	62 249	4 019	57	58 287	15 284	11 071	23 109	19 829	3 663	2 368
1995	91 766	562	91 203	66 888	4 324	64	62 628	16 931	12 206	24 487	21 034	3 748	2 456
1996	98 258	644	97 614	71 866	4 618	64	67 312	18 227	12 719	25 704	21 849	3 823	2 532
CONNECTICUT													
1971	16 175	77	16 098	11 670	481	695	11 885	2 728	1 561	5 283	4 594	3 061	1 388
1972	17 444	76	17 368	12 679	534	734	12 879	2 891	1 674	5 683	4 848	3 070	1 416
1973	19 059	87	18 972	14 026	663	748	14 111	3 143	1 805	6 210	5 350	3 069	1 480
1974	20 772	90	20 682	15 178	751	774	15 202	3 455	2 115	6 753	5 838	3 076	1 511
1975	22 123	81	22 042	15 766	774	837	15 830	3 539	2 754	7 172	6 293	3 085	1 468
1976	24 121	88	24 032	17 215	832	911	17 294	3 865	2 961	7 816	6 775	3 086	1 493
1977	26 642	88	26 554	19 118	915	1 003	19 205	4 308	3 129	8 626	7 470	3 089	1 546
1978	29 760	85	29 675	21 485	1 040	1 149	21 594	4 928	3 238	9 616	8 272	3 095	1 616
1979	33 652	81	33 571	24 178	1 223	1 310	24 265	5 789	3 597	10 856	9 282	3 100	1 675
1980	38 361	85	38 276	26 989	1 375	1 534	27 148	7 070	4 144	12 322	10 471	3 113	1 709
1981	42 959	83	42 876	29 461	1 620	1 670	29 511	8 668	4 781	13 730	11 616	3 129	1 732
1982	46 275	110	46 165	31 399	1 768	1 797	31 428	9 502	5 346	14 742	12 448	3 139	1 731
1983	49 566	111	49 455	33 882	1 899	1 930	33 913	9 907	5 745	15 674	13 509	3 162	1 748
1984	55 314	132	55 182	37 869	2 124	2 078	37 824	11 508	5 982	17 394	15 048	3 180	1 831
1985	59 551	132	59 418	41 371	2 415	2 221	41 177	12 024	6 350	18 603	15 959	3 201	1 889
1986	64 352	145	64 207	44 789	2 671	2 369	44 487	13 111	6 754	19 962	17 004	3 224	1 948
1987	70 370	144	70 226	49 904	2 977	2 516	49 443	13 829	7 099	21 670	18 258	3 247	1 997
1988	77 678	158	77 520	55 281	3 347	2 706	54 641	15 427	7 611	23 741	20 287	3 272	2 050
1989	83 531	145	83 385	58 292	3 589	2 647	57 350	17 761	8 419	25 440	21 799	3 283	2 050
1990	87 180	185	86 995	60 375	3 726	2 913	59 562	18 097	9 521	26 507	22 846	3 289	2 017
1991	88 181	164	88 018	60 670	3 897	2 958	59 731	17 789	10 661	26 810	23 057	3 289	1 940
1992	93 227	191	93 037	63 760	4 023	3 751	63 489	17 314	12 425	28 455	24 096	3 276	1 921
1993	96 440	225	96 214	66 158	4 128	3 641	65 671	17 843	12 926	29 442	24 832	3 276	1 943
1994	99 703	176	99 528	68 309	4 333	3 604	67 580	18 710	13 413	30 462	25 722	3 273	1 928
1995	105 778	170	105 608	71 516	4 564	3 633	70 586	20 801	14 391	32 341	27 063	3 271	1 958
1996	110 916	186	110 730	74 877	4 765	3 927	74 039	22 024	14 853	33 875	27 913	3 274	1 986
DELAWARE													
1971	2 759	40	2 719	2 285	86	-86	2 113	431	215	4 881	4 047	565	280
1972	3 032	51	2 980	2 540	98	-97	2 344	448	239	5 284	4 361	574	293
1973	3 374	98	3 275	2 865	128	-119	2 619	475	280	5 826	4 805	579	305
1974	3 655	85	3 570	3 062	146	-124	2 793	517	345	6 267	5 190	583	302
1975	3 908	95	3 813	3 222	152	-129	2 941	513	454	6 637	5 563	589	292
1976	4 292	86	4 205	3 545	165	-145	3 235	563	494	7 240	5 990	593	296
1977	4 649	58	4 591	3 818	178	-163	3 477	629	543	7 815	6 479	595	296
1978	5 101	63	5 039	4 231	201	-190	3 841	690	571	8 528	7 105	598	304
1979	5 619	56	5 563	4 630	232	-212	4 187	782	651	9 383	7 759	599	312
1980	6 315	14	6 302	5 103	259	-259	4 585	944	786	10 616	8 758	595	312
1981	6 948	42	6 905	5 497	300	-290	4 907	1 157	884	11 658	9 542	596	314
1982	7 459	66	7 392	5 899	328	-321	5 249	1 264	946	12 449	10 339	599	317
1983	7 996	80	7 915	6 345	356	-367	5 621	1 360	1 014	13 206	11 121	605	326
1984	8 758	97	8 661	6 953	389	-412	6 152	1 533	1 073	14 321	12 152	612	341
1985	9 595	105	9 490	7 608	441	-451	6 716	1 728	1 151	15 520	13 184	618	359
1986	10 287	147	10 140	8 082	477	-457	7 147	1 893	1 247	16 393	13 883	628	372
1987	11 147	114	11 032	8 877	516	-521	7 840	1 986	1 321	17 500	14 930	637	389
1988	12 252	185	12 067	9 804	585	-576	8 642	2 169	1 441	18 919	16 243	648	406
1989	13 558	194	13 364	10 780	653	-672	9 455	2 537	1 566	20 596	17 649	658	418
1990	14 485	138	14 346	11 479	693	-735	10 051	2 741	1 693	21 649	18 544	669	422
1991	15 214	130	15 085	11 915	729	-773	10 413	2 901	1 901	22 368	19 277	680	418
1992	15 983	112	15 870	12 430	747	-800	10 883	2 943	2 157	23 178	19 995	690	417
1993	16 683	114	16 569	12 954	781	-870	11 303	3 115	2 265	23 859	20 558	699	424
1994	17 517	109	17 408	13 597	837	-954	11 807	3 266	2 444	24 748	21 215	708	428
1995	18 757	88	18 669	14 496	896	-1 124	12 476	3 655	2 626	26 159	22 417	717	442
1996	20 095	119	19 976	15 446	950	-1 219	13 277	3 948	2 871	27 724	23 549	725	451

YEAR	PERSONAL INCOME (Millions of dollars, except as noted)												TOTAL EMPLOYMENT (Thousands)
	Total	Farm	Nonfarm	Derivation of personal income						Per capita (Dollars)		Population (Thousands)	
				Earnings by place of work	Less: Personal contributions for social insurance	Plus: Adjustment for residence	Equals: Net earnings by place of residence	Dividends, interest, and rent	Transfer payments	Total	Disposable		
DISTRICT OF COLUMBIA													
1971	4 149	0	4 149	6 802	324	-3 494	2 984	530	635	5 528	4 762	751	668
1972	4 522	0	4 522	7 352	357	-3 791	3 203	570	748	6 079	5 202	744	671
1973	4 802	0	4 802	7 822	402	-4 052	3 368	600	833	6 545	5 591	734	664
1974	5 263	0	5 263	8 496	444	-4 411	3 641	653	969	7 302	6 267	721	676
1975	5 745	0	5 745	9 252	478	-4 870	3 904	655	1 187	8 089	6 976	710	680
1976	6 139	0	6 139	10 003	517	-5 325	4 161	713	1 265	8 816	7 487	696	677
1977	6 608	0	6 608	10 841	550	-5 788	4 503	777	1 328	9 692	8 294	682	683
1978	7 017	0	7 017	11 870	600	-6 503	4 767	855	1 395	10 472	8 904	670	696
1979	7 454	0	7 454	12 892	670	-7 284	4 938	957	1 559	11 370	9 546	656	709
1980	7 922	0	7 922	14 028	736	-8 261	5 031	1 107	1 784	12 412	10 450	638	706
1981	8 626	0	8 626	14 892	822	-8 773	5 297	1 355	1 974	13 544	11 239	637	696
1982	9 248	0	9 248	15 760	882	-9 244	5 634	1 508	2 107	14 583	12 130	634	680
1983	9 686	0	9 686	16 767	999	-9 766	6 001	1 529	2 156	15 316	12 902	632	676
1984	10 547	0	10 547	18 287	1 092	-10 604	6 591	1 716	2 239	16 651	14 025	633	699
1985	11 168	0	11 168	19 548	1 222	-11 296	7 029	1 880	2 258	17 599	14 779	635	713
1986	11 788	0	11 788	20 681	1 309	-11 901	7 470	1 976	2 343	18 469	15 512	638	733
1987	12 507	0	12 507	22 434	1 391	-12 942	8 101	1 971	2 434	19 636	16 311	637	746
1988	13 757	0	13 757	24 865	1 542	-14 374	8 949	2 229	2 579	21 822	18 500	630	770
1989	14 649	0	14 649	26 487	1 678	-15 416	9 393	2 634	2 622	23 469	19 810	624	778
1990	15 517	0	15 517	28 410	1 802	-16 578	10 031	2 678	2 809	25 700	21 806	604	787
1991	16 115	0	16 115	29 648	1 907	-17 460	10 281	2 708	3 126	27 091	23 207	595	775
1992	16 815	0	16 815	31 252	1 995	-18 536	10 721	2 702	3 392	28 677	24 731	586	768
1993	17 415	0	17 415	32 564	2 081	-19 366	11 118	2 744	3 553	30 078	25 752	579	768
1994	17 795	0	17 795	33 395	2 140	-20 006	11 249	2 937	3 608	31 327	26 702	568	748
1995	18 021	0	18 021	33 848	2 175	-20 364	11 309	3 114	3 598	32 499	27 780	555	734
1996	18 539	0	18 539	34 298	2 197	-20 637	11 464	3 247	3 829	34 129	29 195	543	716
FLORIDA													
1971	30 570	672	29 897	21 402	942	-13	20 447	6 307	3 816	4 268	3 781	7 163	3 082
1972	35 209	774	34 435	24 854	1 104	-11	23 739	6 972	4 498	4 682	4 073	7 520	3 338
1973	41 278	866	40 412	29 152	1 435	-10	27 707	8 136	5 436	5 207	4 562	7 927	3 666
1974	46 403	939	45 464	32 040	1 588	-2	30 450	9 394	6 558	5 579	4 911	8 317	3 766
1975	50 132	1 038	49 094	33 279	1 578	-10	31 691	10 038	8 403	5 869	5 267	8 542	3 676
1976	55 127	1 074	54 054	36 301	1 719	8	34 590	11 155	9 382	6 340	5 652	8 695	3 730
1977	61 789	1 075	60 714	40 575	1 929	19	38 664	12 722	10 403	6 951	6 172	8 889	3 929
1978	71 747	1 286	70 461	47 078	2 267	21	44 832	15 340	11 575	7 857	6 949	9 132	4 235
1979	83 256	1 367	81 890	53 876	2 715	16	51 177	18 718	13 361	8 791	7 731	9 471	4 457
1980	97 999	1 756	96 243	61 901	3 152	10	58 760	23 306	15 933	9 959	8 716	9 840	4 695
1981	112 989	1 470	111 519	69 132	3 837	34	65 329	29 103	18 557	11 085	9 678	10 193	4 881
1982	121 981	1 902	120 080	73 808	4 237	63	69 634	31 408	20 939	11 649	10 082	10 471	4 969
1983	134 638	2 661	131 977	82 022	4 665	86	77 442	34 422	22 774	12 525	11 075	10 750	5 183
1984	149 148	1 936	147 212	91 653	5 297	131	86 488	38 850	23 811	13 510	12 062	11 040	5 527
1985	163 937	1 946	161 991	100 640	6 104	173	94 709	43 218	26 010	14 442	12 718	11 351	5 807
1986	177 997	2 092	175 905	108 772	6 772	233	102 233	47 744	28 020	15 256	13 380	11 668	6 054
1987	193 029	2 246	190 783	120 430	7 356	299	113 373	49 733	29 923	16 089	14 116	11 997	6 139
1988	210 889	2 865	208 024	132 511	8 363	372	124 520	53 868	32 501	17 137	15 107	12 306	6 452
1989	233 041	2 618	230 423	140 888	9 263	458	132 083	64 923	36 035	18 440	16 231	12 638	6 661
1990	249 766	2 230	247 536	150 436	9 822	558	141 172	68 648	39 946	19 185	16 960	13 018	6 787
1991	260 004	2 724	257 280	154 768	10 347	612	145 032	70 124	44 848	19 563	17 437	13 291	6 785
1992	270 834	2 559	268 275	164 958	11 021	653	154 590	65 703	50 542	20 042	17 825	13 513	6 833
1993	292 533	2 823	289 710	176 441	11 746	441	165 136	73 014	54 383	21 332	18 953	13 714	7 071
1994	306 657	1 941	304 717	184 821	12 614	444	172 651	76 136	57 870	21 959	19 436	13 965	7 315
1995	328 067	1 965	326 103	196 633	13 482	468	183 619	82 455	61 994	23 129	20 425	14 184	7 545
1996	348 849	1 774	347 076	207 974	14 153	512	194 333	89 138	65 378	24 226	21 190	14 400	7 758
GEORGIA													
1971	17 270	484	16 786	14 221	600	-43	13 579	1 907	1 785	3 666	3 261	4 710	2 167
1972	19 433	506	18 927	16 059	692	-36	15 332	2 081	2 021	4 043	3 544	4 807	2 253
1973	22 053	819	21 234	18 235	873	-31	17 331	2 376	2 345	4 494	3 973	4 907	2 356
1974	24 290	704	23 586	19 614	983	-25	18 606	2 768	2 916	4 863	4 299	4 995	2 374
1975	25 972	658	25 314	20 300	1 010	-11	19 279	2 912	3 781	5 134	4 626	5 059	2 313
1976	29 150	644	28 506	23 067	1 134	-24	21 909	3 139	4 102	5 687	5 074	5 126	2 399
1977	32 268	370	31 898	25 720	1 265	-28	24 426	3 486	4 355	6 191	5 490	5 212	2 503
1978	36 766	577	36 189	29 407	1 459	-2	27 946	4 072	4 749	6 955	6 140	5 286	2 622
1979	41 438	616	40 822	32 909	1 698	4	31 215	4 844	5 379	7 686	6 707	5 391	2 704
1980	46 264	58	46 206	35 700	1 932	8	33 776	6 048	6 440	8 433	7 389	5 486	2 747
1981	52 144	518	51 627	39 632	2 275	12	37 369	7 447	7 339	9 364	8 161	5 568	2 785
1982	56 261	682	55 579	42 400	2 490	-29	39 880	8 318	8 063	9 958	8 727	5 650	2 801
1983	61 659	466	61 193	46 438	2 719	-68	43 651	9 284	8 724	10 764	9 424	5 728	2 885
1984	70 283	954	69 329	53 405	3 104	-103	50 198	10 924	9 161	12 045	10 604	5 835	3 080
1985	77 263	777	76 486	58 939	3 577	-118	55 245	12 063	9 954	12 958	11 333	5 963	3 224
1986	84 108	815	83 293	64 402	3 993	-163	60 246	13 188	10 674	13 823	12 114	6 085	3 353
1987	90 610	871	89 738	69 872	4 286	-168	65 418	13 854	11 338	14 594	12 731	6 208	3 454
1988	98 599	1 139	97 459	75 904	4 772	-157	70 974	15 346	12 278	15 611	13 709	6 316	3 572
1989	105 665	1 337	104 328	80 167	5 137	-108	74 922	17 284	13 460	16 482	14 405	6 411	3 635
1990	113 283	1 192	112 090	85 388	5 483	-92	79 814	18 501	14 969	17 411	15 239	6 507	3 681
1991	119 065	1 511	117 554	88 466	5 763	-81	82 621	19 369	17 075	17 973	15 828	6 625	3 650
1992	128 112	1 557	126 556	96 074	6 151	-96	89 827	19 312	18 973	18 931	16 709	6 767	3 729
1993	136 393	1 531	134 862	102 352	6 597	-107	95 648	20 255	20 490	19 749	17 294	6 906	3 898
1994	146 103	1 831	144 273	109 466	7 139	-136	102 191	22 008	21 905	20 686	18 072	7 063	4 057
1995	157 875	1 775	156 100	117 512	7 663	-140	109 709	24 618	23 548	21 901	19 102	7 209	4 215
1996	168 959	1 952	167 007	126 017	8 158	-194	117 666	26 510	24 782	22 977	19 852	7 353	4 344

YEAR	PERSONAL INCOME (Millions of dollars, except as noted)										Per capita (Dollars)		Popu- lation (Thou- sands)	TOTAL EM- PLOY- MENT (Thou- sands)
	Total	Farm	Nonfarm	Earnings by place of work	Less: Personal contribu- tions for social in- surance	Plus: Adjust- ment for resi- dence	Equals: Net earn- ings by place of residence	Dividends, interest, and rent	Transfer payments		Total	Dispos- able		

HAWAII

YEAR	Total	Farm	Nonfarm	Earnings	Less SI	Plus Adj	Net earnings	Div/int/rent	Transfer	Total pc	Disposable pc	Population	Employment
1971	4 112	133	3 979	3 338	159	0	3 180	579	353	5 194	4 508	792	437
1972	4 524	134	4 390	3 667	174	0	3 493	610	420	5 530	4 732	818	453
1973	5 028	138	4 890	4 050	207	0	3 843	702	483	5 973	5 128	842	473
1974	5 762	357	5 404	4 631	238	0	4 393	786	582	6 714	5 796	858	485
1975	6 195	210	5 985	4 904	264	0	4 640	810	744	7 079	6 252	875	499
1976	6 726	175	6 551	5 283	286	0	4 997	855	873	7 537	6 602	892	505
1977	7 287	187	7 101	5 737	313	0	5 425	927	936	7 958	6 924	916	509
1978	8 091	170	7 921	6 333	353	0	5 980	1 093	1 018	8 711	7 532	929	527
1979	9 195	197	8 998	7 154	404	0	6 750	1 319	1 127	9 679	8 347	950	556
1980	10 563	391	10 173	8 169	452	0	7 716	1 543	1 304	10 916	9 427	968	575
1981	11 376	206	11 170	8 528	514	0	8 014	1 844	1 519	11 630	10 032	978	569
1982	12 057	242	11 815	9 074	565	0	8 509	1 878	1 670	12 133	10 681	994	568
1983	13 218	344	12 874	9 855	604	0	9 251	2 120	1 847	13 052	11 457	1 013	579
1984	14 139	233	13 905	10 457	647	0	9 810	2 409	1 920	13 754	12 180	1 028	585
1985	15 103	214	14 889	11 181	700	0	10 481	2 573	2 049	14 527	12 735	1 040	601
1986	16 190	260	15 930	11 983	739	0	11 245	2 757	2 189	15 394	13 495	1 052	616
1987	17 410	231	17 179	13 112	800	0	12 312	2 834	2 264	16 302	14 081	1 068	647
1988	19 260	254	19 006	14 644	913	0	13 731	3 110	2 420	17 836	15 356	1 080	675
1989	21 249	237	21 012	16 130	1 031	0	15 099	3 517	2 633	19 413	16 456	1 095	703
1990	23 991	250	23 741	18 084	1 143	0	16 941	3 916	3 134	21 563	18 373	1 113	730
1991	25 168	207	24 960	19 083	1 228	0	17 855	4 082	3 231	22 279	19 089	1 130	753
1992	26 463	200	26 264	20 328	1 297	0	19 030	3 791	3 642	23 056	19 877	1 148	755
1993	27 666	186	27 480	20 844	1 320	0	19 524	4 183	3 959	23 851	20 589	1 160	751
1994	28 469	180	28 289	21 072	1 354	0	19 718	4 501	4 251	24 278	21 012	1 173	747
1995	29 593	187	29 405	21 144	1 363	0	19 780	5 106	4 706	25 095	21 978	1 179	742
1996	30 072	184	29 888	21 243	1 366	0	19 877	5 321	4 874	25 404	22 065	1 184	742

IDAHO

YEAR	Total	Farm	Nonfarm	Earnings	Less SI	Plus Adj	Net earnings	Div/int/rent	Transfer	Total pc	Disposable pc	Population	Employment
1971	2 747	263	2 483	2 154	87	14	2 080	366	301	3 718	3 324	739	332
1972	3 134	339	2 795	2 487	101	15	2 401	390	343	4 106	3 688	763	347
1973	3 641	468	3 173	2 890	129	17	2 778	472	392	4 656	4 151	782	365
1974	4 290	647	3 643	3 412	152	20	3 280	536	474	5 309	4 698	808	381
1975	4 571	402	4 169	3 544	171	25	3 398	588	585	5 494	4 897	832	393
1976	5 170	357	4 813	4 000	193	31	3 838	664	668	6 033	5 372	857	419
1977	5 655	251	5 404	4 347	214	31	4 163	767	724	6 401	5 683	883	435
1978	6 545	324	6 221	5 074	244	38	4 868	898	779	7 185	6 373	911	460
1979	7 204	234	6 970	5 463	287	43	5 219	1 081	904	7 724	6 836	933	470
1980	8 130	407	7 723	5 987	309	55	5 733	1 314	1 084	8 576	7 594	948	466
1981	8 895	395	8 500	6 349	358	51	6 041	1 615	1 239	9 245	8 100	962	463
1982	9 207	387	8 820	6 318	373	59	6 003	1 785	1 419	9 456	8 367	974	453
1983	9 950	589	9 361	6 981	398	58	6 641	1 803	1 506	10 134	9 049	982	464
1984	10 690	504	10 187	7 521	434	69	7 156	2 000	1 534	10 789	9 674	991	474
1985	11 287	461	10 826	7 890	480	76	7 487	2 118	1 681	11 354	10 139	994	476
1986	11 594	477	11 117	8 016	499	92	7 609	2 207	1 778	11 708	10 509	990	476
1987	12 107	586	11 521	8 499	519	101	8 081	2 207	1 819	12 292	10 976	985	490
1988	12 934	635	12 299	9 204	593	116	8 728	2 266	1 939	13 122	11 670	986	513
1989	14 214	859	13 355	10 142	661	130	9 611	2 517	2 086	14 294	12 559	994	529
1990	15 548	977	14 571	11 137	719	150	10 568	2 702	2 278	15 366	13 490	1 012	552
1991	16 312	802	15 510	11 575	786	165	10 954	2 819	2 539	15 698	13 736	1 039	571
1992	17 763	808	16 955	12 777	849	167	12 094	2 879	2 790	16 650	14 580	1 067	591
1993	19 586	1 136	18 450	14 195	919	148	13 425	3 123	3 038	17 776	15 585	1 102	614
1994	20 732	649	20 082	14 957	1 017	157	14 098	3 412	3 222	18 243	15 959	1 136	651
1995	22 368	673	21 695	15 950	1 100	193	15 043	3 831	3 494	19 181	16 798	1 166	674
1996	23 591	767	22 824	16 714	1 154	220	15 781	4 068	3 742	19 837	17 276	1 189	692

ILLINOIS

YEAR	Total	Farm	Nonfarm	Earnings	Less SI	Plus Adj	Net earnings	Div/int/rent	Transfer	Total pc	Disposable pc	Population	Employment
1971	54 687	929	53 758	43 831	1 872	23	41 982	7 589	5 117	4 880	4 229	11 206	5 105
1972	59 324	1 042	58 282	47 568	2 071	7	45 504	8 057	5 764	5 269	4 505	11 258	5 156
1973	66 436	1 858	64 578	53 091	2 542	-3	50 546	9 114	6 776	5 900	5 088	11 260	5 351
1974	72 781	1 699	71 081	57 583	2 877	-3	54 703	10 349	7 729	6 456	5 545	11 274	5 442
1975	78 721	2 455	76 265	61 211	2 991	-18	58 202	10 774	9 744	6 963	6 058	11 306	5 342
1976	86 291	1 720	84 571	67 023	3 273	13	63 763	11 697	10 831	7 596	6 549	11 360	5 458
1977	95 212	1 751	93 461	74 115	3 567	88	70 636	13 098	11 478	8 347	7 169	11 406	5 587
1978	105 577	1 553	104 024	82 198	4 008	187	78 377	14 979	12 221	9 233	7 922	11 434	5 748
1979	116 428	1 808	114 620	89 924	4 561	283	85 647	17 511	13 270	10 193	8 695	11 423	5 811
1980	126 025	324	125 701	93 513	4 873	386	89 025	20 974	16 026	11 021	9 420	11 435	5 688
1981	139 615	1 680	137 935	101 069	5 599	318	95 789	25 450	18 376	12 200	10 416	11 443	5 684
1982	145 049	829	144 221	102 859	5 881	255	97 233	27 550	20 266	12 698	10 992	11 423	5 581
1983	150 734	-521	151 254	105 810	6 108	230	99 932	29 192	21 609	13 212	11 494	11 409	5 540
1984	166 237	1 059	165 179	118 161	6 697	154	111 618	32 732	21 887	14 567	12 770	11 412	5 744
1985	175 151	1 515	173 636	125 214	7 431	93	117 876	33 996	23 279	15 364	13 430	11 400	5 812
1986	184 420	1 220	183 201	132 027	8 043	40	124 024	36 061	24 335	16 195	14 166	11 387	5 925
1987	194 989	1 233	193 756	141 744	8 591	-43	133 110	36 672	25 207	17 118	14 787	11 391	6 070
1988	207 751	535	207 216	152 156	9 607	-135	142 414	39 039	26 299	18 239	15 863	11 390	6 240
1989	221 909	1 832	220 077	160 123	10 393	-166	149 564	44 328	28 018	19 449	16 792	11 410	6 347
1990	235 039	1 383	233 656	169 228	11 010	-264	157 953	46 899	30 187	20 533	17 727	11 447	6 427
1991	242 666	556	242 110	174 022	11 606	-282	162 134	47 764	32 768	21 072	18 302	11 516	6 422
1992	259 456	1 373	258 083	187 670	12 170	-329	175 171	47 143	37 142	22 374	19 512	11 596	6 406
1993	270 308	1 137	269 172	196 179	12 847	-440	182 891	48 735	38 682	23 163	20 102	11 670	6 497
1994	284 319	1 619	282 700	206 633	13 719	-515	192 400	51 712	40 207	24 230	20 922	11 734	6 677
1995	301 718	418	301 300	216 510	14 488	-557	201 465	57 349	42 904	25 590	22 054	11 790	6 847
1996	318 061	1 704	316 357	227 762	15 132	-573	212 057	60 854	45 150	26 848	22 928	11 847	6 949

YEAR	PERSONAL INCOME (Millions of dollars, except as noted)												TOTAL EMPLOYMENT (Thousands)
				Derivation of personal income						Per capita (Dollars)		Population (Thousands)	
	Total	Farm	Nonfarm	Earnings by place of work	Less: Personal contributions for social insurance	Plus: Adjustment for residence	Equals: Net earnings by place of residence	Dividends, interest, and rent	Transfer payments	Total	Disposable		
INDIANA													
1971	21 449	674	20 775	17 527	700	91	16 918	2 571	1 960	4 086	3 594	5 250	2 290
1972	23 452	584	22 868	19 260	798	123	18 585	2 705	2 163	4 428	3 849	5 296	2 367
1973	26 996	1 291	25 704	22 199	1 008	161	21 352	3 108	2 536	5 066	4 447	5 329	2 483
1974	28 893	796	28 097	23 256	1 135	209	22 330	3 580	2 984	5 401	4 666	5 350	2 492
1975	30 968	1 156	29 812	24 224	1 157	246	23 312	3 911	3 745	5 787	5 097	5 351	2 405
1976	34 746	1 138	33 609	27 476	1 293	287	26 470	4 314	3 962	6 469	5 638	5 372	2 489
1977	38 566	803	37 763	30 554	1 436	335	29 452	4 893	4 220	7 135	6 193	5 405	2 578
1978	43 185	806	42 379	34 251	1 645	385	32 991	5 556	4 639	7 929	6 866	5 446	2 671
1979	47 739	689	47 049	37 412	1 884	452	35 980	6 466	5 293	8 720	7 521	5 475	2 713
1980	51 230	384	50 846	38 254	1 964	574	36 864	7 794	6 572	9 330	8 102	5 491	2 632
1981	55 940	328	55 612	40 815	2 280	619	39 154	9 447	7 339	10 207	8 814	5 480	2 611
1982	57 479	283	57 197	40 702	2 342	685	39 045	10 251	8 183	10 512	9 151	5 468	2 529
1983	60 074	-257	60 331	42 290	2 456	742	40 576	10 726	8 771	11 022	9 686	5 450	2 549
1984	66 656	683	65 974	47 446	2 705	905	45 646	11 918	9 092	12 212	10 783	5 458	2 653
1985	70 261	586	69 675	50 180	3 005	988	48 163	12 543	9 555	12 870	11 317	5 459	2 708
1986	74 000	468	73 531	52 666	3 234	1 082	50 514	13 316	10 170	13 568	11 965	5 454	2 769
1987	78 573	648	77 925	56 846	3 451	1 151	54 546	13 487	10 540	14 356	12 608	5 473	2 865
1988	83 743	159	83 583	60 936	3 861	1 255	58 330	14 195	11 218	15 249	13 415	5 492	2 955
1989	90 091	840	89 251	65 415	4 215	1 343	62 543	15 487	12 061	16 310	14 196	5 524	3 030
1990	95 501	727	94 775	68 732	4 451	1 488	65 769	16 539	13 193	17 192	14 987	5 555	3 083
1991	98 978	124	98 854	70 854	4 722	1 517	67 649	16 697	14 632	17 666	15 458	5 603	3 094
1992	106 333	565	105 768	76 568	5 019	1 669	73 217	16 596	16 520	18 814	16 540	5 652	3 144
1993	112 702	675	112 027	81 405	5 363	1 792	77 834	17 293	17 574	19 749	17 211	5 707	3 217
1994	119 665	555	119 110	86 719	5 805	1 955	82 869	18 549	18 246	20 811	18 032	5 750	3 313
1995	125 805	301	125 504	90 806	6 117	2 209	86 898	20 319	18 588	21 702	18 828	5 797	3 401
1996	132 001	896	131 105	94 929	6 333	2 334	90 930	21 410	19 661	22 601	19 466	5 841	3 437
IOWA													
1971	11 343	1 009	10 334	8 668	375	73	8 367	1 778	1 198	3 977	3 534	2 852	1 297
1972	12 707	1 475	11 231	9 826	417	74	9 483	1 927	1 297	4 442	3 880	2 861	1 316
1973	15 339	2 715	12 624	12 062	523	68	11 607	2 241	1 491	5 356	4 727	2 864	1 374
1974	15 888	1 702	14 186	12 175	613	63	11 625	2 533	1 730	5 540	4 755	2 868	1 407
1975	17 636	1 948	15 688	13 370	659	72	12 783	2 731	2 122	6 120	5 332	2 881	1 407
1976	18 843	1 199	17 644	14 133	720	61	13 474	3 016	2 353	6 489	5 596	2 904	1 455
1977	20 898	1 222	19 676	15 635	779	33	14 889	3 482	2 527	7 171	6 187	2 914	1 488
1978	24 251	2 428	21 823	18 345	879	27	17 492	3 986	2 773	8 308	7 218	2 919	1 514
1979	26 148	1 545	24 603	19 363	1 033	37	18 368	4 667	3 113	8 965	7 711	2 917	1 557
1980	27 655	618	27 036	19 533	1 101	52	18 485	5 495	3 674	9 490	8 131	2 914	1 541
1981	31 371	1 717	29 654	21 654	1 217	76	20 513	6 703	4 156	10 788	9 252	2 908	1 513
1982	31 781	741	31 040	20 644	1 263	136	19 518	7 530	4 733	11 004	9 501	2 888	1 476
1983	32 243	-61	32 304	20 622	1 288	147	19 481	7 703	5 059	11 232	9 749	2 871	1 479
1984	35 637	1 282	34 355	23 584	1 396	168	22 356	8 163	5 118	12 466	11 036	2 859	1 506
1985	36 971	1 534	35 437	24 545	1 515	204	23 234	8 240	5 497	13 066	11 576	2 830	1 502
1986	38 365	1 923	36 443	25 515	1 602	197	24 110	8 520	5 735	13 741	12 241	2 792	1 501
1987	40 219	2 329	37 890	27 577	1 736	193	26 035	8 330	5 853	14 535	12 833	2 767	1 523
1988	41 215	1 348	39 867	28 426	1 936	231	26 720	8 368	6 127	14 888	13 079	2 768	1 568
1989	44 495	2 109	42 386	30 903	2 123	240	29 021	8 959	6 516	16 060	14 007	2 771	1 610
1990	46 965	2 005	44 960	32 427	2 258	261	30 430	9 532	7 003	16 896	14 693	2 780	1 642
1991	48 404	1 451	46 953	33 239	2 378	288	31 148	9 633	7 622	17 340	15 097	2 792	1 664
1992	51 721	2 135	49 587	36 037	2 496	308	33 849	9 671	8 201	18 418	16 133	2 808	1 680
1993	52 410	480	51 930	36 037	2 630	265	33 673	9 976	8 762	18 569	16 270	2 822	1 705
1994	56 787	2 294	54 492	40 138	2 836	260	37 562	10 165	9 059	20 049	17 616	2 832	1 741
1995	59 143	1 489	57 653	41 372	3 010	284	38 645	10 962	9 535	20 802	18 276	2 843	1 790
1996	63 613	3 046	60 568	44 805	3 136	311	41 980	11 619	10 015	22 306	19 503	2 852	1 820
KANSAS													
1971	9 248	700	8 548	6 864	297	419	6 986	1 265	998	4 117	3 658	2 246	1 023
1972	10 337	978	9 358	7 785	340	441	7 886	1 373	1 077	4 583	4 032	2 256	1 049
1973	11 850	1 391	10 459	8 990	423	457	9 024	1 566	1 259	5 233	4 600	2 264	1 091
1974	12 870	1 068	11 802	9 560	485	470	9 544	1 867	1 460	5 675	4 929	2 268	1 123
1975	13 987	816	13 172	10 229	532	483	10 180	2 045	1 763	6 139	5 392	2 279	1 134
1976	15 315	595	14 720	11 206	589	500	11 117	2 233	1 965	6 663	5 838	2 299	1 170
1977	16 744	509	16 235	12 187	628	538	12 097	2 496	2 151	7 224	6 281	2 318	1 209
1978	18 657	296	18 361	13 567	728	587	13 426	2 886	2 344	7 998	6 947	2 333	1 254
1979	21 467	729	20 739	15 700	851	631	15 480	3 402	2 586	9 145	7 870	2 347	1 300
1980	23 538	104	23 434	16 512	940	704	16 276	4 188	3 074	9 936	8 526	2 369	1 314
1981	26 639	276	26 362	18 192	1 099	742	17 834	5 266	3 539	11 170	9 483	2 385	1 328
1982	28 606	561	28 046	19 106	1 169	756	18 693	5 935	3 979	11 913	10 144	2 401	1 312
1983	29 678	317	29 361	19 838	1 214	726	19 350	6 094	4 234	12 286	10 674	2 416	1 329
1984	32 545	712	31 833	22 171	1 331	780	21 621	6 619	4 305	13 426	11 810	2 424	1 372
1985	34 329	770	33 559	23 304	1 458	825	22 671	7 064	4 594	14 142	12 389	2 427	1 377
1986	35 896	891	35 004	24 425	1 559	806	23 672	7 354	4 870	14 756	13 032	2 433	1 377
1987	37 566	1 148	36 418	25 898	1 640	872	25 131	7 391	5 044	15 362	13 429	2 445	1 431
1988	39 536	1 080	38 456	27 321	1 809	879	26 391	7 817	5 328	16 058	14 104	2 462	1 445
1989	41 578	748	40 830	28 389	1 953	924	27 360	8 412	5 806	16 814	14 619	2 473	1 466
1990	44 560	1 349	43 211	30 408	2 067	965	29 306	8 967	6 288	17 963	15 675	2 481	1 484
1991	46 253	968	45 285	31 398	2 194	932	30 135	9 215	6 903	18 564	16 257	2 492	1 502
1992	49 152	1 340	47 811	34 041	2 309	972	32 704	8 896	7 551	19 554	17 228	2 514	1 516
1993	51 245	1 360	49 885	35 605	2 436	1 020	34 189	9 137	7 919	20 242	17 781	2 532	1 538
1994	53 088	1 146	51 941	37 013	2 610	993	35 395	9 274	8 418	20 819	18 221	2 550	1 567
1995	56 218	704	55 514	38 488	2 759	1 020	36 749	10 737	8 732	21 929	19 114	2 564	1 604
1996	59 585	1 118	58 467	40 976	2 895	1 045	39 126	11 410	9 049	23 165	20 015	2 572	1 639

| | PERSONAL INCOME (Millions of dollars, except as noted) | | | | | | | | | | | | TOTAL EMPLOYMENT (Thousands) |
| | | | | Derivation of personal income | | | | | | Per capita (Dollars) | | Population (Thousands) | |
YEAR	Total	Farm	Nonfarm	Earnings by place of work	Less: Personal contributions for social insurance	Plus: Adjustment for residence	Equals: Net earnings by place of residence	Dividends, interest, and rent	Transfer payments	Total	Disposable		
KENTUCKY													
1971	11 062	446	10 616	8 718	369	115	8 463	1 196	1 403	3 354	2 972	3 298	1 360
1972	12 267	558	11 709	9 723	416	110	9 418	1 287	1 562	3 677	3 211	3 336	1 392
1973	13 836	626	13 211	10 965	516	78	10 527	1 450	1 859	4 104	3 629	3 372	1 461
1974	15 603	704	14 898	12 228	595	53	11 687	1 696	2 220	4 566	3 962	3 417	1 495
1975	16 940	512	16 428	12 903	638	47	12 311	1 864	2 765	4 884	4 331	3 469	1 465
1976	19 069	582	18 486	14 635	714	26	13 947	2 070	3 051	5 401	4 771	3 530	1 523
1977	21 500	711	20 789	16 642	796	43	15 890	2 358	3 252	6 014	5 263	3 575	1 579
1978	24 075	637	23 438	18 710	910	57	17 858	2 728	3 489	6 666	5 822	3 611	1 645
1979	27 123	703	26 420	20 869	1 050	54	19 873	3 214	4 036	7 444	6 502	3 644	1 668
1980	29 734	570	29 163	21 935	1 126	80	20 889	3 987	4 858	8 115	7 131	3 664	1 646
1981	33 085	977	32 108	23 875	1 301	78	22 653	4 949	5 483	9 014	7 876	3 670	1 639
1982	34 866	892	33 974	24 572	1 378	77	23 271	5 593	6 003	9 466	8 282	3 683	1 620
1983	35 888	229	35 659	24 853	1 432	110	23 531	5 889	6 468	9 714	8 562	3 694	1 629
1984	40 071	1 091	38 980	28 268	1 590	86	26 764	6 611	6 697	10 843	9 649	3 695	1 682
1985	41 754	834	40 920	29 368	1 765	93	27 695	7 027	7 032	11 301	9 999	3 688	1 706
1986	43 366	592	42 774	30 287	1 893	119	28 513	7 476	7 378	11 759	10 422	3 688	1 741
1987	45 927	698	45 229	32 727	2 036	88	30 779	7 496	7 652	12 469	11 004	3 683	1 774
1988	48 581	668	47 912	34 638	2 275	82	32 446	7 983	8 151	13 201	11 685	3 680	1 828
1989	52 273	1 042	51 231	36 949	2 482	45	34 513	8 874	8 886	14 215	12 485	3 677	1 877
1990	55 776	960	54 815	39 089	2 637	60	36 513	9 478	9 785	15 105	13 246	3 693	1 915
1991	58 567	983	57 584	40 497	2 810	44	37 730	9 673	11 164	15 765	13 887	3 715	1 916
1992	62 883	1 169	61 714	44 158	3 017	-130	41 011	9 590	12 282	16 757	14 798	3 753	1 964
1993	65 652	1 011	64 641	46 313	3 181	-184	42 947	9 711	12 993	17 304	15 257	3 794	2 005
1994	68 670	1 008	67 662	48 723	3 416	-279	45 027	10 160	13 483	17 949	15 801	3 826	2 049
1995	72 739	668	72 071	50 873	3 624	-292	46 957	11 339	14 442	18 860	16 576	3 857	2 104
1996	76 885	1 085	75 800	53 736	3 784	-327	49 625	11 992	15 268	19 797	17 305	3 884	2 134
LOUISIANA													
1971	12 283	332	11 952	9 832	409	-9	9 414	1 396	1 474	3 310	2 968	3 711	1 445
1972	13 454	366	13 088	10 809	460	-21	10 327	1 494	1 632	3 576	3 180	3 762	1 488
1973	15 051	593	14 458	12 097	569	-37	11 491	1 666	1 894	3 972	3 550	3 789	1 550
1974	17 160	622	16 538	13 625	661	-54	12 909	2 028	2 223	4 491	3 979	3 821	1 598
1975	19 168	425	18 743	15 097	737	-82	14 278	2 171	2 719	4 931	4 413	3 887	1 641
1976	21 841	455	21 386	17 366	848	-111	16 407	2 386	3 048	5 527	4 900	3 952	1 702
1977	24 468	452	24 016	19 500	934	-136	18 430	2 699	3 339	6 093	5 381	4 016	1 756
1978	28 130	373	27 758	22 537	1 081	-184	21 272	3 223	3 635	6 906	6 064	4 073	1 848
1979	32 119	511	31 609	25 641	1 267	-227	24 146	3 865	4 109	7 760	6 768	4 139	1 899
1980	37 086	181	36 904	29 002	1 459	-332	27 210	4 943	4 932	8 782	7 633	4 223	1 968
1981	42 699	248	42 451	33 088	1 795	-354	30 939	6 211	5 548	9 969	8 589	4 283	2 036
1982	45 512	254	45 258	34 508	1 920	-332	32 256	6 884	6 372	10 456	9 133	4 353	2 028
1983	47 219	220	47 000	34 816	1 908	-312	32 596	7 464	7 159	10 743	9 518	4 395	1 990
1984	50 324	312	50 012	36 975	2 027	-304	34 644	8 312	7 368	11 436	10 194	4 400	2 031
1985	52 456	225	52 231	37 769	2 171	-274	35 324	8 963	8 170	11 900	10 625	4 408	2 019
1986	52 205	216	51 989	36 505	2 142	-221	34 141	9 149	8 914	11 846	10 740	4 407	1 938
1987	52 285	371	51 914	36 700	2 119	-188	34 392	8 845	9 047	12 036	10 902	4 344	1 914
1988	55 085	564	54 521	38 897	2 321	-171	36 406	9 126	9 553	12 844	11 677	4 289	1 949
1989	57 978	399	57 579	40 363	2 518	-137	37 708	9 938	10 331	13 633	12 315	4 253	1 967
1990	62 416	348	62 067	43 577	2 714	-124	40 739	10 368	11 309	14 800	13 298	4 217	2 018
1991	66 284	420	65 863	46 047	2 914	-132	43 002	10 399	12 882	15 630	14 080	4 241	2 047
1992	70 177	452	69 726	48 536	3 012	-117	45 406	10 160	14 611	16 423	14 873	4 273	2 058
1993	73 794	449	73 345	50 380	3 147	-129	47 104	10 571	16 119	17 205	15 539	4 289	2 105
1994	78 219	514	77 705	53 030	3 406	-130	49 494	11 124	17 602	18 135	16 356	4 313	2 148
1995	82 252	489	81 763	55 875	3 616	-137	52 121	12 220	17 911	18 960	17 083	4 338	2 206
1996	85 548	642	84 907	58 225	3 755	-146	54 323	12 838	18 388	19 664	17 605	4 351	2 247
MAINE													
1971	3 662	70	3 592	2 772	119	-15	2 638	520	504	3 606	3 257	1 016	443
1972	4 006	69	3 937	3 039	131	-18	2 890	550	566	3 871	3 479	1 035	453
1973	4 517	152	4 365	3 417	161	-8	3 248	602	666	4 316	3 849	1 046	470
1974	5 026	200	4 826	3 738	183	-3	3 551	672	803	4 741	4 232	1 060	478
1975	5 365	82	5 283	3 860	196	-14	3 650	705	1 011	4 999	4 506	1 073	475
1976	6 182	166	6 016	4 535	222	-16	4 298	777	1 108	5 672	5 095	1 090	498
1977	6 723	130	6 592	4 901	242	-16	4 643	881	1 198	6 082	5 465	1 105	513
1978	7 444	90	7 354	5 451	276	-13	5 162	991	1 291	6 674	5 971	1 115	532
1979	8 329	76	8 253	6 032	313	-5	5 714	1 163	1 453	7 404	6 593	1 125	546
1980	9 356	46	9 310	6 598	348	-2	6 249	1 412	1 695	8 303	7 368	1 127	555
1981	10 366	118	10 247	7 103	401	1	6 703	1 736	1 926	9 149	8 045	1 133	554
1982	11 103	104	10 998	7 499	434	5	7 070	1 914	2 118	9 768	8 515	1 137	556
1983	11 975	72	11 903	8 087	466	11	7 632	2 060	2 283	10 460	9 243	1 145	568
1984	13 312	117	13 194	9 023	515	19	8 527	2 402	2 383	11 519	10 247	1 156	591
1985	14 352	103	14 250	9 777	581	38	9 234	2 587	2 532	12 342	10 897	1 163	610
1986	15 627	93	15 534	10 655	645	71	10 081	2 896	2 650	13 355	11 719	1 170	634
1987	17 106	134	16 973	11 885	708	87	11 263	3 129	2 714	14 441	12 552	1 185	657
1988	18 734	114	18 620	13 128	807	107	12 429	3 423	2 882	15 562	13 585	1 204	693
1989	20 298	129	20 170	14 125	885	93	13 332	3 870	3 096	16 639	14 529	1 220	708
1990	21 167	157	21 010	14 621	912	94	13 803	3 931	3 433	17 191	15 091	1 231	706
1991	21 440	104	21 335	14 448	936	89	13 600	3 899	3 941	17 352	15 330	1 236	684
1992	22 336	169	22 166	15 040	983	105	14 162	3 842	4 332	18 071	16 014	1 236	687
1993	23 009	151	22 858	15 437	1 032	127	14 531	3 905	4 573	18 577	16 505	1 239	699
1994	23 865	122	23 742	15 873	1 099	161	14 935	4 167	4 763	19 277	17 036	1 238	711
1995	24 966	81	24 885	16 406	1 161	201	15 447	4 520	4 999	20 157	17 842	1 239	720
1996	26 124	109	26 015	17 012	1 204	225	16 034	4 778	5 311	21 011	18 469	1 243	729

YEAR	PERSONAL INCOME (Millions of dollars, except as noted)											Popu-lation (Thousands)	TOTAL EM-PLOY-MENT (Thousands)
	Total	Farm	Nonfarm	Derivation of personal income						Per capita (Dollars)			
				Earnings by place of work	Less: Personal contributions for social insurance	Plus: Adjustment for residence	Equals: Net earnings by place of residence	Dividends, interest, and rent	Transfer payments	Total	Disposable		
MARYLAND													
1971	19 320	118	19 202	13 448	631	2 487	15 305	2 270	1 745	4 803	4 087	4 023	1 729
1972	21 174	154	21 020	14 793	699	2 684	16 778	2 392	2 004	5 188	4 336	4 081	1 781
1973	23 538	233	23 305	16 479	857	2 873	18 495	2 705	2 338	5 728	4 822	4 109	1 846
1974	25 864	188	25 675	17 910	967	3 067	20 010	3 118	2 735	6 257	5 226	4 133	1 868
1975	27 887	228	27 660	18 918	1 025	3 330	21 223	3 297	3 367	6 708	5 698	4 157	1 846
1976	30 583	197	30 386	20 817	1 117	3 574	23 275	3 621	3 688	7 330	6 229	4 172	1 866
1977	33 218	147	33 072	22 554	1 201	3 845	25 198	4 027	3 993	7 919	6 659	4 195	1 919
1978	37 067	204	36 863	25 146	1 349	4 182	27 980	4 687	4 401	8 801	7 406	4 212	2 003
1979	41 196	172	41 024	27 672	1 547	4 523	30 648	5 544	5 004	9 754	8 163	4 212	2 061
1980	46 192	64	46 128	30 126	1 706	4 949	33 369	6 827	5 996	10 926	9 200	4 228	2 074
1981	51 571	140	51 431	32 959	1 955	5 307	36 311	8 385	6 875	12 101	10 075	4 262	2 102
1982	55 247	147	55 100	34 594	2 081	5 740	38 253	9 273	7 720	12 899	10 789	4 283	2 090
1983	59 882	89	59 793	37 663	2 296	6 186	41 554	9 946	8 383	13 883	11 824	4 313	2 158
1984	66 782	271	66 511	42 067	2 562	6 797	46 303	11 683	8 796	15 299	12 987	4 365	2 252
1985	72 801	284	72 517	46 246	2 988	7 374	50 632	12 805	9 364	16 497	14 114	4 413	2 356
1986	78 740	293	78 447	50 182	3 259	7 866	54 790	13 938	10 012	17 549	15 033	4 487	2 443
1987	85 443	299	85 144	55 245	3 473	8 643	60 415	14 536	10 491	18 715	15 824	4 566	2 571
1988	93 649	357	93 292	60 796	3 953	9 641	66 484	15 919	11 246	20 105	17 195	4 658	2 672
1989	101 590	354	101 236	65 173	4 323	10 404	71 254	18 236	12 100	21 490	18 259	4 727	2 729
1990	108 031	338	107 694	69 165	4 601	10 924	75 488	19 309	13 234	22 517	19 184	4 798	2 757
1991	111 424	289	111 135	70 106	4 771	11 420	76 755	19 740	14 929	22 930	19 635	4 859	2 687
1992	115 906	321	115 585	72 897	4 917	12 127	80 107	19 529	16 270	23 609	20 336	4 909	2 661
1993	120 851	299	120 552	75 751	5 105	12 500	83 146	20 508	17 197	24 400	20 985	4 953	2 686
1994	127 014	253	126 761	79 045	5 410	12 855	86 490	21 812	18 712	25 405	21 784	5 000	2 737
1995	133 769	193	133 576	82 198	5 646	13 254	89 806	24 155	19 808	26 547	22 751	5 039	2 790
1996	140 068	318	139 750	85 910	5 859	13 579	93 630	25 365	21 073	27 618	23 491	5 072	2 825
MASSACHUSETTS													
1971	27 570	70	27 499	20 835	847	-103	19 885	4 272	3 413	4 804	4 169	5 739	2 644
1972	29 743	70	29 672	22 595	932	-108	21 555	4 431	3 757	5 162	4 399	5 762	2 697
1973	32 389	77	32 312	24 676	1 136	-131	23 409	4 789	4 190	5 600	4 813	5 784	2 787
1974	35 089	76	35 013	26 217	1 253	-151	24 814	5 315	4 960	6 074	5 218	5 777	2 811
1975	37 427	75	37 352	27 156	1 285	-162	25 709	5 355	6 363	6 495	5 671	5 762	2 728
1976	40 482	83	40 399	29 639	1 373	-188	28 078	5 751	6 653	7 042	6 119	5 749	2 756
1977	44 139	85	44 055	32 559	1 501	-237	30 820	6 386	6 933	7 684	6 635	5 744	2 833
1978	49 021	110	48 911	36 446	1 710	-290	34 446	7 173	7 402	8 536	7 368	5 743	2 959
1979	54 889	94	54 795	40 710	1 992	-365	38 353	8 323	8 213	9 552	8 181	5 746	3 079
1980	61 945	109	61 835	45 168	2 264	-482	42 423	10 109	9 413	10 780	9 192	5 746	3 142
1981	69 096	118	68 978	49 310	2 648	-609	46 053	12 371	10 672	11 978	10 118	5 769	3 155
1982	74 819	133	74 685	52 912	2 892	-733	49 287	13 907	11 624	12 964	11 049	5 771	3 155
1983	81 461	170	81 291	58 384	3 189	-896	54 298	14 799	12 363	14 046	11 974	5 799	3 229
1984	91 854	189	91 665	66 349	3 617	-1 156	61 575	17 440	12 839	15 726	13 470	5 841	3 420
1985	99 335	169	99 166	72 931	4 161	-1 333	67 437	18 621	13 277	16 892	14 371	5 881	3 531
1986	107 441	184	107 256	79 133	4 683	-1 443	73 008	20 248	14 185	18 202	15 417	5 903	3 628
1987	116 673	156	116 517	87 259	5 074	-1 627	80 558	21 339	14 776	19 658	16 569	5 935	3 660
1988	128 253	179	128 074	96 217	5 721	-1 856	88 639	23 648	15 966	21 447	18 362	5 980	3 778
1989	136 291	166	136 125	100 012	6 117	-1 991	91 904	26 582	17 806	22 657	19 340	6 015	3 751
1990	139 918	152	139 766	101 547	6 253	-2 103	93 191	26 977	19 750	23 249	19 852	6 018	3 646
1991	141 926	173	141 753	101 024	6 390	-2 180	92 454	26 875	22 597	23 657	20 279	5 999	3 486
1992	147 654	176	147 477	107 119	6 628	-2 300	98 191	25 828	23 635	24 618	21 074	5 998	3 517
1993	153 282	181	153 101	111 559	6 933	-2 505	102 121	26 795	24 366	25 473	21 725	6 017	3 587
1994	160 247	147	160 101	116 433	7 391	-2 715	106 327	28 327	25 593	26 522	22 486	6 042	3 660
1995	172 008	143	171 864	123 306	7 869	-2 884	112 554	32 381	27 073	28 332	23 901	6 071	3 752
1996	181 505	153	181 352	130 454	8 291	-3 071	119 091	34 468	27 945	29 792	24 810	6 092	3 817
MICHIGAN													
1971	40 150	355	39 795	32 379	1 337	102	31 144	4 865	4 141	4 475	3 900	8 972	3 571
1972	44 595	481	44 114	36 155	1 514	110	34 751	5 149	4 696	4 941	4 228	9 025	3 687
1973	50 049	610	49 439	40 879	1 940	136	39 074	5 651	5 323	5 517	4 763	9 072	3 858
1974	53 593	696	52 896	42 568	2 086	136	40 619	6 408	6 565	5 883	5 106	9 109	3 854
1975	56 603	615	55 989	43 276	2 082	151	41 345	6 759	8 500	6 215	5 472	9 108	3 695
1976	64 063	508	63 555	49 877	2 341	192	47 728	7 456	8 879	7 026	6 097	9 117	3 844
1977	72 279	592	71 686	57 008	2 597	216	54 627	8 422	9 230	7 893	6 781	9 157	4 016
1978	80 924	547	80 377	64 094	2 929	261	61 426	9 708	9 790	8 794	7 504	9 202	4 188
1979	89 173	575	88 598	69 673	3 313	301	66 661	11 304	11 209	9 642	8 231	9 249	4 234
1980	95 312	552	94 761	70 373	3 364	343	67 352	13 301	14 660	10 298	8 919	9 256	4 039
1981	101 867	514	101 353	73 862	3 855	366	70 373	15 873	15 621	11 061	9 537	9 209	3 992
1982	103 644	422	103 222	72 840	3 894	378	69 324	16 880	17 440	11 370	9 916	9 115	3 836
1983	110 081	206	109 874	77 286	4 173	407	73 521	18 103	18 457	12 167	10 625	9 048	3 879
1984	121 946	524	121 423	86 275	4 681	472	82 066	21 201	18 680	13 476	11 812	9 049	4 058
1985	132 288	630	131 658	95 009	5 408	489	90 090	22 817	19 380	14 575	12 652	9 076	4 256
1986	140 667	450	140 218	101 081	5 898	468	95 651	24 578	20 439	15 411	13 394	9 128	4 372
1987	146 465	583	145 883	105 298	6 248	487	99 538	25 307	21 620	15 942	13 828	9 187	4 510
1988	156 456	513	155 943	113 521	6 981	498	107 038	26 840	22 577	16 973	14 791	9 218	4 617
1989	166 610	903	165 707	119 821	7 579	477	112 719	29 927	23 963	18 005	15 569	9 253	4 745
1990	174 396	672	173 724	124 190	7 869	457	116 778	31 627	25 991	18 731	16 297	9 311	4 810
1991	179 174	554	178 620	125 234	8 166	476	117 544	32 330	29 300	19 130	16 688	9 366	4 757
1992	188 722	555	188 167	133 926	8 624	534	125 837	31 974	30 911	20 038	17 538	9 418	4 789
1993	200 695	596	200 099	143 444	9 168	525	134 801	32 903	32 991	21 230	18 524	9 453	4 849
1994	215 266	471	214 795	154 759	10 095	601	145 265	36 563	33 438	22 692	19 699	9 486	5 030
1995	229 544	688	228 856	164 161	10 758	714	154 117	40 244	35 183	24 066	20 877	9 538	5 187
1996	239 330	457	238 872	170 930	11 209	741	160 462	41 939	36 929	24 945	21 474	9 594	5 286

| YEAR | PERSONAL INCOME (Millions of dollars, except as noted) | | | | | | | | | | | Popu-lation (Thou-sands) | TOTAL EM-PLOY-MENT (Thou-sands) |
| | Total | Farm | Nonfarm | Derivation of personal income | | | | | | Per capita (Dollars) | | | |
				Earnings by place of work	Less: Personal contributions for social insurance	Plus: Adjustment for residence	Equals: Net earnings by place of residence	Dividends, interest, and rent	Transfer payments	Total	Dispos-able		
MINNESOTA													
1971	16 315	837	15 478	12 972	551	-29	12 392	2 201	1 722	4 235	3 730	3 852	1 706
1972	17 721	1 012	16 709	14 152	613	-32	13 508	2 305	1 908	4 583	3 968	3 867	1 780
1973	20 868	2 219	18 649	16 836	770	-39	16 027	2 620	2 221	5 371	4 714	3 885	1 878
1974	22 513	1 685	20 827	17 786	889	-35	16 862	3 040	2 611	5 775	4 964	3 898	1 921
1975	24 113	1 301	22 812	18 673	946	-36	17 692	3 296	3 125	6 142	5 322	3 926	1 920
1976	26 282	814	25 467	20 294	1 052	-44	19 197	3 622	3 463	6 642	5 729	3 957	1 977
1977	29 659	1 532	28 127	23 064	1 149	-57	21 858	4 107	3 694	7 452	6 409	3 980	2 034
1978	33 464	1 651	31 813	26 204	1 327	-72	24 805	4 680	3 979	8 356	7 168	4 005	2 123
1979	37 448	1 273	36 175	29 180	1 557	-91	27 532	5 483	4 433	9 274	7 885	4 038	2 222
1980	41 497	919	40 578	31 381	1 711	-100	29 570	6 628	5 299	10 158	8 680	4 085	2 254
1981	45 815	976	44 839	33 768	1 982	-134	31 651	8 088	6 076	11 142	9 485	4 112	2 241
1982	48 687	802	47 885	35 015	2 122	-158	32 735	9 113	6 839	11 785	10 071	4 131	2 200
1983	51 076	77	50 999	36 590	2 295	-186	34 110	9 611	7 355	12 333	10 591	4 141	2 227
1984	58 170	1 376	56 794	42 438	2 539	-246	39 653	10 826	7 690	13 991	12 157	4 158	2 335
1985	61 881	1 244	60 637	45 340	2 844	-295	42 201	11 413	8 268	14 789	12 859	4 184	2 399
1986	65 578	1 534	64 043	48 057	3 079	-336	44 642	12 229	8 706	15 594	13 557	4 205	2 431
1987	69 955	1 995	67 960	52 067	3 307	-387	48 373	12 425	9 157	16 518	14 184	4 235	2 525
1988	73 609	1 154	72 456	55 235	3 703	-471	51 060	12 844	9 705	17 134	14 749	4 296	2 601
1989	79 900	1 982	77 917	59 686	4 042	-457	55 187	14 328	10 384	18 418	15 796	4 338	2 654
1990	85 000	1 887	83 113	63 368	4 306	-484	58 578	15 132	11 290	19 374	16 568	4 387	2 707
1991	88 126	1 089	87 037	65 150	4 559	-497	60 094	15 788	12 244	19 898	17 054	4 429	2 739
1992	94 839	1 163	93 677	70 819	4 874	-535	65 410	16 106	13 324	21 195	18 175	4 475	2 785
1993	97 870	24	97 846	72 679	5 133	-574	66 972	16 718	14 180	21 626	18 442	4 526	2 842
1994	104 727	1 160	103 567	77 992	5 541	-627	71 824	17 948	14 956	22 904	19 504	4 572	2 933
1995	111 031	683	110 347	82 225	5 913	-672	75 641	19 547	15 843	24 061	20 388	4 615	3 026
1996	119 530	1 795	117 735	88 849	6 289	-726	81 834	21 054	16 642	25 663	21 482	4 658	3 084
MISSISSIPPI													
1971	6 424	454	5 970	5 085	211	55	4 929	607	888	2 836	2 589	2 266	939
1972	7 329	517	6 812	5 841	246	69	5 665	658	1 006	3 176	2 855	2 307	979
1973	8 398	711	7 687	6 683	308	90	6 464	762	1 172	3 574	3 238	2 350	1 019
1974	9 259	532	8 727	7 142	356	118	6 904	911	1 445	3 893	3 491	2 379	1 031
1975	9 974	387	9 587	7 450	380	143	7 213	986	1 775	4 156	3 783	2 400	1 001
1976	11 400	581	10 819	8 628	428	173	8 373	1 068	1 959	4 691	4 236	2 430	1 039
1977	12 743	614	12 129	9 678	477	213	9 413	1 197	2 133	5 181	4 694	2 460	1 071
1978	14 205	459	13 746	10 740	558	269	10 451	1 410	2 344	5 709	5 120	2 488	1 102
1979	16 130	718	15 413	12 124	647	326	11 803	1 665	2 662	6 432	5 747	2 508	1 117
1980	17 521	208	17 313	12 484	688	410	12 206	2 125	3 190	6 938	6 195	2 525	1 114
1981	19 630	357	19 273	13 714	802	446	13 358	2 657	3 615	7 731	6 849	2 539	1 110
1982	20 692	422	20 271	14 108	861	457	13 703	3 007	3 982	8 093	7 302	2 557	1 082
1983	21 539	91	21 448	14 453	902	509	14 060	3 110	4 369	8 388	7 548	2 568	1 091
1984	23 545	473	23 072	16 053	982	570	15 641	3 453	4 451	9 133	8 277	2 578	1 121
1985	24 754	435	24 319	16 924	1 085	598	16 437	3 552	4 766	9 565	8 669	2 588	1 129
1986	25 754	185	25 570	17 383	1 175	583	16 791	3 885	5 078	9 930	9 047	2 594	1 136
1987	27 194	535	26 659	18 553	1 217	623	17 959	3 929	5 306	10 506	9 544	2 589	1 147
1988	29 029	663	28 366	19 888	1 360	666	19 194	4 169	5 665	11 250	10 305	2 580	1 176
1989	30 913	505	30 408	20 959	1 504	707	20 161	4 608	6 144	12 008	10 953	2 574	1 196
1990	32 792	334	32 458	22 046	1 588	752	21 210	4 845	6 737	12 724	11 592	2 577	1 208
1991	34 738	460	34 278	23 171	1 680	786	22 277	5 018	7 444	13 402	12 279	2 592	1 217
1992	37 073	525	36 548	24 953	1 793	806	23 966	4 872	8 235	14 192	13 041	2 612	1 242
1993	39 465	418	39 046	26 743	1 940	833	25 636	4 968	8 861	14 955	13 659	2 639	1 297
1994	42 507	643	41 864	29 145	2 140	865	27 871	5 268	9 369	15 931	14 504	2 668	1 347
1995	45 147	496	44 651	30 545	2 285	993	29 252	5 825	10 069	16 745	15 260	2 696	1 379
1996	47 735	842	46 892	32 085	2 378	1 055	30 761	6 139	10 835	17 575	15 986	2 716	1 400
MISSOURI													
1971	19 338	587	18 751	15 914	675	-681	14 559	2 645	2 133	4 095	3 592	4 723	2 200
1972	21 071	746	20 325	17 357	745	-707	15 905	2 845	2 322	4 433	3 837	4 753	2 242
1973	23 545	1 243	22 301	19 327	911	-745	17 671	3 198	2 676	4 931	4 326	4 775	2 325
1974	25 192	668	24 524	20 181	1 016	-776	18 389	3 641	3 163	5 264	4 586	4 785	2 341
1975	27 364	716	26 647	21 390	1 064	-790	19 536	3 877	3 951	5 706	5 038	4 795	2 291
1976	30 278	482	29 796	23 772	1 175	-869	21 728	4 287	4 263	6 277	5 498	4 824	2 365
1977	33 682	719	32 963	26 602	1 288	-1 008	24 306	4 848	4 528	6 952	6 088	4 845	2 424
1978	37 765	935	36 830	29 863	1 466	-1 173	27 223	5 617	4 926	7 753	6 760	4 871	2 513
1979	42 458	1 206	41 252	33 287	1 676	-1 335	30 276	6 612	5 570	8 684	7 542	4 889	2 579
1980	46 116	237	45 879	34 573	1 809	-1 555	31 209	8 154	6 753	9 369	8 143	4 922	2 554
1981	51 514	824	50 690	37 632	2 090	-1 636	33 906	10 042	7 565	10 445	9 039	4 932	2 549
1982	54 253	322	53 931	38 774	2 239	-1 699	34 837	11 139	8 277	11 006	9 446	4 929	2 524
1983	57 723	-133	57 856	41 200	2 390	-1 739	37 070	11 783	8 869	11 676	10 244	4 944	2 570
1984	64 063	363	63 700	46 155	2 650	-1 898	41 606	13 322	9 134	12 876	11 358	4 975	2 678
1985	68 873	712	68 161	49 838	2 974	-2 024	44 840	14 122	9 911	13 774	12 113	5 000	2 752
1986	72 636	469	72 167	52 356	3 222	-2 088	47 046	15 096	10 494	14 461	12 720	5 023	2 816
1987	76 513	653	75 859	55 879	3 437	-2 211	50 231	15 335	10 947	15 131	13 266	5 057	2 853
1988	80 974	582	80 392	59 379	3 789	-2 305	53 285	16 045	11 644	15 934	14 044	5 082	2 907
1989	86 530	844	85 686	62 656	4 094	-2 451	56 111	17 895	12 524	16 981	14 892	5 096	2 959
1990	90 593	600	89 993	65 053	4 281	-2 563	58 209	18 981	13 403	17 672	15 477	5 126	2 987
1991	94 748	480	94 268	66 725	4 483	-2 556	59 685	19 388	15 675	18 373	16 194	5 157	2 964
1992	99 767	655	99 111	71 123	4 696	-2 666	63 761	19 411	16 594	19 228	16 978	5 189	2 981
1993	103 646	312	103 334	73 993	4 930	-2 781	66 282	19 415	17 948	19 806	17 461	5 233	3 062
1994	109 613	564	109 049	78 720	5 328	-2 841	70 551	20 467	18 595	20 779	18 244	5 275	3 138
1995	116 752	71	116 681	82 992	5 697	-3 067	74 228	22 641	19 883	21 949	19 234	5 319	3 216
1996	123 366	811	122 555	87 683	5 944	-3 184	78 554	23 969	20 843	23 022	20 075	5 359	3 274

YEAR	PERSONAL INCOME (Millions of dollars, except as noted)											Population (Thousands)	TOTAL EMPLOYMENT (Thousands)
				Derivation of personal income						Per capita (Dollars)			
	Total	Farm	Nonfarm	Earnings by place of work	Less: Personal contributions for social insurance	Plus: Adjustment for residence	Equals: Net earnings by place of residence	Dividends, interest, and rent	Transfer payments	Total	Disposable		
MONTANA													
1971	2 633	259	2 374	2 035	95	-1	1 940	377	316	3 702	3 306	711	307
1972	3 068	416	2 652	2 413	109	-1	2 304	414	351	4 266	3 764	719	319
1973	3 578	588	2 991	2 810	134	0	2 676	497	405	4 920	4 328	727	333
1974	3 882	475	3 407	2 980	152	1	2 829	576	477	5 266	4 616	737	344
1975	4 241	408	3 833	3 198	164	2	3 036	630	574	5 660	5 007	749	344
1976	4 556	230	4 326	3 397	187	3	3 213	699	644	6 007	5 261	759	359
1977	4 942	70	4 872	3 629	213	4	3 420	813	710	6 407	5 571	771	372
1978	5 870	311	5 559	4 381	242	3	4 142	949	780	7 487	6 575	784	390
1979	6 323	114	6 208	4 585	275	6	4 316	1 130	876	8 012	6 927	789	397
1980	6 945	116	6 829	4 866	297	13	4 582	1 331	1 032	8 805	7 640	789	394
1981	7 850	204	7 646	5 345	342	25	5 028	1 631	1 191	9 870	8 593	795	396
1982	8 278	164	8 114	5 458	361	17	5 114	1 828	1 336	10 297	9 060	804	392
1983	8 664	115	8 549	5 679	377	9	5 311	1 897	1 455	10 643	9 341	814	400
1984	9 214	45	9 169	5 970	406	5	5 570	2 108	1 536	11 225	9 974	821	410
1985	9 443	-70	9 513	6 021	435	3	5 588	2 220	1 634	11 483	10 213	822	409
1986	9 895	242	9 653	6 283	448	-2	5 832	2 307	1 756	12 160	10 876	814	404
1987	10 182	278	9 904	6 516	458	-4	6 054	2 312	1 816	12 647	11 126	805	408
1988	10 372	85	10 287	6 616	507	-3	6 107	2 350	1 916	12 962	11 373	800	419
1989	11 352	403	10 949	7 256	548	-4	6 705	2 558	2 090	14 197	12 334	800	427
1990	12 040	364	11 676	7 643	584	-6	7 054	2 676	2 310	15 053	13 151	800	436
1991	12 922	532	12 391	8 386	634	-16	7 736	2 731	2 455	15 988	14 061	808	447
1992	13 660	412	13 248	8 902	690	-8	8 203	2 789	2 667	16 592	14 553	823	460
1993	14 871	776	14 095	9 854	740	-14	9 100	2 892	2 879	17 678	15 588	841	473
1994	15 137	304	14 833	9 896	788	-13	9 095	3 039	3 002	17 672	15 499	857	497
1995	16 157	325	15 831	10 406	829	-12	9 566	3 356	3 235	18 563	16 382	870	512
1996	16 896	246	16 650	10 832	865	-10	9 957	3 570	3 369	19 214	16 821	879	524
NEBRASKA													
1971	6 177	685	5 492	4 936	202	-106	4 628	941	608	4 106	3 678	1 504	728
1972	6 854	815	6 039	5 480	223	-114	5 142	1 040	672	4 514	3 966	1 518	748
1973	8 007	1 230	6 776	6 424	282	-117	6 026	1 182	799	5 238	4 620	1 529	775
1974	8 357	771	7 586	6 531	321	-125	6 085	1 353	919	5 434	4 731	1 538	793
1975	9 430	1 112	8 318	7 344	343	-131	6 870	1 445	1 115	6 118	5 427	1 541	790
1976	9 907	591	9 316	7 656	376	-138	7 142	1 567	1 198	6 396	5 644	1 549	811
1977	10 746	531	10 215	8 214	403	-135	7 676	1 775	1 295	6 913	6 016	1 554	831
1978	12 533	1 107	11 426	9 707	463	-157	9 087	2 013	1 433	8 030	7 053	1 561	855
1979	13 563	755	12 808	10 357	539	-184	9 634	2 335	1 594	8 670	7 513	1 564	877
1980	14 364	95	14 269	10 490	588	-204	9 698	2 800	1 866	9 136	7 915	1 572	879
1981	16 630	849	15 781	11 972	674	-226	11 073	3 415	2 142	10 535	9 223	1 579	874
1982	17 462	730	16 732	12 264	721	-233	11 310	3 787	2 365	11 039	9 488	1 582	863
1983	18 095	478	17 617	12 566	753	-246	11 568	3 981	2 547	11 421	10 045	1 584	870
1984	20 124	1 102	19 023	14 374	834	-286	13 255	4 244	2 626	12 668	11 317	1 589	889
1985	21 263	1 400	19 864	15 371	927	-312	14 132	4 310	2 821	13 418	11 998	1 585	902
1986	21 934	1 356	20 578	15 778	986	-312	14 480	4 488	2 966	13 932	12 456	1 574	902
1987	22 975	1 648	21 327	16 855	1 062	-311	15 481	4 442	3 052	14 666	13 053	1 567	929
1988	24 399	1 963	22 435	18 087	1 179	-344	16 564	4 621	3 214	15 526	13 823	1 571	954
1989	25 798	1 781	24 017	18 866	1 282	-355	17 229	5 141	3 429	16 381	14 447	1 575	970
1990	27 751	2 148	25 603	20 392	1 367	-371	18 654	5 377	3 720	17 556	15 422	1 581	992
1991	28 729	1 970	26 759	21 091	1 446	-389	19 256	5 451	4 022	18 051	15 855	1 592	999
1992	30 812	2 024	28 788	22 442	1 516	-423	20 502	5 927	4 383	19 210	16 987	1 604	1 006
1993	32 001	1 718	30 283	23 234	1 609	-444	21 182	6 100	4 719	19 817	17 525	1 615	1 028
1994	33 218	1 594	31 624	24 561	1 739	-454	22 368	5 948	4 902	20 435	18 030	1 626	1 070
1995	35 055	1 293	33 763	25 712	1 866	-485	23 360	6 491	5 205	21 385	18 763	1 639	1 099
1996	37 862	2 157	35 704	27 911	1 963	-513	25 435	6 901	5 525	22 917	19 966	1 652	1 124
NEVADA													
1971	2 683	38	2 646	2 227	91	-43	2 093	365	225	5 160	4 559	520	267
1972	3 001	46	2 955	2 481	103	-47	2 330	403	267	5 489	4 813	547	280
1973	3 430	59	3 372	2 846	133	-57	2 656	464	311	6 030	5 303	569	304
1974	3 803	37	3 766	3 097	153	-60	2 884	535	384	6 373	5 589	597	317
1975	4 255	35	4 220	3 407	162	-62	3 183	557	516	6 865	6 176	620	326
1976	4 883	38	4 845	3 912	181	-72	3 659	638	585	7 548	6 676	647	349
1977	5 702	29	5 673	4 588	207	-89	4 292	743	666	8 408	7 396	678	384
1978	6 943	24	6 919	5 616	248	-123	5 245	941	757	9 652	8 425	719	432
1979	8 123	11	8 112	6 492	302	-139	6 051	1 187	885	10 617	9 200	765	468
1980	9 420	60	9 361	7 418	345	-168	6 905	1 440	1 075	11 627	10 124	810	490
1981	10 692	26	10 667	8 233	417	-181	7 636	1 762	1 295	12 614	10 992	848	502
1982	11 235	40	11 195	8 489	439	-181	7 868	1 921	1 446	12 745	11 171	882	497
1983	11 887	32	11 855	8 943	530	-186	8 226	2 084	1 577	13 179	11 698	902	502
1984	13 057	42	13 016	9 769	513	-204	9 051	2 341	1 665	14 117	12 436	925	528
1985	14 226	36	14 190	10 585	584	-212	9 790	2 591	1 845	14 958	13 120	951	550
1986	15 411	32	15 379	11 381	640	-229	10 512	2 846	2 052	15 715	13 743	981	577
1987	16 853	45	16 809	12 600	706	-253	11 641	2 982	2 231	16 469	14 332	1 023	623
1988	19 042	62	18 980	14 407	825	-291	13 291	3 307	2 445	17 713	15 326	1 075	671
1989	21 729	78	21 651	16 163	951	-336	14 876	4 062	2 791	19 104	16 604	1 137	720
1990	24 669	80	24 589	18 309	1 062	-370	16 876	4 612	3 180	20 242	17 560	1 219	763
1991	26 553	74	26 479	19 276	1 136	-373	17 767	4 904	3 882	20 654	18 053	1 286	781
1992	29 073	61	29 012	21 200	1 222	-386	19 592	5 089	4 393	21 795	18 973	1 334	789
1993	31 149	98	31 051	22 961	1 326	-447	21 189	5 306	4 655	22 470	19 385	1 386	831
1994	34 292	65	34 227	25 452	1 494	-496	23 462	5 922	4 908	23 422	20 285	1 464	914
1995	37 951	50	37 900	27 915	1 651	-536	25 728	6 919	5 303	24 748	21 435	1 533	968
1996	41 699	53	41 647	30 802	1 818	-614	28 370	7 628	5 702	26 011	22 280	1 603	1 030

| YEAR | PERSONAL INCOME (Millions of dollars, except as noted) | | | | | | | | | | | | TOTAL EMPLOYMENT (Thousands) |
| | Total | Farm | Nonfarm | Derivation of personal income | | | | | | Per capita (Dollars) | | Population (Thousands) | |
				Earnings by place of work	Less: Personal contributions for social insurance	Plus: Adjustment for residence	Equals: Net earnings by place of residence	Dividends, interest, and rent	Transfer payments	Total	Disposable		
NEW HAMPSHIRE													
1971	3 149	18	3 131	2 199	92	222	2 329	484	336	4 131	3 674	762	336
1972	3 482	20	3 463	2 443	104	243	2 581	529	372	4 455	3 895	782	350
1973	3 934	24	3 910	2 772	132	272	2 912	586	435	4 906	4 346	802	374
1974	4 344	16	4 328	2 985	150	316	3 151	671	522	5 317	4 693	817	381
1975	4 686	19	4 667	3 125	158	347	3 315	711	661	5 646	5 051	830	370
1976	5 339	21	5 317	3 615	178	392	3 829	795	715	6 303	5 594	847	394
1977	6 028	20	6 008	4 100	203	458	4 355	902	771	6 914	6 103	872	418
1978	6 966	21	6 945	4 790	236	539	5 093	1 029	844	7 792	6 836	894	446
1979	8 007	23	7 984	5 473	281	644	5 836	1 210	961	8 781	7 703	912	469
1980	9 166	14	9 151	6 059	315	800	6 543	1 494	1 129	9 917	8 731	924	483
1981	10 371	24	10 348	6 670	371	904	7 202	1 856	1 313	11 073	9 717	937	494
1982	11 251	18	11 233	7 181	413	986	7 753	2 055	1 443	11 872	10 523	948	500
1983	12 502	16	12 486	8 060	460	1 101	8 702	2 257	1 543	13 048	11 520	958	520
1984	14 205	21	14 184	9 105	521	1 312	9 896	2 708	1 602	14 542	12 879	977	556
1985	15 840	26	15 814	10 288	615	1 435	11 108	3 032	1 699	15 891	13 953	997	589
1986	17 565	26	17 539	11 526	702	1 497	12 321	3 443	1 801	17 136	14 896	1 025	621
1987	19 422	44	19 378	13 043	789	1 622	13 877	3 685	1 860	18 422	16 042	1 054	639
1988	21 396	48	21 348	14 409	896	1 770	15 283	4 113	2 000	19 764	17 385	1 083	666
1989	22 735	48	22 687	15 034	962	1 868	15 940	4 581	2 214	20 584	18 136	1 105	666
1990	23 091	42	23 049	14 923	978	1 967	15 912	4 691	2 488	20 768	18 494	1 112	648
1991	23 765	42	23 723	14 770	998	2 034	15 806	4 728	3 231	21 455	19 214	1 108	622
1992	24 882	56	24 826	15 794	1 062	2 108	16 840	4 602	3 440	22 328	19 939	1 114	635
1993	25 706	54	25 652	16 484	1 115	2 198	17 567	4 786	3 353	22 895	20 377	1 123	648
1994	27 532	46	27 486	17 484	1 208	2 295	18 570	5 146	3 816	24 250	21 599	1 135	673
1995	29 510	42	29 468	18 704	1 300	2 368	19 772	5 652	4 086	25 700	22 836	1 148	696
1996	30 939	45	30 894	19 781	1 369	2 471	20 882	6 009	4 047	26 615	23 416	1 162	713
NEW JERSEY													
1971	37 421	106	37 315	26 499	1 177	2 980	28 302	5 504	3 615	5 139	4 530	7 282	3 119
1972	40 593	103	40 490	28 849	1 303	3 157	30 703	5 843	4 046	5 533	4 806	7 337	3 184
1973	44 366	139	44 227	31 711	1 595	3 266	33 383	6 448	4 535	6 048	5 304	7 335	3 288
1974	48 204	152	48 052	34 071	1 782	3 429	35 718	7 170	5 316	6 572	5 743	7 335	3 301
1975	51 575	112	51 463	35 448	1 858	3 669	37 259	7 474	6 842	7 025	6 229	7 341	3 191
1976	56 399	118	56 281	38 906	1 995	3 947	40 858	8 079	7 462	7 680	6 743	7 344	3 248
1977	61 788	126	61 662	42 715	2 175	4 312	44 853	8 969	7 966	8 416	7 298	7 342	3 325
1978	68 925	143	68 782	47 796	2 478	4 884	50 202	10 241	8 482	9 369	8 126	7 356	3 464
1979	77 001	134	76 867	52 869	2 850	5 602	55 621	11 976	9 404	10 444	8 975	7 373	3 555
1980	86 872	124	86 748	58 047	3 156	6 606	61 497	14 581	10 794	11 777	10 103	7 376	3 608
1981	96 827	158	96 669	63 227	3 695	7 188	66 720	17 958	12 149	13 072	11 175	7 407	3 643
1982	104 166	171	103 995	67 395	4 041	7 730	71 084	19 682	13 400	14 018	11 982	7 431	3 650
1983	112 904	203	112 701	73 366	4 404	8 045	77 008	21 489	14 407	15 119	12 992	7 468	3 751
1984	125 541	202	125 339	81 395	4 961	8 455	84 889	25 714	14 939	16 704	14 458	7 515	3 932
1985	135 128	233	134 895	88 527	5 602	8 839	91 765	27 738	15 625	17 861	15 298	7 566	4 047
1986	144 929	235	144 694	95 618	6 280	9 387	98 725	29 737	16 467	19 014	16 270	7 622	4 145
1987	156 919	263	156 656	105 429	6 972	9 976	108 432	31 136	17 350	20 457	17 362	7 671	4 247
1988	172 263	258	172 006	116 947	7 875	10 373	119 445	34 283	18 535	22 336	19 161	7 712	4 355
1989	183 712	251	183 461	122 816	8 383	10 114	124 548	39 165	19 999	23 778	20 468	7 726	4 391
1990	193 391	226	193 165	128 787	8 805	10 511	130 493	40 873	22 024	24 988	21 596	7 740	4 338
1991	197 837	217	197 620	130 235	9 178	10 393	131 450	41 421	24 965	25 471	22 046	7 767	4 209
1992	210 258	215	210 043	138 825	9 669	11 746	140 902	40 795	28 561	26 917	23 274	7 811	4 208
1993	217 788	250	217 538	144 367	9 866	11 700	146 200	41 831	29 757	27 709	23 874	7 860	4 238
1994	225 686	246	225 440	149 969	10 455	11 551	151 065	43 987	30 634	28 547	24 474	7 906	4 279
1995	239 052	252	238 800	156 287	10 888	12 982	158 382	48 119	32 551	30 071	25 826	7 950	4 349
1996	250 295	263	250 033	162 872	11 248	14 200	165 824	50 688	33 784	31 334	26 595	7 988	4 391
NEW MEXICO													
1971	3 586	142	3 445	2 831	125	-21	2 685	448	454	3 405	3 073	1 053	416
1972	4 023	150	3 872	3 182	142	-18	3 021	489	512	3 732	3 341	1 078	440
1973	4 531	193	4 338	3 568	176	-16	3 376	554	601	4 103	3 675	1 104	461
1974	5 102	161	4 940	3 959	206	-14	3 739	638	725	4 517	4 026	1 130	478
1975	5 786	191	5 595	4 455	230	-12	4 214	689	883	4 977	4 514	1 163	491
1976	6 504	135	6 369	5 008	258	-11	4 739	765	1 000	5 442	4 881	1 195	512
1977	7 337	147	7 189	5 678	293	-10	5 376	882	1 078	5 988	5 370	1 225	539
1978	8 427	182	8 245	6 538	338	-10	6 191	1 049	1 187	6 732	5 991	1 252	568
1979	9 591	218	9 373	7 364	394	-8	6 962	1 268	1 361	7 490	6 659	1 281	593
1980	10 807	190	10 617	8 073	445	-3	7 626	1 558	1 623	8 253	7 354	1 309	598
1981	12 223	125	12 097	8 946	533	-1	8 412	1 956	1 854	9 171	8 064	1 333	613
1982	13 235	122	13 113	9 507	582	-1	8 924	2 262	2 049	9 704	8 495	1 364	621
1983	14 067	131	13 936	10 085	673	4	9 416	2 422	2 228	10 088	9 079	1 394	633
1984	15 392	150	15 242	11 051	688	13	10 375	2 689	2 327	10 865	9 778	1 417	658
1985	16 710	215	16 494	11 931	763	18	11 186	2 992	2 532	11 617	10 455	1 438	678
1986	17 369	198	17 171	12 207	806	23	11 425	3 219	2 725	11 874	10 764	1 463	684
1987	18 166	232	17 934	12 765	839	35	11 961	3 279	2 925	12 286	11 026	1 479	703
1988	19 193	315	18 877	13 523	925	44	12 642	3 397	3 154	12 878	11 550	1 490	740
1989	20 496	379	20 117	14 293	1 004	51	13 340	3 718	3 438	13 628	12 199	1 504	755
1990	22 036	413	21 622	15 322	1 073	56	14 305	3 973	3 758	14 497	12 955	1 520	766
1991	23 375	413	22 962	16 364	1 167	59	15 257	3 909	4 210	15 096	13 514	1 548	791
1992	25 003	473	24 531	17 548	1 233	63	16 378	3 963	4 662	15 791	14 148	1 583	804
1993	26 922	538	26 384	18 975	1 329	57	17 703	4 158	5 061	16 627	14 819	1 619	832
1994	28 518	394	28 124	19 975	1 448	63	18 591	4 488	5 439	17 187	15 301	1 659	866
1995	30 781	336	30 445	21 372	1 560	63	19 875	4 921	5 986	18 215	16 278	1 690	900
1996	32 217	352	31 865	22 057	1 612	83	20 528	5 225	6 465	18 803	16 727	1 713	908

| YEAR | PERSONAL INCOME (Millions of dollars, except as noted) | | | | | | | | | | | Popu- lation (Thou- sands) | TOTAL EM- PLOY- MENT (Thou- sands) |
| | Total | Farm | Nonfarm | Derivation of personal income | | | | | | Per capita (Dollars) | | | |
				Earnings by place of work	Less: Personal contributions for social insurance	Plus: Adjustment for residence	Equals: Net earnings by place of residence	Dividends, interest, and rent	Transfer payments	Total	Disposable		
NEW YORK													
1971	95 023	448	94 575	74 869	3 282	-3 212	68 375	14 512	12 136	5 174	4 450	18 365	8 347
1972	101 639	400	101 239	79 966	3 550	-3 417	72 999	15 021	13 619	5 538	4 709	18 352	8 350
1973	108 610	509	108 100	85 238	4 281	-3 566	77 391	16 220	14 998	5 969	5 112	18 195	8 467
1974	116 935	484	116 451	90 113	4 685	-3 732	81 696	17 945	17 295	6 470	5 525	18 073	8 395
1975	124 787	410	124 377	93 905	4 827	-4 013	85 065	18 261	21 462	6 920	5 994	18 032	8 175
1976	133 522	425	133 097	100 283	5 085	-4 347	90 850	19 658	23 014	7 428	6 406	17 975	8 128
1977	144 207	348	143 859	108 408	5 432	-4 819	98 157	21 776	24 274	8 078	6 938	17 852	8 202
1978	157 873	450	157 423	119 192	5 974	-5 466	107 752	24 619	25 502	8 909	7 645	17 720	8 381
1979	173 911	550	173 362	131 019	6 791	-6 264	117 963	28 669	27 279	9 862	8 416	17 634	8 590
1980	193 986	533	193 453	143 997	7 460	-7 376	129 160	33 548	31 277	11 043	9 385	17 567	8 622
1981	216 042	543	215 498	157 768	8 826	-8 319	140 622	40 167	35 253	12 298	10 344	17 568	8 700
1982	232 355	518	231 836	169 360	9 675	-9 123	150 562	43 259	38 534	13 210	11 059	17 590	8 706
1983	248 952	363	248 589	181 057	10 357	-9 670	161 029	46 388	41 535	14 075	11 983	17 687	8 768
1984	277 515	460	277 056	200 941	11 505	-10 362	179 074	54 743	43 699	15 638	13 356	17 746	9 054
1985	296 459	520	295 939	216 859	12 965	-11 022	192 872	57 577	46 010	16 663	14 129	17 792	9 289
1986	317 631	626	317 005	233 657	14 247	-11 860	207 549	61 077	49 005	17 811	15 077	17 833	9 491
1987	338 200	694	337 506	252 993	15 367	-12 696	224 929	62 250	51 020	18 927	15 855	17 869	9 549
1988	367 133	588	366 545	275 144	17 248	-13 502	244 394	68 734	54 006	20 463	17 306	17 941	9 779
1989	392 818	716	392 103	286 977	18 486	-13 343	255 148	79 608	58 063	21 844	18 342	17 983	9 852
1990	416 690	711	415 980	303 542	19 632	-14 145	269 766	83 305	63 619	23 146	19 607	18 003	9 802
1991	426 850	594	426 256	305 907	20 219	-14 025	271 662	83 099	72 089	23 665	20 192	18 037	9 579
1992	450 245	631	449 614	326 927	21 273	-16 249	289 404	79 611	81 230	24 877	21 265	18 099	9 511
1993	463 417	652	462 765	335 073	21 744	-16 234	297 095	80 712	85 610	25 504	21 722	18 170	9 538
1994	479 156	522	478 634	342 641	22 523	-16 135	303 983	85 111	90 061	26 332	22 412	18 197	9 585
1995	505 812	388	505 424	357 918	23 509	-17 474	316 935	92 654	96 222	27 806	23 612	18 191	9 677
1996	530 655	541	530 113	375 519	24 486	-18 980	332 053	97 198	101 404	29 181	24 583	18 185	9 752
NORTH CAROLINA													
1971	18 058	688	17 370	15 072	645	6	14 434	1 878	1 746	3 472	3 063	5 201	2 490
1972	20 428	822	19 606	17 174	743	0	16 430	2 035	1 962	3 857	3 353	5 296	2 602
1973	23 250	1 229	22 021	19 572	936	-3	18 632	2 331	2 287	4 320	3 790	5 382	2 720
1974	25 631	1 172	24 459	21 152	1 068	0	20 084	2 707	2 840	4 693	4 093	5 461	2 743
1975	27 503	1 110	26 393	21 874	1 120	3	20 757	2 885	3 861	4 969	4 436	5 535	2 647
1976	30 776	1 185	29 591	24 602	1 254	4	23 352	3 214	4 211	5 502	4 858	5 593	2 754
1977	33 913	886	33 026	27 098	1 384	8	25 722	3 650	4 540	5 983	5 257	5 668	2 851
1978	38 455	1 171	37 285	30 962	1 598	5	29 369	4 175	4 912	6 699	5 873	5 740	2 948
1979	42 620	776	41 845	33 967	1 848	-1	32 118	4 904	5 598	7 346	6 386	5 802	3 051
1980	47 736	658	47 078	36 961	2 046	-3	34 912	6 120	6 704	8 092	7 033	5 899	3 060
1981	53 625	1 060	52 565	40 749	2 412	-36	38 301	7 621	7 703	9 003	7 803	5 957	3 082
1982	56 893	1 057	55 835	42 621	2 595	-48	39 979	8 340	8 574	9 452	8 303	6 019	3 050
1983	61 933	627	61 307	46 478	2 846	-67	43 566	9 139	9 229	10 191	8 914	6 077	3 137
1984	70 115	1 294	68 821	53 068	3 190	-104	49 773	10 744	9 598	11 375	9 977	6 164	3 305
1985	76 084	1 161	74 922	57 733	3 620	-170	53 943	11 830	10 311	12 166	10 619	6 254	3 409
1986	81 936	1 138	80 798	62 143	4 013	-233	57 897	12 962	11 077	12 961	11 314	6 322	3 511
1987	88 066	1 088	86 978	67 671	4 335	-316	63 019	13 378	11 669	13 752	11 912	6 404	3 630
1988	96 097	1 410	94 687	73 884	4 871	-376	68 637	14 844	12 616	14 828	12 967	6 481	3 777
1989	104 000	1 654	102 346	79 096	5 337	-432	73 328	16 759	13 913	15 840	13 740	6 565	3 865
1990	110 991	2 116	108 875	83 713	5 668	-480	77 565	17 894	15 532	16 673	14 577	6 657	3 918
1991	115 821	2 397	113 424	86 254	5 968	-485	79 802	18 284	17 735	17 149	15 046	6 754	3 893
1992	125 026	2 294	122 733	94 122	6 435	-533	87 153	18 276	19 598	18 277	16 070	6 841	3 995
1993	133 827	2 698	131 130	100 295	6 891	-623	92 781	19 293	21 753	19 228	16 876	6 960	4 121
1994	141 426	2 695	138 731	106 367	7 443	-695	98 230	20 638	22 558	19 979	17 423	7 079	4 241
1995	152 601	2 547	150 054	112 879	7 960	-770	104 149	23 414	25 038	21 188	18 467	7 202	4 370
1996	162 602	2 970	159 632	119 692	8 373	-823	110 496	25 123	26 983	22 205	19 256	7 323	4 463
NORTH DAKOTA													
1971	2 238	414	1 824	1 812	79	-55	1 678	300	261	3 572	3 246	627	284
1972	2 696	662	2 034	2 222	88	-58	2 076	330	290	4 273	3 878	631	288
1973	3 826	1 512	2 315	3 269	112	-61	3 095	405	327	6 051	5 524	632	300
1974	3 788	1 148	2 640	3 138	132	-73	2 933	479	376	5 973	5 275	634	308
1975	3 951	926	3 026	3 190	149	-78	2 963	547	441	6 189	5 477	638	314
1976	3 875	463	3 412	3 035	165	-93	2 778	607	491	6 005	5 300	645	326
1977	4 038	257	3 781	3 052	162	-99	2 791	701	545	6 220	5 520	649	331
1978	5 131	846	4 285	4 039	187	-110	3 742	798	591	7 886	7 001	651	346
1979	5 298	494	4 805	4 070	216	-127	3 727	919	653	8 124	7 188	652	354
1980	5 081	-348	5 430	3 527	242	-141	3 144	1 164	773	7 765	6 724	654	356
1981	6 627	306	6 321	4 655	282	-162	4 212	1 532	884	10 049	8 724	660	360
1982	7 154	275	6 879	4 845	306	-163	4 376	1 786	992	10 694	9 486	669	361
1983	7 497	326	7 171	5 089	319	-167	4 604	1 794	1 099	11 079	9 820	677	367
1984	8 079	550	7 528	5 566	337	-167	5 063	1 855	1 161	11 872	10 664	680	368
1985	8 332	638	7 694	5 751	364	-165	5 222	1 862	1 248	12 308	11 052	677	366
1986	8 464	642	7 822	5 766	382	-162	5 222	1 871	1 371	12 642	11 411	670	359
1987	8 626	645	7 981	5 964	398	-164	5 401	1 786	1 438	13 047	11 700	661	365
1988	7 955	-149	8 104	5 348	431	-168	4 750	1 746	1 459	12 138	10 760	655	369
1989	8 830	325	8 505	6 021	463	-173	5 384	1 857	1 589	13 662	12 100	646	373
1990	9 728	592	9 135	6 614	498	-180	5 936	2 071	1 720	15 262	13 578	637	376
1991	9 830	402	9 428	6 757	532	-189	6 037	1 997	1 797	15 503	13 716	634	385
1992	10 740	759	9 980	7 555	552	-208	6 795	1 989	1 955	16 904	15 077	635	390
1993	10 917	344	10 572	7 581	585	-231	6 765	2 045	2 106	17 136	15 271	637	399
1994	11 661	657	11 004	8 323	620	-246	7 457	2 046	2 159	18 229	16 315	640	414
1995	11 865	121	11 744	8 265	659	-263	7 343	2 267	2 255	18 495	16 526	642	425
1996	13 159	764	12 395	9 352	686	-276	8 390	2 414	2 356	20 448	18 255	644	433

YEAR	PERSONAL INCOME (Millions of dollars, except as noted)									Per capita (Dollars)		Population (Thousands)	TOTAL EMPLOYMENT (Thousands)
	Total	Farm	Nonfarm	Derivation of personal income									
				Earnings by place of work	Less: Personal contributions for social insurance	Plus: Adjustment for residence	Equals: Net earnings by place of residence	Dividends, interest, and rent	Transfer payments	Total	Disposable		
OHIO													
1971	45 937	485	45 452	37 307	1 591	-180	35 536	5 888	4 513	4 279	3 784	10 735	4 627
1972	49 883	581	49 302	40 598	1 746	-185	38 667	6 211	5 005	4 642	4 035	10 747	4 710
1973	55 568	733	54 835	45 301	2 173	-216	42 911	6 897	5 760	5 161	4 497	10 767	4 902
1974	60 880	858	60 022	48 915	2 429	-205	46 281	7 727	6 872	5 655	4 917	10 766	4 964
1975	64 661	863	63 798	50 516	2 443	-186	47 887	8 103	8 670	6 004	5 265	10 770	4 809
1976	71 658	832	70 826	56 360	2 707	-211	53 442	8 781	9 435	6 664	5 816	10 753	4 889
1977	79 534	725	78 809	62 933	3 052	-230	59 650	9 813	10 071	7 384	6 399	10 771	5 034
1978	88 261	676	87 586	69 928	3 467	-252	66 209	11 183	10 869	8 176	7 080	10 795	5 207
1979	97 974	800	97 174	76 822	3 976	-274	72 572	13 057	12 345	9 073	7 807	10 799	5 298
1980	106 854	590	106 264	80 227	4 198	-311	75 719	15 747	15 388	9 893	8 560	10 801	5 215
1981	116 072	142	115 930	84 996	4 806	-369	79 821	19 076	17 174	10 759	9 251	10 788	5 151
1982	120 708	260	120 448	85 729	4 941	-494	80 294	20 513	19 900	11 221	9 752	10 757	4 982
1983	127 531	-89	127 620	89 809	5 193	-611	84 004	22 242	21 285	11 877	10 366	10 738	4 976
1984	140 594	817	139 777	100 342	5 763	-751	93 828	24 766	22 000	13 093	11 517	10 738	5 182
1985	148 984	798	148 187	106 900	6 438	-836	99 625	25 991	23 368	13 878	12 159	10 735	5 314
1986	155 941	602	155 339	111 307	6 895	-871	103 540	27 567	24 834	14 533	12 766	10 730	5 429
1987	163 544	659	162 885	117 889	7 276	-916	109 696	27 822	26 026	15 199	13 233	10 760	5 581
1988	175 040	674	174 366	127 106	8 026	-963	118 117	29 556	27 367	16 210	14 193	10 799	5 726
1989	186 493	1 052	185 441	133 728	8 705	-1 010	124 012	32 800	29 680	17 221	14 986	10 829	5 848
1990	197 109	1 062	196 046	140 661	9 171	-1 077	130 413	34 656	32 040	18 147	15 817	10 862	5 898
1991	203 861	543	203 318	143 659	9 620	-1 113	132 926	35 539	35 396	18 653	16 308	10 929	5 892
1992	215 246	935	214 312	153 173	10 049	-1 180	141 944	34 464	38 838	19 567	17 178	11 000	5 907
1993	225 372	734	224 638	160 558	10 628	-1 254	148 676	36 104	40 592	20 378	17 747	11 059	6 010
1994	237 118	935	236 184	169 881	11 490	-1 328	157 063	37 724	42 331	21 368	18 579	11 097	6 197
1995	251 041	820	250 221	178 238	12 133	-1 489	164 615	41 785	44 641	22 547	19 574	11 134	6 371
1996	262 077	948	261 128	185 451	12 587	-1 547	171 317	44 244	46 515	23 457	20 209	11 173	6 460
OKLAHOMA													
1971	9 651	347	9 303	7 366	317	63	7 112	1 271	1 268	3 686	3 299	2 618	1 132
1972	10 606	440	10 166	8 181	351	72	7 903	1 302	1 401	3 991	3 517	2 657	1 183
1973	12 117	754	11 363	9 334	437	82	8 979	1 546	1 592	4 497	4 005	2 694	1 221
1974	13 523	469	13 053	10 236	508	106	9 834	1 795	1 894	4 949	4 335	2 732	1 256
1975	15 098	417	14 681	11 237	553	140	10 824	1 949	2 324	5 447	4 835	2 772	1 269
1976	16 753	347	16 406	12 452	608	176	12 020	2 150	2 583	5 934	5 250	2 823	1 305
1977	18 659	184	18 476	13 960	689	152	13 423	2 441	2 796	6 511	5 715	2 866	1 359
1978	21 261	182	21 079	16 023	803	149	15 369	2 869	3 022	7 298	6 355	2 913	1 428
1979	24 867	666	24 201	18 762	949	164	17 977	3 438	3 452	8 372	7 278	2 970	1 483
1980	28 764	311	28 453	21 330	1 108	171	20 393	4 357	4 014	9 460	8 166	3 041	1 551
1981	33 589	359	33 230	24 673	1 370	194	23 498	5 518	4 574	10 848	9 218	3 096	1 630
1982	37 287	483	36 804	27 086	1 531	200	25 754	6 373	5 160	11 630	9 795	3 206	1 678
1983	37 950	187	37 763	26 918	1 555	239	25 601	6 708	5 641	11 534	10 095	3 290	1 642
1984	40 692	379	40 313	28 933	1 648	288	27 573	7 350	5 770	12 385	10 921	3 286	1 671
1985	42 253	390	41 864	29 751	1 780	328	28 299	7 786	6 169	12 916	11 419	3 271	1 655
1986	42 164	648	41 516	29 299	1 823	376	27 853	7 713	6 598	12 963	11 756	3 253	1 595
1987	42 035	575	41 460	29 175	1 820	424	27 779	7 359	6 897	13 094	11 686	3 210	1 606
1988	43 858	778	43 080	30 416	1 986	469	28 899	7 590	7 368	13 848	12 357	3 167	1 619
1989	46 318	830	45 488	31 888	2 154	493	30 227	8 233	7 858	14 703	13 022	3 150	1 632
1990	49 202	822	48 380	33 824	2 289	546	32 081	8 656	8 465	15 634	13 622	3 147	1 663
1991	51 102	642	50 459	35 147	2 444	576	33 279	8 553	9 269	16 132	14 193	3 168	1 679
1992	54 119	783	53 336	37 181	2 574	609	35 217	8 647	10 255	16 874	14 962	3 207	1 692
1993	56 552	1 020	55 532	39 094	2 672	623	37 045	8 666	10 841	17 489	15 533	3 234	1 719
1994	58 691	812	57 879	40 174	2 808	673	38 039	9 236	11 416	18 039	15 985	3 254	1 753
1995	61 343	351	60 992	41 269	2 935	701	39 035	9 924	12 384	18 731	16 614	3 275	1 796
1996	64 514	360	64 154	43 300	3 057	735	40 978	10 475	13 061	19 544	17 217	3 301	1 843
OREGON													
1971	9 001	230	8 771	6 972	313	-53	6 607	1 353	1 042	4 187	3 656	2 150	951
1972	10 100	291	9 808	7 905	360	-52	7 492	1 459	1 149	4 601	3 975	2 195	1 001
1973	11 414	398	11 017	8 934	451	-60	8 423	1 638	1 353	5 098	4 423	2 239	1 058
1974	12 934	504	12 430	9 969	518	-72	9 378	1 889	1 667	5 670	4 886	2 281	1 089
1975	14 188	413	13 775	10 660	556	-45	10 059	2 035	2 095	6 103	5 340	2 325	1 105
1976	16 176	388	15 788	12 248	626	-33	11 589	2 284	2 303	6 819	5 911	2 372	1 156
1977	18 141	334	17 807	13 802	715	-96	12 991	2 623	2 527	7 437	6 354	2 439	1 223
1978	20 913	336	20 577	16 011	837	-155	15 019	3 121	2 773	8 333	7 113	2 510	1 297
1979	23 793	399	23 394	18 098	976	-229	16 894	3 786	3 114	9 228	7 852	2 578	1 352
1980	26 315	480	25 834	19 390	1 060	-278	18 052	4 565	3 698	9 963	8 524	2 641	1 353
1981	28 267	388	27 878	19 940	1 189	-268	18 482	5 517	4 267	10 595	9 092	2 668	1 324
1982	28 737	279	28 459	19 658	1 227	-256	18 175	5 760	4 802	10 784	9 264	2 665	1 274
1983	30 431	284	30 147	20 661	1 284	-242	19 135	6 133	5 163	11 470	9 952	2 653	1 300
1984	33 125	409	32 717	22 742	1 406	-284	21 052	6 791	5 282	12 422	10 854	2 667	1 348
1985	34 998	432	34 566	24 208	1 546	-323	22 339	7 044	5 614	13 095	11 384	2 673	1 378
1986	36 826	557	36 268	25 517	1 657	-365	23 495	7 528	5 802	13 723	11 827	2 684	1 414
1987	38 675	494	38 181	27 222	1 777	-422	25 023	7 625	6 027	14 319	12 362	2 701	1 464
1988	42 026	670	41 356	30 045	2 030	-484	27 531	8 068	6 427	15 331	13 406	2 741	1 534
1989	45 768	616	45 152	32 448	2 258	-535	29 656	9 178	6 934	16 401	14 035	2 791	1 587
1990	49 879	657	49 222	35 477	2 433	-629	32 415	9 772	7 691	17 448	15 124	2 859	1 638
1991	52 389	658	51 731	37 072	2 636	-674	33 762	10 070	8 557	17 936	15 442	2 921	1 649
1992	55 762	662	55 100	39 651	2 816	-745	36 089	10 204	9 470	18 727	16 074	2 978	1 668
1993	59 640	824	58 816	42 423	3 011	-888	38 524	10 912	10 204	19 619	16 808	3 040	1 713
1994	63 667	630	63 036	45 457	3 258	-994	41 205	11 799	10 663	20 575	17 530	3 094	1 798
1995	68 806	524	68 282	48 841	3 506	-1 242	44 092	13 185	11 529	21 851	18 698	3 149	1 867
1996	73 922	742	73 180	52 780	3 749	-1 368	47 663	14 208	12 050	23 074	19 612	3 204	1 931

YEAR	PERSONAL INCOME (Millions of dollars, except as noted)												TOTAL EMPLOYMENT (Thousands)
	Total	Farm	Nonfarm	Derivation of personal income						Per capita (Dollars)		Population (Thousands)	
				Earnings by place of work	Less: Personal contributions for social insurance	Plus: Adjustment for residence	Equals: Net earnings by place of residence	Dividends, interest, and rent	Transfer payments	Total	Disposable		
PENNSYLVANIA													
1971	50 862	378	50 484	40 098	1 767	-360	37 970	6 488	6 403	4 280	3 758	11 884	5 159
1972	55 498	398	55 100	43 764	1 956	-361	41 446	6 806	7 245	4 662	4 004	11 905	5 247
1973	61 072	529	60 543	48 202	2 391	-333	45 478	7 546	8 048	5 139	4 448	11 885	5 402
1974	67 125	513	66 613	52 324	2 693	-342	49 289	8 440	9 397	5 658	4 877	11 864	5 419
1975	72 802	471	72 331	55 328	2 815	-372	52 141	8 859	11 803	6 119	5 358	11 898	5 302
1976	80 102	557	79 544	60 588	3 046	-366	57 176	9 725	13 201	6 738	5 881	11 887	5 353
1977	87 896	507	87 390	66 490	3 310	-358	62 823	10 931	14 143	7 398	6 413	11 882	5 429
1978	97 321	550	96 770	73 771	3 690	-362	69 719	12 391	15 211	8 203	7 099	11 865	5 564
1979	108 203	690	107 513	81 300	4 208	-392	76 699	14 400	17 103	9 113	7 852	11 874	5 672
1980	119 050	464	118 587	86 676	4 557	-413	81 706	17 692	19 653	10 031	8 657	11 868	5 638
1981	130 877	671	130 206	92 697	5 238	-386	87 072	21 714	22 091	11 036	9 455	11 859	5 605
1982	138 350	574	137 776	94 601	5 498	-231	88 872	24 242	25 237	11 680	10 071	11 845	5 493
1983	144 750	379	144 372	97 934	5 731	-75	92 129	25 612	27 009	12 228	10 673	11 838	5 452
1984	156 177	840	155 337	106 553	6 375	114	100 292	28 811	27 074	13 218	11 542	11 815	5 603
1985	166 519	837	165 682	112 876	7 038	262	106 101	31 554	28 864	14 147	12 347	11 771	5 712
1986	175 992	882	175 110	118 898	7 703	378	111 573	34 015	30 405	14 936	13 056	11 783	5 806
1987	186 816	859	185 957	128 664	8 181	476	120 960	34 577	31 279	15 817	13 730	11 811	5 996
1988	200 836	701	200 135	139 230	9 143	685	130 771	37 180	32 884	16 954	14 766	11 846	6 171
1989	216 982	942	216 040	148 657	9 868	841	139 630	42 046	35 306	18 286	15 914	11 866	6 270
1990	230 894	907	229 988	157 513	10 434	981	148 060	44 717	38 118	19 410	16 925	11 895	6 343
1991	239 478	606	238 872	161 178	10 935	973	151 216	45 307	42 954	20 047	17 539	11 946	6 275
1992	252 224	1 027	251 196	171 432	11 570	1 085	160 948	44 104	47 172	21 038	18 400	11 989	6 280
1993	262 308	936	261 372	177 944	12 212	1 146	166 877	45 505	49 926	21 799	19 116	12 033	6 315
1994	270 969	744	270 225	184 010	12 890	1 323	172 443	47 444	51 082	22 471	19 672	12 058	6 392
1995	284 963	567	284 396	191 474	13 455	1 367	179 386	52 186	53 391	23 628	20 635	12 060	6 483
1996	299 031	906	298 124	199 478	13 822	1 446	187 102	55 148	56 781	24 803	21 514	12 056	6 552
RHODE ISLAND													
1971	4 110	9	4 101	3 074	151	63	2 986	567	558	4 264	3 758	964	436
1972	4 485	9	4 476	3 380	167	58	3 272	596	617	4 594	4 004	976	447
1973	4 831	7	4 824	3 600	203	72	3 468	661	702	4 940	4 316	978	452
1974	5 144	10	5 135	3 702	219	86	3 569	747	828	5 395	4 709	954	439
1975	5 519	10	5 509	3 833	224	80	3 689	752	1 078	5 831	5 194	946	424
1976	6 083	10	6 073	4 299	245	87	4 141	826	1 116	6 402	5 650	950	442
1977	6 670	9	6 660	4 722	267	102	4 556	932	1 182	6 983	6 168	955	459
1978	7 349	10	7 339	5 238	301	99	5 037	1 049	1 263	7 677	6 696	957	475
1979	8 184	8	8 177	5 823	345	107	5 585	1 201	1 398	8 555	7 384	957	484
1980	9 189	8	9 181	6 344	380	119	6 083	1 497	1 609	9 685	8 413	949	486
1981	10 231	9	10 222	6 804	429	160	6 535	1 852	1 844	10 735	9 352	953	486
1982	10 966	29	10 938	7 143	462	213	6 895	2 044	2 027	11 493	10 063	954	476
1983	11 785	39	11 746	7 701	504	268	7 465	2 164	2 156	12 323	10 888	956	482
1984	13 041	34	13 007	8 532	560	335	8 307	2 536	2 199	13 558	11 970	962	507
1985	13 995	45	13 950	9 203	616	394	8 981	2 642	2 372	14 443	12 723	969	522
1986	15 065	47	15 018	9 977	689	417	9 705	2 878	2 482	15 415	13 472	977	540
1987	16 289	43	16 245	10 933	754	485	10 664	3 037	2 588	16 460	14 242	990	550
1988	17 861	48	17 812	12 042	847	560	11 755	3 359	2 747	17 925	15 659	996	565
1989	19 216	35	19 181	12 705	899	621	12 427	3 825	2 964	19 203	16 766	1 001	566
1990	19 820	33	19 787	12 985	942	662	12 705	3 842	3 273	19 728	17 315	1 005	555
1991	20 119	35	20 084	12 656	975	693	12 374	3 764	3 981	20 028	17 626	1 005	529
1992	20 914	38	20 876	13 415	1 034	721	13 102	3 667	4 145	20 875	18 407	1 002	534
1993	21 836	46	21 790	13 897	1 083	764	13 579	3 793	4 465	21 839	19 229	1 000	539
1994	22 296	33	22 263	14 189	1 140	850	13 899	3 889	4 507	22 383	19 638	996	539
1995	23 541	35	23 506	14 832	1 182	897	14 547	4 223	4 772	23 738	20 856	992	548
1996	24 331	30	24 302	15 243	1 199	969	15 013	4 433	4 885	24 572	21 457	990	550
SOUTH CAROLINA													
1971	8 617	218	8 399	7 052	298	116	6 871	839	908	3 237	2 891	2 662	1 215
1972	9 672	233	9 439	7 951	342	134	7 743	901	1 028	3 558	3 116	2 718	1 262
1973	11 065	317	10 748	9 063	434	147	8 775	1 060	1 229	3 987	3 515	2 775	1 328
1974	12 498	356	12 142	10 112	506	157	9 764	1 190	1 544	4 396	3 866	2 843	1 365
1975	13 503	285	13 218	10 465	527	166	10 105	1 327	2 071	4 656	4 198	2 900	1 326
1976	15 213	239	14 974	11 907	599	196	11 503	1 471	2 238	5 172	4 600	2 941	1 376
1977	16 705	190	16 515	13 078	657	216	12 637	1 667	2 401	5 589	4 953	2 989	1 411
1978	18 940	249	18 691	14 900	756	233	14 377	1 917	2 646	6 228	5 514	3 041	1 467
1979	21 345	267	21 078	16 681	873	253	16 061	2 255	3 029	6 915	6 055	3 087	1 510
1980	23 964	43	23 921	18 155	971	284	17 468	2 823	3 673	7 645	6 715	3 135	1 527
1981	26 902	182	26 720	20 046	1 149	301	19 199	3 477	4 226	8 462	7 390	3 179	1 541
1982	28 393	191	28 202	20 741	1 224	331	19 848	3 892	4 652	8 852	7 803	3 208	1 518
1983	30 816	46	30 770	22 504	1 348	345	21 501	4 347	4 969	9 529	8 400	3 234	1 551
1984	34 426	265	34 160	25 428	1 521	377	24 284	4 992	5 150	10 522	9 323	3 272	1 631
1985	37 068	189	36 878	27 118	1 708	431	25 841	5 532	5 695	11 222	9 925	3 303	1 663
1986	39 504	78	39 426	28 823	1 889	498	27 432	6 013	6 059	11 818	10 467	3 343	1 706
1987	42 426	242	42 183	31 357	2 018	549	29 888	6 226	6 312	12 550	11 080	3 381	1 748
1988	45 998	332	45 666	34 227	2 282	566	32 511	6 727	6 760	13 481	11 997	3 412	1 821
1989	49 052	345	48 707	36 592	2 532	520	34 579	6 881	7 592	14 190	12 496	3 457	1 871
1990	54 047	269	53 778	39 416	2 717	501	37 201	8 311	8 535	15 446	13 670	3 499	1 921
1991	56 047	366	55 681	40 350	2 843	489	37 997	8 437	9 613	15 767	14 058	3 555	1 900
1992	59 259	340	58 919	42 665	2 986	514	40 193	8 391	10 675	16 493	14 765	3 593	1 913
1993	62 484	326	62 158	44 868	3 168	511	42 211	8 815	11 458	17 231	15 365	3 626	1 948
1994	66 019	447	65 572	47 079	3 384	593	44 287	9 445	12 286	18 138	16 116	3 640	1 997
1995	70 208	329	69 878	49 528	3 588	659	46 599	10 537	13 072	19 146	16 934	3 667	2 045
1996	73 890	425	73 465	51 787	3 728	718	48 777	11 161	13 951	19 977	17 584	3 699	2 081

| YEAR | PERSONAL INCOME (Millions of dollars, except as noted) | | | | | | | | | Per capita (Dollars) | | Popu-lation (Thou-sands) | TOTAL EM-PLOY-MENT (Thou-sands) |
| | | | | Derivation of personal income | | | | | | | | | |
	Total	Farm	Nonfarm	Earnings by place of work	Less: Personal contributions for social insurance	Plus: Adjustment for residence	Equals: Net earnings by place of residence	Dividends, interest, and rent	Transfer payments	Total	Dispos-able		
SOUTH DAKOTA													
1971	2 346	397	1 949	1 822	71	6	1 757	319	270	3 494	3 214	671	306
1972	2 718	567	2 152	2 145	80	6	2 071	348	299	4 013	3 698	677	309
1973	3 452	1 027	2 425	2 806	104	7	2 709	398	345	5 085	4 670	679	323
1974	3 444	687	2 758	2 673	122	8	2 559	479	406	5 066	4 580	680	326
1975	3 763	706	3 057	2 869	136	10	2 743	537	483	5 522	5 063	681	326
1976	3 724	278	3 446	2 732	149	12	2 595	592	537	5 422	4 892	687	336
1977	4 224	439	3 785	3 116	154	13	2 975	673	576	6 130	5 606	689	342
1978	4 895	617	4 278	3 659	176	15	3 499	771	626	7 102	6 473	689	355
1979	5 425	656	4 770	4 013	206	16	3 823	895	707	7 874	7 165	689	360
1980	5 428	115	5 313	3 700	220	18	3 498	1 101	829	7 856	7 045	691	354
1981	6 280	400	5 880	4 186	246	14	3 954	1 377	950	9 108	8 198	690	349
1982	6 586	310	6 277	4 206	260	12	3 958	1 570	1 058	9 537	8 532	691	345
1983	6 778	181	6 597	4 336	277	5	4 065	1 576	1 138	9 781	8 870	693	354
1984	7 751	623	7 128	5 197	304	-1	4 892	1 672	1 186	11 116	10 166	697	364
1985	7 995	548	7 447	5 334	335	-3	4 995	1 721	1 279	11 448	10 488	698	366
1986	8 386	589	7 797	5 567	361	-10	5 196	1 846	1 344	12 048	11 041	696	368
1987	8 839	762	8 077	6 036	393	-17	5 626	1 824	1 388	12 699	11 539	696	383
1988	9 204	681	8 523	6 336	434	-24	5 877	1 863	1 464	13 183	12 004	698	390
1989	9 777	677	9 100	6 692	479	-34	6 179	2 010	1 587	14 033	12 674	697	398
1990	10 791	968	9 823	7 510	513	-50	6 947	2 129	1 715	15 490	13 932	697	411
1991	11 356	855	10 501	7 901	552	-61	7 289	2 218	1 849	16 174	14 551	702	423
1992	12 230	934	11 296	8 581	589	-76	7 916	2 284	2 029	17 235	15 526	710	434
1993	12 789	843	11 946	9 018	624	-96	8 297	2 321	2 170	17 831	16 061	717	445
1994	13 602	1 010	12 592	9 772	677	-124	8 972	2 352	2 279	18 783	17 051	724	468
1995	13 981	451	13 530	9 790	727	-148	8 916	2 608	2 457	19 165	17 331	730	481
1996	15 303	1 052	14 252	10 830	758	-157	9 914	2 783	2 606	20 895	18 849	732	488
TENNESSEE													
1971	13 745	297	13 447	11 378	471	-173	10 734	1 470	1 541	3 427	3 060	4 010	1 817
1972	15 459	366	15 093	12 900	545	-199	12 156	1 595	1 708	3 781	3 365	4 088	1 924
1973	17 653	531	17 123	14 679	691	-197	13 791	1 847	2 015	4 266	3 798	4 138	2 025
1974	19 530	356	19 174	15 944	797	-213	14 934	2 135	2 460	4 648	4 144	4 202	2 055
1975	21 108	279	20 829	16 633	825	-218	15 590	2 318	3 200	4 954	4 460	4 261	1 983
1976	23 792	397	23 394	18 877	920	-224	17 733	2 535	3 523	5 496	4 928	4 329	2 052
1977	26 451	324	26 127	21 165	1 040	-280	19 844	2 838	3 769	6 009	5 376	4 402	2 135
1978	30 200	346	29 854	24 315	1 200	-346	22 769	3 304	4 127	6 769	6 035	4 462	2 228
1979	33 848	381	33 467	26 932	1 383	-400	25 149	3 931	4 768	7 467	6 657	4 533	2 282
1980	37 479	239	37 240	28 835	1 504	-469	26 863	4 883	5 733	8 147	7 253	4 600	2 264
1981	41 603	405	41 198	31 392	1 757	-497	29 138	5 975	6 490	8 990	7 998	4 628	2 263
1982	43 825	294	43 531	32 449	1 880	-470	30 098	6 582	7 145	9 433	8 423	4 646	2 224
1983	46 697	-32	46 730	34 578	1 983	-492	32 103	6 944	7 650	10 021	8 973	4 660	2 246
1984	52 168	390	51 777	38 984	2 188	-525	36 270	7 984	7 913	11 131	10 054	4 687	2 353
1985	56 064	315	55 749	42 005	2 471	-555	38 978	8 569	8 517	11 890	10 679	4 715	2 410
1986	60 025	197	59 828	44 903	2 706	-591	41 606	9 238	9 181	12 667	11 406	4 739	2 489
1987	64 608	253	64 355	48 933	2 939	-630	45 365	9 515	9 728	13 508	12 120	4 783	2 591
1988	69 907	304	69 603	52 796	3 269	-663	48 865	10 531	10 511	14 496	13 087	4 822	2 682
1989	74 995	360	74 635	56 053	3 559	-697	51 797	11 799	11 400	15 449	13 899	4 854	2 754
1990	79 850	345	79 505	59 236	3 770	-731	54 735	12 379	12 736	16 327	14 711	4 891	2 790
1991	84 136	403	83 733	61 893	4 011	-723	57 159	12 535	14 442	17 005	15 360	4 948	2 797
1992	91 754	506	91 248	67 957	4 289	-643	63 025	12 506	16 223	18 290	16 518	5 017	2 862
1993	97 704	450	97 254	72 769	4 607	-788	67 374	12 850	17 480	19 199	17 324	5 089	2 957
1994	103 989	511	103 478	77 868	5 019	-886	71 963	13 788	18 237	20 120	18 096	5 168	3 080
1995	111 674	248	111 425	82 535	5 364	-1 021	76 150	15 624	19 900	21 284	19 113	5 247	3 174
1996	116 760	311	116 449	85 929	5 565	-1 063	79 300	16 523	20 938	21 949	19 577	5 320	3 211
TEXAS													
1971	44 414	1 053	43 361	35 792	1 471	-102	34 220	5 938	4 256	3 859	3 430	11 510	5 123
1972	49 277	1 322	47 955	39 803	1 650	-128	38 026	6 457	4 795	4 191	3 680	11 759	5 334
1973	56 191	2 208	53 983	45 343	2 086	-155	43 102	7 354	5 735	4 675	4 122	12 019	5 608
1974	63 574	1 208	62 367	50 685	2 444	-131	48 111	8 599	6 864	5 182	4 535	12 268	5 822
1975	71 930	1 347	70 583	57 058	2 706	-130	54 222	9 224	8 484	5 723	5 068	12 568	5 938
1976	81 723	1 308	80 415	65 386	3 082	-94	62 210	10 102	9 411	6 334	5 569	12 903	6 207
1977	91 772	1 289	90 483	73 941	3 496	-309	70 136	11 391	10 245	6 957	6 059	13 192	6 521
1978	106 380	1 036	105 344	85 752	4 097	-431	81 223	13 726	11 431	7 881	6 898	13 498	6 898
1979	123 696	1 782	121 915	99 340	4 925	-437	93 977	16 729	12 990	8 907	7 708	13 887	7 222
1980	142 474	680	141 793	112 526	5 719	-548	106 259	20 889	15 326	9 937	8 556	14 338	7 511
1981	167 447	2 062	165 385	131 440	7 145	-383	123 912	26 068	17 468	11 355	9 670	14 746	7 925
1982	182 583	1 301	181 282	141 359	7 908	-452	133 000	29 731	19 851	11 909	10 246	15 331	8 096
1983	192 537	1 672	190 865	147 867	8 183	-432	139 251	31 160	22 125	12 223	10 692	15 752	8 086
1984	211 884	1 620	210 264	162 454	8 921	-489	153 045	35 805	23 034	13 237	11 647	16 007	8 466
1985	227 890	1 521	226 369	173 974	10 001	-516	163 457	39 525	24 908	14 004	12 326	16 273	8 718
1986	232 253	1 233	231 020	174 498	10 331	-456	163 711	41 234	27 308	14 024	12 516	16 561	8 558
1987	237 618	1 954	235 664	178 990	10 448	-452	168 089	40 624	28 905	14 296	12 733	16 622	8 771
1988	252 243	1 873	250 370	190 208	11 413	-456	178 340	43 200	30 703	15 134	13 554	16 667	8 943
1989	270 955	1 902	269 053	202 674	12 476	-463	189 735	47 691	33 530	16 122	14 378	16 807	9 065
1990	295 071	2 740	292 332	221 457	13 504	-500	207 454	50 120	37 497	17 310	15 399	17 046	9 287
1991	312 747	2 691	310 056	236 046	14 542	-573	220 930	49 916	41 901	18 008	16 116	17 367	9 467
1992	334 587	3 057	331 531	252 450	15 470	-582	236 397	49 576	48 614	18 906	16 968	17 697	9 550
1993	354 982	3 912	351 070	268 328	16 330	-670	251 328	51 301	52 352	19 650	17 633	18 065	9 854
1994	374 353	2 950	371 403	282 232	17 546	-730	263 956	54 813	55 584	20 308	18 224	18 434	10 192
1995	400 683	2 202	398 481	300 183	18 864	-806	280 513	59 970	60 200	21 311	19 114	18 801	10 533
1996	426 212	1 973	424 239	319 149	20 058	-848	298 244	64 196	63 772	22 282	19 815	19 128	10 798

YEAR	PERSONAL INCOME (Millions of dollars, except as noted)											Popu-lation (Thou-sands)	TOTAL EM-PLOY-MENT (Thou-sands)
				Derivation of personal income						Per capita (Dollars)			
	Total	Farm	Nonfarm	Earnings by place of work	Less: Personal contributions for social insurance	Plus: Adjustment for residence	Equals: Net earnings by place of residence	Dividends, interest, and rent	Transfer payments	Total	Dispos-able		

UTAH

1971	3 943	83	3 860	3 190	151	2	3 042	491	411	3 582	3 205	1 101	467
1972	4 432	97	4 335	3 585	170	5	3 419	542	471	3 906	3 476	1 135	494
1973	4 965	138	4 826	4 033	210	7	3 831	582	552	4 248	3 778	1 169	523
1974	5 576	104	5 472	4 500	244	11	4 267	671	637	4 651	4 126	1 199	545
1975	6 196	73	6 123	4 943	268	13	4 689	717	790	5 022	4 507	1 234	553
1976	7 070	80	6 990	5 689	307	17	5 398	795	876	5 556	4 922	1 272	580
1977	8 015	69	7 946	6 478	351	21	6 148	901	966	6 088	5 368	1 316	613
1978	9 228	77	9 151	7 463	405	27	7 085	1 062	1 081	6 764	5 968	1 364	651
1979	10 523	92	10 432	8 470	489	35	8 016	1 278	1 229	7 431	6 529	1 416	679
1980	11 808	64	11 745	9 307	546	50	8 811	1 535	1 462	8 019	7 062	1 473	689
1981	13 322	40	13 282	10 365	649	57	9 773	1 845	1 704	8 790	7 697	1 515	699
1982	14 321	45	14 276	10 976	701	56	10 331	2 043	1 948	9 190	8 014	1 558	709
1983	15 307	36	15 271	11 658	747	45	10 957	2 232	2 118	9 597	8 579	1 595	721
1984	16 931	62	16 869	13 009	822	41	12 228	2 549	2 154	10 436	9 319	1 622	764
1985	18 133	63	18 070	13 900	899	42	13 043	2 776	2 315	11 037	9 835	1 643	792
1986	18 997	93	18 904	14 458	957	36	13 537	2 950	2 510	11 424	10 168	1 663	805
1987	19 946	125	19 822	15 110	966	26	14 170	3 060	2 716	11 886	10 542	1 678	835
1988	21 051	209	20 842	16 043	1 046	24	15 021	3 178	2 852	12 461	11 029	1 689	871
1989	22 596	203	22 394	17 121	1 140	22	16 003	3 455	3 138	13 246	11 710	1 706	903
1990	24 615	246	24 369	18 748	1 228	15	17 535	3 601	3 479	14 230	12 421	1 730	943
1991	26 364	222	26 141	20 102	1 333	9	18 778	3 716	3 870	14 910	13 062	1 768	968
1992	28 392	271	28 121	21 816	1 432	5	20 389	3 775	4 228	15 654	13 717	1 814	986
1993	30 791	301	30 489	23 605	1 544	0	22 060	4 123	4 608	16 520	14 423	1 864	1 033
1994	33 171	201	32 970	25 662	1 695	-4	23 963	4 450	4 757	17 334	15 029	1 914	1 112
1995	36 166	168	35 998	27 865	1 843	-5	26 017	5 029	5 120	18 468	15 952	1 958	1 169
1996	39 199	181	39 018	30 300	1 989	0	28 312	5 462	5 426	19 595	16 812	2 000	1 224

VERMONT

1971	1 749	67	1 682	1 345	58	-24	1 263	265	221	3 850	3 416	454	206
1972	1 936	75	1 861	1 479	63	-21	1 394	293	249	4 179	3 619	463	211
1973	2 132	78	2 054	1 625	79	-20	1 526	324	282	4 550	3 997	469	220
1974	2 298	64	2 234	1 709	87	-17	1 605	356	337	4 857	4 285	473	222
1975	2 482	65	2 416	1 791	91	-11	1 689	371	422	5 171	4 582	480	220
1976	2 779	81	2 698	2 021	100	-6	1 915	407	457	5 728	5 109	485	228
1977	3 023	69	2 954	2 195	109	-2	2 084	464	476	6 143	5 429	492	236
1978	3 485	98	3 387	2 580	129	-2	2 449	530	506	6 995	6 188	498	252
1979	3 946	108	3 838	2 892	149	5	2 748	625	573	7 803	6 864	506	261
1980	4 423	111	4 313	3 137	164	13	2 985	754	684	8 631	7 569	513	266
1981	4 952	125	4 827	3 427	200	19	3 245	923	783	9 604	8 385	516	271
1982	5 270	122	5 147	3 584	207	24	3 401	999	870	10 151	8 934	519	272
1983	5 679	84	5 595	3 873	216	23	3 680	1 078	921	10 852	9 530	523	278
1984	6 258	81	6 177	4 273	239	29	4 063	1 251	945	11 882	10 484	527	290
1985	6 813	99	6 714	4 725	276	31	4 480	1 344	989	12 854	11 278	530	302
1986	7 360	97	7 263	5 135	306	35	4 863	1 469	1 029	13 781	12 037	534	313
1987	8 003	119	7 884	5 708	338	43	5 412	1 535	1 056	14 813	12 840	540	323
1988	8 786	122	8 664	6 285	386	51	5 950	1 713	1 123	15 981	13 942	550	337
1989	9 616	128	9 488	6 770	427	52	6 395	1 999	1 222	17 242	14 976	558	345
1990	10 003	104	9 899	6 978	446	53	6 585	2 054	1 364	17 720	15 477	564	344
1991	10 195	92	10 103	6 999	465	54	6 588	2 087	1 520	17 949	15 755	568	338
1992	10 825	161	10 664	7 505	491	55	7 069	2 075	1 681	18 952	16 684	571	345
1993	11 239	121	11 118	7 815	516	54	7 353	2 125	1 762	19 533	17 175	575	353
1994	11 787	115	11 671	8 130	547	60	7 643	2 283	1 861	20 299	17 878	581	363
1995	12 595	96	12 499	8 500	579	66	7 987	2 604	2 004	21 538	19 036	585	372
1996	13 227	130	13 097	8 917	606	76	8 386	2 770	2 071	22 470	19 743	589	377

VIRGINIA

1971	19 253	226	19 027	14 906	667	805	15 044	2 298	1 911	4 051	3 499	4 753	2 196
1972	21 452	295	21 157	16 671	758	850	16 763	2 475	2 215	4 443	3 778	4 828	2 263
1973	24 201	390	23 810	18 763	937	916	18 742	2 819	2 640	4 932	4 233	4 907	2 384
1974	27 011	354	26 657	20 633	1 072	1 012	20 573	3 273	3 165	5 426	4 624	4 978	2 451
1975	29 610	299	29 311	21 990	1 142	1 234	22 082	3 555	3 973	5 856	5 056	5 056	2 425
1976	33 017	265	32 751	24 498	1 266	1 414	24 646	3 947	4 424	6 433	5 580	5 133	2 501
1977	36 688	192	36 496	27 175	1 399	1 600	27 376	4 454	4 858	7 048	6 069	5 206	2 584
1978	41 735	316	41 419	30 774	1 579	1 917	31 112	5 264	5 359	7 898	6 759	5 284	2 697
1979	46 902	178	46 723	34 122	1 827	2 259	34 554	6 240	6 108	8 809	7 554	5 325	2 769
1980	53 443	88	53 354	37 650	2 035	2 742	38 356	7 796	7 291	9 955	8 540	5 368	2 802
1981	60 096	303	59 793	41 569	2 369	2 883	42 083	9 630	8 382	11 039	9 401	5 444	2 820
1982	64 597	117	64 480	44 375	2 599	2 910	44 686	10 711	9 200	11 760	10 069	5 493	2 831
1983	70 204	46	70 158	48 406	2 882	2 950	48 474	11 819	9 910	12 616	10 914	5 565	2 904
1984	78 698	316	78 381	54 493	3 183	3 092	54 403	14 035	10 260	13 944	12 170	5 644	3 053
1985	85 411	218	85 192	59 654	3 615	3 166	59 205	15 284	10 922	14 945	12 954	5 715	3 197
1986	92 487	263	92 225	64 971	4 010	3 193	64 154	16 734	11 600	15 914	13 800	5 812	3 333
1987	100 426	365	100 061	71 742	4 387	3 361	70 715	17 498	12 213	16 929	14 548	5 932	3 500
1988	109 198	501	108 697	78 035	4 926	3 726	76 834	19 268	13 095	18 088	15 670	6 037	3 588
1989	117 893	621	117 273	83 527	5 405	3 952	82 076	21 694	14 124	19 263	16 577	6 120	3 685
1990	124 608	639	123 969	87 326	5 689	4 528	86 164	23 027	15 417	20 054	17 363	6 214	3 720
1991	129 238	581	128 657	89 310	5 951	4 918	88 278	23 971	16 988	20 560	17 868	6 286	3 669
1992	136 415	605	135 810	94 747	6 246	5 240	93 740	23 759	18 917	21 354	18 607	6 388	3 688
1993	144 146	496	143 650	99 623	6 568	5 613	98 668	25 328	20 150	22 263	19 332	6 475	3 761
1994	151 487	555	150 932	104 314	6 988	5 804	103 130	27 024	21 332	23 129	19 961	6 550	3 851
1995	160 141	461	159 680	109 375	7 348	5 736	107 763	29 562	22 815	24 208	20 880	6 615	3 934
1996	168 300	479	167 821	115 007	7 675	5 645	112 978	31 285	24 037	25 212	21 600	6 675	4 007

YEAR	PERSONAL INCOME (Millions of dollars, except as noted)											Popu-lation (Thou-sands)	TOTAL EM-PLOY-MENT (Thou-sands)
				Derivation of personal income						Per capita (Dollars)			
	Total	Farm	Nonfarm	Earnings by place of work	Less: Personal contribu-tions for social in-surance	Plus: Adjust-ment for resi-dence	Equals: Net earn-ings by place of residence	Dividends, interest, and rent	Transfer payments	Total	Dispos-able		
WASHINGTON													
1971	15 079	410	14 669	11 364	521	66	10 910	2 204	1 965	4 375	3 917	3 447	1 457
1972	16 309	532	15 777	12 360	576	76	11 860	2 322	2 126	4 732	4 186	3 447	1 481
1973	18 447	780	17 667	14 034	725	93	13 402	2 649	2 395	5 305	4 688	3 477	1 558
1974	20 918	912	20 006	15 803	870	137	15 070	3 011	2 837	5 896	5 217	3 548	1 621
1975	23 447	927	22 520	17 563	983	208	16 787	3 188	3 472	6 479	5 753	3 619	1 659
1976	26 261	769	25 492	19 729	1 074	258	18 913	3 546	3 802	7 116	6 302	3 691	1 739
1977	29 223	616	28 607	22 085	1 174	237	21 148	4 012	4 063	7 747	6 838	3 772	1 815
1978	34 207	774	33 433	26 065	1 385	281	24 962	4 807	4 438	8 802	7 710	3 886	1 939
1979	39 537	755	38 782	30 030	1 645	336	28 721	5 820	4 995	9 853	8 561	4 013	2 061
1980	44 820	890	43 930	33 131	1 834	396	31 693	7 054	6 074	10 788	9 388	4 155	2 109
1981	49 957	845	49 112	35 949	2 147	449	34 252	8 667	7 038	11 794	10 240	4 236	2 126
1982	52 484	767	51 716	37 009	2 276	482	35 215	9 354	7 915	12 272	10 847	4 277	2 101
1983	55 685	1 091	54 594	38 959	2 389	505	37 075	10 117	8 493	12 949	11 586	4 300	2 147
1984	59 769	1 040	58 729	41 534	2 573	560	39 520	11 277	8 972	13 760	12 379	4 344	2 223
1985	63 656	750	62 906	44 113	2 867	605	41 851	12 017	9 788	14 467	12 952	4 400	2 290
1986	68 198	1 067	67 131	47 477	3 142	622	44 958	12 878	10 363	15 316	13 734	4 453	2 364
1987	72 436	1 058	71 378	50 998	3 359	670	48 309	13 304	10 824	15 984	14 213	4 532	2 486
1988	78 451	946	77 506	55 705	3 787	747	52 665	14 203	11 583	16 908	15 046	4 640	2 622
1989	86 530	1 057	85 473	61 052	4 246	830	57 636	16 262	12 632	18 231	16 049	4 746	2 741
1990	96 246	1 085	95 161	68 115	4 680	944	64 380	17 900	13 967	19 637	17 233	4 901	2 862
1991	102 644	1 152	101 491	72 849	5 138	993	68 704	18 218	15 722	20 456	18 028	5 018	2 903
1992	110 684	1 418	109 266	79 306	5 577	1 078	74 807	18 646	17 231	21 503	18 988	5 147	2 932
1993	116 373	1 683	114 690	82 803	5 786	1 077	78 093	19 766	18 514	22 125	19 625	5 260	2 973
1994	121 762	1 162	120 600	86 065	6 155	1 145	81 054	21 184	19 523	22 755	20 112	5 351	3 086
1995	130 350	1 218	129 132	90 797	6 515	1 339	85 621	23 811	20 917	23 927	21 138	5 448	3 148
1996	139 356	1 734	137 623	97 384	6 917	1 426	91 892	25 559	21 905	25 187	22 057	5 533	3 224
WEST VIRGINIA													
1971	5 947	34	5 913	4 711	213	-105	4 393	607	947	3 359	2 974	1 770	670
1972	6 590	41	6 549	5 204	240	-119	4 845	656	1 089	3 667	3 230	1 797	684
1973	7 233	54	7 179	5 618	288	-122	5 209	742	1 282	4 006	3 555	1 805	700
1974	8 045	40	8 005	6 192	326	-137	5 729	863	1 453	4 435	3 894	1 814	711
1975	9 096	23	9 073	6 948	360	-163	6 426	953	1 717	4 942	4 352	1 841	717
1976	10 207	11	10 196	7 859	406	-198	7 256	1 056	1 895	5 437	4 764	1 877	739
1977	11 419	5	11 414	8 871	448	-235	8 188	1 188	2 043	5 992	5 257	1 906	758
1978	12 738	19	12 719	9 906	503	-275	9 128	1 353	2 258	6 633	5 843	1 920	781
1979	14 249	27	14 222	10 916	579	-289	10 049	1 574	2 626	7 348	6 433	1 939	791
1980	15 720	15	15 705	11 676	632	-315	10 728	1 937	3 055	8 056	7 028	1 951	784
1981	16 933	-17	16 950	12 151	718	-300	11 133	2 357	3 443	8 665	7 558	1 954	764
1982	17 695	-27	17 722	12 263	762	-256	11 244	2 672	3 778	9 076	7 949	1 950	743
1983	18 349	-18	18 367	12 329	756	-215	11 357	2 835	4 157	9 433	8 336	1 945	724
1984	19 601	20	19 581	13 210	815	-170	12 226	3 165	4 210	10 168	9 018	1 928	735
1985	20 336	17	20 319	13 638	886	-154	12 597	3 262	4 476	10 665	9 496	1 907	735
1986	21 111	38	21 073	13 904	926	-137	12 841	3 525	4 745	11 215	10 044	1 882	735
1987	21 656	3	21 653	14 299	961	-75	13 263	3 518	4 874	11 658	10 432	1 858	742
1988	22 717	29	22 688	14 948	1 046	-50	13 852	3 710	5 155	12 412	11 215	1 830	755
1989	23 774	56	23 717	15 432	1 118	27	14 341	3 986	5 447	13 159	11 789	1 807	762
1990	25 442	38	25 404	16 497	1 179	72	15 390	4 211	5 841	14 194	12 670	1 792	782
1991	26 711	23	26 688	16 971	1 248	71	15 794	4 347	6 570	14 848	13 287	1 799	784
1992	28 406	47	28 359	17 969	1 311	90	16 748	4 324	7 334	15 718	14 166	1 807	795
1993	29 792	58	29 734	18 661	1 381	93	17 373	4 374	8 045	16 380	14 729	1 819	807
1994	30 973	52	30 921	19 708	1 477	128	18 359	4 536	8 077	16 998	15 250	1 822	829
1995	32 001	14	31 988	20 346	1 535	144	18 955	4 879	8 167	17 532	15 706	1 825	844
1996	33 155	-14	33 169	20 947	1 571	170	19 546	5 116	8 493	18 160	16 179	1 826	853
WISCONSIN													
1971	18 580	737	17 842	14 301	626	259	13 934	2 640	2 006	4 166	3 635	4 460	1 957
1972	20 294	786	19 508	15 711	701	281	15 291	2 771	2 232	4 511	3 888	4 498	2 014
1973	22 720	967	21 752	17 697	876	306	17 127	3 072	2 520	5 028	4 346	4 518	2 116
1974	24 972	857	24 114	19 169	1 003	330	18 496	3 485	2 991	5 503	4 732	4 538	2 159
1975	27 021	910	26 112	20 326	1 058	336	19 604	3 706	3 711	5 913	5 144	4 570	2 148
1976	29 909	800	29 109	22 591	1 136	377	21 833	4 021	4 055	6 524	5 655	4 585	2 211
1977	33 523	1 187	32 336	25 480	1 225	419	24 674	4 490	4 360	7 267	6 253	4 613	2 293
1978	37 632	1 184	36 448	28 618	1 404	472	27 686	5 143	4 803	8 125	6 950	4 632	2 382
1979	42 368	1 453	40 915	31 992	1 637	509	30 864	6 016	5 489	9 080	7 803	4 666	2 465
1980	46 644	1 478	45 166	33 970	1 761	534	32 742	7 230	6 672	9 899	8 523	4 712	2 449
1981	50 645	1 169	49 476	35 721	2 022	583	34 282	8 793	7 570	10 715	9 164	4 726	2 424
1982	53 154	1 030	52 124	36 489	2 111	600	34 979	9 719	8 457	11 240	9 691	4 729	2 381
1983	55 809	443	55 366	37 759	2 122	653	36 290	10 454	9 065	11 820	10 312	4 721	2 384
1984	61 357	950	60 407	41 952	2 307	767	40 412	11 723	9 222	12 957	11 330	4 736	2 478
1985	64 662	942	63 720	44 144	2 519	856	42 480	12 325	9 857	13 620	11 978	4 748	2 509
1986	68 280	1 221	67 059	46 681	2 701	939	44 918	13 081	10 281	14 358	12 593	4 756	2 551
1987	71 955	1 250	70 706	50 002	2 892	1 045	48 155	13 168	10 632	15 060	13 107	4 778	2 620
1988	76 327	743	75 584	53 596	3 268	1 206	51 534	13 752	11 041	15 828	13 737	4 822	2 704
1989	81 800	1 560	80 240	57 434	3 587	1 245	55 092	14 926	11 782	16 843	14 535	4 857	2 760
1990	86 870	1 150	85 721	60 736	3 807	1 325	58 255	15 901	12 715	17 721	15 304	4 902	2 829
1991	90 625	710	89 915	62 877	4 039	1 361	60 199	16 411	14 014	18 315	15 835	4 948	2 862
1992	97 168	789	96 379	68 208	4 334	1 458	65 331	16 649	15 188	19 449	16 830	4 996	2 917
1993	101 931	434	101 497	71 910	4 581	1 487	68 816	17 228	15 887	20 203	17 528	5 045	2 974
1994	107 749	500	107 250	76 372	4 953	1 615	73 034	18 188	16 528	21 192	18 211	5 084	3 070
1995	114 628	270	114 358	80 148	5 254	1 727	76 621	20 489	17 519	22 379	19 228	5 122	3 152
1996	120 325	491	119 834	84 118	5 477	1 823	80 464	21 788	18 073	23 320	19 854	5 160	3 200

	PERSONAL INCOME (Millions of dollars, except as noted)												TOTAL EM-PLOY-MENT (Thousands)
YEAR	Total	Farm	Nonfarm	Derivation of personal income						Per capita (Dollars)		Population (Thousands)	
				Earnings by place of work	Less: Personal contributions for social insurance	Plus: Adjustment for residence	Equals: Net earnings by place of residence	Dividends, interest, and rent	Transfer payments	Total	Disposable		
WYOMING													
1971	1 429	93	1 336	1 122	51	-1	1 070	226	133	4 203	3 726	340	165
1972	1 603	134	1 470	1 287	58	-3	1 226	231	147	4 622	4 143	347	172
1973	1 878	159	1 719	1 513	74	-7	1 432	275	171	5 315	4 697	353	182
1974	2 207	117	2 091	1 788	90	-13	1 685	327	195	6 055	5 251	365	194
1975	2 487	71	2 416	2 021	103	-16	1 903	350	235	6 536	5 752	380	203
1976	2 774	50	2 724	2 259	119	-22	2 118	391	266	7 014	6 083	395	214
1977	3 258	46	3 212	2 679	138	-29	2 513	448	297	7 916	6 882	412	231
1978	3 937	69	3 868	3 256	170	-37	3 049	553	335	9 137	7 938	431	250
1979	4 645	99	4 546	3 850	206	-54	3 591	669	386	10 281	8 792	452	267
1980	5 448	86	5 362	4 462	233	-74	4 155	833	460	11 489	9 851	474	280
1981	6 182	51	6 132	4 984	281	-86	4 618	1 019	546	12 573	10 706	492	290
1982	6 402	33	6 369	5 040	309	-82	4 649	1 126	627	12 641	10 894	506	288
1983	6 324	42	6 282	4 784	267	-59	4 457	1 134	732	12 391	10 936	510	275
1984	6 567	18	6 549	4 964	281	-53	4 630	1 222	714	13 007	11 553	505	277
1985	6 850	22	6 829	5 169	305	-51	4 813	1 272	766	13 709	12 241	500	278
1986	6 706	41	6 665	4 922	299	-40	4 583	1 278	845	13 530	12 190	496	265
1987	6 502	59	6 443	4 691	291	-25	4 375	1 268	858	13 631	12 221	477	260
1988	6 673	49	6 624	4 798	315	-19	4 463	1 313	897	14 347	12 806	465	265
1989	7 133	82	7 052	5 030	334	-13	4 683	1 493	957	15 562	13 698	458	267
1990	7 808	144	7 663	5 448	359	-9	5 081	1 679	1 048	17 220	15 214	453	273
1991	8 438	213	8 226	5 850	387	0	5 463	1 807	1 169	18 426	16 368	458	280
1992	8 722	204	8 518	6 076	409	-9	5 658	1 774	1 291	18 800	16 673	464	282
1993	9 258	276	8 982	6 482	428	-16	6 037	1 833	1 388	19 713	17 423	470	287
1994	9 522	89	9 433	6 580	454	-21	6 105	1 945	1 472	20 013	17 661	476	301
1995	10 035	83	9 951	6 769	472	-21	6 277	2 203	1 555	20 941	18 542	479	307
1996	10 371	61	10 310	6 911	481	-17	6 413	2 309	1 650	21 544	18 961	481	309
NEW ENGLAND													
1971	56 415	311	56 104	41 896	1 748	838	40 986	8 837	6 593	4 703	4 107	11 996	5 454
1972	61 095	319	60 776	45 615	1 933	889	44 571	9 290	7 234	5 054	4 340	12 088	5 573
1973	66 862	424	66 438	50 116	2 373	932	48 674	10 106	8 082	5 504	4 763	12 148	5 783
1974	72 673	456	72 218	53 529	2 643	1 005	51 892	11 217	9 564	5 978	5 177	12 157	5 843
1975	77 601	333	77 268	55 531	2 726	1 076	53 880	11 432	12 289	6 373	5 603	12 176	5 685
1976	84 986	449	84 537	61 324	2 950	1 180	59 555	12 420	13 010	6 962	6 080	12 207	5 811
1977	93 226	402	92 824	67 595	3 238	1 307	65 664	13 873	13 690	7 606	6 617	12 257	6 007
1978	104 026	415	103 611	75 990	3 692	1 483	73 781	15 701	14 544	8 455	7 330	12 303	6 280
1979	117 008	389	116 618	85 108	4 303	1 697	82 501	18 311	16 195	9 478	8 162	12 345	6 515
1980	132 440	373	132 067	94 295	4 847	1 982	91 431	22 336	18 673	10 705	9 186	12 372	6 641
1981	147 975	477	147 498	102 776	5 670	2 144	99 250	27 406	21 319	11 899	10 145	12 436	6 692
1982	159 683	516	159 167	109 718	6 177	2 292	105 834	30 421	23 429	12 808	10 967	12 468	6 691
1983	172 967	492	172 475	119 987	6 734	2 437	115 690	32 266	25 011	13 788	11 892	12 544	6 825
1984	193 984	575	193 409	135 149	7 576	2 617	130 191	37 844	25 949	15 345	13 288	12 642	7 195
1985	209 886	574	209 313	148 296	8 665	2 787	142 417	40 251	27 219	16 474	14 166	12 741	7 444
1986	227 410	592	226 817	161 215	9 696	2 946	154 465	44 045	28 900	17 721	15 148	12 833	7 686
1987	247 863	641	247 222	178 731	10 640	3 126	171 217	46 554	30 092	19 138	16 249	12 951	7 826
1988	272 708	669	272 039	197 362	12 003	3 338	188 697	51 682	32 329	20 842	17 932	13 085	8 095
1989	291 687	651	291 036	206 937	12 880	3 291	197 348	58 617	35 722	22 128	19 026	13 182	8 086
1990	301 179	673	300 507	211 430	13 258	3 586	201 758	59 592	39 829	22 783	19 660	13 220	7 917
1991	305 627	610	305 017	210 566	13 661	3 648	200 554	59 143	45 931	23 146	20 022	13 204	7 598
1992	319 837	792	319 045	222 633	14 222	4 442	212 852	57 328	49 657	24 234	20 862	13 198	7 640
1993	331 512	779	330 734	231 351	14 807	4 279	220 822	59 246	51 444	25 058	21 505	13 230	7 767
1994	345 430	639	344 792	240 418	15 717	4 254	228 956	62 522	53 953	26 040	22 284	13 265	7 873
1995	368 398	568	367 830	253 265	16 654	4 282	240 892	70 181	57 325	27 688	23 582	13 305	8 045
1996	387 042	653	386 389	266 283	17 433	4 598	253 447	74 483	59 112	28 989	24 387	13 351	8 173
MIDEAST													
1971	209 534	1 089	208 445	164 001	7 267	-1 685	155 049	29 736	24 749	4 888	4 238	42 870	19 303
1972	226 457	1 106	225 351	177 263	7 964	-1 825	167 475	31 082	27 901	5 267	4 498	42 992	19 526
1973	245 762	1 509	244 253	192 318	9 653	-1 930	180 735	33 994	31 032	5 737	4 937	42 837	19 973
1974	267 046	1 422	265 624	205 976	10 717	-2 113	193 146	37 843	36 057	6 253	5 362	42 709	19 960
1975	286 706	1 316	285 390	216 073	11 155	-2 386	202 532	39 059	45 115	6 710	5 839	42 728	19 485
1976	311 037	1 384	309 653	234 141	11 924	-2 663	219 554	42 359	49 124	7 290	6 313	42 667	19 568
1977	338 366	1 185	337 180	254 827	12 846	-2 970	239 010	47 108	52 247	7 953	6 841	42 547	19 854
1978	373 303	1 410	371 893	282 007	14 291	-3 455	264 260	53 482	55 561	8 800	7 564	42 421	20 411
1979	413 385	1 601	411 784	310 382	16 298	-4 027	290 057	62 327	61 000	9 759	8 338	42 358	20 899
1980	460 339	1 199	459 140	337 978	17 875	-4 754	315 348	74 700	70 290	10 890	9 295	42 272	20 961
1981	510 892	1 554	509 337	367 039	20 836	-5 273	340 930	90 735	79 227	12 070	10 215	42 329	21 061
1982	546 824	1 476	545 348	387 609	22 506	-5 449	359 654	99 226	87 944	12 902	10 923	42 382	20 936
1983	584 171	1 115	583 056	413 132	24 143	-5 647	383 342	106 324	94 504	13 731	11 781	42 544	21 131
1984	645 320	1 870	643 451	456 196	26 884	-6 012	423 300	124 200	97 820	15 118	13 003	42 687	21 881
1985	691 669	1 980	689 690	491 664	30 255	-6 293	455 116	133 282	103 271	16 163	13 840	42 794	22 476
1986	739 368	2 184	737 184	527 117	33 275	-6 588	487 254	142 635	109 479	17 198	14 719	42 991	22 989
1987	791 031	2 230	788 801	573 641	35 900	-7 063	530 678	146 457	113 896	18 315	15 531	43 190	23 498
1988	859 890	2 088	857 802	626 785	40 348	-7 753	578 685	160 514	120 691	19 797	16 932	43 435	24 153
1989	923 309	2 457	920 853	660 891	43 392	-8 072	609 427	184 225	129 657	21 184	18 059	43 585	24 438
1990	979 009	2 320	976 689	698 896	45 966	-9 042	643 889	193 623	141 497	22 399	19 197	43 708	24 447
1991	1 006 918	1 836	1 005 082	708 989	47 739	-9 473	651 777	195 176	159 965	22 945	19 763	43 884	23 943
1992	1 061 430	2 306	1 059 124	753 762	50 171	-10 627	692 964	189 683	178 783	24 077	20 765	44 085	23 845
1993	1 098 463	2 251	1 096 211	778 653	51 790	-11 124	715 739	194 415	188 309	24 799	21 348	44 294	23 968
1994	1 138 137	1 874	1 136 262	802 657	54 255	-11 366	737 037	204 558	196 542	25 613	22 000	44 437	24 169
1995	1 200 373	1 487	1 198 886	836 221	56 569	-11 360	768 293	223 884	208 196	26 968	23 136	44 511	24 475
1996	1 258 684	2 147	1 256 536	873 523	58 563	-11 612	803 349	235 594	219 741	28 242	24 028	44 568	24 687

YEAR	PERSONAL INCOME (Millions of dollars, except as noted)												TOTAL EMPLOYMENT (Thousands)
				Derivation of personal income						Per capita (Dollars)		Population (Thousands)	
	Total	Farm	Nonfarm	Earnings by place of work	Less: Personal contributions for social insurance	Plus: Adjustment for residence	Equals: Net earnings by place of residence	Dividends, interest, and rent	Transfer payments	Total	Disposable		
GREAT LAKES													
1971	180 803	3 180	177 623	145 346	6 126	294	139 513	23 553	17 736	4 451	3 891	40 622	17 549
1972	197 549	3 475	194 074	159 292	6 830	335	152 797	24 893	19 859	4 839	4 167	40 824	17 933
1973	221 768	5 460	216 309	179 167	8 539	383	171 010	27 843	22 915	5 416	4 695	40 947	18 710
1974	241 118	4 908	236 211	191 491	9 530	468	182 428	31 548	27 142	5 876	5 078	41 037	18 911
1975	257 975	6 000	251 975	199 553	9 731	529	190 350	33 253	34 371	6 276	5 493	41 105	18 399
1976	286 667	4 997	281 670	223 328	10 750	659	213 237	36 268	37 162	6 960	6 039	41 187	18 891
1977	319 114	5 059	314 054	250 090	11 878	827	239 039	40 715	39 359	7 717	6 653	41 353	19 508
1978	355 580	4 766	350 814	279 088	13 452	1 053	266 689	46 569	42 322	8 566	7 363	41 510	20 195
1979	393 683	5 326	388 357	305 823	15 370	1 272	291 724	54 354	47 605	9 461	8 107	41 611	20 520
1980	426 065	3 328	422 737	316 336	16 161	1 526	301 702	65 047	59 317	10 219	8 811	41 694	20 024
1981	464 139	3 834	460 306	336 465	18 562	1 517	319 420	78 641	66 079	11 144	9 567	41 648	19 862
1982	480 035	2 823	477 212	338 619	19 169	1 425	320 875	84 913	74 246	11 569	10 043	41 492	19 309
1983	504 229	-217	504 446	352 954	20 052	1 421	334 323	90 718	79 188	12 189	10 638	41 366	19 329
1984	556 791	4 032	552 759	394 176	22 153	1 547	373 570	102 341	80 880	13 451	11 809	41 393	20 113
1985	591 345	4 470	586 875	421 446	24 801	1 590	398 235	107 671	85 439	14 278	12 485	41 418	20 599
1986	623 309	3 961	619 347	443 761	26 773	1 658	418 647	114 603	90 059	15 036	13 164	41 455	21 045
1987	655 527	4 372	651 155	471 779	28 458	1 725	445 046	116 456	94 025	15 762	13 693	41 590	21 646
1988	699 317	2 625	696 692	507 316	31 742	1 860	477 434	123 382	98 501	16 762	14 626	41 721	22 241
1989	746 903	6 187	740 716	536 520	34 479	1 889	503 930	137 469	105 504	17 838	15 450	41 873	22 731
1990	788 915	4 994	783 921	563 547	36 307	1 928	529 167	145 622	114 125	18 750	16 273	42 077	23 048
1991	815 304	2 486	812 817	576 646	38 153	1 959	540 451	148 742	126 110	19 246	16 766	42 363	23 028
1992	866 926	4 216	862 710	619 545	40 196	2 152	581 500	146 826	138 600	20 321	17 767	42 663	23 163
1993	911 008	3 576	907 432	653 496	42 588	2 111	613 019	152 264	145 725	21 219	18 461	42 934	23 547
1994	964 118	4 079	960 039	694 364	46 062	2 329	650 631	162 736	150 751	22 342	19 346	43 152	24 287
1995	1 022 736	2 497	1 020 239	729 862	48 750	2 604	683 716	180 186	158 835	23 575	20 394	43 381	24 958
1996	1 071 792	4 496	1 067 296	763 190	50 738	2 777	715 230	190 235	166 328	24 575	21 084	43 614	25 331
PLAINS													
1971	67 005	4 630	62 374	52 989	2 251	-373	50 365	9 449	7 190	4 067	3 603	16 475	7 545
1972	74 103	6 255	67 848	58 967	2 507	-390	56 071	10 169	7 864	4 474	3 909	16 563	7 731
1973	86 886	11 337	75 549	69 714	3 124	-431	66 159	11 609	9 118	5 225	4 609	16 628	8 065
1974	92 052	7 730	84 323	72 044	3 579	-469	67 996	13 392	10 665	5 522	4 789	16 672	8 220
1975	100 244	7 523	92 721	77 065	3 830	-470	72 765	14 479	12 999	5 987	5 257	16 743	8 182
1976	108 223	4 422	103 801	82 828	4 227	-571	78 030	15 924	14 269	6 418	5 596	16 864	8 440
1977	119 990	5 208	114 781	91 870	4 563	-715	86 592	18 083	15 315	7 079	6 159	16 950	8 658
1978	136 697	7 881	128 817	105 383	5 225	-885	99 274	20 751	16 673	8 028	6 985	17 028	8 959
1979	151 807	6 657	145 151	115 971	6 078	-1 052	108 841	24 311	18 655	8 879	7 666	17 097	9 249
1980	163 679	1 739	161 940	119 715	6 610	-1 225	111 880	29 531	22 268	9 512	8 202	17 208	9 252
1981	184 877	5 349	179 528	132 059	7 590	-1 326	123 143	36 422	25 312	10 709	9 214	17 264	9 214
1982	194 530	3 741	190 789	134 855	8 079	-1 350	125 426	40 861	28 243	11 250	9 670	17 292	9 081
1983	203 090	1 184	201 906	140 242	8 535	-1 459	130 248	42 541	30 301	11 722	10 215	17 325	9 195
1984	226 368	6 008	220 359	159 486	9 391	-1 649	148 446	46 700	31 221	13 023	11 481	17 382	9 512
1985	239 645	6 844	232 801	169 482	10 417	-1 770	157 296	48 732	33 617	13 771	12 127	17 402	9 664
1986	251 259	7 405	243 854	177 463	11 191	-1 904	164 368	51 404	35 486	14 446	12 748	17 393	9 754
1987	264 693	9 180	255 513	190 275	11 971	-2 027	176 278	51 533	36 881	15 188	13 296	17 428	10 010
1988	276 892	6 659	270 233	200 132	13 282	-2 203	184 647	53 304	38 941	15 792	13 849	17 533	10 233
1989	296 908	8 466	288 441	213 212	14 436	-2 305	196 471	58 601	41 836	16 874	14 707	17 595	10 430
1990	315 386	9 549	305 837	225 772	15 289	-2 422	208 060	62 189	45 137	17 830	15 518	17 688	10 598
1991	327 448	7 215	320 232	232 261	16 145	-2 472	213 645	63 690	50 113	18 399	16 061	17 797	10 675
1992	349 261	9 011	340 250	250 599	17 032	-2 628	230 938	64 284	54 039	19 475	17 055	17 934	10 791
1993	360 877	5 082	355 795	258 147	17 947	-2 841	237 360	65 713	57 804	19 958	17 438	18 082	11 018
1994	382 697	8 427	374 270	276 519	19 351	-3 038	254 130	68 200	60 367	21 005	18 325	18 219	11 330
1995	404 044	4 811	399 233	288 844	20 631	-3 331	264 882	75 253	63 909	22 018	19 147	18 351	11 641
1996	432 418	10 742	421 676	310 406	21 672	-3 501	285 233	80 149	67 036	23 414	20 211	18 468	11 862
SOUTHEAST													
1971	160 484	4 583	155 901	125 916	5 424	925	121 417	20 317	18 751	3 565	3 164	45 013	19 635
1972	180 560	5 366	175 195	142 424	6 230	968	137 162	22 065	21 333	3 924	3 436	46 019	20 523
1973	206 188	7 637	198 551	162 374	7 843	1 033	155 565	25 365	25 258	4 388	3 868	46 992	21 636
1974	230 127	7 002	223 125	177 847	8 937	1 115	170 026	29 540	30 560	4 799	4 215	47 955	22 069
1975	250 262	6 260	244 003	187 459	9 387	1 324	179 396	31 860	39 006	5 130	4 586	48 788	21 642
1976	280 193	6 578	273 615	210 957	10 516	1 486	201 927	35 181	43 085	5 659	5 020	49 514	22 350
1977	311 928	5 943	305 985	235 364	11 695	1 662	225 331	39 857	46 740	6 200	5 478	50 312	23 208
1978	355 903	7 150	348 753	269 171	13 467	1 953	257 657	46 983	51 262	6 963	6 134	51 113	24 308
1979	402 267	7 095	395 172	300 661	15 662	2 276	287 274	56 217	58 776	7 739	6 780	51 977	25 019
1980	454 253	4 432	449 821	328 602	17 483	2 739	313 858	70 210	70 184	8 590	7 517	52 881	25 378
1981	512 453	6 879	505 574	362 811	20 649	2 907	345 069	87 160	80 224	9 556	8 328	53 627	25 676
1982	545 981	6 843	539 138	380 127	22 320	3 064	360 871	95 997	89 112	10 064	8 804	54 249	25 570
1983	587 803	5 025	582 778	407 759	24 020	3 176	386 914	104 260	96 629	10 715	9 451	54 856	26 104
1984	653 412	8 397	645 014	457 382	26 746	3 390	434 026	119 146	100 241	11 770	10 453	55 515	27 387
1985	704 890	7 430	697 460	492 985	30 178	3 535	466 342	130 252	108 295	12 543	11 068	56 199	28 234
1986	752 206	6 843	745 363	524 007	32 861	3 625	494 772	141 621	115 813	13 229	11 687	56 861	28 977
1987	803 893	8 126	795 766	567 700	35 188	3 887	536 400	145 846	121 647	13 972	12 295	57 536	29 705
1988	869 270	10 541	858 728	615 361	39 413	4 314	580 262	158 330	130 677	14 956	13 246	58 120	30 761
1989	938 488	11 036	927 452	653 057	43 136	4 673	614 594	180 845	143 049	15 979	14 078	58 733	31 490
1990	1 003 502	10 196	993 506	693 469	45 812	5 344	653 001	192 501	158 200	16 878	14 912	59 467	32 006
1991	1 050 870	11 985	1 038 885	718 268	48 391	5 784	675 661	197 324	177 884	17 438	15 487	60 262	31 971
1992	1 117 702	12 278	1 105 424	772 303	51 456	6 059	726 905	192 074	198 723	18 296	16 273	61 091	32 458
1993	1 189 022	12 547	1 176 475	818 412	54 730	5 907	769 588	204 817	214 618	19 203	17 033	61 919	33 448
1994	1 255 475	12 567	1 242 907	865 051	58 956	5 967	812 062	216 713	226 699	20 003	17 674	62 764	34 437
1995	1 339 811	11 125	1 328 685	914 981	62 785	5 956	858 152	238 954	242 704	21 076	18 593	63 571	35 443
1996	1 416 289	13 199	1 403 090	964 358	65 677	5 911	904 592	255 420	256 277	22 016	19 288	64 329	36 171

YEAR	PERSONAL INCOME (Millions of dollars, except as noted)												TOTAL EM-PLOY-MENT (Thousands)
				Derivation of personal income						Per capita (Dollars)		Population (Thousands)	
	Total	Farm	Nonfarm	Earnings by place of work	Less: Personal contributions for social insurance	Plus: Adjustment for residence	Equals: Net earnings by place of residence	Dividends, interest, and rent	Transfer payments	Total	Disposable		
SOUTHWEST													
1971	65 438	1 756	63 682	51 944	2 179	-88	49 677	8 940	6 821	3 832	3 410	17 077	7 457
1972	72 852	2 133	70 719	58 058	2 456	-106	55 496	9 674	7 683	4 162	3 659	17 503	7 807
1973	83 222	3 408	79 815	66 252	3 105	-119	63 028	11 096	9 098	4 638	4 102	17 943	8 215
1974	93 915	2 242	91 673	73 803	3 622	-80	70 101	12 917	10 897	5 117	4 487	18 354	8 511
1975	105 279	2 184	103 094	81 834	3 973	-48	77 814	13 855	13 610	5 603	4 981	18 789	8 633
1976	118 993	2 138	116 855	93 128	4 498	24	88 654	15 208	15 131	6 175	5 452	19 270	9 001
1977	133 566	1 902	131 664	105 259	5 124	-222	99 914	17 204	16 447	6 776	5 932	19 710	9 466
1978	154 772	1 735	153 037	122 197	6 005	-359	115 832	20 663	18 277	7 669	6 720	20 180	10 043
1979	180 358	3 077	177 281	141 951	7 204	-351	134 396	25 155	20 808	8 681	7 539	20 777	10 539
1980	207 671	1 676	205 995	160 492	8 331	-459	151 702	31 377	24 591	9 692	8 386	21 426	10 944
1981	242 415	2 980	239 435	185 631	10 313	-202	175 115	39 174	28 125	11 026	9 429	21 985	11 485
1982	263 734	2 318	261 416	199 180	11 365	-258	187 557	44 396	31 781	11 572	9 953	22 791	11 714
1983	278 129	2 320	275 809	208 007	11 884	-184	195 939	47 037	35 153	11 883	10 428	23 405	11 744
1984	305 984	2 705	303 279	229 041	12 932	-179	215 930	53 496	36 558	12 869	11 348	23 776	12 305
1985	329 269	2 647	326 622	245 373	14 466	-147	230 759	58 855	39 654	13 625	12 017	24 166	12 682
1986	338 330	2 577	335 753	248 426	15 082	-15	233 329	61 780	43 221	13 762	12 299	24 585	12 548
1987	348 281	3 395	344 886	256 144	15 354	75	240 865	61 483	45 933	14 073	12 521	24 748	12 857
1988	369 281	3 736	365 545	272 028	16 831	167	255 365	64 887	49 030	14 855	13 280	24 860	13 152
1989	395 502	3 796	391 706	288 405	18 308	249	270 346	71 513	53 643	15 768	14 028	25 083	13 336
1990	427 533	4 614	422 919	312 285	19 665	335	292 956	74 996	59 581	16 837	14 926	25 393	13 623
1991	451 318	4 471	446 847	331 070	21 165	285	310 189	74 741	66 388	17 472	15 575	25 830	13 857
1992	482 037	4 959	477 079	353 704	22 485	332	331 551	74 419	76 067	18 311	16 382	26 325	13 990
1993	512 019	6 294	505 725	376 549	23 784	229	352 994	77 234	81 791	19 059	17 040	26 864	14 436
1994	541 429	4 665	536 765	397 241	25 640	221	371 821	82 651	86 957	19 739	17 630	27 427	14 978
1995	580 326	3 577	576 749	422 886	27 572	175	395 489	90 801	94 036	20 673	18 459	28 071	15 518
1996	617 538	3 372	614 166	449 631	29 254	217	420 594	97 301	99 644	21 614	19 146	28 571	15 943
ROCKY MOUNTAIN													
1971	20 897	1 016	19 881	16 434	713	17	15 738	2 974	2 185	4 023	3 563	5 194	2 343
1972	23 720	1 339	22 381	18 865	819	20	18 066	3 198	2 456	4 419	3 880	5 368	2 482
1973	27 266	1 811	25 454	21 709	1 031	20	20 697	3 706	2 862	4 933	4 332	5 527	2 646
1974	30 764	1 901	28 863	24 325	1 195	22	23 153	4 261	3 351	5 445	4 756	5 650	2 740
1975	33 745	1 440	32 305	26 284	1 294	33	25 023	4 599	4 123	5 836	5 158	5 782	2 778
1976	37 617	1 071	36 546	29 338	1 460	38	27 916	5 097	4 604	6 359	5 581	5 916	2 912
1977	42 101	717	41 384	32 860	1 668	40	31 232	5 816	5 053	6 926	6 043	6 079	3 060
1978	49 030	1 000	48 030	38 500	1 937	51	36 614	6 867	5 549	7 836	6 843	6 257	3 257
1979	55 864	756	55 108	43 544	2 313	51	41 283	8 300	6 281	8 676	7 523	6 439	3 406
1980	63 593	961	62 632	48 594	2 595	71	46 070	10 105	7 417	9 646	8 378	6 592	3 482
1981	72 223	960	71 263	54 236	3 091	53	51 198	12 400	8 624	10 711	9 251	6 743	3 571
1982	77 579	795	76 784	57 330	3 374	53	54 009	13 774	9 797	11 237	9 714	6 904	3 607
1983	82 520	1 129	81 391	60 588	3 519	52	57 121	14 677	10 723	11 730	10 351	7 035	3 653
1984	89 737	1 059	88 678	66 033	3 849	70	62 254	16 450	11 033	12 623	11 190	7 109	3 816
1985	94 680	870	93 810	69 511	4 243	85	65 354	17 516	11 809	13 209	11 686	7 168	3 881
1986	97 841	1 249	96 591	71 127	4 458	106	66 774	18 329	12 738	13 589	12 062	7 200	3 875
1987	101 524	1 534	99 990	73 897	4 550	129	69 477	18 557	13 490	14 090	12 449	7 206	3 907
1988	106 515	1 554	104 961	77 825	4 978	164	73 011	19 259	14 245	14 788	13 051	7 203	4 054
1989	114 681	2 163	112 519	82 938	5 407	197	77 728	21 425	15 527	15 853	13 882	7 234	4 146
1990	123 852	2 641	121 211	89 737	5 810	232	84 159	22 702	16 992	16 969	14 801	7 299	4 258
1991	131 955	2 412	129 543	95 476	6 326	238	89 388	23 748	18 819	17 730	15 474	7 443	4 371
1992	141 527	2 318	139 208	103 419	6 812	236	96 843	23 957	20 726	18 544	16 151	7 632	4 473
1993	153 863	3 454	150 409	112 930	7 355	179	105 754	25 677	22 431	19 615	17 058	7 844	4 660
1994	163 203	1 724	161 479	119 344	7 973	177	111 548	28 131	23 524	20 286	17 552	8 045	4 928
1995	176 490	1 811	174 679	127 878	8 568	220	119 530	31 349	25 610	21 467	18 585	8 222	5 118
1996	188 316	1 899	186 417	136 623	9 106	258	127 774	33 635	26 906	22 490	19 302	8 373	5 282
FAR WEST													
1971	134 239	2 546	131 693	102 987	4 750	-137	98 100	19 957	16 182	4 869	4 321	27 570	12 300
1972	146 974	3 221	143 753	113 810	5 509	-135	108 166	21 159	17 649	5 264	4 589	27 918	12 742
1973	163 287	4 340	158 948	126 493	6 707	-151	119 635	23 841	19 811	5 764	5 070	28 328	13 405
1974	183 285	5 484	177 801	140 602	7 473	-230	132 899	26 943	23 444	6 364	5 585	28 801	13 865
1975	202 573	4 886	197 687	153 566	8 088	-395	145 084	28 395	29 095	6 903	6 125	29 346	14 103
1976	227 726	4 861	222 865	173 374	8 925	-511	163 938	31 370	32 419	7 609	6 691	29 929	14 625
1977	253 443	4 733	248 710	193 377	9 954	-330	183 092	35 336	35 014	8 295	7 243	30 553	15 287
1978	290 929	4 818	286 111	221 947	11 409	-283	210 255	42 555	38 119	9 299	8 092	31 285	16 234
1979	333 287	6 013	327 274	252 905	13 432	-292	239 181	51 920	42 186	10 428	9 023	31 960	17 140
1980	378 319	7 567	370 752	280 870	14 382	-369	266 119	62 738	49 461	11 541	9 981	32 780	17 549
1981	422 165	5 921	416 244	305 110	17 358	-308	287 444	76 919	57 802	12 627	10 931	33 434	17 744
1982	448 758	6 017	442 741	320 925	18 854	-337	301 735	82 923	64 100	13 165	11 488	34 086	17 613
1983	482 341	6 042	476 299	345 677	20 347	-349	324 981	88 897	68 463	13 894	12 218	34 716	18 040
1984	532 836	6 728	526 108	383 818	22 676	-401	360 741	101 609	70 486	15 085	13 275	35 321	18 842
1985	576 027	6 464	569 562	416 089	25 446	-433	390 210	108 191	77 626	15 984	13 979	36 037	19 494
1986	616 624	7 417	609 207	446 685	28 165	-451	418 068	115 462	83 094	16 749	14 645	36 815	20 067
1987	661 286	8 468	652 817	486 434	30 994	-508	454 933	119 042	87 311	17 568	15 189	37 641	20 923
1988	717 779	8 928	708 851	530 871	34 909	-577	495 384	129 225	93 169	18 623	16 183	38 542	21 985
1989	777 912	8 801	768 912	571 031	38 088	-662	532 281	144 407	101 026	19 672	16 917	39 534	22 660
1990	846 717	9 086	837 631	619 160	41 044	-752	577 365	156 975	112 377	20 883	18 027	40 546	23 288
1991	874 106	7 990	866 116	635 486	43 430	-754	591 302	158 208	124 597	21 155	18 419	41 319	23 342
1992	922 202	9 055	913 148	669 475	45 441	-743	623 290	157 363	141 549	21 917	19 209	42 077	23 051
1993	950 857	10 581	940 276	686 770	46 745	-1 576	638 449	162 636	149 772	22 312	19 580	42 616	23 162
1994	984 317	8 858	975 459	707 506	49 039	-1 772	656 695	171 815	155 807	22 867	19 994	43 045	23 648
1995	1 045 697	8 555	1 037 142	741 407	51 068	-1 920	688 418	192 995	164 284	24 052	20 955	43 477	24 247
1996	1 107 835	10 140	1 097 695	784 124	53 398	-2 044	728 682	206 297	172 855	25 173	21 706	44 009	24 867

Notes

Notes

These notes pertain to the data on pages 1 through 334. The notes are arranged by page number, with the pages to which they pertain and the general subject heading shown at the top of each group of notes. The notes provide information about data sources, definitions, methodology, revisions, and sources of additional information.

The tables on pages 1 through 334 are divided into four main parts.

Part I (pages 1 through 126) pertains to the U.S. economy as a whole.

Part II (pages 127 through 234) presents data by industry or industry group, arranged in accordance with the 1987 U.S. Standard Industrial Classification (SIC). The SIC classifies economic activity into divisions such as mining, manufacturing, retail trade, etc., and into a hierarchy of more detailed industry groups within each division. The tables in Part II present data for each SIC division and, within manufacturing, for each major ("two-digit") industry group. Some of these data are repeated from the tables in Part I, giving the user the convenience of a profile of the industry in a single location. Where data are repeated in this way, these notes will normally cross reference earlier discussions of the data, rather than repeat the discussion.

The 1987 SIC is published in Standard Industrial Classification Manual, 1987, Executive Office of the President,

Office of Management and Budget (Washington, DC: U.S. Government Printing Office, 1988). Brief descriptions adapted from the SIC Manual are provided in these notes for the industry groups in Part II. These descriptions list only the main activities for each industry group; the SIC Manual should be consulted for complete detail.

As described in an article in the front of this book, the SIC is being replaced by the North American Industry Classification System (NAICS) as the official U.S. system for the classification of data to be collected in the future. However, since data using the new system have yet to be published, this edition of Business Statistics continues to present data on an SIC basis.

Part III (pages 235-309) contains additional historical data for selected quarterly and monthly series. Quarterly data are shown beginning with 1960 in most cases and monthly data beginning with 1969.

Part IV (pages 311-334) contains data on personal income, population, and employment by state and region. The data are annual and cover 1971 through 1996. More information about these data is given in the introductory note on page 313.

The column headings for the data tables normally indicate that the data are "seasonally adjusted" or "not seasonally adjusted" or "at a seasonally adjusted annual rate." These

headings refer to the monthly or quarterly rather than the annual data. Seasonal adjustment removes from the time series the average impact of variations that normally occur at about the same time each year due to, for example, weather, holidays, and tax payment dates. Data that are presented at annual rates show values at their annual equivalents—the values that would be registered if the rate of activity measured during a particular month or quarter were maintained for a full year.

The statistical method used to achieve the seasonal adjustment may vary from one data set to another. Many of the data are adjusted by a method known as X-11 or by a variant known as X-11 ARIMA, developed by Statistics Canada. A brief description of the X-11 method is found in "Seasonality: Economic Data and Model Estimation," Monthly Labor Review (December 1994).

Most of the data in this volume are from federal government sources and may be reproduced freely. A few are from private sources and are used with permission; further use may be subject to copyright restrictions. A list of data sources, together with complete citations for the government periodicals referred to in these notes, begins on page 383.

The tables in this volume incorporate data revisions and corrections released by the source agencies through August 1997.

Pages 4-8 and 237-246

Gross Domestic Product (GDP); Real GDP; GDP Quantity and Price Indexes; Per Capita Measures

Source: U.S. Department of Commerce, Bureau of Economic Analysis

The GDP components are taken from Tables 1.1, 1.2, 1.3, 1.4, 5.10, and 5.11 of the *National Income and Product Accounts* (NIPA); the quantity and price indexes from Tables 7.1 and 7.2; and the per capita measures from Table 8.3. The data are as published in the 1996 comprehensive NIPA revisions and as subsequently revised and updated through August 1997.

Revisions during 1997

Revised data for 1993 through the first quarter of 1997 were published in the August, September, and October issues of the BEA publication *Survey of Current Business.* Earlier in 1997 data for 1929 through 1958, consistent with the comprehensive 1996 revision of data for 1959 and later years, were released. In addition, data for certain series were revised for all years to make them consistent with BEA's revised estimates of reproducible tangible wealth; series affected included the capital consumption adjustment, the consumption of fixed capital, and the components of national income and personal income that depend on these two series, including total personal income, total national income, proprietors' income, rental income of persons, and corporate profits. (See the May 1997 *Survey of Current Business.*)

The comprehensive 1996 revisions

The results of the most comprehensive NIPA revisions in many years were released in 1996. The revisions incorporated two major conceptual changes: (1) government purchases of structures and equipment are now classified as investment rather than current consumption; and (2) new

chain-weighted price and output measures take account of changes in relative prices and the composition of output over time.

Definitions and notes on the data

Gross domestic product (GDP) is the market value of the goods and services produced by labor and property located in the United States. GDP is the sum of personal consumption expenditures, gross private domestic investment (including change in business inventories and before deduction of charges for consumption of fixed capital), net exports of goods and services, and government consumption expenditures and gross investment.

GDP rather than gross national product (GNP) has been the featured measure of U.S. production since the comprehensive NIPA revisions in 1991. GDP differs from GNP in that GDP refers to production taking place within the geographic boundaries of the United States (including production from capital and labor supplied by nonresidents) while GNP refers to production by labor and property supplied by U.S. residents, whether located in the United States or abroad. GDP is consistent in coverage with other national economic indicators such as employment and productivity. It also is the measure used by almost all other countries and thus facilitates comparison of economic activity in the United States with that of other countries.

Personal consumption expenditures (PCE) is goods and services purchased by persons residing in the United States. Most of PCE consists of purchases of new goods and of services by individuals from business. In addition, PCE includes purchases of new goods and of services by nonprofit institutions, net purchases of used goods by individuals and nonprofit institutions, and purchases abroad of goods and services by U.S. residents traveling or working in foreign countries. PCE also includes purchases for certain services provided by the government—primarily tuition payments for higher education and charges for medical care. Finally, PCE

includes imputed purchases that keep PCE invariant to changes in the way that certain activities are carried out. For example, to take account of the value of the services provided by owner-occupied housing, PCE includes an imputation equal to the estimated rent homeowners would pay if they rented their houses from themselves. (Actual purchases of residential structures by individuals are classified as gross private domestic investment.)

Gross private domestic investment consists of private fixed investment and changes in business inventories.

Private fixed investment consists of both nonresidential and residential fixed investment. It is measured without a deduction for consumption of fixed capital and includes replacements and additions to the capital stock. It covers all investment by business and nonprofit institutions in the United States regardless of whether the investment is owned by U.S. residents. It excludes investment in other countries by U.S. residents. Public purchases of equipment and structures are in the gross government investment account.

Nonresidential private fixed investment consists of new and used structures and producers' durable equipment purchased by private businesses and nonprofit institutions on capital account.

Residential private fixed investment consists of both structures and residential producers' durable equipment—equipment owned by landlords and rented to tenants. Investment in structures consists of new units, improvements to existing units, mobile homes, brokers' commissions on the sale of residential property, and net purchases of used structures from the government.

Change in business inventories is the change in the physical volume of inventories held by business, valued at the average price of the period. It differs from the change in the book value of inventories reported by business; an inventory valuation adjustment converts inventories valued at historical cost to replacement cost.

Net exports of goods and services is exports of goods and services less imports of goods and services. Receipts of factor income are excluded from exports, and payments of factor income are excluded from imports.

Government consumption expenditures is purchases by governments (federal, state, and local) of goods and services for current consumption. It includes compensation of general government employees and an allowance for consumption of general government fixed capital (i.e., depreciation). Receipts for certain services provided by government—primarily tuition payments for higher education and charges for medical care—are defined as government sales, which are treated as deductions from government purchases.

Gross government investment consists of general government and government enterprise expenditures for fixed assets (structures and durable equipment). Government inventory investment is included in government consumption expenditures.

Final sales of domestic product is GDP minus change in business inventories.

Real, or chained (1992) dollar, estimates are estimates from which the effect of price change has been removed. Because the formula for the chain-type quantity indexes uses weights of more than one period, the corresponding chained-dollar estimates are usually not additive; that is, the components in any given table usually do not add to the total. In time periods close to the base year the residual usually is quite small.

Chain-type quantity and price measures use a series of annual weights, chained together, to form a time series that allows for the effect of changes in relative prices over time. This is in contrast to fixed-weight measures, which are calculated with a single set of weights over the entire time period.

Data availability; revision policy

Annual data are available beginning with 1929; quarterly data begin with 1946. Not all data are available for all time periods.

New data normally are released toward the end of each month. The first estimates for each calendar quarter are released in the month after the quarter's end. Revisions for the most recent quarter are released in the second and third months after the quarter's end. In addition, "annual" revisions to the data for the last several years typically occur each July. "Comprehensive" revisions to the data for all time periods typically occur about once every five years.

The most recent data are published each month in the *Survey of Current Business* may be purchased on diskette from BEA, or may be obtained from the BEA internet site (http://www.bea.doc.gov). Full historical data also may be purchased on diskette from BEA or may be obtained from the STAT-USA subscription internet site (http://www.stat-usa.gov).

References

For information about 1997 revisions see the following articles in the *Survey of Current Business:* "Annual NIPA Revision: Newly Available Tables," October 1997; "Annual NIPA Revision: Newly Available Tables," September 1997; and "Annual Revision of the NIPA's: Annual Estimates, 1993-96, and Quarterly Estimates, 1993:I-1997:I," August 1997.

For information about the 1996 comprehensive revisions see: "The Measurement of Depreciation in the U.S. National Income and Product Accounts," July 1997; "Completion of the Comprehensive Revision of the National Income and Product Accounts, 1929-96," May 1997; "BEA's Chain Indexes, Time Series, and Measures of Long-term Economic Growth," May 1997; "BEA's Mid-Decade Strategic Plan: A Progress Report," June 1996; "Index to the NIPA Tables," May 1996; "Improved Estimates of the National Income and

Product Accounts for 1959-95: Results of the Comprehensive Revision," January/February 1996; "Preview of the Comprehensive Revision of the National Income and Product Accounts: New and Redesigned Tables," October 1995; "Preview of the Comprehensive Revision of the National Income and Product Accounts: Recognition of Government Investment and Incorporation of a New Methodology for Calculating Depreciation," September 1995; "Preview of the Comprehensive Revision of the National Income and Product Accounts: BEA's New Featured Measures of Output and Prices," July 1995.

For additional discussion of alternative measures of change in output and prices see the following articles in the *Survey of Current Business*: "BEA's Chain Indexes, Time Series, and Measures of Long-Term Economic Growth," May 1997; "Alternative Measures of Change in Real Output and Prices, Quarterly Estimates for 1959-92," March 1993; "Alternative Measures of Change in Real Output and Prices," April 1992.

Pages 9-11

Composite Indexes of Economic Activity

Sources: U.S. Department of Commerce, Bureau of Economic Analysis and The Conference Board.

The composite indexes of leading, coincident, and lagging indicators are intended to help predict peaks and troughs in the business cycle. They are calculated from sets of component series selected for their utility as indicators of stages of the business cycle. The component series originate with a variety of sources, as indicated below.

Late in 1995 responsibility for compilation and publication of the composite indexes was transferred from the Bureau of Economic Analysis to The Conference Board.

Index components

The *Index of leading economic indicators* consists of the following 10 components, with monthly data seasonally adjusted except as noted.

- *Average weekly hours* are average hours worked per week by production and nonsupervisory workers in manufacturing. Source: Bureau of Labor Statistics. (See the Notes for pages 79-84.)

- *Initial claims, unemployment insurance* are average weekly claims for unemployment insurance under state programs. Data are in thousands. Inverted series. Source: U.S. Department of Labor, Employment and Training Administration. (See the Notes for page 72.)

- *Manufacturers' new orders, consumer goods, and materials* are net new orders in billions of 1992 dollars. Source: Bureau of the Census (see the Notes for pages 147-157), with inflation adjustment by The Conference Board.

- *Vendor performance, slower deliveries diffusion index.* Source: National Association of Purchasing Managers.

- *Manufacturers' new orders, nondefense capital goods* are in billions of 1992 dollars. Source: Bureau of the Census (see the Notes for pages 147-157) with inflation adjustment by The Conference Board.

- *Building permits, new private housing units* is the number of new private housing units (shown in thousands) authorized by local building permits. Monthly data are at a seasonally adjusted annual rate. Source: Bureau of the Census. (See the Notes for page 142.)

- *Stock prices: 500 common stocks* is an index based on 1941-1943=10. Source: Standard and Poor's Corporation.

- *Money supply (M2)* is in billions of 1992 dollars. Source: Federal Reserve Board of Governors (see the Notes for pages 94-95) with inflation adjustment by The Conference Board.

- *Interest rate spread* is equal to the rate on 10-year treasury bonds less the rate on federal funds. Source: Federal Reserve Board of Governors (see the Notes for pages 99-100).

- *Index of consumer expectations* is based on the first quarter of 1966=100. The monthly data are not seasonally adjusted. Source: University of Michigan, Survey Research Center. This is a copyrighted series used by permission; it may not be reproduced without written permission from the source.

The *Index of coincident economic indicators* consists of the following four components, with monthly data seasonally adjusted.

- *Employees on nonagricultural payrolls* are total wage and salary employees in thousands. Source: Bureau of Labor Statistics. (See the Notes for pages 73-78.)

- *Personal income less transfer payments* is in billions of chained 1992 dollars (seasonally adjusted annual rate). Source: Bureau of Economic Analysis (see the Notes for pages 14-17) with inflation adjustment by the Conference Board.

- *Index of industrial production* is an index of the output of mining, manufacturing, and utility sectors of the U.S. economy. The index is based on 1992=100. Source: Federal Reserve, Board of Governors. (See the Notes for pages 22-35.)

- *Manufacturing and trade sales* are in millions of 1992 dollars. Sources: Bureau of the Census (see the Notes for pages 38-41) with inflation adjustment by the Conference Board.

The *Index of lagging economic indicators* consists of the following seven components, with monthly data seasonally adjusted except as noted.

- *Average duration of unemployment* is in weeks. Source: Bureau of Labor Statistics.

- *Ratio: manufacturing and trade inventories to sales* is calculated from sales and inventories in chained 1992 dollars. Source: Bureau of Economic Analysis. (See the Notes for pages 38-41.)

- *Manufacturing labor cost per unit of output* is the smoothed percent changed in this index.

- *Average prime interest rate* is the average percentage rate per annum charged by banks for prime business loans; not seasonally adjusted. Source: Federal Reserve Board of Governors (see the Notes for pages 99-100).

- *Commercial and industrial loans outstanding* is in millions of 1992 dollars. Sources: Federal Reserve Board of Governors (see the Notes for pages 96-98) with inflation adjustment by The Conference Board.

- *Consumer installment credit outstanding* is expressed as a percent of personal income. Sources: Bureau of Economic Analysis and Federal Reserve, Board of Governors. See the Notes for pages 18-19.

- *Consumer price index for services* is the smoothed percent change in this index from the previous month or year. Monthly changes are expressed at a seasonally adjusted annual rate. Source: Bureau of Labor Statistics. (See the Notes for pages 46-52.)

Notes on the data

Each composite index is scaled so that its average monthly value equals 100 in a base year, currently 1992.

Each of the composite indexes measures the average behavior of a group of economic time series that show similar timing at business cycle turns but that represent widely differing activities or sectors of the economy.

The procedures used to construct the indexes are designed to neutralize the tendency of the more volatile series to dominate the average and to enhance the usefulness of the three indexes as a consistent system.

Comprehensive revisions of the composite indexes were introduced in 1996, 1993, and 1989. Changes made to the components of the leading index in the 1996 revision included:

- Adding the interest rate spread as a component ;

- Removing manufacturers' unfilled orders and sensitive material prices as components;

- Replacing contracts and orders for plant and equipment with manufacturers' new orders for nondefense capital goods;

- Showing building permits in thousands of units rather than as an index number.

In addition, all the indexes were moved to 1992 as the base year and deflators the follow BEA's chain-weighting procedures were introduced for all the constant dollar components.

Details about these changes and others that were introduced at the same time can be found in the November and December 1996 and January 1997 issues of The Conference Board's monthly publication, *Business Cycle Indicators*.

Inverted series: These series have their sign reversed for purposes of cyclical analysis calculations.

Smoothed series are smoothed by using a six-month moving average.

Data availability

Data are published each month by The Conference Board. Their monthly report, *Business Cycle Indicators* is available by subscription from: The Conference Board, 845 Third Avenue, New York, NY 10022. A monthly press release is available on The Conference Board internet site (http://

www.tcb-indicators.org). The full historical database is available by subscription from the same internet site.

References

In addition of The Conference Board's *Business Cycle Indicators* (referenced above) see the following articles in the *Survey of Current Business:* "Business Cycle Indicators: Upcoming Revision of the Composite Indexes" (October 1993); "Composite Index of Coincident Indicators and Alternative Composite Indexes" (June 1992); "Leading Indicators and the 'Prime Mover' View" (August 1989); "Business Cycle Indicators: Revised Composite Indexes" (January 1989); "Composite Indexes of Leading, Coincident, and Lagging Indicators" (November 1987). See also *Handbook of Cyclical Indicators* (Bureau of Economic Analysis, 1984).

Page 14-17 and 266-273

Sources and Disposition of Personal Income

Source: U.S. Department of Commerce, Bureau of Economic Analysis

All personal income series were revised in conjunction with the 1996 comprehensive revision of the National Income and Product Accounts. Additional historical revisions, stemming from BEA's revised estimates of reproducible tangible wealth were introduced in 1997. The series affected by the latter revisions include proprietors' income, rental income of persons, and total personal income. (See the May 1997 *Survey of Current Business.*)

Data in this book reflect these revisions and also incorporate the further revisions to the data for 1993-1996 released in July 1997.

Definitions

Personal income is the income received by persons from all sources, that is, from participation in production, from both government and

business transfer payments, and from government interest, which is treated like a transfer payment. *Persons* consists of individuals, nonprofit institutions that primarily serve individuals, private noninsured welfare funds, and private trust funds. Proprietors' income is treated in its entirety as received by individuals. Life insurance carriers and private noninsured pension funds are not counted as persons, but their saving is credited to persons.

Personal income is the sum of wage and salary disbursements, other labor income, proprietors' income with inventory valuation and capital consumption adjustments, rental income of persons with capital consumption adjustments, personal dividend income, personal interest income, and transfer payments to persons, less personal contributions for social insurance.

Personal income differs from national income in that it includes transfer payments and interest received by persons, regardless of source, while it excludes both employee and employer contributions for social insurance, corporate profits tax liability, corporate inventory valuation and capital consumption adjustments, and undistributed corporate profits.

Wage and salary disbursements consists of the monetary remuneration of employees, including the compensation of corporate officers; commissions, tips, and bonuses; voluntary employee contributions to certain deferred compensation plans such as 401(k) plans; and receipts in kind that represent income.

Commodity-producing industries consists of the following Standard Industrial Classification (SIC) divisions: agriculture, forestry, and fishing; mining; construction; and manufacturing. *Distributive industries* consists of the following SIC divisions: transportation (excluding the U.S. Postal Service); communications; electric, gas, and sanitary services; wholesale trade; and retail trade. *Service industries* consists of the restoftheworld sector and the following SIC divisions: finance, insurance, and real estate; and services. *Government* consists of federal, state and local general government and government enterprises.

Other labor income consists of employer payments to private pension and profitsharing plans, private group health and life insurance plans, privately administered workers' compensation plans, supplemental unemployment benefit plans, corporate directors' fees, and several minor categories of employee compensation, including judicial fees to jurors and witnesses, compensation of prison inmates, and marriage fees to justices of the peace.

Proprietors' income with inventory valuation and capital consumption adjustments is the currentproduction income (including income in kind) of sole proprietors and partnerships and of taxexempt cooperatives. The imputed net rental income of owneroccupants of farm dwellings is included. Dividends and monetary interest received by proprietors of nonfinancial business and rental incomes received by persons not primarily engaged in the real estate business are excluded; these incomes are included in dividends, net interest, and rental income of persons. The two valuation adjustments are designed to obtain income measures in which inventory withdrawals and charges for depreciation of fixed capital are valued at replacement cost, the valuation concept underlying national income and product accounting, rather than at historical cost. The capital consumption adjustment also restates depreciation to reflect uniform service lives and a straightline depreciation formula.

Rental income of persons with capital consumption adjustment is the net currentproduction income of persons from the rental of real property, except income of persons primarily engaged in the real estate business; the imputed net rental income of owneroccupants of nonfarm dwellings; and the royalties received by persons from patents, copyrights, and rights to natural

resources. The capital consumption adjustment is described in the preceding paragraph.

Personal dividend income is the dividend income of persons from all sources. It equals net dividends paid by corporations less dividends received by government. Dividends received by government consists of dividends received by state and local general government, primarily by their retirement systems.

Personal interest income is the interest income (monetary and imputed) of persons from all sources. It equals net interest plus interest paid by government less interest received by government plus interest paid by persons. The last item consists of all interest paid by individuals except mortgage interest.

Transfer payments to persons is income payments to persons for which no current services are performed. It consists of business transfer payments to persons and government transfer payments. Government transfer payments consists of benefits from the following social insurance funds: old-age, survivors, and disability insurance (social security); hospital insurance; supplementary medical insurance; unemployment insurance; government employee retirement; railroad retirement; pension benefit guaranty; veterans life insurance; workers' compensation; military medical insurance; and temporary disability insurance. Government transfer payments also includes benefits from certain other programs: veterans benefits, in addition to veterans life insurance; food stamps; black lung; supplemental security income; and public assistance (including Medicaid). Government payments to nonprofit institutions, other than for work under research and development contracts, are also included.

Personal contributions for social insurance, which is subtracted to arrive at personal income, includes payments by employees, selfemployed, and other individuals who participate in the

following programs: old-age, survivors, and disability insurance (social security); hospital insurance; supplementary medical insurance; unemployment insurance; government employee retirement; railroad retirement; veterans life insurance; and temporary disability insurance.

Personal tax and nontax payments is tax payments (net of refunds) by persons residing in the United States that are not chargeable to business expense and certain other personal payments to government agencies (except government enterprises) that are treated like taxes. Personal taxes includes taxes on income, including realized net capital gains; on transfers of estates and gifts; and on personal property. Nontaxes includes donations and fees, fines, and forfeitures. Personal contributions to social insurance is not included.

Disposable personal income is personal income less personal tax and nontax payments. It is the income available to persons for spending or saving. Disposable personal income in chained (1992) dollars represents the inflation-adjusted value of disposable personal income.

Personal outlays is the sum of personal consumption expenditures, interest paid by persons, and personal transfer payments to the rest of the world (net). The last item is personal remittances in cash and in kind to the rest of the world less such remittances from the rest of the world.

Personal saving is personal income less the sum of personal outlays and personal tax and nontax payments. It is the current saving of individuals (including proprietors), nonprofit institutions that primarily serve individuals, life insurance carriers, private noninsured welfare funds, and private trust funds. Personal saving may also be viewed as the sum of the net acquisition of financial assets and the change in physical assets less the sum of net borrowing and of consumption of fixed capital.

Personal consumption expenditures is goods and services purchased by persons residing in the United States. Persons are defined as individuals and nonprofit institutions that primarily serve individuals. Most of personal consumption expenditures (PCE) consists of purchases of new goods and of services by individuals from business. In addition, PCE includes purchases of new goods and of services by nonprofit institutions, net purchases of used goods by individuals and nonprofit institutions, and purchases abroad of goods and services by U.S. residents traveling or working in foreign countries. PCE also includes purchases for certain services provided by the government—primarily tuition payments for higher education and charges for medical care. Finally, PCE includes imputed purchases that keep PCE invariant to changes in the way that certain activities are carried out. For example, to take account of the value of the services provided by owner-occupied housing, PCE includes an imputation equal to the estimated rent homeowners would pay if they rented their houses from themselves. (Actual purchases of residential structures by individuals are classified as gross private domestic investment.)

Durable goods are commodities that can be stored or inventoried and that have an average life of at least three years. *Nondurable goods* are all other commodities that can be stored or inventoried. *Services* are commodities that cannot be stored and that are consumed at the place and time of purchase.

Data availability

Data are released monthly in a BEA press release, normally the first business day following the monthly release of the latest national income and product account (NIPA) estimates. Data are subsequently published each month in the *Survey of Current Business*. Annual and quarterly historical data incorporating the 1997 revisions can be found on pages 164-167 of the August 1997 *Survey*. Full historical data also may be purchased

on diskette from BEA or may be obtained from the STAT-USA subscription internet site (http://www.stat-usa.gov).

References

A discussion of monthly estimates of personal income and its disposition appears in the November 1979 *Survey of Current Business*. A more detailed description of concepts, sources, and methods used in estimating personal consumption expenditures appears in *Personal Consumption Expenditures* (NIPA Methodology Paper No. 6, 1990), available from the National Technical Information Service (NTIS Accession No. PB 90-254244). Information on more recent methodological revisions can be found in the articles listed above under the Notes for pages 4-8.

Pages 18-19

Consumer Installment Credit

Source: Board of Governors of the Federal Reserve System

The consumer installment credit series cover most short and intermediateterm credit extended to individuals through regular business channels, usually to finance the purchase of consumer goods and services or to refinance debts originally incurred for such purposes, and scheduled to be repaid (or with the option of repayment) in two or more installments. Consumer installment credit is categorized by major holders and by major types of credit.

Definitions and notes on the data

Categories of holders include commercial banks, finance companies, credit unions, savings institutions, nonfinancial businesses, and pools of securitized assets. Retailers and gasoline companies are included in the nonfinancial businesses category. *Pools of securitized assets* comprises the outstanding balances of pools upon which securities have been issued; these balances are no longer carried on the balance sheets of the loan originators.

Types of credit include revolving, automobile, and "other." *Revolving credit* includes credit arising from purchases on credit card plans of retail stores and banks, cash advances and check credit plans of banks, and some overdraft credit arrangements. *Automobile credit* represents credit extended for the purchase of new or used passenger automobiles whether or not the credit is specifically secured by the automobile purchased. *"Other" credit* includes mobile home loans and all other installment loans not included in automobile or revolving credit, such as loans for education, boats, trailers, or vacations. These loans may be secured or unsecured.

Debt secured by real estate (including first liens, junior liens, and home equity loans) is excluded. Credit extended to governmental agencies and nonprofit or charitable organizations, as well as credit extended to business or to individuals exclusively for business purposes, is excluded.

The consumer credit series are based on comprehensive benchmark data that become available periodically. Current monthly estimates are brought forward from the latest benchmarks in accordance with weighted changes indicated by sample data. Classifications are made on a "holder" basis. Thus, installment paper sold by retail outlets is included in figures for the banks and finance companies that purchased the paper.

The amount of outstanding credit represents the sum of the balances in the installment receivable accounts of financial institutions and retail outlets at the end of each month. Net change measures the change during the month in the amount of consumer installment credit outstanding. It is defined as the amount of consumer installment credit extended less the amount liquidated (including repayments, chargeoffs, and other credits) during the month. Each monthly change is computed by subtracting the seasonally adjusted amount outstanding at the end of the previous month from the amount outstanding at the end of the current month. Information is not available to make separate estimates of the amount of extensions, liquidations, and chargeoffs of bad debts.

The estimates of the amount of credit outstanding and net change include any finance and insurance charges included as part of the installment contract. Also included in some cases is un-earned income on loans, because some lenders cannot separate the components.

The seasonally adjusted data are adjusted for differences in the number of trading days and for seasonal influences. The seasonal factors used are derived by the X11 ARIMA process.

Revisions

Consumer credit data were revised in August 1997 to incorporate updating of seasonal factors and benchmarking of company components to the June 1996 Survey of Finance Companies. As part of these revisions, the revolving credit category was expanded to include the revolving credit held by finance companies and the "other credit" category was reduced by the same amount.

Data availability

Current data are available monthly, in the Federal Reserve statistical release G.19, "Consumer Credit," and in the *Federal Reserve Bulletin*. The data for earlier years may be purchased on diskette from Publication Services, Board of Governors of the Federal Reserve System. Current and historical data are available on the Federal Reserve internet site (http://www.bog.frb.fed.us/releases/).

Pages 22-35 and 274-277

Industrial Production and Capacity Utilization

Source: Board of Governors of the Federal Reserve System

The industrial production index measures changes in the physical volume or quantity of output of

manufacturing, mining, and electric and gas utilities. *Capacity utilization* is calculated by dividing a seasonally adjusted industrial production index for an industry or group of industries by a related index of capacity.

Around the 15th day of each month, the Federal Reserve issues estimates of industrial production and capacity utilization for the previous month. These estimates are in the form of index numbers reflecting the monthly levels of total output of the nation's factories, mines, and gas and electric utilities. Comprehensive revisions occurred during 1997, when the indexes were placed on a base of 1992=100.

Definitions and notes on the data

The index of industrial production measures a large portion of the output of the national economy on a monthly basis. That portion, together with construction, accounts for the bulk of the variation in output over the course of the business cycle. The index—with its substantial industrial detail—is helpful in illuminating structural developments in the economy.

The index of industrial production is constructed with data from a variety of sources. Current monthly estimates of production in some industries are based on measures of physical output. For industries in which direct measurement is not possible, output is inferred from productionworker hours and the use of electric power.

The weights used in computing the indexes are based on value added—the difference between the value of production and the cost of materials or supplies consumed. Important changes in weighting methods were introduced during 1997 (see *Revisions* below).

The index reflects output changes at all stages within manufacturing and mining industries, including intermediate as well as final products.

The separation of seasonal movements from cyclical and irregular fluctuations and from trend is crucial in the

compilation of the industrial production index. Components of the index are adjusted for two kinds of shorttime recurring fluctuations, i.e., for differences in the number of working days from month to month and for seasonal variation. Beginning with indexes for January 1947, allowances for holiday observances have been made in seasonal factors rather than in working-day adjustments.

Individual series are seasonally adjusted by the X11 ARIMA method.

The index does not cover production on farms, in the construction industry, in transportation, or in various trade and service industries. A number of groups and subgroups include data for individual series not published separately.

The total industrial production index is constructed from more than 200 individual series based on the 1987 Standard Industrial Classification (SIC). These individual series are classified and grouped two ways: by industry groups based on the SIC and by market groups developed by the Federal Reserve. In the market group classification, the individual industrial production series are grouped into final products, intermediate products, and materials. Final products are assumed to be purchased by consumers, businesses, or government for final use. Intermediate products are expected to become inputs in nonindustrial sectors, such as construction, agriculture, and services. Materials are industrial output requiring further processing within the industrial sector. Total products comprise final and intermediate products.

Capacity utilization is calculated by dividing a seasonally adjusted industrial production index for an industry or group of industries by a related index of capacity. The capacity indexes attempt to capture the concept of sustainable practical capacity, which is defined as the greatest level of output that a plant can maintain within the framework of a realistic work schedule, taking account of normal downtime, and assuming sufficient availability of inputs to operate the machinery and equipment in place. The individual capacity indexes are based on a variety of data, including capacity data measured in physical units as compiled by trade associations, surveys of utilization rates and investment, and estimates of growth of the capital stock.

Revisions

Comprehensive revisions were introduced early in 1997, when the reference year of the index was moved from 1987 to 1992=100. The revisions introduced new aggregation methods beginning with the data for 1977 and updated source data for 1992 onward.

Under the new aggregation methods, the value-added weights for each industry are updated annually rather than quinquennially. The more frequent updating takes more accurate account of changes in the relative valuations of the individual industry series and thus provides a more accurate overall index. Because the previous method of updating the weights only once every five years introduced as upward bias into the index, the revised index shows somewhat slower average growth of industrial production. From 1987 to 1996, for example, total industrial production grew at an average pace of about 2.3 percent per year—about one-quarter percentage point less than previously estimated.

Revisions to data for recent years normally occur annually, taking into account additional source data that has become available. Such revisions for the data for 1992 and subsequent years were scheduled to be released in December 1997. These could not be incorporated into this book.

Data availability

Data are available monthly in Federal Reserve release G.17. Selected data are subsequently published monthly in the *Federal Reserve Bulletin.* Historical data may be purchased on diskette from Publications Services, Board of

Governors of the Federal Reserve System. Current and historical data are available on the Federal Reserve internet site (http://www.bog.frb.fed.us/releases/).

References

A description of the 1997 revisions is found in "Industrial Production and Capacity Utilization: Historical Revision and Recent Developments," *Federal Reserve Bulletin*, vol. 83 no.2 (February 1997). For information on seasonal adjustment methods see "A Revision to Industrial Production and Capacity Utilization, 1991-1995," vol. 82 (January 1996). A detailed description of the industrial production index, together with a history of the index, a glossary of terms, and a bibliography is presented in *Industrial Production— 1986 Edition*, available from the Publication Services, Board of Governors of the Federal Reserve System.

Pages 38-41

Manufacturing and Trade Sales and Inventories

Sources: U.S. Department of Commerce, Bureau of the Census (current dollar series) and U.S. Department of Commerce, Bureau of Economic Analysis (constant dollar series)

The current dollar data on these pages draws together summary data from the separate series on manufacturers' shipments, inventories, and orders; merchant wholesalers' sales and inventories; and retail sales and inventories included in Part II of this book. See the Notes to pages 147-157 and 214-218 for information about these data.

Estimates of real sales, inventories, and inventory-sales ratios are published by the Bureau of Economic Analysis. Historical revisions consistent with the comprehensive NIPA revision were released in May 1996.

Data availability

Sales, inventories and inventory-sales ratios for manufacturers, merchant wholesalers, and retailers are published monthly be the Bureau of the Census in a press release entitled "Manufacturing and Trade Inventories and Sales." Sales and inventories in constant dollars are published regularly by the Bureau of Economic Analysis in the *Survey of Current Business.*

References

For information about the 1996 revisions to sales and inventories in constant dollars, see "Real Inventories, Sales, and Inventory-Sales Ratios for Manufacturing and Trade, 1977-95", *Survey of Current Business,* May 1996.

Pages 42-44 and 247-250

Private Fixed Investment by Type

Source: U.S. Department of Commerce, Bureau of Economic Analysis

The data on private fixed investment by type are taken from Tables 5.4 and 5.5 of the National Income and Product Accounts (NIPA) as published in the 1996 comprehensive revisions and as subsequently updated through August 1997.

Definitions

Private fixed investment consists of both nonresidential and residential fixed investment. It is measured without a deduction for consumption of fixed capital and includes replacements and additions to the capital stock. It covers all investment by business and nonprofit institutions in the United States regardless of whether the investment is owned by U.S. residents. It excludes investment in other countries by U.S. residents. Public purchases of equipment and structures are in the gross government investment account.

Nonresidential fixed investment consists of both structures and producers' durable equipment. *Structures* consists of new construction, brokers' commissions on sale of structures, and net purchases of used structures by business and nonprofit institutions from governments. New construction also includes hotels and motels, and mining exploration, shafts, and wells.

Producers' durable equipment consists of private business purchases on capital account of new machinery, equipment, furniture, and vehicles (except for personal-use portions of equipment purchased for both business and personal use), plus dealers' margins on sales of used equipment, and net purchases of used equipment from government, from persons, and from the rest of the world.

Residential fixed investment consists of both structures and residential producers' durable equipment—equipment owned by landlords and rented to tenants. Investment in structures consists of new units, improvements to existing units, mobile homes, brokers' commissions on the sale of residential property, and net purchases of used structures from the government.

Data availability

Current data are released as Tables 5.4 and 5.5 of the monthly release of the latest National Income and Product Account (NIPA) estimates and are subsequently published each month in the *Survey of Current Business*. Revised data for 1993-1996 can be found of the August 1997 *Survey*. Full historical data may be purchased on diskette from BEA or may be obtained from the STAT-USA subscription internet site (http://www.stat-usa.gov).

References

A discussion of the 1996 comprehensive revisions appears in "Improved Estimates of the U.S. National Income and Product Accounts for 1959-95: Results of the Comprehensive Revision," *Survey of Current Business*, January/February 1996. Other sources of general information about the NIPA are listed in the Notes for pages 4-8.

Pages 46-52 and 294-297

Consumer Price Indexes

Source: U.S. Department of Labor, Bureau of Labor Statistics (BLS)

The Consumer Price Index (CPI) is a statistical measure of the average change in the cost of a fixed market basket of consumer goods and services purchased by urban consumers. The indexes in this volume are for all urban consumers (CPI-U) and represent the 1982-84 buying habits of about 80 percent of the noninstitutional population of the United States at that time. An alternative index, the CPI-W, represents the buying habits only of urban wage earners and clerical workers. As described in an article in the front of this book, major revisions to the CPI will be incorporated into the data for January 1998.

Notes on the data

The CPI is based on prices of food, clothing, shelter, fuel, transportation fares, charges for medical care, and other goods and services that people buy for daytoday living. The quantity and quality of these items are kept essentially constant except at times of major revisions so that only price changes will be measured. All taxes directly associated with the purchase and use of items are included in the index.

Data collected from more than 19,000 retail establishments and about 57,000 housing units in 85 urban areas across the country are used to develop the U.S. city average.

A major revision of the indexes became effective with the release of CPI data for January 1987 and another is scheduled with the release of the data for January 1998. These revisions update the content and weights of the market basket of goods and services priced for the CPI; update the statistical sample of urban areas, outlets, and unique items used in calculating the CPI; and improve the statistical methods used for computing a number of CPI components.

The reference base for most indexes currently is 1982-84=100. In January 1999 it will be moved forward to 1993-95=100.

CPI weights for 196477 were derived from reported expenditures of a carefully selected sample of wageearner and clericalworker families and individuals in 196061 and adjusted for price changes between the survey dates and 1963.

Weights for 197886 were derived from a consumer expenditure survey (CES) undertaken over the 197273 period and adjusted for price change between the survey dates and December 1977. Beginning with 1987 the spending patterns reflected in the CPI are derived from a CES undertaken over the 198284 period. The reported expenditures were adjusted for price change between the survey dates and December 1986.

The CES is composed of two separate surveys: an interview survey and a diary survey, both conducted by the Bureau of the Census for BLS. Each expenditure reported in the two surveys is coded to detailed categories which are then combined in expenditure classes and ultimately into seven major groups of expenditures: (1) food and beverages, (2) housing, (3) apparel and upkeep, (4) transportation, (5) medical care, (6) entertainment, and (7) other goods and services. As described in an article in the front of this book, there will be eight major expenditure groups beginning with the data for January 1998.

Beginning January 1966, the BLS has published seasonally adjusted national CPI indexes for selected groups, subgroups, and special groups where there is a significant seasonal pattern of price change. The factors currently in use were derived by the X11ARIMA seasonal adjustment method. Seasonally adjusted indexes and seasonal factors for the preceding five years are updated annually based on data through the previous December. Detailed descriptions of BLS seasonal adjustment procedures are available upon request from the Bureau of Labor Statistics.

Definitions

The *food index* component includes both food at home and food away from home (restaurant meals and other food bought and eaten away from home).

The *housing index* measures changes in rental costs and expenses connected with the acquisition and operation of a home. The CPIU, beginning with data for January 1983, and the CPIW, beginning with data for January 1985, reflect a change in methodology used to compute the homeownership component. A rental equivalence measure replaced the assetprice approach. The central purpose of the change was to separate shelter costs from the investment component of homeownership so that the index would reflect only the cost of shelter services provided by owner-occupied homes.

Fuel and other utilities includes residential telephone, water, sewerage service, and other utilities not shown separately.

The *private transportation index* includes prices paid by urban consumers on such items as new and used automobiles, gasoline, motor oil, tires, repairs and maintenance, insurance, registration fees, driver's licenses, parking fees, etc. City bus, streetcar, subway, taxicab, intercity bus, airplane, and railroad coach fares are some of the components of the public transportation index.

The *medical care index* includes prices for prescription and nonprescription drugs, other medical care commodities, physicians' services, dentists' fees, other professional services, hospital costs, and health insurance. Health insurance is represented by prices for a number of hospital and professional services for which claims are paid, plus a small portion representing the insurer's earnings or "overhead." Effective with the 1987 revision, the presentation of health insurance is changed although the basic pricing method is not. The benefits portion of premiums is allocated to appropriate expenditure categories; the index for

health insurance now represents only the retained earnings portion of the premiums. Effective with the January 1997 data the method of calculating the hospital cost component was changed from the pricing of individual commodities and services to a more comprehensive cost-of-treatment approach. (See the article in the front of this book for more information.)

Data availability

The indexes are initially issued in a press release about two weeks following the month to which the data pertain. The *CPI Detailed Report* is issued about a month after the press release. CPI data also are published monthly in the *Monthly Labor Review*, which also contains periodic articles analyzing price developments. Complete historical data are available on the BLS internet site (http://stats.bls.gov).

References

Two special issues of the *Monthly Labor Review* cover the CPI in detail. The December 1996 issue describes the forthcoming revisions in a series of articles and the December 1993 issue on "The Anatomy on Price Change" includes: "The Consumer Price Index: Underlying Concepts and Caveats"; "Basic Components of the CPI: Estimation of Price Changes"; "The Commodity Substitution Effect in CPI Data, 1982-91"; and "Quality Adjustment of Price Indexes."

For a detailed discussion of the treatment of homeownership, see "Changing the Homeownership Component of the Consumer Price Index to Rental Equivalence," CPI Detailed Report (January 1983).

BLS Handbook of Methods Bulletin 2490 (April 1997), Chapter 17 "Consumer Price Indexes" describes the methodology used in computing the CPI.

Pages 53-57 and 298-301

Producer Price Indexes

Source: U.S. Department of Labor, Bureau of Labor Statistics

Producer Price Indexes (PPI) measure average changes in prices received by domestic producers of commodities in all stages of processing.

Since January 1988, the indexes have been published on a base of 1982=100. Pages 53-57 present data by stage-of-processing. The industry tables in Part II of this book present a number of additional PPI series by commodity and by industry and product.

Definitions

The *stage-of-processing* PPI indexes organize products by class of buyer and degree of fabrication. These have been the featured measures since 1978. The three major indexes are: (1) *finished goods*, commodities that will not undergo further processing and are ready for sale to the ultimate user (e.g., automobiles, meats, apparel, machine tools); (2) *intermediate materials, supplies, and components*, commodities that have been processed but require further processing before they become finished goods (e.g., steel mill products, cotton yarns, lumber, flour) as well as of goods that are physically complete that are purchased by business firms as inputs for their operations (e.g., diesel fuel and paper boxes); and (3) *crude materials* for further processing, products entering the market for the first time that have not been manufactured or fabricated but which will be processed before becoming finished goods (e.g., scrap metals, crude petroleum, raw cotton, livestock).

The traditional *commodity* indexes organize products by similarity of end use or material composition. Each individual product is grouped under one of 15 major commodity groups, two of which comprise the Farm Products and Processed Foods and Feeds Index and the other 13 of which compose the Industrial Commodities Index; the All

Commodities Index is composed of all 15 major commodity groups.

The *industry and product* indexes organize data in accordance with the Standard Industrial Classification (SIC) and the product code extension of the SIC developed by the Bureau of the Census.

Notes on the data

The sample used for calculating the PPI contains (as of mid-1997) about 3,200 commodities and about 80,000 quotations per month, selected to represent the movement of prices of all commodities produced in the manufacturing; agriculture, forestry, and fishing; mining; and gas and electricity and public utility sectors.

To the extent possible, prices used in calculating the PPI represent prices received by domestic producers in the first important commercial transaction for each commodity. These indexes attempt to measure only price changes; i.e., price changes not influenced by changes in quality, quantity, terms of sale, or level of distribution. Most quotations are the selling prices of selected manufacturers or other producers, although a few prices are those quoted on organized exchanges or markets. Transaction prices are sought instead of list or book prices.

Price data are generally collected monthly, primarily by mail questionnaire. Most prices are obtained directly from producing companies on a voluntary and confidential basis. Prices generally are reported for the Tuesday of the week containing the 13th day of the month.

The name "Producer Price Index," became effective when March 1978 data were released, replacing the term "Wholesale Price Index." The change was made to reflect the coverage of the data more accurately. At the same time there was a shift in analytical emphasis from the All Commodities Index and other traditional commodity grouping indexes to the Finished Goods Index and other stageofprocessing indexes.

For analysis of general price trends, stage-of-processing indexes are more useful than commodity grouping indexes. Commodity grouping indexes sometimes produce exaggerated or misleading signals of price changes by reflecting the same price movement through various stages of processing.

The BLS revises the Producer Price Index weighting structure periodically when data from economic censuses become available. Beginning with data for January 1996, the weights used to construct the PPI reflect 1992 shipment values as measured by the 1992 Economic Censuses and other sources. Data for 1992 through 1995 reflect 1987 shipment values; 1987 through 1991 reflect 1982 values; 1976 through 1986 reflect 1972 values; and 1967 through 1975 reflect 1963 values.

BLS has been working for a number of years on a comprehensive overhaul of the theory, methods, and procedures use to construct the PPI. One aspect of this overhaul was the already mentioned shift in emphasis beginning in 1978 to the stage-of-processing measures. Other changes that have been phased in since 1978 include the replacement of judgment sampling with probability sampling techniques; expansion to systematic coverage of the net output of virtually all industries in the mining and manufacturing sectors; a shift from a commodity to an industry orientation; the exclusion of imports from, and the inclusion of exports in, the survey universe; and the respecification of commodities priced to conform to Bureau of the Census definitions. These changes have resulted in a system of indexes that is easier to use in conjunction with data on wages, productivity, and employment and other series that are organized in terms of the SIC and the census product class designations.

Seasonal factors for the PPI are revised annually to take into account the most recent 12 months of data. Seasonally adjusted data for the previous five years are thus subject to annual revision.

Data availability

The indexes are initially issued in a press release about two weeks following the month to which the data pertain and subsequent published in greater detail in the monthly BLS publication, *Producer Price Indexes.* Selected PPI data also are published monthly in the *Monthly Labor Review,* which also contains periodic articles analyzing price developments. Historical data tables providing annual and monthly data for all available periods for all published series are available on request from BLS. Complete historical data are available on the BLS internet site (http://stats.bls.gov).

References

The following *Monthly Labor Review* articles and technical notes contain background information: "Effect of 1992 Weights on Producer Price Indexes" (July 1996); "Hospital Price Inflation: What Does the PPI Tell Us?" (July 1996); "Seasonal Adjustment of Producer Price Index for Passenger Cars" (June 1996); "Effect of Updated Weights on Producer Price Indexes" (March 1993); "Milestones in the Producer Price Index Methodology and Presentation" (August 1989); "New Stage of Process Price System Developed for the Producer Price Index" (April 1988); "Improving the Measurement of Producer Price Changes" (April 1977).

BLS Handbook of Methods Bulletin 2490 (April 1997), Chapter 14 "Producer Prices" describes the methodology used in computing the PPI.

Page 57

Purchasing Power of the Dollar

Source: U.S. Department of Labor, Bureau of Labor Statistics

The purchasing power of the dollar measures changes in the quantity of goods and services a dollar will buy at a particular date compared with a selected base date. It must be defined in terms of: (1) the specific commodities and services that are to be purchased with the dollar; (2) the market level (producer, retail, etc.) at which they are purchased; and (3) the dates for which the comparison is to be made. Thus, the purchasing power of the dollar for a selected period, compared with another period, may be measured in terms of a single commodity or a large group of commodities, for example, all goods and services purchased by consumers at retail, or all finished commodities sold in primary markets.

The BLS publishes two basic price indexes that may be used to calculate the purchasing power of the dollar in the United States: (1) the Producer Price Index (PPI) for Finished Goods, which relates to prices received by the producers of finished commodities at the primary market level, and (2) the Consumer Price Index (CPIW, through 1977; CPIU, beginning 1978), which measures average changes in retail prices of goods and services. These indexes are described in the sections of these notes pertaining to the Producer Price Index and the Consumer Price Index respectively.

The purchasing power of the dollar is computed by dividing the price index number for the base period by the price index number for the date to be compared, and expressing the result in dollars and cents. The base period is the period in which the price index equals 100 (and the purchasing power is $1.00) currently 1982 for the PPI and the average of 1982 through 1984 for the CPI.

Page 58

Prices Received and Paid by Farmers

Source: U.S. Department of Agriculture, National Agricultural Statistics Service (NASS)

The data on prices received and paid by farmers represent prices farmers received for commodities sold as well as prices paid for production input goods and services. Prices are

weighted and aggregated into price indexes. These indexes provide measures of relative price changes for agricultural outputs and inputs. These price measures are based on voluntary reports from agribusiness firms, merchants, dealers, and farmers. Data are collected at regular intervals using mailed inquiries, telephone, and personal enumeration. In January 1995, these data were converted to a reference base of 1990-92=100. As required by law, the "parity ratio" (ratio of prices received to prices paid) also continues to be published on a base of 1910-1914=100. Prices paid indexes were available only quarterly for several years, but have been published monthly beginning January 1996, with monthly indexes for 1995 constructed for historical comparison.

Definitions

Prices received by farmers represent sales from producers to first buyers. They include all grades and qualities. The average commodity price from the survey multiplied by the total quantity marketed theoretically should give the total cash receipts for the commodity.

Prices paid by farmers represent the average costs of inputs purchased by farmers and ranchers to produce agricultural commodities. Conceptually, the average price when multiplied by quantity purchased should equal total producer expenditures for the item.

Ratio of prices received to prices paid is the ratio of the index of prices received for all farm products to the index of prices paid for all commodities and services. (For some years, prices paid are available only for the first month of each quarter. Each month's ratio of prices received to prices paid is based on the latest data available.)

Notes on the data

In 1995, NASS reweighted and reconstructed the prices paid and received indexes. The indexes are now based on five year moving average weights compared with fixed weights

previously. The changes in the construction of the indexes simplified updating component items and reference periods while maintaining appropriate weights. The overall changes to the weighting and construction of the indexes did not have a significant effect on the index levels, and therefore, had little effect on the level of parity prices. Indexes are now published on a 1990-92=100 base. As required by law, the 1910-14=100 base is continued for the parity index.

Prices paid. Beginning 1995, the Prices Paid Survey of items purchased by farm establishments is conducted annually in April. Surveys are conducted for feed, livestock purchases, seed, fertilizer, agricultural chemicals, fuel, and farm machinery. About 135 selected items are priced to represent groups of similar items purchased which make up the major production expenditures categories. The number of input items consumed on farms is so extensive that it is not feasible to collect price data for all of the inputs. Items on the questionnaire are described in the simplest way consistent with definite identification. Firms are requested to report the prices for the item most commonly sold which meets the general specification on the questionnaire.

Reported data are summarized to regional estimates and then weighted to U.S. prices. Weights are based on available consumption or expenditure information. Average prices including state and local taxes are used in computing the indexes and are published in *Agricultural Prices* for the same month as the survey. Regional prices are published for feed, fuel, and fertilizer. U.S. prices are published for the remaining items surveyed.

Bureau of Labor Statistics (BLS), indexes are used to measure price change for the months when no survey data are collected. The BLS indexes measure price changes for farm supplies and repairs, autos and trucks, building materials, and marketing containers. Before 1995, quarterly prices paid surveys were conducted by NASS.

Revisions—prices paid. Indexes are recomputed quarterly to reflect the most recent price changes and include any updated prices or indexes. Prices Paid Indexes including all components and subcomponents are subject to annual revisions as additional data become available. Annual revisions generally are made in the taxes, interest, and rent, and farm services components of the index.

Survey procedures—prices received. Primary sales data used to determine grain prices are obtained from probability samples of mills and elevators. These procedures ensure that virtually all grain moving into commercial channels has a chance of being included in the survey. Livestock prices are obtained from packers, stockyards, auctions, dealers, and market check data. Interfarm sales of grain and livestock are not included since they represent very small percentages of the total marketings. Grain marketed for seed is also excluded. Fruit and vegetable prices are obtained from sample surveys and market check data.

Summary and estimation procedures— prices received. Survey quantities sold are expanded by strata to state levels and used to weight average strata prices to a state average. State prices are then weighted to a U.S. price.

Revisions—prices received. For most items, the current month's price represents a three to five day period around the mid-month. Previous month's prices represent actual dollars received for quantities sold during the entire month. Revisions are published in monthly issues of *Agricultural Prices* and in the annual summary published in July. A schedule of monthly revisions is published in the December issue of *Agricultural Prices* and in the July annual summary.

Reliability— prices received. U.S. price estimates generally have a sampling error of less than one-half percent for the major commodities such as corn, wheat, soybeans, cotton, and rice.

Data availability

Prices paid and received by farmers are available each month in a press release issued around the end of the month. Data are subsequently published monthly in *Agricultural Prices*. Data also are available on the NASS internet site (http://www.usda.gov/nass/).

Reference

"Revised Prices Received and Paid Indexes, United States, 1975-93; for Base Periods 1910-14=100 and 1990-92=100." Statistical Bulletin Number 917, (National Agricultural Statistics Service, February 1995).

Pages 60-61

Employment Cost Indexes

Source: U.S. Department of Labor, Bureau of Labor Statistics (BLS)

The Employment Cost Index (ECI) is a quarterly measure of the change in the cost of labor, free from the influence of employment shifts among occupations and industries. It uses a fixed market basket of labor, similar in concept to the Consumer Price Index's fixed market basket of goods and services, to measure changes over time in employer costs of employing labor. Data are quarterly in all cases; in most cases, index levels have a base period of June 1989 = 100.

Definitions

Total compensation costs include wages, salaries, and the employer's costs for employee benefits. Excluded from wages and salaries and employee benefits are such items as payment-in-kind, free room and board, and tips.

Wages and salaries consist of earnings before payroll deductions, including production bonuses, incentive earnings, commissions, and cost-of-living adjustments.

Benefits include the cost to employers for paid leave, supplemental pay (including nonproduction bonuses), insurance, retirement and savings plans, and legally required benefits

(such as Social Security, workers' compensation, and unemployment insurance).

Private industry workers are workers in private nonfarm industry excluding proprietors, the self-employed, and household workers.

Civilian workers include private nonfarm industry workers and workers in state and local government. Federal workers are excluded.

Notes on the data

Employee benefit costs are calculated as centsperhourworked for benefits ranging from employer payments for Social Security to paid time off for holidays.

The data are collected from a probability sample of about 23,000 occupational observations in about 4,400 sample establishments in private industry and about 6,000 occupational observations in about 1,000 sample establishments in state and local governments. The sample establishments are classified in industry categories based on the 1987 Standard Industrial Classification (SIC). Within an establishment, specific job categories are selected to represent broader occupational definitions. On average, each reporting unit provides wage and compensation information on five well-specified occupations. Data are collected each quarter for the pay period including the 12th day of March, June, September, and December.

Beginning with March 1995, employment weights from the BLS Occupational Employment Statistics survey are used to calculate the indexes. Previous time periods use employment weights from the decennial censuses of population. Use of fixed weights ensures that changes in the indexes reflect only changes in compensation, not employment shifts among industries or occupations with different levels of wages and compensation.

Data availability

Data for the wages and salaries for the private nonfarm economy begin with 1975; those for compensation begin with 1980. The series for state and local government and the civilian nonfarm economy begin with 1981. Historical data are published in the March issue of the BLS periodical *Compensation and Working Conditions*. Complete historical data are available on the BLS internet site (http://stats.bls.gov).

Wage and salary change and compensation cost change data also are available from BLS by major occupational and industry groups, as well as by region and bargaining status. Wage and salary change information is available from 1975 to the present for most of these series. Compensation cost change data are available from 1980 to the present for most series. For 10 occupational and industry series, benefit cost change data are available from the early 1980's to the present. For state and local governments and the civilian economy (state and local governments plus private industry), wage and salary change and compensation cost change data are available for major occupational and industry series. The data for all these series are provided from June 1981 to present.

In most cases, index levels and 3-month and 12-month percent changes are available. Some of the newer industry and occupation series for private industry workers do not have data available back to June 1981.

Updates are available about four weeks following the end of the reference quarter. Reference quarters end in March, June, September, and December.

References

Chapter 8 "National Compensation Measures" *BLS Handbook of Methods* Bulletin 2490 (April 1997); *Employment Cost Indexes and Levels, 1975-1995*, BLS Bulletin 2466 (1995); and the following *Monthly Labor Review* articles: "Is the ECI Sensitive to the Method of Aggregation" (June 1997); "Employment Cost Index Rebased to June 1989" (April 1990); "Measuring the Precision of the Employment Cost Index" (March 1989); "Employment Cost Index to Replace Hourly Earnings Index" (July 1988).

Pages 62-63 and 259-262

Productivity

Source: U.S. Department of Labor, Bureau of Labor Statistics (BLS)

Productivity measures relate real physical output to real input. As such, they encompass a family of measures which include single-factor input measures, such as output per unit of labor input or output per unit of capital input, as well as measures of multifactor productivity (output per unit of combined labor and capital inputs). The indexes published in this book are indexes of labor productivity expressed in terms of output per hour. Data are provided for four sectors of the economy: business, nonfarm business, the nonfinancial corporate sector, and manufacturing.

Historical data were revised during 1996 to introduce output measures consistent with the comprehensive revision of the National Income and Product Accounts (NIPA). Also, consistent with the introduction of annually-weighted output indexes into the NIPA, BLS switched to annually-weighted indexes for the compensation measures underlying the labor productivity estimates.

Definitions

Output per hour of all persons (labor productivity) is the value of goods and services in constant prices produced per hour of labor input.

Compensation per hour is the wages and salaries of employees plus employers' contributions for social insurance and private benefit plans, and the wages, salaries, and supplementary payments for the self-employed—the sum of these divided by hours at work.

Real compensation per hour is compensation per hour deflated by the change in the Consumer Price Index for All Urban Consumers.

Unit labor costs are the labor costs expended in the production of a unit of output and are derived by dividing compensation by output.

Unit nonlabor costs contain all the components of unit nonlabor payments except unit profits.

Hours of all persons are the total hours at work of payroll workers, self-employed persons, and unpaid family workers.

Notes on the data

The output for the business sector is equal to constant dollar gross domestic product less the following: the rental value of owner occupied dwellings, the output of nonprofit institutions, the output of paid employees of private households, and general government. The measures are derived from data supplied by the U.S. Department of Commerce, Bureau of Economic Analysis (BEA), and the Federal Reserve Board of Governors. Quarterly manufacturing output indexes are adjusted by the Bureau of Labor Statistics to annual estimates of manufacturing output (gross product originating) from BEA.

Compensation and hours data are developed from BLS and BEA data. Data on hours at work are obtained from the annual BLS Hours at Work Survey. Hours at work replaced a former measure based primarily on hours paid in 1989. For paid employees, hours at work differs from hours paid in that it excludes paid vacation and holidays, paid sick leave, and other paid personal or administrative leave. When the hours at work concept was introduced in 1989, the historical data were revised to reflect the change in concept.

Although the labor productivity measures relate output to labor input they do not measure the contribution of labor or any other specific factor of production. Rather, they reflect the joint effect of many influences, including changes in technology; capital investment; level of output; utilization of capacity, energy, and materials; the organization of production; managerial skill; and the characteristics and efforts of the work force.

Data availability

Most of the series begin in 1959. Series are available quarterly and annually. Quarterly measures are based entirely on seasonally adjusted data. For some manufacturing series, only annual averages are available. Updates are performed near the end of the first two months of each quarter, reflecting new data from the preceding quarter. Traditionally, all revisions to source data are reflected in the release following the revision. Complete historical data are available on the BLS internet site (http://stats.bls.gov).

BLS also publishes productivity estimates for a number of individual industries. A listing is given in *Productivity Measures for Selected Industries and Government Services*, BLS Bulletin 2440.

References

Chapter 10 "Productivity Measures: Business Sector and Major Subsectors" *BLS Handbook of Methods* Bulletin 2490 (April 1997), and the following *Monthly Labor Review* articles: "Improvements to the Quarterly Productivity Measures" (October 1995); "Hours of Work: A New Base for BLS Productivity Statistics" (February 1990); and "New Sector Definitions for Productivity Series" (October 1976).

Pages 64-66

Corporate Profits and Dividends

Source: U.S. Department of Commerce, Bureau of the Census (since 1983), Federal Trade Commission (prior to 1983), and Securities and Exchange Commission (prior to 1972).

The corporate profits and dividend data are taken from the Quarterly Financial Report (QFR) data set. The QFR, which is based on an extensive sample survey, provides estimates of income and retained earnings, balance sheets, and related financial and operating ratios for industry groups, classified according to the SIC.

Notes on the data

Purpose of the QFR. The main purpose of the QFR is to provide timely, accurate data on business financial conditions for use by government and private sector organizations and individuals. Among its users, the Commerce Department regularly employs QFR data as an important component in determining corporate profits for GNP and National Income estimates, and the Treasury Department estimates corporate tax liability through use of QFR data.

The program designs and maintains on a current basis statistical cross sections (i.e., probability samples) of corporate enterprises; collects, analyzes, and summarizes periodic confidential reports from those corporations; estimates national aggregates based upon the individual company reports; and publishes the resulting aggregates.

Classification by industry. The industry combinations used in the QFR are based on the SIC 1987. A reporting corporation is initially classified into the SIC division accounting for more gross receipts than any other SIC division. To be in scope for the QFR, more gross receipts of the reporting corporation must be accounted for by either (not a combination of) SIC Division B (Mining), Division D (Manufacturing), Division F (Wholesale Trade), or Division G (Retail Trade) than by any other SIC division.

For the most part, after a corporation is assigned to a division, it is further classified by the two-digit SIC major group accounting for more gross receipts than any other two-digit group within the division. In certain cases, corporations are further classified into three-digit SIC groups. QFR data are

published for these major groups when precision criteria are satisfied

Note that these procedures may lead to a conglomerate corporation being assigned to a major group from which only a small proportion of its receipts are obtained. For example, if a corporation obtains 25 percent of its gross receipts from mining activities, 30 percent from manufacturing, 20 percent from wholesale, and 25 percent from retail, it would be classified in the Manufacturing Division. Furthermore, if the 30 percent of manufacturing activity was conducted in two major groups, 20 percent in one and 10 percent in the other, the activities of the corporation as a whole would be classified in the major group accounting for 20 percent of total receipts.

Classification by size. Data are published by asset size classes within industry groups. Since 1973, each reporting manufacturing corporation has been classified and tabulated according to its total assets reported for that quarter. Mining and trade corporations are classified and tabulated according to total assets at time of sample selection. Prior to fourth quarter 1987, they were classified according to total assets at the end of the reference quarter.

Sample. Nearly all corporations whose operations are within the scope of the QFR and which have total assets greater than $50 million are included in the sample. They are permanent sample members. For smaller corporations (as measured by asset size), a replacement scheme is used which provides that oneeighth of the sample be replaced each quarter. Corporations removed are those that have been in the reporting group the longest (usually eight quarters). Therefore, samples of small corporations for adjacent quarters are seveneighths identical. The composition of the sample changes each quarter to reflect the effects of corporate births, deaths, acquisitions, divestitures, mergers, consolidations, and the like.

Comparisons with other statistics. QFR estimates will not necessarily agree with other financial and industrial statistics compilations whether based upon a sample or complete canvass. For example:

- The QFR eliminates multiple counting of interplant and other intra-company transfers included in census establishment statistics.

- The conventional accounting concept of profits is used in the QFR estimates. This differs from the concept of profits employed in the national income and product accounts.

- Corporations' QFR submissions generally embody the accounting conventions adopted for financial reporting purposes. As such, they may differ from those used by corporations for reporting income to the IRS.

- QFR estimates by corporation size are based upon the total assets of consolidated corporate enterprises. They differ from estimates based upon other criteria such as value of shipments or number of employees. They differ also from estimates based upon other reporting units such as establishments, nonconsolidated corporations, or enterprises consolidated differently than in the QFR.

- QFR estimates are based upon a changing sample of audited, unaudited, and estimated reports required to be submitted within 25 days after the end of each quarterly reporting period by corporations. Aggregated for any four consecutive quarters, the QFR estimates will differ from similar aggregations of finalized and audited annual reports.

Changes in the series. A number of changes in accounting, industry classification, and sample design affect the comparability of the QFR data over time. When the QFR series began in 1947, corporations were instructed to consolidate all of their subsidiaries which were taxable under the U.S.

Internal Revenue Code and which were fully consolidated in their latest report to stockholders. The income tax liability rule was expected to eliminate most foreign operations. However, as the number of multinational corporations increased between 1947 and 1973, foreign operations gradually became more significant in the QFR data. New consolidation rules were put into effect in the fourth quarter of 1973 to maximize coverage and minimize the impact of foreign operations on QFR statistics. As a result of these changes, foreign operations are included on an investment basis. The change in consolidation rules and the creation of a line item to reflect equity in earnings from nonconsolidated subsidiaries significantly lessened the comparability of pre and postfourth quarter 1973 reports. There was a net decrease in sales and in net income before taxes. The net effect of the rule changes on net income after taxes was small, as, under both rules, foreign activity should be included above the net income after tax line.

Industry classification from 1959 through the third quarter of 1972 was based on the 1957 SIC (the 1967 SIC revision did not affect the level of aggregation used in the QFR); from the fourth quarter of 1972 through 1987 on the 1972 SIC; and from 1988 forward on the 1987 SIC. Prior to the first quarter of 1974, a corporation was classified as a manufacturer only if 50 percent or more of its gross receipts were derived from manufacturing operations. The new classification rules are more inclusive.

Data availability

QFR data are scheduled for release approximately 75 days after the end of the first, second, and third calendar quarters and approximately 95 days after the end of the fourth calendar quarter. The QFR publishes information on the most recently closed quarter for manufacturing, mining, and wholesaling and the preceding quarter's data for retailing except in the fourth quarter, when the 95day publication lag permits synchronized

presentation. Current data are available in press releases and on the Bureau of the Census internet site (http://www.census.gov). Historical data may be purchased on diskette from the Bureau of the Census.

The QFR is prepared by the Bureau of the Census. The Federal Trade Commission had been responsible for the program from inception in 1947 until December 1982. That responsibility was shared with the Securities and Exchange Commission until 1971.

Pages 68-71 and 278-285

Labor Force, Employment, and Unemployment

Source: U.S. Department of Labor, Bureau of Labor Statistics (BLS)

Note: Due to changes in questionnaire design and survey methodology, data for 1994 and subsequent years are not directly comparable with data for 1993 and earlier years. In addition, data beginning with 1990 incorporate 1990 census-based population controls adjusted for the estimated undercount. See "Notes on the Data" below for additional information.

The labor force, employment, and unemployment data are derived from the Current Population Survey (CPS), a sample survey of households conducted each month by the Bureau of the Census for the Bureau of Labor Statistics. The data pertain to the U.S. civilian noninstitutional population 16 years and over.

Definitions

The *civilian noninstitutional population* comprises all civilians 16 years of age and older who are not inmates of penal or mental institutions, sanitariums, or homes for the aged, infirm, or needy.

Civilian employment includes those civilians who (1) worked for pay or profit at any time during the week which includes the 12th day of the month (the survey week) or who worked unpaid for 15 hours or more in a family-operated enterprise or (2) were temporarily absent from their regular jobs because of because of vacation, illness, industrial dispute, bad weather, or similar reasons. Each employed person is counted only once; those who hold more than one job are counted in the job at which they worked the greatest number of hours during the survey week.

Unemployed persons are all civilians who did not work during the survey week, but were available for work, except for temporary illness, and had made specific efforts to find employment sometime during the prior four weeks. Persons who did not look for work because they were on layoff are also counted as unemployed.

The *civilian labor force* comprises all civilians classified as employed or unemployed.

The civilian *labor force participation rate* represents the proportion of the civilian noninstitutional population (age 16 and over) that is in the civilian labor force.

The *employment to population ratio* represents the proportion of the civilian noninstitutional population (age 16 and over) that is employed.

The long-term unemployed are persons unemployed 15 consecutive weeks or longer. If a person ceases to look for work for two weeks or more (or is employed), the continuity of longterm unemployment is broken.

The civilian *unemployment rate* is the number of unemployed as a percent of the civilian labor force. The unemployment rates for groups within the civilian population (such as, for example, males 20 years and over) are the number of unemployed in a group as a percent of the labor force in that group. The unemployment rates by industry and occupation refer to experienced wage and salary workers and are based on industry or occupation of the last job held.

Civilians in the noninstitutional population, 16 years of age and over, who are not classified as employed or unemployed are defined as "*not in the labor force.*" This group includes those engaged in own home housework, in school, unable to work because of longterm illness, retired, too old, seasonal workers for whom the survey week fell in an "off" season (not reported as unemployed), persons who became discouraged and gave up the search for work, and the voluntarily idle. Also included are those doing only incidental work (less than 15 hours) in a family business during the survey week.

Notes on the data

The CPS data are collected monthly by trained interviewers from sample households selected to represent the U.S. population 16 years of age and older. Sample size was about 60,000 households from mid-1989 to mid-1995, but has since been reduced in two stages to about 50,000 household beginning in January 1996. The data collected are based on the activity or status reported for the calendar week, Sunday through Saturday, that includes the 12th day of the month. Households are interviewed on a rotating basis, so that three-fourths of the sample is the same for any two consecutive months.

Data relating to 1994 and subsequent years are not directly comparable with data for 1993 and earlier years because of the introduction of a major redesign of the survey questionnaire and collection methodology, and the introduction of 1990 census-based population controls, adjusted for the estimated undercount. The redesign included new and revised questions for the classification of individuals as employed or unemployed, the collection of new data on multiple job holding, a change in the definition of discouraged workers, and the implementation of completely automated data collection. Use of 1990 census-based population controls adjusted for the undercount had the effect of raising population estimates and the related labor force estimates. The combined

effect of the changes introduced in 1994 are estimated to have raised the civilian unemployment rate by perhaps 0.2 percentage points.

The 1994 redesign of the CPS was the most extensive in many years. However, there are also several earlier periods of noncomparability in the labor force data, which resulted from the introduction of new decennial census data into the CPS estimation procedures, expansions of the sample, and other improvements made to increase the reliability of the estimates. For strict comparability, the following allowances should be made when making certain data comparisons:

(1) Beginning in 1953, the introduction of 1950 census data added about 600,000 to the population and about 350,000 to the labor force, total employment, and agricultural employment.

(2) Beginning in 1960, the inclusion of Alaska and Hawaii added about 500,000 to the population, about 300,000 to the labor force, and about 240,000 to nonagricultural employment.

(3) Beginning in 1962, the introduction of 1960 census data reduced the population by about 50,000, and the labor force and total employment by about 200,000.

(4) Beginning in 1972, the introduction of 1970 census data added about 800,000 to the population, and a little over 300,000 to the labor force and total employment. A subsequent adjustment in March 1973 (based on 1970 census data), which substantially affected major categories for white and black and other workers, resulted in a net increase of 60,000 in the labor force and total employment.

(5) Beginning in 1978, an expansion in the sample and changes in the estimation procedures added about 250,000 to the labor force and total employment.

(6) Beginning in 1982, changes in the estimation procedures and the introduction of 1980 census data caused substantial increases in the population and estimates of persons in all labor force categories. Rates on labor force characteristics, however, were essentially unchanged. In order to avoid major breaks in series, some 30,000 labor force series were adjusted back to 1970. The effect of the 1982 revisions on various data series and an explanation of the adjustment procedure used are described in "Revisions in the Current Population Survey Beginning in January 1982," in the February 1982 issue of *Employment and Earnings*. The revisions did not, however, smooth out the breaks in series occurring between 1972 and 1979 that are described above.

(7) Beginning in 1986, the population controls used in the estimation procedures were revised to reflect an explicit estimate of the number of undocumented immigrants (largely Hispanic) since 1980 and an improved estimate of the number of legal foreignborn immigrants for the same time period. As a result, the civilian population and labor force estimates were raised by nearly 400,000; civilian employment was increased by about 350,000. The Hispanicorigin civilian population and labor force estimates were raised by about 425,000 and 305,000 respectively, and civilian employment by 270,000. Overall and subgroup unemployment levels and rates were not significantly affected. Because of the magnitude of the adjustments for Hispanics, data were revised back to January 1980 to the extent possible. An explanation of the changes and their effect on estimates appears in "Changes in the Estimation Procedure in the Current Population Survey Beginning in January 1986" in the February 1986 issue of *Employment and Earnings*.

Nonagricultural employment estimates from the CPS differ in levels and trends from estimates compiled from estab-lishment payrolls (described in the Notes for pages 73-78). Factors such as definitions, coverage, and sources account for the differences. The CPS data include domestics and other private household workers, self-employed persons, and unpaid family workers who worked 15 hours or more in the survey week in family-operated enterprises, whereas the payroll or establishment survey covers only employees on payrolls of nonfarm establishments; persons holding more than one job during the survey week are counted once in the household survey, but multiple jobholders are counted each time (i.e., on each payroll) in the establishment survey; and persons with a job but not at work (i.e., absent because of bad weather, work stoppages, personal reasons, etc.) are included in the household survey but are excluded from the payroll survey if on leave without pay for the entire payroll period.

The monthly labor force, employment and unemployment data are seasonally adjusted by the X-11 ARIMA method. Seasonal adjustment factors are revised at the end of each calendar year and the new factors applied to the data for several past years. In February 1997, seasonally adjusted monthly data for 1994 through 1996 were revised.

All seasonally adjusted civilian labor force and unemployment rate statistics, as well as the major employment and unemployment estimates, are computed by aggregating independently adjusted series. For example, the seasonally adjusted levels of total unemployment, civilian employment, the civilian labor force, and the seasonally adjusted unemployment rate are all produced by aggregation of the seasonally adjusted results for component series. The seasonally adjusted level of total unemployment is the sum of the seasonally adjusted levels of unemployment for the four sexage groups (men and women 16 to 19, and men and women 20 years and over). Seasonally adjusted employment is the sum of the seasonally adjusted level of employment for eight sexageindustry groups (men and women 16 to 19, and men and women 20 years and over, employed in nonagricultural and agricultural industries). The seasonally adjusted civilian labor force is the sum of all 12 components. Finally, the seasonally adjusted civilian worker unemployment rate is calculated by taking total seasonally adjusted unemployment as a percent of the total seasonally adjusted civilian labor force.

Data availability

Data for each month usually are released on the first Friday of the following month in a press release that also contains data from the establishment survey (described in the notes to pages 73-78). Data are subsequently published in the BLS monthly periodical *Employment and Earnings*, which also contains detailed explanatory notes. Selected data are published each month in the *Monthly Labor Review*, which also contains frequent articles analyzing labor force, employment, and unemployment developments.

Monthly and annual data beginning with 1948 are available. Historical unadjusted data are published in *Labor Force Statistics Derived from the Current Population Survey*, BLS Bulletin 2307. Historical seasonally adjusted data are available from BLS upon request. Complete historical data are available on the BLS internet site (http://stats.bls.gov).

References

Historical background on the CPS as well as a description of the 1994 redesign are found in three articles in the September 1993 *Monthly Labor Review*: "Why Is It Necessary to Change", "Redesigning the Questionnaire", and "Evaluating Changes in the Estimates." The redesign also is described in the February 1994 issue of *Employment and Earnings*. Information on introduction of the 1990 census-based population controls is found in the March 1996 issue of *Employment and Earnings*. See also Chapter 1 "Labor Force Data Derived from the Current Population Survey" *BLS Handbook of Methods* Bulletin 2490 (April 1997).

Page 72

Insured Unemployment

Source: U.S. Department of Labor, Employment and Training Administration

State programs of unemployment insurance cover operations of regular programs under state unemployment insurance laws. In 1976, the law was amended to extend coverage (effective January 1, 1978) to include virtually all state and local government employees plus many agricultural and domestic workers.

The federal civilian employees unemployment insurance program (UCFE) provides unemployment insurance protection to civilian employees of the federal government or of wholly or partially owned instrumentalities, with the following exceptions: elective officers in the executive and legislative branches of government, certain foreign service personnel, temporary emergency workers, and other small groups.

Unemployment compensation for ex-service members (UCX) provides unemployment insurance protection to veterans under the law of the state in which the claim for compensation is filed.

An *initial claim* is the first claim in a benefit year filed by a worker after losing his job, or the first claim filed at the beginning of a subsequent period of unemployment in the same benefit year. The initial claim establishes the starting date for any insured unemployment that may result if the claimant is unemployed for one week or longer. Transitional claims (filed by persons as they start a new benefit year in a continuing spell of unemployment) are excluded; therefore, the data represent more closely instances of new unemployment.

Monthly averages in this book are averages of the weekly data published by the Employment and Training Administration. Annual data are averages of the monthly data.

Data availability

Data are published in weekly press releases from the Employment and Training Administration. These releases are available on their internet site (http://www.doleta.gov).

Pages 73-78 and 286-289

Nonagricultural Employment

Source: U.S. Department of Labor, Bureau of Labor Statistics (BLS)

The nonagricultural employment data, as well as the hours and earnings data on pages 79-91, are compiled from payroll records. Information is reported monthly on a voluntary basis to the BLS and its cooperating state agencies by more than 350,000 establishments representing all industries except agriculture. These data often are referred to as the "establishment data" or the "payroll data." The data by industry conform to the definitions in the 1987 Standard Industrial Classification (SIC).

Definitions

An *establishment* is an economic unit which produces goods or services (such as a factory or store) at a single location and is engaged in one type of economic activity.

Employed persons are all persons who received pay (including holiday and sick pay) for any part of the payroll period including the 12th day of the month (except in government—see below). Included are all fulltime and parttime workers in nonfarm establishments. Persons holding more than one job are counted in each establishment which reports them. Not covered are proprietors, the selfemployed, unpaid volunteer or family workers, farm workers, domestic workers in households, military personnel, and employees of the Central Intelligence and National Security Agencies; salaried officers of corporations are included.

Persons on an establishment payroll who are on paid sick leave (when pay is received directly from the employer), on paid holiday or vacation, or who work during a portion of the pay period even though they are unemployed or on strike during the rest of the period are counted as employed. Not counted as employed are persons who are laid off, on leave without pay, or on strike for the entire period, or who are hired but have not been paid during the period.

Intermittent workers are counted if they performed any service during the month. BLS considers regular fulltime teachers (private and governmental) to be employed during the summer vacation period whether or not they are specifically paid in those months.

The government division of the SIC includes federal, state, and local activities such as legislative, executive, and judicial functions, as well as all governmentowned and governmentoperated business enterprises, establishments, and institutions (arsenals, navy yards, hospitals, etc.), and government force account construction. Federal government employment is civilian employment only and pertains to the last day of the month. Employees of the Central Intelligence Agency and the National Security Agency are not included.

Nonagricultural employment in these series differs from the measures in the household survey (pages 68-71) in that, among other factors, it excludes domestics and other private household workers, selfemployed persons, and unpaid family workers. Persons holding more than one job during the survey week are counted once in the household survey, but multiple jobholders are counted each time (i.e., on each payroll) in the establishment survey. Persons with a job but not at work (i.e., absent because of bad weather, work stoppages, personal reasons, etc.) are included in the household survey but are excluded from the payroll survey if on leave without pay for the entire payroll period.

Production or nonsupervisory workers. The data refer to the private, nonfarm sector and cover all production and related workers in mining and manufacturing; construction workers in construction; and nonsupervisory workers in transportation, communication, electric, gas, and sanitary services; wholesale and retail trade; finance, insurance, and real estate; and services. These groups account for about four-fifths of the total employment on private nonagricultural payrolls.

Included are fulltime and parttime workers who are on payrolls of private nonfarm establishments and who received pay for all or any part of the pay period that includes the 12th day of the month. Not counted are persons who are laid off, on leave without pay, or on strike for the entire period. Persons who worked in more than one establishment during a single reporting period are counted each time reported, whether the duplication is due to turnover or dual jobholding. The manufacturing series exclude manufacturing operations in government establishments such as arsenals and navy yards; these are included in the government division.

Production and related workers include working supervisors and all nonsupervisory workers (including group leaders and trainees) engaged in fabricating, processing, assembling, inspecting, receiving, storing, handling, packing, warehousing, shipping, trucking, hauling, maintenance, repair, janitorial, guard services, product development, auxiliary production for plant's own use (e.g., power plant), record-keeping, and other services closely associated with these production operations.

Construction workers include the following employees in the construction division of the SIC: working supervisors, qualified craft workers, mechanics, apprentices, laborers, etc., engaged in new work, alterations, demolition, repair, maintenance, etc., whether working at the site of construction or working in shops or yards at jobs (such as precutting and preassembling) ordinarily performed by members of the construction trades.

Nonsupervisory employees include employees (not above the working supervisory level) such as office and clerical workers, repairers, salespersons, operators, drivers, physicians, lawyers, accountants, nurses, social workers, research aides, teachers, drafters, photographers, beauticians, musicians, restaurant workers, custodial workers, attendants, line installers and repairers, laborers, janitors, guards, and other employees at similar occupational levels whose services are closely associated with those of the employees listed.

Notes on the data

Benchmark adjustments. The establishment survey data are adjusted annually to comprehensive counts of employment (called "benchmarks"). Benchmark information on employment, by industry, is compiled by state agencies from reports of establishments covered under state unemployment insurance laws. These tabulations cover about 98 percent of all employees on nonfarm payrolls. Benchmark data for the residual are obtained from the records of the Social Security Administration and a number of other agencies in private industry or government.

The estimates for the benchmark month are compared with new benchmark levels, industry by industry. If revisions are necessary, the monthly series of estimates between benchmark periods are adjusted at levels between the new benchmark and the preceding one, and the new benchmark for each industry is then carried forward progressively to the current month by use of the sample trends. Thus, under this procedure, the benchmark is used to establish the level of employment; the sample is used to measure the monthtomonth changes in the level. Data for all months since the last benchmark to which the series has been adjusted are subject to revision.

Seasonal adjustment. The seasonal movements that recur periodically (such as warm and cold weather, cropgrowing cycles, holidays, vacations, etc.) are generally the largest single component of monthtomonth changes in employ-

ment. After adjusting the data to remove such seasonal variation, the basic trends are more evident. Since the early 1980's the BLS has used the X11 ARIMA procedure to seasonally adjust the establishmentbased series. Seasonal adjustment factors are directly applied to the component levels. Seasonally adjusted totals for employment series are then obtained by aggregating seasonally adjusted components directly, while hours and earnings series represent weighted averages of the seasonally adjusted component series. Seasonally adjusted data are not published for a small number of series characterized by small seasonal components relative to their trendcycle and/or irregular components. These series, however, are used in aggregating to broader seasonally adjusted levels.

Seasonal adjustment factors for federal government employment are derived from unadjusted data that include Christmas temporary workers employed by the Postal Service. The number of temporary census workers for the decennial census are removed, however, prior to the calculation of seasonal adjustment factors.

Revisions of the seasonally adjusted data, usually for the most recent five year period, are made once a year coincident with the benchmark revisions.

Data availability

Employment data by industry division are available beginning with 1919. Data for each month usually are released on the first Friday of the following month in a press release that also contains data from the household survey (described in notes for pages 68-71). Data are subsequently published in the BLS monthly periodical *Employment and Earnings*, which also contains detailed explanatory notes. Selected data are published each month in the *Monthly Labor Review*, which also contains frequent articles analyzing labor force, employment and unemployment developments. Complete historical data are available on the BLS internet site (http://stats.bls.gov).

References

Chapter 2 "Employment, Hours, and Earnings from the Establishment Survey," *BLS Handbook of Methods*, Bulletin 2490 (April 1997).

Pages 79-84 and 290-293

Average Hours Per Week; Aggregate Employee Hours

Source: U.S. Department of Labor, Bureau of Labor Statistics (BLS)

The nonagricultural employment, hours, and earnings data are compiled from payroll records. Information is reported monthly on a voluntary basis to the BLS and its cooperating state agencies by more than 350,000 establishments representing all industries except agriculture. These data often are referred to as the "establishment data" or the "payroll data". The data by industry conform to the definitions in the 1987 Standard Industrial Classification (SIC). See the Notes for pages 73-78 for a general description of the establishment survey.

Definitions

Hours represent the average weekly hours of production or nonsupervisory workers for which pay was received, and are different from standard or scheduled hours. Such factors as unpaid absenteeism, labor turnover, parttime work, and work stoppages cause average weekly hours to be lower than scheduled hours of work for an establishment.

Overtime hours represent the portion of average weekly hours which was in excess of regular hours and for which overtime premiums were paid. Weekend and holiday hours are included only if overtime premiums are paid. Hours for which only shift differential, hazard, incentive, or other similar types of premiums are paid are excluded.

Production or nonsupervisory workers. See the Notes to pages 73-78 for definition.

Notes on the data

Benchmark adjustments. Independent benchmarks are not available for the hours and earnings series. At the time of the annual adjustment of the employment series to new benchmarks, the levels of hours and earnings may be affected slightly by the revised employment weights (which are used in computing the industry averages for hours and earnings), as well as by the changes in seasonal adjustment factors also introduced with the benchmark revision.

Method of computing industry series. "Average weekly hours" for individual industries are computed by dividing production or nonsupervisory worker hours (reported by plants classified in each industry) by the number of production or nonsupervisory workers (reported for the same establishments). Estimates for SIC divisions and major industry groups are averages (weighted by employment) of the figures for component industries.

Seasonal adjustment. Hours and earnings series are seasonally adjusted by applying factors directly to the corresponding unadjusted series. Data for some industries are not seasonally adjusted because the seasonal component is small relative to the trendcycle and/or irregular components and consequently cannot be separated with sufficient precision.

Aggregate hours. Data pertain to production and nonsupervisory workers in nonfarm establishments. The indexes are obtained by multiplying seasonally adjusted production or nonsupervisory worker employment by seasonally adjusted average weekly hours and dividing by the monthly average for the 1982 period. For total private, goodsproducing, serviceproducing, and major industry divisions, the indexes are obtained by summing the seasonally adjusted aggregate weekly employee hours for the component industries and dividing by the monthly average for the 1982 period.

References

Chapter 2 "Employment, Hours, and Earnings from the Establishment Survey," *BLS Handbook of Methods*, Bulletin 2490 (April 1997).

Pages 85-91 and 290-293

Hourly and Weekly Earnings

Source: U.S. Department of Labor, Bureau of Labor Statistics (BLS)

The nonagricultural employment, hours, and earnings data are compiled from payroll records. Information is reported monthly on a voluntary basis to the BLS and its cooperating state agencies by more than 350,000 establishments representing all industries except agriculture. These data often are referred to as the "establishment data" or the "payroll data." The data by industry conform to the definitions in the 1987 Standard Industrial Classification (SIC). See the Notes for pages 73-78 for a general description of the establishment survey.

Definitions

Earnings are the payments production or nonsupervisory workers receive during the survey period, including premium pay for overtime or late-shift work but excluding irregular bonuses and other special payments.

Real earnings are earnings adjusted to reflect the effects of changes in consumer prices. The deflator for this series is derived from the Consumer Price Index for Urban Wage Earners and Clerical Workers (CPI-W).

Production or nonsupervisory workers. See the Notes to pages 73-78 for definition.

Notes on the data

The hours and earnings series are based on reports of gross payroll and corresponding paid hours for full- and part-time production and related workers, construction workers, or nonsupervisory workers who received pay for any part of the pay period that included the 12th of the month.

Total payrolls are before deductions; e.g., for old-age and unemployment insurance, group insurance, withholding taxes, bonds, and union dues. The payroll figures also include pay for overtime, holidays, vacations, and sick leave (paid directly by the employer for the period reported). Excluded from the payroll figures are fringe benefits (health and other types of insurance, contributions to retirement, etc., paid by the employer); bonuses (unless earned and paid regularly each pay period); other pay not earned in the pay period reported (e.g., retroactive pay); tips; and the value of free rent, fuel, meals, or other payment in kind.

Average hourly earnings data are on a "gross" basis; that is, they reflect not only changes in basic hourly and incentive wage rates but also such variable factors as premium pay for overtime and lateshift work, and changes in output of workers paid on an incentive basis. Also, shifts in the volume of employment between relatively highpaid and lowpaid work and changes in workers' earnings in individual establishments affect the general average of hourly earnings.

Averages of hourly earnings should not be confused with wage rates, which represent the rates stipulated for a given unit of work or time, while earnings refer to the actual return to the worker for a stated period of time. The earnings series do not represent total labor cost to the employer because of the exclusion of irregular bonuses, retroactive items, payments of various welfare benefits, payroll taxes paid by employers, and earnings for those employees not covered under the productionworker or nonsupervisoryworker definition. Similarly, average weekly earnings are not the amounts available to workers for spending, since they do not reflect such deductions as those for income and social security taxes, etc.

Method of computing industry series. Average hourly earnings are obtained by dividing the reported total production or nonsupervisory worker payroll by the total production or

nonsupervisory worker hours. Estimates for both hours and hourly earnings for nonfarm divisions and major industry groups are averages (weighted by employment for hours and by aggregate hours for hourly earnings) of the figures for component industries. Average weekly earnings are computed by multiplying average hourly earnings by average weekly hours. In addition to the factors mentioned above, which exert varying influences upon average hourly earnings, average weekly earnings are affected by changes in the length of the work week, part-time work, work stoppages, labor turnover, and absenteeism. Persistent longterm increases in the proportion of parttime workers in retail trade and many of the service industries have reduced average work weeks and have affected the average weekly earnings series.

Independent benchmarks are not available for the hours and earnings series. At the time of the annual adjustment of the employment series to new benchmarks, the levels of hours and earnings may be affected slightly by the revised employment weights (which are used in computing the industry averages for hours and earnings), as well as by the changes in seasonal adjustment factors also introduced with the benchmark revision.

Seasonal adjustment. Hours and earnings series are seasonally adjusted by applying factors directly to the corresponding unadjusted series; seasonally adjusted average weekly earnings are the product of seasonally adjusted hourly earnings and weekly hours. Weekly earnings in constant dollars, seasonally adjusted, are obtained by dividing seasonally adjusted average weekly earnings by the seasonally adjusted Consumer Price Index for Urban Wage Earners and Clerical Workers (CPI-W).

References

Chapter 2 "Employment, Hours, and Earnings from the Establishment Survey," *BLS Handbook of Methods*, Bulletin 2490 (April 1997).

Pages 94-95 and 302-305

Money Stock, Liquid Assets, and Debt;

Components of the Money Stock
Source: Board of Governors of the Federal Reserve System

Estimates of three monetary aggregates (M1, M2, and M3), a broad measure of liquid assets (L), a debt aggregate, and the components of these measures are published weekly. The monthly data are averages of daily figures.

Definitions

M1 consists of (1) currency outside the U.S. Treasury, Federal Reserve Banks, and the vaults of depository institutions; (2) travelers checks of nonbank issuers; (3) demand deposits at all commercial banks other than those due to depository institutions, the U.S. government, and foreign banks and official institutions, less cash items in the process of collection and Federal Reserve float; and (4) other checkable deposits (OCDs), consisting of negotiable order of withdrawal (NOW) and automatic transfer service (ATS) accounts at depository institutions, credit union share draft accounts and demand deposits at thrift institutions.

M2 consists of M1 plus savings deposits (including money market deposit accounts), small-denomination time deposits (time deposits— including retail repurchase agreements (RPs)—in amounts of less than $100,000), and balances in retail money market mutual funds. Excludes individual retirement account (IRA) and Keogh balances at depository institutions and money market funds.

M3 consists of M2 plus large-denomination time deposits (in amounts of $100,000 or more), balances in institutional money funds, RP liabilities (overnight and term) issued by all depository institutions, and Eurodollars (overnight and term) held by U.S. residents at foreign branches of U.S. banks worldwide and at all banking offices in the United Kingdom and Canada. Excludes amounts held by depository institutions, the U.S. government, money funds, and foreign banks and official institutions.

L is a broad measure of liquid assets and consists of M3 plus the nonbank public holdings of U.S. savings bonds, short-term Treasury securities, commercial paper and bankers acceptances, net of money market mutual fund holdings of these assets.

Debt is the outstanding credit market debt of the domestic nonfinancial sectors—the federal sector (U.S. government, not including government-sponsored enterprises or federally related mortgage pools) and the nonfederal sectors (state and local governments, households and nonprofit organizations, nonfinancial corporate and nonfarm noncorporate businesses, and farms). Nonfederal debt consists of mortgages, tax-exempt and corporate bonds, consumer credit, bank loans, commercial paper, and other loans. The data, which are derived from the Federal Reserve Board's flow of funds accounts, are break-adjusted (that is, discontinuities in the data have been smoothed into the series) and month-averaged (that is, the data have been derived by averaging adjacent month-end levels).

Currency consists of currency outside the U.S. Treasury, the Federal Reserve Banks, and the vaults of depository institutions.

Demand deposits consists of demand deposits at commercial banks and foreign-related institutions other than those due to depository institutions, the U.S. government, and foreign banks and official institutions, less cash items in the process of collection and Federal Reserve float.

Other checkable deposits consists of NOW and ATS balances at commercial banks, U.S. branches and agencies of foreign banks, Edge Act corporations, and thrift institutions; credit union share draft balances; and demand deposits at thrift institutions.

Savings deposits include money market deposit accounts.

Small time deposits are those issued at commercial banks and thrift institutions in amounts of less than $100,000. Retail RPs are included. All IRA and Keogh account balances at commercial banks and thrift institutions are subtracted from small time deposits.

Large time deposits are those issued in amounts of $100,000 or more at commercial banks and thrift institutions, excluding those booked at international banking facilities. Deposits held at commercial banks by money market mutual funds, depository institutions, the U.S. government, and foreign banks and official institutions also are excluded.

Notes on the data

Seasonal adjustment. Seasonally adjusted M1 is calculated by summing currency, travelers checks, demand deposits, and OCDs, each seasonally adjusted separately. Seasonally adjusted M2 is computed by adjusting each of its nonM1 components and then adding this result to seasonally adjusted M1. Similarly, seasonally adjusted M3 is obtained by adjusting each of its nonM2 components and then adding this result to seasonally adjusted M2.

Revisions. Money stock measures are revised annually, usually in February, based on a benchmark and seasonal factor review. These revisions typically extend back a number of years. The monetary aggregates were redefined and the liquid asset concept, L, introduced in major revisions in 1980.

There was a minor definitional change in M2 at the time of the 1996 revisions. Overnight wholesale repurchase agreements (RPs) and overnight Eurodollars were removed from M2 and are now included in the non-M2 component of M3. Although the revision lowered M2 for all years since 1969, it had no effect on quarterly and annual percent changes in M2.

Data availability

Estimates are released weekly in Federal Reserve Statistical Release H.6, "Money Stock, Liquid Assets, and Debt Measures." and are subsequently published each month in the *Federal Reserve Bulletin.* Historical data beginning with 1959 are available from Publications Services, Board of Governors of the Federal Reserve System. Current and historical data are available on the Federal Reserve internet site (http://www.bog.frb.fed.us/releases/).

References

The 1997 annual revisions are described in the April 1997 issue of *Federal Reserve Bulletin,* pages 260-264 and the 1996 annual revisions in the April 1996 issue, pages 327-331. An explanation of the redefined monetary aggregates is found in the *Federal Reserve Bulletin* for February 1980.

Page 96

Aggregate Reserves of Depository Institutions and Monetary Base

Source: Board of Governors of the Federal Reserve System

The data presented here are in millions of dollars, seasonally adjusted, and adjusted for changes in reserve requirements ("break-adjusted"). Monthly data are averages of daily figures. Annual data are for December.

Definitions

Total reserves consists of reserve balances with Federal Reserve Banks plus vault cash used to satisfy reserve requirements. Seasonally adjusted break-adjusted total reserves equal seasonally adjusted, break-adjusted required reserves plus unadjusted excess reserves.

Seasonally adjusted, break-adjusted *nonborrowed reserves* equal seasonally adjusted, break-adjusted total reserves less unadjusted total borrowings of depository institutions from the Federal Reserve.

Extended credit consists of borrowing at the discount window under the terms and conditions established for the extended credit program to help depository institutions deal with sustained liquidity pressures. Because there is not the same need to repay such borrowing promptly as there is with traditional short-term adjustment credit, the money market impact of extended credit is similar to that of nonborrowed reserves.

To adjust *required reserves* for discontinuities due to regulatory changes in reserve requirements, a multiplicative procedure is used to estimate what required reserves would have been in past periods had current reserve requirements been in effect. Break-adjusted required reserves are equal to break-adjusted required reserves against transactions deposits.

The seasonally adjusted, break-adjusted *monetary base* consists of (1) seasonally adjusted, break-adjusted total reserves plus (2) the seasonally adjusted currency component of the money stock plus (3), for all quarterly reporters on the "Report of Transaction Accounts, Other Deposits and Vault Cash" and for all those weekly reporters whose vault cash exceeds their required reserves, the seasonally adjusted, break-adjusted difference between current vault cash and the amount applied to satisfy current reserve requirements.

Data availability

Data are released weekly in Federal Reserve release H.3 and subsequently published in the *Federal Reserve Bulletin.* Historical data are available from the Money and Reserves Projections Section, Division of Monetary Affairs, Board of Governors of the Federal Reserve System, Washington, D.C. 20551. Current and historical data also are available on the Federal Reserve internet site (http://www.bog.frb.fed.us/releases/).

Pages 96-98

Assets and Liabilities of Commercial Banks

Source: Board of Governors of the Federal Reserve System

These data series on the assets and liabilities of commercial banks were introduced by the Federal Reserve in March 1994, replacing several discontinued data sets as noted below. Weekly data are Wednesday figures; monthly data are pro rata averages of the weekly figures. Annual data are for December.

Definitions and notes on the data

The current Federal Reserve data set H.8, Assets and Liabilities of Commercial Banks in the United States, was introduced in March 1994. It incorporates key items from three statistical releases that are discontinued: the previous version of the H.8, Assets and Liabilities of Insured Domestically Chartered and ForeignRelated Institutions; the G.7, Loans and Securities at Commercial Banks; and the G.10, Major Nondeposit Funds of Commercial Banks. The new data series are available beginning with 1988.

The new H.8 contains monthly and weekly balance sheets for all commercial banks, domestically chartered banks, small domestic banks, large domestic banks, and foreignrelated institutions. The data are adjusted for known reclassifications between balance sheet items and are presented both seasonally adjusted and not seasonally adjusted. For small and large domestic banks, the data are presented both as reported (actual levels) and after adjustment for mergers between banks in the small and large groups.

The data for *all commercial banks in the United States* covers the following types of institutions in the 50 states and the District of Columbia: domestically chartered commercial banks that submit a weekly report of condition (large domestic); other domestically chartered commercial banks (small domestic); branches and agencies of foreign banks, New York State investment companies, and Edge Act corporations (foreign-related institutions). International banking facilities are excluded. Large domestic banks constitute a universe; small domestic and foreignrelated institutions are estimated based on weekly samples and on quarter-end condition reports. Data are adjusted for breaks caused by reclassifications of assets and liabilities.

Loans and leases in bank credit excludes federal funds sold to, reverse repurchase agreements with, and loans to commercial banks in the United States.

Security loans consists of reverse repurchase agreements with broker-dealers and loans to purchase and carry securities.

Interbank loans consists of federal funds sold to, reverse repurchase agreements with, and loans to commercial banks in the United States.

Cash assets includes vault cash, cash items in process of collection, demand balances due from depository institutions in the United States, balances due from Federal Reserve Banks, and other cash assets.

Other assets and other liabilities exclude the duefrom position with related foreign offices, which is included in net due to related foreign offices.

Total assets excludes unearned income, reserves for losses on loans and leases, and reserves for transfer risk.

Residual: Assets less liabilities. This balancing item is not intended as a measure of equity capital for use in capital adequacy analysis. On a seasonally adjusted basis this item reflects any differences in the seasonal patterns estimated for total assets and total liabilities.

Revisions

In February 1997, data were benchmarked to the September 1996 Call report, and seasonal factors for bank assets and liabilities were reestimated to incorporate data for 1996.

Data availability

Assets and Liabilities of Commercial Banks, Federal Reserve release H.8, is released each Friday around 4:30 P.M. eastern time. Selected data are subsequently published in the *Federal Reserve Bulletin*. Historical data may be purchased on diskette from Publications Services, Board of Governors of the Federal Reserve System. Current and historical data are available on the Federal Reserve internet site (http://www.bog.frb.fed.us/releases/).

Pages 99-100 and 306-309

Interest Rates, Bond Yields, Stock Prices, and Yields

Sources: Board of Governors of the Federal Reserve System; Moody's Investors Service; The Bond Buyer; Dow Jones, Inc.; Standard and Poor's Corporation; New York Stock Exchange.

Definitions and notes on the data

Interest rates and bond yields are percents per year and are averages of business day figures, except as noted.

Federal funds. The daily effective federal funds rate is a weighted average of rates on trades through New York brokers. Monthly figures include each calendar day in the month. Annualized figures use a 360-day year.

The *Federal Reserve discount rate* is the rate for discount window borrowing at the Federal Reserve Bank of New York. Annualized figures use a 360-day year.

Eurodollar deposits. The rate shown is the bid rates for Eurodollar deposits at 11 A.M. London time for one-month deposits.

U.S. Treasury bills, 3-month. The rates shown are auction averages; the monthly averages are computed on an issue-date basis. The rates are quoted on a discount basis and annualized figures use a 360-day year.

Bankers' acceptances, 3-month. The rates shown are representative closing yields for acceptances of the highest rated money center banks. The rates are quoted on a discount basis and annualized figures use a 360-day year.

CDs (secondary market), 3-month. The rates shown are an average of dealer offering rates on nationally traded certificates of deposit. Annualized figures use a 360-day year.

Commercial paper, 6-month. The rates shown are an average of offering rates on commercial paper placed by several leading dealers for firms whose bond rating is AA or the equivalent. The rates are quoted on a discount basis and annualized figures use a 360- day year.

Finance company paper, 6-month. The rates shown are an average of offering rates on paper directly placed by finance companies. The rates are quoted on a discount basis and annualized figures use a 360-day year.

The *bank prime rate* is one of several base rates used by banks to price shortterm business loans. Monthly and annual figures include each calendar day in the month or year.

U.S. Treasury securities. The rates shown for 1-year, 10-year, and 30-year securities are yields on actively traded issues adjusted to constant maturities. Yields on Treasury securities at 'constant maturity' are interpolated by the U.S. Treasury from the daily yield curve. This curve, which relates the yield on a security to its time to maturity, is based on the closing market bid yields on actively traded Treasury securities in the over-the-counter market. These market yields are calculated from composites of quotations reported by five leading U.S. government securities dealers to the Federal Reserve Bank of New York. The constant maturity yield values are read from the yield curve at fixed maturities, currently 1, 2, 3, 5, 7, 10, 20, and 30 years. This method provides a yield for a 10-year maturity, for example, even if no outstanding security has exactly 10 years remaining

to maturity. The *long-term composite* is the unweighted average of rates on all outstanding bonds neither due nor callable in less than 10 years.

Domestic corporate bond yields. The rates shown are for general obligation bonds based on Thursday figures and are provided by Moody's Investors Service and republished by the Federal Reserve.

A-rated utility bonds. The rate shown is an estimate compiled by the Federal Reserve of the yield on a recently offered, Arated utility bond with a maturity of 30 years and call protection of five years; Friday quotations.

State and local bond yields. The rates shown are the Bond Buyer index as republished by the Federal Reserve. The index is based on 20 state and local government general obligation bonds maturing in 20 years or less.

Fixed rate mortgages. The rates shown are contract interest rates on commitments for fixed-rate first mortgages. The rate are obtained by the Federal Reserve from the Federal Home Loan Mortgage Corporation (FHLMC).

Stock price indexes. The Dow Jones industrial average is an average of 30 stocks compiled by Dow Jones, Inc. The Standard and Poor's composite is an index of 500 stocks based on 1941-1943=10 compiled by Standard and Poor's Corporation. The New York Stock Exchange indexes are compiled by the New York Stock Exchange and are based on December 31, 1965=50, except for the utility index, which is based on December 31, 1965=100. The monthly and annual data are averages of daily figures.

Data availability

Interest rates and bond yields are published weekly in the Federal Reserve's H.15 release. Most are subsequently published in the *Federal Reserve Bulletin* as are the stock indexes. The starting dates for individual interest rate series vary; some date back to 1911, and many begin in the 1950's and 1960's.

Historical data may be purchased on diskette from Publications Services, Board of Governors of the Federal Reserve System. Current and historical data are available on the Federal Reserve internet site (http://www.bog.frb.fed.us/releases/).

Pages 102-106 and 255-258

International Transactions

Source: U.S. Department of Commerce, Bureau of Economic Analysis

The U.S. international transactions accounts, or "balance of payments", provide a comprehensive view of economic transactions between the United States and foreign countries. The accounts include estimates of exports and imports of goods and of travel, transportation, and other services; foreign aid; and private and official capital flows, including direct investment. Data in the accounts have undergone extensive revision in the last few years due to the development of improved data sources and methodology. The detailed categories of service exports and imports are shown in the table on pages 121-122 and discussed in the Notes for pages107-122.

Definitions

Credits (+). The following items are treated as credits in the international transactions accounts: exports of goods and services; income received on U.S. assets abroad; unilateral transfers to the United States; capital inflows (i.e., increases in foreign assets in the United States and decreases in U.S. assets abroad); decreases in U.S. official reserve assets; and increases in foreign official assets in the United States.

Debits (-). The following items are treated as debits in the international transactions accounts, indicated by minus signs in the data cells: Imports of goods and services; income payments on foreign assets in the United States; unilateral transfers to foreigners; capital outflows (i.e., decreases in foreign assets in the United States and

increases in U.S. assets abroad); increases in U.S. official reserve assets; and decreases in foreign official assets in the United States.

The *balance on goods* is the excess of exports of goods over imports of goods (a minus sign indicates an excess of imports over exports).

The *balance on services* is the excess of service exports over service imports (a minus sign indicates an excess of imports over exports).

The *balance on goods and services* is the sum of the balance on goods and the balance on services.

The *balance on investment income* is the excess of income receipts on U.S. assets abroad over income payments on foreign assets in the United States (a minus sign indicates an excess of payments over receipts).

The *balance on goods, services, and income* is the excess of exports of goods, services, and income over imports of goods, services, and income (a minus sign indicates an excess of imports over exports). It is equal to the sum of the balance on goods and services and the balance on investment income.

The *balance on unilateral transfers* is equal to unilateral transfers, net.

The *balance on current account* is equal to the sum of the balance on goods, services, and income and the balance on unilateral transfers.

Notes on the data

Exports and imports of goods exclude exports of goods under U.S. military agency sales contracts identified in Census export documents, and imports of goods under direct defense expenditures identified in Census import documents, and reflect various other adjustments (for valuation, coverage, and timing) of Census statistics to a balance of payments basis.

Services include some goods. Mainly, military equipment (included in transfers under military agency sales

contracts); major equipment, other materials, supplies, and petroleum products purchased abroad by U.S. military agencies (included in direct defense expenditures abroad); and fuels purchased by airline and steamship operators (included in other transportation).

Transfers under U.S. military agency sales contracts includes transfers of goods and services under U.S. military grant programs.

Private remittances and other transfers includes taxes paid by U.S. private residents to foreign governments and taxes paid by private nonresidents to the U.S. government beginning in 1982.

Direct investment and direct investment income. Beginning with the data for 1982, direct investment income and the reinvested earnings component of direct investment capital are measured on a current-cost (replacement-cost) basis after adjustment to reported depreciation, depletion, and expensed exploration and development costs. For prior years, depreciation is valued in terms of the historical cost of assets and reflects a mix of prices for the various years in which capital investments were made. See *Survey of Current Business*, June 1992, pages 72ff.

Repayments on U.S. credit and other long-term assets includes sales of foreign obligations to foreigners. The data for 1974 include extraordinary U.S. government transactions with India, described in "Special U.S. Government Transactions," *Survey of Current Business,* June 1974, page 27.

Foreign official assets in the United States. U.S. Treasury securities consists of bills, certificates, marketable bonds and notes, and nonmarketable convertible and nonconvertible bonds and notes; *other U.S. government securities* consists of U.S. Treasury and Export-Import Bank obligations, not included elsewhere, and of debt securities of U.S. government corporations and agencies; *other*

U.S. government liabilities includes, primarily, U.S. government liabilities associated with military agency sales contracts and other transactions arranged with or through foreign official agencies; *other foreign official assets* consists of investments in U.S. corporate stocks and in debt securities of private corporations and state and local governments.

Other foreign assets in the United States; U.S. Treasury securities and U.S. currency flows. As part of the July 1997 revisions, estimates of U.S. currency flows abroad were introduced for the first time. Data for 1974 and subsequent years are affected (see *Survey of Current Business*, July 1997). For 197883, U.S. treasury securities includes foreign currencydenominated notes sold to private residents abroad.

Relation of balance on current account to net foreign investment. Conceptually, "net foreign investment" in the national income and product accounts (NIPAs) is equal to the balance on current account plus allocation of special drawing rights. However, the foreign transactions account in the NIPAs (a) includes adjustments to the international transactions accounts for the treatment of gold, (b) includes adjustments for the different geographical treatment of transactions with U.S. territories and Puerto Rico, and (c) includes services furnished without payment by financial pension plans except life insurance carriers and private noninsured pension plans. A reconciliation of the balance on goods and services from the international accounts and the NIPA net exports appears periodically in the "Reconciliation and Other Special Tables" section of the *Survey of Current Business*. A reconciliation of the other foreign transactions in the two sets of accounts appears in Table 4.5 of the NIPA tables.

Recent revisions

Historical revisions published in July 1997 include:

- improved estimates of U.S. investment income receipts, based on results of a Treasury Department

benchmark survey of U.S. portfolio investment abroad;

- for the first time, estimates of U.S. currency flows abroad, beginning with 1974;

- preliminary results of BEA's 1995 and 1996 annual surveys of international transactions in financial services; and

- preliminary results of BEA's 1996 benchmark survey of selected services (largely business, professional, and technical services).

Data availability

Quarterly and annual data are available. Data first are reported in a press release and subsequently published in the *Survey of Current Business*. Revisions to historical data are published annually. The most recent historical revisions appear in the July 1997 issue of the *Survey*. Complete historical data may be purchased on diskette from BEA. Current data are available on the BEA internet site (http://www.bea.doc.gov).

References

Discussions of the impact of changes in methodology and incorporation of new data sources are found in the June (or, for 1996 and 1997, July) issues of the *Survey of Current Business*, the most recent being "U.S. International Transactions, Revised Estimates for 1974-96" (July 1997).

The Balance of Payments of the United States: Concepts, Data Sources, and Estimating Procedures (1990, NTIS Accession No. PB 90-268715) describes the methodology in detail and provides a list of data sources.

Pages 107-122

Exports and Imports of Goods and Services

Sources: U.S. Department of Commerce, Bureau of the Census and Bureau of Economic Analysis (BEA)

Monthly and annual data on exports and imports of goods are compiled by the Bureau of the Census from documents collected by the U.S. Customs service. BEA makes certain adjustment to these data (described below) to place the estimates on a "balance of payments" basis—a basis consistent with the national and international accounts. Data on exports and imports of services are prepared by BEA from a variety of sources. Monthly data on services are available from the beginning of 1992. Annual and quarterly data for earlier years are available as part of the International Transactions Accounts. Current data on goods and services are available each month in a joint Census-BEA press release.

Definitions—Goods

Goods: Census Basis. The Census basis goods data are compiled from the documents collected by the U.S. Customs Service and reflect the movement of goods between foreign countries and the 50 states, the District of Columbia, Puerto Rico, the U.S. Virgin Islands, and U.S. Foreign Trade Zones. They include government and nongovernment shipments of goods, and exclude shipments between the United States and its territories and possessions, transactions with U.S. military, diplomatic, and consular installations abroad, U.S. goods returned to the United States by its Armed Forces, personal and household effects of travelers, and intransit shipments. The general imports value reflects the total arrival of merchandise from foreign countries that immediately enters consumption channels, warehouses, or Foreign Trade Zones.

For *imports,* the value reported is the U. S. Customs Service appraised value of merchandise, generally, the price paid for merchandise for export to the United States. Import duties, freight, insurance, and other charges incurred in bringing merchandise to the United States are excluded.

Exports are valued at the f.a.s. (free alongside ship) value of merchandise at the U.S. port of export, based on the transaction price including inland freight, insurance and other charges incurred in placing the merchandise alongside the carrier at the U.S. port of exportation.

Goods: Balance of payments (BOP) basis. Goods on a Census basis are adjusted by the BEA to goods on a BOP basis to bring the data in line with the concepts and definitions used to prepare the international and national accounts. Broadly, the adjustments include changes in ownership that occur without goods passing into or out of the customs territory of the United States. These adjustments are necessary to supplement coverage of the Census basis data, to eliminate duplication of transactions recorded elsewhere in the international accounts, and to value transactions according to a standard definition.

The *export* adjustments include *U.S. military sales contracts*. This deduction of U.S. military sales contracts is made because the Census Bureau has included these contracts in the goods data, but BEA includes them in the service category "Transfers Under U.S. Military Sales Contracts." BEA's source material for these contracts is more comprehensive, but has no distinction between goods and services. *Private gift parcels.* This addition is made for parcels mailed to foreigners by individuals through the U.S. Postal Service. (Only commercial shipments are covered in Census goods exports.) *Gold exports, nonmonetary.* This addition is made for gold that is purchased by foreign official agencies from private dealers in the United States and held at the Federal Reserve Bank of New York. The Census data only include gold that leaves the customs territory. *Smaller adjustments.* These include deductions for repairs of goods, exposed motion picture film, and military grant-aid, additions for sales of fish in U.S. territorial waters, exports of electricity to Mexico, and vessels and oil rigs that change ownership for which no export document is filed.

The *import* adjustments include *inland freight in Canada*. The customs value for imports for certain Canadian goods is the point of origin in Canada. The BEA makes an addition for the inland freight charges of transporting these Canadian goods to the U.S. border. *Gold imports, nonmonetary.* This addition is made for gold sold by foreign official agencies to private purchasers out of stock held at the Federal Reserve Bank of New York. The Census data only includes gold that enters the customs territory. *Imports by U.S. military agencies.* This deduction of U.S. military sales contracts is made because the Census Bureau has included these contracts in the goods data, but BEA includes them in the service category "Direct Defense Expenditures." BEA's source material is more comprehensive, but has no distinction between goods and services. *Smaller adjustments.* These include deductions for repairs of goods, and exposed motion picture film; additions for imported electricity from Mexico, conversion of vessels for commercial use, and repairs to U.S. vessels abroad.

Definitions—Services

Services. The statistics are estimates of services transactions between foreign countries and the 50 states, the District of Columbia, Puerto Rico, the U.S. Virgin Islands, and other U.S. territories and possessions. Transactions with U.S. military, diplomatic, and consular installations abroad are excluded because they are considered to be part of the U.S. economy. Services are shown in seven broad categories, described below. For six of these, the categories are the same for imports and exports. For the seventh, exports is "Transfers under U.S. Military Sales Contracts" while for imports the category is "Direct Defense Expenditures."

Travel. Purchases of services and goods by U.S. travelers abroad and by foreign visitors to the United States. A traveler is defined as a person who stays for a period of less than one year in a country of which the person is not a resident. Includes expenditures for food, lodging, recreation, gifts, and other items incidental to a foreign visit.

Passenger fares. Fares paid by residents of one country to residents in other countries. Receipts consist of fares received by U.S. carriers from foreign residents for travel between the United States and foreign countries and between two foreign points. Payments consist of fares paid by U.S. residents to foreign carriers for travel between the United States and foreign countries.

Travel and passenger fares: Break in series. Beginning with data for 1984, these items incorporate results from a survey administered by the U.S. Travel and Tourism Administration. See *Survey of Current Business,* June 1989, pages 57ff.

Other transportation. Charges for the transportation of goods by ocean, air, waterway, pipeline, and rail carriers to and from the United States. Includes freight charges, operating expenses that transportation companies incur in foreign ports, and payments for vessel charter and aircraft and freight car rentals. *Break in series.* Estimates of freight charges for the transportation of goods by truck between the United States and Canada are included in the data beginning with 1986. Reliable estimates for earlier years are not available. See *Survey of Current Business,* June 1994, pages 70ff.

Royalties and license fees. Transactions with foreign residents involving intangible assets and proprietary rights, such as the use of patents, techniques, processes, formulas, designs, know-how, trademarks, copyrights, franchises, and manufacturing rights. The term "royalties" generally refers to payments for the utilization of copyrights or trademarks, and the term "license fees" generally refers to payments for the use of patents or industrial processes.

Other private services. Transactions with affiliated foreigners for which no identification by type is available and transactions with unaffiliated foreigners. (The term "affiliated" refers to a direct investment relationship, which exists when a U.S. person has ownership or control, directly or indirectly, of 10 percent or more of a foreign business enterprise, or when a foreign person has a similar interest in a U.S. enterprise.) Transactions with unaffiliated foreigners consist of education services; financial services; insurance premiums and losses; telecommunications services; and business, professional, and technical services. Included in the last group are advertising services; computer and data processing services; database and other information services; research, development, and testing services; management, consulting, and public relations services; legal services; construction, engineering, architectural, and mining services; industrial engineering services; installation, maintenance, repair of equipment; and other services, including medical services and film and tape rental.

BEA conducts surveys of international transactions in financial services and "selected services" (largely business, professional, and technical services). Beginning with data for 1986, *other private services* includes estimates of business, professional, and technical services from the BEA surveys of selected service. (See *Survey of Current Business*, June 1989, pages 57ff.) The July 1997 revisions to trade in services incorporate preliminary results of the 1995 and 1996 annual surveys of financial services and the 1996 benchmark survey of selected services. See *Survey of Current Business*, July 1997.

Royalties and license fees and other private services: Breaks in series. These items are presented on a gross basis beginning in 1982. The definition of exports is revised to exclude U.S. parents' payments to foreign affiliates and to include U.S. affiliates' receipts from foreign parents. The definition of imports is revised to include U.S. parents' payments to foreign affiliates and to exclude U.S. affiliates' receipts from foreign parents.

Transfers under U.S. military sales contracts (Exports only). Exports of goods and services in which U.S. government military agencies participate. Includes both goods, such as equipment, and services, and repair services and training, that cannot be separately identified.

Direct defense expenditures (Imports only). Expenditures incurred by U.S. military agencies abroad, including expenditures by U.S. personnel, payments of wages to foreign residents, construction expenditures, payments for foreign contractual services, and procurement of foreign goods. Includes both goods and services that cannot be separately identified.

U.S. government miscellaneous services. Transactions of U.S. government nonmilitary agencies with foreign residents. Most of these transactions involve the provision of services to, or purchases of services from, foreigners; transfers of some goods are also included.

Services estimates are based on quarterly, annual, and benchmark surveys and partial information generated from monthly reports. Service transactions are estimated at market prices. Estimates are seasonally adjusted when statistically significant seasonal patterns are present.

Definitions: Area groupings

North America—Canada, Mexico

South/Central America—Anguilla, Antigua and Barbuda, Argentina, Aruba, Bahamas, Barbados, Belize, Bermuda, Bolivia, Brazil, British Virgin Islands, Cayman Islands, Chile, Colombia, Costa Rica, Cuba, Dominica, Dominican Republic, Ecuador, El Salvador, Falkland Islands, French Guiana, Grenada, Guadeloupe, Guatemala, Guyana, Haiti, Honduras, Jamaica, Martinique, Montserrat, Netherlands Antilles, Nicaragua, Panama, Paraguay, Peru, St. Kitts and Nevis, St. Lucia, St. Vincent and the Grenadines, Suriname, Trinidad and Tobago, Turks and Caicos Islands, Uruguay, Venezuela.

Western Europe—Andorra, Austria, Belgium, BosniaHercegovina, Croatia, Cyprus, Denmark, Faroe Islands, Finland, France, Germany, Gibralter, Greece, Iceland, Ireland, Italy, Liechtenstein, Luxembourg, Malta and Gozo, Macedonia, Monaco, Netherlands, Norway, Portugal, San Marino, Slovenia, Spain, Svalbard, Jan Septemberen Island, Sweden, Switzerland, Turkey, United Kingdom, Vatican City, Yugoslavia.

European Union—Austria, Belgium, Denmark, Finland, France, Germany, Greece, Ireland, Italy, Luxembourg, Netherlands, Portugal, Spain, Sweden, United Kingdom.

European Free Trade Association—Iceland, Liechtenstein, Norway, Sweden, Switzerland.

Eastern Europe and former Soviet Republics—Albania, Armenia, Azerbaijan, Belarus, Bulgaria, Czech Republic, Estonia, Georgia, Hungary, Kazakhstan, Kyrgyzstan, Latvia, Lithuania, Moldova, Poland, Romania, Russia, Slovakia, Tajikistan, Turkmenistan, Ukraine, Uzbekistan.

ASEAN—Association of Southeast Asian Nations: Brunei, Indonesia, Malaysia, Philippines, Singapore, Thailand.

MERCOSUR (Southern Common Market)—Argentina, Brazil, Paraguay, Uruguay.

Central American Common Market—Costa Rica, El Salvador, Guatemala, Honduras, Nicaragua.

Newly Industrialized Countries—Hong Kong, South Korea, Singapore, Taiwan.

Organization of Petroleum Exporting Countries (OPEC)—Algeria, Gabon, Indonesia, Iran, Iraq, Kuwait, Libya, Nigeria, Qatar, Saudi Arabia, United Arab Emirates, Venezuela.

Pacific Rim Countries—Australia, Brunei, China, Hong Kong, Indonesia, Japan, Korea, Macao, Malaysia, New Zealand, Papua New Guinea, Philippines, Singapore, Taiwan.

Notes on the data

U.S./Canada data exchange and substitution. The data for U.S. exports to Canada are derived from import data compiled by Canada. The use of Canada's import data to produce U.S. export data requires several alignments in order to compare the two series: *Coverage*—Canadian imports are based on country of origin. U.S. goods shipped from a third country are included. U.S. exports exclude these foreign shipments. U.S. export coverage also excludes certain Canadian postal shipments. *Valuation*—Canadian imports are valued at point of origin in the United States. However, U.S. exports are valued at the port of exit in the United States and include inland freight charges, making the U.S. export value slightly larger. Canada requires inland freight to be reported. When it is not, an estimate of 4.5 percent is used. *Reexports*—U.S. exports include reexports of foreign goods. Again, the aggregate U.S. export figure is slightly larger. *Exchange Rate*—Average monthly exchange rates are applied to convert the published data to U.S. currency.

End-use categories and seasonal adjustment of trade in goods. Goods are initially classified under the Harmonized System (HS) which describes and measures the characteristics of goods traded. Combining trade into approximately 140 export and 140 import enduse categories makes it possible to examine goods according to their principal uses. These categories are used as the basis for computing the seasonal and workingday adjusted data. These adjusted data are then summed to the six enduse aggregates for publication.

The seasonal adjustment procedure is based on a model which estimates the monthly movements as percentages above or below the general level of each enduse commodity series (unlike other methods that redistribute the actual series values over the calendar year). Imports of petroleum and petroleum products are adjusted for the length of the month.

Data availability

Data are released in a joint Census-BEA press release (FT-900) each month about six weeks after the end of the month to which the data pertain. The data on trade in goods by end-use category (BOP basis) and trade in services are subsequently published each month in the *Survey of Current Business.* Additional data and information on goods is obtainable from: Foreign Trade Division, Bureau of the Census, Washington, DC 20233. Additional data and information on services is obtainable from: Balance of Payments Division, Bureau of Economic Analysis, Washington, DC 20230. Current releases and some historical data are available on the Bureau of the Census internet site (http://www.census.gov/ foreign-trade/www/).

Revisions

Data for recent years normally are revised annually. Data on trade in services may be subject to extensive revision as part of BEA's annual revision of the international transactions accounts, usually released each June or July. In July 1997, "other" private service receipts and payments were revised to include preliminary results of BEA's annual surveys of financial services for 1995 and 1996. These were BEA's first annual surveys of financial services, and they update the results of BEA's first benchmark survey, covering 1994. Also incorporated at that time were preliminary results from BEA's 1996 benchmark survey of selected services (largely business, professional, and technical services) and other changes to the trade in services estimates.

References

Discussion of the impact of changes in methodology and incorporation of new data sources are found in discussions of annual revisions of the international transactions accounts in the June or July issue of the BEA publication, *Survey of Current Business,* the most recent being "U.S. International Transactions, Revised Estimates for 1974-96" (July 1997).

Page 122

Export and Import Price Indexes

Source: U.S. Department of Labor, Bureau of Labor Statistics (BLS)

The BLS International Price Program produces monthly and quarterly export and import price indexes for nonmilitary goods traded between the United States and the rest of the world.

Definitions

The *export* price index provides a measure of price change for all products sold by U.S. residents (i.e., businesses and individuals located within the geographic boundaries of the United States, whether or not owned by U.S. citizens) to foreign buyers.

The *import* price index provides a measure of price change for goods purchased from other countries by U.S. residents.

Notes on the data

The product universe for both the import and export indexes includes raw materials, agricultural products, and manufactures. Price data are collected primarily by mail questionnaire, in all but a few cases directly from the exporter or importer.

To the extent possible, the data refer to prices at the U.S. border for exports and at either the foreign border or the U.S. border for imports. For nearly all products, the prices refer to transactions completed during the first week of the month and represent the actual price for which the product was bought or sold, including discounts, allowances, and rebates.

The indexes are weighted indexes of the Laspeyres type. The values assigned to each weight category are based on trade value figures compiled by the Bureau of the Census. The weights currently used refer to 1990. Adjustments are made to account for changes in product characteristics in order to obtain a "pure" measure of price change.

For the export price indexes, the preferred pricing basis is f.a.s. (free alongside ship) U.S. port of exportation. Where necessary, adjustments are made to reported prices to place them on this basis. An attempt is made to collect two prices for imports: f.o.b. (free on board) at the port of exportation and c.i.f. (cost, insurance, and freight) at the U.S. port of importation.

Data availability

Indexes are published monthly in a press release and a more detailed report. Selected data are subsequently published in the *Monthly Labor Review.* Indexes are published for detailed product categories as well as for all commodities. Aggregate import indexes by country or region of origin also are available, as are indexes for selected categories of internationally traded services. Additional information is available from the Division of International Prices, Bureau of Labor Statistics. Complete historical data are available on the BLS internet site (http://stats.bls.gov).

References

"BLS to Produce Monthly Indexes of Export and Import Prices" *Monthly Labor Review* (December 1988) and Chapter 15 "International Price Indexes," *BLS Handbook of Methods* Bulletin 2490 (April 1997).

Pages 124-126

International Comparisons: Production, Prices, Stock Indexes, and Exchange Rates

Source: U.S. Department of Commerce, Bureau of Economic Analysis (BEA) and The Conference Board

These international comparisons, formerly published monthly in the Business Cycle Indicators section of the *Survey of Current Business,* are now published by The Conference Board, which has taken over the business cycle indicators program from BEA (see the Notes to pages 9-11). Original sources of the data are listed below.

Notes on the data

In January 1997 the data for *industrial production, consumer prices, and stock price indexes* were revised to reflect use of the International Monetary Fund (IMF) as the data source and to place all data on a base of 1990=100.

Exchange rates. The exchange value of the U.S. dollar is an index of the weighted-average value of the U.S. dollar against currencies of 10 industrial countries. The data for the other currencies are their exchange rates per U.S. dollar. Data are from the Board of Governors of the Federal Reserve System.

Data availability

Data are published each month by the Conference Board. Their monthly report *Business Cycle Indicators* is available by subscription from: The Conference Board, 845 Third Avenue, New York, NY 10022. Full historical data are available by subscription from The Conference Board internet site (http://www.tcb-indicators.org).

References

Handbook of Cyclical Indicators (Bureau of Economic Analysis, 1984).

Pages 130-134

Mining Industries

Sources: Industrial production and capacity utilization—Board of Governors of the Federal Reserve System (see Notes to pages 22-35); producer prices and employment, hours, and earnings: U.S. Department of Labor, Bureau of Labor Statistics (see Notes to pages 53-57 and 73-91).

Mining (SIC Division B) includes all establishments primarily engaged in mining. The term mining is used in the broad sense to include the extraction of naturally occurring solids (such as coals and ores), liquids (such as crude petroleum), and gases (such as natural gas). Quarrying, well operations, and other preparation customarily done at the mine site are included, as are exploration and development of mineral properties.

Oil and gas extraction (SIC Major Group 13) is classified in mining and includes producing crude petroleum and natural gas, extracting oil from oil sands and shale, producing natural gas and cycle condensate, and producing gas and hydrocarbon liquids from coal at the mine site. Petroleum refining is classified in Manufacturing, Major Group 39. Pipeline transportation of oil and gas is classified in Division E, Transportation.

Notes on the data

Industrial production and capacity utilization. These indexes are for industry groups as defined by the SIC code. The indexes for *total mining* cover SIC Division B as described above; *metal mining* covers Major Group 10, which includes mining for iron, copper, lead, zinc, gold, silver, and ferroalloy ores; *coal mining* covers SIC Major Group 12, which includes mining for bituminous coal and lignite and anthracite coal; *oil and gas extraction* covers Major Group 13, which includes extraction of crude oil and natural gas, production of natural gas liquids, and oil field services; *crude oil and natural gas* covers SIC 131, oil and gas extraction; *natural gas liquids* is SIC 132; and *oil and gas well drilling* is SIC 138, which also includes other oil and gas field services. *Stone and earth minerals* is Major Group 14, which includes mining and quarrying of stone, sand and gravel, clay, and chemical and fertilizer minerals.

The *producer price* indexes and *employment, hours, and earnings* data for metal mining and coal mining cover SICs 10 and 12 respectively; *oil and gas extraction* covers SIC 13; the indexes for crude materials use the stage-of-processing classification. The data for *nonmetallic minerals except fuel* cover SIC 14.

Pages 135

Petroleum and Petroleum Products—Imports and Stocks

Sources: Imports—U.S. Department of Commerce, Bureau of the Census (see Notes to pages 107-122); Stocks—U.S. Department of Energy, Energy Information Administration.

Notes on the data

The import data are published as Exhibit 17, "Imports of Energy-related Petroleum Products, including Crude Petroleum" of the monthly Census-BEA foreign trade press release. *Total energy-related petroleum products* include the following SITC commodity groupings: crude oil, petroleum preparations, and liquified propane and butane gas.

The data on petroleum stocks are derived from the Department of Energy's weekly petroleum supply reporting system and are published in the Energy Information Administration publication "Petroleum Supply Monthly." Stock totals are as of the end of the period. Geographic coverage includes the 50 states and the District of Columbia.

Data availability

Data on stocks are available from the Energy Information Administration internet site (http://www.eia.doe.gov). See the Notes to pages 107-122 for availability of import data.

Page 138-139

Construction Costs, Prices, Employment, Hours, and Earnings

Sources: Construction cost indexes— U.S. Department of Commerce, Bureau of the Census; producer prices; employment, hours, and earnings— U.S. Department of Labor, Bureau of Labor Statistics (see Notes to pages 53-57 and 73-91).

Construction (SIC Division C) includes establishments primarily engaged in construction, including new work, additions, alterations, reconstruction, installations, and repairs. Construction of buildings and heavy construction other than buildings are included. Specialized construction activities, such as plumbing, painting, and electrical work also are included.

General building contractors is SIC Major Group 15 and includes both residential and nonresidential building; heavy construction except building is Major Group16 and includes highways, pipelines, power lines, water mains, and other heavy construction; special trade contractors is Major Group 17 and includes plumbing, painting, carpentry, and other specialized building trades.

The *Construction Cost Indexes* are included in the Bureau of the Census "Construction Put in Place" release (C-30 release). See the Notes to pages 140-141 for additional information on availability.

Pages 140-141

Construction Put in Place

Source: U.S. Department of Commerce, Bureau of the Census

The Census Bureau's estimates of the value of new construction put in place are intended to provide monthly estimates of the total dollar value of construction work done in the U.S.

Definitions and notes on the data

The estimates cover all construction work done each month on new residential and nonresidential buildings and structures, public construction, and improvements to existing buildings and structures. Included are: the cost of labor and materials, cost of architectural and engineering work, overhead costs assigned to the project, interest and taxes paid during construction, and contractor's profits.

The estimates are composites based on mail-out/mail-back and interview

surveys of selected construction project and building owners and estimates developed or compiled from other Census Bureau, federal agency, and private data sources. Five surveys collect data used to estimate 65 percent of total monthly value of construction put in place; other estimates cover the remaining 35 percent of work done.

The Construction Progress Reporting Surveys are mailout/mailback surveys of owners of sampled construction projects that collect data on expenditures for three types of new construction: privatelyowned nonresidential buildings (e.g., office buildings and shopping malls), state and local construction projects (e.g., highways, schools, and housing), and privatelyowned apartment buildings.

Projects are selected using stratified random sample procedures. Private nonresidential and state and local projects are selected from lists compiled by the F.W. Dodge Company (and supplemented with a small sample of projects in nonpermit issuing areas), with strata based on type of construction and estimated project value. Apartment projects are a subsample of multiunit projects identified in the Survey of Construction, with strata based on building location and number of housing units. Owners of selected building projects report on the value of work done each month from project start through completion.

The Consumer Expenditure Survey (CES) and the Survey of Residential Alternations and Repairs (SORAR) collect quarterly data from residential building owners on expenditures for improvements and repairs. The CES is a personal interview survey of home owners. The SORAR is a mailout/ mailback survey of owners of rental or vacant residential buildings identified in the CES. Monthly value in place data are imputed and revised as quarterly results from both surveys become available.

Other estimates are developed or compiled for the value of construction done but not covered by surveys.

Examples include estimates of new home construction activity for houses identified in the Survey of Construction; and data on cable television construction obtained from industry trade association statistics.

Total private construction includes categories not shown separately, including residential improvements, railroads, electric light and power, gas, petroleum pipelines, and farm nonresidential.

Residential construction includes improvements.

Revisions

Data for 1992 and subsequent years were revised in May 1997. Information on the revisions is found in the May 1997 issue of the Bureau of the Census monthly publication "Current Construction Reports—Value of Construction Put in Place" (the C-30 Report). The full report is available on the Bureau of the Census internet site (see below).

Data availability

The construction put in place data are first issued as a monthly press release. A full report (the C-30 Report) follows. Data are shown by type of construction, seasonally adjusted and unadjusted, and in current and constant dollars. Statistics are available at the U.S. level monthly, and by the nine geographic divisions annually for selected categories. The Census Bureau has derived monthly estimates of new construction put in place since 1960.

Expenditures for residential improvements and repairs press releases are issued quarterly. An annual supplement shows data by specific kind of job (e.g., painting), and by region.

Current data and some historical data are available on the Bureau of the Census internet site (http://www.census.gov.const/www/).

Page 142

Housing Starts and Permits; New Home Sales

Source: U.S. Department of Commerce, Bureau of the Census

These data are from two Bureau of the Census Surveys. The *Building Permits Survey* provides current data on new construction, additions and alterations to existing buildings, and demolitions authorized by building permits. The *Survey of Construction* covers housing starts and completions and new home sales.

Notes on the data

The *Building Permits Survey* covers all places that issue permits to authorize new private residential buildings, or changes in or demolition of existing structures. Over 95 percent of all privatelyowned residential buildings constructed are in permitissuing places.

Data collected on permits issued for private projects include: number and permit valuation of housing units authorized by type of structure; number and valuation of additions, alterations, or conversions authorized; and number of residential buildings and housing units and nonresidential buildings authorized for demolition. Data are collected through a mailout/mailback monthly survey of selected permit-issuing places and an annual mail-out/mail-back census of the permit-issuing places that do not report monthly.

The *Survey of Construction* provides current data on starts and completions of new single- and multi-family housing units and sales of new one-family houses. It covers new residential buildings currently authorized by a building permit or started in areas not requiring a building permit. The data collected include start date, completion date, sale date, sales price (for single-family houses only), and physical characteristics of each housing unit, such as square footage and number of bedrooms. Data are collected through telephone or personal interviews.

Data on *mobile home shipments* are compiled from manufacturers' reports to the National Conference of States on Building Codes and Standards (NCSBCS).

Data availability

Housing start and building permit data have been collected by the Bureau of the Census monthly since 1959. Prior to 1959, building permit data were collected by the Bureau of Labor Statistics.

Housing Starts and Building Permits press releases contain the first available start and permit data and are released three weeks after the reference month. New One Family Homes Sold reports are released six weeks after the reference month and provide data on houses sold and for sale, average and median sale prices, and sale prices by type of financing. Both releases contain national and regional data.

Housing Starts reports are available four weeks after the reference period and Housing Units Authorized by Building Permits reports six weeks after. These contain more detailed data than the earlier press releases.

These reports are available on the Bureau of the Census internet site (http://www.census.gov.const/www/).

Pages 144-146

Total Manufacturing: Production, Capacity, Prices, Employment, Hours, and Earnings

Sources: Industrial production and capacity utilization—Board of Governors of the Federal Reserve System (see Notes to pages 22-35); producer prices and employment, hours, and earnings—U.S. Department of Labor, Bureau of Labor Statistics (see Notes to pages 53-57 and 73-91).

Manufacturing (SIC Division D) includes establishments engaged in the mechanical or chemical transformation of materials or substances into new products. These establishments typically are described as plants, factories, or mills. The Division is subdivided into 20 Major Groups, each of which is described briefly at the beginning of the Notes for the pages on which data for the group are presented.

There are numerous borderline cases between manufacturing and other divisions of the SIC. Logging, for example, is included in manufacturing, while threshing and cotton ginning fall under Agriculture, Forestry and Fishing. Dressing of ores and crushing and grinding of sand and gravel are classified under Mining. Production of computer software is classified under Services.

Notes on the data

Many data series divide manufacturing into durable and nondurable goods. *Durable goods* include SIC Major Groups 24, 25, and 32 through 39 (lumber and wood products, furniture and fixtures, stone clay and glass, primary metals industries, fabricated metal products, industrial and commercial machinery and computer equipment, electronic and other electrical equipment, transportation equipment, instruments, and miscellaneous manufactures). *Nondurable goods* include Major Groups 20 through 23 and 26 through 31 (food and kindred products, tobacco products, textile mill products, apparel and related products, paper and allied products, printing and publishing, chemicals, petroleum refining, rubber and miscellaneous plastic products, and leather and leather products).

Industrial production indexes are shown for primary processing and advance processing as well as for durable and nondurable manufacturing. *Primary processing* manufacturing includes textile mill products, paper and products, industrial chemicals, synthetic materials and fertilizers, petroleum products, rubber and plastic products, lumber and products, primary metals, fabricated metals, and stone, clay, and glass products. *Advanced processing* manufacturing includes foods, tobacco products, apparel products, printing and publishing,

chemical products and other agricultural chemicals, leather and products, furniture and fixtures, industrial machinery and equipment, electrical machinery, transportation equipment, instrument, and miscellaneous manufactures.

Pages 147-157

Manufacturers' Shipments, Inventories, and Orders

Source: U.S. Department of Commerce, Bureau of the Census

These data are from the Bureau of the Census monthly M3 survey, a survey covering all manufacturing and intended to provide broad and timely measures of changes in domestic manufacturing activity and indications of future production commitments.

Definitions and notes on the data

Shipments. The value of shipments data represents net selling values, f.o.b. (free on board) plant, after discounts and allowances and excluding freight charges and excise taxes. For multi-establishment companies, the M3 reports typically are company- or division-level reports that encompass groups of plants or products. The data reported are usually net sales and receipts from customers and do not include the value of interplant transfers. The reported sales are used to calculate month-to-month changes which bring forward the universe estimates developed from the Annual Survey of Manufactures (ASM). The value of products made elsewhere under contract from materials owned by the plant is also included in shipments as well as receipts for contract work performed for others, resales, miscellaneous activities such as the sale of scrap and refuse, installation and repair work performed by employees of the plant, and the receipts for research and development performed at the plant.

Inventories. Inventories in the M3 survey are collected on a current cost or pre-LIFO (last in, first out) basis. Because different inventory valuation

methods are reflected in the reported data, the estimates differ slightly from replacement cost estimates. Companies using the LIFO method for valuing inventories report their pre-LIFO value; that is, the adjustment to their base-period prices is excluded. In the ASM, inventories are collected according to this same definition. However, there are discontinuities in the historical data in both surveys. Inventory data prior to 1982 are not comparable to later years due to changes in valuation methods. Until 1982, respondents were asked in the ASM to report their inventories at book values; that is, according to whatever method they used for tax purposes (LIFO, FIFO, and so forth.) Because of this, the value of aggregate inventories for an industry was not precise. The change in instructions for reporting current cost inventories was carried to the monthly survey beginning in January 1987. The data for 1982 to 1987 were redefined (but not recollected) on a pre-LIFO or current cost basis.

Inventory data are requested from respondents by stage of fabrication; that is, finished goods, work in process, and raw materials and supplies. There are several limitations to the quality of these data for two reasons. First, response to the stage of fabrication inquiries is lower than for total inventories because all companies do not keep their data monthly at this level of detail; those companies which do maintain monthly detailed records frequently do not have data for all three stages of fabrication or have quantity (physical volume) data only. Second, a product considered to be a finished good in one industry, such as steel mills shapes, may be reported as a raw material in another industry, such as stamping plants. Therefore, within the two-digit SIC major groups the same type of inventory may be included under different stage of fabrication categories. Like total inventories, stage of fabrication inventories are also benchmarked to the ASM pre-LIFO data, but the stage of fabrication data are benchmarked at the two-digit major group level.

New orders received and unfilled orders. New orders, as reported in the monthly survey, are net of order cancellations and include orders received and filled during the month as well as orders received for future delivery. They also include the value of contract changes which increase or decrease the value of the unfilled orders to which they relate. Orders are defined to include those supported by binding legal documents such as signed contracts, letters of award, or letters of intent, although in some industries this definition may not be strictly applicable. Unfilled orders include orders (as defined above) that have not been reflected as shipments. Generally, unfilled orders at the end of the reporting period are equal to unfilled orders at the beginning of the period plus net new orders received less net shipments.

Coverage. The M3 survey covers companies that have employees and are classified in SIC Division D, Manufacturing. The monthly estimates are based on information obtained from most manufacturing companies with $500 million or more in annual shipments as well as from selected smaller companies.

Benchmarking and revisions

Data beginning with 1982 were revised in mid-1996. The revisions were the result of: (1) benchmarking the shipments and inventory data to the revised, drift adjusted, 1988-1991 ASM; 1992 Census of Manufactures; and 1993-1994 ASM; (2) benchmarking the defense shipments series to the 1992 MC9675, "Shipments to Federal Government Agencies;" (3) adjusting new and unfilled orders to be consistent with the benchmarked shipments and inventory data; (4) correcting monthly data for late receipts, reclassification of reported data, and revisions to previously reported data; (5) updating the trading day adjustment factors for the shipments series; and (6) updating the seasonal adjustment factors for all series, including re-evaluating options used.

Data beginning with 1987 were further revised in April 1997. The revisions reflect benchmarking to the 1994-1995 ASM, revision of seasonal factors, and other adjustments.

Data availability

Data have been collected monthly since 1958.

An Advance Report on Durable Goods Manufacturers' Shipments and Orders is available as a press release about 17 working days after the end of each month. Content includes seasonally and not seasonally adjusted estimates of shipments, new orders, and unfilled orders for durable goods industries.

The Manufacturers' Shipments, Inventories, and Orders reports are released about 22 working days after the end of each month. Content includes revisions to the advance report plus estimates for inventories and nondurable goods industries, tabulations by market category, and ratios of shipments to inventories and to unfilled orders. Revisions include selected data for the two previous months.

Computer diskettes, including data back to 1958, can be purchased from Manufacturing & Construction Division, Manufacturers' Shipments, Inventories, and Orders Branch, Bureau of the Census, Washington, D.C. 20233. (301) 457-4804. The data also are available on the Census Bureau internet site (http://www.census.gov).

References

Bureau of the Census publication M3-1(96), "Manufacturers' Shipments, Inventories, and Orders 1987-1996" contains the 1997 revisions. Report M3-1(95), (July 1996) contains revised data beginning with 1982. These reports can be purchased from Census Bureau's customer services on (301) 457-4100.

Pages 160-161

Lumber and Wood Products

Sources: Industrial production and capacity utilization—Board of Governors of the Federal Reserve System (see Notes to pages 22-35); producer prices and employment, hours, and earnings: U.S. Department of Labor, Bureau of Labor Statistics (see Notes to pages 53-57 and 73-91).

Lumber and wood products (SIC Major Group 24) includes timber and pulpwood cutting, sawmills and other mills engaged in producing basic wooden materials, and manufacture of finished articles made entirely or mostly of wood. However, furniture, office fixtures, musical instruments, toys, and some other wooden articles are classified elsewhere.

Industrial production: Logging (SIC 241) covers timber cutting and production of rough products in the field, including wood chips; *lumber* (SIC 242) covers sawmills and planing mills; *lumber products* includes millwork, veneer, plywood, and structural wood members (SIC 243), wood containers (SIC 244), wood buildings and mobile homes (SIC 245), and miscellaneous wood products (SIC 249); *plywood* includes hardwood and softwood veneer and plywood (SIC 2435, 2436); *manufactured homes* (SIC 245) includes mobile homes (as distinct from motor homes, which are in SIC 371) and prefabricated wood buildings and components.

Pages 161-162

Furniture and Fixtures

Sources: Industrial production and capacity utilization—Board of Governors of the Federal Reserve System (see Notes to pages 22-35); producer prices and employment, hours, and earnings—U.S. Department of Labor, Bureau of Labor Statistics (see Notes to pages 53-57 and 73-91).

Furniture and fixtures (SIC Major Group 25) includes manufacture of household, office, public building, and restaurant furniture and of office and store fixtures.

Industrial production: Household furniture (SIC 251) includes household furniture, including upholstered, made of wood, metal, or other materials.

Pages 163-164

Stone, Clay, and Glass

Sources: Industrial production and capacity utilization—Board of Governors of the Federal Reserve System (see Notes to pages 22-35); manufacturers' shipment, and inventories—U.S. Department of Commerce, Bureau of the Census (see notes to pages 147-157); producer prices and employment, hours, and earnings: U.S. Department of Labor, Bureau of Labor Statistics (see Notes to pages 53-57 and 73-91).

Stone, clay, glass, and concrete products (SIC Major Group 32) includes manufacture of flat glass and other glass products, cement, structural clay products, pottery, concrete and gypsum products, cut stone, abrasive and asbestos products, and other products from materials taken from the earth principally in the form of stone, clay, and sand. When separate reports are available, mining and quarrying are classified in Division B, Mining.

Industrial production: Pressed and blown glass (SIC 322) includes manufacture of pressed, blown, or shaped glass and glassware from glass produced in the same establishment; *glass containers* (SIC 3221) covers manufacture of glass containers for commercial packing and bottling and for home canning; *cement* (SIC 324) covers hydraulic cement, including portland, natural, masonry, and pozzolana cements; *structural clay products* (SIC 325) covers brick and structural clay tile; *concrete and miscellaneous* covers pottery and related products (SIC 326), concrete, gypsum, and plaster products (SIC 327), cut stone and stone products (SIC 328), and abrasive, asbestos, and

miscellaneous nonmetallic mineral products (SIC 329).

Pages 165-169

Primary Metals

Sources: Industrial production and capacity utilization—Board of Governors of the Federal Reserve System (see Notes to pages 22-35); manufacturers' shipments, inventories, and orders—U.S. Department of Commerce, Bureau of the Census (see Notes to pages 147-157); producer prices and employment, hours, and earnings: U.S. Department of Labor, Bureau of Labor Statistics (see Notes to pages 53-57 and 73-91).

Primary metal industries (SIC Major Group 33) includes smelting and refining of ferrous and nonferrous metals from ore, pig, or scrap; rolling, drawing, and alloying metals; manufacture of castings and other basic metal products; and manufacture of nails, spikes, and insulated wire and cable. The production of coke is included. Manufacture of metal forgings or stampings are classified in Major Group 34, Fabricated Metal Products.

Industrial production: iron and steel includes steel works, blast furnaces, and rolling and finishing mills (SIC 331) and iron and steel foundries (SIC 332); *basic steel and mill products* is SIC 331.

Pages 170-171

Fabricated Metal Products

Sources: Industrial production and capacity utilization—Board of Governors of the Federal Reserve System (see Notes to pages 22-35); manufacturers' shipments, inventories, and orders—U.S. Department of Commerce, Bureau of the Census (see Notes to pages 147-157); producer prices and employment, hours, and earnings: U.S. Department of Labor, Bureau of Labor Statistics (see Notes to pages 53-57 and 73-91).

Fabricated metal products, except machinery and transportation equipment (SIC Major Group 34) includes fabricating ferrous and nonferrous metal products, such as metal cans, tinware, hand tools, cutlery, nonelectrical heating apparatus, structural metal products, metal forgings and stampings; ordnance (except vehicles and guided missiles); and a variety of metal and wire products not elsewhere classified. Some important segments of metal fabricating industries, such as machinery, transportation equipment, scientific and controlling instruments, jewelry and silverware, are not included.

Industrial production: metal containers (SIC 341) covers metal cans and shipping containers; *hardware, tools, and cutlery* (SIC 342) covers cutlery, handtools, and general hardware; *hardware and tools* covers hand and edge tools (SIC 3423), saw blades and handsaws (SIC 3425), and hardware, not elsewhere classified (SIC 3429); *structural metal products* (SIC 344) covers fabricated structural metal products including structural metal, doors, plate work, sheet metal work, and ornamental metal work; *other fabricated metal products* includes screw machine products and bolts, nuts, screws, rivets, and washers (SIC 345), metal forgings and stampings (SIC 346), coatings, engraving, and allied services (SIC 347), ordnance and accessories, except vehicles and guided missiles (SIC 348), and miscellaneous fabricated metal products (SIC 349); *fasteners, stampings, etc.* is SIC 345, 346, and 347.

Pages 172-174

Industrial Machinery and Equipment

Sources: Industrial production and capacity utilization—Board of Governors of the Federal Reserve System (see Notes to pages 22-35); manufacturers' shipments, inventories, and orders—U.S. Department of Commerce, Bureau of the Census (see Notes to pages 147-157); producer prices and employment, hours, and earnings: U.S. Department of Labor, Bureau of Labor Statistics (see notes to pages 53-57 and 73-91).

Industrial and commercial machinery and computer equipment (SIC Major Group 35) includes manufacture of industrial and commercial machinery and equipment and computers. Included are manufacture of engines and turbines; farm and garden machinery; construction, mining, and oil field machinery; elevators and conveying equipment; hoists and cranes; metalworking machinery; computer and peripheral equipment; office machinery; and refrigeration machinery. Motor-powered machines ordinarily are included, except for electrical household appliances. Equipment for the generation and transmission of electricity is not included. Hand tools are not included unless powered.

Industrial production: engines and turbines (SIC 351) includes steam, gas, and hydraulic turbines and turbine generator set units and internal combustion engines, not elsewhere classified (aircraft engines and automotive engines, except diesel are classified elsewhere); *construction and allied machinery* (SIC 353) includes construction, mining, and materials handling machinery and equipment; *metalworking machinery* (SIC 354) includes machine tools and accessories, power-driven handtools, rolling mill machinery, and welding and soldering equipment; *special industry machinery* (SIC 355) includes textile machinery, woodworking machinery, paper industries machinery, printing machinery, food products machinery, and others; *general industrial machinery* (SIC 356) includes pumps, bearings, compressors, fans, industrial process furnaces, and others; *computer and office equipment* (SIC 357) includes electronic computers (mainframe, micro, mini, and personal), computer storage devices and peripheral equipment, and calculating machines; *service industry machines* (SIC 358) includes automatic vending machines, commercial laundry machines, air-conditioning and warm air heating equipment, commercial refrigeration equipment and others.

Pages 175-177

Electronic and Electric Equipment

Sources: Industrial production and capacity utilization—Board of Governors of the Federal Reserve System (see Notes to pages 22-35); manufacturers' shipments, inventories, and orders—U.S. Department of Commerce, Bureau of the Census (see Notes to pages 147-157); producer prices and employment, hours, and earnings: U.S. Department of Labor, Bureau of Labor Statistics (see Notes to pages 53-57 and 73-91).

Electronic and other electrical equipment and components, except computer equipment (SIC Major Group 36) includes manufacture of machinery, apparatus, and supplies for the generation, storage, transmission, transformation, and utilization of electrical energy. Included are electricity distribution equipment, electrical industrial apparatus, household appliances, electrical lighting and wiring equipment, radio and television receiving equipment, communications equipment; and other electrical equipment and supplies. Industrial machinery and equipment powered by electric motor are not included nor are measuring and controlling instruments.

Industrial production: electrical machinery is SIC Major Group 36; *major electrical equipment and parts* includes electric transmission and distribution equipment (SIC 361) and electrical industrial apparatus (SIC 362); *electric distribution equipment* is SIC 361; *household appliances* (SIC 363) includes *cooking equipment* (SIC 3551); *refrigerators and freezers* (SIC 3632); *household laundry equipment* (SIC 3633) and *miscellaneous household appliances* (SIC 3634, 3635, and 3639); *audio and video equipment* (SIC 365) includes household radios, TV, tape players, and phonograph records, tapes and disks; *communications equipment* (SIC 366) includes telephone and telegraph apparatus, and broadcasting and communications equipment; *electronic components* (SIC 367) includes tubes, circuit boards, semiconductors, capacitors, resistors, coils, and connectors; *miscellaneous electrical supplies* (SIC 369) includes *storage batteries* (SIC 3691), magnetic and optical recording media (such as blank computer diskettes) and electrical machinery, not elsewhere classified.

Pages 178-183

Transportation Equipment, including Motor Vehicles

Sources: Industrial production and capacity utilization—Board of Governors of the Federal Reserve System (see Notes to pages 22-35); manufacturers' shipments, inventories, and orders—U.S. Department of Commerce, Bureau of the Census (see Notes to pages 147-157); retail sales of cars and trucks—U.S. Department of Commerce, Bureau of Economic Analysis; producer prices, consumer prices, and employment, hours, and earnings—U.S. Department of Labor, Bureau of Labor Statistics (see Notes to pages 53-57, 46-52, and 73-91).

Transportation equipment (SIC Major Group 37) includes manufacture of equipment for transportation of passengers and cargo by land, air, and water, including motor vehicles, aircraft, guided missiles and space vehicles, ships, boats, and railroad equipment. Manufacture of equipment for moving materials on farms and work sites is included in Major Group 35, industrial machinery and equipment.

Industrial production and capacity utilization: Motor vehicles and parts (SIC 371) includes motor vehicles, *motor vehicle parts and accessories* (SIC 3714), truck trailers, and *motor homes* (SIC 3716); *aerospace and miscellaneous transportation equipment* includes *aircraft and parts* (SIC 372), *ships and boats* (SIC 373), and *railroad and miscellaneous* (SIC 374—railroad equipment, 375—motorcycles, bicycles, and parts, 376—guided missiles, space vehicles, and parts, and

379—miscellaneous transportation equipment).

Retail sales and inventories of cars, trucks and buses. These estimates are prepared by the Bureau of Economic Analysis based on data from the American Automobile Manufacturers Association, Ward's Automotive Reports and other sources. Data are available in BEA press releases and on the STAT-USA subscription internet site (http://www.stat-usa.gov).

Page 184

Instruments and Related Products

Sources: Industrial production and capacity utilization—Board of Governors of the Federal Reserve System (see Notes to pages 22-35); manufacturers' shipments and inventories—U.S. Department of Commerce, Bureau of the Census (see Notes to pages 147-157); producer prices and employment, hours, and earnings: U.S. Department of Labor, Bureau of Labor Statistics (see Notes to pages 53-57 and 73-91).

Measuring, analyzing, and controlling instruments; photographic, medical and optical goods; watches and clocks (SIC Major Group 38) includes manufacture of instruments (including professional and scientific) for measuring, testing, analyzing, and controlling, and their associated sensors and accessories; hydrological, hydrographic, meteorological, and geophysical equipment; navigation and guidance systems; surgical and medical instruments, equipment and supplies; photographic equipment and supplies; and watches and clocks.

Industrial production: Scientific and medical instruments includes search, detection, navigation, guidance, aeronautical, and nautical systems, instruments, and equipment (SIC 381); laboratory apparatus and analytical, optical, measuring, and controlling instruments (SIC 382); and surgical, medical, and dental instruments and supplies (SIC 384); *medical instruments* is SIC 384.

Pages 186-187

Food and Beverages

Sources: Industrial production and capacity utilization—Board of Governors of the Federal Reserve System (see Notes to pages 22-35); manufacturers' shipments and inventories—U.S. Department of Commerce, Bureau of the Census (see Notes to pages147-157); producer prices, consumer prices, and employment, hours, and earnings—U.S. Department of Labor, Bureau of Labor Statistics (see Notes to pages 53-57, 46-52, and 73-91).

Food and kindred products (SIC Major Group 20) includes manufacture or processing of foods for human consumption and prepared feeds for animals.

Industrial production: meat products (SIC 201) includes meat packing plants, production of sausages and other prepared meat products, and poultry slaughtering and processing; *dairy products* (SIC 202) includes manufacture of creamery butter, cheese, dry and condensed dairy products, and ice cream and frozen desserts and processing of fluid milk; *canned and frozen foods* (SIC 203) includes canning, freezing, drying, dehydrating, and pickling of fruits, vegetables, and specialty foods; *grain mill products* (SIC 204) includes flour milling, breakfast cereal manufacture, rice milling, prepared mixes and doughs, wet corn milling, and dog and cat food; *bakery products* (SIC 205) includes bread, cookies, crackers, and frozen bakery products; *sugar and confectionery* (SIC 206) includes manufacture and refining of sugar and syrup from cane and sugar beets, candy and confectionery, chocolate and cocoa products, chewing gum, and salted and roasted nuts; *fats and oils* (SIC 207) includes cottonseed, soybean, and vegetable oil mills and manufacture of animal and marine fats and oils; *beverages* (SIC 208) includes alcoholic and nonalcoholic beverages and flavoring extracts and syrups; *coffee and miscellaneous* includes roasted coffee, seafoods, snack foods, macaroni and

spaghetti, and miscellaneous food preparations.

Page 188

Tobacco Products

Sources: Industrial production—Board of Governors of the Federal Reserve (see Notes to pages 22-35); manufacturers' shipments and inventories—U.S. Department of Commerce, Bureau of the Census (see Notes to pages 147-157); producer prices and employment, hours, and earnings—U.S. Department of Labor, Bureau of Labor Statistics (see Notes to pages 53-57 and 73-91).

Tobacco products (SIC Major Group 21) includes manufacture of cigarettes, cigars, smoking and chewing tobacco, and snuff and stemming and redrying of tobacco. Also includes manufacture of nontobacco cigarettes.

Pages 189-190

Textile Mill Products

Sources: Industrial production and capacity utilization—Board of Governors of the Federal Reserve System (see Notes to pages 22-35); manufacturers' shipments and inventories—U.S. Department of Commerce, Bureau of the Census (see Notes to pages 147-157); producer prices and employment, hours, and earnings—U.S. Department of Labor, Bureau of Labor Statistics (see Notes to pages 53-57 and 73-91).

Textile mill products (SIC Major Group 22) includes (1) preparation of fiber and manufacture of yarn, thread, twine, and cordage; (2) manufacture of broad woven, narrow woven, and knit fabrics and carpet and rugs from yarn; (3) dyeing and finishing fiber, yarn, fabrics, and knit apparel; (4) coating, waterproofing, or otherwise treating fabrics; (5) integrated manufacture of finished articles from yarn; and (6) manufacture of felt goods, lace, nonwoven fabrics and miscellaneous textiles.

Industrial production: fabrics (SIC 221, 222, 223, and 224) includes broadwoven and narrow woven fabrics of cotton, wool, silk, and manmade fiber; *knit goods* (SIC 225) includes knitting of hosiery, underwear, and outerwear; *carpeting* (SIC 227) includes manufacture of carpets and rugs from textile materials and from materials such as reeds, sisal, or jute; *yarns and miscellaneous* (SIC 228 and 229) includes yarn and thread mills, coated fabrics (not rubberized), tire cord, nonwoven fabrics, cordage and twine, linen goods, and textiles not elsewhere classified.

Page 191

Apparel

Sources: Industrial production and capacity utilization—Board of Governors of the Federal Reserve System (see Notes to pages 22-35); producer prices, consumer prices, and employment, hours, and earnings—U.S. Department of Labor, Bureau of Labor Statistics (see Notes to pages 53-57, 46-52, and 73-91).

Apparel and other finished products made from fabrics and similar materials (SIC Major Group 23) includes production of clothing and other products by cutting and sewing purchased woven or knit fabrics, leather, rubberized fabrics, plastics, and furs. Also includes manufacture of clothing by cutting and joining (for example, by adhesives) materials such as paper and nonwoven fabrics.

Pages 192-193

Paper and Allied Products

Sources: Industrial production and capacity utilization—Board of Governors of the Federal Reserve System (see Notes to pages 22-35); manufacturers' shipments and inventories—U.S. Department of Commerce, Bureau of the Census (see Notes to pages 147-157); producer prices and employment, hours, and earnings—U.S. Department of Labor, Bureau of Labor Statistics (see Notes to pages 53-57 and 73-91).

Paper and allied products (SIC Major Group 26) includes manufacture of pulps from wood and other cellulose fibers and rags; manufacture of paper and paperboard; and paper products such as bags, boxes, and envelopes. Also included is manufacture of plastic bags.

Industrial production and capacity utilization: Pulp and paper includes pulp mills (SIC 261), paper mills (SIC 262), and paperboard mills (SIC 263); *paper products* includes paperboard containers and boxes (SIC 265) and converted paper and paperboard products, except containers and boxes (SIC 267).

Page 194

Printing and Publishing

Sources: Industrial production and capacity utilization—Board of Governors of the Federal Reserve System (see Notes to pages 22-35); producer prices and employment, hours, and earnings—U.S. Department of Labor, Bureau of Labor Statistics (see Notes to pages 53-57 and 73-91).

Printing, publishing, and allied industries (SIC Major Group 27) includes printing, lithography, and services performed for the printing trade, such as bookbinding and plate making. Also included are publishers of newspapers, books, and periodicals.

Industrial production: Newspapers (SIC 271) includes publishing and printing of newspapers; *commercial printing* (SIC 275) includes lithographic, offset, and gravure printing.

Pages 195-196

Chemicals and Chemical Products

Sources: Industrial production and capacity utilization—Board of Governors of the Federal Reserve System (see Notes to pages 22-35); manufacturers' shipments and inventories—U.S. Department of Commerce, Bureau of the Census (see

Notes to pages 147-157); producer prices and employment, hours, and earnings—U.S. Department of Labor, Bureau of Labor Statistics (see Notes to pages 53-57 and 73-91).

Chemicals and allied products (SIC Major Group 28) includes production of basic chemicals and manufacture of products by predominantly chemical processes. Three general classes of products are included: (1) basic chemicals; (2) chemical products to be used in further manufacture, including synthetic fibers and plastic materials; (3) finished chemical products, including drugs, cosmetics, paints, fertilizers, and explosives. The mining of natural chemicals and fertilizers is classified Division B, Mining.

Industrial production and capacity utilization: Basic chemicals (SIC 281—Industrial Inorganic Chemicals) includes alkalies, chlorine, industrial gases, inorganic pigments, and industrial organic chemicals not elsewhere classified (SIC 2819); *synthetic materials* (SIC 282) includes plastic materials, synthetic resins, and nonvulcanizable elastomers (SIC 2821), synthetic fibers (SIC 2823 and 2824), and synthetic rubber (vulcanizable elastomers); *drugs and medicines* (SIC 283) includes medicinal chemicals and pharmaceutical products; *soaps and toiletries* (SIC 284) includes soap, detergents, cleaning preparations, perfumes, cosmetics, and other toiletries; *industrial organic chemicals* (SIC 286) includes noncyclic organic chemicals, solvents, polyhydric alcohols, synthetic perfumes and flavorings, rubber processing chemicals, plasticizers, synthetic tanning agents, and others; *agricultural chemicals* (SIC 287) includes nitrogenous and phosphatic fertilizers, pesticides, and agricultural chemical not elsewhere classified.

Pages 197-198

Petroleum and Coal Products

Sources: Industrial production and capacity utilization—Board of Governors of the Federal Reserve

System (see Notes to pages 22-35); manufacturers' shipments and inventories—U.S. Department of Commerce, Bureau of the Census (see Notes to pages 147-157); producer prices, consumer prices, and employment, hours, and earnings—U.S. Department of Labor, Bureau of Labor Statistics (see Notes to pages53-57, 46-52, and 73-91).

Petroleum refining and related industries (SIC Major Group 29) includes refining petroleum, manufacturing paving and roofing materials, and compounding lubricating oils and greases from purchased materials. Producing coke and byproducts is classified in Major Group 33, Primary Metals. Gas distribution is classified in public utilities.

Industrial production: Petroleum refining and miscellaneous(SIC 291, 299) includes petroleum refining, blending and compounding lubricating oils and greases, and production of petroleum and coal products not elsewhere classified; paving and roofing materials (SIC 295) includes manufacture of asphalt and tar paving materials and asphalt roofing materials.

Pages 199-200

Rubber and Plastic Products

Sources: Industrial production and capacity utilization: Board of Governors of the Federal Reserve System (see Notes to pages 22-35); manufacturers' shipments and inventories—U.S. Department of Commerce, Bureau of the Census (see Notes to pages 147-157); producer prices and employment, hours, and earnings—U.S. Department of Labor, Bureau of Labor Statistics (see Notes to pages 53-57 and 73-91).

Rubber and miscellaneous plastics products (SIC Major Group 30) includes manufacturing products, not elsewhere classified, from plastic resins and from natural, synthetic, or reclaimed rubber. Many products made from these materials, including boats, toys, buckles, and buttons, are classified elsewhere. Tire manufacture

is included, but recapping and retreading are classified in Services. Manufacture of synthetic rubber and synthetic plastic resins is classified in Chemicals, Major Group 28.

Industrial production: Tires (SIC 301) includes manufacture of pneumatic casings, inner tubes, and solid and cushion tires for all types of vehicles, airplanes, and farm equipment and of tire repair and retreading materials; other rubber products includes manufacture of rubber and plastics footwear (SIC 302), gaskets, packing, and sealing devices and rubber and plastic hosing and belting (SIC 305), and fabricated rubber products not elsewhere classified (SIC 306); plastics products, not elsewhere classified (SIC 308) includes manufacture of unsupported and laminated plastic film, sheet, and profile shapes, plastics pipe, plastics bottles, plastics foam products, and plastics plumbing fixtures.

Page 201

Leather and Leather Products

Sources: Industrial production and capacity utilization—Board of Governors of the Federal Reserve System (see Notes to pages 22-35); producer prices and employment, hours, and earnings—U.S. Department of Labor, Bureau of Labor Statistics (see Notes to pages 53-57 and 73-91).

Leather and leather products (SIC Major Group 31) includes tanning, currying, and finishing hides and skins and manufacturing finished leather and artificial leather products and some similar products made of other materials.

Industrial production: Shoes (SIC 314) includes manufacture of footwear, except rubber or plastic footwear.

Pages 204-207

Transportation, Communications, and Utilities

Sources: Industrial production and capacity utilization—Board of Governors of the Federal Reserve System (see Notes to pages 22-35);

producer prices and employment, hours, and earnings—U.S. Department of Labor, Bureau of Labor Statistics (see Notes to pages 53-57 and 73-91).

Transportation, communications, and electric, gas, and sanitary services (SIC Division E) includes establishments providing to the general public or to other business enterprises passenger and freight transportation, communications services, or electricity, gas, steam, water or sanitary services. The U.S. Postal Service is included as are private courier and delivery services.

Industrial production: electric utilities includes the generation, transmission, and/or distribution of electric energy for sale (SIC 491) and part of SIC 493—combination electric, gas, and other utility services; gas utilities includes natural gas transmission and distribution and manufacture and distribution of liquified petroleum gas (SIC 493) and part of SIC 493.

Employment, hours, and earnings: trucking and warehousing (SIC Major Group 42) includes local and long-distance trucking, warehousing and storage, and courier services (except by air); communications (SIC Major Group 48) includes telephone, telegraph, radio and television, and other communications services; electric, gas, and sanitary services (SIC Major Group 49) includes electricity and gas production and distribution, water supply, sewerage systems, and refuse systems.

Pages 208-209

Electric Power Use

Source: Board of Governors of the Federal Reserve System

Data collected by the Federal Reserve on electric power use in mining and manufacturing are used in the estimation of industrial production. Indexes of electric power use, based on 1992=100, are published monthly in the G.17 release "Industrial Production and Capacity Utilization" (see Notes to pages 22-35).

Pages 212-213

Retail and Wholesale Trade: Employment, Hours, and Earnings

Sources: Employment, hours, and earnings—U.S. Department of Labor, Bureau of Labor Statistics (see Notes to pages 73-91).

Wholesale trade (SIC Division F) includes establishments primarily engaged in selling merchandise to retailers; to commercial, professional, or institutional purchasers; or to other wholesalers. Certain establishments that sell merchandise both for commercial and professional use, such as paint stores and gasoline service stations are classified in Retail Trade. Wholesale trade includes merchant wholesalers—wholesalers who take title to the goods they sell as well as sales branches of manufacturing or mining enterprises (apart from their plants or mines) and commodity brokers and commission merchants. The data in this book pertain to merchant wholesalers only.

Retail trade (SIC Division G) includes establishment primarily engaged in selling merchandise for personal or household consumption and rendering services incidental to the sales of the goods. However, establishments engaged in selling such merchandise as plumbing equipment, electrical supplies, and office furniture are classified in Wholesale Trade, even if a higher proportion of their sales is made to individuals for personal of household use.

General merchandise stores (SIC Major Group 53) includes department stores, variety stores, and general stores; *food stores* (SIC Major Group 54) includes grocery stores, meat markets, bakeries, and other food specialty stores; *auto dealers and service stations* (SIC Major Group 55) includes new and used motor vehicle dealers, auto supply stores, and gasoline service stations; *apparel and accessory stores* (SIC Major Group 56) includes men's, women's, and children's clothing stores, shoe stores,

and accessory stores; *eating and drinking places* (SIC Major Group 58) includes restaurant, carry-outs, institutional food service, bars, and taverns.

Pages 214-218

Retail Sales and Inventories

Source: U.S. Department of Commerce, Bureau of the Census

Each month the Bureau of the Census prepares estimates of retail sales and inventories by kind of business based on a mail-out/mail-back survey of a sample of companies with one or more establishments that sell merchandise and related services to final consumers.

Notes on the data

Inventory data prior to 1980 are not comparable to later years due to changes in valuation methods. Prior to 1980 inventories are book values of merchandise on hand at the end of the period and are valued according to the valuation method used by each respondent. Thus the aggregates are a mixture of LIFO (last-in-first-out) and non-LIFO values. Beginning with 1980 inventories are valued using methods other than LIFO in order to better reflect the current costs of goods held as inventory.

The *survey sample* is stratified by kind of business and estimated sales. All firms with sales above an applicable size cutoff are included. Firms are selected randomly from the remaining strata. To reduce reporting burden, only specially selected panels report each month, with the remainder reporting quarterly in three rotating panels.

Data availability

An *Advanced Monthly Retail Sales* report is released about nine working after the close of the reference month, based on responses from a sub-sample of the complete retail sample. Revised sales estimates and inventory estimates, based on the larger sample are released subsequently.

Combined Annual and Revised Monthly Retail Trade reports are released annually each spring. They include updated seasonal adjustment factors; revised and benchmarked monthly estimates of sales and inventories; monthly data for the most recent 10 years, detailed annual estimates and ratios for the United States by kind of business, and comparable prior-year statistics and year-to-year changes.

Data are available on the Bureau of the Census internet site (http://www.census.gov/econ/www/retmenu.html).

Page 218

Merchant Wholesalers: Sales and Inventories

Source: U.S. Department of Commerce, Bureau of the Census

These data pertain to merchant wholesalers and are based on a monthly survey conducted by the Bureau of the Census.

Notes on the data

Inventory data prior to 1980 are not comparable to later years due to changes in valuation methods and are not included in this book. Prior to 1980 inventories are book values of stocks on hand at the end of the period and are valued according to the valuation method used by each respondent. Thus the aggregates are a mixture of LIFO (last-in-first-out) and non-LIFO values. Beginning with 1980 inventories are valued using methods other than LIFO in order to better reflect the current costs of goods held as inventory.

The survey covers wholesale companies with employment that are primarily engaged in merchant wholesale trade in the U.S. (SIC Division F). These include merchant wholesalers that take title of the goods they sell, and jobbers, industrial distributors, exporters, and importers. Excluded are nonmerchant wholesalers such as manufacturers' sales branches and offices; agents, merchandise or commodity brokers, and commission merchants; and other businesses whose primary activity is other than wholesale trade.

Companies provide data on dollar values of merchant wholesale sales, end-of-month inventories, and methods of inventory valuation.

A survey has been conducted monthly since 1946. A mail-out/mail-back survey of selected wholesale firms is used. Firms are first stratified by merchant wholesale sales, inventories and major kind of business (determined from the latest census of wholesale trade). All firms with wholesale sales or inventories above applicable size cutoffs for each major kind of business are included in the survey. Remaining firms are stratified by major kind of business and estimated sales, and a simple random sample is selected from each stratum. Companies selected with certainty report each month. To minimize reporting burden, randomly selected firms are put in one of three rotating panels and report once each quarter for the two preceding months.

New samples are drawn every five years, and the sample is updated every quarter to reflect "births" and "deaths"; adding new businesses identified in the business and professional classification survey and dropping companies that are no longer active.

Data availability

Monthly Wholesale Trade, Sales and Inventories reports are released six weeks after the close of the reference month. They contain preliminary current month figures and final figures for the previous month. Statistics include sales, inventories, and stock/ sale ratios by three-digit SIC code along with standard errors. Data are both seasonally adjusted and unadjusted.

Combined Annual and Revised Monthly Wholesale Trade reports are released annually each spring. They contain estimated annual sales, monthly and year-end inventories, inventory/sales ratios, purchases, gross

margins, and gross margin/sales ratios by kind of business. Annual estimates are benchmarked to the most recent census of wholesale trade. These reports also present the results of a benchmarking operation that revises monthly sales and inventories estimates. Estimates are both seasonally adjusted and unadjusted.

Data are available on the Bureau of the Census internet site (http://www.census.gov/econ/www/retmenu.html).

Page 220

Finance, Insurance, and Real Estate

Sources: Employment, hours, and earnings—U.S. Department of Labor, Bureau of Labor Statistics (see Notes to pages 73-91).

Finance, insurance and real estate (SIC Division H) includes establishments operating primarily in the fields of finance, insurance, and real estate. *Finance* includes *depository institutions* (SIC Major Group 60), nondepository credit institutions (Major Group 61), and securities brokers and dealers and exchanges (Major Groups 62 and 67). *Insurance* (SIC Major Groups 63 and 64) covers carriers, agents, and brokers of all types of insurance. *Real estate* (SIC Major Group 65) includes buyers, sellers, agents, developers, and owners of real estate.

Pages 221-223

Private Services

Sources: Employment, hours, and earnings—U.S. Department of Labor, Bureau of Labor Statistics (see Notes to pages 73-91).

Services (SIC Division I) includes establishments engaged in providing a wide variety of services to individuals, businesses, government, and other organizations. Personal, business, repair, health, amusement, legal, and engineering services and hotels and

other lodging places are among the categories included.

The SIC Division includes governmental as well as private activities, classified according to the type of service provided. However, the employment, hours, and earnings data shown on these pages pertain only to the private, nonfarm economy.

Agricultural services (SIC Major Group 7) includes soil preparation and crop services, veterinary services, and landscape services; *hotels and other lodging places* (SIC Major Group 70) includes hotels, motels, rooming houses, and RV camps; *personal services* (SIC Major Group 72) includes laundry, photography, hair care, shoe repair, and funeral services; *business services* (SIC Major Group 73) includes *personnel supply services* (SIC 736), *computer and data processing services* (SIC 737), and also advertising, equipment rental, and other business services.

Auto repair, services, and parking (SIC Major Group 75) includes auto rental, parking, and repair; *miscellaneous repair services* (SIC Major Group 76) includes electrical and watch and clock repair, reupholstery and furniture repair, and other repair services.

Motion pictures (SIC Major Group 78) includes motion picture production and distribution, motion picture theaters, and video tape rental; *amusement and recreation* (SIC Major Group 79) includes theaters, sports events, and sports facilities, such as golf courses and health clubs; *legal services* (SIC Major Group 81) includes establishments headed by attorneys; *educational services* (SIC Major Group 82) includes private schools and colleges, libraries, and vocational schools; *social services* (SIC Major Group 83) includes family services, day care, and job training.

Museums, botanical gardens and zoos (SIC Major Group 84) includes museums, galleries, botanical gardens, and zoos; *membership organizations* (SIC Major Group 86) includes business and professional associations, labor unions, and civic, religious, and political organizations; *engineering and management* (SIC Major Group 87) includes engineering, accounting, research, and management services.

Health services (SIC Major Group 80) includes *hospitals* (SIC 806), *offices and clinics of medical doctors* (SIC 801), *nursing and personal care facilities* (SIC 805), *home health care services* (SIC 808), and also dental offices, medical and dental laboratories, and other health care practitioners.

Pages 226-231 and 251-254

Government Receipts and Expenditures

Source: U.S. Department of Commerce, Bureau of Economic Analysis

These data are taken from Tables 3.2, 3.3, 3.7, 3.8, and 3.10 of the National Income and Product Accounts (NIPAs), as published in the 1996 comprehensive NIPA revisions and as subsequently revised and updated through August 1997. The 1996 comprehensive revisions for the first time separated government expenditures into those for current consumption and those for gross investment.

Notes on the data

The data on government receipts and expenditures are an integral part of the national income and product accounts, recording transactions of governments with other U.S. residents and foreigners. Each entry in the government receipts and expenditures account has a corresponding entry elsewhere in the NIPAs. Thus, for example, the sum of personal tax and nontax receipts by federal and state and local governments is equal to personal tax and nontax payments as shown in the personal income table.

The government receipts and expenditures estimates are derived primarily from financial statements on federal, state, and local governments. However, a number of adjustments are made to place the data on the basis

required for the NIPAs. Annual data are placed on a calendar year basis. Data are converted from the cash basis usually found in financial statements to the timing bases required for the NIPAs. In the NIPAs, receipts from businesses generally are on an accrual basis, purchases of goods and services are recorded when delivered; and receipts from and transfer payments to persons are on a cash basis.

The federal receipts and expenditure data from the NIPAs on pages 226-231 thus differs from the federal receipts and outlay data on pages 232-234 in that, among other differences, the latter are by fiscal year and are on a modified cash basis.

Definitions

Personal tax and nontax receipts is tax payments by persons that are not chargeable to business expense and certain other personal payments to government agencies (except government enterprises) that are treated like taxes. Personal taxes includes taxes on income, including realized net capital gains; on transfers of estates and gifts; and on personal property. Nontaxes includes donations and fees, fines, and forfeitures. Personal contributions for social insurance are not included.

Corporate profits tax accruals is the sum of federal, state, and local income taxes on all corporate earnings, including realized net capital gains. These taxes are net of refunds and applicable tax credits.

Indirect business tax and nontax accruals is tax liabilities that are chargeable to business expense in the calculation of profit-type incomes and certain other business liabilities to government agencies (except government enterprises) that are treated like taxes. Examples are sales and property taxes and regulatory and inspection fees. Employer contributions for social insurance are not included.

Contributions for social insurance includes employer and personal contributions for social security, unemployment insurance, government

employee retirement, and other government social insurance programs.

Government consumption expenditures is purchases by governments (federal, state, and local) of goods and services for current consumption. It includes compensation of general government employees and an allowance for consumption of general government fixed capital (i.e., depreciation). Receipts for certain services provided by government—primarily tuition payments for higher education and charges for medical care—are defined as government sales, which are treated as deductions from government purchases.

Transfer payments includes payments to persons for which they do not render current services. Examples are social security benefits, Medicaid, unemployment benefits, and public assistance. U.S. government nonmilitary grants to other countries also are included.

Federal grants-in-aid are net payments from federal to state and local governments to help finances programs such as highway construction, public assistance, and education.

Net interest paid is interest paid to U.S. and foreign persons and businesses and to foreign governments less interest received from business and from foreigners. Interest paid consists of monetary interest paid on public debt and other financial obligations. Interest received consists of monetary and imputed interest received on loans and investments, including the balance of state and local social insurance funds.

Subsidies less current surplus of government enterprises. Subsidies are the monetary grants paid by government to business, including government enterprises at another level of government. The current surplus of government enterprises is their current operating revenue and subsidies received from other levels of government less their current expenses. No deduction is made for depreciation charges and net interest paid.

Surplus or deficit (-), national income and product accounts is the sum of government receipts less the sum of government expenditures.

Gross government investment consists of general government and government enterprise expenditures for fixed assets (structures and durable equipment). Government inventory investment is included in government consumption expenditures.

Capital consumption. Consumption of fixed capital, or depreciation, is included in government consumption expenditures as a partial measure of the value of the services of general government fixed assets; use of depreciation assumes a zero net return on these assets.

Data availability

The most recent data are published each month in the *Survey of Current Business;* may be purchased on diskette from BEA; or may be obtained from the BEA internet site (http:// www.bea.doc.gov). Full historical data also may be purchased on diskette from BEA or may be obtained from the STAT-USA subscription internet site (http://www.stat-usa.gov).

References

For information on the 1996 comprehensive revisions see these articles in the Survey of Current Business: "The Measurement of Depreciation in the U.S. National Income and Product Accounts," July 1997; "Improved Estimates of the National Income and Product Accounts for 1959-95: Results of the Comprehensive Revision," January/February 1996; and "Preview of the Comprehensive Revision of the National Income and Product Accounts: Recognition of Government Investment and Incorporation of a New Methodology for Calculating Depreciation," September 1995. Other sources of general information about the NIPA are listed in the Notes for pages 4-8.

Pages 232-234

Federal Government Receipts and Outlays

Source: U.S. Department of the Treasury

These data on government receipts and outlays are from the *Monthly Treasury Statement* and are on a modified cash basis. Annual data are by federal fiscal years: July 1 to June 30 through 1976 and October 1 to September 30 for subsequent years. There are numerous differences in timing and definition between these estimates and the NIPA estimates on pages 226-231. *Outlays* occur when the federal government liquidates an obligation through a cash payment, when interest accrues on public debt issues, or when a government-owned asset is sold on credit terms. *Outlays by function* present outlays according to the major purpose of the spending. Functional classifications cut across departmental and agency lines.

Data availability

Data are published monthly in the *Monthly Treasury Statement* prepared by the Financial Management Service, U.S. Department of the Treasury. The publication is available on the Financial Management Service internet site (http://www.fms.treas.gov).

Page 234

Government Employment

Source: U.S. Department of Labor, Bureau of Labor Statistics (see Notes to pages 73-91).

The government division of the SIC includes federal, state, and local activities such as legislative, executive, and judicial functions, as well as all governmentowned and governmentoperated business enterprises, establishments, and institutions (arsenals, navy yards, hospitals, etc.), and government force account construction. The figures relate to civilian employment only. BLS considers

regular fulltime teachers (private and governmental) to be employed during the summer vacation period whether or not they are specifically paid in those months.

Employment in federal government establishments represents those who occupied positions the last day of the month. Intermittent workers are counted if they performed any service during the month. Federal government employment excludes employees of the Central Intelligence Agency and the National Security Agency.

Pages 237-246

Selected National Income and Product Account Data

See the Notes for pages 4-8.

Pages 247-250

Private Fixed Investment

See the Notes for pages 42-44.

Pages 251-254

Government Receipts and Expenditures

See the Notes for pages 226-231.

Pages 255-258

U.S. International Transactions

See the Notes for pages 102-106

Pages 259-262

Productivity and Related Data

See the Notes for pages 62-63

Pages 263-265

New Plant and Equipment Spending

Source: U.S. Bureau of Economic Analysis and Bureau of the Census

The data on new plant and equipment spending are from the *Plant and Equipment Survey*. This survey program, which began in 1947, was concluded with the data released in September 1994 and was replaced by a new semi-annual *Investment Plans Survey* (IPS). The IPS was, in turn, discontinued as of March 1996, due to budgetary limitations at the Bureau of the Census. Although an annual capital expenditure survey (ACES) now provides annual data, there is no longer any official survey of capital spending by industry on a less-than-annual basis or of future investment plans. The ACES differs significantly in survey design, scope, and publication detail from the former Plant and Equipment Survey.

To provide a historical time series on new investment by U.S. businesses, the back data from the Plant and Equipment Survey are included in the historical statistics section of this book.

Coverage. The survey covered businesses classified in SIC Divisions A (excluding agricultural producers), B through H, and I (except private households).

Content. Basic data on spending for plant and equipment were collected for each quarter, with additional data obtained for the third and fourth quarters. Quarterly data included actual expenditures for the prior quarter, and planned spending for each of the next three quarters.

Methods. The Census Bureau conducted this survey from the third quarter of 1988 through 1994; the Bureau of Economic Analysis conducted it for prior years. A mailout/mailback quarterly survey of selected large companies, and a mailout/mailback annual survey of additional companies in selected industries was used. The survey panels were benchmarked in 1982. Beginning in 1989, a survey panel maintenance program was used to assess and improve industry coverage based on information from other censuses and surveys. Beginning with 1991, companies not responding to voluntary quarterly survey requests received mandatory annual requests for comparable information.

Data availability

Quarterly and annual data from the Plant and Equipment Survey covering 1947 through mid-1994 are available from the Bureau of the Census.

Pages 266-273

Personal Income

See the Notes for pages 14-17.

Pages 274-277

Industrial Production and Capacity Utilization

See the Notes for pages 22-35.

Pages 278-285

Civilian Population, Labor Force, Employment and Unemployment

See the Notes for pages 68-71.

Pages 286-293

Nonagricultural Employment, Hours, and Earnings

See the Notes for pages 73-91.

Pages 294-297

Consumer Prices Indexes

See the Notes for pages 46-52.

Pages 298-301

Producer Price Indexes

See the Notes for pages 53-57.

Pages 302-305

Money Stock and Selected Components

See the Notes for pages 94-95.

Pages 306-309

Interest Rate, Bond Yields, and Stock Prices

See the notes for pages 99-100.

Pages 315-334

State and Regional Data

See the introductory note on page 313.

Data Sources

Most of the data in this volume are from the government agencies and private sources listed below. The specific source(s) for the individual data sets are identified at the beginning of the Notes for the relevant data pages.

Board of Governors of the Federal Reserve System

20th Street and Constitution Ave., NW
Washington, DC 20551

Data Inquiries:
Publications Services
Mail Stop 127
Board of Governors of the
Federal Reserve System
Washington, DC 20551
Telephone: (202) 452-3244

Monthly Publication:
Federal Reserve Bulletin

Publication Sales:
Available by subscription from
Publications Services at the above
address.

Internet Address:
http://www.bog.frb.fed.us/releases/

Bureau of the Census, U.S. Department of Commerce

Washington, DC 20233

Data Inquiries:
General Information: (301) 457-4100
Foreign Trade Information:
(301) 457-3041

Internet Address:
http://www.census.gov

Bureau of Economic Analysis, U.S. Department of Commerce

Washington, DC 20233

Data Inquiries:
Public Information Office:
(202) 606-9900

Monthly Publication:
Survey of Current Business

Publication Sales:
Available by subscription from the
Superintendent of Documents

Internet Address:
http://www.bea.doc.gov **or**
http://www.stat-usa.gov

Bureau of Labor Statistics, U.S. Department of Labor

2 Massachusetts Ave., NE
Washington, DC 20212

Data Inquiries:
General: (202) 606-5886
24-Hour Hotline: (202) 606-7828

Monthly Publications:
Monthly Labor Review
Employment and Earnings
Compensation and Working Conditions
Producer Price Indexes
CPI Detailed Report

Publication Sales:
Available by subscription from the
Superintendent of Documents

Internet Address:
http://stats.bls.gov

Conference Board, The

845 Third Avenue, New York, NY
10022

Data Inquiries:
Michael Boldin
E-mail: lei@conference-board.org

Publication Sales:
Customer Service: (212) 339-0345

Monthly Publication:
Business Cycle Indicators

Internet Address:
http://www.tcb-indicators.org

Employment and Training Administration U.S. Department of Labor

200 Constitution Avenue, NW
Washington, DC 20210

Data Inquiries:
(202) 219-6871

Internet Address:
http://www.doleta.gov

Energy Information Administration

U.S. Department of Energy
1000 Independence Ave., SW
Washington, DC 20585

Data Inquiries and Publications:
National Energy Information Center
Phone: (202) 586-8800
Fax: (202) 586-0727
E-mail: infoctr@eia.doe.gov

Monthly Publication:
Petroleum Supply Monthly

Internet Address:
http://www.eia.doe.gov

Financial Management Service, U.S. Department of the Treasury

401 14th Street, SW,
Washington, DC 20227

Data Inquiries:
Budget Reports Branch:
(202) 874 -9880

Monthly Publication:
Monthly Treasury Statement

Publication Sales:
Available by subscription from the
Superintendent of Documents

Internet Address:
http://www.fms.treas.gov

National Agricultural Statistics Service U.S. Department of Agriculture

14th & Independence Ave., SW
Washington, DC 20250

Data Inquiries:
Information Hotline: (800) 727-9540

Publication Sales:
Telephone: (800) 999-6779
Fax: (703) 834-0110

Internet Address:
http://www.usda.gov/nass/

To order government publications:
Superintendent of Documents

P.O. Box 371954
Pittsburgh, PA 15250-7954
(202) 512-1800

Index

Index

MANUFACTURING BY INDUSTRY-NONDURABLE GOODS

MANUFACTURING GENERALLY

METALS

MINES AND MINERALS

Recently published by Bernan Press

Handbook of North American Industry: NAFTA and the Economies of Its Member Nations

Jack Cremeans, Editor

At last! A sourcebook full of detailed data on the emerging NAFTA market. Information on the Canadian and Mexican economies—with industry level detail—is presented side by side with comparable U.S. data. Fact-filled articles cover the NAFTA agreement, provide analysis of its effect on U.S. business, and rank various industries in all three NAFTA countries. This volume is full of useful statistics on output, employment, number of establishments, and other details on Canadian and Mexican industries alongside and compared with data for the United States. **A must for everyone selling to, buying from, or interested in the very large new market created by the North American Free Trade Agreement**.

January 1998, Hardback, approx. 600pp, ISBN 0-89059-073-7, $89.00
Standing Order No. 077.64096

1997 County and City Extra: Annual Metro, City and County Data Book

George Hall and Deirdre Gaquin, Editors

Recognized as the definitive source for up-to-date demographic and economic information by geographic area, the *County and City Extra* contains the very latest statistics available for every state, county, metropolitan area, and congressional district, as well as every city with a population of 25,000 or more. This essential volume is filled with detailed tables on: population characteristics, employment, education, income, crime, agriculture, manufacturing, trade, services, federal spending, and local government finance. Ranking tables and colored maps provide ready comparisons across jurisdictions.

"...essential purchase for any library requiring the most current statistics about states, counties, cities, and metropolitan areas."
— Library Journal

May 1997, Hardback, 1,300pp, ISBN 0-89059-071-0, $109.00
Standing Order No. 077.00992

The Bernan Press U.S. DataBook Series™

The Bernan Press U.S. DataBook Series™ is designed to provide essential, yet hard-to-find government statistics in a printed format. Our well-known editors have held high-ranking positions in the Department of Commerce, the Bureau of the Census, the Bureau of Labor Statistics, and other federal and national organizations.

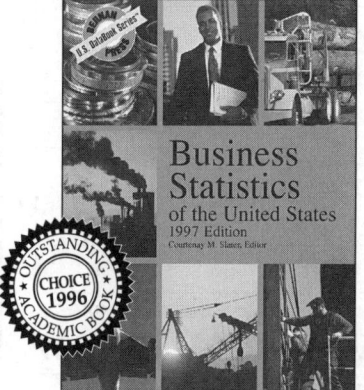

Business Statistics of the United States: 1997 Edition

Courtenay M. Slater, Editor

Based on the popular *Business Statistics*, (formerly published by the Bureau of Economic Analysis), this essential reference work contains 29 years of annual time series data, with monthly data for 1993 through 1996, and an update of key data through the first half of 1997. You'll find current information on: construction and housing; mining, oil, and gas; manufacturing; transportation, communications, and utilities; retail and wholesale trade; services; and government.

It also features a full statistical picture of the overall U.S. economy, including data on: gross domestic product; consumer income and spending; industrial production; money and financial markets; and more. It contains numerous charts and tables illustrating economic trends.

December 1997, Paperback, approx. 420pp, ISBN 0-89059-083-4, $65.00, Standing Order No. 077.05375

Handbook of U.S. Labor Statistics: Employment, Earnings, Prices, Productivity, and Other Labor Data: First Edition

Eva E. Jacobs, Editor

Based on the *Handbook of Labor Statistics*, (formerly published by the Bureau of Labor Statistics), this comprehensive research tool presents historical data on labor market trends through 1995. Topics include: population, labor force, and employment status; consumer prices; producer prices; export and import prices; consumer expenditures; and productivity.

A special feature in this edition is the Bureau of Labor Statistics projections of employment by industry and occupation for 1994-2005.

March 1997, Paperback, 316pp, ISBN 0-89059-062-1, $59.00, Standing Order No. 077.43472

Housing Statistics of the United States: First Edition

Patrick A. Simmons, Editor

This completely new reference work is the first ever comprehensive source for current and historical information on households, housing, and housing finance. Data include: household characteristics; prices, rents, and affordability; housing production and investment; home mortgage lending; housing stock characteristics; and federal housing programs. This is an ideal source for data that can be used for producing or benchmarking market reports, trend analysis, and research.

October 1997, Paperback, 400pp, ISBN 0-89059-065-6, $59.00, Standing Order No. 077.43481

To order, contact Customer Service at (800) 865-3457 or mail/fax the order form on the back page of this book.

Bernan Associates Order Form

4611-F Assembly Drive ■ Lanham, MD 20706 USA

If using a purchase order, please attach this form

Quantity	ISBN	Title	Begin Standing Order?		Price
	0-89059-073-7	Hndbk. of North American Industry, First Ed.	Yes ☐	No ☐	$89.00
	0-89059-071-0	1997 County and City Extra	Yes ☐	No ☐	$109.00
	0-89059-083-4	Business Statistics of the U.S., 1997 Edition	Yes ☐	No ☐	$65.00
	0-89059-062-1	Handbook of U.S. Labor Statistics, First Edition	Yes ☐	No ☐	$59.00
	0-89059-065-6	Housing Statistics of the U.S., First Edition	Yes ☐	No ☐	$59.00

Subtotal	
Postage & Handling*	
Tax**	
Total	

*Add Postage and Handling as follows:
U.S.: 6%, minimum $5.00
Canada and Mexico: 10%, minimum $6.00
Outside North America: 30%, minimum $15.00
**MD, DC, and NY add applicable sales tax;
  Canada add GST

Rush Service
Rush Service is available for an additional $15.

Prices are subject to change

Terms: Net 30 days

Return Policy
You may review any Bernan Press publication for 30 days. If you are not completely satisfied, you may return it for a full refund or credit to your account.

Methods of Payment

Deposit Account
Requires a minimum initial deposit of $100.00 and an ongoing balance of $50.00. Upon receipt of the check or money order, an account will be established and a special account number will be assigned. The cost of ordered publications will be deducted from the funds on deposit.

Invoice Statement Account
Send in the order on an authorized purchase order, and an invoice will be included with the shipment of publications. An account number will be assigned after the first purchase. All future orders can be charged against this account number with an authorized purchase order.

Prepayment
Prepay all orders with a check or money order in U.S. dollars, drawn from a U.S. bank, payable to Bernan Associates.

MAKE RE-ORDERING EASY WITH STANDING ORDERS!

Place your publications on *Standing Order* and you are guaranteed automatic delivery of each new edition as it is published!

☐ **Check here to put the Bernan Press U.S. DataBook Series™ on *Group Standing Order*.**

You'll automatically receive all forthcoming titles in the U.S. DataBook Series as they are published.

☐ Check or Money Order enclosed

☐ Bill Me P.O.#_____ Date_____

☐ MC ☐ Visa ☐ Am Ex Exp. Date_____

Card #_____

Signature _____

YES!
I'd like to open a Deposit Account.
Enclosed is a check for _____
  (minimum $100)
Account # _____
Tax Exempt # _____

Bill To

Name _____
Organization _____
Address _____
_____
Phone _____ Fax _____

Ship To

Name _____
Organization _____
Address _____
_____
Phone _____ Fax _____